"No other guide has as much to offer . . . these books are a pleasure to read."   Gene Shalit on the *Today Show*

". . . Excellently organized for the casual traveler who is looking for a mix of recreation and cultural insight."
Washington Post

★ ★ ★ ★ ★ (5-star rating) "Crisply written and remarkably personable. Cleverly organized so you can pluck out the minutest fact in a moment. Satisfyingly thorough."
Réalités

"The information they offer is up-to-date, crisply presented but far from exhaustive, the judgments knowledgeable but not opinionated."   *New York Times*

"The individual volumes are compact, the prose succinct, and the coverage up-to-date and knowledgeable . . . The format is portable and the index admirably detailed."
John Barkham Syndicate

". . . An abundance of excellent directions, diversions, and facts, including perspectives and getting-ready-to-go advice — succinct, detailed, and well organized in an easy-to-follow style."   *Los Angeles Times*

"They contain an amount of information that is truly staggering, besides being surprisingly current."
Detroit News

"These guides address themselves to the needs of the modern traveler demanding precise, qualitative information . . . Upbeat, slick, and well put together."
Dallas Morning News

". . . Attractive to look at, refreshingly easy to read, and generously packed with information."   *Miami Herald*

"These guides are as good as any published, and much better than most."   *Louisville* (Kentucky) *Times*

Stephen Birnbaum Travel Guides

Acapulco
Bahamas, Turks & Caicos
Barcelona
Bermuda
Boston
Canada
Cancun, Cozumel, and Isla Mujeres
Caribbean
Chicago
Disneyland
Eastern Europe
Europe
Europe for Business Travelers
Florence
France
Great Britain
Hawaii
Ireland
Italy
Ixtapa & Zihuatanejo
London
Los Angeles
Mexico
Miami & Ft. Lauderdale
New York
Paris
Portugal
Rome
San Francisco
South America
Spain
United States
USA for Business Travelers
Venice
Walt Disney World
Western Europe

CONTRIBUTING EDITORS

Judith Harris Ajello, Duncan Anderson, Carmen Anthony, Kathy Arnold, Melvin Benarde, Gunnar Berj, Patricia Bjaaland, Virginia Blackert, Barbara Bowers, Paolo Braghieri, Mark Brayne, John Buskin, Ron Butler, Count Jacob Coudenhove-Kalergi, Ann Campbell-Lord, Linda Carreaga, Rik Cate, Kevin Causey, Paul Century, Stacey Chanin, Vinod Chhabra, Peter Collis, Roger Collis, Charles Cupic, Karen Cure, Stephanie Curtis, Roman Czajkowsky, Jeff Davidson, Linda Davidson, Martha de la Cal, Claire Devener, Thomas S. Dyman, Bjorn Edlund, Bonnie Edwards, Donna Evleth, Jackie Fierman, Brenda Fine, Ted Folke, Joan Gannij, Fradley Garner, Lois Gelatt, Norman Gelb, Jerry Gerber, Andrew Gillman, Mireille Giuliano, Agnes Gottlieb, Do Graff, Patricia Graves, Petar Hadji-Ristic, Jessica Harris, Elizabeth Healy, Margaret Henderso Jack Herbert, Marilyn Bruno Herrera, Ritva Hildebrandt, Brian Hill, Connie Hill, Elva Horva n, David Howley, Julian Isherwood, Bruce Johnston, Jill Jolliffe, Mark Kalish, Anne Kalosh, L th, F. Kauffmann, Virginia Kelley, Alexander Kushnir, André Leduc, Richard Lee, Howell Llew eslie Theodora Lurie, Sirrka Makelainen, Thomas C. Marinelli, Carole Martin, J. P. MacBean, V ellyn, McCune, Jan McGirk, Erica Meltzer, Diane Melville, John Meyer, Anne Millman, Tan rginia Mitchell, Jack Monet, Cara Morris, Martina Norelli, Ottar Odland, Carol Offen, Pat Pat ara K. E. Pedersen, Clare Pedrick, Samuel Perkins, Susan Pierres, Fred Poe, Alemka Porob icof, A. Potok, John Preston, Patricia Tunison Preston, Colin Pringle, Carol Reed, Allen c, Mark Margery Safir, Jerrold L. Schecter, Patricia Schultz, Patrick Schultz, George Semm Rokach, Sessoms, Frank Shiell, Janet Steinberg, Janet Stobbart, Phyllis Stoller, Donald Stroetzer, Hella Thorstad, Nancy Patton Van Zant, Betty Vaughn, Florence Vidal, Paul Wade, Richard Wel, Bruce Claudia Weber, Dennis Weber, David Wickers, Mark Williams, Jennifer Wright, Derri albleigh, Eleni Ziogas, Sonya Zalubowski, Emilia Zino   ck Young,

DIVERSIONS EDITORS
Jeff Davidson, Linda Davidson

SYMBOLS   MAPS
Gloria McKeown   General Cartography Inc., B. Andrew Mudr
                        Folio Graphics Co. Inc.   k,

A Stephen Birnbaum Travel Guide

Birnbaum's EUROPE 1992

Stephen Birnbaum
Alexandra Mayes Birnbaum
EDITORS

Lois Spritzer
EXECUTIVE EDITOR

Laura L. Brengelman
Managing Editor

Mary Callahan
Ann-Rebecca Laschever
Beth Schlau
Dana Margaret Schwartz
Associate Editors

Gene Gold
Assistant Editor

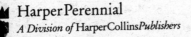

HarperPerennial
A Division of HarperCollins*Publishers*

FIRST EDITION

ISSN: 0749-2561 (Stephen Birnbaum Travel Guides)
ISSN: 0883-2498 (Europe)
ISBN: 0-06-278016-6 (pbk.)

92 93 94 95 96 CC/WP 10 9 8 7 6 5 4 3 2 1

Contents

GETTING READY TO GO

All the practical travel data you need to plan your vacation down to the final detail.

When and How to Go

Preparing

On the Road

FACTS IN BRIEF

A compilation of pertinent tourist information such as entry requirements and customs, sports, language, currency, clothing requirements, and more for 31 European countries.

THE CITIES

Thorough, qualitative guides to each of the 35 cities most often visited by vacationers and businesspeople. Each section, a comprehensive report of the city's most appealing attractions and amenities, is designed to be used on the spot. Directions and recommendations are immediately accessible because each guide is presented in a consistent form.

DIVERSIONS

A selective guide to 21 active and cerebral vacations including the places to pursue them where your quality of experience is likely to be highest.

DIRECTIONS

Europe's most spectacular routes and roads, most arresting natural wonders, most magnificent châteaux and castles, all organized into over 100 specific driving tours.

A Word from the Editor

There is no record of the specific guidebook that Hannibal and his Carthaginian hordes used to chart the route for their elephant trek through the Alps, but you can be sure that they had the help of at least a rudimentary work describing the basics of European geography. For all we know, it may even have included notes on a reliable inn, where the grog was always warm and spicy. Indeed, guides to Europe have existed literally for centuries, so a traveler might logically ask why another one is necessary amid this plenty.

Our answer is that the nature of European travel — and even of the travelers who now routinely make the trip — has changed dramatically of late. For the past 2,000 years or so, travel on the European continent was an extremely elaborate undertaking, one that required extensive advance planning. Even as recently as the late 1950s, a person who had actually been to Europe could dine out on his or her experiences for years, since such adventures were quite extraordinary and usually the province of the privileged alone.

With the advent of jet air travel in the late 1950s, however, and of increased-capacity, wide-body aircraft during the 1960s, travel to and through Europe became extremely common. In fact, in more than 2 decades of nearly unending inflation, airfares may be the only commodity in the world that have actually gone down in price. And as a result, international travel is now well within the budgets of mere mortals.

Attitudes as well as costs have also changed significantly in the last couple of decades. Beginning with the so-called flower children of the 1960s, international travel lost much of its aura of mystery. Whereas their parents might have been happy with just a superficial sampling of Europe — a 14-countries-in-14-days tour, for example — these young people simply picked up and settled in various parts of Europe for an indefinite stay. While living as inexpensively as possible, they adapted to the local lifestyle, and generally immersed themselves in things European.

Thus began an explosion of travel to and through Europe. And over the years, the development of inexpensive charter flights and packages fueled and sharpened the new American interest in and appetite for more extensive exploration of the Continent.

Now, in the 1990s, those same flower children who were in the forefront of the modern travel revolution have undeniably aged. While it may be impolite to point out that they are probably well into their untrustworthy thirties and forties, their original zeal for travel remains undiminished. For them, it's hardly news that the way to get to Switzerland is to head for France, keep on going, and then wait for snow-capped mountains to appear. Such experienced and knowledgeable travelers have decided precisely where they want to go and are more often searching for ideas and insights to expand their already sophisticated travel consciousness. And — reverting to former youthful instincts and habits — they are after a deeper understanding and fuller assimilation of the European milieu. Typically, they visit single countries (or even cities) several times, and may actually do so more than once in a single year. The generation that is currently succeeding this pioneering band also has accepted travel as one of life's givens, and serenely sets off to visit any part of the globe without hesitation.

It is important to note that the European landscape they are likely to encounter has never been more chaotic — or more intriguing and irresistible. Eastern Europe bears virtually no resemblance to that once stolid, stable bloc of nations that so recently presented such a foreboding mien, and the fierce economic cooperation currently being forged in Western Europe is only slightly less revolutionary. These are turbulent times — and wonderfully exciting ones — in the Old World, but the pace of change is so swift that an unprepared sojourner easily can feel out of step and ill at ease.

That's why any 1992 European guidebook worth its price must keep pace with and answer the real needs of today's travelers. That's also why we've tried to create a guide that's specifically organized, written, and edited for today's more demanding modern audience, travelers who need to know how social and political changes have altered local moods and for whom qualitative information is infinitely more desirable than mere quantities of unappraised data. We think that this book — and the other guides in our series — represent a new generation of travel guides, ones that are especially responsive to modern needs and interests.

For years, dating back as far as Herr Baedeker, travel guides have tended to be encyclopedic, seemingly much more concerned with demonstrating expertise in geography and history than with a real analysis of the sorts of things that actually concern a typical modern tourist. But today, when it is hardly necessary to tell a traveler where London is (in many cases, the traveler has been there nearly as often as the guidebook editors), it becomes the responsibility of those editors to provide new perspectives and to suggest new directions in order to make the guide genuinely valuable.

That's exactly what we've tried to do in this series. I think you'll notice a different, more contemporary tone to the text, as well as an organization and focus that are distinctive and more functional. And even a random reading of what follows will demonstrate a substantial departure from the standard guidebook orientation, for we've not only attempted to provide information of a more compelling sort, but we also have tried to present the data in a format that makes it particularly accessible.

Needless to say, it's difficult to decide just what to include in a guidebook of this size — and what to omit. Early on, we realized that giving up the encyclopedic approach precluded our listing every single route and restaurant, a realization that helped define our overall editorial focus. Similarly, when we discussed the possibility of presenting certain information in other than strict geographic order, we found that the new format enabled us to arrange data in a way we feel best answers the questions travelers typically ask.

Large numbers of specific questions have provided the real editorial skeleton for this book. The volume of mail I regularly receive emphasizes that modern travelers want very precise information, so we've tried to organize our material in the most responsive way possible. Readers who want to dine in the best restaurants in Paris or lie on the best beach along the Côte d'Azur will have no trouble extracting that data from this guide.

Travel guides are, understandably, reflections of personal taste, and putting one's name on a title page obviously puts one's preferences on the line. But I think I ought to amplify just what "personal" means. I don't believe in the sort of personal guidebook that's a palpable misrepresentation on its face. It is, for example, hardly possible for any single travel writer to visit thousands of restaurants (and nearly as many hotels) in any given year and provide accurate appraisals of each. And even if it *were* physically possible for one human being to survive such an itinerary, it would of necessity have to be done at a dead sprint, and the perceptions derived therefrom would probably be less valid than those of any other intelligent individual visiting the same establishments. It is, therefore, impossible (especially in a large, annually revised guidebook *series* such as we offer) to have only one person provide all the data on the entire world.

I also happen to think that such individual orientation is of substantially less value to readers. Visiting a single hotel for just one night or eating one hasty meal in a random restaurant hardly equips anyone to provide appraisals that are of more than passing interest. No amount of doggedly alliterative or oppressively onomatopoeic text can camouflage a technique that is essentially specious. We have, therefore, chosen what I like to describe as the "thee and me" approach to restaurant and hotel evaluation and, to a somewhat more limited degree, to the sites and sights we have included in the other sections of our text. What this really reflects is personal sampling tempered by intelligent counsel from informed local sources, and these additional friends-of-the-editor are almost always residents of the city and/or area about which they are consulted.

Despite the presence of several editors, writers, researchers, and local contributors, very precise editing and tailoring keep our text fiercely subjective. So what follows is the gospel according to the Birnbaums, and represents as much of our own taste and instincts as we can manage. It is probable, therefore, that if you like your cities stylish and your mountainsides uncrowded, prefer small hotels with personality to huge high-rise anonymities, and recognize chocolate as the real reason for remaining alive, we're likely to have a long and meaningful relationship. Readers with dissimilar tastes may be less enraptured.

I also should point out something about the person to whom this guidebook is directed. Above all, he or she is a "visitor." This means that such elements as restaurants have been specifically picked to provide the visitor with a representative, enlightening, stimulating, and above all pleasant experience. Since so many extraneous considerations can affect the reception and service accorded a regular restaurant patron, our choices can in no way be construed as an exhaustive guide to resident dining. We think we've listed all the best places, in various price ranges, but they were chosen with a visitor's enjoyment in mind.

Other evidence of how we've tried to tailor our text to reflect modern travel habits is most apparent in the section we call DIVERSIONS. Where once it was common for travelers to spend a European visit imprisoned by a rigid, cathedral- and museum-seeking itinerary, the emphasis today is more on pursuing some athletic enterprise or special interest while seeing the surrounding countryside. So we've organized every activity we could reasonably evaluate and organized the material in a way that is especially accessible to activists of either athletic or cerebral bent. It is no longer necessary, therefore, to wade through a pound or two of superfluous prose just to find the very best crafts shops or the quaintest country inn within a reasonable distance of your destination.

If there is a single thing that best characterizes the revolution in and evolution of current travel habits, it is that most travelers now consider travel a right rather than a privilege. No longer is a trip to the far corners of the country — or to Europe or the Orient — necessarily a once-in-a-lifetime thing; nor is the idea of visiting exotic, faraway places in the least worrisome. Travel today translates as the enthusiastic desire to sample all of the world's opportunities, to find that elusive quality of experience that is not only enriching but comfortable. For that reason, we've tried to make what follows not only helpful and enlightening, but the sort of welcome companion of which every traveler dreams.

Finally, I also should point out that every good travel guide is a living enterprise; that is, no part of this text is carved in stone. In our annual revisions, we refine, expand, and further hone all our material to serve your travel needs better. To this end, no contribution is of greater value to us than your personal reaction to what we have written, as well as information reflecting your own experiences while using the book. We earnestly and enthusiastically solicit your comments about this guide *and* your opinions and perceptions about places you have recently visited. In this way, we will be able to provide the most current information — including the actual experiences of recent travelers — and to make those experiences more readily available to others. Please write to us at 60 E. 42nd St., New York, NY 10165.

We sincerely hope to hear from you.

STEPHEN BIRNBAUM

How to Use This Guide

A great deal of care has gone into the organization of this guide-book, and we believe it represents a real breakthrough in the presentation of travel material. Our aim is to create a new, more modern generation of travel books and to make this guide the most useful and practical travel tool available today.

Our text is divided into five basic sections, in order to present information in the best way on every possible aspect of a European trip. This organization itself should alert you to the vast and varied opportunities available on this continent, as well as indicate all the specific data necessary to plan a successful visit. You won't find much of the conventional "swaying palms and shimmering sand" text here; we've chosen instead to deliver more useful and practical information. Prospective European itineraries tend to speak for themselves, and with so many diverse travel opportunities, we feel our main job is to highlight what's where and to provide basic information — how, when, where, how much, and what's best — to assist you in making the most intelligent choices possible.

Here is a brief summary of the five basic sections and what you can expect to find in each. We believe that you will find both your travel planning and en route enjoyment enhanced by having this book at your side.

GETTING READY TO GO

This mini-encyclopedia of practical travel facts is a sort of know-it-all companion with all the precise information necessary to create a successful journey to and through Europe. There are entries on more than 2 dozen separate topics, including how to get where you're going, what preparations to make before leaving, what to expect in the different countries of Europe, what your trip is likely to cost, and how to avoid prospective problems. The individual entries are specific, realistic, and, where appropriate, cost-oriented.

We expect you to use this section most in the course of planning your trip, for its ideas and suggestions are intended to simplify this often confusing period. Entries are intentionally concise, in an effort to get to the meat of the matter with the least extraneous prose. These entries are augmented by extensive lists of specific sources from which to obtain even more specialized data, plus some suggestions for obtaining travel information on your own.

FACTS IN BRIEF

Here is a compilation of pertinent tourist information, such as entry and customs requirements, languages, currencies, and clothing and climate data on 31 European countries. This section provides easy and immediate access to crucial information to be used at the planning stage as well as on the road.

THE CITIES

Individual reports are presented on the 35 cities most visited by travelers, prepared with the aid of researchers, contributors, professional journalists, and other experts on the spot. Although useful at the planning stage, THE CITIES is really designed to be taken along and used on the spot. Each report offers a short-stay guide within a consistent format: an essay introduces the city as a contemporary place to live and visit; *At-a-Glance* material is actually a site-by-site survey of the most important, interesting, and sometimes most eclectic sights to see and things to do; *Sources and Resources* is a concise listing of pertinent tourism information, meant to answer myriad potentially pressing questions as they arise — from simple things such as the address of the local tourist office, how to get around, which sightseeing tours to take, and when special events occur to something more difficult like where to find the best nightspot or hail a taxi, which are the chic places to shop, and where the best skiing, golf, tennis, fishing, and swimming are to be found. *Best in Town* lists our collection of cost-and-quality choices of the best places to eat and sleep on a variety of budgets.

DIVERSIONS

This section is designed to help travelers find the best places in which to pursue a wide range of physical and cerebral activities, without having to wade through endless pages of unrelated text. This very selective guide lists the broadest possible range of activities, including all the best places to pursue them.

We start with a list of special places to stay and eat, and move to activities that require some perspiration — sports preferences and other rigorous pursuits — and go on to report on a number of more cerebral and spiritual vacation opportunities. In every case, our suggestion of a particular location — and often our recommendation of a specific resort — is intended to guide you to that special place where the quality of experience is likely to be the highest. Whether you seek golf courses or tennis courts, want to go fishing or bicycling, or are searching for romantic château hotels or inspiring cooking schools, each category is the equivalent of a comprehensive checklist of the absolute best in Europe.

DIRECTIONS

Here is a series of more than 100 European itineraries, from the greenest counties of Ireland to the most sunlit Greek islands, covering 31 European countries — both East and West. These itineraries follow Europe's most beautiful routes and roads, past its most spectacular natural wonders, through its most historic cities and countryside. DIRECTIONS is the only section of this book that is organized geographically, and its itineraries cover the touring highlights from Great Britain and Ireland to Czechoslovakia and Hungary in short, independent journeys of 1 to 3 days' duration. Itineraries can be connected for longer trips, or used individually for short, intensive explorations.

Each entry includes a guide to sightseeing highlights; a qualitative guide to accommodations and food along the road (small inns, pensions, *paradores, pousadas,* castle hotels, hospitable farms, country hotels, campgrounds, and off-the-main-road discoveries); and suggestions for activities.

Although each of the book's sections has a distinct format and a special function, they have all been designed to be used together to provide a complete inventory of travel information. To use this book to full advantage, take a few minutes to read the table of contents and random entries in each section to get a firsthand feel of how it all fits together.

Pick and choose needed information. Assume, for example, that you have always wanted to take that typically British vacation, a walking tour through rural England, but you never really knew how to organize it or where to go. Turn first to the hiking section of GETTING READY TO GO, as well as the chapters on planning a trip and accommodations in Europe. These short, informative entries provide plenty of practical information. For specific information on entering and getting around Britain, climate and clothes, shopping, currency, and the like, see FACTS IN BRIEF. But where to go? Turn next to *Great Britain,* DIRECTIONS. Perhaps you choose to walk the 100-odd-mile Cotswold Way. Your trip will almost certainly begin and end in London, and for a complete rundown on that remarkable city you should read the London chapter of THE CITIES. Finally, turn to DIVERSIONS to peruse the chapters on sports, hotels, antiques, and other activities in which you are interested to make sure you don't miss anything in the neighborhood.

In other words, the sections of this book are building blocks designed to help you put together the best possible trip. Use them selectively as a tool, a source of ideas, a reference work for accurate facts, and a guidebook to the best buys, the most exciting sights, the most pleasant accommodations, the tastiest foods — *the best travel experience* that you can possibly have.

GETTING READY TO GO

When and How to Go

What's Where

Europe is the world's second-smallest continent, encompassing a relatively spare 3.7 million square miles, but with a comparatively dense population of 773 million (an average of 209 people per square mile). It is shaped vaguely like a triangle, bounded by Arctic waters and the Atlantic Ocean on the west, the Mediterranean, Aegean, and Black seas to the south, and an eastern border that follows a somewhat imprecise line through the Soviet Union along the Caucasus Mountains, the Caspian Sea, and then north along the Ural Mountains.

Actually, Europe does not conform to the traditional geographical concept of a continent. It is not a self-contained land area surrounded on all sides by water. It is the western fifth of what is commonly known as Eurasia, the giant landmass that stretches from the Atlantic Ocean to the Japanese islands in the Pacific. In the course of its 3,000 years of recorded history, however, cultural, religious, political, and economic influences — along with a sometimes turbulent intermingling of ethnic groups — have defined Europe as an entity, no matter how diverse its parts or geography.

Its dominant influence in Western civilization is due to its location in the North Temperate Zone and the wealth and diversity of its natural resources. The Continent is divided into northern and southern sections by an immense mountain chain — really a series of mountains and valleys — that includes, west to east, the Pyrenees Mountains, the Rhône Valley, the French-Swiss-Austrian Alps, and the curving Carpathian Mountains, which in Romania recede toward Bucharest and the Black Sea. Below this mountainous demarcation line are countries with generally warmer climates and coasts on the southern seas; north of it are countries of highlands and plains with coasts on the northern seas that separate the main body of the Continent from Scandinavia.

Turmoil has never spared Europe, and this century has been as devastating as any. But time and time again, the resourcefulness of its people and the richness of its natural resources — which have led to successful farmers, miners, and industrial development — have helped it recuperate from the ravages of both natural and manmade disaster. And these same strengths gave birth to the amalgam of cultures that forged Western civilization and shaped the world. It easily could be argued that none of the past upheavals even approach the breadth of change that has enveloped Europe since the decade of the 1990s began, but that is just an added element in the mesmerizing European mosaic.

What follows is a short survey of the geography of Europe's nations, starting in the far north and moving roughly counterclockwise.

SCANDINAVIA

Scandinavia refers to that segment of northern Europe consisting of Denmark, Norway, and Sweden — which share close cultural and historical ties and all have at least titular monarchies — and often includes Iceland, a separate island northwest of mainland Europe, as well. Although Finland sometimes is grouped with the Scandinavian countries, and the Scandinavian Tourist Board in New York City represents Finland, it is not, strictly speaking, a Scandinavian country. It is included in this section because it, and bordering nations Norway and Sweden, are separated from central Europe by several straits that wind from the Atlantic Ocean into the North Sea and the Baltic Sea and adjacent gulfs. The northernmost parts of these countries stretch beyond the Arctic Circle, which also touches the northern edges of Iceland.

ICELAND: This North Atlantic island was settled by Norwegians 10 centuries ago, and its Norwegian character still is strong; today, Icelanders speak a language that is basically Old Norse. The 40,000-square-mile island lies east of Greenland, just touching the Arctic Circle; not surprisingly, fishing and the canning and export of seafood products are major industries. The population is sparse (only about 300,000), but has a nearly 100% literacy rate — the highest in the world. Summers are damp and cool; the winters are harsh, but made habitable by the tempering influence of the Gulf Stream. Features of particular interest to visitors are the natural hot springs flowing beneath the island's surface, providing an abundance of thermal heat and the opportunity to savor their soothing waters.

NORWAY: Scandinavia's northwesternmost country, bordering Sweden, Finland, and a tip of the Soviet Union, with a dramatic fjord-splintered Atlantic coast that is lined with sheer and awesome cliffs. The North Cape, the uppermost tip of the country, which reaches deep into the Arctic Circle, is a popular summer cruise destination. Most of the northern region is mountainous, and a quarter of the country is heavily forested. Most of the country's 4.2 million people live in the south, the majority in the coastal region extending from Bergen along the southern Atlantic coast to Oslo, the capital. Some 25,000 Laplanders live in the far north. One of Norway's most important resources is the sea, and the Atlantic Ocean supports much of the country's important fishing industry while the North Sea produces abundant oil. These same waters are warmed by the Gulf Stream, which moderates the coastal climate all year.

SWEDEN: Sweden lies between Norway — with which it shares the Scandinavian Peninsula — and Finland — which borders it on the north but otherwise is separated from it by the Baltic Sea. Sweden is one of the world's most prosperous countries, and its natural resources are highly visible: timberlands that cover half the country; mountains of ore along the Norwegian border; and vast northern glacial fields that melt during the summer and send water coursing through the country's carefully dammed rivers and lakes, providing an ample and reliable source of inexpensive power. Highly productive farms and most of the country's 8.5 million people live in the country's central and southern regions. Most visited is the historic triangle bounded by the coastal cities of Gothenburg on the west, Malmö, near the southern tip of the country, and Stockholm, the capital, on the Baltic Sea. Sweden is spattered with countless lakes, rivers, and waterways.

DENMARK: The smallest and most southerly of the Scandinavian countries covers a total area of 16,600 square miles, extending over several little islands off the coast of north-central Europe and most of the peninsula appropriately known as Jutland — since it actually juts into the straits leading from the North Sea to the Baltic Sea. Because Denmark is made up of flatlands with meager agricultural resources, its people traditionally have depended on trade and conquest for their livelihoods, undertakings made easier by the country's proximity to many of Europe's most important sea lanes. Today it is a highly industrial nation with a population of just over 5 million, famous for chinaware and fine furniture design. The capital, Copenhagen, is a worldwide attraction, known for its convivial and spirited atmosphere. Denmark's international possessions include the Faeroe Islands (lying midway between Scotland and Iceland) and Greenland.

FINLAND: Although Finland shares northern borders with both Norway and Sweden, it shares its longest border with the Soviet Union, and is culturally, linguistically, and even topographically distinct from the rest of Scandinavia. It covers a relatively flat area of 130,120 square miles. The northern Lapland region, within the Arctic Circle, is composed of treeless plains; the central region of the country is densely forested; and the coastal areas along its Baltic Sea gulfs are fertile and most populous. Unlike Norway, Denmark, or Sweden, it has no monarchy, and visitors will observe that the country's almost 5 million citizens take fierce pride in their democracy, perhaps because the country was dominated for centuries, first by Sweden and later by Russia, becoming a republic only after World War I. Major cities — Helsinki (the capital), Turku, Tampere — are highly modern, and Helsinki is a popular jumping-off point (notably by cruise ships) for shore excursions to St. Petersburg and other places in the Soviet Union.

GREAT BRITAIN AND IRELAND

UNITED KINGDOM: The islands that make up the United Kingdom — or the British Isles, as they once were called — lie in the North Atlantic immediately off the northwest coast of France, separated from the Continent by the English Channel, the Strait of Dover, and the North Sea. Dover, on the southwestern tip of England, and Calais, in the northwestern corner of France, are only 25 miles apart. Among the scattering of tiny islands nearby that belong to Great Britain are the Channel Islands, the Isle of Man, and the Orkneys, Hebrides, and Shetlands off the coast of Scotland.

England, Scotland, and Wales are the major entities, together with Northern Ireland (or Ulster), that officially make up the United Kingdom. The first three countries make up the island nearest the Continent — the largest island in Europe. Northern Ireland is in the northeastern part of the island immediately to the west, the rest of which belongs to the Republic of Ireland (or Eire). In total, the United Kingdom covers some 94,000 square miles and has a population of 57 million. Physically, England dominates, covering well over half the area that extends from the southern coast on the English Channel to Newcastle, at the edge of the Scottish Lowlands. Wales abuts England on the west, projecting into the St. George's Channel, which separates it from Ireland. Scotland forms the northern third of the island. The entire island is characterized by hilly terrain — as distinct from truly mountainous — although the celebrated Scottish Highlands occasionally rise 3,000 to 4,000 feet above sea level. The island has been able to draw upon its own resources for livestock breeding, mining, energy, and industry, with large oil reserves in the North Sea (shared with Norway). The climate is subject to prevailing southwesterly winds, which account for its frequently cloudy and damp — but essentially mild — weather all year. These generally inviting physical characteristics complement Great Britain's enormous historical, political, and cultural appeal, and continue to make it one of the most pleasant countries in the world to visit.

Northern Ireland primarily is an agricultural region with many lakes, although much of the land is actually volcanic. Otherwise, Northern Ireland's geographical and physical characteristics are similar to those of the Republic of Ireland. Belfast, the capital, is a fairly new city that boomed during the 19th century — it was dubbed "the Athens of the North" — and now is famed for its linen and shipbuilding industries.

IRISH REPUBLIC: The Republic of Ireland covers some 27,000 square miles, the lion's share of the island it shares with Northern Ireland; its population is 4 million. Highland outcroppings rise to 3,500 feet in places along the country's coasts, but most of the republic is characterized by fertile plains, scenic lakes, and bays, especially along its Atlantic coastline. The famed Shannon River in the southwest is longer than any river in Great Britain. Ireland essentially is an agricultural country, and the same damp, moist air that tempers Britain's climate is responsible for the renowned green associated with the country in song and legend. Gaelic is the official language, although English is the predominant spoken tongue. Dublin, the capital, is located centrally on the island's east coast, facing the Irish Sea and Wales.

THE BENELUX COUNTRIES

The Benelux countries, so named for the acronym formed by the first letters of BElgium, the NEtherlands, and LUXembourg, form a wedge of lowland terrain in the northwestern corner of continental Europe, between Germany and France and the waters of the North Sea. These three small countries all have constitutional monarchies and enjoy a high standard of living.

BELGIUM: Directly north of France, Belgium is heavily industrialized for a country of its modest size (11,781 square miles and just under 10 million people), but it probably is best known as one of Western Europe's major international business and economic centers. Brussels, the capital, is a beautiful city of medieval and Renaissance architecture, with a cosmopolitan atmosphere considerably enhanced by its being the administrative center of the European Economic Community (the EEC, or Common Market). Because of its geographic position, Belgium has been a battleground in more than its fair share of wars, and large numbers of Europeans and North Americans make pilgrimages to its cemeteries and former battlegrounds, which mark some of the most serious confrontations of World Wars I and II.

NETHERLANDS: Much of the Netherlands, or Holland, as it is more commonly known, actually is below sea level, protected from the ravages of the sea by dikes ringing the country's coast. Extending north from Belgium, with an irregular coastline that shelters numerous fishing villages, Holland has had to reclaim much land from the North Sea in order to gain needed farmland (it has an area of 16,041 square miles and a population of 15 million). Amsterdam, the capital, is one of the Continent's liveliest cities, with networks of canals lined by historically and architecturally distinctive homes and numerous museums housing works by Dutch masters and other great European artists.

LUXEMBOURG: Surrounded by Belgium, France, and Germany, Luxembourg is one of Europe's tiniest independent nations (999 square miles and almost 400,000 people) and one of its most fortunate. For not only is it a popular tourist destination, but it also makes a comfortable living from forests in the north and iron mines and prosperous farms in the south. The capital, also called Luxembourg, is a walled town built around a 10th-century castle. It is one of the few countries in the world officially known as a grand duchy — a territorial designation bestowed on it by France and dating from the early 19th century — although Luxembourg long since has been independent.

ATLANTIC EUROPE

France and Spain, two of the giants of Europe, have substantial coastlines on both the Atlantic Ocean and the Mediterranean Sea, and act as virtual dikes by separating those two very distinct bodies of water. Sharing Spain's Atlantic coast is Portugal, and thoroughly landlocked high in the Pyrenees Mountains between France and Spain is tiny Andorra. Another tiny country, Gibraltar, sits at the southwesternmost tip of the Iberian Peninsula, overlooking the straits that connect the Mediterranean to the Atlantic, guarding the entrance to Mediterranean Europe.

FRANCE: Its strategic position between the Atlantic and the Mediterranean has made France the historic crossroads of Europe, witnessing a constant traffic of goods and people. With an area of 211,208 square miles, it is the largest country in Western Europe, a land exceptionally varied and richly productive, with major mountain ranges in the south (the Pyrenees on the border with Spain, the Alps reaching from the Riviera to Switzerland) and a rich basin of farmland in the center. Its famed vineyards grow all around the country, but their grapes are only one item in what may be the most diverse range of agricultural products on the Continent. France has a population of more than 56.4 million people, more than 2 million of whom live in Paris, the capital.

ANDORRA: Sheep raising and tourism are the mainstays of this small country of 175 square miles (49,000 people) set high in the Pyrenees. The major community is Andorra la Vella. The altitude assures snow-capped mountains and chilly evenings year-round, though the days can be surprisingly warm, yet pleasant, during the summer months.

SPAIN: The second-largest country in Western Europe (194,883 square miles) covers the major portion of the Iberian Peninsula, the Continent's southwesternmost segment of land, and includes the Canary and Balearic islands. Spain shares borders with Andorra, France, Gibraltar, and Portugal — which occupies a long rectangle of land separating most of Spain's western border from the ocean. The Atlantic Ocean borders the country along the northwest and southwest; the entire eastern coast of the country faces the Mediterranean, and the southern Andalusian region is popular for its warm climate and for "sun and fun" resorts along the extensive coast. Much of the interior of the country consists of relatively arid, high valleys within ranges of mountains that offer limited areas of arable land. Spain has a total population of 39 million, and Madrid, at the very center of the country, is one of Europe's largest capitals.

PORTUGAL: This southwestern corner of continental Europe occupies a 35,553-square-mile segment of the Iberian Peninsula, bordered by Spain to the north and east and the Atlantic Ocean to the south and west. Portugal also includes the Azores and the Madeira islands. Much of the northern part of the country is mountainous, notably above the Tagus River, which bisects the country and flows into the Atlantic at Lisbon, the capital. Below the Tagus, Portugal is warm and more agricultural, particularly along the growing resort area of the Algarve, the province that lines the country's southern Atlantic coast. The country has a moist and moderate climate, which partly is responsible for the olives and port wine that are among its most famous products, and for the vivid blooms of its trees and plants. Its population is 12 million. In addition to Lisbon and the resort regions, the numerous fishing villages along the coast are popular and colorful tourist attractions.

GIBRALTAR: This 2.25-square-mile piece of land at the southern tip of Spain, creating the passage from the Atlantic into the Mediterranean, is best known for its much-photographed landmark, the Rock of Gibraltar. Now self-governing, it served primarily as a military fortress since 1713, when it became a British possession. Gibraltar is a free port.

MEDITERRANEAN EUROPE

The countries listed below — Monaco, Italy (and San Marino, the tiny country in north-central Italy), Malta, Yugoslavia, Albania, and Greece — all have extensive coasts on the Mediterranean or its tributary seas, the Tyrrhenian, Adriatic, Ionian, and Aegean.

MONACO: With an area of 468 acres, this tiny principality tucked into France's Riviera coast, close to the Italian border, is smaller than New York City's Central Park. From the late 19th century until World War II, it developed and sustained a reputation as a winter social center for royalty and wealthy families. Today, however, the visitor profile has a much more diverse social and economic base, although Monte Carlo — the district that encompasses the famed casinos and several elegant turn-of-the-century hotels — still caters to a chic, international clientele. Monaco's beautiful setting, over-looking the Mediterranean and rising sharply toward the Maritime Alps of France — which border Monaco on the north, east, and west — contributes to its popularity.

ITALY: Italy is the most central European nation of the Mediterranean, sharing its northern borders with France, Switzerland, Austria, and Yugoslavia. It is a boot-shaped peninsula, the second-longest in the world (after Baja California), and covers an area of 116,318 square miles. It is an essentially mountainous country, but several of the most historic port cities of the Western world sit along its coastline, including Genoa, Naples, and Venice. The capital, Rome, is midway down the peninsula, a few miles inland from the western coast, and encompasses Vatican City, a sovereign entity within its municipal boundaries. Except for traditional winter weather in the Alpine region of the north and whipping winds along the coasts in colder months, the climate is moderate to warm throughout the year. Its cities are among the world's most historic. Two major islands, Sicily (at the toe of the peninsula) and Sardinia (west of the mainland across the Tyrrhenian Sea), and the diminutive island of Elba are part of Italy. The country has a population of 57.7 million.

SAN MARINO: Figuratively, this smallest republic in the world (23 square miles and 23,000 people) could be papered over with the postage stamps that, along with tourism, represent its major industries. San Marino is an enclave within the Apennines, a few miles south of Rimini on Italy's Adriatic coast. The capital, also called San Marino, is the site of a church dating from the 10th century.

MALTA: This speck of an island country lies 60 miles south of Sicily, and actually is composed of three islands — the largest of which also is named Malta. It is flat and hot in summer, but its strategic site along the Mediterranean trade routes has subjected it to invading conquerors since the time of the Carthaginians. Its most recent occupants were the British, who maintained it as an important naval base. Malta became an independent republic in 1874. As a tourist destination, it is notable for remnants of fortifications and other structures built during the many centuries of foreign occupancy.

YUGOSLAVIA: The country's long Adriatic coast — and the sprinkling of beaches and islands along it — have made Yugoslavia (until recent ethnic and civil unrest) a prime vacation spot, equally popular with European and other international visitors. The coast stretches from Italy to Albania, and the country also borders Austria, Bulgaria, Greece, Hungary, and Romania. Yugoslavia covers a total area of 99,000 square miles. Though much of the country is hilly or mountainous and encompasses much farmland that is not especially productive, the northeastern region is flatter and has far richer soil. The coastal region is speckled with fishing villages and resorts. The Danube River runs through Belgrade, the capital, in the east-central part of the country. Comprised of six (at press time, contentious) republics, its population of almost 23 million includes people of many ethnic backgrounds, but Serbs predominate.

ALBANIA: Once the recluse among Balkan nations, this is a country of small villages and state farms that even fellow Eastern Europeans had found hard to visit. But for the first time in half a century, the ban on foreigners has at last been lifted. About the size of Maryland — 11,100 square miles, with an estimated population of 3 million — the country has a long Adriatic coast and lies in relation to Yugoslavia and Greece much as Portugal does to Spain. Westerners know it best as the most outspoken of the old Eastern European Communist bloc nations, the country that broke relations with the Soviet Union in 1961. As change has swept the rest of Eastern Europe, Albania has signified that it may be about to review its pervasive xenophobia. Still, Albania's post–World War II history is only the most recent warp in a historical tapestry that has been woven by a series of conquering and invading cultures. By AD 800, Albania was under the control of Bulgaria, and then, with the rest of the Balkan Peninsula, was swept into the Ottoman Turkish Empire from 1478 until 1912, when for a very brief period (until Italy invaded in 1939) it was first a republic and then a monarchy. At the time of this writing Albania was in the process of establishing formal relationships with the West — including the US. Although we do not include Albania in this guide, it is covered in Birnbaum's *Eastern Europe 1992.*

GREECE: This ancient nation is the land terminus of southeastern Europe. Its mountainous mainland borders Albania, Yugoslavia, Bulgaria, and the small continental portion of Turkey; the seas that surround the country on three sides are the setting for the nation's more than 450 historically celebrated islands, of which the largest and most famous are Crete and Rhodes. Including all its islands, Greece has a total land area of 50,960 square miles and a population of 10 million. The overall climate is moderate, which, as in most coastal Mediterranean spots, gives the country a longer than average tourist season. Once outside Athens, the capital, visitors will see that this is not a very prosperous country, since most of the land does not lend itself to agriculture, although half the working population is engaged in some aspect of farming. Shipping, shipbuilding, and tourism are the most lucrative industries in Greece.

CENTRAL EUROPE

In defining central Europe, we throw our net as wide as possible to include all those continental European countries east of France and west of the Soviet Union that do not have coasts on the Mediterranean. Included are Germany and Poland; the landlocked nations of Switzerland, Liechtenstein, Austria, Hungary, and Czechoslovakia; and the Balkan countries of Romania and Bulgaria, both with eastern coastlines on the inland Black Sea. Among these nations, many of which didn't exist as distinct political entities before the First World War, Germany, Poland, Romania, Bulgaria, Hungary, and Czechoslovakia have gone through wrenching changes in just the last few years. It still is not entirely clear how these former Warsaw Pact members will be reconstituted as they move from totalitarian Communist domination to somewhat less oppressive democratic and socialist administration, so what follows describes the state of these countries as we went to press.

GERMANY: The formal unification of East and West Germany took place in October 1990. The area that was known as West Germany (created by the merging of the areas administered by the Americans, British, and French after World War II) extended south from the North Sea and Denmark into the center of the Continent, covering a total area of 96,000 square miles, and bordered six other Western European nations — the Netherlands, Belgium, Luxembourg, France, Switzerland, and Austria — as well as what was East Germany and Czechoslovakia. The most populous country of Europe (61.5 million) outside the Soviet Union, it also is one of the richest, thanks to heavy industrialization, with particular concentration in the Ruhr Valley near the border with the Netherlands and Belgium. Much of the rest of the northern region, however, is a plain devoted to agriculture, and the south of the country is touched by the Bavarian Alps and other mountains in that long chain that bisects the Continent. Southern Germany, a land of considerable charm and beauty, escaped the fate of many of Germany's modern cities, most of which were rebuilt after heavy damage during World War II. Berlin, once again the German capital, sits in the country's northeastern area. The reunified nation is essentially a plains area, and the now combined East and West segments form the most industrially productive country in central Europe.

POLAND: This north-central European state is characterized by relatively even terrain that extends across the northern part of the Continent, although the country's southern border rises into the Carpathian Mountains, which separate it from Czechoslovakia. Poland, bounded by Germany on the west, the Soviet Union and Lithuania on the east, and the Baltic Sea on the north, covers an area of 120,000 square miles, with almost 38 million people. It has firm ethnic and historic roots in central Europe dating from the 9th century, although it went through periods in the 18th century when it virtually disappeared after being divided among the Austrian, Prussian, and Russian empires. The current government, inspired by the Solidarity labor union, succeeds the former Communist regime, and Poland strives to impose a market economy on the old socialist imperatives. Warsaw, its capital, has survived three attempts to annihilate it, first by the Swedes and the Russians, then the French, and more recently the Nazis. Since World War II, the city has been extensively rebuilt.

CZECHOSLOVAKIA: It's hard not to read something of the labyrinthian history of central Europe in Czechoslovakia, which is surrounded by Poland, Austria, Hungary, the Soviet Union, and Germany. The centuries of wars that carved its shape and decided its borders are the history of Europe. Down its center run the Carpathian Mountains; in the west is its capital, Prague, surrounded by good farm country and lined by mineral-rich mountains; in the east are the Tatra Mountains, a continuation of the Carpathian chain. The country covers a total of 49,000 square miles and has a population of 15.5 million. As a republic, Czechoslovakia is relatively young, having been created at the end of World War I from provinces of the former Austro-Hungarian Empire. These provinces — Bohemia, Moravia, and Slovakia (reading from west to east) — still battle for identity, as does the entire nation as it seeks to stabilize its orientation after decades of repressive rule.

SWITZERLAND: This country aptly is referred to as the crest of Europe, with mountain peaks as high as 15,000 feet above sea level. Surrounded by Italy on the south, France on the west, Germany on the north, and Liechtenstein and Austria on the east, Switzerland is completely landlocked, though its glaciers feed the major rivers of the Continent that flow to the North, Baltic, and Mediterranean seas. Switzerland covers an area of 16,000 square miles. Its deep and fertile valleys are not only scenic, but a source of the nation's important dairy products. The capital, Bern, is in the north-central part of the country. Its 6.5 million people are for the most part of German, French, and Italian descent, and all three languages are spoken in the country, though the dominant language is Swiss-German, which is spoken by 65% of the natives. Needless to say, most citizens are at least bilingual; English is widely spoken as well. In the eastern canton of Grisons, the Latin language of Romansh still is spoken.

LIECHTENSTEIN: Nestled at the eastern border of Switzerland along the Rhine River, Liechtenstein is one of the several small (62 square miles; about 29,000 people) principalities of Western Europe that fascinate visitors with their charm and beauty. Despite its tiny size and essentially Alpine topography, it has some farming, though tourism contributes a far greater amount to the national economy. Liechtenstein's principal business, however, is business itself; a carefully maintained tax haven, it attracts a variety of banking and corporate operations to Vaduz, its capital. Today, its diplomatic and communications services are provided by Switzerland, but it has a long and proud history that goes back to the 14th century.

AUSTRIA: Like Switzerland, its western neighbor, Austria is totally surrounded by mountains, but the valleys created by its three Alpine ranges extend the length of the country (its total area is 32,375 square miles). Also like Switzerland, Austria is a major ski resort center and has exceptional scenery, both of which give it year-round tourist appeal. Austria's 7.5 million people are predominantly German, and German is the official language, though very small minorities in the country speak Slovenian, Croatian, and Hungarian. This is an accurate reflection of history, as well as contemporary geography, for Germany is the country's northwestern neighbor, and it also has borders with Yugoslavia and Hungary, as well as with Czechoslovakia, Italy, and Liechtenstein. In many ways, Austria is at the center of the complex history of central Europe; from Vienna, its capital, it served as the center of power of the Hapsburgs for more than 600 years.

HUNGARY: One of several fully landlocked nations of central Europe, Hungary lies below southeastern Czechoslovakia and also borders, from west to east, Austria, Yugoslavia, Romania, and a tip of the Soviet Union. Most of Hungary's 36,000 square miles are highly productive agricultural plains, although industry has absorbed most of the working population (total population is about 10.6 million) since the end of World War II. Hungarians are the product of a mixture of races, notably those ethnic groups from what is now the south-central region of the Soviet Union and Turkey who pushed northwest nearly 2,000 years ago. Budapest, the capital, straddles the Danube and is one of Europe's most historic and romantic cities.

ROMANIA: Legendary mountain ranges — the Transylvanian Alps and Carpathians — forming an arc that divides west and east, are the key physical features of this country. Most of Romania's northern border is along the Ukrainian district of the Soviet Union; the Black Sea is to the east, Bulgaria to the south, and Yugoslavia and Hungary to the west. In total, the country covers 91,700 square miles. Visitors will see pronounced Hungarian and German influences among its 23 million people, although the country's history goes back to the time of the Romans. Bucharest, the capital, is a major attraction for foreign visitors, as well as the local populace, and the Black Sea resort city of Constanta draws visitors from throughout the eastern part of the Continent.

BULGARIA: Like Romania, its northern neighbor, Bulgaria borders the Black Sea on the east and physically is bisected by a mountain range, the Balkans, which runs east to west through the center of the country. Its other borders are with Turkey, Greece, and Yugoslavia. Covering 43,000 square miles, it has a population of just under 9 million. Primarily a Slavic country, nearly 1,000 years ago it dominated the region from the Black Sea west to the Adriatic. The two world wars in this century depleted many of its resources. Sofia is its capital.

EURASIA

SOVIET UNION (AND THE BALTIC STATES): The rapidly altering borders of the Soviet Union cover a land area larger than all of the rest of Europe, about 8.65 million square miles — the Baltic states represent less than a million square miles — and its European section alone is just about half of Europe's total area. The total population is over 286 million. Its western boundary extends along the length of the Continent, from the Barents Sea in the north, where it borders the northeastern tip of Norway and Finland, along the Baltic Sea (where Estonia, Latvia, and Lithuania are situated), Poland, Czechoslovakia, Hungary, and Romania to the Black Sea, the Caucasus, and the Caspian Sea. The Ural Mountains traditionally are considered the dividing line between the European and the eastern (Asian) republics that make up the current Union. As might be expected for a landmass of this size, the terrain is exceptionally diverse. It ranges from glacial fields within the Arctic Circle to huge forests, a great central plain (incorporating the famed Kirghiz Steppe, a fertile agricultural area), and subtropical pockets along certain coastal areas of the Black and Caspian seas. The Caspian Sea actually is the world's largest landlocked lake. Unlike the rest of Europe, however, the climate of Soviet Europe tends to be more humid and cold, lacking the warmth from the Gulf Stream. The Dnieper River, which empties into the Black Sea, and the Volga River, which is the longest in Europe and extends from the center of the country to the Caspian Sea, are the major waterways of the European part of the Soviet Union. Moscow, the capital (with a population of 8 million), and St. Petersburg, the former capital (at the easternmost corner of the Baltic Sea), are the major cities.

When to Go

There really isn't a "best" time to visit Europe. For North Americans, as well as Europeans, the period from mid-May to mid-September has long been — and remains — the peak travel period, traditionally the most popular vacation time. It is important to emphasize that Europe is hardly a single-season destination; more and more travelers who have a choice are enjoying the substantial advantages of off-season travel. Though some of the lesser tourist attractions may have shorter hours or close during the off-season — roughly late September through early May — the major sites remain open and tend to be less crowded with tourists — as are many countries in general. During the off-season, people relax and European life proceeds at a more leisurely pace, and a lively social and cultural calendar flourishes. What's more, travel generally is less expensive.

For some, the most convincing argument in favor of off-season travel is the economic one. Getting there and staying there is more affordable during less popular travel periods, as airfares, hotel rooms, and car rental rates go down and less expensive package tours become available; the independent traveler can go farther on less, too. Europe is not like the Caribbean, where high season and low season are precisely defined and rates drop automatically on a particular date. But many European hotels reduce rates during the off-season, and at certain popular destinations — such as seaside resorts — savings can be as much as 30% to 35%. Although smaller guesthouses, inns, and other establishments in some areas may close during the off-season in response to reduced demand, there still are plenty of alternatives, and, in cities, cut-rate "mini-break" packages — for stays of more than 1 night, especially over a weekend (when business travelers traditionally go home) — are more common.

A definite bonus to visiting during the off-season is that even the most basic services are performed more efficiently. In theory, off-season service is identical to that offered during high season, but the fact is that the absence of demanding crowds inevitably begets much more thoughtful and personal attention. The very same staff that barely can manage to get fresh towels onto the racks during the height of the summer season has the time to chat pleasantly in the spring or fall. And it is not only hotel service that benefits from the absence of the high-season mobs.

There are, however, some notable exceptions to this rule. The general tourism off-season is high season for skiers in the Alps and elsewhere in Europe, meaning higher prices and crowds everywhere there is snow. Most major cities in Europe hold at least one international business or industrial show each year (the *Frankfurt Book Fair* each fall is one example, as are the annual fall and spring fashion shows in Paris and Milan). Particularly in the larger cities, such major trade shows or conferences held at the time of your visit are sure to affect the availability not only of discounts, but even of a place to stay. In countries with harvest festivals (mostly wine-producing countries like France, Germany, Italy, and Spain), off-season autumn discounts also may not exist.

It should be noted that the months immediately before and after the peak summer months — what the travel industry refers to as the shoulder season — often are sought out because they offer fair weather and somewhat smaller crowds. But be aware that very near high-season prices can prevail during these periods, notably in certain popular areas of the Mediterranean — the Greek Islands, several of the more "social" communities of the French Riviera, Spain's Costa del Sol, and Portugal's Algarve.

In short, Europe's vacation appeal, like many other popular destinations, has become multi-seasonal. But it's a big continent, and the noted exceptions notwithstanding, most travel destinations are decidedly less trafficked and less expensive during the winter.

CLIMATE: Here is a brief breakdown of climatic variations by month and/or season at popular European travel destinations. (*Please note that although temperatures usually are recorded on the Celsius scale in Europe, for purposes of clarity we use the more familiar Fahrenheit scale.*)

January, February, March – It's prime ski season, and the central European Alps are the place to be both in terms of challenge and social activity (slopes in Spain, Eastern Europe, and Scandinavia are good destinations for less chic — and less expensive — skiing). During the coldest months, try the southern side of the Alps, which is warmer. Late March and even April skiing can be surprisingly good in the traditional ski centers, which are likely to be less crowded after *Easter* and offer better service — and perhaps even lower prices.

April – Early travelers, particularly Scandinavians on charter flights, head for the Mediterranean, notably Spain's Costa del Sol and the Greek Islands. Tulips, hyacinths, and daffodils are blooming in Holland — until about mid-May. By the way, the guys who wrote "April in Paris" clearly never set foot in the City of Light during damp, dismal, dreary April.

May – The month can be nippy or warm, depending on where you are. If the season isn't too windy or damp, the English countryside can be an attractive destination for a week's drive. Other comfortable spring destinations include Greece, Hungary, and Italy.

June – Most of the Continent has warmed into the 70s F, and it is the first full month of Europe's peak season. Take your pick of any place from the Greek Islands (low 80s F) to Copenhagen (upper 60s F), and don't overlook Iceland, the islands in the lower Baltic Sea, and the Scandinavian capitals, which are fairly well protected from the North Atlantic winds.

AVERAGE TEMPERATURES (in °F)

	January	*April*	*July*	*October*
Albania	35–55	45–65	60–90	50–75
Andorra	40–55	50–70	70–90	45–65
Austria	25–35	40–55	60–75	40–55
Belgium	30–40	40–60	55–75	45–60
Bulgaria	30–45	45–60	65–85	50–70
Czechoslovakia	20–35	40–60	55–80	40–60
Denmark	25–35	35–50	55–70	45–55
Finland	15–30	30–45	55–70	35–50
France	30–45	45–60	60–80	45–60
Germany	25–40	40–60	60–80	45–60
Gibraltar	40–55	50–70	70–90	45–65
Great Britain	35–45	40–60	50–70	45–60
Greece	40–55	50–70	70–90	45–65
Hungary	20–35	50–70	60–80	35–50
Iceland	30–35	35–45	50–60	35–45
Ireland	35–50	40–60	50–70	40–60
Italy	40–50	50–65	65–80	55–70
Liechtenstein	35–45	40–60	55–75	40–55
Luxembourg	30–40	40–60	55–75	45–55
Malta	50–60	55–70	70–85	65–75
Monaco	45–55	55–60	70–80	60–70
Netherlands	30–40	45–55	60–70	50–60
Norway	20–30	35–50	55–70	35–50
Poland	25–35	35–55	55–75	40–55
Portugal	40–55	35–45	70–90	45–65
Romania	20–35	40–65	60–80	45–65
San Marino	40–50	50–65	65–80	55–70
Soviet Union	below 0	25–50	50–70	20–40
Sweden	20–30	35–45	60–70	40–50
Switzerland	35–45	40–60	55–75	40–55
Yugoslavia	25–35	45–65	60–80	45–65

July and August – It's hot in the Mediterranean, but the best time to visit Scandinavia. This also is the best period for cruises to Norway's North Cape and for visits to Moscow and St. Petersburg, as well as for tours of Scotland, the Low Countries (Belgium, Holland, Luxembourg), and France. Central Spain can be surprisingly comfortable, since so much of it is on an elevated plateau. This is traditional vacation time for Europeans, especially the French and Italians — who clear out of the cities in droves in August.

September – North Americans traditionally empty out of the Continent after *Labor Day,* although increasingly greater numbers of visitors are timing their arrivals for the week or two afterward, since the weather remains excellent and many retail establishments on the Continent reopen after summer closings. The weather is very good on the French Riviera, as well as at resorts on the Black Sea.

October – This is the period for manufacturers' exhibitions, fashion shows, international trade fairs, and food festivals. It's also harvest season throughout much of central Europe, and the fairs and festivals that celebrate these events draw heavy crowds of regional visitors, as well as vacationers. The weather tends to be cooler, so pack accordingly.

November and December – Temperatures throughout the Continent are wet and chilly, but not the marrow-freezing cold of the northern US and Canada, except in the northernmost reaches of Europe.

On the preceding page is a chart of seasonal temperature ranges in the countries of Europe. For more climate information, see *Climate and Clothes* (by country) in FACTS IN BRIEF.

Travelers also can get current readings and 3-day Accu-Weather forecasts through *American Express Travel Related Services*' Worldwide Weather Report number. By dialing 900-WEATHER and punching in either the area code for most major cities in the US or an access code for numerous travel destinations worldwide, an up-to-date recording will provide current temperature, sky conditions, wind speed and direction, heat index, relative humidity, local time, highway reports, and beach and boating reports or ski conditions (where appropriate). For locations in Europe, punch in the first three letters of the city. For instance, by entering GEN you will hear the weather report for Geneva — HEL will give you Helsinki; MAD, Madrid; PAR, Paris; ROM, Rome; VIE, Vienna; and so on. This 24-hour service can be accessed from any touch-tone phone in the US and costs 95¢ per minute. The charge will show up on your phone bill. For a free list of the cities covered, send a self-addressed, stamped envelope to *1-900-WEATHER,* 261 Central Ave., Farmingdale, NY 11735.

Traveling by Plane

Flying is the most efficient way to get to Europe, and it is the quickest, most convenient means of travel between different parts of the Continent once you are there. (Cruise ships that call at European ports generally function as hotels for passengers cruising European waters rather than as especially efficient transportation to or between individual destinations.)

The air space between North America and Europe is the most heavily trafficked in the world. It is served by dozens of airlines, almost all of which sell seats at a variety of prices, under a vast spectrum of requirements and restrictions. Since you probably will spend more for your airfare than for any other single item in your travel budget, try to take advantage of the lowest fares offered by either scheduled or charter companies. You should know what kinds of flights are available, the rules under which air travel operates, and all the special package options.

SCHEDULED AIRLINES: Among the dozens of airlines serving Europe from the United States, those offering regularly scheduled flights, many on a daily basis, are *Aer Lingus, Aeroflot, Air France, Air India, Alitalia, American, Austrian Airlines, British Airways, Continental, Czechoslovak Airlines (CSA), Delta, Egypt Air, El Al Israel Airlines, Finnair, Iberia Airlines of Spain, Icelandair, JAT Yugoslav Airlines, KLM Royal Dutch Airlines, LOT Polish Airlines, Lufthansa, Northwest, Olympic, Pakistan International, Sabena, SAS (Scandinavian Air Systems), SwissAir, TAP Air Portugal, Tarom Romanian Air Transport, Turkish Airlines, TWA, United, USAir,* and *Virgin Atlantic.*

Gateways – At present, nonstop flights to Europe depart from Anchorage, Atlanta, Boston, Charlotte, Chicago, Dallas/Ft. Worth, Denver, Detroit, Houston, Los Angeles, Miami, New York, Newark, Orlando, Philadelphia, Pittsburgh, Raleigh, St. Louis, San Francisco, San Diego, Seattle, Tampa, and Washington, DC. Additional direct flights (meaning, usually, that there is no change of flight number between the originating and terminating cities, though there may be one or more stops en route and perhaps a change of plane) depart from some of the above cities and a few others as well. Nonstop or direct, nearly all of these flights land in European capitals or other major cities.

Tickets – When traveling on one of the many regularly scheduled flights, a full-fare ticket provides maximum travel flexibility (although at considerable expense), because there are no advance booking requirements. A prospective passenger can buy a ticket for a flight right up to the minute of takeoff — if a seat is available. If your ticket is for a round trip, you can make the return reservation whenever you wish — months before you leave or the day before you return. Assuming the foreign immigration requirements are met, you can stay at your destination for as long as you like. (Tickets generally are good for a year and can be renewed if not used.) You also can cancel your flight at any time without penalty. However, while it is true that this category of ticket can be purchased at the last minute, it is advisable to reserve well in advance during popular vacation periods and around holiday times.

Fares – Airfares continue to change so rapidly that even experts find it difficult to keep up with them. This ever-changing situation is due to a number of factors, including airline deregulation, volatile labor relations, increasing fuel costs, and vastly increased competition.

Perhaps the most common misconception about fares on scheduled airlines is that the cost of the ticket determines how much service will be provided on the flight. This is true only to a certain extent. A far more realistic rule of thumb is that the less you pay for your ticket, the more restrictions and qualifications are likely to come into play before you board the plane (as well as after you get off). These qualifying aspects relate to the months (and the days of the week) during which you must travel, how far in advance you must purchase your ticket, the minimum and maximum amount of time you may or must remain away, your willingness to decide on a return date at the time of booking — and your ability to stick to that decision. It is not uncommon for passengers sitting side by side on the same wide-body jet to have paid fares varying by hundreds of dollars, and all too often the traveler paying more would have been equally willing (and able) to accept the terms of the far less expensive ticket.

In general, the great variety of fares between the US and Europe can be reduced to four basic categories, including first class, coach (also called economy or tourist class), and excursion or discount fares. A fourth category, called business class, has been added by many airlines in recent years. In addition, Advance Purchase Excursion (APEX) fares offer savings under certain conditions.

In a class by itself is the *Concorde,* the supersonic jet developed jointly by France and Great Britain that cruises at speeds of 1,350 miles an hour (twice the speed of sound) and makes transatlantic crossings in half the time of conventional, subsonic jets. *Air France* offers *Concorde* service from New York to Paris; *British Airways* flies from

Miami, Washington, DC, and New York to London. Service is "single" class (with champagne and caviar all the way), and the fare is expensive, about 20% more than a first class ticket on a subsonic aircraft. Some discounts have been offered, but time is the real gift of the *Concorde*. For travelers to European destinations other than Paris or London, this "gift" may be more or less valuable as compared to a direct flight when taking intra-European connections into account.

A **first class** ticket is your admission to the special section of the aircraft, with larger seats, more legroom, sleeperette seating on some wide-body aircraft, better (or more elaborately served) food, free drinks and headsets for movies and music channels, and above all, personal attention. First class fares are about twice those of full-fare economy, although both first class passengers and those paying full-fare economy fares are entitled to reserve seats and are sold tickets on an open reservation system. An additional advantage of a first class ticket is that if you're planning to visit several cities in Europe, you may include any number of stops en route to or from your most distant destination, provided that certain set restrictions regarding maximum mileage limits and flight routes are respected.

Not too long ago, there were only two classes of air travel, first class and all the rest, usually called economy or tourist. Then **business class** came into being — one of the most successful recent airline innovations. At first, business class passengers were merely curtained off from the other economy passengers. Now a separate cabin or cabins — usually toward the front of the plane — is the norm. While standards of comfort and service are not as high as in first class, they represent a considerable improvement over conditions in the rear of the plane, with roomier seats, more leg and shoulder space between passengers, and fewer seats abreast. Free liquor and headsets, a choice of meal entrées, and a separate counter for speedier check-in are other inducements. As in first class, a business class passenger may travel on any scheduled flight he or she wishes, may buy a one-way or round-trip ticket, and have the ticket remain valid for a year. There are no minimum or maximum stay requirements, no advance booking requirements, and no cancellation penalties, and the fare allows the same free stopover privileges as first class. Airlines often have their own names for their business class service — such as Le Club on *Air France,* Medallion Class on *Delta,* and Ambassador Class on *TWA.*

The terms of the **coach** or **economy** fare may vary slightly from airline to airline, and in fact from time to time airlines may be selling more than one type of economy fare. Coach or economy passengers sit more snugly, as many as 10 in a single row on a wide-body jet, behind the first class and business class sections. Normally alcoholic drinks are not free, nor are the headsets (except on *British Airways,* which does offer these free of charge). If there are two economy fares on the books, one (often called "regular economy") still may include a number of free stopovers. The other, less expensive fare (often called "special economy") may limit stopovers to one or two, with a charge (typically $25) for each one. Like first class passengers, however, passengers paying the full coach fare are subject to none of the restrictions that usually are attached to less expensive excursion and discount fares. There are no advance booking requirements, no minimum stay requirements, and no cancellation penalties. Tickets are sold on an open reservation system: They can be bought for a flight right up to the minute of takeoff (if seats are available), and if the ticket is round-trip, the return reservation can be made anytime you wish. Both first class and coach tickets generally are good for a year, after which they can be renewed if not used, and if you ultimately decide not to fly at all, your money will be refunded. The cost of economy and business class tickets does not vary much in the course of the year between the US and Europe, though on some transatlantic routes they vary from a basic (low-season) price in effect most of the year to a peak (high-season) price during the summer.

Excursions and other **discount** fares are the airlines' equivalent of a special sale, and usually apply to round-trip bookings only. These fares generally differ according to the season and the number of travel days permitted. They are only a bit less flexible than full-fare economy tickets and are, therefore, often useful for both business and holiday travelers. Most round-trip excursion tickets include strict minimum and maximum stay requirements and can be changed only within the specified time limits. So don't count on extending a ticket beyond the prescribed time of return or staying less time than required. Different airlines may have different regulations concerning the number of stopovers permitted, and sometimes excursion fares are less expensive during midweek. The availability of these reduced-rate seats is most limited at busy times such as holidays. Discount- or excursion-fare ticket holders sit with the coach passengers, and, for all intents and purposes, are indistinguishable from them. They receive all the same basic services, even though they may have paid anywhere between 30% and 55% less for the trip. Obviously, it's wise to make plans early enough to qualify for this less expensive transportation if possible.

These discount or excursion fares may masquerade under a variety of names, they may vary from city to city (from the East Coast to the West Coast, especially), but they invariably have strings attached. A common requirement is that the ticket be purchased a certain number of days — usually no fewer than 7 or 14 days — in advance of departure, though it may be booked weeks or months in advance (it has to be "ticketed," or paid for, shortly after booking, however). The return reservation usually has to be made at the time of the original ticketing and cannot be changed later than a certain number of days (again, usually 7 or 14 days) before the return flight. If events force a passenger to change the return reservation after the date allowed, the difference between the round-trip excursion rate and the round-trip coach rate probably will have to be paid, though most airlines allow passengers to use their discounted fares by standing by for an empty seat, even if they don't otherwise have standby fares. Another common condition is a minimum and maximum stay requirement; for example, 1 to 6 days or 6 to 14 days (but including at least a Saturday night). Last, cancellation penalties of up to 50% of the full price of the ticket have been assessed — check the specific penalty in effect when you purchase your discount/excursion ticket — so careful planning is imperative.

Of even greater risk — and bearing the lowest price of all the current discount fares — is the ticket where no change at all in departure and/or return flights is permitted, and where the ticket price is totally nonrefundable. If you do buy a nonrefundable ticket, you should be aware of a new policy followed by many airlines that may make it easier to change your plans if necessary. For a fee — set by each airline and payable at the airport when checking in — you *may* be able to change the time or date of a return flight on a nonrefundable ticket. However, if the nonrefundable ticket price for the replacement flight is higher than that of the original (as often is the case when trading in a weekday for a weekend flight), you will have to pay the difference. Any such change must be made a certain number of days in advance — in some cases as little as 2 days — of either the original or the replacement flight, whichever is earlier; restrictions are set by the individual carrier. (Travelers holding a nonrefundable or other restricted ticket who must change their plans due to a family emergency should know that some carriers may make special allowances in such situations; for further information, see *Medical and Legal Aid and Consular Services,* in this section.)

In the past, some excursion fares offered for travel to Europe came unencumbered by advance booking requirements and cancellation penalties, permitted one stopover (but not a free one) in each direction, and had "open jaws," meaning that you could fly to one city and depart from another, arranging and paying for your own transportation between the two. Excursion fares of this type currently exist only on flights between the US and a few European destinations.

More common is a newer, often less expensive, type of excursion fare, the **APEX**, or **Advance Purchase Excursion**, fare. As with traditional excursion fares, passengers paying an APEX fare sit with and receive the same basic services as any other coach or economy passenger, even though they may have paid up to 50% less for their seats. In return, they are subject to certain restrictions. In the case of most flights to Europe, the ticket usually is good for a minimum of 7 days abroad and a maximum, currently, of 2 to 6 months (depending on the airline and destination); and as its name implies, it must be "ticketed" or paid for in its entirety a certain period of time before departure — usually 21 days. The drawback to an APEX fare is that it penalizes travelers who change their minds — and travel plans. The return reservation must be made at the time of the original ticketing, and if for some reason you change your schedule while abroad, you will have to pay a penalty of $100 or 10% of the ticket value, whichever is greater, as long as you travel within the validity period of your ticket. But if you change your return to a date less than the minimum stay or more than the maximum stay, the difference between the round-trip APEX fare and the full round-trip coach rate will have to be paid. There also is a penalty of anywhere from $75 to $125 or more for canceling or changing a reservation *before* travel begins — check the specific penalty in effect when you purchase your ticket. No stopovers are allowed on an APEX ticket, but it is possible to create an "open-jaw" effect by buying an APEX on a split-ticket basis; for example, flying to Paris and returning from Brussels (or some other city). The total price would be half the price of an APEX to Paris plus half the price of an APEX to Brussels. APEX tickets to Europe are sold at basic and peak rates (peak season is around May through September) and may include surcharges for weekend flights.

There also is a Winter or Super APEX fare, which may go under different names for different carriers (for instance, some airlines call it "Eurosaver"). Similar to the regular APEX fare, it costs slightly less, but is more restrictive. Depending on the airline and destination, it usually is available only for off-peak winter travel and is limited to a stay of between 7 and 21 days. Advance purchase still is required (currently 30 days prior to travel), and ticketing must be completed within 48 hours of reservation. The fare is nonrefundable except in cases of hospitalization or death.

Another type of fare that sometimes is available is the **youth fare**. At present, most airlines flying to Europe are using a form of APEX fare as a youth fare for those through a certain age (which ranges anywhere from 23 to 30). The maximum stay is extended to a year, and the return booking must be left open. Seats usually can be reserved no more than 3 days before departure, and tickets must be purchased when the reservation is made. The return is booked from Europe in the same manner, no more than 3 days before flight time. On most airlines, there is no cancellation penalty, but the fare is subject to availability, so it may be difficult to book a return during peak travel periods, and as with the regular APEX fare, it may not even be available for travel to or from some countries during high season and may be offered only on selected routes.

Standby fares, at one time the rock-bottom price at which a traveler could fly to Europe, have become elusive. At the time of this writing, most major scheduled airlines did not regularly offer standby fares on most direct flights to Europe. Because airline fares and their conditions constantly change, bargain hunters should not hesitate to ask if such a fare exists at the time they plan to travel. If a standby fare is not offered on direct flights to your desired destination, inquire about the possibility of connecting flights through other European countries.

While the definition of standby varies somewhat from airline to airline, it generally means that you make yourself available to buy a ticket for a flight (usually no sooner than the day of departure), then literally stand by on the chance that a seat will be empty. Once aboard, however, a standby passenger has the same meal service and frills (or lack of them) enjoyed by others in the economy class compartment.

Something else to check is the possibility of qualifying for a **GIT** (Group Inclusive Travel) fare, which requires that a specific dollar amount of ground arrangements be purchased, in advance, along with the ticket. The requirements vary as to number of travel days and stopovers permitted, and the minimum number of passengers required for a group. The actual fares also vary, but the cost will be spelled out in brochures distributed by the tour operators handling the ground arrangements. In the past, GIT fares were among the least expensive available from the established carriers, but the prevalence of discount fares has caused group fares to all but disappear from some air routes. Travelers reading brochures on group package tours to Europe will find that, in almost all cases, the applicable airfare given as a sample (to be added to the price of the land package to obtain the total tour price) is an APEX fare, the same discount fare available to the independent traveler.

The major airlines serving Europe from the US may also offer individual excursion-fare rates similar to GIT fares, which are sold in conjunction with ground accommodation packages. Previously called ITX, and sometimes referred to as individual tour-basing fares, these fares generally are offered as part of "air/hotel/car/transfer packages," and can reduce the cost of an economy fare by more than a third. The packages are booked for a specific amount of time, with return dates specified; re-scheduling and cancellation restrictions and penalties vary from carrier to carrier. At the time of this writing, this type of fare was offered by *Aer Lingus, Air France, Alitalia, American, British Airways, Delta, Iberia, Northwest, TWA,* and *United,* and although their offerings did not represent substantial savings over the standard economy fare, it is worth checking at the time you plan to travel. (For further information on package options, see *Package Tours,* in this section.)

Travelers looking for the least expensive possible airfares should, finally, scan the pages of their hometown newspapers (especially the Sunday travel sections) for announcements of special promotional fares. Most airlines offer their most attractive special fares to encourage travel during slow seasons, and to inaugurate and publicize new routes. Even if none of these factors applies, prospective passengers can be fairly sure that the number of discount seats per flight at the lowest price is strictly limited, or that the fare offering includes a set expiration date — which means it's absolutely necessary to move fast to enjoy the lowest possible price.

Among other special airline promotional deals for which you should be on the lookout are discount or upgrade coupons, sometimes offered by the major carriers and found in mail-order merchandise catalogues. For instance, airlines sometimes issue coupons that typically cost around $25 each and are good for a percentage discount or an upgrade on an international airline ticket — including flights to Europe. The only requirement beyond the fee generally is that a coupon purchaser must buy at least one item from the catalogue. There usually are some minimum airfare restrictions before the coupon is redeemable, but in general these are worthwhile offers. Restrictions often include certain blackout days (when the coupon cannot be used at all), usually imposed during peak travel periods. These coupons are particularly valuable to business travelers who tend to buy full-fare tickets, and while the coupons are issued in the buyer's name, they can be used by others who are traveling on the same itinerary.

It's always wise to ask about discount or promotional fares and about any conditions that might restrict booking, payment, cancellation, and changes in plans. Check the prices from neighboring cities. A special rate may be offered in a nearby city but not in yours, and it may be enough of a bargain to warrant your leaving from that city. Ask if there is a difference in price for midweek versus weekend travel, or if there is a further discount for traveling early in the morning or late at night. Also be sure to investigate package deals, which are offered by virtually every airline. These may include a car rental, accommodations, and dining and/or sightseeing features, in addition to the basic airfare, and the combined cost of packaged elements usually is considerably less than the cost of the exact same elements when purchased separately.

If in the course of your research you come across a deal that seems too good to be true, keep in mind that logic may not be a component of deeply discounted airfares — there's not always any sane relationship between miles to be flown and the price to get there. More often than not, the level of competition on a given route dictates the degree of discount, and don't be dissuaded from accepting an offer that sounds irresistible just because it also sounds illogical. Better to buy that inexpensive fare while it's being offered and worry about the sense — or absence thereof — while you're flying to your desired destination.

When you're satisfied that you've found the lowest possible price for which you can conveniently qualify (you may have to call the airline more than once, because different airline reservations clerks have been known to quote different prices), make your booking. Then, to protect yourself against fare increases, purchase and pay for your ticket as soon as possible after you've received a confirmed reservation. Airlines generally will honor their tickets, even if the operative price at the time of your flight is higher than the price you paid; if fares go up between the time you *reserve* a flight and the time you *pay* for it, you likely will be out of luck. Finally, with excursion or discount fares, it is important to remember that when a reservations clerk says that you must purchase a ticket by a specific date, this is an absolute deadline. Miss the deadline and the airline may automatically cancel your reservation without telling you.

■ **Note:** Another wrinkle in the airfare scene is that if the fares go *down* after you purchase your ticket, you *may* be entitled to a refund of the difference. However, this is only possible in certain situations — availability and advance purchase restrictions pertaining to the lower rate are set by the airline. If you suspect that you may be able to qualify for such a refund, check with your travel agent or the airline.

Frequent Flyers – Most of the leading carriers serving Europe — including *American, British Airways, Continental, Delta, Northwest, TWA, United,* and *USAir* — offer a bonus system to frequent travelers. After the first 10,000 miles, for example, a passenger might be eligible for a first class seat for the coach fare; after another 10,000 miles, he or she might receive a discount on his or her next ticket purchase. The value of the bonuses continues to increase as more miles are logged. Once you are signed up for such a program, if flying to Europe on *Aer Lingus, Air France, Alitalia, Iberia, KLM Royal Dutch Airlines, Lufthansa, Sabena, SAS, SwissAir,* or another Europe-based airline, ask if the miles to be flown may be applied toward your collective bonus mileage account with a US carrier.

Bonus miles also may be earned by patronizing affiliated car rental companies or hotel chains, or by using one of the credit cards that now offers this reward. In deciding whether to accept such a credit card from one of the issuing organizations that tempt you with frequent flyer mileage bonuses on a specific airline, first determine whether the interest rate charged on the unpaid balance is the same as (or less than) possible alternate credit cards, and whether the annual "membership" fee also is equal or lower. If these charges are slightly higher than those of competing cards, weigh the difference against the potential value in airfare savings. Also ask about any bonus miles awarded just for signing up — 1,000 is common, 5,000 generally the maximum.

For the most up-to-date information on frequent flyer bonus options, you may want to send for the monthly newsletter *Frequent.* Issued by Frequent Publications, it provides current information about frequent flyer plans in general, as well as specific data about promotions, awards, and combination deals to help you keep track of the profusion — and confusion — of current and upcoming availabilities. For a year's subscription, send $33 to Frequent Publications, 4715-C Town Center Dr., Colorado Springs, CO 80916 (phone: 800-333-5937).

There also is a monthly magazine called *Frequent Flyer,* but unlike the newsletter mentioned above, its focus is primarily on newsy articles of interest to business travelers and other frequent flyers. Published by Official Airline Guides (PO Box 58543, Boulder, CO 80322-8543; phone: 800-323-3537), *Frequent Flyer* is available for $24 for a 1-year subscription.

Low-Fare Airlines – Increasingly, in today's economic climate, the stimulus for special fares is the appearance of new airlines associated with bargain rates. On these airlines, all seats on any given flight generally sell for the same price, which is somewhat below the lowest discount fare offered by the larger, more established airlines. It is important to note that tickets offered by the smaller airlines specializing in low-cost travel frequently are not subject to the same restrictions as the lowest-priced ticket offered by the more established carriers. They may not require advance purchase or minimum and maximum stays, may involve no cancellation penalties and may be available one way or round trip. A disadvantage to many of the low-fare airlines, however, is that when something goes wrong, such as delayed baggage or a flight cancellation due to equipment breakdown, their smaller fleets and fewer flights mean that passengers may have to wait longer for a solution than they would on one of the equipment-rich major carriers.

One airline offering a consistently low fare to Europe is *Virgin Atlantic* (phone: 800-862-8621 or 212-242-1330), which flies daily from New York (Newark Airport) to London (Gatwick Airport). The airline sells tickets in several categories, including business or "upper" class, economy, APEX, and nonrefundable variations on standby. Fares from New York to London include Late Saver fares — which must be purchased no less than 7 days prior to travel — and Late Late Saver fares — which are purchased no later than 1 day prior to travel. Travelers to destinations other than Great Britain will have to take a second flight from London, but still may save money. To determine the potential savings, add the cost of the transatlantic fare and the cost of connecting flights to come up with the total ticket price.

In a class by itself is *Icelandair,* a scheduled airline long known as a good source of low-cost flights to Europe. *Icelandair* flies from Baltimore/Washington, New York, and Orlando, via Reykjavik, Iceland, to Copenhagen (Denmark), Glasgow and London (Great Britain), Gothenburg (Sweden), Helsinki (Finland), Luxembourg (in the country of the same name), and Oslo (Norway). In addition, the airline increases the options for its passengers by offering "thru-fares" on connecting flights to Athens (Greece), Frankfurt (Germany), or Nice or Paris (France), coupled with free bus service to many German cities. (The price of the intra-European flights — aboard Luxembourg's *Luxair* — is included in the price *Icelandair* quotes for the transatlantic portion of the travel to these farther destinations.)

Icelandair sells tickets in a variety of categories, from unrestricted economy fares to a sort of standby "3-days-before" fare (which functions just like the youth fares described above but has no age requirement). Travelers should be aware, however, that most *Icelandair* flights stop in Reykjavik for 45 minutes — a minor delay for most, but one that further prolongs the trip for passengers who will wait again in Luxembourg to board connecting flights to their ultimate destinations. For reservations and tickets, contact a travel agent or *Icelandair* (phone: 800-223-5500 or 212-967-8888).

Intra-European Fares – The cost of the round trip across the Atlantic is not the only expense to be considered. Flights between European cities, when booked in Europe, can be quite expensive. But discounts recently have been introduced on routes between some European cities, and other discounts do exist.

Recent Common Market moves toward airline deregulation are expected to lead gradually to a greater variety of budget fares. In the meantime, however, the high cost of fares between most European cities can be avoided by careful use of stopover rights on the higher-priced transatlantic tickets — first class, business class, and full-fare economy. If your ticket doesn't allow stopovers, ask about PEX, Super PEX, APEX, and other excursion fares. If you are able to comply with applicable restrictions and can use them, you may save as much as 35% to 50% off full-fare economy. Note that these fares, which once could be bought only after arrival in Europe, are now sold in the US and can be bought before departure.

It is not easy to inform yourself about stopover possibilities by talking to most airline reservations clerks. More than likely, an inquiry concerning any projected trip will prompt the reply that a particular route is nonstop aboard the carrier in question, thereby precluding stopovers completely, or that the carrier does not fly to all the places you want to visit. It may take additional inquiries, perhaps with the aid of a travel agent, to determine the full range of options regarding stopover privileges.

Travelers might be able to squeeze in visits to Lisbon and Madrid on a first class ticket to Nice, for instance; Amsterdam and Brussels can be visited on a ticket to Paris; and Paris might be only the first of many free European stopovers possible on a one-way or round-trip ticket to a city in Eastern Europe or points beyond. The airline that flies you on the first leg of your trip across the Atlantic issues the ticket, though you may have to use several different airlines in order to complete your journey. First class tickets are valid for a full year, so there's no rush.

Among current discounted intra-European fares are those offered by *Air Inter*, France's major domestic airline. *Air Inter* offers reduced rates to families, married couples, senior citizens, students, youths, and children of various ages — all of which are available to French citizens as well as foreign visitors buying their tickets after arrival in France. In addition, for foreigners only, the airline offers discounted "Visit France" fares, which must be bought in the US in conjunction with a transatlantic ticket to France (both the international flight, which can be aboard any carrier, and the intra-France flight must be issued on the same ticket). *Air Inter* also offers a discount pass, the France Pass, which permits unlimited travel for any 7-day period within a given month. The pass can be used on all of the airline's routes with the exception of certain peak-hour flights (the "red flights" used mostly by business travelers). Further information on ticketing for *Air Inter*'s current airfare packages is available from *Air France* (*Air Inter*'s general sales agent in the US) or from *Jet Vacations* (phone: 800-JET-0999 or 212-247-0999).

For travel within Spain, *Iberia* offers the "Visit Spain" air pass, which allows purchasers to fly *Iberia* or *Aviaco* (a major domestic airline) to as many as 30 Spanish destinations on the mainland or in the Balearic Islands — and gives these passengers 60 days to complete the travel — all for one price. As with the Visit France fares, the Visit Spain pass must be bought in the US in conjunction with a transatlantic round-trip ticket to Spain (of which at least the eastbound portion must be aboard *Iberia*). Although the pass holders must choose the Spanish cities to be visited at the time of purchase (with an option to skip any city as long as the original sequence of remaining cities is maintained), reservations for specific flight dates need not be made in advance and pass holders have the flexibility to spend as much time as they wish (within the 60-day validity period) at each destination. For further information and current pass prices, contact *Iberia Airlines of Spain* (phone: 800-772-4642).

British Airways also offers an economical pass plan, which provides substantial savings on flights within the United Kingdom. A traveler can buy anywhere from 3 to 12 flights, with a fixed fee per flight (depending on the distance to be flown). Tickets have to be purchased prior to leaving the US or Canada, and an itinerary must be selected and paid for 7 days prior to the first flight. To get these discounted flights it is necessary for a traveler to have a round-trip transatlantic ticket — although this ticket does not have to be on *British Airways*. For information, contact *British Airways* (phone: 800-AIRWAYS).

Finnair offers a Holiday Ticket which allows an unlimited number of flights on any of *Finnair*'s routes in Finland during a 15-day period. The pass can be purchased at any time prior to leaving the US through a travel agent, and pass holders can wait until they are in Finland before deciding on specific destinations and making reservations. For information, contact *Finnair* (phone: 800-950-5000).

Other, although perhaps less impressive, discounted transatlantic and intra-European airfare packages may be offered by carriers in other countries. Ask a travel agent or the airline when making reservations.

Great Britain has been a leader in pushing for liberalization of intra-European airfares, and a great variety of bargain fares are available out of London, especially to Amsterdam and Dublin, and to a lesser extent to Belgium, Germany, Luxembourg, and Switzerland. Another recourse for those seeking savings on intra-European fares are the London "bucket shops" (discount travel agencies selling air tickets for less than the amount at which the airlines themselves would sell them), a flourishing industry given the British government's pro-consumer stance on airline competition. Bucket shops, both in London and the US, can be found most easily in the travel sections of Sunday newspapers. (For further information, see "Consolidators and Bucket Shops," below.)

Taxes and Other Fees – Travelers who have shopped for the best possible flight at the lowest possible price should be warned that a number of extras will be added to that price and collected by the airline or travel agent who issues the ticket. These taxes *usually* (but not always) are included in the prices quoted by airline reservations clerks.

The $6 International Air Transportation Tax is a departure tax paid by all passengers flying from the US to a foreign destination. A $10 US Federal Inspection Fee is levied on all air and cruise passengers who arrive in the US from outside North America (those arriving from Canada, Mexico, the Caribbean, and US territories are exempt). Still another fee is charged by some airlines to cover more stringent security procedures, prompted by recent terrorist incidents. The 8% federal US Transportation Tax applies to travel within the US or US territories, as well as to passengers flying between US cities en route to a foreign destination if the trip includes a stopover of more than 12 hours at a US point. Someone flying from Los Angeles to New York and stopping in New York for more than 12 hours before boarding a flight to Geneva, for instance, would pay the 8% tax on the domestic portion of the trip.

Reservations – For those who don't have the time or patience to investigate personally all possible air departures and connections for a proposed trip, a travel agent can be of inestimable help. A good agent should have all the information on which flights go where and when, and which categories of tickets are available on each. Most have computerized reservation links with the major carriers, so that a seat can be reserved and confirmed in minutes. An increasing number of agents also possess fare-comparison computer programs, so they often are very reliable sources of detailed competitive price data. (For more information, see *How to Use a Travel Agent,* in this section.)

When making reservations through a travel agent, ask the agent to give the airline your home phone number, as well as your daytime business phone number. All too often the agent uses the agency number as the official contact for changes in flight plans. Especially during the winter, weather conditions hundreds or even thousands of miles away can wreak havoc with flight schedules. Aircraft are constantly in use, and a plane delayed in the Orient or on the West Coast can miss its scheduled flight from the East Coast the next morning. The airlines are fairly reliable about getting this sort of information to passengers if they can reach them; diligence does little good at 10 PM if the airline has only the agency's or an office number.

Reconfirmation is strongly recommended for all international flights (though it is not usually required on US domestic flights) and, in the case of flights to Europe, it is a good idea to confirm your round-trip reservations — especially the return leg — as well as any point-to-point flights within Europe. Some (though increasingly fewer) reservations to and from international destinations are automatically canceled after a required reconfirmation period (typically 72 hours) has passed — even if you have a confirmed, fully paid ticket in hand. It always is wise to call ahead to make sure that the airline did not slip up in entering your original reservation, or in registering any changes you may have made since, and that it has your seat reservation and/or special meal request in the computer. If you look at the printed information on the ticket, you'll see the airline's reconfirmation policy stated explicitly. Don't be lulled into a false sense of security by the "OK" on your ticket next to the number and time of the flight. This only means that a reservation has been entered; a reconfirmation still may be necessary. If in doubt — call.

If you plan not to take a flight on which you hold a confirmed reservation, by all means inform the airline. Because the problem of "no-shows" is a constant expense for airlines, they are allowed to overbook flights, a practice that often contributes to the threat of denied boarding for a certain number of passengers (see "Getting Bumped," below).

Seating – For most types of tickets, airline seats usually are assigned on a first-come, first-served basis at check-in, although some airlines make it possible to reserve a seat at the time of ticket purchase. Always check in early for your flight, even with advance seat assignments. A good rule of thumb for international flights is to arrive at the airport *at least* 2 hours before the scheduled departure to give yourself plenty of time in case there are long lines.

Most airlines furnish seating charts, which make choosing a seat much easier, but there are a few basics to consider. You must decide whether you prefer a window, aisle, or middle seat. On flights where smoking is permitted, you also should specify if you prefer the smoking or nonsmoking section.

The amount of legroom provided (as well as chest room, especially when the seat in front of you is in a reclining position) is determined by something called "pitch," a measure of the distance between the back of the seat in front of you and the front of the back of your seat. The amount of pitch is a matter of airline policy, not the type of plane you fly. First class and business class seats have the greatest pitch, a fact that figures prominently in airline advertising. In economy class or coach, the standard pitch ranges from 33 to as little as 31 inches — downright cramped.

The number of seats abreast, another factor determining comfort, depends on a combination of airline policy and airplane dimensions. First class and business class have the fewest seats per row. Economy generally has 9 seats per row on a DC-10 or an L-1011, making either one slightly more comfortable than a 747, on which there normally are 10 seats per row. Charter flights on DC-10s and L-1011s, however, often have 10 seats per row and can be noticeably more cramped than 747 charters, on which the seating normally remains at 10 per row.

Airline representatives claim that most aircraft are more stable toward the front and midsection, while seats farthest from the engines are quietest. Passengers who have long legs and are traveling on a wide-body aircraft might request a seat directly behind a door or emergency exit, since these seats often have greater than average pitch, or a seat in the first row of a given section, which offers extra legroom — although these seats are increasingly being reserved for passengers who are willing (and able) to perform certain tasks in the event of emergency evacuation. It often is impossible, however, to see the movie from these seats, which are directly behind the plane's exits. Be aware that the first row of the economy section (called a "bulkhead" seat) on a conventional aircraft (not a widebody) does *not* offer extra legroom, since the fixed partition will not permit passengers to slide their feet under it, and that watching a movie from this first-row seat can be difficult and uncomfortable. These bulkhead seats do, however, provide ample room to use a bassinet or safety seat and often are reserved for families traveling with children.

A window seat protects you from aisle traffic and clumsy serving carts and also provides a view, while an aisle seat enables you to get up and stretch your legs without disturbing anyone. Middle seats are the least desirable, and seats in the last row are the worst of all, since they seldom recline fully. If you wish to avoid children on your flight or if you find that you are sitting in an especially noisy section, you usually are free to move to any unoccupied seat — if there is one.

If you are overweight, you may face the prospect of a long flight with special trepidation. Center seats in the alignments of wide-body 747s, L-1011s, and DC-10s are about 1½ inches wider than those on either side, so larger travelers tend to be more comfortable there.

Despite all these rules of thumb, finding out which specific rows are near emergency exits or at the front of a wide-body cabin can be difficult because seating arrangements on two otherwise identical planes vary from airline to airline. There is, however, a quarterly publication called *Airline Seating Guide* that publishes seating charts for most major US airlines and many foreign carriers as well. Your travel agent should have a copy, or you can buy the US edition for $39.95 per year and the international edition for $44.95. Order from Carlson Publishing Co., Box 888, Los Alamitos, CA 90720 (phone: 800-728-4877 or 213-493-4877).

Simply reserving an airline seat in advance, however, actually may guarantee very little. Most airlines require that passengers arrive at the departure gate at least 45 minutes (sometimes more) ahead of time to hold a seat reservation. They may cancel seat assignments and may not honor reservations of passengers who have not checked in some period of time — usually around 45 minutes, depending on the airline and airport — before scheduled departure time, and they *ask* travelers to check in at least 2 hours before international flights. It pays to read the fine print on your ticket carefully and plan ahead.

A far better strategy is to visit an airline ticket office (or one of a select group of travel agents) to secure an actual boarding pass for your specific flight. Once this has been issued, airline computers show you as checked in, and you effectively own the seat you have selected (although some carriers may not honor boarding passes of passengers arriving at the gate less than 10 minutes before departure). This also is good — but not foolproof — insurance against getting bumped from an overbooked flight and is, therefore, an especially valuable tactic at peak travel times.

Smoking – One decision regarding choosing a seat has been taken out of the hands of many travelers who smoke. Effective February 25, 1990, the US government imposed a ban that prohibits smoking on all flights scheduled for 6 hours or less within the US and its territories. The new regulation applies to both domestic and international carriers serving these routes.

In the case of flights to Europe, these rules do not apply to nonstop flights from the US, or those with a *continuous* flight time of over 6 hours between stops in the US or its territories. Smoking is not permitted on segments of international flights where the time between US landings is under 6 hours — for instance, flights that include a stopover (even with no change of plane) or connecting flights. To further complicate the situation, several individual carriers are banning smoking altogether on certain routes. (As we went to press, this ban had not yet extended to carriers flying between the US and Europe.)

On those flights that do permit smoking, the US Department of Transportation has determined that nonsmoking sections must be enlarged to accommodate all passengers who wish to sit in one. The airline does not, however, have to shift seating to accommodate nonsmokers who arrive late for a flight or for travelers flying standby, and in general not all airlines can guarantee a seat in the nonsmoking section on international flights. Cigar and pipe smoking are prohibited on all flights, even in the smoking sections.

For a wallet-size guide, which notes in detail the rights of nonsmokers according to these regulations, send a self-addressed, stamped envelope to *ASH (Action on Smoking and Health),* Airline Card, 2013 H St. NW, Washington, DC 20006 (phone: 202-659-4310).

Meals – If you have specific dietary requirements, be sure to let the airline know well before departure time. The available meals include vegetarian, seafood, kosher, Muslim, Hindu, high-protein, low-calorie, low-cholesterol, low-fat, low-sodium, diabetic, bland, and children's menus. There is no extra charge for this option. It usually is necessary to request special meals when you make your reservations — check-in time is too late. It's also wise to reconfirm that your request for a special meal has made its way into the airline's computer — the time to do this is 24 hours before departure. (Note that special meals generally are not available on intra-European flights on small local carriers. If this poses a problem, try to eat before you board, or bring a snack with you.)

Baggage – Travelers from the US face two different kinds of rules. When you fly on a US airline or on a major international carrier, US baggage regulations will be in effect. Though airline baggage allowances vary slightly, in general all passengers are allowed to carry on board, without charge, one piece of luggage that will fit easily under a seat of the plane or in an overhead bin, and whose combined dimensions (length, width, and depth) do not exceed 45 inches. A reasonable amount of reading material, camera equipment, and a handbag also are allowed. In addition, all passengers are allowed to check two bags in the cargo hold: one usually not to exceed 62 inches when length, width, and depth are combined, the other not to exceed 55 inches in combined dimensions. Generally no single bag may weigh more than 70 pounds. This weight restriction, however, may vary on transatlantic flights on some European airlines, ranging from as much as 88 pounds permitted for first class passengers to as little as 50 pounds for economy class — so check with the specific carrier in advance.

On many intra-European flights, baggage allowance may be subject to the old weight determination, under which each economy or discount passenger is allowed only a total of 44 pounds of luggage without additional charge. First class or business class passengers are allowed a total of 66 pounds. (If you are flying from the US to Europe and connecting to a domestic flight, you generally will be allowed the same amount of baggage as on the international flight. If you break your trip and then take a domestic flight, the local carrier's weight restrictions apply.)

Charges for additional, oversize, or overweight bags usually are made at a flat rate; the actual dollar amount varies from carrier to carrier. If you plan to travel with any special equipment or sporting gear, be sure to check with the airline beforehand. Most have specific procedures for handling such baggage, and you may have to pay for transport regardless of how much other baggage you have checked. Golf clubs and skis may be checked through as luggage (most airlines are accustomed to handling them), but tennis rackets should be carried onto the plane. Aqua-lung tanks, depressurized and appropriately packed with padding, and surfboards (minus the fin and padded) also may go as baggage. Snorkeling gear should be packed in a suitcase, duffle bag, or tote bag. Some airlines require that bicycles be partially dismantled and packaged (see *Camping and Caravanning, Hiking and Biking,* in this section).

Airline policies regarding baggage allowances for children vary and usually are based on the percentage of full adult fare paid. Although on many US carriers children who are ticket holders are entitled to the same baggage allowance as a full-fare passenger, some carriers allow only one bag per child, which sometimes must be smaller than an adult's bag (around 39 to 45 inches in combined dimensions). Often there is no luggage allowance for a child traveling on an adult's lap or in a bassinet. Particularly for international carriers, it's always wise to check ahead. (For more information, see *Hints for Traveling with Children,* in this section.)

To reduce the chances of your luggage going astray, remove all airline tags from previous trips, label each bag inside and out — with your business address rather than your home address on the outside, to prevent thieves from knowing whose house might be unguarded. Lock everything and double-check the tag that the airline attaches to make sure that it is correctly coded for your destination: CDG for Charles de Gaulle in Paris, FCO for Fiumicino in Rome, HTH for Heathrow in London, HEL for Vantaa in Helsinki, MAD for Barajas in Madrid, and so on.

If your bags are not in the baggage claim area after your flight, or if they're damaged, report the problem to airline personnel immediately. Keep in mind that policies regarding the specific time limit within which you have to make your claim vary from carrier to carrier. Fill out a report form on your lost or damaged luggage and keep a copy of it and your original baggage claim check. If you must surrender the check to claim a damaged bag, get a receipt for it to prove that you did, indeed, check your baggage on the flight. If luggage is missing, be sure to give the airline your destination and/or a telephone number where you can be reached. Also take the name and number of the person in charge of recovering lost luggage.

Most airlines have emergency funds for passengers stranded away from home without their luggage, but if it turns out your bags are truly lost and not simply delayed, do not then and there sign any paper indicating you'll accept an offered settlement. Since the airline is responsible for the value of your bags within certain statutory limits ($1,250 per passenger for lost baggage on a US domestic flight; $9.07 per pound or $20 per kilo for checked baggage, and up to $400 per passenger for unchecked baggage on an international flight), you should take some time to assess the extent of your loss (see *Insurance,* in this section). It's a good idea to keep records indicating the value of the contents of your luggage. A wise alternative is to take a Polaroid picture of the most valuable of your packed items just after putting them in your suitcase.

Considering the increased incidence of damage to baggage, it's now more than ever a good idea to keep the sales slips that confirm how much you paid for your bags. These are invaluable in establishing the value of damaged baggage and eliminate any arguments. A better way to protect your precious gear from the luggage-eating conveyers is to try to carry it on board wherever possible.

Be aware that airport security increasingly is an issue all over Europe, and is taken very seriously. Heavily armed police patrol the airports, and unattended luggage of any description may be confiscated and quickly destroyed. Passengers checking in at a European airport may undergo at least two separate inspections of their tickets, passports, and luggage by courteous but serious airline personnel — who ask passengers if their baggage has been out of their possession between packing and the airport or if they have been given gifts or other items to transport — before checked items are accepted.

Airline Clubs – US and some foreign carriers have clubs for travelers who pay for membership. These are not solely for first class passengers, although a first class ticket *may* entitle a passenger to lounge privileges. Membership (which, by law, requires a fee) entitles the traveler to use the private lounges at airports along their route, to refreshments served in these lounges, and to check-cashing privileges at most of their counters. Extras include special telephone numbers for individual reservations, embossed luggage tags, and a membership card for identification. Airlines serving Europe that offer membership in such clubs include the following:

> *American:* The *Admirals Club.* Single yearly membership $125 (plus a onetime $50 initiation fee), spouse an additional $70 per year.
> *British Airways:* The *Executive Club.* Membership is complimentary. There are three levels of membership (Blue Card, Silver Card, and Gold Card), each based on a combination of class chosen and mileage flown.
> *Continental:* The *President's Club.* Single yearly membership $140 for the first year; $90 yearly thereafter; spouse an additional $25 per year.

Delta: The *Crown Club.* Single yearly membership $150; spouse an additional $50 per year.

Northwest: The *World Club.* Single yearly membership $150 (plus a onetime $25 initiation fee); spouse an additional $45 per year; 3-year and lifetime memberships also available.

TWA: The *Ambassador Club.* Single yearly membership $150; spouse an additional $25 per year; lifetime memberships also available.

United: The *Red Carpet Club.* Single yearly membership $100 (plus a onetime $100 initiation fee), spouse an additional $50; 3-year and lifetime memberships also available.

USAir: The *USAir Club.* Single yearly membership $125; spouse an additional $25 per year.

Note that such companies do not have club facilities in all airports. Other airlines also offer a variety of special services in many airports.

Getting Bumped – A special air travel problem is the possibility that an airline will accept more reservations (and sell more tickets) than there are seats on a given flight. This is entirely legal and is done to make up for "no-shows," passengers who don't show up for a flight for which they have made reservations and bought tickets. If the airline has oversold the flight and everyone does show up, there simply aren't enough seats. When this happens, the airline is subject to stringent rules designed to protect travelers.

In such cases, the airline first seeks ticket holders willing to give up their seats voluntarily in return for a negotiable sum of money or some other inducement, such as an offer of upgraded seating on the next flight or a voucher for a free trip at some other time. If there are not enough volunteers, the airline may bump passengers against their wishes.

Anyone inconvenienced in this way, however, is entitled to an explanation of the criteria used to determine who does and does not get on the flight, as well as compensation if the resulting delay exceeds certain limits. If the airline can put the bumped passengers on an alternate flight that is *scheduled to arrive* at their original destination within 1 hour of their originally scheduled arrival time, no compensation is owed. If the delay is more than 1 hour but less than 2 hours on a domestic US flight, they must be paid denied-boarding compensation equivalent to the one-way fare to their destination (but not more than $200). If the delay is more than 2 hours after the original arrival time on a domestic flight or more than 4 hours on an international flight, the compensation must be doubled (not more than $400). The airline also may offer bumped travelers a voucher for a free flight instead of the denied-boarding compensation. The passenger may be given the choice of either the money or the voucher, the dollar value of which may be no less than the monetary compensation to which the passenger would be entitled. The voucher is not a substitute for the bumped passenger's original ticket; the airline continues to honor that as well.

Keep in mind that the above regulations and policies are only for flights leaving the US, and do *not* apply to charters or to inbound flights originating abroad, even on US carriers. Airlines carrying passengers between foreign destinations are free to determine what compensation they will pay to passengers who are bumped because of overbooking. They generally spell out their policies on airline tickets. Some foreign airline policies are similar to the US policy; however, don't assume all carriers will be as generous.

To protect yourself as best you can against getting bumped, arrive at the airport early, allowing plenty of time to check in and get to the gate. If the flight is oversold, ask immediately for the written statement explaining the airline's policy on denied-boarding compensation and its boarding priorities. If the airline refuses to give you this information, or if you feel they have not handled the situation properly, file a complaint with both the airline and the appropriate government agency (see "Consumer Protection," below).

Delays and Cancellations – The above compensation rules also do not apply if the flight is canceled or delayed, or if a smaller aircraft is substituted due to mechanical problems. Each airline has its own policy for assisting passengers whose flights are delayed or canceled or who must wait for another flight because their original one was overbooked. Most airline personnel will make new travel arrangements if necessary. If the delay is longer than 4 hours, the airline may pay for a phone call or telegram, a meal, and, in some cases, a hotel room and transportation to it.

■ **Caution:** If you are bumped or miss a flight, be sure to ask the airline to notify other airlines on which you have reservations or connecting flights. When your name is taken off the passenger list of your initial flight, the computer usually cancels all of your reservations automatically, unless *you* take steps to preserve them.

CHARTER FLIGHTS: By booking a block of seats on a specially arranged flight, charter operators offer travelers air transportation for a substantial reduction over the full coach or economy fare. These operators may offer air-only charters (selling transportation alone) or charter packages (the flight plus a combination of land arrangements such as accommodations, meals, tours, or car rentals). Charters are especially attractive to people living in smaller cities or out-of-the-way places, because they frequently leave from nearby airports, saving travelers the inconvenience and expense of getting to a major gateway.

From the consumer's standpoint, charters differ from scheduled airlines in two main respects: You generally need to book and pay in advance, and you can't change the itinerary or the departure and return dates once you've booked the flight. In practice, however, these restrictions don't always apply. Today, although most charter flights still require advance reservations, some permit last-minute bookings (when there are unsold seats available), and some even offer seats on a standby basis.

Though charters almost always are round trip, and it is unlikely that you would be sold a one-way seat on a round-trip flight, on rare occasions one-way tickets on charters are offered. Although it may be possible to book a one-way charter in the US, giving you more flexibility in scheduling your return, note that US regulations pertaining to charters may be more permissive than the charter laws of other countries. For example, if you want to book a one-way foreign charter back to the US, you may find advance booking rules in force.

Some things to keep in mind about the charter game include the following:

1. It cannot be repeated often enough that if you are forced to cancel your trip, you can lose much (and possibly all) of your money unless you have cancellation insurance, which is a *must* (see *Insurance,* in this section). Frequently, if the cancellation occurs far enough in advance (often 6 weeks or more), you may forfeit only a $25 or $50 penalty. If you cancel only 2 or 3 weeks before the flight, there may be no refund at all unless you or the operator can provide a substitute passenger.

2. Charter flights may be canceled by the operator up to 10 days before departure for any reason, usually underbooking. Your money is returned in this event, but there may be too little time for you to make new arrangements.

3. Most charters have little of the flexibility of regularly scheduled flights regarding refunds and the changing of flight dates; if you book a return flight, you must be on it or lose your money.

4. Charter operators are permitted to assess a surcharge, if fuel or other costs warrant it, of up to 10% of the airfare up to 10 days before departure.

5. Because of the economics of charter flights, your plane almost always will be full, so you will be crowded, though not necessarily uncomfortable.

There is, however, a new movement among charter airlines to provide flight accommodations that are comfort-oriented. Four charter airlines — a couple of which are the charter arms of well-known scheduled European-flag carriers — are offering charter flights that have a special section featuring substantially increased levels of comfort:

Balair: This Swiss-based charter arm of *SwissAir* offers "Relax Class" seats on flights from Miami, New York, and San Francisco to Switzerland.

Condor: This German airline — which flies from a number of US gateways to Frankfurt, Munich, and Stuttgart (Germany) — calls its less crowded service "Comfort Class."

LTU: A Germany-based airline — which flies from Los Angeles, Miami, New York, and San Francisco to Düsseldorf, Hamburg, and Munich (Germany) — offers less confining seating.

Tower Air: This US-based charter airline provides the equivalent of a business class section on its charter flights from the US to Rome.

For an extensive list of charter carriers, see below.

To avoid problems, *always* choose charter flights with care. When you consider a charter, ask your travel agent who runs it and carefully check the company. The Better Business Bureau in the company's home city can report on how many complaints, if any, have been lodged against it in the past. Protect yourself with trip cancellation and interruption insurance, which can help safeguard your investment if you or a traveling companion is unable to make the trip and must cancel too late to receive a full refund from the company providing your travel services. (This is advisable whether you're buying a charter flight alone or a tour package for which the airfare is provided by charter or scheduled flight.)

Bookings – If you do fly on a charter, read the contract's fine print carefully and pay particular attention to the following:

Instructions concerning the payment of the deposit and its balance and to whom the check is to be made payable. Ordinarily, checks are made out to an escrow account, which means the charter company can't spend your money until your flight has safely returned. This provides some protection for you. To ensure the safe handling of your money, make out your check to the escrow account, the number of which must appear by law on the brochure, though all too often it is on the back in fine print. Write the details of the charter, including the destination and dates, on the face of the check; on the back, print "For Deposit Only." Your travel agent may prefer that you make out your check to the agency, saying that it will then pay the tour operator the fee minus commission. It is perfectly legal to write the check as we suggest, however, and if your agent objects too vociferously (he or she should trust the tour operator to send the proper commission), consider taking your business elsewhere. If you don't make your check out to the escrow account, you lose the protection of that escrow should the trip be canceled. Furthermore, recent bankruptcies in the travel industry have served to point out that even the protection of escrow may not be enough to safeguard a traveler's investment. More and more, insurance is becoming a necessity. The charter company should be bonded (usually by an insurance company), and if you want to file a claim against it, the claim should be sent to the bonding agent. The contract will set a time limit within which a claim must be filed.

Specific stipulations and penalties for cancellations. Most charters allow you to cancel up to 45 days in advance without major penalty, but some cancellation dates are 50 to 60 days before departure.

Stipulations regarding cancellation and major changes made by the charterer. US rules say that charter flights may not be canceled within 10 days of departure except when circumstances — such as natural disasters or political upheavals — make it impossible to fly. Charterers may make "major changes," however, such as in the date or place of departure or return, but you are entitled to cancel and receive a full refund if you don't accept these changes. A price increase of more than 10% at any time up to 10 days before departure is considered a major change; no price increase is allowed during the 10 days immediately before departure.

Among the charter operators flying between the US and Europe are the following:

Air Charter (888 7th Ave., New York, NY 10106; phone: 800-JET-9999).

Air Europa (136 E. 57th St., Suite 1602, New York, NY 10022; phone: 212-888-7010).

American Trans Air (PO Box 51609, Indianapolis, IN 46251; phone: 317-243-4150).

Balair (608 5th Ave., New York, NY 10020; phone: 212-581-3411).

Club de Vacaciones (777 5th Ave., Suite 200, Huntington, NY 00173; phone: 800-648-0404).

Condor (875 Michigan Ave., Suite 3221, Chicago, IL 60611; phone: 312-951-0055).

Council Charter (205 E. 42nd St., New York, NY 10017; phone: 800-223-7402 or 212-661-0311).

LTU (6033 W. Century Blvd., Suite 1000, Los Angeles, CA 90045; phone: 800-888-0200).

Tower Air (Hangar 8, JFK International Airport, Jamaica, NY 11430; phone: 718-917-4306).

Unitravel (1177 N. Warson Rd., St. Louis, MO 63132; phone: 800-325-2222 or 314-569-2501).

For the full range of possibilities at the time you plan to travel, you may want to subscribe to the travel newsletter *Jax Fax,* which regularly features a list of charter companies and packagers offering seats on charter flights and may be a source for other charter flights to Europe. For a year's subscription send a check or money order for $12 to *Jax Fax,* 397 Post Rd., Darien, CT 06820 (phone: 203-655-8746).

DISCOUNTS ON SCHEDULED FLIGHTS: Promotional fares often are called discount fares because they cost less than what used to be the standard airline fare — full-fare economy. Nevertheless, they cost the traveler the same whether they are bought through a travel agent or directly from the airline. Tickets that cost less if bought from some outlet other than the airline do exist, however. While it is likely that the vast majority of travelers flying to Europe in the near future will be doing so on a promotional fare or charter rather than on a "discount" air ticket of this sort, it still is a good idea for cost-conscious consumers to be aware of the latest developments in the budget airfare scene. Note that the following discussion makes clear-cut distinctions among the types of discounts available based on how they reach the consumer; in actual practice, the distinctions are not nearly so precise.

Courier Travel – There was a time when traveling as a courier was a sort of underground way to save money and visit otherwise unaffordable destinations, but more and more, this once exotic idea of traveling as a courier is becoming a very "establishment" exercise. "Courier" means no more than a traveler who accompanies freight of one sort or another, and typically that freight replaces what otherwise would be the traveler's checked baggage. Be prepared, therefore, to carry all your own personal travel gear in a carry-on bag. In addition, the so-called courier usually pays only a portion of the total airfare — the freight company pays the remainder — and the courier also may be assessed a small registration fee. Note that many courier flights can be booked in advance (sometimes as much as 3 months) and that flights usually are round trip.

There are dozens of courier companies operating actively around the globe, and several publications provide information on courier opportunities:

A Simple Guide to Courier Travel, by Jesse L. Riddle, is a particularly good reference guide to courier travel. Published by the Carriage Group (PO Box 2394, Lake Oswego, OR 97035; phone: 800-344-9375), it's available for $14.95, including postage and handling.

Travel Secrets (PO Box 2325, New York, NY 10108; phone: 212-245-8703). Provides information useful to those considering traveling as a courier and often lists specific US and Canadian courier companies. Monthly; a year's subscription costs $33.

Travel Unlimited (PO Box 1058, Allston, MA 02134-1058; no phone). Lists courier companies and agents worldwide. Monthly; for a year's subscription send $25.

World Courier News (PO Box 77471, San Francisco, CA 94107; no phone). Provides information on courier opportunities, as well as useful tips. Each issue highlights a different destination. Monthly; for a year's subscription send $20.

Among the companies that regularly send couriers to Europe are the following:

Courier Travel Service (530 Central Ave., Cedarhurst, NY 11516; phone: 800-922-2FLY or 516-374-2299).

Discount Travel International (152 W. 72nd St., Suite 223, New York, NY 10023; phone: 212-655-5151).

Excaliber International Courier (c/o *Way to Go Travel*, 3317 Barham Blvd., Hollywood, CA 90068; phone: 213-851-2572).

World Courier (13742 Guy Brewer Blvd., Jamaica, NY 11434; phone: 718-978-9552).

In addition, *Now Voyager* (74 Varick St., Suite 307, New York, NY 10013; phone: 212-431-1616) is a referral agency that matches up would-be couriers with courier companies.

Net Fare Sources – The newest notion for reducing the costs of travel services comes from travel agents who offer individual travelers "net" fares. Defined simply, a net fare is the bare minimum amount at which an airline or tour operator will carry a prospective traveler. It doesn't include the amount that normally would be paid to the travel agent as a commission. Traditionally, such commissions amount to about 10% on domestic fares and from 10% to 20% on international fares — not counting significant additions to these commission levels that are paid retroactively when agents sell more than a specific volume of tickets or trips for a single supplier. At press time, at least one travel agency in the US was offering travelers the opportunity to purchase tickets and/or tours for a net price. Instead of earning income from individual commissions, this agency assesses a fixed fee that may or may not provide a bargain for travelers; it requires a little arithmetic to determine whether to use the services of a net travel agent or those of one who accepts conventional commissions. One of the potential drawbacks of buying from agencies selling travel services at net fares is that some airlines refuse to do business with them, thus possibly limiting your flight options.

Travel Avenue is a fee-based agency that rebates its ordinary agency commission to the customer. For domestic flights, they will find the lowest retail fare, then rebate 7% to 10% (depending on the airline selected) of that price minus a $10 ticket-writing charge. The rebate percentage for international flights varies from 5% to 16% (again depending on the airline), and the ticket-writing fee is $25. The ticket-writing charge is imposed per ticket; if the ticket includes more than eight separate flights, an additional $10 or $25 fee is charged. Customers using free flight coupons pay the ticket-writing charge, plus an additional $5 coupon-processing fee.

Travel Avenue will rebate commissions on all tickets, including heavily discounted fares and senior citizen passes. Available 7 days a week, reservations should be made far enough in advance to allow the tickets to be sent by first class mail, since extra charges accrue for special handling. It's possible to economize further by making your own airline reservation, then asking *Travel Avenue* only to write/issue your ticket. For travelers outside the Chicago area, business may be transacted by phone and purchases charged to a credit card. For further information, contact *Travel Avenue* at 641 W. Lake St., Suite 201, Chicago, IL 60606-1012 (phone: 312-876-1116 in Illinois; 800-333-3335 elsewhere in the US).

Consolidators and Bucket Shops – Other vendors of travel services can afford to sell tickets to their customers at an even greater discount because the airline has sold the tickets to them at a substantial discount (usually accomplished by sharply increasing commissions to that vendor), a practice in which many airlines indulge, albeit discreetly, preferring that the general public not know they are undercutting their own "list" prices. Airlines anticipating a slow period on a particular route sometimes sell off a certain portion of their capacity at a very great discount to a wholesaler, or consolidator. The wholesaler sometimes is a charter operator who resells the seats to the public as though they were charter seats, which is why prospective travelers perusing the brochures of charter operators with large programs frequently see a number of flights designated as "scheduled service." As often as not, however, the consolidator, in turn, sells the seats to a travel agency specializing in discounting. Airlines also can sell seats directly to such an agency, which thus acts as its own consolidator. The airline offers the seats either at a net wholesale price, but without the volume-purchase requirement that would be difficult for a modest retail travel agency to fulfill, or at the standard price, but with a commission override large enough (as high as 50%) to allow both a profit and a price reduction to the public.

Travel agencies specializing in discounting sometimes are called "bucket shops," a term fraught with connotations of unreliability in this country. But in today's highly competitive travel marketplace, more and more conventional travel agencies are selling consolidator-supplied tickets, and the old bucket shops' image is becoming respectable. Agencies that specialize in discounted tickets exist in most large cities, and usually can be found by studying the smaller ads in the travel sections of Sunday newspapers.

Before buying a discounted ticket, whether from a bucket shop or a conventional, full-service travel agency, keep the following considerations in mind: To be in a position to judge how much you'll be saving, first find out the "list" prices of tickets to your destination. Then do some comparison shopping among agencies. Also bear in mind that a ticket that may not differ much in price from one available directly from the airline may, however, allow the circumvention of such things as the advance-purchase requirement. If your plans are less than final, be sure to find out about any other restrictions, such as penalties for canceling a flight or changing a reservation. Most discount tickets are non-endorsable, meaning they can be used only on the airline that issued them, and they usually are marked "nonrefundable" to prevent their being cashed in for a list-price refund.

A great many bucket shops are small businesses operating on a thin margin, so it's a good idea to check the local Better Business Bureau for any complaints registered against the one with which you're dealing before parting with any money. If you still do not feel reassured, consider buying discounted tickets only through a conventional travel agency, which can be expected to have found its own reliable source of consolidator tickets — some of the largest consolidators, in fact, sell only to travel agencies.

A few bucket shops require payment in cash or by certified check or money order, but if credit cards are accepted, use that option. Note, however, if buying from a charter operator selling both scheduled and charter flights, that the scheduled seats are not protected by the regulations — including the use of escrow accounts — governing the charter seats. Well-established charter operators, nevertheless, may extend the same protections to their scheduled flights, and when this is the case, consumers should be sure that the payment option selected directs their money into the escrow account.

Among the numerous consolidators offering discount fares to Europe are the following:

Bargain Air (655 Deep Valley Dr., Suite 355, Rolling Hills, CA 90274; phone: 800-347-2345 or 213-377-2919).

Council Charter (205 E. 42nd St., New York, NY 10017; phone: 800-223-7402 or 212-661-0311).

Euro Asia Express (475 El Camino Real, Millbrae, CA 94030; phone: 800-782-9624 or 415-692-9966 in California; 800-782-9625 elsewhere in the US).

International Adventures (60 E. 42nd St., New York, NY 10165; phone: 212-599-0577).

Maharaja/Consumer Wholesale (393 Fifth Ave., 2nd Floor, New York, NY 10016; phone: 212-213-2020 in New York State; 800-223-6862 elsewhere in the US).

TFI Tours International (34 W. 37th St., 12th Floor, New York, NY 10001; phone: 212-736-1140).

Travac Tours and Charters (989 Sixth Ave., New York, NY 10018; phone: 212-563-3303).

25 West Tours (2490 Coral Way, Miami, FL 33145; phone: 305-856-0810; 800-423-6954 in Florida; 800-252-5052 elsewhere in the US).

Union Vacations (3175 N. Lincoln St., Chicago, IL 60657; 312-868-0100).

Unitravel (1177 N. Warson Rd., St. Louis, MO 63132; phone: 314-569-0900 in Missouri; 800-325-2222 elsewhere in the US).

■**Note:** Although rebating and discounting are becoming increasingly common, there is some legal ambiguity concerning them. Strictly speaking, it is legal to discount domestic tickets, but not international tickets. On the other hand, the law that prohibits discounting, the Federal Aviation Act of 1958, is consistently ignored these days, in part because consumers benefit from the practice and in part because many illegal arrangements are indistinguishable from legal ones. Since the line separating the two is so fine that even the authorities can't always tell the difference, it is unlikely that most consumers would be able to do so, and in fact it is not illegal to *buy* a discounted ticket. If the issue of legality bothers you, ask the agency whether any ticket you're about to buy would be permissible under the above-mentioned act.

OTHER DISCOUNT TRAVEL SOURCES: An excellent source of information on economical travel opportunities is the *Consumer Reports Travel Letter,* published monthly by Consumers Union. It keeps abreast of the scene on a wide variety of fronts, including package tours, rental cars, insurance, and more, but it is especially helpful for its comprehensive coverage of airfares, offering guidance on all the options from scheduled flights on major or low-fare airlines to charters and discount sources. For a year's subscription send $37 ($57 for 2 years) to *Consumer Reports Travel Letter* (PO Box 53629, Boulder, CO 80322-3629; phone: 800-999-7959). For information on other travel newsletters, see *Books, Newspapers, Magazines, and Newsletters,* in this section.

Last-Minute Travel Clubs – Still another way to take advantage of bargain airfares is open to those who have a flexible schedule. A number of organizations, usually set up as last-minute travel clubs and functioning on a membership basis, routinely keep in touch with travel suppliers to help them dispose of unsold inventory at discounts of between 15% and 60%. A great deal of the inventory consists of complete package tours and cruises, but some clubs offer air-only charter seats and, occasionally, seats on scheduled flights.

Members pay an annual fee and receive a toll-free hotline telephone number to call for information on imminent trips. In some cases, they also receive periodic mailings with information on bargain travel opportunities for which there is more advance notice. Despite the suggestive names of the clubs providing these services, last-minute travel does not necessarily mean that you cannot make plans until literally the last minute. Trips can be announced as little as a few days or as much as 2 months before departure, but the average is from 1 to 4 weeks' notice.

Among the organizations regularly offering such discounted travel opportunities to Europe are the following:

Discount Club of America (61-33 Woodhaven Blvd., Rego Park, NY 11374; phone: 800-321-9587 or 718-335-9612). Annual fee: $39 per family.

Discount Travel International (Ives Building, 114 Forrest Ave., Suite 205, Narberth, PA 19072; phone: 800-334-9294 or 215-668-7184). Annual fee: $45 per household.

Encore Short Notice (4501 Forbes Blvd., Lanham, MD 20706; phone: 301-459-8020; 800-638-0930 for customer service). Annual fee: $48 per family.

Last Minute Travel (1249 Boylston St., Boston, MA 02215; phone: 800-LAST-MIN or 617-267-9800). No fee.

Moment's Notice (425 Madison Ave., New York, NY 10017; phone: 212-486-0503). Annual fee: $19.95 per family.

Spur-of-the-Moment Tours and Cruises (10780 Jefferson Blvd., Culver City, CA 90230; phone: 213-839-2418 in California; 800-343-1991 elsewhere in the US). No fee.

Traveler's Advantage (3033 S. Parker Rd., Suite 1000, Aurora, CO 80014; phone: 800-548-1116). Annual fee: $49 per family.

Vacations to Go (2411 Fountain View, Suite 201, Houston, TX 77057; phone: 800-338-4962). Annual fee: $19.95 per family.

Worldwide Discount Travel Club (1674 Meridian Ave., Miami Beach, FL 33139; phone: 305-534-2082). Annual fee: $40 per person; $50 per family.

Generic Air Travel – Organizations that apply the same flexible-schedule idea to air travel only and sell tickets at literally the last minute also exist. The service they provide sometimes is known as "generic" air travel, and it operates somewhat like an ordinary airline standby service except that the organizations running it offer seats on not one but several scheduled and charter airlines.

One pioneer of generic flights is *Airhitch* (2790 Broadway, Suite 100, New York, NY 10025; phone: 212-864-2000), which arranges flights to Europe from various US gateways. Prospective travelers register by paying a fee (applicable toward the fare) and stipulate a range of acceptable departure dates and their desired destination, along with alternate choices. The week before the date range begins, they are notified of at least two flights that will be available during the time period, agree on one, and remit the balance of the fare to the company. If they do not accept any of the suggested flights, they lose their deposit; if, through no fault of their own, they do not ultimately get on any agreed-on flight, all of their money is refunded. Return flights are arranged the same way.

Bartered Travel – Suppose a hotel buys advertising space in a newspaper. As payment, the hotel gives the publishing company the use of a number of hotel rooms in lieu of cash. This is barter, a common means of exchange among hotels, airlines, car rental companies, cruise lines, tour operators, restaurants, and other travel service companies. When a bartering company finds itself with empty airline seats (or excess hotel rooms, or cruise ship cabin space, and so on) and offers them to the public, considerable savings can be enjoyed.

Bartered-travel clubs often offer discounts of up to 50% to members who pay an annual fee (approximately $50 at press time) that entitles them to select the flights, cruises, hotel rooms, or other travel services that the club obtained by barter. Members usually present a voucher, club credit card, or scrip (a dollar-denomination voucher negotiable only for the bartered product) to the hotel, which in turn subtracts the dollar amount from the bartering company's account.

Selling bartered travel is a perfectly legitimate means of retailing. One advantage to club members is that they don't have to wait until the last minute to obtain flight or room reservations.

Among the companies specializing in bartered travel, several that frequently offer members travel services to and in Europe include the following:

IGT (In Good Taste) Services (1111 Lincoln Rd., 4th Floor, Miami Beach, FL 33139; phone: 800-444-8872 or 305-534-7900). Annual fee: $48 per family.

Travel Guild (18210 Redmond Way, Redmond, WA 98052; phone: 206-861-1900). Annual fee: $48 per family.

Travel World Leisure Club (225 W. 34th St., Suite 2203, New York, NY 10122; phone: 800-444-TWLC or 212-239-4855). Annual fee: $50 per family.

CONSUMER PROTECTION: Consumers who feel that they have not been dealt with fairly by an airline should make their complaints known. Begin with the customer service representative at the airport where the problem occurs. If he or she cannot resolve your complaint to your satisfaction, write to the airline's consumer office. In a businesslike, typed letter, explain what reservations you held, what happened, the names of the employees involved, and what you expect the airline to do to remedy the situation. Send copies (never the originals) of the tickets, receipts, and other documents that back your claims. Ideally, all correspondence should be sent via certified mail, return receipt requested. This provides proof that your complaint was received.

Passengers with consumer complaints — lost baggage, compensation for getting bumped, violations of smoking and nonsmoking rules, deceptive practices by an airline, charter regulations — who are not satisfied with the airline's response should contact the US Department of Transportation (DOT), Consumer Affairs Division (400 Seventh St. SW, Room 10405, Washington, DC 20590; phone: 202-366-2220). DOT personnel stress, however, that consumers initially should direct their complaints to the airline that provoked them.

Travelers with an unresolved complaint involving a foreign carrier also can contact the US Department of Transportation. DOT personnel will do what they can to help resolve all such complaints, although their influence may be limited.

Consumers with complaints against specific European airlines or other travel-related services can write to the appropriate government agency; the national tourist office (see *Tourist Information Offices,* in this section) should be able to provide this information. Outline the specifics in the native language of the country — French for France, Italian for Italy, and so on — in as much detail as possible. (Keep in mind, if a translator is required, this correspondence could get expensive.) The agency will try to resolve the complaint or, if it is out of their jurisdiction, will refer the matter to the proper authorities, and will notify you in writing (in their own language) of the result of their inquires and/or any action taken.

Remember, too, that the federal Fair Credit Billing Act permits purchasers to refuse payment for credit card charges where services have not been delivered, so the onus of dealing with the receiver for a bankrupt airline falls on the credit card company. Do not rely on another airline to honor the ticket you're holding, since the days when virtually all major carriers subscribed to a default protection program that bound them to do so are long gone. Some airlines may voluntarily step forward to accommodate the stranded passengers of a fellow carrier, but this is now an entirely altruistic act.

The deregulation of US airlines has meant that a traveler must find out for himself or herself what he or she is entitled to receive. The US Department of Transportation's informative consumer booklet, *Fly Rights,* is a good place to start. To receive a copy, send $1 to the Superintendent of Documents (US Government Printing Office, Washington, DC 20402-9325; phone: 202-783-3238). Specify its stock number, 050-000-00513-5, and allow 3 to 4 weeks for delivery.

■ **Note:** Those who tend to experience discomfort due to the change in air pressure while flying may be interested in the free pamphlet *Ears, Altitude and Airplane Travel;* for a copy send a self-addressed, stamped, business-size envelope to the *American Academy of Otolaryngology* (One Prince St., Alexandria, VA 22314; phone: 703-836-4444). And for when you land, *Overcoming Jet Lag* offers some helpful tips on minimizing post-flight stress; it is available from Berkeley Publishing Group (PO Box 506, Mail Order Dept., East Rutherford, NJ 07073; phone: 800-631-8571) for $6.95, plus shipping and handling.

Traveling by Ship

 There was a time when traveling by ship was extraordinarily expensive, time consuming, utterly elegant, and was utilized almost exclusively for getting from one point to another. Alas, the days when steamships reigned as the primary means of transatlantic transportation are gone, days when England, France, Germany, Italy, the Netherlands, Norway, and Sweden — and the US — had fleets of passenger liners that offered week-plus trips across the North Atlantic. Only one ship (*Cunard*'s *Queen Elizabeth 2*) continues to offer this kind of service between the US and Europe with any degree of regularity; others make "positioning" cruises a few times a year at most. At the same time, the possibility of booking passage to Europe on a cargo ship is becoming less practical. Fewer and fewer travelers, therefore, first set foot on European soil with sea legs developed during an ocean voyage.

Although fewer travelers to Europe are choosing sea travel as a means of transport to a specific destination, more and more people are cruising *around* Europe. No longer primarily pure transportation, cruising currently is riding a wave of popularity as a leisure activity in its own right, and the host of new ships (and dozens of rebuilt old ones) testifies dramatically to the attraction of vacationing on the high seas. And due to the growing popularity of travel along coastal and inland waterways, more and more travelers — particularly repeat travelers — are climbing aboard some kind of water-borne conveyance once they've arrived in Europe, and are touring as part of an intra-European cruise, from coastal waterways, from the banks of a river, or from the towpath of a canal.

Many modern-day cruise ships seem much more like motels-at-sea than the classic liners of a couple of generations ago, but they are consistently comfortable and passengers often are pampered. Cruise prices are quite reasonable, and since the single cruise price covers all the major items in a typical vacation — transportation, accommodations, all meals, and entertainment, and a full range of social activities, sports, and recreation — a traveler need not fear any unexpected assaults on the family travel budget.

When selecting a cruise, your basic criteria should be where you want to go, the time you have available, how much you want to spend, and the kind of environment that best suits your style and taste (in which case price is an important determinant). Rely on the suggestions of a travel agent — preferably one specializing in cruises (see "A final note on picking a cruise," below) — but be honest with the agent (and with yourself) in describing the type of atmosphere you're seeking. Ask for suggestions from friends who have been on cruises; if you trust their judgment, they should be able to suggest a ship on which you'll feel comfortable.

There are a number of moments in the cruise-planning process when discounts are available from the major cruise lines, so it may be possible to enjoy some diminution of the list price almost anytime you book passage on a cruise ship. For those willing to commit early — say 4 to 6 months before sailing — most of the major cruise lines routinely offer a 10% reduction off posted prices, in addition to the widest selection of cabins. For those who decide to sail rather late in the game — say, 4 to 6 weeks before departure — savings often are even greater — an average of 20% — as steamship lines try to fill up their ships. The only negative aspect is that the choice of cabins tends to be limited, although it is possible that a fare upgrade will be offered to make this limited selection more palatable. In addition, there's the option of buying from a discount travel club or a travel agency that specializes in last-minute bargains; these discounters and other discount travel sources are discussed at the end of *Traveling by Plane,* above.

Most of the time, the inclusion of air transportation in the cruise package costs significantly less than if you were to buy the cruise separately and arrange your own air transportation to the port. If you do decide on one of these economical air/sea packages, be forewarned that it is not unusual for the pre-arranged flight arrangements to be less than convenient. The problems often arrive with the receipt of your cruise ticket, which also includes the airline ticket for the flight to get you to and from the ship dock. This is normally the first time you see the flights on which you have been booked and can appraise the convenience of the departure and arrival times. The cruise ship lines generally are not very forthcoming about altering flight schedules, and your own travel agent also may have difficulty in rearranging flight times or carriers. That means that the only remaining alternative is to ask the line to forget about making your flight arrangements and to pay for them separately by yourself. This may be more costly, but it's more likely to give you an arrival and departure schedule that will best conform to the sailing and docking times of the ship on which you will be cruising.

Cruise lines promote sailings to and around Europe as "get away from it all" vacations. But prospective cruise ship passengers will find that the variety of cruises is tremendous, and the quality, while generally high, varies depending on shipboard services, the tone of shipboard life, the cost of the cruise, and operative itineraries. Although there are less expensive ways to see Europe, the romance and enjoyment of a sea voyage remain irresistible for many, so a few points should be considered by such sojourners before they sign on for a seagoing vacation (after all, it's hard to get off in mid-ocean). Herewith, a rundown on what to expect from a cruise, a few suggestions on what to look for and arrange when purchasing passage on one, and some representative sailings to and around Europe.

CABINS: The most important factor in determining the price of a cruise is the cabin. Cabin prices are set according to size and location. The size can vary considerably on older ships, less so on newer or more recently modernized ones, and may be entirely uniform on the very newest vessels.

Shipboard accommodations utilize the same pricing pattern as hotels. Suites, which consist of a sitting room–bedroom combination and occasionally a private small deck that could be compared to a patio, cost the most. Prices for other cabins (interchangeably called staterooms) usually are more expensive on the upper passenger decks, less expensive on lower decks; if a cabin has a bathtub instead of a shower, the price probably will be higher. The outside cabins with portholes cost more than inside cabins without views and generally are preferred — although many experienced cruise passengers eschew the more expensive accommodations for they know they will spend very few waking hours in their cabins. As in all forms of travel, accommodations are more expensive for single travelers. If you are traveling on your own but want to share a double cabin to reduce the cost, some ship lines will attempt to find someone of the same sex willing to share quarters (see *Hints for Single Travelers,* in this section).

FACILITIES AND ACTIVITIES: You may not use your cabin very much — organized shipboard activities are geared to keep you busy. A standard schedule might consist of swimming, sunbathing, and numerous other outdoor recreations. Evenings are devoted to leisurely dining, lounge shows or movies, bingo and other organized games, gambling, dancing, and a midnight buffet. Your cruise fare includes all of these activities — except the cost of drinks.

Most cruise ships have at least one major social lounge, a main dining room, several bars, an entertainment room that may double as a discotheque for late dancing, an exercise room, indoor games facilities, at least one pool, and shopping facilities, which can range from a single boutique to an arcade. Still others have gambling casinos and/or slot machines, card rooms, libraries, children's recreation centers, indoor pools (as well as one or more on open decks), separate movie theaters, and private meeting rooms. Open deck space should be ample, because this is where most passengers spend their days at sea.

Usually there is a social director and staff to organize and coordinate activities. Evening entertainment is provided by professionals. Movies are mostly first-run and drinks are moderate in price (or should be) because a ship is exempt from local taxes when at sea.

■ **Note:** To be prepared for possible illnesses at sea, travelers should get a prescription from their doctor for medicine to counteract motion sickness. All ships with more than 12 passengers have a doctor on board, plus facilities for handling sickness or medical emergencies.

Shore Excursions – These side trips almost always are optional and available at extra cost. Before you leave, do a little basic research about the European ports you'll be visiting and decide what sights will interest you. If several of the most compelling of these are some distance from the pier where your ship docks, chances are that paying for a shore excursion will be worth the money.

Shore excursions usually can be booked through your travel agent at the same time you make your cruise booking, but this is worthwhile only if you can get complete details on the nature of each excursion being offered. If you can't get these details, better opt to purchase your shore arrangements after you're on board. Your enthusiasm for an excursion may be higher once you are on board because you will have met other passengers with whom to share the excitement of "shore leave." And depending on your time in port, you may decide to eschew the guided tour and venture out on your own.

Meals – All meals on board almost always are included in the basic price of a cruise, and the food generally is abundant and quite palatable. Evening meals are taken in the main dining room, where tables are assigned according to the passengers' preferences. Tables usually accommodate from 2 to 10; specify your preference when you book your cruise. If there are two sittings, you also can specify which one you want at the time you book or, at the latest, when you board the ship. Later sittings usually are more leisurely. Breakfast frequently is available in your cabin, as well as in the main dining room. For lunch, many passengers prefer the buffet offered on deck, usually at or near the pool, but again, the main dining room is available.

DRESS: Most people pack too much for a cruise on the assumption that their daily attire should be chic and every night is a big event. Comfort is a more realistic criterion. Daytime wear on most ships is decidedly casual. Evening wear for most cruises is dressy-casual. Formal attire probably is not necessary for 1-week cruises, optional for longer ones. (For information on choosing and packing a basic wardrobe, see *How to Pack,* in this section.)

TIPS: Tips are a strictly personal expense, and you *are* expected to tip — in particular, your cabin and dining room stewards. The general rule of thumb (or palm) is to expect to pay from 10% to 20% of your total cruise budget for gratuities — the actual amount within this range is based on the length of the cruise and the extent of personalized services provided. Allow $2 to $5 a day for each cabin and dining room steward (more if you wish), and additional sums for very good service. (*Note:* Tips should be paid by and for each individual in a cabin, whether there are one, two, or more.) Others who may merit tips are the deck steward who sets up your chair at the pool or elsewhere, the wine steward in the dining room, porters who handle your luggage (tip them individually at the time they assist you), and any others who provide personal service. On some ships you can charge your bar tab to your cabin; throw in the tip when you pay it at the end of the cruise. Smart travelers tip twice during the trip: about midway through the cruise and at the end; even wiser travelers tip a bit at the start of the trip to ensure better service throughout.

Although some cruise lines do have a no-tipping policy and you are not penalized by the crew for not tipping, naturally, you aren't penalized for tipping, either. If you can restrain yourself, it is better not to tip on those few ships that discourage it. However, never make the mistake of not tipping on the majority of ships, where it is a common, expected practice. (For further information on calculating gratuities, see *Tipping,* in this section.)

SHIP SANITATION: The US Public Health Service (PHS) currently inspects all passenger vessels calling at US ports, so very precise information is available on which ships meet its requirements and which do not. The further requirement that ships immediately report any illness that occurs on board adds to the available data.

The problem for a prospective cruise passenger is to determine whether the ship on which he or she plans to sail has met the official sanitary standard. US regulations require the PHS to publish actual grades for the ships inspected (rather than the old pass or fail designation), so it's now easy to determine any cruise ship's status. Nearly 4,000 travel agents, public health organizations, and doctors receive a copy of each monthly ship sanitation summary, but be aware that not all travel agents fully understand what this ship inspection program is all about. The best advice is to deal with a travel agent who specializes in cruise bookings, for he or she is most likely to have the latest information on the sanitary conditions of all cruise ships (see "A final note on picking a cruise," below). To receive a copy of the most recent summary or a particular inspection report, contact Chief, Vessel Sanitation Program, Center for Environmental Health and Injury Control, 1015 N. America Way, Room 107, Miami, FL 33132 (phone: 305-536-4307).

TRANSATLANTIC CROSSINGS: There are a number of cruise lines that sail between the US and Europe. If none of the operative itineraries offered at the time you plan to travel visits your intended destination, consider disembarking at another European port and proceeding by ship, plane, train, or car.

For seagoing enthusiasts, *Cunard*'s *Queen Elizabeth 2* is one of the largest and most comfortable vessels afloat and each year the *QE2* schedules approximately a dozen round-trip transatlantic crossings between June and, usually, December. This ship normally sets its course from New York to Southampton, England (a 5-day trip), and then sails directly back to the US, although on a few of the crossings it proceeds from Southampton to Cherbourg, France, or to other European ports before turning back across the Atlantic. (Similarly, on some crossings, the ship calls at various East Coast

US ports in addition to New York, thus giving passengers a choice of where to embark or disembark.) Europe-bound travelers on crossings not scheduled to call at their desired destination can take an intra-European flight, and later take a transatlantic flight home. Another alternative is to take one of the ferries departing from Southampton or Cherbourg.

For those sailing to Europe on the *QE2* and flying home, another option is based on the validity period of the return ticket. Following the transatlantic crossing, passengers have a specified time — up to 40 days for first class passengers and 15 days for the less expensive fares — during which they can tour Europe. Usually the included transatlantic flight must be to selected US gateways served by *British Airways,* but passengers may return to other gateways by paying a supplement. Those who want to splurge can apply the air allowance included in such air/sea packages toward a ticket aboard *British Airways'* supersonic *Concorde,* although the difference between the basic allowance and the *Concorde* fare is substantial. There are no maximum stay restrictions for passengers who upgrade to a return flight on the *Concorde.*

Cunard also offers various European tour packages applicable to the basic air/sea offer. Among the tours offered last year were combination Paris/London packages, including 3 days and 2 nights in each city; a 10-day Andalusian Express tour, which stops in London, then in Córdoba, Granada, Marbella, and Seville (Spain), including 2-days of traveling aboard the famed *Andalusian Express* train; a 14-day Alpine Splendor package featuring stops in Innsbruck (Austria), the Italian Dolomites, Paris (France), Munich, Oberammergau, Rothenburg, Wiesbaden (Germany), London (Great Britain), Amsterdam (the Netherlands), Lucerne and St. Moritz (Switzerland); a 17-day Shamrock tour, which tours Great Britain and Ireland; and a Best of Europe package, including a trip on the famed *Venice Simplon–Orient Express* train. For further information, check with your travel agent or contact *Cunard* (555 Fifth Ave., New York, NY 10017; phone: 800-221-4770 or 800-5-CUNARD).

Positioning Cruises – Another interesting possibility for those who have the time is what the industry calls a positioning cruise. This is the sailing of a US- or Caribbean-based vessel from its winter berth to the city in Europe from which it will be offering summer cruise programs. Eastbound positioning cruises take place in the spring; westbound cruises return in the fall. Since ships do not make the return trip until they need to position themselves for the next cruise season, most lines offering positioning cruises have some air/sea arrangement that allows passengers to fly home economically — though the cruises themselves are not an inexpensive way to travel.

Typically, the ships set sail from Florida or from San Juan, Puerto Rico, and cross the Atlantic to any one of a number of European ports where the trip may be broken — Barcelona, Cherbourg, Genoa, Le Havre, Lisbon, London, Málaga, Piraeus, Southampton, Venice — before proceeding to cruise European waters (for example, the Mediterranean, the Baltic Sea, the Black Sea, the Norwegian fjords). Passengers can elect to stay aboard for the basic transatlantic segment alone or for both the crossing and the subsequent European cruise. Ports of call on such crossings and subsequent itineraries may vary substantially from year to year. For the most current information on operative itineraries, ask your travel agent or contact the cruise line directly.

Among the lines that offer positioning cruises to Europe are the following:

Cunard (555 Fifth Ave., New York, NY 10017; phone: 800-872-4770, 800-221-4770, or 800-5-CUNARD). The *Vistafjord* makes 10-day transatlantic positioning cruises between Ft. Lauderdale and Lisbon (Portugal) that call at the island of Madeira (off Portugal). *Cunard*'s luxurious *Sea Goddess I* makes a positioning cruise from St. Thomas in the Caribbean to Málaga (Spain), calling at Madeira and Vilamoura (Portugal); the reverse itinerary is offered in the fall. The *Princess* also makes a positioning cruise from Ft. Lauderdale to Málaga.

Crystal Cruises (2121 Ave. of the Stars, Los Angeles, CA 90067; phone: 800-446-6645). Offers a 12-day cruise aboard the *Crystal Harmony* that sails between Ft. Lauderdale and Lisbon (Portugal); ports of call include the Canary Islands (Spain) and Madeira (Portugal).

Princess Cruises (10100 Santa Monica Blvd., Los Angeles, CA 90067; phone: 800-421-0522). The *Royal Princess* makes an 8-day positioning cruises between New York and Southampton (England).

Royal Cruise Line (One Maritime Plaza, Suite 1400, San Francisco, CA 94111; phone: 800-792-2992 or 415-956-7200 in California; 800-227-4534 elsewhere in the US). Offers a 21-day transatlantic positioning cruise aboard the *Golden Odyssey* from either Aruba (in the Caribbean) or San Juan (Puerto Rico) to Venice (Italy), that calls at ports in France, Greece, Italy, Portugal, Spain, and Yugoslavia. The *Crown Odyssey* makes a 21-day trip from San Juan to Athens (Greece), with stops in Monaco, Italy, Spain, and Portugal. The *Crown Odyssey* also makes a 20-day cruise between Buenos Aires (Argentina) and Lisbon (Portugal).

Royal Viking Line (95 Merrick Way, Coral Gables, FL 33134; phone: 800-422-8000). Makes a 14-day crossing from Ft. Lauderdale to Rome (Italy) aboard the *Royal Viking Sun* that calls at ports in France, Portugal, and Spain. The *Royal Viking Queen* makes 12-day cruises between Barbados (in the Caribbean) and Seville (Spain) that call at Madeira (Portugal).

Sea Bourn Cruise Line (55 Francisco St., San Francisco, CA 94133; phone: 800-351-9595). The *Sea Bourn Spirit* makes 12-day positioning cruises from Ft. Lauderdale to Bordeaux (France) that call at the Azores (Portugal); passengers can disembark, or opt to continue on any of several subsequent Mediterranean cruises. The *Sea Bourn Pride* makes a 9-dày transatlantic positioning cruise between Barbados and Lisbon (Portugal), and a 10-day cruise between London and New York.

Sun Line (1 Rockefeller Plaza, Suite 315, New York, NY 10020; phone: 800-445-6400 or 212-397-6400). The *Stella Solaris* makes a 21-day cruise from Ft. Lauderdale to Piraeus (Greece) that calls at ports in France, Italy, Portugal, and Spain.

Windstar (PO Box C34013, Seattle, WA 98124-1013; phone: 800-626-9900 or 206-281-3535). The *Wind Star,* a 440-foot cruise ship, makes 10- to 22-day sailings between Antigua (in the Caribbean) and Nice (France).

INTRA-EUROPEAN CRUISES: For travelers seeking cruises out of British and continental ports, the opportunities are limitless. Northern European waters are particularly popular in summer, with Amsterdam and Copenhagen major embarkation centers, notably for sailings along Norway's fjord-lined coast as well as to major Baltic ports like Helsinki, St. Petersburg, and Stockholm. July is the month of the midnight sun; cruises to witness this phenomenon are available out of Bergen, Norway.

Still other major ports for summer cruises within Europe are Calais and Nice in France; Genoa and Venice in Italy; Mainz, Germany, and Basel, Switzerland, for Rhine River boat trips; and Piraeus, the famed port of Athens (Greece), from which there are innumerable daily sailings for single-day or week-plus cruises to the Aegean Islands (see *Classic Cruises and Wonderful Waterways,* DIVERSIONS).

The following list of cruise lines, ships, and sailings is a sampling of the countless itineraries offered throughout Europe.

Club Med (3 E. 54th St., New York, NY 10022; phone: 800-CLUB-MED). The 617-foot *Club Med I* makes 7-day round-trip sailings from Toulon (France). It calls at ports in France and Italy. Also offered is an 11-day Iberian Peninsula trip that sails from Toulon to Lisbon (Portugal), calling at ports in Spain.

Costa Cruises (PO Box 01614, Miami, FL 33101-9865; phone: 305-358-7330). Offers a 10-day cruise aboard the *Eugenio Costa* that sails round trip from Genoa (Italy) and stops in Italy, Portugal, and Spain. Another 10-day sailing aboard the same ship also begins and ends in Genoa and stops in Italy and Greece. The *Enrico Costa* makes 7-day round-trip cruises from Venice (Italy) that stop in several Greek ports of call and also calls at Dubrovnik (Yugoslavia). The *Costa Marina* makes 8-day round-trip cruises from Genoa that stop in France, Italy, and Spain. *Costa Marina* makes 8-day round-trip cruises from Genoa that stop in Gibraltar, as well as ports in Spain. The *Danae* makes 11-day round-trip cruises from Venice that stop in Albania, Greece, Italy, and Yugoslavia.

Crystal Cruises (2121 Ave. of the Stars, Los Angeles, CA 90067; phone: 800-446-6645). Offers a baker's dozen of 13-day cruises aboard the *Crystal Harmony* that call at ports throughout Europe. Among these itineraries are a Lisbon (Portugal) to Rome (Italy) cruise that stops in France, Italy, and Spain. Another is a Mediterranean/Black Sea cruise that sails from Rome to Athens (Greece) and calls on ports in Italy, the Soviet Union, Turkey, and Yugoslavia. Also offered is a North Cape cruise between Lisbon and Copenhagen (Denmark), calling at ports in England, France, the Netherlands, Norway, the Soviet Union, and Sweden.

Cunard (555 Fifth Ave., New York, NY 10017; phone: 800-872-4770 or 800-5-CUNARD). The particularly luxurious and exclusive *Sea Goddess I* and *Sea Goddess II* both offer a 7-day cruise between Monte Carlo (Monaco) and Venice (Italy) with stops in Italy. The following itineraries are offered aboard the *Sea Goddess I:* a 7-day Iberia tour that begins and ends in Málaga, stopping in Spanish ports and Gibraltar; 5- to 12-day cruises stopping in Gibraltar and Spain; 7- to 11-day cruises between Rome (Italy) and Monte Carlo (Monaco), calling at ports in France and Italy; an 11-day cruise between London and Pauillac (France), Sardinia (Italy), Monte Carlo, and Ibiza (Spain); and a 10-day cruise between London and Copenhagen (Denmark), visting ports of call throughout Scandinavia. Sailings aboard the *Sea Goddess II* include: a 7-day Riviera cruise round-trip from Monte Carlo with stops in France, Italy, and Spain; a 10-day Mediterranean/Black Sea cruise between Venice and Istanbul (Turkey), stopping in Romania, the Soviet Union, and Yugoslavia; a 10-day Greek Isles/Turkey cruise that sails from Istanbul to Haifa (Israel), stopping in Turkey and Yugoslavia, as well as at several Greek islands. *Cunard's Princess* makes 14-day cruises between Athens (Greece) and Venice, calling at a number of Greek islands and Dubrovnik (Yugoslavia), and a 14-day Canary Islands cruise from Málaga (Spain), calling at Gibraltar, Madeira (Portugal), and several ports in the Canary Islands (Spain). The *Vistafjord* offers a 13-day Baltic/Russia round-trip cruise from Hamburg (Germany) that stops in Denmark, England, Finland, Norway, the Soviet Union, and Sweden. Also offered is a 14-day Baltic/Western Mediterranean trip sailing from Hamburg to Genoa (Italy), stopping in Denmark, England, Gibraltar, Norway, Poland, Portugal, and Spain.

Epirotiki Lines (551 Fifth Ave., New York, NY 10176; phone: 212-221-2470 or 212-599-1750). Offers 7- to 14-day cruises around the Greek islands aboard the *Jason,* the *Oceanos,* and the *World Renaissance.* The *Odysseus* makes 14-night cruises between Venice and Genoa (Italy), stopping in Italy, Bulgaria, several islands in Greece, the Soviet Union, Turkey, and Yugoslavia.

Ocean Cruise Lines (1510 SE 17th St., Ft. Lauderdale, FL 33316; phone: 305-764-3500). Offers cruises aboard the *Ocean Princess* through the Mediterranean, either round-trip from Nice or between Nice and Venice; these call at French,

Greek, Italian, and Spanish ports. Other itineraries include North Sea cruises (round trip from Copenhagen, Denmark), and cruises through the Baltic Sea that call at ports in Denmark, Finland, the Soviet Union, and Sweden.

Paquet French Cruises (1510 SE 17th St., Ft. Lauderdale, FL 33316; phone: 800-556-8850). From Le Havre (France), the *Mermoz* makes a 10-day cruise that stops in England, Portugal, and Spain. Wine is spotlighted, and besides shore excursions visiting wine cellars in the port and sherry regions there may be lectures, wine tastings, and wine-related contests aboard ship. The *Mermoz* also makes 18-day Music Festival round-trip sailings from Toulon (France) that visit Greece and Italy; it also makes a theater cruise for French-speaking passengers only. Also offered are an 18-day Baltic Capitals cruise and 10- and 12-day cruises through the Norwegian fjords that call at ports in Denmark, Iceland, and Norway.

P&O Cruises (c/o *Express Travel Services,* Empire State Building, Suite 7718, 350 Fifth Ave., New York, NY 10118; phone: 212-629-3630 in New York State; 800-223-5799 elsewhere in the US). Based in Southampton (England), where all their European trips begin and end. The *Canberra* makes a 13-day Renaissance & Rivieras cruise calling at French, Italian, and Spanish ports. Their Mediterranean cruises include a 13-day Best of the Mediterranean trip aboard the *Canberra* that calls at Barcelona and Vigo (Spain). The 12-day Islands in the Sun cruise stops in Lisbon and Madeira (Portugal) and Spain's Canary Islands. An Indian Summer cruise aboard the *Sea Princess* stops in Portugal and Spain. Among the numerous other intra-European itineraries offered aboard these ships are Baltic Treasures; Cradles of Civilization; Historic Cities and Idyllic Isles; the Lands of the Vikings; To the Midnight Sun; and Northern Capitals.

Princess Cruises (10100 Santa Monica Blvd, Los Angeles, CA 90067; phone: 800-421-0522). The *Crown Princess* makes 14-day cruises between Athens (Greece) and London (England), with stops in France, Gibraltar, Italy, Portugal, and Spain. The *Crown Princess* also makes 14-day cruises between Venice (Italy) and Athens, stopping in Greece, Turkey, the Soviet Union, and Yugoslavia. And 12-day cruises aboard either the *Royal Princess* or *Crown Princess* between Barcelona (Spain) and Venice stop in France, Greece, Italy, and Yugoslavia. The *Royal Princess* also makes 13-day cruises between Barcelona (Spain) and London, stopping in France, Italy, Portugal, and Spain.

Raymond & Whitcomb (400 Madison Ave., New York, NY 10017; phone: 212-759-3960). The *Argonaut* makes 14-day Voyage to Byzantium cruises between Venice (Italy) and Istanbul (Turkey), stopping at Italian, Greek, and Turkish ports of call. A 12-night voyage aboard the *Argonaut* sails between Genoa (Italy) and Lisbon (Portugal); this ship also makes 15-day sailings between Genoa and Venice. In conjunction with the Smithsonian Institute, this line also offers a Black Sea Passage 14-day round-trip cruise from Istanbul, which stops in ports in Bulgaria, Romania, and the Soviet Union.

Royal Cruise Line (One Maritime Plaza, Suite 1400, San Francisco, CA 94111; phone: 800-792-2992 or 415-956-7200 in California; 800-227-4534 elsewhere in the US). The *Crown Odyssey* makes 12-day Great Capitals of Europe between Venice (Italy) and Tilbury (near London, England), stopping in France, Italy, Portugal, Spain, and Yugoslavia. This ship also makes a 13-day round-trip cruise, beginning and ending in Tilbury, and exploring Denmark, Finland, Germany, the Netherlands, Norway, the Soviet Union, and Sweden. Both the *Crown Odyssey* and the *Golden Odyssey* also make 12-day Gala Mediterranean cruises between Lisbon (Portugal) and Athens (Greece), stopping in France, Italy, and Spain. The *Golden Odyssey* also sails on a 12-day Best of Italy, France, and the Greek Isles cruise between Venice and Nice (France) that stops in Greece, Italy, and Monaco, and on a 21-day Magnificent Odyssey cruise, stopping in Gibraltar, Italy, Monaco, Portugal, and Spain.

Royal Viking Line (95 Merrick Way, Coral Gables, FL 33134; phone: 800-422-8000). The *Royal Viking Queen* makes a 14-day Bagpipes and Shamrock cruise between London (England) and Copenhagen (Denmark) that calls at Irish and Scottish ports; a 14-day Best of Europe cruise between London and Monte Carlo (Monaco), stopping in Spanish and Portuguese ports; a Mediterranean/*Expo '92* cruise between Seville (Spain) and Venice (Italy); and 14-day sailings between Monte Carlo and Istanbul (Turkey). The *Royal Viking Sun* makes 12-day cruises between Lisbon (Portugal) and Venice that call at ports in France, Italy, Spain, and Yugoslavia. This ship also cruises between London and Barcelona (Spain), Bordeaux (France) and Venice, and leaves from Tilbury (near London) on 14-day North Cape or Connoisseur's Europe sailings.

Sea Bourn Cruise Line (55 Francisco Street, San Francisco, CA 94133; phone: 800-351-9595). The luxurious *Sea Bourn Pride* and the *Sea Bourn Spirit* both offer a variety of intra-European cruises each year. The *Sea Bourn Pride* makes a 7-day Mediterranean cruise departing from Venice (Italy) with ports of call in Italy, the Maltese Islands, and Yugoslavia; 13-day sailings between London and Bordeaux (France) that call at British and Irish ports; and an 11-day cruise between Lisbon (Portugal) and Nice (France). The *Sea Bourn Spirit* sails from Piraeus (Greece) on 14-day Black Sea cruise stopping in Greece, the Soviet Union, Turkey, and Yugoslavia, as well as on a 7-day Mediterranean cruise departing from Venice that also calls at Civitavecchia (the port for Rome).

Sun Lines (1 Rockefeller Plaza, Suite 315, New York, NY 10020; phone: 800-445-6400 or 212-397-6400). The *Stella Maris* makes a 7-day round-trip cruise between Venice (Italy) and Nice (France), calling on Italian ports. The *Stella Oceanis* makes 3- to 4-day cruises through the Greek islands.

Swan Hellenic Cruises (c/o *Esplanade Tours,* 581 Boylston St., Boston, MA 02116; phone: 800-426-5492 or 617-266-7465). The *Orpheus* makes numerous cruises (over 40 separate itineraries) throughout Europe; many sailings focus on art or natural history. Among their offerings is a 9-day Shores of Ireland cruise that calls at Irish and Scottish ports.

Wind Star Cruises (PO C34013, Seattle, WA 98124-1013; phone: 800-250-7245). Offers 7-day round-trip cruises aboard the *Wind Star.* These cruises depart from Nice (France) and stop in Calvi (Corsica), Monte Carlo (Monaco), and Portofino and Portovenere (Italy).

In addition, the *International Cruise Center* (250 Old Country Rd., Mineola, NY 11501; phone: 516-747-8880 in New York State; 800-221-3254 elsewhere in the US) is the general sales agent for several European lines.

FREIGHTERS: An alternative to conventional cruise ships is travel by freighter. These are cargo ships that also take a limited number of passengers (usually about 12) in reasonably comfortable accommodations. The idea of traveling by freighter has long appealed to romantic souls, but there are a number of drawbacks to consider before casting off. Once upon a time, a major advantage of freighter travel was its low cost, but this is no longer the case. Though freighters usually are less expensive than cruise ships, the difference is not as great as it once was. Accommodations and recreational facilities vary, but freighters were not designed to amuse passengers, so it is important to appreciate the idea of freighter travel itself. Schedules are erratic, and travelers must fit their timetable to that of the ship. Passengers have found themselves waiting as long as a month for a promised sailing, and because freighters follow their cargo commitments, it is possible that a scheduled port could be omitted at the last minute or a new one added.

Anyone contemplating taking a freighter from a US port across the Atlantic should be aware that at press time only a few freighter lines were carrying passengers on such crossings. Such freighter lines and sailings include the following:

Bank Line Freighters of Britain (contact *Freighter World Cruises;* address below). Offers 110- to 130-day around-the-world sailings, which leave from Antwerp (Belgium) and end in Rotterdam (the Netherlands). Passenger quarters are above average in terms of luxury and facilities (private baths, VCRs, and so on).

Bergen Line (505 Fifth Ave., New York, NY 10017; phone: 212-986-2711 in New York; 800-323-7436 elsewhere in the US). Offers 11-day round-trip sailings around the Norwegian coastline, departing from Bergen, Norway. A 10- or 12-day air/sea package from New York also is offered.

Cast Shipping (contact *Freighter World Cruises;* address below). Sails from Montreal (Canada) to Antwerp (Belgium), with a capacity of 12 passengers, taking 16 days eastward (to Europe) and 12 days westward (back to Canada). Ships depart two or three times a month between April and October.

Container Ships Reederi (contact *Freighter World Cruises;* address below). Departs approximately every once a month and, with a capacity of 9 passengers, sails from Long Beach, California, via the Panama Canal to Felixstowe (England), Le Havre (France), and Rotterdam (the Netherlands), taking 23 to 24 days to make the trip.

Egon Oldendorff (contact *Norton, Lilly & Co.,* 245 Monticello Arcade, Suite 15, Norfolk, VA 23510; phone: 804-622-7035). Offers 12- to 15-day sailings from the US Gulf — Mobile (Alabama), Tampa (Florida), and New Orleans (Louisiana) — and the East Coast — Baltimore (Maryland), Philadelphia (Pennsylvania), and Norfolk (Virginia) — to Amsterdam (the Netherlands), Bordeaux (France), Hamburg (Germany), or Rotterdam (the Netherlands).

Losinjska Plovidba (PO Box 135, Rijeka 51001, Yugoslavia; no phone). Sails from Rijeka (Yugoslavia) to several ports in Greece, Italy, and Turkey.

Lykes Lines (300 Poydras, New Orleans, LA 70130; phone: 800-535-1861 or 504-523-6611). Sails from New Orleans and Norfolk (Virginia) to Antwerp (Belgium), Felixstowe (England), Le Havre (France), Bremerhaven (Germany), and Rotterdam (the Netherlands), and from Galveston (Texas) to Livorno and Naples (Italy), and to ports in the Middle East. The ships carry up to 8 passengers, the trips last from 12 to 16 days, and ships leave every 8 to 14 days year-round.

Mediterranean Shipping Co. (contact *Sea the Difference,* 96 Morton St., New York, NY 10014; phone: 800-666-9333 or 212-691-3760). Sails from Baltimore, Boston, Port Elizabeth (New Jersey), and Newport News (Virginia) to Antwerp (Belgium), Felixstowe (England), Le Havre (France), and Bremen and Hamburg (Germany), taking 18 to 19 days for the trip. The ships can carry 12 passengers and leave twice a month year-round. Prices vary substantially, based on departure point and destination.

Mineral Shipping (contact *Freighter World Cruises;* address below). Leaves from Savannah (Georgia) to Rotterdam (the Netherlands), taking several weeks; the full round trip takes 33 days. It also sails from Savannah to Rotterdam via Jamaica. The ships sail up to twice monthly year-round and can hold up to 12 passengers.

Polish Ocean Lines (contact *Gdynia America Line,* 39 Broadway, 14th Floor, New York, NY 10006; phone: 212-952-1280). Once a week, freighters accommodating 6 passengers in 3 double cabins leave on voyages approximately 8 to 10 days in length from Port Newark (New Jersey) to Le Havre (France), Rotterdam (the Netherlands), and Bremerhaven (Germany). Passengers also can board in Baltimore, Maryland, or Wilmington, North Carolina (for a supplement).

United Baltic Corp. Ltd. (Dexter House, 2 Royal Mt. Court, London, England EC3N 4XX; phone: 44-71-265-0808). Offers frequent 10- or 21-day sailings from Great Britain to Finland.

Yugoslav Great Lakes Line (contact *TravLTips Cruise and Freighter Travel Association;* address below). Sails from Montreal (Canada) to a variety of European ports including Genoa, Livorno, Naples, and Trieste (Italy).

The following specialists deal only (or largely) in freighter travel. They provide information, schedules, and, when you're ready to sail, booking services.

Freighter World Cruises, Inc. (180 S. Lake Ave., Suite 335, Pasadena, CA 91101; phone: 818-449-3106). A freighter travel agency that acts as general agent for several freighter lines. Publishes the twice-monthly *Freighter Space Advisory,* listing space available on sailings worldwide. A subscription costs $27 a year, $25 of which can be credited toward the cost of a cruise.

Pearl's Travel Tips (9903 Oaks La., Seminole, FL 34642; phone: 813-393-2919). Run by Ilse Hoffman, who finds sailings for her customers and sends them off with all kinds of valuable information and advice.

TravLtips Cruise and Freighter Travel Association (PO Box 188, Flushing, NY 11358; phone: 800-872-8584 or 718-939-2400). A freighter travel agency and club ($15 per year or $25 for 2 years) whose members receive the bimonthly *TravLtips* magazine of cruise and freighter travel.

Those interested in freighter travel also may want to subscribe to *Freighter Travel News,* a publication of the *Freighter Travel Club of America.* A year's subscription to this monthly newsletter costs $18. To subscribe, write to the club at 3524 Harts Lake Rd., Roy, WA 98580.

Another monthly newsletter that may be of interest to those planning to cruise European waters is *Ocean and Cruise News,* which offers comprehensive coverage of the latest on the cruise ship scene. A year's subscription costs $24. Contact *Ocean and Cruise News,* PO Box 92, Stamford, CT 06904 (phone: 203-329-2787).

INLAND WATERWAYS: Cruising the canals and rivers of Europe is becoming more and more popular, probably in reaction to the speed of jet travel and the normal rush to do as much as possible in as little time as possible. A cabin cruiser or converted barge averages only about 5 miles an hour, covering in a week of slow floating the same distance a car would travel in a few hours of determined driving. Passengers see only a small section of countryside, but they see it in depth and with an intimacy simply impossible any other way.

There are two ways to cruise the inland waterways: by renting your own self-drive boat or by booking aboard a hotel-boat. If you choose to skipper your own diesel-powered cruiser, you will be shown how to handle the craft and told whom to call if you break down. But once you cast off, you and your party — the boats sleep from 2 to 10 people — will be on your own. You help lockkeepers operate the gates and do your own cooking (in addition to village markets, the lockkeepers themselves often have fresh provisions) or eat at cafés and restaurants along the way. The cost of the rental can vary considerably, depending on the size of the boat, the season, and the area. (And note that fuel is not included.)

The alternative is to cruise on a hotel-boat — often a converted barge. These can carry anywhere from 6 to 24 guests, occasionally even more, as well as the crew. You can charter the boat and have it all to yourself or join other guests aboard. Cruises usually last from 3 days to a week; accommodations can be simple or quite luxurious, and most meals usually are included. When reading the brochure, note the boat's facilities (most cabins have private washbasins, showers, and toilets, but bathrooms also can be separate and shared), as well as the itinerary and any special features, such as sightseeing excursions, that may be offered. Many of the European cruises have a special emphasis such as food and wine, and include tasting excursions to vineyards and wine cellars; others make a point of visiting historic spots. Again, prices can vary substantially, depending on the season, operative itinerary, and level of luxury.

The travel firms listed below, including the operators of hotel-boat cruises and representatives of self-drive boat suppliers, can provide information or arrange your whole holiday afloat in Europe.

Abercrombie & Kent/Continental Waterways (1520 Kensington Rd., Suite 103, Oak Brook, IL 60521; phone: 708-954-2944 in Illinois; 800-323-7308 elsewhere in the US). Runs hotel-boat cruises in France, Great Britain, Holland, and Belgium.

Anglo Welsh Waterways Holidays (The Canal Basin, Market Harborough, Leicester LE16 7BJ, England; phone: 44-81-730-9600). Rents canal boats in England and Wales.

Bargain Boating, Morgantown Travel Service (PO Box 757, Morgantown, WV 26507-0757; phone: 800-637-0782 or 304-292-8471). Books self-skippered boats in Belgium, Denmark, France, Great Britain, Ireland, and the Netherlands.

Blakes Vacations (4918 Dempster St., Skokie, IL 60077; phone: 708-982-0561 in Illinois; 800-628-8118 elswhere in the US). Books self-skippered boats in France, Great Britain, Ireland, Italy, and Spain.

Esplanade Tours (581 Boylston St., Boston, MA 02116; phone: 800-628-4893 or 617-266-7465). Books hotel-boat cruises in France.

Etoile de Champagne (89 Broad St., Boston, 02110; phone: 800-666-1620 or 617-426-1776). Offers luxury chartered hotel-boat cruises thoughout the inland waterways of Belgium, France, and the Netherlands.

Floating Through Europe (271 Madison Ave., New York, NY 10016; phone: 800-221-3140 or 212-685-5600). Operates hotel-boat cruises in Belgium, France, and Great Britain.

French Country Waterways, Ltd. (PO Box 2195, Duxbury, MA 02331; phone: 617-934-2454 or 800-222-1236 throughout the continental US). Books hotel-boat cruises in France; a number of trips also include hot-air balloon rides.

French Experience (370 Lexington Ave., Suite 812, New York, NY 10017; phone: 800-28-FRANCE or 212-986-3800). Books self-drive boats throughout France.

Hideaways International (15 Goldsmith St., PO Box 1270, Littleton, MA 01460; phone: 800-843-4433 or 508-486-8955). Books skippered barge trips on the inland waterways of Belgium, France, and the Netherlands.

Hoseasons Holidays Ltd. (Sunway House, Lowestoft, Suffolk NR32 3LT, England; phone: 44-502-500505). Offers self-skippered boats in France, Great Britain, and the Netherlands.

KD German Rhine Line (contact *Rhine Cruise Agency,* 170 Hamilton Ave., White Plains, NY; phone: 914-948-3600 or 800-346-6525 in the Eastern US; or 323 Geary St., San Francisco, CA 94102; phone: 415-392-8817 or 800-858-8587 in the Western US, including Alaska and Hawaii). Books hotel-boat cruises on the Rhine and Elbe rivers in Germany, as well as in France, the Netherlands, and Switzerland.

Skipper Travel Services (210 California Ave., Palo Alto, CA 94306; phone: 415-321-5658). Books self-drive boats and hotel-boat cruises in France, Great Britain, Ireland, and the Netherlands.

French Cruise Lines (FCL) also offers inland cruises on the French Rhône, Saône, and Seine rivers aboard two 100-passenger ships, the *Arlène* and the *Normandy.* Ports of call include Paris, Rouen, and Villequier. Round-trip fares for the 6- and 7-night river cruises include all meals, but not wine — only the finest French vintages are served. For information, contact *French Cruise Lines,* 701 Lee St., Des Plaines, IL 60016 (phone: 800-222-8664).

Another source of information are associations concerned with the use and mainte- nance of European inland waterways and canals. For instance, Britain's *Inland Water- ways Association* (114 Regent's Park Rd., London NW1 8UQ, England; phone: 44-71- 586-2510), which maintains and monitors the country's extensive canal system, also can provide detailed information on its over 25,000 members, who incude boaters, as well as lockkeepers. And the Irish Republic's Office of Public Works, Waterways Division (51 St. Stephen's Green, Dublin 2, Ireland; phone: 353-1-613111), which maintains and monitors Ireland's inland waterways, also can provide detailed information for those interested in sailing these waters.

■ **A final note on picking a cruise:** A "cruise-only" travel agency can best help you choose a cruise ship and itinerary. Cruise-only agents are best equipped to tell you about a particular ship's "personality," the kind of person with whom you'll likely be traveling on a particular ship, what dress is acceptable (it varies from ship to ship), and much more. Travel agencies that specialize in booking cruises usually are members of the *National Association of Cruise Only Agencies (NACOA).* For a listing of the agencies in your area (requests are limited to three states), send a self-addressed, stamped envelope to *NACOA,* PO Box 7209, Freeport, NY 11520, or call 516-378-8006.

FERRIES: Numerous ferries link European ports, and nearly all of them carry both passengers and cars — you simply drive on and drive off in most cases — and most routes are in service year-round. Some operators offer reduced rates for round-trip excursions, midweek travel, or off-season travel. Space for cars should be booked as early as possible, especially for July and August crossings, even though most lines schedule more frequent departures during the summer months. Note that long jour- neys, of 8 to 10 hours or more, tend to be scheduled overnight.

Most ferry arrivals and departures are well served by connecting passenger trains or buses, and passengers can buy through train tickets that include the sea portion of the trip. The Paris to London route on through services by train/*Hovercraft*/train, for example, takes an average 5½ hours; from Paris to London on through services by train/ferry/train can take from 7 to 9 hours by day, depending on the route, or about 9½ to 10½ hours overnight. And the new *Hoverspeed* fleet of even faster catamaran ferries cuts the actual channel crossing time down even further — by another 15 to 20 minutes. (And the effect of the pending completion of the Eurotunnel between France and Great Britain on such connecting service remains to be seen.)

Traveling by Train

Perhaps the most economical, and often the most satisfying, way to see a lot of a foreign country in a relatively short time is by rail. It certainly is the quickest way to travel between two cities up to 300 miles apart (beyond that, a flight normally would be quicker, even counting the time it takes to get to and from the airport). But time isn't always the only consideration. Traveling by train is a way to keep moving and to keep seeing at the same time. The fares usually are reasonable, and with the special discounts available to visitors, it can be an almost irresistible bargain. You only need to get to a station on time; after that, put your watch in your pocket and relax. You may not get to your destination exactly at the appointed hour (although European trains are quite punctual for the most part), but you'll have a marvelous time looking out the window and enjoying the ride.

TRAINS: While North Americans have been raised to depend on their cars, Europeans have long been able to depend on public transportation. Some of the special trains you may encounter in Europe include the *EuroCity (EC)* trains, which have ushered in a new phase of European train service. These trains are largely international and are operated by several of Europe's national railway companies. The *EC* network, introduced in May 1987, has by now all but replaced the *Trans-Europe Express (TEE),* which provided the European Economic Community with fast, efficient, luxurious train service between major cities since the 1950s. *TEE*s have been all but phased out in Europe; in fact, many *EuroCity* and *InterCity* (see below) trains are former *TEE*s to which second class has been added.

*EC*s currently are the prestige trains of Europe and maintain high standards. They use modern, air conditioned coaches, are punctual and clean, and travel at a minimum speed of 54 miles per hour (the average includes time for station stops). All *EC* trains also have dining facilities and bilingual personnel on board. With the exception of some first class–only trains (such as those running between Paris and Brussels), the *EC*s generally offer both first and second class service and require payment of a supplement for all departures. The supplement includes the price of a reserved seat, which is obligatory on any *EC* crossing borders but not on trips within a country. The *EC* network includes 200 connections within the 12 participating countries: Austria, Belgium, Denmark, France, Germany, Italy, Luxembourg, the Netherlands, Norway, Spain, Sweden, and Switzerland.

If there are no *EC*s on a route, the next best trains are likely to be *InterCity (IC)* trains, which are similar to *EC*s in that they provide a high standard of service, have both first and second class cars, and usually require payment of a supplement. There are both national and international *IC* trains. As mentioned above, some are former *TEE*s to which second class cars have been added; a great many more already existed as part of the rail networks of certain countries (Germany, for instance, has a highly developed *IC* system). Supplements must be paid to ride all continental *IC* trains except the Swiss ones (other exceptions are the *IC* trains of Great Britain, whose railway system has not yet been integrated with the continental system), while reservations are obligatory only on those crossing borders. Another train offering the same high quality of service as the *IC*s is the *Trans Euro Night (TEN),* an overnight train with sleeping quarters — these are aptly named, as they run literally "across" Europe.

The next step in the development of this network is a link across the English Channel. At the time of this writing, the Eurotunnel (also referred to as the "Chunnel") was still under construction and the official scheduled completion date (and current popular estimate) is early 1994. This addition will connect the British railway with French and other continental service and will open the way for an additional *ICE* network linking London, Paris, and Brussels. That network is expected to be further extended to Cologne and Amsterdam — the current estimate for this addition is 1995.

France's railway system encompasses the world's fastest train, the *TGV* (*Train à Grande Vitesse*), which represents the state of the art in train technology. Though *TGV*s are capable of speeds of up to 317 mph (511 kph), their maximum speed in commercial operation is limited to 186 mph (298). They run on a so-called dedicated track, which has so far been laid between Paris and Lyons and to the Atlantic coast — serving points south and west of Paris, including the Spanish border. Another new line this year will be running between Paris and the Tarentaise Valley, near where the *1992 Winter Olympics* will be held. Because *TGV*s are capable of running on conventional track, as well as on their own special track, you also can take it on other routes, such as from Paris to Switzerland.

*TGV*s carry first and second class passengers, supplements must be paid for travel during rush hours and on peak days, and reservations are obligatory. Reservations can be made in the US from 2 months to 15 days before departure; in France, the reservation period ranges from 6 months in advance by mail to a few minutes before departure by using *TGV* Réservation Rapide machines in train stations. The reservation fee is a flat amount per seat (at press time, $8 if made in the US). For tickets, reservations, and information, contact any of the *Rail Europe* offices listed at the end of this section.

Other European countries also offer high-speed rail service. For instance, Italy's *Pendolino* runs between Milan and Rome at 180 mph (288 kph), offering first class service only. Great Britain's highspeed *IC*s include the *Intercity 125* (which travels at 125 mph) and the even faster and more luxurious *InterCity 225* (which travels at 140 mph). And joining other European countries in the addition of high-speed rail service, the *Spanish National Railways* will be offering a speedy new *IC*-type service starting in April of this year — called *Alta Velocidad Español (AVE)* — between Seville and Madrid, which will run at 186 mph (298 kph). And *Germany Rail*'s new high-speed *InterCity Express (ICE)* trains are now running at 165 mph (264 kph) between Hamburg — via Frankfurt — and Munich. Other national railways are expected to follow suit in the near future.

These special trains are but a small part of Europe's highly developed rail service. Hundreds of towns across the Continent are served by "regular" express and local trains. These trains generally have first and second class cars and meal service. (Those that make long overnight trips also offer various sleeping facilities, which must be reserved during peak travel periods.) In addition, special train excursions and itineraries are offered aboard trains such as the *Venice Simplon–Orient Express* and the *Anna Karenina;* for information on these and other special package offerings, see *Package Tours,* in this section.

ACCOMMODATIONS, FARES, SERVICES: Fares on European trains are based on a combination of the distance traveled and the quality of accommodations the passenger enjoys. You pay on the basis of traveling first or second class; for express trains — such as the *EC, IC,* some *TGV* trains, and other expresses such as *Rapidos* in Italy and Portugal, and *Talgos* in Spain — you also will have to pay a supplement. Traditionally, seating is arranged in compartments, with three or four passengers on one side facing a like number on the other side, but increasingly, in the newer cars, compartments have been replaced by a central-aisle design.

Tickets can be purchased through travel agents or national railway offices in the US (addresses below) or abroad, as well as at train stations, where domestic and international tickets usually are sold separately and lines can be long. The fare structure differs from country to country, but short hauls always are more expensive on a per-mile basis than longer runs. Most ticket and reservations systems are computerized and efficient.

Both first and second class seats on most European trains can be reserved in advance for a flat fee per seat. Reservations reduce flexibility, but they are advisable during the summer on popular routes — particularly long-distance routes. They also are advisable at holiday times (but note that reservations — except for the obligatory ones — may not be accepted for trains departing around *Christmas* or *Easter*) and at any time of the year if it is imperative that you be on a particular train.

In the US, the reservation period usually runs around 2 months to 15 days before departure. For most trains, the reservation fee is about $3 per seat. If the reservation is made in the US, the reservation fee is a flat amount per seat ($8, including communications charges). As these fees add up, consider buying tickets here and making reservations, even those that are obligatory, after you arrive in Europe.

Sleeping accommodations are found on overnight trains going long distances. Two types of arrangements are possible on European trains: "couchettes" and sleepers.

Couchettes, available in both first and second class versions, basically are the coach seats of a compartment converted to sleeping berths, with pillows, sheets, and blankets. First class compartments contain four couchettes (an upper and a lower on each side of the aisle); second class compartments contain six (an upper, middle, and lower on each side). Note that only second class couchettes are offered in some countries — the exceptions include France and Italy. Couchettes cost a standard charge (at present, around $15 to $20 in either class if reserved in the US) above the first or second class fare; they are a relatively inexpensive way to get a night's rest aboard the train. However, they provide privacy only for those traveling with a family or other group that can use the whole compartment; individual travelers usually are mixed with strangers of either sex.

Sleepers are actual bedroom compartments providing one to three beds with a mattress, pillow, sheets, and blanket, plus a washbasin with hot and cold water. Several kinds of compartments are available, though not always on every train. Singles, specials, and doubles are all first class accommodations. The special is the least expensive, and is a slightly smaller individual compartment than the single; the double is for two people who have booked it together. Tourist compartments (T2 and T3) are second class compartments for two and three people traveling together or for strangers, though unlike couchette accommodations, strangers of the opposite sex are segregated. Sleeper accommodations require payment of the basic first or second class fare plus a supplement that varies with the type of compartment and the distance traveled. From the least to the most expensive, sleeper arrangements can cost anywhere from twice the price of a couchette to as much as eight times more.

The wide range of dining facilities runs from prix fixe menus served in dining cars or at your seat to self-service cafeteria-style cars and ambulatory vendors dispensing snacks, sandwiches, and beverages. In-seat and dining car lunch and dinner reservations either are made in advance or after boarding by visiting the dining car or through the train steward. If you're sure you will want to eat en route, it's a good idea to inquire beforehand exactly what meal service is offered on the train you'll be taking and whether advance dining reservations are required.

A standardized pictorial code has been fashioned to indicate the many amenities offered at train stations. These include restaurants, as well as showers, post and telegraph offices, exchange bureaus, and diaper changing facilities. Most large cities have two or more stations, with service to different parts of the country leaving from different stations, so make sure you know the name of the station for your train.

Naturally, it is best to travel light. More and more modern trains are equipped with a place to put luggage just inside the doors, but otherwise you will have to hoist your suitcase up onto the overhead rack. There also may be a per-passenger baggage restriction and you may have to pay for anything over this amount. If you have too much luggage to handle yourself, it often can be sent as registered baggage. Note that such checked baggage may not travel on the same train that you do; if it is not at the station when you arrive, it may be on the next train — but just in case it actually has been lost or stolen, ask a conductor. As a general rule, baggage can be checked through to your destination between any two stations *within* a country, but not between two different countries, because of customs inspections.

Baggage can be checked overnight at most stations, and some stations also provide 24-hour luggage lockers where you can temporarily free yourself of surplus bags. Due to recent bomb scares, however, luggage lockers are increasingly less common in European railroad stations, and in some countries — such as Great Britain — lockers have been eliminated altogether. In some stations, you'll find self-service luggage carts at your disposal — although both these and porters frequently are in short supply.

Those planning driving routes should be aware that most European railways have some form of auto ferry that allows car owners to take to the rails for long distances while their car travels with them on a flatcar. Note that such service usually can be booked only in Europe, and it is quite popular with Europeans, especially in the peak summer months. Your best bet is to make reservations as soon as you get to Europe, the earlier the better.

Other useful services include the convenience of renting a car at a railroad station. Passengers may be able to reserve a car before boarding the train and find it waiting for them at their destination. (For information on a combination rail pass and rental car program, see "Passes," below.) Similar services also exist for bicyclists.

PASSES: Rail passes are offered by most European railroad companies. They allow unlimited train travel within a set time period, frequently include connecting service via other forms of transportation, and can save the traveler a considerable amount of money, as well as time. The only requirement is validation of the pass by an information clerk on the day of your first rail trip; thereafter, there is no need to stand in line — and lines can be very long during peak travel periods — to buy individual tickets for subsequent trips. Designed primarily for foreign visitors, these passes generally must be bought in the US (or some other foreign location) prior to arrival in Europe. Although these passes can be among the best bargains around, be sure to look into the comparable cost of individual train tickets which — depending on the number of days you plan to travel — may work out to be less expensive.

The Eurailpass, the first and best known of all rail passes, is valid for travel through 17 countries — Austria, Belgium, Denmark, Finland, France, Germany, Greece, Holland, Hungary, the Irish Republic, Italy, Luxembourg, Norway, Portugal, Spain, Sweden, and Switzerland. It entitles holders to 15 or 21 days or 1, 2, or 3 months of unlimited first class travel, plus many extras, including free travel or substantial reductions on some ferry crossings (within and between countries in the Eurail network), river trips, lake steamers, and transportation by bus and private railroads, as well as scheduled *Europabus* services, and airport to city center rail connections. Since the Eurailpass is a first class pass, Eurail travelers can ride just about any European train they wish, including special express trains, without paying additional supplements. The only extras are the nominal reservation fee and sleeper and couchette costs.

A Eurailpass for children under 12 is half the adult price (children under 4 travel free) but includes the same features. The Eurail Youthpass, for travelers under 26 years of age, is slightly different, in that it is valid for travel in second class only.

The Eurail Saverpass resembles the basic Eurailpass, except that it provides 15 days of unlimited first class travel for three people traveling together during peak season; two people traveling together qualify if travel takes place entirely between October 1 and March 31. The Saverpass provides savings of approximately $100 per ticket as compared to the price of a 15-day Eurailpass.

Another option is the Eurail Flexipass, which can be used for first class travel on any 5 days within a 15-day period, 9 days within a 21-day period, or 14 days within a 30-day period. All of these passes must be bought before you go, either from a travel agent or from a US office of the French, German, Italian, or Swiss railway companies. A Eurail Aid office in Europe will replace lost passes when proper documentation is provided; a reissuance fee is charged. (A list of Eurail Aid offices throughout Europe is provided when you buy a Eurailpass; you also can ask at any national railway office in Europe for the nearest location.)

Also note that both the 7-day Eurailpass and the 9-day Eurail Flexipass can be combined with 3 to 8 days of car rental through *Hertz*. The program, marketed under the name *Hertz* EurailDrive Escape, includes a car rental with unlimited mileage, basic insurance, and taxes, as well as some drop-off options within most of the countries of rental. Reservations must be made in the US at least 7 days in advance by calling *Hertz* at 800-654-3001.

The Eurailpass is a bargain for those who will be traveling widely throughout Europe; however, if you're going to tour one country extensively, inquire about national discount plans (before leaving the US in case the plan requires purchase abroad). Many countries issue passes similar to the Eurailpass that allow unlimited travel for defined periods of time over the national transportation network. In addition, there is an endless array of special discount tickets, rail and bike plans, rail and road plans, and other bargains. Most national railroads also offer discounts to those over 60 or 65, those under 26, and children under 12; younger children may ride free.

Although Eurailpasses are not valid in Great Britain, *BritRail* passes, which include transportation throughout England, Scotland, and Wales, come in versions similar to the Eurailpass. For those planning to travel throughout both Great Britain and France, the BritFrance Railpass covers train travel in just these two countries, as well as round-trip transportation aboard the *Hoverspeed Hovercraft* across the English Channel. France's own pass, the France Railpass, offers unlimited train travel, again within a set number of days, on the country's extensive rail network. Other similar single-country passes include Italy's Italian Tourist Ticket (or *BTLC*) and Italian Kilometric Ticket (or *BC*), Portugal's discounted Tourist Ticket, and Spain's Tourist Pass (also called a Spanish Rail Pass). Ireland's Rambler Ticket is good for travel in the Irish Republic and the Rail Runabout Ticket applies to travel in Northern Ireland only, while the Emerald Isle Card is valid for travel in both Northern Ireland and the Irish Republic.

Other areawide programs also exist: The Benelux Tourail ticket, for instance — which can be purchased only in the Benelux countries — allows unlimited travel in Belgium, Luxembourg, and the Netherlands for any 5 days within a 17-day period; this fare is offered on a seasonal basis (approximately March through September). The Holland Railpass is valid for 3 days of unlimited travel during any 10-day period. The Scandinavian Rail Pass is good for 15, 21, or 30 days of first or second class travel on trains throughout Denmark, Finland, Norway, and Sweden and over certain ferry routes as well. It can be bought at any railroad station in Scandinavia.

Rail passes offered in Eastern Europe include Poland's Polrailpass and the Hungary Pass. The relatively new European East Pass entitles holders to 5 days of first class rail travel in Austria, Czechoslovakia, Hungary, and Poland during a 15-day period. A longer version allows 10 days travel during 1 month. (Note that Hungary also is the only Eastern European country included in the Eurail network.)

FURTHER INFORMATION: Some books you may want to consult before embarking on an extensive rail trip in Europe include the *Eurail Traveler's Guide* (which contains a railroad map) and the *Eurail Timetable.* Both are free from Eurailpass (Box 10383, Stamford, CT 06904-2383), as well as from the Eurail Distribution Centre (Box 300, Succursale R, Montreal, Quebec H2S 3K9, Canada). The *Eurail Guide,* by Kathryn Turpin and Marvin Saltzman, is available in most travel bookstores; it also can be ordered from Eurail Guide Annuals (27540 Pacific Coast Hwy., Malibu, CA 90265; phone: 213-457-7286) for $14.95, plus shipping and handling. *Europe by Eurail,* by George Wright Ferguson, is available from Globe Pequot Press (PO Box Q, Chester, CT 06412; phone: 203-526-9571) for $14.95, plus shipping and handling. The latter two guides discuss train travel in general, contain information on countries included in the Eurail network (the Saltzman book also discusses Eastern Europe and the rest of the world), and suggest numerous sightseeing excursions by rail from various base cities.

You also may want to buy the *Thomas Cook European Timetable,* a weighty and detailed compendium of European international and national rail services that constitutes the most revered and accurate railway reference in existence. The *Timetable* comes out monthly, but because most European countries switch to summer schedules at the end of May (and back to winter schedules at the end of September), the June edition offers the first complete summer schedule (and October the first complete winter schedule). The February through May editions, however, contain increasingly more definitive supplements on upcoming summer schedules that can be used to plan a trip.

The *Thomas Cook European Timetable* is available in some travel bookstores or can be ordered from the *Forsyth Travel Library* (PO Box 2975, Shawnee Mission, KS 66201-1375; phone: 800-367-7984 or 913-384-0496) for $12.95, plus shipping and handling; credit card orders also are accepted by phone.

Following are addresses for the national railway offices in the US and Canada that sell tickets and passes and make reservations:

BritRail Travel International
New York State: 1500 Broadway, New York, NY 10017 (phone: 212-575-2667).
Canada: 94 Cumberland St., Toronto, Ontario M5R 1A3, Canada (phone: 416-929-3333); 409 Granville St., Vancouver, British Columbia V6C 1T2, Canada (phone: 604-683-6896).

German Rail
California: 11933 Wilshire Blvd., Los Angeles, CA 90025 (phone: 213-479-2772).
Georgia: 3400 Peachtree Rd. NE, Lenox Towers, Suite 1299, Atlanta, GA 30326 (phone: 404-266-9555).
Illinois: 9575 Higgins Rd., Suite 505, Rosemont, IL 60018 (phone: 312-692-4209).
Massachusetts: 625 Statler Office Bldg., Boston, MA 02116 (phone: 617-542-0577).
New York State: 747 Third Ave., New York, NY 10017 (phone: 212-308-3100).
Texas: 222 W. Las Colinas, Suite 1050, Irving, TX 75039 (phone: 214-402-8377).
Canada: 1290 Bay St., Toronto, Ontario M5R 2C3, Canada (phone: 416-968-3272).

Irish Republic
California: *CIE Tours International,* c/o Ms. D. O'Neil, 118 42nd St., Newport Beach, CA 92663 (phone: 714-645-3508).
Illinois: *CIE Tours International,* c/o Ms. M. Flanagan, 8 S. Michigan Ave., Suite 2012, Chicago, IL 60603 (phone: 312-372-4497).
New Jersey: main office: *CIE Tours International,* 108 Ridgedale Ave., Morristown, NJ 07960 (phone: 800-CIE-TOUR or 201-292-3438).

Northern Ireland Railways
New York State: Northern Ireland Tourist Board, 40 W. 57th St., New York, NY 10019 (phone: 212-686-6250).

Italian State Railways
California: 6033 W. Century Blvd., Suite 980, Los Angeles, CA 90045 (phone: 213-338-8620 or 800-CIT-RAIL in California).
New York State: 594 Broadway, Suite 307, New York, NY 10012 (phone: 212-274-0590).
Canada: 1450 City Councillors, Montreal, Quebec H3A 2E6, Canada (phone: 514-845-9101); 111 Avenue Rd., Suite 808, Toronto, Ontario M5R 3J8, Canada (phone: 416-927-7712).

In addition, *Rail Europe* is the North American representative of the national railways of Austria, Czechoslovakia, Denmark, France, Hungary, the Netherlands, Norway, Poland, Portugal, Spain, Sweden, Switzerland, and Yugoslavia. The following offices provide helpful information for travelers throughout Europe, sell Eurailpasses, and make reservations and sell tickets for rail service within and connecting service between a number of European countries:

California: 360 Post St., San Francisco, CA 94108 (phone: 415-982-1993).
Florida: 800 Corporate Dr., Suite 108, Ft. Lauderdale, FL 33334 (phone: 305-776-2729).

Illinois: 11 E. Adams St., Suite 906, Chicago, IL 60603 (phone: 312-427-8691).
New York State: 226-230 Westchester Ave., White Plains, NY 10604 (phone: 800-345-1990 or 914-682-5172).
Texas: 6060 N. Central Ave., Suite 220, Dallas, TX 75206 (phone: 214-691-5573).
Canada: 2087 Dundas East, Suite 204, Mississauga, Ontario L4X 1M2, Canada (phone: 416-602-4195); 643 Notre Dame Ouest, Suite 200, Montreal, Quebec HC3 1H8, Canada (phone: 514-392-1311); 409 Granville St., Suite 452, Vancouver, British Columbia B6C 1T2, Canada (phone: 604-688-6707).

Finally, although any travel agent can assist you in making arrangements to tour Europe by rail, you may want to consult a train travel specialist, such as *Accent on Travel,* 1030 Curtis St., Suite 201, Menlo Park, CA 94025 (phone: 415-326-7330 in California; 800-347-0645 elsewhere in the US).

Traveling by Car

 Driving certainly is the most flexible way to explore out-of-the-way regions of Europe. The privacy, comfort, and convenience of touring by car can't be matched by any other form of transport. Trains often whiz much too fast past too many enticing landscapes, tunnel through or pass between hills and mountains rather than climb up and around them for a better view, frequently deposit passengers in an unappealing part of town, and don't permit many spur-of-the-moment stops and starts. In a car you go where you want when you want, and can stop along the way as often as you like for a meal, a photograph, or a particularly appealing view.

Europe is ideally suited for driving tours. Distances between points of interest usually are reasonable, and the historical and cultural density is such that the flexibility of a car can be used to maximum advantage. A traveler can cover large amounts of territory visiting major sites or spend the same amount of time motoring from one small village to another while exploring the countryside. (See DIRECTIONS for our choices of the most interesting driving routes.)

In most parts of Europe, travelers who wish to cover a country from end to end can count on a good system of highways to help them make time. Those choosing to explore only one region will find that the secondary and even lesser roads are well surfaced and generally in good condition; even farther off the beaten track, this usually is the case. Either way, there is plenty of satisfying scenery en route.

But driving isn't an inexpensive way to travel. Gas prices are far higher in Europe than in North America, and car rentals seldom are available at bargain rates. Keep in mind, however, that driving becomes more economical with more passengers. Because the price of getting wheels abroad will be more than an incidental expense, it is important to investigate every alternative before making a final choice. Many travelers find this expense amply justified when considering that rather than just the means to an end, a well-planned driving route can be an important part of the adventure.

Before setting out, make certain that everything you need is in order. If at all possible, discuss your intended trip with someone who already has driven the route to find out about road conditions and available services. If you can't speak to someone personally, try to read about others' experiences. Automobile clubs (see below) and government tourist offices in the US can be good sources of travel information, although when requesting brochures and maps, be sure to specify the areas you are planning to visit. (Also see "Roads and Maps," below.)

Driving – A valid driver's license from his or her state of residence enables a US citizen to drive throughout Europe. In Hungary, Italy, and the Soviet Union, an

International Driving Permit (IDP) also is required. In addition, Spain requires US citizens to have an IDP to drive a rental car. Other European countries (such as Bulgaria) require merely that a US license is accompanied by a translation (and the IDP is the best form for this) or *strongly* recommend that American drivers obtain an IDP, especially if they plan to do a lot of driving. Although it is advisable to comply with these requirements and recommendations, regulations are not always enforced, and foreign drivers are known to have driven in countries where an IDP is required without incident using only their regular license.

An IDP essentially is a translation of the driver's US license into 9 languages and it must be accompanied by your US license to be valid. You can obtain an IDP before you leave from most branches of the *American Automobile Association (AAA)*. Applicants must be at least 18 years old, and the application must be accompanied by two passport-size photos (some *AAA* branches have a photo machine available), a valid US driver's license, and a fee of $10. The IDP is good for 1 year.

Proof of liability insurance also is required and is a standard part of any car rental contract. (To be sure of having the appropriate coverage, let the rental staff know in advance about the national borders you plan to cross.) If buying a car and using it abroad, the driver must carry an International Insurance Certificate, known as a Green Card. Your insurance agent or carrier can arrange for a special policy to cover you in Europe, and will automatically issue your Green Card.

Some countries, however, may require that you obtain a specific policy available only in these countries *on arrival.* For instance, in the Soviet Union, Green Cards are not recognized and drivers are required to purchase insurance from the state insurance agency, *Ingosstrakh,* which has offices in most major cities, and at many border crossings. Your insurance carrier or the national tourism office can provide information on such special requirements and application procedures.

Driving is on the right side of the road in most of Europe and passing is on the left. Unless otherwise indicated, those coming from the right at intersections have the right of way, but streetcars usually have priority over other vehicles. Pedestrians at designated crosswalks (often marked by diagonal stripes or other similar markings on city streets) often have priority over all vehicles. Exceptions to the rule of "priority to the right" are priority roads, marked by a sign with a yellow diamond; these have the right of way until the diamond reappears with a black bar and the right of way reverts to those coming from the right. Another exception is the limited form of "priority to the left" (or *priorité à gauche*) that has been introduced at selected traffic circles in France (marked by a sign showing arrows going around in a circle, meaning that cars already in those circles have priority over cars entering). In Great Britain, Ireland, and Malta, driving is on the left side of the road and all rules are reversed. On Swiss and other mountain passes, traffic going up has priority over traffic coming down.

Also note that highway signs showing distance from point to point usually are in kilometers rather than miles (1 mile equals approximately 1.6 kilometers; 1 kilometer equals approximately .62 mile). And speed limits are in kilometers per hour, so think twice before hitting the gas when you see a speed limit of 100. That means 62 miles per hour. (In countries such as Great Britain and Ireland which have not yet fully converted to the metric system, however, distances and speed still may be expressed in miles — or in both miles and kilometers.) When touring along Europe's scenic roadways, it is all too easy to inch up over the speed limit. *Be forewarned:* Particularly in Eastern European countries, speed limits are strictly enforced and violators are subject to hefty fines and possibly even jail sentences.

And use alcohol sparingly prior to getting behind the wheel. Europeans are zealous in prosecuting those who commit infractions under the influence. Even in those countries that have a somewhat casual attitude and a marked lack of restrictions regarding the sale of wine and liquor — such as France and Italy — the laws and penalties regarding driving while intoxicated are just as severe. The Scandinavian countries, those of Eastern Europe, and France, Great Britain, and Ireland routinely administer Breathalyzer tests and are rigorous in imposing fines and jail sentences. In many European countries, the use of seat belts is compulsory for the driver and front-seat passenger, and in some countries (such as France) children under a certain age may not sit in the front seat unless the car has no back seat. Some countries also require that motorcycle drivers wear helmets. Use the horn sparingly — only in emergencies and when approaching blind mountain curves. In some towns and cities honking is forbidden; flash your headlights instead. And watch out for bicycles and motor scooters — they are everywhere.

Pictorial direction signs are standardized under the International Roadsign System and their meanings are indicated by their shapes — triangular signs indicate danger; circular signs give instructions; and rectangular signs are informative. Driving in European cities can be a tricky proposition, since many of them do not have street signs at convenient corners, but instead identify their byways with plaques attached to the walls of corner buildings. They often are difficult to spot until you've passed them, and since most streets don't run parallel to one another, taking the next turn can lead you astray. Fortunately, most European cities and towns post numerous signs pointing the way to the center of the city, and plotting a course to your destination from there may be far easier. In Italy, look for the signs that read CENTRO CITTÀ; in France, CENTRE VILLE; in Spain, CENTRO; and in Germany, ZENTRUM or INNENSTADT.

■ **Note:** Pay particular attention to parking signs in large cities throughout Europe, especially those indicating "control zones," where an unattended parked car presents a serious security risk. If you park in a restricted zone, unlike in the US (where you chance only a ticket or being towed), you may return to find that the trunk and doors have been blown off by overly cautious security forces. More likely, however, you'll return to find one of the car's wheels "clamped," a procedure that renders your car inoperable and involves a tedious (and costly) process to get it freed.

Roads and Maps – Europe's network of highways is as well maintained as any in North America, with a system comparable to the American highway system: expressways, first class roads, and well-surfaced secondary roads (which in outlying areas like Scandinavia's Arctic region may be dirt or gravel but will be carefully maintained, in any case). Every European country maintains its own highway system.

Traffic congestion is at its worst on main roads, particularly those radiating from major cities. Look for signs pointing out detours or alternative routes to popular holiday destinations. In some countries, service stations, information points, and tourist offices distribute free maps of the alternate routes, which may be the long way around but probably will get you to your destination faster in the end.

Except for free stretches in the vicinity of cities, most European autoroutes are toll roads, and they are fairly expensive. They save time, gas, and wear and tear on the car, but they are obviously not the roads to take if you want to browse and linger along the way. Most other main roads, including national roads and secondary or regional roads are free, well maintained, and much more picturesque, while minor roads have their own charm.

Three decades ago, a pan-European commission established standards for international European routes, called E roads. Most European maps note E-route numbers together with national route numbers. For example, autoroute A1 in France could also be called E5, but Germany's A1 would have a different E number. Both designations appear on Michelin's newest maps, but expect discrepancies between the old and new numbers in maps, guidebooks, and brochures for some time to come. Other single-country maps generally use only a national number.

Excellent road maps of Europe — including Austria, Belgium, France, Germany,

Great Britain, Holland, Ireland, Italy, Portugal, Spain, Switzerland, and Yugoslavia — are published by Michelin, the French tire company. All Michelin publications — red and green guides, as well as road maps (by far the best for visitors touring) — are readily available in bookstores and map shops throughout the US and all over Europe, and also can be ordered from the company's US headquarters, Michelin Guides and Maps (PO Box 3305, Spartanburg, SC 29304-3305; phone: 803-599-0850 in South Carolina; 800-423-0485 elsewhere in the US). A new edition of each map appears every year; if you're not buying directly from the publisher, make sure that the edition you buy is no more than 2 years old by opening one fold and checking the publication date, given just under the black circle with the map number.

Other good sources of current information on European roads and routes are the atlases, maps, and guides published by Rand McNally. Rand McNally publications are available in most bookstores or can be bought directly from the following Rand McNally retail stores: 444 N. Michigan Ave., Chicago, IL 60611 (phone: 312-321-1751); 150 S. Wacker Dr., Chicago, IL 60606 (phone: 312-332-2009); 150 E. 52nd St., New York, NY 10022 (phone: 212-758-7488); 595 Market St., San Francisco, CA 94105-2803 (phone: 415-777-3131).

The *Freytag & Berndt* excellent series of 28 road maps ($8.95 each) covers most major destinations throughout Europe. Published in country, city, and regional versions, they are among the most extensive and detailed European maps available. The US distributor of these maps and a good source of just about any other map available is *Map Link* (25 E. Mason St., Suite 201, Santa Barbara, CA 93101; phone: 805-965-4402). You may want to order their comprehensive guide to maps worldwide, *The World Map Directory* ($29.95). If they don't have the map you want in stock, they will order it for you.

The *American Automobile Association (AAA)* also provides several useful reference sources, including an overall Europe planning map, regional maps of Europe, the 600-page *Travel Guide to Europe* (the price varies from branch to branch), and the 64-page *Motoring Europe* ($7.25). These are available from most local *AAA* offices (see below). Another invaluable guide, *Euroad: The Complete Guide to Motoring in Europe,* is available for $8.80, including postage and handling, from *VLE Limited,* PO Box 444, Fort Lee, NJ 07024 (phone: 201-585-5080 or 212-580-8030).

Road maps also are sold at gas stations throughout Europe. Stateside, some free maps can be obtained from the national tourist offices of the countries you plan to visit (see *Tourist Information Offices,* in this section, for addresses).

Automobile Clubs and Roadside Assistance – Most European automobile clubs offer emergency service to any breakdown victim, whether a club member or not; however, only members of these clubs or affiliated clubs may have access to certain information services and receive discounted or free towing and repair services.

Members of the *American Automobile Association (AAA)* often are automatically entitled to a number of services from foreign clubs. With over 31 million members in chapters throughout the US and Canada, the *AAA* is the largest automobile club in North America. *AAA* affiliates throughout the US provide a variety of travel services to members, including a travel agency, trip planning, fee-free traveler's checks, and reimbursement for foreign roadside assistance. They will help plan an itinerary, send a map with clear routing directions, and even make hotel reservations. These services apply to travel in both the US and Europe. Although *AAA* members receive maps and brochures for no charge or at a discount, non-members also can order from an extensive selection of highway and topographical maps at most *AAA* branches. You can join the *AAA* through local chapters (listed in the telephone book under *AAA*) or contact the national office at 1000 AAA Dr., Heathrow, FL 32746-5063 (phone: 407-444-8544).

If you break down on the road, immediate emergency procedure is to get the car off the road. If the road has a narrow shoulder, try to get all the way off, even if you have to hang off the shoulder a bit. Better yet, try to make it to an area where the shoulder is wider — if you are crawling along well below the speed limit, use your emergency flashers to warn other drivers. To signal for help, raise the hood, and tie a white handkerchief or rag to the door handle or radio antenna. Don't leave the car unattended, and don't try any major repairs on the road.

Motor patrols usually drive small cars painted a uniform color (which varies from country to country). Call boxes are located on many major autoroutes for stranded travelers to dial for roadside assistance. On secondary roads, emergency phones may be posted with phone numbers of local garages providing towing and basic repair services, although on very rural routes, these boxes may be few and far between. A number of countries also have a single national number to dial for roadside assistance.

Aside from these options, a driver in distress will have to contact the nearest service center by pay phone. And although English is spoken widely in Europe, if language is a barrier in explaining your dilemma, your best bet may be to reach an international operator who can stay on the line as an interpreter. (For further information on calling for help, see *Mail, Telephone, and Electricity* and *Medical and Legal Aid and Consular Services,* both in this section.) Car rental companies also make provisions for breakdowns, emergency service, and assistance; ask for a number to call when you pick up the vehicle.

Gasoline – Gasoline is sold by the liter on the Continent and by either the liter or British or "imperial" gallon in the United Kingdom and Ireland. A liter is slightly more than 1 quart; aproximately 3.8 liters equal 1 US gallon. One imperial gallon equals 1.2 US gallons. Regular or leaded gas generally is sold in two grades. Diesel also is widely available, but unleaded fuel is only now being introduced in Europe and may be difficult (or even impossible) to find.

Gas prices everywhere rise and fall depending upon the world supply of oil, and an American traveling overseas is further affected by the prevailing rate of exchange, so it is difficult to say exactly how much fuel will cost when you travel. It is not difficult to predict, however, that gas prices will be substantially higher than you are accustomed to paying in the US.

Particularly when traveling in rural areas, fill up whenever you come to a gas station. It may be a long way to the next open station. (Even in more populated areas, it may be difficult to find an open station on Sundays or holidays.) You don't want to get stranded on an isolated stretch — so it is a good idea to bring along an extra few gallons in a steel container. (Plastic containers tend to break when a car is bouncing over rocky roads. This, in turn, creates the danger of fire should the gasoline ignite from a static electricity spark. Plastic containers also may burst at high altitudes.)

Considering the cost of gas in Europe relative to US prices, gas economy is of particular concern. The prudent traveler should plan an itinerary and make as many reservations as possible in advance in order not to waste gas figuring out where to go, stay, or eat. Drive early in the day, when there is less traffic. Then leave your car at the hotel and use local transportation whenever possible after you arrive at your destination.

Although it may be as dangerous to drive at a speed much below the posted limit as it is to drive above it — particularly on toll autoroutes, superhighways where the speed limit may be as high as 130 kph (81 mph) — at 88 kph (55 mph) a car gets 25% better mileage than at 112 kph (70 mph). The number of miles per liter or gallon also is increased by driving smoothly.

RENTING A CAR: Although there are other options, such as leasing or outright purchase, most travelers who want to drive in Europe simply rent a car. Travelers to Europe can rent a car through a travel agent or international rental firm before leaving home, or from a local company once they are in Europe. Another possibility, also arranged before departure, is to rent the car as part of a larger travel package (see "Fly/Drive Packages," below, as well as *Package Tours,* in this section).

Renting a car in Europe is not inexpensive, but it is possible to economize by determining your own needs and then shopping around among the car rental companies until you find the best deal. As you comparison shop, keep in mind that rates vary considerably, not only from city to city, but also from location to location within the same city. For instance, it might be less expensive to rent a car in the center of a city than at the airport. Ask about special rates or promotional deals, such as weekend or weekly rates, bonus coupons for airline tickets, or 24-hour rates that include gas and unlimited mileage.

Rental car companies operating in Europe can be divided into three basic categories: large international companies; national or regional companies; and smaller local companies. Because of aggressive local competition, the cost of renting a car can be less expensive once a traveler arrives in Europe compared to the prices quoted in advance in the US. Local companies usually are less expensive than the international giants.

Given this situation, it's tempting to wait until arriving to scout out the lowest-priced rental from the company located the farthest from the airport high-rent district and offering no pick-up services. But if your arrival coincides with a holiday or a peak travel period, you may be disappointed to find that even the most expensive car in town was spoken for months ago. Whenever possible, it is best to reserve in advance, anywhere from a few days in slack periods to a month or more during the busier seasons.

Renting from the US – Travel agents can arrange foreign rentals for clients, but it is just as easy to call and rent a car yourself. Listed below are some of the major international rental companies represented in Europe that have information and reservations numbers that can be dialed toll-free from the US:

Avis (phone: 800-331-1084). Offers rentals in Austria, Belgium, Bulgaria, Czechoslovakia, Denmark, Finland, France, Germany, Great Britain, Greece, Hungary, Ireland, Italy, Luxembourg, the Maltese Islands, the Netherlands, Norway, Poland, Portugal, Romania, the Soviet Union, Spain, Sweden, Switzerland, and Yugoslavia.

Budget (phone: 800-527-0700). Offers rentals in Austria, Belgium, Czechoslovakia, Denmark, Finland, France, Germany, Great Britain, Greece, Hungary, Ireland, Italy, Luxembourg, the Maltese Islands, Monaco, the Netherlands, Poland, Portugal, Spain, Sweden, Switzerland, and Yugoslavia. (At at the time of this writing this company was negotiating to open branches in the Soviet Union.)

Dollar Rent-a-Car (known throughout most of Europe as *Eurodollar;* phone: 800-800-6000). Offers rentals in Austria, Belgium, Denmark, Finland, France, Germany, Great Britain, Greece, Ireland, Italy, Luxembourg, the Netherlands, Norway, Portugal, Sweden, and Yugoslavia.

Hertz (phone: 800-654-3001). Offers rentals in Austria, Belgium, Bulgaria, Czechoslovakia, Denmark, Finland, France, Germany, Great Britain, Greece, Hungary, Ireland, Italy, Luxembourg, the Netherlands, Norway, Poland, Portugal, Romania, the Soviet Union, Spain, Sweden, Switzerland, and Yugoslavia.

National (known in Europe as *Europcar;* phone: 800-CAR-EUROPE). Offers rentals in Andorra, Austria, Belgium, Bulgaria, Czechoslovakia, Denmark, Finland, France, Germany, Gibraltar, Great Britain, Greece, Hungary, Iceland, Ireland, Italy, Luxembourg, the Maltese Islands, Monaco, Norway, the Netherlands, Poland, Romania, the Soviet Union, Spain, Sweden, Switzerland, and Yugoslavia.

Thrifty Rent-A-Car (phone: 800-367-2277). Has locations in Denmark, France, Germany, Greece, Ireland, Luxembourg, Norway, Portugal, and Scotland.

Note that *Avis* also offers two helpful free services for customers traveling in Europe: the "Know Before You Go" US hotline (phone: 212-876-AVIS); and an "On Call

Service" for customers calling once in Europe. Both provide travelers with tourist information on Austria, Belgium, Czechoslovakia, Denmark, France, Germany, Great Britain, Ireland, Italy, Luxembourg, the Netherlands, Poland, Portugal, Spain, Sweden, and Switzerland. Topics may range from questions about driving (distances, gasoline prices, and license requirements) to queries about currency, customs, tipping, and weather. (Callers to the US number then receive a personal letter confirming the information discussed.) For the European service, there is a different toll-free number in each country; the numbers are given to you when you rent from *Avis* (personnel at these numbers speak English).

Another special service is *Avis*'s Europe Message Center, which operates like any answering service in that it will take phone messages any time of the day or night for *Avis* customers. *Avis* renters are given a telephone number in Europe that they can leave with anyone who wants to contact them while they are touring; if your rental car comes with a car phone, *Avis* will give this number to callers (with your permission). The tourers themselves can call a toll-free number to pick up messages or leave word for family, friends, or business colleagues. To utilize the service, a renter picks up his or her car at an *Avis* outlet in Europe, and then simply calls the Message Center and registers using the rental agreement number. It's even possible to leave an itinerary — which can be altered later if necessary — making messages easy to leave and/or pick up.

It also is possible to rent a car before you go by contacting any of a number of smaller or less well known US companies that do not operate worldwide. These organizations specialize in European auto travel, including leasing and car purchase in addition to car rental, or actually are tour operators with a well-established European car rental program. These firms, whose names and addresses are listed below, act as agents for a variety of European suppliers, offer unlimited mileage almost exclusively, and frequently manage to undersell their larger competitors by a significant margin.

There are legitimate bargains in car rentals provided you shop for them. Call all the familiar car rental names whose toll-free numbers are given above (don't forget to ask about their special discount plans), and then call the smaller companies listed below. In the recent past, the latter have tended to offer significantly lower rates, but it always pays to compare. Begin your comparison shopping early, because the best deals may be booked to capacity quickly and may require payment 14 to 21 days or more before picking up the car.

Auto Europe (PO Box 1097, Camden, ME 04843; phone: 207-236-8235; 800-223-5555 throughout the US; 800-458-9503 in Canada). Offers rentals in Austria, Belgium, Bulgaria, Czechoslovakia, Denmark, Finland, France, Germany, Great Britain, Greece, Hungary, Ireland, Italy, Luxembourg, the Netherlands, Norway, Poland, Portugal, Romania, the Soviet Union, Spain, Sweden, Switzerland, and Yugoslavia.

Europe by Car (One Rockefeller Plaza, New York, NY 10020; phone: 212-581-3040 in New York State; 800-223-1516 elsewhere in the US; and 9000 Sunset Blvd., Los Angeles, CA 90069; phone: 800-252-9401 or 213-272-0424). Offers rentals in Austria, Belgium, Denmark, France, Germany, Great Britain, Greece, Hungary, Ireland, Italy, Luxembourg, the Netherlands, Portugal, Spain, Sweden, Switzerland, and Yugoslavia.

European Car Reservations (349 W. Commercial St., Suite 2950, East Rochester, NY 14445; phone: 800-535-3303). Offers rentals in Austria, Belgium, Denmark, Finland, France, Germany, Great Britain, Greece, Hungary, Ireland, Italy, Luxembourg, the Netherlands, Portugal, Spain, Sweden, Switzerland, and Yugoslavia.

Foremost Euro-Car (5430 Van Nuys Blvd., Suite 306, Van Nuys, CA 91401; phone: 800-272-3299 or 818-786-1960). Offers rentals in Austria, Belgium, Denmark, France, Germany, Great Britain, Hungary, Ireland, Italy, Luxembourg, the Netherlands, Portugal, Spain, Switzerland, and Yugoslavia.

Kemwel Group (106 Calvert St., Harrison, NY 10528; phone: 800-678-0678 or 914-835-5555). Offers rentals in Austria, Belgium, Czechoslovakia, Denmark, Finland, France, Germany, Great Britain, Greece, Holland, Hungary, Iceland, Ireland, Italy, Luxembourg, Malta, Norway, Poland, Portugal, Spain, Sweden, Switzerland, and Yugoslavia.

Meier's World Travel (6033 W. Century Blvd., Suite 1080, Los Angeles, CA 90045; phone: 800-937-0700). In conjunction with a number of major car rental companies (such as *Hertz*) arranges economical rentals in Austria, Czechoslovakia, Denmark, France, Great Britain, Hungary, Ireland, Italy, the Netherlands, Norway, Spain, Sweden, and Switzerland. Also arranges rentals in Germany for touring throughout Eastern Europe (except the Soviet Union).

One of the ways to keep the cost of car rentals down is to deal with a car rental consolidator, such as *Connex International* (23 N. Division St., Peekskill, NY 10566; phone: 800-333-3949 or 914-739-0066). *Connex*'s main business is negotiating with virtually all of the major car rental agencies for the lowest possible prices for its customers. This company arranges rentals throughout Europe, including numerous locations in cities and towns in Austria, Belgium, Czechoslovakia, Denmark, Finland, France, Germany, Great Britain, Greece, Hungary, Ireland, Italy, Luxembourg, Norway, Portugal, Spain, Sweden, Switzerland, and Yugoslavia.

The Soviet Union has become increasingly open to rental car tourism — more than 12,000 miles of main and secondary roads now are open to travelers. At present, rental cars picked up in nearby countries can be driven into the Soviet Union at certain border points, and *Auto Europe, Hertz,* and *National* cars also can be picked up once in the Soviet Union. Generally cars can be rented for independent touring directly from these companies (in which case you will need to register your route with *Intourist,* the official government travel agency) or from *Intourist,* either with or without an *Intourist* chauffeur-guide. Be advised, however, that regulations change quite often, so be sure to check the situation prior to departure. For further information, write for *Tour the USSR by Car,* free from *Intourist* (Suite 658, 630 Fifth Ave., New York, NY 10111; phone: 212-757-3884). And for information on US travel agents that offer car rentals as part of fly/drive packages to Eastern Europe, see *Package Tours,* in this section.

■ **Extra Special:** For travelers for whom driving is more than just a means of getting from here to there, *Auto Exclusiv* (2 Frankfurter Str., Heusenstamm D-6056, Germany; phone: 49-06104-3060; fax: 49-06104-65960) rents the very best cars manufactured in Germany. From their headquarters in Heusenstamm, very near the Frankfurt airport, they provide top-of-the-line Mercedes, BMWs, and Porsches for a driving tour that has an extra element of excitement — and speed. Prices are hardly inexpensive, but many feel the pleasure of being behind the wheel of a BMW 750iL or a Porsche Carrera 4 is worth the cost. Now, in conjunction with *Leading Hotels of the World, Auto Exclusiv* offers a dozen planned touring programs, as well as customized itineraries. Another company that offers similarly exciting models in some countries is *European Car Reservations* (349 W. Commercial St., Suite 2950, East Rochester, NY 14445; phone: 800-535-3303).

Local Rentals – It has long been common wisdom that the least expensive way to rent a car is to make arrangements in Europe. This is less true today than it used to be. Many medium to large European car rental companies have become the overseas suppliers of stateside companies such as those mentioned previously, and often the stateside agency, by dint of sheer volume, has been able to negotiate more favorable rates for its US customers than the European firm offers its own. Still, lower rates may be found by searching out small, strictly local rental companies overseas, whether at less than prime addresses in major cities or in more remote areas. But to find them you must be willing to invest a sufficient amount of vacation time comparing prices on the scene. You also must be prepared to return the car to the location that rented it; drop-off possibilities are likely to be limited.

The brochures of some of the smaller car rental companies, often available from European tourist board offices in the US, can serve as a useful basis for comparison. Once overseas, local tourist authorities may be able to supply the names of local rental companies, and the local phone book (if you can read the native language) is another a good place to begin. (For further information on local rental companies, see the individual reports in THE CITIES.)

Also bear in mind that *French National Railways (SNCF)* offers a car rental service in conjunction with *Avis* at train stations throughout France. This service also is included in the France Rail 'N Drive Pass, another joint offering of *Avis* and *French National Railways.* As with most rail passes, it must be bought in the US, even though, when in France, pass holders are free to reserve the car with only 24 hours' notice. A rail-and-drive pass offered by *Hertz,* EurailDrive Escape, is valid in all the countries that are included in the Eurail network. (For further information on rail-and-drive packages, see *Traveling by Train,* above.)

Requirements – Whether you decide to rent a car in advance from a large international rental company with European branches or wait to rent from a local company, you should know that renting a car is rarely as simple as signing on the dotted line and roaring off into the night. If you are renting for personal use, you must have a valid driver's license (as well as an International Driving Permit, in some countries; see "Driving," above) and will have to convince the renting agency that (1) you are personally creditworthy, and (2) you will bring the car back at the stated time. This will be easy if you have a major credit card; most rental companies accept credit cards in lieu of a cash deposit, as well as for payment of your final bill. If you prefer to pay in cash, leave your credit card imprint as a "deposit," then pay your bill in cash when you return the car.

If you are planning to rent a car once in Europe, *Avis, Budget, Hertz,* and other US rental companies usually *will* rent to travelers paying in cash and leaving either a credit card imprint or a substantial amount of cash as a deposit. This is not necessarily standard policy, however, as other international chains, and a number of local and regional European companies will *not* rent to an individual who doesn't have a valid credit card. In this case, you may have to call around to find a company that accepts cash.

Also keep in mind that although the minimum age to drive a car in most European countries is 18 years, the minimum age to rent a car is set by the rental company. (Restrictions vary from company to company, as well as at different locations.) Many firms have a minimum age requirement of 21 years, some raise that to 23 or 25 years, and for some models of cars it rises to 30 years. The upper age limit at many companies is between 69 and 75; others have no upper limit or may make drivers above a certain age subject to special conditions.

Costs – Finding the most economical car rental will require some telephone shopping on your part. As a *general* rule, expect to hear lower prices quoted by the smaller, strictly local companies than by the well-known international names, with those of the national European companies falling somewhere between the two.

Comparison shopping always is advisable, however, because the company that has the least expensive rentals in one country may not have the least expensive in another, and even the international giants offer discount plans whose conditions are easy for most travelers to fulfill. For instance, *Budget* and *National* offer discounts of anywhere from 10% to 30% off their usual rates (according to the size of the car and the duration of the rental), provided that the car is reserved a certain number of days before departure (usually 7 to 14 days, but it can be less), is rented for a minimum period (5 days or, more often, a week), is paid for at the time of booking, and, in most cases, is returned to the same location that supplied it or to another in the same country. Similar discount plans include *Hertz*'s Affordable Europe and *Avis*'s Supervalue Rates Europe.

If driving short distances for only a day or two, the best deal may be a per-day, per-mile (or per-kilometer) rate: You pay a flat fee for each day you keep the car, plus a per-mile (or per-kilometer) charge. An increasingly common alternative is to be granted a certain number of free miles or kilometers each day and then be charged on a per-mile or per-kilometer basis over that number.

A better alternative for touring the countryside may be a flat per-day rate with unlimited free mileage; this certainly is the most economical rate if you plan to drive over 100 miles (160 km). Make sure that the low, flat daily rate that catches your eye, however, is indeed a per-day rate: Often the lowest price advertised by a company turns out to be available only with a minimum 3-day rental — fine if you want the car that long, but not the bargain it appears if you really intend to use it no more than 24 hours for in-city driving. Flat weekly rates also are available, and some flat monthly rates that represent a further saving over the daily rate. (Note: When renting a car in Europe, the term "mileage" may refer either to miles or kilometers.)

Other factors influencing cost naturally include the type of car you rent. Rentals are based on a tiered price system, with different sizes of cars — variations of budget, economy, regular, and luxury — often listed as A (the smallest and least expensive) through F, G, or H, and sometimes even higher. Charges may increase by only a few dollars a day through several categories of subcompact and compact cars — where most of the competition is — then increase by great leaps through the remaining classes of full-size and luxury cars and passenger vans. The larger the car, the more it costs to rent and the more gas it consumes, but for some people the greater comfort and extra luggage space of a larger car (in which bags and sporting gear can be safely locked out of sight) may make it worth the additional expense. Be warned, too, that relatively few European cars have automatic transmissions, and those that do are more likely to be in the F group than the A group. Similarly, cars with air conditioning are likely to be found in the more expensive categories only. Most expensive are sleek sports cars, but, again, for some people the thrill of driving such a car — for a week or a day — may be worth it.

Electing to pay for collision damage waiver (CDW) protection will add considerably to the cost of renting a car. You may be responsible for the *full value* of the vehicle being rented, but you can dispense with the possible obligation by buying the offered waiver at a cost of about $11 to $13 a day. Before making any decisions about optional collision damage waivers, check with your own insurance agent and determine whether your personal automobile insurance policy covers rented vehicles; if it does, you probably won't need to pay for the waiver. Be aware, too, that increasing numbers of credit cards automatically provide CDW coverage if the car rental is charged to the appropriate credit card. However, the specific terms of such coverage differ sharply among individual credit card companies, so check with the credit card company for information on the nature and amount of coverage provided. Business travelers also should be aware that, at the time of this writing, *American Express* had withdrawn its automatic CDW coverage from some corporate *Green* card accounts — watch for similar cutbacks by other credit card companies.

Overseas, the amount renters may be liable for should damage occur has not risen to the heights it has in the US. In addition, some European car rental agreements include collision damage waiver coverage. In this case, the CDW supplement frees the renter from liability for the *deductible* amount — as opposed to the standard CDW coverage, described above, which releases the driver from liability for the full value of the car. In Europe, this deductible typically ranges anywhere from $1,500 to $5,000 at present, but can be much higher for some luxury car groups. As with the full collision damage waiver, the cost of waiving this liability — which can be as high as $25 a day — is far from negligible, however. Drivers who rent cars in the US often are able to decline the CDW because many personal car insurance policies (subject to their own deductibles) extend to rental cars; unfortunately, such coverage usually does not extend to cars rented for use outside the US and Canada. Similarly, CDW coverage provided by some credit cards if the rental is charged to the card may be limited to cars rented in the US or Canada.

When inquiring about CDW coverage and costs, you should be aware that a number of the major international car rental companies now are automatically including the cost of this waiver in their quoted prices. This does not mean that they are absorbing this cost and you are receiving free coverage — total rental prices have increased to include the former CDW charge. The disadvantage of this inclusion is that you probably will not have the option to refuse this coverage, and will end up paying the added charge — even if you already are adequately covered by your own insurance policy or through a credit card company.

Additional costs to be added to the price tag include drop-off charges or one-way service fees. The lowest price quoted by any given company may apply only to a car that is returned to the same location from which it was rented. A slightly higher rate may be charged if the car is to be returned to a different location (even within the same city), and a considerably higher rate may prevail if the rental begins in one country and ends in another.

A further consideration: Don't forget that all car rentals are subject to Value Added Tax (VAT). This tax rarely is included in the rental price that's advertised or quoted, but it always must be paid — whether you pay in advance in the US or pay it when you drop off the car. There is a wide variation in this tax rate from country to country: In France, the VAT rate on car rentals currently is 28%; in Belgium it is 25%; in Italy, $19%; in Germany, 14%; in Spain and Luxembourg, 12%; and in Switzerland, no tax is charged.

One-way rentals bridging two countries used to be exempt from tax, but that is no longer the case. In general, the tax on one-way rentals is determined by the country in which the car has been rented, so if your tour plans include several countries, you should examine your options regarding the pick-up and drop-off points. Even if you intend to visit only one country, you still might consider a nearby country as a pick-up point if it will provide a substantial savings. For instance, for a tourer planning to explore the eastern regions of France, there's a strong financial incentive to pick up his or her rental car in Switzerland and then drive across the nearby French border (at a 28% car rental cost saving!).

Some rental agencies that do not maintain their own fleets use a contractor, whose country of registration determines the rate of taxation. An example is *Kemwel Group*, whose one-way rentals from all countries except Germany, Italy, the Netherlands, Portugal, and Sweden are taxed at the Danish rate of 22%. *Kemwel*'s special programs offer savings to the client planning to tour Europe (particularly through countries where the tax rate is higher). Offered throughout Europe, their rates include full insurance coverage (with a $100 deductible) and all European VAT, plus unlimited mileage. If part of a fly/drive package (see below) booked through *Kemwel*, rates may be even lower. Bookings must be reserved and paid for at least 7 days before delivery of the car, and the vehicle must be returned to the *Kemwel* garage from which it was originally rented. For further information, contact *Kemwel Group*, 106 Calvert St., Harrison, NY 10528 (phone: 800-678-0678 or 914-835-5555).

Also don't forget to factor in the price of gas. Rental cars usually are delivered with a full tank of gas. (This is not always the case, however, so check the gas gauge when picking up the car, and have the amount of gas noted on your rental agreement if the tank is not full.) Remember to fill the tank before you return the car or you will have to pay to refill it, and gasoline at the car rental company's pump always is much more expensive than at a service station. This policy may vary for smaller local and regional companies; ask when picking up the vehicle. Before leaving the lot, also check that the rental car has a spare tire and jack in the trunk.

Finally, currency fluctuation is another factor to consider. Most brochures quote rental prices in US dollars, but these dollar amounts frequently are only guides; that is, they represent the prevailing rate of exchange at the time the brochure was printed. The rate may be very different when you call to make a reservation, and different again when the time comes to pay the bill (when the amount owed may be paid in cash in foreign currency or as a charge to a credit card, which is recalculated at a still later date's rate of exchange). Some companies guarantee rates in dollars (often for a slight surcharge), but this is an advantage only when the value of the dollar is steadily declining overseas. If the dollar is growing stronger overseas, you may be better off with rates guaranteed in the local currency.

Fly/Drive Packages – Airlines, charter companies, car rental companies, and tour operators have been offering fly/drive packages for years, and even though the basic components of the package have changed somewhat — return airfare, a car waiting at the airport, and perhaps a night's lodging all for one inclusive price used to be the rule — the idea remains the same. You rent a car *here* for use *there* by booking it along with other arrangements for the trip. These days, the very minimum arrangement possible is the result of a tie-in between a car rental company and an airline, which entitles customers to a rental car for less than the company's usual rates, provided they show proof of having booked a flight on that airline.

Slightly more elaborate fly/drive packages are listed under various names (go-as-you-please, self-drive, or, simply, car tours) in the independent vacations sections of tour catalogues. Their most common ingredients are the rental car plus some sort of hotel voucher plan, with the applicable airfare listed separately. You set off on your trip with a block of prepaid accommodations vouchers, a list of hotels that accept them (usually members of a hotel chain or association), and a reservation for the first night's stay, after which the staff of each hotel books the next one for you or you make your own reservations. Naturally, the greater the number of establishments participating in the scheme, the more freedom you have to range at will during the day's driving and still be near a place to stay for the night.

The cost of these combination packages generally varies according to the size of the car and the quality of the hotels; there usually is an additional drop-off charge if the car is picked up in one city and returned in another. Most packages are offered at several different price levels, ranging from a standard plan covering stays in hotels to a budget plan using acccommodations such as small inns, farmhouses, or bed and breakfast establishments. Airlines also have special rental car rates available when you book their flights, often with a flexible hotel voucher program. Less flexible car tours provide a rental car, a hotel plan, and a set itinerary that permits no deviation because the hotels all are reserved in advance. For information on packagers of car tours, see *Package Tours,* in this section.

LEASING: Anyone planning to be in Europe for 3 weeks or more should compare the cost of renting a car with that of leasing one for the same period. While the money saved by leasing — rather than renting for a 23-day (the minimum) or 30-day period — may not be great, what is saved over the course of a long-term lease — 45, 60, 90 days, or more — amounts to hundreds, even thousands, of dollars. Part of the savings is due to the fact that leased cars are exempt from the stiff taxes applicable to rented cars. In addition, leasing plans provide for collision insurance with no deductible amount, so there is no need to add the daily cost of collision damage waiver protection (an option offered by rental companies — see above). A further advantage of a car lease — actually a financed purchase/repurchase plan — is that you reserve your car by specific make and model rather than by group only, and it is delivered to you fresh from the factory.

Unfortunately, leasing as described above is offered only in Belgium and France, and the savings it permits can be realized to the fullest only if the cars are picked up and returned in those countries. While leased cars can be delivered to other countries, the charge for this service can be very high, and on top of this must be added an identical return charge. If you don't intend to keep the car very long, the two charges can nullify the amount saved by leasing rather than renting, so you will have to do some arithmetic. It is possible to lease a car in countries other than Belgium and France, but most of the plans offered are best described as long-term rentals at preferential rates. They differ from true leasing in that you will pay tax and collision damage waiver protection (though it may be included in the quoted price), and the cars usually are late model used cars rather than brand-new.

One of the major car leasing companies is *Renault,* offering leases of new cars for 23 days to 6 months. The cars are exempt from tax, all insurance is included, and there is no mileage charge. There is no pick-up or drop-off charge for some locations in France; charges for other locations throughout Europe vary substantially. For further information and reservations, ask your travel agent or contact *Renault USA,* 650 First Ave., New York, NY 10016 (phone: 212-532-1221 in New York State; 800-221-1052 elsewhere in the US).

Peugeot also offers a similar leasing arrangement, called the "Peugeot Vacation Plan." In acccordance with the standard type of financed purchase/repurchase plan, travelers pick up the car in France, paying at the time of pick-up to use the car for a specified period of time (anywhere between 22 and 175 days), and at the end of this pre-arranged period return it to *Peugeot.* The tax-free temporary "purchase" includes unlimited mileage, factory warranty, full collision damage waiver coverage (no deductible), and 24-hour towing and roadside assistance. Pick-up and drop-off locations and charges are similar to *Renault*'s. *Peugeot*'s "European Delivery" program is a full-purchase program, including shipment of the car to the US, as discussed below. For further information, contact *Peugeot Motors of America* (1 Peugeot Plaza, Lyndhurst, NJ 07071; phone: 201-935-8400). Some of the car rental firms listed above — *Auto Europe, Europe by Car, Foremost Euro-Car,* and *Kemwel* — also arrange European car leases.

BUYING A CAR: If your plans include both buying a new car of European make and a driving tour of Europe, it's possible to combine the two ventures and save some money on each. By buying the car abroad and using it during your vacation, you pay quite a bit less for it than the US dealer would charge and at the same time avoid the expense of renting a car during your holiday. There are two basic ways to achieve this desired end, but one, factory delivery, is far simpler than the other, direct import.

Factory delivery means that you place an order for a car in the US and then pick it up in Europe, often literally at the factory gate. It also means that your new car is built to American specifications, complying with all US emission and safety standards. Because of this, only cars made by manufacturers who have established a formal program for such sales to American customers may be bought at the factory. At present, the list includes Audi, BMW, Jaguar, Mercedes-Benz, Peugeot, Porsche, Saab, Volkswagen, and Volvo, among others (whose manufacturers generally restrict their offerings to those models they ordinarily export to the US). The factory delivery price, in US dollars, usually runs about 5% to 15% below the sticker price of the same model at a US dealership and includes US Customs duty, but the cost of the incidentals, and the insurance necessary for driving the car around Europe, are extra, except in BMW's plan.

One of the few disadvantages of factory delivery is that car manufacturers make only a limited number of models available each year, and for certain popular models you may have to get in line early in the season. Another is that you must take your trip when the car is ready, not when you are, although you usually will have 8 to 10 weeks' notice. The actual place of delivery can vary; it is more economical to pick up the car at the factory, but arrangements sometimes — but not always — can be made to have it delivered elsewhere for an extra charge. For example, Jaguars (now owned by Ford) must be ordered through a US dealer and picked up at the factory in Coventry, England, however, they also can be dropped off for shipment home in any number of European cities. For information, write to *Jaguar Cars,* 555 MacArthur Blvd., Mahwah, NJ 07430 (phone: 201-818-8500).

Cars for factory delivery usually can be ordered either through one of the manufacturer's authorized dealers in the US or through companies — among them *Europe by Car, Foremost Euro-Car,* and *Kemwel* (see above for contact information) — that specialize in such transactions. (Note that *Foremost Euro-Car* services all of the US for rentals and leasing, but they arrange *sales* only for California residents.) Another company arranging car sales abroad is *Ship Side Tax Free World on Wheels BV,* 600B Lake St., Suite A, Ramsey, NJ 07446 (phone: 201-818-0400).

Occasionally an auto manufacturer offers free or discounted airfare in connection with a European delivery program. This year, Mercedes-Benz has a program including discounted round-trip airfare ($500 for two economy fare seats or one business class seat) from any US gateway served by *Delta, Lufthansa,* or *SwissAir,* to Stuttgart (where the buyer picks up the car), plus a 2-night stay at the local *Hilton* or *Ramada* hotel, and 15 days' free comprehensive road insurance. For details, contact *Mercedes-Benz of North America,* 1 Mercedes Dr., Montvale, NJ 07645 (phone: 800-458-8202).

The other way to buy a car abroad, **direct import**, sometimes is referred to as "gray market" buying. It is perfectly legal, but not totally hassle-free. Direct import means that you buy abroad a car that was meant for use abroad, not one built according to US specifications. It can be new or used, and may even include — in Great Britain or Ireland — a steering wheel on the right side. The main drawback to direct import is that the process of modification to bring the car into compliance with US standards is expensive and time consuming; it typically costs from $5,000 to $7,000 in parts and labor and takes from 2 to 6 months. In addition, the same shipping, insurance, and miscellaneous expenses (another $2,000 to $5,000, according to estimates) that would be included in the factory delivery price must be added to the purchase price of the car, and the considerable burden of shepherding it on its journey from showroom to home garage usually is borne by the purchaser. Direct import dealers do exist (they are not the same as your local, factory-authorized foreign car dealer, with whom you are now in competition), but even if you use one, you still need to do a great deal of paperwork yourself.

Once upon a time, the main advantage of the direct import method — besides the fact that it can be used for makes and models not available in factory delivery programs — was that much more money could be saved importing an expensive car. Given today's exchange rates, however, the method's potential greater gain is harder to realize and must be weighed against its greater difficulties. Still, if direct importing interests you, you can obtain a list of those makes and models approved for conversion in this country, and of the converters licensed to bring them up to US specifications, by contacting the Environmental Protection Agency, Manufacturers' Operations Division, EN-340-F, Investigations/Imports Section, 401 M St. SW, Washington, DC 20460 (phone: 202-382-2479).

If you have special problems getting your car into the US, you might consider contacting a specialist in vehicle importation, such as Daniel Kokal, an independent regulatory consultant. His address is 15014 Kamputa Dr., Centerville, VA 22020 (phone: 703-818-9009).

Package Tours

 If the mere thought of buying a package for travel to and through Europe conjures up visions of a race through ten countries in as many days in lockstep with a horde of frazzled fellow travelers, remember that packages have come a long way. For one thing, not all packages necessarily are escorted tours, and the one you buy does not have to include any organized touring at all — nor will it necessarily include traveling companions. If it does, however, you'll find that people of all sorts — many just like yourself — are taking advantage of packages today because they are economical and convenient, save you an immense amount of planning time, and exist in such variety that it's virtually impossible not to find one that fits at least the majority of your travel preferences. Given the high cost of travel these days, packages have emerged as a particularly wise buy.

In essence, a package is an amalgam of travel services that can be purchased in a single transaction. A package (tour or otherwise) to and through Europe may include any or all of the following: round-trip transatlantic transportation, local transportation (and/or car rentals), accommodations, some or all meals, sightseeing, entertainment, transfers to and from the hotel at each destination, taxes, tips, escort service, and a variety of incidental features that might be offered as options at additional cost. In other words, a package can be any combination of travel elements, from a fully escorted tour offered at an all-inclusive price to a simple fly/drive booking allowing you to move about totally on your own. Its principal advantage is that it saves money: The cost of the combined arrangements invariably is well below the price of the same elements if bought separately, and particularly if transportation is provided by charter or discount flight, the whole package could cost less than just a round-trip economy airline ticket on a regularly scheduled flight. A package provides more than economy and convenience: It releases the traveler from having to make individual arrangements for each separate element of a trip.

Note that travelers to Eastern Europe — particularly first-time visitors — are strongly advised to buy package arrangements — whether escorted or locally hosted. A la carte travel arrangements have a tendency to come unglued in countries that for many years worked only through central planning. Eastern European government travel agencies (some are in the process of privatization) are notorious for putting the interest of traveling groups ahead of those of individuals. In addition, the shortage of hotel rooms, transport, restaurants, and other tourist necessities make highly necessary an intermediary who thoroughly knows the ropes.

Tour programs generally can be divided into two categories — "escorted" (or locally hosted) and "independent." An escorted tour means that a guide will accompany the group from the beginning of the tour through to the return flight; a locally hosted tour means that the group will be met upon arrival at each location by a different local host. On independent tours, there generally is a choice of hotels, meal plans, and sightseeing trips in each city, as well as a variety of special excursions. The independent plan is for travelers who do not want a totally set itinerary, but who do prefer confirmed hotel reservations. Whether choosing an escorted or independent tour, always bring along complete contact information for your tour operator in case a problem arises, although US tour operators often have European affiliates who can give additional assistance or make other arrangements on the spot.

To determine whether a package — or more specifically, *which* package — fits your travel plans, start by evaluating your interests and needs, deciding how much and what you want to spend, see, and do. Gather whatever package tour information is available for your schedule. Be sure that you take the time to read the brochure *carefully* to determine precisely what is included. Keep in mind that travel brochures are written to entice you into signing up for a package tour. Often the language is deceptive and devious. For example, a brochure may quote the lowest prices for a package tour based on facilities that are unavailable during the off-season, undesirable at any season, or just plain nonexistent. Information such as "breakfast included" (as it often is in packages to Europe) or "plus tax" (which can add up) should be taken into account. Note, too, that the prices quoted in brochures almost always are based on double occupancy: The rate listed is for each of two people sharing a double room, and if you travel alone, the supplement for single accommodations can raise the price considerably (see *Hints for Single Travelers,* in this section).

In this age of erratic airfares, the brochure most often will *not* include the price of an airline ticket in the price of the package, though sample fares from various gateway cities usually will be listed separately as extras to be added to the price of the ground arrangements. Before figuring your actual cost, check the latest fares with the airlines, because the samples invariably are out of date by the time you read them. If the brochure gives more than one category of sample fares per gateway city — such as an individual tour-basing fare, a group fare, an excursion, APEX, or other discount ticket — your travel agent or airline tour desk will be able to tell you which one applies to the package you choose, depending on when you travel, how far in advance you book, and other factors. (An individual tour-basing fare is a fare computed as part of a package that includes land arrangements, thereby entitling a carrier to reduce the air portion almost to the absolute minimum. Though it always represents a saving over full-fare coach or economy, lately the individual tour-basing fare has not been as inexpensive as the excursion and other discount fares that also are available to individuals. The group fare usually is the least expensive fare, and it is the tour operator, not you, who makes up the group.) When the brochure does not include round-trip transportation in the package price, don't forget to add the cost of round-trip transportation from your home to the departure city to come up with the total cost of the package.

Finally, read the general information regarding terms and conditions and the responsibility clause (usually in fine print at the end of the descriptive literature) to determine the precise elements for which the tour operator is — and is not — liable. Here the tour operator frequently expresses the right to change services or schedules as long as equivalent arrangements are offered. This clause also absolves the operator of responsibility for circumstances beyond human control, such as floods, or injury to you or your property. In reading, ask the following questions:

1. Does the tour include airfare or other transportation, sightseeing, meals, transfers, taxes, baggage handling, tips, or any other services? Do you want all these services?
2. If the brochure indicates that "some meals" are included, does this mean a welcoming and farewell dinner, two breakfasts, or every evening meal?
3. What classes of hotels are offered? If you will be traveling alone, what is the single supplement?
4. Does the tour itinerary or price vary according to the season?
5. Are the prices guaranteed; that is, if costs increase between the time you book and the time you depart, can surcharges unilaterally be added?
6. Do you get a full refund if you cancel? If not, be sure to obtain cancellation insurance.
7. Can the operator cancel if too few people join? At what point?

One of the consumer's biggest problems is finding enough information to judge the reliability of a tour packager, since individual travelers seldom have direct contact with the firm putting the package together. Usually, a retail travel agent is interposed between customer and tour operator, and much depends on his or her candor and cooperation. So ask a number of questions about the tour you are considering. For example:

- Has the travel agent ever used a package provided by this tour operator?
- How long has the tour operator been in business? Check the Better Business Bureau in the area where the tour operator is based to see if any complaints have been filed against it.
- Is the tour operator a member of the *United States Tour Operators Association (USTOA;* 211 E. 51st St., Suite 12B, New York, NY 10022; phone: 212-944-5727)? The *USTOA* will provide a list of its members on request; it also offers a useful brochure, *How to Select a Package Tour.*
- How many and which companies are involved in the package?
- If air travel is by charter flight, is there an escrow account in which deposits will be held; if so, what is the name of the bank?

This last question is very important. US law requires that tour operators place every charter passenger's deposit and subsequent payment in a proper escrow account. Money paid into such an account cannot legally be used except to pay for the costs of a particular package or as a refund if the trip is canceled. To ensure the safe handling of your money, make your check payable to the escrow account — by law, the name of the depository bank must appear in the operator-participant contract, and usually is found in that mass of minuscule type on the back of the brochure. Write the details of the charter, including the destination and dates, on the face of the check; on the back, print "For Deposit Only." Your travel agent may prefer that you make your check out to the agency, saying that it will then pay the tour operator the fee minus commission. But it is perfectly legal to write your check as we suggest, and if your agent objects too strongly (the agent should have sufficient faith in the tour operator to trust him or her to send the proper commission), consider taking your business elsewhere. If you don't make your check out to the escrow account, you lose the protection of that escrow should the trip be canceled or the tour operator or travel agent fail. Furthermore, recent bankruptcies in the travel industry have served to point out that even the protection of escrow may not be enough to safeguard your investment. Increasingly, insurance is becoming a necessity (see *Insurance,* in this section), and payment by credit card has become popular since it offers some additional safeguards if the tour operator defaults.

■ **A word of advice:** Purchasers of vacation packages who feel they're not getting their money's worth are more likely to get a refund if they complain in writing to the operator — and bail out of the whole package immediately. Alert the tour operator or resort manager to the fact that you are dissatisfied, that you will be leaving for home as soon as transportation can be arranged, and that you expect a refund. They may have forms to fill out detailing your complaint; otherwise, state your case in a letter. Even if difficulty in arranging immediate transportation home detains you, your dated, written complaint should help in procuring a refund from the operator.

SAMPLE PACKAGES TO EUROPE: There are so many packages available to Europe today that it's probably safe to say that just about any arrangement anyone might want is available for as long as it is wanted, whether it's to hit the highlights of a number of countries, explore a selected region in depth, or to visit several major cities. The keynote is flexibility.

Escorted Tours – Those seeking the maximum in structure will find that the classic sightseeing tour by motorcoach, fully escorted and all-inclusive (or nearly), has withstood the test of time and still is well represented among the programs of the major tour operators. Typically, these itineraries begin in a major city — such as London, Paris, Rome, and so on — and take anywhere from 1 to 3 weeks, or more, to trace a route through the country (or through several countries) covering highlighted attractions en route. Such escorted tours are particularly attractive to travelers interested in discovering Eastern Europe — where making your own arrangements still is difficult at best.

Hotel accommodations in these packages usually are characterized as first class or better, with private baths or showers accompanying all rooms, although more than a few tour packagers offer less expensive alternatives by providing more modest lodgings. These packages tend to be all-inclusive, although the number of included meals may vary considerably and wine (or other alcoholic beverage) is included only when the tour literature clearly states so. Among such packages are the following:

Abercrombie & Kent (1520 Kensington Rd., Suite 212, Oak Brook, IL 60521; phone: 708-954-2944 in Illinois; 800-323-7308 elsewhere in the US). Offers all-inclusive package tours that take care of just about everything — right down to a traveling bellhop to handle your baggage. These tours include packages to Austria, Denmark, France, Great Britain, Hungary, Ireland, Italy, Norway, Portugal, Spain, and Sweden.

Abreu Tours (317 E. 34th St., New York, NY 10016; phone: 800-223-1580 or 212-661-0555). Offers escorted motorcoach tours of Portugal and Spain.

AESU (248 W. Quadrangle, Village of Cross Keys, Baltimore, MD 21210; phone: 800-638-7640 or 301-323-4416). Offers escorted motorcoach tours of Austria, Belgium, Denmark, Finland, France, Germany, Great Britain, Greece, Hungary, Italy, Liechtenstein, Monaco, the Netherlands, the Soviet Union, Spain, Sweden, Switzerland, and Yugoslavia.

AIB Tours (3798 Flagler, Coral Gables, FL 33134; phone: 305-442-0246; 800-232-0242 in Florida; 800-242-8687 elsewhere in the US). Offers tours of Portugal and Spain.

Amelia Tours (280 Old Country Rd., Hicksville, NY 11801; phone: 800-742-4591 or 516-433-0696). Offers escorted motorcoach tours in Italy.

American Express Travel Related Services (offices throughout the US; phone: 800-241-1700 for information and local branches). Their numerous escorted motorcoach itineraries tour Austria, Belgium, Czechoslovakia, Denmark, Finland, France, Germany, Great Britain, Greece, Hungary, Ireland, Italy, Luxembourg, the Netherlands, Norway, Poland, Portugal, Spain, Sweden, and Switzerland. This tour operator prefers that bookings be made through travel agents.

American Media Tours (16 W. 32nd St., Suite PH, New York, NY 10001; phone: 800-969-6344 or 212-465-1630). Offers escorted motorcoach tours of France and the Soviet Union.

American Travel Abroad (250 W. 57th St., New York, NY 10107; phone: 212-586-5230 in New York State, 800-228-0877 elsewhere in the US). This company offers a wide variey of escorted itineraries throughout Eastern Europe.

Atlas Ambassador (60 E. 42nd St., New York, NY 10165; phone: 212-297-6767). Offers multi-country, one-country, and regional escorted tours of Hungary, Poland, the Soviet Union, and Yugoslavia.

Balkan Holidays USA (41 E. 42nd St., Suite 606, New York, NY 10017; phone: 212-573-5530). Offers escorted motorcoach tours of Bulgaria, Czechoslovakia, Greece, Hungary, Poland, Romania, the Soviet Union, and Yugoslavia.

Baltic Tours (77 Oak St., Suite 4, Newton, MA 02164; phone: 617-965-8080). Offers tours throughout the Soviet Union and the Baltic states of Estonia, Latvia, and Lithuania, as well as of Denmark, Finland, Norway, Poland, and Sweden.

Bennett (270 Madison Ave., New York, NY 10016; phone: 800-221-2420 or 212-532-5060). Offers escorted motorcoach tours of Austria, Denmark, Finland, Germany, Iceland, the Netherlands, Norway, and Switzerland.

Brendan Tours (15137 Califa St., Van Nuys, CA 91411; phone: 800-421-8446 or 818-785-9696). Offers escorted motorcoach tours of Austria, Belgium, Bulgaria, Czechoslovakia, Denmark, Finland, France, Germany, Great Britain, Greece, Hungary, Italy, Liechtenstein, Luxembourg, Monaco, the Netherlands, Norway, Poland, Portugal, Romania, San Marino, the Soviet Union, Spain, Sweden, Switzerland, and Yugoslavia.

Brian Moore International (116 Main St., Medway, MA 02053; phone: 800-982-2299 or 508-533-6683). Offers escorted motorcoach tours of Great Britain and Ireland.

Caravan Tours (401 N. Michigan Ave., Chicago, IL 60611; phone: 800-621-8338 or 312-321-9800). Offers escorted motorcoach tours of Austria, Belgium, Denmark, Finland, France, Germany, Gibraltar, Great Britain, Greece, Hungary, Ireland, Italy, Liechtenstein, Luxembourg, Monaco, the Netherlands, Norway, Portugal, San Marino, the Soviet Union, Spain, Sweden, Switzerland, and Yugoslavia.

Cavalcade Tours (450 Harmon Meadow Blvd., Secaucus, NJ 07094; phone: 800-356-2405). Offers escorted motorcoach tours of Great Britain, Portugal, and Spain.

Celtic International (161 Central Ave., Albany, NY 12206; phone: 800-833-4373 or 518-463-5511). Offers escorted motorcoach tours of Great Britain and Ireland.

CIE Tours International (108 Ridgedale Ave., Morristown, NJ 07960; phone: 800-CIE-TOUR or 201-292-3438). Offers escorted motorcoach tours of Great Britain and Ireland.

Collette Tours (162 Middle St., Pawtucket, RI 02860; phone: 800-832-4656, 800-752-2655 in New England). Offers escorted tours of Austria, Czechoslovakia, Denmark, France, Germany, Great Britain, Hungary, Iceland, Ireland, Italy, Norway, Poland, Portugal, Spain, Sweden, and Switzerland.

Contiki Holidays (1432 E. Katella Ave., Anaheim, CA 92805; phone: 714-937-0611 or 800-624-0611 in California; 800-626-0611 elsewhere in the US). Offers escorted motorcoach tours — geared to the younger set (18 to 35 year olds) — of Austria, Belgium, Bulgaria, Czechoslovakia, Denmark, Finland, France, Germany, Great Britain, Greece, Ireland, Italy, Liechtenstein, Monaco, the Netherlands, Norway, Poland, the Soviet Union, Spain, Sweden, Switzerland, and Yugoslavia.

Donna Franca Tours (470 Commonwealth Ave., Boston, MA 02215; phone: 617-227-3111 in Massachusetts; 800-225-6290 elsewhere in the US). Offers escorted motorcoach tours in Italy. This tour operator prefers that bookings be made through travel agents.

Esplanade Tours (581 Boylston St., Boston, MA 02116; phone: 800-426-5492 or 617-266-7465). Offers escorted motorcoach tours in Italy.

Five Star Touring (60 E. 42nd St., Suite 612, New York, NY 10165; phone: 800-792-7827 or 212-818-9140). Offers escorted tours of France, Great Britain, and the Soviet Union.

Four Winds Travel (175 Fifth Ave., New York, NY 10010; phone: 800-248-4444 or 212-777-0260). Offers escorted tours throughout Eastern Europe.

General Tours (770 Broadway, 10th Floor, New York, NY 10003; phone: 800-221-2216 or 212-598-1800). Offers 9- to 24-day tours of Bulgaria, Czechoslovakia, Germany, Hungary, Poland, and Romania.

Globus-Gateway and Cosmos (95-25 Queens Blvd., Rego Park, NY 11374; phone: 800-221-0090; or 150 S. Los Robles Ave., Pasadena, CA 91101; phone: 818-449-2019 or 800-556-5454). These affiliated agencies offer escorted tours throughout Europe. Note that bookings must be made through a travel agent.

Grimes Travel (250 W. 57th St., New York, NY 10107; phone: 212-307-7797 in New York State; 800-832-7778 elsewhere in the US). Offers escorted motorcoach tours of Austria, Belgium, Denmark, Finland, France, Germany, Great Britain, Greece, Hungary, Iceland, Ireland, Italy, Liechtenstein, Luxembourg, the Maltese Islands, the Netherlands, Norway, Portugal, Spain, Sweden, Switzerland, and Yugoslavia.

Insight International Tours (745 Atlantic Ave., Suite 720, Boston, MA 02111; phone: 800-582-8380 or 617-426-6666). Offers escorted motorcoach tours of Austria, Belgium, Czechoslovakia, Denmark, France, Germany, Great Britain, Greece, Hungary, Ireland, Italy, Liechtenstein, Luxembourg, Monaco, the Netherlands, Norway, Poland, Portugal, Romania, the Soviet Union, Spain, Sweden, Switzerland, and Yugoslavia. As this tour operator is a wholesaler, bookings must be made through a travel agent.

Isram Travel (630 Third Ave., New York, NY 10017; phone: 800-223-7460 or 212-922-1022). Has greatly expanded its Eastern Europe offerings and now goes to every Eastern European country (except Albania). Its programs include a 12-day Best of the Soviet trip to Moscow, Kiev, and St. Petersburg.

ITS Tours and Travel (1055 Texas Ave., Suite 104, College Station, TX 77840; phone: 800-533-8688 or 409-764-9400). Offers 9- to 19-day escorted tours of Austria, Czechoslovakia, Germany, Hungary, Poland, the Soviet Union, and Yugoslavia, as well as customized tours throughout Eastern Europe.

Kobasniuk Travel (157 Second Ave., New York, NY 10003; phone: 212-254-8779). Offers escorted tours throughout Eastern Europe.

Koch Overseas (157 E. 86th St., New York, NY 10028; phone: 212-369-3800). Offers a 7-day tour of Germany.

Kompas International (630 Fifth Ave., Suite 219, New York, NY 10111; phone: 800-233-6422 or 212-265-8210). Operates a wide variety of tours throughout Eastern Europe and specializes in Yugoslavia.

Legend Tours (3990 Old Town Ave., Suite 100C, San Diego, CA 92110; phone: 800-333-6114 or 619-293-7040). Offers escorted tours to all Eastern European countries (except Bulgaria and Turkey).

Leisure Resource (58 River St., Milford, CT 06460; phone: 800-999-1152). Offers escorted motorcoach tours of Andorra, Austria, Belgium, Bulgaria, Czechoslovakia, Denmark, Finland, France, Germany, Gibraltar, Great Britain, Greece, Hungary, Iceland, Ireland, Italy, Liechtenstein, Luxembourg, the Maltese Islands, Monaco, the Netherlands, Norway, Poland, Portugal, Romania, San Marino, the Soviet Union, Spain, Sweden, Switzerland, and Yugoslavia.

Littoral Travel (613 Hope Rd., Eatontown, NJ 07724; phone: 800-327-7457 or 908-389-2160). Offers tours to Bulgaria, Czechoslovakia, Hungary, Romania, and Yugoslavia, specializing in fitness and rejuvenation.

Lismore Tours (106 E. 31st St., New York, NY 10016; phone: 800-547-6673 or 212-685-0100). Offers escorted motorcoach tours of Great Britain and Ireland.

Love Holidays/Uniworld (15315 Magnolia Blvd., Suite 110, Sherman Oaks, CA 91403; phone: 800-456-5683 or 213-873-7991). Offers tours throughout Eastern Europe, including a number of tours of the Soviet Union and a package that visits both Albania and Yugoslavia. As this tour operator is a wholesaler, consult a travel agent.

Lynott Tours (350 Fifth Ave., Suite 2619, New York, NY 10118; phone: 212-760-0101 in New York State; 800-221-2474 elsewhere in the US). Offers escorted motorcoach tours of Great Britain and Ireland.

Maupintour (PO Box 807, Lawrence, KS 66044; phone: 800-255-4266). Offers escorted motorcoach tours of Austria, Belgium, Bulgaria, Czechoslovakia, Denmark, Finland, France, Germany, Great Britain, Greece, Hungary, Iceland,

Ireland, Italy, Liechtenstein, Luxembourg, Monaco, the Netherlands, Norway, Poland, Portugal, Romania, the Soviet Union, Spain, Sweden, Switzerland, and Yugoslavia.

Meier's World Travel (6033 W. Century Blvd., Suite 1080, Los Angeles, CA 90045; phone: 800-937-0700). Offers tours of Austria, Czechoslovakia, Germany, Hungary, Switzerland, and Yugoslavia.

Melia International (450 Seventh Ave., Suite 1805, New York, NY 10103; phone: 212-967-6565 in New York State; 800-848-2314 elsewhere in the US). Offers escorted motorcoach tours of Austria, Belgium, Czechoslovakia, Denmark, Finland, France, Germany, Great Britain, Greece, Hungary, Italy, Liechtenstein, Luxembourg, Monaco, the Netherlands, Norway, Poland, Portugal, the Soviet Union, Spain, Sweden, Switzerland, and Yugoslavia.

Mill-Run Tours (20 E. 49th St., New York, NY 10017; phone: 212-486-9840 in New York State, 800-MILL-RUN elsewhere). Offers tours of Portugal and its islands, the Azores and Madeira.

Olson Travel World (1334 Parkview Ave., Suite 210, Manhattan Beach, CA 90266; phone: 800-421-5785 or 213-546-8400). Offers escorted motorcoach tours of Austria, Belgium, Czechoslovakia, Denmark, Finland, France, Germany, Gibraltar, Great Britain, Greece, Hungary, Ireland, Italy, Liechtenstein, Luxembourg, Monaco, the Netherlands, Norway, Poland, Portugal, the Soviet Union, Spain, Sweden, Switzerland, and Yugoslavia.

Orbis (342 Madison Ave., Suite 1512, New York, NY 10173; phone: 212-867-5011). Offers a 15-day tour of Poland.

Perillo Tours (577 Chestnut Ridge Rd., Woodcliff Lake, NJ 07675; phone: 800-431-1515). Offers escorted motorcoach tours of Italy.

Putnik Travel (39 Beechwood, Manhasset, NY 11030; phone: 800-669-0757 or 516-627-2636). Offers a range of escorted tours of Czechoslovakia and Yugoslavia, plus multi-country programs to most other Eastern European countries.

Rahim Tours (12 S. Dixie Hwy., Lake Worth, FL 33460: phone: 800-556-5305 or 407-585-5305). Offers tours of the Soviet Union.

Russian Travel Bureau (225 E. 44th St., New York, NY 10017; phone: 800-847-1800 or 212-986-1500). Offers 11- to 24-day tours of the Soviet Union.

Skyline Travel Club (666 Old Country Rd., Suite 205, Garden City, NY 11530; phone 516-222-9090 or 800-645-6198). Offers escorted tours of Portugal and Spain.

Solrep (2524 Nottingham, Houston, TX 77005; phone: 713-529-5547 in Texas; 800-231-0985 elsewhere in the US). Offers escorted motorcoach tours of Austria, Belgium, Denmark, France, Germany, Great Britain, Ireland, Italy, Liechtenstein, Monaco, the Netherlands, Poland, the Soviet Union, Spain, Sweden, and Switzerland.

Sovereign Tourism (411 W. Putnam Ave., Suite 105, Greenwich, CT 06830; phone: 800-832-3228 or 203-629-3900). Offers tours throughout Great Britain.

STI (8619 Reseda Blvd., Suite 103, Northridge, CA 91324; phone: 800-525-0525 or 818-886-0633). Offers escorted motorcoach tours — some geared for the younger set — of Austria, Belgium, Czechoslovakia, Denmark, France, Germany, Great Britain, Greece, Hungary, Ireland, Italy, Liechtenstein, Luxembourg, Monaco, the Netherlands, Poland, Portugal, the Soviet Union, Switzerland, and Yugoslavia.

Trafalgar Tours (11 E. 26th St., New York, NY 10010; phone: 212-689-8977 in New York City; 800-854-0103 elsewhere in the US). Offers escorted motorcoach tours of Austria, Belgium, Bulgaria, Czechoslovakia, Denmark, Finland, France, Germany, Great Britain, Greece, Hungary, Ireland, Italy, Liechtenstein, Monaco, the Netherlands, Norway, Poland, Portugal, Romania, the Soviet Union, Spain, Sweden, Switzerland, and Yugoslavia. Bookings are made through travel agents, but you can contact *Trafalgar Tours* directly for information.

Travcoa (PO Box 2630, Newport Beach, CA 92658; phone: 800-992-2004 or 714-476-2800 in California; 800-992-2003 elsewhere in the US). Offers a lineup of all-inclusive, escorted motorcoach tours of Austria, Bulgaria, Czechoslovakia, Denmark, Finland, France, Germany, Gibraltar, Great Britain, Greece, Hungary, Iceland, Ireland, Italy, Liechtenstein, Luxembourg, Monaco, the Netherlands, Norway, Poland, Portugal, Romania, the Soviet Union, Spain, Sweden, Switzerland, and Yugoslavia.

Travel Bound (599 Broadway, Penthouse, New York, NY 10012; phone: 800-456-8656 or 212-334-1350). Offers escorted motorcoach tours of Austria, Belgium, Bulgaria, Czechoslovakia, Denmark, Finland, France, Germany, Gibraltar, Great Britain, Greece, Hungary, Ireland, Italy, Liechtenstein, Luxembourg, Monaco, the Netherlands, Norway, Poland, Portugal, San Marino, the Soviet Union, Spain, Sweden, Switzerland, and Yugoslavia.

Travel Time (17 N. State St., Chicago, IL 60602; phone: 800-621-4725). Offers escorted motorcoach tours of Austria, France, Great Britain, Italy, the Netherlands, and Switzerland.

TWA Getaway Tours (phone: 800-GETAWAY). Offers escorted motorcoach tours of Austria, Belgium, Bulgaria, Czechoslovakia, Denmark, Finland, France, Germany, Gibraltar, Great Britain, Greece, Hungary, Ireland, Italy, Liechtenstein, Monaco, the Netherlands, Norway, Poland, Portugal, the Soviet Union, Spain, Sweden, Switzerland, and Yugoslavia.

Unitours (8 S. Michigan Ave., Chicago, IL 60603; phone: 800-621-0557 or 312-782-1590). Offers escorted motorcoach tours of Austria, Belgium, Bulgaria, Czechoslovakia, Finland, France, Germany, Great Britain, Greece, Hungary, Ireland, Italy, Luxembourg, Monaco, the Netherlands, Poland, Romania, the Soviet Union, and Switzerland.

Value Holidays (10224 N. Port Washington Rd., Mequon, WI 53092; phone: 800-558-6850 or 414-241-6373). Offers escorted motorcoach tours of Austria, France, Germany, Great Britain, Ireland, and Switzerland.

Yugotours (350 Fifth Ave., Suite 2212, New York, NY 10118; phone: 800-223-5298 or 212-563-2400). Operates multi-country tours in all the Eastern European countries.

Independent Tours – Less restrictive arrangements for travelers who prefer more independence than that found on escorted tours are listed in the semi-escorted and hosted sections of tour catalogues. These may combine some aspects of an escorted tour, such as moving from place to place by motorcoach, with longer stays in one spot, where participants are at liberty but a host or hostess — that is, a representative of the tour company — is available at a local office or even in the hotel to answer questions and assist in arranging activities and optional excursions.

Another equally common type of package available to Europe is the car tour or fly/drive arrangement, often described in brochures as a self-drive or go-as-you-please tour. These are independent vacations, geared to travelers who want to cover as much ground as they might on an escorted group sightseeing tour but who prefer to do it on their own. The most flexible plans include no more than a map, a rental car, and a block of as many prepaid hotel vouchers as are needed for the length of the stay (the packages typically are 4 or 7 days long, extendable by individual extra days or additional package segments), along with a list of participating hotels at which the vouchers are accepted. In most cases, only the first night's accommodation is reserved; from then on, travelers book their rooms one stop ahead as they drive from place to place, creating their own itinerary as they go. When the hotels are members of a chain or association — which they usually are — the staff of the last hotel will reserve the next one for you. In other cases, there may be a choice of reserving all accommodations before departure — usually for a fee. Operators offering these packages usually sell vouchers in more than one price category: Travelers may have the option of upgrading hotel accommodations by paying a supplement directly to more expensive hostelries or can economize by choosing to stay in a modest inn, guesthouse, or bed and breakfast establishment. Another type of fly/drive arrangement is slightly more restrictive in that the tour packager supplies an itinerary that must be followed day by day, with a specific hotel to be reached each night. Often these plans are more deluxe as well.

Fly/drive packages to and around Europe include the following:

Abercrombie & Kent International (1520 Kensington Rd., Suite 212, Oak Brook, IL 60521; phone: 708-954-2944 in Illinois; 800-323-7308 elsewhere in the US). Their customized self-drive or chauffeured tours of Europe include stays in hotels that are converted manor houses, castles, and other stately homes. These packages are offered to Austria, Denmark, France, Great Britain, Hungary, Ireland, Italy, Norway, Portugal, Spain, and Sweden.

American Express Travel Related Services (offices throughout the US; phone: 800-241-1700 for information and local branches). Offers fly/drive packages to Great Britain, France, and Italy.

AutoVenture (425 Pike St., Suite 502, Seattle, WA 98101; phone: 206-624-6033 in Washington State; 800-426-7502 elsewhere in the US). This company's deluxe car tours are available in either a self-drive or chauffeured version. Their itineraries often feature overnight stays in hotels that are elegant converted manor houses, villas, old and distinctive country inns, or otherwise noteworthy. These packages are offered to Austria, Belgium, Bulgaria, Czechoslovakia, Denmark, Finland, France, Germany, Gibraltar, Great Britain, Greece, Hungary, Iceland, Ireland, Italy, Liechtenstein, Luxembourg, Monaco, the Netherlands, Norway, Poland, Portugal, Romania, the Soviet Union, Spain, Sweden, Switzerland, and Yugoslavia.

Bentley Tours (1649 Colorado Blvd., Los Angeles, CA 90041; phone: 800-821-9726 or 213-258-8451). Offers fly/drive packages in Great Britain and Ireland.

Brendan Tours (15137 Califa St., Van Nuys, CA 91411; phone: 800-421-8446 or 818-785-9696). Offers fly/drive packages to France, Germany, Great Britain, Ireland, and the Netherlands.

Brian Moore International (116 Main St., Medway, MA 02053; phone: 800-982-2299 or 508-533-6683). Offers fly/drive packages to Great Britain and Ireland.

Celtic International (161 Central Ave., Albany, NY 12206; phone: 800-833-4373 or 518-463-5511). Offers fly/drive packages to Great Britain and Ireland.

CIE Tours International (108 Ridgedale Ave., Morristown, NJ 07960; phone: 800-CIE-TOUR or 201-292-3438). Offers fly/drive packages to Great Britain and Ireland.

Collette Tours (162 Middle St., Pawtucket, RI 02860; phone: 800-832-4656, 800-752-2655 in New England). Offers fly/drive packages to Austria, Denmark, France, Germany, Great Britain, Iceland, Ireland, Italy, Norway, Portugal, Spain, Sweden, and Switzerland.

David B. Mitchell & Company (200 Madison Ave., New York, NY 10016; phone: 800-372-1323 or 212-889-4822). Also offers luxurious self-drive or chauffeured tours, which include stays in elegant *Relais & Châteaux* member establishments (see our discussion of accommodations, in *On the Road,* in this section). Among their offerings are fly/drive packages to Austria, France, Germany, Great Britain, Ireland, Liechtenstein, and Switzerland. Also arranges customized tours.

Extra Value Travel (683 S. Collier Blvd., Marco Island, FL 33937; phone: 800-255-2847). In conjunction with international car rental companies, offers fly/drive packages to Austria, Belgium, Bulgaria, Denmark, France, Germany, Great Britain, Greece, Hungary, Ireland, Italy, Liechtenstein, Luxembourg, the Maltese Islands, the Netherlands, Norway, Portugal, Spain, Sweden, Switzerland, and Yugoslavia.

European Car Vacations (9 Boston St., Suite 10, Lynn, MA 01904; phone: 800-223-6764 or 617-581-0844). Offers fly/drive packages to Andorra, Austria, Belgium, Bulgaria, Denmark, France, Germany, Great Britain, Greece, Hungary, Ireland, Italy, Liechtenstein, Luxembourg, the Maltese Islands, the Netherlands, Norway, Spain, Sweden, Switzerland, and Yugoslavia.

Europe Express (588 Broadway, Suite 505, New York, NY 10012; phone: 800-927-3876 or 212-334-0836). Offers fly/drive packages to Austria, Belgium, Denmark, Finland, France, Germany, Great Britain, Ireland, Italy, the Netherlands, Norway, Portugal, Spain, Sweden, and Switzerland.

The French Experience (370 Lexington Ave., New York, NY 10017; phone: 800-28-FRANCE or 212-986-1115). Offers fly/drive packages to France.

Ibero Travel (109-21 72nd Rd., Forest Hills, New York, NY 11375; phone: 800-654-2376 in New York State; 800-882-6678 elsewhere in the US). Offers fly/drive packages to Portugal and Spain.

H.S. & Associates (160 E. 26th St., Suite 5H, New York, NY 10010; phone: 800-927-4765 or 212-689-5400). Specializes in packages to France, including fly/drive packages.

Kompas International (630 Fifth Ave., Suite 219, New York, NY 10111; phone: 800-233-6422 or 212-265-8210). Offers fly/drive packages throughout Eastern Europe.

Legend Tours (3990 Old Town Ave., Suite 100C, San Diego, CA 92110; phone: 800-333-6114 or 619-293-7040). Offers fly/drive packages in all Eastern European countries (except Turkey).

Lismore Tours (106 E. 31st St., New York, NY 10016; phone: 800-547-6673 or 212-685-0100). Offers fly/drive packages to Great Britain and Ireland.

Lynott Tours (350 Fifth Ave., Suite 2619, New York, NY 10118; phone: 212-760-0101 in New York State; 800-221-2474 elsewhere in the US). Offers fly/drive packages to Great Britain and Ireland.

Marsans International (19 W. 34th St., Suite 302, New York, NY 10001; phone: 212-239-3880 in New York State; 800-777-9110 elsewhere in the US). Offers fly/drive packages to Portugal and Spain. Note that their specialty is arranging tours for Spanish-speaking clients.

Plus Ultra Tours (174 7th Ave., New York, NY 10011; phone: 800-242-0394 or 212-242-0393). Offers fly/drive packages to Portugal and Spain.

Putnik Travel (39 Beechwood, Manhasset, NY 11030; phone: 800-669-0757 or 516-627-2636). Offers fly/drive packages in Czechoslovakia and Yugoslavia.

Travel Bound (599 Broadway, Penthouse, New York, NY 10012; phone: 800-456-8656 or 212-334-1350). Offers fly/drive packages to Austria, Belgium, Bulgaria, Czechoslovakia, Denmark, Finland, France, Germany, Gibraltar, Great Britain, Greece, Hungary, Ireland, Italy, Liechtenstein, Luxembourg, Monaco, the Netherlands, Norway, Poland, Portugal, Romania, San Marino, the Soviet Union, Spain, Sweden, and Yugoslavia.

Value Holidays (10224 N. Port Washington Rd., Mequon, WI 53092; phone: 800-558-6850 or 414-241-6373). Offers fly/drive packages to Austria, France, Germany, Great Britain, and Switzerland.

Yugotours (350 Fifth Ave., Suite 2212, New York, NY 10118; phone: 800-223-5298 or 212-563-2400). Offers fly/drive packages in a number of Eastern European countries.

Stay-Put City and Resort Packages – A further possibility for independent travelers is a "stay-put" package in Europe. These appeal to travelers who want to be on their own and remain in one place for the duration of their vacation, although it is not unusual for travelers to buy more than one package at a time.

Basically, a city package — no matter what the city — includes round-trip transfers between airport and hotel, a choice of hotel accommodations (usually including continental breakfast) in several price ranges, plus any number of other features that you may not need or want but would lose valuable time arranging if you did. Common package features are 1 or 2 half-day guided tours of the city; passes for unlimited travel by underground (subway) or bus; discount cards for shops, museums, and restaurants; temporary membership in and admission to clubs, casinos, discotheques, or other nightspots; and car rental for some or all of your stay. Other features may be anything from a souvenir travel bag to a tasting of local wines or dinner and a show.

These packages usually are a week long — although 4-day and 14-day packages also are available, and most packages can be extended by extra days — and often are hosted; that is, a representative of the tour company may be available at a local office or even in the hotel to answer questions, handle problems, and assist in arranging activities and optional excursions. A similar stay-put resort package generally omits the sightseeing tour and may offer some sort of daily meal plan if accommodations are in hotels; accommodations in apartment hotels with kitchenettes are another common alternative.

Among the stay-put packages offered in Europe are the following:

American Express Travel Related Services (offices throughout the US; phone: 800-241-1700 for information and local branches). Offers city packages to Amsterdam, Athens, Barcelona, Berlin, Brussels, Copenhagen, Dublin, Edinburgh, Florence, Frankfurt, Geneva, Hamburg, Innsbruck, Lisbon, London, Lucerne, Lyons, Madrid, Milan, Munich, Paris, Rome, Salzburg, Stockholm, Venice, Vienna, and Zurich, as well as stay-put resort packages on the French Riviera. Although there usually is a 3-day minimum, packages can be arranged for as long as you like.

Bennett (270 Madison Ave., New York, NY 10016; phone: 800-221-2420 or 212-532-5060). Offers 3-night or longer city packages to Amsterdam, Athens, Berlin, Brussels, Budapest, Copenhagen, Dublin, Edinburgh, Florence, Geneva, Helsinki, Istanbul, Innsbruck, Lisbon, London, Lucerne, Madrid, Munich, Nice, Oslo, Paris, Prague, Rome, Salzburg, Stockholm, Venice, Vienna, Warsaw, and Zurich.

Brendan Tours (15137 Califa St., Van Nuys, CA 91411; phone: 800-421-8446 or 818-785-9696). Offers 9-day city packages to London, Paris, and Rome, as well as a variety of 8- to 16-day combination packages including Amsterdam, London, Paris, and Rome.

British Airways Holidays (phone: 800-AIRWAYS). Offers a London/Paris city package, including 3 nights in each city. Their London Plus package includes a minimum stay of 3 days in London, along with a 3-day stay in any one of the following cities: Amsterdam, Athens, Copenhagen, Berlin, Madrid, Paris, Rome, Venice, Vienna, and Zurich. The Four City Classic package includes 3 days in London and 3 days each in Florence, Rome, and Venice. Transportation between the cities is by air and rail; extended-stay options are available for all packages.

Cavalcade Tours (450 Harmon Meadow Blvd., Secaucus, NJ 07094; phone: 800-356-2405). Offers city packages to Barcelona, Granada, Ibiza, Lisbon, London, Madrid, and Paris.

Châteaux Accueil (c/o *DMI Tours*, 14340 Memorial Dr., Houston, TX 77079;

phone: 800-553-5090). Offers stay-put packages at private châteaux in France. Owners are in residence, often functioning as hosts, and in many cases English is spoken.

CIE Tours International (108 Ridgedale Ave., Morristown, NJ 07960; phone: 800-CIE-TOUR or 201-292-3438). Offers a 3-night Dublin Fair City package that includes theater tickets.

DER Tours (11933 Wilshire Blvd., Los Angeles, CA 90025; phone: 800-937-123 or 213-479-4411). Offers 3-night or longer city packages to Amsterdam, Barcelona, Berlin, Brussels, Budapest, Florence, Frankfurt, Geneva, Hanover, Hamburg, London, Lucerne, Madrid, Munich, Nice, Nuremberg, Paris, Rome, Salzburg, Venice, Vienna, and Zurich, as well as stay-put packages on Spain's Costa del Sol.

Europe Express (588 Broadway, Suite 505, New York, NY 10012; phone: 800-927-3876 or 212-334-0836). Offers 3-night or longer city packages to Amsterdam, Barcelona, Brussels, Dublin, Edinburgh, Florence, Frankfurt, Geneva, Heidelberg, Helsinki, Lisbon, London, Lucerne, Madrid, Milan, Munich, Nice, Oslo, Paris, Rome, Stockholm, Venice, and Vienna.

General Tours (770 Broadway, 10th Floor, New York, NY 10003; phone: 800-221-2216 or 212-598-1800). Offers city packages throughout Eastern Europe.

Isram Travel (630 Third Ave., New York, NY 10017; phone: 800-223-7460 or 212-922-1022). Offers city packages throughout Eastern Europe.

Jet Vacations (1775 Broadway, New York, NY 10019; phone: 800-JET-0999 or 212-247-0999). Offers city packages to Amsterdam, Cannes, Copenhagen, Edinburgh, Düsseldorf, Florence, Frankfurt, Geneva, the Hague, Helsinki, Innsbruck, Lisbon, London, Lucerne, Lugano, Lyons, Madeira, Madrid, Milan, Monte Carlo, Munich, Nice, Oslo, Paris, Rome, Salzburg, St.-Tropez, Stockholm, Stuttgart, Venice, Vienna, and Zurich, as well as châteaux stays throughout France and stay-put resort packages on Spain's Costa del Sol.

Kompas International (630 Fifth Ave., Suite 219, New York, NY 10111; phone: 800-233-6422 or 212-265-8210). Offers city packages in Belgrade, Budapest, Dubrovnik, Prague, and Zagreb.

Legend Tours (3990 Old Town Ave., Suite 100C, San Diego, CA 92110; phone: 800-333-6114 or 619-293-7040). Offers city packages in all Eastern European countries (except Turkey).

Marsans International (19 W. 34th St., Suite 302, New York, NY 10001; phone: 212-239-3880 in New York State; 800-777-9110 elsewhere in the US). Offers 5-day city packages to London, Madrid, Paris, and Rome, as well as customized stay-put packages in other cities. Note that their specialty is arranging packages for Spanish-speaking clients.

Meier's World Travel (6033 W. Century Blvd., Suite 1080, Los Angeles, CA 90045; phone: 800-937-0700). Arranges 3-night or longer customized city packages to Amsterdam, Berlin, Budapest, Düsseldorf, Florence, Frankfurt, Hamburg, London, Munich, Paris, Prague, Rome, Salzburg, Venice, Vienna, and Zurich.

Petrabax Tours (97-45 Queens Blvd., Suite 505, Rego Park, NY 11374; phone: 718-897-7272 in New York State; 800-367-6611 elsewhere). Offers 4-day or longer city packages throughout Europe for Spanish-speaking clientele.

Spanish Heritage Tours (116-47 Queens Blvd., Forest Hills, NY 11375; phone: 718-520-1300 or 800-221-2580). Offers 6-night or longer city packages in Barcelona, Lisbon, Madrid, and Seville, as well as customized city packages throughout Portugal and Spain.

SuperCities (7855 Haskell Ave., Van Nuys, CA 91406; phone: 800-633-300 or 818-988-7844). Offers 2-night or longer city packages to Amsterdam, Athens, Barcelona, Bergen, Brussels, Copenhagen, Florence, Frankfurt, Lisbon, London, Lucerne, Madrid, Munich, Nice, Oslo, Paris, Rome, Salzburg, Stockholm, Venice, Vienna, and Zurich.

TWA Getaway Tours (phone: 800-GETAWAY). Offers numerous 8-day city packages throughout Europe, including London Theatre Week, London Theatre Spectacular, Paris Rendezvous, Roman Holiday, and Royal Madrid packages, as well as a variety of combination city packages.

Unitours (8 S. Michigan Ave., Chicago, IL 60603; phone: 800-621-0557 or 312-782-1590). Offers 3-night or longer city packages to Amsterdam, Budapest, the Hague, Prague, Salzburg, and Vienna.

U.S. & International Travel & Tours (117 S. Main St., Mishawaka, IN 46544; phone: 219-255-7272 or 800-759-7373). Offers city packages throughout Eastern Europe.

Value Holidays (10224 N. Port Washington Rd., Mequon, WI 53092; phone: 800-558-6850 or 414-241-6373). Offers 3-night or longer city packages to Berlin, Paris, and Vienna.

Volare (1560 Broadway, Suite 808, New York, NY 10036; phone: 212-768-1313). Offers city packages throughout Eastern Europe.

Voyage International (366 Second St. Pike, Southampton, PA 18966; phone: 800-468-4012 or 215-364-4300). Specializes in stay-put packages in and around Paris.

Yugotours (350 Fifth Ave., Suite 2212, New York, NY 10118; phone: 800-223-5298 or 212-563-2400). Offers city packages throughout Eastern Europe.

Special-Interest Packages – Special-interest tours are a growing sector of the travel industry. These are similar to the packages discussed above, with the exception that the package — whether it be of the all-inclusive motorcoach, fly/drive, or stay-put variety — is designed with a particular focus in mind, such as a specific sport, cultural events, history, or fine food and wines.

Programs focusing on food and wine are prominent among packages of this sort put together for visitors to Europe. Note, though, that they tend to be quite structured arrangements rather than independent ones, and they rarely are created with the budget traveler in mind. Also note that inclusive as they may be, few food and wine tours include *all* meals in the package price. This is not necessarily a cost-cutting technique on the part of the packager; rather, because of the lavishness of some of the meals, others may be left to the discretion of the participants, not only to allow time for leisure, but also to allow for differing rates of metabolism. Similarly, even on wine tours that spend entire days in practically full-time tasting, unlimited table wine at meals may not be included in the package price. The brochures usually are clear about what comes with the package and when.

Among the various food and wine tours, groups on *Bacchants' Pilgrimages'* annual 3-week Southern France Classic visit châteaux, vineyards, and wine cellars from the Loire Valley to Cognac, Bordeaux, the Côtes du Rhône, Burgundy, Champagne, and Paris, tasting all the way. Included are winery-hosted luncheons, picnics, two dinners in three-star restaurants, and other luncheons and dinners in restaurants of lesser fame. Similar packages are offered to the Maltese Islands, Portugal, and Spain. Bookings are through travel agents or *Bacchants' Pilgrimages,* 345 California St., Suite 2570, San Francisco, CA 94104 (phone: 415-981-8518).

For groups of 10 or more travelers, *Travel Concepts* (62 Commonwealth Ave., Suite 3, Boston, MA 02116; phone: 617-266-8450) offers a variety of custom-designed food and wine packages to Denmark, France, Germany, Great Britain, Ireland, Italy, Spain, and Switzerland. They also design other customized tours.

There also are special-interest packages catering to travelers particularly interested in the arts and/or cultural studies. Among these are the packages for classical music and opera lovers offered by *Dailey-Thorp* (315 W. 57th St., New York, NY 10019; phone: 212-307-1555). Their tours focus on various European musical events and the roster is always changing. Itineraries also include music-related activities such as visits to sites associated with composers or their works. These packages are offered to Austria, Belgium, Czechoslovàkia, Denmark, Finland, France, Germany, Great Britain, Greece, Hungary, Ireland, Italy, Monacò, the Netherlands, Norway, Poland, Portugal, the Soviet Union, Spain, Switzerland, and Yugoslavia.

For art enthusiasts, *Prospect Art Tours* (454-458 Chiswick High Rd., London W45TT, England; phone: 44-81-995-2151 or 44-81-995-2163) offers 5- to 15-day tours visiting key museums, private galleries, and art collections throughout Europe, including Austria, Belgium, Czechoslovakia, Denmark, France, Germany, Great Britain, Greece, Hungary, Ireland, Italy, the Netherlands, Poland, Portugal, Spain, and Switzerland. Their tours often emphasize a specific artistic theme — such as the work of a particular artist or the art or architecture of a particular region or period.

Artwork of France's earliest inhabitants can be explored through *Past Time Tours*' Cave Art of France package. The 14-day tour includes educational lectures and a look at some of the world's most intriguing prehistoric ritual art and symbols. Leaving from Paris, the tour begins in Toulouse and continues on to Foix and Les Eyzies. They also offer a similar 7- to 10-day tour of Spain. For information, contact *Past Time Tours* (800 Larch La., Sacramento, CA 95864-5042; phone: 916-485-8140). And *Far Horizons* (PO Box 1529, 16 Fern La., San Anselmo, CA 94960; phone: 415-457-4575) specializes in archaeological and cultural special-interest packages.

The Heritage Roots Tours offered by *Celtic International Tours* (161 Central Ave., Albany, NY 12206; phone: 800-833-4373 or 518-463-5511) are for travelers of Irish extraction who wish to know more about their ancestors. Other special-interest packages to Ireland include *Aer Lingus*'s Pub Tour of Ireland and the Shop Ireland package offered by *Matterhorn Travel Service* (2450 Riva Rd., Annapolis, MD 21401; phone: 301-224-2230 in Maryland; 800-638-9150 elsewhere in the US).

The *Battle of Normandy Foundation* in conjunction with *HIP Tours* (134 Golf Club Dr., Longwood, FL 32779-4693; phone: 800-869-9576 or 407-862-4556) offers tours of World War II battlegrounds in France, Belgium, Germany, and Luxembourg. At the time of this writing, *Galaxy Tours* (997 Old Eagle School Rd., #207, PO Box 234, Wayne, PA 19087-0234; phone: 800-523-7287 or 215-964-8010), a specialist in veterans' tours, also was planning some tours of Eastern Front battlefields.

Since Europe is a land of pilgrimage, it also is the destination of tours geared to Roman Catholic travelers. One company specializing in such tours is *Catholic Travel* (10018 Cedar La., Kensington, MD 20895; phone: 301-564-1904). Lead by a spiritual director, pilgrimages are offered to France, Great Britain, Ireland, Italy, Portugal, Spain, and Yugoslavia. Other companies offering trips with an religious focus include *Kompas International* (630 Fifth Ave., Suite 219, New York, NY 10111; phone: 800-233-6422 or 212-265-8210), *Putnik Travel* (39 Beechwood, Manhasset, NY 11030; phone: 800-669-0757 or 516-627-2636), and *Yugotours* (350 Fifth Ave., Suite 2212, New York, NY 10118; phone: 800-223-5298 or 212-563-2400). All three operate tours to Medjugorje, Yugoslavia — a major point of pilgrimage since the Virgin Mary appeared to a group of children in 1981.

For Jewish travelers, the *American Jewish Congress* (15 E. 84th St., New York, NY 10028; phone: 212-879-4588 in New York State; 800-221-4694 elsewhere in the US) regularly arranges tours to Europe. Their broad range of itineraries visits Belgium, Bulgaria, Czechoslovakia, Denmark, Germany, Gibraltar, Great Britain, Greece, Hungary, Italy, the Netherlands, Norway, Poland, Portugal, the Soviet Union, Spain, Sweden, and Switzerland. *Isram Travel* (630 Third Ave., New York, NY 10017; 800-223-7460 or 212-922-1022) also offers Jewish Heritage packages to Bulgaria, Hungary, and Poland.

For travelers interested in touring by rail, the legendary *Orient Express* of old, the luxury hotel on wheels that carried tourists and tycoons, kings and conspirators from London and Paris via Eastern Europe to Istanbul, has been revived as the *Venice Simplon–Orient Express*. Twice weekly year-round (except December and January), this train runs between London and Venice, giving passengers a nostalgic taste of the golden age of rail travel aboard sumptuously restored carriages of the 1920s. Stops en route include Innsbruck, Salzburg, and Vienna (Austria), Paris (France), Munich (Germany), Milan and Verona (Italy), Basel, Lausanne, and Zurich (Switzerland). For information, contact *Venice Simplon–Orient Express,* 1155 Ave. of the Americas, 30th Floor, New York, NY 10036 (phone: 800-524-2420).

And those who are interested in touring the Soviet Union by private rail car should contact *Abercrombie & Kent* (1520 Kensington Rd., Suite 212, Oak Brook, IL 60521; phone: 708-954-2944 in Illinois; 800-323-7308 elsewhere in the US). Two different itineraries are offered aboard the company's exclusive train, the *Anna Karenina*. The first is a 12-day tour of the ancient cities of Old Russia, including St. Petersburg and Moscow, and the second is a 17-day journey across Siberia.

The ballooning packages offered by the *Bombard Society* (6727 Curran St., McLean, VA 22101; phone: 800-862-8537 or 703-448-9407) explore Austria, France, Italy, and Switzerland — both from on high and with feet on the ground. The packages include daily flights via hot-air balloon (flown by pilots, not tour participants), sightseeing, hotel accommodations, and meals, many of which are candlelit buffets served after the day's flight.

And for those with somewhat ghoulish tastes, *Littoral Travel* (613 Hope Rd., Eatontown, NJ 07724; phone: 800-327-7457 or 908-389-2160) offers an 8-day Dracula Tour for Halloween in Transylvania (Romania), with a Halloween party in a castle.

Sports Packages – Ski packages are foremost among the sports-related packages to Europe. The foundation of the package usually is a week or two of hotel or condominium accommodations at a ski resort, and for those choosing the hotel rather than the apartment, the price often includes a meal plan of breakfast and dinner daily. The other features of a ski vacation — round-trip bus, train, or rental car transportation between the airport and the resort, ski passes, baggage handling, taxes and tips — are included in varying combinations according to the packager. If transatlantic transportation is by charter flight (not unusual on ski packages), airfare, too, will be included in the price. If not, the applicable "group ski" or other fare will be listed separately. Among the numerous packagers offering ski packages to Europe are the following:

Adventures on Skis (815 North Rd., Westfield, MA 01085; phone: 800-628-9655 or 413-568-2855). Offers ski packages to Austria, France, Italy, and Switzerland.

Alpine Skiing and Travel (534 New State Hwy., Raynham, MA 02767; phone: 508-823-7707; 800-551-8822 in Massachusetts; 800-343-9676 elsewhere in the US). Offers ski packages to Austria, France, Italy, and Switzerland.

Central Holiday Tours (206 Central Ave., Jersey City, NJ 07307; phone: 800-526-6045). Offers ski packages in Austria, France, Italy, and Switzerland.

Club Med (40 W. 57th St., New York, NY 10019; phone: 800-CLUB-MED). Vacation packages at the *Club Med* ski resort in France, Italy, and Switzerland include lessons at the *Club*'s private ski school and all lift passes.

Steve Lohr's Skiworld and Travel (206 Central Ave., Jersey City, NJ 07307; phone: 201-798-3900 in New Jersey; 800-223-1306 elsewhere in the US). Offers ski packages to Austria, France, Italy, the Soviet Union, and Sweden.

Tour Center (1281 Patterson Point Rd., Secaucus, NJ 07094; phone: 800-222-1170 or 201-348-2244). Offers ski packages to Austria, France, Italy, and Switzerland.

Golf tours are a staple for many countries — particularly Ireland and Scotland. The main ingredient of these tours is the opportunity to play at some of the most celebrated courses in the world. A fly/drive arrangement usually is involved, with rental car, hotel accommodations for a week or two, often dinner each day, and some greens fees included. Some packages provide an entire week at one course or a choice of courses, some combine a golfing holiday in Ireland with a visit to Scottish courses, and some are offered in other European countries, less well known for their greens, but still offering challenging courses. In addition, although some packagers offer structured golf tours (motorcoach or independent), others recommend courses and a basic itinerary, letting you design the package.

Among the numerous packagers offering golf vacations to Europe are the following:

Adventure Golf Holiday (815 North Rd., Westfield, MA 01085; phone: 800-628-9655 or 413-568-2855). Offers packages to Austria, France, Germany, Ireland, Italy, Portugal, Spain, Switzerland, and Scotland.

Adventures in Golf (29 Valencia Dr., Nashua, NH 03062; phone: 603-882-8367). Offers packages to France, Great Britain, Ireland, Portugal, and Spain.

Atlantic Golf (235 Post Rd. W., Westport, CT 06880; phone: 800-443-8075 or 203-454-0090). Offers packages to Ireland.

Fourth Dimension Tours (1150 NW 72nd Ave., Miami, FL 33126; phone: 800-343-0020 or 305-477-1525). Offers packages to Portugal and Spain.

Golfing Holidays (231 E. Millbrae Ave., Millbrae, CA 94030; phone: 415-697-0230). Offers packages to Andorra, Austria, Belgium, Bulgaria, Czechoslovakia, Denmark, Finland, France, Germany, Gibraltar, Great Britain, Greece, Hungary, Iceland, Ireland, Italy, Liechtenstein, Luxembourg, the Maltese Islands, Monaco, the Netherlands, Norway, Poland, Portugal, Romania, San Marino, the Soviet Union, Spain, Sweden, Switzerland, and Yugoslavia.

Golf International (275 Madison Ave., New York, NY 10016; phone: 212-986-9176). Offers packages to France, Great Britain, Ireland, and Monaco.

Golfpac (Box 940490, 901 N. Lake Destiny Dr., Suite 192, Maitland, FL 32794-0490; phone: 800-327-0878 or 407-660-8277). Offers packages to Great Britain and Ireland.

Grasshopper Golf Tours (403 Hill Ave., Glen Ellyn, IL 60137; phone: 708-858-1660). Offers packages to Great Britain.

Henry Hudson Tours (Box 155, Malden on Hudson, NY 12453; phone: 800-431-6064 or 914-246-8453). Offers packages to Ireland.

InterGolf (PO Box 819, Champlain, NY 12919 or 1980 Sherbrook St. W., Suite 210, Montreal, Quebec H3H 1E8, Canada; phone: 514-933-2772). Offers packages to Austria, France, Germany, Great Britain, Greece, Ireland, Monaco, the Netherlands, Portugal, Spain, and Switzerland.

Ireland Golf Tours (251 E. 85th St., New York, NY 10028; phone: 800-346-5388 or 212-772-8220). Offers packages to Ireland.

Isle Inn Tours (113 S. Washington St., Alexandria, VA 22314; phone: 800-237-9376 or 703-739-2277). Offers packages to Ireland.

ITC Golf Tours (4439 Atlantic Ave., Suite 205, Long Beach, CA 90807; phone: 800-257-4981 or 213-595-6905). Offers packages to Austria, France, Great Britain, Ireland, Portugal, and Spain.

Marsans Intercontinental (19 W. 34 St., New York, NY 10001; phone: 212-239-3880 in New York State; 800-777-9110 elsewhere in the US). Offers packages to France, Great Britain, Ireland, Monaco, Portugal, and Spain. Note that their specialty is arranging tours for Spanish-speaking clients.

Owenoak International (3 Parklands Dr., Darien, CT 06820; phone: 800-426-4498 or 203-655-2531). Offers packages to Great Britain.

Perry Golf (8302 Dunwoody Pl., Suite 305, Atlanta, GA 30350; phone: 404-394-5400 or 800-344-5257). Offers packages to Ireland, Portugal, and Spain.

Scottish Golf Holidays (9403 Kenwood Rd., Cincinnati, OH 45242; phone: 800-284-8884 or 513-984-0414). Offers packages to Ireland and Scotland.

Value Holidays (10224 N. Port Washington Rd., Mequon, WI 53092; phone: 800-558-6850 or 414-241-6373). Offers packages to Austria, Great Britain, and Ireland.

Wide World of Golf (PO Box 5217, Su Vecino Court, Carmel, CA 93921; phone: 408-624-6667). Offers packages to Austria, Belgium, Denmark, Finland, France, Germany, Gibraltar, Great Britain, Greece, Iceland, Ireland, Italy, Luxembourg, Monaco, the Netherlands, Norway, Portugal, San Marino, the Soviet Union, Spain, Sweden, Switzerland, and Yugoslavia.

Tennis and golf tours operated in conjunction with canal cruises are organized by *Grand Slam Tennis Tours* (PO Box 5132, La Quinta, CA 92253; phone: 619-564-5443). The latest additions to their programs are two Tennis Experience tours. The first, from the last week of May through mid-June, includes center-court seats to the *French Open International Tennis Championship* in Paris; the second, Château Tennis, a week-long program, runs several times between May and October, and includes stays at three different châteaux (2 nights at each). The company also arranges independent tours to the *French Open*.

Sports enthusiasts may want to attend this year's *Winter* and *Summer Olympics,* hosted, respectively, by Albertville (in the French Alps) and Barcelona (Spain). *Olson Travelworld* (1334 Parkview Ave., Suite 210, Manhattan Beach, CA 90266; phone: 800-421-5785 or 213-546-8400) is the official tour operator for this year's *Olympics* and is offering packages including local accommodations and tickets to individual sporting events and the opening and closing ceremonies. In addition, *Powder Ski Adventures* (24196 Alicia Parkway, Mission Viejo, CA 92691; phone: 800-888-6262 or 714-859-7919) offers 7-night ski packages that include tickets to some of the *Olympic* ski events. Other companies, such as *Melia International* (450 Seventh Ave., Suite 1805, New York, NY 10103; phone: 212-967-6565 in New York State; 800-848-2314 elsewhere in the US) are offering similar packages. If you are considering attending the *Olympics,* be sure to check with a travel agent well in advance.

Among other sports-oriented packages are those focused on — and guaranteeing entrance in — marathons. *Marathon Tours* (108 Main St., Charlestown, MA 02129; phone: 617-242-7845) offers packages including races in Austria, Belgium, Denmark, Finland, France, Germany, Great Britain, Greece, Iceland, Ireland, Italy, the Netherlands, Norway, the Soviet Union, Spain, Sweden, Switzerland, and Yugoslavia. In addition, *Grimes Travel* (250 W. 57th St., New York, NY 10019; phone: 212-307-7797 in New York State; 800-832-7778 elsewhere) sends runners to Ireland for the *Dublin Marathon* in October.

Horseback riding holidays are the province of *FITS Equestrian* (2011 Alamo Pintado Rd., Solvang, CA 93463; phone: 805-688-9494). The choices — not for beginners — include week-long riding packages in Austria, France, Germany, Great Britain, Greece, Hungary, Iceland, Ireland, Italy, Portugal, the Soviet Union, and Spain. *Equitour* (PO Box 807, Dubois, WY 82513; phone: 307-455-3363 in Wyoming; 800-545-0019 elsewhere in the US) also offers horseback riding packages in Austria, France, Germany, Great Britain, Greece, Hungary, Iceland, Ireland, Italy, Portugal, the Soviet Union, and Spain. And *Discover Expeditions* (31 Madeline Rd., Ridge, NY 11961; phone: 800-242-5554) operates an 11-day ride in Roztocze in Eastern Poland.

And for marksmen and fisherfolk, *Frontiers International* (PO Box 959, Pearce Mill Rd., Wexford, PA 15090; phone: 412-935-1577 or 800-245-1950) offers hunting and fishing packages in Czechoslovakia, Denmark, Finland, Great Britain, Hungary, Iceland, Ireland, Norway, the Soviet Union, Sweden, and Yugoslavia. For the serious hunter, *Kleinburger World Wide Travel* (3627 First Ave. S., Seattle, WA 98134; phone 206-343-9699 or 800-232-3708) arranges hunts and hunting throughout Eastern European. The most popular game right now is Marco Polo sheep in Russia.

Also for fisherfolk are the packages offered by *Fishing International* (Hilltop Estate, 4010 Montecito Ave., Santa Rosa CA 95404; phone: 800-950-4242 or 707-542-4242). Their week-long packages include accommodations in small country inns, hotels that are converted castles, and other distinctive settings, as well as all meals, personal guides, and the opportunity to exchange fish stories about the one that got away with fellow enthusiasts. Their enticing offerings span the waters of Austria, France, Great Britain, Iceland, Ireland, Norway, Portugal, Scotland, the Soviet Union, and Spain. They also design customized tours.

For those interested in wildlife, *Discover Expeditions* (31 Madeline Rd., Ridge, NY 11961; phone: 800-242-5554) operates adventure and wildlife tours in Poland. The 11-day Bierbrza River Wildlife Trip travels through some of the greatest wetland areas of Europe. *Wilderness Travel* (801 Allston Way, Berkeley, CA 94710; phone: 800-368-2794 or 510-548-0420) offers a Last Wolves of Europe package, spending 10 days in the forests of northern Poland.

And for those seeking a relaxing vacation focusing on physical health and beautification, spa packages cover arrangements at Europe's thermal resorts. These usually are 1 week long and provide accommodations, some or all meals, and one or two treatments daily (classic spa treatments such as manual or hydromassage, mud baths, and so on), often with the option of a beauty program rather than the basic spa regimen. *Health and Fitness Vacations* (2911 Grand Ave., Suite 3A, Mayfair in the Grove, Miami, FL 33133; phone: 305-445-3876), a specialist in spa vacations offers packages throughout Europe. *Spa Trek International* (470 Park Ave. S., 14th Floor, New York, NY 10016; phone: 800-272-3480 or 212-779-3480) books clients at spas in Austria, Czechoslovakia, France, Germany, Great Britain, Hungary, Italy, Portugal, Romania, Spain, Switzerland, and Yugoslavia. Other companies offering European spa vactions include *Atlas Ambassador* (60 E. 42nd st., New York, NY 10165; phone: 212-297-6767), which concentrates on the spas of Yugoslavia; and *Hungarian Hotels Sales Office* (6033 W. Century Blvd., Suite 670, Los Angeles, CA 90045; phone: 213-649-5960), which books Hungarian establishments.

Special-interest tours for practitioners and spectators of other sports include many biking and hiking tours of varying levels of difficulty. For the names and addresses of their organizers, see *Camping and Caravanning, Hiking and Biking,* in this section.

PACKAGES BOOKED IN EUROPE: Those who may want to add a tour or package program after they are in Europe should know that package tours can be booked at all major capitals and other metropolitan areas. Besides the excitement of adding a vacation within a vacation to your itinerary, these Europe-based packages represent an economical way of getting from one point in Europe to another (and back).

The most popular place in which to book while abroad is London. North American travelers find British tours particularly attractive because they're mostly for English-speaking groups and often are accompanied by English-speaking escorts and/or guides. In addition, many British tour operators cater to the budget end of the market. Not long ago, for less than half the price of a scheduled air ticket from London to Athens and back, the smart shopper was able to pick up the flight plus a week's worth of adequate, if spartan, accommodations, and even some meals. These days, the bargains are not quite as great, but many British operators continue to cater to the budget end of the market, and they still manage to put together a good deal that becomes even better at times when the exchange rate is favorable to Americans.

If your interest is a tour of Great Britain, note that most of these companies, with their local clientele in mind, tend to specialize in tours from London to the Continent, and the assortment of budget tours of their own country is less broad. A number of these packagers do offer a selection of 3- or 4-day mini-tours covering a limited area of Britain, which can make a welcome excursion in the midst of an otherwise independent stay in London.

The following are some of Britain's major high-volume or economy-minded tour operators. Some have become familiar names in this country because they maintain US offices and market some or all of their tour offerings directly to the American public; booking one of their packages is no different than booking the package of a US tour operator. Almost all of the rest have at least a representative in the US to handle bookings. Note that most of these offices or representatives prefer to deal with travel agents rather than individuals. Note also that because of the extra costs involved in making arrangements from this end, packages booked here can run 5% to 15% more than if booked in Britain; and if you attempt to book through the British office by mail, your request will most likely be referred to the US representative. Clearly, you will save money by waiting until you are in England to book, but there's a chance that the package you want will not be available at the last minute.

Cosmos (*In London:* 180 Vauxhall Bridge Rd., London SW1V 1ED, England; phone: 44-71-834-7412. *In the US:* 95-25 Queens Blvd., 3rd Floor, Rego Park, NY 11374; phone: 718-268-7000; 800-221-0090 from the eastern US; 800-556-5454 from the western US, including Alaska and Hawaii). This firm specializes in low-cost motorcoach tours of Europe. This tour operator is a wholesaler, so bookings must be made through a travel agent.

Eurobout (*In London:* 27 Cockspur St., 4th Floor, London SW1Y 5BN, England; phone: 44-71-930-1138. *In the US:* c/o *Leisure Resource,* 58 River St., Milford, CT 06460; phone: 800-999-1152; or *Solrep Inc.,* 2524 Nottingham, Houston, TX 77005; phone: 713-529-5547 in Texas; 800-231-0985 elsewhere in the US). Smaller than *Cosmos* and less of a bargain specialist, *Eurobout* offers economical tours of Europe. This tour operator is a wholesaler; make bookings through a travel agent.

Frames Rickards (*In London:* 11 Herbrand St., London WC1N 1EX, England; phone: 44-71-837-3111. *In the US:* c/o *Trophy Tours,* 1810 Glenville Dr., Suite 124, Richardson, TX 75081; phone: 214-690-3875 in Texas; 800-527-2473 elsewhere in the US). Offers reasonably-priced coach tours of the Continent, Ireland, and Great Britain, including a series of low-cost mini-tours of England, Scotland, and Wales. Their US agent, *Trophy Tours,* prefers that bookings be made through a travel agent.

Globus-Gateway (London and US addresses and phone numbers are the same as those of *Cosmos;* see above). Offers numerous motorcoach tours of the Continent, as well as packages to Great Britain and Ireland. Independent city tours are among the standard offerings. This tour operator is a wholesaler; make bookings through a travel agent.

Insight International Tours (*In London:* 26 Cockspur St., Trafalgar Sq., London SW1Y 5BY, England; phone: 44-71-930-7444. *In the US:* 745 Atlantic Ave., Suite 720, Boston, MA 02111; phone: 800-582-8380 or 617-426-6666). Known as a good source for packaged travel buys, in addition to numerous longer tours (from a week to 37 days) of Great Britain and/or Ireland, Europe, and the Middle East, their offerings include a series of 2- to 5-day mini-tours of Britain. The US office accepts bookings from travel agents only.

Thomas Cook (*In London:* 45 Berkeley St., Piccadilly, London W1A 1EB, England; phone: 44-71-499-4000. Also has offices throughout the US.) Among the best known British tour operators, *Cook*'s tours span the world, with itineraries ranging from deluxe to moderate, along with some of the budget variety. Although this company is a wholesaler, you can book a tour directly through any of its offices in major cities in North America or through travel agents.

Thomson Holidays (*In London:* Greater London House, Hampstead Rd., London NW1 7SD, England; phone: 44-71-387-9321. No US office.) One of Great Britain's largest tour operators, *Thomson* has its own airline, *Britannia Airways,* and its coach tours travel from home turf to Europe and venture as far afield as the Himalayas. This company also is known for a broad selection of Mediterranean holiday packages that include round-trip airfare (from Britain) and a week or more of villa or apartment rental.

Trafalgar Tours (*In London:* 15 Grosvenor Pl., London SW1X 7HH, England; phone: 44-71-235-7079. *In the US:* 11 E. 26th St., New York, NY 10010; phone: 212-689-8977 in New York City; 800-854-0103 elsewhere in the US). This agency offers an extensive selection of first class tours of Europe, plus a group of budget-conscious CostSaver tours that include inexpensive accommodations. Bookings are made through travel agents, but you can contact *Trafalgar Tours* directly for information.

Camping and Caravanning, Hiking and Biking

CAMPING: Europe welcomes campers, whether they come alone or with a group, with tents or in recreational vehicles — generally known in Europe as "caravans" (a term that technically refers to towable campers as opposed to fully motorized vehicles known as "minibuses" or "minivans"). Camping probably is the best way to enjoy the countryside. And fortunately campgrounds are plentiful throughout Europe. They are used by millions of people a year, many of them foreigners.

Where to Camp – Caravanning is extremely popular with European vacationers, and many parks cater more to the caravanner than to the tent dweller. Sites for camping and caravanning are run by government tourist agencies, automobile associations, provinces and municipalities, and private companies. Some campgrounds have minimal facilities, and others are quite elaborate, with a variety of amenities on the premises. Most sites are open from about *Easter* through October.

Language barrier aside, directors of campgrounds often have a great deal of information about their region, and some even will arrange local tours or recommend sports facilities or attractions in the immediate area. Campgrounds also provide the atmosphere and opportunity to meet other travelers and exchange useful information. Too much so, sometimes — the popularity of European campgrounds causes them to be quite crowded during the summer, and campsites can be so close together that any attempt at privacy or getting away from it all is sabotaged. As campgrounds fill quickly throughout the season, and the more isolated sites always go first, it's a good idea to arrive early in the day and reserve your chosen spot — which leaves you free to explore the area for the rest of the day. (Whenever possible, try to call ahead and arrange a "pitch" in advance. At the height of the season, if you do not have advance reservations, you may be lucky to get even a less desirable site.)

In many countries, neither campers nor caravanners are restricted to the official sites. It may be possible to camp free on other public grounds. Ask the city police or local tourist information office about regulations. To camp on private property you first must obtain the permission of the landowner or tenant — and assume the responsibility of leaving the land exactly as you found it in return for the hospitality. When in difficulty, remember that tourist information offices throughout Europe will gladly direct visitors to sites in the areas they serve.

European campgrounds are well marked and rates usually are posted at the entrance. Still, it's best to have a map or check the information available in one of the numerous comprehensive guides to sites across the Continent and/or the sources listed below. It also may be difficult to find camping facilities open before June or after September, so a guide that gives this information comes in particularly handy off-season.

In the US, camping maps, brochures, and lists of sites are distributed by the tourist offices of individual countries, and a variety of useful publications also are available from American and European automobile clubs and other associations. The *American Automobile Association (AAA)* offers a number of useful resources, including its 600-page *Travel Guide to Europe* and the 64-page *Motoring Europe,* as well as a variety of useful maps; contact the nearest branch of *AAA* or the national office (see *Traveling by Car,* in this section). In addition, the *Automobile Association of Great Britain (AA)* publishes a comprehensive guide, *Camping and Caravanning in Europe* ($14.95), which lists over 4,000 sites throughout Europe, as well as other information of interest to campers. The *AA* also publishes a guide focusing on the British Isles, *Camping and Caravanning in Britain* ($11.75). Both are available from the *AA;* to order, contact AA Publishing (Fanum House, Basingstoke, Hampshire RG21 2EA, England; phone: 44-256-20123). The Britain guide also is available from the *British Travel Bookshop* (40 W. 57th St., New York, NY 10019; phone: 212-765-0898), for $12.95 (when ordering, add a $3 handling charge), as well as from other travel bookstores. Other useful guides include *The Campers Companion to Northern Europe* (Williamson; $13.95) and *Camper's Companion to Southern Europe* (out of print; check in your library).

The French international camping organization *Fédération Internationale de Camping et Caravaning* issues a pass, called a *carnet,* that entitles the bearer to a modest discount on camping fees throughout Europe, and is actually required at some European campgrounds. It is available in the US from the *National Campers and Hikers Association* (4804 Transit Rd., Bldg. 2, Depew, NY 14043; phone: 716-668-6242) for a fee of $30, which includes membership in the organization, as well as camping information.

Other European camping associations include the following:

France: Both the *Association Camping Club de France* (218 Bd. St.-Germain, Paris 75008, France; phone: 33-1-45-48-30-03) and *Fédération Française de Camping et de Caravaning* (78 Rue de Rivoli, Paris 75004, France; phone: 33-1-42-72-84-08) provide specific information on member campgrounds. *Association Camping Qualité France* (105 Rue Lafayette, Paris 75010, France; phone: 33-1-48-78-13-77) publishes a guide rating campgrounds by stars. And the *Fédération Nationale des Gîtes Ruraux de France* (35 Rue Godot-de-Mauroy, Paris 75009, France; phone: 33-1-47-42-25-43) issues a list of farms where camping is permitted.

Great Britain and Ireland: *Camping and Caravanning Club of Great Britain and Ireland* (Greenfields House, Westwood Way, Coventry CV4 8JH, England; phone: 44-203-694995) offers a free annual guide to its own and other British and Irish sites. Another source of useful information is the *Caravan Club Ltd.* (East Grinstead House, East Grinstead, West Sussex RH19 1UA, England; phone: 44-342-326944).

Italy: *Federcampeggio* (Via Vittorio Emanuele, Casella Postale 11, Calenzano 23-50041, Florence, Italy; phone: 39-55-882391) provides information on campgrounds and can reserve sites either before you go (preferable) or once you are in Italy (a chancy venture).

Camping et Caravaning France is a comprehensive Michelin guide covering more than 2,000 campgrounds throughout France; unfortunately it currently is published only in French. It is available for $12.95 in bookstores throughout France and in some travel bookstores and French-language bookstores in the US, and can be ordered from Michelin Guides and Maps, PO Box 3305, Spartanburg, SC 29304-3305 (phone: 803-599-0850 in South Carolina; 800-423-0485 elsewhere in the US).

The Portuguese National Tourist Office offers a useful brochure called *Roteiro Campisto,* which is available in English, as is the National Tourist Office of Spain's comprehensive *Guía de Campings.* The Northern Ireland Tourist Board's free booklet *Northern Ireland: Camping and Caravan Parks* lists more than 100 sites (it is available from the British Tourist Authority in the US). Annual guides, including detailed information on rated campgrounds, are available from the British Tourist Authority *(Caravan & Camping Parks)* and the Irish Tourist Board *(Caravan & Camping Sites).* The *Automobile Club d'Italia (ACI;* 261 Via Cristoforo Colombo, Rome 00185, Italy; phone: 39-6-5106; or 8 Via Marsala, Rome 00185, Italy; phone: 39-6-49981) publishes the paperback book *Campeggi in Italia,* a succinct and specific outline of facilities at Italian campgrounds, organized by localities.

Most experienced campers prefer to bring their own tried and true equipment, but camping equipment is available for sale or rent throughout Europe. For information on outfitters, consult the above-mentioned guides to camping and caravanning or contact the national tourist offices in the US which may be able to refer you to reliable European dealers.

Keep in mind that accessible food will lure scavenging wildlife, which may invade tents and vehicles. Also, even if you are assured that the campground where you are staying provides potable water, it is safer to use bottled, purified, or boiled water for drinking. To purify tap water, either use a water purification kit (available at most camping supply stores) or bring the water to a full, *rolling* boil over a camp stove. It also is inadvisable to use water from streams, rivers, or lakes — even purified.

Organized Camping Trips – A packaged camping tour abroad is a good way to have your cake and eat it, too. The problems of advance planning and day-to-day organizing are left to someone else, yet you still reap the benefits that shoestring travel affords and can enjoy the insights of experienced guides and the company of other campers. Be aware, however, that these packages usually are geared to the young, with ages 18 to 35 as common limits. Transfer from place to place is by bus (as on other sightseeing tours), overnights are in tents, and meal arrangements vary. Often there is a kitty that covers meals in restaurants or in the camp; sometimes there is a chef, and sometimes the cooking is done by the participants themselves. When considering a packaged camping tour, be sure to find out if equipment is included and what individual participants are required to bring.

The *Specialty Travel Index* (305 San Anselmo Ave., Suite 313, San Anselmo, CA 94960; phone: 415-459-4900) is a directory for special-interest travel and an invaluable resource. Listings include tour operators specializing in camping, as well as myriad other interests that combine nicely with a camping trip, such as biking, motorcycling, horseback riding, ballooning, and boating. The index costs $6 per copy, $10 for a year's subscription of two issues.

Among such packages are the camping tours of Europe offered by the following:

Autotours (20 Craven Ter., London W2, England; phone: 44-71-258-0272). Their camping trips depart from London and range from 3 to 10 weeks. A broad range of European itineraries is available, including camping packages to Austria, Belgium, Bulgaria, Czechoslovakia, Denmark, Finland, France, Germany, Gibraltar, Great Britain, Greece, Hungary, Italy, Liechtenstein, Monaco, the Netherlands, Norway, Poland, Portugal, Romania, San Marino, the Soviet Union, Spain, Sweden, Switzerland, and Yugoslavia.

Contiki Holidays (1432 E. Katella Ave., Anaheim, CA 92805; phone: 714-937-0611; 800-624-0611 in California; 800-626-0611 elsewhere in the continental US, and 11 E. 26th St., New York, NY 10010; phone: 800-FOR-TIKI). Operates camping tours of Scandinavia and Russia.

Himalayan Travel (PO Box 481, Greenwich, CT 06836; phone: 800-225-2380). Offers a variety of camping trips throughout Europe, including Austria, Belgium, Bulgaria, Czechoslovakia, France, Germany, Great Britain, Greece, Hungary, Iceland, Italy, Poland, Romania, the Soviet Union, Spain, Switzerland, and Yugoslavia.

Nouvelles Frontières (87 Bd. de Grenelle, Paris 75015, France; phone: 33-1-42-73-05-68; and 12 E. 33rd St., 11th Floor, New York, NY 10016; phone: 800-366-6587 or 212-779-0600). This French agency specializes in adventure travel/hiking and canoe/kayak trips, as well as sailing, diving, and horseback riding vacations which, for the most part, leave from Paris for locations outside France and include camping.

World Tracks Limited (12 Abingdon Rd., London W8 6AF, England; phone: 44-71-937-3028). Offers a number of motorcoach camping trips that traverse Europe, including Austria, Belgium, Bulgaria, Czechoslovakia, Denmark, Finland, France, Germany, Gibraltar, Great Britain, Greece, Hungary, Italy, Monaco, the Netherlands, Norway, Poland, Portugal, San Marino, the Soviet Union, Spain, Sweden, Switzerland, and Yugoslavia.

Also note that a number of packagers listed below under "Hiking" and "Biking" may offer these pursuits in combination with camping — it pays to call and ask when planning your trip.

Recreational Vehicles – Known in Europe as caravans, recreational vehicles (RVs) will appeal most to the kind of person who prefers flexibility of accommodation — there are countless campgrounds throughout Europe and many of them provide RV hookups — and enjoys camping with a little extra comfort.

An RV undoubtedly saves a traveler a great deal of money on accommodations; in-camp cooking saves money on food as well. However, it is important to remember that renting an RV is a major expense; also, any kind of RV increases gas consumption considerably.

Although the term "recreational vehicle" is applied to all manner of camping vehicles, whether towed or self-propelled, generally the models available for rent in Europe are either towable campers (caravans) or motorized RVs. The motorized models usually are either minivans or minibuses — vans customized in various ways for camping, often including elevated roofs — or larger, coach-type, fully equipped homes on wheels, requiring electrical hookups at night to run the TV set, air conditioning, and kitchen appliances. Although most models are equipped with standard shift, occasionally automatic shift vehicles may be available for an additional charge.

Towed vehicles can be hired overseas, but usually are not offered by US or international companies. Motorized models are available from international and regional car rental companies in the major cities (see *Traveling by Car,* earlier in this section), although you probably will have to do some calling around to find one.

If you are planning to caravan all over Europe, make sure that the appliances in the vehicle you choose are equipped to deal with the electrical and gas standards of all countries on your itinerary. There are differences, for instance, between the bottled stove gas supplied in various countries. You should have either a sufficient supply of the gas your camper requires or equipment that can use more than one type. When towing a camper, note that something towed is not automatically covered by the liability insurance of the primary vehicle, so the driver's Green Card must carry a specific endorsement that covers the towed vehicle.

Whether driving a camper or towing, it is essential to have some idea of the terrain you'll be encountering en route. Not only are numerous mountain passes closed in winter, but grades often are too steep for certain vehicles to negotiate and some roads are off limits to towed caravans. Car tunnels, or "piggyback" services on trains can help bypass those summits too difficult to climb, but they also may impose dimension limitations and often charge high fees. The *AAA* and other guides noted above provide detailed information on the principal passes and tunnels. Your best source of information on specific weather and road conditions may be national automobile clubs (where they exist). Local police and tourist offices are other good sources of road information.

Among the companies offering RV rental in Europe are the following:

Auto Europe (PO Box 1907, Camden, ME 04843; phone: 207-236-8235 in Maine; 800-223-5555 elsewhere in the US). Offers minibus and minivan rentals in France, Germany, and Great Britain.

Avis Car Away (6 Rue de Caen, Paris 92400, France; phone: 33-1-43-34-15-81). Affiliated with *Avis* car rentals, this company rents fully equipped motorhomes in France.

Avis Rent-A-Car (6128 E. 38th St., Tulsa, OK 74135; phone: 800-331-1084, ext. 7719). This division of *Avis* offers minibus rentals at numerous locations throughout Europe, including Austria, Belgium, Czechoslovakia, Finland, France, Germany, Gibraltar, Great Britain, Greece, Hungary, Iceland, Ireland, Italy, Luxembourg, Monaco, Norway, Poland, Portugal, the Soviet Union, Spain, Sweden, Switzerland, and Yugoslavia.

Connex International (23 N. Division St., Peekskill, NY 10566; phone: 800-333-3949 or 914-739-0066). Rents minibuses in Czechoslovakia, Hungary, Spain, and Yugoslavia, and motorized RVs in Germany, Great Britain, and the Netherlands.

Europe by Car (One Rockefeller Plaza, New York, NY 10020; phone: 212-581-3040 in New York State; 800-223-1516 elsewhere in the US; and 9000 Sunset Blvd., Los Angeles, CA 90069; phone: 800-252-9401 or 213-272-0424). Rents minibuses and RVs in Austria, Belgium, Denmark, France, Germany, Great Britain, Greece, Hungary, Ireland, Italy, Luxembourg, the Netherlands, Norway, Portugal, Spain, Sweden, Switzerland, and Yugoslavia.

FCI Location (Zone Industrielle de Saint-Brendan, Quentin 22800, France; phone: 33-96-74-08-36). Rents motorized RVs in France.

Foremost Euro-Car (5430 Van Nuys Blvd., Suite 306, Van Nuys, CA 91401; phone: 800-272-3299 or 818-786-1960). Rents minibuses and RVs in Austria, Belgium, France, Germany, Great Britain, Ireland, Italy, Luxembourg, the Netherlands, Portugal, Spain, and Switzerland.

Kemwel Group (106 Calvert St., Harrison, NY 10528; phone: 800-678-0678 or 914-835-5555). Rents minibuses throughout Europe.

Trois Soleils (Maison Trois Soleils, 2 Rte. de Paris, Ittenheim 67117, France; phone: 33-88-69-17-17). Rents motorized RVs, as well as some basic campers in France.

The general policy with the above agencies is to make reservations far enough in advance to receive a voucher required to pick up the vehicle at the designated location in Europe. RV rentals also may be arranged on arrival from a number of other European companies. For additional rental sources, ask at local car rental companies and national tourist board offices. Whether arranging the rental before leaving the US or once in Europe, make reservations as early as possible as the supply of RVs is limited and the demand great.

Useful information on RVs is available from the following sources:

Living on Wheels, by Richard A. Wolters. Provides useful information on how to choose and operate a recreational vehicle. As it's currently out of print, check your library.

Recreational Vehicle Industry Association (RVIA; PO Box 2999, Reston, VA 22090-2999). Issues a useful complimentary package of information on RVs, as well as a 24-page magazine-size guide, *Set Free in an RV* ($3), and a free catalogue of RV sources and consumer information. Write to the association for these and other publications.

Recreational Vehicle Rental Association (RVRA; 3251 Old Lee Hwy., Suite 500, Fairfax, VA 22030; phone: 800-336-0355 or 703-591-7130). This RV dealers group publishes an annual rental directory, *Who's Who in RV Rentals* ($7.50).

TL Enterprises (29901 Agoura Rd., Agoura, CA 91301; phone: 818-991-4980) publishes two monthly magazines for RV enthusiasts: *Motorhome* and *Trailer Life.* A year's subscription to either costs $22; a combined subscription to both costs $44. Members of the *TL Enterprises' Good Sam Club* can subscribe for half price and also receive discounts on a variety of other RV services; membership costs $19 per year.

Trailblazer (1000 124th Ave. NE, Bellevue, WA 98005; phone: 206-455-8585). A recreational-vehicle and motorhome magazine. A year's subscription costs $24.

And for those who can read French, the RV-enthusiast magazine *Le Monde du Camping-Car* includes recommendations on routes and campgrounds, itineraries, feature articles, and other general RV information, including local sales and rental companies. A 1-year subscription of 10 issues costs 220F (approximately $37 US at press time); this must be paid in francs by international money order, available at US banks and post offices. To subscribe, write to Monique Deregard, *Le Monde du Camping-Car,* 15-17 Quai de l'Oise, Paris 75019, France (phone: 33-1-40-34-22-07).

Although most RV travelers head off independently, traveling in a "caravan" where several RVs travel together offers the best of both worlds for an RV trip: Since caravan members are provided with detailed itineraries and directions, they can, if they wish, travel independently — or with one or two other RVs — to and from pre-arranged destinations, yet when the full caravan convenes, they can enjoy the fellowship of the group and participate in planned activities. Caravans usually include from 20 to 40 vehicles, which are led by a "wagonmaster," who functions as tour escort, keeping things running smoothly and on schedule. The wagonmaster's assistant, the "tailgunner," brings up the rear and handles any mechanical problems. The caravan tour operator takes care of trip planning and routing, insurance, campground reservations and fees, and so forth. Besides the planned sightseeing, social activities can include group dinners, shows and other entertainment, and cookouts at campsites, but again, caravan members always have the option of spending as much time by themselves as they wish.

One such operator of RV caravan trips is *Creative World Rallies and Caravans* (606 N. Carrollton Ave., New Orleans, LA 70119; phone: 800-732-8337 or 504-486-7259). Their caravanning tours span Austria, Czechoslovakia, Denmark, Finland, France, Germany, Great Britain, Hungary, Liechtenstein, Luxembourg, Norway, Poland, Sweden, Switzerland, and Yugoslavia.

HIKING: If you would rather eliminate all the gear and planning and take to the outdoors unencumbered, park the car and go for a day's hike. By all means, cover as much area as you can by foot; you'll see everything in far more detail than you would from the window of any conveyance.

Marked hiking trails abound in Europe. Germany alone has some 80,000 miles of them in addition to 9,000 Alpine trails. On Britain's Pennine Way, one of the country's official long-distance footpaths and its roughest, you can walk 270 lonely miles up the backbone of England to the Scottish border, a trip recommended only for experienced hikers equipped with maps and compass to steer them through remote moorland and probable bad weather. Less practiced but more gregarious hikers can join the weekend crowds for a short stretch of one of France's easiest *sentiers de grande randonnée,* the Sentier de l'Ile-de-France, a 375-mile route ringing Paris. Equally popular (lodging along the way for July and August is booked months in advance) but much more difficult is the spectacularly scenic Tour du Mont-Blanc, a 100-mile route around the mountain massif taking in three countries — France, Italy, and Switzerland. Many tourist authorities distribute information sheets on walking and mountaineering, and there are numerous other sources for those intent on getting about on their own.

The British Tourist Authority's information sheet *Walking* describes national parks, long-distance footpaths, and other walking areas in England, Wales, Scotland, and Northern Ireland. Britain's Ordnance Survey and *Automobile Association* jointly publish the useful guide *Walks and Tours in Britain* ($13.95). The Irish Tourist Board and the Northern Ireland Tourist Board both distribute information sheets useful to hikers. The *Open Forest,* a guide to state parks and forests, is available free from tourism offices in Ireland, as is *Hill Walking and Rock Climbing.* The four regional guidebooks of the *Irish Walk Guides* series are available for IR£5 (about $7.50) from Gill and Macmillan (Golden Bridge, Inchichore, Dublin 8, Ireland; phone: 353-1-531005).

The Swiss National Tourist Office recommends *Walking Switzerland — The Swiss Way,* by Marcia and Philip Lieberman ($10.95 from Mountaineers Books, 1011 SW Klickitat Way, Suite 107, Seattle, WA 98134; phone: 800-553-4453 or 206-223-6303). Also available is *Postbus: The Best High-Altitude and Panoramic Walks,* a booklet detailing various scenic routes whose jumping-off points can be reached via the Swiss postbus service. Another useful guide, providing information on Austrian, French, Italian, and Swiss mountain treks is *100 Hikes in the Alps* by Ira Spring and Harvey Edwards (The Mountaineers, 1985; $10.95). For those exploring the Italian side, there's *Backpacking and Walking in Italy* by Stefano Ardito (Bradt Publishers; $15.95) and *Dolomites of Italy: A Travel Guide* by James and Ann Goldsmith (Hunter Publishing; $17.95); both are available from the *Tattered Cover* (2955 E. First Ave., Denver, CO 80206; phone: 800-833-9327 or 303-322-7727).

Books on France's vast trail network include *Walking in France* by Rob Hunter (Oxford Illustrated Press paperback; $9.95), *Long Walks in France* by Adam Nicolson (Harmony Books; out of print but check your library), and *Walking in the Footpath of Europe: Dordogne; Pyrénées; Provence* by Robertson MacCarta (Seven Hills Book Distributor; $18.95 each). Serious hikers may want to check at their library for the very comprehensive but out of print *On Foot Through Europe: A Trail Guide to France & the Benelux Nations* by Craig Evans, which includes information about guides and guidebooks, weather, lodgings, equipment, useful addresses, long-distance footpaths, cross-country skiing possibilities, national and regional parks, and individual provinces and the resources specific to each.

For touring Portugal afoot, see *Landscapes of Madeira* (Hunter; $9.95) by John and Pat Underwood. And for those wandering Spanish byways, there is *Trekking in Spain* (Lonely Planet; $11.95) by Marc Dubin.

Another useful set of guidebooks, which focuses on more casual strolls, is the *Walking Through* series, which includes volumes on Amsterdam, Barcelona, Brussels, London, Madrid, Munich, Paris, Rome, Seville, Stuttgart, Vienna, and Zurich. These are available from VLE Limited (PO Box 444, Ft. Lee, NJ 07024; phone: 201-567-5536 or 212-580-8030) for $3 each. And be sure to see our own new 1992 European titles, *Birnbaum's Barcelona, Florence, London, Paris, Rome, Venice* ($10 each), edited by Stephen Birnbaum and Alexandra Mayes Birnbaum, which include walks to and through some of Europe's most spectacular sites and little-known corners; available in most bookstores, these also can be ordered from HarperCollins Publishers (Order Dept., Keystone Park, Scranton, PA 18512; phone: 800-242-7737).

Even those tourist offices that do not have literature on hand (or have little in English) can direct you to associations in their countries that supply maps, guides, and further information. For long visits, membership in a local club is suggested. The following hiking, mountaineering, and rock climbing clubs provide information on their respective countries:

France: *Fédération Française de la Randonnée Pédestre (FFRP)* (9 Av. Georges-V, Paris 75008, France; phone: 33-1-47-23-62-32) and the *Club Alpin Français, Commission de Randonnées* (9 Rue La Boétie, Paris 75008, France; phone: 33-1-47-42-38-46).

Germany: *Deutsch Oppenvereins* (26-IV Hirtenstr., Munich 8000, Germany; phone: 49-89-594357).

Great Britain: *British Mountaineering Council* (Crawford House, Precinct Centre, Booth St. E., Manchester M13 9RZ, England; phone: 44-61-273-5835) and the *Ramblers Association* (1-5 Wandsworth Rd., London SW8 2XX, England: phone: 44-71-582-6878).

Ireland: *Mountaineering Council of Ireland* (c/o *Association of Adventure Sports,* Longmile Rd., Dublin 12, Ireland; phone: 353-1-509845).

Italy: *Club Alpino Italiano* (3 Via Ugo Foscolo, Milan 20121, Italy; phone: 39-2-72-023085) and *Touring Club Italiano* (10 Corso Italia, Milan 20122, Italy; phone: 39-2-852-6225).

■ **A word of warning:** It is particularly important to wear socks, long pants, and long-sleeve shirts when hiking in heavily wooded areas — particularly in the Black Forest of southern Germany — due to the danger of Neuro Borreliosis, which is spread through the bite of the deer tick and other ticks. First diagnosed years ago in Europe, this disease recently has become familiar to Americans as Lyme Borreliosis (also known as Lyme Tick disease). A strong insect repellent designed to repel ticks also may be helpful. The initial symptoms of this disease often are a swelling and/or a rash, generally accompanied by flu-like symptoms — such as fever and aching muscles. Readily curable in the early stages through antibiotics, if left untreated it can lead to serious complications. For information on areas of contagion, precautions, and treatment, contact the *Lyme Borreliosis Foundation* (PO Box 462, Tolland, CT 06084; phone: 203-871-2900). A number of helpful hints also is provided in *Ticks and What You Can Do About Them,* which is available from Wilderness Press (2440 Bancroft Way, Berkeley, CA 94704; phone: 800-443-7227 or 510-843-8080).

Organized Hiking Trips – Those who prefer to travel as part of an organized group should contact the following organizations:

Above the Clouds Trekking (PO Box 398, Worcester, MA 01602; phone: 508-799-4499 or 800-233-4499. Offers treks in Czechoslovakia and Poland.

Alternative Travel Groups (69-71 Banbury Rd., Oxford OX2 6PE, England; phone: 800-527-5997). The motto of this company is "The best way to see a country is on foot." Among its numerous itineraries worldwide are walking tours in France, Great Britain, Italy, Ireland, Portugal, and Spain.

American Youth Hostels (PO Box 37613, Washington, DC 20013-7613; phone: 202-783-6161). Their numerous European itineraries change from year to year, so check at the time you plan to travel.

Avenir Adventures (PO Box 2730, Park City, UT 84060; phone: 800-367-3230, 801-649-2495, or 801-249-7430). Offers hiking tours of Greece.

Baumeler Tours (10 Grand Ave., Rockville Centre, New York, NY 11570-9861; phone: 516-766-6160 in New York State; 800-6-ABROAD elsewhere in the US). Offers hiking trips in France, Germany, Great Britain, Italy, and Switzerland.

Breakaway Vacations (164 E. 90th St., #2Y, New York, NY 10128; phone: 212-722-4221). Offers walking tours of Great Britain.

British Coastal Trails (150 Carob Way, Coronado, CA 92118; phone: 800-473-1210 or 619-437-1211). Offers 28 different 8- to 12-day itineraries throughout Great Britain and Ireland.

Butterfield & Robinson (70 Bond St., Suite 300, Toronto, Ontario M5B 1X3, Canada; phone: 800-387-1147 or 416-864-1354). Most of their numerous hiking tours emphasize easy exercise and the finest in dining and accommodations — definitely not "roughing it." Destinations explored include Austria, Bulgaria, Denmark, France, Germany, Great Britain, Hungary, Ireland, and Italy.

Country Cycling Tours (140 W. 83rd St., New York, NY 10024; phone: 212-874-5151). Offers 7- to 8-day walking tours in France and Italy.

Discover Expeditions (31 Madeline Rd., Ridge, NY 11961; phone: 800-242-5554). Offers outdoor expeditions, including hiking in Eastern Europe, especially Poland.

Distant Journeys (PO Box 1211, Camden, ME 04843; phone: 207-799-5507 from June 1 to October 15, 207-236-9788 during the rest of the year). Offers hiking tours of the Mont-Blanc region in France, Italy, and Switzerland, as well as walking tours in Great Britain.

English Wanderer (6 George St., Ferryhill, County Durham DL17 0DT, England; phone: 44-740-653169; and 13 Wellington Court, Spencers Wood, Reading RG7 1BN, England; phone: 44-734-882515). Offers tours in Great Britain and Ireland.

Europeds (883 Sinex Ave., Pacific Grove, CA 93950; phone: 408-372-1173). Offers inn-to-inn walking tours in France, Great Britain, and Switzerland.

Exodus (9 Weir Rd., London SW2 OLT, England; phone: 44-81-675-5550; or c/o *Force 10 Expeditions,* PO Box 34354, Pensacola, FL 32507; phone: 800-492-6661 or 904-462-6661). This adventure specialist offers inn-to-inn walking tours in Andorra, France, Greece, Hungary, Italy, Poland, Romania, the Soviet Union, Spain, Switzerland, and Yugoslavia.

Forum Travel International (91 Gregory, #21, Pleasant Hill, CA 94523; phone: 510-671-2900). Offers a number of enticing itineraries in Austria, Belgium, Czechoslovakia, France, Germany, Great Britain, Greece, Hungary, Ireland, Italy, Liechtenstein, Luxembourg, the Maltese Islands, the Netherlands, Poland, the Soviet Union, Spain, and Switzerland. Their tours are graded in four levels of difficulty — the most energetic grade covering as many as 20 miles a day and geared to those already accustomed to hard mountain walking.

Genet Expeditions (PO Box 230861, Anchorage, AK 99523 (phone: 800-33-GENET or 907-561-2123). Offers a hiking/climbing tour that includes the Italian side of Mont-Blanc in the Alps.

Himalayan Travel (PO Box 481, Greenwich, CT 06836; phone: 800-225-2380). Offers inn-to-inn walking tours in France, Great Britain, Greece, Italy, Romania, Spain, and Switzerland.

Mountain Travel-Sobek (6420 Fairmount Ave., El Cerrito, CA 94530; phone: 415-527-8100 in California; 800-227-2384 elsewhere in the US). This adventure-trip specialist offers treks through the Alps (including the famous Tour du Mont-Blanc mentioned above) and the Pyrenees, as well as hiking trips in Austria, Czechoslovakia, France, Germany, Great Britain, Greece, Italy, Norway, Poland, the Soviet Union, Spain, and Switzerland.

New England Hiking Holidays (PO Box 1648, North Conway, NY 03860; phone:

800-869-0949 or 603-356-9696). Offers walking tours in Austria, Great Britain, and Switzerland.

Outdoor Bound (18 Stuyvesant Oval, #1A, New York, NY 10009; phone: 212-505-1020). Offers inn-to-inn walking tours of Britain's Lake District.

Progressive Travel (1932 First Ave., Suite 1100, Seattle, WA 98101; phone: 800-245-2229). Itineraries include 5-8 day walking tours of England, France, Ireland, and Switzerland.

Sierra Club (Outing Department, 730 Polk St., San Francisco, CA 94109; phone: 415-776-2211). Offers a selection of trips each year, usually about 2 weeks in length. Some are backpacking trips, moving to a new camp each day; others make day hikes from a base camp. Recent itineraries included hikes in Czechoslovakia, France, Great Britain, Greece, Iceland, Italy, Portugal, Romania, the Soviet Union, Spain, and the Swiss Alps. Other trips combine hiking with biking.

The Wayfarers (172 Bellevue Ave., Newport, RI 02840; phone: 401-849-5087). Offers walking tours in Great Britain.

Wilderness Travel (801 Allston Way, Berkeley, CA 94710; phone: 800-368-2794 or 510-548-0420). Offers a wide range of hiking trips throughout Eastern and Western Europe, including Bulgaria, France, Great Britain, Ireland, Italy, Norway, Portugal, Romania, the Soviet Union, Spain, Switzerland, and Yugoslavia.

Yamnuska (PO Box 1920, Canmore, Alberta, Canada T0L 0M0; phone: 403-678-4164). Offers a 12-day Mont-Blanc tour of the French, Italian, and Swiss Alps.

An alternative to dealing directly with the above companies is to contact *All Adventure Travel,* a specialist in hiking and biking trips worldwide. This company, which acts as a representative for numerous special tour packagers offering such outdoor adventures, can provide a wealth of detailed information about each packager and programs offered. They also will help you design and arrange all aspects of a personalized itinerary. This company operates much like a travel agency, collecting commissions from the packagers. Therefore, there is no additional charge for these services. For information, contact *All Adventure Travel,* PO Box 4307, Boulder, CO 80306 (phone: 800-537-4025 or 303-499-1981).

BIKING: For young and/or fit travelers, the bicycle offers a marvelous tool for exploring Europe, especially those countries where terrains are especially conducive to easy cycling like the Benelux nations, much of Britain, and parts of Scandinavia. Throughout the Continent, secondary roads thread through picturesque stretches of countryside. Biking does have its drawbacks: Little baggage can be carried, travel is slow, and cyclists are exposed to the elements. However, should a cyclist need rest or refuge from the weather, there always is a welcoming tavern or comfortable inn around the next bend.

Besides being a viable way to tour Europe — and to burn calories to make room for larger portions of continental food — biking is a great way to meet people. When traveling in non-English-speaking nations, however, remember that although many Europeans speak some English, this is not likely to be the case in rural areas, so pack a good copy of a foreign phrase book if your command of the native language is not up to par.

A good book to help you plan a trip is *Bicycle Touring in Europe,* by Karen and Gary Hawkins available for $11.95 from Pantheon Books (201 E. 50th St., New York, NY 10022; phone: 800-726-0600). It offers information on buying and equipping a touring bike, useful clothing and supplies, and helpful techniques for the long-distance biker. Another good general book is *Europe by Bike,* by Karen and Terry Whitehall ($10.95; Mountaineers Books; 1011 SW Kickitat Way, Suite 107, Seattle, WA 98134; phone: 800-553-4453).

If you are headed for France, *Expeditions in France: Bicycle Tours of the Wine Country* by Sally Taylor (Sally Taylor & Friends; $9) is available in some travel bookstores. *Cyclist's Britain,* produced by a cycling group in England, outlines several tours of England, Scotland, and Wales; it is available in the US (for $14.95, plus postage and handling) through Hunter Publishing (300 Raritan Center Pkwy., Edison, NJ 08818; phone: 201-225-1900). The British Tourist Authority's booklet *Cycling in Britain* provides information on various aspects of biking in Britain and also describes several routes. Another excellent guide is *The CTC Route Guide to Cycling in Britain and Ireland* by Christa Gausden and Nicholas Crane (Penguin Books; $12.95).

Another source of information on bicycling in the Republic of Ireland is the *Federation of Irish Cyclists* (Halson St., Dublin 7, Ireland; phone: 353-1-727524); for Northern Ireland, consult the *Ulster Cycling Federation* (Ms. Carmel Ann Hunter, 108 Moneymore Rd., Cookstown, County Tyrone, Northern Ireland; phone: 44-6487-63214). The Northern Ireland Tourist Board also distributes a free leaflet *Cycling in Northern Ireland.* The *Royal Dutch Touring Club (ANWB;* 220 Wassenaarseweg, 2596 EC, the Hague, the Netherlands; phone: 31-70-326-4426) publishes a series of detailed maps charting Holland's excellent bike paths. Some of these also are available at the Netherlands Board of Tourism. Other tourist boards — such as the French Government Tourist Board — also provide a list of suggest itineraries on request.

Michelin maps (on a scale of 1:200,000) cover most of Europe and provide detailed and clear road references. They are available from Michelin Guides and Maps (PO Box 3305, Spartanburg, SC 29304-3305; phone: 803-599-0850 in South Carolina; 800-423-0485 elsewhere in the US). Maps of the Bartholomew Leisure Map series (on a scale of 1:100,000) cover Great Britain and Ireland. This company also offers numerous other maps, atlases, and route planners for these and other countries throughout Europe. If unavailable locally, they can be ordered from the US representative, Hammond, Inc. (515 Valley St., Maplewood, NJ 07040; phone: 201-763-6000) or by contacting Bartholomew directly (at 12 Duncan St., Edinburgh EH9 1TA, Scotland; phone: 44-31-667-9341).

One of the best sources for detailed topographical and just about any other type of map (of just about anywhere in the world) is *Map Link* (25 E. Mason St., Santa Barbara, CA 93101; phone: 805-965-4402). Their comprehensive guide *The World Map Directory* ($29.95) includes a wealth of sources, and if they don't stock a map of the area in which you are interested (or the type of map best suited to your outdoor exploration), they will order it for you. They carry numerous maps of Europe, including a wide range of topographical maps.

Choosing, Renting, and Buying a Bike – Although many bicycling enthusiasts choose to take along their own bikes, bicycles can be rented throughout Europe. Long and short rentals are available; however, particularly in rural areas, it may pay to check ahead. Cities such as Amsterdam, where biking is a way of life, provide complete cycling services. Throughout Europe, national railways often have bicycles for rent at train stations, often at a discount for ticket holders. Many also feature "rent it here, leave it there" programs, allowing you to take your bike on the train to another town without returning it to the station from which it was rented. Almost all European trains have facilities for bike transport at nominal fees.

As an alternative to renting, you might consider buying a bicycle in Europe. Bicycle shops that rent bikes also usually sell them and buying a used bike might be even less expensive than a long-term rental. For information on bicycle rental shops in European cities, see *Sources and Resources* in the individual city reports of THE CITIES.

If you do buy a bike and plan on taking it home, remember that it will be subject to an import duty by US Customs if its price (or the total of purchases in Europe) exceeds $400. When evaluating this cost, take into account additional charges for shipping. A European bicycle purchased in the US should have proof-of-purchase papers to avoid potential customs problems. Even the smallest towns usually have a bike shop, so it's not difficult to replace or add to gear; however, because tires and tubes are sized to metric dimensions in Europe, when riding your own bike, bring extras from home.

Airlines going from the US (or elsewhere) to Europe generally allow bicycles to be checked as baggage; they require that the pedals be removed, handlebars be turned sideways, and the bike be in a shipping carton (which some airlines provide, subject to availability — call ahead to make sure). If buying a shipping carton from a bicycle shop, check the airline's specifications and also ask about storing the carton at the destination airport so you can use it again for the return flight. Although some airlines charge only a nominal fee, if the traveler already has checked two pieces of baggage, there may be an additional excess baggage charge of $70 to $80 for the bicycle. As regulations vary from carrier to carrier, be sure to call well before departure to find out your airline's specific regulations. As with other baggage, make sure that the bike is thoroughly labeled with your name, a business address and phone number, and the correct airport destination code.

Biking Tours – A number of organizations offer bike tours in Europe. Linking up with a bike tour is more expensive than traveling alone, but with experienced leaders, an organized tour often becomes an educational, as well as a very social, experience.

One of the attractions of a bike tour is that the shipment of equipment — the bike — is handled by organizers, and the shipping fee is included in the total tour package. Travelers simply deliver the bike to the airport, already disassembled and boxed; shipping cartons can be obtained from most bicycle shops with little difficulty. Bicyclists not with a tour must make their own arrangements with the airline, and there are no standard procedures for this (see above). Although some tour organizers will rent bikes, most prefer that participants bring a bike with which they are already familiar. Another attraction of *some* tours is the existence of a "sag wagon" to carry extra luggage, fatigued cyclists, and their bikes, too, when pedaling another mile is impossible.

Most bike tours are scheduled from May to October, last 1 or 2 weeks, are limited to 20 or 25 people, and provide lodging in inns or hotels, though some use hostels or even tents. Tours vary considerably in style and ambience, so request brochures from several operators in order to make the best decision. When contacting groups, be sure to ask about the maximum number of people on the trip, the maximum number of miles to be traveled each day, and the degree of difficulty of the biking; these details should determine which tour you join and can greatly affect your enjoyment of the experience. Planning ahead is essential because trips often fill up 6 months or more in advance.

Among the companies offering biking tours to Europe are the following:

Backroads Bicycle Touring (1516 Fifth St., Berkeley, CA 94710-1713; phone: 800-245-3874 or 510-527-1555). Offers superior food and accommodations on its tours through France, Great Britain, Ireland, and Italy. Tours are geared to beginning and intermediate riders.

Baumeler Tours (10 Grand Ave., Rockville Center, NY 11570-9861; phone: 516-766-6160, collect, in New York State; 800-6-ABROAD elsewhere in the US). Specializing in bicycling tours, both individual and escorted, this company offers tours in Austria, Czechoslovakia, Denmark, France, Germany, Hungary, Italy, and Switzerland.

Breakaway Vacations (164 E. 90th St., No. 2Y, New York, NY 10128; phone: 212-722-4221). Offers 9-day inn-to-inn biking tours of Great Britain.

Butterfield & Robinson (70 Bond St., Suite 300, Toronto, Ontario M5B 1X3, Canada; phone: 800-387-1147 or 416-864-1354). Offers a number of first class biking tours, many quite sophisticated in focus and including luxurious accom-

modations and fine dining en route. Trips are geared to various age groups and
are rated at four levels of difficulty. Among their offerings are tours of Austria,
Denmark, France, Germany, Great Britain, Hungary, Ireland, Italy, Portugal,
and Spain.

Châteaux Bike Tours (Box 5706, Denver, CO 90217; phone: 800-678-BIKE or
303-393-6910). Offers biking tours of France, Italy, and Switzerland.

Classic Bicycle Tours and Treks (PO Box 668, Clarkson, NY 14430; phone:
800-777-8090 or 716-637-5970). Offers cycling trips through France, Great
Britain, Greece, and Ireland.

Country Cycling Tours (140 W. 83rd St., New York, NY 10024; phone: 800-284-
8954 or 212-874-5151). Offers a variety of biking tours to France, Great Britain,
Ireland, Italy, and the Netherlands.

Cycle France, Cycle Portugal, and Cycle Spain (c/o *Roatan Charter*, PO Box 877,
San Antonio, FL 33576; phone: 904-588-4132 or 800-245-4226). Offer tours on
two wheels of these three countries.

Easy Rider Tours (PO Box 1384, E. Arlington, MA 02174; phone: 617-643-8332).
Offers biking tours of Portugal and Spain, as well as Ireland (where tours feature
evenings in local pubs with guest storytellers).

Earth Ventures (2625 N. Meridien St., Suite 612, Indianapolis, IN 46208-7705;
phone: 317-926-0453). Itineraries include 6- to 49-day biking tours of France
and Italy, 8-day tours of Austria and Great Britain, and 8- to 10-day packages
just in France, which include a combination of either ballooning, canoeing, or
sailing.

Eurobike (PO Box 40, DeKalb, IL 60115; phone: 800-252-1990 or 815-758-8851).
Offers biking trips in Austria, Belgium, Czechoslovakia, Denmark, France,
Germany, Great Britain, Hungary, Ireland, Italy, Luxembourg, the Nether-
lands, Portugal, Spain, and Switzerland.

Europeds (883 Sinex Ave., Pacific Grove, CA 93950; phone: 800-321-9552 or
408-372-1173). Offers 5- to 14-day biking tours of France and Switzerland.

Forum Travel International (91 Gregory, #21, Pleasant Hill, CA 94523; phone:
415-671-2900). Offers both group and self-guided biking tours to Austria,
France, Germany, Great Britain, Ireland, Italy, and Switzerland, as well as
countries in Eastern Europe.

Gerhard's Bicycle Odysseys (4949 SW Macadam, Portland, OR 97201; phone:
503-223-2402). Offers 2-week hotel-to-hotel biking trips to Austria, France,
Germany, Ireland, and Switzerland.

Himalayan Travel (PO Box 481, Greenwich, CT 06836; phone: 800-225-2380).
Offers hotel-to-hotel biking tours in France.

International Bicyle Tours (Box 754, 7 Chamblin Sq., Essex, CT 06426; phone:
203-767-7005). Offers biking tours in Austria, France, Germany, Great Britain,
and the Netherlands.

Progressive Travel Ltd. (1932 First Ave., Suite 1100, Seattle, WA 98101; phone:
800-245-2229 or 206-443-4225). Their biking itineraries are offered in France,
Great Britain, Ireland, Italy, the Netherlands, and Switzerland.

Rocky Mountain Cycling Tours (PO Box 1978, Canmore, Alberta T0L 0M0,
Canada; phone: 800-661-2453 or 403-678-6770). Organizes bike trips in France,
Germany, Italy, Norway, and Sweden.

Travent International (PO Box 305, Waterbury Center, VT 05677-0305; phone:
800-325-3009 or 802-244-5153). Offers biking tours in France, Great Britain,
Ireland, Italy, the Netherlands, Sweden, and Switzerland.

Value Holidays (10224 N. Port Washington Rd., Mequon, WI 53092; phone:
800-558-6850 or 414-241-6373). Offers biking tours of Czechoslovakia, Italy,
and Spain.

Vermont Bicyle Touring (PO Box 711, Bristol, VT 05443; phone: 802-453-4811). Offers several biking tours in France, Great Britain, Ireland, and the Netherlands.

Other useful sources of information on bicycling in Europe include the following:

American Youth Hostels (PO Box 37613, Washington, DC 20013-7613; phone: 202-783-6161). A number of biking tours are sponsored annually by this nonprofit organization and its local chapters. Membership is open to all ages and departures are geared to various age groups and levels of skill and frequently feature accommodations in hostels — along with hotels for adults and campgrounds for younger participants.

Bicycle Adventure Club (3904 Groton St., San Diego, CA 92110-5635; phone: 619-226-2175). This bicycling club sponsors a variety of tours for members. Although the itineraries vary from year to year, recent tours included France, Great Britain, Hungary, Ireland, Italy, Monaco, the Soviet Union, Spain, and Yugoslavia. Membership costs $30 per year and is open to those 21 and older.

Cyclists' Touring Club (*CTC;* Cotterell House, 69 Meadrow, Godalming, Surrey GU7 3HS, England; phone: 44-483-41-7217). Britain's largest cycling association, this group organizes tours of numerous countries, including Czechoslovakia, France, Germany, Great Britain, Ireland, Italy, the Netherlands, Norway, and Spain. *CTC* has a number of planned routes available in pamphlet form for bikers on their own and helps members plan their own tours. The club also publishes a yearly handbook, as well as magazines.

International Bicycle Touring Society (*IBTS;* PO Box 6979, San Diego, CA 92166-0979; phone: 619-226-TOUR). This nonprofit organization regularly sponsors low-cost bicycle tours of Austria, Denmark, France, Germany, Great Britain, Ireland, the Netherlands, and Switzerland. Tours are led by member volunteers, and participants must be over 21. For information, send $2 plus a self-addressed, stamped envelope.

League of American Wheelmen (190 W. Ostend St., Suite 120, Baltimore, MD 21230; phone: 301-539-3399). This organziation publishes *Tourfinder,* a list of organizations that sponsor bicycle tours worldwide. The list is free with membership ($25 individual, $30 family) and can be obtained by non-members who send $5. The *League* also can put you in touch with biking groups in your area.

Preparing

Calculating Costs

$ A realistic appraisal of your travel expenses is the most crucial bit of planning you will undertake before any trip. It also is, unfortunately, one for which it is most difficult to give precise, practical advice.

After several years of living relatively high on the hog, travel from North America to Europe dropped off precipitously in 1987 in response, among other considerations, to the relative weakness of the US dollar on the Continent. Many Americans who had enjoyed bargain prices while touring through Europe only a couple of years before, found that disadvantageous exchange rates really put a crimp in their travel planning. But even though the halcyon days of dollar domination seem over for the present, discount fares and the availability of charter flights can greatly reduce the cost of a European vacation. Package tours can even further reduce costs, as European providers of travel services try to win back their American clients in the 1990s.

Europe always has been one of the most popular destinations for both the first-time and the seasoned traveler, and it is certainly one where the competition for American visitors often works to inspire surprisingly affordable travel opportunities. Nevertheless, most travelers still have to plan carefully before they go and manage their travel funds prudently.

In Europe, estimating travel expenses depends on the mode of transportation you choose, the part or parts of the Continent you plan to visit, how long you will stay, and in some cases, what time of year you plan to travel. In addition to the basics of transportation, hotels, meals, and sightseeing, you have to take into account seasonal price changes that apply on certain air routings and at popular vacation destinations, as well as the vagaries of currency exchange.

Prices, inflation, and exchange rates are hardly uniform across Europe. Traditionally, northern and central European countries — Scandinavia, the Benelux nations, Germany, Switzerland, Austria — are more expensive and usually have less favorable exchange rates for the dollar than do the Mediterranean and Eastern European countries. In general, all European countries have a saving grace: Though their capitals — like our own major cities — suffer from a high cost of living, travel in the surrounding countryside can be more reasonable, and even inexpensive (depending on your choice of accommodations and means of transport). The dollar normally goes farthest of all in Yugoslavia, Greece, Ireland, and Portugal in southern and Western Europe, and Poland in the East.

In general, it's also a good idea to organize your trip so that you pay for as much of it as you can in Europe, using currency purchased from local banks (which, barring interim variations, generally offer a more advantageous rate of exchange than US sources). That means minimizing the amount of advance deposits paid in US greenbacks and deferring as many bills as possible until you arrive in Europe, although the economies possible through prepaid package tours and other special deals may offset the savings in currency exchange. (For further information on managing money abroad, see *Credit and Currency,* in this section.)

DETERMINING A BUDGET: When calculating costs, start with the basics, the major expenses being transportation, accommodations, and food. However, don't forget such extras as local transportation, shopping, and such miscellaneous items as laundry and tips. The reasonable cost of these items usually is a positive surprise to your budget. Ask about special discount passes that provide unlimited travel by the day or the week on regular city transportation. Entries in the individual city reports in THE CITIES give helpful information on local transportation options.

Other expenses, such as the cost of local sightseeing tours, will vary from city to city. Tourist information offices are plentiful throughout Europe, and most of the better hotels will have someone at the front desk to provide a rundown on the costs of local tours and full-day excursions in and out of the city. Travel agents also can provide this information. Government tourist offices, as well as railway offices, can provide information on current discount offerings (for offices in the US, see *Tourist Information Offices* and *Traveling by Train,* both in this section). Entries in the individual city reports in THE CITIES also give helpful information on local transportation options.

Budget-minded families can take advantage of some of the more economical accommodations options to be found across the Continent (see our discussion of accommodations in *On the Road,* in this section). Campgrounds are particularly inexpensive and they are located throughout Europe (see *Camping and Caravanning, Hiking and Biking,* in this section). Picnicking is another way to cut costs, and Europe abounds with well-groomed parks and idyllic pastoral settings. A stop at a local market can provide a feast of regional specialties at a surprisingly economical price compared to the cost of a restaurant lunch.

In planning any travel budget, it also is wise to allow a realistic amount for both entertainment and recreation. Are you planning to spend time sightseeing and visiting museums? Do you intend to spend your days skiing at a popular resort? Is daily golf or tennis a part of your plan? Will your children be disappointed if they don't sail on a *bateau-mouche* in Paris or take a gondola ride in Venice? Finally, don't forget that if haunting clubs, discotheques, or other nightspots is an essential part of your vacation, or you feel that one performance of the city's top ballet troupe, orchestra, or theater company may not be enough, allow for the extra cost of nightlife.

If at any point in the planning process it appears impossible to estimate expenses, consider this suggestion: The easiest way to put a ceiling on the price of all these elements is to buy a package tour. A totally planned and escorted one, with almost all transportation, rooms, meals, sightseeing, local travel, tips, and a dinner show or two included and prepaid, provides a pretty exact total of what the trip will cost beforehand, and the only surprise will be the one you spring on yourself by succumbing to some irresistible, expensive souvenir. And keep in mind, particularly when calculating the major expenses, that costs vary according to fluctuations in the exchange rate — that is, how much of a given foreign currency a dollar will buy.

■ **Note:** The volatility of exchange rates means that between the time you originally make your hotel reservations and the day you arrive, the price in US dollars may vary substantially from the price originally quoted. To avoid paying more than you expected, it's wise to confirm rates by writing directly to hotels or by calling their representatives in the US.

Planning a Trip

123 Travelers fall into two categories: those who make lists and those who do not. Some people prefer to plot the course of their trip to the finest detail, with contingency plans and alternatives at the ready. For others, the joy of a voyage is its spontaneity; exhaustive planning only lessens the thrill of anticipation and the sense of freedom.

For most travelers, however, any week-plus trip to Europe can be too expensive for an "I'll take my chances" type of attitude. Even perennial gypsies and anarchistic wanderers have to take into account the time-consuming logistics of getting around, and even with minimal baggage, they need to think about packing. Hence, at least some planning is crucial.

This is not to suggest that you work out your itinerary in minute detail before you go, but it's still wise to decide certain basics at the very start: where to go, what to do, and how much to spend. These decisions require a certain amount of consideration. So before rigorously planning specific details, you might want to establish your general travel objectives:

1. How much time will you have for the entire trip, and how much of it are you willing to spend getting where you're going?
2. What interests and/or activities do you want to pursue while on vacation? Do you want to visit one, a few, or several different places?
3. At what time of year do you want to go?
4. What kind of geography or climate would you prefer?
5. Do you want peace and privacy or lots of activity and company?
6. How much money can you afford to spend for the entire vacation?

You now can make almost all of your own travel arrangements if you have time to follow through with hotels, airlines, tour operators, and so on. But you'll probably save considerable time and energy if you have a travel agent make arrangements for you. The agent also should be able to advise you of alternate arrangements of which you may not be aware. Only rarely will a travel agent's services cost a traveler any money, and they may even save you some (see *How to Use a Travel Agent,* below).

If it applies to your schedule and destination, pay particular attention to the dates when off-season rates go into effect. In major tourism areas, accommodations may cost less during the off-season (and the weather often is perfectly acceptable at this time). Off-season rates frequently are lower for car rentals and other facilities, too. In general, it is a good idea to be aware of holiday weeks, as rates at hotels generally are higher during these periods and rooms normally are heavily booked.

Make plans early. During the summer season and other holiday periods, make hotel reservations at least a month in advance in all major cities. If you are flying at peak times and want to benefit from the savings of discount fares or charter programs, purchase tickets as far ahead as possible. Many European hotels require deposits before they will guarantee reservations, and this most often is the case during peak travel periods. (Be sure you have a receipt for any deposit or use a credit card.) Religious and national holidays also are times requiring reservations well in advance throughout Europe.

Before your departure, find out what the weather is likely to be at your destination. Consult *When to Go,* in this section, for information on climatic variations and a chart of average temperatures in various countries in Europe. See *How to Pack,* in this section, for some suggestions on how to decide what clothes to take. Also see FACTS IN BRIEF, as well as THE CITIES for information on special events that may occur during your stay. These chapters also provide essential information on language, currency, local transportation, and other services and resources.

Make a list of any valuable items you are carrying with you, including credit card numbers and the serial numbers of your traveler's checks. Put copies in your purse or pocket, and leave other copies at home. Put a label with your name and home address on the inside of your luggage for identification in case of loss. Put your name and business address — *never your home address* — on a label on the outside of your luggage. (Those who run businesses from home should use the office address of a friend or relative.)

Review your travel documents. If you are traveling by air, check that your ticket has been filled in correctly. The left side of the ticket should have a list of each stop you will make (even if you are only stopping to change planes), beginning with your departure point. Be sure that the list is correct, and count the number of copies to see that you have one for each plane you will take. If you have confirmed reservations, be sure that the column marked "status" says "OK" beside each flight. Have in hand vouchers or proof of payment for any reservation for which you've paid in advance; this includes hotels, transfers to and from the airport, sightseeing tours, car rentals, and tickets to special events.

Although policies vary from carrier to carrier, it's still smart to reconfirm your flight 48 to 72 hours before departure, both going and returning; reconfirmation is particularly recommended for point-to-point flights within Europe. If you will be driving while in Europe, bring your driver's license and any other necessary documentation — such as proof of insurance.

Before traveling to any non-English-speaking European country, you should consider learning some basic words in its language. Although you can get by in most countries speaking only English — particularly if you stick to the major resort areas and other popular tourist destinations — your trip will be much more rewarding and enjoyable (and, in some instances, safer) if you can communicate with the people who live in the areas you will be visiting. Europeans will not make you feel silly or stupid if you don't pronounce words properly — in fact they will openly appreciate your efforts if you do try to converse.

Some adult education programs and community colleges offer courses in the languages spoken in Eastern and Western European countries. Berlitz, among others, has a series of teach-yourself language courses on audiocassette tapes. They are available for $15.95 each from Macmillan Publishing Co. (100 Front St., Riverside, NJ 08075; phone: 800-257-5755) in the following languages: Danish, Dutch, Finnish, French, German, Greek, Hungarian, Italian, Norwegian, Polish, Portuguese, Russian, Serbo-Croatian (Yugoslavia), Spanish, and Swedish. And for those visiting a number of countries, Berlitz offers a European Pack of two audiocassettes for $19.95, that teaches basic phrases in Danish, Dutch, Finnish, French, German, Greek, Italian, Norwegian, Polish, Portuguese, Spanish, Russian, Serbo-Croatian, and Swedish.

Finally, you always should bear in mind that despite the most careful plans, things do not always occur on schedule. If you maintain a flexible attitude and try to accept minor disruptions as less than cataclysmic, you will enjoy yourself a lot more.

How to Use a Travel Agent

 A reliable travel agent remains the best source of service and information for planning a trip abroad, whether you have a specific itinerary and require an agent only to make reservations or you need extensive help in sorting through the maze of airfares, tour offerings, hotel packages, and the scores of other arrangements that may be involved in a trip to Europe.

Know what you want from a travel agent so that you can evaluate what you are getting. It is perfectly reasonable to expect your agent to be a thoroughly knowledgeable travel specialist, with information about your destination and, even more crucial, a command of current airfares, ground arrangements, and other wrinkles in the travel scene.

Most travel agents work through computer reservations systems (CRS). These are used to assess the availability and cost of flights, hotels, and car rentals, and through them they can book reservations. Despite reports of "computer bias," in which a computer may favor one airline over another, the CRS should provide agents with the entire spectrum of flights available to a given destination and the complete range of fares in considerably less time than it takes to telephone the airlines individually — and at no extra cost to the client.

Make the most intelligent use of a travel agent's time and expertise; understand the economics of the industry. As a client, traditionally you pay nothing for the agent's services; with few exceptions, it's all free, from hotel bookings to advice on package tours. Any money the travel agent makes on the time spent arranging your itinerary — booking hotels or flights, or suggesting activities — comes from commissions paid by the suppliers of these services — the airlines, hotels, and so on. These commissions generally run from 10% to 15% of the total cost of the service, although suppliers often reward agencies that sell their services in volume with an increased commission, called an override. In most instances, you'll find that travel agents make their time and experience available to you at no cost, and you do not pay more for an airline ticket, package tour, or other product bought from a travel agent than you would for the same one bought directly from the supplier.

Exceptions to the general rule of free service by a travel agent are the agencies beginning to practice net pricing. In essence, such agencies return their commissions and overrides to their customers and make their income by charging a flat fee per transaction instead (thus adding a charge after a reduction for the commissions has been made). Net fares and fees are a growing practice, though hardly widespread.

Even a conventional travel agent sometimes may charge a fee for special services. These chargeable items may include long-distance telephone or cable costs incurred in making a booking, reserving a room in a place that does not pay a commission (such as a small, out-of-the-way hotel), or special attention such as planning a highly personalized itinerary. A fee also may be assessed in instances of deeply discounted airfares.

Choose a travel agent with the same care with which you would choose a doctor or lawyer. You will be spending a good deal of money on the basis of the agent's judgment, so you have a right to expect that judgment to be mature, informed, and interested. At the moment, unfortunately, there aren't many standards within the travel agent industry to help you gauge competence, and the quality of individual agents varies enormously.

At present, only nine states have registration, licensing, or other forms of travel agent–related legislation on their books. Rhode Island licenses travel agents; Florida, Hawaii, Iowa, and Ohio register them; and California, Illinois, Oregon, and Washington have laws governing the sale of transportation or related services. While state licensing of agents cannot absolutely guarantee competence, it can at least ensure that an agent has met some minimum requirements.

Perhaps the best-prepared agents are those who have completed the CTC Travel Management program offered by the *Institute of Certified Travel Agents (ICTA)* and carry the initials CTC (Certified Travel Counselor) after their names. This indicates a relatively high level of expertise. For a free list of CTCs in your area, send a self-addressed, stamped, #10 envelope to *ICTA,* 148 Linden St., Box 82-56, Wellesley, MA 02181 (phone: 617-237-0280 in Massachusetts; 800-542-4282 elsewhere in the US).

An agent's membership in the *American Society of Travel Agents (ASTA)* can be a useful guideline in making a selection. But keep in mind that *ASTA* is an industry organization, requiring only that its members be licensed in those states where required; be accredited to represent the suppliers whose products they sell, including airline and cruise tickets; and adhere to its Principles of Professional Conduct and Ethics code. *ASTA* does not guarantee the competence, ethics, or financial soundness of its members, but it does offer some recourse if you feel you have been dealt with unfairly. Complaints may be registered with *ASTA* (Consumer Affairs Dept., PO Box 23992, Washington, DC 20026-3992; phone: 703-739-2782). First try to resolve the complaint directly with the supplier. For a list of *ASTA* members in your area, send a self-addressed, stamped, #10 envelope to *ASTA,* Public Relations Dept., at the address above.

There also is the *Association of Retail Travel Agents (ARTA),* a smaller but highly respected trade organization similar to *ASTA.* Its member agencies and agents similarly agree to abide by a code of ethics, and complaints about a member can be made to *ARTA's* Grievance Committee, 1745 Jeff Davis Hwy., Arlington, VA 22202-3402 (phone: 800-969-6069 or 703-553-7777).

Perhaps the best way to find a travel agent is by word of mouth. If the agent (or agency) has done a good job for your friends over a period of time, it probably indicates a certain level of commitment and competence. Always ask not only for the name of the company but also for the name of the specific agent with whom your friends dealt, for it is that individual who will serve you, and quality can vary widely within a single agency. There are some superb travel agents in the business, and they can facilitate vacation or business arrangements.

Entry Requirements and Documents

As we went to press, only Romania and the Soviet Union still required US citizens to obtain visas for entry. (At the time of this writing, however, Yugoslavia was considering reinstating its visa requirement.) Given the uncertain political state of the Eastern European nations, it is entirely possible that this requirement — and/or the procedures to adhere to it — may change during the shelf-life of this guide. It would be wise to double-check.

Where visas are not required, a valid US passport is the only document required, and that same passport also is needed to re-enter the US. However, immigration officers in Western European airports *may* want to see that you have sufficient funds for your trip (for example, traveler's checks, credit cards, and so on) and a return ticket to the US. As a general rule, possession of a US passport entitles the bearer to remain in most European countries as a tourist for up to 90 days. For resident aliens of the US, the requirements are determined by their country of origin, and they should inquire at the nearest consulate or embassy of each country they plan to visit to find out what documents they need to enter Europe.

Vaccination certificates are required only if the traveler is entering from an area of contagion as defined by the World Health Organization and, as the US is considered an area "free from contagion," an international vaccination certificate no longer is required for entering Europe for a short period of time. Because smallpox is considered eradicated from the world, only a few countries continue to require visitors to have a smallpox vaccination certificate. You certainly will not need one to travel to Europe or return to the US.

VISAS: In most European countries, visas are required for study, residency, work, or stays of more than 3 months, and US citizens should address themselves to the appropriate embassy or consulate well in advance of a proposed trip (for addresses see *European Embassies and Consulates in the US,* in this section). Visas of this type are available for stays in Europe for various periods, usually up to 1 year. The ready processing of a visa application may be based on the duration of the visa you are requesting — visas for studying in Europe for several months are likely to be processed more quickly than year-long residency visas. Proof of substantial means of independent support during the stay also is pertinent to the acceptance of any long-term-stay application.

At least two items are necessary to apply for a visa: a valid passport and a completed visa form. (These forms may be obtained by sending a written request with a self-addressed, stamped envelope to the appropriate consulate.) Other requirements vary from country to country. Generally, cash, a money order, or certified check may be used for payment if applying in person, a money order or certified check if applying by mail. Visas normally are issued on the spot; however, if there is a backlog, you may have to return to pick it up a few days later. To avoid frustration and wasted time, it is a good idea to call ahead to check during what hours and days visa requests are accepted. If applying by mail, expect to wait 1 week or longer for return by regular mail; you may want to ask about special delivery options (such as *Federal Express*) which will cost more but may be worth it for the time saved.

Note: The government tourism offices of those Eastern European countries requiring visas can provide application forms but cannot actually issue the visas. (These tourism offices are listed in *Tourist Information Offices,* in this section, as well as in FACTS IN BRIEF, which also provides specific information on visa requirements for each country.) In addition, it is possible to obtain a visa at the borders of these countries — with the exception of the Soviet Union — but this procedure is not recommended due to the potential for long delay in the processing of your application. It is far better to arrive with a visa in hand.

PASSPORTS: While traveling in Europe, carry your passport with you at all times (for an exception to this rule, see our note "When Checking In," below). If you lose your passport while abroad, immediately report the loss to the nearest US consulate or embassy (see *Medical and Legal Aid and Consular Services,* in this section, for locations in Europe). You can get a 3-month temporary passport directly from the consulate, but you must fill out a "loss of passport" form and follow the same application procedure — and pay the same fees — as you did for the original (see below). It's likely to speed things up if you have a record of your passport number and the place and date of its issue (a photocopy of the first page of your passport is perfect). Keep this information separate from your passport — you might want to give it to a traveling companion to hold or put it in the bottom of your suitcase.

US passports are now valid for 10 years from the date of issue (5 years for those under age 18). The expired passport itself is not renewable, but must be turned in along with your application for a new and valid one (you will get it back, voided, when you receive the new one). Normal passports contain 24 pages, but frequent travelers can request a 48-page passport at no extra cost. Every individual, regardless of age, must have his or her own passport. Family passports no longer are issued. Passports can be renewed by mail with forms obtained at designated locations only if the expired passport was issued no more than 12 years before the date of application for renewal and it was not issued before the applicant's 16th birthday. The rules for renewal regarding teens under 16 and younger applicants may vary depending on age and when their previous passport was issued. Those who are eligible to apply by mail must send the completed form with the expired passport, two photos (see description below), and $55 (no execution fee required) to the nearest passport agency office. Delivery can take as little as 2 weeks or as long as 6 weeks during the busiest season — from approximately mid-March to mid-September.

Adults applying for the first time and younger applicants who must apply for a passport in person (as well as those who cannot wait for mail application turnaround) can do so at one of the following places:

1. The State Department passport agencies in Boston, Chicago, Honolulu, Houston, Los Angeles, Miami, New Orleans, New York City, Philadelphia, San Francisco, Seattle, Stamford, CT, and Washington, DC.
2. A federal or state courthouse.

3. Any of the 1,000 post offices across the country with designated acceptance facilities.

Application blanks are available at all these offices and must be presented with the following:

1. Proof of US citizenship. This can be a previous passport or one in which you were included. If you are applying for your first passport and were born in the United States, an original or certified birth certificate is the required proof. If you were born abroad, a Certificate of Naturalization, a Certificate of Citizenship, a Report of Birth Abroad of a Citizen of the United States, or a Certification of Birth is necessary.
2. Two 2-by-2-inch, front-view photographs in color or black and white, with a light, plain background, taken within the previous 6 months. These must be taken by a photographer rather than a machine.
3. A $65 passport fee ($40 for travelers under 16), which includes a $10 execution fee. *Note:* Your best bet is to bring the exact amount in cash (no change is given) or a separate check or money order for each passport (although a family can combine several passport fees on one check or money order).
4. Proof of identity. Again, this can be a previous passport, a Certificate of Naturalization or of Citizenship, a driver's license, or a government ID card with a physical description or a photograph. Failing any of these, you should be accompanied by a blood relative or a friend of at least 2 years' standing who will testify to your identity. Credit cards or social security cards do not suffice as proof of identity — but note that since 1988, US citizens *must* supply their social security numbers.

As getting a passport — or international visa — through the mail can mean waiting as much as 6 weeks or more, a new mini-industry has cropped up in those cities where there is a US passport office. The yellow pages currently list quite a few organizations willing to wait on line to expedite obtaining a visa or passport renewal; there's even one alternative for those who live nowhere near the cities mentioned above. In the nation's capital there's an organization called the *Washington Passport and Visa Service*. It may be the answer for folks in need of special rapid action, since this organization can get a passport application or renewal turned around in a single day. What's more, their proximity to an embassy or consulate of every foreign country represented in the US helps to speed the processing of visa applications as well. The fee for a 5- to 7-day turnaround is $30; for next-day service the charge is $50; and for same-day service they charge $90. For information, application forms, and other prices, contact *Washington Passport and Visa Service* (2318 18th St. NW, Washington, DC 20009; phone: 800-272-7776). Another company in Washington providing this service is *Travisa* (2100 P St. NW, Washington, DC 20037; phone: 800-222-2589).

If you need an emergency passport, it also is possible to be issued a passport in a matter of hours by going directly to your nearest passport office (there is no way, however, to avoid waiting in line). Explain the nature of the emergency, usually as serious as a death in the family; a ticket in hand for a flight the following day also will suffice. Should the emergency occur outside of business hours, all is not lost. There's a 24-hour telephone number in Washington, DC (phone: 202-634-3600) that can put you in touch with a State Department duty officer who may be able to expedite your application.

■ **When Checking In:** Some European hotels may ask you to surrender your passport for 24 hours. While we all get a little nervous when we're parted from our passports, the US State Department's passport division advises that it's a perfectly acceptable procedure. The purpose usually is to check the validity of the passport and ascertain whether the passport holder is a fugitive or has a police record. Many hotels merely will ask that you enter your passport number on your registration card. If a hotel does take your passport, make sure it's returned to you the next day.

DUTY AND CUSTOMS: As a general rule, the requirements for bringing the majority of items into Europe is that they must be in quantities small enough not to imply commercial import.

Each country has strict regulations regarding the amount of specific goods that may be imported without duty, as well as the duty that must be paid if the quantity exceeds these limits. Restrictions generally apply to a broad range of items, including the following: alcoholic beverages; cigarettes, cigars, and loose tobacco; coffee and tea; cologne and perfume; and items designated as gifts (valued at a specified amount). When planning a trip to Europe, contact the government tourist authority of each country you plan to visit (for offices in the US, see *Tourist Information Offices,* in this section) for information on procedures, the type and quantity of goods regulated, and duties imposed on overages.

If you are bringing along a computer, camera, or any other electronic equipment for your own use that you will be taking back to the US, you should register the item with the US Customs Service in order to avoid paying duty both entering and returning from Europe. (Also see *Customs and Returning to the US,* in this section.) For information on this procedure, as well as for a variety of pamphlets on US customs regulations, contact the local office of the US Customs Service or the central office, PO Box 7407, Washington, DC 20044 (phone: 202-566-8195).

■ **One rule to follow:** When passing through customs, it is illegal not to declare dutiable items; penalties range from stiff fines and seizure of the goods to prison terms. So don't try to sneak anything through — it just isn't worth it.

Insurance

 It is unfortunate that most decisions to buy travel insurance are impulsive and usually are made without any real consideration of the traveler's existing policies. Therefore, the first person with whom you should discuss travel insurance is your own insurance broker, not a travel agent or the clerk behind the airport insurance counter. You may discover that the insurance you already carry — homeowner's policies and/or accident, health, and life insurance — protects you adequately while you travel and that your real needs are in the more mundane areas of excess value insurance for baggage or trip cancellation insurance.

TYPES OF INSURANCE: To make insurance decisions intelligently, however, you first should understand the basic categories of travel insurance and what they cover. Then you can decide what you should have in the broader context of your personal insurance needs, and you can choose the most economical way of getting the desired protection: through riders on existing policies; with onetime short-term policies; through a special program put together for the frequent traveler; through coverage that's part of a travel club's benefits; or with a combination policy sold by insurance companies through brokers, automobile clubs, tour operators, and travel agents.

There are seven basic categories of travel insurance:

1. Baggage and personal effects insurance
2. Personal accident and sickness insurance
3. Trip cancellation and interruption insurance
4. Default and/or bankruptcy insurance

5. Flight insurance (to cover injury or death)
6. Automobile insurance (for driving your own or a rented car)
7. Combination policies

Baggage and Personal Effects Insurance – Ask your insurance agent if baggage and personal effects are included in your current homeowner's policy, or if you will need a special floater to cover you for the duration of a trip. The object is to protect your bags and their contents in case of damage or theft anytime during your travels, not just while you're in flight and covered by the airline's policy. Furthermore, only limited protection is provided by the carrier. Baggage liability varies from carrier to carrier, but generally speaking, on domestic flights, luggage usually is insured to $1,250 — that's per passenger, not per bag. For most international flights, including domestic portions of international flights, the airline's liability limit is approximately $9.07 per pound or $20 per kilo (which comes to about $360 per 40-pound suitcase) for checked baggage and up to $400 per passenger for unchecked baggage. These limits should be specified on your airline ticket, but to be awarded any amount, you'll have to provide an itemized list of lost property, and if you're including new and/or expensive items, be prepared for a request that you back up your claim with sales receipts or other proof of purchase.

If you are carrying goods worth more than the maximum protection offered by the airline, bus, or train company, consider excess value insurance. Additional coverage is available from airlines at an average, currently, of $1 to $2 per $100 worth of coverage, up to a maximum of $5,000. This insurance can be purchased at the airline counter when you check in, though you should arrive early to fill out the necessary forms and to avoid holding up other passengers.

Major credit card companies also provide coverage for lost or delayed baggage — and this coverage often also is over and above what the airline will pay. The basic coverage usually is automatic for all cardholders who use the credit card to purchase tickets, but to qualify for additional coverage, cardholders generally must enroll.

American Express: Provides $500 coverage for checked baggage; $1,250 for carry-on baggage; and $250 for valuables, such as cameras and jewelry.

Carte Blanche and Diners Club: Provide $1,250 free insurance for checked or carry-on baggage that's lost or damaged.

Discover Card: Offers $500 insurance for checked baggage and $1,250 for carry-on baggage — but to qualify for this coverage cardholders first must purchase additional flight insurance (see "Flight Insurance," below).

MasterCard and Visa: Baggage insurance coverage set by the issuing institution.

Additional baggage and personal effects insurance also is included in certain of the combination travel insurance policies discussed below.

■ **A note of warning:** Be sure to read the fine print of any excess value insurance policy; there often are specific exclusions, such as cash, tickets, furs, gold and silver objects, art, and antiques. And remember that insurance companies ordinarily will pay only the depreciated value of the goods rather than their replacement value. The best way to protect the items you're carrying in your luggage is to take photos of your valuables and keep a record of the serial numbers of such items as cameras, typewriters, laptop computers, radios, and so on. This will establish that you do, indeed, own the objects. If your luggage disappears en route or is damaged, deal with the situation immediately. If an airline loses your luggage, you will be asked to fill out a Property Irregularity Report before you leave the airport. If your property disappears at other transportation centers, tell the local company, but also report it to the police (since the insurance company will check with the police when processing the claim). When traveling by train, if you are sending excess luggage as registered baggage, remember that some trains may not have provisions for extra cargo; if your baggage does not arrive when you do, it may not be lost, just on the next train!

Personal Accident and Sickness Insurance – This covers you in case of illness during your trip or death in an accident. Most policies insure you for hospital and doctor's expenses, lost income, and so on. In most cases, it is a standard part of existing health insurance policies, though you should check with your broker to be sure that your policy will pay for any medical expenses incurred abroad. If not, take out a separate vacation accident policy or an entire vacation insurance policy that includes health and life coverage.

Two examples of such comprehensive health and life insurance coverage are the travel insurance packages offered by *Wallach & Co:*

HealthCare Global: This insurance package, which can be purchased for periods of 10 to 180 days, is offered for two age groups: Men and women up to age 75 receive $25,000 medical insurance and $50,000 accidental injury or death benefit; those from age 76 to 84 are eligible for $12,500 medical insurance and $25,000 injury or death benefit. For either policy, the cost for a 10-day period is $25.

HealthCare Abroad: This program is available to individuals up to age 75. For $3 per day (minimum 10 days, maximum 90 days), policy holders receive $100,000 medical insurance and $25,000 accidental injury or death benefit.

Both of these basic programs also may be bought in combination with trip cancellation and baggage insurance at extra cost. For further information, write to *Wallach & Co.,* 243 Church St. NW, Suite 100-D, Vienna, VA 22180 (phone: 703-281-9500 in Virginia; 800-237-6615 elsewhere in the US).

Trip Cancellation and Interruption Insurance – Most charter and package tour passengers pay for their travel well before departure. The disappointment of having to miss a vacation because of illness or any other reason pales before the awful prospect that not all (and sometimes none) of the money paid in advance might be returned. So cancellation insurance for any package tour is a must.

Although cancellation penalties vary (they are listed in the fine print of every tour brochure, and before you purchase a package tour you should know exactly what they are), rarely will a passenger get more than 50% of this money back if forced to cancel within a few weeks of scheduled departure. Therefore, if you book a package tour or charter flight, you should have trip cancellation insurance to guarantee full reimbursement or refund should you, a traveling companion, or a member of your immediate family get sick, forcing you to cancel your trip or *return home early.*

The key here is *not* to buy just enough insurance to guarantee full reimbursement for the cost of the package or charter in case of cancellation. The proper amount of coverage should be sufficient to reimburse you for the cost of having to catch up with a tour after its departure or having to travel home at the full economy airfare if you have to forgo the return flight of your charter. There usually is quite a discrepancy between a charter fare and the amount charged to travel the same distance on a regularly scheduled flight at full economy fare.

Trip cancellation insurance is available from travel agents and tour operators in two forms: as part of a short-term, all-purpose travel insurance package (sold by the travel agent); or as specific cancellation insurance designed by the tour operator for a specific charter tour. Generally, tour operators' policies are less expensive, but also less inclusive. Cancellation insurance also is available directly from insurance companies or their agents as part of a short-term, all-inclusive travel insurance policy.

Before you decide on a policy, read each one carefully. (Either type can be purchased from a travel agent when you book the charter or package tour.) Be certain that your policy includes enough coverage to pay your fare from the farthest destination on your itinerary should you have to miss the charter flight. Also, be sure to check the fine print for stipulations concerning "family members" and "pre-existing medical conditions," as well as allowances for living expenses if you must delay your return due to bodily injury or illness.

Default and/or Bankruptcy Insurance – Although trip cancellation insurance usually protects you if *you* are unable to complete — or begin — your trip, a fairly recent innovation is coverage in the event of default and/or bankruptcy on the part of the tour operator, airline, or other travel supplier. In some travel insurance packages, this contingency is included in the trip cancellation portion of the coverage; in others, it is a separate feature. Either way, it is becoming increasingly important. Whereas sophisticated travelers have long known to beware of the possibility of default or bankruptcy when buying a charter flight or tour package, in recent years more than a few respected scheduled airlines have unexpectedly revealed their shaky financial condition, sometimes leaving hordes of stranded ticket holders in their wake. Moreover, the value of escrow protection of a charter passenger's funds lately has been unreliable. While default/bankruptcy insurance will not ordinarily result in reimbursement in time to pay for new arrangements, it can ensure that you will get your money back, and even independent travelers buying no more than an airplane ticket may want to consider it.

Flight Insurance – Airlines have carefully established limits of liability for injury to or the death of passengers on international flights. For all international flights to, from, or with a stopover in the US, all carriers are liable for up to $75,000 per passenger. For all other international flights, the liability is based on where you purchase the ticket: If booked in advance in the US, the maximum liability is $75,000; if arrangements are made abroad, the liability is $10,000. But remember, these liabilities are not the same thing as insurance policies; every penny that an airline eventually pays in the case of injury or death may be subject to a legal battle.

But before you buy last-minute flight insurance from an airport vending machine, consider the purchase in light of your total existing insurance coverage. A careful review of your current policies may reveal that you already are amply covered for accidental death, sometimes up to three times the amount provided for by the flight insurance you're buying in the airport.

Be aware that airport insurance, the kind typically bought at a counter or from a vending machine, is among the most expensive forms of life insurance coverage, and that even within a single airport, rates for approximately the same coverage vary widely. Often policies sold in vending machines are more expensive than those sold over the counter, even when they are with the same national company.

If you buy your plane ticket with a major credit card, you generally receive automatic insurance coverage at no extra cost. Additional coverage usually can be obtained at extremely reasonable prices, but a cardholder must sign up for it in advance. (Note that rates vary slightly for residents of some states.) As we went to press, the travel accident and life insurance policies of the major credit card companies were as follows:

American Express: Automatically provides $100,000 in insurance to its *Green, Gold,* and *Optima* cardholders, and $500,000 to *Platinum* cardholders. With *American Express,* $4 per ticket buys an additional $250,000 worth of flight insurance; $6.50 buys $500,000 worth; and $13 provides an added $1 million worth of coverage.

Carte Blanche: Automatically provides $150,000 flight insurance. An additional $250,000 worth of insurance is available for $4; $500,000 costs $6.50.

Diners Club: Provides $350,000 free flight insurance. An additional $250,000 worth of insurance is available for $4; $500,000 costs $6.50.

Discover Card: Provides $500,000 free flight insurance. An additional $250,000 worth of insurance is available for $4; $500,000 costs $6.50.

MasterCard and Visa: Insurance coverage set by the issuing institution.

Automobile Insurance – Public liability and property damage (third-party) insurance is compulsory in Europe, and whether you drive your own or a rental car you must carry insurance. Car rentals in Europe usually include public liability, property damage, fire, and theft coverage and, sometimes (depending on the car rental company), collision damage coverage with a deductible.

In your car rental contract, you'll see that for about $11 to $13 a day, you may buy optional collision damage waiver (CDW) protection. (If partial coverage with a deductible is included in the rental contract, the CDW will cover the deductible in the event of an accident, and can cost as much as $25 per day.) If you do not accept the CDW coverage, you may be liable for as much as the full retail value of the rental car, and by paying for the CDW you are relieved of all responsibility for any damage to the car. Before agreeing to this coverage, however, check with your own broker about your existing personal automobile insurance policy. It very well may cover your entire liability exposure without any additional cost, or you automatically may be covered by the credit card company to which you are charging the cost of your rental. To find out the amount of rental car insurance provided by major credit cards contact the issuing institutions.

You also should know that an increasing number of the major international car rental companies automatically are including the cost of the CDW in their basic rates. Car rental prices have increased to include this coverage, although rental company ad campaigns may promote this as a new, improved rental package "benefit." The disadvantage of this inclusion is that you may not have the option to turn down the CDW — even if you already are adequately covered by your own insurance policy or through a credit card company.

Your rental contract (with the appropriate insurance box checked off), as well as proof of your personal insurance policy, if applicable, are required as proof of insurance. If you will be driving your own car in Europe, you must carry an International Insurance Certificate (called a Green Card), available through insurance brokers in the US.

This certificate is valid in all European countries except the Soviet Union, which does not recognize it. Drivers will have to buy separate insurance for the country from *Ingosstrakh,* the insurance company of the Soviet Union, which has representatives at border crossings. Further information is available from *Ingosstrakh,* Pjatnitskaja ul #12, Moscow M35, Soviet Union (phone 7095-231-1677, fax: 7095-230-2518).

Combination Policies – Short-term insurance policies, which may include a combination of any or all of the types of insurance discussed above, are available through retail insurance agencies, automobile clubs, and many travel agents. These combination policies are designed to cover you for the duration of a single trip.

Policies of this type include the following:

Access America International: A subsidiary of the Blue Cross/Blue Shield plans of New York and Washington, DC, now available nationwide. Contact *Access America,* 600 Third Ave., PO Box 807, New York, NY 10163 (phone: 800-284-8300 or 212-490-5345).

Carefree: Underwritten by The Hartford. Contact *Carefree Travel Insurance,* Arm Coverage, PO Box 310, Mineola, NY 11501 (phone: 800-645-2424 or 516-294-0220).

NEAR Services: In addition to a full range of travel services, this organization offers a comprehensive travel insurance package. An added feature is coverage for lost or stolen airline tickets. Contact *NEAR Services,* 450 Prairie Ave., Suite 101, Calumet City, IL 60409 (phone: 708-868-6700 in the Chicago area; 800-654-6700 elsewhere in the US and Canada).

Tele-Trip: Underwritten by the Mutual of Omaha Companies. Contact *Tele-Trip Co.,* PO Box 31685, 3201 Farnam St., Omaha, NE 68131 (phone: 402-345-2400 in Nebraska; 800-228-9792 elsewhere in the US).

Travel Assistance International: Provided by Europ Assistance Worldwide Services, and underwritten by Transamerica Occidental Life Insurance. Contact *Travel Assistance International,* 1333 15th St. NW, Suite 400, Washington, DC 20005 (phone: 202-331-1609 in Washington, DC; 800-821-2828 elsewhere in the US).

Travel Guard International: Underwritten by the Insurance Company of North America, it is available through authorized travel agents, or contact *Travel Guard International,* 1145 Clark St., Stevens Point, WI 54481 (phone: 715-345-0505 in Wisconsin; 800-826-1300 elsewhere in the US).

Travel Insurance PAK: Underwritten by The Travelers. Contact *The Travelers Companies,* Ticket and Travel Plans, One Tower Sq., Hartford, CT 06183-5040 (phone: 203-277-2319 in Connecticut; 800-243-3174 elsewhere in the US).

WorldCare Travel Assistance Association: This organization offers insurance packages underwritten by Transamerica Occidental Life Insurance Company and Transamerica Premier Insurance Company. Contact *WorldCare Travel Assistance Association,* 605 Market St., Suite 1300, San Francisco, CA 94105 (phone: 800-666-4993 or 415-541-4991).

How to Pack

 No one can provide a completely foolproof list of precisely what to pack, so it's best to let common sense, space, and comfort guide you. Keep one maxim in mind: Less is more. You simply won't need as much clothing as you think, and you are far more likely to need a forgotten accessory — or a needle and thread or scissors — than a particular piece of clothing.

As with almost anything relating to travel, a little planning can go a long way.

1. Where are you going — city, country, or both?
2. How many total days will you be gone?
3. What's the average temperature likely to be during your stay?

The goal is to remain perfectly comfortable, neat, clean, and adequately fashionable, but to pack as little as possible. Learn to travel light by following two firm packing principles:

1. Organize your travel wardrobe around a single color — blue or brown, for example — that allows you to mix, match, and layer clothes. Holding firm to one color scheme will make it easy to eliminate items of clothing that don't harmonize.
2. Never overpack to ensure a supply of fresh clothing — shirts, blouses, underwear — for each day of a long trip. Use hotel laundries to wash and clean clothes. If these are too expensive, self-service laundries are found in most towns of any size.

CLIMATE AND CLOTHES: Exactly what you pack for your trip will be a function of where you are going and when and the kinds of things you intend to do. A few degrees can make all the difference between being comfortably attired and very real suffering, so your initial step should be to find out what the general weather conditions are likely to be in the areas you will visit.

Every country in Europe has distinct seasonal changes, but the degree, duration, and extent of the changes vary widely. Although most of Europe is farther north than the US — Paris, sitting astride latitude 48° 52', and London, at 51° 30', are respectively about even with and slightly north of Quebec's Gaspé Peninsula — the climate generally is milder. The exceptions include mountainous regions — such as the Swiss Alps — where you can expect somewhat colder weather year-round. The farther north you go (closer to the Arctic Circle), the more the weather resembles that of the northernmost US and Canada.

These exceptions aside, for the most part residents of the US will find that the same wardrobe they would wear in the Middle Atlantic United States will, with a few adjustments, also be appropriate for most parts of Europe in the same season. Anyone going to Europe from the late fall through the early spring, however, should take into account that while central heating is prevalent, interiors often are not heated to the same degree they would be in the US. Thus most people probably will feel more comfortable wearing heavier clothing indoors than they might at home — for instance, sweaters rather than lightweight shirts and blouses.

More information about the climate in Europe, along with a chart of average low and high temperatures for different countries, is given in *When to Go,* in this section; see also the individual country listings in FACTS IN BRIEF.

Keeping temperature and climate in mind, consider the problem of luggage. Plan on one suitcase per person (and in a pinch, remember it's always easier to carry two small suitcases than to schlepp one that is roughly the size of the downtown Detroit). Standard 26- to 28-inch suitcases can be made to work for 1 week or 1 month, and unless you are going for no more than a weekend, never cram wardrobes for two people into one suitcase. Hanging bags are best for dresses, suits, and jackets.

FASHION: On the whole, Europe is no more formal than North America, so be guided by your own taste. On the Left Bank in Paris, for example, anything goes; on the Right Bank, wear what you would in any cosmopolitan American city. Although Europeans do enjoy dressing up, formal attire is necessary only for the most elegant occasions — such as opening night at Milan's *La Scala* opera house (though European students have been attending the opera in blue jeans for years).

Before packing, lay out every piece of clothing you think you might want to take. Select clothing on the basis of what can serve several functions (wherever possible, clothes should be chosen that can be used for both daytime and evening wear). Pack clothes that have a lot of pockets for traveler's checks, documents, and tickets. Eliminate items that don't mix, match, or coordinate with your color scheme. If you can't wear it in at least two distinct incarnations, leave it at home. Accessorize everything beforehand so you know exactly what you will be wearing with what.

Layering is the key to comfort — particularly when touring in parts of the countryside where mornings and evenings can be chilly even when the days are mild. No matter where you are traveling in Europe, however, layering is a good way to prepare for atypical temperatures or changes in the weather. For unexpectedly cold days or for outings in the countryside, recommended basics are a lightweight wool or heavy cotton turtleneck, which can be worn under a shirt, and perhaps a third layer, such as a pullover sweater, jacket, or windbreaker. In warmer weather, substitute T-shirts and lightweight cotton shirts or sweaters for the turtleneck and wool layers. As the weather changes, you can add or remove clothes as required.

A versatile item of clothing that travelers will find indispensable while traveling in Europe is a raincoat, preferably one with a zip-out lining — and maybe a hood or rain hat. (If you do decide to take an umbrella, a compact telescoping model is best.) Other useful apparel includes a warm wool sweater or jacket, because even in the summer, warm clothing will be welcome for exploring caves in Spain, champagne cellars in France, or catacombs in Italy. And finally — since the best touring of Europe's castles, churches, and countryside is done on foot — it is essential to bring comfortable shoes (often this means an old pair, already broken in).

Your carry-on luggage should contain a survival kit with the basic things you will need in case your luggage gets lost or stolen: a toothbrush, toothpaste, all medications, a sweater, nightclothes, and a change of underwear. With these essential items at hand, you will be prepared for any sudden, unexpected occurrence that separates you from your suitcase. If you have many 1- or 2-night stops scheduled, you can live out of your survival case without having to unpack completely at each hotel.

Sundries – If you are traveling during the summer and will be spending a lot of time outdoors, bring along a sun hat (to protect hair as well as skin) and sunscreen. Also, if you are heading for a holiday on skis, do not underestimate the effect of the sun's glare off snowy slopes, especially in higher altitudes — the exposed areas of your face and neck are particularly susceptible to burning. Other items you might consider packing are a pocket-size flashlight with extra batteries, a small sewing kit, a first-aid kit (see *Staying Healthy,* in this section, for recommended components), binoculars, and a camera or camcorder (see *Cameras and Equipment,* also in this section).

■ **Note:** For those on the go, *Travel Mini Pack* offers numerous products — from toilet articles to wrinkle-remover spray — in handy travel sizes, as well as travel accessories such as money pouches, foreign currency calculators, and even a combination hair dryer/iron. For a catalogue, contact *Travel Mini Pack,* PO Box 571, Stony Point, NY 10980 (phone: 914-429-8281).

PACKING: The basic idea of packing is to get everything into the suitcase and out again with as few wrinkles as possible. Simple, casual clothes — shirts, jeans and slacks, permanent press skirts — can be rolled into neat, tight sausages that keep other packed items in place and leave the clothes themselves amazingly unwrinkled. However, for items that are too bulky or delicate for even careful rolling, a suitcase can be packed with the heaviest items on the bottom, toward the hinges, so that they will not wrinkle more perishable clothes. Candidates for the bottom layer include shoes (stuff them with small items to save space), a toilet kit, handbags (stuff them to help keep their shape), and an alarm clock. Fill out this layer with things that will not wrinkle or will not matter if they do, such as sweaters, socks, a bathing suit, gloves, and underwear.

If you get this first, heavy layer as smooth as possible with the fill-ins, you will have a shelf for the next layer — the most easily wrinkled items, like slacks, jackets, shirts, dresses, and skirts. These should be buttoned and zipped and laid along the whole length of the suitcase with as little folding as possible. When you do need to make a fold, do it on a crease (as with pants), along a seam in the fabric, or where it will not show (such as shirttails). Alternate each piece of clothing, using one side of the suitcase, then the other, to make the layers as flat as possible. Make the layers even and the total contents of your bag full and firm to keep things from shifting around during transit. On the top layer put the things you will want at once: nightclothes, an umbrella or raincoat, a sweater.

With men's two-suiter suitcases, follow the same procedure. Then place jackets on hangers, straighten them out, and leave them unbuttoned. If they are too wide for the suitcase, fold them lengthwise down the middle, straighten the shoulders, and fold the sleeves in along the seam.

While packing, it is a good idea to separate each layer of clothes with plastic cleaning bags, which will help preserve pressed clothes while they are in the suitcase. Unpack your bags as soon as you get to your hotel. Nothing so thoroughly destroys freshly cleaned and pressed clothes as sitting for days in a suitcase. Finally, if something is badly wrinkled and can't be professionally pressed before you must wear it, hang it for several hours in a bathroom where the bathtub has been filled with very hot water; keep the bathroom door closed so the room becomes something of a steamroom. It really works miracles.

SOME FINAL PACKING HINTS: Apart from the items you pack as carry-on luggage (see above), always keep all necessary medicines, valuable jewelry, and travel or business documents in your purse, briefcase, or carry-on bag — *not in the luggage you will check.* Tuck a bathing suit into your handbag or briefcase, too; in the event of lost baggage, it's frustrating to be without one. And whether in your overnight bag or checked luggage, cosmetics and any liquids should be packed in plastic bottles or at least wrapped in plastic bags and tied.

Golf clubs and skis may be checked through as luggage (most airlines are accustomed to handling them), but tennis rackets should be carried onto the plane. Some airlines require that bicycles be partially dismantled and packaged (see *Camping and Caravanning, Hiking and Biking,* in this section). Check with the airline before departure to see if there is a specific regulation concerning any special equipment or sporting gear you plan to take.

Hints for Handicapped Travelers

 From 40 to 50 million people in the US alone have some sort of disability, and over half this number are physically handicapped. Like everyone else today, they — and the uncounted disabled millions around the world — are on the move. More than ever before, they are demanding facilities they can use comfortably, and they are being heard.

PLANNING: Collect as much information as you can about your specific disability and facilities for the disabled in Europe. Make your travel arrangements well in advance and specify to all services involved the exact nature of your condition or restricted mobility, as your trip will be much more comfortable if you know that there are accommodations and facilities to suit your needs. The best way to find out if your intended destination can accommodate a handicapped traveler is to write or call the local tourist authority or hotel and ask specific questions. If you require a corridor of a certain width to maneuver a wheelchair or if you need handles on the bathroom walls for support, ask the hotel manager. A travel agent or the local chapter or national office of the organization that deals with your particular disability — for example, the *American Foundation for the Blind* or the *American Heart Association* — will supply the most up-to-date information on the subject. The following organizations offer general information on access:

ACCENT on Living (PO Box 700, Bloomington, IL 61702; phone: 309-378-2961). This information service for persons with disabilities provides a free list of travel agencies specializing in arranging trips for the disabled; for a copy send a self-addressed, stamped envelope. Also offers a wide range of publications, including a quarterly magazine ($8 per year; $14 for 2 years) for persons with disabilities.

Comité National Français de Liaison pour la Réadaptation des Handicapés (*CNFLRH;* 38 Bd. Raspail, Paris 75007, France; phone: 33-1-45-48-90-13), a French organization affiliated with *Mobility International USA* (see listing below), is a central source of information to contact if your itinerary includes a trip to France (if you visit in person, call beforehand for an appointment). The

CNFLRH also publishes, in French, *Touristes Quand Même!,* a city-by-city listing of local services accessible to the handicapped such as banks, churches, pharmacies, and pools, as well as some tourist sites, medical specialists for the physically disabled — physical therapists, orthopedists, and so on — and sources of wheelchair rental and repair. Last updated in 1987, it includes a volume covering Paris alone. To obtain a copy, contact a branch of the French Government Tourist Office or *CNFLRH.*

Information Center for Individuals with Disabilities (Fort Point Pl., 1st Floor, 27-43 Wormwood St., Boston, MA 02210; phone: 800-462-5015 in Massachusetts; 617-727-5540/1 elsewhere in the US; both numbers provide voice and TDD — telecommunications device for the deaf). The center offers information and referral services on disability-related issues, publishes fact sheets on travel agents, tour operators, and other travel resources, and can help you research your trip.

Mobility International USA (*MIUSA;* PO Box 3551, Eugene, OR 97403; phone: 503-343-1284; both voice and TDD). This US branch of *Mobility International* (the main office is at 228 Borough High St., London SE1 1JX, England; phone: 44-71-403-5688), a nonprofit British organization with affiliates worldwide, offers members advice and assistance — including information on accommodations and other travel services, and publications applicable to the traveler's disability. *Mobility International* also offers a quarterly newsletter and a comprehensive sourcebook, *A World of Options for the 90s: A Guide to International Education Exchange, Community Service and Travel for Persons with Disabilities* ($14 for members; $16 for non-members). Membership includes the newsletter and is $20 a year; subscription to the newsletter alone is $10 annually. Among this organization's European affiliates are the following:

- *Associazone per L'Assistenza* (29 Via San Barnaba, Milano I-20122, Italy; phone: 39-25-512009).
- *Irish Wheelchair Association* (Aras Chuchulain, Blackheath Dr., Clontars, Dublin 3, Irish Republic; phone: 353-1-338241).
- *Mobility International Germany* (c/o *BAG-C,* 5 Eupenerstrasse, D-6500 Mainz, Germany; phone: 49-61-31-22-5506).
- *Mobility International Switzerland* (Hard 4, Winterthur 8408, Switzerland; phone: 41-52-256825).
- *Trivsel and Tryghed* (4 Driftskontoret Sydskraenten, Kalundborg DK-4400, Denmark; phone: 45-03-50-9611).

Paralyzed Veterans of America (*PVA;* PVA/ATTS Program, 801 18th St. NW, Washington, DC 20006; phone: 202-416-7708 in Washington, DC; 800-424-8200 elsewhere in the US). The members of this national service organization all are veterans who have suffered spinal cord injuries, but it offers advocacy services and information to all persons with a disability. *PVA* also sponsors *Access to the Skies (ATTS),* a program that coordinates the efforts of the national and international air travel industry in providing airport and airplane access for the disabled. Members receive several helpful publications, as well as regular notification of conferences on subjects of interest to the disabled traveler.

Royal Association for Disability and Rehabilitation (*RADAR;* 25 Mortimer St., London W1N 8AB, England; phone: 44-71-637-5400). Offers a number of publications for the handicapped, including *Holidays in the British Isles 1992: A Guide for Disabled People* and *Holidays and Travel Abroad 1991/92 — A Guide for Disabled People,* a comprehensive guidebook focusing on international travel. These publications can be ordered by sending payment in British pounds to *RADAR*. As we went to press, they cost just over £4.50 and £3 respectively; call for current pricing before ordering.

Society for the Advancement of Travel for the Handicapped (*SATH;* 26 Court St., Penthouse, Brooklyn, NY 11242; phone: 718-858-5483). To keep abreast of developments in travel for the handicapped as they occur, you may want to join *SATH,* a nonprofit organization whose members include consumers, as well as travel service professionals who have experience (or an interest) in travel for the handicapped. For an annual fee of $45 ($25 for students and travelers who are 65 and older) members receive a quarterly newsletter and have access to extensive information and referral services. *SATH* also offers two useful publications: *Travel Tips for the Handicapped* (a series of informative fact sheets) and *The United States Welcomes Handicapped Visitors* (a 48-page guide covering domestic transportation and accommodations that includes useful hints for travelers with disabilities abroad); to order, send a self-addressed, #10 envelope and $1 per title for postage.

Travel Information Service (Moss Rehabilitation Hospital, 1200 W. Tabor Rd., Philadelphia, PA 19141-3099; phone: 215-456-9600 for voice; 215-456-9602 for TDD). This service assists physically handicapped people in planning trips and supplies detailed information on accessibility for a nominal fee.

Blind travelers should contact the *American Foundation for the Blind* (15 W. 16th St., New York, NY 10011; phone: 212-620-2147 in New York State; 800-232-5463 elsewhere in the US) and *The Seeing Eye* (Box 375, Morristown, NJ 07963-0375; phone: 201-539-4425); both provide useful information on resources for the visually impaired. *Note:* Entry requirements for dogs, including Seeing Eye dogs, vary throughout Europe. Most countries require a certificate guaranteeing that the animal is rabies-free. The animal must be vaccinated against rabies within a specific period — usually not less than 20 days or more than 11 months before departure. Vaccination certificates must be signed by the veterinarian administering the vaccination and certified and stamped by a veterinarian who is designated as an inspector by the US Department of Agriculture (USDA). For the location of the nearest regional USDA-certified office providing this service, as well as for other useful information, contact the US Department of Agriculture, APHIS, VS, 2568A Riva Rd., Room 207, Annapolis, MD 21401. The *American Society for the Prevention of Cruelty to Animals* (*ASPCA;* Education Dept., 441 E. 92 St., New York, NY 10128; phone: 212-876-7700) offers a useful booklet, *Traveling With Your Pet,* which lists inoculation and other requirements by country. It is available for $5 (including postage and handling).

Note: Any dog brought into the British Isles, including Northern Ireland and the Irish Republic, must spend 6 months in quarantine; Finland, Norway, and Sweden require 4 months in quarantine; Gibraltar and Iceland prohibit the entry of dogs from the US (and some other countries); and Malta prohibits the importation of any animal.

In addition, there are a number of publications — from travel guides to magazines — of interest to handicapped travelers. Among these are the following:

Access in London, by William Forester (London: Robert Nicholson Publications), is a detailed accessibility guide to London sites and accommodations. It costs $7.95 and is available at the *British Travel Bookshop,* 40 W. 57th St., New York, NY 10019 (phone: 800-448-3039 or 212-765-0898).

Access to the World, by Louise Weiss, offers sound tips for the disabled traveler. Published by Facts on File (460 Park Ave. S., New York, NY 10016; phone: 212-683-2244 in New York State; 800-322-8755 elsewhere in the US; 800-443-8323 in Canada), it costs $16.95. Check with your local bookstore; it also can be ordered by phone with a credit card.

The Diabetic Traveler (PO Box 8223 RW, Stamford, CT 06905; phone: 203-327-5832) is a useful quarterly newsletter. Each issue highlights a single destination or type of travel and includes information on general resources and hints for diabetics. A 1-year subscription costs $15. When subscribing, ask for the free fact sheet including an index of special articles; back issues are available for $4 each.

Guide to Traveling with Arthritis, a free brochure available by writing to the Upjohn Company (PO Box 307-B, Coventry, CT 06238), provides lots of good, commonsense tips on planning your trip and how to be as comfortable as possible when traveling by car, bus, train, cruise ship, or plane.

Handicapped Travel Newsletter is regarded as one of the best sources of information for the disabled traveler. It is edited by wheelchair-bound Vietnam veteran Michael Quigley, who has traveled to 93 countries around the world. Issued every 2 months (plus special issues), a subscription is $10 per year. Write to *Handicapped Travel Newsletter,* PO Box 269, Athens, TX 75751 (phone: 214-677-1260).

Handi-Travel: A Resource Book for Disabled and Elderly Travellers, by Cinnie Noble, is a comprehensive travel guide full of practical tips for those with disabilities affecting mobility, hearing, or sight. To order this book, send $12.95, plus shipping and handling, to the *Canadian Rehabilitation Council for the Disabled,* 45 Sheppard Ave. E., Suite 801, Toronto, Ontario M2N 5W9, Canada (phone: 416-250-7490; both voice and TDD).

The Itinerary (PO Box 2012, Bayonne, NJ 07002-2012; phone: 201-858-3400). This bimonthly travel magazine for people with disabilities includes information on accessibility, listings of tours, news of adaptive devices, travel aids, and special services, as well as numerous general travel hints. A subscription costs $10 a year.

The Physically Disabled Traveler's Guide, by Rod W. Durgin and Norene Lindsay, rates accessibility of a number of travel services and includes a list of organizations specializing in travel for the disabled. It is available for $9.95, plus shipping and handling, from Resource Directories, 3361 Executive Pkwy., Suite 302, Toledo, OH 43606 (phone: 419-536-5353 in the Toledo area; 800-274-8515 elsewhere in the US).

Ticket to Safe Travel offers useful information for travelers with diabetes. A reprint of this article is available free from local chapters of the *American Diabetes Association.* For the nearest branch, contact the central office at 505 Eighth Ave., 21st Floor, New York, NY 10018 (phone: 212-947-9707 in New York State; 800-232-3472 elsewhere in the US).

Travel for the Patient with Chronic Obstructive Pulmonary Disease, a publication of the George Washington University Medical Center, provides some sound practical suggestions for those with emphysema, chronic bronchitis, asthma, or other lung ailments. To order, send $2 to Dr. Harold Silver, 1601 18th St. NW, Washington, DC 20009 (phone: 202-667-0134).

Traveling Like Everybody Else: A Practical Guide for Disabled Travelers, by Jacqueline Freedman and Susan Gersten, offers the disabled tips on traveling by car, cruise ship, and plane, as well as lists of accessible accommodations, tour operators specializing in tours for disabled travelers, and other resources. It is available for $11.95, plus postage and handling, from Modan Publishing, PO Box 1202, Bellmore, NY 11710 (phone: 516-679-1380).

Travel Tips for Hearing-Impaired People, a free pamphlet for deaf and hearing-impaired travelers, is available from the *American Academy of Otolaryngology* (One Prince St., Alexandria, VA 22314; phone: 703-836-4444). For a copy, send a self-addressed, stamped, business-size envelope to the academy.

Travel Tips for People with Arthritis, a free 31-page booklet published by the *Arthritis Foundation,* provides helpful information regarding travel by car, bus, train, cruise ship, or plane, planning your trip, medical considerations, and ways to conserve your energy while traveling. It also includes listings of helpful resources, such as associations and travel agencies that operate tours for disabled travelers. For a copy, contact your local *Arthritis Foundation* chapter, or write to the national office, PO Box 19000, Atlanta, GA 30326 (phone: 404-872-7100).

A few more basic resources to look for are *Travel for the Disabled,* by Helen Hecker ($9.95), and by the same author, *Directory of Travel Agencies for the Disabled* ($19.95). *Wheelchair Vagabond,* by John G. Nelson, is another useful guide for travelers confined to a wheelchair (hardcover, $14.95; paperback, $9.95). All three titles are published by Twin Peaks Press, PO Box 129, Vancouver, WA 98666 (phone: 800-637-CALM or 206-694-2462).

Other good sources of information include the tourist offices of the countries you plan to visit. The Danish Tourist Board's *Access in Denmark — A Tourist Guide for the Disabled* and the Netherlands Board of Tourism's *The Handicapped* are two particularly comprehensive publications for the disabled, both available in English. The Swedish National Tourist Office and the Irish Tourist Board publish guides to accessible accommodations and restaurants and also may be able to provide assistance with escorts. The accommodations guide published by the Norwegian Tourist Board notes which hotels are accessible for travelers in wheelchairs. The British Tourist Authority also carries pamphlets on disabled access in Great Britain.

For accessibility information and European escort services, contact one of the following organizations (arrangements should be made well in advance):

France: *Paris Airport Authority* (10 E. 21st St., Suite 600, New York, NY 10010; phone: 212-529-8484).

Italy: *Italian Spastic Society* (4/H Via Sipro, Rome 00136, Italy; phone: 39-6-389604); and *ANMIC* (2 Via Crescenzio, Rome 00110, Italy; phone: 39-6-8077831).

Spain: *The National Institute of Social Services* (Ministry of Labour, Health and Social Security, Nuevos Ministerios, Paseo de la Castellana, S/N, Madrid 28071, Spain; phone: 34-1-253-6000, -253-7600, or -233-7995).

Sweden: *Swedish Central Committee for Rehabilitation, Swedish Institute for the Handicapped* (Box 303, S-161 Bromma 26, Sweden; phone: 46-8-620-1700).

Switzerland: *Holiday Guides for the Handicapped through Switzerland, c/o Mobility International* (Hard 4, Winterthur 8408, Switzerland; phone: 41-52-256825).

In the Republic of Ireland, the *National Rehabilitation Board* (25 Clyde Rd., Ballsbridge, Dublin 4, Ireland; phone: 353-1-689618) is the central source of information on facilities for the handicapped, and the *Union of Voluntary Organisations for the Handicapped* (29 Eaton Sq., Monkstown, Co. Dublin; phone: 353-1-809251) will provide addresses and phone numbers of local volunteer organizations serving the handicapped. In Northern Ireland, the *Northern Ireland Council on Disability* (2 Annadale Ave., Belfast BT7 3JR, Northern Ireland, UK; phone: 44-232-491011) is the central source of information for the handicapped, and in conjunction with the Northern Ireland Tourist Board, publishes and distributes the free booklet *The Disabled Tourist in Northern Ireland: Things to See, Places to Stay,* which provides useful information on everything from access for wheelchair visitors to overnight accommodations and facilities for the hearing-impaired and for visually handicapped people. The Irish Tourist Board (in the Republic) also publishes an annual *Guide to Hotels and Guesthouses,* indicating handicapped accessibility, but its *Accommodation and Restaurant Guide for*

Disabled Persons, available free from US offices, is an access guide and is much more useful.

Two organizations based in Great Britain offer information for handicapped persons traveling throughout Europe. *Tripscope* (63 Esmond Rd., London W4 1JE, England; phone: 44-81-994-9294) is a telephone-based information and referral service (not a booking agent) that can help with transportation options for journeys throughout Europe. It may, for instance, be able to recommend outlets leasing vehicles adapted to accommodate wheelchairs. *Tripscope* also provides information on cassettes for blind or visually impaired travelers, and accepts written requests for information from those with speech impediments. And for general information, there's *Holiday Care Service* (2 Old Bank Chambers, Station Rd., Horley, Surrey RH6 9HW, England; phone: 44-293-774535), a first-rate, free advisory service on accommodations, transportation, and holiday packages throughout Europe for disabled visitors.

Other services for the handicapped in Great Britain include *Carelink* and *Airbus,* weekday minibus services adapted to take wheelchairs that connect with main *BritRail* stations and Heathrow Airport; for information, contact London Regional Transport Unit for Disabled Passengers (55 Broadway, London SW1H 0BD, England; phone: 44-71-222-5600). *Artsline* (5 Crowndale Rd., London NW1 1TU, England; phone: 44-71-388-2227) offers free telephone advice on disabled access, programs, and facilities at London theaters and art venues (it does not make bookings); a monthly magazine and cassette tape also are available.

Regularly revised hotel and restaurant guides use the symbol of access (a person in a wheelchair; see the symbol at the beginning of this section) to point out accommodations suitable for wheelchair-bound guests.

PLANE: The US Department of Transportation (DOT) has ruled that US airlines must accept all passengers with disabilities. As a matter of course, US airlines were pretty good about accommodating handicapped passengers even before the ruling, although each airline has somewhat different procedures. Foreign airlines also are generally good about accommodating the disabled traveler, but again, policies vary from carrier to carrier. Ask for specifics when you book your flight.

Disabled passengers should always make reservations well in advance, and should provide the airline with all relevant details of their condition. These details include information on mobility and equipment that you will need the airline to supply — such as a wheelchair for boarding or portable oxygen for in-flight use. Be sure that the person to whom you speak fully understands the degree of your disability — the more details provided, the more effective help the airline can give you.

On the day before the flight, call back to make sure that all arrangements have been prepared, and arrive early on the day of the flight so that you can board before the rest of the passengers. It's a good idea to bring a medical certificate with you, stating your specific disability or the need to carry particular medicine.

Because most airports have jetways (corridors connecting the terminal with the door of the plane), a disabled passenger usually can be taken as far as the plane, and sometimes right onto it, in a wheelchair. If not, a narrow boarding chair may be used to take you to your seat. Your own wheelchair, which will be folded and put in the baggage compartment, should be tagged as escort luggage to assure that it's available at planeside upon landing rather than in the baggage claim area. Travel is not quite as simple if your wheelchair is battery-operated: Unless it has non-spillable batteries, it might not be accepted on board, and you will have to check with the airline ahead of time to find out how the batteries and the chair should be packaged for the flight. Usually people in wheelchairs are asked to wait until other passengers have disembarked. If you are making a tight connection, be sure to tell the attendant.

Passengers who use oxygen may not use their personal supply in the cabin, though it may be carried on the plane as cargo when properly packed and labeled. If you will need oxygen during the flight, the airline will supply it to you (there is a charge) provided you have given advance notice — 24 hours to a few days, depending on the carrier.

Useful information on every stage of air travel, from planning to arrival, is provided in the booklet *Incapacitated Passengers Air Travel Guide*. To receive a free copy, write to the *International Air Transport Association* (Publications Sales Department, 2000 Peel St., Montreal, Quebec H3A 2R4, Canada; phone: 514-844-6311). Another helpful publication is *Air Transportation of Handicapped Persons*, which explains the general guidelines that govern air carrier policies. For a copy of this free booklet, write to the US Department of Transportation (Distribution Unit, Publications Section, M-443-2, Washington, DC 20590) and ask for "Free Advisory Circular #AC-120-32." *Access Travel: A Guide to the Accessibility of Airport Terminals*, a free publication of the *Airport Operators Council International*, provides information on more than 500 airports worldwide — including major airports throughout Europe — and offers ratings of 70 features, such as accessibility to bathrooms, corridor width, and parking spaces. For a copy, contact the Consumer Information Center (Dept. 563W, Pueblo, CO 81009; phone: 719-948-3334).

Among the major US carriers serving Europe, the following airlines have TDD toll-free lines in the US for the hearing-impaired:

American: 800-582-1573 in Ohio; 800-543-1586 elsewhere in the US.
Continental: 800-343-9195.
TWA: 800-252-0622 in California; 800-421-8480 elsewhere in the US.
United: 800-942-8819 in Illinois; 800-323-0170 elsewhere in the US.
USAir: 800-245-2966.

SHIP: Among the ships calling at European ports, *Cunard*'s *Queen Elizabeth 2*, *Crystal Cruises*' *Crystal Harmony*, and *Royal Cruise Line*'s *Crown Odyssey* are considered the best-equipped vessels for the physically disabled. Handicapped travelers are advised to book their trip at least 90 days in advance to reserve specialized cabins.

For those in wheelchairs or with limited mobility, one of the best sources for evaluating a ship's accessibility is the free chart issued by the *Cruise Lines International Association* (500 Fifth Ave., Suite 1407, New York, NY 10110; phone: 212-921-0066). The chart lists accessible ships and indicates whether they accommodate standard-size or only narrow wheelchairs, have ramps, wide doors, low or no doorsills, handrails in the rooms, and so on. (For information on ships cruising around Europe, see *Traveling by Ship*, in this section.)

GROUND TRANSPORTATION: Perhaps the simplest solution to getting around is to travel with an able-bodied companion who can drive. Another alternative in Europe is to hire a driver/translator with a car — be sure to get a recommendation from a reputable source. The organizations listed above may be able to help you make arrangements — another source is your hotel concierge.

If you are accustomed to driving your own hand-controlled car and are determined to rent one, you may have to do some extensive research, since in Europe it is difficult to find rental cars fitted with hand controls. If agencies do provide hand-controlled cars, they are apt to be few, offered only on a limited basis in major metropolitan areas, and in high demand. The best course is to contact the major car rental agencies listed in *Traveling by Car*, in this section, well before your departure; but be forewarned: You still may be out of luck. Other sources for information on vehicles adapted for the handicapped are the organizations discussed above.

The *American Automobile Association (AAA)* publishes a useful booklet, *The Handicapped Driver's Mobility Guide*. Contact the central office or your local *AAA* club for availability and pricing, which may vary at different branch offices.

Although taxis and public transportation also are available in Europe, accessibility for the disabled varies and may be limited in rural areas, as well as in some cities. Check with a travel agent or tourist authorities for information.

TRAIN: Train travel for the wheelchair-bound is becoming more feasible in Europe. All *TGV* trains, for example — France's very high speed trains, which happen to be the fastest trains in the world — have doors at platform level so that passengers can roll on and off, and spaces have been set aside where they can stay in their wheelchairs. A booklet describing *Société Nationale des Chemins de Fer Français, (SNCF; French National Railways)* services for the handicapped can be picked up in major railroad stations in France, primarily in Paris. Unfortunately, it is issued in French only. Ask for *Le Supplément au Guide Pratique du Voyageur à l'Attention des Personnes à Mobilité Réduite.* Another useful booklet is the *Guide des Transports à l'Usage des Personnes à Mobilité Réduite,* available from the *Comité National Français de Liaison pour la Réadaptation des Handicapés (CNFLRH),* 38 Bd. Raspail, Paris 75007, France (phone: 33-1-45-48-90-13).

Other trains in Europe are not as well adapted to wheelchairs, but timetables often specify which departures are accessible. And on trains that cannot accommodate wheelchairs, depending on the type of train, special arrangements sometimes may be made in advance through the station manager — for instance, wheelchair-bound travelers may be able to travel in the guard's car. For further information on European trains, contact the specific country's rail service representatives in the US (addresses are listed in *Traveling by Train,* in this section) or ask for information at regional rail offices abroad.

BUS: In general, bus travel is not recommended for travelers who are totally wheelchair-bound unless they have someone along who can lift them on and off or they are members of a group tour designed for the handicapped and are using a specially outfitted bus. If you have some mobility, however, you'll find local personnel usually quite happy to help you board and exit.

TOURS: Programs designed for the physically impaired are run by specialists who have researched hotels, restaurants, and sites to be sure they present no insurmountable obstacles. The following travel agencies and tour operators specialize in making group and individual arrangements for travelers with physical or other disabilities.

Access: The Foundation for Accessibility by the Disabled (PO Box 356, Malverne, NY 11565; phone: 516-887-5798). A travelers' referral service that acts as an intermediary with tour operators and agents worldwide, and provides information on accessibility at various locations.

Accessible Journeys (412 S. 45th St., Philadelphia, PA 19104; phone: 215-747-0171). Arranges for traveling companions who are medical professionals — registered or licensed practical nurses, therapists, or doctors (all are experienced travelers). Several prospective companions' profiles and photos are sent to the client for perusal, and if one is acceptable, the "match" is made. The client usually pays all travel expenses for the companion, plus a certain amount in "earnings" to replace wages the companion would be making at his or her usual job. This company also offers tours and cruises for people with special needs, although you don't have to take one of their tours to hire a companion through them.

Accessible Tours/Directions Unlimited (720 N. Bedford Rd., Bedford Hills, NY 10507; phone: 914-241-1700 in New York State; 800-533-5343 elsewhere in the continental US). Arranges group or individual tours for disabled persons traveling in the company of able-bodied friends or family members. Accepts the unaccompanied traveler if completely self-sufficient.

Dialysis at Sea Cruises (611 Barry Place, Indian Rocks Beach, FL 34635; phone: 800-544-7604 or 813-596-7604). Offers cruises that include the medical services of a nephrologist (a specialist in kidney disease) and a staff of dialysis nurses. Family, friends, and companions are welcome to travel on these cruises, but the number of dialysis patients usually is limited to roughly ten travelers per trip.

Evergreen Travel Service (4114 198th St. SW, Suite 13, Lynnwood, WA 98036-6742; phone: 206-776-1184 or 800-435-2288 throughout the continental US and Canada). Offers worldwide tours and cruises for the disabled (Wings on Wheels Tours), sight-impaired/blind (White Cane Tours), and hearing-impaired/deaf (Flying Fingers Tours). Most programs are first class or deluxe, and include a trained escort.

Flying Wheels Travel (143 W. Bridge St., Box 382, Owatonna, MN 55060; phone: 800-535-6790 or 507-451-5005). Handles both tours and individual arrangements.

The Guided Tour (613 W. Cheltenham Ave., Suite 200, Melrose Park, PA 19126; phone: 215-782-1370). Arranges tours for people with developmental and learning disabilities and sponsors separate tours for members of the same population who also are physically disabled or who simply need a slower pace.

Handi-Travel (First National Travel Ltd., Thornhill Sq., 300 John St., Suite 405, Thornhill, Ontario L3T 5W4, Canada; phone: 416-731-4714). Handles tours and individual arrangements.

Sprout (893 Amsterdam Ave., New York, NY 10025; phone: 212-222-9575). Arranges travel programs for mildly and moderately developmentally disabled teens and adults.

USTS Travel Horizons (11 E. 44th St., New York, NY 10017; phone: 800-487-8787 or 212-687-5121). Travel agent and registered nurse Mary Ann Hamm designs trips for individual travelers requiring all types of kidney dialysis and handles arrangements for the dialysis.

Whole Person Tours (PO Box 1084, Bayonne, NJ 07002-1084; phone: 201-858-3400). Handicapped owner Bob Zywicki travels the world with his wheelchair and offers a lineup of escorted tours (many conducted by him) for the disabled. *Whole Person Tours* also publishes *The Itinerary,* a bimonthly newsletter for disabled travelers (see the publication source list above).

Travelers who would benefit from being accompanied by a nurse or physical therapist also can hire a companion through *Traveling Nurses' Network,* a service provided by Twin Peaks Press (PO Box 129, Vancouver, WA 98666; phone: 800-637-CALM or 206-694-2462). For a $10 fee, clients receive the names of three nurses, whom they can then contact directly; for a $125 fee, the agency will make all the hiring arrangements for the client. Travel arrangements also may be made in some cases — the fee for this further service is determined on an individual basis.

A similar service is offered by *MedEscort International* (ABE International Airport, PO Box 8766, Allentown, PA 18105; phone: 800-255-7182 in the continental US; elsewhere, call 215-791-3111). Clients can arrange to be accompanied by a nurse, paramedic, respiratory therapist, or physician through *MedEscort.* The fees are based on the disabled traveler's needs. This service also can assist in making travel arrangements.

A special guiding service is offered by Oxford historian William Forrester, who became London's first fully qualified and registered guide in a wheelchair. He escorts travelers for entire holidays, or just helps in planning an independent tour suited to each traveler's particular interests and mobility. Contact William Forrester, 1 Belvedere Close, Manor Rd., Guildford, Surrey GU2 6NP, England (phone: 44-483-575401).

Hints for Single Travelers

Just about the last trip in human history on which the participants were neatly paired was the voyage of Noah's Ark. Ever since, passenger lists and tour groups have reflected the same kind of asymmetry that occurs in real life, as countless individuals set forth to see the world unaccompanied (or unencumbered, depending on your outlook) by spouse, lover, friend, or relative.

The truth is that the travel industry is not very fair to people who vacation by themselves. People traveling alone almost invariably end up paying more than individuals traveling in pairs. Most travel bargains, including package tours, accommodations, resort packages, and cruises, are based on *double-occupancy* rates. This means that the per-person price is offered on the basis of two people traveling together and sharing a double room (which means they each will spend a good deal more on meals and extras). The single traveler will have to pay a surcharge, called a single supplement, for exactly the same package. In extreme cases, this can add as much as 30% to 55% to the basic per-person rate.

Don't despair, however. Throughout Europe, there are scores of smaller hotels and other hostelries where, in addition to a cozier atmosphere, prices still are quite reasonable for the single traveler. Some cruise lines have begun to offer special cruises for singles, and some resorts cater to the single traveler.

The obvious, most effective alternative is to find a traveling companion. Even special "singles' tours" that promise no supplements usually are based on people sharing double rooms. Perhaps the most recent innovation along these lines is the creation of organizations that "introduce" the single traveler to other single travelers, somewhat like a dating service. Some charge fees, others are free, but the basic service offered is the same: to match an unattached person with a compatible travel mate, often as part of the company's own package tours. Among such organizations are the following:

Jane's International (2603 Bath Ave., Brooklyn, NY 11214; phone: 718-266-2045). This service puts potential traveling companions in touch with one another. No age limit, no fee.

Odyssey Network (118 Cedar St., Wellesley, MA 02181; phone: 617-237-2400). Originally founded to match single women travelers, this company now includes men in its enrollment. *Odyssey* offers a quarterly newsletter for members who are seeking a travel companion, and occasionally organizes small group tours. A newsletter subscription is $50.

Partners-in-Travel (PO Box 491145, Los Angeles, CA 90049; phone: 213-476-4869). Members receive a list of singles seeking traveling companions; prospective companions make contact through the agency. The membership fee is $40 per year and includes a chatty newsletter (6 issues per year).

Travel Companion Exchange (PO Box 833, Amityville, NY 11701; phone: 516-454-0880). This group publishes a newsletter for singles and a directory of individuals looking for travel companions. On joining, members fill out a lengthy questionnaire and write a small listing (much like an ad in a personal column). Based on these listings, members can request copies of profiles and contact prospective traveling companions. It is wise to join well in advance of your planned vacation so that there's enough time to determine compatibility and plan a joint trip. Membership fees, including the newsletter, are $36 for 6 months or $60 a year for a single-sex listing; $66 and $120, respectively, for a complete listing. Subscription to the newsletter alone costs $24 for 6 months or $36 per year.

Also note that certain cruise lines offer guaranteed share rates for single travelers, whereby cabin mates are selected on request. Two cruise lines that provide such rates are *Cunard* (phone: 800-221-4770) and *Royal Cruise Line* (phone: 800-792-2992 or 415-956-7200 in California; 800-227-4534 elsewhere in the US).

In addition, a number of tour packagers cater to single travelers. These companies offer packages designed for individuals interested in vacationing with a group of single travelers or in being matched with a traveling companion. Among the better established of these agencies are the following:

Contiki Holidays (1432 E. Katella Ave., Anaheim, CA 92805; phone: 714-937-0611; 800-624-0611 in California; 800-626-0611 elsewhere in the continental US). Specializes in vacations for 18- to 35-year-olds. Packages to Europe frequently are offered. As this packager is a wholesaler, reservations must be booked through a travel agent.

Cosmos: This tour operator offers budget motorcoach tours of Europe with a guaranteed-share plan whereby singles who wish to share rooms (and avoid paying the single supplement) are matched by the tour escort with individuals of the same sex and charged the basic double-occupancy tour price. Contact the firm at one of its three North American branches: 95-25 Queens Blvd., Rego Park, NY 11374 (phone: 800-221-0090 from the eastern US); 150 S. Los Robles Ave., Pasadena, CA 91101 (phone: 818-449-0919 or 800-556-5454 from the western US); 1801 Eglinton Ave. W., Suite 104, Toronto, Ontario M6E 2H8, Canada (phone: 416-787-1281).

Gallivanting (515 E. 79th St., Suite 20F, New York, NY 10021; phone: 800-933-9699 or 212-988-0617). Caters to singles from 25 to 55 and offers trips featuring the history, archaeology, architecture, and art of Europe; also arranges custom tours. Single-share guarantee when bookings are paid for 75 days in advance.

Grand Circle Travel (347 Congress St., Boston, MA 02210; phone: 800-221-2610 or 617-350-7500). Arranges extended vacations, escorted tours, and cruises for the over-50 traveler, including singles. Membership, which is automatic when you book a trip through *Grand Circle,* includes travel discounts and other extras, such as a Pen Pals service for singles seeking traveling companions.

Insight International Tours (745 Atlantic Ave., Boston MA 02111; phone: 800-582-8380 or 617-482-2000). Offers a matching service for single travelers. Several tours are geared for travelers in the 18 to 35 age group.

Saga International Holidays (120 Boylston St., Boston MA 02116; phone: 800-343-0273 or 617-451-6808). A subsidiary of a British company specializing in older travelers, many of them single, *Saga* offers a broad selection of packages for people age 60 and over or those 50 to 59 traveling with someone 60 or older. Although anyone can book a *Saga* trip, a $15 club membership includes a subscription to their newsletter, as well as other publications and travel services — such as a matching service for single travelers.

Singles in Motion (545 W. 236th St., Suite 1D, Riverdale, NY 10463; phone: 212-884-4464). Offers a number of packages for single travelers, including tours, cruises, and excursions focusing on outdoor activities such as hiking and biking.

Singleworld (401 Theodore Fremd Ave., Rye, NY 10580; phone: 914-967-3334 or 800-223-6490 in the continental US). For a yearly fee of $25, this club books members on its tours and cruises, and arranges shared accommodations, allowing individual travelers to avoid the single supplement charge; members also receive a quarterly newsletter. *Singleworld* offers package tours for singles with departures categorized by age group (for those 35 or younger, or for all ages).

Solo Flights (127 S. Compo Rd., Westport, CT 06880; phone: 203-226-9993).

Represents a number of packagers and cruise lines and books singles on individual and group tours.

STI (8619 Reseda Blvd., Suite 103, Northridge, CA 91324; phone: 800-525-0525 or 818-886-0633). Specializes in travel for 18 to 30 year olds. Offers multi-country escorted tours ranging from 2 weeks to 2 months, including itineraries in Europe.

Suddenly Single Tours (161 Dreiser Loop, the Bronx, NY 10475; phone: 212-379-8800). Specializes in group tours for singles; many participants are over 40.

Travel in Two's (239 N. Broadway, Suite 3, N. Tarrytown, NY 10591; phone: 914-631-8409). This company books solo travelers on packages offered by a number of companies (at no extra cost to clients), offers its own tours, and matches singles with traveling companions. Many offerings are listed in their quarterly *Singles Vacation Newsletter,* which costs $7.50 per issue or $20 per year.

A good book for single travelers is *Traveling On Your Own,* by Eleanor Berman, which offers tips on traveling solo and includes information on trips for singles, ranging from outdoor adventures to educational programs. Available in bookstores, it also can be ordered by sending $12.95, plus postage and handling, to Random House, Order Dept., 400 Hahn Rd., Westminster, MD 21157 (phone: 800-733-3000).

Single travelers also may want to subscribe to *Going Solo,* a newsletter that offers helpful information on going on your own. Issued eight times a year, a subscription costs $36. Contact Doerfer Communications, PO Box 1035, Cambridge, MA 02238 (phone: 617-876-2764).

Single travelers interested in meeting Europeans may want to consider *Club Med,* which operates scores of resorts in more than 37 countries worldwide and caters to singles, as well as couples and families. Though the clientele often is under 30, there is a considerable age mix: the average age is 37 and the majority of these guests are European. There is 1 *Club Med* resort in Bulgaria; 12 in France; 5 in Greece; 1 in Ireland; 4 in Italy; 1 in Portugal; 4 in Spain; and 2 in Yugoslavia. *Club Med* offers single travelers package-rate vacations including airfare, food, lodging, entertainment, and athletic facilities. The atmosphere is relaxed, the dress informal, and the price reasonable. For information, contact *Club Med,* 3 E. 54th St., New York, NY 10022 (phone: 800-CLUB-MED).

For other possibilities that include an opportunity to visit with Europeans and accommodations alternatives suitable for single travelers, see our discussion of accommodations in *On the Road,* in this section.

WOMEN AND STUDENTS: Two specific groups of single travelers deserve special mention: women and students. Countless women travel by themselves in Europe, and such an adventure need not be feared.

One lingering inhibition many female travelers still harbor is that of eating alone in public places. The trick is to relax and enjoy your meal and surroundings; while you may run across the occasional unenlightened waiter, dining solo is no longer uncommon.

Studying Abroad – A large number of single travelers are students. Travel *is* education. Travel broadens a person's knowledge and deepens his or her perception of the world in a way no media or "armchair" experience ever could. In addition, to study a country's language, art, culture, or history in one of its own schools is to enjoy the most productive method of learning.

By "student" we do not necessarily mean a person who wishes to matriculate at a foreign university to earn an academic degree. Nor do we necessarily mean a younger person. A student is anyone who wishes to include some sort of educational program in a trip to Europe.

There are many benefits for students abroad, and the way to begin to discover them is to consult the *Council on International Educational Exchange (CIEE).* This organization, which runs a variety of well-known work, study, and travel programs for students, is the US sponsor of the International Student Identity Card (ISIC). Reductions on airfare, other transportation, and entry fees to most museums and other exhibitions are only some of the advantages of the card. To apply for it, write to *CIEE* at one of the following addresses: 205 E. 42nd St., New York, NY 10017 (phone: 212-661-1414); 312 Sutter St., Suite 407, San Francisco, CA 94108 (phone: 415-421-3473); and 919 Irving St., Suite 102, San Francisco, CA 94122 (phone: 415-566-6222). Mark the letter "Attn. Student ID." Application requires a $14 fee, a passport-size photograph, and proof that you are a matriculating student (this means either a transcript or a letter or bill from your school registrar with the school's official seal; high school and junior high school students can use their report cards). There is no maximum age limit, but participants must be at least 12 years old. The *ID Discount Guide,* which gives details of the discounts country by country, is free with membership. Another free publication of *CIEE* is the informative annual 64-page *Student Travel Catalog,* which covers all aspects of youth-travel abroad for vacation trips, jobs, or study programs, and also includes a list of other helpful publications. You can order the catalogue from the Information and Student Services Department at the New York address given above.

Another card of value in Europe, and also available through *CIEE,* is the Federation of International Youth Travel Organizations (FIYTO) card, which provides many of the benefits of the ISIC card. In this case, cardholders need not be students, merely under age 26. To apply, send $14 with a passport-size photo and proof of birth date to *CIEE* at one of the addresses above.

CIEE also sponsors charter flights to Europe that are open to students and non-students of any age. Flights between New York and Paris or London (with budget-priced add-ons available from Boston, Chicago, Denver, El Paso, Los Angeles, Las Vegas, Minneapolis, St. Louis, Salt Lake City, San Diego, San Francisco, Seattle, and several other US cities) arrive and depart daily from Kennedy (JFK) or Newark airports during the high season. Regularly scheduled direct flights also are offered from Boston to Brussels. Youth fares also may be offered by some scheduled airlines offering transatlantic service to Europe. To find out about current discounts and restrictions, contact the individual carriers. (Also see *Traveling by Plane,* in this section.)

A number of transportation discounts are available to students throughout Europe. *British Rail,* for example, offers discounts to students and youths. The *BritRail* Youth Pass, for anyone age 16 through 25, permits unlimited, economy class train travel throughout England, Scotland, and Wales for periods of 8, 15, or 22 days or 1 month. To buy a pass, contact your travel agent or *BritRail Travel International* offices in North America (for addresses and phone numbers, see *Traveling by Train,* in this section). The national rail companies of France, Ireland, and many other countries also offer discounts to students and youths.

For extensive travel throughout Europe, there is a version of the Eurailpass restricted to travelers (including non-students) under 26 years of age. The Eurail Youthpass entitles the bearer to either 1 or 2 months of unlimited second class rail travel in 17 countries. In addition, it is honored on many European steamers and ferries (including ferry crossings between Ireland and France on the *Irish Continental Line*) and on railroad connections between the airport and the center of town in various cities. The pass also entitles the bearer to reduced rates on some bus lines in several countries. The Eurail Youthpass can be purchased only by those living outside Europe or North Africa, and it must be purchased before departure. Eurailpasses can be bought from a US travel agent or from the national railway offices of the countries in the Eurail network (for further information, see *Traveling by Train,* in this section).

Students and singles in general should keep in mind that youth hostels exist in many cities throughout Europe. They always are inexpensive, generally clean and well situated, and they are a sure place to meet other people traveling alone. Hostels are run by the hosteling associations of 68 countries that make up the *International Youth Hostel Federation (IYHF);* membership in one of the national associations affords access to the hostels of the rest. To join the American affiliate, *American Youth Hostels (AYH),* contact the national office (PO Box 37613, Washington, DC 20013-7613; phone: 202-783-6161), or the local *AYH* council nearest you. As we went to press, the following membership rates were in effect: $25 for adults (between 18 and 54), $10 for youths (17 and under), $15 for seniors (55 and up), and $35 for family membership. *Hostelling North America,* which lists hostels in the US and Canada, comes with your *AYH* card (non-members can purchase the handbook for $5, plus postage and handling); the *Guide to Budget Accommodation, Volume 1,* covers hostels in Europe (*Volume 2* covers the rest of the world) and must be purchased ($10.95, plus postage and handling).

Those who go abroad without an *AYH* card may purchase a youth hostel International Guest Card (usually for under $20), and obtain information on local youth hostels by contacting one of the national youth hostel associations in Europe. Other sources of information include European tourist boards, which may provide information sheets on hostels in their areas (see the individual city reports in THE CITIES for locations).

Another option is *Campus Holidays USA* (242 Bellevue Ave., Upper Montclair, NJ 07043; phone: 201-744-8724 in New Jersey; 800-526-2915 elsewhere in the US), which offers accommodations at universities in England and Scotland. It includes single, twin, and even triple rooms for friends or families traveling together.

In Great Britain, the *YMCA* and the *YWCA* also run economical accommodations. You can get a list of *Y*s in Britain by writing to *YMCA/YWCA Accommodations, National Council of YMCAs* (640 Forest Rd., Walthamstow, London E17 3DZ, England; phone: 44-81-520-5599), or the *Young Women's Christian Association of Great Britain* (52 Cornmarket St., Oxford OX1 3EJ, England; phone: 44-865-726110). These agencies will not book rooms for travelers, however, so reservations must be made directly with the *Y* of your choice.

Those interested in campus stays should know about the *U.S. and Worldwide Travel Accommodations Guide,* which lists colleges and universities throughout Europe that offer simple, but comfortable, accommodations in their residence halls, primarily during the summer season. The accommodations vary from single and double rooms to full apartments and suites with kitchens, and the rooms can be booked by the day, week, or month. Prices range from $12 to $24 per night, with an average of about $20. An added bonus of this type of arrangement is that visitors usually are free to utilize various campus sport and recreation facilities. For a copy of the guide, which describes services and facilities in detail, send $12.95 to *Campus Travel Service,* PO Box 8355, Newport Beach, CA 92660 (phone: 714-720-3729).

And there's always camping. Virtually any area of the countryside in Europe has a place to pitch a tent and enjoy the scenery. (For more information, see *Camping and Caravanning, Hiking and Biking,* in this section.)

Opportunities for study range from summer or academic-year courses in a language and civilization of a European country designed specifically for foreigners (including those whose school days are well behind them) to long-term university attendance by those intending to take a degree.

Complete details on more than 3,000 available courses abroad (including at European universities) and suggestions on how to apply are contained in two books published by the *Institute of International Education* (IIE Books, Publications Office, 809 UN Plaza, New York, NY 10017; phone: 212-984-5412): *Vacation Study Abroad*

($26.95, plus shipping and handling) and *Academic Year Abroad* ($31.95, plus shipping and handling). A third book, *Teaching Abroad,* costs $21.95, plus shipping and handling. IIE Books also offers a free pamphlet called *Basic Facts on Study Abroad.*

The *National Registration Center for Study Abroad (NRCSA;* PO Box 1393, Milwaukee, WI 53201; phone: 414-278-0631) also offers a publication called the *Worldwide Classroom: Study Abroad and Learning Vacations in 40 Countries: 1991-1992,* available for $5, plus $3 shipping and handling, which includes information on over 160 schools and cultural centers that offer courses for Americans with the primary focus on foreign language and culture.

Those who are interested in a "learning vacation" abroad also may be interested in *Travel and Learn* by Evelyn Kaye. This guide to educational travel discusses a wide range of opportunities — everything from archaeology to whale watching — and provides information on organizations that offer programs in these areas of interest. The book is available in bookstores for $23.95; or you can send $26 (which includes shipping charges) to Blue Penguin Publications (147 Sylvan Ave., Leonia, NJ 07605; phone: 800-800-8147 or 201-461-6918). *Learning Vacations* by Gerson G. Eisenberg also provides extensive information on seminars, workshops, courses, and so on — in a wide variety of subjects. Available in bookstores, it also can be ordered from Peterson's Guides (PO Box 2123, Princeton, NJ 08543-2123; phone: 800-338-3282 or 609-243-9111) for $11.95, plus shipping and handling.

Work, Study, Travel Abroad: The Whole World Handbook, issued by the *Council on International Educational Exchange (CIEE),* is an informative, chatty guide on study programs, work opportunities, and travel hints, with a particularly good section on Europe. It is available for $10.95, plus shipping and handling, from *CIEE* (address above).

AFS Intercultural Programs (313 E. 43rd St., New York, NY 10017; phone: 800-AFS-INFO or 212-949-4242) sets up exchanges between US and foreign high school students on an individual basis for a semester or a whole academic year.

National Association of Secondary School Principals (NASSP; 1904 Association Dr., Reston, VA 22091; phone: 703-860-0200), an association of administrators, teachers, and state education officials, sponsors *School Partnership International,* a program in which secondary schools in the US are linked with partner schools abroad for an annual short-term exchange of students and faculty.

If you are interested in a home-stay travel program, in which you learn about European culture by living with a family, contact the *Experiment in International Living.* Its *School for International Training* offers academic semesters for college students at a number of European universities. The organization's short-term home-stay programs also are educational in focus and are offered in over 40 countries, including locations throughout Europe. For further information, contact *Experiment in International Living,* PO Box 676, Brattleboro, VT 05302-0676 (phone: 802-257-7751 in Vermont; 800-451-4465 elsewhere in the continental US).

Another organization specializing in travel as an educational experience is the *American Institute for Foreign Study (AIFS;* 102 Greenwich Ave., Greenwich, CT 06830; phone: 800-727-AIFS, 203-869-9090, or 203-863-6087). Students can enroll for the full academic year or for any number of semesters. *AIFS* caters primarily to bona fide high school or college students, but its non-credit international learning programs are open to independent travelers of all ages (approximately 20% of *AIFS* students are over 25).

WORKING ABROAD: Jobs for foreigners in Europe are not easy to come by and in general do not pay well enough to cover all the expenses of a trip. They do provide an invaluable learning experience, however, while helping to make a trip more affordable.

For a complete list of work/study programs administered by institutions in Europe, contact the government tourist offices in North America (see *Tourist Information Offices,* in this section, for addresses).

Hints for Older Travelers

Special discounts and more free time are just two factors that have given Americans over age 65 a chance to see the world at affordable prices. Senior citizens make up an ever-growing segment of the travel population, and the trend among them is to travel more frequently and for longer periods of time.

PLANNING: When planning a vacation, prepare your itinerary with one eye on your own physical condition and the other on a topographical map. Keep in mind variations in climate, terrain, and altitudes, which may pose some danger for anyone with heart or breathing problems.

Older travelers may find the following publications of interest:

The Discount Guide for Travelers Over 55, by Caroline and Walter Weintz, is an excellent book for budget-conscious older travelers. It is available by sending $7.95, plus shipping and handling, to Penguin USA (Att. Cash Sales, 120 Woodbine St., Bergenfield, NJ 07621); when ordering, specify the ISBN number: 0-525-48358-6.

Going Abroad: 101 Tips for Mature Travelers offers tips on preparing for your trip, commonsense precautions en route, and some basic travel terminology. This concise, free booklet is available from *Grand Circle Travel,* 347 Congress St., Boston, MA 02210 (phone: 800-221-2610 or 617-350-7500).

The International Health Guide for Senior Citizen Travelers, by Dr. W. Robert Lange, covers such topics as trip preparations, food and water precautions, adjusting to weather and climate conditions, finding a doctor, motion sickness, jet lag, and so on. Also includes a list of resource organizations that provide medical assistance for travelers. It is available for $4.95 postpaid from Pilot Books, 103 Cooper St., Babylon, NY 11702 (phone: 516-422-2225).

The Mature Traveler is a monthly newsletter that provides information on travel discounts, places of interest, useful tips, and other topics of interest for travelers 49 and up. To subscribe, send $21.95 to GEM Publishing Group, PO Box 50820, Reno, NV 89513 (phone: 702-786-7419).

Travel Easy: The Practical Guide for People Over 50, by Rosalind Massow, discusses a wide range of subjects — from trip planning, transportation options, and preparing for departure to avoiding and handling medical problems en route. It's available for $6.50 to members of the *American Association of Retired Persons (AARP),* and for $8.95 to non-members; call about current charges for postage and handling. Order from *AARP* Books, c/o Customer Service, Scott, Foresman & Company, 1900 E. Lake Ave., Glenview, IL 60025 (phone: 708-729-3000).

Travel Tips for Older Americans is a useful booklet that provides good, basic advice. This US State Department publication (stock number: 044-000-02270-2) can be ordered by sending a check or money order for $1 to the Superintendent of Documents (US Government Printing Office, Washington, DC 20402) or by calling 202-783-3238 and charging the order to a credit card.

Unbelievably Good Deals & Great Adventures That You Absolutely Can't Get Unless You're Over 50, by Joan Rattner Heilman, offers travel tips for older travelers, including discounts on accommodations and transportation, as well as a list of organizations for seniors. It is available for $7.95, plus shipping and handling, from Contemporary Books, 180 N. Michigan Ave., Chicago, IL 60601 (phone: 312-782-9181).

HEALTH: Health facilities in Europe generally are excellent; however, an inability to speak the language can pose a serious problem, not in receiving treatment at large hospitals, where many doctors and other staff members will speak English, but in getting help elsewhere or in getting to the place where help is available. A number of organizations exist to help travelers avoid or deal with a medical emergency overseas. For information on these services, see *Medical and Legal Aid and Consular Services,* in this section.

Pre-trip medical and dental checkups are strongly recommended. In addition, be sure to take along any prescription medication you need, enough to last *without a new prescription* for the duration of your trip; pack all medications with a note from your doctor for the benefit of airport authorities. If you have specific medical problems, bring prescriptions and a "medical file" composed of the following:

1. A summary of medical history and current diagnosis.
2. A list of drugs to which you are allergic.
3. Your most recent electrocardiogram, if you have heart problems.
4. Your doctor's name, address, and telephone number.

DISCOUNTS AND PACKAGES: Since guidelines change from place to place, it is a good idea to inquire in advance about discounts for transportation, hotels, concerts, movies, museums, and other activities. The tourist offices in the US and the local tourist information offices in Europe can give the most up-to-date information about discounts and programs for older travelers (for addresses see *Tourist Information Offices,* in this section, as well as the individual city reports in THE CITIES).

Many hotel chains, airlines, cruise lines, bus companies, car rental companies, and other travel suppliers offer discounts to older travelers. US airlines such as *American, Continental, Northwest, TWA, United* and *USAir* offer those age 62 and over (and one traveling companion per qualifying senior citizen) discounts on flights from the US to Europe. Foreign airlines such as *Alitalia, British Airways, KLM, LOT Polish Airlines, Lufthansa, SAS,* and *TAP Air Portugal* also offer discounts for passengers age 60 (or 62) and over, which also may apply to one traveling companion. For information on current prices and applicable restrictions, contact the individual carriers.

In France, the *Carte Vermeil* entitles anyone over 60 to a variety of discounts, including a 60% discount on rail fares in France during off-peak hours if the ticket is bought in France. The card, which is available only in France, can be obtained by filling out a form at a major railroad station and presenting it, along with one's passport, to the designated official at the station, and is valid for 1 year.

In Great Britain, *British Rail* offers a Senior Citizen Pass for those 60 and older. It permits unlimited first class train travel through England, Scotland, and Wales at less than the cost of a regular first class *BritRail* pass. Both are available for 8, 15, or 22 days or 1 month and must be purchased before entering Great Britain. *Northern Irelands Railways'* Rail Runabout Ticket, bought in Northern Ireland and good for 7 consecutive days of unlimited train travel, is half price to senior citizens. In Italy, the *Carta d'Argento* (Silver Card) entitles men and women over 60 to a 30% discount on rail fares in Italy. This card can be bought in Italy at rail stations, *CIT* offices (see *Traveling by Train,* in this section), and certain other travel agencies on presentation of a passport, and is valid for 1 year.

On *British Airways,* seniors can apply for a Privilege Traveler Card which costs $10 and entitles them to 10% discounts on all fares and waives any penalties. Seniors also are offered 10% off *Cunard* cruises, rail travel abroad the *Venice Simplon–Orient Express,* if arrangements are made through *British Airways.* This card also covers a companion who is 55 or older. Keep in mind that it takes 4 to 6 weeks to process new card applications. For information, call *British Airways* (phone: 800-AIRWAYS).

Some discounts, however, are extended only to bona fide members of certain senior citizens organizations. Because the same organizations frequently offer package tours to both domestic and international destinations, the benefits of membership are twofold: Those who join can take advantage of discounts as individual travelers and also reap the savings that group travel affords. In addition, because the age requirements for some of these organizations are quite low (or nonexistent), the benefits can begin to accrue early.

In order to take advantage of these discounts, you should carry proof of your age (or eligibility). A driver's license, membership card in a recognized senior citizen's organization, or a Medicare card should be adequate. Among the organizations dedicated to helping older travelers see the world are the following:

American Association of Retired Persons (*AARP;* 1909 K St. NW, Washington, DC 20049; phone: 202-872-4700). The largest and best known of these organizations. Membership is open to anyone 50 or over, whether retired or not; dues are $5 a year, $12.50 for 3 years, or $35 for 10 years, and include spouse. The *AARP* Travel Experience Worldwide program, available through *American Express Travel Related Services* offers members tours, cruises, and other travel programs worldwide designed exclusively for older travelers. Members can book these services by calling *American Express* at 800-927-0111 for land and air travel, or 800-745-4567 for cruises.

Mature Outlook (Customer Service Center, 6001 N. Clark St., Chicago, IL 60660; phone: 800-336-6330). Through its *Travel Alert,* tours, cruises, and other vacation packages are available to members at special savings. Hotel and car rental discounts and travel accident insurance also are available. Membership is open to anyone 50 years of age or older, costs $9.95 a year, and includes a bimonthly newsletter and magazine, as well as information on package tours.

National Council of Senior Citizens (1331 F St., Washington, DC 20005; phone: 202-347-8800). Here, too, the emphasis is on keeping costs low. This nonprofit organization offers members a different roster of package tours each year, as well as individual arrangements through its affiliated travel agency *(Vantage Travel Service).* Although most members are over 50, membership is open to anyone (regardless of age) for an annual fee of $12 per person or couple. Lifetime membership costs $150.

Certain travel agencies and tour operators offer special trips geared to older travelers. Among them are the following:

Evergreen Travel Service (4114 198th St. SW, Suite 13, Lynnwood, WA 98036-6742; phone: 206-776-1184 or 800-435-2288 throughout the continental US and Canada). This specialist in trips for persons with disabilities recently introduced Lazybones Tours, a program offering leisurely tours for older travelers. Most programs are first class or deluxe, and include an escort.

Gadabout Tours (700 E. Tahquitz, Palm Springs, CA 92262; phone: 619-325-5556 or 800-521-7309 in California; 800-952-5068 elsewhere in the US). Offers a number of escorted tours and cruises for singles to Europe, including Austria, Great Britain, Ireland, and Spain.

Grand Circle Travel (347 Congress St., Boston, MA 02210; phone: 800-221-2610 or 617-350-7500). Caters exclusively to the over-50 traveler and packages a large variety of escorted tours, cruises, and extended vacations. Membership, which is automatic when you book a trip through *Grand Circle,* includes discount certificates on future trips and other travel services, such as a matching service for single travelers and a helpful free booklet, *Going Abroad: 101 Tips for Mature Travelers* (see the source list above).

Grandtravel (6900 Wisconsin Ave., Suite 706, Chevy Chase, MD 20815; phone: 301-986-0790 in Maryland; 800-247-7651 elsewhere in the US). An agency that specializes in trips for grandparents and their grandchildren (aunts and uncles are welcome, too), bringing the generations together through travel. Several itineraries coincide with school vacations and emphasize historic and natural sites. Transportation, accommodations, and activities are thoughtfully arranged to meet the needs of the young and the young-at-heart.

Insight International Tours (745 Atlantic Ave., Boston, MA 02111; phone: 800-582-8380 or 617-482-2000). Offers a matching service for single travelers. Several tours are geared for mature travelers.

OmniTours (1 Northfield Plaza, Northfield, IL 60093; phone: 800-962-0060 or 708-441-5250). Offers combination air and rail group tours designed for travelers 50 years and older.

Saga International Holidays (120 Boylston St., Boston MA 02116; phone: 617-451-6808 or 800-343-0273). A subsidiary of a British company catering to older travelers, *Saga* offers a broad selection of packages for people age 60 and over or those 50 to 59 traveling with someone 60 or older. Although anyone can book a *Saga* trip, a $15 club membership includes a subscription to their newsletter, as well as other publications and travel services.

Yugotours (350 Fifth Ave., Suite 2212, New York, NY 10118; phone: 800-223-5298 or 212-563-2400). This tour operator offers packages to Spain and Yugoslavia designed for older travelers.

Many travel agencies, particularly the larger ones, are delighted to make presentations to help a group of senior citizens select destinations. A local chamber of commerce should be able to provide the names of such agencies. Once a time and place are determined, an organization member or travel agent can obtain group quotations for transportation, accommodations, meal plans, and sightseeing. Larger groups usually get the best breaks.

Another choice open to older travelers is a trip that includes an educational element. *Elderhostel,* a nonprofit organization, offers programs at educational institutions worldwide, including Austria, Denmark, France, Germany, Great Britain, Greece, Ireland, Italy, the Netherlands, Norway, Portugal, the Soviet Union, Spain, and Switzerland. The foreign programs generally last about 2 weeks, and include double-occupancy accommodations in hotels or student residence halls and all meals. Travel to the programs usually is by designated scheduled flights, and participants can arrange to extend their stay at the end of the program. Elderhostelers must be at least 60 years old (younger if a spouse or companion qualifies), in good health, and not in need of special diets. For a free catalogue describing the program and current offerings, write to *Elderhostel* (75 Federal St., Boston, MA 02110; phone: 617-426-7788). Those interested in the program also can borrow slides at no charge or purchase an informational videotape for $5.

Interhostel, a program sponsored by the Division of Continuing Education of the University of New Hampshire, sends travelers back to school at cooperating institutions in 25 countries on 4 continents, including Austria, Czechoslovakia, France, Germany, Great Britain, Greece, Holland, Hungary, Ireland, Italy, Norway, Poland, Portugal, the Soviet Union, Sweden, and Switzerland. Participants attend lectures on the history, economy, politics, and cultural life of the country they are visiting, go on field trips to pertinent points of interest, and take part in activities meant to introduce them to their foreign contemporaries. Trips are for 2 weeks; accommodations are on campus in university residence halls or off campus in modest hotels (double occupancy). Groups are limited to 35 to 40 participants who are at least 50 years old (or at least 40 if a participating spouse is at least 50), physically active, and not in need of special diets. For further information or to receive the three free seasonal catalogues, contact *Interhostel*, UNH Division of Continuing Education, 6 Garrison Ave., Durham, NH 03824 (phone: 800-733-9753 or 603-862-1147).

Hints for Traveling with Children

 What better way to encounter the world's variety than in the company of the wide-eyed members of your family? Their presence does not have to be a burden or an excessive expense. The current generation of discounts for children and family package deals can make a trip together quite reasonable.

A family trip will be an investment in your children's future, making geography and history come alive to them, and leaving a sure memory that will be among the fondest you will share with them someday. Their insights will be refreshing to you; their impulses may take you to unexpected places with unexpected dividends.

PLANNING: Here are several hints for making a trip with children easy and fun.

1. Children, like everyone else, will derive more pleasure from a trip if they know something about the country before they arrive. Begin their education about a month before you leave. Using maps, travel magazines, and books, give children a clear idea of where you are going and how far away it is.

2. Children should help to plan the itinerary, and where you go and what you do should reflect some of their ideas. If they already know something about the sites they'll visit, they will have the excitement of recognition when they arrive.

3. Children also will enjoy learning some phrases in the languages of the countries you will be visiting — a few basics like "hello," "good-bye," and "thank you."

4. Familiarize the children with foreign currencies. Give them an allowance for the trip, and be sure they understand just how far it will or won't go.

5. Give children specific responsibilities: The job of carrying their own flight bags and looking after their personal things, along with some other light chores, will give them a stake in the journey.

6. Give each child a diary or scrapbook to take along.

Audiocassettes may make European countries come alive for children. One useful resource to which you may want to refer is the *Berlitz Jr.* instructional series for children, which is available in French and Spanish editions. The series combines an illustrated storybook with a lively 60-minute audiocassette. Each book features a character, Teddy, who goes to school and learns to count and spell and speak foreign phrases. The book/cassette package is available for $19.95, plus shipping and handling, from Macmillan Publishing Company, Front and Brown Sts., Riverside, NJ 08075 (phone: 800-257-5755).

Children's books about Europe provide an excellent introduction to the continent and its various cultures. Some particularly good titles include the following:

> *Art For Children* is a delightful series by Ernest Raboff (HarperCollins; $11.95 hardcover; $5.95 paperback) designed to introduce children ages 5 to 12 to famous artists and their works. There are 16 books in the series, each one concentrating on a different artist.
>
> *Atlas of Ancient Greece and Atlas of Ancient Rome,* by Anton Powell (Facts on File; $17.95 each), are part of a series that explores ancient civilizations. Fully illustrated, they are packed with information and will add excitement to any ruins that children may encounter in Europe.
>
> *Castle,* by David Macaulay (Houghton Mifflin; $14.95 hardcover; $6.95 paper-

back). Using text and drawings, this book shows how castles were built in the 13th century, and is particularly suited to helping children from kindergarten to grade 5 learn about the castles they may see in Europe.

Cathedral: The Story of Its Construction, by the same author (Houghton Mifflin; $14.95 hardcover; $6.95 paperback). Another interesting and informative book — a must for those visiting St. Peter's in the Vatican in Italy; Chartres, Notre-Dame, and Sacré-Coeur in France; and other great cathedrals in Europe.

Great Painters, by Pierra Ventura (G. P. Putnam & Sons; $20.95), is a beautifully illustrated introduction to English, Flemish, French, and Italian painting for older children (ages 12 and up).

Walls: Defenses Throughout History, by James Giblin (Little, Brown; $14.45), discusses the walled city of Carcassonne, Hadrian's Wall in England, and the great defensive walls of World Wars I and II, among others.

These and other children's books can be found at many general bookstores and libraries. Bookstores specializing in children's books include the following:

Books of Wonder (132 7th Ave., New York, NY 10011; phone: 212-989-3270; or 464 Hudson St., New York, NY 10014; phone: 212-645-8006). Carries both new and used books for children.

Cheshire Cat (5512 Connecticut Ave. NW, Washington, DC 20015; phone: 202-244-3956). Specializes in books for children of all ages.

Eeyore's Books for Children (2212 Broadway, New York, NY 10024; phone: 212-362-0634; or 25 E. 83rd St., New York, NY 10028; phone: 212-988-3404). Carries an extensive selection of children's books; features a special travel section.

Reading Reptile, Books and Toys for Young Mammals (4120 Pennsylvania, Kansas City, MO 64111; phone: 816-753-0441). Carries books for children and teens to age 15.

Red Balloon (891 Grand Ave., St. Paul, MN 55105; phone: 612-224-8320). Carries both new and used books for children.

White Rabbit Children's Books (7755 Girard Ave., La Jolla, CA 92037; phone: 619-454-3518). Carries books and music for children (and parents).

Another source of children's books perfect to take on the road is *The Family Travel Guides Catalogue.* This detailed booklet contains informative and amusing titles focusing on numerous countries. For instance, the *Travel Papers,* a series of short articles full of useful facts for families, covers several European countries, including France, Great Britain, and Italy. The *Travel Papers* and the catalogue are available from Carousel Press (PO Box 6061, Albany, CA 94706; phone: 510-527-5849), which also is the mail-order supplier of all titles listed in the catalogue.

And for parents, *Travel With Your Children* (*TWYCH;* 80 Eighth Ave., New York, NY 10011; phone: 212-206-0688) publishes a newsletter, *Family Travel Times,* that focuses on families with young travelers and offers helpful hints. An annual subscription (10 issues) is $35 and includes a copy of the "Airline Guide" issue (updated every other year), which focuses on the subject of flying with children. This special issue is available separately for $10.

Another newsletter devoted to family travel is *Getaways.* This quarterly publication provides reviews of family-oriented literature, activities, and useful travel tips. To subscribe, send $25 to *Getaways,* Att. Ms. Brooke Kane, PO Box 11511, Washington, DC 20008 (phone: 703-534-8747).

Also of interest to parents traveling with their children is *How to Take Great Trips With Your Kids,* by psychologist Sanford Portnoy and his wife, Joan Flynn Portnoy. The book includes helpful tips from fellow family travelers, tips on economical accommodations and touring by car, recreational vehicle, and train, as well as over 50 games to play with your children en route. It is available for $8.95, plus shipping and handling, from Harvard Common Press, 535 Albany St., Boston, MA 02118 (phone: 617-423-5803). Another title worth looking for is *Great Vacations with Your Kids,* by Dorothy Jordan (Dutton; $12.95).

A series of books called "Kidding Around" includes a Paris volume and a London volume. Each book starts with an overview of the city, along with some interesting background information, and then is divided into areas, with descriptions of the various attractions in the general order in which you might encounter them. These books can be ordered directly from the publisher by sending $9.95, plus shipping, to John Muir Publications, PO Box 613, Santa Fe, NM 87504, or by calling 800-888-7504 or 505-982-4078.

Another book on family travel, *Travel with Children,* by Maureen Wheeler, offers a wide range of practical tips on traveling with children, and includes accounts of the author's family travel experiences. It is available for $10.95, plus shipping and handling, from Lonely Planet Publications, Embarcadero West, 112 Linden St., Oakland, CA 94607 (phone: 415-893-8555).

Finally, parents arranging a trip with their children may want to deal with an agency specializing in family travel such as *Let's Take the Kids* (1268 Devon Ave., Los Angeles, CA 90024; phone: 800-726-4349 or 213-274-7088). In addition to arranging and booking trips for individual families, this group occasionally organizes trips for single-parent families traveling together. They also offer a parent travel network, whereby parents who have been to a particular destination can evaluate it for others.

GETTING THERE AND GETTING AROUND: Begin early to investigate all available discount and charter flights, as well as any package deals and special rates offered by the major airlines. Booking sometimes is required up to 2 months in advance. You may well find that charter plans offer no reductions for children, or not enough to offset the risk of last-minute delays or other inconveniences to which charters are subject. The major scheduled airlines, on the other hand, almost invariably provide hefty discounts for children (for specific information on fares and in-flight accommodations for children, also see *Traveling by Plane,* in this section).

PLANE: When you make your reservations, tell the airline that you are traveling with a child. Children ages 2 through 12 generally travel at about a half to two-thirds of the regular full-fare adult ticket prices on most international flights. This children's fare, however, usually is much higher than the excursion fare, which is applicable to any traveler regardless of age. On many international flights, children under 2 travel at about 10% of the adult fare if they sit on an adult's lap. A second infant without a second adult would pay the fare applicable to children ages 2 through 11.

Although some airlines will, on request, supply bassinets for infants, most carriers encourage parents to bring their own safety seat on board, which then is strapped into the airline seat with a regular seat belt. This is much safer — and certainly more comfortable — than holding the child in your lap. If you do not purchase a seat for your baby, you have the option of bringing the infant restraint along on the off-chance that there might be an empty seat next to yours — in which case some airlines will let you use that seat at no charge for your baby and infant seat. However, if there is no empty seat available, the infant seat no doubt will have to be checked as baggage (and you may have to pay an additional charge), since it generally does not fit under airplane seats or in the overhead racks. The safest bet is to pay for a seat.

Be forewarned: Some safety seats designed primarily for use in cars do not fit into plane seats properly. Although nearly all seats manufactured since 1985 carry labels indicating whether they meet federal standards for use aboard planes, actual seat sizes may vary from carrier to carrier. At the time of this writing, the FAA was in the process of reviewing and revising the federal regulations regarding infant travel and safety devices — it was still to be determined if children should be *required* to sit in safety seats and whether the airlines will have to provide them.

If using one of these infant restraints, you should try to get bulkhead seats which will provide extra room to care for your child during the flight. You also should request a bulkhead seat when using a bassinet — again, this is not as safe as strapping the child in. On some planes bassinets hook into a bulkhead wall; on others it is placed on the floor in front of you. (Note that bulkhead seats often are reserved for families traveling with children.) As a general rule, babies should be held during takeoff and landing.

Request seats on the aisle if you have a toddler or if you think you will need to use the bathroom frequently. Carry onto the plane all you will need to care for and occupy your children during the flight — formula, diapers, a sweater, books, favorite stuffed animals, and so on. Dress your baby simply, with a minimum of buttons and snaps, because the only place you may have to change a diaper is at your seat or in a small lavatory. The flight attendant can warm a bottle for you.

On most US carriers, you also can ask for a hot dog or hamburger instead of the airline's regular dinner if you give at least 24 hours' notice. Some, but not all, airlines have baby food aboard. While you should bring along toys from home, also ask about children's diversions. Some carriers have terrific free packages of games, coloring books, and puzzles.

When the plane takes off and lands, make sure your baby is nursing or has a bottle, pacifier, or thumb in its mouth. This sucking will make the child swallow and help to clear stopped ears. A piece of hard candy will do the same thing for an older child.

Parents traveling by plane with toddlers, children, or teenagers may want to consult *When Kids Fly,* a free booklet published by Massport (Public Affairs Department, 10 Park Plaza, Boston, MA 02116-3971; phone: 617-973-5600), which includes helpful information on airfares for children, infant seats, what to do in the event of overbooked or cancelled flights, and so on.

■**Note:** Newborn babies, whose lungs may not be able to adjust to the altitude, should not be taken aboard an airplane. And some airlines may refuse to allow a pregnant woman in her 8th or 9th month to fly. Check with the airline ahead of time, and carry a letter from your doctor stating that you are fit to travel — and indicating the estimated date of birth.

SHIP AND TRAIN: Some shipping lines offer cruises that feature special activities for children, particularly during periods that coincide with major school holidays like *Christmas, Easter,* and the summer months. On such cruises, children may be charged special cut-rate fares, and there are youth counselors to organize activities. Occasionally, a shipping line even offers free passage during the summer months for children under age 16 occupying a stateroom with two (full-fare) adult passengers. Your travel agent should know which cruise lines offer such programs.

If you plan to travel by train when abroad, note that on some European railways, children under 4 (accompanied by an adult) travel free, provided they do not occupy a seat; children under 4 occupying a seat and from ages 4 through 11 also often travel at a lower fare. Policies vary greatly from country to country. In Switzerland, for instance, children under 16 (traveling with at least one parent) travel free. The Eurailpass, which is good for unlimited train travel throughout Europe, is half price for children ages 4 through 11. For further information, see *Traveling by Ship* and *Traveling by Train.*

CAR: Touring by car allows greater flexibility in traveling and packing. You may want to stock the car with a variety of favorite snacks. Games and simple toys, such as magnetic checkerboards or drawing pencils and pads, also provide a welcome diversion. Frequent stops so that children can run around make car travel much easier.

ACCOMMODATIONS AND MEALS: Often a cot for a child will be placed in a hotel room at little or no extra charge. If you wish to sleep in separate rooms, special rates sometimes are available for families; some places do not charge for children under a certain age. In many of the larger chain hotels, the staffs are more used to children. These hotels also are likely to have swimming pools or gamerooms — both popular with most youngsters. Many large resorts also have recreation centers for children. Cabins, bungalows, condominiums, and other rental options offer families privacy, flexibility, some kitchen facilities, and often lower costs.

You might want to look into accommodations along the way that will add to the color of your trip. For instance, country inns, farmhouses, and cottages throughout Europe provide a delightful experience for the whole family and permit a view of European life different from that gained in a conventional hotel. And don't forget castles, châteaux, old manor houses, and palaces — many of which double as hotels. Children will love them.

Among the least expensive options is a camping facility; many are situated in beautiful, out-of-the-way spots, and generally are good, well equipped, and less expensive than any hotel. For further information on accommodations options for the whole family, see our discussions in *On the Road,* and for information on camping facilities, see *Camping and Caravanning, Hiking and Biking,* both in this section.

Better hotels in Europe may be able to arrange for a sitter for the times you will want to be without the children — for an evening's entertainment or a particularly rigorous stint of sightseeing. Whether the sitter is hired directly or through an agency, ask for and check references.

At mealtime, don't deny yourself or your children the delights of a new style of cooking. Encourage them to try new things. Children like to know what kind of food to expect, so it will be interesting to look up European dishes before leaving. And don't forget about picnics. Note that although milk is pasteurized and water is potable in large cities throughout Europe, it's wise to stick to bottled water for small children and for those with sensitive stomachs.

Things to Remember

1. If you are spending your vacation touring many places, pace the days with children in mind. Break the trip into half-day segments, with running around or "doing" time built in. Keep travel time on the road to a maximum of 4 to 5 hours a day.
2. Don't forget that a child's attention span is far shorter than an adult's. Children don't have to see every sight or all of any sight to learn something from their trip; watching, playing with, and talking to other children can be equally enlightening.
3. Let your children lead the way sometimes; their perspective is different from yours, and they may lead you to things you would never have noticed on your own.
4. Remember the places that children love to visit: aquariums, zoos, amusement parks, beaches, nature trails, and so on. Among the activities that may pique their interest are bicycling, snorkeling, boat trips, horseback riding, visiting children's museums, and viewing natural-habitat exhibits.

Staying Healthy

The surest way to return home in good health is to be prepared for medical problems that might occur on vacation. Below, we've outlined some things you need to think about before you go.

Older travelers or anyone suffering from a chronic medical condition, such as diabetes, high blood pressure, cardiopulmonary disease, asthma, or ear, eye, or sinus trouble, should consult a physician before leaving home. Those with conditions requiring special consideration when traveling should consider seeing, in addition to their regular physician, a specialist in travel medicine. For a referral in a particular community, contact the nearest medical school or ask a local doctor to recommend such a specialist. Dr. Leonard Marcus, a member of the *American Committee on Clinical Tropical Medicine and Travelers' Health,* provides a directory of more than 100 travel doctors across the country. For a copy, send a 9- by 12-inch self-addressed, stamped envelope, plus postage, to Dr. Marcus at 148 Highland Ave., Newton, MA 02165 (phone: 617-527-4003).

FIRST AID: Put together a compact, personal medical kit including Band-Aids, first-aid cream, antiseptic, nose drops, insect repellent, aspirin, an extra pair of prescription glasses or contact lenses (and a copy of your prescription for glasses or contact lenses); sunglasses; over-the-counter remedies for diarrhea, indigestion, and motion sickness; a thermometer; and a supply of those prescription medicines you take regularly.

In a corner of your kit, keep a list of all the drugs you have brought and their purpose, as well as duplicate copies of your doctor's prescriptions (or a note from your doctor). As brand names may vary in different countries, it's a good idea to ask your doctor for the generic name of any drugs you use so that you can ask for their equivalent should you need a refill.

It also is a good idea to ask your doctor to prepare a medical identification card that includes such information as your blood type, your social security number, any allergies or chronic health problems you have, and your medical insurance information. Considering the essential contents of your kit, keep it with you, rather than in your checked luggage.

SUNBURN: The burning power of the sun can quickly cause severe sunburn or sunstroke. To protect yourself against these ills, wear sunglasses, take along a broad-brimmed hat and cover-up, and use a sunscreen lotion.

WATER SAFETY: Europe is famous for its beaches, but it's important to remember that the sea, especially the wild Atlantic and the Mediterranean, can be treacherous. A few precautions are necessary. Beware of the undertow, that current of water running back down the beach after a wave has washed ashore; it can knock you off your feet and into the surf. Even more dangerous is the riptide, a strong current of water running against the tide, which can pull you out to sea. If you get caught offshore, don't panic or try to fight the current, because it will only exhaust you; instead, ride it out while waiting for it to subside, which usually happens not too far from shore, or try swimming away parallel to the beach.

Sharks are sometimes sighted, but they usually don't come in close to shore, and they are well fed on fish. Should you meet up with one, just swim away as quietly and smoothly as you can, without shouting or splashing. Although not aggressive, eels can be dangerous when threatened. If snorkeling or diving in coastal waters or freshwater lakes or streams, beware of crevices where these creatures may be lurking. The tentacled Portuguese man-of-war and other jellyfish also may drift in quiet salt waters for food and often wash up onto the beach; the long tentacles of these creatures sting whatever they touch — a paste made of household vinegar and unseasoned meat tenderizer is the recommended treatment.

If complications, allergic reactions (such as breathlessness, fever, or cramps), or signs of serious infection result from any of the above circumstances, *see a doctor.*

INSECTS AND OTHER PESTS: Flies and mosquitoes can be troublesome, so it is a good idea to use some form of topical insect repellent — those containing DEET (N,N-diethyl-m-toluamide) are among the most common and effective. The US Environmental Protection Agency (EPA) stresses that you should not use any pesticide that has not been approved by the EPA (check the label) and that all such preparations should be used in moderation. If picnicking or camping, burn mosquito coils or candles containing allethrin, pyrethrin, or citronella, or use a pyrethrum-containing flying-insect spray. For further information about active ingredients in repellents, call the *National Pesticide Telecommunications Network*'s 24-hour hotline number: 800-858-7378.

If you do get bitten — by mosquitoes, horse or black flies, or other bugs — the itching can be relieved with baking soda, topical first-aid cream, or antihistamine tablets. Should a bite become infected, treat it with a disinfectant or antibiotic cream.

Though rarer, bites from snakes or spiders can be serious. If possible, always try to catch the villain for identification purposes. If bitten by these creatures or *any* wild animal, the best course of action may be to head directly to the nearest emergency ward or outpatient clinic of a hospital. Cockroaches, waterbugs, and termites thrive in warm climates, but pose no serious health threat.

If you are bitten and you develop a rash and flu-like symptom, you may have been bitten by a tick carrying what is known as Lyme Borreliosis (known as Lyme Tick disease) and you should consult a physician. Many Americans believe that this disease is unique to the US; however, it was first diagnosed in Europe — where it is called Neuro Borreliosis — and has been a problem there for years. Caution should be taken in all wooded areas. For further information on this rapidly spreading problem, see *Camping and Caravanning, Hiking and Biking,* in this section.

FOOD AND WATER: Tap water generally is clean and potable throughout most of Europe. You may want to drink bottled water, however, as do the Europeans, at least at the beginning of the trip. This is not because there is something wrong with the water, as far as the residents are concerned, but because new microbes in the digestive tract to which you have not become accustomed may cause mild stomach or intestinal upsets. Particularly in rural areas, the water supply may not be thoroughly purified, and local residents either have developed immunities to the natural bacteria or boil it for drinking. You also should avoid drinking water from freshwater streams, rivers, or pools. In campgrounds water usually is indicated as drinkable or for washing only — again, if you're not sure, ask.

Milk is pasteurized throughout Europe, and dairy products are safe to eat, as are fruit, vegetables, meat, poultry, and fish. Because of Mediterranean pollution, however, fish and shellfish should be eaten cooked, and make sure it is *fresh,* particularly in the heat of summer, when inadequate refrigeration is an additional concern.

Following all these precautions will not guarantee an illness-free trip, but should minimize the risk. As a final hedge against economic if not physical problems, make sure your health insurance will cover all eventualities while you are away. If not, there are policies designed specifically for travel. Many are worth investigating. As with all insurance, they seem like a waste of money until you need them. For further information, see *Insurance* and *Medical and Legal Aid and Consular Services,* both in this section.

HELPFUL PUBLICATIONS: Practically every phase of health care — before, during, and after a trip — is covered in *The New Traveler's Health Guide,* by Drs. Patrick J. Doyle and James E. Banta. It is available for $4.95, plus postage and handling, from Acropolis Books Ltd., 13950 Park Center Rd., Herndon, VA 22071 (phone: 800-451-7771 or 703-709-0006).

The *Traveling Healthy Newsletter,* which is published six times a year, also is brimming with health-related travel tips. For a year's subscription, which costs $24, contact Dr. Karl Neumann (108-48 70th Rd., Forest Hills, NY 11375; phone: 718-268-7290). Dr. Neumann also is the editor of the useful free booklet *Traveling Healthy,* which is available by writing to the *Travel Healthy Program* (PO Box 10208, New Brunswick, NJ 08906-9910; phone: 215-732-4100).

For more information regarding preventive health care for travelers, contact the

International Association for Medical Assistance to Travelers (*IAMAT:* 417 Center St., Lewiston, NY 14092; phone: 716-754-4883). The Centers for Disease Control also publishes an interesting booklet, *Health Information for International Travel.* To order send a check or money order for $5 to the Superintendent of Documents (US Government Printing Office, Washington, DC 20402), or charge it to your credit card by calling 202-783-3238. For information on vaccination requirements, disease outbreaks, and other health information pertaining to traveling abroad, you also can call the Centers for Disease Control's 24-hour International Health Requirements and Recommendations Information Hotline: 404-332-4559.

On the Road

Credit and Currency

 It may seem hard to believe, but one of the greatest (and least understood) costs of travel is money itself. Your one single objective in relation to the care and retention of your travel funds is to make them stretch as far as possible. When you do spend money, it should be on things that expand and enhance your travel experience, with no buying power lost due to carelessness or lack of knowledge. This requires more than merely ferreting out the best airfare or the most charming budget hotel. It means being canny about the management of money itself. Herewith, a primer on making money go as far as possible overseas.

CURRENCY: The value of European currencies in relation to the US dollar fluctuates daily, affected by a wide variety of phenomena. A country-by-country listing of foreign currencies throughout Europe, as well as other useful information, is given in FACTS IN BRIEF.

Although US dollars may be accepted in Europe (particularly at points of entry), you certainly will lose a percentage of your dollar's buying power if you do not take the time to convert it into the local legal tender. By paying for goods and services in the local currency, you save money by not negotiating invariably unfavorable exchange rates for every small purchase, and avoid difficulty where US currency is not readily — or happily — accepted. *Throughout this book, unless specifically stated otherwise, prices are given in US dollars.*

FOREIGN EXCHANGE: Because of the volatility of exchange rates, be sure to check the current value of the currencies of the countries you plan to visit before finalizing any travel budget. And before you actually depart on your trip, be aware of the most advantageous exchange rates offered by various financial institutions — US banks, currency exchange firms, or foreign banks.

For the best sense of current trends, follow the rates posted in the financial section of your local newspaper or in such international newspapers as the *International Herald Tribune.* You can check with your own bank or with *Thomas Cook Foreign Exchange* (for the nearest location, call 800-972-2192 in Illinois; 800-621-0666 elsewhere in the US). *Harold Reuter and Company,* a currency exchange service in New York City (200 Park Ave., Suite 332 E., New York, NY 10166; phone: 212-661-0826) also is particularly helpful in determining current trends in exchange rates. *Ruesch International* offers up-to-date foreign currency information and currency-related services (such as converting foreign currency VAT refund checks into US dollars; see *Duty-Free Shopping and Value Added Tax,* in this section). *Ruesch* also offers a pocket-size *Foreign Currency Guide* (good for estimating general equivalents while planning) and a helpful brochure, *6 Foreign Exchange Tips for the Traveler.* Contact *Ruesch International* at one of the following addresses: 3 First National Plaza, Suite 2020, Chicago, IL 60602 (phone: 312-332-5900); 1925 Century Park E., Suite 240, Los Angeles, CA 90067 (phone: 213-277-7800); 608 Fifth Ave., "Swiss Center," New York, NY 10020 (phone:

212-977-2700); or 1350 Eye St. NW, 10th Floor and street level, Washington, DC 20005 (phone: 800-424-2923 or 202-408-1200).

In Europe, you will find the official rate of exchange posted in banks, airports, money exchange houses, hotels, and some shops. As a general rule, expect to get more local currency for your US dollar at banks than at any other commercial establishment. Exchange rates may change from day to day, and most banks offer the same (or very similar) exchange rates. In a pinch, the convenience of exchanging money in your hotel — sometimes on a 24-hour basis — *may* make up for the difference in the exchange rate. Don't try to bargain in banks or hotels — no one will alter the rates for you.

Money exchange houses are financial institutions that charge a fee for the service of exchanging dollars for local currency. When considering alternatives, be aware that although the rate again varies among these establishments, the rates of exchange offered are bound to be slightly less favorable than the terms offered at nearby banks — again, don't be surprised if you get less foreign currency for your dollar than the rate published in the papers.

Travelers to Eastern Europe should be aware that these general rules of comparative rates do not apply as the currency of most of these countries is not freely traded (see Rule Number Two, below). Published exchange rates really have no practical impact. Until very recently there were "official" rates of exchange that were strictly enforced by the various governments, and travelers from Western countries were obliged to exchange (at that artificial rate) a specific amount in dollars for each day they'd be staying in an Eastern European country. With all the recent upheavals, however, these currency regulations are changing almost daily, and while exchange rates remain artificially supported, there's more of an air of reality about the process. Even so, consulting the sources discussed above for current exchange rates will give you widely varying rates for Eastern European currencies. Since you currently can't take the foreign currency into these countries — you must buy it when you get there — you would do best to budget your trip expenses according to the exchange rates quoted by the national tourist offices.

That said, however, the following rules of thumb are worth remembering.

Rule number one: Never (repeat: *never*) exchange dollars for foreign currency at hotels, restaurants, or retail shops. If you do, you are sure to lose a significant amount of your dollars' buying power. If you do come across a storefront exchange counter offering what appears to be an incredible bargain, there's too much counterfeit specie in circulation to take the chance (see Rule number three, below).

Rule number two: Estimate your needs carefully; if you overbuy, you lose twice — buying and selling back. Every time you exchange money, someone is making a profit, and rest assured it isn't you. In countries with foreign exchange restrictions (some Eastern European countries), you will be required to turn in local currency when you leave. And even in countries with no such restrictions, you will have to declare and pay taxes on anything over a specified amount. Use up foreign notes before leaving, saving just enough for last-minute incidentals, and tips.

Rule number three: Don't buy money on the black market. The exchange rate may be better, but it is a common practice to pass off counterfeit bills to unsuspecting foreigners who aren't familiar with the local currency. It's usually a sucker's game, and you almost always are the sucker; it also can land you in jail.

Rule number four: Learn the local currency quickly and keep abreast of daily fluctuations in the exchange rate. These are listed in the English-language *International Herald Tribune* daily for the preceding day, as well as in every major newspaper in Europe. Rates change to some degree every day. For rough calculations, it is quick and safe to use round figures, but for purchases and actual currency exchanges, carry a small pocket calculator to help you compute the exact rate. Inexpensive calculators specifically designed to convert currency amounts for travelers are widely available.

When changing money, don't be afraid to ask how much commission you're being charged, and the exact amount of the prevailing exchange rate. In fact, in any exchange of money for goods or services, you should work out the rate before making any payment.

TIP PACKS: It's not a bad idea to buy a *small* amount of foreign coins and banknotes before your departure. But note the emphasis on "small," because, for the most part, you are better off carrying the bulk of your travel funds to Europe in US dollar traveler's checks (see below). Still, the advantages of tip packs are threefold:

1. You become familiar with the currency (really the only way to guard against making mistakes or being cheated during your first few hours in a new country).
2. You are guaranteed some money should you arrive when a bank or exchange counter isn't open or available. You don't have to depend on hotel desks, porters, or taxi drivers to change your money.

A "tip pack" is the only foreign currency you should buy before you leave. If you do run short upon arrival, US dollars often are accepted at points of entry. In other areas, they either *may* be accepted, or someone may accommodate you by changing a small amount — though invariably at a less than advantageous rate.

TRAVELER'S CHECKS: It's wise to carry traveler's checks while on the road instead of (or in addition to) cash, since it's possible to replace them if they are stolen or lost; you usually can receive partial or full replacement funds the same day if you have your purchase receipt and proper identification. Issued in various denominations and available in both US dollars and foreign currencies, with adequate proof of identification (credit cards, driver's license, passport) traveler's checks are as good as cash in most hotels, restaurants, stores, and banks.

Don't assume, however, that restaurants, small shops, and other establishments are going to be able to change checks of large denominations. Worldwide, more and more establishments are beginning to restrict the amount of traveler's checks they will accept or cash, so it is wise to purchase at least some of your checks in small denominations — say, $10 and $20. Also, don't expect to cash them into US dollars except at banks and international airports.

Although traveler's checks are available in foreign currencies, the exchange rates offered by the issuing companies in the US generally are far less favorable than those available from banks both in the US and abroad. Therefore, it usually is better to carry the bulk of your travel funds abroad in US dollar–denomination traveler's checks.

Every type of traveler's check is legal tender in banks around the world, and each company guarantees full replacement if checks are lost or stolen. After that the similarity ends. Some charge a fee for purchase, others are free; you can buy traveler's checks at almost any bank, and some are available by mail. Most important, each traveler's check issuer differs slightly in its refund policy — the amount refunded immediately, the accessibility of refund locations, the availability of a 24-hour refund service, and the time it will take for you to receive replacement checks. For instance, *American Express* guarantees replacement of lost or stolen traveler's checks in under 3 hours at any *American Express* office — other companies may not be as prompt. (Note that *American Express*'s 3-hour policy is based on the traveler's being able to provide the serial numbers of the lost checks. Without these numbers, refunds can take much longer.)

We cannot overemphasize the importance of knowing how to replace lost or stolen checks. All of the traveler's check companies have agents around the world, both in their own name and at associated agencies (usually, but not necessarily, banks), where refunds can be obtained during business hours. Most of them also have 24-hour toll-free telephone lines, and some even will provide emergency funds to tide you over on a Sunday.

Be sure to make a photocopy of the refund instructions that will be given to you by the issuing institution at the time of purchase. To avoid complications should you need to redeem lost checks (and to speed up the replacement process), keep the purchase receipt and an accurate list, by serial number, of the checks that have been spent or cashed. You may want to incorporate this information in an "emergency packet," also including your passport number and date of issue, the numbers of the credit cards you are carrying, and any other bits of information you shouldn't be without. Always keep these records separate from the checks and the original records themselves (you may want to give them to a traveling companion to hold).

Although most people understand the desirability of carrying funds in the form of traveler's checks as protection against loss or theft, an equally good reason is that US dollar traveler's checks invariably get a better rate of exchange than cash does — usually by at least 1% (although the discrepancy has been known to be substantially higher). The reasons for this are technical, but potential savings exist and it is a fact of travel life that should not be ignored.

That 1% won't do you much good, however, if you already have spent it buying your traveler's checks. Several of the major traveler's check companies charge 1% for the acquisition of their checks. To receive fee-free traveler's checks you may have to meet certain qualifications — for instance, *Thomas Cook*'s checks issued in US currency are free if you make your travel arrangements through its travel agency. *American Express* traveler's checks are available without charge to members of the *American Automobile Association.* Holders of some credit cards (such as the *American Express Platinum* card) also may be entitled to free traveler's checks. The issuing institution (e.g., the particular bank at which you purchase them) may itself charge a fee. If you purchase traveler's checks at a bank in which you or your company maintains significant accounts (especially commercial accounts of some size), the bank may absorb the 1% fee as a courtesy.

American Express, Bank of America, Citicorp, MasterCard, Thomas Cook, and *Visa* all offer traveler's checks. Here is a list of the major companies issuing traveler's checks and the numbers to call in the event that loss or theft makes replacement necessary:

> *American Express:* To report lost or stolen checks in the US, call 800-221-7282. In Europe, *American Express* advises travelers to call 44-273-571600 (in Brighton, England) collect. You also can call 801-968-8300 (in the US), collect, or contact the nearest *American Express* office.
>
> *Bank of America:* To report lost or stolen checks in the US, call 800-227-3460; elsewhere worldwide, call 415-624-5400 or 415-622-3800, collect.
>
> *Citicorp:* To report lost or stolen checks in the US, call 800-645-6556. In Europe and elsewhere worldwide, call 813-623-1709 or 813-626-4444, collect.
>
> *MasterCard:* To report lost or stolen checks in the US, call 800-223-9920. In Europe, call the New York office, 212-974-5696, collect, and they will direct you to the nearest branch of *MasterCard.*
>
> *Thomas Cook MasterCard:* To report lost or stolen checks in the US, call 800-223-7373. In Europe, call the US office, 609-987-7300, collect, and they will direct you to the nearest branch of *Thomas Cook.*
>
> *Visa:* To report lost or stolen checks in the continental US, call 800-227-6811. In Europe, call 415-574-7111 (in the US) or 44-71-937-8091 (in London), collect.

CREDIT CARDS: Some establishments you encounter during the course of your travels may not honor any credit cards and some may not honor all cards, so there is a practical reason to carry more than one. Most US credit cards, including the principal bank cards, are honored in Europe; however, keep in mind that some cards may be issued under different names in Europe. For example, *MasterCard* may go under the name *Access* or *Eurocard,* and *Visa* often is called *Carte Bleue* — wherever these equivalents are accepted, *MasterCard* and *Visa* may be used. The following is a list of credit cards that enjoy wide domestic and international acceptance:

American Express: Cardholders can cash personal checks for traveler's checks and cash at *American Express* or its representatives' offices in the US up to the following limits (within any 21-day period): $1,000 for *Green* and *Optima* cardholders; $5,000 for *Gold* cardholders; and $10,000 for *Platinum* cardholders. Check cashing also is available to cardholders who are guests at participating hotels (up to $250) and for holders of airline tickets at participating airlines (up to $50). Free travel accident, baggage, and car rental insurance if ticket or rental is charged to card; additional insurance also is available for additional cost. For further information or to report a lost or stolen *American Express* card, call 800-528-4800 throughout the continental US; in Europe, contact a local *American Express* office or call 212-477-5700, collect.

Carte Blanche: Free travel accident, baggage, and car rental insurance if ticket or rental is charged to card; additional insurance also is available at additional cost. For medical, legal, and travel assistance worldwide, call 800-356-3448 throughout the US; in Europe, call 214-680-6480, collect. For further information or to report a lost or stolen *Carte Blanche* card, call 800-525-9135 throughout the US; in Europe, call 303-790-2433, collect.

Diners Club: Emergency personal check cashing for cardholders staying at participating hotels and motels (up to $250 per stay). Free travel accident, baggage, and car rental insurance if ticket or rental is charged to card; additional insurance also is available for an additional fee. For medical, legal, and travel assistance worldwide, call 800-356-3448 throughout the US; in Europe, call 214-680-6480, collect. For further information or to report a lost or stolen *Diners Club* card, call 800-525-9135 throughout the US; in Europe, call 303-790-2433, collect.

Discover Card: Offered by a subsidiary of Sears, Roebuck & Co., it provides cardholders with cash advances at numerous automatic teller machines and *Sears* stores throughout the US. For further information and to report a lost or stolen *Discover* card, call 800-DISCOVER throughout the US; in Europe, call 302-323-7652, collect.

MasterCard: Cash advances are available at participating banks worldwide. Check with your issuing bank for information. *MasterCard* also offers a 24-hour emergency lost-card service; call 800-826-2181 throughout the US; 314-275-6690, collect, from abroad.

Visa: Cash advances are available at participating banks worldwide. Check with your issuing bank for information. *Visa* also offers a 24-hour emergency lost-card service; call 800-336-8472 throughout the US. In Europe, call 415-574-7700, collect.

One of the thorniest problems relating to the use of credit cards abroad concerns the rate of exchange at which a purchase is charged. Be aware that the exchange rate in effect on the date that you make a foreign purchase or pay for a foreign service has nothing at all to do with the rate of exchange at which your purchase is billed to you when you get the invoice (sometimes months later) in the US. The amount which the credit card company charges is either a function of the exchange rate at which the establishment's bank processed it or the rate in effect on the day your charge is received at the credit card center. (There is a 1-year limit on the time a shop or hotel can take to forward its charge slips.)

The principle at work in this credit card–exchange rate roulette is simple, but very hard to predict. You make a purchase at a particular dollar versus local currency exchange rate. If the dollar gets stronger in the time between purchase and billing, your purchase actually costs you less than you anticipated. If the dollar drops in value during the interim, you pay more than you thought you would. There isn't much you can do about these vagaries except to follow one very broad, very clumsy rule of thumb: If the dollar is doing well at the time of purchase, its value increasing against the local currency, use your credit card on the assumption it still will be doing well when billing takes place. If the dollar is doing badly, assume it will continue to do badly and pay with traveler's checks or cash. If you get too badly stuck, the best recourse is to complain, loudly. Be aware, too, that most credit card companies charge an unannounced, un-itemized 1% fee for converting foreign currency charges to US dollars.

SENDING MONEY ABROAD: If you have used up your traveler's checks, cashed as many emergency personal checks as your credit card allows, drawn on your cash advance line to the fullest extent, and still need money, have it sent abroad via one of the following services:

American Express (phone: 800-543-4080). Offers a service in Europe called "Moneygram," completing money transfers in anywhere from 10 minutes to 2 days. The sender can go to any *American Express* office in the US and can transfer money by presenting cash, a personal check, money order, or credit card — *Discover, Mastercard, Visa,* or *American Express Optima Card* (no other *American Express* or other credit cards are accepted). *American Express Optima* cardholders also can arrange for this transfer over the phone. The minimum transfer charge is $25, which rises with the amount of the transaction; the sender can forward funds of up to $10,000 per transaction (credit card users are limited to the amount of pre-established credit line). To collect at the other end, the receiver must show identification (passport, driver's license, or other picture ID) at an *American Express* office in Europe. This service is offered in Austria, Belgium, Denmark, France, Germany, Great Britain, Greece, Holland, Ireland, Italy, Luxembourg, Monaco, Poland, Spain, Sweden, and Switzerland.

Western Union Telegraph Company (phone: 800-325-4176). To send money to Europe, a friend or relative can go, cash in hand, to any *Western Union* office in the US, where, for a *minimum* charge of $13 (it rises with the amount of the transaction), the funds will be wired directly to one of their branch offices, to one of *Western Union*'s correspondent banks, or to the main post office in the nearest major city of the country you're visiting. (This service is available in Austria, Belgium, Bulgaria, Czechoslovakia, Denmark, France, Germany, Great Britain, Greece, Holland, Hungary, Ireland, Italy, Luxembourg, Poland, Portugal, Romania, Spain, Switzerland, and Yugoslavia.) When the money arrives in Europe, you will not be notified — you must go to the *Western Union* branch office, bank, or post office to inquire. Transfers generally take from 10 to 15 minutes, if wired directly to one of their branch offices, but may take anywhere from 2 to 5 business days if *Western Union* does not have any local branches. The funds will be turned over in local currency, based on the rate of exchange in effect on the day of receipt. For a higher fee, the US party to this transaction may call *Western Union* with a *MasterCard* or *Visa* number to send up to $2,000, although larger transfers will be sent to a predesignated location.

If you are literally down to your last cent, the nearest US consulate (see *Medical and Legal Aid and Consular Services,* in this section) will let you call home to set these matters in motion.

CASH MACHINES: Automatic teller machines (ATMs) are increasingly common worldwide. If your bank participates in one of the international ATM networks (most do), the bank will issue you a "cash card" along with a personal identification code or number (also called a PIC or PIN). You can use this card at any ATM in the same electronic network to check your account balances, transfer monies between checking and savings accounts, and — most important for a traveler — withdraw cash instantly. Network ATMs generally are located in banks, commercial and transportation centers, and near major tourist attractions.

Some financial institutions offer exclusive automatic teller machines for their own customers only at bank branches. At the time of this writing, ATMs which *are* connected generally belong to one of the following two international networks:

Cirrus: Has over 55,000 ATMs in more than 22 countries worldwide, including over 300 locations throughout Denmark, France, and Great Britain. *Master-Card* holders also may use their cards to draw cash against their credit lines. For a free booklet listing the locations of these machines and further information on the *Cirrus* network, call 800-4-CIRRUS.

Plus System: Has over 56,000 automatic teller machines worldwide, including over 200 locations throughout Great Britain and Ireland. *MasterCard* and *Visa* cardholders also may use their cards to draw cash against their credit lines. For a free directory listing the locations of these machines and further information on the *Plus System* network, call 800-THE-PLUS.

Accommodations

From elegant, centuries-old castle resorts and modern, functional high-rises to inexpensive inns and modest bed and breakfast establishments, it's easy to be comfortable and well cared for on almost any budget in Europe. Admittedly, the Mediterranean coast is full of deluxe establishments providing expensive services to people with money to burn, but more affordable alternatives always have been available, particularly in the countryside.

On the whole, deluxe and first class accommodations in Europe, especially in the large metropolitan centers (London, Paris, Rome, and so on), are more expensive than the same types of accommodations in the US. When the dollar is strong, such top-of-the-line establishments are within the range of a great number of travelers who previously would not have been able to afford them. But lately, the generally unfavorable rate of exchange has rendered princely accommodations very pricey.

Once upon a time, such things as the superiority of New World plumbing made many of the numerous less expensive accommodations alternatives unacceptable for North Americans. Today, the gap has closed considerably, and in most countries the majority of hostelries catering to the tourist trade are likely to be adequate in their basic facilities.

Before you go, consult brochures and booklets available free from European tourist offices in the US (see *Tourist Information Offices,* in this section, for addresses). Other publications can be purchased from the travel bookstores listed in *Books, Newspapers, Magazines, and Newsletters,* also in this section.

HOTELS, INNS, AND GUESTHOUSES: European **hotels** may be large or small, part of a chain or independent, new and of the "international standard" type or well established and traditional. There are built-for-the-purposes premises and converted stately homes and villas, resort hotels offering plenty of opportunities for recreation, and smaller tourist hotels offering virtually none.

One way to select the type of hotel that fits your finances and personal needs is to become familiar with the official hotel grading systems used in the countries you plan to visit. Not all European governments grade hotels, but most do. Most systems categorize accommodations, assigning a letter or a certain number of stars to each according to specific criteria, such as the number of rooms, the percentage of rooms with private bathrooms, and the presence of other amenities. Behind these grades may be found anything from a luxurious, turreted castle redolent of European history to a large, modern, and functional high-rise or a simple, family-run hostelry. While the results of these assessments may not tally with your own judgments, and while the five-star (deluxe) or one-star (plain but comfortable) hotels of one country may not measure up to those of another, by knowing the rating in advance you'll have a reasonable idea of the type of accommodations to expect — and their price. The national tourist offices of countries that grade hotels should be able to furnish you with a general price range for each category in their system.

Inns are of particular interest to travelers attracted by the prospect of sampling the lodgings of another age. There are inns dating from medieval times and many more not quite so old that have nevertheless been in business for centuries. An inn was, first of all, a wayside watering place for travelers passing on foot, horseback, or by coach, but laws requiring the innkeeper to provide food for the drinkers and accommodations for the diners turned innkeepers into hoteliers. The focal point of an inn often still is its public bar; the number of rooms may be, therefore, limited, and some in city centers do not provide accommodations at all. What remains of bygone days is the charm of thatch or slate roofs, timbered or stone façades, cobblestone courtyards, beamed ceilings, and the occasional four-poster bed. Heating and hot and cold water in the rooms usually have been added, though private bathrooms normally are lacking.

Guesthouses (called "pensions" on the Continent) often are rated on a scale similar to the one used for hotels. Though it is sometimes difficult to distinguish between some of the smaller, family-run hotels and the guesthouses, the latter almost always are family enterprises and tend to be more informal and personal in their hospitality. The official dividing line is the meal service: Unlike hotels, guesthouses do not provide meals for non-guests, and unlike inns, they often are not licensed to serve alcohol. Guesthouses cater exclusively to their guests, and in some cases will serve breakfast only (generally a full one, which is included in the room price), though usually a partial- or full-board plan by the day or the week will be available. Guesthouses, too, can vary in atmosphere from old, converted Georgian residences to brand-new, built-for-the-purpose premises. Bathroom facilities vary considerably: In a top-graded hotel, most rooms will have private bathrooms; in a top-graded guesthouse, some rooms with private bath may be available. (In either hotel or guesthouse where a private bath is lacking, the room often will have hot and cold running water.) Again, the government tourist boards are the best source of publications and information on these establishments.

In addition to the general cost guidelines provided by such grading systems, some European hotels actually display minimum and maximum prices on the front door, where they are easily legible from the street. The posted prices generally include service and, except in a few cases, all taxes, so that receiving the bill at the end of a stay is rarely a cause for shock. The prices also usually are for double rooms (since in Europe, as elsewhere, there are more double than single rooms), and the price of a double usually holds whether it's occupied by one or two people. The price of breakfast — which may be obligatory or optional — also often is posted by the reception desk.

Hotel Chains – A great many hotels in Europe are members of chains or hotel associations. Among the well-known, international names with properties throughout Europe, particularly in major cities, are the following (with toll-free reservations numbers to call in the US):

Best Western (phone: 800-528-1234). Has nearly 1,000 properties in Andorra, Austria, Belgium, Denmark, Finland, France, Germany, Great Britain, Hungary, Ireland, Italy, Luxembourg, the Netherlands, Norway, Portugal, Spain, and Sweden.

Conrad (phone: 800-445-8667). The international division of *Hilton* hotels; has 1 property in Ireland (Dublin), 1 in Great Britain (London), and 1 in Monaco (Monte Carlo).

Forte Hotels International (formerly *Trusthouse Forte;* phone: 800-225-5843). Has over 500 properties in Great Britain, and 35 in Belgium, France, Germany, Ireland, Italy, the Maltese Islands, Monaco, the Netherlands, Norway, Portugal, Spain, Sweden, and Switzerland.

Hilton International (phone: 800-445-8667). Owned by the Ladbroke's gambling group of Great Britain, there is no proprietary connection with the US *Hilton* chain. Has over 80 properties in Austria, France, Germany, Great Britain, Hungary, Italy, the Netherlands, Spain, and Switzerland.

Holiday Inn (phone: 800-465-4329). Has 95 properties in Belgium, France, Germany, Gibraltar, Great Britain, Greece, Iceland, Italy, the Maltese Islands, the Netherlands, Poland, Portugal, Spain, Switzerland, and Yugoslavia.

Hyatt Regency (phone: 800-233-1234). Has 10 properties in France, Germany, Gibraltar, Great Britain, Hungary, Spain, and Switzerland.

Inter-Continental (phone: 800-327-0200). Has 50 properties in Austria, Belgium, Czechoslovakia, Finland, France, Germany, Great Britain, Greece, Hungary, Italy, Luxembourg, the Netherlands, Poland, Portugal, Romania, Spain, the Soviet Union, Switzerland, and Yugoslavia.

Marriott (phone: 800-228-9290). Has 10 European properties, in Austria, France, Germany, Great Britain, Greece, the Netherlands, and Poland.

Meridien (phone: 800-543-4300). Has 6 properties in France, Great Britain, Greece, and Portugal.

Minotels Europe (phone: 800-336-4668). Has over 625 properties in Andorra, Austria, Belgium, Denmark, Finland, France, Germany, Great Britain, Greece, Hungary, Ireland, Italy, Luxembourg, the Maltese Islands, the Netherlands, Norway, Portugal, Spain, Sweden, Switzerland, and Yugoslavia.

Radisson (phone: 800-333-3333). Has 1 property in the Soviet Union (Moscow) and 1 in Hungary (Budapest).

Ramada (phone: 800-272-6232). Has almost 30 properties in Austria, Belgium, Finland, Germany, Great Britain, Hungary, Italy, Spain, Sweden, and Switzerland.

Sheraton (phone: 800-325-3535). Has over 30 properties in Austria, Belgium, Bulgaria, Denmark, Germany, Great Britain, Italy, Luxembourg, Portugal, Spain, Sweden, and Switzerland.

Among the larger European chains — whose names may be less familiar but many of whom nevertheless have a US office that will provide information and take reservations — is the *Pullman International* group of approximately 125 hotels in Austria, Belgium, Denmark, France, Germany, Great Britain, Holland, Italy, the Soviet Union, and Spain. For information and reservations, contact *Pullman International* (1500 Broadway, New York, NY 10036; phone: 800-223-9862 or 212-719-9363). Another group, *Utell International* (810 N. 96th St., Omaha, NE; 68114-2594; phone: 800-44-UTELL) represents over 2,000 properties in Austria, Belgium, Czechoslovakia, Denmark, Finland, France, Germany, Gibraltar, Great Britain, Greece, Hungary, Ireland, Italy, Luxembourg, the Soviet Union, Sweden, Switzerland, and Yugoslavia.

Other European hotel chains include *Ibis, Novotel, Mercure,* and *Sofitel* which together have a wide range of properties in Andorra, Austria, Belgium, Bulgaria, Czechoslovakia, Denmark, Germany, Great Britain, Greece, Holland, Hungary, Ireland, Italy, Poland, Portugal, the Soviet Union, Spain, and Sweden. All four are represented by *Resinter Reservations* (2 Overhill Rd., Scarsdale, NY 10583; phone: 800-221-4542).

Note, finally, that *Marketing Ahead* (433 Fifth Ave., New York, NY 10016; phone: 212-686-9213) represents numerous independent hotels in France, Portugal, and Spain. There also are numerous stateside representatives for individual European hotels. The appropriate government tourist offices in the US should be able to tell you who in the US represents a particular property.

■ **Reservation Services:** Though not all travelers would face the prospect of arriving in a strange city without a reservation with equal sangfroid, in Europe there are services that help book empty rooms for those who risk it. Generally, information on these services is available at the airport information desk or from the local tourist board office.

SPECIAL PLACES: Among the most interesting accommodations in Europe are those truly distinctive and frequently historic facilities whose ambience and style reflect something special of the country they are in. Examples of these are the country inns, manor houses, and bed and breakfast establishments of Britain and Ireland; the famed *relais* of France; converted castles in Germany; the architecturally distinctive *paradores* of Spain and *pousadas* of Portugal; the resort health spas of southeastern Europe; and Italy's *pensioni*, virtually a cultural institution within that country, although this style of accommodation has long been available throughout the Continent. Many of these unique hostelries are included in the *Best in Town* sections of the individual reports in THE CITIES and in *Best en Route* in DIRECTIONS, as well as in various sections of DIVERSIONS.

British Castles and Country-House Hotels – Found throughout the British Isles, these establishments specialize in the traditional atmosphere, service, and hospitality of the great English country estates. Many once were country homes, ancestral manor houses, or castles, and a number are noteworthy for architectural features, surrounding gardens or parks, river- or lakeside settings, or locations in dell, dale, or mountains. The real attraction, however, is the history associated with so many of them and their antique decors. Most have modern amenities (television sets, private baths) along with traditional features such as fireplaces and sitting rooms. Much sought out by the British as weekend retreats, so weekend reservations are a must. Midweek reservations also are strongly recommended during high season and around the holidays. For information, contact the British Tourist Authority (for addresses, see *Tourist Information Offices*, in this section).

Relais & Châteaux – Most members of this association are in France, but the group has grown to include dozens of establishments in many other countries. Three groups of members — *Relais de Campagne, Châteaux-Hôtels,* and *Relais Gourmands* — belong to the *Relais & Châteaux* association, including approximately 322 establishments throughout Western Europe.

The first two groups are of particular interest to travelers who wish lodgings reflecting the ambience, style, and, frequently, the history of the places they are visiting. Some properties actually are palaces or ancient castles — several dating back to the 13th century — that have been converted into hotels. Others are old inns (*relais* means a posthouse or inn), manor houses, even converted mills, convents, and monasteries. A few well-known city and resort establishments are included, such as the *Crillon* in Paris, the *Marbella Club* in Spain, and the *Lord Byron* in Rome, but most are in quiet country surroundings, and frequently are graced with parklands, ponds, and flowering gardens.

Members of the *Relais & Châteaux* group often are expensive, though no more than you would pay for deluxe, authentically elegant accommodations and service anywhere in the world (and many are not all that costly). Accommodations and service from one *relais* or château to another can range from simple but comfortable to elegantly deluxe, but they all maintain very high standards (the kitchens are uniformly first-rate) in order to retain their memberships, as they are appraised annually.

The third group of members, *Relais Gourmands,* is composed of exceptionally fine restaurants. These establishments also may have rooms for rent, but the establishments are *not* rated on the basis of their accommodations, so they may not match (or even come close to) the standards of room quality maintained by the others.

An illustrated catalogue of all the *Relais & Châteaux* properties is published annually and is available for $5 from *Relais & Châteaux* (2400 Lazy Hollow, Suite 152D, Houston, TX 77063) or from *David B. Mitchell & Company* (200 Madison Ave., New York, NY 10016; phone: 800-372-1323 or 212-696-1323). The association also can provide information on member properties. Reservations can be made directly with the establishments, through *David B. Mitchell & Company,* or through a travel agency.

Gast im Schloss – Germany's contribution to high style and historic accommodations is this association of hotels and restaurants in castles, mansions, and historic buildings. (The name is literally translated as "Guest in Castle.") Most of these properties have exceptionally picturesque settings and surroundings — on hills overlooking the Rhine, alongside lakes, or in densely wooded parks and parklands. Though stylish and often grand, there nonetheless is a prevailing sense of informality in most of the hotels. All have modern facilities and many offer numerous activities — tennis, riding, hunting, fishing, swimming, golf — either on the property or nearby. Prices are moderate to expensive, the atmosphere friendly and hospitable, and many of the properties present the romantic appeal of dinner before an open fireplace and a room in a castle turret. Special itineraries have been designed for motorists who want to visit several hotels in the association. These are described in the publication *Gast im Schloss: Castle Tours,* while the accommodations themselves are the focus of *Gast im Schloss: Castle Hotels;* both are available from the German National Tourist Office (see *Tourist Information Offices,* in this section, for addresses).

Paradores and Pousadas – Since 1928 the Spanish government has been renovating abandoned castles, palaces, convents, and other historic structures, as well as building new establishments — to create its excellent system of *paradores.* Guests can stay in a 15th-century castle, Renaissance palace, Muslim fortress, or splendidly ornate hunting chalet, all fitted out with modern facilities, and yet prices often are very reasonable. Within the Spanish system of grading hotels, *paradores* are mainly 3- to 4-star establishments (a few 2- and 5-star places exist). Portugal has a similar network of state-run inns called *pousadas.* Although only some *pousadas* are in historic buildings (such as palaces and monasteries), all are in scenic areas and in regional styles of architecture that complement their surroundings; all have modern conveniences and restaurants. *Pousadas* are graded independently from the rest of Portugal's accommodations; they are divided into three categories (B, C, and CH, corresponding to inexpensive, moderate, and deluxe historic building). For further information, contact the Spanish and Portuguese national tourist offices (for addresses, see *Tourist Information Offices,* in this section), or *Marketing Ahead* (433 Fifth Ave., New York, NY 10016; phone: 212-686-9213), which also makes reservations for these establishments.

Pensioni – Italy's contribution to continental accommodations happily remains part of the entire European travel scene. The chief attractions of *pensioni* (the anglicized spelling is pensions) are family-style quarters for a limited number of visitors, meals for those who wish to dine in-house, and lower prices than one would pay at a hotel. In other words, *pensioni* offer a more personal type of living — and economy. Whatever may be sacrificed in the way of front desk and other services at regular hotels usually is compensated for at *pensioni* by an element of charm. Although in the past these establishments required that guests register for a minimum stay and take one or both of their main meals in the house, most no longer discourage 1-night stays and many have dispensed with meal requirements (and less expensive pensions may serve only breakfast). Private baths are likely to be offered in only the more expensive pensions. According to the official grading system used by the Italian Government Travel Office (ENIT), there is no longer an official distinction between hotels and *pensioni,* and most brochures no longer list them separately. Further information and detailed lists of accommodations in Italy's main cities that include information on *pensioni* is available from the US offices of the Italian Government Travel Office (for addresses, see *Tourist Information Offices,* in this section).

BED AND BREAKFAST ESTABLISHMENTS AND OTHER ACCOMMODATIONS: In the British Isles, bed and breakfast establishments (commonly known as B&Bs) are a staple of the low-cost lodging scene and are found wherever there are extra rooms to let in a private home and a host or hostess willing to attend to the details of hospitality. On the Continent they are increasingly common, and not only in rural areas.

Bed and breakfast establishments provide exactly what the name implies. It is unusual for a bed and breakfast establishment to offer the extra services found in the other hostelries, so the bed and breakfast route often is the least expensive way to go.

Beyond these two fundamentals, nothing else is predictable about bed and breakfast establishments. The bed may be in an extra room in a family home, in an apartment with a separate entrance, or in a free-standing cottage elsewhere on the host's property. Some homes have only one room to let, whereas others may be large enough to have another party or two in residence at the same time. In European B&Bs, private baths are the exception rather than the rule. The breakfast most often will be a version of the standard continental breakfast: fruit plus juice; toast, croissant, roll, or homemade bread, with jam or marmalade; and coffee or tea. However, particularly in rural areas, it may be a heartier one, and as often as not (any language barrier aside) served along with family history to add to the local lore. If you're in a studio with a kitchenette, you may be furnished with the makings and have to prepare it for yourself. Despite their name, some B&Bs offer an evening meal as well — by prior arrangement and at extra cost.

Some hosts enjoy helping guests with tips on what to see and do and even serve as informal tour guides, while in other places your privacy won't be disturbed. Whichever the case, the beauty of bed and breakfast establishments is that you'll always have a warm reception and the opportunity to meet many more inhabitants of the region than you otherwise would, which means that you'll experience their hospitality in a special fashion.

Bed and breakfast establishments range from humble country cottages to elegant manor houses. To avoid disappointment, find out as much as you can before you book. European government tourist offices are an excellent source of information. For instance, the British Tourist Authority publishes a leaflet explaining the bed and breakfast idea, and the national tourist boards of the United Kingdom and other organizations publish annual B&B guides. The French Government Tourist Office also distributes a brochure explaining their system of bed and breakfast establishments (known as *gîtes* in France), as well as a guide listing a selection of about 200 of these; further information is available from the *Fédération Nationale des Gîtes Ruraux de France* (35 Rue Godot-de-Mauroy, Paris 75009, France; phone: 33-1-47-42-25-43). In addition, most tourist information centers abroad provide information on bed and breakfast establishments nearby.

For information on British B&Bs, the *Worldwide Bed and Breakfast Association* publishes *The Best Bed & Breakfast in the World 1992–93,* a guide to over 800 member establishments throughout England, Scotland, and Wales. The book costs $15.95, and purchase includes an $18 discount that may applied toward the cost of a stay in London. Found in bookstores, it also can be ordered from the distributor, Globe Pequot Press (138 W. Main St., Box Q, Chester, CT 06412; phone: 800-243-0495). The *World-*

wide Bed & Breakfast Association also acts as a booking service for the properties listed; contact the association at PO Box 134, London SW10 9EH, England (phone: 44-81-742-9123 for information and reservations, 24 hours).

Although most hosts may be contacted directly, as in the US, some prefer that arrangements be made through a reservations organization. The general procedure for making reservations through bed and breakfast services is that you contact them with your requirements, and they help find the right place, then confirm your reservations upon receipt of a deposit. Any further information needed will be provided by either the service or by the owner of the bed and breakfast establishment.

Reservations for bed and breakfast accommodations in Europe also are handled by the following companies:

Anglo-American Reisebüro (AAR; 13 Bodelschwinghstr., Westerkappeln 4535, Germany; phone: 49-54-042570). Represents bed and breakfast properties throughout Western and Eastern Europe. (Note that they have English-speaking personnel, but you may have to call more than once to reach one.)

British Travel Associates (PO Box 299, Elkton, VA 22927; phone: 800-327-6097 or 703-298-2232). Handles bed and breakfast accommodations in England, Scotland, and Wales.

The Bulldog Club (35 The Chase, London SW4 0NP, England; phone: 44-71-491-0066). This club books members into some of the finest bed and breakfast establishments in Great Britain; the annual membership fee is $40 per person.

Chez Vous (220 Redwood Hwy., Suite 129, Mill Valley, CA 94941; phone: 415-331-2535). Handles bed and breakfast establishments in France.

French Experience (370 Lexington Ave., New York, NY 10017; phone: 212-986-1115). Represents the French bed and breakfast association, *Café Couette,* which includes bed and breakfast establishments throughout France.

Hometours International (1170 Broadway, New York, NY 10001; phone: 800-367-4668 or 212-689-0851). All properties represented are categorized according to the quality of accommodations and facilities. This company represents bed and breakfast establishments in France, Great Britain, and Ireland.

IBV Bed and Breakfast Systems (13113 Ideal Dr., Silver Springs, MD; phone: 301-942-3770). Handles bed and breakfast establishments in Czechoslovakia and the Soviet Union.

Independent Traveller Thorverton (Exeter EX5 5NU, England; phone: 44-392-860807). Handles bed and breakfast accommodations throughout England and Ireland.

ITS Tours and Travel (1055 Texas Ave., Suite 104, College Station, TX 77840; phone: 800-533-8688 or 409-764-9400). Handles bed and breakfast accommodations in the Soviet Union.

Leander Travel Inc. (2715 Garland La., Plymouth, MN 55447; phone: 612-473-2911). Handles bed and breakfast accommodations throughout the British Isles.

Travellers B&B Reservation Service (PO Box 492, Mercer Island, WA 98040; phone: 206-232-2345). Handles bed and breakfast accommodation in Great Britain and Ireland.

Another useful source of information on bed and breakfast establishments overseas is the *Bed & Breakfast Reservations Services Worldwide,* a trade associations of B&B reservations services, which provides a list of its members for $3. To order the most recent edition, contact them at PO Box 39000, Washington, DC 20016 (phone: 800-842-1486).

Farmhouses – In the country, city people rediscover the sounds of songbirds and the smell of grass. Suburbanites get the chance to poke around an area where the nearest neighbor lives miles away. Parents can say to their children, "No, milk does not originate in a cardboard carton," and prove it. Youngsters can meet people who live differently, think differently, and have different values. But even if there were no lessons to be learned, a stay at a farm would be a decidedly pleasant way to pass a couple of weeks, so it's no wonder that all over Europe there are numerous farms welcoming guests.

Farm families in Europe often put up guests on a bed and breakfast basis — for a night or two or by the week, with weekly half-board plans available. Travelers can pick a traditional or a modern farm, a dairy farm over a sheep farm, one with ponies to ride, or one near a river for fishing. If the peace and quiet and the coziness of the welcome are appealing, a farmhouse can be an ideal base from which to explore a region by car or by foot and an especially good idea for those traveling with children. For information on farm stays in Europe, contact the appropriate government tourist office in the US (for addresses, see *Tourist Information Offices,* in this section).

Rental Options – An attractive alternative for the visitor content to stay in one spot for a week or more is to rent one of the numerous properties available throughout Europe. These offer a wide range of luxury and convenience, depending on the price you want to pay. One of the advantages of staying in a house, apartment (usually called a "flat" overseas), or other rented vacation home is that you will feel much more like a visitor than a tourist.

Known to Europeans as a "holiday let" or a "self-catering holiday," a vacation in a furnished rental has both the advantages and disadvantages of living "at home" abroad. It can be less expensive than staying in a first class hotel, although very luxurious and expensive rentals are available, too. It has the comforts of home, including a kitchen, which can mean potential savings on food. Furthermore, it gives a sense of the country being visited that a large hotel often cannot. On the other hand, a certain amount of housework is involved because if you don't eat out, you have to cook, and though some rentals (especially the luxury ones) include a cleaning person, most don't. (If the rental doesn't include daily cleaning, arrangements often can be made with a nearby service.)

For a family, two or more couples, or a group of friends, the per-person cost — even for a luxurious rental — can be quite reasonable. Weekly and monthly rates are available to reduce costs still more. But best of all is the amount of space that no conventional hotel room can equal. As with hotels, the rates for properties in some areas are seasonal, rising during the peak travel season, while for others they remain the same year-round. To have your pick of the properties available, you should begin to make arrangements for a rental at least 6 months in advance.

There are several ways of finding a suitable rental property. A number of tourist boards issue region-by-region guides to apartments, bungalows, cottages, houses, chalets, castles, and villas for rent that meet some range of minimum standards. Many tour operators regularly include a few rental packages among their offerings; these generally are available through a travel agent. In addition, a number of companies specialize in rental vacations. Their plans typically include rental of the property (or several properties, but usually for a minimum stay per location), a rental car, and airfare.

The companies listed below rent a wide range of properties in Europe. They handle the booking and confirmation paperwork and can be expected to provide more information about the properties than that which might ordinarily be gleaned from a short listing in an accommodations guide.

At Home Abroad (405 E. 56th St., Apt. 6H, New York, NY 10022; phone: 212-421-9165). Their offerings include apartments, modest to luxurious houses, castles, and villas in France, Great Britain, Ireland, Italy, Portugal, and Spain. Photographs of properties can be requested by mail for a $50 registration fee.

B & D De Vogue Travel Services (PO Box 1998, Visalia, CA 93279; phone:

800-338-0483); or *Paris Séjour Réservations,* 90 Av. des Champs-Elysées, Paris 75008, France; phone: 33-1-42-56-30-00). Rents apartments, private homes, and châteaux throughout Belgium, France, Germany, Italy, and Portugal.

Blake's Vacations (4918 Dempster St., Skokie, IL 60077; phone: 800-628-8118). Rents country houses and villas in France, Great Britain, Ireland, Italy, and Spain.

British Travel Associates (PO Box 299, Elkton, VA 22927; phone: 800-327-6097 or 703-298-2232). Arranges apartment and cottage rentals, as well as stays in castles and country mansions in France, Great Britain, and Italy.

Castles, Cottages and Flats (7 *Faneuil Hall Marketplace,* Boston, MA 02109; phone: 617-742-6030). Their specialty is cottages in England's heartland, but also featured are properties elsewhere in England, Scotland, Wales, and Ireland, as well as country houses and villas in France and Italy. Small charge ($5) for receipt of main catalogue, refundable upon booking.

Chez Vous (220 Redwood Hwy., Suite 129E, Mill Valley, CA 94941; phone: 415-331-2535). Offers country homes and villas throughout France.

Coast to Coast Resorts (860 Solar Building, 1000 16th St. NW, Washington, DC 20036; phone: 800-368-5721 or 202-293-8000). Handles country homes and villas in France, as well as more modest properties in Austria, Germany, Great Britain, Holland, Italy, Luxembourg, Spain, Switzerland, and Yugoslavia.

Coast to Coast Tours (PO Box 431920, Miami, FL 33243; phone: 800-622-1520). Handles condominiums and apartments around Paris.

Country Holidays (Spring Mill, Stonybank Rd., Earby, Lancashire BB8 6RW, England; phone: 44-282-844284). Handles rental properties throughout Great Britain.

Eastone Overseas Accommodations (198 Southampton Dr., Jupiter, FL 33458; phone: 407-575-6991). Handles apartments, cottages, houses, castles, and villas in Austria, France, Germany, Great Britain, Ireland, Italy, Portugal, Spain, Switzerland, and Yugoslavia.

Europa-Let (PO Box 3537, Ashland, OR 97520; phone: 800-462-4486 or 503-482-5806). Offers apartments, castles, cottages, mansions, and villas in Austria, France, Germany, Great Britain, Greece, Italy, Portugal, Spain, and Switzerland.

French Experience (370 Lexington Ave., New York, NY 10017; phone: 212-986-1115). Rents apartments, country cottages, houses, and villas in France.

Grandluxe Internatonal (165 Chestnut St., Allendale, NJ 07401; phone: 201-327-2333). Rents apartments, country houses, castles, and villas in Austria, France, Germany, and Italy.

Heart of England Cottages (PO Box 878, Eufala, AL 36072-0878; phone: 205-687-9800). Just what the name says.

Heritage of Ireland (22 Railroad St., Great Barrington, MA 01230; phone: 413-528-6610). Represents a wide range of properties — from castles to cottages — throughout Ireland. A catalogue is available for $5.

Hideaways International (15 Goldsmith St., PO Box 1270, Littleton, MA 01460; phone: 800-843-4433 or 508-486-8955). Rents apartments, manor houses, and villas in France, Great Britain, Greece, Ireland, Italy, Portugal, Spain, and Yugoslavia.

Hometours International (1170 Broadway, New York, NY 10001; phone: 800-367-4668 or 212-689-0851). Handles apartments, country houses, and villas in England, France, and Italy.

Independent Traveller Thorverton (Exeter EX5 5NU, England; phone: 44-392-860807). Handles apartments and cottages in Great Britain and Ireland.

In the English Manner (4092 N. Ivy Rd., Atlanta, GA 30342; phone: 404-231-5837; or 900 Wilshire Blvd., Suite 830, Los Angeles, CA 90017; phone: 800-422-0799 or 213-629-1811). This company specializes in large, elegant properties — castles, manor houses, stately homes — throughout Great Britain.

International Lodging Corp. (300 1st Ave., Suite 7C, New York, NY 10009; phone: 212-228-5900). Handles flats, cottages, country houses, and villas in France, Germany, Great Britain, Greece, Ireland, Italy, Portugal, and Spain.

Interhome (124 Little Falls Rd., Fairfield, NJ 07004; phone: 201-882-6864). Rents apartments, chalets, and villas in Austria, Belgium, France, Germany, Holland, Hungary, Italy, Portugal, Spain, and Switzerland.

Livingstone Holidays (1720 E. Garry Ave., Suite 236, Santa Ana, CA 92705; phone: 714-476-2823). Handles cottages and flats in France, Great Britain, and Italy. Small charge ($2) for larger brochures.

London Apartments, Ltd. (5 Hidden Valley Rd., Lafayette, CA 94549; phone: 800-366-8748 or 415-283-4280). Rents flats in London.

Rent a Vacation Everywhere (*RAVE;* 328 Main St. E., Suite 526, Rochester, NY 14604; phone: 716-454-6440). Rents moderate to luxurious apartments, cottages, castles, and villas in France, Great Britain, Greece, Ireland, Italy, Portugal, Spain, and Switzerland.

Vacances en Campagne and Vacanze in Italia (PO Box 297, Falls Village, CT 06031; phone: 800-533-5405). The former branch of this company represents properties in France and Great Britain; the latter rents apartments and houses in Italy. A catalogue is available for $5.

VHR Worldwide (235 Kensington Ave., Norwood, NJ 07648; phone: 201-767-9393, locally; 800-NEED-A-VILLA, elsewhere). Rents apartments, country homes, and villas in France, Great Britain, Greece, Italy, Portugal, and Spain.

Villas International (605 Market St., Suite 510, San Francisco, CA 94105; phone: 800-221-2260 or 415-281-0910). Offers a good selection of simple cottages, some windmills, apartments, châteaux, and other gracious properties in Austria, Belgium, Czechoslovakia, France, Germany, Great Britain, Greece, Holland, Hungary, Ireland, Italy, Portugal, Spain, and Yugoslavia.

And for further information, including a general discussion of all forms of vacation rentals, evaluating costs, and information on rental opportunities throughout Europe, see *A Traveler's Guide to Vacation Rentals in Europe.* Available in general bookstores, it also can be ordered from Penguin USA (120 Woodbine St., Bergenfield, NJ 07621; phone: 800-526-0275 and ask for cash sales) for $11.95, plus postage and handling.

In addition, a useful publication, the *Worldwide Home Rental Guide,* lists properties throughout Europe, as well as their managing agencies. Issued twice annually, single copies may be available at larger newsstands for $10 an issue. For a year's subscription, send $18 to *Worldwide Home Rental Guide,* PO Box 2842, Sante Fe, NM 87504 (phone: 505-988-5188).

When considering a particular vacation-rental property, look for answers to the following questions:
- How do you get from the airport to the property?
- If the property is on the shore, how far is the nearest beach? Is it sandy or rocky and is it safe for swimming?
- What size and number of beds are provided?
- How far is the property from whatever else is important to you, such as a golf course or nightlife?
- How far is the nearest market?

- Are baby-sitters, cribs, bicycles, or anything else you may need for your children available?
- Is maid service provided daily?
- Is air conditioning and/or a phone provided?
- Is a car rental part of the package? Is a car necessary?

Before deciding which rental is for you, make sure you have satisfactory answers to all your questions. Ask your travel agent to find out or call the company involved directly.

HOME EXCHANGES: Still another alternative for travelers who are content to stay in one place during their vacation is a home exchange: The Smith family from Chicago moves into the home of the Jiménez family in Madrid, while the Jiménez family enjoys a stay in the Smiths' home. The home exchange is an exceptionally inexpensive way to ensure comfortable, reasonable living quarters with amenities that no hotel possibly could offer; often the trade includes a car. Moreover, it allows you to live in a new community in a way that few tourists ever do: For a little while, at least, you will become something of a resident.

Several companies publish directories of individuals and families willing to trade homes with others for a specific period of time. In some cases, you must be willing to list your own home in the directory; in others, you can subscribe without appearing in it. Most listings are for straight exchanges only, but each of the directories also has a number of listings placed by people interested in either exchanging or renting (for instance, if they own a second home). Other arrangements include exchanges of hospitality while owners are in residence or youth exchanges, where your teenager is put up as a guest in return for your putting up their teenager at a later date. A few house-sitting opportunities also are available. In most cases, arrangements for the actual exchange take place directly between you and the foreign host. There is no guarantee that you will find a listing in the area in which you are interested, but each of the organizations given below includes European homes among its hundreds or even thousands of foreign listings.

Home Base Holidays (7 Park Ave., London N13 5PG, England; phone: 44-81-886-8752). For $42 a year, subscribers receive four listings, with an option to list in all four.

Intervac US/International Home Exchange Service (Box 190070, San Francisco, CA 94119; phone: 415-435-3497). For $45 (plus postage), subscribers receive copies of the three directories published yearly, and are entitled to list their home in one of them; a black-and-white photo may be included with the listing for an additional $10. A $5 discount is given to travelers over age 62.

Loan-A-Home (2 Park La., Apt. 6E, Mt. Vernon, NY 10552; phone: 914-664-7640). Specializes in long-term (4 months or more — excluding July and August) housing arrangements worldwide for students, professors, businesspeople, and retirees, although its two annual directories (with supplements) carry a small list of short-term rentals and/or exchanges. $35 for a copy of one directory and one supplement; $45 for two directories and two supplements.

Vacation Exchange Club (PO Box 820, Haleiwa, HI 96712; phone: 800-638-3841). Some 10,000 listings. For $50, the subscriber receives four directories per year and is listed in one. For $35, the subscriber receives all four directories but no listing.

World Wide Exchange (1344 Pacific Ave., Suite 103, Santa Cruz, CA 95060; phone: 408-476-4206). The $45 annual membership fee includes one listing (for house, yacht, or motorhome) and three guides.

Worldwide Home Exchange Club (13 Knightsbridge Green, London SW1X 7QL, England; phone: 44-71-589-6055; or 806 Brantford Ave., Silver Spring, MD

20904; no phone). Handles over 1,500 listings a year worldwide. For $25 a year, you will receive two listings, as well as supplements.

Better Homes and Travel (formerly *Home Exchange International*), with an office in New York, and representatives in Los Angeles, London, Paris, and Milan, functions differently in that it publishes no directory and shepherds the exchange process most of the way. Interested parties supply the firm with photographs of themselves and their homes, information on the type of home they want and where, and a registration fee of $50. The company then works with its other offices to propose a few possibilities, and only when a match is made do the parties exchange names, addresses, and phone numbers. For this service, *Better Homes and Travel* charges a closing fee, which ranges from $150 to $500 for switches from 2 weeks to 3 months in duration, and from $300 to $600 for longer switches. Contact *Better Homes and Travel* at 30 E. 33rd St., New York, NY 10016 (phone: 212-689-6608).

HOME STAYS: If the idea of staying in a private home as the guest of a foreign family appeals to you, check with the *United States Servas Committee,* which maintains a list of hosts throughout the world willing to throw open their doors to foreigners, entirely free of charge — including about 4,000 hosts throughout Europe.

The aim of this nonprofit cultural program is to promote international understanding and peace, and every effort is made to discourage freeloaders. *Servas* will send you an application form and the name of the nearest of some 200 interviewers around the US for you to contact. After the interview, if you're approved, you'll receive documentation certifying you as a *Servas* traveler. There is a membership fee of $45 per person, as well as a deposit of $25 to receive the host list, refunded on its return. The list gives the name, address, age, occupation, and other particulars of the each host, including languages spoken. From then on, it is up to you to write to them directly, and *Servas* makes no guarantee that you will be accommodated.

Servas stresses that you should choose only people you really want to meet, and that during your stay (which normally lasts between 2 nights and 2 weeks) you should be interested mainly in your hosts, not in sightseeing. It also suggests that one way to show your appreciation once you've returned home is to become a host yourself. The minimum age of a *Servas* traveler is 18 (however, children under 18 may accompany their parents), and though quite a few are young people who've just finished college, there are travelers (and hosts) in all age ranges and occupations. Contact *Servas* at 11 John St., Room 407, New York, NY 10038 (phone: 212-267-0252).

Another organization arranging home stays is *In the English Manner,* which specializes in home stays with British families — but also has a number of Irish families — who open their homes to guests. Prospective hosts have been visited by the company to assure that only those genuinely interested in meeting foreigners and making their stay a memorable experience participate. Hosts, in fact, are probably better screened than guests, who need merely supply the company with family members' names and ages, occupations, special interests, and other pertinent data, such as allergies. The company then selects a few possible hosts and lets the client make the final decision. There is a minimum stay of 3 nights, which can be divided among three different families if desired, but no maximum stay except what is mutually agreeable to both hosts and guests. The entire cost of the stay is paid in advance. Meals that guests decide upon in advance also are prepaid; meals and other extras decided upon during the stay are paid in cash on departure (to avoid embarrassment, the company advises clients beforehand what the hosts charge). The program is not for budget travelers (the double occupancy rate ranges from expensive to very expensive) and the homes are not ordinary; they include several country houses, some larger stately homes, and a castle. Single rates are available, and there are reductions for children. Contact *In the English Manner,* 4092 N. Ivy Rd., Atlanta, GA 30342 (phone: 404-231-5837); or 900 Wilshire Blvd., Suite 830, Los Angeles, CA 90017 (phone: 800-422-0799 or 213-629-1811).

For further information on home stays in Great Britain, see the British Tourist Authority's informative, free booklet *Stay with A British Family,* which lists agencies that arrange for foreigners to stay in a British home, as well as a listing of many specific homes with brief descriptions and pertinent information. Another publication that lists home stay opportunities is *Wolsey Lodges: Welcome to an Englishman's Home.* This brochure lists private homes, mostly in village and country locations, linked by the "Wolsey Lodges" banner. For a copy of this publication, write to *Wolsey Lodges,* 17 Chapel St., Bildeston, Suffolk 1P7 7EP, England.

An organization offering home stays with French families is *Friends in France.* Travelers can choose from over 40 homes, ranging from simple country homes to stately châteaux. Prices for a double room vary substantially (depending on the level of elegance), although breakfast always is included. In this sense these resemble bed and breakfast accommodations rather than the traditional home stay arrangement, however, the host families are from a diverse spectrum of backgrounds and occupations, and their participation in the program generally is indicative of an interest in people and an eagerness to share their own little corner of France with their visitors. Through a detailed questionnaire, plus follow-up contact, *Friends in France* helps select the most suitable home or homes for your stay. There is a minimum stay of 3 nights and a maximum of 2 weeks with any one family; you can visit one or several homes during the course of your stay. About half the host families have an English-speaking member and the visitor's knowledge of French is taken into account when selecting the host family. A free brochure describing the program and a booklet for $7 describing the participating properties are available from *Friends in France* at PO Box 1044, Rocky Hill, CT 06067 (phone: 203-563-0195).

One of the fringe benefits of *glasnost* is the formation of a company called *American-Soviet Homestays,* which also arranges for Americans to spend some time in Soviet homes. As with the home stay programs discussed above, this type of vacation lets visitors bypass the sometimes impersonal rigidity of a package tour and enjoy the warmth of becoming absorbed in the daily life of their Soviet hosts. The trips are 17 to 21 days long and consist of visits to two different families in two different cities for 1 week each. The pairs of cities vary, but include Moscow and/or St. Petersburg, plus Alma Ata (Khazakhstan), Frunze (Kirghizia), Kiev (Ukraine), Riga (Latvia), Tallinn (Estonia), or Vilnius (Lithuania). Other destinations offered include Prague (Czechoslovakia), Berlin (Germany), and Budapest (Hungary). The company has counterparts in the Soviet Union with whom they work, and certain policies have been established, such as the following: At least one member of the host family must speak English; a separate room in the apartment is to be set aside for the guests; and the hosts must take time off from work during the visits. The guests will enjoy hearty Russian home cooking, and the hosts always are happy to take their new American friends sightseeing, shopping, or visiting. Departures for this program are from New York or Los Angeles, and an escort accompanies the travelers throughout the trip. While in the Soviet Union, the escort always is available by phone to solve any problems. The program runs May through September, and the company also arranges for Soviet visitors to spend time with American families. For further information, contact *American-Soviet Homestays, Inc.,* Route 1, Box 68, Iowa City, IA 52240 (phone: 319-626-2125).

You also might be interested in a publication called *International Meet-the-People Directory,* published by the *International Visitor Information Service.* It lists several agencies in a number of foreign countries (37 worldwide, 18 in Europe) that arrange home visits for Americans, either for dinner or overnight stays. To order a copy, send $5.95 to the *International Visitor Information Service* (733 15th St. NW, Suite 300, Washington, DC 20005; phone: 202-783-6540). For other local organizations and services offering home exchanges, contact the local tourist authority.

Time Zones, Business Hours, and Public Holidays

TIME ZONES: The countries of Europe fall into three time zones. Greenwich Mean Time — the time in Greenwich, England, at longitude 0°0′ — is the base from which all other time zones are measured. Areas in zones west of Greenwich have earlier times and are called Greenwich Minus; those to the east have later times and are called Greenwich Plus. For example, New York City — which falls into the Greenwich Minus 5 time zone — is 5 hours earlier than Greenwich, England. When it is noon in Greenwich, it is 7 AM in New York and Washington, DC.

The countries of Europe fall into the following time zones:

Greenwich Mean Time: The time is the same as in Greenwich, England, in the rest of Great Britain, Iceland, Ireland, and Portugal.

Greenwich Plus 1: The time is 1 hour later than in Greenwich, England, in Andorra, Austria, Belgium, Czechoslovakia, Denmark, France, Germany, Gibraltar, Holland, Hungary, Italy, Liechtenstein, Luxembourg, the Maltese Islands, Monaco, Norway, Poland, San Marino, western parts of the Soviet Union, Spain, Sweden, Switzerland, and Yugoslavia. (This time zone also is referred to as "Central European Time.")

Greenwich Plus 2: The time is 2 hours later than in Greenwich, England, in Bulgaria, Finland, Greece, Romania, and some eastern parts of the Soviet Union.

Almost all European nations move their clocks ahead an hour in the spring and back an hour in the fall, corresponding to the US's daylight savings time, although in both cases the date of the change tends to be a couple of weeks earlier than the dates we have adopted in the US. For about 2 weeks in the spring, then, the time difference between the US and many European countries is 1 hour greater than usual; for a 2-week period in the fall, there is 1 hour less differential.

European timetables use a 24-hour clock to denote arrival and departure times, which means that hours are expressed sequentially from 1 AM. By this method, 9 AM is recorded as 0900, noon as 1200, 1 PM as 1300, 6 PM as 1800, midnight as 2400, and so on. For example, the departure of a train at 7 AM will be announced as "0700"; one leaving at 7 PM will be noted as "1900."

BUSINESS HOURS: Travelers who are used to the American workday may be surprised to find that the Europeans follow a more eccentric schedule. Businesses open on weekdays between 8 and 9 AM and, in the northern European countries, continue through the day until 4 or 5 PM. The central and southern European countries tend to close for a 2- to 2½-hour lunch break (although the trend is currently moving toward shorter, 1-hour breaks) starting at 12:30 or 1 PM, and therefore close later in the evening — between 5:30 and 7. There are variations, of course.

Banks close an hour or two earlier than businesses as a rule but tend to open on weekdays at about the same time and, in some countries, selected branches also are open for a half or full day on Saturdays. If it's vital to you, check in advance because there are some exceptions. For more information, see *Banking/Business Hours* for the individual countries in FACTS IN BRIEF.

PUBLIC HOLIDAYS: Holidays also vary within countries, but if generalization can be attempted it is that (1) all businesses close down for a national day at least once a year and (2) religious holidays are more widely celebrated in Europe than in the US. *Easter* often is a 4-day celebration — *Good Friday* through *Easter Monday* — and

Ascension Day, Whitmonday or *Pentecost, The Assumption, All Saints' Day, Christmas Day,* and the following day (December 26, called *Boxing Day* in the United Kingdom) all are broadly observed. For information on holidays throughout Europe, see *Holidays/Special Events* in FACTS IN BRIEF.

Mail, Telephone, and Electricity

MAIL: European post offices generally are open during the week at the same hours as banks and other businesses, often offering Saturday morning hours as well (see "Business Hours," above); in large cities there may be a branch or two open 24 hours a day. As in the US, stamps usually can be bought both at post offices and at some stores, and letters also can be mailed from private and public mail boxes. It always is advisable, however, to send packages directly from post offices.

The number of digits in postal codes varies from country to country, and while some countries use numerals only (as in US zip codes), others may use a combination of numbers and letters (as in Canadian postal codes). The postal code always should be specified. This may merely speed delivery, but sometimes — because many small towns in Europe have the same or similar names — delivery of a letter may depend on it. If you do not have the correct postal code, the appropriate tourist board or European consulate or embassy should be able to look it up for you. Alternatively, you could call the addressee directly — if you have the telephone number — and although this will be costly, it may be worth it to ensure delivery of your correspondence.

Letters sent from Europe to the US always should be sent via airmail — otherwise they may end up going the *long* way by boat. Although letters have been known to arrive in as short a time as 5 days, it is a good idea to allow *at least* 10 days for delivery in either direction. If your correspondence is important, you may want to send it via one of the special courier services: *Federal Express, DHL,* and other international services are available throughout Europe. The cost is considerably higher than sending something via the postal service — but the assurance of its timely arrival is worth it.

There are several places that will receive and hold mail for travelers in Europe. Mail sent to you at a hotel and clearly marked "Guest Mail, Hold for Arrival" is one safe approach. Post offices in most countries also will extend this service to you if the mail is addressed to the European equivalent of US general delivery, most often called *Poste Restante,* particularly in Western European countries (the government tourist board of the country you plan to visit can tell you the correct term). This probably is the best way for travelers to have mail sent if they do not have a definite address. Although in some countries the central or main post office in each city or town handles *Poste Restante,* in others, such mail may be delivered to any one of a number of branch offices (particularly in major cities). Therefore, it is best to make sure that the address and/or specific name of the office be indicated (not just the name of the city), and travelers should be sure to call at the correct office when inquiring after mail. Also, don't forget to take your passport with you when you go to collect it. Most post offices require formal identification before they will release anything; there also may be a small charge for picking up your mail.

If you are an *American Express* customer (a cardholder, a carrier of *American Express* traveler's checks, or traveling on an *American Express Travel Related Services* tour), you can have mail sent to its offices in cities along your route. Letters are held free of charge — registered mail and packages are not accepted. You must be able to show an *American Express* card, traveler's checks, or a voucher proving you are on one of the company's tours to avoid paying for mail privileges. Those who aren't clients must pay a nominal charge each time they inquire if they have received mail, whether or not they actually have a letter. There also is a forwarding fee, for clients and non-clients alike. Mail should be addressed to you, care of *American Express,* and should be marked "Client Mail Service." Additional information on its mail service and addresses of *American Express* offices in Europe are listed in the pamphlet *Services and Offices,* available from any US branch of *American Express.*

While US embassies and consulates abroad will not under ordinary circumstances accept mail for tourists, they may hold mail for US citizens in an emergency situation or if the papers are especially important. It is best to inform them either by separate letter or cable, or by phone (particularly if you are in the country already), that you will be using their address for this purpose.

TELEPHONE: European telephone systems are not too different from our own. For the most part, direct dialing within the country, between nations, and overseas in possible throughout most of Europe. The number of digits in European telephone numbers, however, may vary from country to country, as well as within countries, and to further confuse matters, in some areas a city code may not be required or may be included in the digits quoted as the "local" number. If you dial a number directly and your call does not go through, either the circuits are busy, or you may need to add or delete one or several digits. If you have tried several times and are sure that you have the correct number, have an international operator place the call — however, this will be more expensive than dialing directly. (To reach an international operator in the US, dial "0" for a local operator and ask him or her to connect you.)

The procedure for calling anywhere in Europe from the US is as follows: dial 011 (the international access code) + the country code + the city code + the local number. For example, to place a call from anywhere in the US to Athens, Greece, dial 011 + 30 (the country code) + 1 (the city code) + the local number.

The procedure for calling the US from most European countries is as follows: Generally you will have to dial an international access code and a country code for the US before the area code and local number. For instance, to call directly to New York from anywhere in Spain, dial 07 (the international access code) + 1 (the US country code) + 212 + the local number.

As in the US, the general rule for dialing within a country is that if you are calling within the same city code (similar to a US area code), you simply dial the local number. If you are dialing from one city code coverage area to a number in another city, dial the city code + the local number. Note that this procedure and the procedure for calling the US from Europe described above are meant as general guidelines; find out the applicable procedures either from government tourist offices in the US before you go or when you arrive in Europe.

The procedure for reaching a local operator also varies from country to country, as does that for reaching an international operator. For operator-assisted calls between European nations or to the US, generally you will dial one direct number or the international access code followed by the number for the operator. For a country-by-country list of numbers to call in the event of an emergency, see *Medical and Legal Aid and Consular Services,* in this section.

Making connections in Europe (particularly in Eastern Europe) sometimes can be hit or miss — all exchanges are not always in operation on the same day. If the number dialed does not go through, try later or the next day. So be warned: Those who have to make an important call — to make a hotel reservation in another city, for instance — should start to do so a few days ahead.

As in the US, in Europe public pay phones are found in transportation centers (airports, train stations, and so on), at post offices, hotels, restaurants, commercial centers, and in booths on the street. The majority of European pay phones still take coins, but phones that take major credit cards (see *Credit and Currency,* in this section) or that take specially designated phone cards are increasingly common, particularly in metropolitan areas and at major tourist destinations.

These phone cards have been instigated to cut down on vandalism, as well as to free callers from the necessity of carrying around a pocketful of change, and generally are sold in various local currency denominations. The units per card, like message units in US phone parlance, are a combination of time and distance. To use such a card, you insert it into a slot in the phone and dial the number you wish to reach. A display gradually will count down the value that remains on your card. When you run out of units on the card, you can insert another.

Phone card systems have been introduced in a number of European countries, including France, Great Britain, Italy, Ireland, Portugal, Scandinavia, and Spain; others are expected to follow suit in the near future. Phone cards can be purchased at post offices, transportation and other commercial centers, at designated shops (usually sporting a sign in the window indicating this service), as well as from some tourist board offices. For further information, contact the government tourist boards of these countries (see *Tourist Information Offices,* in this section).

Although you can use a telephone-company credit card number on any phone, pay phones that take major credit cards are increasingly common worldwide, particularly in transportation and tourism centers. Also now available is the "affinity card," a combined telephone calling card/bank credit card that can be used for domestic and international calls. Cards of this type include the following:

> *AT&T/Universal* (phone: 800-662-7759). Cardholders can charge calls to the US from overseas.
>
> *Executive Telecard International* (phone: 800-950-3800). Cardholders can charge calls to the US from overseas, as well as between most European countries.
>
> *Sprint Visa* (phone: 800-446-7625). Cardholders can charge calls to the US from overseas.

Similarly, *MCI VisaPhone* (phone: 800-866-0099) can add phone card privileges to the services available through your existing *Visa* card. This service allows you to use your *Visa* account number, plus an additional code, to charge calls on any touch-tone phone in the US and Europe.

Hotel Surcharges – A lot of digits are involved once a caller starts dialing beyond national borders, but avoiding operator-assisted calls can cut costs considerably and bring rates into a somewhat more reasonable range — except for calls made through hotel switchboards. One of the most unpleasant surprises travelers encounter in many foreign countries is the amount they find tacked on to their hotel bill for telephone calls, because foreign hotels routinely add on astronomical surcharges. (It's not at all uncommon to find 300% or 400% added to the actual telephone charges.)

Until recently, the only recourse against this unconscionable overcharging was to call collect from abroad or to use a telephone credit card — available through a simple procedure from any local US phone company. (Note, however, that even if you use a telephone credit card, some hotels still may charge a fee for line usage.) Now, *American Telephone and Telegraph (AT&T)* offers *USA Direct,* a service that connects users, via a toll-free number, with an *AT&T* operator in the US, who will then put the call through at the standard international rate. Another new feature of this service is that travelers abroad can reach US toll-free (800) numbers by calling a *USA Direct* operator, who will connect them. Charges for all calls made through *USA Direct* appear on the caller's regular US phone bill. As we went to press, this service was available throughout Western Europe; in Eastern Europe it was available only in Czechoslovakia, Hungary, Poland, and Yugoslavia. For a brochure and wallet card listing toll-free numbers by country, contact International Information Service, *AT&T Communications* (635 Grant St., Pittsburgh, PA 15219; phone: 800-874-4000).

AT&T also has put together *Teleplan,* an agreement among certain hoteliers that sets a limit on surcharges for calls made by guests from their rooms. *Teleplan* currently is in effect in selected hotels throughout Europe. *Teleplan* agreements stipulate a flat, low rate for credit card or collect calls, and a flat percentage on calls paid for at the hotel. For further information, contact *AT&T*'s International Information Service (address above).

Until such services become universal, it's wise to ask the surcharge rate *before* calling from a hotel. (Also note that even in areas where these services are available, some European hotels may block guests' access to them in order to collect full surcharges.) If the rate is high, it's best to use a telephone credit card, make a collect call, or place the call and ask the party to call right back. If none of these choices is possible, to avoid surcharges make international calls from the local post office or one of the special telephone centers located throughout Europe. Another way to keep down the cost of telephoning from Europe is to leave a copy of your itinerary and telephone numbers with people in the US so that they can call you instead.

A particularly useful service for travelers to Europe is *AT&T*'s Language Line Service. By calling 800-628-8486, you will be connected with an interpreter in any one of 143 languages and dialects, who will provide on-line interpretive services for $3.50 a minute. From the US, this service is particularly useful for booking travel services in Europe where English is not spoken — or not spoken fluently. Once in Europe, this number can be reached by using the *USA Direct* toll-free (800) number connection feature described above — it will enable you to make arrangements at foreign establishments or to reach emergency or other vital services with which you would otherwise have trouble communicating due to the language barrier. For further information, contact *AT&T* at the address above or call 800-752-6096.

Other Resources – Particularly useful for planning a trip is *AT&T*'s *Toll-Free 800 Directory,* which lists thousands of companies with 800 numbers, both alphabetically (white pages) and by category (yellow pages), including a wide range of travel services — from travel agents to transportation and accommodations. Issued in a consumer edition for $9.95 and a business edition for $14.95, both are available from *AT&T Phone Centers* or by calling 800-426-8686. Other useful directories for use before you leave and on the road include the *Toll-Free Travel & Vacation Information Directory* ($4.95 postpaid from Pilot Books, 103 Cooper St., Babylon, NY 11702; phone 516-422-2225) and *The Phone Booklet,* which lists the nationwide, toll-free (800) numbers of travel information sources and suppliers — such as major airlines, hotel and motel chains, car rental companies, and tourist information offices (send $2 to *Scott American Corporation,* Box 88, W. Redding, CT 06896).

ELECTRICITY: The US runs on 110-volt, 60-cycle alternating current; most of Europe runs on 220- or 240-volt, 50-cycle alternating current, although 115- and 125-volt current still exists in some areas. (The voltage rarely is indicated on the outlet or anywhere else in hotel rooms, so it's always best to ask each time you change addresses.) The difference between US and European voltage means that, without a converter, the motor of a US appliance used overseas at 220 or 240 volts would run at twice the speed at which it's meant to operate and would quickly burn out. For specific information on electrical standards, see *Electric Current* in the individual country entries in FACTS IN BRIEF.

Travelers can solve the problem by buying a lightweight converter to transform foreign voltage into the US kind (there are several types of converters, depending on the wattage of the appliance) or by buying dual-voltage appliances, which convert from one to the other at the flick of a switch (hair dryers of this sort are common). The difference between the 50- and 60-cycle currents will cause no problem — the American appliance simply will run more slowly — but it still will be necessary to deal with differing socket configurations before plugging in. To be fully prepared, bring along an extension cord (in older or rural establishments the electrical outlet may be farther from the sink than the cord on your razor or hair dryer can reach), and a wall socket adapter with a full set of plugs to ensure that you'll be able to plug in anywhere.

One good source for sets of plugs and adapters for use worldwide is the *Franzus Company* (PO Box 142, Beacon Falls, CT 06403; phone: 203-723-6664). *Franzus* also publishes a useful brochure, *Foreign Electricity Is No Deep Dark Secret,* which provides information about converters and adapter plugs for electric appliances to be used abroad but manufactured for use in the US. To obtain a free copy, send a self-addressed, stamped envelope to *Franzus* at the above address; a catalogue of other travel accessories is available on request.

Medical and Legal Aid and Consular Services

MEDICAL AID ABROAD: Nothing ruins a vacation or business trip more effectively than sudden injury or illness. You will discover, in the event of an emergency, that most tourist facilities — transportation companies, hotels, and resorts — are equipped to handle the situation quickly and efficiently. Most European towns and cities of any size have a public hospital and even the tiniest hamlet has a medical clinic or private physician nearby. All hospitals are prepared for emergency cases, and many hospitals also have walk-in clinics to serve people who do not really need emergency service, but who have no place to go for immediate medical attention. The level of medical care in Western Europe generally is excellent, providing the same basic specialties and services that are available in the US. (Note that in Eastern European countries, medical standards may fall far short of our expectations.)

Before you go, be sure to check with your insurance company about the applicability of your hospitalization and major medical policies while you're abroad; many policies do not apply, and others are not accepted in Europe. Older travelers should know that Medicare does not make payments outside the US, and — contrary to lingering popular belief — free public health services (in those countries that have them — Great Britain, for example) do not provide free medical or dental care to visitors, except in (and only in) a few instances. If your medical policy does not protect you while you're traveling, there are comprehensive combination policies specifically designed to fill the gap. (For a discussion of medical insurance and a list of inclusive combination policies, see *Insurance,* in this section.)

If a bona fide emergency occurs, in some countries an inability to speak the native language can pose a serious problem in getting help or in getting to the place where help is available. The fastest way to receive attention may be to go directly to the emergency room of the nearest hospital. An alternative is to dial the local emergency number (see the country-by-country list at the end of this section) used to summon the police, fire trucks, and ambulances.

Most emergency services send out well-equipped and well-staffed ambulances, although in some areas, ambulances may not be equipped with the advanced EMS technology found in the US. Since ambulance dispatchers often are accustomed to taking calls from doctors only, state immediately that you are a foreign tourist and then describe the nature of your problem and your location. In non-English-speaking countries, however, the ambulance dispatcher probably will not be bilingual, and unless you speak the language, he or she will be unable to determine the nature of the emergency, what equipment will be needed, or even where to send the ambulance. Travelers with little or no foreign language ability should try to get someone else to make the call. If the situation is desperate, an international operator may be able to make the call to the local emergency service and stay on the line as interpreter. (You should find out what number to dial for an international operator as soon as you arrive in a new country.)

If a doctor is needed for something less than an emergency, there are several ways to find one. If you are staying in a hotel or at a resort, ask for help in reaching a doctor or other emergency services, or for the house physician, who may visit you in your room or ask you to visit an office. Even in countries where a foreign language is spoken, travelers staying at a hotel of any size probably will find that the doctor on call speaks at least a modicum of English — if not, request one who does. When you register at a hotel, it's not a bad idea to include your home address and telephone number; this will facilitate the process of notifying friends, relatives, or your own doctor in case of an emergency.

Dialing the emergency number also may be of help in locating a doctor in a non-emergency situation (again, if you can speak the language). Callers often will be given the name of a general practitioner, since private doctors (usually specialists) may see patients upon referral only. You might also check at the local post office, where neighborhood emergency physicians may be listed (though they often aren't), as well as in the local telephone directory. If you are already at the hospital, you may see the specialist there, or you may make an appointment to be seen at his or her office.

In addition, though general practitioners deliver primary care, there is no violation of protocol in approaching a specialist directly; call the appropriate department of a teaching hospital or the nearest US consulate or embassy (see "Legal Aid and Consular Services," below), which also maintains a list of doctors. Remember that if you are hospitalized, you will have to pay, even in an emergency.

There should be no problem finding a 24-hour drugstore (called a "chemist" in Great Britain; *pharmacie* in France; *Apotheke* in Germany; *farmacia* in Italy for drugs only and *profumeria* for cosmetics and toiletries; *farmacia* in Spain; and *apotek* in Sweden) in any major European city. In many areas, pharmacists who close are required to post in the window the addresses of the nearest all-night drugstores or the evening's on-call pharmacy (night duty may rotate among pharmacies in some areas). A call to the emergency room of the local hospital also may produce this information. In small towns, where none may be open after normal business hours, you may be able to have one open in an emergency situation — such as a diabetic needing insulin — although you may be charged a fee for this off-hour service.

Bring along a copy of any prescription you may have from your doctor in case you should need a refill. In the case of minor complaints, European pharmacists *may* agree to fill a foreign prescription; however, do not count on this. In most cases, you probably will need a local doctor to rewrite the prescription. Even in an emergency, a traveler will more than likely be given only enough of a drug to last until a local prescription can be obtained.

Americans also will notice that some drugs sold only by prescription in the US are sold over the counter in Europe (and vice versa). Though this can be very handy, be aware that common cold medicines and aspirin that contain codeine or other controlled substances will not be allowed back into the US.

Emergency assistance also is available from the various medical programs designed for travelers who have chronic ailments or whose illness requires them to return home:

International Association of Medical Assistance to Travelers (*IAMAT;* 417 Center St., Lewiston, NY 14092; phone: 716-754-4883). Entitles members to the services of participating doctors around the world, as well as clinics and hospitals in various locations. Participating physicians agree to adhere to a basic charge of around $40 to see a patient referred by *IAMAT*. To join, simply write to *IAMAT;* in about 3 weeks you will receive a membership card, the booklet of members, and an inoculation chart. A nonprofit organization, *IAMAT* appreciates donations; with a donation of $25 or more, you will receive a set of worldwide climate charts detailing weather and sanitary conditions. (Delivery can take up to 5 weeks, so plan ahead.)

International SOS Assistance (PO Box 11568, Philadelphia, PA 19116; phone: 800-523-8930 or 215-244-1500). Subscribers are provided with telephone access — 24 hours a day, 365 days a year — to a worldwide, monitored, multilingual network of medical centers. A phone call brings assistance ranging from a telephone consultation to transportation home by ambulance or aircraft, or, in some cases, transportation of a family member to wherever you are hospitalized. Individual rates are $35 for 2 weeks of coverage ($3.50 for each additional day), $70 for 1 month, or $240 for 1 year; couple and family rates also are available.

Medic Alert Foundation (2323 N. Colorado, Turlock, CA 95380; phone: 800-ID-ALERT or 209-668-3333). If you have a health condition that may not be readily perceptible to the casual observer — one that might result in a tragic error in an emergency situation — this organization offers identification emblems specifying such conditions. The foundation also maintains a computerized central file from which your complete medical history is available 24 hours a day by phone (the telephone number is clearly inscribed on the emblem). The onetime membership fee (between $25 and $45) is based on the type of metal from which the emblem is made — the choices range from stainless steel to 10K gold-filled.

TravMed (PO Box 10623, Baltimore, MD 21204; phone: 800-732-5309 or 301-296-5225). For $3 per day, subscribers receive comprehensive medical assistance while abroad. Major medical expenses are covered up to $100,000, and special transportation home or of a family member to wherever you are hospitalized is provided at no additional cost.

■ **Note:** Those who are unable to take a reserved flight due to personal illness or who must fly home unexpectedly due to a family emergency should be aware that airlines may offer a discounted airfare (or arrange a partial refund) if the traveler can demonstrate that his or her situation is indeed a legitimate emergency. Your inability to fly or the illness or death of an immediate family member usually must be substantiated by a doctor's note or by the name, relationship, and funeral home from which the deceased will be buried. In such cases, airlines often will waive certain advance purchase restrictions or you may receive a refund check or voucher for future travel at a later date. Be aware, however, that this bereavement fare may not necessarily be the least expensive fare available and, if possible, it is best to have a travel agent check all possible flights through a computer reservations system (CRS).

Emergency Numbers in Europe – As discussed above, in the event of an accident or other medical emergency, call the applicable number listed below (as you would dial 911 throughout the US). State immediately that you are a foreign tourist and then the nature of your problem and your location.

Andorra: Dial 182-0020 for an ambulance or 21222 for the police.
Austria: Dial 144 for an ambulance or 133 for the police.
Belgium: Dial 100 for an ambulance or 101 for the police.

Bulgaria: Dial 150 for an ambulance or 911 for the police.

Czechoslovakia: Dial 155 for an ambulance or 158 for the police.

Denmark: Dial 000 for emergency assistance.

Finland: Dial 000 for emergency assistance.

France: Dial 17 for emergency assistance.

Germany: Dial 110 for emergency assistance.

Gibraltar: Dial 199 for emergency assistance.

Great Britain: Dial 999 for emergency assistance.

Greece: Dial 100 for emergency assistance, 150 for an ambulance, or 171 for the police.

Hungary: Dial 04 for an ambulance or 07 for the police.

Iceland: In Reykjavik, dial 11100 for an ambulance or 11166 for the police; elsewhere in Iceland, dial 02 for an operator who will connect you to the police or other emergency services.

Ireland: Dial 999 for emergency assistance.

Italy: Dial 113 for an ambulance or 112 for the police.

Liechtenstein: Dial 144 for an ambulance or 117 for the police.

Luxembourg: Dial 012 for emergency assistance.

Maltese Islands: Dial 196 for an ambulance or 191 for the police.

Monaco: Dial 933-01945 for an ambulance or 17 for the police.

Netherlands: In Amsterdam, dial 559-9111 for emergency assistance; elsewhere in Holland, dial 008 for an operator who will connect you to the police or other emergency services.

Norway: Dial 003 for an ambulance or 002 for the police.

Poland: Dial 999 for an ambulance or 997 for the police.

Portugal: Dial 115 for emergency assistance.

Romania: In Bucharest, dial 061 for an ambulance or 055 for the police; elsewhere in Romania, dial 091 for an operator who will connect you to the police or other emergency services.

San Marino: Dial 113 for emergency assistance.

Soviet Union: Dial 03 for an ambulance or 02 for the police.

Spain: Dial 091 for emergency assistance.

Sweden: Dial 90000 for emergency assistance.

Switzerland: Dial 144 for an ambulance or 117 for the police.

Yugoslavia: Dial 94 for an ambulance or 92 for the police.

LEGAL AID AND CONSULAR SERVICES: There is one crucial place to keep in mind when outside the US, namely, the American Services section of the US consulate. If you are injured or become seriously ill, the consulate will direct you to medical assistance and notify your relatives. If, while abroad, you become involved in a dispute that could lead to legal action, the consulate, once again, is the place to turn.

It usually is far more alarming to be arrested abroad than at home. Not only are you alone among strangers, but the punishment can be worse. Granted, the US consulate can advise you of your rights and provide a list of lawyers, but it cannot interfere with the local legal process. Except for minor infractions of the local traffic code, there is no reason for any law-abiding traveler to run afoul of immigration, customs, or any other law enforcement authority.

The best advice is to be honest and law-abiding. If you get a traffic ticket, pay it. If you are approached by drug hawkers, ignore them. The penalties for possession of marijuana, cocaine, and other narcotics are even more severe abroad than in the US. (If you are picked up for any drug-related offense, do not expect US foreign service officials to be sympathetic. Chances are they will notify a lawyer and your family and that's about all. See "Drugs," below.)

In the case of minor traffic accidents (such as a fender bender), it often is most expedient to settle the matter before the police get involved. If, however, you are involved in a serious accident, where an injury or fatality results, the first step is to contact the nearest US consulate (for addresses, see below) and ask the consul to locate a lawyer to assist you. If you have a traveling companion, ask him or her to call the consulate (unless either of you has a local contact who can help you quickly). Competent English-speaking lawyers practice throughout Europe, and it is possible to obtain good legal counsel on short notice.

The US Department of State in Washington, DC, insists that any US citizen who is arrested abroad has the right to contact the US embassy or consulate "immediately," but it may be a while before you are given permission to use a phone. Do not labor under the illusion, however, that in a scrape with foreign officialdom the consulate can act as an arbitrator or ombudsman on a US citizen's behalf. Nothing could be farther from the truth. Consuls have no power, authorized or otherwise, to subvert, alter, or contravene the legal processes, however unfair, of the foreign country in which they serve. Nor can a consul oil the machinery of a foreign bureaucracy or provide legal advice. The consul's responsibilities do encompass "welfare duties," including providing a list of lawyers and information on local sources of legal aid, informing relatives in the US, and organizing and administering any defense monies sent from home. If a case is tried unfairly or the punishment seems unusually severe, the consul can make a formal complaint to the authorities. For questions about US citizens arrested abroad, how to get money to them, and other useful information, call the *Citizens' Emergency Center* of the Office of Special Consular Services in Washington, DC, at 202-647-5225. (For further information about this invaluable hotline, see below.)

Other welfare duties, not involving legal hassles, cover cases of both illness and destitution. If you should get sick, the US consul can provide names of doctors and dentists, as well as the names of all local hospitals and clinics; the consul also will contact family members in the US and help arrange special ambulance service for a flight home. In a situation involving "legitimate and proven poverty" of a US citizen stranded abroad without funds, the consul will contact sources of money (such as family or friends in the US), apply for aid to agencies in foreign countries, and in a last resort — which is *rarely* — arrange for repatriation at government expense, although this is a loan that must be repaid. And in case of natural disasters or civil unrest, consulates around the world handle the evacuation of US citizens if it becomes necessary.

The consulate is not occupied solely with emergencies and is certainly not there to aid in trivial situations, such as canceled reservations or lost baggage, no matter how important these matters may seem to the victimized tourist. The main duties of any consulate are administering statutory services, such as the issuance of passports and visas; providing notarial services; distributing VA, social security, and civil service benefits to US citizens; taking depositions; handling extradition cases; and reporting to Washington the births, deaths, and marriages of US citizens living within the consulate's domain.

We hope that none of the information in this section will be necessary during your stay in Europe. If you can avoid legal hassles altogether, you will have a much more pleasant trip. If you become involved in an imbroglio, the local authorities may spare you legal complications if you make clear your tourist status. And if you run into a confrontation that might lead to legal complications developing with a citizen or with local authorities, the best tactic is to apologize and try to leave as gracefully as possible. Do not get into fights with residents, no matter how belligerent or provocative they are in a given situation.

Following is a list of US embassies and consulates in Europe. (If you are not a US citizen, contact the consulate of your own nation.) The first address listed is that of the US embassy; where there are additional locations listed, these are consulates in cities other than the one in which the embassy is located. Note that mailing addresses may be different — so call before sending anything to these offices. Also note that, unlike elsewhere in GETTING READY TO GO, we have not included country codes in these telephone numbers, as it is most likely that you will be calling these offices while in Europe.

Austria: 16 Boltzmanngasse, Vienna 1090 (phone: 222-315511); A-5020 Giselakai, Salzburg 51 (phone: 662-28-601).

Belgium: 27 Bd. du Régent, Brussels B-1000 (phone: 2-513-3830); Rubens Center, 5 Nationalestraat, Antwerp B-2000 (phone: 3-225-0071).

Bulgaria: 1 Stamboliski Blvd., Sofia (phone: 2-884801, 2-884802, or 2-884803).

Czechoslovakia: 15 Triste, 12548 Prague 1 (phone: 2-536641 through 49).

Denmark: 24 Dag Hammerskjölds Alle, Copenhagen 2100 (phone: 31-423144).

Finland: 14 Itainen Puistotie, Helsinki 00140 (phone: 0-171931).

France: 2 Av. Gabriel, Paris 75382 (phone: 1-42-96-12-02 or 1-42-61-80-75); 22 Cours du Maréchal-Foch, Bordeaux 33080 (phone: 56-52-65-95); 7 Quai Général-Sarrail, Lyons 69454 (phone: 78-24-68-49); 12 Bd. Paul-Peytral, Marseilles 13286 (phone: 91-54-92-00); 15 Av. d'Alsace, Strasbourg 67082 (phone: 88-35-31-04).

Germany: Deichmanns Au, 5300 Bonn 2 (phone: 228-3391); 170 Clayallee, D-1000 Berlin 33 (Dahlem; phone: 30-81-97543); 21 Siesmayerstr., 6000 Frankfurt 1 (phone: 69-753-50); 27 Alster Ufer, 2000 Hamburg 36 (phone: 40-411710); 5 Königinstr., 8000 Munich 22 (phone: 89-2-8881); 7 Urbanstr., Stuttgart 7000 (phone: 711-21-450).

Great Britain: 24-31 Grosvenor Sq. W., London W1A 1AE (phone: 71-499-9000); Queen's House, 14 Queen St., Belfast BT1 6EQ (phone: 232-328239); 3 Regent Ter., Edinburgh EH7 5BW (phone: 31-556-8315).

Greece: 921 Queen Sophias Ave., Athens 10160 (phone: 1-721-29-51); 59 Leoforos Nikis, Thessaloníki GR-546-22 (phone: 31-266-121).

Hungary: 1054 Szabadsag Tér. 12, Budapest (phone: 1-126450).

Iceland: 21 Laufasvegur, Reykjavik (phone: 1-29100).

Ireland: 42 Elgin Rd., Ballsbridge, Dublin 4 (phone: 1-688-777).

Italy: 119/A Via Veneto, Rome 00187 (phone: 6-46741); Banca d'America e d'Italia Bldg., 6 Piazza Portello, Genoa 16124 (phone: 10-282741 through 5); 2-10 Via Principe Amedeo, Milan 20121 (phone: 2-290-04559); Piazza della Repubblica, Naples 80122 (phone: 81-761-4303); 38 Lungarno Amerigo Vespucci, Florence (phone: 55-2398276).

Luxembourg: 22 Bd. Emmanuel-Servais, Luxembourg 2535 (phone: 460123 through 7).

Netherlands: 102 Lange Voorhout, the Hague (phone: 70-362-4911); 19 Museumplein, Amsterdam (phone: 20-6645661).

Norway: 18 Drammensveien, Oslo 2 (phone: 2-448550).

Poland: 29-31 Aleje Ujazdowskie, Warsaw (phone: 2-6283041).

Portugal: Av. das Forças Armadas, Sete Rios, Lisbon 1600 (phone: 1-725600).

Romania: 7-9 Strada Tudor Arghezi, Bucharest (phone: 0-104040).

Soviet Union: 19-21-23 Ulitsa Chaykovskogo, Moscow (phone: 95-252-2451 through -2459); 15 Ulitsa Petra Lavrova, St. Petersburg (phone: 812-274-8235).

Spain: 75 Serrano, Madrid 28006 (phone: 1-577-4000); 33-4 Via Laietana, Barcelona (phone: 3-319-9550).

Sweden: 101 Strandvagen, Stockholm S-115-27 (phone: 8-783-5300).

Switzerland: 93 Jubilaeumstr., Bern 3005 (phone: 31-43-70-11); 11 Rte. de Pregny, Chambesy/Geneva 1292 (phone: 22-738-7613); 141 Zolliikerstr., Zurich 8008 (phone: 1-552566).

Yugoslavia: 50 Kneza Milosa, Belgrade (phone: 11-645-655); 2 Braće Kavurića, Zagreb (phone: 41-444-800).

If your itinerary includes any country not on the above list, its national tourist office can tell you which consulate or embassy abroad is charged with responsibility for Americans there.

You can obtain a booklet with addresses of most US embassies and consulates around the world by writing the Superintendent of Documents (US Government Printing Office, Washington, DC 20402; phone: 202-783-3238) and asking for publication #78-77, *Key Offices of Foreign Service Posts.*

As mentioned above, the US State Department operates a *Citizens' Emergency Center,* which offers a number of services to American travelers abroad and their families at home. In addition to giving callers up-to-date information on trouble spots, the center will contact authorities abroad in an attempt to locate a traveler or deliver an urgent message. In case of illness, death, arrest, destitution, or repatriation of a US citizen on foreign soil, it will relay information to relatives at home if the consulate is unable to do so. Travel advisory information is available 24 hours a day to people with touch-tone phones (phone: 202-647-5225). Callers with rotary phones can get travel advisory information at this number from 8:15 AM to 10 PM (eastern standard time) on weekdays; 9 AM to 3 PM on Saturdays. In the event of an emergency, this number also may be called during these hours. For emergency calls only, at all other times, call 202-634-3600 and ask for the Duty Officer.

Drinking and Drugs

DRINKING: It is more than likely that some of the warmest memories of a trip to Europe will be moments of conviviality shared over a drink in a neighborhood pub, a *Weinstube,* or a sunlit café. As in the US, national taxes on alcohol affect the prices of liquor in Europe. In general, local wine, beer, and other liquor are the best buys, so take this opportunity to savor them at the source.

With the exception of European beer, which at around 5% has a slightly higher alcoholic content than that of North America, European beverages are no stronger than those found in the US: Wines and champagne contain a standard 12% alcohol; fortified wines such as sherry, port, and the aperitifs have anywhere between 12% and 18%; and brandies and hard liquor between 40% and 50% (80 to 100 proof). The potency of such famed liquors as Russian vodka, Scandinavian aquavit, and Yugoslavian *slivovitz* derives from the fact that they are often taken fast and neat rather than that they have high alcoholic content.

Europe offers a wide variety of alcoholic drinks, and you should taste as many as you can. A short survey of some of the favorites:

Austria – Here the classic drink combination (especially in summer) is a shot of schnapps followed by a chaser of beer. Schnapps is a general term for a wide range of liquors, distilled from grain at about 80 proof. Enjoyed in a *Gasthaus,* schnapps is served straight up.

Bulgaria – A bar is a *bar* (same spelling), and the favorite drink is a small, chilled glass of *slivovitz,* a flavorful spirit made from plums.

France – Wine by the glass or carafe is the trademark of Parisian cafés, where the house choice (*vin de la maison*) usually is reasonably priced and palatable.

Germany – The size of many German waistlines testifies to the overriding popularity of *Bier,* served by the *viertel liter* (one-quarter liter) in a *Taverne* or *Bier Keller* (beer cellar).

Great Britain – Scotch whisky and English ale are the favorites in England's pubs.

Whisky may be tempered with a little water (never ice), and ale comes at room temperature — except when it is called lager, which usually is chilled. Other sweeter brews include hard cider, which is served in two versions — sweet (slightly alcoholic) and hard (more potent) — and mead, a traditional, syrupy, honey liqueur.

Greece – High-proof *ouzo* is the drink of choice. The best is made from grapes, tasting faintly of licorice (it's flavored with anise), and is served on the rocks or with water in a *kafenio* (coffeehouse). Another widely imbibed favorite is *retsina,* a traditional resin-flavored wine.

Ireland – Guinness stout, a dark, syrupy ale with a thick, creamy head and a pronounced bitterness from hops, is the favorite in local pubs.

Italy – Along with wine, the popular drink at a local *caffè* is Campari, usually served on the rocks with soda and a twist.

Poland – Polish vodka, traditionally served neat and slightly chilled in a liqueur glass, is distilled from grain. Available in *bars* (same spelling), it often is served with a grind of fresh pepper or a twist of lemon.

Scandinavia – Without a doubt, the regional drink is aquavit, a flavored neutral spirit, sometimes derived from potatoes, sometimes from grain. Served icy cold in a tulip-shape glass, occasionally with a side of beer, aquavit almost always is imbibed with meals. In fancy restaurants, the bottle is brought to the table encased in a jacket of ice.

The Soviet Union – Vodka is the overwhelming drink of choice.

Spain – In addition to a glass of red wine (*a tinto*), the *gente* enjoy a wide range of excellent sherries. Most people will order a glass of sherry (*a fino*), served in a small glass to be sipped leisurely in an outdoor *café* or *bar* (same spelling).

Switzerland – On the French side, drinking habits run along Gallic lines; that is, wine is preferred. On the German side, a cup of coffee with schnapps or a mug of beer is popular.

Yugoslavia – Once again, the taste is for plums, and *slivovitz,* served in a *gostina* (bar), is considered the national drink.

As in the US, national taxes on alcohol in the Common Market countries affect the prices of liquor there, not — as used to be the case — the fact that they are manufactured in other countries. Any alcoholic beverage is expensive in Denmark, Norway, and Sweden because it is highly taxed. In France, if a drink costs a lot, it's because the café prices it that way. Gin is as cheap in Italy as in Great Britain. However, in Austria, not a Common Market country, taxes make imported liquor exorbitant, so it is best to drink whatever alcoholic beverage is produced locally.

Whiskey and gin are not indigenous to the Continent, and as a general rule, mixed drinks are expensive. If you like a drop before dinner, a good way to save money is to buy a bottle of your favorite brand at the airport before leaving the US and enjoy it in your hotel before setting forth.

Most European countries allow a quart or more of hard liquor and at least one bottle of wine to be brought in duty-free; check with government tourist offices in the US for the limit (for addresses, see *Tourist Information Offices,* in this section). If you are buying any quantity of alcohol (such as a case of wine) in Europe and traveling through a number of countries, you will have to pass through customs and pay duty at each border crossing, so you might want to arrange to have it shipped home. Whether bringing it with you or shipping, you will have to pay US import duties on any quantity over the allowed 1 liter (see *Customs and Returning to the US,* in this section).

DRUGS: For the most part, illegal narcotics are as prevalent in Europe as in the US, but the moderate legal penalties and vague social acceptance that marijuana has gained in the US have no equivalents in Europe (with the exception of Amsterdam, where marijuana has a quasi-legal status). Due to the international war on drugs, enforcement of drug laws is becoming increasingly strict throughout the world. Local European narcotics officers and customs officials are renowned for their absence of understanding and lack of a sense of humor — especially where foreigners are concerned.

Opiates and barbiturates, and other increasingly popular drugs — "'white powder" substances like heroin, cocaine, and "crack" (the cocaine derivative) — continue to be of major concern to narcotics officials. Most European countries have toughened laws regarding illegal drugs and narcotics, and it is important to bear in mind that the type or quantity of drugs involved is of minor importance. The maximum penalties may be imposed for possessing even *traces* of illegal drugs. There is a high conviction rate in these cases, and bail for foreigners is rare. Persons arrested are subject to the laws of the country they are visiting, and there isn't much that the US consulate can do for drug offenders beyond providing a list of lawyers. The best advice we can offer is this: Don't carry, use, buy, or sell illegal drugs.

Those who carry medicines that contain a controlled drug should be sure to have a current doctor's prescription with them. Ironically, travelers can get into almost as much trouble coming through US customs with over-the-counter drugs picked up abroad that contain substances that are controlled in the US. Cold medicines, pain relievers, and the like often have codeine or codeine derivatives that are illegal, except by prescription, in the US. Throw them out before leaving for home.

■ **Be forewarned:** US narcotics agents warn travelers of the increasingly common ploy of drug dealers asking travelers to transport a "gift" or other package back to the US. Don't be fooled into thinking that the protection of US law applies abroad — accused of illegal drug trafficking, you will be considered guilty until you prove your innocence. In other words, do not, under any circumstances, agree to take anything across the border for a stranger.

Tipping

Throughout Europe you will find the custom of including some kind of service charge — generally 12% to 15% — in the bill for a meal or accommodations more common than in the US. This can confuse Americans not familiar with the custom. On the one hand, many a traveler, unaware of this policy, has left many a superfluous tip. On the other hand, travelers aware of this policy may make the mistake of assuming that it takes care of everything. It doesn't. While "service included" in theory eliminates any question of how much and whom to tip, in practice there still are occasions when on-the-spot tips are appropriate. Among these are tips to show appreciation for special services, as well as tips meant to say "thank you" for services rendered.

In restaurants, the service charge may appear in one of two ways: It either already is calculated in the prices listed or will be added to the final bill. For the most part, if you see a notation at the bottom of the menu — such as *service compris* or *s.c.* (French), *Eingeschlossen* (German), *compreso* or *incluso* (Italian), and so on — without a percentage figure, the charge should be included in the prices; if a percentage figure is indicated, the service charge has not yet been added. To further confuse the issue, not every restaurant notes if its policy is to include service and at what point the charge is added. If you are at all unsure, you should feel no embarrassment about asking a waiter.

The service charge generally ranges from 12% to 15%. If it isn't added, a 15% tip — just as in the US — usually is a safe figure, although one should never hesitate to penalize poor service or reward excellent and efficient attention by leaving less or more. If the tip has been added, no further gratuity is expected — though it's a common practice in Europe for diners to leave a few extra coins on the table for the waiter. The emphasis is on *few,* and the local equivalent of $1 usually is quite adequate.

Although it's not necessary to tip the maître d' of most restaurants — unless he has been especially helpful in arranging a special party or providing a table (slipping him something in a crowded restaurant *may* get you seated sooner or procure a preferred table) — when tipping is desirable or appropriate, the least amount should be around the current equivalent of $5. In the finest restaurants, where a multiplicity of servers are present, plan to tip 5% to the captain. In some countries, the sommelier (wine waiter) is tipped a standard gratuity of approximately $2 per bottle of wine; in others he is tipped only if he has selected the wine for you, in which case it is customary to tip 10% of the price of the bottle — so use your own discretion.

In British pubs, where you simply pay the bartender the price of drinks, there generally is no tipping — unless you care to offer him or her an occasional drink — not a bad policy to follow in other countries. Where a "tab" is run up and a bill presented — in bars, cafés, cocktail lounges, nightclubs, pubs, and so on — tipping is similar to restaurants: Service often is included, but you may want to leave a few extra coins on the table.

In allocating gratuities at a restaurant, pay particular attention to what has become the standard credit card charge form, which now includes separate places for gratuities for waiters and/or captains. If these separate boxes are not on the charge slip, simply ask the waiter or captain how these separate tips should be indicated. Be aware, too, of the increasingly common, devious practice of placing the amount of an entire restaurant bill (in which service already has been included) in the top box of a charge slip, leaving the "tip" and "total" boxes ominously empty. Don't be intimidated: Leave the "tip" box blank and just repeat the total amount next to "total" before signing. In some establishments, tips indicated on credit card receipts may not be given to the help, so you may want to leave tips in cash.

As in restaurants, visitors usually will find a service charge of 12% to 15% included in their final bill at most hotels. No additional gratuities are required — or expected — beyond this billed service charge. It is unlikely, however, that a service charge will be added to bills in small family-run guesthouses, inns, or bed and breakfast establishments. In these cases, guests should let their instincts be their guide; no tipping is expected by members of the family who own the establishment, but it is a nice gesture to leave something for others — such as a dining room waiter or a maid — who may have been helpful. A gratuity of around $1 per night is adequate in most cases.

If a hotel does not automatically add a service charge, it is perfectly proper for guests to ask to have an extra 10% to 15% added to their bill, to be distributed among those who served them. This may be an especially convenient solution in a large hotel, where it's difficult to determine just who out of a horde of attendants actually performed particular services.

For those who prefer to distribute tips themselves, a chambermaid generally is tipped at the rate of around $1 per day. Tip the concierge or hall porter for specific services only, with the amount of such gratuities dependent on the level of service provided. For any special service you receive in a hotel, a tip is expected — the current equivalent of $1 being the minimum for a small service.

Bellhops, doormen, and porters at hotels and transportation centers generally are tipped at the rate of around $1 per piece of luggage, along with a small additional amount if a doorman helps with a cab or car. Once upon a time, taxi drivers in Europe would give you a rather odd look if presented with a tip for a fare, but times have changed, and 10% to 15% of the amount on the meter is now a standard gratuity.

Miscellaneous tips: Tipping ushers in a movie house, theater, or concert hall varies from country to country, but in general a few coins for being shown to a seat is appropriate. In some countries, the program is not free and in lieu of a tip it is common practice to purchase a program from the person who seats you. Sightseeing tour guides also should be tipped. If you are traveling in a group, decide together what you want to give the guide and present it from the group at the end of the tour ($1 per person is a reasonable tip). If you have been individually escorted, the amount paid should depend on the degree of your satisfaction, but it should not be less than 10% of the total tour price. Museum and monument guides also are usually tipped, and it is a nice touch to tip a caretaker who unlocks a small church or turns on the lights in a chapel for you in some out-of-the-way town.

In barbershops and beauty salons, tip as you would at home, keeping in mind that the percentages vary according to the type of establishment — 10% in the most expensive salons; 15% to 20% in less expensive establishments. (As a general rule, the person who washes your hair should get a small additional tip.) The washroom attendants in these places, or wherever you see one, should get a small tip — they usually set out a little plate with a coin already on it indicating the suggested denomination. And for further information on calculating gratuities, see *Tipping* in the individual country entries in FACTS IN BRIEF.

Tipping always is a matter of personal preference. In the situations covered above, as well as in any others that arise where you feel a tip is expected or due, feel free to express your pleasure or displeasure. Again, never hesitate to reward excellent and efficient attention or to penalize poor service. Give an extra gratuity and a word of thanks when someone has gone out of his or her way for you. Either way, the more personal the act of tipping, the more appropriate it seems. And if you didn't like the service — or the attitude — don't tip.

Duty-Free Shopping and Value Added Tax

DUTY-FREE SHOPS: Because of the newly integrated European economy, there were some questions at the time of this writing as to the fate and number of duty-free shops that would be maintained in international airports in European Economic Community (EEC) member countries. It appears, however, that those traveling between EEC countries and any country *not* a member of the Common Market will still be entitled to buy duty-free items. Since the United States is not a Common Market member, duty-free purchases by US travelers will, presumably, remain as is even after the end of 1992.

If common sense says that it always is less expensive to buy goods in an airport duty-free shop than to buy them at home or in the streets of a foreign city, travelers should be aware of some basic facts. Duty-free, first of all, does not mean that the goods travelers buy will be free of duty when they return to the US. Rather, it means that the shop has paid no import tax acquiring goods of foreign make because the goods are not to be used in the country where the shop is located. This is why duty-free goods are available only in the restricted, passengers-only area of international airports or are delivered to departing passengers on the plane. In a duty-free store, travelers save money only on goods of foreign make because they are the only items on which an import tax would be charged in any other store. There usually is no saving on locally made items, but in countries that impose Value Added Taxes (see below) that are refundable to foreigners, the prices in airport duty-free shops also are minus this tax, sparing travelers the often cumbersome procedures they otherwise have to follow to obtain a VAT refund.

Beyond this, there is little reason to delay buying locally made merchandise and/or souvenirs until reaching the airport (for information on local specialties, see the individual city chapters in THE CITIES and *Shopping Spree: Europe for the Savvy,* in DIVER-SIONS). In fact, because airport duty-free shops usually pay high rents, the locally made goods sold in them may well be more expensive than they would be in downtown stores. The real bargains are foreign goods, but — let the buyer beware — not all foreign goods are automatically less expensive in an airport duty-free shop. You can get a good deal on even small amounts of perfume, costing less than the usually required minimum purchase, tax-free. Other fairly standard bargains include spirits, smoking materials, cameras, clothing, watches, chocolates, and other food and luxury items — but first be sure to know what these items cost elsewhere. Terrific savings do exist (they are the reason for such shops, after all), but so do overpriced items that an unwary shopper might find equally tempting. In addition, if you wait to do your shopping at airport duty-free shops, you will be taking the chance that the desired item is out of stock or unavailable.

Duty-free shops are located in most major international airports throughout Europe. Two of Europe's best known duty-free shops are at Ireland's Shannon Airport, the oldest, and at Amsterdam's Schiphol Airport, the largest. You can get a catalogue of the Amsterdam shop — useful for price comparisons — by writing to the *Amsterdam Airport Shopping Centre* (PO Box 7501, 1118 ZG Schiphol Airport, Amsterdam, Holland; phone: 31-20-601-0966 for information; 31-20-601-2497 for catalogues). Shannon Airport also operates a mail-order service that can be used long after you've left Europe; pick up the catalogue as you pass through Shannon or request it from *Shannon Development* (757 Third Ave., 19th Floor, New York, NY 10017; phone: 212-371-5550).

■ **Buyer Beware:** In some countries you may come across shops *not* at airports that call themselves duty-free shops. These require shoppers to show a foreign passport but are subject to the same rules as other stores, including paying import duty on foreign items. What "tax-free" means in the case of these establishments is something of an advertising strategy: They are announcing loud and clear that they do, indeed, offer the VAT refund service — sometimes on the spot (minus a fee for higher overhead). Prices may be no better at these stores and could be even higher due to the addition of this service.

VALUE ADDED TAX: Commonly abbreviated as VAT, this is a tax levied by various European countries and added to the purchase price of most goods and services. The standard VAT rate in Europe ranges from a low of around 6% on food purchases to a high of 33.33% on luxury goods such as watches, jewelry, furs, glass, and cameras. (Food served at a restaurant and transportation are exempt.) Note that these figures are a broad range, and the actual percentage of tax imposed is determined by each nation.

The tax is meant to apply only to residents (and is already included in the price tag), but visitors are required to pay it, too, unless they have purchases shipped directly to an address abroad by the store. If visitors pay the tax and take purchases with them, however, they usually are entitled to a refund under retail export schemes that have been in operation throughout Europe for several years. In the past, returning travelers have complained of delays in receiving the refunds and of difficulties in converting checks written in foreign currency into dollars, but new services have recently been introduced that greatly streamline the refund procedure. Refund options may be limited, however, by restrictions set on certain items, minimum purchase amounts required to qualify (as in France, where the minimum purchase is 1,200F), and the vendor's participation in one of these programs or cooperation regarding necessary paperwork. Another wrinkle is that you only may be entitled to a partial refund of the tax — as in Austria, where VATs range from 20% to 32%, but the maximum refund is 16.66%.

Most Western European countries participating in these refund schemes have similar policies, usually requiring the buyer's submission of documents (in most cases provided by the store) to customs officials when returning to the US. Sometimes the customs official will merely stamp or authorize the documents and you will have to mail the paperwork either to a central facility or to the store where you purchased the goods (addressed envelopes usually are provided) and then wait for their refund check to arrive in the mail. In other countries — such as Finland, France, Germany, Great Britain, Ireland, Italy, and Sweden — you may be able to obtain the refund in cash at the airport.

Remember, restrictions on these tax-refund schemes vary from country to country, and participation among establishments also may vary, so before making any major purchase, first determine if you are entitled to and will be able to receive a refund. As the tax can add substantially to the purchase price, you may want to consider shopping elsewhere if you will not be reimbursed.

One of the drawbacks of most VAT refunds is that you may have to wait months before you receive the refund. A refund by dollar check or credited to a credit card account is relatively hassle-free, but should you receive a check in a foreign currency, you'll probably find that your US bank will assess a fee, as much as $15 or more, for converting it into US dollars. Far less costly is sending the foreign currency check (after endorsing it) to *Ruesch International,* which will convert it to a check in US dollars for a $2 fee (deducted from the dollar check). Other services include commission-free traveler's checks and foreign currency which can be ordered by mail. Contact *Ruesch International* at one of the following addresses: 191 Peachtree St., Atlanta, GA 30303 (phone: 404-222-9300); 3 First National Plaza, Suite 2020, Chicago, IL 60602 (phone: 312-332-5900); 1925 Century Park E., Suite 240, Los Angeles, CA 90067 (phone: 213-277-7800); 608 Fifth Ave., "Swiss Center," New York, NY 10020 (phone: 212-977-2700); and 1350 Eye St. NW, 10th Floor and street level, Washington, DC 20005 (phone: 800-424-2923 or 202-408-1200).

An additional method of reimbursement is possible if the purchases in Europe are made by credit card. The store may agree to make two credit card charges, one for the price of the goods, the other for the amount of the tax. Then, when the stamped copy of the form arrives from customs, the store simply tears up the charge slip for the sales tax and the amount never appears on your account.

Religion on the Road

 Europe is predominantly Christian, and every town, right down to the most isolated village, has its own church. And in larger, more heavily populated areas, some amount of religious variety is reflected in the houses of worship of other denominations.

The surest source of information on religious services in an unfamiliar country is the desk clerk of the hotel or guesthouse in which you are staying; the local tourist information office, a US consul, or a church of another religious affiliation also may be able to provide this information. If you aren't in an area with services held in your own denomination, you might find it interesting to attend the service of another religion. You also might enjoy attending a service in a foreign language — even if you don't understand all the words. Some of the most beautiful churches in the world are found in Europe, and few things are more inspiring than a high mass set amidst medieval arches and stained glass.

Customs and Returning to the US

 Whether you return to the United States by air or sea, you must declare to the US Customs official at the point of entry everything you have bought or acquired while in Europe. The customs check can go smoothly, lasting only a few minutes, or can take hours, depending on the officer's instinct. To speed up the process, keep all your receipts handy and try to pack your purchases together in an accessible part of your suitcase. It might save you from unpacking all your belongings.

DUTY-FREE ARTICLES: In general, the duty-free allowance for US citizens returning from abroad is $400. This limit includes items used or worn while abroad, souvenirs for friends, and gifts received during the trip. A flat 10% duty based on the "fair retail value in country of acquisition" is assessed on the next $1,000 worth of merchandise brought in for personal use or gifts. Amounts over the basic allotment and the 10% dutiable amount are dutiable at a variety of rates. The average rate for typical tourist purchases is about 12%, but you can find out rates on specific items by consulting *Tariff Schedules of the United States* in a library or any US Customs Service office.

Families traveling together may make a joint declaration to customs, which permits one member to exceed his or her duty-free exemption to the extent that another falls short. Families also may pool purchases dutiable under the flat rate. A family of three, for example, would be eligible for up to a total of $3,000 at the 10% flat duty rate (after each member had used up his or her $400 duty-free exemption) rather than three separate $1,000 allowances. This grouping of purchases is extremely useful when considering the duty on a high-tariff item, such as jewelry or a fur coat.

Personal exemptions can be used once every 30 days; in order to be eligible, an individual must have been out of the country for more than 48 hours. If any portion of the exemption has been used once within any 30-day period or if your trip is less than 48 hours long, the duty-free allowance is cut to $25.

There are certain articles, however, that are duty-free only up to certain limits. The $25 allowance includes the following: 10 cigars (not Cuban), 60 cigarettes, and 4 ounces of perfume. Individuals eligible for the full $400 duty-free limit are allowed 1 carton of cigarettes (200), 100 cigars, and 1 liter of liquor or wine if the traveler is over 21. Alcohol above this allowance is liable for both duty and an Internal Revenue tax. Antiques, if they are 100 or more years old and you have proof from the seller of that fact, are duty-free, as are paintings and drawings if done entirely by hand. To avoid paying duty twice, register the serial numbers of foreign-made watches and electronic equipment with the nearest US Customs bureau before departure; receipts of insurance policies also should be carried for other foreign-made items. (Also see the note at the end of *Entry Requirements and Documents,* in this section.)

Gold, gold medals, bullion, and up to $10,000 in currency or negotiable instruments may be brought into the US without being declared. Sums over $10,000 must be declared in writing.

The allotment for individual "unsolicited" gifts mailed from abroad (no more than one per day per recipient) is $50 retail value per gift. These gifts do not have to be declared and are not included in your duty-free exemption (see below). Although you should include a receipt for purchases with each package, the examiner is empowered to impose a duty based on his or her assessment of the value of the goods. The duty owed is collected by the US Postal Service when the package is delivered (also see below). More information on mailing packages home from abroad is contained in the

US Customs Service pamphlet *Buyer Beware, International Mail Imports* (see below for where to write for this and other useful brochures).

CLEARING CUSTOMS: This is a simple procedure. Forms are distributed by airline or ship personnel before arrival. (Note that a $5-per-person service charge — called a user fee — is collected by airlines and cruise lines to help cover the cost of customs checks, but this is included in the ticket price.) If your purchases total no more than the $400 duty-free limit, you need only fill out the identification part of the form and make an oral declaration to the customs inspector. If entering with more than $400 worth of goods, you must submit a written declaration.

Customs agents are businesslike, efficient, and not unkind. During the peak season, clearance can take time, but this generally is because of the strain imposed by a number of jumbo jets simultaneously discharging their passengers, not because of unwarranted zealousness on the part of the customs people.

Efforts to streamline procedures used to include the so-called Citizens' Bypass Program, which allowed US citizens whose purchases were within their duty-free allowance to go to the "green line," where they simply showed their passports to the customs inspector. Although at the time of this writing this procedure still is being followed at some international airports in the US, most airports have returned to an earlier system. US citizens arriving from overseas now have to go through a passport check by the Immigration & Naturalization Service (INS) prior to recovering their baggage and proceeding to customs. (US citizens will not be on the same line as foreign visitors, but this additional wait does delay clearance on re-entry into the US.) Although all passengers have to go through this passport inspection, those entering with purchases within the duty-free limit may be spared a thorough customs inspection; however, inspectors still retain the right to search any luggage they choose — so don't do anything foolish.

It is illegal not to declare dutiable items; not to do so, in fact, constitutes smuggling, and the penalty can be anything from stiff fines and seizure of the goods to prison sentences. It simply isn't worth doing. Nor should you go along with the suggestions of foreign merchants who offer to help you secure a bargain by deceiving customs officials in any way. Such transactions frequently are a setup, using the foreign merchant as an agent of US Customs. Another agent of US Customs is TECS, the Treasury Enforcement Communications System, a computer that stores all kinds of pertinent information on returning citizens. There is a basic rule to buying goods abroad, and it should never be broken: *If you can't afford the duty on something, don't buy it.* Your list or verbal declaration should include all items purchased abroad, as well as gifts received abroad, purchases made at the behest of others, the value of repairs, and anything brought in for resale in the US.

Do not include in the list items that do not accompany you, i.e., purchases that you have mailed or had shipped home. As mentioned above, these are dutiable in any case, even if for your own use and even if the items that accompany your return from the same trip do not exhaust your duty-free exemption. It is a good idea, if you have accumulated too much while abroad, to mail home any personal effects (made and bought in the US) that you no longer need rather than your foreign purchases. These personal effects pass through US Customs as "American goods returned" and are not subject to duty.

If you cannot avoid shipping home your foreign purchases, however, the US Customs Service suggests that the package be clearly marked "Not for Sale," and that a copy of the bill of sale be included. The US Customs examiner usually will accept this as indicative of the article's fair retail value, but if he or she believes it to be falsified or feels the goods have been seriously undervalued, a higher retail value may be assigned.

FORBIDDEN ITEMS: Narcotics, plants, and many types of food are not allowed into the US. Drugs are totally illegal, with the exception of medication prescribed by a physician. It's a good idea not to travel with too large a quantity of any given prescription drug (although, in the event that a pharmacy is not open when you need it, bring along several extra doses) and to have the prescription on hand in case any question arises either abroad or when re-entering the US.

Any authentic archaeological find or other artifacts considered by a European government to be a "national treasure" cannot be exported. They will be confiscated at the border, and the violator runs the risk of being fined or imprisoned. People interested in anything that might qualify as such an item should check with the customs agency of the country of origin.

Tourists have long been forbidden to bring into the US foreign-made US trademarked articles purchased abroad (if the trademark is recorded with customs) without written permission. It's now permissible to enter with one such item in your possession as long as it's for personal use.

The US Customs Service implements the rigorous Department of Agriculture regulations concerning the importation of vegetable matter, seeds, bulbs, and the like. Living vegetable matter may not be imported without a permit, and everything must be inspected, permit or not. Approved items (which do not require a permit) include dried bamboo and woven items made of straw; beads made of most seeds (but not jequirity beans — the poisonous scarlet and black seed of the rosary pea); cones of pine and other trees; roasted coffee beans; most flower bulbs; flowers (without roots); dried or canned fruits, jellies, or jams; polished rice; dried beans and teas; herb plants (not witchweed); nuts (but not acorns, chestnuts, or any nuts with outer husks); dried lichens, mushrooms, truffles, shamrocks, and seaweed; and most dried spices.

Other processed foods and baked goods usually are okay. Regulations on meat products generally depend on the country of origin and manner of processing. As a rule, commercially canned meat, hermetically sealed and cooked in the can so that it can be stored without refrigeration, is permitted, but not all canned meat fulfills this requirement. Be careful when buying European-made pâté, for instance. Goose liver pâté in itself is acceptable, but the pork fat that often is part of it, either as an ingredient or a rind, may not be. Even canned pâtés may not be admitted for this reason. (The imported ones you see in US stores have been prepared and packaged according to US regulations.) So before stocking up on a newfound favorite, it pays to check in advance — otherwise you might have to leave it behind.

The US Customs Service also enforces federal laws that prohibit the entry of articles made from the furs or hides of animals on the endangered species list. Beware of shoes, bags, and belts made of crocodile and certain kinds of lizard, and anything made of tortoiseshell; this also applies to preserved crocodiles, lizards, and turtles sometimes sold in gift shops. And if you're shopping for big-ticket items, beware of fur coats made from the skins of spotted cats. They are sold in Europe, but they will be confiscated upon your return to the US, and there will be no refund. For information about other animals on the endangered species list, contact the Department of the Interior, US Fish and Wildlife Service (Publications Unit, 4401 N. Fairfax Dr., Room 130, Arlington, VA 22203; phone: 703-358-1711), and ask for the free publication *Facts About Federal Wildlife Laws.*

Also note that some foreign governments prohibit the export of items made from certain species of wildlife, and the US honors any such restrictions. Before you go shopping in any foreign country, check with the US Department of Agriculture (G110 Federal Bldg., Hyattsville, MD 20782; phone: 301-436-8413) and find out what items are prohibited from the country you will be visiting.

The US Customs Service publishes a series of free pamphlets with customs information. It includes *Know Before You Go,* a basic discussion of customs requirements pertaining to all travelers; *Buyers Beware, International Mail Imports; Travelers' Tips on Bringing Food, Plant, and Animal Products into the United States; Importing a Car; GSP and the Traveler; Pocket Hints; Currency Reporting; Pets, Wildlife, US Customs;*

Customs Hints for Visitors (Nonresidents); and *Trademark Information for Travelers.*
For the entire series or individual pamphlets, write to the US Customs Service (PO Box
7407, Washington, DC 20044), or contact any of the seven regional offices, in Boston,
Chicago, Houston, Long Beach (California), Miami, New Orleans, and New York. The
US Customs Service has a tape-recorded message whereby callers using touch-tone
phones can get more information on various topics; the number is 202-566-8195. These
pamphlets provide great briefing material, but if you still have questions when in
Europe, contact the nearest US embassy or consulate in the particular country you're
visiting (for addresses, see *Medical and Legal Aid and Consular Services,* above).

Sources and Resources

Tourist Information Offices

 European tourist authorities in North America generally are the best sources of travel information, and most of their publications are free for the asking. When requesting brochures and maps, state the areas you plan to visit, as well as your particular interests: accommodations, restaurants, special events, tourist attractions, guided tours, and facilities for specific sports and other activities. There is no need to send a self-addressed, stamped envelope with your request, unless specified. Offices generally are open on weekdays, during normal business hours.

The best places for tourist information in each European city are listed in the *Sources and Resources* section of the individual city reports in THE CITIES; the central offices of the national tourist information bureaus in each European country are listed in FACTS IN BRIEF. Below is a list of European tourist authorities in the US.

Andorra
Andorra Tourism: Mr. Gilberto Garcia, 6800 N. Knox Ave., Lincolnwood, IL 60646 (phone: 708-674-3091).

Austria
Austrian National Tourist Office:
- 500 N. Michigan Ave., Suite 1950, Chicago, IL 60611 (phone: 312-644-5556).
- 1300 Post Oak Blvd., Suite 960, Houston, TX 77056 (phone: 713-850-9999).
- 11601 Wilshire Blvd., Suite 2480, Los Angeles, CA 90025-1760 (phone: 213-477-3332).
- 500 Fifth Ave., Suite 2009, New York, NY 10110 (phone: 212-944-6880).

Belgium
Belgian National Tourist Office: 745 Fifth Ave., New York, NY 10151 (phone: 212-758-8130).

Bulgaria
Balkan Holidays/USA/Ltd.: 41 E. 42nd St., Suite 606, New York, NY 10017 (phone: 212-573-5530).

Czechoslovakia
Cedok, Czechoslovak Travel Bureau: 10 E. 40th St., Suite 1902, New York, NY 10016 (phone: 212-689-9720).
Embassy of Czechoslovakia: 3900 Linnean Ave. NW, Washington, DC 20008 (phone: 202-363-6308).

Denmark
The following offices of the *Scandinavian Tourist Board* provide tourist information for Denmark:

- 8929 Wilshire Blvd., Suite 212, Beverly Hills, CA 90211 (phone: 213-657-4808).
- 150 N. Michigan Ave, Suite 2145, Chicago, IL 60601 (phone: 312-726-1120).
- 655 Third Ave., New York, NY 10017 (phone: 212-949-2333).

Finland
The following office of the *Scandinavian Tourist Board* provides tourist information for Finland:
- 655 Third Ave., New York, NY 10017 (phone: 212-949-2333).

France
French Government Tourist Office:
- 645 N. Michigan Ave., Suite 630, Chicago, IL 60611-2836 (phone: 312-337-6301).
- 2305 Cedar Springs Rd., Suite 205, Dallas, TX 75201 (phone: 214-720-4010).
- 9454 Wilshire Blvd., Suite 303, Beverly Hills, CA 90212-2967 (phone: 213-271-6665).
- 610 Fifth Ave., New York, NY 10020-2452 (requests by mail only); walk-in office on street level: 628 Fifth Ave., New York, NY 10020 (phone: 212-757-1125).

Germany
German National Tourist Office:
- 747 Third Ave., 33rd Floor, New York, NY 10017 (phone: 212-308-3300).
- 444 S. Flower St., Suite 2230, Los Angeles, CA 90071 (phone: 213-688-7332).

Gibraltar
Gibraltar Information Bureau: 1155 15th Street NW, Washington, DC 20005 (phone: 202-452-1108).

Great Britain
British Tourist Authority:
- 2580 Cumberland Pkwy., Suite 470, Atlanta, GA 30339 (phone: 404-432-9635).
- 625 N. Michigan Ave., Suite 1510, Chicago, IL 60611 (phone: 312-787-0490).
- World Trade Center, 350 S. Figueroa St., Suite 450, Los Angeles, CA 90071 (phone: 213-628-3525).
- 40 W. 57th St., Suite 320, New York, NY 10019 (phone: 212-581-4700).

Greece
Greek National Tourist Organization:
- 168 N. Michigan Ave., Suite 600, Chicago, IL 60601 (phone: 312-782-1084).
- 611 W. Sixth St., Suite 2198, Los Angeles, CA 90017 (phone: 213-626-6696).
- 645 Fifth Ave., 5th Floor, New York, NY 10022 (phone: 212-421-5777).

Hungary
Hungarian Travel Bureau (IBUSZ): 1 Parker Plaza, Suite 1104, Ft. Lee, NJ 07024 (phone: 201-592-8585).

Iceland
The following office of the *Scandinavian Tourist Board* provides tourist information for Iceland:
- 655 Third Ave., New York, NY 10017 (phone: 212-949-2333).

Irish Republic
Irish Tourist Board:
- 757 Third Ave., New York, NY 10017 (phone: 212-418-0800).
- 160 Bloor St. E., Suite 934, Toronto M4W 1B9, Canada (phone: 416-929-2777).

Northern Ireland
Northern Ireland Tourist Board: 276 Fifth Ave., Suite 500, New York, NY 10001 (phone: 212-686-6250).
(Also see the listings for the *British Tourist Authority,* above, which no longer promotes tourism in Northern Ireland, but does provide publications that include useful information on that country.)

Italy
Italian Government Travel Office (Ente Nazionale Italiano di Turismo; ENIT):
- 500 N. Michigan Ave., Chicago, IL 60611 (phone: 312-644-0990).
- 630 Fifth Ave., Suite 1565, New York, NY 10111 (phone: 212-245-4822).
- 360 Post St., Suite 801, San Francisco, CA 94108 (phone: 415-392-6206).

Liechtenstein
Note that there is no official Liechtenstein government tourist office in the US, but the *Swiss National Tourist Office* (see below) handles requests for travel information.

Luxembourg
Luxembourg National Tourist Office: 801 Second Ave., New York, NY 10017 (phone: 212-370-9850).

Malta
Note that there is no official Maltese government tourist office in the US, but the embassy and consulate of Malta (see *European Embassies and Consulates in the US,* below) handle requests for travel information.

Monaco
Monaco Government Tourist and Convention Bureau:
- 542 S. Dearborn St., Suite 550, Chicago, IL 60605 (phone: 312-939-7863).
- 845 Third Ave., 19th Floor, New York, NY 10022 (phone: 212-759-5227).

The Netherlands
Netherlands Board of Tourism:
- 225 N. Michigan Ave., Suite 326, Chicago, IL 60601 (phone: 312-819-0300).
- 355 Lexington Ave., New York, NY 10017 (phone: 212-370-7367).
- 90 New Montgomery St., Suite 305, San Francisco, CA 94105 (phone: 415-543-6772).

Norway
The following offices of the *Scandinavian Tourist Board* provide tourist information for Norway:
- 8929 Wilshire Blvd., Suite 212, Beverly Hills, CA 90211 (phone: 213-657-4808).
- 150 N. Michigan Ave., Suite 2145, Chicago, IL 60601 (phone: 312-726-1120).
- 655 Third Ave., New York, NY 10017 (phone: 212-949-2333).

Poland
Orbis Polish Travel Agency: 342 Madison Ave., Suite 1512, New York, NY 10173 (phone: 212-867-5011).

Polish National Tourist Office: 333 N. Michigan Ave., Suite 228, Chicago, IL 60601 (phone: 312-236-9013).

Portugal

Portuguese National Tourist Office:
- 590 Fifth Ave., 4th Floor, New York, NY 10036-4704 (phone: 212-354-4403).
- 4120 Yonge St., Suite 414, Willowdale, Ontario M2P 2B8, Canada (phone: 416-250-7575).

Romania

Romanian National Tourist Office: 573 Third Ave., New York, NY 10016 (phone: 212-697-6971).

San Marino

Note that there is no official San Marino government tourist office in the US, but the San Marino consulates (see *European Embassies and Consulates in the US,* below) handle requests for travel information.

The Soviet Union and the Baltic States

Intourist Travel Information Office: 630 Fifth Ave., Suite 868, New York, NY 10111 (phone: 212-757-3884).

Spain

National Tourist Office of Spain:
- Water Tower Place, 845 N. Michigan Ave., Suite 915E, Chicago, IL 60611 (phone: 312-642-1992).
- San Vincente Plaza Bldg., 8383 Wilshire Blvd., Suite 938, Beverly Hills, CA 90211 (phone: 213-658-7188).
- 1221 Brickell Ave., Suite 1850, Miami, FL 33131 (phone: 305-358-1992).
- 665 Fifth Ave., New York, NY 10022 (phone: 212-759-8822).
- 102 Bloor St. W., 14th Floor, Toronto, Ontario M5S 1M8, Canada (phone: 416-961-3131 or 416-961-4079).

Sweden

The following offices of the *Scandinavian Tourist Board* provide tourist information for Sweden:
- 8929 Wilshire Blvd., Suite 212, Beverly Hills, CA 90211 (phone: 213-657-4808).
- 150 N. Michigan Ave., Suite 2145, Chicago, IL 60601 (phone: 312-726-1120).
- 655 Third Ave., New York, NY 10017 (phone: 212-949-2333).

Switzerland

Swiss National Tourist Office:
- 150 N. Michigan Ave., Suite 2930, Chicago, IL 60601 (phone: 312-630-5840).
- 222 N. Sepulveda Blvd., Suite 1570, El Segundo, CA 90245 (phone: 213-335-5980).
- 608 Fifth Ave., New York, NY 10020 (phone: 212-757-5944).
- 260 Stockton St., 2nd Floor, San Francisco, CA 94108 (phone: 415-362-2260).

Yugoslavia

Yugoslav National Tourist Office: 630 Fifth Ave., Mezzanine Level, New York, NY 10111 (phone: 212-757-2801). Note that, at press time, this office was closed indefinitely due to civil and political unrest.

European Embassies and Consulates in the US

European governments maintain embassies and consulates in the US. One of their primary functions is to provide visas for certain resident aliens (depending on their country of origin) and for Americans planning to visit for extended periods, or to study, reside, or work in Europe. Consulates also are empowered to sign official documents and to notarize copies or translations of US documents, which may be necessary for those papers to be considered legal abroad. Listed below are the European embassies and consulates in the US.

Andorra
Consular services are provided by *Andorra Tourism,* Mr. Gilberto Garcia, 6800 N. Knox Ave., Lincolnwood, IL 60646 (phone: 708-674-3091).

Austria
Embassy: 2343 Massachusetts Ave. NW, Washington, DC 20008 (phone: 202-483-4474).
Consulates:
- 400 N. Michigan Ave., Suite 707, Chicago, IL 60611 (phone: 312-222-1515).
- 11859 Wilshire Blvd., Suite 501, Los Angeles, CA 90025 (phone: 213-444-9310).
- 31 E. 69th St., New York, NY 10021 (phone: 212-288-1727).

Belgium
Embassy: 3330 Garfield St. NW, Washington, DC 20008 (phone: 202-333-6900).
Consulates:
- 800 Peachtree Center, South Tower, Atlanta, GA 30303 (phone: 404-659-2150).
- 333 N. Michigan Ave., Room 2000, Chicago, IL 60601 (phone: 312-263-6624).
- 6100 Wilshire Blvd., Suite 1200, Los Angeles, CA 90048 (phone: 213-857-1244).
- 50 Rockefeller Plaza, Room 1104, New York, NY 10020 (phone: 212-586-5150).

Bulgaria
Embassy and Consulate: 1621 22nd St. NW, Washington, DC 20008 (phone: 202-387-7969 for the Embassy; 202-483-5885 for the Consulate).

Czechoslovakia
Embassy: 3900 Linnean Ave. NW, Washington, DC 20008 (phone: 202-363-6308).

Denmark
Embassy: 3200 Whitehaven St. NW, Washington, DC 20008-3683 (phone: 202-234-4300).
Consulates:
- 875 N. Michigan Ave., Suite 3430, Chicago, IL 60611 (phone: 312-787-8780).
- 3440 Wilshire Blvd., Suite 904, Los Angeles, CA 90010-2183 (phone: 213-387-4277).
- 825 Third Ave., New York, NY 10022 (phone: 212-223-4545).

Finland
Embassy: 3216 New Mexico Ave., Washington, DC 20016 (phone: 202-363-2430).
Consulates:
- 1900 Ave. of the Stars, Suite 1025, Los Angeles, CA 90067 (phone: 213-203-9903).
- 380 Madison Ave., New York, NY 10017 (phone: 212-573-6007).

France
Embassy: 4101 Reservoir Rd. NW, Washington, DC 20007-2176 (phone: 202-944-6000).
Consulates:
- *For visa applications:* 20 Park Plaza (in the Statler Office Bldg.), Suite 1123, Boston, MA 02116 (phone: 617-451-6755/6). *All other business:* 3 Commonwealth Ave., Boston, MA 02116 (phone: 617-266-9413).
- Olympia Center, 737 N. Michigan Ave., Suite 2020, Chicago, IL 60611 (phone: 312-787-5359, 312-787-5360, or 312-787-5361; recorded visa information: 312-787-7889).
- 2727 Allen Pkwy., Suite 976, Houston, TX 77019 (phone: 713-528-2181).
- 10990 Wilshire Blvd., Suite 300, Los Angeles, CA 90024 (phone: 213-479-4426).
- 1 Biscayne Tower, Suite 1710, 2 S. Biscayne Blvd., Miami, FL 33131 (phone: 305-372-9798).
- 3305 St. Charles Ave., New Orleans, LA 70115 (phone: 504-897-6381/2).
- *Main office and to apply by mail for a visa:* 934 Fifth Ave., New York, NY 10021 (phone: 212-606-3688; recorded visa information: 212-606-3680).
- 540 Bush St., San Francisco, CA 94108 (phone: 415-397-4330).

Germany
Embassy: 4645 Reservoir Rd. NW, Washington, DC 20007-1998 (phone: 202-298-4000).
Consulates:
- 285 Peachtree Center Ave. NE, Marquis Two Tower, Atlanta, GA 30303-1221 (phone: 404-659-4760).
- 3 Copley Pl., Suite 500, Boston, MA 02116 (phone: 617-536-4414).
- 104 S. Michigan Ave., Chicago, IL 60603-5957 (phone: 312-263-0850).
- 660 Plaza Dr., Edison Plaza, Suite 2100, Detroit, MI 48226-1849 (phone: 313-962-6526).
- 1330 Post Oak Blvd., Suite 1850, Houston, TX 77056-3818 (phone: 713-627-7771).
- 6222 Wilshire Blvd., Suite 500, Los Angeles, CA 90048 (phone: 213-930-2703).
- 100 N. Biscayne Blvd., Suite 2210, Miami, Fl 33132 (phone: 305-358-0290).
- 460 Park Ave., New York, NY 10022 (phone: 212-308-8700).
- 1960 Jackson St., San Francisco, CA 94109 (phone: 415-775-1061).
- One Union Sq., Suite 2500, 600 University St., Seattle, WA 98101 (phone: 206-682-4313).

Gibraltar
Consular services are provided by *Gibraltar Information Bureau,* 1155 15th Street NW, Washington, DC 20005 (phone: 202-452-1108).

Great Britain
Embassy: 3100 Massachusetts Ave. NW, Washington, DC 20008 (phone: 202-462-1340).

Consulates:
- Marquis I Tower, Suite 2700, 245 Peachtree Center Ave., Atlanta, GA 30303 (phone: 404-524-5856).
- Federal Reserve Plaza, 600 Atlantic Ave., 25th Floor, Boston, MA 02210 (phone: 617-248-9555).
- 33 N. Dearborn St., Chicago, IL 60602 (phone: 312-346-1810).
- 55 Public Sq., Suite 1650, Cleveland, OH 44113-1963 (phone: 216-621-7674).
- 813 Stemmons Tower W., 2730 Stemmons Fwy., Dallas, TX 75207 (phone: 214-637-3600).
- Dresser Tower, Suite 2250, 601 Jefferson, Houston, TX 77002 (phone: 713-659-6270).
- 3701 Wilshire Blvd., Suite 312, Los Angeles, CA 90010 (phone 213-385-7381).
- Brickell Bay Office Tower, Suite 2110, 1001 S. Bayshore Dr., Miami, FL 33131 (phone: 305-374-1522).
- 321 St. Charles Ave., 10th Floor, New Orleans, LA 70130 (phone: 504-586-8300).
- 845 Third Ave., New York, NY 10022 (phone: 212-745-0200).
- c/o Mather & Co., 226 Walnut St., Philadelphia, PA 19106 (phone: 215-925-0118).
- 3515 SW Council Crest Dr., Portland, OR 97201 (phone: 503-227-5669).
- 1 Sansome St., Suite 850, San Francisco, CA 94104 (phone: 415-981-3030).
- 820 First Interstate Center, 999 Third Ave., Seattle, WA 98104 (phone: 206-622-9255).

Greece
Embassy: 2221 Massachusetts Ave. NW, Washington, DC 20008 (phone: 202-667-3168).
Consulates:
- 3340 Peachtree Rd. NE, Tower Place, Suite 1670, Atlanta, GA 30326 (phone: 404-261-3313).
- 20 Park Plaza, Suite 526, Boston, MA 02116 (phone: 617-542-3240).
- 168 N. Michigan Ave., Chicago, IL 60601 (phone: 312-372-5356).
- 1360 Post Oak Blvd., Suite 2480, Houston, TX 77056 (phone: 713-840-7522).
- 3255 Wilshire Blvd., Suite 1103, Los Angeles, CA 90010 (phone: 213-385-1447).
- 2318 World Trade Center, 2 Canal St., New Orleans, LA 70130 (phone: 504-523-1167).
- 69 E. 79th St., New York, NY 10021 (phone: 212-988-5500).
- 2441 Gough St., San Francisco, CA 94123 (phone: 415-775-2102).

Hungary
Embassy: 3910 Shoemaker St. NW, Washington, DC 20008 (phone: 202-362-6730).
Consulate: 223 E. 52nd St., New York, NY 10022 (phone: 212-879-4127).

Iceland
Embassy: 2022 Connecticut Ave. NW, Washington, DC 20008 (phone: 202-265-6653).
Consulate: 370 Lexington Ave., Suite 505, New York, NY 10017 (phone: 212-686-4100).

Ireland

Embassy: 2234 Massachusetts Ave. NW, Washington, DC 20008 (phone: 202-462-3939).

Consulates:
- 535 Boylston St., Boston, MA 02116 (phone: 617-267-9330).
- 400 N. Michigan Ave., Suite 911, Chicago, IL 606011 (phone: 312-337-1868).
- 515 Madison Ave., 18th Floor, New York, NY 100022 (phone: 212-319-2555).
- 655 Montgomery St., San Francisco, CA 94111 (phone: 415-392-4214).

Note: The above embassy and consulates pertain to the Irish Republic only. The British embassy and consulates in the US handle all consular matters for Northern Ireland.

Italy

Embassy: 1601 Fuller St. NW, Washington, DC 20009 (phone: 202-328-5500).

Consulates:
- 100 Boylston St., Suite 900, Boston, MA 02116 (phone: 617-542-0483).
- 500 N. Michigan Ave., Chicago, IL 60611 (phone: 312-467-1550).
- Buhl Bldg., 535 Griswold, Suite 1840, Detroit, MI 48226 (phone: 313-963-8560).
- 1300 Post Oak Rd., Suite 660, Houston, TX 77056 (phone: 713-850-7520).
- 12400 Wilshire Blvd., Suite 300, Los Angeles, CA 90025 (phone: 213-820-0622).
- 630 Camp St., New Orleans, LA 70130 (phone: 504-524-2271).
- 690 Park Ave., New York, NY 10021 (phone: 212-737-9100).
- 421 Chestnut St., Philadelphia, PA 19106 (phone: 215-592-7329).
- 2590 Webster St., San Francisco, CA 94115 (phone: 415-931-4924).

Liechtenstein

Consular services for Liechtenstein are provided by the *Swiss Embassy* and *Consulates* (see below).

Luxembourg

Embassy: 2200 Massachusetts Ave. NW, Washington, DC 20008 (phone: 202-265-4171).

Consulates:
- 8215 Roswell Rd., Bldg. 600, Atlanta, GA 30350 (phone: 404-668-9811).
- 180 N. LaSalle St., Suite 1400, Chicago, IL 60601 (phone: 312-726-0355).
- 200 S. Biscayne Blvd., Suite 3240, Miami, FL 33131 (phone: 305-373-1300).
- 1429 Atlantic St., N. Kansas City, MO 64116 (phone: 816-474-4761).
- 8012 Oak St., New Orleans, LA 70118 (phone: 504-881-3743).
- 801 Second Ave., 13th Floor, New York, NY 10017 (phone: 212-370-9870).
- 1 Sansome St., Suite 830, San Francisco, CA 94104 (phone: 415-788-0815).

Malta

Embassy: 2017 Connecticut Ave. NW, Washington, DC 20008 (phone: 202-462-3611).

Consulate General: 249 E. 35th St., New York, NY 10016 (phone: 212-725-2345).

Monaco

Consulate: 845 Third Ave., 19th Floor, New York, NY 10022 (phone: 212-759-5227).

Note: The French consulates (see above) also often handle consular matters for Monaco.

The Netherlands

Embassy: 4200 Linnean Ave. NW, Washington, DC 20008-3896 (phone: 202-244-5300).

Consulates:
- 303 E. Wacker Dr., Suite 410, Chicago, IL 60601 (phone: 312-856-0110).
- 2200 Post Oak Blvd., Suite 610, Houston, TX 77056-4783 (phone: 713-622-8000).
- 3460 Wilshire Blvd., Suite 509, Los Angeles, CA 90010-2270 (phone: 213-380-3440).
- 1 Rockefeller Plaza, 11th Floor, New York, NY 10020-2094 (phone: 212-246-1429).

Norway
Embassy: 2720 34th St. NW, Washington, DC 20008 (phone: 202-333-6000).
Consulates:
- 2777 Allen Parkway, Suite 1185, Houston, TX 77019 (phone: 713-521-2900).
- 5750 Wilshire Blvd., Suite 470, Los Angeles, CA 90036 (phone: 213-933-7717).
- 229 Foshay Tower, Minneapolis, MN 55402 (phone: 612-332-3338).
- 825 Third Ave., 17th Floor, New York, NY 10022 (phone: 212-421-7333).
- 2 Embarcadero Center, Suite 2930, San Francisco, CA 94111 (phone: 415-986-0766).

Poland
Embassy: 2640 16th St. NW, Washington, DC 20009 (phone: 202-234-0626).
Consulates:
- 1530 N. Lake Shore Dr., Chicago, IL 60610 (phone: 312-337-8166).
- 233 Madison Ave., New York, NY 10016 (phone: 212-889-8360).
- 3460 Wilshire Blvd., Suite 470, Los Angeles, CA 90036 (phone: 213-365-7900).

Portugal
Embassy: 2125 Kalorama Rd. NW, Washington, DC 20008 (phone: 202-328-8610).
Consulates:
- 899 Boylston St., 2nd Floor, Boston, MA 02115 (phone: 617-536-8740).
- 1180 Raymond Blvd., Suite 222, Newark, NJ 07102 (phone: 201-622-7300).
- 628 Pleasant St., Suite 204, New Bedford, MA 02740 (phone: 508-997-6151).
- 630 Fifth Ave., Suite 655, New York, NY 10111 (phone: 212-246-4580).
- 56 Pine St., 6th Floor, Providence, RI 02903 (phone: 401-272-2003).
- 3298 Washington St., San Francisco, CA 94115 (phone: 415-346-3400).

Romania
Embassy: 1607 23rd St. NW, Washington, DC 20008 (phone: 202-232-4747).

San Marino
Consulates:
- 350 Fifth Ave., Suite 3107, New York, NY 10018 (phone: 212-465-1012).
- 186 Leher Ave., Elmont, NY 11003 (phone: 516-437-4699).
- 1685 E. Big Beaver Rd., Troy, MI 48083 (phone: 313-528-1190, Wednesdays and Saturdays only).
- 1899 L St. NW, Suite 500, Washington, DC 20036 (phone: 202-223-3517).

The Soviet Union
Embassy: 1125 16th St. NW, Washington, DC 20036 (phone: 202-628-7551).
Consulates:
- 2790 Green St., San Francisco, CA 94123 (phone: 415-922-6642).
- 1825 S. Phelps Pl. NW, Washington, DC 20008 (phone: 202-939-8917).
Note: For information on the newly independent Baltic states, see below.

Spain

Embassy: 2700 15th St. NW, Washington, DC 20009 (phone: 202-265-0190).
Consulates:

- 545 Boylston St., Suite 803, Boston, MA 02116 (phone: 617-536-2506).
- 180 N. Michigan Ave., Suite 1500, Chicago, IL 60601 (phone: 312-782-4588).
- 151 Sevilla Ave., 2nd Floor, Coral Gables, FL 33134 (phone: 305-446-5511).
- 1800 Bering Dr., Suite 660, Houston, TX 77057 (phone: 713-783-6200).
- 6300 Wilshire Blvd., Suite 1434, Los Angeles, CA 90048 (phone: 213-658-6050).
- 2102 World Trade Center, 2 Canal St., New Orleans, LA 70130 (phone: 504-525-4951).
- 150 E. 58th St., 16th Floor, New York, NY 10155 (phone: 212-355-4080).
- 2080 Jefferson St., San Francisco, CA 94123 (phone: 415-922-2995).

Sweden

Embassy: 600 New Hampshire Ave. NW, Suite 1200, Washington, DC 20037 (phone: 202-944-5600).
Consulates:

- 150 N. Michigan Ave., Suite 1250, Chicago, IL 60601-7593 (phone: 312-781-6262).
- 10808 Wilshire Blvd., Suite 505, Los Angeles, CA 90024-4314 (phone: 213-470-2555).
- 1 Dag Hammarskjold Plaza, 45th Floor, New York, NY 10017-2201 (phone: 212-751-5900).

Switzerland

Embassy: 2900 Cathedral Ave. NW, Washington, DC 20008 (phone: 202-745-7900).
Consulates:

- 1275 Peachtree St. NE, Suite 425, Atlanta, GA 30309 (phone: 404-872-7874).
- Olympia Center, Suite 2301, 737 N. Michigan Ave., Chicago, IL 60611 (phone: 312-915-0061).
- First Interstate Bank Plaza, 1000 Louisiana St., Suite 5670, Houston, TX 77002 (phone: 713-650-0000).
- 3440 Wilshire Blvd., Suite 817, Los Angeles, CA 90010-2176 (phone: 213-388-4127).
- 665 Fifth Ave., 8th Floor, New York, NY 10022 (phone: 212-758-2560).
- 456 Montgomery St., Suite 1500, San Francisco, CA 94104 (phone: 415-788-2272).

Yugoslavia

Embassy: 2410 California St. NW, Washington, DC 20008 (phone: 202-462-6566).
Consulates:

- 307 N. Michigan Ave., Suite 1600, Chicago, IL 60601 (phone: 312-332-0169).
- 1700 E. 13th St., Park Center, Suite 4R, Cleveland, OH 44114 (phone: 216-621-2093).
- 767 Third Ave., 17th Floor, New York, NY 10017 (phone: 212-838-2300).
- 1375 Sutter St., Suite 406, San Francisco, CA 94109 (phone: 415-776-4941).
- 625 Fenwick St., Suite 1605, Pittsburgh, PA 15222 (phone: 412-471-6191).

At press time the Baltic states were in the process of establishing a consulary presence in the US.

Estonia: Was establishing an embassy in Washington, DC. Meanwhile information is available from the Estonian Consulate General, 9 Rockefeller Center, New York, NY 10020 (phone: 212-247-1450).

Latvia: The Legation of Latvia (4325 17th St. NW, Washington, DC 20011; phone: 202-234-5860) is the precursor to Latvia's not-yet-established embassy.

Lithuania: The Legation of Lithuania (2622 16th St. NW, Washington, DC 20009; phone: 202-234-2860) is the precursor to Lithuania's embassy. Information also is available from the Lithuanian Consulate General, 41 W. 82nd St., New York, NY 10024 (phone: 212-877-4552).

Theater and Special Event Tickets

In more than one section of this book you will read about events that spark your interest — everything from music festivals and special theater seasons to sporting championships — along with telephone numbers and addresses to which to write for descriptive brochures, reservations, or tickets. The various tourist authorities can supply information on these and other special events and festivals that take place in Europe, though they cannot in all cases provide the actual program or detailed information on ticket prices.

Since many of these occasions often are fully booked well in advance, you should think about having your reservation in hand before you go. In some cases, tickets may be reserved over the phone and charged to a credit card, or you can send an international money order or foreign draft. If you do write, remember that any request from the US should be accompanied by an International Reply Coupon to ensure a response (send two of them for an airmail response). These international coupons, money orders, and drafts are available at US post offices.

For further information, write for the *European Travel Commission*'s extensive list of events scheduled for the entire year for its 24 member countries. For a free copy, send a self-addressed, stamped, business-size (4 x 9½) envelope to "European Events," *European Travel Commission,* PO Box 1754, New York, NY 10185.

Books, Newspapers, Magazines, and Newsletters

Throughout GETTING READY TO GO, numerous books and brochures have been recommended as good sources of further information on a variety of topics. In many cases, these are publications of the various tourist authorities and are available at any of their offices both here and abroad. Additional ones are published by other European and US government agencies, specialty clubs and organizations, tour operators, and other travel service suppliers, and are available directly from these sources or found in the travel section of any good general bookstore or any sizable public library. If you still can't find something, the following stores and/or mail-order houses also specialize in travel literature. They offer books on Europe along with guides to the rest of the world and in some cases, even an old Baedeker or two.

Book Passage (51 Tamal Vista Blvd., Corte Madera, CA 94925; phone: 415-927-0960 in California; 800-321-9785 elsewhere in the US). Travel guides and maps to all areas of the world. A free catalogue is available.

The Complete Traveller (199 Madison Ave., New York, NY 10016; phone: 212-685-9007). Travel guides and maps. A catalogue is available for $2.

Forsyth Travel Library (PO Box 2975, Shawnee Mission, KS 66201-1375; phone:

800-367-7984 or 913-384-3440). Travel guides and maps, old and new, to all parts of the world, including Europe. Ask for the "Worldwide Travel Books and Maps" catalogue.

Gourmet Guides (2801 Leavenworth Ave., San Francisco, CA 94133; phone: 415-771-9948). Travel guides and maps, along with cookbooks. Mail-order lists available on request.

Phileas Fogg's Books and Maps (87 *Stanford Shopping Center*, Palo Alto, CA 94304; phone: 800-533-FOGG or 415-327-1754). Travel guides, maps, and language aids.

Tattered Cover (2955 E. First Ave., Denver, CO 80206; phone: 800-833-9327 or 303-322-7727). The travel department alone of this enormous bookstore carries over 7,000 books, as well as maps and atlases. No catalogue is offered (the list is too extensive), but a newsletter, issued three times a year, is available on request.

Thomas Brothers Maps & Travel Books (603 W. Seventh St., Los Angeles, CA 90017; phone: 213-627-4018). Maps (including road atlases, street guides, and wall maps), guidebooks, and travel accessories.

Traveller's Bookstore (22 W. 52nd St., New York, NY 10019; phone: 212-664-0995). Travel guides, maps, literature, and accessories. A catalogue is available for $2.

In addition, the following bookstores and mail-order houses, which specialize in information on specific countries or in English-language translations of foreign travel publications of interest to visitors to Europe, are a further resource.

British Gifts (PO Box 26558, Los Angeles, CA 90026; phone: 213-666-7778). Mail order only. Stocks a large selection of maps and books on Great Britain, including *Automobile Association of Great Britain (AA)* and British Tourist Authority publications.

British Market (2366 Rice Blvd., Houston, TX 77005; phone: 800-448-0907 or 713-529-9889). Specializes in Great Britain. Stocks maps and British Tourist Authority literature, as well as a wide range of guidebooks published both in the United Kingdom and the US. Selected price lists are available.

British Travel Bookshop (40 W. 57th St., 3rd Floor, New York, NY 10019; phone: 800-448-3039 or 212-765-0898). Carries a complete line of books and maps on all areas of Great Britain, including those of the Britain's *Automobile Association (AA)* and the British Tourist Authority, as well as other books by major and little-known publishers. A book list is available.

Irish Books and Graphics (580 Broadway, Room 1103, New York, NY 10012; phone: 212-274-1923). Sells a variety of Irish books (both new and out of print), records, cassettes, posters, prints, and maps. This store, the largest supplier of books in Gaelic outside of Dublin, covers just about every subject pertaining to Ireland — including art, architecture, literature, history, and travel.

Irish Books & Media (1433 Franklin Ave. E., Minneapolis, MN 55404; phone: 612-871-3505). This mail-order supplier specializes in all kinds of books from and about Ireland — history, fiction, biographies, as well as travel.

Lectorum (137 W. 14th St., New York, NY 10011; phone: 212-929-2833). Specializes in Spanish books, none in translation, including a variety of travel books and Spanish classics.

Librairie de France/Libreria Hispanica (French and Spanish Book Corporation) (610 Fifth Ave., New York, NY 10020; phone: 212-581-8810 and 115 Fifth Ave., New York, NY 10003; phone: 212-673-7400). Specializes in language dictionaries and French and Spanish fiction and nonfiction; carries some French-language guidebooks published in France.

Luso Brazilian (PO Box 170286, Brooklyn, NY 11217; phone: 718-624-4000).

Specializes in Portuguese books, many in English translation, with a wide selection of travel material. The store has a mail-order facility.

Rizzoli International Bookstore & Gallery (31 W. 57th St., New York, NY 10019; phone: 212-759-2424; additional branches in New York City, as well as Boston, Chicago, Costa Mesa, CA, and Williamsburg, VA). Carries a wide range of art and architecture books, as well as travel guides to various countries, particularly English- and Italian-language guides to Italy.

In addition, *Culturgrams* is a handy series of pamphlets that provides a good sampling of information on the people, cultures, sights, and bargains to be found in over 90 countries around the world. Each four-page, newsletter-size leaflet covers one country. Almost every Eastern and Western European country is included in the series (the exceptions include Andorra, Albania, Liechtenstein, Malta, Monaco, and San Marino). The topics included range from customs and courtesies to lifestyles and demographics. These fact-filled pamphlets are published by the David M. Kennedy Center for International Studies at Brigham Young University; for an order form contact the group c/o Publication Services (280 HRCB, Provo, UT 84602; phone: 801-378-6528). When ordering from 1 to 5 *Culturgrams,* the price is $1 each; 6 to 49 pamphlets cost 50¢ each; and for larger quantities, the price per copy goes down proportionately.

Another source of cultural information is *Do's and Taboos Around the World,* compiled by the Parker Pen Company and edited by Roger E. Axtell. It focuses on protocol, customs, etiquette, hand gestures and body language, gift giving, the dangers of using US jargon, and so on, and can be fun to read even if you're not going anyplace. It's available for $10.95 in bookstores or through John Wiley & Sons, 1 Wiley Dr., Somerset, NJ 08875 (phone: 908-469-4400).

In non-English-speaking countries, you often will have the frustrating experience of being presented with a menu that might be written in Martian, for all the information you can extract from it. An excellent pocket-size guide available in bookstores is the Berlitz *European Menu Reader,* which will help you decode menus in 14 European languages. It also deals with the differences from American and British terminology. It is available at bookstores or can be ordered from Berlitz Publications, Inc. (900 Chester Ave., Delran, NJ 08075; phone: 800-526-8047) for $6.95, plus postage and handling.

NEWSPAPERS AND MAGAZINES: A subscription to the *International Herald Tribune* is a good idea for dedicated travelers. This English-language newspaper is written and edited mostly in Paris, and is *the* newspaper read most regularly and avidly by Americans abroad to keep up with world news, US news, sports, the stock market (US and foreign), fluctuations in exchange rates, and an assortment of help-wanted ads, real estate listings, and personals, global in scope. Published 6 days a week (no Sunday paper), it is available at newsstands throughout the US and in cities worldwide. Larger hotels may have copies in the lobby for guests — if you don't see a copy, ask the hotel concierge if it is available. A 1-year's subscription in the US costs $349. To subscribe, write or call the Subscription Manager, *International Herald Tribune,* 850 Third Ave., 10th Floor, New York, NY 10022 (phone: 800-882-2884 or 212-752-3890).

Among the major US publications that can be bought in Europe (generally a day or two after distribution in the US) in many of the larger cities and resort areas, at hotels, airports, and newsstands are *The New York Times, USA Today,* and the *Wall Street Journal.* Note that some papers may cost more than in the US.

Europe is well known for its fine food, and sampling the regional fare is likely to be one of the highlights of any visit. You will find reading about local edibles worthwhile before you go or after you return. *Gourmet,* a magazine specializing in food, frequently features mouth-watering articles on the foods of Europe, although its scope is much broader. It is available at newsstands throughout the US for $2.50 an issue or for $18 a year from *Gourmet,* PO Box 53780, Boulder, CO 80322 (phone: 800-365-2454).

Before or after your trip, you may want to subscribe to various publications devoted exclusively to a particular European city or country. For information on such publications, contact the appropriate tourist authority or see "Local Coverage" in THE CITIES. There are numerous additional magazines for every special interest available; check at your library information desk for a directory of such publications, or look over the selection offered by a well-stocked newsstand.

NEWSLETTERS: Throughout GETTING READY TO GO we have mentioned specific newsletters which our readers may be interested in consulting for further information. One of the very best sources of detailed travel information is *Consumer Reports Travel Letter*. Published monthly by Consumers Union (PO Box 53629, Boulder, CO 80322-3629; phone: 800-999-7959), it offers comprehensive coverage of the travel scene on a wide variety of fronts. A year's subscription costs $37; 2 years, $57.

The following travel newsletters also provide useful up-to-date information on travel services and bargains:

Entree (PO Box 5148, Santa Barbara, CA 93150; phone: 805-969-5848). This newsletter caters to a sophisticated, discriminating traveler with the means to explore the places mentioned. Subscribers have access to a 24-hour hotline providing information on restaurants and accommodations around the world. Monthly; a year's subscription costs $59.

The Hideaway Report (Harper Associates, PO Box 50, Sun Valley, ID 83353; phone: 208-622-3193). This monthly source highlights retreats — including European idylls — for sophisticated travelers. A year's subscription costs $90.

Romantic Hideaways (217 E. 86th St., Suite 258, New York, NY 10028; phone: 212-969-8682). This monthly newsletter leans toward those special places made for those traveling in twos. A year's subscription costs $65.

Travel Smart (Communications House, 40 Beechdale Rd., Dobbs Ferry, NY 10522; phone: 914-693-8300 in New York; 800-327-3633 elsewhere in the US). This monthly covers a wide variety of trips and travel discounts. A year's subscription costs $44.

In addition, the following are a sampling of the countless newsletters devoted exclusively to a single country or area of Europe.

La Belle France: The Sophisticated Guide to France (Travel Guide, PO Box 3485, Charlottesville, VA 22901; phone: 804-295-1200). This 8-page monthly newsletter contains hotel and restaurant reviews, as well as shopping information for Paris and other cities, and often includes short articles spotlighting a luxury destination. A year's subscription costs $67.

British Travel Letter (824 E. Baltimore St., Baltimore, MD 21202; (phone: 800-787-0138 or 301-494-9791). This monthly newsletter provides useful information on off-the-beaten track attractions throughout Britain. A year's subscription costs $39, and includes *Cheers,* a guide to 100 of the best British pubs, and *London Confidential,* an insider's view of London. (Subscribers also receive a 10% discount on the purchase of any of the *Personal Courier* series of cassettes, which provide audio tours of Great Britain.)

Exploring Ireland (318 Pershing Ave., Roselle, NJ 07204; phone: 908-298-0315) This bimonthly newsletter covers all aspects of traveling in Ireland. It provides useful information on package tours, accommodations, cultural and historical sites, and the exploration of Ireland's islands. A year's subscription costs $29; a free sample issue will be sent on request.

France Today (1051 Divisadero St., San Francisco, CA 94115; phone: 415-921-5100). Focuses on French politics, business, and culture, as well as travel and events. A year's subscription (10 issues) costs $27.

Gemütlichkeit (UpCountry Publishing, 2892 Chronicle Ave., Hayward, CA 94542; 800-521-6722 or 415-538-0628). This monthly newsletter focuses primarily on Austria, Germany, and Switzerland, providing information on transportation options and hotels and restaurants, as well as interesting articles. A year's subscription costs $57.

Inside Ireland (Rookwood, Stocking La., Ballyboden, Dublin 16, Irish Republic; phone: 353-1-931906). Published independently by Brenda Weir, this is a quarterly newsletter that reports on a wide variety of topics — shopping, real estate, the arts, restaurants and pubs, retirement in Ireland, and the like. A subscription also entitles readers to use the publication's information service, to receive special supplements, and to a variety of discounts. A year's subscription costs $35; sample copies of the newsletter are available for $5.

Letter from London (63 E. 79th St., Apt. 4A, New York, NY 10021; no phone). This 8-page newsletter is published independently roughly once a month by Mary Anne Evans, a native Londoner. She reports on a wide variety of topics — hotels and restaurants, shopping, current and upcoming gallery exhibitions and theater productions, and the like. Each issue also contains a "Country Letter," featuring an event or place out of town. A year's subscription (10 issues) costs $69; send $5 for a sample issue.

London Outlook (PO Box 498E, Millwood, NY 10546; phone: 914-941-5989). A 10-page newsletter devoted to London specifically, and Great Britain in general. A year's subscription costs $45 (10 issues); send $3.50 for a sample issue.

■**Computer Services:** Anyone who owns a personal computer and a modem can subscribe to a database service providing everything from airline schedules and fares to restaurant listings. Two such services of particular use to travelers are *CompuServe* (5000 Arlington Center Blvd., Columbus, OH 43220; phone: 800-848-8199 or 614-457-8600; $39.95 to join, plus usage fees of $6 to $12.50 per hour) and *Prodigy Services* (445 Hamilton Ave., White Plains, NY 10601; phone: 800-822-6922 or 914-993-8000; $12.95 per month's subscription, plus variable usage fees). Before using any computer bulletin-board services, be sure to take precautions to prevent downloading of a computer "virus." First install one of the programs designed to screen out such nuisances.

Weights and Measures

When traveling in Europe, you'll find that just about every quantity, whether it is distance, length, weight, or capacity, will be expressed in unfamiliar terms. In fact, this is true for travel almost everywhere in the world, since the US is one of the last countries to make its way to the metric system. Your trip to Europe may serve to familiarize you with what one day may be the weights and measures at your local grocery store.

There are some specific things to keep in mind during your trip. Fruits and vegetables at a market generally are recorded in kilos (kilograms), as is your luggage at the airport and your body weight. (This latter is particularly pleasing to people of significant size, who instead of weighing 220 pounds hit the scales at a mere 100 kilos.) A kilo equals 2.2 pounds and 1 pound is .45 kilos. Body temperature usually is measured in degrees centigrade or Celsius rather than on the Fahrenheit scale, so that a normal body temperature is 37C, not 98.6F, and freezing is 0 degrees C rather than 32F — although in Great Britain, the Irish Republic, and in some parts of the Continent, the Fahrenheit scale still may be in use. Other quirks of the British system include measuring body weight in stone (one stone equals 14 pounds).

Gasoline is sold by the liter (approximately 3.8 liters to 1 gallon) although in the United Kingdom gas may be sold by the British or "imperial" gallon, which is 20% larger than the US gallon. Tire pressure gauges and other equipment measure in kilograms per square centimeter rather than pounds per square inch. Highway signs usually are written in kilometers rather than miles (1 mile equals 1.6 kilometers; 1 kilometer equals .62 mile). And speed limits are in kilometers per hour, so think twice before hitting the gas when you see a speed limit of 100. That means 62 miles per hour.

The tables and conversion factors listed below should give you all the information you will need to understand any transaction, road sign, or map you encounter during your travels.

CONVERSION TABLES
METRIC TO US MEASUREMENTS

Multiply:	by:	to convert to:
LENGTH		
millimeters	.04	inches
meters	3.3	feet
meters	1.1	yards
kilometers	.6	miles
CAPACITY		
liters	2.11	pints (liquid)
liters	1.06	quarts (liquid)
liters	.26	gallons (liquid)
WEIGHT		
grams	.04	ounces (avoir.)
kilograms	2.2	pounds (avoir.)

US TO METRIC MEASUREMENTS

LENGTH		
inches	25.0	millimeters
feet	.3	meters
yards	.9	meters
miles	1.6	kilometers
CAPACITY		
pints	.47	liters
quarts	.95	liters
gallons	3.8	liters
WEIGHT		
ounces	28.0	grams
pounds	.45	kilograms

TEMPERATURE

$$°F = (°C \times 9/5) + 32 \qquad °C = (°F - 32) \times 5/9$$

APPROXIMATE EQUIVALENTS		
Metric Unit	**Abbreviation**	**US Equivalent**
LENGTH		
meter	m	39.37 inches
kilometer	km	.62 mile
millimeter	mm	.04 inch
CAPACITY		
liter	l	1.057 quarts
WEIGHT		
gram	g	.035 ounce
kilogram	kg	2.2 pounds
metric ton	MT	1.1 tons
ENERGY		
kilowatt	kw	1.34 horsepower

Cameras and Equipment

 Vacations are everybody's favorite time for taking pictures and home movies. After all, most of us want to remember the places we visit — and show them off to others. Here are a few suggestions to help you get the best results from your travel photography or videography.

BEFORE THE TRIP

If you're taking your camera or camcorder out after a long period in mothballs, or have just bought a new one, check it thoroughly before you leave to prevent unexpected breakdowns or disappointing pictures.

1. Still cameras should be cleaned carefully and thoroughly, inside and out. If using a camcorder, run a head cleaner through it. You also may want to have your camcorder professionally serviced (opening the casing yourself will violate the manufacturer's warranty). Always use filters to protect your lens while traveling.
2. Check the batteries for your camera's light meter and flash, and take along extras just in case yours wear out during the trip. For camcorders, bring along extra Nickel-Cadmium (Ni-Cad) batteries; if you use rechargeable batteries, a recharger will cut down on the extras.
3. Using all the settings and features, shoot at least one test roll of film or one videocassette, using the type you plan to take along with you.

EQUIPMENT TO TAKE ALONG

Keep your gear light and compact. Items that are too heavy or bulky to be carried comfortably on a full-day excursion will likely remain in your hotel room.

1. Invest in a broad camera or camcorder strap if you now have a thin one. It will make carrying the camera much more comfortable.
2. A sturdy canvas, vinyl, or leather camera or camcorder bag, preferably with

padded pockets (not an airline bag), will keep your equipment organized and easy to find. If you will be doing much shooting around the water, a waterproof case is best.

3. For cleaning, bring along a camel's hair brush that retracts into a rubber squeeze bulb. Also take plenty of lens tissue, soft cloths, and plastic bags to protect equipment from dust and moisture.

■**Note:** If you are planning on using your camcorder in Europe, note that most European countries operate on a different electrical current than the US, so you should make sure that the battery charger that comes with your camcorder is compatible with the current in the countries you're visiting. You'll also need a plug adapter kit to cope with the variations in plug configurations found in Europe. And don't expect to be able to play back your tape through a European TV set or VCR. The US and Canada use a different television standard than most European countries; these systems are incompatible with each other and multiple-standard TV sets are rare.

FILM AND TAPES: If you are concerned about airport security X-rays damaging undeveloped film (X-rays do not affect processed film) or tapes, store them in one of the lead-lined bags sold in camera shops. In the US and Canada, incidents of X-ray damage to unprocessed film (exposed or unexposed) are few because low-dosage X-ray equipment is used virtually everywhere. However, when crossing international borders, travelers should know that foreign X-ray equipment used for carry-on baggage may deliver higher levels of radiation and that even more powerful X-ray equipment may be used for checked luggage, so it's best to carry your film on board. If you're traveling without a protective bag, you may want to ask to have your photo equipment inspected by hand. In the US, Federal Aviation Administration regulations require that if you request a hand inspection, you get it, but overseas the response may depend on the humor of the inspector.

One type of film that should never be subjected to X-rays is the very high speed ASA 1000; there are lead-lined bags made especially for it — and, in the event that you are refused a hand inspection, this is the only way to save your film. The walk-through metal detector devices at airports do not affect film, though the film cartridges may set them off. Because cassettes have been favorite carriers for terrorist explosives over the years, airport officials probably will insist that you put these through the X-ray machine as well. If you don't have a choice, put them through and hope for the best.

You should have no problem finding film or tapes throughout Europe. When buying film, tapes, or photo accessories the best rule of thumb is to stick to name brands with which you are familiar. Different countries have their own ways of labeling camcorder tapes, and although the variations in recording and playback standards won't affect your ability to use the tape, they will affect how quickly you record and how much time you actually have to record on the tape. The availability of film processing labs and equipment repair shops will vary from area to area.

If taking photographs in Eastern Europe, bring your own film from the US or Western Europe for use. *Intourist,* for example, warns that film bought in the Soviet Union should be processed there as it is incompatible with most Western developing processes. For other local quirks, it's best to check with the government tourist offices.

■**A note about courtesy and caution:** When photographing individuals in Europe (and anywhere else in the world), ask first. It's common courtesy. Furthermore, some governments have security regulations regarding the use of cameras and will not permit the photographing of certain subjects, such as particular government and military installations. When in doubt, ask.

FACTS IN BRIEF

Facts in Brief

The tourist authority addresses listed below are for information within each country. For US addresses of national tourist authorities, see *Tourist Information Offices*, GETTING READY TO GO. We also feel obliged to say that much of Eastern Europe remained in the midst of very significant change as we went to press. That means that matters of visa/entry requirements, currency exchange, and even national holidays are quite likely to change during the 12-month life of this book. The dates noted here were correct at press time, but the vagaries of Eastern Europe in particular make double-checking especially prudent during 1992.

Andorra

TOURIST INFORMATION: The center for assistance is the *Conselleria de Turisme i Esportes Govern d'Andorra,* Andorra La Vella, c/o Senyor Sergi Nadal/Director of Tourism and Sports (phone: 29345; fax: 60184).

ENTRY REQUIREMENTS: Andorra has none, but France and Spain have checkpoints on their sides of the border and will request a current US passport. If you plan to arrive or leave via the French border, you don't need a visa for crossing into or out of France.

GETTING THERE/GETTING AROUND: Buses – Seasonal bus service between La Tour de Carol, France, and the main centers in Andorra is provided by *Autos Viuda Pujol Huguet.* There also are daily buses from Barcelona, Spain. Microbuses serve the principal Andorran villages from Andorra la Vella.

Cars – Winter snows can close the main French Route 20 to Andorra. The alternate, all-weather route is Spain's Route C1313 from Puigcerdá to Seu d'Urgell, where it connects with Route C145 to Andorra.

Trains – Andorra is one of the few countries in Europe without an inch of train track on its territory. The nearest station in Spain is at Puigcerdá, from which bus connections are available to Seu d' Urgell and Andorra la Vella. If you're traveling from Madrid, take the train to Lleida, then connect with a bus to Seu d'Urgell and Andorra.

From France, the French railway stops at Ax-les-Thermes, Hospitalet-près-l'Andorre, and La Tour de Carol. From these towns, bus connections are available to Andorra la Vella.

CLIMATE AND CLOTHES: All 175 square miles of Andorra are tucked into a few folds high up in the eastern Pyrenees between Spain and France. The altitude assures snow-capped mountains and chilly evenings year-round, but the temperature on June, July, and August days easily can reach 80F (25C) before plunging at nightfall, so pack cottons, as well as heavy sweaters.

LANGUAGE: Catalan, spoken in neighboring Spain, is the official tongue, but French and Spanish are equally common. Shopkeepers and hoteliers speak English.

ELECTRIC CURRENT: 220 volts, AC.

MONEY: The French franc, which equals 100 centimes, and Spanish peseta, which equals 100 centimos, both are legal tender.

TIPPING: Sometimes restaurants and hotels include service charges, sometimes not. From 10% to 15% is the expected tip.

BANKING/BUSINESS HOURS: Banks are generally open from 9 AM to 1 PM and from 3 to 5 PM weekdays, and from 9 AM to noon on Saturdays. Banks are closed on Sundays. Most other businesses are open from 9 AM to 1 PM and from 3 to 7 PM weekdays.

HOLIDAYS/SPECIAL EVENTS: *New Year's Day* (January 1), *Epiphany* (January 6), *Easter Monday* (April 20), *Pentecost Monday* (June 8), *Benediction of the Automobiles* (July 10), *Carnival of St. John* (June 23), *Feast of La Verge de Meritxell* (September 8), *All Saints' Day* (November 1), and *Christmas Day* (December 25). The *Feste de Andorra la Vella* is celebrated on the first Saturday, Sunday, and Monday in August.

SHOPPING: On weekends, the roads leading through Andorra la Vella are as clogged with shoppers as *Macy's* aisles during *Christmas*. Tax-free merchandise (often a euphemism for smuggled goods) is the goal, and cars bulging with purchases can barely pass one another on the narrow thoroughfare. Cigarettes, sheepskin jackets, liquor, Parisian fashions, gasoline, canned goods, and perfume are just a few of the bargains that lure the shopper. Most stores are open from 9 AM to 8 PM daily; some close between 1 and 3 PM.

Austria

TOURIST INFORMATION: Literature can be obtained from the *Austrian National Tourist Office* (*Oesterreichische Fremdenverkehrswerbung;* 1 Margaretemstr., Vienna A-1040; phone: 222-588660). Regional information is provided by state tourist offices found in the capital cities of the nine states and called either *Landesfremden-verkehrsverband* or *Fremdenverkehrsverband.*

ENTRY REQUIREMENTS: US citizens with current US passports need no visas for visits of 3 months or less.

GETTING THERE/GETTING AROUND: Airlines – *Austrian Airlines* and *Delta* both offer nonstop service to Vienna from New York. At press time, *Pan American* also offered nonstop flights to Vienna from New York. *Austrian Airlines,* as well as many other European airlines, connect most major European cities with Vienna and other Austrian destinations. *TWA* has service to Vienna via Frankfurt. *Austrian Airlines* offers daily domestic service from Vienna to Graz, Klagenfurt, Linz, and Salzburg; *Tyrolean Airways* has service from Innsbruck to Vienna, Amsterdam, Frankfurt, and Zurich Mondays through Fridays.

Cars – European makes can be rented from the usual array of international and local firms in all major Austrian cities. The tax rate on rental cars is 21% unless the car is kept 22 days or longer, in which case the tax rate is 33%. The *Austrian Federal Railways,* in cooperation with *Avis* and *Inter-Rent,* offers car rentals for pickup at certain stations, including Vienna, Graz, Innsbruck, and Salzburg. The reservation must be made at least 2 hours prior to arrival at the station where the car will be picked up. Reservations may be made at any railroad station, *OeBB*-appointed travel agencies, or with the conductor on express trains; maximum rental period is 3 days. Road condition information in English can be obtained daily from 6 AM to 10 PM by calling 711997 in Vienna; outside the capital dial the Vienna city code (0222) first.

Trains – *Austrian Federal Railways* (*OeBB*) offers the Austrian Network Pass, which provides unlimited travel on trains in Austria for 1 month. This pass can be purchased at all Austrian railroad stations. Senior citizen discounts of 50% are available to travelers over 60 (women) and 65 (men) on trains, the postal buses, and buses operated by the *Federal Railways* (not local transit). An application form may be picked up at the railroad stations throughout Austria, as well as those in Frankfurt, Munich, and Zurich. Also available at Austrian rail stations is the Rabbit Card, which allows 4 days of unlimited train travel. It must be used within 10 days from the date of purchase.

CLIMATE AND CLOTHES: Mountains cover over 70% of the country and altitude rather than latitude determines temperature. Be prepared for summer showers. On the whole, the climate is moderate with summer daytime averages in the 70s F (20C) and nights cooling to the 50s F (10C). Winter days are in the 30s F (0 degrees C) and 40s F (5C). Comfortable sporting gear is standard. For Vienna, take something reasonably elegant for a gala evening on the town.

LANGUAGE: German (*Hochdeutsch*) is the written language and is taught in the schools, but numerous and pronounced regional dialects exist. English is taught as the second language and is understood in major tourist areas.

ELECTRIC CURRENT: 220 volts, AC.

MONEY: The Austrian schilling (AS internationally, S in Austria) is divided into 100 groschen.

TIPPING: Service charges run between 10% and 15% on restaurant and hotel bills, with the higher percentage included in luxury establishment bills. Leave a small amount of change for the waiter or the maid. Porters and bellmen should receive 10 schillings per bag, doormen about 5, and taxi drivers 10% of the fare.

BANKING/BUSINESS HOURS: Banks are generally open from 8 AM to 3 PM weekdays, and until 5 or 5:30 PM on Thursdays; branch offices close from 12:30 to 1:30 PM but otherwise keep the same hours as main offices. The Meinl Bank AG in Vienna (8a Stephanspl.), however, stays open until 5 PM every weekday. Money can be changed from 7 AM to 10 PM daily at the capital's Westbahnhof and Südbahnhof railway stations and at the airport around the times of international flights. An automatic money changer has been installed on Vienna's Kärntnerstrasse (across from the *Opera House*) which will change major denominations of European currency into Austrian schillings. Most other businesses are open from 8 AM to 4 PM, Mondays through Thursdays, and until noon on Fridays.

HOLIDAYS/SPECIAL EVENTS: *New Year's Day* (January 1), *Epiphany* (January 6), *Easter Monday* (April 20), *Labor Day* (May 1), *Ascension Day* (May 28), *Whitmonday* (June 8), *Corpus Christi Day* (June 18), *Feast of the Assumption* (August 15), *Flag Day* (October 26), *All Saints' Day* (November 1), *Feast of the Immaculate Conception* (December 8), *Christmas Day* (December 25), and *St. Stephen's Day* (December 26).

Austria's most famous music festivals are the *International Music Festival of Vienna,* May and June, reservations from the *Austrian Travel Agency* (7 Friedrichstr., Vienna A-1010; phone: 58-8000); the *Carinthian Summer Festival* in Ossiach and Villach, July through August (reservations are available from 76 Gumpendorfer Str., Vienna A-1060; phone: 568198); the *Bregenz Festival on Lake Constance* in July and August (for reservations contact *Kartenbüro,* Postfach 311, Bregenz A-6901; phone: 5574-49200); and the *Salzburg Festival,* also in July and August, reservations procedure varies according to event. To ensure that you get the tickets you want to these and other festivals, contact the *Austrian National Tourist Office* in the US for full details on how to order tickets well before your departure.

SHOPPING: Dirndls, lederhosen, Alpine hats with a rakish feather or enameled emblem, and fabric printed with folkloric patterns are all evocative of provincial Austria and can be purchased regionally at *Heimatwerk* shops, which generally have the best selection of local artisans' work. Other specialties include the ubiquitous enamelware, loden cloth coats and jackets, well-designed sweaters, Viennese petit-point articles, precious jewelry, porcelain, and glassware. Sleek Austrian skiwear is a bargain only for those already paying top dollar.

Stores are open between 8 AM and 6 PM; some close for 2 hours at noon for lunch. Most are closed Saturday afternoons, and all day Sundays. To obtain a VAT refund, ask the *Austrian National Tourist Office* for a copy of the booklet *Tax Refunds for Shopping in Austria.* The procedure is complicated.

Belgium

TOURIST INFORMATION: Town Hall, Grand Place, Bruxelles (Brussels) 1000, is the address for *Tourist Information Brussels* (*TIB;* phone: 513-8940); tourist information for the city and country: 61 Rue Marché-aux-Herbes (phone: 504-0390). Tourist offices in all other cities are called either *Syndicat d'Initiative* or *Dienst voor Toerisme.*

ENTRY REQUIREMENTS: A current US passport is good for visits of 3 months or less by US citizens.

GETTING THERE/GETTING AROUND: Airlines – *Sabena* flies nonstop from Anchorage, Atlanta, Boston, Chicago, New York, Montreal, and Toronto to Brussels. *Delta* and *TWA* fly nonstop from New York to Brussels.

Bus – *Europabus* is a network of tourist bus services operated by the European railways. Both scheduled services and tours are offered. Contact *Debock,* 105 Rue Marché-aux-Herbes, Brussels 1000 (phone: 513-6154).

Cars – Motoring information, as well as breakdown service is provided by the *Touring Club de Belgique* (44 Rue de la Loi, Brussels 1040; phone: 233-2211), and the *Royal Automobile Club de Belgique,* which also has an SOS breakdown number (call the number above for the specific breakdown number for the area you are traveling in). The small yellow cars of the touring *secours* (literally, "help") patrol offer assistance to motorists in need.

Trains – Belgium's rail network is said to be the world's most comprehensive. The *Société Nationale Chemin de Fer Belge* (*SNCB*) offers several reduced-fare plans and also the Benelux Tourrail Pass, good for 5 days of travel in a 17-day period on the Belgian, Dutch, and Luxembourg railways.

CLIMATE AND CLOTHES: The sea is the predominant influence on the weather and the gently undulating hills that cover a good part of the country's interior don't stop the prevailing westerlies. In the Ardennes, morning fogs near the shore turn into evening mists (a raincoat and umbrella can come in handy). The climate is temperate with few extremes. Temperatures reach 70F (21C) in summer and drop to the low 40s (near 0 degrees C) in winter. Dress is cosmopolitan and French in style. Bikinis are much in evidence on Belgium's west coast beaches, but none are St.-Tropez–style, and whatever swimming attire you wear you must keep on. In the capital of Brussels, women should *never* wear shorts.

LANGUAGE: French is spoken by inhabitants of the Walloon area south of Brussels — about 32% of the population. Brussels itself is primarily French-speaking but lies in Flanders, where the official language is Flemish, an accented version of Dutch. German is the third national language but is spoken by less than 1% of the inhabitants. English is widely understood.

ELECTRIC CURRENT: 220 volts, AC.

MONEY: The Belgian franc (BF) equals 100 centimes.

TIPPING: A 16% service charge is added to most restaurant bills and also is included on taxi meters. More and more hotels are including service charges on their bills. If they are not included, 50 BF should suffice for bellmen (per bag) and 100 BF for chambermaids (per day). Restaurant and café tabs usually include a gratuity. Railway station porters charge a fixed fee of 20 to 25 BF per bag. Taxi fares include the tip. Restroom attendants expect at least 7 BF; coatroom attendants, 20 to 50 BF per article. Barber and beauty shop bills often include the tip. Ushers at movie theaters expect 10 BF per person.

BANKING/BUSINESS HOURS: Banks are generally open Mondays through Fridays from 9 AM to 3 or 4 PM; some banks are open later on Fridays. Most other businesses are open weekdays from 9 AM to 5 PM, and are closed for an hour between noon and 2 PM.

HOLIDAYS/SPECIAL EVENTS: *New Year's Day* (January 1), *Easter Monday* (April 20), *Labor Day* (May 1), *Ascension Day* (May 28), *Whitmonday* (June 8), *Independence Day* (July 21), *Assumption Day* (August 15), *All Saints' Day* (November 1), *Armistice Day* (November 11), *Christmas* (December 25 and 26).

Belgian folkloric pageants and processions are famed and numerous. *Carnival* in Binche climaxes on *Shrove Tuesday* with costumed and ostrich-plumed "Gilles" pummeling the crowds with oranges. *Ascension Thursday* in May is celebrated in Bruges by the famed *Procession of the Holy Blood;* also in May, the *Cat Festival* of Iper features costumes, floats, and the tossing of plush cats from the town's belfry.

SHOPPING: Chocolate is a Belgian specialty. *Godiva* (owned by the US *Campbell Soup Company*) has its own stores in Belgium, but is by no means the only source for fine chocolates. The true devotee also should seek out the Neuhaus, Corne de la Toison d'Or, and Wittamer brands.

Pewter, manufactured by Les Potstainiers Hugo in Huy and Meestertingieters in Tongeren, and Val St.-Lambert crystal are good buys. Belgian linen and lace are justifiably famous.

The beautifully balanced sporting guns of the Fabrique Nationale in Herstal, among the aristocracy of shotguns, can be specially ordered with scenes hand etched by local craftsmen.

Larger Belgian stores are open from 9:15 AM to 6 PM. Smaller shops that close for lunch usually remain open until 8 PM. The Belgian VAT varies from 10% to 33%, depending on the item.

Bulgaria

TOURIST INFORMATION: *Balkantourist,* the country's largest travel company, is currently being privatized. Their headquarters is at 1 Vitosha Boulevard in Sofia (phone: 43331). Local tourist information offices throughout the country provide maps and other materials and assistance. For more information on travel to Bulgaria and the rest of central and Eastern Europe, contact *Balkan Holidays/USA/Ltd.* (161 E. 86th St., New York, NY 10028; phone: 212-573-5530).

ENTRY REQUIREMENTS: US citizens need a current passport to enter the country, but no visa is required for stays of up to 30 days. Visas are required for US citizens staying longer than 30 days; they are available within 7 to 10 business days of filling out the appropriate forms. The cost is $23 (a rush fee of $9 may also be applied). Delivery by *Federal Express* is available for a $15.50 charge; the express mail charge is $10. Contact the Bulgarian Embassy (1621 22nd St. NW, Washington, DC 20008; phone: 202-387-7969). Visas also may be obtained in Bulgaria at the Consular Office of the Ministry of Foreign Affairs in Sofia (phone: 41441).

GETTING THERE/GETTING AROUND: Airlines – At press time, *Jes Air,* a new Bulgarian airline, had just launched the first direct service between Sofia, the capital, and New York. The weekly flights depart on Wednesdays. *Balkanair* flies between major cities in Bulgaria and connects Sofia to all European capitals.

Bus – Tours run by *Balkantourist* are accompanied by multilingual guides, alleviate the language problem, and are suggested for sightseeing.

Cars – Probably the best bet for the tourist. Cars can be rented in Bulgaria's major cities through *Avis* (phone: 800-331-1084), *Dollar Rent-a-Car* (known in Bulgaria as

Eurodollar; phone: 800-421-6878), *Hertz* (phone: 800-654-3001), and *National* (phone: 800-CAR-EUROPE). Free emergency assistance is provided by road aid cars that patrol the highways or can be called (phone: 146).

Trains – The *BDG* (*Bulgarian State Railway*) service between Sofia and Varna on the Black Sea is frequent and efficient, but most other trains are locals and crowded. There also is service between Sofia and other major capitals, such as Istanbul and Vienna.

CLIMATE AND CLOTHES: The Balkan Mountains (highest range is the Rila Dagh, at more than 9,000 feet) crisscross the country to reach straight to the edge of the Black Sea and its golden beaches. Summers are dry but not oppressively hot (80s F, high 20s C) and winters cold, dry, and relatively windless with temperatures in the 30s F (around 0 degrees C). Informality is the keynote in summer dress. Jackets and ties (and warm coats) are best for fall and winter in Sofia, the capital.

LANGUAGE: Bulgarian, a South Slavic tongue, is similar to Russian and uses the Cyrillic alphabet. You can just navigate the tourist circuit with English (Russian is the second language) and should consider the use of English-speaking guides if you wish to communicate in the countryside.

ELECTRIC CURRENT: 220 volt, AC.

MONEY: The lev equals 100 stotinki. It is illegal to import or export Bulgarian currency.

TIPPING: In theory tips are not accepted; in practice they are. About 10% of a restaurant bill would suffice.

BANKING/BUSINESS HOURS: Generally from Mondays through Fridays from 9 AM to 5 PM.

HOLIDAYS/SPECIAL EVENTS: *New Year's Day* (January 1), *National Liberation Day* (March 3), Greek Orthodox *Easter* (April 26), *Cyrillic Alphabet Holiday* (May 24), and *Christmas Day* (December 25).

Bulgaria is the world's leading exporter of attar of roses and one of the biggest festivals occurs the first Sunday in June celebrating the harvest of the huge rose crop, which covers a 20-mile swath in the Kazanlŭk area.

Slunchev Bryag, best known as Sunny Beach, on Bulgaria's Riviera hosts a pop music festival called *Golden Orpheus* in early June, which brings entertainers and groups from all over the world. In a more serious vein, Sofia's continuous musical weeks in May and June concentrate on the classical, and Plovdiv has chamber music concerts throughout the month of June. Humor is the focus of Gabrovo's biennual (odd-numbered years only) comedic extravaganza, which brings tourists from all over the world to this centrally located town for 10 days in mid-May.

SHOPPING: Attar of roses in hand-carved wooden containers is the most popular Bulgarian souvenir, but larger purchases could include leather goods or the rugs made in Kotel (in general, a center for crafts), which come in a variety of colorful designs, or those of Chiprovtsi. The *Bulgarian Artists Union* runs shops around the country featuring products of the membership, and the state-run foreign currency *Corecom* stores are a good source for other Bulgarian products including silks and sheepskin coats. Normal store hours are 8:30 AM to 7 PM Mondays through Saturdays, with a 2-hour break at midday. In small towns, stores may close early on Saturdays.

Czechoslovakia

TOURIST INFORMATION: *Cedok*'s blue sign with the white bird in flight signifies general tourist services at some 150 locations throughout the country. (*Cedok* is in the process of being privatized.) Its main office is at 18 Na Příkopě, Prague 1, 11135 (phone:

212-7111), and its accommodations service is at 5 Panská, Prague. Larger cities also have tourist information centers.

ENTRY REQUIREMENTS: US citizens need only a current passport for visits of up to 30 days. Visas are not required.

GETTING THERE/GETTING AROUND: Airlines – *CSA,* the Czechoslovak airline, flies the New York–Prague route with Ilyusin 62s nonstop in summer and from Montreal year-round. *Delta* flies to Prague via Frankfurt or Vienna. Prague is the hub from which domestic flights on *CSA* radiate to 13 airports, including Brno, Bratislava, Košice, Ostrava, Piešťany (for spas), and Poprad in the Tatras (for skiing and mountaineering).

Bus – Next to the airlines, express bus service to Germany, Austria, Poland, Yugoslavia, and Hungary, as well as domestic service aboard *CSD* coaches, is probably the fastest way of traveling in and out of and throughout Czechoslovakia.

Cars – Rentals are available from *Pragocar,* with outlets in the major cities. The Yellow Angels in four-wheel-drive vehicles of the *Ustredni Automotoklub* provide emergency service for motorists. Gas coupons are sold at frontier crossings, at the automobile club office in Prague (29 Opletalova; phone: 223544), and at Zivnostenska Bank (20 Na Příkopě, Prague).

Trains – There's frequent service aboard trains of the *Ceskoslovenské Státní Dráhy* (*CSD*), and various European expresses stop at Prague, Bratislava, and Brno.

CLIMATE AND CLOTHES: Czechoslovakia really is three contiguous areas snaking across central Europe — Bohemia, Moravia, and Slovakia — and temperatures are about the same in all three. Average temperatures are around 70F (21C) in summer, and the low 20s F (a little below 0 degrees C) in winter, although mountains are chillier in both seasons. Prague has cold, damp winters (average temperature is 30F/−1C); and warm summers (70F/21C).

Dress is casual but conservative. Evenings at luxury resorts such as Karlovy Vary (Carlsbad) and Mariánské Lázně (Marienbad) call for reasonably dressy clothes.

LANGUAGE: Czech is spoken by those living in the Czech Republic (a combination of the Bohemian and Moravian regions), who make up about two-thirds of the population. Slovak, the native language of the rest of the population, is spoken in the eastern Slovak Republic. Both languages are Slavic and very similar. Those engaged in tourism speak English.

ELECTRIC CURRENT: 220 volts, AC.

MONEY: One koruna (Kčs) consists of 100 halers. It is illegal to import or export Czechoslovak currency.

TIPPING: Restaurant bills don't include service charges, and at least 10% should be added; taxi drivers also expect 10% tips; 5 to 10 korunas should be given to porters and doormen.

BANKING/BUSINESS HOURS: Banks are generally open from 8 AM to 4 PM weekdays; some are open until 6 PM twice a week and once a week until noon. Most other businesses are open from 8 AM to 4 PM weekdays.

HOLIDAYS/SPECIAL EVENTS: *New Year's Day* (January 1), *Easter Monday* (April 20), *Labor Day* (May 1), *Anniversary of Liberation* (May 9), *National Holiday* (July 5), *Proclamation of Czechoslovak Republic* (October 28), *Christmas Day* (December 25), and *Boxing Day* (December 26).

Fine international performances are part of Prague's annual spring music festival, *Prague Spring* (Pražské Jaro), beginning May 12, the anniversary of the Czech composer Bedřich Smetana's death, and continuing through June 1. Two colorful folk festivals offer grand displays of typical costumes, music, and dances of the republic's two states: the *Moravian Fete* held in Strážnice in June, and the *Slovakian Festival* in Východná in July.

SHOPPING: Antiques are a lure, and the small shops in Prague delight the collector and window-shopper alike. As we went to press, antiques still had to be purchased at

Tuzex-approved shops to be eligible for export. *Tuzex* shops sell a wide range of crafts and tourist goods, such as Bohemian glass and porcelain and fine quality records, for foreign currency. However, given the political changes, Czech authorities could not confirm whether or not these *Tuzex* shops would remain state supported. Modern applied arts are sold at *Art Centrum* in Prague and special folk art outlets for hand-painted *Easter* eggs, straw *Christmas* ornaments, jewelry, woven linen, and the like, are found in many towns. Shops are open Mondays through Fridays from 8 or 9 AM to 6 PM, Saturdays from 9 AM to 1 PM.

Denmark

TOURIST INFORMATION: The central office of the *Danish National Tourist Office* (22 H.C. Andersens Blvd. at the *Tivoli* entrance by Town Hall; phone: 33-11325) or the *Tourist Association of Copenhagen* in the *Magasin du Nord* department store (Kongens Nytorv; phone: 33-114433) has maps, brochures, and literature (all in English) on touring the entire country, as well as Greenland and the Faeroe Islands; regional tourist offices in Denmark's major cities are equally well stocked. Innumerable local *turistbureaus* are distinguished by the international tourist logo, a sign with a lowercase *i* on a green background.

ENTRY REQUIREMENTS: A current US passport is good for visits of 3 months or less.

GETTING THERE/GETTING AROUND: Airlines – *SAS* flies nonstop to Copenhagen from Anchorage, Chicago, Los Angeles, Newark, New York, and Seattle. *Icelandair* has regularly scheduled flights from New York to Copenhagen (with a stop in Reykjavik); *TWA* flies nonstop and direct from New York to Copenhagen. *Delta* flies nonstop from Atlanta to Copenhagen. *Danair*'s domestic flights leave Copenhagen's Kastrup Airport for Bornholm, Funen, and nine airports in Jutland and the Faeroe Islands. *SAS* has service to Greenland from Copenhagen. In the winter, inexpensive charters carry sun-starved Scandinavians to warmer Mediterranean shores such as Greece, Israel, and Majorca.

Cars – There are no toll roads in Denmark. Emergency call boxes for breakdown assistance are located along *motorvejs* (major highways).

Ferries – The *DSB* ferries are an integral part of the highway and rail system and, though they have been supplemented by bridges, they are still an essential part of the major crossing between Funen and Zealand, called the Store Baelt (Great Belt).

Trains – The modern *Intercity, IC3,* and *L* (*Lyntog*) expresses cover the country at great speeds, navigating the crossing between Zealand and Funen aboard huge, hand-some ferries. At other junctions, you leave the train, cross by boat, and board another train to continue. The *Dansk Statsbaner* or *DSB* (*Danish State Railway*) is one of the sponsors of the Scandinavian Rail Pass and also honors the Eurailpass, Eurail Youth-pass, and Eurail Saverpass.

CLIMATE AND CLOTHES: Thanks to the Gulf Stream, winters are relatively mild with daytime temperatures averaging 34F (about 0 degrees C) in February, the coldest month. The changeable summer weather often includes rainstorms and the long sum-mer nights can be chilly, but summer days average about 70F (21C). Recent summers in Copenhagen have been exceptionally sunny and warm; sunshine lasts long into the evening due to the city's northerly latitude, but once the sun goes down, it does get cool, so bring a sweater. Winters in Copenhagen can be damp and foggy; don't forget to bring a raincoat and umbrella.

As far as dress is concerned, the Danes do not stand on ceremony, and informal attire is acceptable in most theaters and restaurants. Men should bring a tie and jacket if they are planning to dine at the more exclusive restaurants.

LANGUAGE: Danish, but English has been compulsory in secondary schools since World War II and is spoken and understood throughout the country.

ELECTRIC CURRENT: 220 volts, 50 cycles, AC.

MONEY: The Danish krone (DKr) equals 100 øre.

TIPPING: Railway porters and washroom attendants receive tips, but otherwise they are not expected unless a special service has been provided. Service charges always are included in restaurant and hotel bills, and in taxi fares.

BANKING/BUSINESS HOURS: Banks are generally open Mondays through Fridays from 9:30 AM to 4 PM; some banks are open to 6 PM on Thursdays. Most other businesses are open weekdays from 8 AM to 4 PM; government offices usually close at 2 PM on Fridays.

HOLIDAYS/SPECIAL EVENTS: *New Year's Day* (January 1), *Maundy Thursday* (April 16), *Good Friday* (April 17), *Easter Monday* (April 20), *Common Prayers Day* (May 15), *Ascension Day* (May 28), *Constitution Day* (June 5), *Whitmonday* (June 8), *Christmas Day* (December 25), and *Boxing Day* (December 26).

In July and August, Odense re-creates local boy Hans Christian Andersen's fairy tales. Frederikssund's *Viking Festival* in June and July is a fine historical pageant. An array of first class cultural events is held all summer long at Copenhagen's *Tivoli* amusement park, open from May to mid-September.

SHOPPING: Shopping in Copenhagen is a trip in itself. Bing & Grøndahl and Royal Copenhagen porcelain, Holmegaard glass, Georg Jensen silver, and furs from A. C. Bang and Birger Christensen are but a few of the products that make the dedicated shopper shiver with delight. Some better buys are Bornholm ceramics, handmade woolens from Tönder and the Faeroe Islands, and Lego toys. Herring, ham, and the national drink, aquavit, can always cheer you up when you contemplate your empty wallet back home. Denmark has a stiff value added tax (MOMS) of about 22%, but part of it can be saved by shopping at stores that display the Tax Free sign (minimum purchase per shop for this service is DKr. 600).

In general, stores are open weekdays between 10 AM and 5:30 PM and on Saturday mornings.

Finland

TOURIST INFORMATION: The *Finnish Tourist Board* (*MEK*) is based in Helsinki, with a tourist information office at 26 Unioninkatu, Helsinki, 00130 (phone: 403-01300). *MEK* headquarters is at 11 Töölönkatu, Helsinki, 00100 (phone: 403011). All cities and towns have city tourist offices (*Matkailutoimisto*), identified by a lowercase *i* on a green background.

ENTRY REQUIREMENTS: A current US passport is required for visits of 3 months or less by US citizens.

GETTING THERE/GETTING AROUND: Airlines – Daily *Finnair* flights link New York with Helsinki nonstop. *Delta* also has service to Helsinki from New York either nonstop or with a stop in Stockholm. *SAS* flies from New York to Helsinki via Copenhagen and Stockholm. Domestically, *Finnair* serves 23 cities at some of the lowest fares in Europe. *Finnair* offers a Holiday Ticket good for 15 days of unlimited domestic air travel, as well as family and senior citizen discounts.

Cars – Car rentals are readily available in Helsinki. The 519-mile (830-km) trip between Helsinki and Rovaniemi, the capital of Lapland on the Arctic Circle, takes about 12 hours by car over well-maintained, year-round roads.

Ferries, Ships, and Other Transport – The series of interconnecting lakes in western, central, and southeastern Finland seems to take up more room than the landmass there. A varied fleet, from hydrofoils to small lake steamers, provides service in this unique area. Buses are the primary surface transport, as well as being a major means of transit in the northern region of Lapland. Contact *Oy Matkahuolto Ab* (3 Simonkatu, Helsinki 00100; phone: 642744) for overseas bus depots, reservations, and ticket sales in Finland.

Trains – *Valtionrautatiet (VR)* provides excellent equipment and relatively inexpensive service and offers a selection of discount tourist plans including the Finnrail Pass, for various periods of unlimited travel; the Tourist Ticket, which includes bus, boat, air, and train travel, valid for a year; and the Scandinavian Rail Pass and Eurailpass. The railroad's northern terminus is Kolari, far above the Arctic Circle.

CLIMATE AND CLOTHES: In the south, snow covers the country from December to mid-April, when it begins melting. Winter comes earlier to the north, around the end of October, and stays later, until mid-May. Midday temperatures in Helsinki average 72F (22C) in July, the warmest month, and 25F (−7C) in February, the coldest. At Ivalo, to the far north, warm July days average 66F (18C) and cool February days, 17F (−3C). Weather in Helsinki can be cold and gray in winter. The cold is no different from that of the US Great Lakes area in winter. A heavy coat and sweater (wool dresses and/or a suit, for women), a pair of lined boots, and good wool- or silk-lined gloves will see you through the outdoors in fine shape. Don't worry about the heating indoors; hotels and restaurants are comfortably warm.

Informal dress is frowned upon in the better restaurants, where jackets and ties are expected. In general, the tenor is slightly more conservative than in other Scandinavian countries. Women should pack a couple of cocktail dresses. In summer or winter, pants suits are popular here.

For hot weather, lightweight cotton or drip-dry clothes are ideal. Bring a bathing suit or two; add a sweater and a raincoat, to play it safe. The thermometer in summer can rise from a coolish 50F to 60F (10C to 16C) to the hot 90s (about 30C to 32C). At this time of year, tourists are treated to a bonus — almost 19 hours of daylight.

A note on the midnight sun and the winter darkness: The area of northern Finland that lies within the Arctic Circle has 2 months of midnight sun (June and July) and 2 of winter darkness (December and January). In southern Finland (which includes Helsinki), midsummer offers about 5 hours of nocturnal twilight.

LANGUAGE: Finland's two official tongues are Finnish, spoken by 93% of the Finnish people, which like Hungarian and Estonian is a Finno-Ugric language; and Swedish, an Indo-European language spoken by about 6.2% of the people. Lappish, also Finno-Ugric, is the native speech of about 2,000 citizens. English is found in the major tourist centers and is the country's most widely spoken foreign language.

ELECTRIC CURRENT: 220 volts, AC.

MONEY: The Finnish markka (FIM) equals 100 pennis.

TIPPING: Restaurants add a 14% service charge during the week and on Saturdays, and 15% on Sundays and holidays, but you can leave a bit extra for the waiter, and make sure to tip about 3 Fmks to the restaurant doorman. Hotel bills also include the service. Porters receive 3 Fmks but others, including cab drivers, don't expect tips.

BANKING/BUSINESS HOURS: Banks are open weekdays from 9:15 AM to 4:15 PM. Most other businesses are open weekdays from 8:30 AM to 4 or 4:30 PM, but government office hours are 8 AM to 4:15 PM (3:15 in summer).

HOLIDAYS/SPECIAL EVENTS: *New Year's Day* (January 1), *Good Friday* (April 17), *Easter Monday* (April 20), *Walpurgis Night* (April 30), *May Day* (May 1), *Ascen-*

sion Day (May 28), *Midsummer's Eve* (June 19) and *Midsummer's Day* (June 20), *All Saints' Day* (November 1), *Independence Day* (December 6), *Christmas Eve* (December 24), *Christmas Day* (December 25), and *Boxing Day* (December 26).

All Finland is a festival between June and September, with many diverse cultural events. Music is the theme of most, with the performing arts celebrated in Helsinki throughout the summer.

In late February the *Salpausselkä Skiing Championships* feature cross-country ski races at Lahti. Also in February is the 75-km *Finlandia Ski Race* between Hämeenlinna and Lahti. The beginning of March brings the *Kuopio Skating Marathon* in Kuopio. Reindeer roundups in Lapland are in progress from October to January.

SHOPPING: The Finnish genius for modern design has made Marimekko fabrics, Arabia ceramics, and Iittala glassware international household names. Lapponia jewelry, fusing gold and silver in stylized replicas of natural forms, is highly regarded, as is the Aarikka line of wooden jewelry. Multicolored patterned rya rugs come from Finland, as do the orange-handled scissors made by Fiskars, which also makes a fine line of steel cutlery. Traditional decorated Puukko sheath knives make perfect presents for outdoor people. For an overall view of Finnish products, stop at the *Museum of Applied Arts,* 23 Korkeavuorenkatu, in Helsinki.

The Finnish 16% sales tax (VAT) can be avoided (via a refund in the mail) by having stores send purchases to your departure point or directly home. Or you can save between 11% and 13% — to be refunded at your point of departure — and take the package with you, sealed, under Finland's tax-free program. Summer shopping hours are generally 8:30 AM to 5 PM Mondays through Thursdays, until 8 PM on Fridays, and 9 AM to 3 PM on Saturdays.

France

TOURIST INFORMATION: The main *Office du Tourisme* is at 127 Av. des Champs-Elysées, Paris 75008 (phone: 472-08898 for information in English; 472-36172 in French), with branches at the major train stations, such as the Gare du Nord, Gare de l'Est, Gare de Lyon, and Gare d'Austerlitz, and at major airports throughout France. Local *Syndicats d'Initiative (SI)* supply literature in cities and towns. Regional information is available in Paris from the more than 20 provincial tourist bureaus, called collectively *Maisons de Province à Paris,* scattered around the city.

ENTRY REQUIREMENTS: The only requirement for American citizens to enter France is a current US passport. Visas are required for stays longer than 90 days.

GETTING THERE/GETTING AROUND: Airlines – *Air France* has daily *Concorde* flights between New York and Paris. *Concorde* flights take 3 hours and 45 minutes from New York to Paris. Tickets cost about 20% more than subsonic first class fares. *Air France* also flies nonstop to Paris from Anchorage, Boston, Chicago, Houston, Los Angeles, Miami, Newark, New York, Philadelphia, San Francisco, and Washington, DC, and from New York to Nice; *TWA* flies nonstop from Boston, Los Angeles, New York, St. Louis, and Washington, DC. *Delta* flies nonstop from Atlanta and Cincinnati; *American* has nonstops from Chicago, New York, Dallas/Ft. Worth, and Raleigh/Durham; *Continental* flies nonstop from Newark to Paris, and *UTA* from San Francisco. *Delta* has nonstop service from New York, Miami, and Washington, DC, to Paris, and from New York to Nice. *Air Inter,* the national domestic carrier, serves all of France, including Corsica.

Cars – French toll roads, *autoroutes,* are well patrolled, and breakdown service is readily available — many major autoroutes are equipped with 24-hour information centers that can arrange for assistance to motorists. Emergency call boxes are available on other routes and continually are being installed in new locations.

Trains – With over 22,000 miles of track, France has the largest rail network on the Continent, and, with crack Corail and turbotrains and the *TGV* (*train à grande vitesse*), the fastest trains. Although the *TGV* has set records, in commercial operation its speed is 186 mph. It cuts the trip from Paris to Lyons to 2 hours, and there are numerous round trips daily. The *TGV Atlantique* line offers service to points south and west of Paris, including Bordeaux, Nantes, Quimper, Rennes, Tours, and the Spanish border. The *TGV Sud-Est* line goes from the Lyons Station in Paris to Albertville, where the *1992 Winter Olympics* will be held. The trip takes 3 hours and 36 minutes; there will be approximately 30 trains per day on this route during the games. Other train lines also will increase service to the region during the *Olympics*.

The France Railpass offers unlimited travel over the entire *Société Nationale des Chemins de Fer Français* (*SNCF*) railway system. Available for either first or second class travel, for periods of 4 or 9 days within 15 days (for the 4-day pass) or one month (for the 9-day pass), it must be purchased before going abroad, either from a travel agent or from *Rail Europe* offices in the US. Bonuses include round-trip rail transfer from the Paris airports (Orly or de Gaulle) to downtown, a 1-day Metropass, and various discounts. For train information in English in Paris, call 050-25050; elsewhere, add the city code: 1. For information, contact *Rail Europe,* 230 Westchester Ave., White Plains, NY 10604 (phone: 914-682-5172 or 800-848-7245).

CLIMATE AND CLOTHES: It's generally fair and warm in the summertime, particularly in the south. Winters are mild, with overall daytime averages in the 40s F (about 5C), rising to highs of around 55F (12C) in January and February along the Riviera. Paris has about the same weather as US Middle Atlantic states, though it's usually not warmer than 75F (24C) or colder than 30F (−1C). It rains frequently year-round, so a raincoat and folding umbrella are absolute musts. Air conditioning is still rather rare, and thermostats are usually set relatively low in winter. Whoever wrote about the glories of April in Paris clearly never spent a spring in Paris's chilly gray damp.

The celebrated French sense of style is best illustrated by the manner of dress. Visitors will certainly not feel ill at ease dressed casually and comfortably, but you may find a visit to Paris the perfect opportunity to practice a little Parisian chic.

LANGUAGE: French is spoken with verve and pride and, while you normally can get by in English, use whatever French words and phrases you know. Residents of Paris have a reputation for dealing coldly with non-French speakers. This is only partially justified, and in the provinces visitors will find few who speak English but an enormous amount of cordiality and patience.

ELECTRIC CURRENT: 220 volts, AC.

MONEY: The French franc (F) equals 100 centimes.

TIPPING: Hotel and restaurant bills include a 12% to 15% service charge. The doorman should receive 5F per piece, for help with suitcases; the room service waiter 10F; the chambermaid should get 10F per person, per day. Taxi drivers are rarely tipped by the French but may expect it from an American; 15% will suffice.

BANKING/BUSINESS HOURS: Banks are open weekdays from 9 AM to 5 PM. Business hours generally run from 9 AM to 6 PM, with a generous break of up to 2½ hours for lunch beginning at noon or 1 PM.

HOLIDAYS/SPECIAL EVENTS: *New Year's Day* (January 1), *Easter Monday* (April 20), *Labor Day* (May 1), *VE Day* (May 8), *Ascension Day* (May 28), *Whitmonday* (June 8), *Bastille Day* (July 14), the *Feast of the Assumption* (August 15), *All Saints' Day* (November 1), *Armistice Day* (November 11), and *Christmas Day* (December 25).

The *Festival d' Avignon,* a theater festival held annually in July and August, has no peer in France. Some wonderful, purely musical festivals take place each summer, among them the Strasbourg *International Music Festival* in early June, the *International Festival of Lyric Art and Music* in mid-July in Aix-en-Provence, and the *Biennale de la Musique Française* (formerly the *Berlioz Festival*) in September in Lyons.

Famous sporting events include the *Le Mans* 24-hour race in mid-June and the *Tour de France,* the world's premier bicycle race, the first 3 weeks in July. The *Air Show* at Le Bourget Airport takes place in June of odd-numbered years and the *Auto Show* in Paris in October of even-numbered years. This year, the *Winter Olympics* will take place in Albertville, February 6–23.

Dijon's *Gastronomic Fair* in early November is followed by the *Three Days of Glory* in Clos-de-Vougeot, Beaune, and Meursault nearby. The *Cannes Film Festival* is held annually in May.

SHOPPING: Boutiques, no matter how beautiful, are pricey. You will do much better in wholesale outlets or stores that carry seconds, discontinued lines, and overstocks. The savings are significant. Decent prices on housewares can be found in large Parisian department stores or their branches, as well as at the usually less expensive *Prisunic* and *Monoprix* chains.

For the ultimate in bric-a-brac shopping stop at any hamlet, no matter how small, on market day. Regional products include faïence pottery from Quimper and Vallauris and porcelain from Limoges, as well as truffles from Périgord, mustards from Dijon, and herbs from Provence, also the home of lovely printed fabrics, exemplified by the Souleido cottons.

Most department stores are open Mondays through Saturdays from 9:30 AM to 6:30 PM, with one or two late-night closings. Boutiques close on Sundays, and some on Mondays.

The French VAT (TVA) ranges from 5.5% (on some food purchases) to 33.33% (on luxury items), but typically is about 18.6%. If you buy goods from one shop worth more than 1,200 francs, you are eligible for a refund. Refund forms are provided by the store at the time of purchase; however, stores are not required to participate in the refund program.

Germany

TOURIST INFORMATION: The *German National Tourist Board* (*Deutsche Zentrale für Tourismus; DZT*) is at 69 Beethovenstrasse, D-6000 Frankfurt am Main, 1 (phone: 69-75720). There usually is a small charge for regional publications, available at local tourist offices (called *Verkehrsverein* or *Verkehrsamt*) found in train stations, city halls, tourist kiosks, and storefronts throughout the country. In Berlin, the main tourist office is in the large complex of shops and restaurants at *Europa-Center* (entrance on Budapaserstr.; phone: 849-262-6031; fax: 849-212-32520). The main tourist office is open daily from 7:30 AM to 10:30 PM, and a branch office at Tegel Airport is open daily from 8 AM until 10:30 PM.

ENTRY REQUIREMENTS: No visa is necessary for periods of 3 months or less for US citizens with current US passports.

GETTING THERE/GETTING AROUND: Airlines – *Lufthansa* regularly schedules nonstop flights to Berlin and Frankfurt from Atlanta, Boston, Chicago, Dallas, Los Angeles, Miami, Newark, New York, San Francisco, and Washington, DC; to Munich from New York; to Cologne and Hamburg from Newark; and to Düsseldorf from Chicago, Los Angeles, Miami, and New York. Direct service is available from Chicago and Los Angeles to Munich via Düsseldorf; Philadelphia to Frankfurt via New York or Montreal; and to Frankfurt from Houston via Atlanta. There also are numerous connecting flights to Nuremberg, and other major cities. *TWA* flies nonstop to Frankfurt from New York and St. Louis, and *Delta* has nonstop service from Atlanta to Munich and Frankfurt plus nonstop service to Berlin, Frankfurt, Hamburg, and Munich and direct flights to Stuttgart, all from New York. *Northwest* has nonstop service from Boston and Detroit to Frankfurt. *American* offers nonstop service to Frankfurt, Munich, and Düsseldorf from Chicago. *KLM* and *SAS* both have connections from New York to Berlin's Schönefeld Airport — *KLM* through Amsterdam; *SAS* via Stockholm.

Cars – The exceptionally large range of models available for rent runs the gamut from VWs to a selection of motor homes. Money-saving rentals of 30 days or more, called leases, are good values.

Cruises – Advance reservations are essential for the exceedingly popular 2-, 3-, 4-, and 5-day Rhine cruises run by the *Koln-Düsseldorfer German Rhine Line* or *K-D* (Frankenwerft, Cologne 15,5000, Germany). Book in the US through *Rhine Cruise Agency* (170 Hamilton Ave., White Plains, NY 10601; phone: 914-948-3600; 800-858-8587 in the western US; 800-346-6525 in the eastern US).

Trains – The Germanrail Pass is good for 4, 9, or 16 days of unlimited travel over the *Deutsche Bundesbahn*'s (*DB*) 15,000-mile rail network. Included with all but the 4-day pass is a discount for travel to Berlin. The pass can be obtained in the US and in Germany, but it is available only to those whose permanent residence is outside Germany. *DB* also sells youth tickets and offers discounts to senior citizens. (Eurailpasses are valid on the *DB*.) *Deutsche Reichsbahn* (*DR*) trains run frequently and many have automobile transport facilities, particularly useful if you're making connections with the car and passenger ferries crossing the Baltic between Warnemünde and Gedser, Denmark, or Sassnitz and Trelleborg, Sweden.

CLIMATE AND CLOTHES: Generally moderate temperatures prevail from the shores of the North Sea south over the forests and river valleys to the slopes of the Bavarian Alps. Summer days average a comfortable 70F (21C), but be prepared for chilly evenings that sometimes dip to the low to mid-50s F (about 10C). In some parts of the country, climatic changes can be abrupt as a result of the combination of the moist northern Baltic maritime climate with that of the mountains to the south and west. Rain can fall at any time of the year. Frankfurt often is overcast and frequently foggy and rainy, so a raincoat is recommended in all seasons. Berlin's air tends to be fresh and less damp because of the lake-studded woodlands surrounding the city, but smog does set in at times.

Dress is conservative in the cities, though not forbiddingly so. Ties for men are absolutely required only in the casinos and better restaurants; jackets will suffice in most first class establishments. There are some nude beaches; except for these, keep your suit on.

LANGUAGE: High German is the written language and the one that's commonly spoken, albeit with different accents, throughout the country. Regional dialects, Bavarian for one, are on the wane but are still found in small towns and rural areas. *Platt* (or low) *Deutsch* is spoken in the north and the Saxon dialect is common in the south. About 300,000 Sorbs (Wends) live in Lusatia and speak a Slavic tongue.

English, mandatory in German schools since World War II, is common among the younger generations and is the second language of the country today.

ELECTRIC CURRENT: 220 volts, AC.

MONEY: The deutsche mark (DM) equals 100 pfennigs.

TIPPING: A 10% to 12% service charge is customarily included in restaurant checks. Superior service may warrant something in addition. Porters receive 1 deutsche mark per bag. Taxi drivers should get about 15% of the fare.

BANKING/BUSINESS HOURS: In Berlin, banks are generally open from 9 AM to 1 PM weekdays and also from 3:30 to 6 PM Tuesdays and Thursdays. Throughout the city various bank branches operate from 9 AM to 6 PM weekdays and on Saturday mornings. The Berliner Bank at Tegel Airport is open from 8 AM to 10 PM daily. In Munich, banks are generally open weekdays from 8:30 AM to 12:30 PM and again from 1:30 to 3:30 PM; on Thursdays they close at 5:30 PM. The bank at the city's main train station is open daily from 6 AM to 11:30 PM. Most other businesses throughout the country operate weekdays from 9 AM to 5 PM.

HOLIDAYS/SPECIAL EVENTS: *New Year's Day* (January 1), *Good Friday* (April 17), *Easter Monday* (April 20), *Labor Day* (May 1), *Ascension Day* (May 28), *Whitmonday* (June 8), *German Unity Day* (October 3), *Day of Prayer and Repentance* (November 18), *Christmas Day* (December 25), and *Boxing Day* (December 26).

The *Richard Wagner Opera Festival* in Bayreuth takes place in July and August every year. The prudent will order direct from Bayreuth at least a year in advance. (The deadline is November 15 of the year preceding the concert date.) Write: *Festspielleitung Bayreuth* (Postfach 100262, Bayreuth 8580). Leipzig's industrial fairs originated over 800 years ago and are held semiannually in the spring and fall. Hotel space is limited and reservations should be made 6 months in advance. If there is no space in Leipzig, you may be luckier in Halle, 20 minutes away. The *German National Tourist Board's Calendar of Events* is insurance against missing any of the fairs, folk festivals, concerts, and the like, that take place throughout the country each year.

SHOPPING: You can save something like $2,000 to $6,000 on the US purchase price of any Mercedes diesel model if you order it in advance from a US dealer or overseas delivery specialist to be picked up in Germany. Making a more modest dent in your wallet are excellent German steel cutlery, goose-down comforters, Rosenthal china and glassware, cameras, optical goods, and toys (wooden ones for the younger set or, for the more sophisticated, multicomponent structural types such as Fischer technik).

Inquire locally about rebates on the German 14% VAT sales tax. Stores are open weekdays from 9 AM to 6 PM; some close from 12:30 to 3 PM for lunch. They follow the same hours the first Saturday of every month but close at 2 PM the other three Saturdays.

Gibraltar

TOURIST INFORMATION: The *Gibraltar Government Tourist Office* is at Cathedral Square (phone: 350-76400) on the Rock; write for literature to Cathedral Square, PO Box 303, Gibraltar.

ENTRY REQUIREMENTS: US citizens can enter this British colony with a current US passport and can stay for up to 3 months.

GETTING THERE/GETTING AROUND: *GB Airways, British Airways,* and *Air Europe* fly from London in 2½ hours. *GB Airways* also operates frequently scheduled 20-minute flights to Tangiers. There also is catamaran service to Tangiers. Entry from Spain presents no problem: The border is open 24 hours daily and visitors may walk or drive across easily.

On the Rock, touring is done on foot or by minibus, taxi, or rental car. Driving is on the right.

CLIMATE AND CLOTHES: Hot summer temperatures in the high 80s and low 90s (mid-20s to low 30s C) are kept comfortable both by southeasterly sea breezes and by dips in the Mediterranean. Lightweight, light-colored clothes are pro forma. The rainy season is during the cooler — mid-60s to low 70s (16C to 22C) — winter months.

LANGUAGE: Gibraltar residents are British subjects and English is the official language, but Spanish is commonly spoken.

ELECTRIC CURRENT: 240 volts, AC.

MONEY: The British pound sterling (£) equals 100 pence. Gibraltar also prints its own bank notes, which only can be used locally.

TIPPING: Most restaurant bills include service. If not, 10% to 15% is expected.

BANKING/BUSINESS HOURS: Banks are open Mondays through Thursdays 9 AM to 3:30 PM and on Fridays it stays open till 4:30 PM. General business hours are Mondays through Fridays 9 AM to 3 PM.

HOLIDAYS/SPECIAL EVENTS: *New Year's Day* (January 1), *Good Friday* (April 17), *Easter Monday* (April 20), *Queen's Birthday* (June 15), *Late Summer Bank Holiday* (last Monday in August; August 31 this year), *Christmas Day* (December 25), and *Boxing Day* (December 26).

A self-governing British colony, Gibraltar celebrates a few anniversaries like the *Battle of Trafalgar Day,* in October, and *Remembrance Day,* in November. The Changing of the Guard takes place at 11 every Tuesday morning outside the governor's residence. The main religious festival in this predominantly Catholic colony is *Holy Week,* when outdoor processions and special services are held. Deep-sea and pier fishing competitions take place year-round, and shark angling competitions are held twice yearly.

SHOPPING: Gibraltar has very good shopping for tourists, with duty-free facilities at the air terminal and at a few shops. Also, there is no VAT. It's a bargain bonanza for British products such as whiskey, woolens, and linen, as well as such international goods as gold jewelry, pearls, leather goods, fishing tackle, sporting goods, and watches. North African mementos including camel saddles and djellabas can be picked up at one of the raffish bazaars that coexist with the more stately boutiques. Cigarettes, tobacco and, yes, Havana cigars are very nicely priced.

Normal shopping hours are 9 AM to 1 PM and 3 to 7 PM weekdays and 9 AM to 1 PM on Saturdays. However, whenever a cruise ship is in port the stores are open.

Great Britain

TOURIST INFORMATION: Over 700 *Tourist Information Centres* (*TIC*s) provide accommodations listings, as well as literature throughout England, Wales, Scotland, and Northern Ireland. The central London office is the *British Travel Centre,* 12 Regent St., Piccadilly Circus, London SW1 (phone: 71-730-3400).

ENTRY REQUIREMENTS: A current US passport is the only requirement for stays of 3 months or less by US citizens.

GETTING THERE/GETTING AROUND: Airlines – *British Airways* flies to London from Anchorage, Atlanta, Boston, Chicago, Dallas, Detroit, Houston, Los Angeles, Miami (*Concorde* and subsonic service), New York (*Concorde* and subsonic service), Newark, Philadelphia, Pittsburgh, Orlando, San Juan, San Francisco, Seattle, Tampa, and Washington, DC (*Concorde* and subsonic service). US carriers with nonstop service to London are *Delta* from Atlanta; *TWA* from Boston, Chicago, Los Angeles, New York, and St. Louis; *American* from Dallas/Ft. Worth; *Northwest* from Boston and Minneapolis; and *Continental* from Newark, Houston, Denver, and Miami. *TWA* also flies to London on a connecting flight out of Philadelphia. Additional service is provided by *Virgin Atlantic Airways* (from Newark, New Jersey), *Air India* (from New York), and *Air New Zealand* (from Los Angeles).

At least 10 domestic airlines serve the major cities and islands. *British Airways* runs many shuttle flights daily between Glasgow, Edinburgh, Belfast, Manchester, and London.

Cars – Yes, they still drive on the left-hand side of the road. If you're a member of the *AAA* in the US, you might be entitled to reciprocal membership privileges with the *RAC* or *AA,* two British automobile clubs.

Trains – *BritRail*'s 125 intercity and 225 high-speed trains offer superb service, and *BR*'s numerous bargain plans for travelers couldn't be more tempting: the *BritRail* Pass; the *BritRail* Youth Pass for those under 26; and the Senior Citizen Pass, available for reduced-rate first class travel for those 60 or over. The *BritRail* FlexiPass entitles travelers in each of these categories to 4 days of train travel within an 8-day period, 8 days within a 15-day period, or 15 days within 1 month.

CLIMATE AND CLOTHES: Daily temperatures average in the low to mid 60s F (about 16C) in summer and hover around 40F (6C) in December, January, and February. Winter is wetter than summer, with 15 or 16 rainy days a month as opposed to summer's 12 or 13. The seasons are well defined though not as extreme as those in the northeastern United States. Dress accordingly. A finely tuned sense of fashion is terrific in London but not necessary in the country. Bring a raincoat and a folding umbrella.

LANGUAGE: English is the national language, but Welsh is widely spoken in Wales, as is Gaelic in the Outer Islands in Scotland. Regional dialects are often heard in Scotland, Yorkshire, and Cornwall.

ELECTRIC CURRENT: 240 volts, AC.

MONEY: The pound sterling (£) is divided into 100 pence.

TIPPING: Service charges of between 10% and 15% usually are included in hotel bills but make sure. Otherwise the tipping standard is between 10% and 15% in restaurants and taxis, and 50 pence per bag for bellmen and porters.

BANKING/BUSINESS HOURS: In Edinburgh, the Bank of Scotland is open on weekdays from 9:30 AM to 4:45 PM and on Thursdays until 5:30 PM. The Royal Bank of Scotland is open weekdays from 9:30 AM to 3:30 PM (also, from 4:30 to 5:30 PM on Thursdays). In London, banks are open weekdays from 9:30 AM to 3:30 PM, and some major branches of Barclays, National Westminster, and Midland are open Saturday mornings from 9 AM to noon. (There also are 24-hour money-exchanging facilities at London's airports and one at the Victoria train station that is open from 7:45 AM to 10 PM.) Most other businesses throughout the country operate from 9 or 9:30 AM to 5 or 5:30 PM on weekdays.

HOLIDAYS/SPECIAL EVENTS: *New Year's Day* (January 1), *Good Friday* (April 17), *Easter Monday* (April 20), the first and last Monday in May and the last Monday in August (bank holidays), *Christmas Day* (December 25), and *Boxing Day* (December 26).

The country hosts a mind-boggling array of special events, with the theater the primary focus of many. The *Royal Shakespeare Company* performances begin in Stratford in late March or early April and continue through January. The *Royal National Theatre* on London's South Bank has performances year-round. The *Edinburgh Festival,* Scotland's all-cultural bash, which coincides with the *Military Tattoo,* runs for 3 weeks in August. Opera performances at Glyndebourne, East Sussex, from the end of May to mid-August, are elegant, dressy occasions.

Dates for some of the more famous sporting events? June for the *Derby* in Epsom, Surrey, and the *Royal Ascot* races in Ascot, Berkshire; late June to early July for the *All England Lawn Tennis Championships* (better known as *Wimbledon*) in London, and for the *Henley Regatta* in Henley-on-Thames; July for the *British Grand Prix* and early August for *Cowes' Sailing Week,* on the Isle of Wight; and every 2 years (even-numbered) in September for the *Farnborough Air Show* in Hampshire.

The *Queen's Official Birthday* is saluted by mounted guards "Trooping the Color" in London, the second Saturday in June.

SHOPPING: There are still a few antiques left, in spite of the shiploads consigned to US dealers, and it's fun to hunt for them. In London try Tower Bridge Road (*New*

Caledonian Market) — a dealer's market — very early Friday mornings and Portobello Road on Saturday mornings. However, you don't have to look far to find china from quality suppliers such as Minton, Royal Doulton, Aynsley, and Wedgwood.

Harris tweeds, Liberty prints in cotton and silk, and ancestral tartans are sold by the yard and are made up into fashionable clothes. Burberry and Jaeger are good labels, and there are less expensive durable sport clothes at *Marks & Spencer* stores around the country. Main sale months are January and July.

Sales tax (VAT) is 15%. Most stores will arrange to refund VAT to foreign buyers who take the goods out of the country.

Shops open weekdays and Saturdays from 9 AM to 5:30 PM. Hours may differ in small towns, where shops sometimes close at noon 1 day a week, and in London, where most shops open and close later.

Greece

TOURIST INFORMATION: The *National Tourist Organization of Greece* (*EOT* in Greek) has its main office at 2 Amerikis Street in Athens (phone: 222-3111). There are ten regional branches and four bureaus at frontier crossings. In most cities and towns, special tourist police provide information, as well as assistance.

ENTRY REQUIREMENTS: A current US passport is good for visits of up to 3 months.

GETTING THERE/GETTING AROUND: Airlines – *Olympic Airlines* and *TWA* have nonstop service from New York to Athens. Domestic flights radiate from *Olympic*'s Hellinikon Airport near Athens to about 20 cities and islands at the season's height.

Cars – The *Automobile and Touring Club* (*ELPA*) mans road patrols and highway stations, as well as an emergency number (phone: 104) good within a 38-mile (60-km) range of major cities.

Trains – Three international expresses reach Athens through Belgrade. However, because Yugoslavia is not included in the Eurail system, those with Eurailpasses enter Greece via ferry from Brindisi, Italy. The *Hellenic State Railway* (*OSE*) uses buses, as well as trains to offer frequent service throughout the country. These routes are supplemented by privately run bus companies.

CLIMATE AND CLOTHES: The country boasts more than 3,000 hours of sunshine a year. Hot summers, with averages in the low 90s F (about 30C), are mitigated somewhat by the *meltemia* breezes. In Athens, even during July and August when the temperatures exceed 90F (32C), cool evening breezes make the heat bearable. During May, June, September, and October, days are somewhat cooler, with temperatures ranging from 60F to 80F (between 16C and 31C). The beaches are less crowded then, and the water still is warm enough for swimming. In spring, the hills come to life with gentle hues of green and colorful wildflowers. Winters are mild, with temperatures in the 40s and 50s F (between 5C and 13C), damper air, and more rain than any other season. In the north, the temperature is about 10 degrees lower.

Lightweight white and pastel clothes are appropriate summerwear. Pack something dressy for the captain's dinner if planning a cruise; ties are required for men only for admittance to one of the country's three gambling casinos. For the spring and fall, a light jacket or coat is advisable. You can use a winter coat during the cold months, but another good way to counter the penetrating dampness is by wearing a few layers of sweaters. Seeing the city of Athens any time of year makes demands on your feet —

bring comfortable walking shoes. *Note:* The city's air pollution is justifiably notorious, especially during summer. Otherwise, the air is similar to that in Los Angeles, and sometimes considerably better.

LANGUAGE: Greek; English is spoken on the tourist circuit.

ELECTRIC CURRENT: 220 volts, AC.

MONEY: The drachma (Dr) is divided into 100 lepta.

TIPPING: The minimum tip for a small service is 20 drachmas. Service charges are included in most bills, but it is customary to add 5% to 10%.

BANKING/BUSINESS HOURS: Most banks are open weekdays from 8 AM to 2 PM. Government offices generally operate from 7:30 or 8 AM to 2:30 or 3 PM; private businesses are usually open from 8 or 9 AM to 4 or 5 PM.

HOLIDAYS/SPECIAL EVENTS: *New Year's Day* (January 1), *Shrove Monday* (March 9), *National Independence Day* (March 25), *Good Friday* (April 17), *St. George's Day* (April 20), *Labor Day* (May 1), *Feast of the Assumption* (August 15), *National Day* (October 28), *Christmas Day* (December 25) and *Boxing Day* (December 26).

The annual *Athens Festival* is held every day in the Odeon, built by Herod Atticus in AD 161, from June through September. Superb Greek dramas are presented in the amphitheater at Epidaurus on weekends from the end of June until the end of September. Schedules and tickets for both are available from the *Athens Festival Box Office* (4 Stadiou St., Athens; phone: 322-1459 or 322-3111, ext. 240), which also sells tickets to the daily sound-and-light shows in English at the Acropolis from April through October.

SHOPPING: To educate yourself in the range and variety of crafts produced in Greece before making a purchase, visit one of the *EOMMEX* (National Organization of Hellenic Handicrafts) showrooms in Athens and 13 other major Greek cities. Unfortunately they display but don't sell handmade wares. There also is a permanent exhibit of ceramics at Maroussi, where Greek pottery is sold, as well as displayed.

Caftans, shirts, and dresses made from striped and textured *sedoni* cotton, which originally was used as sheeting, as well as from the heavier grades of colored cloth are widely available. Traditional fishermen's clothes, including wool undershirts and navy blue hats, are trendy additions to a wardrobe. Two small items in great favor with the incurably anxious are worry beads and evil eyes.

During the summer, gift and craft shops are open daily except Sundays from 8 AM to 9 PM. Regular stores are open Mondays, Wednesdays, and Saturdays from 8 AM to 2:30 PM and Tuesdays, Thursdays, and Fridays from 8 AM to 1:30 PM and 5 to 8 PM.

Hungary

TOURIST INFORMATION: Branches of *IBUSZ,* the country's now privatized travel company, are found in all major cities. The central office is at 5 Felszabadulás tér, Budapest 1364 (phone: 118-6866). *IBUSZ* also has a 24-hour accommodations service at 3 Petőfi tér, 1052 in Budapest (phone: 184842 or 183925). Tourist offices in smaller cities and towns are called *Idegenforgalmi Hivatal.*

ENTRY REQUIREMENTS: A valid US passport is needed for stays of up to 90 days. A visa is required for stays longer than 3 months; the fee is $15. For visa application forms, contact *IBUSZ Hungarian Travel* (1 Parker Plaza, Suite 1104, Ft. Lee, NJ 07024; phone: 201-592-8585); the Hungarian Embassy, Consular Section (3910 Shoemaker St. NW., Washington, DC 20008; phone: 202-362-6733); or the Hungarian

Consulate (8 E. 75 St., New York, NY 10021; phone: 212-879-4125, 212-879-4126, or 212-879-4127).

GETTING THERE/GETTING AROUND: Airlines – *Malev,* the Hungarian national airline, flies nonstop from New York to Budapest. Other flights to Budapest are offered from New York by *KLM,* via Amsterdam; *Lufthansa,* via Munich and Düsseldorf; *SAS,* via Copenhagen; *British Airways,* via London; *Air France,* via Paris (with a change of airport); and *Finnair,* via Helsinki. *Malev* has service between Ferihegy Airport, Budapest, and 40 major cities in Europe and the Middle East.

Cars – International firms and *IBUSZ* rent European models. Some words of caution: The law against driving after drinking is carefully enforced; you are breaking the law if found driving with *any* alcohol in the blood.

Trains – Budapest is a transfer point for some 25 international expresses, including the *Nord Orient Express* and the *Wiener Walzer.* Nationally, the *MAV* (*Magyar Allamvasutak*) diesel or electric express trains run often and are comfortable. Hungary is a member of the *Eurail* network. From the US, *Eurail* information for Hungary can be obtained through French, Italian, Swiss, or German railroads.

CLIMATE AND CLOTHES: Hungary is a small — 35,910-square-mile — nation bisected by the Danube River. Lake Balaton to the west is Europe's second-largest lake and a good place to cool off during the typically hot summers, with temperatures averaging 86F (30C). Winters are cold (about 30F, −1C) and dry. In Budapest, the wooded Buda hills protect the city against extremes of heat and cold, but summers can be hot and humid. In summer the average temperature is about 72F (22C); in winter it is about 34F (1C). Dress in Hungary tends to be more informal than in the US. Men usually wear open-neck shirts, except in theaters and fine restaurants, where ties and dark suits are the norm.

LANGUAGE: Hungarian, a Finno-Ugric tongue, is the native language of 95% of the population. German is the second language (a heritage of the Austro-Hungarian Empire) but English is becoming increasingly common.

ELECTRIC CURRENT: 220 volts, AC.

MONEY: The forint (Ft) equals 100 fillér.

TIPPING: Add 15% to restaurant bills; 20 forints is the usual small tip for taxi drivers, porters, and hairdressers.

BANKING/BUSINESS HOURS: Banks and many offices are open weekdays from 8 or 9 AM to 2 or 4 PM. Currency exchange facilities outside the banks are numerous.

HOLIDAYS/SPECIAL EVENTS: *New Year's Day* (January 1), *Anniversary of the 1848 Revolution* (March 15), *Easter Monday* (April 20), *Labor Day* (May 1), *St. Stephen's Day* (August 20), *Christmas Day* (December 25), and *Boxing Day* (December 26).

Feasts and gaiety are traditional when the wine harvest begins in the fall. Important vineyard areas include Tokay; the Badacsony Mountain slopes near Balaton; Eger (where the red "Bulls' Blood" is made); Sopron; and parts of the Puszta. Fall also starts the season at Budapest's opera house, the *Academy of Music.* The *Budapest Spring Festival* is held in late March. During the summer you can hear music of native sons Franz Liszt, Béla Bartók, or Franz Lehár in Budapest's Margaret Island open-air theater.

SHOPPING: Embroidery patterns and techniques, startling in their color and complexity, vary from region to region, and those of the Kalocsa, Mezökövesd, Pálóc, and Sárköz areas are highly regarded. Painted and carved wooden vessels and objects originally made by shepherds are still fashioned today, as is peasant earthenware. Village potters produce traditional local patterns as well as more modern styles. *Folkart and Handicraft Cooperatives* around the country sell these products for forints or they can be bought with hard currency from *Intertourist* shops.

Stores are open weekdays from 8 AM to 5 PM; Thursdays they often stay open until 7 or 8 PM. On Saturdays, stores are open half-days, from 8 AM to 1 PM.

Iceland

TOURIST INFORMATION: The *Iceland Tourist Board*'s head office is at 3 Laekgagata, Reykjavik (phone: 27488).

ENTRY REQUIREMENTS: US citizens need only a current passport for visits of 3 months or less.

GETTING THERE/GETTING AROUND: Airlines – *Icelandair* has nonstop service from New York to Keflavík Airport, about 45 minutes from the capital. Reykjavik is the hub of *Icelandair*'s domestic flights to 16 cities in the nation. These flights, by the way, cost very little more than bus service to the same destinations.

Buses – *BSI* (*Bifreidastod Island,* or *Iceland Coach Company*) is the umbrella group for most of the national bus companies and is headquartered at the *Umferdarmidstodin* (bus station) in Reykjavík (phone: 22300). There are a total of about 8,000 miles of road, about 4,500 of which are covered by the coaches. In 1974 the road encircling the island and known as the ring route was completed, although parts of it remain unpaved. Coach passes for this road, as well as passes good for unlimited travel anywhere in the country, are available from *BSI.*

Cars – There are plenty of car rental firms, with most supplying four-wheel-drive vehicles. Be advised that many roads are unpaved and surfaced in dirt or crushed volcanic matter.

Trains – There are no trains in Iceland.

CLIMATE AND CLOTHES: While far more temperate in winter than might be expected — 31F (0 degrees C) is the average January temperature in Reykjavik — summers are cool, with July averages in the low 60s F (10C).

Daylight is continuous from mid-May through August but gradually lessens until there are only 3 or 4 hours of daylight in each 24-hour period from November through January. Careful attention is paid to fashion. Jeans are fine for Saturday night discoing but won't do for dinner in the more staid restaurants.

LANGUAGE: Modern Icelandic hasn't changed much from the Old Norse spoken by the ancient Vikings who colonized the island 1,100 years ago. Danish is the second language, and English is compulsory in high school and is widely spoken, particularly by the younger generation.

ELECTRIC CURRENT: 220 volts, AC.

MONEY: The Icelandic krona (IKr) equals 100 aurar.

TIPPING: Service charges are added to most bills and extra tips are not expected.

BANKING/BUSINESS HOURS: Banking hours are generally Monday through Friday from 9:15 AM to 4 PM, and on Thursday banks reopen from 6 to 7 PM. Most other businesses are open Monday through Friday 9 AM to 6 PM.

HOLIDAYS/SPECIAL EVENTS: *New Year's Day* (January 1), *Maundy Thursday* (April 16), *Good Friday* (April 17), *Easter Sunday* (April 19), *Easter Monday* (April 20), *First Day of Summer* (April 23), *Labor Day* (May 1), *Ascension Day* (May 28), *Whitsunday* (June 7), *Whitmonday* (June 8), *Independence Day* (June 17), *Shop and Office Workers Holiday* (August 3), *Christmas Eve* (December 24), *Christmas Day* (December 25), and *Boxing Day* (December 26).

June 17 heralds the widely celebrated *National Day.* In early August, the Westman Islands (a small group of islands south of Iceland) hold a summer festival featuring bonfires and open-air entertainment. One of the most famous events is the biennial *Reykjavik Arts Festival* (to be held in June this year), featuring top artists in opera, ballet, and theater, as well as famous sculptors and painters from around the world.

SHOPPING: The fluffy, earth-colored Lopi wool blankets, outerwear, and accessories are synonymous with Iceland. Sheep also are the source of the shearling coats, jackets, and hats made here.

Several fine potters hand-throw earthenware containers in natural colors. Crushed lava is a common addition to highly glazed ceramic pieces popular as souvenirs.

The *Icemart* shop at Keflavík Airport sells all of these products.

Stores are open weekdays from 9 AM to 6 PM and some, but not all, from 10 AM to noon on Saturdays.

Ireland

TOURIST INFORMATION: The lowercase *i* identifies tourist information offices in some 80 locations around the country. *Irish Tourist Board* (*Bord Fáilte*) publications also are available in regional offices and in Dublin at 14 Upper O'Connell St., Dublin 1 (phone: 747733).

ENTRY REQUIREMENTS: US citizens require only a current passport.

GETTING THERE/GETTING AROUND: Airlines – *Aer Lingus* flies nonstop from Boston, Chicago, and New York into Ireland's Shannon International Airport, always continuing to Dublin, and also provides domestic service between Dublin and Cork. At press time, *Aer Lingus* flights from Los Angeles were scheduled to begin this spring. *Delta* flies nonstop to Shannon from Atlanta. *Aer Arann* schedules flights between Galway and the Aran Islands in Galway Bay, and *Ryan Air* flies from London to Dublin and Waterford.

Cars – Driving is on the left. Mobile homes, as well as cars, can be rented here and the *Irish Tourist Board* has mapped out a number of scenic tours for the motorist.

Ferries – Car- and passenger-carrying ferries connect Great Britain with Ireland. The ferries run between Holyhead and Dún Laoghaire, Holyhead and Dublin, Liverpool and Dublin, Fishguard and Rosslare, and Cork and Swansea. Between Britain and Ireland, the operators are the *B&I Line* (in the US, book through *Lynott Tours,* phone: 212-760-0101 in New York; 800-221-2474 elsewhere), *Sealink Ferries* (in the US, book through *BritRail,* phone: 212-599-5400), and *P&O European Ferries* (in the US, phone: 800-221-3254). The *Irish Ferries'* ships sail between Rosslare and Le Havre, Rosslare and Cherbourg, and Cork and Le Havre (book through *CIE Tours,* phone: in the US, 800-243-7687; in New York, 212-697-3914). *Brittany Ferries* operate between Cork and Roscoff, France (in the US, book through *P&O European Ferries,* phone: 800-221-3254).

Trains – *Córas Iompair Eireann* (*CIE*), the national transport company, with its supertrain intercity service, manages railroads, as well as bus routes. Rambler tickets good for 8 or 15 days are an inexpensive way to cover the Irish Republic and the 15-day Overlander or Emerald Isle Card includes travel in Northern Ireland. These tickets can be used for either bus or train travel.

CLIMATE AND CLOTHES: Summer highs are in the mid-60s F (around 18C) and winter averages in the 40s F (around 4C). This is partially explained by the chilling east winds. Make sure you have a warm wool sweater or jacket even in summer. Tweeds are worn year-round and lend a conservative cast to what is essentially a casual mode of dress. A raincoat and umbrella always are useful.

LANGUAGE: Though Irish, or Gaelic, is the national language, English is spoken more widely today except in those few areas — primarily on the west coast — where Gaelic is still dominant.

ELECTRIC CURRENT: 220 volts, AC.

MONEY: The Irish pound (IR£) equals 100 pence. Be aware that the Irish pound (punt) and the British pound are no longer tied to one another and are not interchangeable. Each has its own value in relation to world currencies, and the Irish pound lately has been trading at a level roughly 15% to 20% less than its British counterpart.

TIPPING: Check to make sure the customary 10% to 15% service charge is added to restaurant and hotel bills. If so, no further tip is necessary. Taxi drivers get 10% to 15% and porters about 50 pence per bag.

BANKING/BUSINESS HOURS: Banks are generally open from 10 AM to 3 PM weekdays; to 5 PM Thursdays. Most other businesses are open weekdays from 9 AM to 5 PM, some until 6 PM. Bank of America, Bank of Nova Scotia, Chase, Citibank, and First National Bank of Chicago all have branches in the St. Stephen's Green/ Grafton Street area of Dublin.

HOLIDAYS/SPECIAL EVENTS: *New Year's Day* (January 1), *St. Patrick's Day* (March 17), *Good Friday* (April 17), *Easter Monday* (April 20), bank holidays (the first Monday in June and August, and the last Monday in October), *Christmas Day* (December 25), and *St. Stephen's Day* (December 26).

The Royal Dublin Society organizes the *Dublin Horse Show,* an outstanding sporting and social event in August, as well as the *Spring Show and Industries Fair,* a trade and livestock exhibition in May. Traditional Irish ballads are celebrated during the *Fleadh Cheoil na hEireann,* Ireland's premier cultural festival, held in August at a different site each year. Other major festivals are the *Rose of Tralee Festival* in late August at Tralee, and the *Cork International Choral and Folk Dance Festival* in April. Rarely performed 18th- and 19th-century operas are presented at the *Wexford Opera Festival,* a must if you're near Wexford in late October. Also in late October is the *Guinness Jazz Festival* in Cork, drawing talented musicians from around the world. St. Patrick gets his due during a week of celebrations throughout the country in mid-March. New plays by Irish authors are featured at the *Dublin Theatre Festival,* held from late September to October.

September culminates both of Ireland's most popular spectator sport seasons in Dublin with the *All Ireland Hurling Finals* followed by the *All Ireland Football Finals.*

SHOPPING: Crafts are thriving in Ireland. Products in the traditional and modern international styles and combinations of the two are found in craft centers, workshops, and stores throughout the country. Details are in the *Irish Crafts* information sheet from *Irish Tourist Board* offices in the US. The traditional and highly prized wool Aran sweaters and hats, earthenware in modern but natural shapes, and exceedingly well executed jewelry in contemporary styles are typical of the work currently being done.

Pearly Belleek china, luminous Waterford crystal, and Irish lace endow any table with elegance. Irish smoked salmon goes well in such a setting.

The Value Added Tax (VAT) is 10% or 23% in the Irish Republic (the higher rate is applied to luxury items such as watches, jewelry, and cameras), and 17% in Northern Ireland. Visitors may avoid paying the VAT by having products shipped directly home.

Stores are open between 9 AM and 5:30 PM daily except Sundays, with 1 early closing day in rural areas — usually either Mondays or Wednesdays. Some stores in Dublin are closed Mondays. Dublin's stores and most shopping centers around the country are open late Thursday nights.

Italy

TOURIST INFORMATION: Publications and assistance are provided on a region-by-region basis by various *Assessorati e Aziende Regionali del Turismo (ART)* offices; in provinces by the *Enti Provinciali per il Turismo (EPT)*; and in towns and resort areas from assorted *Aziende Autonome di Soggiorno e Turismo (AAST)* offices.

ENTRY REQUIREMENTS: US citizens require only a current US passport for visits of 3 months or less.

GETTING THERE/GETTING AROUND: Airlines – *Alitalia* flies nonstop from Chicago, Los Angeles, and New York to Milan. To Rome, there's nonstop service from New York, Boston, Chicago, and Miami, and direct service, via Milan, from Chicago and Los Angeles. To Venice, there's direct service from New York, via Milan. There also is summertime direct service from New York to Palermo via Rome. *TWA* flies from Boston (via New York), Chicago (via New York), and New York (nonstop) to both Milan and Rome. *Delta* offers nonstop service from New York to Milan and Rome. Service within Italy is provided by *Alitalia* and *ATI*.

Cars – Italy's toll roads are excellent, but be prepared for the high-speed traffic.

Trains – Kilometer for kilometer, among the least expensive in Europe. Travel is fastest on *rapidi* (including *TEE* and *IC* trains), which connect major cities; *espressi* are the next fastest. A high-speed line links Rome and Florence, as well as Rome and Milan.

CLIMATE AND CLOTHES: Hot summers get hotter the farther south you go (high 80s F or about 30C), but are mitigated by shore breezes along Italy's 5,000-mile coastline. Northern Alpine areas are exceedingly cold in winter as are the Apennines, but temperatures are in the relatively mild 40s F (around 7C) and even warmer along the Italian Riviera and the Amalfi and Sicilian coasts. Florence's climate can be rather severe: cold and damp in winter and stifling in summer. Spring and fall are the best times to visit, particularly when it doesn't happen to rain. The hottest time is from mid-June to mid-September, when temperatures range from 60F (15C) to 90F (32C). Temperatures rarely drop below freezing in winter — the range is 36F (2C) to 52F (11C) from December through mid-March, but the cold is often gripping. Average temperatures in Rome in July and August hover around 82F (27C), but a heavy sirocco wind from the African deserts often brings the maximum above 100F (38C). (Don't always expect air conditioning.) Residents of Milan, Italy's fashion capital, dress chicly, though they are more conservative than Romans, who follow every fashion fad. Florence, too, is a fashion center. Stylishly casual resort wear is perfect for the beach areas and jeans are fine for the hill country. Fortunately, Romans are quite informal, except for very special occasions, and men rarely wear jackets or ties in the summer. Women should be careful when visiting churches, where immodest dress (bare shoulders included) is frowned upon if not downright forbidden. Rain gear is often handy in winter throughout the country.

LANGUAGE: Italian is universally spoken but Italy's original city-states each had their own dialect and literature and in some places these dialects — Sardinian, Sicilian, Neapolitan, Venetian, and Milanese — still are spoken.

ELECTRIC CURRENT: 220 volts, AC, but there are some 110-volt outlets. Sometimes both voltages are found in hotel guestrooms, so beware.

MONEY: The Italian currency unit is the lira (abbreviated either as L. or Lit.); the plural of lira is lire.

TIPPING: Keep a handful of lire notes ready. In spite of 15% to 18% service charges at your hotel and the 15% usually added to restaurant bills, you'll be expected to give about 1,000 to 1,500 lire or more to chambermaids for each night you stay, and at least 1,500 lire to bellhops for each bag they take, and so on. Waiters and wine stewards get an extra 10% of the bill. When eating or drinking at a café counter, the procedure is to pay at the cash register first, then take the small receipt over to the counter, where you leave it with from 100 to 200 lire (depending on what you're having). Then place your order with the barman. You may have a hard time getting served if you don't follow this procedure. Taxi drivers receive 15% of the meter, hairdressers 15% of the bill. Even service station attendants expect about 1,000 or more lire for cleaning windshields and giving directions. Theater ushers are tipped 1,000 lire.

BANKING/BUSINESS HOURS: Bank hours vary, particularly in the afternoon, but most are open weekdays from 8:30 AM to 1:30 PM, closed for lunch, and open again from 3:30 to 4:15 PM. Some others open in the afternoon from 2:30 to 3:30 PM. On days preceding holidays, banking hours are from 8:30 to 11:30 AM. Government offices generally operate from 8 AM to 2 PM. Most other businesses are open from 9 AM to 1 PM and again from 3:30 or 4 to 7:30 or 8 PM. (A few remain open all day, but these generally close at 6:30 PM.)

HOLIDAYS/SPECIAL EVENTS: *New Year's Day* (January 1), *Epiphany* (January 6), *Easter Monday* (April 20), *Liberation Day* (April 25), *Labor Day* (May 1), *Ferragosto* or *August Holiday* (August 15), *All Saints' Day* (November 1), *Feast of the Immaculate Conception* (December 8), *Christmas Day* (December 25), and *St. Stephen's Day* (December 26).

Summer outdoor performances of Italian operas are held in July and August in Rome's *Terme di Caracalla;* from mid-July through mid-August in Verona's *Arena;* and in July at the *Arena Sferisterio* in Macerata. The regular opera season at such notable houses as *La Scala* in Milan, *San Carlo* in Naples, and the *Opera* in Rome runs from December to June. Two festivals of note that feature concerts, ballet, opera, and drama are Spoleto's *Festival of Two Worlds,* between mid-June and mid-July, and Florence's *Maggio Musicale Fiorentino* in May and June.

Colorful pageants that feature medieval costumes include Gubbio's *Race of the Candles* on May 15; Siena's *Il Palio,* a horse race in medieval garb, held annually on July 2 and August 16; Venice's *Il Redentore,* a gondola procession and race the third Sunday in July; and Marostica's *Living Chess Game,* held in September of even-numbered years.

SHOPPING: Italian leather goods, textiles, jewelry, and ceramics are fine buys. Most elegantly hand-stitched sheets, carefully worked boots, stunningly designed silk ties and scarves, and subtly knit fabrics fill the boutiques of Rome and Milan. *Upim, Standa, Coin,* and *Rinascente* chain stores are great for inexpensive, locally made finds. Florence is known especially for handicrafts. Baskets from the straw market in Florence are terrific to tote your purchases around in, including perhaps rolls of the gorgeous Florentine papers, appropriate for lining drawers or covering notebooks.

Store hours generally are from 9 AM to 1 PM and 3:30 or 4 to 7:30 or 8 PM; stores in northern Italy have shorter lunch hours and earlier closing times.

Liechtenstein

TOURIST INFORMATION: Locally available at the *Liechtenstein Tourist Office,* 37 Städtle, 9490 Vaduz, Principality of Liechtenstein (phone: 75-21443).

ENTRY REQUIREMENTS: If entering from Switzerland, there are no border formalities whatsoever. US citizens can visit the country as tourists for up to 3 months with a current US passport.

GETTING THERE/GETTING AROUND: There are no flights into this tiny country simply because it has no airport. After flying into Zurich, Switzerland, you travel by train to Sargans or Buchs, Switzerland. The rail line between Zurich and Vienna passes through Liechtenstein, but not Vaduz, the capital. Express trains make stops at Buchs and at Feldkirch, Austria, with postal buses providing the link between these stations and Vaduz.

CLIMATE AND CLOTHES: This tiny country is a land of mountains and valleys. The eastern two-thirds of its 61 square miles are covered by mountains of moderate height; these drop to the beautiful and fertile Rhine Valley in the west, and the entire country, like its neighbors Switzerland and Austria, is cooled and made temperate by the *Föhn,* the famous south wind of this section of central Europe. Travelers will feel perfectly comfortable in informal clothes throughout Liechtenstein.

LANGUAGE: Liechtenstein's official language is German, but many citizens speak a dialect similar to that of southwestern Germany and Alsace, and accents vary from village to village. Most people involved in any way with tourists speak English.

ELECTRIC CURRENT: 220 volts, AC.

MONEY: The Swiss franc (Sfr) is made up of 100 centimes.

TIPPING: A 15% service charge is included in all hotel and restaurant bills.

BANKING/BUSINESS HOURS: Banks are generally open Monday through Friday 8 AM to noon and 1:30 to 4:30 PM. Most other businesses are open Monday through Friday 8 AM to noon and 2 to 5 PM.

HOLIDAYS/SPECIAL EVENTS: *New Year's Day* (January 1), *Good Friday* (April 17), *Easter Monday* (April 20), *Ascension Day* (May 28), *Pentecost Day* (June 8), *Christmas Day* (December 25), and *Boxing Day* (December 26).

The prince's birthday on August 15 is celebrated as a national holiday. The first Sunday of *Lent* signals *Bonfire Sunday* with the lighting of fires and torches followed by traditional pancake suppers.

SHOPPING: Beautiful postage stamps and prestamped postcards are collector's items, inexpensive souvenirs, and also a leading local industry. Swiss watches, optical goods, and music boxes are reasonably priced. Shops are open weekdays from 8 AM to noon and from 1:30 to 6:30 PM, with Saturday closings at around 4 PM.

Luxembourg

TOURIST INFORMATION: The *Office National du Tourisme* (*ONT*), with general information on the country, is at 77 Rue d'Anvers, PO Box 1001, Luxembourg City, L-1010 (phone: 496666). The *Syndicat d'Initiative* in most towns provides local information. It is based at the Place d'Armes in Luxemburg City (phone: 22809). *ONT* and *Syndicat* offices are identified by the national information logo of a blue knight on a white background.

ENTRY REQUIREMENTS: US citizens can stay in Luxembourg indefinitely with a current US passport.

GETTING THERE/GETTING AROUND: Airlines – *Icelandair* provides direct service (via Reykjavik) from New York, Baltimore/Washington, DC, and Orlando. Findel Airport is just outside Luxembourg City.

Cars – Luxembourg car rental fleets probably have the cheapest rates on the Continent for periods of a week or more. If you pick up and deliver your car there, you probably will pay less than the rate for the same car rented in Belgium and dropped off in Paris. The VAT on car rentals is 12%.

Trains – The *Chemin de Fer Luxembourgeois* (*CFL*) offers a number of reduced-fare plans, including weekend excursion rates, flat-fee 1-day, 5-day, and 1-month network passes, and senior citizen half-fare tickets. The Benelux Tourrail Pass, good for any 5 days of travel in a 17-day period in Belgium, Luxembourg, and the Netherlands, is available at the main railway stations in Luxembourg City.

CLIMATE AND CLOTHES: Hilly and forested in the north, Luxembourg has a storybook look, with pastoral farms stretching in the south along the banks of the Moselle River, which separates the country from neighboring Germany. Temperatures are moderate: summer days in the low 70s F (20s C) and winter days in the 40s F (around 5C). Dress for the weather, not for society, and carry a wool sweater or jacket in the summer in the Ardennes and sturdy shoes for hiking in the mountains.

LANGUAGE: It's a trilingual country: French is the official language, but German is spoken by most people, and Letzeburgesch, a Low German dialect, by all. English, compulsory in high school, is understood everywhere.

ELECTRIC CURRENT: 220 volts, AC.

MONEY: The Luxembourg franc (Lux. F.) equals 100 centimes. Belgian and Luxembourg francs can be used interchangeably, but the Luxembourg franc is not widely accepted outside the country. Change francs for other currencies before leaving.

TIPPING: A 15% service charge is included in hotel, restaurant, and bar bills. Porters and bellmen receive about 20 francs per bag and taxi drivers 15% of the meter charge.

BANKING/BUSINESS HOURS: Bank hours are Monday through Friday 9 AM to noon or 1 PM, and 1 or 2 to 5 PM. Most other businesses are open 9 AM to 6 PM Monday through Friday, with a closing during lunch hour.

HOLIDAYS/SPECIAL EVENTS: *New Year's Day* (January 1), *Shrove Monday* (March 9), *Easter Monday* (April 20), *Labor Day* (May 1), *Ascension Day* (May 28), *Whitmonday* (June 8), *National Holiday* (June 23), *Assumption Day* (August 15), *All Saints' Day* (November 1), *Christmas Day* (December 25), and *Boxing Day* (December 26).

The *Octave,* an annual pilgrimage to Our Lady of Luxembourg, takes place the fifth Sunday after *Easter* in both Luxembourg City and Diekirch, with the royal family of Luxembourg participating in the closing procession; the *St. Willibrord's Dancing Procession* is held on *Whitsun Tuesday* about a month later in Echternach. *Remembrance Day* honors General George Patton, Jr. early each July in Ettelbrück; and Grevenmacher holds its *Grape and Wine Festival* (one of the many towns along the Moselle to do so) in mid-September. .

SHOPPING: The beautiful porcelain and crystal of Villeroy & Boch are produced in Septfontaines, where the factory store is open to visitors. A regional specialty is the earthenware pottery of Nospelt, northwest of Luxembourg City, where there's a 2-week exhibit of local work each August. They are sold locally in leading shops.

Stores are open Mondays through Saturdays from 8:30 or 9 AM to noon and from 2 to 6 PM; Mondays from 2 to 6 PM. All stores are closed Sundays; some are closed Mondays as well. VAT varies between 7% and 12% and can be avoided by presenting purchases to customs at the airport with a special form supplied by the store.

The Maltese Islands

TOURIST INFORMATION: The *Malta National Tourist Office* is in Valletta (phone: 224444 or 228282), on the main island of Malta.

ENTRY REQUIREMENTS: US citizens require a current US passport for visits of up to 3 months.

GETTING THERE/GETTING AROUND: Airlines – *Air Malta* has daily nonstop flights from London and Rome (twice daily during the summer) to Luqa Airport outside Valletta. Other destinations served twice weekly or weekly include Amsterdam, Cairo, Copenhagen, Frankfurt, Lyons, Munich, Paris, and Zurich. The islands of Malta and Gozo are linked by frequent car and passenger ferries. The third Maltese island, Comino, less than a square mile in area, has only one hotel, no cars, and is connected by scheduled boat service to the island of Malta.

Cars – A variety of cars can be rented in Malta, as well as in Rabat, the capital of the island of Gozo. Driving on the left-hand side of the road is a custom inherited from the British.

CLIMATE AND CLOTHES: Vibrantly clear and sunny weather makes Malta very appealing to tourists. What rain there is falls between November and February, also the period of highest winds. Temperatures climb into the 90s F (30s C) in the heat of the Mediterranean summer, but otherwise hover in the 70s F (20s C). A holiday mood prevails throughout the country and informality is the keynote, though bikinis, fine for the beach, should not be worn off the sands.

LANGUAGE: Maltese is a Semitic language derived from Phoenician, and uses the Latin alphabet instead of the Arabic in its printed form. It is influenced by Italian (Sicily is only 60 miles to the north) and English (Malta was a British colony for some 160 years). Today, both Italian and English are spoken by almost all inhabitants.

ELECTRIC CURRENT: 220 volts, AC.

MONEY: The Maltese lira (LM) is divided into 100 cents.

TIPPING: The norm is 10%. Sometimes it is included in restaurant bills.

BANKING/BUSINESS HOURS: Banks are open Monday through Friday 8 AM to noon, and Saturday from 8 to 11:30 AM. Most other businesses are open Monday through Friday 8:30 AM to 1 PM and 2:30 to 5:30 PM, and Saturday from 8:30 AM to 1 PM.

HOLIDAYS/SPECIAL EVENTS: *New Year's Day* (January 1), *Feast of St. Paul's Shipwreck* (February 10), *Feast of St. Joseph* (March 19), *Freedom Day* (March 31), *Good Friday* (April 17), *Workers' Day* (May 1), *Sette Giugno* (June 7), *Feast of St. Peter and St. Paul* (June 29), *Feast of the Assumption* (August 15), *Victory Day* (September 8), *Independence Day* (September 21), *Feast of the Immaculate Conception* (December 8), *Republic Day* (December 13), and *Christmas Day* (December 25).

Two-day *festas,* honoring the patron saint of different Maltese villages, provide plenty of local color and gaiety in this exceedingly Catholic republic. They're concentrated in the summer months and feature processions of saints' images through village streets, accompanied by bands, marchers, and a lot of fireworks. Valletta's *Carnival* is celebrated by the whole country on the second weekend in May with a float parade and enormous papier-mâché characters, as well as much merrymaking.

SHOPPING: An overview of the country's typical handicrafts can be obtained from a visit to the *Centru Snajja Maltim* (Malta Crafts Center) opposite St. John's Cathedral in Valletta. However, you shouldn't miss the *Crafts Village,* at Ta Qali near Mdina, where you can see the products being made as well as purchase them on the spot. The heavy lacework is in the traditional mode. Decorative glass is manufactured here and so are Persian-style rugs. Maltese gold and silver filigree jewelry is beautiful. Stores open at 9 AM and close at 7 PM (8 PM on Saturdays) with a 3- to 4-hour lunch break.

Monaco

TOURIST INFORMATION: The *National Office of Tourism* is at 2A Bd. des Moulins, Monte Carlo, Monaco 98030 (phone: 933-08701).

ENTRY REQUIREMENTS: There is no frontier between France and Monaco, and French immigration regulations apply. If you plan to arrive or leave via France you do not need a visa for crossing into or out of France.

GETTING THERE/GETTING AROUND: With the exception of a few local bus routes, Monaco relies on France for transportation and other services.

Airlines – *Air France* and *Delta* fly nonstop from New York to Nice. *British Airways* provides service from New York to Nice via London; *Sabena* via Brussels; and *Iberia* by way of Madrid. *Heli Air,* Monaco's helicopters, connect Monte Carlo with the airport, as well as with other destinations on the Riviera. There also is bus service between the airport and Monaco.

Cars – The principality easily is reached from Autoroute A8 or from the scenic Route de la Moyenne Corniche. The *Automobile Club of Monaco* (23 Bd. Albert-I, Monte Carlo; phone: 933-03220) provides information for motorists, as well as details on the *Grand Prix.*

Trains – The *Gare de Monaco/Monte Carlo* is on the *SNCF*'s (*Société Nationale des Chemins de Fer Français*) Riviera line. Several international trains make stops there such as the overnight *Train Bleu* from Paris. *SNCF*'s *Métrazur* shuttles along the Côte d'Azur between Cannes and Menton, stopping at Monaco every 30 minutes. Both the Eurailpass and *SNCF*'s France Railpass include Monaco.

CLIMATE AND CLOTHES: Monaco claims 305 days of sun every year, with averages for water temperature and air temperature about the same: in the high 70s F (20s C) in summer, dropping to the mid-50s F (around 10C) in winter. For clothes, what goes on the French Riviera is appropriate here but going topless is allowed only at the *Beach Club.* Casual dress suffices in the *Casino de Monte Carlo's* American Room, but coat and tie are required in the other rooms. You always can dress up more if you wish.

LANGUAGE: French is spoken, but the singular Monégasque dialect, a mixture of Italian and Niçois, is officially encouraged and mandatory in grade school. English also is taught in the schools and is spoken in hotels, restaurants, and at the casinos.

ELECTRIC CURRENT: 220 volts, AC.

MONEY: The French franc (F), made up of 100 centimes, is the most popular currency. French bank notes are legal tender here, but Monégasque coins bearing Prince Rainier's likeness are circulated domestically and can be exchanged for French francs in France.

TIPPING: All bills — hotel, restaurant, and taxi — include a 15% service charge. Tips are not expected, but if you consider the service extraordinary, they are accepted.

BANKING/BUSINESS HOURS: Banks are open 9 AM to noon and 2 to 4 PM Monday through Friday. Most other businesses are open 8:30 AM to 6 PM Monday through Friday.

HOLIDAYS/SPECIAL EVENTS: *New Year's Day* (January 1), *Good Friday* (April 17), *Easter Monday* (April 20), *Labor Day* (May 1), *Ascension Day* (May 28), *Whit-monday* (June 8), *Assumption Day* (August 15), *All Saints' Day* (November 1), *National Day* (November 19), *Feast of the Immaculate Conception* (December 8), and *Christmas Day* (December 25).

January brings sports cars in abundance for the *Monte Carlo Rallye,* and the *International Circus Festival* comes in February. April is the month for the *International Tennis World Championships.* The *Grand Prix de Monaco* is held in May, when futuristic Formula 1 racing cars take to the Belle Epoque streets of Monte Carlo. Several nights in late July and early August are enlivened by the *International Fireworks Festival;* the elegant *Monégasque Red Cross Gala* is held on the first Friday in August.

SHOPPING: All the international names in perfume, jewelry, and clothing are carried by the chic shops surrounding the casino. Local embroidery, ceramics, and other handcrafted products are sold at *Boutique du Rocher,* the proceeds of which go to charity. Monégasque stamps are highly prized by collectors. Stores are open 9 AM to 7 PM Monday through Saturday; some close from noon to 2 PM for lunch. Some stores are open Sunday afternoons.

The Netherlands

TOURIST INFORMATION: The main offices of the ubiquitous *VVV* (*Vereniging voor Vreemdelingen Verkeer*) are in Amsterdam at 10 Stationsplein (phone: 626-6444) and

106 Leidersestraat (phone: 551-2512). Offices, easily identified throughout the country by a triangular logo of three Vs, provide lists of accommodations, as well as information services. Many restaurants even offer low-priced tourist menus — look for the "VVV" sign.

ENTRY REQUIREMENTS: US citizens require only a current US passport for stays up to 3 months.

GETTING THERE/GETTING AROUND: Airlines – *KLM* flies to Amsterdam's Schiphol Airport nonstop from Atlanta, Baltimore, Chicago, Houston, Los Angeles, Minneapolis, New York, and Orlando. Domestically, *KLM*'s City Hoppers connect Amsterdam and Eindhoven, Enschede, Groningen, Rotterdam, and Maastricht, as well as other Dutch and some Belgian cities.

Cars – Emergency road service is provided by the yellow cars of the *Royal Dutch Touring Club*'s (*ANWB*) *Wegenwacht* service.

Cruises – Rhine River trips of 2 days or more begin in Amsterdam and Rotterdam. Two-, three-, and four-country cruises are available, with stops in France, Germany, and Switzerland. Schedules and reservation information are available from *K-D Rhine* headquarters (15 Frankenwerft, Cologne 5000, Germany); or *Rhine Cruise Agency* (170 Hamilton Ave., White Plains, NY 10601; phone: 914-948-3600; 800-858-8587 in the western US; 800-346-6525 in the eastern US). *VVV* has details on local boat trips.

Trains – Service is extensive and frequent. The claim is made that all towns in Holland have trains in both directions at least once an hour. Discount plans offered by the *Nederlandse Spoorwegen* (*NS*) include 3- and 7-day Rail Ranger Passes. (Note that the 3-day pass can only be obtained at the US branches of the *Netherlands Board of Tourism.*) The *NS* also sells the Benelux Tourrail Pass for any 5 days of travel in a 17-day period in the three-country area.

CLIMATE AND CLOTHES: In Holland, they say you can often experience four seasons in 1 day. The influence of the surrounding North Sea results in a temperate, if damp, climate. June through September are the warmest months, with daytime highs around 70F (21C), and July through November is the rainiest time. Winter lows are in the 30s F (around 0 degrees C). Dress is casual, and rain gear always comes in handy. In Amsterdam you can dress lightly, but bring along an extra jacket, and a wool scarf to brace against the wind year-round.

LANGUAGE: The national language is Dutch, but English is spoken by many people.

ELECTRIC CURRENT: 220 volts, AC.

MONEY: The guilder (also called florin; both are abbreviated Fl.) is made up of 100 cents.

TIPPING: A 15% service charge is included in hotel and restaurant bills; if the service is good, leave an extra 5%. The porters at train stations get 1 guilder; bellmen expect less. Taxi drivers don't expect tips, but a tip of around a guilder is appropriate for long rides. A guilder also is the usual tip for other small services.

BANKING/BUSINESS HOURS: Banks are generally open from 9 AM to 4 PM, but larger branches of Amro and ABN banks stay open until 5. Foreign exchange offices in Amsterdam are open daily and have slightly longer hours: 31A Leidseplein, 8:30 AM to 10 PM; Schiphol Airport, 7 AM to 11 PM; and the Central Railway Station, 7 AM to 10:45 PM (open at 8 AM on Sundays). Most other businesses are open 9 AM to 5 PM Mondays through Fridays.

HOLIDAYS/SPECIAL EVENTS: *New Year's Day* (January 1), the *Queen's Birthday* (April 15), *Good Friday* (April 17), *Easter Monday* (April 20), *Ascension Day* (May 28), *Whitmonday* (June 8), and *Christmas Day* (December 25).

Crocuses, daffodils, tulips, and hyacinths flower in awesome profusion at the famed *Keukenhof* (Kitchen Garden) in Lisse from the end of March through the third week of May. The equally colorful displays of commercial bulb growers are free for the looking in areas east, north, and south of Amsterdam.

Famous cheese markets are held at Alkmaar on Fridays from May through September and at Gouda on Thursdays from mid-June through August. They start at 9:30 or 10 AM and end midday; check with local hotel or tourist offices for exact hours. The second Saturday in May is *Windmill Day,* with some 400 mills testing their sails; in July and August, 17 mills near Kinderdijk are in operation from 2:30 to 5:30 PM on Saturdays. The *Holland Festival,* the nation's cultural bash, is held throughout June, with various cities holding events. Available by mail from the Chicago office of the *Netherlands Board of Tourism* or through *KLM* packages are two travel bonus programs. The Holland Leisure Card ($15) is good for discounts on car, train, and plane travel; on selected accommodations; on canal cruises; on shopping at selected stores and diamond polishers; and on admissions to major tourist attractions. The Holland Leisure Card-Plus ($39) features free access to more than 375 museums, as well as all the discounts offered with the Holland Leisure Card.

SHOPPING: Amsterdam is one of the world's diamond cutting centers, but before you purchase, a few words of caution: Not only have diamond prices skyrocketed because of speculation in recent years, but there often is a dramatic difference between Dutch and US appraisals of the same diamond, with US estimates of value often lower than Dutch. Less controversial purchases? Dröste chocolates, in the ever-popular sectioned apple shape, make a nice small gift. Equally delicious and long-lasting are the whole (unsectioned) edam and gouda cheeses. Art prints are reasonable here and Dutch reproductions are of high quality. Blue Delftware is produced by Porceleyne Fles in Delft. A softer hued blue porcelain is made in Makkum in Friesland. Check the *Vroom en Dreesman* (*V en D*) chain of stores throughout the country for locally manufactured goods in a wide range of prices. *Hema* is another chain of department stores where travelers can find necessities at good prices — from stockings and film to cosmetics and umbrellas. (*Hema* coffee shops also are a bargain for lunch.) Shops generally are open from 8:30 or 9 AM to 5:30 or 6 PM. In Amsterdam, most shops stay open until 9 PM on Thursdays. They're closed Sundays and another half day during the week, usually Monday mornings or Wednesday afternoons. Schiphol Airport's duty-free shops are open to departing passengers daily from 7 AM until the last scheduled flight.

Norway

TOURIST INFORMATION: The central organization is the *Norwegian Tourist Board* (Havnelageret, 1 Langkaia, Oslo 0105; phone: 2-427044). Regional tourist offices called *Reiselivsrad* (*TTK*s) are in major cities and towns.

ENTRY REQUIREMENTS: US citizens require a current US passport for stays of up to 3 months.

GETTING THERE/GETTING AROUND: Airlines – *SAS* has direct service from New York to Oslo and from Chicago to Oslo via Copenhagen. Flights also are available from New York on *Icelandair* via Reykjavik. *TWA* has nonstop service from New York to Oslo. Plane travel is common in this long, narrow land, and three lines, *Widerøe's Flyveselskap, Braathen's SAFE,* and *SAS,* cover the routes.

Cars – The Arctic Highway runs 1,564 miles from Oslo to Kirkenes but is hardly an expressway. Hard-surface, winding roads are fine for exploring but not for covering a lot of ground in a short time. Snow closes certain passes in winter, making May through September prime driving time.

Cruises – Ships provide two kinds of travel: express coastal steamer trips (up to 11 days), with stops at various ports between Bergen and Kirkenes; and cruises along one or several fjords. Inquire about the coastal steamer excursions at the *Bergen Line* (505 Fifth Ave., New York, NY 10017; phone: 800-323-7436). Nine different cruise lines offer trips to the fjords, North Cape, and various Norwegian islands. For information, contact the *Norwegian Tourist Board* (655 Third Ave., New York, NY 10017; phone: 212-949-2333).

Trains – The routes are well engineered and magnificently scenic with modern equipment and a notably comfortable second class. The Oslo-Bergen trip across the Hardanger plateau is particularly breathtaking. *Norges Statsbaners* (*NSB*) participates in the Scandinavian Railpass and has discounts for senior citizens and families.

CLIMATE AND CLOTHES: Above the Arctic Circle in Kirkenes near the Russian border, during round-the-clock days in summer temperatures average in the mid-50s F (10C) and throughout the long winter nights temperatures hover in the mid-teens F (0 degrees C to −10C). Oslo's southern summer temperatures average in the low 70s F (about 20C). Since the sun shines 24 hours a day during midsummer above the Arctic Circle, some visitors may want to bring a sleeping mask or some other device to prevent the brightness from disturbing their rest. It also can be quite rainy along the coast during the summer. Medium-weight clothing and a light raincoat are most practical. The fjords are warm enough for summer swimming. Plan on some pretty dresses and spiffy jackets for the 14-day North Cape cruises but otherwise, throughout Norway, dress is casual and comfortable.

LANGUAGE: Norwegian is the national language. English is commonplace among the younger generation and those in the tourist industry. However, don't expect to chat with northern farmers and fishermen unless you speak Norwegian.

ELECTRIC CURRENT: 220 volts, AC.

MONEY: The Norwegian krone (NOK) equals 100 øre.

TIPPING: Between 2 and 3 NOK is the usual small tip for bellmen, porters, chambermaids (per night), and cloakroom personnel. A 15% service charge usually is added to restaurant bills.

BANKING/BUSINESS HOURS: Banks are generally open weekdays from 8:15 AM to 3:30 PM, Thursdays until 5. During the summer (June through August) they close at 3 PM on weekdays and at 5 PM on Thursdays. Most other businesses are open from 8 or 9 AM to 3 or 4 PM.

HOLIDAYS/SPECIAL EVENTS: *New Year's Day* (January 1), *Maundy Thursday* (April 16), *Good Friday* (April 17), *Easter Monday* (April 20), *Labor Day* (May 1), *Constitution Day* (May 17), *Ascension Day* (May 28), *Whitmonday* (June 8), *Christmas Day* (December 25), and *Boxing Day* (December 26).

The century-old *Holmenkollen Ski Festival* outside Oslo at the beginning of March attracts top talent and underscores Norway's role as the cradle of modern skiing. Other leading cross-country races include downtown Oslo's *Monolith* in January and Lillehammer's *Birkebeiner* in March. Jazz is a mania for many in Scandinavia and for none more so than the Norwegians, who hold four international festivals annually: in Bergen late May to early June; at Kongsberg in early July; Molde the end of July; and Voss in March. Classical music, together with ballet, opera, and drama, makes up the *Bergen International Festival,* which runs from late May to early June. The Nobel Peace Prize is presented in Oslo in December.

SHOPPING: The colorful, intricately patterned hand-knit Norwegian sweaters never wear out. Wood-handled, stainless steel Norwegian cutlery is exceptionally stylish, as are blond bentwood chairs of impeccable design. Sports equipment is well known and well made: rods, spools, hand-tied flies, and O. Mustad & Son hooks for the fisherman; Bonna, Epoke, Skilom, and Asnes cross-country skis, and Rottefella bindings for cross-country skiers. Stores generally are open weekdays from 8:30 AM to 5 PM (Thursday nights until 7 PM) and Saturdays until 3 PM. In major cities and towns, shopping malls stay open until 8 PM.

Poland

TOURIST INFORMATION: *Informacja Turystyczna* (*IT*) centers are everywhere: hotels, at the frontier, along highways, and at airports, railway stations, and seaports. *Orbis,* the national travel bureau, has its headquarters at 16 ul-Bracka, Warsaw 00028 (phone: 260271).

ENTRY REQUIREMENTS: A valid passport is required for US citizens; no visa is required for stays of up to 90 days. Visas for stays of longer than 90 days may be obtained within Poland or prior to departure at Polish consulates in the US. Applying for the visa necessitates a current passport, two photos, and a visa fee of $23. An express visa can be obtained within 24 hours for an additional $15. Details are available from the *Polish National Tourist Office* (333 N. Michigan Ave., Suite 228, Chicago, IL 60601; phone: 312-236-9013) or from the Consular Division of the Polish Embassy (2224 Wyoming Ave. NW, Washington, DC 20008; phone: 202-234-2501; 233 Madison Ave., New York, NY 10016; phone: 212-889-8360; or 1530 N. Lake Shore Dr., Chicago, IL; phone: 312-337-8166).

GETTING THERE/GETTING AROUND: Airlines – *LOT,* the Polish national airline, flies nonstop from Chicago and New York to Warsaw. *Lot* also offers charter flights to Poland from Los Angeles. *Delta* offers nonstop service from New York to Warsaw and direct via Frankfurt. Within Poland, *LOT*'s reasonably priced flights connect Warsaw with 10 cities and also Cracow and Katowice to Gdansk, Poznau, and Szczecin.

Cars – Both self-drive and chauffeured Fiats and Fords are rented by *Orbis Rent-a-Car* (*Forum Hotel,* ul. 27 Nowogrodzka, Warsaw; phone: 293875). *PZM* (*Polish Automobile and Motorcycle Association*) is the organization to contact for routings, reservations, and emergency assistance. The *Office of Motor Tourism* is at 63 al-Jerozolimskie, Warsaw 00697 (phone: 294550).

Trains – Polish train fares are relatively inexpensive by most Western European standards. The *Polskie Koleje Panstwowe* or *PKP*'s Polrailpass for 8, 15, 21, or 30 days of unlimited rail travel is a bargain. The modern expresses, which provide frequent intercity service, are the best-equipped trains.

CLIMATE AND CLOTHES: Autumn, normally crisp and sunny, is a long, lovely season, especially in the forests and hills that cover about a third of the country. Snow covers the Carpathian Mountains by mid-December and lasts until April. Winter temperatures hover around 26F (-3C), while summers are warm and dry, with an average temperature of 68F (20C). Beware of severe pollution in many of Poland's cities. Rainwear is essential during most of the year, especially in Warsaw. Blue jeans are okay for daytime touring and shopping, but evenings at the theater and best restaurants call for dresses and ties.

LANGUAGE: Polish, Slavic in origin, is the official language, but German and some English also are spoken.

ELECTRIC CURRENT: 220 volts, AC.

MONEY: The zloty (Zl) is made up of 100 groszy. When entering and leaving Poland, you must declare how much currency (of any country) you have with you; no import or export of Polish currency is allowed. Unused zlotys must be left at the border — there are exchange counters at most transportation centers.

TIPPING: The usual tip is 10% of hotel, restaurant, hairdresser, and taxi bills. Service charges are not included in most bills.

BANKING/BUSINESS HOURS: Banks are generally open from 8 AM to 4 PM weekdays. Most other businesses keep the same hours.

HOLIDAYS/SPECIAL EVENTS: *New Year's Day* (January 1), *Easter Monday* (April

20), *May Day* (May 1), *National Independence Day* (July 22), *All Saints' Day* (November 11), and *Christmas* (December 25 and 26).

The *Chopin Piano Competition* is held every 4 years in Warsaw (the next is scheduled for fall 1994). If you can't make it, there are spring and summer Chopin concerts in Warsaw's lovely Lazienki Park and a month devoted to his music at the Duszniki Spa each August. More music? In August, organists from all over the world come to Oliwa on the Baltic coast to give concerts on the cathedral's superb organ, and Warsaw hosts an internationally famous *Modern Music Festival* each September. Warsaw's *Jazz Jamboree* is an October event drawing fans from everywhere.

The *Poster Biennale* — a competition of graphic art posters depicting various events, people, and places, held in Warsaw's largest art galleries in June of even-numbered years — is one of the most prestigious contests of its kind. *CEPELIA,* national folk art cooperatives located throughout Poland, have an enormous display and sale of regionally made products each June.

In March, Zakopane, a resort in the Tatra Mountains, holds the most important Nordic and Alpine ski races of the season. And in May all attention is focused on the big, international *Berlin-Warsaw-Prague Bicycle Race.*

SHOPPING: The *DESA* shops specialize in fine arts and quality merchandise such as crystal and Wloclawkek pottery. *CEPELIA,* the crafts co-op, has the best regional wares, including Baltic amber beads and jewelry, kilim-style flat weave rugs, sheepskin outerwear — especially those decorated with Zakopane embroidery — and Silesian lace.

Shops usually are open weekdays from 11 AM to 7 PM, and are closed Saturdays. Major department stores are open from 8 AM to 6 PM weekdays, and from 8 AM to 1 PM on Saturdays.

Portugal

TOURIST INFORMATION: Portugal's main tourist information agency, *Instituto de Promoçao Turistica,* is at 51 Rua Alexandre Herculano, 2nd Floor, Lisbon (phone: 681174). *Postos de Turismo* (Tourist Posts) provide tourist information at offices throughout the country. The main branches in Lisbon are at the Palácio Foz (Praça dos Restauradores (phone: 3463624), at the airport (phone: 893689), and at Santa Apolónia train station (phone: 867848). For information (in English), call 3463314.

ENTRY REQUIREMENTS: US citizens need only a current US passport for stays of up to 60 days.

GETTING THERE/GETTING AROUND: Airlines – *Delta, TAP Air Portugal,* and *TWA* fly nonstop from New York to Lisbon. *TAP* flies nonstop from Boston to Ponta Delgada in the Azores, and some other flights stop there, too. Domestically, *TAP* has jet service to Porto and Faro, Terceira, and San Miguel in the Azores, and Funchal and Porto Santo in Madeira. Within Portugal, scheduled *LAR* flies to Bragança, Faro, and Vila Real.

Cars – Services for the stranded motorist include call boxes, a frequent sight along major routes. If someone is injured, call 115 anywhere in Portugal; operators also speak English.

Trains – Because the track gauge is an unusually wide 9 inches (in Spain as well), the cars on the efficient and modern *CP* (*Companhia dos Caminhos de Ferro Portugueses*) are wider and extremely comfortable. The *CP*'s electric trains make frequent runs from Lisbon to Sintra and Cascais. Reservations are suggested on the express trains to Porto and the Algarve, the *International Sud-Express* to Paris, and the twice-daily trains to Madrid.

The *CP* sells economical Tourist Tickets good for unlimited travel for periods of 5, 10, or 15 days and has other discount plans for groups. The Senior Citizen's discount is 50%.

CLIMATE AND CLOTHES: The weather is mostly sunny, mild, and lacking in extremes, with temperatures ranging between 50 and 75F (10 to 24C) year-round on the mainland and in the Azores. Madeira, off the African coast to the southwest, is a bit warmer and attracts sun and sand lovers in all seasons, but the tourist trade peaks December through April. April in Portugal is usually one of the rainiest months. It is invariably cool after the sun goes down, so even in summer a sweater will come in handy. Almost any kind of attire is acceptable, but if you are visiting Lisbon, be sure to bring a pair of comfortable shoes for the city's cobblestone streets.

LANGUAGE: Portuguese, though English is spoken in major tourist areas.

ELECTRIC CURRENT: 220 volts, AC.

MONEY: The escudo is abbreviated with a dollar sign, which takes the place of the decimal point in our currency (for example, 1$00), and equals 100 centavos.

TIPPING: Tips in the 10% to 15% range are expected even though a 10% service charge normally is included on hotel and restaurant bills. Porters and bellmen should receive from 20$00 to 25$00 per bag.

BANKING/BUSINESS HOURS: Banks are open weekdays from 8:30 AM to 2:45 PM. Most other businesses operate on weekdays from 9 AM to 1 PM, and from 3 to 7 PM.

HOLIDAYS/SPECIAL EVENTS: *New Year's Day* (January 1), *Mardi Gras* (March 3), *Good Friday* (April 17), *Freedom Day* (April 25), *Labor Day* (May 1), *Camões Day* (June 10), *Assumption Day* (August 15), *Day of the Republic* (October 5), *All Saints' Day* (November 1), *Independence Day* (December 1), *Feast of the Immaculate Conception* (December 8), and *Christmas Day* (December 25).

The streets erupt with color and pageantry during celebrations commemorating various saints. Tradition calls for folk dancing, fireworks, processions, and bullfights. Of particular note is the *Festa de Santo Antonio* held in mid-June in Lisbon's Moorish Alfama section and the *Festa de São Silvestre* on *New Year's Eve* in Madeira, where elaborate fireworks are set off from barges in the harbor. A running of the bulls is part of the festivities at Vila Franca de Xira in July. And for local color nearer Lisbon, Mercês, just outside Sintra, holds a fair annually at the end of October featuring food and crafts.

SHOPPING: Hand-painted *azulejos* were once used as ballast for ships crossing the Atlantic — they now weigh down suitcases on international jets. Tiles in myriad designs are made by *Sant'Anna, Viúva Lamego,* and *Sacavem* in or near Lisbon. *Vista Alegre* makes exquisite porcelain in both antique and modern designs. Craftsmen's skills are considered a precious resource in Portugal, where apprentices are carefully nurtured in order to sustain this shopper's paradise of tin and copperware, wrought-iron products, hand-stitched Arraiolos rugs, and filigree in silver and gold.

White port wine, difficult to find in the US, as well as red port and fine old madeiras are elegant and warming souvenirs.

Stores are open from 9 AM to 1 PM and 3 to 7 PM weekdays and 9 AM to 1 PM on Saturdays. Shopping center hours are from 10 AM to 9 PM daily.

Romania

TOURIST INFORMATION: *Carpati,* the national tourist office, is currently being privatized. It covers all phases of travel and is headquartered in Bucharest (7 Magheru Blvd.; phone: 145160). In towns where there is no *Carpati* office, county tourist offices

(*Oficiul Judetean de Turism*) provide travel assistance. In addition, several hundred travel agencies have opened in Romania during the past 2 years.

ENTRY REQUIREMENTS: Though subject to change because of continuing turbulent political events, at press time tourist visas, good for visits of up to 60 days, cost $30 and require a current US passport for documentation. They're available at Romanian diplomatic offices in the US (Romanian Consular Office, 1607 23rd St. NW, Washington, DC 20008: phone: 202-232-4748 or 202-232-4749), or upon arrival at the border or at Otopeni Airport in Bucharest.

GETTING THERE/GETTING AROUND: Airlines – *TAROM, Romanian Air Transport,* has direct flights from New York to Bucharest via Vienna and Luxembourg (note, however, that this airline is not recommended due to poor service). Several other major airlines have connecting flights from Europe. Domestically, *TAROM* has one or more flights a day between Bucharest and 14 destinations.

Cars – *Carpati,* the national tourist office, and its branches in the major cities offer car rentals (currently limited to the nationally produced Dacia 1300 and 2000 and the Oltcit-Club), accommodations, itineraries, and road assistance.

Cruises – The Danube (Dunărea) River enters the Black Sea from southern Romania, forming a natural boundary with Yugoslavia and Bulgaria. River cruises from Vienna to the Black Sea and the Danube Delta, and shorter trips between Romanian towns are run by *NAVROM* (contact local tourist offices in Romania for information).

Trains – *Căile Ferate Române (CFR),* the *Romanian Railway Company,* with diesel and electrically equipped trains, accepts Interail Passes but not Eurail. International expresses connect Romania with both Eastern and other European countries.

CLIMATE AND CLOTHES: The mode of dress reflects the atmosphere: It's relaxed and casual. Black Sea bathing resorts are informal, in keeping with the summer heat (daytime temperatures average around 82F/28C in July and August). Carpathian ski resorts, usually blanketed in 3 feet of snow during the high season (December to March), have temperatures in the mid to upper 30s F (around 0 degrees C). Overall, the four seasons are clearly defined and the climate is similar to New York City's.

LANGUAGE: Romanian, a Romance language derived directly from Latin, shows some Slavic influences. French, the second language until after World War II, is not spoken much now; English is becoming more common.

ELECTRIC CURRENT: 220 volts, AC.

MONEY: The leu (L) equals 100 bani. At press time, the Romanian government reportedly had plans to replace the leu with a new, as-yet-unnamed currency. It still is illegal to enter or leave the country with Romanian currency.

TIPPING: Though not expected, tips are accepted for special services.

BANKING/BUSINESS HOURS: Banks are open Monday through Friday from 8:30 or 9 AM to 4:30 or 5 PM. Most other businesses are open Monday through Friday 8 AM to 4:30 PM.

HOLIDAYS/SPECIAL EVENTS: *New Year's* (January 1 and 2), Greek Orthodox *Easter* (April 26), *Labor Day* (May 1), *National Day* (December 1), and *Christmas* (December 25 and 26). (At press time, Romania was about to draw up a new constitution; it is expected that new national holidays will be announced.)

Centuries-old folk customs are very much alive today and festivals are colorful displays of dances, costumes, and folk art. *Carpati* publishes a calendar with histories of major celebrations. Most noteworthy are the *Simbra Oilor* at Oas (the first Sunday in May), marking the return of the sheep to the pasture; the *Girls Fair* at Mount Gaina, originally more of a mating game for singles than a fair, has grown into a major folk festival on the third Sunday in July; and the *Hora de la Prislop,* with a galaxy of dances and costumes, the second Sunday in August at Mount Prislop.

SHOPPING: Given the continuing strength of folkloric traditions it's not surprising that crafts are carefully nurtured and handmade products highly prized. Pottery is produced at over 200 locations; noteworthy are the black pottery of Marginea in

Bukovina, the Corund near Moldavia, the Vama in Oas, and particularly the pottery of the Oltenia provinces. Potters' fairs provide grand selections from a variety of craftspeople and regions. Rugs run the gamut from the flatwoven or *scoarta* style exemplified by Moldavian and Banat rugs to Persian hand-knotted, high-pile rugs. Glass paintings from the 18th and 19th centuries have inspired a modern generation of glass painters. The best examples of Romanian art can be viewed and purchased at government-sponsored *Galeriile de Arta* boutiques. Keep an eye out for silk dresses in subdued, abstract patterns hand-painted by leading artists, a scarce but stunning find. *COMTURIST* shops sell a wide range of products for foreign exchange, including caviar from sturgeon caught in the Danube Delta.

Smaller shops have shorter hours of 9 AM to 1 PM and again from 4 PM to 8 PM; department stores stay open from 9 AM to 6 PM; food markets from 7 AM to 6 PM, with some open until 9 PM. Stores are closed on Sundays.

San Marino

TOURIST INFORMATION: The *Government Tourist Board* is near the walls of the city at the Palazzo del Turismo (Cont. Omagnano, Republic of San Marino 47031 — via Italy; phone: 992101). It's crucial to write "via Italy" on the envelope to avoid mail being sent to California.

ENTRY REQUIREMENTS: There are no border formalities between San Marino and Italy; your current US passport is all that is required for 3 months or less.

GETTING THERE/GETTING AROUND: Airlines – Rimini, Italy, 14 miles (22 km) to the east, has the nearest airport and is the closest stop for trains and express buses. Local buses make frequent connections between Rimini and San Marino.

Cars – Take the Rimini exit off autostrada A14 and proceed about 11 miles (18 km) west. Drive right up Monte Titano to the capital or leave your car below and take the cable car (*funivia*) or the shuttle buses to the ramparts.

CLIMATE AND CLOTHES: Summer days average around 82F (28C) in spite of the republic's setting on craggy peaks high above the Romagna plain. Relatively mild winters in the 40s F (4 to 9C) are chilled by the constant presence of the somewhat unsettling *garbino* wind blowing from the south. Dress is very informal everywhere.

LANGUAGE: The Sammarinese dialect is commonly used but Italian is the official tongue. English is spoken by about 30% of the population.

ELECTRIC CURRENT: 220 volts, AC.

MONEY: The Italian lira (L. or Lit.) circulates in San Marino, but some local coins and medallions are minted as souvenirs.

TIPPING: Service charges usually are added but check to make sure. Tips of between 1,000 and 2,000 lire should be given for small services.

BANKING/BUSINESS HOURS: Banks are open 8 AM to 2:30 PM on weekdays. Other businesses are open 8 AM to 2:30 PM on weekdays; some offices, particularly government offices, are also open on Monday and Thursdays from 3:15 to 6 PM.

HOLIDAYS/SPECIAL EVENTS: *New Year's Day* (January 1), *Epiphany* (January 6), *Anniversary of the Liberation of San Marino* (February 5), *St. Joseph Day* (March 19), *Anniversary of the Arengo* (March 25), *Good Friday* (April 17), *Easter Monday* (April 20), *Labor Day* (May 1), *Ascension Day* (May 28), *Feast of Corpus Domini* (June 18), *St. Peter and St. Paul Day* (June 29), *Fall of Fascism* (July 28), *Assumption of Holy Virgin* (August 14–16), *San Marino Day* (September 3), *Anniversary of Rovereta* (October 14), *All Saints' Day* (November 1), *Commemoration of the Dead* (November 2), *Immaculate Conception* (December 8), *Christmas* (December 24–26), *New Year's Eve* (December 31).

September 3 is the feast day of the country's patron saint, Saint Marino, with a crossbow contest among members of the *Crossbowmen's Corps,* who dress in traditional Renaissance costumes.

Two captain's regents rule San Marino for periods of only 6 months at a time and their investiture ceremonies, every April 1 and October 1, are elaborate affairs with costumed guards and foreign representatives in attendance.

During the summer of odd-numbered years the *International Art Biennale* takes place in San Marino, and an international grand prix is held annually near San Marino, in April.

SHOPPING: San Marino stamps are a major source of revenue and have considerable value among collectors. Both modern and traditional ceramic pieces are popular and unique souvenirs. And even this miniscule land produces its own wine — a tasty muscatel (*moscato*). Shops generally are open from 9 AM to 5 PM on weekdays. Some open on Saturdays during the summer.

The Soviet Union
(And Estonia, Latvia, and Lithuania)

TOURIST INFORMATION: *Intourist,* the company for foreign travel, that operates most hotels, many restaurants, and other businesses in the Soviet Union, arranges many trips there and to the recently independent Baltic states of Estonia, Latvia, and Lithuania through its appointed travel agents in the US. The head office is 16 Marx Prospekt, Moscow 103009 (phone: 203-6962). *Intourist* also has branches in most Soviet cities, as well as in New York (630 Fifth Ave., Suite 868, New York, NY 10111; phone: 212-757-3884). While *Intourist* used to make all travel arrangements for US visitors, it now is possible to make arrangements directly with an increasing number of cooperatives and other types of independent businesses in the Soviet Union and the Baltic states, and through travel agencies in the US.

ENTRY REQUIREMENTS: At the time of this writing, visas are required to the Soviet Union, and to Lithuania, Estonia, and Latvia. At present, there are three kinds of visas: tourist, "ordinary" (for business or family visits), and transit. All need advance planning. Once your trip has been confirmed by *Intourist* in Moscow, your travel agent must file your visa application with a consular office in the US a minimum of 14 days before your arrival in the Soviet Union. An itinerary complete with dates must be submitted along with a $20 processing fee (there is an aditional $10 fee for so-called rush jobs) and other documents (including proof of pre-arranged accommodations, a letter of invitation from a Soviet associate for business travel, and so on) to the Consular Division of the Soviet Embassy (1825 Phelps Ave. NW, Washington, DC 20008; phone: 202-939-8900). *Intourist* offices can furnish procedural details. Contact *Intourist* in the US (at the address above).

GETTING THERE/GETTING AROUND: Flexibility in travel arrangements is still somewhat limited, and visitors are expected to stick to predetermined itineraries. Restrictions on accessible routes and modes of transportation remain in effect in the Soviet Union, but have lifted in the Baltic states. Once you arrive, it's possible to extend your stay, provided the hotel has rooms available.

Airlines – *Aeroflot* flies to Moscow from Montreal, Washington, DC, and New York; all flights include a stopover in Canada except for one nonstop flight from New York. *Finnair* flies to Moscow and St. Petersburg (formerly Leningrad) from New York and Los Angeles via Helsinki. In addition, many major foreign carriers (*Air Canada, Air France, Austrian Airlines, KLM, Sabina, Swissair, SAS*) offer connecting flights to the Soviet Union from the Continent. *Aeroflot* has thousands of domestic flights to cities in all the republics, independent or not, at reasonable rates. At press time, *Aeroflot* continued to serve the now independent Baltic states.

Cars – You can drive a rental car or your own automobile into the Soviet Union at certain border points and also may rent Russian makes from *Intourist* in certain cities. A growing number of international and independent rental companies are cropping up in Moscow, St. Petersburg, Riga (in Latvia), and Vilnius (in Lithuania). Although an increasing amount of flexibility in driving itineraries is being allowed, the restricted driving routes in the country still are determined and fully arranged through *Intourist,* which also provides the necessary papers for car touring and insurance. One word to the wise motorist: Obey Russian rules of the road — they're strictly enforced.

Trains – The Moscow-St. Petersburg route is quickly traveled on the Soviet railway's *Sovyetskaya Zheleznaya Doroga* (*SZD*), while the *Trans-Siberian Railroad* covers 6,250 miles of the old USSR, going through over 65 towns and villages. The entire *Trans-Siberian* trip — from Moscow to Nakhodka — takes about 8 days. Overall, the trains aren't terribly fast, but most are comfortable. Passage is arranged through *Intourist,* as well as through US agents handling Soviet travel.

CLIMATE AND CLOTHES: Make no mistake, it's warm in summer and very, very cold in winter, but Moscow is at least dry, crisp, and often sunny even when your breath steams the air. This guide deals exclusively with the European portion of the Soviet Union, where winter temperatures average 20F (-7C), often lower, and summers rarely get above the 70s F (20s C). St. Petersburg is near the Gulf of Finland and the Baltic Sea and, although farther north, tends to be warmer. The temperatures average 16F to 19F (-9 to -7C) during January and in the mid-60s F (16 to 18C) during July, with about 6 to 13 days of precipitation per month. The Republic of Georgia enjoys a mild, almost Mediterranean climate throughout most of the year. In the Baltic states of Estonia, Latvia, and Lithuania, temperatures average 25 to 35F (-4C to 0 degrees C) from December through February and in the mid-80s F (around 30C) in July. Boots, warm socks, heavy coats, and lined gloves are essential in winter. You also will want something festive for the inevitable farewell gala if you're part of a group tour. In warmer weather, a raincoat with a removable lining or a sweater and raincoat will suffice. Visitors need not dress up in Moscow or St. Petersburg, but on the other hand, shorts are in poor taste and blue jeans are inappropriate for evenings out. You are expected to check your coat when entering any public building or restaurant. All garments are hung on hooks, so it is a good idea to sew a chain or heavy loop into your coat collar in order to prevent damage — and dark looks from the cloakroom attendant.

LANGUAGE: More than 100 ethnic groups live in the Soviet Union's fast-breaking-away republics and in the Baltic states. Russian, an East Slavic language, is still the preeminent tongue. *Intourist* personnel and workers in the hotel and restaurant industries speak English.

ELECTRIC CURRENT: 220 volts, AC.

MONEY: One ruble (R or Rub) is made up of 100 kopecks. Rubles cannot be taken into or out of the Soviet Union. When initially exchanging currency, a customs certificate is issued that must be presented to exchange rubles for dollars. Money can be exchanged only through outlets of the State Bank of the Soviet Union. When you leave the country, any remaining Russian currency can be changed into dollars at the bank of the last border point — provided that you have bank receipts of previous transactions. Major credit cards are widely accepted, as are traveler's checks issued by American Express, Bank of America, Barclay's Bank, and Citibank.

■**Note:** As we went to press, the volatile state of the Soviet economy made it impossible to provide an exchange rate for the ruble that was likely to be of any practical use to travelers. Not even the Soviet Embassy and *Intourist* (the Soviet's own government-run tourism organization) could agree on the "official" rate of exchange between the ruble and the US dollar. We can only advise travelers to check the exchange rate immediately prior to departure; the government has officially stated that it will henceforth match the rate offered on the all-too-active currency black market (which has historically offered a far greater number of rubles for a US dollar than any official source). In addition, the newly independent Baltic states of Estonia, Latvia, and Lithuania are in the process of introducing their own currency.

TIPPING: Tipping is not officially sanctioned, though tips are not refused.

BANKING/BUSINESS HOURS: There are banking branches for currency exchange at major *Intourist* hotels, open weekdays from 9 AM to 5 PM. In Moscow, a foreign exchange bank, Vneshekonombank of the Soviet Union, is located between the *National* and *Intourist* hotels on Tverskaya Street (formerly Gorky St.); it is open from 8:45 AM to noon, and from 12:50 to 7:50 PM. Most other businesses are open weekdays from 9 AM to 5 or 6 PM.

HOLIDAYS/SPECIAL EVENTS: *New Year's Day* (January 1), Russian Orthodox *Christmas* (January 7), *International Women's Day* (March 8), *May Day* (May 1 and 2), *Victory Day* (May 9), *October Revolution* (November 7).

Among a number of government-sponsored cultural events, Moscow's *Russian Winter Festival* from December 27 through January 2 offers a repertoire of the country's finest ballet, opera, symphonic, and theatrical companies; the spectacular Moscow circus with its dancing bears; and horse-pulled sleigh (*troika*) rides. Other folk and classical music festivals include *Kiev Spring* in May, and *White Nights* in St. Petersburg in June.

SHOPPING: Fine performances by Soviet virtuosos and orchestras are captured on the technically excellent Meloydia records. Good opera glasses make appropriate gifts for the culturally inclined and fur hats and lined gloves for those living in cold climes.

Caviar's not only an antidote to the often less-than-exciting fare but a luxurious memento. Exquisitely painted and lacquered *palekh* boxes, reputedly a dying art, represent the height of refinement and are lovely souvenirs. Purchases can be made with foreign currency at the *Beryozka* shops in major hotels or with rubles at stores such as *GUM* and *Melodia* in Moscow.

Shopping hours for department stores are from 8 AM to 9 PM, and in smaller shops from 10 AM to 7 PM; most shops are closed Sundays, and some close for lunch.

Spain

TOURIST INFORMATION: *Oficinas de Información y Turismo* are found in all major cities, train stations, and airports. In addition to dispensing literature and giving travel assistance, some sell inexpensive tourist insurance policies covering medical expenses, accidents, and baggage theft.

ENTRY REQUIREMENTS: A current US passport is good for visits of 6 months or less.

GETTING THERE/GETTING AROUND: Airlines – *Iberia Airlines* of Spain operates nonstops to Madrid from Los Angeles, Miami, and New York, as well as nonstops between New York and Barcelona. Other airlines serving Spain include *Delta* with nonstop service from New York to Madrid, *TWA* with nonstops from New York to Madrid and Barcelona, and connecting flights from Los Angeles, and *American,* which flies nonstop from Dallas/Ft. Worth to Madrid. *Aeroméxico* has nonstop service from Miami to Madrid. Early morning arrival schedules enable easy connections to cities throughout mainland Spain, the Canary and Balearic Islands. *Iberia*'s economical Visit

Spain AirPass, which must be purchased in conjunction with an *Iberia* transatlantic flight, offers unlimited travel throughout Spain and the Balearic Islands in a 60-day period on *Iberia* and *Aviaco,* Spain's domestic carrier. *Iberia*'s "air bridge" (*Puente Aereo*) shuttle has flights between Madrid and Barcelona departing every 30 minutes throughout the day.

Cars – Rental rates are particularly reasonable and one-way Iberian rentals that allow pickup in Spain and drop-off in Portugal (or vice versa) are useful for touring. The VAT on car rentals is 12%.

Trains – It is possible to take high-speed, air conditioned trains like the *Talgo* to Paris, Marseilles, Geneva, and Rome without changing at the borders. *RENFE*'s (*Spanish National Railways*) best equipment usually is found on the longer distance runs between major cities and are widely recommended. However, some second class trains can be slower, more crowded, and often poorly equipped. Buses are best for short hauls and excursions. Rail passes for 8 or 15 days of travel are sold through *Rail Europe* (see *Traveling by Train* in GETTING READY TO GO for addresses in the US), and at any *RENFE* offices and stations in Spain.

CLIMATE AND CLOTHES: Surrounded by the sea, the Iberian Peninsula is dominated by the vast interior central plateau where river valleys have formed lateral depressions interspersed with mountain ranges. In Spain, the result of this diversity is a varied climate: Coolest and most humid along the north Mar Cantábrico coast, with winters averaging 26F (– 3C) and summer temperatures of around 77F (25C); dry and arid in the central regions; tremendously hot during summers in Andalusia to the south (up to 95F, 35C); and year-round temperate (66F, 19C), sunny days abound on the Costa del Sol and in the Balearic and Canary islands.

The fashionable Spanish dress with enviable panache, so in leading cities wear your chicest clothing. Generally, casual clothes, suitable for the climate, are acceptable tourist attire, and in the resorts, most anything goes.

LANGUAGE: Castilian Spanish is the official tongue, but other regional languages are Catalán (Catalonia), Basque (Basque Country which, in Basque, is *Euskadi*), Gallego (Galicia), Valenciano (Levant provinces), and Mallorquín (the Balearic Islands). English is understood in principal resorts, hotels, restaurants, and shops — but not too far off the tourist track.

ELECTRIC CURRENT: 220 volts, AC.

MONEY: The peseta (Pta) is the unit of currency.

TIPPING: Though service charges of 15% are included in restaurant bills, extra tips of between 5% and 10%, depending on the attention you receive, are expected. Taxi drivers receive 5% of the meter and, in most cases, 50 to 100 pesetas is enough for porters, bellmen, and per night for chambermaids.

BANKING/BUSINESS HOURS: Banks are generally open from 9 AM to 2 PM Mondays through Fridays and from 9 AM to 1:30 PM Saturdays; many banks are closed on Saturdays during the summer. Most other businesses are open weekdays from 9 AM to 2 PM and from 4:30 to 7 PM, although some have changed to an 8 AM to 3 PM schedule.

HOLIDAYS/SPECIAL EVENTS: *New Year's Day* (January 1), *Epiphany* (January 6), *St. Joseph's Day* (March 19), *Maundy Thursday* (April 16), *Good Friday* (April 17), *Easter Monday* (April 20), *Día del Trabajo* (May 1), *San Isidro Day* (May 15), *Corpus Christi* (June 18), *St. James's Day* (July 25), *Assumption Day* (August 15), *Columbus Day* (October 12), *All Saints' Day* (November 1), *Immaculate Conception* (December 8), and *Christmas Day* (December 25).

All cities and towns in Spain hold fairs or fiestas (*ferias*), some more colorful and exciting than others. Undoubtedly the three most famous are Valencia's *Fallas de San José* in mid-March, when groups of huge figures (*ninots*) are composed into satirical groups (*fallas*), paraded, and finally set on fire; the *Feria de Sevilla* in late April, with the citizenry parading on horseback in elegant regional dress to the accompaniment of music and flamenco dancing; and the *Feria de San Fermín* in Pamplona the second week of July, with the historic running of the bulls.

The most splendid *Holy Week* (Semana Santa) observances take place in Andalusia, with particularly notable processions in Seville and Málaga. The sherry wine harvest is celebrated in Jerez de la Frontera in mid-September.

This year, *Expo '92,* a world's fair involving over 100 countries, will be held in Seville from April 20 to October 12. The *1992 Summer Olympics* will be held in Barcelona from July 25 through August 9. A number of special events will be held throughout the year in Madrid, the European Cultural Capital for 1992.

SHOPPING: Leather goods, from supple suede gloves and elegant calf handbags to wineskins (*botas*) that require careful curing, are excellent purchases, with perhaps the best selection found in Madrid. Designer clothes, including those of Pertegaz and Balenciaga, are the height of fashion. Costume jewelry is imaginative, and the black and white pearls labeled Perlas Majórica are world famous.

Other exceptional buys are shoes, from classic calf pumps to provincial cloth espadrilles; porcelain by Lladró and pottery by regional craftsmen; and wool rugs using technologies translated from tapestry makers or simple cotton-rag throws. Spanish sherry is unequaled and *fino* is a fine buy, as are brandies. Saffron is a tasty addition to your Spanish recipes.

Shops usually are open from 9:30 or 10 AM to 1 or 1:30 PM and from 4:30 or 5 to 8 or 8:30 PM on weekdays and are closed Saturday afternoons and Sundays. Department stores now stay open through the traditional 3-hour siesta, and most are open all day Saturday, from 9:30 or 10 AM to 7:30 or 8 PM. Some stores are open Sundays as well.

The VAT in Spain is 6% on practical goods and 12% on luxury items.

Sweden

TOURIST INFORMATION: The identifying logo of the over 200 *Turistbyrå* is the international lowercase white *i* against a green background. Regional information is provided by the *Swedish Tourist Board,* Sverigehuset, Hammgatan, Stockholm (phone: 789-2000).

ENTRY REQUIREMENTS: For visits of 3 months or less, a current US passport is all that is necessary.

GETTING THERE/GETTING AROUND: Sweden is about 1,000 miles long from top to toe. Transportation on clean, modern equipment with an enviable on-time record makes all areas, from Malmö in the south to beyond the Arctic Circle, easily accessible.

Airlines – *SAS* flies nonstop from New York to Stockholm. In addition, there are connecting flights to Stockholm via Copenhagen from Chicago, Los Angeles, and Seattle. *TWA* has nonstop service to Stockholm from New York; *American Airlines* flies direct from Chicago to Stockholm; *TWA* also has direct service via Brussels. Thirty-two cities in Sweden are connected by the domestic airline, *Linjeflyg.*

Cars – Most major US car rental firms are represented in Sweden. For a motoring map with suggested itineraries, contact the *Swedish Tourist Board,* 655 Third Ave., New York, NY 10017 (phone: 212-949-2333).

Trains – *Staten Järnvägar* (*SJ*) diesel and electric trains are comfortable and fast. Service in the north is augmented by postal buses that carry passengers to outlying areas. The *SJ* network is part of the Scandinavian Railpass, good for 15 or 21 days or 1 month of unlimited travel in first or second class on all trains and several ferry lines, and also for 50% discounts on other specified ferry runs.

CLIMATE AND CLOTHES: July and August temperatures range in the low to mid

60s F (about 18C) around the sea-level cities of Malmö, Gothenburg, and Stockholm. January and February, the coolest months, average 26F (− 3C) in Stockholm, slightly warmer in the south. The well-styled, yet comfortable and functional, clothing of the Swedes mirrors their refined sense of design and informal, outdoor orientation. Warm underwear, a heavy topcoat, warm gloves, and sensible footwear are recommended. Casual dress is fine in summer but in fall and winter, you'll want a more cosmopolitan look.

LANGUAGE: Swedish, but many people have a firm command of English.

ELECTRIC CURRENT: 220 volts, AC.

MONEY: The Swedish krona (SEK) equals 100 øre.

TIPPING: A 13% service charge is automatically tacked on to restaurant tabs and hotels add 15%.

BANKING/BUSINESS HOURS: Banks are generally open weekdays from 9:30 AM to 3 PM, with some centrally located banks open to 5 PM. Smaller branches of the central banks also are open from 4:30 to 6 PM one evening per week. Most other businesses are open from 7:30 or 9 AM until 4 or 5:30 PM. Stores are open from 9:30 AM to 6 PM weekdays, and from 9:30 AM to 1 or 2 PM Saturdays.

HOLIDAYS/SPECIAL EVENTS: *New Year's Day* (January 1), *Twelfth Day* (January 6), *Good Friday* (April 17), *Easter Monday* (April 20), *Ascension Day* (May 28), *Whitmonday* (June 8), *Labor Day* (the Saturday between October 31 and November 6), *All Saints' Day* (November 1), *Christmas Day* (December 25), and *Boxing Day* (December 26).

Summer is greeted with great gaiety on the weekend closest to the summer solstice in late June. Maypoles, garlands, flower-decked houses, dancing, and special midsummer dishes typify this most popular festival. *St. Lucia's Day,* December 13, ushers in *Christmas,* with young girls and women wearing crowns of candles and distributing traditional pastries at dawn.

The rococo *Drottningholm Court Theater* outside Stockholm presents primarily 18th-century operas, ballets, and classical music mid-May to mid-September.

SHOPPING: The famed crystal of Orrefors and Kosta Boda can be bought in Stockholm and around the country, or you can visit the glass district near Växjo, where 36 of the nation's 44 glassworks are concentrated. Seconds are sold at shops adjoining the factories.

Swedish cotton and woolen fabrics are used to advantage by designers such as Katja. If you're thinking mink, it's a good buy here.

Beautifully designed kitchenware and utensils, in a variety of materials, are quality items, as is furniture. Avoid the 23% VAT (called MOMS) by having the store send merchandise directly to your home. Also, many stores throughout Sweden participate in the Scandinavian Tax-free program. An export receipt is issued at the time of purchase and is then presented at designated airport and ferry terminals for a partial VAT refund.

Shops generally are open weekdays from 9:30 or 10 AM to 6 PM and on Saturdays from 10 AM until anywhere between 1 and 4 PM.

Switzerland

TOURIST INFORMATION: The headquarters of the *Swiss National Tourist Office* (*Schweizerische Verkehrszentrale*) is at 38 Bellariastrasse, Zurich CH-8027 (phone: 288-1111). All but the tiniest Swiss towns have efficient and well-prepared tourist offices, and regional centers have region-wide information.

ENTRY REQUIREMENTS: A current US passport. No visa is required for visits of less than 3 months.

GETTING THERE/GETTING AROUND: The transportation network is beautifully integrated and famed for the punctuality of its moving parts. The key to its workings is the *Official Timetable* available for $16 from *Avos Travel* (608 Fifth Ave., Suite 410, New York, NY 10020; phone: 212-245-1150). Note that anyone driving on the super-highways in Switzerland must buy a special car sticker, used in lieu of tolls. Cars rented in Switzerland usually have these stickers; if you're driving into the country, they can be purchased for 30 SFr. (about $22) at border crossings.

Airlines – *Swissair* has daily nonstop service to Zurich and Geneva from New York. There also are nonstop flights from Atlanta, Boston, and Chicago to Zurich and a direct flight from Chicago to Geneva via Zurich. *American* flies nonstop from Chicago to Zurich and *Delta* offers nonstop service from New York to Zurich. *TWA* flies direct from New York to Geneva and Zurich via Paris.

Cars – Road service and information are provided by the *Automobile Club de Suisse* (39 Wasserwerkgasse, 3000 Bern 13; phone: 031-224722), and the *Touring Club Suisse* (9 Rue Pierre-Fatio, 1211 Geneva 3; phone: 022-371-2812). For breakdown service, call 140, and for road conditions, call 163 from anywhere in the country. The national Swiss number for information in English is 111.

Trains – This small country has 3,100 miles of electrified track covering its terrain. The *SBB* (*Schweizerische Bundesbahnen*) offers the Swiss Pass, allowing unlimited trips on trains, boats, and postal buses and a discount of 25% on mountain railways and cable cars. The Pass also includes free transportation, within 25 cities, on the public transportation system. Other transportation bargains include the Swiss Card. For information on all discount cards, contact any of the Swiss National Tourist Office (SNTO) branches in the US before you go.

CLIMATE AND CLOTHES: Famous for its snow-capped mountains — at 15,217 feet the Dufourspitze on Monte Rosa is the highest — Switzerland also boasts a sun belt along Lake Maggiore (890 feet above sea level) complete with palm trees. These contrasts indicate not only a variety of climates but also abrupt changes in the weather. However, normal summer daytime highs average in the mid-70s F (24C).

Swiss dress is generally conservative in color and style. However, you'll be at ease if you dress according to the activities you pursue.

LANGUAGE: There are four. German is spoken by 65% of the population; French by 19%, Italian by 12%, and Romansh, derived from Latin, by less than 1%. Swiss dialects, called collectively Schweizerdeutsch, vary from region to region. English is widely understood.

ELECTRIC CURRENT: 220 volts, AC.

MONEY: The Swiss franc (SFr) is made up of 100 centimes (French) or rappen (German).

TIPPING: A 15% service charge is included in hotel, restaurant, and bar bills, and is automatically included in taxi fares, so that only porters and bellmen require tipping, about 1 franc per bag.

BANKING/BUSINESS HOURS: Banks are generally open weekdays from 8:30 AM to 4:30 PM. Most other businesses are usually open weekdays from 9 AM to 5 PM, but many offices are closed between noon and 2 PM.

HOLIDAYS/SPECIAL EVENTS: *New Year's Day* and the day after (January 1 and 2), *Good Friday* (April 17), *Easter Monday* (April 20), *Ascension Day* (May 28), *Whitmonday* (June 8), *Independence Day* (August 1), *Jeûne Fédéral* (Fasting Day, the first Thursday in September), and *Christmas* (December 25 and 26).

The list of Swiss festivals goes on and on and there's something for everyone, whether your interest lies in music, history, industry, or sports. World-renowned occasions, such as Geneva's 10-day *International Motor Show* in March and the *Lucerne Music*

Festival of musical events in August are most enjoyable, but don't overlook the patriotic and folkloric observances that give a clear sense of Swiss culture. The major national event of this kind is celebrated all around Switzerland on August 1, when fireworks light the sky to commemorate the founding of the Swiss Confederation. A complete roster of special events is available at *SNTO* offices.

SHOPPING: Switzerland is synonymous with watches and the wondrous array awaiting your choice is overwhelming. The watchmaker's sweetest rival in Switzerland is the chocolatier. Be sure to try many a connoisseur's favorites — Lindt or Tobler. Not surprisingly, quality music boxes, precision tools, optical goods, and drafting sets are good buys. Multibladed and multipurpose red Swiss Army knives are universally popular.

Caran d'Ache pastels, crayons, colored pencils, and pens are treasured by children, as well as professional artists. Also art books, most notably the Skira series — an exemplary collection — are published here.

Stores in the major cities are open from 8 AM to 6:30 PM on weekdays except on Monday mornings, when they often are closed. Stores close at 4 or 5 PM on Saturdays and all day on Sundays. In smaller towns, closing for an hour and a half at noon is common.

Yugoslavia

TOURIST INFORMATION: Major cities have *Tourist Information Offices,* identified by the internationally recognized green sign with the white *i.* The two main tourist information offices in Belgrade are at the railway station and in the subway at Terazije Street next to the Albania Building (phone: 635343 or 635622). The *Tourist Association of Belgrade* can be reached at 339696 or 327834. The words *Turist Biro* and *Drustvo* denote information locations.

ENTRY REQUIREMENTS: In recognition of the European Year of Tourism, Yugoslavia suspended its usual visa requirements from April 1991 to April 1992. A current US passport is the only document needed for stays of less than 30 days. Those who plan to stay longer than 30 days must report to the local authorities (usually the nearest office of the Secretariat for Internal Affairs, known as *SUP*) to receive additional documentation. At press time, the Yugoslavian government had not yet made a decision as to whether visas will be required after April of this year.

GETTING THERE/GETTING AROUND: Airlines – *JAT* (*Jugoslovenske Aerotransport*) and *Yugoslav Airlines* fly nonstop from Chicago and New York to Belgrade. *JAT* also has service from Los Angeles via Chicago. *Delta* flies from New York to Belgrade via Frankfurt. The extensive domestic service is rated a bargain by European standards.

Cars – Probably the best way to view the scenic Adriatic coast. Rentals are readily available and gas coupons — available at border crossings — save 5% over regular prices but only if your car has foreign plates. If a breakdown occurs, call 987, an emergency number manned by the *SPI* (local automobile club).

Trains – The *Jugoslovenski Zeljeznice* (*JZ*) rail line runs inland from north to south, with occasional spurs east to cities along the coast. Planes, the Adriatic Highway, and the sea are the best ways to get to and between points on the Istrian and Dalmatian coasts and islands and to the southern Adriatic coast. The jewel in the *JZ*'s crown is the 325-mile line between Belgrade and Bar on the Montenegro coast. It's an engineering tour de force — 254 tunnels and 234 bridges had to be built in order to complete the line. The fastest, most comfortably equipped are the business trains (*Poslovni voz*).

CLIMATE AND CLOTHES: Swimming is comfortable along the Adriatic coast from

May through October, when water temperatures hit the mid-60s F (about 18C) (at least from Dubrovnik south). They rise to the mid-70s F (24C) in summer, when air temperatures hit the low 80s F (28C). Inland summers are hot; winters in the mountains are cold, with snows beginning in December and lingering through April.

Dressing or undressing is your choice on the many nude beaches found along the Istrian Peninsula. Belgrade and Zagreb require the most conservative clothes and Dubrovnik and Sveti Stefan are scenes of the more chic looks.

LANGUAGE: Serbo-Croatian is the official language in four of the six republics: Croatia, Bosnia-Herzegovina, Montenegro, and Serbia. Although all citizens speak virtually the same language, it has two written versions: The Serbs, affiliated with the Eastern Orthodox church, use the Cyrillic alphabet and the Croats, mostly Roman Catholics, use a modified Latin version. Macedonian and Slovenian are the languages of Macedonia and Slovenia. More and more students are choosing English as their second language and it is spoken frequently by the young, as well as those associated with the tourist industry.

ELECTRIC CURRENT: 220 volts, AC.

MONEY: The dinar (Din) equals 100 paras.

TIPPING: Discretionary at hotels and restaurants, as service charges of 10% to 15% are put on the bills, but it's best to give a few dinars extra. Porters receive 50 dinars per bag.

BANKING/BUSINESS HOURS: Banks are generally open 8 AM to 6 PM Mondays through Fridays. Most other businesses are open 7:30 AM to 3:30 PM on weekdays.

HOLIDAYS/SPECIAL EVENTS: *New Year's Day* (January 1), *Memorial Day* (July 4), *Republic Day* (November 29), and *Christmas Day* (December 25).

Summer here is a festival of culture and folklore. The most elaborate event is the *Dubrovnik Summer Festival,* an artistic extravaganza in mid-July through August, with performances set in historic locales and parks. Others include: Zagreb's *International Revue of Original Folklore* in July, with over 80 groups the world over plus Yugoslavian troupes competing in a stunning exhibition of regional dances and costumes; Split's *Melodies of the Adriatic* festival in early July; and Korcula's celebration featuring the *Moreska Sword Dance,* Thursdays from May through September.

SHOPPING: Yugoslavia is well known for primitive art. The works of leading artists are widely reproduced and internationally acclaimed. The delicate, colorful, and detailed paintings on glass are exquisite. Check the major cities for exhibitions and dealers.

Many stores specialize in the fine native handicrafts, such as embroidery, sweaters, leatherware, woodcarvings, ceramics, and the bright and cheerfully colored Bosnian and Serbian rugs.

The town of Samobor near Zagreb lends its name to the country's finest crystal.

Shops are open from 7 or 8 AM to noon and 2 or 3 to 7 or 8 PM on weekdays; Saturdays, from 8 AM to 2 or 3 PM. Stores are closed Sundays.

THE
CITIES

AMSTERDAM

More than any other major city in Europe, Amsterdam seems to have been designed with people in mind. It is a city built to human scale, refreshingly free of high-rise monuments to corporate egotism. It does not overawe or oppress. Its small streets, graceful canals, and narrow buildings invite exploration. Even its mansions — the elegant 17th-century houses built on the canals by earlier generations of the great and wealthy — are grand without being grandiose.

Emerging from Amsterdam's Central Station to face a welter of taxis, trams, bicycles, boats and bridges, commuters and traffic, one might not believe that it is a soothing city. But cross the traffic and follow any of the canals that lace the city like the concentric tiers of a football stadium, and you will discover its serenity. The four largest and most historic canals — Singel, Herengracht, Keizersgracht, and Prinsengracht — pass near almost everything worth seeing at some point in their grand perambulation around the city.

These canals and the buildings that line them were the heart of Holland's thriving trade for centuries, and as you walk your eye will begin to pick out the details that distinguish the city's singular traditional architecture — unique gables and spires atop the attenuated and tipsy houses that delineate 17th- and 18th-century Amsterdam from the modern city. The finest old houses, built by rich traders, are along the Herengracht (aptly, "Gentlemen's Canal"). On the Singel, at the Munt, is the flower market, with flower-filled boats and barges moored along the canal. And a few blocks from where the Singel leaves the port are two "cat boats," filled with some of Amsterdam's stray cats. And most canals are dotted picturesquely with houseboats. Walking the canals not only is unavoidable in Amsterdam, it is one of the chief joys of city life. And being a sensible lot, when Amsterdammers are in a hurry, they prefer to navigate the narrow canal streets by bicycle. Where cars get stuck for hours behind vans and trucks, bikes whiz through. Of a population of 700,000, some 600,000 people have bicycles, and any visitor can join them for the price of a rental and the willpower to ignore hectic traffic. But be aware that cars and taxis have the right-of-way, even though many daring cyclists often ignore red lights.

Amsterdam has plenty of historical structures — more than 7,000 on the government-designated list of protected monuments. And though its beautiful 17th-century central area has been preserved largely intact, and the city must rank among the world's tops in museums per capita — some 55 at last count — it is no architectural mausoleum. You will find that most of these protected 17th- and 18th-century buildings are carrying on business pretty much as usual today. They house small firms, families, cluttered shops, cafés, prostitutes — or all of them together. This is the genius of Amsterdam. In a word, the city has spirit.

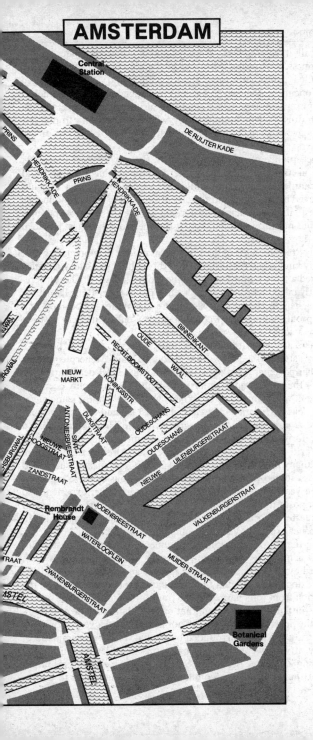

The Dutch call it *gezelligheid,* a special quality that translates inadequately as "coziness." It means intimacy, of the sort offered by the traditional, dark-walled cafés with their shaded lamps and Persian-carpeted tables, but also openness, the easygoing, informal sociability that characterizes so many Amsterdammers. It is a quality that informs all aspects of life in the city, from dress — which almost everywhere is eclectic — to politics. Amsterdammers are not concerned with dictating beliefs, behavior, or appearance to others.

This casual acceptance of different standards, the city's famed tolerance, is firmly rooted in its Calvinist past. Amsterdam always has been first and foremost a mercantile city, built on middle class values and money. This has by no means proved a bad thing, and the city always has exerted an influence disproportionate to its size, placing Amsterdam among the ten most popular tourist destinations in Europe, and making it Europe's fourth largest financial center.

The city's early "regent" class of merchants was unique in appreciating that intolerance of any kind is bad for business, and throughout its history Amsterdam has displayed a truly admirable reluctance to persecute whichever heretics were currently in vogue. As the great French philosopher René Descartes put it while living here in 1631, "Everybody here except me is in business and so absorbed by profit making that I could spend my entire life here without being noticed by a soul."

Amsterdammers are not without convictions, however. One of the city's few monuments, a statue of a dockworker at Jonas Daniël Meijerplein, commemorates the heroic general strike of 1941 protesting Nazi deportations of the city's Jews — the only demonstration of its kind to occur in any occupied country, and one in which many of the strikers were shot. On the same *plein,* or square, is the *Jewish Historical Museum,* and just around the corner from the *Anne Frank House,* on the Keizersgracht, is the Homomonument, a sculpture in the form of a pink triangle that commemorates homosexuals killed during World War II. By the end of the war, Amsterdammers were hiding nearly as many fugitives in their homes as the Germans had succeeded in rounding up for forced labor camps. The most famous of these fugitives, of course, was 14-year-old Anne Frank, who documented her experience so unforgettably for posterity in her diary; the house where the Frank family and friends were sequestered for 2 years is now one of the major tourist sights in Amsterdam — a heartrending visit for young and old alike.

But it is fitting that the earliest known document mentioning Amsterdam by name, from which the city traditionally dates its founding, had to do with commerce. Issued by the Count of Holland in 1275 and on view today at the city archives, the document granted the inhabitants around the "dam on the Amstel" exemption from toll charges on the transport of locally made goods.

In spite of this important concession, that original dam, the site of today's Dam Square in the heart of the city, could not have seemed a very promising location to its first occupants. Surrounded by the flat, marshy swampland of the river estuary, it was swept regularly by storms that blew in unimpeded from the bordering Zuiderzee (Southern Sea). It was so lacking in resources of any kind that the wood for the community's first houses had to be imported.

But, as the Dutch like to boast, while God made the world, they made the Netherlands, and today the Zuiderzee is gone, walled out by a massive, 19-mile dike completed in 1932 and supporting Highway E-10, which now links the provinces of North Holland and Friesland. In the sea's place is the reclaimed Flevoland polder and the immense freshwater Ijsselmeer. And the uninviting landscape has disappeared beneath the capital itself, most of whose buildings are supported by an estimated 5 million wooden piles driven deep into the soggy ground.

Amsterdam's convenient central location for trade was virtually its only natural resource, and Amsterdammers, who soon became known for their acute (and frequently ruthless) business practices, were quick to take advantage of the fact. By the dawn of the 16th century, the early settlement had grown into a thriving city of about 12,000. This original city center, still referred to locally as the *walletjes* for the early walls surrounding it, is better known nowadays as the famous red-light district, with prostitutes, porno shops, and sex clubs incongruously housed in a picturesque quarter of preserved 17th- and 18th-century homes and warehouses, secondhand bookstores, boutiques, and Chinese restaurants.

Amsterdam reached the peak of its fortune during the Golden Age of the 17th century, when it became the center of a worldwide maritime empire and the base of the country's emergence as a major world power in spite of (in fact, largely because of) an almost perpetual state of war. With characteristic aplomb, the city carried on a highly profitable trade with both its enemies and allies, even going so far at one point as to insure enemy ships against destruction by Dutch forces. It also offered sanctuary to a stream of skilled refugees from other cities — again to its own considerable profit — and it was during this period that work was completed on the rapidly expanding city's crowning glory: the elegant network of canals ringing it, along which the great and newly rich constructed magnificent homes. Today Amsterdam has more canals than Venice — 165 — containing more than 60 miles of waterways and spanned by some 1,000 bridges.

The period following the Golden Age was one of decline for both the city and the country. By the dawn of the 19th century, Holland was a French province under Napoleon. After the emperor's defeat, it became a Dutch monarchy for the first time in 1815 under King Willem I. After 1875, the country experienced a strong economic revival with the construction of the North Sea Canal, the *Rijksmuseum,* and the *Concertgebouw* (Concert Hall). World War I, however, bypassed the country, and by the time it was invaded by Nazi forces in World War II, Holland had become one of the most backward nations in Europe.

Today it is one of the most progressive, and much of the credit for this must go to Amsterdam. For this great and unique city, which even the Dutch themselves don't really understand and tend to dismiss as "difficult," has never lost its sense of pride or determined independence. Today, thanks largely to its opportunistic burghers and the liberal traditions they helped to establish, Amsterdam remains a city, more than anything else, of possibilities. It is open, *gezellig,* vibrant, tolerant in the extreme, fascinating, and — above all — alive. Certainly it is a city to be seen but, even more, a city to settle into, if only for a few days.

AMSTERDAM AT-A-GLANCE

SEEING THE CITY: During summer months, the towers of two of Amsterdam's most historic churches offer the best views of the old city center areas. The Oude Kerk (Old Church), which dates from the early 14th century, is in the heart of the *walletjes* district in the oldest part of the city at Oudekerksplein (open daily except Sundays from 10 AM to 4 PM; phone: 625-8284). The Westerkerk (Western Church; phone: 684-2705), Rembrandt's burial place, was completed in 1631 and is amid Amsterdam's Golden Age canals in the most beautiful part of the city at the Westermarkt. Boasting the city's tallest church tower (at more than 250 feet), with its distinctive gold crown, it usually can be visited from 2 to 5 PM on Tuesdays, Wednesdays, Fridays, and Saturdays from June 1 until September 15.

At the harbor next to Central Station is the modern Harbor Building housing the *MartInn* restaurant (7 De Ruiterkade; phone: 625-6277), from which you can enjoy a panoramic view of the harbor and canals in comfort. Open weekdays for lunch and dinner until 9:30 PM; reservations necessary. For a spectacular view of Amsterdam's newer southern fringe area, visit the elegant *Ciel Bleu* French restaurant atop the 23-story luxury *Okura* hotel (175 Ferdinand Bolstraat; phone: 678-7111). Open daily from 6:30 PM to 1 AM; reservations advised. Another place to see the rooftops and canal configurations is the coffee shop on the sixth floor of the *Metz* department store (455 Keizersgracht; phone: 624-8810). Open during regular store hours: 10 AM to 6 PM daily, except Mondays from 1 PM, and Thursdays to 9 PM.

Taking a boat tour of Amsterdam's canals has become a virtual tourist cliché, but it's still the best way to make a first acquaintance with the city. Several operators along the Rokin, the Damrak, Prins Hendrikkade, and the Nassaukade run the tours, which last about an hour. Try *Lovers* (opposite Central Station; phone: 622-2181) or *Kooij* (phone: 623-3810), near the Dam on the Rokin at the intersection with Spui. Tours depart every few minutes. Or take a cultural excursion on the *Museum Boat* (phone: 625-6464) that shuttles between several of the city's prominent museums, such as the *Rijksmuseum* and the *Scheepvaart* (Maritime) *Museum*. At ground level, six do-it-yourself walking tours from the VVV, the tourist office (opposite Central Station; phone: 626-6444), make it easy and fun to explore on foot.

SPECIAL PLACES: The major sights of Amsterdam are grouped conveniently around a few principal areas, all within walking distance of one another. The city's central landmark and natural focal point is Dam Square, or simply, the Dam. At the end of the Damrak — a short street leading from the harbor and Central Station — the busy square is dominated by the distinctive war memorial constructed there in 1956. In good weather, the steps ringing the monument are a sea of young people — residents and tourists — resting, singing, making plans. The open plaza of the square opposite the monument often attracts a variety of spontaneous and organized activities, festivals, and jazz concerts, and free puppet shows are staged there on one or two afternoons a week during the summer. Beware: Sadly, there often are pickpockets and drug dealers loitering around the square, too. There are now uniformed "city watchmen" on duty daily at the city's hot spots (Rembrandtsplein, Leidseplein, and Waterlooplein) who can assist visitors from 9 AM to 5 PM.

Royal Palace – Hailed as the "eighth wonder of the world" after its completion in 1662 because of the 13,659 wooden piles holding it up. Its regal interior, decorated by the leading artists of the time, can be viewed daily during the summer from 12:30 to 4 PM and on Wednesdays in winter at 1:45 PM by arrangement. Don't expect to see the queen unless she is receiving official visitors that day; she lives in the Royal Palace in The Hague. Admission charge. On Dam Square, opposite the war memorial across the plaza (phone: 626-6444).

Nieuwe Kerk (New Church) – An imposing late Gothic church dating from around 1500 and the traditional place of inauguration of new monarchs. Following 2 decades of restoration, the church reopened in time for the coronation of Queen Beatrix in 1980 and now features concerts and exhibitions. Open weekdays 11 AM to 4 PM, Sundays noon to 5 PM, with an organ concert at 3 PM; closed January and February. On Dam Square, next to the Royal Palace (phone: 626-8168).

De Drie Fleschjes (The Three Bottles) – A historic, cask-lined tasting house unchanged since it first opened for business in 1650. Make sure you sample some of the traditional "old Holland" liqueurs (the best-known brands are Bols and Hoppe) that are its specialty. Open daily except Sundays from noon to 8:30 PM. No admission charge. Behind the Nieuwe Kerk at 16 Gravenstraat (phone: 624-8443).

Canals – More than any other, Amsterdam is a city to stroll through. Not to be missed is its most beautiful section — the concentric rings of canals known as the Singel (Moat), Herengracht (Gentlemen's Canal), Keizersgracht (Emperor's Canal), and Prinsengracht (Prince's Canal). To see what the elegant homes lining the canals originally looked like, visit the *Willet-Holthuysen Museum,* open daily from 11 AM to 5 PM; admission charge. 605 Herengracht (phone: 626-4290).

Beurs van Berlage – Designed at the end of the 19th century by noted Dutch architect H.P. Berlage, this was Amsterdam's third stock exchange building, and it now houses architecture exhibits. It's also the home of the *Netherlands Philharmonic Orchestra.* There also is an excellent Art Deco café. Open daily when architecture exhibitions are on. Admission charge to exhibits. 3 Beursplein, on the Dam between Central Station and Dam Square (phone: 626-5257).

Anne Frank House – A short way west of the Dam and just around the corner from the Westerkerk is the house containing the secret annex where the Frank family and their friends hid from the Nazis for 2 years. No matter how prepared you are, you will be shocked by the size and vulnerability of the quarters that housed 14-year-old Anne, her parents and sister, their friends the Van Daans and their teenage son Peter, and a dentist named Dussel. You'll go in behind a bookcase that disguised the entrance to the upstairs hideout and see the simple artifacts, photos, and newspaper clippings that speak so mutely and eloquently of tragic times.

Anne's father, Otto Frank (who was the lone survivor of the Gestapo raid in August 1944 that sent the whole group to extermination camps), received Anne's diary from one of the Dutch people who helped hide the family. The diary has become one of the great cultural documents of this century.

Downstairs is an excellent video show and changing exhibitions on current issues related to racism and discrimination. A visit to Anne's house is an excellent way to introduce young people to the horrors of the Holocaust. Open daily from 9 AM to 5 PM, Sundays from 10 AM, and to 7 PM from June through August. Admission charge. 263 Prinsengracht (phone: 626-4533).

Jordaan – Amsterdam's colorful working class district. Devote a day to simply exploring the maze of narrow streets and alleys with their innumerable small boutiques and arts and crafts shops sprinkled among the more traditional businesses — and several nights to experiencing the Jordaaners themselves in their characteristic neighborhood cafés, unlike any others in Amsterdam (see *Nightclubs and Nightlife*). The major part of the Jordaan is bordered by the Rozengracht, Lijnbaansgracht, Brouwersgracht, and Prinsengracht, with the most interesting shops concentrated at 2e Anjeliersdwarsstraat, 2e Tuindwarsstraat, and 2e Egelantiersdwarsstraat. For a taste of 17th-century Amsterdam, visit the Monday market on the Noordermarkt, and bargain with its lively Dutch vendors.

Walletjes – Immediately to the east of the Dam is the picturesque Old City center named for the medieval walls that once surrounded it. This attractive area includes a number of purely historic sites, described in the entries that follow, and is worth a daytime walk. Ironically, perhaps, the area now is best known as the red-light district, a European capital of public sex. And it really is public; everything is out in the open, with no effort at concealment. (Once Paris was the world's sex capital; now it looks tame in comparison with once-puritanical cities like Copenhagen and Amsterdam). Almost 1,000 "girls," many of them extremely attractive, line OZ Voorburgwal, the Oudezijds Achterburgwal, and the small neighboring streets, standing in windows with real red lights, on the streets, and often riding bicycles. There are live sex shows and sex shops all along OZ Voorburgwal. As would be wise in any city's "Times Square" area, watch out for pickpockets and street criminals.

The Zeedijk, the old sailors' quarter, is being restored to its 17th-century grandeur, with the *Golden Tulip Barbizon Palace* hotel (see *Checking In*) and smart shops as its focal points. Amsterdam's Chinese community celebrates both *New Year's Eve* and the *Chinese New Year* with a huge display of fireworks on the bridge by the Zeedijk.

Amstelkring Museum – The 17th century was a period of repression of Catholics, and at least 26 clandestine churches were built in city attics by 1681. This one, nicknamed "Our Dear Lord in the Attic" and extending through the joined attics of three houses, is equipped with everything from organ to baroque altar. The entry house was set up in 1663 and has one of the few completely preserved classical 17th-century living rooms still existing in Amsterdam. Open daily from 10 AM to 5 PM, Sundays from 1 PM. Guided tours by appointment; English guides available by request. Admission charge. In the heart of the *walletjes* district at 40 Oude Zijds Voorburgwal (phone: 624-6604).

Artis – This 150-year-old zoo has a beautifully landscaped garden, as well as some fascinating inhabitants. There also is a planetarium, conservatory, and coffee shop/buffet. Open daily from 9 AM to 5 PM. Admission charge. 4U Plantage Kerklaan (phone: 623-1836).

Hortus Botanicus – Just minutes from the zoo and city center, this botanical garden is a little oasis that provides a break from the city's bustle. Open daily. Admission charge. 2 Plantage Middenlaan (phone: 525-5405).

Waag (Weigh-House) – Part of a gate and a fragment of the Old City walls dating from 1488, the Waag later was converted into a weighing house. Anatomy lessons were given here from 1619 until 1939, an early one of which was the subject of Rembrandt's famous painting *The Anatomy Lesson of Dr. Tulp.* The public is not admitted but the house can be viewed from the Nieuwmarkt.

Schreierstoren (Weepers' Tower) – Dating from 1569, this is another fragment of the original city walls. Henry Hudson departed from here on his voyage to the New World in 1609. Tradition has it that the tower got its name from the sailors' wives who used to see off their husbands from here. Between the *walletjes* district and Central Station at the corners of Prins Hendrikkade and Geldersekade.

Flea Market – This is Amsterdam's famous open-air secondhand market. A major part of the fun used to be haggling over the price of treasures unearthed from the random mounds, but a surfeit of affluent visitors has spoiled the dealers somewhat, and these days there are few treasures to be found. The market has returned to the original Waterlooplein location (for which it was originally named), next to the City Hall and *Opera House.* Open daily except Sundays from 10 AM to 4 PM.

Rembrandt House – The house where Rembrandt lived and worked from about 1639 to 1658 is fully restored and furnished much as it must have appeared to him. Virtually all of his 250 etchings are on display here. Open daily from 10 AM to 5 PM, Sundays from 1 PM. Admission charge. Near the flea market at 4-6 Jodenbreestraat (phone: 624-9486).

Munt (Mint) – A short street called the Rokin leads to the Munt. Although named for the coining use it was put to after the French occupation, this monument, which dates from 1490, is interesting as another piece of the original city walls.

Rembrandtsplein – Turning left at the Munt takes you into the Reguliersbreestraat, which leads directly into the concentration of piano bars, nightclubs, and casinos around the Rembrandtsplein. Once the city's butter market, Rembrandtsplein now is a pedestrian-only precinct and a leading center of nightlife, known particularly for striptease clubs and topless bars, which line the adjoining Thorbeckeplein. An open-air art market is held on Sundays. If you enter the Rembrandtsplein from Amstelstraat, a street on your right, called Engelse Pelgrimsteeg, is where some of the English Pilgrims lived before leaving for the New World.

Try to catch a film at the *Tuschinski,* just before the square. This ornate Art Deco theater, one of Europe's most beautiful, is worth seeing regardless of what's playing. Tours are available during the summer. 26 Reguliersbreestraat (phone: 626-2633).

Begijnhof – The best known of the 75 *hofjes* (enclosed courtyards) still scattered around Amsterdam and unobtrusively concealed behind ordinary doors in the walls of residential buildings. Founded in 1346 as a cloister, it is now, like the other *hofjes,* an idyllic inner-city residential block for the elderly, but anyone may take advantage of the oasis of tranquillity provided by the courtyard. The Begijnhof also contains Amsterdam's English church, which regularly holds classical music performances, as well as its oldest surviving house at No. 34, built in about 1470. The easy-to-miss entrance is on a short street called Spui, leading from the Rokin.

Leidseplein – One of the city's major centers of nightlife; in the summer its open terrace also is a favorite daytime gathering place for dedicated people watchers and beer drinkers; in winter, its open-air ice skating rink is popular. Next door is the *Stadsschouwburg,* a leading municipal theater. 26 Leidseplein (phone: 624-2311).

Vondel Park – Amsterdam's beautiful main park, with 120 acres of woodland, waterways, grassy fields, the *Netherlands Film Museum* (see *Museums*), and one of the best jogging tracks in town. In summer, it is transformed into just the kind of colorful human zoo Amsterdam would be expected to produce, with a number of open-air events presented on an almost daily basis (see *Special Events*). It is best to go before dark. Bordered by Constantijn Huygensstraat, Overtoom, Amstelveenseweg, and Koninginneweg/Willemsparkweg.

Rijksmuseum – This world-famous museum is probably best known for Rembrandt's *Night Watch,* but it also has the world's greatest collection of Dutch masters and other painters from the 15th to the 19th century. From December 4, 1991, through March 1 of this year, a special Rembrandt exhibit features many works by the artist, as well as his pupils. Tickets to the special exhibit must be purchased in advance at Amsterdam's tourist offices (VVV; see *Tourist Information*) or in the United States through the Chicago office of the Netherlands Board of Tourism (225 N. Michigan Ave., #326, Chicago, Illinois 60601; phone: 312-819-0300; fax: 312-819-1740). Tickets are $15; credit cards *only* accepted. During the special exhibition, museum hours will be extended from 10 AM to 8 PM daily, except *New Year's Day.* The sculpture and applied arts collections are open regular hours: Tuesdays through Saturdays from 10 AM to 5 PM, Sundays from 1 PM. Admission charge. 42 Stadhouderskade (phone: 673-2121).

Tram Museum – A fleet of old electric tram cars are on display at the site of the old steam train station near the Olympic Stadium. Restored cars provide rides to the Amsterdam Woods. Open from April to October on Sundays and holidays only; in July and August open daily except Mondays and Fridays. Admission charge. 264 Amstelveenseweg (phone: 673-7538).

Stedelijk Museum – Amsterdam's museum of modern art, with paintings and sculptures dating from the mid-19th century as well as changing exhibitions of contemporary international artists. Open from 11 AM to 5 PM daily. Admission charge. 13 Paulus Potterstraat (phone: 573-2911).

Van Gogh Museum – Grouped with the *Rijksmuseum* and the *Stedelijk* along Amsterdam's appropriately named Museumplein, this newest of the city's big three museums opened in 1972. Its ultramodern facilities feature an unrivaled collection of 200 paintings and 400 drawings by the famous Dutch artist, as well as changing exhibitions of paintings related to his work. On Sundays from 2 to 4 PM, adults can take art lessons, complete with live models. Open weekdays (except Mondays) from 10 AM to 5 PM, Sundays from 1 PM. Admission charge. 7 Paulus Potterstraat (phone: 570-5200).

RAI – Amsterdam's modern congress and exhibition center has a regularly changing schedule of major international trade fairs and expositions. 8 Europaplein, reachable by tram or train from Schiphol Airport (phone: 541-1411).

Albert Cuyp Market – Amsterdam's largest and most colorful street market, with rows of stalls selling food, flowers, clothing, books, and practically everything else imaginable. It extends for blocks along the street for which it is named, starting at the Ferdinand Bolstraat, not far from the Museumplein. Closed Sundays; not to be missed whether or not you buy, but do be aware of pickpockets.

Aviodome Museum – A perfect way to fill in waiting time at Schiphol Airport, with exhibits on everything to do with flight, from a model of the first flying reptile of 150 million years ago to a replica of the Wright Brothers' plane, a mockup of a modern jet cabin, and a half-scale model of the Apollo Moon Lander. Open 10 AM to 5 PM; closed Mondays. Admission charge. Schiphol International Airport, about 6 miles (10 km) from Amsterdam on Highway E-10 to The Hague (phone: 617-3640).

Scheepvaart (Maritime) Museum – This collection pays tribute to the country's 3 centuries of globe-girdling exploits. Displays include ship models, nautical paintings, and charts. A replica of the historic trading ship the *Amsterdam* is permanently moored here, too. Open Tuesdays through Fridays from 10 AM to 5 PM; Sundays from 1 to 5 PM. Admission charge. 1 Kattenburgerplein (phone: 523-2311).

World Trade Center – This colossal complex of offices, shops, and exhibition halls caters to the international businesses that are the lifeblood of the city. 1 Strawinskylaan; take the train from Schiphol Airport (phone: 575-9111).

Jewish Historical Museum – At a complex of four former German synagogues, the extensive collection focuses on the Holocaust, as well as the customs and festivals of Jewish people in the Netherlands. Open daily from 11 AM to 5 PM. Admission charge. 2-4 Jonas Daniël Meijerplein (phone: 626-9945).

Muziektheater – Overlooking the Amstel River, this 1,600-seat, very contemporary complex, serves as the city's opera house — home to the *Netherlands Opera Company* and the *Dutch National Ballet* — and adjoins Amsterdam's City Hall (Stadhuis; 3 Amstel; phone: 625-5455). Drop in the *Waterloo Grand Café* (15 Zwanenburgwal) for indoor or terrace dining and snacks.

Heineken Brewery – Although the brewery itself is no longer in operation at this location, visitors can tour the old premises and see a video presentation and exhibits that give a historical overview of this brewing dynasty. Afterward, guests receive a sample of the brew. From May 15 to September 15 tours are available at 9 AM and 1 PM. (Visitors should arrive at least 10 minutes early to be assured a place in the morning tour.) During the rest of the year, only morning tours are offered. Admission charge. Tram Nos. 16, 24, and 25 stop near the entrance. 78 Stadhouderskade (phone: 523-9239).

■**EXTRA SPECIAL:** Most of the attractions around the world that require rising before dawn are usually not worth it. A notable exception is the morning flower auctions held in Aalsmeer, just outside Amsterdam. Both the place and the activity are unique.

  The flower auctions are held in a building said to be the largest under a single roof on this planet — occupying an area greater than 50 football fields. Acres and acres of freshly cut, fragrant roses set beside equal acreages of tulips, carnations, freesia, and other blossoms. There are cut flowers as far as the eye can see: a scene that overwhelms the senses.

Operations at Aalsmeer begin before dawn, with the six auction rooms going into action around 7 AM. The bidding "clocks" involve hundreds of bidders who occupy the steep grandstands above the constant parade of carts full of blooms upon which bids are accepted. More than 4,000 flower growers are part of this immense cooperative, and it's a sight that is both beautiful and aromatic. The flower auction is held weekdays from 7:30 to 11:30 AM. Any hotel in Amsterdam can help arrange transportation.

SOURCES AND RESOURCES

TOURIST INFORMATION: For brochures, general information, and inexpensive maps showing all the major sights, lists of many of the city's hotels and restaurants, and similar materials, go to the city tourist offices (VVV) in the *Coffee House* (opposite the Central Station or at 106 Leidsestraat). Open weekdays and Saturdays from 9 AM to 8:30 PM, Sundays from 10 AM to 5:30 PM (phone: 626-6444).

Before leaving home, pick up a Holland Leisure Card (about $13), which provides discounts on car, train, and plane travel as well as breaks on shopping and attractions in the Netherlands. For details, contact the Netherlands Board of Tourism, Information Dept., 355 Lexington Ave., New York, NY 10017 (phone: 212-370-7367).

The most detailed commercial map (which includes the entire public transport system) is the *Falkplan,* available at any newsstand or at the tourist office.

The US Embassy is at Lange Voorhout in The Hague (phone: 70-362-4911). The US Consulate is in Amsterdam (19 Museumplein; phone: 664-5661).

Local Coverage – The best guide to what's happening is the bi-weekly *What's On in Amsterdam,* available from the VVV. The *Amsterdam Times* also contains listings of museums and other sights, as well as general information and useful tips.

The English-language monthly magazine *Holland Herald* covers activities of interest to visitors throughout the country and runs features on restaurants, shopping, special attractions, and Dutch life in general. It is available on *KLM* flights.

Most of Amsterdam's bookshops have books in English on various aspects of the city and the rest of the Netherlands. For the best selection, try *Scheltema Holkema Vermeulen* (16-18 Koningsplein; phone: 626-7212); *Athenaeum* (14 Spui; phone: 622-6248), which has an adjacent newsstand with long hours, including Sundays; *W.H. Smith* (152 Kalverstraat; phone: 638-3821), the English book and magazine store; or any of the *AKO* establishments around town. *Premsela* (78 Van Baerlestraat; phone: 662-4266) and *Art Book* (645 Prinsengracht; phone: 625-9337) have stunning art volumes, as do many of the major museums. The *American Discount Book* (185 Kalverstraat; phone: 625-5537), which has an English tearoom downstairs (open Sundays), is devoted primarily to American publications. *Van Gennep* (283 Spuistraat; phone: 624-7033) specializes in remaindered art, jazz, and literature books.

Food – *What's On,* published by the tourist bureau and available at the city tourist offices (VVV), has restaurant listings, but note that the establishments listed pay to be included.

TELEPHONE: The country code for Holland is 31; the city code for Amsterdam is 20. Note that as of March 1991, all 6-digit phone numbers are preceded by a 6.

GETTING AROUND: Airport – Schiphol Airport, which handles both domestic and international carriers, is about a 25-minute ride from the center of Amsterdam (or about double that time during rush hours); taxi fare to downtown should run about 55 to 60 Dutch guilders (about $29 to $32). *Schiphol Line* trains leave every 15 minutes for the Amsterdam South railway terminals at the World Trade Center and the RAI Congress Hall (both close to the city center), the terminal by the Fashion Trade Center, and Central Station; cost is about 4.50 guilders ($2.40) one way. *KLM* provides bus service from the airport to several central hotels for about 16.50 guilders ($8.70) each way. Buses leave every 30 minutes.

Bicycle – If you have nerves of steel, do as the Dutch do and rent a bike, but make sure you leave it securely locked! One source is *Rent-a-Bike* at Central Station (33 Stationsplein; phone: 624-8391). Deposit (200 guilders/$105) required. Bike tours are available through the VVV (phone: 626-6444).

Boat – A boat tour of the canals is the best way to get the feel of the city. In addition to the glass-top sightseeing boats already mentioned under *At-A-Glance,* water taxis accommodating up to 8 people can be hired or flagged down year-round for transportation or sightseeing (at a flat group rate of about 95 guilders/$50 an hour, or by the meter at about 25 guilders/$13 for 15 minutes; phone: 622-2181). The *Museum Boat* (phone: 625-6464) departs in front of the Central Station, near the VVV, and follows a fixed route with stops at several prominent museums, such as the *Rijksmuseum* and the *Scheepvaart* (Maritime) *Museum;* the cost is about $6.25. Canal bikes (pedal boats) for 2 to 4 persons can be rented opposite the *Rijksmuseum,* next to the *Anne Frank House,* and at various spots around town, April to October (phone: 626-5574).

Bus, Train, and Tram – The Central Railway Station (1 Stationsplein, at the end of Damrak), also is the hub for the city's local trams and buses. For train information, call 620-2266; for buses and trams, 627-2727. Most hotels have free copies of the *City Transport Welcome Folder,* which lists all pertinent information in English.

The workhorse of Amsterdam's exemplary public transportation system is its network of frequently running trams (streetcars), supplemented by bus routes and a metro (subway) line. The city is divided into tariff zones. Buy a day card (*dagkaart*) from the driver for 9.35 guilders (about $5) or a multiple "strip card" at any tobacco shop or the bus office at Central Station, which can be used for short trips during the week. Tell the driver your destination, and he will stamp the appropriate strip for that zone. Most places in the city center require two strips. Cards also can be purchased at reduced prices from the GVB (city transport) office in front of Central Station, where simplified maps of the system are available as well. All cards are good for unlimited transfers within the same zone for 1 hour after being stamped. If transferring, you can enter trams by the rear door. Persons over 65 and under 10 travel at half fare. After the normal system shuts down (around midnight), the night bus network (*nachtbus*), covering the main routes through the city, is in service. Since the trams run on an honor system, tram police often board unannounced and ask to see tickets. If you're caught without one, the embarassing — and costly — fine is 100 guilders (about $53). The metro, or Dutch subway, runs from Central Station to the city suburbs and generally is used by commuters only.

Car Rental – *Avis, Budget,* and *Hertz* and many smaller firms are well represented at Schiphol Airport and in the city, but driving in Amsterdam is no way to have a happy holiday. If you do, here are some basic survival tips: (1) Trams have absolute right-of-way and enjoy exercising it; (2) all other traffic coming from the right usually has priority and the Dutch regard yielding as a matter of dent before dishonor; (3) stay out of marked cycle lanes and watch out for kamikaze cyclists who ignore red lights; (4) taxis are allowed to drive on tram tracks; and (5) keep a good book handy to spare your blood pressure. Rules of the road are contained in the *Welcome* *to Holland* brochure, published by the Netherlands Board of Tourism and available from most VVVs.

Taxi – Service is moderately expensive, and taxis normally don't cruise, although you sometimes can flag down an empty one. The best place to get one is at one of the many taxi stands around the center of town. Or call *Taxi Central* (phone: 677-7777).

LOCAL SERVICES: Dentist (English-Speaking) – Most dentists in Amsterdam speak English fairly well; call the *Central Dental Service* at 679-1821.

    Dry Cleaner/Tailor – *Palthe* (57 Vijzelstraat and other locations; phone: 623-0337); *Cleaning Shop Express* (22 Huidenstraat; phone: 623-1219).

Limousine Service – *Doelen* (13 Schakelstraat; phone: 682-7126); *Jishé,* day or night (phone: 21-591-3076); *Van Delden & Son,* 24-hour service (68 Admiraal de Ruyterweg; phone: 612-6846).

Medical Emergency – *Vrije University Hospital First Aid* (1117 de Boelelaan; phone: 548-9111); *Central Doctors' Service* (phone: 664-2111).

Messenger Service – *Randstad Koeriersdienst,* 24-hour service. 48 Andreas Schelfhoutstraat (phone: 617-3622).

National/International Courier – *Abacus Couriers,* service day and night (phone: 484-4236); *DHL International,* near Schiphol Airport (phone: 606-0552).

Office Equipment Rental – *Wilson Office Machines* (70 Utrechtsestraat; phone: 623-8395); *Ruad,* carries audiovisual equipment (33 Kuiperbergweg; phone: 697-8191).

Pharmacy – For prescriptions: *Dam* (2 Damstraat; phone: 624-4331); *Apollo* (19 Beethovenstraat; phone: 662-8108). Pharmacies are open from 8:30 AM to 5 PM Mondays through Fridays; they operate on a rotation basis for night and weekend service. Non-prescription items are found at the *drogist;* ask your concierge for the nearest one.

Photocopies – *Rank Xerox Copy Bureau* (665 A. J. Ernststraat; phone: 644-7404; also other locations); *Printerette* (70 Vijzelstraat; phone: 625-4604; also other locations); *Copy Copy,* open on Saturdays and Sundays, has telex and fax services (47 Herengracht; phone: 620-9503).

Post Office – The main branch is open weekdays from 8:30 AM to 6 PM, until 9 PM on Thursdays, and on Saturdays from 9 AM to noon. 250 Singel (phone: 555-8911).

Teleconference Facilities – For conference calls, dial the *PTT* at 305-55555 to make arrangements for up to 21 connections.

Telex – Telecommunications of all types are processed through *PTT Telehouse,* open 24 hours. 48-50 Raadhuisstraat (phone: 674-3653).

Translator – *Institute Amsterdam* (191 Willemsparkweg; phone: 676-4220); *Language Solution* (11 Corellistraat; phone: 675-4698).

Other – Business services: *ManPower,* an international company providing temporary services (World Trade Center, 901 Strawinskylaan; phone: 662-5626); *Executive Services Amsterdam,* also provides word processing (29 Ruysdaelkade; phone: 671-6566); *Eurobusiness Center,* also provides temporary office space, multilingual staff (three locations: 62 Keizersgracht; phone: 626-5749; 8 Parklaan, Rotterdam; phone: 10-436-5113; and 95 Martinolaan, Maastricht; phone: 43-617499). Florist (it's considered a social blunder to visit a Dutch home without bringing flowers): *Ivy's* (35 Leidseplein; phone: 623-6561); *Pompon* (8 Prinsengracht; phone: 622-5137). Men's formal attire rental: *John Kennis* (76 Vijzelstraat; phone: 623-3680); *Joh Huijer* (153 Weteringschans; phone: 623-5439). Professional photographer: *Capital Press and Photo* (35 Schipholdijk, Bldg. 106, Schiphol Airport; phone: 604-1046); *Nationaal Foto* (7 Heinzestraat; phone: 676-0555). Relocation services: *Formula Two,* for short-term housing, orientation, itinerary preparation, and other services necessary to doing business in the Netherlands (120A Vondelstraat; phone: 612-9121). Hair salon for men and women: *Simcha's,* 178 Stadionweg (phone: 662-9790).

SPECIAL EVENTS: *New Year's Eve* in Amsterdam is a wild extravaganza, with fireworks exploding throughout the city. The *Queen's Birthday,* April 30, is a time of uninhibited celebration throughout the land. In Amsterdam, festivities include street fairs with live music and ethnic food stands on the Dam, as well as a citywide "yard sale" of secondhand goods. During June, the annual *Holland Festival* is a day-and-night cultural extravaganza crammed with dance, music, and theater performances by top Dutch and foreign companies; July is the month for showcasing young talent with the *Summer Festival.* Throughout the summer, various music, mime, dance, theater, and special children's programs for all tastes are presented free on many days of the week in the Vondel Park. The *Uitmarkt* is a free performing arts festival held at various locations the last weekend of August; simultaneously, all concert and theater organizations offer special low prices to introduce the new season. At the beginning of September, the world's largest floral procession departs from Aalsmeer, site of the world's biggest flower auction (see *Extra Special*), winding its way to Dam Square by late afternoon. In mid-September, Jordaaners celebrate their own district and way of life with markets, fairs, cabarets, and other festivities during the 2-week *Jordaan Festival.* In mid-November, thousands line the streets as St. Nicholas, the original Santa Claus, makes his grand entry into Amsterdam. The parade begins by Central Station, heads down the Dam, and loops around town. While 1990 was the year of Van Gogh in Amsterdam, 1991-92 features a comprehensive exhibition of Rembrandt's work. From December 4, 1991, to March 1 of this year, the *Rijksmuseum* is presenting a major Rembrandt exhibition (for more information see *Special Places,* above).

 MUSEUMS: Amsterdam has about 50 altogether. For considerable savings, buy a museum card (about $20), which offers "unlimited" entry to almost all museums in the Netherlands, excluding special exhibitions; cards can be purchased at any museum. Additional museums of interest not mentioned under *Special Places* include the following:

Allard-Pierson Museum – An archaeological collection spanning several thousand years of classical culture. Open 10 AM to 5 PM Tuesdays through Fridays. Admission charge. 127 Oude Turfmarkt (phone: 525-2556).

Amsterdam Historical Museum – In a former orphanage dating from 1414, with changing exhibitions as well as permanent displays about the history of Amsterdam. Open daily from 11 AM to 5 PM. Admission charge. 92 Kalverstraat (phone: 523-1822).

Biblical Museum – Devoted to the origins of the history of the "book of books," it also includes archaeology exhibits in two elegantly restored 17th-century canal houses. Don't miss the models of the ancient tabernacle. Closed Mondays. Admission charge. 366 Herengracht (phone: 624-7949).

't Kromhout – One of the oldest shipyards in Amsterdam, it still operates and offers exhibitions, plus a demonstration of 19th-century shipbuilding. Open weekdays from 10 AM to 4 PM. Admission charge. 147 Hoogte Kadijk (phone: 627-6777).

Madame Tussaud's Waxworks Museum – An affiliate of the London branch, it displays wax models of famous people. It reopened in September after extensive renovations. Open daily from 10 AM to 6 PM; 9 AM to 7 PM in July and August (Sundays from 10 AM). Admission charge. On Dam Square (phone: 622-9949).

Museum Van Loon – This opulent house, built in 1672, was occupied during the 19th century by merchant-prince Hendrik Van Loon. It now offers a vivid example of how wealthy Dutch families lived during the Golden Age. Open Mondays only from 10 AM to 5 PM. Admission charge. 672 Keizersgracht (phone: 624-5255).

Netherlands Film Museum – Continuing exhibits on the history of film, as well as two daily showings of classic international films. Stop in at *Café Vertigo* here between films. Open daily. Separate admission charges for screenings and museum exhibits. 3 Vondelpark (phone: 683-1646).

Nint Technology Museum – Modern technology, from physics to computers. Open weekdays 10 AM to 5 PM; weekends 11 AM to 5 PM. Admission charge. 129 Tolstraat (phone: 664-6021).

Piggy Bank Museum – Some 2,000 money boxes are the focus of the permanent exhibition. Open Mondays through Fridays from 1 to 4 PM. Admission charge. 12 Raadhuisstraat (phone: 556-7425).

Theater Museum – A collection of historical objects relating to Dutch theater, displayed in a fine 18th-century interior. Open from 11 AM to 5 PM; closed Mondays. Admission charge. 168 Herengracht (phone: 623-5104).

Tropen (Royal Tropical) Museum – A showcase for culture and developments in the Third World. Open 10 AM to 5 PM weekdays; 12 to 5 PM on weekends. Admission charge. 2 Linnaeusstraat (phone: 568-8200).

Also worth a visit are the Noorderkerk (Northern Church), dating from 1623, at the Noordermarkt; Zuiderkerk (Southern Church), dating from 1611, on Zandstraat; Portuguese Synagogue, dating from 1675, at Jonas Daniël Meijerplein; and Montelbaanstoren, a city-wall fragment dating from 1512, at the corner of Oude Schans and Oude Waal.

 SHOPPING: The world's largest duty-free shopping center is at Amsterdam's Schiphol Airport. City shops are closed Sundays and Monday mornings, some all day Mondays. Normal hours are from 9 AM to 5:30 or 6 PM, with a slightly earlier closing time on Saturdays. Large stores and many smaller shops, especially in the center, remain open until 9 PM on Thursdays. *Avondverkoops,* or night shops, generally are open evenings from 4 PM to 1 AM. Found throughout the city, they sell fresh fruits and vegetables, prepared foods, wines, and staples. Two of the best are *Sterk,* across from the *Muziektheater* on the Waterlooplein, and *Baltus* (127 Vijzelstraat).

Amsterdam's finest stores are along the P. C. Hooftstraat, adjacent Van Baerlestraat, and on the Rokin. The Leidsestraat, between the Spui and Leidseplein, and the pedestrian-only Kalverstraat, from the Dam to the Munt, are other busy shopping districts. Some of the best shops also can be found on the small side streets connecting the canals — Herenstraat, Prinsenstraat, Runstraat, Huidenstraat — and along the Utrechtsestraat, Wolvenstraat, and Berenstraat.

Amsterdam has had a long history as a center of the diamond industry, and a number of old firms are happy to show visitors around their works. Whether you can afford to buy diamonds or not, you may want to see how the precious gems are polished to perfection. Contact *Amsterdam Diamond Centre* (1-5 Rokin; phone: 624-5787); *Gassan Diamond House* (173-75 Nieuw Uilenberstraat; phone: 622-5333); *Coster Diamonds* (2-4 Paulus Potterstraat; phone: 676-2222); *Herman Schipper* (3 Heiligeweg; phone: 623-6572); *Holshuysen-Stoeltie* (13-17 Wagenstraat; phone: 623-7601); and *Van Moppes Diamonds* (2-6 Albert Cuypstraat; phone: 676-1242). Pick up an introductory brochure about diamonds from the city tourist office.

Other good buys besides diamonds are famous Delftware, handicrafts, tulip bulbs, and antiques (watch out, however, for abundant fake diamonds or fake antiques; to be safe, stick to recommended merchants). The greatest concentration of antiques shops is to be found along the Nieuwe Spiegelstraat, Spiegelgracht, and adjacent streets near the *Rijksmuseum.* There also is an indoor antiques market at 38 Looiersgracht, between the Leidseplein and Jordaan, open Mondays through Thursdays and Saturdays from 11 AM to 5 PM (phone: 624-9038). Stamps and coins are featured every Wednesday and Saturday afternoon on the Nieuwezijds Voorburgwal between the Dam and the Spui, and old books are on sale daily (except Sundays) at the historic Oudemanhuispoort, between Oude Zijds Achterburgwal and Kloveniersburgwal. At the Noordermarkt, a bird market and *boerenmarkt* (farmers' market) take place Saturdays until 3 PM, and a popular flea market and textiles sale take place Mondays until 1 PM. For other Amsterdam markets and the Jordaan, see *Special Places*.

The following shops are especially recommended:

Authentic Ship Models – A fascinating array of wooden model ships and maritime antiques. A variety of "do-it-yourself" model kits featuring windmills and da Vinci machinery as well as ships. 191 Bloemstraat (phone: 624-6601).

De Bijenkorf (The Beehive) – Amsterdam's renowned department store concentrates on the finest in contemporary fashions and furnishings. At the Dam (phone: 621-8080).

Bonebakker – This is the place for diamonds; the oldest and most respected gem merchant in the Netherlands, founded in 1792. Although the premises are elegant, prices aren't a bit higher than anywhere else. 88-90 Rokin (phone: 623-2294).

Christmas World – Just behind the New Church, this cheerful shop sells unique *Christmas* items year-round. 137 Nieuwezijds Voorburgwal (phone: 622-7047).

Christopher Clarke – An English designer who creates unique earrings and accessories in a shop that looks like an exquisite jewelry box. 4 Molsteeg (phone: 620-0017).

Condomerie "Golden Fleece" – Only in Amsterdam would you find a condom boutique/art gallery catering to the health consciousness of the 1990s. Operated by two Dutch women who provide a pleasant atmosphere, along with straight-forward information on their products. 141 Warmoestraat off the Damrak (phone: 627-4174).

Focke & Meltzer – Headquarters for famous European china and crystal since 1823. 65 P. C. Hooftstraat (phone: 664-2311).

Hajenius – "Everything for the smoker" since 1826, including custom-rolled cigars. 92-96 Rokin (phone: 623-7494).

Hema – A basic department-variety store with high-quality items and low prices on clothing, umbrellas, film, sundries, and food items. Several locations throughout the city, including 174 Nieuwendijk (phone: 624-7264) and 10 Reguliersbreestraat (phone: 624-6506).

Hoeden Atelier (Hat Studio) – Monica van Dam sells her lovely hats here, along with antique hat pins. Open Tuesdays through Saturdays from noon to 5:30 PM. 256 Prinsengracht (phone: 627-4742).

Klompenboer – You can watch wooden shoes being made here. 20 Nieuwezijds Voorburgwal (phone: 623-0632).

De Knopen Winkel – Its name means "Button Shop" and it's located on a charming shopping street behind the Royal Palace. This tiny spot has buttons of every kind — from glass to silk. Open Tuesdays through Saturdays. 14 Wolvenstraat (phone: 624-0479).

De Kookboekhandel – An infinite variety of cookbooks from around the world, many in English. Closed Sundays and Mondays. 26 Runstraat (phone: 622-4768).

Maison de Bonneterie – This elegant, chandelier-hung Amsterdam institution, dating from the 19th century, specializes in quality fashion. 183 Kalverstraat (phone: 626-2162).

Mouwes – A simple walk-in market with a variety of kosher foods. Closed Saturdays. 73 Utrechtsestraat (phone: 623-5053).

Pompon – For plants and flowers arranged and sold with a personal touch. 8 Prinsengracht (phone: 622-5137).

Porceleyne Fles – Good for Delft blue. 12 Muntplein at the base of the Munt (phone: 623-2271).

Tesselschade – Handmade dolls and typical crafts. 33 Leidseplein (phone: 623-6665).

Vroom and Dreesman – Amsterdam's second department store, carrying a wide range of goods. 201 Kalverstraat (phone: 622-0171) and other locations.

 SPORTS AND FITNESS: Sports facilities in the city are much in demand and largely restricted to members. Those listed here are open to members *and* the general public alike, but call first to make sure there's a place for you. Additional facilities outside Amsterdam are included in *The Netherlands,* DIRECTIONS.

Boating – *'t Kompas Loosdrecht,* in Loosdrecht, outside Amsterdam, has sailing equipment (phone: 2158-1431). *Robinson* (6 Dorpsstraat, Landsmeer; phone: 2809-1346) has rowing equipment.

Bowling – *Knijn,* 3 Scheldeplein (phone: 664-2211).

Cycling – There are special paths for exploring the Amsterdamse Bos woodland park south of the city, where bikes can also be rented (phone: 644-5473).

Fishing – At the *Bosbaan* in the Amsterdamse Bos, but you have to go through the formality of getting a license first, obtainable from any post office (phone: 643-1414).

Fitness Centers – The *Sonesta Splash Club* (1 Kattengat; phone: 627-1044) and the *Marriott Health Club* (21 Stadhouderskade; phone: 683-5151) are both open to the public and offer saunas, whirlpool baths, Turkish baths, and massages. The *Americain* (97 Leidsekade; phone: 624-5322) has a gym and a sauna, and the *Hôtel de l'Europe* (2-8 Nieuwe Doelen; phone: 623-4836) has a health club and a pool.

Golf – The *Amsterdam Golf Club* is at 4 Zwarte Laantje (phone: 694-3650). Non-members must bring an official handicap from their home course to play on this 9-hole green. Amsterdam's newest golf complex is *Golf Center Amstelborgh* (phone: 697-5000), 20 minutes from the city center off Highway A-2 (Amsterdam-Utrecht; Oude Kerk aan de Amstel exit). It has a 9-hole course, plus the largest driving range in Europe. Equipment is available for rental, and there is a restaurant, as well as meeting and locker rooms. Open Mondays through Fridays from 7 AM to 11 PM and on Saturdays and Sundays from 8 AM to 9 PM.

Horseback Riding – *Amsterdamse Manege* (25 Nieuwe Kalfjeslaan, Amsterdam; phone: 643-1342), has indoor and ring riding only. Horses can be rented at *Boszicht Manege* (25 Bosrandweg; phone: 641-3054).

Jogging – Try Vondel Park in the city center (entrance at Stadhouderskade and Vossiusstraat); or run along the Amstel River or in the Bos (wood) on the southern edge of town (take tram No. 12 to the river; bus Nos. 170, 171, or 172; No. 65 to the Bos).

Skating – *Jaap Eden Rink,* from November to February (64 Radioweg; phone: 694-9894) or the public Leidseplein rink, which is open only in the winter months. You also can skate on the canals in winter when they freeze over.

Soccer – Amsterdam is the home of the world-famous *Ajax* soccer team. It's easier to get tickets to heaven than to home games, but if you're feeling blessed, you always can try at *Olympic Stadium,* 20 Stadionplein (phone: 671-1115).

Swimming – The *Marnixbad* is a public pool at 5 Marnixplein (phone: 625-4843).

Tennis and Squash – *Frans Otten Stadium* has courts (10 Stadionstraat; phone: 662-8767). Indoor and outdoor courts are available at *Gold Star* (20 Karel Lotssyaan; phone: 644-5483). Squash courts are at *Squash City* (near Central Station at 6 Ketelmakerstraat; phone: 622-3575).

 THEATER: There are several resident English-language companies presenting contemporary plays in Amsterdam. One of the best is *Stalhouderij* (4 Bloemdwarsstraat; phone: 626-2282). The *Shaffy Theater* (324 Keizersgracht; phone: 623-1311) hosts dance programs and, on occasion, English groups on tour. The *Carré* (115-125 Amstel; phone: 622-5225) frequently has top international productions, performers, and groups. Current schedules are listed for all of these in the *What's On in Amsterdam* guide, and the VVV also will accept bookings (in person only). The VVV theater booking office, just in front of Central Station, is open Mondays through Saturdays from 10 AM to 4 PM.

MUSIC: The driest month for first-rate cultural events is July, when the great orchestras are touring or taking a well-earned rest, although some excellent concerts are offered during the summer at Vondel Park and at various theaters, churches, and cafés. At other times of the year, the best in classical music usually is performed at the *Concertgebouw* (98 Van Baerlestraat; phone: 671-9871), or the *Beurs van Berlage,* the former stock exchange building on the Damrak that is now home to the *Nederlands Philharmonic Orchestra* (62 Damrak; phone: 626-5257). There is a regular series of concerts, on Saturday afternoons at the English Church (in the Begijnhof; phone: 624-9665) as well as frequent concerts of all kinds at the *Waalse Church* (157 Oude Zijds Achterburgwal; phone: 623-2074), and at the *Mozes & Aaron Church* (57 Waterlooplein; phone: 622-1305). Sunday morning coffee concerts and other entertaining events take place at the *Round Lutheran Church,* now a cultural annex of the *Sonesta* hotel (1 Kattengat; phone: 621-2223). The *Ijsbreker* (23 Weesperzijde; phone: 668-1805) features new music in the classic and contemporary form, à la John Cage. The café is a popular spot and one of the best places to look out on the Amstel in warm weather. On the first Sunday of each month, the *Anthony Theater* (30 Oudezijds Voorburgwal; phone: 622-4793) in the red-light district features Yiddish music in its small, but cozy space. Pop concerts, featuring top international groups, are held at the *Jaap Edenhal* (on the Radioweg; phone: 694-9652). Rock, salsa, and new music concerts by well-known groups are held at the *Paradiso* (6 Weteringschans; phone: 626-4521), and the *Melkweg* (234 Lijnbahnsgracht; phone: 624-1777). Popular jazz clubs are *Bimhuis* (73-77 Oudeschans; phone: 623-3373), where international artists and aspirants hold sessions, and *Café Alto* (115 Korte Leidsedwarsstraat; phone: 626-3249), where good local players are showcased. Though there's no cover charge, management stands firm on the two-drinks-per-set policy. The cozy *Piano Bar Le Maxim* (35 Leidsekruisstraat; phone: 624-1920) features a variety of music. Current performances are listed in *What's On.* For bookings and further information, contact the VVV or the *Uitburo* ticket office (26 Leidseplein; phone: 621-1211).

NIGHTCLUBS AND NIGHTLIFE: The greatest concentration of cafés, nightclubs, and discotheques is around the Leidseplein, Rembrandtsplein, and adjoining Thorbeckeplein, and many clubs keep going until 3AM or later. Popular discos are *Mazzo* (114 Rozengracht; phone: 626-7500); *Escape* (11-15 Rembrandtsplein; phone: 622-3542); *Roxy* (465 Singel; phone: 620-0354); and *Juliana's,* at the *Hilton International* (138 Apollolaan; phone: 673-7313). There is generally a $5 to $20 cover charge, and at *Juliana's,* a dress code. Visitors can try their luck at the *Hilton's Casino Amsterdam* (138 Apollolaan; phone: 664-9911), or at the new *Holland Casino Amsterdam* (on Kleingartmenplantsoen, near the Leidseplein), which at press time was scheduled to open in the *Lido Complex,* a collection of shops, restaurants, and theaters.

What really distinguishes Amsterdam's nightlife is its unique cafés (highly recommended is *Amsterdam Pub Guide* by Ben ten Holter). A full listing of the best would fill this volume, but the representative sample that follows will get you started. For other recommended places, see the jazz cafés listed under *Music* and those serving food under *Eating Out. Hoppe,* dating from 1670, is the most famous and most "in" of the traditional "brown" (small, dark, Old World, intimate, lively, convivial) cafés (18-20 Spui; phone: 623-7849); *Gollem,* a minuscule place especially famed among those in the know for its wide variety of Belgian Trappist beers (4 Raamsteeg; phone: 626-6645);

Papeneiland, tracing its ancestry back to a coffin-maker who sold drinks at the beginning of the 17th century, claims to be the oldest café in Amsterdam. It is distinguished by a tunnel entrance in its cellar that formerly led under the canal and was used by 17th-century Catholics as a secret way of getting together for worship (2 Prinsengracht; phone: 624-1989). *De Klepel* has a loyal clientele that has come to play chess for the past 20 years. Light snacks are served; chamber music and jazz sessions are held on alternate Sundays, except during summer, from 5 to 8 PM (22 Prinsenstraat; phone: 623-8244). *Café de Prins* is one of the better "eet cafés" in the city. Across from the *Anne Frank House,* it is especially good for dinner or Sunday brunch (124 Prinsengracht; phone: 624-9382). *Nol* is a typical Jordaan café that comes alive nightly in a special "Old Amsterdam" way, complete with animated sing-alongs. Not to be missed if you enjoy people uninhibitedly enjoying themselves (109 Westerstraat; phone: 624-5380). For drinks mixed with music, visit *De Twee Zwaantjes,* where for several generations the local brew has been served accompanied by a song (114 Prinsengracht; phone: 625-2729). Note that most Amsterdam cafés normally close at 1 AM on weekdays, an hour later on weekends. Many serve an important function as congenial daytime gathering places as well, and quite a few start the day (with excellent coffee, if you prefer), but not until 10 or 11 AM. There also are some "night cafés" that are open from 10 PM to 3 or 4 AM. Stop in at *Koophandel,* which comes alive after 1 AM and features the best in Belgian beer, bottled or on tap (49 Bloemgracht, in the Jordaan area).

BEST IN TOWN

CHECKING IN: Visitors arriving without a hotel reservation (not recommended), should go to the VVV, which, for a nominal fee (a little over a dollar), almost always will be able to find a room in one of Amsterdam's more than 200 hotels. Reservations can be made through the Netherlands Reservation Centre (NRC; PO Box 404, Leidschendam 2260 AK, the Netherlands; phone: 70-320-2500). Note that while the larger hotels and restaurants accept major international credit cards (primarily American Express, Diners Club, MasterCard, and Visa), plastic payment is not widely accepted in Holland. (It is becoming more prevalent, however, and businesses displaying the Eurocard logo also accept MasterCard and Visa.)

The Netherlands Board of Tourism (355 Lexington Ave., New York, NY 10017; phone: 212-370-7367) offers an accommodations brochure covering all of Holland, with price categories indicated. Their Amsterdam vacation brochure is even more useful, as it includes categorized listings of hotels in the city.

Rates in most hotels vary according to the time of year and the size of individual rooms. In general, Amsterdam hotels are not inexpensive. Expect to pay $150 or more for a double room in those places listed as expensive, $80 to $100 for those we have rated moderate, and under $60 for inexpensive accommodations. All telephone numbers are in the 20 city code unless otherwise indicated.

The big international hostelries add a charge for breakfast, but the more traditional Dutch hotels still include it as part of the basic room rate. It may be either continental (coffee and rolls) or Dutch (heartier, with bread, cheese, and a soft-boiled egg).

Americain (or American) – It is difficult to explain precisely what makes this 1882 landmark right on Leidse Square so special, but its ornate Art Nouveau café-restaurant, protected as a historical monument, is certainly part of the answer. Both Dutch and visiting celebrities find their way here eventually (Madonna , Eric

Clapton, and Gloria Estefan have slept here) — as does everyone else in Amsterdam. A glass of beer, served by black-suited waiters, costs about the same as anywhere else in town and the clientele ranges from jeans-clad students to the jet set. More than any other hotel (it has 108 rooms), this one captures the indefinable essence of the city. It features a fitness center with a sauna. Business facilities include room service from 6:30 AM to midnight, meeting rooms for up to 400, foreign currency exchange, secretarial services in English, audiovisual equipment, photocopiers, computers, cable television news service, and translation services. 28 Leidseplein (phone: 623-4813; fax: 625-3236; telex: 12545). Expensive.

Amstel Inter-Continental – The grande dame of Amsterdam hotels since it opened in 1866 on the beautiful river of the same name. Celebrities and royalty stay here, and so should you if you want to find out what Old World opulence and service are really all about. The hotel has just finished renovations and will open in the spring with 80 suites, as well as a complete fitness club and a business center with meeting rooms for up to 150. 1 Professor Tulpplein (phone: 622-6060). Expensive.

Apollo – The English country-house atmosphere of this 217-room hostelry is enhanced by its lobby, which faces the water. Its special feature is a waterside bar and outdoor terrace with panoramic views of five canals. There's also a nonsmoking floor, laundry and dry cleaning services, valet, and free use of bicycles. Managed by Trusthouse Forte. Business facilities include 24-hour room service, meeting rooms for up to 200, concierge, foreign currency exchange, secretarial services in English, audiovisual equipment, photocopiers, computers, cable television news service, and translation services. 2 Apollolaan (phone: 673-5922; fax: 673-9771; telex: 14084). Expensive.

Golden Tulip Barbizon Palace – Nineteen landmark 17th-century homes that once belonged to prosperous Dutch merchants were unified and incorporated into this 268 room hotel 4 years ago. Close to the Central Station and the picturesque inner harbor, this luxury property combines some of the city's most historic façades with an ultramodern interior. Behind one of the facades once was a 15th-century sailors' flophouse called the "Monkey House." Today it houses once of the hotel's best suites. The *Vermeer* restaurant is especially good (see *Eating Out*), and the café-restaurant, *Brasseria,* serves a fine Sunday brunch. There's also a shopping arcade and fitness center. Business facilities include 24-hour room service, meeting rooms for up to 375, concierge, foreign currency exchange, secretarial services in English, audiovisual equipment, photocopiers, computers, cable television news service, translation services, and express checkout. 59-72 Prins Hendrikkade, at Zeedijk (phone: 556-4564; fax: 624-3353; telex: 10187). Expensive.

Grand – This building has quite a history, having functioned at different times as a 15th-century nunnery, the Town Hall, and the home of Medici royalty. After a complete renovation, it recently opened its doors as a 5-star deluxe hotel featuring 178 rooms, all elegantly furnished with phones, private baths, mini-bars, and color television sets. Business facilities include 24-hour room service, meeting rooms for up to 300, foreign currency exchange, a business center with secretarial services, audiovisual equipment, cable television news, and translation services. The *Admiralty* restaurant serves fish specialties. 197 Oudezijds Voorburgwal (phone: 626-1109; fax: 626-6286). Expensive.

Grand Hotel Krasnapolsky – Built at the turn of the century, over the years, the "Kras" has grown from a unique coffee shop (begun by a Polish immigrant) to an Amsterdam institution, and the complete renovation of its 330 rooms did not destroy its character or its atmosphere. Many of the spacious guestrooms offer picture-postcard views; try to book No. 1026, which overlooks Dam Square and the Royal Palace. There is a good Japanese steakhouse, and the buffet breakfast served in the winter garden is gratis to hotel guests. Business facilities include

24-hour room service, meeting rooms for up to 2,000, concierge, foreign currency exchange, secretarial services in English, audiovisual equipment, photocopiers, computers, cable television news, translation services, and express checkout. The site is on the edge of Amsterdam's red-light district, and this is the only hotel actually on the Dam, at No. 9 (phone: 554-9111; fax: 600-8607). Expensive.

Hilton International – With 265 rooms, this rather ordinary canalside hotel is decorated with some original Dutch paintings. In addition to executive floors, it offers the room that John Lennon and Yoko Ono occupied in 1969, now the "John and Yoko Honeymoon Suite," which is decorated in pure white with parts of Lennon's songs hand-painted on the ceiling; the suite also has a whirlpool bath. The hotel restaurant offers a luncheon buffet; there also is a bar, and a disco for evening entertainment. Business facilities include 24-hour room service, meeting rooms for up to 630, concierge, foreign currency exchange, secretarial services in English, audiovisual equipment, photocopiers, computers, cable television news service, translation services, and express checkout. 138 Apollolaan (phone: 678-0780; fax: 662-6688). Expensive.

Holiday Inn Crowne Plaza – The first deluxe European property opened by the ubiquitous American chain began operations in 1987 with 270 rooms, which were recently redecorated. Right in the city center. Amenities include a health club, swimming pool, 2 saunas, whirlpool bath, several restaurants, a lobby bar, and a typical Dutch café. Business facilities include 24-hour room service, meeting rooms for up to 250, concierge, foreign currency exchange, secretarial services in English, audiovisual equipment, photocopiers, computers, cable television news service, translation services, and express checkout. 5 Nieuwezijds Voorburgwal (phone: 620-0500; fax: 620-1173). Expensive.

Hôtel de l'Europe – An honorable alternative to the *Amstel,* this elegant Belle Epoque, 180-room establishment traces its origins to a fortress built in 1481 to defend the city. It was completely rebuilt in 1895 and has retained the grandeur of that extravagant period. Its waterside restaurant, the *Excelsior,* serves fine continental fare (see *Eating Out*), and a second dining spot, *La Terrace,* has a patio, offering an Amstel River view. The hotel has a health club and a pool. Business facilities include 24-hour room service, meeting rooms for up to 500, concierge, foreign currency exchange, audiovisual equipment, photocopiers, computers, and cable television news service. 2-8 Nieuwe Doelenstraat (phone: 623-4836; fax: 624-2962; telex: 12081). Expensive.

Okura – A 23-story hotel with 768 beds, owned and operated by a Japanese concern. The *Ciel Bleu Penthouse* features French food to accompany a panoramic view; there is also a fine sushi bar and a Japanese grillroom, plus 2 coffee shops, a sauna, and a shopping arcade. Business facilities include 24-hour room service, meeting rooms for up to 1,250, concierge, foreign currency exchange, secretarial services in English, audiovisual equipment, photocopiers, computers, cable television news service, translation services, and express checkout. At 333 Ferdinand Bolstraat (phone: 678-7111; fax: 671-2344). Expensive.

Pulitzer – Between 1968 and 1971 Peter Pulitzer, the grandson of US newspaper mogul Joseph Pulitzer, converted a group of 24 historic canal houses into an attractive mix of old and new. The 241 rooms and 8 apartments are modern, but by no means uniform, since their layout has been determined by the original architecture. The original roof beams also have been retained. Guests can enjoy (for a fee) the afternoon champagne cruise in the hotel's canal boat, which is docked right out front. Business facilities include 24-hour room service, meeting rooms for up to 160, foreign currency exchange, secretarial services in English, audiovisual equipment, photocopiers, computers, cable television news service, and translation services. 315-331 Prinsengracht (phone: 523-5235). Expensive.

SAS Royal – Opened in the spring of 1990, it's in the heart of Amsterdam. Offering luxury with a Scandinavian flair, it has 250 rooms and 15 suites, a 7-story atrium with a Japanese garden and waterfall, a restaurant, café, and bar. The presidential suite has its own sauna. Operated by *SAS Airlines,* the hotel has an *SAS* check-in counter. Business facilities include 24-hour room service, meeting rooms for up to 250, concierge, foreign currency exchange, secretarial services in English, audio-visual equipment, photocopiers, computers, cable television news service, translation services, and express checkout. Between the Dam and the opera house, just 5 minutes from the Rokin, 13 Russland (phone: 520-8300; fax: 520-8200). Expensive.

Scandic Crown Victoria – Across from the Central Station, this property has been in existence since 1890 and was recently taken over by the Scandic Crown chain, which renovated the hotel and added a new wing and business center. Luxury, comfort, and friendly service are emphasized. The 321 rooms all have a telephone, color TV set, mini-bar, private bath, radio, hair dryer, and trouser press. Some rooms are reserved for nonsmokers and disabled guests. There's a Swedish restaurant serving smörgasbord, a terrace café, and a comfortable bar. The fitness center has complete facilities, including a swimming pool, sauna, solarium, and Turkish bath. Underground parking is just opposite the hotel. Business facilities include foreign currency exchange, secretarial services in English, and cable television news service. 1-6 Damrak (phone: 623-4255; fax: 625-2997; telex: 16625). Expensive to moderate.

Ambassade – A pleasant, old-fashioned, traditional Dutch hotel whose 46 rooms, all with baths, telephones, and TV sets, are in a historic canal house furnished with antiques. About three-quarters of the rooms are now accessible by elevator. Business facilities include 24-hour room service, foreign currency exchange, and photocopiers. 341 Herengracht (phone: 626-2333; fax: 624-5321). Moderate.

Classic – Housed in a former distillery in the city center between the Damrak and the Royal Palace, this is one of Amsterdam's newer hotels. The 33 rooms have private bath, phone, color TV sets, and radios. 14-16 Gravenstraat (phone: 623-3716; fax: 638-1156). Moderate.

Concert Inn – Just opposite the century-old *Concertgebouw* (Concert Hall), this family-run hotel has 24 rooms with private bath, telephone, color TV set, and mini-bar. 11 De Lairessestraat (phone: 675-0051; fax: 675-3934). Moderate.

Dikker & Thijs – In the heart of the city by the Leidseplein, this unique hostelry has only 25 rooms with private bath, color TV sets, telephones, mini-bars, and radios. Under the same roof are three famous eateries in a restaurant/brasserie/delicatessen complex. Service is personal and friendly. 444 Prinsengracht (phone: 626-7721; fax: 625-8986; telex: 13161). Moderate.

Jan Luyken – In the heart of the concert and museum quarter, this first class 63-room hotel combines modern amenities with traditional Dutch hospitality. Room service from 7 AM to 11 PM. 54-58 Jan Luykenstraat (phone: 573-0730 or 573-0717; fax: 676-3841). Moderate.

Pullman Hotel Capitool – Centrally located opposite a tram line just minutes from the Central Station and historic Amsterdam, it offers a variety of rooms and suites, including some for handicapped guests. The high-ceilinged guestrooms have private bath, color TV set, telephone, mini-bar, radio, trouser press, and hair dryer. The fitness room has a sauna and solarium. A Dutch buffet breakfast is included in the rate. The hotel's social center is the plush *Pullman Bar,* fitted out with the original fittings taken from grand old trains — the drinks are named after famous trains of the past. Business facilities include concierge, meeting rooms for up to 200, foreign currency exchange, secretarial services in English, audiovisual equipment, and photocopiers. 67 Nieuwezijds Voorburgwal (phone: 627-5900; fax: 623-8932; telex: 14494). Moderate.

Toren – Centrally located near the historic Jordaan quarter and minutes from the *Anne Frank House,* it features comfortable, clean rooms and a bar/restaurant. Rates include breakfast. 164 Keizersgracht (phone: 622-6352; fax: 626-7905). Moderate.

Wiechmann – Owned by a former Oklahoman, a Mr. Boddy, this 30-room hotel (only 12 rooms have bath or shower) is friendly, comfortable, and reasonable. It has a bar and a breakfast room; no elevator. 328-330 Prinsengracht (phone: 626-3321; fax: 626-8962). Moderate.

Roemer Visscher – Just minutes from the Leidseplein shops and restaurants, this unique hotel offers studio-parlor rooms equipped with telephones, color TV sets, and private baths. 10 Roemer Visscherstraat (phone: 612-5511; telex: 12326). Moderate to inexpensive.

Esperance – A small (6 rooms) family hostelry, between the *Rijksmuseum* and the Heineken Brewery. Room rates include breakfast. 49 Stadhouderskade (phone: 671-4049). Inexpensive.

Hoksbergen – Situated on the beautiful Singel Canal in the heart of the city, the rooms have private bath with shower, TV sets, and telephones. 301 Singel (phone: 626-6043). Inexpensive.

Keizershof – A true Dutch atmosphere is offered at this cozy and friendly 6-room hostelry operated by the De Vries family. The 17th-century house, located on the picturesque Keizersgracht Canal, has a spiral staircase connecting 4 floors (alas, no elevator), and there is a grand piano in the parlor. A tasty Dutch breakfast is included in the rates. 618 Keizersgracht (phone: 622-2855). Inexpensive.

Singel – Converted from a 17th-century house on the Singel Canal, this stylish hostelry has modern rooms with private bath, telephone, and color TV set. Dutch breakfast is included. 13 Singel (phone: 626-3108; fax: 620-3777). Inexpensive.

EATING OUT: Amsterdam is justly famed for its restaurants — more than 200 specializing in foreign food alone — and especially renowned for its Indonesian import, rijsttafel (rice table). In a traditional rijsttafel, the ceremonial Indonesian feast adopted by Dutch colonials, a large dish of rice is surrounded by up to 20 smaller dishes of meat and chicken with a variety of sauces, prawns, meat kebabs (or *satay*) in peanut sauce, fried bananas, cucumber in sour sauce — and many, many other dishes, some spicy and some bland. It is a treat. If you want lighter fare, try *bami goreng,* stir-fried noodles with strips of vegetables and meat, or *nasi goreng,* a plate of rice with vegetables and meat. All are served in Amsterdam's ubiquitous Indonesian restaurants, and some can be modified for vegetarians.

Traditional Dutch foods and drinks also should be sampled. You probably already are familiar with gouda and edam, the popular Dutch cheeses. Vendors in the many open-air stalls around the city also hawk salted raw herring, a Dutch favorite, for about $2. Dutch dishes also worth sampling are the snackfoods *poffertjes,* which are small pancakes normally served with ice cream or a fruit topping, or *pannekoeken,* larger crêpe-like concoctions with toppings of rum or liqueur. Either of these is wonderful with just a bit of butter and sugar, and stands offering these delicious treats exist all around Amsterdam.

Meals in Holland are designed to stick to your ribs and to warm you in winter. Especially good in cold weather (if you need an excuse) is classic Dutch split-pea soup, or *erwtensoep.* Also good are *capucijners,* an indigenous Dutch bean; Dutch beef stew (*hutspot*); and kale with potatoes and sausage (*boerenkool met rookworst*).

Dutch beer is almost uniformly excellent, although many afficionados prefer the rich variety of Trappist beers from Belgium and the ales from Germany. The native liquor is *jenever* (gin); *oude jenever* is aged gin, milder and mellower; *jonge jenever* is stronger and plainer in taste.

For the best in inexpensive eating, try one of our recommended cafés ($20 or less for two) or a traditional *broodjeswinkel* (sandwich shop, not to be confused with modern junk-food snack bars). There are, too, window snack bars that sell Dutch fast-food, such as croquettes and *satays*.

At the restaurants we have rated as expensive, be prepared to part with $115 or more for a complete dinner for two, including wine and coffee. You can get away with considerably less, however, if you choose carefully from the varied menus. Places in the moderate category range between $50 and $75 for everything; at those listed as inexpensive, expect to pay about $35 (with the simplest about half that).

Note that any restaurant displaying the blue Tourist Menu sign (there are several in Amsterdam) must provide a three-course meal for the fixed price of about $10 to $12 (not including drinks). In Amsterdam, service charges and local taxes are usually included in the bill. All places accept major credit cards, unless otherwise indicated. All telephone numbers are in the 20 city code.

Beddington's – Jeanne Beddington has been called a chef's chef because of her innovative cuisine. The room has clean modern lines and does not upstage the food in this "power" dining spot. Open for lunch Tuesdays through Fridays; for dinner, Mondays through Saturdays. Reservations necessary. 6-8 Roelof Hartstraat (phone: 676-5201). Expensive.

Christophe – This intimate, decidedly chic restaurant has earned one Michelin star. Closed Sundays. Reservations necessary. 46 Leliegracht (phone: 625-0807). Expensive.

De Dikkert – A 300-year-old windmill just outside the city limits in bordering Amstelveen is the setting for surprisingly elegant fare. The menu changes with the seasons, but this is a good place to sample game and fowl and, in the spring, try the white asparagus "prepared any way you like." The interior decor is warm and comfortable — tables set spaciously apart — and the service able and friendly. Closed Sundays. Major credit cards accepted. 104a Amsterdamseweg (phone: 411378). Expensive.

Excelsior – Imaginatively prepared food that has been awarded a star from Michelin is served at this stylish restaurant set on the waterside overlooking the Amstel. The vegetarian can dine well here; try the vegetable consommé. There is a fine wine list and tempting desserts. Open daily for lunch and dinner. Reservations necessary. In the *Hotel de l'Europe;* 2-8 Nieuwe Doelenstraat (phone: 623-4836). Expensive.

Halvemaan – Considered one of Amsterdam's best chef's for decades, John Halvemaan has opened a waterside dining establishment in the Amsterdam suburbs. It has the tranquillity of a Japanese tearoom and a kitchen inspired by France, Italy, and the Orient. Halvemaan's wife, Esther, is responsible for the beautiful interior, including a half-moon motif in homage to their translated name. Open Mondays through Fridays for both lunch and dinner; open Saturdays for dinner only. Reservations essential. In the suburb of Buitenveldert; 20 Van Leyenberghlaan (phone: 644-0348). Expensive.

De Kersentuin (Cherry Orchard) – Quintessential nouvelle cuisine (with many ingredients flown in daily from France) served in the lush surroundings of a room out of a Chekhov play. Food, service, and decor are among the most distinctive in town. One Michelin star. Open weekdays for lunch, daily except Sundays for dinner. Reservations advised. In the *Garden Hotel,* 7 Dijsselhofplantsoen (phone: 664-2121). Expensive.

De Trechter – Call for a reservation the minute you arrive in town and perhaps you will be lucky enough to get one of the nine tables at this haute cuisine French restaurant. Chef Jan de Wit has already earned this establishment one Michelin star and is working on a second. Every dish is cooked to order — and to perfection. The service is excellent and the wine list versatile and fairly priced. Dinner only; closed Sundays and Mondays. Reservations necessary. 63 Hobbemakade (phone: 671-1263). Expensive.

Vermeer – The pride of the *Golden Tulip Barbizon Palace,* this elegant dining room's decor was inspired by the master painter, and much of the original 17th-century atmosphere has been retained. Seasonal fish and game dishes are the specialty, and there is an extensive wine list, which includes a variety of half-bottles and champagnes. Open daily from 6:30 PM. Reservations necessary. Prins Hendrikkade (phone: 556-4564). Expensive.

Silveren Spiegel – Picturesque and charming are the only words to describe this intimate, antiques-furnished dining place set in two very crooked houses dating from 1614. The food is international; the service, excellent. Ask the owner-host Ben van de Nieuwboer to make a selection from the impressive wine list, since he is a respected wine expert. Closed Sundays. Reservations advised. 4 Kattengat (phone: 624-6589). Expensive to moderate.

D'Vijff Vlieghen (Five Flies) – It's a bit of an adventure just finding this place, which is owned by the *Grand Hotel Krasnapolsky.* The main door doesn't open, so you must enter by way of a side street, called D'Vijff Vlieghen. Once inside, you are transported to the 17th century by a series of delightful dining rooms built in that era, complete with real Rembrandt drawings on the walls. Try the typical Dutch dishes using fresh, local ingredients. Up a steep set of stairs is an intimate *jenever* bar. Open daily for dinner. Reservations advised. 294 Spuistraat (phone: 624-8369). Expensive to moderate.

Café Luxembourg – On the historic Spui square, its menu features appetizers supplied by top restaurants in the city and good wines by the glass. Open daily. No reservations. 22 Spui (phone: 620-6264). Moderate.

Corneille – Fine French food is served in elegant, yet simple, surroundings. Good wines, fair prices, and attentive service. Dinner only; closed Sundays and Mondays. Reservations advised. 25 Herenstraat (phone: 638-0148). Moderate.

Entrecôte – True to its name, this elegant spot on Amsterdam's stylish shopping street serves fine beef and veal, which comes with a salad and crispy *pommes frites.* Dinner only; closed Sundays and Mondays. Reservations advised. 70 P. C. Hooftstraat (phone: 673-7776). Moderate.

L'Entresol – Between Central Station and the red-light district, it features authentic Flemish food and attracts a loyal clientele. Open Wednesdays through Sundays for dinner only. Reservations advised. 29 Geldersekade (phone: 623-7912). Moderate.

Oesterbar – This is the place for serious fish eaters: nothing fancy, just remarkably fresh fish and shellfish of all kinds, cooked simply, but to perfection. Solo diners can enjoy a meal seated at the counter near the ovens or at the one near the fish tanks. If you prefer eating at a conventional table, reserve one downstairs. Open daily. Reservations advised. 10 Leidseplein (phone: 623-2988). Moderate.

Pier 10 – Just behind the Central Station, it's set dockside and serves first-rate international fare. Open daily for lunch and dinner. Reservations advised. 10 De Ruyterkade Steiger (phone: 624-8276). Moderate.

Le Provençal – French lunch and dinner specialties, premium service, and pleasant atmosphere. Open weekdays for lunch, daily for dinner. Reservations advised.

Opposite the *Rijksmuseum* near the Spiegelgracht, at 91 Weteringschans (phone: 623-9619). Moderate.

Tom Yam – A trip to the Far East inspired respected chef Jos Boomgardt to open this elegant Thai eatery, which offers five different menus. Open daily, except Mondays, for dinner. Reservations advised. 22 the Staalstraat (phone: 622-9533). Moderate.

De Blauwe Hollander – It features authentic cooking just as any Dutch grandmother makes, from a typical *hutsput* (a stew made with leeks, carrots, potatoes, and beef) to the classic mashed potatoes and endives. Open daily for dinner. Reservations advised. In the Leidseplein district, 28 Leidsekruistraat (phone: 623-3014). Moderate to inexpensive.

Café Descartes – An authentic French place hidden in the *Maison Descartes* cultural center, it seats 25-30 patrons in the 17th-century building's original kitchen. Soup, salads, and house specialties such as *coq au vin,* rabbit stew, and cassoulet are offered at café prices. Lunch and dinner menu changes daily. Closed weekends. Reservations advised. Next to the French consulate at 2 Vijzelgracht (phone: 622-1913). Moderate to inexpensive.

Lonny's – Here is elegant dining, reasonably priced. Lonny is one of the city's veteran chefs. Take-out available. Open daily for dinner. Reservations advised. 48 Rozengracht (phone: 623-8950). Moderate to inexpensive.

Sluizer – The good, solid fish served in this Old World restaurant with marble-topped tables and fringed lampshades makes it popular with Amsterdammers and visitors alike. The restaurant next door shares the same name and offers a menu with meat dishes. In warm weather, patrons can dine on the terrace in a secluded garden. Open daily. No reservations. 45 Utrechtsestraat (phone: 626-3557). Moderate to inexpensive.

Toscanini – Simple Italian food is served in a simpatico environment where the pasta is more interesting than the main dishes, and the Italian wines are fairly priced. Closed Tuesdays. Reservations necessary since the place almost always is full of loyal regulars. 52 Goudsbloemstraat (phone: 623-2813). Moderate to inexpensive.

La Baguette – Just a bridge away from the Rembrandtsplein, this *croissanterie-potagerie* specializes in sandwiches and soup in the French style. Open daily. No reservations. No credit cards accepted. 534 Herengracht (phone: 625-0853). Inexpensive.

Broodje van Kootje – The most famous of Amsterdam's traditional sandwich shops. The food is varied, wholesome, and inexpensive. Recommended for a quick lunch or snack. For breakfast, try an *uitsmijter* (basically a ham or beef sandwich topped with a fried egg). Open daily from 9:30 AM to 1:30 AM. No reservations. No credit cards accepted. 20 Leidseplein (phone: 232046), 12 Rembrandtsplein (phone: 623-6513) and 28 Spui (phone: 623-7451). Inexpensive.

Green Cuisine – Run by a savvy mother and son, this spot features excellent fish and vegetarian dishes with ethnic variations. Dinner only; closed Tuesdays. Reservations unnecessary. No credit cards accepted. 9 Beulingstraat (phone: 627-5755). Inexpensive.

Greenwoods – A little oasis set along an Amsterdam canal, this café is operated by two ladies from Australia and England who serve breakfast, lunch, and afternoon tea with all the trimmings. It's a good place for a quick and healthy bite between sightseeing excursions. Open Mondays through Fridays from 10 AM to 7 PM, and on Saturdays and Sundays from 11 AM to 7 PM. No reservations. 103 Singel (phone: 230-7071). Inexpensive.

Pancake Corner – Plate-size pancakes are served with a variety of toppings. Also worth a try is the kettle of mussels, served with salad and *pommes frites.* Open daily for lunch and dinner. No reservations. Across from the Leidseplein, 51 Kleine Gartmanplantsoen (phone: 627-6303). Inexpensive.

Poentjak Pas – The place serves one of the best *rijsttafels* in the city, as well as other Indonesian dishes. Also try the omelette with vegetables or the spicy string beans. Open daily (except Mondays) for dinner only. No reservations. 366 Nassaukade, by the Leidseplein (phone: 618-0906). Inexpensive.

Pompadour – A plush tearoom in which to sample handmade chocolates by the piece and creamy pastries made daily. Closed Sundays. No reservations. No credit cards accepted. 12 Huidenstraat (phone: 623-9554). Inexpensive.

Sie Joe – An Indonesian snack shop near Dam Square, it's a good place to experiment before taking on a large *rijsttafel* (rice table). Try the *satay* (skewers of beef or chicken with a spicy peanut sauce) or the *bami goreng*. Open from 11 AM to 7 PM; closed Sundays. No reservations. No credit cards accepted. 24 Gravenstraat (phone: 624-1830). Inexpensive.

ATHENS

Athens is the site of the greatest achievements of the classical age of Greece. Its architectural, social, artistic, and political triumphs have become a universal legacy. Against its ancient standards are measured the cultural, intellectual, and spiritual development of all Western civilizations.

In Athens the units of this measure are everywhere apparent. Drive down a wide thoroughfare and you pass the Temple of the Olympian Zeus, masterfully carved Corinthian columns still intact, honoring the highest of Greek gods. Turn a corner in *Monastiraki,* the flea market, and you come upon the Agora, the ancient marketplace crowned by the Theseion, one of the best-preserved Doric temples, sacred to blacksmiths, who worked here 2,000 years ago; follow the Panathenaic Way, the grand ceremonial path of Ancient Athens, and like centuries of Athenians before you, you approach the Acropolis, the crown of Greek culture high on a rock above Athens.

For more than 2,000 years the Acropolis has dominated the city — first as a spiritual center and fortress; later as the site of the Parthenon, a temple honoring Athena, the patron goddess of Athens; still later as the locus of churches, mosques, and even harems as it was transformed by different conquerors. Today, stripped of the many statues that once lined the way, with drums and columns strewn about, the Acropolis remains, even in ruins, majestic and monumental.

The setting inspires contemplation, its starkness somehow appropriate. Bared to its essentials, you can only imagine the golden age of Greece (in the middle of the 5th century BC) when Pericles had the Parthenon built — every column curving slightly inward in order to appear perfectly straight at a distance — when the dramas of Aeschylus and Sophocles were performed for the first time in the Theater of Dionysus below; when democracy first brought all citizens together to decide their common fate on the Pnyx hill to the west.

The Acropolis commands an excellent view of the surrounding Attic plain and overlapping layers of Western civilization. Immediately below the walls lies the Agora; adjacent is the Plaka district, the 19th-century area frequented by Lord Byron when he lived in Athens. In the distance to the north rises Mt. Parnes, the highest mountain in Attica, and Mt. Pentelikon, where Pentelic marble is quarried. Between the mountains spreads the Mesogheia Valley, where grapes for resinated wine (*retsina*) are harvested. To the south lies the Saronic Gulf; slightly west of there a smokestack marks the offshore island of Salamis, where the Greeks defeated the Persians in the famous naval battle of 480 BC.

To the east lies the modern city, spread out around the Acropolis almost like an afterthought. Planned by German architects for King Otto in 1840, Athens was designed to accommodate a maximum of 200,000 people. Today some 3.5 million people inhabit greater Athens, which extends past the port of Piraeus. Most roads are narrow and inadequate for the ever-increasing number of automobiles. Traffic is horrendous, with streets congested during seemingly interminable rush hours. The indefatigable breeze blowing in from the sea doesn't manage to keep the air fresh, for Athens is blanketed, winter and summer, with *nefos,* a hazy and hazardous cloud of pollution. To combat both the traffic and pollution problems, only half of Athens's vehicles are permitted into the city's center on any given day (odd license-plate numbers on odd-numbered days, even numbers on even days). In addition, many narrow downtown streets are being converted to pedestrian walkways. Mayor Antonis Tritsisma has announced plans to further improve the city's environment by building an archaeological park that will link the city's main historical structures, adding an electric streetcar system, and banning many vehicles from driving on downtown streets. In the meantime, more greenery has been added, and the government is striving to provide cleaner fuel.

Although the city's intransigently modern problems have yet to be completely resolved, the splendid natural advantages here still draw hordes of visitors. Athens's perfect Mediterranean climate — the sun shines brilliantly most of the year and the air is dry even in midsummer — endows the city with a relaxed atmosphere and outlook.

Athenians embrace their environment with relish. The cream-colored, terraced marble apartments built into the hills are sunny and airy. Athenians take to the beaches lining the coasts year-round for sun, sea, and vigorous, noisy games. As early as April, a few leathery-looking old men paddle around in the water — and are joined by everyone else quite comfortably from May to October. In Syntagma (Constitution), Kolonaki, and Fokionos Negri Squares, residents spend hours over cups of coffee — the thick, muddy Greek variety — discussing life and politics or just people watching. Athenian workers break in the afternoons for a few hours, return to work, and head out to dinner quite late, about 10 PM. Even on weeknights, *tavernas* — informal restaurants — are full past midnight. In many *bouzoukia* — nightclubs in which traditional bouzouki music is played — the entertainment does not really start until midnight. Despite the big-city veneer, people take their time.

Travelers will find this both engaging and perplexing. The lifestyle is quite pleasant, but it takes its toll on the economy. Greece has mastered a few industries — its shipping fleet is the largest in the world, and tourism has been a well-organized business — but still Greece has one of the lowest gross national products among the major countries in Europe. A member of the European Economic Community (EEC) only since January 1, 1981, Greece entered as its tenth and poorest member. Greek economic analysts hoped that this action would boost the economy. But Greek industries and workers, previously sheltered by import restrictions, now face stiffer competition from Common Market countries, and the government is balking continually at conforming to standing EEC regulations, many of which favor the northern European members. However, some benefits are beginning to roll in, and Greece stands to obtain billions of dollars worth of agricultural and regional development subsidies from the newly integrated European economy.

The most populous and advanced city in Greece, Athens is caught between the incongruities of a valiant past and a problematic present. The dilemma

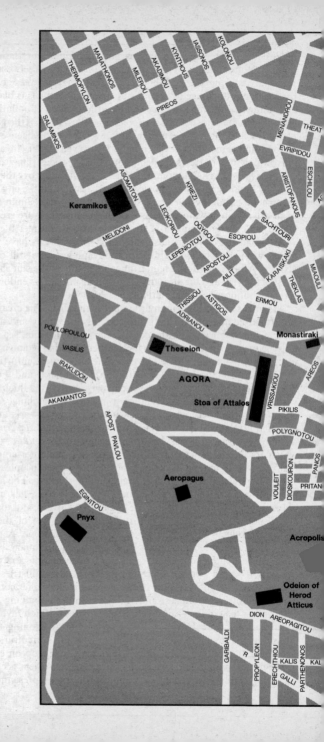

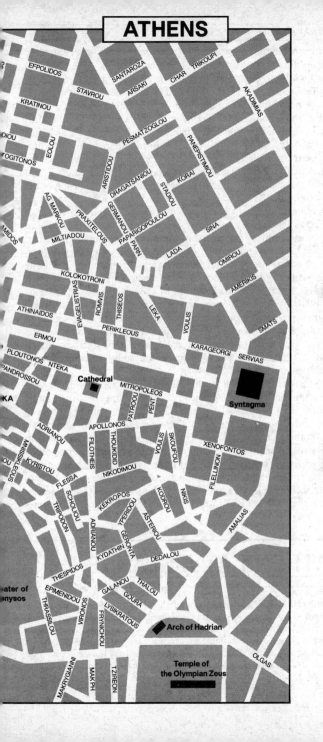

ATHENS

EFPOLIDOS
SANTAROZA
CHAR TRIKOUPI
KRATINOU
STAVROU
ARSAKI
AKADIMAS
EOLOU
PESMATZOGLOU
DIOU
PANEPISTIMIOU
OGITONOS
ARISTIDOU
DRAGATSANIOU
KORAI
STADIOU
AG. MARKOU
PRAXITELOUS
GERMANOU
PAPARIGOPOULOU
SINA
AMIDOS
MILTIADOU
PAPN
LADA
OMIROU
KOLOKOTRONI
AMERIKIS
ATHINAIDOS
EVAGELISTRIAS
ROMVIS
THISEOS
LEKA
ERMOU
PERIKLEOUS
VOULIS
SMATS
PLOUTONOS
NTEKA
KARAGEORGI
SERVIAS
PANDROSSOU
Cathedral
MITROPOLEOS
KA
PATROU
PENT
Syntagma
ADRIANOU
APOLLONOS
THOUKIDID
STILIOU
XENOFONTOS
MNISIKLEOUS
FILOTHEIS
SKOUFOU
KYRISTOU
NIKODIMOU
FLELLINON
OU
FLESSA
KEKROPOS
NIKIS
SCHOLIOU
YPERIDOU
KOUROU
TRIPODON
ADRIANOU
ASTERIOU
AMALIAS
KYDATHIN
GERONTA
DEDALOU
THESPIDOS
EPIMENIDOU
GALANOU
THALOU
ater of
VIRONOS
GOURA
onysos
THRASSILOU
FRYNICHOU
LYSIKRATOUS
Arch of Hadrian
MAKRYGIANNI
MAKPH
TZIREON
OLGAS
**Temple of
the Olympian Zeus**

is in part historic. After the classical age of Greece, Athens was conquered and dominated by foreign powers. Though the early rulers were relatively benign, Athens lost the freedom and democratic structure that nurtured its greatest cultural achievements. First conquered by the Macedonians and later by the Romans, Athens remained an important seat of learning until the Edict of Justinian closed the schools of philosophy in AD 529. Under Byzantine rule, many temples were modified for Christian use, and Athens became just another provincial city. After the fall of Constantinople in 1453, the Ottomans seized the city and ruled for almost 400 years, during which time the most sacred sites of the Acropolis were damaged and desecrated.

Athens became the capital of a liberated Greece after the conclusion of the War of Independence in 1829. The country suffered heavy loss of life during the Nazi occupation of 1941–45 and again during the Greek Civil War of 1946. It was ruled as a monarchy until 1967, when King Constantine fled after failing to topple the military dictatorship established earlier in the year. Papadopoulos and his junta endured for 7 long, bitter years; a civilian government finally was restored in 1974 and the monarchy abolished by plebiscite in favor of a republic. With the election of Andreas Papandreou in 1981, Greece had its first Socialist government. But by the late 1980s, the administration was troubled by economic woes and political and personal and scandals. Elections in April 1990 brought a conservative, pro-Western regime to power. Measures are being taken by Prime Minister Constantine Mitsotakis of the New Democracy party to rescue the economy in time for the evolving single European market: Taxes and food prices are going up, while school budgets and salaries are being cut.

In a sense, Athens has come full circle. Though its ancient history is very ancient indeed, Athens is entirely new as a modern democracy, with an almost burdensome history and a future still unmade. Perhaps this split in its history has created the ambivalent nature of modern Athens — a city somewhat overshadowed by the glories of its past. Greece in general — and Athens in particular — has had more than its share of contemporary problems, many of them a by-product of the geographic fact of being very near the center of the world's most virulent and violent conflicts. But the determined government is urgently seeking solutions that are consistent with the Greek view of the globe. While they still remain to be found, the will to search continues to be strong.

ATHENS AT-A-GLANCE

SEEING THE CITY: Lycabettus, the city's highest hill, opens up a panorama of Athens — Syntagma Square and the National Gardens, the Acropolis and its surrounding hills, and in the distance, the Saronic Gulf. The 912-foot summit is crowned by the tiny 19th-century chapel of St. George, visible from other parts of the city and worth a closer look. A café halfway up and a restaurant at the top provide unsurpassed views, refreshments, and meals. Approaches to the summit include roads, a funicular, and footpaths that afford ever-expanding views of

Athens. Open daily (the funicular operates from 8 AM to midnight). Entrance at Ploutarchou and Aristipou in Kolonaki (no phone). Accessible by bus No. 023 from Kaningos and Kolonaki Squares, but walking is a more scenic alternative for the energetic.

SPECIAL PLACES: Most of the interesting sights of Athens are within easy walking distance of one another. Archaeological sites are concentrated around the Acropolis. The narrow, winding streets of the immediately adjacent areas of the Plaka district and *Monastiraki* lend themselves to walking. The National Gardens, with its maze of winding, tree-lined paths, also is a pleasant place to walk (see below). Syntagma Square, the center of modern Athens, is a 20-minute walk or short cab ride away.

Acropolis – Dominating the Athenian landscape, this monument of Western civilization is unsurpassed in its beauty, architectural splendor, and historical importance. Situated on a massive 512-foot-high limestone rock, 300 feet above the general level of the city, this naturally strategic location has been inhabited since neolithic times. In about 1500 BC, a Mycenean ruler crowned the height with a citadel; during the same period, the first in a series of temples honoring Athena, the goddess of the city, was built — a tradition that continued over the centuries. In 480 BC, the Persians sacked the city and destroyed the Acropolis. Some 35 years later, Pericles, the renowned Athenian statesman, conceived a plan to rebuild the Acropolis on a grand scale as the true capital of Greek civilization. Under the direction of the architects Iktinos and Kallikrates, structures were erected that endure today. The Propylea, the monumental entrance on the west, was constructed between 449 and 444 BC. Though the roof was destroyed by a Venetian cannon volley in 1687, the rows of columns — Doric on the outside (without bases) and Ionic on the inside (with bases and more elaborate capitals) — still line the way. On the south side of the Propylea stands the temple of the Wingless Victory, Athena Nike, built between 425 and 422 BC in monolithic Ionic columns. On the north side of the entrance is a Roman tower built in the 1st century AD as a votive offering by Agrippa, nephew of Emperor Augustus.

Beyond the Propylea, on the highest part of the hill, stands the Parthenon, the main temple of the Acropolis, built between 447 and 432 BC of white Pentelic marble. This is the virgin Athena's most sacred temple, and everything about it is a celebration of perfect order, from its Doric columns to the metopes — friezes with reliefs of mythological battles — that decorate it. The Greek government continues to wage a feisty campaign, fraught with much bureaucracy, against the *British Museum* in London to get it to return many missing metopes, taken by Lord Elgin nearly 200 years ago and now called the Elgin marbles. From a distance the columns appear perfectly parallel and straight, an illusion that is sustained only by a minor miracle of engineering, the turning of each column slightly inward to create an image of perfect harmony. To the north is the Erechtheion, a temple honoring both Athena and Poseidon, god of the sea, who in ancient times lost out to Athena in the battle for the worship of the Athenians. The Ionic structure contains several architectural novelties, including the Karyatids, sculptures of lovely maidens that support a porch and stylized sculptural decor of little friezes of palm flowers between the capitals and columns that influenced the later Corinthian style. Because of environmental damage, five of the six original Karyatids have been replaced by copies. Four of the originals can be seen at the *Acropolis Museum.* Athena is the patron of Athens because she gave mankind the gift of the olive, and her olive tree stands at the west side of the temple; a saltwater spring to represent Poseidon is said to have sprung inside the temple in ancient times. Close inspection of the supporting wall directly north of the Erechtheion reveals several drums that survive from the first Acropolis; their purpose is to keep alive the memory of the catastrophic sack of Athens by the Persians.

Over the years, the Acropolis has undergone many alterations at the hands of conquerors. The Parthenon and the Erechtheion were converted into churches during the Byzantine era. During the Turkish occupation, the Parthenon was used as a mosque and the Erechtheion as a harem.

Even today, air pollution and the high sulfur content of rainwater are turning the marble to soft gypsum. The work of reconstruction is well under way. Rehabilitation of the Erechtheion has been completed; the limestone Acropolis rock base is being stabilized; architects began a 10-year renovation of the Parthenon in 1983 and soon will follow with reconstruction of the Propylea. Despite hardships, the Acropolis has endured thousands of years as one of the highest accomplishments of Western civilization.

The *Acropolis Museum* houses most of the works of art discovered in the Acropolis since excavation began in 1835. Highlights of the collection include fragments of the Parthenon frieze and numerous sculptures — the *Kritian Boy,* the *Calf Bearer,* the *Rider and the Running Hound,* and the *Kourai* maidens. Open weekdays from 8 AM to 5 PM, weekends from 8:30 AM to 3 PM. Admission charge. Entrance on Areopagitou St. (phone: 321-0219). From Syntagma Square, take bus No. 230 from Amalias Avenue and Othonos Street, or take a leisurely walk there, as done in ancient times.

Pnyx – This hill on the west side of the Acropolis, which now serves as the theater for the sound and light show, is the true cradle of Athenian democracy. Here, in classical times, Athenians assembled to decide issues. All free male citizens were summoned to the hill. Officers carrying ropes covered with fresh paint would round up those who didn't come and mark them so that they could be identified and fined. No such penalties are incurred today for those who don't attend the sound and light show. The script delivers a dramatized history of the Acropolis in ridiculously overblown language. But the view of the Acropolis is spectacular. Shows in English are held nightly at 9 PM from April 1 to October 31. Admission charge. Entrance on Areopagitou St. opposite the Acropolis.

Areopagus – The highest court of ancient Athens convened on this hill below the Acropolis. According to Aeschylus, Orestes was tried here for the murder of his mother, Klytemnestra. The jury split and Athena broke the tie by throwing her support behind Orestes. Legend has it that he had been chased by the Furies — mythological creatures with women's heads and birds' bodies. In AD 51, St. Paul delivered his Sermon of the Unknown God from this site. Open daily. No admission charge. Just below the west slope of the Acropolis.

Mouseion Hill – In 1687, a Venetian cannon fired from this hill severely damaged the Parthenon. At the top, there's a monument of Philopappos, a prominent Athenian of the 2nd century AD. Open daily. No admission charge. Areopagitou west of the Acropolis.

Hephaisteion – Also called the Theseion or the Temple of Hephaistos, it was built between 444 and 442 BC and was the first structure completed in Pericles's ambitious program. The Theseion is one of the best preserved Doric temples in existence, despite the missing roof and worn Parian marble sculptures. Its architect was Kallikrates, who also built the Athena Nike. The Doric hexagonal structure with slender columns offers good views of other great surrounding works; to the south along Ailou is the Roman Forum, an eastward extension of the Agora (see below), commissioned by Julius Caesar. The unique octagonal structure seen from Hephaisteion is the Tower of the Winds, built during the 1st century BC as a combined weather vane and clock. During the 7th century AD, the Hephaisteion was first adapted to Christian use; it became the Church of St. George around 1300. No admission charge. The entrance is from the Agora (no phone).

Agora (Stoa of Attalos) – The commercial and public center of ancient Athens spreads out below the Acropolis, which was the town's spiritual and military center. Situated at the junction of the three main roads of the time — from Piraeus, the

Mesogheia Valley, and the mountains — the Agora was the main marketplace. Leaders, philosophers, and common people gathered here to discuss current events and metaphysics. During the classical age of Greece, Sophocles taught here, and the plays of Aeschylus were performed in the theater. Much of what remains — columns, statues — is in ruins, but you can re-create the scene imaginatively. You needn't work too hard on the reconstructed *Stoa of Attalos.* Originally built in the 2nd century BC by Attalos II, King of Pergamon, the marble-colonnaded structure was rebuilt with funds from private American donors. Once an arcade of shops, the *Stoa* is now a museum housing Mycenaean artifacts excavated from the site, including early plans for the building and the Acropolis and a collection of marble statues and sculptures, along with coins and vases. The Theseion, or Temple of Hephaistos, sits atop the highest point of the Agora (see above). Most of the ruins are scattered between the *Stoa* and the Theseion. Open daily; museum open Tuesdays through Sundays from 8:30 AM to 3 PM. Admission charge. Entrance on Adrianou (phone: 321-0185).

Keramikos – The cemetery of ancient Athens has some original graves in place, including the Memorial of Dexilos, honoring a knight killed in action at Corinth in the 4th century BC. Other graves, as well as sculptures and vases found on the site, are in the *Oberlaender Museum,* just beside the cemetery entrance. Open Tuesdays through Sundays from 8:30 AM to 3 PM. Admission charge. 148 Ermou St., below *Monastiraki* (phone: 346-3552).

Theater of Dionysos – Built in the 4th century BC, this is the oldest of the Greek theaters. The plays of Sophocles, Euripides, Aristophanes, and Aeschylus were first performed here. Open daily. Admission charge. Dionisiou Areopagitou St., on the slope of the Acropolis (phone: 322-4625).

Odeion of Herod Atticus – Athens's other ancient theater was built in AD 160 by a rich Athenian philosopher. The structure illustrates the Roman influence on later Greek architecture. This theater is now the setting of the annual, summer-long *Athens Festival,* which features opera, ballet, and concerts performed by first-rate companies from Europe and the US. Open daily. No admission charge. On the southern slope of the Acropolis (phone: 922-6330).

Temple of the Olympian Zeus – Honoring Zeus, the supreme god of heaven and earth, this massive temple, also known as the Olympeion, was built over a 700-year period beginning in the 6th century BC. The temple was the largest constructed in the elaborate Corinthian style. Only 14 columns remain intact; one is fallen — all are beautifully carved. Although it's surrounded by noisy streets, the historic location still provides a quiet haven for reflection. Open daily except Mondays from 8:30 AM to 3 PM. Admission charge. Vasilissis Olgas and Amalias (phone: 922-6330).

Arch of Hadrian – Roman Emperor Hadrian had this arch built in AD 132 to demarcate the city he built from the earlier city, which was said to have been erected by the mythological King Theseus. Open daily. No admission charge. Vasilissis Olgas and Amalias (phone: 922-6330).

Olympic Stadium – On the site of the ancient Panathenean Stadium, opposite the eastern side of the Zappeion Gardens, this white marble structure was the stadium for the first modern *Olympic* games in 1896. Open daily. No admission charge. Vasileos Konstantinou and Agras.

Plaka District – Hugging the north and northeast slopes of the Acropolis, this section of 19th-century Athens retains its essential nature. The narrow, winding streets are lined with restored 1- and 2-story houses; shops selling popular Greek art, pottery, jewelry, textiles, and ouzo; and lively *tavernas.* One of the best places to go for dinner and evening entertainment is *Xynos* (4 Angelou Geronda; phone: 322-1065. For a full description of this and other Plaka district restaurants, see *Eating Out.*) At the west side of the Plaka district are the Roman Agora and the unusual Tower of the Winds Monument. Dating from the 1st century BC, this marble octagonal structure has eight reliefs, each personifying a wind blowing from a different direction. Open daily. No admission charge. Between Ermou and the north slope of the Acropolis.

Monastiraki – Also known as the *Athens Flea Market*, it features the traditions of leatherworking and metalsmithing first carried on within the city walls of the adjacent Agora. Numerous shops carry a wide variety of items, including antiques, jewelry, leather goods, copper, and bronze. You can see coppersmiths work in the back of their shops. Bargaining for goods is an acceptable practice at some of the stores, but shop carefully since many of the goods (and prices) are targeted specifically toward tourists eager to buy. For more information, see *Shopping*. Open daily. No admission charge. Off Monastiraki Sq., on and around Ifestou.

Greek Orthodox Cathedral – This has been the headquarters of the Greek Orthodox church since 1864. The structure is actually composed of stones from 72 demolished cathedrals, and the interior is impressively ornate. Note the lovely 12th-century Byzantine church immediately to the south. Open daily. Mitropoleos, between Syntagma and Monastiraki Sqs.

Syntagma Square – The center of modern Athens, this is prime territory for watching the world go by. Sitting at one of the cafés, you can watch foreign businesspeople rushing in and out of the luxurious *NJV Méridien* and *Grande Bretagne* hotels, office workers heading home, and a special breed of Greek men called *kamaki* (harpooners) trying to pick up female tourists. The House of Parliament and Memorial to the Unknown Soldier flank the east side of the square. Twenty minutes before every hour, *evzones,* soldiers in traditional dress, perform the Changing of the Guard ceremony; Sundays at 11 AM the entire regiment comes out in full regalia. No admission charge. Between Arageorgi Servias and Othonos.

National Gardens – They were designed some 140 years ago at the urging of Queen Amalia, wife of King Otto. Peacocks and waterfowl are at home here, nightingales sing in the spring, and hundreds of homeless cats seem to peacefully coexist with them all. Adjacent to the gardens is the Zappeion, Athens's version of the Tuileries, with broad promenades and a formal design. Open daily. No admission charge. Entrances on Amalias, Vasilissis Sofias, and Irodou Attikou.

Benaki Museum – Set on the site of Antonios Benaki's former townhouse, a short walk from Syntagma (Constitution) Square, an eclectic collection from his private holdings on display — costumes, ceramics, furniture, and arms. Some of the highlights are Lord Byron's writing desk, Muslim woodcarvings, and delicate Byzantine miniatures. Open daily, except Tuesdays, from 8:30 AM to 2 PM. Admission charge. 1 Koumbari at Vasilissis Sofias (phone: 361-1617).

National Archaeological Museum – One of the world's greatest museums, this institution houses a treasure of art spanning 2,500 years of ancient Greek civilization. The scope and breadth of the collection are staggering — rooms and rooms of Greek vases, statues, and sculpture. Some of the highlights are the *Death Mask of Agamemnon;* a statue of Anavissos Kouros, the finest of the tradition of *kouroi,* beautiful youths represented nude in a rigid stance with their left feet slightly forward and their arms at their sides; the bronze statue of Poseidon, god of the sea, discovered at Cape Artemisium in 1928; the statue of the *Youth from Marathon;* recently discovered Minoan findings from excavations on Santorini; and the sculpture of the bronze *Jockey and Horse of Artemisium.* Open Mondays from 11 AM to 5 PM, Tuesdays through Fridays from 8 AM to 5 PM, and weekends from 8:30 AM to 3 PM. Admission charge. 1 Tositsa St. (phone: 821-7717).

■**EXTRA SPECIAL:** When you've had your fill of the city, head for Sounion and the Temple of Poseidon, 40 miles (64 km) south of Athens along the southwest coast. Though the road is somewhat congested in the summer, the route follows the Saronic Gulf, and the view is Greece at its most elemental — sun, rock, and sea. The closer you get to Sounion, the better it gets, as the road winds around steep cliffs overlooking spectacular vistas.

High on a cliff above the sea stands the Temple of Poseidon. Only 15 Doric columns remain, but the temple of the sea god is beautiful in all its starkness. The setting, the ever-changing light, the crashing waves, inspired no less a personage than Byron to engrave his name in the marble. Later he wrote in "Don Juan," "Place me on Sunium's marble steep/Where nothing save the waves and I/May hear our mutual murmurs sweep . . ." Open daily from 10 AM to sunset. Admission charge (phone: 29-239363).

En route you can stop off for a swim in the little town of Vouliagmeni, home of the *Astir Palace* (phone: 896-0211; fax: 896-25820), one of Europe's great resorts. Built on a hill above Vouliagmeni Beach, the hotel has a marble terrace with a spectacular view, 384 rooms and 77 luxury bungalows on the beach, and a variety of fine restaurants.

SOURCES AND RESOURCES

TOURIST INFORMATION: The National Tourist Organization of Greece (NTOG; its Greek acronym is EOT; 2 Amerikis St., near Syntagma Sq.; phone: 322-2545 or 323-4130, ext. 342) provides all manner of information — free maps, brochures, and pamphlets — and supervises tourist services, from the classification of hotels and restaurants to the operation of public beaches. The NTOG also runs an information desk at Hellinikon, Athens's international airport. Another source of tourist information and aid is the Tourist Police, a branch of the Metropolitan Police that helps travelers find accommodations. For information 24 hours a day in several languages, call the special number — 171. The headquarters of the Tourist Police is at 7 Syngrou (phone: 921-4392); other offices are at Larissis Railway Station (phone: 412-27900), Hellinikon Airport (phone: 981-4093), and Piraeus (phone: 452-3670).

The US Embassy and Consulate are at 91 Vasilissis Sofias (phone: 721-2951 or 721-8401).

Local Coverage – The *Athens News* is the daily local English-language paper; the weekly *Greek News* also provides local coverage in English. Most leading foreign newspapers and magazines, including the *International Herald Tribune,* are available at hotels and Syntagma or Kolonaki news kiosks. The *Athenian* is a monthly magazine in English with articles on contemporary Greece and thorough listings of entertainment events, points of interest, and restaurants. *This Week in Athens,* distributed by the NTOG, is a weekly pamphlet with information on current activities as well as general information. *Greece's Weekly,* a newsmagazine, focuses on national and international politics.

For additional English-language guides to Athens and Greece, try Athens's oldest bookstore, *Eleftheroudakis Books* (4 Nikis St., near Syntagma Sq.; phone: 322-1231 or 322-9388), or *Compendium Bookshop* (28 Nikis St.; phone: 322-1248).

Food – Check the Restaurants and Entertainment sections of the *Athenian* or the *Athens News.*

TELEPHONE: The country code for Greece is 30; the city code for Athens is 1.

GETTING AROUND: Airport – Athen's Hellinikon Airport is about 6½ miles (10 km) from Syntagma Square in the center of the city, about a half-hour drive. Taxi fare should run about 1,400 to 1,500 drachmas (about $7.90 to $8.40), plus 200 drachmas (about $1.10) extra for each piece of luggage. Airport buses from both the West (for *Olympic Airways*) and East (foreign airlines) terminals will take you to Syntagma Square for less than 100 drachmas (about 60¢). From Athens, take express buses *A* and *O* from Syntagma Square or Omonia Square, or buses No. 133, No. 122, and No. 167 to the West terminal; express buses *A* and *O* to the East terminal leave from Syntagma Square and Omonia Square every 20 minutes from 6 AM to midnight, while bus No. 121 leaves every 40 minutes from Vasilissis Olgas Avenue.

Bus – There are some 40 bus and trolley routes serving central Athens and the outlying areas. Buses and electric trolleys run from 5 AM to 12 or 12:30 AM. They afford a convenient, inexpensive, and fairly comfortable way to get around, provided you avoid them during rush hours: 7 to 9 AM, 2 to 3 PM, 5 to 6 PM, and 8 to 10 PM. The fare is 40 drachmas (about 20¢) to any point in the Athens-Piraeus area, provided there is no transfer. Bus routes are outlined on the NTOG map of Athens, but you always can check with the NTOG or Tourist Police (phone: 171) for information.

Car Rental – All major car rental companies have offices in Athens. A valid international driver's license is required for Americans. Some of the most reliable agencies are: *Avis* (48 Amalias; phone: 322-4951); *Budget* (8 Syngrou; phone: 921-4771); *Hellascars* (7 Stadiou; phone: 923-5352); and *Hertz* (12 Syngrou; phone: 922-0102). *Peris* (921-6371 or 923-9829) offers luxury car rental service. *The Greek Automobile Club (ELPA)* can provide foreign motorists with information on road conditions and road service, insurance, legal advice, hotel reservations, and camping. Call 174 in Athens and Thessaloniki. For a list of gas stations open after 7 PM, dial 104.

Subway – Until Athens builds two proposed subway lines, the city's only line passes through central Athens, linking Piraeus, the major port, with the suburb of Kifissia. The line goes underground only downtown and emerges outside town. The fare is 40 drachmas (about 20¢), no matter how far you go. Trains run frequently between 5:30 AM and midnight.

Taxi – Cab fares in Athens are inexpensive when compared to those in other major European cities. Most cabs are individually owned, but rates are standardized, so if you want to avoid being taken for a ride, ask the hotel desk or tourist office how much your trip usually costs. You can pick up a cab at stands near the main squares, major hotels, or railway stations, or hail one in the street, though it's difficult to find one during rush hours. To hail one, you must clearly shout your destination (hotel or area) and stand on a street with traffic going in that direction. Sharing a cab is a common practice, but you pay your full fare even if you share. Extra fare is charged for luggage. To call for a taxi 24 hours a day, dial 432-3000.

Tours – Various companies offer sightseeing tours of Athens by air conditioned bus as well as half- and full-day excursions to attractions within a few hours of the city — Cape Sounion, Delphi, Corinth, Mycenae, Epidaurus, and so on. Two of the best companies are *Chat Tours* (4 Stadiou; phone: 323-6582, 322-3137), and *Key Tours* (2 Ermou; phone: 322-2886). If you would like to hire a government-trained guide, contact the NTOG, a travel agent such as *American Express,* or the hotel concierge.

Train – Stathmos Larissis, the main train station (phone: 522-2491), is a short cab ride from downtown that costs about 240 drachmas (about $1.35). For information about trains to the Peloponnesus, which leave from the station on Pelopos Street (behind the main station), call 362-4402. For schedules of trains departing from Athens to other parts of Greece, dial 145; to other parts of Europe, 147.

LOCAL SERVICES: Dentist (English-Speaking) – Dr. Phil Rossi and Dr. Maria Anninou, 9A-25th Martiou (phone: 933-4961).

 Dry Cleaner/Tailor – *Star Dry Cleaning,* 67 Panepistimiou (phone: 321-4721).

Limousine Service – *Carey* for 24-hour service (phone: 323-4120 or 323-1638).

Medical Emergency – *Hygeia Hospital* (Kifissias Ave. and 4 Erythros Stavros; phone: 682-7940); for 24-hour medical emergency assistance, dial 166.

Messenger Service – *DHL International* is used for local deliveries (see below).

National/International Courier – *DHL International* (28 Philellinon, Syntagma Sq.; phone: 982-9691); *TNT Skypak* (40 Vouliagmenis Ave.; phone: 995-0803).

Office Equipment Rental – *Executive Services Ltd.* (Athens Tower B, Suite 506, 2 Messogion St.; phone: 770-1062).

Pharmacy – *Pharmacy Safliani E. Efkleidou* (20 Akadimias at Voukourestiou; phone: 361-1010); *Pharmacy Panos Zamaloykas* (4 Stadiou St.; phone: 324-9589).

Photocopies – *Andrew Antoniou* (61 Stadiou St.; phone: 324-4043); *Kalliopi Volti* (downstairs at 4A Valaoritou; phone: 363-8827); *Foto-Astir* (17 Amerikis St.; phone: 363-0449).

Post Office – The main office (100 Aeolou; phone: 321-6023) and a branch (Syntagma Sq. at Mitropoleos; phone: 323-7573) are open from 7:30 AM to 10 PM.

Secretary/Stenographer (English-Speaking) – *Executive Services Ltd.* (Athens Tower B, Suite 506, 2 Messogion St.; phone: 770-1062 or 778-3698).

Telex – *Executive Services Ltd.* (Athens Tower B, Suite 506, 2 Messogion St.; phone: 778-3698 or 770-1062); *Greek Telecommunications Organization* (phone: 155 to send a telex within Greece; 165 to send it abroad).

Translator – *Executive Services Ltd.* (Athens Tower B, Suite 506, 2 Messogion St.; phone: 770-1062); *IBS International Business Services* (29 Michalakopoulou; phone: 721-0774).

Other – *American-Hellenic Chamber of Commerce and Business Library* (17 Valaoritou; phone: 361-8385); *Commercial Library* (American Embassy, 91 Vasilissis Sofias; phone: 721-2951).

SPECIAL EVENTS: On *Good Friday,* one of the most solemn religious holidays (March or April), an impressive candlelight *Epitaph Procession* leads from the Greek Orthodox Cathedral on Mitropoleos to Syntagma Square and back. The *Athens Festival* is an international arts festival presenting a full summer of theater, music, opera, and ballet performed by renowned artists from Greece, Europe, and the US. Most of the events are held in the Herod Atticus Odeion, a Roman amphitheater built in AD 160 at the foot of the rock of the Acropolis — a setting that enhances the contemporary entertainment by creating links with the rich artistic heritage of Greece. Tickets are available at 4 Stadiou in the arcade (phone: 322-3111, ext. 240, or 322-1459), or at the theater just before the performance. The *Athens Wine Festival* offers a good time for both Athenians and tourists from mid-July to early September. Held in a lovely pine-wooded park at Daphni, 7 miles (11 km) from Athens, admission entitles you to unlimited access to wine produced in all different regions of Greece. Inexpensive drinking glasses are for sale that make nice souvenirs. A few concessions and *tavernas* provide snacks and meals — barbecued chicken and souvlaki. Groups perform traditional and popular music and dances that get pretty merry as the night wears on. The *Athens Open International Marathon,* usually held the fourth Sunday in October, follows the route of Pheidippidis from near the Tomb of Marathon to *Olympic Stadium,* site of the first modern *Olympics* in 1896.

MUSEUMS: For a complete description of the *National Archaeological Museum,* the *Acropolis Museum,* the *Benaki Museum,* and the *Agora Museum (Stoa of Attalos)* see *Special Places.* Other interesting museums are listed below. All charge admission unless otherwise indicated.

Byzantine Museum – Religious art and icons dating from the period of Byzantine occupation, from the 3rd to 15th century. Closed Mondays. 22 Vasilissis Sofias (phone: 721-1027).

Dimitris Pieridis Museum of Modern Art – Paintings, sculpture, and engravings by Greek and Cypriot artists. Open Mondays through Fridays from 6 to 9 PM; Saturdays and Sundays from 10 AM to 1 PM. 29 St. George Ave., Glyfada (phone: 894-8287).

Goulandris Natural History Museum – Greece's plant and animal life, geology, and paleontology. Closed Fridays. 13 Levidou in Kifissia (phone: 801-5870).

Historical and Ethnological Museum – Portraits, arms, and mementos of the heroes of the 1821 War of Independence, plus Lord Byron's sword and helmet. Closed Mondays. 13 Stadiou on Kolokotronis Sq., in the former Parliament House (phone: 323-7617).

Historical Greek Costume Museum – Traditional costumes from all over Greece. Open Mondays, Wednesdays, and Fridays from 10 AM to 10 PM. No admission charge. 7 Dimokritou, Kolonaki Sq.(phone: 362-9513).

Jewish Museum of Greece – Judeo-Greek and Sephardic religious and folk art are represented. Closed Saturdays. 36 Amalias (phone: 323-1577).

Kanellopoulos Museum – A private collection of pre- and post-Christian art and artifacts. Closed Tuesdays. Theorias and Panos in the Plaka district (phone: 321-2313).

Museum of Cycladic and Ancient Greek Art – Two thousand years of the Bronze Age Cycladic civilization, whose simple geometric lines and austere marble shapes have a strong influence on 20th-century sculpture. Closed Tuesdays and Sundays. 4 Neofytou Douka in Kolonaki (phone: 724-9706).

Museum of Greek Popular Art – Traditional arts and crafts, including embroidery, carved wooden objects, and paintings. Closed Mondays. 17 Kidathinaion in the Plaka district (phone: 322-9031).

Railway Museum – Old trains and related objects, including steam locomotives from the 1800s and the personal car of a sultan of Turkey. Open Wednesdays and Fridays; other days by appointment only. 301 Liossion St. (phone: 524-1323).

War Museum – Weapons, uniforms, regimental flags, medals, and more. Closed Mondays. Vasilissis Sofias and Rizari (phone: 723-5263).

SHOPPING: Goods from all over Greece are available in stores in Athens. Specialties include gold and silver jewelry, embroidered shirts and dresses, fabrics, *flokati* rugs of fluffy sheep's wool, pottery, onyx, marble, alabaster, and leather goods. These are available in the main shopping area downtown around Syntagma, Omonia, and Kolonaki Squares as well as in *Monastiraki,* the flea market, where shopping sometimes involves bargaining. The best pottery is available in Maroussi at shops along Kifissias Boulevard. Two good shopping streets for something other than typical souvenirs are Voukourestiou and Tsakalof, which have pedestrian-only malls. For flowers, stop in *Flerianos* (3 Stadiou St.; phone: 322-1514); there also are several flower stalls behind the Parliament Building off Syntagma Square on Vasilissis Sofias Street.

Before you buy handicrafts, visit the *National Organization of Hellenic Handicrafts* (9 Mitropoleos; phone: 322-1017), where items are exhibited to give some standard notions of quality and price. Except for carpets, goods are not for sale.

Another thing to keep in mind is where the regional specialties originate. Some of the best jewelry comes from Ioannina; interesting ceramics from Sifnos and Skopelos;

and highly original embroidery from Skyros, Crete, Lefkas, and Rhodes. The Thessaly and Epirus regions specialize in *flokati* rugs.

Downtown stores usually are open Mondays, Wednesdays, and Saturdays from 8 AM to 2:30 PM; Tuesdays, Thursdays, and Fridays from 8 AM to 1:30 PM and from 5 to 8 PM. Shops around Monastiraki Square remain open on Sundays from 8 AM to 12:30 PM.

Benaki Museum – The place to pick up prints and jewelry with reproductions of themes and designs in the museum's collection. A wide variety of items — from matchbooks, scarves, and tablecloths to needlepoint kits — also is available. Closed Tuesdays. 1 Koumbari at the corner of Vasilissis Sofias (phone: 361-1617).

Dora Furs – Specialists in a variety of furs. 31-33 Voulis St. (phone: 323-2727).

Greek Women's Institution – Exquisite embroidery and handwoven fabrics from the islands are on sale here, along with reproductions of old embroidery patterns from the *Benaki Museum* collection. 13 Voukourestiou (phone: 362-4038).

Karamichos-Mazarakis – Specializes in *flokati* rugs and other rugs from around the world. Low prices and worldwide shipping and delivery are available. Near Syntagma Sq. at 31 Voulis St. (phone: 322-4108).

Lallaounis – This internationally known jeweler does original and traditional Greek designs in gold and silver. 12 Voukourestiou (phone: 361-1371) and 6 Panepistimiou (phone: 362-4354).

Lyceum of Greek Women – Woven fabrics, embroidery, bedspreads, rugs, curtains, and pillowcases are sold along with ceramics and jewelry. 17 Dimokritou (phone: 363-7698).

Minion – Greece's largest department store with over 60,000 items, from bathing suits to carpets. 13 Patission St. (phone: 523-8901).

Monastiraki – A flea market section that is a bargainer's heaven, where you can find just about anything for any price, depending on your bargaining skills. Myriad small stalls carry everything from first class junk to quality copper, brass, antique jewelry, icons, old books, and leather goods, sandals and embroidered shirts and dresses. On Sundays an open-air bazaar is held from 8 AM to noon, when many vendors sell new junk instead of old, and there's more browsing than buying. Open daily. Off Monastiraki Sq., on and around Ifestou.

National Welfare Organization – This nonprofit organization runs three shops that carry a wide variety of crafts, from moderately priced copper and woven products to embroideries, jewelry, and rugs. 6 Ypatias (phone: 322-2146), 46 Vasilissis Sofias, in the lobby of the *Hilton* hotel (phone: 646-0603 or 646-0921), and 24 Voukourestiou (phone: 361-1443).

Papapetrou – High-quality handbags at reasonable prices. 128 Patission St. (phone: 823-6918).

Parthenis – A star among Greek designers, he is the first to export Greek women's fashions successfully on a large scale to the US and Europe. His designs are avant-garde and medium-priced. Dimokritou and Tsakalof in Kolonaki (phone: 363-0020 or 363-3158) and Nikis near the Plaka district.

Periptero – These small kiosks at street corners carry an eclectic assortment of goods — newspapers, chocolate, pens, pencils, film, cosmetics, books, dolls, and pharmaceutical items. For 10 drachmas (about 6¢), you can use the telephone.

Studio Mocassino – A fine selection of stylish shoes for men and women. 7 Ermou (phone: 323-4744).

Trussardi – A variety of leather accessories. Closed Sundays. 15 Tsakalof St. (no phone).

XEN – The *YWCA* store has a small but attractive collection of handmade embroideries. 11 Amerikis (phone: 362-4231).

Zolotas – An internationally renowned jeweler who does both original and traditional designs in silver and gold. 10 Panepistimiou (phone: 361-3782).

SPORTS AND FITNESS: The Mediterranean climate, a long coastline, and well-organized beaches combine to make Athens good territory for those who enjoy sports.

Cycling – The *Greek Cycling Federation* offers cycling tours throughout the country. 28 Bouboulinas St. (phone: 883-1414).

Fitness Centers – *Caravel Executive Club,* in the *Caravel* hotel (2 Vasileos Alexandrou Ave.; phone: 729-0721), has a gym, jogging track, and sauna; *Nautilus Gym* (30 Ioan. Metaxa, Glyfada; phone: 894-2111), is a small coed health studio. *Chic* (Syntagma Sq.; phone: 322-4108) has beauty and fitness centers for women only throughout the country. Many large hotels, such as the *Hilton* and *Inter-Continental,* also have fitness centers.

Golf – At the 18-hole *Glyfada Golf Club* (8 miles/13 km from the center of Athens; phone: 894-6875), you can challenge par 72 on a gradually sloping course in the foothills of Mt. Hymettus, overlooking the Saronic Gulf. The 6,808-yard course has well-maintained fairways lined with pine trees. Clubs and carts are available for rent and a city bus links the course with downtown.

Hiking – *Ipethrios Zoi,* a mountaineering club, organizes outings every weekend at a minimal cost. No special equipment is necessary, except good hiking shoes and a backpack. 9 Vasilissis Sofias (phone: 361-5779).

Horseback Riding – The *Tatoi Riding Club* welcomes travelers to its four open-air tracks (Varimbombi; phone: 801-4513). Slightly less expensive, and open to visitors, is the *Athens Riding Club* (Gerakas, Aghia Paraskevi; phone: 661-1088).

Jogging – The National Gardens, next to the Parliament Building in the center of town, is honeycombed with dirt tracks. For a real workout try the hills around the Acropolis.

Sailing – Quite popular, particularly in Piraeus, where many residents maintain private boats in Mikrolimano, the small harbor, or in the larger Zea Marina. Many sailing regattas are held throughout the year. For information, contact *Sailing Federation,* 15A Xenofontos (phone: 323-6813 or 323-5560).

Swimming – The beaches to the north and south of Athens are some of the cleanest you'll find so close to any major city. Within an hour's bus or cab ride from downtown, you can swim and sunbathe at attractive beaches that have lovely natural settings and complete facilities — changing rooms, refreshment stands, playgrounds, canoe and paddleboat rentals, and tennis, basketball, and volleyball courts. The NTOG operates a large, clean beach 25 miles (40 km) to the north at Porto Rafti (phone: 0299-72572). There are two good NTOG beaches to the south, both 10 miles (16 km) from downtown at Voulas Alipedou (phone: 895-3248 and 895-9590); Vouliagmeni, 16 miles (26 km) from the center (phone: 896-0906), a long and popular beach jutting out between sea and bay; and Varkiza, 24 miles (38 km) from town, where bungalows are available (phone: 897-2102). Glyfada, 10 miles (16 km) from Athens, is a fashionable resort area with good beaches. Beaches are open year-round, though most people swim between May and October. There's a small admission charge at the NTOG beaches. Bear in mind that because of Greece's lack of treatment plants for sewage and industrial waste, the farther from the city, the cleaner the water.

Tennis – The NTOG beaches listed above have outdoor tennis courts; only the court at Varkiza is open daily year-round. No equipment is provided and a modest fee is charged. The courts at the *Agios Kosmas Athletic Center* in Attica (phone: 981-2112) are open to non-members.

Water Skiing – Several training centers in Vouliagmeni provide instruction for beginners and equipment for those with experience: *Naval Club* (Vouliagmeni Bay;

phone: 896-2416); *Lipiterakou School* (Akti Vouliagmeni Beach; phone: 896-0743); and
G. *Kasidokosta School* (Astir Vouliagmeni Beach; phone: 896-0820).

THEATER: Athens has a fairly active theater scene, but plays are presented
almost exclusively in Greek. The state theatrical company, the *National
Theater* in Athens (20 Agiou Constantinou; phone: 522-3242 or 522-5501),
performs modern and classical plays as well as works by foreign playwrights
(translated into Greek). During the summer, the company performs in the ancient
Epidauros amphitheater as part of the *Athens Festival.*

Language is no barrier to appreciating the folk dances performed by the renowned
Dora Stratou Dance Company of Athens. Performances are held nightly from early
May until the end of September at the theater on Philopappou Hill (phone: 324-4395
from 8 AM to 2 PM; 921-4650 after 5:30 PM).

MUSIC: The *Athens State Orchestra* gives classical concerts during the
winter and spring, and *Lyriki Skini,* the *National Opera Company,* performs
operas with foreign guest stars during the winter and spring at the *Olympia
Theater* (59 Akadimias; phone: 361-2461). During the summer, both groups
participate in the *Athens Festival. Parnassos Hall* (8 Agiou Georgiou Karits; phone:
323-8745), has regular recitals throughout the year which offer a look at Greek musical
culture. The *Atheneum International Cultural Center* houses the *Maria Callas Concert
Hall,* which hosts international music competitions and other cultural events (8 Amerikis St.; phone: 363-3701). The *Athens Music Hall and Opera House,* formerly the *Athens
Concert Hall,* features a variety of concerts in the hall, which has movable ceilings,
wings and stage, along with six dazzling chandeliers said to be the heaviest in the world
(Vasilissis Sofias St., next to the US Embassy; phone: 729-0637 or 729-0391). The
Lycabettus Amphitheater at the foot of Lycabettus Hill in the center of Athens is the
site of an annual music festival every June or July. For traditional Greek bouzouki
music, see *Nightclubs and Nightlife.*

NIGHTCLUBS AND NIGHTLIFE: Athens has an active nightlife. Athenians
tend to dine late, so very often things don't get rolling until after 10 PM.
Whether you're interested in a simple evening sitting around a café or more
elaborate dining and entertainment (which can get rather costly), you'll find
numerous places to go and plenty of company. Bars and other nightspots close at 2
AM weekdays, 3 AM Sundays.

The most celebrated of Greek social institutions are the *tavernas* — restaurant-cafés
that come in all sizes and styles, with or without entertainment. In summer, the dining
is alfresco beneath the stars and wandering vines. The emphasis is on eating, but there's
often a variety of entertainment: clubs featuring local singers or groups that generally
perform folk songs and popular music (the Plaka district is one of the liveliest, with
a profusion of *tavernas* and *boîtes*). Among the most popular *tavernas* are *Xynos* (4
Angelou Geronda in the Plaka district; phone: 322-1065), which features guitarists
performing Greek songs; *Anixi* (272 Vouliagmenis Ave.; phone: 973-5012); and *Epis-
trefe* (in Nea Kifissias, west of the National Rd.; phone: 246-8166), for bouzouki and
balalaika music. Best bets for *boîtes* are concentrated in the Plaka district: *Apanemia*
(4 Tholou; phone: 324-8580); *Diagonios* (111 Andrianou; phone: 323-3644); *Esperides*
(6 Tholou; phone: 322-5482); and *Zoom* (37 Kydathineon; phone: 322-5920).

If you're interested in a frenetic nightlife scene, try *bouzoukia* (establishments where
the emphasis is on traditional bouzouki music) or nightclubs. Most open at 10 PM and
close around 2 or 3 AM. As the volume of the music increases, so does the pace: People
burst balloons, toss flowers, throw plates, and break into impromptu dances as the level
of energy becomes almost as high as the tab for drinks, dinner, entertainment, and

broken plates. For classic bouzouki by renowned composers and singers and *rembetika* — the Greek version of blues — try *Harama* (Endos Skopeftiriou in Kesariani; phone: 766-4869). Reservations are necessary. Though the doors open at about 10 PM, the excitement really starts around midnight and keeps building. Two excellent *bouzoukia* clubs in Glyfada are *Neraida* and *Deliua.*

For a more subdued evening, you can spend hours over coffee, drinks, and pastry at *Dionysos Zonar*'s and *Floka,* two well-known cafés off Syntagma, on Panepistimiou. Or sip drinks at *Ratka,* a fashionable Kolonaki bar (22 Haritos; phone: 729-0746). Popular *tavernas* in the Plaka district include *To Terani* (at the intersection of Ragkava Tripodon and Epixarmov Sts.), and *Kafe Plaka* (Tripodon at Flessa and Lysion Sts.). *Brettos* (Kydathineon St.; phone: 323-2110), also in the Plaka district, has an almost unlimited selection of ouzo, wines, and distilled specialties. The genial proprietor speaks enough English to assist in your selection. Take your camera to capture the ambience.

If you're interested in trying your luck, the *Mont Parnes Casino* (22 miles/35 km from Athens; phone: 322-9412) in the *Mont Parnes* hotel, operates games of chance — baccarat, chemin de fer, blackjack, and roulette. There's also a club for dining and dancing. You can drive to the top of the mountain or leave your car at the parking lot and reach the hotel entrance by cable car.

Saturday night fever is a fundamental part of Athens nightlife. Among the classiest discos are *Barbarella* (253 Syngrou; phone: 942-5601); *14 Disco* (14 Kolonaki Sq.; phone: 724-5938); *Bolpanema* (2 Diadochou Pavlou St., Glyfada; phone: 894-3072); *Rigel* (behind the *Hilton,* 39 Michalakopoulou St.; phone: 724-1418); *Medousa* (2 Makri St.; phone: 921-8120); and *Make Up* (beginning of Panepistimiou, in an arcade just west of Voukourestiou; phone: 364-2160). Make reservations. Less exclusive, but still hot, is *Athens* (253 Syngrou Ave., in Nea Smyrni; phone: 942-5602).

BEST IN TOWN

 CHECKING IN: Athens has a wide variety of hotels. The chic *Athenaeum Inter-Continental* and the renowned *Grande Bretagne* top the list, which also includes the *Athens Hilton International* and *Ledra Marriott,* as well as less plush — but no less pleasant — accommodations. The NTOG is still in the process of changing over to an international star ratings system, but in the meantime it divides hotels into five categories — Deluxe, A, B, C, and D. Listed below are our choices for the best hotels in all categories, from the most posh to least expensive (though still comfortable) rooms. Hotel prices in Greece compare very favorably to those elsewhere in Europe. In all categories, Greek hotels generally offer good value; many moderately priced and inexpensive hotels have lots of class — swimming pools and rooftop sun decks, gardens, or bars with panoramic views of the city. In peak season, expect to pay $130 to $250 a night for a double room in the expensive category (deluxe hotels); around $50 to $100 in the moderate; and $40 or less for inexpensive lodging. A number of hotels lower their rates by as much as 20% off-season, from November through March. Rates often include continental breakfasts; half board is compulsory at many hotels on the islands. All telephone numbers are in the 1 city code unless otherwise indicated.

Astir Palace – One of the most tastefully decorated hotels in Athens, this property faces the House of Parliament and is within an easy walk of the smart shops of Kolonaki. Catering mainly to a well-heeled business clientele, it has 79 beautiful, air conditioned rooms that look onto a small sunken garden studded with ruins of ancient Athens that were uncovered during the excavation. The hotel also has a restaurant and a coffee shop. Business facilities include meeting rooms for up to 500, foreign currency exchange, secretarial services in English, audiovisual equipment, photocopiers, computers, cable television news service, and translation services. Syntagma Sq. (phone: 364-3112; fax: 364-2825; telex: 222380). Expensive.

Athenaeum Inter-Continental – A luxury spot that's a study in space and light: A massive glass atrium fills the huge, beige marble lobby with light, and picture windows illuminate separate living and sleeping areas in all 597 rooms. Furnishings are modern and comfortable. French and continental food is served at *La Rôtisserie,* and the *Café Pergola,* which opens onto a terrace with a free-form swimming pool, serves the best Sunday brunch in Athens. For Asian fare, there's *Kublai Khan* (see *Eating Out*). Other amenities include a pub, tea lounge, and disco. Business facilities include 24-hour room service, meeting rooms for up to 1,500, concierge, foreign currency exchange, secretarial services in English, audiovisual equipment, photocopiers, computers, cable television news service, translation services, and express checkout. 89-93 Syngrou Ave. (phone: 902-3666; fax: 921-7653; telex: 221554). Expensive.

Athens Hilton International – Something of a landmark, if not of Greek history, then of luxury, comfort, and services. During the warmest months, an international set hangs out around the large outdoor swimming pool, the best in Athens, and for the fitness-minded there is a health club. The 473 air conditioned rooms are modern and nicely appointed, with views of the Acropolis or the mountains to the north. The *Kellari* specializes in Greek food and wine, while the *Byzantine* offers a salad bar and buffet of hot dishes (open for breakfast, lunch, and dinner). The new *Polo Club* bar features live piano music in a clubby atmosphere. Airport shuttle service is available to all guests. Business facilities include 24-hour room service, meeting rooms for up to 1,200, English-speaking concierge, foreign currency exchange, audiovisual equipment, and express checkout. 46 Vasilissis Sofias (phone: 722-0201; fax: 721-3110; telex: 215808). Expensive.

Grande Bretagne – A grand old hotel built in 1826, it recently was taken over by CIGA, which, hopefully, will restore some of the old-fashioned elegance and once superior service. The lobby and public rooms are spacious, with marble floors, Oriental carpets, valuable paintings, and mahogany armchairs. Right on Syntagma Square in the heart of the city, with 394 rooms and 25 palatial suites (some with Acropolis views), the hotel still is the scene of state receptions and its guest list includes the most prominent personalities of the last 150 years. Among the facilities are an elegant dining room and a coffee shop. The hotel is air conditioned throughout. The Ionian Bank is on the hotel premises. A new executive floor offers 3 large suites, a lounge, and a highly trained staff to provide extra services for the business traveler. Other business facilities include 24-hour room service, meeting rooms for up to 450, English-speaking concierge, foreign currency exchange, secretarial services in English, audiovisual equipment, photocopiers, and cable television news service. 1 Vasileos Georgiou Ave., on Syntagma Sq. (phone: 325-0701; fax: 322-8034; telex: 219615). Expensive.

Ledra Marriott – Attractive, with a marble lobby and fresh flowers throughout its public spaces, it also boasts notably attentive service. The 258 rooms are quite large, and each has a marble bath, 3 telephones, mini-bar, and movies on the color TV sets. Athens's only Polynesian restaurant, the *Kona Kai,* is here, as are the *Ledra Grill,* serving continental fare, and the family-style *Zephyron.* The hotel's rooftop pool (and whirlpool bath) offers a splendid view of the Acropolis. Business facilities include 24-hour room service, meeting rooms for up to 500, concierge, foreign currency exchange, secretarial services in English, audiovisual equipment, photocopiers, computers, cable television news, translation services, and express checkout. 115 Syngrou Ave. (phone: 934-7711; fax: 935-8603; telex: 223465). Expensive.

NJV Meridien – One of the newest additions to Syntagma Square, this 182-room property is a marvel of French sophistication, modern efficiency, and exquisite taste. Marble, mirrors, and leather are the hallmarks of the elegant public spaces. Superior rooms have balconies overlooking the square. Facilities include 2 restaurants, a bar, shops, air conditioning, satellite TV, and mini-bars. Syntagma Sq. (phone: 255-3019). Expensive.

Amalia – Across from the National Gardens and just a few steps from Syntagma Square and the Greek Parliament, this popular hotel is known for its friendly service. The 100 modern rooms have private bath and telephone, and some have balconies. There's a restaurant, bar, and tearoom. Airport bus service. 10 Amalias Ave. (phone: 323-7301). Moderate.

Arethusa – The 87 rooms have air conditioning, private bath, and telephone. Short walking distance to the Plaka in the Syntagma Square neighborhood. No restaurant. 12 Nikis St. (phone: 322-9431). Moderate.

Athens Chandris – Convenient to the airport and Piraeus, it's just 15 minutes from the city center. Rooms are modern, and facilities include a rooftop swimming pool, a restaurant, and bar. Shuttle buses take guests into town hourly up until 10 PM. 385 Syngrou Ave. (phone: 941-4824). Moderate.

Athens Gate – Overlooking the Arch of Hadrian and the Temple of Zeus, this modern, brightly furnished place offers excellent value. The 106 rooms have balconies, private baths, and good views. The rooftop sun deck commands a panoramic view of Athens — from the Parliament, Lycabettus, the *Olympic Stadium,* and the Acropolis to the Saronic Gulf in the distance. The *Athenian* restaurant serves traditional Greek dishes and international specialties, too. There's also a well-appointed bar decorated in marble, leather, and chrome. 10 Syngrou (phone: 923-8302). Moderate.

Attika Palace – A modern, 8-story property in the heart of town, it is a convenient and comfortable place to stay. Though the lobby is small, the 78 rooms are large, airy, and nicely furnished, with private baths, air conditioning, and telephones. Many have balconies, and the rooms on the top two floors have sweeping views of the city and the Acropolis. Spacious hallways and lounges, restaurant and bar. 6 Karageorgi Servias, off Syntagma Sq. (phone: 322-3007). Moderate.

Divani Zafolia-Alexandras – Near the *Archaeological Museum,* this place has a neo-Byzantine decor, a much-frequented swimming pool, and a roof garden. The 192 rooms have private baths, balconies, and air conditioning. The *Grand Byzantine* is a large bar, and the restaurant serves international fare. Underground garage. 87-89 Alexandras (phone: 644-9012; fax; 644-2040). Moderate.

Electra – Another first-rate establishment in the center of the city, the 110 rooms are simply and comfortably furnished and air conditioned. Good views of the Acropolis are provided from the rooftop swimming pool. The bar is good for a quick drink or a more leisurely cocktail after a day's sightseeing. The restaurant serves both Greek and international specialties. Service is first rate. 5 Ermou, just off Syntagma Sq. (phone: 322-3223; fax: 322-0310). Moderate.

Park – This luxurious hotel is in a quiet section of town convenient to the *National Archaeological Museum.* The building is topped off with a swimming pool and a roof garden bar that offer good views of the Acropolis and Lycabettus Hill. The 146 air conditioned rooms are fully equipped with radios and TV sets, private baths, and refrigerator bars. The *Latina,* one of 2 restaurants, serves Italian specialties; snacks are available 24 hours a day at the coffee shop. There are boutiques, shops, and a bank. 10 Alexandras (phone: 883-2712). Moderate.

Titania – Between the city's two main squares, Syntagma and Omonia, this 398-room hotel is stylish both inside and out. Atop the 8-story structure are a bar and terrace with stunning views. Rooms are done in bright colors and contemporary designs. All have air conditioning, phones, and bathrooms. Other facilities include a 24-hour coffee shop, a restaurant, and a piano bar. 52 Panepistimiou (phone: 360-9612). Moderate.

Athenian Inn – Very little traffic passes by this exceptionally clean and attractive pension on a side street in the chic Kolonaki quarter. The 28 rooms, as well as the small bar and dining room, are outfitted with the dark rustic furniture and fabrics of the Greek countryside. 22 Haritos (phone: 723-9552; telex: 224092). Moderate to inexpensive.

Ava – This small, no-frills, family-operated hostelry is clean, quiet, and (beware) extremely simple (spartan, even). Its main advantage is the ideal location just below the Acropolis in the Plaka district. All rooms have private bath, and some family suites with kitchens are available. No restaurant. 9 Lissi Kratous St. (phone: 323-6618). Inexpensive.

Byron – A small, unpretentious hotel in the heart of the Plaka, yet on a quiet street. No restaurant. 19 Vironos St. (phone: 323-0327). Inexpensive.

Ermeion – Right in the center of Athenian life, this hostelry is 5 minutes from central Syntagma Square and the *Monastiraki* flea market. Friendly proprietors run this clean, 29-room property. 66 Ermou (phone: 321-2753). Inexpensive.

Museum – Near the *National Archaeological Museum,* it has 58 clean and comfortable rooms, a large lobby, a bar, and a recreation room. 16 Bouboulinas and Tossitsa (phone: 360-5612). Inexpensive.

Myrto – Near Syntagma Square, this simple hostelry offers clean, basic rooms. No restaurant. 40 Nikis St. (phone: 322-7237). Inexpensive.

Nefeli – In the shadow of the Acropolis, this attractive property has 18 simply furnished rooms with private baths and telephones. Other facilities include a coffee shop and roof garden facing the Acropolis. Hyperidou St. in the Plaka district (phone: 322-8044). Inexpensive.

Niki – Another excellent value, this small hotel near Syntagma Square has 24 clean, standard rooms. 27 Nikis (phone: 322-0913). Inexpensive.

 EATING OUT: Visitors to Athens from Chicago, New York, Toronto, and other places with large Greek communities soon will understand why so many transplanted Greeks take to restauranting. In Greece, eating out is a way of life. Restaurants are more than places to have a bite before an evening's entertainment; very often they *are* the entertainment. Whether in a local *taverna* or one of the more elegant restaurants in town, Greeks take their time over food. Breakfast is light; lunch is eaten in midafternoon; and dinner usually doesn't start until at least 9 PM, when the *tavernas* begin to open. Then the parade of Greek food begins: *mezedakia* (appetizers) — *horiatikosalata* (tomato, cucumber, olives, and feta cheese salad), *taramosalata* (a fish roe spread), *plaki* (a bean dish), *melitsanosalata* (eggplant salad), *spanakopita* (small spinach pies), *tiropita* (cheese pies), *dolmadakia* (grape leaves stuffed with meat, rice, and onions, served with a lemon sauce). Next is the entrée: There's a choice of grilled meat — baby lamb or beef, veal, or chicken — and a wide assortment of seafood — octopus, squid, red snapper, lobster, or *youvetsi* (a casserole). *Retsina,* a resinated wine, traditionally accompanies *taverna* meals, although locally brewed beers have become popular. Greeks indulge their love for rich pastries and thick, strong coffee at cafés. Adventurous meat lovers should visit the Athens meat market arcade (on Aristoghitonos St., near Omonia Sq.). There are two 24-hour eateries here that cook traditional dishes in a genuine Greek atmosphere. *Stipfado* (stew), tripe, and various soups are the favorites of regulars who make this the last stop after a night at the bouzouki clubs. Be aware that it's best to visit the meat market with a group, since it's located in a rather rough section of town. Market closed Sundays.

What makes all these eating establishments even more attractive is the relatively modest tab. Expect to pay around $30 and up for a dinner for two in the places listed as expensive; $20 or less in those listed as moderate; and $10 and under in the inexpensive category. Prices include drinks and tips. Many restaurants are open only for dinner, so telephone beforehand. All restaurants accept most major credit cards, unless otherwise indicated. All telephone numbers are in the 1 city code unless otherwise indicated.

L'Abrevoir – The oldest French dining place in Athens, it also is one of the best, serving marvelously light soufflés, snails, steak tartare, and tender swordfish steaks. In summer, dine in the garden under mulberry trees. It is the perfect spot for a secluded lunch for two. Open daily. Reservations necessary at night only. 51 Xenokratous, Kolonaki (phone: 722-9106). Expensive.

Bayazzo – Owned by a German chef named Klaus, who once cooked for the Shah of Iran, this is the only restaurant serving nouvelle cuisine in Athens. It is also, by far, the most elegant (with a little theater of mechanized, antique china clowns), the best, and the most expensive. But it's worth every drachma. Imagine a "dialogue of veal with mushrooms and green apple" or a cocotte of "swordfish in disguise" topped with puff pastry. The desserts are truly sinful and deserve a visit just for themselves. Dinner only; closed Sundays and *Christmas*. Reservations advised. 35 Ploutarchou St. at Dimokratou, Kolonaki (phone: 729-1420). Expensive.

Athenaeum – Housed on the ground floor of the *Atheneum International Cultural Center,* this soignée spot with marble pillars is frequented by a sophisticated crowd for snacks, lunch, and candelit dinners. The menu offers everything from smoked salmon and caviar to steak tartare and pasta. Open only from September through June; closed Sundays. Reservations necessary. 8 Amerikis St. (phone: 363-1125). Expensive to moderate.

Dionyssos – The two restaurants by this name have similar menus and different, though equally splendid, views — one offers a panorama from the top of Lycabettus; the other, the Acropolis. Such views make the visit worthwhile, but the varied menu usually is only mediocre. When in doubt, stick to the *mezedakia* (hors d'oeuvres), such as spinach and cheese pies, and the *tzatziki,* a yogurt made with garlic and cucumbers. The waiters at both are multilingual. Open daily. Reservations unnecessary. Dionisiou Areopagitou, just opposite the Acropolis (phone: 923-1936), and Mt. Lycabettus, accessible by the funicular that starts at the top of Ploutarchou, above Kolonaki Sq. (phone: 722-6374). Expensive to moderate.

Kublai Khan – Located in the *Athenaeum Inter-Continental* hotel, it features Asian specialties. Try the Mongolian barbecue or the weekly Szechuan and Thai feasts from the buffet. Open daily. Reservations advised. 89-93 Syngrou Ave. (phone: 902-3666). Expensive to moderate.

Act I – Right in the center of town, this cozy restaurant/cocktail lounge is reminiscent of a New York piano bar. Evenings, a pianist plays old American favorites as well as contemporary Greek hits. The food is plentiful and good, including Greek and American specialties. Open daily. Reservations advised. 18 Akadimias (phone: 360-2492). Moderate.

Ellinikon – This sophisticated little place, one of the many trendy café-restaurants on Kolonaki Square, is said to be "where the elite meet." Indeed, fashionable young men and women, as well as visiting executives from the US and around the Continent, are the usual clientele. The restaurant serves a variety of continental and local dishes, the best of which is lamb blanketed with a rich egg and lemon sauce spiked with wine. The pastries also are quite good. Open daily. Reservations unnecessary. 19-20 Kolonaki Sq. (phone: 361-5866). Moderate.

Flame Steak House – Near the *Hilton* hotel, the specialty here is (what else?) charcoal-grilled steaks and chops. Open daily from 10 AM to 1 AM. Reservations advised. 9 Hadziyanni Mexi St. (phone: 723-8540). Moderate.

Hermion – Just south of the Greek Orthodox cathedral on Mitropoleos, this stylish tavern is tucked away in an appealing cul-de-sac. The food always is fresh, imaginative, and light on the oil. Be sure to try the eggplant croquettes. Open daily. Reservations unnecessary. 15 Pandrossou, off Kapnikareas near the Adrianou St. square (phone: 324-6725 or 324-7148). Moderate.

Palia – Established in 1896, this traditional *taverna* features delicous Greek specialties and live music. Closed Sundays. Reservations advised. 35 Markou Mousourou, on the hill behind the *Olympic Stadium* (phone: 752-2396). Moderate.

Papakia – In one of the few 19th-century houses left in Athens, it features outdoor dining in summer, with specials including duckling *à l'orange*. Open daily. Reservations advised. 5 Pondou (phone: 779-3072). Moderate.

Ta Kalamia – One of the most famous *tavernas* in Greece (its name translates as "bamboo"), moved from polluted central Athens to a breezy northern suburb. The first course here, a mixture of wonderful *mezedakia*, is followed by a variety of imaginative meat dishes. In summer, dine alfresco in a garden lined with live bamboo. Open daily. Reservations unnecessary. Aghiou Georgiou and 26 Aiskilou, Halandri (phone: 681-0529). Moderate.

Aerides – Located above the Plaka district by the Tower of the Winds, this *taverna* has a diverse menu of Greek specialties. The lively crowd is comprised of locals and tourists alike. Open for breakfast, lunch, and dinner from 8 AM to midnight. No reservations. 3 M. Auriliou, Plaka (phone: 322-6266). Moderate to inexpensive.

Xynos – Though much of the rest of the Plaka district has become highly commercialized, this old, well-known *taverna* retains a fair measure of authenticity. The place is always lively with guitarists playing popular Greek songs and plenty of good *retsina* to go around. Food is typically Greek and good — veal *hasapi,* lamb *youvetsi,* Greek salads, shish kebab, and spicy appetizers. During the summer, the action takes place in the garden; in winter, inside where the walls are lined with amusing murals of Greek life. Closed Sundays. Reservations advised. 4 Angelou Gerondos (phone: 322-1065). Moderate to inexpensive.

Apotsos – Near Syntagma Square, this cozy indoor *ouzerie* is popular with locals who enjoy the simple but tasty Greek dishes and the low prices. The atmosphere is casual and cluttered, and the *taverna's* walls a collage of old signs, photographs, and other memorabilia. Closed Sundays. Reservations unnecessary. In an arcade at 10 Panepistimiou, just west of Voukourestiou (phone: 363-7046). Inexpensive.

Brazilian – This café in the middle of Athens specializes in tasty sandwiches made with crunchy rolls. The menu also features pastries and a variety of rich, fresh coffees and teas — all served by an amiable staff of Greek women. Closed Sundays. No reservations. No credit cards accepted. 1 Voukourestiou (phone: 323-5463). Inexpensive.

Delphi – A no-frills eatery in the Plaka district, it serves fresh and light Greek dishes. Try the moussaka and the tangy yogurt dip, *tzatziki.* Open daily. Reservations advised. 13 Nikis St. (phone: 323-4869). Inexpensive.

Nick's American Coffee Shop – Modeled after a typical coffee shop in 1950s middle America, this is a welcome oasis for those who've had one too many moussakas and are longing for a taste of home. Grilled cheese sandwiches, omelettes, salads, and other US fare are on the large menu. Open daily for breakfast, lunch, and dinner from 7 AM to midnight. Reservations unnecessary. 1 Nikis St. (phone: 322-8724). Inexpensive.

O Platanos – One of the oldest *tavernas* in the Plaka district, this place is off a small street away from the hectic crowd. It is simply decorated, but has a large and well-prepared selection of Greek foods and unbeatable prices. Closed Sundays. No reservations. No credit cards accepted. 4 Diogenous (phone: 322-0666). Inexpensive.

Socrates' Prison – The owners of this unpretentious *taverna* — a former prison — claim it really was the site of Socrates' internment. Good food, house wine, and boisterous conversation make it a jolly spot. Closed Sundays. Reservations unnecessary. No credit cards accepted. 20 Mitseon, across from *Herod Atticus* theater (phone: 922-3434). Inexpensive.

STOA Coffee Fever – An authentic espresso bar with efficient service and a frenetic atmosphere, it offers good sandwiches, pastries, and great coffee. Closed Sundays. No reservations. Located in a shopping arcade near Syntagma Sq., 7 Bou (phone: 324-7866). Inexpensive.

Themistoklis – Delicious Greek food is served in a brightly lit family atmosphere popular with locals. Sample the *mezedakia* (appetizers), which include *tzatziki* (yogurt, cucumbers, and garlic salad), and the green vegetable dish *horta.* Open daily. No reservations. 31 Vasilissis Georgiou in the Pangrati neighborhood, near the *Hilton* hotel (phone: 721-9553). Inexpensive.

■**Note:** Mikrolimano is a little port in Piraeus that harbors a row of seafood restaurants. Fishermen get up at 3 AM to catch the sweet and succulent daily fare, such as *garides* (prawns), *octapodi* (octopus), *astako* (crawfish, lobster, or langouste), *barbounia* (red mullet), and *garides youvetsi* (a shrimp, cheese, wine, and tomato casserole that most of the restaurants along the port claim to have invented). The usual procedure here is to go into a restaurant and make your selection straight from the refrigerator. In summer, you would then saunter back outside and dine beside the small yachts, right on the quay where musicians and flower vendors stroll. Because of the decrease in catches of late, however, most restaurants have turned to using frozen fish — often without admitting it. Check first with a sniff, or a look at the eyes for brightness. Fish is quite expensive these days in Greece, so be aware when ordering fish sold by the kilogram.

Good places right on the small port include *Kuyu-Kaplanis* (Alexandrou Koumoundourou; open daily; credit cards accepted; phone: 411-1623) for red snapper baked with shrimp, mushrooms, and whiskey; shellfish in delicate sauces; and stuffed eggplant. *The Black Goat* (Alexandrou Koumoundourou; open daily; credit cards accepted;phone: 427626), a popular yachtsmen's rendezvous, serves a great selection of fresh fish. Other good spots are *Argo* (22 Akti Koumoundourou; phone: 411-9861), *Captain John's* (16 Akti Koumoundourou; phone: 417-7589), *El Greco* (24 Akti Koumoundourou; phone: 412-7324), and *Zorba's* (14 Akti Koumoundourou; phone: 411-1663). No reservations needed at any of the Mikrolimano fish *tavernas.* All range in price from expensive to moderate.

If you're interested in a unique gastronomic experience, head a few miles east out of Athens on the road that leads up Mt. Hymettus. You'll come to Kareas, a small town on the mountain, which is inhabited chiefly by Romanian refugees. They have set up several restaurants along the road serving unusual dishes — *stipfado* (hare stew with small onions in tomato sauce) and grilled meat including baby lamb and goat. As you eat, you can enjoy the cool mountain air, which provides welcome relief on hot summer days, and an excellent view of Athens. Expensive to moderate.

BARCELONA

Seeing a circle of men and women move in simple, slow steps to the music of flute and drum around a sun-drenched square on a Sunday afternoon provides an almost visceral understanding of Barcelona and its people. This regional dance, the *sardana* — once described by a poet as a dance "of people going forth holding hands" — is indicative of the sense of community and passion for music that is typical of Barcelona.

The *sardana* appears to happen spontaneously. People walking back from mass or a Sunday stroll begin to linger in the cathedral square. Seemingly from nowhere, a band gathers and begins to play what sounds like rhythmic dirges. People set aside purses, prayer books, and hymnals, then join hands to form large circles. Slowly, the circles revolve as the dancers step out the intricately counted measures on tiptoe, and soon they are caught up in the intensity of the music. They hold their hands high; some close their eyes. The music continues in melodic tones. Then, almost abruptly, the *sardana* is over. The dancers nod to their neighbors, gather up their belongings, and continue on their way home.

Witnessing this, you will see the soul of Barcelona, the strong communal feeling that tempers Catalonia's legendary individualism. Not only has Barcelona long been a great Mediterranean port and Spain's "Second City," but it also has long been the capital of the Catalan people, a stronghold of Catalan nationalism in more repressive times, the locus of Catalan representation vis-à-vis the government of Madrid in freer ones. There always has been a strong regional identity and pride here. After the death of Francisco Franco in 1975, the native Catalan language, no longer suppressed, quickly regained its place as the dominant one of the region. Streets and place names were changed back from Castilian to Catalan, and with the democratic constitution of King Juan Carlos, the region of Catalonia — encompassing the provinces of Barcelona, Gerona (Girona in Catalan), Lérida (Lleida), and Tarragona — was designated one of the country's 17 *comunidades autónomas* (autonomous communities).

Given its position across the Pyrenees from France, on the Mediterranean Sea south of the Costa Brava (literally, "wild coast"), Barcelona has a history and language that link it as much to France as to Spain. Catalan, the lilting language of the region, is derived from the French *langue d'oc,* or Provençal, and is spoken in French Catalonia as well.

The history of Barcelona dates back to 218 BC, when Hamilcar Barça, a powerful Carthaginian (and Hannibal's father), founded Barcino. The Romans developed the town, throwing up walls, parts of which can still can be seen. The Visigoths fought over it in the 5th century, the Moors in the 8th century, and in 801 it was the turn of Charlemagne, who included it in the Spanish March — a Frankish province serving as the dividing line between

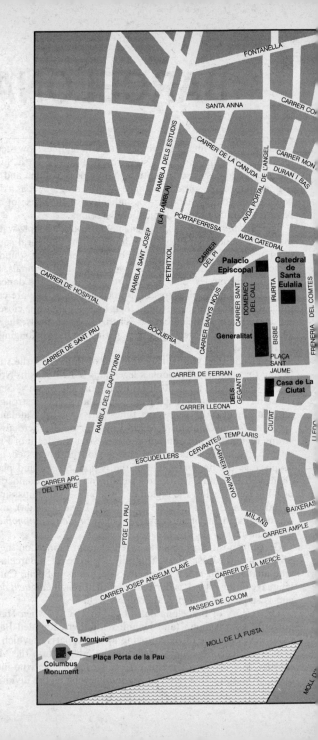

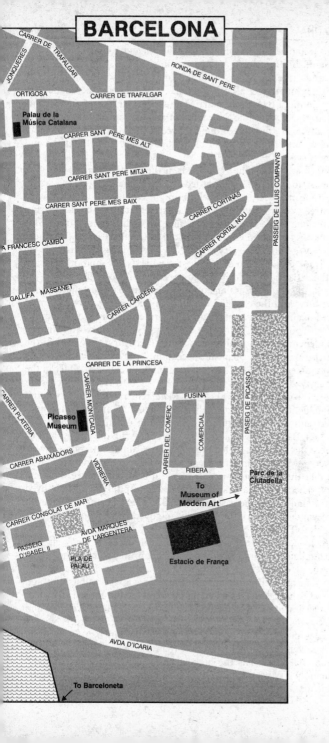

BARCELONA

CARRER DE TRAFALGAR

JONQUERES

RONDA DE SANT PERE

ORTIGOSA

CARRER DE TRAFALGAR

Palau de la Música Catalana

CARRER SANT PERE MÉS ALT

CARRER SANT PERE MITJA

CARRER SANT PERE MES BAIX

CARRER CORTINAS

A FRANCESC CAMBÓ

CARRER PORTAL NOU

PASSEIG DE LLUIS COMPANYS

GALLIFA   MASSANET

CARRER CARDERS

CARRER DE LA PRINCESA

CARRER PLATERIA

CARRER MONTCADA

FUSINA

Picasso Museum

CARRER DEL COMERC

COMERCIAL

CARRER ABAIXADORS

VIDRIERIA

RIBERA

PASSEIG DE PICASSO

To Museum of Modern Art →

Parc de la Ciutadella

CARRER CONSOLAT DE MAR

AVDA MARQUES DE L'ARGENTERA

PASSEIG D'ISABEL II

PLA DE PALAU

Estació de França

AVDA D'ICARIA

To Barceloneta ↙

Christian Europe and Muslim Spain. During the 9th and 10th centuries, local lords, the Counts of Barcelona, became strong enough to establish their independence and drive the Moors from the lands to the south, and by 1100 Barcelona had dominion over all of Catalonia. When Ramón Berenguer IV, a 12th-century Count of Barcelona, married an Aragonese heiress and became King of Aragon, the city became the capital of the combined Catalonian and Aragonese kingdom. It grew to be a major force in the Mediterranean before it was assimilated into the new Spain of Ferdinand and Isabella at the end of the 15th century.

At one point, it was said that "every fish in the Mediterranean wore the red and yellow stripes of the kingdom led by Catalonia." Barcelona was a major Mediterranean power, a force whose might can be felt even today in the medieval streets of the city's old Gothic quarter, the Barri Gòtic. During the 1400s, Barcelona rivaled Genoa and Venice in Mediterranean trade. But although Columbus (Colón in Castilian, Colom in Catalan) sailed from here on his historic voyage, the discovery of the New World proved disastrous for Catalonia. As trade moved from east to west, Seville, Cádiz, and other Spanish ports on the Atlantic rose in importance, and Barcelona declined.

Thereafter, the question of Catalan autonomy became a consistent theme in Barcelona's history, and the city and region often picked the wrong team in making a stand against the rest of Spain. They rose up against the Spanish crown during the Thirty Years War in the 17th century and failed in an attempt to set up an independent nation. In the early 18th century, they backed the Hapsburgs in the War of the Spanish Succession, prompting the victorious Bourbons to put an end to what Catalonian autonomy remained. Only in the late 19th and early 20th centuries did Barcelona begin to recoup. Success in industry fostered a cultural revival — the *Renaixença* — and a newfound sense of Catalan identity. Architects such as Antoni Gaudí and his contemporaries designed and raised buildings of astonishing creativity in new city quarters — in fact, Barcelona was as much a center of Art Nouveau as Paris or Vienna, but here the style was called *modernisme.* Catalan and non-Catalan artists such as Joan Miró, Pablo Picasso, and Juan Gris, attracted by the city's life and color and the spirit of its people, made it a meeting place. Political radicalism flourished, and Barcelona became the capital of a short-lived autonomous Catalan government set up in 1932. Then, during the Spanish Civil War, it became the seat of the Republican government from November 1937 until its fall to Franco's Nationalists in January 1939.

Today, Barcelona, the most European of Spanish cities, is big, rich, and commercial. Catalans are famous throughout Spain for their business acumen, and young people seeking commercial advancement are drawn here from all parts of the Iberian Peninsula. Barcelona is the publishing and literary capital of Spain, as well as its major port and second-largest city (pop. 1,755,000). Government offices, boulevards, and fountains here are large and pompous exhibitions of civic pride; Catalans walk the city streets with a swagger and a confidence that boasts, "We are different, better educated, more culturally aware, and much better off than the rest of Spain." It is no coincidence that Barcelona has the highest literacy rate in Spain, and can claim to be the only city where the patron saint's day is celebrated with gifts of books to friends. "There's a bookshop and a bank on every block," they claim, and bellhops and shoeshine boys often are buried in books that on closer inspection turn out to be French, German, or English classics, rather than Spanish mystery novels.

The seaport atmosphere is felt throughout the city, but it is most apparent in the area closest to the waterfront. With all the charms of the rest of the city, the harbor remains a focal point: a place to watch the comings and goings of cruise ships and tankers; to hire motorboats or other pleasure craft for cruises along the coast; to photograph the 200-foot monument to Christopher Columbus; or merely to be part of the bustle of the docks.

Barcelona has become a favored destination for Europeans who like their big cities to have more than just a cathedral and an art museum. Scores of good restaurants attest to the Barcelonan love of good food and the variety of the regional dishes. Chic designer fashion boutiques (the city police uniforms were designed by couturier Antoni Miró!) attract visitors, as do some of the finest modernist buildings in Europe, including not only the works of Gaudí but also the Palau de la Música Catalana, which attests to the Catalan love of music in this city where many people belong to choral societies and choirs, and the young usually join societies to learn regional dances such as the *sardana.*

Recent Catalan prosperity has restored the ancient, revamped the old, and forged the new. And it's third time lucky for the city that was turned down as host for both the 1924 and 1972 *Olympic Games,* as it readies itself to host the *1992 Summer Games.* In addition to being a feast of sport, the games have triggered a massive clean-up and rebuilding: Working class areas like Vall d'Hebron have new sports facilities, and the 200-acre formerly decayed waterfront has been transformed into the Olympic Village, and will remain as a living community after the world's athletes have left. In addition, the city is spending over $100 million on the construction of 20 new hotels and has built a new, $150 million terminal at El Prat Airport that is capable of handling over 12 million passengers a year. These and other multibillion-dollar projects, however, are not geared to the requirements of the *Olympics* alone, but are designed to be permanent, expanding the city's tourism and sports facilities for the post-*Olympic* 21st century, referred to locally as "Barcelona 2000."

But all the *Olympic*-inspired construction is hardly the essence of Barcelona. You'll realize this if you are fortunate enough to be walking through the Barri Gòtic some evening at dusk, and hear voices softly singing a medieval madrigal as though the spirits of the past were alive. Just pause and savor the moment: You will have found the true spirit of Barcelona.

BARCELONA AT-A-GLANCE

SEEING THE CITY: There are excellent panoramic views of Barcelona, its harbor, the foothills of the Pyrenees, and the Mediterranean from the top of Tibidabo, a 1,745-foot hill on the northwest edge of the city. Covered with pines, it's topped with an amusement park, a church that is lit up at night, and, to celebrate the upcoming *Olympics,* a needle-like 800-foot-tall telecommunications tower, symbolic of Barcelona's perception of itself as "the city of the future." To get to Tibidabo, take the *FFCC* train to Avinguda del Tibidabo, change to the *tramvia blau* (blue tram), and take it one stop to Peu del Funicular, where you can take the funicular to the *Tibidabo Amusement Park*. Check the park's opening hours with the tourist office before setting out, however, because it's not open every day and it closes fairly early. At other times (or if you're interested more in the view than the park anyway), do as the locals do and get off after the tram ride and walk across the square to the smart but pricey restaurant, *La Venta* (Plaça Dr. Andreu; phone: 212-6455). Or stop for drinks at one of the bars (the *Mirablau* has panoramic picture windows). At night, the lights of the city below create a spectacular sight.

SPECIAL PLACES: The city's oldest buildings of historic and artistic interest are located in the Barri Gòtic, the old medieval heart of Barcelona, an area that is crisscrossed by alleyways weaving among ancient palaces, churches, and apartment blocks. When the walls of the old city were pulled down during the 19th century, Barcelona expanded north and west into the Eixample (Ensanche in Castilian — literally "enlargement"), a grid pattern of wide streets and boulevards. Avinguda Diagonal and Gran Via de les Corts Catalanes, modern Barcelona's major streets, cut across this chessboard, which is the city's special pride because of the unparalleled late 19th- and early-20th-century architecture found here, including Gaudí's most interesting works. To the south of the Barri Gòtic and the Eixample is Montjuïc, called the "Hill of the Jews" because a Jewish cemetery once was located here. This is the city's playground, a sports and recreation area and the site of the *1992 Olympic* complex. Buildings put up to house exhibitions for the *1929 World's Fair* still scale its slopes, and at the summit, a huge castle overlooks the sea.

BARRI GÒTIC

Catedral de Barcelona – Barcelona's cathedral, dedicated to Santa Eulàlia, the 4th-century Barcelona-born martyr who is the city's patron saint, is an excellent example of Catalan Gothic architecture. It was begun in 1298 on the site of an 11th-century Romanesque cathedral that one of the Counts of Barcelona, Ramón Berenguer I, had founded to replace an even earlier church damaged by the Moors. It was largely finished in the mid-15th century, except for the façade and two towers, which were not constructed until the end of the 19th century, although they follow the original plans. The interior is laid out in classic Catalan Gothic form, with three aisles neatly engineered to produce an overall effect of grandeur and uplift. The church is comparatively light inside, with the flickering of thousands of votive candles adding a cheery note, and on the saint's day, February 12, it is full of flowers.

In the enclosed choir are beautifully carved 14th- and 15th-century wooden stalls; the coats of arms painted on them, dated 1518, belong to the Knights of the Golden Fleece, who met here that year. The Grand Master of the group, Holy Roman Emperor Charles V, included the Kings of Hungary, France, Portugal, Denmark, and Poland in this "club," and Henry VIII of England had a stall on the emperor's right. Note also the *trascoro,* the white marble choir screen that forms the back of the choir, beautifully carved in the 16th century with scenes from the saint's life. Her remains are in an impressive white alabaster tomb in the crypt, which is down the stairs in front of the massive High Altar. Also buried in the church are the founder of the Romanesque cathedral, Ramón Berenguer, and his wife, Almodis, in plush-covered caskets on the wall to the side of the High Altar (look up). The chapel of St. Benedict (the third one beyond the caskets) is among the more notable of many in the cathedral; it contains the nine-panel Altarpiece of the Transfiguration by the 15th-century Catalan artist, Bernat Martorell. The fourth chapel before the caskets houses another of the cathedral's treasures, the 15th-century polychrome tomb of St. Raymond of Penyafort.

The adjoining cloister is a homey surprise. Reached through the cathedral, through the Santa Llúcia chapel, and through doors from the street, it is an oasis of greenery, full of palm trees and inhabited by numerous pigeons and a gaggle of geese who reside beside fountains and a pool. Off the cloister, in the chapter house, is the small *Museu de la Catedral,* containing, among other exhibits, *La Pietat,* a 15th-century painting on wood by Bartolomé Bermejo. The cathedral is open daily from 7:30 AM to 1:30 PM and from 4 to 7:30 PM; the museum is open from 11 AM to 1 PM. Admission charges to the enclosed choir and to the museum. Plaça de la Seu (phone: 315-3555).

Palau de la Generalitat (Palace of Government) – This 15th-century Gothic structure was the seat of the ancient Catalonian parliament and now houses the executive branch of Catalonia's autonomous government. Inside are a 15th-century Flamboyant Gothic chapel, the Chapel of St. George, with splendid 17th-century vaulting, the 16th-century Saló de Sant Jordi (St. George Room), in which the most important decisions of state have been handed down over the centuries, and other notable rooms. Unfortunately, this is a working building and is not at present open to the public, but arrangements can be made to see it, weekends only, by appointment. Contact the Protocolo (public relations) office. Plaça de Sant Jaume (phone: 301-8364).

Casa de la Ciutat (City Hall) – Like the Palau de la Generalitat across the square, this structure, also known as the Ajuntament, is another fine example of Gothic civil architecture. The façade on the square is 19th-century neo-classical, however. Walk along the Carrer de la Ciutat side to see the building's original 14th-century Flamboyant Gothic façade. Since this, too, is a working building and closed to the public, its interior, including the restored Saló del Consell de Cent (Chamber of the Council of One Hundred) and the Saló de Sesion (Session Chamber), can be seen on weekends and by appointment only. Plaça de Sant Jaume (phone: 302-4200).

Palau Reial Major (Great Royal Palace) – The former palace of the Counts of Barcelona, who later became the Kings of Aragon. Built in the 14th century, it actually is a complex of buildings, of which one large room, the Saló del Tinell, a magnificent banquet hall, is the nucleus. Legend has it that on his return from the New World, Christopher Columbus was presented to King Ferdinand and Queen Isabella here. The room is closed to the public unless there is a concert or exhibition; then it is worth the price of admission just to see it and the stylized painting of the Catholic Monarchs sitting on the palace's great steps, surrounded by the heroic Columbus and the American Indians he brought home on his return voyage. Plaça del Rei.

Museu d'Història de la Ciutat (Museum of City History) – The city's history museum, at the opposite end of Plaça del Rei, is housed in the Casa Clariana-Padellàs, a 16th-century Gothic merchant's house that actually was moved stone by stone from a nearby street and rebuilt on the present site. Begin a tour in the basement, where pathways thread through an actual excavated section of Roman Barcelona, past remains of houses, storerooms, columns, walls, and bits of mosaic pavement. Upstairs rooms contain paintings, furniture, and municipal memorabilia, including the 16th-century Gran Rellotge, one of the six clocks that have occupied the cathedral bell tower. The museum also incorporates part of the Palau Reial Major: that is, the 14th-century Capella de Santa Agata, which is bare except for the *Altarpiece of the Epiphany,* painted in 1465 by Jaume Huguet. Open Tuesdays through Saturdays from 9 AM to 8:30 PM, Sundays from 9 AM to 1:30 PM, and Mondays from 3:30 to 8:30 PM. Admission charge. Entrance on Carrer del Veguer (phone: 315-1111).

Museu Frederic Marès – Set up in another part of the Palau Reial Major, this is an important collection of medieval art, particularly medieval sculpture, donated to the city by the museum's namesake, a prominent local sculptor. The painted wooden religious statues, peculiar to this part of Spain, are outstanding. On the upper floors, a display of artifacts ranging from costumes and combs to pipes and purses invites visitors to discover what everyday life was like in old Catalonia. Open Tuesdays through Saturdays from 9 AM to 2 PM and from 4 to 7 PM, open mornings only on Sundays; closed Mondays. Admission charge. 5-6 Plaça de Sant Iu (phone: 325-5800).

Museu Picasso – Housed in the beautiful 15th-century Palau Agüilar, which is of nearly as much interest as the master's works, this is not strictly within the Barri Gòtic, although it's quite near. A lovely Gothic-Renaissance courtyard opens to the roof, surrounded by tiers of galleries arcaded with pointed arches and slender columns. Lithographs and early works from the artist's years in Málaga and Barcelona (1889–1905) constitute most of the collection, but there are a few special pieces. One is the large exhibition of 44 variations of *Las Meninas*, the famous Velázquez painting in Madrid's *Prado*. Also notice examples of Picasso's warm and unpretentious ceramic work, including brightly painted plates and jugs. Open Tuesdays through Sundays and holidays from 10 AM to 8 PM; closed Mondays. Admission charge. 15 Carrer de Montcada (phone: 319-6310).

Palau de la Música Catalana – Also not far from the Barri Gòtic, although very distant from it spiritually, this is quintessential modernism, the Catalan variation on the Art Nouveau theme. Designed by Lluís Domènech i Montaner and built from 1905-1908, this concert hall is every bit as colorful as anything designed by the more famous Gaudí, but it's also less bizarre and, therefore, in the opinion of many, more beautiful — Gaudí himself is said to have likened it to what heaven must be like. The interior of the auditorium, topped by a stained glass dome, covered with mosaics, and rife with ceramic rosettes, garlands, and winged pegasuses, can be seen only by attending a performance. Those not wishing or unable to get tickets can amble in with the crowd and admire the foyer, itself a lovely space full of brick pillars that rise to ceramic capitals decked with ceramic rosettes. There's an elegant bar in the middle adorned with more stained glass. In summer, when there are no concerts, don't fail to walk by the equally colorful exterior. Carrer d'Amadeu Vives (phone: 301-1104).

EIXAMPLE

Passeig de Gràcia – Running from Plaça de Catalunya to Plaça de Juan Carlos I, where it is cut off by Avinguda Diagonal, this is the widest boulevard in the grid-patterned enlargement that grew up in the 1860s and 1870s after Barcelona's old walls were torn down. Lined with boutiques, banks, hotels, cinemas, and art galleries, it links the Barri Gòtic to what once was the old village of Gràcia, and it provides a pleasant backdrop for a stroll. Characteristic of the street are the *fanals-banc*, combined lampposts and mosaic benches designed by the modernist architect Pere de Falqués and dating from 1900. Of much greater interest, however, are the modernist buildings located here, three of them in one block alone, between Carrer del Consell de Cent and Carrer d'Aragó, the so-called *mançana de la discórdia* or "block of discord." Locals, shocked by the clashing of avant-garde styles, gave it this nickname, a pun on the word *mançana*, which means both city block and apple — the reference to the mythological apple of discord is the sort of sophisticated joke Barcelonans enjoy.

Casa Lleó-Morera – On the corner of Passeig de Gràcia and Carrer del Consell de Cent, this is one of the three noteworthy modernist buildings occupying the "block of discord." Designed by Lluís Domènech i Montaner and built in 1905, at the peak of the Catalan modernist movement, it has stone balconies carved in flower designs and winged lions. The façade is monochromatic, but step across the street to see the ventilator on top, like an elaborate bonnet with a green, pink, and yellow flowered hat band. The ground floor is occupied by a *Loewe* boutique; upstairs the building houses the headquarters of the Patronat de Turisme. 35 Passeig de Gràcia.

Casa Amatller and Casa Batlló – Making up the remainder of the "block of discord," the Casa Amatller (41 Passeig de Gràcia) was designed by Josep Puig i Cadafalch in 1900 and has a Dutch look, with a stepped-gable front inlaid with tiles and green lacy shutters in its windows. It contrasts dramatically with its neighbor, the

Casa Batlló (43 Passeig de Gràcia), which dates from 1904-1906 and is a typical design by Antoni Gaudí, the leader of the modernist movement. With mask-shape balconies, sensuous curves in stone and iron, and bits of broken tile in its upper levels, it's a fairy-tale abode looking for all the world as though it were inhabited by giant mice. Casa Amatller is a library, so it's possible to tiptoe in, but Casa Batlló is closed to the public.

Casa Milá – Only a short way up Passeig de Gràcia, this apartment house, dating from 1906-1910, is regarded as the classic example of Gaudí's modernist architecture. Popularly known as La Pedrera (the "stone quarry"), it seems to be making an almost sculptural attempt to distance itself from the harsh, square lines of its turn-of-the-century neighbors. Notice the intricately swirling ironwork of the balconies, the melting, "soft" sinuousness of the building's horizontal lines as it wraps around the corner. The famous roof terrace has more strange formations covering the chimneys and ventilators. Conducted tours of the rooftop take place Mondays through Fridays at 10 AM, 11 AM, and noon and at 4 and 9 PM; Saturdays at 10 AM, 11 AM, and noon only. There is no charge — just turn up. There is no elevator, but the 6 flights of stairs are worth the effort to see details of doorknobs and banisters en route. 91 Passeig de Gràcia (phone: 215-3398 or 319-7700).

Fundació Antoni Tàpies (Antoni Tàpies Foundation) – Along with the *Museu Picasso* and the *Fundació Joan Miró* on Montjuïc, this is Barcelona's third, and newest, museum dedicated to a single artist. Opened in 1990 in a refurbished 19th-century modernist building designed by Lluís Domènech i Montaner, it houses a major collection of the still-living Catalan artist's works — paintings, drawings, sculpture, assemblage, ceramics — previously stored in warehouses and in private collections, including his own. There is also a research library and space for shows by other contemporary artists, but perhaps the main attraction is the huge Tàpies sculpture of metal wire and tubing on the roof of the building, taking up the entire width of the façade and adding 40-plus feet to its height. It's called *Cloud and Chair*, and you may love this bizarre construction or hate it, but if you're walking along the street, near Passeig de Gràcia, you certainly won't fail to notice it. Open daily from 11 AM to 8 PM; closed Monday. Admission charge. 255 Carrer d'Aragó (phone: 487-0315).

Parc Güell – Constructed between 1900 and 1914, this originally was planned as a real estate development by Gaudí and his friend Count Eusebio Güell, a noted Barcelona industrialist and civic leader. Only two plots of this garden city ever were sold, however (one to Gaudí himself), and the city purchased the property in 1926. It now is a public park. Two gingerbread-style houses — entry pavilions intended as the porter's lodge and an office building — flank the entrance gate; between them a staircase sweeps up to a "hall" or "forest" of mock-classical columns that would have been the development's marketplace. They support a raised plaza covered with gravel and entirely edged with an undulating bench whose backrest is a mosaic quilt of colored ceramic tiles. This extraordinary outdoor space originally was meant to be a recreation center, which is more or less the function it serves today. Also within the park is the *Casa-Museu Gaudí* (Gaudí House-Museum), installed in the house in which the architect lived from 1906 to 1926 (it was designed by another architect, Francesc Berenguer); on display are personal objects, including his bed, and furniture designed by Gaudí and others — most interestingly, some of the original built-in closets from Casa Milá and a large sliding door from Casa Battló. The park is open during daylight hours; the museum is open from 10 AM to 2 PM and from 4 to 6 PM; closed Saturdays. Admission charge to the museum. Bus No. 24 up Passeig de Gràcia leads to the Carretera del Carmel entrance, which is close to the museum, and also not far from the main entrance (with pavilions) located at Carrer de Llarrad and Carrer d'Olot.

La Sagrada Familia (Church of the Holy Family) – Antoni Gaudí was killed in a tram accident in 1926 before he could complete this religious edifice, his most famous and controversial work. One of Spain's most extraordinary buildings (its full name is Temple Expiatori de la Sagrada Família), it still is essentially a building site, unencumbered by a roof. Begun in 1884, the church originally was designed by Francesc del Villar in the neo-Gothic style. When Gaudí was commissioned to take over the project in 1891, he changed the design considerably. Of the two façades and eight towers that are complete, only the famous Nativity Façade, on the Carrer de Marina side, was finished when Gaudí died. Carved to suggest molten stone, it has four tall spires, blue-green stained glass windows, and a porch filled with sculpted figures, including the Virgin Mary, Joseph, and the infant Christ above the main portal. The Passion Façade, on the Carrer de Sardenya side, was begun in 1952. Still to come are a central dome, to rise more than 500 feet and represent Christ, along with several smaller domes representing the Virgin Mary and the Evangelists. Work continues slowly, and few expect the church's completion before the middle of the 21st century. Take the elevator (or the stairs) up the Nativity side to the dizzy heights of the spires for views of the city and close-ups of the amazing architectural details. Steps go even higher, but beware if you suffer from vertigo! The audiovisual show in the *Museu Monogràfic*, located in the crypt (which also was finished at the time of Gaudí's death), traces the history of the church, as do the architect's models. Open daily, June through August, from 8 AM to 9 PM; September through May, from 9 AM to 7 PM. Admission charge, plus an additional charge for the elevator (which keeps shorter operating hours than the site as a whole). Plaça de la Sagrada Família; entrance on Carrer de Sardenya (phone: 255-0247).

MONTJUÏC

Fonts Lluminoses – These illuminated fountains, designed for the *1929 World's Fair*, look like Hollywood special effects. Colored lights play on jets of water that rise and fall to music broadcast by loudspeakers — all against a backdrop of the Palau Nacional, which was the Spanish pavilion for the same fair. It sounds like kitsch, but it's quite a show! The fountains are in operation in summer on Thursdays, Saturdays, and Sundays from 9 PM to midnight (with music from 10 to 11 PM), and in winter on Saturdays and Sundays from 8 to 11 PM (with music from 9 to 10 PM). No shows from January through March. Between Plaça d'Espanya and Montjuïc.

Poble Espanyol (Spanish Village) – Also built for the *1929 World's Fair* and revitalized (as is everything else in the city) for this year's *Olympics,* this is a 5-acre model village whose streets and squares are lined with examples of traditional buildings from every region of Spain, most of them re-creations of actual structures. There is a Plaza Mayor, a Calle de la Conquista, and a Plaza de la Iglesia, just as might be found in any Spanish town or city, and numerous restaurants, bars, and nightspots. A walk through "town" illustrates the diversity of Spanish architecture and offers a chance to see traditional artisans at work; their carvings, pottery, glass, leather, and metalworks are sold in the village's 35 shops. The grounds are open daily from 9 AM until the wee hours, closing at 2 AM Sundays and Mondays and at 4 AM the remaining days, but note that shops, restaurants, and other enterprises within the village keep their own, shorter hours. Admission charge. Avinguda del Marquès de Comillas (phone: 325-7866).

Museu d'Art de Catalunya (Museum of Catalonian Art) – The museum's home is the massive imitation Renaissance-baroque Palau Nacional that was the Spanish pavilion in the *1929 World's Fair.* It has been undergoing a complete remodeling of its interior, and currently only a small portion of the main treasures is on display in the one section that remains open. The rest of the museum was closed at press time, and is expected to reopen after the *Summer Olympics.* Often referred to as "the *Prado* of Romanesque art," the museum contains a splendid collection of Romanesque panel paintings and sculpture, in addition to its chief treasure, a series of frescoes removed from small churches of the Pyrenees region. The museum also is renowned for its

Gothic holdings, as well as for canvases by such greats as Velázquez, Zurbarán, and El Greco. Open from 9:30 AM to 2 PM; closed Mondays. No admission charge. Mirador del Palau, Parc de Montjuïc (phone: 223-1824).

Fundació Joan Miró (Joan Miró Foundation) – Set up in an ultramodern building designed by Josep Lluís Sert, the late Catalan architect, this is a light, airy tribute to Catalonia's surrealist master, who also was an outstanding sculptor and weaver, as his *Tapis de la Fundació* demonstrates. Numerous painted bronze sculptures are displayed on terraces of the museum's upper level; in the galleries are works in various styles and mediums, including a haunting *Self Portrait,* which the artist began in 1937 and did not finish until 1960. The museum hosts frequent special exhibitions, and also has a library and well-stocked art bookstore. Open Tuesdays through Saturdays, from 11 AM to 8 PM; Sundays and holidays, from 11 AM to 2:30 PM. Admission charge. Plaça Neptú, Parc de Montjuïc (phone: 329-1908).

Museu Arqueològic (Archaeological Museum) – Exhibits include relics found in the excavation of the Greco-Roman city of Empúries nearby, various jewels and miniatures, and other remnants of Spain's prehistoric cultures, as well as a fine collection of Greek, Carthaginian, and Roman statues and mosaics. Open Tuesdays through Saturdays, from 9:30 AM to 1 PM and from 4 to 7 PM; Sundays, from 9:30 AM to 1 PM; and holidays, from 10 AM to 2 PM. Admission charge. Carrer de Lleida (phone: 423-2149).

Anell Olímpic (Olympic Ring) – Montjuïc has been designated the principal site for this year's *Summer Olympics,* which are scheduled to take place from July 25 to August 9. The sports facilities within the *Olympic Ring* include the main, 70,000-seat *Estadi Olímpic* (Olympic Stadium), a complete restructuring of a stadium originally built for the *1929 World's Fair.* The opening and closing ceremonies and track and field events will be held here; tours begin at the Marathon Entrance between 10 AM and 3 PM on weekends (phone: 424-0508). Also within the ring are the new 17,000-seat domed *Palau d'Esports Sant Jordi* (St. George Sports Palace), by the Japanese architect Arata Isozaki; the *Piscines Municipals B. Picornell* (B. Picornell Municipal Pools), open-air pools with seating for 5,000; and baseball, rugby, and practice fields, all within walking distance of one another. There are numerous bicycle and jogging paths, too, and they are such popular exercise sites that it may seem the whole city is getting in shape for the *Olympics.*

Museu Militar (Military Museum) – From time immemorial there has been a fortress at the top of Montjuïc, and the castle occupying the spot today, built largely in the 17th century and expanded in the 18th, has been restored and pressed into service as a museum. The belvedere on the grounds provides stunning views of Barcelona — of the port below and across the city to Tibidabo. On display inside are military uniforms, toy soldiers, models of forts, and a collection of 17th- to 19th-century guns. The castle can be reached by road as well as aboard the Montjuïc *telèferic,* a cable car that takes over where the Montjuïc funicular leaves off (see *Getting Around*) and carries passengers up and over the *Parc d'Atraccions de Montjuïc* (Montjuïc Amusement Park) to the top of the mountain, where the castle, the belvedere, and a panoramic restaurant are located. The museum is open Tuesdays through Saturdays from 10 AM to 2 PM and from 4 to 7 PM, Sundays and holidays from 10 AM to 7 PM. Admission charge. The *telèferic* is in operation daily in summer, on Saturdays, Sundays, and holidays in winter. Parc de Montjuïc (phone: 329-8613).

ELSEWHERE

La Rambla – This is the city's favorite — and liveliest — promenade, brimming with activity. Originally a drainage channel, it runs from the harbor to Plaça de Catalunya, changing its name en route (Rambla dels Caputxins, Rambla de Sant Josep, Rambla de Canaletes, and so on). Traffic moves up one side and down the other, and in the middle is a wide, tree-lined pedestrian esplanade. A brisk 20-minute trot would cover it all, but the whole idea is to take it much more slowly, examining the flower stands, thumbing through the books at the book stalls, reading a favorite newspaper or magazine at a sidewalk café, or merely strolling and chatting with friends. Look for the sidewalk mosaic by Miró at the Plaça de Boquería; stroll to the nearby Mercat de Sant Josep (St. Joseph's market, better known as the *Boquería*); and be sure to visit the *Gran Teatre del Liceu,* one of the world's great opera houses, at the corner of La Rambla and Carrer de Sant Pau. The no-expenses-spared restoration confirms this as one of the world's largest and most majestic auditoriums. Tours are conducted September through June, Mondays through Fridays, from 11:30 AM to 12:15 PM. Admission charge. Also see Gaudí's first major work, the Palau Güell, 3 Carrer Nou de la Rambla (phone: 317-3974), a few steps off La Rambla and now serving as the *Museu de les Arts de l'Espectacle* (Museum of Theater Arts), open from 10 AM to 1 PM and from 5 to 7 PM; closed Sundays and holidays. Admission charge. Just off the port, the triangle between La Rambla and the Avinguda del Paral-lel, with its little alleyways, is known as the Barri Xinès, literally "Chinese district," but is actually the red-light district. These areas, however, are reputedly being cleaned up for the *Olympics.*

The Waterfront – Barcelona's historic seagoing tradition has made it one of the most important cities on the Mediterranean, one that today serves as a nearly compulsory port of call for major international cruise ships. But its industrial waterfront only lately has been cleaned up and reclaimed for the pleasure of the people. The Moll de la Fusta, the quay where the Barri Gòtic meets the harbor, now boasts a pedestrian promenade, palm trees, and park benches, as well as several outdoor restaurants and bars known as *chiringuitos.* Most locals consider most of these restaurants too expensive to patronize, so just stop in for a drink.

Monument a Colom (Columbus Monument) – At the harbor end of the La Rambla, anchoring one end of the Moll de la Fusta, this is the tallest tribute in the world to the noted explorer. It was erected in 1886 and consists of a statue of Columbus standing atop an orb atop a pillar, pointing seaward. Take the elevator to the top floor for an extraordinary view. Open late June to late September from 9 AM to 9 PM daily; the rest of the year, open Tuesdays through Saturdays from 10 AM to 2 PM and from 3:30 to 6:30 PM; Sundays and holidays from 10 AM to 7 PM. Admission charge. Plaça Porta de la Pau.

Museu Marítim (Maritime Museum) – The old low, stone buildings with the gables behind the Columbus Monument are examples of medieval Catalan industrial architecture. They were built in the 14th century as the Drassanes Reials (Royal Shipyards); ships that carried the red-and-yellow Catalan flag to the far corners of the world were launched from these yards years before Columbus's bold discovery. Fittingly, the city's *Maritime Museum* now occupies the yards. On display are old maps and compasses, ships' figureheads, models of ancient fishing boats, freighters, and other vessels, and a full-size reproduction of the *Real,* the galley that was Don Juan de Austria's victorious flagship in the Battle of Lepanto in 1571. Open Tuesdays through Saturdays from 9:30 AM to 1 PM and from 4 to 7 PM; Sundays and holidays from 10 AM to 2 PM. 1 Plaça Porta de la Pau (phone: 301-1871).

Barceloneta – The lively "Little Barcelona" district is a long finger of land lying across Barcelona harbor, between the city and the Mediterranean. The Passeig Nacional, lined with bars and every kind of eating establishment imaginable, forms the area's waterfront promenade on the city side. Behind it, a grid of streets strung with laundry drying from balconies and encompassing a few leafy plazas stretches to the beach on the Mediterranean side, the Platja de la Barceloneta. The area is famous for its numerous tiny seafood restaurants — in summer, tables are put right on the beach and dining goes on into late evening. Somewhat to the north is Vall d'Hebron, a massive redevelopment zone that is the site of the new Olympic Village. To reach Barceloneta, walk all the way around the waterfront past the Moll d'Espanya, take the subway to the Barceloneta stop and walk from there, take any of several buses, or take the Barceloneta *telèferic*.

Parc de la Ciutadella – This open space was created just over 100 years ago for the *Universal Exhibition of 1888*. It's popular with Barcelonans, not just for the park itself, but for the added attractions such as the zoo (phone: 309-2500) and the Palau de la Ciutadella, which houses the Parlament de Catalunya. Next door is the *Museu d'Art Modern* (phone: 319-5728 or 310-6308), devoted to Catalan artists little known outside the region. The museum is open Tuesdays through Saturdays from 9 AM to 7:30 PM, Sundays until 2 PM, and Mondays from 3 to 7:30 PM. No admission charge. The zoo is open from 10 AM to 5:30 PM daily. Admission charge.

■**EXTRA SPECIAL:** The Sierra de Montserrat lies 40 miles (64 km) northwest of Barcelona, in the geographical and spiritual heart of Catalonia. The many legends that surround Montserrat, which inspired Wagner's opera *Parsifal,* undoubtedly arose from the strangely unreal appearance of these impressive mountain peaks. Tucked within is the Benedictine monastery whose Marian shrine has attracted pilgrims for over 700 years. *La Moreneta* (The Black Madonna), a polychrome statue of the Virgin Mary, represents the spiritual life of the province and is central to Catalan unity. Legend has it that St. Luke carved the statue and presented it to St. Peter in Barcelona in AD 50. Actually, the tall, slim carving dates from the 12th century. The Virgin sits impassively in a small chamber above the main altar of the monastery's basilica, accepting pilgrims' reverential kisses on her outstretched right hand, which holds a sphere of the world. The basilica is open daily from 8 AM to 8 PM. No admission is charged, but a donation is welcome. The monastery's famous *Escolania,* a boys' choir claiming to be the oldest in the world, sings at 1 PM each Sunday and on special occasions. There is also a museum at the site, open daily from 10 AM to 2:30 PM and from 3:30 to 6 PM. Admission charge (phone: 835-0251). From the monastery, paths and funiculars lead to the Santa Cova, the cave where the statue is supposed to have been found, and to the isolated hermitages of Sant Miguel, Sant Joan, and Sant Jeroni. The belvedere at the latter, 4,061 feet above sea level, provides views that stretch from the Pyrenees to the Balearic Islands and are as breathtaking as they are vertiginous.

SOURCES AND RESOURCES

TOURIST INFORMATION: Brochures, maps, and general information are available from the Patronat Municipal de Turisme de Barcelona (Barcelona Tourist Bureau, 35 Passeig de Gràcia; phone: 215-4477), open Mondays through Fridays, from 9 AM to 2:30 PM and from 3:30 to 5:30 PM. There are also tourist information offices at 658 Gran Via de les Corts Catalanes (phone: 301-7443), open Mondays through Fridays from 9 AM to 7 PM and Saturdays until 2 PM; and in the Barri Gòtic (at the Ajuntament, Plaça de Sant Jaume; phone: 318-2525), open Mondays through Fridays from 9 AM to 9 PM, Saturdays until 2 PM. The information offices at the Moll de la Fusta (phone: 310-3716) and at Barcelona Sants Central Railway Station (phone: 250-2592) are both open daily from 8 AM to 8 PM, while the office at El Prat Airport international arrival hall (phone: 325-5829) is open Mondays through Saturdays from 9:30 AM to 8 PM, Sundays until 3 PM. The "Casacas Rojas," red-jacketed tourist guides who patrol popular areas such as the Barri Gòtic, the Passeig de Gràcia, and La Rambla, supply on-the-spot information from approximately mid-June to mid-September.

The US Consulate is at 33 Via Laietana (phone: 319-9550).

Local Coverage – The tourist offices provide good free maps and brochures. The weekly *Guía del Ocio* and monthly Barcelona city magazine, *Vivir en Barcelona,* both available at newsstands, provide comprehensive listings of museums, nightspots, restaurants, and other attractions, although not in English (the latter does include some information in English in high-season editions). Watch the news in English on TV3 during the summer. Alternatively, dial 010 for Barcelona Information, a telephone "what's on" service where English-speaking operators occasionally can be found.

 TELEPHONE: The country code for Spain is 34; the city code for Barcelona is 3. If calling from within Spain, dial 93 before the local number.

 GETTING AROUND: Airport – Barcelona's airport for both domestic and international flights is El Prat (phone: 379-2762), located 7½ miles (12 km) southwest of the city, or about 30 minutes from downtown by taxi; the fare ranges from about $15 to $20. Trains run between the airport and Barcelona Sants Central Railway Station, connecting with the subway lines, every 20 minutes; the trip takes 15 minutes and the fare is approximately $1. *Iberia's* shuttle (*Puente Aereo*) has flights to and from Madrid every hour throughout the day. There is an *Iberia* office at 30 Passeig de Gràcia (phone for domestic reservations: 301-6800; for international reservations: 302-7656; for information: 301-3893).

Boat – Ferries operated by *Trasmediterránea* leave Barcelona for the Balearic Islands daily in summer, less frequently in winter. The company is located at 2 Via Laietana (phone: 319-8212); departures are from the Moll de Barcelona pier near the Columbus Monument. *Golondrinas,* or "swallow boats," making brief sightseeing jaunts in the harbor (out to the breakwater and back) depart from directly in front of the monument from 10 AM to 8 PM in summer and from 10:30 AM to 1 PM and from 3 to 5 PM in winter. The trip takes only about 15 minutes; buy the ticket from the office at the water's edge (phone: 310-0342).

Bus – Although more than 50 routes crisscross the city, the system is easy to use, since stops are marked with a map of each route that passes there. The best deal for the visitor is *Bus Cien,* the No. 100 bus that constantly circles around 12 well-known sites such as the cathedral, the Sagrada Familia, and so on. The flat-rate full-day ticket (bought on the bus) lets you get on and off as often as you like, and also entitles the bearer to a discount at museums ($3 for 1 day, $8.50 for 3 days, $12.50 for 5 days). The route operates only in high season, however, from approximately mid-June to mid-September. At other times, buy the 10-ride ticket (T-1, or Targeta Multiviatge) for 380 pesetas (about $3.50). It's valid on all buses as well as on the subway, the funicular to Montjuïc, and the *tramvia blau* (blue tram) to Tibidabo. (A T-2 ticket is good for the subway, the funicular, and the *tramvia blau,* but not for the bus.) Buy the ticket at the public transport kiosk in Plaça de Catalunya (where the *Guía del Transport Públic de Barcelona* also is available) or at any subway station. After boarding the bus (enter through the front doors), insert the ticket in the date-stamping machine. For city bus information, call 336-0000.

Long-distance domestic and international buses also serve the city. For information on tickets and departure points, phone 336-0000 or 241-1990.

Car Rental – Cars are useful for day trips outside Barcelona, but usually are more trouble than they are worth for touring within the city. All the major international and local car rental firms have offices at the airport.

Funiculars and Cable Cars – In addition to the funicular to Tibidabo (see *Seeing the City*), there is a funicular making the climb from the Parallel subway stop up to Montjuïc, where it connects with the Montjuïc *telèferic,* a cable car that swings out over the *Montjuïc Amusement Park* and makes one interim stop before depositing passengers at the castle, belvedere, and restaurant at the top. The funicular, cable car, and amusement park are in operation daily in summer; in winter, only on Saturdays, Sundays, and holidays. Both the T-1 and T-2 tickets are valid on the funicular, but neither is valid on the cable car, which requires an extra fare. Another *telèferic* connects Barceloneta with Miramar, at the foot of Montjuïc, making an interim stop at the Torre de Jaume I on the Moll de Barcelona. The trip is a spectacular one across the harbor — passengers swing out over the cruise ships and hang over the water as though in a slow-moving airplane. Rides begin at 10 AM in summer and 11 AM in winter; T-1 and T-2 tickets are not valid.

Subway – A "Metro" sign indicates an entrance to Barcelona's modern, clean subway system. There are four lines (*L1, L3, L4,* and *L5*), all easy to use. Individual rides cost 65 pesetas (about 60¢), but the 10-ride ticket (T-2, or Targeta Multiviatge) is a better buy for multiple trips; it costs 325 pesetas (about $3) at any subway station, and is valid on the funicular to Montjuïc and the *tramvia blau* as well, but not on the buses.

Taxi – Taxis can be hailed while they cruise the streets or picked up at one of the numerous *paradas de taxi,* taxi ranks, throughout the city. For *Radio Taxi,* call 300-3811. During the day, *Lliure* or *Libre* in the window indicates that a cab is available; at night, a green light shines on the roof. The city is divided into various fare zones, and fares generally are moderate.

Train – Barcelona is served by trains operated by *RENFE* (Spanish National Railways) and by trains operated by *Ferrocarrils de la Generalitat de Catalunya* (*FFCC*). There are four railway stations, all undergoing long-term refurbishment as part of the *Olympic* face-lift. Local, national, and international departures constantly are being changed, so it is vital to check and double-check before any journey. The stations are Estació Central Barcelona Sants, at the end of Avinguda de Roma, the main station for long-distance trains; Estació de França, on Avinguda Marquès de l'Argentera; Estació Passeig de Gràcia, on Passeig de Gràcia at Carrer d'Aragó; and Estació Plaça de Catalunya. For fare and schedule information, contact *RENFE* at Barcelona Sants or call the 24-hour-a-day information service (phone: 490-0202).

 LOCAL SERVICES: Dentist – Ask the US Consulate or your hotel concierge for recommendations.

Dry Cleaner – *Tintorería Guilera,* 10 Santa Rosa (phone: 218-9141).

Limousine Service – *International Limousine System,* 47 Ronda Sant Pere (phone: 229-1388; contact Miguel Regol Font).

Medical Emergency – *Hospital de la Santa Creu i de Sant Pau* (167 Sant Antoni María Claret; phone: 347-3133 or 348-1144); ambulance (phone: 311-2121 or 302-3333).

Messenger Service – *Mensajerías Barcelona Express,* 4 Carrer de Berlín (phone: 322-2222).

National/International Courier – *DHL International,* 332-334 Carrer de Entença (phone: 321-4561; for pickup, 321-7316).

Office Equipment Rental – *Rigau,* rents typewriters (Gran Via de les Corts Catalanes; phone: 318-7040); *Exit* rents audiovisual equipment (58 Carrer de Numancia; phone: 322-3166).

Pharmacy – *Farmàcia Valls* (314 Carrer del Consell de Cent; phone: 317-1944). Pharmacies operate on a rotating basis 24 hours a day; check newspapers for listings.

Photocopies – There are photocopy shops all over town.

Post Office – Central de Correus, open weekdays from 8 AM to 10 PM; Saturdays from 9 AM to 2 PM; Sundays and holidays from 10 AM to noon. Plaça Antoni López (phone: 318-3831).

Secretary/Stenographer (English-Speaking) – *TEASA* (168 Carrer de Bailén;

phone: 257-4709 or 257-3589; contact Carmen Trias); *OTAC* (45-47 Carrer de Sepúlveda; phone: 325-2546; contact José Luís Laborda).

Tailor – *Baleta,* 21 Passeig de Gràcia; phone: 301-0304).

Telex – Central de Correus, open 24 hours a day. Plaça Antoni López (phone: 318-3831).

Translator – *TEASA* (168 Carrer de Bailén; phone: 257-4709 or 257-3589; contact Carmen Trias); *OTAC* (45-47 Carrer de Sepúlveda; phone: 325-2546; contact José Luís Laborda); *Rosario Tauler de Canals* (50 Passeig de Sant Joan; phone: 301-7181).

Other – Convention facilities: *Palacio de Congresos* (Convention Center), at the Barcelona Fair Grounds, features every meeting and convention facility, including an auditorium that holds 1,200 (Av. María Cristina; phone: 423-3101). Convention information: *Barcelona Convention Bureau,* providing information for meetings and conventions at restaurants and historical sites around the city (35 Passeig de Gràcia; phone: 215-4477). Men's formalwear rental: *Trajes Etiqueta* (7 Plaça d'Adriá; phone: 201-9260); *Diagonal 523* (phone: 205-4956).

SPECIAL EVENTS: Although religious holidays and saints' days are occasions for numerous festivities in Barcelona, this year will be highlighted by the *1992 Summer Olympics* (see below). April 23 is the *Festa de Sant Jordi* (Feast of St. George), patron saint of Catalonia. Flower stands overflow with roses, and bookstalls on La Rambla are bustling, because this is the day for lovers, and its gifts are a flower and a book. Bonfires, fireworks, dancing, and revelry mark the nights before the feast days of *Sant Joan* (St. John) and *Sant Pere* (St. Peter), on June 23 and 28 respectively. On Thursdays from June through September, the Guardia Urbana (City Police) don scarlet tunics and white plumed helmets for a riding exhibition at 9 PM at the Pista Hipica La Fuxarda, Montjuïc. September 11 is Catalonia's national day, *La Diada,* while September 24 is the *Festa de la Mercè* (Feast of Our Lady of Mercy), honoring the city's patron saint; the week building up to it is fun, noisy, exhausting, full of folk dancing, fireworks displays, and general gaiety, which includes teams of men forming *castellers* (human pyramids). *Christmas* is heralded by the 2-week *Fira de Santa Llúcia,* when stalls selling greenery, decorations, gifts, and the figures for *Christmas* crèches, are set up in front of the cathedral and the Sagrada Família. One of the traditional figures on sale strikes an impudent pose — to say the least.

■ **1992 Summer Olympics:** Barcelona has spent the past 3 years vigorously preparing itself for the *Summer Olympics.* From July 25 to August 9 the city will be bustling with activity, from archery, basketball, and badminton to equestrian competitions, judo, swimming, and yachting. The **Opening Ceremony** is on July 25 at the *Montjuïc Olympic Stadium.* **Closing Ceremonies** are set for August 9, at the *Montjuïc Olympic Stadium.*

Package Ticket Sales in the US are available through *Olson Travel World,* Olympic Division, PO Box 1992, El Segundo, CA 90245 (phone: 213-615-0711 or 800-US4-1992; fax: 213-640-1039).

MUSEUMS: Barcelonans love museums, and the city has many more to be proud of than those listed in *Special Places.*

Museu dels Autómates (Museum of Automatons) – A display of mechanical dolls and animals. Open only when the amusement park in which it is located is open: Thursdays and Fridays from noon to 2 PM and from 3 to 5:45 PM; Saturdays, Sundays, and holidays from noon to 3 PM and from 4 to 7:45 PM.

Admission charge to the park includes the museum. Parc del Tibidabo (phone: 211-7942).

Museu del Calçat Antic (Shoemakers' Museum) – Antique shoes, including 1st-century slave sandals and 3rd-century shepherd's footwear, and a collection of famous people's shoes. Open Tuesdays through Sundays and holidays from 11:30 AM to 2 PM. Admission charge. Plaça Sant Felip Neri (phone: 9302-2680).

Museu de la Ciència (Science Museum) – A popular, hands-on kind of place with changing exhibitions (e.g., "The Return of the Dinosaurs"); permanent rooms illustrating optics, the universe, mechanics, perception; and a planetarium. Open Tuesdays through Sundays and holidays from 10 AM to 8 PM. Admission charge. 55 Carrer Teodor Roviralta, off Avinguda del Tibidabo (phone: 212-6050).

Museu del Futbol Club Barcelona (Barcelona Soccer Museum) – Trophies and videos highlighting the local soccer club's illustrious history — one of the most popular attractions in town. Open Tuesdays through Fridays from 10 AM to 1 PM and from 4 to 6 PM, mornings only on Saturdays and holidays. Admission charge. *Estadi Camp Nou,* Carrer Arístides Maillol (phone: 330-9411).

Museu Monestir de Pedralbes (Pedralbes Monastery and Museum) – A 14th-century Gothic church known for stained glass windows, choir stalls, and an unusual 3-story cloister. Open Tuesdays through Sundays from 9:30 AM to 2 PM. No admission charge. 9 Baixada del Monestir (phone: 203-9282).

Museu de la Música – An odd collection of antique musical instruments. Open Tuesdays through Sundays from 9 AM to 2 PM. No admission charge. 373 Avinguda Diagonal (phone: 217-1157).

Museu Taurí (Museum of Bullfighting) – A collection of bullfighters' costumes — suits of light — and other memorabilia. Open daily from April through September from 10 AM to 1 PM and from 3:30 to 7 PM. Admission charge. 749 Gran Via de les Corts Catalanes (phone: 245-5803).

Palau Reial de Pedralbes (Pedralbes Royal Palace) – Mainly Italian antiques including fans, Murano chandeliers, and tapestries, housed in the former palace of Alfonso XIII; also a collection of ceramics (previously housed at the Palau Nacional on Montjuïc) is impressive for its range — from early Moorish and Catalan ware through 18th-century tiles and even contemporary designs. Open Tuesdays through Fridays from 10 AM to 1 PM and from 4 PM to 7 PM, Saturdays, Sundays, and holidays from 10 AM to 1:30 PM. No admission charge. 686 Avinguda Diagonal (phone: 203-7501).

SHOPPING: Barcelona has been a textile center for centuries, and it always has been a good place to buy leather goods. Now, it's become a source of up-to-the-minute fashion as well, with bright, young designers coming to the fore. Fashion-conscious Barcelonans believe that their city has more in common with Paris than Madrid, providing them with contemporary chic right at home. Passeig de Gràcia and Rambla de Catalunya are lined with elegant shops selling leather goods, furs, accessories, and jewelry for men and women, as well as with boutiques carrying Spain's *moda joven* (young fashion). More boutiques are housed in shopping centers or indoor arcades, of which the best known is the *Bulevard Rosa* (55 Passeig de Gràcia), which has shops selling everything from clothing and hats to unusual jewelry and paper goods. Also located here is the government-sponsored *Centre Permanent d'Artesania* (phone: 215-7178 or 215-5814), where changing exhibitions of crafts by contemporary Catalan artists and artisans are held. What's on display is for sale, although it can't be taken away until the show closes. For crafts, however, don't fail to visit the *Poble Espanyol,* the model village on Montjuïc, where there are some 35 stores featuring pottery, carvings, glassware, leather goods, and other typical folk crafts made by artisans from every region of Spain. Also visit the Ribera-El Born quarter around the *Picasso Museum* on Carrer de Montcada, known as the artists' and craftsmen's quarter. There are two *El Corte Inglés* stores (Plaça de Catalunya; phone: 301-3256; and 617 Avinguda Diagonal; phone: 322-0012). Part of the Spain-wide department store chain, they're known for quality in everything from Lladró porcelain and leather gloves to other clothing, records, and books; best of all, they are open during the long Spanish lunch hour. In general, department stores are open from 10 AM to 8:30 PM; smaller shops close between 2 and 4:30 PM. All are closed — the sign says *Tancat* in Catalan — on Sundays.

As for the markets, a visit to at least one is a colorful must, whether the daily *Boquería* food market just off La Rambla, where the fresh, tempting produce puts big city supermarkets to shame, or one of the weekly meeting places for enthusiasts of coins, stamps, or bric-a-brac. Bargain hard at *Els Encants,* the flea market at Plaça de les Glòries Catalanes (Mondays, Wednesdays, Fridays, and Saturdays, dawn until dusk); spend Sunday mornings in Plaça Reial among the stamp and coin collectors (10 AM to 2 PM) or at Ronda Sant Antoni, leafing through old books (10 AM to 2 PM.) Plaça del Pi hosts an antiques market on Thursdays from 9 AM to 8 PM.

Artespanya – A high-quality choice of Spanish crafts, from handmade glass to tables and chairs. 75 Rambla de Catalunya (phone: 215-2939).

Adolfo Domínguez – Menswear from one of Spain's internationally recognized designers. 89 Passeig de Gràcia (phone: 215-7638).

Camper – Women's shoes and handbags, the latest in styles and colors. 248 Carrer Muntanyer (phone: 201-3188).

Francesc Tasies i Ginesta – Handmade rope-soled espadrilles; an old-fashioned craft brought up to date by the use of contemporary colors and designs. 7 Carrer d'Avinyó (phone: 301-0172).

Groc – The second-floor salon where trendy designer Tony Miró sells his chic and expensive ladies' evening and daywear. Will make-to-order in 15 days, but 20% is added to ready-to-wear prices. 103 Rambla de Catalunya (phone: 216-0089).

Jean Pierre Bua – Fashion by young designers, from Catalunya and elsewhere in Europe. Look for Roser Marcé's "modern classics" for men and women. 469 Avinguda Diagonal (phone: 439-7100).

Jorge Juan – Well-priced women's shoes and handbags in distinctive designs. 125 Rambla de Catalunya (phone: 217-0840).

Loewe – A branch of Spain's best-known and most expensive purveyor of fine leather goods. 35 Passeig de Gràcia (phone: 216-0400).

Matrícula – The latest in men's and women's clothing and accessories from Yamamoto and Rifat Ozbek, among other names. 12 Carrer del Tenor Viñas (phone: 201-9706).

Margarita Nuez – Elegant women's clothing in the finest fabrics. 3 Carrer de Josep Bertránd (phone: 200-8400).

Tema – Fashions by Spanish designers Manuel Piña, Jesús del Pozo, and Jorge Gonsalves (a favorite of Queen Sofía). 19 Carrer Ferrán Agulló (phone: 209-5165).

Trau – Where society girls go for posh glad rags. 6 Carrer Ferrán Agulló (phone: 201-3268).

2 Bis – Amusing "popular art" pieces, including overweight terra cotta bathing beauties and papier-mâché infantas; also, some serious glassware and plates. Near the cathedral, at 2 Carrer del Bisbe (phone: 315-0954).

Vigares – A small, but good selection of leather goods at tempting prices (including riding boots for not much more than $100). 16 Carrer de Balmes (phone: 317-5898).

 SPORTS AND FITNESS: For the last few years, Barcelona has been busy preparing for its role as host to the *1992 Summer Olympic Games* (see *Special Events*), and at press time, more than 100,000 volunteers from all over Spain were busy assisting the Barcelona Olympic Organizing Committee in its task. But the city already boasted many major facilities, including the 120,000-seat *Camp Nou Stadium,* Europe's largest, and the *B. Picornell Municipal Pools* on Montjuïc, before construction of the new *Olympic Ring* facilities began. Other possibilities for the sports-minded include the following:

Bullfighting – Catalans claim to abhor bullfighting and, in fact, most of the spectators in the arena are Spaniards who have moved to the area — or tourists. The gigantic *Plaça Monumental* (Gran Via de les Corts Catalanes) has fights on Sundays from April to late September at 5 PM (6 PM if it's very hot). Additional fights are on Thursdays in August. Advance tickets are available at 24 Gran Via de les Corts Catalanes, at the corner of Carrer d'Aribau (phone: 245-5803). The city's other bullring, *Les Arenes,* at the other end of the same avenue, is now used for pop shows and exhibitions.

Fitness Centers – *Squash Diagonal* (193 Carrer de Roger de Flor; phone: 258-0809) has a pool, sauna, and gym, in addition to squash courts. *Sport Dyr* (388 Carrer de Castillejos; phone: 255-4949) has four gyms, including weight room, sauna, and massage. A gym for women only (2 Avinguda de Roma; phone: 325-8100) also offers a sauna, a swimming pool, and a solarium, as well as aerobics sessions and beauty treatments.

Golf – There are several golf courses around Barcelona, including the *Real Club de Golf El Prat* (10 miles/16 km southwest of town near the airport; phone: 379-0278), which is the best course, used by the European pro tour; *Club de Golf Sant Cugat* (Sant Cugat del Vallès 12½ miles/20 km away and hard to find in the hilly suburbs to the west; phone: 674-3908); and *Club de Golf Vallromanes* (15½ miles/25 km along the Masnou-Granollers road; phone: 568-0362).

Jogging – Parc de la Ciutadella, near the center of town, has a good track. The paths surrounding Montjuïc also are popular jogging spots.

Soccer – The *Olympics* notwithstanding, soccer is the major passion. The *Futbol Club (F.C.) Barcelona* embodies the spirit of Catalonia, especially when the opponent is longtime rival *Real Madrid.* The world's greatest stars are signed up to play for the club, and infants are enrolled as club members from birth. More than 120,000 fans regularly attend home games, played at the *Estadi Camp Nou* (Camp Nou Stadium), which also will host the *Olympics* soccer final. *Espanyol,* the other, less popular, "major league" club in town, plays at *Sarrià Stadium.*

Swimming – Take a dip in the waters that will host the *Olympic* swimming events at *Piscines Municipals B. Picornell* (on Montjuïc, near the main stadium; phone: 325-9281). Although the locals go to Barceloneta to the beach, the water is really rather polluted and it's not recommended to swim near the city.

Tennis – Courts may be available at the *Real Club de Tenis Barcelona* (5 Carrer de Bosch i Gimpera; phone: 203-7758) or *Real Club de Tenis de Turó* (673 Avinguda Diagonal; phone: 203-8012).

 THEATER: The city has a strong theatrical tradition in Catalan, but it still embraces foreign playwrights such as Shakespeare and Chekhov. At the *Teatre Lliure* (Free Theater; Carrer Leopold Alas; phone: 218-9251), Fabia Puigserver's cooperative troupe is so dynamic that language is no barrier when the works are familiar. Another Catalan troupe, the *Companiya Flotats,* led by Josep María Flotats, whose repertoire tends to be lighter, though still socially aware, has moved into the new national theater, part of the Plaça de les Arts complex which has been built near the Plaça de les Glòries Catalanes. Experimental theater can be seen in the impressive *Mercat de les Flors* (59 Carrer de Lleida; phone: 426-1875), the old Flower Hall built on Montjuïc for the *1929 World's Fair.* Higher up the hill, the *Teatre Grec* (phone: 243-0062), an open-air amphitheater, hosts a festival every June and July, with classic Greek tragedies and other works. Popular musicals and vaudeville-type shows are at the *Apolo* (59 Avinguda del Paral-lel; phone: 241-4006) and the *Victoria* (65 Avinguda del Paral-lel; phone: 241-3985). The sporting side of the *Olympics* begins this summer, but Barcelona began preparing the cultural calendar back in 1988. Many companies from around the world are making an appearance. The *Gran Teatre del Liceu* (facing La Rambla with the box office at 1 Carrer de Sant Pau; phone: 318-9122) hosts opera and ballet with international stars as well as local favorite Montserrat Caballé (for more information, see *Special Places*).

 MUSIC: Barcelona is a music center year-round. From November through May, opera and ballet dominate, but there is a festival of some sort every month, from medieval music in May to the *International Music Festival* in October. Two new concert halls have been built in the Plaça de les Arts complex, located near Plaça de les Glòries Catalanes. The *Palau de la Música Catalana* (just off Via Laietana, at the corner of Carrer de Sant Pere Més Alt and Carrer d'Amadeu Vives; phone: 301-1104) is a gem of Art Nouveau style by architect Lluís Domènech i Montaner. The *Orquestra Ciutat de Barcelona* (Barcelona Municipal Orchestra) can be heard here, among other groups.

 NIGHTCLUBS AND NIGHTLIFE: Barcelona has plenty of action, but beware while roaming through the most popular after-dark centers, since the city also has its share of muggers and purse snatchers. Be wary of thieves on motorcycles and minibikes, who snatch purses from pedestrians and out of cars parked or stopped at traffic signals. The city's pubs, bars, and cafés begin to fill up between 10 and 11 PM, but these establishments merely serve as a warm-up for the clubs and discotheques, which open even later and only kick into high gear at 1 or 2 AM. A Las Vegas–style nightclub, *Scala Barcelona* (47 Passeig de Sant Joan; phone: 232-6363) presents elaborate dinner shows and dancing. For flamenco, try *El Cordobés* (35 Rambla; phone: 317-6653), *Andalucía* (27 Rambla; phone: 302-2009), and *El Patio Andaluz* (242 Carrer d'Aribau; phone: 209-3375). Shows are continuous from 10 PM to 3 AM, but really get going after midnight, when the performers and the audiences are warmed up. Popular discotheques include *Bikini,* which features rock and Latin beats (571 Avinguda Diagonal; phone: 230-5134); the *Up and Down,* with loud music downstairs and a restaurant and a more "sophisticated" club upstairs (179 Carrer de Numancia; phone: 204-8809); and *Studio 54,* a weekends-only favorite, boasting lots of elbow room and the best light show in town (64 Avinguda del Parallel; phone: 329-5454). For hot jazz, try the live jams at *La Cova del Drac* (30 Carrer de Tuset, phone: 216-5642). The *Gran Casino de Barcelona* (Sant Pere de Ribes, 26 miles/42 km from the city near the seaside town of Sitges; phone: 893-3666). You have to be over 18, with a passport for identification, to enjoy the dining and gambling in a 19th-century setting.

BEST IN TOWN

 CHECKING IN: Barcelona always has been short on hotel space; not surprisingly, the drive has been to double the number of beds available in time for this year's *Summer Olympics.* Five thousand new hotel rooms have been added to the city's previous 14,000-room-plus hotel capacity. These are meant not only to accommodate *Olympics* visitors, but also to serve as permanent expansions that will meet the demands of tourism into the 21st century. The *Arts* hotel, a brand-new establishment managed by the Ritz-Carlton Company is opening in May in the Olympic Village area on the waterfront, and will offer every imaginable amenity. In an already noisy city, the sounds of *Olympic*-inspired construction have become an added intrusion, so ask for a quiet room. Note that with the *Olympics* in town, prices are rocketing. Expect to pay more than $350 a night for a double room at a hotel listed below as very expensive (a category that, in Barcelona, includes only the *Ritz* — not to be confused with the aforementioned Ritz-Carlton–managed property), between $150 and $250 for a double room at a hotel listed as expensive, $100 to $130 at one listed moderate, and less than $100 at an inexpensive hotel. All telephone numbers are in the 3 city code unless otherwise indicated.

Ritz – Built in 1919, this deluxe aristocrat boasts a new face, and once again lives up to its reputation for superb service in an elegant, charming atmosphere. A favorite meeting place — especially during afternoon tea, which is served in the lounge with a string quartet softly playing — this is the hotel of choice of many international celebrities. All 314 rooms have high ceilings and air conditioning. There also is a fine restaurant. Amenities include 24-hour room service; 8 meeting rooms that hold from 20 to 500 people; an English-speaking concierge; foreign currency exchange; English-speaking secretarial services; audiovisual equipment; photocopiers; a translation service; and express checkout. 668 Gran Via de les Corts Catalanes (phone: 318-5200; fax: 378-0148; telex: 52739 RITZOTEL). Very expensive.

Almirante – This small, modern hostelry is in the center of the city near the cathedral. There are 80 oversize rooms with luxury bathrooms and TV sets. Amenities include 24-hour room service; 6 meeting rooms for up to 80; an English-speaking concierge; foreign currency exchange; English-speaking secretarial services; a photocopier; and translation services. 42 Via Laietana (phone: 319-9500). Expensive.

Avenida Palace – Polished brass and fancy carpets lend a tasteful, Old World atmosphere to this deluxe property. The 229 rooms are air conditioned, cheerful, and quiet, with color television sets and mini-bars. The public areas are adorned with sedate paintings, fine reproductions, and interesting antiques. There is a gymnasium and a sauna; 5 meeting rooms that hold up to 300; an English-speaking concierge; foreign currency exchange; English-speaking secretarial services; audiovisual equipment; photocopiers; computers; translation services; 24-hour room service; and express checkout. The staff is well trained and extremely attentive. 605 Gran Via de les Corts Catalanes (phone: 301-9600; fax: 318-1234; telex: 54734 APTEL E). Expensive.

Barcelona Hilton – Relatively new, with 300 rooms, including several executive floors, of which one is reserved exclusively for women. The business center with 15 meeting rooms for up to 1,000, English-speaking concierge, foreign currency exchange, English-speaking secretarial services, audiovisual equipment, photocopiers, computers, translation services, plus the health club all confirm that this is aimed at the business market. There also is 24-hour room service and express checkout. 589 Avinguda Diagonal (phone: 410-7499; fax: 322-5291; telex: 99623). Expensive.

Calderón – Another longtime Barcelona favorite with the business crowd, but with a bright new image. The generously proportioned 244 rooms are air conditioned, and most have been equipped with the conveniences and services frequent business travelers expect. There are 10 meeting rooms; an English-speaking concierge; foreign currency exchange; English-speaking secretarial services; audiovisual equipment; photocopiers; translation services; and express checkout. The rooftop swimming pool, sauna, and sun terrace command a splendid view of the city. 26 Rambla de Catalunya (phone: 301-0000; fax: 317-3157; telex: 99529 or 51549). Expensive.

Colón – A recently renovated old favorite in the Barri Gòtic, right in front of the cathedral. Clean, pleasantly decorated, it has 166 air conditioned, high-ceilinged rooms, including 10 on the sixth floor with terraces (3 of these — two doubles and a single — face the cathedral). Amenities include 24-hour room service; 1 meeting room for up to 100 people; an English-speaking concierge; foreign currency exchange; and translation services. 7 Avinguda de la Catedral (phone: 301-1404; fax: 317-2915; telex: 52654, callback COLONOTEL). Expensive.

Condes de Barcelona – Modernist outside and modern inside, it's in a striking Art Nouveau building that was transformed into a luxury hotel in the mid-1980s, and proved so popular that it is already undergoing an expansion. The 180 air conditioned rooms and suites contain all the expected amenities. Its location in the heart of the Eixample is ideal, the *Brasserie Condal* restaurant, excellent. There are 5 meeting rooms with a capacity of 20 to 225 people; an English-speaking concierge; foreign currency exchange; English-speaking secretarial services; audiovisual equipment; photocopiers; and translation services. 75 Passeig de Gràcia (phone: 487-3737; fax: 216-0835; telex: 51531). Expensive.

Derby – Older sister to the *Gran Derby,* this is an elegant establishment done up in hushed colors, with diffused lighting and impressive wood trim and ornamentation. The 116 air conditioned rooms have private baths; those on the top floor have large terraces. There are 3 meeting rooms for up to 50 people; an English-speaking concierge; foreign currency exchange; English-speaking secretarial services; a photocopier; and translation services. The intimate piano bar adds an extra special touch. Affiliated with Best Western. 21 Carrer de Loreto (phone: 322-3215; fax: 410-0862; telex: 97429 DEHO). Expensive.

Diplomatic – Dedicated to businesspeople with its excellent conference facilities, this modern 213-room establishment is conveniently located near the Pedrera and the Passeig de Gràcia shops. There is 24-hour room service, 5 meeting rooms that hold up to 500 people; an English-speaking concierge; foreign currency exchange; English-speaking secretarial services; audiovisual equipment, photocopiers; computers; translation services; and express checkout. 122 Carrer de Pau Claris (phone: 317-3100; fax: 318-6531; telex: 54701, callback DIPLOTEL). Expensive.

Duques de Bergara – Stepping into the foyer, you'll find yourself 100 years back in time. Marble floors, pillars, cut-glass mirrors, and molded ceilings make this a charming hotel, located next to the Plaça de Catalunya. The 56 rooms are modern and stylish. Amenities include 24-hour room service; 2 meeting rooms; an English-speaking concierge; foreign currency exchange; English-speaking secretarial services; and photocopiers. 11 Bergara (phone: 301-5151; fax: 317-3442; telex: 98717 APHO-E). Expensive.

Gran Derby – An apartment hotel, with 43 air conditioned suites and duplexes, each containing a sitting room, color television set, bar, and refrigerator. Facilities include 4 meeting rooms seating up to 100; an English-speaking concierge; foreign currency exchange; English-speaking secretarial services; photocopiers; computers; and translation services. The very fashionable marble decor and the helpful staff make up for a somewhat inconvenient location away from the city center. 28 Carrer de Loreto. (phone: 322-2062; fax: 410-0862; telex: 97429 DEHO). Expensive.

Majestic – A Barcelona classic affiliated with Best Western, with 335 air conditioned rooms endowed with color television sets, in-room English-language movies, built-in hair dryers, and mini-bars. There also is a gymnasium, sauna, and rooftop swimming pool, plus 24-hour room service; 9 meeting rooms; an English-speaking concierge; foreign currency exchange; English-speaking secretarial services; audiovisual equipment; and photocopiers. The location, in the heart of the Eixample (opposite the *Condes de Barcelona*), amid restaurants, shops, and Art Nouveau buildings, couldn't be better. 70 Passeig de Gràcia (phone: 215-4512; fax: 215-7773; telex: 52211, callback MAJESTICOTEL). Expensive.

Meliá Barcelona Sarrìa – Near Plaça de Francesc Macià, this is a favorite with businesspeople. All 312 rooms are air conditioned and have king-size beds. The executive Piso Real floor features its own concierge. There is 24-hour room service; 9 meeting rooms; an English-speaking concierge; foreign currency exchange; English-speaking secretarial services; audiovisual equipment; photocopiers; and translation services. 50 Avinguda de Sarrìa (phone: 410-6060; fax: 321-5179; telex: 51033 or 51638 HMBS, callback MELIA BARNA). Expensive.

Presidente – Recently renovated, this 161-room modern, luxury establishment is located away from the center of town but is, nevertheless, busy with businesspeople, film stars, and personalities. There is 24-hour room service; 3 meeting rooms holding up to 150; an English-speaking concierge; foreign currency exchange; English-speaking secretarial services; audiovisual equipment; photocopiers; and translation services. 570 Avinguda Diagonal (phone: 200-2111; fax: 209-5106; telex: 52180, callback HUSA). Expensive.

Princesa Sofía – Big, bustling, and modern, this convention-oriented hotel has an indoor swimming pool, a gym, a sauna, and restaurants. It could be anywhere in the world, but is out near the university and the *Camp Nou Stadium*. The 514 air conditioned rooms, decorated in contemporary style, have large, tile bathrooms, direct-dial telephones, color television sets, and mini-bars. Other amenities include 24-hour room service; 28 meeting rooms; an English-speaking concierge; foreign currency exchange; English-speaking secretarial services; audiovisual equipment; photocopiers; computers; translation services; and express checkout. Plaça de Pius XII (phone: 330-7111; fax: 330-7621; telex: 51683 or 51032). Expensive.

Ramada Renaissance – Previously the grand old *Manila* and now upgraded to a big (210-room), imposing member of the international group, providing expected standards of comfort and service including 24-hour room service; an English-speaking concierge; foreign currency exchange; English-speaking secretarial services; audiovisual equipment; photocopiers; computers in its business center; translation services; 10 meeting rooms; and express checkout; the Renaissance Club rooms on the top 4 floors are the top accommodations, featuring Minitel computer terminals. Ideally located near the Barri Gòtic, it has 2 restaurants. 111 Rambla (phone: 318-6200). Expensive.

Regente – This gem among Barcelona's smaller establishents is located on a quiet extension of La Rambla. The 78 rooms are comfortable, with private baths and color television sets, as well as smartly decorated: Door handles, wall panels, windows, and other fixtures reflect an Art Nouveau affinity. Facilities include a rooftop pool, a meeting room for up to 120; an English-speaking concierge; foreign currency exchange; English-speaking secretarial services; photocopier; private garage; and a cozy bar. 76 Rambla de Catalunya (phone: 215-2570; fax: 487-3227; telex: 51939). Expensive.

Gala Placidia – An economical apartment complex, it has 28 suites with sitting rooms (fireplaces, too), dining areas, and refrigerators, in addition to the small bedrooms. 112 Via Augusta (phone: 217-8200; telex: 98820 HGPL). Moderate.

Oriente – Right on the Rambla, so reserve a room at the back. Built in 1842, with fancy public rooms, its Old World charm has worn a bit, but its central location just about compensates. 140 rooms. 45 Rambla (phone: 302-2558; fax: 412-3819; telex: 54134, callback LIHOTEL). Moderate.

Rialto – In the heart of the Barri Gòtic, this simple but stylish place has 128 rooms, all air conditioned. 42 Carrer de Ferrán (phone: 318-5212; fax: 315-3819; telex: 97206 ATT. H. RIALTO). Moderate.

Espanya – A budget hotel with an Art Nouveau dining room in a 19th-century building. It has antique plumbing, but it's clean, with 84 rooms on the edge of the Barri Gòtic. 9 Ronda de Sant Pau (phone: 318-1758; telex: 50574). Inexpensive.

Gaudí – Renovated and rather bare, but handy for Montjuïc, the port, and the Barri Gòtic. There are 71 rooms; those on the top floor have great views of Montjuïc and the cathedral. 12 Carrer Nou de la Rambla (phone: 317-9032; telex: 98974 HGPL) Inexpensive.

EATING OUT: Catalans take pride in their regional cuisine, which is more sophisticated and closer to French cooking than that of the rest of Spain. Portions are generous and meals are quite frequent: Coffee and a pastry for breakfast, an omelette or a ham-and-cheese sandwich between 11 and noon, a late lunch, a round of *tapas* (see below) later in the day to take the edge off the appetite, and an even later dinner, beginning at 10 or 10:30 PM. (In the heat of summer, and on weekends, this could be 11 PM!) As Catalan self-pride has mushroomed, so have Catalan-style restaurants, exploiting the richness of the Mediterranean fish, as well as bountiful local orchards, fields, and vineyards inland. Try the *sarsuela,* a soup or stew of lobster, crayfish, squid, mussels, and whitefish of various types. The most basic Catalan dish is *escudella i carn d'olla,* a hearty stew of sausage, beans, meatballs, and spices. The ubiquitous caramel custard, *crema catalana,* made with eggs, milk, sugar, and cinnamon, usually concludes a meal. Check for the daily special — *menú del día,* usually a three-course meal with bread and wine — which restaurants are required to offer at a set price. Expect to pay $75 or more for a dinner for two in restaurants classified as expensive, $35 to $65 in the moderate range, and under $30 in the inexpensive places. *Note:* During the *Olympics,* some August closings may be waived. All telephone numbers are in the 3 city code unless otherwise indicated.

Agut d'Avinyó – A favorite for both lunch and dinner, this beautiful multilevel restaurant in the Barri Gòtic has whitewashed walls, oak plank floors, and antique furnishings. Its traditional Catalan food — especially the duck with figs — is excellent. The award-winning owner-hostess, Mercedes Giralt, lends her considerable charm to it all. Closed Sundays, *Holy Week,* and the month of August. Reservations necessary. Major credit cards accepted. 3 Carrer de la Trinitat (phone: 302-6034). Expensive.

Azulete – Imaginative international dishes are served here, and the house, with its gardens and fountain, is a delight. The dining room of this former mansion is actually a glass-enclosed garden, with tables arranged around a decorative pool, surrounded by lush vegetation. Specialties include tiny medallions of pork, crowned with mushroom purée, and broiled *lubina* (sea bass) with fresh dill. For dessert, try figs with strawberry-scented honey. Closed Saturdays at lunch, Sundays, holidays, the first 2 weeks in August, and from *Christmas* through *New Year's.* Reservations advised. Major credit cards accepted. 281 Via Augusta (phone: 203-5943). Expensive.

Beltxenea – When he opened it on the premises of the former *Ama Lur* restaurant, owner-chef Miguel Ezcurra was reviving the tradition of Basque cooking in Barcelona. His new approach to the typical dishes of northwest Spain makes a change from Catalan food. Fish in spicy sauce is a specialty. Closed Sundays, Saturday lunch, and *Easter.* Reservations necessary. Major credit cards accepted. 275 Carrer de Mallorca (phone: 215-3848). Expensive.

El Dorado Petit – Owner Luis Cruañas is a star in a city where eating is a serious pastime. Influenced by the simplicity of Italian cooking, he gave Catalan dishes a lighter touch, relying on the high quality of fresh, local produce. The result is a sophisticated restaurant, with dishes that constantly tempt even regular customers: delicate carrot and champagne soup; black rice, Palafrugell-style; rockfish filets with a tomato *coulis* and shallot vinaigrette; partridge stuffed with prunes and chestnuts; fresh roasted goose liver with sherry vinegar; all followed by homemade ice cream and petits fours. The Catalan white wines, rioja reds, and local sparkling *cavas* complement one of Spain's finest dining experiences. Closed August 8–27. Reservations essential. Major credit cards accepted. 51 Carrer de Dolors Monserdá (phone: 204-5153). Expensive.

Florián – Rosa Grau cooks while her husband, Xavier, minds the front, where pictures line the walls. Pasta with sea urchin sauce, ravioli stuffed with four cheeses, and red mullet with black olives are examples of Rosa's flair with local products. Closed Sundays, *Holy Week,* 2 weeks in August, and *Christmas.* Reservations necessary. Major credit cards accepted. 20 Carrer de Bertrán i Serra (phone: 212-4627). Expensive.

Jaume de Provença – Innovative chef Jaume Bargues reacts well to what's available at the market. Frequent specialties include crab lasagna, sea bass stuffed with fresh salmon, and pigs' trotters with roquefort cheese sauce. Closed Sunday nights and Mondays, *Holy Week,* the month of August, and 2 weeks in September. Reservations necessary. Major credit cards accepted. 88 Carrer de Provença (phone: 230-0029). Expensive.

Neichel – Strictly French, like the owner-chef, whose efforts have won two Michelin stars (there's no more highly rated restaurant in town) and a dedicated local following. The constant flow of inventive new dishes has put exotic little parcels of raw and smoked salmon with caviar, and salads of lobster with mustard vinaigrette on the menu along with more straightforward sea bass with a mousseline of truffles, monkfish in clam sauce, and pigeon with lentils and bacon. Add a selection of 30 desserts from the trolley, fine Spanish wines, and excellent service, and this is a place for a celebration. Closed Sundays, holidays, *Christmas* week, *Holy Week,* and the month of August. Reservations necessary. Major credit cards accepted. 16 *bis* Avinguda de Pedralbes (phone: 203-8408). Expensive.

Quo Vadis – Muted paneling, soft lights, and harmonious decor provide a pleasing ambience at this top establishment. Service is solicitous and the highly original international cuisine is excellent. Closed Sundays. Reservations advised. Major credit cards accepted. 7 Carrer de Carmen (phone: 317-7447). Expensive.

Reno – Another impressive kitchen that uses local recipes in a classic way, its specialties include sole with freshwater crayfish, hake with anchovy sauce, and roast duck with honey and sherry vinegar. The *Menù Reno* offers a sampling of the house's most popular dishes. Open daily, year-round. Reservations advised. Major credit cards accepted. 27 Carrer de Tuset (phone: 200-9129). Expensive.

Arcs de Sant Gervasi – One of Barcelona's newer favorites, in the bustling neighborhood near Plaça de Francesc Macià. Try the gratin of eggplant, ham, and tiny shrimp, or the slices of rare duck with zucchini mousse and sliced pears. Open daily. Reservations advised. Major credit cards accepted. 103 Carrer de Santaló (phone: 201-9277). Moderate.

Blau Mari – A chic new spot on the Barcelona waterfront, featuring fresh fish, seafood, and paellas. Open daily. Reservations unnecessary. Major credit cards accepted. Moll de la Fusta (phone: 218-9222). Moderate.

Brasserie Flo – The atmosphere is Parisian; the meat dishes, especially the barbecue, are outstanding. A favorite place for café society, in jeans or black tie, it's open late for the after-theater crowd. Open daily. No reservations. Major credit cards accepted. 10 Carrer de les Jonqueres (phone: 317-8037). Moderate.

Casa Isidre – The morning market determines the selection of standard-setting Catalan dishes in this Barcelona landmark, once a favorite of Joan Miró. There also is an intelligently stocked wine cellar. Only 10 tables, so reservations are essential and should be made *at least* 2 days in advance. Closed Sundays, holidays, *Christmas* week, *Holy Week,* and during the month of August. Major credit cards accepted. 12 Carrer de les Flors (phone: 241-1139). Moderate.

Los Caracoles – At first glance this bustling, jovial place looks like a tourist trap, but the good solid Catalan cooking is most impressive. Try *los caracoles* (snails); the *langostinos* are fresh and delicious. Open daily. Reservations necessary (but, even so, you'll have to wait during rush hours). Major credit cards accepted. 14 Carrer dels Escudellers (phone: 302-3185). Moderate.

La Dorada – On an average day, this popular eatery serves 1,200 meals! The dining room is fitted with nautical relics, which complement the menu of mostly seafood dishes (and the recipes are more national than regional). Among the favorites are Galician scallops and *sarsuela* (seafood stew). Service is deft and, despite the crowds, never rushed. Closed Sundays. Reservations advised. Major credit cards accepted. 44 Travessera de Gràcia (phone: 200-6322). Moderate.

Senyor Parellada – Located near the *Museu Picasso,* this refined and ambitious restaurant serves traditional Catalan cooking at very reasonable prices. Try the *escalivada,* a cold salad of red peppers, onions, eggplant, and thin slices of cod; or breast of duck with tarragon vinegar. Closed Sundays and holidays. Reservations advised. Major credit cards accepted. 37 Carrer Argenteria (phone: 315-4010). Moderate.

Set Portes – Near the waterfront and a Barcelona favorite since it opened in 1836, it still retains its original decor and charm. Catalan cuisine, including great seafood and homemade desserts, is served in abundant proportions, and the large dining rooms are packed on weekends. Open daily. Reservations advised. Major credit cards accepted. 14 Passeig Isabel II (phone: 319-3033). Moderate.

La Bona Cuina – The decor looks a bit like a modernist parlor, with walls paneled in dark wood, lace curtains at the windows, and a huge Art Nouveau mirror, all gold swirls with a golden peacock on top, dominating the room. In the Barri Gòtic, behind the cathedral, it unabashedly caters to tourists, but delivers good food (Catalan, especially fish and seafood) and good value. Open daily. Reservations advised. Visa accepted. 12 Carrer Pietat (phone: 315-4156). Moderate to inexpensive.

La Cuineta – Under the same management as *La Bona Cuina* and quite close by in the Barri Gòtic, this is set up in 17th-century wine vaults. Open daily. Reservations advised. Visa accepted. 4 Carrer Paradis (phone: 315-0111). Moderate to inexpensive.

Can Costa – Only the freshest of fish and seafood is served at this delightful establishment, one of a number of restaurants side by side on the Barceloneta beachfront. The fish and vegetables are piled high on tables on the sidewalk, and guests walk past the hubbub of the kitchen to a large room open to the sea. In summer, the tables and benches spill out onto the sand. Open daily. No reservations. Major credit cards accepted. 12 Platja de Sant Miguel, Barceloneta (phone: 315-1903). Inexpensive.

Les Corts Catalanes – A wonderful vegetarian delicatessen, located 1 block from the Passeig de Gràcia, serving everything from vegetable lasagna to cheese or spinach empanadas (pot pies). Open daily. No reservations. Visa accepted. 603 Gran Via de les Corts Catalanes (phone: 301-0376). Inexpensive.

Egipte – Very popular and definitely bohemian, serving students and artists. It's located behind the *Boquería* market, so order the dish of the day for the freshest food in town. Closed Sundays, Mondays, and religious holidays. No reservations. Visa accepted. 12 Carrer de Jerusalén. Second location at 79 de la Rambla (phone: 317-7480). Inexpensive.

Quatre Gats – The third incarnation of the popular Barri Gòtic café. The original, which opened in 1897, was a hangout for artists and writers of the Catalan modernist movement, and Picasso had his first show here. There's café society ambience still: Art Nouveau lamps, wrought-iron and marble tables, potted palms, and candelabra on the baby grand. The menu is a limited one of unpretentious

Catalan dishes (try the *Especial 4 Gats* salad for a new twist on diet food). Open daily. No reservations. Visa accepted. 3 Carrer de Montsió (phone: 302-4140). Inexpensive.

 TAPAS BARS: The Catalans did not invent *tapas,* the Spanish equivalent of hors d'oeuvres; it's said the Andalusians did. But they've become as adept as the rest of the Spaniards at the *tapeo,* which consists of making the rounds of *tapas* bars, downing a drink at each, and sampling these delicious snacks — the Spanish version of the treasure hunt, some might say. Barcelona has numerous *tapas* bars, the most colorful of which are located along La Rambla and in the area surrounding the *Picasso Museum.* Some of the more popular choices are beyond this zone, however, including *Flish Flash,* well off the beaten tourist path (25 Carrer de la Ciutat de Granada; phone: 237-0990), where more than 70 types of tortillas attract a good crowd. *Jamón Jamón* (off Plaça de Francesc Macià at 4 Carrer del Mestre Nicolau; phone: 209-4103) serves what its name (which means "Ham Ham") implies — and it serves the best, from Jabugo. *Mundial* (1 Plaça Sant Agustín; phone: 331-2516) specializes in seafood. *Belvedere* (in a quiet alleyway off Paseig de Gràcia, 3 Passatge Mercader; phone: 215-9088) offers a nice terrace and a wide selection. At *Bodega Sepúlveda* (173 Carrer de Sepúlveda; phone: 254-7094), the proprietor's own wine accompanies cheese in oil and little salads. The *Cava de Olimpia* (10 Carrer de Loreto; phone: 239-1073), near the *Derby, Gran Derby,* and *Meliá Barcelona Sarrìa* hotels, takes its name from *cava,* the Spanish answer to champagne. It's part of a recent vogue of *xampanerias* where corks are popped at reasonable prices.

BELGRADE

The long-smoldering ethnic and nationalistic tensions among the Serbs, Croats, and Slovenes (among others) erupted dramatically during the past year. As a result, the US State Department issued a warning to US visitors against travel to Yugoslavia. Prospective travelers should check more recent developments with the US State Department's Citizens' Emergency Center (202-647-5225) prior to departure. You should also be aware that the Yugoslavia National Tourist Office in New York City closed indefinitely last summer. We offer the following in the hope that Yugoslavia's problems will end sometime soon, and that it once again becomes a safe place to visit.

At sunset, a cool breeze disperses the day's accumulation of dust and grime. At twilight, the citizens of Belgrade converge on the pedestrian street of Knez Mihailova to indulge in their traditional evening stroll, the *korzo*. Although the stores along Knez Mihailova stay open until 10 PM, Belgraders aren't here to shop. They come to relax, to chat, to be seen. The crowd in this capital city is not dressed in the drab clothes associated with Yugoslavia's once stolid neighbors in the Soviet bloc; the women wear brightly colored lipstick and flashy fashions, and many of the men are in jeans. Couples fill the cafés, where they drink small cups of strong, sweet Turkish coffee and watch the passersby.

From the looks of this relaxed and well-heeled crowd, it's hard to imagine that ethnic and political tensions are tearing Yugoslavia apart. Despite the conflicts that beset this nation of 23 million, Belgraders seem to manage to enjoy life. Though the city lacks the beauty of such other Eastern European capitals as Prague or Cracow, it has a palpable charm. The people — not the architecture — are the soul of the city. Belgraders pride themselves on being raconteurs and gourmets, and they love a good play or concert. They're also fanatical sports fans. When Belgrade lost its bid to host the *1988 Summer Olympics,* it was a national disaster — a tragedy somewhat mitigated by the city's recent successful drive to host the *1994 World Basketball Championships.* (Yugoslavs are among Europe's most avid hoops fans, and have sent several players to the NBA.) In fact, of all the conversations a foreigner is most likely to overhear during the *korzo,* one of the likeliest is the fate of the *Red Stars,* Belgrade's basketball team.

The red star of communism rose and set briefly in Belgrade, but in the grand scale of things, that was a minor event. This is a city with a long memory. During the 2,300 years since it was founded, Belgrade has been destroyed and rebuilt at least 40 times. Little has survived those cataclysms. From an architectural standpoint, Belgrade is a wasteland: There are no grand cathedrals or mosques, no medieval cloisters, no Renaissance palaces. Aside from the imposing fortress of Kalemegdan, built by the Austrians, and the rather kitschy 19th-century bohemian district known as Skadarlija, the city has few historic buildings.

The vast expanse of cement blocks known collectively as Novi Beograd (New Belgrade) are particularly hard on the eye. Built across the Sava River from the Old Town, Novi Beograd is dominated by a superlatively grim structure: the 24-story headquarters of the Central Committee of the Federal Executive Council.

But Belgrade has begun to lose its reputation as a dusty Balkan backwater. For years, residents joked that the city should be called Sivigrad (Gray City) instead of Belgrade (White City) because of its grimy, unpainted façades. Then, in preparation for the 1989 Conference of Non-Aligned Nations, the capital got a new coat of paint — and several new buildings. Four luxury hotels, including a new *Hyatt* (see *Checking In*), were built to house the delegates. The Knez Mihailova was turned into a pedestrian walkway, and new cafés and privately owned restaurants opened. Though Belgrade still has more in common with Beijing than with Brussels or Bologna, it's starting to come alive.

The irony is that as Belgrade becomes more appealing, Yugoslavia is falling apart. Belgrade is the nation's capital, and, with 1.5 million inhabitants, the largest city in Yugoslavia. Yet the thousands of government bureaucrats who live and work in Novi Beograd may soon be at a loss for what and whom to govern. The country, which has existed as a unified nation only since 1918, is rapidly being torn apart by the centrifugal forces of ethnic nationalism. Of the six republics, only Serbia (including Macedonia) and Montenegro were independent states before World War I; the rest were part of the Austro-Hungarian empire. (The name "Yugoslavia" was not itself adopted until 1929 — until then the nation had been known as the "Kingdom of the Serbs, Croats, and Slovenes.") The movement for independence and unification — and the assassination by Serbian nationalist forces of Austria-Hungary's Archduke Francis Ferdinand — was the catalyst for the war.

Given the extraordinary diversity of all of its people, it's no wonder that Yugoslavia is disintegrating. Five major ethnic groups coexist here: Serbs, Croats, Slovenes, Macedonians, and Montenegrins. Most of the population is Slavic, but there are several vocal non-Slavic minorities, including immigrants from neighboring Albania and Hungary. Yugoslavia is a linguistic Babel: Dozens of languages and dialects are spoken, including four major ones. Some Yugoslavs write with Cyrillic letters; others use the Roman alphabet. The population also is divided along religious lines: Some Yugoslavs are Roman Catholic, others are Serbian Orthodox, and still others are Muslim.

Most Belgraders are Serbs. They use Cyrillic script — a fact not lost on first-time visitors from the West, who generally find the street signs unintelligible — and attend Eastern Orthodox churches. The Serbs spearheaded the drive for unification, and they dominated the pan-Slavic nation that was founded in 1918. Other ethnic groups — particularly the Croatians — resented Serbia's hegemony, and strife between the groups broke out in bloody conflict during World War II. After the war, Josip Broz Tito, whose father was a Croatian blacksmith, and his mother a Slovene, assumed control over a new federal government with the blessing of leaders from the Soviet Union, Britain, and the United States. Tito created two additional autonomous provinces within Serbia: Kosovo and Vojvodina.

During his lifetime, Tito managed to contain Yugoslavia's ethnic rivalries

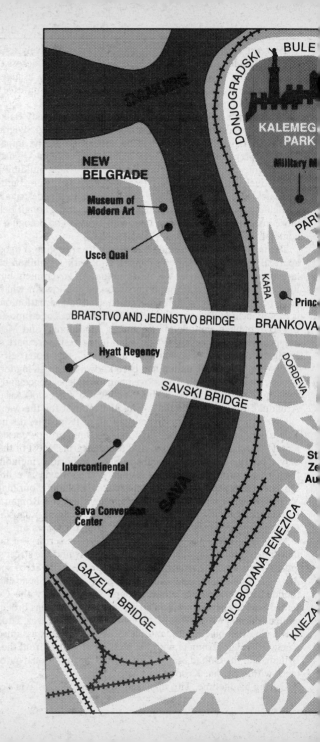

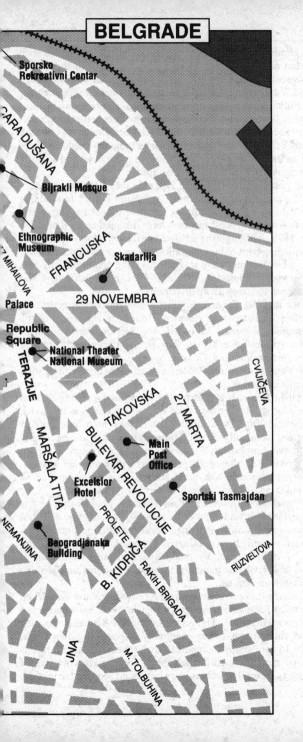

BELGRADE

Sporsko Rekreativni Centar

CARA DUŠANA

Bijrakli Mosque

Ethnographic Museum

27 MIHAILOVA

FRANCUSKA

Skadarlija

29 NOVEMBRA

Palace

Republic Square

National Theater
National Museum

TERAZJE

TAKOVSKA

CVJUČEVA

27 MARTA

MARŠALA TITA

BULEVAR REVOLUCIJE

Main Post Office

Excelsior Hotel

Sportski Tasmajdan

NEMANJINA

Beogradjanaka Building

PROLETE KČA

RAKIH BRIGADA

B. KIDRIČA

RUZVELTOVA

JNA

M. TOLBUHINA

and curb Serbia's grand designs. The barrel-chested leader commanded such respect (or fear) that no one dared cross him. Opponents found themselves hounded by Tito's secret police — or facing a firing squad. Despite Tito's autocratic leanings, Yugoslavia eventually became the most flexible member of the Communist bloc. Farms were not collectivized, as they were in most of the rest of Eastern Europe, and Tito's system of worker self-management became a model for socialists in both East and West. Censorship was relaxed to some degree, and Yugoslavs were permitted some religious freedom. These reforms have had an impact on Belgraders, who are more open and friendly than, say, the average citizen of Bucharest or Sofia.

A spurt of rapid postwar growth turned Belgrade into a bustling modern city; in the past 15 years, though, economic stagnation has set in. Saddled with a $21 billion debt to Western creditors, the government has imposed a deeply resented austerity plan. Real incomes have declined more than 40% since their peak in 1979. Although the stringent currency reform introduced in 1989 ended a damaging bout of hyperinflation, prices are now on a par with those in the West, while incomes have stagnated. Living conditions are difficult, particularly for young Belgraders, who, even after they finish college and marry, often are forced to live with their parents.

After Tito's death in 1980, the six republics found themselves embroiled in quarrels that often escalated into violence. Under the leadership of the charismatic Communist Slobodan Milŏsević, the Serbian Party began to lobby for a greater role in government. The rich, independently minded northern republics of Slovenia and Croatia called for democracy and the transformation of Yugoslavia into a loose, economically driven federation similar to the Common Market.

Milŏsević also pushed economic reform, but he wanted a strong Serbian elite to control the process. Rather than take Western countries as its model, President Milŏsević said Yugoslavia should pattern itself after Singapore or Taiwan — prosperous, nominally democratic countries that are essentially authoritarian. Milŏsević's proposals, intended to unite the country in a common purpose, have riven it further. Serbs see him as a pragmatician who can restore the foundering economy. Non-Serbs see him as a demagogue and a power-hungry populist who wants to restore Serbian tyranny.

There is one thing about Milŏsević that no Yugoslav doubts: that he has aroused Serbian nationalism and used it to reshape the country. His first target was the Albanians of Kosovo Province. Serbia's heartland since medieval times, Kosovo has recently been dominated by non-Slavic Albanians, who outnumber Serbs by eight to one. By mobilizing a massive contingent of nationalistic Serbs, Milŏsević has managed to bring Vojvodina and Kosovo under ever tighter Serbian control.

The cost of Milŏsević's move to reincorporate Kosovo is still unclear. When Kosovo was welcomed back into the Serbian fold in 1989, Serbs sang and danced in the streets of Belgrade. Thousands of angry Albanians also took to the streets, and though riot police eventually imposed a sullen truce, tensions seem ready to flare at any moment. Early last year, ultra-nationalists opposed to Milŏsević demonstrated in the capital, and the army was called in to crush the protests. Several marchers were killed and scores were injured.

Yugoslavia's tumultuous present is rooted in its past. Belgrade, located in a strategic spot at the confluence of the Sava and Danube rivers, has been fought over for centuries. Archaeologists have found that the area has been occupied continuously for several thousand years. During the 3rd century BC, bands of Celts settled in the river valleys. Roman legions conquered the region in the 1st century AD and garrisoned their troops in a fortress named Singidunum, the site of modern Belgrade. When the Roman Empire split in AD 395, the troops at Singidunum found themselves straddling the border between the two new entities. It was a precarious position. As the empire collapsed, barbarian tribes sacked the fortress repeatedly. The Huns razed Singidunum in the 5th century, and it remained abandoned for more than a century, until the Emperor Justinian ordered it rebuilt.

Slavs first migrated to the region in the mid-7th century. The city's Slavic name, Belgrade, was mentioned in a letter written by Pope John VIII to Bulgarian Prince Boris Mikhailo in 878. During the next few centuries, the town was at the center of a struggle between Hungarians sweeping in from the north and the Byzantine army advancing from the south. In 1127, the Hungarians built the citadel of Zemun on the right (north) bank of the Danube, using stones taken from buildings in Belgrade; later, Byzantine soldiers retook Zemun and used the same stones to rebuild Belgrade. When the Byzantine Empire collapsed, the Hungarians and Bulgarians fought for control of the city.

The Serbians became contenders in the early Middle Ages. The Serbian King Dragutin wrested Belgrade from the hands of the Hungarians in 1284, then lost it again shortly thereafter. In 1521, Belgrade was taken by Turkish armies, under the command of Suleiman the Magnificent. The Turks soon transformed the town from a flea-bitten garrison into a flourishing market town with 100,000 inhabitants. The Austrians captured the city briefly in 1683 and took it again in 1717, building the fortifications at Kalemegdan to protect it. The town was soon flooded with immigrants: Germans, Hungarians, French, Czechs, Slovaks. But the garrisons at Kalemegdan did little to stave off the Turks, who reoccupied the city in 1739, razing its monuments, transforming churches into mosques, and forcibly converting Belgrade's citizens to Islam.

More than a century later, in 1867, the Serbs succeeded in toppling their Turkish overlords, and Belgrade became the capital of an independent Serbian Republic. Freed from the Ottoman yoke, the city grew apace; the first trains chugged into Belgrade Station in 1884, and electricity arrived 8 years later.

When World War I broke out in 1914, Belgrade was bombed steadily by the Austrians for 4 months before surrendering; the Austrians held the city for only 13 days. In 1915, after another bloody battle, the Austrians occupied it a second time. At the end of the war, Belgrade became the capital of the Independent Kingdom of the Serbs, Croats, and Slovenes. (The name was changed to Yugoslavia in 1929.)

The city grew rapidly between the two world wars, but progress was short-lived. On the morning of *Palm Sunday* on April 6, 1941, the city was pounded with German bombs. Though Yugoslavia was officially neutral and

Hitler did not formally declare war against the Yugoslavs, his intention was clear: destroy civilian morale by wreaking maximum destruction. More than 25,000 people were killed on that bloody Sunday. During the German occupation, more than 80,000 Yugoslav resistance fighters were shot by Nazi firing squads at Jajinci on the outskirts of Belgrade. The Germans finally withdrew when the Soviet Red Army and the Yugoslav Communists liberated the capital on October 20, 1944.

As it has been so many times in the past, Yugoslavia is once again threatened by ethnic strife. Although Yugoslavs generally are pro-Western and tourist-savvy, they may not take kindly to criticisms of their country. Should you find yourself in a café on Knez Mihailova chatting with some locals, think twice before you raise a political question. The ever-volatile Yugoslavs harbor a particular passion for politics, and unless you want your chat to turn into a general shouting match, you may be best off sticking to a discussion of the weather.

BELGRADE AT-A-GLANCE

 SEEING THE CITY: The most spectacular view is from the Ušće Quai on the Sava River looking up at the fortress at Kalemegdan. A good vantage spot for the same view is the *Museum of Modern Art* there, which is open daily except Tuesdays. The best view of downtown is from atop the Beogradjanaka Building located at 5 Masarikova (the 24-story skyscraper, which used to be the headquarters of the Central Committee of the Federal Executive Council, is now a business center — just take an elevator to the top floor).

 SPECIAL PLACES: Knez Mihailova is the city's heart and soul. It begins near the *Moskva* hotel (see *Checking In*) on Terazije Square (which isn't a square at all, but a broad boulevard), and runs northwest through the Old Town to Kalemegdan Park. Once an ancient Roman road, Knez Mihailova was the central axis of the first town plan, drawn up in 1867 by Emilijan Josimovic, a professor at the Lyceum. The street was named Mihailova in 1872, after Serbian Prince Mihailo Obrenović, and is now Belgrade's main shopping street.

OLD BELGRADE (STARI GRAD)

Kalemegdan Fortress (Tvrdjava Kalemegdan) – This strategic redoubt is Belgrade's most important historic monument, and the site of the city's largest and most popular park. The core of the Old City was once located on the bluff near the fort. Near the end of the 1st century AD, the Romans built a fortress on the hill; it eventually became the permanent headquarters of the Fourth Flavian Legion. Invading Huns and Goths destroyed the Roman fortifications, and Avars and Slavs demolished its massive walls. Byzantine Emperor Michael Comnenus built a new garrison atop the rubble in the 12th century. Three hundred years later, Serbian chief Stefan Lazarevic expanded and strengthened the fort, and built a palace and a dock on the Sava River; a town soon sprang up within the ramparts of the fort.

Although most of the fort's walls date from the 19th century, a few signs of its venerable history remain. Visitors enter through a baroque gate built by Prince Eugene of Savoy, who temporarily liberated the city from the Turks in 1717. Inside, there is a Roman bath, a 16th-century Turkish fountain, and the Ružica Orthodox Church, built in 1730.

Kalemegdan is a favorite leisure spot among Belgraders. There are tennis and basketball courts, open-air cafés and restaurants, a good *Military Museum* (Vojni Muzej; open 10 AM to 5 PM; closed Mondays; admission charge), a *Hunting and Forestry Museum* (Muzej šumarstva i lova), the zoo (*zooloski vrt*), and the *Cvijeta Zuzoric Art Pavilion* (open 10 AM to 6 PM, Sundays to 2 PM, closed Mondays; admission charge), where contemporary Serbian painters and sculptors hold exhibitions. Busts and statues of Serbian writers, artists, politicians, and public figures grace the park, where townspeople often perform impromptu folk dances on Sunday afternoons.

Serbian Orthodox Cathedral (Srpske Prazoslazne Crkve) – Located at the foot of the fortress at Kalemegdan, the church was built between 1837 and 1845 and is dedicated to the Archangel Michael. The architecture is neo-classical, embellished with baroque flourishes. Inside are tombs of several Serbian princes. Before the monarchy was abolished, Serbian kings were crowned in the cathedral. To this day, patriarchs of the Serbian Orthodox church are elected and installed here.

Bijrakli Mosque (Bajrakli Dzamija) – Up the street from the cathedral is the city's only remaining mosque. At the height of Ottoman influence during the 18th century, Belgrade's Muslims worshipped in 20 different mosques. This survivor is of negligible architectural import. The locals call it the Mosque of the Flag, in remembrance of the days when a signal flag was flown from its dome five times a day to call the *imams* (in Islam, religious teachers) of the city to prayer.

Princess Ljubica's Palace (Konak Knjeginje Ljubice) – At the corner of Sime Maricovića and 7 Jula Streets stands Belgrade's best surviving example of a 19th-century Balkan palace. Built for Prince Miloš's wife in 1831, and furnished in the opulent style of the time, it is now a museum. Open weekdays 10 AM to 5 PM, weekends 9 AM to 4 PM; closed Mondays. Admission charge.

Skadarlija – This is Belgrade's equivalent to Paris's Montmartre, or so the locals say. It certainly attracts similar hordes of tourists; more than 20,000 jam the streets each day. The district has a charm that the rest of the city lacks. The neighborhood was settled in the 1830s by Gypsies, who built their homes in the shadow of the old Turkish ramparts. Their flimsy dwellings were later torn down and replaced with brick buildings, artisan workshops, and cafés. By the turn of the century, Skadarlija was attracting a bohemian set of actors, painters, and members of the literati. Stroll about and enjoy the cafés, restaurants, Gypsy street-singers, folk dancers, open-air theaters, and cabarets. In summer, the main cobblestone street is lined with food stands and crafts stalls.

Terazije Square – Technically, it's not a square at all, but one of the city's major thoroughfares. (Belgraders refer to it simply as "Terazije," without further embellishment.) Knez Mihailova, the city's main shopping street, begins here. On the far side of this pedestrian area is the *Moskva* hotel, with its popular café. It is here that the longest and widest street in Old Belgrade, the 4-mile-long Bulevar Revolucije (Boulevard of the Revolution) begins. The boulevard skirts Yugoslavia's Parliament, an undistinguished neo-classical building dating from 1936, and continues past a bustling commercial zone to Tašmajdan Park and the Church of Sveti Mark. Four tremendous pillars support the towering dome of the church; King Alexander and Queen Draga, who were brutally murdered by terrorists in 1903, are buried inside.

Republic Square (Trg Republike) – Located just off Knez Mihailova, it is the city's grandest square. Built in the latter part of the 19th century, when Stambol Gate was torn down to make room for the new *National Theater,* this is where the road to Istanbul began. (Stambol Gate was reviled by the nationalistic Serbs, for it was here that the Turks executed victims, impaling the heads of those who dared to defy Ottoman rule.) An equestrian statue of Prince Mihailo Obrenović, a Serbian leader, stands in the center of the square. On one side is the *National Museum,* on another is the *National Theater.*

NEW BELGRADE (NOVI BEOGRAD)

Once a barren marsh, the area north of the Sava River has become a thriving commercial center. No one would say that Novi Beograd has style, unless Stalinist architecture is your idea of high art. But it is here that the nation's bureaucracy ticks along, and where visitors convene at the ultramodern *Sava Convention Center* and *Belgrade Fairgrounds.* The fairgrounds (on Vojvode Mišića Blvd.) cover an area of 99 acres and have 14 exhibition halls. The large convention center is located at 9 Milentija Popovića (phone: 222-4322 or 222-4323). The city's two most modern hotels, the *Hyatt Regency* and the *Intercontinental* (see *Checking In* for both), are located near the center of Novi Beograd.

St. Sava Cathedral (Katedrala Svetog Save) – When completed, it will be the largest Eastern Orthodox church in the world. Ground was broken for the church — modeled after the Byzantine Hagia Sophia in Istanbul (which is now a mosque) — in 1953, and after a long hiatus under the Communists, construction resumed in 1986. The notion of building a cathedral dedicated to St. Sava (1175–1235), the father of Serbian culture, was first proposed in 1895. Priests already conduct services in the half-finished church, and there are guided tours. Kataníceva St.

Josip Broz Tito Memorial Center – Located a few miles south of the city center (at 10A Bulevar Oktobarske Revolucije), this was the home and office of Marshal Tito, Yugoslavia's longtime Communist leader. After his death in 1980, Tito was buried here in a massive tomb, and the villa was turned into a museum; the exhibitions give an in-depth picture of Yugoslavia's most famous modern political figure. Be forewarned: Tito, once revered to the point of fanaticism, has now fallen out of favor, and there is talk of closing the memorial. The center can be reached by trolley buses Nos. 40 and 41, and is open every day except Monday from 9 AM to 4 PM. Admission charge. In the Kuća Cveća (House of Flowers; phone: 687409).

ENVIRONS

Zemun – This charming suburb, north of the city on the Danube, has an authentic Austrian flavor. While all the settlements south of the Danube, including Belgrade, were long under Turkish control, Zemun straddled the borders between the Ottoman and Austro-Hungarian empires. On sunny Sundays, many Belgraders stroll along the riverbank to the town. In the summer, regattas are launched from Zemun, and windsurfers disport near the shore. The town has some of the best restaurants in Yugoslavia (see *Eating Out*), and there is a large open-air market near the river. Visitors can walk to the town or take bus No. 17, which departs from the main market at Zeleni venac (Green Garland) in downtown Belgrade.

Iron Gates (Zeljezna Kapija) – After the Sava joins the Danube at Belgrade, the river flows for some 65 miles through the fertile Serbian plains to the Romanian border. Just before the frontier, the river flows into a 2-mile stretch of spectacular rapids. Until a massive dam (the Iron Gates) was built in 1963, innumerable lives were lost in the turbulent waters. Roads to the Iron Gates are in poor condition; the best way to visit the falls is to take a hydrofoil from Belgrade from Kladovo. Most agencies arrange tours through the *Beogradbrod Travel Agency* at 8 Karadjordjeva on the Belgrade harbor (phone: 622279).

■ **EXTRA SPECIAL:** Gypsy Island (Ada Ciganlija). Belgrade summers can be swelteringly hot. Many residents of the city escape to this small island in the middle of the Sava River to sun or sail. Don't expect luxury (there are restaurants, but no hotels). No one would dare compare the beaches to those along the Adriatic, but all the same the island offers a welcome break from the bustle of the city. Boats can be rented, and there's even a nudist beach. Take a No.23 bus from the center of town.

SOURCES AND RESOURCES

TOURIST INFORMATION: Guided tours, maps, and information on cultural events are available from the city's central tourist office, located on Knez Mihailova in the Albania underpass at Terazije Square. It is open daily from 8 AM to 8 PM (phone: 635343, 635662, or 182382). There also are tourist information offices at the Central Railroad Station (phone: 646240), which is open daily except Sundays from 7 AM to 10 PM. English-speaking guides can be hired at the tourist office at 21 Studentski Square (phone: 629811 or 628791). In addition to the information available from the official tourist offices, Belgrade has several travel agencies that offer various services. Most run their own car-rental agencies, and some have their own hotels. The largest are *Putnik* (1 Dragoslava Jovanovića; phone: 352591); *Yugotours* (31 Djure Djakovića; phone: 764622); *JAT-Air Lift* (1 Moše Pijade; phone: 326503); and *InexTurist* (5 Trg Republike; phone: 622360).

The US Embassy is located at 50 Kneza Miloša (phone: 645655). Along with the US Consulate (at the same location), it is open Mondays to Fridays from 7 AM until noon.

Local Coverage – A weekly edition of the Belgrade daily *Politika* is published in English. But beware: The paper, once the most respected in the country, has been turned into a pro-Serbian propaganda sheet by President Slobodan Milošević. Details on cultural and sporting events are available in the monthly English edition of *Beospektar.* Western newspapers and magazines — such as the *International Herald Tribune, Time,* and *Newsweek* — are readily available. The best newsstands for foreign publications are in the *Intercontinental, Hyatt, Jugoslavija, Metropol,* and *Slavija* hotels; at the Central Railway Station; at Terazije in front of the *Moskva* hotel, and in the pedestrian subway near the *Beograd* cinema.

TELEPHONE: The country code for Yugoslavia is 38; the city code for Belgrade is 11. The telephone system seems to work better here than anywhere else in Eastern Europe, and there is direct dialing to the US.

GETTING AROUND: Belgrade is a good city for walkers, particularly in the downtown pedestrian area. It's also large, and has spread out considerably in recent years, so at some point you'll probably need to use public transportation or cabs. The subway is still unfinished.

Airport – The Belgrade Airport is just 11 miles (18 km) from the city center, and there are direct flights to most major cities in Europe, North America, Asia, the Middle East, and North Africa. *JAT,* the Yugoslav state airline, makes regular trips from here to most Yugoslav cities. Internal flights were once ridiculously inexpensive — just $20 or so one way from Belgrade to Dubrovnik. Under the government's austerity plan, however, domestic plane fares have skyrocketed: The trip to Dubrovnik now costs around $100 one way. For information on departures and arrivals, call 675992 or 601424.

Taxis can get to the city center from the airport in only 20 minutes, but the fare is steep: about $30. *JAT* runs buses every 10 minutes from 4 AM to 9 PM from its office on 17 Bulevar Revolucije (phone: 330310). The fare is about $1.

Boat – The Port of Belgrade is located on the right bank of the Danube and handles 3 million tons of cargo and 10,000 containers each year. The passenger terminal (8 Karadjordjeva) and docks are a few blocks north from the train station, on the right bank of the Sava, near its confluence with the Danube. Passenger and excursion ships going from Vienna and Budapest to the Black Sea stop here. The hydrofoils that skim up the Danube to the Romanian border and the Iron Gates (See *Special Places*) also depart from here; for schedules and ticket information, call the *Beogradbrod Travel Agency* (phone: 622279).

Bus – The main bus station is located right next to the railway station (4 Zeleznička; phone: 624751 or 627049). The bus company is a public monopoly called *GSP*. Buses going to all the major towns in the country leave from the station, which also is a stopover for several international coach lines. Buy tickets for the bus at tobacco (*duvan*) shops — if you buy them on the bus they will cost twice as much. A single-price ticket is good for one trip, with no transfers. It's most economical and efficient to buy a six-strip ticket, good for six trips. Validate the ticket onboard, because there are spot checks, and stiff fines for violators.

Car Rental – *Hertz, Avis, Europcar,* and all other major international rental companies are represented. *Hertz* has two offices, one at the airport (phone: 601555, ext. 2754); the other at the *Jugoslavija* hotel (3 Bulevar Edvarda Karadjordjeva; phone: 692339). *Avis* has five offices: at the airport (phone: 601555, exts. 2920 and 2924); at the Central Railway Station (phone: 683007); at the *Intercontinental* (10 Vladmira Popovića; phone: 131910); and two downtown (at 25 Obilićev venac; phone: 629423 or 620362; and 30 Maksima Gorkog; phone: 444-5366 and 457677). All the rental agencies' fleets include a wide variety of vehicles, from standard European models to large American-made limousines. (Native-built Yugos are available, too, but they aren't terribly reliable; since the driving in Yugoslavia can be tough, they are not recommended.)

Taxi – Belgrade used to be a great taxi town, with easy-to-find cabs and inexpensive fares. There still are plenty of taxis, but fares have skyrocketed. Hail one in the street, and make sure the driver starts the meter. Cabs also may be ordered by phoning *Radio Taxi* (phone: 444-3443, 417377, or 622796).

Train – Belgrade is a crossroads for trains coming from Italy, Austria, and Hungary to the north and west and Sofia, Istanbul, Thessaloníki, and Athens to the south. The main railway station, which handles almost all traffic except trains to Romania, is located downtown (1 Trg Bratstva i Jedinstixa; phone: 645822, 645843, or 646636). Trains to Romania depart from the Danube Railway Station (39 Djure Djakovića; phone: 763880).

 LOCAL SERVICES: Dentist (English-Speaking) – A dental clinic is located at 15 Ivana Milutinovića (phone: 443491); you'll find someone who speaks English there.

 Dry Cleaner – Best bet is your hotel.

Limousine Service – Inquire at your hotel, or some of the private car rental agencies.

Medical Emergency – Telephone number is 94. The hospital is at the *Boris Kidriča Health Center,* 1 Pasterova (phone: 683755).

National/International Courier – *DHL International,* 6 Vladimira Popovića (phone: 222-4825).

Office Equipment Rental – Contact the Yugoslav Chamber of Commerce (23 Terazije; phone: 339461); the *Hyatt Regency Belgrade* provides excellent business services (see *Checking In*).

Pharmacy – The newspapers publish a list of after-hours pharmacies.

Photocopies – There are quite a few private shops in the center of town; look for a sign saying "Photocopies."

Post Office – The main post office is at 6 Takovska (open Mondays to Fridays 7 AM to 8 PM and Saturdays 9 AM to 4 PM.

Secretary/Stenographer (English-Speaking) – Contact the Chamber of Commerce or the *Hyatt* hotel.

Tailor – Inquire at your hotel for the closest tailor (*krojač*).

Translator – Contact the Chamber of Commerce or the *Hyatt* hotel.

 SPECIAL EVENTS: In recent years, Belgrade's cultural scene has grown livelier. It peaks in October, when the city hosts *BITEF,* a theater festival that features avant-garde and experimental theater from around the globe; and *BEMUS,* a classical music festival with foreign orchestras, choirs, operas, and ballet troupes. October also is the time of the *Joy of Europe,* an annual children's art festival that is attended by young folks from Eastern and Western Europe. In January, the city hosts *FEST,* an international film festival; every November, the *Belgrade Jazz* (*Beograski Dzez*) *Festival* takes place. For information: 22 Makedenska, Belgrade 11000 (phone: 320127).

 MUSEUMS: Belgrade doesn't have a *Louvre* or a *Prado,* but there are still a fair number of artworks to see. Hours vary according to season, but museums generally are open from 9 AM to 4 PM. Most museums are closed Mondays.

Ethnographic Museum (Enografski Muzej) – Displays of Serbian costumes, textiles, and rugs, as well as traditional utensils and farming equipment, ritual objects, and paintings of events from Serbian history. There also is a collection of 19th-century photography. Open 10 AM to 5 PM; Thursdays until 7 PM; Saturdays from 9 AM; closed Mondays. Admission charge. 13 Studentski Trg (phone: 181888).

Frescoes Gallery (Galerija Fresaka) – Contains replicas of the finest medieval frescoes from Serbian and Macedonian monasteries. The oldest Serbian frescoes date from the 11th century; though these aren't the real thing, they are exceptional copies, and since most of the monasteries are difficult to reach, the museum at least gives a sense of the treasures they contain. Open 10 AM to 5 PM; Thursdays and Saturdays open until 7 PM; closed Mondays. Admission charge. 20 Cara Urosa St. (phone: 621491).

Military Museum (Vojni Muzej) – Has exhibits of four periods: the 6th to the 13th centuries and the Ottoman conquest; the period of Turkish rule from the 14th to the 19th centuries; the Serbian struggle for independence, which began with the uprising of 1804 and ended in 1918; and the Resistance movement during World War II. There also are open-air displays of 18th- and 19th-century cannon, heavy artillery and field guns, and equipment used by World War II Resistance fighters. Open 10 AM to 5 PM; closed Mondays. Admission charge. Located inside the Kalemegdan fortress (phone: 620722).

Museum of Modern Art (Muzej Savremene Umetnosti) – It has 6,000 paintings, prints, and other works by 20th-century Yugoslav artists in its permanent collection. There also are frequent special installations. The view from the museum across the Sava River to the Kalemegdan fortress is spectacular. Open 10 AM to 5 PM; closed Tuesdays. Admission charge. In Novi Beograd on the Quai Ušće (phone: 326544).

Museum of the Serbian Orthodox Church (Muzej Srpske Pravoslavne Crkve) – Founded in 1856, the museum houses a collection of 9,300 objects, of which 530 are on permanent display. They include ecclesiastical portraits, engravings, manuscripts, liturgical vestments and objects, and medieval Byzantine seals and historical documents. 5 Sedmog Jula (phone: 635699).

National Museum (Narodni Muzej) – The ground floor is devoted to archaeology; the second, to painting. Skip the archaeology and head upstairs. The museum has an excellent collection of French Impressionists, including 40 works by Renoir and 20 by

Degas. There also are paintings by Tintoretto, Rubens, Breughel, Monet, and Picasso. If you still have the energy, head back downstairs to see the fragments of medieval frescoes from Serbian monasteries and the superb icons from Ohrid. Open 10 AM to 5 PM; Thursdays until 7 PM; Saturdays from 9 AM; Sundays until 2 PM; closed Mondays. Admission charge. Trg Republike (phone: 624322).

 SHOPPING: There are no great bargains here; prices are equal to those in Western Europe. The best buys are on handmade native goods: wool sweaters, folk art, and jewelry. Many have an appealing Oriental air. Look for them at the *Yugo Export* and the *Narodna Radinost* shops, both of which can be found along Knez Mihailova, the pedestrian shopping street. Handicrafts also are sold in lively open-air markets, where everything from fresh produce to kitchen utensils to clothes is on display. The largest and most colorful market is at Zeleni venac, down the street from the *Moskva* hotel. But beware: The quality here is not as high as it is at *Yugo Export* and *Naradna Radinost.* The markets are open daily from 5 AM. Other shops are open from 8 AM to 8 PM, with a midday break. Many shops on Knez Mihailova stay open until 10 PM.

 SPORTS AND FITNESS: Belgrade is a great sports city for participants and spectators alike. The city has several hundred sports clubs and associations, and the stadiums and public facilities are excellent. Favorite sports here are soccer and basketball.

Basketball – Belgrade's own *Red Stars* are the most famous team. They play at *Košarkaški Stadium* (2 Kalemegdan; phone: 623-5000). Most sports clubs also have basketball courts. Among the best are *Sportski Tašmajdan* in Tašmajdan Park (26 Georgi Dimitrova; phone: 331353); *Sporsko Rekreativni Centar Zvezdara* (11 Vjekeslava Kovaca; phone: 414901); and *Stadion JNA* (JNA Army Stadium; 1 Humska; phone: 648222).

Fitness Centers – The city boasts several all-purpose sports complexes, featuring everything from exercise rooms to soccer stadiums and swimming pools. Among them are *Tašmajdan* (26 Georgi Dimitrova St.; phone: 347430); *Pionir* (39 Carli Caplina St.; phone: 766566); *Banjica* (4 Crnotravska St.; phone: 668700 or 667999); *Pinki* (2 Gradski Park; phone: 615422); and *Vračar* (1 Sjenika St.; phone: 452342).

Horse Racing – The *Belgrade Hippodrome* opened in 1914 and is the city's oldest track. Horse racing has been a popular organized sport here since 1863. The season runs from early June until late September. Careva cuprija (phone: 559858).

Soccer – *Red Star Stadium* (1 Ljutice Bodana; phone: 662341) is the largest in the Balkans; with room for 105,000 spectators, it hosts the *Crvena Zvezda* (Red Army) team. The other major arena, the *JNA Army Stadium,* is nearby (1 Humska; phone: 648222); it has a seating capacity of 55,000, and hosts the *Partizan* team.

Swimming – The *Hyatt* (phone: 222-1234), *Intercontinental* (phone: 222-3333), and *Jugoslavija* hotels (phone: 600222) all have good pools, saunas, and massage rooms. There is an Olympic-size pool at Tašmajdan Park (26 Georgi Dimitrova; phone: 331353 or 340901). Some sports centers also have regulation-size pools. You also can swim (in the nude, if you like) at the beaches on the Ada Ciganlija, the small island in the Sava River.

Tennis – The *Intercontinental* has both indoor and outdoor courts (phone: 222-3333). Most sports clubs have courts of some sort.

 THEATER: Belgraders are serious theatergoers: The city has eight professional repertory theaters, which stage a total of 50 premieres and 3,000 performances each year. The *National Theater* (2 Trg Republike; phone: 628640), the oldest in the city, also hosts local opera and ballet. The theater staged its first play in 1869; its first opera, Puccini's *Madame Butterfly,* premiered in 1920. For avant-garde productions, the best bets are *Atelje 212* (21 Lole Ribara; phone: 346146), *Teatar Pozoriste "Dušan Radović"* (1 Aberdareva; phone: 332072), and *Bitef Teatar* (1 Drinčićeva; phone: 320608). Tickets are available at the individual box offices.

MUSIC: Belgrade has four professional symphonies: the *Belgrade Philharmonic* at Sala Kolarac (5 Studenski Trg; phone: 659277); the *Belgrade Radio and Television Symphony Orchestra and Choir;* the *JNA Army Symphony Orchestra and Choir;* and the *Belgrade Opera,* which performs at the *National Theater* (2 Trg Republike; phone: 628640). The *Kolo Folk Dance Group* performs national songs and dances. Tickets are available at the box office or from hotel reception desks.

NIGHTCLUBS AND NIGHTLIFE: Belgraders love to dance. Almost all the good hotels have a bar with dancing. On summer evenings, there's often dancing in the streets in Skadarlija. Recommended restaurants that offer a chance to take a turn around the floor include the *Citadela* (outside of town at Banovci; phone: 228-5220); the *Topčiderska noc* (Bulevar Vojvode Mišića bb; phone: 652299); *Crvena Zvezda* (Kalemegdan; phone: 620500); *Jezero* (Ada Ciganlija; phone: 544455); *Pri Majolki* (5 Palmira Toljatija in Novi Beograd; phone: 604774); *Resava* (24 General Zdanova; phone: 333192); and *Stadion* (1 Humska; phone: 648573). The *Metropol* and *Jugoslavija* hotels each has a casino, open from 9 PM to 3 AM (see *Checking In*).

BEST IN TOWN

CHECKING IN: Lodging is not as dire a problem here as it once was. There are at least a dozen commendable hotels, but count on paying Western prices. The best, the *Hyatt* and the *Intercontinental,* have plenty of amenities, but they are inconveniently located in Novi Beograd, across the river from the Old Town. The best lodgings downtown are the *Slavija Lux* and the *Moskva.* Most downtown hotels are higher on charm than comfort. Expect to pay $140 to $180 for a double room in hotels listed as expensive, about $100 to $130 for moderate accommodations, and $60 to $90 for inexpensive ones. (There are less expensive hostelries, but unless the *YMCA* is your idea of luxury, they're not worth patronizing.) All telephone numbers are in the 11 area code unless otherwise indicated.

Beograd Intercontinental – Until the *Hyatt* came along, this was the only authentically deluxe establishment in town. Near the *Sava Center* in Novi Beograd, its neo-modernist architecture is a long way from the kind that projects warmth and welcome. There are 420 rooms with color satellite TV, 24-hour room service, laundry and dry cleaning, and direct-dial phones. Guests can choose from among 4 restaurants; there's also a nightclub. The recreation center has indoor and outdoor tennis courts, 2 squash courts, a swimming pool, sauna, massage room, solarium, and steamroom. Conference rooms also are available. 10 Vladimira Popovića (phone: 222-3333 or 800-327-0200). Expensive.

Hyatt Regency Belgrade – Belgrade's newest — and finest — property, it's located on Dimitrije Tucovíc Square, right next to the *Sava Center* in Novi Beograd. Giving new meaning to the word luxury as it applies in the Balkans, it has an elegant lobby with a sunken garden and waterfall and 308 antiques-filled rooms, including 86 suites (the Presidential Suite goes for $800 a night). All the rooms have air conditioning units that can be individually controlled — a must during the hot, humid summer months. Each room has a mini-bar and color satellite TV set. There also is a day-care service and a business center with fax machines, photocopiers, and offices and translators for hire. The hotel has a gym, massage room, solarium, and swimming pool, as well as a good Italian restaurant and a jazz club. 5 Milentija Popovića (phone: 222-1234 or 800-233-1234). Expensive.

Jugoslavija – Belgrade's largest property, it has a total of 473 rooms, suites, and apartments, all air conditioned. Though half its rooms overlook the Danube, the location next to a busy highway is less than appealing. Call it Stalinist-style luxury, but at least there's a casino. 3 Bulevar Edvarda Kardelja (phone: 600222). Expensive.

Moskva – Belgrade's elite establishment for many years before a devastating bombing raid in April 1941, this former grande dame could stand a major overhaul; nevertheless, it does retain some of its Old World charm. Constructed in 1906 and now a historic monument, it has 132 rooms and suites (none of them air conditioned), including 6 residential apartments. There is a restaurant (see *Eating Out*), and the café, with its pleasant outdoor terrace, is a popular meeting place for locals. 1 Balkanska (phone: 686255). Expensive.

Slavija Lux – Located downtown on Dimitrije Tucović Square, this modern hostelry has 100 rooms, including 64 doubles, 24 singles, and 11 suites. All the rooms have direct-dial telephone, air conditioning, color TV sets, and mini-bars. There's a 7th-floor restaurant with an outdoor terrace, and a piano bar and an aperitif bar just off the main lobby; also a sauna and fitness center. 2 Svetog Save (phone: 444-1422). Expensive.

Excelsior – Located in the center of town, just around the corner from the *JAT* bus terminal and 10 minutes from the railway and city bus stations, this 1923 property has 86 rooms and 6 suites. There's a restaurant that seats 100 (the food is pretty good) and a conference room that can accommodate 40 people. The hotel is one of the city's architectural landmarks, though it could use a face-lift. 5 Kneza Milosa (phone: 331381). Moderate.

Majestic – A charmer that could use a featherdusting, this was one of Belgrade's most elegant hotels half a century ago. Its location, just off Knez Mihailova, is super. Many of its 90 rooms still have pre–World War II furniture; there are 8 suites. Locals love the café, which serves terrific iced coffee. 28 Obilićev venac (phone: 636022). Moderate.

Metropol – A concrete-block behemoth in Tašmajdan Park, with 218 rooms and 6 suites. The giant *Arhiv* restaurant (see *Eating Out*) can serve up to 800 people at one sitting. The hotel has a casino, and a pleasant outdoor terrace overlooks the park. 69 Bulevar Revolucije (phone: 330910). Moderate.

Palace – Situated in the oldest part of town, next to a little park, this old-fashioned dowager has 63 rooms and 15 suites, all with color television sets; there are 2 large restaurants. 23 Topličin venac (phone: 637222). Moderate.

Slavija – This bleak, Iron Curtain–style property dominates Dimitrije Tucović Square. There are 268 single rooms, 226 doubles, 16 suites, and an annex with an additional 178 rooms. It specializes in handling large groups, so if you're not keen on crowded lobbies, stay away. 1 Svetog Save (phone: 450842). Moderate to inexpensive.

Astoria – Built in 1936, this 77-room hostelry recently has been spiffed up, but don't expect the *Ritz*. Near the railway and bus stations. 1 Milovana Milovanovića (phone: 645422). Inexpensive.

Balkan – Recommended only for its nifty location, right on Terazije Square. Rooms — there are 25 singles and 45 doubles — can be tatty. The garden restaurant is pleasant, though, and there is a billiard room. 2 Prizrenska (phone: 687466). Inexpensive.

Beograd – Offering basic lodging near the train station, it has 58 rooms and 4 suites. 52 Balkanska (phone: 645199). Inexpensive.

Kasina – This place overlooks Terazije Square and has an outdoor café. 25 Terazije (phone: 335574). Inexpensive.

Park – A 130-room hostelry located downtown, next to the old flower market. 4 Njegoševa (phone: 334722). Inexpensive.

Splendid – Nearby the Knez Mihailova shopping district, it has 18 single and 31 double rooms. Though hardly deserving of its name, it is decent. 5 Dragoslava Jovanovića (phone: 335444). Inexpensive.

Union – Another aging downtown property with 75 rooms, near the pedestrian district. 11 Kosovska (phone: 187036). Inexpensive.

 EATING OUT: Don't think fancy. If Serbs try to copy French haute cuisine, they invariably fail. Kept simple, though, the food can be delicious. Grilled meat — *cevapcici* (grilled spicy ground beef sausages) and kebabs — are local favorites. There also is excellent spit-roasted spring lamb or suckling pig. Stuffed peppers and spicy meat patties also are good. Everything is served in heaping portions with carafes of Yugoslav wine, which ranges from palatable to good.

There are dozens of good restaurants in Belgrade, and enterprising families are opening new ones almost daily. Avoid the pretentious spots in the big hotels. The modest eateries are much cheerier, and, generally, the simpler the setting, the better the food. Look for a place with singers and musicians, or if the weather is fair, something with an outdoor terrace. The most popular places are in the bustling Skadarlija area. Unfortunately, they're often packed to the rafters with tourists. A good meal should cost no more than $20 a person.

Accidental tourists who would rather be at home watching the *Red Sox* can find solace in a Big Mac. Two *McDonald's* have opened in Belgrade; both are tremendously popular. The one in Slavija Square opened in 1988, the first *McDonald's* in the Soviet bloc; the other is on Terazije across from the *Moskva* hotel. Everything is locally made, right down to the ketchup, which is tough to find in this part of the world. (Yugoslavs have plenty of tomato paste, tomato purée, and tomato sauce, but nothing that resembles ketchup.) The burgers are no worse — or no better, depending on your taste — than their stateside counterparts. Dinner for two in a restaurant listed as expensive will cost about $40; in a moderate place, $30; and in an inexpensive one, under $25. All telephone numbers are in the 11 area code unless otherwise indicated.

SKADARLIJA

Dva Bela Goluba – Featuring good local fare, this place also offers live music. Reservations unnecessary. Major credit cards accepted. 18 Skadarska (phone: 339079). Expensive.

Dva Jelena – One of the newest in the city, it serves regional meat and fish dishes. Reservations unnecessary. Major credit cards accepted. 32 Skadarska (phone: 334834). Expensive.

Ima Dana – For alfresco dining. Reservations unnecessary. Major credit cards accepted. 38 Skadarska (phone: 334422). Expensive.

Skadarlija – This place also offers alfresco dining. Reservations unnecessary. Major credit cards accepted. 17 Cetinjska (phone: 334983). Expensive.

Tri Sešira – Serves traditional Serbian cooking, including a mixed grill of ham, steak, liver, and sausage. Top off the meal with a glass of red vranac wine. Reservations advised. Major credit cards accepted. 31 Skadarska (phone: 347501). Expensive.

Zlatni Bokal – This dining spot features regional fare and offers live music. Reservations unnecessary. Major credit cards accepted. 26 Skadarska (phone: 334834). Expensive.

DOWNTOWN

Restoran Hotela Moskva – Good Serbian specialties, but short on atmosphere. Reservations advised. Major credit cards accepted. At the *Moskva Hotel*, 1 Balkanska (phone: 324613). Expensive.

Arhiv – Named after the nearby *Serbian National Archives*, this restaurant, decorated with turn-of-the-century photographs, offers traditional Serbian dishes and friendly service. Reservations necessary. Major credit cards accepted. Located in the *Metropol Hotel*, 69 Revolucije Blvd. (phone: 513-30911; fax: 332991). Moderate.

Dva Ribara – One of the best seafood restaurants in Belgrade. The prices are surprisingly low. Not far from the *Moskva* hotel. Reservations unnecessary. Major credit cards accepted. 21 Narodnog fronta (phone: 686471). Moderate.

Peking – For those who are desperate for Chinese food. No reservations. Major credit cards accepted. 2 Vuka Karadzica (phone: 181931). Moderate.

Tabor – A find. This great privately owned place has excellent grilled meat. The locals love it. A bit far from the center of town, but worth the hike. Reservations advised. Major credit cards accepted. 348 Bulevar Revolucije (phone: 412464). Moderate.

Kod Crepajca – A typical small-town Yugoslavian restaurant, it offers traditional Serbian food and prompt service. If you happen to be here on a Saturday when a portion of the place has been rented out to a wedding party, you also could enjoy traditional Serbian music — sometimes cheery, sometimes nostalgic, and often sung by all the patrons. Reservations unnecessary. 16 Svetozara Miletica, Pancevo, 10 miles (16 km) northeast of Belgrade (no phone). Moderate to inexpensive.

McDonald's – The golden arches grace two locations in Belgrade. Their locally made Big Macs and fries should stave off any homesickness. Two locations: Terazije Sq. and Slavija Sq. (no phones). Inexpensive.

ZEMUN

This suburb has two of the finest — and most expensive — private restaurants in Yugoslavia. American diplomats tend to congregate here.

Daka – 39 Hercegovacka (phone: 101319). Expensive.

Zlatnik – 26 Slavonska (phone: 101365). Expensive.

RIVERBOAT DINING

A wonderful way to dine in Belgrade is to board one of the riverboats that have been permanently moored and turned into restaurants.

Barakuda – Near the beach at 3 Ada Ciganlija (phone: 544344). Moderate.

Dijalog – Great downtown location on Ušće Quai (phone: 768626). Moderate.

Kazablanka – At Ada Ciganlija bb (phone: 545654). Moderate.

Savski Galeb – Moored in the Sava River at Ušće Save (phone: 150900). Moderate.

■ **Not for members only:** Many of Belgrade's best restaurants are located in clubs run by local associations. They are open to the public and some are reasonably priced. They're also a good place to get a glimpse of local life.

Klub Privrednika (Entrepreneurs Club) – The locale is hardly elegant — it's in a basement — but this recently refurbished club offers charm, good service, and well-prepared food. Reservations advised. Major credit cards accepted. Not far from the *Moskva* hotel at 34 Terazije (phone: 658739). Expensive.

Klub Knjizevnika (Writers Club) – A celebrated venue for journalists and writers, located in the basement of a villa. The atmosphere is boisterous — and bibulous, too. Reservations unnecessary. Major credit cards accepted. 7 Fancuska (phone: 627931). Moderate.

Klub Bojan Stupica – Located behind the *Yugoslav Drama Theater,* it really comes alive after a performance. The food's not great, but this is the place to see the "in" crowd. No reservations. Major credit cards accepted. 50 Maršala Tita (phone: 686285). Inexpensive.

 CAFÉS: Belgrade has innumerable cafés, many with outdoor terraces. Among the best — and most popular — are the two that front the *Majestic* and *Moskva* hotels. Sit back and sip a cup of strong, sweet Turkish coffee, or if you're at the *Majestic,* try an iced coffee, a delectable concoction of coffee, vanilla ice cream, and whipped cream. As the popularity of the drink suggests, Belgraders are passionately fond of ice cream. Even on the chilliest winter days, street vendors do a brisk business selling cones.

BERLIN

From early October to early November of 1989, the entire world watched in rapt awe as East Berliners and citizens in other East German cities took to the streets almost daily to demand the basic democratic freedoms that had been denied to them for decades. At virtually the same time, tens of thousands of other citizens of the German Democratic Republic (East Germans) were making their way to the West through the gaps in the Iron Curtain that were increasingly widening in Budapest, Prague, and Warsaw. Using any means of conveyance possible, the East Germans made it abundantly clear to their leaders that totalitarian domination over their lives was at an end.

When Mikhail Gorbachev made it clear that Soviet troops would not be used to support the ruling Communist clique in East Germany, the Socialist Unity party (the regime that had ruled East Germany since 1945) suddenly announced, on the evening of November 9, 1989, that the Berlin Wall would come down. Surprisingly, the East German regime was as good as its word; by *Christmas* 1989, Berliners from both East and West could finally walk through the historic Brandenburg Gate on their way from one sector of the long-divided city to the other.

The 30-mile-long Wall has now been completely dismantled and Checkpoint Charlie was "brought in from the cold" in June 1990. Germans in general — and Berliners in particular — now enjoy free access to all of Berlin for the first time since the city was partitioned at the conclusion of World War II. And in June 1991, Germany's Parliament voted to move the seat of the federal government from Bonn to Berlin, the country's historic capital.

Berlin symbolizes the rebirth of freedom in a city (and an entire nation) where the Wall was for years the most tangibly monstrous monument of the Cold War. In 1963, when John F. Kennedy told thousands of cheering Germans that he, too, was a Berliner, he made a political statement of rare depth and resonance. Not only did it sum up the then current state of the Cold War — very frigid, indeed, since the building of the Berlin Wall 2 years earlier — but its unspoken promise of a worldwide community of sympathy for the plight of Berliners managed to touch and soothe the profound anxiety of the city and its residents.

For 15 years, West Berliners lived in an isolation made more desolate by the overpowering cultural and historic importance of their city before World War II. Long gone was the Imperial Berlin that ruled Germany until World War I; gone, too, was the devil-may-care Berlin of the 1920s and early 1930s, so admirably captured by Christopher Isherwood in its mad gaiety and decadence; gone even were the days of the terrible power of the Third Reich. Berlin was a capital city without a country. And then in 1961 the city was irreversibly truncated, and West Berliners saw the few treasured historic buildings that had survived the war disappear behind the blank and pitiless concrete face of the Wall. As the Wall went up, they lost family, friends, city, and heritage overnight. This radical surgery left a wave of shock, an anger that had hardly begun to dissipate when President Kennedy visited in 1963. It also left a stubborn determination to remain free, which more than any other emotion from that dark period still drives the city today.

The division of Berlin, a fact of life for 45 years for West Berlin's 2.1 million and East Berlin's 1.2 million people, began in 1944, when the US, Great Britain, France, and the Soviet Union, meeting in London, divided not only the city, but all of Germany, into occupied zones.

Because no written Soviet guarantee of access from West Germany existed, the Western Allies were unable to prevent Moscow from launching a land blockade of West Berlin in 1948. It took a whole year of a massive Allied airlift to force the Soviets to back down. West Berlin had been saved from slow starvation, but 70 Allied airmen and 8 German workers died trying to keep West Berlin's lifeline open.

The city divided along Cold War political lines into two separate municipal entities. Soviet threats against West Berlin, which continued throughout the 1950s, culminated in the overnight erection of the Wall by the East German Communist regime on August 13, 1961. The concrete barrier effectively sealed off the 185 square miles of West Berlin from the 156 square miles of East Berlin. The city's location made the Wall particularly problematic for West Berlin, since it existed right in the heart of East Germany — 110 miles from the nearest West German border, and the same distance from the Baltic Sea in the north and Czechoslovakia in the south. (Berlin is only 52 miles from the Polish border, which means that it is closer to Warsaw than to Munich.) The ugly 9-foot-high symbol that ailed Europe's body politic kept the people of West Berlin separated from East Berlin. Nevertheless, thousands of Berliners on either side of the dividing line continued to maintain bonds of blood and friendship.

This effort was made easier in 1971 when the three Western Allies met with the Soviet Union and produced the Four Power Agreement on Berlin to reduce East-West tensions over the city. Afterward, access to West Berlin from West Germany was assured, and both halves of the city settled down to a relatively normal existence. Nevertheless, West Berlin continued to be the only city in Europe under military occupation. In the Western sectors, sovereignty was still exercised by the Americans, the British, and the French; and the 13,000 Allied troops here were a visible reminder for the West Berliners that Western guarantees enabled them to live and work in freedom. In September 1990, a treaty ended the 45-year occupation of Berlin and other German territory, and gave Germany full sovereignty. And since reunification on October 3, 1990, the Soviet Union has dropped its objections to a united Germany joining NATO.

One of the initial far-reaching changes for the reunited country was the re-introduction of all-German elections on December 2, 1990, which placed Chancellor Helmut Kohl and his Christian Democratic party at the head of the new Germany. Today, for Germans on both sides of what was the Iron Curtain, the rapid pace of change continues. Once again, as in the days of the

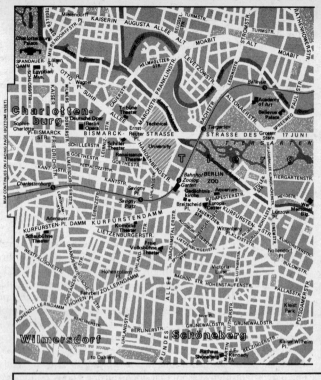
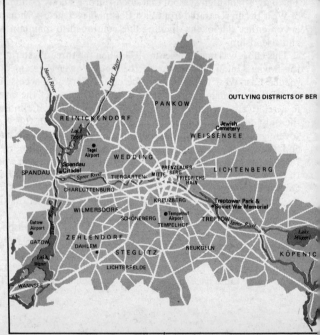

BERLIN

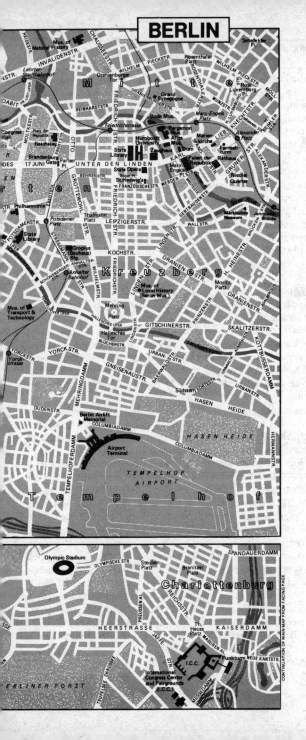

Soviet blockade more than 40 years ago, Berlin is a focal point of international attention.

The re-established capital, once in the vanguard of Cold War tension and later reduced to the role of a "political wallflower," is now the center of Germany's transition. It is in Berlin, where two different social and economic systems have contrasted so sharply — and will continue to do so for some time — that the post-1989 changes are more noticeable than anywhere else in the country. While the West German deutsche mark (DM) replaced the East German mark in the summer of 1990, it will take years for the two sides to become fully integrated and for the scars of Berlin's stormy postwar history to heal. Difficulties have arisen, chiefly in the economic sector. Although western Berlin continues to flourish, eastern Berlin struggles with severe financial problems. Make no mistake, in many ways the city remains divided culturally and sociologically. For the first time in a generation, however, Berlin has the opportunity to develop into the German metropolis of tomorrow. It is, after all, the capital and the center of a metropolitan area of 5 million people — the largest economic region between the Ruhr basin and Moscow.

Architecturally, postwar eastern Berlin and ancient Imperial Berlin are curiously intermixed. On the site of the modern Palast der Republik (where the former East German Parliament used to meet), the Hohenzollerns built a palace and ruled first as Electors of Brandenburg (from the early 15th century), then as Kings of Prussia, and finally as German emperors. They made their small capital an architectural jewel, lining the main street, Unter den Linden, with magnificent baroque palaces and other noble edifices. Although World War II destroyed or severely damaged every one of these historic monuments, the Communist regime attempted to restore many of them to their former splendor. And unlike West Berlin, which had to substitute economic prosperity for the loss of its hinterland, East Berlin was closely linked to the quiet, lake-studded, and forested countryside surrounding it, the Mark of Brandenburg.

While World War II and its aftermath gave the heart of the Old City to East Berlin, the new, truncated West Berlin, rising from the ashes of the war, created its own urban essence. That it succeeded in this massive enterprise is an understatement. Since the war devastated West Berlin, construction of new buildings greatly changed the appearance of the city. A small part of the architecture of the past — the majestic Charlottenburg and Bellevue palaces, for example — were somewhat damaged by the war, but largely salvageable. But Tegel Airport, as well as numerous hospitals, schools, factories, businesses, and housing projects, were all built in a kind of anonymous contemporary style — many of the buildings are high-rises — and at a pace that continues unabated. In 1987, the city's International Building Exhibition, a massive program that entailed the reconstruction and renovation of many war-struck districts in West Berlin, was completed. The glitz and the glitter of Kurfürstendamm, West Berlin's prestigious international thoroughfare, was its trademark.

What makes today's Berlin an outstanding place in which to live and to visit is its culture. Continuing its prewar role, the rejoined city remains a

cultural center of the very first order. It has some 30 theaters, and two companies, the *Schaubühne* and the *Berliner Ensemble,* said by critics to be two of the world's best German-speaking troupes. Also of international rank are the famed *Berlin Philharmonic Orchestra* and numerous museums like the great *Dahlem Museum,* the *New National Gallery,* and the *Bauhaus Museum,* as well as the magnificent museum complex on Berlin's famed Museumsinsel (Museum Island). There is a kind of creative ferment here and a cult of quality that has attracted writers, artists, composers, architects, and actors for centuries.

Berlin is not only a cultural but an educational center, and one of the finest in Europe. The Free University, Technical University, and Humboldt University, where many young Germans study, enjoy excellent reputations. Despite the great many older citizens living in Berlin, this is a city of — and for — the young, a city of pop music, experimental movies and theaters, and student hangouts. Berlin is Germany's largest industrial center, with many firms headquartered there. The city's large foreign population — more than 250,-000 non-Germans live and work here — once added a special spice to the melting pot. But for some, the recent flood of Eastern Europeans has begun to spoil the stew.

The people who live in Berlin are pleasant and polite. Wherever visitors go — museums, hotels, restaurants — they are treated with courtesy. It is hard to do justice in mere words to the remarkable variety of life here. In constant flux, Berlin is a place for people who thrive on exchanges of high energy. Perhaps Christopher Isherwood would feel at home in this new, highly sophisticated, and ever-changing Berlin, after all. The indomitable spirit of the courageous, pugnacious, and worldly wise Berliners would certainly remind him of the city he wrote about more than half a century ago.

BERLIN AT-A-GLANCE

SEEING THE CITY: The tallest structure in Berlin is the slender spire of the Fernsehturm (television tower), which climbs to a height of 1,209 feet above the city. Built in 1969, it is Europe's second-tallest tower. A revolving sphere at 655 feet is decked out with studio and transmission facilities, as well as with a restaurant and café, from which there is a magnificent view of the city. Open daily. Admission charge. Between Alexanderplatz and Marx-Engels-Platz (phone: 9-212-3333).

The Funkturm, Berlin's radio tower, is a steel-latticed spire 453 feet above the town. An elevator ascends the structure to a viewing platform that, weather permitting, offers a good view of Germany's largest city. Platform open daily from 10 AM to 11:30 PM; restaurant level open 10 AM to 11 PM. Admission charge. Messedamm (phone: 849-303-82996).

Although not as high, the top floor of *Europa-Center* offers a more breathtaking view of this fascinating city, since it is in the middle of the downtown area. The building, a business center with numerous shops and restaurants, was erected in 1965 and is grouped around two courtyards. Its 22-story tower is 270 feet high. On the top floor are the *I-Punkt* restaurant and a café and a nightclub. The roof terrace commands an extensive panoramic view, especially impressive after dark. The sparkling lights of the broad Kurfürstendamm give you an inkling of what Berlin is all about. Open daily until midnight. No admission charge. Breitscheidplatz (phone: 849-261-1014 and 849-262-7670).

SPECIAL PLACES: Berlin is easy to get around. Most of the downtown area was laid out in the late 19th century, and the streets form a sensible grid. You can see much of that part of the city by foot, if you familiarize yourself with the main thoroughfares. Running from east to west in the western part of the city are Kurfürstendamm (the closest thing to Main Street), Hardenbergstrasse, Kantstrasse, and Strasse des 17 Juni; the chief north-to-south connections are Potsdamer Strasse, Joachimstaler Strasse, and Wilmersdorfer Strasse. In Berlin's eastern section, the important downtown streets are Friedrichstrasse, which runs north to south, and Unter den Linden (which becomes Strasse des 17 Juni in "West" Berlin) and Karl-Marx-Allee, both running east to west. Berlin's historical center is on an island in the Spree River. To reach outlying areas of the city, use the *U-Bahn* (subway), buses, streetcars, or *S-Bahn* (aboveground trains). For more information, see *Getting Around*.

Various operators offer a wide range of sightseeing tours through Berlin. For times and places of the daily departures, consult the tourist office (see *Sources and Resources*) or your hotel.

Unter den Linden – Some 1,500 yards long and almost 70 yards wide, this avenue is in the very heart of what was East Berlin. Originally laid out to connect the royal palace with the hunting preserve, the Tiergarten, it got its name from the rows of linden trees that were planted on both sides (and in the center) of the wide boulevard. In the 18th and 19th centuries, a number of magnificent structures were built along the boulevard. Although many were bombed during World War II, the government has faithfully restored those that survived.

Zeughaus (Arsenal) – Built between 1695 and 1706, this lovely baroque structure is the oldest on Unter den Linden. Set on the Spree, it overlooks historic Museum Island (Museumsinsel). Originally an arsenal (hence the name), the building now houses the *Museum für Deutsche Geschichte* (Museum of German History). Closed Fridays. No admission. 2 Unter den Linden (phone: 9-200-0591).

Neue Wache (New Guard House) – Built in 1818, this has been a monument to the victims of fascism and militarism since 1960. Open daily. No admission charge. 4 Unter den Linden (no phone).

Humboldt University – Erected in the mid-18th century, it became Friedrich Wilhelm University in 1810. Since 1949, this, the largest university in what was East Germany, has been known by its present name. Famous teachers included Hegel, Max Planck, and Einstein; Marx and Engels were students here. 6 Unter den Linden (phone: 9-20930).

Deutsche Staatsbibliothek (German State Library) – Built in the early 20th century, the library occupies the site of the former Prussian State Library; the latter's stock of books that remained in Berlin during the war has been stored here. The rest are at the Staatsbibliothek. Open daily. No admission charge. 8 Unter den Linden (phone: 9-20378435).

Brandenburger Tor (Brandenburg Gate) – There is very little of historical interest between the Deutsche Staatsbibliothek and this massive Berlin landmark at the western end of Unter den Linden. The Brandenburg Gate, formerly inaccessible to cars and pedestrians because of the Wall, now is fully accessible; the Gate turned 200 years old in the summer of last year. The Quadriga, a beaten copper replica of the goddess of victory in a chariot drawn by four horses, was restored to the top of the Gate during the anniversary ceremonies in August 1991. The triumphal arch is brilliantly lit at night. Pariser Platz.

Tiergarten – This beautiful public park — far more extensive than the zoological gardens, which are at its western fringe — originally was the royal hunting preserve. It now is one of the world's largest and most beautifully landscaped urban parks and is dotted with charming lakes and ponds. The Tiergarten extends from the zoo to within several hundred yards of the Brandenburg Gate, about 2 miles (3 km) away.

House of World Cultures – Formerly the Congress Hall, it was a gift of the American people in 1957. The ultramodern structure stands in the Tiergarten, on the banks of the Spree. Always controversial because of its bold design, it suffered a major setback in 1980, when the roof collapsed, but it was repaired and the building reopened in 1987. It now offers exhibitions, concerts, and theater devoted to the world's ethnic minorities. In addition to exhibition halls and conference rooms, it has a charming riverside restaurant and café-bar (both closed Mondays). Nearby is a 140-foot-tall carillon, whose 68 bells resound daily at noon and 6 PM. Open daily. No admission charge (phone: 849-394-2377).

Reichstag – At the eastern edge of the Tiergarten, just north of the Brandenburg Gate, is Germany's once and future Parliament building, built in the late 19th century in Italian High Renaissance style. Gutted by fire by Hitler's supporters in 1933, it was rebuilt and currently is used for political conclaves. A permanent display is devoted to recent German history. It will take several years to renovate the building to accommodate the Bundestag — the seat of Germany's government. Closed Mondays. No admission charge. Pl. der Republik (phone: 849-39770).

Philharmonie – The home of the world-renowned *Berlin Philharmonic Orchestra* is just a few blocks south of the Reichstag, at the southern fringe of the Tiergarten. The building's asymmetrical architecture has been controversial ever since it was completed in 1963. It has been closed for repairs, but is slated to reopen early this year. Until then, the *Berlin Philharmonic* performs next door in the *Kammermusiksaal* (Chamber Music Hall; Matthäikirchpl.; phone: 849-261-4383), a near-mirror image of the *Philharmonie,* and at the *Schauspielhaus* (Concert Hall; Pl. der Akademie; phone: 9-849-227-2129 or 9-227-2122). For tickets, call 849-254880.

Museum of Musical Instruments – This museum holds an intriguing collection of European instruments that date from the 16th century. Music lovers will particularly enjoy such rarities as Frederick the Great's flute and Edvard Grieg's piano. Closed Mondays. No admission charge. 1 Tiergartenstr. (phone: 849-254810).

Museum of Arts and Crafts – Next door to the *Philharmonie,* in the city's developing cultural center, is this imposing museum that houses a unique collection of German artifacts from the past 900 years. Closed Mondays. No admission charge. 6 Tiergartenstr. (phone: 849-266-2911).

Altes Palais (Old Palace) – On the south side of Unter den Linden, this is the first historic structure visitors see. Built in 1836, it was the residence of Emperor William I during the last 50 years of his life. It is now used by Humboldt University. 9 Unter den Linden.

Alte Bibliothek (Old Library) – The Prussian State Library was here until 1914. Built in the late 18th century, it is now part of Humboldt University. Set back from Unter den Linden, on Bebelplatz. (Formerly Opernplatz, made famous during the Nazi burning of books in 1933.)

St. Hedwigs Kathedrale – This Roman Catholic cathedral dates from the late 18th century and was built according to plans laid down by Frederick the Great (who was, by all appearances, impressed by the Pantheon in Rome). Gutted in the war, it has been just as carefully restored as most other Unter den Linden landmarks. Bebelplatz.

Deutsche Staatsoper (German State Opera) – The opera house was built in 1743 and burned down 100 years later. Rebuilt, it was twice destroyed by bombs during the last war. Almost 1,500 people can attend performances here (for ticket information see "Music," *Sources and Resources*). 7 Unter den Linden.

Palais Unter den Linden – Originally built in the 17th century, it was known as the Kronprinzenpalais until 1945. The rebuilt façade, however, is modeled on the one added in 1857. Two German emperors were born here, and during the Weimar Republic it was used as a museum of contemporary art; today the government maintains it as an official guesthouse. 1 Unter den Linden.

Staatsratsgebäude – Though not in use at press time, this modern structure is still worth seeing from the outside; it's where the former East German government, the State Council, used to meet in the days of Communist boss Erich Honecker's rule. The centerpiece is one of the portals from the former royal palace. South side of Marx-Engels-Platz.

Museumsinsel – On the north side of Marx-Engels-Platz, surrounded on three sides by the Spree River, is one of the world's largest and most magnificent museum complexes. The buildings date to the 19th and early 20th centuries. The *Altes Museum* accommodates contemporary paintings and the former *Cabinet of Engravings*, containing 135,000 prints by German and foreign masters (15th to 18th century); among the latter treasures are Botticelli's illustrations of scenes from Dante's *Divine Comedy*. Across the street is the *New National Gallery*, which houses 19th- and early-20th-century art. Behind this is the *Pergamon Museum*, whose collection of antique art is one of the most important in the world. Its showpieces are the huge *Pergamon Altar* and the remarkable *Roman Market Gate of Miletus*, both 2nd century BC. The entrance gate to the ancient city of Babylonia and the adjacent procession street also are overwhelming sights. In this building, too, are the *Far Eastern Collection*, the *Museum of Ethnography*, the *Near Eastern Museum*, and the *Islamic Museum*.

At the northernmost tip of this island of museums is the *Bode Museum*, once the famed *Kaiser Friedrich Museum*. It now houses the *Egyptian Museum* (there's another museum of the same name which houses the bust of Queen Nefertiti; see *Museums*, below), the *Early Christian and Byzantine Collection*, the *Picture Gallery*, the *Sculpture Collection*, the *Cabinet of Coins*, and the *Museum of Pre- and Proto-History*. Among the treasures here are such masterpieces of German sculpture as the 12th-century *Naumburg Crucifix* and the *Winged Altarpiece* from Minden Cathedral (15th century).

Except for the *Near Eastern Museum* and part of the antique collection, both at the *Pergamon Museum*, the Museumsinsel is closed Mondays and Tuesdays. Admission charge to each museum.

Marienkirche (St. Mary's Church) – Just past the Museumsinsel, in the shadows of the Fernsehturm, is St. Mary's, Berlin's second-oldest church. First erected in 1240, it is a pleasant combination of Gothic and neo-classical styles. Karl-Liebknecht-Str.

Nicolai Quarter – A charming 16th-century neighborhood, destroyed by bombs in World War II and later rebuilt, it's perfect for a leisurely stroll through narrow streets, replete with gas lanterns and several period taverns, as well as for a visit to the city's oldest church, Nikolaikirche (ca. 1230) or to the Ephraim Palais (1766). Between the Spree and City Hall (Rathaus).

Jüdischer Friedhof Weissensee (Jewish Cemetery) – In the Weissensee district, this is said to be the largest Jewish cemetery in Europe. Restored by the former East German government, it contains thousands of graves, most marked by large, ornate tombstones in late-19th- and early-20th-century style. Male visitors must wear hats. Closed Fridays after 2 PM and on Saturdays. 45 Herbert-Baum-Str.

Kaiser Wilhelm Gedächtniskirche – This huge neo-Romanesque church was built toward the end of the 19th century, but it was almost completely destroyed by Allied bombing during World War II and has been only partially rebuilt. Its hexagonal bell tower and the octagonal church are new. The old west tower, 207 feet tall, was preserved in its ruined state. Partially new, partially old, partially preserved, and partially destroyed, it has become a symbol of the city and Berliners consider it the focal point of the western part of the city. Breitscheidpl.

Zoologischer Garten – On the west side of the city, 1 block north of the Gedächt-niskirche, is one of Berlin's two zoos (Tierpark is the other; see below). Germany's first, the zoological gardens were laid out in 1841 and still have more species than any other zoo in the world. Open daily. Admission charge. 8 Hardenbergpl. (phone: 849-254010).

Aquarium – Next door to the Zoologischer Garten, it has the most comprehensive collection in the world. The prewar building has been completely renovated, but it still has the tropical hall in which you can watch large numbers of alligators and crocodiles in their own environments; your vantage point is a bridge a mere 10 feet or so above the bloodthirsty creatures. Open daily. Admission charge. 32 Budapester Str. (phone: 849-254010).

New National Galerie – Designed by Ludwig Mies van der Rohe, this striking building houses the city's collections of late-19th- and 20th-century art. Jazz concerts are held in the sculpture garden during the summer months. Closed Mondays. No admission charge. 50 Potsdamerstr. (phone: 849-266-2666).

Staatsbibliothek – Directly opposite the *New National Gallery* is the starkly modern State Library, Berlin's successor to the Prussian State Library. Its collection of more than 3 million volumes makes it one of the world's largest. Exhibitions and lectures also are presented. Closed Sundays. No admission charge. 33 Potsdamerstr. (phone: 849-2661).

War Memorial – Plaques and impressive statuary are grouped in the courtyard of this building near the Tiergarten and *New National Gallery,* which housed the German Armed Forces Supreme Command during World War II, to honor the German officers who were shot here for the ill-fated uprising against Hitler on July 20, 1944. There also is a historical document center. Open daily. No admission charge. 14 Stauffenbergstr. (phone: 849-260-42202). Also interesting is the Plötzensee Memorial, Hüttigpfad. (phone: 849-344-3226).

Prinz Albrecht Gelände (Topography of Terror) – On this site next to where the Wall stood was the headquarters of Nazi terror mechanisms: the Gestapo and the SS. It now houses a moving and informative documentary exhibition devoted to the victims of the Hitler regime. Open daily, except Mondays, from 10 AM to 6 PM. No admission charge. 110 Stresemannstr. (phone: 849-254-86703).

Museum of Transport and Technology – Across the Landwehr Canal and a bit east is this growing showplace, which houses a very interesting collection devoted to the historic development of the railroad, the automobile, the bicycle, and the airplane. Closed Mondays. Admission charge. 9 Trebbiner Str. (phone: 849-254840).

Rathaus Schöneberg – More than a mile (1.6 km) due south is City Hall, which also functions as the seat of government for the borough of Schöneberg. At press time, the mayor was expected to move his offices to the former East Berlin City Hall this fall, and other government officials will likely follow. There is a good panoramic view from the top of the spireless tower, which contains a replica of the American Liberty Bell, presented to the Berliners by General Lucius Clay in 1950. On June 26, 1963, President John F. Kennedy made his "Ich bin ein Berliner" speech from the balcony here to a gathering of over 450,000 citizens. The tower can be ascended Wednesdays and Sundays from April to September. No admission charge. John-F.-Kennedy-Pl. (phone: 849-7831).

Schloss Charlottenburg – A few miles to the northwest is this truly majestic palace, the best example of royal Prussian architecture in Berlin. Begun in 1695, it took 100 years to build. The historic royal chambers, completely restored since the massive destruction of the last war, are open daily, except Mondays, for an admission charge.

The palace also houses the *Prehistoric Museum* and the Romantic gallery of early-19th-century art (closed Fridays; no admission charge). The beautifully laid out park behind the palace is one of the nicest areas in the city. Luisenpl. (phone: 849-320911).

International Congress Center and Fairgrounds – About a mile and a half (2 km) southwest of the palace is the modern ICC, as it is called. Across the street from this looming building, and connected to it by a covered pedestrian walkway, are the rambling fairgrounds, the site of the year-round fairs and exhibitions, which include international *Green Week* (an agricultural exhibition) and the German radio and TV exhibition. On the fairgrounds is the Funkturm or radio tower (see *Seeing the City*). Masurenallee and Messedamm (phone: 849-30381).

Olympic Stadium – Another 2 miles (3 km) to the west, this huge sports arena casts its shadow over the low-lying houses of a pleasant residential area. It was built for the *1936 Olympic Games,* and if you look hard, you can still make out the "royal" box, from which Hitler and his cohorts took in the spectacle. It is open daily to the public when no sports events are on. Admission charge. Olympischer Pl. (phone: 849-304-0676).

Spandau Citadel – Even farther west, on the Havel River, is the historic Spandau Citadel. The oldest edifice on the grounds, the Julius Tower, dates from the 14th century. The citadel, which had served as a fortification, a prison, and the royal treasury, now is a local history museum. The Nazi war criminals were not housed here, but at the prison in Wilhelmstrasse, in the middle of Spandau. The citadel is closed Mondays. Admission charge. Am Juliusturm (phone: 849-33911).

Dahlem Museum Center – To the south, in the fashionable and lovely section of Dahlem, is one of Berlin's largest museum complexes. (The others are at Charlottenburg Palace, near the Tiergarten, and on the Museumsinsel.) Its extensive buildings accommodate several institutions, and you can spend at least a full day going through them: the *Painting Gallery,* an important collection of European painting from the Middle Ages to the 18th century, with good pieces of fanciful rococo art; the *Sculpture Department,* with Byzantine and European sculpture from the 3rd to the 18th century; the *Ethnographic Museum,* with one of the world's most complete collections; *Museums of Islamic, Indian, and Far Eastern Art;* and the *Department of Prints and Engravings.* All are closed Mondays; no admission charge. 8 Lansstr. (phone: 849-83011).

Botanical Gardens – No more than half a mile to the east are the largest botanical gardens in Germany, and one of the world's most significant collections of flora. Of special interest in the 104-acre gardens are the geographical gardens, where plants from various parts of the world flourish in carefully maintained native environments. There is a fascinating botanic display at the museum, next to the entrance of the gardens. The gardens are open daily; the museum is closed Mondays. Admission charge to both museum and gardens. 6 Königin-Luise-Str. (phone: 849-830060).

Sowjetisches Ehrenmal – In the suburbs of eastern Berlin, within the confines of verdant Treptower Park and not far from the left bank of the Spree, is this huge Soviet War Memorial. Dedicated in 1949, it honors more than 5,000 Soviet soldiers who fell in the battle for Berlin in 1945. Much of the material used came from the ruins of Hitler's Reich Chancellery. Open daily. Entrance from Puschkinallee and Am Treptower Park.

Tierpark – Also in the city's suburbs, this zoo was opened in 1955 on the grounds of Friedrichsfelde Palace. As much as possible, the animals are shown in herds or family groups, in spacious enclosures that blend with the landscape. Open daily. Admission charge. 125 Am Tierpark (phone: 9-0111).

■ **EXTRA SPECIAL:** Largely unknown to most tourists, who rarely leave the downtown area, the outlying districts of Berlin are mostly forests and waterways, which include the Havel, Tegeler See, Wannsee, and Spree rivers, as well as the Grune-wald, Tegel, and Spandau forests. To see the Havel and the forests, on the west side, board one of the 70 ships that make daily trips on the Havel. Boats leave eight times a day from *Easter* until the end of September. There are many Havel ship lines; the largest is *Stern and Kreisschiffahrt,* 60 Sachtleben Str. (phone: 849-810-0040).

Along the way, get off at any number of points and explore to your heart's content, then reboard a subsequent boat. Stopping-off points include Grunewald Tower, formerly Kaiser Wilhelm Tower, dating from the 19th century and affording a good view from the top; Lindwerder Island, with restaurants offering snacks of beer, coffee, and cake; Pfaueninsel (Peacock Island), a beautiful example of an 18th-century formal garden with small pavilions, ponds, and a château dating from 1796 that is open to the public; and Potsdam, the former Prussian royal residence, just outside the city. All stops on this trip are well provisioned with restaurants and beer gardens. (The only catch is that since these boats are mostly for Berliners and rarely cater to foreign visitors, English usually is not spoken by the guides).

The sights passed on the Havel also may be approached by land (subway, streetcar, *S-Bahn,* or bus). Bear in mind that many of the sights are closed on Mondays and Tuesdays.

A similar tour is offered on the Spree River, whose tributaries flow through the city for a total of 20 miles before joining the Havel. The *Weisse Flotte,* a fleet of 60 white excursion ships, plies the Spree and its tributaries everyday from March to September (phone: 9-27120). You can get on and off the *Weisse Flotte* boats as often as you wish. Along the way you might want to stop off at these sights: the Müggelturm, a 98-foot-high tower near Berlin's largest lake, Müggelsee; the Rathaus of Köpenick; and the Mecklenburger Dorf in Köpenick, a replica of a 19th-century north German village, featuring typical snacks and beverages at very reasonable prices. Boats depart eight times a day from the piers on the Spree at the Treptower Park *S-Bahn* station. (This trip is mostly for Germans, so English is rarely spoken on board.)

SOURCES AND RESOURCES

TOURIST INFORMATION: The tourist office (Verkehrsamt) is in the large complex of shops and restaurants at *Europa-Center* (entrance on Budapesterstr.; phone: 849-262-6031; fax: 849-212-32520). It also maintains a branch at Tegel Airport (both open daily until 10:30 PM, as well as at the foot of Ferensehturm, at Bahnhof Zoo train station, and at the Dreilinden autobahn entrance to the city. The tourist offices will supply you with all sorts of free information in English about Berlin. This includes a general tourist map and numerous brochures. One of the best-detailed and most up-to-date local maps of Berlin is the *Berlin Stadtatlas,* available at many bookstores and larger newsstands, for about $10. Another source of information is *Dial Berlin,* a private tourism consortium that has a telephone hotline in the US (800-237-5469).

The US Embassy is at 4-5 Neustädtische Kirch Str. (phone: 9-220-2741 or 9-229-1338). The US Consulate is at 170 Clayallee (phone: 849-832-4087).

Local Coverage – There is no newspaper in English, but a monthly calendar of events called *Berlin Programm* is available at the tourist office and at newsstands; some of the information is in English.

Food – *Berlin Programm* has limited restaurant listings (in German). The tourist office can provide dining information in English.

TELEPHONE: Despite unification, at press time Berlin (and all of Germany) planned to maintain separate phone systems, at least until late this year. To call "East" Berlin from the US, dial 011 (international access code) + 37 (country code) + 2 (city code) + the local number; to call "West" Berlin from the US, dial 011 (international access code) + 49 (country code) + 30 (city code) + the local number.

Calling within a now unified Germany is somewhat involved: When calling "East" Berlin from "West" Berlin, dial 9 + the local number. To place a call from "East" Berlin to "West" Berlin, dial 849 + the local number. From elsewhere in "West" Germany to "East" Berlin, dial 372 + the local number. From elsewhere in "East" Germany to "West" Berlin, dial 30 + the local number. From elsewhere in "West" Germany to "West" Berlin, dial 030 + the local number. And from elsewhere in "East" Germany to "East" Berlin, dial 0372 + the local number.

All phone numbers listed in this chapter are preceded by these codes — 9 for an "East" Berlin number or 849 for a "West" Berlin number. (When dialing from outside Berlin, follow the procedures outlined above and do not dial these in-city codes.)

GETTING AROUND: Airport – Tegel Airport, a 20- to 30-minute ride from downtown, handles most domestic and international flights. Taxi fare to the center of the city from Tegel Airport should run about $18. The No. 9 bus provides service from the airport to downtown and leaves from just outside Gate 8 every 15 minutes between 5:30 AM and midnight. Schöenfeld Airport, just outside the city and about a 45-minute drive to downtown, handles some international traffic; taxi fare to downtown costs about $24. For information about buses to this airport, call 9-301-8028. Tempelhof Airport, in the city center, caters to a limited number of domestic carriers; it's 15 minutes by taxi from downtown, with a fare of about $6. The No. 19 bus also runs to Tempelhof, as does the *U-Bahn* from the Platz der Luftbrücke station.

Car Rental – The major American firms are represented, as well as several European companies. Information can be obtained at any hotel.

Subway and Bus – Berlin has one of the world's most efficient public transportation systems. The subway, or *U-Bahn,* with its snappy little yellow cars, has been a fact of life here since 1902, and its 8 lines serve almost every part of the city. The *U-Bahn* is fast, clean, convenient, and one of the least expensive in Germany, as is the 100-year-old *S-Bahn,* the "el"; both lines travel to points in eastern Berlin. A ticket for 3 DM (about $1.80) is valid for a trip from one end of the city to the other, and you can transfer as often as you wish within the *U-Bahn* system, the elevated *S-Bahn,* and to any of the many bus and streetcar lines that ply Berlin's streets. A *carnet,* valid for five rides, is available. The Berlin Transport Authority also sells a ticket (10 DM/about $6) valid for 24 hours on all *U-Bahn, S-Bahn,* and bus lines traveling throughout Berlin. A 6-day tourist ticket, which costs 26 DM (about $16), also is available.

Taxi – Taxis can be hailed in the streets, and there are cabstands all over town and at the major hotels. Fares are posted near the stands. (To call a cab, dial 849-6902 or 849-261026.)

Train – The main railroad station is Bahnhof-Zoologischer Garten at Hardenbergplatz. For schedules and fare information, call 849-19419.

LOCAL SERVICES: Dentist (English-Speaking) – Most German dentists speak English. However, the US Consulate (phone: 849-832-4087) has a list of English-speaking dentists (and physicians). For emergency service in western Berlin, dial 849-1141; in eastern Berlin, 9-1259.

Dry Cleaner/Tailor – *Horst Marschall* (80 Uhlandstr.; phone: 849-861-4374); *Hermeneit* (134B Kantstr.; phone: 849-313-8113).

Limousine Service – *Minex,* 64A Detmolderstr. (phone: 849-853-3091).

Medical Emergency – Each of the city's hospitals has an emergency room; the biggest are at *Klinikum-Steglitz* (30 Hindenburgdamm; phone: 849-7981), and *Klinikum-Charlottenburg* (130 Spandauer Damm; phone: 849-3031). For emergency service in western Berlin, dial 849-310031; in eastern Berlin, 9-1259.

Messenger Service – *Be-Be-Car,* 17 Crailsheimerstr. (phone: 849-774-6072).

National/International Courier – *DHL International,* 62 Unter den Eichen (phone: 849-831-5026).

Office Equipment Rental – *Eischleb* (129 Uhlandstr.; phone: 849-860491); *Wegert Photographers,* for audiovisual equipment (124 Potsdamerstr.; phone: 849-250020).

Pharmacy – *Europa-Apotheke* (*Europa-Center* at the Tauentzienstr. entrance). To find out which pharmacies are open at night, over the weekend, or on holidays, dial 849-1141.

Photocopies – *Copy-Center,* 40 Bayreutherstr. (phone: 849-211-3411).

Post Office – At Bahnhof Zoo train station (street level), open 24 hours daily, and at Tegel Airport, open daily from 6:30 AM to 9 PM.

Secretary/Stenographer (English-Speaking) – *Bürotel,* 180 Kurfürstendamm (phone: 849-882-7031).

Telex – The post office at 21 Winterfeldtstr. (phone: 849-2181).

Translator – *Bundesverband der Dolmetscher und Übersetzer,* or *BDÜ,* the Association of Interpreters and Translators (phone: 849-826-4100).

Other – Tuxedo and evening gown rental: *Runge* (99 Bismarckstr.; phone: 849-312-1187). Costumes: *Hinz* (29/30 Wilmersdorferstr.; phone: 849-341-7988).

SPECIAL EVENTS: *Green Week,* an annual agricultural fair, takes place at the fairgrounds toward the end of January. The *Berlin Film Festival,* another annual fixture, is in February. A *Festival of German Drama* is performed every May, and once a year in September the city puts on its ambitious *Festival of the Arts.* A *Jazz Festival* attracts international soloists to Berlin every year during the first week of November.

MUSEUMS: The *Prussian State Museums* in Dahlem, at Charlottenburg Palace, and near the Tiergarten are described in *Special Places,* as are the Zeughaus, which houses the *Museum of German History,* and the museums in the Museumsinsel complex. Other exhibits worth seeing include the following:

Egyptian Museum – Directly opposite Charlottenburg Palace is this unusual collection whose priceless treasures include the world-renowned bust of Queen Nefertiti and the magnificent *Kalabsha Gate.* Closed Fridays. No admission charge. 70 Schloss-str. (phone: 849-320911).

Märkisches Museum – One of the best of its kind in Europe, it surveys Berlin's history. Closed Mondays and Tuesdays. Admission charge. 5 Am Köllnischen Park (phone: 9-270-0514).

Museum of Local Art and History – Paintings, documents, and sculptures on the history of Berlin are housed in a beautiful 18th-century rococo building, once the Prussian Supreme Court, which has been lovingly restored. Visit the beer cellar, which features traditional Berlin snacks and beverages. Closed Mondays. Admission charge. 14 Lindenstr. (phone: 849-258-62839).

■**Note:** As you stroll through the city you probably will see the old Grand Synagogue of Berlin covered with scaffolding (on Oranienburger Str. between Tucholsky Str. and Krausnick Str.). On *Kristallnacht,* November 9, 1938, the synagogue was burned in one of the incidents marking the onset of the holocausts, and was further destroyed by bombs during World War II. When restoration is completed, probably in 1993, it will reopen as the *Museum of Judaism.* For additional information, contact Irene Runge at the Berlin Jewish Community Center (phone: 849-448-5928).

 SHOPPING: Berlin has an abundance of interesting shops. There is hardly anything you cannot buy here, and some of the items offered for sale are truly unique. The best shopping is in the western part of the city. If you just want to browse before making up your mind, go through *Europa-Center,* at the foot of Kurfürstendamm in the middle of the downtown area. This city within a city has scores of small shops and boutiques offering a variety of typical German specialties. German cameras, including those by Leica, Rollei, and Zeiss, are available here, but it is necessary to do very careful comparison shopping. The same brands often are less expensive in the US. Optical goods such as binoculars, telescopes, and microscopes also are German specialties, and there are good buys in china and porcelain; great names in the latter are Meissen, Rosenthal, and KPM (State Porcelain Manufactory). Women's and men's fashions, toys, cutlery, and clocks are good buys, too. Although you might want to do some exploring on your own, here is a small sample of recommended stores:

Antiquitäten Döbler – Porcelain, crystal, and pewter. 8 Keithstr. (phone: 849-211-9344).

Bouvier – A bookstore with a very good international selection. Spandauer Str. (phone: 849-210-9431).

Dürlich – Antique furniture. 5 Keithstr. (phone: 849-243660).

Gronert – Antiques. 10 Keithstr. (phone: 849-241585).

Horn's – The latest in women's fashions. 213 Kurfürstendamm (phone: 849-881-4055).

J. A. Henckels – Cutlery. 33 Kurfürstendamm (phone: 849-881-3315).

Jil Sander Boutique – Chic women's wear. 48 Kurfürstendamm (phone: 849-883-3730).

Ka De We – Germany's largest, grandest, and best-stocked department store, with simply everything, including an enormous food shop with a score of lunch counters (sixth floor). 21-24 Tauentzienstr. (phone: 849-21210).

Marga Schoeller – English and American books. 33 Knesebeckstr. (phone: 849-881-1112).

Staatliche Porzellan Manufaktur Berlin (*KPM*) – Beautiful china. The factory is at 1 Wegelystrasse, the salesroom at 205 Kurfürstendamm (phone: 849-390090).

Vom Winde Verweht (**Gone with the Wind**) – An Anglo-American kite emporium featuring fascinating European kites at low prices. 81 Eisenacher Str. (phone: 849-784-7769 or 849-788-1992).

SPORTS AND FITNESS: Bicycling – You can rent a bicycle by the hour for a jaunt through the expansive Grunewald forest from *F. Damrau,* Schmetterlingspl. (phone: 849-811-5829; call before 9 AM).

   Fitness Center – *Fitness-Studio,* 182-183 Kurfürstendamm (phone: 849-882-6301).

Golf – The *Golf und Landclub* has a 9-hole golf course. Stölpchenweg, Berlin-Wannsee (phone: 849-805-5075).

Ice Hockey – From November through April, you can see professional games at the *Eissporthalle.* Jafféstr. (phone: 849-30381).

Ice Skating – In the winter, there are various public rinks in the city. Consult the tourist office for sites and hours.

Jogging – Best is the central Tiergarten park. Farther out, runners prefer Grunewald forest.

Soccer – A very special sport here, as "West Germany" won the *1990 World Cup*. *Hertha* and *Blau-Weiss,* Berlin's professional soccer teams, play on autumn Saturdays at the *Olympic Stadium.* Olympischer Pl. (phone: 849-304-0676).

Swimming – Aquatic sports can be enjoyed at a number of indoor and outdoor pools; each of Berlin's 23 boroughs has at least one public facility. There is a sandy beach lining crystal water at Glienicker See, a lake at the westernmost fringe of the city.

Tennis – In addition to several private clubs, the city has a number of public courts. For locations and hours of admission, consult the tourist office.

Trotting Races – Every Wednesday and Sunday there is racing at the trotting course in *Mariendorf.* 222 Mariendorfer Damm (phone: 849-74011).

THEATER: Theater in Berlin, still Germany's theatrical metropolis, is an all-German affair. For a look at the classical repertoire, go to the *Schiller Theater* (110 Bismarckstr.; phone: 849-319-5236), *Deutsches Theater* (13A Schumannstr.; phone: 9-287-1225), and — at the same address — the intimate *Kammerspiele,* which was founded in 1906 by Max Reinhardt (phone: 9-287-1226). Another small stage, the *Maxim Gorki Theater,* also performs plays from the classical repertoire, as well as dramas by the Russian playwright Ann Festungsgraben (phone: 9-207-1790). What is probably one of the most important German-language theaters in the world is a three-stage complex, *Schaubühne am Lehniner Platz* (153 Kurfürstendamm; phone: 849-890023). For Brecht fans, a visit to the *Berliner Ensemble* — which the German dramatist founded in 1948 — is a must (Bertolt-Brecht-Platz; phone: 9-282-3160). Genuine political and social satire can be enjoyed at the *Distel,* whose shows are performed at two small theaters (101 Friedrichstr.; phone: 9-207-1291; and 9 Degnerstr.; phone: 9-376-5174). Other prominent theaters are *Renaissance Theater* (6 Hardenbergstr.; phone: 849-312-4202); *Freie Volksbühne* (24 Schaperstr.; phone: 849-881-3742); *Theater am Kurfürstendamm* (206 Kurfürstendamm; phone: 849-882-3789); *Komödie* (206 Kurfürstendamm; phone: 849-882-7893); *Tribüne* (18-20 Otto-Suhr-Allee; phone: 849-341-2600). One of Europe's most successful children's theaters is *Grips* (22 Altonaer Str.; phone: 849-391-4004). Tickets to most theater performances in the city can be bought directly at the box offices; they also can be ordered at the ground-floor theater and concert ticket counter of the theaters' visitors service (closed Sundays) at the *Palast* hotel (Spandauer Str.; phone: 9-212-5258 or 9-212-5902).

MUSIC: Berlin is one of the world's musical centers, with performances of everything from classical to pop and rock. The *Berlin Philharmonic Orchestra,* led by Claudio Abbado, will perform at the *Kammermusiksaal* (Chamber Music Hall; Matthäikirchpl.; phone: 849-261-4383) and at the *Schauspielhaus* (Pl. der Akademie; phone: 9-227-2129 or 9-227-2122), until repairs on the orchestra's permanent home, the *Philharmonie* (next door to the *Kammermusiksaal*), are completed this summer. The *Schauspielhaus,* built in 1820, also hosts other world-famous orchestras. The *Radio Symphony Orchestra* gives most of its concerts at *Sender Freies Berlin,* the radio station (8-14 Masurenallee; for tickets, dial 9-302-7242). Concerts and recitals of classical music can be heard at the *Hochschule der Künste* (College of Arts; 1 Fasanenstr.; phone: 849-318-52374). One of the world's leading opera houses, the *Deutsche Oper,* has daily performances; ballet is scheduled once a week (34-37 Bismarckstr.; phone: 849-341-4449). Another internationally known opera house is the 18th-century *Deutsche Staatsoper* (7 Unter den Linden; phone: 9-205-4556). No less renowned, the *Komische Oper* (55-57 Behrenstr.; phone: 9-229-2555) has a much more modern approach. Operettas and musicals are launched at *Theater des Westens* (12

Kantstr.; phone: 849-312-1022). Pop concerts, many by visiting international stars, are performed at the *International Congress Center* (see *Special Places*), the *Metropol* (see *Nightclubs and Nightlife*), and the *Deutschlandhalle* (Messedamm; phone: 849-303-84387). For the latest in jazz and rock music, attend one of the concerts that are frequently given at *Quartier Latin* (96 Potsdamerstr.; phone: 849-261-3707). For the latest listings, consult the *Berlin Programm.*

 NIGHTCLUBS AND NIGHTLIFE: For live music and dancing, try some of these popular places: *Loretta* (89 Lietzenburger Str.; phone: 849-882-3354); *Salsa* (13 Wielandstr.; phone: 849-324-1642); and *Joe's Biersalon* (225 Kurfüstendamm; phone: 849-882-7871). Two relatively lively nightspots are the *Moskva-Bar* (34 Karl-Marx-Allee; phone: 9-279-2869) — there's a cover charge — and *Lindencorso* (17 Unter den Linden; phone: 9-220-2461); there's live music in the *Konzertcafé* and interesting musical shows and revues in the first floor *Nachtbar Havanna* (closed Tuesdays and Wednesdays; cover charge). It is not only the young crowd that likes to dance at these clubs: *Café Keese* (108 Bismarckstr.; phone: 849-312-9111); *Big Apple* (13 Bundesallee; phone: 849-881-2887); *Level* (15 Joachimstaler Str.; phone: 849-882-5488); and *Bristol-Bar* (in the *Kempinski Hotel,* 27 Kurfürstendamm; phone: 849-884-34756).

Discotheques hit this city with a big splash in the late 1970s and they are still jumping. For the youngsters, *Dschungel* is really "in" (53 Nürnberger Str.; phone: 849-246698), and singles gather at the *Pinguin Bar* (39 Rosa-Luxemburg-Str.; phone: 9-282-7432) and *Checkpoint* (55 Leipziger Str.; phone: 9-208-2995). The following discos are popular with people from all age groups: *Empire* (30 Hauptstr.; phone: 849-784-8565); *Far Out* (156 Kurfürstendamm; phone: 849-320-00723); *Abraxas* (134 Kantstr.; phone: 849-312-9493); *Pool* (19 Motzstr.; phone: 849-247529); *Annabell's* (64 Fasanenstr.; phone: 849-883-5220); *Metropol* (5 Nollendorfpl.; phone: 849-216-2787); *VIP-Club* (top of the *Europa-Center,* Breitscheidpl.; phone: 849-261-2452); and *Big Eden* (202 Kurfürstendamm; phone: 849-323-2016).

Talking about shows, one cannot forget Berlin's cabarets. Both *Stachelschweine* (*Europa-Center;* phone: 849-261-4795) and *Wühlmäuse* (Lietzenburgerstr. corner of Nürnberger Str.; phone: 849-213-7047) put on interesting performances, devoted chiefly to literary and political satire. At *Kartoon* (24 Französische Str.; phone: 849-229-9305), the waiters, who both serve and perform, specialize in skits that satirize the recent political changes in Germany. Nightclubs featuring transvestite shows have long been a German specialty. If you like this sort of thing — and even if you do not — you may be pleasantly surprised; visit *La Vie en Rose* (*Europa-Center;* phone: 849-323-6006), or *Chez Nous* (14 Marburger Str.; phone: 849-213-1810). Jazz buffs have several very popular clubs at their disposal, each of them featuring live music: *Quasimodo* (12A Kantstr.; phone: 849-312-8086), *Flöz* (37 Nassauische Str.; phone: 849-861-1000), *Lohmeyer's* (24 Eosanderstr.; phone: 849-342-9660), and *Badenscher Hof* (29 Badensche Str.; phone: 849-861-0080). Folk music from Ireland reigns supreme at the *Irish Harp Pub* (15 Giesebrechtstr.; phone: 849-882-7739), and at *Go In* (17 Bleibtreustr.; phone: 849-881-7218).

Berlin is known for its multitude of small, intimate, pub-like bars, which offer no more than excellent drinks, a few snacks, and lots of *Gemütlichkeit* (congeniality). Those worthy of mention include *Die Kleine Weltlaterne,* which caters to an arty crowd (22 Nestorstr.; phone: 849-892-6585); *Lutter & Wegener,* a wine cellar of note (55 Schlüterstr.; phone: 849-881-3440); *Zwiebelfisch,* a favorite haunt for journalists and students (7-8 Savignypl.; phone: 849-317363); *Raabediele* (open daily; in Ermeler Haus, 10-12 Märkisches Ufer; phone: 9-275-5103); and *Zur letzten Instanz* (closed Sundays; 16-17 Waisenstr.; phone: 9-212-5528). If gambling is one of your sins, visit the city's one and only licensed casino, on the ground floor at the Budapester Strasser side of *Europa-Center,* for roulette, baccarat, and blackjack. It's open daily from 3 PM to 3 AM (phone: 849-250-0890).

BEST IN TOWN

CHECKING IN: Visitors can choose from among one of the best assortments of hotels in all of Germany. At press time, hotels in the city's eastern section were still being privatized, but it is unlikely that any of those we have listed will close as a consequence. Since there always seems to be something happening in this scintillating city, overnight accommodations are often hard to find and it is advisable to make advance reservations — either directly with the hotel of your choice or through the city's efficient tourist office; *Dial Berlin* can also help here (see *Tourist Information*).

Our selection includes some of the luxury hotels, as well as establishments that can be classified as moderate and inexpensive. Many of the latter are exciting little houses, noted for their charm. A word of caution: Hotel accommodations in Germany are expensive, and Berlin is no exception. Should you prefer more modest, although somewhat less comfortable, rooms, the tourist office is the place to which to turn. The hotels in our selection have a bath or a shower in every room, and in almost every case the rooms have telephones. For a double room in those hotels we have classed as expensive, expect to pay $190 and up; from $85 to $185 in the moderate category; under $85 in the inexpensive class. Breakfast is included in the rates at hotels below, unless otherwise indicated. All telephone numbers listed below are preceded by the city codes — 9 for "East" Berlin and 849 for "West" Berlin. These codes are used only when calling from "East" Berlin to "West" Berlin and vice versa. (For more information on calling from outside Berlin, follow the procedures described in *Telephone,* above.)

Am Zoo – When Thomas Wolfe came to Berlin in the early 1930s, he stayed at this 145-room hotel, one of the traditional downtown establishments. Business facilities include 24-hour room service, meeting rooms for up to 200, English-speaking concierge, foreign currency exchange, secretarial services in English, audiovisual equipment, photocopiers, computers, cable television news, translation services, and express checkout. 25 Kurfürstendamm (phone: 849-884370; fax: 849-884-37714; telex: 183835). Expensive.

Bristol Kempinski – Berlin's most traditional and classiest hotel, this 358-room establishment has a tradition of noblesse oblige. Its present location in the middle of the city's golden mile — the Kurfürstendamm — makes it ideal for sightseeing. It also boasts a renowned restaurant, the *Kempinski Grill* (see *Eating Out*), and the *Bristol Bar*. Business facilities include 24-hour room service, meeting rooms for up to 600, English-speaking concierge, foreign currency exchange, secretarial services in English, audiovisual equipment, photocopiers, computers, cable television news, translation services, and express checkout. Breakfast not included. 27 Kurfürstendamm (phone: 849-884340; fax: 849-883-6075; telex: 183553). Expensive.

Domhotel – This new, beautifully designed property in the eastern part of the city opened in late 1990. The hotel overlooks the German and French cathedrals (thus its name — *Dom* means "cathedral"), along with the 19th-century Platz der Akademie and the *Schauspielhaus* concert hall. The 392 rooms are all luxuriously appointed. Several restaurants, taverns, and bars, as well as a swimming pool, sauna, and fitness center were slated to open as we went to press. Business facilities include 24-hour room service, meeting rooms for up to 350, English-speaking concierge, foreign currency exchange, secretarial services in English, audiovisual equipment, photocopiers, computers, cable television news, translation services, and express checkout. 30 Mohrenstr. (phone: 9-20980; fax: 9-209-8269). Expensive.

Grand – Right in the middle of the historic downtown area in what was East Berlin, it offers authentic luxury and comfort. The 350 well-appointed rooms, the spacious lobby, and the 14 restaurants (especially good is *Zur Goldenen Gans;* see *Eating Out*) and cafés all seem so "Western" that it's hard to avoid a little disorientation at these elegant premises in the middle of what used to be a workers' state. Business facilities include 24-hour room service, meeting rooms for up to 100, English-speaking concierge, foreign currency exchange, secretarial services in English, audiovisual equipment, photocopiers, computers, cable television news, translation services, and express checkout. 158-164 Friedrichstr. (phone: 9-20920; fax: 9-229-4095; telex: 113401). Expensive.

Grand Hotel Esplanade – With 400 rooms, plus 17 suites, this fine hostelry is idyllically set on a canal — but it's downtown Berlin, not Amsterdam, that's just around the corner. The rooms, service, and other amenities are well above standard, and several restaurants are on the premises. Business facilities include 24-hour room service, meeting rooms for up to 450, English-speaking concierge, foreign currency exchange, secretarial services in English, audiovisual equipment, photocopiers, computers, cable television news, translation services, and express checkout. Breakfast not included. 15 Lützowufer (phone: 849-261011; fax: 849-262-9121; telex: 185986). Expensive.

Inter-Continental – A landmark (it was the *Hilton* until 1978), this 600-room establishment continues to offer luxurious accommodations in an area a bit removed from the city's hustle and bustle. Although only a stone's throw from the center of activities, it overlooks the Tiergarten and has several restaurants, as well as a popular ballroom. Business facilities include 24-hour room service, meeting rooms for up to 1,600, English-speaking concierge, foreign currency exchange, secretarial services in English, audiovisual equipment, photocopiers, computers, cable television news, translation services, and express checkout. Breakfast not included. 2 Budapester Str. (phone: 849-26020; fax: 849-260-280760; telex: 184280). Expensive.

Metropol – This handsome 340-room high-rise was built in the mid-1970s by a Swedish firm. Extras are a fine dining room (see *Eating Out*), a sauna, and a garage. In former East Berlin, the hotel has always appealed to those used to Western European luxury. Business facilities include 24-hour room service, meeting rooms for up to 120, English-speaking concierge, foreign currency exchange, secretarial services in English, audiovisual equipment, photocopiers, computers, cable television news, translation services, and express checkout. 150-153 Friedrichstr. (phone: 9-22040; telex: 114141). Expensive.

Palace – Just behind the Gedächtniskirche and within the orb of the *Europa-Center,* this imposing downtown hostelry has a large number of apartments and 160 well-appointed rooms, as well as a swimming pool and a sauna. Business facilities include 24-hour room service, meeting rooms for up to 600, English-speaking concierge, foreign currency exchange, secretarial services in English, audiovisual equipment, photocopiers, computers, cable television news, translation services, and express checkout. 42 Budapester Str. (phone: 849-269111; fax: 849-262-6577; telex: 184825). Expensive.

Palast – A 600-room hotel in the city's eastern section, it provides first class service, luxurious accommodations, and a good view of the city. Its restaurants serve a variety of ethnic cooking, from Asian to French. Business facilities include 24-hour room service, meeting rooms for up to 780, English-speaking concierge, foreign currency exchange, secretarial services in English, audiovisual equipment, photocopiers, computers, cable television news, translation services, and express checkout. 5 Karl Liebknecht Str. (phone: 9-2410; fax: 9-212-7273; telex: 115050). Expensive.

Penta – With 425 rooms, this is one of Berlin's largest and most modern properties. On the premises are a restaurant, bar, beer cellar, swimming pool, sauna, solarium, and an underground garage. Business facilities include 24-hour room service, meeting rooms for up to 350, English-speaking concierge, foreign currency exchange, secretarial services in English, audiovisual equipment, photocopiers, computers, cable television news, translation services, and express checkout. Breakfast not included. Centrally located at 65 Nürnberger Str. (phone: 849-210070; fax: 849-213-2009; telex: 182877). Expensive.

Schweizerhof – This 441-room establishment is opposite the *Inter-Continental* and is managed by that same chain. The ongoing motif is Swiss, as the name implies, and the service is excellent. There is a restaurant. Breakfast not included. 21-31 Budapester Str. (phone: 849-26960; fax: 849-269-6900; telex: 185501). Expensive.

Seehof – Only 2½ miles (4 km) down the road from the downtown area, on the lovely Lietzensee, this 80-room hotel overlooks a small park. Business facilities include 24-hour room service, meeting rooms for up to 600, English-speaking concierge, foreign currency exchange, secretarial services in English, audiovisual equipment, photocopiers, computers, cable television news, translation services, and express checkout. 11 Lietzensee Ufer (phone: 849-320020; fax: 849-320-02251; telex: 182943). Expensive.

Steigenberger – This modern, comfortable establishment with 400 rooms — plus several restaurants and bars, a swimming pool, sauna, and shopping arcade — is a link in one of Germany's largest hotel chains. The location is prime. Business facilities include 24-hour room service, meeting rooms for up to 600, English-speaking concierge, foreign currency exchange, secretarial services in English, audiovisual equipment, photocopiers, computers, cable television news, translation services, and express checkout. Breakfast not included. Downtown, facing lovely Los Angeles Platz (phone: 849-21080; fax: 849-210-8117; telex: 181444). Expensive.

Berolina – Pleasantly set back from bustling Karl-Marx-Allee, this 300-plus-room property in the city's eastern end offers first class service and comfort. Restaurant and cozy grill/bar on the premises. Business facilities include 24-hour room service, meeting rooms for up to 40, English-speaking concierge, foreign currency exchange, secretarial services in English, audiovisual equipment, photocopiers, computers, cable television news, translation services, and express checkout. Breakfast not included. 31 Karl-Marx-Allee (phone: 9-210-9541; telex: 114331). Expensive to moderate.

Stadt Berlin – In the eastern downtown area, its 994 rooms make it one of the largest in the city. It has a fine restaurant — the *Panorama* (see *Eating Out*) — a sauna, and a garage. Right behind the hotel is Alexanderplatz; closed off to automobile traffic, the square is ringed by restaurants, stores, the Fernsehturm, and other public buildings. Business facilities include 24-hour room service, meeting rooms for up to 400, English-speaking concierge, foreign currency exchange, secretarial services in English, audiovisual equipment, photocopiers, computers, cable television news, translation services, and express checkout. Alexanderpl. (phone: 9-2190; telex: 114111). Expensive to moderate.

Am Studio – A modern place offering a magnificent view of the city from each of its 78 rooms. English-speaking concierge. 80 Kaiserdamm (phone: 849-302081; fax: 849-301-9578; telex: 182825). Moderate.

Berlin Excelsior – Just off Kurfürstendamm in the center of town, this pleasant property offers 325 rooms with refrigerators; public rooms include a breakfast room, restaurant, bar, and banquet room. Business facilities include 24-hour room service, meeting rooms for up to 120, English-speaking concierge, foreign currency exchange, secretarial services in English, audiovisual equipment, photocopiers, computers, cable television news, translation services, and express checkout. 14 Hardenbergstr. (phone: 849-31991; fax: 849-319-92849; telex: 184781). Moderate.

Börse – Right in the middle of downtown Berlin, this 38-room hotel offers little peace and quiet. But it's surrounded by shops, cafés, restaurants, theaters, and movie houses. Business facilities include 24-hour room service, English-speaking concierge, foreign currency exchange, and photocopiers. 34 Kurfürstendamm (phone: 849-881-3021). Moderate.

Domus – Located on a charming side street in the city center, this pleasant establishment offers 70 comfortable rooms. No restaurant, but a generous buffet breakfast. 49 Uhlandstr. (phone: 849-882041; fax: 849-882-0410). Moderate.

Novotel – With 187 rooms, and right next to Tegel Airport, it provides efficiency without any sacrifice of comfort. Sauna, solarium, and swimming pool on the premises. Business facilities include meeting rooms for up to 25, English-speaking concierge, and foreign currency exchange. 202 Kurt-Schumacher Damm (phone: 849-41060; fax: 849-410-6700; telex: 181605). Moderate.

Plaza – Just around the corner from Kurfürstendamm is this 131-room alternative to more expensive accommodations. Business facilities include an English-speaking concierge and foreign currency exchange. 63 Knesebeckstr. (phone: 849-884130; fax: 849-884-13754). Moderate.

Riehmer's Hofgarten – This offbeat hostelry, which looks out onto the courtyard of a large turn-of-the-century apartment complex, is located in Kreuzberg, a neighborhood popular with artists. Guests enjoy comfort without frills. Breakfast is provided, but there is no restaurant. 83 Yorckstr. (phone: 849-781011; telex: 786-6059). Moderate.

Econtel – Midway between Tegel Airport and downtown and near the *Deutsche Oper* and Charlottenburg Palace, it puts its accent on comfort rather than luxury, but doesn't sacrifice modern facilities. Business facilities include meeting rooms for up to 25, an English-speaking concierge, and foreign currency exchange. Breakfast not included. 24-26 Sömmeringstr. (phone: 849-344001; fax: 849-344-7034). Inexpensive.

Hospiz am Bahnhof Friedrichstrasse – Near the rail entry to what was East Berlin, this clean, well-run hospice has no frills, but its 110 rooms are comfortable and reasonably priced. Concierge speaks little English. Breakfast not included. 8 Albrechtstr. (phone: 9-284030). Inexpensive.

Sachsenhof – A 65-room hostelry that can be a bit musty, but it's right in the middle of what was Christopher Isherwood's Berlin. He lived around the corner at 17 Nollendorfstrasse. Business facilities include an English-speaking concierge, foreign currency exchange, photocopiers, and express checkout. 7 Motzstr. (phone: 849-216-2074). Inexpensive.

 EATING OUT: German food is hearty and can be very good or, at its worst, as heavy as lead. Main courses usually consist of roasted or stewed meat with boiled potatoes or dumplings (called *Knödel,* which are very heavy) and sauerkraut, cabbage, or other vegetables, like string beans. Wiener schnitzel and sauerbraten are well-known specialties.

Like other continentals, Germans like rolls for breakfast, occasionally the sweet, cruller-like pastries called *Krapfen* and *Berliner Pfannkuchen.* Then at mid-morning they often have a snack of sausages and bread called *Brotzeit* or "breadtime."

Sausages are the specialty in Germany at any time of day or night; they are made from pork, veal, and game. The frankfurter, which originated in Vienna, is longer, slimmer, and better than the American variety. *Weisswurst* is white sausage made mostly of veal; *Bratwurst* is pork sausage; a *Regensburger* is a spicy pork sausage.

Interesting appetizers include herring, which is very popular and comes in many varieties, and *Hase im Topf,* a delicious rabbit pâté. Soups are popular and very substantial: *Leberknödelsuppe* (liver dumpling soup), *Erbsensuppe* (pea soup), and *Kohlsuppe* (cabbage soup) are just a few. *Schwarzbrot,* or dark bread, is very tasty, especially Westphalian pumpernickel.

Although Berlin restaurants serving traditional German fare offer many of these dishes, they are more commonly served throughout other regions of the country. For a typical Berlin treat, try a *Konditorei,* a little shop that offers excellent cakes and pastries with coffee or tea. Special desserts are *Schwarzwälder Kirschtorte,* a Black Forest cherry cake with whipped cream; *Baumkuchen,* a towering cake with icing; *Kugelhupf,* a marvelous coffee cake; or *Käsekuchen,* a cheesecake. Other Berlin specialties include *Eisbein* (pigs' knuckles) and *Erbsensuppe* (pea soup).

Germans are justifiably famous for their beer and wine, too. In south Germany, light beer (*helles*) and dark (*dunkles*) come in many sizes and varieties. Most beers come from Munich, but you might want to try *Berliner Weisse* in the summer, a whitish beer made from wheat and often served *mit Schuss,* or raspberry juice. North Germans drink pilsener beer. *Bierkeller* (beer restaurants) serve food as well as beer.

Germany produces a lot of wine, some of it very good. You may be disappointed in *Liebfraumilch,* which is not a place name (it means "Milk of Our Lady") and thus not reliable. Best bets are the Moselles — light, pleasant, and often cheap — like *Wehlener Sonnenuhr, Piesporter,* or *Zeltinger.* Rhine wines, of course, are famous — some of the best are *Niersteiner, Oppenheimer,* and *Schloss Johannisberger.* Baden wines are equally renowned, especially *Weissherbst,* a rosé.

Note that at press time, all restaurants in what was East Berlin were still in the process of being privatized, so the quality of many of these establishments may very well improve under more competitive circumstances. Privatization also has caused many eateries to close or be replaced, and the situation will probably continue, so it is especially necessary to call before you go.

Expect to pay $100 or more at restaurants in the expensive category; between $50 and $75 in the moderate range; and less than $50 at places classed as inexpensive. Prices are for a dinner for two, not including drinks and wine. Tips are included in the bill. All restaurants below accept major credit cards, unless otherwise indicated. All telephone numbers listed below are preceded by the city codes — 9 for "East" Berlin and 849 for "West" Berlin. These codes are used only when calling from "East" Berlin to "West" Berlin and vice versa. (For more information on calling from outside of Berlin, follow the procedures described in *Telephone,* above.)

Bamberger Reiter – Creative nouvelle Austro-French cuisine, served in a cozy atmosphere. The menu is composed of two fixed "tastings," one of five courses, the other of seven (don't despair; portions are modest). There also is a wide selection of French and German wines. The garden at the front is a very pleasant place to dine in spring and summer. Dinner only; closed Sundays and Mondays. Reservations advised. 7 Regensburger Str. (there are two such streets in Berlin; this is the one on the corner of Bamberger Str.; phone: 849-244282). Expensive.

Chalet Corniche – A special place is this beautiful former country mansion in the Grunewald section, on the western fringe of the city. Not only does the impressive architecture (the house was built around a big old tree) give you the feeling of bonhomie, but the view through the tall windows onto wide lawns and a beautiful lake is as soul-satisfying as the food. We recommend the veal steaks and the seafood specialties. Open daily. Reservations advised. 5B Königsallee (phone: 849-892-8597). Expensive.

Frühsammer's – For inspired continental cuisine, this is the place — well worth the sojourn to the suburbs. Closed Sundays. Reservations advised. 101 Matterhornstr. (phone: 849-803-8023). Expensive.

Globe – One of the best hotel dining rooms in town (it's in the *Berlin* hotel), with continental dishes served in elegant surroundings. You can dine either in the main dining room or in the smaller grillroom. Lunch is less expensive than dinner. Grillroom closed Sundays. Reservations advised. 62 Kurfürstenstr. (phone: 849-26050). Expensive.

Panorama – A fitting name for a restaurant on the 37th floor of the *Stadt Berlin* hotel. The food almost equals the marvelous view. Try the daily specialties. Open daily. Reservations necessary. Alexanderplatz (phone: 9-219-4347). Expensive.

Restauration 1900 – Of all the new restaurants to have opened in eastern Berlin since the Wall came down, this one's undoubtedly the best. Located in Prenzlauer Berg, Berlin's Greenwich Village, it was named for the famous Bertolucci film. The city's cultural elite come here to dine and look. The food is continental-Mediterranean. Try the bouillabaisse. Dinner only. Closed Sundays and Mondays. Reservations necessary. 1 Husemannstr. (phone: 9-449-4052). Expensive.

Rockendorf's – Although a bit off the beaten track, this restaurant is well worth the trip. It's in a turn-of-the-century villa in the suburb of Waidmannslust. Nostalgia is trump here, as well as imaginatively prepared continental dishes and a very good choice of wines. Closed Sundays, Mondays, and 3 weeks in August. Reservations advised. 1 Düsterhauptstr. (phone: 849-402-3099). Expensive.

Zur Goldenen Gans – The "Golden Goose" is the pride of the *Grand* hotel. The food and decor are Thuringian, with such specialties as roast goose and grilled sausages with bacon-laden potato salad. Native red wines are featured. Open daily. Reservations necessary. 158-164 Friedrichstr. (phone: 9-20920). Expensive.

Alt-Luxemburg – The nouvelle cuisine at this cozy bistro near the city center has attracted its share of well-deserved attention. The seafood specialties, in particular, are worthy of serious consideration. Closed Sundays, Mondays, and 3 weeks in July. Reservations advised. 70 Pestalozzistr. (phone: 849-323-8730). Expensive to moderate.

Conti Fischstuben – As the name implies, this is for lovers of seafood. A small dining room in the *Ambassador* hotel with an exclusive flair. Dinner only. Closed Sundays. Reservations advised. 42 Bayreuther Str. (phone: 849-2190-2362). Expensive to moderate.

Daitokai – This genuine Japanese haunt is close to the Kurfürstendamm. The food is good and the service friendly. Guests can sit on the floor Japanese-style. Closed Mondays. No reservations. *Europa-Center* (phone: 849-261-8099). Expensive to moderate.

Ermeler Haus – If you prefer to avoid the hustle and bustle of the immediate downtown area, this spot's for you. The beautiful structure, originally built in 1703 on an island opposite, was rebuilt here after the original site was razed following wartime damage and Communist confiscation. It's one of the few historic buildings left, aside from those on Unter den Linden. The interior is all rococo, as is the second-floor restaurant, which offers good continental dishes in intimate surroundings. The *Raabe-Diele* beer cellar and the first floor café also are popular here. Open daily. Reservations advised. 10-12 Märkisches Ufer (phone: 9-275-5103). Expensive to moderate.

Fernsehturm – Europe's second-tallest tower (described in *Seeing the City*) has a revolving café-restaurant from which, at a height of 655 feet, you get a breathtaking all-around view of Berlin. The food is also good. There is a $3 admission charge, and you have to be finished within an hour. Open daily. Reservations advised from 10 AM to 2 PM. Between Alexanderplatz and Marx-Engels-Platz (phone: 9-212-3333 or 9-210-4232). Expensive to moderate.

Ganymed – On the Spree, near Bahnhof Friedrichstrasse (handy if you arrive by subway or *S-Bahn*). As at many restaurants in town, there is background music. The atmosphere is comfortable and intimate, the food continental, and the wines good. Open daily; closed Monday lunch. Reservations advised. 5 Schiffbauerdamm (phone: 9-282-9540). Expensive to moderate.

Grand Slam – Named for the current tennis craze in Germany, this eatery is located in a quiet, leafy suburb, about 7 miles (11 km) from downtown Berlin. The food is excellent; try the cream of spinach soup with a side dish of black truffle slices, or the many succulent lamb creations. This is one of the few restaurants in town that requires male guests to wear a tie at the table. Open for lunch and dinner; closed Sundays and Mondays. Reservations advised. 47-55 Gottfried von Cramm Weg (phone: 849-825-3810). Expensive to moderate.

Kardell – Specialties are leg of lamb, game, steaks, and fish. Herr Kardell, the owner, still runs the place with obsessive attention to detail. Open daily; supper only Saturdays. Reservations advised. 24 Gervinusstr. (phone: 849-324-1066). Expensive to moderate.

Kempinski Grill – The candlight glow, creamy decor, and piano music are all serenely old-fashioned in Berlin's number one hotel dining room. The menu features lobster (a Berlin obsession) in salad, soup, and sauce. Grilled fish and steaks also are recommended. Round off the evening with a stop at the hotel's soothing *Bristol Bar*. Closed Sundays. Reservations advised. 27 Kurfürstendamm (phone: 849-884-34792). Expensive to moderate.

Metropol – This hotel dining room, tastefully decorated, features rustic *Gemütlichkeit*. The food is continental and good. Open daily. Reservations advised. 150-153 Friedrichstr. (phone: 9-22040 or 9-203070). Expensive to moderate.

Moskva – Worth a visit just to sample its Russian specialties. Open daily. Reservations necessary. 34 Karl-Marx-Allee (phone: 9-279-2869). Expensive to moderate.

Paris-Moskau – Not far from the Reichstag, in a somewhat undistinguished neighborhood, is this distinguished restaurant. Its three dining rooms are in a charming 2-story house, all done in white. In addition to excellent continental cuisine and drinks served by a young, dedicated team, it features a very pleasant atmosphere, heightened by an artistic decor and two terraces. Open daily. Reservations advised. 141 Alt-Moabit (phone: 849-394-2081). Expensive to moderate.

Anselmo – A must for devotees of Italian fare, this intimate spot has an imaginative and well-run kitchen, rustic decor, and a pleasant atmosphere. Closed Mondays. Reservations advised. 17 Damaschkestr. (phone: 849-323-3094). Moderate.

Aphrodite – A new dining establishment in the Prenzlauer Berg district, it offers continental dishes and wines at reasonable prices. Try the lamb filet with a glass of chardonnay. Dinner only. Closed Sundays and Mondays. Reservations advised. 61 Schönhauser Allee (phone: 9-448-1707). Moderate.

Ax-Bax – The beautiful people often hang out in this nicely designed bar that has no identifying sign on the door. In addition to the drinks and glitter, it also has good food. Open daily from 7:30 PM; closed Saturdays. Reservations advised. 34 Leibnizstr. (phone: 849-313-8594). Moderate.

Blockhaus Nikolskoe – For fans of German history and good continental food, this place, high above the wide Havel River, looks like a Russian dacha. It was built in log cabin fashion in 1819 by Prussian King Friedrich Wilhelm III for his daughter, Charlotte, and her husband, Grand Duke Nicholas (later Russian Czar Nicholas I). Closed Thursdays and in the winter after 7 PM. Reservations advised. It is in a forested area, with no street address; ask directions when you make reservations (phone: 849-805-2914). Moderate.

Exil – This out-of-the-way place is well worth the trip. On a canal in Kreuzberg, it features well-prepared Viennese dishes. You can dine at the bower-like terrace, weather permitting. The service also is charmingly Viennese. Dinner only; closed Mondays. Reservations advised. No credit cards accepted. 44a Paul-Lincke-Ufer (phone: 849-612-7037). Moderate.

Florian – A finely tuned crew maintains this admirable dining spot. The menu emphasizes French, Austrian, and Bohemian fare, and the wines and the service are as good as the food. The neighborhood is currently "in," so the place is frequented by artists, film people, and the so-called New Wave set. Dinner only. Closed December 24–31. Reservations advised. 52 Grolmanstr. (phone: 849-313-9184). Moderate.

Fofi's – A Greek-style bistro that has become a magnet for the "in" crowd, and indeed the attractions here are the Greek food and the clientele. Open daily for dinner; closed December 24. Reservations advised. 70 Fasanenstr. — look for the *"estiatorio"* sign (phone: 849-881-8785). Moderate.

Hongkong – The kitchen staff here knows how to make the tantalizing most of basic Cantonese cooking, with an extensive menu and excellent service to go with a convenient location. Open daily. Reservations advised. 210 Kurfürstendamm (phone: 849-881-5756). Moderate.

I-Punkt – The international menu is adequate, but most people come here for the spectacular view. On the 20th floor of the *Europa-Center* complex, it offers one of the best panoramic views of Berlin and is especially impressive after dark. Open daily. Reservations unnecessary. *Europa-Center* at Breitscheidpl. (phone: 849-261-1014). Moderate.

Mundart – In Kreuzberg, a former working class district that has gone arty, it features French cuisine, though Jacques, the imaginative chef, is no disciple of nouvelle. The decor, service, and excellent wines are also highly commendable. Dinner only; closed Mondays and Tuesdays and during July. Reservations advised. No credit cards accepted. 33-34 Muskauer Str. (phone: 849-612-2061). Moderate.

November – On the south bank of the Landwehrkanal, oppposite the *New National Gallery*, this intimate, bistro-like place is a favorite of writers, artists, and others belonging to the cultural scene. The sophisticated ambience is in charming contrast to the up-market tone of the cuisine offered by an extremely obliging staff. Try the leg of lamb or game dishes. Open daily for dinner only. Reservations advised. 65 Schoeneberger Ufer (phone: 849-261-3882). Moderate.

Offenbach Stuben – Intimate and cozy, this is one of the few eateries in the city's eastern section that always has been privately run. The German and continental fare are fine, as are the beverages. Closed Sundays and Mondays. Reservations essential. 8 Stubbenkammerstr. (phone: 9-448-4106). Moderate.

Paris-Bar – A traditional bistro that is a magnet for students and artists drawn by the French cuisine, as well as the paintings on the walls. Closed Sundays. Reservations advised. 152 Kantstr. (phone: 849-313-8052). Moderate.

Im Reichstag – One wing of this late-19th-century building, the former (and future) seat of the German Parliament (see *Special Places*), has been set aside as a restaurant. Solid German food in a historic setting. Closed Mondays. Reservations advised. No credit cards accepted. Platz der Republik (phone: 849-397-7172). Moderate.

Schipkapass – A rustically decorated Czech eatery, featuring those two mainstays of every good Bohemian kitchen: Prague ham and pilsener beer. You can feast on the large portions. Open daily for dinner. Reservations advised. No credit cards accepted. 185 Hohenzollerndamm (phone: 849-871941). Moderate.

Zum Stilbruch – Once a traditional Berlin tavern, now a small and cozy restaurant. The continental dishes are well prepared and efficiently served at prices that prevailed in Germany 25 years ago. The specialties are the Eastern European dishes (upon request). Closed weekends. Reservations advised. 84 Florastr. (phone: 9-349-0066). Moderate.

Gastmahl des Meeres – Fish is the only dish served in this conveniently located place in the city center. Slightly more expensive is *Rendezvous für Feinschmecker,* the fancy grill 1 floor below street level where fish also reigns supreme. (One of Berlin's largest bookstores, *Bouvier* — see *Shopping* — is right above the ground-floor dining room.) Open daily. Reservations unnecessary. Spandauer Str., at the corner of Karl-Liebknecht-Str. (phone: 9-212-3296). Moderate to inexpensive.

Möwe – Across the Spree from Bahnhof Friedrichstrasse and down the road a bit is this intimate, tastefully appointed grill-restaurant. The name, German for "dove," is the symbol of the local artists' association, whose club this formerly was. This pleasant place is frequented by an intelligent, lively crowd. The kitchen is praiseworthy: continental cuisine, with a nod to the East. Closed Mondays. Reservations advised. No credit cards accepted. 18 Hermann-Matern-Str. (phone: 9-282-5741). Moderate to inexpensive.

Müggelsee-Perle – The fish, fowl, and game dishes are best; also try the Berlin pea soup. On the shore of the Grossen Müggelsee, the restaurant is accessible by excursion ship (see *Extra Special*) as well as by bus and car. Open daily. Reservations advised. Am Grossen Müggelsee (phone: 9-66020). Moderate to inexpensive.

El Bodegón – This lively Spanish *finca,* featuring a wide range of Iberian dishes, is much frequented by students, musicians, and artists. The atmosphere is genuinely Iberian, including guitar music, chiefly flamenco. Open daily for dinner. Reservations unnecessary. 61 Schlüterstr. (phone: 849-312-4497). Inexpensive.

Brasserie – You will find a true French bistro here. The decor, food, and wine are typical of the Gallic provinces. There also is a small enclosed terrace. Open daily. Reservations unnecessary. 3 Wittenbergpl. (phone: 849-245786). Inexpensive.

Café Möhring – This traditional German *Konditorei* has two locations on the city's busy Kurfürstendamm. Here you can enjoy rich cakes, light Danish pastry, and other wonders from their own bakery to go along with your coffee or tea. Light hot meals also are available. Open daily; closes at noon on December 24. Reservations unnecessary. 213 and 234 Kurfürstendamm (phone: 849-881-2075 and 882-3844). Inexpensive.

Einstein – The high-ceilinged and mirrored dining room in this turn-of-the-century villa is a perfect setting for an afternoon's Viennese coffee and pastry. Open daily until 2 AM. No reservations. No credit cards accepted. 58 Kurfürstenstr. (phone: 849-261-5096). Inexpensive.

Häagen-Dazs – A refreshing taste from home, its name notwithstanding. The same good ice cream (you won't have any trouble translating from the German *Eiscrem*); ask for one *Kugel* (scoop) or two *Kugeln.* Open daily. No credit cards accepted. 224 Kurfürstendamm (phone: 849-882-1207). Inexpensive.

Hardtke – Two traditional restaurants with traditionally hearty German food such as fresh *leberwurst* and *blutwurst.* All meat dishes come from its own butcher shops. Rustic, friendly atmosphere, and very good value. Open daily. Reservations advised. 27 and 27B Meinekestr. (phone: 849-881-9827). Inexpensive.

Hollandstüb'l – Dutch fare, with the accent on dishes from the East Indies (*nasi goreng,* rijsttafel, and so on). The decor is a holdover from the 1920s, when this was one of Berlin's more popular restaurants. Open daily. No reservations. 11 Martin-Luther-Str. (phone: 849-248593). Inexpensive.

Jimmy's Diner – Right out of *American Graffiti,* this spot in the heart of town is a larger-than-life replica of the good old American diner, complete with canned music piped in everywhere, even in the WC. The menu is what you'd expect: luscious cheeseburgers, coleslaw (the only place in town that serves it), pasta, salads, sandwiches, and steaks. For dessert, have a slice of apple pie and a cup of coffee. Open daily. No reservations, and it's crowded in the evening. 41 Pariser Str. (phone: 849-882-3141). Inexpensive.

Litfass – Not far from the Kurfürstendamm and the famous *Schaubühne* theater is this unpretentious Portuguese place. Among the specialties are shark steaks and potted chicken in garlic sauce. Open daily for dinner. No reservations. No credit cards accepted. 49 Sybelstr. (phone: 849-323-2215). Inexpensive.

Shell Café-Restaurant – For casual but hearty fare that is served all hours of the day, this centrally located eatery is a real find. Set in a former gas station (and named for the oil company), it features brunch with American-style bacon and eggs. Open daily. Reservations unnecessary, but the place gets very crowded after 4 PM, so expect a wait. 22 Knesebeckstr. (phone: 849-312-8310). Inexpensive.

BRUSSELS

As the headquarters of NATO, the Common Market, the Benelux Union, and the European Atomic Energy Community, Brussels not only is the capital of Belgium and of the Belgian province of Brabant, it is in many ways the capital of all Europe. Three distinct sets of ambassadors reside in the city: one for Belgium, one for NATO, and one for the Common Market. It is a familiar joke that if someone were to yell "Fire!" in a Brussels theater, half the audience would run out to safety, and the other half would call their home governments for instructions.

Brussels is a fast-paced modern city of 971,000 people (including suburbs), rivaling New York City in its often ruthless destruction of the old in favor of the new. There are skyscrapers, traffic problems, and broad avenues with underpasses and overpasses. Much of the city is starkly modern; what is not modern is frankly medieval, and of that, happily, much remains.

The Grand' Place, the magnificent square that justly is the city's pride and joy, was a prosperous marketplace in the Middle Ages, when it was known as the Grote Markt. Splendid old baroque guild houses, with façades ornately decorated in gold, line the square, its noble 15th-century Gothic Hôtel de Ville in the southwest facing the palatial 18th-century *Maison du Roi,* now the municipal museum. Nearby, the still narrow and cobbled streets bear quaint medieval names reminiscent of the market that was held there: Bread Street, Pepper Street, Street of the Herb Market, and Little Street of the Butchers. Besides produce, goods such as lace, tapestries, jewelry, crystal, and leather are, as they have always been, the staples of the city's trade. The heart of the city is enclosed by a rough hexagon of boulevards that run along its 14th-century ramparts. Within this belt of ancient streets lies almost all of historic Brussels. Much of the history of the city — and to some degree, the very history of all Europe — can be traced in its growth from Grote Markt to Common Market.

Brussels lies just northeast of the geographic center of Belgium, surrounded by vast forests. Sitting on the crucial intersection of a north-south river (the Senne River now runs underground through the city) and an east-west land route (between Bruges and Cologne, Germany), Brussels's destiny as a marketplace was inevitable. Today's city, which celebrated its millennium in 1979, traces its origins to the earliest known written records of the area, which date from 979; but on the eastern edge of town, near the Common Market headquarters, excavations have uncovered Stone Age burial mounds that reveal that a thriving community was on the spot in 5000 BC. The historic town was known as Bruocsella, a bustling Christian community in the 7th century that within 200 years had become an established market for produce from the Senne River valley. The city's character as a center of trade and business already was established. By 1288 Brussels was important enough to

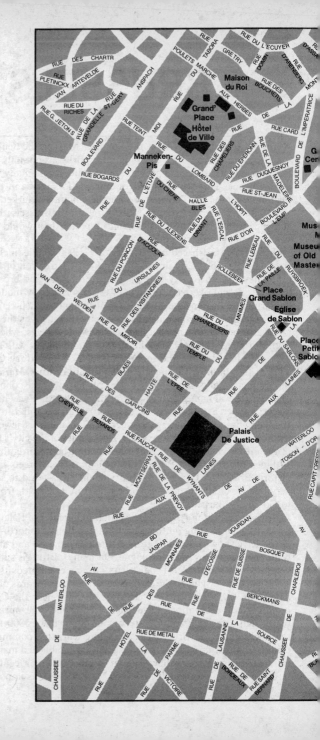

BRUSSELS

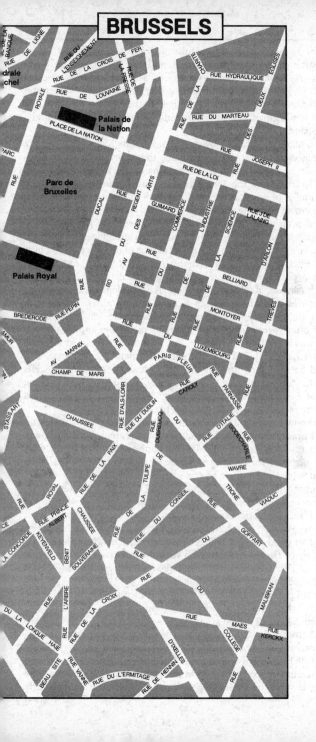

be the object of a pitched battle by the Duke of Brabant, Jean le Victorieux, who won the battle of Woeringen against Renalt the Bellicose in order to protect the city. As nobles of the city married into the ruling houses of Europe, Brussels seesawed between the great powers of Europe — sometimes in one sphere of influence, sometimes in another. In the course of its long and troubled history, it was allied with or controlled by Spain, Austria, Burgundy, France, and Holland.

Although dominated by foreign powers for most of its history and subject to wars, rebellions, and invasions for centuries, the canny Belgian burghers learned early on to prosper even in adversity. This knack of riding the tides of history came to fruition in the 15th and 16th centuries under the political domination of Philip of Burgundy and Charles V of Spain. This was the golden age of Flemish painting, tapestry, and lace.

Finally in 1830, after centuries of foreign rule, the people of Brussels began the revolution against the Hollanders that made them an independent nation. It happened in a strange way: During a performance of an opera, *La Muette de Portici* by Daniel François Auber, at the *Théâtre Royal de la Monnaie* (Mint Theater), a patriotic song aroused the audience to leave the opera house, take to the streets, and begin the fight. After independence, the first King of Belgium was Leopold of Saksen-Koburg, a naturalized Englishman and Queen Victoria's "dearest uncle" and confidant. He was followed by Leopold II, who often is remembered for his many mistresses and for the fact that the Congo was his personal property, but who was determined to make Brussels a truly royal capital. Town planning, not painting or music, fascinated him and he dedicated himself to what he called "outside art." His nephew, Albert I, was Belgium's great hero during World War I. Next came the controversial Leopold III, who was king during World War II and abdicated in favor of his son, Baudouin, the present king.

Brussels has known little tranquillity in its long history. For centuries Spain, Austria, France, and Holland made Belgium an arena for their power politics; in this century, Germany invaded Belgium during both world wars and used it as a highway for its armies. Twice in this century the Germans have set up field kitchens for their troops in the Grand' Place.

Like many European cities, Brussels has thrived despite such vicissitudes. Its people have not only endured, but have amassed great fortunes while doing it, and garnered the sophistication and taste to use their money to best advantage. The result is an unusually rich tapestry of a city, well endowed with good food and good art — two passions that most Belgians share. The food of Brussels rivals that of France, from which it is derived. And it is said that if a resident of Brussels loses wife or job, he neither gets drunk nor calls out his rival. He goes out for a good dinner.

A clue to the Belgian character can be found in Flemish art. The greatest Belgian artists are the Breughels, elder and younger; Hans Memling; and Peter Paul Rubens. And the worlds that these men portrayed — the peasant simplicity of the Breughels' lusty canvases, the mysticism of Memling, and Rubens's deft combination of things of the spirit and things of the flesh — reflect an aspect of life in Brussels and the attitude of its residents.

Although Belgium's place in the world is firmly established, a domestic problem remains that has been plaguing the country for centuries. The early tribes that settled Belgium were Latin and Germanic, and the country today is a mixture — not a blend — of the two heritages. Linguistically and culturally, the two never have fused. The bitterness between the two factions has led to a series of political crises that continue to this day. The Walloons, French-speaking Belgians, live in Belgium's four southwestern provinces; the Flemish, who speak Flemish (or Nederlands), a form of Dutch, are in the north and northeast. The government, a democratic republic, is an uneasy coalition between the two groups. Brussels sits in Brabant, the central province, and, as a compromise, every street sign here is in both languages, just as every official speech or decree has to be in French and Flemish. One solution for people is to speak the ubiquitous third language, a good British English.

This 1,000-year-old cosmopolitan and international city is a delightful and restorative place to visit, with its variety of excellent restaurants, the wealth of great Flemish paintings in its *Museum of Old Masters,* and the exquisite and ubiquitous Art Nouveau architecture. Brussels is, above all, an art-loving city, and it hosts nearly 100 museums and a number of gracious parks. The ebullient creativity of the Bruxellois is evident everywhere, even in the subways: In a city where riders are treated daily to views of works by such leading Belgian artists as Paul Delvaux, it should come as no surprise that this also is the comic-strip capital of the world. Whatever else you do, you will find yourself returning again and again to the Grand' Place. Some people prefer it in the early morning, when it is given over to a vast flower market and the sun drenches the colors splashed across the cobblestones. Others prefer it at night, when floodlights lace the centuries-old buildings with gold. Day or night, taken in from the comfort of one of the cafés that ring it, the Grand' Place is a sight one never forgets.

BRUSSELS AT-A-GLANCE

SEEING THE CITY: The Palais de Justice, at Place Poelaert, is on a hill from which you can see the city, especially the older section of town. The Palais was one of the largest monuments built in Europe during the 19th century.

SPECIAL PLACES: Most of the interesting sights in town are situated within the inner circle of boulevards that enclose the central sections of town; a great majority lie in the rather small area between the Grand' Place and Parc de Bruxelles and can easily be covered on foot.

IN TOWN

Grand' Place – Reputed to be Europe's most beautiful square and an irresistible magnet to everyone, Grand' Place is the historic heart of Brussels. It doesn't matter whether you see it for the first time by day or by night. Just wander around it and get the feel of the place. Then go back a second time for your serious sightseeing. And don't miss the bird market and the flower market, both on Sunday mornings.

It is hard to believe that this beautiful square was destroyed by Louis XIV's armies in 1695 during a 35-hour bombardment. Most of the square, including the spire of the Town Hall, burned down, but within 3 years the people of Brussels had rebuilt it all.

In the square are the guild houses, the King's House (see below), and the Town Hall, unquestionably the most beautiful building in Brussels. Its spire is topped by a statue of St. Michael, patron saint of Brussels. Construction was begun in the 15th century and its style is pure Gothic. Inside is an excellent collection of tapestries. The building is considered a symbol of the city's freedom and it is rated as one of Europe's finest examples of 15th-century architecture. Closed Saturdays and Mondays. Admission charge (phone: 512-7554).

The other buildings around the square are guildhalls built between 1696 and 1698, after the originals were destroyed in the 1695 bombardment. Among the guilds represented are the bakers, coopers, archers, boatmen, haberdashers, butchers, and brewers.

Wander through the narrow, medieval streets leading off the Grand' Place. Their names are straight out of the Middle Ages: Street of the Herring, Stove Street, Pepper Street, Butter Street, Street of the Cheese Market — all dating from when this area was one vast marketplace.

Maison du Roi (King's House) – This historic building, on the site of a 13th-century bread market, was rebuilt in the 1870s. It houses the *Musée Communal* (Municipal Museum of the City of Brussels), which has exhibitions on the history and archaeology of the city. There also are examples of the applied arts of Brussels, such as tapestries, lace, and goldsmiths' work, and here are displayed the clothing and uniforms for the *Manneken-Pis* (see below). Closed weekend afternoons. Admission charge. Grand' Place (phone: 511-2742).

Maison des Brasseurs (Brewery Museum) – Set in the building of the ancient brewers' guild, right in the Grand' Place, is a collection of old beer making equipment. Next door is a charming drinking house where you can taste the various beers. Closed Saturday afternoons, Sundays, and the week between *Christmas* and *New Year's*. Admission charge. 10 Grand' Place (phone: 511-4987).

Manneken-Pis – Southwest of the Grand' Place is the small bronze 17th-century statue by Jérôme Duquesnoy. This impudent little boy making water is considered symbolic of the city's irreverent spirit. There are many guesses as to its origin, but all that anybody knows for sure is that it has been here since 1619. Periodically, he is stolen and then returned safely. His dazzling wardrobe, which he sometimes wears, is on display at the King's House. He has over 400 suits of clothing, given to him by everybody from Louis XV of France to the Boy Scouts of America and the Allied Armies of World War II. Rue de l'Etuve, just off the Grand' Place.

Jeanneke-Pis – The female counterpart to *Manneken-Pis,* the fountain was created in 1985 by Denis Adrien Debouvrie to symbolize loyalty. A couple who throws a coin into the water is purportedly guaranteed mutual fidelity. In a little alley off the Rue des Bouchers, Impasse de la Fidelité.

Galeries St.-Hubert – Built in 1847, just north of the Grand' Place, this is the oldest arcade in Europe and has been a fashionable promenade since it was built. There are elegant shops and restaurants here, and the surrounding streets, such as the quaint and narrow Petite Rue des Bouchers, are known for their many fine restaurants. Rue du Marché-aux-Herbes.

Parc de Bruxelles (Brussels Park) – Near the fine arts complex, this historic park originally was the hunting ground of the Dukes of Brabant. It was laid out in the formal French manner during the 18th century, when it was a fashionable promenade. In 1830, the park was the scene of heavy fighting between Dutch troops and patriots. The Palais du Roi, the office of the sovereign, overlooks the park just east of the Place Royale. The Rue Ducale boasts a row of aristocratic mansions. Byron lived at No. 51 when he composed the Waterloo stanzas of "Childe Harold."

Place Royale (Royal Square) – Between the palace and the fine arts complex is this elegantly proportioned neo-classical square, built during the 18th century. The statue of Charles of Lorraine was removed by anti-Royalists during the French Revolution and replaced by one of Godfrey of Bouillon, leader of the first Crusade.

Musée d'Art Ancien (Museum of Old Masters) – This is a very large collection of paintings, mostly Flemish, from the 14th to the 17th century. Included are the works of Rubens, the Breughels, and Van Dyck, among others. Closed Mondays and public holidays. No admission charge. 3 Rue de la Régence (phone: 513-9630).

Musée d'Art Moderne (Museum of Modern Art) – Next to the *Musée d'Art Ancien,* this building — with underground levels — is a dramatic showcase for an extensive collection of art that spans the period from 1880 to the present, including works by Belgium's greatest modern artists — among them Paul Delvaux, James Ensor, and René Magritte. When taken together, the two-museum complex (known as the *Royal Museums of Fine Arts*), comprises one of Europe's most impressive art museums. No admission charge. Closed Mondays and public holidays. 1 Pl. Royale (phone: 513-9630).

Church of Notre-Dame-des-Victoires-du-Sablon – Right near the fine arts complex, this 15th-century church is an outstanding example of late Gothic architecture. According to tradition, a Brussels woman had a vision that she should bring a statue of the Virgin Mary from Antwerp to Brussels; when she did so, her boat was guided by angels. She presented the statue to the crossbowmen, and their chapel became a popular place for pilgrimage. So many people crowded the chapel that in 1400 work began on the present church. Pl. du Petit-Sablon.

Place du Grand-Sablon (Grand Sablon Square) – Below the church, the heart of the antiques center of Brussels is the scene of a book and antiques market on weekends. The streets of this bustling area are lined with art galleries, antiques shops, cafés, restaurants, and the city's most esteemed bakery, *Wittamer.* Just off the square is the Romanesque Church of Notre-Dame-de-la-Chapelle, burial place of painter Pieter Brueghel the Elder and the philosopher Spinoza.

Place du Petit-Sablon (Petit Sablon Square) – This square is dotted with 48 small bronze statues representing the medieval trade guilds. A formal garden slopes down the square from the church above and contains statues of the Counts of Egmont and Hoorn, two of Brussels's martyrs of independence. In 1568 these great Flemish (Catholic) noblemen were beheaded in the Grand' Place for protesting to Philip II of Spain about the persecution of Protestants. Egmont's courage was celebrated in a play by Goethe and an overture by Beethoven. Nearby, his home, the 16th-century Egmont Palace, now is the scene of many international receptions. Off the Place du Petit-Sablon is the Rue des Six-Jeunes-Hommes, which has some lovely old houses.

Cathédrale de St.-Michel (St. Michael's Cathedral) – Sitting majestically on top of a hill near the center of town, the national cathedral of Belgium is one of the oldest buildings in Brussels. Begun in the 13th century, it's in typical Belgian Gothic style. Its 16th-century stained glass windows were donated by Emperor Charles V. The baroque pulpit and the mausoleums also are worthy of note. Bd. de l'Impératrice at Pl. Ste.-Gudule.

Colonne du Congrès (Congress Column) – Near the cathedral, the column was built in 1850 to honor the national congress that promulgated the Belgian constitution, after the 1830 revolution. On top of the column is a statue of King Leopold I. In front is the eternal flame that burns in memory of the unknown soldiers from both world wars. From the esplanade there is a good view of the entire city. Rue Royale, north of St. Michael's Cathedral at Pl. du Congrès.

Musées Royaux d'Art et Histoire (Royal Museums of Art and History) – In the Parc du Cinquantenaire at the eastern end of town, this is one of the largest museums of its kind. Its exhibits include ancient civilizations, particularly Egyptian and Greco-Roman, Belgian history and folklore, and the useful and decorative arts in Europe. Closed Mondays and certain holidays. No admission charge. 10 Parc du Cinquantenaire (phone: 733-9610).

Art Nouveau in Brussels – Surprisingly few foreigners are aware that Brussels is home to more important examples of buildings designed in the graciously curvilinear, turn-of-the-century architectural style known as Art Nouveau than any other city in the world. In addition to the museum/workshop of Victor Horta (*Horta Museum;* 25 Rue Américaine; phone: 537-1692), one of Art Nouveau's foremost proponents, a number of period buildings still stand in Brussels. The Hôtel Solvay (224 Av. Louise), Maison Stoclet (281 Av. de Tervuren), and Hôtel Tassel (6 Rue Paul-Emile Janson, now the Mexican Embassy) are probably the most famous of the private residences. Special group visits to the Hôtel Solvay and Hôtel Tassel occasionally are arranged by the *Horta Museum;* the Maison Stoclet cannot be visited. Among the public Art Nouveau buildings worth visiting are two hotels — the *Pullman Astoria* (103 Rue Royale; phone: 217-6290) and the *Métropole* (31 Pl. de Brouckère; phone: 217-2300) — a restaurant, *De Ultième Hallucinatie* (316 Rue Royale; phone: 217-0604), and the *Falstaff Café* (25-27 Rue Henri-Maus; phone: 511-8789). Excellent specialized tours can be arranged through *ARAU* (phone: 513-4761).

OUT OF TOWN

Since Belgium is such a small country (only 11,750 square miles), even its major cities of Bruges, Antwerp, and Ghent are within a short distance of Brussels.

Maison d'Erasme (Erasmus's House) – In the southwestern suburb of Anderlecht, this was not, in fact, Erasmus's house, but the home of a friend where the "Prince of Humanists" stayed in about 1521. Nevertheless, this is a beautiful patrician residence, immensely evocative of the personality of the man. Rooms are richly furnished in 16th-century style; there's a library and a quiet walled garden as well as documents to illustrate the life and work of Erasmus. The house also includes a small but excellent collection of Renaissance paintings, including Hans Holbein's portrait of Erasmus and works by Roger van der Weyden and Hieronymus Bosch. Closed Tuesdays and Fridays. Admission charge. 31 Rue du Chapitre, Anderlecht (phone: 521-1383).

Church of St. Pierre and St. Guidon – Also in Anderlecht, at Place de la Vaillance (phone: 521-8415), not far from Erasmus's House, you might want to look at the 15th-century Gothic Church of St. Pierre and St. Guidon with its ancient crypt and Renaissance wall paintings. Just north of the church on the Rue du Chapelain is a small, interesting Flemish convent (*béguinage*), founded in 1252 and restored in 1956 to its original appearance, with the mother superior's room, kitchen, courtyard, and so on. 4 Rue du Chapelain, Anderlecht.

Atomium – The Parc du Centenaire, in a northern suburb of Brussels, was the site of the *1958 World's Fair.* The symbol of the fair is the Atomium, which represents the molecule of a crystal of iron magnified 165 billion times. There's an elevator to a restaurant at the top and escalators to various spheres that contain exhibitions — most of them now dated — on the peaceful uses of atomic energy. There also is a vast group of exhibition halls dating from the *1935 and 1958 World's Fairs.* Also on the site is the Bruparck, comprised of the *Oceadium,* an indoor, aquatic amusement park; *Kinepolis,* with 23 movie theaters under one roof; the Village, whose cafés, restaurants, shops, and playground all evoke Brussels of the past; and Mini-Europe, with 400 models (scaled 1:25) of the Old World's most famous landmarks. Open daily. Admission charge. Heysel, Laeken (phone 477-0977).

Waterloo – On the night before the battle, the Duchess of Richmond gave a huge ball on Brussels's Rue Royale that was immortalized in Lord Byron's "Childe Harold's Pilgrimage" and Thackeray's novel *Vanity Fair.* The site of the famous battle is only 12 miles (19 km) south of the city and is accessible by public bus and by coach excursions. If you climb the lion monument (Butte du Lion), you can see a somewhat obstructed view of the battlefield itself. There is a museum of battle nearby. Open daily. Admission charge. 90 Chemin des Vertes-Bornes (phone: 384-3139).

A better sense of the battle can be gained from a visit to another museum in the town of Waterloo, which is about 2 miles (3 km) north of the battlefield and once was Wellington's headquarters. *Wellington Museum* (closed the week between *Christmas and New Year's*). Admission charge. 147 Chaussée de Bruxelles (phone: 354-5954).

Villers-la-Ville – About 15 miles (24 km) south of Waterloo are the awe-inspiring ruins of a 12th-century Cistercian abbey, complete with dining hall and brewery. Open Sundays and holidays only, October through mid-March; daily the rest of the year. Admission charge (phone: 71-879555).

Beersel Castle – This early-14th-century château-fort is 10 miles (16 km) south of Brussels. The brick building, with three towers and set in the middle of a moat, has no furnishings but does have the obligatory drawbridge, lookout tower, and torture room. Visitors (especially those with small children) should be careful around the castle since there are lots of open windows and few safety rails. Open daily from March to mid-November, weekends only the rest of the year; closed in January. Admission charge (phone: 376-2924).

Gaasbeek Castle – This historic 13th-century castle (many times restored) is 6 miles (10 km) southwest of Brussels. Though its exterior, with seven round towers, is medieval, its interior contains Renaissance furnishings and valuable tapestries, furniture, and objets d'art. There's a 100-acre park. The view from the terrace in the garden was painted by Pieter Breughel the Elder. Closed Mondays from April through October and Fridays year-round. No admission charge. 12 Groenstr., Lennik (phone: 532-4372).

■**EXTRA SPECIAL:** Take a 1¼-hour train ride to Bruges (in Flemish, Brugge), often called Die Scone, "the beautiful." This is one of Europe's best-preserved medieval cities, a place of rare charm: narrow cobbled streets with picturesque canals spanned by more than 50 bridges. The maze of winding streets makes driving difficult, but most of the places in town can be reached on foot.

Everything centers around the Grote Markt, or main square; you can enjoy a 40-minute tour of the city by the canal boats that are anchored just southeast of the Grote Markt or rent a horse-drawn carriage right in the square. Also on the Grote Markt is the tourist office. Don't miss the famous belfry, very tall — 353 feet — with a carillon of 49 bells. Concerts are held year-round.

Bruges is famous as a lace making center, and the finest examples of the art are exhibited in the *Gruuthuse Museum* (17 Dijver; phone: 50-339911), a 15th-century palace with fine furniture and a superb collection of old Flemish lace. Other outstanding places are the *Groeninge Museum* (12 Dijver; phone: 50-339911), containing a great many fine examples of Flemish art; the graceful 13th-century Gothic cathedral; and the *Memling Museum* (38 Mariastr.; phone: 50-332562) at St. Jans Hospital, containing the oldest pharmacy in the world as well as many important works of the great 15th-century painter.

Bruges has many other sights, not least of which are the streets themselves, narrow and winding and lined with gabled houses. You can see the town in one rather strenuous day or, if you choose, stay overnight at one of the charming hotels, such as the *Duc de Bourgogne,* 12 Huidenvettersplein (phone: 50-332038).

SOURCES AND RESOURCES

TOURIST INFORMATION: Basic information about Brussels is available in the US from the Belgian National Tourist Office (745 Fifth Ave., New York, NY 10151; 212-758-8130). In Brussels, be sure to visit the main office (61 Rue Marché-aux-Herbes; phone: 512-3030) for excellent maps and leaflets, calendars of tourist events, and aid of any sort, or the Brussels Tourist Office (in the Hôtel de Ville, Grand' Place; phone: 513-8940). At the airport, contact a multilingual hostess in the baggage area, or call 722-3000.

The US Embassy is at 27 Bd. du Régent (phone: 513-3830).

Local Coverage – The best English-language publication is *The Bulletin,* a weekly in a newsmagazine format. It's available at local newsstands.

Food – The tourist office puts out a booklet, *Gourmet Restaurants,* available for a small fee. It includes a gastronomic rating of more than 100 restaurants as decided by "five of the best food critics in Brussels."

 TELEPHONE: The country code for Belgium is 32; the city code for Brussels is 2.

 GETTING AROUND: Airport – Brussels National Airport at Zaventem is a 20-minute drive from downtown. Taxi fare should run about 1,000 Belgian francs (about $32). At press time the airport was under expansion; plans included the addition of 55 gates and an underground train system leading directly to the new 4-story terminal. Greater Brussels taxis (*Autolux,* phone: 425-6020; *Taxis Oranges,* phone: 513-6200) are more economical than those parked at the airport. An efficient train service links the airport directly with center city; it operates every 20 to 30 minutes from 5:39 AM to 11:46 PM. City buses marked BZ or 3586 run from Zaventem to the North Station.

Bus, Tram, and Métro – A clear, detailed map is available at the tourist office. Rides are inexpensive, and you can buy a five- or ten-ride card at a savings. There is a special 1-day unlimited ticket for about $5.

Car Rental – *Avis* (145 Rue Américaine; phone: 537-1280) and *Hertz* (8 Bd. Lemonnier; phone: 513-2886) rent cars. Offices of other major rental agencies also are found at the airport.

Taxi – Taxis are plentiful but quite expensive. The tip is included in the fare. You can order a cab from *Taxis Verts* (Green Taxis) by calling 511-2244, or pick one up at a taxi stand.

 LOCAL SERVICES: Dentist (English-Speaking) – Dr. G. Trice (8 Bd. Brand-Whitlock; phone: 733-3314); or call the dental help service, *service de garde dentaire,* (phone: 426-1026).

Dry Cleaner/Tailor – *DeGeest,* 41 Rue de l'Hôpital (phone: 512-5978).

Limousine Service – *François Jacobs,* for chauffeured Mercedes-Benzes and Rolls-Royces. 60 Rue F.-Séverin (phone: 215-9859).

Medical Emergency – *CUL, Cliniques Universitaires St.-Luc* (10 Av. Hippocrates; phone: 764-1111). For emergency service, dial 100.

Messenger Service – *Eurocolis* (10A Rue P.-Gassée; phone: 425-3801). Brussels taxi drivers also perform this service; call *Taxi Verts* (phone: 347-4747).

National/International Courier – *DHL International Express* (210 Kosterstr., Diegem; phone: 720-9500); *Federal Express* (Freight Building 2, Brussels National Airport; phone: 722-7777).

Office Equipment Rental – *IOP,* 38b Bd. Bischoffsheim (phone: 218-4444).

Pharmacy – *Grande Pharmacie de Brouckère* (10-12 Passage du Nord; phone: 218-0575). Pharmacies are open from 9 AM to 6 PM weekdays and on Saturday mornings; they operate on a rotation basis for night and weekend service (at least one per neighborhood is on weekend duty).

Photocopies – *D-Copy,* 17-25 Rue des Vièrges (phone: 512-7010).

Post Office – *Monnaie Center,* open Mondays through Saturdays from 8 AM to 8

PM (Pl. de la Monnaie; phone: 219-3860); *Gare du Midi,* 24-hour service (48A Av. Fonsny; phone: 538-4000).

Secretary/Stenographer (English-Speaking) – *Gregg* (43 Cantersteen; phone: 513-6710); *Wings* (51 Rue de Joncker; phone: 537-7240).

Teleconference Facilities – *Hilton International Brussels* (see *Best in Town,* below).

Telex – *Régie des Télégraphes et des Téléphones,* open from 8 AM to 10 PM, 19 Bd. de l'Impératrice (phone: 513-4490).

Other – Business services: *Burotel Belgium,* also provides office space (4-5 Rue de la Presse; phone: 217-8080); *European Business Facilities* (20-22 Rue du Commerce; phone: 511-7290). Tuxedo and fur rental: *Francy-Tailor* (50 Bd. Emile-Jacqmain; phone: 217-8494); and *John Kennis* (12 Av. Marnix; phone: 513-2303).

SPECIAL EVENTS: Each year in February, the *Palais des Beaux-Arts* hosts the *Foire des Antiquaires de Belgique,* a 2-week antiques fair featuring a magnificent array of pieces collected by antiques dealers around the country; for more information contact the *Palais des Beaux-Arts* (23 Rue Ravenstein; phone: 512-5045). Every spring, usually in May, the Royal Palace Greenhouses are open to the public. In Laeken, just a few miles north of downtown Brussels, the indoor gardens feature exotic flowering trees and plants, many of them native to Zaire, once the Belgian colony called the Congo. Call the tourist office for exact dates and hours (phone: 512-3030).

Starting officially in late June, but actually a month earlier, with a series of preliminary park concerts dubbed "kiosks à musique," is the annual *Festival Musical d'Eté.*

The *Ommegang* pageant takes place in the Grand' Place on the first Thursday in July at 9 PM. It is a centuries-old spectacle commemorating the miraculous arrival of a statue of the Virgin Mary in the Sablon church. The word *ommegang* means "to walk around," which is done much as it was in the 16th century for Charles V and his court. The oldest and noblest families take part in the procession, representing their ancestors who took part in the original pageant. This colorful, splendid tradition is one of Belgium's most popular attractions. Tickets for bleacher seats go fast; see the tourist office.

During August, September, and early October, Brussels is part of the *Festival of Flanders,* one of Europe's major music festivals, featuring internationally known orchestras, soloists, operas, and dance companies — and tickets are reasonably priced. For information write the *Festival of Flanders* (18 Eugène Flageyplein, Brussels 1050; phone: 648-1484). Not to be outdone, Wallonia has its own music festival beginning in June. Contact the *Festival of Wallonia* (11 Rue sur-les-Foulons, Liège 4000; phone: 41-223248) for details. There's also a month-long fair in summer (mid-July to mid-August) on the Boulevard du Midi, featuring rides and local foods.

In August, when the royal couple take their holiday, the ornate sitting rooms and splendid ballroom of the Royal Palace are open for inspection by one and all. No admission charge. Pl. des Palais.

Every other year in September and October since 1969, Brussels has produced its own international arts festival, *Europalia,* in which the events focus on a specific nation. Art exhibitions; music, dance, and theater performances; film screenings; and literary conferences all attract the top names in their respective fields. In 1991 the festival was devoted to the arts of Portugal, and next year it will focus on Mexico.

MUSEUMS: Besides those mentioned in *Special Places,* some of the more interesting museums include the following:

Autoworld – A spectacular collection of vintage cars. Featured are curious old Peugeots and Model-T Fords, along with the Cadillacs of FDR and

JFK. Closed *Christmas* and *New Year's Day*. Admission charge. Esplanade du Cinquantenaire, Etterbeek (phone: 736-4165).

Bibliothèque Royale Albert I (Royal Library) – More than 3 million volumes as well as coins, maps, and splendid illuminated manuscripts. Closed Sundays, holidays, and the last week of August. No admission charge. Mont des Arts (phone: 519-5311).

Musée Communal des Beaux Arts d'Ixelles (Museum of Fine Arts of Ixelles) – Splendid Dürers, Toulouse-Lautrec posters, and works of French and Belgian Impressionists. Closed Mondays, weekday mornings, and public holidays. No admission charge to the permanent collection. 71 Rue Jean-Van-Volsem, Ixelles (phone: 511-9084).

Musée Horta (Horta Museum) – The home and studio of the Art Nouveau architect Victor Horta. Open daily except Mondays and public holidays, from 2 to 5:30 PM. Admission charge. 25 Rue Américaine (phone: 537-1692).

Musée Instrumental (Museum of Musical Instruments) – Housing 5,000 instruments from the Bronze Age to the present. Open Sunday mornings; Tuesday, Thursday, and Saturday afternoons; and Wednesday evenings. 17 Pl. du Petit-Sablon (phone: 512-0848).

Musée Royale de l'Afrique Centrale (Royal Museum of Central Africa) – The brainchild of colonialist King Leopold II, it has an interesting art gallery and a panorama of African life. A formal French garden sits behind the museum. Open daily. No admission charge. 13 Leuvensesteenweg, Tervuren (phone: 767-5401).

Musée de Sciences Naturelles (Museum of Natural Science) – Noteworthy for its collection of well-preserved dinosaur skeletons, unearthed in western Belgium in 1878. Open daily. Admission charge. 29 Rue Vautier, Ixelles (648-0475).

Pavillon Chinois (Chinese Pavilion) – A first-rate collection of 17th- and 18th-century Chinese and Japanese porcelain. Closed Mondays and public holidays. No admission charge. 44 Av. Van Praet Laeken (phone: 268-1608).

 SHOPPING: Brussels is not a city for bargain hunters, but you will get top quality for the price you pay. In Brussels, or any other Belgian city, look for Val St. Lambert, one of the world's finest crystals. Pewter and linen also are excellent values. Leather goods and women's clothing are terribly chic and equally *cher*. All the top couturiers are represented here, including Dior, Armani, and Valentino.

Lace is the product you will see most often, especially in the souvenir shops around the Grand' Place. Some of the little old ladies who made Brussels lace world famous still are working, but alas, much of the lace now is machine-made in Hong Kong. This lace usually is used on cocktail napkins and placemats, which make small, inexpensive, and easily portable gifts. Look carefully at tags to know what you are buying.

Belgian carpets usually are of a very high standard. In most cases, they are mechanically produced and offer a wide variety of styles and materials. Copies of Oriental designs are said to be the biggest sellers now — even in the Middle East. To ensure quality, look for the "T" mark on the carpet backing.

Antiques most often are of excellent quality. The streets surrounding the Place du Grand Sablon (Rue Watteau, Rue Lebeau, Rue Ernest-Allard) are full of interesting shops. Or try the Saturday and Sunday market at the Place du Grand Sablon. Usually there are some lovely things there, so it's fun even if you are only "just looking." There also is a book market at the same place.

Although there are fine shops all over the city, there are two main shopping districts. The more modestly priced is the one in the area including the Boulevard Adolphe-Max, the Boulevard Anspach, Rue Neuve, Rue Marché-aux-Herbes, and Galeries St.-Hubert. The other, uptown, where the chic boutiques are located, is the Avenue Louise,

Avenue de la Toison d'Or, and the Boulevard de Waterloo. *Les Jardins du Sablons* (at 36 Pl. du Sablon and 6 Rue des Minimes) houses 36 shops and a tearoom under its skylit cupola. Anderlecht, a suburb of Brussels, has one of the largest covered suburban shopping centers in Europe.

Flea market shoppers enjoy the daily Marché de la Brocante at the Place du Jeu-Balle. Bimonthly auctions, featuring high-quality items from carpets and antiques to art and jewelry, are held at the *Galerie Moderne* (3 Rue du Parnasse; phone: 513-9010). Another reputable auction house is *Nova* (35 Rue du Pépin; phone: 512-2494).

A good place to get a sampling of everything is at *L'Innovation* (also known as *Inno*), Brussels's finest department store (111 Rue Neuve; phone: 211-2111).

Art et Sélection – Famous Val St.-Lambert crystal. 83 Rue Marché-aux-Herbes (phone: 511-8448).

Biot-Believre – Linen tablecloths and the like, hand embroidered on request. 8 Rue de Naples (phone: 512-9571).

CBRS – The best of Belgian carpets from a variety of manufacturers. 431 Bd. Emile-Bockstael (phone: 479-9944).

Corné Toison d'Or – Belgian chocolates for the connoisseur. 12 Av. de la Toison d'Or, 24-26 Galerie du Roi, and several other locations (phone: 512-8947 or 512-4984).

Degand Tailleur-Chemisier – Fine men's suits, shirts, and accessories by Chester Barrie, Zimmerli, and Ballantyne, as well as clothes tailor-made on the premises. Degand's mother, Yvonne, runs the women's shop on the top floor. 415 Av. Louise (phone: 649-0073).

Delvaux – *The* place for leather goods. 31 Galerie de la Reine, 22-24 Bd. Adolphe-Max, and 24a Av. de la Toison-d'Or (phone: 512-7198, 217-4234, and 513-0502, respectively).

Dujardin – Fashionable, well-made clothing for children. 8-10 Av. Louise (phone: 513-6070).

Madymous – Official distributor of Huy pewter, considered Belgium's best. Look for the Huy hallmark (the town's castle mark) to be sure. 42B-C-D Rue du Noyer (phone: 733-5065).

Manufacture Belge de Dentelles – Lace and lace making. 6-8 Galerie de la Reine (phone: 511-4477).

Rose's Lace – A boutique for blouses and lingerie made of Belgian lace and linen. 1 Rue des Brasseurs (phone: 512-1126).

Textilux Center – Brussels tapestries in traditional and modern designs. 41 Rue du Lombard, near the *Manneken-Pis* (phone: 513-5015).

Wittamer – Delectable chocolates and pastries. 12-13 Pl. du Grand-Sablon (phone: 512-3742).

Wolfers – Fine jewelry and diamonds. 82 Av. Louise (phone: 511-6525).

 SPORTS AND FITNESS: Fitness Centers – The facilities at the *Brussels Hilton* (38 Bd. de Waterloo; phone: 513-8877), and the *Brussels Sheraton* (3 Pl. Rogier; phone: 219-3400), can be used for a fee. The *Woluwé* sports center (near Forêt de Soignes at 87 Av. Mounier; phone: 762-8522), has an Olympic-size swimming pool and also charges admission.

Golf – The *Royal Golf Club de Belgique* is the royal diplomats' club (Château de Ravenstein, Tervuren; phone: 767-5801). The clubhouse is in one of the buildings belonging to the Ravenstein Château property. The facilities are first-rate and only 7 miles (11 km) from downtown Brussels.

Horseback Riding – Try *Royal Etrier Belge* (19 Chaussée du Vert-Chasseur; phone: 374-2860), or contact the *Fédération Royale Belge des Sports Equestres* (38 Av. Hamoir; phone: 374-4734).

Jogging – Best is Brussels Park, opposite the Royal Palace and bordered by Rue Royale. More expansive is Cinquantenaire Park (take the métro to Schuman and you'll spot the park just ahead). About a mile away on Avenue de Tervuren is the hilly Woluwé Park (take tram No. 44 from the Montgomery métro station). Farther afield is the Forêt de Soignes (Royal Forest), just outside the city (take tram No. 44 and signal the driver to stop as the woodland comes into sight). Because of the traffic, jogging is not recommended on the streets of Brussels. Real enthusiasts will enjoy the annual 20-km race held in June at the Cinquantenaire Park or the annual *Brussels Marathon,* held each September.

Soccer – Known as *football,* this is the most popular spectator sport. Major games are played at *Heysel Stadium,* 135 Av. du Marathon (phone: 478-9300).

Swimming – At *Bains de Bruxelles* (28 Rue du Chevreuil; phone: 511-2468); *Calypso* (60 Av. L.-Wiener, Boitsfort; phone: 673-3929); and *Poséidon* (2 Av. des Vaillants, Woluwé-St.-Lambert; phone: 771-6655).

Tennis – Try the *Brussels Lawn Tennis Club* at 890 Chaussée de Waterloo (phone: 374-9259).

 THEATER: The marionette theater, *de Toone,* is a must. Popular plays are performed by puppets in Brussels slang nightly except Sundays (21 Petite Rue des Bouchers; phone: 513-5486). Most modern plays are in French or Flemish, though occasionally there is some amateur theater in English. Brussels has more than 20 theaters staging a variety of plays; check the daily newspapers for schedules.

 MUSIC: One of the world's most prestigious music competitions is the *Concours Reine Elisabeth,* named for the grandmother of the present king. It takes place in May and usually is covered by TV and radio.

The *Théâtre Royal de la Monnaie* (Pl. de la Monnaie; phone: 218-1202), has been renovated in splendid fashion. The *Monnaie* is the home of opera and ballet in Brussels, but it also is an important part of its history. The original building dated from the late 17th century and was built on the site of the old mint (hence the name). The present building dates from 1817. In 1830, at a performance of Auber's opera *La Muette de Portici* at the *Monnaie,* one of the patriotic songs ("Sacred love of the fatherland, give us courage and pride") so inflamed the audience that they streamed out of the opera house and unleashed the rebellion that ultimately led to Belgium's independence. Recitals and concerts by world-famous musicians are given throughout the year, usually in the *Palais des Beaux-Arts* (23 Rue Ravenstein; phone: 512-5045). Sunday morning concerts, usually by string quartets, are offered at the *Astoria* hotel's *Boîte à Musique* (103 Rue Royale; phone: 513-0965).

NIGHTCLUBS AND NIGHTLIFE: As in most large cities, the nightclubs often are tourist traps, so be prepared to spend a lot of money if you go to them. *En Plein Ciel* (38 Bd. de Waterloo; phone: 513-8877), the rooftop restaurant of the *Hilton* hotel, has a small dance floor. The atmosphere is pleasant; the view, on a starry night, impressive. Reservations are necessary. *Le Mozart* (541 Chaussée d'Alsemberg; phone: 344-0809), is a pub that serves jazz as well as food until 5 AM. You can have dinner up until 6 AM at *Safir,* the classic all-night spot (23 Petite Rue des Bouchers; phone: 511-8478). Reservations unnecessary. Live jazz late into the night in a requisite smoky atmosphere is the Saturday-night staple at *Bierodrome* (21 Pl. Fernand-Cocq; phone: 512-0456). Popular discos include *Le Crocodile Club,* at the *Royal Windsor* hotel (5 Rue Duquesnoy; phone: 511-4215), closed Sundays; *Le Garage* (16-18 Rue Duquesnoy; phone: 512-6622), for trendy but blaring New

Wave; and Brussels's most outrageous disco, *Le Mirano Continental* (38 Chaussée de Louvain; phone: 218-5772), open Saturdays only.

Brussels also has some superb café-bistros, including *'T Spinnekopke* (1 Pl. du Jardin aux Fleurs; phone: 511-8695), and *De Ultième Hallucinatie* (316 Rue Royale; phone: 217-0614), an Art Nouveau marvel where fine food is served on weekends. For a pleasant nightcap, try *Au Roi d'Espagne* (in the Grand' Place; phone: 513-0807) or *Au Bon Vieux Temps* (12 Rue Marché-aux-Herbes; phone: 218-1546). The *Café Métropole* (31 Place de Brouckère) has an Art Nouveau interior and an outdoor café heated for year-round dining (phone: 219-2384). Reservations unnecessary. The *Falstaff Bistro* (near the Grand' Place at 17-23 Rue Maus; phone: 511-8789) has turn-of-the-century decor and a lively clientele. Scores of English beers are available for sampling at *La Houblonnière* (4 Pl. de Londres; phone: 502-1597), where Dixieland jazz is heard on Sunday nights, *La Lunette* (3 Pl. de la Monnaie; phone: 218-0378), or *Le Jugement Dernier* (165 Chaussée de Haecht; phone: 217-9597).

BEST IN TOWN

CHECKING IN: Accommodations in Brussels reflect the level of quality appropriate for Europe's diplomatic and commercial capital — and so do the prices. A double room and bath in a very expensive Brussels hotel will cost from $435 to $465; a double room in an expensive hotel usually runs from $145 to $200 and more; a moderately priced hotel charges between $80 and $125; an inexpensive hotel (rare in this city) can be $50 to $80. Rates include a 16% service charge and VAT. Significantly lower rates prevail on weekends and during July and August. All telephone numbers are in the 2 city code unless otherwise indicated.

Royal Windsor – In the Grand' Place area, this 300-room hotel is Tudor in style and its *Quatre Saisons* restaurant offers a splendid menu (see *Eating Out*). Its atmosphere is British; its ambience modern and quite pleasant; soundproofed rooms have TV sets, unusual paneling, and handwoven fabrics. Underground parking garage. Business facilities include 24-hour room service, meeting rooms for up to 250, English-speaking concierge, foreign currency exchange, secretarial services in English, audiovisual equipment, photocopiers, computers, cable television news, translation services, and express checkout. 5-7 Rue Duquesnoy (phone: 511-4215; fax: 511-6004; telex: 62905). Very expensive.

Amigo – Gracious and comfortable, in an ideal location, only one street away from the Grand' Place. It has the charm (and sometimes the noise) of the square and an aristocratic interior with velvet upholstery and silk wainscoting. There's a garage, a restaurant, a bar, and 183 spacious rooms and suites. Best are the sixth-floor apartments with terraces. Business facilities include 24-hour room service, meeting rooms for up to 200, English-speaking concierge, foreign currency exchange, audiovisual equipment, photocopiers, and cable television news. 1-3 Rue de l'Amigo (phone: 511-5910; fax: 513-5277; telex: 21618). Expensive.

Brussels Sheraton – Brussels's largest property (530 rooms) has several dining rooms, including *Les Comtes de Flandres*, serving haute cuisine (see *Eating Out*), and a coffee shop. It's a sleek, modern, 31-story affair with a handsome lobby, well-appointed, good-size rooms, a discotheque, a fitness center, and a pool. Business facilities include 24-hour room service, meeting rooms for up to 1,000, English-speaking concierge, foreign currency exchange, secretarial services in English, audiovisual equipment, photocopiers, cable television news, and translation services. 3 Pl. Rogier (phone: 219-3400; fax: 218-6618; telex: 26887). Expensive.

Hilton International Brussels – Another of the city's large (369 rooms) establishments, near the Avenue Louise shopping area, and where the international business set frequently hangs out. All rooms have TV sets and air conditioning; duplexes have balconies and full kitchens. The roof garden restaurant affords a superb view of the city, and there is an authentic French restaurant (see *Eating Out*), an English pub, and a bar-discotheque patronized by locals. Business facilities include 24-hour room service, meeting rooms for up to 450, English-speaking concierge, foreign currency exchange, secretarial services in English, audiovisual equipment, computers, cable television news, and express checkout. 38 Bd. de Waterloo (phone: 504-1111; fax: 504-2111; telex: 22744). Expensive.

Holiday Inn Brussels Airport – Like any other member of the chain, this large (228-room) place is clean, convenient, and standardized. It has tennis courts, a pool, and a sauna. Courtesy buses run to the airport and into town. Business facilities include 24-hour room service, meeting rooms for up to 500, English-speaking concierge, foreign currency exchange, secretarial services in English, audiovisual equipment, photocopiers, computers, cable television news, translation services, and express checkout. 7 Holiday St., near the airport in Diegem (phone: 720-5865; fax: 720-4145; telex: 24285). Expensive.

Jollyhotel Atlanta – Taking its name from the heyday of *Gone With the Wind,* this link in the Jolly chain has a rooftop restaurant, *La Veranda* (see *Eating Out*), with a good view of the city. The hotel is downtown, and some of the 244 rooms can be noisy. Business facilities include meeting rooms for up to 50, English-speaking concierge, foreign currency exchange, secretarial services in English, audiovisual equipment, and translation services. 7 Bd. Adolphe-Max (phone: 217-0120; fax: 217-3758; telex: 21475). Expensive.

Métropole – The city's last remaining 19th-century establishment, it has 410 rooms decorated in styles ranging from Art Deco to modern. The lobby, café, and restaurant (see *Eating Out*) have been restored but still retain last century's charm. Business facilities include 24-hour room service, meeting rooms for up to 500, English-speaking concierge, foreign currency exchange, secretarial services in English, audiovisual equipment, photocopiers, cable television news, translation services, and express checkout. 31 Pl. de Brouckère (phone: 217-2300; fax: 218-0220; telex: 21234). Expensive.

Palace – Tastefully renovated, this 360-room hotel was built in 1910 and overlooks the Botanical Gardens. Business facilities include meeting rooms for up to 500, English-speaking concierge, foreign currency exchange, secretarial services in English, audiovisual equipment, photocopiers, cable television news, and translation services. 3 Rue Gineste (phone: 217-6200; fax: 218-7651; telex: 65604). Expensive.

Pullman Astoria – Smaller (128 rooms), with a lovely staircase and quiet, comfortable rooms, this hostelry is a souvenir of the Belle Epoque. The bar is decorated to represent a Pullman compartment. Business facilities include 24-hour room service, meeting rooms for up to 320, English-speaking concierge, foreign currency exchange, secretarial services in English, audiovisual equipment, photocopiers, computers, translation services, and express checkout. 103 Rue Royale (phone: 217-6290; fax: 217-1150; telex: 25050). Expensive.

SAS Royal – Opened in 1989, this 281-room property, a stone's throw from the Grand' Place and the Rue Neuve shopping area, has been creatively designed around an inner atrium bursting with light and plant life. Guests can choose from different room styles, including Art Deco Italian, Oriental, or Scandinavian. There is a piano bar, a 1950s American–style bar and grill, a restaurant serving Belgian and Scandinavian specialties, and the *Sea Grill,* a highly regarded seafood restaurant (see *Eating Out*). Business facilities include 24-hour room service, meeting rooms for up to 250, English-speaking concierge, foreign currency exchange, secretarial services in English, audiovisual equipment, photocopiers, computers, cable television news, translation services, and express checkout. 47 Rue du Fossé-aux-Loups (phone: 219-2828; fax: 219-6262; telex: 62904). Expensive.

Scandic Crown – Formerly the *Hyatt Regency,* it's one of the city's more gracious modern hotels, with 315 rooms, including 4 duplexes, 7 junior suites, 2 presidential suites, and 15 executive suites; all were redecorated in 1990. *Hugo's* restaurant serves French fare (see *Eating Out*), and there also is a breakfast room. The hotel also has complete health club facilities. Business facilities include 24-hour room service, meeting rooms for up to 350, English-speaking concierge, foreign currency exchange, secretarial services in English, audiovisual equipment, photocopiers, computers, cable television news, translation services, and express checkout. 250 Rue Royale (phone: 220-6611; fax: 217-8444; telex: 61871). Expensive.

Stéphanie – Close to one of the best shopping districts in Brussels, this 142-room hostelry is convenient for shoppers, but its front rooms can be noisy. Children under 12 stay free in adult's room. Business facilities include 24-hour room service, meeting rooms for up to 180, English-speaking concierge, foreign currency exchange, secretarial services in English, audiovisual equipment, photocopiers, translation services, and express checkout. 91-93 Av. Louise (phone: 539-0240; fax: 538-0307; telex: 25558). Expensive.

City Garden – Modern, spacious, and comfortable, this 96-room residential hotel offers kitchenettes and proximity to the métro and Common Market headquarters. Business facilities include meeting rooms for up to 20, English-speaking concierge, foreign currency exchange, secretarial services in English, photocopiers, and express checkout. 59 Rue Joseph-II (phone: 230-0945; fax: 230-6437; telex: 63570). Moderate.

Novotel – Conveniently located 1 block from the Grand' Place and within walking distance of many prime downtown sites, this 136-room property is a quiet place to stay, in spite of its busy location. Belgian and international dishes are served in the reasonably priced restaurant. Children under 16 stay free with their parents. Business facilities include meeting rooms for up to 30, English-speaking concierge, foreign currency exchange, audiovisual equipment, photocopiers, computers, and cable television news. 120 Rue Marché-aux-Herbes (phone: 514-3333; fax: 511-7723; telex: 20377). Moderate.

La Légende – Small (32 rooms) and centrally located in the city, just a short walk from the *Manneken-Pis.* The concierge speaks some English. 33 Rue de l'Etuve (phone: 512-8290). Moderate to inexpensive.

 EATING OUT: Brussels's pride in good food extends from the most fashionable to the simplest restaurants, from the most elaborate haute cuisine to simply prepared fresh produce. A good restaurant in Brussels goes to exceptional lengths to please a patron who enjoys good food. If you order pâté, for example, you won't get by without sampling several varieties, while the restaurateur beams at every sign of pleasure that you show. Belgium's cooks are some of the best in the world, and Belgian food, once a stepchild of French cuisine, has developed its own specialties. These include the inevitable Brussels sprouts; asparagus from Malines; red cabbage prepared *à la flamande* (with apple); *carbonnades flamandes* (beef braised in beer); *boudin* (blood and white sausage); *waterzooi de volaille* (chicken in a vegetable and cream soup); *anguilles au vert* (eels, served with herbs); and mussels served in a variety of ways. Belgian pastries are excellent, especially *pain à la grecque,* a very light, sweet rusk; *gaufres* (waffles); and tarts made with custard, sugar, or rice. And don't miss *pralines,* the famous Belgian chocolate with a variety of fillings. Bruxellois, the people of Brussels, will tell you that their chocolate is the best in the world — and they may be right. Beer is special here, too, including, among others, Faro, Gueuze-Lambic, Kriek-Lambic, and Trappiste.

There are about 1,700 restaurants in the city, and the best of them rate as virtual national monuments. It's all too easy to spend a small fortune for a good meal, but it's not absolutely necessary. It is unusual to have a bad meal anywhere. A dinner for two, including wine (and remember, most wine is imported), in an expensive restaurant averages $145 to $200; in a moderately priced restaurant, it comes to between $80 and $140; and in an inexpensive one, $75 or less. Unless otherwise noted, Brussels's restaurants take major credit cards. All telephone numbers are in the 2 city code unless otherwise indicated.

L'Alban Chambon – In the Art Nouveau setting of the *Métropole* hotel, chef Dominique Michou of the Académie Culinaire de France offers a wide selection of French specialties. Closed Saturdays, Sundays, and holidays. Reservations necessary. 31 Pl. de Brouckère (phone: 217-2300). Expensive.

Barbizon – This charming villa is in the midst of the Forêt de Soignes and serves such specialties as aspic-coated lobster, smoked salmon and asparagus, and duck and endive salad. Closed Tuesdays, Wednesdays, all of February, and mid-July to early August. Reservations necessary. 95 Willeriekendreef (phone: 657-0462). Expensive.

Bernard – You initially may believe that you have wandered into a grocery store by mistake, but go up one flight to the small dining room where the tables are tucked nose to nose. It looks unpretentious, but it caters mostly to knowledgeable Belgian gastronomes. Closed Sundays, holidays, Monday evenings, and July. Reservations necessary. 93 Rue de Namur (phone: 512-8821). Expensive.

De Bijgaarden – Imaginative fare combines with superb management at this impeccable suburban dining spot. *Pheasant Smitane* and *sole Hôtellerie* share the menu with other creative house specialties. Closed Sundays, Saturday lunch, *Easter,* and the last half of August. Reservations advised. 20 Isidoor Van Beveren Str., Groot Bijgaarden (phone: 466-4485). Expensive.

Bruneau – One of Brussels's finest restaurants, boasting three Michelin stars, it serves excellent French cuisine against a pleasant background approaching Art Deco style. Try the *menu de dégustation,* which includes wines chosen to perfectly complement this sampling of the house specialties. Closed Tuesday nights, Wednesdays, mid-June to mid-July, and *Christmas* to *New Year's Day.* Reservations necessary. 73-75 Av. Broustin (phone: 427-6978). Expensive.

Comme Chez Soi – From the outside, this small townhouse looks inconsequential; inside is one of the best dining places in Belgium, and one of the few outside France to earn three Michelin stars. Try the mussels, fish, venison, foie gras, and pastries. Closed Sundays, Mondays, the week of Christmas, and July. Reservations essential. 23 Pl. Rouppe (phone: 512-2921). Expensive.

Les Comtes de Flandres – The restaurant of the *Brussels Sheraton* serves fine French fare from a seasonal menu. Closed Saturdays, Sundays, and August. Reservations necessary. 3 Pl. Rogier (phone: 219-3400). Expensive.

La Cravache d'Or – Small and elegant, this restaurant offers a varied repertoire of foods from land and sea. Closed Saturdays for lunch, Sundays, major holidays, the first 3 weeks in August, and the first week of January. Reservations necessary. 10 Pl. Albert-Leemans (phone: 538-3746). Expensive.

Au Duc d'Arenberg – A 17th-century house with white walls and lots of paintings is the setting for this cheerful restaurant, best known for duck and Normandy crêpes. Closed Sundays and the last week of December. Reservations advised. 9 Pl. du Petit-Sablon (phone: 511-1475). Expensive.

L'Ecailler du Palais Royal – Unpretentious from the outside, it serves superbly prepared seafood dishes in a 16th-century guild house in the Grand Sablon. Try turbot, lobster, and oysters in season. Closed Sundays, public holidays, and August. Reservations necessary. 18-20 Rue Bodenbroek (phone: 511-9950). Expensive.

Eddie Van Maele – Set in an unpretentious villa north of Brussels, this small establishment decorated in pale pinks and grays serves imaginative creations prepared by one of Belgium's master chefs. If you have trouble choosing a dessert, the Van Maeles will serve you an artistically arranged sampling of them all. Closed Saturday lunch, Sundays, and Mondays. Reservations essential. Near *Heysel Stadium,* 964-966 Chaussée Romaine, Wemmel (phone: 460-6145). Expensive.

Hugo's – In an intimate dining room at the *Scandic Crown* hotel, chef Michel Addons, recipient of a Silver Bocuse Award, offers prize-winning French fare, plus a different menu every Sunday. Closed Saturday lunch and mid-July to mid-August. Reservations necessary. 250 Rue Royale (phone: 220-6611). Expensive.

La Maison du Cygne – Making its home in an exquisite 16th-century building, this elegant place is especially proud of such creations as lobster cassoulet, pheasant with chicory, and milk-fed lamb. Closed Saturday lunch, Sundays, *Christmas, New Year's Day,* and 1 week in August. Reservations necessary. 2 Rue Charles-Buls, Grand' Place (phone: 511-8244). Expensive.

Les Quatre Saisons – The *Royal Windsor* hotel's award-winning French restaurant is as elegant in ambience as it is in cuisine. Try the duck liver, pigeon breasts, or sole prepared creatively by the prize-winning chef Gert Jan Raven. Open daily for lunch and dinner; closed 3 weeks July through August. Reservations advised. 5 Rue Duquesnoy (phone: 511-4215). Expensive.

Romeyer – Boasting a third Michelin star, it's actually a country lodge in the Forêt de Soignes, just a few miles outside the city. Specialties include lobster sausage and stuffed crayfish. Special prix fixe menus feature seasonal items (wild game in winter) and include wines chosen by chef Pierre Romeyer to complement his creations. Closed Sunday evenings, Mondays, February, and the first half of August. Reservations necessary. 109 Steenweg op Groenendaal, Hoeilaart (phone: 657-0581). Expensive.

Sea Grill – The highly reputed French seafood chef Jacques Le Divellec comes to Brussels once a month to prepare food for the *SAS Royal* hotel's dining room, which overlooks the atrium. There is a wonderful variety of fish and shellfish from which to choose. Closed Saturday lunch and Sundays. Reservations necessary. 47 Rue du Fossé-aux-Loups (phone: 219-2828). Expensive.

Le Trèfle à Quatre – Set on the picturesque shore of Genval Lake, this elegant dining establishment won a Brussels Iris de la Gastronomie award in 1990 for chef Michel Haquin's imaginative fare. Closed Mondays, Tuesdays, and mid-January to mid-February. Reservations necessary. Château du Lac, 87 Av. du Lac, Genval (phone: 654-0798). Expensive.

Villa Lorraine – Probably the country's most famous restaurant. The setting is a lovely villa just outside the city center; the service is impeccable, the decor sumptuous, the food the sort of French-style stuff of which dreams are made. Try the hot lobster pâté or the sole. Closed Sundays and most of July. Reservations necessary. 75 Av. du Vivier-d'Oie (phone: 374-3163). Expensive.

Les Années Folles – A tiny, friendly bistro with a menu that often has been imitated. A reasonably priced fixed menu always is available. Duck breast salad and veal *escalope* with calvados are recommended. Closed Saturday lunch and Sundays. Reservations necessary. 17 Rue Haute (phone: 513-5858). Moderate.

Aux Armes de Bruxelles – This is one of the traditional Brussels restaurants on one of the narrow little streets leading off the Grand' Place. Its specialty is fish. Closed Mondays and the second half of June. Reservations advised. 13 Rue des Bouchers (phone: 511-5598). Moderate.

Auberge de Boendael – Although this isn't downtown, it's definitely worth the ride for its delicious meat and fish specialties, grilled over a wood fire. Try to save room for a dessert of homemade coffee ice cream (*café glace*) and sorbets. Closed weekends and mid-July to mid-August. Reservations necessary. 12 Sq. du Vieux-Tilleul (phone: 672-7055). Moderate.

Bellemolen – This country mill house built in 1149 and charmingly restored with a warm, rustic atmosphere, is well worth the 15-mile (24-km) drive northwest of Brussels. The prix fixe menu offers seasonal specialties, artfully prepared and efficiently served. During summer, seating also is available in the garden. Closed Sunday evenings and Mondays. Reservations advised. Exit 19A off the E40; turn left across the bridge and continue one-quarter mile to 11 Stationstr., Essene-Affligem (phone: 53-666238). Moderate.

Maison du Boeuf – In the *Brussels Hilton,* overlooking the gardens of the Egmont Palace, it specializes in shellfish as well as beef. Open daily. Reservations advised. 38 Bd. de Waterloo (phone: 513-8877). Moderate.

L'Ogenblik – A small eatery with the feel of a Paris bistro. All the waiters wear floor-length aprons, and the menu changes daily to offer astonishing variety. The house specialty, bouillabaisse, is chock full of half a dozen kinds of seafood. Closed Sundays. Reservations advised. 1 Galerie des Princes (phone: 511-6151). Moderate.

La Veranda – Overlooking Brussels, the rooftop restaurant of the *Jollyhotel Atlanta* serves a menu of fine meat and fish entrées, all prepared with an Italian twist. Closed Saturdays, Sundays, and 2 weeks at *Christmas* and *New Year's.* Reservations advised. 7 Bd. Adolphe-Max (phone: 217-0120). Moderate.

Chez Jean – Usually packed with regulars, this simple establishment just off the Grand' Place serves tasty Belgian fare. Daily specials are scrawled in soap on wall mirrors. Closed Sundays and Mondays. Reservations advised. 6 Rue Chapeliers (phone: 511-9815). Inexpensive.

'T Kelderke – Congenial and rustic, this bistro serves hearty Belgian fare such as rabbit stewed in beer and *waterzooi,* a hearty soup-like mixture of boiled chicken and vegetables. Open daily. No reservations. 15 Grand' Place (phone: 513-7344). Inexpensive.

St.-Pierre – A modest little place tucked away off the Grand' Place. The service is good and the quality of the food reliable. Open daily for lunch and dinner. Reservations advised. 76 Marché-aux-Herbes (phone: 511-8291). Inexpensive.

Au Vieux Saint-Martin – A favorite place for artists, it is bright and cheerful, with newspapers and magazines to read if you are dining alone. The menu is simple, with Belgian specialties. Open daily. No reservations. No credit cards accepted. 38 Pl. du Grand-Sablon (phone: 512-6476). Inexpensive.

Le Vimar – Tucked into the corner of a busy square near Common Market headquarters, this small spot has long been a favorite of the Bruxellois. Seafood is the specialty: Try the turbot with leeks, mussels in white wine sauce, or seafood casserole. Closed weekends and late July to mid-August. Reservations advised. 67 Pl. Jourdan (phone: 231-0949). Inexpensive.

Vincent – On one of the narrow, cobblestone streets near the Grand' Place, this is the place to go for Belgian specialties. *Moules à l'escargot* (mussels cooked in a butter and garlic sauce) is a tasty starter; steaks are a good main course. Closed the month of August. Reservations advised. 8 Rue des Dominicains (phone: 511-2303). Inexpensive.

BUCHAREST

Bucharest is a vivid blend of old and new — prelude and aftermath — the ancient part of the city dating back to the 14th century, the new manifested in the remains of the revolution of December 1989. In between, the city has survived (just barely) one of the most oppressive (and insane) regimes in Eastern Europe. In many ways, it's a wonder that there's any city here at all.

A full 3 years after the world's first live televised people's revolution — weeks of uprisings finally consummated by an army coup d'état — pre-revolutionary graffiti still remains on façades, and government buildings, their windows broken and surfaces riddled with bullet holes, are cordoned off and secured by police. But the tricolor Romanian flag — *sans* its Communist red star, sometimes with a jagged hole in its place — flies proudly over this city of 2.2 million people. In almost every sense, the scene is bizarre and the operative ambience is *Alice in Wonderland* combined with some surrealistic horror show.

In addition to being the capital of Romania since 1862, Bucharest is the capital (since 1659) of the southern region of Walachia, which spans the foothills of the Carpathian Mountains across the southern Danube plain to the lush, white beaches of the Black Sea. The other two major regions of the country are Transylvania, bounded by the Carpathians in the west, and Moldavia, bordering the Soviet Union in the east. Though Transylvania has a large ethnic Hungarian minority (whose ancestors were imported as colonists in the 13th century by the Hungarian monarchy, which had great influence in the area), the language and culture of Romania as a whole have their origins in the Roman conquest of the area's Thracian tribes during the 1st century. This is why Romanians, unique among Eastern Europeans, speak a Romance language that evolved from Latin between the 7th and 10th centuries, and so is related to French, Italian, and Spanish.

Romania's capital was first officially called Bucharest in a 1459 document signed by Prince Vlad Tepeş. The son of Prince Vlad Dracul (Vlad the Devil), Vlad Tepeş became known as Vlad the Impaler (because of a propensity to impale his enemies) and Dracula (Son of the Devil). Mentions of a settlement called Dîmboviţa Citadel, located astride the Dîmboviţa River, date back to 1368. According to folklore, a shepherd named Buchur (thus the name Bucharest) settled at a bend in the river in the 11th or 12th century, and built a Christian church. The Eastern Orthodox form of Christianity had been introduced in the area by invading Bulgars in the 9th century, and ever since Romania's history has been closely aligned with that of Eastern Orthodoxy, whose local epicenter became Bucharest's Cathedral of the Patriarch.

From the 3rd through the 12th centuries, the territories of what was later to become Romania were repeatedly swept by Germanic and Slavic invaders; they then came under the domination of the Hungarians. After the 15th

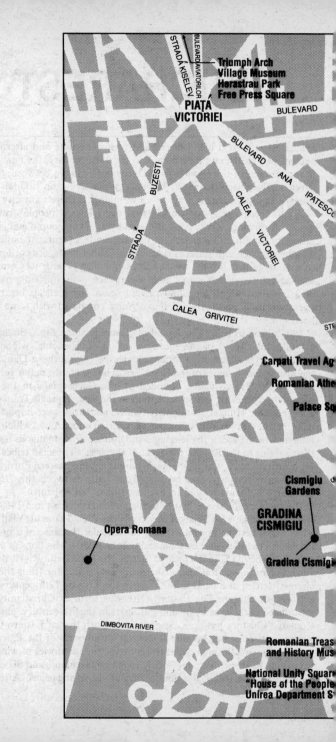

STRADĂ KISELEV
BULEVARDAVIATORILOR

Triumph Arch
Village Museum
Herastrau Park
Free Press Square

PIAȚA
VICTORIEI

BULEVARD

BUZESTI

BULEVARD

ANA

IPATESCU

CALEA

VICTORIEI

STRADĂ

CALEA GRIVITEI

STF

Carpati Travel Ag

Romanian Athe

Palace Sq

Cismigiu
Gardens

GRADINA
CISMIGIU

Opera Romana

Gradina Cismig

DIMBOVITA RIVER

Romanian Treas
and History Mus

National Unity Square
"House of the People
Unirea Department S"

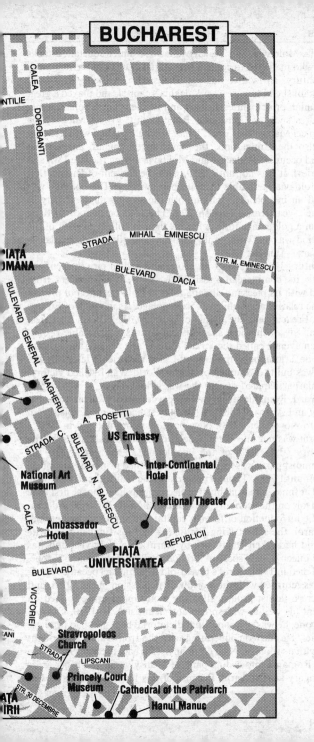

BUCHAREST

CALEA

ĂNTILIE

DOROBANTI

STRADĂ   MIHAIL   EMINESCU

PIAȚA
ROMANĂ

STR. M. EMINESCU

BULEVARD   DACIA

BULEVARD   GENERAL

MAGHERU

A. ROSETTI

STRADA C.

BULEVARD

US Embassy

Inter-Continental
Hotel

National Art
Museum

CALEA

N. BALCESCU

National Theater

Ambassador
Hotel

REPUBLICII

PIAȚA
UNIVERSITATEA

BULEVARD

VICTORIEI

Stravropoleos
Church

STRADA

LIPSCANI

ÇANI

Princely Court
Museum

Cathedral of the Patriarch

STR. 30 DECEMBRIE

PIAȚA
IRII

Hanul Manuc

century, Walachia, Moldavia, and Transylvania were under constant attacks from the Turks, who managed to control substantial chunks of territory well into the 19th century. In fact, it was the Turks who, working with local Roman rulers, established Bucharest as Walachia's capital, and played a great part in the Romanian principalities' history and politics. These rulers, sometimes heroic figures such as Constantin Brîncoveanu, Prince Michael the Brave, and Stefan cel Mare ("the Great"), had to juggle dealing with not only the Turks but also the Hungarians, the kingdom of Poland, and Czarist Russia (which had occupied Walachia and Moldavia during the late 18th and early 19th centuries). It was not until 1859, with the consent of Russia, that Walachia and Moldavia were able to unite permanently. The country was officially declared an independent nation with the signing of the Treaty of Berlin, ending the 2-year Russo-Turkish War. The 1881 coronation of King Carol I ushered in a golden age for Bucharest, though not for the rest of the country. The period was not without its financial difficulties and popular — particularly peasant — unrest.

Nineteenth-century Bucharest was an exotic and stylish city that enticed businessmen with its commercial possibilities, as well as travelers from around the world with its pleasant climate, folklore, and tradition of princes and kings, and the relative accessibility of its language. As in much of Europe at the time, the French held the monopoly on style here, and Bucharest affected a Parisian air, with wide, spacious boulevards, fashionable restaurants and cafés, an avenue called the Stradă Paris (Paris Street), and eventually even an Arc de Triomphe at the head of Calea Victoriei (Victory Boulevard). The arch was built to commemorate the World War I Allied victory, in which Romania participated during the war's final days.

After World War I, Romania struggled to recover from its wartime occupation by Germany and Austria-Hungary (Bucharest had been occupied from December 1916 to November 1918). New parties sprang up, and in 1921 a limited land reform was put into effect which produced some benefits for the country's peasantry (then 80% of the population). That same year, the Romanian Communist party was formed, but it remained primarily an underground movement until 1948. Though progress in the political and economic spheres was fitful at times, a reasonably free election was held for the first time in 1927, and controls on the economy were eased, allowing for greater decentralization and the introduction of foreign capital. During this same period, Crown Prince Carol, the son of King Ferdinand and his English-born wife Queen Marie (who had taken New York by storm on a 1926 visit and was dubbed the "real queen of café society"), renounced his rights to the throne. When Ferdinand died in 1927, Carol's 6-year-old son Michael became regent.

Economic crises returned with the worldwide depression in the 1930s, and in this atmosphere a fascist group called the Iron Guard arose to feed on popular discontent (as well as widespread anti-Semitism). In 1930, Carol II reclaimed the throne; he was of a somewhat dictatorial bent and had little use for political parties. He started cooperating with the Iron Guard and sought rapprochement with its sponsor, Nazi Germany. This backfired in 1940, when Hitler pressured Romania into ceding parts of Transylvania and other areas to his allies, Hungary and Bulgaria. Because of this humiliation, Carol was forced to abdicate, and power was given by his son, King Michael, to Marshal Ion Antonescu, who turned the country into a fascist state in alliance with the Axis powers.

Though the fascists had been initially abetted by King Michael, as the war turned against the Axis and Soviet troops closed in around Romania, he helped engineer a coup that deposed the Antonescu regime in August 1944. Michael himself was forced to abdicate in 1947 as the Soviet-sponsored Communists (under Gheorghe Gheorghiu-Dej) consolidated their hold over the country. The aristocracy of Bucharest was displaced, private enterprise and tourism were all but obliterated, and the elegant establishments "liberated for the people" quickly fell into neglect and decay. The city's famed hotel and restaurant trade fell away, too, a victim of the general apathy produced by lack of competition. Once a city of princes, the Paris of the Balkans gradually deteriorated into just another fading monument to doctrinaire Communism, patrolled by the Securitate, the regime's feared secret police.

In 1965, Nicolae Ceaușescu took over the leadership of the Romanian Communist party, beginning a 24-year reign which saw a gradual leaning toward association with some Western countries, particularly West Germany. Bucharest was ostensibly given a face-lift; dozens of dilapidated old buildings that housed the city's increasingly deprived masses were destroyed in order to build grandiose government palaces and monuments to socialism. Many of these are still unfinished, except for their impressive façades.

The Romanian people (today a nation 23 million strong) paid the price for Ceaușescu's extravagences. Profits from the textile and poultry industries were used to pay for Ceaușescu's shrines to himself, while food shortages were commonplace. There was a psychological price to be paid as well. Censorship was the norm; even ownership of a typewriter was illegal. The 1989 overthrow of the Ceaușescu regime helped bring about fundamental reforms: Food appeared on store shelves again, birth control was permitted — and typewriters allowed. The first free elections in Romania since World War II were held in May 1990. Ion Iliescu was elected president, and as leader of the National Salvation Front, Petre Roman became Prime Minister of the Parliament. At press time, plans for privatization were being discussed, but were delayed due to disagreements between the Parliament and the presidency.

The city still retains a faded fin-de-siècle air, though a number of buildings are still under scaffolding or bear scars from the December 1989 upheavals. The Ceaușescus didn't quite raze all of gracious Old Bucharest, though, and now many of the beautiful mansions, palaces, villas, parks, vineyards, and marinas that had been reserved for the Ceaușescu family's exclusive use are open to the public.

The southern zone of Bucharest is the most interesting and historic. It is here that you will find the remnants of the Princely Court, on the banks of the Dîmbovița. Several blocks away is the Gradina Cismigiu, a grand park that affords a picturesque 19th-century garden retreat from the urban bustle. To the northwest is Piață Victoriei, the capital's main plaza, from which its major avenues — Calea Victoriei, Bulevard Ilie Pintilie, Bulevard Ana Ipatescu, Stradă Buzesti, Stradă Kiselev, Bulevard Aviatorilor — radiate. The embankments of the Dîmbovița have been landscaped, and their promenades offer pleasant and scenic areas for strolling, along with open-air restaurants, cafés, and gardens. Even the river itself, once rather heavily polluted, has been cleaned up. Though Bucharest long ago had to forgo its claim as the Paris of the Balkans, visitors still might come across some of that old *je ne c'est quoi*.

BUCHAREST AT-A-GLANCE

 SEEING THE CITY: There is really no one spot from which to behold all of Bucharest, but the courtyard of the Cathedral of the Patriarch — perched on a quiet hillside overlooking the city just south of the Princely Court — does offer a nice view of the Old Quarter. Perhaps the best panoramic view of the city as a whole is from the *Balada* restaurant on the 22nd floor of the *Inter-Continental* hotel (see *Checking In*).

SPECIAL PLACES: The vivid mood of post-revolutionary Bucharest is one of the most exciting aspects of the city. Right now the streets still pulsate with an intensity that will soon fade into everyday life. A visit to Bucharest affords an opportunity to witness a piece of history — though visitors must be willing to expend some initiative and energy, and endure considerable discomfort. It's not all difficult, as you will find many people eager to share their experiences with you. Hire an English-speaking guide and/or driver and car through *Carpaţi*, the state travel agency, and ask to be taken on a tour of the sites of the 1989 revolution. With a little luck, your guide/driver might be a member of the generation that sparked the fires of the December uprising. He or she can be your key to insights into the heart of Bucharest, which the official tours, heavy on ancient history, will never reveal.

Old Bucharest – The core of this district is the Princely Court (now a museum), the central part of the original Dîmboviţa Citadel. Portions of the ruins of the medieval citadel and its surrounding streets are being reconstructed; parts of the area are open for viewing.

Other attractions of the Old City are the Lipscani trading area, with several old houses of worship, such as the 16th-century Curtea Veche (Old Court Church), where visitors can witness Orthodox masses daily, and Stavropoleos Church, a prime example of a uniquely Romanian architectural style named after the illustrious 18th-century Walachian Prince Constantin Brâncoveanu. This curvy Brâncovenesc style, executed in both wood and stone, is a fusion of late Renaissance, Byzantine, and Romanian folk-art designs.

Cathedral of the Patriarch (Basilica Patriarhiei) – Built during the 17th century, the seat of the Patriarch of the Romanian Orthodox church was later enlarged when the patriarchate was transferred from the province of Moldavia to Walachia. Inside, groups of old women dressed in black can be seen sitting on the floor sharing a lunch of bread, cheese, and melon; later they clean and decorate the cathedral with flowers. Though never closed by the Communist regime, eventually it, like many places of worship in the area, was slated for demolition and saved only by the 1989 revolution. The courtyard and cemetery, erected during the mid–19th century in memory of bishops and monks already dead for 3 centuries, are filled with headstones and crosses inscribed in ornate Old Slavonic. The cathedral is open for daily services at 10 AM and sometimes in the evening. 21 Alçea Patriarhiei (phone: 163455).

Romanian National Parliament (Parlamentul National) – Situated across from the cathedral, this long, gray, neo-classical structure was built in 1907. Formerly the seat of the rubber-stamp Grand National Assembly under the Communist regime, the building is open to the public when Parliament is in session (from September through July); parliamentary sessions themselves also are open to the public. The entrances are guarded by friendly Romanian soldiers dressed in sharp new khakis that replaced the old Soviet-style green uniforms. Aleea Marii Adunari Nationale.

Princely Court (Palatul Voyavodal) – Once the home of the Kings and Princes of Walachia, it is now a historical museum, located almost entirely underground, showing the progressive building of the citadel from the 15th to the 18th century. The outlines of the original citadel are preserved in stone; later additions are brick. From the outside, only chimneys and archways are visible, but inside are artifacts and portions of the original citadel. The museum is open daily from 10 AM to 5 PM except Mondays; admission charge. 31 Stradă 30 Decembrie.

Lipscani Street (Stradă Lipscani) – Just 2 blocks from the Princely Court is the most historical part of Bucharest, the principal trading street of the Old City. A wonderful place to walk for its myriad small shops and outdoor stands, and also because the narrow lane so teems with people, pushcarts, bicycles, and even horses, sheep, and fowl that it is next to impassable for cars. Merchants and farmers from all over the Balkans used to bring their wares to trade in the district, which dates from the 18th century.

Hanul Manuc – A medieval inn — still in business (see *Checking In*) — with a courtyard entered from the street through a set of enormous wrought-iron gates. The 1812 peace treaty between Turkey and Russia, which handed part of Moldavia (called Bessarabia) over to Russia, was signed here. 62 Stradă 30 Decembrie. *Note:* At press time this street was expected to be renamed.

Romanian Stock Exchange (Burse Româbească) – One of the most ornate pieces of architecture in Bucharest, the Burse was built in 1880 and restored by the Ceaușescu government 100 years later. No longer used for its original purpose, a new stock exchange opened last year at another location. The style reflects Byzantine and Romanesque features: Magnificent marble columns are topped with dosserets (a sort of secondary capital) of hammered copper, the floor is of patterned stone, the octagonal ceiling is a mosaic of leaded glass stained in vibrant shades of blue. Iron gates, cherubs, and other finely carved statuary preside over the variety of shoe and cosmetics stores now housed here. 18 Stradă Lipscani.

University Square (Piață Universitatea) – North of Lipscani, at the intersection of Nicolae Bălcescu and Republicii boulevards, this plaza, the seat of Bucharest's university, was the site of much of the fighting of the December Revolution. Demonstrators, unhappy with the new government, continue to gather here to voice their dissent.

Palace Square (Piață Palatului; formerly Piață Gheorghe Gheorghiu-Dej) – Just northeast of University Square, this plaza was named for the former royal palace, which became a government building and half of which now houses the *Museum of National Art*. Across from the palace is the monumental Civic Center, formerly the Communist party headquarters, from whose roof the Ceaușescus temporarily escaped by helicopter during the 1989 uprising. In front of the building (which is cordoned off and protected by armed guards) are shrines to the victims of the revolution. One of these is a massive cross brought by an Orthodox priest and his followers from Timișoara, the city where the revolution began. Citizens decorate the shrine daily with fresh flowers and votive candles.

Victory Boulevard (Calea Victoriei) – Once referred to as the Champs-Elysées of Bucharest, the Calea Victoriei runs from Piață Victoriei (Victory Square) at its north end southward to Piață Unirii (National Unity Square). Just southeast of the boulevard are a group of beautifully landscaped center islands with lovely fountains dividing another wide thoroughfare, Alçea Fintinilor (formerly the Boulevard of the Victory of Socialism).

At the head of the Calea Victoriei is an imposing red marble palace; designed for public gatherings and presidential speeches, it was still under construction — at a cost of up to $3 million — when Ceauşescu fell. Many buildings (including residences) were torn down to make way for the old regime's flamboyant showpiece, which was vandalized during the revolution. Today, this "House of the People" is only 90% finished and the giant cobblestone square in front has become a free-for-all through which cars and taxis zigzag in crazy patterns and wedding parties careen, blowing their horns, just for the fun of it.

Free Press Square (Piaţă Presei Libere) – This plaza used to be named for *Scintei,* the Communist party journal which was published here for 40 years, until the 1989 revolution (now it is the site of a non-Communist paper). It took two cranes 4 days to remove the 7,000-pound bronze statue of Lenin that stood here. Rumors are that a Japanese firm purchased the statue and planned to melt it down to its original — and now more valuable — state.

Victory Square (Piaţă Victoriei) – This is the point from which most of Bucharest's main streets emanate. Across the plaza is Stradă Kiselev, bordered on either side by parkland and leading through the Arcul de Triumf (Triumphal Arch) past Free Press Square into Herăstrău Park, Bucharest's largest nature preserve.

Forest Parks – Bucharest is blessed with extensive greenery and spacious parks, including several nature preserves and recreation areas. Perhaps the best known is Herăstrău Park, whose 1½-square-mile expanse is home to a large lake, more than a half-dozen pleasant restaurants, and an outdoor museum. The latter, the *Muzeul Satului* (Village Museum), is a collection of houses, churches, and other structures from throughout Romania (open daily; admission charge). The pastoral settings provide a pleasant respite from urban Bucharest, and the museum displays a good cross section of the very different architectural styles found in the various regions of the country. If you hadn't planned to travel outside the capital, a visit to this museum might change your mind. In summer the museum hosts crafts demonstrations, including weaving, carving, wool spinning, and making *nai* (wooden wind instruments). For those who want to take photographs, the 2-lei (less than 5¢) entry fee is raised to 5 or 6 lei (depending on whether you enter for the whole day or just an afternoon).

Băneasa Forest, located within the city limits to the north of Herăstrău, has areas for picnicking and such outdoor games as volleyball and badminton, as well as the *Băneasa Forest* restaurant, which offers outdoor dining and Romanian folk shows.

OUTSIDE THE CITY

Snagov Lake and Monastery (Lacul si Minastriea Snagov) – A lovely recreation area located 15 miles (24 km) north of Bucharest, Snagov is very popular with the residents of the capital for family outings (as well as with the Romanian national sculling team for training). It's about a 30- to 40-minute drive from downtown, depending on how many Gypsy carts, herds of sheep, or gaggles of geese make you yield the right of way.

Snagov Island is in the middle of the lake and was formerly closed to the public because Ceauşescu had built a villa on its western shore; the island now is open to all and can be reached via an 85-person ferry (see below). Also on the small island is the 15th-century church and monastery founded by Vlad Tepeş (better known as Vlad the Impaler or Dracula), who is buried in the crypt here. In the portrait of him that rests before the altar, the prince is long-lashed, wide-eyed, and somewhat demented looking. (Though certainly fierce and ruthless, even by the standards of 5 centuries past, Vlad is revered throughout Romania as one of the country's greatest rulers, and was not literally a bloodsucker; Count Dracula was a 19th-century fictional exaggeration dreamed up by Irish author Bram Stoker. Vlad did, however, earn the sobriquet "The Impaler," due to his fondness for skewering the bodies of invading Turks on their own swords — nearly 20,000 of them.)

The original monastery and church, dating from the 6th century, were christened the Church of Princes in 1383 and fortified, serving until 1418 as a fortress to defend Walachia. Vlad Tepeş built the current Snagov Monastery and fortifications in 1456 (including an underground escape tunnel to the shore which is now in disrepair and unusable). The church's altar table is from the original 6th-century structure and has never been moved, as is customary in the Orthodox faith. On display in the church are a number of ancient ecclesiastical documents, including copies of the first Romanian bible, printed at Snagov toward the end of the 17th century (the original is in Bucharest's Romanian Academy). The monastery is still home to four monks, and Sunday and holiday services are held at 9 AM (Sunday mass is open to the public).

Also along the lakeshore are a number of small cafés, outdoor food stands selling barbecued meat and *mititei* (lamb sausage), and a restaurant at the Snagov Lake recreation area. Rowboats can be rented for 20 lei (about $1) per hour (don't try to row all the way out to the island, though, since there's no place to dock). A number of small villas on the island offer interesting tourist accommodations, which can be booked through *Carpaţi* (phone: 145160).

A note on the ferry: It operates during the summer on no particular schedule — just whenever the captain feels there are enough passengers for a run to the island, generally once every hour. It can be chartered, though, for around $45 per hour. *Carpaţi* will tell you it's impossible to visit the island during the winter, but you can arrange private passage with one of the weekly supply boats (again, on no particular schedule; you simply have to show up at the dock and ask around, or ask your guide to find out what day the boat leaves).

Mogoşoaia Palace – A visit to the elegant 18th-century estate of Prince Constantin Brâncoveanu, 9 miles (13 km) through the parks and forests to the northwest of the city, is one of Bucharest's finest day trips. Now a museum of medieval art and artifacts, the palace itself overshadows its contents. A formal structure, it was built on the scale of a Venetian palazzo, with ornately arched colonnades, a stately, close-cropped garden, and a quiet reflecting pond. Open daily. Admission charge. 1 Valea Parcului (phone: 685560).

■ **EXTRA SPECIAL:** The most exotic and typical example of traditional Romanian life is found outside the capital. Just a few miles from the center of Bucharest are villages where peasants still live off the land; where Gypsies roam the countryside in tarpaulin-covered wagons pulled by horses or oxen; and public wells are sheltered by brilliantly painted shrines.

Worthwhile excurions include the 2-hour ride through rural Walachia to reach the lovely medieval monastery at Curtea de Argeş, once the seat of Walachia's rulers; the extensive ruins of the 1st-century Roman settlement at Sarmizegatusa (in the Jiu Valley between Transylvania and Walachia); and the lovely, red-roofed, medieval Transylvanian town of Braşov, some 115 miles (184 km) north of Bucharest.

Stays in some of Moldavia's beautiful working monasteries and convents are available on a very limited basis. All prospective visitors must be screened well in advance for a stay of 2 to 3 days. Quarters are modest and clean, and the environment is one of complete peace and serenity. Apply through *Carpaţi* (and be persistent).

SOURCES AND RESOURCES

 TOURIST INFORMATION: In Bucharest, the main branch of the *Carpaţi-Bucureşti* National Tourist Office is located at 7 Calea General Magheru (phone: 145160). In the United States, information is available from the Romanian National Tourist Board (600 Third Avenue, New York, NY 10017; phone: 212-697-6971). Hours and days of operation can be somewhat erratic, so be sure to call ahead. The tourist offices also will make hotel and other reservations for you, but in many cases it may be safer to book through your own travel agent.

The US Embassy is located at 14 Stradă Tudor Arghezi, just behind the *Inter-Continental* hotel (phone: 104040).

Local Coverage – The most prominent local newspaper is *Romănia Libera;* if you read any other Romance language, you may pick out headlines and some words. English-language newspapers and magazines are still difficult (or impossible) to obtain. Often a *Carpaţi* guide will be happy to listen to the nightly news and fill you in the next morning. Or bring your own portable shortwave radio.

 TELEPHONE: The country code for Romania is 40; the city code for Bucharest is 0. The public phones generally work, and are easily operable with 1-lei coins. Overseas calls must be made from private or hotel phones.

 GETTING AROUND: Bucharest's roughly 43 square miles are easy to navigate, and are best covered on foot or in a rental or chauffeured car (parking spaces generally are available). Taxis are a good option, too; they're inexpensive, and drivers will often wait for you. The most difficult area to navigate is Lipscani, where you probably should plan to walk.

Airport – Buses leave Otoponi International Airport and Bănesea (domestic) Airport for Bucharest about every hour from 5 AM to 10 PM and cost the equivalent of 25¢. To get out to the airport, catch the buses which depart from the *Tarom* airlines office in downtown Bucharest (10 Stradă Brezoianu) about 12 times a day (7 times on Sunday). The taxi fare to or from Bănesea is about 100 lei (about $5), and slightly higher to Otoponi (both are just under a half hour from the city center).

Bus, Trolley, and Streetcar – They crisscross the city and are inexpensive (1 to 2 lei — less than a nickel), but crowded and dirty. Buses are the least reliable form of transportation; often you will see crowds of people waiting for buses that never arrive. Two-lei tickets are purchased and validated on board.

Car Rental – Automobiles, with or without drivers, are available through *Carpaţi.* Though costs are reasonable, you may be able to get an even better bargain by hiring a *Carpaţi* driver independently to take you around the city for a day. *Hertz* and *Avis* have outlets at major hotels, and *VIP Tours,* a private rental agency, has opened behind the *Athénée Palace* hotel. Payment is in hard currency or by credit card only. Many private travel agencies in Bucharest also rent cars — a complete list can be found at the Ministry of Tourism, 17 Apolodor St.

Metro – Three interconnected lines serve Bucharest: The first travels around the city in a circle, the second traverses the city, and the third serves the outlying industrial areas. A 2-lei coin admits a passenger through the turnstile. The system, called *Metrou,* is clean and efficient and runs all night (which is more than can be said even for such Western European capitals as Paris and London). No maps are available, though there are some diagrams affixed to the walls in the stations (along with the intriguing bonus of graffiti left over from the revolution).

Taxi – State taxis, distinguishable by their yellow license plates, will take you anywhere in the city for 35 to 50 lei (about $1.75 to $2.50; they can be ordered by phone from anywhere in Bucharest by dailing 053). Private, state-licensed taxis have white plates and signs in the window reading "P Taxi" or "Taxi Particular." They generally charge three to four times more than the state taxis, but they're also more readily available. Unlicensed cabs with no signs also will stop to pick up passengers — particularly handy at night, when there's a scarcity of regular taxis. Travel this way at your own risk, however; if the cab has no meter, agree on a price *before* getting in. The best way to hail any taxi is still by palming a package of Kent cigarettes (Bucharest's brand of choice). Though the fare is generally in lei, drivers won't turn down dollars or other hard currency.

Train – The main railway station, through which 90% of the rail traffic passes, is the Gară de Nord, which occupies an entire city block on Calea Grivitei. There are a handful of lesser stations that provide service only to a few small towns around Bucharest. It's best to book train reservations and pay in advance with *Carpați* before leaving the US if you want to be assured of private, first class accommodations (if you really want to meet the Romanian people, consider traveling what is known as regular class). The local trains make a lot of stops, they don't take reservations, and are generally quite crowded, but eventually you'll find a seat. For train schedule information dial 052 in Bucharest.

LOCAL SERVICES: Dentist (English-Speaking) – Most hospitals have dental services, and many of their dentists speak some English. Inquire at your hotel for more information.

    Dry Cleaner – In addition to the hotels, there is a network called *Nufarul;* most dry cleaning will take 2 or 3 days.

Limousine Service – Through *Carpați.*

Medical Emergency – Telephone number is 061. The *Hospital of Urgency* (*Spidalul de Urgenta*) handles all emergencies in Bucharest. On Stefan cel Mare Blvd.

Messenger Service – Available from any of the large hotels. The service is free if it is a matter of 5 or 10 minutes, but they charge for longer deliveries.

National/International Courier – *DHL International* is offered through *International Romexpresx Service.* 47 Stradă Eminescu (phone: 191580).

Office Equipment Rental – Available from the larger hotels.

Pharmacy – To find the all-night pharmacy closest to your hotel, call the 24-hour pharmacy hotline 065. Most pharmacies have someone who speaks some English.

Photocopies – At the *Inter-Continental* hotel (4-6 Calea Nicolae Bălcescu; phone: 137040 or 140400); some storefront services also are opening up — inquire at your hotel.

Post Office – The main post office is 37 Calea Victoriei. Open from 8 AM to 6 PM.

Secretary/Stenographer (English-Speaking) – Contact the Chamber of Commerce. 22 Calea Nicolae Bălcescu (phone: 154707).

Tailor – Inquire at your hotel for the closest tailor.

Telex – Most hotels and the main post office have telex and fax facilities.

Translator – Through *Carpați* or the Chamber of Commerce (address and phone above).

SPECIAL EVENTS: A music festival featuring the works of Romanian composer Georges Enesco is held at the *Romanian Athenium* (1 Stradă Franklin; phone: 156875) in September. An international trade show primarily geared for businesses takes place twice a year, in May and in October

(1 Piață Presei Libere; phone: 183183; in the US call the Romanian Trade Mission: 212-682-9120). International festivals are held several times a year at the *Village Museum.* On the *Feast of Saint Dimitru* (in June — the date changes each year; ask at *Carpați*), the saint's coffin is taken from the Cathedral of the Patriarch and carried through the streets so that the faithful can see and touch it. But the most colorful and unusual events generally take place in the provincial villages, not in Bucharest. The *Feast of the Goat* is a masked winter carnival held in many villages from *Christmas Eve* through *Epiphany* (January 6).

MUSEUMS: Besides the museum of the Princely Court listed in *Special Places,* other museums of interest include the following.

National Musuem of Art (Muzeul National de Arta) – Although closed for a time because of damage from the recent revolution, the museum's superb collection of Romanian and European painting and sculpture is once again open to the public. The works of such local artists as the 19th-century painter Grigorescu are hung beside those of such European giants as Rubens and Van Gogh. Sculpture also is represented, including works of the world-renowned Romanian-born sculptor Constantin Brancusi (1876–1957). Open from 9 AM to 5 PM; closed Mondays. Admission charge. Piață Revolutiei.

Romanian Treasury and History Museum (Muzeul de Historie si Trezorie) – The worthwhile part of this museum is on the ground floor (upstairs is mostly empty); to get in you will have to relinquish all cameras, notebooks, and anything else the soldiers standing guard think you might use to compromise Romania's national treasures. There is an exquisite collection of gold and jewelry dating as far back as the 5th century BC: headdresses, icons, goblets, coins, and military and religious ornaments from the Dacian and Roman eras through the 19th century. Displays are marked in Romanian and English. Open from 10 AM to 6 PM; closed Mondays. Admission charge. 12 Calea Victoriei.

SHOPPING: A wide selection of Romanian products — such as gorgeous leaded crystal, handmade lace, woodcarvings, embroidery, pottery (including the beautiful shiny black Margina pottery), wool sweaters, hats, and blankets — are available at *Comturist* shops located in major hotels throughout Bucharest and the rest of the country. These shops offer some decent bargains, especially on crystal. Payment is in hard currency *only* — cash or credit card. Most of what you'll probably want to take home from Romania will be bulky or breakable, so plan to leave some extra room in your luggage.

Stores where Romanians shop (and pay in lei) also can offer some interesting finds. Store hours are generally from 8 AM to 4 PM, though some open from 8 AM to noon, close until 4 PM, then reopen from 4 to 8 PM. Food and department store hours are from 6 AM to 9 PM.

Amzei Market – This huge indoor/outdoor market is open year-round, and in late summer and fall sells the fresh fruit and vegetables so noticeably absent at most restaurants. There also are booths for crafts, including hand-knit wool sweaters, blankets, and throws, as well as the bright red and black embroidered table runners that decorate homes and restaurant walls. Stradă Amzei Biserica (behind the *Bucureşti* hotel).

Biblioteca – The name simply means "library." Both Romanian and foreign books are sold here, the latter mostly in German and Russian (including some beautifully illustrated 20th-century texts). 54 Stradă 30 Decembrie.

Bruitere – A jewelry shop with a good selection of ivory pins and inexpensive costume jewelry, as well as outdated Eastern-bloc camera equipment. 122 Calea Victoriei.

Cogsignatia – Any one of several consignment stores among the wonderful little shops along Stradă Lipscani. They sell everything from antiques to Western goods imported from Turkey and Greece. As you enter the street from the east, an alleyway on the left leads into a cobblestone courtyard with iron-shuttered windows, part of the original 15th-century marketplace. The shops are about eight doors down on the left-hand side of the courtyard. Stradă Lipscani.

Photo Muzică – Wonderful woodcarvings and ceramics at absurdly low prices. Also record albums and cassette tapes. Corner of Stradă Sçoală Floreasco and Calea Dorobanti.

State Post Office (Oficiu Poştal) – Not only are stamps sold here, but also picture postcards and decorative envelopes. Open 7 AM to 8 PM. 150 Calea Dorobanti.

Union of Plastic Artists (Uniunea Artistilor Plastici) – Look for this sign on the doors of a series of small art galleries located in the courtyard off Stradă Lipscani. They sell cards and small prints, oil lamps, ceramics, jewelry, glassware, and paintings. Be sure to get a receipt from the shopkeeper that will allow you to take original art out of the country.

Unirea – The city's central department store, with a good souvenir department. Sometimes you'll find handmade wool rugs, scarves, and national costumes and blouses. 1 Piaţă Unirii, just south of Stradă Lipscani.

 SPORTS & FITNESS: Physical fitness and sports activities are considered a fundamental activity for all Romanians — at school, in the factories, and in the villages. International recognition has come to a few Romanians; who can forget the darling of the *1976 Summer Olympics* in Montreal, Nadia Comaneci? In the tennis world, players Ion Tiriac and Ilie 'Nasty' Nastase have had their share of aces. As elsewhere in Europe, soccer is the national game here, and matches are played during summer and fall at several stadiums in Bucharest, including the *Dinamo* (2 Stefan cel Mare; phone 121470). Fitness centers and swimming pools can be found at the *Inter-Continental* and *Bucureşti* hotels.

 THEATER: Tickets to shows and musical events are generally quite inexpensive and can be obtained at box offices, through most hotels, *Carpaţi,* or at ticket agencies around town (there are two right near the *National Art Museum,* for example). The *Romanian Athenium* (1 Stradă Franklin; phone: 156875) is the home of the *Bucharest Philharmonic Orchestra and Madrigal,* which performs here during the winter. The *Caragiale National Theater* (2 N. Calea Nicolae Bălcescu; phone: 147171) stages Romanian classics, Shakespeare, and other plays. Native son Eugène Ionescu's works are popular in Bucharest, and have been frequently presented at the *Theater of Comedy* (2 Stradă Mandinesti). Opera and ballet fans should check the September-through-May schedule at the *Opera Romana* (70 Blvd. 6 Martie). The only theaters open during the summer season (mid-June through mid-September) are puppet and comedy theaters; they offer satire, very popular with Romanians.

MUSIC: The *Rapsodia Romana Artistic Ensemble Hall* (53 Stradă Lipscani; phone: 131300) offers folkloric song and dance from Walachia, Moldavia, and Transylvania. Those with more contemporary tastes can take in pop and jazz concerts at the *Hall of the Radio and Television Building* (191 Calea Dorobanti). The *Bucharest Radio-Television Orchestra* also gives classical performances here featuring many guest artists. Watch especially for Alexandru Andrias, a favorite balladeer since his underground days before the 1989 revolution.

NIGHTCLUBS AND NIGHTLIFE: The nightclub scene, especially later in the evening, is generally oriented toward cabarets and floor shows at the large hotels. Popular among locals, especially the under-30 crowd, is the *Salion Spaniol* (116 Calea Victoriei), with offerings ranging from amateur entertainment to special guest stars (such as John Jewell, a folksinger from California who recently was the local rage). For a blend of cabaret, vaudeville, and satire that can be entertaining even if you don't speak Romanian, try *Tanasr* (174 Calea Victoriei) and the *Savoy Theater* (Stradă Academie).

BEST IN TOWN

CHECKING IN: Although some effort is being made to renovate or upgrade accommodations for the first time in more than 4 decades, Romania's economic difficulties still dog the country's hotel industry, with tourists sometimes turned away due to shortages of such basics as lightbulbs. Hotels in Bucharest and Romania's other major cities are the most inexpensive in Eastern Europe, and their quality is adequate to good, though hardly comparable to their "deluxe" counterparts in Western Europe. Double rooms in hotels listed here as expensive range in price from about $95 to $155; moderate accommodations run about $56 to $80. Inexpensive establishments, which often lack private baths, are $50 or less. Advance reservations are particularly important during the summer months. All telephone numbers are in the 0 area code unless otherwise indicated.

Ambassador – Built in 1937, this is a typical example of the Stalinesque cement-block style. The 13-story hostelry is eminently serviceable, as well as conveniently located near Piață Universitatea and *Carpați's* main office. There is a good restaurant and a wonderful pastry shop. Rooms are adequate, with bulky phones and TV sets. As for room service, it exists, but be patient. 10 Blvd. General Magheru (phone: 110440 or 159080). Expensive.

Athénée Palace – Once grand, and now merely atmospheric. Many of its rooms were damaged during the December 1989 revolution, but most had been restored at press time. There are 2 restaurants (one featuring musical entertainment), and a good take-out pastry shop in the lobby. Major credit cards accepted. 1-3 Episcopiei St. (phone: 140899; telex: 11162). Expensive.

București – An Old World–style, yet modern 448-room establishment located on one of Bucharest's main thoroughfares and convenient to most sites in the city center. Its rooms and suites are small but comfortable. There's a good restaurant (see *Eating Out*) with a nightly Romanian music show, a brasserie, snack bar, and hard-currency beer bar. Other amenities include indoor and outdoor swimming pools, saunas, a hairdresser, one of the only Western-style fitness centers in Romania, typewriter rental, photocopying service, and even a dental clinic. 63-11 Calea Victoriei (phone: 142177 or 155850). Expensive.

Flora-Cure – A pleasant 4-story hotel with a lovely setting in pastoral Herăstrău Park on the outskirts of Bucharest. In addition to a restaurant, brasserie, cafeteria, and bar, facilities include a swimming pool and sauna. For jet-lagged travelers, skin-care and anti-aging treatments are available for an additional fee. 1 Calea Poligrafiei (phone: 184640 or 114438). Expensive.

Inter-Continental – Bucharest's most modern property boasts 417 rooms at a great downtown location, but none of the Old World charm of the *București*. Many of the amenities are similar, though, including a pool and fitness center, and 3 good restaurants serving Romanian and international food. 4-6 Calea Nicolae Bălcescu (phone: 137040 or 140400). Expensive.

Lebăda – A hotel with conference facilities, tennis courts, and a bowling alley. It's on the site of a recently razed monastery on an island in Lake Pantelimon. Hwy. 3, near the eastern edge of the city (phone: 243000). Expensive.

Capitol – The 80 rooms here are a bit plain and even run down, but the location — just off Piaţa Universitatea — is terrific, and the price is right. Rooms have phones and television sets, and there is a restaurant and coffee shop on the premises. 29 Calea Victoriei (phone: 158030). Expensive to moderate.

Grivita – Thanks to very reasonable prices and a convenient location near the Gară de Nord train station, all 62 rooms here are often full. Amenities are minimal, but there is a passable restaurant. 130 Calea Grivitei (phone: 505380 or 502327). Moderate.

Hanul Manuc – Built as an inn 300 years ago around a courtyard forming part of the city's old Princely Court, this historic 2-story wooden structure was first renovated in the 19th century. Today it has 32 rooms with phones or television sets; there also is a hair salon on the premises. The on-site *Cramma* restaurant serves Romanian and continental fare, as well as a wide variety of Romanian vintages (*manuc* means "wine cellar"). Stradă Sepcari (also listed as 62 Stradă 30 Decembrie; phone: 131415). Moderate.

Opera – An old-style establishment where guests sometimes have small sinks in their rooms, but must share bathrooms; rooms do have phones and television sets. The lack of a restaurant is made up for by its proximity to some of Bucharest's best eating establishments and to the theater district. 37 Stradă Brezoianu (phone: 141075). Moderate.

Palas – A pleasant 173-room hostelry also located within walking distance of Bucharest's theater district, it has a decent restaurant and cafeteria, as well as a *Comturist* hard-currency shop. 24 Stradă Brezoianu (no phone; book through *Carpaţi*). Moderate.

Parc – Located in Herăstrău Park, next door to the *Flora-Cure,* this 257-room property is not quite as exclusive, but comfortable nonetheless, with modern amenities including a pool and a sauna, a restaurant, a cafeteria, a brasserie, and a bar with nightly entertainment. Skin treatments can be had here, too. 3 Calea Poligrafiei (phone: 180950). Moderate.

La President – Away from the downtown area and located in a quiet rose and statue garden surrounded by a wrought-iron fence, this privately run red stone and brick 3-story hostelry was opened in 1990. Originally built in 1938 to house the mistress of King Carol II, its rooms are furnished in 19th-century style; suites boast Oriental carpets and antiques. A favorite among members of the foreign diplomatic corps, particularly for its lovely restaurant (see *Eating Out*). 12 Stradă Kiselev (phone: 184110). Moderate.

EATING OUT: Though Bucharest was once a gastronomic capital rivaling Paris, the city is struggling to regain even a soupçon of its former reputation. Happily, things are slowly improving, and there are a handful of restaurants that are a cut above the rest.

Authentic Romanian food is usually simple but varied, due to multifarious cultural influences — Slavic, Germanic, and French among them. Fish dishes abound. The favorite appetizer is *mititei,* a small skinless lamb or pork sausage spiced with garlic and herbs and grilled. *Ciorbă* is a hearty soup which comes in many varieties, among them *ciorbă de perişoare* (a milky broth with meatballs and vegetables) and *ciorbă de burta* (a creamed soup with veal tripe, rice, and vegetables, highly seasoned with vinegar and garlic). Perhaps the primary national staple is *mămăligă,* a creamy corn porridge which accompanies the entrée at lunch or is eaten by itself as a light supper, served with fresh unsalted cheese and sour cream. (It's a good substitute for the soggy French fries most restaurants serve.) Perhaps the best Romanian dishes are the desserts, like cream-filled chocolate pastries, mocha- or fruit-filled strudel, and rich Austrian-style tortes and honey-nut pies. Wash all this down with a selection of quite good red and white wines from Transylvania, Moldavia, and the Black Sea area. Murfatlar wines (mostly white) have won medals in worldwide competitions, and cotnari, a northern Moldavian white, was a favorite of the 15th-century Moldavian Prince Stefan cel Mare (the Great). Another national drink is țuică, an aromatic (and very potent) plum eau-de-vie.

The major meal of the day in Romania is generally taken at noon, though many restaurants, including those listed here, serve a full menu at both lunch and dinner. Lunch usually is served from noon to 3 PM, and dinner from 7 to 10 PM.

Restaurant meals in Romania are a bargain by European — and even Eastern European — standards. Most restaurants charge only about $12 for even the most lavish, three-course extravaganza for two. At more moderately priced establishments, expect to pay between $6 and $8. Payment is in lei unless otherwise noted. All telephone numbers are in the 0 area code unless otherwise indicated.

Berlin – For a break from Romanian fare, try an authentic German *Biergarten* that serves everything from Wiener schnitzel to salads with real lettuce (a rarity here) — and even American-style cheeseburgers. Romanian food also is served. The East German staff is gone now, but the menu seems to have held up well enough. There's also an outdoor terrace and an elegant downstairs dining room complete with crystal chandeliers, a grand piano, and even live parakeets in the window. The crowd is informal and congenial. Reservations advised. All major credit cards accepted. 4 Stradă Constantin Mille/7 Calea Victoriei (phone: 144652). Expensive.

Bucureşti – In the hotel of the same name, meals here are well prepared, with fresh, if not particularly imaginative, fare such as beef Stroganoff, roast pork, and lamb chops. A wonderful tradition left over from 19th-century Bucharest is the "show table," which allows diners to peruse the specials of the day before ordering (a boon for non-Romanian speakers). Desserts are creamy and irresistible. Entertainment includes a Romanian pop-rock band and folkloric song and dance. Reservations advised. Credit cards and hard currency accepted. 63-11 Calea Victoriei (phone: l42177 or 155850). Expensive.

La President – One of the establishments that is trying hard — and succeeding — to restore some of the luster to the culinary arts in Bucharest. Romanian dishes mix with continental specialties, including superb chateaubriand, pâté, fresh fruit, and cakes and pastries that taste as heavenly as they look. Reservations necessary. Credit cards or hard currency only. At *La President Hotel,* 12 Stradă Kiselev (phone: 184110). Expensive.

Capşa – Founded around the turn of the century by a Parisian restaurateur, this became the city's premier culinary institution, as well as an artistic and literary salon and magnet for Bucharest's aristocratic elite. Red velvet banquettes, gold-framed beveled mirrors, crystal chandeliers, and pink marble columns suggest some of the grandeur of a lost age. The food is continental, with a variety of Romanian specialties, and the kitchen makes as much use as possible of fresh local produce. Reservations necessary (but can only be made in person or in advance through *Carpați*). Credit cards accepted by advance arrangement through *Carpați.* 36 Calea Victoriei (phone: 134482). Expensive to moderate.

Casa Lido – Originally built in 1890 with later neo-classical touches, its decorative focal point is a grand spiral staircase. The Romanian food is adequate rather than inspired, but the service is quite elegant, and there is a good selection of wines and cognacs (but no țuică). Entrance is through a courtyard on a side street. Reservations necessary. Credit cards accepted by advance arrangement through *Carpați*. 13 Stradă C.A. Rosetti (phone: 135680 or 155085). Moderate.

Casa Romana – Romanian specialties, plus pizza and other Italian dishes, as well as steaks. Occasionally a shipment of Italian wine or German beer livens up the menu. Serves continuously from 11 AM to midnight. No reservations. 2 Calea Victoriei (phone: 146808). Moderate.

Nan Ging – Bucharest's only Chinese eatery was once run by Chinese, but the current Romanian staff does a decent job of keeping the Oriental flame alive, serving great dumplings with four sauces and fair to good (if a bit greasy and salty) dishes such as spring rolls and pork with peanuts. Service can be slow, however. Reservations advised. At the *Minerva Hotel,* corner of Calea Anai Ipatescu and Stradă Loc Dimitru Lemnea (phone: 506010). Moderate.

Paduar Baneasa – A popular indoor/outdoor place in a park setting, with a good menu. Recommended Romanian specialties include cold stuffed vegetable appetizers. Entertainment is provided by a five-piece band and there's a folkloric show. A bit touristy, but you might spot a few Romanians here, too. Reservations advised and should be made in person. In Băneasa Forest (no phone). Moderate.

Pescăruș – A large, 2-story dining spot (whose name means "seagull"), situated on a lovely lake in Herăstrău Park. It's well-suited for large groups, and evening folkloric shows can be arranged. The fare is a combination of international and Romanian dishes. Reservations necessary. Calea Aviatorilor (phone: 794640). Moderate.

Podul Magosoare – No music and not much atmosphere, but the Romanian specialties are as close to homemade as you're likely to find anywhere. A favorite dinner spot for locals. Corner of Calea Victoriei and Stradă Lemnea (no phone). Moderate.

Warshowia – A Polish place, it specializes in the fare of the capital, as its name implies. Good bets are stuffed Warsaw duck (with apples, raisins, and bread stuffing), steaks, and pork with mushrooms and sour cream. There's a good wine list, including some Polish vintages. Breakfast also is served. Reservations advised. 98 Calea Dorobanti (phone: 795180). Moderate.

BUDAPEST

The Danube, central Europe's great river — which flows for 1,770 miles from the Black Forest to the Black Sea, through Ulm, Regensburg, Linz, and Vienna — is particularly wide and beautiful when it reaches Budapest. Arriving from Vienna on the hydrofoil — a 4½-hour trip around the Danube Bend — visitors see Budapest at its most splendid. Buda and Pest, two of the city's three parts (along with smaller Obuda), both face that mighty river, forming the physical and spiritual center of the Hungarian capital.

Sprawling over the rolling hills of Buda and the almost endless plain of Pest, the two halves of the city form strophe and antistrophe around the Danube. Buda rises and falls along its hills in a swelling reprise of medieval cobblestone streets and ancient buildings, crowned by the neo-Gothic tower of Matthias Church. The streets of Pest — the governmental and commercial center of the city — run in rings and radials around grand squares of monumental buildings and dramatic statues and memorials. The hilly parts of Buda have much cleaner air than busy Pest, which is quite noisy and polluted. Inhabitants of the city say that the more pollution is produced in Pest, the better the producer can afford to live in Buda. Buda and Pest have been united only since 1873, and one has the feeling that the marriage has not yet settled into comfortable middle age. From the river, an observer clearly sees the two buildings that best characterize Budapest's two halves: Matthias Church in Buda, where generations of Hungarian kings were crowned; and Pest's neo-Gothic Parliament, towering like a huge wedding cake on the banks of the river. It is as if both parts of the city relate to the Danube more comfortably than to each other. Budapest also is a capital of sculptures, and there are more than 500 life-size statues — from political leaders to poets — throughout the city.

So beautiful is this city of 2 million people — one-fifth of the country's population — that visitors might not suspect that Budapest, like other European cities, has a history of recurrent invasion, destruction, and reconstruction that only intensified in this century, including a siege and heavy bombing in World War II in which 33,000 buildings and all the city's bridges were demolished. Before, and since, Hungary has been no stranger to social and political turmoil.

The Hungarian nation was founded by Arpád, a semi-legendary chief of the Magyars, who brought his people from the Urals in the 9th century. Before this time, in the 3rd century BC, the Celts established a town called Ak-In (ample water), and in the 1st century AD it became a Roman town of considerable size called Aquincum. The Magyar cities of Buda and Pest grew as trade and craft centers, thriving especially under Hungary's first king, St. Stephen (who reigned from 997 to 1038). But a bloody invasion by the Mongols in 1241 destroyed both Buda and Pest. The cities were rebuilt and became even more splendid. King Béla IV granted Pest the right to build a fortified castle, and in Buda, by royal charter, he established the municipality.

The Ottoman Turks arrived in the 16th century, bringing 150 years of decay, poverty, and captivity to Buda. The country fell to the Hapsburg Empire in 1686. And although a liberal revolt started in Pest in March a century and a half later in 1848, czarist troops brutally suppressed the revolt the following year, at Vienna's request. In 1867 the Austro-Hungarian Empire was established, granting Budapest greater home rule, but the Hapsburg Empire maintained control over the country until the end of World War I.

During the early days of the Hapsburg rule, Pest was a commercial center inhabited by Germans, while Buda developed as an imperial garrison. From the time of the 1848 uprising to 1918, the population of Budapest increased from 100,000 to 1 million. Industries developed, and by the end of the century the city became almost totally populated by Magyars, after thousands of peasants arrived there to become factory workers. Other groups, lured by Budapest's economic success, also migrated here. The Serbs, who basically ran the Danube's shipping industry, and the Greeks and other Balkan peoples became merchants here. A large number of Jews also came from the eastern provinces, where they had been prohibited from owning land; in Budapest they became merchants and bankers. By 1900 there were almost 200,000 Jews in Budapest, where they prospered until World War II, when the Nazi occupation destroyed their community — and their lives.

Under the bitterly resented Trianon Peace Treaty (1920), Hungary lost a third of its territory to the new states of Czechoslovakia, Romania, and Yugoslavia. A former admiral in the imperial navy, Miklós Horthy, set up an oppressive right-wing regime that later allied itself with Nazi Germany. Then Germany occupied Hungary from 1944 until the country's liberation by the Soviet army in April 1945. Another oppressive regime soon followed, this time Communist.

In May of 1989, Hungary gained the attention of the world when it opened its border with Austria and allowed tens of thousands of East Germans, who had filled refugee camps in Hungary, to leave the country freely. The following October the Communist party changed its structure and its name to the Socialist party, making Hungary the first Eastern European country to formally abandon communism. Hungary's first free elections since 1947 were held in March of 1990. On the 33rd anniversary of its 1956 anti-Communist uprising — quashed almost immediately by Soviet tanks — Hungary once again declared itself an independent republic, but this time without military retribution. In August 1990, the country's first post-Communist Parliament elected Arpád Göncz president for a 5-year term. The full effects of the country's fledgling social democracy remain to be seen. By the end of 1990 the inflation rate had reached 30%, and today, Hungarians are learning to economize on everything from food to footwear. While Hungary has a long way to go in healing its ailing economy, dramatic changes continue to surface, including the privatization of many state-owned enterprises.

In the absence of an aristocratic elite, Hungary venerates its artists, writers, and musicians, and today's Budapest is a place where a tourist is likely to encounter a city that loves good living. Rock 'n' roll, jeans, provocative

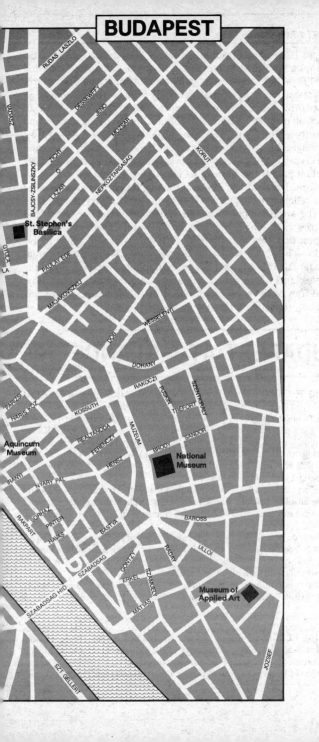

BUDAPEST

RUDAS LASZLO

VADASZ

DESSEWFFY

JENO

MOZSAR

ZICHY

O

KORUT

LAZAR

BAJCSY-ZSILINSZKY

NEPKOZTARSASAG

GYULA
LA

**St. Stephen's
Basilica**

PAULAY EDE

MAJAKOVSZKIJ

WESSELENYI

DOB

DOHANY

RAKOCZI

PUSKIN

SZENTKIRALY

PARISI

TREFORT

HARIS KOZ

KOSSUTH

REALTANODA

MUZEUM

SANDOR

**Aquincum
Museum**

FERENCZI

BRODY

**National
Museum**

IRANYI

HENSZ

NYARY PAL

SORHAZ

BASTYA

BAROSS

PINTER

RAKPART

HAVAS

ULLOI

SZABADSAG

GONTA

RADAY

SZABADSAG HID

ERKEL

SZAMUELY

**Museum of
Applied Art**

MATYAS

JOZSEF

SZT GELLERT

T-shirts in various languages, a tradition of satire, Western magazines, fads, and foods have long been evident on the city's streets. Budapest's rich and diverse cultural life includes 28 theaters (where admission, thanks to government subsidies, is sometimes the equivalent of only 50¢), two opera houses, an operetta theater, three concert halls, a puppet theater, and more than 20 museums. In fact, all manner of Hungarian cultural life can be found here, and most of the country's inhabitants who come to Budapest discover they must compete with foreigners for places in theaters and a quiet corner in a museum. Bookstores and Gypsy violinists seem to be everywhere. And meeting at a café is still an important part of the fabric of social and intellectual life.

Hungarian cuisine has absorbed Turkish, French, Italian, Slavic, and other influences into a deliciously unique blend. The wines of Hungary, particularly the whites, like the world-famous tokay, are very popular and very good, and Hungarian pastries rank among the best in the world. There is a popular saying in Budapest that goes something like, "If only we could afford to live as well as we do — how well we would live."Budapest's slightly irreverent humor is characteristic of a city that has listened to tales sweeping down the river for centuries, and where living well is in part pleasure and part duty, a tribute to centuries of the good life provided by Budapest and its psychic source, the ancient, untroubled Danube.

BUDAPEST AT-A-GLANCE

SEEING THE CITY: The best view of Budapest is from the top of Gellért Hill (Gellért hegy) on the Buda side, which can be climbed from Gellért Square (Gellért tér). From the balustrades of a stone fort built in 1850 you will enjoy a panorama of the Danube with its bridges — Margaret Bridge to Margaret Island in the middle of the Danube, the recreational center of the city; the historic Chain Bridge to Castle Hill on the Buda side, the oldest part of town; and the Elizabeth Bridge that connects Buda with the Inner City on the Pest side, the busy downtown commercial and shopping center.

In front of the fort, or Citadella, is the gigantic Liberation Monument, a statue of a woman holding an olive branch, which is sometimes called Budapest's Statue of Liberty; it commemorates the Soviet liberation of Budapest from Nazi occupation in 1945.

Since Buda is built on seven hills, there are several views of the city. One of the best is from the *Hilton International,* in the Castle District, from where the Danube, Margaret Island, and the flat Pest side of the river, including the spectacular façade of the Hungarian Parliament, are all clearly visible.

Budapest is divided into numerous districts designated by a Roman numeral before the street address. "Utca," "ut," and "utja" mean "street" in Hungarian; "tér" means "square."

SPECIAL PLACES: Budapest, once actually three cities — Buda, Obuda, and Pest — sprawls along both banks of the Danube River and is difficult to explore on foot because of the distances involved. To make matters worse, the streets of Pest run in circles; Buda's streets are hilly and cobbled. A map is strongly advised (see *Sources and Resources*). Public transportation, though crowded, is good, and fares are low.

Castle District – Topped by monuments, this hill is the heart of medieval Budapest, with cobbled streets, narrow alleys, and lovely squares. Homes are painted in pastel colors, each marking the trade of its owner. Its baroque and classical public buildings, also painted in lovely pastel shades, now house famous restaurants, writers' studios, a student quarter, and many landmarks of old Budapest. Unfortunately, few Hungarians live in this area anymore, since the charming medieval district has become a visitor's paradise in which almost everyone speaks a foreign language. Much of the area was badly damaged during World War II, and restorations include a 19th-century funicular railway (Budavári Sikló) that climbs up the hill from the Danube. The railway leaves from Clark Adám tér, from 7:30 AM to 10 PM daily; round-trip tickets cost about $1.50; the trip takes 50 seconds each way.

Budapest Hilton – It is not even faintly ironic that the first sight to see in medieval Budapest is the *Hilton* (phone: 175-1000). It took 10 years to build, primarily because it occupies one of the most historic sites in Buda, high on Castle Hill, looking down on the Danube. As excavation for the hotel proceeded, archaeologists kept uncovering ruins and artifacts dating from the 13th century, and in the end the hotel elected — in response to strong local pressure — to include many of these ruins in its own design.

As a result, its modern stone and glass façade includes the walls and tower of a 13th-century Dominican church and a Jesuit monastery. Part of the front of the hotel is a 17th-century baroque building, once a Jesuit college. Inside, the thoroughly modern decor has been adapted to incorporate Gothic columns, Roman milestones, bas-reliefs, and shards found during excavation. Reflected in a rosy glass wall of the hotel is the famous Fishermen's Bastion, a neo-Romanesque series of arches and towers overlooking the Danube (see below). Its Miklós Tower (on the street side), once a church tower, has been converted into a casino. The Matthias Church is next door.

Fishermen's Bastion – So named because the fishermen of the city had to protect this northern side of the Royal Castle from siege in medieval times, the bastion is a turn-of-the-century *Disneyland*-type version of Romanesque ramparts and turrets, affording another vantage point of the Danube and the city.

Matthias Church – This neo-Gothic edifice atop Castle Hill, where King Matthias was married twice, dates from the 13th century, although it has been rebuilt many times, most recently after severe damage during World War II. Its correct name is Church of Our Lady. With its Gothic spires and colored tile roof, this coronation church of Hungarian kings has one of Europe's most memorable silhouettes. During the Turkish occupation of Hungary in the 16th and 17th centuries, the church served as a mosque.

Especially noteworthy are the baroque gilt and splendor of the nave and the baroque and Renaissance chalices and vestments in the treasury. Sunday morning mass is celebrated with music, and there are frequent organ recitals. I, 2 Szentháromság tér.

Café Ruszwurm – Just down the block from Matthias Church is this fabulous 1827 pastry shop, still serving the best baked goods in central Europe. With displays of old utensils once used by pastry chefs, 19th-century signs, and Biedermeier cherrywood furniture with striped silk upholstery, *Ruszwurm* has been designated a historic monument. Its pastries, known all over Europe, are miraculously light and rich. You can hardly go wrong: Try *rétes,* or strudel; vanilla slices; or *Ruszwurm* cake, a chocolate cake filled with chocolate cream and seasoned with orange peel and rum. I, 7 Szentháromság tér (phone: 175-5284).

Royal Palace – Reduced to rubble by bombs in 1944–45, the palace has carefully been rebuilt to incorporate all the styles of its historic past. That was not its first reconstruction, however. Prior to the bombing, it existed primarily as an 18th-century building with some baroque touches; before that it had been destroyed and rebuilt several times since it was first constructed as a castle. It now houses the *Historical Museum of Budapest* and the *National Gallery*. I, 2 Szent György tér.

Historical Museum of Budapest – In Wing E (the southern wing) of the Royal Palace, the museum contains archaeological remains of the ancient town and the history of the construction of the palace. It displays splendid furniture, sculpture, ceramics, glass, and china; the halls, dating from the 15th century, have Renaissance doorcases carved in red marble. To appreciate the richness of this collection, one must remember that Hungary's King Matthias had a greater income at the end of the 15th century than either the English or the French king. I, 2 Szent György tér (phone: 156-0727).

Hungarian National Gallery – Housed in the Royal Palace, this museum displays the works of the greatest Hungarian artists of the 19th and 20th centuries. English-language guides are available. I, 17 Dísz tér, Wings B, C, and D.

Aquincum Museum – One of the most significant excavations of a Roman urban area outside Italy, Aquincum (meaning "ample water") in its heyday had almost 100,000 inhabitants. Its streets, homes, temple, and amphitheater have been unearthed 4 miles upstream of the city center on the western bank of the Danube. The museum on the site has mosaics depicting public baths, jewelry, glass, and inscribed stones. Open from May to October. III, 139 Szentendrei utca (phone: 168-7650).

Margaret Island (Margitsziget) – This resort and recreation island lies right in the middle of the river, accessible from both banks by the Margaret Bridge (Margit híd). Cars and trains enter from Árpád Bridge to the north; on summer weekends, a bus runs between the southern end of the island and the hotels near Árpád Bridge. The whole island is a park, with a sports stadium, a large municipal swimming pool, a rose garden, a fountain, several hotels, restaurants, and spas. During the summer months, when theaters close, the performances move to outdoor quarters here; you can see plays, concerts, films, and sports events. For specific programs, inquire at the tourist office, *IBUSZ* (see *Sources and Resources*).

Inner City Parish Church (Belvárosi Templom) – This is the oldest building in Pest, begun in the 12th century. It shows evidence of many styles of construction, including a Romanesque arch, a Gothic chancel, a Muslim prayer niche, and a Roman wall. V, 15 Március (March 15) tér.

St. Stephen's Basilica – The largest church in the city, with its large dome and two tall spires, the basilica (officially known as St. Stephen's Parish Church) dominates the flat landscape of Pest. Built in the 19th century, its murals and altarpieces are by leading Hungarian painters and sculptors. V, Bajcsy-Zsilinszky utca.

Hungarian National Museum – This oldest and most important museum in Budapest houses the greatest historical and archaeological collections of the country. The first collections were bequeathed to the museum in 1802, and the buildings were erected between 1837 and 1847. One of the prehistoric exhibitions displays the most ancient remnant of European man, the skull from Vértesszölös. There are also Roman ceramics, Avar gold and silver work, and the famous Hungarian Crown of St. Stephen and other historic crown jewels. Among the gold objects are a chiseled Byzantine crown (called the Crown of Monomachos) and the gold baton of Franz Liszt. There also is an exhibition of minerals. VIII, 14-16 Múzeum körút (phone: 113-4400).

Museum of Applied Arts – Another one of the great museums of Budapest; its most important collections are European and Hungarian ceramics, the work of goldsmiths and silversmiths from the 15th to 17th century, Italian Renaissance textiles, Turkish carpets, and Flemish tapestries from the 17th century. The museum's artifacts were a gift of Odön Lechner and Gyula Pártos in 1896. IX, 33-37 Üllői utca (phone: 117-5222).

Parliament – Mirrored in the Danube, these impressive buildings on the Pest side are reminiscent of London's Houses of Parliament. Finished in 1902, they were built over a period of 17 years. A maze of 10 courtyards, 29 staircases, and 88 statues,

Parliament is a favorite haunt for lovers after dark. In 1950, the Communist party placed a giant red star atop the Parliament building. During the 1989 revolt, it took workers 2 months to remove it. Along Széchenyi rakpart and backed by Kossuth Lajos tér.

Andrássy ut – Named after a 19th-century statesman and also known as Embassy Row, this noble avenue, which extends from near the Basilica to Heroes' Square, has known many names that reflect Budapest's stormy past — among them Sugár (Radial) in the 19th century, Andrássy in the early 20th century, Stalin Avenue and Avenue of Hungarian Youth in 1956, Népköztársaság (People's Republic) in 1957, and Andrássy again in 1990. The avenue is lined with palaces on both sides, many of which were designed by the architect Miklós Ybl in the 1870s and 1880s; among these buildings are the *State Opera House* and several theaters. No. 60 once housed the Gestapo and the Communist secret police.

Heroes' Square (Hősök tér) – At the end of Népköztársaság is a large square marked with the Millennial Monument, which was begun in 1896 to celebrate Hungary's thousand years. A semicircular colonnade displays a pantheon of Hungarian historical figures; on top of the 119-foot pillar in the middle of the square is a statue of the Angel Gabriel who, according to legend, offered a royal crown to King Stephen I, founder of the kingdom. On this square are the *Museum of Fine Arts* and the *Art Gallery*.

Museum of Fine Arts – Here is the greatest collection of its kind in the country. The building is at the entrance of Városliget (City Park), on the left as you face the Millennial Monument. More than 100,000 works of art are housed in this neo-classical structure. Among the masterpieces are seven paintings by El Greco and five by Goya. The Italian and Dutch sections have many world-famous paintings, including the *Madonna Esterházy* by Raphael and the *Sermon of St. John the Baptist* by Pieter Breughel, the Elder. The museum also has permanent exhibitions of Egyptian antiquities, Greco-Roman antiquities, and modern European painting and sculpture. XIV, Hősök tér (phone: 142-9759).

City Park (Városliget) – This large park just behind Heroes' Square contains an artificial lake; the Széchenyi Baths (a public spa); a zoo; a botanical garden; an amusement park; and Vajdahunyad Castle, built in the early 1900s in a conglomeration of Hungarian architectural styles.

Café Gerbeaud (Cukrászda) – In the heart of Pest, facing a beautifully restored square bustling with tourists and street entertainers, this is no mere pastry shop; it is an institution. As in Vienna, the coffeehouses of Budapest have traditionally served as social and literary centers, and this one, with its decadent pastries and leisured atmosphere reminiscent of days gone by, is the best in town. V, 7 Vörösmarty tér (phone: 118-6823).

Korona – Another pastry shop, convenient for strollers in the Castle District, this is also a gathering place for literary types and tourists, featuring poetry readings and other literary events, often in foreign languages. I, 16 Dísz tér (phone: 175-6139).

Obuda – The Fő tér, or Main Square, of this district is an island of charming old houses and taverns in a sea of large estates. Concerts and exhibitions are held in the Zichy Palace at No. 3, but the numerous surrounding restaurants — many with outdoor seating — are an even bigger attraction.

Imre Varga Collection – Portrait monuments by the internationally famous sculptor are scattered throughout his native Hungary. Samples of his work are on permanent exhibition here, and sometimes the artist himself is on hand. III, 7 Laktanya utca (phone: 180-3274).

Spas – Hungary is famous for its thermal spas. Budapest spas — there are some 20 in the city today — date from the Roman era and from the Turks, who built several baths in the city in the 16th century, among them the Rudas (I, 9 Döbrenti tér; dating from 1566 and completely renovated in 1987) and Király (I, 84 Főo) spas in Buda, both still functioning. Although these spas treat people who are suffering from respiratory, rheumatic, and circulatory ailments, they are purportedly restorative for almost anyone, especially anyone suffering from obesity or simple fatigue. Treatments include drinking cures (mineral waters), baths in lukewarm or very hot mineral pools, mud packs, and massages, all directed by specialists under the direction of doctors. However, there is a large caveat about Budapest spas: They are not all hygienic. For this reason the spas around Hungary's Lake Balaton are more famous and more widely patronized by Westerners. If you are interested in Budapest spas, try the *Thermál Hotel Margitsziget* (phone: 131-1100) or its recently built neighbor, the *Ramada Grand* hotel (phone: 111-1000), on Margaret Island, or contact the tourist office, *IBUSZ,* for help in making a judicious selection (see *Sources and Resources*).

Kerepesi Cemetery – Once you've tired of walking from monument to church to museum, visit the Kerepesi Cemetery, an oasis in the heart of the city. Wealthy Hungarians spent fortunes building mausoleums adorned with sculptures and decorations, and the century-old trees here offer pleasant shade. At one side of the cemetery are monuments to people who died during the 1919 revolution and the 1956 uprising.

■**EXTRA SPECIAL:** A boat trip on the beautiful Danube is an experience you will not soon forget. From May to September, *IBUSZ* offers several day tours to the Danube Bend area, about 31 miles north of Budapest, where the Danube makes a hairpin turn that changes from a west-east to a north-south course into an area rich in scenery, with limestone hills and volcanic mountains, and in history, with river communities that date from Roman times. Tours depart Wednesdays and Saturdays at 8:30 AM from the Vigadó tér landing dock; cost is $35 (phone: 118-1223; 129-5844; or call *IBUSZ;* phone: 118-1223). From the beginning of April through October, there are daily hydrofoil trips between Budapest and Vienna; for information, contact *MAHART* (V, Belgrád rakpart; phone: 118-1953 or 118-1706).

SOURCES AND RESOURCES

TOURIST INFORMATION: For general information, brochures, and maps, contact *IBUSZ* — Hungary's largest travel agency, formally run by the state but now privately owned (V, 5 Felszabadulás tér; phone: 118-6866 or 3 Petőofi tér; phone: 118-5707), open 24 hours; or the Budapest Tourist Office (V, 5 Roosevelt tér; phone: 117-3555). Or contact *Tourinform* (V, 2 Sütőo utca; phone: 117-9800), open from 8 AM to 8 PM. Of the many travel agencies offering sightseeing tours of the country, *IPV Tourisme* offers particularly imaginative packages with an accent on Hungarian culture and history (22 Angol utca, Budapest H-1149; phone: 163-3406). English-language guidebooks to Budapest and elsewhere in Hungary are sold in the city's hotel shops and in bookstores. City maps, booklets on Budapest attractions, and other information are available from the US office of *IBUSZ* (1 Parker Plaza, Suite 1104, Ft. Lee, NJ 07024; phone: 201-592-8585 or 800-367-7878).

The US Embassy is at V, 12 Szabadság tér (phone: 112-6450).

Local Coverage – A comprehensive free monthly bulletin in German and English, *Programme in Hungary,* is available at hotel desks. An illustrated daily paper in English and German, the *Daily News,* is available at newsstands and hotels. Major international papers, such as the London *Times* and the *International Herald Tribune,* are available at some newspaper stores in the center.

Food – *Budapest: A Critical Guide* by András Török, published in Budapest by Park/Officina Nova and available only in Hungary, is the best source of restaurant information, along with an excellent discussion of the city's architecture. *Programme in Hungary* lists a few restaurants, but not in detail.

TELEPHONE: The country code for Hungary is 36; the city code for Budapest is 1.

GETTING AROUND: Airport – Ferihegy Airport handles all international flights (there is no domestic service in Hungary). A second terminal handles *MALEV* (the Hungarian national carrier) flights (phone: 118-4333). The drive from the airport to downtown Budapest takes about a half hour, and a taxi ride should cost approximately 500 forints (Fts.; about $8). The airport bus service to the International Bus Station on Engels Square is much less. It runs every half hour and takes 30 minutes to reach Bus Terminal 1 (about $3) and 40 minutes to Terminal 2 (about $4). For information on air travel, contact *MALEV* (V, 2 Roosevelt tér; phone: 118-9033 or V, 2 Dorottya utca; phone: 118-4333 or 118-5913). For airport information, call 157-9123.

Bus, Tram, and Subway – Public transportation is efficient and very cheap. Tickets are sold at tobacco shops, kiosks, and ticket offices, but not on the vehicles. Each ticket, valid for one trip, must be punched in the machines inside the vehicles. Yellow tickets are good on the metro (subway), trams, and trolleybuses; blue tickets are good for bus transportation only.

Bus Tours – You might wish to get acquainted with Budapest by taking the 3-hour tour (about $13) of the city offered daily by *IBUSZ* (VII, 3/C Tanács krt.; phone: 114-23140 for tour information); or contact the branch offices listed above or the Budapest Tourist Office. A 4-hour *IBUSZ* tour, conducted Wednesdays at 2 PM from Engels Square, offers a look at the city's cultural life, with art studio and museum visits and concerts ($15).

Car Rental – *IBUSZ-Avis* (V, 8 Martinelli tér; phone: 111-84685, and V, 5 Türr István utca; phone: 117-9299); *Fötaxi-Hertz* (VII, 24 Kertész utca; phone: 111-6116); *Budget* (43 Ferenc krt.; phone: 113-1466). There are branches of *Budget, Avis,* and *Hertz* at the airport.

Motorboat – The *Dunatúra* water taxi service offers individualized Danube tours from May through September. They can be booked through hotels or at the boat dock at Petőofi Square.

Taxi – There are taxi stands throughout the city; rates are low and a 10-15% tip is customary. Budapest's taxi companies include *Fötaxi* (phone: 122-2222) and *Volántaxi* (phone: 166-6666); both companies offer drivers for guided tours of the city. *Budataxi* (phone: 120-0200) runs a fleet of more comfortable cars which are not made in Eastern Europe.

Train – The main office of the *Hungarian State Railways* (*MAV;* VI, 35 Andrássy ut; phone: 122-8049) handles tickets, reservations, and general train information. Major stations are the Eastern (Keleti; Baross tér; phone: 113-6835), for eastbound and most international trains; and the Western (Nyugati; Marx tér; phone: 149-0115), for trains headed west. A fast, dependable *EuroCity* train — the *Lehár* — runs between Budapest and Vienna in under 3 hours. For international information service, call 122-4052.

LOCAL SERVICES: In Budapest, the larger hotels are the best bet for businesspeople who would like lots of services under one roof. Most of these hotels provide dry cleaning and tailoring, telex, photocopying, and more, along with a concierge who will help find anything the hotel can't supply.

Dentist (English-Speaking) – *Fogpótlástani Klinika* (Dental Clinic; 5 Mikszájh Kálmán tér; phone: 113-1639). The dental clinic in the *Volga* hotel (65 Dózsa György utca; phone: 290200) is open daily from 8 AM to 6 PM.

Dry Cleaner/Tailor – *Cooperative Dry Cleaning* (6-9 Flórián tér, *Flórián Shopping Center*); the *Patyolat* dry-cleaning chain (look for the swan logo) can be found all over the city; major hotels also offer dry-cleaning service.

Limousine Service – Budapest has no "limousine" rental companies, but you can rent a car with a driver from *IBUSZ-Avis* (8 Martinelli tér, Budapest 1052; phone: 118-4240 or 118-4158) or *Főtaxi* (24 Kertész utca; phone: 122-1471).

Medical Emergency – Emergency cases are handled by hospitals on a rotating basis. Dial 04 for the ambulance, and it will take you to the facility on duty.

Messenger Service – Ask your hotel concierge.

National/International Courier – *DHL International,* 4 Peter Bod Lejto (phone: 186-1776).

Office Equipment Rental – Check with the main hotels that offer conference rooms and other business services.

Pharmacy – There is 24-hour service at five pharmacies (VI, 91 Lenin körút; VIII, 86 Rákóczi utca; II, 22 Frankel Leó utca; IX, 3 Borános tér; and XII, 1-6 Alkotás).

Photocopies – At all major hotels.

Post Office – Post office No. 62 (VI, 105-107 Lenin körút, near the Western Railway Station) and post office No. 70 (VII, 1 Verseny utca, at the Eastern Railway Station) both have 24-hour service.

Secretary/Stenographer (English-Speaking) – Ask your hotel concierge.

Telex – The post office at V, 17-19 Petőfi Sándor utca.

Translator – *IBUSZ* (5 Felszabadulás tér; phone: 186866) or inquire at your hotel.

 SPECIAL EVENTS: The *Budapest Spring Festival,* 10 days in March, is the highlight of the cultural season and features concerts, folk dance, and other performances. In 1986, Hungary became the host country for the annual *Formula 1 Grand Prix* on the *Hungaroring* at Mogyoród, about a half-hour's drive from Budapest. This international auto race takes place every year in August. Tickets are available at the *Forma-1 GT-1PV* box office (V, 2 Vigadó tér; phone: 117-5067). *Budapest Music Weeks,* in early fall, include international competitions for various types of musicians and many concerts. For information about this and other special events, contact *IBUSZ* (see above).

Besides *Christmas, Boxing Day* (December 26), *New Year's Day,* and *Easter Monday,* Hungarians celebrate political anniversaries on April 4 (*Liberation from the Nazis*), May 1 (*Labor Day*), and August 20 (*St. Stephen's Day,* for the first King of Hungary; now *Constitution Day*), when the hills of Buda, particularly the citadel there, are the stage for a gigantic fireworks show. In 1989 a new national holiday was declared: *March 15,* marking the beginning of the Hungarian Revolution of 1848, a date sacred to Hungarian patriots. In addition to official celebrations, peaceful marches and demonstrations organized by opposition groups are the order of the day; motorists take note. Budapest has announced plans to host a *World's Fair* in 1996.

 MUSEUMS: Several museums provide an introduction to Hungary's rich religious heritage: *Collections of Ecclesiastical Treasures* at the Matthias Church (I, Szentháromság tér) and at St. Stephen's Basilica (V, Szent István tér); the *National Evangelical Museum* (V, 4 Deak tér); and the *Bible Museum* (IX, 28 Ráday utca). In addition to these museums and the museums listed in *Special Places,* the following are worth a visit:

Béla Bartók Memorial House – Concerts are presented here on occasion. II, 29 Csalán utca (phone: 116-4123).

Ethnographic Museum – A glimpse into the country's past. V, 12 Kossuth tér (phone: 132-6349).

Ferenc (Franz) Liszt Museum – Set up in Liszt's apartment in the old Academy of Music; a site for piano recitals. VI, 35 Vörösmarty utca (phone: 122-9804).

Jewish Museum – The history of Hungarian Jewry through liturgical objects and other documents. VII, 8 Dohány utca (phone: 142-8949).

Museum of Hungarian Commerce and Catering – I, 4 Fortuna utca (phone: 175-6242).

Museum of Postage Stamps – An extensive collection that includes some very rare stamps. VII, 47 Hársfa utca (phone: 142-0960).

Musical History Museum – Historical instruments. An exhibition called Béla Bartók's Workshop traces the composer's creative process. A concert series is presented here. I, 7 Táncsics Mihály utca (phone: 175-9282).

Semmelweis Museum of the History of Medicine – A fascinating look at the development of European and Hungarian medicine from Roman times to the present. Dr. Ignác Semmelweis, the man responsible for the cure for childbed fever, was born in the building that now houses the museum. I, 1-3 Apród utca (phone: 175-3533).

 SHOPPING: At press time most shops were still state-owned, although stores slowly are being privatized, and changes in retail businesses already are being felt. Most items in Budapest department stores still appear shabby by Western standards. However, the *Intertourist, Utastourist,* and *Konsumtourist* shops sell a considerably better array of gifts for hard currency only. Here you can find colorful pottery, Herend and Alföldi porcelain, Matyó and Kalocsa embroideries, which can be used for wall hangings or even framed as folk art. The country is famous for its peasant blouses, dolls in regional costumes, and embroidered sheepskin jackets. There also are herdsmen's carvings on wood and horn. There are *Intertourist Shops* in all the major hotels and on Kigyó utca in Pest. Budapest also has shops and cooperatives devoted exclusively to folk art: these include the beautifully remodeled *Folk Art Center* at several locations (V, 14 Váci utca; V, 12 Régiposta utca; V, 2 Kossuth Lajos utca; and XIII, 26 Szent István krt.).

A big bargain in Budapest is custom-made clothing, both suits for men and dresses for women. The workmanship and style are excellent, but it is best to bring your own material, as there is little good fabric around. Ask your hotel porter for the nearest tailor or dressmaker or try the *Klára Rotschild Salon,* V, 12 Váci utca (phone: 118-4090).

At any grocery store you can buy an authentic, inexpensive, and very portable souvenir — a packet of Hungarian paprika, the real stuff, not the red dust generally sprinkled on as a decorative touch in the US. Or buy a bottle of Hungarian wine at one of the many delicatessens. One of the ethnographic prints sold at *Photography Gallery* (7 Váci utca) also makes a good souvenir.

Near the Astoria metro stop there is a small flea market where Eastern European migrants offer their national goods; other items, such as Western cigarettes, also are sold.

Antikvárium – In the middle of the pedestrian district, this secondhand book store offers 16th- and 17th-century books in Latin, and old maps, prints, and photos. 281 Váci utca (phone: 118-5673).

Bianca – A variety of fashionable Hungarian- and Italian-made clothing for men and women. 2 Sütö utca.

Helia D Studio – An array of cosmetics that make great gifts. English-speaking staff. V, 19-21 Váci utca.

Herbária – For a wonderful selection of herbal teas, spices, and natural cosmetics. V, 4 Tolbuhin krt.

Luca Folklor Shop – A tiny treasure trove of gift items. Open daily. V, 7-9 Régiposta utca.

National Center of Museums Shop – Reproductions of museum objects. V, 7 József Nádor tér.

Rózsavölgyi – Hungarian classical and folk music. V, 5 Martinelli tér.

Zsuzsa Lörincz – Genuine folk costumes and pottery, mostly from Transylvania. V, 14 Régiposta utca.

SPORTS AND FITNESS: Boating – By arrangement with *IBUSZ* (see above), you can rent a sailboat, sailing dinghy, motorboat, small hydrofoil, and even water skis by the hour or by the day. It is the very best way to enjoy the Danube.

Fishing – Licenses are issued by the *National Federation of Hungarian Anglers* (*MOHOSZ;* V, 6 Október utca; phone: 132-5315); and at the fishing information bureau (II, 1 Bem József utca).

Fitness Centers – The facilities at both the *Forum* (12-14 Apáczai Csere János utca; phone: 117-8088) and the *Atrium Hyatt* (2 Roosevelt tér; phone: 138-3000) are open to non-guests for a charge. Budapest is renowned for its medicinal baths; among the best are the *Gellért* (XI, 4 Kelenhegyi utca), and the *Lukács* (II, 25-29 Frankel Leó utca).

Golf – Minibuses transport guests to a 9-hole course set amid oak and acacia trees on an island in the Danube, just north of the city limits (Kisoroszi, Szentendrei-sziget; for information call the *Hilton* at 175-1000 or 175-1230). The *Vörös Csillag* (Red Star Hotel; XII, 21 Rege utca; phone: 175-0416) has a mini-golf course.

Greyhound Racing – On the Danube embankment, just outside Budapest, there are races from May to September. Inquire at *IBUSZ* for details (see above).

Horse Racing – There are trotting races at the track at Ugetópálya (VIII, 9 Kerepesi utca), and flat racing at the track at X, 9 Albertirsai utca.

Horseback Riding – A very popular pastime in this land of horsemen. There are schools and stables in and around Budapest, including the *Petneházy Riding School* (II, 5 Feketefej utca; phone: 164267). Information on riding tours is provided by *IBUSZ* (see above), or *Pegazus Tours* (V, 5 Károlyi Mihály utca; phone: 117-1552).

Jogging – Margitsziget (Margaret Island), in the center of the city in the Danube River, is the best place to run. The island is roughly 2 miles long and half a mile wide, and most of it is given over to sports facilities. Either take a cab to the island's *Thermál* hotel and choose a path from there, or jog over on the pedestrian-only Margaret Bridge. Running is also pleasant along the foothills near the *Budapest* hotel (II, 47-49 Szilágy Erzsébet fasor). For information on jogging, call the *Futapest Club* (XIII, 14/6 Fürst Sándor utca; phone: 132-8739).

Skating – There is a large outdoor ice skating rink in City Park, near Vajdahunyad Castle (XIV, Népstadion utca). Skating competitions and other athletic events take place at the *Budapest Sports Hall* (XIV, 1-3 Istvánmezei utca; phone: 163-6430).

Skiing – The Buda hills right in and around Budapest, accessible by bus and funicular, have several slopes, the most popular of which is the Szabadsághegy.

Soccer – As in many European countries, soccer (called football) is the most popular spectator sport. The largest city stadium is the *People's Stadium* (Népstadion) near City Park in Pest, seating 96,000 spectators (XIV, 3-5 Istvánmezei utca; phone: 169-9122). Information on games and other sports events is available from the ticket bureau (at VI, 6 Andrássy ut; phone: 112-4234).

Swimming – Budapest has many indoor and outdoor pools. People swim in the Danube, but it is not too clean (though not nearly as dirty as, say, the Hudson River in New York) and sometimes has strong currents. The largest public facility — both indoor and outdoor — is the *National Swimming Pool* on Margaret Island. In addition, many hotels have pools, both ordinary and thermal. The stately *Gellért,* for example, has an outdoor pool with artificial waves, in a park setting (XI, 1 Szt. Gellért tér). In the Városliget (City Park), the turn-of-the-century *Széchenyi Baths* include three large outdoor pools, also open in winter (XIV, 11 Allatkerti krt.).

Tennis – There are tennis courts near *Dózsa Stadium* on Margaret Island; at *FTC Sporttelep* (Sports Grounds; 129 Ullői utca); and on Szabadság Hill, near the *Olympia Hotel;* 40 Eötvös utca). The *Flamenco* hotel has an indoor court (XI, 7 Tas vezér utca; phone: 252250), and the *Novotel Budapest* (XII, 63-67 Alkotás utca) also has courts.

THEATER: In Budapest everyone goes to the numerous theaters that are subsidized by the state and are very inexpensive. Most performances are in Hungarian, but you might enjoy seeing a Shakespearean or some other familiar play in Hungarian. If not, the *Municipal Operetta Theater* (VI, 19 Nagymezőo utca in Pest) has performances of Kálmán, Lehár, Romberg, and other great operetta composers whose works need no translation. The *Main Puppet Theater* (VI, 69Népköztársaság útja) presents everything from the *Three Little Pigs* to *The Miraculous Mandarin* for children and revues and satires for adults. The *Municipal Grand Circus,* open weekdays, is in the City Park (XIV, 7 Allatkerti körút; phone: 142-8300).

For tickets and more details see the current *Programme in Hungary,* contact *IBUSZ* (see above), or call the *Central Booking Agency for Theaters,* VI, 18 Andrássy ut (phone: 112-0000).

MUSIC: Budapest has a rich musical life; this city of Bartók and Kodály has two opera houses, several symphony orchestras, and a great many chamber groups. The renovated *Hungarian State Opera House* (VI, 22 Andrássy ut; phone: 153-0170), and the *Erkel Theater* (VIII, 30 Köztársaság tér; phone: 133-0540) offer operas and ballets. Concerts are given at the *Academy of Music* (VI, 8 Liszt Ferenc tér; phone: 142-0179) and at the *Pest Concert Hall* (V, 1 Vigadó tér; phone: 118-9167 or 118-9909), facing the Danube. The Matthias Church also has concerts. There is a *Concert Ticket Office* (V, 1 Vörösmarty tér; phone: 117-6222). On Sundays at 11 AM concerts are held at the *Ethnographic Museum* (V, 12 Kossuth tér) sometimes featuring children's folk dancing.

In the summer, the music moves outdoors to Margaret Island. For tickets and information, contact *IBUSZ* or the *Central Booking Agency* (see *Theater*).

NIGHTCLUBS AND NIGHTLIFE: Though much more lively than that of other Eastern European cities, Budapest's nightlife is somewhat limited. There are great cabarets in such hotels as the *Bellevue* in the *Duna Inter-Continental* and the *Troubadour* in the *Budapest Hilton* (see *Checking In*). Others worth a visit are the *Maxim Varieté* (VII, 3 Akácfa utca), *Moulin Rouge* (VI, 17 Nagymezőo utca) *Casanova* (I, 4 Batthyány tér), and the nightclub program of the *Lidó* (V, 5 Szabadsajtó utca), a famous café at the turn of the century and now a restaurant with entertainment. All stay open until at least 4 AM, most until 5 AM. After that, there is always a Turkish bath or a sauna.

In the hotels, try the *Béke Orfeum,* at the *Béke* (VI, 97 Lenin krt.) and *Horoszkóp,* at the *Buda-Penta* (I, 41-43 Krisztina krt.), which appeals to a younger crowd. Gamblers can try their luck at the *Hilton*'s elegant *Casino,* using hard currency; open daily from 5 PM (phone: 175-1000). The two other casinos in Hungary are at the *Thermál* hotel in Hévíz and in the western town of Sopron, on the Austrian border. For jazz, stop in at *Fregatt Söröző* (V, 26 Molnar utca).

BEST IN TOWN

 CHECKING IN: Although new hotels constantly are being built, there often is a shortage of hotel rooms in Budapest, especially during the summer. It is advisable to make reservations well in advance, either through your own travel agent or through *IBUSZ* (see *Sources and Resources*).

Hotel prices in Budapest, however, are quite reasonable compared with those of other European capitals. We have listed as expensive hotels that charge from $100 to $200 and up for a double; $45 to $100 as moderate; and $20 to $40 as inexpensive. Note that *IBUSZ* rents rooms in private homes (usually with shared bath) from $12 per day. All telephone numbers are in the 1 city code unless otherwise indicated.

Aquincum – Located on the Buda side of the Danube near the Arpád Bridge, this hotel features 312 rooms with balconies. It operates a nightclub, and a restaurant called the *Ambrosia,* which serves Hungarian fare. Business facilities include a business center equipped with a fax machine and computers, secretarial services, foreign currency exchange, and express checkout. Meeting rooms are available for up to 200. Arpád Fejedelem útja 94 (phone: 188-6360; fax: 168-8872; telex: 222160). Expensive.

Atrium Hyatt – A central courtyard densely lined with hanging greenery is the focus of this 357-room luxury establishment. It has a top-floor **VIP Regency Club,** a swimming pool, and a health club. Its *Old Timer* restaurant has international cuisine, the *Tokaj* has Hungarian fare and Gypsy music; the *Atrium Terrace* is its coffee shop, and the rustic *Clark Brasserie* is very popular for snacks accompanied by draft beer (see *Eating Out*). Business facilities include 24-hour room service, meeting rooms for up to 300, audiovisual equipment, photocopiers, and cable television news. V, 2 Roosevelt tér (phone: 138-3000; fax: 118-8271; telex: 225485). Expensive.

Béke Radisson – A reconstructed old hotel with a turn-of-the-century ambience, evident particularly in its beautiful *Zsolnay Café.* Business facilities include 24-hour room service, meeting rooms for up to 200, and cable television news. VI, 97 Lenin krt. (phone: 132-3300; fax: 153-3380; telex: 225748). Expensive.

Budapest Hilton International – This 323-room property sits on a hill in Buda's Castle District, behind the Fishermen's Bastion, overlooking the Danube, adjacent to the Matthias Church. The hotel includes ruins of a 13th-century church of the Dominican Order (where concerts are presented on warm summer evenings) and a Jesuit monastery. A walkway with a glass wall allows guests to see the restored cloisters. There's a restaurant called *Halászbástya* (see *Eating Out*); a wine cellar dubbed *Dr. Faust;* a coffee shop with rustic decor; a 2-level espresso bar with an outdoor terrace; the colorful *Kalocsa* restaurant; and the *Codex Bar,* which occupies the site of the country's first printing workshop, opened in the 15th century. Business facilities include 24-hour room service, meeting rooms for up to 1,000, audiovisual equipment, photocopiers, cable television news, and translation services. I, 1-3 Hess András tér (phone: 175-1000; fax: 156-0285; telex: 225984). Expensive.

Duna Inter-Continental – This deluxe 350-room hotel is on Pest's riverside Corso, a traditional promenade between the Chain and Elizabeth bridges. All rooms have a view of Buda Castle on the opposite bank. A renovation endowed this already well-accoutered hotel with a pool, fitness center, squash court, solarium, and a sauna. Among the restaurants: the peasant-inn-style *Csárda,* the *Rendezvous,* and the *Bellevue,* in addition to the *Intermezzo* terrace café, the *Tokaj* wine cellar, and a nightclub. Business facilities include 24-hour room service, meeting rooms for up to 1,000, audiovisual equipment, photocopiers, cable television news, and translation services. V, 4 Apáczai Csere János utca (phone: 117-5122; fax: 118-4973; telex: 225277). Expensive.

Forum – A first class, 408-room property next to the *Hyatt,* featuring wonderful river views, an efficient staff, and a lavish breakfast buffet. These days, more wheeler-dealer talk is heard in the lobby than in the locker room of the *Harvard Club.* It boasts a swimming pool and a health club with a bar. For dining, choose between the elegant *Silhouette* restaurant and the informal *Forum Grill* (open from 6 AM to 2 AM). For pastries and coffee, stop by the *Viennese Café.* Business facilities include 24-hour room service, meeting rooms for up to 240, audiovisual equipment, photocopiers, cable television news, and translation services. V, 12-14 Apáczai Csere János utca (phone: 117-8088; fax: 117-9808; telex: 224178). Expensive.

Gellért – On the Buda side of the Danube near Liberation Memorial Park, this 240-room Old World hotel at the foot of Gellért Hill is completing some much-needed renovation. It has 3 swimming pools with medicinal waters, a thermal bath, and a sun terrace. Famous for Hungarian cooking served in a restaurant with Gypsy music; there's also an espresso bar, a beer hall, and a nightclub. Business facilities include meeting rooms for up to 400, audiovisual equipment, photocopiers, and cable television news. XI, 1 Szt. Gellért tér (phone: 185-2200). Expensive.

Helia – This new 8-story hotel with 256 rooms is set on the Pest side of the Danube embankment, just opposite Margaret Island. It has 2 restaurants, the *Jupiter,* a buffet-style eatery, and the *Saturnus,* with an à la carte menu. Recreational pluses include a pool, tennis courts, sauna, and solarium, and a bridge that leads from the hotel to the island. Business facilities include meeting rooms for up to 200, audiovisual equipment, and cable television news. 62-64 Karpat utca (phone: 129-8650; fax: 120-1429; telex: 202539). Expensive.

Korona – Best Western runs this new property, which is situated in the main shopping and business area. The two wings of the hotel are connected by a bridge, and the 8-story building features a swimming pool, solarium, and sauna. Business facilities include photocopy and fax services, as well as meeting rooms for up to 100. 12-14 Kecskemeti utca (phone: 117-4111; fax: 118-3867; telex: 223622). Expensive.

Ramada Grand Hotel Margitsziget – A renovated spa dating from the 19th century, it now is a resort-hotel, and its *Thermál* hotel is connected by an underground passage. Business facilities include conference rooms for up to 180. XIII, Margaret Island (phone: 111-1000; fax: 153-3029; telex: 226682). Expensive.

Thermál Hotel Margitsziget – This 340-room luxury spa hotel has health facilities with diagnostic and treatment centers and equipment for hydrotherapy and physiotherapy. It has a swimming pool, solarium, sauna, and fitness rooms, and offers special inclusive packages with spa treatments and diet plans. Business facilities include conference rooms for up to 180. XIII, Margaret Island (phone: 131-1100; fax: 153-3029; telex: 2246682). Expensive.

Nemzeti – Another Old World (1880s) establishment, it was restored a few years ago but could use additional touching up. This 76-room place has an elegant restaurant with Gypsy music and a beer hall. Beware: The location is noisy. Cable television news is available. 4 József krt. (phone: 133-9160; fax: 114-0019; telex: 227710). Expensive to moderate.

Astoria – Another renovated old hostelry (it was built in 1911), this one has a marvelous café and probably is the best of the moderately priced hotels. Business facilities include a conference room for up to 15. V, 19 Kossuth Lajos utca (phone: 117-3411; fax: 118-6798; telex: 224205). Moderate.

Buda-Penta – Near the Southern Railway Station and Underground Terminal in Buda, it has 392 rooms plus 7 apartments, all with air conditioning, plus a swimming pool and health club, a restaurant, coffee shop, beer hall, and nightclub. Business facilities include a conference room for 6, audiovisual equipment, and photocopiers. I, 41-43 Krisztina körút (phone: 156-6333; fax: 155-6964; telex: 225495). Moderate.

Erzsébet – An attractive modern property on the site of a much older one. The *János Beer Cellar* has kept the furnishings of its popular predecessor. Business facilities include conference rooms for up to 100, audiovisual equipment, and photocopiers. V, 11-15 Károlyi Mihály utca (phone: 138-2111; fax: 118-9237; telex: 227494). Moderate.

Grand Hotel Hungaria – Opposite the Eastern Railway Station stands a bustling hotel — the biggest in the country — with 529 rooms (beware, the walls are paper thin), a restaurant, beer hall, wine cellar, *Jugendstil* (Art Nouveau) café, and nightclub. Business facilities include conference rooms for up to 300, audiovisual equipment, and photocopiers. VII, Rákóczi utca (phone: 122-9050; fax: 122-8029; telex: 224987). Moderate.

Olympia – Somewhat on the outskirts of town in the residential Buda hills, this pleasant place has a swimming pool, health club, tennis court, and restaurants. There's also a nightclub. Business facilities include conference rooms for up to 120 and photocopiers. XII, 40 Eötvös utca (phone: 156-3575; fax: 156-8720; telex: 226368). Moderate.

Novotel Budapest – A quick drive from the city center, it has 324 rooms, a small pool, tennis courts, restaurants, and bars. The *Budapest Convention Center* is next door. Business facilities include a conference room for up to 15 and cable television news. XII, 63-67 Alkotás utca (phone: 186-9588; fax: 166-5636; telex: 225496). Moderate.

Taverna – The main pedestrian shopping street in Pest boasts a well-designed, post-modern hotel with 224 rooms, a restaurant, beer hall, pastry shop, fast-food eatery, and a champagne bar. Conference room for up to 130. V, 20 Váci utca (phone: 138-4999; fax: 118-7188; telex: 227707). Moderate.

 EATING OUT: The justly celebrated cuisine of Hungary dates from ancient times. The most celebrated ingredient is paprika, the red pepper that comes in different strengths and is used copiously, most notably in *paprikás csirke* (paprika chicken) and in sauces. (Don't worry about paprika dishes being too hot; any restaurant will be glad to spice to your taste.) Another culinary characteristic is the use of pork drippings, which in concert with the ubiquitous sour creams, makes here meals so conspicuously caloric. Various Hungarian dishes have become world famous, particularly goulash (*gulyás*), which will not be what you expect if you have eaten it outside Hungary. Here, it is a very thick soup with meat (usually beef or pork), onions, carrots, sour cream, and a lot of paprika. If you like fish, try Hungarian bouillabaisse (*halászlé*), a clear soup made with *fogas* (a unique pike-perch caught only in Lake Balaton) or bream, seasoned with onions and many spices including paprika. *Kolozsvári rakott káposzta,* or layered cabbage, includes eggs and sausage, heaps of sour cream, and crisp pork chops.

Hungarian rye bread is superb, and a biscuit called *pogácsa,* a flaky pastry strewn with bits of crackling pork, is delicious. Hungarian pastries are absolutely fabulous; Budapest is the place to let that diet go. You might start with *rétes* (strudel) or *dobos torta,* the famous many-layered cake — but the sky is the limit. Filled with apricot preserves and *lekvár* (prune preserves), walnuts, hazelnuts, crushed poppy seeds, and chocolate, they are all sinfully delectable.

Hungarian wines are wonderful, especially tokay, which is often sweet; *tokaji szamo-*

rodni and *tokaji aszú* are famous dessert wines made from hand-picked, shriveled, "noble rot" grapes. A popular choice with meals is *egri bikavér* (bull's blood), a heavy red wine. *Leányka* is a delicious white wine.

Hungarians love to linger over small cups of strong coffee, called *eszpresszó*, or over *dupla kava*, which is strong double mocha brew. These are available everywhere — in pastry shops, cafés, and the *Mackó* shops, whose symbol is a bear cub.

Budapest has over 2,000 restaurants, cafés, pastry shops, wine and beer cellars, and taverns. A few of the highlights are listed below. There is an important distinction to be made among eating establishments in Budapest: Whenever possible, try to determine if a restaurant is privately owned or still state-run. The food at private establishments is generally of a higher quality and the service is better. And the most genuine Hungarian food often is found at places which use the native word for "restaurant," *étterem*, where Hungarians are served traditional spicy dishes, unmodified to meet the milder tastes of tourists. The concierge at your hotel should be able to help in this regard. For a dinner for two with wine, expect to pay $50 to $60 in restaurants listed as expensive; $20 to $30 in those categorized as moderate; and $10 to $20 in inexpensive places. Restaurants below accept major credit cards unless otherwise noted. All telephone numbers are in the 1 city code unless otherwise indicated.

Alabárdos – In one of the most beautiful Gothic buildings in the Castle District. Try the house specialty, flambéed meat served with great ceremony on a sword. Closed Sundays. Reservations necessary. American Express and Visa accepted. I, 2 Országház utca (phone: 156-0851). Expensive.

Gundel – Perhaps the most famous chef in Budapest's history was Károly Gundel, and his restaurant is now owned by the Hungarian-born American, restaurateur/entrepreneur George Lang. This large, near-sacred dining spot will be fully renovated (and its garden restored) and reopened by spring. The menu will emphasize elegant native fare: *fogas*, Lake Balaton's famous whitefish, game dishes, delicious desserts — we hope Károly's legendary crêpe filled with hazelnuts and cream and covered by a bittersweet chocolate sauce will again make mouths marvel. The decor will celebrate its country with Hungarian antiques and paintings. Ties required. Open daily. Reservations necessary. XIV, 2 Allatkerti ut, in the Városliget (phone: 122-1002). Expensive. Note: During *Gundel*'s renovation, *Bagolyvár*, the landmark eatery next door will remain open under the new name *Kis-Gundel* (Little Gundel) and will serve meals prepared by *Gundel*'s new chefs.

Halászbástya – Next to the *Hilton*, inside one of the towers of the Fishermen's Bastion (see *Special Places*), with a fabulous view of the Parliament building and the town. Hungarian food and Gypsy music are featured. Open daily. Reservations necessary. I, Fishermen's Bastion (phone: 156-1446). Expensive.

Hungária – For that big night on the town, this evocative eatery wins the laurels. A Budapest institution since 1894, when it was known as the *Café New York*, it is palatial in every respect. The baroque decor, gilt columns, frosted glass globes, and glittering mirrors will probably remind you more of an opera house or a royal palace than a restaurant. If opulence and its concomitant ambience is what you seek, by all means visit. However, if food is your primary interest, a downturn in its near-legendary gastronomic reputation may dissuade you. Among the specialties still well worth trying are *kengurufarokleves* (kangaroo tail soup), *crêpes à la Hortobágy* (crêpes stuffed with meat and served with a paprika sauce), *sertésborda magyarovári módra* (pork cutlet with mushrooms, ham, and cheese), and a dessert called *omelette surprise* (parfait in sponge cake baked in a froth of egg white). The *Hungária* is not only a restaurant but a coffeehouse, café, and nightclub. Don't be put off by the incongruous, Soviet-style chandeliers. Open daily. Reservations necessary. VII, 9-11 Erzsébet körút (phone: 122-3849). Expensive.

Légrádi Testvérek (Légrádi Brothers) – Make reservations at least a week in advance (only 30 persons, maximum) for this outstanding private dining place. Traditional Hungarian specialties are prepared at the table. Dinner only, weekdays. Reservations necessary. V, 23 Magyar utca (phone: 118-6804). Expensive.

Ménes Csárda – This small, cozy establishment with an equestrian decor became an instant hit after it opened in 1982. It serves unusual Hungarian specialties — often prepared at your table — in attractive ceramic dishes made for the restaurant by a local artist. Try the stuffed filet of pork with *tápióbicskei hozzávaló* and the cherry or cottage cheese (*túrós*) strudel. Good, light wines are available. While you dine, a Gypsy *cimbalom* player performs. Open daily. Reservations necessary. V, 15 Apáczai Csere János utca (phone: 117-0803). Expensive.

Rézkakas – One of the more recent additions to the city's selection of fine dining establishments, this spot offers a good selection of game and fish dishes, as well as particularly fine wines. The service is excellent. Open daily. Reservations necessary. 3 V Veres Pálné utca (phone: 118-0038). Expensive.

Vadrózsa – In a private villa with a shady garden, it features charcoal-broiled specialties such as goose liver and pike-perch, plus other tempting dishes. This place is frequented by diplomats and, perhaps diplomatically, no longer lists prices on the menu. Very friendly service. Closed Mondays. Reservations necessary. II, 12 Pentelei Molnár utca (phone: 113-5111). Expensive.

Vén Buda (Old Buda) – Serving traditional Hungarian dishes, this dining place has become a firmly established favorite in recent years. Closed weekends. Reservations necessary. II, 22 Erőod utca (phone: 115-3396). Expensive.

Kárpátia – Traditional Hungarian specialties are served under vaulted ceilings with musical interludes (especially aimed at tourists) in the evenings. Open daily. Reservations advised. V, 4-8 Károlyi Mihály utca (phone: 117-0303). Expensive to moderate.

Vasmacska – Popular with out-of-towners, the interior of this restaurant evokes the atmosphere of an officers' wardroom on a ship. The house specialty is a hearty bean dish with different kinds of smoked meat. Downstairs is a less expensive beer hall. Open daily. Reservations advised. No credit cards accepted. III, 3-5 Laktanya utca (phone: 188-7123). Expensive to moderate.

Aranybárány Borozó – The "Golden Lamb Wine Bar" specializes, naturally, in lamb dishes, served in a cellar decorated with shepherd motifs. Open daily. Reservations advised on weekends. No credit cards accepted. V, 4 Harmincad utca (phone: 117-2703). Moderate.

Aranymókus Kertvendéglőo (Golden Squirrel Garden) – Traditional game dishes (but no squirrel, in case you care). A short taxi ride from the center. Closed Mondays. Reservations advised on weekends. No credit cards accepted. XII, 25 Istenhegyi utca (phone: 155-6728 or 155-9594). Moderate.

Borkóstoló (Gresham Wine Bar) – Near the Houses of Parliament, here you can taste fine Hungarian wines such as tokay, which is often sweet; *egri bikavér* (bull's blood), a marvelous dry red wine believed to have medicinal value; and *leányka,* a good white wine. Closed Sundays. Reservations advised on weekends. No credit cards accepted. V, Mérleg utca (phone: 117-2502). Moderate.

Kiskakukk – An extensive year-round menu of game dishes, served in noisy, plain surroundings. Closed Sundays during summer. Reservations advised. XIII, 12 Pozsonyi utca (phone: 132-1732). Moderate.

Kispipa – A brasserie atmosphere — bright lights, red tablecloths, and friendly chatter by diners who all seem to know each other — prevails at this private eatery. It features an extensive menu of Hungarian specialties and almost anything else you might wish to eat. It's a 5-minute taxi ride from the major hotels in Pest. Closed Sundays. Reservations necessary. 38 Akácfa utca (phone: 142-2587). Moderate.

Mátyás Pince – Tourists are not the only people drawn to this romantic beer cellar in central Pest, where the real commodities are copious quantities of wine and even richer servings of Gypsy music and old Budapest spirit. If you actually get hungry, its fish dishes are well known around the city. Open daily. Reservations advised on weekends. No credit cards accepted. V, 7 Március 15 tér (phone: 118-1650). Moderate.

Régi Országház – This old inn on the north side of the castle in Buda offers many rooms with different decors, a wine cellar, Gypsy music, and jazz. Open daily. Reservations advised on weekends. No credit cards accepted. I, 17 Országház utca (phone: 175-0650). Moderate.

Sipos Halászkert – Known as the *New Sipos* — to distinguish it from the original *Régi Sipos Halászkert* (Old Sipos; 46 Lajos utca; phone: 686480) — this is a case of new quarters for an old standby — a fish restaurant with a tradition that began half a century ago. There is music and a garden. Reservations advised on weekends. Fő tér in the Obuda district (phone: 188-8745). Moderate.

Százéves (100-éves) – Actually more than a half-century older than the 100 years its name indicates, it's in a lovely baroque town palace in the center of the city. Its atmosphere is intimate and the food enjoyable, though service can be slow at lunchtime, when it's very crowded. Open daily. Reservations advised on weekends. V, 2 Pesti Barnabás utca (phone: 118-3608). Moderate.

Apostolok – This old brasserie is centrally located and very popular, especially for lunch. Open daily. Reservations advised on weekends. No credit cards accepted. V, 4-6 Kígyó utca (phone: 118-3704). Moderate to inexpensive.

Dunakorzó – Near the riverside cluster of deluxe hotels. Undistinguished decor but known among hearty eaters for its heaping portions of solid Hungarian fare. Open daily. Reservations advised on weekends. No credit cards accepted. V, 3 Vigadó tér (phone: 118-6362). Moderate to inexpensive.

Kisbuda – A charming place, with good Hungarian food, a cozy interior, and a large garden. Open daily. Reservations advised on weekends. Frankel Leó utca (phone: 115-2244). Moderate to inexpensive.

Pest-Buda – Operating in the same building in the Castle District since 1880, when it had a local carriage trade and attracted visitors from as far away as Vienna. It is not suited for big functions or balls, but rather is a place for family suppers, with romantic, vaulted dining rooms and period furnishings. Try the Wiener schnitzel. Open daily. Reservations advised on weekends. No credit cards accepted. I, 3 Fortuna utca (phone: 156-9849). Moderate to inexpensive.

Pilvax – An old café-restaurant in the heart of the Inner City of Pest, it is noted for its chicken broth, pastries, and cakes. Gypsy music accompanies the meal. Reservations advised on weekends. No credit cards accepted. V, 1-3 Pilvax köz (phone: 117-5902). Moderate to inexpensive.

Alföldi – This is where Hungarians come for Sunday lunch; it's noisy and offers simple, traditional fare. Reservations unnecessary. No credit cards accepted. V, 4 Kecskeméti utca (phone: 117-4404). Inexpensive.

Clark Brasserie (Söröző) – Stop here for a glass of beer or wine and a fast light meal, such as a bowl of mushroom soup (*vargánya leves*). The cabbage strudel (*káposztás rétes*) is a must. A particular specialty is the Nomad Roast — a sirloin and veal roast grilled on a slab of stone at the table (for two people). Reservations unnecessary. No credit cards accepted. V, 15 Apáczai Csere János utca (phone: 117-0803). Inexpensive.

Halászárda – Especially popular with Hungarians, this casual place serves a delicious version of fish soup. The eatery features a small orchestra for dancing. Reservations unnecessary. No credit cards accepted. 15 Népszinház utca (no phone). Inexpensive.

COPENHAGEN

In the early mornings of 1848 in Copenhagen's old waterfront district, Nyhavn, a tall, top-hatted figure often could be seen emerging from the elegant portals of No. 67B. A few books underneath his arm, the figure would walk in the direction of the docks, with the apparent intention of inspecting the wooden sailing ships moored there. However, he had other things on his mind.

The figure was Hans Christian Andersen, Denmark's beloved raconteur of fairy tales and the country's most famous citizen. A poor shoemaker's son who allegorized the remarkable tale of his own life in *The Ugly Duckling,* Andersen often found inspiration during these morning walks around Nyhavn, where he lived for some 20 years. The stately old merchants' townhouses, the shabby sailors' bars, the tattoo parlors, and all the other assorted arcana of dockside life — so much of which is the same today — must have provided good soil for his fertile imagination. Once, when questioned about his literary methods, he replied, "It came without incentive — while I was walking on the street the thought came to me."

Thus it is no surprise to discover that Andersen's first literary success, a fantastic tale in the E. T. A. Hoffmann tradition, bore the title *A Walk from Holmen's Canal to the East Point of the Island of Amager in the Years 1828 and 1829.*

During that same period, a mere 10 blocks away from Andersen, one might find that dour theologian and progenitor of existentialism, Søren Kierkegaard, out taking *his* morning constitutional. Kierkegaard and Andersen were literary contemporaries, and although they had about as much in common as Hamlet and Victor Borge, their writings bear witness to the fact that they both loved their walks in Copenhagen.

The largest city in Scandinavia, with a population of about 1.5 million, Copenhagen is on the northeastern shore of Zealand, the largest of Denmark's approximately 500 islands. Here the Danes have somehow managed to synthesize the urban sophistication of a large continental city with the friendly charm of a small village. And Copenhagen remains a pedestrian's paradise. Lively Strøget (the Strolling Street) is Europe's oldest and longest "walking street." The backbone of the city, Strøget links Kongens Nytorv, the largest square in the harbor, with Rådhuspladsen, the largest square in the downtown area. You can find just about anything you could want on Strøget — with its modern department stores, tiny boutiques, ice cream stands, bars, theaters, sex shops, street musicians, park benches, and infinite opportunities for idle conversation — just about anything, that is, except cars and automotive pollution.

This congenial and idyllic atmosphere might lead the casual observer to believe that Copenhagen has been lucky enough to occupy some turgid backwater of history, far from the dynamic fury of world events. On the contrary, Copenhagen has had a rich and dramatic history, a history of which the Danes are justly proud. Because of its strategic location on the Oresund, a narrow seaway connecting the North and the Baltic seas (and separating Denmark from Sweden), Copenhagen has been besieged by the Swedes, leveled by the English, and occupied by the Germans.

According to Danish tradition, København (literally, "Merchants' Harbor") was founded in 1167 by a Bishop Absalon during the reign of Valdemar the Great. Absalon built a fortress on the island of Slotsholmen to protect the port, and the ruins of this fortress are still visible in the cellars of the parliament building Christiansborg.

In 1416, King Erik of Pomerania made Copenhagen the capital of Denmark, but it was not until the reign of Christian IV (1588-1648) and the Danish Renaissance that Copenhagen acquired some of the features one associates with it today. Christian IV was a great builder, and many of his contributions still stand — the Stock Exchange, Rosenborg Castle, the Round Tower, Kongens Have Park, and the residential districts of Nyboder and Christianshavn.

Disaster struck Copenhagen during the following century: The great fire of 1728 destroyed two-fifths of the houses in the city. Wood and straw thatch buildings were particularly combustible, and the narrow streets and alleys made firefighting all but impossible. A second great fire in 1795 reduced another fifth of the city to ashes.

Efforts at reconstruction were delayed by war. In 1801, the Danes found themselves confronted by a large English fleet under the command of Lord Nelson. Legend has it that the Danes hoisted a cease-fire flag after a heavy bombardment, whereupon Nelson raised his telescope to his blind eye and ordered the attack intensified. The subsequent Danish resistance was a high-water mark in the patriotic lore of Copenhagen. The English retired, only to send a larger fleet in 1807 to finish the job. A fierce rocket assault left most of Copenhagen in flames, and the city capitulated — for the first time in modern history.

Displaying their remarkable recuperative powers, the Danes quickly rebuilt the city. The Danish golden age of the mid-19th century followed, a time in which social progress, as evidenced by the parliamentary constitution of 1849, was accompanied by a flourishing of the arts. Many of the buildings one sees today are remnants of the Danish golden age. Fittingly, the old ramparts were removed during this era and replaced with a lush and verdant belt of parks.

Denmark lost its border provinces to Prussia in a war in 1864 but managed to steer clear of any other major conflicts; it was neutral in World War I — and remained so until the 5-year German occupation during World War II. From April 9, 1940, to May 5, 1945, the heroic resistance of the Danish people to the Nazis was nearly unanimous. When the Danish merchant fleet was ordered by the Germans to make for a neutral port at the time of the occupation, more than 90% of the seamen (about 5,000 men) chose to answer the appeal of London radio to sail to an Allied port and join the war. Of the 5,000, 600 died and 60% of the ships were sunk. Back in Copenhagen, the underground press flourished and isolated incidents of resistance were numer-

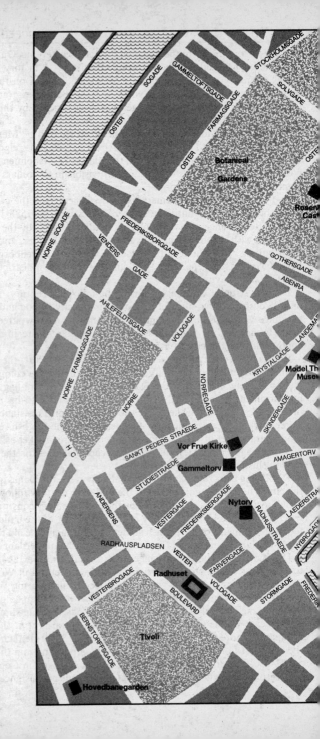

COPENHAGEN

DELFINGADE

ELSDYRSGADE

SUENSONSGADE

GRØNNINGEN

HAREGADE

RIGENSGADE

ESPLANADEN

FREDERICIAGADE

ADELGADE

BORGERGADE

STORE KONGENSGADE

**Museum of
Decorative Art**

KRONPRINSESSEGADE

DRONNINGENS TVAERGADE

BREDGADE

**Amalienborg
Castle**

ADELGADE

BORGERGADE

AMALIENGADE

NY ØSTERGADE

BREMERHOLM

KONGENS
NYTORV

NYHAVN

NYHAVN

ØSTERGADE

HERLUF TROLLES GADE

HEIBERGSGADE

PEDER

NIKOLAJGADE

TORDENSKJOLDSGADE

HOLBERGSGADE

ADMIRALGADE

NIELS JUELS GADE

SKRAMS

KAN

HOLMENS

HAVNEGADE

orvaldsens
Museum

VED STRANDEN

hristiansborg
Castle

KNIPPELS BRO

BRYGGE

CHRISTIANS

INDERHAVNEN

ous, reaching a climax on August 29, 1943, when the Danish government unanimously and unqualifiedly said no to German ultimatums. Open resistance began: sabotage by underground groups, arms supplies, intelligence activities, and, most dramatically, escape routes for Jews and other war victims. About 7,000 persons were successfully evacuated to Sweden, and only 450 arrested and taken to Germany. The Danes paid a price for their courageous actions: Their resistance was met with violent Nazi countermeasures — arrests, deportations, executions, and random shootings. Yet the Danes remained so active in resisting Hitler that Denmark generally was recognized as a de facto ally.

Postwar Copenhagen is a unique blend of historical charm and modern efficiency. Enlightened social reform and respect for aesthetic and sentimental values make Copenhagen one of the most delightful cities in Europe. The brutal new skyscrapers that loom over the horizon of many European cities have been exiled to the suburbs here, and one is hard pressed to find any symptoms of urban blight.

Denmark is a highly advanced country politically and socially. Its government, which resembles England's, is a constitutional monarchy with Queen Margrethe II on the throne and a parliament of 179 members called the Folketing. Widely known as a nation that cares for its citizens, Denmark has a comprehensive social security system and national health insurance, and is known for offering a high standard of living. But its cost of living is higher than that of the US or Germany. In recent years, Denmark has run up a colossal foreign debt, with annual net interest payments in the billions of kroner. This deficit was accompanied by high unemployment, which reached double digits in the 1960s, and inflation. In an effort to deal with these problems, the government instituted wage and price controls and gave several more twists to the tax screw, simultaneously freezing total expenditures in real terms. Taxes today are among the world's highest. Copenhagen is currently emerging from its slump, however. Unemployment has fallen to 8%, exports are booming, and oil from the North Sea has reduced the country's dependence on foreign oil. With the consolidation of trade within the Common Market, too, the Danes are poised to cash in on increased international trade.

Aside from its political prominence as the capital of Denmark, Copenhagen is also the site of a major shipyard and design center, and is the home of the Carlsberg and Tuborg breweries, which produce one of Denmark's leading exports — beer.

The Danish people enjoy a reputation for being masters of recreational pursuits; in fact, Copenhagen is known among more reserved Scandinavians as being more than a little libertine. This reputation is not entirely unjustified, as Copenhagen is a place to have a good time, sinful or otherwise.

Ever since the Vikings left their women responsible for the farms when they went out on plundering raids, Danes have had an unusually liberal attitude toward sex. In 1967, Denmark became the first country in the world to abolish all restrictions on the sale of pornographic literature to adults. After an initial boom, the sales of pornography actually went down, as did the number of sex crimes. Male tourists who expect Danish women to be especially promiscuous may be disappointed; there is probably no greater level of promiscuity in Denmark than in any other country in Europe.

Whatever your pleasure, whether it be pornography or the *Royal Danish Ballet,* you will find much to enjoy in Copenhagen. A statue of the town's symbol, the *Little Mermaid,* perches petite and green on the waterfront to greet all visitors. Commissioned by Carlsberg magnate Carl Jacobsen in 1913, the statue was completed in 1915 and has survived the repeated humiliations of being doused in red paint, then in blue paint, and even decapitated. The *Mermaid* was erected by the Danes to express their gratitude to Hans Christian Andersen for his love of fantasy and of his fellow man.

In Andersen's tale, a mermaid falls hopelessly in love with a mortal prince who, alas, loves another. Begging to have feet so she can walk like a human, the mermaid suffers great physical pain whenever she takes a step, as well as emotional anguish when she finds that her prince's romantic interests lie elsewhere. In the end she must pay the penalty of dissolving into an incorporeal spirit whose function is to help mortals navigate in perilous waters.

The spirits of the mermaid, the snow queen, the nightingale, and the ugly duckling seem to haunt the picture book streets of the Copenhagen that Hans Christian Andersen loved so dearly. And no wonder. Even today, in spite of its dominant role as Denmark's political and commercial center, Copenhagen's skyline is still much the same as it was in his day — a fairy-tale conglomeration of ancient church steeples, spiraling golden towers, massive domes, and staircased gables silhouetted against a copen blue sky.

COPENHAGEN AT-A-GLANCE

SEEING THE CITY: There are no World Trade Centers or Eiffel Towers in Copenhagen, but a far more authentic alternative exists in the Round Tower. Built in 1642 by the monarch Christian IV as an observatory, it offers a panorama of the spires and steeples of the Old Town of Copenhagen. Peter the Great of Russia reportedly led a carriage containing the Czarina Catherine to the top of the Round Tower in the 18th century, but today's visitors will unfortunately have to climb the 687-foot spiral walkway. Be advised, however, that the observatory on the roof is open only in clear weather. Open daily; admission charge. The Round Tower (Rundetårn) is on Købmagergade.

Several of Copenhagen's churches also provide views of the city, including the bizarre baroque tower of Vor Frelsers Kirke (Our Saviour's Church; on Sankt Annaegade at Prinsessegade), which also is open to visitors. Here the spiral stairway is on the outside of the tower, so bring a sweater if it's chilly. Admission charge to the tower.

A spectacular view of Copenhagen is afforded by the *Top of Town* restaurant on the 25th floor of the *Scandinavia Hotel,* 70 Amager Blvd.

SPECIAL PLACES: Copenhagen is a pedestrian's paradise, and it is relatively easy to get oriented after finding Strøget, the "strolling" street, which is made up of five connecting pedestrian streets, none of them named Strøget. (From Rådhuspladsen, the names are Frederiksberggade, Nygade, Vimmelskaftet, Amagertorv, and Ostergade.) The medieval street plan of the Old Town is irregular, however, and once you leave the downtown area and familiar landmarks, it is possible to get lost. Danes generally are very helpful, and, as nearly everyone seems to speak English, it is very difficult to get hopelessly lost. In addition to the tourist office, banks and many stores give away city maps with street guides, both in English.

DOWNTOWN

Slotsholmen Island, Christiansborg Palace, and Thorvaldsen's Museum – In the central part of Copenhagen it is possible to visit the island where Absalon built his fortress in 1167, founding the city. The best way to get there is to walk from Rådhuspladsen down Vester Voldgade, left on Stormgade, and across the bridge leading into Porthusgade, where you will be confronted with *Thorvaldsen's Museum* to your left and, to your right, Christiansborg Palace, with the seat of the Danish parliament on one side and royal reception rooms on the other. Bertil Thorvaldsen was the most famous Danish sculptor; in 1838 he donated all of his work to the city of his birth, and in turn, the city built the museum to house his variations on classical themes. The museum is open daily, except Mondays, from 10 AM to 5 PM year-round; no admission charge. English-language guided tours are available at 4 PM on Sundays and Wednesdays from June through September (phone: 33-321532).

Christiansborg was completed in 1740, burned in 1794, rebuilt in 1828, and burned down once more. The present palace, in a mixed baroque/rococo design by Thorvald Jorgenson, was built from 1906 to 1928 (although the buildings around the riding ground date from the 1740s, and were under renovation at press time). Guided English-language tours of the royal reception rooms take place at 11 AM and 1 PM, except Mondays and Saturdays, February through April; at 11 AM and at 1 and 3 PM, except Mondays, May through September; and at 11 AM and 1 PM on Tuesdays, Thursdays, and Sundays from October through December (phone: 33-926492). Underneath the palace, ruins of Absalon's fortress and its successor, Copenhagen Castle, are open from 9:30 AM to 3:30 PM daily (closed Saturdays in winter). Admission charge.

Vor Frue Kirke (Our Lady's Church) – Using Rådhuspladsen as a starting point, you reach the old section of Copenhagen by taking a left down Vester Voldgade and then taking a right on Studiestraede. Up ahead you will see Vor Frue Kirke, Copenhagen's neo-classic cathedral, which was completed in 1829. Statues of the 12 disciples guard the porticoes inside, and a kneeling angel holds a seashell baptismal font. Open daily (phone: 33-144128).

Gammeltorv – If you take a right on Nørregade in front of the cathedral, you will enter the oldest part of the city — the marketplace of Gammeltorv, on which the fortress on Slotsholmen was built to defend in 1167. In addition to being the first marketplace in Copenhagen, Gammeltorv has been the site of jousting tournaments and public executions and still is a center for social activity. Nytorv was added in 1606 as an extension of Gammeltorv. *Caritas* (Charity), the city's oldest fountain, donated by King Christian IV in 1609, is here.

Dukketeatermuseet (Model Theater Museum) – At the end of Skindergade, the street that runs through the Latin Quarter, Copenhagen's university area, this museum has a historical collection of toy theaters. Open Tuesdays, Thursdays, Fridays, and Saturdays from 12:30 to 5 PM. Admission charge. 52 Købmagergade (phone: 33-151579).

Eksperimentarium (Science Center) – One of Copenhagen's newest attractions offers visitors the chance to use computer technology to better understand science. Some 225 lively and interesting demonstrations on topics ranging from the earth's ozone layer to food's fat and calorie content have made this imaginative center a hit, especially with children. There are changing exhibits. Open daily. Admission charge. In the old bottling plant of the Tuborg Brewery at 7 Tuborg Havnevej (phone: 39-273333).

Botanisk Have (Botanical Gardens) – A park and greenhouses sport both tropical and subtropical plants; in the summer, the "wildlife" on view includes topless sunbathers. Open daily. No admission charge. Entrance at Gothersgade and Sølvgade. 128 Gothersgade (phone: 33-127460).

Rosenborg Slot (Rosenborg Castle) – This Renaissance castle was built by Christian IV over the 11-year period from 1606 to 1617. Its fine interiors contain the crown jewels and treasures of the Danish royal family from the 15th to the 19th century. Be sure to see the dazzling porcelain and crystal closets and the tiled bathroom with running water that King Christian installed in 1616. Open daily from June until late October; open Tuesdays, Fridays, and Sundays the rest of the year. Admission charge. 4A Øster Voldgade (phone: 33-153286).

Amalienborg Palace – The residence of the Danish royal family since 1794, Amalienborg is another spectacular example of Danish rococo, with four identical palaces set perfectly against the harbor background. Unfortunately, it can be seen only from the outside. When the royal family is in residence, however, there is plenty of pomp for all to see during the daily Changing of the Guard. The Royal Guard leaves the Rosenborg Castle at 11:30 AM and marches through the streets, to arrive at the Amalienborg Palace at noon.

The Harbor – The harbor area, or Nyhavn, favorite haunt for sailors from around the world and home of Hans Christian Andersen for many years, is a fascinating area where you can run into all manner of characters ranging from sleek fashion models walking their Afghan hounds to the proverbial drunken sailors who may have just been decorated at Tattoo Jack's. For an interesting tour, start at the *Royal Theater* at Kongens Nytorv, then follow the left-hand side of Nyhavn Canal toward the water. En route you can look at the sturdy fishing boats and sailing ships. The right-hand side of Nyhavn, also known as the Charlottenborg side, has been an elegant residential area for many years. It was here, in No. 67, that Andersen lived between 1845 and 1864 and wrote many of his famous fairy tales. In recent years, a number of good, small restaurants have emerged on both sides of Nyhavn; the sailors' bars here — *Cap Horn,* the *Brooklyn,* and others — may seem exotic, but generally are no bargain, and seem to survive by enticing inebriated Swedes on their way to the ferry back to Sweden.

Kunstindustrimuseet (Museum of Decorative and Applied Art) – Founded in 1890, the museum contains European and Oriental applied art from the Middle Ages to modern times, including a fine collection of contemporary decorative art. Wonderful furniture, porcelain, and crystal are displayed in room after room. The modern wing offers a good overview of the talents of today's best Danish designers. Open daily, except Mondays, from 1 to 4 PM. No admission charge on weekdays except during July and August. 68 Bredgade (phone: 33-149452).

Frihedsmuseet (Resistance Museum) – In Churchill Park just outside the entrance to Kastellet — or the Citadel, Copenhagen's old harbor fortifications (open from 6 AM to sundown) — the *Frihedsmuseet* contains relics from the resistance movement during the German occupation of 1940–45. Closed Mondays. No admission charge. Churchill Park at Langelinie (phone: 33-137714).

Ny Carlsberg Glyptotek (New Carlsberg Scuplture Museum) – Gorgeous marble and mosaics adorn this solid building, which has a lush green, glass-covered courtyard in its center. In addition to halls with Egyptian mummies and rows of Greek, Etruscan, and Roman statues, there's a respectable collection of 19th- and 20th-century European art, including works by Gauguin and Van Gogh. Open daily, except Mondays, year-round. No admission charge on Wednesdays and Sundays. 7 Dantes Plads (phone: 33-911065).

Langelinie Pavilion and Promenade – One of the loveliest spots in Copenhagen is just opposite the Citadel, overlooking the harbor — the Langelinie *Pavilion* and Promenade. The *Pavilion* (phone: 33-121214) is an elegant (and pricey) restaurant-where you can gaze at the moonlit waters and dine and dance until the wee hours on Fridays and Saturdays. Should you want a breath of fresh air, you can always suggest a walk along the promenade to take a look at *Den Lille Havfrue* (Little Mermaid), erected in 1913 thanks to a grant from Carlsberg Brewery magnate Carl Jacobsen.

Medicinsk-Historisk Museum (Medical History Museum) – Reputed to be the world's largest medical history repository, this is a bizarre and fascinating collection housed in Copenhagen's former medical college. Dental, psychiatric, obstetrical, pharmacological, and surgical tools are on exhibit, and a guide explains past medical treatments, many of which seem outrageous in light of today's scientific knowledge. Open for guided tours only. English-language tours available at 2 PM on Tuesdays, Thursdays, and Sundays year-round. No admission charge. 62 Bredgade (phone: 33-152501).

Carlsberg Brewery – In case you're wondering how they make the stuff that everybody seems to be drinking, you will be happy to learn that guests are welcome at the Carlsberg Brewery, a 20-minute walk from Rådhuspladsen, or take the No. 6 bus. Danes take their beer as seriously as the Irish take Guinness stout, and be advised that Elephant Beer, the world-famous Danish brew by Carlsberg, is about twice as strong as regular American beer (or even the Elephant Beer marketed in the US). Closed weekends; free tours conducted on weekdays at 11 AM and 2:30 PM. 140 Ny Carlsbergvej (phone: 31-211221; for groups of 10 or more, ask for ext. 1312).

Tuborg Brewery – Tuborg, which can be reached by bus No. 1, also welcomes visitors on weekdays. Free tours in English at 10 AM and 12:30 and 2:30 PM comprise an hour of walking and a half hour of quaffing. 54 Strandvejen (phone: 31-293311, ext. 2212).

Tivoli – Copenhagen's most famous recreational area is found on the south side of Rådhuspladsen. Built in 1843 on top of the old city ramparts, it's a tantalizing (though some may find it a bit less than dazzling) hybrid of an amusement park, gardens (160,000 flowers), lakes, theaters, dance halls, and restaurants, illuminated at night by over 100,000 colored lights. Whether you are looking for a first class restaurant such as *Belle Terasse* or *Divan I and II,* or a hot or cold open sandwich at *Grøften,* or the tawdry company of a one-armed bandit, *Tivoli* has it all.

The season runs from late April to mid-September, from 10 AM to midnight daily. Internationally known artists perform on an outdoor stage every night. The concert hall features nightly concerts with orchestras and soloists, often free of charge. Other entertainment includes the *Tivoli Boy Guard* marching band, the *Pantomime Theater,* children's theater, promenade concerts every night around the gardens, and amusement park rides. A highlight is the fireworks show at 11:45 PM Wednesdays, Fridays, and Saturdays, and at 11:30 PM on Sundays. Vesterbrogade, near Town Hall Square (phone: 33-151001).

Scala – Somewhat like an upscale US mall, but with a distinctly Danish flavor, this multistory shopping, dining, and entertainment complex offers a wide assortment of cafés, small ethnic eateries, boutiques, cinemas, live music, and even a fitness center. It's a wonderful place to eat lunch, get an inexpensive snack (the homemade Italian *gelati* is delicious), window shop, or people watch. Across the street from *Tivoli.* 2 Axeltorv (phone: 33-151215).

Søpavillion (Lake Pavilion) – A 10-minute walk from Town Hall Square, the old pavilion on Lake Peblinge offers live music, cabaret, art shows, and international food and drink year-round. Søpavillion has much the same magic as *Tivoli's* 19th-century *Pantomime Theater* — the same architect designed both. Three picture-perfect lakes draw sailors in summer, skaters in winter, and joggers doing laps in all seasons. Go even if just for coffee and the view. Open daily from 11:30 AM to 2 AM. Admission charge for shows. 24 Gyldenløvesgade (phone: 33-151224).

Tycho Brahe Planetarium – Named for the famous 16th-century Danish astronomer, this planetarium features an impressive computer-controlled Zeiss star projector, capable of simulating a voyage through a glittering firmament. The planetarium's 275-seat theater also features Omnimax films on a 360-degree screen in the planetarium dome. Shows are presented hourly, but due to the great popularity, it may be necessary to purchase tickets days in advance or put your name on a waiting list. There are exhibitions on astronomy and space exploration, and a restaurant, bar, and gift shop. Open from 8:30 AM (from 10:30 AM Sundays and Mondays) until 9 PM (to 10 PM on Fridays and Saturdays). Admission charge, plus an additional charge for films. 10 Gl. Kongevej (phone: 33-121224).

Christiania – The dreams of the 1960s may have died sometime in the early 1970s, and the media would have us believe that the Age of Love has become the Age of Rap; however, the news has not yet reached Copenhagen. Christiania, a sprawling section of Copenhagen that covers about 10 square blocks in the Christianshavn district, can be found easily by walking toward the towering golden spire of the aforementioned Vor Frelser Kirke. The casual visitor will be assaulted by a helter-skelter patchwork of theatrical spectacles, conceptual art pieces, strung-out hippies, stray children and dogs, psychedelic paintings, and, yes, whatever you want to smoke, if such is your bent. Although this community has been the subject of hot debate in Copenhagen, its very existence is indicative of the Danes' civic tolerance.

OUTSIDE THE CITY

Dragør – Dragør is an enchanting fishing village south of Copenhagen that dates from the 16th century and is still in vintage condition. Its streets are paved with cobblestones, and 65 of its quaint, old, red-roofed houses are protected historical sites, making an address here both fashionable and expensive. On the tip of the island of Amager, Dragør is about a 30-minute ride from Rådhuspladsen on bus No. 30 or No. 33, and worth the trip if you want to see a village straight from the pages of Hans Christian Andersen.

The oldest house in the village is the home of the *Dragør Museum* (4 Strandlinien; phone: 31-534106), open daily except Mondays, May through September (admission charge). Two old inns, the *Dragør Kro* (23 Kongev; phone: 31-530187) and the *Café Beghuset* (14 Strandg.; phone: 31-53036), offer bars for relaxing and restaurants that serve Danish and French specialties. Both are open daily, year-round, with a small admission charge. The most pleasant way to get here is by boat; there are ferry connections from Dragør to the town of Limhamn in Sweden.

Frilandsmuseet (Open-Air Museum) – This is a half-hour ride outside the city on the No. 184 bus, or by *S-train* to Sorgenfri station, and is an elaborate tribute to the joys of being down on the farm in the Danish countryside. (Just more proof that the Danes are incurable romantics.) Old houses from the various regions of Denmark have been dismantled and moved here, piece by piece, and efforts even have been made to re-create the ecological environment of each kind of farm. Interiors also have been re-created, and during the summer the visitor can watch sheep being sheared, wool being carded, garments being spun, and other examples of agrarian toil. There is a modern restaurant, but if you have not had your fill of pastoral splendor, there also are picnic tables and benches. The *Open-Air Museum* is open daily, except Mondays, March through November. Admission charge. 100 Kongevejen, Sorgenfri, Kgs. Lyngby (phone: 42-850292).

Helsingør (Elsinore) – About a 45-minute train ride north of Copenhagen lies the famous castle (phone: 49-213078) that's supposed to have been the site of Hamlet's endless brooding. In case you're looking forward to roaming its ramparts in search of the ghost, you may be disappointed to learn that the present castle, named Kronborg, is not the original, but was built during the 16th and 17th centuries. The Danes insist that Hamlet did exist, however, and refer the curious to the medieval Danish historian

Saxo Grammaticus's epic work, *Gesta Danorum,* for further details. Some rooms, including the king's and queen's apartments, are open daily for an admission charge. Also on the Kronborg grounds, and included in the admission charge, is the *Mercantile and Maritime Museum* (phone: 49-210685). Perhaps the best thing about the castle is the magnificent view of the sound from the ramparts. Occasionally, visiting theatrical groups perform *Hamlet* in the courtyard. The eastern outskirts of Helsingør are not far from the ferry docks (phone: 49-210685).

Fredensborg – About 5 miles (8 km) southwest of Helsingør is Fredensborg Palace, the spring and autumn home of the Danish royal family. The palace is open for tours only in July, but the magnificent Versailles-style grounds and gardens are open to the public year-round. A short walk from the palace is the *Store Kro* inn, a charming place to stop for lunch or the night. Part of it dates from 1723, and over the years the elegant 72-room hotel has been the scene of official receptions and royal weddings. 1-6 Slots-gade (phone: 42-280047).

Louisiana Modern Art Museum – In the town of Humlebaek, 22 miles (about 35 km) north of Copenhagen, in a park overlooking the sea, it has the most important collection of modern Danish art in Europe, as well as works by Andy Warhol and other internationally renowned artists. Don't miss the special temporary exhibits; Dalí, Picasso, Chagall, and other greats have been featured in the past. More exhibition space has been added, including a wing dedicated to graphic arts, so if you haven't visited in a while, it's time to return. Originally the private collection of art patron Knud W. Jensen, the *Louisiana* was opened to the public in 1958. If you like well-displayed modern art and beautiful scenery — another plus is the lovely views afforded by the museum's picture windows — stop en route to Helsingør. Open daily. Admission charge for adults (over age 18). All-inclusive tickets for transportation and museum admission are sold at the Central Station. Take the train to Humlebaek or the No. 388 bus from Klampenborg station. 13 Gammel Strandvej, Humlebaek (phone: 42-190719).

Roskilde – About 19 miles (30 km) west of Copenhagen is an ancient city that was the capital of Denmark until the 15th century. During the 13th century it was one of the premier cities in Europe and, prior to that, it was the site of the first Danish church (a short-lived wooden affair erected by Harald Bluetooth in 980), Roskilde is a treasure trove of Viking artifacts and other items of archaeological interest. Roskilde Cathedral was built in the 1170s by Bishop Absalon on top of Harald's church, and aside from being the first Gothic cathedral in Denmark, it is the burial place of 38 Danish kings and queens. The tour in the cathedral will lead you from one spectacular marble sarcophagus to another. Try to be on hand when the church's St. George and the dragon clock strikes on the hour and the figure moves. The cathedral, or Domkirke, is open daily for a small admission charge; it is closed during religious services. Take the train to Roskilde or bus No. 123 (phone: 42-352700).

A relic of heathen culture, the *Vikingeskibshallen* (Viking Ship Museum) contains five reconstructed Viking ships that were sunk off Roskilde around AD 1000. Aside from this magnificent bit of salvage work, the museum offers detailed descriptions of Viking seafaring techniques and life on board. An English-language film describes the salvage efforts. Using dendrochronology (the study of tree rings), scientists have made the exciting discovery that one of the ships was built in Dublin, a former Viking stronghold. When seeing the vessels, it is somewhat awe inspiring to remember that Vikings sailed across the Atlantic to Greenland and Newfoundland in them. Open daily. Admission charge. At the end of Strandengen. By the water, Roskilde (phone: 42-356555).

Oldtidsbyen – In Lejre, 7 miles (about 11 km) southwest of Roskilde, the Oldtids-byen is a reconstruction of an Iron Age village. Run by the Historical Archaeological Research Center, the Oldtidsbyen was created with grants from the Carlsberg Founda-tion and the government for the purpose of studying Iron Age life. Open daily May through September and October 13–21. Admission charge. Take the train or bus No. 233 to Lejre (phone: 42-380245).

Bornholm – Should the summer be extremely warm or should you just be suffering from a stiff dose of the urban blues, why not follow the example of the Danes and beat a retreat to Bornholm, a beautiful island in the Baltic between Denmark and Sweden. An overnight ferry trip from Copenhagen, Bornholm is the secret summer paradise for the nature-loving Danes and Swedes, and offers over 200 Viking burial mounds, 40 rune stones, and 4 round churches from the early Middle Ages. There also are several spectacular beaches. *Pelle the Conqueror,* the 1989 Oscar winner for best foreign language picture, was filmed here. For more information, write to the Bornholm Tourist Office, 21 Snellemark, DK-3700 Rønne, Denmark (phone: 53-958566; fax: 53-953466; telex: 48174).

■**EXTRA SPECIAL:** About 23 miles (36 km) north of Copenhagen, at Hillerød, lies the remarkable Frederiksborg Castle (not to be confused with Fredensborg Palace, still a royal residence) — a building that many consider to be Europe's most beautiful Renaissance castle. Built on the grounds of an old manor by Christian IV, between 1600 and 1620, most of the structure was gutted by fire in 1859. It was then reconstructed from the original drawings, thanks chiefly to funding from the Carlsberg Foundation. Since 1878, the castle has been the *National Historical Museum,* in which collections of Danish artifacts, including costumes, armor, artwork, and furniture, are arranged in the rooms as though they were still a part of daily life in an earlier time. Particularly noteworthy is the chapel — one of the few rooms untouched by the fire. Since it continues to be used as the chapel of the Danish Orders of Chivalry, its walls are lined with the crests of heads of state, industry, and the arts. The altar is made of silver and ornately carved ebony; the organ (ca. 1600) has its original pipes and still is played. The throne room includes a throne "elevator," which permitted the king to make rather dramatic appearances as he emerged through the floor. Castle grounds and museum are open daily. Admission charge. From Copenhagen, take the *S-train* to Hillerød (phone: 42-260439).

SOURCES AND RESOURCES

TOURIST INFORMATION: For general information, brochures, and maps, contact the Danish National Tourist Office (655 Third Ave., New York, NY 10017; phone: 212-949-2333). In Copenhagen, contact the Danish Tourist Board (22 H. C. Andersen Blvd. at the *Tivoli* entrance by Town Hall; phone: 33-111325). Students may wish to consult the Youth Information Center (13 Rådhusstraede; phone: 33-156518). For assistance in finding accommodations, a room service is at Kiosk P in Copenhagen's main rail station (see "Getting Around," below).

The US Embassy is at 24 Dag Hammarskjöld Allé (phone: 31-423144).

Local Coverage – The Copenhagen Tourist Office should be able to keep you abreast of events of interest. *Copenhagen This Week,* available at hotels and the tourist offices, also is helpful. Unfortunately, there are no English-language newspapers in Copenhagen. If you miss news from home, buy the traveler's daily blessing, the *International Herald Tribune* (about $2.50), or listen to the 8:10 AM English news (weekdays) on Radio Denmark, Program I.

Food – The Danish Tourist Board publishes a brochure, *Restaurants in Copenhagen,* which lists and advertises a number of dining options. Eating places also are listed in *Copenhagen This Week.*

TELEPHONE: The country code for Denmark is 45; the city codes for Copenhagen are 31 through 49.

GETTING AROUND: Airport – The completely remodeled Kastrup International, with its upgraded restaurants, terrific (but pricey) duty-free boutiques, and other attractions, has been christened "Europe's most beautiful airport." It handles both international and domestic flights and is a 20-minute taxi ride from the center of town (an average fare is about $17). Bus service operates every 15 minutes, starting on the hour, between the airport and Copenhagen's main railway station. Fare: 26 kroner (about $4).

Bicycle – If you want your own means of transport, why not follow the example of the Danes and get a bicycle? Nearly all streets have separate lanes for bicycle traffic, and except for the worst winter months, it is often easier to ride a bicycle than drive a car on Copenhagen's narrow streets. A new company, *Bycyclen* (City Bike) provides 5,000 bikes that can be borrowed for a 20-kroner (about $3) refundable deposit from service racks located throughout the city. Bicycles can be rented at *Københavns Cyklebørs* (at the Central Station, 11 Reventlowsgade entrance; phone: 33-140717) or from *Dan Wheel* (3 Colbjørnsensgade; phone: 31-212227); both places charge about $10 a day with a $35 deposit.

Bus – Though Copenhagen is small enough to be seen on foot, the bus system offers an inexpensive and efficient alternative if your feet are weary from the cobblestones. The city bus system (*HT/Copenhagen Transport*) is excellent and is supplemented by electric *S-trains* to the suburbs. Local buses and *S-trains* start running at 5 AM (6 on Sundays), and the last regular departures from downtown are at about 12:30 AM. All buses and railways in Copenhagen and environs operate under a collective fare system. This means within defined zones, tickets are good for a full hour's travel by bus or train with unlimited transfers. Buy your tickets from bus drivers or at train stations. Discount tickets, good for ten trips, can be bought at stations, *HT* ticket offices, or from bus drivers. You stamp your ticket yourself by running it through the automatic machine at the front of the bus, where you board; when taking the train, you will see the machine on the platform. This is important, as an invalid or unstamped ticket can cost you 250 kroner (about $39) or more, and they are checked now and again. For more bus information, call 31-951701; for *S-train* information, 33-141701.

The Copenhagen Card, available for 1, 2, or 3 days, provides unlimited travel by bus or train in the metropolitan area, substantial reductions on fares for crossings to Sweden, and free admission to more than 40 museums. The card can be purchased at hotels, major railway stations, travel agencies, and the tourist information office; it costs 105 kroner (about $16), 170 kroner ($26), or 215 kroner ($33); half price for children under 12.

Canal Tours – A great way to see the city is *from* the water. *Canal Tours Copenhagen* offers four different types of tours, with or without guides, in open-air boats through the city's waterways. The grand guided tour travels through the harbour and canals, passing castles, churches, and other sights. Another tour, without guide, travels directly to the *Little Mermaid* and the Langelinie Promenade. The season lasts from late April to mid-September. Tours cost from 24 kroner (about $3.70) to 36 kroner ($5.60). The ticket office is at Gammel Strand (phone: 33-133105).

Car Rental – To rent a car, you must be at least 20 years old, although some firms set 25 as the age limit. Reputable companies include *Avis* (1 Kampmannsgade; phone:

33-152299), *Hertz* (3 Ved Vesterport; phone: 33-127700), and *InterRent/Europcar* (6 Jernbanegade; phone: 33-116200).

Taxi – Taxis are expensive but fast, and can be hailed on the streets. They are available when the green light on top is on, and the tip is included in the fare. To call a taxi, phone 31-353535.

Train – The city's main railway station is Hovedbanegaarden, on Vesterbrogade (phone: 33-141701, for fares and schedules).

LOCAL SERVICES: Dentist (English-Speaking) – Kirsten and Franklin Laessø (1 Herlev Torv, Herlev; phone: 42-940920); *Tandlaegevagten* (14 Oslo Plads; phone: 31-380251) is a clinic for dental emergencies.

Doctor (English-Speaking) – *Laegevagt* (Doctor's Watch; phone: 32-840041), a taxi radio service, dispatches quick medical assistance in Greater Copenhagen from 4 PM to 8 AM daily.

Dry Cleaner/Tailor – *Schleisner* (12 Vester Voldgade; phone: 33-110037); *Brødrene Andersen,* tailor (7-9 Østergade; phone: 33-151577).

Limousine Service – *Copenhagen Limousine Service,* 9-11 Halmtorvet (phone: 31-311234).

Medical Emergency – Treatment at any hospital emergency room *(skadestue)* is free. *Kommunehospitalet* (5 Østerfarimagsgade; phone: 33-938500); *Rigshospitalet* (9 Blegdamsvej; phone: 31-386633).

Messenger Service – *Radio Codan Bilen,* for deliveries by taxi (phone: 31-353001).

National/International Courier – *World Courier Service,* 7 Kirstinehøy (phone: 31-515031).

Pharmacy – *Steno Apotek,* 6C Vesterbrogade (phone: 33-148266).

Photocopies – *Xerox Copy Center* (5 Trommesalen; phone: 31-314400); there's also a copy center in the Central Station (11 Reventlowsgade).

Post Office – The main post office (37 Tietgensgade; phone: 33-932510) and the central post office (33 Købmagergade; phone: 33-321212) are open from 9 AM to 6 PM weekdays and until 1 PM Saturdays. For information about both branches, call 33-146298. There's also a branch in Central Station, which is open even later and on Sundays.

Secretary/Stenographer (English-Speaking) – *A-1 Service,* 3 Rebaek Søpark (phone: 31-474547 or 31-474537).

Translator – *Translatør-Centret,* 1 Vingelodden (phone: 35-820144).

Other – Tuxedo rental: *Amorin,* 45 Vesterbrogade (phone: 31-212021 or 31-212158).

SPECIAL EVENTS: The advent of spring in Copenhagen is heralded by the opening of *Bakken,* Scandinavia's oldest (500 years old) festive amusement park in the Deer Park north of Copenhagen (late March) and *Tivoli* in late April (see *Special Places).* The century-old *Benneweis Circus* (8 Jernbanegade; phone: 33-142192), begins its season in late April and ends in mid-September. Each June, Copenhagen celebrates *Carnival* with costumes, music, and parades. Then there's the swinging *Copenhagen Jazz Festival* in midsummer.

MUSEUMS: In addition to those mentioned in *Special Places,* Copenhagen boasts a number of other well-organized museums, the most notable of which are the following:

Børsen (Stock Exchange) – Closed to the public, but definitely one of Copenhagen's most striking buildings, it is more than the dramatic Danish adaptation of Dutch Renaissance that catches the eye: What initially appears to be an intricately interwoven steeple is actually a wooden spire comprised of four brilliantly entwined golden dragons' tails. Check the base of the spire for the dragons' heads and bodies; the tangled tails point heavenward. Børsgade.

Det Danske Filmmuseum (Danish Film Museum) – A comprehensive archive of films and related books. Closed Wednesdays and weekends. No admission charge. 4 Store Søndervoldstraede (phone: 31-576500).

Geologisk Museum (Geological Museum) – Meteorites, fossils, and minerals. Closed Mondays. No admission charge. 5-7 Oster Voldgade (phone: 33-135001).

Københavns Bymuseum og Søren Kierkegaard-Samlingen (Copenhagen's City Museum and the Søren Kierkegaard Collection) – The city's 800 years in pictures and mementos; also Søren Kierkegaard curios. Closed Mondays. No admission charge. 59 Vesterbrogade (phone: 31-210772).

Legetøjsmuseet (Toy Museum) – Toys from generations ago. Closed Fridays. Admission charge. 13 Valkendorfsgade (phone: 33-141009).

Nationalmuseet (National Museum) – Historical and ethnographical collections, from prehistory up to the turn of the century, including Viking exhibits. Closed Mondays. No admission charge. 12 Frederiksholms Kanal (phone: 33-134411).

Statens Museum for Kunst (Royal Museum of Fine Arts) – Danish and European works of art, including a Matisse collection. Out front, a group of funny-figured statues is known locally as the "Muppet Show" (its formal name is the *Human Wall*). Closed Mondays. No admission charge. Sølvgade at Oster Voldgade (phone: 33-912126).

Zoologisk Museum (Zoological Museum) – Animal life explained through exhibitions, models, and dioramas. Closed Mondays. No admission charge. 15 Universitetsparken (phone: 31-354111).

SHOPPING: With all its perambulating pedways, Copenhagen is ideal for the consumer. Keep in mind that the 22% sales tax in Denmark is included in the price. To obtain a partial refund of this tax, have the goods delivered to you at the airport, or present the sales slips and article(s) at the customs counter there for the 16.5% refund. If you have the items shipped directly to the US, make a note of the store's name and address, keep your receipt, and insure all goods against damage.

Denmark is world famous for beautifully designed wares for the home — furniture, of course; sterling silver by *Georg Jensen* and others; and porcelain by *Bing & Grøndahl* and *Royal Copenhagen.* Also, Copenhagen is northern Europe's main fur trading center. It might be wise to check the prices of these items before you leave home, as savings may not be substantial in Denmark.

Another Danish claim to fame is pastry, though in Denmark the doughy, sticky pastry we know as danish bears little resemblance to the crispy, buttery concoctions Danes call *wienerbrod* (Vienna bread). Follow your taste buds into the nearest bake shop for a whiff of those *kanelstaenger, snegle, tebirkes, borgmesterstaenger,* and their caloric ilk. In the core of the old town, Copenhagen's oldest active bakery, *Hos Kurt Lorenz* (29 Skt. Pedersstr.; phone: 33-111129) — which traces its owner-family history back to 1652 — has them all. Also on the culinary front, at *J. Chr. Andersen's Eftf.* (32 Købmagergade; phone: 33-121345) you'll find from 450 to 500 different kinds of cheese, many of them homemade — or at least home-aged. If you fancy chocolate or Gran Marnier cheese, this is the place. Purchases can be vacuum-packed for the trip home.

You might wish to stroll down Strøget, the most famous of the city's shopping streets, three-quarters of a mile long. Strøget is not one but actually five connecting streets, none of them named Strøget (see *Special Places*). This stretch abounds in department stores and specialty shops. And take a look at the side streets as well.

Other pedestrian streets are Fiolstraede and Købmagergade in the old Latin Quarter, once the student quarter and now more cosmopolitan, the place to go for antiques and rare books as well as boutiques and specialty shops.

Be sure to investigate the extension of Pistolstraede, just off the Ostergade section of Strøget. It has a charming little arcade with a Danish pastry shop and other food stores, and branches of such fashion legends as *Chanel* and *Louis Vuitton*. Don't miss the shopping, dining, and entertainment complex called *Scala* (see *Special Places*), across the street from *Tivoli*. For folks who like their shopping a lot less formal, Copenhagen boasts a very appealing, low-pressure flea market that functions most Saturdays (in good weather) at the Israel Plads (at Romersgade). All shops listed below accept major credit cards.

A. C. Bang – A fine place for furs. 27 Ostergade.

Bang and Olufsen – Superb and superbly designed TV sets and sound equipment. 3 Ostergade (phone: 33-150422) and in the *Hotel Scandinavia*, 70 Amager Blvd. (phone: 31-574520).

A. Michelsen – High-quality silver. 40 Ostergade (phone: 33-114080).

Anthon Berg – Irresistible Danish chocolates, many filled with marzipan or liqueurs. 1 Ostergade (phone: 33-111564).

Bing & Grøndahl – World-famous porcelain. 4 Amagertorv (phone: 33-122686).

Birger Christensen – Perhaps the best furrier in Scandinavia. 38 Ostergade (phone: 31-115555).

Bjørn Wiinblads Hus – Prints, porcelain, and decorations by Denmark's distinctive contemporary artist. 11 Ny Ostergade (phone: 33-151245).

Boghallen – For English-language paperbacks and the latest hardcovers. Also Denmark's largest selection of travel books. 37 Rådhuspladsen (phone: 33-118511).

Georg Jensen Silver – Needs no introduction. 40 Ostergade (phone: 33-114080).

Hans Hansen Sølv **(Silver)** – Similar quality and lower prices than *Georg Jensen*, plus more contemporary designs. 16 Amagertorv (phone: 33-156067).

Illum's – A large, popular department store with selections of all typical Danish wares; also a fine restaurant. Don't miss the basement food hall selling freshly baked breads, pastries, seafood, and deli specialties. 52 Ostergade (phone: 33-144002).

Illums Bolighus – World-renowned furnishings center of modern design. 10 Amagertorv (phone: 33-141941).

In Circus – A consortium of a dozen-plus Danish designers provide the trendiest of ready-to-wear and costume jewelry. 7 Hyskenstraede (phone: 33-913392).

Den Kongelige Porcelainsfabrik – The Royal Copenhagen Porcelain Factory is the maker of perhaps the most exquisite (and expensive) porcelain — especially the Flora Danica pattern. Tours of the factory are available in English. 6 Amagertorv (phone: 33-137181).

Magasin du Nord – The city's largest, oldest, and best-known department store; every variety of Danish merchandise is well displayed. 13 Kongens Nytorv (phone: 33-114433).

Paustian House – Marvelously modern furniture and related accoutrements by such renowned Scandinavian designer/architects as Anders Hermansen, Philippe Starck, and Alvar Aalto. The prize-winning building was designed by Danish architect Joern Utzon (who designed the *Sydney Opera House*). Check US prices before purchasing. On Copenhagen's northernmost harborfront, 2 Kalkbraenderiløbskaj; take the *S-train* east to Nordhavn and walk (phone: 31-184511)).

Rosenthal Studio Haus A/S – Elegant porcelain. 21 Frederiksberggade (phone: 33-142101).

 SPORTS AND FITNESS: Copenhagen does not have the variety of sports facilities found in many American cities, but the few sports popular in Denmark are *very* popular. Call the *Idraettens Hus* (Sports House) for information on most sports organizations (phone: 42-455555).

Bicycle Racing – Due to the Danish mania for bicycles, this is one of Denmark's biggest international sports. *Ordrup Cykelbane* is open 1 day a week; contact *Brøndby Stadion* for information (phone: 42-455800); *Brannersvej* and *Charlottenlund* are open from May to September, usually Tuesdays and Sundays. In addition, every year around the last week in January the exciting *Copenhagen Six-Day International Cycle Race* is held.

Fitness Centers – *Form & Figur* (21 Amagertorv; phone: 33-143202) accepts non-members on a temporary basis (3-month minimum), as do *Copenhagen Squash Club,* Vestersøhus (58-60 Vestersøgade; phone: 33-118638), and *Københavns Bold-klub* — a tennis club — (147 Peter Bangsvej; phone: 31-714180). Also check the fitness center at *Scala* (2 Axeltorv; phone: 33-151215).

Horse Racing – Not many horses in Denmark, but the Danes enjoy gambling. Head to *Klampenborg Galopbane* (Klampenborgvej, Klampenborg; phone: 31-637898). Races are on Saturdays between mid-April and mid-December, except in July when they are on Tuesdays.

Jogging – The parks, Kongens Have and Faelledparken, as well as the Central Lakes (Søerne), are all good spots, 10 minutes from Town Hall Square.

Soccer – Known in Denmark as *fodbold,* there are matches every weekend from April to June and August to November. The Danish national team also plays *World Cup* matches in Copenhagen at Idraetsparken, Osterbro.

Swimming – The coast north of Copenhagen has many beaches, and the water is relatively warm in the latter part of the summer. In the northern suburb of Klampenborg, Bellevue Strandpark, a city beach, is very popular. South of Copenhagen, Køge Bay Strandpark is an area of beaches, marinas, and dunes. Topless, if not nude, bathing is the norm in Denmark, especially for the young. There are also a number of excellent Olympic-size public pools, both indoor and outdoor. Between May 15 and August 31, try Bavnehøj Friluftsbad (90 Enghavevej; phone: 31-214900). For year-round indoor swimming, try Kildeskovshallen (25 Adolfsvej, Gentofte; phone: 31-682822).

THEATER: Because the arts in Denmark are government subsidized, tickets are normally inexpensive. The famous *Det Kongelige Teater* (Royal Theater) at Kongens Nytorv is worth a visit. The *Danish National Theater* and national opera company perform here, in Danish, as does the *Royal Danish Ballet,* one of the world's foremost dance companies. There are two stages: the Old Stage (Gamle Scene) and the New Stage (Nye Scene). The season at *Det Kongelige Teater* is being extended this year; for information on exact dates and for all bookings, contact the tourist office or box office (phone: 33-141002). In the summer there are lighter diversions, like cabarets at *Tivoli,* beer hall entertainment at *Bakken,* and international acts at the *Benneweis Circus.* The *Mermaid Theater* (27 Skt. Pedersstr.; phone: 33-114303) is Scandinavia's only permanent English-language stage, presenting Scandinavian plays in summer and British and American works in winter. A cabaret in the style of an old English musical is presented during *Christmastime.*

MUSIC: Besides opera at the *Royal Theater* (see above) there are classical music concerts, performed by the *Radio Symphony Orchestra* in *Radio House Concert Hall* and *Zealand Symphony Hall* in *Tivoli.* Students of the Royal Danish Academy of Music give regular concerts, usually free, at 1 Niels Brocksgade. During the winter season there also are modern music concerts at *Ny Carlsberg Glyptotek* and *Louisiana Museum* (see *Special Places*). Excellent jazz and big-name guest stars often are available at *Montmartre,* the northern European jazz capital (41 Nørregade; phone: 33-136966). The world's best rock bands often give extraordinary performances in Copenhagen, as the audiences tend to be very responsive, at *Falkonér Teatret* (9 Falkonér Allé; phone: 31-198001). If you want to make bookings for musical or theatrical events and you can't make it to the theater, contact the ticket agent *Saga Ticket Center* (23 Vesterbrogade; phone: 31-238800).

NIGHTCLUBS AND NIGHTLIFE: Popular traditional nightspots with food, live music, and dancing are the *Scandinavia* hotel's *After 8* (70 Amager Blvd.; phone: 33-112324), and *Nautilus* (24-28 Toldbodgade; phone: 33-118282), in the *Copenhagen Admiral* hotel. *La Brasserie* (*Hotel d'Angleterre*, 34 Kongens Nytorv; phone: 33-320122), has a trendy bar and is the spot to see and be seen.

More informal are *Den Røde Pimpernel* (7 Hans Christian Andersen Blvd.; phone: 33-122032), and the lively *HongKong* (7 Nyhavn; phone: 33-129272). If you like discotheques, there are several alternatives, but nothing that measures up to New York's finest. Most of them require specific dress, and their pretensions of exclusivity often extend to asking you to buy a phony membership card at the door. The best of the lot are *Annabel's* (16 Lille Kongensgade; phone: 33-112020) and *On the Rox,* (12-14 Pilestraede; phone: 33-123912). Visitors interested in risking a few kroner can try their luck out at the new *Casino Copenhagen* in the *Scandinaire* hotel. There's a 40 kroner (about $6) entrance fee. Jacket and tie required for men. Open daily at 4 PM.

The music cafés are a much better deal, and are much friendlier. The best are, in addition to the aforementioned *Montmartre, New Daddy's Dance Hall* for rock and punk (5 Axeltorv; phone: 33-114679), and *La Fontaine* (11 Kompagnistraede; phone: 33-116098). This place specializes in jazz, but is perhaps best known for being the place *everyone* goes to for morning coffee after a night on the town. Another late-night bar-restaurant-café, just behind the *Royal Theater,* is *Brønnum* (Kongens Nytorv; phone: 33-930365), open from late afternoon to 5 AM. For folk music and a younger crowd, try *Vognhjulet* (67 Thorsgade; phone: 31-831570).

BEST IN TOWN

CHECKING IN: There are a few large luxury hotels in Copenhagen, and not only are they expensive, but too often the rooms are on the small side with service that can only be described as indifferent. When booking rooms, check whether you will have a shower or a bath and whether breakfast is included. Also, look for weekend, off-season discounts. Expect to pay $250 or more for a double in those hotels we classify as very expensive; $180 to $245 at expensive; 100 to $175, moderate; and under $100 in the inexpensive range. All rates include tax and, unless otherwise indicated, breakfast (usually a generous buffet). Now that Copenhagen has several new hotels the days of severe room shortages during peak summer season may be over, but it is still wise to book in advance, if possible. If you arrive without reservations, you'll fare better by consulting the accommodations service at Kiosk P in the central rail station than by contacting hotels on your own. The service charges a nominal fee, but it often can get you special room rates. Also, be forewarned that many of the less-expensive establishments are closed during the *Christmas-New Year's* holidays. All telephone numbers are in the 33 through 49 city codes unless otherwise indicated.

d'Angleterre – Built in 1775, this 126-room hostelry is the oldest and still the most venerable in town. The old-fashioned paneled rooms and the location near Nyhavn give something of the sensation of being on an old ocean liner — albeit one that could use better housekeeping service. There's a good, reasonably priced French restaurant, an "in" eatery, *La Brasserie* (see *Eating Out*), and a bar called *The Bar.* Breakfast is not included in rates. Business facilities include 24-hour room service, meeting rooms for up to 250, English-speaking concierge, foreign currency exchange, secretarial services in English, audiovisual equipment, photocopiers, and cable television news. 34 Kongens Nytorv (phone: 33-120095; fax: 33-121118). Very expensive.

SAS Royal – Primarily a businessperson's hotel, it has little charm (the rooms are rather generic), but what this high-rise lacks in personality it makes up for in special facilities for the business traveler. There is also a café, bistro, and formal restaurant, plus shops, and the *Fellini* nightclub. Request a room with a view of the *Tivoli* lights. Business facilities include 24-hour room service, meeting rooms for up to 200, concierge, audiovisual equipment, and express checkout. 1 Hammerichsgade (phone: 33-141412; or in the US, 800-4UTELL; fax: 33-141421; telex: 27155). Very expensive.

Scandinavia – This 542-room modern skyscraper run by *SAS* is the largest in town. On the 25th floor is the *Top of Town* restaurant, which affords spectacular views of the city, while downstairs is *After 8*. Gambling guests might enjoy the new *Casino Copenhagen*. Like the *Sheraton Copenhagen,* the hotel caters basically to the needs and tastes of businesspeople on the move. Business facilities include 24-hour room service, meeting rooms for up to 1,200, English-speaking concierge, secretarial services in English, audiovisual equipment, photocopiers, computers, cable television news, translation services, and express checkout. 70 Amager Blvd. (phone: 33-112324; fax: 31-570193). Very expensive.

Sheraton Copenhagen – An alternative to the above, with 470 rooms, a pleasant view of the city, and the *King's Court Bar.* Business facilities include 24-hour room service, meeting rooms for up to 1,200, English-speaking concierge, secretarial services in English, audiovisual equipment, photocopiers, cable television news, and translation services. 6 Vester Søgade (phone: 33-143535; fax: 33-321223). Very expensive.

Grand – This fully renovated, classic 142-room hotel is conveniently located a few blocks from *Tivoli* and Rådhuspladsen, and is right near the central railway station. Well-appointed rooms, a French-inspired sidewalk café, and an elegant Danish restaurant are among its many features. Business facilities include meeting rooms for up to 40, English-speaking concierge, and cable television news. 9 Vesterbrogade (phone: 31-313600; fax: 31-313350). Very expensive to expensive.

Palace – This turn-of-the-century hotel, with a newly renovated façade, is right where the action is — overlooking Copenhagen's central Town Hall Square, and only a 2-minute walk to *Tivoli.* The 159 rooms are comfortably furnished, and there is a popular Danish buffet lunch or dinner. 57 Rådhuspladsen (phone: 33-144050; fax: 33-145279). Very expensive to expensive.

Phoenix – Set in a graceful 17th-century building, this luxurious new property offers 212 well-appointed rooms, including 3 suites with Jacuzzis and 52 executive rooms with their own fax machines, marble baths, and gold-plated fixtures. The hotel also offers a sauna and indoor pool (a rarity in Copenhagen). Along with a first class international restaurant, there is a traditional Danish eatery, British pub, and a bar. Breakfast is not included in the rates. Business facilities include 24-hour room service, meeting rooms for up to 120, English-speaking concierge, audiovisual equipment, photocopiers, cable television news, and express checkout. 37 Bredgade (phone: 33-330033; fax: 33-339833; telex: 40068). Very expensive to expensive.

Plaza – If finely wrought antique furnishings, mahogany paneling, and luxurious comfort appeal to you, consider reserving one of the 96 rooms at this Art Nouveau monument. The unusually high quality of accoutrements and service make it a favorite of famous visiting artists. You will need to reserve well ahead of your intended arrival. The wood-paneled *Library Bar* is a cozy spot for a drink, and the *Alexander Nevski* is the only Russian restaurant in town (see *Eating Out*). Business facilities include room service from 7 AM to 11 PM, meeting rooms for up to 60, English-speaking concierge, audiovisual equipment, photocopiers, and cable television news. 4 Bernstorffsgade (phone: 33-149262; fax: 33-939362; telex: 15330). Very expensive to expensive.

Kong Frederik – In the heart of town, just a stone's throw from *Tivoli* and Town Hall, are 110 rooms in a charmingly renovated hotel. Color TV sets, videos, and hair dryers are among the amenities. The tiled restaurant is a good (and popular) spot for lunch or dinner, as is the *Queen's Pub*. 25 Vester Voldgade (phone: 33-125902; fax: 33-935901). Expensive.

Neptun – Formerly a sailor's hostel, this 66-room inn has been restored to offer first class amenities while retaining its 130-year-old charm. In a lovely section of Nyhavn, near Kongens Nytorv. 18 Sankt Annae Plads (phone: 33-138900; fax: 33-141250). Expensive to moderate.

Opera – Located just behind the *Royal Theater,* this Old World hotel was formerly an apartment building. The 87 rooms have been redecorated, but many are small, so request a suite if spacious accommodations are a priority. The *Opera Bar* off the lobby has comfortable red leather chairs and a gentlemen's club atmosphere, and there is a good Danish-French restaurant. Business facilities include meeting rooms for up to 30, audiovisual equipment, photocopiers, and cable television news. 15 Tordenskjoldsgade (phone: 33-121519; fax: 33-321282; telex: 15812). Expensive to moderate.

Altea Hotel Scala – Operated by the French Pullman chain, this sleek, new property has 134 bright, modern rooms with convenient extras such as trouser presses and hair dryers. There's also a breakfast room, café, and bar. Business facilities include meeting rooms for up to 70, audiovisual equipment, photocopiers, and cable television news. The property is contributing to the gentrification of the former pornography district near the Central Station. 13 Colbjørnsensgade (phone: 31-221100 or in the US, 800-44UTELL; fax: 31-222199; telex: 21100). Moderate.

Avenue – A 68-room property in western Copenhagen, converted from a 4-story residential building. Closed between December 23 and January 1. 29 Aboulevarden (phone: 31-373111; fax: 31-373486). Moderate.

Copenhagen Admiral – In an old corn warehouse on the waterfront near the *d'Angleterre* (and a good deal less expensive), it has 366 modern rooms, a sauna, bar, restaurant, and the congenial *Nautilus* nightclub downstairs. Business facilities include room service for breakfast, meeting rooms for up to 230, English-speaking concierge, audiovisual equipment, photocopiers, and cable television news. Breakfast is not included in the rates. 24 Toldbodgade (phone: 33-118282 or 800-223-9868 in the US; fax: 33-325542). Moderate.

Osterport – Though this long, low hotel alongside the railroad tracks looks rather odd, it provides comfortable accommodations and a good *smørrebrød* lunch. Business facilities include meeting rooms for up to 10, English-speaking concierge, photocopiers, and cable television news. 5 Oslo Plads (phone: 33-112266; fax: 33-122555). Moderate.

Absalon – Named for the city's founder, this is a clean hotel on the harbor for those on a limited budget. The 260 rooms, most with private bath, rent for a wide variety of prices. 19 Helgolandsgade (phone: 31-242211; fax: 31-243411). Moderate to inexpensive.

Cosmopole – Just a block south of *Tivoli,* with 245 beds and a wide variety of rooms and rates, this spot is a particularly good bargain for the single traveler. 11 Colbjørnsensgade (phone: 31-213333; fax: 31-313399). Moderate to inexpensive.

Ibsens – Here is a decent alternative to the *Absalon* (above), a 46-room hotel on a quiet side street near the Botanical Gardens. 23 Vendersgade (phone: 33-131913; fax: 33-131916). Moderate to inexpensive.

Viking – An honorable old salt's hotel near Nyhavn, this 91-room property provides an address in the heart of the city's harbor section. 65 Bredgade (phone: 33-124550; fax: 33-124618). Moderate to inexpensive.

EATING OUT: The Danes enjoy good food as well as good beer and "snaps" (aquavit), and there are a number of classy old restaurants with capital continental cuisine — especially French. There also are many small taverns/inns, or *kro,* with Danish specialties like open-face sandwiches or *smørrebrød.* Increasingly popular are the little croissant shops that are popping up all over the city. An inexpensive croissant sandwich at lunch is a good way to stretch the budget in order to afford a splurge at dinner.

A Dane will never refuse a snaps with herring — and there are plenty of other reasons to indulge as well. Snaps usually is imbibed icy cold, by the glass or the bottle, and is often chased by one of the many wonderful Danish beers. The best snaps are Aalborg's Jubileum and Harald Jensen.

The proper way to toast is to raise your glass to eye level, say *"skål,"* and look your companions in the eye. Toss back the entire shot — if you're hardy enough — and, before returning the glass to the table, hold it at eye level again. Aquavit also may be drunk in the form of "punch" (heated and sweetened with a sugar cube) or in coffee.

Reservations usually are not a problem, but it always is wise to call. Be advised that liquor is heavily taxed and likely to be about twice as expensive as at home — your bill in general may seem a bit high, but remember that the 15% service charge is included in the price. Danes seldom leave any additional amount unless service is really superb. Expect to pay at least $90 to $100 for a meal for two at a restaurant in our expensive category; $60 to $85 in the moderate range; and $40 to $55 in any restaurant listed as inexpensive. Prices don't include wine and drinks, which easily can double the tab. All restaurants listed below accept major credit cards. All telephone numbers are in the 31 through 49 city codes, unless otherwise indicated.

Kong Hans – Under the vaulted, whitewashed ceiling of a 14th-century wine cellar is possibly the best and most elegant restaurant in town. Young chef Daniel Letz proudly presides over silky pickled or smoked salmon (smoked right on the premises), stuffed *langoustes, côte de boeuf,* and a selection of splendid desserts. The atmosphere is sophisticated, but Letz makes sure that everyone feels relaxed and comfortable. Superb service. Dinner only. Closed Sundays and holidays, and July. Reservations necessary. 6 Vingaards (phone: 33-116868). Very expensive.

Alexander Nevski – The only Russian dining establishment in town, it's pricey, but the quality of the food is excellent. In a dark, plush dining room, guests can savor caviar with delicate *blinis* and other tsarian specialties. There's also a selection of 20 vodkas, as well as tea served from a samovar. Save room for one of the incredibly rich desserts made with fresh berries. Open daily. Reservations necessary. In the *Plaza Hotel,* 4 Bernstorffsgade (phone: 33-149262). Expensive.

Belle Terrasse – The most elegant restaurant in *Tivoli.* Lush gardens, live music, very romantic ambience. An experience, though an expensive one. Closed September through April. Reservations advised. *Tivoli* (phone: 33-121136). Expensive.

Egoisten – A traditional restaurant with an enduring reputation for its haute cuisine. Closed weekends. Reservations advised. 12 Hovedvagtsg. (phone: 33-127971). Expensive.

Els – The murals date from the mid-19th century, when the restaurant was a coffeehouse. The menu is nouvelle-inspired Danish and French. Closed December 24, 25, and 31, and January 1. Reservations necessary. 3 Store Strandstraede (phone: 33-141341). Expensive.

Les Etoiles et une Rose – An exciting addition to the Copenhagen dining scene, it specializes in lovingly prepared fish and game. Five- and seven-course tasting menus change daily, while the à la carte list varies with the seasons. Closed Saturdays for lunch and Sundays. Reservations advised. 43 Dronningens Tvaergade (phone: 33-150554). Expensive.

Kommandanten – A 17th-century house, consisting of several enchanting doll-size rooms painted in copen blue, is the setting for classic dining. Though the menu is not in English, a friendly waiter will happily translate the chef's offerings: possibly a frothy, hot lobster soup with sorrel and a perfectly grilled piece of salmon (part of a three-course "fish menu"), or a six-course menu that will give you a taste of the best of old and new Danish cooking. Open for lunch and dinner. Closed Sundays. Reservations necessary. 7 Ny Adelgade (phone: 33-120990). Expensive.

Langelinie Pavillonen – In the harbor north of Amalienborg Castle, with a magnificent view of the waterfront. Music, dancing . . . and the *Little Mermaid*. The food is overpriced and ordinary, but worth it for the setting. There's dancing on Fridays and Saturdays. Open daily for dinner; closed December 22 through 31; no music on Sundays. Reservations necessary. Langelinie (phone: 33-121214). Expensive.

Saison – Just a few miles north of the city in the village of Skovshoved is this fine eatery serving freshly caught fish and seafood treats such as oysters in parsley bouillon, and turbot and forest mushrooms served with potatoes. Closed Sundays. Reservations advised. 267 Strandvejen (phone: 31-640028). Expensive.

Copenhagen Corner – Ask for a window table for a good view of pedestrian traffic past Rådhuspladsen (City Hall Square). Traditional Danish dishes are served in this pleasant spot, which always is packed. Closed December 24 and 25 and January 1. Reservations advised for dinner. Rådhuspladsen (phone: 33-914545). Expensive to moderate.

La Brasserie – The *d'Angleterre* hotel's trendy, informal eatery has a varied menu, including enticing hot and cold hors d'oeuvres, "quick meals," and complete dinners of fish, pheasant, and pork tenderloin. It also has a bar that hops with young Danes. Closed Sundays. Reservations unnecessary. 34 Kongens Nytorv (phone: 33-320122). Moderate.

Café Grønnegade – A variety of nooks and crannies in the basement and ground floor of a 305-year-old townhouse is the setting for the informal and friendly "Greenstreet Café." Piping hot onion soup and the freshest of local fish and vegetables are fine choices. Open daily for dinner only. Reservations unnecessary. 39 Grønnegade (phone: 33-933133). Moderate.

Dahua – Chinese food in Copenhagen is not bad, and this place is among the best. Closed *Christmas Eve*. Reservations unnecessary. 8 Gammel Torv (phone: 33-157855). Moderate.

Den Gyldne Fortun – This spot serves *smørrebrød* for lunch only and is popular with big groups (a minimum of 20 people is required). Open daily. Reservations necessary for smorgasbord. 18 Ved Stranden (phone: 33-122011). Moderate.

Krogs – Across the canal from Christiansborg, it serves the best seafood in Copenhagen. The bouillabaisse is an excellent choice, but is rather pricey. Closed Sundays and from December 20–January 7. Reservations advised. 38 Gammel Strand (phone: 33-158915). Moderate.

Påfuglen – If you want to dine in *Tivoli* for more reasonable rates, try this family-style place. Closed September to May. Reservations unnecessary. *Tivoli* (phone: 33-129540). Moderate.

Slotskaelderen – Known locally as *Gitte Kik* (the name of the owner and granddaughter of the founder) and favored by politicians and businessmen, this basement spot is the ideal place to sample true *smørrebrød*. An ample selection of cold, open-face sandwiches (try the roast beef topped with soft fried onions), a variety of herring, and several hot dishes are among the choices, along with good Danish beer. Lunch only. Closed Sundays. Reservations unnecessary. 4 Fortunstraede (phone: 33-111537). Moderate.

Wessels Kro – Want to partake of the famous Danish *store kolde bord* ("the great cold table")? There's a wide assortment of Danish hams and other cold cuts at this quaint old tavern. Closed *New Year's Eve.* Reservations unnecessary. 7 Svaertegade (phone: 33-126793). Moderate.

Peder Oxe – This popular meeting place has a little something for everybody's tastes, but the specialties are meat dishes and serve-yourself salads. A bottle of house wine is provided at every table, and guests are charged according to the amount they drink. It's very "in," so book ahead. Closed *Christmas Eve.* 11 Gråbrødre Torv (phone: 33-110077). Moderate to inexpensive.

Greens – Formerly *Cranks,* it offers a vegetarian buffet that even a dyed-in-the-wool carnivore will enjoy. Popular dishes include eggplant parmesan and meatless moussaka. Closed Sundays and major holidays. (A take-out shop is open weekdays only.) No reservations. 12-14 Grønnegade, Pistolstr. (phone: 33-151690). Inexpensive.

Mongolian Barbecue – Among the best in the latest crop of its kind, this dining spot offers all you can eat from a choice of lamb, chicken, pork, and beef, for a fixed price. Open for dinner only; closed *Christmas.* Reservations unnecessary. Downstairs at 66 St. Kongensgade (phone: 33-146466). Inexpensive.

Parnas – A crazy, dark, and smoky place with a piano bar, it's a friendly artists' haven otherwise. Hash with béarnaise sauce is a specialty. Open from noon until 3 AM; closed Sundays, *Christmas Eve,* and *New Year's Eve.* No reservations. 16 Lille Kongensgade (phone: 33-114910). Inexpensive.

DUBLIN

Dublin is a friendly city steeped in a history sometimes splendid, and often troubled; a city of wide Georgian streets, elegant squares, and magnificent doorways; of ancient churches and cathedrals that thrust their hallowed spires and towers against the skyline; of memorable sunsets that bathe the 18th-century red brick façades in a fiery glow, turning windows into sheets of gold; a city where the English language acquires a special dimension and where dark, creamy-headed Guinness stout flows abundantly in companionable pubs. There is no other European capital like this one, set like a jewel in the sweep of Dublin Bay. Behind, to the south, rise the Dublin hills and the Wicklow Mountains. Through the city the River Liffey — James Joyce's Anna Livia Plurabelle — wends its leisurely way to the sea, spanned as it passes through Dublin by 11 bridges.

Once there was only one bridge. Indeed, it was not so much a bridge as a mere ford in the river, and it stood approximately where the Father Matthew Bridge stands today. It was built by the first Celtic inhabitants of what is now Dublin. When they came here, we cannot be sure; what is certain is that by AD 140 they were well established on this site. The Celts themselves probably referred to the spot by a name that endures to this day — the official Gaelic *Baile Atha Cliath* (town of the ford of the hurdles).

It was not, however, until the coming of the Vikings in the 9th century that Dublin as we now know it began to take shape. The old Celtic settlement had at no time been a place of national importance; its only significance was as a ford of the Liffey en route to the ancient royal capital of Tara. In AD 837, 65 Viking longboats sailed into Dublin Harbor and up the mouth of the River Liffey. These early Viking settlers established themselves a little downstream from the old Celtic settlement, on a spot where the Poddle, which now flows underground, entered the Liffey, causing it to form a dark pool, or *dubh linn*. The Vikings referred to their settlement by these two Gaelic words, and the anglicized version became the city's modern English name. Dublin rapidly became the focal point of the Viking invasion of Ireland. Then, as the Vikings began to see that trading was ultimately more profitable than plunder, and as they began to settle and intermarry in their new homeland, Dublin became a major center for their extensive European trade. Not long after their arrival, the Vikings were converted to Christianity and in 1034 erected a cathedral, which became the nucleus of modern Christ Church. The cathedral stood in the center of Viking Dublin and allows us to place the ancient city accurately.

Just over 3 centuries after the coming of the Vikings, new invaders swept Ireland. In 1169 the first contingent of Normans landed on the beach of Bannow, in County Wexford. Two years later, the powerful Baron Richard Gilbert de Clare, otherwise known as Strongbow, arrived at the gates of Dublin with 1,000 men. The city was taken by storm; its Viking king and

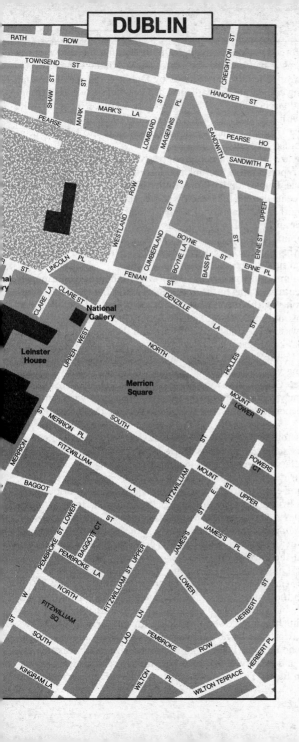

inhabitants were forced to flee. Thereafter Dublin became the center of the English conquest, as it had become the center of the Viking conquest.

Not long afterward, the city was fortified by Dublin Castle, built not far from the old Viking cathedral. The cathedral had been taken over by Strongbow and a new and larger edifice had been erected in its place. The city walls were built along with the castle. (Their remains can be seen at St. Audeon's Arch, below Christ Church.) Thus medieval Dublin began to take shape, a small area surrounded by walls.

In shape and in size Dublin did not alter greatly until the arrival of a new viceroy, or king's representative, in 1662 heralded the city's rise to definitive national importance. Dublin, under James Butler, Duke of Ormonde, became and remained the central arena for Ireland's social, political, and cultural life.

Butler, believing that the stability of a government should be reflected in public works, began municipal improvements almost immediately. The solitary, medieval Dublin Bridge was joined by four new bridges across the river; Phoenix Park (to this day the largest enclosed urban park in the world) was walled; and several new streets were built.

While Dublin's importance as a city and as a seaport increased enormously in the late 17th century, it was in the 18th century that the city truly flourished, becoming one of the most vibrant and sparkling capitals in all of Europe. The strong movement toward parliamentary independence that took place at this time was reflected in the construction of the splendid Parliament House (now the Bank of Ireland in College Green). Begun in 1729, it was the first in a series of great public buildings built during this time. In addition, extensive rebuilding was carried out on Dublin Castle and Trinity College, and the Wide Streets Commission was set up. It was as if the city were proudly preparing for the new position of importance it would occupy when, in 1782, parliamentary independence was conceded to Ireland by the British Parliament.

Great buildings followed one another in dizzying succession — Leinster House, the Royal Exchange, the Mansion House, the Four Courts, the Custom House. Irish classical architecture, in all its gravity, beauty, and balance, reached full maturity. It flowered in public buildings and private houses, spacious squares and elegant streets. This was Georgian Dublin (various King Georges sat on the British throne in the period): the Dublin of Henry Grattan, Jonathan Swift, David Garrick, Peg Woffington, Oliver Goldsmith, Bishop Berkeley, and Edmund Burke. Handel himself conducted the world première of his "Messiah" in this glittering city, whose center was the area between Dublin Castle and the Parliament House.

Architecturally, Dublin reached its zenith in the 18th century. Later, its brilliance would be embodied in the written word rather than in stone. In the 19th century, with the dismantling of the Parliament, Dublin's political and social life suffered a blow from which it was not to recover easily. By contrast, the city's literary life began to flower in the late 19th and early 20th centuries with the birth of two great literary movements — the Irish literary renaissance and the Gaelic League. The two movements revived and romanticized the early legends and history of Ireland. The literary renaissance — spearheaded by William Butler Yeats, Lady Augusta Gregory, Douglas Hyde, and

John Millington Synge, to name but a few — placed a splendid and indelible mark on 20th-century English literature. (Equally renowned are Irish or Ireland-born writers of the era who were not directly associated with either Irish literary renaissance, such as Samuel Beckett, who was born in Dublin in 1906 and won the Nobel Prize for literature in 1969; George Bernard Shaw, who wrote in England but was born in Dublin; and the Irish playwright Brendan Behan.) The movement found its greatest expression in the creation of the *Abbey Theatre,* associated forever with the brilliant plays of Sean O'Casey. For many years the *Abbey* was the most famous theater in the world. The Gaelic League had more popular appeal; with its dream of the restoration of the Gaelic language and the reestablishment of a separate Irish cultural nation, it provided a great deal of the inspiration for the Easter Rebellion of 1916.

The Easter Rebellion, concentrated in Dublin, sparked the 5-year War of Independence, which culminated in the Anglo-Irish Treaty of 1921 (whereby Ireland gained the status of free state). The signing of the treaty was followed by civil war in 1922–23, during which many buildings that had escaped damage in the 1916 rebellion suffered badly. Today, happily, all the heirlooms of the 18th century have been restored to their original grandeur.

Dublin today, with a population of just over 1 million people, is far larger than it has been at any other stage of its history. Nevertheless, it still is an eminently walkable city. The crossroads of medieval and 18th-century Dublin remain the center of interest. Within a half-mile radius of the Bank of Ireland on College Green lie the cathedrals, the museums, Dublin Castle, the great Georgian public buildings, the parks, and the shops. All are neatly enclosed by the Royal Canal to the north and the Grand Canal to the south.

Thanks to the *Dublin Millennium* celebrations in 1988, the downtown area of the city now enjoys a number of permanent enhancements, including ten new sculptures by modern Irish craftspersons. The most notable pieces include a free-standing "liberty bell" in St. Patrick's Cathedral Park, a replica of a Viking ship on Essex Quay, and a double arch on a traffic island in Merrion Row, near St. Stephen's Green. In the heart of the city on O'Connell Street there also now is an elaborate fountain, with 40 spouts, designed to represent the course of the River Liffey. The river itself is represented by a larger-than-life sculpture of a reclining female nude, *Anna Livia.*

Another recent urban improvement has been the transformation of Grafton Street into a pedestrian shopping area, with brick walkways, benches, and plants. The shops along Grafton and nearby also have been rejuvenated, with smart new façades and signs.

In addition to sightseeing, visitors should be sure to sample Dublin's abundant cultural offerings. This year promises to be especially interesting, as Trinity College will be celebrating its 400th anniversary with a full program of lectures, concerts, and other activities (see *Special Events*).

But the true focal point of Dubliners' social life is the pub, and it is there that a visitor must go to find it. Dublin can be a comfortable, "down home" place to visit, so slow down and enjoy it. It has an endearing earthiness, a quality that inspired James Joyce to refer affectionately to his native city as a "strumpet city in the sunset" and "dear, dirty Dublin."

DUBLIN AT-A-GLANCE

SEEING THE CITY: Views of this essentially flat city are best from a number of restaurants in the surrounding hills; particularly nice is *Killakee House* in Rathfarnham (Killakee Rd.; phone: 932645 or 932917). Or see Dublin from afar from the neighboring Wicklow Mountains.

SPECIAL PLACES: Central Dublin is very compact. Since traffic can move slowly, by far the best way to see the city is on foot. Making full use of Dublin's splendid, signposted *Tourist Trail,* the determined sightseer should set off on foot to see and experience as much of Dublin as time allows. Walk the wide Georgian squares and avenues, meander down the cobblestone lanes near the Liffey Quays, stroll through the sylvan paths of St. Stephen's Green or along bustling Grafton Street — Dublin's shoppers' paradise — and stop at *Bewley's* (78-79 Grafton St.; phone: 776761) for a cup of coffee or at the *Shelbourne* hotel (27 St. Stephen's Green; phone: 766471) for a proper afternoon tea.

SOUTH DOWNTOWN

Merrion Square – This is the loveliest of Dublin's Georgian squares, a study in balance and elegance that evokes the graciousness of a vanished age. Note particularly the variety of fanlights on doorways. At No. 1, the young Oscar Wilde lived with his celebrated parents, the surgeon Sir William Wills Wilde and poetess Speranza; No. 42 was the home of Sir Jonah Barrington, 18th-century barrister and raconteur; at No. 58 lived Daniel O'Connell, the "Liberator" who won Catholic emancipation in 1829; No. 70 was the home of tragic Sheridan Le Fanu, author of sinister tales such as *Uncle Silas* and *Through a Glass Darkly* (after his wife's death in 1858, he shut himself up there, appearing only after nightfall to walk in the shadows of Merrion Square); at No. 82 lived William Butler Yeats, poet and Nobel Prize winner. Today, the only house in the square used as a private dwelling is No. 71, where well-known couturière Sybil Connolly has her home and studio.

Leinster House – When young Lord Kildare, Earl of Leinster, chose to build a mansion here in 1745, all of fashionable Dublin protested, for at that time the north side of the city was the fashionable side. Undaunted, he went ahead with his plan, asserting prophetically, "Where I go, fashion will follow." The house Lord Kildare built is said to resemble (and may have inspired) the White House, whose architect, James Hoban of Carlow, studied in Dublin after the completion of Leinster House. The building was purchased in the 19th century by the Royal Dublin Society, and in 1921 the Parliament of the new Irish Free State chose the building as its meeting place. Leinster House continues to be the meeting place of the Dáil (House of Representatives) and Seanad (Senate). When the Dáil is in session, visitors may watch from the visitors' gallery. Sessions are held Tuesdays through Thursdays, except in July, August, and September. Apply for tickets at the main gate or by writing in advance. No admission charge. Kildare St., Merrion Sq. (phone: 789911).

National Museum – When Leinster House belonged to the Royal Dublin Society, it became the nucleus of a complex of cultural buildings — the *National Gallery* (phone: 615133), the National Library (phone: 618811), the *Museum of Natural History* (phone: 618811), and the *National Museum.* These all are worth visiting, but the *National Museum* especially should not be missed. Its collection of gold objects dating from the Bronze Age to early Christian times is almost without parallel in Western Europe. The *National Museum* is closed Mondays. There is an admission charge for special exhibits. Kildare St. (phone: 765521).

Genealogical Office and Heraldic Museum – Formerly in Dublin Castle, this is the domain of Ireland's chief herald (the official in charge of genealogy, heraldic arms, and the like), and the ideal starting point for an ancestry hunt. Open weekdays. No admission charge, but there is a fee for genealogical consultations. 2 Kildare St. (phone: 608670).

St. Stephen's Green – A couple of blocks southwest of Merrion Square lies St. Stephen's Green, the loveliest of Dublin's many public parks. Its 22 acres contain gardens, a waterfall, and an ornamental lake. In summer, it's an excellent place to sit and watch working Dublin take its lunch; bands play on the bandstand in July and August.

Mansion House – Dublin preceded London in building a Mansion House for its lord mayor in 1715. In the Round Room, the Declaration of Irish Independence was adopted in 1919, and the Anglo-Irish Treaty of 1921 was signed here. The Round Room usually is open to visitors. No admission charge. Dawson St. (phone: 762852).

Trinity College – Dawson Street descends to meet Trinity College, the oldest university in Ireland (celebrating its 400th anniversary this year), founded by Elizabeth I of England on the site of the 12th-century Monastery of All Hallows. Alumni of the college include Oliver Goldsmith, Edmund Burke, Jonathan Swift, Bishop Berkeley (pronounced *Bark*-lee) — who also lent his name to Berkeley in California — William Congreve, Thomas Moore, Sheridan Le Fanu, Oscar Wilde, and J. P. Donleavy. No trace of the original Elizabethan structure remains; the oldest surviving part of the college dates from 1700. The Long Room, Trinity's famous library, is the longest single-chamber library in existence. It contains a priceless collection of 800,000 volumes and 3,000 ancient manuscripts and papyri. The library's chief treasure is the *Book of Kells,* an 8th-century illuminated manuscript of the four gospels described as the "most beautiful book in the world." Closed Saturday afternoons and Sundays. Admission charge April to October. College Green (phone: 772941).

Trinity College also is the home of "The Dublin Experience," a 45-minute multimedia sound and light show that traces the history of Dublin from earliest times to the present. It is shown daily, on the hour, from 10 AM to 5 PM, May through October, in the *Davis Theatre.* Admission charge. Entrance on Nassau St. (phone: 772941, ext. 1177).

Parliament House – Facing Trinity College is the monumental Parliament House, now the Bank of Ireland. Built in 1729 and regarded as one of the finest examples of the architecture of its period, this was the first of the great series of 18th-century public buildings in Dublin. As its name implies, it was erected to house the Irish Parliament in the century that saw the birth of Home Rule. Closed Sundays. No admission charge. College Green (phone: 776801).

Dublin Castle – Dame Street leads westward from College Green toward the older part of the city, where the early Viking and Norman settlers established themselves.

Castles have gone up and down on the site of the present castle. A Celtic *rath* (a medieval earthen fort) was almost certainly followed by a wooden Viking fortress, and this in turn was supplanted by the great stone castle erected by John of England in the 13th century. The castle was for 400 years the center of English rule in Ireland; for much of this time it had as grim a reputation as the Tower of London. Although the present building dates primarily from the 18th century, one of the four towers that flanked the original moated castle survives as the Record Tower. The 15th-century Bedford Tower was the state prison; the Georgian State Apartments, formerly the residence of the English viceroys, were beautifully restored between 1950 and 1963, and again in 1990. They now are used for state functions. St. Patrick's Hall in the State Apartments was the scene of the inauguration of Ireland's first president, Douglas Hyde; here, too, President John F. Kennedy was declared a freeman of Dublin.

Open daily. There's an admission charge for the Bedford Tower, the Chapel Royal, and the State Apartments. Dame St. (phone: 777129).

Christ Church Cathedral – Not far from Dublin Castle, the massive shape of Christ Church Cathedral crowns the hill on which the ancient city stood. Founded in 1038 by Viking King Sitric Silkenbeard of Dublin, Christ Church was demolished in the 12th century and rebuilt by the Norman Richard Gilbert de Clare (Strongbow), who is buried within its walls. The cruciform building has been much restored through the centuries, but the beautiful pointed nave and the wonderful stonework remain virtually unchanged. These walls have witnessed many dramatic scenes in the course of Irish history. Christ Church today is the Church of Ireland (Protestant) cathedral for the diocese of Dublin. The vaulted crypt remains one of the largest in Ireland. In front of this cathedral Dubliners traditionally gather to ring in the *New Year*. The cathedral and crypt are open daily. There's no admission charge, but a small donation is requested. Christ Church Pl. (phone: 778099).

St. Audeon's Arch and the City Walls – The 13th-century Church of St. Audeon is Dublin's oldest parish church. It was founded by early Norman settlers, who gave it the name St. Ouen, or Audeon, after the patron saint of their native Rouen. Close to the church is a flight of steps leading down to St. Audeon's Arch, the sole surviving gateway of the medieval city walls. Open daily. No admission charge, but donations are welcome. High St. (phone: 679-1855).

The Irish Life Viking Adventure – This living-history museum is the Irish answer to colonial Williamsburg. Buildings, music, sound effects, lighting, and aromas recreate the Viking/Irish culture of Dublin 1,000 years ago. Visitors may walk through the museum and interact with costumed interpreters. A multi-image show, "The Flame on the Hill," presents a look at Ireland before the coming of the Vikings. Open April through October; closed Sundays and Mondays. Admission charge. On the lower level of St. Audeon's Church, High St. (phone: 679-7099). Note: This attraction is scheduled to move to the Church of St. Michael and St. John, Essex Quay, sometime this year. Call the museum or the Dublin Tourism Office (phone: 747733) for information.

St. Patrick's Cathedral – Christ Church stood within the old walled city. John Comyn, one of Dublin's 12th-century archbishops, felt that while he remained under municipal jurisdiction he could not achieve the temporal power for which he thirsted. Accordingly, he left the city walls and built a fine structure within a stone's throw of Christ Church. Today St. Patrick's is the national cathedral of the Church of Ireland. By the 19th century both cathedrals were in a state of considerable disrepair. Henry Roe, a distiller, came to the aid of Christ Church, restoring it at his own expense; Sir Benjamin Lee Guinness of the famous brewing family came to the assistance of St. Patrick's — hence the saying in Dublin that "Christ Church was restored with glasses, St. Patrick's with pints!"

The early English interior of St. Patrick's is very beautiful; the nave is the longest in Ireland. The cathedral also has a wealth of monuments, including the Geraldine Door, the Cork Memorial, and the monument to Dame St. Léger. The most interesting aspect of St. Patrick's, however, is its association with Jonathan Swift, author of *Gulliver's Travels* and dean of the cathedral for 32 years. Within these walls he is buried, beside his loving Stella. On a slab near the entrance is carved the epitaph Swift composed for himself, which Yeats described as the greatest epitaph in literature: "He lies where furious indignation can no longer rend his heart." Open to visitors daily. Admission charge. Patrick St. (phone: 754817).

Guinness Brewery – Founded in 1759 by Arthur Guinness with a mere £100, Guinness's today is the largest exporting stout brewery in the world. The *Guinness Hopstore* (on Crane St. adjacent to the main brewery) once was the storage building for the ingredients of the world-famous dark stout, and the aroma remains. Now it is a public hall showcasing traveling displays, art shows, technological works, and contemporary arts. The visitors' center shows an audiovisual presentation about the making of the famous brew, complete with free samples. Also of note in the visitors' center are the *Guinness Museum* and the *Cooper's Museum.* Closed Saturdays and Sundays. Admission charge. Crane St. (phone: 536700).

Royal Hospital – One of Ireland's oldest public buildings, this 17th-century treasure was restored for IR£20 million and reopened in 1985 on its 300th anniversary. Originally built as a home for aged veterans, it is now Ireland's *National Centre for Culture and the Arts.* Displays range from *National Museum* pieces to traveling art exhibitions from as far away as China. The restoration of the Grand Hall/dining room has been rated as one of the finest such projects in Europe in this century. It also is used for public concerts, recitals, and lectures (check the Dublin newspapers). Surrounding the building are 50 acres of grounds, including an 18th-century formal garden, a courtyard, a sculpture park, and Bully's Acre, the resting place of many 11th-century Irish chieftains. Closed Mondays. Admission charge. Kilmainham (phone: 718666 or 719147).

NORTH DOWNTOWN

Four Courts – Almost across the river from the Guinness Brewery lies the stately Four Courts of Justice, dating from the apogee of the 18th century. The design of the building was begun by Thomas Cooley and completed by James Gandon, the greatest of all the Georgian architects. Supreme and High Court sittings are open to the public on weekdays. No admission charge. Inns Quay (phone: 725555).

St. Michan's Church – Not far from the Four Courts is St. Michan's, a 17th-century church built on the site of a 10th-century Viking church. The 18th-century organ is said to have been played by Handel when he was in Dublin for the first public performance of "Messiah."

Of perhaps greater interest is the extraordinary crypt, with its remarkable preservative atmosphere: Bodies have lain here for centuries without decomposing, and vistors can, if they feel so inclined, shake the leathery hand of an 8-foot-tall Crusader. Open weekdays and Saturday mornings. Admission charge. Church St. (phone: 724154).

Irish Whiskey Corner – With so many pubs on every street of the city, it's no wonder that Irish whiskey, like Guinness stout, is big business in Ireland. The story of the legendary liquid, known in Gaelic as *uisce beatha* (the water of life), is illustrated in this former distillery warehouse. One-hour tours include a short introductory audiovisual presentation, a visit to an exhibition area with archival photographs and distillery memorabilia, and a whiskey making demonstration. The tour ends at a pub-style "tasting room," where visitors can sample the various brands being brewed today. Tours are available Mondays through Fridays at 3:30 PM. Admission charge. Bow St. (phone: 725566).

Moore Street – Near the historic General Post Office (2 blocks west of Henry Street) is Moore Street. Here, among the fruit and flower sellers, the true voice of Dublin is audible — lively, warm, voluble, speaking an English that is straight out of Sean O'Casey.

Municipal Gallery of Modern Art – Beyond the Garden of Remembrance (a memorial to those who died for Irish freedom), on the north side of Parnell Square, is Charlemont House. Lord Charlemont, for whom the house was designed by Sir William Chambers in 1764, was a great patron of the arts; it is fitting, therefore, that his house has become the *Municipal Gallery of Modern Art.* The gallery should not be missed; it has an outstanding collection of Impressionist paintings, as well as works by Picasso, Utrillo, Bonnard, and such prominent Irish painters as Sir William Orpen, John B. Yeats (the poet's father), and Jack Yeats (the poet's brother). Closed Mondays. No admission charge. Parnell Sq. (phone: 741903).

Abbey Theatre – Alas, the original *Abbey Theatre,* founded by Yeats and Lady Gregory on the site of the old city morgue, is no more. In 1951, at the close of a performance of O'Casey's *Plough and the Stars* — a play that ends with Dublin blazing in the aftermath of rebellion — the theater itself caught fire and was burned to the ground. The new *Abbey,* designed by Michael Scott, one of the country's foremost architects, opened in 1966 on the site of the original building. The lobby, which can be seen daily except Sundays, contains interesting portraits of those connected with the theater's early successes. Performances nightly except Sundays. Abbey St. (phone: 744505 or 787222).

Custom House – This masterpiece of Georgian architecture adorns the north bank of the Liffey, to the east of O'Connell St. It was the *chef d'oeuvre* of James Gandon and is one of the finest buildings of its kind in Europe. Now occupied by government offices and closed to the public, it should nonetheless be seen at close range: The carved riverheads that form the keystones of the arches and entrances are splendid. Custom House Quay (phone: 742961).

Custom House Quay Development – There's something new on the Dublin skyline. This major urban renewal project — covering a 27-acre site adjacent to the historic Custom House in the city's dockside area — is scheduled to be completed in stages over the next few years. Architectural work is in the hands of Benjamin Thompson and Associates, the US firm that designed New York's *South Street Seaport* and Boston's *Faneuil Hall.* At the core of the site is the Dublin Financial Services Centre, a network of international banking, brokerage, and insurance firms, many of which are establishing a base in Ireland for the first time to provide a link to the new European community. In addition to the financial hub, which debuts this year, future plans include a hotel and conference facility, shops, restaurants, museums, and entertainment outlets. It's definitely worth a stroll along the Liffey to see how the project is progressing. Custom House Quay (phone: 363122).

SUBURBS

Phoenix Park – Northwest of the city center, this is the largest enclosed urban park in the world. Within its walls are the residences of the President of the Republic and the US Ambassador. The park covers 1,760 acres, beautifully planted with a great variety of trees. Among the attractions are the lovely People's Gardens, a herd of fallow deer, and the Zoological Gardens. Dublin Zoo is said to be the most beautiful zoo in Europe; it also has a most impressive collection of animals and holds several records for lion breeding. The park and zoo are open daily. Admission charge for the zoo. Entrance on Park Gate St. (phone: 213021 or 771425).

Chester Beatty Library – Founded by an American-born, naturalized British resident in Ireland, this library is considered to be the most valuable and representative private collection of Oriental manuscripts and miniatures in the world. The "copper millionaire with a heart of gold," Chester Beatty willed his marvelous library to the people of Dublin. Open Tuesdays through Saturdays. No admission charge. 20 Shrewsbury Rd., Ballsbridge (phone: 269-2386).

Malahide Castle – In a north city suburb of Dublin, Malahide Castle (now open to the public), was for 8 centuries the home of the Talbots of Malahide. Magnificently furnished in mostly 18th-century style with part of the very valuable National Portrait Collection on view, it is well worth a visit. Also on display is the Fry Model Railway, one of the largest modern railway exhibits in the world, which includes 300 model trains, trams, and items of Irish railway history dating from 1834. Open daily. Admission charge. Malahide (phone: 845-2337 or 845-2655).

Newbridge House and Park – Built in 1740, this country mansion is full of memorabilia of the Cobbe family, including their original hand-carved furniture collection, portraits, memoirs, daybooks, travel memorabilia from around the world, and an extensive doll collection. Downstairs, visitors can view a kitchen and laundry room from 1760, complete with ancient implements. The wooded grounds (365 acres) are constantly being enhanced with new attractions, including Tara's Palace, a huge, 25-room dollhouse incorporating the façades of three great 18th-century Irish mansions

(Leinster, Carton, and Castletown), and Newbridge Farm, a 20-acre prototype of a Victorian farm with indigenous Irish livestock (Kerry Cows, Jacob Sheep, Shannon goats, and Connemara ponies) and produce. There also are numerous picnic areas and walking trails. Five miles north of Dublin Airport and 12 miles from the city center, Newbridge can be comfortably combined with an excursion to nearby Malahide Castle. Open 10 AM to 5 PM weekdays, 2 to 6 PM Sundays, April through October; 2 to 5 PM Sundays, November through March. Admission charge. Off the Dublin-Belfast road, N1, at Donabate (phone: 436534 or 436535).

■ **EXTRA SPECIAL:** The beautiful Boyne Valley is one of Ireland's most storied and evocative sites, and it makes an easy and interesting day trip. Leave Dublin by the Navan road, passing through Dunshaughlin (which takes its name from a church founded by St. Seachnall, a companion of St. Patrick). Six miles south of Navan, signposted to the left, is the Hill of Tara. Although only some grassy mounds and earthworks recall a splendid past, it is impossible to remain unmoved by the site's history: This is Royal Tara, where the High Kings of Ireland were crowned on the Lia Fail (Stone of Destiny) in prehistoric times. And it was here, at the tribes' great triennial Feis of Tara, that laws were enacted and revised. Now, as Moore wrote in his immortal song, "No more to chiefs and ladies bright / The harp of Tara swells / The chord alone that breaks at night / Its tale of ruin tells."

Returning to the Navan road, you will pass the striking ruins of 16th-century Athlumney Castle on the east bank of the Boyne, about 1½ miles from Navan. Continue through Donaghmore, with its remains of a 12th-century church and a round tower. Nearby, below the Boyne Bridge, lies Log na Ri (Hollow of the King), where people once swam their herds of cattle ceremonially across the river to protect them from the "little people" and from natural disasters.

The village of Slane lies on one of the loveliest stretches of the Boyne. There are some delightful Georgian houses, but the history of this small town goes back far beyond the 18th century. On the hill that overlooks Slane, St. Patrick lit the paschal fire on *Holy Saturday,* AD 433, and drew upon himself the wrath of the high king's druids. Patrick emerged victorious from the ensuing confrontation, and Christianity began its reign in Ireland. On the slopes of the hill are the remains of an ancient earthen fort and the ruins of a 16th-century church. Apart from archaeological interest, the climb up Slane Hill is well worth the effort — rewarding the energetic with fine views across the tranquil Boyne Valley to Trim and Drogheda. Just outside the town lies the estate of Slane Castle, a 19th-century castellated mansion in which the present occupant, Lord Mountcharles, has opened a fine restaurant (phone: 412-4207).

Downstream from Slane is Brugh na Boinne (the Palace of the Boyne), a vast necropolis more than 4,000 years old. Here, beneath a chain of tumuli (ancient burial mounds), Kings of Ireland were laid to rest in passage graves of remarkable complexity. The tumuli of Dowth, Knowth, and Newgrange are of particular interest, for both their extent and the amazing diversity of their sculptured ornamentation. Newgrange, one of the finest passage graves in all of Western Europe, has been opened to the public. There's a permanent archaeological exhibition on the site. Guided tours are available. Closed Mondays. Admission charge (phone: 412-4274).

Farther down the Boyne Valley is Drogheda, an ancient town that has witnessed many dramatic scenes in the course of Irish history, most involving the contention of Royalists and Puritans for the English throne. Oliver Cromwell burned the city to the ground during a vicious siege in the 1640s, and James II was defeated by William of Orange on July 12, 1690. Reminders of Drogheda's past (all clustered in an area on the outskirts of town) include the 13th-century St. Laurence's Gate, the only survivor of the original ten gates in this once-walled city; the ruins of 13th-century St. Mary's Abbey; the Norman motte-and-bailey of Millmount and the fine *Millmount Museum;* and St. Peter's Church, where the head of St. Oliver Plunkett, martyred Archbishop of Armagh, is enshrined.

Five miles north of Drogheda is Monasterboice, an ancient monastic settlement noteworthy for one of the most perfect high crosses in Ireland — the intricately carved 10th-century Cross of Muireadach. Southwest of Monasterboice are the impressive ruins of Mellifont Abbey. Dating from 1142, this was the first Cistercian foundation in Ireland and heralded a whole new style of ecclesiastical architecture. Note especially the remains of the gate house and the octagonal lavabo (water basin).

Return to Dublin via N1.

SOURCES AND RESOURCES

 TOURIST INFORMATION: For information, brochures, and maps before departure, contact the Irish Tourist Board (757 Third Ave., New York, NY 10017; phone: 212-418-0800). For on-the-spot information and assistance, call the Dublin Tourism Office (at Dublin Airport; phone: 376387, or 14 O'Connell St.; phone: 747733). The tourist board personnel offer advice on all aspects of a stay in Ireland and can make theater bookings and hotel reservations anywhere in the country.

The Irish Tourist Board publishes several useful guides, which are available at tourist board offices and at most bookstores. They include *Dining in Ireland, The Dublin Guide,* and *Tourist Trail,* an excellent city walking guide. The best city map is the Ordnance Survey Dublin Map; less detailed but generally adequate maps are also available.

The US Embassy is at 42 Elgin Rd., Ballbridge (phone: 688777).

Local Coverage – *In Dublin,* published biweekly, covers every conceivable activity in Dublin, including theater, cinema, music, exhibitions, sports, and cabarets. The *Dublin Event Guide,* available at no charge at hotels, shops, and tourist offices, is another good resource. Large daily newspapers are the *Irish Times,* the *Irish Independent,* and the *Irish Press;* evening papers are the *Evening Herald* and the *Evening Press.*

 TELEPHONE: The country code for Ireland is 353. The city code for Dublin and the immediate vicinity is 01 if you are dialing within the country and 1 if you are dialing from abroad. Be aware that Dublin phone numbers are being changed from 6 digits to 7 digits, a process that will continue through 1994. If you dial a number that has been changed since press time, a recording should inform you of the new number; otherwise, check with the local operator or the tourist office.

GETTING AROUND: Airport – Dublin Airport is north of the city at Collinstown. In normal traffic, a trip from the airport to downtown takes 35 to 40 minutes, with an average taxi fare of $18 to $27. *CIE (Córas Iompair Eireann, National Transport Company)* operates bus service (see below), timed to meet all flights, between the airport and the central bus station.

Bus and Train – *Bus Eireann* and *Irish Rail,* divisions of *CIE,* operate bus and rail services not only in Dublin but nationwide. Cross-city bus routes are extensive. The bus fare is collected after the passenger is seated (exact fare is not required). Although

Dublin has no subway, a commuter rail system, *Dublin Area Rapid Transit (DART)*, runs from central Dublin along the bay as far north as Howth and as far south as Bray. It is swift, dependable, and safe at all hours. The train fare is collected at entry points.

For extended stays, purchase an Explorer Pass, which provides unlimited use of the *DART* system and of all buses and trains within a 20-mile radius. The cost for 4 consecutive days is about $14.

All information regarding bus and rail travel throughout the republic can be obtained by calling 787777. Official *Bus Eireann* and *Irish Rail* timetables are available at newsstands.

Car Rental – Many international companies, such as *Avis, Budget, Hertz,* and *National,* as well as a variety of local firms, offer excellent self-drive opportunities. *Dan Dooley* (42 Westland Row; phone: 772733; at the airport 842-8355), and *Murray's* (Baggot Street Bridge; phone: 681777; and at the airport; phone: 378179) both are dependable. More information and brochures are available from the tourist board.

Taxi – There are taxi stands throughout the city, especially near main hotels, and cabs also can be hailed in the streets. Among the companies that have 24-hour radio service are *Blue Cabs* (phone: 761111), *Co-op Taxis* (phone: 766666), and *National Radio Cabs* (phone: 772222).

Tours – A good way to get one's bearings in Dublin is to take a guided tour. *Bus Eireann* operates half-day motorcoach tours through the city and the nearby country-side, and full-day tours to more distant points, with prices averaging about $13 for a half-day trip, and about $23 for a full-day tour. All tours leave from the Central Bus Station (Store St.; phone: 787777). *Gray Line* (3 Clanwilliam Ter.; phone: 619666) also offers a limited number of tours.

Walking tours are conducted by several individuals and small firms. *Old Dublin Walking Tours* offers 2-hour tours around the Liberties area, departing from Christ Church Cathedral, daily during summer and on weekends during the rest of the year. The cost is about $7; for reservations and information, call 532407. Babette Walsh, a guide registered with the Irish Tourist Board, knows every nook and cranny of the city and offers customized tours, including escorted shopping sprees. She is an irresistible storyteller, and her often salty dialogue more than makes up for her occasionally creative view of Irish history. Ms. Walsh leads from 2 to 20 people on private jaunts for between $60 and $75 for a half day and from $90 to $110 for a full day. Contact Ms. Walsh in advance (at the *Cottage,* Balscaddon Rd., Howth, Co. Dublin; phone: 391869). The *Dublin Literary Pub Crawl* leads guests to old haunts of the city's illustrious literary figures, such as Samuel Beckett, James Joyce, Brendan Behan, and Patrick Kavanaugh, a journalist who wrote about the area. The tour costs about $7.75 and begins at the *Bailey Pub* (Duke St.) on Tuesdays, Wednesdays, and Thursdays, June through August. To book a tour or to obtain additional information, call 540228.

Horse-drawn carriage tours are among Dublin's newest and most popular form of sightseeing excursion. The carriages vary in size and style (some are open and others closed), and can accommodate from two to five passengers plus a driver/guide. Tours depart from the Grafton Street corner of St. Stephen's Green. Visitors have their choice of a quick trip around the Green; a half-hour Georgian tour past the *National Museum,* Mansion House, the Government buildings, Merrion Square, Grand Canal, and Leeson Street; and an hour-long historic route that takes in St. Patrick's Cathedral, Christ Church Cathedral, the Four Courts, and Dublin Castle. Rates range from $9 to $45 per carriage ride. Rides are available daily and some evenings, depending on the weather. No reservations necessary; tours are on a first-come, first-served basis. For more information, contact Bernard Fagan (phone: 726968).

Last year, *Liffey Tours Ltd.* began running waterbus tours on the River Liffey. The glass-enclosed luxury cruiser departs from Butte Bridge and travels under O'Connell Bridge and the Ha'penny Bridge, along the quays of the city, and past the Guinness

Brewery and the historic Four Courts and Customs House. Commentary during the 1-hour trip is provided by Dublin raconteur Eamonn Mac Thomais. The tour is approximately $9 for adults and $4.50 for children (phone: 538364).

LOCAL SERVICES: Dentist – Frank Allen (45 Fitzwilliam Sq.; phone: 762160); McDonagh Bros. (106 Marlboro St.; phone: 729721).

Dry Cleaner/Tailor – *Grafton Cleaners* (32 S. William St.; phone: 679-4309); *Baggot Dry Cleaners* (33 Upper Baggot St.; phone: 681286); *City Tailors* (42 Mary St.; phone: 734268); *Alteration Centre* (28 S. Anne St.; phone: 776258).

Limousine Service – *Murray's Europe Car* (Baggot St. Bridge; phone: 681777); *Vincent Russell* (42 Dromartin Park; phone: 982922).

Medical Emergency – *St. Vincent's Hospital* (Elm Park; phone: 694533).

Messenger Service – *A-1 Courier Service* (*Palmerstown Shopping Centre,* Unit 16, Kennelsfort Rd.; phone: 626-7633); *Shamrock Couriers* (41 Lower Baggot St.; phone: 612800).

National/International Courier – *DHL International* (Airways Industrial Estate, Santry; phone: 424622); *City Skyway Express* (Unit 93, Newtown Industrial Estate, Coolock; phone: 484111); *Federal Express* (Unit 1, Willsborough Industrial Estate, Clonshaugh; phone: 482299); *UPS* (Walsh-Western Ltd., Santry Hall, Santry Industrial Estate; phone: 427766); *TNT Skypak* (143 Lower Drumcondra Rd.; phone: 373716).

Office Equipment Rental – *Executive Rentals* (Woodchester House, Golden La.; phone: 756691); *Dublin Office Service* (58 Haddington Rd.; phone: 681355).

Pharmacy – *Hamilton Long,* open until 6 PM (5 Lower O'Connell St.; phone: 743352); *O'Connell Pharmacy,* open until 10 PM (310 Harold's Cross Rd.; phone: 973977); *Roches,* open until 7:30 PM Mondays through Saturdays and 11 AM to 1:30 PM Sundays (165 Upper Rathmines Rd.; phone: 972693).

Photocopies – *Rank Xerox Copy Bureau* (Stephen Ct.; phone: 760461); *Prontaprint,* two locations (38 Upper Baggot St., phone: 609500; and 3 Lower Leeson St., phone: 605480).

Post Office – Main branch, open 8 AM to 8 PM Mondays through Saturdays and 10:30 AM to 6:30 PM Sundays. Lower O'Connell St. (phone: 748888).

Secretary/Stenographer – *Active Business Partner Ltd.* (Haddington Hall, 80 Haddington Rd.; phone: 681748); *CO-SEC Secretarial Services* (IDA Enterprise Center, Pearse St.; phone: 775655).

Teleconference Facilities – *Convention Bureau of Ireland,* Baggot St. Bridge (phone: 765871).

Telex – *Bord Telecom* (6-8 College Green; phone: 778222).

Other – Men's formal attire rental: *Dawson's Formal Wear* (20 Dawson St.; phone: 616707); *McGrath's Dress Hire* (13 Aston's Quay; phone: 775307); *Wicklow St. Dress Hire* (33 Wicklow St.; phone: 716533). Cellular car phone rental: *Cellrent* (Dublin Airport; phone: 424700).

SPECIAL EVENTS: Trinity College marks its 400th anniversary this year, and Dublin will celebrate with a wide variety of special events throughout the year, involving the arts, culture, and history; for information on specific programs contact the Irish Tourist Board (757 Third Ave., New York, NY 10017; phone: 212-418-0800). Other outstanding annual events include *St. Patrick's Day,* March 17, with a parade and many other festivities; the *Spring Show,* a social and agricultural gathering in May; the *Festival in Great Irish Houses* in June, featuring concerts by international celebrities in Georgian mansions near Dublin; *Bloomsday,* June 16, when James Joyce aficionados gather from around the world to follow the circuitous path through Dublin that Leopold Bloom took from morning until late at night in *Ulysses;* the *Horse Show,* the principal sporting and social event of the year, held at the Royal Dublin Society grounds in Ballsbridge in July or August; the *Dublin Theatre Festival* in September and October, featuring new plays by Irish authors; and the *Dublin Marathon,* the last Monday in October. For details about these and other events, inquire at the tourist board (see "Tourist Information" above).

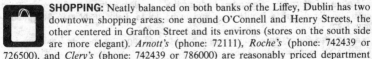

MUSEUMS: The *National Museum,* the *Heraldic Museum,* and the Royal Hospital are described in "Special Places." Dublin also is the home of several smaller museums:

Dublin Civic Museum – Adjacent to the *Powerscourt Town House Centre,* it contains artifacts and memorabilia — from old maps and prints to street signs and wooden water mains — reflecting 1,000 years of Dublin history. Closed Mondays. No admission charge. 58 S. William St. (phone: 771642).

Dublin Writers' Museum – Dedicated to Dublin's rich literary heritage, this museum commemorates the work of some of its most famous native scribes, including Oscar Wilde, Jonathan Swift, George Bernard Shaw, Samuel Beckett, and especially James Joyce, whose works so faithfully reveal and reflect the city. Set in two adjacent Georgian houses, the museum has a collection of rare editions, original manuscripts, and memorabilia. The museum also includes a center for living writers, providing a place for them to work and meet with their peers. Open daily. Admission charge. 18-19 Parnell Sq. (phone: 747733).

George Bernard Shaw Museum – The playwright was born in this house in 1856 and lived here for the first decade of his life. The museum, which is scheduled to open this year, will include original furnishings and memorabilia. Call for hours. 33 Synge St. (phone: 756166).

Irish Jewish Museum – Housed in a former synagogue, this museum traces the history of Jews in Ireland over the last 500 years. Documents, photographs, and memorabilia are on display. Open Sundays, Tuesdays, and Thursdays; Sundays only in winter. No admission charge, but donations are welcome. 3-4 Walworth Rd., off Victoria St. (phone: 283-2703).

Irish Museum of Modern Art – The first of its kind in Ireland, this new facility has a permanent collection of contemporary and avant-garde works by Irish and non-Irish artists. The museum, part of the Royal Hospital complex, also hosts visiting contemporary art exhibitions. Closed Mondays. No admission charge. Kilmainham (phone: 718666).

Museum of Childhood – Exhibits include dolls, dollhouses, and doll carriages from all over the world, dating from 1730 to 1940. There also are antique toys and rocking horses. Schedule varies, so call in advance. Admission charge. The Palms, 20 Palmerstown Park, Rathmines (phone: 973223).

National Wax Museum – Life-size wax figures of important Irish historical, political, literary, theatrical, and sports figures, as well as international newsmakers from Pope John Paul II to Michael Jackson, are displayed. Open daily. Admission charge. Granby Row, off Parnell Sq. (phone: 726340).

SHOPPING: Neatly balanced on both banks of the Liffey, Dublin has two downtown shopping areas: one around O'Connell and Henry Streets, the other centered in Grafton Street and its environs (stores on the south side are more elegant). *Arnott's* (phone: 72111), *Roche's* (phone: 742439 or 726500), and *Clery's* (phone: 742439 or 786000) are reasonably priced department stores in the O'Connell and Henry Streets area; *Brown Thomas* (phone: 679-5666) and *Switzer's & Company* (phone: 776821) are the main department stores on Grafton Street. *Powerscourt Town House Centre,* just off Grafton Street, has a number of clothing, antiques, and crafts shops in a courtyard built around a pretty townhouse. The city's two newest shopping complexes are the *Royal Hibernian Way* on Dawson

Street and *St. Stephen's Green Shopping Centre* (housed behind a re-created Regency façade) on the green. Good buys in Dublin include chunky Aran sweaters, Donegal tweeds, Waterford and Galway crystal, and Belleek china. The following are some recommended shops (unless otherwise indicated, the stores are closed on Sundays):

Best of Irish – A wide range of Irish goods — crystal, china, hand-knit goods, jewelry, linen, and tweeds. Open daily May through September; closed Sundays the rest of the year. Two locations: Next to the *Westbury Hotel,* on Harry St., off Grafton St. (phone: 679-1233); and 5 Nassau St. (phone: 679-9117).

Bewley's Café Ltd. – A Dublin landmark, it's an emporium of coffees and teas of all nations, with a tempting candy selection as well. Sampling is encouraged. There are 5 shops in the Dublin area, but only the one on Grafton Street has waitress service. Open daily. 78-79 Grafton St. (phone: 776761).

Blarney Woolen Mills – A branch of the Cork-based family enterprise, this huge new shop is known for its very competitive prices. It stocks all the visitor favorites, from tweeds and hand-knits to crystal, china, pottery, and souvenirs. Open daily. 21-23 Nassau St. (phone: 710068).

Cleo Ltd. – For more than 50 years one of Dublin's most fashionable sources for hand-knit and handwoven cloaks, caps, suits, coats, and shawls. 18 Kildare St. (phone: 761421).

Doll Store – Antique and modern, mass-produced and limited editions, dolls of all sizes and stripes are available at this shop. This also is the place to buy dollhouses, and doll clothes, hats, shoes, stands, wigs, eyes. . . 62 S. Great George's St. (phone: 783403).

Eason & Son Ltd. – Jam-packed with tomes and paperbacks, maps, records, and stationery. 40-42 Lower O'Connell St. (phone: 733811).

Fergus O'Farrell – For more than 25 years, this has been a showcase for top-quality Irish crafts — from woodcarvings and brass door knockers to beaten copper art; also handmade candles, stationery, and prints from 19th-century woodcuts. 62 Dawson St. (phone: 770862).

Fred Hanna – Bookseller to Trinity College and one of the finest bookstores in the country. New and used volumes; excellent books and maps on Ireland. 28-29 Nassau St. (phone: 771255).

Hardy's – For new and antique jewelry and timepieces. 11 Johnson's Court (phone: 715587).

Heraldic Artists – A good source for family crests, flags, scrolls, and genealogical books. 3 Nassau St. (phone: 762391).

H. Johnston Ltd. – Traditional blackthorn walking sticks. 11 Wicklow St. (phone: 771249).

Hodges Figgis – Another terrific bookstore, this one has an exceptional selection of paperbacks. 57-58 Dawson St. (phone: 774764).

House of Ireland – Top-quality Irish and European goods — from Aynsley, Lladró, Spode, Wedgwood, Hummel, and Waterford crystal and china to hand-knits, kilts, linen, and shillelaghs. Open daily in summer; closed Sundays the rest of the year. 64-65 Nassau St. and 6465 Dawson St. (phone: 714543).

House of Names – For more high-quality genealogical items; sweaters can be custom-ordered with a family crest and name. Open daily. 26 Nassau St. (phone: 679-7287).

Kapp and Peterson – Tobacco and hand-carved pipes for men *and* women. 117 Grafton St. (phone: 714652).

Kevin & Howlin Ltd. – Men's ready-to-wear and made-to-measure clothing. The store carries some women's tweeds. 31 Nassau St. (phone: 770257).

Laura Ashley – Fashion and fabrics for the home, women, and children. 60 Grafton St. (phone: 679-5433).

Malton Gallery & Bookshop – Focusing on Ireland of old, this shop specializes in prints by 18th-century artist James Malton. His watercolor collection, titled "Views of Dublin," has been transformed into prints, engravings, placemats, coasters, greeting cards, and postcards. Other wares on sale here include hand-marked silver, pewterware, crystal, and books. 23 St. Stephen's Green (phone: 766333).

Margaret Joyce – Women's sweaters, hand-knit in wool or cotton. *Powerscourt Town House Centre* (phone: 679-8037).

Marks & Spencer – A branch of the famous London emporium, this department store offers a wide array of clothing, household items, and souvenirs of Ireland, Britain, and the rest of Europe. Grafton St. at Lemon St. (phone: 679-7855).

Mullins of Dublin – Coats of arms emblazoned on parchment, plaques, and even doorknockers. 36 Upper O'Connell St. (phone: 741133).

Pat Crowley – Silky, seductive blouses and dresses. 3 Molesworth Pl. (phone: 615580).

Patrick Flood – Silver and gold jewelry in traditional Irish designs. Unit 14C, 1st floor, *Powerscourt Town House Centre* (phone: 679-4256).

Sheepskin Shop – Just the spot to stock up on high-quality sheepskin and lambskin suits and coats. The shop also has a varied selection of leather trousers, suits, and jackets. 20 Wicklow St. (phone: 719585).

Sleater's – A charming jewelry shop tucked in an alley between Grafton Street and *Powerscourt Town House Centre*. 9 Johnson's Court (phone: 777532).

Sweater Shop – A good source of sweaters of all kinds, colors, styles, fibers, and patterns. Other high-quality Irish knitwear garments also are stocked. 9 Wicklow St., off Grafton St. (phone: 713270).

Sybil Connolly – Ireland's reigning couturière; her romantic ball gowns of finely pleated Irish linen are special indeed. Open weekdays and by appointment. 71 Merrion Sq. (phone: 767281).

Tower Design Craft Centre – Once a sugar refinery, this renovated 1862 tower houses the workshops of more than 30 innovative craftspeople, with work ranging from heraldic jewelry, Irish oak woodcarvings, and hand-cut crystal to *Chez Nous* Irish chocolates, stained glass, toys, and fishing tackle. There's also a self-service restaurant. An ideal stop for a rainy day. Pearse St. (phone: 775655).

Trinity College Library Shop – Specializing in scholarly works and books on Irish subjects, this shop also carries reproductions, posters, and prints from the *Book of Kells*. Throughout this year, this spot also will be the best source of souvenir items and crafts relating to the 400th anniversary of Trinity College. Open weekdays, also open Saturdays from March through December. Nassau St. (phone: 772941).

Waltons Musical Instrument Galleries – Bagpipes and Irish harps as well as records. 2-5 N. Frederick St. (phone: 747805).

Waterstone & Co. – Another great bookshop, a branch of the British firm of the same name, this is a haven for buying and browsing, with an array of volumes on international topics, as well as ceiling-high shelves on Irish history, literature, language, politics, cookery, and crafts. Open daily. 7 Dawson St. (phone: 679-1415).

Weir & Sons – A tradition in Dublin, this classy shop offers the best in jewelry, gold, silver, antiques, glass, china, and leather goods. 96-97 Grafton St. (phone: 779678).

 SPORTS AND FITNESS: Bicycling – Irish Raleigh Industries operates *Rent-a-Bike* at a number of city firms (phone: 626-1333). Two downtown shops offering bicycle rentals are *USIT Rent-A-Bike* (58 Lower Gardiner's Row; phone: 725349) and *McDonald's* (38 Wexford St.; phone: 752586). Charges average $9 per day or $36 per week.

Gaelic Games – Football and hurling are two fast, enthralling field sports; important matches are played at *Croke Park* (Jones Rd; phone: 363222). For details, see the calendar of events in *In Dublin*.

Golf – More than 30 golf courses are within easy reach of Dublin; visitors are welcome at all clubs on weekdays, but gaining admission can be more difficult on weekends. Two of the finest courses in the world, *Portmarnock* (phone: 323082) and *Royal Dublin* (phone: 336346), are just north of the city and should not be missed.

Greyhound Racing – An exciting spectator sport, you can go to the dogs regularly at two tracks, *Shelbourne Park Stadium* and *Harold's Cross Stadium* each an 8-minute ride from the city center. Details in *In Dublin* or at the tourist board.

Horse Racing – Six miles south of the city in Foxrock is the *Leopardstown* race-course, a modern track with glass-enclosed viewing areas. The best-known course in the Dublin vicinity is *Curragh* (phone: 45-41025), about a mile outside the town of Kildare in County Kildare, less than an hour's drive from Dublin. This modern complex hosts the *Irish Derby* in June and other high-stakes races throughout the year. *Leopardstown* (phone: 896307) can provide information on all local racing events. Note: the *Phoenix Park* racecourse on the western edge of the city closed last year.

Horseback Riding – A list of riding establishments close to Dublin is available at the tourist board.

Tennis – Ireland has a first-rate international facility, the *Kilternan Tennis Centre* (phone: 953729 or 955559), which is about a 15-minute taxi ride from the city center. With 4 indoor and 4 outdoor courts, it is open daily from 7 AM to midnight, year-round. Equipment may be rented at *Pro Shop Kilternan* at the tennis center. There are a few public courts, generally outdoors, in and around Dublin, where visitors can play for a small fee. The most central is Herbert Park (Ballsbridge; phone: 684364).

 THEATER: For complete program listings see the publications listed in *Tourist Information,* above. There are at least ten main theaters in the city center; smaller theater troupes perform in the universities, in suburban theaters, and occasionally in pubs and hotels. The main theaters are the *Abbey,* featuring works by contemporary Irish playwrights as well as revivals of the plays of Synge, Beckett, O'Casey, Yeats, and Behan; the *Peacock,* which specializes in new and experimental works (both at Lower Abbey St.; phone: 744505 or 787222); the *Gate,* the theater of Michael MacLiammoir and Hilton Edwards (Cavendish Row; phone: 744045); the *Gaiety* (S. King St.; phone: 771717), mostly for revues, musicals, and opera; the *Olympia* (Dame St.; phone: 778962), for everything from revues to straight plays; the *John Player Theatre* (S. Circular Rd; phone: 532707) for contempo-rary drama; the *Focus* (Pembroke Pl.; phone: 763071), for Russian and Scandinavian works; and the very avant-garde *Project Arts Centre* (39 E. Essex St.; phone: 712321).

The three newest stages are the *Andrews Lane Theatre* (12-16 Andrews La.; phone: 679-5720) for contemporary off-Broadway–style productions; the *Tivoli Theatre* (135-138 Francis St.; phone: 544472) for controversial Irish plays and imports from London; and the *New Eblana Theatre* (Store St.; phone: 679-8404), a revived "pocket" theater in the basement of Busaras, the central bus station, and a venue for contemporary plays.

For children, the *Lambert Mews Puppet Theatre* in the suburb of Monkstown will prove irresistible. Clifden La., Monkstown (phone: 280-0974).

It is always advisable to make reservations for theater performances in Dublin. You can make bookings at theaters, the tourist board, and the information desks of *Switzer's* and *Brown Thomas* stores (both on Grafton St.). Most of the theaters accept telephone reservations and credit cards.

 MUSIC: The *National Concert Hall* (Earlsfort Ter.; off St. Stephen's Green; phone: 711888), is the center of Dublin's active musical life and the home of the *RTE (Radio Telefis Eireann) Symphony Orchestra. RTE* perform-ances are held regularly, as are a variety of other concerts. For a schedule, phone the concert hall or check local publications. In April and September the *Dublin Grand Opera Society* holds its spring and winter seasons at the *Gaiety Theatre* (S. King

St.; phone: 771717). For big-name rock concerts, such as *U2* performances, the popular new venue is the *Point Theatre* (at East Link Bridge; phone: 363633), a renovated depot with state-of-the-art acoustics. The *Olympia* (Dame St.; phone: 778962) also hosts occasional rock gigs.

Traditional Irish music is a must. Sessions (*seisiún*) are held at many places around the city by an organization called *Comhaltas Ceoltóirí Eireann* (phone: 280-0295); ballad sessions are held nightly except Sundays in the *Barn* on the ground floor of the *Abbey Tavern* (Howth, 10 miles north of the city on the coast; phone: 322006 or 390307). Many pubs offer music informally — *O'Donoghue's* (15 Merrion Row; phone: 614303) is one of the most famous (and least comfortable). Others to try: *Toner's* (Lower Baggot St.; phone: 763090); the *Baggot Inn* (Lower Baggot St.; phone: 761430); *Kitty O'Shea's* (23-25 Upper Grand Canal St.; phone: 609965); and *Foley's* (1 Merrion Row; phone: 610115). Many other pubs are listed in *In Dublin.*

NIGHTCLUBS AND NIGHTLIFE: There is little in the way of large-scale cabaret-cum-dancing in Dublin; swinging Dublin tends to congregate on the discotheque scene. Premises range from the large, lively places where an escort is not necessarily required to small, intimate clubs. Most discotheques have only wine licenses.

Among the more established discotheques on a rapidly changing scene are the large and lively *Annabel's* in the *Burlington* hotel (Leeson St.; phone: 60522), *Raffles* in the *Sachs* (Northampton Rd.; phone: 680995), *Blinkers* at *Leopardstown* racecourse (phone: 896307), and *Rumours* (O'Connell St.; phone: 722850). Smaller, more intimate clubs are mainly to be found in the Leeson Street area: *Styx* (phone: 761560) and *Cats* (phone: 616151) are two. The most famous traditional cabaret in Dublin is the established *Jurys Cabaret,* nightly except Mondays from April through October (*Jurys Hotel,* Northumberland Rd.; phone: 605000). Also good are the *Braemor Rooms* (Churchtown; phone: 981016); *Doyle's Irish Cabaret,* presented from April through October at the *Burlington* (Leeson St.; phone: 605222); and the *Clontarf Castle* dinner show (Castle Ave.; phone: 332271).

BEST IN TOWN

CHECKING IN: With the recent opening of three new first class hotels and the refurbishment of several others, Dublin's hotels have risen significantly in quality, but they still are not at the top of world class standards. Expect to pay $250 and up for a double room in hotels classified as very expensive; $180 to $250 for those classified as expensive; $90 to $180 in those listed as moderate; and less than $90 for an inexpensive room. A room with Irish breakfast for two in a private home in a residential neighborhood will cost $65 or less.

Note: The tourist board offers a list of hotels it has inspected and graded; it also offers a computerized reservation service all over Ireland (see *Tourist Information,* above). Reservations for many of the hotels may be made through international reservations services; the applicable numbers are listed in individual hotel entries below. All telephone numbers are in the 1 city code unless otherwise indicated.

Berkeley Court – The flagship of the Doyle group and the first Irish member of the Leading Hotels of the World group. Close to the city in the leafy suburb of Ballsbridge, it combines graciousness with modern efficiency. Contemporary and antique furnishings harmonize, and the service is exceptionally warm and friendly. There are 210 rooms and 6 suites (all with Jacuzzis), including a 6-room, $2,000-a-night penthouse suite. There also is an excellent dining room, the *Berkeley Room* (see *Eating Out),* a conservatory-style coffee shop, a health center with indoor pool and saunas, and a shopping arcade. Business facilities include 24-hour room service, 7 meeting rooms for up to 400, concierge, foreign currency exchange, secretarial services, audiovisual equipment, photocopiers, translation services, and express checkout. Lansdowne Rd. (phone: 601711, 800-223-6800 or 800-44-UTELL from the US; fax: 617238; telex: 30554). Very expensive.

Conrad – Dublin's newest international hotel — opened in 1990 by the US Hilton hotel chain — is in the heart of the city, opposite the *National Concert Hall* and across from St. Stephen's Green. It offers 192 bright and airy guestrooms (including 10 suites), all with bay windows. Each room has an executive desk, 2 or 3 telephones, mini-bar, color TV set, and a large marble bathroom. One floor is reserved for nonsmokers. Other facilities include a fully equipped health club, hair salon, a car rental desk, and a garage. The *Alexandra* (see *Eating Out*) is the hotel's most elegant restaurant; there also is an informal brasserie, and a lively pub. Business facilities include 24-hour room service, 8 meeting rooms for up to 370, concierge, foreign currency exchange, secretarial services, audiovisual equipment, photocopiers, translation services, and express checkout. Earlsfort Ter. (phone: 765555 or 800-HILTON from the US; fax: 765424). Very expensive.

Shelbourne – This venerable establishment, a nice mixture of the dignified and the lively, now is more polished than ever after a $5-million face-lift. Some of the 167 rooms are truly splendid, particularly the front rooms on the second floor. Many are supremely comfortable, if compact. But the sense of history in the creaky-floored hallways, the glittering function rooms, and the varied clientele — from socialites to literati — make this establishment especially appealing. The *Horseshoe Bar* is one of the livelier fixtures of Dublin pub life, while the main restaurant, with its 1826 plasterwork and trio of Waterford crystal chandeliers, is a showcase for modern Irish cuisine. Business facilities include 24-hour room service, 8 meeting rooms for up to 400, concierge, foreign currency exchange, secretarial services, audiovisual equipment, photocopiers, translation services, and express checkout. 27 St. Stephen's Green (phone: 766471 or 800-223-5672 from the continental US or Canada; fax: 616006; telex: 93653). Very expensive.

Westbury – The fashionable centerpiece of a chic mall of shops and restaurants, this hotel is a member of the Doyle group. The management emphasizes elegance, and the 206 rooms have canopied beds and an abundance of mahogany and brass furnishings. Private suites with Jacuzzis also are available. Public facilities include a restaurant, coffee shop, seafood pub, and a lobby lounge with pianist. There also is an arcade of shops and underground parking. Business facilities include 24-hour room service, 5 meeting rooms for up to 300, concierge, foreign currency exchange, secretarial services, audiovisual equipment, photocopiers, translation services, and express checkout. Grafton St. (phone: 679-1122; 800-223-6800 or 800-44-UTELL from the US; fax: 679-7078; telex: 91091). Very expensive.

Jurys – In Ballsbridge opposite the American Embassy, this modern complex has a multi-story, skylit lobby area and a dome-shape central atrium. The main hotel offers 290 rooms, each with well-equipped bathroom. In addition, 100 extra-large rooms and suites are in a newer, separate but connected 8-story wing. Known as the *Towers,* this section offers the most advanced and comprehensive hotel services in Ireland. Each of the computer-key-accessible rooms has a bay window, a mini-bar, 3 telephone lines, work area, satellite TV, marble and tile bathroom, walk-in closet, and either king- or queen-size beds. All the *Towers'* rooms are decorated with designer fabrics and specially styled furnishings, such as rocking recliner chairs. Two floors are designated as nonsmoking. The *Towers* has its own hospitality lounge, separate elevators, and entrance. There also are 2 restaurants, a 23-hour coffee shop, 2 bars, an indoor/outdoor swimming pool, and health center. For entertainment, there is *Jurys Cabaret,* Ireland's longest running variety show. Business facilities include 24-hour room service, 12 meeting rooms for up to 850, concierge, foreign currency exchange, secretarial services, audiovisual equipment, photocopiers, translation services, and express checkout. Northumberland Rd. (phone: 605000, 800-44-UTELL or 800-THE-OMNI from the US; fax: 605540; telex: 93723). Very expensive (*Towers*) to expensive (main hotel).

Bloom's – Centrally located, this intimate spot (a member of the Quality Inn Choice Hotels group) has a high commitment to service. Its 86 rooms have color TV sets, air conditioning, trouser presses, free mixers and ice, and direct-dial telephones. Every corridor has an ice cabinet and a shoeshine machine. There's also a grill-room, two lounges, and enclosed parking. Business facilities include 24-hour room service, a meeting room for up to 100, concierge, foreign currency exchange, secretarial services, audiovisual equipment, and photocopiers. Anglesea St. (phone: 715622 or 800-221-2222 from the US; fax: 715997; telex: 93815). Expensive.

Burlington – Ireland's largest property, with 500 rooms, was completely refurbished in 1989. Restaurants include an international dining room, the *Sussex,* and the cozy *Diplomat* for beef and seafood. The trendy *Burlington Bar,* with its cheery hanging plants, globe lights, and brass, has a popular lunch buffet. A musical revue is performed at *Doyle's Irish Cabaret* on summer evenings, and there's year-round entertainment in *Annabel's* nightclub. Business facilities include 24-hour room service, 9 meeting rooms for up to 2,500, concierge, foreign currency exchange, secretarial services, audiovisual equipment, and photocopiers. Leeson St. (phone: 605222; 800-223-0888 or 800-44-UTELL from the US; fax: 608496; telex: 93815). Expensive.

Gresham – Once considered one of the grandest of Dublin hotels, it has changed ownership a number of times and recently came to rest in the Ryan Holdings group. Though you hardly could call it grand these days, this 200-room hostelry once attracted lots of luminaries. Business facilities include 24-hour room service, 6 meeting rooms for up to 200, concierge, foreign currency exchange, secretarial services, audiovisual equipment, and photocopiers. Upper O'Connell St. (phone: 746881; 800-223-0888 or 800-44-UTELL from the US; fax: 787175; telex: 32473). Expensive.

Mont Clare – One of the city's oldest hotels, this 6-story Georgian-style property was totally revamped and refurbished in 1990. It sits in the heart of the business district, at the corner of Clare Street overlooking Merrion Square, close to Trinity College, the Irish government buildings, and museums. There are 80 rooms, each with bath, phone, TV set, radio, hair dryer, mini-bar/refrigerator, tea- and cof-fee-making facilities, and trouser press. A restaurant, lounge, and enclosed parking lot are on the premises. Business facilities include 24-hour room service, 5 meeting rooms for up to 250, concierge, foreign currency exchange, secretarial services, audiovisual equipment, and photocopier. Merrion Sq. (phone: 616799, or 800-44-UTELL from the US; fax: 615663; telex: 91471). Expensive.

Stephen's Hall – An alternative to the traditional hotel or guesthouse, this new property offers apartment-style accommodations on a short-term basis — ideal for travelers who want to entertain or do business in Dublin, or for those who want to save money by cooking for themselves. The exterior is a replica of a Georgian building that formerly stood on the site, and the interior is modern and functional. Each of the 37 suites consists of a sitting room, dining area, well-equipped kitchen, bathroom, and 1 or 2 bedrooms with phone. Services include daily cleaning and maintenance, and underground parking. 14-17 Lower Leeson St., Earlsford Ter. (phone: 610585 or 800-223-6510 from the US; fax: 610606). Expensive to moder-ate.

Longfields – Located on one of the city's most fashionable streets, this small hostelry offers all the charm of a Georgian home with modern comforts. It is comprised of two 18th-century Georgian townhouses, originally owned by Richard Long-field, also known as Viscount Longueville, a member of the Irish Parliament over 200 years ago. Completely restored and refurbished over the last 3 years, it now has 26 rooms all with private baths, and a decor that reflects both the Georgian period and more modern influences. Each room has a phone, color TV set, mini-bar, clock radio, and hair dryer. Business facilities include a board-style meeting room with a capacity of up to 20, foreign currency exchange, secretarial services, and photocopier. 10 Lower Fitzwilliam St. (phone: 761367; fax: 761542). Moderate.

Montrose – Similar to but larger than the *Tara Tower,* this establishment is near the National Radio and Television studios and across the road from the Belfield campus of University College, Dublin. About 10 minutes' drive from the city center, on a well-serviced bus route, its 190 bedrooms are comfortable, and it has a good restaurant. There's a grill, a bar, a health center, a hairdressing salon, and a souvenir shop. Business facilities include 24-hour room service, 3 meeting rooms for up to 80, concierge, foreign currency exchange, secretarial services, audiovisual equipment, and photocopier. Stillorgan Rd. (phone: 269-3311, or 800-223-0888 from the US; fax: 269-1164; telex: 91207). Moderate.

Russell Court – Two former Georgian houses have been transformed into this convenient place less than a block from St. Stephen's Green. The decor in the public areas is Art Deco, and the 22 modern bedrooms, all with bath, are decorated in light woods and pastel tones. Facilities include a restaurant, lounge, and night-club. 21-23 Harcourt St. (phone: 784991, or 800-521-0643 from the US; fax: 784066; telex: 91880). Moderate.

Skylon – Midway between downtown and the Dublin Airport, this modern north-side hostelry has 100 rooms all decorated in a colorful Irish motif. The hotel also features a restaurant/grill that stays open until midnight. Upper Drumcondra Rd. (phone: 379121 or 800-223-0888 from the US; fax: 372778; telex: 90790). Moderate.

Tara Tower – Modern, comfortable, very reasonably priced, and just 10 minutes' drive from the city center, on a well-serviced bus route. The 100 bedrooms have radio, television sets, and telephone, and many overlook Dublin Bay. The lobby is small, but the hotel's good restaurant/grill is open until midnight. Business facilities include 24-hour room service, 2 meeting rooms for up to 250, concierge, foreign currency exchange, secretarial services, audiovisual equipment, and photocopiers. Merrion Rd. (phone: 269-4666, or 800-223-0888 from the US; fax: 269-1027; telex: 90790). Moderate.

Anglesea Townhouse – Near the American Embassy, this Edwardian residence is the home of Helen Kirrane, who spoils her guests with hearty breakfasts of fresh fish, homemade breads and scones, fresh juices, baked fruits, and warm cereals. Heirlooms and family antiques add to the ambience of this jewel of a bed and breakfast guesthouse. All 7 rooms have private bath/shower, TV sets, and direct-dial telephones. 63 Anglesea Rd., Ballsbridge (phone: 683877; fax: 683461). Moderate to inexpensive.

Ariel House – A homey guesthouse with 15 rooms and a restaurant with a wine license. One block from the *DART* station for easy commuting to the city center. Room rates include full breakfast. 52 Lansdowne Rd. (phone: 685512; fax: 685845). Moderate to inexpensive.

Fitzwilliam – Situated at the corner of Fitzwilliam and Baggot Streets in the heart of Georgian Dublin within walking distance of St. Stephen's Green, this spacious townhouse dates back to the mid-1700s. Originally a private residence, it has been restored and converted into a 12-room guesthouse, owned and operated by the Reddin family. Each room is furnished with antiques and equipped with a phone, TV set, and modern bathroom. Facilities include a restaurant and a cozy parlor with a marble fireplace. 41 Upper Fitzwilliam St. (phone: 600448; fax: 767488). Moderate to inexpensive.

Georgian House – Recently renovated, this centrally located guesthouse is less than 2 blocks south of St. Stephen's Green. It offers 11 bedrooms with private bath/ shower, phone, and TV set, but no elevator. There also is a restaurant and an enclosed parking area. 20 Lower Baggot St. (phone: 604300 or 618832). Moderate to inexpensive.

Egan's House – Another comfortable guesthouse, offering 23 rooms, all with private baths. There is also a small restaurant. 7 Iona Park (phone: 303611; fax: 303312). Inexpensive.

Iona House – A guesthouse with 11 rooms, all with private bath, and a restaurant/ coffee shop serving breakfast to late-night snacks. 5 Iona Park (phone: 306217; fax: 606732). Inexpensive.

Mount Herbert – Close to the city center in a quaint neighborhood, this well-run, family-owned Georgian mansion has 88 rooms (77 with private baths), a health facility, and a fairly good restaurant. No bar (wine license only) but a very pleasant atmosphere. Business facilities include 24-hour room service, 7 meeting rooms for up to 150, and audiovisual equipment. 7 Herbert Rd. (phone: 684321 fax: 607077; telex: 92173). Inexpensive.

 EATING OUT: Where food is concerned, Ireland, first and foremost an agricultural country, has outstanding raw materials. But truly distinctive and innovative Irish cuisine really does not exist. Traditional dishes such as Irish stew, Dublin coddle, and bacon and cabbage are served, but this kind of dish is a *rara avis* on the menu of most better restaurants, being looked down upon as too common to prepare for discriminating diners.

When it comes to meals prepared with the finest produce, however, Ireland's top restaurants can compare with the best anywhere. Dublin offers a wide range of first class restaurants, a somewhat more restricted range of moderately priced establishments, and a number of fast-service, inexpensive eating places.

Dinner for two, excluding drinks, will cost $110 and up in expensive restaurants; $75 to $100 in moderate places; and under $65 in inexpensive ones. Reservations always are recommended, especially at expensive and moderate establishments. Unless noted otherwise, most are closed Sundays and holidays. All telephone numbers are in the 1 city code unless otherwise indicated.

Alexandra – Small and intimate, this dining spot in the *Conrad* hotel is somewhat like a private club, with open fireplaces, panelled walls, crystal chandeliers, brass fittings, and oil paintings. The imaginative menu includes such dishes as salmon *paupiettes* in cabbage and spinach leaves; loin of lamb with truffle and caper juice; and medallions of veal in ginger. Closed Sundays. Reservations advised. Major credit cards accepted. *Conrad Hotel,* Earlsford Ter. (phone: 765555). Expensive.

Berkeley Room – One of Dublin's best hotel dining rooms, it is elegant and lavishly appointed; its prize-winning chef produces highly satisfactory fare, including rack of lamb, roast duckling, and prime ribs carved at tableside. Open daily. Reservations advised. Major credit cards accepted. *Berkeley Court Hotel,* Lansdowne Rd. (phone: 601711). Expensive.

Le Coq Hardi – This gracious Georgian establishment is run by owner/chef John Howard, twice gold-medal winner in the prestigious *Hotelympia/Salon Culinaire* contest. Its extensive à la carte menu offers many house specialties, including

Howard's renowned ducking *à l'orange.* Closed Sundays. Reservations necessary. Major credit cards accepted. 35 Pembroke Rd., Ballsbridge (phone: 689070). Expensive.

Dobbins – A wine-cellar atmosphere prevails at this relaxed bistro with a sawdust-strewn floor, wooden benches, and checkered linen. On warm days there is additional seating in a tropical patio area with a sliding-glass roof. The varied international menu includes salmon and sole with prawn tails and spinach soufflé, beef teriyaki, and breast of chicken with garlic and vodka butter. There often is live Irish harp music on weekends. Closed Sundays. Reservations advised. Major credit cards accepted. Stephen's La. (phone: 76479). Expensive.

Ernie's – This place earned its far-reaching reputation under the direction of master seafood chef Ernie Evans. Though Ernie has passed away, his family carries on the restaurant's fine tradition. The menu still features *fruits de mer,* including Valencia scallops, garlic prawns, and fresh salmon. Open for lunch and dinner; closed Sundays and Mondays. Reservations necessary. Major credit cards accepted. Mulberry Gardens, Donnybrook (phone: 269-3300). Expensive.

Grey Door – Open since 1978, this restaurant has achieved an enviable reputation for fine Russian and Finnish cuisine. The wine list is good and the more adventurous imbiber can sample such rarities as Russian champagne. The setting behind this elegant doorway in the heart of Georgian Dublin is intimate, rather like dining in a private home. Closed Sundays. Reservations advised. Major credit cards accepted. 23 Upper Pembroke St. (phone: 763286). Expensive.

King Sitric – This superb small dining place, right on the bay, serves perfectly cooked fish and excellent wines in a tastefully restored old house. It also specializes in game birds such as grouse and snipe. The service is very good. Closed Sundays. Reservations necessary. Major credit cards accepted. East Pier, Howth (phone: 325235). Expensive.

Locks – A French provincial eatery on the banks of the Grand Canal near Portobello Bridge. Only the freshest produce is used for such dishes as wild salmon and breast of pigeon. Closed Sundays. Reservations necessary. Major credit cards accepted. 1 Windsor Ter., Portobello (phone: 538352 or 543391). Expensive.

Lord Edward – Strictly for seafood lovers (no meat on the menu), this place is set in a tall Victorian building opposite historic Christ Church Cathedral, in the older part of the city. The food is prepared and served in the classic French style. Closed Sundays and Mondays. Reservations necessary. Major credit cards accepted. 23 Christ Church Pl. (phone: 542420). Expensive.

Old Dublin – This cozy eatery has rose-colored linen and walls and roaring fireplaces. Specialties on the menu include Scandinavian-style fish, which owner Eamonn Walsh learned to love while in Finland. For meat eaters there's filet à la Novgorod — chateaubriand sliced and served on sauerkraut alongside fried kasha (buckwheat groats), spicy mushrooms, caviar, and sour cream. There also is a good wine list. Open weekdays for lunch and dinner; Saturdays for dinner only; closed holidays. Reservations advised. Major credit cards accepted. 91 Francis St. (phone: 542028 or 542346). Expensive.

Patrick Guilbaud – A trendy place for nouvelle cuisine that draws an equally stylish crowd. Specialties include breast of duck in cider sauce, veal kidneys and sweetbreads, lamb's tongue and brill, and bacon in curry sauce. Closed Sundays. Reservations essential. Major credit cards accepted. 46 James Pl., off Baggot St. (phone: 764192). Expensive.

White's on the Green – An elegantly appointed gathering place for media stars, celebrities, and expense-account diners, it has the air of a Georgian garden. Dublin's "in" spot features *cuisine moderne* and the finest of service traditions. Menu ranges from veal sweetbreads with fennel and celery to roast wild salmon or *panaché* of lamb with fresh tarragon. Closed Sundays. Reservations essential. Major credit cards accepted. 119 St. Stephen's Green (phone: 751975). Expensive.

Shannons – Dubliners looking for a view of the city's Grand Canal have put this place at the top of their lists. It is bright and airy, with many plants, flowers, and wide picture windows. The menu features the freshest of Irish seafood, produce, and prime meat; unique combination dishes include breast of chicken layered with salmon, and trout with turbot. Service is first-rate. Closed Sundays. Reservations advised. Major credit cards accepted. Portobello Harbour, Portobello (phone: 782933). Expensive to moderate.

Coffers – Around the corner from *Bloom's* hotel, this small, comfortable eatery specializes in steaks — varying from a plain filet to a pork steak cooked in fresh apples and Pernod. It features a special pre-theater dinner daily except Sundays. Open for dinner daily, weekdays for lunch. Reservations advised. Major credit cards accepted. 6 Cope St. (phone: 715900 or 715740). Moderate.

Gallery 22 – A pleasant, garden-like atmosphere pervades this dining spot near the *Shelbourne* hotel. The innovative menu includes seafood pancakes, rack of lamb, sea trout, and filet steak with vermouth sauce. Vegetarian dishes also are served. A pre-theater dinner is offered. Closed Sundays. Reservations necessary. Major credit cards accepted. 22 St. Stephen's Green (phone: 616669). Moderate.

La Grenouille – A French-style bistro next to the *Powerscourt Town House Centre.* Each dish on the limited menu is cooked to order. Choices range from rack of lamb or chicken in bleu cheese sauce to steaks and duck, all served with an array of fresh vegetables. Open daily for dinner year-round; lunch on weekdays April through December. Reservations advised. Major credit cards accepted, except American Express. 64 S. William St. (phone: 779157). Moderate.

Kilmartin's – Originally owned by a turf accountant (a bookie), this bar retains both its name and its racing decor under new owners. Run by two young women, both *Cordon Bleu* chefs, Kilmartin's specializes in poached salmon and crispy duck. The house wine is particularly good. Open for lunch and dinner weekdays; dinner only on Saturdays and Sundays. Reservations advised. Major credit cards accepted. 19 Upper Baggot St. (phone: 686674). Moderate.

McGrattans' in the Lane – An elegant Georgian door is the entrance to this restaurant, tucked in an alley between Lower Baggot Street and Merrion Square. The interior is equally inviting, with a cozy living room–like cocktail area and a skylit and plant-filled dining room. The menu melds French recipes and Irish ingredients: poached salmon florentine, *canard aux noix* (crispy duck with walnuts and honey sauce), *poulet* William (breast of chicken in pastry with citrus sauce), noisettes of lamb diable (roast lamb with mustard and tarragon sauce). Open daily. Reservations advised. Major credit cards accepted. 76 Fitzwilliam La. (phone: 618808). Moderate.

Mitchell's – This place, in the cellar of *Mitchell's Wine Merchants,* is where swinging Dubliners lunch. The menu is somewhat limited, but the helpings are large, the cooking quite good, and the desserts mouth-watering. Alas, it's not open in the evenings. Get here before 12:30 PM, or you'll find yourself in for a long wait (which you can while away by sampling some of their splendid wines). Closed Sundays. No reservations. American Express and Visa accepted. 21 Kildare St. (phone: 680367). Moderate.

Oisin's – Named for a legendary Irish warrior hero, this restaurant is owned by the much-traveled Feargal O'hUiginn, who aims to provide an Irish dining experience both in atmosphere and in applying haute-cuisine standards to traditional Irish fare. The menu, which is printed in Gaelic and English, includes Dublin coddle (sausage and bacon in a stock of apples and onions; a dish beloved by Jonathan Swift), Irish stew, corned beef and cabbage, as well as rack of lamb with fresh fruit sauces, salmon in seaweed sauce, and lobster. All dishes are garnished with edible flowers and herbs from the restaurant's garden. Open for dinner only. Closed Sundays and Mondays (occasionally open Sundays and Mondays in summer). Reservations advised. Major credit cards accepted. 31 Upper Camden St. (phone: 753433). Moderate.

Osprey's – Around the corner from *Jurys* and the American Embassy, this cozy candlelit restaurant has two small dining rooms, each with a fireplace. Flambé cooking is a specialty here, as are such international dishes as beef Wellington, salmon *en croûte,* chicken Madeira, Wiener schnitzel, and Dover sole. Closed Sundays. Reservations advised. Major credit cards accepted. 41-43 Shelbourne Rd. (phone: 608087). Moderate.

Polo One – Less than a block from St. Stephen's Green and tucked between Kildare and Dawson Streets, this dining place is close to all the major sights and shops. The white and blue modern decor is enhanced by a fine collection of paintings by local artists. The menu, a hybrid of Italian, Spanish, and American influences, emphasizes fresh Irish ingredients, local cheeses, seafood, and fruit. The diverse selections include wild salmon and tiger shrimp, farm-raised chicken, *fettuccine primavera,* and paella. Closed Sundays. Reservations advised. Major credit cards accepted. 5-6 Molesworth Pl. (phone: 766442 or 763362). Moderate.

La Vie en Rose – Definitively French, right down to the no-English menu, this relatively new bistro offers good value with all-inclusive prices for three- and four-course meals. The food is presented both imaginatively and in substantial portions. Although the menu changes daily, entrées often include red mullet, sea bass, duckling, and breast of capon. Among the desserts, *pavé au chocolat* (a chocolate wedge) wins raves from all but the strictest dieters. Closed Sundays and Mondays. Reservations advised. Major credit cards accepted. Upper Stephen's St., off George's St. (phone: 781771). Moderate.

Gallagher's Boxty House – Casual and unpretentious, this spot is a haven for Irish country cooking, from Irish stew to boiled cabbage and bacon. As its name implies, it also is a good place to try the traditional dish called "boxty," a potato pancake rolled like a burrito around a variety of fillings such as chicken and ham, or vegetables. All dishes are accompanied by boiled potatoes, carrots, and other fresh Irish produce. Open daily. No reservations. Major credit cards accepted. 20-21 Temple Bar (phone: 772762). Moderate to inexpensive.

Rudyards – On 3 floors of a tall, narrow house in Crown Alley, this spot offers a combination of mildly exotic continental dishes, including spinach-stuffed pancakes, *navarin* of lamb, tomato pie, pasta, and beef in orange sauce. Closed Sundays. Reservations unnecessary. Major credit cards accepted. 15 Crown Alley, off Dame St. (phone: 710846). Moderate to inexpensive.

Unicorn – Established in 1939, this small Italian bistro is a favorite with Irish politicians and literati. All pasta and sauces are made by owners Renato and Nina Sidoli. Open from 10AM to 10 PM except Sundays. Reservations advised. No credit cards accepted. Merrion Ct., off Merrion Row (phone: 762182 or 688552). Moderate to inexpensive.

Bad Ass Café – One of the brightest, and liveliest eateries to hit town in some time. It's famed as much for its (loud) rock music and videos as for its great pizza. Steaks are another specialty. Open daily. Reservations unnecessary. Major credit cards accepted. 9-11 Crown Alley, behind the Central Bank on Dame St. (phone: 712596). Inexpensive.

Beshoff – Owned by a family long known as purveyors of fresh fish, this is a classy version of the traditional Dublin fish-and-chips shop, with a black-and-white marble decor. The menu features chips (French fries) with salmon, shark, squid, turbot, or prawns, as well as the humble cod. Open daily, noon to midnight.

Reservations unnecessary. No credit cards accepted. 14 Westmoreland St. (phone: 778781). Inexpensive.

Captain America's – Specializes in "genuine American hamburgers," Tex-Mex, and barbecue dishes, served with American beer and rock music. Open daily. Reservations unnecessary. No credit cards accepted. Grafton Ct., 1st floor, Grafton St. (phone: 715266). Inexpensive.

Casper's Bar & Grill – A lively eatery with some traditional Irish dishes, such as Irish stew (not always easy to come by in local restaurants). There's also an exotic range of cocktails and a selection of international beers. Open daily; brunch served Saturdays and Sundays. Reservations advised. Major credit cards accepted. 6 Wicklow St. (phone: 679-4347). Inexpensive.

SHARING A PINT: Until you have been in a pub, you have not experienced Dublin. Here Dubliners come to pursue two serious occupations: drinking and conversation. Many pubs are ugly and modern, complete with Muzak and plastic, but plenty of traditional pubs remain — noisy, companionable places for the pursuit of friendly ghosts of bygone Dublin in an unhurried atmosphere. Some favorites are the *Horseshoe Bar* in the *Shelbourne* hotel (St. Stephen's Green; phone: 766471), favored by the uppity, horsey set; the *Bailey* (2 Duke St.; phone: 772760), a literary pub that actually displays the door of nearby 7 Eccles Street, where Joyce's Molly and Leopold Bloom lived; *O'Donoghue's* (Merrion Row, off St. Stephen's Green; phone: 614303) for Irish ballads; the *Palace Bar* (21 Fleet St.; phone: 779290), a traditional haunt of journalists and literati; the award-winning *Dubliner* in *Jurys* hotel (Northumberland Rd.; phone: 605000), which offers an airy atmosphere with a fireplace and a section called the "Press Room," serving (lethal) seasonal drinks; *Mulligans* (8 Poolbeg St.; phone: 775582), renowned for the quality of its pint, appreciated equally by the dock workers and students (from nearby Trinity College), who form its main clientele; the *Stag's Head* (1 Dame Ct.; phone: 679-3701), a great haunt of the legal profession, which serves hearty hot lunches at reasonable prices; *Neary's* (1 Chatham St.; phone: 778586), which offers delicacies like smoked salmon and oysters in season; the *Brazen Head* (Bridge St.; phone: 779549) and *Davy Byrne's* (21 Duke St.; phone: 775217) for plain drinking and gab; *Doheny and Nesbitt* (5 Lower Baggot St.; phone: 762945), which is always called just "Nesbitts" (try the bar, not the modernized upstairs lounge); and last, but very far from least, the utterly delightful *Ryans* (28 Parkgate St.; phone: 776097), with its shining mirrors, courteous barmen, and snugs where guests can drink quietly and enjoy first-rate pub grub.

EDINBURGH

Other beautiful and famous urban centers such as Rome or San Francisco may share the distinction of being built on hills, but Edinburgh, a stark and in some ways still medieval city whose streets have often flowed with blood, alone can claim to be built on extinct volcanoes.

Astride one of these, high above the houses where Edinburgh's 433,480 inhabitants dwell, looms Edinburgh Castle, a portentous fairy-tale structure that often makes visitors gasp the first time they see it. It seems almost supernatural, with ancient stonemasonry rising out of volcanic rock as if there were no dividing line between the two.

From the 7th century on, there was a fortress where Edinburgh Castle now stands, and as life in the Middle Ages became more civilized, life within the fortress spilled onto the long sloping ridge — carved by glaciers ages after the volcanic era — that runs down from Edinburgh Castle to the foot of Arthur's Seat, another extinct volcano, crowning Edinburgh's central park. The ridge, with its clusters of high stone and wood tenements, its one thin, snakelike public street, its cathedral, and its tolbooth, was (and still is) the securing knot at the center of Scotland's legal, commercial, and artistic fiber.

Walking around central Edinburgh today is sheer joy. There's very little need for a map; it's hard to get lost. Every time you reach a hilltop, there's a glorious vista of the sweeping fusion of earth, sky, and sea, and every glance up an alley reveals fantastic steeples, jagged, smoking, chimney-potted skylines, or beauteous rotund domes. The city lights its most imposing public buildings at night, and they are legion, spread out over a series of precipices and valleys. Nature provides incredible sunsets, the product of Scotland's unique slowly fading evening light (the "gloaming") and rapid change in the evening temperature. Legend and romance are at every hand. Somebody famous lived in almost every residence.

At the head of the legend and romance brigade are the arch Presbyterian John Knox and Mary, Queen of Scots, who together dominated life in the Edinburgh of the late 16th century. (Not that they dominated it together. When Mary arrived in Edinburgh in the autumn of 1561 as Scotland's very young and very Catholic new queen, Knox described the event in his diary as God having fouled the air with black fog and seeping rain.) The political and religious strife attendant upon Mary's reign is notorious, as are her two marriages and the three deaths associated with them, the last of these her own (she was beheaded by her cousin Queen Elizabeth I of England, to whom she had fled for asylum). Mary lived in Holyrood Palace, by the abbey at the base of Arthur's Seat. John Knox lived up the ridge from her near St. Giles's Cathedral, within the city gates. Both residences still stand, and are open to the public today.

Their Edinburgh reached its full flower around the end of the 17th century, when the tenements along the ridge had grown 15 (or more) tottering stories high and housed uncounted numbers of people, all of whom threw their garbage into the central street, warning those below with nothing more than the terse cry *"Gardez-loo!"* Buildings frequently collapsed. Water could be had only from one of the city's six wells, called "pennywells" (their sites are still marked today), and inhabitants would line up with buckets from 3 AM on to be sure of some water.

These cramped and malodorous conditions, plus a plethora of alehouses and a police force made up of decrepit Highlanders back from European wars, no doubt had something to do with the locals' favorite sport, rioting on fete days, parade days, and the king's birthday. Riots occasioned by more serious events were frequent also and occurred regularly in every age up to the Victorian and even beyond. Famous instances are the assassination of a wealthy councillor, John MacMorran, by dissatisfied youths at the Royal High School (16th century); "Cleanse the Causeway," a battle in the streets between two noble families, the Douglases and Hamiltons (17th century); the Jenny Geddes affair, in which a Presbyterian fishwife caused pandemonium by throwing a stool at a dean who was reading the new Episcopal service book in St. Giles's Cathedral — the first event in the British Civil War (17th century); the Porteous Riots, immortalized by Sir Walter Scott in *The Heart of Midlothian* (18th century); and the trial of William Burke, whose sale of his victims' corpses to the University of Edinburgh's medical luminaries did so much to further the international reputation of that great institution (19th century). Religious riots have scarred the city's history repeatedly, although the last one was in the 1930s.

Obviously this wizened medieval town had to spread out somehow, and luckily, in the second half of the 18th century, its by now thoroughly Protestant God sent it an increase in trade and prosperity. City fathers erected a wealth of new buildings on another ridge to the north — known as the New Town, connected to the Old Town by bridges. The classically proportioned beauty of New Town buildings, many of which were designed by the world-renowned British architect Robert Adam, is a testament to what is generally regarded as Edinburgh's golden age, part of the so-called Scottish Enlightenment. It was a great age not only for architects but for writers, publishers, philosophers, and politicians. Throughout the city, taverns became the sites of ongoing seminars. Among many other well-known people of the time, David Hume, Adam Smith, and James Boswell were Edinburgh men.

Today's Edinburgh has lost some of its traditional vibrancy and color, though it is certainly safer and cleaner. The near stranglehold the Presbyterian Church of Scotland attained on the social institutions during Queen Victoria's reign meant that industriousness, temperance, and respectability — all the middle class virtues — took supreme command of the city. About 60% of the present inhabitants are white-collar workers, an unusually high proportion, which helps keep the local flavor staid.

Nonetheless, signs are that things are livening up. Since 1979, an avalanche of flashy pubs, nightspots, and restaurants has shattered the city's sober air. Edinburgh has always been favored by geography, situated as it is on the Firth of Forth, an inlet in the North Sea, and surrounded by woods, rolling hills,

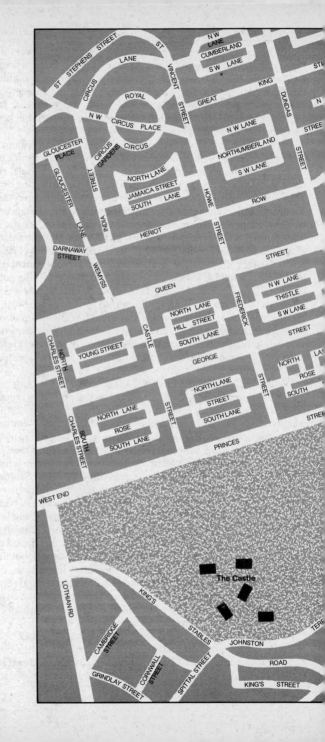

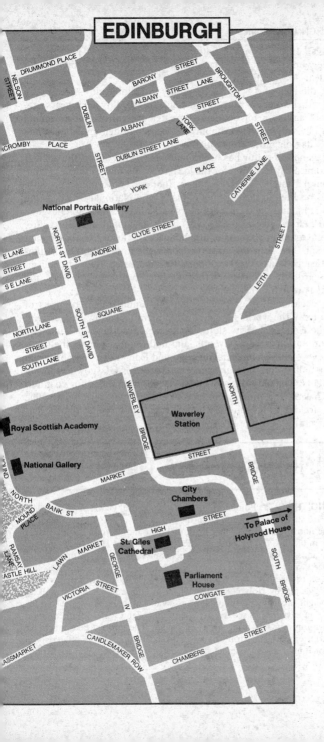

and lochs (lakes). It is not only a national capital but a port whose chief exports include whisky, coal, and machinery; a large brewing center; and a center for nuclear and electronics research.

And though the idea of a Scottish Assembly at Edinburgh — favored by a majority of Scottish voters — was set aside on a technicality a few years ago, a groundswell of agitation for Scotland's greater control of its own affairs remains. Who can say whether Edinburgh's second golden age is at hand? Perhaps not all its volcanoes are extinct.

Certainly the smell of sulfur has been ominously in the air, as the ancient capital has become a battleground for the local repercussions of former Prime Minister Margaret Thatcher's bitter conflicts. Increased government pressure on the BBC has resulted in the shelving of plans for a National Broadcasting Centre for Scotland, and the transfer of news and current affairs to Glasgow. The *Edinburgh Festival* (see *Extra Special*) has been caught in the crossfire, threatened by government slashing of arts budgets and local Labour Council charges of elitism. The *Festival,* however, continues to maintain high standards and has reached out to embrace populism, increased internationalism, and the avant-garde. It would seem that, despite continuing pressure, the theater pageant is reviving, rejuvenated.

If anything, occasional disasters heighten the innumerable triumphs of what is undoubtedly the world's greatest arts festival. The low-budget *Film Festival* can't be Cannes, but its stature increases steadily. Unfortunately, mismanagement, anti-apartheid boycotts, and underfunding made the *Commonwealth Games* of 1986 a financial disaster, and Edinburgh's complacency has been additionally jolted by a growing preference for Glasgow as the site for sporting events. The old Glasgow taunt that Edinburgh is "fur coat and nae knickers" has all too much relevance in a cold financial climate. The capital has had to look to its laurels, which means, among other things, that tourists are currently taken far less for granted.

EDINBURGH AT-A-GLANCE

 SEEING THE CITY: Edinburgh has many wonderful views; on a clear day, there are striking panoramas from the top of any of its extinct volcanoes. To the north lies the sparkling Firth of Forth and, beyond it, the ancient kingdom of Fife. To the south are the lovely Pentland Hills and surrounding plowed farmlands. Look eastward, where the giant Bass Rock, off the coast of Berwickshire, meets your eye. Look westward to see across the whole nation to Ben Lomond, nearly on the west coast of Scotland! If you have a car, drive up Arthur's Seat (the road begins just by Holyrood Palace), park at Dunsapie Loch, and walk to the uppermost height (a steep and furzy climb — wear flat shoes and watch out for falling sheep). If you have no car, see the city from Edinburgh Castle. Another option is to take an open-top tour bus from Waverley Bridge. The journey takes about 50 minutes round-trip, or you can stroll around and reboard at stops as often as you wish. For additional information, contact *Lothian Region Transport,* Waverly Bridge (phone: 220-4111).

SPECIAL PLACES: The "Royal Mile" is the name given to the oldest part of the city, the road that runs downhill from Edinburgh Castle to Holyrood Palace. It comprises four contiguous streets: Castle Hill, the Lawnmarket, High Street, and the Canongate. Since the entire citizenry of Edinburgh lived and worked for centuries either on or just off these four streets, the Royal Mile is practically groaning with objects and sites of historic fascination: 16th- and 17th-century houses, well preserved, with their adjacent courtyards and closes; residences of famous writers and distinguished thinkers; St. Giles's Cathedral, the High Kirk of Edinburgh, with its 17th-century spire in the shape of the Scottish crown; excellent museums; the classical City Chambers; and the building where Scotland's Parliament met from 1639 until union with England's in 1707.

THE ROYAL MILE

Edinburgh Castle – The oldest building in Edinburgh is part of the castle structure, a tiny ethereal chapel built by Queen Margaret, the wife of the Malcolm who features in *Macbeth*. King James VI of Scotland (later James I of England) was born here. The Scottish Regalia, including Sceptre and Crown, are on display. These disappeared after the union of Scotland with England and were found, over 100 years later, by Sir Walter Scott (who was leading a government commission appointed to look for them) in an old locked box. Emotion ran so high that his daughter, who was present on the occasion, fainted when he lifted the lid. Also in the castle is the Scottish National War Memorial, honoring Scots who died in the two world wars. Open Mondays through Saturdays from 9:30 AM to 6 PM and on Sundays from 11 AM to 6 PM during the summer and Mondays through Saturdays from 9:30 AM to 5 PM and on Sundays from 12:30 to 5 PM during the winter (phone: 225-9846).

Outlook Tower and Camera Obscura – A short distance east of the castle, climb up 98 steps, walk outside, and find yourself face to face with church spires. The camera obscura, actually a periscope, throws a revolving image of nearby streets and buildings onto a circular table, while one of the tower's denizens gives an excellent historical talk. There also are exhibitions of holography and pin-photography — tiny photos taken through matchboxes. Downstairs is a very good book shop carrying everything from Lady Antonia Fraser's best-selling biography of Mary, Queen of Scots, to gleaming coffee-table volumes about one of the national obsessions, Scotch whisky. Open Mondays through Fridays from 9:30 AM to 6 PM and on Saturdays and Sundays from 10 AM to 6 PM April 1 through September 1, and Mondays through Fridays from 9:30 AM to 5 PM and Saturdays and Sundays from 10 AM to 5 PM during the winter. Admission charge. Castle Hill (phone: 226-3709).

Parliament House – Built from 1632 to 1640, after Charles I suggested that it replace the Collegiate buildings of St. Giles's Cathedral, this historic sanctum once housed Scotland's Parliament and is today the country's supreme court. Until 1982, tourists could enter only by written request. Its showpiece is the Great Hall, with a fine hammer-beam roof and walls laden with portraits by Raeburn and other famous Scottish artists. Also of interest is the Signet Library, a splendid example of interior decoration, with an exquisite ceiling. Written permission of the librarian is required to visit, however. Open Mondays through Fridays from 10 AM to 4 PM year round. Admission charge for library. Upper High St. (phone: 225-2595).

St. Giles's Cathedral – A church of some sort has stood here for over 1,000 years. The medieval building here was named for the Athenian saint Egidius (Giles). St. Giles's has often been showered by flying religious fur, especially at the time of the Reformation. In 1559–60 soldiers were put on guard at the church and many of its treasures hidden in private Catholic homes; Protestant nobles nonetheless ravaged the altars. Later, English troops came to their aid and stripped St. Giles's from top to bottom. It was at this stage that John Knox, a prime mover in this sequence of events, was made minister of St. Giles's. His unmarked grave is believed to be under Parliament Square, just outside St. Giles's. Upper High St. (phone: 225-4363).

Mercat Cross, or Market Cross – Near the east door of St. Giles's stands a monument restored in 1885 by W. E. Gladstone, prime minister of Britain off and on from 1868 to 1894. Here was the crossroads at which proclamations were read out and public hangings took place, until well into the 19th century. It was also the commercial focal point of old Edinburgh, the place being so thick with butchers, bakers, merchants, burgesses, lawyers, tinkers, tailors, farmers, drovers, and fishmongers that the town council issued ordinances requiring each trade to occupy its own separate neighboring street or close (hence the names you see on the entrances to the closes as you go down the Royal Mile: Fleshmarket Close, Advocates' Close, and so on). City tradesmen never obeyed these ordinances, however, and the Mercat Cross remained as colorful as ever until the city began to spread out in the second half of the 18th century. High St., by St. Giles's.

Advocates' Close and Anchor Close – These are typical of the many narrow alleys that gave access to the inns and taverns that were so much a part of Edinburgh's 18th-century cultural life. Doors to these places (taverns no longer) were topped by stone architraves dating from the 16th century and bearing inscriptions like "Blissit Be God of Al His Gifts" or "Spes Altera Vitae" (these two examples are still in Advocates' Close today). In Anchor Close was *Douglas's,* where the poet Robert Burns habitually drank. Entrances of both closes are from High St.

John Knox's House – Legend says that Scotland's fieriest preacher of all time lived here, but historians say no. However, legend has won, and this attractive 15th-century dwelling was preserved when most of its neighbors were razed during the widening of High Street in 1849. Open October through March, 10 AM to 5 PM. Closed Sundays. Admission charge. 45 High St. (phone: 556-2647).

Acheson House – When King Charles I was crowned at Edinburgh in 1633, Sir Archibald Acheson, baronet, was his secretary of state. Acheson built this house, a small courtyard mansion, the only one of its kind in Edinburgh, in the same year. It was the height of elegance in its day, yet 100 years later it had become a popular brothel and 200 years after that was inhabited by 14 families, though it had been built to house one. It was bought and restored by the Marquess of Bute in 1935, whereupon, despite its history, it was leased to the Canongate Kirk for a manse! Although today it is once again under private ownership, it is well worth seeing from the outside. 140 Canongate.

Canongate Kirkyard – Opposite Acheson House. Pause long enough to read the long list — mounted on a plaque — of notables buried here. Canongate.

Brass Rubbing Centre – Visitors may rub any of the brasses or stones on show. Materials are provided for a fee that probably won't come to more than $8. The brass commemorating Robert the Bruce, King of Scotland from 1306 to 1329, is very impressive. In addition to being nice souvenirs, your own finished products make beautiful gifts. In Trinity Apse, Chalmers Close, off High St. (phone: 556-4364).

Holyrood Palace – A royal retreat since the beginning of the 16th century, the palace is where Queen Elizabeth II stays when she is in residence in Edinburgh. It is made of stone, a huge, imposing round-towered edifice befitting kings and queens. Most of what you see of it now was built by Charles II from 1671, but it is chiefly associated with Mary, Queen of Scots, who lived in it well before that for 6 contentious, sensational years. The old part, still extant, contains her bedroom and the supper room in which David Riccio, her secretary, was brutally murdered before her very eyes by a gang of armed men that included her jealous husband, her cousin Lord Darnley. By the side of the palace, within its spacious grounds, are the picturesque ruins of Holyrood Abbey and the lodge known as Queen Mary's Bath House, where she reputedly bathed in red wine. A guide will take you through it all, sparing no gory details. Closed when the queen is in town. Admission charge. At the bottom of the Canongate (phone: 556-1096).

Scotch Whisky Heritage Centre – Just next door to the entrance to the Edinburgh Castle, this tourist attraction features an hour-long tour, in an electric barrel-car, that shows the role of whisky in Scotland's turbulent past. The sounds and even the smells of the distilling industry are tantalizingly reproduced. You will emerge knowing exactly how to make whisky. The heritage shop stocks over 60 brands of malt and blended whiskies. Open daily, 10 AM to 5 PM. 358 Castlehill (phone: 220-0441).

Scottish Poetry Library – For anyone who visits Britain to explore America's literary ancestry, an hour or two browsing here should bring rich pleasure. An extensive collection of books, magazines, and tapes with Scottish works in English, Scots, and Gaelic is housed in this 18th-century building in a courtyard off the Royal Mile. The building was formerly owned by Edinburgh's most famous burglar, Deacon William Brodie, a respectable town councillor by day and a criminal by night, who was hanged in 1788. Open Mondays through Saturdays from noon to 6 PM (noon to 8 PM on Thursdays). No admission charge. 14 High St. (phone: 557-2876).

BEYOND THE ROYAL MILE

Princes Street Gardens – Princes Street is modern Edinburgh's Main Street, its Broadway, and its Fifth Avenue. The gardens stretch nearly the street's whole length on the south side, where the old Nor' Loch, which was used in medieval times as the castle moat, once stood. The city spends thousands of pounds every year to keep the gardens opulent with flowers. In summer months (June–September) there are concerts, children's shows, variety acts, and do-it-yourself Scottish country dancing (to professional bands) here. Gates close at dusk. Princes St.

National Gallery of Scotland – Smack in the middle of Princes Street Gardens, on a manmade embankment called the Mound, is this exquisite museum, opened in 1859. It contains paintings by British and European masters from the 14th century to Cézanne. Closed Sunday mornings. Admission charge. The Mound (phone: 556-8921).

Scott Monument – Sir Walter Scott is certainly one of Edinburgh's favorite sons — his face even decorates all Bank of Scotland notes, even though he was the most famous bankrupt in Scottish history. The elaborate 200-foot Gothic monument, which recently underwent extensive restorations, on the east end of Princes Street Gardens, helps make Edinburgh's skyline the ornamental marvel it is. Its 287 steps take you to the summit. (Don't attempt it if you suffer from vertigo.) Closed Sundays. Admission charge. Princes St. (phone: 225-2424, ext. 6596).

New Town – To the north of Princes Street lies the largest neo-classical townscape in Europe, built between the 1760s and 1830s. Assiduous conservation means that little has changed externally into these streets, squares, and crescents. Three of the more interesting ones are Charlotte Square (designed by Robert Adam), Moray Place, and Ann Street. The New Town Conservation Centre conducts personalized tours Mondays through Fridays; call in advance to arrange a time. The center also offers exibitions, a reference library, and various publications. 13A Dundas St. (phone: 557-5222).

Georgian House – On the most gracious square in the elegant New Town, the National Trust for Scotland has furnished a house in period style and opened it to the public. The kitchen is a wonderland of utilitarian objects that would have belonged to a typical high class late-18th-century ménage. Fascinating audiovisual sessions on the history and topography of the New Town come with the admission price. Open daily April through October (Mondays through Saturdays, 10 AM to 5 PM; Sundays, 2 to 5 PM); closed November through March. 7 Charlotte Sq. (phone: 225-2160).

Edinburgh Zoo – Opposite the Pentland Hills, away from the city center, en route to the western suburb of Corstorphine, is a zoo with a view and the world's most famous penguins, the largest colony in captivity. Every afternoon at 2:30, from April through

September, they perform their delightful Penguin Parade through the park grounds. Open daily from 9 AM to 6 PM. Admission charge. Corstorphine Rd., Murrayfield (phone: 334-9171).

Grassmarket – This ancient street is flanked by many cozy eateries, elegant shops, and seedy-looking flophouses. The West Bow, off the street's east end, has some intriguing boutiques. Leading from the Grassmarket is Cowgate, with the 16th-century Magdalen Chapel (phone the Scottish Reformation Society to see it: 220-1450).

Dean Village – This 800-year-old grain milling town on the Water of Leith is over 100 feet below the level of much of the rest of the city and a good place to soak up local color. In summer the woodland walk along the river is popping with bohemians who live in the next village, Stockbridge. End of Bell's Brae (turn left off Queensferry St. onto Bell's Brae as you approach Dean Bridge from the west end of Princes St.).

Water of Leith Walkway – The Walkway extends from the outlying Edinburgh district of Colinton, on the southwest side of the city, near the Water of Leith's source, to the mouth of the Water of Leith at Edinburgh's chief seaport, a distance of over 10 miles. The Stockbridge section of the Walkway, including the woodland path from Dean Village, features St. Bernard's Well, so named to honor 12th-century St. Bernard of Clairvaux, said to have restored himself to health with the Well's healing waters after a frosty reception by the Scottish court, which followed his attempt to raise a Scottish army for the Second Crusade. The Well is encased in an impressive Doric rotunda featuring a marble statue of Hygeia, Goddess of Health.

Greyfriars Kirk – This historic Presbyterian church, dedicated on *Christmas Day* in 1620, was the site of a pre-Reformation Franciscan friary. It is also where Presbyterians declared their opposition to the prescribed Episcopalianism of Charles I by signing the National Covenant in blood in 1638. Open March through September. The Kirkyard (graveyard) is open daily from 10 AM to 6:30 PM. Sunday services are given in English and in Gaelic. George IV Bridge (phone: 225-1900).

Edinburgh Crystal Visitors Centre – Cut-glass items sell like hotcakes in the Edinburgh shops, and here's a chance to see how the objects are made. Operating in a town about 12 miles south of Edinburgh, the *Centre* offers guided tours on weekdays; guests can see the glass blown, sheared, and cut. There is also a factory shop and a restaurant. Open from 9:15 AM to 3:30 PM. Children under 10 are not allowed. At Eastfield near Penicuik; take Straiton Rd. south from town (phone: 968-75128).

■ **EXTRA SPECIAL:** The *Edinburgh International Festival* is held every year during the last 3 weeks of August. It features the best-known, most highly regarded performers in opera, music, theater, and dance. Each year brings different orchestras, soloists, theater and opera companies — all are usually topnotch.

Accompanying the festival proper is the phenomenal *Edinburgh Festival Fringe,* an orgy of over 900 productions by amateur and lesser-known professional companies from Europe, Great Britain, and the US who come to Edinburgh at their own expense to strike a blow for art — and for themselves. The *Edinburgh Military Tattoo,* a spectacular concert in full Highland dress by the massed pipe bands of Her Majesty's Scottish regiments, blasts forth most nights during the festival on the Castle Esplanade.

Coinciding with the first 2 weeks of the *International Festival* is the *Edinburgh International Film Festival.* Entries are screened at 88 Lothian Road, where the rest of the year *Filmhouse* (phone: 228-2688) offers a varied diet of classics and art movies in bijou surroundings with restaurant and bar facilities. The *Edinburgh International Jazz Festival* convenes during the second week of the festival. Pick up the succession of lively concerts at the *Edinburgh Festival Club,* in the Edinburgh University Staff Club (9-15 Chambers St.; phone: 226-5639).

Those interested are advised to reserve tickets — and hotel space — as far in advance as possible, especially for the most popular attractions such as the *Tattoo.* A detailed *Festival* brochure is available at the British Tourist Authority in the US (see *Sources and Resources*) by May or June. Book reservations through a travel agent or write directly to the individual events. For the *International Festival,* it's the *Festival Box Office* (21 Market St., Edinburgh EH1 1BW; phone: 226-4001); for the *Tattoo,* the *Ticket Centre* (31-33 Waverley Bridge, Edinburgh EH1 1QB; phone: 225-3732); and the *Edinburgh Festival Fringe Society* (180 High St.; phone: 226-5257 or 226-5259). The film and jazz festivals are more informal and easier to get tickets for once you're in Edinburgh.

SOURCES AND RESOURCES

TOURIST INFORMATION: The City of Edinburgh Tourist Centre (3 Princes St., Edinburgh EH2 2QP; phone: 557-1700), offers information, maps, and leaflets, and stocks all City of Edinburgh publications. On sale there is the *Edinburgh Official Guide,* updated annually. In it is a reasonable working map of downtown areas, with places of interest marked. A good, more detailed map is the Edinburgh edition of the *Geographia Street Atlas and Index* series, on sale at most local bookshops. The pamphlets on Edinburgh history and legend at the *Outlook Tower and Camera Obscura* bookshop (see *Special Places*) will add greatly to your appreciation of what you see of the city. Each costs about $2.50. For a selection of other publications of local interest, also check the *Ticket Centre* (Waverley Bridge; phone: 225-8616), open weekdays 10 AM to 4:30 PM; Saturdays, 10 AM to 12:30 PM; during high summer, open later and on the weekends.

The US Consulate is at 3 Regent Ter. (phone: 556-5213).

The tourist center also has leaflets on guided walking tours available in Edinburgh, including tours of the Royal Mile, the New Town, Leith, and a Robert Louis Stevenson trail. Among the offerings is a small foray into the dark side of Edinburgh's history entitled Ghosts, Ghouls, Gallows.

For information concerning travel in other parts of Scotland, drop by the Scottish Travel Centre on South St. Andrew St. (phone: 332-2433).

Local Coverage – The *Scotsman,* morning daily; the *Edinburgh Evening News,* evening daily; *What's On,* published monthly by the city, listing forthcoming happenings; another *What's On,* a free, privately owned monthly, available in most hotel lobbies; and *The List,* a comprehensive Glasgow and Edinburgh events guide (phone: 558-1191). Also see the *Festival Times* during the *Edinburgh Festival.*

Food – See *Eating and Drinking in Edinburgh,* sold by the tourist board, *Waverley Market,* 3 Princes St.

TELEPHONE: The country code for Scotland is 44; the city code for Edinburgh is 31.

GETTING AROUND: Airport – Edinburgh Airport is about a half hour from the center of town; the average taxi fare is $12. An *Airlink* bus, No. 100, travels from the airport to Waverley Bridge, making stops en route at Haymarket and Murrayfield (phone: 226-5087). The tourist desk at Edinburgh Airport (phone: 333-1000) will provide information.

Bus – *Lothian Region Transport* headquarters is at 14 Queen St. (phone: 554-4494), parallel to Princes Street, 2 blocks away. Route maps, except those that run from St. Andrew Square (phone: 556-8464), are available from the City Transport Information desk at the *Ticket Centre* on Waverley Bridge (phone: 226-5087). Passengers can reach most places from Princes Street; exact fare required. The tourist board office can provide information on bus tours of the city and countryside. Longer-distance buses leave from St. Andrew Square Bus Station (St. Andrew Sq.). The Edinburgh Tourist-card provides unlimited bus travel for 2, 5, or 9 days, and may be purchased at either the *Lothian Region Transport* office or the *Ticket Centre.* The *Edinburgh Airbus,* a 30-minute service between the airport and the city center stops at most of the major hotels (phone: 556-2244).

Car Rental – All major national firms are represented at the airport and in town.

Taxi – There are cabstands at St. Andrew Square Bus Station, Waverley Station (off Princes St.), in front of the *Caledonian* hotel (west end of Princes St.), and in front of the *Cameron Toll Shopping Centre* (Lady Rd.). To call a cab, contact *City Cabs* (phone: 228-1211), *Central Radio Taxis* (phone: 229-2468), or *Radiocabs* (phone: 225-6736 or 225-9000).

Train – The main railway station is Waverley Station at Princes Street and Waverley Bridge (phone: 556-2451). All trains *not* bound for London also stop at Haymarket Station, about 3 blocks west of Princes St. To catch a train here, add about 4 minutes to departure time from Waverley Station. There also is a 24-hour *British Rail* information service (phone: 556-2451).

LOCAL SERVICES:
 Dentist – Dental emergencies are treated for a nominal charge at *Western General Hospital* (Crewe Rd.; phone: 332-2525) and at the *Dental Hospital* (31 Chambers St.; phone: 225-9511).

Dry Cleaner/Tailor – *Pullar's,* 2-hour dry cleaning (23 Frederick St.; phone: 225-8095); *Quick Stitch,* for quick repairs, is just around the corner from *Pullar's* (79 Rose St.; phone: 225-5840).

Limousine Service – *W. L. Sleigh,* 6 Devon Rd. (phone: 337-3171).

Medical Emergency – *Royal Infirmary,* Emergency Ward, Lauriston Pl. (phone: 229-2477).

Messenger Service – *QED,* operates 24 hours daily at *Dundonald House,* 5-7 Dundonald St. (phone: 557-3877; fax: 556-0215).

National/International Courier – *QED* (see above); *Pony Express,* 31A Albany St. (phone: 557-4303).

Office Equipment Rental – *Reception Business Administrative Services* (21 Lansdowne Crescent; phone: 226-2830); also rents office space on a short-term basis.

Pharmacy – *Boots* (48 Shandwick Pl.; phone: 225-6757) is open from 8:45 AM to 9 PM Mondays through Saturdays and from 11 AM to 4:30 PM Sundays.

Photocopies – *Rank Xerox* (27 George St.; phone: 225-4388); *Rondes Duplicating Agency* (61 Queen St.; phone: 225-7063) also word-processes handwritten material.

Post Office – The main post office is open from 9 AM to 5:30 PM Mondays through Thursdays, from 9:30 AM to 5:30 PM on Fridays, and from 9 AM to 12:30 PM on Saturdays. 2 Waterloo Pl., east of Princes St. (phone: 550-8229).

Secretary/Stenographer – *Reception Business Administrative Services,* 21 Lansdowne Crescent (phone: 226-2830).

Teleconference Facilities – Edinburgh can now handle five-party calls. To make an appointment, call *British Telecom* weekdays from 8:30 AM to 5 PM. Dial 100 and ask for Woodcraft Telephone Exchange.

Telex – *Waverley Business Services,* 11 Cumberland St. (phone: 557-4880).

Other – Tuxedo rental: *Dormie Menswear* (46 Frederick St.; phone: 225-2625). Should the occasion arise, they also have full Highland dress available for rent.

SPECIAL EVENTS: *New Years' Eve,* or "hogamonay," is celebrated after midnight by visiting the homes of friends and acquaintances (it is customary to take a half-bottle of whisky or another favorite tipple to share with your hosts). The *Edinburgh Folk Festival* occurs in early spring. For details, contact the *Folk Festival Office* (16A Fleshmarket Close; phone: 220-0464). The world's only international science festival, the *Edinburgh Science Festival,* has been held for the past 3 years here in early April; it includes films, walks, talks, and conferences on superconductivity, high-tech wine making, genetic engineering, and more. For more details contact the *Science Festival Box Office* (20 Torphicen St., Edinburgh EH1 1QS; phone: 228-4756). The *Scottish Antiques Fair* and the *Edinburgh Annual Antiques Fair* are held in April, July, and November; both are hosted by the *Roxburghe* hotel (Charlotte Sq.; phone: 547-4464; Linda Hay has details). The *Edinburgh International Festival* and the concurrent *Edinburgh Festival Fringe,* the *Edinburgh Military Tattoo,* the *Edinburgh International Film Festival,* and the *Edinburgh International Jazz Festival* are held every year during the last 3 weeks in August. (For details, see *Extra Special.*)

MUSEUMS: The city runs two museums of local history: *Huntly House* (142 Canongate; phone: 225-2424, ext. 6689) and the *Lady Stair's House,* a Burns, Scott, and Stevenson museum (Lawnmarket; phone: 225-2424, ext. 6593). Both are open Mondays through Saturdays, 10 AM to 5 PM. The *National Gallery of Scotland,* one of the three Scottish national galleries, is described in *Special Places.* Other museums include the following:

Central Library – An outstanding collection of maps, prints, photographs, books, and newspapers. The Reference, Scotland, and Edinburgh rooms are invaluable. Opening times vary. George IV Bridge (phone: 225-5584).

De Marco Gallery – Headquarters for avant-garde art. Closed Sundays. Open 10:30 AM to 6 PM. 17-21 Blackfriars St. (phone: 557-0707).

Lauriston Castle – A fine 16th-century tower enlarged to become a historic home, the castle overlooks the estuary of the Firth of Forth. The interior is filled with period furniture and collections of Derbyshire Blue Hogn, Crossley wool mosaics, and objets d'art. Visits with guided tours only. Admission charge. Open on Saturdays and Sundays only during the winter; closed Fridays during the spring and summer. Call in advance for tour information. Off Cramond Rd. S. (phone: 336-2060 or 225-2424, ext. 6689).

Museum of Childhood – A treasure house of historic toys, dolls, and children's clothing, it also features a time tunnel with reconstructions of a schoolroom, a street scene, a fancy dress party, and a late 19th-century nursery. Its founder, a bachelor who intended the museum for adults only, so disliked little ones that he once replied to a radio interviewer that he couldn't tolerate children between meals. Nevertheless, the museum has always been immensely popular with small fry. Open Mondays through Saturdays from 10 AM to 6 PM; closed Sundays except in August (open from 2 to 5 PM) from June 1 through September 30, and open Mondays through Saturdays from 10 AM to 5 PM from October 1 through May 31. 38 High St. (phone: 225-2424, ext. 6645).

National Library of Scotland – Exhibits on Scotland's literati through the ages. Temporary admission to the reading room may be obtained by serious inquirers. Open Mondays through Fridays from 9:30 AM to 8:30 PM and on Saturdays from 9:30 AM to 1 PM. George IV Bridge (phone: 226-4531).

The People's Story – Tells the tale of the working class of Edinburgh through the centuries, including sections on the development of trade unions, health, welfare, and leisure. Opening hours are the same as the *Museum of Childhood.* At the Canongate Tolbooth, 163 Canongate (phone: 225-2424, ext. 6638).

Royal Museum of Scotland – A museum of natural history, science, and technology that houses Scotland's collection of decorative arts from around the world. Displays range from primitive art to space-age material, and the working models in the Hall of Power are great for kids. Open Mondays through Saturdays from 10 AM to 5 PM and Sundays from 2 to 5 PM. Chambers St. (phone: 225-7534).

Russell Collection of Historial Musical Instruments – A feast for those who appreciate early keyboard music. Housed in *Saint Cecilia's Hall,* a restored 18th-century concert hall, the collection of 1,000 instruments is owned by Edinburgh University. Open Wednesdays and Saturdays from 2 to 5 PM. Admission charge. Corner of Cowgate and Niddry Sts. (phone: 650-1000, ext. 2805).

Scottish National Gallery of Modern Art – Scotland's finest collection of 20th-century painting, sculpture, and graphic art that includes works by Picasso, Matisse, Moore, Hockney, Campbell, and Conroy. Open Mondays through Saturdays from 10 AM to 5 PM, and on Sundays from 2 to 5 PM. Belford Rd. (phone: 556-8921).

Scottish National Portrait Gallery – Features paintings and sculptures of Mary, Queen of Scots, Robert Burns, Sir Walter Scott, and more. Open Mondays through Saturdays from 10 AM to 5 PM, and on Sundays from 2 to 5 PM. 1 Queen St. (phone: 556-8921).

 SHOPPING: Princes Street is Edinburgh's main shopping street, chockablock with a variety of stores. In addition, at the east end of Princes Street is *Waverley Market,* a large, modern shopping mall with Waverley Station at its base and the tourist office on the roof. Open daily until 6 PM, except Thursdays until 7 PM. The best buy is in Scottish tartans and woolens. Also worth a look are antiques — particularly Victoriana — in the area around St. Stephen's Street in Stockbridge. Bone china and Scottish crystal are attractive, and don't miss the shortbread, which is on sale everywhere. St. Mary's Street, leading off the Royal Mile, is rapidly becoming famous for shops selling secondhand clothes, jewelry, and objets d'art. We especially recommend the following shops:

Debenham's – A branch of the London firm, with clothes, accessories, cosmetics, and more. 109-112 Princes St. (phone: 225-1302).

Edinburgh Woollen Mill – Good, inexpensive alternative to the *Scotch House,* with three locations: 62 Princes St. (phone: 225-4966); 453 Lawnmarket (phone: 225-1525); and 139 Princes St. (phone: 226-3840).

Eric Davidson – Antique furniture, ceramics, paintings, and clocks. 4 Grassmarket (phone: 225-5815).

James Pringle's Woolen Mill – If it's made of wool, it's probably sold here. Offering low prices for top-quality goods is the policy of this factory outlet, which also provides free taxi service from your hotel to their door. 70-74 Bangor Rd. (phone: 553-5161).

Jenner's Department Store – Sells everything, especially bone china and Scottish crystal. A particularly good selection of fine food items, ideal for packing fancy picnics. Princes and St. David's Sts. (phone: 225-2442).

John R. Martin – An unusual and ever-changing assortment of merchandise, from gold thimbles to stuffed elephants. 96 West Bow (phone: 226-7190).

Joseph H. Bonnar – For a wide assortment of jewelry, including antique pieces. 72 Thistle St. (phone: 226-2811).

Kinloch Anderson Ltd. – Serving the royal family, it's the place where Prince Charles, among others, obtains his kilts (for more details see "Shopping Spree" in *For the Experience,* DIVERSIONS). 4 Dock St. (phone: 555-1392).

Mrs. Baxter's Victorian Kitchen – Fine foods and homemade jams are available in this re-created 19th-century kitchen, the central feature of which is the magnificent, old-fashioned cooking range. Rose St. (phone: 226-2022).

Pitlochry Knitwear – Bargains in Scottish products, especially sweaters, kilts, and ladies' suits. 28 North Bridge (phone: 225-3893).

Scotch House – Classy, expensive woolens such as kilts, sweaters, tweeds, scarves, shawls, and mohairs. 60 Princes St. (phone: 556-1252).

Scottish Craft Centre – Attractive handmade items. Canongate St.

Scottish Gallery – The oldest gallery in Scotland, it dates back to 1842 and sells contemporary Scottish paintings and crafts. 94 George St. (phone: 225-5955).

Whisky Shop – This connoisseurs' paradise claims to have the largest selection of whiskies anywhere in the world. *Waverley Market* (phone: 558-1588).

SPORTS AND FITNESS: Biking – If you have the urge to pedal, rentals are available at about $8.25 a day from *Central Cycle Hire,* 13 Lochrin Pl., Tolcross (phone: 228-6363).

Fitness Center – *Meadowbank Sports Centre* (139 London Rd.; phone: 661-5365), has a large gym with weights and exercise equipment, a 400-meter track, and classes in archery, boxing, fencing, and judo. For other sports, consult the *Edinburgh Official Guide* and the Edinburgh Tourist Centre's *What's On.*

Golf – Scotland's national mania. A letter from your home club president or pro should get you into any of the city's 22 courses (you'll usually need it only for the posh, private ones like *Royal Burgess, Bruntsfield,* both in suburban Barnton, and *Muirfield* — home of the world's oldest group of players, the *Honourable Company of Edinburgh Golfers* — in nearby Gullane). Make tee-times at these clubs ahead of arrival. Golf clubs can be rented. Full details on public courses are listed in the *Edinburgh Official Guide,* on the map *Golf Courses of Scotland,* and in the free leaflet *Golf Courses in Scotland,* all available at the tourist office.

Jogging – A good bet is *Holyrood Park,* near the huge stone palace at the foot of Canongate. An especially popular run is around Arthur's Seat, the extinct volcano in the center of the park.

Skiing – *Hillend Ski Centre* on the Pentland Hills is the largest manmade slope in Great Britain. Equipment can be rented, and instruction is available. Open daily during winter from 9:30 AM to 10 PM, and in summer from 9:30 AM to 9 PM on weekdays, and to 5 PM on weekends (phone: 445-4433).

Swimming – Have a dip in the luxurious *Royal Commonwealth Pool,* built for the 1970 *Commonwealth Games.* Also here is the only indoor rowing tank in Great Britain, where you can flex your muscles and pretend that you are competing in *Eights Week* at Oxford, and Nautilus, Europe's largest water slide, with re-created river rapids, a twister, and a stingray. Open weekdays, 9 AM to 9 PM, weekends, 10 AM to 4 PM. Dalkeith Rd. (phone: 667-7211).

THEATER: The *King's* (2 Leven St.; phone: 229-1201), and the *Royal Lyceum* (Grindlay St.; phone: 229-9697), are Edinburgh's two main venues. The *Royal Lyceum* reopened after extensive renovations in 1991. The *King's* presents everything from occasional touring productions of the finest of London's *National Theatre* to boring, patronizing junk. On the other hand, the *Royal Lyceum* has been gaining an increasingly high reputation for presenting interesting productions, primarily of established plays. Pop stars and extravaganzas are frequently presented at the *Edinburgh Exhibition Centre* (Ingliston; phone: 333-3036) or at the *Playhouse* (20 Greenside Pl.; phone: 557-2590), a converted cinema where musical productions are staged. The *Traverse* (112 West Bow; phone: 226-2633) is a small theater which has become internationally known for its productions of avant-garde pieces and for presenting the work of new playwrights from all over the world. The *Netherbow* (43 High St.; phone: 556-9579), and *Theatre Workshop* (34 Hamilton Pl.;

phone: 225-7942), mount small-scale, artistic productions. Schedules are in the dailies and in *The List.*

MUSIC: Classical music is the city's overriding passion. Highbrow musical events are held at *Usher Hall* (Lothian Rd.; phone: 228-1155), where the *Scottish National Orchestra* holds performances on Friday nights at 7:30. The *Scottish Opera Company,* which maintains good standards, has seasons at the *King's,* and also at the *Playhouse* (see *Theater* for addresses), where other famous names in both classical and non-classical music give concerts. Concerts also are held at *Saint Cecilia's Hall* (Canongate; no phone). For chamber music and occasional jazz, try *Queen's Hall* (Clerk St.; phone: 668-3456). At St. Mary's Cathedral (Palmerston Pl.; phone: 225-6293), evensong is sung on weekday afternoons at 5:15 by a trained choir with boy sopranos. Also, countless amateur groups swell the city's halls and churches. Details are available in the dailies and in *The List.*

NIGHTCLUBS AND NIGHTLIFE: Edinburgh isn't exactly Las Vegas; it isn't even Philadelphia. Discos here usually are filled with a very young crowd, but you could risk the following if you're under 30: *Madisons* (Lothian Rd.; phone: 229-7670), which has the most modern light show in Scotland; *Zenatec* (56 Fountainbridge; phone: 229-7733); *Cinderellas Rockerfellers* (99 St. Stephen St.; phone: 556-0266); *Buster Brown's Disco* (25 Market St.; phone: 226-4224); the *Red Hot Pepper Club* (3 Semple St.; phone: 229-7733); the *Network Night Club* (3 W. Tollcross; phone: 228-3252); and *Outer Limits* — teenagers leave at 11 PM so others can roll up to an after-hours bar (W. Tollcross; phone: 228-3252). *Amphitheatre,* in a deconsecrated movie theater, is officially a nightclub and *the* place to go (it's on the Lothian Rd. between *Usher Hall* and Princes St.; phone: 229-7670). Jazz and folk music can be heard at bars and hotels around the city; check the *Evening News*'s "Nightlife" page, *What's On* magazine, or *The List.*

BEST IN TOWN

CHECKING IN: In Scotland, it is practically impossible to get a room without an accompanying kippers-to-nuts Big Scottish Breakfast (you pay for it whether you eat it or not). Expect to shell out $155 and up for a double room with breakfast in the hotels listed below as expensive; $90 to $155 for those in the moderate category; between $55 and $90 for the cheapies-but-goodies in the inexpensive range. Unless otherwise noted, hotels accept all major credit cards. Should you find it impossible to get into any of our selected hotels, the City of Edinburgh District Council at the airport and in town at the tourist center, *Waverley Market* (3 Princes St.; phone: 557-1700), has an accommodations service covering all of Edinburgh and the surrounding district. All telephone numbers are in the 31 area code unless otherwise indicated.

Balmoral Edinburgh – At the turn of the century, two rival railway companies raced to be the first to erect its own hotel; the North British railway company won, and its establishment began receiving guests in 1902. After a £23 million refurbishment, the hotel reopened in 1991. The Victorian features of this architectural landmark have been retained, although it has been revamped for the 21st century. Business facilities include 24-hour room service, meeting rooms for up to 400, concierge, foreign currency exchange, secretarial services, audiovisual equipment, photocopiers, computers, cable television news, translation services, and express checkout. Princes St. (phone: 556-2414; fax: 557-3747; telex: 727282). Expensive.

Caledonian – A large Edwardian former railroad hotel with 237 rooms, 2 dining rooms, and 3 bars. Recently completely refurbished, it boasts great views of Edinburgh Castle. The decor is very engaging, and the rooms have been made infinitely more appealing. Celebrities love it. The "Caley" has always been associated with refined society, although it once forgot itself sufficiently to allow Roy Rogers to bring his horse, Trigger, into the lounge and parade him up the Grand Staircase. Although rumors spread that the equine wonder took his repose in the Versailles Suite, he was led away in the early hours of the morning to nearby stables. The new *Carriages* restaurant rivals the hotel's *Pompadour* dining room, with its first class fare (see *Eating Out*). Business facilities include 24-hour room service, meeting rooms for up to 250, concierge, foreign currency exchange, secretarial services, audiovisual equipment, photocopiers, translation services, and express checkout. West end of Princes St. (phone: 225-2433; fax: 225-6632; telex: 72179). Expensive.

Carlton Highland – Remarkably transformed from an old department store into a grand and sophisticated Victorian hotel with 207 rooms, 2 dining rooms, and a bar. Health facilities include squash courts, a gym, saunas, and Jacuzzi, and there is live entertainment and dancing nightly at the hotel's *Minus One* nightclub. North Bridge, off Princes St. (phone: 556-7277). Expensive.

Channings – Once a fine Georgian residence in the West End of Edinburgh, this elegant townhouse is located down a quiet cobbled lane within walking distance of Princes Street. There are 48 beautifully appointed rooms with modern amenities, and the bar and brasserie offer Scottish and international dishes. Business facilities include 24-hour room service, meeting rooms for up to 20, concierge, foreign currency exchange, secretarial services, audiovisual equipment, photocopiers, and computers. Channings South Learmonth Gardens; phone: 315-2226; fax: 332-9631). Expensive.

Dalhousie Castle – Originally built during the 12th century and enlarged ever since (Queen Victoria once stayed here). Now it's a luxury country-house hotel with 24 rooms. About 8 miles south of Edinburgh (phone: 87-520153). Expensive.

Edinburgh Sheraton – Honey-colored, just off Princes Street, it seems architecturally incongruous in the neighborhood, but can't be beat for its range of modern amenities: 263 well-equipped rooms (including suites that overlook Festival Square, where you can sit at the window and watch the pipes and drums of the Scots Guards playing below as Edinburgh Castle looms in the background), a health club and gym, a sauna and whirlpool bath, a swimming pool, parking, a bar, and a restaurant. 1 Festival Sq. (phone: 229-9131). Expensive.

George – Located in the New Town between Charlotte and St. Andrew squares, this gracious establishment originated as apartments for the aristocracy when the New Town of Edinburgh was created by architect Robert Adam and his pupils, and it still retains a luxurious ambience. It has 195 bedrooms (phones in rooms), 2 dining rooms, and the *Long Gathering of the Clans* bar. Business facilities include 24-hour room service, meeting rooms for up to 250, concierge, foreign currency exchange, secretarial services, audiovisual equipment, photocopiers, teletext, and express checkout. 19-21 George St. (phone: 225-1251; fax: 226-5644; telex: 72570). Expensive.

Hilton National – Flashy, contemporary, away from the center of things but with a beautiful view of the Water of Leith and close to Dean Village and the *Museum of Modern Art*. There are 144 rooms and 2 restaurants. Business facilities include 24-hour room service, meeting rooms for up to 140, concierge, foreign currency exchange, secretarial services, audiovisual equipment, photocopiers, teletext, and express checkout. 69 Belford Rd. (phone: 332-2545; fax: 322-3805; telex: 727979). Expensive.

King James Thistle – An oasis of charm and friendliness in *St. James* (a shopping center — otherwise known as Edinburgh's leading eyesore). Guests are treated graciously by the staff of this 147-room hotel; the *St. Jacques* restaurant offers Scottish food prepared *à la français*. Business facilities include 24-hour room service, meeting rooms for up to 250, concierge, foreign currency exchange, secretarial services, audiovisual equipment, photocopiers, teletext, translation services, and express checkout. Top of Leith Walk at Princes St. (phone: 556-0111; fax: 557-5335; telex: 727200). Expensive.

Norton House – Set in a secluded parkland on the edge of Edinburgh, this ornate Victorian mansion was once the home of the Ushers (they founded the brewing firm). Dine in the lovely conservatory restaurant or the more informal *Norton Tavern,* located in what once was the walled garden. Business facilities include 24-hour room service, meeting rooms for up to 400, concierge, foreign currency exchange, secretarial services, audiovisual equipment, photocopiers, teletext, and express checkout. In Ingilston, near Edinburgh Airport (phone: 333-1275; fax: 333-5305; telex: 727232). Expensive.

Post House – Ultramodern, all-conveniences affair, this is a good place to be if you have a car (it's beside the zoo, outside the city center). Its low-priced coffeehouse is less stuffily British than almost anywhere else. Breakfast optional. All 208 rooms have phones. Business facilities include 24-hour room service, meeting rooms for up to 150, concierge, foreign currency exchange, secretarial services, audiovisual equipment, photocopiers, teletext, translation services, and express checkout. Corstorphine Rd. (phone: 334-0390; fax: 334-9237; telex: 727103). Expensive.

Roxburghe – A distinguished, tranquil oasis at the West End of Princes Street. The hotel is one of the best examples of Robert Adam's townhouse architecture in his showpiece, Charlotte Square. Scottish seafood and game are the specialties in the *Consort* restaurant. There are 75 well-appointed guestrooms. Business facilities include 24-hour room service, meeting rooms for up to 300, concierge, foreign currency exchange, secretarial services, audiovisual equipment, photocopiers, and express checkout. Charlotte Sq. (phone: 225-3921; fax: 220-2518; telex: 727054). Expensive.

Royal Scot – This 252-room modern structure is the epitome of the faultless airport hotel. Direct access to M8 for Glasgow. Business facilities include 24-hour room service, meeting rooms for up to 300, concierge, foreign currency exchange, secretarial services, audiovisual equipment, photocopiers, and telextext. 111 Glasgow Rd. (phone: 334-9191). Expensive.

Scandic Crown – Located halfway between Edinburgh Castle and the Royal Mile in Edinburgh's Old Town, this new establishment has an antiquated air, which goes well with the neighboring architecture. Rooms have heated floors, security safes, satellite TV, free in-house movies, and mini-bars. The 2 restaurants serve a combination of Scandinavian and Scottish fare. There's also a health club with Finnish saunas. Business facilities include 24-hour room service, meeting rooms for up to 80, concierge, secretarial services, audiovisual equipment, photocopiers, computers, translation services, and express checkout. 80 High St. (phone: 557-9797; fax: 557-9789). Expensive.

Howard – Its flower-filled window boxes are the last word in winsomeness. It has 25 rooms, with phones (and, surprisingly for a hostelry this size in Edinburgh, private baths). 32-36 Great King St. (phone: 557-3500). Expensive to moderate.

Royal British – One of the few hotels actually located in Princes Street, this establishment is just across the road from the Waverley railway station and shopping center (Edinburgh Castle looms beyond). There are 77 guestrooms, many of which have four-poster beds. Traditional Scottish high teas are served in the early evening. The *Claymore* restaurant serves good Scottish fare. Business facilities include 24-hour room service, meeting rooms for up to 150, concierge, foreign currency exchange, secretarial services, audiovisual equipment, and photocopiers. 20 Princes St. (phone: 556-4901; fax: 557-0510; telex: 57476). Expensive to moderate.

Braid Hills – Muriel Spark fans will remember that this is where Miss Jean Brodie, by then past her prime, took tea. An old, established, family-run, 68-room hotel in the southern suburbs toward the Pentland Hills. 134 Braid Rd. (phone: 447-8888). Moderate.

Donmaree – This establishment recently underwent extensive renovations. There still are 17 rooms, but a new conservatory overlooks the gardens. The restaurant offers good, traditional dishes. 21 Mayfield Gardens (phone: 667-3641). Moderate to inexpensive.

Galloway Guest House – Just off the panoramic Dean Bridge, all 10 rooms have color TV sets; 6 have a private bath; and none has a phone. Room rate includes breakfast. Guests also have access to tea and coffee facilities. On-street parking. No credit cards accepted. 22 Dean Park Crescent (phone: 332-3672). Inexpensive.

EATING OUT: Reports on Scottish food vary from calling it a joke to claiming it is at least superior to English cooking. Still, visitors might want to try some of the following specialties: cock-a-leekie soup (chicken and leek), salmon, haddock, trout, and Aberdeen Angus beef. Skip any offering of haggis (spicy intestines), except on a purely experimental basis. Scones originated in Scotland, and shortbread shouldn't be missed. Restaurants usually keep the city's formal hours (lunch until 2:30, dinner anywhere from 6 on). Expect to pay $80 and up for dinner for two, excluding wine and tips, in establishments listed as very expensive; $55 to $75 for expensive; $30 to $50 in moderate establishments; and under $30 in inexpensive places. All telephone numbers are in the 31 area code unless otherwise indicated.

Pompadour – The fascinating lunch menu is a steadily unfurling history of Scottish cooking, while dinner features French dishes (some of the recipes were used in the Palace of Holyroodhouse when Mary, Queen of Scots married the heir to the French throne). Closed Saturdays and Sundays for lunch. Reservations advised. In the *Caledonian Hotel,* Princes St. (phone: 225-2433). Very expensive.

L'Auberge – A discreet, indeed positively diplomatic, dining spot that serves French fare, most notably fish and game. Open daily. Reservations unnecessary. 58 St. Mary's St. between Cowgate and Canongate (phone: 556-5888). Expensive.

Beehive Inn – Among the fittings in this Old Town place is a cell door from the very Old Town jail. Steaks and fish are served from an open charcoal grill and are followed by luscious desserts. Closed Sundays. Reservations advised. 18 Grassmarket (phone: 225-7171). Expensive.

Cosmo's – Edinburgh's link to Rome. Everybody who works here is fiercely Italian, as is the menu, with seafood and veal dishes among the favorites. The cocktail bar is made of imported Italian marble. Closed Sundays and Mondays. Reservations necessary. 58A Castle St. (phone: 226-6743). Expensive.

Howtowdie – White tablecloths and glass cases full of taxidermists' birds set the tone at this Highland-style establishment long famed for its ritzy image and traditional Scottish cooking. Closed Sundays, October to April. Reservations advised. 24A Stafford St. (phone: 225-6291). Expensive.

Merchant's – Trendy and French, with white tablecloths, silver, crystal, arfd decorated in the style of a French country house; there's also a green parrot that sleeps at lunchtime and can be pacified at dinner with a monkey-nut. Closed Sundays. Reservations unnecessary. 17 Merchant St. (phone: 225-4009). Expensive.

Prestonfield House – A 300-year-old country estate within its own peacock-laden park grounds. Candlelit dinners in rooms with tapestries, paintings, and blazing open fires. French cooking. Open daily. Reservations necessary. Off Priestfield Rd. (phone: 668-3346). Expensive.

Arches – The dining room adjoining this bustling university-area bar has very good lunches and elegant dinners. Open daily. Reservations advised. 66-67 South Bridge (phone: 556-0200). Moderate.

Bay of Bengal – Excellent Indian dishes are cooked from scratch with delicate spices, and the wait for your meal is well worth it. Open daily. Reservations advised. 146 High St. (phone: 225-2361). Moderate.

Lorenzo's – Delightful cellar restaurant near Edinburgh Castle, this charming Italian spot offers Roman cooking and romantic corner tables. Open daily. Reservations advised. 5 Johnston Terrace (phone: 226-2426). Moderate.

Skipper's Bistro – A jolly waterfront seafood spot in Leith, justly known for its imaginative preparations and the freshness of its ingredients. Closed Sundays. Reservations necessary. 1A Dock Pl., Leith (phone: 554-1018). Moderate.

Helios Fountain – Among other specialties featured at this trendy café are a selection of vegetarian pies and goulashes invented each morning by the proprietors; the dishes are ready in time for lunchtime guests. It's a great spot for eavesdropping on intellectual conversations or for watching people browse over the books and jewelry making materials also sold here. Open Mondays through Saturdays, 10 AM to 6 PM. Reservations unnecessary. 7 Grassmarket (phone: 229-7884). Inexpensive.

Henderson's Salad Table – This cafeteria-style vegetarian's heaven-on-earth may keep diners standing in line for as long as 15 minutes, but it's worth it. Piles of salads, hot pots, opulent desserts available continuously day and evening. Closed Sundays. No reservations. 94 Hanover St. (phone: 225-2131). Inexpensive.

SHARING A PINT: Until recently, boozing was restricted to puritanical hours. But now it's possible to imbibe from 11 AM to 11 PM, and a few places have opened up where the taps keep flowing until the wee hours. Among the best pubs: the *Abbotsford* (3 Rose St.) is a haunt of Scotland's "Makars" (playwrights and poets) and journalists; *Bennet's* (Leven St.) is a noisy but atmospheric theater-district pub with a Victorian hangover; the *Beau Brummel* (99 Hanover St.) is a neo-Regency plush artifact in mid-city; and the *Tilted Wig* (1-2-3 Cumberland St.), facetiously known as the Wilted Twig, is notable for its uncompromising trendiness and has a clientele of bar-hogging English smoothies, whom you can scatter at a stroke by standing in the doorway shouting, "Nigel, your MG's on fire!" And for enjoyable courtyard drinking facilities, join the crowd of university students at the *Pear Tree* (36 W. Nicolson St., off Buccleuch St.). If you enjoy folk music, try the *Fiddler's Arms* (9-11 Grassmarket).

Rutherford's (Drummond St., off South Bridge opposite Old College) was much frequented by Robert Louis Stevenson and Arthur Conan Doyle when they were Edinburgh University students in the 1870s, although while within its portals they never knowingly met. *Stewart's,* across the road, is a fine working class pub, and if the private back room is free, you and your friends can occupy it for an old-fashioned disputatious Scottish enquiry into philosophy — see Scott's *Guy Mannering. Preservation Hall* (9 Victoria St., opposite the *Bookfare* bookshop) is large, commodious, ornamented with fine epigraphs against drink, and offers rock and jazz music evenings. *Mather's* (25 Broughton St.) is the ecumenical watering hole for left-wing labour, nationalist, and sexual politicos. Opulent barges sometimes carry licenses in tourist season on the Leith waterfront. Find out at the *Waterfront Wine Bar* (1C Dock Pl., Leith). Also try *The Malt Shovel* (57 The Shore, Leith). Both offer bar lunches.

FLORENCE

Florence, city of the arts, jewel of the Renaissance, symbol of the Tuscan pride in grace and refinement, is for many an acquired taste. Rome has romance, Venice intrigue, and Naples a poignant gaiety; Florence may seem too austere, too serious, too severe. The elegance that is Florence does not seize you immediately — not like the splashing fountains of Rome, the noisy laughter and song of Naples, the pastel chandeliers peeking out of patrician palaces along Venice's Grand Canal.

Next to the mellow tangerine hues of Rome, the pinks of Venice, and the orgy of color that is Naples, Florence is a study in neutral shades: blacks and whites, beiges and browns, a splattering of dark green. Its people seem less spontaneous and exuberant than Romans or Neapolitans, more hardworking and reserved, with a sort of innate sense of dignity and pride.

Florentine palaces are more like fortresses, at first glance rather forbidding and uninviting to the visitor; the city's somber streets are lined with solid, direct architecture; its civic sculpture is noble and restrained. But this is only a superficial view of Florence. Step into the palaces and you will be awed by the beauty of fine details as well as by some of the world's greatest art treasures. Look at the fine Florentine crafts in gold and leather and exquisite fabrics in the elegant but classically serious shops. It won't take long before you will understand why the culture and art of Florence have attracted people from around the world through the centuries, and why it is as much a favorite of artists, students, and expatriates today as it was at its apogee under the Medicis in the 15th century.

Florence was the home of Cimabue and Giotto, the fathers of Italian painting; of Brunelleschi, Donatello, and Masaccio, who paved the way for the Renaissance; of the Della Robbias, Botticelli, Leonardo da Vinci, and Michelangelo; of Dante Alighieri, Petrarch, and Boccaccio; of Machiavelli and Galileo. Art, science, and life found their finest, most powerful expression in Florence, and records of this splendid past fill the city's many galleries, museums, churches, and palaces, demanding attention.

Florence — *Firenze* in Italian — probably originated as an Etruscan center, but it was only under the Romans in the 1st century BC that it became a true city. Like so many other cities of its time, Roman Florence grew up along the fertile banks of a river, in this case the Arno, amid the rolling green hills of Tuscany. Its Latin name, *Florentia* ("flowering"), probably referred to the city's florid growth, although some ancient historians attributed it to Florinus, the Roman general who besieged the nearby Etruscan hill town of Fiesole in 63 BC.

During the Roman rule, Florence became a thriving military and trading center, with its share of temples, baths, a Town Hall, and an amphitheater, but few architectural monuments of that epoch have survived.

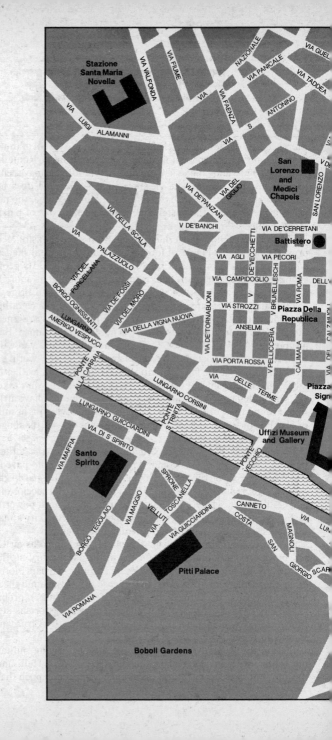

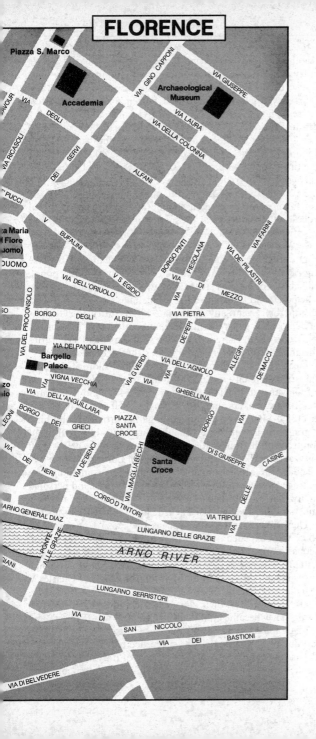

After the fall of the Roman Empire, Florence sank into the decadence of the Dark Ages, and despite a temporary reprieve during Charlemagne's 8th- and 9th-century European empire, it did not really flourish again until the late 11th century. It was then that the great guilds were developed and the florin-based currency began to appear, and Florence became a powerful, self-governing republic.

In the 12th century, interfamily feuds were widespread, and over 150 square stone towers — built for defense by influential families right next to their houses — dominated the city's skyline. Even so, during that and the next century, the Florentine population of about 60,000 (twice that of London at the time) was busily engaged in trade with the rest of the Mediterranean. The amazing building boom that followed, bringing about the demolition of the fortified houses in favor of more gracious public and private palazzi and magnificent churches, reflected the great prosperity of the city's trading and banking families, its wool and silk industries, and the enormous strength of the florin.

As a free city-state or *comune,* Florence managed to maintain a balance between the authority of the Germanic emperors and that of the popes, overcoming the difficulties of internal struggles between the burgher Guelphs (who supported the pope) and the aristocratic Ghibellines (who were behind the Holy Roman Emperor). Eventually, by the late 13th century, the Guelphs won power and a democratic government was inaugurated with the famous Ordinances of Justice. So began Florence's ascent, which spanned 3 centuries and reached its height and greatest splendor under the Medici family.

Owing in large measure to the patronage of the Medicis, Florence became the liveliest and most creative city in Europe. While this certainly pertained during the time of Giovanni di Bicci de' Medici (1360–1429) and his illustrious dynasty of merchants, bankers, and art patrons, as well as that of his son Cosimo the Elder (1389–1464), who continued to gather artists around him, it was Cosimo's grandson Lorenzo the Magnificent (1449–1492) who put Florence in the forefront of the Italian Renaissance. An elaborate celebration will take place this year to mark the 500th anniversary of Lorenzo's death (see *Special Events*). Today, the Medici might be thought of as something of a political machine, since they controlled — through their wealth and personal power alone — a city that was, in theory at least, still a democratic republic governed by members of the trade guilds. Their de facto rule was not uncontested, however. They suffered reversals, such as the Pazzi Conspiracy in 1478, and twice they were expelled — from 1494 to 1512, when a revolution brought the religious reformer Savonarola briefly to power (and an attempt was made to reestablish democracy), and again from 1527 to 1530, when another republic was set up, only to fall to the troops of Emperor Charles V and lead to the Medici restoration.

Finally, in the late 16th century, their glory days behind them, the Medici gained an official title. They became grand dukes (Cosimo I was the first), and Florence became the capital of the grand duchy of Tuscany. In the 18th century, the grand duchy of the Medici was succeeded by that of the house of Lorraine, until Tuscany became part of the kingdom of Italy in 1860. From 1865 to 1871, Florence reigned as temporary capital of the kingdom, but with the capital's transfer to Rome, the history of Florence merges with that of the rest of Italy.

Two catastrophes in this century have caused inestimable damage to Florence's art treasures. In 1944, all the beloved bridges crossing the Arno — except for the Ponte Vecchio — were blown up by the Nazis. Reconstruction began as soon as the Germans retreated. Then, 2 decades later, in November 1966, the Arno burst its banks, covering the historic center with a muddy slime. Over 1,400 works of art, 2 million valuable books, and countless homes were damaged by floodwaters that reached depths of 23 feet. The people of Florence, with help from all over the world, rose to the challenge. Before the floodwaters had receded, they began the painstaking chore of rescuing their treasures from 600,000 tons of mud, oil, and debris.

Today, the city of Florence — with a population of slightly less than half a million — still is a vital force in the arts, in culture, and in science, as well as an industrial, commercial, and university center and a leader in the fields of handicrafts and fashion. Note, indeed, how the Florentines dress, their fine attention to detail and the remarkable sense of style that turns an ordinary outfit into something personal and very special. And note the almost arrogant local swagger. Then realize that these are people who wake up every morning to the marvels of Michelangelo, who literally live in a 15th-century Renaissance textbook. Their artistic and cultural heritage is unsurpassed, truly unique in the world. No doubt you'll agree that they have every reason to be proud.

FLORENCE AT-A-GLANCE

SEEING THE CITY: The picture-postcard view of Florence is the one from Piazzale Michelangelo, on the far side of the Arno. From here, more than 300 feet above sea level, the eye embraces the entire city and neighboring hill towns as far as Pistoia, but it is the foreground that rivets the attention. The Arno, with all its bridges, from Ponte San Niccolò to Ponte della Vittoria, the Palazzo Vecchio, with its tower and crenelations, the *Uffizi,* the flank of Santa Croce, numerous spires and domes — all are in the picture. And looming over the whole, like a whale washed ashore in the land of Lilliput, is the massive Duomo, with its bell tower and giant red cupola. The *piazzale* is reached by a splendid tree-lined avenue, called the Viale dei Colli, which begins at Ponte San Niccolò and winds up to the enormous square under the name of Viale Michelangelo. It then proceeds beyond the square as far as the Porta Romana under the names of Viale Galileo and Viale Machiavelli. From the bridge to the Roman Gate is a scenic 4-mile walk, but it's also possible to trace the same route aboard bus No. 13 from the station. Another extraordinary view, of Florence and the entire Arno Valley, can be enjoyed from the lookout terrace just before the Church of St. Francis, perched on a hill studded with cypress trees and sumptuous villas in neighboring Fiesole (see *Special Places*).

SPECIAL PLACES: The Arno is a good orientation point for first-time visitors to Florence. Most of the city sits on the north, or right, bank of the river, including its principal squares: Piazza del Duomo, the religious heart of Florence; Piazza della Repubblica, its bustling commercial center; and Piazza della Signoria, the ancient political center and today a favorite meeting place because of its outdoor cafés. The most elegant shopping street, Via Tornabuoni, runs from the Arno to Piazza Antinori. The other side of the river is known as the Oltrarno, literally, "beyond the Arno." Sights here include the *Pitti Palace* and Boboli Gardens, the churches of Santo Spirito and Santa Maria del Carmine, and Piazzale Michelangelo.

THE CATHEDRAL (DUOMO) COMPLEX

Il Duomo (The Cathedral) – The Cathedral of Santa Maria del Fiore was begun in 1296 by the Sienese architect Arnolfo di Cambio and took 173 years to complete. Dominating a large double square, it is the fourth-longest church in the world (after St. Peter's in Rome, St. Paul's in London, and the Duomo of Milan) and is said to be capable of holding over 20,000 people. The gigantic project was financed by the Florentine republic and the Clothmakers Guild in an age of faith when every city-state aspired to claim the biggest and most important cathedral as its own. Besides religious services, the Duomo has served as the site of major civic ceremonies and many noteworthy historical events, such as the Pazzi Conspiracy, when Giuliano de' Medici was assassinated in 1478. The original façade, never completed, was destroyed in the 16th century and replaced in the late 19th century. Whereas the exterior walls are encased in colorful marble (white from Carrara, green from Prato, and pink from Siena), the interior seems plain and cold by comparison, a brownish-gray sandstone called *pietra forte* and soberly decorated in keeping with the Florentine character. Most of the original statuary that adorned the Duomo, including Michelangelo's unfinished *Pietà*, has been moved to the *Museo dell'Opera del Duomo* (see below). The remains of the ancient Church of Santa Reparata, the original cathedral of Florence, which came to light under the Duomo during the extensive excavation after the 1966 flood, are very interesting (take the staircase near the entrance on the right side of the nave). The crypt is particularly haunting. Closed Sunday and holiday afternoons; admission charge.

The public competition for the design of the dome was won by a Florentine, Filippo Brunelleschi, who had marveled at the great engineering feat of ancient Rome, the dome of the Pantheon. The Renaissance architect's mighty cupola, built between 1420 and 1436, the first since antiquity, subsequently inspired Michelangelo as he faced the important task of designing the dome of St. Peter's in Rome. Brunelleschi's dome surpasses both the Pantheon and St. Peter's, although today it is seriously cracked and monitored by computer. Over 371 feet high and 148 feet across, it has double walls between which a 463-step staircase leads to a lantern at the top (also a Brunelleschi design). Restorations have been under way for more than a decade and, due to the necessity of scaffolding — not to mention the huge green canvas drape — there is little available light for viewing the dome's immense fresco (begun by Vasari). Still, the 40-minute climb up and down is well worth the effort for the breathtaking panorama from the top and for a true sense of the awesome size of this artistic and technical masterpiece. No, Virginia, there is no elevator. Closed Sundays and holidays. Admission charge.

Il Campanile (Bell Tower) – The graceful freestanding belfry of the Duomo, one of the most unusual in Italy, was begun by Giotto in 1334 (when he was 67) and eventually completed by Francesco Talenti. The bas-reliefs adorning the base are copies of originals by Giotto and Luca della Robbia that have been removed to the *Duomo Museum*, as have the statues of the Prophets (done by various artists, including Donatello) that stood in the niches. The 414-stair climb to the top leads to a terrace with another bird's-eye view of Florence. There's no elevator. Closed Sunday and holiday afternoons; admission charge.

Il Battistero (The Baptistry) – Dedicated to St. John the Baptist, the patron saint of Florence, the baptistry is a unique treasure, the origins of which are lost in time. The octagonal building may date to the 4th century, contemporary with the Church of Santa Reparata, while the exterior of white and green marble dates to the 12th century and is typical of the Tuscan Romanesque style, with an Oriental influence. To this day, the baptistry still is used for baptisms, and many a famous Florentine (such as Dante Alighieri) has been baptized here. On the *Feast of St. John* (June 24), the relics of the saint are displayed in the building and candles are lit in his honor (see *Special Events*). The interior is covered with magnificent Byzantine mosaics by 13th- and 14th-century Florentine and Venetian masters, but it is the three gilded bronze doorways that are the main tourist attraction. The South Door, by Andrea Pisano, is the oldest, dating from the early 14th century. In the Gothic style, it has 28 panels with reliefs of the life of St. John the Baptist and the cardinal and theological virtues. The North Door (1403–1424), in late Gothic style, was the result of a competition in which the unanimous winner was Lorenzo Ghiberti (Brunelleschi was among the competitors). It, too, is divided into 28 panels depicting scenes from the life of Christ, the Evangelists, and the Doctors of the Church. Ghiberti's East Door, however, facing the cathedral, is his masterpiece. In full Renaissance style, it was defined by Michelangelo as worthy of being the "gate of paradise." Begun in 1425 and completed in 1452, when Ghiberti was 74 years old, it consists of 10 panels illustrating Old Testament stories and medallions containing self-portraits of Ghiberti and his adopted son, Vittorio (who designed the frame), as well as portraits of their principal contemporaries.

Museo dell'Opera del Duomo (Duomo Museum) – Masterpieces from the cathedral, the baptistry, and the bell tower are here, especially sculpture: Michelangelo's unfinished *Pietà* (third of his four), Donatello's *Mary Magdalene,* the famous choir lofts (*cantorie*) by Luca della Robbia and Donatello, the precious silver altar frontal from the baptistry, fragments from the original cathedral façade, even the original wooden scale model of Brunelleschi's dome. Closed Sunday afternoons; admission charge. 9 Piazza del Duomo (no phone).

ELSEWHERE DOWNTOWN

Galleria degli Uffizi (Uffizi Museum and Gallery) – Italy's most important art museum is in a Renaissance palace built on the site of an 11th-century church (San Piero Scheraggio, the remains of which are incorporated in the palazzo and may still be seen. The splendor of this museum derives not only from the great works it contains but also from the 16th-century building itself, which was commissioned by Cosimo I and designed by Vasari (completed by Buontalenti) to house the Medicis' administrative offices, or *Uffizi*. In 1581, Francesco I began converting the top floor into an art museum destined to become one of the world's greatest. The three corridors, with light streaming through their great windows, are a spectacle in themselves, and the collection they contain is so vast — the most important Italian and European paintings of the 13th through the 18th century — that we suggest taking along a good guide or guidebook (Luciano Berti's is excellent) and comfortable shoes. Remember also to allow more time for a visit here than you think you'll need. At the top of the monumental staircase (there also is an elevator) on the second floor is the Prints and Drawings Collection; the museum proper (painting and sculpture) is on the third floor. Fifteen rooms are devoted to Florentine and Tuscan masterpieces, including the work of Cimabue, Giotto, Fra Filippo Lippi, Paolo Uccello, Fra Angelico, Da Vinci, and Michelangelo, not to mention such other non-Florentine masters as Raphael, Titian, Tintoretto, Caravaggio, Rubens, Van Dyck, and Rembrandt. The Botticelli Room contains the master's *Birth of Venus* and his restored *Allegoria della Primavera* (Allegory of Spring) as well as other allegorical and mythological works that make this the most important Botticelli collection in the world. Open Tuesdays through Saturdays from 9 AM to 7 PM. Admission charge. Piazza della Signoria (phone: 218341).

For diehards, there is an important collection of self-portraits lining the Corridoio Vasariano (Vasari Corridor) that may be visited by special arrangement. The portraits include those of Raphael, Rubens, Van Dyck, Velázquez, Bernini, Canova, Corot,

Fattori, and Chagall. Even without the portraits, the half-mile walk would be fascinating. The corridor actually is a raised passageway built in the 1560s to allow members of the Medici court to move from their old palace and offices (Palazzo Vecchio and Uffizi) to their new palace (*Palazzo Pitti*) without having to resort to the streets. It crosses the river on the tops of shops on the Ponte Vecchio and affords splendid views of the Arno, the Church of Santa Felicità, and the Boboli Gardens. Closed Mondays and Sunday and holiday afternoons; admission charge. To visit the Vasari Corridor, write to the *Uffizi* well in advance of your arrival (there's no extra fee). 6 Loggiato degli Uffizi (phone: 218341).

Palazzo della Signoria or Palazzo Vecchio (Old Palace) – This fortress-like palace, built by Arnolfo di Cambio between 1298 and 1314 as the seat of Florence's new democratic government of *priori,* or guild leaders, began as Florence's Town Hall and is still just that. From 1540 to 1550, it was temporarily the residence of the Medicis as they progressed from their ancestral home, the Medici-Riccardi Palace, to their new home in the *Palazzo Pitti.* Although in a rather severe Gothic style, it is at once powerful and graceful, with a lofty tower 308 feet high. Beyond its rusticated façade is an elaborately ornate courtyard highlighted by Verrocchio's delightful fountain of a bronze cherub holding a dolphin (1476). The medieval austerity of the exterior also contrasts with the sumptuous apartments inside. The massive Salone dei Cinquecento (Salon of the Five Hundred) on the first floor, built in 1496 for Savonarola's short-lived republican Council of Five Hundred, is decorated with frescoes by Vasari. Also, don't miss Vasari's *studiolo,* Francesco de' Medici's gem of a study, with magnificent *armadio* doors painted by artists of the schools of Bronzino and Vasari. On the third floor is an exhibition of 140 works of art removed from Italy by the Nazis and recovered by Rodolfo Siviero, the famed Italian art sleuth. Open Mondays through Fridays from 9 AM to 7 PM; no admission charge Sundays. Piazza della Signoria (phone: 276-8465).

Loggia dei Lanzi or Loggia della Signoria – Built between 1376 and 1382 for the election and proclamation of public officials and other ceremonies, it took its name in the 16th century from Cosimo I's Germano-Swiss mercenary soldiers (known in Italian as *lanzichenecchi*), who were stationed here. Today the loggia is a delightful open-air museum with masterpieces of sculpture from various periods under its arches. Particularly noteworthy are Cellini's *Perseus* and Giambologna's *Rape of the Sabines.* Piazza della Signoria.

Ponte Vecchio – The "old bridge" is indeed Florence's oldest and the only one to survive the Nazi destruction in 1944, although the houses at either end were blown up by the Germans. Built on the site of a Roman crossing, the first stone version was swept away in a flood in 1333 and rebuilt in 1345 as it is now, with rows of shops lining both sides (the backs of which, supported on brackets, overhang the Arno). They were occupied by butchers until Cosimo I assigned them to gold- and silversmiths in the late 16th century.

Palazzo Pitti e Galleria Palatina (Pitti Palace and Palatine Gallery) – On the side of the Arno opposite the *Uffizi,* and a few blocks from the riverbank, is a rugged, austere, 15th-century palace built to the plans of Brunelleschi, originally for the Pitti family. When it was bought by Cosimo I and his wife, Eleonora of Toledo, in the 16th century, it was enlarged and became the seat of the Medici grand dukes and later of the Savoy royal family until 1871. The enormous building now houses several museums: The *Galleria Palatina,* upstairs on the first floor and one of the must-sees, is devoted to 16th- and 17th-century art — works by Raphael (11 in all), Rubens, Murillo, Andrea del Sarto, Fra Filippo Lippi, Titian, Veronese, and Tintoretto, to name a few (there are over 650) — arranged in no apparent order. The gallery, in fact, still resembles a sumptuous apartment in a palace more than a museum. Priceless masterpieces seem to hang at random in elaborately decorated rooms filled with tapestries, frescoes, and gilded stuccoes. The Appartamenti Monumentali (Royal Apartments), in another wing of the same floor and once inhabited in turn by the Medici, Lorraine, and Savoy families, reopened in 1989 after 2 years of restoration work. The *Museo degli Argenti* (Silver Museum), occupying 16 rooms on the ground floor and another must-see, is filled not only with silverware but also with gold, jewels, cameos, tapestries, furniture, crystal, and ivory of the Medicis. Still another museum, the *Galleria d'Arte Moderna,* on the second floor, houses mainly 19th-century Tuscan works. There is also a *Coach and Carriage Museum* (temporarily closed). An entrance on the left side of the palace leads to the Boboli Gardens, which extend for acres and are open until dusk. A delightful example of a 16th-century Italian garden, they were laid out for Eleonora of Toledo and are studded with cypress trees, unusual statuary, grottoes, and foun- tains — plus the *Museo delle Porcellane* (Porcelain Museum) and the *Galleria del Costume* (Costume Gallery) in the Palazzina della Meridiana.

The *Palatine Gallery* (phone: 210323), the *Gallery of Modern Art* (phone: 287096), the *Silver Museum* (phone: 212557), and the *Costume Gallery* (phone: 287096) are open Mondays through Saturdays from 9 AM to 2 PM; Sundays from 9 AM to 1 PM. One admission charge covers the *Palatine Gallery,* the *Silver Museum,* and the Royal Apartments. The *Gallery of Modern Art* charges a separate admission. No admission charge to the Boboli Gardens (phone: 213440), *Porcelain Museum,* and *Costume Gal- lery.* Piazza dei Pitti (phone: 213440).

Chiesa di Santo Spirito (Church of the Holy Spirit) – This is one of Brunelleschi's last works, and a gem, though you'll notice the church's stark façade is very different from its interior. Brunelleschi died before he could complete what is generally acknowl- edged as one of the finest examples of a Renaissance church, so a team of architects finished it. Inside there are 2 dozen chapels, with masterpieces by Donatello, Ghirland- aio, Filippino Lippi, Sansovino, and others. Piazza Santo Spirito itself is a charming quiet spot, surrounded by 16th-century buildings — the perfect place to escape from the bustle on the other side of the Arno. Open daily from 8:30 AM to noon and 3:30 to 6:30 PM. Piazza Santo Spirito (phone: 210030).

Palazzo del Bargello e Museo Nazionale (Bargello Palace and National Mu- seum) – The *Bargello* is to sculpture what the *Uffizi* is to painting, yet for some reason it is visited far less frequently by tourists. Its most noteworthy piece just might be Florence's second-most famous *David* — the bronze by Donatello — sculpted in 1530. The building, the Palazzo del Podestà, is one of the finest and best-preserved examples of Florence's 13th- and 14th-century medieval architecture. Inside, all of the schools of Florentine and Tuscan sculpture are represented: Donatello, Verrocchio, Cellini, Michelangelo, the Della Robbias, and others. Open Tuesdays through Saturdays from 9 AM to 12:30 PM; Sundays from 9 AM to 1:30 PM. Admission charge. 4 Via del Proconsolo (phone: 210801).

Santa Croce (Church of the Holy Cross) – Italy's largest and best-known Francis- can church, Santa Croce was begun late in the 13th century and was enriched over the centuries with numerous works of art as well as tombs of many famous Italians, including Michelangelo, Machiavelli, Rossini, and Galileo (there is a funeral monu- ment to Dante here, but he is buried in Ravenna). Under Santa Croce are the remains of an earlier chapel founded by St. Francis of Assisi in 1228. The church is particularly noteworthy for a wooden crucifix by Donatello, for chapels with frescoes by Taddeo and Agnolo Gaddi, and above all for the fresco cycles by Giotto in the Bardi and Peruzzi chapels. Go outside the church and turn left to visit the 14th-century cloister and the 15th-century Pazzi Chapel, a Renaissance gem by Brunelleschi, designed at the height of his career. During the 1966 flood, the waters reached the top of the cloister's arches and damage here was particularly severe. Piazza Santa Croce (phone: 244619).

Galleria dell'Accademia (Academy of Fine Arts Gallery) – Michelangelo's origi- nal *David* was brought here from Piazza della Signoria (where one of many first-rate copies takes its place) in 1873. Since then, millions of visitors have come just to see this monumental sculpture (about a million a year now — one of whom smashed a toe on *David's* left foot last fall; it was being pedicured at press time) carved from a single block of Carrara marble and, in the same room, the four unfinished *Slaves* that Michelangelo meant to adorn Pope Julius II's unrealized tomb for St. Peter's in Rome. In the summer, lines form down the street and the doors often close when it gets too crowded. Unfortunately, many visitors ignore the rich collection of Florentine paintings — from 13th-century primitives to 16th-century mannerists — and the five rooms opened in 1985 to display works that had never before been shown to the public. These include 14th- and 15th-century paintings and an extraordinary collection of Russian icons brought to Florence by the Lorraines when they succeeded the Medicis during the first half of the 18th century. Open Tuesdays through Saturdays from 9 AM to 2 PM; Sundays to 1 PM. Admission charge. 60 Via Ricasoli (phone: 214375).

Convento di San Marco (Museum of St. Mark) – Vasari described this monastery as a perfect example of monastic architecture. It was built in the 15th century by the Medici architect Michelozzo (who actually rebuilt a more ancient Dominican monastery) and its walls — as well as more than 40 monks' cells — were frescoed by Fra Angelico (and his assistants), who lived here as a monk from 1438 to 1445. Now a Fra Angelico museum, it contains panel paintings brought from various churches and galleries in addition to the painter's wonderful *Crucifixion* (in the chapter house across the cloister) and his exquisite *Annunciation* (at the top of the stairs leading to the dormitory). In addition to the cells decorated by Fra Angelico, see the one used by the reforming martyr Savonarola. There also are paintings by Fra Bartolomeo (see his portrait of Savonarola), Ghirlandaio, Paolo Uccello, and others. Open Tuesdays through Saturdays from 9 AM to 2 PM; Sundays to 1 PM. Admission charge. 1 Piazza San Marco (phone: 210741).

Piazza della Santissima Annunziata (Square of the Most Holy Annunciation) – This square best preserves the essence of the Florentine Renaissance spirit. It has porticoes on three sides, a 16th-century palace (by Ammannati) on the fourth, plus an early-17th-century equestrian statue of Ferdinando I de' Medici by Giambologna in the middle. Most interesting is the portico on the east side, that of the Spedale degli Innocenti (Hospital of the Innocents), built in the early 15th century by Brunelleschi as a home for orphans and abandoned children, one of Florence's oldest charity institutions and the world's first foundling hospital. Except for the two imitations at either end, the ceramic tondos of swaddled babies are by Andrea della Robbia. Inside, the *Galleria dello Spedale degli Innocenti* (closed Wednesdays; admission charge) contains works by Ghirlandaio and others.

The Chiesa della Santissima Annunziata (Church of the Most Holy Annunciation), on the north side of the square, is much loved by Florentine brides, who traditionally leave their bouquets at one of its altars after the wedding ceremony. The church was founded in the 13th century, but rebuilt in the 15th century by Michelozzo. The left door of the church portico leads into the Chiostro dei Morti (Cloister of the Dead), which contains the *Madonna del Sacco,* a famous fresco by Andrea del Sarto. The middle door leads into the church via the Chiostrino dei Voti (Little Cloister of the Vows), with frescoes by several famous artists of the 16th century, including Del Sarto, Pontormo, and Rosso Fiorentino. Of the numerous artworks in the church itself, Andrea del Castagno's fresco of the Trinity, over the altar of the second chapel on the left, is one of the most prized.

Chiesa di San Lorenzo (Church of St. Lawrence) – This 15th-century Renaissance building was designed by Brunelleschi as the Medici parish church. A later façade, by Michelangelo, was never completed. Make your way to the Sagrestia Vecchia (Old Sacristy), the earliest part of the church and one of Brunelleschi's most notable early creations, remarkable for the purity and harmony of the overall conception. It contains, besides decorations by Donatello, the tombs of several Medicis, including Giovanni di Bicci. Be sure to go outside and through a doorway to the left of the façade to the Chiostro di San Lorenzo and to the Biblioteca Mediceo-Laurenziana (Laurentian Library; closed Sundays and holidays), a Michelangelo masterpiece designed to hold the Medici collection of manuscripts — 10,000 precious volumes. Piazza San Lorenzo (phone: 216634).

Mercato di San Lorenzo – This colorful open-air market has stalls where everything — from a special wooden rolling pin for making ravioli to a handmade mohair sweater — is sold. And because this is Florence, the leather goods can be a good buy, especially belts, jackets, and handbags. There also is a 2-story covered building with a lovely glass dome, where all kinds of food products are on sale, including local meat, cheeses, and produce, and fresh eggs and homemade wine brought in by peasant farmers from the Tuscan countryside. The indoor market is closed Sundays. Piazza San Lorenzo.

Cappelle Medicee (Medici Chapels) – Once part of San Lorenzo, these famous Medici funerary chapels now have a separate entrance. The first of the chapels, the Cappella dei Principi (Chapel of the Princes), where Cosimo I and the other grand dukes of Tuscany lie, is the later of the two, and it is a family burial vault supreme: The elaborate baroque interior took all of the 17th and 18th centuries to complete. Note the fine examples of Florentine mosaic, fine inlay done with semi-precious stones. But the real attraction here is the other chapel, the Sagrestia Nuova (New Sacristy), a companion piece to the Sagrestia Vecchia (see above). This magnificent show is by Michelangelo, who was commissioned by Cardinal Giulio de' Medici (later Pope Clement VII) and Pope Leo X (another Medici) to design both the interior — Michelangelo's first architectural job — and the statuary as a fitting resting place for members of their family. Michelangelo worked on it from 1521 to 1533 and left two of the projected tombs incomplete, but those he finished — the tomb of Lorenzo II, Duke of Urbino, with the figures of Dawn and Dusk, and the tomb of Giuliano, Duke of Nemours, with the figures of Night and Day, are extraordinary. (Lorenzo il Magnifico and his brother Giuliano, the latter murdered in the Duomo, are buried in the tomb opposite the altar, which bears a splendid *Madonna with Child* by Michelangelo.) The Sagrestia Nuova was being restored at press time as part of the 500th anniversary celebration of Il Magnifico's death. Don't miss the feeling of this room as a whole; with its square plan and imposing dome (especially its unusual trapezoidal windows), one almost has a sensation of soaring upward! Open Tuesdays through Saturdays from 9 AM to 2 PM; Sundays to 1 PM. Admission charge. Piazza Madonna degli Aldobrandini (phone: 213206).

Palazzo Medici-Riccardi (Medici-Riccardi Palace) – Not far from San Lorenzo is the palace where the Medici family lived until 1540, when they moved to the Palazzo Vecchio. When Cosimo the Elder decided to build a mansion for the family, he first asked Brunelleschi to design it but rejected the architect's plans as too luxurious and likely to create excessive envy. So Michelozzo was the master responsible for what was to be the first authentic Renaissance mansion — as well as a barometer of the proper lifestyle for a Florentine banker. Be sure to visit the tiny chapel to see Benozzo Gozzoli's wonderful fresco of the Three Kings on their way to Bethlehem; admission charge. At press time, the palazzo was being restored for the Medici anniversary celebration. Open daily except Wednesdays from 9 AM to noon and from 3 to 5 PM; Sundays from 9 AM to noon. 1 Via Cavour (phone: 217601).

Santa Maria Novella – Designed by two Dominican monks in the late 13th century and largely completed by the mid-14th century (except for the façade, which was designed by Leon Battista Alberti and finished in the late 15th century), this church figures in Boccaccio's *Decameron* as the place where his protagonists discuss the plague of 1348, the Black Death. Michelangelo, at the age of 13, was sent here to study painting under Ghirlandaio, whose frescoes adorn the otherwise gloomy interior, as do others by Masaccio, Filippino Lippi, and followers of Giotto. See the Gondi and Strozzi chapels and the great Chiostro Verde (Green Cloister), so called for the predominance of green in the decoration by Paolo Uccello and his school. Piazza Santa Maria Novella (phone: 282187).

Orsanmichele – This solid, square 14th-century structure once housed wheat for emergency use on its upper floors, while the ground floor was a church, and the whole was adopted by the city's artisans and guilds and used as an oratory — an unusual combination. Outside, the 14 statues in the niches representing patron saints of the guilds were sculpted by the best Florentine artists of the 14th to 16th centuries. The interior is dominated by a huge 14th-century tabernacle of colored marble by Andrea Orcagna. On *St. Anne's Day,* July 26, the building is decorated with flags of the guilds to commemorate the expulsion of the tyrannical Duke of Athens from Florence on July 26, 1343. Via dei Calzaiuoli.

Sinagoga (Synagogue) – Built in the late 19th century by the Florentine Jewish community in the Sephardic-Moorish style, this is one of the world's most beautiful synagogues. It was severely damaged during the 1966 floods but was lovingly and accurately restored. Visits are permitted from 9 AM until half an hour before rites. Ring the bell at the smaller of the two gates, and an English-speaking woman will take you around. 4 Via Farini (phone: 284715).

Mercato Nuovo (Straw Market) – This covered market near Piazza della Signoria dates from the 16th century. It holds an amazing assortment of handbags, sun hats, and placemats in traditional Florentine straw and raffia, wonderful embroidery work, typical gilt-pattern wooden articles, and other souvenirs, although the focus in recent years has been more on goods from African countries. The symbol of the market is the *Porcellino,* an imposing and slightly daunting bronze statue of a wild boar. Rub its shiny nose and toss a coin into the fountain to ensure a return visit. Open daily. Piazza del Mercato Nuovo.

ENVIRONS

San Miniato al Monte – Near Piazzale Michelangelo, this lovely church beloved by the Florentines dominates the hill of the same name and looks out over a broad panorama of Florence and the surrounding hills — a romantic setting that makes it a particular favorite for weddings. One of the best examples of Tuscan Romanesque architecture and design in the city, it was built from the 11th to the 13th century on the spot where St. Miniato, martyred in the 3rd century, is reputed to have placed his severed head after carrying it up from Florence. The façade is in the typical green and white marble of the Florentine Romanesque style, as is the pulpit inside, and the geometric patterns on the inlaid floor are Oriental. Art treasures include Michelozzo's Crucifix Chapel, with terra cotta decorations by Luca della Robbia; Spinello Aretino's frescoes in the sacristy; and the Chapel of the Cardinal of Portugal, a Renaissance addition that contains works by Baldovinetti, Antonio and Piero del Pollaiolo, and Luca della Robbia. The church was being restored as we went to press, in preparation for the festivities to mark the 500th anniversary of the death of Lorenzo de' Medici. The monks of San Miniato repeat vespers in Gregorian chant every day from 4:45 to 5:30 PM. Tourists are welcome if they plan to attend the entire mass (before the service, a monk asks visitors to leave if their time is short). By all means stop by the adjoining cemetery, a wonderful collection of Italian funerary art (the English painter Henry Savage Landor and Carlo Lorenzini, a.k.a. Carlo Collodi, author of *Pinocchio,* are buried here). The fortifications surrounding the church were designed by Michelangelo against the imperial troops of Charles V. Viale Galileo (phone: 234-2731).

Forte Belvedere – A 15-minute walk, or a short bus ride from the center of Florence will take you to this imposing 16th-century fort — built by the famous Florentine architect Buontalenti — which forms part of the Old City walls. There are splendid views of the city below and the fortress itself often has exhibitions of painting and sculpture inside. In summer the grounds become a makeshift open-air movie theater.

It's a pleasant walk either up through the Boboli Gardens or up the steep Costa San Giorgio from the Ponte Vecchio. Alternatively, take bus Nos. 12 or 13 from the center. Open daily from 9 AM to 8 PM. Admission charge. Costa San Giorgio (phone: 234-2822).

Fiesole – This beautiful village on a hill overlooking Florence and the Arno was an ancient Etruscan settlement and, later, a Roman city. The Duomo, begun in the 11th century and radically restored in the 19th, is on the main square, Piazza Mino da Fiesole, and just off the square is the *Teatro Romano,* built about 80 BC, where classical plays are sometimes performed, especially during the summer festival (*L'Estate Fiesolana*), which is devoted primarily to music. Take the picturesque Via San Francesco leading out of the square and walk up to the Church of St. Francis, passing the public gardens along the way and stopping at the terrace to enjoy the splendid view of Florence. The church, built during the 14th and 15th centuries, contains some very charming cloisters, especially the tiny Choistrino di San Bernardino. Visit the monks' cells, furnished as they were in the 15th century. Fiesole's tourist office is at 37 Piazza Mino (phone: 598720). Fiesole is 5 miles (8 km) north of Florence and can be reached by bus No. 7 from the railway station or Piazza San Marco (be careful, as this bus is a notorious venue for pickpockets).

Certosa di Galluzzo – Southwest of downtown is this monastery 7 miles (11 km) away, where the monks have been growing herbs and making liqueurs from them for centuries. Visitors can tour this splendid working facility, set in a magnificent country-side of rolling Tuscan hills, and buy some of their products to take home. There also is a small museum with some beautiful frescoes, most notably those by Pontormo from the 16th century. The No. 37 bus from the center goes directly to the *certosa* (monastery). By car, it is a 15-minute trip. Follow the signs for Galluzzo, and you'll see the monastery loom up in front of you. Open daily except Mondays from 9 AM to noon and 3 to 5 PM; admission charge. Galluzzo (phone: 204-9226).

Casa di Machiavelli – In the small village of Sant'Andrea in Percussina, 12 miles (20 km) and a half-hour drive from the city, is this house (known as Albergaccio) where Niccolò Machiavelli lived after being exiled from Florence by the Medicis. He wrote his masterpiece *Il Principe* (The Prince) here. The house is furnished as it was when Machiavelli was in residence. Open daily from 9 AM to 12:30 PM and 3:30 to 6 PM. Admission charge. Across the road (you can't miss it) is a small trattoria where the writer apparently was wont to repair for a jug of wine in between chapters. It still serves an excellent dish of Tuscan beans and very good peasant bread. A private bus company, *Sita* (phone: 48365 weekdays, 211487 weekends), runs from Piazza Santa Maria Novella to the village; by car, take SS2 heading toward Siena and turn off at San Casciano Val di Pesa. The village is signposted from there. Sant'Andrea in Percussina (no phone).

■**EXTRA SPECIAL:** Scattered about the Florentine countryside are a number of stately villas of the historic aristocracy of Florence, three of which are associated with the Medici family. On the road to Sesto Fiorentino, about 5 miles (8 km) north of the city, are the 16th-century Villa della Petraia (originally a castle of the Brunelleschi family, rebuilt in 1575 for a Medici cardinal by Buontalenti) and, just down the hill, the 15th-century Villa di Castello, which was taken over by the Medicis in 1477. Both have lovely gardens and fountains by Tribolo. The Villa Medici at Poggio a Caiano, at the foot of Monte Albano, about 10 miles (16 km) northwest of Florence, was rebuilt for Lorenzo the Magnificent by Giuliano da Sangallo from 1480 to 1485. The gardens of all three villas usually are open daily except Mondays; the interiors of the Petraia and Poggio a Caiano villas also may be visited (but hours and policies change; call 451208 for information regarding the former, 877012 for the latter). *Agriturist* runs organized excursions to the villas, as well as to country estates in the neighboring wine growing region. For information, contact *Agriturist,* 3 Piazza San Firenze (phone: 287838).

SOURCES AND RESOURCES

TOURIST INFORMATION: The Ente Provinciale per il Turismo (16 Via Alessandro Manzoni; phone: 247-8141/2/3/4/5) will provide general information, brochures, and maps of the city and the surrounding area. It is open Mondays through Saturdays from 8:30 AM to 1:30 PM. There's also a tourist information booth just outside the train station as well as an office at 15 Via Tornabuoni (phone: 217459), open Mondays through Saturdays from 9 AM to 1 PM. For information on Tuscany, contact the Regional Tourist Office (26 Via di Novoli; phone: 438-2111). Helpful for younger travelers is the *Student Travel Service* (*STS;* 18r Via Zannetti; phone: 268396 or 292067).

The US Consulate is at 38 Lungarno Amerigo Vespucci (phone: 298276).

Numerous maps and pocket-size guidebooks to Florence, such as the *Storti Guides,* are published in Italy and are available at newsstands throughout the city. Excellent guides in English available in bookstores are by Luciano Berti and by Rolando and Piero Fusi. Background reading before your trip might include Mary McCarthy's classic *The Stones of Florence* (Harcourt), a discussion of the history and character of the city as seen through its art, Christopher Hibbert's *The House of Medici: Its Rise and Fall* (Morrow), a study of the city's most influential family, and new this year, our own *Birnbaum's Florence* (HarperCollins).

Local Coverage – Check the brochure *Florence Concierge Information,* available at most hotels, or pick up a copy of *Florence Today* at the tourist information office. *Vista,* a free English-language magazine published every 3 months, also lists activities of interest to visitors. It is found at major hotels and tourist offices. Florence's daily newspaper is *La Nazione.* A national newspaper, *La Republicca,* has a section on Florence in which there is a daily calendar of events in English.

TELEPHONE: The country code for Italy is 39; the city code for Florence is 55. When calling from within Italy, dial 055 before the local number.

GETTING AROUND: Most visitors find Florence one of the easiest of European cities to navigate. Although it is fairly large, the scale is rather intimate, and it's easy to get just about anywhere on foot. Almost all the major sites are on the north side, or right bank, of the river, but most of those on the Oltrarno side ("beyond the Arno") are within easy walking distance of the center. Part of the city's center is closed to traffic, except for those with permits, making it quite pleasant for pedestrians. Visitors sometimes are confused by the numbers on Florentine buildings, for houses are numbered according to a double system. Black (*nero*) numbers indicate dwellings, while red (*rosso*) numbers — indicated by an "r" after the number in street addresses — are commercial buildings (shops and such). The black and the red have little relationship to each other, so you may find a black 68 next to a red 5.

Airport – Florence has no international airport; the closest one is Pisa's Galileo Galilei Airport (phone: 50-28088), a 1-hour train ride from the city, but too often closed due to nearly ubiquitous early morning fog. Travelers destined for flights from Pisa's airport can check bags through to their final destination from Florence's train station, where a Pisa airport check-in counter has been set up on Quai 5. It's far safer, though, to take the train to Rome and fly out of Italy from there (although there are flights from Milan, in winter, it is fog-bound even more frequently than Pisa). From Florence's main train station, the minibus operated by *Auto Alberghi* (phone: 261624) stops at most of the city's hotels for a fee.

Florence does have a domestic aiport, Peretola Civic Airport (11 Via del Termine; phone: 373498), with some flights to Milan, Rome, Venice, Turin, and Trieste. Service to this airport has been expanded, with scheduled international flights arriving from Brussels, Frankfurt, London, Munich, Nice, Paris, Stuttgart, and Vienna. Peretola is a 10-minute drive from downtown; taxi fare into the city will run about $10.

Bicycles, Mopeds, and Motorbikes – *Ciao & Basta* (33 Via Bardi; phone: 234-2726), rents bicycles; *Bici-Città* (phone: 499319 or 296335) will furnish two free bikes for 2 hours upon presentation of a *SCAF* car park coupon, and has three locations: Fortezza da Basso, Piazza Pitti, and Stazione Centrale on Via Alamanni (by the stairway). Motorbikes are available from *Program* (135r Borgo Ognissanti; phone: 282916), *Motorent* (9r Via San Zanobi; phone: 490113), and *Sabra* (8 Via Artisti; phone: 576256 or 579609), which also rents mopeds. Ride carefully!

Buses – *ATAF* is the city bus company, running about 40 city and suburban routes. Bus routes are listed in the yellow pages of the telephone directory. Tickets — which should be purchased before boarding — can be bought at tobacco counters, in bars, and at some newsstands; they cost about $1 and can be used more than once, with a 1½-hour time limit. Children under 1 meter (39 inches) tall ride free. As there are no ticket collectors (only automatic stamping machines), many passengers do not buy tickets, but anybody caught without one by the occasional controller is fined on the spot. The back door of the bus is for boarding, the middle for disembarking; the front door is only for season ticket holders. At rush hour, buses are impossibly crowded and it's sometimes difficult to get off at the desired stop. Walking often is faster and more enjoyable, but pedestrians are cautioned to watch out for buses and taxis in special lanes permitting them to travel the wrong way on many one-way streets.

Car Rental – *Avis* (128r Borgo Ognissanti; phone: 289010 or 213629); *Europcar* (53 Borgo Ognissanti; phone: 293444); *Europedrive* (35-37 Via Bisenzio; phone: 437-6862 or 422-2839); *Garage S. Lucia* (9r Via Orti Oricellari; phone: 216583); *Hertz* (33 Via Maso Finiguerra; phone: 298295); *InterRent Autonoleggio* (1r Via il Prato; phone: 218665); *Italy by Car* (*Budget;* 134r Borgo Ognissanti; phone: 293021); *Maggiore* (11 Via Maso Finiguerra; phone: 210238); and *Program* (135r Borgo Ognissanti; phone: 289010). Be aware that parking is difficult in the center and the one-way system can be maddening. An alternative is to leave your car at one of the attended parking lots outside the center or at your hotel, and walk or take a taxi.

Taxi – You can hail a cruising taxi (it's available if the light on top is lit) or pick one up at one of the numerous cabstands around the city. You can call for a taxi by dialing 4798 or 4390. Cabs are metered, but there are extra charges for night rides, luggage, station pickups, and the like. It is customary to give a small tip. A general rule is to round off the fare to the nearest 1,000 lire (about 80¢).

Train – Stazione Centrale Santa Maria Novella, the city's main railway station, is near the church of the same name, at Piazza Stazione. Call 278785 from 7 AM to 9 PM for information.

 LOCAL SERVICES: Dentist (English-Speaking) – Dr. Mario De Leo (1 Via Roma; phone: 215030); Dr. Giano Ricci (26 Via Gino Capponi; phone: 247-9471).

Dry Cleaner/Tailor – *Augusta,* 1-hour dry cleaning (16r Via delle Belle

Donne and other locations; phone: 210249); *Sartoria Maiano,* for men's tailoring only (2 Piazza Antinori; phone: 284146).

Limousine Service – *Barocchi* (9 Via Orti Oricellari; phone: 216583); *Far-Autonoleggio,* also has minibus service (101 Via San Gallo; phone: 483410).

Medical Emergency – *Ambulanze Misericordie* (phone: 212222) or *Fratellanza Militare* (phone: 215555). For emergency heart problems, call the *Unità Coronarica Mobile* (Mobile Coronary Unit; phone: 283394). English-speaking doctors can be reached 24 hours a day at *Tourist Medical Service* (59 Via Lorenzo Il Magnifico; phone: 475411), or *Santa Chiara Clinic* (11 Piazza Indipendenza; phone: 496312 or 475230).

Messenger Service – *Amico Espresso,* Via Ponte All'asse (phone: 375108 or 375136).

National/International Courier – *DHL International* (243-45 Via della Cupola; phone: 318031); *Federal Express* (200 Via Sansovino; phone: 706460); *Universal Express* (1 Piazza Goldoni; phone: 296525).

Office Equipment Rental – *Sabbatini & Co.,* typewriters and calculators for a 15-day minimum. 16r Via Banchi (phone: 210103).

Pharmacy – *Taverna* (20r Piazza San Giovanni; phone: 284013); *Molteni* (7r Via Calzaiuoli; phone: 263490); *Comunale No. 13* (Stazione Santa Maria Novella; phone: 263435). All are open daily, 24 hours.

Photocopies – *Landini* (87/L Via Novoli; phone: 431308); *Centro 2P* (30 Via G. Bastianelli; phone: 417709 or 430783); *Eliocopia* (138r Via Cavour; phone: 210004). Some stationers (*cartolerie*) also provide this service.

Post Office – *PTT,* open weekdays from 8:15 AM to 7 PM and Saturdays from 8:15 AM to noon. 3 Via Pellicceria (phone: 211147).

Telex – *PTT,* open 24 hours. 3 Via Pellicceria (phone: 215364).

Translators/Interpreters – *International Service Inc.* (20 Via Palazzuolo; phone: 575371); *Tradv-Co* (27 Via Marconi; phone: 579657).

Other – Office space rental: *Centro Uffici Redco,* furnished and equipped. 11 Lungarno B. Cellini (phone: 681-1893).

 SPECIAL EVENTS: Florence is bathed in medieval splendor each year for festivities surrounding the *Festa di San Giovanni Battista* (Feast of St. John the Baptist), June 24. Part of the tradition for the past several hundred years has been the *Calcio in Costume,* which consists of more than 500 men wearing colorful 16th-century costumes — with modern T-shirts — and playing a very rough game of soccer. Actually, because there are four teams, representing the old rival neighborhoods of San Giovanni, Santo Spirito, Santa Croce, and Santa Maria Novella (distinguishable by their green, white, blue, and red costumes, respectively), three games are played, two preliminaries and a final. One is usually scheduled on June 24 and the other two within a week or two before or after that date. The game, which resembles wrestling, rugby, and soccer, with the round leather ball thrown more often than kicked, originated in the Roman *arpasto,* played on sandy ground by soldiers training for war. It evolved through the Middle Ages and the Renaissance (in 1530 there was a most famous match played by the Florentines in defiance of the imperial troops of Charles V who were besieging the city), lapsed for about a century and a half, and then was revived in 1930. Also revived was the preliminary parade of Florentine guild officials, followed by the four teams led by their resident noblemen on horseback (the best known of whom is the Marchese Emilio Pucci di Barsento, the fashion designer). Because the game and its 8,000 or so spectators constitute some danger to the fountains and statuary of Florence's historic piazze, it was moved at one point to the Boboli Gardens, only to be banned there, too. This year (and probably every year to come) it will be held at its original site, Piazza Santa Croce.

Among the other folkloric events is the centuries-old ceremony called the *Scoppio del Carro,* literally "bursting the cart," which takes place traditionally on *Easter*

Sunday in celebration of a Christian victory in one of the Crusades and culminates in a great fireworks display. A large cart drawn by white oxen is brought to Piazza del Duomo and connected to the main altar of the cathedral by a metal wire. At the stroke of noon, when the bells announce the Resurrection of Christ, the Cardinal Archbishop of Florence sets off a dove-shaped rocket that runs along the wire to the cart filled with firecrackers. When the cart explodes, the Florentine spectators jump with joy, taking the event and the flight of the "dove" as a good omen for the future. Occasionally the dove doesn't make it and sighs of something worse than disappointment fill the square, as this is considered a bad omen indeed. On *Ascension Day* each May, Florentines celebrate the *Festa del Grillo* by going to the Cascine, a park along the Arno at the edge of the center, and buying crickets in cages, only to set them free. The *Festa delle Rificolone,* September 7, is celebrated with a procession along the Arno and across the Ponte San Niccolò with colorful paper lanterns and torches.

At the *Fortezza del Basso* in June is the *Mostra Mercato degli Antiquari Toscani* where regional Tuscan antiques dealers sell everything from Etruscan relics to 19th-century antiques. The *Biennale Dell'Antiquariato,* an important international antiques fair, is held in odd-number years in the fall at the Palazzo Strozzi.

From April through the summer of this year, a series of events will take place to commemorate the 500th anniversary of the death of Lorenzo de' Medici — one of Florence's most famous and best-loved citizens. A series of exhibitions, talks, concerts, and costume parades will be held in the city and continue through the summer. Highlights include an exhibit at the *Palazzo Medici* of paintings, sculptures, majolica, and furnishings — collected from various museums around the world — that were part of Lorenzo's collection when he lived there. Another exhibit (the place had not been determined at press time) will re-create the workshops of some of the major artists who worked during Il Magnifico's lifetime, including Botticelli, Lippi, Ghirlandaio, and Perugino. For a detailed program of the festivities, contact the tourist office.

MUSEUMS: Since museums are possibly the city's top attraction, quite a few have already been described under *Special Places.* A few more of the 70 or so museums in the city are listed here, along with additional churches and palaces whose artwork makes them, in effect, museums, too. As hours may vary, contact the tourist information office (phone: 217459) or the Superintendent of Museums and Galleries (phone: 218341) for information about hours.

Badia Fiorentina – The church of a former Benedictine abbey (*badia*), with a part-Romanesque, part-Gothic campanile, it was founded in the 10th century, enlarged in the 13th, and rebuilt in the 17th. Opposite the *Bargello.* Via del Proconsolo (no phone).

Casa Buonarroti – The small house Michelangelo bought for his next of kin, containing some of the master's early works, as well as works done in his honor by some of the foremost artists of the 16th and 17th centuries. Open Tuesdays through Saturdays from 9:30 AM to 1:30 PM, Sundays from 9:30 AM to 12:30 PM. Admission charge. 70 Via Ghibellina (phone: 241752).

Casa di Dante – A small museum in what is believed to have been Dante's house, it documents his life, times, and work. Open from 9:30 AM to 12:30 PM and 3:30 to 6:30 PM, Sundays from 9:30 AM to 12:30 PM. Closed Wednesdays. No admission charge. 1 Via Santa Margherita (phone: 283343).

Casa Guidi – Robert and Elizabeth Barrett Browning lived on the first floor of this 15th-century palazzo at the corner of the *Pitti Palace* from shortly after their secret marriage in 1846 until Elizabeth's death in 1861. Now called the *Browning Institute,* it is an unfinished museum and a memorial to both poets. It's best to ask the tourist office about when the museum is open. Admission charge. 8 Piazza San Felice (no phone).

Cenacolo di Sant'Apollonia – The refectory of a former convent, containing Andrea del Castagno's remarkable fresco of the Last Supper (ca. 1450). Closed Mondays. Admission charge. 1 Via XXVII Aprile (phone: 287074).

Museo di Antropologia ed Etnologia (Museum of Anthropology and Ethnology) – First of its genre in Italy, continually enlarged, now with more than 30 rooms and a vast collection divided by race, continent, and culture. Open Thursdays, Fridays, and Saturdays from 9 AM to 1 PM and the third Sunday of the month (except July through September). Admission charge. 12 Via del Proconsolo (phone: 296449).

Museo Archeologico (Archaeological Museum) – This fascinating museum contains a permanent jewelry exhibit of gold and gems from the Medici. There also is a collection of Etruscan, Greek, and Roman art housed in six halls (damaged during the 1966 flood) that were reopened after a lengthy, costly restoration. A topographical section features objects from ancient Etruria; and an Egyptian area has mummies, statues, and a well-preserved chariot found in Thebes. Open Tuesdays through Saturdays from 9 AM to 2 PM, Sundays from 9 AM to 1 PM. Admission charge. 38 Via Colonna (phone: 247-8641).

Museo Archeologico di Fiesole – A fine selection of treasures from both the Etruscan and Roman periods of Fiesolan history, including an especially rich collection of Etruscan pottery. The museum is part of a complex that also has a Roman theater — used for concerts in the summer — and the remains of an Etruscan temple. Open daily from 9AM to 7 PM. Admission charge. Piazza Mino, Fiesole (phone: 59477).

Museo Bardini – Sculpture, tapestries, bronzes, furniture, and paintings. Open from 9 AM to 2 PM, Sundays from 9 AM to 1 PM. Closed Wednesdays. Admission charge. 1 Piazza dei Mozzi (phone: 234-2427).

Museo Firenze Com'Era (Florence "As It Was" Museum) – Collection of mainly 19th-century maps, paintings, documents, and photos illustrating aspects of the city over the centuries. There also is a permanent exhibition of works by the 20th-century artist Ottone Rosai. Open from 9 AM to 2 PM, Sundays from 9 AM to 1 PM. Closed Thursdays. Admission charge. 24 Via dell'Oriuolo (phone: 217305).

Museo della Fondazione Horne (Horne Museum) – A jewel of a museum — paintings, drawings, sculptures, furniture, ceramics, coins, and unusual old household utensils, the collection of an Englishman, Herbert Percy Horne, bequeathed to the city in 1916 and set up in his 15th-century *palazzetto.* Open from 9 AM to 1 PM. Closed Sundays and holidays. Admission charge. 6 Via de' Benci (phone: 244661).

Museo Stibbert – Vast collection (about 50,000 pieces) of art objects, antiques, arms from all over the world, and other curiosities left by the English collector Stibbert, with his villa and gardens. Open from 9 AM to 1 PM, Sundays from 9 AM to 12:30 PM. Closed Thursdays. Admission charge. 26 Via Federico Stibbert (phone: 486049).

Museo di Storia Naturale (Museum of Natural History) – Also known as "La Specola," it has a weird but interesting collection of wax anatomical models from the late 18th century. There also is an exhibit of waxed and stuffed animals. Open daily except Sundays from 9 AM to noon; second Sunday of the month from 9:30 AM to 12:30 PM. No admission charge. 17 Via Romana (phone: 222451).

Museo di Storia della Scienza (Museum of the History of Science) – Scientific instruments, including Galileo's telescopes, and odd items documenting the development of modern science from the Renaissance to the 20th century. Open Tuesdays, Thursdays, and Saturdays from 9:30 AM to 1 PM; Mondays, Wednesdays, and Fridays from 9:30 AM to 1 PM and from 2 to 5 PM. Admission charge. 1 Piazza de' Giudici (phone: 293493).

Ognissanti (All Saints' Church) – Built in the 13th century and rebuilt in the 17th, it contains extraordinary frescoes by Ghirlandaio and Botticelli and is the burial place of the latter as well as of the family of Amerigo Vespucci. 42 Piazza d'Ognissanti (phone: 239870).

Palazzo Davanzati – A well-preserved 14th-century palace with 15th-century furniture, tapestries, and ceramics, also known as the *Museo della Casa Fiorentina Antica* (Florentine House Museum). Open from 9 AM to 1 PM. Closed Saturdays. Admission charge. 13 Via Porta Rossa (phone: 216518).

Palazzo Strozzi – This masterpiece of Renaissance architecture is the scene of a biennial international antiques show, held in the fall (in odd-number years). Open from 9:30 AM to 1 PM and 3 to 7 PM. Closed Mondays. Admission charge. Piazza Strozzi (phone: 215990).

Santi Apostoli (Church of the Holy Apostles) – Built in the 11th century, redecorated in the 15th and 16th centuries, and restored in the 1930s, it holds the flints said to have been brought back from Jerusalem during the Crusades and still used to light the Holy Fire in the Duomo for the *Scoppio del Carro* at *Easter* (see *Special Events*).

Santa Maria del Carmine – Dating from the second half of the 13th century, this Carmelite church was mostly destroyed in a fire in 1771, but the Corsini and Brancacci chapels were spared. The latter, reopened after 10 years of restoration, contains the Masaccio frescoes that inspired Renaissance painters from Fra Angelico to Raphael. Piazza del Carmine.

Santa Trinita (Church of the Holy Trinity) – One of the oldest churches in Florence, built in the 11th century with a 16th-century façade. See the Ghirlandaio frescoes in the Sassetti Chapel — one shows the church with its original Romanesque façade. Piazza Santa Trinita.

SHOPPING: Shopping is absolutely wonderful in Florence, arguably Italy's most fashionable city. For clothing, the smartest streets are Via Tornabuoni, Via della Vigna Nuova, Via Calzaiuoli, and Via Roma. The shops lining the Ponte Vecchio have been selling beautiful gold and silver jewelry since 1593. Antiques, leather goods, and handmade lingerie are other specialties of Florentine shops. Winter store hours are 9 AM to 1 PM and 3:30 to 7:30 PM Tuesdays through Saturdays; 3:30 to 7:30 PM on Mondays. The summer finds these stores closed on Saturday afternoons rather than Monday mornings, and the evening closing hour is extended by a half hour to 8. Some shops that are geared to tourists (fashion, leather, souvenirs, and so on) stay open all day. Food shops traditionally close on Wednesdays.

Alex – The best in designer clothes for women — Gianni Versace, Yamamoto, Byblos, Claude Montana, Basile, Thierry Mugler. 19r and 5r Via della Vigna Nuova (phone: 210446).

Antico Setificio Fiorentino – Fabulous fabrics, all handloomed. 97r Via della Vigna Nuova (phone: 282700).

Befani & Tai – Quality gold craftsmanship at good prices. 13r Via Vacchereccia (phone: 287825).

Beltrami – A chain of elegant, expensive leatherwear shops: shoes, bags, jackets, pants, and other items. 31r, 44r, and 202r Via Calzaiuoli (phone: 212418); 1r Via dei Pecori (phone: 216321); 11r Via Calimala (phone: 212288); and 28 Via Tornabuoni (phone: 287779).

Benetton – Colorful, reasonably priced casualwear for the young at heart. 66-68r Via Por Santa Maria (phone: 287111) and 2r Via Calimala (phone: 214878), and other locations.

Bijoux Cascio – Moderately priced jewelry, particularly in gold; the designs are the shop's own. 32r Via Tornabuoni (phone: 284709) and other locations).

BM – An English-language bookstore. 4r Borgo Ognissanti (phone: 294575).

Bottega Veneta – Exquisite leather goods, especially handbags. 3-4r Piazza Ognissanti (phone: 294265).

Cartier – Fantastic jewelry. 1 Piazza Santa Trinita (phone: 292347).

Casa de' Tessuti – *The* place to go to find wonderful Italian fabrics, including wool, silk, and linen. 20-24r Via de' Pecori (phone: 215961).

Cellerini – High-quality bags and suitcases made by a craftsman in a workshop above the store. 9 Via del Sole (phone: 282533).

Cirri – Lovely linen. 38-40r Via Por Santa Maria (phone: 296593).

C.O.I. – Gold jewelry sold by weight at affordable prices. 8 Via Por S. Maria (phone: 283970 or 293424).

David – Leather bags, luggage, shoes, clothes. 11-13r Via Roma (phone: 211884).

Emilio Paoli – Straw market with class — locally produced gift articles and imports. 26r Via della Vigna Nuova (phone: 214596).

Emilio Pucci Boutique – Pucci fashions — back in style. Palazzo Pucci, 6 Via de' Pucci (phone: 287622).

Falai – Florence is known for its jewelry shops, but this one will also copy much-loved items or help you design new ones from drawings or descriptions. 28r Via Por S. Maria (phone: 261688).

Feltrinelli – Art books. 12-20r Via Cavour (phone: 219524).

Ferragamo – The famous shoemaker's headquarters in Italy, with the widest selection of styles and colors. 12-16r Via Tornabuoni (phone: 292123).

Gants – Gloves of the highest quality; they make their own. 78r Via Porta Rossa.

Gerard – Way-out, punk, and exotic fashions for men and women. 18-20r Via Vacchereccia (phone: 215942).

Gherardini – A century-old leather shop, also selling sunglasses and perfume, run by an old Florentine family (the subject of the *Mona Lisa* was a Gherardini). 57r Via della Vigna Nuova (phone: 215678) and other locations.

Giulio Giannini e Figlio – This father-and-son store is one of the oldest selling the famous hand-crafted Florentine paper products, and its selection is one of the best in town. 37r Piazza Pitti (phone: 215342).

Gori Boutique – Santa Croce Leather School products, as well as articles by Italy's top-name designers. 13r Piazza Santa Croce (phone: 242935).

Gucci – The parent store of Italy's best known leather and fashion purveyor. Less expensive than in the US, but hardly inexpensive. 57-73-75r Via Tornabuoni (phone: 264011).

Happy Jack – A good, men's boutique; alterations done quickly. 7-13r Via della Vigna Nuova (phone: 284329).

Libreria Franco Maria Ricci – Fine books selected by the publishers of *FMR* magazine. 41r Via delle Belle Donne (phone: 283312).

Libreria Salimbeni – Specializes in art books. 14r Via Matteo Palmieri (phone: 234-0904).

Lily of Florence – Italian shoes in American sizes. 2r Via Guicciardini (phone: 294748).

Loretta Caponi – Exquisite handmade lingerie and linen by this second-generation shop that designs for Nina Ricci and Dior. 38-40r Borgo Ognissanti (phone: 213668).

Luisa Spagnoli – Women's high-quality clothing, made from the purest cotton and wool, at moderate prices. 20 Via Strozzi (phone: 211978).

Madova – Italy's most competent and incomparable glovemaker. 1r Via Guiccardini (phone: 296526).

Mario Buccellati – Fine jewelry and silverware in traditional Florentine designs. 71r Via Tornabuoni (phone: 296579).

Mario Valentino – Designer shoes and bags. 67r Via Tornabuoni (phone: 261338).

Melli – Antique jewelry, ivory, silver, and clocks. 48 Ponte Vecchio (phone: 211413).

Mercato Nuovo (Straw Market) – The covered market, with all sorts of items made of straw, wood, and leather, as well as goods from Florence's growing immigrant community. Piazza del Mercato Nuovo.

Mujer – Original fashions for the adventurous woman. 6r Via Vacchereccia (phone: 210057).

Neuber – British and Italian wools. 32r Via Strozzi (phone: 215763).

Papiro – *Papier à cuve,* or marbled paper, a method of hand-decoration invented in the 17th century; lovely stationery. 55 Via Cavour (phone: 215262) and other locations.

Parson – Trendy women's boutique. 16-18r Via Tosinghi (phone: 282590).

La Pelle – Leather clothes made to order in two stores. 11-13r and 11-14r Via Guicciardini (phone: 292031).

Pineider – Italy's most famous stationers. 13r Piazza della Signoria (phone: 284655) and 76r Via Tornabuoni (phone: 211605).

Pratesi – Elegant and expensive linen. 8-10 Lungarno Amerigo Vespucci.

Primi Mesi – Embroidered crib and carriage sets; maternity, infants, and toddlers wear. 23r Via dei Cimatori (phone: 296372).

Principe – A small but elegant department store. 21-29r Piazza Strozzi (phone: 216821).

Renard – Leather, suede, and sheepskin clothing. 21-23r Via dei Martelli (phone: 284566).

Rosetta Belli – Specializes in handbags, and at relatively reasonable prices. 9r Via dei Fossi (phone: 293567).

Santa Croce Leather School – Top-quality leather goods (boxes, gloves, handbags, wallets, clothing, and shoes) from the school and shop inside the Monastery of Santa Croce. 16 Piazza Santa Croce or (through the garden) 5r Via San Giuseppe (phone: 244533 or 247-9913).

Schwicker – Quality gifts by Florentine artisans. 40r Piazza Pitti (phone: 211851).

Seeber – English-language bookshop. 70 Via Tornabuoni (phone: 215697).

Stefanel – Colorful casualwear. Via Borgo San Lorenzo (phone: 312578).

Tanino Crisci – The most stylish shoe shop (for men and women) in town. 43-45 Via Tornabuoni (phone: 216741).

Torrini – Exquisite jewelry. 10r Piazza Duomo (phone: 284506).

U. Gerardi – Best selection of coral jewelry in town. 5 Ponte Vecchio (phone: 211809).

Ugo Poggi – Florentine handicrafts in silver, china, glass. 26r Via degli Strozzi (phone: 216741).

Ungaro Parallèle – High fashion for women. 30r Via della Vigna Nuova (phone: 210129).

UPIM – A large, moderately priced department store. Piazza della Repubblica (phone: 298544).

Valmar – Tapestry items perfect for everything from upholstery to women's belts. 53r Via Porta Rossa (phone: 284493).

Zanobetti – Classic clothing and leather goods for men and women. 20-22r Via Calimala (phone: 210646).

SPORTS AND FITNESS: Check with your concierge to find out which sports facilities currently are open to the public. Most are private clubs, but a day visit often can be arranged for a fee.

Fitness Centers – *Indoor Club* (15 Via Bardazzi; phone: 430275); *Palestra Savasana* (26 Via J. da Diaccetto; phone: 287373); *Sauna Finlandese* (108 Via Cavour; phone: 587246); *Tropos* (20a Via Orcagna; phone: 661581).

Golf – There is a good 18-hole course (closed Mondays) at *Golf dell'Ugolino,* in nearby Impruneta, 3 Via Chiantigiana (phone: 230-1096).

Horseback Riding – For information, call *Piazzale Cascine* (phone: 360056) or *Agriturist* (phone: 287838). Just outside the city is *Badia Montescalari* (129 Via Montescalari at La Panca; phone: 959596).

Jogging – The best place to run is the Cascine, a very long, narrow park along the Arno west of the center. To get there, follow the river to Ponte della Vittoria.

Soccer – See the *Fiorentina* in action from September to May at the *Stadio Comunale,* designed by Pier Luigi Nervi. 4-6 Viale Manfredo Fanti (phone: 572625).

Squash – Courts can be reserved at the *Centro Squash Firenze;* 24-29 Viale Piombino (phone: 710055).

Swimming – Swimmers will do best to stay at one of the following hotels: *Crest, Croce di Malta* (although the pool is very small), *Jolly Carlton, Kraft, Minerva, Park Palace, Villa Belvedere, Villa Medici,* or *Villa sull'Arno* or, outside the city, at the *Grand Hotel Villa Cora, Villa La Massa, Villa San Michele,* or the *Villa Villoresi.* There also are a few indoor and outdoor public pools, including *Piscina Costoli* (Viale Paoli; phone: 669744); *Piscina Le Pavoniere,* an outdoor pool in a pleasant park (Viale degli Olmi; phone: 367506); and *Zodiac Sport* (2 Via A. Grandi; phone: 202-2847).

Tennis – Play tennis at the semi-public *Circolo Tennis alle Cascine* (1 Viale Visarno; phone: 356651); *Assi-Giglio-Rosso* (64 Viale Michelangelo; phone: 681-2686 or 687858); *Il Poggetto* (24/B Via Michele Mercati; phone: 460127); and *Match Ball* (Via della Massa; phone: 631752).

 THEATER: If you'd like to see a play in Italian, the principal theaters in Florence are the *Teatro della Pergola* (32 Via della Pergola; phone: 247-9651); the *Teatro Niccolini* (5 Via Ricasoli; phone: 213282); and *Tenda Città di Firenze* (Via de Nicola; phone: 650-4112). *Teatro Variety* (47 Via del Madonnone; phone: 660632) offers singers and humorous contemporary pieces. Films in English are shown frequently at the *Cinema Astro* (Piazza San Simone near Santa Croce; phone: 222388).

 MUSIC: Opera begins earlier in Florence than in most Italian cities. The season at the *Teatro Comunale* (Corso Italia; phone: 27791), the principal opera house and concert hall, runs from October to early January, with ballet in July. The annual *Maggio Musicale Fiorentino* festival, which attracts some of the world's finest musicians and singers, also is held here in May and June. Tickets can be purchased at the theater; *Universal Turismo* (7r Via Speziali; phone: 217241); or *Box Office* (10A/r Via della Pergola; phone: 241881). The *Teatro della Pergola* (see *Theater*) is the scene of Saturday afternoon concerts from autumn through spring. The *Orchestra da Camera Fiorentina* (Florentine Chamber Orchestra; 6 Via E. Poggi; phone: 470027) regularly stages classical concerts. Open-air concerts are held in the cloisters of the Badia Fiesolana (in Fiesole) and of the Ospedale degli Innocenti on summer evenings, and occasionally in other historic monuments such as the restored Church of Santo Stefano al Ponte Vecchio, now the seat of the *Regional Tuscan Orchestra.*

 NIGHTCLUBS AND NIGHTLIFE: A Florentine evening usually begins with an *aperitivo* at one of the cafés on Piazza della Signoria (such as *Caffè Rivoire,* an elegant watering hole with wood-paneled walls and marble-top tables) or Piazza della Repubblica, at *Harry's Bar* (22r Lungarno Amerigo Vespucci; phone: 296700), or at *Bar Donatello,* on the main floor of the *Excelsior* hotel, the pre-dinner gathering place for Florence's smart set. Because nightspots come and go so quickly — and since most are closed at least 1 night of the week — it always is a good idea to check with your hotel concierge before going out. Discos and piano bars are among the most popular forms of evening entertainment, and tops among the former are *Tenax* (46 Via Pratese; phone: 373050) and *Jackie-O'* (24/A Via dell'Erta Canina; phone: 234-2442). Other discos include *Yab Yum* (5r Via Sassetti; phone: 282018); *Full-Up* (21r Via della Vigna Vecchia; phone: 293006); and *Plegyne* (26r Piazza Santa Maria Novella; phone: 211590). For the very young crowd, dancing happens at *Space Electronic* (37 Via Palazzuolo; phone: 293082). If a quieter evening is called for, there are numerous lovely piano bars from which to choose, such as the elegant *Loggia Tornaquinci,* nestled atop a 16th-century Medici building (6r Via Tornabuoni; phone: 219148). Others include the *Caffè* (9 Piazza Pitti; phone: 296241); *Oberon* (12r Via dell'Erta Canina; phone: 216516), and *Prezzemolo* (5r Via della Caldaie; phone: 211530), a champagne bar for night owls. The elegant *Oliviero* (51r Via della Terme; phone: 287643), is a restaurant with piano bar, the place for a romantic evening. There also are piano bars at some of the hotels, such as the *Anglo-American,* the *Londra,* the *Majestic,* and the *Savoy. Il Salotto* is a "private" club open to everyone. Situated in a 15th-century palazzo at 33 Borgo Pinti, it's not surprising that it boasts a clientele of Florentine nobility, artists, and wealthy merchants. Popular for drinks is the *Caffè Strozzi* (16-19 Piazza Strozzi; phone: 212574), with outdoor tables for good people watching. Three other local favorites are *Gilli,* a Belle Epoque café with a lively outdoor terrace (39r Piazza della Repubblica; phone: 296310); *Giacosa* (83 Via Tornabuoni; phone: 296226), where the elite meet over truffle-paste sandwiches; and *Procacci* (33 Via Tornabuoni), a café/bar serving white truffle-paste sandwiches and other elegant snacks to a chic local crowd.

BEST IN TOWN

 CHECKING IN: Florence is well organized for visitors, with more than 400 hotels to accommodate more than 20,000 travelers. Still, somehow, it's hard to find a room in high season. The hotel count above and the list below include former *pensioni,* something like boardinghouses, but now officially designated as "hotels." A few still require that some meals be taken, a feature that is specified for those that do. (Half board means you must take breakfast and either lunch or dinner at the establishment.) A very expensive hotel can cost above $500 a night. At an expensive hotel, plan on spending from $210 to more than $470 a night for a double room. Moderate-priced establishments cost between $95 and $210; inexpensive lodging ranges from $60 to $95. All telephone numbers are in the 55 city code unless otherwise indicated.

Villa Cora – A neo-classical villa built during the period when Florence was the capital of Italy. The name comes from one of the many former owners, an ambassador. As a private villa, it hosted Napoleon's widow, Eugénie, as well as Tchaikovsky's patron, the Baroness Von Meck. It offers spacious rooms and suites (56 rooms) decorated in the original style, grand public rooms, and a magnificent garden with heated pool, all about 2 miles (3 km) from the chaotic city center. On the other side of the Boboli Gardens. Business facilities include 24-hour room service, meeting rooms for up to 120, English-speaking concierge, foreign currency exchange, secretarial services in English, audiovisual equipment, photocopiers, computers, cable television news, translation services, and express checkout. 18 Viale Machiavelli (phone: 229-8451; fax: 229086; telex: 570604). Very expensive.

Villa San Michele – Dramatically set about 5 miles (8 km) from Florence, on the slopes below Fiesole. Originally an ancient monastery, built by the Davanzati family in the late 15th century and designed in part by Michelangelo, it became a private villa during Napoleon's day and was transformed into one of Tuscany's most romantic hotels in the 1950s. (Brigitte Bardot honeymooned here in the 1960s.) Restored to its former glory, it now has 28 rooms (most with Jacuzzis), intimate dining indoors or in the open-air loggia, fragrant gardens with splendid views, a pool, and limousine service into the city. Business facilities include 24-hour room service, meeting rooms for up to 40, English-speaking concierge, foreign currency exchange, secretarial services in English, audiovisual equipment, photocopiers, computers, cable television news, translation services, and express checkout. Half board required. Open from March to mid-November. 4 Via Doccia, Fiesole (phone: 59451; in the US, 800-237-1236; fax: 598734; telex: 570643). Very expensive.

Excelsior – Beside the Arno, just a short walk from the city center, traditional in both style and service. Part of the reliably luxurious and efficient CIGA chain. The excellent terrace restaurant, *Il Cestello,* has a splendid view when the stained glass windows are opened. The 205-room hotel is a favorite of Florentines and their guests. Business facilities include 24-hour room service, meeting rooms for up to 350, English-speaking concierge, foreign currency exchange, secretarial services in English, audiovisual equipment, photocopiers, computers, cable television news, translation services, and express checkout. 3 Piazza Ognissanti (phone: 264201; fax: 210278; telex: 570022). Expensive.

Grand – Across the street from the *Excelsior,* this 109-room hostelry was renovated in 1990 to re-create its original 15th-century elegance. Brunelleschi is said to have designed the palazzo as a residence for one of Florence's noble families. Part of the CIGA chain, it has meeting and banquet rooms and a restaurant. Business facilities include 24-hour room service, meeting rooms for up to 230, English-speaking concierge, foreign currency exchange, secretarial services in English, audiovisual equipment, photocopiers, computers, cable television news, translation services, and express checkout. 1 Piazza Ognissanti (phone: 278781; fax: 217400; telex: 570055). Expensive.

Helvetia & Bristol – Considered one of Florence's best in the 19th century, this hotel has now been restored to all its former glory, with antique furniture, velvet drapes, and original oil paintings. All 50 rooms and suites are decorated in different styles, ranging from chinoiserie to Art Nouveau, and all have Jacuzzis. Ideally located on a tranquil street behind the Piazza della Repubblica. Business facilities include 24-hour room service, meeting rooms for up to 70, English-speaking concierge, foreign currency exchange, secretarial services in English, audiovisual equipment, photocopiers, computers, cable television news, translation services, and express checkout. 2 Via dei Pescioni (phone: 287814; fax: 288353; telex: 572696). Expensive.

Hotel de la Ville – Dark, quiet, and somber, the perfect place for light sleepers. Its double doors and storm windows provide a peaceful oasis in the center of Florence, just off the elegant Via Tornabuoni. There are 96 rooms. Business facilities include 24-hour room service, meeting rooms for up to 75, English-speaking concierge, foreign currency exchange, secretarial services in English, audiovisual equipment, photocopiers, computers, cable television news, translation services, and express checkout. 1 Piazza Antinori (phone: 261806; fax: 261809; telex: 570518). Expensive.

Regency Umbria – Small (31 rooms) patrician villa set in a quiet residential area and decorated with exquisite taste. Like its sister in Rome (the *Lord Byron*), it offers calm and privacy, discreetly displaying its Relais & Châteaux crest at the entrance. There is a charming garden and an excellent restaurant (see *Eating Out*). Business facilities include 24-hour room service, meeting rooms for up to 20, English-speaking concierge, foreign currency exchange, secretarial services in English, audiovisual equipment, photocopiers, computers, cable television news, translation services, and express checkout. 3 Piazza Massimo d'Azeglio (phone and fax: 245247; telex: 571058). Expensive.

Savoy – A classic gem in the heart of Florence, with most of its 100 rooms decorated in Venetian style. It also has a popular piano bar. Business facilities include 24-hour room service, meeting rooms for up to 150, English-speaking concierge, foreign currency exchange, secretarial services in English, audiovisual equipment, photocopiers, computers, cable television news, translation services, and express checkout. 7 Piazza della Repubblica (phone: 283313; fax: 284840; telex: 570220). Expensive.

Sheraton – Situated 3 miles (5 km) south of Florence, this 321-room member of the worldwide chain has tennis courts and an outdoor swimming pool (perfect for a dip after a hot day's sightseeing). A van transports guests into the city. Business facilities include 24-hour room service, meeting rooms for up to 1,300, English-speaking concierge, foreign currency exchange, secretarial services in English, audiovisual equipment, photocopiers, computers, cable television news, translation services, and express checkout. Just off the Firenze Sud autostrada exit. 33 Via G. Agnelli (phone: 64901; fax: 680747; telex: 575860). Expensive.

Torre di Bellosguardo – The majestic, cypress-framed site on a hill overlooking Florence's terra cotta roofs makes this handsome, 16-room hostelry a special place to stay. A sunny verandah, lush gardens, and a swimming pool — plus rooms whose ceilings are punctuated by rough hewn beams and each of which is individually decorated with antiques — add to the charm. There is an English-speaking concierge and 24-hour room service. 2 Via Roti Michelozzi (phone: 229-8145). Expensive.

Villa Medici – A reconstruction of the 18th-century Sonnino de Renzis Palace, halfway between the railroad station and the River Arno. Many of the 110 charming, spacious rooms have balconies affording panoramic views. The grand public rooms, tranquil gardens, and elegant service all are worthy of a hotel of this class. The swimming pool is a bow to contemporary tastes. Business facilities include 24-hour room service, meeting rooms for up to 100, English-speaking concierge, foreign currency exchange, secretarial services in English, audiovisual equipment, photocopiers, computers, cable television news, translation services, and express checkout. 42 Via del Prato (phone: 261331; fax: 261336; telex: 570179). Expensive.

Anglo-American – Between the train station and the river, very near the *Teatro Comunale*, with 118 refurbished rooms. Business facilities include 24-hour room service, meeting rooms for up to 150, English-speaking concierge, foreign currency exchange, secretarial services in English, audiovisual equipment, photocopiers, computers, cable television news, translation services, and express checkout. 9 Via Garibaldi (phone: 282114; fax: 268513; telex: 570289). Expensive to moderate.

Croce di Malta – Housed in a former convent close to Santa Croce, the site actually harks back to Roman times — you'll see Roman columns and an ancient brick vaulted roof, all carefully restored by the hotel's architect-owner. There are 98 rooms, a pretty garden, and a small swimming pool — a luxury for a hotel in the center of town. Business facilities include 24-hour room service, meeting rooms for up to 70, English-speaking concierge, foreign currency exchange, secretarial services in English, audiovisual equipment, photocopiers, computers, cable television news, translation services, and express checkout. 7 Via della Scala (phone: 282600 or 211740; fax: 287121; telex: 570540). Expensive to moderate.

Fenice Palace – Recently renovated and restored, the 67 guestrooms occupy 4 floors in a 19th-century palazzo near the Duomo. The accommodations offer considerable comfort and some magnificent views of the city's major monuments. Business facilities include 24-hour room service, English-speaking concierge, foreign currency exchange, secretarial services in English, audiovisual equipment, photocopiers, computers, translation services, and express checkout. 10 Via Martelli (phone: 289942; fax: 210087; telex: 575580). Expensive to moderate.

Jolly Carlton – Large and modern, this 167-room member of the efficient Jolly chain has a pool and a wonderful view from the terrace. It's near the Cascine park. Business facilities include 24-hour room service, meeting rooms for up to 120,

English-speaking concierge, foreign currency exchange, secretarial services in English, audiovisual equipment, photocopiers, computers, cable television news, translation services, and express checkout. 4/A Piazza Vittorio Veneto (phone: 2770; fax: 292794; telex: 571523). Expensive to moderate.

Kraft – This modern 66-room hotel in a nice area near the *Teatro Comunale* has a roof-garden restaurant sporting umbrella pines and a cypress tree as well as a splendid panorama and a rooftop swimming pool. Business facilities include 24-hour room service, meeting rooms for up to 60, English-speaking concierge, foreign currency exchange, secretarial services in English, audiovisual equipment, photocopiers, computers, translation services, and express checkout. 2 Via Solferino (phone: 284273; fax: 298267; telex: 571523). Expensive to moderate.

Lungarno – Comfortable, functional, and cheerful. Set between the Ponte Vecchio and the Ponte Santa Trinita on the Oltrarno side of town, with 70 modern rooms, the best of which have terraces and balconies overlooking the Arno (be sure to book one of these in advance). There also is a garage. Business facilities include 24-hour room service, meeting rooms for up to 60, English-speaking concierge, foreign currency exchange, secretarial services in English, audiovisual equipment, photocopiers, computers, cable television news, translation services, and express checkout. 14 Borgo San Jacopo (phone: 264211; fax: 268437; telex: 570129). Expensive to moderate.

Minerva – The 107 rooms here are large and comfortably furnished, all with private modern baths. The staff is pleasant, and the hotel is near the train station, convenient to shopping and the major museums. Business facilities include 24-hour room service, meeting rooms for up to 70, English-speaking concierge, foreign currency exchange, secretarial services in English, audiovisual equipment, photocopiers, computers, cable television news, translation services, and express checkout. 16 Piazza Santa Maria Novella (phone: 284555; fax: 268281; telex: 570414). Expensive to moderate.

Palazzo Antellesi – Visitors planning at least a 1-week stay in Florence might want to consider renting an apartment in this exquisite palazzo on Piazza Santa Croce. The owners have converted it into several self-contained units that can sleep from two to five people. It is one of the few buildings in the city with a frescoed façade and some of the apartments also have frescoes. All are beautifully furnished, most have fireplaces, and some have terraces. There also is a garden and several courtyards, making this place an oasis of peace when Florence is at its hottest and most crowded. 21-22 Piazza Santa Croce (phone: 244456; fax: 234-5552). Expensive to moderate.

Tornabuoni Beacci – This delightful former pensione occupies the top floors of a 14th-century palace on Florence's most elegant street. It's traditional yet cheerful and sunny, provides excellent service, and has a charming terrace. Guests are required to take breakfast and another meal (half board) during high season. 3 Via Tornabuoni (phone: 212645; telex: 570215). Expensive to moderate.

Baglioni – A traditional hotel in refined Tuscan taste: parquet floors, solid furnishings, handsome carpets, sober — even somber — atmosphere and service, with nearly 200 rooms. It's near the railway station and only a short walk from the best shopping. The roof garden restaurant has an enviable view of the historic city. Business facilities include 24-hour room service, meeting rooms for up to 210, English-speaking concierge, foreign currency exchange, secretarial services in English, audiovisual equipment, photocopiers, computers, cable television news, translation services, and express checkout. 6 Piazza dell'Unità Italiana (phone: 218441; fax: 215695; telex: 580525). Moderate.

Continental – In an ideal, albeit sometimes noisy, spot overlooking the Ponte Vecchio, this is as efficient as its sister hotel across the river, the *Lungarno,* which you can see from the terrace. No restaurant. Business facilities include 24-hour room service, English-speaking concierge, and cable television news. 2 Lungarno Acciaiuoli (phone: 282392; fax: 268557; telex: 580525). Moderate.

Monna Lisa – On a tiny side street, this hostelry in an old renovated building offers Old World charm and style with modern comforts. Some of the 20 guestrooms have Jacuzzis. There is private parking for no extra charge during low season. 27 Borgo Pinti (phone: 247-9751). Moderate.

Villa Villoresi – About 5 miles (8 km) from the center of Florence, it's another noble home away from home. It dates to the 12th century, but for the last 200 years it has been the property of the Villoresi family, who turned it into a hotel in the 1960s. With only 28 rooms, they manage to impart a sense of family as well as history. Bedroom walls have frescoes and meals are good. There is a pool in the garden among the olive trees. 2 Via Ciampi, Località Colonnata, Sesto Fiorentino (phone: 448-9032; telex: 580567). Moderate.

Loggiato dei Serviti – Well located on the charming Piazza SS Annunziata, the 20 rooms in this Renaissance palazzo are a bargain, especially by Florentine standards. Most are furnished with antiques. Be sure to book well in advance. 3 Piazza SS Annunziata (phone: 219165; telex: 575808). Moderate to inexpensive.

Balestri – A clean, no-frills stopping place overlooking the Arno. It has 50 rooms, no restaurant. 7 Piazza Mentana (phone: 214743). Inexpensive.

Bencistà – This 35-room 15th-century villa, an inn among the olive trees near Fiesole, is a beautiful bargain for those whose shoestrings do not stretch as far as the *Villa San Michele.* Half board is required. No phones in the rooms. A free minibus service is available to take guests into Florence. Open mid-March to November. 4 Via Benedetto da Maiano, between Fiesole and San Domenico (phone: 59163). Inexpensive.

Morandi alla Crocetta – A small but charming 15-room hotel, run by an English-woman and her Italian-born son in what used to be a Dominican convent. Rooms are furnished with Tuscan antiques and many guests become friends of the family, returning year after year. 50 Via Laura (phone: 234-4747; fax: 248-0954). Inexpensive.

Pendini – An old-style, family-run place, in operation for over 100 years in a building far older, but renovated. 2 Via degli Strozzi (phone: 211170; fax: 282179; telex: 570007). Inexpensive.

Porta Rossa – Said to be one of Florence's oldest (14th century, with a 13th-century tower), and perhaps in need of a little sprucing up. Balzac and Stendhal, they say, slept here. It has Renaissance public rooms (good for meetings in the commercial center of the city) and a terrace overlooking the Ponte Vecchio. 19 Via Porta Rossa (phone: 287551). Inexpensive.

Quisisana Ponte Vecchio – Between the Ponte Vecchio and the *Uffizi,* with a view of the former from a charming terrace. This was the setting for the film *A Room with a View,* adapted from E.M. Forster's novel. 4 Lungarno Archibusieri (phone: 216692; fax: 268303). Inexpensive.

La Residenza – A small, renovated hotel, with a lovely terrace, on Florence's best shopping street. Half board is required during high season. 8 Via Tornabuoni (phone: 284197; telex: 570093). Inexpensive.

Silla – A quiet, charming, and friendly place, with 3 large newer rooms on the third floor. Its large flowered terrace overlooks the river and a park on the Oltrarno side of town. No restaurant; usually closed in December. 5 Via dei Renai (phone: 234-2889). Inexpensive.

EATING OUT: Back in the 16th century, Catherine de' Medici married King Henry II of France, and her cousin Maria de' Medici married Henry IV. The women took their cooks and their recipes for creams, sauces, pastries, and ice creams to the French court — along with their trousseaus. As an Elizabethan poet once said, "Tuscany provided creams and cakes and lively Florentine women to sweeten the taste and minds of the French."

Following their departure, the fanciness went out of Florentine food, and French cooking began to shine. But today, Florentine cooking, while simpler and more straightforward than it was during the Renaissance, is still at the top of the list of Italy's many varied regional dishes. No small contributing factor to this culinary art is the quality of the ingredients. Tuscany boasts excellent olive oil and wine, exquisite fruits and vegetables, good game in season, fresh fish from its coast, as well as salami, sausages, and every kind of meat. A *bistecca alla fiorentina,* thick and juicy on the bone and traditionally accompanied by new potatoes or white beans drenched in pure golden olive oil, is a meal fit for the fussiest of kings. Diners can roughly gauge the price of a restaurant before entering by the cost per kilo (2.2 pounds) of its Florentine steaks on the menu displayed outside. Fortunately, one steak is usually more than enough for two persons, and it is not considered a gaffe to order one steak for two or more.

Mealtimes in Florence begin earlier than in Rome, beginning by 12:30 or 1 PM for lunch, and by 8 PM for dinner. Many of the typical mamma 'n' papa restaurants are small, popular, and crowded. If you don't book, be prepared to wait and eventually share a table (single guests are often seated at a communal table — a respectable way of meeting residents). Also unlike Rome, you won't be encouraged to linger over your dessert wine if there are people waiting for your table. Food, like most everything else in Florentine life, is taken seriously; do your business and socializing elsewhere. A meal for two at the very expensive *Enoteca Pinchiorri* will vary (but will be at least $200), depending on what you eat and what wine you order. A full meal for two, including the house wine or the low-priced (but excellent) local chianti, at an expensive restaurant will cost between $95 and $180. Expect to pay between $60 and $95 at a moderate restaurant and under $60 at an inexpensive one. All telephone numbers are in the 55 city code unless otherwise indicated.

Enoteca Pinchiorri – In the 15th-century Ciofi-Iacometti Palace, with a delightful courtyard for dining alfresco, this is possibly Italy's best restaurant and certainly the place for that grand dinner in Florence. The service, however, can be very unfriendly — a major minus, considering the size of the check. The four chefs prepare exquisite traditional and nouvelle dishes with a Franco-Italian flavor, perhaps a mosaic of sweet and sour fish, sweetbread salad with shrimp sauce, ricotta and salami pie, or medallions of veal with capers and lime. The wine collection (60,000 bottles) is outstanding, understandably so, since the restaurant actually began as a wine showroom. Closed Sundays, Mondays at lunch, and August. Reservations necessary. Major credit cards accepted. 87 Via Ghibellina (phone: 242777). Very expensive.

Campidoglio – White tablecloths and elegant service set this attractive place apart from most Florentine trattorie, and the excellent Italian fare makes it worth the tab. Closed Thursdays. Reservations advised. Major credit cards accepted. 8r Via Campidoglio (phone: 287770). Expensive.

Il Cenacolo – "The Last Supper" continues to be the rage in refined restaurants. The ambience is ultra-cool, with a lovely garden for alfresco dining in fine weather. The cuisine is both traditional and new, featuring some old Florentine recipes with an innovative flair and a light touch for today's health-conscious patrons. There also is a bar in which to drown your sorrows after you settle the tab. Closed Sundays all day and Mondays at lunch. Reservations necessary. Major credit cards accepted. 34 Via Borgo Ognissanti (phone: 219493). Expensive.

Harry's Bar – No relation to the famed eatery in Venice, but Americans tend to flock here just the same. Italian specialties are best, though it's also the place to find a hamburger and French fries. Closed Sundays and mid-December to mid-January. Reservations advised. Major credit cards accepted. 22r Lungarno Amerigo Vespucci (phone: 296700). Expensive.

Relais le Jardin – Located in the *Regency Umbria* hotel, well-heeled Florentines like to dine here, especially in summer when the tables are moved into the garden. The tone is one of understated elegance, with first class service and faultless Florentine cooking. The menu changes frequently, and the chef turns out some interesting pasta variations. Open daily. Reservations advised. Major credit cards accepted. 3 Piazza Massimo d'Azeglio (phone: 245247). Expensive.

Sabatini – Once Florence's top dining room, but thoroughly outclassed in recent years. It's still quiet, dignified, and noted for its traditional fare, but the quality has slipped. Some may find the standard menu far less interesting than those of less expensive trattorie. Closed Mondays. Reservations advised. Major credit cards accepted. 9/A Via Panzani (phone: 211559 or 282802). Expensive.

Cantinetta Antinori – Not quite a restaurant, but a typically rustic yet fashionably chic cantina, with food designed to accompany the Antinori wines. Perfect for a light lunch of salami or *finocchiona* with bread, *crostini* (chicken liver canapés), soup, or a modest hot dish such as tripe or *bollito* (mixed boiled meat). Closed weekends and August. Reservations unnecessary. No credit cards accepted. 3 Piazza Antinori (phone: 292234). Expensive to moderate.

Cibreo – Also named after a historic Florentine dish, one so good it is said to have given Catherine de' Medici near fatal indigestion from overeating. Although the menu offers interesting old Tuscan dishes, it does not limit itself to the traditional Florentine fare it does so well. Genoese minestrone, eggplant parmesan from the south, polenta from the Veneto, plus savory appetizers such as walnut and *pecorino* cheese salad, soups, seafood with an unusual twist (mussel terrine, squid stew), and homemade desserts are all available, as are good wines. In summer, there's alfresco dining. Closed Sundays and from late July to mid-September. Reservations necessary. Major credit cards accepted. 118r Via de' Macci (phone: 234-1100). Expensive to moderate.

Coco Lezzone – Another Florentine favorite, serving authentic local food using the best ingredients and no pretenses. Try the *pappa al pomodoro,* a thick soup made of fresh tomatoes, herbs, and bread. This restaurant is crowded and hurried; don't expect to linger. Closed Sundays, Saturdays in the summer and Tuesdays in the winter, the last week in July, and August. Reservations advised. No credit cards accepted. 26r Via del Parioncino (phone: 287178). Expensive to moderate.

Taverna del Bronzino – Rustic yet elegant, set in a 16th-century palazzo furnished with antiques and a garden for alfresco dining in season. *Crostini ai funghi porcini* (wild mushroom canapés), *tortelloni al cedro,* and renowned Florentine beef with green peppers are specialties. Closed Sundays. Reservations advised. Major credit cards accepted. 25-27r Via delle Ruote (phone: 495220). Expensive to moderate.

La Vecchia Cucina – A bit out of the way, but with a *nuova cucina* worth trying when you've had your fill of wonderfully traditional Tuscan food. The innovative menu of a half-dozen first and second courses and three desserts is recited by the owner (tricky if you don't speak Italian), and it changes every week. Interesting wine list. Closed Sundays and August. Reservations advised. Major credit cards accepted. 1r Viale Edmondo De Amicis (phone: 660143). Expensive to moderate.

Buzzino – The perfect place for lunch or dinner after a cultural feast at the *Uffizi,* which is just a block away. The setting is warm, the waiters friendly, and the food good enough to put tired museumgoers back on their feet. The bill is sweetened by the arrival of the free *vin santo* (a sweet dessert wine). Open daily. Reservations advised. Major credit cards accepted. 8 Via dei Leoni (phone: 239-8013). Moderate.

Cammillo – An appealing, bustling spot near the Ponte S. Trinita, offering authentic dishes such as tripe *alla fiorentina* and, in season, pasta with white truffles. Closed Wednesdays and Thursdays. Reservations unnecessary. No credit cards accepted. 57r Borgo San Jacopo (phone: 212427). Moderate.

La Carabaccia – Named after an antique Florentine dish (none other than onion soup) loved by the Medicis, the menu changes daily according to what's good at the market. Five starters and five main courses generally are offered, occasionally featuring parts of an animal you never thought you could eat (don't ask!). Very popular, informal, and unrushed. Closed Sundays, Mondays at lunch, and August. Reservations advised. No credit cards accepted. 190r Via Palazzuolo (phone: 214782). Moderate.

Le Cave – A delightful stop in Fiesole and sheer magic in early summer and fall, when it's great to lunch under the linden trees and gaze out over the splendid valley. Indoors is warm, cozy, and rustic, as is the country-style cooking, beginning with excellent prosciutto, *finocchiona,* and other local salami, chicken and truffle croquettes, canapés of mozzarella and mushrooms, *crespelle* or ravioli, and the house specialty, *gallina al mattone,* spring chicken grilled on an open fire and seriously seasoned with black pepper and the purest of virgin olive oils. Closed Thursdays, Sunday evenings, and August. Reservations necessary. No credit cards accepted. 16 Via delle Cave, Località Maiano, Fiesole (phone: 59133). Moderate.

Da Ganino (Ex-Mario) – Long a Florentine favorite, this typically tiny Tuscan trattoria is run by a family. It still is small and cozy in the winter, with alfresco dining on the small square in fine weather. Here is some of the best Florentine *cucina,* including fresh mushrooms and truffles in season and a justifiably famous cheesecake. Closed Sundays, 3 weeks in August, and Christmas. Reservations advised. Major credit cards accepted. 4r Piazza dei Cimatori (phone: 214125). Moderate.

Garga – The unusual specialties of this establishment include *zuppa di cavoli neri* (soup of a bitter green local vegetable), risotto of leeks and bacon, and *gnocchetti verdi* (pasta of spinach and ricotta) — all exquisitely prepared. Absolutely terrific. Closed Sundays and Monday lunch. Reservations necessary. No credit cards accepted. 48-52 Via del Moro (phone: 239-8898). Moderate.

Il Latini – This popular eatery, in the former stables of the historic Palazzo Rucellai, serves such solid and abundant fare as hearty Tuscan soup, unpretentious meat platters, grilled fish, fresh vegetables, and traditional desserts. Not for romantic evenings, here you sit at long communal tables and the food keeps arriving. Good value. Closed Mondays and at lunch on Tuesdays. Reservations unnecessary. No credit cards accepted. 6r Via Palchetti (phone: 210916). Moderate.

La Loggia – On the most spectacular site in Florence, with a view over the entire city, it's run by some former *Sabatini* waiters who, by employing traditional Tuscan cuisine and efficient service despite the crowds, have transformed a once-mediocre restaurant into a Florentine favorite. The panorama from the terrace makes it especially pleasant during the summer. Closed Wednesdays. Reservations advised. Major credit cards accepted. 1 Piazzale Michelangelo (phone: 287032 or 234-2832). Moderate.

Omero – The menu here hasn't changed in decades, and all the regulars who flock to this eatery are grateful. In the front is a grocery store where Florentines buy staples or stop for a glass of wine. The restaurant in the back has beautiful views of the Tuscan hills, and the small garden downstairs is wonderful for summer dining, although the service tends to be slow and the sound of the insect zapper may be distracting. Still, the exceptional *fettunta* (Tuscan garlic bread), ravioli, grilled chicken, ubiquitous *bistecca alla fiorentina,* fried artichokes or zucchini blossoms (in season), and meringue dessert are worth the wait. Closed Tuesdays and August. Reservations advised. Major credit cards accepted. 11r Via Pian dei Guillari (phone: 220053). Moderate.

Osteria da Quinto – A longtime favorite with Florentines, in large part because owner Leo Codacci is a great music lover and often treats customers to bursts of song when the mood strikes him. The *bistecca alla fiorentina* is among the biggest and best in town. It's always packed, so be sure to reserve ahead. Closed Mondays. Major credit cards accepted. 5 Piazza Peruzzi (phone: 213323). Moderate.

Pallottino – One of Florence's newest, this rising star on the gastronomic scene offers a good selection of Tuscan food, including many hard-to-find dishes. Specialties like spaghetti with fresh tomatoes and arugula, stuffed chicken neck (tastes much better than it sounds), and *bistecca alla fiorentina* are not to be missed. Closed Mondays and Tuesdays for lunch. Reservations necessary. Major credit cards accepted. 1r Via Isola delle Stinche (phone: 289573). Moderate.

Pierot – The specialty is seafood, especially on Tuesdays and Fridays. The menu is long and ever changing, depending on the availability of ingredients, but if you spot the traditional squid and beet dish called *inzimino di calamari e bietoline,* try it; ditto the chestnut ice cream for dessert. Open later than most. Closed Sundays and the last 3 weeks of July. Reservations advised. Major credit cards accepted. 25r Piazza Taddeo Gaddi (phone: 702100). Moderate.

La Sostanza – Popularly called *Troia,* literally a hog (also a woman of easy virtue), this is one of Florence's oldest and most cherished trattorie, serving some of the best steaks in town. If you haven't had a *bistecca alla fiorentina* with Tuscan beans, get here early. The place is picturesquely plain and tiny, the turnover as fast as the service (which can be rude if you try to linger). Communal tables. Closed Saturday evenings, Sundays, and August. Reservations necessary. 25r Via del Porcellana (phone: 212691). Moderate.

Trattoria del Francescano – Lovers of hearty Florentine fare such as *tagliatelle con funghi porcini* (wide noodles with mushrooms) and *pappa al pomodoro* (thick fresh tomato and bread soup) will appreciate this family-run place. Great store is set by fresh ingredients and time-honored recipes. Closed Wednesdays. Reservations necessary. Major credit cards accepted. 26r Via San Giuseppe (phone: 241605). Moderate.

Tredici Gobbi – Once known for Hungarian cooking, which still simmers on the back burner, Tuscan specialties have come to the fore. Closed Sunday evenings, Mondays, and August. Reservations advised. Major credit cards accepted. 9r Via del Porcellana (phone: 298769). Moderate.

Antico Fattore – In the shadow of the *Uffizi,* it's famous for its *ribollita,* a vegetable soup so thick with broccoli, bread, and white beans a spoon stands up in it. The rest of the menu is equally hearty peasant fare. Closed Sundays, Mondays, and mid-July to early August. Reservations advised. Major credit cards accepted. 1r Via Lambertesca (phone: 261215). Moderate to inexpensive.

Angiolino – Very good potluck and very economical. This is on the Pitti side of the river and the ambience is cozy. Closed Sundays and Mondays. Reservations unnecessary. No credit cards accepted. 36r Via di Santo Spirito (phone: 239-8976). Inexpensive.

Cinghiale Bianco – Cozy and hospitable, this trattoria serves great pasta and other tasty Florentine specialties at very reasonable prices. Don't miss the *fettunta farcita,* an old peasant recipe of garlic-rubbed bread layered with spinach and white beans. Closed Tuesdays, Wednesdays, and January. Reservations advised. No credit cards accepted. 43r Borgo San Jacopo (phone: 215706). Inexpensive.

Fagioli – A cheery, rustic ambience and a full bar. Enjoy the *passato di fagioli con pasta,* a thick soup of white beans and pasta. Closed weekends and August.

Reservations unnecessary. No credit cards accepted. 47r Corso Tintori (phone: 244285). Inexpensive.

Le Mossacce – Still largely frequented by habitués, it's filled with long paper-covered tables and serves good country cooking. Try the *ribollita,* a thick and hearty vegetable soup. Closed Saturday nights, Sundays, and August. Reservations unnecessary. No credit cards accepted. 55r Via del Proconsolo (phone: 294361). Inexpensive.

Ruggero – This simple trattoria serves some of the best Florentine food in the city — well-prepared, rustic fare. The *pasta alla carrettiera* (in a spicy tomato sauce), the traditional *pappa al pomodoro* (thick tomato soup), *ribollita,* and meat dishes are all tasty. The tables are filled with members of the Florentine nobility during Sunday lunchtime. Closed Tuesdays, Wednesdays, and July 7 to August 7. Reservations necessary. No credit cards accepted. 89 Via Senese (phone: 220542). Inexpensive.

Trattoria da Graziella – When you are tired of Florentine fare, head to this eatery in Fiesole where Sardinian-born Ugo Salis offers well-cooked island dishes, such as the spectacular and mouth-watering suckling pig. There are good Sardinian wines to wash down the meal, though chianti fans also will be satisfied. There is a large terrace for alfresco dining. Closed Mondays. Reservations advised. Major credit cards accepted. 20 Via Cave di Maiano, Fiesole (phone: 599963). Inexpensive.

Vecchia Bettola – A typical Tuscan trattoria with quality home-style cooking and marble tabletops. Closed Mondays and Tuesdays. Reservations unnecessary. No credit cards accepted. 32-34r Viale Ariosto (phone: 224158). Inexpensive.

Note: When the urge for something delectably *dolce* becomes irresistible, we head for one of our two overwhelming favorites. *Vivoli* (7 Via Isola della Stinche) serves some of the best gelati in town, in flavors from chocolate to grapefruit, fresh strawberry to tea. Another good place is *Perchè No* (19r Via dei Tavolini), on a side street near Piazza della Signoria, where all the fruit flavors are made with fresh fruit. *Rivoire* (on the Piazza della Signoria), a combination coffeehouse/candy shop, sells a confection of creamed chocolate that you literally eat with a spoon. It's sold in individual boxes — with spoon attached! And if for some reason your tastebuds get homesick, head for *CarLie's* (12r Via della Brache). Started by two Smith College graduates, these Yankees offer brownies, cupcakes, strawberry shortcake, and at *Thanksgiving,* pumpkin or apple pie.

FRANKFURT

Trade and traffic have formed Frankfurt's destiny since its earliest existence as a community, more than 1,200 years ago. Its location on the Main River at the heart of the European continent made it the crossroads of prehistoric trade routes linking northern Europe with the Mediterranean areas, and Eastern with Western Europe. The city grew, spreading out to meet the imperial forest of Dreieich in the south and the wooded Taunus Mountains encircling the broad plain formed by the Main as it flows toward the Rhine. Frankfurt today is a bustling commercial city with a genuine international flair. It also is a city with many parks and museums. Look behind the imposing glass and steel of modern Frankfurt and you will find lovingly restored landmarks that highlight the city's long history.

The Celts were here first, but were forced west across the Rhine by migrating German tribes. Romans had settled along the Main by the 1st century AD, but they fled the Saxon tribes, who, in turn, were driven out by the Franks in 496. The little settlement on the Main became the site of the Franks' ford — where Saxons from south of the river could cross over to trade.

Ludwig the German, first ruler of the German Empire and a grandson of Charlemagne, made Frankfurt his capital, and from 1356 to 1792 Frankfurt was where the Holy Roman emperors were elected. Frankfurt was granted the right to mint money in the 16th century, and since that time finance and trade have been synonymous with it. The Rothschild financial dynasty started here with Meyer Amschel Rothschild (1743–1812); his sons who succeeded him were known as "the five Frankfurters."

Frankfurt also claims Germany's greatest poet, Johann Wolfgang von Goethe, as its own. Goethe was born here in 1749. St. Paul's Church, where Germany's first National Assembly met in 1848, has become a symbol of German liberalism.

In this century, Frankfurt once again earned a reputation as a center of liberalism, as pockets of opposition to the Nazis were centered here. Although a massive Allied air attack during World War II destroyed much of the city, Frankfurt was quick to rebuild after the war and never really stopped. The city has made a conscious attempt to relieve the coldness of modern skyscrapers with attractive pedestrian precincts for shopping and strolling or simply relaxing in an outdoor café. The city's parks and forest and neighboring green belts are much used by Frankfurt's urban population.

Frankfurters sometimes refer to their city as "Mainhattan" (Manhattan on the Main). Around 630,000 people live in Frankfurt proper, but the greater Frankfurt area, extending across the fertile Main Valley and up into the Taunus Mountains, has a population of more than a million. Frankfurt's citizens work in its financial center and in the chemical, electronics, machine tool, and printing industries. They are cosmopolitan and used to sampling the

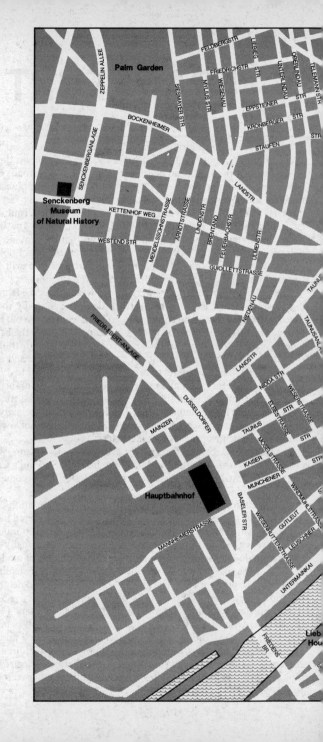

FRANKFURT

Stock Exchange

Hauptwache

Goethe's House

Romerberg

RIVER MAIN

Museum of Arts and Crafts

Museum of Ethnology

Postal Museum

adel Museum
stitute of Art

ESCHERSHEIMER
IM
TRUTZ
GARTNER
WEG
FRANKFURT
BOCKENHEIMER
ld
era
use
LANDSTR
OEDER WEG
ESCHENHEIMER
ANLAGE
ANLAGE
PETERS STR
BLEICH STR
VILBELER STR
HOCH STR
TAUBENSTR
STIFT STR
STEPHAN STR
GR FRIEDBERGER STR
ESCHERSHEIMER
ZEIL
FAHRGASSE
JUNGHOFSTR
HOLZGRABEN
HASENGASSE
TONGESGASSE
GALLUSSTRASSE
FRIEDENSTRASSE
HIRSCHGR
LANDSTR
BERLINER STR
STR
BRAUBACH STR
FAHRGASSE
MAINZER
BETHMANN
WEIFSSFRAUNSTR
MAINKAI
ALTE BRUCKE
STR
UNTERMAIN ANLAGE
EISSINERSTEG
UNTERMAIN BR
SCHAUMAIN KAI
METZLER STR
SCHWEIZER STR
WALTER KOLB STR
SCHIFFER STR
STR
STADEL STR
STR
DANNECKER STR
DURER STR
GARTEN
GUTZKOW STR
BRUCKEN STR
KENNEDY ALLEE
SCHWANTHALER STR
STR
HOLBEN STR
TEXTOR STR
HEDDERICH STR

world's best goods as the result of the role Frankfurt plays as an international trade center. Like many Germans, some Frankfurters are anxious about the adverse effects German unification may have on their local economy (and pocketbooks), but for the present there seems to be no noticeable difference in their standard of living.

Frankfurt still is a city of superlatives: the city has faster trains, more cars per capita, more banks, a larger airport, and more skyscrapers than almost any other German city. Europe's tallest office building, the 52-story, 842-foot-high Messeturm (fairgrounds tower) designed by the Chicago-based, German-born architect Helmut Jahn, opened here in 1990. In spite of their efficiency, money making, and slightly smug air of success, Frankfurters have maintained a casual approach to life that exists almost nowhere else in Germany. This is, after all, the city that shuts down for an afternoon each spring (the Tuesday following *Whitmonday*) so that its citizens can walk in the woods.

FRANKFURT AT-A-GLANCE

SEEING THE CITY: You get a sweeping view of the Main Valley, the Taunus Mountains, and the city from the glass-enclosed observation deck of the 1,086-foot Europaturm television tower (Western Europe's tallest) near Rosa Luxemburgstrasse in the Ginnheim section of northwest Frankfurt. There is a cafeteria and a revolving restaurant in the tower (see *Eating Out*). Open daily. Admission charge for the observation platform.

SPECIAL PLACES: Central Frankfurt is on the right bank of a bend in the Main. Most of the commercial and historic areas are in a small area ringed by a series of green parks that follow the Old City walls. Across the Main is a district called Sachsenhausen. Both these areas are ideal for exploring on foot. But you also can see Frankfurt on weekends by riding the *Ebbelwei Express,* gaily painted streetcars that begin circle tours of the city every 30 minutes between 1:30 and 5:30 PM. With your ride you'll get music, and you can buy some of Frankfurt's famous apple wine (*Apfelwein*) to sip along the way. Hop aboard at any of the 18 *Ebbelwei Express* stops, including those in the Theaterplatz, at the main railroad station, or at the intersection of Gartenstrasse and Schweizerstrasse in Sachsenhausen. It costs about $3 for an hour's ride; call 213-22425 for information.

DOWNTOWN

Hauptwache – This beautifully reconstructed baroque building, once a sentry house dating from 1730, and the little square over which it presides are considered the heart of Frankfurt. There is a lovely outdoor café in which you can enjoy coffee and cake while you get your bearings. Just in front of the café is an escalator leading from the street to a huge underground shopping mall. Before leaving the square, though, you may want to visit St. Katharine's Church (Katharinenkirche), where the poet Goethe was christened and confirmed. An der Hauptwache.

Goethe's House and Museum – A few blocks southwest of the Hauptwache is the boyhood home of Frankfurt's favorite son. Faithfully reconstructed after the war and furnished with many original possessions of the poet's family, the house offers a fascinating peek at 18th-century life in a wealthy, commercial city. In an adjoining museum are documents on Goethe's life and work as well as pictures and sculpture by well-known artists of his era. Open daily. Admission charge. 23 Grosser Hirschgraben (phone: 282824).

Römerberg – South of the Hauptwache, on a broad square with a statue of Justice, are three adjoining burghers' houses that have served as Frankfurt's City Hall since 1405. The three gabled façades and the row of seven medieval houses across the street are the symbol of this city. History comes alive in the Kaisersaal (Imperial Hall) where banquets were held to celebrate the coronations of the Holy Roman Emperors. East of Römerberg Platz is the Cathedral of St. Bartholomew (the Dom), built between the 13th and 15th centuries on a Carolingian foundation dating from 852. The cathedral's outstanding feature is a 15th-century dome and lantern tower. Between Römerberg and the cathedral is the *Kunsthalle,* a series of exhibition halls.

Der Historische Garten (Historical Garden) – In 1953, the remains of a Roman settlement and a Carolingian imperial palace were found at this site in front of the main entrance to the Dom. It's the oldest site in Frankfurt. Open daily. No admission charge (no phone).

Alt-Sachsenhausen – A few steps from Römerberg, near where the ancient Franks forded the river, the Eiserner Steg footbridge leads across the river into another old section of the city. (*Sachsenhausen* means "Saxons' houses.") Here you can enjoy the jumble of half-timbered houses and rough cobbled streets with their inviting pubs and restaurants, and the charming little squares and pretty fountains that are particularly lively meeting places at night and on weekends. Visit the local pubs for the special apple cider called *Stöffche* and the Frankfurt dishes *Rippchen* (pork ribs) or *Haxen* (pork foot and sauerkraut). For listings of pubs to visit in Alt-Sachsenhausen, see *Nightclubs and Nightlife.*

Palmengarten (Palm Garden) – One of Europe's most famous botanical gardens, these 55 acres of trees, meadows, ponds, gardens, and footpaths offer a welcome sanctuary from the bustling city. Over 12,000 varieties of plants grow in the park and thousands of orchids and cacti are displayed in its conservatories. A traditional Sunday afternoon entertainment in Frankfurt is a stroll through the flower gardens, perhaps pausing to listen to one of the concerts, followed by an elaborate ice cream sundae on the flower-bedecked terrace of the *Palmengarten* restaurant. Open daily. Admission charge. Entrance at Palmengartenstr. (phone: 212-33382).

Zoologischer Garten (Frankfurt Zoo) – This is one of Europe's oldest zoos, but nonetheless one of its most up to date. Founded in 1858, the zoo is noted for its beautifully landscaped open-air enclosures and for its success in breeding rare species. Open daily. Admission charge. 16 Alfred-Brehm-Pl. (phone: 212-33731).

Frankfurter Wertpapierbörse (Frankfurt Stock Exchange) – Frankfurt is one of the most important financial centers in the world. Nearly 400 German and overseas banks have headquarters or subsidiaries in the city. Although open to the public less than an hour on any given day, no tour of the financial district would be complete without a visit to the spectators' gallery to watch the activity on the floor. Open weekdays, 11:30 AM to 12:15 PM. No admission charge. Börsenpl. (phone: 219-7382).

Städelsches Kunstinstitut und Städtische Galerie (Städel Museum Institute of Art and Municipal Gallery) – Famous works of Flemish primitives and German masters of the 16th century are on display in the second-floor picture gallery. Open daily except Mondays, 10 AM to 5 PM. Admission charge. 63 Schaumainkai (phone: 605-0980).

Alte Oper (Old Opera House) – A victim of wartime bombing, this 100-year-old landmark was finally rebuilt in 1981. Although no opera is performed here, the ultra-modern complex of rooms and halls now is used for concerts and conferences. The façade and the vestibule (now a café) were fully restored. Opernpl. (phone: 134-0400).

SUBURBS

Deutsches Ledermuseum (Leather Museum) – Exhibitions of the history of shoes and handbags are displayed in a wonderfully fragrant museum in Offenbach just 5 miles (8 km) southeast of Frankfurt. Open daily. Admission charge. 86 Frankfurterstr., in Offenbach (phone: 813021).

■**EXTRA SPECIAL:** The charming old town of Marburg an der Lahn, remarkable for its university, its castle, and the first Gothic church ever built in Germany (between 1235 and 1285), is 59 miles (94 km) north of Frankfurt in the Hesse region. The church is dedicated to St. Elizabeth of Hungary, who lived and performed good works here. The university is a center for Protestant theology. On the market square in the old quarter of town, you can see several old half-timbered houses dating from the mid-16th century. As you wander the twisting alleys of the old quarter, you may meet country people in traditional costume, particularly if your visit coincides with market days, Wednesdays and Saturdays.

SOURCES AND RESOURCES

TOURIST INFORMATION: For information, maps, brochures, hotel and restaurant listings, plus special sightseeing tours and tickets to local events, see the Frankfurter Verkehrsamt (Frankfurt Tourist Association). It has information bureaus on the north side of the main train station, opposite track 23 (phone: 212-38849 or 212-38851), and at 27 Römberg (phone: 212-38708 or 212-387090). There also is a tourist information office at the airport in the arrivals hall (phone: 693153). All tourist information bureaus are open daily.

Frankfurt Guide of the City, by Franz Lerner, is the best guide published in English. It is filled with city history and interesting facts as well as a variety of walking tours. It is available at bookstores and some newsstands.

The US Consulate is at 21 Siesmayerstrasse (phone: 75350).

Local Coverage – *Seven,* an English-language weekly that carries a calendar of events throughout Germany, is available at newsstands.

Food – *Seven* also has restaurant listings.

TELEPHONE: The country code for Germany is 49; the city code for Frankfurt is 69.

GETTING AROUND: Frankfurt has a clean, efficient, and quiet rapid transit system of buses, streetcars, subways, and trains. The trip from the Rhine-Main Airport to Frankfurt's main railway station takes only 12 minutes by train. Use the same kind of ticket for the entire system. Buy tickets from automatic dispensers before boarding or purchase a special 1-day, cut-rate ticket at the tourist information bureaus. Maps and timetables are conveniently posted throughout the system.

Airport – Frankfurt's Rhine-Main Airport handles both domestic and international flights. It's about a 20-minute drive from the airport to downtown, and a taxi will cost about $23. Various lines of the *S-Bahn* inter-urban train system speed their way to downtown Frankfurt in just 11 minutes (look for signs to the *S-Bahn,* and take the trains headed for Hauptbahnhof).

Buses and Streetcars – City buses (*Stadtbus*) and streetcars (*Strassenbahn*) transport passengers inexpensively to all parts of the city and to many suburbs.

Car Rental – All major international firms are represented. But if driving a special German vehicle — Porsche, BMW, Mercedes — on the autobahn at top speed is one reason you're visiting Germany, get in touch with *Auto Exclusiv,* in Heusenstamm, about 20 minutes from the Frankfurt Airport. They rent ultra-high-performance vehicles (phone: 6104-3060; fax: 6104-65960).

Subways and Trains – The subway system, called the *U-Bahn,* and the fast trains to outlying areas, *S-Bahn,* get you where you want to go quickly and comfortably. The main stops are at Hauptwache and the railway station.

Taxi – There are stands near major hotels, stations, and at some intersections. Most public telephone booths have a taxi call-number posted. But taxis are expensive.

 LOCAL SERVICES: Dentist (English-Speaking) – Most German dentists speak English; however, the US Consulate (phone: 75350) has a list of English-speaking dentists (and physicians). For emergency service, dial 660-7271.

Dry Cleaner – *Descoteaux,* 127 Mainzer Landstr. (phone: 252859).

Limousine Service – *Classic Limousines,* 3 Am Siebenstein, Dreieich-Buchschlag (phone: 610-362324).

Medical Emergency – All hospitals in Frankfurt have emergency rooms. For emergency service, dial 110; to obtain a doctor at any time of day or night, call 11500.

National/International Courier – *DHL International,* Kelsterbach, 5A Fasanensweg (phone: 610-77540).

Office Equipment Rental – *Böhler* (Sulzbach, 12A Wiesenstr.; phone: 619-671981); *Neithold,* for audiovisual equipment (10 Schillerstr.; phone: 284626).

Pharmacy – *Hirsch-Apotheke* (111 Zeil; phone: 281565). To find out which pharmacies are open at night, on weekends, or on holidays, dial 11500.

Photocopies – *Richter,* 72 Mendelssohnstr. (phone: 740981).

Post Office – The post office at Hauptbahnhof (the train station) is open 24 hours (phone: 261-5113).

Secretary/Stenographer (English-Speaking) – *Büro-Service International,* 37 Hermannstr. (phone: 555813).

Tailor – *Flesch,* 7 Martin-Luther-Str. (phone: 444777).

Telex – The post office at 14 Grosse Eschenheimerstr. (phone: 2111).

Translator – *Bundesverband der Dolmetscher und Ubersetzer* (*BDU;* the Association of Interpreters and Translators) 148 Wolfsgangstr.

Other – Tuxedo and fur rental: *Amor,* 43 Zeil (phone: 284271).

 SPECIAL EVENTS: Frankfurt is at its busiest during the more than a dozen trade fairs that draw some 1.2 million visitors to the city each year. The biggest of these are the *International Frankfurt Fairs* held in spring and fall and the *Book Fair* in October. Most of these events are held at the fairgrounds (*Messegelände*), a huge exhibition center near the main railway station. The tradition of trade fairs in Frankfurt dates back 800 years. There also are numerous public fairs, such as the *Main Fair,* in August, in the streets between the river and St. Paul's Church; and *Dippemess,* a big country fair held in April and again in September, with colorful stalls of crockery the main attraction. One other very special local holiday deserves mention: *Wäldchestag.* On the Tuesday following *Whitmonday,* most Frankfurters leave the city to walk in the neighboring woods, eat sausages and drink beer, and dance in the Forest House (*Oberforsthaus*).

MUSEUMS: In addition to those mentioned in *Special Places*, Frankfurt has a number of interesting museums (most of which charge no admission). They all are closed Mondays.

Deutsches Architektur Museum (Museum of German Architecture) – Exhibits of contemporary architecture, as well as presentations on theoretical issues pertaining to architecture (ecology, responsibility to people, and more). 43 Schaumainkai (phone: 212-38844).

Deutsches Postmuseum (German Postal Museum) – Exhibits relating to the history of the post office and the telephone company, including a large collection of stamps. 53 Schaumainkai (phone: 60600).

Film Museum – Covers a wide variety of international films. 41 Schaumainkai (phone: 212-38830).

Historisches Museum (History Museum) – Frankfurt over the years. 19 Saalgasse am Römerberg (phone: 212-35599).

Jüdisches Museum (Jewish Museum) – Jewish life in Germany, through exhibitions, seminars, readings, and films. 14-15 Untermainkai (phone: 212-35000).

Liebieghaus (Liebieg House) – Ancient and modern sculpture. 71 Schaumainkai (phone: 212-38617).

Museum für Kunsthandwerk (Museum of Arts and Crafts) – Over 30,000 European and Asian handicrafts. 17 Schaumainkai (phone: 212-34037).

Museum of Modern Art – The newest addition to Frankfurt's museums has collected works of American and German artists, as well as from around Europe. 10 Domstr. (phone: 212-30447).

Museum für Völkerkunde (Museum of Ethnology) – Changing exhibitions, with emphasis on Third World countries. 29 Schaumainkai (phone: 212-35390).

Naturmuseum Senckenberg (Senckenberg Museum of Natural History) – Animals, plants, fossils, and geological items, including an impressive collection of dinosaurs and prehistoric whales. 25 Senckenberganlange. The exception, it is open daily (phone: 75421).

Schirn Kunsthalle – A museum of modern art. Am Römerberg (phone: 299-8820).

SHOPPING: As befits Europe's major transportation hub, Frankfurt is filled with goods from all over the world. It is said that more money passes through the cash registers of the well-stocked department stores on the Zeil than on any other street in Europe. The best-known department stores are *Kaufhof* (116 Zeil) and *Hertie* (90 Zeil). There are several pedestrian streets besides the Zeil, including Grosse Bockenheimerstrasse, with its chic boutiques and elegant apparel shops. Incidentally, this street is known locally as Fressgasse (a rough English equivalent is "Gluttony Alley") because it is lined with so many restaurants, wine bars, and delicatessens. The best buys are the well-known German cutlery, expensive but superbly made leather clothing, and Frankfurt's distinctive blue and gray pottery. Another street, Goethestrasse, offers a tempting variety of designer clothing stores.

Bellak – The best in German handicrafts. 20 Goethestr. (phone: 292793).

Henckels – Finest in German cutlery. 11 Rossmarkt.

Lorey – Hummel, Meissen, and Rosenthal figurines. 16 Schillerstr. (phone: 299950).

Rosenthal am Kaiserplatz – World-renowned porcelain. 9 Kaiserstr. (phone: 283726).

Toni Schiesser – Fashionable women's wear. 2 Friedensstr. (phone: 282519).

SPORTS AND FITNESS: One out of every six Frankfurt residents belongs to some type of sports club, and walking and jogging along the river or the marked paths in the city forest and in the nearby Taunus Mountains have reached epidemic proportion. Physical fitness is even sponsored by the state government, which maintains *Trimm Dich* facilities ("keep yourself trim"), a 1.5-mile (2.5-km) illustrated course of exercises and jogging in the city forest. Frankfurt is a major soccer city, with professional matches held in the *Waldstadion* (362 Mörfelder Landstr.; phone: 678040). There's also a 6-day bicycle race each year at the *Festhalle* at the fairgrounds.

Bicycling – Besides the 6-day race, numerous cycling events are scheduled during summer months, and there are paths in the city parks and the forest. Bicycles can be rented at *Fahrrad Burger,* 6 Bornheimer Handstr. (phone: 491807).

Fitness Center – Many major hotels have fitness facilities on their premises (see *Checking In*).

Golf – The 18-hole course at *Frankfurter Golfclub* is just west of *Waldstadion* at 41 Golf Str. (phone: 666-2317/8).

Horse Racing – Flat races and steeplechase races are held at *Frankfurt-South Racecourse* in suburban Niederrad, on Schwarzwaldstr. (phone: 678-7018).

Ice Skating – You can skate or just watch other people at various rinks, including one at the *Waldstadion* (see above), or the spacious *Eissporthalle Frankfurt* (Bornheimer Hand; phone: 419141).

Jogging – Stadtwald, south of the Main River and 4 miles (6 km) from downtown; take streetcar No. 14; exit Oberschweinstiege.

Soccer – *Eintracht* is Frankfurt's professional club. You can join the enthusiastic supporters at *Waldstadion* nearly every other weekend during the season (for tickets, phone: 678040).

Swimming – Several hotels have swimming pools, and there are numerous indoor and outdoor pools throughout the city. For indoor swimming, visit *Rebstockbad* (7 August-Euler-Str.; phone: 708078/9). *Stadtbad Mitte* has warm and cold pools as well as saunas (4-8 Hochstr., phone: 212-35238).

Tennis – Exhibition matches are played at *Waldstadion* and the *Festhalle.* It is difficult for visitors to get court time at parks and clubs because of local demand.

THEATER: Frankfurt has more than 20 theaters. Most performances are in German, but there are some English-speaking theaters, including the *American Playhouse* (150 Hansa Allee; phone: 151835) and the *English Theater* (52 Kaiserstr.; phone: 242-3160). *The City Theater* is in temporary quarters: a large stage (Bockenheimer Warte; phone: 212-37435) and a small stage (2 Hofstr.; phone: 212-37395). The *Fritz Rémond-Theater* is at the Frankfurt Zoo (16 Alfred Brehm Pl.; phone: 435166), and often produces current British and American hits in German. The *Theater am Turm* (*TAT*) offers drama (2 Eschersheimer Landstr.; phone: 154-5110), and you'll find light comedy the specialty at *Die Kömodie* (18 Neue Mainzer Str.; phone: 284580).

MUSIC: Whatever your taste in music, from opera and jazz to punk, you'll hear it in Frankfurt. The *City Opera* performs on the stage of the theater in the Städtische Buhnen arts complex on Theaterplatz (phone: 212-37434). There are frequent choral, symphony, and chamber music concerts at *Hessischer-Rundfunk* (8 Bertramstr.; phone: 155-2382), at the huge *Jahrhunderthalle* in suburban Höchst (phone: 360-1240), and at the *Old Opera House* (Opernpl.; phone: 134-0400). Jazz lovers will love Frankfurt, which is purported to have more than 100 daily performances, ranging from traditional New Orleans to modern jazz. *Der Jazzkeller* (18a Kleine Bockenheimerstr.; phone: 288537), is the best-known club, but you also should try *Jazzkneipe* (70 Berlinerstr.; phone: 287173); *Sinkkasten Arts Club* (9 Brönnerstr.; phone: 280385); *Jazzhaus* (12 Kleine Bockenheimerstr.; phone: 287194); *Jazz-Life Podium* (22 Kleine Rittergasse; phone: 626346), and *Lorbascher Tal* (49 Grosse Rittergasse; phone: 616459). Upcoming music events are posted on billboards around the city and in the daily newspaper.

NIGHTCLUBS AND NIGHTLIFE: All of the city's big hotels offer music and dancing, and discotheques are cropping up all over the city. *Tangente* (87 Bockenheimer Landstr.; phone: 745773) features a pub upstairs and a disco in the cellar. One of the trendiest discos is *Dorian Gray* (at the airport; phone: 690-2212), modeled after New York's late *Studio 54*. *Blue Infinitum* in the *Marriott* hotel (2-10 Hamburger Allee; phone: 795-52315) features floor shows as well as dancing, as do *St. John's Inn* (20 Grosser Hirschgraben) and *Varieté-Tiger-Palast* (16-20 Heiligkreuzgasse; phone: 20770). Other good clubs include *Chamäleon* (13 Kaiserhofstr.; phone: 289977), *Cooky's* (4 Am Salzhaus; phone: 287662), *Funkadelic* (11 Brönnerstr.; phone: 283808), *Omen* (14 Junghofstr.; phone: 282233), *Le Jardin* (6 Kaiserhofstr.; phone: 288956), *Frankfurt Music-Hall,* and *Plastic* (14 Seilerstr.; phone: 285055). Pub hopping in Sachsenhausen gets merrier and merrier as the night wears on. Look for the traditional green wreath hanging over the door to identify taverns that serve Frankfurt's special apple wine. Among the most authentic are *Zum Fichtekraenzi* (5 Wallstr.; phone: 612778), which serves homemade *Sülze mit Bratkartoffeln* (sliced pork in aspic with baked potatoes); *Zum Gemalten Hause* with a garden (67 Schweizerstr.; phone: 614559); *Apfelweinwirtschaft Wagner* (71 Schweizerstr.; phone: 612565); *Zum Eichkatzerl,* which has its own apple winery and delicious wine and cheese (29 Dreieichstr.; phone: 617480); *Zur Germani* and *Zum Kanonesteppel,* together known as "the island," (16 Textorstr.; phone: 613336); *Lorsbacher Tal,* which has its own apple winery (in the center of Sachsenhausen, 49 Grosse Rittergasse; phone: 616459); and *Zu den Drei Steuber* (28 Dreieichstrasse; phone: 622229). Most pubs are open from 6 PM to 12 AM.

BEST IN TOWN

 CHECKING IN: Although Frankfurt has a total of 200 hotels and pensions, with over 14,000 beds, only the most confident traveler comes here without a reservation. Space always is tight, and empty hotel rooms are nearly nonexistent during the big trade fairs, when, incidentally, the highest prices normally prevail. At an expensive hotel, expect to pay from $160 to $225 a night for a double room. Moderate hotels charge from $60 to $160; anything below must be considered inexpensive. Virtually all hotels in Frankfurt, regardless of price, share the German virtue of cleanliness. All telephone numbers are in the 69 city code unless otherwise indicated.

Arabella Grand – With 378 spacious, modern rooms, this new luxury property is conveniently located in the city center. Close to the Zeil, the main shopping street, the hotel has a swimming pool, massage, and several restaurants, including *Dynasty* (see *Eating Out*). Business facilities include 24-hour room service, meeting rooms for up to 400, English-speaking concierge, foreign currency exchange, secretarial services in English, audiovisual equipment, photocopiers, computers, cable television news, and translation services. 7 Konrad-Adenauer-Str. (phone: 29810; fax: 2981810). Expensive.

Frankfurt Inter-Continental – One of Europe's largest, with American-style service. It has a swimming pool, sauna, and solarium, a glittering nightclub, and several restaurants. Ask for a room on the river side. Business facilities include 24-hour room service, meeting rooms for up to 800, English-speaking concierge, foreign currency exchange, secretarial services in English, audiovisual equipment, photocopiers, and express checkout. 43 Wilhelm-Leuschnerstr. (phone: 26050; fax: 697-72418; telex: 417-0417). Expensive.

Frankfurt Marriott – The tallest hotel in Germany is near the fairgrounds, but its decor is more sophisticated than you might expect from a place that caters to conventioneers. There is a bakery on the premises, a small disco, and a seductive piano bar, *Die Bibliotheke.* Business facilities include 24-hour room service, meeting rooms for up to 1,450, English-speaking concierge, foreign currency exchange, secretarial services in English, audiovisual equipment, photocopiers, and express checkout. 2-10 Hamburger Allee (phone: 79550; fax: 795-52432; telex: 412573). Expensive.

Frankfurt-Sheraton – Walk right in from the airport's central terminal. An extension has made this one of Germany's largest hotels, with 820 rooms. In addition to the usual amenities, there is a comfortable restaurant, *Papillon,* with an extensive menu and good wine list. The *Red Baron* nightclub is a popular late-night stop. Business facilities include 24-hour room service, meeting rooms for up to 1,200, English-speaking concierge, foreign currency exchange, audiovisual equipment, photocopiers, and express checkout. Central terminal, Rhine-Main Airport (phone: 69770; fax: 697-72418; telex: 4170417). Expensive.

Mövenpick Park Frankfurt – Typical of small European-style luxury establishments, including what many Frankfurters consider "the best table in town" in its restaurant, *La Truffe* (see *Eating Out*). Conveniently near the main train station. 28-38 Wiesenhüttenpl. (phone: 26970; fax: 269-78849). Expensive.

Steigenberger Frankfurter Hof – In the tradition of grand European hotels; it was refurbished and restored to its pre-war charm after serving as headquarters for the Allied occupation forces. It's easy to find an attractive spot here where a waiter will bring a drink, a newspaper, or a message. International movers and shakers from the political and financial worlds dine in the *Français* restaurant (see *Eating Out*). The less expensive *Hofgarten Grill* has an extensive menu and offers excellent service. An indoor swimming pool, solarium, sauna, and nightclub also are on the premises. Bicycle rental is available. Business facilities include 24-hour room service, meeting rooms for up to 650, English-speaking concierge, foreign currency exchange, secretarial services in English, audiovisual equipment, photocopiers, translation services, and express checkout. 17 Kaiserpl. (phone: 21502; fax: 697-52505). Expensive.

Admiral – In a nice location near the zoo, this 67-room hostelry offers good service and reasonable rates. Business facilities include concierge and photocopiers. 25 Hölderlinstr. (phone: 448021; fax: 439402). Moderate.

Am Berg – Once a private villa and now a designated historical monument, this property offers 20 large rooms, rebuilt after World War II to their original 1900 style. 23 Grethenweg (phone: 612021). Moderate.

Dom – Although in the historic downtown area, this smallish hostelry is an oasis of quiet. 3 Kannengiessergasse (phone: 282141). Moderate.

Frankfurt – A motel in the city center is a rarity in Germany. This one, with 66 rooms, is convenient and offers good service and reasonable rates. 204 Eschersheimer Landstr. (phone: 568011). Moderate.

Haus Hübner – Small, and in a pleasant neighborhood not far from the main train station. 23 Westendstr. (phone: 746044). Moderate.

Holzenparkhaus – The charm of this small hotel is its location on a quiet street facing a small park north of the city center. Seven languages are spoken here, making it a favorite of international visitors. 62 Holzhausenstr. (phone: 152-0900). Moderate.

Mozart – Charming 35-room hostelry next to the US military headquarters. Note that the quieter rooms are in the back. Business facilities include a concierge, foreign currency exchange, photocopiers, and cable television news. 17 Parkstr. (phone: 550831). Moderate.

Diana – With 24 rooms, this small place is near the city center. No frills, but standard comfort. Breakfast is not included in the room rate. 83 Westendstr. (phone: 747007). Moderate to inexpensive.

Maingau – In Sachsenhausen, on the south bank of the Main River, this is a particularly reasonably priced hotel. 38-40 Schifferstr. (phone: 617001). Moderate to inexpensive.

Weisses Haus – This small, pleasant hotel is conveniently located just outside the city center. No frills here, but there is a restaurant on the premises, and the rooms certainly live up to German standards for comfort and cleanliness. 18 Jahnstr. (phone: 554605). Inexpensive.

 EATING OUT: Though Frankfurt is not noted for its culinary artistry, local specialties are prepared just as well in restaurants as in private homes. The large population of foreign-born residents inspires a wide spectrum of European and Asian cuisines. Lunch often is the main daily meal, and in most places it is served between 11 AM and 3 PM. Restaurants then close until about 5:30 PM. Except in big hotel restaurants, it is difficult to just drop in anywhere for a late lunch. However, there is a late afternoon Kaffee ritual, at which Frankfurters fortify themselves with coffee and pastry or a snack at a *Konditorei.* A local specialty that is a perfect nosh with beer or wine is *Handkäs mit Musik:* soft limburger cheese mixed with vinegar, oil, a bit of onion, and a few caraway seeds. And whether the frankfurter originated here or not, you still can buy the best franks in Frankfurt, on the freshest rolls, from a cart right outside the *Kaufhof* department store. You'll pay $80 or more for two, not including drinks or extras, at restaurants in the expensive category; $50 to $80 in the moderate range; and under $50 at inexpensive places. All restaurants below accept major credit cards. All telephone numbers are in the 69 city code unless otherwise indicated.

Dynasty – Excellent Chinese food is served in the *Arabella Grand* hotel. Specialties include the dynasty duck, deep-fried and served with vegetables. The restaurant is spacious and can accommodate large groups. There are some tables in the garden, too. Open daily. Reservations advised. 7 Konrad-Adenauer-Str. (phone: 293041). Expensive.

Erno's Bistro – French, with checkered tablecloths and superior cooking. It's apt to be crowded, but worth the wait for a table. Closed weekends and mid-June to mid-July. Reservations advised. 15 Liebigstr. (phone: 721997). Expensive.

La Femme – An elegant Art Nouveau bistro with an old-fashioned wine cellar, it serves nouvelle fare prepared according to Swabian recipes. Closed Sundays. Reservations advised. 5 Am Weingarten (phone: 707-1606). Expensive.

Français – Game and French cuisine and excellent service have made this dining room at the *Frankfurter Hof* a particular favorite of people used to eating the best. Closed Sundays and holidays and for 4 weeks during summer. Reservations advised. 17 Kaiserpl. (phone: 21502). Expensive.

Humperdinck – Not your typical Hansel and Gretel atmosphere nor your typical German fare. Instead, this establishment in the fashionable Westend district concocts wonderful nouvelle cuisine dishes, with an emphasis on seafood and lamb. Closed Saturdays until 7 PM, Sundays, and during the summer school vacation. Reservations advised. 95 Grüneburgweg (phone: 722122). Expensive.

Kikkoman – An elegant Japanese restaurant. Dinner only on Saturdays, Sundays, and holidays. Zoo Passage, 1 Anlage Friedberger (phone: 4990021). Expensive.

Mövenpick-Baron de la Mouette – Opposite the *Old Opera House,* this spot serves very good French fare. Reservations advised. 2 Opernplatz (phone: 20680). Expensive.

La Truffe – In the *Mövenpick Park* hotel, this dining room is decorated in almost as classically elegant a fashion as its traditional French cuisine. Try the truffle dishes, the delicious cheeses, and the fine wines. Closed for Saturday lunches and on Sundays. Reservations necessary. 36 Wiesenhüttenpl. (phone: 269-78830). Expensive.

Weinhaus Brückenkeller – Set in old vaults furnished with precious antiques, it serves good French and local fare. A fiddler sometimes strolls from table to table taking requests from guests. Dinner only. Closed on Sundays and holidays and for 3 weeks in July. Reservations advised. 6 Schützenstrasse (phone: 284238). Expensive.

Windows im Europaturm – For magnificent views of Frankfurt, dine in the rotating restaurant of the Europe-tower, Western Europe's tallest office building (see *Seeing the City*). The menu offers international fare. Open daily. Reservations advised. 20 Wilhelm-Epstein-Str. (phone: 533077). Expensive.

Le Midi – An intimate place serving excellent French fare at reasonable prices. Closed weekends and during the summer school holidays. Reservations advised. 47 Liebigstr. (phone: 721438). Expensive to moderate.

Rôtisserie – This elegant dining spot in the *Inter-Continental* hotel is first class, especially when game is in season. Closed Sundays. Reservations advised. 43 Wilhelm Leuschnerstr. (phone: 260-2425). Expensive to moderate.

Alte Brückenmühle – On the Sachsenhausen side of the river, this cozy eatery's decor is in the traditional, Old German style. The menu features the choicest cuts of veal, beef, pork, poultry, game, and fish — all prepared in accordance with old Frankfurt recipes. Lunch specials are especially reasonable in price. Closed for lunch on Saturdays. Reservations advised. 10 Wallstr. (phone: 612543). Moderate.

Aubergine – A small, cozy eatery serving French food prepared with seasonal ingredients. Dinner only on Saturdays. Reservations advised. 14 Alte Gasse (phone: 287843). Moderate.

Börsenkeller – In the financial district, serving delicious roast pork and other local specialties in a large rustic room decorated with wood tables, wrought-iron lamps, and candles. Closed Sundays. Reservations advised for lunch. 11 Schillerstr. (phone: 281115). Moderate.

Frankfurter Stubb – German specialties are beautifully prepared in this well-appointed cellar restaurant at the *Frankfurter Hof.* When white asparagus (*Spargel*) from the Schwetzinger area south of Frankfurt is in season, in May, it is presented here in an imaginative array of dishes, served with wine chosen to complement its delicate flavor. Closed Sundays. Reservations advised. 33 Bethmannstr. (phone: 215830). Moderate.

Gargantua – Despite its name, this charming bistro is an intimate place that usually attracts a crowd that prefers first class continental cuisine at reasonable prices. Closed Sundays, Mondays, and July; no lunch on weekends. Reservations advised. 3 Friesengasse (phone: 776442). Moderate.

Knoblauch – The name means garlic in German, an ingredient used with a deft hand in the fragrant, hearty, delicious French food. A warm, noisy, cheerful place, it is actually a pub-restaurant and art gallery. Closed Saturdays and Sundays. Reservations advised. 39 Staufenstr. (phone: 722828). Moderate.

Mövenpick-Orangerie – Offering a fine view of the *Old Opera House,* this is a good place to stop for lunch while shopping. Swiss and continental specialties, delicious cakes, and ice cream are on the menu. Dinner reservations advised. 2 Opernplatz (phone: 20680). Moderate.

Altes Zollhaus – Travelers who could not make it through the Frankfurt city gates in time found refuge for the night in this former customs house, dating from the

18th century, which now specializes in local dishes. Closed Mondays. Reservations advised. 531 Friedberger Landstr. (phone: 472707). Inexpensive.

Künstlerkeller – In the cellar of a former Carmelite monastery dating from the 13th century. Hearty food, and the convivial patrons will make you feel both comfortable and welcome. Be sure to ask the hostess for her wine recommendations. Closed Mondays. No reservations. 1 Müngasse (phone: 292242). Inexpensive.

GENEVA

Probably the most international of all cities, Geneva is where world leaders often have gathered in order to negotiate agreements and dream of peace. It is the birthplace and headquarters of the International Red Cross, founded in 1863 by Henri Dunant, a native son. The Geneva Convention, binding nations to care for all sick and wounded in war, was signed here in 1864. Home to the defunct League of Nations, center of the European United Nations, Geneva has hosted Big Four foreign ministers' conferences in 1954 and 1959 — as well as the noted Reagan-Gorbachev talks in 1985 — and has been the site of the nuclear disarmament talks.

Geneva's international role is a historical one, certainly due in part to its central location at one of Europe's crossroads. Near the French border and not far from Italy, where the Rhône River flows into its 45-mile-long lake, called Lake Geneva in English and Lac Léman in French, the city has had a very long and distinguished history. "Gen-eva," a Ligurian word (or "Genoa,") means "emerging from the waters." Waters were important in the city's history, since Geneva was the site of the only bridge across the Rhône for many centuries, a bridge that had been built and rebuilt many times even before the Romans took the city from the Celts in 58 BC.

Because of its strategic location, Geneva also was the site of many feuds and wars, from the rivalry between its prince bishop and the Duke of Savoy during the 15th century to Napoleon's occupation from 1798 to 1815. The year 1815 marked Geneva's entry into the Swiss Confederation to protect its long-fought-for independence and peace.

During the Middle Ages, Geneva, as host to a series of international fairs, took up its international vocation. The Protestant Reformation left a deeper mark on Geneva than on any other city, since John Calvin himself chose it as his headquarters, earning for Geneva the title of "the Rome of the Protestants." Here Calvin preached and prayed but also acted as a dictatorial ruler, building new ramparts, creating his own laws, and even burning his enemy, Miguel Serveto, at the stake for his incompatible religious opinions. Calvin's most influential move was the founding of the University of Geneva in 1559: For 2 centuries thereafter, Geneva became the schoolmaster for all of Protestant Europe. So austere and rigid was the tone of this Calvinist city that many of its own citizens, the most famous of whom was Jean-Jacques Rousseau, opted to flee. The great 18th-century philosopher never returned to his birthplace after his books were burned here.

Other celebrities found Geneva more congenial, notably Rousseau's great rival Voltaire and that great Swiss writer and personality Madame de Staël. And virtually all the romantics flocked to the city and its surrounding lake: Chateaubriand, Byron, Dostoyevsky, Goethe, and Victor Hugo were just a few. And parts of Diderot's great encyclopedia were printed here, as well.

GENEVA

LAKE
GENEVA

PROMENADE DU LAC

Jardin
Anglais

GÉNÉRAL GUISAN

RUE DU RHONE

D'ITALIE

RIVE

RUE

ROND-POINT
DE RIVE

DALCROZE

AVALLEE

FERDINAND

Museum
of
Art and
History

Museum of
Old
Musical
Instruments

BOULEVARD

RUE

LEFORT

RUE DE MONNETIERRUE

RUE
CHARLES

GALLAND

RUE MONT DE SION

BOULEVARD DES TRANCHEES

RUE DE LA SCIE

RUE VERSONNEX

RUE PIERRE FATIO

BD HELVETIQUE

RUE

AMI
LULLIN

HODLER

QUAI

RUE
DU
LAC

RUE
MUZY

RUE DES GLACIS DE RIVE

DU PARC

RUE ST-LAURENT

RUE ADRIEN LACHENAL

QUAI GUSTAVE ADOR

GUSTAVE ADOR

RUE DU ROVERAY

RUE DES EAUX-VIVES

RUE DU TRENTE - ET-UN-DECEMBRE

BLANVALET

RUE
DE

MAIRIE

RUE DE MONCHOISY

RUE DU NANT

AV DE FRONTENEX

RUE DE LA TERRASSIERE

RUE
DE
VILLEREUSE

RTE DE MALAGNOU

**To Parc
de la Grange**

Today, with more than 160,000 inhabitants, Geneva is rather small for a major international city. Human in scale, its sights can easily be seen on foot. Its two most characteristic landmarks are the Jet d'Eau, said to be the tallest fountain in the world, with its water rising to a height of between 400 and 500 feet from May to October; and the Flower Clock in the Jardin Anglais, with its face made of flowers and its hands keeping perfect time — as befits a city that is the home of the leading watchmakers of the world.

Whether you want to buy a watch; walk along the quais, particularly the Quai du Mont-Blanc with its panoramic view of the Alps; visit this capital of the Reformation with its Old Town clustered in narrow streets around the Cathedral of St. Pierre; or, as many do, use Geneva as a base for exploring the Alps or the lake — Geneva, the international city, will warmly extend toward you its traditional hospitality.

GENEVA AT-A-GLANCE

SEEING THE CITY: The best view of the town and its surroundings is from the North Tower of Cathédrale St.-Pierre; on a clear day it is well worth the 153 steps and the admission charge; the panorama of city, lake, Alps, and Jura Mountains is spectacular. Another superb view — and the one most often photographed — is from the Quai du Mont-Blanc near the bridge; on the sailboat-dotted lake you can see the famous Jet d'Eau, pride of Geneva, with the Alps as background.

SPECIAL PLACES: The Old Town, built on a hill around its famous Reformation Cathedral, was important in medieval times as the site of international fairs. The few streets in the immediate vicinity of the Bourg de Four are easily explored on foot. Just stroll down the narrow, cobblestone streets, discovering delightful corners like Place Bourg de Four, the former market square, have coffee or snacks in one of the cafés, and browse in the antiques stores. In summer there are regular walks in the Old Town with English-speaking guides; ask at the tourist office (see *Sources and Resources*) for details.

Carouge – Within the city limits is a little old town where time stands still and people live their quiet lives independent of busy Geneva, between its low houses, shady squares, fountains, and pubs. Enchanting! Carouge is becoming more and more popular after dark, though, when its cafés and small theaters fill up.

DOWNTOWN

Cathédrale St.-Pierre – Built in the 12th to 13th century on the site of earlier churches, Cathédrale St.-Pierre was reconstructed later; John Calvin preached here, and his chair can be seen in the austere interior. The archaeological excavations under the church, which date from the 4th century, were opened to the public in 1986. Open daily; closed at lunchtime. Cour St.-Pierre.

Calvin Auditorium – Next door to Cathédrale St.-Pierre is a Gothic church where John Knox used to preach; it was restored in 1959 for John Calvin's 450th anniversary. Rue de la Taconnerie.

Maison Tavel – A few steps from Calvin Auditorium is the oldest house in Geneva, already in existence by 1303. Inside, the *Museum of Old Geneva* features a collection of historic engravings as well as changing exhibitions on Old Geneva. Closed Mondays. 6 Rue du Puits-St.-Pierre.

Old Arsenal – Across the street from the Maison Tavel is the arsenal dating from the days of Napoleon. (Its cannon were seized by the Austrians in 1814.) On the wall are three modern mosaics by Cingria. Rue de l'Hôtel de Ville.

Hôtel de Ville – Geneva's Town Hall, where the Geneva Convention was signed in 1864 in the Alabama Court. (The room where the signing took place may be visited by applying to the guardian.) Its oldest part is Baudet Tower, erected in 1455. Rue de l'Hôtel de Ville.

St. Germain Church – On the site of an early Christian basilica, with beautiful modern stained glass windows, it is an example of 15th-century Gothic architecture. Rue des Granges.

Reformation Monument – Under the ramparts that used to surround the town, in a pleasant park belonging to the university, is a long, plain wall, erected in 1917, with statues of the main Reformation leaders — Calvin, Knox, Farel, de Bèze — flanked by other, less prominent personages; bas-reliefs and tablets tell the story of Calvin, one of the world leaders of the Protestant Reformation. Promenade des Bastions.

Promenade on the Quais – Both sides of the lake are interesting. You might start at Quai du Mont-Blanc (see *Seeing the City*). Here are several top hotels, a landing pier, and a monument to the Duke of Brunswick who left his fortune to the town about 100 years ago (with the condition that he get a monument like the Scaligeri in Verona); see the panoramic table on the quai, a map of nearby and distant peaks that are especially beautiful in the afternoon when the sun sets on the Alps. If you go north, the quai ends at the Botanical Garden, in a succession of beautifully manicured city parks. However, following the river westward from the Pont (Bridge) du Mont-Blanc is the Quai des Bergues, with the charming, small Rousseau Island just off it. This is a wonderful place for a rest, under large trees and the statue of Geneva's famous son.

On the opposite side of the bridge (Pont du Mont-Blanc) is the Jardin Anglais (English Garden), with a huge clock whose face is composed of flowers, the hands giving the exact time — typically Genevois.

Parc de la Grange – From the Jardin Anglais, the Quai Gustave-Ador eventually runs into the delightful Parc de la Grange, with one of the finest rose gardens in Europe (overpowering in June) and the even larger Parc des Eaux-Vives.

Palais des Nations – The former League of Nations palace, as big as Versailles, now houses the European section of the UN as well as a small museum of diplomatic history and a *Philatelic Museum*. Several impressive halls in the palace were decorated by European and African artists. There are daily guided tours. Closed at the end of December for 14 days. Admission charge. Av. de la Paix (phone: 734-6011). In surrounding buildings are other international offices, such as the World Health Organization (phone: 791-2111) and the International Red Cross (phone: 734-6001). Especially striking is the building that houses the International Labor Office. This impressive structure has a luxurious marble interior and artistic decorations from all over the world (phone: 799-6111). Group visits to the above three organizations can be arranged by special request.

Museum of Art and History – The important archaeological section features medieval furniture, sculpture, an armory, and an excellent fine arts collection; one of the most interesting paintings is Conrad Witz's *Miraculous Fishing*, painted in 1444 for an altar of the cathedral with a background depicting medieval Geneva. Closed Monday mornings. No admission charge. 2 Rue Charles-Galland (phone: 290011).

Musée de l'Horlogerie (Watch Museum) – This is an exquisite collection of watches, clocks, and enamelworks from the 16th century on, with emphasis on artisans from Geneva, which is a worldwide watchmaking center. The setting is a charming townhouse and park, now owned by the city. Closed Monday mornings. No admission charge. 15 Rte. de Malagnou (phone: 736-7412).

Baur Collections – In the home of the original owner, with a small garden, this is a private collection of superb Chinese and Japanese ceramics. Open afternoons only; closed Mondays. Admission charge. 8 Rue Munier-Romilly (phone: 461729).

Barbier-Mueller Museum – An outstanding private collection of primitive art, it has twice-yearly exhibits of African, Indonesian, Pacific, and pre-Columbian items. Open afternoons only; closed Sundays and Mondays. Admission charge. Rue Jean-Calvin (phone: 786-4646).

Musée d'Instruments Anciens de Musique (Museum of Old Musical Instruments) – This private collection was bought by the city, but its former owner still is the curator. All the instruments, however old, still can be played, and on occasion visiting musicians do just that. Open Tuesdays, Thursdays, and Fridays; check opening hours. Admission charge. Next to the Russian church at 23 Rue Lefort (phone: 469565).

Musée de l'Histoire des Sciences (Museum of the History of Science) – A collection of instruments and souvenirs mainly of Swiss scientists (mathematical, medical, astronomical, physics, and other items) is in a lovely setting. The museum reopened last fall after a complete renovation. Closed in the morning and from November to April. No admission charge. Villa Bartholoni, 128 Rue de Lausanne (phone: 731-6985).

Institut et Musée Voltaire – The beautiful residence of Voltaire, with his furniture, art objects, manuscripts, correspondence, and works, is open every weekday afternoon. No admission charge. 25 Rue des Délices (phone: 447133).

Musée Internationale de la Croix-Rouge (International Red Cross Museum) – Geneva's newest museum opened late in 1988 and displays documents of the Red Cross over the course of its history, since 1863. Closed Tuesdays. Admission charge. 17 Av. de la Paix (phone: 734-5248).

Jean-Jacques Rousseau Museum – The manuscripts, letters, pictures, and death mask of Rousseau can be seen here daily, except on Saturday afternoons and Sundays. No admission charge. The Public and University Library, Salle Lullin, Promenade des Bastions (phone: 208266).

OUT OF TOWN

Bodmerian Library – In the bewitching setting of the luxurious villa of Zurich millionaire Martin Bodmer, in the suburb of Cologny (about 2 miles/3 km from Geneva), with a panoramic view of the lake and the town, this is a unique private collection of rare manuscripts, first editions, and incunabula; the villa also houses a research institute. The exhibitions of the collection change occasionally. Open Thursday afternoons. Admission charge. Rte. du Guignard, Cologny (phone: 736-2370).

Château de Penthes – This 18th-century private château is in a lovely park and features views of the Alps and lake. It houses the *Museum of Swiss Expatriates,* where documents from the Middle Ages to the 1980s are found. The *Geneva Military Museum* is in an adjoining pavilion; a second pavilion has a pleasant coffee shop. Closed Mondays. Admission charge. 18 Chemin de l'Impératrice, Pregny-Chambésy, about a mile (1.6 km) outside the city (phone: 734-9021).

Boat Ride on the Lake and the Rhône River – Beautiful Lake Geneva (Lac Léman), 45-miles-long with Geneva on its western end, Lausanne in the middle, and Vevey and Montreux to the east, has been popular with nature lovers at least since the days of Rousseau. Its southern shore is in France; the northern shore in Switzerland is the more famous part. The romantics loved Lake Geneva, particularly the area around Vevey and Montreux, and the list of greats who've lived here is formidable: Byron, Goethe, Victor Hugo, and Balzac are just a few.

The Château de Chillon — celebrated by Byron in "The Prisoner of Chillon" in 1816 — can be visited by boat. This 9th-century castle held François Bonivard prisoner; he was chained to a pillar for 4 years (1532–36) for delivering Protestant sermons.

A trip on the lake is a must, with its vineyards, châteaux, and old towns. Cruises of varying lengths are offered several times a day (except in winter) by three different companies. There also are daily trips down the unspoiled, wooded shores of the Rhône. For details, inquire at the tourist office (see *Sources and Resources*) or at *Navigation Mouettes Genevoises* (8 Quai du Mont-Blanc; phone: 732-2944).

Château de Coppet – About 7 miles (11 km) from Geneva, on the lake, in the charming little town of Coppet, is the castle and park of the famous Madame de Staël, the meeting place of some of the greatest minds of the 18th and early 19th centuries. Madame de Staël led a complicated and unconventional life, which is described in her famous autobiography; she was separated from her husband for the love of the novelist Benjamin Constant. She wrote several successful novels and a study of German Romanticism that so enraged Napoleon that he destroyed an entire edition as "un-French," and she was forced to flee to England and Russia. Closed November to February and Mondays. Admission charge (phone: 776-1028).

■**EXTRA SPECIAL:** Mt. Salève, the "house mountain" of Geneva, is only about 4 miles (6 km) away in France. Salève's peak is 4,000 feet high; in fall and winter, when the city often is deep in fog, Salève towers above it all.

Go by car or by the No. 8 bus from Geneva (catch it at the Gare Cornavin, the main train station) to Veyrier, where the cable car affords a magnificent view at any time of the Valley of the Arve, Geneva, and Mont-Blanc. There are scores of walks, including the steep Pas de l'Echelle from Veyrier to Monnetier, a picturesque village with a number of good restaurants. If you wish, you can continue to Rocher-de-Faverges in France. (Don't forget to take your passport!)

In warm weather — for the more daring or just for spectators — Mt. Salève is a center for hang gliding.

SOURCES AND RESOURCES

 TOURIST INFORMATION: For general information, brochures, and maps, contact the Office du Tourisme, at Gare Cornavin (the main train station, phone: 738-5200). In the US, contact the Swiss National Tourist Office (608 Fifth Ave., New York, NY 10020; phone: 212-757-5944).

The US Consulate is in the northern suburb of Chambésy, on the western shore of Lake Geneva. 1-3 Av. de la Paix (phone: 738-7613).

Local Coverage – *This Week in Geneva,* a bilingual publication, is helpful for practical information, cultural programs, and advertisements; it also contains a concise "guided tour" of the city. (You also can get it separately in a pamphlet without the advertising.)

There are no local newspapers in English, but the daily *International Herald Tribune* is available for world news.

Food – Restaurants are advertised in *This Week in Geneva.*

 TELEPHONE: The country code for Switzerland is 41; the city code for Geneva is 22.

GETTING AROUND: Airport – Cointrin Airport (phone: 799-3111 for flight information) handles both domestic and international traffic. It's about a 15-minute drive from downtown, and taxi fare will run from 25 to 35 Swiss francs (about $15 to $22). There also is train service to and from Gare Cornavin, the main railroad station.

Bus – There are many buses and they run frequently. You must buy a ticket from a vending machine, found at all stops. (You cannot buy a ticket on the bus, and you are fined if found without one.) Information booklets with bus routes are available for a small fee at the main train station. On No. 1 at Cornavin (the railroad station) you can take a circular sightseeing tour in English, returning as No. 11 to the same spot. You also can buy an economical 1-, 2-, or 3-day pass for unlimited transportation on buses and trolleys for about $3.90, $7.15, and $9.10 respectively. Swiss Pass holders (for unlimited rail, bus, and boat travel in Switzerland) do not have to pay an additional fee for city transport in Geneva.

Car Rental – All major firms are represented at the airport and in the city. Note that the rates are among the highest in Europe. *Avis* (44 Rue Lausanne; phone: 731-9000; and the airport; phone: 798-2300); *Budget* (37 Rue Lausanne; phone: 732-5252; and the airport; phone: 798-2253); and *Autolocation Leman* (6 Rue Amat; phone: 732-0143).

Taxi – Taxis are much more expensive than in the US, but the tip is included in the fare. They can be hailed all over the city; the light on top indicates availability.

Train – The main train station is Gare Cornavin, at Pl. Cornavin (phone: 731-6450).

LOCAL SERVICES: Dentist (English-Speaking) – *Alliance des Cliniques Dentaires* provides names and addresses around the clock. 5 Rue Mallombré (phone: 466444).

Dry Cleaner/Tailor – *Baechler,* 3 Pl. Molard (phone: 216039) and other locations.

Limousine Service – *Globe SA,* 36 Rue de Zurich (phone: 731-0750).

Medical Emergency – *Hôpital Cantonal Universitaire* (24 Rue Michel-du-Crest; phone: 226111 or 46921). *Permanence Medicale,* dispensary and surgery open 24 hours; major credit cards accepted (21 Rue de Chantepoulet; phone: 731-2120).

Messenger Service – *DHL International,* 40 Av. Aïre (phone: 444400).

National/International Courier – *DHL International,* 40 Av. Aire (444400).

Office Equipment Rental – *Thiéry* (8 Rue des Corps-Saints; phone: 7324911); also, ask you hotel concierge.

Pharmacy – *Pharmacie Centrale,* 9 Rue du Mont-Blanc (phone: 731-9740).

Photocopies – *TEX SA,* 1 Pl. St.-Gervais (phone: 732-6704).

Post Office – The main post office is open from 7:30 AM to 10:45 PM. 36-40 Rue Montbrillant (phone: 739-2111).

Secretary/Stenographer (English-Speaking) – *Manpower* (4 Rue Winkelried; phone: 731-6800); *Recipa* (14 Rue de la Corraterie; phone: 289188).

Telex – Main post office (36-40 Rue Montbrillant; phone: 739-2111), and other post offices (18 Rue du Mont-Blanc and at Rue du Stande, Pl. de la Poste). Go to the telegram window at each location.

Translator – *Intercongress* (54 *bis,* Rte. des Acacias; phone: 435179); *Traducta* (2 Rue Môle; phone: 732-6393).

Other – Tuxedo rental: *Balestra,* by appointment. 20 Av. Mail (phone: 284140).

SPECIAL EVENTS: The *International Motor Show,* for 10 days in early March, is one of the most important in Europe, keeping all Geneva excited and its hotels packed. The *First of August, Independence Day,* is a national holiday commemorating the founding of the Swiss Confederation, with bonfires on the hills. *Fête de Genève* is a long weekend in mid-August, with fairs and processions, culminating in magnificent fireworks on the lake. The *Montres et Bijoux* (Watch and Jewelry Show), with a display of the latest products, is held in October of odd-numbered years. The *Escalade,* on or around December 13, the most typically Genevois celebration, commemorates the city's 1602 victory over the Savoyard enemy with a colorful evening torchlight pageant in the darkened streets, with medieval costumes and all-night partying.

MUSEUMS: In addition to the museums described in *Special Places,* the following also are interesting.

Musée d'Etnographie (Ethnographic Museum) – A rich worldwide collection. 65-67 Bd. Carl-Vogt (phone: 281218).

Musée d'Histoire Naturelle (Natural History Museum) – The most modern natural history display in Europe. 1 Rte. de Malagnou (phone: 735-9130).

Musée Rath – Temporary exhibits only: try to catch the watch and jewelry one when it comes through. Pl. Neuve (phone: 285616).

Museum of the Reformation – A monument to the most important figures of the Reformation. Public and University Library, Salle Lullin. Promenade des Bastions (phone: 208266).

Petit Palais – Art from 1890 to the present, especially Renoir and Picasso. 2 Terr. St.-Victor (phone: 461433).

SHOPPING: The main shopping area, offering the best and most expensive stores, is around Rue du Rhône and its parallel and side streets. Other shopping streets are *les rues basses,* literally "downhill streets": A few of these are Rue du Marché, Rue de la Confédération, and Rue de Rive. Also, many new (and expensive) boutiques and gift shops recently have opened up in the small streets around Place du Bourg-de-Four in the Old Town.

Geneva's version of New York City's Trump Tower, *Centre Commercial de la Confédération,* opened in 1986. It features several levels of shops, from designer boutiques to cafés, in an attractive Art Nouveau decor. Rue de la Confédération.

Geneva's best buys are watches — the most famous in the world — jewelry, toys, clothes, and the nearly ubiquitous Swiss Army knives. There is a flea market on Wednesdays and Saturdays on the Plain de Plainpalais and a flower and vegetable market on Saturday mornings on the streets of *les rues basses.*

To sample everything, try Geneva's best-known department stores, *Placette* (phone: 731-7400) at 9 Rue Grenus and *Grand Passage* (phone: 206611) at 50 Rue du Rhône.

A la Bonnonnière – The place to find Geneva's best chocolates. 11 Rue de Rive (phone: 216196).

Bon Génie – Fashion for men and women. At several locations, including the *Inter-Continental Hotel,* 7-9 Chemin du Petit-Saconnex (phone: 733-4545).

Bucherer – Watches and jewelry. 26 Quai Général-Guisan (phone: 216266).

Au Chalet Suisse – Lace blouses and tablecloths; hand-embroidered accessories. 18 Quai de Général-Guisan (phone: 218210).

Chocolat Arn – Another of the city's luscious chocolate shops. 12 Pl. Bourg-de-Four (phone: 204094).

Chocolaterie du Rhône – World-class sweets, including perhaps the quintessential chocolate truffle. 3 Rue de la Confédération (phone: 215614).

Collet – Still more fine jewelry. 8 Pl. du Molard (phone: 210877).

Confiserie Hautlé – Another windfall for the chocoholic. At 21 Pl. du Bourg-de-Four (phone: 203773).

Davidoff – The original home of these famous cigars. 2 Rue de Rive (phone: 289041).

Galerie Catherine van Notten – Swiss paintings. 17 Grande Rue (phone: 280-3932).

Gérard Père & Fils – A paradise for cigar smokers. At the *Noga-Hilton,* 19 Quai du Mont-Blanc (phone: 732-6511).

Gübelin – More fine watches and jewelry. 1 Pl. du Molard (phone: 288655).

Hermès – The famous French firm, specializing in expensive ties, leather goods, scarves, and saddlery. 43 Rue du Rhône (phone: 217677).

Librarie des Amateurs – English, German, and French classic books. 15 Grande Rue (phone: 213313).

Ludwig Muller – Original jewelry designs. Rue de Chaudronniers (phone: 202930).

Aux Mille Cadeaux – Lovely gifts, music boxes, cuckoo clocks. 11 Rue Céard (phone: 213010).

Naville – The biggest international bookstore in Geneva has four branches. 5 Rue de la Confédération (phone: 292133) and 5-7 Rue Lévrier (phone: 732-2400) are the most central. The other two are at 11 Rue Prince (phone: 280111) and 61 Rte. Flourissant (phone: 470075).

Patek Philippe – The famous timepieces and jewelry. 22 Quai du Général-Guisan (phone: 200366).

Piaget – More timepieces and jewelry. 40 Rue du Rhône (phone: 287388).

Salomé – Art Deco and contemporary furnishings and accessories. 5 Rue de Chaudronniers (phone: 210370).

Schmitt – An antiques shop in the Old Town specializing in English furniture, silverware, plates, and lamps. 3 Rue de l'Hôtel-de-Ville (phone: 283540).

Spengler – Reasonably priced clothes for men, women, and children (not designer names). 26 Bd. Georges-Favon (phone: 214511).

Sturzenegger – Fine Swiss embroidery and linen. 3 Rue du Rhône (phone: 289534).

Tabbah – Pricey jewelry and other trifles. 25-27 Rue du Rhône (phone: 281860).

Uniprix – The *Woolworth's* of Geneva. 4 Rue Croix-d'Or (phone: 286166).

Van Cleef & Arpels – A branch of the world-famous jeweler. 12 Quai de Général-Guisan (phone: 288166).

 SPORTS AND FITNESS: Fitness Center – *John Valentine Fitness Club* (12 Rue Gautier; phone: 732-8050) offers a 1-day pass for visitors.

Golf – The 18-hole *Golf Club of Geneva* (phone: 735-7540), in a magnificent setting in Cologny, is private but accepts guests who write or call in advance. Open March to December. Geneva has no public courses.

Ice Skating – Indoor and outdoor skating is offered only in winter, at *Les Vernets* skating rink at Quai des Vernets.

Jogging – Best for running are Parc Mont Repos, Parc Bertrand, Parc des Eaux-Vives, and the quais on both sides of the lake.

Sailing – The most obvious sport in Geneva; rentals are all along the quais, especially Quais Mont-Blanc, Wilson, and Gustave-Ador.

Skiing – There are excellent runs, very crowded on weekends, within 1 hour of Geneva in the marvelous resorts of Haute Savoie in France. The best known are Chamonix and Megève, about an hour away; the newest resort, Flaine, is even closer. The closest good skiing in Switzerland is in Champéry or on the glacier of Les Diablerets, about 1½ hours away.

Soccer – Called football in Europe, soccer is very popular here. Games are in different stadiums, including *Stade des Charmilles.*

Swimming – Beaches on the lake are open in summer, like the Geneva Beach on Quai Gustave-Ador and Pâquis Beach on the Quai du Mont-Blanc (and two beaches on the Rte. de Lausanne). The indoor pool of *Les Vernets* is in the suburb of Acacias, 4-6 Rue Hans-Wilsdorf (phone: 438850).

Tennis – There are several clubs; courts must be reserved in advance. Try the *Geneva Tennis Club* at Parc des Eaux-Vives (phone: 735-5350).

THEATER: The major theaters are the *Théâtre de Carouge* (Rue Joseph-Girard) and *Le Caveau* (Av. Ste.-Clotilde). Performances are in French except for some visiting companies. International theatrical shows occasionally are presented at the *Grand Casino* at the *Noga-Hilton* hotel (19 Quai du Mont-Blanc).

MUSIC: Operas are performed in the *Grand Théâtre* (Pl. Neuve; phone: 212311) from October to May (not daily), with one production per month and greatly varying quality. There also are excellent popular and classical concerts. The *Orchestre de la Suisse Romande* gives regular performances with many renowned guest artists. Tickets are somewhat difficult to get. Most performances are at *Victoria Hall* (Rue Hornung; phone: 288121). There also are frequent concerts and recitals in churches, and open-air concerts in season. During the summer, free concerts are held at 12:30 PM at the *Museum of the Red Cross* (17 Av. de la Paix; phone: 734-5248). For further details about concert activity, contact the tourist office's concert line (phone: 786-3611).

While the *Montreux International Jazz Festival* is going on in July, a number of the performers appear in concert or in clubs in Geneva. Contact the concert telephone number above for information. If you want to attend the festival in person, a short train ride from the Cornavin station makes the 50-mile (80-km) trip to Montreux (for more information about the *Montreux Festival,* see *Europe's Magnificent Music Festivals,* DIVERSIONS).

NIGHTCLUBS AND NIGHTLIFE: Geneva has the most active nightlife in Switzerland (which does not mean all that much) — enjoyed mainly by visiting and resident foreigners. The best are the private clubs. *Griffins* (36 Bd. Helvétique; phone: 735-1218) is a favorite and has good food. Among a dozen places with shows, the most popular and international are *Ba-Ta-Clan,* the best-known striptease spot (15 Rue de la Fontaine; phone: 296498); or *Pussy Cat Saloon,* another striptease spot (in the same building as the *Club 58* nightclub; at 15 Glacis de Rive; phone: 735-1515); *Maxim's,* with a music hall show and dining run by Bob Azzam (2 Rue Thalberg; phone: 732-9900); and *La Garçonnière,* which offers a transvestite show (22 Pl. Bémont at Cité; phone: 282161). Several of the better hotel restaurants have dance floors, such as the *Richemond* (Jardin Brunswick). *Régine's,* a member of the chic, international discotheque chain, is attached to the *Noga-Hilton's Grand Casino* (19 Quai du Mont-Blanc; phone: 731-5735). At the *Hilton* and other Swiss casinos, only minimum bets are allowed (about 5 Swiss francs), so most gamblers go to Divonne in France, 12½ miles (20 km) away.

BEST IN TOWN

CHECKING IN: There are many hotels, but small, charming, inexpensive ones with atmosphere are almost nonexistent; the rule is either old-time luxury or functional modern. Many hotels are clustered around the main railroad station, only a few minutes from the lake; there also are some excellent hotels along the water. All the hotels listed here have telephones in rooms; most also have radio and television sets. Reservations are strongly advised. The range for a double with a bath and/or shower in the expensive category is $240 and up; moderate, $120 to $185; inexpensive, $75 to $120. More moderate rates can be found on the outskirts of town. All telephone numbers are in the 22 city code unless otherwise indicated.

Les Armures – In a 17th-century building in the Old Town, this is considered by many the most charming hotel in Geneva. There are 24 rooms and 4 suites. Decor is rustic-elegant: beamed ceilings, vaulted doors. Its popular restaurant is the oldest in Geneva (see *Eating Out*). Major credit cards accepted. 1 Rue du Puits-St.-Pierre (phone: 289172; fax: 289846; telex: 421129). Expensive.

Beau-Rivage – This place has retained its Old World charm in spite of relatively recent renovations; there are 120 rooms, some with superb lakefront views. Its justifiably famous restaurant is called *Chat Botté* (see *Eating Out*). Business facilities include 24-hour room service, meeting rooms for up to 200, English-speaking concierge, foreign currency exchange, secretarial services in English, audiovisual equipment, photocopiers, computers, cable television news, and translation services. Major credit cards accepted. 13 Quai du Mont-Blanc (phone: 731-0221; fax: 7389847; telex: 412539). Expensive.

Des Bergues – A grand, splendidly renovated property in a choice location, downtown near the lake. It has 109 rooms, 8 suites, the elegant *Amphitryon* restaurant (see *Eating Out*), and room service from 6 AM to midnight. Business facilities include meeting rooms for up to 500, English-speaking concierge, foreign currency exchange, secretarial services in English, audiovisual equipment, photocopiers, computers, cable television news, and translation services. 33 Quai des Bergues (phone: 731-5050; fax: 732-1989; telex: 412540). Expensive.

La Cigogne – One of the newer and most unusual hotels in the city center; 100 yards from the lake, it was built in 1903 as a bordello. The decor of each of its 50 rooms is different, and some are furnished with collectors' items, such as the beds of onetime visitors Cary Grant and Barbara Hutton. Room service is available around the clock. Major credit cards accepted. 17 Pl. Longemalle (phone: 214242; fax: 214065; telex: 421748). Expensive.

Geneva Penta – Equidistant from the airport and downtown, this recently built property has 320 rooms, and a fitness center with a sauna. Business facilities include meeting rooms for up to 650, secretarial services in English, and audiovisual equipment. 75-77 Av. Louis-Casai (phone: 798-4700; fax: 798-7758; telex: 415571). Expensive.

Inter-Continental – Close to the European headquarters of the UN and *Palexpo*, the new exhibition center, this hostelry overlooks Geneva's lakeshore and the city center. All 353 rooms, 60 of which are suites, are air conditioned, with color television sets equipped with 18 cable programs in 5 languages. The restaurant, *Les Continents*, boasts a Michelin star and serves fine French food. There also is a coffee shop, a piano bar, and a bar next to the swimming pool. Other amenities include a shopping arcade, a fitness canter, a *SwissAir* desk, and a beauty salon. Business facilities include 24-hour room service, meeting rooms for up to 450, English-speaking concierge, audiovisual equipment, photocopiers, computers, and translation services. 7-9 Chemin Petit-Saconnex (phone: 734-6091; fax: 734286; telex: 412921). Expensive.

Noga Hilton – Sleek and modern, with 300 rooms, right on Lake Geneva, this is currently the most expensive property in the city. Guests can enjoy a sauna, heated pool, boutiques, a nightclub, a discotheque, and numerous restaurants (among them *Le Cygne,* one of the best in town; see *Eating Out*). Business facilities include 24-hour room service, meeting rooms for up to 1,400, English-speaking concierge, foreign currency exchange, secretarial services in English, audiovisual equipment, photocopiers, computers, cable television news, translation services, and express checkout. Parking available. 19 Quai du Mont-Blanc (phone: 731-9811; fax: 738-6432; telex: 412337). Expensive.

Du Rhône – A favorite of vacationers and businesspeople alike, this recently renovated modern establishment has 350 cheerful rooms, most with a view, 2 restaurants, and a terrace. The fifth floor is reserved for nonsmokers. The famous wine cellar houses 200,000 bottles of mostly French and Swiss wines. The hotel is headquarters for the International Wine Academy and frequently hosts the *Trophée des Barmen,* an international wine-tasting competition held in *Le Neptune* restaurant (see *Eating Out*). Business facilities include 24-hour room service, meeting rooms for up to 200, English-speaking concierge, foreign currency exchange, secretarial services in English, audiovisual equipment, photocopiers, computers, cable television news, and translation services. Quai Turretini (phone: 731-9831; fax: 732-4558; telex: 22213). Expensive.

Le Richemond – Still the most prestigious hotel in town, abounding with understated elegance; its rooms generally are full. The restaurant, *Le Gentilhomme,* is first-rate, with dance music at night (see *Eating Out*). Business facilities include 24-hour room service, meeting rooms for up to 500, English-speaking concierge, foreign currency exchange, secretarial services in English, audiovisual equipment, photocopiers, computers, cable television news, and translation services. Major credit cards accepted. Jardin Brunswick (phone: 731-1400; fax: 731-6709; telex: 412560). Expensive.

Amat-Carlton – A very comfortable, modern property with pleasant, spacious rooms with balconies. Apartments with kitchens for longer stays (10-day minimum) are available. Major credit cards accepted. 22 Rue Amat (phone: 731-6850; fax: 732-8247; telex: 412546). Moderate.

Du Midi – In an excellent location, this pleasant, modern hotel has 80 comfortable rooms, some with river views; cafés and restaurants. Major credit cards accepted. Pl. Chevelu (phone: 731-7800; fax: 731-0020; telex: 412552). Moderate.

La Tourelle – About 10 minutes from the center of town (direct bus service) in luxurious, residential Vésenaz, featuring 24 attractive, comfortable rooms in a villa with a garden and a view of the lake. Closed December and January. Most credit cards accepted. 26 Rte. d'Hermance, Genève-Vésenaz (phone: 752-1628). Moderate to inexpensive.

Le Grenil – Connected with the *YMCA,* this modern hotel is not far from the city center, with a snack restaurant; an excellent value. Most of its 50 rooms have showers and private toilets. There are meeting rooms for up to 200. Major credit cards accepted. 7 Av. Ste.-Clotilde (phone: 283055; telex: 429307). Inexpensive.

Lido – A "best buy," this is an excellently run 32-room, no-frills hotel in a central location. Major credit cards accepted. 8 Rue de Chantepoulet (phone: 731-5530). Inexpensive.

Des Tourelles – (No connection with *La Tourelle.*) This is a very modest, family-type, centrally located hotel with 24 rooms *without* private showers (or toilets), but they are available on every floor. The place is pleasant and sunny and offers a view of the river. No credit cards accepted. 2 Bd. James-Fazy (phone: 732-4423). Inexpensive.

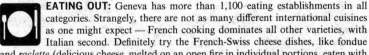 **EATING OUT:** Geneva has more than 1,100 eating establishments in all categories. Strangely, there are not as many different international cuisines as one might expect — French cooking dominates all other varieties, with Italian second. Definitely try the French-Swiss cheese dishes, like fondue and *raclette* (delicious cheese, melted on an open fire in individual portions, eaten with tiny potatoes) served in special inexpensive pubs. Also, try the excellent lake fish, like *perche* (perch) and, if available, the rare *omble chevalier* (grayling), found only in Lac Léman. When ordering, ask to see the *carte,* as *menu* applies only to the daily set meal. Tips are included in bills, but it is customary to add a bit. Our price range is for a three-course dinner for two, without drinks, wine, or coffee. Count on $100 to $150 and up for expensive places, $65 to $90 for moderate, and $40 to $55 for an inexpensive

meal. Set lunch menus are considerably less expensive in many restaurants. All telephone numbers are in the 22 city code unless otherwise indicated.

Girardet – *Extra special:* In Crissier, a tiny town only 36 miles (60 km) from Geneva (just outside Lausanne), superbly talented chef Fredy Girardet has created a restaurant that simply is the best in Europe. Be sure to write for dinner reservations, but no more than 2 months ahead; call for lunch weeks ahead. If you splurge only once during your European stay, do it here. Closed Sundays, Mondays, parts of August, and *Christmas.* No credit cards accepted. 1 Rte. d'Yverdon, Crissier (phone: 021-634-0505). Very expensive.

Amphitryon – Fine French food is served in this elegant dining place at *Des Bergues* hotel. Closed Saturdays and Sundays. Reservations advised. Major credit cards accepted. 33 Quai Bergues (phone: 731-5050). Expensive.

Le Béarn – Small and elegant, it is among the best in town, serving fresh, imaginative dishes and delicious warm desserts. Closed Saturdays at lunchtime, Sundays, and mid-July through mid-August. Reservations necessary. Most credit cards accepted. 4 Quai de la Poste (phone: 210028). Expensive.

Le Chat Botté – Set in the *Beau Rivage* hotel, this notable eatery rates a Michelin star. Specialties include mousseline of lobster and artichokes. Closed Saturdays, Sundays, holidays, and for 2 weeks at the end of March and beginning of April, as well as over the *Christmas-New Year* holidays. Reservations necessary. Major credit cards accepted. 13 Quai du Mont-Blanc (phone: 731-6532). Expensive.

Le Cygne – Another Michelin star, this one to a restaurant in the *Noga Hilton* hotel. Scottish grouse in season is the specialty. Open daily. Reservations advised. Major credit cards accepted. Jardin Brunswick (phone: 731-9811). Expensive.

Le Gentilhomme – One of the most celebrated eating places in a city of fine restaurants. The menu offers an absolutely unbeatable selection of caviar, and there is a wide selection of meat and fish dishes. Closed Saturdays and Sundays. Reservations advised. Major credit cards accepted. In the *Richemond Hotel,* Jardin Brunswick (phone: 731-1400). Expensive.

Le Lion D'Or – Elegant dining with a lovely view overlooking the lake. Try the "blue lobster salad" (their seafood is a house specialty) — but everything is good. Closed weekends. Reservations necessary (preferably way in advance). Most credit cards accepted. 5 Pl. Gauthier (phone: 736-4432). Expensive.

Le Neptune – In the *Hôtel du Rhône,* this elegant dining spot is a member of the Chaîne des Rôtisseurs and a favorite of Geneva businesspeople. It features creative variations on classic French food. There is an open-air terrace and private dining rooms may be reserved. Closed Saturdays and Sundays. Reservations advised. Major credit cards accepted. Quai Turretini (phone: 731-9831). Expensive.

La Perle du Lac – On the lake, in Parc Mon Repos; in summer you can dine outside with the ravishing view; in winter it is intimate, elegant, and candlelit. A less expensive café adjoins the restaurant. Closed Mondays. Reservations necessary. Most credit cards accepted. 128 Rue de Lausanne (phone: 731-7935). Expensive.

Tse Fung – In *La Réserve* hotel at the city limits, this is one of the best Chinese restaurants in Europe. Open daily. Reservations necessary. Major credit cards accepted. 301 Rte. de Lausanne, Bellevue (phone: 774-1736). Expensive.

Chez Valentino – A lively Italian place, 3 miles (5 km) from the city center, with fabulous hors d'oeuvres and featuring a flower-filled terrace in spring and summer. Closed Mondays and Tuesdays at lunch and August. Reservations advised. Major credit cards accepted. 63 Rte. de Thonon, Vésenaz (phone: 752-1440). Expensive to moderate.

La Favola – The best of French and Italian accents is found in the cuisine served in this friendly and relaxed restaurant in the Old Town. Owner-chef Gabriel Martinoli makes his own pasta and risotto and takes full advantage of seasonal produce. Closed Saturdays, Sundays, and July. Reservations advised. Major credit cards accepted. 15 Rue Jean-Calvin (phone: 217437). Expensive to moderate.

L'Olivier de Provence – An intimate, elegant French dining spot in the charming setting of Carouge. In summer it has a big, tree-shaded garden. Closed Sundays. Reservations advised. Major credit cards accepted. 13 Rue Jacques-Dalphin (phone: 420450). Expensive to moderate.

Auberge de la Mère Royaume – A cozy, paneled "Old Geneva style" place with French specialties. Closed Saturday lunch and Sundays. Reservations advised. Major credit cards accepted. 9 Rue des Corps-Saints (phone: 732-7008). Moderate.

Edelweiss – A Swiss chalet with folk music and regional specialties. Open daily. Reservations unnecessary. Major credit cards accepted. 2 Pl. de la Navigation (phone: 731-3658). Moderate.

La Fenice – Tasty Venetian specialties served in a chummy, homey atmosphere. Closed Sundays, Mondays, and the first 2 weeks in August. Reservations necessary. Major credit cards accepted. 78 Avenue de Châtelaine (phone: 797-0370). Moderate.

Hostellerie de la Vendée – The interior is functional and sober, but the service and food are outstanding. Frequented by a chic local clientele, it offers seasonal specialties. On the outskirts of town. Dinner only. Closed Sundays. Reservations advised. Major credit cards accepted. 28 Chemin de la Vendée, Petit Lancy (phone: 792-0411). Moderate.

Les Armures – The oldest restaurant in Geneva, rich in atmosphere, this is a good place for *raclette,* fondue, or even pizza. Closed Monday lunch. Reservations advised. Major credit cards accepted. In *Les Armures Hotel* in the heart of the Old Town at 1 Rue du Puits-St.-Pierre (phone: 283442). Moderate to inexpensive.

Cave Valaisanne et Chalet Suisse – Cozy and friendly, it offers an excellent fondue, as well as other good cheese dishes. Open daily. Reservations unnecessary. Major credit cards accepted. 23 Bd. Georges-Favon (phone: 281236). Moderate to inexpensive.

Café des Beaux-Arts – Modest, but very lively, this bistro is very popular with locals. Potato au gratin is a specialty. Closed Mondays and the second Sunday of the month. Reservations unnecessary. No credit cards accepted. 32 Rue de Carouge (phone: 291501). Inexpensive.

Café du Centre – This pleasant brasserie is on historic Place du Molard, and serves a huge variety of dishes till well after midnight. (There is a more expensive section upstairs.) Open daily. Reservations unnecessary. No credit cards accepted. 5 Pl. du Molard (phone: 218586). Inexpensive.

Palais de Justice – An unassuming little place with lots of local color, on the romantic square of the Old Town. Closed Sundays. Reservations advised. No credit cards accepted. 8 Pl. Bourg-de-Four (phone: 204254). Inexpensive.

HELSINKI

On the southern coast of Finland lies Helsinki, the Daughter of the Baltic, a city almost as close to Russia geographically and culturally as to Scandinavia. Helsinki overlooks the Gulf of Finland on the Baltic Sea; across the gulf lie the restless Soviet republics of Lithuania, Estonia, and Latvia, and at the far eastern end of the gulf is St. Petersburg, the recently renamed Leningrad.

Midway between Stockholm to the west and St. Petersburg to the east, Helsinki reflects both Eastern and Western influences. The Eastern presence in Finland dates back to the 1st century, when nomadic Finnish-speaking fishermen and hunters migrated to the area from Eastern Europe, forcing the Lapps, the original inhabitants, to move north to what is now Lapland. Even the Finnish language is most closely related, not to the Scandinavian languages, as one might imagine, but to Estonian.

Hemmed in by Sweden and Russia — Finland shares a 335-mile border with Sweden on the west, a 788-mile border with the Soviet Union on the east — it is no wonder that Finland became the buffer and the buffeted in wars between these two great rival powers. From the 13th century, when Finland was conquered by the Swedes, through the 19th century, when Russia took over — and until the Finnish nation declared its independence in 1917 — Finland suffered in the recurring wars between the two countries.

In 1812, shortly after the Russians conquered Finland in the Napoleonic Wars, Czar Alexander I moved the capital to Helsinki from Turku, a city on the west coast. In 1828, the university was moved from Turku, and Helsinki became an intellectual as well as a political center.

Around the same time, in 1808, the city was ravaged by a fire that totally demolished its crowded wooden buildings. When subsequently rebuilt as the nation's capital, Helsinki was well planned and deliberately spacious. Carefully charted by Johan Albrecht Ehrenström and executed by the noted architect Carl Ludvig Engel, the reconstruction was completed by 1840. The neo-classical buildings in the old center of town date from this period. Many of them, now renovated, house shops, restaurants, and cafés.

The skyline of this pollution-free city is accented by the imposing dome of the Lutheran cathedral (1840) and the onion-shaped domes of the Russian Orthodox church (1868). Helsinki's gleaming pastel buildings, many of which were designed by distinguished architects and built of local pale granite, have earned it the title of White City of the North. But this is a place to see interesting modern architecture as well; the Finnish nation, world renowned for its achievements in modern design, has produced such notables as Eliel Saarinen and Alvar Aalto, and many striking examples of their work can be seen here. Surely the most dramatic of Helsinki's many fine specimens of modern architecture is Temppeliaukio Church, blasted from solid rock, designed by two Finnish brothers, Timo and Tuomo Suomalainen. Helsinki also is noted for its wide streets and its parks and squares, which often are graced by magnificent sculptures.

Surrounded by water on three sides (to the north are green fields, forests, and lakes), Helsinki has a natural seaport that is kept open most of the winter by icebreakers. The port once was protected by the fortifications on Suomenlinna, a group of five rocky islands south of the city's center. Helsinki's harbor, Finland's largest, handles the bulk of the nation's maritime activity. Finland's imports of petroleum products, vehicles, and consumer goods just exceed its exports of paper, wood, metal products, and machinery.

Although it is a capitalist nation bordering on the Soviet Union, Finland is fanatically neutral. The government is a parliamentary republic, headed by a president who is elected for a 6-year term. Finland's standard of living is higher than the Soviet Union's and almost as high as that of neighboring Sweden or the US. Like other Scandinavians, Finns are culturally advanced. Many Finns speak English, which has replaced Swedish as the second language taught in schools. Illiteracy is unknown, social welfare is extensive, and all the proceeds from gambling are allocated to public charity. Some 60% of the nation's people live in cities — with half a million, over 10%, in Helsinki — making their livings from manufacturing and service industries.

Though by nature shy and reserved, sometimes a brooding people, Finns are passionate underneath — the music of native son Jean Sibelius expresses this hidden intensity — and they can surprise you with their wry humor. They are lovers of pleasure (dining out as much as their budgets allow), appreciators of great music, and mad about dancing, whether it be disco or cheek-to-cheek.

The Finns also love nature and the outdoors. With 188,000 lakes in the country, everyone swims and many families have a boat, be it a canoe or luxury yacht. Summer, from June to September, finds the bulk of the population at the family cottage along a waterfront of lake, river, or sea, often commuting to work when not on vacation. And in winter everyone — young and old — skis.

Cleanliness is a Finnish virtue. The streets, homes, shops, hotels, and restaurants of Helsinki are spotless. The Finns themselves take particularly good care of their bodies, hardly surprising when you consider that one of the great Finnish pastimes is the sauna.

It is estimated that there are nearly 1½ million saunas in Finland, and certainly there are plenty in and around Helsinki; nearly every hotel has at least one. Four of the most popular are at the *Hesperia, Kalastajatorppa, Inter-Continental,* and *Strand Inter-Continental* hotels; since anyone can go and many do, it is advisable to book in advance. You may wish to partake of some "sauna sausage" and beer after the event, as the natives do.

The sauna takes place in a wood-lined room, heated by a special stove to about 176F-212F. The intense heat is pleasant rather than suffocating. The sauna's users, clad in bathing suits and robes, sit on benches around a table, sipping bottled water, chatting, and conducting other affairs — many Finnish business deals are transacted in this relaxed atmosphere. Water is thrown on a layer of stones on the stove in order to produce *löyly,* or steam, which causes perspiration. Light whisking with birch twigs acts to increase the body's

HELSINKI

circulation. Ideally, the sauna user cools off with a dip in a lake, the sea, or a swimming pool. In winter, many Finns take a dip in a hole in the ice, which they call *avanto*.

Would-be polar bear or not, you surely will experience a euphoric sense of total relaxation and well-being after the sauna. Don't miss it.

HELSINKI AT-A-GLANCE

 SEEING THE CITY: From the steps of Helsinki's majestic cathedral, an observer's eyes can span the old part of the city and in a sweeping glance draw a capsule understanding of the city's history. In front of the church is the spacious Senate Square, designed during the early 19th century in neo-classical style to form a homogeneous whole. The Sederholm residence, built in 1755–57, is the oldest building in the city. On the west side of the square, always in harmony with the design, is Helsinki University; on the east side is the Government Building. Nearby is Esplanadi Park (Esplanadipuisto), center of Helsinki's business activities. Beginning at the Market Place, the tree-lined avenue, with a wide promenade for strollers and ample room for traffic on either side, ends several blocks north at Mannerheimintie (Mannerheim Street).

A tourist soon realizes that the Finns' dedication to nature is no myth. There is no crowding in Helsinki. As many as 240 parks, of all sizes, dot the city's landscape, leaving almost 30% of the metropolitan area open. Throughout Helsinki, the working people, the retired, the students, and the newcomers, too, find squares, triangles, and parks of all kinds to stop at for a rest.

On a summer walking tour in this part of town, it's fun to take time out at the *Kappeli* restaurant (see *Eating Out*), a charming old dining place at the edge of Esplanadi Park, for lunch or coffee in the afternoon. In a tranquil setting, foreign visitors soon fall into the casual, lighthearted mood of the Finns, many of whom gravitate there at lunch hour to enjoy the leisure of drinking beer outdoors and listening to a potpourri of music played by modern and traditional bands in the gazebo-like bandstand in the park or to watch folk dances.

 SPECIAL PLACES: Trams and buses run frequently in all directions (see *Sources and Resources*), but most foreign visitors prefer to explore the city by foot. Fortunately, downtown Helsinki is rather compact. Chances are you will be staying in a hotel that is centrally located, so you will be within walking distance of many of the city's attractions.

DOWNTOWN

Finlandia Hall – Either as part of a sightseeing tour or, even better, to attend a performance, you should not miss this $9-million marble edifice, the last architectural triumph of the country's great Alvar Aalto, world acclaimed for his simple yet elegant design. The sleek, white concert and congress hall is set in Hesperia Park on Mannerheimintie, almost directly across from the *National Museum.* You can't miss it. Check at your hotel desk for a free copy of *Helsinki This Week* to learn the program schedule. No admission charge for tour. 4 Karamzininkatu (phone: 40241).

Sibelius Monument – Dedicated in 1967 to Finland's revered composer, Jean Sibelius, this monument is a giant sculpture of tubular steel pipes. To the side of this impressive work, which dwarfs visitors, the sculptress Eila Hiltunen molded a head of the composer. Lighted at night, the bold monument is a gripping sight. Sibelius Park.

Cathedral – The cornerstone of Carl Ludwig Engel's Lutheran cathedral was laid in 1830, and the cathedral was consecrated in 1852. Today it remains a parish church, but it also is the scene of national festive services. Open daily from 9 AM to 7 PM, Sundays from noon. Senate Sq. (no phone).

Uspenski Cathedral – This classic example of Byzantine-Slavic brick architecture was completed in 1868 and restored for its 100th anniversary. Open Wednesdays from 2 to 6 PM and Thursdays from 9 AM to 1 PM. 1 Kanavakatu (no phone).

Temppeliaukio Church – Known as the Rock Church, this unique house of worship was designed by two brothers, Timo and Tuomo Suomalainen. Carved out of solid rock, it is topped with a copper dome that spans 70 feet. It occupies most of a block and from the street or air only the dome is visible. The interior is pink and gray granite with vertical glass strips cut into the ceiling that allow light to enter in dramatic shafts. Breathtakingly beautiful in its simplicity. Open daily. 3 Lutherinkatu (phone: 494698).

Parliament House – Visitors are welcome except when Parliament is in recess. You can join a guided tour at certain hours or attend plenary sessions in the galleries. No admission charge. 30 Mannerheimintie (phone: 4321).

National Museum – Founded in 1893, this large museum also includes an extensive library. The government-owned building was designed in 1910 by the noted Finnish architects Saarinen, Gesellius, and Lindgren. Collections include archaeological, historical, and ethnological displays. There are 19,000 archaeological items from the Stone, Bronze, and Iron Ages in Scandinavia and the Soviet Union; 80,000 historical items include Finnish interiors, costumes, textiles, weapons, metals, and coins; Finnish, Ugric, and Lapp ethnic collections include 15,300 items on hunting, textiles, folk art, and furniture. Open Mondays through Saturdays and Tuesday evenings. Admission charge. 34 Mannerheimintie (phone: 40251).

Art Museum of the Ateneum – Paintings, sculptures, drawings, and etchings — mostly modern Finnish but also foreign and classical — housed in a neo-Renaissance building. Recently reopened after a 6-year renovation, the collection now also includes older works from the Finnish archives. Closed Mondays. No admission charge Saturdays. Near Railway Sq. (phone: 694-5933).

Seurasaari – This charming park and open-air museum provide a representative picture of early Finland, complete with farm and manor houses that were transported from all over the country and reassembled here. You might want to picnic outdoors. The museum, which sits on Seurasaari Island, offers some entertainment in the summer, mostly folk dancers in colorful native garb. Bus No. 24 will take you there, and you enter by a footbridge. Open daily, May 2 to August 30. No admission charge Wednesdays. Seurasaari Island (phone: 484712).

Helsinki Zoo – In 1988, this largest of Finland's zoos marked its 100th birthday. Most animals are housed in their natural environment on Korkeasaari Island near the city. Besides northern animals, the collection includes llamas, bison, bears, and lions, and a number of endangered species, among them the rare snow leopard. Weather permitting, guests can have lunch in an open-air café and gaze out to sea toward Helsinki's skyline and South Harbor. In the summer, ferry service is available from the shore of Market Square, and motorboat service brings visitors here from the shore of Hakaniemi Square. The zoo also is accessible by bridge via bus No. 16 to Mustikkamaa, from where there is a 1-mile walk through Mustikkamaa Island, across the pedestrian bridge to Korkeasaari .Open daily year-round. Admission charge (phone: 135-20222).

Suomenlinna – An intriguing island, the largest of a group of five rocky islands to the south of the city center, only a 15-minute boat ride from South Harbor. This 18th-century fortification, reputed to be the largest sea fortress in the world, is well worth a visit. Built in 1748, when Finland was part of Sweden, the fortress was planned and directed by Marshal Augustin Ehrensvärd. Called the Gibraltar of the North, the fortress capitulated to the Russians in 1808 and defended itself successfully against an Anglo-French fleet in 1855, during the Crimean War.

A visitor can explore the fortifications of Susisaari (Wolf Island), reached by crossing a footbridge, and Kustaanmiekka (Gustav's Sword) with their forts and casements, parks and walks.

On the island of Susisaari, the *Ehrensvärd Museum* exhibits Suomenlinna's history (open May through September; Saturdays and Sundays only in September; phone: 668131). The *Armfelt Museum* on the island of Kustaanmiekka shows the life of the 19th-century Finnish gentry (open Saturdays and Sundays; phone: 668154); also on Kustaanmiekka are the *Coast Defense Artillery Museum* and the World War II submarine *Vesikko* (open daily between May and August; no phone).

The islands also have art exhibitions and a restaurant, *Walhalla* (on Suomenlinna), open in the summer.

The ferry from Market Square to Suomenlinna leaves hourly on the half-hour and takes about 15 minutes. In summer, tours start at the information kiosk (phone: 668341 in summer or 668154 in winter).

Design Forum – A gallery showcasing changing exhibitions of Finnish designers' textiles and other applied arts. Open Mondays through Fridays and occasional weekends. No admission charge. 8 Etelaesplanadi (phone: 629290).

Senate Square – In order to appreciate Helsinki's rich history, a visit to the complex of neo-classical buildings built between 1818 and 1852 is a must: The cathedral, government palace, city administration, and university buildings are now surrounded by modern shops and cafés.

Stadium Tower – The *Olympic Stadium* with its 236-foot-high tower was designed by Yrjö Lindegren and Toivo Jäntti. In front is Wäinö Aaltonen's statue of gold medal runner Paavo Nurmi. 3 Eteläinen Stadionintie (phone: 440363).

Botanical Gardens of the University – Established in 1833, this lush park holds Finland's largest botanical collection. There are a variety of trees, shrubs, and grasses common to Finland; the greenhouses showcase exotic tropical plants. Open daily. Admission charge. 44 Unioninkatu (phone: 650188).

Presidential Palace – Once the Heidenstrauch mansion, the imposing palace was designed by Pehr Granstedt and completed in 1814. It served as the czar's residence when he visited Finland and became the Presidential Palace when Finland gained its independence. Closed to the public. 1 Pohjoisesplanadi.

Kauppatori Market Square – At the foot of the esplanade at South Harbor is the open-air marketplace, one of the most visited spots in Helsinki. Open daily except Sundays, it is filled with brightly colored stalls, manned by old and young alike, that sell everything from fresh flowers and vegetables and fruit to trinkets and freshly caught fish. Bustling and bursting with color, it's a place to see and a place to mingle with the Finns. Browse or buy, but be sure to stop long enough to taste the freshly brewed coffee and munch on the delicate Finnish pastries. From May 15 to August 30, the evening market is open 3:30 to 8 PM Mondays through Fridays.

Hietalahti – Be sure to take your camera to this popular flea market, known by locals as *Hietsu*, which attracts a loyal and colorful following. There are bargains on old books, toys, clothing, military uniforms, and Russian goods. Closed Sundays. Walk across the Esplanadi, cross Mannerheimintie, and head to the end of Tarja Blvd.

Linnanmäki – Helsinki's answer to Copenhagen's *Tivoli* is patronized by Finns from all parts of the country, as well as residents and tourists. It's more than an amusement park; only 30% of its visitors are children. This popular amusement park includes 25 different rides, an indoor and an open-air theater, restaurants, two small cafés, a dancing pavilion, and assorted kiosks. Special rides are the gigantic Big Dipper and a carousel built in 1892 with hand-carved animals. The *Peacock Theater* seats 906 indoors and features internationally known comedians, clowns, acrobats, musicians, and marionettes. The open-air auditorium offers similar entertainments plus high-wire acrobatic acts.

A special aspect of *Linnanmäki* is that its proceeds, often exceeding $2 million a year, are donated to various children's charities, hence the title "the park with the heart." Open daily except Mondays, May through August. Admission charge; rides extra (phone: 750391).

Heureka – This science center, which opened in 1989 in Vantaa, near the Helsinki Airport, offers a wide range of exhibitions on modern technology. Visitors can conduct their own experiments or stop in the theater, which shows a variety of science films. Restaurant, café, and bar. Admission charge. 1 Tiedepuisto (phone: 857999).

SUBURBS

Tapiola – Called the Garden City of Finland, it's a utopian suburb designed in the 1950s to emphasize the quality of living in harmony with the surrounding nature. Tapiola, taken from the Finnish national epic *Kalevala*, was an imaginary place where the fabled people lived. It was built step by step by a group of private nonprofit organizations, and it still is not considered complete. About 17,000 people share the 670 acres, which include their own newspapers, clubs, shopping centers, a marina, a sports arena, libraries, and an outdoor glassed-in swimming pool. Within a short distance of Tapiola is another interesting architectural sight, the Technical University in Otaniemi, designed by Alvar Aalto. Don't miss Dipoli, the campus clubhouse.

You might want to check with the Helsinki City Tourist Office (see *Sources and Resources*) for a sightseeing tour. Tapiola is a short but expensive cab ride from downtown Helsinki, or take a bus marked Tapiola from the bus station.

■ **EXTRA SPECIAL:** Since Finland is a country of 188,000 lakes and 180,000 islands, it would be sheer folly to make it to this land and not experience some part of the visit on water. Get another perspective on the capital from a boat. There are leisurely paced sightseeing and lunch cruises and archipelago tours that depart daily from Market Square from June 1 to August 31, taking you past innumerable little islands and around peninsulas. You can choose between a ride that lasts 1¼ hours or one that runs for 5 hours, including lunch. You'll enjoy this respite on a warm summer day.

For those who have the time, plan to arrive in style from Stockholm on the *Silja Lines* deluxe cruise ship. The overnight excursion features fine dining and entertainment for about $200 per person, including a stateroom and tour of Helsinki. Other ships sail to interesting locales such as Turku, Finland's former capital, and St. Petersburg. For more information contact the Helsinki City Tourist Office (phone: 169-3757).

SOURCES AND RESOURCES

TOURIST INFORMATION: For general information, brochures, and maps, contact the Finland Tourist Board (655 Third Ave., New York, NY 10017; phone: 212-949-2333), or the Helsinki City Tourist Office (19 Pohjoisesplanadi; phone: 169-3757 and 174088). "Helsinki Today" (phone: 58) gives recorded programs (in English) of events in the city.

The US Embassy is at 14 Puistotie (phone: 171931).

Local Coverage – *City Magazine,* the quarterly publication written for English-speaking visitors, is available free at kiosks around town and at the airport. No English-language newspapers are published in Helsinki. The *International Herald Tribune* is available at the better hotels, newsstands, and the airport. *The Academic Book Store,* (39 Pohjoisesplenadi) carries a large selection of newspapers and magazines in many languages.

Food and Drink – A little red book, *Where to Eat in Helsinki,* gives restaurants from one to five stars; it's published by the Gastronomic Society of Finland and is available at the *Academic Book Store.* Also indispensable is *Food from Finland,* a Finnish cookbook that contains recipes and text written in English by Anna-Maija and Juha Tanttu.

As in many Nordic countries, the sale of wine, beer, and spirits is operated under a monopoly. Retail sales are handled through the state-run *Alko* stores (open Mondays through Fridays; Saturdays only from October through April) located throughout the city.

 TELEPHONE: The country code for Finland is 358; the city code for Helsinki is 0.

 GETTING AROUND: Airport – Helsinki-Vantaa Airport, 12 miles (19 km) north of the city, handles both domestic and international traffic. Taxi fare from the airport to downtown runs about $25. *Finnair* buses travel between the airport and the air terminal adjoining the *Inter-Continental* hotel (21 Töölönkatu; phone: 818-7770), or from the new city terminal at the central train station (3 Asema Aukio; phone: 818-7980). The buses run two to five times every hour and cost about $5 one way.

Car Rental – Besides *Avis, Budget,* and *Hertz,* there are *InterRent, Europcar,* and others. Car rental desks are found at the airport and in many hotel lobbies.

Taxi – Cabstands, clearly marked "Taksi," are at every few corners, with plenty of cabs waiting their turns. Cabs are plentiful, except around midnight when bars close and long lines begin to form at taxi stands. Fares are not inexpensive; the meter starts at about $2.55, and there is an extra charge from 10 PM to 6 AM. You can hail a cab when the sign is illuminated. No tip is expected.

Train – The city's main train station is Rautatieasema (13 Vilhonkatu; phone: 7071 or 659411). With its splendid Art Nouveau architecture and good restaurants, the station is a destination in itself.

Tram and Bus – Trams 3T and 3B, which can be boarded anywhere along their route, offer a tour of the business and residential areas of the capital, with a taped commentary in English during the summer months. In addition, a 24-hour tourist ticket, available at the Helsinki City Tourist Office, entitles you to unlimited travel on trams and buses for about $10. The Helsinki Card ($15 to $24) provides unlimited travel on trams, buses, subways (linking the city center and the eastern suburbs), and ferries, as well as free admission to 40 museums, discount theater and concert tickets, and special weekend discounts at hotels. It can be purchased at the airport, the Helsinki City Tourist Office, or *Stockmann's* department store (52 Aleksanterinkatu). Tram, bus, and metro tickets are priced at 6 Finnish marks (about $1.50). Call the bus station for information: 602122.

If you wish to travel beyond the city, comfortable motor coaches provide transportation to cities such as Tampere and Turku (phone: 692-2088).

LOCAL SERVICES: Dentist (English-Speaking) – *Forum Dentists' Centre* (20 Mannerheimintie; phone: 694-4133); for 24-hour emergency service, call 736166.

    Dry Cleaner/Tailor – *Lindström Oy* (City Passage, 2nd Floor; phone: 657251); also, ask your hotel concierge.

Limousine Service – *Pentti Lindfors/International Limousine System* (32H Alku-tie; phone: 744577); *Nordic Promotion* is a good taxi service for tourists (20A Manner-heimintie; phone: 611252).

Medical Emergency – *Helsinki University Hospital* (4 Haartmaninkatu; phone: 4711). To contact a doctor (they all speak English) in an emergency, dial 008 or 000; for 24-hour information about medical services, call 735001.

Messenger Service – *Stadin Kuriiri,* 5 Kotisaarenkatu (phone: 756-8815).

National/International Courier – *DHL International,* 3 Läkkisepänkuja (phone: 799877).

Office Equipment Rental – *AV-Point,* for audiovisual equipment (9 Eljaksentie; phone: 565-3633); *Helsinki Business Center* rents fully equipped offices with secretarial services and can arrange international teleconferencing (17A Salomonkatu; phone: 694-7711).

Pharmacy – *Yliopiston Apteekki,* open 24 hours daily. 96 Mannerheimintie (phone: 415778).

Photocopies – *Stockmann's* (52 Aleksanterinkatu; phone: 1211); most hotels also have photocopiers.

Post Office – The main post office is open Mondays from 9 AM to 6 PM, Tuesdays through Fridays 9 AM to 5 PM (11 Mannerheimintie; phone: 195-5117); *Poste Restante* (general delivery) hours are from 8 AM to 10 PM Mondays through Saturdays, and from 11 AM to 10 PM Sundays (phone: 195-5123).

Secretary/Stenographer (English-Speaking) – *Toimialapalvelu* (4A Mais-traatinportti; phone: 145011); *Sihteeriyhdistys* (26A Kalevankatu; phone: 693-2150).

Telex – *Teleservice,* at the main post office, is open daily from 7 AM to 11 PM (11B Mannerheimintie; phone: 661126); a telex can also be sent at any time by dialing 21.

Translator – Andrew McGafferty (phone: 874-3584).

Other – Business services: *Business Center Finland* (16A Melknokatu; phone: 670344); *Office Forum* is open 24 hours daily and also provides office space (20 Mannerheimintie; phone: 694-8455). Formal wear rental: *Juhla-Asu* (4A Kaisaniemen-katu; phone: 666024). Professional photographer: *Lehtikuva Press Photo Agency & Studio* (6-8 Ludviginkatu; phone: 1221). News in English: dial 40.

 SPECIAL EVENTS: More than a decade ago, Finland introduced over 800 summer festivals, produced and presented in various sections of the country. The idea was to attract foreign visitors and to familiarize them with the Finnish people and their achievements and, at the same time, to entertain them with local professional talent and international luminaries. The events run from symphonic concerts and opera performances given in a 15th-century castle courtyard to rock, folk, jazz, and pop music; to art exhibits; to seminars on world problems — cultural fare for everyone, including the small fry. For information, contact *Finland Festivals* 3A Vuorikatu, 17th floor. (phone: 607386 or 669695).

The *Finland Festival* chain of dozens of programs generally starts in mid-June and runs till mid-August. These are followed by the big *Helsinki Festival,* which includes as many as 100 presentations between late August and early September. For complete program information, contact *Helsinki Festival,* 28 Unioninkatu (phone: 659688).

Visitors also might like to catch the *Changing of the Guard* at the Main Guard Post, behind the President's Palace every day at 1 PM.

 MUSEUMS: In addition to the museums described in *Special Places,* the following are noteworthy.

Ainola – Once the home of composer Jean Sibelius. Open Wednesdays through Sundays, May through September. Admission charge. Järvenpää (phone: 287322).

City Museum – The history of the city from its founding to the present is on display at two locations. The main collection of pictures and objects is housed in a private villa at 6 Tomisto Dagmarinkatu, the rest can be seen at 2 Karamzininkatu. Open weekdays from 9 AM to 3 PM (same phone for both: 169-3444).

Gallen-Kallela – The castle-like studio-home of Akseli Gallen-Kallela, Finland's national painter. Open daily. Reachable by tram No. 4 to Munkkiniemi, then either walk about a mile to Espoo or take bus No. 33 (weekdays only). Espoo (phone: 513388).

Hvitträsk – The former studio and residence of architects and designers Eliel Saarinen, Armas Lindgren, and Herman Gesellius now serves as a cultural center and is open year-round. Bus No. 166 from platform 62 at the central bus station will get you there in 40 minutes. The restaurant serves excellent seasonal Finnish cuisine (phone: 297-6033) and the gift shop sells unique handicrafts. Closed Mondays November through March; admission charge. Luoma, Kirkkonummi (phone: 90-297-5779).

Mannerheim Museum – Originally the home of Finland's great war hero and president, Marshal Mannerheim. Open Fridays, Saturdays, and Sundays from 11 AM to 3 PM. Admission charge. In Kaivopuisto Park, 14 Kalliolinnantie (phone: 635443).

Museum of Applied Arts – Finnish industrial design and native handicrafts. Closed Mondays. Admission charge. 23 Korkeavuorenkatu (phone: 174455).

Museum of Finnish Building – Archives and exhibitions of Finnish architecture, past and present. Open Tuesdays through Sundays. Admission charge. 24 Kasarmikatu (phone: 661918).

Photographic Museum of Finland – Exhibitions of work by Finnish and international photographers. Open daily 11 AM to 4 PM. Admission charge. 6 Keskuskatu (phone: 658544).

Urho Kekkonen Museum (Tamminiemi) – The home of Urho Kekkonen, Finland's late president, from 1956 to 1986, it opened as a museum in 1987. Open daily. Admission charge. Adjacent to the *Seurasaari Open-Air Museum* (phone: 480684).

SHOPPING: Shopping can be fun and profitable in Finland. You'll run into some of the best buys in Europe if you're interested in textiles, ceramics, glassware, jewelry, handicrafts, furs, and leather goods. Jewelry includes gold items fashioned after centuries-old ornaments as well as bold modern designs in silver and wood. Famed rya rugs woven in fine wools are bargains. Furs are great in Finland, and the most famous designers create astonishing — and expensive — works of art from mink, fox, and lynx, among others. *Marimekko and Vuokko* clothes and fabrics, *Arabia* glass and pottery, and *Aarikka* wooden toys also are exceptional items (check below for details on all three). *Note:* Before you go shopping, visit the *Finnish Design Center* (19 Kasarmikatu; phone: 626388), a permanent exhibition of Finnish handicrafts and industrial design.

The main shopping area in Helsinki is in the vicinity of the large hotels, particularly along Aleksanterinkatu and Esplanadi Park and their side streets. *Kauppatori* is the city's open-air market, where vendors offer a wide array of items including inexpensive furs, handmade goods, and local produce. It's at the far end of the esplanade at South Harbor. The *Senatti Center* is a complex of bazaars, art galleries, shops, restaurants, and cafés in the revived Old Town Empire buildings at Aleksanterinkatu, Unioninkatu, Sofiankatu. And for flea-market followers, *Hietalahti* (see *Special Places*) offers colorful sights as well as bargains.

Keep in mind that a VAT of 16% to 18% is added to the price of many items bought in Helsinki. However, department stores and finer shops will provide an 11% to 13% tax refund receipt for both cash and credit card purchases by foreign visitors; it can be cashed at the airport or on board ships sailing between Finland and Sweden. Most shops and boutiques are open on weekdays from 9 AM to 5 PM, and department stores are open on weekdays from 9 AM to 8 PM and until 2 PM on Saturdays.

Aarikka – Toys, jewelry, animals, and other articles in wood and silver designed by Kaija Aarikka. 27 Pohjoisesplanadi (phone: 652277).

Academic Book Store – One of the world's largest bookstores, designed by Alvar Aalto. Visit the *Café Aalto* (on the premises) between book buying. 39 Pohjoisesplanadi (phone: 901-2141).

Agora – A shopping patio surrounded by elegant boutiques filled with jewelry, crystal, sculpture, furs, fashions, and Finland's only genuine tearoom. 30 Unioninkatu.

Akanoirta – Wonderful wool sweaters in fall colors. At the *Senatti Center*.

Arabia – For Helsinki's best selection of Iittala glass, as well as ceramics, crystal, and exquisite china. 25 Pohjoisesplanadi (phone: 170055). Visit the *Arabia Factory Store* for discounted prices. 135 Hämeentie.

Artek – Housed in the Rautatalo building, designed by architect Alvar Aalto, it offers Aalto home furnishings, including furniture, lamps, textiles, and assorted design products. 3 Keskuskatu.

Forum – A modern shopping plaza packed with boutiques and shops displaying novelty items. Its 4 floors also offer restaurants, cafés, and a delicatessen. 20 Mannerheimintie.

Galerie Björn Weckström – This reputable sculptor is the principal designer of the avant-garde Lapponia jewelry that's often made with gold nuggets and spectrolite from Lapland. 30 Unioninkatu.

Iittala Shop – Glass, crystal, giftware, and kitchen utensils. 27 Pohjoisesplanadi (phone: 663305).

Kalevala-Koru – Extensive selection of traditional folk jewelry in gold, silver, and bronze. 25 Unioninkatu (phone: 171520).

Kankurin Tupa – Handmade clothing, woven rugs, jewelry, crystal, wall hangings, and kitchen accessories. 40 Mannerheimintie.

Karvinen Annikki – The best textiles in Helsinki, including handwoven blankets, pillows, wall hangings, and placemats. 33 Pohjoisesplanadi (phone: 633837).

Marimekko – The internationally famous designer's brightly colored fabrics and clothing. 31 Pohjoisesplanadi (phone: 177944).

Pentik – Exclusive clothing designs in leather. Two central locations: *Forum Mall*, 20 Mannerheimintie (phone: 694-8817) and 27 Pohjoisesplanadi (phone: 625-558).

***Old Harbor Market* (Wanha Satama)** – Two historic warehouses built in 1897 have been beautifully restored and now house boutiques, restaurants, and crafts exhibitions. At the harbor, near the Presidential Palace.

Rahikainen Boutique – Fine selection of Finnish furs, including many one-of-a-kinds by the acclaimed Finnish designer. 48 Kasarmikatu.

Sauna Shop – For wonderful bath accessories, including robes, soaps, and towels. In the *Senatti Center*, 28 Aleksanterinkatu (phone: 634733).

Schröder, Hellbom and Degerlund – For the serious fisherman, it offers a wide variety of reasonably priced Rapala fishing lures. 23 Unioninkatu (phone: 656656).

Stockmann's – The leading, the largest, and the oldest (founded in 1862) department store, it carries a wide range of Finnish-made goods and food products. 52 Aleksanterinkatu.

Tarja Niskanen – Ms. Niskanen is reputed to be the best furrier in the city. 33 Pohjoisesplanadi (phone: 624022).

Vuokko – Bold new fashions for men and women. 25 Pohjoisesplanadi (phone: 750144).

Wahlmans – A variety of hats, including fur in Russian styles. 35 Pohjoisesplanadi.

 SPORTS AND FITNESS: Because of its climate, Finland is a paradise for all varieties of winter sports. Lovers of nature and the outdoors, Finns go in for boating and bicycling as well as skiing.

Bicycling – Finland is big on bicycling. There are prescribed routes, but you can plan out your own by using maps. Those around Helsinki and other cities run partly on special bicycle lanes. There also are some old country roads in good cycling condition. Check with the Helsinki City Tourist Office for details, including where to rent a bike.

Boating – There are many yachting clubs on the islands right outside Helsinki. A boat or canoe can be rented, but the reefy waters are rather tricky. Check with the *Yachting Association* or the *Motor Boat Association* (both at 20 Radiokatu; phone: 1581). The *Nautic Center* (9 Itälahdenkatu; phone: 670271), rents boats with or without a crew.

Bowling – For information about the 79 bowling alleys in Finland, contact the *Finnish Bowling Federation,* 3 Ruusulankatu (phone: 409133).

Fishing – It's possible to fish at sea and in local inland waters year-round. General fishing licenses can be obtained for about $8 at banks and post offices, Mondays through Fridays. For further information, check with the Finland Tourist Board (655 Third Ave., New York, NY 10017; phone: 212-949-2333), or the Helsinki City Tourist Office (19 Pohjoisesplanadi; phone: 169-3757 or 174088).

Fitness Centers – *Nautilus Sports Center* (17B Salomonkatu; phone: 694-5833); *Forum Gym* (23B Yrjönkatu; phone: 602702).

Golf – Finland boasts some 72 courses, and the best part of golfing in this country is that in summer you can tee off as late as 10 PM and finish all 18 holes in daylight because there are almost 24 hours of light. For course information, contact the *Finnish Golf Union* (20 Radiokatu; phone: 144284). Visitors should bring their club membership cards from home. Many top hotels, including the *Hesperia* (phone: 43101), have golf simulators — a computer system that shows the player how the ball would go if played on a real golf course.

Jogging – Finns are health oriented and are on the jogging kick, too. Americans dedicated to the daily ritual will find paths close to *Olympic Stadium* and in the Kaivopuisto park in the southern part of the city or around Hesperia Park near the city center.

Horseback Riding – You won't have trouble finding a horse to ride. Check with the *Finnish Equestrian Federation,* 20 Radiokatu (phone: 158-2315).

Hunting – Finland's big game is moose. Three- to four-day packages, including tests at shooting areas, licenses, insurance, comfortable accommodations, and full board are available to those who want to join in the sport. The season runs from late October to December. Contact the *Hunter's Central Organization* (phone: 877-7677).

Saunas – Most hotels have their own saunas; it's best to book them in advance. Public saunas usually do not accept reservations. Contact the Helsinki City Tourist Office for further information.

Skiing – Skiing is to Finns as baseball is to Americans. In Finland skiing means mostly cross-country skiing, for which its terrain is ideal. All over the country there are marked and often illuminated ski trails of varying lengths and difficulty. There are also numerous downhill slopes with ski lifts. The peak season for skiing in south and central Finland is from January to March; in Lapland it runs from late autumn through May. (A bonus for skiers in May is a deep suntan, which is produced by 14 to 16 hours of sunshine.)

Ski equipment can be rented at *Stadion Retkeilymaja* (3B Pohjois Stadionintie; phone: 496071), and all ski centers.

You can — and many Finns do this on weekends — just put on your skis and follow tracks on the Gulf of Finland to the islands. There are ski tracks all around Helsinki. Or you may prefer a weekend or week-long ski package at one of the many winter sports centers all over Finland. Resorts offer cross-country skiing, of course, as well as ski lifts, downhill slopes, marked and illuminated ski trails, keep-fit rooms, guided excursions, saunas, evening entertainment, and ski instruction. Two popular areas near Helsinki are Messilä (65 miles/100 km) near the site of international skiing competitions in February, and Hyvinkää (about 40 miles/64 km). The *Peurama Ski Center* (phone: 298-1011), just a half-hour ride from Helsinki, attracts downhill and cross-country enthusiasts.

Further information about skiing is available from the local sports association, *Suomen Latu* (7 Fabianinkatu; phone: 170101); the Helsinki City Tourist Office (see above); or from any travel agent in Helsinki.

Veteran skiers may enter the *Finlandia Ski Race* (cross-country) in early March or any of a number of ski races. Inquire at the Finland National Tourist Office, 19 Pohjoisesplanadi.

Soccer – In summer there are games between Finland and other countries. Check *Helsinki This Week* for schedules.

Squash – For information on the 600 squash courts throughout Finland, contact the *Finnish Squash Racquets Association,* 20 Radiokatu (phone: 158-2400).

Tennis – Tennis is popular in Scandinavia. Helsinki alone has more than 30 clubs. It's best to bring your own racket. For booking a court and other information, call the *Finnish Tennis Association,* 20 Radiokatu (phone: 1581).

Winter Sports and Activities – A unique experience in Lapland is a reindeer safari, often complete with a Lapp guide; participants travel by reindeer sledge across the fells and spend the night in a modern log cabin. For information about such winter tours, contact the *Finland Travel Bureau Ltd.* 10A Kaivokatu, Helsinki 00100 (phone: 18261).

 THEATER: The top three theaters in town are the *Kansallisteatteri* (Finnish National Theater; Asema-aukio, Railway Station Plaza; phone: 652763); *Kaupunginteatteri* (City Theater; 5 Eläintarhantie; phone: 394022); and the *Svenska Teatern* (Swedish Theater; 2 Pohjoisesplanadi; phone: 170654). You may not understand Finnish or Swedish, which are the languages of practically all productions, but you might want to take in one performance just for fun. In summer there are only open-air performances.

 MUSIC: There's always an excellent choice of concerts by symphony orchestras, chamber groups, and jazz artists. Many name performers from Europe, the US, and other countries can be seen, so don't be surprised if you find a group of Japanese instrumentalists playing one concert and the *New York Philharmonic* at another. Major concert halls include: *Finlandia Hall* (4 Karamzininkatu; phone: 40241); *Kulttuuritalo* (House of Culture; 4 Sturenkatu; phone: 77081 or 768119) *Sibelius Academy* (9 P. Rautatiekatu; phone: 135-2539); *Ritarihuone* (House of Nobility; 3 Aleksanterinkatu); and *Finnish National Opera* (23-27 Bulevardi; phone: 129255. Operas are sung in their original languages.) *Musiikki-Fazer* (11 Aleksanterinkatu; phone: 56011), is the main agency for concert and opera tickets. At press time a new opera house was under construction on Mannerheimintie at the edge of Hesperia Park; it is slated to open late this year, with the official season beginning in 1993.

 NIGHTLIFE AND NIGHTCLUBS: Finns are nightlifers, especially the under-50 segment of the population, who are endowed with limitless endurance. The disco has won points in this city, and the proof is in the crowds that flock to "nightclubs," as discos are called here, at various locales around the city. There usually are lines to get into the clubs, since most places close at 1 AM. Be patient and enjoy the people watching, but be aware that even if you're willing to pay the cover charge, a doorman usually decides who can enter. Dress conservatively, and expect to tip the people who grant you entrance, check your coat, and call a taxi. Two of the liveliest spots in the city are *Old Baker's* (12 Mannerheimintie; phone:

605607), and the *Fizz* (next door at 10 Mannerheimintie; phone: 641717). For more elegant surroundings, try *Café Metropol* (Kaivopiha; phone: 666966) and *Berlin* (3 Töölönkatu; phone: 499002) or the discos at the *Hesperia, Inter-Continental,* and *Strand Inter-Continental* hotels, all open to 3 AM. *Café Adlon* (phone: 664611) is one of the city's most sophisticated nightclubs. The best place to enjoy a drink and an incredible view of the city rooftops is from the *Ateljee* bar in the *Torni* hotel tower (5 Kalevankatu; phone: 131131). Roulette, which is restricted to a limit of 25¢ per chip, is popular here. You'll find roulette wheels in many hotels and nightspots.

BEST IN TOWN

CHECKING IN: Most of the city's accommodations are centrally located, modern, and equipped with all the amenities that make for a comfortable stay (and all of the hotels listed below have at least one sauna). Although there is something of a hotel building boom going on in Helsinki, reservations still should be made in advance, especially during the peak of the summer season. For those traveling to Finland in summer, seasonal discount accommodations coupons, called Finncheques, are available. These coupons reduce hotel rates considerably and are good at any of 160 hotels across the country; a full breakfast is also included. Finncheques can be purchased in the US from *Holiday Tours of America,* (40 E. 49th St., New York, NY 10017; phone: 212-832-9072 or 800-223-0567). For travelers on a budget who want a glimpse of Finnish life, the Finland Tourist Board and local travel agencies can arrange farm holidays.

Expect to pay $125 and up a night for a double room in a hotel in the expensive category; $80 to $120 in the moderate category; and $75 and under in the inexpensive category. Credit cards are accepted everywhere. All telephone numbers are in the 0 city code unless otherwise indicated.

Hesperia – This luxury property is across the street from Hesperia Park and a stone's throw from *Finlandia Hall.* Its good location, fine service, outstanding Russian restaurant (See *Eating Out*), and French-style grillroom, boutiques, disco, sauna, and swimming pool make it a popular choice. There's also roulette in the lobby for those who follow the sportin' life. Suites available. Business facilities include room service from 6:30 to 2:30 AM, meeting rooms for up to 450, English-speaking concierge, foreign currency exchange, secretarial services in English, audiovisual equipment, photocopiers, computers, cable television news, translation services, and express checkout. 50 Mannerheimintie (phone: 43101; fax: 431-0995; telex: 122115). Expensive.

Inter-Continental – With 555 rooms and 30 luxury suites, this is Scandinavia's largest establishment. The sauna on the top floor offers a chance to look out over the city from the adjoining terrace. Roulette may be played in the *Baltic Lounge* on the main floor or on the ninth floor lounge with a panoramic view. Elegant seafood dishes are served at *Galateia,* also on the ninth floor (see *Eating Out*). Take time to saunter through the shopping arcade in the lobby or swim in the pool. Business facilities include 24-hour room service, meeting rooms for up to 450, English-speaking concierge, foreign currency exchange, secretarial services in English, audiovisual equipment, photocopiers, computers, cable television news, translation services, and express checkout. The *Finnair* bus terminal conveniently adjoins the rear entrance. 46-48 Mannerheimintie (phone: 441331 or 40551; fax: 405-5255). Expensive.

Kalastajatorppa – Outside the city center, and in a perfect setting in a park bordered by the blue waters of the Gulf of Finland, "Fisherman's Cottage," as its name translates, is spacious and ultramodern, with 235 rooms. Its annex is designed so that windows from double rooms overlook the sea. Several handsome suites are available. This latest addition to the hotel connects to the older section via a whitewashed rock tunnel, brilliantly lighted for walking. A romantic formal garden invites a stroll between dancing sessions in the main dining room or *Red Room* disco. Lots of activity, including tennis courts, a private beach, and 2 indoor pools. Business facilities include room service from 7 AM to 11:30 PM, meeting rooms for up to 55, English-speaking concierge, foreign currency exchange, secretarial services in English, audiovisual equipment, photocopiers, and translation services. 1 Kalastajatorpantie (phone: 45811; fax: 458-1668; telex: 121571). Expensive.

Marski – In the center of town, across from *Stockmann's* department store. Check in on the main floor, which is in an office building. Rooms begin on the third floor. It's a little more like a business traveler's hotel, but equipped with most desired facilities, including 2 saunas. The restaurant is very good, and the *Fizz* bar behind the reception desk is popular for cocktails in the late afternoon and for disco dancing at night. Business facilities include 24-hour room service, meeting rooms for up to 1,500, English-speaking concierge, foreign currency exchange, secretarial services, audiovisual equipment, photocopiers, computers, cable television news, and translation services. 10 Mannerheimintie (phone: 68061; fax: 642377). Expensive.

Palace – This gracious place is near the South Harbor and the Market Place. An older hostelry with only 59 rooms, it has been beautifully renovated; the accommodations are most comfortable (there are 3 saunas) and the service fine. The Italian *La Vista* restaurant on the second floor and the *Gourmet* dining room on the ninth floor serve excellent fare (see *Eating Out*), and the *American Bar* on the top floor is a delight. In summer you can take your drinks and lunch on the terrace and enjoy the wide expanse of sea, watching ships come and go. Business facilities include 24-hour room service, meeting rooms for up to 200, English-speaking concierge, foreign currency exchange, secretarial services in English, audiovisual equipment, photocopiers, cable television news, translation services, and express checkout. 10 Eteläranta (phone: 134561; fax: 654786). Expensive.

Ramada Presidentti – A luxurious establishment that's centrally located with 500 rooms, sauna and a swimming pool. It has a good steakhouse and several other restaurants. Business facilities include room service to 1 AM, meeting rooms for up to 400, foreign currency exchange, secretarial services in English, audiovisual equipment, photocopiers, cable television news, translation services, and express checkout. 4 Eteläinen Rautatiekatu (phone: 6911; fax: 694-7886). Expensive.

SAS Royal – The first member of the SAS chain in Finland opened last summer with 260 deluxe rooms, 2 restaurants, and accommodations for the disabled. Business facilities include meeting rooms for up to 500, English-speaking concierge, secretarial services in English, audiovisual equipment, photocopiers, and computers. 2 Runeberginkatu (phone: 69580; fax: 695-87100; telex: 122112). Expensive.

Strand Inter-Continental – Elegant and intimate, this 200-room hotel opened in 1989 on the waterfront, near the Old City center. The top floor has 4 saunas, each with its own terrace, and a swimming pool; there also is an elegant glass atrium and an excellent choice of restaurants (see *Eating Out*). Business facilities include 24-hour room service, meeting rooms for up to 250, English-speaking concierge, foreign currency exchange, secretarial services in English, audiovisual equipment, photocopiers, computers, cable television news, translation services, and express checkout. *Finnair* passengers can check luggage and receive boarding passes in the lobby. 4 John Stenberginranta (phone: 39351; fax: 761362). Expensive.

Seurahuone-Socis – Across from the railway station, it has traditional Old World charm and has been beautifully renovated. It also has a good restaurant, a classic Art Deco café and pub, and 118 rooms with modern conveniences. Business facilities include foreign currency exchange, secretarial services in English, audiovisual equipment, photocopiers, computers, cable television news, and translation services. 12 Kaivokatu (phone: 170441; fax: 664170). Expensive to moderate.

Anna – A quiet, comfortable place, it has 60 rooms with shower, color TV set, and mini-bar. 1 Annankatu (phone: 648011; fax: 602664). Moderate.

Aurora – In the heart of Helsinki, this small, dependable place has a restaurant, a bar, a swimming pool, and a sauna. 50 Helsinginkatu (phone: 717400; fax: 714240). Moderate.

Helka – Located in the center of town, this Best Western property has 164 comfortable, modern rooms, a lobby bar, restaurant, sauna, Jacuzzi, and solarium. 23 Pohjoinen Rautatiekatu (phone: 440581; fax: 441087). Moderate.

Klaus Kurki – Frequented mostly by businesspeople, it has comfortable rooms, a quiet bar, a pleasant restaurant, and an unpretentious wine cellar serving quick, moderately priced lunches. The hotel prides itself on personal, friendly service. Business facilities include room service from 7 AM to midnight, meeting rooms for up to 16, English-speaking concierge, foreign currency exchange, audiovisual equipment, photocopiers, and express checkout. 2-4 Bulevardi (phone: 618911; fax: 608538). Moderate.

Rivoli Jardin – Charming and cozy, with 54 rooms, it is well run and centrally located. There is a bar, a café, and a winter garden, plus a fitness room and a sauna. Snacks are available through room service (until midnight), but there's no full-service restaurant. 40 Kararmikatu (phone: 177880; fax: 656988). Moderate.

Hospiz – This *YMCA* hotel near the center of town has 163 rooms and a restaurant (no liquor license); good for a family on a budget. 17 Vuorikatu (phone: 170481; fax: 626880). Moderate to inexpensive.

Marttahotelli – Near the business district, this 45-room hotel run by the *Finnish Housewives' Association* is quiet and has a restaurant without a liquor license. 24 Uudenmaankatu (phone: 646211). Inexpensive.

■**Note:** During June, July, and August, the university's student quarters are for rent. They offer more modest accommodations and services than ordinary hotels but are quite comfortable and reasonably priced. For general hotel bookings in Finland contact the *Hotel Booking Center* (Railway Station, Helsinki 00100; phone: 171133; fax: 175524), or the *Finnish Travel Association* (25 Mikonkatu; phone: 170868), which also provides camping information. For youth and family hostels, contact the *Hotel Booking Center* (38B Yrjönkatu; phone: 694-0377; fax: 693-1349).

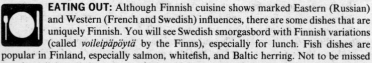 **EATING OUT:** Although Finnish cuisine shows marked Eastern (Russian) and Western (French and Swedish) influences, there are some dishes that are uniquely Finnish. You will see Swedish smorgasbord with Finnish variations (called *voileipäpöytä* by the Finns), especially for lunch. Fish dishes are popular in Finland, especially salmon, whitefish, and Baltic herring. Not to be missed are the delicious little native crayfish, which taste like American lobster but are even better; they are in season from about July 20 until September.

You also might want to try reindeer meat, which is served in many forms — as steaks, chops, and in stews, for example — but especially tasty is reindeer tongue, served smoked or in a madeira sauce. *Vorshmack* is a hearty dish that blends herring, mutton, beef, and onions, and is served with sour cream and a baked potato. Fried Baltic herring is also quite tasty.

Another typical dish is *karjalanpiirakka,* a pastry dough of rye flour (rye bread is big in Finland), filled with rice or potato; also *kalakukko,* a fish and pork pie.

The national dessert is Finnish crêpes, called *ohukainen.* Also delicious are fresh berries, especially strawberries and cloudberries (yellowish raspberries), and the chewy Lapp cheese, which is served warm with a berry sauce.

Finns drink their own high-quality beer and vodka (often served, as the Russians do, ice cold with hors d'oeuvres); also brandy, Scotch, and Campari. Try Finnish after-dinner liqueurs made with berries, particularly *mesimarja* (from brambleberries), *lakka* (from cloudberries), and *karpalo* (from cranberries).

There are many small, upbeat restaurants in Helsinki, not to mention cafeterias, snack bars, hamburger joints, and pizzerias for eating on the run. But Helsinki still lacks any good American-style restaurants that serve salads, steaks, and baked potatoes.

Dress is informal, but jackets and ties are required for men in the evening. Women can wear casual or cocktail dresses. If you feel like dressing up, by all means do. You won't be alone.

Note: There are a number of charming, strictly summer restaurants in Helsinki that are near water or on small islands; great for dinner and dancing. The *Walhalla* on the island fortress of Suomenlinna is one of the most charming. Check at the concierge's desk at your hotel, or get a list from the Helsinki City Tourist Office.

Remember, there is no tipping in restaurants; a service charge is included in your bill. However, leaving a small additional gratuity is a common practice. The obligatory cloakroom fee to restaurant doormen is usually clearly indicated; if not, it is about $1.

Restaurant prices are comparable to those in other European countries; expect to pay $90 to $150 for dinner for two with one drink at an expensive restaurant; $50 to $85 is moderate; $25 to $45 is inexpensive (with beer). Due to government regulation of alcoholic beverages, prices are very high except at *Alko,* the state liquor stores found through Finland. Finally, if you want to look up an eating place in the phone book, the Finnish word for restaurant is *ravintola.* All places below accept most major credit cards. All telephone numbers are in the 0 city code.

Alexander Nevski – The decor is elegant and the service attentive at this Russian dining place. Closed Sundays. Reservations advised. 17 Pohjoisesplanadi (phone: 639610). Expensive.

Galateia – The *Inter-Continental*'s elegant seafood dining room on the ninth floor, with a panoramic city view and a luminous interior. Reservations advised. 46-48 Mannerheimintie (phone: 441331). Expensive.

George – A sophisticated spot, in the heart of Helsinki, known for consistently high culinary standards — it's the only restaurant in Finland to have earned a star from Michelin. The decor is timeless and unpretentious. Closed Sundays. Reservations necessary. 17 Kalevankatu (phone: 647662). Expensive.

Havis Amanda – This cellar restaurant with charming atmosphere and good service enjoys a reputation for excellence. Table d'hôte and à la carte menus showcase fresh seafood. Save some room for the luscious desserts. Closed Sundays. Reservations advised. 23 Unioninkatu (phone: 666882). Expensive.

Hesperia Russian Room – Reviving culinary traditions from the time of the czars, this dining room in the *Hesperia* hotel offers exciting taste experiences and old-time Russian atmosphere. The menu offers traditional Russian dishes, as well as international ones prepared à la Russe. Open daily. Reservations advised. 50 Mannerheimintie (phone: 43101). Expensive.

Palace Gourmet – One of the *Palace* hotel's two restaurants, it is considered among the city's best. International and Finnish fare are featured. Closed weekends. Reservations necessary. 10 Eteläranta (phone: 657474). Expensive.

Pamir – Finnish fish and game dishes served in a tranquil setting, with muted colors and Saarinen furniture. In summer there's waterfront terrace dining. Closed Sundays. Reservations advised. In the *Strand Inter-Continental,* 4 John Stenberginranta (phone: 39351). Expensive.

Savoy – In the center of town at the top of an office building designed by Alvar Aalto. One of the better patronized dining places for intimate luncheons. Continental, international menus, Finnish specialties, and a good *vorschmack.* Closed weekends. Reservations advised. 14 Eteläesplanadi (phone: 176571). Expensive.

Bellevue – Not too far from Market Square near the Russian Orthodox church, this humble establishment is considered one of the best of several Russian restaurants in Helsinki. Closed for dinner on Saturdays and Sundays and during January and February. Reservations advised. 3 Rahapajankatu (phone: 179560). Expensive to moderate.

Kappeli – This large establishment has several dining rooms, a coffeehouse, and a beer cellar, with outdoor service in summer. Its atmosphere is part of its attraction. Near the colorful Market Square. A lively concert from the bandstand across the adjoining park accompanies your lunch. Dancing at night. Open daily. Reservations advised. Esplanadipuisto (Esplanadi Park; phone: 179242). Expensive to moderate.

Katariina – Across from the Lutheran cathedral in one of the city's oldest buildings, this family-operated place combines the French and Finnish cuisines. Recent reports indicate that the quality isn't quite up to par. Good wines by the glass, unusual for Finland. Closed Mondays. Reservations advised. 22-24 Aleksanterinkatu (phone: 656722). Expensive to moderate.

Kosmos – A slice of Finnish bohemian life — the patrons are painters, poets, and philosophers — with a versatile bistro menu. The beefy men at the door act as bouncers and check coats; local protocol dictates that you tip them 4 marks (about $1). Closed Saturdays and Sundays. Reservations necessary. 3 Kalevankatu (phone: 607717). Expensive to moderate.

Kynsilaukka – Garlic is the specialty of this restaurant where everything — soup, reindeer filets, and ice cream — is prepared with a touch of the clove. Go with someone you love. Open daily. Reservations advised. 22 Fredrikinkatu (phone: 651939). Expensive to moderate.

Piekka – Both the food and the atmosphere are authentically Finnish. The menu features rich soups, fresh fish and game according to season, and tasty desserts of local berries and cheeses. Open daily. Reservations advised. 68 Mannerheimintie (phone: 493591). Expensive to moderate.

Säkkipilli and The Old Baker's – A busy downtown spot with two restaurants, a pub, and a disco. Closed weekends. Reservations advised. Corner of 2 Kalevankatu and 12 Mannerheimintie (phone: 605607). *Säkkipilli,* expensive; *Old Baker's,* moderate.

Saslik – A favorite spot for day-trippers from Stockholm who rub elbows with locals and their foreign guests. Russian specialties are served in a labyrinth of rooms (along with live music). Try the beef and vegetable platter and a shot of chilled vodka. Closed Sundays. Reservations necessary. Major credit cards accepted. 12 Neitsytpolka (phone: 170544). Expensive to moderate.

Bulevardia – A bohemian bastion. The drinks and the people watching are a little more exciting than the food, which is tasty and not too pricey. Open daily. Reservations necessary. 34 Bulevardi (phone: 645243). Moderate.

Elite – Striking Functionalist decor was restored with loving care to create this restaurant frequented by artists and writers. Order local specialties like Baltic herring or *vorschmack,* or just try the soup and salad bar. Open daily. Reservations necessary. Excellent house wines. 22 Et. Hesperiankatu (phone: 495542). Moderate.

Wellamo – Locals come here for hearty soups and daily specials of the season according to the whim of the proprietress. The art on the walls is for sale and changes monthly. Closed Mondays. Reservations advised. 9 Vyokatu (phone: 663139). Moderate.

Happy Days – A no-frills coffee shop in the center of town. Open daily. Reservations unnecessary. 2 Pohjoisesplanadi (phone: 624023). Moderate to inexpensive.

Kasvisravintola – A basic vegetarian eatery, with a health food shop on the premises. Open daily. Reservations unnecessary. 3 Korkeavuorenkatu (phone: 179212). Moderate to inexpensive.

Aurora – A tearoom, serving light fare in a cozy atmosphere. Open daily. Reservations unnecessary. 50 Helsinginkatu (phone: 717400). Inexpensive.

Le Buffet – Drop in during a day of shopping to relax and enjoy seafood, fresh salads, or just a snack. Closed Sundays. Reservations unnecessary. *Forum Shopping Center,* 20 Mannerheimintie (phone: 694-1319). Inexpensive.

Café Ekberg – A Helsinki institution for breakfast, lunch, or simply tea. The baked goods are made daily on the premises. Closed Sundays. Reservations unnecessary. 9 Bulevardi (phone: 605269). Inexpensive.

Café Ursula – A café alongside the Kaivopuisto shore with a harbor view (phone: 652-817). Open daily. No reservations. Inexpensive.

Fazer – One of several tearooms/sweetshops run by the famed chocolate manufacturer, which also serves light meals and the best ice cream in town. Closed Sundays. No reservations. 3 Kluuvikatu (phone: 666597). Inexpensive.

Wanhan Kahuila – This student hangout is a good place to quaff a beer and have a chat. Terrace dining in summer. Open daily. No reservations. 3 Mannerheimintie (phone: 667376). Inexpensive.

LISBON

Lisbon is a bit like the heroine of an old movie who faces the gravest of perils in every reel — but emerges in the end still beautiful. During its more than 2,000 years of history, the city has undergone devastating earthquakes, plagues, fires, floods, invasions by barbarians, sackings, revolutions, and, more recently, the incursion of ugly urban development and pollution. But Lisbon remains beautiful, if a trifle faded and disheveled. At certain times of the day, the sun casts a golden reflection so intense that the broad expanse of estuary facing the city seems literally to live up to its popular name, Mar da Palha, or "Sea of Straw." And as the sun moves across the sky, the pastel buildings, tree-lined boulevards, cobblestone streets, and mosaic sidewalks of this city built in tiers on seven hills are bathed again and again in new perspectives of light.

Legend says that Lisbon was founded by Ulysses, who gave it the name Olisipo. Less romantic historians say that the ancient name was Phoenician in origin and that the city grew up gradually as a port town on the estuary of the Tagus River, where traders from many lands drew their boats to shore to sell their wares — or perhaps to raid. Gradually, safety-conscious inhabitants moved to the top of the hill where the old St. George's Castle stands today, and then, little by little, occupied the surrounding hills.

Over the centuries, many people came and went: Celts, Phoenicians, Carthaginians, Romans, Visigoths, and Moors, until the 12th century, when the city was taken by the Christian Portuguese. As Portugal built its vast empire during the 15th and 16th centuries, citizens from many diverse lands came to live in Lisbon. And when decades of dictatorship ended in 1974 and the country dissolved the remnants of its empire, a new wave of immigrants arrived from Angola, Mozambique, Timor, and the Cape Verde Islands.

More than 1.6 million people live in Lisbon and its environs today, and yet, in some ways, this westernmost capital of Europe is still a small town. The lisboetas, accustomed to foreigners, are tolerant of their visitors' ways, their dress, and their inability to speak Portuguese. They usually can give directions in English. Sometimes they will even drop what they are doing and take a visitor where he or she wants to go.

Lisbon has known moments of glory. The Romans, who arrived in 205 BC, made it, after Mérida in Spain, the most important city on the Iberian Peninsula, a place with baths, a theater, a 6-mile-long aqueduct (not the one standing today), and Roman roads stretching out in all directions. In their turn, the Moors, whose stay lasted from 714 to 1147, gathered their most brilliant thinkers, scientists, and writers at Aschbouna — as they renamed the city — and made it a renowned center of learning. Lisbon began to come into its own as Portuguese, however, only after its recapture from the Moors during the 12th century (Dom Afonso Henriques, Portugal's first king, and an army of crusaders from northern Europe besieged the castle for 17 weeks to accomplish that), and after King Afonso III's transfer of the court from Coimbra in 1260. By the 14th century, Lisbon had nearly 4 miles of walls, with 77 towers and 38 entranceways.

The city's greatest glory came during the 15th and 16th centuries. At a time when the world's seas were uncharted and darkness and superstition ruled people's imaginations, Lisbon was sending forth Portuguese caravels into the unknown, and her explorers were bringing the world's riches back from Africa, India, Brazil, and China. The Age of Discovery, as it is called, was ushered in by Prince Henry the Navigator (1394–1460), the son of King João I and his English wife, Philippa of Lancaster. During the early 15th century, Prince Henry established a school of navigation at Sagres, in southwest Portugal, and from there ships sailing under his authority explored the coast of Africa, making great strides in the study of geography, map making, and shipbuilding. His contributions to the advancement of exploration led, at the end of the century, not only to the epochal voyage of Christopher Columbus, but also to the voyages of Bartholomeu Dias, who rounded the Cape of Good Hope in 1488, and of Vasco da Gama, who sailed out from Lisbon in 1497 and returned 2 years later after reaching the Indies. Portugal's so-called Spice Age had begun.

Trade with India, and later with Brazil — discovered by Pedro Alvares Cabral in 1500 — made Lisbon immensely rich. By the 16th century, the city was a great commercial and maritime power, the "Queen of the Tagus," ruling from one of the best harbors in Europe. Churches and palaces were built. In 1502, King Manuel I, wishing to erect a memorial to Portugal's explorers, began construction of one of Lisbon's greatest monuments, the Jerónimos Monastery in Belém, the Lisbon suburb from which Vasco da Gama had set sail. The ropes, anchors, and seaweed carved on this building (and on others of the period) are typical of the uniquely Portuguese decorative style that came to be known as Manueline.

But all was not joyful. Persecution of Jews began during the late 15th century, and the Inquisition was introduced during the early 16th century, to endure some 200 years. Thousands were tortured in the Palace of the Inquisition in the Rossio, and many others died in the *autos-da-fé* held in the public squares of the city. In 1580, Philip II of Spain annexed the country and became Philip I of Portugal; Spanish rule lasted until 1640, when the Spanish governor of Lisbon was deposed by a group of Portuguese noblemen. Lisbon then revived its profitable trade with the rest of the world, and a spate of new building began. This time, given the discovery of gold in Brazil during the late 17th century, the characteristic decorative element of the period was richly gilded baroque woodwork (it is possible that the name of the baroque style may have come from the Portuguese word *barroco*, meaning "rough pearl"). The reign of João V (1706–50) was known for its magnificence.

Then, on *All Saints' Day* morning, November 1, 1755, while most of Lisbon was at mass, one of the worst earthquakes ever known shook the city like a straw in the wind. Within minutes, two-thirds of Lisbon was in ruins. A 40-foot tidal wave rose on the Tagus and slammed into the city. Fires, begun by tapers lighted in the churches for the feast day and fanned by a violent

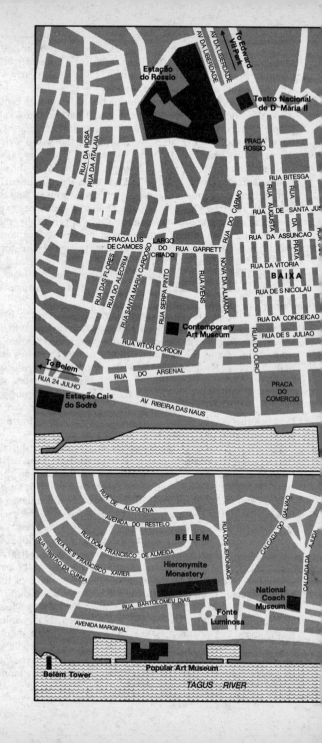

LISBON

RUA DA VERONICA

C DA GRACA

CAMPO DE SANTA CLARA

Castelo
São Jorge

São Vincente
de Fora

RUA DOS REMEDIOS

RUE DOS

RUA JARDIM DO TOBACO

ALFAMA

RUA JOAO EVANGELISTA

RUA DO BARAO

S MAMEDE

NEGRAS

Sé Catedral

S BACALHOEIROS

ALFANDEGA

TAGUS RIVER

windstorm, burned what the quake had left intact. As many as 40,000 people perished — causing philosophers, among them Voltaire, to conclude that this was not, after all, the most perfect of all worlds.

The prime minister, the Marquês de Pombal, quickly and efficiently set out to rebuild Lisbon on the rubble covering the valley floor between two of its hills. The stately plan of the city's classical squares and boulevards was traced out, and the straight lines and 18th-century proportions of the quarter called the Baixa — lower town — grew up in place of the previous medieval jumble. The Baixa's parallel streets are lined with nearly uniform, 5-story buildings.

Pombal is best remembered for this accomplishment, not for the reign of terror that he instituted against his enemies that made Lisbon a city of fear. Political turmoil marked the rest of the 18th century and the 19th. In 1908, King Carlos I and his son were assassinated in Praça do Comércio. In 1910, radical republicans overthrew the monarchy, forcing King Manuel II into exile. The political turbulence of the ensuing democratic republic gave way to dictatorship in 1926 and the rise to power of António de Oliveira Salazar, a professor of finance from Coimbra University, who ruled Portugal until 1968. He put the country's finances in order and kept Portugal out of World War II, but during the nearly half century he and his successor, Marcello Caetano, remained in power, Portugal was turned gradually into a police state.

On the 25th of April, 1974, a group of young officers staged a coup in Lisbon and helped set up a democratically elected government. It was a revolution in which few lives were lost, but it altered the face of the capital. As the streets became the scene of demonstrations by newly formed labor unions and political parties, once-pristine buildings and monuments were spray-painted with slogans, and mosaic sidewalks that used to be scoured daily became grubby. Up to this time, Lisbon had been the capital of the world's last colonial empire, but with the breakup of the empire following the revolution, nearly a million refugees poured into the city. The government housed some in hotels; others lived in shanties. Their crated belongings lined the banks of the Tagus.

Within a few years, the situation stabilized. The refugees were miraculously absorbed into the life of the city and helped make Lisbon a more dynamic place. The city's beauty began to reemerge from under the posters and slogans and grime. Many of the old buildings — the greater part of Lisbon's stock is from the late 18th and 19th centuries, with much plain, utilitarian architecture added during this century — are molding away from neglect. But some of the more important ones are getting a face wash and repairs. Post-modernist buildings, in glass and bright colors, mostly the work of architect Tomás Taveira, also have appeared.

Portugal joined the European Economic Community (Common Market) in 1986, bringing in new investment funds and new products for Lisbon's shelves. Anyone who knows the city, but has been absent for a while, will find that Lisbon today is not the same as it was even a very few years ago. Many of the streets in the Baixa are being closed to traffic and turned into pedestrian malls paved with cobblestones. Musicians entertain the strollers, and sidewalk artists sketch inexpensive portraits. Artisans offer jewelry, leatherwork, embroidery, and other wares from little stalls. There are many attractive open-air cafés and restaurants. Hotels have been renovated and more new accommodations for visitors seem to be added each year. The delights of Lisbon again are apparent; maybe that's why tourism is flourishing.

LISBON AT-A-GLANCE

SEEING THE CITY: A city built on hills frequently surprises visitors with lovely views that emerge without warning around unexpected corners. Lisbon is such a place. It has 17 natural balconies — called *miradouros* — from which to view the city. Foremost of these is the hilltop on which the ruins of St. George's Castle stand. All of the squares are laid out beneath: Praça do Comércio by the banks of the Tagus; the Rossio with its fountains and flower stalls; Praça da Figueira, the bustling market square; Praça dos Restauradores with its monument to Portugal's independence; the circular Praça Marquês de Pombal at the end of the broad Avenida da Liberdade; and beyond that, the lovely Parque Eduardo VII. On a clear day, it is possible to see the castles of Sintra far to the west. Another vantage point that's worth a pause is Largo de Santa Luzia, in the Alfama district, just downhill from the castle, between it and Lisbon's cathedral. Although the view from here — over the Alfama's red-roofed buildings down to the port — is less broadly panoramic than the one from the castle, the esplanade is charming, lined with *azulejos,* or glazed tiles, and endowed with flower beds, and a trellis-topped colonnade. (For those who prefer not to walk, it's reached by one of Lisbon's picturesque, vintage *eléctricos,* or trolleys — the No. 28.) A third *miradouro* is the terrace on Rua de São Pedro de Alcântara, on the opposite hill across the city in the Bairro Alto. From here there is a picture postcard view of the castle, with the Alfama district spread down the slopes below its walls.

Another breathtaking view is from the bridge across the Tagus, known since the 1974 revolution as Ponte 25 de Abril, but previously named for Salazar, who built it in the 1960s. The third-longest suspension bridge in the world, it is particularly spectacular at night, when its cables, the ships in the river, and the city are all brightly lit. On the other side, there is a marvelous panorama of the Tagus estuary from the top of the statue of Cristo Rei (Christ the King), a gift to Portugal from Brazil. (Open daily from 10 AM to 6 PM; there is an admission charge, and an elevator takes visitors up.) Those without a car can cross the river by ferry from Praça do Comércio and take a bus from Cacilhas to the statue.

SPECIAL PLACES: In ancient times, and later under the Moors, Lisbon was contained within walls that surrounded the hill where St. George's Castle now stands. Today, that area is the Alfama, the oldest part of the city, where traces of the picturesque Judiaria (Jewish Quarter) and Mouraria (Moorish Quarter) still can be seen, along with Roman remains. The Alfama has been destroyed several times by earthquakes, but it always was rebuilt along the same plan, its tortuous, narrow streets spiraling down from the top of the hill to the Baixa below. The Baixa, to the west of the Alfama, is the main shopping and commercial district of Lisbon. Built after the earthquake in a grid fashion, it stretches northward from Praça do Comércio by the river to the top of the Rossio, one of the city's main squares, and includes such aptly named streets as Rua Aurea (its official name — confusingly, it's generally known and shown on most maps as Rua do Ouro, which means the same thing — Gold Street) and Rua da Prata (Silver Street), which are lined with fine jewelers and banks. Up the hill and west of the Rossio is the part of the Baixa known locally as the Chiado — not much more than 10 square blocks. This also is a popular shopping district dotted with coffeehouses and outdoor cafés, but a disastrous fire in September 1988 destroyed a great number of the shops — including two of Europe's oldest department stores — and other landmarks. Happily, most of the façades of the burned buildings remained standing after the flames were put out, even though the interiors were gutted, and recently announced rebuilding plans call for restoration of the district, rather than wholesale modernization. The plan, which includes turning the shell of one of the former department stores into an exclusive hotel and the other into a shopping and cultural center, is expected to take six years to complete.

Higher up is the Bairro Alto, or High Quarter, above and to the west of Praça dos Restauradores and the Rossio. At one time a wealthy (and later a seedy) residential district, it has been taken over by the avant-garde and become the center of nightlife in downtown Lisbon, with fine restaurants, typical *tascas* (taverns or small eating places), and *fado* houses, where sad Portuguese folk songs are sung. West of the Bairro Alto are the Madragoa and Lapa districts, residential areas where restaurants, government buildings, embassies, and several museums and art galleries also can be found. Modern Lisbon, with museums, the zoo, and new quarters, stretches to the north and east of the downtown area.

The Belém quarter is along the riverbank west of all of the above. Because it suffered very little in the 1755 earthquake, many of its fine palaces and monuments are still standing. Belém also is home to several museums, as well as many restaurants.

ST. GEORGE'S CASTLE AND THE ALFAMA

Castelo de São Jorge (St. George's Castle) – Built on one of Lisbon's highest hills, this castle with ten towers is considered the cradle of the city. An Iron Age *castro,* or fortified hilltop town, probably was located here, succeeded by Roman fortifications (Roman walls and other remains are being excavated), a fortress built by the Visigoths during the 5th century, and later, a Moorish fortified town. The present castle was built during the 12th century. Within the grounds are lovely gardens where peacocks roam free, the remains of an Arabian palace where the Kings of Portugal lived from the 14th to the 16th century, and a restaurant, the *Casa do Leão* (locals consider it overpriced for the quality of the food, although the locale is attractive). From the terrace on the south and west sides and from the walk around the towers, the views of Lisbon are extensive. Open daily from 9 AM to 9 PM (7 PM from October through March). No admission charge. Rua Costa do Castelo.

Alfama – This Old Quarter slopes downhill from St. George's Castle. A cobbled labyrinth with some streets so narrow that pedestrians must walk in single file, it is one of the most colorful spots in Europe. Its streets are overhung with balconies ablaze with scarlet geraniums and lined with little taverns decorated with strings of peppers, garlic, and cheese. By day, caged canaries on the balconies sing in the sun; at night, wrought-iron lamps light the scene; and on washdays, the buildings are strung with clotheslines and drying laundry. Although some medieval mansions and Moorish buildings exist, most of the houses date from the late 18th century, after the earthquake. The best times to see the Alfama are in the morning when the markets are open, late in the afternoon when the streets and squares are alive with people, or on a moonlit evening. The quarter stretches north to south from the castle to the banks of the Tagus, and west to east from the cathedral to the vicinity of the church of São Vicente de Fora.

Sé (Cathedral) – Lisbon's oldest church, built just after the Christian Reconquest of the 12th century, suffered enormous earthquake damage in 1755, but was rebuilt during the 18th century and restored during this one. It is a typical fortress-church of solid, massive construction, with battlements and towers. The plain façade is Romanesque, the ambulatory chapels and the cloister are pure Gothic, and the choir is baroque. In the *azulejo*-lined enclosure just inside the door is the baptismal font of St.

Anthony of Padua, Portugal's patron saint, who was born here (although he spent much of his life in Italy), and in the chapel to the left is a *presépio* (Nativity scene) by Joaquim Machado de Castro. Relics of St. Vincent, patron saint of Lisbon, also are in the cathedral, but are brought out only on special occasions. There is a museum of religious vestments and ecclesiastical gold, currently closed for repairs. The cloister is open from 9 AM to 1 PM and from 2 to 4 PM; closed Mondays (cathedral open Mondays, however). Admission charge to the cloister. Largo da Sé (phone: 866752).

Museu-Escola de Artes Decorativas (Museum-School of Decorative Arts) – Located just around the bend from the Largo de Santa Luzia *miradouro* and housed in a 17th-century palace that survived the earthquake, this museum contains collections of Portuguese porcelain, silver, crystal, paintings, tapestries, and furniture, mostly of the 17th and 18th centuries. They're not arranged museum-style, but much more beguilingly as the furnishings of an aristocratic Lisboan home of yesteryear. The objects once were the property of Dr. Ricardo Espírito Santo Silva, who set up a foundation both to create a museum and to preserve the skills and tools of traditional Portuguese craftsmanship. The foundation runs a school and workshops for the reproduction and restoration of antiques — furniture, books, fabrics, and so on — adjacent to the museum, which visitors may tour. An appointment is required for the workshops (phone: 872183). The museum is open Tuesdays through Saturdays from 10 AM to 1 PM and 2:30 to 5 PM. Admission charge. 2 Largo das Portas do Sol (phone: 862184).

Igreja de São Vicente de Fora (Church of St. Vincent Outside the Walls) – From Largo das Portas do Sol, follow the *eléctrico* tracks down Escadinhas de São Tomé and then up again to this church, which was built during the late 16th and early 17th centuries by Filippo Terzi and sports a mannerist façade. A remnant of an old monastery, it is notable for its cloisters, lavishly lined with 18th-century *azulejos*. Beyond, set up in the old monastery refectory, is the Panteão Real (Royal Pantheon), the mausoleum of the Bragança family, which ruled Portugal from 1640 to 1910. Most of the Bragança kings and queens, including Portugal's last monarchs, are buried here. Open from 10 AM to 5 PM; closed Mondays. Admission charge to the cloisters and pantheon also gains entrance to an ornate sacristy, lined with inlaid marble. Largo de São Vicente (phone: 876470).

Igreja de Santa Engrácia – Begun during the 17th century but not completed until 1966, when it also was restored, this church gave rise to a Portuguese expression, *"obras de Santa Engrácia,"* used to describe a seemingly never-ending task. The grandiose structure, with a baroque façade and an interior richly decorated in marble, now serves as the Panteão Nacional (National Pantheon), containing the tombs of three Portuguese presidents and three writers, as well as memorials to other famous figures — including Prince Henry the Navigator, Luís de Camões, and Vasco da Gama — who are not buried here. This is within easy walking distance of São Vicente, but on Tuesdays and Saturdays, you may be detained by the flea market that's set up on the street between the two. Open from 10 AM to 5 PM; closed Mondays. Admission charge. Campo de Santa Clara (phone: 871529).

Museu Militar (Military Museum) – Housed in an 18th-century arsenal (the huge, saffron-yellow building in front of the Santa Apolónia train station), it contains cannon, guns, swords, armor, and uniforms, as well as paintings, sculptures, coin collections, and other mementos of Portugal's wars. One room is dedicated to the discoveries of Vasco da Gama. Open Tuesdays through Saturdays from 10 AM to 4 PM; Sundays, from 11 AM to 5 PM. Admission charge. Largo dos Caminhos de Ferro (phone: 867135).

Igreja da Madre de Deus (Church of the Mother of God) – Although the convent complex here was founded in 1501, most of what is seen today was built during the 18th century. The church is resplendent with ornate, gilded baroque woodwork, oil paintings, and *azulejos,* but the church is only part of the attraction, because the *Museu*

Nacional do Azulejo is installed in the convent complex, and it's a must-see for tile lovers. Exquisite examples of the art, both Portuguese and foreign, from the 15th century to the present, are displayed in rooms around two cloisters, one of them a small gem. In addition to its other treasures, the museum possesses a long tile frieze dating from approximately 1730 depicting a panorama of Lisbon before the earthquake. There's also a pleasant cafeteria, decorated with 19th-century kitchen tiles. Open from 10 AM to 5 PM; closed Mondays. Admission charge. Bus No. 13A from Praça do Comércio goes to the convent. Rua da Madre de Deus (phone: 814-7747).

Nossa Senhora da Conceição Velha – Built during the early 16th century on the site of Lisbon's ancient synagogue, this was completely devastated in the 1755 earthquake, but its original Manueline portal survived. The beautiful doorway, richly carved with limestone figures, was retained for the new church — which, however, has little of note inside. Rua da Alfândega.

Casa dos Bicos (House of Pointed Stones) – When it was built during the 16th century, this house belonged to the family of Afonso de Albuquerque, a famous Portuguese viceroy to India. The earthquake reduced the 4-story structure to only several feet of foundations, but it has been completely rebuilt. The façade is covered with pyramidal stones, similar to the Casa de los Picos in Segovia, Spain, and the Palazzo dei Diamanti in Ferrara, Italy. The house is now used as an art gallery and is open to the public only when there are special exhibitions. Rua dos Bacalhoeiros (phone: 877330).

BAIXA

Praça do Comércio – This impressive riverside square, laid out after the earthquake by the Marquês de Pombal, is edged on three sides by arcaded neo-classical buildings. It's also known as Terreiro do Paço (Palace Square), after the royal palace that stood here in pre-earthquake days, and, to the English, as Black Horse Square, after the bronze equestrian statue of King José I, a design by the 18th-century sculptor Joaquim Machado de Castro, standing in the middle. The triumphal arch on the north side of the square, leading to Rua Augusta and the rest of the Baixa, was finished during the late 19th century. The square was the scene of the assassination of King Carlos I and his son in 1908.

Rossio – Officially called Praça de Dom Pedro IV, after the 18th-century king who is the subject of the statue in the center, this is the heart of the city and the northern limit of the Baixa. As early as the 13th century, this was the city's marketplace, but like Praça do Comércio and the rest of the Baixa, it was destroyed by the earthquake of 1755; the square was then newly laid out by Pombal. On the north side is the 19th-century *Teatro Nacional de Dona Maria II,* standing on the site of a onetime royal palace that during the 16th century, became the seat of the Inquisition. The square is much cheerier now, graced with flower stalls, fountains, and open-air cafés.

Elevador de Santa Justa (Santa Justa Elevator) – This lacy gray iron structure reminiscent of the Eiffel Tower — and often erroneously attributed to Eiffel — was designed by Raoul Mesnier, a Portuguese engineer of French descent, and erected in 1898. It not only spares visitors' feet the climb from Rua do Ouro (Rua Aurea) to Largo do Carmo in the Chiado, but also provides a panoramic view of the city from the top, and as you exit, you pass under a flying buttress of the Igreja do Carmo. The elevator runs from 7 AM to 11 PM (from 9 AM on Sundays).

Igreja do Carmo (Carmo Church) – Built during the 14th century, this was an imposing, majestic structure that overlooked the city until it was largely destroyed by the 1755 earthquake. The shell, with Gothic arches and a Gothic doorway, remains, and is floodlit at night. The ruins have been turned into the *Museu Arqueológico do Carmo,* containing prehistoric, Roman, Visigothic, and medieval artifacts, as well as medieval sculpture, *azulejos,* and inscriptions. Open from 10 AM to 1 PM and from 2 to 5 PM (July through September, 10 AM to 6 PM); closed Sundays. Admission charge. Largo do Carmo (phone: 346-0473).

BAIRRO ALTO

Solar do Vinho do Porto – This comfortable bar run by the Port Wine Institute is the next best thing to a trip to Portugal's northern capital. It's stocked with all types and vintages of porto — the official name for port wine — which visitors can order by the glass. There are about 160 different kinds, so go early or, better, often. Open daily, from 10 AM to 11:30 PM. 45 Rua de São Pedro de Alcântara (phone: 347-5707).

Igreja de São Roque (Church of St. Rock) – This 16th-century church has a flat wooden ceiling painted to look like a vaulted one, but it's best known for the baroque Capela de São João Baptista, the fourth chapel on the left. The chapel was commissioned during the mid-18th century by King João V, designed in Rome and assembled there, blessed by the pope — and then dismantled, to be shipped to Portugal and rebuilt at its present address. The lapis lazuli, porphyry, marble, alabaster, ivory, and other precious and semi-precious building materials cost the king dearly, but the workmanship was impeccable, as can be seen in the *Baptism of Christ,* which looks like an oil painting but is actually an exquisitely fine mosaic. The *Museu de São Roque* adjoining the church contains paintings and liturgical objects and richly embroidered vestments. Admission charge to the museum, which is open from 10 AM to 5 PM; closed Mondays. Church remains open after museum closes. Largo Trindade Coelho (phone: 346-0361).

NORTHERN AND WESTERN LISBON

Parque Eduardo VII (Edward VII Park) – Downtown Lisbon's largest green space is this formally landscaped park at the northern end of Avenida da Liberdade, just beyond Praça Marquês de Pombal. From the esplanade at the top of the park, the view extends over the lower town to the Tagus. In the northwest corner is the charming Estufa Fria (Cold Greenhouse), where lush tropical plants grow in abundance among streams, pools, and waterfalls. A slatted roof protects them from the extremes of summer and winter. Within the Estufa Fria is a hothouse, the Estufa Quente. Open daily from 9 AM to 6 PM (5 PM in winter); the Estufa Quente closes a half-hour earlier. Admission charge (phone: 682278).

Museu Calouste Gulbenkian (Gulbenkian Museum) – When the Armenian oil tycoon Calouste Sarkis Gulbenkian died in 1955, he left most of his estate and his enormous art collection to Portugal, the country to which he had fled during World War II and where he spent the last years of his life. The result was the Calouste Gulbenkian Foundation, a modern building that houses not only this museum, but also auditoriums, a library, and exhibition space. Don't miss the museum, a repository of 50 years of astute collecting — 3,000 pieces including works Gulbenkian bought from the *Hermitage Museum* in the 1920s when the Soviet Union needed foreign currency. The treasures include fine European paintings, sculpture, 18th-century French furniture, Chinese vases, Greek coins, medieval ivories, illuminated manuscripts, Middle Eastern carpets and ceramics, and more. There also is a marvelous collection of small Egyptian pieces and a unique collection of Art Nouveau jewelry by René Lalique. Open June through November from 10 AM to 5 PM; closed Mondays (winter hours are the same except for Wednesdays and Saturdays, when the museum opens at 2 PM and closes at 7 PM). Admission charge. 45 Avenida de Berna (phone: 793-4068).

Centro de Arte Moderna (Modern Art Center) – In the gardens behind the *Gulbenkian Museum,* it has an impressive collection of 19th- and 20th-century Portuguese paintings and sculpture, including paintings by José de Almada Negreiros. A cafeteria overlooks the gardens. The hours are the same as those of the *Gulbenkian Museum.* Admission charge. Rua Dr. Nicolau de Bettencourt (phone: 793-4068).

Jardim Zoológico (Zoo) – Set in a 65-acre park, the zoo is home to some 2,000 animals, including an elephant who rings a bell for money. Other distractions include pony rides for children, rowboats, and a small train. Open daily, from 9 AM to 8 PM, from April through October (closes at 6 PM the rest of the year). Admission charge. Parque das Laranjeiras (phone: 726-8041).

Palácio dos Marqueses da Fronteira – West of the zoo, on the edge of the Parque Florestal de Monsanto, is an interesting palace built during the second half of the 17th century and originally used by its aristocratic owners as a hunting lodge. It's notable for the great number of *azulejos* that cover its walls — both inside and outside in the formal gardens — many of them depicting historical events. The palace still is privately owned but open to visitors on Mondays and Wednesdays from 10 AM to noon and on Saturdays from 3 to 6:30 PM. Admission charge. 1 Largo de São Domingos de Benfica (phone: 782023).

Aqueduto das Aguas Livres – Built during the first half of the 18th century to bring water from Caneças (11 miles/18 km northwest of Lisbon) to a reservoir near the present-day Amoreiras complex, the Aguas Livres Aqueduct miraculously survived the 1755 earthquake and still supplies the city with drinking water. It consists of 109 stone arches, some of them underground, but an impressive stretch of it (with one arch 214 feet high) runs through the Parque Florestal de Monsanto and the Campolide section of town, and can be seen from the road (N7) that leads to Estoril and Sintra. With special permission, it is possible to visit the inside of the aqueduct, with its fountains and statuary; inquire at the tourist office.

Basílica da Estrela (Basilica of the Star) – Built by Queen Maria I between 1779 and 1790, it fulfilled a vow she had made while petitioning God to grant her a son. The dome is one of Lisbon's landmarks; the tomb of the founder is inside. This church reflects the style of the school of sculpture founded at Mafra by the Italian sculptor Alessandro Giusti, one of whose Portuguese pupils, Joaquim Machado de Castro, was responsible for the manger figures here. Open daily. Praça da Estrela.

Museu Nacional de Arte Antiga (National Museum of Ancient Art) – One of the most important of Lisbon's museums, this is housed partly in a 17th-century palace that once belonged to Pombal and partly in an adjacent 20th-century building. Although it contains numerous foreign works, such as a celebrated Bosch triptych, *The Temptation of St. Anthony,* the museum is most notable for its paintings of the Portuguese school, especially of the 15th and 16th centuries. The prize in this group — perhaps the most famous painting in Portugal — is the six-panel polyptych known as the *Panéis de São Vicente de Fora* (St. Vincent Panels), a masterpiece by Nuno Gonçalves, the most important Portuguese painter of the 15th century. The polyptych is precious not only for its artistic merit (and because it's the only Gonçalves painting still extant), but also because it constitutes a document of Portuguese society of the time. Also in the museum are sculptures; Portuguese, European, and Oriental ceramics; objects in silver and gold; jewelry, furniture, and tapestries; and the entire gilt-and-tile laden Saint Albert Chapel, an architectural leftover from a Carmelite convent that once occupied the spot. A tea garden overlooking the river is open in summer. Open from 10 AM to 1 PM and from 2:30 to 5 PM; closed Mondays. Admission charge. 95 Rua das Janelas Verdes (phone: 672725).

BELÉM

Mosteiro dos Jerónimos (Hieronymite Monastery) – One of Lisbon's great landmarks, this white marble monastery was founded in 1502 by King Manuel I to give thanks for the successful return of Vasco da Gama's fleet from the Indies and to commemorate all the great voyages of Portugal's explorers during the Age of Discovery. Because Vasco da Gama had sailed from Belém in 1497, to return 2 years later, the site of a small mariners' chapel here seemed a fitting one for the memorial, about which it is said that it was "built by pepper," since it was paid for by riches brought by the spice trade. The sea motifs — seashells, ropes, anchors, and other symbols — that are carved throughout in great profusion are the characteristic decorative elements of the Manueline style of architecture, a uniquely Portuguese style that represented a transition from Gothic to Renaissance and eventually took its name from the king, Dom Manuel. The monastery is considered the country's finest example of Manueline architecture: The two portals, the extremely slender columns and characteristic network vaulting of the church, and the richly sculpted 2-story cloister are exceptionally beautiful. King Manuel I and several other monarchs are buried in the church, as is Vasco da Gama, whose tomb, just inside the entrance, is marked by a caravel. Opposite it, marked by a lyre and quill pen, is a monument to Luís de Camões, whose bones may or may not be inside (he died in Africa, and the wrong bones may have been brought back). The long galleries to the west of the monastery, neo-Manueline from the 19th century, contain the *Museu Nacional de Arqueologia e Etnologia* (open from 10 AM to 2 PM and from 2 to 5 PM; closed Mondays; admission charge) and, around the corner, the *Museu da Marinha* (see below). More modern annexes across the courtyard from the entrance to the latter contain its collection of real boats rather than models and the *Planetario Calouste Gulbenkian,* which has presentations several days a week (times are posted outside; admission charge). The monastery is open from 10 AM to 6:30 PM, July through September (to 5 PM the rest of the year); closed Mondays. Admission charge to the cloister. Praça do Império (phone: 617020).

Museu da Marinha (Naval Museum) – In the 19th-century galleries attached to the monastery, plus a modern extension to handle the overflow, this museum contains small models of boats from all eras of Portuguese history, from the earliest caravels of the Age of Discovery to warships, trading ships, and submarines — along with naval uniforms and other marine paraphernalia. Real boats are exhibited in the hangar-like extension. Of them the late-18th-century *galeota,* or galley, built for the wedding of Crown Prince João (who became João VI) to a Spanish princess and rowed by 71 red-coated figures, is the star. Examples of traditional boats from various regions include a *rabelo* boat from the Douro River, a *moliceiro* from the Ria de Aveiro, and fishing boats from the Algarve. Open from 10 AM to 5 PM; closed Mondays. Admission charge. Praça do Império (phone: 362-0010).

Museu Nacional dos Coches (National Coach Museum) – Probably the finest coach collection in the world, housed in a building that was once the riding school of the Palácio de Belém, formerly a royal palace and now the presidential palace. The collection contains coaches ranging from the 16th through 19th centuries, and although a few are simple (such as the first one as you enter, which carried Philip III of Spain when he came to claim the throne as King Philip II of Portugal), most are beautifully carved, gilded works of art suitable for transporting royal personages or their emissaries (note the three Italian-made 18th-century baroque extravaganzas used by the Portuguese Ambassador to the Holy See). Open from 10 AM to 1 PM and from 2:30 to 6:30 PM (closes at 5:30 PM from October through May); closed Mondays. Admission charge. Praça Afonso de Albuquerque (phone: 363-8022).

Padrão dos Descobrimentos (Monument to the Discoveries) – On the river in front of the monastery, this is a modern monument, put up in 1960 to commemorate the 500th anniversary of the death of Prince Henry the Navigator. It's shaped like the prow of a Portuguese caravel, with the prince as a figurehead leading a sculptured frieze of the personages of the time seaward. Inside, besides exhibition space, there's an elevator to a belvedere on top, from where the view extends up and down the Tagus and over formally laid-out green lawns to the Mosteiro dos Jerónimos and the rest of Belém. Open Tuesdays through Sundays from 9 AM to 7 PM (to 6 PM October through February); opens at 2 PM on Mondays; admission charge to the belvedere. Praça do Império.

Torre de Belém (Tower of Belém) – This quadrangular, 5-story tower, which looks like a huge chess piece, stands on the banks of the Tagus, west of the Monument to the Discoveries. The Portuguese consider it a symbol of their brave past, and its image often is used on official papers. Built during the 16th century to protect the river from pirates (because land has been reclaimed from the river since then, the tower was at one time farther out, surrounded by water), it later functioned as a prison. This is another example of Manueline architecture, richly decorated with sea motifs, statues, stone tracery, and Moorish balconies. Inside is a permanent exhibition of 15th- and 16th-century armaments and navigational instruments. Visitors may climb to the top for a view of the Tagus from the outside terrace. Open from 10 AM to 6:30 PM (to 5 PM from October through May); closed Mondays. Admission charge. Off Avenida Marginal (phone: 301-6982).

Palácio Nacional da Ajuda – In the hills behind Belém, this former royal palace was built during the early 19th century and is full of furniture, paintings, sculpture, and objets d'art left much as they were when royalty still occupied the premises. The widow of King Luís, Maria Pia of Savoy, who died in 1911, was its last royal inhabitant, but the palace is still used occasionally by the Portuguese government for state dinners. Open from 10 AM to 5 PM; closed Mondays. Admission charge. Largo da Ajuda (phone: 363-7095).

ENVIRONS

Estoril – This seaside suburb about 15½ miles (25 km) west of Lisbon became internationally famous during World War II when both Allied and Axis spies were tripping over each other, notably at the *Palácio* hotel. Since Portugal was neutral, there was a gentlemen's agreement: Allied diplomats could play golf at the local clubs on certain days, Axis diplomats on others. Immediately after the war, Estoril became home for numerous members of Europe's exiled royalty, giving it a touch of glamour. The crowned heads are gone now, but Estoril, with its bars and cafés and its gambling casino, is still a glamorous place. Its large turn-of-the-century mansions, hidden away behind spacious lawns and gardens flanking winding, hilly streets and wide avenues, lend it a definitely Old World air. The Parque do Estoril, a lovely garden of stately palm trees and purple-red bougainvillea, faces the seaside esplanade and the beach. The modern, elegant *Casino Estoril* sits at the top of the park. The residential district of Monte Estoril is west of the park, tending to merge with Cascais. Estoril can be reached easily by train from Lisbon's Cais do Sodré station or via the beach highway (Estrada Marginal).

Cascais – Once a simple fishing village whose picturesque, brightly painted boats headed out to sea each morning, Cascais (pronounced Kash-ka-*ish*) evolved during this century into a beach resort and the home of thousands of European — especially British — expatriates and, like Estoril, deposed royalty and dictators. Today, the fast-growing town, just west of Estoril, makes its living largely from tourism, although fishermen remain and the sight of fish being auctioned off at the market (on weekday evenings) by the beach is worth seeing. Cascais has few monuments to detain sightseers: There is one important church, the Manueline Nossa Senhora da Assunção, notable for its 18th-century *azulejos* and for its paintings by Josefa d'Obidos; the Citadel, a 17th-century military building; and the *Museu-Biblioteca Condes de Castro Guimarães*, with paintings, sculpture, furniture, and objets d'art set up in an old mansion (open 10 AM to 5 PM; closed Tuesdays; no admission charge). It has plenty of other distractions, however. The bullfights held on summer Sundays at the Monumental de Cascais attract many visitors. Water sports and sailing are available from its beaches; there are also riding stables, tennis courts, and golf courses in the vicinity. The town (and the coast around it) are famous for their seafood restaurants, many of which overlook the bay and the sea. There is no dearth of nightlife, either, as Cascais is full of bars and discos.

Along the coast west of town is the Boca do Inferno (Mouth of Hell), a set of rocky cliffs full of caves and smaller cavities through which the sea storms and rages — an awesome sight. Farther along the coast road, 5½ miles (9 km) from Cascais, is Praia do Guincho, an immense stretch of sand between two promontories where the wind howls (*guincho* means "shriek"), the sea is rough, and the undertow dangerous; it is popular with brave surfers. Still farther along is a headland, Cabo da Roca, the western-most point of continental Europe, where there is a lighthouse. Cascais can be reached by train from Lisbon's Cais do Sodré station.

Queluz – This town 7½ miles (12 km) northwest of Lisbon is known for its lovely pink rococo Palácio Nacional, where official guests of the Portuguese government usually are housed. The palace was begun in 1747 by the Infante Dom Pedro, who became Pedro III, consort of Queen Maria I, an unfortunate queen who lived here after going mad following Pedro's death and that of her oldest son. Designed by Mateus Vicente de Oliveira, a pupil of the architect of the Mafra Monastery, the royal residence took decades to finish and has been restored after being partially destroyed by fire in this century. Its rooms are filled with Portuguese furnishings and tapestries, Italian glassware and marble, Dutch tiles, Chinese screens, Austrian porce-lain, and other exquisite antiques; its gardens are laid out to resemble those of Ver-sailles (Queen Maria had been engaged to Louis XV), with fountains, statuary, and *azulejos*. Among the more striking rooms are the Throne Room, the Hall of Mirrors, the Hall of the Ambassadors, the Music Salon, and the Queen's Dressing Room. Chamber music concerts and other cultural events take place here during the sum-mer. The palace is open from 10 AM to 1 PM and from 2 to 5 PM; closed Tuesdays. Admission charge (phone: 435-0039). Queluz can be reached by train from Lisbon's Rossio station.

■**EXTRA SPECIAL:** The beauty of Sintra, a town on the north slope of the Serra de Sintra about 17½ miles (28 km) northwest of Lisbon, has been sung through the ages, most notably by Portugal's most famous poet, Camões, in *The Lusiads,* and by Lord Byron, who called it a "glorious Eden" in "Childe Harold." The town has an enchanting setting, swathed in towering trees, dense ferns, and plants and flowers of every description brought by the Portuguese from all corners of their once far-flung empire — all kept green by water gushing from the rocks in springs and little waterfalls tumbling everywhere down the mountain. Mists from the nearby Atlantic often envelop its heights and lend it an ethereal and unreal air (as well as give it a pleasant climate in summer while, on occasion, obscuring its majestic views). Among the oldest towns in Portugal, it was occupied by the Moors, who built two castles, one of them winding around the side of the mountain from pinnacle to pinnacle and the other in the center of the present town. After Sintra was taken from the Moors in the 12th century, it became a favorite summer residence of the Portuguese monarchs. Over the centuries, they built the imposing National Palace in town on the site of one of the Moorish castles and the whimsi-cal, *Disneyland*-like Pena Palace on the very peak of the mountain, where it can be seen from as far away as Lisbon and the Arrábida Peninsula.

Sintra is very crowded in summer and on weekends. It can be reached by car on N117 and N249 or by train from the Rossio station. Those who come by train can take a taxi to visit the palaces that are located at some distance from the center; otherwise, the tourist office at Praça da República (phone: 923-1157) provides maps for those who want to walk. There also are horse-drawn carriages that take visitors sightseeing around town. Good restaurants and hotels abound, as do excellent shops selling handicrafts, especially rugs, porcelain, and straw goods. The Feira de São Pedro de Sintra, a market that takes place on the second and fourth Sundays of every month, sells everything imaginable. During the *Sintra*

Music Festival, held from mid-June to mid-July, concerts take place in the palaces and other public buildings.

The Palácio Nacional de Sintra, in the main square, was built on the foundations of a Moorish palace by King João I in the late 14th century and added to by King Manuel I in the early 16th century. Later, it received still further additions, making the enormous structure a survey of styles from Moorish through Mudéjar, Gothic, Manueline, and Renaissance to baroque. Outside, besides the twin conical chimneys that dominate the town, the most notable feature of the palace are the characteristic Manueline windows. Inside, its most important features are the *azulejos* facing its walls throughout, some of the finest to be seen in the country. One of the most interesting rooms is the Sala dos Brazoës (Hall of the Coats of Arms), built during Manuel's reign; its ceiling is an octagonal wooden cupola whose painted panels show the coats of arms of the king, his 8 children, and the 72 noble familes of Portugal at the time. (The blue-and-white wall tiles depicting hunting scenes are from the 18th century.) In the Sala das Pêgas (Hall of the Magpies), the ceiling is decorated with 136 magpies — painted, so the story goes, on the orders of João I after his wife, Philippa of Lancaster, caught him kissing one of the ladies-in-waiting. (There were 136 ladies-in-waiting at court, and the idea was to put an end to gossip among them.) The largest room is the Sala dos Cisnes (Hall of Swans), so named because of the ceramic swans decorating it and the painted ones on the ceiling. The palace is open from 10 AM to 1 PM and from 2 to 5 PM; closed Wednesdays. Admission charge (phone: 923-4118).

The Palácio Nacional da Pena, standing on the highest peak above Sintra, is reached up a spectacular road of hairpin curves through beautiful parks and woods. After religious orders were expelled from Portugal in 1832, Ferdinand of Saxe-Coburg-Gotha, consort of Queen Maria II, bought a small 16th-century monastery that stood on this spot and commissioned a German architect, Baron Eschewege, to create a new medieval palace around it. Inspired by the Bavarian castles in his own country, the architect combined their styles with Moorish, Gothic, and Manueline elements to create a fantastic building complete with gold-topped domes, turrets, crenelated walls, parapets, and a drawbridge. The cloister and chapel of the monastery were preserved; the latter has a black alabaster and marble altarpiece executed in the 16th century by Nicolas Chanterene, although its stained glass windows are 19th-century German. The rooms of the palace proper are filled with furniture and ornaments of many different periods and are particularly noteworthy because they have been left much as they were when last occupied by the royal family, which fled into exile in 1910. The views from the palace verandahs are spectacular, and the Parque da Pena surrounding it, planted in the 19th century, also is impressive, containing plants and trees from all over the world. The palace is open from 9 AM to 6 PM (to 5 PM in winter); closed Mondays. Admission charge (phone: 923-0227).

Still another of Sintra's palaces, the *Palácio dos Seteais,* has been turned into a luxury hotel (see *Checking In*), but there are other sights to see, including the Castelo dos Mouros, or Moorish Castle, located off the same road that leads to the Pena Palace, about halfway up the mountain. It was originally built by the Moors in the 8th or 9th century and was restored after the Christian Reconquest of the 12th century and later by King Fernando I. It has five rather dilapidated towers, a keep, and long walls that undulate over a great part of the mountain. Elsewhere is the Quinta de Monserrate, a palace and park built by a 19th-century Englishman, Sir Francis Cook, about 2 miles (3 km) from Sintra via N375. The palace is an odd-looking, three-domed structure, but it is the wonderful gardens, landscaped on a steep slope, that are the prime attraction (open daily, from 9 AM to sunset; admission charge). Another sight is the Convento dos Capuchos, 4 miles

(6 km) from town via N247-3. Built in the 16th century, it is a peculiar place in that the monks' cells are carved out of rock and lined with cork to keep out the damp. (Ring the bell and the caretaker will open the door.)

SOURCES AND RESOURCES

TOURIST INFORMATION: Maps, brochures, shopping guides, listings of monthly events, and other information can be obtained from any of the Postos de Turismo (Tourist Posts) run by the Direcção-Geral do Turismo (Directorate General for Tourism), which is headquartered at 86 Avenida António Augusto de Aguiar. A tourist post is located at the same address (phone: 575086), but perhaps the most convenient one in downtown Lisbon is the one at Palácio Foz (Praça dos Restauradores; phone: 346-3624). Other branches are at Lisbon Airport (phone: 885974), at the Santa Apolónia train station (phone: 867848), and at the Alcântara boat dock (phone: 600756). English-speaking staff is available to answer questions and help make hotel reservations. It is possible to hire English-speaking guides through the tourist offices or by calling the guides union, the Sindicato Nacional da Actividade Turistica, Tradutores e Intérpretes (phone: 343-3298).

The US Embassy is on Avenida das Forças Armadas (phone: 726-6600).

Local Coverage – The leading daily is the *Diário de Notícias,* a morning paper. *Seminario* and *Expresso* are two of the most prestigious weekly papers. English-language newspapers and magazines are on sale at most newsstands.

TELEPHONE: The country code for Portugal is 351; the city code for Lisbon is 1. If calling from within Portugal, dial 01 before the local number.

GETTING AROUND: Although various sections of the city, such as the Alfama, are ideal for strolling, remember that Lisbon is built on seven hills; visitors probably will want to ride from one section to another. Parking is problematic, so public transportation and taxis are the best bet.

Airport – Lisbon's airport for both domestic and international flights, Portela de Sacavém (phone: 802060), is only 5 miles (8 km) northeast of the center, a 15- to 30-minute drive, depending on traffic. Taxi fare to most hotels should come to about $7. The *Linha Verde* (Green Line) express bus runs between the airport and the Santa Apolónia train station, stopping at major downtown points. *TAP Air Portugal* has a local address (3A Praça Marquês de Pombal; phone: 544080 or 575020). For information on *TAP*'s subsidiary, *Linhas Aéreas Regionais* (*LAR*), which has flights to many cities in Portugal, call 848-7119 or 848-0637.

Boat – Ferryboats, carrying both passengers and cars, cross the Tagus every few minutes from the Praça do Comércio and Cais do Sodré for Cacilhas, Barreiro, and other points. There also is a river service to Cascais. Short cruises on the Tagus take place from April through October.

Bus – City buses and trams are run by *CARRIS* (*Companhia Carris de Ferro de Lisboa*). Maps and other information can be obtained at the window at the side of the Santa Justa Elevator, just off Rua do Carmo. Bus and tram fares vary according to the zone; the basic fare is 100 escudos (about 65¢). Get on the bus by the front door, buy a ticket from the driver, and cancel it in the machine. Tourist passes for 4 or 7 days of unlimited travel by bus, tram, subway, ferryboat, and the Santa Justa Elevator can be bought at the Praça dos Restauradores and Praça Marquês de Pombal subway stations and at the Santa Justa Elevator. Lisbon's trams are not only vintage vehicles and picturesque in themselves, but many go through the more historic parts of the city, providing a cheap way to take a tour. Long-distance bus service is provided by *Rodoviária Nacional,* the state-owned bus company, whose terminal is at Casal de Ribeiro (phone: 545439).

Car Rental – Most major firms have offices in Lisbon and at the airport: *Avis* (12C Avenida Praia da Vitória; phone: 561177; at the airport; phone: 894836; at the Santa Apolónia train station; phone: 876887; *Penta* hotel; phone: 726-5629; and at the *Ritz* hotel; phone: 692020); *Hertz* (10 Avenida 5 de Outubro; phone: 579077; at 10 Avenida Visconde Seabra; phone: 772944; and at the *Novotel Hotel,* 1642 Avenida José Malhoa; phone: 726-7221); *Budget* (6 Avenida Fontes Pereira de Melo; phone: 537717, and at the airport; phone: 801785 or 803981).

Elevator – The Elevador de Santa Justa takes passengers from Rua do Ouro (Rua Aurea) in the Baixa to Largo do Carmo in the Chiado. The Portuguese also refer to several streetcars that travel a steep route as "elevators," among them the Glória Elevator, running from Calçada da Glória, on the west side of Praça dos Restauradores, to the Bairro Alto. The unlimited-travel tourist pass is valid on elevators; individual rides cost 22.50 escudos (about 15¢).

Subway – The underground system serving Lisbon is called the *Metropolitano.* A large "M" aboveground designates the stations — Rossio and Restáuradores are the most central ones. The fare is 50 escudos (about 33¢ — or 40 escudos if bought in a machine) to any point. The unlimited-travel tourist pass is valid underground. Beware of pickpockets.

Taxi – Cabs are metered and inexpensive — a ride to almost any part of the city will cost less than $6. For trips outside Lisbon, a set rate per kilometer is charged beyond the city limits. Taxis can be hailed on the street or picked up at cabstands conveniently scattered around town. (Note that by law, passengers must get in and out on the sidewalk side, not the street side. Also by law, drivers may charge extra for luggage, but the regulation is vague and amounts are sometimes excessive.) To call a cab, dial 793-2756 or 825061.

Train – Frequent, fast electric trains connecting Lisbon with Belém, Estoril, and Cascais leave from the Estação Cais do Sodré (phone: 370181), by the river near Praça do Comércio. Trains to Queluz and Sintra operate from the Estação do Rossio (phone: 877092), just off the Rossio. (It's the 19th-century building with the charming, elaborately carved neo-Manueline façade just across from the side of the *Teatro Nacional.* Confusingly, it's hardly ever referred to by its real name, Estação Central, which is carved in neo-Manueline letters around its circular doors.) Trains for most of the rest of Portugal and elsewhere in Europe leave from Estação Santa Apolónia (phone: 876025), which is located along the river east of the Alfama district, not within walking distance of the center — take a bus or tram. The station for trains to the Algarve is Estação Sul e Sueste (phone: 877179), on the east side of Praça do Comércio. These southbound trains actually leave from Barreiro, on the south bank of the Tagus, but tickets include the price of the ferry ride from the station. Trains between Lisbon, Porto, and Faro have air conditioned coaches with bar and restaurant service.

LOCAL SERVICES: Dentist (English-Speaking) – The US Embassy has a list of English-speaking practitioners. Avenida das Forças Armadas (phone: 726-6600).

Dry Cleaner/Tailor – *Lavandarias AmoreiraSec,* Shop 1003, *Amoreiras Shopping Center,* Avenida Eng. Duarte Pacheco (phone: 692384).

Medical Emergency – Lisbon has three hospitals with emergency facilities: *Hospital São Jose* (phone: 872240); *Hospital de Santa Maria* (phone: 793-2762); and *Hospital São Francisco Xavier* (phone: 617351).

Messenger Service – *Pony Express,* 18-1 Avenida Marques de Tomar (phone: 574684).

National/International Courier – *DHL International,* Rua D, Building 121, Portela Airport (phone: 808520 or 808570).

Office Equipment Rental – *Inforgal,* 321 Avenida 5 de Outubro (phone: 793-2650 or 793-4057).

Pharmacy – *The Farmacia Azevedo* is in Lisbon's central square, the Rossio; 31 Praça de Dom Pedro IV (phone: 342-7478). Pharmacies take turns for weekend and after-hours service; each one posts the names of the shops on duty on its door.

Photocopies – *Rank Xerox Centro de Copias* (106 Avenida Antonio Augusto Aguiar; phone: 577110). Simple facilities also are widely available in stationery shops.

Post Office – There are two main downtown post offices. One (Praça dos Restauradores) is open weekdays from 8 AM to 10 PM, and the other (Praça do Comércio) is open weekdays from 8:30 AM to 6:30 PM.

Secretary/Stenographer (English-Speaking) – *Intess* (62 Rua São Julião; phone: 879947); *American Typing Services* (phone: 539650). Both companies also can supply translators.

Telex – At two post office locations. One (Praça dos Restauradores) is open weekdays from 9 AM to 7 PM, and the other (48-C Av. Fontes Pereira de Melo; phone: 524030) is open from 9 AM to 7 PM daily.

Translator – Lynn de Albuquerque (phone: 419-2383); *Intess* (phone: 879947); *American Typing Services* (phone: 539650).

Other – Tuxedo rental: *Guarda Roupa Anahory,* Rua Madalena (phone: 872046).

SPECIAL EVENTS: In ancient times, the *Festas dos Santos Populares* (Feasts of the Popular Saints), held in June, were celebrations of the summer solstice, but they are now Christian rites in honor of Santo António (St. Anthony), São João (St. John), and São Pedro (St. Peter). The *Feast of St. Anthony,* June 13 and the night before, is a bit like *New Year's Eve* and *New Year's Day.* Although most people associate St. Anthony (of Padua) with Italy, he actually was born in the Alfama in Lisbon, and people here make much ado about it. The Old Quarter comes alive on the eve: Dances are held in streets festooned with colored lanterns, and throughout the night gallons of good, rough wine are drunk to wash down mountains of sardines roasted on open barbecues. The saint is a powerful matchmaker, so this is the night when the city's young girls hope to meet their future husbands. Street stalls sell little pots of a spicy-smelling green herb called *manjerico,* each pot holding a message of advice or consolation for lovers. In the Baixa, neighborhood associations bedecked in traditional costumes parade down Avenida da Liberdade, each attempting to outdo the display of the others. For the *Feast of St. John,* on June 23 and 24, people make bonfires sprinkled with scented herbs and thistles and jump over them to show their daring, an ancient rite connected with fertility. The final celebration is the *Feast of Saint Peter,* on June 29. In little towns around Lisbon, such as Montijo, there is a running of the bulls and a blessing of ships on this day.

MUSEUMS: In addition to those discussed in *Special Places,* Lisbon also has the following museums that may be of interest. Note that most museums are closed on Mondays, and that many that ordinarily impose an admission charge are free on Sundays.

Museu da Cidade (City Museum) – Maps, engravings, and other objects telling Lisbon's history, set up in an 18th-century palace. Open from 10 AM to 1 PM and from 2 to 6 PM; closed Mondays. Admission charge. 245 Campo Grande (phone: 759-1617).

Museu Nacional do Teatro (National Theater Museum) – Costumes, scenery, drawings, programs, posters, and other theatrical memorabilia. Open from 10 AM to

1 PM and from 2:30 to 5PM; closed Mondays. Admission charge. 10-12 Estrada do Lumiar (phone: 758-2547).

Museu Nacional do Traje (National Costume Museum) – Changing exhibitions of Portuguese and foreign costumes, accessories, and fabric, in a lovely old suburban house located about a mile north of the *City Museum*. Open from 10 AM to 1 PM and from 2:30 to 5 PM; closed Mondays. Admission charge. 5 Largo São João Baptista, Parque de Monteiro-Mor, Lumiar (phone: 759-0318).

Museu Rafael Bordalo Pinheiro – Devoted to the works of the 19th-century caricaturist, ceramist, and painter of the same name. Open from 10 AM to 1 PM and from 2 to 6 PM; closed Mondays. Admission charge. 382 Campo Grande (phone: 759-0816).

SHOPPING: The most important shopping area in Lisbon is the Baixa, the zone between the Rossio and the river, with the mosaic-paved, pedestrian street, Rua Augusta, as its backbone. Another shop-heavy street, Rua do Carmo, leads from this area to the part of the Baixa known as the Chiado, where many fashionable shops still are located, even though some of the more famous ones, along with two department stores, burned down when fire ravaged much of this area in 1988. The damaged blocks are being rebuilt, but at present shoppers either take the Santa Justa Elevator to the Chiado or make their way from Rua do Carmo to Rua Garrett, the backbone of the area, via temporary scaffolding erected over the debris. Antiques row also is located in this part of the city: Rua Dom Pedro V, in the Bairro Alto, is the heart of it, but shops also congregate along Rua do Alecrim, Rua da Misericórdia, Rua São Pedro de Alcântara, and Rua da Escola Politécnica. Shops in the downtown area are open Mondays through Fridays, from 9 AM to 1 PM and 3 to 5 PM, Saturdays from 9 AM to 1 PM; many *centros comerciais* (shopping centers) stay open until midnight. The most famous, with sophisticated shops of all kinds — more than 300 of them — is the *Centro Comercial das Amoreiras,* a post-modernist complex (on Avenida Engenheiro Duarte Pacheco) with huge towers in pinks and greens and glass, designed by architect Tomás Taveira. At the other extreme is the *Feira da Ladra* (Thieves' Market), a flea market held Tuesdays and Saturdays (on Largo de Santa Clara) at the edge of the Alfama. Among the best buys in Lisbon are gold, silver, and jewelry — it is relatively inexpensive and the guaranteed content of the gold and silver make many pieces a bargain. There has been a renaissance in painting, tapestry making, and ceramics, with the accompanying opening of many new galleries. A revival in tile making, often in reproduction of 17th- and 18th-century designs, also has taken place, and many of the stores selling these wares will pack and ship. Rugs from Arraiolos and lace from Madeira, beautiful glass and crystal, copperware, fishermen's sweaters, and baskets are other good buys, along with fashionable clothing, shoes, and leather goods. Note that many of the shops below have branches in the *Amoreiras Shopping Center.*

Almorávida – A wide variety of regional crafts, pottery, and filigree jewelry plus an extensive collection of Portuguese-style, custom-made rugs. 10-14 Rua do Milagre de Sto. António (phone: 862261).

Ana Salazar – Clothes by Ana Salazar, Portugal's most famous avant-garde designer for women. 87 Rua do Carmo (phone: 347-2289).

Artesanato Arameiro – A wide variety of regional handicrafts — lace, rugs, ceramics, copperware, and filigree. 62 Praça dos Restauradores (phone: 342-0238).

Atlantis – Crystal tableware from Alcobaça. *Centro Comercial das Amoreiras* (phone: 693670).

Augustus – Elegant clothes for women. *Centro Comercial das Amoreiras* (phone: 693479).

Casa dos Bordados da Madeira – Embroidery and lace from Madeira and a wide selection of other Portuguese handicrafts. 135 Rua Primeiro de Dezembro (phone: 342-1447).

Charles – A very wide selection of shoes. 105 Rua do Carmo (phone: 320700) and 109 Rua Augusta (phone: 342-6584).

Charlot – Considered a very fashionable boutique, with designer labels from Portugal, Italy, and France. 28 Rua Barata Salgueiro (phone: 573665).

Diadema – Lovely gold and silver jewelry. 166 Rua do Ouro (phone: 342-1362).

Fábrica de Cerâmica Viúva Lamego – Makes and sells reproductions of old tiles; its bird and animal motifs are famous, but it also makes high-quality modern designs. 25 Largo do Intendente Pina Manique (phone: 521401).

Fábrica de Loiça de Sacavém – Fine porcelain in traditional and modern patterns. 57 Avenida da Liberdade (phone: 342-3902).

Galeria Comicos – A good gallery showing avant-garde paintings. 1B Rua Tenente Raul Cascais (phone: 677794).

Galeria Sesimbra – Lisbon's second oldest art gallery, known for hand-stitched Agulha tapestries, made from designs by leading contemporary Portuguese artists. 77 Rua Castilho (phone: 560291).

Galeria 111 – The longest established of Lisbon's art galleries, selling the best of today's Portuguese artists. 111 Campo Grande (phone: 767406).

Helio – Top-quality shoes for men and women. 93 Rua do Carmo (phone: 342-2725).

Livraria Bertrand – An enormous selection of books. Corner of Rua Garrett and Rua Anchieta (phone: 342-0081).

Livraria Buchholz – A large stock of foreign books as well as Portuguese ones. 4 Rua do Duque de Palmela (phone: 547358).

Madeira Gobelins – Embroidery, woven tapestries, and carpets from Madeira. 40 Rua Castilho (phone: 563708).

Madeira House – Lisbon's oldest shop dealing in genuine Madeira embroidery and lace, it also sells less expensive embroidered linens. 131 Rua Augusta (phone: 342-0557).

New York – A classy shop with the latest in women's clothes. 206 Rua do Ouro (phone: 342-1764).

Ourivesaria Pimenta – Fine jewelry, watches, and silver. 257 Rua Augusta (phone: 342-4564).

Porfirios – For young and trendy dressers. 63 Rua da Vitória (phone: 346-8274).

Quintão – Beautiful handmade Arraiolos rugs that are works of art. 30 Rua Ivens (phone: 346-5837).

Rosa & Teixeira – A highly ranked tailor selling his own designs for men and women. 204 Avenida da Liberdade (phone: 542063).

Sant'Anna – Reproductions of 17th- and 18th-century tiles, made in the shop's own factory. 95 Rua do Alecrim (phone: 342-2537). The factory, at 96 Calçada da Boa Hora, can be visited, but call first (phone: 363-8292).

Vista Alegre – The makers of Portugal's finest porcelain. 52-54 Rua Ivens (phone: 342-8612) and 18 Largo do Chiado (phone: 346-1401).

 SPORTS AND FITNESS: Bullfighting – Portuguese bullfighting, quite different from the Spanish version, is more a spectacle of horsemanship than a fight. Bulls are never killed in the ring here, and the fighting is done mostly on horseback, with the *cavaleiros* wearing magnificent 18th-century costumes as they ride against the bulls. After the horseman finishes with a mock kill, the *forcados* — eight young men dressed in brown pants, white shirts, cummerbunds, and tasseled caps — jump over the barrier and line up to wrestle the bull: the most popular part of the bullfight. Their leader taunts the bull to charge and when it does, the leader grabs it around the neck and they all wrestle it to the ground. Although there is a bullfight at *Easter,* the season begins in earnest in June and generally runs through September, with contests usually held on Thursdays, Sundays, and holidays. The most important fights take place in Lisbon at the *Praça*

de Touros do Campo Pequeno (Campo Pequeno Bullring), a mosque-like structure with minarets all around its walls (Avenida da República; phone: 793-2093), and at the *Monumental de Cascais.*

Fishing – Boats for deep-sea fishing can be rented from local fishermen at Sesimbra, a fishing village 27 miles (43 km) south of Lisbon, or at Cascais.

Fitness Centers – *Health Club Soleil,* a chain, is in the *Sheraton* hotel (1 Rua Latino Coelho; phone: 527353); the *Palácio* (in Estoril; phone: 468-8184); the *Estoril-Sol* (in Cascais; phone: 489-5086); and at *Squash Soleil* (*Centro Comercial das Amoreiras,* Avenida Engenheiro Duarte Pacheco; phone: 692907).

Golf – The *Clube de Golfe do Estoril* (on Avenida da República in Estoril; phone: 468-0176) has 27 holes; caddies and clubs can be rented, and lessons by professionals are available. Also in the Estoril–Cascais area are the *Estoril-Sol Golf Club* (Estrada da Lagoa Azul; phone: 923-2461), with 9 holes belonging to the *Estoril-Sol* hotel; and the *Clube de Golfe da Marinha,* an 18-hole Robert Trent Jones course (in the Quinta da Marinha tourist development at Cascais; phone: 486-9881). The British *Lisbon Sports Club* has an 18-hole course (at Casal da Carregueira, on the Belas–Sabugo road, about 15½ miles/25 km northwest of Lisbon; phone: 431-0077). The *Clube de Campo de Lisboa* (Lisbon Country Club; Quinta da Aroeira, Fonte da Telha; phone: 226-1802 or 226-1358) has 18 holes on the coast, 9½ miles (15 km) south of Lisbon.

Horseback Riding – Equestrians can be accommodated at the *Clube de Campo de Lisboa* (south of Lisbon; phone: 226-1802 or 226-1060); at the *Clube da Marinha* (at Cascais; phone: 289282); at the *Pony Club Cascais* (Quinta da Bicuda; phone: 284-3233); and at the *Clube de Campo Dom Carlos I* (Estrada Areia, Praia do Guincho; phone: 285-1403).

Jogging – Attractive as it may seem, jogging in Lisbon's central Parque Eduardo VII is not recommended, especially alone or at night. Instead, run along the riverside between the Ponte 25 de Abril and Belém. Another good place is the fitness circuit in the *Estadio Nacional* (National Stadium) area on the outskirts of the city on the way to Estoril, where the track winds through pleasant pine woods. (But do not jog alone.) The park in Estoril and the seafront in Cascais are also good.

Soccer – This is Portugal's most popular sport by far, and it's ruled by a triumvirate of three top clubs: *Sporting* and *Benfica,* from Lisbon, and *Porto,* from the northern capital of Porto. Any game in which one of these teams takes part should be worth watching, as the rivalries are very intense. (Note that the crowds are not unruly here and there has been no hooliganism, as in some other parts of Europe.) The season runs from June until the end of August, and matches are played on Sundays at various stadiums; tickets can be obtained with the help of the hotel desk.

Swimming – The entire coast west of the city and south of it across the river is banded with sandy beaches, and many hotels have private swimming pools. However, water pollution has become a problem on some of the beaches between Lisbon and Estoril, so check first about possible health hazards. (Don't go in the water unless the blue safety flag is flying.) In Estoril, the *Tamariz* restaurant, on the beach, has changing rooms.

Tennis – Courts are available at Estoril's *Clube de Tênis* (Avenida Amaral; phone: 468-6669); at the *Clube de Campo Dom Carlos I* (Estrada Areia, Praia do Guincho; phone: 285-2362); and at the *Lisbon Sports Club* (Casal da Carregueira, 15½ miles (25 km) northwest of Lisbon near Belas; phone: 431-0077).

 THEATER: Classic and contemporary plays are presented year-round except during July at the *Teatro Nacional de Dona Maria II* (Praça Dom Pedro IV; phone: 347-1087). Performances take place in Portuguese, of course. The *revista,* or revue, a popular Lisbon tradition embracing topical sketches, satire, music, and dancing reminiscent of old-fashioned vaudeville, can make for a lively evening even for those who don't understand the language. The best revues are presented in small theaters in the rather ramshackle Parque Mayer theater district, just off Avenida da Liberdade.

MUSIC: Lisbon's opera house, the *Teatro Nacional de São Carlos,* is near the Chiado district downtown (9 Rua Serpa Pinto; phone: 346-8408 or 346-8664). Built in the 18th century, it is one of Europe's prettiest, with an apricot-colored interior set off by touches of green and gold. The season runs from mid-December until May. Various ballet companies also perform at the opera house, but the *Gulbenkian Foundation Ballet Company,* sponsored by the foundation, is one of the best ballet companies in Europe at the moment, performing both classical and modern dance. Performances take place at the auditorium of the Gulbenkian Foundation building (45 Avenida de Berna; phone: 793-4068). Symphony and chamber music concerts can also be heard here and at the *Teatro Municipal de São Luís* (Rua António Maria Cardoso; phone: 342-7172).

NIGHTCLUBS AND NIGHTLIFE: A good place to begin an evening with a pre-dinner glass of dry, white port is *A Brasileira* (122 Rua Garrett), one of Lisbon's traditional old cafés. Take a seat at one of the tables outdoors and watch the world go by; the gentleman in bronze, occupying the bronze table, flanked by bronze chairs, is Fernando Pessoa (1888–1935), a Portuguese man of letters — this statue of him was placed here on the 100th anniversary of his birth. A second old café popular among the old guard is *Café Nicola,* on the Rossio.

Lisbon's popular *fado* houses — restaurants with *fado* music — are scattered throughout the old Alfama and Bairro Alto districts. *Fado,* which means "fate" or "destiny," is the name given to the anecdotal, satirical, sentimental, or occasionally happy songs performed, usually by a woman swathed in black (the *fadista*), to the accompaniment of one or more 12-stringed guitars. Although *fado* has become commercialized and many restaurants beef up their shows with folk dancing and popular music, a visitor may be lucky enough to be on hand some night when the singers and the musicians are in the mood to revive the real thing. Do not make a sound during the singing — neither the singers nor the spectators permit it. Some particularly good spots are *Senhor Vinho* (18 Rua do Meio à Lapa; phone: 672681), where the *fado* is pure; *O Faia* (54 Rua da Barroca; phone: 342-1923), one of the best known; *Adega Machado* (91 Rua do Norte; phone: 346-0095), entertaining because it offers spirited folk dancing; *Lisboa à Noite* (69 Rua das Gáveas; phone: 346-8557); and *A Severa* (51-61 Rua das Gáveas; phone: 346-4006). All are in the Bairro Alto, except *Senhor Vinho,* which is in the Lapa district west of the Bairro Alto. Those who are not dining should go after 10 PM. Reservations are essential.

The top discotheques are sometimes difficult to get into for all but regular customers (they're often frequented by local socialites), and many impose an expensive cover charge. Some of the best are *Banana Power* (52 Rua Cascais; phone: 631815), in the Alcântara dock area west of the center toward Belém; the *Fragil Bar* (128 Rua da Atalaia; phone: 346-9587), in the Bairro Alto; *Ad Lib* (18 Rua Barata Salgueiro; phone: 561717); *Stones* (1 Rua do Olival; phone: 396-4545); *Whispers* (35 Avenida Fontes Pereira de Melo; phone: 575489); *Trumps* (104-B Rua da Imprensa Nacional; phone: 671059), which has a huge dance floor; and *Springfellows* (Avenida Oscar Monteiro Torres; phone; 793-2944), which is very fancy and on 3 floors. *Procópio* (21-21A Avenida Alto São Francisco; phone: 652851) is a lively bar but doesn't have live music; *Loucuras* (37 Avenida Pedro Alvares Cabral; phone: 681117) offers live music. African music — especially from Cape Verde — is heard all over town. *Clave di Nos* (100 Rua do Norte; phone: 346-8420), a restaurant with good food, has a good Cape Verdian band.

Bars to try in Estoril include the *Founder's Inn* (11D Rua Dom Afonso Henriques;

phone: 468-2221); and the *English Bar* (Estrada Marginal, Monte Estoril; phone: 468-0413). In Estoril, however, don't miss a night at the world-famous *Casino Estoril* (phone: 268-4521), a shiny, modern building in the Parque Estoril. It's open every day (to those over 21 endowed with a passport) from 3 PM to 3 AM, and has all the classic European and American games: roulette, baccarat, chemin de fer, blackjack, French bank, slot machines, bingo. The roulette stakes are higher than in Portugal's other casinos, and the slot machines sometimes spit out jackpots of more than $200,000. But gambling is only one of the attractions. The glittering restaurant-nightclub resembles the *Lido* in Paris, with balconies and a main floor seating 800 and the only really international show in the country.

Cascais has a spirited nightlife, with many bars and cafés such as the *John Bull,* an English-style pub (32 Praça Costa Pinto; phone: 483-3319); *Tren Velho,* a converted train coach sitting beside the station (Avenida Duquesa de Palmela; phone: 486-7355); *Bar 21,* an attractive cocktail lounge (1A Travessa da Misericórdia; phone: 486-7518); and *Cutty Sark* (6 Travessa da Ressureição). The list of popular discos includes *Coconuts* (7 Boca do Inferno; phone: 284-4109), with an outdoor terrace by the sea; *Julianas* (10 Avenida 25 de Abril; phone: 486-4052); and the very snooty *Van Gogo* (9 Travessa da Alfarrobeira; phone: 483-3378). For *fado* in Cascais, try *Forte Dom Rodrigo* (Estrada de Birre; phone: 285-1373), or *Picadeiro Maria d'Almeida* (Quinta da Guia, Torre; phone: 486-9982).

BEST IN TOWN

CHECKING IN: A visitor's primary decision will be whether to stay right in Lisbon, to commute (with thousands of *lisboetas*) from Estoril or Cascais via the clean, inexpensive trains that run into the city about every 20 minutes, or even to stay in Sintra. Whichever your choice, a double room with a private bath will cost from $80 to $130 a night in a hotel in the expensive category, from $50 to $70 in the moderate range, and $30 to $40 in the inexpensive range. Reservations are necessary. All telephone numbers are in the 1 city code unless otherwise indicated.

LISBON

Alfa – A very modern 350-room luxury high-rise near the zoo and the *Gulbenkian Museum.* It has 3 restaurants (one with a panoramic view), a swimming pool, a sauna, shops, and a hairdresser. Business facilities include 24-hour room service, meeting rooms for up to 230, English-speaking concierge, foreign currency exchange, audiovisual equipment, and photocopiers. Avenida Columbano Bordalo Pinheiro (phone: 726-2121 or 726-4516; fax: 7263031; telex: 18377). Expensive.

Altis – This 9-story ultramodern hotel of steel, glass, and concrete has 305 rooms, a nice view from its rooftop grill, and a heated indoor swimming pool. Business facilities include 24-hour room service, meeting rooms for up to 400, English-speaking concierge, foreign currency exchange, secretarial services in English by prior arrangement, audiovisual equipment, photocopiers, and translation services. It's located about halfway between the Rossio train station and Parque Eduardo VII. 11 Rua Castilho (phone: 522496; fax: 548696; telex: 13314). Expensive.

Diplomático – Well situated near Parque Eduardo VII, it has 90 rooms equipped with air conditioning, mini-bars, and TV sets, plus a restaurant, bar, and private parking. Business facilities include 24-hour room service, meeting rooms for up to 80, English-speaking concierge, foreign currency exchange, audiovisual equipment, and photocopiers. 74 Rua Castilho (phone: 562041; fax: 522155; telex: 13713). Expensive.

Lisboa Plaza – Centrally located off Avenida da Liberdade, newly redecorated by a leading Portuguese designer, and elegant, this is family owned and operated. It has 93 air conditioned, soundproofed rooms (with mini-bars, TV sets, and all the rest), in addition to the *Quinta d'Avenida* restaurant; the bar, done in Art Nouveau style, is a popular meeting place. Business facilities include 24-hour room service, English-speaking concierge, foreign currency exchange, secretarial services in English, photocopiers, and translation services by prior arrangement. 7 Travessa do Salitre (phone: 346-3922; fax: 347-1630; telex: 16402). Expensive.

Lisboa Sheraton – One of the best of the chain in Europe, this 400-room high-rise offers comfortable accommodations, marble bathrooms, and elegant public areas and lounges. All rooms are air conditioned, and there is a heated, open-air swimming pool, plus several restaurants (including the 29th-floor *Panorama*), bars, shops, and a health club. Business facilities include 24-hour room service, meeting rooms for up to 550, English-speaking concierge, foreign currency exchange, secretarial services in English, audiovisual equipment, photocopiers, computers by previous arrangement, and translation services. It's located a bit away from the city center, a few blocks north of Praça Marquês de Pombal. 1 Rua Latino Coelho (phone: 575757; fax: 547164; telex: 12774). Expensive.

Meridien – A sparkling addition to Lisbon's complement of modern luxury hotels, it overlooks Parque Eduardo VII. The decor runs to chrome, marble, and splashing fountains, and the restaurants feature French cooking, hardly unusual in a hotel run by a subsidiary of *Air France*. Business facilities include 24-hour room service, English-speaking concierge, foreign currency exchange, secretarial services in English, audiovisual equipment, photocopiers, computers, cable television news, and translation services. 149 Rua Castilho (phone: 690900; fax: 693231; telex: 64315). Expensive.

Penta – Large, modern, and just a short cab ride from the center of town, beyond the *Gulbenkian Museum*. It has restaurants and bars, a disco, shops, a swimming pool on the grounds, and a shuttle service to the city center and the airport; the 592 rooms are fully equipped, with private baths, balconies, color TV sets, video, radio, and direct-dial telephones. Business facilities include meeting rooms for up to 600, English-speaking concierge, foreign currency exchange, secretarial services in English, audiovisual equipment, photocopiers, cable television news, and translation services. Major credit cards accepted. 1600 Avenida dos Combatentes (phone: 726-4054; fax: 726-4418; telex: 18437). Expensive.

Ritz Inter-Continental – On a hill overlooking Parque Eduardo VII, next door to the *Meridien,* this luxury establishment is contemporary on the outside (built in the 1950s), but traditional within. The appointments are dazzling — silks, satins, and suedes — and some of its 260 rooms and 40 suites are furnished with reproductions of antiques. It has large public rooms and a lovely piano bar overlooking the park, fine shops, a tearoom, coffee shop, disco, and beauty parlor, as well as the *Grill Room* (see *Eating Out*), one of the most fashionable restaurants in Lisbon. Bedrooms are air conditioned, soundproofed, and equipped with mini-bars, TV sets, radio, and in-house movies; some have balconies overlooking the park. Business facilities include 24-hour room service, meeting rooms for up to 700, English-speaking concierge, foreign currency exchange, secretarial services in English, audiovisual equipment, photocopiers, computers, cable television news, and translation services. Major credit cards accepted. 88 Rua Rodrigo da Fonseca (phone: 692020; fax: 691783; telex: 12589). Expensive.

Tivoli – Well situated, with 350 rooms and suites. Because it's so convenient, right on the main avenue downtown, the lobby is a popular meeting place for businesspeople as well as tourists (and the excellent bar just off the lobby is a favorite of local journalists). There is a restaurant, plus a popular rooftop grillroom, a small pool set in a garden, and tennis courts. Business facilities include 24-hour room service, meeting rooms for up to 200, English-speaking concierge, secretarial services in English, audiovisual equipment, photocopiers, cable television news, and translation services. Major credit cards accepted. 185 Avenida da Liberdade (phone: 530181; fax: 579461; telex: 12588). Expensive.

Flórida – Near Praça Marquês de Pombal, it has 120 air conditioned rooms with all the facilities (bath, telephone, TV set, radio); no restaurant, but there's a bar, a gift shop, and a hairdresser. Business facilities include 24-hour room service, meeting rooms for up to 100, English-speaking concierge, foreign currency exchange, photocopiers, and translation services. Major credit cards accepted. 32 Avenida Duque de Palmela (phone: 576145; fax: 543584; telex: 12256). Expensive to moderate.

Príncipe Real – A small downtown hotel with a traditional flavor, located off Avenida da Liberdade in the vicinity of Parque Mayer and the Botanical Garden. There are 24 rooms, all with air conditioning and a TV set, nearly all with a balcony. The top-floor dining room has a swath of picture window looking across the city to St. George's Castle. 53 Rua da Alegria (phone: 346-0116). Expensive to moderate.

Rex – Modern, with 70 rooms, and on the edge of Parque Eduardo VII, near the more prestigious *Ritz* and *Meridien* hotels. All rooms have air conditioning, a TV set, and a radio; half have balconies overlooking the park. There are 2 restaurants (one with a panoramic view) and a bar. Business facilities include meeting rooms for up to 200, foreign currency exchange, audiovisual equipment, photocopiers, and translation services. Major credit cards accepted. 169 Rua Castilho (phone: 682161; fax: 687581; telex: 18120). Expensive to moderate.

York House – One of the most attractive places to stay in Lisbon, although it is some distance west of the heart of the city, close to the *Museu Nacional de Arte Antiga*. Housed in a 17th-century building that was once a convent, this lovely, 45-room, antiques-filled *pensão* has a restaurant, and a nice bar with tables in the garden — a particular favorite of British visitors, writers, and embassy personnel. Across and down the street a bit, in an 18th-century house (No. 47) that once belonged to the writer Eça de Queirós, there's an equally old-fashioned and aristocratic 17-room annex to this small hostelry, making a total of 62 rooms (not all with private bath). Business facilities include English-speaking concierge, foreign currency exchange, and photocopiers. Major credit cards accepted. 32 Rua das Janelas Verdes (phone: 396-2435; fax: 672793; telex: 16791). Expensive to moderate.

Dom Carlos – A comfortable place to stay at Praça Marquês de Pombal. The 73 rooms are air conditioned and equipped with private baths, TV sets, and mini-bars. No restaurant, but there is a breakfast room and a bar. Business facilities include 24-hour room service, English-speaking concierge, foreign currency exchange, and photocopiers. Major credit cards accepted. 121 Avenida Duque de Loulé (phone: 539071; fax: 352-0728; telex: 16468). Moderate.

Eduardo VII – Not far from Praça Marquês de Pombal, it has 110 air conditioned rooms with private baths and other conveniences. There also is an excellent rooftop restaurant with a view of the city. Business facilities include meeting rooms for up to 40, English-speaking concierge, foreign currency exchange, secretarial services in English, audiovisual equipment, and photocopiers. Major credit cards accepted. 5 Avenida Fontes Pereira de Melo (phone: 530141; fax: 533879; telex: 18340). Moderate.

Flamingo – Small, conveniently located, with 39 rooms — some of them air conditioned. All have soundproofing, TV sets, and mini-bars. The hotel also has a good restaurant and a bar. Business facilities include English-speaking concierge, foreign currency exchange, and photocopiers. Major credit cards accepted. 41 Rua Castilho (phone: 532191; fax: 352-1216; telex: 14736). Moderate.

Príncipe – Northeast of Parque Eduardo VII, it has 70 air conditioned rooms, each with a private bath, a TV set, and a telephone, plus a restaurant and bar. 201 Avenida Duque de Avila (phone: 536151). Moderate.

Senhora do Monte – Like the *York House,* this is an insider's inn. Small, located up in the old Graça quarter northeast of St. George's Castle, it has good views of Lisbon from some of its 27 rooms (all with private baths). It's not the best location for access, but old hands swear by it. Business facilities include English-speaking concierge and foreign currency exchange. Major credit cards accepted. 39 Calçada do Monte (phone: 862846; fax: 877783). Moderate.

Tivoli Jardim – On a quieter street behind its sister, the *Tivoli,* and therefore, a much quieter hotel. Modern, it has 120 rooms (each with a private bath and many with balconies), a restaurant, bar, snack bar, and car park. The service is first rate, and guests have access to the *Tivoli*'s pool and tennis courts. Business facilities include 24-hour room service, meeting rooms for up to 200 at the *Tivoli* hotel next door, English-speaking concierge, foreign currency exchange, secretarial services in English (also at the *Tivoli*), photocopiers, and translation services. Major credit cards accepted. 7-9 Rua Júlio César Machado (phone: 539971; fax: 556566; telex: 12172). Moderate.

Dom Manuel – Modern and efficient (64 rooms, each with a private bath), and just around the corner from the *Gulbenkian Museum.* The rooms are small, but comfortably appointed, with air conditioning, TV sets, and video. There is a breakfast room and a bar, but no restaurant. Business facilities include meeting rooms for up to 12, English-speaking concierge, foreign currency exchange, and photocopiers. Major credit cards accepted. 189 Avenida Duque de Avila (phone: 576160; fax: 576985; telex: 43558). Moderate to inexpensive.

Miraparque – In a quiet location facing Parque Eduardo VII, it has 100 rooms with private baths, a restaurant, and a bar. Business facilities include English-speaking concierge, foreign currency exchange, and photocopiers. Major credit cards accepted. 12 Avenida Sidónio Pais (phone: 578070; fax: 578920; telex: 16745). Moderate to inexpensive.

Insulana – In the Baixa, this exceedingly central, friendly *albergaria* (inn) has 32 rooms, each with a private bath. Business facilities include English-speaking concierge and foreign currency exchange. Major credit cards accepted. 52 Rua Assunção (phone: 342-3131). Inexpensive.

Torre – This modern, attractive little place is a 15-minute taxi ride from the center of Lisbon, but convenient for sightseeing in Belém, where it's right beside one of Lisbon's best known sights — the Jerónimos Monastery. There are 50 rooms with private baths, a bar, and a restaurant. Business facilities include English-speaking concierge and foreign currency exchange. Major credit cards accepted. 8 Rua dos Jerónimos (phone: 363-7332; fax: 645995). Inexpensive.

ESTORIL

Atlántico – In the pleasant residential district of Monte Estoril, this is a modern spot on the sea (or rather, nearly on the sea, since the electric train tracks run between it and the beach). There are 175 air conditioned rooms (some with balconies overlooking the Atlantic), a terrace with a large saltwater swimming pool, an excellent restaurant, bar, nightclub, and billiards room. Business facilities include meeting rooms for up to 80, English-speaking concierge, foreign currency exchange, audiovisual equipment, and photocopiers. Major credit cards accepted.

Estrada Marginal, Monte Estoril (phone: 468-5170; fax: 468-3619; telex: 18125). Expensive.

Lennox Country Club – A hillside *estalagem* (inn) standing in a garden setting overlooking the coast. There are 32 rooms with private baths, some in the main building, which was once a private home, and some in modern additions, plus a very good restaurant with excellent service, a kidney-shape, heated outdoor swimming pool, and a tennis court. The inn emphasizes golf — golfing memorabilia decorate it, there is a putting green, and free transportation is provided to courses in the area, as well as to area riding stables. Major credit cards accepted. 5 Rua Engenheiro Alvaro Pedro de Sousa (phone: 468-0424; fax: 467-0859; telex: 13190). Expensive.

Palácio – Imagine Allied and Axis spies peeping around pillars during World War II and the jewels of exiled royalty glinting in the light of crystal chandeliers; that's the essence of this gracious Old World hotel by the park. The public rooms are majestic, the staff the sort that seems to remember everyone who has ever stayed here, and the 200 rooms and suites, with traditional and contemporary furnishings, are air conditioned. In addition to the dining room, there is the adjoining, superlative *Four Seasons Grill* (see *Eating Out*). A heated swimming pool and cabañas are in the lovely gardens behind the hotel; the beach on the Atlantic is a 5-minute walk away. Temporary membership in the nearby *Estoril Golf Club* is available (hotel guests don't pay greens fees); there are tennis courts next door. Business facilities include 24-hour room service, meeting rooms for up to 300, English-speaking concierge, foreign currency exchange, secretarial services in English, audiovisual equipment, photocopiers, and translation services. Major credit cards accepted. Parque Estoril (phone: 468-0400; fax: 468-4867; telex: 12757). Expensive.

Grande – On a hill overlooking the sea in Monte Estoril, this is a modern establishment with 73 rooms with private baths (some with balconies), a bar, a restaurant, and a covered swimming pool. Business facilities include foreign currency exchange and photocopiers. Major credit cards accepted. Avenida Sabóia, Monte Estoril (phone: 468-4609; fax: 468-4834; telex: 13807). Expensive to moderate.

Praia – This modern property is near the park in front of the *Palácio*. It has 91 air conditioned rooms, some with balconies, a panoramic restaurant on the seventh floor, a bar, and a swimming pool. Business facilities include 24-hour room service, meeting rooms for up to 40, English-speaking concierge, foreign currency exchange, and photocopiers. Major credit cards accepted. Estrada Marginal (phone: 468-1811; fax: 468-1815; telex: 16007). Expensive to moderate.

Alvorada – Another modern hostelry, near the casino, it has 51 rooms, each with private bath and a balcony. There's no swimming pool, but there is a solarium on top, and the hotel is only 200 yards from the beach. Breakfast room and bar; no restaurant. Business facilities include English-speaking concierge, foreign currency exchange, and photocopiers. Major credit cards accepted. 3 Rua de Lisboa (phone: 468-0070; fax: 468-7250; telex: 13573). Moderate.

Founder's Inn – British-owned and also known as the *Estalagem do Fundador,* it has 14 pleasant rooms with private baths, each furnished differently. The restaurant serves excellent English cooking; there's also a bar, with music, that's a local nightspot. A freshwater pool is on the grounds, which are on a hillside, set back from the beachfront. There is an English-speaking concierge and foreign currency exchange. Major credit cards accepted. 11 Rua Dom Afonso Henriques (phone: 468-222!; fax: 468-8779). Moderate.

Inglaterra – A charming, turn-of-the-century private home-turned-hotel, set in gardens near the *Palácio.* Inside, the 45 rooms (each with a private bath) are spare and contemporary, rather than old-fashioned in style; there's a bar, restaurant, and swimming pool, an English-speaking concierge, foreign currency exchange, and photocopiers. Major credit cards accepted. 1 Rua do Porto (phone: 468-4461; fax: 468-2108; telex: 65235). Moderate.

Lido – A very comfortable, modern hostelry in a quiet spot on a hillside away from the beach, but not far from the casino and park. The 62 rooms and suites all have private baths and balconies, telephones, and radios; there is a restaurant, a bar, a large swimming pool, a solarium, and a terrace with a view of the ocean. Business facilities include English-speaking concierge, foreign currency exchange, and photocopiers. Major credit cards accepted. 12 Rua do Alentejo (phone: 468-4098). Moderate.

Pica-Pau – A good *pensão* in a nice old white-painted villa with a red tile roof, near the *Lido* and the *Founder's Inn*. The 48 rooms with private baths are completely modern; there is a bar, a restaurant, and a swimming pool. Also, an English-speaking concierge and foreign currency exchange. Major credit cards accepted. 48 Rua Dom Afonso Henriques (phone: 468-0556; fax: 468-0664). Moderate to inexpensive.

Smart – Another *pensão,* in a very large old house. It has 16 rooms, most with television sets and private baths (the rest have washbasins), a breakfast room (no restaurant), and a garden with palm trees. It's not far from the beach. English-speaking concierge. No credit cards. 3 Rua José Viana (phone: 468-2164). Inexpensive.

CASCAIS

Albatroz – A luxury property perched on the rocks at the water's edge. The location is choice, which is not hard to understand since the core of this hotel was built during the 19th century as a villa for the royal family. Between the original building and a newer balconied addition, there are 40 rooms with bath. An excellent restaurant (see *Eating Out*) and bar, both surrounded by windows overlooking the sea, and a swimming pool with plenty of room for sunbathing are further attractions. Business facilities include meeting rooms for up to 30, English-speaking concierge, foreign currency exchange, secretarial services in English, audiovisual equipment, photocopiers, and translation services. Major credit cards accepted. 100 Rua Frederico Arouca (phone: 483-2821; fax: 284-4827; telex: 16052). Expensive.

Cidadela – Near the center of town, with 140 rooms and some apartments, each with its own sea-view balcony. Facilities include a good restaurant, a bar, and a swimming pool set amid attractive gardens. Business facilities include 24-hour room service, meeting rooms for up to 100, English-speaking concierge, foreign currency exchange, audiovisual equipment, photocopiers, and translation services. Major credit cards accepted. Avenida 25 de Abril (phone: 483-2921; fax: 486-7226; telex: 66895). Expensive.

Estoril-Sol – The biggest on the coast, with 347 rooms and suites. It's east of town, between the center of Cascais and Monte Estoril, and is separated from the water only by the electric train tracks (an underground passage leads directly to the beach). The hotel is rife with facilities: an Olympic-size swimming pool, a children's pool, 5 bars, a large, panoramic rooftop restaurant, a disco, shops, a health club, sauna, squash courts, a bowling alley, and its own 9-hole golf course in lovely surroundings nearby. Business facilities include 24-hour room service, meeting rooms for up to 1,200, English-speaking concierge, foreign currency exchange, secretarial services in English, audiovisual equipment, photocopiers, cable television news, and translation services. Major credit cards accepted. Parque Palmela (phone: 483-2831; fax: 483-2280; telex: 15102). Expensive.

Farol – A charming *estalagem* (inn) in a building that was once the private house of an aristocratic family. It's located by the sea, just west of the center along the road to Boca do Inferno and Praia do Guincho. It has 20 rooms with bath, a swimming pool, tennis court, bar, snack bar, and a restaurant that overlooks the water. There's an English-speaking concierge and foreign currency exchange. Major credit cards accepted. 7 Estrada da Boca do Inferno (phone: 483-0173; fax: 284-1447; telex: 14658). Expensive.

Guincho – The waves crash on three sides of this restored 17th-century fortress that looks out to sea from a rocky promontory 5½ miles (9 km) northwest of Cascais. The location is spectacular, with beach on both sides, although walking on the beach is recommended more than going in the water, due to the treacherous undertow here, near the westernmost point of continental Europe. The 36 rooms and suites in this elegant establishment all have private baths, old brick-vaulted ceilings, telephones, mini-bars, and TV sets, and some have balconies. There is a bar and a panoramic restaurant (see *Eating Out*). Business facilities include English-speaking concierge, foreign currency exchange, secretarial services in English, audiovisual equipment, photocopiers, and translation services. Major credit cards accepted. Praia do Guincho (phone: 285-0491; fax: 285-0431; telex: 43138). Expensive.

Baia – Right on the beach, in the heart of town, where the local fishermen tie up their painted boats. There are 85 rooms in this modern hotel, most with balconies; restaurant and terrace bar. Business facilities include English-speaking concierge, foreign currency exchange, and photocopiers. Major credit cards accepted. Avenida Marginal (phone: 483-1033; fax: 483-1095; telex: 43468). Expensive to moderate.

Dom Carlos – This *pensão* in the center of Cascais occupies a restored house built in 1640, and the breakfast room and chapel maintain the decorations of that period. There are 18 rooms with private baths, a TV salon, and a tree-filled garden. 8 Rua Latino Coelho (phone: 486-8463). Moderate.

Nau – The location is convenient — in front of the train station and only 150 yards or so from the beach. Modern, it has 56 rooms with private baths and balconies, plus a TV room, a bar, and a restaurant with a terrace. An English-speaking concierge and foreign currency exchange are on hand. No credit cards. 14 Rua Dra. Iracy Doyle (phone: 483-2861; telex: 42289). Moderate.

Valbom – An *albergaria* (inn) in the center of Cascais, near the train station, it's better looking inside than from the outside. There are 40 rooms with private baths; there's a bar, but no restaurant (breakfast is served). There is an English-speaking concierge and a foreign currency exchange. No credit cards. 14 Avenida Valbom (phone: 483-2831). Inexpensive.

SINTRA

Palácio dos Seteais – One of the loveliest and most romantic hotels in Europe. Built at the end of the 18th century for the Dutch consul in Lisbon, it was sold to the fifth Marquês de Marialva and was often visited by royalty. Marble gleams underfoot and murals line the walls of the public rooms; the 18 guestrooms are beautifully decorated with antiques, handwoven rugs, and tapestries, but no TV sets and no mini-bars to destroy the neo-classical illusion. Located just outside Sintra, the hotel does have a television lounge, a bar, and a well-known restaurant (see *Eating Out*) overlooking spacious gardens, a formal, windowed salon with views of the Sintra Valley, and a swimming pool and tennis courts. Business facilities include 24-hour room service, meeting rooms for up to 40, English-speaking concierge, foreign currency exchange, secretarial services in English, audiovisual equipment, photocopiers, and translation services. Major credit cards accepted. 8 Rua Barbosa do Bocage (phone: 923-3200; fax: 923-4277; telex: 14410). Expensive.

Tivoli Sintra – The best in town, this is situated off the main square of Sintra, right by the National Palace. The modern building has all the modern conveniences, along with traditional Portuguese touches in the decor. There are 75 air conditioned rooms with private baths, balconies, TV sets, and telephones. A highly regarded restaurant with a view (see *Eating Out*), lounges, bars, a hairdresser, and a garage are among the facilities. Business facilities include 24-hour room service, meeting rooms for up to 220, English-speaking concierge, foreign currency exchange, secretarial services in English, audiovisual equipment, photocopiers, cable television news, and translation services. Major credit cards accepted. Praça da República (phone: 923-3505; fax: 923-1572; telex: 42314). Expensive.

Central – Short on rooms (only 11, all with private bath), it's long on charm, and it's on the main square, in front of the palace. There is a tearoom, a bar, and a pleasant restaurant with a terrace for lunch in the summer. 35 Praça da República (phone: 923-0963). Moderate.

Sintra – In São Pedro de Sintra, a 10-minute walk from downtown. This *pensão* has 13 rooms (10 with private baths), a swimming pool, TV room, and a breakfast room (no restaurant). There is an English-speaking concierge and a foreign currency exchange. No credit cards accepted. Travessa dos Avelares, São Pedro de Sintra (phone: 923-0738). Inexpensive.

Portugal's *Tourism in the Country* program — a network of elegant old aristocratic estates and manor houses (categorized as *Turismo de Habitação* properties), simpler but still fine country homes (*Turismo Rural*), and farmhouses (*Agroturismo*) that take in small numbers of paying guests — is most active in the rural north, but travelers interested in this type of accommodation do have some choices in the Lisbon area. Among them is the charming *Casal de São Roque,* by the sea in Estoril. Built at the beginning of the century and furnished accordingly, it has 6 rooms for guests, 4 with private baths; the hosts will serve meals upon request. Contact *Casal de São Roque* (Avenida Marginal, Estoril 2765; phone: 268-0217). In the center of Cascais, there's the *Casa da Pérgola* (13 Avenida Valbom, Cascais 2736; phone: 284-0040), set in lovely gardens, offering a luxurious suite and 5 bedrooms with private baths.

Sintra has three properties. The *Quinta de São Tiago* (Sintra 2710; phone: 923-2923) is an imposing noble house several centuries old, surrounded by vast lawns with a swimming pool, near the *Palácio dos Seteais.* There are 7 double bedrooms, luxuriously furnished with antiques; the owners (an Englishman and his Spanish wife) serve meals on request. The *Quinta da Capella* (Estrada de Monserrate, Sintra 2710; phone: 929-0170) is another impressive old noble house surrounded by gardens, located beyond Seteais and the Quinta de Monserrate. One suite and 4 beautifully furnished bedrooms with private baths — or 2 independent apartments — are available. Finally, the *Vila das Rosas* (2-4 Rua António Cunha, Sintra 2710; phone: 923-4216) is a large, white 19th-century house with a red tile roof on the northern outskirts of Sintra; 4 double rooms with bath, a suite of 3 rooms with a private bath, and a cottage in the garden are available. In summer, breakfast is served in the cool wine cellar; other meals are served on request. The *Quinta de São Tiago* and the *Quinta da Capella* are in the expensive price category; the remaining three are moderate. Reservations for the above houses can also be made through certain central booking agencies (see *Accommodations,* GETTING READY TO GO).

EATING OUT: Portuguese food offers a surprising variety of tastes. Over the centuries, this seagoing nation's cuisine has come under the influence of far-flung countries in Asia, Africa, and the Americas, as well as neighboring Spain and nearby France. Lisbon's restaurants reflect this heritage (and all its regional permutations). Fish and seafood abound and usually are fresh and delicious. Those who want to splurge should order steamed lobster or grilled prawns, or dishes such as *arroz de marisco* (rice with shellfish). Stuffed crab and boiled sea spider (eaten by cracking it open with a wooden mallet) are flavorful, and codfish is a great local favorite — it's said the Portuguese have as many ways to prepare it as there are days in the year, one of the best being *bacalhau à Gomes de Sá,* named for a Porto restaurant owner. The best restaurants serve delicious smoked swordfish, sliced very thin, with lemon and capers, but for something uniquely Portuguese, sample the charcoal-grilled sardines sold in the street. Lisbon's meat is best grilled, but typical dishes such as *cozido à portuguesa* (a stew of boiled vegetables, sausages, and different types of meat, popular in the north) and *iscas à portuguesa* (thin slices of calf's liver marinated in wine, garlic, and bay leaves, and cooked in a shallow earthenware dish) are worth trying. Desserts, mostly based on eggs, sugar, and almonds, tend to be too sweet for some palates, but there are good cheeses — *queijo da Serra,* from northeastern Portugal, and Serpa, from the Alentejo, among the best. Wines from all over the country appear on the city's wine lists. The rule is to choose those that are more than 5 years old (except for northern *vinhos verdes,* which should be less than 2 years old, but which are not often found in Lisbon). Pungent, fruity bairrada wines, mellow, woody Dão wines, and flowery douro wines are all good. Bucelas is an excellent white from a small demarcated zone north of Lisbon.

Dinner for two, with a local wine, averages from $50 to $70 at restaurants listed below as expensive, from $30 to $50 at moderate establishments, and from $20 to $30 at inexpensive restaurants. Customary dining time is no earlier than 7:30 PM, but many restaurants close their kitchens at 11 PM. Lunch is served between noon and 2:30 PM. All telephone numbers are in the 1 city code unless otherwise indicated.

LISBON

Antonio Clara – Located in a 19th-century, Art Nouveau mansion that is now a municipal monument, this dining spot run by the same owners as *Clara* (below) specializes in Portuguese fare and fine fish dishes. It also boasts a good wine cellar. Open Mondays through Saturdays for lunch and dinner. Reservations necessary. Major credit cards accepted. 46 Avenida de República (phone: 766380). Expensive.

Aviz – One of the best dining places in town. When the old *Aviz* hotel — where the multimillionaire Calouste Gulbenkian spent the final days of his life in Lisbon — was torn down, Chef Alberto Rapetti and some of his staff opened this restaurant just off Largo do Chiado, bringing with them all the elegance and flair that had made the old hostelry an international favorite. The decor is very Belle Epoque, the food excellent, and the service flawless. Closed Saturdays at lunch and on Sundays. Reservations advised. Major credit cards accepted. 12B Rua Serpa Pinto (phone: 342-8391). Expensive.

Casa da Comida – This discreetly elegant restaurant is in a converted house, with tables set around a charming enclosed garden and an adjoining period bar. The food is delicious and beautifully presented. Closed Saturdays at lunch and Sundays. Reservations advised. Major credit cards accepted. 1 Travessa das Amoreiras (phone: 685376). Expensive.

Chester – Although this attractive little spot near the *Ritz* specializes in steaks, it also has shellfish alive in tanks for the choosing and the fish is always fresh. Closed Sundays. Reservations advised. Major credit cards accepted. 87 Rua Rodrigo da Fonseca (phone: 657347). Expensive.

Clara – Very elegant and spacious, serving excellent regional Portuguese and international food — one of Lisbon's best. It's in an old house with gardens that are illuminated at night. Closed Sundays. Reservations advised. Major credit cards accepted. 49 Campo dos Mártires de Pátria (phone: 570434). Expensive.

Escorial – A famous dining place in a district, near Praça dos Restauradores, that's noted for seafood. Elegantly decorated, with a nice bar, and known for good service, it also serves excellent international cuisine. Closed only on the 1st of May — *Labor Day* in Europe. Reservations advised. Major credit cards accepted. 47 Rua das Portas de Santo Antão (phone: 346-3758). Expensive.

Gambrinus – Famous for fish and seafood, with numerous small dining rooms that fan out from the open blue-tiled kitchen. In the heart of the city, it usually is jammed with businessmen at lunchtime. Open daily. Reservations necessary. Major credit cards accepted. 25 Rua das Portas de Santo Antão (phone: 342-1466). Expensive.

Gare Marítima Restaurante Michel – Staffed by students of Michel, Portugal's preeminent chef, who also runs a restaurant under his name in the Alfama (see below). Portuguese nouvelle cuisine is served in a beautifully restored waterfront setting at the old passenger ship terminal. Impeccable service and an excellent wine list make for pleasant repasts. Closed Saturdays for lunch, Sundays, and public holidays. Reservations necessary. Major credit cards accepted. Gare Marítima, Alcântara Sul (phone: 676335). Expensive.

Michel – The owner, a well-known cook on television in Portugal, specializes in nouvelle cuisine, Portuguese-style, although traditional French dishes also are served. Handsomely decorated, this is in the Alfama, just below St. George's Castle. Closed Saturdays at lunch and Sundays. Reservations necessary. Major credit cards accepted. 5 Largo de Santa Cruz do Castelo (phone: 864358). Expensive.

Ritz Grill Room – The restaurant of the *Ritz* hotel prepares unusually good food and is a fashionable gathering place for Lisbon businesspeople. Open daily. Reservations advised. Major credit cards accepted. 88 Rua Rodrigo da Fonseca (phone: 692020). Expensive.

Tágide – A beautiful staircase leads from the small dining room on the first floor to a second-floor dining area where picture windows afford a great view of the Tagus, a must for visitors who want to see the city and eat well at the same time. Portuguese and international dishes share the menu; the service is impeccable, yet pleasant. Closed Sundays. Reservations necessary. Major credit cards accepted. 18 Largo da Biblioteca Pública (phone: 342-0720). Expensive.

Tavares – Lisbon's oldest, it began as a café in 1784 and became a luxurious restaurant in 1861. After celebrating its 200th birthday, this city landmark had its gold leaf walls redone, its mirrors replated, its armchairs reupholstered, and more, so the light from its crystal chandeliers shines on a scene that's as opulent as ever, the haunt of businesspeople, government officials, and the like, and the perfect setting for excellent food and fine wine. Closed Saturdays at lunch and on Sundays. Reservations advised. Major credit cards accepted. 37 Rua da Misericórdia (phone: 342-1112). Expensive.

Conventual – The menu is based on old Portuguese convent and monastery recipes, some of which go back to the 17th century, and objects from churches decorate the premises. Typical dishes include *bacalhau com coentros* (cod with coriander) and *ensopado de borrego* (lamb stew). Closed Saturdays at lunch and Sundays. Reservations advised. Major credit cards accepted. 44 Praça das Flores (phone: 609196). Expensive to moderate.

Restaurante 33 – Good food and a pleasant atmosphere prevail in this well-appointed restaurant behind an elegant clapboard façade, not far from the *Ritz*. Closed Sundays. Reservations advised. Major credit cards accepted. 33 Rua Alexandre Herculano (phone: 546079). Expensive to moderate.

Sua Excelência – In the Madragoa quarter, near the embassy residences. Knock on the door to gain entry, and the attentive owner will read out the entire menu in English, if so desired. He serves a very good *açorda* (a sort of "dry" soup, or stew, a combination of seafood, bread, eggs, and coriander) and Mozambique prawns with a peppery sauce. Closed Wednesdays and the month of September. Reservations unnecessary. Major credit cards accepted. 42 Rua do Conde (phone: 603614). Expensive to moderate.

Caseiro – A good restaurant among the many near the Jerónimos Monastery in Belém. It is typically Portuguese, specializing in regional dishes and seafood, and attractively decorated. Closed Mondays. Reservations advised. Major credit cards accepted. 5 Rua de Belém (phone: 463-8803). Moderate.

Faz Figura – Overlooking the Tagus in the Alfama quarter, its wood paneling and leather chairs give it the atmosphere of an exclusive club, but there is also a verandah where diners can sit and watch the ships on the river. Fish and seafood, Portuguese and international dishes, are available. Closed Sundays. Reservations unnecessary. Major credit cards accepted. 15B Rua do Paraíso (phone: 868981). Moderate.

Gondola – A long-established Italian eatery near the *Gulbenkian Museum,* and a favorite with visitors. There's a lovely vine-covered garden for summer dining. Closed Saturday evenings and Sundays. Reservations advised. Major credit cards accepted. 64 Avenida de Berna (phone: 770426). Moderate.

Laçerda – Also near the *Gulbenkian Museum,* this small place used to be a butcher shop and is still devoted to meat (choose a cut from the hook by the door). Photos of celebrities who have dined here decorate the walls, and strings of garlic and onions hang from the ceiling. Closed Sundays. Reservations unnecessary. No credit cards accepted. 36 Avenida de Berna (phone: 774057). Moderate.

Pap'Açorda – The entrance to this Bairro Alto bakery-turned-restaurant is through an old wood-paneled bar. Inside, there is a very attractive enclosed garden banked with green plants. The mixed fish grilled on a skewer is very good, but the specialty of the house is the porridgy seafood-bread-eggs-and-coriander mixture known as *açorda.* Closed Saturdays at lunch and Sundays. Reservations advised. Major credit cards accepted. 57 Rua da Atalaia (phone: 346-4811). Moderate.

Varina da Madragoa – An old tavern turned into a blue-and-white tiled restaurant, near Parliament. Good Portuguese food, including excellent *bacalhau,* or codfish. Closed Saturdays at lunch and Mondays. Reservations unnecessary. Major credit cards accepted. 36 Rua das Madres (phone: 665533). Moderate.

Bomjardim – Considered tops in preparing *frango na brasa,* chicken that's charcoal-broiled on a rotating spit and, if it's desired, accompanied by a fiery chili sauce (*piri piri*). This is one of Lisbon's most popular — and least expensive — culinary delights. There are two *Bomjardim* restaurants facing each other just off Praça dos Restauradores. Noisy and crowded at lunchtime; open daily. No reservations or credit cards accepted. 10-11 Travessa de Santo Antão (phone: 342-7424). Inexpensive.

Bota Alta – Traditional Portuguese cooking, served in a cheery bistro atmosphere. It's in the midst of all the Bairro Alto nightlife, and usually very busy. Closed Sundays. Reservations advised — or go early. Major credit cards accepted. 35-37 Travessa da Queimada (phone: 342-7959). Inexpensive.

Porto d'Abrigo – Although not imposing in appearance, this tiny eatery is one of Lisbon's culinary landmarks. Famous for its Portuguese specialties, it's usually very crowded at lunchtime. Closed Sundays. Reservations advised. Major credit cards accepted. 16 Rua dos Remolares (phone: 346-0875). Inexpensive.

Xico Carreira – In the picturesque, rather shabby theater district off Avenida da Liberdade, it's off the beaten track for most people and full of local color. A former bullfighter owns it; posters and mementos of the sport decorate it. Try the *bife a cortador* (a big grilled steak) or the *cozido transmontano* (boiled dinner of vegetables, sausages, and meats). Crowded at lunchtime. Closed Sundays. Reservations unnecessary. Major credit cards accepted. Parque Mayer (phone: 346-3805). Inexpensive.

ESTORIL

Casino Estoril – The glittering, balcony-lined restaurant here is known for its international show — at 11:30 PM every night, with stars such as Julio Iglesias and Dionne Warwick — but it's no less recommendable for food and service, both excellent. It has a long menu listing Portuguese and international dishes. Open daily. Reservations advised. Major credit cards accepted. Parque Estoril (phone: 468-4521). Expensive.

Choupana – On a cliff overlooking the sea a bit over a mile (2 km) east of Estoril, this specializes in seafood, but has a varied menu of other dishes as well. The dining room is large, panoramic, and air conditioned. Later at night, there is a show and music until all hours. Open daily. Reservations advised. Major credit cards accepted. Estrada Marginal, São João do Estoril (phone: 468-3099). Expensive.

Four Seasons Grill – A very elegant place for the finest dining in Estoril. The long menu of Portuguese and international dishes changes four times a year, according to the seasons, and when it does, so does the china, the decor, and the waiters' uniforms. It is run by the *Palácio* hotel, which is next door, and can be entered using either its own street entrance or the hotel lobby. Open daily. Reservations advised. Major credit cards accepted. *Hotel Palácio,* Parque Estoril (phone: 468-0400). Expensive.

English Bar – This brown-and-white building overlooks the water, with windows all around. It's cozily decorated in the English manner (and has a popular bar), but serves very good Portuguese and international dishes. Closed Sundays. Reservations unnecessary. Major credit cards accepted. Estrada Marginal, Monte Estoril (phone: 269-0413). Expensive to moderate.

A Maré – By the sea with a lovely panoramic view and a varied menu. There is a large air conditioned dining room and, in summer, an outside barbecue. Open daily. Reservations unnecessary. Major credit cards accepted. Estrada Marginal, Monte Estoril (phone: 468-5570). Expensive to moderate.

Ferra Mulinhas – Portuguese and Hungarian cooking. It's open only for dinner and is closed Tuesdays. Reservations unnecessary. Major credit cards accepted. 5A Rua Viveiro (phone: 468-0005). Moderate.

Garrafão – A fish and seafood spot with its own vivarium, on the outskirts of Estoril. Closed Thursdays. Reservations unnecessary. Major credit cards accepted. Amoreira (phone: 468-4195). Inexpensive.

CASCAIS

Albatroz – This outstanding restaurant — the dining room of the hotel of the same name — is set on rocks at the edge of the sea. It's known for a varied menu of well-prepared dishes, including good seafood, and the picture windows that surround it make it exceedingly fine for its views as well. Open daily. Reservations necessary. Major credit cards accepted. 100 Rua Frederico Arouca (phone: 483-2821). Expensive.

Baluarte – By the sea, with 2 air conditioned dining rooms featuring splendid views. It specializes in seafood, but also has a long menu of other Portuguese and international dishes. Open daily. Reservations advised. Major credit cards accepted. 1 Avenida Marechal Carmona (phone: 486-5471). Expensive.

Hotel do Guincho – The restaurant here, in a cliff-top hotel that was once a fortress guarding continental Europe's westernmost extremity, is surrounded by windows looking onto the crashing Atlantic. The location alone makes it a wonderful lunch or dinner spot for those on a day's outing along the coast, but the excellence of the food — with emphasis on seafood — and of the service would recommend it even without the view. Located 5½ miles (9 km) northwest of Cascais. Open daily. Reservations advised. Major credit cards accepted. Praia do Guincho (phone: 285-0491). Expensive.

João Padeiro – From its beginnings a number of years ago as a simple eatery, this has become one of the most renowned seafood restaurants in Cascais. Old stone grinding wheels and pieces from windmills decorate the three dining rooms most attractively. Closed Tuesdays. Reservations necessary. Major credit cards accepted. 12 Rua Visconde da Luz (phone: 483-0232). Expensive.

Muchaxo – In an *estalagem* of the same name, this is one of the most famous seafood spots on the Lisbon coast. The inn is by the sea, so there is a marvelous view over the water. Open daily. Reservations unnecessary. Major credit cards accepted. Praia do Guincho (phone: 285-0221). Expensive.

Pescador – A charming place near the fish market, it is decorated with a fishermen's motif. Fish and seafood are very good here. Open daily. Reservations unnecessary. Major credit cards accepted. 10B Rua das Flores (phone: 483-2054). Expensive to moderate.

O Batel – Nicely decorated in a rustic fashion, this is another good seafood restaurant, near the fish market. Open daily. Reservations unnecessary. Major credit cards accepted. 4 Travessa das Flores (phone: 483-0215). Moderate.

Beira Mar – One of the longest established of the seafood eateries near the fish market. Decorated with blue and white tiles, it serves international fare in addition to good seafood. Open daily. Reservations unnecessary. Major credit cards accepted. 6 Rua das Flores (phone: 483-0152). Moderate.

Burladero – By the bullring, it is large, air conditioned, and specializes in grilled meat. Closed for lunch on Wednesdays and Thursdays. Reservations unnecessary. Major credit cards accepted. Praça de Touros (phone: 486-8751). Moderate.

John Bull – A well-known English pub with a good little restaurant attached; international fare is served. Open daily. Reservations unnecessary. Major credit cards accepted. 31 Praça Costa Pinto (phone: 483-3319). Moderate.

O Pipas – A smart seafood spot in the center of town, near the fish market, it consists of a small air conditioned dining room decorated with wine barrels and hanging garlic braids and sausages. Open daily. Reservations unnecessary. Major credit cards accepted. 1B Rua das Flores (phone: 486-4501). Moderate.

A Taverna de Gil Vicente – This cozy little restaurant has a fireplace and features international cooking. Closed Wednesdays. Reservations unnecessary. Major credit cards accepted. 22 Rua dos Navegantes (phone: 483-2032). Moderate.

Galegos – Near the center of town, this simple place serves Portuguese and northern Spanish dishes. Open daily. Reservations unnecessary. Major credit cards accepted. 3 Avenida Valbom (phone: 483-2586). Inexpensive.

QUELUZ

Cozinha Velha – The name means "Old Kitchen" — and this is the former royal kitchen of the National Palace at Queluz, now turned into a restaurant with considerable atmosphere. It has high stone arches, a 15-foot-long marble worktable, a walk-in fireplace, enormous spits, and walls lined with copper pots and utensils, many of them originals. Excellent food, combined with the splendor of the setting, make this an experience to remember. Air conditioned; open daily. Reservations necessary. Major credit cards accepted. Palácio Nacional de Queluz (phone: 848-1221). Expensive.

Poço – Large, with 3 air conditioned dining rooms where good Portuguese food is served. Closed Mondays. Reservations unnecessary. Major credit cards accepted. 33 Avenida da República (phone: 435-7737). Inexpensive.

SINTRA

Monserrate – The floor-to-ceiling windows of this air conditioned hotel restaurant afford a panoramic view of the valley below Sintra. The menu features international dishes. Open daily. Reservations necessary. Major credit cards accepted. *Hotel Tivoli Sintra*, Praça da República (phone: 923-3505). Expensive.

Palácio dos Seteais – An 18th-century palace makes a lovely setting for lunch on a sunny day, especially a leisurely Sunday, and especially when the restaurant has an adjoining garden terrace on which to indulge in after-dinner coffee. This very elegant restaurant, serving well-prepared Portuguese and international dishes, is located outside Sintra, in the hotel of the same name. Open daily. Reservations necessary. Major credit cards accepted. 8 Rua Barbosa do Bocage (phone: 923-3200). Expensive.

Cantinho de São Pedro – Also in São Pedro de Sintra, this rustic restaurant has 2 large dining rooms and a wine cellar. Try it for seafood, game, or one of the many French dishes on the menu. Closed Mondays and Thursday evenings. Reservations advised. Major credit cards accepted. 18 Praça Dom Fernando II, São Pedro de Sintra (phone: 923-0267). Moderate.

Dos Arcos – Typical Portuguese dishes are served in an attractive setting that includes a waterfall. In an old part of town, a 10-minute walk from downtown. Open daily. Reservations unnecessary. Major credit cards accepted. 4 Rua Serpa Pinto, São Pedro de Sintra (phone: 923-0264). Moderate.

Galeria Real – Above a gallery of antiques shops in São Pedro de Sintra, this is a lovely dining room, filled with antiques. The menu features Portuguese and French food. Open daily. Reservations unnecessary. Major credit cards accepted. Rua Tude de Sousa, São Pedro de Sintra (phone: 923-1661). Moderate.

Solar de São Pedro – Two large dining rooms with fireplaces and a menu of French and Portuguese selections keep this place busy. Closed Tuesday evenings and Wednesdays. Reservations advised. Major credit cards accepted. 12 Praça Dom Fernando II, São Pedro de Sintra (phone: 923-1860). Moderate.

Adega do Saloio – The rustic decor, the strings of onions and garlic hanging from the ceiling, the fireplaces, and the open kitchen tell visitors that this "countryman's winery" is aptly named. Meats, fish, and seafood grilled on the spit are the specialties. Located at the entrance to Sintra from Lisbon or Estoril. Closed Tuesdays. Reservations unnecessary. No credit cards accepted. Chão de Meninos (phone: 923-1422). Moderate to inexpensive.

Portelinho – Small, air conditioned, with a bar, it serves a variety of Portuguese regional dishes at reasonable prices. Open daily. Reservations unnecessary. Major credit cards accepted. 66-70 Avenida Movimento das Forças Armadas (phone: 923-3857). Inexpensive.

LONDON

British author and journalist V. S. Pritchett noted that the essence of London was contained in the very sound of its name: Lon-don, a weighty word, solid, monumental, dignified, even ponderous. London is a shapeless city without a center; it sprawls anarchically over 620 square miles and brims over with a variety of neighborhoods and people. One of its sharpest observers, Daniel Defoe, portrayed London in the 18th century much as it could be described today: "It is . . . stretched out in buildings, straggling, confused . . . out of all shape, uncompact and unequal; neither long nor broad, round or square."

London can best be understood not as one city but as a conglomeration of villages that were incorporated whole, one by one, as the monster expanded — Chelsea, Battersea, Paddington, and Hampstead are just a few. Fortunately, all of its important parks and squares have remained inviolate, but not without a struggle, for London's merchant class — its backbone and its pride — often resisted and defeated town planners, ever since Parliament turned down Sir Christopher Wren's splendid plan to rebuild after the fire of 1666. It was royalty and aristocracy who created and preserved the parks — St. James's Park, Hyde Park, Kensington Gardens, Regent's Park, and Kew Gardens were all royal parks — and their enthusiasm became contagious. The passionate regard of Londoners for their green spots has been one of the city's saving graces as it grew so helplessly and recklessly, more in the spirit of commerce than of urban planning.

Today's London — though marred by soulless high-rise intruders of glass and concrete — boasts more greenery than any metropolis could reasonably hope to retain in these philistine times. Aside from its many garden squares and the meticulously tended plots of so many Londoners' homes, the city is punctuated by a series of large parks and commons; besides those already mentioned, there are Wimbledon Common, Richmond Deer Park, Primrose Hill, Hampstead Heath — the list goes on and on. And to make even more certain that citification does not intrude too far into London life, a green belt, almost 100 square miles of forest and grassland, virtually encircles the city and, to the chagrin and impatience of developers, is meticulously preserved by law.

London's other natural resource, the river Thames, has not been so fortunate. As any glance at a map will show, London follows the serpentine meanderings of the Thames, England's principal river. Nearly everything of interest in London is on or near the Thames, for London is London because it is a natural port. The river has always been London's mainstay, for centuries its only east-west road, and it has justifiably been said that "every drop of the Thames is liquid history." At the site of the Naval College in Greenwich, for example, there once stood a royal palace where Henry VIII and

Elizabeth I were born, and where tournaments, pageants, and banquets were held.

A great river port and a city of gardens, London is also a city of stately squares and monuments, of royalty with its pomp and ceremony, a cosmopolitan city of the first rank. Until World War II, it was the capital of the mammoth and far-flung British Empire upon which, it was said, the sun never set. For many centuries, a powerful Britannia ruled a considerable section of the globe — the largest since Roman times — and the English language spread from the inconsiderable British Isles to become the dominant language all over the world, from North America to India.

If the British Empire has contracted drastically, it has done so gracefully, among memories of its greatest days. And if once-subject peoples hated their oppressor, they still love London, and many have chosen to live there. London is still the center of the Commonwealth of independent nations that were once British colonies, and its cosmopolitan atmosphere owes a great deal to the ubiquity of former colonials. Their presence is felt in the substantial Indian-Pakistani community in the Southall district of West London; in the strong Caribbean flavor in Brixton; in Chinatown in and around Gerrard Street — a hop, skip, and a jump from Piccadilly Circus; in the Cypriot groceries and bakeries of Camden Town; and in the majestic mosque on the fringe of Regent's Park.

A tantalizing diversity of accents flavors the English language here — accents from Australia and Barbados, Bangladesh and Nigeria, Canada and Malaysia, Kenya and South Africa, Sri Lanka and Ireland, Hong Kong and the US. And then the various inflections of Britain itself also are to be heard in the streets of London — the lilt and rasp of cockney, Oxford, Somerset, Yorkshire, the Scottish Highlands, and the Welsh mining towns.

London's somewhat onomatopoeic name derives from the Celtic term *Llyn-din,* meaning "river place," but little is known of London before it was renamed *Londinium* by the Romans in AD 43. The rather fantastical 12th-century historian Geoffrey of Monmouth may have originated the myth widespread in Shakespeare's day — that London was founded by Brute, a direct descendant of Aeneas in 1108 BC, who named it Troynovant, New Troy, or Trenovant. Even in medieval times, London had grandiose notions of its own importance — a prideful self-image that has been amply justified by history. Nevertheless, yet another chunk of Roman London recently has been uncovered by archaeologists from the *Museum of London.* While excavating the foundation of the 15th-century Guildhall chapel, they found Roman works more than 1 meter wide that have been identified as Roman London's missing amphitheater. This, however, is not viewable, though part of the old Roman city wall may be seen near the Tower of London, as can some segments that are in the *Museum of London* (phone: 71-600-3699).

The city was sufficiently prominent for the Norman invader William the Conqueror to make it his capital in 1066. During the Middle Ages, the expansion of trade, population growth, and the energetic activities of its guilds of merchants and craftsmen promoted London's prosperity. Indisputably, London's golden age was the English Renaissance, the 16th century, the time of Queen Elizabeth I, Shakespeare, and Drake's defeat of the Spanish Ar-

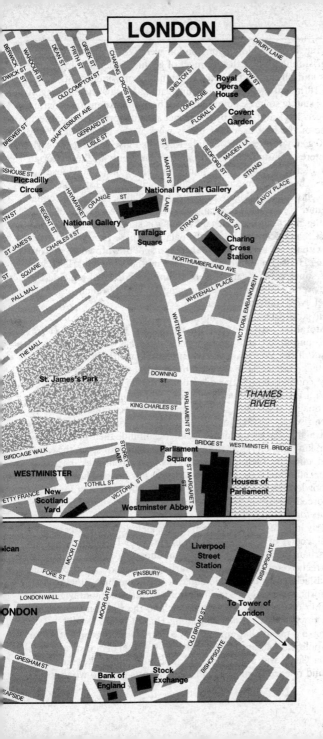

mada. Most of the Tudor buildings of London were wiped out in the great fire of 1666. Christopher Wren, the architect of genius, undertook to rebuild many buildings and churches, the most outstanding of which is St. Paul's Cathedral. The 18th century, a highly sophisticated age, saw the building of noble homes and stately squares, culminating in the grand expansion program developed between 1811 and 1820 by the prince regent's principal architect, John Nash. One of the best examples of his work is the terrace of largely crown-owned Regency houses surrounding Regent's Park. During the early 19th century, interest continued in homes and squares; only in the Victorian age, the height of the Empire, were public buildings like the Houses of Parliament redesigned, this time in grand and fanciful neo-Gothic style.

London has seen whole catalogues of heroes and villains, crises and conflagrations, come and go, sometimes swallowed whole in the passage of time, sometimes leaving relics. Still on elegant display is stately Hampton Court Palace, the most magnificent of England's palaces, where Henry VIII lived now and again with five of his six wives. There is a spot downtown — in front of the Banqueting House on Whitehall — where another king, Charles I, was beheaded by his subjects, who calmly were committing dreaded regicide 140 years before the presumably more emotional and explosive French across the English Channel even contemplated such a gesture.

London has lived through the unbounded permissiveness of the flamboyantly royal Restoration period (1660–85), when even King Charles II frequented brothels and didn't care who knew it, and it has survived the stern moral puritanism of the Victorian era, when it was downright rude to refer to a *breast* of chicken or a piano *leg*. And more recently, London stood up with exemplary courage under the devastating effects of Nazi bombings, which destroyed a great many buildings and killed thousands of people.

Many of our images of London, taken from old movies, actually mirror its realities: Big Ben rises above the Houses of Parliament, somberly striking the hour; ramrod-straight, scarlet-uniformed soldiers half hide their faces in towering black bearskin hats; clerks at the Bank of England still sport the kinds of top hats and tailcoats their predecessors wore for centuries; barristers (lawyers) in court still don wigs and black robes. A few images, however, are outdated: The bowler hat has been slipping steadily out of fashion for years, and rigidly enforced environmental regulations have made London's once-famous pea soup fog a thing of the past.

London's nearly infinite variety of urban moods includes the sturdy edifices lining Whitehall, center of the British government, with Trafalgar Square at its head and Parliament at its foot; the elegant shopping areas of Knightsbridge, Bond Street, Kensington, and the Burlington Arcade; suburban chic in Barnes and Blackheath; handsome squares in Bloomsbury; melancholy mystery in Victoria and Waterloo train stations with their spy-movie atmosphere; the vitality of East End street markets; and the riparian tranquillity of Thames-side towpaths in Putney and along Hammersmith Mall.

The British have a talent that amounts to a genius for government — for democracy and political tolerance — a talent that has been demonstrated ever since the Magna Carta was signed in 1215, and one that makes London's ambience easy and relaxed for individualists of all sorts. It is no wonder that the eccentric and inveterate Londoner of the city's 18th-century heyday, Dr. Samuel Johnson, once declared, "When a man is tired of London, he is tired of life, for there is in London all that life can afford."

Johnson's opinion, though somewhat overblown (and open to challenge today), essentially was shared by one of several modern American writers who chose to live in London. Disillusioned with New York, Boston, and Paris, Henry James decided in favor of London in 1881. Somehow he concluded that London was a place eminently suited to human life: "It is not a pleasant place; it is not agreeable, or cheerful, or easy, or exempt from reproach. It is only magnificent. You can draw up a tremendous list of reasons why it should be unsupportable. The fogs, the smoke, the dirt, the darkness, the wet, the distances, the ugliness, the brutal size of the place, the horrible numerosity of society . . . but . . . London is on the whole the most possible form of life."

LONDON AT-A-GLANCE

 SEEING THE CITY: London has, for the most part, resisted the temptation to build high. Aside from a handful of modest gestures toward skyscraping, there aren't many towering structures to obscure panoramic overviews of the city from its higher vantage points, which include the following:

London Hilton International – There were discreet noises of disapproval from Buckingham Palace when it was realized that the view from the roof bar of the *Hilton* included not only the palace grounds but, with high-powered binoculars, the inside of some of the royal chambers as well. In fact, the view over Mayfair, Hyde Park, and Westminster is breathtaking. 22 Park La., W1A 2HH (phone: 71-493-8000).

Westminster Cathedral – Not to be confused with Westminster Abbey. The top of the bell tower of London's Roman Catholic cathedral looks down on a broad expanse of the inner city. An elevator takes visitors up for a token charge (from April to September only). Off Victoria St. near the station, at Ashley Pl., SW1 (phone: 71-834-7452).

Hampstead Heath – Climb to the top of Parliament Hill, on the southern rim of this "wilderness" in north London. On a clear day, the view south from the Heath makes the city look like a vast village.

South Bank Arts Center – On the south bank of Waterloo Bridge is the bunker-like complex of cultural buildings, including the *Royal Festival Hall,* the *Royal National Theatre,* the *National Film Theatre,* the *Hayward Gallery,* and other cultural attractions. For a view of London, look across the Thames — upriver to the Houses of Parliament, downriver to St. Paul's Cathedral.

Tower Bridge Walkway – The upper part of one of London's famous landmarks is open to visitors. In addition to the viewing gallery, there is an exhibition on the history of London's bridges and a museum that includes the bridge's Victorian steam pumping engines. Open November through March, 10 AM to 4:45 PM; April through October, 10 AM to 6:30 PM. Admission charge. Tower Hill Underground Station (phone: 71-403-3761 or 71-407-0922).

St. Paul's Cathedral – The reward for climbing the 538 steps up to the dome of this cathedral — the largest in the world after St. Peter's in Rome — is a panoramic view of London. Galleries are open 10 AM to 4:15 PM weekdays; 11 AM to 4:15 PM

Saturdays; closed Sundays and for special services. Admission charge to galleries. St. Paul's, Mansion House Underground Stations (phone: 71-248-2705).

Docklands – The development of this area is so extensive that it even includes its own railroad; new apartment, commercial, and office buildings stretch seemingly without end. The *Docklands Light Railway,* a high-tech, overhead train, runs from Tower Hill to Greenwich, speeding over the fast-developing and fascinating terrain. If food shopping is on your agenda, visiting the Docklands will put to rest forever the image of British homemakers buying the family's food in tiny neighborhood greengrocers and small butcher shops. There's a market here called the *Super Store,* a British interpretation of a California supermarket, and the *Billingsgate Market,* originally on Lower Thames Street, has moved here. It's the place where some of London's premier chefs pick out their produce and fresh fish early in the morning, and it's the best place to pick up a side of smoked Scottish salmon to cart home. And the Docklands also is home to the *Design Museum* (admission charge; Butlers Wharf SE1 2YD; phone: 71-407-6265). Walking tours of the Rotherhithe district, where the *Mayflower* returned from its journey in 1621, are offered by local historian Jim Nash; for details contact *Karisma Travel* (21 Hayes Wood Ave., Hayes, Bromley, Kent BR2 7BG; phone: 81-462-4953; call a week in advance). Further development plans for the Docklands extend to 1998, which will include the completion of *Canary Wharf* — including the tallest building in Europe; so there is always something new popping up in this burgeoning community.

SPECIAL PLACES: Surveying London from the steps of St. Paul's Cathedral at the turn of the 19th century, a visiting Prussian general commented to his English host: "What a place to plunder!" Even those who are less rapacious will appreciate the extraordinary wealth of sights London displays for visitors to inspect. Though some are dispersed in various corners of this vast city, most are clustered reasonably close together in or near the inner districts of Westminster, the City, and Kensington. Twenty Photospot locations — places to stand to get the best photographs of famous sights — have been indicated throughout Westminster with blue and white signs fixed to lampposts.

WESTMINSTER

Changing of the Guard – An American who lived in London once said, "There's just no better way to convince yourself that you're in London!" This famous ceremony takes place daily from April to mid-August (alternate days in winter) promptly at 11:30 AM in the Buckingham Palace forecourt, at 11:15 AM at St. James's Palace, and at 11:30 AM at the Tower of London. (In very wet weather, it may be canceled.) St. James's Park, Green Park, and Victoria Underground Stations.

Horse Guards – If you haven't had enough, you can see a new guard of 12 members of the Household Cavalry troop in with trumpet and standard, daily at 11 AM, Sundays at 10 AM, on the west side of Whitehall. Incidentally, they come from stables not far from Hyde Park and make a daily parade along the south roadway of Hyde Park, past Buckingham Palace, and then on to Trafalgar Square to turn into Whitehall. Their progress is as much fun to watch as the actual ceremony. Westminster, Charing Cross, and Embankment Underground Stations.

Buckingham Palace – The royal standard flies from the roof when the monarch is in residence at her London home. Although George III bought the palace in 1762, sovereigns officially still lived in St. James's Palace around the corner in Pall Mall, and Buckingham Palace did not become the actual principal regal dwelling until 1837, when Queen Victoria moved in. The palace, unfortunately, is open only to invited guests (the *Queen's Gallery* and Royal Mews are open to the public; see below). The queen's summer garden parties are held on the palace lawns. The interior contains magnificently decorated apartments, a superb picture gallery, and a throne room (66 feet long), where foreign ambassadors are received and knights are knighted. The palace grounds contain the largest private garden in London (40 acres). And the gate that originally was built for the entrance, too narrow for the coaches of George IV, now marks the Hyde Park end of Oxford Street and is known as Marble Arch. Victoria, St. James's Park, Green Park Underground Stations.

State Visits – If you aren't going to be in London for the queen's official birthday in June, you might want to see her greet a foreign dignitary in full regalia. This happens quite frequently and is announced in the royal calendar in the *Times.* The queen meets her guest at Victoria Station, and they ride to Buckingham Palace in a procession of horse-drawn coaches, followed by the colorful Horse Guards. Meanwhile, at Hyde Park Corner, the cannoneers on horseback perform elaborate maneuvers before their salute thunders through the whole city.

Queen's Gallery – Treasures from the royal art collection are on public display only in this room of the palace. Open Tuesdays through Saturdays from 10:30 AM to 5 PM; Sundays from 2 to 5 PM; closed when exhibitions are being changed, about once a year. Admission charge. Buckingham Palace Rd., SW1 (phone: 71-799-2331).

Royal Academy – Housed in a building that resembles a combined mausoleum, railroad station, and funeral parlor are the works of the established, leading fashionable painters of the past. It's also the place where some of the major exhibitions to visit London are mounted. Admission charge. Burlington House, Piccadilly, W1 (phone: 71-439-7438).

Royal Mews – The mews is a palace alley where the magnificent bridal coach, other state coaches, and the horses that draw them are stabled. The public is admitted on Wednesdays and Thursdays from 2 to 4 PM. Admission charge. Buckingham Palace Rd., SW1 (phone: 71-799-2331).

St. James's Park – Parks are everywhere in London and Londoners love them. This is one of the nicest, where at lunch hour on a sunny day you can see the impeccably dressed London businessmen lounging on the grass, their shoes off and their sleeves rolled up. With its sizable lake (designed by John Nash) inhabited by pelicans and other wild fowl, St. James's was originally a royal deer park, drained under Henry VIII in 1532 and laid out as a pleasure ground for Charles II.

The Mall – The wide avenue (pronounced *Mal*), parallel to Pall Mall, is lined with lime trees and Regency buildings and leads from Trafalgar Square to Buckingham Palace. This is the principal ceremonial route used by Queen Elizabeth and her escort of Household Cavalry for the State Opening of Parliament (October/November) and the *Trooping the Colour* (see *Special Events*). It is closed to traffic on Sunday afternoons.

Trafalgar Square – One of London's most heavily trafficked squares is built around the towering Nelson's Column — a 145-foot-high monument bearing a 17-foot statue that honors Lord Nelson, victor at the naval Battle of Trafalgar in 1805. At the base of the monument are four huge bronze lions and two fountains. Flanked by handsome buildings, including the *National Gallery* and the 18th-century Church of St. Martin in the Fields (have lunch or tea in the café in the crypt), the square is a favorite gathering place for political demonstrations, tourists, and pigeons.

Piccadilly Circus – Downtown London finds its center here in the heart of the theater district and on the edge of Soho. This is the London equivalent of Times Square — lots of it is just as tacky — and at the center of the busy "circus," or traffic circle, is the restored statue of Eros (moved about 40 feet from its original perch), which actually was designed in 1893 as *The Angel of Christian Charity,* a memorial to the charitable Earl of Shaftesbury — the archer and his bow were meant as a pun on his name. The *Trocadero,* a converted 3-story shopping and entertainment complex, has lent Piccadilly a new level of bustle. A recent addition is *Rock Circus* (phone: 71-734-0943), housed on the top 4 floors of the London Pavilion. Rock music's immortals — from the *Beatles* to the *Who* — are brought to life with surprisingly impressive lighting, narration, and music; it also includes Europe's largest revolving auditorium, where "performances" are offered by rather remarkable robotic figures. It's not quite real life, but a pretty fair approximation. Open Mondays, Wednesdays, and Thursdays from 11 AM to 9 PM; Tuesdays noon to 9 PM; Fridays and Saturdays 11 AM to 10 PM. Another popular exhibition is the *Guinness World Records* display. Open daily from 10 AM to 10 PM. Separate admission charges (phone: 71-439-7331).

National Gallery – One of the world's great art museums, this is an inexhaustible feast for art lovers. In the vast collection on display are works by such masters as Uccello, da Vinci, Titian, Rembrandt, Rubens, Cranach, Gainsborough, El Greco, Renoir, Cézanne, and Van Gogh. The just opened Sainsbury Wing highlights Giotto, van Eyck, and Boticelli, among others. The museum has undertaken the rehanging of its entire collection in chronological order. Open daily, 10 AM to 6 PM; Sundays, 2 to 6 PM. No admission charge. Trafalgar Sq., WC2 (phone: 71-839-3321).

National Portrait Gallery – Right behind the *National Gallery* sits this delightful museum. Nearly every English celebrity from the last 500 years is pictured here, with the earliest personalities at the top and the 20th-century notables at the bottom. Open Mondays through Fridays, 10 AM to 5 PM; Saturdays, 10 AM to 6 PM; Sundays, 2 to 6 PM. Admission to special exhibitions only. 2 St. Martin's Pl., WC2 (phone: 71-306-0055).

Whitehall – A broad boulevard stretching from Trafalgar Square to Parliament Square, lined most of the way by government ministries and such historic buildings as the Banqueting House (completed in 1622, with a ceiling painted by Rubens) and the Horse Guards (whose central archway is ceremonially guarded by mounted troopers).

Detective novel fans may be interested to know that from 1890 to 1967 Scotland Yard occupied the Norman Shaw Building at the Trafalgar end of Whitehall; it now houses offices for members of Parliament. The Yard has moved to Victoria Street near St. James's Park.

Downing Street – Off Whitehall, a street of small, unpretentious Georgian houses includes the official residences of the most important figures in the British government, the Prime Minister at No. 10 and the Chancellor of the Exchequer (Britain's secretary of the treasury) at No. 11.

Cabinet War Rooms – Constructed to resemble its wartime appearance (and filled with its original furnishings), this underground complex of 20 rooms was Winston Churchill's auxiliary command post during World War II, which he used most often during the German Luftwaffe's blitz on London. Of special note are the map room, with maps pinpointing the positions of Allied and German troops in the final stages of the war, the room where the prime minister met with his staff, and the cramped transatlantic telephone room (No. 63) used only by Churchill himself. The Cabinet War Rooms are an auxiliary site of London's *Imperial War Museum* (see below). Open daily from 10 AM to 6 PM. Admission charge. Beneath the government building on the corner of Great George's St. and Horse Guard Rd., SW1 (phone: 71-930-6961).

Westminster Abbey – It's easy to get lost among the endlessly fascinating tombs and plaques and not even notice the Abbey's splendid architecture, so do look at the structure itself and don't miss the cloisters, which display its Gothic design to advantage. Note also the fine Tudor chapel of Henry VII, with its tall windows and lovely fan-tracery vaulting, and the 13th-century chapel of St. Edward the Confessor, containing England's Coronation Chair and Scotland's ancient coronation Stone of Scone.

Ever since William the Conqueror was crowned here in 1066, the Abbey has been the traditional place where English monarchs are crowned, married, and buried. You don't have to be an Anglophile to be moved by the numerous tombs and memorials with their fascinating inscriptions — here are honored (not necessarily buried) kings and queens, soldiers, statesmen, and many other prominent English men and women. Poets' Corner, in the south transept, contains the tombs of Chaucer, Ben Jonson, Tennyson, Browning, and many others — plus memorials to nearly every English poet of note and to some Americans, such as Longfellow and T. S. Eliot.

The Abbey is itself a lesson in English history. A church has stood on this site since at least AD 170; in the 8th century, it was a Benedictine monastery. The current early–English Gothic edifice, begun in the 13th century, took almost 300 years to build.

Guided tours are offered six times every weekday and three times on Saturdays. The nave and cloisters are open daily from 8 AM to 6 PM; Wednesdays 8 AM to 7:45 PM. The Royal Chapel is open weekdays from 9 AM to 4:45 PM; Saturdays 9:20 AM to 2:45 PM and from 3:45 to 5:45 PM. Closed Sundays. Admission charge to the royal chapels, Poets' Corner, and to some other sections as well. Broad Sanctuary SW1, off Parliament Sq. (phone: 71-222-5152).

Houses of Parliament – The imposing neo-Gothic, mid-19th-century buildings of the Palace of Westminster, as it is sometimes called, look especially splendid from the opposite side of the river. There are separate chambers for the House of Commons and the House of Lords, and visitors are admitted to the Strangers' Galleries of both houses by lining up at St. Stephen's Entrance, opposite Westminster Abbey. Big Ben, the world-famous 13½-ton bell in the clock tower of the palace, which is illuminated when Parliament is in session, still strikes the hours. Although the buildings are closed to the public, there are limited tours outside session hours (weekday mornings and Friday evenings). To make tour arrangements, write in advance to The Public Information Office (1 Derby Gate, London SW1A 1DG). Particularly impressive are Westminster Hall, with its magnificent hammer-beam roof, and the gold and scarlet House of Lords. No admission charge. St. Margaret St., SW1 (phone: 71-219-3000).

Tate Gallery – London's fine art museum includes an impressive collection of British paintings from the 16th century to the dawn of the 20th century, as well as modern British and international art. Best of all are masterpieces by Turner, Constable, Hogarth, and Blake. Nicholas Serota, the museum's director, has continued the reorganization of the gallery, arranging the works in chronological order rather than by skill or style. The Turner collection is housed exclusively in the ultramodern Clore Gallery extension. Open Mondays through Saturdays from 10 AM to 6 PM and on Sundays from 2 to 6 PM. Admission charge to special exhibitions only. Millbank, SW1 (phone: 71-821-1313).

Soho – This area of London is full of character; lively, bustling, and noisy by day; indiscreetly enticing by night. Its name comes from the ancient hunting cry used centuries ago when the area was parkland. The hunting, in a way, still goes on, particularly by undercover detectives. Soho lacks the sophistication and glamor of its counterparts in Europe, but it's not all sleazy either. The striptease clubs vie for customers with the numerous restaurants, most serving moderately priced food (mostly Italian and Chinese). Soho offers a diversity of entertainments: Shaftesbury Avenue is lined with theaters and movie houses. Gerrard Street abounds with Chinese restaurants, and it is the place to go for *Chinese New Year* celebrations. London's liveliest fruit and vegetable market is on Berwick Street (if you shop here, never touch the produce, as the vendors will get furious). Frith Street is a favorite Italian haunt, the best place for a foaming cappuccino and a view of Italian TV at the *Bar Italia*. Old Compton Street has several good delicatessens, perfect places to buy a picnic lunch to take to Soho Square.

Covent Garden – Tucked away behind the Strand, *Covent Garden* was the site of London's main fruit, vegetable, and flower market for over 300 years. The area was immortalized in Shaw's *Pygmalion* and the musical *My Fair Lady* by the scene in which young Eliza Doolittle sells flowers to the ladies and gents emerging from the *Royal Opera House*. The *Opera House* is still here, but the market moved south of the river in 1974 and the *Garden* has since undergone extensive redevelopment. The central market building has been converted into London's first permanent late-night shopping center, with an emphasis on all-British goods. In the former flower market is the *London Transport Museum,* whose exhibits include a replica of the first horse-drawn bus and a steam locomotive built in 1866 (open daily from 10 AM to 6 PM; phone: 71-379-6344). Boutiques selling quality clothes for men and women are springing up all over, along with discos, wine bars, and brasserie-style restaurants. On weekends the whole area is packed with young people. One nice touch: Just to remind everyone of the *Old Covent Garden,* there are about 40 of the original wrought-iron trading stands from which the home-produced wares of English craftspeople are sold.

Bloomsbury – Well-designed squares — Bloomsbury Square, Bedford Square, Russell Square, and others — surrounded by pretty, terraced houses form this aristocratic district. Within its confines are the *British Museum* and the Centre of the University of London. The Bloomsbury group of writers and artists included Virginia Woolf, her husband Leonard Woolf, her sister Vanessa Bell and her husband Clive Bell, Lytton Strachey, E. M. Forster, Roger Fry, and John Maynard Keynes. Living nearby and peripheral to this central group were D. H. Lawrence, Bertrand Russell, and others. Unfortunately, none of the original buildings in Bloomsbury Square have survived, but the garden is still here, and nearby Bedford Square remains complete. Virginia Woolf lived at 46 Gordon Square before her marriage.

. **British Museum** – One of the world's largest museums offers a dazzling array of permanent exhibitions — including the legendary Elgin Marbles (from the Parthenon) and the Rosetta Stone. Seven sculpture galleries exhibit some 1,500 Greek and Roman treasures. This magnificent collection includes two of the seven wonders of the ancient world: the Mausoleum of Halicarnassus and the Temple of Artemis at Ephesus. There is an equally impressive parade of temporary displays. The Egyptian and Mesopotamian galleries are especially stunning. The manuscript room of the British Library, within the museum, displays an original copy of the Magna Carta, together with the signatures of a great many famous authors — Shakespeare, Dickens, Austen, and Joyce among them — and numerous original manuscripts, including *Alice's Adventures in Wonderland.* The British Library has an enormous collection, since every book published in Britain must be sent here. If you wish to use the library, consult a copy of the library's catalogue, stocked by major world libraries. Send in your requests with call numbers; many books often take 2 days to arrive from storage or other branches. The library also has a remarkable, gigantic Victorian Reading Room with a huge dome made of papier-mâché, measuring 140 feet across and 106 feet high. Many of the world's great thinkers and writers worked here, including Marx, Lenin, Gandhi, Yeats, and Dickens. Access to the Reading Room is limited; you must call or write to the museum's British Library Readers' Admissions Office for permission. Open Mondays through Saturdays, 10 AM to 5 PM; Sundays, 2:30 to 6 PM. Admission charge to special exhibitions only. Great Russell St. WC1 (phone: museum, 71-636-1555; library, 71-636-1544).

Oxford, Regent, Bond, and Kensington High Streets – London's main shopping streets include large department and specialty stores (*Selfridges, Debenhams, John Lewis, Liberty, D. H. Evans*), chain stores offering good value in clothes (*Marks & Spencer, C & A, British Home Stores, Littlewoods*), and scores of popular clothing chains (*The Gap, Laura Ashley, Benetton, Principles*).

Burlington Arcade – A charming covered shopping promenade dating from the Regency period (early 19th century), the arcade contains elegant, expensive shops selling cashmere sweaters (we've seen some here that were 10-ply!), antique jewelry, and other expensive items. One entrance is on Piccadilly (the street, not the circus), the other near Old Bond St., W1.

. **Hyde Park** – London's most famous patch of greenery (361 acres) is particularly well known for its Speakers' Corner at Marble Arch, where crowds gather each Sunday afternoon to hear impromptu diatribes and debates. Among the park's other attractions are sculptures by Henry Moore; an extensive bridle path; a cycle path; the Serpentine Lake, where boats for rowing and sailing can be rented and where there's swimming in the summer; a bird sanctuary; vast expanses of lawn; and the recently opened *Serpentine* restaurant (phone: 71-402-1142).

Madame Tussaud's – The popularity of this wax museum is undiminished by the persistent criticism that its effigies are a little bland, and visitors are quite likely to find themselves innocently addressing a museum attendant — or a waxwork murderer. Madame moved to London from Paris in 1802, when she was 42, crossing the Channel with her waxwork effigies of heads that had rolled during the French Revolution. The current museum includes many modern and historical personalities and the gory Chamber of Horrors, with its murderers and hangmen. Open daily from 10 AM (9:30 AM on Saturdays) to 5:30 PM. Admission charge. Marylebone Rd., NW1 (phone: 71-935-6861).

London Planetarium – During their 30-minute shows, visitors travel through space and time under a huge starlit dome. Interesting commentary accompanies the display. The first show begins at 12:20 PM, and they continue every 40 minutes thereafter, with the last one at 4:20 PM (on Saturdays and Sundays, the first is at 10:20 AM and the last at 5 PM). There is also a Laserium show at varying times in the evening. Guests can save money by purchasing a combination ticket to the planetarium and *Madame Tussaud's* — both at the same address, Marylebone Rd., NW1. Open daily (phone: 71-486-1121).

THE CITY

The difference between London and the City of London can be confusing to a visitor. They are, in fact, two distinctly different entities, one within the other. The City of London, usually called only the City, covers the original Roman London. It is now the "square mile" financial and commercial center of the great metropolis. With a Lord Mayor (who only serves in a ceremonial capacity), a police force, and rapidly growing new developments, it is the core of Greater London. The governing council, the London Residuary Body, administers 32 boroughs including the City.

St. Paul's Cathedral – The cathedral church of the London Anglican diocese stands atop Ludgate Hill and is the largest church in London. This Renaissance masterpiece by Sir Christopher Wren took 35 years to build (1675–1710). Its domed exterior is majestic and its sparse decorations are gold and mosaic. The interior contains particularly splendid choir stalls, screens, and inside the spectacular dome, the "Whispering Gallery," with its strange acoustics. Nelson and Wellington are buried beneath the main floor, and there is a fine statue of John Donne, metaphysical poet and dean of St. Paul's from 1621 to 1631 — he stands looking quite alive on an urn in an up-ended coffin which, typically, he bought during his lifetime and kept in his house. Wren himself was buried here in 1723, with his epitaph inscribed beneath the dome in Latin: "If you seek his monument, look around you."

A gorgeous monument it remains; though damaged by bombs during World War II, it became a rallying point for the flagging spirits of wartime Londoners. More recently, St. Paul's raised British spirits as the site for the wedding of Prince Charles and Lady Diana Spencer in July 1981. The Golden Gallery at the top of the dome, 542 steps from the ground, offers an excellent view of the city. The cathedral is open to tourists on weekdays from 10 AM to 4:15 PM and on Saturdays from 11 AM to 4:15 PM. Admission charge to galleries. St. Paul's Churchyard, EC4 (phone: 71-248-2705).

Old Bailey – This is the colloquial name for London's Central Criminal Court, on the site of the notorious Newgate Prison. Visitors are admitted to the court, on a space-available basis, to audit the proceedings and to see lawyers (called barristers, in court) and judges clad in wigs and robes. Open weekdays 10:30 AM to 1 PM and 2 PM to 4 PM. No children under 14 years of age admitted. No admission charge. Old Bailey, EC4 (phone: 71-248-3277).

Museum of London – Exhibits and displays depict London history from the Roman occupation to modern times. The museum is in the Barbican area and was opened in 1976. It includes Roman remains, Anglo-Saxon artifacts, Renaissance musical instruments, a cell from old Newgate prison, Victorian shops and offices, audiovisual recreation of the 1666 Great Fire, and the Lord Mayor's Golden Stage Coach. Closed Mondays. Open Tuesdays through Saturdays, 10 AM to 6 PM; Sundays, 2 to 6 PM. No admission charge. 150 London Wall, EC2 (phone: 71-600-3699).

Barbican Centre for Arts and Conferences – Served by underground stations Barbican, St. Paul's, and Moorgate, the *Barbican,* which opened in 1982, includes 6,000 apartments, the Guildhall School of Music and Drama, and the restored St. Giles's Church (built in 1390). The *Barbican* also features the 2026-seat *Barbican Hall* doubling as conference venue (with simultaneous translation system), and *Concert Hall* (*London Symphony Orchestra*); the 1166-seat *Barbican Theatre* (the *Royal Shakespeare Company*'s London performance venue); a 200-seat studio theatre; sculpture courtyard; art exhibition galleries; seminar rooms; three cinemas; two exhibition halls; a municipal lending library; restaurants and bars. Faced with rising costs there has been a question as to whether the *RSC* can maintain its London home. At press time, however, there were no plans for the company to leave the *Barbican.* Silk St. EC2 (phone: for guided tours and general information, 71-638-4141, ext. 218; recorded information, 71-628-2295 or 71-628-9760; box office, 71-638-8891).

Bank of England – Banker to the British government, holder of the country's gold reserves in its vaults, controller of Britain's banking and monetary affairs, the "Old Lady of Threadneedle Street" is the most famous bank in the world. Bathed in tradition as well as the mechanics of modern high finance, its porters and messengers wear traditional livery. Visits by appointment only. The *Bank of England Museum* here is open daily from 10 AM to 5 PM (from 11 AM on Saturdays and Sundays). No admission charge. Threadneedle St., EC2 (phone: 71-601-4444 for the bank; 71-601-5792 for the museum).

Mansion House – The official residence of the Lord Mayor of London, containing his private apartments, built in the 18th century in Renaissance style. It is difficult to gain admission to the house, but you may request permission by writing, well in advance of your visit, to the Principal Assistant Office (Mansion House, London EC4N 8EH). Mansion House St., EC4 (phone: 71-626-2500).

Lloyd's – A strikingly dramatic, futuristic building now houses the world's most important seller of international maritime and high-risk insurance. The exhibition gallery overlooking the trading floor is open only to groups who have booked a tour in advance. Corner of Lime and Leadenhall Sts., EC3 N7 DQ (phone: 71-327-5786).

Stock Exchange – The second-largest exchange in the world is no longer open to the public. Old Broad St., EC2 (phone: 71-588-2355).

The Monument – A fluted Doric column, topped by a flaming urn, was designed by Sir Christopher Wren to commemorate the Great Fire of London (1666) and stands 202 feet tall. (Its height was determined because it was allegedly 202 feet from the bakery on Pudding Lane where the fire began.) The view from the top is partially obstructed by new buildings. Open April through September, weekdays 9 AM to 6 PM, Saturdays and Sundays 2 to 6 PM; October through March, open Mondays through Saturdays 9 AM to 4 PM, closed Sundays. Admission charge. Monument St., EC3 (phone: 71-626-2717).

Tower of London – Originally conceived as a fortress to keep "fierce" Londoners at bay and to guard the river approaches, it has served as a palace, a prison, a mint, and an observatory as well. Today, the main points of interest are the Crown Jewels; the White Tower (the oldest building), with its exhibition of ancient arms, armor, and torture implements; St. John's Chapel, the oldest church in London; the Bloody Tower, where the two little princes disappeared in 1483 and Sir Walter Raleigh languished from 1603 to 1616; an exhibit of old military weapons; Tower Green, where two of Henry VIII's queens — and many others — were beheaded; and Traitors' Gate, through which boats bearing prisoners entered the castle. The yeoman warders ("Beef-eaters") still wear historic uniforms. They also give excellent recitals of that segment of English history that was played out within the tower walls. You can see the wonderful Ceremony of the Keys here every night at 9:30 PM; reserve tickets several months ahead. (Send a stamped, self-addressed envelope to Resident Governor Constable's Office, HM Tower of London, EC3N 4AB.) Open March through October, Mondays through Saturdays 9:30 AM to 6:30 PM, Sundays 2 to 6 PM; November through February, open Mondays through Saturdays 9:30 AM to 5 PM; closed Sundays. Admission charge (phone: 71-709-0765, general inquiries; 71-488-5718, for recorded information).

Fleet Street – Most native and foreign newspapers and press associations once had offices here — in the center of London's active newspaper world — but none remain because of the exodus to more technologically advanced plants elsewhere. The street also boasts two 17th-century pubs, the *Cock Tavern* (No. 22) and *Ye Olde Cheshire Cheese* (just off Fleet St. at 5 Little Essex St.), where Dr. Samuel Johnson held court for the literary giants of his day.

Johnson's House – In nearby Gough Square is the house where Johnson wrote his famous *Dictionary;* the house is now a museum of Johnsoniana. Open May through September, daily from 11 AM to 5:30 AM; October through April, 11 AM to 5 PM; closed Sundays. Admission charge. 17 Gough Sq., EC4 (phone: 71-353-3745).

Inns of Court – Quaint and quiet precincts house the ancient buildings, grounds, and gardens that mark the traditional center of Britain's legal profession. Only the four Inns of Court — Gray's, Lincoln's, and the Inner and Middle Temples — have the right to call would-be barristers to the bar to practice law. Especially charming is the still-Dickensian Lincoln's Inn, where young Dickens worked as an office boy. It was in its great hall that the writer later set parts of his fictional law case of Jarndyce v. Jarndyce in *Bleak House.* John Donne once preached in the Lincoln's Inn chapel, designed by Inigo Jones. The chapel can be seen on weekdays between 12:30 and 2:30 PM; ask at the Gatehouse (Chancery La., WC2; phone: 71-405-1393). Also lovely are the gardens of Lincoln's Inn Fields, laid out by Inigo Jones in 1618. The neo-Gothic Royal Courts of Justice in the Strand, better known as the Law Courts, are home to the High Court and the Court of Appeal of England and Wales, which pass judgment on Britain's most important civil cases. These courts, unlike the Old Bailey, are closed to the public.

OTHER LONDON ATTRACTIONS

Regent's Park – The sprawling 472 acres just north of the city center has beautiful gardens, vast lawns, a pond with paddleboats, and one of the finest zoos in the world. (Unfortunately, at press time threats were voiced about the zoo's possible closure due to financial problems.) Crescents of elegant terraced homes border the park. No admission charge to the park. London Zoo open daily November through February, from 10 AM to 4 PM; March through October, from 9 AM to 6 PM; open until 7 PM on Sundays and bank holidays. Admission charge (phone: 71-722-3333).

Camden Passage – This quaint pedestrian alleyway, lined with antiques and specialty shops, has an open-air market — pushcarts selling curios and antiques — on Tuesdays, Wednesday mornings, and Saturdays. Just off Upper St. in Islington, north of the city, N1.

Hampstead Heath – The north London bucolic paradise of wild heathland, meadows, and wooded dells is the highest point in London. Kenwood House, a 17th-century estate on the heath, is the home of the Iveagh Bequest, a collection of art (Gainsborough, Rembrandt, Turner, and others; see "Museums" in *For the Mind,* DIVER-

SIONS) assembled by the first Earl of Iveagh. Lakeside concerts, both classical and jazz, are held on the grounds in summer (for details, call 71-734-1877). Hampstead Underground Station.

Kew Gardens – Here are the Royal Botanic Gardens, with tens of thousands of trees and other plants. The gardens' primary purpose is to serve the science of botany by researching, cultivating, experimenting, and identifying plants. There are shaded walks, floral displays, and magnificent Victorian glass greenhouses — especially the Temperate House, with some 3,000 different plants, including a 60-foot Chilean wine palm. Open daily March through September 9:30 AM to 6:30 PM; October through February 9:30 AM to 4 PM (phone: Kew Road, Kew, Richmond; 81-9401171). Admission charge.

Portobello Road – This area is famous for its antiques shops, junk shops, and outdoor pushcarts; it is one of the largest street markets in the world. The pushcarts are out only on Fridays and Saturdays, which are the best and most crowded days for the market. Less well known is *Bermondsey Market* (Long La. at Tower Bridge Rd. SE1) on Fridays from 7 AM on; this is where many of the antiques found on Portobello Road or Camden Passage were probably purchased.

Victoria and Albert Museum – Born of the *1851 Exposition,* the museum contains a vast collection of fine and applied arts (probably the largest collection of the latter in the world) — an amalgam of the great, the odd, and the ugly. Especially delightful are the English period rooms. There are superb collections of paintings, prints, ceramics, metalwork, costumes, and armor in the museum, which also contains English miniatures and famous Raphael cartoons. The museum's Henry Cole Wing (named after its founder) houses a broad selection of changing exhibitions, as well as an interesting permanent display of printmaking techniques. The Nehru Gallery, opened in 1990, has the finest collection of Indian art outside of India. Jazz concerts and fashion shows are held in the Italianate Pirelli Garden at the heart of the museum. Open daily from 10 AM to 6 PM; Sundays 2:30 to 6 PM. Entry donation suggested. Cromwell Rd., SW7 (phone: 71-938-8500; exhibitions information: 71-938-8349).

Imperial War Museum – A collection of tanks, planes, cannon, submarines, rockets, artifacts, and war paintings bridging the history of war from Flanders to the Falklands is housed in this 4-floor museum (originally Bethlem Royal Hospital, hence the word "bedlam"). There are telephones that visitors can pick up to hear people describing their firsthand wartime experiences; and historical films and videos further help to bring wartime events alive. The 20-minute-long "Blitz Experience" confines groups of 20 people to a damp, cramped re-creation of a bomb shelter during a World War II air raid; and "Operation Jericho" is a bumpy simulation of a WWII bombing raid (additional charge for each). Also see the WWI "Trench Experience" (no charge). There is a souvenir shop and a café for light meals and snacks. Open daily from 10 AM to 6 PM; closed *Christmas Eve, Christmas, Boxing Day,* and *New Year's Day.* Admission charge, except on Fridays. Lambeth Rd., SE1 (phone: 71-735-8922).

Greenwich – This Thames-side borough is traditionally associated with British seapower, especially when Britain "ruled the waves." Here, along Romney Road, is the Royal Naval College whose beautiful painted hall and chapel are open daily except Thursdays (when the college is is session) from 2:30 to 5 PM. No admission charge (phone: 81-858-2154). Also here is the *National Maritime Museum,* celebrating Britain's illustrious nautical past (see *For the Mind,* in DIVERSIONS) and the *Queen's House,* designed by Inigo Jones for Queen Henrietta Maria, wife of Charles I, reopened in 1990 after extensive restoration. Up the hill is the *Old Royal Observatory* with astronomical instruments. These three are open April through September, Mondays through Saturdays, 10 AM to 6 PM; Sundays 2 to 6 PM; October through March, Mondays through Saturdays 10 AM to 5 PM; Sundays noon to 5 PM (phone: 81-858-4422). Admission charge to each, but a money-saving "Passport" includes entry to these plus the *Cutty Sark,* a superbly preserved 19th-century clipper ship. Open April through September,

Mondays through Saturdays 10 AM to 6 PM; Sundays noon to 6 PM; October through March Mondays through Saturdays 10 AM to 5 PM; Sundays noon to 5 PM. Cutty Sark Gardens, SE 10 (phone: 81-858-3445). Greenwich Park is 200 acres of greenery with splendid views from the hill across to the Docklands and the rest of London. Greenwich Station, *British Rail.*

Richmond Park – The largest urban park in Britain is one of the few with herds of deer roaming free. (Hunting them is illegal, though this was once a royal hunting preserve established by Charles I.) It also has large oaks and rhododendron gardens. From nearby Richmond Hill there is a magnificent view of the Thames Valley. Richmond tube stop or *British Rail.*

Manor Houses – Six beautifully maintained historic homes are in Greater London. Notable for their architecture, antiques, grounds, and in the case of Kenwood, an 18th-century art collection, these homes are all accessible by bus and subway: Kenwood House (Hampstead tube stop or *British Rail,* Hampstead Heath; open daily; no admission charge; phone: 81-348-1236); Ham House (Richmond tube stop or *British Rail;* closed Mondays; admission charge; phone: 81-940-1950); Chiswick (Turnham Green or Chiswick Park tube stop; open daily; admission charge; phone: 81-995-0508); Syon House (Gunnersbury tube stop, then a No. 237 or No. 267 bus, or *British Rail,* Brentford Central; open daily except Fridays and Saturdays from *Easter* through September; admission charge; phone: 81-560-0881); and Osterley Park House (Osterley tube stop; closed Mondays; admission charge; phone: 81-560-3918). Apsley House, home of the Duke of Wellington, houses the *Wellington Museum.* It contains many fine paintings, including portraits of the Iron Duke's fellow commanders from the victorious campaign against the French, and a nude (!) statue of Napoleon Bonaparte. Open Tuesdays through Sundays from 10 AM to 5 PM; admission charge (149 Piccadilly, W1; phone: 71-499-5676).

Spencer House – This 1756 mansion owned by the Spencer family — the Princess of Wales is the former Lady Diana Spencer — has recently been restored and opened to the public. There are nine state rooms filled with artwork and furniture from the family's wide collection. The neo-classical state rooms were among the first to be so designed in Europe. Open Sundays for pre-arranged tours only from 11:30 AM to 5:30 PM; closed during August and January. Admission charge. St. James's Place, Piccadilly W1 (phone: 71-499-8620).

Hampton Court Palace – On the Thames, this sumptuous palace and gardens are in London's southwest corner. Begun by Cardinal Wolsey in 1514, the palace was appropriated by Henry VIII and was a royal residence for 2 centuries. Its attractions include a picture gallery, tapestries, state apartments, Tudor kitchens — newly restored to the grandeur of Henry VIII's day, re-creating the *Feast of St. John the Baptist* on a midsummer day in 1542 — the original tennis court, a moat, a great vine (2 centuries old), gardens, and a maze. The quickest way to get here is by *British Rail* (32 minutes from Waterloo Station), but you can take a bus or even a boat from Westminster Pier or Richmond during the summer. Open daily from March through October, from 9:30 AM to 6 PM. November through February, daily from 9:30 AM to 4:30 PM. Admission charge. East Molesey, Surrey (phone: 81-977-8441).

Freud Museum – This house was the north London home of the seminal psychiatrist after he left Vienna in 1938. His antiquities collection, library, desk, and famous couch are all on display. Open Wednesdays through Sundays, noon to 5 PM. Admission charge. 20 Maresfield Gardens, NW3 (phone: 71-435-2002).

Highgate Cemetery – The awe-inspiring grave of Karl Marx in the eastern cemetery (open daily from 10 AM to 4:45 PM during the summer, 10 AM to 3:45 PM during the winter) attracts countless visitors. Entrance to the western cemetery, with its overgrown gravestones and catacombs of the not-so-famous, is by guided tour only. Admission charge. Highgate Hill, NW3 (phone: 81-340-1834 for times).

Thames Flood Barrier – A massive and intriguing defense structure across the river at Woolwich Reach near Greenwich. Boats regularly leave Barrier Gardens Pier (or the riverside promenade nearby) for visits up close. Visitors are not allowed on the barrier itself, but audiovisual displays at the visitors' center, on the river's south bank just downstream, explain its background and illustrate the risk to London of exceptionally high tides. Open weekdays from 10:30 AM to 5 PM, weekends to 5:30 PM. Admission charge. Accessible from London by road, by river (from Westminster Pier to Barrier Gardens Pier), and by rail (to Charlton Station). 1 Unity Way, Woolwich (phone: 81-854-1373).

■**EXTRA SPECIAL:** Windsor Castle is the largest inhabited castle in the world. It is the queen's official residence, and was built by William the Conqueror in 1066 after his victory at the Battle of Hastings. Among the royal sovereigns buried here are Queen Victoria and Albert, her beloved consort. Windsor looks like a fairy-tale castle in a child's picture book: The huge Norman edifice looms majestically above the town; visitors feel awed and enchanted as they climb up the curving cobblestone street from the train station, past pubs and shops, toward Henry VIII's Gateway. The castle precincts are open daily, and there's a regular changing of the guard. The State Apartments, which can be toured when they're not in use, are splendidly decorated with paintings, tapestries, furniture, and rugs. There is also an exhibition of drawings by Leonardo da Vinci, Michelangelo, and Raphael, and a room displaying Queen Mary's dollhouse. Separate admission charges. For information, call 753-386-8286.

The castle is bordered by 4,800 acres of parkland on one side and the town on the other. The Savill Gardens — 35 acres of flowering shrubs, rare flowers, and woodland, make for a lovely summer walk. Open daily. Admission charge (phone: 784-35544). While the town still has a certain charm, heavy tourism is beginning to have a deleterious effect. Across the river is Eton — considered by some to be the more attractive town — which is the famous home of the exclusive boys' school founded by Henry IV in 1440.

The train from Paddington stops right in the center of Windsor (travel time is 39 minutes), or there's a *Green Line* coach from Victoria (1½ hours).

Don't miss taking one of the many boat trips along the Thames to places like Marlow, Cookham, or Henley (where the first rowing regatta in the world was held in 1839). The Royal Windsor Safari Park is also located southwest of London. It's an easy 45-minute car ride (exit 3 off the M3; exit 6 off the M6). Once a royal hunting ground, it's now a drive-through zoo, whose residents include baboons, camels, rhinos, cheetahs, and Bengal tigers. Be forewarned: In summer the park is very popular and traffic is bumper-to-bumper. An alternative would be to take the safari bus. Open daily. Admission charge (phone: 753-869841).

For a spectacular side trip out of London, there is nothing quite like Oxford and Stratford-upon-Avon, Shakespeare's birthplace — both of which can be seen in a 1-day organized bus tour. Otherwise you can choose one; the regular bus from Victoria Coach Station to Stratford (90 miles) travels via Oxford (65 miles), so you can catch a glimpse of the ancient colleges if you try hard (for information call *National Express Coach;* phone: 71-730-0202).

Shakespeare's birthplace is still an Elizabethan town, and even if there's no time to see a play at the *Shakespeare Memorial Theatre,* the Tudor houses, with their overhung gables and traditional straw roofs, are a very pleasant sight. The poet's birthplace is a must, as is the grave at charming Holy Trinity Church. The Great Garden of New Place, said to contain every flower that Shakespeare mentioned in his plays, and Anne Hathaway's Cottage are both enjoyable (for tourist information, call 789-293127).

Oxford is England's oldest university town; its fine Gothic buildings have cloistered many famous Englishmen. Most of the great colleges are on High Street (the High) or Broad Street (the Broad). See Queen's College, Christ Church, Trinity College, the Bodleian Library, and the marvelous *Ashmolean Museum of Art;* be sure to look in a bookstore, too — *Blackwell's* on Broad Street is one of the finest in the world. Students usually guide the university tours (for tourist information, call 865-726871).

Another highly recommended day trip, less ambitious than Stratford and Oxford, is Cambridge, only 1 hour from London by train. Cambridge is even more delightful than Oxford because the town takes full advantage of the river Cam. So don't fail to walk along "the Backs" — the back lawns of several colleges, leading down to the river; or better yet, rent a canoe or a punt, a flat-bottomed boat that is propelled by a long pole. (It's easier than it sounds.) The town has two parallel main streets that change their names every 2 blocks; one is a shopping street and the other is lined with colleges. Don't miss *Heffers* on Trinity Street; it's the biggest branch of the best bookstore in Cambridge. Stroll through the famous colleges — King's, Trinity, Queens, Jesus, Magdalene, and Clare. King's College Chapel is a 15th-century Gothic structure that is a real beauty. Also see at least one garden and one dining hall (for tourist information, call 223-322640).

SOURCES AND RESOURCES

TOURIST INFORMATION: In the US, contact the British Tourist Authority (40 W. 57th St., New York, NY 10019; phone: 212-581-4700). The London Visitor and Convention Bureau is the best source of information for attractions and events once you get to London. Its information center on the forecourt of Victoria British Rail Station is open Mondays through Saturdays, 8 AM to 7 PM; Sundays, 8 AM to 5 PM, later in peak summer months. Many leaflets and brochures about the city's landmarks and events are available; staff people are also on hand to answer questions on what to do, how, and when. Other branches are at the tube station at Heathrow Airport Terminals 1, 2, and 3 (8 AM to 6:30 PM), *Harrods* and *Selfridges* stores (during store hours), and the Tower of London (*Easter* to November only). A telephone information service is offered weekdays, 9 AM to 6 PM (phone: 71-730-3488), but it is very busy. Accommodations and tours can be reserved by telephone using credit cards, Mondays through Fridays 9 AM to 6 PM (phone: 71-824-8844).

The British Travel Centre books travel tickets, reserves accommodations and theater tickets, and sells guidebooks. They have numerous free leaflets that include fascinating information (for movie trivia buffs, pick up the "Movie Map," which guides you to famous film locations). It offers a free information service, including an information hotline covering the whole of Britain. There also is an All-Ireland Information Desk, a Welsh Tourist Office, and a National Trust Shop. Open 9 AM to 6:30 PM weekdays; 9 AM to 5 PM Saturdays; 10 AM to 4 PM Sundays. 4 Lower Regent St. (phone: 71-730-3400).

Among the most comprehensive and useful guidebooks to London are the *Blue Guide to London* (Benn); *London Round the Clock* (CPC Guidebooks); *Londonwalks* (Holt, Rinehart & Winston); and a series of guides available from *Time Out* (Time Out Ltd.). *Naked London* (Queen Anne Press) lists the city's more unusual, less visited sights for dedicated sleuths. The annual *Good Food Guide* and *Egon Ronay's* hotel and restaurant guide are available in most bookstores. For detailed information on 200 London museums, including maps, consult the *London Museums and Collections Guide* (CPC Guidebooks). The *Shell Guide to the History of London* (Michael Joseph) bristles with exciting, accurate details on the city. *London: Louise Nicholson's Definitive Guide* (Bodley Head) comes surprisingly close to the claims of the title. Susie Elms's *The London Theatre Scene* (Frank Cook) gives fair coverage of an essential aspect of the city. For incurable Anglophiles, *The London Encyclopedia* (by Benjamin Weinreb) is a must. A new guide called *Permanent Londoners: An Illustrated Guide to the Cemeteries of London* lists the locations of the graves, along with biographical notes, of some of the more famous Londoners buried in the city. The book is available from Chelsea Publishing Co. (PO Box 130, Post Mills, VT 05058-0130; phone: 802-333-9073). Another new book called *Amazing London,* published by the British Tourist Authority, lists numerous bargains to help a tourist's dollars go farther. It also provides discounts up to 50% in certain shops, restaurants, and tourist attractions. For a free copy contact the British Tourist Authority (40 W. 57th St., New York, NY 10019; phone: 212-581-4708). The *Travel Bookshop* (25 Cecil Court, WC2N 4EZ; phone: 71-836-9132) has a wide selection of guidebooks and travel information. It's possible to get secondhand books here and to trade your own books as well.

London A-Z and *Nicholson's Street Finder,* inexpensive pocket-size books of street maps (available in bookstores and from most "newsagents"), are very useful for finding London addresses. Also helpful are maps of the subway system and bus routes and the *London Regional Transport Visitors Guide* — all available free from the London Transport information centers at several stations, including Victoria, Piccadilly, Charing Cross, Oxford Circus, and Heathrow Central, and at the ticket booths of many other stations (phone: 71-222-1234 for information).

The US Embassy is at 24-31 Grosvenor Sq. W1. (phone: 71-499-9000).

Local Coverage – Of London's several newspapers, the *Times,* the *Sunday Times,* the *Observer* (Sundays only), the *Guardian,* the *Independent,* and the *Daily Telegraph* are the most useful for visitors. Also helpful are the weekly magazines *City Limits, Time Out,* and *New Statesman.* The *Evening Standard* is the paper most read by Londoners. For business news, read the *Financial Times* (daily) and the *Economist* magazine (weekly).

 TELEPHONE: The country code for the United Kingdom is 44. London has two area codes. The area code for inner London is 71; for outer London, 81. All telephone numbers listed in this chapter, therefore, include the correct city code. When calling from one area code to another within London or from elsewhere within Great Britain, dial either 071 or 081 before the local number.

To dial from many pay phones in London (and elsewhere in Great Britain) today, you will need something other than a pocketful of change — one of two telephone credit cards from *British Telecom* or *Mercury.* Many coin operated pay phones have been supplemented and sometimes replaced with telephones that take a phone card. (For detailed information, see *Mail, Telephone, and Electricity* in GETTING READY TO GO.)

 GETTING AROUND: Airports – London now has four airports. The two main airports are Heathrow (phone: 81-759-4321) and Gatwick (phone: 293-28822), both of which handle international and domestic traffic. Heathrow is 15 miles and about 50 minutes from downtown; a taxi into town will cost about $30 to $40 unless you share: Two passengers to the West Central district, for example, pay about $15; three pay $12 each; four $11 each; and five (the maximum) $10 each. (When sharing, the cab meter is turned off and passengers agree beforehand on the order of destinations. There's a shared-cab rank at Terminal 1, and they're also available at London's 200 taxi stands.) If you aren't carrying heavy luggage, the trip downtown can be made easily on the London underground (subway) from two stations at Heathrow: One serves terminals 1, 2, and 3; the other serves Terminal 4. *Piccadilly Line* trains leave every 4 to 10 minutes and operate between 5 AM (6:45 on Sundays) and 11:30 PM; the trip takes about 1 hour. Stops are convenient to most of London's main hotel areas, and the line feeds into the rest of the London underground network. *Airbus A1* runs between Heathrow and Victoria Station (one of the city's main and most central railway terminals); *Airbus* A2 goes from the airport to Euston Station. Both stop at major airport hotels en route. Get a pamphlet at any airport London Transport Information Desk. Disabled facilities are available; US currency accepted (phone: 81-995-8092).

Gatwick Airport is 27 miles and 1½ hours from downtown. Express buses leave every 15 minutes and cost about $5. Gatwick is not connected to the underground system, but it does have its own rail station, with express trains leaving for Victoria Station every 15 minutes from 6 AM to 10 PM during the day and hourly through the rest of the night; the cost is about $11. The journey takes about 30 minutes and is by far the best transportation alternative between airport and town. A taxi into the city will cost about $70 and up! *Green Line* bus No. 777 travels between Gatwick Airport and Victoria Station (phone: 81-668-7261 for information) and costs about $5.50 for the 70-minute trip.

London's newest air terminal is the upgraded Stanstead Airport, 30 miles northeast of the city. A shuttle-train connects it to Liverpool Street Rail Station (45 minutes). Connections to Scotland, major cities in Belgium, France, and Holland are relieving pressure on the other London airports.

The London "City" airport is 4 miles from downtown; the 15-minute taxi ride to the airport costs about $16. Riverboat service from either Chelsea Harbour or Charing Cross costs about $4.

Boat – The *RiverBus Partnership,* a high-speed riverboat service, links east London to west, between London City Port and Chelsea Harbour (including the London "City" Airport). It runs at approximately 20-minute intervals, weekdays from 7 AM to 10 PM, calling at eight piers. Exchange Tower, 1 Harbour Exchange Sq., E14 (phone: 71-512-0555).

For a leisurely view of London from the Thames, tour boats leave roughly every half hour from Westminster Pier (at the foot of Westminster Bridge) and from Charing Cross Pier (on Victoria Embankment); they sail (*Easter* through September) upriver to Kew or downriver to the Tower of London, Greenwich, and the massive Thames flood barrier. An inclusive ticket covering a round-trip boat ride from central London to Greenwich and entry to the *National Maritime Museum,* the Old Royal Observatory, and the *Cutty Sark* clipper is available for about $10 from the British Travel Centre, the Victoria Tourist Information Centre, and at Charing Cross, Westminster, and Tower piers. A journey along Regent's Canal through north London is offered (summers only) by *Jason's Trip* (opposite 60 Blomfield Rd., Little Venice W9; phone: 71-286-3428). For further information about these and other boat trips, contact the London Tourist Board or the Convention Bureau's River Boat Information Service (phone: 71-730-4812).

Bus and Underground – The London public transport system seems to be getting more and more sluggish these days, and you'll hear many Londoners complaining about it, but it is still reasonably efficient and will get you where you're going. The subway, called the underground or tube, and bus lines, cover the city pretty well — though buses suffer from traffic congestion, and the underground is notoriously thin south of the Thames. (Avoid rush-hour traffic, which is hideous, from 8:30 to 9:30 AM and from 5 to 6 PM.) The tops of London's famous red double-decker buses do, however, offer some delightful views of the city and its people. The underground is easy to understand and to use, with clear directions and poster maps in all stations. Pick up free bus and underground maps from tourist offices or underground ticket booths.

The fares on both trains and buses are set according to length of the journey. On most buses, conductors take payment after you tell them where you're going; some require that you pay as you enter. Underground tickets are bought on entering a station. Retain your ticket; you'll have to surrender it when you get off (or have to pay again), and bus inspectors make spot checks to see that no one's stealing a free ride. There also are *Red Arrow* express buses, which link all the mainline *British Rail* stations, but you'll have to check stops before you get on. With just a few exceptions, public transport comes to a halt around midnight; it varies according to underground line and bus route. If you're going to be traveling late, check available facilities. For 24-hour travel information, call 71-222-1234.

A London Transport Visitor Travelcard can be purchased in the US from travel agents and *BritRail Travel International* offices in New York, Dallas, and Los Angeles, or in London from *London Regional Transport* travel information centers. The card provides unlimited travel on virtually all of London's bus and underground networks and costs about $4 for 1 day (available only in London), $15 for 3 days, $21 for 4 days, and $35 for 7 days. If purchased in the US, a book of discount vouchers for many of the city's sights is included; for purchase in London, a passport-size photo must be provided.

One of the least expensive and most comprehensive ways to tour the city is to take the *Original London Transport Sightseeing Tour,* a 2-hour unconducted bus tour, which leaves every hour from four sites: Marble Arch, Piccadilly Circus, Baker Street tube station, and Victoria Station (phone: 71-227-3456). Other guided bus tours are offered by *American Express* (phone: 71-930-4411), *Frames* (phone: 71-837-6311), *Harrods* (phone: 71-581-3603), and *Thomas Cook* (phone: 71-499-4000).

Car Rental – Most rental agencies have desks at the airports. Some London rental agencies include *Hertz* (at Marble Arch; phone: 71-402-4242) and *Avis* (35 Headford Pl. SW1; phone: 71-245-9862). *Eurodollar* (224 Fulham Palace Rd.; phone: 71-385-5515) and *Thrifty* (39 Finchley Lane; phone: 81-202-0093) are less expensive, or try *Guy Salmon Car Rentals* (7-23 Bryanston St., Marble Arch; phone: 71-408-1255), or *Europcar,* formerly *Godfrey Davis* (Davis House, Wilton Rd. SW1; phone: 71-834-8484). In addition, *Budget Rent-A-Car* has four reservation desks at Heathrow Airport terminals (phone: 81-759-2216). And for riding in style, call *Avis Luxury Car Services* (220 Norwood Crescent, Hounslow; phone: 81-897-2621) for chauffeur-driven Rolls-Royces, Daimlers, Mercedes, and limousines.

Helicopter Flights – See London from the air. Sightseeing tours are available (prices vary and start at around $250). The standard flight includes an aerial tour of the major London sites; special views available on request. Make a reservation with *C.B. Helicopters,* Battersea (phone: 71-228-3232).

Taxi – Those fine old London cabs are gradually being supplemented with more "practical" models. It is one of life's great tragedies. Although dashboard computers in cabs are becoming increasingly more common, too, London cabbies seem generally pleased with the new system; the computers allow communication between driver and dispatcher so that the cab's home office knows who's empty and who's closest to a prospective fare. Riders will be happy to know that the computer also allows drivers to check on possible traffic problems and to obtain basic route instructions. Whether you end up in a computerized or "regular" cab, taxi fares in London are increasingly expensive (though you don't mind the price so much if you're riding in the big, old comfortable vehicles), and a 15% tip is customary.

Tell a London cabbie where you're going *before* entering the cab. When it rains or late at night, an empty cab (identifiable by the glow of the roof light) is often very difficult to find, so it is wise to carry the telephone number of one or more of the cab companies that respond to calls by phone. There are also many "minicab" companies that do not respond when hailed on the street, nor do they use meters. They operate on a fixed fare basis between their home base and your destination, and you have to call their central office to book one. Hotel porters or reception desks usually can make arrangements to have such a car pick you up at a specified time and place. Be aware that taxi rates are higher after 8 PM (and sometimes even higher after midnight) and on weekends and holidays.

Several firms and taxi drivers offer guided tours of London; details are available at information centers. You can arrange for the personal services of a member of London's Guild of Guides by phoning the London Visitor and Convention Bureau's Guide Dept. (phone: 71-730-3450).

London Taxi Video Tours provides a unique service in which a knowledgeable and obliging driver/guide will escort from 1 to 5 people on a 3-hour tour of London, driving them from place to place in one of the city's wonderful, old, big, black cabs. The guide videotapes his group, capturing them strolling London's streets, visiting historic sites, talking to a London policeman, watching the Changing of the Guard. The videotape, which includes perky background music, is later presented to travelers in a system compatible with American VCRs. The tour, including the video, costs about $205 (extra copies are about $33). An all-day tour also is available for about $330. Special theme tours (Victorian and macabre London, the haunts of the "Elephant Man," and "Sweeney Todd" territory) or custom-designed tours also are available. Reservations advised. 25 Stanway Rd., Benfleet, Essex SS7 5UX (phone: 268-566330).

Train – London has 11 principal train stations, each the starting point for trains to a particular region, with occasional overlapping of routes. The ones you are most likely to encounter include King's Cross (phone: 71-278-2477), the departure point for northeast England and eastern Scotland, including Edinburgh; Euston (phone: 71-387-7070), serving the Midlands, north Wales, including connections to Northern Ireland and the Republic, northwest England, and western Scotland, including Glasgow; Paddington (phone: 71-262-6767), for the West Country and south Wales, including Fishguard and ferries to Rosslare, Ireland; Victoria (phone: 71-928-5100), for Gatwick Airport and, along with Charing Cross Station (phone: 71-928-5100), for departures to southeast England; and Liverpool St. Station (phone: 71-928-5100), for departures to East Anglia and to Harwich for ferries to the Continent and Scandinavia. All of these stations are connected via London's underground.

BritRail's Travelpak transportation program is intended for travelers who wish to venture out of London. It includes round-trip journeys from Gatwick or Heathrow airports to central London; the London Explorer; and a 4-day *BritRail* pass for unlimited train travel within Britain. Maps and timetables are also included. *BritRail* Travelpaks must be obtained before leaving the US from any North American *BritRail* office. Write *BritRail,* 630 Third Ave., New York, NY 10017 (phone: 212-599-5400).

For a special treat, take a day trip on the luxurious British *Pullman* cars of the *Venice Simplon–Orient Express.* You can see the spas, castles, and more in southwest England on trips to Bath, Bristol, and Salisbury. Or take the trip through beautiful Kent, enjoying a sumptuous, 4-course luncheon as you wind through the countryside. For additional information: 1155 Avenue of the Americas, New York, NY 10036 (phone: 800-524-2420; 212-302-5006 in New York City; 71-834-8122 in London).

Walking Tours – A trained guide can show you Shakespeare's London or that of Dickens or Jack the Ripper — many different themes are offered. These reasonably priced tours last up to 2 hours, generally in the afternoon or evening. *City Walks* offers several tours, including a Sherlock Holmes Trail of Mystery and Whodunit Tour departing from the Baker Street underground station, Baker St. exit, on Tuesdays at 10:30 AM (phone: 71-937-4281). *Citisights* (phone: 81-806-4325) start from many places, including the *Museum of London* (London Wall). *Streets of London* (phone: 81-882-3414) start from various underground stations. *Londoner Pub Walks* (phone: 81-883-2656) start from Temple underground station (*District* and *Circle* lines) on

Fridays at 7:30 PM. *London Walks* (phone: 71-435-6413) provides tours leaving from a variety of points. A tour of the Docklands' Rotherhite district is offered by local historian Jim Nash (see the "Docklands," above). Informative books on London walking tours include *London Walks* (Holt, Rinehart & Winston), *Guide to Literary London* (Batford) by George Williams, and our own new *Birnbaum's London* (HarperCollins). *Time Out* also has day-by-day listings of walks in each issue.

Especially for Kids – If you're traveling *en famille* and have the urge to be alone but don't want to deprive your offspring (all ages) of what London and its immediate countryside have to offer, *Take-a-Guide* may be the answer. They will provide a car with a driver-guide especially knowledgeable in the ways and wiles of young folk for half- or full-day tours. It's costly: in London, $212 for a half day; $350 for a full day; or in the countryside, $250 for a half day; $500 for a full day. Contact them in the US at 800-223-6450; 212-628-4823 in New York City; 71-221-5475 in London.

 LOCAL SERVICES: Dentist – *Eastman Dental Hospital,* 256 Gray's Inn Rd., WC1 (phone: 71-837-3646).

    Dry Cleaner/Tailor – *Jeeves* (8-10 Pont St. SW1; phone: 71-235-1101); *Anderson Sheppard* (30 Savile Row, W1; phone: 71-734-1420).

Limousine Service – *Guy Salmon,* 23 Bryanston St. (phone: 71-408-1255).

Medical Emergency – *Middlesex Hospital* is the most central of London's hospitals and provides 24-hour emergency service (Mortimer St., W1; phone: 71-636-8333). In cases of extreme emergency, dial 999.

Messenger Service – *Quicksilver,* 227 Liverpool Rd., N1 (phone: 71-734-6126).

National/International Courier – *DHL International* (181 The Strand, London WC2; phone: 81-890-9000 and Orbital Park, Great South West Rd., Hounslow, Middlesex; phone: 81-890-9000); *Federal Express* (9 Elms La., Unit 4, London SW8 5BP; phone: 81-5949811 or toll-free in England, 800-123-800); *British Airways* operates *Speedbird Express* (World Cargo Centre, Hounslow, Middlesex; phone: 81-562-6279 or 81-562-6229).

Office Equipment Rental – *Office Installations,* 11A The Mall, W5 (phone: 81-579-6771).

Pharmacy – *Boots* (Piccadilly Circus; phone: 71-734-6126). The local police stations have lists of 24-hour pharmacies in their neighborhoods.

Photocopies – *Kall Kwik,* at several locations, including 21 Kingly St., W1 (phone: 71-434-2471).

Post Office – The main post office is open from 8 AM to 8 PM Mondays through Saturdays, and from 10 AM to 5 PM Sundays. 24 William IV St., Trafalgar Sq., WC2 (phone: 71-930-9580).

Secretary/Stenographer – *Drake Business Centre,* 136 Regent St., W1 (phone: 71-437-6900).

Teleconference Facilities – The *Inter-Continental* hotel (1 Hamilton Pl.; phone: 71-409-3131) has a worldwide teleconference link in its Mercury video conferencing studio (phone: 71-491-7824, direct line).

Telex – *Kensington Business Centre* is open from 8:30 AM to 8 PM. 9-11 Kensington High St., W8 (phone: 71-938-1721 or 71-938-2151).

Other – Business services: *Business Centre* (next to Terminal 2, Heathrow Airport; phone: 81-759-2434); *Channel 5,* also provides direct mail services (331 Goswell Rd., EC1; phone: 71-833-2732). Camera rental and repair: *Keith, Johnson, and Pelling* (Great Marlborough St., W1; phone: 71-439-8811). Jewelry rental: *Robert White* (22 Tavistock St., WC2; phone: 71-240-3111). Unisex hair salon: *Vidal Sassoon* (60 S. Molton St., W1; phone: 71-491-8848). Tuxedo rental: *Moss Bros.* (Bedford St., WC2; phone: 71-240-4567). Fur rental: *Herman* (30 Maddox St., W1; phone: 71-734-3804).

SPECIAL EVENTS: Dates vary marginally from year to year and should be checked — together with details — with the London Visitor and Convention Bureau. In late March/early April, the Oxford and Cambridge rowing "eights" race through the waters from Putney to Mortlake, an important competition for the two universities, whose respective teams practice for months beforehand. The world-famous *Chelsea Flower Show* takes place in late May. In early June, enjoy the annual *Trooping the Colour,* England's most elaborate display of pageantry — a Horse Guards' parade, with military music and much pomp and circumstance — all in celebration of the queen's official birthday. You can see some of the parade without a ticket, but for the ceremony you must book before March 1 by writing to the Brigade Major (Headquarters, Household Division, Horseguards, Whitehall SW1) — do not send money. The 2-week-long *Greenwich Festival,* also held in June, includes mime and dance performances, poetry readings, a wide variety of music, and children's events. (For more details see "The Best Festivals" in *For the Mind,* DIVERSIONS.) The *Grosvenor House Antiques Fair* is held for 10 days every June at the hotel on Park Lane. Late June heralds the *Wimbledon Lawn Tennis Championship* — the world's most prestigious — complete with a member of the royal family presenting the prizes. The *City of London Festival* is held for 2½ weeks in July within the old city's square mile. It features choirs, orchestras, chamber groups, and leading soloists of international repute, along with a popular jazz program, dance, street theater, and a wide range of exhibitions. The *Henley Royal Regatta,* in early July (at Henley-on-Thames, a 1-hour train ride from London), is an international rowing competition and one of the big social events of the year. Watch from the towpath (free) or from within the *Regatta* enclosure (fee). The *Royal Tournament,* a military pageant, takes place at Earl's Court for 3 weeks in July. The *Early Music Centre Festival* — featuring orchestral, chamber, and choral music — is usually held sometime between the end of September and early November. October or November is the time for the *State Opening of Parliament; Guy Fawkes Day* is on November 5, when fireworks and bonfires mark the anniversary of the plot to blow up both Houses of Parliament and King James I in 1605; and on the second Saturday in November, the *Lord Mayor's Procession* is held in which the new lord mayor, who rides in a golden carriage, is followed by bands and wacky, colorful floats. On the first Sunday in November, the *London-To-Brighton Veteran Car Run* features shiny antique autos undertaking the 50-mile drive. On *Remembrance Sunday,* the Sunday following November 11 (*Armistice Day*), a moving and solemn parade of veterans passes before the queen and lays red poppy wreaths at the base of the Cenotaph, on Whitehall.

MUSEUMS: Many of London's museums and galleries have no admission charge; others charge $1.50 to $3. A number of the museums are described in *Special Places.* Others of note include the following:

Bethnal Green Museum of Childhood – Impressive collection of more than 4,000 toys, including dolls and dollhouses, games, and puppets. Open Mondays through Thursdays and Saturdays from 10 AM to 5:50 PM; Sundays 2:30 to 5:50 PM. No admission charge. Cambridge Heath Rd., E2 (phone: 81-980-3204).

Courtauld Institute Galleries – A remarkable collection of French Impressionist and post-Impressionist paintings is now in a new home. Open Mondays through Saturdays 10 AM to 6 PM; Sundays 2 to 6 PM. No admission charge. Somerset House, the Strand, WC1 (phone: 71-873-2538).

Design Museum – Examples of everyday items from today's consumer society are on display at this museum in the Docklands. Tea kettles, tables and chairs, cars and bikes are all part of the permanent exhibit explaining the development of such items' design. There is also a library, lecture theater, and riverside café. Open daily, except Mondays, from 11:30 AM to 6:30 PM. Admission charge. Butler's Wharf, SE1 (phone: 71-403-6933).

Dickens's House – Manuscripts of early works, first editions, and personal memorabilia. Open Mondays through Saturdays 10 AM to 5 PM. Admission charge. 48 Doughty St., WC1 (phone: 71-405-2127).

Dulwich College Picture Gallery – Works by European masters in one of England's most beautiful art galleries. The college itself boasts such famous alumni as P.G. Wodehouse and Raymond Chandler. Open Tuesdays through Fridays 10 AM to 1 PM and 2 to 5 PM; Saturdays 11 AM to 5 PM; Sundays 2 to 5 PM. Admission charge. College Rd., SE21 (phone: 81-693-5254).

Ecological Museum – The history of the earth is represented in tremendous collections of rocks, fossils, and exhibits on the latest theories. Open Mondays through Saturdays 10 AM to 6 PM; Sundays 11 AM to 6 PM. Admission charge. Exhibition Rd., SW7 (phone: 71-938-8765).

Florence Nightingale Museum – Opened in 1989, this museum is not for nurses only. It offers a fascinating look at the life of the "Lady with the Lamp." Open Tuesdays through Sundays, including bank holidays, from 10 AM to 4 PM (last admission). Admission charge. 2 Lambeth Palace Rd., SE1 (phone: 71-620-0374).

Hayward Gallery – Temporary exhibitions of British and international art. Open Tuesdays and Wednesdays from 10 AM to 8 PM; other days from 10 AM to 6 PM. Admission charge. At the South Bank Centre on Belvedere Rd, SE1 (phone: 71-928-3144).

Institute of Contemporary Arts – Exhibitions of up-to-date British art, film, theater, manifesto. Open daily, noon to 10 PM. Admission charge. Nash House, Duke of York Steps, the Mall, SW1 (phone: 71-930-3647).

Jewish Museum – Art and antiques illustrating Jewish history. Closed Mondays, Saturdays, and Jewish and bank holidays. No admission charge. Woburn House, Upper Woburn Pl., WC1 (phone: 71-388-4525).

London Toy and Model Museum – This charming Victorian building houses a fine collection of model trains and mechanical toys. Open Tuesdays through Saturdays from 10 AM to 5:30 PM; Sundays from 11 AM to 5:30 PM. Admission charge. October House, 23 Craven Hill, W2 (phone: 71-262-7905).

Museum of Garden History – Set in tiny St. Mary-at-Lambeth Church, the museum houses a collection of antique gardening tools and horticultural exhibits. A 17th-century–style garden (out back) contains a tulip tree and trumpet honeysuckle. Captain Bligh — who lived down the road — is buried right in the garden's center! Open Mondays through Fridays from 11 AM to 3 PM and on Sundays from 10:30 AM to 5 PM, the first Sunday in March to the second Sunday in December. No admission charge. On Lambeth Palace Rd., SE1, across the Thames from Parliament (phone: 71-373-4030).

Museum of Mankind – Ethnographic exhibitions. Open Mondays through Saturdays from 10 AM to 5 PM; Sundays 2:30 to 6 PM. No admission charge. 6 Burlington Gardens, W1 (phone: 71-323-8043).

Museum of the Moving Image – The museum has over 50 exhibits and over 1,000 clips from various old and recent films and TV shows. There's also a good bit of movie memorabilia, including Charlie Chaplin's hat and cane and fine movies ignored by big distributors. Open Tuesdays through Saturdays, 10 AM to 8 PM; Sundays, 10 AM to 6 PM; closed Mondays. Admission charge. South Bank, underneath the Waterloo Bridge, next to the *Royal Festival Hall* (phone: 71-928-3535).

Musical Museum – One of Europe's most comprehensive collections of pianos and mechanical musical instruments, all in good working condition. Open April through October on Saturdays and Sundays from 2 to 5 PM. Admission charge. 368 High St., Brentford, Middlesex (phone: 81-560-8108).

Natural History Museum – Exhibits of native wildlife, plants, fossils, and minerals. Open Mondays to Saturdays from 10 AM to 6 PM; Sundays from 11 AM to 6 PM. Admission charge. Cromwell Rd., SW7 (phone: 71-589-6323).

Royal Air Force Museum – A full exhibition of planes from the time of the Wright Brothers to the present. Open daily from 10 AM to 6 PM. Admission charge. Grahame Park Way, NW9 (phone: 81-205-2266).

Science Museum – The development of science and industry, including an "Exploration of Space" exhibit. Open Mondays through Saturdays 10 AM to 6 PM; Sundays 11 AM to 6 PM. Admission charge. Exhibition Rd., SW7 (phone: 71-589-3456).

Sir John Soane's Museum – Its collection includes Hogarth's series *The Rake's Progress.* Open Tuesdays through Saturdays from 10 AM to 5 PM. No admission charge. 13 Lincoln's Inn Fields, WC2 (phone: 71-405-2107).

Theatre Museum – Britain's newest collection of theatrical material has been given its own home. Everything from circus to pop, grand opera to mime, straight theater to Punch and Judy and pantomime is here, as well as an excellent informal café-restaurant on the main floor. Open Tuesdays through Sundays 11 AM to 7 PM. Admission charge. 1E Tavistock St., WC2 (phone: 71-836-7891).

Wallace Collection – Sir Richard Wallace's fine collection of European paintings, sculpture, porcelain, and armor. Open Mondays through Saturdays from 10 AM to 5 PM; Sundays from 2 to 5 PM. No admission charge. Hertford House, Manchester Sq., W1 (phone: 71-935-0687).

Whitechapel Art Gallery – An East End haven for modern art, including works by Moore, Hepworth, and Hockney. Temporary exhibitions range from contemporary British artists to Third World and ethnic minority artists. Open from 11 AM to 5 PM, Wednesdays to 8 PM; closed Mondays and bank holidays. No admission charge. 80 Whitechapel High St., E7 (phone: 71-377-0107).

 SHOPPING: Stores generally are open from 9 AM to 5:30 or 6 PM, daily except Sundays, but the shops in the West End stay open until about 7:30 PM on Thursdays, and *Covent Garden* stays open until 7 PM Mondays through Saturdays. Although London is traditionally one of the most expensive cities in the world, savvy shoppers still can find good buys. The current lure, however, is more for fine British workmanship and style than very low prices.

The favorite items on any shopping list in London are cashmere and Shetland knitwear; fabric (tweeds, blends, men's suitings); riding gear; custom-made men's suits, shirts, shoes, and hats; shotguns; china and crystal; umbrellas; antiques; sporting goods; English food specialties (jams and marmalade, various blended teas, stilton cheese, shortbread, and others). Books published by British houses, once a fine buy, are now far higher in price, and you probably will do better to buy the US editions. For secondhand books, though, London still hides treasures. Charing Cross Road is a good place to start, and even pricey establishments may have basements with long out of print paperbacks in good condition, along with unfashionable Victoriana at very inexpensive prices. See Sheppard's *Directory of Second-Hand and Antiquarian Bookshops of the British Isles* for tips. But as all bargain hunters know, there is no substitute for your own voyages of discovery.

Devoted bargain hunters recognize that the best time to buy British is during the semi-annual sales that usually occur from *Boxing Day* (December 26) through the early part of the new year and again in early July. The *Christmas/New Year* sales offer by far the best bargains in the city, and the crowds can be the equal of the low prices. Many stores remain open on *New Year's Day* to accommodate the bargain hunters, and the best-publicized single sale is that held by *Harrods* for 3 weeks beginning the first Wednesday in January. That opening day is an event in itself.

Be sure to take your passport when you shop, and always inquire about the VAT refund application forms when your total purchases in a shop are over £50, about $83. The VAT (Value Added Tax) is a 17.5% surcharge payable at the sales counter, but foreign customers usually will be reimbursed for it at home. *Chequepoint* money exchange in London will cash VAT refund checks 24 hours a day, but you'll have to pay for the privilege; there are three branches: 548 Oxford St., 222 Earl's Court Rd., and 71 Gloucester Rd. For purchases at any of the 10,000 shops displaying the London Tax Free Shopping logo, retailers issue vouchers that will be stamped by Customs when you leave the country and then posted to LTFS (21-24 Cockspur St., SW1); a refund is issued in local currency in as few as 4 days.

Though scattered about the city, the most appealing shops tend to center in the West End area, particularly along Old and New Bond Streets, Oxford, South Molton, Regent, and Jermyn Streets, and Piccadilly. Other good shopping areas are the Kings Road, Kensington High Street, and Kensington Church Street, along with Knightsbridge and *Covent Garden.*

This is a city of markets; we have already described Portobello Road and Camden Passage in *Special Places.* Also worthy of note is *Camden Lock Market* (Camden High St., NW1) on Saturdays and Sundays for far-out clothes, leather items, antiques, and trinkets. The restored *Jubilee Market,* on the south side of *Covent Garden* piazza, is one of the largest indoor markets in the country. It features antiques and a flea market on Mondays; housewares, clothing, and jewelry Tuesdays through Fridays; and crafts on weekends. Another good choice for the real antiques connoisseur is the *Bermondsey–New Caledonian Market,* open on Fridays before dawn — bring a flashlight (at Bermondsey St. and Long La., off Tower Bridge Rd.). Or get up early on a Sunday morning and head for the East End to sample a typically English transport café ("caff") breakfast at *Fred's* (40 Aberfeldy St., E14; phone: 71-987-6084) before tackling the very famous Petticoat Lane for food, inexpensive clothes, crockery, and even the proverbial kitchen sink.

The following stores are only a sampling of London's treasure houses.

Alexander Juran – This business, started in Prague during the reign of Emperor Franz Josef II, has unattractive showrooms but wonderful merchandise, including textiles, rugs, and carpets. 74 New Bond St., W1 (phone: 71-629-2550).

Anderson and Sheppard – Reputable "made-to-measure" tailor for men's clothes. 30 Savile Row, W1 (phone: 71-734-1420).

Antiquarius Antique Market – Wide variety of antique items from over 170 vendors. 135-141 King's Rd., SW3 (phone: 71-351-5353).

Antique Porcelain Company Ltd. – For 18th-century English porcelain and other varieties. 149 New Bond St., W1 (phone: 71-629-1254).

Aquascutum – Famous for raincoats and jackets for men and women. 100 Regent St., W1 (phone: 71-734-6090).

Asprey & Company – Fine jewelry, silver, and luggage. 165-169 New Bond St., W1 (phone: 71-493-6767).

Austin Reed – Classic English menswear, plus an old-fashioned barber shop in the basement. Some women's wear, too. 103 Regent St., W1 (phone: 71-734-6789).

Bates – A gentlemen's hatter, and our favorite. Check out the eight-part caps. 21A Jermyn St., SW1 (phone: 71-734-2722).

Body Shop – More than 150 different beauty products (perfume, soap, hair and skin care products — famous for not having been tested on animals), from the worldwide chain that started in Brighton. There are several locations throughout the city. One of the main stores is at 32 Great Marlborough St., W1 (phone: 71-437-5137).

Bond Street Antique Centre – Everything from antique jewelry and watches to silver and porcelain. 124 New Bond St., W1 (phone: 71-351-5353).

Browns – Designer clothes for men and women in seven shops along the tiny, pedestrians-only South Molton St., W1 (phone: 71-491-7833).

Burberrys – Superb, expensive, men's and women's raincoats and traditional clothes, and home of the now nearly ubiquitous plaid that began life as a raincoat lining. 18 Haymarket, SW1 (phone: 71-930-3343).

Caroline Charles – Perfect women's styles for *Ascot* and other very social events. 56-57 Beauchamp Pl., SW3 (phone: 71-589-5850).

Chelsea Antique Market – London's first antiques market still has a fine selection and reputation. 253 King's Rd., SW3 (phone: 71-352-1424).

Church's Shoes – Superior men's shoes in various locations, including 58-59 Burlington Arcade, W1 (phone: 71-493-8307).

Collets – One of the best places to find musical recordings from Eastern Europe, particularly folk tunes. 129-31 Charing Cross Rd., WC2 (phone: 71-734-0782).

Conran's – Terence Conran has transformed the beautiful Michelin Building into a larger, more exclusive and expensive version of his well-known *Habitat* stores. However, the export of larger furniture and furnishings is probably better arranged through a US branch. After some heavy shopping, stop into the *Bibendum Oyster Bar* on the ground floor for a light meal. 81 Fulham Rd., SW3 (phone: 71-589-7401).

Cordings – Sportswear for the quintessential country squire. They've also recently added a fine line of women's wear, from linen suits to riding gear. 19-20 Piccadilly, W1 (phone: 71-734-0830).

Courtenay House – Pricey but elegantly designed women's wear; particularly beautiful ladies' sweaters and silky lingerie. 22 Brook St., W1 (phone: 71-629-0542).

David Shilling – His one-off (a tad eccentric) hat creations always create a stir at *Ascot.* 44 Chiltern St., W1 (phone: 71-935-8473).

Dillon's – London's most scholastic bookstore, partly owned by London University. 1 Malet St., WC1 (phone: 71-636-1577).

Douglas Hayward – A reputable made-to-order tailor. 95 Mount St., W1 (phone: 71-499-5574).

Dress Circle – If the music of show biz is what you're after, here are original recordings from big and small hits (and total flops), plus pressings of Judy Garland, Bing Crosby, Peggy Lee. 57-59 Monmouth St. (phone: 71-240-2227).

Farlows – Perhaps the best spot in London to buy the completely waterproof and windproof Barbour jackets and hats. 5 Pall Mall (phone: 71-839-2423).

Feathers – French and Italian designer clothing for women. 40 Hans Crescent, SW1 (phone: 71-589-0356).

58 Dean Street Records – Offers a wide selection of show tunes and movie soundtracks, and the staff is very helpful. 58 Dean St., W1 (phone: 71-734-8777).

Filofax Shop – The famous brand name personal organizers. 21 Conduit St., W1 (phone: 71-499-0457).

Floris – Old-fashioned English scents, soaps, potpourri, and more in a charming Victorian shop. 89 Jermyn St., SW1 (phone: 71-930-2885).

Fortnum & Mason – Boasts designer originals (of the rather dowdy variety), an appealing soda fountain-cum-restaurant, and one of the most elegant grocery departments in the world (where the staff wears striped morning trousers and swallowtail coats). 181 Piccadilly, W1 (phone: 71-734-8040).

Foyle's – London's largest bookstore. 119 Charing Cross Rd., WC2 (phone: 71-734-8040).

Grays Antique Market – The hundreds of stalls here and at the annex down the street sell everything from antique playing cards to 16th-century furniture. 1-7 Davies Mews, W1, and 58 Davies St., W1 (phone: 71-629-7034).

Grosvenor Prints – Over 100,000 prints on many subjects. 28-32 Shelton St., *Covent Garden,* WC2 (phone: 71-836-1979).

Gucci – Outposts of the famous Italian fashion, leather goods, and shoe manufacturer are found at 27 Old Bond St., W1 (phone: 71-629-2716), and at 17-18 Sloane St., SW1 (phone: 71-235-6707).

Habitat – Up-to-the-minute designs with realistic prices for furniture and household goods. 196 Tottenham Court Rd., W1 (phone: 71-631-3880), and 206 King's Rd., SW3 (phone: 71-351-1211).

Hackett: These elegant, but warmly welcoming, shops cater to men's sartorial and tonsorial needs. From togs for the most formal occasion, to a first class shave. There are several branches: 65b New Kings Rd., SW6 (phone: 71-731-2790), 26 Eastcheap, EC3 (phone: 71-626-0707), and 1-2 Holborn Bars, EC1 (phone: 71-405-1767).

Halcyon Days – The best place to find authentic enameled Battersea boxes — both antique and brand-new. 14 Brook St., W1 (phone: 71-629-8811).

Hamleys – The largest toy shop in the world. 200 Regent St., W1 (phone: 71-734-3161).

Harrods – The ultimate department store, although it does tend to be quite expensive. It has everything, even a mortuary and a bank, and what it doesn't stock it will get for you. The "Food Halls" particularly fascinate visitors, and traditional British merchandise is available in abundance. For those interested in trendy styles, it has the *Way In* boutique. Its annual January sale is legendary. 87-135 Brompton Rd., Knightsbridge, SW1 (phone: 71-730-1234).

Harvey Nichols – Lady Di's favorite luxury department store, specializing in women's haute couture. Knightsbridge, SW1 (phone: 71-235-5000).

Heal's – Furniture and fabrics in the best modern designs. (It also has a popular lunch-meeting restaurant.) 196 Tottenham Court Rd., W1 (phone: 71-636-1666).

Henry Sotheran Ltd. – Now incorporates *Cavendish Rare Books*. The large stock includes books on voyages and travel, Weinrab architectural books, finely bound literature, early English and continental titles. 2 Sackville St., W1 (phone: 71-439-6151).

Herbert Johnson – Men's and women's hats. 30 New Bond St., W1 (phone: 71-408-1174).

Irish Linen Co. – Plain and fancy bed and table linen and handkerchieves. 35 Burlington Arcade, W1 (phone: 71-493-8949).

Jaeger – Tailored (and expensive) men's and women's clothes. 204 Regent St., W1 (phone: 71-494-3101) and 163 Sloane St., SW1 (phone: 71-235-2505).

James Lock and Company, Ltd. – The royal hatters. They fitted a crown for the queen's coronation, and they'll happily fit you for your first bowler. Plus hats for fishermen, hunters, groundskeepers. 6 St. James's St., SW1 (phone: 71-930-8874).

James Purdey and Sons – The place to go for custom-made shotguns and other shooting gear. 57 S. Audley St., W1 (phone: 71-499-1801).

James Smith and Sons – Believed to be the oldest umbrella shop in Europe, it was opened in 1830 by James Smith, and in 1857 it moved to its current address. Besides umbrellas, it also carries walking sticks and whips. A couple of blocks from the *British Museum*, 53 New Oxford St., WC1 (phone: 71-836-4731).

Jasper Conran – Top British designer clothes from Sir Terence Conran's son. 303 Brompton Rd., SW3 (phone: 71-823-9134).

John Keil – Lovely, expensive antiques. 154 Brompton Rd., SW3 (phone: 71-589-6454).

John Lewis – Good, basic department store, "never knowingly undersold" and particularly noted for its fabrics and household goods. 278 Oxford St., W1 (phone: 71-629-7711).

John Lobb – World-famous for men's made-to-order shoes — at stratospheric prices — that will last 10 years or more, with proper care. 9 St. James's St., SW1 (phone: 71-930-3664).

Joseph – One of the trend-setting shopping spots selling everything from luggage and housewares to men and women's clothing, now with several branches around London. Try the largest, 77 Fulham Rd., SW3 (phone: 71-823-9500) or the one at 26 Sloane St., SW1 (phone: 71-235-5470).

Justin De Blank – Excellent specialty foods, especially cheese and take-out dishes. 42 Elizabeth St., SW1 (phone: 71-730-0605).

Kent & Curwen – The place to buy authentic cricket caps, Henley club ties, and all sorts of similarly preppy raiment. 39 St. James's St., SW1 (phone: 71-409-1955), and 6 Royal Arcade (for *Wimbledon* wear), W1 (phone: 71-493-6882).

Laura Ashley – A relatively inexpensive women's boutique specializing in romantically styled skirts, dresses, and blouses. 256 Regent St., W1 (phone: 71-437-9760) plus other branches including 47-49 Brompton Rd., SW (phone: 71-823-9700).

Liberty – Famous for print fabrics. Scarves and ties a specialty. 210 Regent St., W1 (phone: 71-734-1234).

Lillywhites – The whole gamut of sporting goods. Piccadilly Circus, SW1 (phone: 71-930-3181).

London Silver Vaults – An extraordinary maze of antique silver and jewelry shops below ground, housed in what once were real vaults. (A few shops sell new silver or silver plate, too.) Browse around first; prices range from astronomical to affordable, some shops offer items at considerably lower prices than similar pieces fetch on New Bond and Conduit Streets. 53-54 Chancery La., WC2 (phone: 71-242-3844).

Lucy B. Campbell – Decorative prints from the 17th to the 19th century. 80 Holland Park Ave., W11 (phone: 71-229-4252).

Mallet and Son – Specializes in fine English antique furniture, but carries a wide variety of other items, too. 40 New Bond St., W1 (phone: 71-499-7411).

Mandy's – For all kinds of Irish music — *Clancy Brothers, ceilidh,* country, and *Chieftains*-style. 161 High Rd., NW10 (phone: 81-459-2842).

Marks & Spencer – Locally nicknamed "Marks & Sparks," this chain specializes in clothes for the whole family, made to high standards and sold at very reasonable prices. Its sweaters (especially cashmere and Shetland) are among the best buys in Britain; plus linens and their own cosmetics line. 458 Oxford St., W1, and many other branches (phone: 71-935-7954).

McAfee – Good selection of fine men's shoes. 17-18 Old Bond St., W1 (phone: 71-499-7343).

Moss Bros. – Men's formal attire (including dress tartans) and high-quality riding clothes for sale and hire. 88 Regent St., W1 (phone: 71-494-0666) and 27 King St., WC2 (phone: 71-497-9354).

Partridge Ltd. – Fine (but expensive) antiques. 144 New Bond St., W1 (phone: 71-629-0834).

Paul Smith – Britain's number one men's designer has two adjacent shops in *Covent Garden.* 43-44 Floral St., WC2 (phone: 71-379-7133).

Peter Jones – Another good, well-stocked department store, offering moderately priced, tasteful goods. Sloane Sq., SW1 (phone: 71-730-1234).

Pickering and Chatto – For antiquarian books on many topics. 17 Pall Mall, SW1 (phone: 71-930-8634).

Prestat – The best chocolates in all of London. Try the truffles. 14 Princes Arcade, SWI (phone: 71-629-4838).

Reject China Shop – Good buys in slightly (invisible) irregular, name-brand china. Glassware, crystal, and flatware, too. For a fee, the shop will ship your purchases back home. 33-35 Beauchamp Pl., SW3 (phone: 71-581-0737), or 134 Regent St., W1 (phone: 71-434-2502).

Scotch House – Famous for Scottish cashmeres, sweaters, tartans — a wide selection of well-known labels. 2 Brompton Rd., SW1 (phone: 71-581-2151), and many branches.

Selfridges – This famous department store offers somewhat less variety than *Harrods,* but it has just about everything, too — only a little less expensive. The extensive china and crystal department carries most patterns available. Oxford St., W1 (phone: 71-629-1234).

Shellys Shoes – Wide selection of trendy street-fashion footwear, from thigh-high suede boots to platform shoes. 159 Oxford St., W1 (phone: 71-439-8717).

Shirin – The best designer cashmeres in town. 51 Beauchamp Pl., SW3 (phone: 71-581-1936).

Simpson (Piccadilly) – Classic and safe English looks for men and women, including their own famous "Daks" label. 203 Piccadilly, W1 (phone: 71-734-2002 or toll-free in the UK, 800-282-188).

S. J. Phillips – Silver, jewelry, and more from the 16th to the early 19th centuries. 139 New Bond St., W1 (phone: 71-629-6261).

Smythson of Bond Street – The world's best place to buy diaries, notepads, and calendars, many in Florentine marbled paper; also exotic ledgers in which to record odd data. 54 New Bond St., W1 (phone: 71-629-8558).

Sotheby Parke Bernet – The world's oldest art auctioneer, interesting to look at even if you don't plan to buy. They auction books, porcelain, furniture, jewelry, and works of art; at times, even such odd items as vintage cars and wines. Viewing hours are between 9:30 AM and 4:30 PM on weekdays, at 34 New Bond St., W1 (phone: 71-493-8080).

Swaine, Adeney, Brigg, and Sons – Riding gear and their famous pure silk umbrellas. 185 Piccadilly, W1 (phone: 71-734-4277).

Temple Gallery – Specializes in Byzantine, Greek, and early Russian icons. 6 Clarendon Cross, W11 (phone: 71-727-3809).

Thomas Goode and Company – London's best china and glass shop first opened in 1827. Even if you don't plan to buy anything, you may want to look at their beautiful 1876 showroom, browse through their Irish linen boutique, and admire the fantastic fresh or dried floral arrangents for sale in one corner. 19 S. Audley St., W1 (phone: 71-499-2823).

Turnbull and Asser – Famous for their made-to-order shirts, but they also sell ready-made luxury menswear and women's wear next door. 71-72 Jermyn St., SW1 (phone: 71-930-0502).

Twinings – Tea — and (almost) nothing but — in bags, balls, and bulk. 216 Strand, WC2 (phone: 71-353-3511).

Vigo-Sternberg Galleries – For tapestries from the 16th to the 19th centuries. 37 S. Audley St., W1 (phone: 71-629-8307).

Waterstone's – Look for the maroon canopy of this huge chain of bookstores, whose instant success is due mainly to enterprising, well-informed staff and late, late hours (it's open till midnight in Edinburgh, for example). There are many branches, including ones on Hampstead High St. (phone: 71-794-1098), Old Brompton Rd. (phone: 71-581-8522), Charing Cross Rd. (phone: 71-434-4291), and High St., Kensington (phone: 71-376-2028).

W. Bill Ltd. – Shetland sweaters, knit ties, argyle socks, club mufflers, gloves. Two locations: 28 Old Bond St., W1 (phone: 71-629-2554) and 93 Old Bond St., W1 (phone: 71-629-2837).

Wedgwood – Porcelain. 158 Regent St., W1 (phone: 71-734-7262).

Westaway and Westaway – Cashmere and Shetland wool kilts, sweaters, scarves, and blankets. 65 Great Russell St., WC1, and around the corner at 29 Bloomsbury, WC1 (phone: 71-405-4479).

Whiteleys of Bayswater – Once a department store rivaling *Harrods,* the original building has undergone a total renovation and is now a beautiful, enclosed Edwardian mall housing a branch of just about every shop found on Bond Street or Piccadilly. The top tier holds a "Food Court," offering cafés, bars, and restaurants. Both stores and restaurants are open daily (from 10 AM to 10 PM and 10 AM to midnight, respectively). Queensway, W2 (phone: 71-229-8844).

SPORTS AND FITNESS: Soccer (called football hereabouts) and cricket are the most popular spectator pastimes, but London offers a wide variety of other sports.

Cricket – The season runs from mid-April to early September. The best places to watch it are at *Lord's Cricket Ground* (St. John's Wood Rd., NW8; phone: 71-289-1615), and *The Oval* (Kennington, SE11; phone: 71-582-6660).

Fishing – Several public ponds right in London are accessible to the angler. A permit is required from the Royal Parks Department (The Storeyard, Hyde Park, W2; phone: 71-262-5484). The department also can provide information on where to fish.

Fitness Centers – *Barbican Health & Fitness Centre* (97 Aldersgate St., EC2; phone: 71-374-0091); *Pineapple Dance Studios* (7 Langley St., WC2; phone: 71-836-4004) and several other locations around town, as well as in several hotels.

Golf – Aside from private clubs, for which membership is required, there are several municipal courses, some of which rent clubs. Try *Pickett's Lock Centre* (Pickett's Lock La., N9; phone: 81-803-3611), *Addington Court* (Featherbed La., Addington, Croydon; phone: 81-657-0281), and *Beckenham Place Park* (Beckenham, Kent; phone: 81-650-2292). *Wentworth* (Virginia Water, Surrey; phone: 344-2201) and *Sunningdale* (Ridgemount Rd., Sunningdale, Berkshire; phone: 990-21681) are two of the best courses in England and are within driving distance of London. A letter from your home club pro or president (plus a polite phone call) may gain access to their courses during the week.

Greyhound Racing – *Wembley Stadium* (Stadium Way, Wembley; phone: 81-902-8833, ext. 3346), and others. There are evening races, so check the afternoon newspapers for details.

Horse Racing – Nine major racecourses are within easy reach of London, including *Epsom,* where the *Derby* (pronounced *Dar*-by) is run, and *Ascot,* where the *Royal Ascot* races take place — both in June. The flat racing season is from March to November; steeplechasing, August to June. Call the *Jockey Club* (42 Portman Sq., W1; phone: 71-486-4921) for information.

Horseback Riding – Try *Bathurst Riding Stables* (63 Bathurst Mews, W2; phone: 71-723-2813) and *Ross Nye's Riding Establishment* (8 Bathurst Mews, W2; phone: 71-262-3791).

Ice Skating – There is the *Queen's Ice Skating Club* (17 Queensway, W2; phone: 71-229-0172) and *Silver Blades Ice Rink* (386 Streatham High Rd., SW16; phone: 81-769-7861). Skates are for rent at both rinks.

Jogging – Most pleasant for running are Hyde Park, bordered by Kensington Road, Park Lane, and Bayswater Road; Hampstead Heath, North London; and Regent's Park, bordered by Prince Albert Road, Albany Street, Marylebone Road, and Park Road. Do not jog after dark.

Rugby – An autumn-through-spring spectacle at *Rugby Football Ground,* Whitton Rd., Twickenham (phone: 81-892-8161).

Soccer – *The* big sport in Britain. The local football season is autumn to spring and the most popular local clubs are *Arsenal* (*Highbury Stadium,* Avenell Rd., N5; phone: 71-226-0304); *Chelsea* (Stamford Bridge, Fulham Rd., SW6; phone: 71-381-6221); and *Tottenham Hotspur* (White Hart La., N17; phone: 81-808-8080). As a spectator, be careful at games. Buy a seat rather than standing space. Violence and overcrowding have been major problems in recent years.

Swimming – Several excellent indoor public pools include: *Swiss Cottage Center* (Adelaide Rd., NW3; phone: 71-586-5989); *Putney Swimming Baths* (376 Upper Richmond Rd., SW15; phone: 81-789-1124); and *The Oasis* (167 High Holborn,, WC1; phone: 71-836-9555). There is outdoor swimming in the Hyde Park Serpentine, and Hampstead Heath, in the summer.

Tennis – Aside from private clubs, more than 50 London public parks have tennis courts available to all. Get information from the London Visitor and Convention Bureau (phone: 71-730-3488).

THEATER: London remains the theater capital of the world, with about 50 theaters regularly putting on plays in and around its West End theater district and a vigorous collection of "fringe" theaters in various parts of town. Best known, and most accomplished, are the two main repertory theater companies — the *Royal National Theatre Company* at the *Royal National Theatre* (South Bank, SE1; phone: 71-928-2252) and the *Royal Shakespeare Company (RSC)* at the *Barbican Centre* (The Barbican, EC2; phone: 71-638-8891); from time to time, both present dazzling versions of classics and new plays, although they sometimes trade on their reputations — the *National* mistaking dreariness for realism, and the *RSC*, stuffiness for stability. (For reliable critical reviews, consult *Time Out* magazine and the *Guardian*'s Michael Billington.) Shakespearean plays also are performed in summer at the open-air theater in Regent's Park, NW1 (phone: 71-935-5756).

In the West End, presentations include both first class and second-rate drama and comedy, a fair sprinkling of farce (for which the British have a particular fondness), and the best imports from the American stage. Visitors from the US often find attending theater in London easier — and a little less expensive — than it is at home. Except for the small handful of runaway box office successes, tickets usually are available for all performances. In most cases, you can reserve by telephone, but tickets must be picked up well before curtain time. *The West End Theatre Society* operates a half-price ticket kiosk in Leicester Square. It posts a list of shows for which remaining seats may be purchased at half-price on the day of the performance. Ticket agencies that offer tickets to all shows, charging a small commission, include *Keith Prowse & Co.* (phone: 81-741-9999; in the US, 800-669-7469; in New York City, 212-398-1430), *Ticketmaster* (phone: 71-379-4444), *London Theatre Bookings* (96 Shaftesbury Ave.; phone: 71-439-3371/4061), and *First Call* (phone: 71-240-7200). A phone service, *Theatreline,* offers information on a wide variety of West End performances (phone: 836-430959 for plays; 836-430960 for musicals; 836-430961 for comedies; 836-430962 for thrillers; 836-430963 for children's shows; 836-430964 for opera, ballet, and dance); calls can be placed from anywhere in Great Britain, and there is a service charge per call — about 60¢ to 80¢ in Great Britain, depending on the time of day. Another service, *Theatre Tonight,* offers tickets for sold-out performances. Available from noon to 6 PM, tickets can be bought by phone with a Visa card for same-night performances; no booking fee or ticket surcharge (phone: 71-753-0333).

The quality of London's fringe theater varies from accomplished and imaginative to amateurish. Theaters in pubs are at the *King's Head* (115 Upper St., Islington, N1; phone: 71-226-1916), and at the *Bush* (in the *Bush Hotel,* Shepherd's Bush Green, W6; phone: 81-743-3388). The *Riverside Studios* (Crisp Rd., Hammersmith, W6; phone: 81-748-3354), the *Tricycle Theatre* (269 Kilburn High Rd., NW6; phone: 71-328-1000), and the *New End Theatre* (27 New End, Hampstead, NW3; phone: 71-794-0022), have established reputations for the excellence of their productions, which often move on to the West End and sometimes even directly to Broadway. Also keep an eye on the *Donmar Warehouse* for major transfers from the *Edinburgh Festival Fringe* or for exciting avant-garde companies such as *Cheek by Jowl* (41 Earlham St., *Covent Garden,* WC2; phone: 71-240-8230). Lunchtime fringe theater presentations offer an alternative to sightseeing on rainy days.

A visit to *St. Martin's* is now tantamount to seeing a major London landmark, as it houses the late Agatha Christie's *The Mousetrap;* transferred from the *Ambassadors* next door, there's a fresh cast each year, and it's been running since 1952 — the longest run ever in nightly theater. The play is an exciting, tantalizing, and mildly frightening mystery-thriller. If you tell whodunit, you are ruined socially. West St., Cambridge Circus, WC2 (phone: 71-836-1443).

For those interested in musical nostalgia, the recently refurbished *Players Theatre* (in Villiers St., just off the Strand at Charing Cross station; phone: 71-839-1134) offers old-fashioned Victorian music hall entertainment.

Check *Time Out* or *City Limits* for comprehensive lists, plot summaries, and theater phone numbers. Daily papers list West End performances.

Show tours to London are very popular in season; see your travel agent for package deals. If you want to reserve specific tickets before you arrive in London, there are agencies in the US that keep a listing of what's on in London. For a service charge of about $5 per ticket, they will sell you the best seats only. Contact *Edwards & Edwards* (One Times Square Plaza, New York, NY 10036; phone: 212-944-0290 or 800-223-6108) or *Keith Prowse & Co.* (234 W. 44th St., New York, NY 10036; phone: 212-398-1430 or 800-669-7469).

■**Note:** For more London theatre listings see "The Performing Arts" in *For the Mind,* DIVERSIONS.

The best of London's ballet performances are presented at *Covent Garden,* the *Coliseum,* and at *Sadler's Wells* (Roseberry Ave., EC1; phone: 71-278-8916), though the original company has moved to Birmingham, as well as at *The Place* (17 Dukes Rd., WC1; phone: 71-387-0031), home of the *London Contemporary Dance Theatre* and the *London School of Contemporary Dance.* Details about concert, recital, opera, and ballet performances are listed in the arts sections of the Sunday newspapers. Tickets to London ballet performances can be obtained in the US by contacting *Edwards & Edwards* (One Times Square Plaza, New York, NY 10036; phone: 212-944-0290 or 800-223-6108).

 CINEMA: London may not be the equal of Paris as a movie metropolis, but many say it's stronger when it comes to very good, little-known films, often from the US or Commonwealth countries. British film is startling in both similarities and contrasts to that of the US. In Great Britain, Chaplin, Hitchcock, and Laughton are regarded as English. The *British Film Institute* (21 Stephen St., W1; phone: 71-255-1444) has an incomparable British and international film library, administers the National Film Archive, contains first class documentation and filmographic material, and publishes the monthly *Film Bulletin* and the quarterly *Sight and Sound,* as well as running the *London Film Festival* (November), which takes place in the *National Film Theatre* (*NFT*) on the South Bank near Waterloo Station and Bridge (phone: 71-928-3232). Membership is required at the *NFT* (about 80¢ a day or $15.70 for a year), but it's well worth it for its two cinemas; wide variety of old and new British, US, and international movies; good film bookshop; and eating facilities. The success of the *NFT*'s *London Film Festival* in past years testifies to the high caliber of London's critics, who include the *Evening Standard*'s Alexander Walker, the *Guardian*'s Derek Malcolm, the *Financial Times*'s Nigel Andrews, and above all, the *Observer*'s Philip French; the *Film Festival* appoints one of them as its *supremo* of the year.

As with the theater, there are big divisions between West End and fringe (or independent) cinema. The West End strives for probable box-office smash hits, so look out for long lines at Friday openings, and head for early showings, some of which begin not long after noon. Monday admission prices are less expensive. One word of warning: West End movie house prices are not inexpensive. Admission to a long-running film (at a theater on the Haymarket) cost us £6.50 last winter. The widest selection of films under one roof can be found at *Whiteleys,* an enclosed mall with eight cinemas (Queensway, W2; phone: 71-792-3303). For sheer comfort, the *Curzon Mayfair* (on Mayfair's Curzon St., W1 in the West End; phone: 71-465-8865) is unbeatable for both low-budget and commercial films. The most exciting film fare usually is found in independents, and sometimes you must travel to remote parts of London to see outstanding work in an almost empty cinema. If independent films interest you, check what's showing in places like *Everyman* (at Hampstead; phone: 71-435-1525); the luxurious, comfortable *Barbican Centre Cinemas* (phone: 71-638-8891); *Screen* (Baker St., W1; phone: 71-935-2772); *Screen on the Green* (at Islington; phone: 71-226-3520); and

Screen on the Hill (in Hampstead; phone: 71-435-3366). All feature late-night showings and children's screenings on Saturdays (as do the *Barbican and NFT*). In some cases you may have to pay moderate club fees. Most British cinemas now ban smoking. Telephone the theaters for show times.

The *Museum of London,* near the *Barbican* (phone: 71-600-3699) and the *Museum of the Moving Image* (phone: 71-928-3535), alongside the *National Film Theatre,* also show films. Since showings are not regular, it is best to call ahead or to check in *Time Out.*

 MUSIC: Few cities offer a greater variety of musical performances — both classical music and the many varieties of popular music. For classical fare, the focus of attention is the *South Banks Arts Centre* with its three concert halls — *Royal Festival Hall, Queen Elizabeth Hall,* and the *Purcell Room* — (phone: 71-928-3191 for all three); the *Barbican Hall,* home of the *London Symphony Orchestra* (phone: 71-638-4141); and the *Royal Albert Hall* (Kensington Gore, SW7; phone: 71-589-8212). The latter is the home of the *Henry Wood Promenade Concerts,* or more simply, the *Proms,* an 8-week series of orchestral concerts that has been a popular feature of the London summer scene (July to September) for decades. Tickets are inexpensive because the Proms came into being to give students and other people who are not affluent an opportunity to dress up and be part of a grand musical event. The performances are tops (some broadcast live by the BBC), and the SRO audience is large and enthusiastic. *Wigmore Hall* (Wigmore St., W1; phone: 71-935-2141), is best known for recitals of chamber music and performances by some of the world's most accomplished instrumental and vocal soloists. Concerts also are often held in the dignified, splendid setting of St. John's Church (Smith Sq., SW1; phone: 71-222-1061). During the summer, outdoor concerts are given at Kenwood, Crystal Palace, and Holland Park, and bands play in many of London's parks.

Operas at *Covent Garden Royal Opera House* (Floral St., WC2; phone: 71-240-1066), are internationally famous. The *English National Opera Company,* whose performances are always in English, is at the *London Coliseum* (St. Martin's La., WC2; phone: 71-836-3161). If you wish to obtain opera tickets before departing from the US, contact the agency *Edwards & Edwards* (One Times Square Plaza, New York, NY 10036; phone: 212-944-0290 or 800-223-6108).

Although superstar musicians and vocalists usually appear in the city's larger halls, good live popular music can be heard in London's music pubs. Among the best of them are the *Dublin Castle* (94 Parkway, NW1; phone: 71-485-1773); *King's Head* (4 Fulham High St., SW6; phone: 71-736-1413); *Hare and Hounds* (181 Upper St., N1; phone: 71-226-2992); and *Half Moon* (93 Lower Richmond Rd, SW15; phone: 81-788-2387).

If you are interested in purchasing tickets in the US to see pop and rock musicians who will be appearing in London, contact *Keith Prowse & Co. (USA),* 234 W. 44th St., New York, NY 10036 (phone: 800-669-7469 or 212-398-1430 in New York City).

 NIGHTCLUBS AND NIGHTLIFE: There was a time when they virtually rolled up the sidewalks in London at 11 PM. Now there's a very lively and often wild nightlife, including nightclubs, jazz clubs, historical feast entertainments, and gambling casinos. Some wind up around midnight; most go on until well into the early morning hours. In *Covent Garden* and still-trendy-after-all-these-years Chelsea, particularly along King's and Fulham roads, are fashionable pubs, wine bars, and restaurants. Two nightclubs with cabarets are *The Talk of the Town* (Drury La., WC2; phone: 71-408-1001) and *L'Hirondelle* (199 Swallow St., W1; phone: 71-734-1511). The best jazz clubs are *Ronnie Scott's* (47 Frith St., W1; phone: 71-439-0747), and *The 100 Club* (100 Oxford St., W1; phone: 71-636-0933). For jazz and a slice, try *Pizza Express* (10 Dean St., W1; phone: 71-437-9595), or *Pizza on the Park* (11 Knightsbridge, SW1; phone: 71-235-5550). *Dingwalls* (Camden Lock, Chalk Farm Rd., NW1; phone: 71-267-4967) and the *Town and Country Club* (9 Highgate Rd., NW5; phone: 71-284-0303) have a continually changing program of much-acclaimed performers of rock music.

For a special (if touristy) treat, London offers the Medieval Banquet, complete with traditional meals served by costumed waiters and waitresses. Menus resemble those of traditional Elizabethan feasts, and there is period music, horseplay, occasional mock sword fights, Shakespearean playlets, and other light entertainment. Try *Tudor Rooms* (17 Swallow St., W1; phone: 71-240-3978); *Beefeater* (St. Katherine Dock, E1; phone: 71-408-1001); and *Cockney Cabaret* (6 Hanover St., W1; phone: 71-408-1001).

The disco scene is an ever changing one, and many places — such as expensive and exclusive *Annabel's* (44 Berkeley Sq., W1; phone: 71-629-3558) — are open only to members. Clubs of the moment include: the *Hippodrome* (Charing Cross Rd., WC2 (phone: 71-437-4311); *Stringfellows* (16-19 Upper St. Martin's La., WC2; phone: 71-240-5534); *Legend's* (29 Old Burlington St., W1; phone: 71-437-9933); *Crazy Larry's* (Lots Rd., SW10; phone: 71-376-5555); *Tramp* (40 Jermyn St., SW1; phone: 71-734-0565), where the chic social set meets to disco (members only); and *Limelight* (136 Shaftesbury Ave., W1; phone: 71-434-0572). A smart addition to the West London night scene is the *Broadway Boulevard* club in Ealing, particularly convenient for guests at the nearby Heathrow hotels (phone: 81-840-0616).

Female impersonators regularly perform at the *Jongleurs Cabaret Club* (at the *Coronet,* Lavender Gardens, SW11; phone: 71-585-0955) and *Black Cap* (171 Camden High St., NW1; phone: 71-485-1742). Phone for details.

BEST IN TOWN

 CHECKING IN: Visitors arriving in London between early spring and mid-autumn without hotel reservations are in for an unpleasant experience. For many years now, there has been a glaring shortage of hotel rooms in the British capital during the prime tourist season, which each year seems to begin earlier and end later. (For a small fee, the Tourist Information Centre at Victoria Station Forecourt, or at the underground station in Heathrow, will try to help you locate a room. For credit card reservations, call 71-824-8844 Mondays through Fridays 9 AM to 6 PM.) This fact, plus years of general inflation and the difficulty of finding suitable hotel staff, are largely responsible for often excessive hotel charges, generally out of keeping with other costs in Britain. As a rule, very expensive and expensive hotels do not include any meals in their prices; moderate and inexpensive·hotels generally include continental breakfasts. Prices — with bath, English breakfast, VAT, and a 10% service charge sometimes included — are $350 and up (sometimes way up) for a double room in a very expensive hotel; $200 to $325 for a double room in an expensive hotel; $135 to $190 in moderate; and $85 to $130, inexpensive. All telephone numbers in inner London are in the 71 area code; in outer London, in the 81 area code, unless otherwise indicated.

More and more small hotels have opened up in converted townhouses. Some offer bed and breakfast only, while others have restaurants. The *Aster House* and *Pembridge Court* are hostelries that have received top ratings from the British Tourist Authority (see below for additional information on both). The BTA (phone: 212-581-4700, for information in the US) has a useful list of bed and breakfast hotels.

As an alternative to conventional hotel accommodations, it's easy to stay in one of

500 private homes and apartments through a program called "Your Home in London." These vary from a single in a bed and breakfast establishment for $30 a night to a 2-bedroom apartment in central London for $140 a night. For information in the US, call 301-269-6232. The *Bulldog Club* is yet another resource for very upscale bed and breakfast accommodations, and functions exclusively for its members (annual membership costs about $50 per person). It has contacts with a variety of period homes in London's busy city center or calmer, surrounding neighborhoods. For additional information: 35 The Chase, London SW4 0NP (phone: 71-622-6935; fax: 71-720-2748). Or contact their North American office: 6 Kittredge Ct., Richmond Hill, Ontario, Canada L4C 7X3 (phone: 416-737-2798; fax: 416-737-3179).

Members of the *English-Speaking Union* are eligible for a 30% discount at the *Chesterfield* hotel, as well as for discounts on numerous functions at the *Union's* headquarters in London and other *E-SU* offices around the world. For more information regarding membership and activities contact the *English-Speaking Union* in the US (16 E. 69th St., New York, NY 10021; phone: 212-879-6800) or in London (Dartmouth House, 37 Charles St., W1, London WIX 8LX; phone: 71-491-2622).

If you are particularly interested in service flats (furnished apartments with close-to-traditional hotel services — mostly daily maid service), contact *Eastone Overseas Accommodations,* 6682 141st Lane N., Palm Beach Gardens, FL 33418 (phone: 407-575-6991) or *Hometours International* (1170 Broadway, New York, NY 10001; phone: 212-689-0851 or 800-367-4668). Service flats range from the very elegant to the very modest at a bed and breakfast establishment.

Berkeley – Remarkably understated, this 160-room hotel manages to preserve its impeccably high standards while keeping a low profile. Soft-spoken service complements the tastefully lavish, traditional English decor. There also is a health club and a new gymnasium. Business facilities include 24-hour room service, meeting rooms for up to 220, concierge, foreign currency exchange, secretarial services, translation services, photocopiers, cable television news, and express checkout. Wilton Pl., Knightsbridge, SW1 (phone: 71-235-6000; fax: 71-235-4330; telex: 919252). Very expensive.

Claridges – This plush 190-room outpost for visiting royalty, heads of state, and other distinguished and/or affluent foreigners is an Art Deco treasure. The line of chauffered limousines outside the main entrance sometimes makes traffic seem impenetrable. Wrought-iron balconies and a sweeping foyer staircase help provide a stately setting for one of London's most elegant hostelries. Liveried footmen serve afternoon tea. Business facilities include 24-hour room service, meeting rooms for up to 250, concierge, foreign currency exchange, secretarial services, audiovisual equipment, photocopiers, computers, cable television news, translation services, and express checkout. Brook St., W1 (phone: 71-629-8860; fax: 71-499-2210; telex: 21872). Very expensive.

Connaught – A touch too sober for high livers; a trifle too formal for the rough-and-ready crowd. But there aren't many hotels left in the world that can rival it for welcome, elegance, and comfort — particularly in its luxurious suites. The food served in the restaurant and *The Grill,* rated one Michelin star, is an experience all its own (see *Eating Out*). Business facilities include 24-hour room service, 2 private dining rooms, concierge, and foreign currency exchange. Carlos Pl., W1 (phone: 71-491-0688; fax: 71-495-3262). Very expensive.

Dorchester – The grande dame is back after a 2-year closure for a total face-lift, and she looks better than ever. All 252 rooms and 55 suites were refurbished and redecorated (the bed linen is extra special; the bathrooms superbly designed). Behind the scenes, renovation involved hidden necessities like wiring, plumbing, triple-glazing on the Park Lane side, and air conditioning. Best of all, the service is topnotch. Once again you can take tea in the pink marble *Promenade* and eat in the *Grill* and *Terrace* restaurants. Additions include the *Oriental* restaurant, which specializes in authentic Cantonese food, and the exclusive basement night-spot — the *Dorchester Club,* which requires membership 48 hours in advance. Business facilities include 24-hour room service, meeting rooms for up to 1,000, concierge, foreign currency exchange, secretarial services, audiovisual equipment, photocopiers, computers, cable television news, translation services, a health club, and express checkout. Park La., W1 (phone: 71-629-8888; fax: 71-409-0114; telex: 887704). Very expensive.

Forty-Seven Park Street – One of our most cherished secrets, these 54 suites, or "service flats," are a favorite of folks who are staying for more than a few days; the accommodations are not-so-small apartments perfect for extended visits. Breakfast alone is worth crossing the Atlantic, since "room service" here is pro-vided by the elegant *Le Gavroche* restaurant, which flourishes downstairs (see *Eating Out*). Owned by the Roux Brothers, who also own the restaurant (and the *Wayside Inn* out in Bray), the furnishings are luxurious in the best English taste. The location, roughly between Hyde Park and Grosvenor Square, also is ideal. Business facilities include 24-hour room service, meeting rooms for up to 24, concierge, foreign currency exchange, secretarial services, photocopiers, comput-ers, and translation services. 47 Park St., W1 (phone: 71-491-7282; fax: 71-491-7281; telex: 22116). Very expensive.

Grosvenor House – This 454-room grande dame facing Hyde Park has a health club, a swimming pool, some interesting shops, the much-lauded *Pavilion* restau-rant (see *Eating Out*), the *Park Lounge,* which serves traditional afternoon teas, and the exclusive *Crown Club* on the top floor for members only — usually busi-nesspeople who require special services — with rooms, suites, a lounge, and com-plimentary extras. Business facilities include 24-hour room service, meeting rooms for up to 1,500, concierge, foreign currency exchange, secretarial services, audio-visual equipment, photocopiers, translation services, and express checkout. Park La., W1 (phone: 71-499-6363; fax: 71-629-9337; telex: 24871). Very expensive.

Inn on the Park – Don't be deceived by the modern exterior; everything is tradi-tional (and wonderful) within. A fine example of the superb service routinely offered by members of the Four Seasons chain, the 228 rooms are comfortable, tastefully furnished, and spacious. The breakfast buffet is delightful; the restaurant is first rate. Business facilities include 24-hour room service, meeting rooms for up to 450, concierge, foreign currency exchange, secretarial services, audiovisual equipment, photocopiers, computers, translation services, and express checkout. Hamilton Pl., Piccadilly, W1 (phone: 71-499-0888; fax: 71-499-5572; telex: 22771). Very expensive.

Inter-Continental – Smack-dab in the middle of the West End, right on Hyde Park Corner, with windows overlooking the route of the Royal Horse Guards as they go cantering off for the Changing of the Guard each morning. Its 490 well-proportioned rooms are equipped with refrigerated bars. Modern and comfortable, particularly the Art Deco *Le Soufflé* restaurant, but the location is the chief lure. Business facilities include 24-hour room service, meeting rooms for up to 1,000, concierge, foreign currency exchange, secretarial services, audiovisual equipment, photocopiers, computers, translation services, and express checkout. 1 Hamilton Pl., Hyde Park Corner, W1 (phone: 71-409-3131; fax: 71-493-3476; telex: 25853). Very expensive.

Lanesborough – This brand-new luxury hotel at Hyde Park Corner just steps from the Wellington Gate in the tony Belgravia area, is built within the landmark structure that was St. George's Hospital from 1734 to 1980. The interior design recreates the feeling of an elegant 19th-century residence. There are 95 superbly appointed guestrooms which include 46 suites, some with steam showers and

Jacuzzis. The more formal *Dining Room* offers traditional English food, while the *Conservatory* serves light meals for breakfast and lunch, and traditional afternoon tea. The Library and the Withdrawing Room both have bars. The location is one of the best in the city. Business facilities include 24-hour room and butler service, concierge, secretarial services, in-room fax machines, 2-line telephones, and cable television news. Knightsbridge and Grosvenor Crescent (phone: 214-871-5400, for information). Very expensive.

Langham Hilton – Originally opened in 1865 as "the first grand hotel of London," it was known for its "rising rooms" (elevators) and famous guests, including Mark Twain, Toscanini, and Oscar Wilde. Following World War II, it was converted to BBC offices and studios, but after a multimillion-dollar renovation, restoring many original Victorian features, it reopened last year as a 385-room hotel. Several restaurants include the *Palm Court,* serving light meals and snacks around-the-clock, and *Tsar's,* specializing in vodka and caviar. Business facilities include 24-hour room service, meeting rooms for up to 500, concierge, foreign currency exchange, secretarial services, audiovisual equipment, photocopiers, computers, cable television news, translation services, and express checkout. Portland Pl., W1N 3AA (phone: 71-636-1000; in the US, 800-223-1146; fax: 71-323-2340; telex: 21113). Very Expensive.

London Hilton International – Well situated off Hyde Park Corner, near shopping and theater, this contemporary high-rise offers comfortable accommodations (392 rooms) and spectacular views of the park and the city. Special attention to executives includes a multilingual switchboard, secretarial staff, office equipment, and private dining rooms. There's every conceivable service, plus 3 restaurants — *Windows on the World,* with a view; *Trader Vics* (Polynesian); and the *Brasserie.* Business facilities include 24-hour room service, meeting rooms for up to 1,000, concierge, foreign currency exchange, secretarial services, audiovisual equipment, photocopiers, computers, translation services, and express checkout. 22 Park La., W1 (phone: 71-493-8000; 71-493-4957; telex: 24873). Very expensive.

Park Lane – If you don't mind the noise of the city streets, the site of this hotel, in the heart of the West End, is appealing. Some of the 320 rooms have views of Green Park across the street. *Bracewell's* restaurant is an elegant dining spot. Business facilities include 24-hour room service, meeting rooms for up to 500, concierge, foreign currency exchange, secretarial services, audiovisual equipment, photocopiers, computers, translation services, and express checkout. Piccadilly, W1 (phone: 71-499-6321; fax: 71-499-1965; telex: 21533). Very expensive.

Ritz – The fellow who was heard to mutter snootily, "Nobody stays at the *Ritz* anymore" was off base, especially since renovations have restored much of the old luster and certainly got the "bugs" out. With 130 rooms, it now ranks among London's finest stopping places, and it's hard to find another hotel in London with more elegant surroundings. Tea here is a very pleasant experience; in probably the most formal and elegant tearoom in the city, gracious white-tied waiters carry silver trays to serve guests in the lovely Louis XIV–style *Palm Court* (reservations necessary at least 2 weeks in advance for weekends and 1 week in advance for weekdays.) The dining room is equally splendid, with its elegant interior columns, opulent ceiling frescoes, and the view of Green Park. Once again, after a bit of a slump, the fare almost matches the elegant surroundings. Business facilities include 24-hour room service, meeting rooms for up to 50, concierge, foreign currency exchange, secretarial services, audiovisual equipment, photocopiers, computers, cable television news, and translation services. Piccadilly, W1 (phone: 71-493-8181; fax: 71-493-2687; telex: 257200). Very expensive.

St. James's Club – For about $400 per year ($250 thereafter) and an introduction by a member, you can join this exclusive residential club in the heart of London (though you don't need to bother for your first stay). Guests have full use of club suites. Some very good food is served in the downstairs dining room. Business facilities include 24-hour room service, meeting rooms for up to 30, concierge, foreign currency exchange, secretarial services, audiovisual equipment, photocopiers, computers, and translation services. 7 Park Pl., SW1 (phone: 71-629-7688; fax: 71-491-0987; telex: 298519). Very expensive.

Savoy – A favorite of film and theater performers, some of whom check in for months, the hotel celebrated its 100-year anniversary in 1989. Still one of London's top addresses, its 200 rooms are overseen by armies of chambermaids and porters, and the reputation of its famous *Savoy Grill* (see *Eating Out*) has been restored through a beautiful resuscitation of the decor and a revitalization of the kitchen. More casual than the *Savoy Grill*, the *Upstairs Bar* serves primarily seafood and offers 44 different vintages of wine. The *River* restaurant has a wonderful view of the gardens and the Thames. Tea is served in the spacious Thames Foyer, where guests relax in posh, comfortable sofas and chairs in a garden-theme setting with a pianist playing background music; hotel guests are served in an exclusive tearoom. The Thames Suites are the most beautiful accommodations in the city. Business facilities include 24-hour room service, meeting rooms for up to 500, concierge, foreign currency exchange, secretarial services, computers, cable television news, translation services, and express checkout. The Strand, WC2 (phone: 71-836-4343 or 71-836-3719; fax: 71-872-8894; telex: 24234). Very expensive.

22 Jermyn Street – London's fashionable menswear street also has had a fashionable hotel since 1990. Wedged up a long passageway between a hatmaker and a shirtmaker, there are 18 rooms which are really suites, furnished with antiques, elegant curtains, and marble bathrooms. It's so English that guests expect valets at the guestroom doors — and get them! There's no restaurant, but many of London's best eateries are moments away. Business facilities include 24-hour room service, concierge, secretarial services, fax machines in the rooms, and photocopiers. 22 Jermyn St., SW1Y 6HL (phone: 71-734-2353; fax: 71-734-0750; telex: 261085). Very expensive.

Windsor – This brand-new Ritz-Carlton property is opening this May in what was the *Great Central* hotel, built in 1899. It has 308 guestrooms, which include 58 suites. The rooms all have marble baths, safe deposit boxes, thick bathrobes, and color television sets, and many have working fireplaces. There is a restaurant, café, and lobby lounge serving tea and drinks, as well as a swimming pool and health and fitness center. The Club level offers a private lounge and concierge staff, complimentary continental breakfast, light lunch, afternoon tea, cocktails with hors d'oeuvres, and late evening sweets and cordials. Business facilities include 24-hour room service, meeting rooms for up to 200, concierge, secretarial services, audiovisual equipment, photocopiers, and translation services. 222 Marylebone Rd., London (phone: 71-499-4050; fax: 71-409-0880). Very expensive.

Abbey Court – In the Notting Hill Gate area near Portobello Market, this elegant hotel has 22 bedrooms of various sizes, all with private bath, TV sets, hair dryers, and trouser presses. The flowers on display in the common areas are especially lovely. Breakfast is served in the room, and 24-hour room service also is available. No restaurant. Business facilities include 24-hour room service, concierge, secretarial services, and photocopiers. 20 Pembridge Gardens, W2 (phone: 71-221-7518; fax: 71-792-0858; telex: 262172). Expensive.

Basil Street – A relic with a reputation for graceful, old-fashioned service and beautiful antique furnishings to match. It draws a faithful international clientele who, if they can reserve one of its 94 smallish rooms, prefer staying here to patronizing any of the modern, impersonal, newer hotels. It has a women's health club and sits just down the street from *Harrods*. Business facilities include 24-hour room service, meeting rooms for up to 300, concierge, foreign currency exchange, audiovisual equipment, and photocopiers. 8 Basil St., SW3 (phone: 71-581-3311; fax: 71-581-3693; telex: 28379). Expensive.

Beaufort – Tranquil and very elegant, it is composed of two Victorian houses in Beaufort Gardens, the heart of fashionable Knightsbridge. It offers 28 comfortable and attractively decorated rooms, each with a plenitude of facilities: stereo/cassette player; TV set; direct-dial phone; hair dryer; magazines and books; a decanter of brandy; and even a teddy bear for the youngsters. Breakfast is brought on a tray each morning. Convenient to restaurants and shops (*Harrods* is just around the corner). Business facilities include concierge and photocopiers. 33 Beaufort Gardens, SW3 (phone: 71-584-5252; fax: 71-589-2834; telex: 929200). Expensive.

Blakes – A row of Victorian townhouses has been transformed into this charming 52-room hotel, where many employees wear stylish uniforms. There's black antique furniture on the lower level, while the upper floors are decorated in pale gray and pastels. The bathrooms are made of marble, and business facilities include a topnotch restaurant, laundry service, 24-hour room service, concierge, foreign currency exchange, secretarial services, and photocopiers. Popular with show-biz folk. 33 Roland Gardens, SW7 (phone: 71-370-6701; fax: 71-373-0442; telex: 813500). Expensive.

Britannia – Mahogany furniture, velvet armchairs, rooms painted in colors you might choose at home — all very tasteful and solid, despite the anonymity of the spacious foyer with the pretentious chandeliers. This is where the American Embassy — also on the square — often puts up visiting middle-ranking State Department officials. The 354 rooms all have private bath. A link in the Inter-Continental chain. Business facilities include 24-hour room service, meeting rooms for up to 120, concierge, foreign currency exchange, secretarial services, audiovisual equipment, photocopiers, computers, cable television news, translation services, and express checkout. Grosvenor Sq., W1 (phone: 71-629-9400; fax: 71-629-7736; telex: 23941). Expensive.

Brown's – As English as you can get, retaining pleasing, quaint, Victorian charm, and not at all marred by heavy, sturdy furniture or the somewhat hushed atmosphere. Strong on service. If it's an English tea you're after, this is the place (tie and jacket required). Business facilities include 24-hour room service, meeting rooms for up to 80, concierge, foreign currency exchange, and photocopiers. Dover St., W1 (phone: 71-493-6020; fax: 71-493-9381; telex: 28686). Expensive.

Cadogan Thistle – Very comfortable, older, 69-room place, redolent of Edwardian England. Oscar Wilde was arrested here, and Lillie Langtry, who was having an affair with the Prince of Wales (later Edward VII), lived next door. The furniture and decor are original, but modern conveniences are offered as well. Business facilities include 24-hour room service, meeting rooms for up to 40, concierge, foreign currency exchange, secretarial services, photocopiers, and express checkout. 75 Sloane St., SW1 (phone: 71-235-7141; fax: 71-245-0994; telex: 267893). Expensive.

Capital – Only a stone's throw from *Harrods,* this 45-room hotel has been beautifully refurbished and is a member of the prestigious Relais & Châteaux group. All rooms have air conditioning, color TV sets, radios, and elegantly appointed bathrooms — and the beds have the best pillows in England! There is an intimate lounge, a lively bar, and an excellent French restaurant (see *Eating Out*). Business facilities include 24-hour room service, meeting rooms for up to 24, concierge, foreign currency exchange, secretarial services, photocopiers, and cable television news. 22 Basil St., Knightsbridge, SW3 (phone: 71-589-5171; in the US, 800-926-3199; fax: 71-225-0011; telex: 919042). Expensive.

Chesterfield – In the heart of Mayfair and near Hyde Park, this small, rebuilt

Georgian mansion has a certain exclusive elegance. Its 110 bedrooms are thoroughly modernized and well equipped. Amenities include a restaurant, a wood-paneled library, and a small bar that opens onto a flower-filled patio. Business facilities include 24-hour room service, meeting rooms for up to 150, concierge, foreign currency exchange, photocopiers, and express checkout. 35 Charles St., W1 (phone: 71-491-2622; fax: 71-491-4793; telex: 269394). Expensive.

Churchill – Always thought of as an 'American' style hotel, though no longer quite as popular with visitors from the US. Inside, a turn-of-the-century mood is reflected in the discreet decor, which is undergoing a $50 million dollar roof-to-roadway renovation. This is a well-run, efficient 430-room place, with a pleasant restaurant and a snack room that serves the best bacon and eggs in London. Business facilities include 24-hour room service, meeting rooms for up to 200, concierge, foreign currency exchange, secretarial services, photocopiers, computers, cable television news, translation services, and express checkout. Portman Sq., W1 (phone: 71-486-5800; fax: 71-486-1255; telex: 264831). Expensive.

Conrad Chelsea Harbour – Hilton hotels (the US branch, not the international chain) has opened in Chelsea Harbour, overlooking the Thames. Each of the 160 suites has a living room, 3 telephones, and a mini-bar. Guests can take advantage of the hotel's health club, complete with a heated indoor swimming pool, saunas, and steamrooms. There are 18 shops and restaurants, including the *Compass Rose,* which serves international and continental fare, or the less formal *Broadwood Lounge,* for breakfast and light meals. *Drakes* bar is open nightly. Business facilities include 24-hour room service, meeting rooms for up to 200, concierge, foreign currency exchange, secretarial services, photocopiers, computers, cable television news, and express checkout. Chelsea Harbour, SW10 (phone: 71-823-3000; 800-HILTONS in the US; or 800-268-9275 in Canada; fax: 71-351-6525; telex: 919222). Expensive.

Draycott – The 26 rooms here are each distinctively decorated. While there's no restaurant, there is 24-hour room service, as well as a drawing room. Staying here is like living in a fashionable London townhouse, and guests must register as members upon their first visit. Business facilities include meeting rooms for up to 15, concierge, foreign currency exchange, secretarial services, photocopiers, and computers. 24-26 Cadogan Gardens, SW3 (phone: 71-730-6466; fax: 71-730-0236). Expensive.

Drury Lane Moat House – Near the theater district and fashionable *Covent Garden,* this 153-room hotel is ultramodern with a cool, sophisticated decor and an elegant bar. Business facilities include 24-hour room service, meeting rooms for up to 100, concierge, foreign currency exchange, secretarial services in English, audiovisual equipment, photocopiers, computers, translation services, and express checkout. 10 Drury La., High Holborn, WC2 (phone: 71-836-6666; 71-831-1548; telex: 881395). Expensive.

Dukes – Despite its modest size (only 36 rooms and 26 suites), this is an establishment where nobility and prestige shine through. The exterior has an exquisite Edwardian façade, there's a peaceful flower-filled courtyard, and some suites are named for former dukes. A virtual total reconstruction has produced accommodations of great taste and warmth, and the snug location, down a quiet cul-de-sac, does its best to make guests feel protected and private. Afternoon tea is a formal affair served in the elegant dining room. Piccadilly, Buckingham Palace, Trafalgar Square, Hyde Park Corner, and the shops of Bond Street and the Burlington Arcade are all within walking distance. Now owned by Cunard, which also operates the nearby *Ritz* and *Stafford.* Business facilities include 24-hour room service, meeting rooms for up to 150, concierge, foreign currency exchange, secretarial services, audiovisual equipment, photocopiers, translation services, and express checkout. 35 St. James's Pl., SW1A (phone: 71-491-4840; fax: 71-493-1264; telex: 28283). Expensive.

Edwardian International – The first 5-star hotel at Heathrow Airport manages to deliver an English country-house feel despite its location and size (460 rooms, 17 suites). *Henley's* restaurant serves British favorites (steak and kidney pie), as well as Italian and French dishes. The *Brasserie* is open from 6:30 AM to 11 PM for light, quick meals, while the Leisure Centre has a full gym, a swimming pool, a sauna, and hairdressing facilities. Business facilities include 24-hour room service, concierge, foreign currency exchange, secretarial services, audiovisual equipment, photocopiers, computers, cable television news, and translation services. Bath Rd., Hayes, Middx. UB3 5AW (phone: 81-759-6311; fax: 81-759-4559; telex: 23925; in the US, 800-447-7011). Expensive.

Forte Crest St. James' – Formerly the *Cavendish* and now a member of the Forte group, this very modern property offers one of the most attractive locations in central London, near Piccadilly. Its 254 rooms are comfortable, though hardly elegant. There are 2 restaurants and a pleasant bar. Business facilities include 24-hour room service, meeting rooms for up to 200, concierge, foreign currency exchange, secretarial services, audiovisual equipment, photocopiers, computers, cable television news, translation services, and express checkout. Jermyn St., SW1 (phone: 71-930-2111; fax: 71-839-2125; telex: 263187 CAVHTL G). Expensive.

Halcyon – A $15-million restoration brought the two Belle Epoque mansions that are the foundations of this property back to their original glamor. Some of the 44 guestrooms feature four-poster beds and Jacuzzis, plus all modern conveniences. Its *Kingfisher* restaurant is among London's best hotel dining spots. Business facilities include 24-hour room service, meeting rooms for up to 120, concierge, foreign currency exchange, secretarial services, audiovisual equipment, photocopiers, translation services, and express checkout. 81 Holland Park, W11 (phone: 71-727-7288; fax: 71-229-8516; telex: 266721). Expensive.

Halkin – This intimate, newly constructed property in the Belgravia area, right near Buckingham Palace and Hyde Park, boasts 41 individually designed rooms and suites, furnished with a mixture of contemporary and antique pieces. The hotel's restaurant looks over a pretty garden, and serves fine French food. Business facilities include 24-hour room service, meeting rooms for up to 50, concierge, secretarial services, photocopiers, cable television news, fax machines in each room, and translation services. 5-6 Halkin St., SW1 (phone: 71-333-1000; in the US, 800-345-3457; fax: 71-333-1100). Expensive.

Hyde Park – The only hotel set in Hyde Park, this establishment — formerly apartments during Victorian times — played host to Rudolph Valentino in the 1920s and George VI and Queen Elizabeth in 1948. The recently redecorated 186 spacious bedrooms and suites are furnished with antique furniture and modern bathrooms. Some rooms also have spectacular views of the park (some have air conditioning). Marble stairs, chandeliers, and plants are all part of the hotel's elegant decor. Visit the *Park Room,* with huge windows providing panoramic views of Hyde Park, for delicious meals, including breakfast and afternoon tea. There is also a grillroom, and a drawing room. Business facilities include 24-hour room service, meeting rooms for up to 250, concierge, foreign currency exchange, secretarial services, audiovisual equipment, photocopiers, and translation services. 66 Knightsbridge, SW1 (phone: 71-235-2000; fax: 71-235-4552; telex: 262057). Expensive.

London Marriott – Close to the American Embassy and West End shopping, it's bright and busy, and it has a full range of facilities — lounge, bar, 2 restaurants, shops, 223 very comfortable rooms, and good service. Business facilities include 24-hour room service, meeting rooms for up to 1,000, concierge, foreign currency exchange, secretarial services, audiovisual equipment, photocopiers, computers, cable television news, and translation services. Grosvenor Sq., W1 (phone: 71-493-1232; fax: 71-491-3201; telex: 268101). Expensive.

Londonderry – Overlooking Hyde Park, its 3 penthouse suites and 150 rooms have just undergone a renovation, and there is a new health club. Business facilities include 24-hour room service, meeting rooms for up to 130, concierge, foreign currency exchange, secretarial services, photocopiers, and express checkout. Park La., W1 (phone: 71-493-7292; fax: 71-495-1395; telex: 263292). Expensive.

Mayfair Holiday Inn – Renovation hasn't damaged the hotel's Regency style, unusual for this chain. Sitting in London's most prestigious neighborhood, it has 192 rooms, the à la carte *Berkeley* restaurant, and an evening pianist in the *Dauphin* cocktail bar. Business facilities include 24-hour room service, meeting rooms for up to 70, concierge, foreign currency exchange, secretarial services, photocopiers, and computers. 3 Berkeley St., W1 (phone: 71-493-8282; fax: 71-629-2827; telex: 24561). Expensive.

Le Meridien – Located between the Royal Academy and Piccadilly Circus, the lofty, Edwardian marble entrance hall leads to the 284 rooms and 24 suites. Many of the accommodations here are on the smallish side. The *Terrace* restaurant, on the second floor, has a glass roof, and the space beneath the hotel has been transformed into a very good health club. There is also a less formal restaurant, a bar, and a cocktail lounge. Afternoon tea in the lounge is accompanied by a harpist. Business facilities include 24-hour room service, meeting rooms for up to 100, concierge, foreign currency exchange, secretarial services, audiovisual equipment, photocopiers, computers, cable television news, translation services, and express checkout. Piccadilly, W1 (phone: 71-734-8000; fax: 71-437-3574; telex: 25795). Expensive.

Montcalm – A smaller, elegant hostelry that has a lovely façade, a warm-toned and understated interior, and topnotch service. Its 114 rooms have all the usual comforts, and its 6 suites are especially luxurious. There's a bar, and chef Gary Houiellbecq brings to bear all the skills he employed at the acclaimed *Compleat Angler* in Marlow in *Les Célébrités* restaurant. Business facilities include 24-hour room service, meeting rooms for up to 70, concierge, foreign currency exchange, secretarial services, audiovisual equipment, photocopiers, computers, and express checkout. Great Cumberland Pl., W1 (phone: 71-402-4288; fax: 71-724-9180; telex: 28710). Expensive.

Mountbatten – The life and times of Earl Mountbatten of Burma is the theme throughout this refurbished, wonderfully eccentric hotel's public rooms, all with exhibitions of various mementos from India. All 127 rooms feature Italian marble bathrooms, satellite color TV and in-house movies, while 7 suites have whirlpool baths. A purely vegetarian tea (scones without animal fat) is served in the country-house–style drawing room decorated with oak paneling and a fireplace. Business facilities include 24-hour room service, meeting rooms for up to 75, concierge, foreign currency exchange, secretarial services, audiovisual equipment, photocopiers, computers, and translation services. Monmouth St., *Covent Garden,* WC2 (phone: 71-836-4300; fax: 71-240-3547; telex: 298087). Expensive.

Pelham – These two mid-Victorian townhouses in South Kensington offer 35 stylish (though smallish) rooms and 2 suites — all individually decorated and all with private bath, a TV set, and telephone. There is also a restaurant and 2 lounges. Business facilities include 24-hour room service, a small meeting room, concierge, foreign currency exchange, and secretarial services. Cromwell Place, SW7 2LA (phone: 71-589-8288; fax: 71-584-8444; telex: 8814714). Expensive.

Royal Court – Clean and comfortable, the 102-room establishment has a courteous, helpful staff, at the head of London's fashionable Chelsea shopping and residential district and within quick, easy reach of the rest of the action in town. Business facilities include 24-hour room service, meeting rooms for up to 40, concierge, foreign currency exchange, secretarial services, audiovisual equipment, photocopiers, computers, and express checkout. Sloane Sq., SW1 (phone: 71-730-9191; fax: 71-824-8381; telex: 296818). Expensive.

Selfridges – Just behind the department store of the same name, it's modern in both furnishings and tone, but its housekeeping needs upgrading. 298 rooms. Convenient for shopping. Business facilities include 24-hour room service, meeting rooms for up to 200, concierge, foreign currency exchange, secretarial services, audiovisual equipment, photocopiers, translation services, and express checkout. Orchard St., W1 (phone: 71-408-2080; fax: 71-409-2295; telex: 22361). Expensive.

Stafford – In a surprisingly quiet side street close to the city center, this is where many American television and newspaper organizations often lodge visiting correspondents to give them efficient, friendly, British small-hotel management at its best. Owned by Cunard, the hostelry's 62 rooms have been refurbished in smashing style. Enjoy tea in the cozy drawing room, complete with fireplaces and comfortable furniture. Business facilities include 24-hour room service, meeting rooms for up to 30, concierge, foreign currency exchange, secretarial services, photocopiers, computers, and cable television news. 16 St. James's Pl., SW1 (phone: 71-493-0111; fax: 71-493-7121; telex: 28602). Expensive.

Sterling Heathrow – A first-rate addition to Heathrow Airport, with its own covered walkway to Terminal 4. Designed by Michael Manser, it is shaped like a steel parallelogram, with a 5-story glass atrium enclosing a waterfall, as well as 3 restaurants. The 400 rooms have everything from trouser presses to an in-room review of accounts and express checkout — on your TV screen. The health club has a pool, gym, steamroom, and a sauna. Business facilities include 24-hour room service, meeting rooms for up to 200, concierge, foreign currency exchange, secretarial services, audiovisual equipment, photocopiers, cable television news, and express checkout. Terminal 4, Heathrow Airport, Hounslow, Middx. TW6 3AF (phone: 81-759-7755; fax: 81-759-7579). Expensive.

White's – What used to be three 19th-century merchant bankers' private homes have been transformed into one of London's most charming small hostelries, with 54 rooms. It has personality that the larger ones lack — a cobbled forecourt, a glass-and-iron-covered entryway, even a wood-paneled writing room where tea is served in the afternoon. Choose a room at the front, overlooking Hyde Park, and take breakfast on the balcony. Business facilities include 24-hour room service, meeting rooms for up to 30, concierge, foreign currency exchange, secretarial services, audiovisual equipment, photocopiers, and computers. Lancaster Gate, W2 (phone: 71-262-2711; fax: 71-262-2147; telex: 24771). Expensive.

Dorset Square – Set on a lovely garden square (formerly Thomas Lord's own private cricket grounds) in the heart of London, this Georgian house is one of the city's more charming hotels. Guests can choose from 37 rooms. There is 24-hour room service and photocopiers. 39-40 Dorset Sq., NW1 (phone: 71-723-7874; fax: 71-724-3328; telex: 263964). Expensive to moderate.

Fenja – In this classic Victorian townhouse, each of the 14 bedrooms is named for a writer or artist with associations in the locality (Jane Austen, Hilaire Belloc, Henry James, John Singer Sargent). There are private baths/showers with luxury fittings, and crystal decanters filled with liquor. Business facilities include meeting rooms for up to 14, foreign currency exchange, secretarial services, and photocopiers. 69 Cadogan Gardens, SW3 (phone: 71-589-7333; fax: 71-581-4958; telex: 934272). Expensive to moderate.

Hilton International Kensington – A bit out of the way, this modern 605-room hotel offers a great deal of comfort at prices below those of most Hiltons. An executive floor was added in 1990, which offers separate check-in and checkout and complimentary breakfast in a private lounge. Facilities include a traditional restaurant with a lavish Sunday brunch, piano lounge, a Japanese restaurant. Rooms are well designed and well maintained. Business facilities include 24-hour room service, meeting rooms for up to 250, concierge, foreign currency exchange, secretarial services, audiovisual equipment, photocopiers, computers, and express checkout. 179-199 Holland Park Ave., W11 (phone: 71-603-3355; fax: 71-602-9397; telex: 919763). Expensive to moderate.

Number Sixteen – Housed in four adjoining townhouses, this is a delightfully comfortable spot with an accent on personal service. The 36 rooms feature fresh flowers and full baths/showers. Continental breakfast is served in all rooms, some of which have terraces leading to the conservatory and garden. There is a small bar. Because of its quiet atmosphere, it is not suitable for small children. Photocopiers available. 16 Sumner Place, SW7 (phone: 71-589-5232; fax: 71-584-8615; telex: 266638). Expensive to moderate.

Academy – Not far from the University of London and the *British Museum,* this 32-room property scores for its handy location. Colorful modern art and pretty floral curtains and bedspreads make rooms cheery whether they are on the ground floor or upstairs (in what was once the attic). Paperbacks can be borrowed from the library that overlooks a small patio garden at the back. The stylish restaurant and bar are in the basement. 17-21 Gower St., WC1 (phone: 71-631-4115; 800-678-3096, in the US; fax: 71-636-3442; telex: 24364). Moderate.

Copthorne Tara – Situated on a quiet corner of Kensington, this 831-room giant is just minutes from the bustling High Street and within walking distance of the *Albert Hall,* the *Victoria & Albert Museum,* the *Natural History Museum,* and just a short jog from Kensington Gardens. The rooms are on the small side, but all have color TV sets and many have hair dryers. There are 4 restaurants, a night-club, baby-sitting service, and a garage. Business facilities include 24-hour room service, meeting rooms for up to 500, concierge, foreign currency exchange, secretarial services, audiovisual equipment, photocopiers, computers, and express checkout. Wright's La., W8 (phone: 71-937-7211; fax: 71-937-7100; telex: 918834). Moderate.

Cranley – Sister hotel of *One Cranley Place* (see below), this is larger, with 41 rooms and plusher furnishings. The unusual decor is bolder than most townhouse hotels, described by the American owner as "gutsy." With CNN on TV, microwaves in the kitchenettes, plus showers and firm mattresses straight from the US, the aim is to make you feel at home. Secretarial services and photocopiers are available. 10-12 Bina Gardens, SW5 (phone: 71-373-0123; fax: 71-373-9497; in the US, phone: 800-553-2582 or 313-995-4400; fax: 313-995-1050). Moderate.

Diplomat – Small and charming, with an 1882 white façade, it has 27 rooms — all with private baths. It is comfortable, friendly, and affordable. There is a breakfast room, but no restaurant. In Belgravia at 2 Chesham St., SW1 (phone: 71-235-1544; fax: 71-259-6153; telex: 926679). Moderate.

Durrants – This elegant Regency-style hotel has a splendid location behind the *Wallace Collection,* and is only a few minutes' walk from the Oxford Street shopping district. It has been family-run for over 70 years, and all 95 rooms have retained their character while being kept comfortably up to date. Business facilities include 24-hour room service, meeting rooms for up to 45, concierge, foreign currency exchange, audiovisual equipment, and photocopiers. George St., W1 (phone: 71-935-8131; fax: 71-487-3510; telex: 894919). Moderate.

Embassy House – This Edwardian building, on a wide tree-lined street in Kensington, is very near the *Albert Hall,* the *Victoria & Albert Museum,* and the *Natural History Museum,* and an easy walk from *Harrods* and Hyde Park. There are 69 rooms, and although the decor is modern, there are elaborate high ceilings and elegant staircases. There's also a restaurant and bar. Business facilities include 24-hour room service, concierge, foreign currency exchange, secretarial services, and photocopiers. 31 Queens Gate, SW7 (phone: 71-584-7222; fax: 71-589-8193; telex: 914893). Moderate.

Gatwick Hilton International – Part of the airport's expansion program, this 552-room hotel provides much-needed accommodations for the ever-increasing number of visitors using the Gatwick gateway. Connected to the terminal by an enclosed walkway. Business facilities include 24-hour room service, meeting rooms for up to 400, concierge, foreign currency exchange, secretarial services, audiovisual equipment, photocopiers, computers, and express checkout. There also are 2 restaurants, bars, a health club, and lounge service. Gatwick Airport (phone: 293-518080; fax: 293-28980; telex: 877021). Moderate.

Gore – Ten-foot-tall potted palms and a collection of 5,000 prints on the walls set the tone in this 54-room hostelry, just 5 minutes from *Albert Hall* and the shopping on Kensington's High Street. Wall safes are an unusual addition to conveniences such as hair dryers and mini-bars in the rooms. Ask to see, if not stay in, the Judy Garland room, with its carved medieval-style bed. The *Bistro 190* on the ground floor is a popular dining spot. Business facilities include 24-hour room service, meeting rooms for up to 20, concierge, foreign currency exchange, secretarial services, audiovisual equipment, photocopiers, and express checkout. 189 Queen's Gate, SW7 (phone: 71-584-6601; fax: 71-589-8127; telex: 296244). Moderate.

Harewood – Small and modern, this property is well maintained by a pleasant and efficient staff. Some of its 93 rooms have private terraces. Restaurant and wine bar. Business facilities include 24-hour room service, meeting rooms for up to 100, concierge, foreign currency exchange, secretarial services, audiovisual equipment, and photocopiers. Harewood Row, NW1 (phone: 71-262-2707; fax: 71-262-2975; telex: 297225). Moderate.

Hazlitts – Formerly the nurses' quarters for the Royal Women's Hospital during Victorian times, this row of three adjacent terrace houses now serves as a cozy bed and breakfast establishment. The National Trust building has 23 rooms, each individually decorated in Victorian flavor and each with private bath. Hung on the walls are 2,000 prints depicting Victorian London. Photocopiers are available. 6 Frith St., W1 (phone: 71-434-1771; fax: 71-439-1524). Moderate.

L'Hotel – Owned by the same folks that own the wonderful *Capital* just a few steps away, this comfortable 12-room bed and breakfast hotel has a New England colonial–style decor, with pine furniture and a huge patchwork quilt hung over the stairs. All rooms have mini-bars and kettles for making tea or coffee; 4 rooms have fireplaces. Breakfast is served in *Le Metro* bistro next door, and laundry and dry cleaning services are available. Business facilities include meeting rooms for up to 24, foreign currency exchange, secretarial services, audiovisual equipment, photocopiers, translation services, and express checkout. 28 Basil St., SW3 (phone: 71-589-6286; fax: 71-225-0011). Moderate.

One Cranley Place – Set among a row of Regency houses, this charming and personal establishment is like a private home. Unique antique pieces furnish the individually decorated rooms (from double rooms to luxury double suites), and fireplaces in rooms and common areas make for an exceptionally cozy atmosphere. Some rooms overlook the quiet mews at the back and there is a small garden. Breakfast is served in the dining room or guests' rooms; tea and light snacks also are available. Business facilities include 24-hour room service, concierge, secretarial services, and photocopiers. 1 Cranley Place, S. Kensington, SW7 (phone: 71-589-7944; fax: 71-225-3931; in the US, phone: 800-553-2582 or 313-995-4400; fax: 313-995-1050). Moderate.

Pastoria – In the very center of the West End, near all theaters, this pleasant, comfortable little hotel has 58 rooms, all with baths and TV sets; it has a bar and a restaurant. Business facilities include 24-hour room service, meeting rooms for up to 60, concierge, foreign currency exchange, secretarial services, photocopiers, and translation services. St. Martin's St., WC2 (phone: 71-930-8641; fax: 71-925-0551; telex: 25538). Moderate.

Pembridge Court – Recommended by bed and breakfast aficionados, this cozy Victorian townhouse has a variety of room sizes, from large doubles to tiny singles. Each room has a private bath and phone. The hotel is particularly pleasant for cat lovers, since two resident ginger cats normally greet new arrivals. The bistro serves English breakfasts and French fare for dinner. Business facilities include meeting rooms for up to 20, concierge, foreign currency exchange, secretarial services, and photocopiers. 34 Pembridge Gardens (phone: 71-229-9977; fax: 71-727-4982; telex: 298363). Moderate.

Portland Bloomsbury – Around the corner from the entrance to the *British Museum*, this little gem opened in 1990. All 26 bedrooms and the 1 suite have plush furnishings and white tiled bathrooms with hair dryers. The elegant basement restaurant serves Italian food and looks out onto a small garden. Business facilities include 24-hour room service, meeting rooms for up to 20, concierge, foreign currency exchange, secretarial services, photocopiers, translation services, and express checkout. 7 Montague St., WC1 (phone: 71-323-1717; fax: 71-636-6498). Moderate.

Portobello – Antiques are a main feature in this hostelry, converted from two Victorian rowhouses, located near the Portobello antiques market. The 25 rooms come in all shapes and sizes, and most have simple but attractive military-style mahogany furniture; the "Special Rooms" have four-poster beds. Bathrooms tend to be quite small. There is an informal restaurant and bar in the basement. The atmosphere is friendly and relaxing throughout. Business facilities include 24-hour room service, secretarial services, photocopiers, and express checkout. 22 Stanley Gardens, W11 (phone: 71-727-2777; fax: 71-792-9641; telex: 268349 Port G). Moderate.

Ramada Inn – All 501 rooms have private baths and in-house movies. There's also a comfortable Victorian pub. Business facilities include meeting rooms for up to 1,750, concierge, foreign currency exchange, secretarial services, audiovisual equipment, photocopiers, computers, translation services, and express checkout. Lillie Rd., SW6 (phone: 71-385-1255; fax: 71-381-4450; telex: 917728). Moderate.

Royal Horseguards Thistle – Overlooking the Thames and offering good views of the South Bank, its 376 rooms provide a good base for those interested in the changing of the Buckingham Palace guard, Westminster Abbey, and the Houses of Parliament. Riverside rooms have balconies, and there's a pleasant terrace. Business facilities include 24-hour room service, meeting rooms for up to 100, concierge, foreign currency exchange, secretarial services, audiovisual equipment, photocopiers, computers, translation services, and express checkout. 2 Whitehall Ct., SW1 (phone: 71-839-3400; fax: 71-925-2263; telex: 917096). Moderate.

White House – A very big place with 577 rooms, converted from apartments, it's in a quiet spot near Regents Park. Modernized and efficiently run, it has a coffee shop and wine bar. Business facilities include 24-hour room service, meeting rooms for up to 100, concierge, foreign currency exchange, secretarial services, audiovisual equipment, photocopiers, computers, translation services, and express checkout. Albany St., NW1 (phone: 71-387-1200; fax: 71-388-0091; telex: 24111). Moderate.

Wilbraham – A charming, 52-room bed and breakfast establishment, just around the corner from Sloane Square. Business facilities include foreign currency exchange, secretarial services, and photocopiers. 1 Wilbraham Place, SW1 (phone: 71-730-8296). Moderate.

Claverley – Named the "Best Bed and Breakfast Hotel" in 1987 by the British

Tourist Authority, this establishment, in the middle of London, has 36 rooms, 30 of which have private baths; some rooms have four-poster beds. All bedrooms have floral decor, and each has a heated towel rack in the bathroom. Guests are invited to help themselves to newspapers, coffee, tea, and cookies in the reading room. A fine British breakfast is served in the morning. Just a block from *Harrods.* Photocopiers are available. 13 Beaufort Gardens, SW3 (phone: 71-589-8541; fax: 71-730-6815). Moderate to inexpensive.

Aster House – One of the top bed and breakfast properties (according to the BTA) in London, this unpretentious, family-run establishment has 14 rooms with private shower; 1 has a four-poster bed and fireplace. Enjoy breakfast in the conservatory under blooming bougainvillea. In South Kensington on 3 Sumner Place, SW7 (phone: 71-581-5888; fax: 71-584-4925). Inexpensive.

Blandford – Another pleasant bed and breakfast establishment, this one has 33 rooms, decorated in pastel greens and pinks, each with a color TV set and direct-dial telephone. An English breakfast is served in the morning, and complimentary newspapers are offered. There is 24-hour room service available. 80 Chiltern St, W1M (phone: 71-486-3103; fax: 71-487-2786; telex: 262594). Inexpensive.

Delmere – Nearly 200 years old, this lovely hostelry was designed by architect Samuel Pepys Cockerell, a student of Benjamin H. Latrobe, who designed the south wing of the Capitol building in Washington, DC. Its 40 rooms are equipped with private showers or baths, hair dryers, and the makings for tea and coffee. There is also a bar and a restaurant, *La Perla,* serving Italian food. The staff, mostly from Holland, is very friendly. Paddington Station, where trains depart to Bath and south Wales, is a mere 5-minute walk away. Business facilities include 24-hour room service, small meeting rooms, concierge, foreign currency exchange, secretarial services, photocopiers, and computers. 130 Sussex Gardens, Hyde Park, W2 (phone: 71-706-3344; fax: 71-262-1863; telex: 8953857). Inexpensive.

Ebury Court – A small hotel with smallish but cozy rooms and an intimate atmosphere (the owners dine with guests in the restaurant). Its faithful clientele testifies to its comfort, suitability, and "country house in London" touches. Hard to beat — all things considered — in a town where hotel prices tend to be unreasonable. Fewer than half of the 39 rooms have a private bath or shower. There are meeting facilities for up to 40; a concierge, and photocopiers. 26 Ebury St., SW1 (phone: 71-730-8147; fax: 71-823-5966). Inexpensive.

Hotel 167 – Another bed and breakfast place, it is housed in a brick Victorian building and has been lovingly and uniquely furnished with both modern and antique pieces, along with a color scheme of soft grays and creams. Double rooms include private bath, and singles have baths opposite the rooms. Conveniently located near good shopping on Fulham Road, the *Victoria and Albert Museum,* and the Gloucester Road underground station. 167 Old Brompton Rd., SW5 (phone: 71-373-0672; fax: 71-373-3360). Inexpensive.

Hotel la Place – Fine bed and breakfast establishment with 24 rooms, including private baths, TV sets, and king-size or two double beds; some rooms also have mini-bars. British breakfast is served in the morning. Business facilities include 24-hour room service, meeting rooms for up to 20, concierge, secretarial services, and photocopiers. 17 Nottingham Place, W1M (phone: 71-486-2323). Inexpensive.

Observatory House – Once owned by Count Dangerville of France (and many members of royalty have slept here since), this bed and breakfast establishment has been renovated in Victorian decor. All 26 rooms have private showers, color TV sets, telephones, trouser presses, and tea and coffee supplies. Some rooms are for nonsmokers only. Business facilities include foreign currency exchange, secretarial services, photocopiers, and computers. 37 Hornton St., Kensington, W8 (phone: 71-937-1577; fax: 71-938-3585; telex: 9149172). Inexpensive.

St. Giles – Formerly a *YMCA* hostel, the lodging facilities have been transformed, renovated, and expanded into a hotel of over 600 rooms. Guests have free use of the pool at the *Y*, and access to the sauna and other facilities, all located in the lower section of the building containing the hotel. Close to the *British Museum* and Oxford Street shopping district. There are photocopiers and a concierge. Bedford Ave., WC1 (phone: 71-636-8616; fax: 71-631-1031; telex: 22683). Inexpensive.

Winchester – Near Victoria Station, this bed and breakfast place is in an old townhouse with a Victorian-style façade. The 18 bedrooms include modern bathrooms with showers, color TV sets, and radios. Guests are treated to an English breakfast in the morning. 17 Belgrave Rd., Victoria, SW1 (phone: 71-828-2972; fax: 71-828-5191; telex: 26974). Inexpensive.

 EATING OUT: Once upon a time, few London restaurants were ever known for the excellence of their cooking — and some visitors of times past might call that a charitable understatement. But there's been a notable transformation in recent years. While restaurants offering really good English cooking — and not simply "chips with everything" — are still not easy to find (some are listed below), there has been a veritable explosion of good foreign restaurants in town (many of which are also noted below). A new telephone service, *Dining By Numbers*, offers 24-hour information on hundreds of London restaurants, grouped by region. A map is available from *Direct Dialing* (29 Dean St., W1V 6LL; phone: 71-287-3287). For restaurants in central London call 71-839-12345-1; inner London, call 71-839-12345-2, and outer London, call 71-839-12345-3.

A meal for two will cost $150 and up at a restaurant listed as very expensive; $100, expensive; $50 to $75 is moderate; and $40 and under, inexpensive. Prices do not include drinks, wine, or tips. Most London restaurants have developed the continental habit of automatically adding a service charge to the bill, so make certain you're not tipping twice. Reservations are necessary in all restaurants below. All telephone numbers in inner London are in the 71 area code; in outer London, in the 81 area code, unless otherwise indicated.

Bibendum – Located on the second floor of the former Michelin building, it was stylishly renovated by Sir Terence Conran of the *Habitat* chain of stores. Chef Simon Hopkinson's good taste evokes English dreams of France, and he serves the best roast beef in town. Open daily for lunch and dinner. Reservations necessary. Major credit cards accepted. Michelin House, 81 Fulham Rd., SW3 (phone: 71-581-5817). Very expensive.

Connaught Grill – Although there are two dining rooms at the *Connaught* hotel that share the same kitchen, it is the *Grill* that has one Michelin star. Very dignified and very proper, it has a fine reputation for both its fine food and elegant service. Frankly, these guys carry stuffy to sometimes excessive lengths, but it's hard not to appreciate the masterful culinary performance; and though the wine list is conservative, you won't find more expertly prepared liver and bacon in the city. The setting — lots of rich paneling and crystal chandeliers — matches the distinction of the menu. Closed weekends and bank holidays. Reservations essential. Major credit cards accepted. At the *Connaught Hotel*, Carlos Pl., W1 (phone: 71-499-7070). Very expensive.

Le Gavroche – Probably the best French restaurant in London and, according to *Guide Michelin*, one of the best in the entire country, with three stars to its credit (only one other establishment in Britain has received such a high rating). The food is classic French; many of the dishes by those chefs extraordinaires, the Roux brothers, qualify as genuine masterpieces. Try the *pot au feu Albert*, a fine, rich casserole. Closed weekends. Reservations essential (well in advance). Major credit cards accepted. 43 Upper Brook St., W1 (phone: 71-408-0881). Very expensive.

L'Arlequin – A tiny establishment that offers unusual and innovative Gallic cooking by proprietor Christian Delteil, who reputedly makes the best sorbets in London. Also try either the ravioli of lobster or the divine stuffed cabbage. Closed weekends, 3 weeks in August, and 1 week in winter. Reservations essential. Major credit cards accepted. 123 Queenstown Rd., SW8 (phone: 71-622-0555). Expensive.

Le Bistroquet – A chic, French-ish brasserie. Ceiling fans rotate and spiky-haired waiters and waitresses whiz between tables as fish dishes cooked in parchment are cut open, filling the air with the scent of capers and fresh fennel. Open daily. Reservations necessary. Major credit cards accepted. 273-275 Camden High St., NW1 (phone: 71-485-9607). Expensive.

Capital Hotel Restaurant – The elegant, comfortable, small dining room in this hotel near *Harrods* offers well-chosen, admirably prepared French dishes. Some discriminating Londoners consider it the best place to dine in town. Shuns the aren't-you-lucky-to-get-a-table attitude flaunted by some other better London restaurants. Open daily for lunch and dinner. Reservations necessary. Major credit cards accepted. 22-24 Basil St., SW3 (phone: 71-589-5171). Expensive.

Cavaliers' – Sue and David Cavaliers' restaurant, south of the river in upwardly mobile Battersea, serves French fare prepared by an accomplished British chef. Closed Sundays and Mondays. Reservations essential. Major credit cards accepted. 129 Queenstown Rd., SW8 (phone: 71-720-6960). Expensive.

Chez Nico – London's rage for the new has a leader in Nico Ladenis, England's first love-to-be-hated culinary star. This temperamental talent specializes in gutsy flavors and ample portions that have earned this eatery two Michelin stars. (For a less formal atmosphere, try *Very Simply Nico;* see below.) Closed Saturdays and Sundays. Reservations essential. Major credit cards accepted. 35 Great Portland St., W1 (phone: 71-436-8846). Expensive.

Gay Hussar – Among the best Hungarian restaurants this side of Budapest, its substantial menu offers a varied selection: chicken ragout soup, goulash, roast pork, and lots more. The food here is extremely filling as well as delicious. Informal atmosphere, with a regular clientele drawn from London's newspaper and publishing world. Closed Sundays. Reservations essential. Major credit cards accepted. 2 Greek St., W1 (phone: 71-437-0973). Expensive.

Greens – Pinstripes and bowlers rule at this establishment, which serves the best oysters in London, and some would say the best English food. Open daily. Reservations necessary, at least 4 days in advance during the week. Major credit cards accepted. 36 Duke St., SW1 (phone: 71-930-4566). Expensive.

Greig's Grill – Formerly the *Guinea Grill,* this small, unimposing restaurant substitutes displays of its fresh food — steaks, chops, fresh vegetables — for a menu. The food, cooked with care, is as good as ever — the Scottish beef is the best in London — but the service is right out of "Fawlty Towers." Closed Sundays. Reservations necessary. Major credit cards accepted. 26 Bruton Pl., W1 (phone: 71-629-5613). Expensive.

Harvey's – The current wild boy — long hair, bad language, and all — is the chef at this eatery, Marco Pierre White. If he's in the right mood, he'll cook up a dream: oysters with *tagliatelle* and pigeon from Bresse. Open Tuesdays through Saturdays for lunch and dinner. Reservations essential. Major credit cards accepted. 2 Bellevue Rd. (phone: 81-672-0114). Expensive.

Hilaire – Once serving only superb French food, this spot now also offers impressive English dishes, imaginatively prepared and charmingly served. Closed Saturdays for lunch and Sundays. Reservations essential. Major credit cards accepted. 68 Old Brompton Rd., SW7 (phone: 71-584-8993). Expensive.

Ivy – Since 1911, this has been one of *the* restaurants of London's theater elite. A change of ownership has brought it a new lease on life, plus specially commissioned works of contemporary art that contrast with the stained glass and oak paneling. International specialities are served along with British classics like grilled Dover sole, Cumberland sausages, and smoked salmon with scrambled eggs. Open daily from noon to 3 PM and from 5:30 PM to midnight. Reservations essential. Major credit cards accepted. 1 West St., WC2 (phone: 71-836-4751). Expensive.

Ken Lo's Memories of China – The premier Chinese eatery in London, where well-known Chinese author and tennis player Ken Lo and his chefs prepare a wide range of fine dishes from all regions of China, from *dim sum* to Szechuan-style food. Closed Sundays and bank holidays. Reservations advised. Major credit cards accepted. 67 Ebury St., SW7 (phone: 71-730-7734); and a new location at Harbour Yard, Chelsea Harbour, SW 10 (phone: 71-352-4953). Expensive.

Leith's – A fine continental restaurant in an out-of-the-way Victorian building northwest of Kensington Gardens, this spot serves very good entrées, hors d'oeuvres, and desserts as part of a fine prix fixe dinner. An excellent vegetarian menu is also available, and its wine selection is very good. Open daily for dinner. Reservations essential. Major credit cards accepted. 92 Kensington Park Rd., W11 (phone: 71-229-4481). Expensive.

Pavilion – In the *Grosvenor House* hotel, it serves English fare, including Dover sole, salmon, and lamb; the starter buffet features such treats as king-size prawns, cold salmon, and salads. Situated at the front of the hotel, the spacious, bright, and airy dining room offers a fine view of Hyde Park. Open daily for breakfast, lunch, and dinner. Reservations advised for lunch and dinner on Sundays. Major credit cards accepted. *Grosvenor House,* Park La., W1 (phone: 71-499-6363). Expensive.

Rue St. Jacques – Lavishly decorated with huge gold-framed mirrors. The food is marked by rich cream sauces. A delicous vegetarian main course also is available. Pricey, but well worth it. The formality stretches to jacket-and-tie requirement and a doorman who provides parking service. Closed Saturdays for lunch and Sundays. Reservations necessary. Major credit cards accepted. 5 Charlotte St., W1 (phone: 71-637-0222). Expensive.

Savoy Grill – Renowned as a celebrity watching ground, but actually inhabited mostly by a male, business clientele. Although the menu features some classic French dishes, the English grills and roasts are its specialty. The lovely, restored decor resembles a luxurious ship's dining room (first class, natch) of 50 years ago. Perfect for after theater. Closed Saturday lunch and Sundays. Reservations essential. Major credit cards accepted. At the *Savoy Hotel,* The Strand, WC2 (phone: 71-836-4343). Expensive.

Sutherlands – Don't be put off by the plain exterior. This place is for serious food lovers and has been awarded a Michelin star for innovative dishes that range from *courgette* (zucchini) flowers stuffed with chicken mousse and ringed with wild mushroom sauce to a chocolate truffle torte with marmalade mousse. Fine wine list. Closed Saturday lunch and Sundays. Reservations essential. Major credit cards accepted. 45 Lexington St., W1 (phone: 71-434-3401). Expensive.

Tante Claire – Run by chef Pierre Koffman and his wife, Annie, this establishment has been awarded two Michelin stars, as well as many other honors. While fish dishes are the chef's specialty, everything — especially the duck, calves liver, and *pied de cochon farci aux morilles* (pig's foot stuffed with foie gras and mushrooms) — is excellent. The prix fixe lunch is a remarkably good value at around $45. Closed weekends. Reservations essential. Major credit cards accepted. 68 Royal Hospital Rd., SW3 (phone: 71-352-6045). Expensive.

Wilton's – Good food, skillfully prepared, elegantly served in a plush, rather formal Victorian setting. Game, fish, oxtail, steak and kidney pie — what the best of English cooking can be all about. Closed Saturday lunch, Sundays, and 3 weeks in August. Reservations necessary. Major credit cards accepted. 55 Jermyn St., SW1 (phone: 71-629-9955). Expensive.

Langan's Brasserie – Still trendy after all these years, and still a haunt for celebrities. Ask for a downstairs table and take your time studying the lengthy menu. (For a lighter menu, try *Langan's Bistro;* see below.) Closed Saturdays and Sundays for lunch. Reservations necessary. Major credit cards accepted. 1 Stratton St., W1 (phone: 71-493-6437). Expensive to moderate.

Alastair Little – This spot is not so new but still chic, and many find the chef here to be the most natural cook in the city, offering an eclectic menu featuring French, Japanese and Italian dishes. Open for lunch and dinner Mondays through Fridays; Saturdays for dinner only; closed Sundays. Reservations advised. No credit cards accepted. 49 Frith St., W1 (phone: 71-734-5183). Moderate.

Bloom's – Specializing in Jewish food, it has a bright and bustling atmosphere, a bit like the dining room of a large hotel, with waiters who almost — but not quite — throw the food at you. The popular take-out counter serves the best hot salt beef (like corned beef) sandwiches in town. House wine is Israeli. Closed Friday evenings and Saturdays. Reservations advised. Major credit cards accepted. 130 Golders Green Rd., NW11 (phone: 81-455-1338) and 90 Whitechapel High St., E1 (phone: 71-247-6001). Moderate.

Bombay Brasserie – At lunchtime there is an Indian buffet; at dinner, classic cooking from the Bombay region. Parsi dishes, rarely found outside of India itself, are also included. And the setting is lovely, with lots of banana plants, wicker chairs, and ceiling fans. Popular with both the American and British show-biz colonies. Open daily. Reservations essential. Major credit cards accepted. Courtfield Close, Courtfield Rd., SW7 (phone: 71-370-4040). Moderate.

Camden Brasserie – The daily specials are posted on a board outside this restaurant, located in an increasingly fashionable part of town. Among the selections are meat and fish grilled over an open fire. Open daily for lunch and dinner. Reservations necessary. Major credit cards accepted. 216 Camden High St., NW1 (phone: 71-482-2114). Moderate.

Chuen Cheng Ku – At this huge restaurant in the heart of Chinatown, the overwhelming majority of the clientele is Chinese. The specialty here is dim sum, served every day until 6 PM. Also try the pork with chili and salt, duck webs, steamed lobster with ginger, and shark fin soup. Open daily. Reservations necessary. Major credit cards accepted. 17 Wardour St., W1 (phone: 71-437-1398). Moderate.

Clarke's – It's London's answer to the Bay Area's *Chez Panisse,* set dinner menus of California-style cooking in a lovely, light, basement eatery. Open Mondays through Fridays for lunch and dinner; closed weekends. Reservations necessary. Major credit cards accepted. 124 Kensington Church St., W8 (phone: 71-221-9225). Moderate.

Kensington Place – One of the hot tickets in town, set behind a huge glass front, so you can see and be seen. A mix of "Californian new English" cookery from partridge and cabbage to foie gras, oysters, and delicious desserts. Frenzied atmosphere, sensible wine list. Open daily. Reservations necessary. Major credit cards accepted. 201 Kensington Church St., W8 (phone: 71-727-3184). Moderate.

Langan's Bistro – Serves slightly simpler and less expensive dishes prepared in the same style as *Langan's Brasserie.* Closed Sundays and Saturdays for lunch. Reservations advised. Major credit cards accepted. 26 Devonshire St., W1 (phone: 71-935-4531). Moderate.

Porters – A very English eatery in *Covent Garden,* it's famous for home-cooked pies — steak, mushroom, and vegetable are the specialties (and an acquired taste). The kitchen, bar, and basement are more spacious since the restaurant's total redecoration. Open daily. Reservations advised, especially for lunch. Major credit cards accepted. 17 Henrietta St., WC2 (phone: 71-836-6466). Moderate.

River Café – The eloquent northern Italian dishes and the Thames-side location here are best appreciated at lunch. Open daily except Mondays for lunch, and Saturdays and Sundays for dinner. Reservations essential. Major credit cards accepted. Thames Wharf, Rainville Rd., W6 (phone: 71-381-8824) Moderate.

Rules – Approaching its bicentennial, this eatery has been at the same site since 1798. The Lillie Langtry Room upstairs, where the actress dined with Edward VII, is reserved for private parties. The downstairs retains its Victorian atmosphere and decor. Walls are covered with signed photographs and cartoons of actors and authors. Once a *must* for visitors to London, the quality of its food has seesawed over recent years. The menu remains decidedly British, from feathered game amd game fish in season to treacle sponge pudding. Open daily from noon to midnight. Reservations essential. American Express, MasterCard, and Visa accepted. 35 Maiden La., WC2 (phone: 71-836-5314). Moderate.

Shezan – Just below street level, this quiet brick and tile spot prepares some very fine Pakistani food. Specialties include marinated-in-yogurt *murg tikka Lahori* (chicken cooked in tandoori, or clay, ovens) and *kabab kabli* (minced spiced beef). An enthusiastic staff will explain the intricacies of tandoori cooking, help with your order, and lavish excellent service upon you. Closed Sundays. Reservations necessary. Major credit cards accepted. 16 Cheval Pl., SW7 (phone: 71-589-7918). Moderate.

Stephen Bull – For value, it was the most successful opening back in 1989. This clean-cut, modern eatery offers creatively prepared food, as well as service pared to essentials for true enjoyment and sensible tabs. Open for lunch and dinner Mondays through Fridays; for dinner only on Saturdays; closed Sundays. Reservations necessary. Major credit cards accepted. 5-7 Blandford St., W1 (phone: 71-486-9696). Moderate.

Sweetings – A special London experience, this traditional fish restaurant is one of the great lunchtime attractions in London's financial district. You may have to sit at a counter with your lobster, brill, or haddock, but it will be fresh and perfectly prepared. Open weekday lunchtime only; no reservations, so expect a wait. Major credit cards accepted. 39 Queen Victoria St., EC4 (phone: 71-248-3062). Moderate.

Tate Gallery Restaurant – Who would expect one of London's better dining establishments to be in a fine art museum? But here it is — a genuine culinary outpost (leaning toward French cuisine), with a very good wine list. Enjoy the famous Rex Whistler murals as you sip. Lunch only. Closed Sundays. Reservations essential. No credit cards accepted. *Tate Gallery.* Millbank, SW1 (phone: 71-834-6754). Moderate.

Thai Pavilion – The staff may have limited familiarity with English at this place in Soho, but the decor is pretty, and the beef with sesame, fish cakes in chili sauce, or chicken with peanut sauce are worth the effort to be understood. Try one of the Thai beers to cool off the roof of your mouth. Open daily. Reservations advised. Major credit cards accepted. 42 Rupert St., W1 (phone: 71-287-6333). Moderate.

Trattoo – An airy, attractive eatery, just off Kensington High Street, it serves very good northern Italian food — from a variety of pasta to *saltimbocca* or *fegato all veneziana.* Closed Sundays for lunch. Reservations advised. Major credit cards accepted. 2 Abingdon Rd., W8 (phone: 71-937-4448). Moderate.

La Trattoria dei Pescatori – A busy atmosphere pervades this place, whose decor includes a boat, terra cotta tiles, copper pans, and chunky ceiling beams. The menu is enormous, with trout, halibut, salmon, shrimp, turbot, and lobster appearing in several guises. A typical specialty is *misto dei crostacei alla crema* — Mediterranean prawns, scallops, shrimp, and mussels sautéed with onions and herbs, simmered in fish stock and asti, with a touch of cream. Closed Sundays. Reservations necessary. Major credit cards accepted. 57 Charlotte St., W1 (phone: 71-580-3289). Moderate.

Treasure of China – In a landmark Georgian building in historic Greenwich, it's a leader in original Peking and Szechuan cooking. Owners Tony Low and Roger Norman offer a selective daily menu, as well as superb banquets celebrating Chinese festivals. Open daily. Reservations essential. Major credit cards accepted. 10 Nelson Rd., SE10 (phone: 81-858-9884). Moderate.

Very Simply Nico – It's Nico Ladenis's not-so-snooty steak-and-chips joint. Open for lunch and dinner; closed Sundays. Reservations necessary. Major credit cards accepted. 48A Rochester Row, SW1 (phone: 71-630-8061). Moderate.

Wheeler's – One of the chain of London seafood restaurants with the same name, this is the original and the best of the lot. It's an old-fashioned, narrow establishment, on 3 floors, which specializes in a variety of ways of preparing real Dover sole. The oyster bar on the ground floor is our favorite perch for savoring bivalves and smoked salmon. Closed Sundays. Reservations advised. Major credit cards accepted. Duke of York St. at Apple Tree Yard, SW1 (phone: 71-930-2460). Moderate.

Chiang Mai – Thai restaurants used to be a rarity in London. This one has always been easy to spot since it's the only eatery in Soho (and probably the whole of Britain) with a carved wooden elephant poised on the sidewalk. The menu offers such dishes as coconut chicken and *galanga* soup. Those unfamiliar with northern Thai cooking should inquire about the spiciness of individual dishes before ordering. Open daily. Reservations advised. Major credit cards accepted. 48 Frith St., W1 (phone: 71-437-7444). Moderate to inexpensive.

HQ – Live jazz is the main attraction at this restaurant/wine bar in trendy Camden Lock. Its location above the arts and crafts shops affords guests good views of the canal and weekend street performers. Open daily for dinner. Reservations necessary. Major credit cards accepted. Commercial Pl., SW1 (phone: 71-485-6044). Moderate to inexpensive.

Kalamaras Taverna – A small friendly eatery with authentic Greek food, prepared under the watchful eye of the Greek owner. The menu here is more varied than in most of the other Greek/Cypriot restaurants in London. Open Mondays through Saturdays for dinner. Reservations advised. Major credit cards accepted. 76 and 66 Inverness Mews, W2, off Queensway. No. 66 has no liquor license (phone: 71-727-5082 or 71-727-9122). Moderate and inexpensive, respectively.

Kettner's – As you check your coat, you have to make your choice — a bottle of champagne at the bar (25 labels in stock), a humble but tasty salad in the brasserie-style café, or a pizza in the beautifully furnished dining room reminiscent of an Edwardian hotel. Open daily, noon to midnight. Reservations unnecessary. Major credit cards accepted. 29 Romilly St., Soho, W1 (phone: 71-437-6437). Moderate to inexpensive.

Khyber – A wide selection of Indian Punjabi specialties, as well as tasty vegetarian dishes, are served here. Try the *pannir,* mild cheese cooked with peas, meat, and spices, and the *aloo gobi,* a cauliflower dish. Open daily. Reservations advised. Major credit cards accepted. 56 Westbourne Grove, W2 (phone: 71-727-4385). Moderate to inexpensive.

Last Days of the Raj – This popular eatery on the eastern fringe of *Covent Garden* serves dishes from India's Punjabi region. Punjabi cuisine is rather mild, and one of its specialties is meat prepared tandoori style — marinated in yogurt and spices, then baked in a special tray oven. Some kind of tandoori cooking is usually on the menu in addition to other specials, which change every few months. The exotic mango-based cocktails are powerful, and the service is extremely friendly. Be sure to dine at the Drury Lane *Raj,* as other restaurants are now trading on the original restaurant's good name. Open daily. Reservations essential. Major credit cards accepted. 22 Drury La., WC2 (phone: 71-836-1628). Moderate to inexpensive.

Smolensky's Balloon – This American-owned cocktail bar/restaurant with a 1930s piano-bar atmosphere is guaranteed to make you feel homesick. Steaks and fries figure importantly on the menu, offset by some interesting vegetarian dishes. Real family fun. Open daily, noon to 11:45 PM; Sundays noon to 10:30 PM. Reservations unnecessary. Major credit cards accepted. 1 Dover St., W1 (phone: 71-491-1199). There is a second branch at 105 Strand, WC2 (phone: 71-497-2101). Both moderate to inexpensive.

Street Fish Shop – For decent salmon, as well as traditional fish and chips. Open for lunch and dinner; closed Monday evenings and Sundays. Reservations unnecessary. Major credit cards accepted. 324 Upper St. (phone: 71-359-1401). Moderate to inexpensive.

Bangkok – Known for its *saté* — small tender slices of beef marinated in a curry and soy sauce and served with a palate-destroying hot peanut sauce. From your butcher block table you can watch your meal being prepared in the windowed kitchen. Closed Sundays. Reservations unnecessary. Major credit cards accepted. 9 Bute St., SW7 (phone: 71-584-8529). Inexpensive.

Calabash – West African fare gives this place a unique position on London's restaurant map, especially since it's in the bubbling *Covent Garden* district. The service is accommodating and helpful, and the food is both good and different. Closed Sundays. Reservations advised. Major credit cards accepted. Downstairs at London's *Africa Centre*, 38 King St., WC2 (phone: 71-836-1976). Inexpensive.

Chicago Pizza Pie Factory – A decade ago, an American advertising executive turned his back on the US ad world to bring London deep-dish pizza Windy City–style, along with Budweiser beer and chocolate cheesecake. Londoners beat a path to his door and haven't yet stopped clamoring to get in. Open daily. Reservations unnecessary. Major credit cards accepted. 17 Hanover Sq., W1 (phone: 71-629-2669). Inexpensive.

Cosmoba – A small and friendly family-run Italian restaurant that is basic in every respect — except for its food. Tucked down a tiny alleyway and always packed with regulars. Closed Sundays. Reservations advised. Major credit cards accepted. 9 Cosmo Pl., WC1 (phone: 71-837-0904). Inexpensive.

Cranks – There are several branches of this self-service vegetarian restaurant. All are popular and serve good homemade desserts, as well as salads, quiches, and other hot food. Drop in for coffee or afternoon tea. Some of the more central branches include: 8 Marshall St., W1 (phone: 71-437-9431), open for dinner Mondays through Saturdays; 11 The Market, *Covent Garden*, WC1 (phone: 71-379-6508), open daily; Tottenham St., W1 (phone: 71-631-3912), closed Sundays; Unit 11, Adelaide St., WC2 (phone: 71-836-0660), closed Sundays; 23 Bartlett St., W1 (phone: 71-495-1340), closed Sundays; and Gt. Newport St., Leicester Sq. (phone: 71-83605226), open daily. Reservations advised. Major credit cards accepted. Inexpensive.

Dove – Boasting a nice riverside spot, it serves good as well as filling pub grub and good Fullers beer. Open daily. Reservations unnecessary. Major credit cards accepted. 19 Upper Mall, Hammersmith, W6 (phone: 81-748-5405). Inexpensive.

Dumpling Inn – This Peking-style restaurant serves excellent Oriental dumplings, and most of the other dishes are equally good. Try the fried seaweed; it's got lots of vitamins and tastes terrific. The service, though efficient, is a bit brisk. Open daily. Reservations unnecessary. Major credit cards accepted. 15A Gerrard St., W1 (phone: 71-437-2567). Inexpensive.

Geales' – Truly fresh English fare, including fish and chips, is served in a setting that looks like a 1930s tearoom. Go early, because this spot is no secret. Closed

Sundays and Mondays and the last 3 weeks in August. Reservations unnecessary. Major credit cards accepted. 2 Farmer St., W8 (phone: 71-727-7969). Inexpensive.

Hard Rock Café – The original. An American-style eating emporium with a loud jukebox and good burgers. It's always crowded, and the lines stretch well out into the street. As much a T-shirt vendor (at the shop around the corner) these days as a restaurant. Open daily. No reservations. Major credit cards accepted. 150 Old Park La., W1 (phone: 71-629-0382). Inexpensive.

My Old Dutch – This authentic Dutch pancake house serves endless varieties of sweet and savory pancakes on genuine blue Delft plates. Loud music. Open daily. Reservations necessary only for parties of eight or more. Major credit cards accepted. 132 High Holborn, WC1 (phone: 71-242-5200). Inexpensive.

Standard – Possibly the best Indian restaurant value in London, so it tends to get crowded quickly. Open daily. Reservations advised. Major credit cards accepted. 23 Westbourne Grove, W2 (phone: 71-727-4818). Inexpensive.

Tuttons – Serving food all day, it's a very popular and lively brasserie in a former *Covent Garden* warehouse, and a handy snack spot for theatergoers. Open from 10 AM to 11:30 PM Sundays through Thursdays; 10 AM to midnight Fridays and Saturdays. Reservations advised. Major credit cards accepted. 11 Russell St., WC2 (phone: 71-836-4141). Inexpensive.

Widow Applebaum – Not an authentic New York delicatessen, but this place serves pretty good herring, cold cuts, chopped liver, potato salad, dill pickles, and apple pie. Closed Sundays. Reservations unnecessary. Major credit cards accepted. 46 S. Molton St., W1 (phone: 71-629-4649). Inexpensive.

SHARING A PINT: There are several thousand pubs in London, the vast majority of which are owned by the six biggest brewers. Most of these pubs have two bars: the "public," which is for the working man who wants to get on with the business of drinking, and the "saloon" or "lounge," which makes an attempt at providing comfort and may serve food and wine as well as beer. Liquor at the latter may cost more. Among the means by which pubs are appraised is the brand and variety of draft brews that spew forth from its taps. The extraordinary variety can easily perplex the uninitiated. There's ale: bitter, mild, stout; and lager, whose varying tastes provide a perfect excuse to linger longer in pubs you find particularly convivial. Eating in a crowded pub is not always easy because the limited number of tables are barely large enough to hold all the empty beer glasses, let alone food. Pub food is hearty but not especially imaginative: a ploughman's lunch, which is a hunk of bread and cheese plus a pickle; cottage pie, which is ground meat with mashed potatoes on top, baked in the oven; sausages; and sandwiches. The number (and quality) of pubs serving more upscale food is increasing, since British law has recently expanded opening hours for pubs offering food; the law used to require pubs to close for several hours during late afternoon to early evening, whereas now most open at 10:30 or 11 AM and remain open until 11 PM.

Here are the names of pubs where we like to raise a pint or two: *Dirty Dick's* (202 Bishopsgate, EC2) is offbeat but popular, with fake bats and spiders hanging from the ceilings, sawdust on the floor, and good bar snacks; and *Sherlock Holmes* (10 Northumberland St., WC2; phone: 71-930-2644) is the pub that Holmes's creator, Arthur Conan Doyle, used to frequent when it was still the *Northumberland Arms,* and which he mentioned in *Hound of the Baskervilles.* A glass-enclosed replica of Holmes's Baker Street study is there, along with Holmes memorabilia. The *Audley* (41 Mount St., W1) is our favorite luncheon stop in the high-rent district, with fine sandwiches and salad plates in an atypically hygienic environment. Other fine spots include *The Antelope* (22 Eaton Terrace, SW1), where the Bellamys (or even Hudson, their butler) might have sipped a lager on the way home to nearby 165 Eaton Place; *The Grenadier* (18 Wilton

Row, SW1) perhaps the poshest pub site in town, just off Belgravia Square; *Admiral Codrington* (17 Mossop St., SW3) is large and Victorian, with brass beer pumps, engraved mirrors, and good food; *Dickens Inn* by the Tower (St. Katherine's Way, E1) is a converted warehouse overlooking a colorful yacht marina and serving shellfish snacks; *George Inn* (77 Borough High St., SE1) dates from 1676 and retains the original gallery for viewing Shakespearean plays in the summer; *The Flask* (77 Highgate West Hill, N6) serves drinks at three paneled bars and on its outside patio; *The Lamb* (94 Lambs Conduit St., WC1) is also paneled and hung with photos of past music hall performers; *Museum Tavern* (49 Great Russell St., WC1) is across the road from the *British Museum* and decorated with hanging flower baskets; *Princess Louise* (208 High Holborn, WC1) has live music, cabaret, and a wine bar upstairs with good food; *Bull and Bush* (North End Way, NW3) owes its fame to the Edwardian music-hall song "Down at the Old Bull and Bush." Former customers include Thomas Gainsborough and Charles Dickens. It has an outdoor bar and barbecue for balmy summer evenings. *Prospect of Whitby* (57 Wapping Wall, E1), the oldest riverside pub in London, was once the haunt of thieves and smugglers (now it draws jazz lovers); *Ye Olde Cheshire Cheese* (5 Little Essex St., EC4, just off Fleet St.) is a 17th-century pub, with paneled walls and sawdust floors that's popular with the Fleet Street set. On the south bank of the Thames, in the district of the Docklands called Rotherhithe, are two special pubs, the *Mayflower* and the *Angel;* the former has been around since the days in the 17th century when the *Mayflower* left for the New World and returned to Rotherhithe; today, the partially rebuilt Tudor inn is still a good spot to enjoy beer and ale. The *Angel* is set on stone pillars overlooking the Thames, and the cozy, dark interior hasn't changed much since the days when it was patronized by Samuel Pepys and Captain Cook.

 WINE BARS: Growing in popularity on the London scene, they serve wine by the glass or bottle, accompanied by such light fare as quiche and salad, and occasionally full meals. Prices tend to be lower in wine bars than in restaurants, and tables can often be reserved in advance. Here's a selection of the finest: *Café Suze* (1 Glentworth St., NW1) combines rustic decor with good homemade food; *Cork and Bottle* (44-46 Cranbourn St., WC2) is patronized by the London wine trade and has a classical guitarist providing background music; *Draycott's* (114 Draycott Ave., SW3) has tables grouped outside on the pavement and is frequented by the smart London set; *Ebury Wine Bar* (139 Ebury St., SW1), in the heart of Belgravia, serves good food (try the English pudding) and offers live music nightly; *Le Bistroquet* (273-275 Camden High St., NW1) is one of London's trendiest spots, popular with the city's yuppies; *Shampers* (4 Kingly St., W1) is near the famous *Liberty* department store, and sometimes has a classical guitarist in the evenings; *Skinkers* (42 Tooley St.) is an atmospheric spot with sawdust on the floor, serving hearty food; *Crown Passage Vaults* (20 King St.) is renowned for its potted shrimp — to be eaten with a glass of montagny or pouilly vinzelles; *Bar des Amis* (11-14 Hanover Pl., WC2) is a crowded watering hole in fashionable *Covent Garden; Crawford's* (10-11 Crawford St., W1) is a lively basement bar serving full cold buffet lunches and suppers; *Brahms and Liszt* (19 Russell St., WC2) always has good wines, food, and music; *Julie's* (137 Portland Rd., W11) has become a landmark for aging flower children; *El Vino* (47 Fleet St., EC4), once a journalists' haunt famous for refusing to serve women at the bar, is now full of legal eagles and PR folk in a nice Old World atmosphere.

MADRID

When King Philip II proclaimed Madrid the capital of Spain and all her colonies in 1561, he said that he chose it because of the "healthy air and brilliant skies" and because, "Like the body's heart, it is located in the center of the Peninsula." Philip was right. Madrid's air is delightfully dry and invigorating. Its "Velázquez skies" that so inspired the court painter are dramatically bright, with more than 3,000 hours of sunshine annually. As a result of Philip's proclamation, what had been an insignificant Castilian town of 17,000 suddenly burst into being as the cosmopolitan nucleus of the Spanish Empire — upon which, in those days, the sun never set. One of Europe's youngest capitals, Madrid grew fast, as if making up for lost time. A comment by a Spanish poet in 1644 continued to be true until just a few decades ago: "Each day, new houses are being built, and those that used to be on the outskirts are now in the middle of the town."

Today, the city has blossomed into a glamorous metropolis of 4.3 million, and it thrives on its own vitality. More than ever, it is ebullient, outgoing, fun-loving, proud, stylish, and creative, a city intensely lived in and adored by its varied mosaic of inhabitants. Throughout its history, a great proportion of its residents have been born elsewhere in Spain, a country of various and diverse cultures. Yet soon after their arrival, they feel "adopted" and become as genuinely *madrileño* as native sons and daughters.

According to a saying as meaningful to *madrileños* as the Cibeles Fountain, "the next best place after Madrid is heaven, but with a peephole for looking down at it." The city has a way of enticing foreigners as well. Visitors invariably feel at home in Madrid — much more so, of course, if they speak Spanish. Another popular saying, often seen on bumper stickers, boasts that Madrid is *"el pórtico al cielo"* ("the gateway to heaven"). The city is, in fact, the highest capital in Europe — 2,135 feet above the sea level of the Mediterranean at Alicante, affirmed by a plaque at Puerta del Sol.

Despite its high-tech, high-fashion, streamlined skyscrapers up the Castellana, and its unparalleled flurry of activities as 1992's European Cultural Capital — designated as such by the European Economic Community (EEC) — Madrid still endearingly refers to itself as a "town," or *villa*. Its official name during the 16th century was the "Very Noble, Loyal, Heroic, Imperial, and Distinguished Village and Court of Madrid, Capital of Spain," or, simply, "Villa." The City Hall, for example, is Casa de la Villa, the modern concert-theater-exhibition center is *Centro Cultural de la Villa,* and the summer-long program of concerts, fairs, and entertainment is called *"Veranos en la Villa."*

Madrileños love to be out on the streets, where walking or strolling — the *paseo* — is an activity in itself, rather than just a means of getting somewhere. And they enjoy crowding together. In spring, summer, and fall, thousands of outdoor *terrazas* (cafés), set up on sidewalks and in squares and parks, teem day and night with convivial people chatting, eating, drinking, gossiping (locals love to gossip), and simply looking at each other. There's always eye contact and usually a friendly or witty greeting — *madrileños* also admire a quick wit — even to those who are just buying a newspaper.

Madrid's artistic-creative surge of the late 1970s and early 1980s — *la movida* — sparked a rebirth of indoor and outdoor café society. Stylish *madrileños* congregate at *terrazas* along Paseo de Recoletos and the Castellana from dusk until practically dawn. Crowded late-night, Spanish-style pubs, specializing in high-decibel rock or soothing classical music, line Calle de las Huertas, one of the liveliest streets in the old part of town. Amazingly, this street is also occupied by the early-17th-century Convent of the Trinitarias, where cloistered nuns live and embroider, and where Miguel de Cervantes is buried. In the typical old section of Lavapiés, entire families gather to eat, drink, and chat with their neighbors at simple restaurants with sidewalk tables. The *tertulia,* an age-old Madrid custom, brings experts and devotees together for informal discussions about their favorite subjects. Visitors will surely find *tertulias* about theater or literature at the *Café Gijón,* art at the *Círculo de Bellas Artes* lounge, and bullfighting and breeding at the bar of the *Wellington* hotel, to name a random few.

When it's time for the midday *aperitivo* around 1 PM (when stores, offices, and many museums close), thousands of *tapas* bars, *tabernas,* and swank cafés become jammed for a couple of hours until lunchtime, when they suddenly empty and the restaurants fill up. Around 4 or 5 PM (when the stores, offices, and museums reopen), the restaurants become vacant — it's customary to go somewhere else for coffee or cognac — and the bars and cafés are reactivated. They reach another peak when it's *aperitivo* time again, around 8 PM (as stores, offices, and museums close for the day), before dinner around 10 PM, when the restaurants fill up once more. Then it's time for a movie, concert, theater performance, jazz at a café, or simply a stroll.

Madrid boasts the longest nights of any Spanish city — even though in midsummer the sun doesn't set until almost 11 PM. Discotheques don't get started until 1 or 2 AM, and at many, the action continues until 7 AM. Then it's time for a typical Madrid breakfast of thick hot chocolate with *churros* (sticks or loops of crisp fried dough), elbow to elbow with others just beginning their day. Nevertheless, *madrileños* don't mistake their city for a vacation spot and are fully aware that it is indeed a place for hard work.

There are many Madrids. In fact, the city is sometimes referred to in the plural — *los madriles* — because of its various facets. In addition to nocturnal Madrid, daytime Madrid, and seasonal Madrid, there are different architectural and historical Madrids.

Not much remains of medieval Moorish Madrid, and even less is known — although legends abound. In 852, the Emir of Córdoba, Muhammad I, chose the strategic ravine top above the Manzanares River (where the Royal Palace now stands) as the site for a fortified Alcázar (castle) to guard the route between Toledo and Alcalá de Henares against the reconquering Christians. The Moors described their settlement alongside the Alcázar as "a village bordered by the Manzanares River on one side and the brilliant sky on the

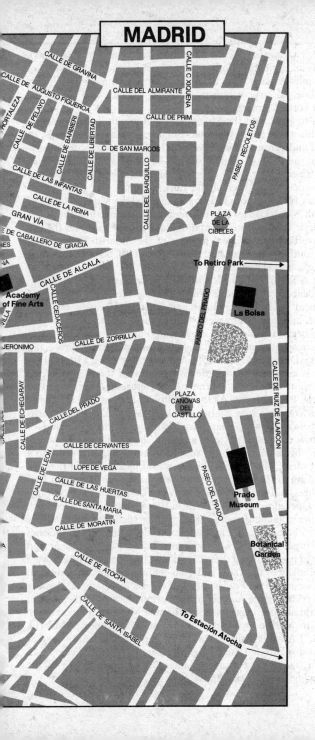

MADRID

CALLE DE GRAVINA

CALLE DE AUGUSTO FIGUEROA

CALLE DEL ALMIRANTE

CALLE C XIQUENA

CALLE DE PRIM

CALLE DE GRACIA

HORTALEZA

CALLE DE PELAYO

CALLE DE BARBIERI

CALLE DE LIBERTAD

C DE SAN MARCOS

CALLE DE LAS INFANTAS

CALLE DEL BARQUILLO

PASEO RECOLETOS

CALLE DE LA REINA

GRAN VÍA

DE CABALLERO DE GRACIÁ

ES

NA

CALLE DE ALCALA

CALLE CEDACEROS

PLAZA DE LA CIBELES

To Retiro Park →

Academy of Fine Arts

VILLA

La Bolsa

PASEO DEL PRADO

CALLE DE ZORRILLA

JERONIMO

CALLE DEL PRADO

CALLE DE ECHEGARAY

PLAZA CANOVAS DEL CASTILLO

CALLE DE RUIZ DE ALARCON

CALLE DE CERVANTES

CALLE DE LEON

LOPE DE VEGA

CALLE DE LAS HUERTAS

CALLE DE SANTA MARIA

PASEO DEL PRADO

Prado Museum

CALLE DE MORATIN

Botanical Garden

CALLE DE ATOCHA

CALLE DE SANTA ISABEL

To Estación Atocha →

other." They called it Magerit (later mispronounced as Madrid by Castilians), meaning delicious and "plentiful flowing water," not for the meager water of the Manzanares, but for water from the nearby Sierra de Guadarrama. (This water from the Lozoya River continues to supply the city, and is also the brand name of a bottled mineral water).

Magerit began to grow, and the Moors built and rebuilt walls to enclose it, keeping up with its random expansion. Fragments of these old walls, as well as sections of underground passageways to the Alcázar, have been uncovered as recently as the 1970s — a major site can be seen at Cuesta de la Vega, near the Royal Palace. Other well-preserved remnants of medieval Moorish Magerit are the house and tower of the Lujanes family and the adjacent Periodicals Library building, both at Plaza de la Villa; the Mudéjar tower of the Church of San Nicolás de los Servitas, slightly to the north of the plaza; the equally Mudéjar tower of the Church of San Pedro el Viejo, on the site of what may have been the original mosque of the Moorish Quarter (La Morería), to the south of the plaza; and the Morería itself, a zone of winding alleys around Plaza del Alamillo.

In 1083, King Alfonso VI and his Christian troops reconquered Madrid and took up residence in the Alcázar. The *madrileño* melting pot expanded with the subsequent influx of Christians into what then became medieval Christian Madrid, and more walls were built to surround it.

The city really began to take shape when King Philip II of the Hapsburg House of Austria raised its rank to capital of Spain and moved the throne and court from Toledo. During his reign (1556–98) and those of his 17th-century successors, what is known as Madrid de los Austrias, or the Madrid of the Hapsburgs, was built. This is the charming and picturesque section of Old Madrid around the Plaza Mayor. As the nobility built mansions, the clergy founded churches, convents, monasteries, and hospitals, and merchants, artisans, and innkeepers set up shop. Hapsburg Madrid grew into a labyrinth of meandering narrow cobblestone streets and tiny squares lined with severe buildings of stone, brick, and masonry, topped by roofs that blended into a burnt-red "sea of tiles." The Spanish Empire was at its zenith, and the *siglo de oro* (Golden Age) of Renaissance literature flourished in Hapsburg Madrid. Streets, squares, and statues bear the names of Cervantes, Lope de Vega, Tirso de Molina, Quevedo, and Calderón de la Barca, all of whom lived here.

The city continued fanning southward, creating such delightful *barrios* (neighborhoods) as Lavapiés and Embajadores, lively with *tabernas, mesones* (inns), vendors, organ-grinders, and artisans. The *castizo* (genuine) and uniquely *madrileño* personality of these barrios and their colorful people were the inspiration of many of the 18th- and 19th-century *zarzuelas* (traditional Spanish musical dramas), *La Verbena de la Paloma,* for example, that are presented outdoors during the summer at La Corrala, located in the heart of this *castizo* Madrid at Plaza Agustín Lara. (Lara, a Mexican composer who had never been to Madrid, wrote the city's unofficial anthem, "Madrid, Madrid, Madrid.") Anyone visiting Madrid during the first half of August should be sure to stroll around these *barrios castizos* to see *madrileños* of all ages bedecked in traditional costumes, dancing the graceful *chotis* in the streets, and enjoying the *verbenas* (fairs).

When the Hapsburg dynasty died out at the end of the 17th century, King Philip V, grandson of France's King Louis XIV, was the chief claimant to the throne of Spain. After a war of succession, he established the Bourbon dynasty as the legitimate heir to the kingdom in 1770. The Bourbon monarchs began the new century by setting out to create a splendid new European capital worthy of their neo-classical French models. When the Alcázar burned down, Philip V commissioned top architects (Spaniard Ventura Rodríguez and Italian Francesco Sabatini) to replace it with a grandiose palace comparable to Versailles. Systematic expansion to the east of old Hapsburg Madrid, with wide avenues and large squares laid out in geometric configuration, transformed Madrid into a model city of the Enlightenment — the Madrid de los Borbones, or Madrid of the Bourbons. The city's urban renewal, embellishment, and social progress culminated with the reign of *madrileño* King Carlos III, "the Construction King of the Enlightenment," known affectionately as the "King-Mayor." Carlos commissioned Juan de Villanueva to design the neo-classical *Natural Science Museum,* which later became the *Prado Museum,* and the adjacent Botanical Gardens. The exquisite tree-lined Paseo del Prado, with its Neptune, Apollo, and Cibeles fountains by Ventura Rodríguez, and the monumental Puerta de Alcalá (then marking the eastern end of the city) are among the legacies of Carlos III.

The steady progress of the city and the country foundered, however, in 1808, when Napoleon was encouraged to invade Spain because of the weakness of Carlos IV, the next Bourbon king. The French succeeded in the invasion after ruthlessly executing Spanish resisters on the night of May 2, a tragedy immortalized by Goya in his famous paintings now in the *Prado.* At the Plaza de la Lealtad on Paseo del Prado, a memorial obelisk with an eternal flame commemorates *el dos de mayo.*

Napoleon forced the crowning of his brother, Joseph Bonaparte, as King of Spain. "Pepe Botella" (Bottle Joe), as he was called (either for his drinking habits or for having put a tax on liquor), in his quest for open space for ongoing urban renewal, tore down picturesque chunks of Hapsburg Madrid, including much of the Retiro Park Palace and a church in the small Plaza de Ramales that contained the grave of Velázquez. But the Spanish War of Independence led to the expulsion of the French and the return to the throne of a Bourbon king, Fernando VII, in 1813.

In the last third of the 19th century, Romantic Madrid spread farther northward. Aristocratic palatial mansions graced the elegant Salamanca district, where today some of Madrid's finest shops and boutiques line Calles Serrano and Velázquez. Paseo del Prado extended north to become Paseo de Recoletos and, still farther north, Paseo de la Castellana. By the early 20th century, a transportation problem arose: There was no street connecting the new outlying districts of Salamanca and Argüelles. The solution was to chop through part of Old Madrid and construct a new thoroughfare, the Gran Vía.

The instability of the monarchy during the early 20th century led to further political upheaval. Alfonso XIII finally abdicated in 1931 to avoid a civil war. But the Socialist Republican government's decentralization plan and reform measures aroused strenuous right-wing opposition, which resulted in insurrection and, in 1936, the Spanish Civil War. Much of Madrid, which remained aligned with the Republican government, was blown to pieces at the hands of Generalísimo Francisco Franco's Nationalist forces. During the nearly 40 years of Franco's dictatorship, Madrid's spirit and creativity were stifled. Franco's death in 1975, the restoration of the monarchy, and the institution of a representative, democratic government brought about a dramatic multifaceted surge of activity ranging from construction to culture. As if making up for those 40 years of lost time, *madrileños,* with their newfound affluence and freedom of expression, have made their city one of Europe's most energetic and trendsetting, in art, fashion, music, and theater. The late Mayor Enrique Tierno Galván, whose irrevocable moniker is "The Best Mayor of Madrid," inspired his fellow citizens with such an affection for the city's own traditions and lore, promoted the arts with such enthusiasm, and fomented the *movida madrileña* with such verve that he became a revered figure — so much so that after his death in 1986, a *zarzuela* was written about him.

During this momentous year for Spain — the multifarious celebrations of the 500th anniversary of the discovery of America — Madrid plays a leading role worthy of its designation as 1992's European Capital of Culture. Sharing the spotlight with Barcelona, capital of Catalonia and host of the *1992 Summer Olympics,* and with Seville, capital of Andalusia and site of *Expo '92,* Madrid is enjoying another "golden age" with 366 days and nights (it's leap year!) of nonpareil scheduled cultural and entertainment events, and the culmination of major permanent city projects. A new logo identifies Madrid '92: a Gothic "M" outlined with a circle and a square, based on the 500-year-old design by Dürer.

The Triángulo del Arte (Triangle of Art) encompasses, within a 1-kilometer area, the newly reopened *Centro de Arte Reina Sofía-Museo Nacional de Arte Moderno y Contemporáneo,* now a premier museum of modern and contemporary art; the refurbished *Prado Museum,* with a series of special exhibitions; and the *Prado*'s *Palacio de Villahermosa* annex, remodeled and reopened this year to permanently exhibit the Thyssen-Bornemisza Collection, considered to be the world's second most important private art collection after that of the Queen of England. Next to the new *Auditorio Nacional* on Calle Principe de Vergara, the brand-new *Museo de la Ciudad* (Museum of the City) exhibits testimonials to the evolution of Madrid. Flanking the Plaza Mayor (Main Square), where major spectacles are being staged throughout the year, the 17th-century *Casa de la Panadería* has been refurbished and opened as a cultural center. The 19th-century Palacio de Linares in the Plaza de Cibeles has just been restored and converted into the *Museo de América* (Museum of America), a cultural and diplomatic center devoted to Spain's relationship with Latin America. Commemorating Columbus's discovery, a spectacular 302-foot-high permanent monument in the form of an armillary sphere (an old astronomical instrument) has been erected in the new Valdebernardo section southeast of downtown. Opening in initial phases are sections of the *Convention and Exhibit Center* of Campo de las Naciones, a vast, multifaceted urban project near Barajas International Airport geared for the year 2000. After 5 years of renovation and transformation, the *Teatro Real* will reopen (hopefully at the end of this year) as one of Europe's premiere opera houses.

And Madrid finally has a completed cathedral. The Catedral de la Almudena, named for the patroness of the city and under construction now for an entire century, is being completed this year and will be the oldest "new" cathedral in Europe, located in the Plaza de la Armería facing the Royal Palace.

Madrileños who can't stand being away from home can zoom to Seville for the day on *RENFE*'s new bullet train that makes the trip in less than 3 hours to visit *Expo '92*. They also can board one of *Iberia*'s *Puente Aereo* (Air Bridge) 1-hour flights — as frequent as 10 minutes apart — to take in the *Olympics* in Barcelona, and return home in time to stroll around Old Madrid where organ grinders still play on the cobblestone streets.

MADRID AT-A-GLANCE

SEEING THE CITY: For a wonderfully romantic view of Madrid, watch the sun set from the 25th-floor roof garden and pool of the *Plaza* hotel. The sharp "Velázquez sky," portrayed in the artist's famous paintings, is usually tinted with a golden hue. Looking over the "sea of tile" rooftops, visitors will see a fine view of the Royal Palace and, to the north, the distant Sierra de Guadarrama. The hotel's terrace and pool are open daily during the summer months. Admission charge. 2 Plaza de España (phone: 247-1200).

SPECIAL PLACES: The bustling Puerta del Sol, "kilometer zero" of the Spanish road network, and the Plaza de Cibeles traffic circle are two focal points at the heart of Madrid, which actually lies within the city's southwestern area. The Atocha railroad station and traffic circle mark the southern extremity of this zone, the Royal Palace and Parque del Retiro form its western and eastern borders respectively, and Plaza de Colón marks its northern limit. One major tree-lined avenue, with three names, bisects the entire city from top to bottom. Its southern section, between Atocha and Plaza de Cibeles, is called Paseo del Prado. From Cibeles north to Plaza de Colón, its name is Paseo de Recoletos. At Plaza de Colón, it becomes the long Paseo de la Castellana, which runs through modern Madrid to the north end of the city beyond Plaza de Castilla and the Chamartín railroad station. The two major east–west arteries are Calle de Alcalá and the Gran Vía; the latter angles northwest to Plaza de España.

For a basic overview, take a half-day motorcoach tour of the city or an excursion to surrounding sights with *Julía Tours* (68 Gran Vía; phone: 541-9125); *Pullmantur* (8 Plaza de Oriente; phone: 541-1805); or *Trapsatur* (23 Calle San Bernardo; phone: 542-6666). *Julía Tours* also can be booked in the US through their US representative *Bravo Tours* (182 Main St., Ridgefield Park, NJ 07760; phone: 800-272-8764). The best way to see Madrid, however, is by walking; many picturesque areas can be seen only on foot. Rest assured that, at least in the center of the city, things are much closer than they seem from the inside of a motorcoach or taxi. A good stroll, for starters, is from Puerta del Sol to Plaza Mayor, then downhill to Plaza de Oriente. Good maps of the city are provided free of charge at the tourist offices. Keep in mind that most museums close on Mondays, some close at midday, and smaller ones for the entire month of August.

Plaza Mayor – Oddly enough, this grandiose main square, which is closed to vehicular traffic, is easily missed if you don't aim for it and enter through one of the nine arched entryways. Built during the 17th century by order of King Philip III, it is the quintessence of Hapsburg Madrid — cobblestones, tile roofs, and imposing austere buildings. Before the king commissioned Juan Gómez de Mora to "straighten it out," the perfectly rectangular, perfectly flat plaza shared the irregularity of the surrounding architectural chaos. After its completion, the plaza became the stage for a wide variety of 17th- and 18th-century spectacles — audiences of over 50,000 witnessed hangings, burnings, and the decapitation of heretics, as well as canonizations of saints (such as St. Teresa and St. Isidro, Madrid's patron saint), jousting tournaments, plays (including those of Lope de Vega), circuses, and even bullfights. The 477 balconies of the surrounding buildings served as spectator "boxes" — not for the tenants, but for royalty and aristocrats. Beautifully refurbished, the Plaza Mayor is still lively, but with tamer entertainment — strolling student minstrels (*la tuna*), other amateur musicians, artists, and on-the-spot portrait painters selling their works, as well as summer concerts and ballets, and outdoor cafés for watching it all. Myriad shops, many over a century old, line the arcades around the plaza. On Sunday mornings, philatelists and numismatists set up shop in the arcades, to the delight of stamp and coin collectors. Visitors can easily lose their sense of direction inside this vast enclosure, so it's helpful to know that the bronze equestrian statue of Philip III in the center is facing east (toward the *Prado Museum*). The legendary Arco de Cuchilleros entrance is at the southwest corner.

Puerta del Sol – This vast oblong plaza is the bustling nerve center of modern Madrid life. Ten streets converge here, including the arteries of Alcalá, San Jerónimo, Mayor, and Arenal. The name of the square, "Gate of the Sun" in English, comes from a long-disappeared medieval city wall carved with a sunburst. On the south side, the 18th-century Comunidad government building, originally the Central Post Office, is topped by a clock tower. At midnight on *New Year's Eve,* thousands gather here to hear the clock strike and swallow one grape at each stroke to ensure 12 months of good fortune during the new year. Near the curb in front of the building's main entrance, a famous (yet inconspicuous) emblem in the sidewalk marks "kilometer zero," the central point from which all Spanish highways radiate, and from which their distance is measured. Directly across the plaza stands the venerated bronze statue of the *Oso y el Madroño* (the bear and the madrona berry tree), the symbol and coat of arms of Madrid since the 13th century.

Museo Nacional del Prado (Prado Museum) – One of the world's supreme art museums, the *Prado* is a treasure house of over 4,000 universal masterpieces, most of which were acquired over the centuries by art-loving Spanish monarchs. The wealth of Spanish paintings includes famous works by El Greco (including the *Adoration of the Shepherds*), Zurbarán, Velázquez (including *The Spinners* and *Maids of Honor*), Murillo, Ribera (including the *Martyrdom of St. Bartholomew*), and Goya (including his renowned *Naked Maja* and *Maja Clothed*). On the ground floor, a special section is devoted to the tapestry cartoons designed by Goya for the palace-monastery at San Lorenzo de El Escorial (see *Extra Special*) and to his extraordinary *Disasters of War* etchings, which represent his thoughts and comments on Spain's War of Independence. Visitors also will find Goya's stunning *Second of May* and *Third of May* canvases. Vast rooms are devoted to Italians Fra Angelico, Botticelli, Raphael, Correggio, Caravaggio, Titian, Tintoretto, and Veronese. Other rooms display paintings by Flemish and German masters such as Rubens, van der Weyden, Hieronymus Bosch (including *The Garden of Earthly Delights*), Memling, Dürer, and Van Dyck. From the Dutch are works by Rembrandt, Metsu, and Hobbema. French art is represented by Poussin, Lorrain, and Watteau, and the English by Reynolds, Gainsborough, and Lawrence.

The neo-classical *Prado* building was originally a natural science museum, conceived by Carlos III, the Enlightenment "King-Mayor," who ordered its construction by architect Juan de Villanueva. In 1819, King Fernando VII converted it into a museum to house the royal art collection. A bronze statue of Velázquez stands before the main façade, a statue of Goya at the north façade, and one of Murillo at the south side. In addition to the main *Prado,* or Villanueva building, the museum also includes two annexes. One, the Casón del Buen Retiro, resembles a small Greek temple, and is just up a hill from the Goya statue. It was once the stately ballroom of the 17th-century Royal Retiro Palace complex, which was destroyed during the French occupation of Madrid. It now contains, up the stairs, the *Museum of 19th-Century Spanish Painting* and, on the other side, facing the Parque del Retiro, with a separate entrance, a wing devoted to Picasso's monumental *Guernica,* which portrays the horrors of the Spanish Civil War and the devastating bombardment of that Basque town. The other annex, the splendid *Villahermosa Palace,* is diagonally across Plaza Cánovas del Castillo (the square with the Neptune Fountain) from the main building. Its spacious interior has been redesigned to house a major portion of the vast Thyssen-Bornemisza Collection, here on long-term loan, and which many consider the most important privately owned art collection in the world.

The *Prado* long ago outgrew its walls. Thus, the main building underwent a major refurbishment program, opening some 2 dozen remodeled rooms to display works previously in storage or on loan to other Spanish museums. Expansion plans for additional exhibit space include the acquisition in the mid-1990s of the nearby 17th-century Salón de Reinos building, which currently houses the *Museo del Ejército* (Army Museum). Still in the planning stages is the final relocation of *Guernica,* and the drawings related to it, to the *Queen Sofía Art Center-National Museum of Modern and Contemporary Art* which is devoted to contemporary art.

The *Prado* collection is so vast that it is impossible to savor its wonders in a single visit. If time is limited, it is best to select a few galleries of special interest, or enlist the services of the extremely knowledgeable government-licensed free-lance guides at the main entrance. The guides are more readily available in the early morning, and their fee is about $15 per hour. Reproductions from the *Prado*'s collection, postcards, and fine arts books are sold at the shop inside the museum. There also is a bar-restaurant on the premises. The *Prado* is open Tuesdays through Saturdays, from 9 AM to 6:45 PM; Sundays, 10 AM to 1:45 PM. Closed holidays. One admission charge grants access to the main building and the annexes. Paseo del Prado (phone: 420-2836).

Palacio Real (Royal Palace) – The Moors chose a strategic site overlooking the Manzanares River to build their Alcázar, or castle-fortress. After the 11th-century Reconquest, Christian leaders renovated it and moved into it, and Philip II made it the royal residence after proclaiming Madrid the capital of Spain in 1561. During the reign of Philip V, Spain's first Bourbon monarch, the Alcázar was destroyed by fire on Christmas Eve, 1734. The king then commissioned top Spanish and Italian architects to construct a glorious new palace in neo-classical style on the very same rugged steep site. It took 26 years to build the colossus of granite and white limestone, with walls 13 feet thick, over 2,800 rooms, 23 courtyards, and magnificently opulent interiors. "King-Mayor" Carlos III finally became the first royal resident. The east façade faces the grand Plaza de Oriente; at the north side are the formal Sabatini Gardens; and down the slopes on the west side is the Campo del Moro — 20 acres of forest, manicured gardens, and fountains, now a public park. The palace's main entrance is on the south side, through the tall iron gates leading into an immense courtyard called the Plaza de la Armería (armory), a setting for the pageantry of royal occasions. The imposing structure at the courtyard's south end is the Catedral de la Almudena, honoring the patroness of the city. Under construction for nearly a century, it will finally be completed this year, making it the oldest *new* cathedral in the world!

The palace is seen by guided tour, with different sections shown on different tours; both Spanish- and English-speaking National Patrimony guides lead the tours. Note that the King and Queen of Spain live in the Palacio de la Zarzuela, on the outskirts of Madrid, but the Palacio Real still is used for official occasions and is closed to the public at those times, which are not always announced in advance. Normally, opening hours are Mondays through Saturdays, from 9:30 AM to 5:15 PM; Sundays and holidays, from 9:15 AM to 2:15 PM. Admission charge. Plaza de Oriente (phone: 248-7404).

Plaza de Oriente – To the disappointment of Asian tourists, its name in Spanish simply means East (*oriente*) Square, because it faces the east façade of the Royal Palace (which also is sometimes referred to, in turn, as the Palacio de Oriente). Across the plaza from the palace is the *Teatro Real* (Royal Theater), which, after a major 2-year revamping of its interior, is scheduled to reopen this year as one of Europe's finest opera houses. In the center of the plaza stands the 9-ton bronze equestrian statue of King Philip IV, based on a drawing by Velázquez. Philip's horse is rearing up, supported solely by its hind legs, posing an equilibrium problem for Florentine sculptor Pietro Tacca. He consulted none other than the illustrious Galileo, whose solution was to make the front end of the statue hollow and the rear end solid.

Centro de Arte Reina Sofía-Museo Nacional de Arte Moderno y Contemporáneo (Queen Sofía Art Center-National Museum of Modern and Contemporary Art) – This gargantuan 18th-century building was Madrid's Hospital General de San Carlos until 1965. Following a tremendous reconstruction project, the building was inaugurated in 1986 as a museum devoted to contemporary art, named in honor of the present Queen of Spain. Following a long-term program of expansion within its already vast space, the museum reopened in November 1990 (after a 22-month closure) to take its place among the world's leading contemporary art galleries and modern art museums. The entire collection of the former *Museo Español de Arte Contemporáneo* (Spanish Contemporary Art Museum) was transferred here, and comprises 3,000 paintings, 9,000 drawings, and 400 sculptures, including works by Picasso, Miró, Dalí, Gris, and Julio Gonzáles. In addition to its still-growing permanent collection, it contains the most important contemporary art libraries in Spain with state-of-the-art computerized braille reading facilities, as well as videos (*videoarte*), photography collections, research facilities, and workshops. Throughout the year, several prominent exhibitions are scheduled at *CARS* (the museum's much-needed acronym) and at its two landmark annexes in Retiro Park, the *Palacio de Velázquez* and *Palacio de Cristal*. Open from 10 AM to 9 PM; closed Tuesdays. Admission charge: 52 Calle Santa Isabel (phone: 467-5062).

Plaza de Cibeles – Dominating Madrid's favorite traffic circle is the fountain and statue of the Greek fertility goddess Cibeles, astride her chariot drawn by two rather friendly looking lions. A Madrid custom requires that visitors "say hello to La Cibeles" upon arrival in town. Almost drowning out the vision of the Cibeles Fountain with its massiveness, the wedding-cake, turn-of-the-century Palacio de Comunicaciones (now the city's post office) on the plaza is so imposing that *madrileños* often refer to it as "Our Lady of Communications." Both Cibeles and the monumental arches of the Puerta de Alcalá (Alcalá Gate) up the street at Plaza de la Independencia are 18th-century endowments of the Bourbon "King-Mayor" Carlos III. On the southwest side of Plaza de Cibeles is the Banco de España; on the northwest side, the Palacio de Buenavista, which houses the Ministry of Defense.

Parque del Retiro (Retreat Park) – During the early 17th century, it was a royal retreat and the grounds of both a royal palace complex and a porcelain factory, then on the outskirts of town. Now Madrid's public park, right in the city, the Retiro covers 300 peaceful acres of forest, manicured gardens, statuary, fountains, picnic grounds, and cafés. It is a delightful place for strolling, jogging, a horse-and-carriage ride, or a boat ride around the lake, which is overlooked by the huge semicircular monument to King Alfonso XII. Art exhibitions are held at the park's Palacio de Cristal, a 19th-century jewel of glass and wrought iron, and at the Palacio de Velázquez, named for its architect, not for the painter. During the summer, at 10 PM and midnight, classical and flamenco concerts are staged in the Cecilio Rodríguez Gardens (Menéndez Pelayo entrance), and the outdoor cinema (entrance on Alfonso XII) features Spanish and foreign (including US) films. The park's loveliest entrance is through the wrought-iron gates at Plaza de la Independencia, also referred to as the Puerta de Alcalá.

Plaza de la Villa – One of Madrid's most charming squares, its architectural diversity makes it especially interesting. Dominating the west side, the 17th-century neoclassical Casa de la Villa, also called the Ayuntamiento (City Hall), was designed by Juan Gómez de Mora, the same architect who planned the Plaza Mayor. Adding to the *madrileño* atmosphere, its carillon chimes the hour with *zarzuela* melodies and plays 20-minute concerts every evening. Along the back of the square is the 16th-century Plateresque Casa de Cisneros palace, built by the nephew and heir of the cardinal regent of the same name. On the east side are the old Periodicals Library, with a large Mudéjar doorway, and the massive medieval Lujanes Tower, one of the oldest in Madrid and full of legends (one of its prisoners was King Francis I of France). Separating these two structures, the tiny Calle de Codo (Elbow Street) angles down to the tranquil Plaza del Cordón, which is surrounded by historic noble mansions. The bronze statue in the center of Plaza de la Villa honors Admiral Alvaro de Bazán, who fought — as did Cervantes — against the Turks in the Battle of Lepanto in 1571. The City Hall's splendid museum collection is open to the public every Monday (except holidays), from 5 to 7 PM, with free tours escorted by guides from the Madrid Tourist Board. Plaza de la Villa (phone: 588-0002).

Museo de la Real Academia de Bellas Artes de San Fernando (Museum of the San Fernando Royal Academy of Fine Arts) – Housed in a splendid 18th-century palace just east of the Puerta del Sol, the academy's permanent collection comprises some 1,500 paintings and over 800 sculptures. There are works by El Greco, Velázquez, Zurbarán, Murillo, Goya, and Sorolla, to name a few, as well as by Italian and Flemish masters. The only painting of George Washington in Spain is here; the portrait commemorates the Treaty of Friendship between Spain and the US. Closed to the public for 12 years, the museum reopened in 1986 and is gradually regaining the international renown it deserves — not only for its permanent collection, but for prestigious scheduled exhibitions held throughout the year. Open Tuesdays through Saturdays, from 9 AM to 7 PM; Sundays and Mondays, from 9 AM to 2 PM; during the summer, 9 AM to 2 PM daily. Admission charge. 13 Calle de Alcalá (phone: 532-1546).

Convento de las Descalzas Reales (Convent of the Barefoot Carmelites) – Behind its stark stone façade is an awesomely opulent interior filled with an astonishing wealth of artistic treasures and ornamentation bestowed by kings and noblemen. Princess Juana of Austria, sister of Philip II, opened this convent of the Royal Barefoot Carmelite Nuns in 1559. It welcomed disconsolate empresses, queens, princesses, and *infantas,* including Juana's sister María, Empress of Germany. The grandiose stairway is a breathtaking example of *barroco madrileño,* every centimeter lavishly decorated with frescoes and carved wood. Art treasures include works by El Greco, Zurbarán, Titian, and Sánchez Coello, as well as Rubens tapestries. From the windows of the upper floor is a lovely view over the tranquil rooftop garden, where the cloistered nuns still grow their vegetables just as they have for centuries, unaffected by the bustling Gran Vía just 1 block north, or the gigantic *El Corte Inglés* department store practically alongside. Visitors are escorted by resident Spanish-speaking National Patrimony guides; tours in English should be arranged in advance through the *Office of Museums* (phone: 248-7404). Hours vary according to the season, and are limited because the cloistered nuns often use the museum sections in their daily life; in general, however, opening hours are Tuesdays through Saturdays, from 10 AM to 1:30 PM. The admission charge includes the tour. Plaza de las Descalzas Reales (phone: 248-7404).

Convento de la Encarnación (Convent of the Incarnation) – Built by order of Queen Margarita of Austria, wife of King Philip III, this Augustinian convent was blessed in 1616. Designed in the severe classical style by Juan Gómez de Mora, its façade gives no clue to the bounteous religious and secular art treasures inside. The dazzling reliquary room displays some 1,500 religious relics contained in priceless gold and silver urns and jeweled cases. Among them, a legendary vial contains the blood of St. Pantaleón, which is said to liquefy every year on his birthday, July 27. A contrasting neo-classical 18th-century church designed by Ventura Rodríguez is set back in the center of the convent façade, and a statue of Lope de Vega graces its peaceful front garden. Like the Descalzas Reales, this is an active cloistered convent, and individuals and groups must be escorted by resident guides; tours in English can be arranged in advance through the *Office of Museums* (phone: 248-7404). Open Tuesdays through Saturdays, from 10 AM to 1:30 PM. The admission charge includes the tour. Plaza de la Encarnación (phone: 247-0510).

Museo Municipal – Devoted to the history of Madrid, this fine museum will enhance any visitor's awareness of the city's evolution, culture, and personality. It is filled with art, furnishings, porcelains, photographs, engravings, and meticulously detailed maps and models of the city during the 17th, 18th, and 19th centuries. The museum building, declared a National Monument in 1919, was originally an 18th-century hospital, and its elaborately ornate Churrigueresque-style entrance is in itself a worthwhile sight. Open Tuesdays through Saturdays, from 10 AM to 2 PM and 5 to 9 PM; Sundays, from 10 AM to 2:30 PM. Admission charge. 78 Calle Fuencarral (phone: 522-5732).

Mercado Puerta de Toledo – What used to be Madrid's old Central Fish Market (*mercado*) has been transformed into a sparkling showcase of fine Spanish handicrafts, art, antiques, jewelry, fashion, and interior design — everything from soup to nuts, in fact, since the premises include *El Abanico Gastronómico,* a combined restaurant and store featuring fine foods and wines from every region of Spain. Within the complex, the *Café del Mercado* is a lively nightspot. The market also is the setting for concerts, recitals, and art and photography exhibitions. Regularly scheduled video projections include a "bird's-eye view" of Madrid past and present. At the courtyard entrance is a functional Monument to Time: a giant sculptured combination sundial and lunar clock, considered the world's largest. The market is adjacent to the Puerta de Toledo, one of the ancient city gates, dominated by a 19th-century neo-classical triumphal arch. Joseph Bonaparte initiated construction of the arch; ironically, its completion celebrated the ousting of the French in the War of Independence, and the "welcome back" of Bourbon King Fernando VII. Open daily with dining, drinking, and entertainment going on into the wee hours. No admission charge. 1 Ronda de Toledo (phone: 266-7200).

Jardín Botánico (Botanical Garden) – The garden was designed in 1774 by Juan de Villanueva, the same architect who designed the *Prado Museum,* whose south façade it faces. Twenty manicured acres contain some 30,000 species of plants and flowers from Spain and throughout the world. Carlos III commissioned the project as part of his urban refurbishment program. By his order, therapeutic and medicinal plants and herbs were distributed free to those in need. Between the *Prado* and the entrance to the garden is the small Plaza de Murillo, which has a bronze statue of the 17th-century painter and the "Four Fountains" of mythological triton cherubs playing with dolphins. Open daily, from 10 AM to 7 PM (later in summer). Admission charge. On Paseo del Prado at Plaza de Murillo (phone: 420-3568).

Real Fábrica de Tapices (Royal Tapestry Factory) – Established early in the 18th century, this factory-museum continues to use authentic traditional techniques in producing handmade Spanish tapestries and rugs. In addition to the permanent collection, visitors can see the workshops and watch master artisans at work weaving tapestries from cartoons by Goya and other artists, knotting luxuriant rugs, or doing intricate restoration work. Rugs and tapestries can be purchased by special order, and they can even be custom-made from the customer's own design. Open Mondays through Fridays, from 9:30 AM to 12:30 PM; closed August. Admission charge. 3 Calle Fuenterrabía (phone: 551-3400).

Museo del Ejército (Army Museum) – Everything imaginable related to battle throughout Spain's history is here in an amazing array of over 27,000 items — uniforms, armor, cannon, swords (including one belonging to El Cid), stupendous collections of miniature soldiers, and portraits of heroines and heroes (such as Cervantes, when he lost his hand in the Battle of Lepanto). Downstairs, a curious collection of damaged carriages and automobiles whose illustrious passengers were assassinated en route recounts Madrid's turbulent political history. It's all chockablock within the vast and lavishly baroque interior of one of the two surviving buildings of the 17th-century Royal Retiro Palace complex (the other is the adjacent Casón del Buen Retiro, which the museum's pleasant bar overlooks). Whatever your interests, this is well worth seeing — while it lasts. Plans have been laid for the ever-expanding *Prado Museum* to take over this palatial building, and for the collection to be moved in the mid-1990s to a new venue at the Ministry of Defense complex in the Moncloa district. Open from 10 AM to 2 PM; closed Mondays. Admission charge. 1 Calle Méndez Núñez (phone: 531-4624).

Museo Arqueológico Nacional (National Archaeological Museum) – The star among the Iberian and classical antiquities is the enigmatic *Dama de Elche,* a dramatic Iberian bust of a priestess, or perhaps an aristocrat, estimated to have been sculpted during the 4th century BC. Also on display are basket weavings and funeral objects of early Iberians, as well as neolithic, Celtic, ancient Greek, Roman, and Visigothic artifacts and handicrafts. In the garden at the entrance is an underground replica of the famous Altamira Cave and its prehistoric paintings. Open Tuesdays through Saturdays, from 9:30 AM to 8:30 PM; Sundays and holidays, from 9:30 PM to 2:30 PM. The admission charge includes entrance to the *National Library* (see below), at the opposite side of the same building. 13 Calle Serrano (phone: 577-7912).

Biblioteca Nacional (National Library) – With over 6 million volumes, this is one of the world's richest libraries, truly a researcher's paradise. It was inaugurated in 1892 to commemorate the quadricentennial of the Discovery of America. Statues of Cervantes, Lope de Vega, and other illustrious Spaniards of letters stand at the classical columned entrance. Scheduled and seasonal exhibits of publications and graphics are held in the ground floor galleries. Open Tuesdays through Saturdays, from 10 AM to 9 PM; Sundays and holidays, 10 AM to 2 PM. The admission charge includes entrance to the *National Archaeological Museum* at the opposite side of the same building. 20 Paseo de Recoletos (phone: 575-6800).

Casa de Campo – Once the private royal hunting grounds, this 4,300-acre forested public park on the right bank of the Manzanares River is a playground for *madrileños* and visitors alike. It has a zoo (complete with a panda), picnic and fair grounds (important trade fairs and conventions are held here), and a giant amusement park, *Parque de Atracciones,* with rides and entertainment at an outdoor theater rife with a spirited carnival atmosphere. Other highlights include a concert stadium, an all-encompassing sports complex, a small lake, and the bullpens of La Venta de Batán (for bullfight practice and previews of the bulls). The park is easily reached by bus, metro, taxi, or the *teleférico* (cable car) that runs from Paseo del Pintor Rosales in Parque del Oeste (not far from Plaza de España). The zoo is open daily, April through September; Saturdays, Sundays, and holidays only, October through March. The amusement park is closed in winter and closed Mondays the rest of the year. Admission charge to attractions. Casa de Campo (phone: 463-2900).

Basílica de San Francisco el Grande – A few blocks south of the Royal Palace, this neo-classical church is one of the largest and most richly decorated in Madrid. Another project of King Carlos III, it was designed by the city's finest 18th-century architects. Six side chapels (the first on the left was painted by Goya) line its circular interior, which is topped by a cupola 108 feet in diameter. The museum inside the church contains a wealth of religious art. Museum hours are Tuesdays through Saturdays, from 11 AM to 1 PM and 4 to 7 PM; closed holidays. Admission charge to the museum. Plaza de San Francisco (phone: 265-3800).

■**EXTRA SPECIAL:** Some 30 miles (48 km) northwest of Madrid, the colossal monastery-palace of El Escorial symbolizes the grandeur of the Spanish Empire during its 16th-century Golden Age. King Philip II ordered its construction on a foothill of the Sierra de Guadarrama to commemorate Spain's victory over France at St.-Quentin, Flanders, and also to serve as a pantheon for his father, Holy Roman Emperor Charles V, and himself. It took more than 1,500 workmen 21 years to complete this extraordinary, austere monument designed by Juan de Herrera. The gray granite edifice, with hundreds of rooms and thousands of windows, is a sight never to be forgotten. The guided tour includes visits to the royal apartments, the museums (with paintings by Titian, Ribera, Velázquez, Tintoretto, Dürer, Lucas Jordan, and others), the library (with 40,000 priceless volumes and 4,700 manuscripts), the basilica, the royal pantheon with its tombs of Spanish monarchs, and the adjacent pantheon where their progeny are entombed. To reach the monastery-palace by car, take the N-VI national highway northwest to Guadarrama, then head south on C600; or take the more scenic country route, C505. There is frequent train and bus service between Madrid and the contiguous town of San Lorenzo de El Escorial, which is charming and well worth seeing. Open from 10 AM to 1 PM and 3 to 6 PM; closed Mondays. Admission charge (phone: 890-5903).

Nearby, to the north, is the Valle de los Caídos (Valley of the Fallen), an astonishing memorial to those who died in the Spanish Civil War. A huge basilica containing the tombs of soldiers from both sides has been hollowed into a mountain. Generalísimo Francisco Franco, who ordered the monument's construction, also is buried here. A granite cross stands 500 feet in the air atop the mountain peak. Open Tuesdays through Sundays, 10 AM to 6 PM. No admission charge, but there is a small parking fee (phone: 890-5611).

SOURCES AND RESOURCES

 TOURIST INFORMATION: Information, maps, and brochures can be obtained from the Oficina Municipal de Turismo (Municipal Tourist Office; 3 Plaza Mayor; phone: 266-5477). Information on the city, the rest of the province, and all of Spain also is available from the tourist information office of the Comunidad de Madrid (Province of Madrid, 2 Duque de Medinaceli; phone: 429-4951), near the *Palace* hotel. Other information offices run by the province are at Torre de Madrid, Plaza de España (phone: 541-2325), at Barajas Airport, and at the Chamartín train station.

The US Embassy is at 75 Calle Serrano (phone: 576-3400 or 3600).

Local Coverage – *ABC* and *El País,* among Spain's most important Spanish-language dailies, cover local, national, and international events, plus arts and entertainment listings. The *Guía del Ocio* ("Leisure Guide"), in Spanish, is the most complete weekly guide to restaurants, entertainment, culture, and sports.

TELEPHONE: The country code for Spain is 34; the city code for Madrid is 1. If calling from within Spain, dial 91 before the local number.

GETTING AROUND: Airport – Aeropuerto de Barajas, 10 miles (16 km) from downtown Madrid, handles both international and domestic flights. It is about a 20-minute taxi ride from the center of the city, depending on traffic; the fare will run about $15. (Note that taxis charge an additional 50¢ for picking up passengers at the airport, as well as another 25¢ per bag. There also is a 50¢ surcharge for all rides at night (11:30 PM to 6 AM) and all day on Sundays and holidays. Public buses run every 15 minutes between the airport and the air terminal in the center of the city under Plaza de Colón; the buses are yellow and are marked "Aeropuerto." The main *Iberia Airlines* office is at 130 Calle Velázquez (phone for domestic reservations: 411-1011; phone for international reservations: 563-9966). *Iberia*'s *Puente Aereo* (Air Bridge) runs 1-hour flights to Barcelona, leaving every 10 minutes.

Bus – Excellent, bus service is available throughout Madrid. Normal service operates from 6 AM to midnight; between midnight and 6 AM, there is service every 30 minutes from Plaza de Cibeles and Puerta del Sol. Signs clearly marking the routes are at each bus stop. Individual bus tickets are bought from the driver and cost 115 pesetas per ride. Discounted "bonobus" passes, good for ten rides, cost 450 pesetas, and can be bought at *Empresa Municipal de Transportes* (*EMT*) kiosks all over the city including one on the east side of Puerta del Sol and another at the south side of Plaza de Cibeles; upon boarding the bus, insert the pass into the date-stamping machine behind the driver. For information on the city bus system, call *EMT* at 401-9900. Madrid has no central bus station from which long-distance buses depart, but the Estación Sur de Autobuses (17 Calle Canarias; phone: 468-4200), serving Andalusia and other points south, is the largest of several.

Car Rental – All major international and Spanish firms are represented; most have offices at Madrid's Aeroporto de Barajas, and some at Chamartín and Atocha train stations. Agencies in the city include *América* (23 Calle Cartagena; phone: 246-7919); *Atesa* (59 Gran Vía; phone: 247-0202; and 25 Calle Princesa; phone: 241-5004); *Avis* (60 Gran Vía; phone: 247-2048; and in the airport terminal under Plaza de Colón; phone: 576-2862); *Europcar* (29 Calle Orense; phone: 445-9930; and 12 Calle García de Paredes; phone: 448-8706); *Hertz* (88 Gran Vía; phone: 248-5803; and in the *Castellana Inter-Continental* hotel (49 Paseo de la Castellana; phone: 319-0378); and *Ital* (31 Calle Princesa; phone: 241-9403).

Subway – Madrid's metro is efficient and clean and in operation from 6 AM to 1:30 AM. Stops along all ten lines are clearly marked, and color-coded maps are easy to read. Tickets are purchased from machines and inserted into electronic turnstiles, or they're bought at pass-through booths. (Do not discard the ticket until the end of the ride.) Discounted ten-ride tickets also are available (410 pesetas); buy these at metro stations. For subway information, call 435-2266.

Taxi – Metered cabs are white with a diagonal red line. If a cab is available, it will have a windshield sign that says *libre* and an illuminated green light on its roof. Fares are moderate. Taxis can be hailed on the street, picked up at cabstands, or summoned by phone: *Radio-Teléfono Taxi* (phone: 247-8200); *Radio-Taxi* (phone: 404-9000); *Tele-taxi* (phone: 445-9008).

Train – The two major stations of the *RENFE* (Spanish National Railway) are Chamartín at the north end of Madrid and Atocha at the south end. Both serve long-distance trains, as well as commuter trains to surrounding areas (*cercanías*). West of Plaza de España, a third station, Principe Pío (also called Estación del Norte), serves some lines to northern Spain. *RENFE*'s main city ticket office is located at 44 Calle de Alcalá (phone: 429-0518 for information; 429-8228 for reservations). Tickets also can be purchased at the train stations and at *RENFE's* Nuevos Ministerios and Recoletos stations.

On Saturdays and Sundays from May through October, *RENFE* operates a series of tourist trains offering 1- and 2-day excursions to nearby places of interest. Museum entrance fees, guided tours, motorcoach sightseeing, and, in some cases, meals are included in the cost of the transportation; hotel accommodations are included in the 2-day packages, which travel to more distant destinations. The specially named 1-day excursion trains head for Aranjuez (*Tren de la Fresa,* or "Strawberry Train"); Toledo (*Ciudad de Toledo*); Avila (*Murallas de Avila*); Sigüenza (*Doncel de Sigüenza*); and the Piedra River and Monastery in Aragon (*Monasterio de Piedra*). The cost is approximately $15–$20, with discounts for children under 12. Trains departing on 2-day excursions, leaving Saturday mornings and returning Sunday nights, make trips to Cáceres (*Ciudad Monumental de Cáceres*); Burgos (*Tierras del Cid*); Cuenca (*Ciudad Encantada de Cuenca*); Valladolid (*Cuna del Descubrimiento*); Salamanca (*Plaza Mayor de Salamanca*); Soria (*Camino de Soria*); Zamora (*Románico de Zamora*); and Palencia (*Camino de Santiago Palentino*). Prices range from about $70 to $135, depending on the train and choice of hotel. *RENFE*'s new bullet trains make the trip to Seville in less than 3 hours. Reservations should be made in advance at *RENFE* offices or through one of the many travel agencies scattered throughout Madrid. (Check the list of destinations for additional cities upon arrival in Madrid, because the innovative tourist train idea has been so successful that new destinations are added each season.)

 LOCAL SERVICES: Dentist (English-Speaking) – Ask at the US Embassy (phone: 576-3400 or 576-3600) or your hotel concierge.

Dry Cleaner – *El Corte Inglés* department store, also does laundry. 3 Preciados (phone: 532-1800).

Limousine Service – *American Express* makes arrangements with English-speaking drivers. 2 Plaza de las Cortes (phone: 429-5775).

Medical Emergency – *British American Hospital* (1 Paseo de Juan XXIII; phone: 234-6700); *Red Cross Central Hospital* (22 Av. Reina Victoria; phone: 233-3900; Emergency, phone: 233-7777); *La Paz Hospital* (Paseo de la Castellana; phone: 734-2600). The national police emergency number is 091; the municipal police is 092.

Messenger Service – *Mensajeros Express,* 5 Calle Berlín (phone: 255-3300).

National/International Courier – *DHL International* (17 Torres Quevedo, Polígono Fin de Semana; phone: 747-7711); *Federal Express* (13 Calle Arrastari, Polígono Las Mercedes; phone: 329-0460).

Office Equipment Rental – *El 7,* for typewriters (39 Hortaleza; phone: 522-5943); *Telson,* for audiovisual equipment (64 Pradillo; phone: 413-4463).

Pharmacy – To find the all-night pharmacy closest to your hotel, call the 24-hour pharmacy hotline 098. Pharmacy hours also are listed in the newspapers; look under "Farmacias de Guardia."

Photocopies – There are shops throughout the city. Outstanding is *Prontaprint,* open Mondays through Fridays 10 AM to 7 PM. Two locations: 15 Jacometrezo, just off the Gran Vía, between Plaza Callao and Plaza Santo Domingo (phone: 248-9958) and 56 María de Molina (phone: 411-0823).

Post Office – The main post office is Palacio de Comunicaciones at Plaza de la Cibeles (phone: 521-4004 or 521-8195). Hours vary according to the service provided; stamps can be purchased from 9 AM to 10 PM.

Secretary/Stenographer (English-Speaking) – *Intercom English SA* (19 General Martínez Campos; phone: 445-4751); *CADRESSA* (33 General Margallo; phone: 270-3077).

Tailor – *Galeote M. Córdova* (10 Manuel de Falla; phone: 457-7539); *Fernando Hervas* (27 Príncipe; phone: 429-6331).

Telex – *Palacio de Comunicaciones* (Plaza de la Cibeles; phone: 521-4004 or 521-8195); *Telefónica* will receive and hold telexes sent to 41663 or 41664. They can be picked up as a type of general delivery. The telex department is open from 9 AM to 9 PM daily (Plaza Colón; phone: 410-3186).

Translator – *CADRESSA* (33 General Margallo; phone: 270-3077); *Siasa* (134 Paseo de la Habana; phone: 457-4891); *Intercom English SA* (19 General Martínez Campos; phone: 445-4751).

Other – Convention facilities: *Palacio de Congresos* (99 Paseo de la Castellana; phone: 555-1600 or 555-4906) has 2 auditoriums that can be joined for a total capacity of 2,684 people, an amphitheater for up to 900, 8 meeting rooms for up to 320, audiovisual equipment, closed-circuit TV, cafeteria, banquet hall, and private dining rooms for 100; total capacity is 10,000 people. *Casa de Campo* has facilities on its fairgrounds and in its auditorium space for hundreds of stands, and the meeting hall has a capacity for 608; located on the outskirts of Madrid (for information: *Auditorio del Recinto de la Casa de Campo,* Avenida Portugal; phone: 463-6334). The *Madrid Convention Bureau* offers full assistance for every aspect of meeting and convention arrangements (69 Mayor; phone: 588-2930).

Communications services: *Telefónica* (locations at 30 Gran Vía, Plaza de las Cibeles, and Plaza Colón. Long-distance calls can be paid by Visa or MasterCard. The Gran Vía location is open 24 hours; the offices at Gran Vía and Colón have AT&T "USA Direct" phone service for collect or phone credit card calls to the US).

Tuxedo rental: *Cornejo* (2 Magdalena; phone: 239-1646).

 SPECIAL EVENTS: Madrid has a distinctive, exuberant way of celebrating Spain's national holidays, as well as its own year-long calendar of local fairs and festivals. And the city's cultural calendar will be extra full for the next 12 months because of Madrid's designation as the European Cultural Capital of the Year. *Madrileños* go all out for *Carnaval* frolic, frocks, and parades in February, ending on *Ash Wednesday* with the allegorical *Entierro de la Sardina* (Burial of the Sardine). The *International Festival of Theater and Film* is held in April. On the *Second of May,* at Plaza 2 de Mayo in the Malasaña district, processions and events commemorate the city's uprising against the massacring French, which Goya portrayed so dramatically. But even more *madrileño* are the *Fiestas de San Isidro* — 10 days of nonstop street fairs, festivals, concerts, special daily bullfights, and more, all in celebration of Madrid's patron saint, whose feast day is on May 15. (This age-old tradition of picnics and merrymaking at the Meadows of San Isidro alongside the Manzanares River also was depicted by Goya.) On June 13, the *Verbena de San Antonio* (St. Anthony's Fair) takes place at the shrine of San Antonio de la Florida, with outdoor singing and dancing and traditional drinking from the fountain. It's also customary to throw pins into the holy water; young "spinsters" dip in, and their chances for acquiring a mate depend on the number of pins that stick in their hands.

Madrid is extra-lively during the summer, despite the mass exodus by summer vacationers. During July, August, and early September, the city government presents *Veranos en la Villa* (Summers in the "Village"), 2-plus months of countless cultural events featuring international superstars and local talent — ballet, symphonic music, opera, jazz, rock, pop, salsa, *zarzuelas,* films, and many diverse exhibitions — in open-air and theater settings throughout the city. Fitting in neatly with all this are colorful *verbenas* (street parties) honoring the feast days of three of Madrid's most popular saints: San Cayetano (August 3), San Lorenzo (August 5), and La Virgen de la Paloma (August 15). In the *barrios castizos* (authentically typical neighborhoods, such as Lavapiés, Embajadores, Puerta de Toledo), *madrileños,* from toddlers to great-grandparents, dress in the traditional attire of *chulos* and *chulapas* reminiscent of 19th-century *zarzuelas.* They gather at lively street fairs to eat, drink, and dance the *chotis* and *pasodoble,* enjoying musical groups, folk music performances, organ-grinders, processions, *limonada* (not lemonade, but a kind of white-wine sangria), and their own innate ebullience. The world class *Madrid International Jazz Festival* is held in late October and/or early November. From October to the beginning of December, the *Fiesta de Otoño* (Autumn Festival), also organized by the city government, presents an abundance of concerts and performances by top international and Spanish companies at Madrid theaters and concert halls. November 9 celebrates the day of Madrid's patroness, La Virgen de la Almudena. During the *Christmas* season, the city is bedecked with festive lights, and the Plaza Mayor fills with countless stands selling decorations, figurines for Nativity scenes, candies, wreaths, and *Christmas* trees. On *New Year's Eve,* throngs gather at the Puerta del Sol to swallow one grape at each stroke of the clock at midnight, wishing for 12 months of good luck in the new year. The *Christmas* season lasts until *Epiphany,* January 6, on the eve of which children delight at the *Cabalgata de los Reyes,* the procession through the city streets by the gift-giving Three Wise Men. As if all of this weren't enough, each barrio expresses its individual personality with its own fiestas and *festivales* throughout the year.

 MUSEUMS: Many museums are described in *Special Places* (above). Included in the following list of additional museums are certain churches that, because of their high artistic quality, should not be overlooked. Note that the *Museo de América* (America's Museum; 6 Avenida Reyes Católicos), housing Latin American crafts and folk art along with pre-Columbian artifacts, currently closed for restoration, is scheduled to reopen this year (possibly in a new location). Also closed for restoration, but scheduled to reopen this year, is the *Casa-Museo de Lope de Vega* (Lope de Vega House-Museum, 11 Calle Cervantes; phone: 239-4605), consisting of the home and garden of Spain's great Golden Age dramatist; it ordinarily is open Tuesdays and Thursdays only, from 10AM to 2 PM, and closed in summer. Admission charge. Keep in mind that the hours of many museums may vary during the summer, and smaller museums may be closed during July and August. The *Office of Museums* will be able to supply the latest information (phone: 248-7404).

Basílica de San Miguel – An unusual 18th-century church with an air of Italian baroque in its convex façade and graceful interior. Open daily. 4 Calle de San Justo.

Catedral de San Isidro – This imposing 17th-century church was *temporarily* designated the Cathedral of Madrid in 1885, pending the completion of the Catedral de la Almudena — which has been under construction for over a century. The entombed remains of St. Isidro, patron saint of Madrid, and those of his wife, Santa María de la Cabeza, sit on the altar. Open daily. 37 Calle Toledo.

Círculo de Bellas Artes (Fine Arts Circle) – Several galleries of this art, design, and photography center display works by students and prominent teachers. Open daily; exhibits and events are scheduled at varying hours; pick up a monthly program at the tourist office. Admission charge to most exhibits. 42 Calle de Alcalá (phone: 531-7700).

Estudio y Museo Sorolla (Sorolla Studio and Museum) – The house in which Joaquín Sorolla, the Valencian Impressionist "Painter of Light," lived, worked, and died in 1923. Contents include a collection of his works; the studio and library remain intact. Open from 10 AM to 3 PM; closed Mondays. Admission charge. 37 Calle General Martínez Campos (phone: 410-1584).

Fundación Casa de Alba (House of Alba Foundation) – The magnificent 18th-century Palacio de Liria, former residence of the Duchess of Alba, containing the family's priceless private collection of art, tapestries, archives, and furnishings. Admission (free) must be requested well in advance by writing to: Fundación Casa de Alba, 20 Calle Princesa, 28008 Madrid (phone: 247-5302).

Iglesia y Convento de San Jerónimo el Real (Church and Convent of San Jerónimo) – This giant Gothic temple overlooking the *Prado* was built by order of

King Ferdinand and Queen Isabella in 1503. It is closed for massive renovation, and is not scheduled to reopen until the mid-1990s. 19 Calle Ruiz de Alarcón.

Museo Cerralbo – The palatial 19th-century mansion of the Marqués de Cerralbo houses an important collection of art, antiques, ceramics, tapestries, and ancient artifacts. Outstanding among the paintings are works by El Greco, Ribera, Velázquez, Zurbarán, and Van Dyck. Open from 10 AM to 2 PM and 4 to 6 PM; closed Mondays and in August. Admission charge. 17 Calle Ventura Rodríguez (phone: 247-3647).

Museo de la Ciudad (Museum of the City) – This brand-new museum exhibits testimonials to the evolution of Madrid. 140 Calle Principe de Vergara. For more information, call 588-6500.

Museo de Escultura Abstracta al Aire Libre (Outdoor Museum of Abstract Sculpture) – Contemporary Spanish sculptures permanently placed in a pedestrian area on the Castellana, under the Calles Eduardo Dato–Juan Bravo overpass. Open continuously; no admission charge. Paseo de la Castellana (no phone).

Museo de Figuras de Cera (Wax Museum) – An international gallery of historic personages, including celebrity bullfighters and such fictional Spanish notables as Don Quixote and Sancho Panza. Open daily, from 10:30 AM to 1:30 PM and 4 to 8 PM. Admission charge. Centro Colón (phone: 308-0825).

Museo Lázaro Galdiano – Named for its founder, whose palatial mansion houses his extraordinary collection of art, jewelry, ivory, and enamel. Open from 10 AM to 2 PM; closed Mondays and in August. Admission charge. 122 Calle Serrano (phone: 261-6084).

Museo Nacional de Artes Decorativas (National Museum of Decorative Arts) – Four floors of furniture, porcelains, jewelry, Spanish tiles and fans, a full Valencian kitchen, and handicrafts from the 16th through 19th centuries. Open Tuesdays through Fridays, from 10 AM to 3 PM; Saturdays and Sundays, from 10 AM to 2 PM; closed in summer. Admission charge. 12 Calle Montálban (phone: 521-3440).

Museo Nacional Ferroviario (National Railroad Museum) – Madrid's first train station, Estación de las Delicias, now is a museum complete with intact antique trains, royal cars, and other predecessors of the modern railroad. From May through October, the restored 19th-century "Strawberry Train" (*Tren de la Fresa*) departs here on 1-day excursions to Aranjuez. Open Tuesdays through Saturdays, from 10 AM to 5 PM; Sundays and holidays, from 10 AM to 2 PM. Admission charge. 61 Paseo de las Delicias (phone: 227-3121).

Museo Naval (Maritime Museum) – Models of ships and ports, nautical instruments, and maps, including Juan de la Cosa's historic *mapa mundi*, the first map to include the New World, drawn in 1500. Open from 10:30 AM to 1:30 PM; closed Mondays and in August. Admission charge. 2 Calle Montálban (phone: 521-0419).

Museo Panteón de Goya (Pantheon of Goya, also called Ermita de San Antonio) – Goya painted the magnificent religious frescoes on the dome and walls of this small 18th-century church, which was to become his tomb. Open Tuesdays through Fridays, from 10 AM to 1:30 PM and 4 to 7 PM; weekends and holidays, from 10 AM to 1:30 PM. No admission charge. Glorieta de San Antonio de la Florida (phone: 542-0722).

Museo Romántico (Romantic Museum) – Paintings, furniture, and decor of 19th-century Madrid, housed in an 18th-century mansion. Open Tuesdays through Saturdays, from 10 AM to 6 PM; Sundays, from 10 AM to 2 PM. Closed August. Admission charge. 13 Calle San Mateo (phone: 448-1071).

Museo Taurino (Bullfighting Museum) – An important collection of bullfighting memorabilia, including photographs, celebrity bullfighters' "suits of lights," and even taxidermic trophies of ears, tails, and entire bulls. Open Mondays through Fridays, from 9 AM to 3 PM; during bullfighting season (May through October), open Sundays, closed Mondays. Admission charge. Plaza de Toros Monumental de las Ventas, 237 Calle de Alcalá (phone: 255-1857).

Templo de Debod – A gift from the Egyptian government in the 1970s, this 2,500-year-old Egyptian temple was shipped to Madrid in 1,359 cases and reassembled, towering over a reflecting pool. Theater and music performances are held here in summer. Open daily, from 10 AM to 1 PM; holidays, from 10 AM to 3 PM. No admission charge. Parque del Oeste.

SHOPPING: Madrid's 54,000 stores and shops offer everything imaginable, from high fashion to flamenco guitars. Handicrafts, fine leather goods, embroidery, ceramics, Lladró porcelains, art, and antiques are among the enticing buys available throughout the city. Everything goes on sale twice a year — after *Christmas* (which in Spain means January 7, the day after *Epiphany*) and during the summer. The big summer sales (*rebajas*) begin in July, and prices are reduced even more during the first 3 weeks of August. Shops generally open at 9:30 AM, close from 1:30 to 4:30 PM for lunch and the siesta, and close for the night at 8 PM. The huge flagship stores of Spain's two major department store chains are next to each other in the pedestrian shopping area between the Gran Vía and Puerta del Sol: *El Corte Inglés* (3 Calle Preciados; phone: 532-8100) and *Galerías Preciados* (1 Plaza de Callao; phone: 522-4771). Unlike most retailers, they remain open during the lunch and siesta hours, and they provide special services for tourists, such as English-speaking escorts to accompany shoppers and coordination of shipping services to hotel or home. Branch stores of *El Corte Inglés* are at 56 Calle Princesa, 76 Calle Goya, and 79 Calle Raimundo Fernández Villaverde (the biggest of all, just off the Castellana). Branches of *Galerías Preciados* are at 10-11 Calle Arapiles, 87 Calle Goya, 47 Calle Serrano, and at the *Madrid 2 Shopping Center* (also known as *La Vaguada*) in northern Madrid.

Near the two department stores, four stores specializing in fine china, porcelain (especially Lladró), and Majórica pearls, line the Gran Vía: *Souvenirs* (11 Gran Vía, near Calle de Alcalá; phone: 521-5119); *Vinvinda* (44 Gran Vía, near Plaza de Callao; phone: 213-0514); *Regalos A.R.* (46 Gran Vía; phone: 522-6869); and *La Galette* (67 Gran Vía, near Plaza de España; phone: 248-8938). Window shopping is a favorite pastime along Calle Serrano, which is full of elegant boutiques and galleries; the Plaza Mayor area is another place to look for appealing shopping opportunities.

Other places to browse or buy include the rebuilt *Mercado Puerta de Toledo* (see *Special Places*), where over 150 shops, boutiques, and galleries are stuffed with the finest in Spanish handicrafts, art, fashion, antiques, jewelry, housewares, and food products. Easy-to-operate computer terminals reveal what and where everything is in this sparkling complex, which is all under one roof (1 Ronda de Toledo; phone: 266-7200). *La Galería del Prado* (phone: 429-7551), a recent addition to the *Palace* hotel (7 Plaza de las Cortes), is a glamorous assembly of 38 top fashion boutiques, art galleries, jewelers, and gift shops, as well as a fancy food shop, a beauty salon, bookstore, and a buffet-style restaurant. Still another shopping mall, in modern Madrid, just off the Castellana, is *Moda Shopping* (40 Avenida General Perón), with over 60 establishments selling everything from high fashion to sporting goods, and with plenty of restaurants and bars to enjoy during shopping breaks.

El Rastro, Madrid's legendary outdoor flea market, (open Sundays and holiday mornings only) spreads for countless blocks in the old section of the city, beginning at Plaza de Cascorro and fanning south to Ronda de Toledo. Hundreds of stands are set up to sell everything from canaries to museum-piece antiques, and bargaining, preferably in Spanish, is customary. (Guard wallets and purses from pickpockets.) Open daily, year-round, is the *Cuesta de Moyano,* a stretch of Calle de Claudio Moyano (along the south side of the Botanical Gardens) with a string of bookstalls selling new, used, and out of print "finds" of everything imaginable that's been published.

Adolfo Domínguez – The boutique of the innovative Spanish celebrity designer, whose daring women's fashions set the "wrinkles (in the fabric, that is) are beautiful" trend. 4 Calle Ortega y Gasset (phone: 276-0084).

Antigua Casa Talavera – Authentic regional handcrafted ceramics and dinnerware from all over Spain form an overwhelming display in this small, family-owned shop just off the Gran Vía, near Plaza de Santo Domingo. 2 Calle Isabel la Católica (phone: 247-3417).

Artespaña – Government run, with a wide range of handicrafts and home furnishings from all over Spain. 3 Plaza de las Cortes, 14 Calle Hermosilla, 33 Calle Don Ramón de la Cruz, and *Centro Comercial Madrid 2–La Vaguada* (phone for all locations: 413-6262).

Ascot – An excellent women's boutique selling haute couture and ready-to-wear fashions by María Teresa de Vega, who clothes some of Madrid's most beautiful people. 88 Calle Serrano (phone: 431-3712).

El Aventurero – A small bookstore specializing in guidebooks, maps, books on the art of bullfighting, and outstanding "coffee-table" tomes on Spanish subjects, with an ample selection in English, too. Just off Plaza Mayor at 15 Calle Toledo (phone: 266-4457).

Boutique Granada – A small shop selling leather goods of the highest quality. 12 Calle de Vergara (phone: 241-0746).

Canalejas – Top-quality men's shirtmakers, specializing in the classic European formfitting cut. 20 Carrera de San Jerónimo (phone: 521-8075).

Casa de Diego – Founded in 1858, this old-time store makes hand-painted fans — and frames for displaying them — as well as canes and umbrellas. Two locations: 12 Puerta del Sol (phone: 522-6643), and 4 Calle Mesonero Romanos (phone: 531-0223).

Casa Jiménez – Another classic store specializing in fans and *mantones de manila,* fine lace shawls. 42 Calle Preciados (phone: 248-0526).

Casa del Libro – Madrid's biggest book store. 29 Gran Vía (phone: 521-1932). A brand-new branch, on 4 floors, is at 3 Calle Maestro Vitoria (phone: 521-4898).

Cortefiel – Leading men's and women's fashions and accessories are carried at 40 Calle Serrano (phone: 431-3342). Branches at 178 Paseo de la Castellana (phone: 259-5713) and 27 Gran Vía (phone: 247-1701) specialize in men's fashions only, while those at 146 Paseo de la Castellana (phone: 250-3638) and 13 Calle Preciados (phone: 522-6567) cater exclusively to women.

El Corte Inglés Record Department – The latest in Spanish classical, pop, and flamenco music on record, tape, and compact disc, as well as a complete selection of every other type of recorded music. They even carry *sevillanas* dance lessons on videocassette. Across the street from the main store at 3 Calle Preciados (phone: 532-8100).

Elena Benarroch – Stylish designs in women's furs. This well-known furrier also has a shop in New York. 24 Calle Monte Esquinza (phone: 308-2816).

Gil, Sucesor de Anatolín Quevedo – Spanish and international celebrities purchase work-of-art shawls, mantillas, and embroidery at this generations-old establishment. 2 Carrera de San Jerónimo (phone: 521-2549).

Gritos de Madrid – A fine ceramics shop owned by master craftsman Eduardo Fernández, and featuring his works. He is responsible for the restoration of Madrid's interesting hand-illustrated tile street signs, and his famous ceramic mural of 17th-century Madrid hangs in the City Hall's museum collection. 6 Plaza Mayor (phone: 265-9154).

Joaquín Berao – Fine jewelry by the young Spanish designer — earrings, bracelets, rings, and pendants in ultramodern designs. 13 Calle Conde de Xiquena (phone: 410-1620).

Lepanto – Fashions, luggage, and accessories, in leather. 3 Plaza de Oriente (phone: 242-2357).

Loewe – Fine leather fashions for men and women, as well as accessories and luggage. At several locations: 8 Gran Vía, 26 Calle Serrano, and at the *Palace* hotel; a shop at 34 Calle Serrano carries men's fashions exclusively (phone for all locations: 435-3023).

Maty – For dance enthusiasts: authentic regional (including flamenco) costumes for men, women, and children, and dance shoes and boots as well. 2 Calle Maestro Vitoria (phone: 479-8802).

Seseña – Always in style in Spain, capes are becoming the "in" thing for evening-wear everywhere, and this store, founded in 1901, manufactures a fine line for men and women. (It also instructs clients on the fine art of wearing a cape.) 23 Calle Cruz (phone: 531-6840).

 SPORTS AND FITNESS: Basketball – Madrid plays host to much of the finest basketball in Europe. The city is represented by such teams as *Real Madrid* and *Estudiantes* and also is the home of the Spanish National and *Olympic* squads. The most important games are played at the *Palacio de Deportes* (99 Calle Jorge Juan; phone: 401-9100), and at the *Polideportivo Magariños* (127 Calle Serrano; phone: 262-4022).

Bullfighting – Although not universally appreciated, bullfighting is the most re-nowned sport of Spain — Spaniards insist it is an art — and the largest bullfighting ring in Madrid is *Plaza de Toros Monumental de las Ventas,* which seats 22,300 people. There also is a smaller ring, *Plaza de Toros de Carabanchel,* near the Vista Alegre metro stop. The season runs from mid-May through October. Tickets may be purchased the day of the event at a counter at 3 Calle Vitoria (near the Puerta del Sol), at the bullring, or through a hotel concierge.

Fishing – There are fishing reserves along the Lozoya, Madarquillos, Jarama, and Cofio rivers not far from Madrid. They are populated mostly by trout, carp, black bass, pike, and barbel. The Santillana reservoir is particularly good for pike. For season and license information, contact the *Dirección General del Medio Rural,* 39 Calle Jorge Juan (phone: 435-5121).

Fitness Centers – Madrid has 27 municipal gymnasiums; for information on the one nearest your hotel, call 464-9050.

Golf – The Madrid area boasts several excellent private golf courses, such as the two 18-hole courses at the *Real Club de la Puerta de Hierro* (Avenida Miraflores; phone: 316-1745); the 18-hole and 9-hole courses at the *Club de Campo Villa de Madrid* (Carretera de Castilla; phone: 207-0395); the Jack Nicklaus–designed 18-hole course of the *Club de Golf La Moraleja* (7 miles/11 km north of town along the Burgos–Madrid highway; phone: 650-0700); and the 18 holes of the *Nuevo Club de Golf de Madrid* (at Las Matas, 16 miles/26 km west of town via the Carretera de La Coruña; phone: 630-0820). The *Federación Española de Golf* (9 Calle Capitán Haya; phone: 555-2682) has details on most of the area's facilities; hotels also can provide information regarding the use of the clubs by non-members.

Horse Racing – The *Hipódromo de la Zarzuela* (4 miles/7 km north of the center, along Carretera de La Coruña) features Sunday-afternoon races during spring and fall meetings. Buses for the track leave from the corner of Calles Princesa and Hilarión Eslava (phone: 207-0140).

Jogging – Parque del Retiro and Casa de Campo both have jogging tracks.

Skiing – *Puerto de Navacerrada,* a mountain resort (just 37 miles/60 km north of Madrid; phone: 852-1435) has 12 ski runs and 6 lifts.

Soccer – One of Spain's most popular teams, the capital's *Real Madrid,* plays its home games at the *Estadio Santiago Bernabéu* (1 Calle Concha Espina; phone: 250-0600), while its rival, *Atlético de Madrid,* takes the field at the *Estadio Vicente Calderón* (6 Paseo Virgen del Puerto; phone: 266-4707).

Swimming – Many hotels have pools, but Madrid also has 150 public swimming pools, including those indoors and outdoors at *Casa de Campo* (Avenida del Angel; phone: 463-0050). Another nice pool is at *La Elipa* (Avenida de la Paz; phone: 430-3358), which also has an area set aside for co-ed nude sunbathing. For information on other municipal pools, call 463-5498.

Tennis – Among the hundreds of public and private tennis courts in town are the 35 courts at the *Club de Campo Villa de Madrid,* Carretera de Castilla (phone: 207-0395), and the 28 courts of the *Club de Tenis Chamartín* (2 Calle Federico Salmón; phone: 250-5965).

THEATER: Theater productions are in Spanish. Anyone fluent and interested in the Spanish classics should check the *Guía del Ocio* for what's on at the *Teatro Español* (25 Calle del Príncipe; phone: 429-6297), which stages the classics of the Golden Age; at the nearby *Teatro de la Comedia* (14 Calle del Príncipe; phone: 521-4931), where the *Compañía Nacional de Teatro Clásico* (National Classical Theater Company) also puts on a fine repertoire of classic Spanish plays, as well as modern ones and foreign adaptations; and at the *Teatro Nacional María Guerrero* (4 Tamayo y Baus; phone: 319-4769), still another venue for both modern plays and classics of the Spanish and international repertoires. For the strictly modern and avant-garde, there's the *Centro Nacional de Nuevas Tendencias Escénicas* (National Center of New Theater Trends), housed at the *Sala Olimpia* (Plaza de Lavapiés; phone: 237-4622). Madrid is a city of film buffs, but if you feel like taking in a film and your Spanish is not good enough for the latest Almodóvar, note that foreign films usually are not dubbed into Spanish — look for "V.O.," meaning '*versión original*" in the ad. *Cine Doré,* known as the Filmoteca Española (3 Calle Santa Isabel; phone: 227-3866), has all the avant-garde foreign films; *Alphavilla* (14 Calle Martín de los Heros; phone: 248-4524) is another possibility. Ballets, operas, and *zarzuelas* (or operettas — some *zarzuelas* resemble musical comedy, others light opera), present fewer difficulties for nonspeakers of Spanish. Check listings for the restored *Teatro Nuevo Apolo Musical de Madrid* (1 Plaza Tirso de Molina; phone: 369-0637), home base for director José Tamayo's *Nueva Antología de la Zarzuela* company; *Teatro Lírico Nacional de la Zarzuela* (4 Calle Jovellanos; phone: 429-8225), which also hosts opera, ballet, and concerts, in addition to traditional *zarzuela;* and the *Centro Cultural de la Villa* (Plaza de Colón; phone: 575-6080), which presents both theater and *zarzuela.*

MUSIC: Bolero and fandango are the typically Castilian dances and flamenco is Andalusian, but it is the latter most tourists want to see and hear, so there are numerous excellent flamenco *tablaos* (cabarets) in Madrid. Some of the best are *Corral de la Morería* (17 Calle Morería; phone: 265-1137); *Café de Chinitas* (7 Calle Torija; phone: 248-5135); *Torres Bermejas* (11 Calle Mesonero Romanos; phone: 532-3322); and, *Venta del Gato* (about 5 miles/8 km outside Madrid on the road to Burgos, 214 Avenida de Burgos; phone: 776-6060). *Café Central* (10 Plaza del Angel; phone: 468-0844) offers live music nightly (jazz, classical, salsa, or folk) as well as late dinner. Madrid's main hall for classical concerts is the new *Auditorio Nacional de Música* (146 Calle Príncipe de Vergara; phone: 337-0100), the home of the *Orquestra Nacional de España* and the *Coro Nacional de España* — the Spanish National Orchestra and the Spanish National Chorus. At present, the *Teatro Real,* formerly the city's premier concert hall, at Plaza de Oriente, is being converted into the *Teatro de la Opera,* scheduled to open late this year. Classical music also can be heard at several other locations, including the *Fundación Juan March* (77 Calle Castelló; phone: 435-4250). For a list of theaters presenting *zarzuela,* Spain's traditional form of operetta, see *Theater* above.

 NIGHTCLUBS AND NIGHTLIFE: Nightlife in Madrid can continue all night. Cover charges at cabarets and nightclubs include one drink, dancing, and floor shows that are becoming more risqué by the minute. Top choices include *Scala-Meliá Castilla* (43 Calle Capitán Haya; phone: 571-4411) and *Florida Park* (in the Parque del Retiro; phone: 573-7804). For a night of gambling, dining, dancing, and entertainment, the *Casino Gran Madrid* has it all (it's 20 minutes from downtown at Torrelodones, with free transportation from 6 Plaza de España; phone: 856-1100). The latest dance rage in Madrid is the *sevillanas. Madrileños* have adopted the delightful dance music of their Andalusian cousins as their own and, by popular demand, *sevillanas* music plays at many discos; dozens of *salas rocieras* — nightclubs dedicated to dancing and watching *sevillanas* — attract teens, married couples, and diplomats alike. Among the best are *El Portón* (25 Calle Lopez de Hoyos; phone: 262-4956), *Al Andalus* (19 Calle Capitán Haya; phone: 556-1439), *La Caseta* (13 Calle General Castaños; phone: 419-0343), and *Almonte* (35 Calle de Juan Bravo; phone: 411-6880). *La Maestranza* (16 Calle Mauricio Legendre, near Plaza de Castilla; phone: 315-9059) features star *sevillanas* performers in its floor shows and also serves outstanding Andalusian cuisine. Some discotheques and boîtes run two sessions a night, at 7 and 11 PM until the wee hours. Among the more popular are *Pachá* (11 Calle Barceló; phone: 446-0137) and *Joy Eslava* (11 Calle Arenal; phone: 266-3733), where ballroom dancing is now the fad. Striptease shows are the attraction at *Alazán* (24 Paseo de la Castellana; phone: 435-8948). There's late dining and an energetic downstairs disco at *Archy* (11 Calle Marqués de Riscal; phone: 308-2736), while the latest gathering spot for the glitterati is *Teatriz* (15 Calle Hermosilla; phone: 577-5379). The *Cervecería Alemana* (6 Plaza Santa Ana; phone: 429-7033), a tavern that's an old Hemingway hangout, remains a favorite nightspot. In the *Mercado Puerta de Toledo,* the *Café del Mercado* swings with late-night live jazz, and salsa dancing starts at 2 AM on weekends (1 Ronda de Toledo; phone: 265-8739); *Cock* (16 Calle Reina; no phone) draws an avant-garde set. *Madrileños* love to *pasear,* or stroll along the streets, and from April through October thousands of *terrazas* — outdoor cafés lining plazas, parks, and avenues — are jumping with nocturnal activity. Late revelers usually cap the evening with thick hot chocolate and *churros* at *Chocolatería de San Ginés* (in the alley behind San Ginés church), open all night.

BEST IN TOWN

 CHECKING IN: Modern Madrid boasts over 50,000 hotel rooms, with accommodations ranging from "grand luxe" to countless *hostales* and *pensiones.* Reservations are nonetheless recommended, especially between May and September and during such special events as national and local festivals, expositions, and conventions. And, because of the city's designation as this year's European Capital of Culture, accommodations will be at an even greater premium. Expect to pay $550 or more a night for a double room in a hotel listed as very expensive, from $170 to $300 in an establishment listed as expensive, from $65 to $160 in a moderately priced hotel, and $50 or less in an inexpensive one. All telephone numbers are in the 1 city code unless otherwise indicated.

Ritz – The epitome of elegance, luxury, and Belle Epoque grace, this impeccably maintained classic opened in 1910. It was built at the behest of King Alfonso XIII, and its construction and decoration were overseen by César Ritz himself. No two of the 156 air conditioned rooms and suites are alike, but all are adorned with paintings, antiques, and tailored handwoven carpeting from the Royal Tapestry Factory. Jacket-and-tie attire is appropriate for men in the bar and the exquisite *Ritz* restaurant, one of Madrid's finest (see *Eating Out*). The casual *Ritz Garden Terrace* also offers delightful dining, cocktails, and *tapas*. Business facilities include 24-hour room service, meeting rooms for up to 500, English-speaking concierge, foreign currency exchange, secretarial services in English, audiovisual equipment, photocopiers, computers, cable television news service, translation services, and express checkout. 5 Plaza de la Lealtad (phone: 521-2857; fax: 232-8776). Very expensive.

Santo Mauro – This exquisite addition to Madrid's supreme echelon of *gran lujo* hotels was inaugurated last year in what was originally the turn-of-the-century palatial mansion of the Duques de Santo Mauro, and later became the Philippine Embassy. Centrally located in the elegant Almagro-Castellana section, the French-style building was faithfully restored to its original style. The new interior decor, however, created by Madrid's hottest designers, is the last word in Art Deco. There are public salons and a stately patio-garden. Although there are only 36 rooms, mostly suites, all feature a compact disc and cassette stereo system and satellite TV (VCRs are available on request). Other facilities include 24-hour room service, a sauna, indoor swimming pool, summer terrace restaurant, and in the mansion's original library, the *Belagua* restaurant (see *Eating Out*). Business facilities include 24-hour room service, English-speaking concierge, foreign currency exchange, photocopiers, translation services, and express checkout. 36 Zurbano (phone: 319-6900; fax: 308-5417). Very expensive.

Villa Magna – Taken over by Hyatt hotels in 1990, this 194-room property has had a sterling reputation since its construction in the early 1970s. The modern, yet stately, building of glass and marble is set amid landscaped gardens in the heart of aristocratic Madrid. A multimillion-dollar remodeling project added unequaled luster — and technology — to the spacious, air conditioned rooms; high quality personal service enhances the hotel's casual elegance. The *Champagne Bar* boasts one of Europe's finest selections of bubbly beverages, and the, *Villa Magna* restaurant is celebrated for its imaginative specialties (see *Eating Out*). Richly decorated private salons accommodate meetings and banquets. Business facilities include 24-hour room service, meeting rooms for up to 250, English-speaking concierge, foreign currency exchange, secretarial services in English, audiovisual equipment, photocopiers, computers, cable television news service, translation services, and express checkout. 22 Paseo de la Castellana (phone: 578-2000; fax: 575-3158, for reservations; fax: 575-9504, to reach hotel guests). Very expensive.

Villa Real – Among Madrid's newer establishments, its design and atmosphere embody Old World grace; marble, bronze, and hand-crafted wood, works of fine art and antique furnishings create a seignorial interior decor. All 115 luxurious rooms and suites are air conditioned and feature satellite television sets, mini-bars, and 3 or more high-tech telephones. Elegantly furnished top-floor duplexes have 2 bathrooms — 1 with a sauna, the other with a Jacuzzi — and large private balconies overlooking the Spanish Parliament Palace, the Neptune Fountain, and the *Prado Museum's* Villahermosa Palace. There is 24-hour room service and a friendly, competent staff. The hotel's choice setting — between Paseo del Prado and Puerta del Sol — couldn't be better. Business facilities include 24-hour room service, meeting rooms for up to 300, English-speaking concierge, foreign currency exchange, secretarial services in English, audiovisual equipment, photocopiers, computers, cable television news service, translation services, and express checkout. 10-11 Plaza de la Cortes (phone: 420-3767). Very expensive to expensive.

Apart-Suites Foxá – Sparkling new and near the Chamartín train station and Plaza de Castilla, this apartment-style hostelry in two adjacent buildings features 282 well-furnished suites that accommodate up to four people (the separate living rooms have sofa beds). Breakfast is included in the room rate. Amenities include air conditioning, color TV sets, a parking garage, a restaurant, and a coffee shop. Business facilities include 24-hour room service, meeting rooms for up to 400, English-speaking concierge, foreign currency exchange, secretarial services in English, audiovisual equipment, photocopiers, computers, cable television news service, translation services, and express checkout. Foxá 25 and Foxá 32 (phone: 733-7064; fax: 314-1165). Expensive.

Apart-Suites Orense – Near the *Convention Center* and the Castellana, this modern apartment-style property, under the same management as the above *Apart-Suites Foxá*, has 141 suites with color TV sets, air conditioning, a restaurant, and a coffee shop. Business facilities include 24-hour room service, meeting rooms for up to 400, English-speaking concierge, foreign currency exchange, secretarial services in English, audiovisual equipment, photocopiers, computers, cable television news service, translation services, and express checkout. Orense 38 (phone: 597-1568; fax: 597-1295). Expensive.

Barajas – The raison d'être of this 230-room hotel is its proximity to Madrid's Barajas International Airport. All rooms are air conditioned and have color television sets. Guests can enjoy the garden swimming pool, bar, restaurant, and health club. Half-day rates are available for meetings or jet-lag therapy. Free transportation is provided to and from the airport terminals. Business facilities include 24-hour room service, meeting rooms for up to 675, English-speaking concierge, foreign currency exchange, secretarial services in English, audiovisual equipment, photocopiers, computers, cable television news service, translation services, and express checkout. 305 Avenida Logroño (phone: 747-7700). Expensive.

Castellana Inter-Continental – Opened in the early 1950s as the *Castellana Hilton,* this has been a traditional favorite of Americans traveling to Madrid for business or pleasure. Its 310 air conditioned rooms, all containing modern accoutrements, are large and nicely decorated in pleasant pastels. Adjacent to the stately, marble-pillared lobby are car rental, airline, and tour desks, boutiques, a health club, and a business services department. *Los Continentes* restaurant and *La Ronda* piano bar are pleasant for meeting and eating. Business facilities include 24-hour room service, meeting rooms for up to 350, English-speaking concierge, foreign currency exchange, secretarial services in English, audiovisual equipment, photocopiers, computers, cable television news service, translation services, and express checkout. 49 Paseo de la Castellana (phone: 410-0200; in the US, 800-327-5853; fax: 319-5853). Expensive.

Eurobuilding – An extremely well designed modern complex off the northern section of the Castellana near the *Convention Center* and *Estadio Santiago Bernabéu.* Within the complex, in addition to the 421-room hotel building, the *Eurobuilding 2* tower comprises 154 apartment-style units. All rooms and apartments are air conditioned. There also are 2 swimming pools, a health club, a hair salon, stores, and 4 restaurants. Business facilities include 24-hour room service, meeting rooms for up to 900, English-speaking concierge, foreign currency exchange, secretarial services in English, audiovisual equipment, photocopiers, computers, cable television news service, translation services, and express checkout. 23 Calle Padre Damián (phone: 457-1700). Expensive.

Holiday Inn Madrid – Typical of the US Holiday Inn chain, this modern and busy establishment with 344 air conditioned rooms, has a swimming pool, health club, gymnasium, shopping arcade, and restaurants. A perfect place for anyone who wants to be near the Azca shopping and commercial complex, the *Convention Center, Estadio Santiago Bernabéu,* and the Castellana. Business facilities include meeting rooms for up to 450, English-speaking concierge, foreign currency exchange, secretarial services in English, audiovisual equipment, photocopiers, computers, cable television news service, translation services, and express checkout. 4 Plaza Carlos Trías Bertrán (phone: 597-0102). Expensive.

Meliá Castilla – Nearly 1,000 air conditioned rooms in a modern high-rise just off the Castellana in northern Madrid's business section. Facilities and meeting rooms cater primarily to executive travelers. There also is a swimming pool, gymnasium, sauna, shopping arcade, several restaurants and bars, and the *Scala Meliá Castilla,* a Las Vegas–style nightclub. Business facilities include 24-hour room service, meeting rooms for up to 800, English-speaking concierge, foreign currency exchange, secretarial services in English, audiovisual equipment, photocopiers, computers, cable television news service, translation services, and express checkout. 43 Calle Capitán Haya (phone: 571-2211; fax: 571-2210). Expensive.

Meliá Madrid – Ideally located near the Plaza de España and very well run. The 266 air conditioned rooms in this gleaming white, modern building are tastefully decorated in various styles, and have color television sets. The dining room, grill, bar, and *Bong Bing* discotheque are popular meeting places. There also is a gymnasium, sauna, and conference facilities complete with state-of-the-art audiovisual equipment. Business facilities include 24-hour room service, meeting rooms for up to 380, English-speaking concierge, foreign currency exchange, secretarial services in English, audiovisual equipment, photocopiers, computers, cable television news service, translation services, and express checkout. 27 Calle Princesa (phone: 541-8200; fax: 541-1988). Expensive.

Miguel Angel – Conveniently located on Paseo de la Castellana, this 304-room property combines modern luxuries with classic decor; 17th-, 18th-, and 19th-century paintings, tapestries, and furniture decorate the lobby and suites. Most rooms have balconies, and all offer color television sets. Facilities include a health club, with sauna, Jacuzzi, gymnasium, and heated, indoor swimming pool. Guests can enjoy fine food at the *Florencia* restaurant, afternoon tea and cocktails at the *Bar Farnesio,* and dinner, dancing, and live entertainment at the *Boite Zacarías* restaurant. Business facilities include 24-hour room service, meeting rooms for up to 650, English-speaking concierge, foreign currency exchange, secretarial services in English, audiovisual equipment, photocopiers, computers, cable television news service, translation services, and express checkout. 31 Calle Miguel Angel (phone: 442-8199). Expensive.

Monte Real – Located in a tranquil residential district about 20 minutes from the city center, this luxurious establishment is near the *Puerta de Hierro Golf Club.* All 77 rooms are air conditioned and have color television sets. Facilities include a swimming pool, sauna, lovely gardens, a restaurant, and a bar. Business facilities include meeting rooms for up to 350, English-speaking concierge, foreign currency exchange, secretarial services in English, audiovisual equipment, photocopiers, computers, translation services, and express checkout. 17 Calle Arroyo del Fresno, Puerta de Hierro (phone: 316-2140). Expensive.

Palace – Inaugurated in 1920, this aristocratic Madrid landmark was, like the *Ritz,* built by personal order of King Alfonso XIII. Its Old World Belle Epoque elegance and decor are faithfully maintained, while the utmost of modern facilities makes for true luxury in the spacious 518 air conditioned rooms and suites. Located in the heart of the city, the hotel overlooks the Neptune Fountain and Paseo del Prado. The lobby, embellished with trompe l'oeil painting, leads to the elegant, cozy lounge, which is topped by an immense painted-glass rotunda — an inviting setting for cocktails or informal dining at *El Ambiqú,* with a musical backdrop of piano and violin until 2 AM.. A recent addition, on the ground floor, is the *Galería del Prado,* a collection of 38 fine boutiques, galleries, and shops, as well as *La*

Plaza, a self-service restaurant. Business facilities include 24-hour room service, meeting rooms for up to 1500, English-speaking concierge, foreign currency exchange, secretarial services in English, audiovisual equipment, photocopiers, computers, cable television news service, translation services, and express checkout. 7 Plaza de las Cortes (phone: 429-7551; fax: 429-8655). Expensive.

Wellington – Classic and nicely located in the Salamanca district, with fine boutiques, galleries, and the Parque del Retiro practically at the doorstep. The owner raised brave bulls; a stuffed triumphant one, named Cucharito, resides in the lounge amid the antique tapestries. Bullfighters, breeders, and aficionados stay and congregate here. All of the spacious 258 rooms are air conditioned, with color television sets. In summer, the outdoor swimming pool and the garden, with its restaurant, bar, and health club, are lively gathering spots. Business facilities include 24-hour room service, meeting rooms for up to 250, English-speaking concierge, foreign currency exchange, secretarial services in English, audiovisual equipment, photocopiers, computers, translation services, and express checkout. 8 Calle Velázquez (phone: 575-4400; fax: 576-4164). Expensive.

Suecia – Expansion of this Swedish-managed (hence its name) hotel has added modern rooms and suites within the same building, but the original ones are still well maintained and very comfortable. All 67 rooms, old and new, are air conditioned, with color television sets, mini-bars, and safes. Hemingway lived here, enjoying the great advantage of the location — on a quiet street just west of Paseo del Prado, around the corner from Calle de Alcalá. Smoked salmon and smorgasbord are main attractions in the *Bellman* restaurant. Business facilities include meeting rooms for up to 150, English-speaking concierge, foreign currency exchange, secretarial services in English, audiovisual equipment, computers, and translation services. 4 Calle Marqués de Casa Riera (phone: 531-6900; fax: 521-7141). Expensive to moderate.

Tryp Fénix – This Madrid aristocrat has been refurbished and reborn and once again is considered among the city's finest. Ideally situated on the tree-lined Castellana at Plaza de Colón, it has 216 air conditioned rooms and up-to-the-minute amenities enhanced by an air of sparkling elegance. Business facilities include 24-hour room service, meeting rooms for up to 200, English-speaking concierge, foreign currency exchange, secretarial services in English, audiovisual equipment, photocopiers, computers, translation services, and express checkout. 2 Calle Hermosilla (phone: 431-6700). Expensive to moderate.

Alcalá – Right on the north edge of Parque del Retiro and Plaza de la Independencia, in the genteel Salamanca district, it is within easy walking distance of fine shops and restaurants on Calle Serrano, as well as the *Prado* and other museums. All 153 air conditioned rooms have color television sets. The restaurant serves enticing Basque specialties. Business facilities include meeting rooms for up to 60, English-speaking concierge, foreign currency exchange, secretarial services in English, audiovisual equipment, photocopiers, computers, and translation services. 66 Calle de Alcalá (phone: 435-1060; fax: 435-1105). Moderate.

Arosa – Although it's on the bustling Gran Vía, it has the charm, peaceful mood, and personalized service of a small luxury establishment. The 126 air conditioned rooms, no two exactly alike, are tastefully decorated; luxurious bathrooms feature built-in hair dryers, fabulous showers in the bathtubs, and other treats, such as soothing bath salts. The atmosphere is delightful in the bar, lounge, and restaurant. Doormen at the small, elegant side-street entrance know guests by name. Business facilities include English-speaking concierge, foreign currency exchange, and translation services. 21 Calle de la Salud (phone: 532-1600; fax: 531-3127). Moderate.

Carlton – A complete renovation has raised the comfort level here. In a unique location — the southern part of central Madrid — it is near the Atocha train station complex, as well as within easy walking distance of the *National Museum Queen Sofía Art Center* and, a little farther north, the Botanical Gardens and the *Prado*. All of the 133 air conditioned rooms have color television sets. Business facilities include 24-hour room service, meeting rooms for up to 200, English-speaking concierge, foreign currency exchange, secretarial services in English, audiovisual equipment, photocopiers, computers, and translation services. 26 Paseo de las Delicias (phone: 239-7100; fax: 227-8510). Moderate.

Chamartín – The single advantage of this 378-room property is the fact that it is located within the modern Chamartín train station complex at the north end of the city. All rooms are air conditioned, have color television sets, and offer excellent views. Business facilities include meeting rooms for up to 525, English-speaking concierge, foreign currency exchange, secretarial services in English, audiovisual equipment, photocopiers, translation services, and express checkout. Estación de Chamartín (phone: 733-7011). Moderate.

Emperador – Centrally located right on the Gran Vía. All 232 rooms are air conditioned and have color television sets. Unusual among the many hotels in the immediate area, it boasts a rooftop garden with a swimming pool and excellent views of the city. Business facilities include 24-hour room service, meeting rooms for up to 200, English-speaking concierge, foreign currency exchange, secretarial services in English, audiovisual equipment, photocopiers, computers, and translation services. 53 Gran Vía (phone: 413-6511). Moderate.

Escultor – Conveniently located near the Castellana in a quiet residential area, its 82 air conditioned, apartment-style units offer separate sitting rooms with color television sets, complete kitchens, and mini-bars. Business facilities include meeting rooms for up to 250, English-speaking concierge, foreign currency exchange, secretarial services in English, audiovisual equipment, photocopiers, computers, and translation services. 5 Calle Miguel Angel (phone: 410-4203). Moderate.

Mayorazgo – Excellent service and 200 well-appointed, comfortable, air conditioned rooms just a step from the central Gran Vía. The decor provides a retreat to a pleasant Castilian past. Business facilities include meeting rooms for up to 300, English-speaking concierge, foreign currency exchange, secretarial services in English, audiovisual equipment, photocopiers, computers, and translation services. 3 Calle Flor Baja (phone: 247-2600; fax: 541-2485). Moderate.

Plaza – Located within the gigantic Edificio España landmark building of the early 1950s, this hotel with 306 rooms (all air conditioned) is usually swarming with tour groups. The 26th-floor swimming pool and terrace restaurant offer marvelous panoramic views of the city. Business facilities include 24-hour room service, meeting rooms for up to 500, English-speaking concierge, foreign currency exchange, secretarial services in English, audiovisual equipment, photocopiers, computers, and translation services. 2 Plaza de España (phone: 247-1200). Moderate.

Reina Victoria – After acquisition by the Tryp hotel chain and a total remodeling of its interior in 1990, this Madrid classic is once again worthy of its royal namesake (wife of King Alfonso XIII and grandmother of the present King Juan Carlos). Built in 1923 and designated a building of National Historic Interest, its unaltered 6-story façade, elaborate with pilasters, turrets, wrought-iron balconies, and bay windows, dominates the entire west side of the picturesque Plaza Santa Ana, a prime Old Madrid location. The 201 rooms and suites all have modern amenities (at less than regal prices). The *Bar Taurino* revives the hotel's decades-old tradition as a rendezvous for bullfighters, breeders, and aficionados. Business facilities include meeting rooms for up to 500, English-speaking concierge, foreign currency exchange, secretarial services in English, audiovisual equipment, photocopiers, computers, and translation services. 14 Plaza Santa Ana (phone: 531-4500). Moderate.

Serrano – Small and tasteful, refined and immaculate, on a quiet street between the

Castellana and the boutique-lined Calle Serrano. Its marble-floored lobby is comfortably furnished and richly decorated with antiques (including a large 17th-century tapestry) and huge arrangements of fresh flowers. All 34 rooms are air conditioned and have color television sets. No restaurant, but snacks and sandwiches are available at the bar. Business facilities include English-speaking concierge, foreign currency exchange, and translation services. 8 Calle Marqués de Villamejor (phone: 435-5200). Moderate.

Tryp Ambassador – This restored 6-story noble mansion was converted into a fine 181-room hotel only recently. It has all the latest conveniences, and its unique location, close to the *Teatro Real* opera house, and also to Plaza de Oriente and the Royal Palace, makes it especially appealing. The restaurant serves Spanish and international fare. Business facilities include 24-hour room service, meeting rooms for up to 290, English-speaking concierge, foreign currency exchange, secretarial services in English, audiovisual equipment, photocopiers, computers, translation services, and express checkout. 5 Cuesta Santo Domingo (phone: 541-6700) Moderate.

Carlos V – Conveniently located, with 67 air conditioned rooms, right in the lively pedestrian area between the Gran Vía and Puerta del Sol, near the Convento de las Descalzas Reales and *El Corte Inglés* department store. Business facilities include English-speaking concierge and foreign currency exchange. 5 Calle Maestra Vitoria (phone: 531-4100; fax: 531-3761). Moderate to inexpensive.

Don Diego – A well-kept *pensión* near the Parque del Retiro in Madrid's lovely Salamanca district. The 58 rooms are nicely furnished, and several have ample balconies. There is a television lounge and a bar that serves sandwiches and breakfast. 45 Calle Velázquez (phone: 435-0760). Moderate to inexpensive.

Galiano – A converted mansion, complete with marble floors, antique paintings, tapestries, and carved-wood furniture in the lobby and lounge. On a tranquil side street just off the Castellana and Plaza de Colón, it has 29 comfortable singles, doubles, and suites. Breakfast and color television sets are optional. There is an English-speaking concierge. 6 Calle Alcalá Galiano (phone: 319-2000). Moderate to inexpensive.

Puerta de Toledo – Away from major hotel clusters, it is located on the fringe of picturesque Old Madrid, facing the Triumphal Arch of the Puerta de Toledo and near the new Mercado Puerta de Toledo. Its 160 rooms are air conditioned, comfortable, and well maintained. 4 Glorieta Puerta de Toledo (phone: 474-7100). Moderate to inexpensive.

Jamic – A small pension centrally located across the street from the *Palace* hotel and near the *Prado*. 4 Plaza de las Cortes (phone: 429-0068). Inexpensive.

Lisboa – This well run residential *hostal* has 23 rooms, all with private baths and telephones, plus maid service, a television lounge, and an elevator. The location is terrific: just off the Plaza Santa Ana in charming Old Madrid, yet a short walk to the *Palace*, the *Ritz*, and the *Prado*. English is spoken and credit cards are accepted. Fine restaurants of all price ranges line the street. 17 Calle Ventura de la Vega (phone: 429-9894). Inexpensive.

 EATING OUT: *Madrileños* eat the main meal of their day during the work break from 2 to 4 PM. An early-evening snack (*merienda*), such as wine and those typically Spanish tidbits called *tapas, chocolate con churros,* or coffee and sweets takes the edge off appetites until a light supper is eaten after 10 PM. For those who can't adjust to the Spanish schedule, there are always *cafeterías* and snack bars, and many restaurants start serving dinner at about 8:30 PM to accommodate non-Spaniards. Restaurants listed below as very expensive will charge $175 or more for a dinner for two with wine; similar fare will cost $90 to $150 at restaurants listed as expensive, between $40 and $80 at moderate eateries, and $35 or less at inexpensive ones. Most restaurants offer a set menu (*menú del día*), a complete meal for an economical price. Some restaurants include the 6% Value Added Tax in their menu prices. Check beforehand whether the menu says *IVA incluido* or *IVA no incluido.* All telephone numbers are in the 1 city code unless otherwise indicated.

Horcher – Operated for generations by the Horcher family, this remains one of Madrid's most elegant dining places, serving continental fare with an Austro-Hungarian flavor. Dining here is an indulgence that should include such delicacies as *chuletas de ternasco a la castellana* (baby lamb chops), endive salad (with truffles), and crêpes Sir Holten for dessert. Diners might even try the classic goulash. Closed Sundays. Reservations are necessary for lunch and dinner. American Express, Visa, and Diners Club accepted. 6 Calle Alfonso XII (phone: 522-0731). Very expensive.

Jockey – A Madrid classic, intimate and elegant, and a recipient of the National Gastronomy Award. The continental cuisine is superb, as are traditional dishes such as *cocido madrileño,* a multifaceted savory stew, the broth of which is served as a side dish. Other specialties include *perdiz española* (partridge), *lomo de lubina* (filet of sea bass), and *mousse de anguila* (eel mousse). Closed Sundays and August. Reservations necessary. Major credit cards accepted. 6 Calle Amador de los Ríos (phone: 319-1003). Very expensive.

Ritz – The sumptuous restaurant of the luxurious *Ritz* hotel, serving French cuisine befitting the Limoges dinnerware and Louis XV silver service. Chamber music adds to the regal rapture. Open daily for breakfast, lunch, and dinner. Reservations necessary. Major credit cards accepted. (The separate *Ritz Garden-Terrace* offers more casual dining, or simply afternoon tea or *tapas.*) 5 Plaza de la Lealtad (phone: 521-2857). Very expensive.

Villa Magna – The remodeling of Madrid's *Villa Magna* hotel has placed its restaurant among the city's finest. Cristóbal Blanco, the prize-winning chef, designs such nouvelle delicacies as grilled scallops with caviar in basil sauce, while the china on which they are served was designed by Paloma Picasso. The *Champagne Bar* dispenses 252 French and Spanish vintages. (By the way, those precious place settings — plates plus silverware — cost $600 each, so be careful!) Open for breakfast, lunch, and dinner. Reservations necessary. Major credit cards accepted. 22 Paseo de la Castellana (phone: 261-4900). Very expensive.

Zalacaín – Probably the finest restaurant in all of Spain, it was the first in the country to win three Michelin stars and still shares that honor only with *Arzak,* in San Sebastián. It serves highly imaginative Basque and French haute cuisines, particularly seafood, and the service — by loyal employees who adore owner Jesús Oyarbide — is perfection. Luxurious decor, gleaming silverware and glasses, fresh flowers, and an irresistible dessert cart all contribute to the dining experience. Closed Saturdays for lunch, Sundays, August, *Easter Week,* and holidays. Reservations necessary (call at least 2 days in advance). American Express, Visa, and Diners Club accepted. 4 Calle Alvarez de Baena (phone: 261-4840). Very expensive.

La Basílica – Once an old baroque church, this is now a baroque and elegant restaurant. Sophisticates enjoy international, nouvelle, and Spanish cuisines in the see-and-be-seen main dining room or in secluded alcoves. It's located on a narrow street in Old Madrid, near Plaza Mayor. Closed Saturdays at lunch and all day Sundays. Reservations essential. Major credit cards accepted. 12 Calle de la Bolsa (phone: 521-8623). Expensive.

Belagua – When it reopened last year in the new *Santo Mauro* hotel, this renowned eatery already had an elite *madrileño* following from its previous location in the *Sanvy* hotel. The same Basque-Navarre fare that has long attracted locals is served in the sophisticated atmosphere of the restored library of a turn-of-the-century French palatial mansion, redecorated in glowing Art Deco. Traditional specialties include monkfish and spider crab stew, entrées with oxtail, pig's feet, lobster, or blood sausage, not to mention the exquisite desserts. Open daily; Sundays exclusively for hotel guests. Reservations advised. Major credit cards accepted. 36 Zurbano (phone: 319-6900). Expensive.

Cabo Mayor – The owner and chef both have won the National Gastronomy Award, and for good reason: Their fresh seafood from the province of Santander is imaginatively prepared, and the vegetable dishes are superlative. If it's on the menu, try the *cigalas y langostinos con verduras al jerez sibarita* (crayfish and prawns with green vegetables in sherry sauce). Closed Sundays, the last 2 weeks of August, *Christmas Week, New Year's Week,* and *Easter Week.* Reservations advised. American Express, Diners Club, and Visa accepted. 37 Calle Juan Ramón Jiménez (phone: 250-8776). Expensive.

El Cenador del Prado – Favored by aficionados of nouvelle cuisine and artistically decorated in a style reminiscent of an elegant conservatory, allowing indoor dining under the stars. Try *patatas a la importancia con almejas* (potatoes with clams) or the *pato al vinagre de frambuesas* (duck with raspberry vinegar). Politicians from the nearby Spanish Parliament may be at the next table. Closed for lunch on Saturdays and all day Sundays. Reservations necessary. Major credit cards accepted. 4 Calle del Prado (phone: 429-1561). Expensive.

La Dorada – Fresh seafood of every imaginable variety is flown in daily from the Mediterranean to this mammoth establishment, which serves Andalusian fare. (There also are two *Doradas* in Seville, one in Barcelona, Marbella, and another in Paris.) Particularly noteworthy is the fish baked in a crust of salt, an Andalusian practice that results, surprisingly, in a dish that's not salty. Closed Sundays and August. Reservations are essential, as this place is always crowded — and you'll enjoy the food even more if you reserve one of the private dining rooms. Major credit cards accepted. 64-66 Calle Orense (phone: 270-2002). Expensive.

Fortuny – Relatively recent on Madrid's restaurant scene, it soon established its place among the preferred, with outstanding international haute cuisine. Housed in an aristocratic 19th-century mansion, it offers private dining rooms for banquets or intimacy. There also is a terrace with a waterfall, for outdoor summer dining. Closed Sundays and holidays. Reservations necessary. Major credit cards accepted. 34 Calle Fortuny (phone: 308-3268). Expensive.

La Gamella – The owner-chef-host is Richard Stephens, an American who also is an instructor at Madrid's Alambique School of Gastronomy. His intimate restaurant here, in the building in which philosopher José Ortega y Gasset was born, is dedicated to new Spanish cuisine — and it's one of Madrid's best. The creative appetizers and main dishes — try the *pastel de chorizo fresco y pimientos rojos* (Spanish sausage and red pepper quiche), the irresistible desserts, and the fine wine list add up to an adventure in taste, and the *colorista* design and art of the decor enhance the experience. A private dining room downstairs seats 10. Closed Sundays, holidays, and August. Reservations advised. Major credit cards accepted. 4 Calle Alfonso XII (phone: 532-4509). Expensive.

Gure-Etxea – One of the best for Basque dishes in Madrid, serving specialties such as *porrusalda* (leek and potato soup with cod) and a variety of fish dishes. Both the atmosphere and the service are pleasant. Closed Sundays and August. Reservations advised. American Express and Visa accepted. 12 Plaza de la Paja (phone: 265-6149). Expensive.

Lhardy – A *madrileño* institution since 1839, and the decor, atmosphere, and table settings haven't changed much since then. One specialty in the upstairs dining rooms and private salons is *cocido madrileño,* the typical stew. At *merienda* time in the late afternoon, the street-entrance restaurant and stand-up bar fill with regulars who serve themselves the *caldo* (broth) of the *cocido* from a silver tureen, and also enjoy finger sandwiches, canapés, cold cuts, pastries, cocktails, or coffee. Closed Sunday and holiday evenings and the month of August. Reservations essential for the private dining rooms. Major credit cards accepted. Carrera de San Jerónimo (phone: 521-3385). Expensive.

O'Pazo – The morning catch from the Cantabrian Sea — lobster, hake, turbot, endemic sea bass, and varieties of shellfish — is flown in wiggling fresh and prepared with loving care to delight the clientele, who fill the place for both lunch and dinner. Closed Sundays and August. Reservations advised. MasterCard and Visa accepted. 20 Calle Reina Mercedes (phone: 253-2333). Expensive.

Paradís Madrid – Barcelona's well-known eatery opened a branch here last year (after establishing one in New York City) in a turn-of-the-century mansion alongside Plaza de las Cortes. The menu is primarily Catalán-Mediterranean — mushrooms served in several delicious ways (one stuffed with duck liver), five variations of *bacalao* (cod), and a "catch of the day." A separate menu entitled "Homage to the Great Chefs" features original dishes of illustrious Basque (Juan Mari Arzak) and Catalán (Santi Santamaría) chefs. For *tapas* and typical Catalán *pan con tomate* (bread spread with tomato), the *Bodiguilla* bar serves until 1:30 AM. Closed for Sunday dinner. Reservations advised. Major credit cards accepted. 14 Marqués de Cubas (phone: 429-7303). Expensive.

Platerías – Its intimate low-key elegance in the heart of Old Madrid creates a pleasant atmosphere for enjoying authentic Spanish dishes, such as *callos madrileños* (succulent tripe, Madrid style), *chipirones* (cuttlefish in its own ink), and remarkable vegetable plates. Closed Sundays. Reservations advised. Major credit cards accepted. 11 Plaza Santa Ana (phone: 429-7048). Expensive.

Príncipe de Viana – Fine seasonal Basque-Navarrese specialties are served in a relaxed, elegant atmosphere. Closed Saturdays for lunch, Sundays, and from mid-August through the first week of September. Reservations advised. American Express and Visa accepted. 5 Calle Manuel de Falla (phone: 259-1448). Expensive.

La Trainera – Another favorite of seafood lovers. The owner prizes his flown-in catch and serves fish and shellfish as nature intended. No fishing village in the world can compete with the grilled sole served here. Closed Sundays and August. Reservations advised. MasterCard and Visa accepted. 60 Calle Lagasca (phone: 276-8035). Expensive.

Café de Oriente – Anything from *tapas* to French haute cuisine can be enjoyed here in a delightful *madrileño* atmosphere. It is an ideal place for afternoon tea or cocktails at a sidewalk table overlooking the square and the Royal Palace or inside the café (reservations unnecessary); for fine Castilian dining downstairs in the vaulted 17th-century Sala Capitular de San Gil (reservations advised); or for superb French-Basque cuisine in the adjacent restaurant (reservations advised) or one of the private dining rooms frequented by royalty and diplomats (reservations essential). Closed Mondays for lunch, Sundays, and August. Major credit cards accepted. 2 Plaza de Oriente (phone: 247-1564). Expensive to moderate.

El Abanico Gastronómico – The "Gastronomic Fan" is a combination restaurant and food shop located within the *Mercado Puerta de Toledo* (see *Special Places*). Regional cuisines, wines, and delicacies from all over Spain are the stock in trade. Open from 11:30 AM to midnight; closed Mondays. Reservations unnecessary. No credit cards accepted. 1 Ronda de Toledo (phone: 576-0009). Moderate.

Antigua Casa Sobrino de Botín – Also known as *Casa Botín,* this is one of Madrid's oldest restaurants — founded in 1725. It is famous for its Castilian-style roast suckling pig and baby lamb, one of which is usually featured on the *menú del día*. Lunch and dinner each seem to fall into two "shifts," with the early-eating tourists first, followed by *madrileños,* whose normal dining hours are after 2 and 9 PM, respectively. Open daily. Reservations unnecessary. Major credit cards accepted. 17 Calle Cuchilleros (phone: 266-4217). Moderate.

Café Gijón – This 100-year-old Madrid institution is a traditional meeting and greeting place for intellectuals and artists, who gather here to enjoy good food and conversation. During the summer, the sidewalk café is one of the city's liveliest. Open daily. No reservations. Visa and MasterCard accepted. 21 Paseo de Recoletos (phone: 532-5425). Moderate.

El Callejón – A bust of Hemingway and walls chockablock with celebrity photos attest to those who have enjoyed the friendly atmosphere and home-cooked food here in the past. An informal Old Madrid place, it serves a different regional specialty each day of the week, but *callos madrileños* is always on the menu, and *tapas* abound. Open daily. Reservations unnecessary. Major credit cards accepted. 6 Calle Ternera (phone: 531-9195). Moderate.

Casa Lucio – This casual restaurant has become an institution among the elite (and that includes members of the royal family), who enjoy fine Spanish food — especially seafood. Its location in Old Madrid adds to the flavor. Closed Saturdays for lunch and during August. Reservations essential. American Express and Visa accepted. 35 Calle Cava Baja (phone: 265-3252). Moderate.

Casa Paco – The steaks served in this old tavern are excellent. Other specialties include typical *madrileño* dishes. Closed Sundays and August. No reservations. Visa accepted. 11 Calle Puerta Cerrada (phone: 266-3166). Moderate.

La Chata – This totally typical *mesón* bears the nickname of Madrid's adored Infanta Isabel (the only child of Queen Isabel II), who is depicted on the wonderful hand-painted tile façade by artist Eduardo Fernández. Delicious morsels are served at the *tapas* bar, and the small restaurant specializes in roast suckling pig and lamb dishes. Closed Sunday evenings and Wednesdays. No reservations or credit cards accepted. 25 Calle Cava Baja (phone: 266-1458). Moderate.

El Cuchi – The Spanish link of Mexico's famous *Carlos 'n' Charlie's* chain, with specialties of both worlds served by a gregarious staff. It's casual, and jammed with humorous paraphernalia. One of its claims to fame: "Hemingway never ate here." Open daily. Reservations unnecessary. Major credit cards accepted. 3 Calle Cuchilleros (phone: 255-4424). Moderate.

Los Galayos – A typical tavern serving fine Castilian roast suckling pig and lamb, with a *tapas* bar and an outdoor café right alongside the Plaza Mayor. Open daily. Reservations unnecessary. Major credit cards accepted. 1 Plaza Mayor (phone: 265-6222). Moderate.

La Galette – Outstanding vegetarian and non-vegetarian dishes and Viennese pastries are served in a delightful atmosphere at a good location in the elegant Salamanca district. Its popularity makes reservations essential. Closed Sundays. MasterCard and Visa accepted. 11 Calle Conde de Aranda (phone: 276-0641). Moderate.

El Ingenio – This unpretentious, family-run restaurant is decorated with Don Quixote and Sancho Panza memorabilia, and its menu delights diners who fall into either category of physique. The seafood is impeccably fresh since it is flown in from the Bay of Biscay, and the pork, lamb, and beef are all locally farm-grown. Closed Sundays and holidays. Reservations unnecessary. Major credit cards accepted. Just off the Plaza de España at 10 Calle Leganitos (phone: 541-9133). Moderate.

La Maestranza – Andalusian in its cooking, atmosphere, and decor, with great *sevillanas* music groups playing for professional dancers and the customers who know this Andalusian folk dance, which has become Madrid's latest rage. Closed Sundays. Reservations advised. Major credit cards accepted. 16 Calle Mauricio Legendre (phone: 315-9059). Moderate.

El Mentidero de la Villa – Inventive French cuisine by Japanese chef Ken Sato, in a delightful modern-art decor. Specialties include *rollo de primavera con puerros y gambas* (spring rolls with leeks and shrimp). Closed Sundays. Reservations advised. Major credit cards accepted. 6 Calle Santo Tomé (phone: 419-5506). Moderate.

La Mesa Redonda – A small eatery on one of Old Madrid's most charming little streets. Its American owners serve the best *Thanksgiving* dinner in town. Other specialties include beef bourguignon and stews. Dinner only; closed Sundays. Reservations unnecessary (except for *Thanksgiving*). No credit cards accepted. 17 Calle Nuncio (phone: 265-0289). Moderate.

La Plaza – Within the sparkling new *Galería del Prado* at the *Palace* hotel, amid the exquisite boutiques and galleries, this combination buffet-style and self-service restaurant dispenses enticing salads, entrées, and pastries. Serve yourself a multi-course meal or just a snack, to eat in a choice of surrounding settings. The adjacent bar serves cocktails and coffee. Closed Sundays. No reservations or credit cards accepted. 7 Plaza de las Cortes (phone: 429-7551). Moderate.

Posada de la Villa – Although the 3-story building is relatively new, this authentic eatery dates back to 1642, when it was originally a *posada* (inn) for out-of-towners. It has retained its tradition of hospitality and still offers fine typical dishes such as *cocido madrileño* and roast pig and lamb. Closed Sunday evenings. Reservations unnecessary. Major credit cards accepted. 9 Calle Cava Baja (phone: 266-1860). Moderate.

La Quinta del Sordo – The façade of this award-winning restaurant is adorned with fine hand-painted tile mosaics. Its name means "house of the deaf man," referring to the place where Goya lived in Madrid. Reproductions of Goya art and memorabilia add to the decor. An array of fine Castilian dishes offers memorable dining in a pleasant atmosphere. Closed Sunday evenings. Reservations unnecessary. Major credit cards accepted. 10 Calle Sacramento (phone: 248-1852). Moderate.

Riazor – An unpretentious turn-of-the-century establishment with a cordial atmosphere, fine traditional fare, and a cornucopia of hot and cold *tapas* served with verve at the bar. The upstairs dining room has panels adjustable to fit a size range of banquet parties. Open daily. Reservations unnecessary, except for groups. Visa accepted. Located 1 short block south of Plaza Mayor at 19 Calle Toledo (phone: 266-5466). Moderate.

Taberna del Alabardero – A Madrid classic, this was the tavern of the Royal Palace guards (*alabardero* means "halberdier," or a soldier armed with a halberd — a 15th- and 16th-century weapon combining a pike and an ax). There is a wonderful *tapas* bar, and succulent Spanish and Basque dishes are served in cozy dining rooms reminiscent of 19th-century Madrid. Open for lunch and dinner daily. Reservations unnecessary. Major credit cards accepted. (Father Lezama, the famous and popular Basque priest-restaurateur-owner, also has a version of this restaurant in Washington, DC.) 6 Calle Felipe V (phone: 541-5192). Moderate.

Foster's Hollywood – It's a *restaurante americano*, complete with a variety of hamburgers and barbecued spareribs. But far from being a *yanqui* fast-food joint, this small chain of pleasant restaurants offers good service and atmosphere. Open daily at all locations. No reservations. Major credit cards accepted. Several locations: 1 Calle Magallanes (phone: 488-9165); 3 Calle Apolonio Morales (phone: 457-7911); 1 Calle Tamayo y Baus (phone: 231-5115); 16 Calle del Cristo (phone: 638-6791); 14-16 Avenida de Brasil (phone: 455-1688); 80 Calle Velázquez (phone: 435-6128); and 100 Calle Guzmán el Bueno (phone: 234-4923). Inexpensive.

El Granero de Lavapiés – Good vegetarian food in one of Old Madrid's most typical neighborhoods. No reservations or credit cards accepted. 10 Calle Argumosa (phone: 467-7611). Inexpensive.

Mesón Museo del Jamón – Any restaurant with 4,000 hams dangling from its ceiling and draping its walls deserves the name "Ham Museum," and there are four such pork paradises in central Madrid. Fine hams from the regions of Jabugo, Murcia, Salamanca, and Extremadura are served in various ways, including sandwiches, at the stand-up bars and at dining tables. Also featured are an array of cheeses, a great deli, and roast chicken. Any dish can also be prepared to take out. No reservations or credit cards accepted. 6 Carrera San Jerónimo (phone: 521-0340); 72 Gran Vía (phone: 541-2023); 44 Paseo del Prado (phone: 230-4385); and 54 Calle Atocha (phone: 227-0716). Inexpensive.

La Salsería – Befitting its name, this small bar with an outdoor café specializes in sauces — 15 kinds, served in the holes of a conveniently held artist's palette, in the center of which are ruffled fried potatoes for dipping. Try *spaghetti a la siciliana* as well. Closed Mondays. No reservations or credit cards accepted. Across the traffic circle from the Mercado Puerta de Toledo. 2 Calle Ronda de Toledo (phone: 266-0890). Inexpensive.

Taberna de Antonio Sánchez – Genuinely typical of Old Madrid, it has been a venerated favorite ever since it was founded by a legendary bullfighter more than 150 years ago. The small, unpretentious dining rooms are charming, the realm of wonderful food — seafood, Spanish cuisine, salads, and desserts — served with care. Closed Sunday evenings. No reservations. Visa accepted. 13 Calle Mesón de Paredes (phone: 239-7826). Inexpensive.

 TAPAS BARS: The uniquely Spanish snacks known as *tapas* probably originated in Seville, when a slice of ham or a piece of bread was discovered to be a convenient *tapa* (lid) to keep flies out of a glass of wine. Today, the drink departs little from the time-tested standard, but the inventiveness of the Spanish chef knows no bounds when it comes to *tapas*. The definition embraces everything from a little plate of green olives through an array of cheeses, sausages, hams, seafood, eggs, and vegetables that have been sliced, diced, wrapped, filled, marinated, sauced, sautéed, or otherwise cooked for hot or cold consumption, to a variety of tidbits swallowed raw and naked as nature made them. *El tapeo* (enjoying *tapas*) is a way of life in Spain, especially in Madrid, where there are literally thousands of places to do so. Practically every bar (not to be confused with pubs or *bares americanos,* which are for drinks only) serves *tapas,* as do *tabernas, mesones, tascas, cervecerías,* and even *cafeterías.* And most establishments specializing in *tapas* also have a few tables or even dining rooms in addition to their stand-up bar. Toothpicks and fingers are the most common utensils; shrimp, langoustine, mussel, and clam shells, olive pits, napkins, and almost everything else are dropped on the floor, which is swept and scoured after each surge (from 1 to 3 PM and 7 to 9 PM, more or less — usually more).

A *chato* (glass of wine) or *caña* (draft beer) customarily is served with a free *tapita.* If you want more and if the vast array of *tapas* on display is overwhelming, just point to what you want. If you prefer a larger portion, ask for a *ración,* which can be a small meal in itself. Don't pay until you've completely finished; the bartender probably will remember everything you consumed, even if you don't. He'll deliver your change on a saucer; leave a few *duros* (5-peseta coins) as a tip, and always say *gracias* and *adiós* when you depart.

Tapas bar hopping is at its best in the central and old sections of Madrid. One of the city's best is *La Trucha* (with two locations, both just off Plaza Santa Ana: 3 Calle Manuel Fernández y González; phone: 259-1448; and 6 Calle Nuñez de Arce; phone: 532-0882). They're jammed at *tapa* time, and with good reason: Everything from bull tails to succulent red pimentos, as well as *trucha* (trout), is served with gusto (closed Sunday nights, and they take turns for July and August vacations). Nearby, the *Cervecería Alemana* (6 Plaza Santa Ana; phone: 429-7033) is, despite its name ("German Beer Parlor"), thoroughly *madrileño,* which is why the ubiquitous Hemingway frequented it and artists, intellectuals, and students continue to flock here. Among the *tapas* are good hams, sausages, and cheeses (closed Tuesdays and August). Around Puerta del Sol are *Casa Labra* (12 Calle Tetuán; phone: 532-1405), which was founded in 1860 and has been jam-packed ever since — among the specialties is fluff-fried *bacalao* (cod) that melts in the mouth, and *Mejillonería El Pasaje* (3 Pasaje de Matheu; phone: 521-5155), which deals in mussels exclusively, fresh from Galicia, served in any quantity, and prepared in various delicious ways. *La Torre del Oro* (26 Plaza Mayor; phone: 266-5016) is a lively Andalusian bar appropriately decorated with stunning bullfight photos and memorabilia (including a mounted earless bull's head), with recorded *sevillanas* music adding to the ambience; the *tapas* include such delicacies as baby eels and fresh anchovies, fried or marinated. In the same vicinity, *Valle del Tietar* (5 Calle Ciudad Rodrigo; phone: 248-0511), in the northwest arcade entrance to the plaza, offers *tapas,* Avila style, with suckling pig and kid specialties, while *El Oso y el Madroño* (4 Calle de la Bolsa; phone: 532-1377) is as *madrileño* as its name, which refers to the "bear and the madrona tree" on the city's coat of arms; the nonstop hand-cranked hurdy-gurdy and jovial local clientele make for authentic atmosphere. *El Shotis* (11 Calle Cava Baja; phone: 265-3230) is south of Plaza Mayor. Named after Madrid's traditional 19th-century couple's dance (which you'll hear playing on the jukebox, this unpretentious tavern is as typical as can be (closed Mondays and August). Elsewhere, there's *Monje Cervecería* (21 Calle del Arenal; phone: 248-3598), a showcase of fresh seafood, and lamb sweetbreads as well, and *La Mi Venta* (7 Plaza Marina Española; phone: 248-5091), where a friendly neighborhood atmosphere prevails and fine hot and cold *tapas* and *raciones* are served, with select hams as the specialty. At *Bocaito* (6 Calle Libertad; phone: 532-1219), north of the Gran Vía and Calle de Alcalá, animated *tapas* makers behind the bar prepare a limitless selection of outstanding treats, and giant Talavera ceramic plates on the walls are painted with fine reproductions of Goya's "Wine Harvest." Adjacent is a deli and small dining room with communal tables.

MARSEILLES

Some cities pass through a chrysalis stage as important ports before they emerge into greatness as commercial centers or industrial powers. Not so Marseilles. As it has been for 25 centuries, since before the Greeks controlled the wine-dark seas of the Mediterranean, modern Marseilles is above all else a port city. In 600 BC, Phocaean Greeks from Asia Minor founded the city, calling it Massalia, and then, as now, it acted as port of entry for goods, people, ideas, and most of all, history. (A commemorative block near Marseilles's thriving Vieux Port proclaims with perfect accuracy and stunning lack of modesty: "They founded Marseilles, from which civilization reached the West.")

With a population just brushing 900,000, Marseilles is France's second-largest city. But that may say more about the importance of the Mediterranean to France than of France's influence on Marseilles. Landlocked Paris, so gay in springtime and so gray in winter, is another country, 500 miles away, every mile of which must be traveled on land. It is a journey that traditional Marseillais, otherwise so effusive and warm, are reluctant to make. Marseilles and its people face steadfastly toward the sea, from which they have always drawn such strength.

When the city provisioned the Crusaders and welcomed back their booty, it was trading with Africa, the Near East, and the Far East. Today the names have changed, but France's major port does business with the same countries, and a lot more besides. Marseillais have as much in common with Italians and Greeks — fellow Mediterraneans — as they do with Parisians.

Unlike Paris, which has become predictable and bourgeois by comparison, Marseilles is France's connection to the sensuous, boisterous world of the Mediterranean. Sailors from all over the world roam the Canebière, the famous street leading up from the Vieux Port (Old Port), in search of women, excitement, or perhaps a little bit of smuggling on the side on their next tour of duty. And frequently violence still erupts, as it did in the gangland murder at the *Bar du Téléphone* not too many years ago. The milieu of the French underworld endures as a presence, for Marseilles remains, as both Interpol and Hollywood would have it, "the French connection." Even though many of the drug middlemen have moved on to Amsterdam or Berlin, Gene Hackman still would recognize the place. But an odd question lingers: Do we consider port cities wicked because of Marseilles, or do we feel such thrilling wickedness in Marseilles because it is so much the port city of our dreams?

As in all great port cities, numerous foreigners and immigrants have settled in Marseilles — particularly industrial workers from the island of Corsica and a large number of North Africans. Often poor, many Algerians, Tunisians, and Moroccans live in slums around the Porte d'Aix and the Rue Ste.-Barbe, where shops sell inexpensive North African items, but where few people feel comfortable wandering after dark. The area is perfectly safe in the daytime, however, and it's worth a visit for the colors and smells alone.

Life is lived boisterously in the Marseilles streets, particularly in the area around the Vieux Port, which now is a harbor for pleasure boats and for sidewalk restaurants offering bouillabaisse. Although the Germans dynamited much of the picturesque but seedy old quarter during World War II (because it was a center for the Résistance), some reminders of Marseilles's tradition still survive.

From the beginning, the city prospered at the hands of the Greek traders, declined under Roman rule, and was revived by the Crusaders, whom Marseilles supplied with food and weapons. Devastated by the great plague in 1720, in which 50,000 of its citizens perished, Marseilles rose again to support the French Revolution with enthusiasm. In 1792, 500 volunteers marched to Paris, singing a new war song composed at Strasbourg by a young officer named Rouget de Lisle. All the way to Paris, the Marseillais sang the new song with Mediterranean exuberance. Practice improved their performance, so that when the troops reached Paris, their expert chorus electrified all listeners. The song caught on and became France's stirring national anthem, named not for the city but for those staunch choristers, "La Marseillaise."

One hundred years later, the opening of the Suez Canal virtually assured the continued maritime success of Marseilles, and commercial traffic abandoned the small Vieux Port for a new one directly to the north. The new port was also destroyed during World War II, but it was rebuilt and expanded. Flat, nondescript, and soulless buildings have risen on the once vibrant site of the Old Quarter. Ironically, every new groundbreaking brings the possibility of unearthing still more traces of earlier civilizations, like the Roman docks discovered in the 1940s or the Greek ramparts found in 1967. Medieval churches now stand side by side with steel and glass apartment buildings. The excavations at the Centre Bourse are open to visitors.

Many visitors to Marseilles are heading off to the Côte d'Azur and are in the city only to change trains at the recently rebuilt Gare St.-Charles or planes at the modern Aéroport de Marignane. But there's sufficient reason to linger. Step into a café on the Vieux Port as the burning Mediterranean sun starts to sink in the sky and order a milky white *pastis,* an anise-flavored aperitif. (Or duck into the less seedy *La Samaritaine* on Bd. de la République.) Around you are spectacular white limestone hills and in front, a harbor filled with the cries and accents of far-off lands. Drink it all in, along with your *pastis.* Who knows? You may, like the American writer M.F.K. Fisher, fall in love with Marseilles and stay longer, soaking in its rich Mediterranean atmosphere and exploring its abundant historic remains.

MARSEILLES AT-A-GLANCE

 SEEING THE CITY: Take the No. 60 bus up to this hilly city's most imposing height, a 531-foot limestone bluff crowned by the Basilica of Notre-Dame-de-la-Garde, known to the Provençal as La Bonne Mère. There's an extraordinary view — particularly at sunset — from the terrace: The boats on the Vieux Port, the white rocky islands, and the densely built city stretch out below. The half-Roman, half-Byzantine basilica itself, topped by a huge gilded statue of the

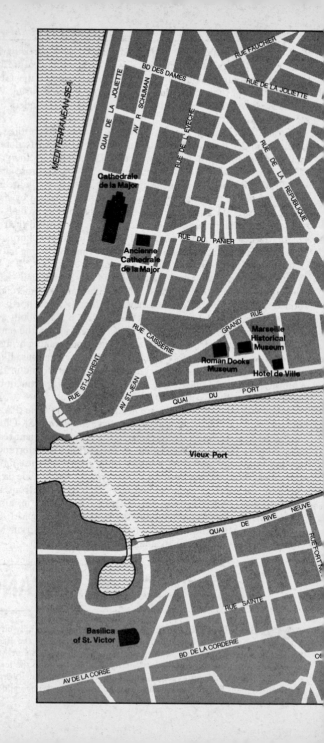

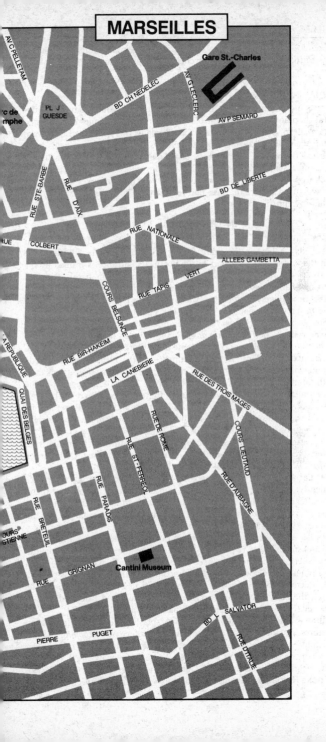

MARSEILLES

Gare St.-Charles

AV C.PELLETAM

PL J GUESDE

rc de mphe

BD CH.NEDELEC

AV G.LECLERC

AV P.SEMARD

RUE STE-BARBE

RUE D'AIX

BD DE LIBERTE

RUE

COLBERT

RUE NATIONALE

ALLEES GAMBETTA

COURS BELSUNCE

RUE TAPIS

VERT

RUE BIR-HAKEIM

LA CANEBIERE

RUE DES TROIS MAGES

A REPUBLIQUE

QUAI DES BELGES

RUE DE ROME

COURS LIEUTAUD

RUE ST-FERREOL

RUE D'AUBAGNE

OURS STIENNE

RUE BRETEUIL

RUE PARADIS

RUE

GRIGNAN

Cantini Museum

PIERRE

PUGET

BD L. SALVATOR

RUE D'ITALIE

Virgin, is far less of a draw than its view, but inside it does have interesting hand-painted offerings to the Virgin as thanks for curing various ailments. Pl. du Colonel Eden.

 SPECIAL PLACES: If you walk down the Gare St.-Charles's monumental staircase and continue on the Boulevard d'Athènes, you'll come to a busy central shopping street, the Canebière. Visitors are sometimes disappointed at the modern, occasionally tacky appearance of this celebrated boulevard that runs into the Vieux Port. During the Middle Ages there were hemp fields here, or *chénevières* (hence the name Canebière); the broad plane-tree-lined concourse is still the key artery — and essential reference point — of Marseilles. During December, it becomes the backdrop for the colorful *santons* fair, where folk art takes center stage in the form of clay figures, some 2 to 3 feet tall, representing both the *Christmas* story and Provençal life in centuries past.

IN THE CITY

Vieux Port – Follow the Canebière down to the Quai des Belges and you'll arrive at the Vieux Port. Today a harbor for small fishing boats and yachts, it's far more picturesque than the burgeoning new port to the north. Its entrance is framed by the 17th-century forts of St. Jean and St. Nicolas (a Foreign Legion base). Terraced restaurants featuring bouillabaisse (at staggering prices) overlook the animated marina. A fresh-fish market does a lively business every morning. This is the heart of Marseilles. It still is possible to ferry from one side of the Vieux Port to the other, as in Marcel Pagnol's films. Ferries make the trip every 2 or 3 minutes from 7 AM to 6 PM daily. There also is a sightseeing train — *Le Petit Train de la Bonne Mère* — that leaves frequently from the Vieux Port to the Basilica of Notre-Dame-de-la-Garde from 2:15 to 6:15 PM.

Musée des Beaux-Arts (Fine Arts Museum) – In the 19th-century Palais de Longchamp — noteworthy in its own right for impressive fountains and gardens (and even a zoo) — the museum offers a considerable display of art. Paintings from the Italian, Flemish, Dutch, and French (David, Courbet, Ingres) schools share the palace's left wing with works by Marseilles natives Honoré Daumier and Pierre Puget and by other Provençal artists. On the ground floor is a charming children's museum. The right wing of the palace contains a natural history museum. The *Beaux-Arts* is open daily from 10 AM to 5 PM; the natural history museum is open Wednesdays through Mondays from 10 AM to noon and 2 to 6 PM. Separate admission charge for each museum. Pl. Bernex (phone: *Beaux-Arts,* 91-62-21-17; natural history museum, 91-62-30-78).

Musée Grobet-Labadié – Near the Longchamp Palace, this l9th-century showplace is furnished opulently, exactly as it was when the musician Louis Grobet lived there. Stop by before or after visiting the *Fine Arts Museum.* Open Mondays through Saturdays from 10 AM to 5 PM; Sundays from noon to 7 PM. Admission charge. 140 Bd. Longchamp (phone: 91-62-21-82 or 91-08-96-04).

Outdoor Markets – Wander through the city's raucous market areas and take in their vivid sights and smells. They're particularly alive in the mornings on the Quai des Belges, where the fishermen and their wives sell their catch directly. Also, note the food market on Rue Longue des Capucins (at Rue Vacon, near the Canebière); the flea markets near the Porte d'Aix (that is, the triumphal arch in Pl. Jules-Guesde at the end of Rue d'Aix); the daily book market on Le Cours Julien; and Rue St.-Barbe in the Algerian quarter (but avoid this racially troubled area after dark).

Le Cours Julien – This unique public square has splashing fountains, interesting boutiques, bookstores, restaurants, and an innovative art gallery (see *Shopping*). It will take an hour to explore the whole plaza, but allow yourself the pleasure of real contact with the youth, vigor, and creativity of Marseilles. To get here, walk north from the Old Port, up the Canebière, then East onto Bd. Garibaldi, which crosses Le Cours Julien.

Musée des Docks Romains – An unexpected benefit came from the Germans' 1943 bombing of the old quarter. Fascinating remains of long-buried Roman docks and statuary were unearthed in the course of rebuilding the area, and the museum incorporates the original setting plus objects retrieved offshore. Open daily from 10 AM to 5 PM. Admission charge. 28 Pl. Vivaux (phone: 91-91-24-62).

Musée d'Histoire de Marseille – The excavations of the ancient Greek port and ramparts are now a museum. The open-air archaeological dig features the remains of a boat excavated on the site. Open daily from noon to 7 PM. Closed Sundays. Admission charge. Pl. Belsunce (phone: 91-90-42-22).

Le Panier – From the Quai du Port, the narrow streets climb toward what little remains of Old Marseilles. Reminiscent of Paris's Montmartre (and likewise beginning to suffer the same "renewal" fate), the Panier quarter is a maze of tiny streets reverberating with the exuberant sounds of daily life in a Provençal neighborhood. It is not lacking for art galleries or interesting bistros. Behind the Hôtel de Ville, climb the steps to the left of Notre-Dame-des-Accoules's bell tower, the remains of a 12th-century church.

La Vieille Charité – Located in the Panier district, this baroque building of rose stone with an egg-shaped cupola was designed as a prison hospital by Pierre Puget and took 75 years to build — from 1640 to 1715. Abandoned in the early part of this century, it was taken over by squatters until 1986, when a vast renovation restored the building to its original state. It currently is home to several research institutes and houses temporary exhibitions of predominantly contemporary art as well as Egyptian and Greek artifacts. Open Mondays through Fridays from 10 AM to 5 PM; Saturdays and Sundays from noon to 7 PM. Admission charge. 2 Rue de la Charité (phone: 91-56-28-38).

Cathédrales de la Major – Reminiscent of Muslim mosques, the cathedrals' domes and cupolas dominate the Quai de la Tourette. The sadly battered Ancienne (Old) Major was built in the 12th century in pure Romanesque style on the ruins of the Roman Temple of Diana. The huge, ostentatious cathedral next to it was built in the 19th century in a Romanesque-Byzantine style. Pl. de la Major.

Abbaye St.-Victor – The present fortified Gothic church dates from the 11th to the 14th century, but the real interest lies below, in its crypt, which actually is an ancient basilica founded in the 5th century in honor of the 3rd-century martyr St. Victor. This abbey contains a chapel and the tomb of two 3rd-century martyrs in addition to pagan and early Christian catacombs. The church also hosts concerts; call for the program. The abbey is open daily from 9 AM to noon and from 2 to 6 PM. Crypt closed Sundays. Admission charge. At the end of Rue Sainte (phone: 91-33-25-86).

Cité Radieuse – Designed by the renowned Le Corbusier, the 17-story housing development — or *unité d'habitation* — was avant-garde for its time (1947–52) and is still a landmark in modern functional architecture. There is a moderately priced hotel with a number of shops on the premises. 280 Bd. Michelet.

Parc Borély – This is a lovely stretch of greenery where you can take some sun by the lake or rent a bicycle. There's also a quaint racetrack on the same site. The park itself closes after dark. Promenade de la Plage and Av. Clot-Bey.

Château Gombert – This neighborhood just inside the city limits claims the *Musée des Arts et Traditions Populaires du Terroir Marseillais* (Museum of Popular Art and Traditions), 5 Pl. des Héros (phone: 91-68-14-38). Among its exhibitions are pottery, pewter, and glass displays. Open only on Saturday, Sunday, and Monday afternoons from 2 to 6 PM. Admission charge. In summer the town holds a festival of Provençal folklore. Follow the autoroute north toward Lyons and exit at La Rose.

OUT OF TOWN

Promenade de la Corniche – This scenic coast road that winds for some 3 miles (5 km) south of the Vieux Port passes in its course Marseilles's most spectacular homes and a breathtaking view of the sea and the islands, including the Château d'If and the Frioul Islands (see below). Also known as the Corniche Président-J.-F.-Kennedy, it passes a picture-postcard fishing port, Vallon des Auffes, and lovely rocky coves before it becomes the Promenade de la Plage (with Parc Borély) and continues toward Cassis, a beautiful fishing town, now also a summer resort, that was celebrated by Derain, Vlaminck, Matisse, and Dufy. Cassis is 14 miles (22 km) from Marseilles. Beautiful, sandy Prado Beach is also along the Corniche road; watch for signs. Pick up Corniche Président-J.-F.-Kennedy at Rue des Catalans.

Château d'If. – Set on a rocky island, this beautiful castle was built in the 16th century for defense, and then turned into a state prison whose most famous "guest" was Alexandre Dumas's Count of Monte Cristo. Inside some cells are carvings by Huguenot prisoners. Open daily; admission charge. The château can be reached by boats that leave about every 15 minutes for a 20-minute ride from the Quai des Belges (phone: 91-55-50-09).

Allauch – On a cliff with a church on top and windmills all around, the town offers a good view of Marseilles and the harbor and is known for *suce-miel,* a type of lollipop made of honey, and *croquants aux amandes,* almond biscuits. To get here, take Boulevard de la Libération out of Marseilles and follow signs north to St. Barnabé/Allauch.

Frioul Islands – These islands southwest of Marseilles have sparkling creeks that provide an idyllic retreat from the city's sometimes torrid atmosphere. Boats leave for the islands from the Quai des Belges every hour (in winter, every 1½ hours). Les Armateurs Côtiers (phone: 91-55-50-09).

■ **EXTRA SPECIAL:** For unsurpassed and unspoiled natural beauty, don't leave the region without seeing its spectacular *calanques* along the coast between Marseilles and Cassis. The *calanques* are crystal-clear narrow creeks running between stark white limestone cliffs that soar up to 650 feet, much like small fjords. They can be approached only by foot (about 1½ hours each way) or by boat, thereby ensuring a minimum number of tourists. The closest *calanques* — Sormiou and Morgiou — can be reached from Roy d'Espagne (take bus No. 44) and Les Baumettes (No. 22), respectively. For information on organized hiking ventures, visit *Les Excursionnistes Marseillais* (16 Rue de la Rotonde; phone: 91-84-75-52), Tuesdays through Saturdays from 6 to 8 PM. Otherwise, leave by boat from Quai des Belges.

SOURCES AND RESOURCES

TOURIST INFORMATION: The English-speaking staff of the Office du Tourisme (4 La Canebière; phone: 91-54-91-11) provides hotel reservations, maps, guides, and advice; also ask for *La Charte de la Bouillabaisse,* which gives the real recipe for this much maligned and poorly imitated fish soup and provides a list of those restaurants serving the authentic concoction. A second tourist office is at Gare St.-Charles (phone: 91-50-59-18).

For a closer look at Marseilles, read *A Considerable Town,* by the American M.F.K. Fisher; it's a charming and personal account of a city she loves.

A good street-indexed map is the *Carte et Plan Frézet,* available at major bookstores along the Canebière. They also carry general English-language guidebooks, but no local English publications exist. Also, pick up a copy of *A Tout Marseille,* a new bimonthly magazine in French of what's happening, put out by the tourist office and distributed free of charge.

From late May to October, 3-hour guided bus tours of Marseilles are available in English from *Protour* (4 Bd. Baille; phone: 91-94-00-44), for about $18.

Local Coverage – The local newspapers, *Le Méridional* and *Le Provençal,* are available at any newsstand.

 TELEPHONE: The country code for France is 33; the city code for Marseilles is 91, which is incorporated into all local 8-digit numbers. (*Note:* The area code for the airport is 42.) When calling a number in Marseilles from the Paris region (including the Ile-de-France), dial 16, wait for the dial tone, then dial the 8-digit number. When calling a number from outside Paris, dial only the 8-digit number. When calling from the US, dial 33 (which is the country code), followed by the 8-digit number.

 GETTING AROUND: Airport – Marseilles-Marignane Airport is about 18 miles (29 km) northwest of the city (phone: 42-78-21-00). International and domestic terminals are adjacent in the main airport concourse. For a taxi into town, 24 hours a day, call 42-78-24-44; the 20- to 30-minute ride will cost about 200F ($33). There are buses every 20 minutes in both directions from 6 AM to 9:50 PM and according to flight schedules; the approximate time to Gare St.-Charles, the main train station, is 30 minutes, and the fare is about 36F ($6). For information on regular bus service to the airport from Marseilles, call 91-50-59-34.

Boat – Boats leave for the Frioul Islands (see *Special Places*) from the Quai des Belges approximately every hour. Les Armateurs Côtiers (phone: 91-55-50-09).

Bus and Métro – Marseilles's attractive subway system is coordinated with the buses, allowing easy — and free — transfers between systems. The métro goes in only two directions, so it's difficult to get lost. Buy a *carnet* (packet) of six tickets instead of the single ticket. The métro shuts down each night at 9 PM, though there are many buses that run later, some offering service throughout the night. For information, call 91-91-92-10. For information about regular bus service to Marseilles-Marignane Airport, call 91-50-59-34.

Car Rental – Major international firms are represented.

Ferry – For ferries to Corsica, inquire at *SNCM,* 61 Bd. des Dames (phone: 91-56-62-05 or 91-56-32-00).

Taxi – There are cabstands around the city, or call *Taxi Tupp* (phone: 91-05-80-80), *Marseille Taxi* (phone: 91-02-20-20), *Maison du Taxi* (phone: 91-95-92-50), or *Taxi Radio France* (phone: 91-49-91-00).

Train – Marseilles's train station is Gare St.-Charles (phone: 91-08-50-50 for information, 91-08-84-12 for reservations). The extension of the Paris-Lyons high-speed *TGV* line to Valence, which has experienced considerable resistence from locals who want to preserve the environment, will (if and when completed) cut travel time between Paris and Marseilles to just over 3 hours; until then, it takes about 4½ hours.

 LOCAL SERVICES: In town, the *Centre Méditerranéen de Commerce International,* known as *CMCI* (Rue Henri-Barbusse; phone: 91-08-60-00), is a one-stop center for the visiting businessperson operated by the Chamber of Commerce. Available under one roof are individual offices for rent; meeting and conference rooms; telex, photocopying, and word processing services; multilingual secretarial help; translation services; ultramodern teleconference and telecommunications facilities; and professional business advice and information on the Marseilles region. It is within walking distance of the Stock Exchange (Bourse) and the Old Port in the heart of the business and commercial center of the city.

Dentist (English-Speaking) – *Dr. Simon,* 14 Av. de Toulon (phone: 91-78-34-63).

Dry Cleaner/Tailor – *Pressing,* open from 8 AM to 5:15 PM. 22 Av. du Prado (phone: 91-37-40-02).

Limousine Service – *René Dissaux,* 20 Rue Mazenod (phone: 91-91-36-10 or 91-57-43-42).

Medical Emergency – *SAMU (Service d'Aide Médicale Urgente;* phone: 91-49-91-91), an emergency medical service with a specially equipped ambulance, is for serious emergencies only and is available 24 hours a day. Two other services are *SOS Médicins* (phone: 91-52-91-52) and *SOS Dentistes* (phone: 91-25-77-77).

Messenger Service – *Marseille Courses,* 147 Rue Paradis (phone: 91-37-57-82).

National/International Courier – *DHL International,* Cil la Bastide Blanche, Quartier du Griffon, Vitrolles (phone: 78-90-80-80).

Office Equipment Rental – *Bureaux & Machines,* 33 Bd. Vauban (phone: 91-81-78-60).

Pharmacy – *Grande Pharmacie Castellane,* open from 8 AM to 9 PM (11 Pl. Castellane; phone: 91-48-70-20). Open all night is the *Pharmacie de Garde* — the drugstore on duty — the location of which is posted on the window of all pharmacies.

Photocopies – At most photographic stores in the city. Also at *Service 2A* (at the airport), and at *CMCI* (Rue Henri-Barbusse; phone: 91-08-60-00).

Post Office – The main post office is open Mondays through Fridays from 8 AM to 7 PM, and on Saturdays from 8 AM to noon. 13 Rue Henri-Barbusse (phone: 91-95-40-00).

Secretary/Stenographer (English-Speaking) – *Manpower,* 96 Rue de la République (phone: 91-91-09-22).

Teleconference Facilities – At *CMCI* (Rue Henri-Barbusse; phone: 91-08-60-00).

Telex – At the post office, 1 Rue Henri-Barbusse, and at *CMCI* (Rue Henri-Barbusse; phone: 91-08-60-00).

Translators/Interpreters – Contact the Chamber of Commerce (Palais de la Bourse; phone: 91-39-33-33) or the *CMCI* (Rue Henri-Barbusse; phone: 91-08-60-00).

SPECIAL EVENTS: There's an *International Folklore Festival* in early July at the Château Gombert (Pl. des Héros) as well as a live crèche at *Christmas.* The best events during the rest of the year are the *Santons Fair,* during which the traditional hand-painted clay statuettes fill *Christmas* crèches all over the city (December 1 to January 6); *La Fête de Mai,* when the Cours Julien and Place Carli are closed to cars and open to circus acts, theater troupes, and singers (late May); the *Garlic Fair,* when mounds of garlic cover the sidewalks of Cour Belsunce (June 15 to July 15); and the *L'Eté Marseillais* (inaugurated in 1990) which is an extension of the traditional *Islands Festival* (July and August). The fete runs from mid-June to mid-September and includes a wide range of peformances — from classical music and dance to jazz and theater — that take place in the city's parks, churches, monuments, and on the islands off the port of Marseilles.

MUSEUMS: Besides those described in *Special Places,* there are three other notable Marseilles museums:

Musée Cantini – Provençal ceramics and often outstanding contemporary art exhibitions. Open daily from 10 AM to 5 PM; Saturdays and Sundays from noon to 7 PM. Admission charge. 19 Rue Grignan (phone: 91-54-77-75).

Musée de la Moto – Opened in 1990, the collection of motorcycles here includes a De Dion Bouton (1898), a Moto Guzzi (1947), a Motosacoche 215cc (1904), and many more. Open daily except Tuesdays from 10 AM to 6 PM. Admission charge. Traverse St.-Paul, Quartier le Merlan (phone: 91-02-29-55).

Musée du Vieux Marseille – A folklore museum set up in a 16th-century house, the Maison Diamantée (Diamond House), so called for the shape of its stone facing and best known for its *santon* collection (see *Shopping*). Open daily from 10 AM to 5 PM. Admission charge. Rue de la Prison (phone: 91-55-10-19).

SHOPPING: Major department stores, elegant couturier and gift shops, and enough shoe shops to make a centipede happy are clustered in the frenetic area around the Canebière (Rue de Rome, Rue Paradis, and the pedestrian-only Rue St.-Ferréol, where some of the trendiest shops are found). The flashy and trendy *Centre Bourse* is a shopping center north of the Canebière. Less expensive shops, usually selling North African items, are in the vicinity of the Porte d'Aix (Arc de Triomphe).

Typical Marseillais souvenirs include clay *santons,* which can be found in tourist shops or at numerous booths set up for the *Christmas Santons Fair* on the Canebière. The word *santon* is derived from the Italian *santibelli,* "the beautiful saints." These small, naively modeled and brightly colored figurines represent both biblical figures and traditional characters of Provence life such as the Gypsy, the shepherd, and the milkmaid.

Les Arcenaux – A bookstore and publishing house that sells new and old editions. It also has a tearoom, a restaurant, and an antiques shop. 25 Cours Estienne d'Orves (phone: 91-54-39-37).

Le Four des Navettes – Try some *navettes* (half-bread, half-cake loaves, which stay fresh for months) from this remarkable 200-year-old bakery. 136 Rue Sainte (phone: 91-33-32-12).

Galerie Roger Pailhas – An art gallery that promotes the work of international artists, including some of Marseilles's most original ones. 61 Cours Julien (phone: 91-42-18-01).

Hermès – Among the best-known names in elegant and expensive French accessories, including their famous *carré* silk scarves, ties, and handbags. 93 Rue Paradis (phone: 91-53-24-57).

Parenthèses – Jazz bookstore and publisher, it's a storehouse of books on music, the arts, and architecture. 72 Cours Julien (phone: 91-48-74-44).

Soleiado – A bright boutique featuring the gay, Provençal print fabrics of its namesake, as well as skirts, quilted bags and accessories, placemats, and tablecloths. 101-103 Rue Paradis (phone: 91-37-83-16).

Au Tastevin – A slightly cluttered, old-fashioned shop where wines of the nearby Cassis and Bandol regions can be bought, as well as foie gras, truffles, and a limited selection of Fauchon food products. 8 Rue Edmond-Rostand (phone: 91-37-10-62).

 SPORTS AND FITNESS: Professional sports include auto racing, basketball, horse racing, ice hockey, rugby, and soccer. Inquire at the tourist office.
     Fishing – Notably for gilt-head and mackerel: off the Corniche, in the *calanques,* the Frioul Islands, and in nearby fishing villages.

Golf – Tee off at *Golf de la Salette,* a new 18-hole course less than 5 miles (8 km) from central Marseilles (phone: 91-27-12-16). To get there, take the autoroute east and exit at La Valentine. About 14 miles (22 km) from the city is the *Golf Club Aix-Marseille* (Domaine de Riquetti, Les Milles, Aix-en-Provence; phone: 42-24-20-41).

Horseback Riding – Inquire at the *Centre Equestre de la Ville de Marseille,* 33 Carthage (phone: 91-73-72-94).

Jogging – Take bus No.21 to Domaine de Luminy, about 4 miles (6 km) from the city center. Or try Parc Borély, 3 miles (5 km) south of the city by the Promenade de la Corniche.

Sailing – Contact *Centre Municipal de Voile* (Plage due Roucas-Blanc; phone: 91-76-31-60) or *Centre Nautique Roucas-Blanc* (Plage du Roucas-Blanc; phone: 91-22-72-49).

Swimming – *Piscine Luminy,* Rte. Léon Lachamp (phone: 91-41-26-59).

Tennis and Squash – Try the courts at *Tennis Municipaux* (Allée Ray-Grassi; phone: 91-77-83-89) or *Tennis Didier* (81 *bis* François-Mauriac; phone: 91-26-16-05). Both *Set-Squash Marseille* (265 Av. de Mazargues; phone: 91-71-94-71) and *Prado Squash* (26 *bis* Bd. Michelet; phone: 91-22-83-90) provide facilities for tennis as well as squash.

Water Sports – For information, call or visit the *Fédération des Sociétés Nautiques des Bouches du Rhône,* 10 Av. de la Corse (phone: 91-54-34-88).

 THEATER: Theater is booming in Marseilles, with more than 10 new stages opening in the past few years. There's a surprisingly good choice of theater activity year-round. The choices range from the intimate *Centre Culturel* for theater and music (33 Cours Julien; phone: 91-92-02-16) to the *Café-Théâtre du Vieux Panier* (52 Rue Ste.-Françoise; phone: 91-91-00-74) and the *Théâtre de Poche* (see above) to the more ambitious national theater, *La Criée* (30 Quai de Rive-Neuve; phone: 91-54-74-54 or 91-54-70-54), where reservations are necessary. An especially interesting program is offered by the *Théâtre du Gyptis* (136 Rue Loubon; phone: 91-08-10-18). The *Théâtre Toursky* (16 Passage du Théâtre; phone: 91-02-58-35) re-opened in 1990 and features a wide variety of contemporary and classic performances. The *Théâtre Massalia* (60 Rue Grignan; phone: 91-55-66-06) has been converted into a unique marionette theater featuring performances by marionette companies from all over Europe. For experimental theater, visit *Théâtre de Poche* (see above) and *Théâtre de Lenche* (4 Pl. de Lenche; phone: 91-91-55-56 or 91-91-52-22). (*Note:* Those who don't speak French will endure no handicap while enjoying operettas or mime performances, which are presented frequently.) In addition, the *Opéra de Marseille* is the home of the *Compagnie Roland Petit,* France's well-known ballet company. For theater information and tickets, visit the office of the *FNAC* at *Centre Bourse,* north of the Canebière.

 MUSIC: The Marseillais know good opera and ballet as well as they know bouillabaisse. The sometimes outstanding *Opéra de Marseille* (Pl. de l'Opéra; phone: 91-55-00-70 or 91-55-14-99) and the *Théâtre de Recherche de Marseille* (*TRM;* Espace Massalia, 60 Rue Grignan; phone: 91-55-66-06) both have devoted followings. Chamber music and organ recitals are frequent at major churches and occasionally outdoors on the Vieux Port. Popular music doesn't fare nearly as well.

 NIGHTCLUBS AND NIGHTLIFE: Marseilles does not suffer from inactivity after dark, with action ranging from the sedate to the frenetic. In the former category, visitors will find soothing piano bars such as *Le Beauvau* in the *Pullman Beauvau* hotel (9 Rue Beauvau; phone: 91-54-91-00), whose barman really knows his trade. The most "in" nightspots include *Bunny's Club* (2 Rue Corneille; phone: 91-54-09-02), with a packed dance floor and an excellent sound system; *Abbaye de la Commanderie* (20 Rue Corneille; phone: 91-33-45-56), a cabaret that draws its neighbor's overflow with a *sympathique* evening of nonstop songs; and *London Club* (73 Corniche Président-J.-F.-Kennedy; phone: 91-52-64-64), a friendly nightclub/disco. At the moment, the young set favors *Le Rock A Billy* (5 Rue Molière; phone: 91-54-70-36) and the famous, as well as the would-bes, congregate at *Le Juke* (6 Rue Lully; phone: 91-33-14-88). Other current popular nightspots include *L'Ascenseur* (22 Pl. Thiars; phone: 91-33-13-27); *Le Golf* (3 Rue Sénac; phone: 91-48-59-76); and *Roll's Club* (76 Corniche Président-J.-F.-Kennedy; phone: 81-52-21-21). Unique *Espace Julien* (33 Cours Julien; phone: 91-47-09-64) offers jazz occasionally and an open cabaret where anyone can perform; it's also a learning center for everything from musical instruments to dance to gymnastics.

BEST IN TOWN

CHECKING IN: Marseilles traditionally has had a meager selection of good hotels. With a recent spurt of hotel construction there's now an overabundance of higher priced, ultramodern rooms, but not much improvement in the lower price ranges. Expect to pay $130 and up for a double room (not including breakfast) in a very expensive hotel; $90 to $120 in an expensive one; $60 to $90 for moderate; and under $60 for an inexpensive one.

Le Petit Nice – Small (18 rooms and suites in 2 buildings) and gracious, it was built in the 19th century as a private villa. There's a shaded garden and a superb two-star Michelin restaurant (see *Eating Out*), all looking out over the Mediterranean from a magnificent position on the Corniche. The restaurant is closed Mondays, and Tuesdays during the winter; the hotel is closed during January and the first week in February. Business facilities include foreign currency exchange, secretarial services in English, and express checkout. Major credit cards accepted. 160 Corniche Président-J.-F.-Kennedy (phone: 91-59-25-92; fax: 91-59-28-08; telex: 401565). Very expensive.

Concorde Palm Beach – A supermodern spot by the sea, with an outdoor pool and a good restaurant, *La Réserve*. Business facilities include meeting rooms for up to 500, English-speaking concierge, foreign currency exchange, secretarial services in English, audiovisual equipment, photocopiers, translation services, and express checkout. Major credit cards accepted. 2 Promenade de la Plage (phone: 91-76-20-00; fax: 91-77-37-83; telex: 401894). Expensive.

Mercure – Just a 5-minute walk from the Old Port, the former *Altéa* hotel, has been taken over by the Mercure chain. It distinguishes itself by its taste, pleasant piano bar, and an outstanding restaurant, *L'Oursinade* (see *Eating Out*). Its 200 rooms have all the expected luxury hotel amenities. Business facilities include 24-hour room service, meeting rooms for up to 450, foreign currency exchange, audiovisual equipment, and photocopiers. Major credit cards accepted. Rue Neuve-St.-Martin (phone: 91-39-20-00; fax: 91-56-24-57; telex: 401886). Expensive.

Pullman Beauvau – Next to the tourist office and just down the street from the *Opéra,* this is one of Marseilles's best properties. Most of its 72 rooms face the Vieux Port. Business facilities include meeting rooms for up to 30, English-speaking concierge, foreign currency exchange, audiovisual equipment, and photocopiers. Major credit cards accepted. 4 Rue Beauvau (phone: 91-54-91-00; fax: 91-54-15-76; telex: 401778). Expensive.

Sofitel Vieux Port – Magnificent and modern, with a splendid view from its perch above the entrance to the Old Port, near the *Palais du Pharo.* It has some 200 rooms, air conditioning, a heated outdoor pool, a cozy bar, and a fine restaurant, *Les Trois Forts* (see *Eating Out*). Business facilities include 24-hour room service, meeting rooms for up to 150, English-speaking concierge, audiovisual equipment, photocopiers, translation services, and express checkout. Major credit cards accepted. 36 Bd. Charles-Livon (phone: 91-52-90-19; fax: 91-59-28-08; telex: 401270). Expensive.

Astoria – One of a number of small, old, Marseilles hostelries that have been renovated, this turn-of-the-century relic now has a bright, skylit lobby filled with plants, and contemporary furnishings in the guestrooms. Major credit cards accepted. 10 Bd. Garibaldi (phone: 91-33-33-50; fax: 91-54-80-75; telex: 402175). Moderate.

Bompard – In a quiet park on a hill not far from the sea, only a 5-minute drive (on the coastal road) from the bustle of the Vieux Port. Some of its 40-plus rooms —

in the main building or surrounding bungalows — have kitchenettes. No restaurant. Business facilities include 24-hour room service, meeting rooms for up to 40, English-speaking concierge, foreign currency exchange, audiovisual equipment, photocopiers, and express checkout. Major credit cards accepted. 2 Rue des Flots-Bleus (phone: 91-52-10-93; fax: 91-31-02-14). Moderate.

St.-Ferréol – Located just off the main pedestrian shopping street near the Canebière and the Old Port. This newly renovated 19-room hotel is stylish and comfortable with extras such as a Jacuzzi in some rooms, marble baths, elegant fabrics, and a cozy little bar for breakfast and drinks. An excellent value. Major credit cards accepted. 19 Rue Pisançon (phone: 91-33-12-21; fax: 91-54-29-97). Moderate.

Hermès – Recently renovated with a neo-Greek theme, the main attractions of this 30-room hostelry are its location just off the quai, its reasonable prices, and its fifth-floor rooms with terraces that overlook the Old Port. Major credit cards accepted. 2 Rue Bonneterie (phone: 91-90-34-51; fax: 91-91-14-44). Moderate to inexpensive.

Alizé – This renovated 35-room portside hotel with a yellow stone façade is a welcome addition to the lower-price hostelries. Ask for a room with a view of the Old Port. Major credit cards accepted. 7 Quai des Belges (phone: 91-33-66-97; fax: 91-54-80-06). Inexpensive.

Capitainerie de Vieux Port – Formerly the *Urbis,* this modern hotel has 148 rooms, a restaurant, a bar, and conference facilities. Close to the Vieux Port and 1 block above the Cours d'Estienne d'Orves. Business facilities include meeting rooms for up to 60, foreign currency exchange, audiovisual equipment, and photocopiers. Major credit cards accepted. 46 Rue Sainte (phone: 91-54-73-73; fax: 91-54-77-77). Inexpensive.

Grand Hôtel de Genève – Old, but now modernized, it is in a quiet pedestrian precinct just behind the Old Port. No restaurant. Major credit cards accepted. 3 *bis* Rue Reine-Elizabeth (phone: 91-90-51-42; fax: 91-90-76-24). Inexpensive.

 EATING OUT: What it has traditionally lacked in hotels, Marseilles always has made up for in restaurants; they are among France's finest, and that is saying a lot. Besides classic French cuisine, be sure to try Provençal (from Provence — the southern region of France that straddles the Rhône River) specialties. The city virtually is synonymous with bouillabaisse, a dish not to be missed. In its classical form, this soup is based on Mediterranean rockfish (called *rouget*), but other fish and shellfish usually are added, particularly lobster and crab. The seasoning (cayenne, garlic, tomatoes, herbs) is very special, but the star ingredient is saffron, which gives bouillabaisse its golden color. It often is served with rouille, a relish made of red pepper, garlic, and fish broth, as well as with aioli, a delicious olive-oil-based garlic mayonnaise. Another dish common on menus in Marseilles is bourride, a fish stew that some prefer to bouillabaisse.

Other regional specialties include *anchoïade,* anchovies and olive oil mashed into a paste that accompanies raw vegetables; *poutargue,* fish eggs grated in oil, then pressed and dried to become a sort of white caviar; *navettes,* flat biscuits flavored with orange-flower water; and *fougasses,* flat, salty breads in leaf designs, flavored with walnuts, olives, bacon, or cheese.

You also may wish to sample *pastis,* the anise-flavored aperitif that tastes something like licorice. Usually colorless, *pastis* is served diluted with ice water, which turns it cloudy white. Also try wines from Provence, particularly the dry, pleasant rosé.

Expect to pay $80 and considerably higher in the expensive category (for two without wine); from $50 to $80 in the moderate range; and under $50 in the inexpensive category. Prices include a service charge.

Calypso – This outstanding dining room offers a classic sea view and, some still swear, Marseilles's best bouillabaisse — although it lost its Michelin star in 1991).

No meat or vegetables here, just impeccably served seafood. But the quality and quantity leave nothing to be desired. Its twin and peer — *Michel* — is across the street. Open daily. Reservations necessary. Major credit cards accepted. 3 Rue des Catalans (phone: 91-52-64-00). Expensive.

Chaudron Provençal – Copper cauldrons hang from wide ceiling beams in this rustic little fish restaurant located in the Panier district. Diners choose from the day's fresh fish displayed in baskets next to the tiny open kitchen; you pay by weight. The quality is high, with prices to match. Closed Saturday lunch and Sundays. Reservations advised. Major credit cards accepted. 48 Rue Caisserie (phone: 91-91-02-37). Expensive.

Chez Brun (Aux Mets de Provence) – At this venerable family-run place, you'll eat in the *ancienne* style. Up to 20 dishes of the true Provençal cuisine, which means fish and olive-spiced specialties. Closed Sundays, Mondays, and holidays. Reservations necessary. Major credit cards accepted. 18 Quai du Rive-Neuve, on the 2nd Floor; the entrance is hard to find, so watch closely (phone: 91-33-35-38). Expensive.

Chez Fonfon – In an old fishing club, it's heavy on local color and boat scenes, real bouillabaisse, and other fish dishes. Closed Saturdays, Sundays, and 2 weeks at *Christmastime.* Reservations unnecessary. Major credit cards accepted. 140 Vallen des Auffes (phone: 91-52-14-38). Expensive.

Michel (Les Catalans) – Across the street from the *Calypso.* The menu is short and the seafood is succulent, even though its Michelin star was taken away in 1991. Don't miss the bouillabaisse. Closed Tuesdays and Wednesdays. Reservations unnecessary. Major credit cards accepted. 6 Rue des Catalans (phone: 91-52-30-63). Expensive.

Miramar – Touted by locals as one of the best sources on the quai of the Old Port for authentic bouillabaisse, this modern dining place also serves a wide variety of other fish dishes and regional specialties. Closed Sundays, Saturday lunch, and during August. Reservations unnecessary. Major credit cards accepted. 12 Quai du Port (phone: 91-91-10-40). Expensive.

Le Petit Nice – A two-star Michelin establishment that deserves a third rosette. Our favorite dining spot in Marseilles; the view alone is worth the price of admission. The tomato tart appetizer is the most beautiful single menu item we've ever had on our *plats,* and the lobster ragout is equally impressive. Closed Mondays, and Tuesdays during the winter. Reservations necessary. Major credit cards accepted. 160 Corniche Président-J.-F.-Kennedy (phone: 91-59-25-92). Expensive.

New York – For seafood again, try this restaurant in the old harbor area. Especially good are the fish terrine and the bourride. The owner fell in love with New York when he was a sailor — thus the name. Open daily. Reservations unnecessary. Major credit cards accepted. 7 Quai des Belges (phone: 91-33-60-98 or 91-33-91-79). Expensive to moderate.

L'Oursinade – In the *Mercure* hotel, this place serves very fine Provençal dishes in an atmosphere of understated elegance. Closed Sundays and late July through August. Reservations unnecessary. Major credit cards accepted. Rue Neuve-St.-Martin (phone: 91-39-20-00). Expensive to moderate.

Les Trois Forts – You'll find a panoramic view of the Old Port here, and such inventive dishes as lamb's liver braised with melon and honey. Open daily. Reservations unnecessary. Major credit cards accepted. *Sofitel Vieux Port,* 36 Bd. Charles-Livon (phone: 91-52-90-19). Expensive to moderate.

L'Avant-Scène – The food here runs to fairly light French, and the place actually is a café/art gallery/theater/magazine shop all rolled into one. The theater is downstairs, and there's a fashion designer's atelier upstairs. Open Tuesdays through Saturdays from 8 PM to 2 AM. Reservations unnecessary. Major credit cards accepted. 59 Cours Julien (phone: 91-42-19-29). Moderate.

Chez Caruso – Where the locals go when they crave some delicious Italian food. Closed Sunday nights, Mondays, and from mid-October through mid-November. Reservations unnecessary. Major credit cards accepted. 158 Quai du Port (phone: 91-90-94-04). Moderate.

Cousin, Cousine – Interesting nouvelle cuisine is served here, along with good local wines. Try the hot oysters with broccoli and pheasant in wine sauce. Closed Sundays and Mondays. Reservations unnecessary. Major credit cards accepted. 102 Cours Julien (phone: 91-48-14-50). Moderate.

Au Pescadou – On entering, you'll be dazzled immediately by the spectacular array of fresh oysters, clams, mussels, and other seafood delicacies. With ingredients like these, only the simplest preparation is needed. Closed Sunday nights and July and August. Reservations advised. Major credit cards accepted. 19 Pl. Castellane (phone: 91-78-36-01). Moderate.

Les Platanes (Restaurant des Abattoirs) – By the slaughterhouse, at the city's northern extreme, this immense old café is where the butchers themselves eat. Choose from beef, pork, veal, and a great selection of sausages. Closed Saturdays and Sundays. Reservations advised. Major credit cards accepted. 7 Av. Journet (phone: 91-60-93-17). Moderate.

Texas Fiesta – Run by a Frenchman who used to live in Houston, this lively spot serves up Tex-Mex food, margaritas, American beer, and, on Tuesday nights, country music. Open daily. Reservations unnecessary. Major credit cards accepted. 70 Cours Julien (phone: 91-48-49-24). Moderate.

Aux Baguettes d'Or – Located just behind the *Opéra,* it offers authentic Vietnamese food and friendly service, and sometimes is frequented by singers after performances. Closed Sundays. Reservations advised. Major credit cards accepted. 65 Rue Francis-Davso (phone: 91-54-20-39). Moderate to inexpensive.

Dimitri – Hungarian and Russian specialties are the order of the day. Closed Sundays and Mondays. Reservations advised. Major credit cards accepted. 6 Rue Meolan (phone: 91-54-09-68). Inexpensive.

La Kahenas – This Tunisian eatery offers daily specials, mint tea, pastries, and is crowded at lunch. Closed Sundays. No reservations. No credit cards accepted. 2 Rue de la République (phone: 91-90-61-93). Inexpensive.

Tarte Julie – Every pie imaginable, sweet or salty, is here, along with pizza and salads. Closed Sundays. No reservations. Major credit cards accepted. 14 Av. du Prado (phone: 91-37-23-45). Inexpensive.

 BARS AND CAFÉS: At 5 PM the old Marseillais (barely a woman in sight) gather for *pastis* and tall tales at *Au Vieux Panier,* a café just outside Marseilles (52 Rue Ste.-Françoise). Facing the Vieux Port is *Le Petit Pernod* (30 Rue des Trois Mages) where the bourgeoise congregate. *Place Thiars* (38A Pl. Thiars) is an artists' haunt that becomes even more popular in the summer, when it attracts tourists and theater people to its alfresco dining. The barman really knows his stuff at *Le Beauvau* (9 Rue Beauvau).

MILAN

Milan is the financial and commercial hub of Italy, and one of the most important business centers in the world. At first glance, it is a city of cold, uninspired skyscrapers, a city whose energizing force is money. Even the museum devoted to Leonardo da Vinci here testifies as much to his scientific and technical genius as to his artistic spirit. The people of Milan are industrious, sophisticated, chic, serious — not inclined to watch the world pass by from a sunny café table.

Although with nearly 1.6 million people Milan is a distant second in size to Rome, many Milanese think of their city as Italy's real capital; it is arguably more powerful than Rome. It boasts 400 banks and a silk market that rivals the one in Lyons. Its *International Trade Fair* each spring draws hundreds of thousands of businesspeople from all over the world, as do its autumn and spring showings of luxury fashions. Milan is the home of the prestigious Luigi Bocconi Commercial University, whose graduates include successful international economists, bankers, and company presidents. The city also is the center of Italian publishing and of trendsetting furniture design.

Still, Milan's economic preoccupation is tempered by an appreciation of less mundane pursuits. It is the *La Scala* opera house, with its perfect acoustics and grand traditions, not the Milan Stock Exchange (Borsa Valori), that is the pride of the city. The opening of the opera season each December is a national event, when newspapers print even the menus for the traditional midnight supper parties in the tony restaurants.

The very heart of Milan is its rose-tinted white marble Gothic Duomo; the spires of Milan's magnificent cathedral seem to soar in defiance of the less ethereal buildings around it, though many of them often boast lovely fin de siècle architectural details and delightful, secret courtyard gardens. At the same time, Milan is the gateway to the Lombardy lake region, to ski resorts along the Swiss border to the north, and to the mist-veiled charm of the broad Po River — with its rice paddies, fishermen, and even a school of naïf painters — to the south.

So it is unfortunate that many visitors who look for the Italy of sunny skies, outdoor cafés, and quaint villages may hurry through Milan. The early-19th-century French writer Stendahl lived here for 4 decades; when he died in 1842, there were instructions for his tombstone to read: "Arrigo [Henri] Beyle [his real surname], Milanese — Lived, Wrote, Loved." Stendahl's enthusiasm for Milan, which in 1800 was one of Europe's wealthiest and most luxurious cities, was boundless: "For me this city is the most beautiful place on earth," he wrote. The Milanese themselves passionately ascribe to this view. They point with pride to the city's symbols of its illustrious past: the 16 Corinthian columns outside the 4th-century San Lorenzo Basilica, the remains of the

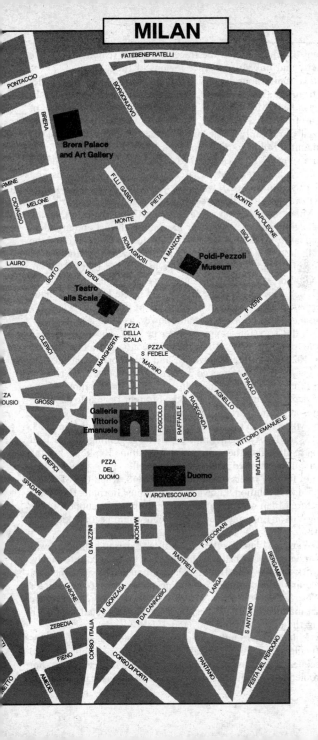

MILAN

FATEBENEFRATELLI

PONTACCIO

BORGONUOVO

BRERA

Brera Palace
and Art Gallery

MONTE NAPOLEONE

F LLI GABBA

DI PIETA

RMINE

MELONE

CIOVASSO

MONTE

BIGLI

ROMAGNOSI

LAURO

G VERDI

BOITO

A MANZONI

Poldi-Pezzoli
Museum

Teatro
alla Scala

P VERRI

CLERICI

PZZA
DELLA
SCALA

PZZA
S FEDELE

S MARGHERITA

MARINO

ZA
DUSIO

GROSSI

Galleria
Vittorio
Emanuele

FOSCOLO

S RAFFAELE

S RADEGONDA

AGNELLO

S PAOLO

VITTORIO EMANUELE

OREFICI

PZZA
DEL
DUOMO

Duomo

PATTARI

SPADARI

V ARCIVESCOVADO

G MAZZINI

MARCONI

F PECORARI

RASTRELLI

BERGAMINI

UNIONE

M GONZAGA

P DA CANNOBIO

LARGA

ZEBEDIA

S ANTONIO

FIENO

CORSO ITALIA

CORSO DI PORTA

PANTANO

FESTA DEL PERDONO

AMEDEI

ETTO

16th-century Spanish ramparts, and the traces of *navigli* (canals) that once crisscrossed the city and linked it to other regions of Italy.

Milan has had a tumultuous history. Invading armies continually descended upon it from the time it was a Celtic settlement. The Romans subdued the city they called "Mediolanum" in 222 BC, and it was the capital of the Roman Empire from AD 286 to 402. In AD 313, Constantine the Great officially recognized Christianity in the famous Edict of Milan, and with the coming of Christianity, Milan found a spiritual father in Bishop Ambrose (later proclaimed a saint), who accomplished the seemingly impossible task of conciliating church and state. After a series of invasions by Huns and Goths, the Lombards (Lungobardi), who had originated in northwest Germany, pushed their way southward to cross the Alps and invade the Po Valley towns, including Milan, in 568. They ruled for more than 2 centuries, giving their name to the region, and they left their imprint on the art and architecture, language, and laws. Tyrranical Frankish rulers followed, but around the year 1000 the Milanese bishops wrested temporal power from them, and Milan became one of the first Italian city-states to be ruled by the church. Constant wars followed, and after a 9-month siege Milan fell to Frederick Barbarossa. In 1176, all the cities in the area united in the Lombard League to defeat the German invader and win recognition of its independence.

This ushered in a century of prosperity and power, as local family dynasties, beginning with the Torriani, assumed power in 1260. The Visconti then seized power from them in 1277. Under the Visconti, particularly Gian Galeazzo (1345–1402), Milan grew in wealth and splendor. When the Visconti died out in 1447, Milan experienced 3 years of Republican government before Francesco Sforza proclaimed himself duke. The most famous of the Sforzas was Ludovico il Moro (1451–1508), who brought Leonardo da Vinci, Donato Bramante, and other artists to Milan to enhance the city. After Ludovico's death, Milan fell to the invading French, to the Spanish in 1535, and, then, in 1713, to the Austrian Empire. At the beginning of the 19th century, Napoleon made Milan the capital of the Cisalpine Republic, but the tyrannic Austrian rulers returned when Napoleon fell.

The succession of foreign rulers began to ebb in 1848, when the Milanese staged a glorious 5-day revolution, known as the Cinque Giornate. But it was nearly 10 years before Milan was liberated and could throw its support to the Piedmontese King Victor Emmanuel of Savoy, who would become king of a unified Italy in 1860.

During World War II, Milan was the site of bitter partisan fighting; it was bombed 15 times and many of its historic buildings were damaged extensively. But restoration work and new construction began immediately after the war. Bomb damage required the complete rebuilding of about half the region's factories, which proved a blessing in disguise since the new plants were extremely modern manufacturing entities, making them especially competitive and spawning the boom of the 1950s and 1960s.

Contemporary Milan is surrounded by a massive, smoke-belching industrial belt — producing auto parts, chemicals, manmade fibers, appliances and rubber. The consequent smog has been somewhat reduced in recent years, but still remains a problem, as do polluted waterways. The city's air is constantly monitored, and when it reaches the risky level, automobile driving is severely curtailed. A large downtown stretch of shopping area is totally traffic-free. Milan is a virtual maze of four-lane highways connecting it with the other northern industrial cities — Genoa, Turin, Venice, and Brescia — and, by the Autostrada del Sole, to Rome and southern Italy.

The center of Italy's publishing and advertising industry and private TV networks, Milan specializes in innovative industrial design and avant-garde graphics. Its textile design and fashions are on a par with those of Paris. The city itself is prosperous and elegant; its people enjoy a high standard of living and a stimulating cultural and intellectual life. Whether you come on business, to attend the opera, to patronize the elegant Milanese fashion houses, or to admire the city's art treasures, you will find Milan's sophistication equal to that of London or Paris or New York, but always uncompromisingly Italian.

MILAN AT-A-GLANCE

SEEING THE CITY: For a grand view of Milan, the surrounding Lombard plain, the Alps, and the Apennines, climb the 166 steps, or take an elevator, to the roof of the cathedral (see *Special Places*). From here, more stairs take you to the topmost gallery at the base of the cathedral's central spire, 354 feet from the ground. The stairway to the roof is entered from the south transept near the Medici tomb; the elevator is entered from outside the church, on the north side (toward the *Rinascente* department store); an elevator on the south side is sometimes also in operation. Both are open daily and charge admission. A new seventh-floor addition to *Rinascente* boasts a café whose vast windows bring the Duomo's gargoyles within, it would seem, sipping distance of your *aperitivo*. Here your admission charge for a unique view is the price of a cup of coffee. There is also a 350-foot viewing tower in Sempione Park, just beyond the Castello Sforzesco (see *Special Places*).

SPECIAL PLACES: The huge Piazza del Duomo (Cathedral Square), with its perennial pigeons and ever-present pensioners, is one of the city's few pedestrian oases and the heart of this bustling metropolis. Leading north from Piazza del Duomo to Piazza della Scala is the elegant glass-domed arcade, the *Galleria Vittorio Emanuele.* Built between 1865 and 1877 under the direction of architect Giuseppe Mengoni, it has for decades been considered the *salotto,* or salon, of Milan for its exclusive shops, bookstores, cafés, and restaurants.

Some of the city's tourist attractions are too far from the center to reach comfortably on foot, but *ATM,* the local bus and tram system, connects these sites efficiently, as does the relatively new and clean subway system.

DOWNTOWN

Il Duomo (Cathedral) – The most magnificent Milanese monument is the shimmering marble cathedral, with 135 spires and more than 2,200 sculptures decorating its exterior. From the roof, reached by an elevator or a 166-step climb, you can study the details of its pinnacles and flying buttresses. The interior of the cathedral, divided into five main aisles by an imposing stand of 58 columns, contains another 2,000 sculptures. The cathedral, on the site of an early Christian church located in the center of the then

Roman city of Mediolanum, is considered the finest example of Gothic architecture in northern Italy, although its own architectural peculiarities — it was begun in 1386 but not completed until 1813 — prevent it from being pure Gothic. Only St. Peter's in Rome is larger. Next to the cathedral at 14 Piazza del Duomo is the *Museo del Duomo,* which beautifully displays Milanese artifacts from the early Middle Ages, including illuminated manuscripts, parchments, statuary, architectural plans, and tapestries. A plus is the air conditioned *ambiente.* Open Tuesdays through Sundays from 9:30 AM to 12:30 PM and 3 to 6 PM. Admission charge. Piazza del Duomo.

Teatro alla Scala (La Scala) – The most famous opera house in the world was built between 1776 and 1778 on the site of the Church of Santa Maria della Scala. It was here that works by Donizetti, Rossini, Bellini, and Verdi were first acclaimed and where Arturo Toscanini conducted and was artistic director for many years. The neo-classic building, damaged extensively during World War II, was reopened in 1946. Its acoustics are perfect. Traditionally, *La Scala*'s season begins on December 7, the feast day of Milan's patron saint, St. Ambrose, and lasts until the end of May. The box office (phone: 807041/42/43/44) is open daily, 10 AM to 1 PM and 3:30 to 5:30 PM (until 9:30 PM on the day of a performance); closed Mondays. (For information, call 809129; for credit card purchases, call 809126.) Agencies do not exist, and opera tickets are extremely difficult to obtain (even for Milanesi), but the theater can be visited by appointment (phone: 887-9377). A sure way to get tickets is to give large amounts of lire to the *portiere* at your hotel. The adjacent *Museo della Scala* (La Scala Museum) houses a rich collection of manuscripts, costumes, and other memorabilia from the theater's history. Open Mondays through Fridays from 9 AM to noon and 2 to 6 PM; Saturdays from 9 AM to noon and 2 to 3:30 PM; Sundays from 9 AM to noon from May through September. Admission charge. The theater and museum are north of Piazza del Duomo, through the *Galleria Vittorio Emanuele,* on Piazza della Scala (phone: 805-3418).

Museo Poldi-Pezzoli (Poldi-Pezzoli Museum) – The Milanese nobleman Gian Giacomo Poldi-Pezzoli bequeathed his home and exquisite private art collection to the city in 1879. It includes some prime examples of Renaissance to 17th-century paintings and sculpture, Oriental porcelain, Persian carpets, and tapestries. There also are a Botticelli portrait of the Madonna, paintings by Giovanni Battista Tiepolo, Pollaiolo and Fra Bartolomeo, as well as Giovanni Bellini's *Pietà.* Open Mondays through Fridays from 9:30 AM to 12:30 PM and 2:30 to 6 PM; Saturdays from 9:30 AM to 12:30 PM and 2:30 to 7:30 PM. Admission charge. A short walk from *La Scala.* 12 Via Manzoni (phone: 794889).

Palazzo e Pinacoteca di Brera (Brera Palace and Art Gallery) – One of the most important state-owned galleries in Italy, and Milan's finest, is housed in the 17th-century Brera Palace. Its 38 rooms contain a broad representation of Italian painting, with particularly good examples from the Venetian and Lombard schools, including such masterpieces as Andrea Mantegna's *Dead Christ,* Raphael's *Wedding Feast of the Virgin,* and Caravaggio's *Dinner at Emmaus.* The palace also has an important library (founded in 1770) of incunabula and manuscripts, plus a collection of all books printed in the Milanese province since 1788. In the courtyard is a monumental statue of Napoleon I, depicted as a conquering Caesar. The art gallery is open Mondays through Saturdays from 9 AM to 1:45 PM; Sundays from 9 AM to 12:45 PM; closed the last Tuesday of each month. Admission charge. The library is closed Sundays. A few blocks north of *La Scala.* 28 Via Brera (phone: 808387).

Castello Sforzesco e Museo d'Arte Antica (Sforza Castle and Museum of Antique Art) – In the mid-15th century, Duke Francesco Sforza built this large, square brick castle on the site of a castle of the Visconti that had been destroyed. It became a fortress after the fall of the Sforzas and was damaged repeatedly in sieges before restoration began in the 19th century. Further damaged during World War II, it has been repaired, and today houses the *Museo d'Arte Antica* (Museum of Antique Art) whose treasures include the unfinished *Rondanini Pietà,* the last work of Michelangelo. The museum is entered from the courtyard of the residential part of the castle, the Corte Ducale. Open Tuesdays through Sundays from 9:30 AM to 12:30 PM; closed the last Tuesday of each month. No admission charge. West of the Brera. Piazza Castello (phone: 6236, ext. 3940).

The castle also houses exhibits of art, musical instruments, and manuscripts. Well-publicized temporary exhibitions often are set up in other rooms. (Same hours as the *Museo d'Arte Antica.*) Beyond the castle is the beautiful 116-acre Parco Sempione (Sempione Park), with an aquarium, sports arena, and neo-classic Arco della Pace (Arch of Peace), a triumphal arch with statues and bas-relief. The arch, on the model of Septimius Severus at Rome, marks the beginning of the historic Corso Sempione (Simplon Road) through the Alps to France, which was built by order of Napoleon.

Basilica e Museo di Sant'Ambrogio (St. Ambrose's Basilica and Museum) – The basilica was founded in the 4th century by Bishop Ambrose (later St. Ambrose), who baptized St. Augustine here. The bas-relief on the doorway dates from the time of St. Ambrose, and the two bronze doors are from the 9th century. The basilica was enlarged in the 11th century, and its superb atrium was added in the 12th century. Two other early Christian saints — Gervase and Protasius — are buried with St. Ambrose in the crypt. The ceiling of the apse is decorated with 10th-century mosaics. Above the portico is the *Museo di Sant'Ambrogio* (Museum of St. Ambrose), where you can see a 12th-century cross, a missal of Gian Galeazzo Visconti, and other religious treasures. The museum is open Wednesdays, Thursdays, Fridays, and Mondays from 10 AM to noon and 3 to 5 PM; Saturdays and Sundays from 3 to 5 PM; closed in August. Admission charge. South of the Sforza Castle. 15 Piazza Sant'Ambrogio (phone: 872059).

Santa Maria delle Grazie (The Church of St. Mary of Grace) – The interior of this restored brick and terra cotta church, representing a period of transition from Gothic to Renaissance, is decorated with some fine 15th-century frescoes. But the church, though beautiful in itself, usually is visited because Leonardo da Vinci's *The Last Supper* (known as the *Cenacolo Vinciano*) is on a wall of the refectory of the former Dominican convent next to it. *The Last Supper* was painted in tempera, which is not particularly durable, and though it has been restored several times, it has suffered considerable deterioration. The current restoration keeps viewers at a frustrating distance from the dim painting, and the nearly ubiquitous scaffolding doesn't help; meanwhile, the refectory remains open to visitors. Open Tuesdays through Saturdays from 9 AM to 1:15 PM and 2 to 6:15 PM; Sundays and Mondays from 9 AM to 1:15 PM. Admission charge. A few blocks northwest of Sant'Ambrogio. Piazza Santa Maria delle Grazie (phone: 498-7588).

ENVIRONS

Certosa di Pavia (Carthusian Monastery) – Gian Galeazzo Visconti founded this monastery in 1396 as a family mausoleum. With its façade of multicolored marble sculpture and its interior heavily decorated with frescoes, baroque grillwork, and other ornamentation, the monastery is one of the most remarkable buildings in Italy. It is conveniently reached from Milan by coach excursion or by road. Closed Mondays. No admission charge, but donations are welcome. Sixteen miles (26 km) from Milan, just off the Milan-Pavia Road (call 925613 for information on guided tours).

Pavia – On the banks of the Ticino, this gracious city was the capital of the Lombard kingdom and later a free commune, until it fell to the Visconti in 1359. The famous University of Pavia was officially founded in the same century, although its origins go back to the 9th century. The 15th-century Duomo (with a 19th-century façade, however) is flanked by an 11th-century tower and backed by the 16th-century Broletto

(Town Hall). An admirable church (Leonardo da Vinci and Bramante helped with the plans), it is nevertheless a relative newcomer — not far away is the Romanesque Basilica di San Michele, a 12th-century rebuilding of the 7th-century church where Charlemagne and Frederick Barbarossa were crowned Lombard kings. Still another Romanesque church, San Pietro in Ciel d'Oro, holds the tomb of St. Augustine. Pavia's main street, the Strada Nuova, is lined with elegant shops and ends at the river, which is crossed by a postwar reconstruction of a 14th-century covered bridge. Five miles (8 km) south of the Certosa di Pavia.

Monza – The world-famous Monza *Autodromo* is the scene of the Italian *Grand Prix Formula One* race early in September each year. Except during race preparation times, visitors can drive around the course, with its well-known seven corners (admission charge). The *Autodromo* is in a splendid park that was once part of the Villa Reale (Royal Villa), and now has golf courses, a racecourse, and a swimming pool, as well as the auto track. The historic cathedral at Monza (Piazza del Duomo) also is worth a visit. Built during the 13th and 14th centuries, it has a façade of white, green, and black marble, notable for its harmonious proportions and decorations. The *Museo Serpero* (Piazza del Duomo; phone: 393-23404) houses an interesting collection of precious medieval works in gold from the cathedral. It is open daily, except Sunday mornings and Mondays, from 9 AM to noon and 3 to 5 PM; admission charge. Monza is easily reached by bus or train; by road, it is 7 miles (11 km) northeast of Milan on SS 36.

> ■**EXTRA SPECIAL:** Until the early part of this century, Milan was crisscrossed by canals (*navigli*). Today only two remain, and their environs (it's a fair walk; from the Piazza del Duomo take Via Torino and Corso di Porta Ticinese) are perhaps the most picturesque in Milan. A stroll through this quarter provides a marked contrast to the rest of this modern, bustling city. On the last Sunday of every month, there is a huge and fascinating antiques market, the *Mercatone del Naviglio*, along the *navigli*.

SOURCES AND RESOURCES

TOURIST INFORMATION: General tourist information is available at the extremely helpful Provincial Tourist Board (Ente Provinciale per il Turismo, or EPT), conveniently located at corner of the Piazza del Duomo (12 Via Marconi; phone: 809662 or 870016), and at the central train terminal (phone: 669-0432 or 669-0532)). The EPT will make hotel reservations within Milan (phone: 706095) and provide information on current exhibits and events in the city, and to a lesser extent, on other regions of Italy. A good way to be introduced to the city is to view the free video presentation at the EPT office by the Duomo (address above).

Agenzia Autostradale conducts a 3-hour bus tour in English of the city that leaves daily from the Piazzetta Reale. Tickets are available from most hotels and travel agencies, or directly on board. From April to October, the company also offers an all-day tour of the Lombardy lakes. Pick-up points are at Piazza Castello and the Stazione Centrale (the main train station). For information on prices and hours for both tours, call 801161. The *Gestione Governative Navigazione Laghi* (21 Via Ariosto; phone: 481-6230 or 481-2086) arranges boat trips on the lakes.

A welcome convenience to travelers low on lire are automatic foreign exchange machines where you can change $5, $10, and $20 bills (as well as many other currencies) into local tender. The exchange rate is usually about what banks offer and there is a fixed commission charge comparable to what financial institutions charge. A few of the many locations for these ATMs are at the airports; the tourist office (1 Via Marconi); and the Banca Cesare Ponti (19 Piazza Duomo).

The US Consulate is at 2-10 Piazza Amedeo (phone: 290-09841).

Local Coverage – The tourist board can provide copies of *Milan Is,* a useful guide in English, which includes activities, facts, phone numbers, and listings of restaurants and discos. The monthly *Night & Day Milano,* distributed by many hotels, has bulletins on special events, and *Viva Milano,* a weekly entertainment newspaper in Italian, provides up-to-date information on shops, fairs, restaurants, and discos. Other publications, such as the monthly *Milano Mese* and *Un Ospite di Milano* (A Guest in Milano), produced by the Hotel Concierges Association, often are available in hotels. *Yes please* is an English-language monthly about Milan, available at newsstands.

The *Milan Trade Fair Center* is at 1 Largo Domodossola (phone: 49971). During fair events, an office is set up at Linate Airport (phone: 738-2431).

Food – There are several books in Italian that provide listings of restaurants and food and wine shops throughout Italy. Some of the better guides are *La Guida d'Italia* (published annually by *L'Espresso*), *I Ristoranti di Bell'Italia* (published annually by *Mondadori*), and *Gambero Rosso* (published by *Il Manifesto*). They all are sold on newsstands.

 TELEPHONE: The country code for Italy is 39; the city code for Milan is 2. When calling from within Italy, dial 02 before the local number.

 GETTING AROUND: Much of the center of Milan has been closed to traffic, so it is far more convenient for visitors to use public transportation. Inexpensive day tickets that allow unlimited travel on the public transportation system can be purchased at the *ATM* Ufficio Abbonamenti at the Piazza del Duomo subway station, at the Stazione Centrale, and at the EPT on Via Marconi.

Airports – Malpensa Airport is about 28 miles (45 km) and less than an hour's drive from the center of Milan; a taxi ride into town can cost as much as $70. Buses to Malpensa leave from Stazione Centrale, on the east side of the *Galleria delle Carrozze,* every half hour and cost about $7 (phone: 868008 or 331-797480). They also stop at the east entrance of Porta Garibaldi Station en route. For flight information, call 748-52200, and for lost luggage, call 748-54215.

Linate Airport handles domestic traffic, as well as some international — but not intercontinental — flights. Linate is 5 miles (8 km) and 15 minutes (longer if traffic is heavy) from downtown Milan; taxi fare into the center of the city is about $16. *ATM* bus No. 73 leaves for the airport from Corso Europa (near Piazza San Babila), and Porta Garibaldi Station every 10 minutes between 5:40 AM and midnight, and costs about $1 (phone: 748-52200). For lost luggage, call 748-54215. *Doria Agenzia* has buses that leave from Stazione Centrale every 20 minutes from 5:40 AM to 8:30 PM. Tickets cost about $2.

Although there is no regular transportation between Malpensa and Linate airports, *Alitalia* occasionally provides group transfers when two connecting *Alitalia* flights are involved. For information on domestic flights, call 28361; for international flights, call 28371.

Bus and Tram – The local bus and tram service, *ATM,* efficiently connects various points of this sprawling city. Tickets are sold at tobacconists and newsstands throughout the city and must be purchased in advance. They are valid for 75 minutes, thus permitting transfer to other lines, and can be used for the subway as well.

Car Rental – Most international firms are represented. *Avis, Europcar, Hertz,* and

Maggiore all have counters at both Malpensa and Linate airports and at several locations in the city. Central reservations numbers are *Avis* (phone: 6981); *Europcar* (phone: 607-1051); *Hertz* (phone: 20483 or 654929); *Maggiore* (phone: 760-04238). Also try *Budget* (13 Via Vittorio Pisani; phone: 670-3151) and at Malpensa (phone: 868221) and Linate (phone: 738-5639); *InterRent* (4 Corso Como; phone: 657-0477 or 659-9417) and at Malpensa (phone: 868124) and Linate (phone: 733585). *Avis, Hertz,* and *Maggiore* also have branches at the train station. Note that Malpensa Airport has desks at which tourists may buy coupons that can be redeemed at gas stations around Italy. Coupons must be purchased in foreign currency. Another option is *Limousine Service* (phone: 344752).

Subway – The efficient, clean *Metropolitana Milanese* (*MM*) now has three lines (a third was inaugurated last year). The most useful for tourists is line M3, which directly links the main railway station, through Piazza del Duomo, and the Porta Romana. Tickets are sold at coin-operated machines in each station and at many tobacconists.

Taxi – Taxis can be hailed while cruising, picked up at a cabstand, or called by radio taxi (phone: 8388, 8585, 6767, or 5251). Meters begin at about $5 plus arrival and waiting time if the cab is called by phone. Do not be surprised if the driver asks for a surcharge after 10 PM or on Sundays or holidays. There is an additional small charge for baggage.

Train – Milan's main train station is Stazione Centrale (Piazzale Duca d'Aosta; phone: 67500). Several smaller stations serve local commuter lines. The largest of these is Porta Garibaldi, the departure point for trains to Turin, Pavia, Monza, Bergamo, and other points (phone: 655-2078). Several new, comfortable, high-speed trains make the trip to Rome in 5 hours or less. The *Pendolino* clocks it in 4 hours, and the ticket price includes dinner. Some of the fast trains (the *rapidi*) have comfortable second class accommodations. Book ahead.

 LOCAL SERVICES: Credit Card Offices – *American Express* (3 Via Brera; phone: 85571; for lost traveler's checks, phone: 1678-720-0024, toll-free in Italy); *Diners Club* (32 Piazza della Repubblica; phone: 669-81203); *Master-Card* and *Visa* (toll-free phone: 1678-68086); *AT&T* (for calls to the US, dial 172-1011).

Dentist (English-Speaking) – Dr. Lucia Calinescu (7 Piazza Giovanni delle Bande Nere; phone: 406241); Dr. Massimo Rossi (121 Porta Romana; phone: 546-4664).

Dry Cleaner – *Guritz,* 7-9 Via Sant'Andrea (phone: 760-02129).

Limousine Service – *Garage Principe e Savoia* (1 Via Cartesio; phone: 650220); *Autonoleggi Del Sole* (120 Viale Umbria; phone: 714023); *Auto VIP* (7 Via Aldrovandi; phone: 204-9817).

Medical Emergency – *Ospedale Maggiore Policlinico* (35 Via Francesco Sforza; phone: 551-1655); *Ospedale Fatebenefratelli* (23 Corso di Porta Nuova; phone: 63631). In cases of extreme emergency, call 3883 for a house call, 7733 or 113 for an ambulance or medical assistance. Two English-speaking physicians are Dr. Larry Burdick (4 Corso XXII Marzo; phone: 204-9167) and Dr. Bettina Sturlese (19 Via S. Eufemia; phone: 805-7831 or 279167).

Messenger Service – *Rinaldi* (10 Via Sant'Andrea; phone: 796851; fax: 782160); *Agenzia Scutto* (21 Via Bramante; phone: 316441); *Pony Express* (39 Via Bernardino Vero; phone: 8441); *City Cross* (phone: 404-8241).

National/International Courier – *DHL International* (15 Via Agnello and 21 Via Fantoli; phone: 50781); *Emery Air Freight* (in Segrate; phone: 213-4613); *Italcargo* (214 Via Cassanese, Segrate; phone: 213-99510); *Moto Mondo* (phone: 738-3310); *Federal Express* (10 Via Albricci; phone: 863222 or 506-4076; fax: 502341).

Office Equipment Rental – Most of the city's better hotels can arrange for short-term rental (a day or two) of typewriters and other items. Companies that rent such equipment usually do so only on a monthly basis. For long-term rental, contact *ARS* (5 Piazza della Repubblica; phone: 799151); *Executive Services Business Center* (8 Via Monti; phone: 345-2211, and 14 Via Leopardi; phone: 498-2251); *Managing Center* (12 Via Washington; phone: 481-93012).

Pharmacy – The main floor of Stazione Centrale (the main railway station), *Galleria delle Partenze,* has a 24-hour pharmacy (phone: 669-0735). *Cooperative Farmaceutica* (1 Via Orefici, Piazza del Duomo; phone: 872266) is open day and night but closed at mealtimes. Call 192 for information regarding pharmacies that are open at night, Sundays, and holidays (*farmacia di turno*). Local newspapers list which pharmacies are open on holidays.

Photocopies – *Fotocolors Duplicating Service* (6 Largo Promessi Sposi; phone: 846-5176); *Fotoriproduzione Documenti* (Via Larga; phone: 862319); *De Poli* (27 Corso Vercelli; phone: 487438); *Copisteria Tecnocopy* (17 Via Grossich; phone: 236-0475), which stays open in August. Some photocopy centers also will send and receive faxes.

Post Office – The main post office is open weekdays from 8 AM to 8 PM and Saturdays from 8 AM to noon (4 Piazza Cordusio; phone: 160). The railway post office is open for registered letters weekdays from 8 AM to 10 PM and Saturdays from 8 AM to noon (8-10 Via Aporti; phone: 663-0649).

Secretary/Stenographer (English-Speaking) – *Congress Service* (7 Piazza Massari; phone: 608-0983); *Copisteria Manara* (28 Porta Vittoria; phone: 540-1047).

Tailor – *Caraceni* (16 Via Fatebenefratelli; phone: 655-1972); *Luisa Corvino* (6 Corso Concordia; phone: 795147).

Telex/Telefaxes – Main post office (4 Piazza Cordusio; phone: 869-2874), open 24 hours daily. For information about telefax service, call 866702.

Translator – *Associazione Italiana Traduttori Interpreti* (*ANTI,* 75 Via B. d'Alviano; phone: 415-9846); *Centro Serbelloni* (1 Via Serbelloni; phone: 760-00248); *Congress Service* (7 Piazza Massari; phone: 608-0983); *Translator/Interpreter Center* (10 Via Lambrate; phone: 287-0336); *Pronto-Mondo,* telephone interpreter (phone: 669-84862); *Simultanea* (phone: 720-01266).

Other – Milan has numerous "congress centers" that are equipped with audiovisual devices, simultaneous translation systems, and other services: *Athena* (4 Via Serbelloni; phone: 741253); *Centro Congressi Milanofiori* (Viale Milano Fiori, Assago; phone: 825-2969 or 824791); *Castello di Macconago Meeting Center,* a 14th-century castle 15 minutes from downtown (38 Via Macconago; phone: 539-1053 or 569-4819); *Centro Mitec* (49 Via Vittorio Colonna; phone: 439-0383); and *Tekno Congress* (1 Via Marazzini; phone: 282-2730). Fully equipped offices can be rented through *Executive Service* (8 Via V. Monti; phone: 345-2211); *International Business Centre* (12 Corso Europa; phone: 545-6331); *Centro Bonsaglio* (1a Via Borromei; phone: 805-1898); *Centro Italiano Congressi* (121/A Corso di Porta Romana; phone: 551-87057); *ES Assistance* (8 Corso Venezia; phone: 784812). Other helpful places for business travelers: *US International Marketing Center* (5 Via Gattamelata; phone: 469-6451); *Camera di Commercio Americana in Italia* (12 Via Agnello; phone: 869-0661). Formal wear rental: *Lo Bosco Casa d'Arte* (7 Corso Venezia; phone: 760-00585).

 SPECIAL EVENTS: The annual *International Trade Fair* held in late April since the 1920s has put Milan squarely on the international business map. Although this is the city's biggest, there are various other trade fairs and exhibitions (including the showings of designer collections, the twice yearly fashion fair, and the September furniture fair) almost every month except July and August, making advance hotel reservations essential. Information, a copy of the useful bilingual periodical *In Fiera,* and a year-round calendar of events can be obtained from the main *Trade Fair* office (1 Largo Domodossola; phone: 49971). In July and August, the city sponsors a variety of outdoor cultural events; sometimes restaurants join in by serving regional specialties in the parks. The opening of the opera season at *La Scala,* which takes place each year on December 7, is the city's major cultural event.

MUSEUMS: In addition to those listed in *Special Places,* there are several other museums in Milan worth a visit. All, except the Basilica di San Lorenzo Maggiore, have an admission charge.

Basilica di San Lorenzo Maggiore – This 4th-century church is the oldest in the West. 39 Corso di Porta Ticinese.

Galleria d'Arte Moderna (Modern Art Gallery) – Open Wednesdays through Mondays from 9:30 AM to 7:30 PM. Villa Comunale, 16 Via Palestro (phone: 702819).

Museo e Casa di Manzoni (Manzoni Museum and House) – The former home of Alessandro Manzoni, author of the 19th-century classic *I Promessi Sposi* (The Betrothed). Open Tuesdays through Fridays from 9 AM to noon and 2 to 4 PM. 1 Via Morone (phone: 871019).

Museo di Milano (Museum of Milan) – Open Tuesdays through Sundays from 9:30 AM to 7:30 PM; closed the last Tuesday of each month. 6 Via Sant' Andrea (phone: 706245).

Museo del Risorgimento Nazionale (National Museum of the Risorgimento) – Open daily from 9:30 AM to 7:30 PM. 23 Via Borgonuovo (phone: 869-3549).

Museo della Scienza e della Tecnica Leonardo da Vinci (Leonardo da Vinci Museum of Science and Technology) – Open daily except Mondays from 9:30 AM to 4:50 PM. 21 Via San Vittore (phone: 480-10040).

Museo di Storia Contemporanea (Museum of Contemporary History) – Open Tuesdays through Sundays from 9:30 AM to 7:30 PM; closed the last Tuesday of each month. 6 Via Sant' Andrea (phone: 760-06245).

Palazzo Reale (Royal Palace) – A beautiful 18th-century building that houses the *Museum of Contemporary Art* and prestigious temporary exhibitions. Open daily from 9:30 AM to 7:30 PM. Piazza del Duomo (phone: 6236).

GALLERIES: Milan also has scores of art galleries with interesting shows. They generally are open from 10:30 AM to 1 PM and 4 to 8 PM except Mondays. The following offer an excellent selection of contemporary and early-20th-century Italian art:

Arte Centro – 11 Via Brera (phone: 865888).

Centro Annunciata – 44 Via Manzoni (phone: 796026).

Christie's – 9 Via Borgogna (phone: 794712).

Galleria Fonte d'Abisso – 7 Via del Carmine (phone: 873050).

Salvatore Ala – 3 Via Mameli (phone: 716500).

Sotheby's – 3 Via Montenapoleone (phone: 783907).

Studio Marconi – 15-17 Via Tadino (phone: 294-04373 or 225543).

Toselli – 9 Via del Carmine (phone: 805-0434).

SHOPPING: With the explosion of Italian design and fashion over the last 20 years, Milan is an international style center full of enticing, if expensive, shops, including showrooms and boutiques of many of Italy's major contemporary clothing designers, such as Milan's own *Mila Schön* (2 Via Montenapoleone); her store for men is a few steps away. It also is a center for antiques and home furnishings. The main shopping area comprises the streets near Piazza del Duomo and *La Scala,* particularly the elegant Via Montenapoleone, Via della Spiga, and Via Sant'Andrea. Here you'll find the boutiques of top Italian designers *Giorgio Armani* (9 Via Sant'Andrea); *Gianni Versace* (4 and 25 Via della Spiga); *Enrico Coveri*

(Via San Pietro all'Orto); *Missoni* (1 Via Montenapoleone); *Ferragamo* (3 Via Montenapoleone); and *Krizia* (23 Via della Spiga), most of whom are based in Milan. The *Galleria Vittorio Emanuele* (between the Piazza del Duomo and the Piazza della Scala) is a good place to window shop and stop at one of its many cafés for a coffee or cool drink in summer. Boutiques offering modern fashions and antique clothes also are scattered throughout the old Brera quarter — Milan's Left Bank — and around St. Ambrose's Basilica. *Caffè Moda Durini* (14 Via Durini), the only mini-shopping mall in the city, is filled with fashions by designers such as Valentino (for men); there's also a café on the lower level. Shop hours generally are from 9 or 9:30 AM to 12:30 PM and 3:30 to 7:30 PM. Most shops are closed Sundays and Monday mornings.

Milan also has several outdoor markets. Tuesday mornings and Saturdays, there are clothing stalls on Viale Papiniano and Via V. Marcello. On the third Saturday of the month the *Mercato di Brera* sells antiques, real and otherwise, from 10 AM to 11 PM in and around Piazza Formentini. Early in December, a flea market and fair near the *Basilica e Museo di Sant'Ambrogio* features a wide selection of clothes, antiques, old books, and knickknacks.

Accademia – Fine menswear and accessories. 11 Via Solferino.

Alberto Subert – Fine Italian and imported antiques. 22 Via della Spiga.

Arflex – Armchairs and chaises that are produced by top designers and are among the best known in Italy. 28 Via Durini.

Arte Antica – One of the city's best-known antiques stores, with French porcelain, clocks, and furniture. 11 Via Sant'Andrea.

Beltrami – Shoes, handbags, and beautifully styled, ready-to-wear. 16 Via Montenapoleone.

Bottega Veneta – Basket-woven fine leather goods are the hallmark of this famed store. 5 Via della Spiga.

Brigatti – Considered Milan's finest men's sportswear shop. Also has a ski boutique for the entire family. 15 Corso Venezia.

Bulgari – World-famous high-style jewelry designer, offering masterpieces made from gold, silver, platinum, and precious stones. 6 Via Sant'Andrea.

Calderoni – Exquisite jewelry and silver. 8 Via Montenapoleone.

Carrano – Stylish women's shoes. 21 Via Sant'Andrea.

Centenari – Fine old prints and paintings. 92 *Galleria Vittorio Emanuele II.*

Cignarelli – Wonderful homemade herbal liqueurs. 65 Corso Buenos Aires.

Decomania – Art Deco objects and furniture. 5-9 Via Fiori Chiari.

Dispensa Gualtiero Marchesi – The maestro of Italian nouvelle cooking sells culinary items from pâté to placemats. 6 Via San Giovanni sul Muro.

Ermenegildo Zegna – Designer menswear. 3 Via Verri.

Fendi – High-fashion silk shirts, purses, and furs designed by Karl Lagerfeld. 16 Via Sant' Andrea.

Fontana – Furniture with a flair by the famous avant-garde Memphis Milano School. 3 Via Montenapoleone.

Franco and Aldo Lorenzi – Elegant travel and smoking accessories for men. 9 Via Montenapoleone.

Frette – Luxurious linen for bed and bath, as well as silk negligees. 21 Via Montenapoleone.

Galtrucco – Shimmering silks from Como, by the meter or ready-to-wear. 27 Via Montenapoleone.

Gherardini – Florentine leather goods and sportswear. 8 Via della Spiga.

Guanti Berni – Beautiful leather gloves for men and women. Via Sant'Andrea.

Gucci – Leatherwear, clothing, and shoes from the famous maker. 5 Via Montenapoleone.

Mario Buccellati – Jeweler famed for his finely chased, engraved gold. Inside the courtyard at 12 Via Montenapoleone.

Mastro Geppetto – Dolls, toys, models, plus a life-size Pinocchio. 14 Corso Matteotti.

Moschino – High fashion ready-to-wear for women. 12 Via Sant'Andrea.

Naj-Oleari – Vibrant-colored animal prints. 8 Via Brera.

Officina Alessi – The ultimate in wooden and stainless steel household objects, in a tiny shop designed by Sottsass, Italy's most famous architect. 9 Corso Matteotti.

L'Oro dei Farlocchi – The place for unique presents — ivory penknives, crystal knickknacks, and so on. 5 Via Madonnina.

Orsi – A small but highly regarded antiques shop, with lovely 17th- and 18th-century furniture. 14 Via Bagutta.

Peck – This fancy food store should not be missed, especially by those eager for the best in dried *porcini* mushrooms, truffles, and other Italian specialties. Its restaurant is next door (see *Eating Out*). 9 Via Spadari.

Philippe Daverio – Prestigious antiques dealer. 6/A Via Montenapoleone.

Prada – Fashion insiders know that this is the place for shoes with the shape of things to come. 1 Via della Spiga.

Pratesi – Luxurious linen. 21 Via Montenapoleone.

Provera – Top-quality wines sold in a 1920s' shop that specializes in wines from the north. Sold by the bottle or the glass; there are a few tables for tasting. 7 Corso Magenta.

Richard Ginori – Fine bone china in traditional or contemporary styles, such as the popular "Italian Fruit" design. 1 Corso Matteotti.

Rubinacci – Top French designers and the store's own elegant line of women's fashions. 10 Via Sant'Andrea.

Salviati – Exquisite hand-blown Venetian glass in decorator bottles, designer desk lamps, and vases. Corner of Via Manzoni and Via Montenapoleone.

Scavia – Sleek and supemely elegant jewelry, especially the satin-smooth gold bracelets in a variety of widths. 9 Via Spiga.

Shara Pagano – The bijoux are not the real thing, but are gems nonetheless. 7 Via della Spiga.

Stationery – The city's best-stocked stationery store, with interesting gadgets and office accessories. 3 Via Solferino.

T & J Vestor – For Missoni's carpets and wall hangings, and tablecloth and napkin sets. 38 Via Manzoni.

Tanino Crisci – The best in finely crafted men's and women's footwear. 3 Via Montenapoleone.

Trussardi – High-fashion leatherwear, luggage, and briefcases for men and women. 7 Via Sant'Andrea.

Valentino Donna – Women's clothing by the famous designer. 3 Via Santo Spirito. Men's fashions sold at *Valentino Uomo.* 20 Via Montenapoleone.

Venini – Hand-blown glass — from perfume bottles to chandeliers, made by one of Venice's foremost artisans. 9 Via Montenapoleone.

Vittorio Siniscalchi – One of Milan's best custom shirtmakers for men. 8 Via Gesù.

DISCOUNT SHOPS

If you're one of those — like us — who tries to make every lira go a long, long way, here are some select discount outlets where fine Italian goods and fashions are often found at far less than the prices in fancier shops. For indefatigable bargain hunters, a good guide is *Bargain Hunting in Milan, Le Occasioni di Milano,* available at some newsstands and bookstores.

Diecidecimi – Men's and women's fashions, all discounted 50%, including a large selection of leather jackets and sheepskin coats. 34 Via Plino.

Emporio – Discounted classic, spirited clothing from previous and current seasons; *not* part of *Emporio Armani.* 11 Via Prini, near Corso Sempione.

Emporio Armani – His less expensive line. 24 Via Durini.

Mimosa – Samples from the salons of name designers. 12 Piazza Santo Stefano.

Misul – Women's clothes in luxurious fabrics, often sold at far less than retail prices. Call for an appointment. 3 Via San Calocero.

Niki – Elegant women's clothes at half the usual price. 78 Viale Montenero.

Il Salvagente – Armani, Valentino, and other famous designer clothes for men, women, and children; in a warehouse-like store offering excellent discounts. 16 Via Fratelli Bronzetti and 28 Via Balzaretti.

 SPORTS AND FITNESS: Downtown Milan is small, and has little green space, few gyms, and a scarcity of public parks. But it has an efficient municipal sports organization. For specific information on what sports are offered, and where, contact the Ufficio Sport e Tempo Libero (2 Via Marconi; phone: 6236) to consult their listings on golf courses, horseback riding, squash courts, etc. The staff (some English-speaking) either will make reservations for you (in the case of municipal tennis courts) or explain how you can do it yourself (alternatively, ask your hotel concierge to do it for you). The closest and largest green space for jogging, paddling a boat, swimming in a large public pool, picnicking, sunbathing, and café sitting with Milanese families is the Idroscalo Parco Azzurro (Azzurro Park and Boat Landing), whose artificial lake served the city's seaplanes until the 1970s. The waters are now filtered and reportedly not polluted. The city bus No. ID leaves from Piazza Fontana for the park at frequent intervals, including on Sundays.

Bicycling – Rentals by the hour, day, or month at *Vittorio Comizzoli* (60 Via Washington; phone: 498-4694) and *Cooperativa Il Picchio* (49 Corso San Gottardo; phone: 837-7926 or 837-2757).

Fitness Centers – *Skorpion Center* (24 Corso Vittorio Emanuele; phone: 796098); *Club Francesco Conti* (7 Via de Toqueville; phone: 657-0297, and 4 Via Cerva; phone: 760-00141); *American Contourella* (six locations, including 10 Via Montenapoleone; phone: 760-05290); *Health Center Club* (33 Via Kramer; phone: 272372); *Skorpion Center* (24 Corso Vittorio Emanuele; phone: 796098).

Golf – There are several golf courses in the Milan area, the largest and most accessible of which is the 27-hole course at the *Golf Club Milano,* in the park at nearby Monza (phone: 39-703081/2).

Horseback Riding – There are two riding stables in Milan: the *Centro Ippico Lombardo* (21 Via Fetonte; phone: 408-4270) and the *Centro Ippico Milanese* (20 Via Macconago; phone: 539-2013). For more information, get in touch with the Milan branch of *ANTE,* the national equestrian society (44/B Via Piranesi; phone: 738-4615).

Horse Racing – Thoroughbred and trotting races are run at the internationally famous *Ippodromo San Siro* (phone: 452-1854), on the eastern outskirts of Milan.

Ice Skating – There is a rink in operation from September through May at the Palazzo del Ghiaccio (14 Via Piranesi; phone: 7398). Skates can be rented at *Saini* (136 Via Corelli; phone: 738-0841).

Jogging – Try Parco Sempione, the Giardini Pubblici (Public Gardens), or the Idroscala Parco Azzurro.

Soccer – From September to May, both *Inter* and *Milan* play at *Stadio Comunale Giuseppe Meazza* (5 Via Piccolomini; phone: 454123 or 408-4123).

Squash – Courts are available at the *Giambellino Squash Club,* 5 Via Giambellino; (phone: 422-5979).

Swimming – Public indoor pools include *Cozzi* (35 Viale Tunisia); *Mincio* (13 Via Mincio); and *Solari* (11 Via Montevideo). Open-air pools include *Lido* (15 Piazzale Lotto, near the *San Siro Stadium;* phone: 7398); *Romano* (35 Via Ponzio); *Piscina Olimpica* (in the park at Monza); and *Argelati* (6 Via Segantini; phone: 835-0012).

Tennis – Public courts should be booked well ahead of time. Some of the main courts are at *Bonacossa* (74 Via Mecenate; phone: 506-1277); *Centro Polisportivo* (48 Via Valvassori Peroni; phone: 236-6254); *Lido di Milano* (15 Piazzale Lotto; phone: 391667); and *Ripamonti* (4 Via Iseo; phone: 645-9253).

 THEATER: You can take in classical Italian theater productions, including ones by world-famous director Giorgio Strehler, at the *Piccolo Teatro* (2 Via Rovello; phone: 869-0631); the *Manzoni* (40 Via Manzoni; phone: 790543); the *Salone Pier Lombardo* (14 Via Pier Lombardo; phone: 584410); or the *Teatro Lirico* (14 Via Larga; phone: 866418). For avant-garde and experimental theater, try the *Carcano* (63 Corso di Porto Romana; phone: 551-81377); or the *Centro Ricerca Teatro* (7 Via Ulisse Dini; phone: 846-6592 or 846-5693). Three theaters now offer English-language films: *Anteo* (9 Via Milazzo; phone: 659-7773) on Mondays; *Arcobaleno* (11 Viale Tunisia; phone: 294-06054) on Wednesdays; and *Mexico* (57 Via Savona; phone: 479802) on Thursdays.

 MUSIC: The renowned *La Scala* (see *Special Places*) is an obvious must for an opera fan lucky enough to have tickets in hand (or to have made the acquaintance of a sharp concierge who knows the ropes), but ballet and concerts also are held here; Piazza della Scala (phone: 807041). Concerts also are held at the *Auditorium Angelicum* (2 Piazza Sant'Angelo; phone: 632748), and the *Conservatorio di Musica* (12 Via Conservatorio; phone: 760-01755). Tickets to the *Angelicum* are sold at 4 Via Gustavo Favo or at *Ricordi Music Shop* (2 Via Berchet).

 NIGHTCLUBS AND NIGHTLIFE: Milan has a variety of nightclubs offering both dinner and dancing. The most popular of these include *Charley Max* (2 Via Marconi; phone: 871416); *Caffè Roma* (4 Via Ancona; phone: 876960); and *Nepentha,* open until 3 AM (1 Piazza Diaz; phone: 804837). Top discos include *American Disaster* (48 Via Boscovich; phone: 225728); *Good Mood* (29 Via Turati; phone: 669349); *Plastic* — a favorite with the young, avant-garde crowd — (120 Viale Umbria; phone: 733993); and *Calipso Club* (120 Viale Umbria; phone: 256-0553). Live music, including jazz, can be heard regularly at numerous clubs, among them *Capolinea* (119 Via Ludovico il Moro; phone: 428602), the city's oldest jazz spot, where internationally acclaimed musicians perform; *Ca'Bianca,* an excellent music and cabaret spot near the Naviglio Grande (117 Via Ludovico il Moro); and the loud, loud *Le Scimmie* (49 Via Ascanio Sforza; phone: 839-1874). The latter also has rock or blues, as does *Live Music* (4 Via Ciaia; phone: 668-8738). Milanese folk tunes and ballads are performed at *Osteria Amici Miei* (14 Via Nicola d'Apulia; phone: 285-0001). *Apollo Danze* (17 Via Procaccini), a 25-year-old dance hall, has live music on Monday afternoons (at cut rates), Saturday nights, and Sundays.

Milan has many cozy piano bars that are ideal for a late drink and snack. Try *Bistrot Piano Bar di Gualtiero Marchesi* (Piazza del Duomo; phone: 877120); *Golden Memory* (22 Via Lazzaro Papi; phone: 548-4209); *Gershwin's* (10 Via Corrado il Salico; phone: 849-7722); or the elegant *Momus* (8 Via Fiori Chiari; phone: 896227). There are striptease shows at *Teatrino* (3 Corsia dei Servi; phone: 793716), *Maschere* (7 Via Borgogna; phone: 705584), *Venus* (1 Via Giardino; phone: 805-0330); and *Smeraldo* (Piazza 25 Aprile; phone: 662768).

BEST IN TOWN

CHECKING IN: As an international business center, Milan offers a wide range of accommodations for the visitor, from traditional, old-fashioned hotels to efficient, modern, commercial ones. The number of hotels grew last year, just in time to help the city promote its bid to host the *2000 Olympic Games*. Because of the many fairs and fashion showings, some hotels are fully booked in peak periods a year ahead. Summer reservations are easier to obtain. Milan's hotel prices are quite high. In high season (summer, *Easter*), very expensive hotels here will cost $550 or more a night for a double room; expensive hotels will cost from $350 to $500 a night; moderate hotels charge $200 to $350 for a double; and inexpensive hotels will charge between $100 and $200. Off-season rates are about 10% lower. Unless otherwise noted, all Milan hotels accept major credit cards. All telephone numbers are in the 2 city code unless otherwise indicated.

Excelsior Gallia – Built by the Gallia family in the early 1930s, this luxury place — decorated in the grand style — with 241 rooms and 12 suites is spacious, efficient, and friendly. Its restaurant ranks among the city's very finest (see *Eating Out*). Near the central train station. Business facilities include meeting rooms for up to 400, English-speaking concierge, foreign currency exchange, secretarial services in English, audiovisual equipment, photocopiers, computers, translation services, and express checkout. 9 Piazza Duca D'Aosta (phone: 6785; fax: 656306; telex: 311160GALLIA I). Very expensive.

Pierre Milano – Slightly off the beaten track, nevertheless, this luxurious 47-room hotel is a favorite of the VIP business crowd. There is an American bar on the premises, but no restaurant. Business facilities include 24-hour room service, meeting rooms for up to 20, English-speaking concierge, foreign currency exchange, secretarial services in English, audiovisual equipment, photocopiers, cable television news, translation services, and express checkout. 32 Via de Amicis (phone: 805-6221; fax: 805-2157; telex: 333303PIER MI). Very expensive.

Duomo – Much favored by the movers and shakers of Italian commerce. Bi-level rooms provide a businesslike sitting room, while touches of marble and Oriental carpets add swank to the contemporary decor. In the heart of town, just off Piazza del Duomo, but on a pedestrian street that ensures quiet. Business facilities include 24-hour room service, meeting rooms for up to 20, English-speaking concierge, foreign currency exchange, secretarial services in English, audiovisual equipment, photocopiers, computers, and translation services. 1 Via San Raffaele (phone: 8833; fax: 864-62027; telex: 312086). Expensive.

Hilton International – An attractive 332-room hotel in the new commercial center facing the main railway station, about a mile north of the center and the cathedral, it is tastefully decorated in a mixture of Italian provincial and modern styles. There is also a colorful, moderately priced Italian restaurant and a discotheque. The service is first-rate. Business facilities include 24-hour room service, meeting rooms for up to 240, English-speaking concierge, foreign currency exchange, secretarial services in English, audiovisual equipment, photocopiers, computers, cable television news, translation services, and express checkout. 12 Via Galvani (phone: 698331; fax: 607-1904; telex: 330433HILTEL I). Expensive.

Palace – Transformed by a $2.5-million renovation, each floor has a different color scheme and the rooms are decorated in ultramodern style. The smaller new wing is more conventional than the renovated old wing. Dining is on the roof garden or in the famous and attractive *Casanova Grill,* with its refined decor. 20 Piazza della Repubblica (phone: 6336; fax: 654485). Expensive.

Principe di Savoia – An ambitious renovation recently took place at this classic deluxe hotel, including a new façade, lobby, and reception areas. Enlarged and redecorated guestrooms boast antiques, thick rugs, marble baths, and air conditioning. There are kitchenette apartments with balconies in the new wing. The location is excellent: just north of the cathedral on a fashionable street away from the busy main road, yet within walking distance of Milan's boutique-lined Via Montenapoleone. 17 Piazza della Repubblica (phone: 6230). Expensive.

Spadari al Duomo – Under new management (and formerly called the *Lord Internazionale*), this tiny hostelry is on a busy little shopping street near the cathedral. All 18 rooms are decorated with Memphis-style furniture, with attention paid to architectural details. Although the guestrooms are soundproofed, be sure to ask for one on the top floor — the plumbing is quite noisy farther down. There is no restaurant, but a small café serves light meals. Business facilities include 24-hour room service, meeting rooms for up to 30, cable television news, translation services, and express checkout. It also is possible to have a fax machine in your room. 11 Via Spadari (phone: 720-02371; fax: 720-02371). Expensive.

Blaise & Francis – New and conveniently close to the main train station (and 10 minutes from the center), it has 110 rooms, but no restaurant. It also has a garage. Business facilities include 24-hour room service and meeting rooms for up to 250. 9 Via Butti (phone: 668-02366; fax: 668-02909). Expensive to moderate.

Bonaparte – Formerly a residential hotel (now fully refurbished), this smallish property (56 rooms) is luxuriously appointed. 13 Via Cusani (phone: 8560; fax: 869-3601). Expensive to moderate.

Century Tower – This new, very comfortable, 198-room hotel has a garden, restaurant, and bar. 25/B Via Fabio Filzi (phone: 67504; fax: 669-80602). Expensive to moderate.

Executive – Next to the old airport bus terminal, about a mile from downtown Milan, this American-style hotel has a pleasant staff, deluxe rooms, a good restaurant and bar, saunas, and a swimming pool. 45 Via Don Luigi Sturzo (phone: 6294). Expensive to moderate.

Fiera Milano – Across the street from the fairgrounds, this 238-room hostelry has air conditioning and private parking. Business facilities include meeting rooms for up to 50, English-speaking concierge, foreign currency exchange, secretarial services in English, audiovisual equipment, photocopiers, cable television news, translation services, and express checkout. 20 Viale Boezio (phone: 3105; fax: 314119; telex: 331426HOTFIE). Expensive to moderate.

Jolly President – So centrally located that you can see the gargoyles on top of the Duomo from some windows, it has 201 comfortable rooms and a restaurant. 10 Largo Augusto (phone: 7746; fax: 783449). Expensive to moderate.

Europeo – Not far from the center of town, this fine hotel has its own peaceful garden and pool, all the modern conveniences, and very good service. 38 Via Canonica (phone: 331-4751; fax: 331-05410). Moderate.

Ibis Ca'Grande – Not centrally located, but new, with 132 rooms, a restaurant, bar, and garden. It has parking facilities, and also is well connected to the city center by bus. 13-15 Viale Suzzani (phone: 661-03000; fax: 661-02797). Moderate.

Manin – This small, first class hostelry is about a half mile from *La Scala.* Some of the rooms have been redecorated in a modern style; the older rooms are not impressive but are spacious and comfortable. There's also a very good restaurant and bar. Business facilities include meeting rooms for up to 100, English-speaking concierge, foreign currency exchange, audiovisual equipment, photocopiers, cable television news, and express checkout. 7 Via Manin (phone: 659-6511; fax: 655-2160; telex: 320385MANIN I). Moderate.

Mirage – Renovated last year, this high-quality, 50-room establishment has a bar, but no restaurant. 61 Via Casella (phone: 392-10471; fax: 392-10589). Moderate.

Nasco – An American-style place, it's an excellent choice when downtown hotels are full. Business facilities include meeting rooms for up to 150, English-speaking concierge, foreign currency exchange, audiovisual equipment, and photocopiers. 40 Via Spallanzani (phone: 204-3841). Moderate.

Novotel Milano Est Aeroporto – Near Linate Airport, this Fiat investment has 208 rooms and is one of the few to offer a swimming pool and garden, as well as a restaurant. Business facilities include meeting rooms for up to 320, English-speaking concierge, foreign currency exchange, secretarial services in English, audiovisual equipment, photocopiers, computers, cable television news, translation services, and express checkout. 12 Via Mecenate (phone: 580-11085; fax: 580-11086; telex: 331237NOVMIE). Moderate.

Novotel Milano Nord – Another newcomer, with 172 rooms, swimming pool, garden, restaurant, and bar. Business facilities include meeting rooms for up to 500, English-speaking concierge, foreign currency exchange, secretarial services in English, audiovisual equipment, photocopiers, computers, cable television news, translation services, and express checkout. 13 Viale Suzzani (phone: 661-01861; fax: 566-101961; telex: 331292). Moderate.

Manzoni – Small, pleasant and quiet, it's right in the city's center, and boasts a garage. No restaurant, but room service provides snacks. There's a shopping mall nearby. No credit cards accepted. 20 Via Santo Spirito (phone: 794045). Moderate to inexpensive.

Antica Locanda Solferino – Delightful tiny place, with only 11 rooms, in the old Brera quarter a few blocks north of *La Scala*. This once was a tavern and retains much of the Old World fin-de-siècle charm in its furniture and decor. No credit cards accepted. Book far in advance. 2 Via Castelfidardo (phone: 657-0129). Inexpensive.

Casa Svizzera – Near the Duomo, well maintained, and with air conditioning to boot. This 45-room place is a good value for the money and location. 3 Via San Raffaele (phone: 869-2246; fax: 349-8190). Inexpensive.

Centro – A small budget hotel in the heart of downtown Milan. 46 Via Broletto (phone: 875232; fax: 875578). Inexpensive.

EATING OUT: It is a time of special grace for dining out in Milan. Its restaurants today are among the world's finest. Milanese food, like much of northern fare, differs from other Italian food in that butter is used more often than olive oil. Look for special dishes made with the fabulous *tartufi bianchi* (Italian white truffles) from the neighboring Piedmont region, when they are in season between September and *Christmas*. Rice from the region's own plantations is used as a food base, with saffron-perfumed *risotto alla milanese* the favorite provender — best eaten with a steaming osso buco (veal shank). The Milanese also love fresh fish and know how to prepare it. In September, try delicious white peaches. Expect to pay $200 or more for dinner for two at one of Milan's expensive restaurants — among the most expensive in Italy; $80 to $130 at a moderately priced restaurant; and $50 to $75 at an inexpensive one. Prices don't include drinks, wine, or tips. It is a good idea to check whether the restaurant you select accepts credit cards. All telephone numbers are in the 2 city code unless otherwise indicated.

Antica Osteria del Ponte – At last, a real challenge to *Gualtiero Marchesi*, 10 miles (16 km) outside Milan in an old-fashioned inn by a bridge along a picturesque *naviglio*. Here since 1976, it is one of only two restaurants in Italy (both, significantly, in Milan) to be awarded three Michelin stars. It's a family affair — Ezio Santin and his son Maurizio perform wonders in the kitchen and wife Renata is hostess in the intimate dining room with a fireplace and antique furnishings. Look for expert, creative ways with the classic risotto and ravioli — including one dish that has them stuffed with lobster and covered with a lobster sauce — and new and interesting ways of preparing fine fresh fish. Truffles in season make their appearance, and for lovers of sweets, a hot chocolate soufflé arrives blanketed in a white chocolate sauce. Closed *Christmas* to January 12 and August. Reservations necessary. Major credit cards accepted. 9 Piazza G. Negri, Cassinetta di Lugagnano (phone: 942-0034). Very expensive.

Gualtiero Marchesi – Owned by one of Italy's most eminent chefs (Michelin has given him three stars), this restaurant provides an elegant setting for an Italian nouvelle cuisine that many consider the best in Italy — though some critics fault the tiny portions and somewhat staid atmosphere. The open-face ravioli are a triumph, the risotto sublime, though the edible gold-leaf topping is a real case of gilding the lily. A single dish can be ordered as a sampler. Closed Sundays, Mondays for lunch, and August. Reservations necessary. Major credit cards accepted. 9 Via Bonvesin della Riva (phone: 741246). Very expensive.

El Toulà – One of Milan's finest dining places, created by the noted restaurateur Alfredo Beltrame and situated behind *La Scala.* The pasta specialty is *manicaretti,* but the chef, Daniel Droudaine is French; so is much of the menu. Closed Sundays, from June to August; closed Saturdays in winter. Reservations necessary. Major credit cards accepted. 6 Piazza Paolo Ferrari (phone: 870302). Very expensive.

Aimo and Nadia – A husband and wife team from Tuscany run this restaurant, one of Italy's top ten and renowned for its creative fare, in an unprepossessing area of Milan. *Ovoli* (mushrooms) and Alba truffles abound, but the real culinary triumph is the risotto with zucchini blossoms and truffles; the desserts are luscious. Closed Sundays and August. Reservations necessary. Major credit cards accepted. 6 Via Montecuccoli (phone: 416886). Expensive.

Biffi Scala – A favorite place for late-night suppers, particularly after the opera. The decor is extravagant, the fare Lombard and international. Closed Sundays, last 2 weeks in August, and *Christmas* week. Reservations necessary. Major credit cards accepted. Piazza della Scala (phone: 866651). Expensive.

Calajunco Milano – The Aeolian Islands inspire its fine Sicilian restaurant's menu, which includes zucchini blossom–stuffed ravioli with squid sauce and, for an antipasto, seashell "plates" brimming with linguini in a mixed shellfish sauce. The unique fish sausage also is worth trying. There is a fixed price sampler menu (*menù degustazione*). Closed Sundays and some holidays. Reservations necessary. Major credit cards accepted. 5 Via Stoppani (phone: 204-6003). Expensive.

Gallia's – Some of Milan's hotels provide fine dining, and here is one of the best. At the *Excelsior Gallia,* diners can savor traditional dishes, such as the delicious tournedos Rossini, in an elegant setting. Open daily. Reservations necessary. Major credit cards accepted. Piazza Duca d'Aosta (phone: 6785). Expensive.

Giannino – So famous that some people reserve 6 months in advance, this is a beloved bastion of traditional Italian fare, including homemade pasta and pastries. The fish also is excellent. Elegant private dining rooms can be provided. Closed Sundays and August. Reservations necessary. Major credit cards accepted. 8 Via Amatore Sciesa (phone: 545-2948). Expensive.

Saint Andrews – This elegant downtown dining place with dark paneled walls and plush upholstery is a favorite of Milanese executives. Romantic atmosphere and an imaginative menu. Closed Sundays and August. Reservations advised. Major credit cards accepted. 23 Via Sant'Andrea (phone: 793132). Expensive.

Savini – Everything here, from the service to the decor, including the crystal chandeliers and silk lampshades, is classic and exquisite. After a brief lapse, the restaurant is once again topnotch, with mostly Lombard fare (although there is a smattering of international dishes), excellent fresh fish, and fine wines. VIPs like the private rooms; Onassis and Callas dined together in the small, gilded downstairs room. Closed Sundays and August. Reservations necessary. Major credit cards accepted. 11 *Galleria Vittorio Emanuele* (phone: 805-8343). Expensive.

La Scaletta – The Italian *nuova cucina* at this outstanding, elegantly appointed 2-room restaurant is so popular among Milanese diners that reservations are essential. Closed Sundays, Mondays, *Christmas, New Year's,* and August. No credit cards accepted. 3 Piazza Stazione Porta Genova (phone: 581-00290). Expensive.

Alfio – It has a central location, an enclosed winter garden, and very good antipasti, risotto, and fish and meat dishes. Closed Saturdays, Sunday lunch, and August. Reservations advised. Major credit cards accepted. 31 Via Senato (phone: 780731). Expensive to moderate.

Da Alfredo Gran San Bernardo – Alfredo Valli serves some of the best regional cooking in town in this large and friendly place. Try the *risotto alla milanese,* the veal cutlet, or the classic Lombardy stew of pork, sausages, carrots, and white wine, *casseoeula,* served with corn bread, or polenta. Closed weekends and August. Reservations advised. Major credit cards accepted. 14 Via Borgese (phone: 331-9000). Expensive to moderate.

Boeucc – Artists dine next to financiers in this traditional downtown restaurant. In the local dialect, the name means "hole-in-the-wall," but the clientele, service, traditional menu (here's the place for the real Milanese, saffron-perfumed risotto), and vast wine list belie the name. Closed Saturdays. Reservations advised. Major credit cards accepted. 2 Piazza Belgiojoso (phone: 790224). Expensive to moderate.

La Briciola – High-fashion models, journalists, and young Milanese-about-town enjoy the light touch of host Gianni Valveri's homemade pasta, salads, and fresh fish. Good value for the money. Closed Sundays and Monday afternoons. Reservations necessary. Major credit cards accepted. 25 Via Solferino (phone: 655-1012). Expensive to moderate.

Don Lisander – On summer evenings, downtown diners can enjoy the courtyard garden at this reliable old favorite. It offers a sampler menu of impeccably prepared traditional Italian dishes year-round. Closed Saturday evenings and Sundays. Reservations advised. Major credit cards accepted. 12/A Via Manzoni (phone: 790130). Expensive to moderate.

Gli Orti di Leonardo – In this smart, brick-vaulted eatery, fish hors d'oeuvres are served and followed by "little risotti," made with surprising ingredients. A rich choice of wines is available. Closed Sundays and most of August. Reservations advised. Major credit cards accepted. 6-8 Via Aristide de Togni (phone: 498-3476). Expensive to moderate.

Osteria del Binari – Elegant, with an impressive choice of traditional dishes from several Italian regions. The hot soup is topped with an incredibly light puff pastry. Closed Sundays and mid-August. Reservations advised. Major credit cards accepted. 1 Via Tortona (phone: 894-09428). Expensive to moderate.

Peck – Around the corner from the Duomo, this is an offshoot of the eponymous, elegant, food emporium. With its masterful blend of the classics and the creative, it is taking over the block, with an adjacent delicatessen (see *Shopping*), a pricey takeout, and separate counter service also worth trying. Closed the first 3 weeks of July and in early January. Reservations advised. Major credit cards accepted. 4 Via Victor Hugo (phone: 876774). Expensive to moderate.

Il Porto – The specialties at this family-run eatery are fresh fish and friendly service. Closed Sundays and August. Reservations necessary. Major credit cards accepted. Piazzale Cantore (phone: 832-1481). Expensive to moderate.

Stendhal – Named for the French author (who lived in the area), the menu offers

Brera's finest dining. It's everything a fancy restaurant should be: intimate, candle-lit, beautiful. The French antiques are authentic; so is the cuisine — from fresh *porcini* mushrooms to delectable desserts. Closed Saturday lunch and Sundays. Reservations necessary. Major credit cards accepted. Via San Marco near Via Ancona (phone: 653917 or 655-5587). Expensive to moderate.

Torre del Mangia – The tennis pros and other movers and shakers like the healthy approach to food here, such as the fresh fish prepared by Tuscan chef Peppino. Try the *tagliolini allo scorfano,* stuffed pasta with fish sauce, and light fried zucchini. Closed Sunday evenings and Mondays. Reservations necessary. Major credit cards accepted. 27 Via Procaccini (phone: 314871). Expensive to moderate.

Bice – Years ago, Tuscan-bred Bice Mungai opened a tiny shop in which she served staples from home, such as *la ribollita* (vegetable soup made with purple cabbage). From such beginnings came an evolution into one of Milan's chicest restaurants, with branches in Paris and New York, and today's wide menu of both meat and fish specialties, including *risotto al pesce* (risotto with fish). In season, wild mushrooms, stuffed pheasant, and truffle toppings are also served. Closed Mondays, Tuesday lunch, and July 22 to August 30. Reservations advised. Major credit cards accepted. 23 Via Borgospesso (phone: 760-02572). Moderate.

La Brisa – In the heart of the city, though hidden away, with a garden and a first class kitchen. Popular with financiers and artists. Closed for lunch on weekends. Reservations advised. Major credit cards accepted. 15 Via Brisa (phone: 864-50521). Moderate.

Canovianio – Right in the Duomo's shadow, highly creative dishes are served in a stunning interior. Closed Saturday lunch and Sundays. Reservations advised. Major credit cards accepted. 6 Via Hoepli (phone: 864-60147). Moderate.

Cavallini – With a garden for summer dining, this cosmopolitan trattoria reflects decades of sober culinary industry. Fresh fish is served daily, and the *tortellini in brodo* (small stuffed pasta in broth) is outstanding. Closed Sundays, during mid-August, and some holidays. Reservations advised. Major credit cards accepted. 2 Via Mauro Macchi (phone: 669-3174). Moderate.

Le Colline Pisane – This lively Tuscan trattoria serves fine food in pleasant sur-roundings. Closed Sundays and August. Reservations advised. Major credit cards accepted. 5 Largo La Fobba (phone: 659-9136). Moderate.

Decio Carugati – The food critic and author Decio himself is the host here. His creative, adventurous culinary compositions and fine wines are widely admired. Closed Sundays. Reservations advised. Major credit cards accepted. 2 Via Corsica at the corner of Via Vigevano (phone: 832-3970). Moderate.

Al Garibaldi – An unpretentious eatery catering to Milan's young professional crowd. The kitchen dispenses topnotch inventive food with great professionalism. Closed Fridays, *Christmas,* and August. Reservations advised. Major credit cards accepted. 7 Viale Montegrappa (phone: 659-8006). Moderate.

Alle Langhe – A family-style, popular trattoria serving Piedmontese fare that makes visitors feel welcome. Closed Sundays. Reservations advised. Major credit cards accepted. 6 Corso Como (phone: 655-4279). Moderate.

Malatesta Il Punto – Quail eggs with truffles, eel pâté with pine nuts, and Chinese fondue for two are among the specialties of this popular restaurant, one of several in Milan offering a fixed price sampler menu (*menù degustazione*). Closed Sundays and part of August. Reservations advised. Major credit cards accepted. 29 Via Bianca di Savoia (phone: 546-1079). Moderate.

Al Materel – It's rustic Lombardy at its best, with old family recipes, homemade pasta, and wild game and wild mushrooms in season. Closed Tuesdays. Reservations advised. No credit cards accepted. Corner of Via Laura Solera Montegazza and Corso Garibaldi (phone: 654204). Moderate.

Osteria di Porta Cicca – In one of the oldest parts of the city, with only 11 tables, be prepared for truly innovative dining. Favorites are *tagliolini* with zucchini blossoms and chunks of salmon, and poppy-seed-coated salmon steaks served with a whipped horseradish cream. Closed Sundays and alternate Mondays when the restaurant offers cooking classes, January 1 to 10, and August. Reservations advised. Major credit cards accepted. 51 Ripa di Porta Ticinese (phone: 581-04451). Moderate.

Osteria del Vecchio Canneto – It's definitely the place to try wonderful seafood and fine wines from Abruzzi. There is only a prix fixe menu. Closed Sundays and August. Reservations advised. Major credit cards accepted. 56 Via Solferino, but the entrance is around the corner on Via del Porto Nuovo (phone: 659-8498). Moderate.

La Pantera – Near Milan University, this Tuscan-style restaurant is run with loving care by Tina Lucchesi and her family. The *involtini* (stuffed veal slices), *farro* (a staple grain eaten by the ancient Romans), chick-peas in olive oil, and *la ribollita* (hearty vegetable soup) are among the specialties. Closed Tuesdays. Reservations advised. Major credit cards accepted. 12 Via Festa del Perdono (phone: 583-307408). Moderate.

Paper Moon – The city's first high-style pizzeria, where the show business, fashion business, and business business crowds rub elbows. Very trendy, and the people watching makes up for the slow service. Closed Sundays, 3 weeks in August, and 2 weeks around *Christmas*. Reservations advised. No credit cards accepted. 1 Via Bagutta (phone: 760-222297). Moderate.

Al Piccolo Teatro – Milan insiders enjoy this casual, traditional, and reliable trattoria, which they describe as simpatico (congenial). Especially good for lunch. Closed Sundays. Reservations advised. Major credit cards accepted. 8 Viale Pasubio (phone: 657-5648). Moderate.

Prospero – Though this eatery has been around since 1900, its dining room now is sleek and modern. The *ravioloni* with eggplant, bacon, and *porcini* mushrooms or the *risotto saltato* are great starters for lunch or dinnner. Closed Sundays. Reservations advised. Major credit cards accepted. 20 Via Chiosetto (phone: 551-87646). Moderate.

Quattro Mori – Near the Sforza Castle, this elegant, family-run eatery serves traditional Milanese food. It has a garden. Closed Saturday lunch, Sundays, and August. Reservations advised. Major credit cards accepted. 2 Via San Giovanni sul Muro (phone: 870617). Moderate.

Ribot – Set in a splendid garden, here's where the horsey set comes before the races at nearby *Ippodromo San Siro;* pictures of horses adorn the dark, paneled walls. In season, the spaghetti comes with the prized wild mushrooms, *ovoli.* Steaks are a specialty, and the chef makes his own cookies. Closed Mondays and most of August. Reservations necessary. Major credit cards accepted. 41 Via Cremosano (phone: 330-01646). Moderate.

Rigolo – A large, friendly place that's a favorite of local journalists and businesspeople, it serves Tuscan specialties (such as thick, grilled steaks) and a superb selection of homemade desserts. Closed Mondays and August. Reservations advised. Major credit cards accepted. 11 Via Solferino (phone: 864-63220). Moderate.

Il Sole – A favorite with Milanese, thanks to its relaxed atmosphere and air conditioning. Try the ricotta-based *gnocchetti* (little dumplings) in herb butter and homemade *tagliatelle* in a yellow bell pepper cream sauce. Dinner only. Closed Mondays. Reservations advised. Major credit cards accepted. 5 Via Curtatone (phone: 551-88500). Moderate.

Solferino – Milanese tradition holds sway in this pleasant eatery in La Brera, the artists' quarter. The potato soup with wild mushrooms is intriguing. Also try the house specialty, *risotto alla milanese* (rice doused in saffron), and the real thing when it comes to the Milanese cutlet. Closed Saturday lunch, Sundays, and the last 2 weeks in August. Reservations advised. Major credit cards accepted. 2 Via Castelfidardo (phone: 659-9886). Moderate.

Torre di Pisa – Everybody dines here, jamming into five rooms to enjoy host Romano's trendy fare of Tuscan specialties. Closed Saturday lunch, Sundays, and the first 3 weeks of August. Reservations necessary. Major credit cards accepted. 26 Via Mercato (phone: 874877). Moderate.

L'Ulmet – Milanese adore this place for its successful combination of traditional and creative Italian fare. Built on ancient Roman foundations, its roof incorporates a 1,600-year-old plinth. Wild game is served in season. For dessert, try the crêpes with honey and pine nuts. Closed Sundays and Mondays for lunch. Reservations advised. Major credit cards accepted. At the corner of Via Disciplini and Via Olmetto (phone: 805-9260). Moderate.

Il Verdi – *The* place for lunch these days. The menu offers a choice of 24 salads, ranging from the seafaring *innamorata* with trout, octopus, and potatoes to a mango, corn, and bamboo-based *orientale*. There is a full regular menu as well, and the restaurant also is open for dinner. Closed Saturday lunch and Sundays. No reservations. No credit cards accepted. 5 Piazza Mirabello (phone: 651412). Moderate.

La Vittoria – Opened in 1905, this friendly *ristorante* has kept pace with the times. It offers an ever-changing menu, and the selection of olive oils makes salad dressings an adventure. Closed Saturday lunch and Sundays. Reservations advised. Major credit cards accepted. 6 Via Anfiteatro (phone: 860726). Moderate.

Il Brigadino – The menu includes a variety of creative dishes, including fruit-based risottos. A prix fixe lunch makes this a popular spot with fashion models and photographers. Closed Sundays. Reservations unnecessary. No credit cards accepted. 14 Via Savona (phone: 835-4812). Moderate to inexpensive.

Giardino – Near the banks of the Naviglio River, this restaurant in the 19th-century courtyard spreads out under surrounding trees in summer and is enlivened by passing musicians. The food is simple but delicious and the atmosphere is reminiscent of a 19th-century Milanese tavern or *osteria*. Closed Tuesdays. Reservations unnecessary. No credit cards accepted. 36 Alzaia Naviglio Grande (phone: 894-09321). Moderate to inexpensive.

El Pouliereu – Summer diners delight in the century-old trees in the garden here, and in winter guests savor the mixed boiled meat. Fish, game, and other hearty, well-prepared dishes also are served. Closed Wednesdays and in mid-August. Reservations unnecessary. No credit cards accepted. 337 Via Rapiamonti (phone: 569-0954). Moderate to inexpensive.

San Fermo – The main lure is a wide selection of fixed price lunches, as well as its signature *insalatone*. Closed Sundays and Monday lunch from September through mid-June; Saturday nights and Sundays from mid-June through August. Reservations advised. Major credit cards accepted. 1 Via San Fermo della Battaglia (phone: 655-1784). Moderate to inexpensive.

La Topaia – Run by a multi-ethnic couple, the menu includes specialties from the Liguria region (near Genoa), Yugoslavia, and the French countryside. This spot is a summertime favorite. Dinner only. Closed Sundays. Reservations advised. Major credit cards accepted. 46 Via Argelati (phone: 837-3469). Inexpensive.

Along with its fine restaurants, Milan now boasts some of Italy's best *paninerie* (sandwich shops), which offer a variety of hot and cold sandwiches of sometimes unusual combinations. Try *Bar Magenta* (13 Via Carducci; phone: 805-3808) or *Paninomania* (Corso Porta Romana; phone: 576827). Most frequented by local office and fashion industry workers are the tiny coffee bars inside some of downtown Milan's charming courtyards. They also offer inexpensive, pleasant lunches — a plate of pasta, a cooked vegetable, and a glass of wine. Try the *Montanelli American Bar* (inside the courtyard by *Buccellati* at 12 Via Montenapoleone).

For Milan's best coffee, visit *Marches* (Via Meravighi); customers must stand at the bar, but they linger over hand-dipped chocolates and the Milanese *Christmas* specialty, the *panettone* (fruitcake). For tea and chocolates, the *Sant'Ambroeus* (7 Corso Matteotti) is the place to go — big, old-fashioned, and charming, with immense Venetian chandeliers and matrons in furs. The 164-year-old *Cova* (near *La Scala* at 8 Via Montenapoleone) similarly has pink damask tablecloths and waiters in black tie; try the hand-dipped *kikingerli*-filled (sour cherry) chocolates, and take home some candied violets. *Babington's* (8 Via Sant'Andrea), a sister to the English tearoom in Rome, has just opened. Conveniently located in the shopping district, it's off a courtyard and has Victorian decor. At the *Café Radetzky* (105 Corso Garibaldi), a 15-minute walk from downtown, the atmosphere of Milan 150 years ago when the Austrians ruled has been lovingly re-created in a coffee shop with style. *Note:* After a full day of gallery-hopping or nonstop shopping, unwind at *Cucchi* (closed Mondays; 1 Corso Genova), and sip a Bellini (fresh peach juice and champagne) outdoors in summer, or in winter nurse a Negroni (red vermouth and gin) surrounded by pink velvet and chandeliers. Should you want to start your day with a fresh-from-the-oven brioche, stop by at 7:45 AM.

MOSCOW

The eyes and ears of the world were abruptly focused on Moscow during August of 1991. First came word that the KGB and Kremlin hardliners had taken over the government and ousted Mikhail Gorbachev (who was away on vacation in the Crimea) in a not atypical coup d'état. The era of *glasnost* and *perestroika* seemed ready to be relegated to a field of dreams.

But as the tanks rolled in, Muscovites thronged into the city's streets. Boris Yeltsin, the first freely elected (in June 1991) President of the Russian Republic, exorted Soviet citizens to hold fast.

Then, unbelievably, just 72 hours later, the coup was reversed; a stunned Mikhail Gorbachev returned to Moscow. Within days, the death knell rang for the Communist Party, the old hammer and sickle were consigned to history, and the pre-Revolutionary flag of Russia was unfurled and flown from Moscow's rooftops. Communism was the casualty, democracy the winner, and although Gorbachev remained in office, Yeltsin was clearly the man of the hour.

For many Westerners — in spite of all the recent and extraordinary politburo pyrotechnics — Moscow is so closely associated with Soviet hegemony that it seems as much a political philosophy as a place. Visitors to Moscow, the city, however, are exposed to a feast of sights, a rich selection of cultural activities, and contact with warm, generous, and responsive people. The new atmosphere in Moscow, for however long it lasts, has made Muscovites more communicative and accessible to visitors.

Moscow has always been on the periphery of Europe. Situated on the Moskva River deep in the northwestern region of what is the world's largest state in area, it was impervious to outside cultural and economic influences for centuries. The original Moscow architecture, for example, developed in the 15th century when imported Byzantine traditions were forced into conformity with the native arts of northwestern Russia. The bulbous domes that are a characteristic feature of Russian churches are apparently a native Russian form.

A bit of history helps explain the city better. There is archaeological evidence that people occupied this area along the Moskva as early as the neolithic period, but the first mention of the tiny village of Moscow is found in Russian chronicles of 1147. Yuri Dolgoruky, a Prince of Suzdal, had established a small wooden fortress on a hill overlooking the river, in the same vicinity as the present Kremlin. (The word *kremlin* is a transliteration of the old Russian word for fortress.) At first merely a stop on the river trade route between the Baltic Sea and the Black Sea, Moscow became the capital of the principality in the 13th century and was the center of power in the northern area when Mongol Tartars overran the Russian lands.

The present brick walls of the Kremlin were firmly in place by the late 15th century, but they could not prevent the town growing up outside the fortress from being destroyed by the Crimean Tartars in 1571 and again by the Poles in the 17th century. Following these troubled times, Moscow began to expand and establish itself as a powerful city under a long line of Romanov czars. The most famous Romanov was Peter I, called Peter the Great, who was much enamored of Holland and Western Europe. In 1714, he moved the capital from Moscow to a new city he was building on the Gulf of Finland to reflect the taste and culture of the West.

Although the capital was moved to St. Petersburg, Moscow remained an important center of the Orthodox church and, as they had done since the reign of Ivan the Terrible, Russian czars continued to return to the Assumption (Uspensky) Cathedral in the Kremlin for their coronations. During the 18th and 19th centuries, Moscow established its university and its major theaters and continued to expand its boundaries. As the city spread out from the Kremlin complex, the ring of fortress monasteries and convents that had served as Moscow's protective perimeter became an integral part of the city itself. A contemporary city map reflects this gradual expansion in ever-widening rings from the Kremlin–Red Square center.

In his zeal to ensure that his new capital would have no rival, Peter the Great decreed that no stone buildings be erected anywhere in Russia except in St. Petersburg. So even though Napoleon's armies failed to conquer Moscow in 1812, nearly three-quarters of the city was destroyed in the fires set in the wake of the French occupation. A special commission was set up by Alexander I to reconstruct Moscow in 1825, and several magnificent buildings were constructed in the imperial style, including the renowned *Bolshoi Theater.*

After the 1917 Revolution, the new Bolshevik government returned the capital to Moscow, and the Kremlin once again became the seat of power. Since then, Moscow has undergone a series of transformations. Between 1926 and 1939, the population doubled; today it exceeds 8 million. New offices, and later skyscrapers, filled in the city's contemporary skyline. Streets were widened and old areas of the city were razed to make way for modern hotels and offices. In 1935, the first part of Moscow's extensive metro (subway) system was completed. During World War II, 75 Nazi divisions massed against the city but were unable to conquer it. Moscow handed the German armies their first major defeat as the Russian people bore the brunt of the most ferocious German attacks while the Western European Allies organized their strategy with the US.

Moscow today is about three-quarters the size of Los Angeles. A circular bypass highway, about 16 miles from the city's center, marks its present boundaries. Beyond the bypass are miles of slender white birch trees and, occasionally, one of the quaint wooden houses with intricately carved façades once typical of this area. The generally flat country surrounding Moscow has facilitated the construction and maintenance of a railway network that makes Moscow a manufacturing and industrial hub as well as the center of government. It is, indeed, the center (if no longer the heart) of the Soviet Union, its most powerful and important city. You can comprehend the ethnic diversity and disparity of the Soviet Union merely by walking along Moscow's streets.

Ukrainians, Armenians, Caucasians, Georgians, central Asians — they all come here, as visitors, to shop or to bring their goods to sell at farmers' markets throughout the city.

A first-time visitor will be surprised at the change in the formerly stoic façade of the typical Muscovite's public demeanor. Locals long to talk to Westerners these days, and exchange points of view. Eavesdrop on a wedding reception in your hotel or visit the circus or racetrack or dine at one of the local restaurants and you will find — despite continuing internal ethnic dissension — the zest and exuberance with which Russians celebrate life. The bureaucratic complexity of dealing with everyday existence continues, however, and may dampen enthusiasm during working hours, but when it's time to play, Russian spirits revive rapidly.

Even before the abortive coup, much had changed. *Glasnost* ("openness") and *perestroika* ("restructuring") created a greater tolerance of creative activity that is reflected in the theater and art world, and now, particularly, television and the press have been freed of party control. The effort to change and renew the moribund Soviet economy and adjust to a democratic way of life—as republic after republic announces its intention to break away—will be a Herculean task at best, but observing the process is fascinating and a once-in-a-lifetime opportunity. And greater change even than that occuring as we went to press will inevitably follow.

The Soviet Union's economic and political conditions didn't change much in 1991, as unrest in most of the republics continued while food supplies, industrial production, and general consumer confidence did not improve. Mr. Gorbachev may be in power, but his power base seems to have grown shakier.

To the Western eye, Moscow always may be more imposing than beautiful. Its appearance may change with new construction or the shift in seasons, and its character has now taken on new color: It is a city that exudes energy, a city that pulsates with power, and a city that leaves any visitor feeling that he or she has gained new insight into the Soviet psyche.

MOSCOW AT-A-GLANCE

 SEEING THE CITY: The lookout point in front of Moscow State University in Lenin Hills affords the best panorama of the city. Below you is the Moskva River and the *Luzhniki* sports complex, while in the distance you can see the gold and silver domes of Novodevichy Convent and the Kremlin complex (see *Special Places*) and seven look-alike skyscrapers. The university is near the Leninskie Gory metro stop. There's a fine view of Red Square and the Kremlin from the *Rossia* restaurant on the top floor of the 21-story tower wing of the *Rossia Hotel* at 6 Varvarka St. (phone: 298-1562 or 298-5400).

Note: The following information on sights and sites was accurate as we went to press, but it is more than possible that statues will have been toppled, streets and squares renamed, and hotels and restaurants have changed hands. So do as the locals are doing: Watch history change before your eyes and look upon a visit this year as an extraordinary experience.

SPECIAL PLACES: Moscow grew up in concentric rings around the Kremlin, and much of what is of interest to the visitor is within the area bounded by the Boulevard Ring, Bulvarnoye Koltso. However, there is also much to explore in the area between the Boulevard Ring and the more outlying Garden Ring, Sadovoye Koltso, which roughly duplicates an old earthen wall that was demolished early in the last century. Gorky Street has been renamed Tverskaya Street; it runs from Revolyutsii (Revolution) Square northwest to Tverskaya Zastava Square and the railway terminus for trains from Western Europe, and is considered Moscow's main street. Near the Kremlin, Arbat Street, which runs for less than a mile, is closed to vehicles. It has become a meetingplace for amateur and professional musicians and artists who paint portraits, strum guitars, and attract crowds of young people and the curious, particularly on weekends. There are open-air food shops, street clowns, and pantomime performers in good weather. The Arbat's new atmosphere is an outgrowth of *glasnost,* and not to be missed.

INSIDE THE KREMLIN

Kremlin Complex – Kremlins, or fortresses, can be found in a number of old Russian towns. None, however, is as well known as the Moscow Kremlin, which occupies 69 acres overlooking the Moskva and is the seat of the central Soviet government. The entire complex is surrounded by a red fortress wall studded with towers. Atop five of these towers are gigantic red stars that are lighted at night. Buried in the Kremlin walls are the ashes of various Russian heroes and two Americans — John Reed, whose book, *Ten Days That Shook the World,* is an eyewitness account of the Russian Revolution, and William ("Big Bill") Haywood, founder of the International Workers of the World (IWW), forerunner of the American Communist Party. There are guided tours of the Kremlin complex, or you can walk through the grounds on your own. Open daily.

Cathedral Square – The central square in the Kremlin takes its name from the three principal cathedrals situated here. The largest one, Assumption (Uspensky) Cathedral, with its white limestone walls and five gilded domes, was built around 1475. This was the private cathedral of the czars, many of whom were crowned here, but when Napoleon occupied Moscow his men used it for a stable and burned some of its icons for firewood. Annunciation (Blagoveshchensky) Cathedral had three cupolas when it was built in early-Moscow style between 1484 and 1489. But when six new domes were added during reconstruction after a fire in the 16th century, it became known as the "golden-domed" cathedral. The five domes of Archangel Michael (Arkhangelsky) Cathedral, built between 1505 and 1509, are painted silver. All the czars from Ivan Kalita to Peter the Great, except for Boris Godunov, are buried here. Also on the square is the Palace of Facets (Granovitaya Palata), the oldest public building in Moscow, dating from 1473 to 1491; the Belltower of Ivan the Great, and several other early cathedrals. A kiosk sells tickets for the major cathedrals; some are museums and others are places of worship. Closed Thursdays.

Grand Kremlin Palace – Once the residence of the imperial family in Moscow, the palace is a government building where the Supreme Soviet of the USSR and of the Russian Federation met until last summer's abortive coup. Built from 1838 to 1849, the yellow-and-white-walled palace appears from the outside to have 3 floors. Actually, there are only 2; the second floor has 2 tiers of windows. Not open to the general public except by special tour (phone: 928-5213).

Armory (Oruzheinaya Palata) – The luxury of court life in czarist Russia is manifest in the halls of this museum next to the Grand Kremlin Palace. Wonderful treasures of gold and silver, Fabergé eggs, royal carriages, ball gowns, and other royal regalia are preserved here. If you are lucky, you may be able to join one of the very small tour groups admitted to the Diamond Fund (Almaznyi Fond), open daily except Thursdays (tours are given in English). This section of the armory holds Catherine II's diamond-encrusted crown, her scepter with its Orlov diamond, and her golden orb as well as other precious gems. Advance arrangement for this tour must be made through *Intourist* (see *Sources and Resources*). Open 10 AM to 5 PM; closed Thursdays; admission charge (phone: 921-4720). The Diamond Fund is open 10 AM to 5 PM; closed Thursdays; admission charge (phone: 229-2036).

OUTSIDE THE KREMLIN

Red Square (Krasnaya Ploshchad) – This enormous square — 2,280 feet long and 426 feet wide — is the heart of Moscow and the Soviet Union. It is bounded on the west by the Kremlin wall and the Lenin Mausoleum, on the south by St. Basil's Cathedral, on the east by the mammoth department store, *GUM,* and on the north by the *State History Museum.* The chief festivals — *May Day* on May 1 and *Revolution Memorial Day* on November 7 — take place here amid much flag waving.

V.I. Lenin Mausoleum (Mausolei V.I. Lenin) – The body of V. I. Lenin, the Russian revolutionary and founder of Bolshevism, was still displayed in its glass sarcophagus as we went to press. But his days of rest, in this huge red and black, stepped mausoleum in front of the Kremlin wall seem numbered. Still, an impressive changing of the guard ceremony was taking place in front of the mausoleum every hour. New guards goose-step out of the Kremlin through the main gate at 2 minutes before the hour and replace the old guards in front of the tomb as the clock in the Kremlin's Spassky Tower chimes the hour. Incredible numbers of people pass through the mausoleum each week to view Lenin's body. With the death of the Communist Party, however, Mr. Lenin's remains may be removed before too long. Closed Mondays and Fridays. Open 10 AM to 3 PM, Sundays; 10 AM to 1 PM, other days. On Red Sq. (phone: 224-5115).

St. Basil's Cathedral (Pokrovsky Sobor) – St. Basil's is to Moscow what the Eiffel Tower is to Paris and the Statue of Liberty is to New York — a symbol uniquely expressive of the city. The gay colors and fanciful patterns of the cupolas of the cathedral's nine chapels have fascinated visitors since St. Basil's was built at the bidding of Ivan the Terrible in the mid-16th century to celebrate the liberation of the Russian state from the Tartar yoke. Legend has it that terrible Ivan had the architects blinded when it was finished, so that they could never build a finer church. Take time to go inside and wander through the narrow passages to the tiny, but extensively frescoed chapels. St. Basil's no longer has a religious function; it is a museum. Closed Tuesdays and the first Monday of the month. Open from 10:30 AM to 3:30 PM during winter and from 9:30 AM to 5 PM during summer. Admission charge. On Red Sq. (phone: 298-3304).

GUM – One of the best-known — and largest (but poorly stocked) — department stores in the world, *GUM* (an acronym, pronounced *Goom*) was built in the late 19th century as an arcade for nearly 1,000 small shops. It is said that some 350,000 shoppers wander through the 3 levels of this government-operated store each day. Closed Sundays; open 8 AM to 8 PM. On Red Sq. (phone: 921-5763 or 921-5692).

Central V. I. Lenin Museum (Tsentralny Musei V. I. Lenin) – Photographs of early revolutionary leaders and documents relating to Lenin's rise to power are housed in this red brick parliament (Duma) building on Revolution Square, just north of Red Square. Among the thousands of exhibits in the museum's 22 halls are many of Lenin's manuscripts, letters, and personal belongings, including a 1920 Rolls-Royce. Current conditions in the Soviet Union may soon change this museum's focus and function. Open Tuesdays through Thursdays, 10:30 AM to 7 PM; Fridays through Sundays, 9:30 AM to 6 PM. Closed Mondays. No admission charge. 4 Revolution Sq. (phone: 925-4808).

Central Market (Tsentralny Rynok) – Flowers and produce are available year-round at this open-air market. Farmers from the now nominally independent southern republics come to Moscow weekly to sell their goods in the free enterprise markets here and elsewhere around the city — great places to see Muscovites with their defenses down. Open 7 AM to 6 PM. 15 Tsvetnoi Prospekt; Metro: Tsvetnoi Blvd. (phone: 923-8687).

Metro – Moscow's subway system is one of the city's most interesting museums in addition to being a clean, efficient means of transportation. Each of its more than 100 stations has its own aesthetic scheme: stained glass windows, mosaics set with gold, crystal chandeliers, marble and stainless steel columns, bronze statues. The first line of the metro was opened in 1935; the newer the station, the less ornate it is likely to be. Some of the station platforms, reached by fast escalators, are as much as 300 feet underground. For a single, very small fare (5 kopecks) you can ride the entire system, getting off at every station for a look. Since trains arrive every 2 to 4 minutes, you can cover much of the system in a short time. The most central stop is a junction of three stations — Revolution Square, Teatralnaya Square, and Okhotnii Ryad — joined by underground passages. Open daily, 5:30 to 1:15 AM.

New Maiden Convent (Novodevichy Monastyr) – Founded in 1524 to commemorate the liberation of Smolensk, this richly endowed convent was part of a ring of fortress-monasteries and convents that formed a protective circle around the Kremlin. Boris Godunov was proclaimed czar from this convent; Peter I's sister, Sophia, was imprisoned here when she encouraged rebellion against him; noble families sent their unmarried daughters and widowed, or unwanted, wives to live here. There is a functioning Russian Orthodox church here, but the convent's *Smolensk Cathedral* now serves as a museum of Russian applied arts from the 16th and 17th centuries. Chekhov, Gogol, Prokofiev, Stanislavski, Khrushchev, and other famous Russians are buried in a cemetery to the south of the convent. Open 10 AM to 5 PM. Closed Tuesdays and the first Monday of the month. Admission charge. Near the Sportivnaya metro station. Also reached by trolleys No. 11 and No. 15 or buses No. 64, No. 132, and No. 808. 1 Novodevichy Proezd (phone: 246-8526).

Moscow State University – South of the convent, across the Moskva, the monumental university towers above the city from its 415-acre site in Lenin Hills. Statistics offer the best summary of the world's largest university. The new buildings put up during the late Stalinist period between 1949 and 1953 contain 45,000 rooms connected by some 90 miles of corridors. The main building is 787 feet tall and its façade is 1,470 feet long. The university was founded in 1755 by Russian scientist Mikhail Lomonosov and officially bears his name. Near the Universitet and Leninskije Gory metro stops. Also reached by bus and trolley. Universitetskij Prospekt (phone: 939-1000).

Pushkin Museum of Fine Arts (Gosudarstvenni Musei Izobrazitelnikh Iskusstv im. A. S. Pushkina) – Originally built as an educational museum, the *Pushkin* still has a large study collection of plaster casts of world sculpture. However, its most important works are in its rich collection of ancient Oriental and Renaissance art and its collection of 19th- and early-20th-century French paintings, including the work of Paul Cézanne, Claude Monet, and Pierre-Auguste Renoir. Open Wednesdays, Thursdays, and Fridays, 12 noon to 7 PM; Saturdays, 10 AM to 6 PM; Tuesdays reserved for group visits only. Closed Mondays and the last Friday of the month. Admission charge. 12 Volkhonka St. (phone: 203-7998 or 203-6974).

Moscow Circus – The capital's circus is noted for its music, lights, breathtaking aerial feats, special animal acts, and spectacular finales, but it is perhaps best known for its clowns. The role of the clowns in the Russian circus is central to the entire evening. The master clown is seen between each act, filling time with silly skits and riotous routines while equipment is being rearranged. Performances start at 7 PM (7 Vernadskogo Prospekt; phone: 930-2815). There also is a circus at 13 Tsvetnoi Boulevard (phone: 200-0668). To book tickets, call the State Foreign Tourist Office's special number (phone: 203-7581).

USSR Exhibition of Economic Achievements (Vistavka Dostizheny Narodnogno Khozyaistva SSSR-VDNKH) – This is sort of the *Smithsonian Institution* of the Soviet Union. All aspects of Soviet life — agriculture, industry, culture, and science — are detailed by the exhibits at this 553-acre park and pavilion site in northwest Moscow. The park, which has a zoo and a circus, is a popular place for Muscovites to spend a free day. In winter there is skiing, skating, and riding in a *troika,* the Russian horse-drawn sleigh. Outside the main entrance is an impressive monument to the Soviet space effort, a gleaming rocket trail in titanium called *Conquerors of Space.* The famous sculpture *The Worker and the Collective Farm Woman,* created by Vera Mukhina for the 1937 *Paris Fair,* stands at the North Gates entrance. The various buildings have different hours and closing days. The VDNKH metro stop is just beside the main entrance. Mira Prospekt (phone: 181-9162).

ENVIRONS

Kolomenskoye Estate-Museum – Established as a country estate for the ruling family in the 14th century, Kolomenskoye is on a hill beside the Moskva River about 10 miles (16 km) southeast of the Kremlin. The first stone church in the Russian "tent roof" style was erected here by Ivan Kalita in 1532, and several churches and buildings from the 16th and 17th century can also be seen here. The museum has interesting exhibitions of door locks and keys, ceramic tiles and stones, and carved-wood architectural details (open 10 AM to 5 PM, closed Mondays and Tuesdays; admission charge). The buildings can be seen from the main road, but the entrance is from a dirt road off the Kashirskoye Chaussée (Highway). 39 Andropov Prospekt (phone: 112-5217 or 115-2384).

Kuskovo Estate – One of the best collections of 18th-century Russian art can be found in the palace of this estate that once belonged to the Sheremetiev family, one of the oldest Russian noble families. The palace has pine-log walls faced with painted boards and was built by serf craftsmen. Since 1932, it has been known as the *State Museum of Ceramics,* with collections of Russian porcelain, glass, china, and majolica. A 70-acre formal French garden completes the ensemble. Open 10 AM to 4 PM; closed Mondays, Tuesdays, and last Wednesday of each month. 2 Junosti St. (phone: 370-0160). The estate is about 6 miles (10 km) from central Moscow, along the Ryazanskoye Highway.

Arkhangelskoye Estate – The museum in the palace of this estate, which usually exhibits a collection of European painting and sculpture, is closed for restoration until 1995, but we still recommend a visit to the property to see the lovely grounds and pleasant setting beside the Moskva. The park is in the French style, with statues and monuments lining the avenues. Arkhangelskoye is 10 miles (16 km) from Moscow and can be reached by taking Leningradsky Prospekt to the Volokolamskoye Highway and then taking the left fork onto Petrovo-Dalniye Highway. 143420 Moskovskaya Oblast (phone: 561-9456).

■**EXTRA SPECIAL:** Northeast of Moscow, there are two old cities — Sergiyev Posad (formerly known as Zagorsk) and Suzdal — that hold special attraction for a visitor. Arrangements to visit them are best made well in advance through *Intourist.*

Sergiyev Posad: This little town (whose medieval name was recently restored) on the Koshura and Glimitza rivers is the center of the handmade toy industry. Its *Toy Museum* (123 Krasnoi Armiyi Prospekt; phone: 254-44101) has a wonderful collection of toys from the Bronze Age to the present. Open 10 AM to 5 PM; closed Mondays, Tuesdays, and the last Friday of each month. The reason most visitors come here, however, is to see the Trinity Monastery of St. Sergius (Troitskio-Sergievskaya Lavra), one of the most important surviving medieval monasteries in the Soviet Union. Founded by St. Sergius in 1340, the monastery has important historical significance as well as importance as a center of art and learning. During the Time of Troubles in the mid-19th century, it withstood a 16-month siege by Polish troops. Today it is the center for Russian Orthodoxy and a major pilgrimage site.

The monastery's Trinity Cathedral (Troitsky Sobor), built between 1422 and 1427, holds the tomb of St. Sergius and many beautiful icons. Assumption (Uspensky) Cathedral is best known for its stunning blue domes decorated with gold stars. Boris Godunov and members of his family are buried in tombs beside the cathedral. In the museums housed in other monastery buildings you can see rich collections of Russian ecclesiastical art, portraits, rare fabrics, and Russian handicrafts; the monastery comprises three museums: the *Museum of Art,* open 10 AM to 6 PM; closed Mondays, Thursdays, and the last Wednesday of each month; the *Historical Museum,* open 10 AM to 6 PM; closed Mondays, Fridays, and the last Tuesday of each month; and the *Sacristy,* which only offers daily guided tours (none in English) that depart every 15 minutes from 11 AM to noon and from 2:15 PM to 5:30 PM. For more information, call 8-254-45356. Sergiyev Posad is about 45 miles (72 km) from central Moscow. Follow Mira Prospekt onto the Jaroslavskoje Highway, which will take you to Sergiyev Posad. There also is frequent local train service from Kazansky Station in central Moscow (travel time is about 1 hour).

Suzdal: A settlement since at least the 10th century, Suzdal has become a museum-city of ancient monasteries, churches, and convents and secular buildings spanning the centuries. Inside the walls of the Suzdal Kremlin beside the Kamenka River, you'll find the Nativity of the Virgin (Rozhdestvensky) Cathedral, built between 1222 and 1225. Its star-studded blue domes are similar to those at the Assumption Cathedral in Sergiyev Posad. The *Suzdal Local Museum* is in the Archbishop's Palace near the cathedral and features collections of early Russian icons, clothing, and jewelry. Open 10 AM to 5 PM. Closed Mondays. (phone: 21805 or 21594). More recently, representative 18th- and 19th-century buildings have been brought to Suzdal from various regions of the country and installed in the open-air *Museum of Wooden Architecture* beside the river.

Suzdal is 22 miles (35 km) due north of Vladimir, another ancient city worth a visit. You may want to make a 2-day excursion from Moscow and use Vladimir as a base for your trip to Suzdal. If you leave Moscow by Entusiastov Prospekt, it runs into Gorkovskoye Highway, which will take you to Vladimir, 114 miles (182 km) to the northeast. If you plan to go directly to Suzdal, drive north along the Klasma River out of Vladimir. There also are frequent trains from Moscow's Kursk railway station to Vladimir.

SOURCES AND RESOURCES

TOURIST INFORMATION: *Intourist* is the largest travel agency in the Soviet Union. It owns hotels and restaurants and deals with all types of foreign travel, though no longer maintains a monopoly on tourism to and through the Soviet Union. In Moscow, the *Intourist* office is at 16 Okhotnii Ryad (phone: 292-8876; telex: 41-1211 SU). There are two other travel agencies in the Soviet Union: the *Tourist Council of the Trade Unions* (phone: 271-2737), which organizes visits by trade union delegations, and *Sputnik* (15 Kosugina St.; phone: 939-8065), which organizes group tours for young people. *Intourist* provides English-speaking guides for general and specific sightseeing, but for your own enjoyment, take the time to learn the Russian (Cyrillic) alphabet and the sound of each of its characters. When you sound out the signs you see, you will recognize many English and French cognates.

The US Embassy is at 1921-23 Chaikovskovo St. (phone: 252-2451/9).

Although good transportation and city maps are available at hotel kiosks in Moscow, comprehensive travel guides in English should be purchased before you leave the US. One of the most useful general guides is *The Complete Guide to the Soviet Union,* by Victor and Jennifer Louis (St. Martin's Press; $29.95). *The Blue Guide*'s look at Moscow and Leningrad — now St. Petersburg (W. W. Norton; $19.95) is another good travel handbook.

The *Falkplan City Map of Moscow* (Hamburg: Falk-Verlag; $7.95) is a valuable backup for local maps and is available in bookstores throughout the US. It is an excellent, handy pocket map with a street name index, public transportation routes, and lists of hotels, museums, and theaters.

Local Coverage – An English edition of the weekly paper *Moscow News* usually is available at hotels. The *International Herald Tribune* and some Western European and North American dailies and weeklies can sometimes be purchased at kiosks and hard currency shops, although not on a regular basis. During the past year, the Hearst newspaper corporation and *Izvestia,* the Soviet daily newspaper, have distributed several issues of the first ever Soviet-American newspaper, *We/Mbl.* If you are desperate for news of the world, stop by the American Embassy for an update. Otherwise, bring along a shortwave radio or be content with blissful ignorance. (If you read Russian, you'll discover that the Soviet newspapers — formerly just propanganda sheets — have improved greatly.)

Food – For a listing of 100 cooperative restaurants, consult the guide *Cooperative Restaurants & Cafes of Moscow,* published by Fakt in English and Russian and available from sidewalk and subway vendors for 1.85 rubles.

 TELEPHONE: It is now possible to dial Moscow direct from the US. The country code for the Soviet Union is 7; the city code for Moscow is 095.

A word about telephones: The Soviet telephone system is notoriously bad. Telephone directories seem to be one of Russia's rarest commodities, but you can get assistance at your hotel's desk or service bureau. The service bureau can book long-distance calls for you, but it is advisable to arrange the call at least an hour before you wish to make connections. To use the pay phones, deposit a 2-kopeck coin in the slot before lifting the receiver. Dial when you hear a continuous buzzing sound.

 GETTING AROUND: Moscow has a very efficient and exceptionally inexpensive public transportation system. From late spring through early fall, you might also take one of the low-priced boats that cruise along the Moskva River, stopping in different parts of the city.

Airports – Sheremetevo I (domestic flights) and Sheremetevo II (international flights) are about 40 minutes from downtown by taxi; the fare is about 10 rubles. Three other airports, Domodedovo, Bykovo, and Vnukovo, serve domestic flights and are located from 40 minutes (Bykovo and Unukovo) to 1 hour (Domodedovo) from downtown Moscow. To book tickets by phone, call 155-5003.

Bus, Tram, and Trolley – These transport lines operate from 6 AM to 1 AM (trams) or to 1:30 AM (trolley and bus) and cost only 5 kopecks. Bus tickets can be obtained from the driver in units of 10 or from a hotel newsstand. Riders punch their own tickets and retain them until the end of the ride. (There are periodic inspections to enforce the honor system of paying the fare.) Maps showing the routes for all lines are available at hotel kiosks.

Car Rental – Automobiles, with or without chauffeurs, may be rented through *Intourist* (phone: 203-0096) for use in the city. Rentals must be paid for in foreign currency or with a credit card. Chauffeur-driven Japanese–made cars can be hired from *INIS* (phone: 927-1187 or 200-3207). *Hertz,* under the licensee *MTD Service,* rents cars, with or without drivers, in the city center (phone: 800-654-3001). Other rental agencies include *Inturtrans* (15 Petrovka St.; phone: 921-8968 or 927-1152); *Intouravto* (28A Riabinovaya St.; phone: 446-7434 or 446-3002); and *Moscow Rent Service* (79 Krasnobogatirskaya St.; phone: 963-9173 or 963-8727). Several hotels also have car rental facilities (see *Checking In*).

Metro – The subway has several interconnected lines. One runs in a rough circle; the others radiate out to different parts of the city. Trains arrive and depart at the various stations frequently and operate from 6 AM to 1 AM.

Taxi – Taxi fare is uniform for the entire country: 20 kopecks per kilometer, plus 20 kopecks per passenger. Normally, they can only be found at cabstands — marked with a "T" and a checkered pattern similar to the one on taxi doors — or at hotels. They can be ordered in advance, however, through your hotel service bureau or, if you speak Russian, by calling 927-0000 or 927-2108; calling a taxi costs 5 rubles extra during the day, 10 rubles more at night. It is best to order a taxi at least an hour in advance. If you are on the street and taxis do not stop, try raising two fingers, which means that you will pay twice the fare on the meter — a standard practice in Moscow. Also, American cigarettes are highly prized by most Moscow taxi drivers so waving a pack may have a dramatic effect on a cabby's willingness to take you where you want to go.

Train – Moscow supports over a dozen train stations. Check at any *Intourist* hotel for information about locations, fares, and schedules.

 LOCAL SERVICES: Most hotels will try to arrange for any special services a business traveler might require, such as a translator. (Also see *Checking In.*)

 SPECIAL EVENTS: Last year marked the first time that the Soviet government recognized *Christmas* (the Russian Orthodox *Christmas* is on January 7) and *Easter Friday* as official public holidays. *International Women's Day,* March 8, commemorates the Second International Conference of Socialist Women, which took place in Copenhagen in 1910. April 22 is *Lenin's birthday,* which (given the recent turn of political events), may no longer be a cause for celebration when you read this. Because pictures of the ceremonies in Red Square are transmitted around the world, the *International Labor Day* celebration, with its parades and demonstrations every May 1, is one of the best-known events in Moscow. May 2 also is a national holiday. Another major public holiday is *Victory Day,* May 9, when veterans meet and parade in the parks and squares. The *Moscow Film Festival* is held annually in June and July. *Constitution Day* is celebrated on October 7, and the anniversary of the *1917 Russian Revolution* is celebrated with parades and demonstrations on November 7 (November 8 also is a national holiday). The *Russian Winter Festival,* a major festival of the arts, runs from December 25 to January 5. *New Year's* is celebrated in the evening on December 31 and on January 1.

 MUSEUMS: Besides those mentioned in *Special Places,* Moscow has numerous museums devoted to Russian art and folk craft, the work of famous writers and composers who lived here, and various aspects of Russian history. All museums below have no admission charge.

Andrei Rublev Museum of Old Russian Art – In Moscow's oldest cathedral, a good collection of restored icons. Open from 11 AM to 6 PM; closed Wednesdays and the last day of the month. 10 Pryamikova Sq. (phone: 278-1429).

Central Exhibition Hall, or "Manege" (Tsentralni Vistavochni Sal) – Art exhibitions in the former stables of the czars. It was slated to close sometime this year for renovations, so call ahead first. Open from 11 AM to 8 PM. 50 Manezhnaya Sq. (phone: 202-9304).

Chekhov Museum – Exhibitions relating to Russia's greatest playwright. Open from 11 AM to 7 PM; closed Mondays and the last day of the month. 6 Sadovaya-Kudrinskaya St. (phone: 291-6154).

Darwin Museum – A zoological collection is the focus at this merchant's house that was built in the early 20th century. At press time, this museum was closed for repairs, and no reopening date had been set. 1 Malaya Pirogovskaya St. (phone: 246-6470).

Dostoyevsky Apartment-Museum – Memorabilia of the great author. Open from 4 to 8:30 PM on Wednesdays and Fridays; 11 AM to 5:30 PM on Thursdays, Saturdays, and Sundays; closed the last day of the month. 2 Doestoyskovo St. (phone: 281-1085).

Glinka State Central Museum of Musical Culture (Gosudarstvenni Tsentralni Musei Musikalnoi Kulturi im. M. I. Glinki) – Compositions by Russian composers, along with 1,500 instruments. Open from 1 to 7:30 PM on Wednesdays and Fridays; 11 AM to 5:30 PM, Thursdays, Saturdays, and Sundays; closed the last day of the month. 4 Fadeev St. (phone: 972-3237).

Gorky Museum – The writer's life in letters, manuscripts, and pictures. Open from 1 to 7:30 PM on Tuesdays and Thursdays; from 11 AM to 6:30 PM Wednesdays, Fridays, and weekends; closed the last day of the month. 25A Vorovskovo St. (phone: 290-5130).

Lenin Funeral Train Pavilion-Museum – The railway car that transported Lenin's coffin to his funeral; it exhibits Lenin memorabilia. Subject to possible redefinition by the new powers-that-be. Located at the Paveletsky Station. Open daily, except Tuesdays, from 9 AM to 6 PM. Closed the last Wednesday of the month. 1 Lenina Sq. (phone: 235-2898).

Leo Tolstoy Home (Filial Museya L. H. Tolstovo) – The restored home of the writer, who lived here from 1882 to 1909. Open from 10 AM to 4 PM October through March; 10 AM to 5:30 PM April through September; closed Mondays and the last Friday of the month. 21 Leva Tolstovo St. (phone: 246-9444).

Leo Tolstoy Museum (Gosudarstvenni Literaturni Musei L. H. Tolstovo) – In the former Lopukhin mansion, it contains manuscripts and other memorabilia. Open 11 AM to 6 PM; closed Mondays and the last Friday of the month. 11 Kropotkinskaya St. (phone: 202-2190).

Museum of Folk Art (Musei Narodnovo Iskusstva) – Folk arts, such as embroidery, enamelwork, and woodcarvings. Open from noon to 7:30 PM Tuesdays and Thursdays; from 11 AM to 5:30 PM Wednesdays, Fridays, and weekends; closed the last day of the month. 7 Stanislavskovo St. (phone: 291-8718).

Museum of the Revolution (Tsentralni Musei Revolyutsii SSSR) – Documents the 1905 revolution; the revolt of February 1917; and the Great October Socialist Revolution. Open from 11 AM to 7 PM Wednesdays and Fridays; 10 AM to 6 PM other days. Closed Mondays. 21 Tverskaya St. (phone: 299-5217).

State History Museum – Moscow's oldest museum, it was closed indefinitely at press time for renovations. 1-2 Red Sq. (phone: 928-8452). Check with *Intourist* (phone: 292-8876) or at your hotel for reopening information (phone: 292-1111).

State Museum of Oriental Art (Gosudarstvenni Musei Iskusstv Narodov Vostoka) – Crafts of the Soviet Far East, plus Chinese, Indian, and Japanese arts. Open from 11 AM to 7 PM. 12A Suvorovskii Blvd. (phone: 202-4953 or 202-4555).

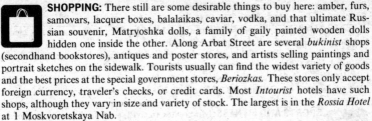 **SHOPPING:** There still are some desirable things to buy here: amber, furs, samovars, lacquer boxes, balalaikas, caviar, vodka, and that ultimate Russian souvenir, Matryoshka dolls, a family of gaily painted wooden dolls hidden one inside the other. Along Arbat Street are several *bukinist* shops (secondhand bookstores), antiques and poster stores, and artists selling paintings and portrait sketches on the sidewalk. Tourists usually can find the widest variety of goods and the best prices at the special government stores, *Beriozkas.* These stores only accept foreign currency, traveler's checks, or credit cards. Most *Intourist* hotels have such shops, although they vary in size and variety of stock. The largest is in the *Rossia Hotel* at 1 Moskvoretskaya Nab.

Soviet department stores usually are open from 8 AM to 9 PM; food stores, however, may remain open later. Be warned that the selection and quality of merchandise in these stores often is disappointing. If you decide instead to use Russian currency and shop where the Muscovites do, here are some suggestions:

Antikvar – Rare works of Russian art. Open from 11 AM to 7 PM. Closed Sundays. 6 Hudojestvennogo Teatra Proezd (phone: 292-8705 or 292-5114).

Cvetnie Kamni **(Colored Stones)** – A wonderful assortment of semi-precious stones and jewelry. Open from 10 AM to 7 PM; closed Sundays. 17 Berzarina St. (phone: 192-9018).

Detsky Mir – The name translates to "Children's World," and this shop is particularly noted for its wonderful toys. Open 8 AM to 8 PM. 2 Okhotnii Ryad St. (phone: 927-2007).

Dom Farfora **(House of Porcelain)** – A good assortment of porcelain dishes, figurines, and vases. Open from 11 AM to 7 PM; closed Sundays. 36 Leninskii Prospekt (phone: 137-6023).

Dom Knigi – Beautiful souvenir books about Moscow and the Soviet Union and colorful Russian posters and postcards can be purchased at this "House of Books." Open from 11 AM to 8 PM; closed Sundays. 26 Novii Arbat St. (phone: 290-4507).

GUM – Moscow's huge, government-run department store (see *Special Places*). Open from 8 AM to 8 PM. 3 Red Sq. (phone: 926-3471).

Iskusstvo – Books, posters, souvenirs, and boxes. Open 10 AM to 7 PM. 4 Arbat St. (phone: 291-7067 or 291-7444).

Izmailovo Park – An outdoor art market on Saturdays and Sundays offers a wide range of contemporary paintings by both amateurs and accomplished artists. Arts, crafts, jewelry, antiques, and curios also are for sale. Be prepared to bargain and beware of forgeries. There seems to be very little control. Barbecue kebabs and street jazz add to the exciting atmosphere here. Five-minute walk from the Izmailovo Park metro; 17 Narodny Prospekt (phone: 166-7909).

Lancôme – A branch of the famous French cosmetics firm. Closed Sundays. Open 11 AM to 2 PM and 3 to 8 PM. 7 Okhotnii Ryad St. (phone: 292-1194).

Luks – A cooperative selling fashionable (by local standards) dresses from some of Moscow's best designers. Open daily from 9 AM to 8 PM. 4 Pelshe St. (phone: 437-6438).

Melodia – As its name suggests, this is the place to buy records of some of those marvelous Russian folk songs you've been hearing since you arrived. Open from 9 AM to 9 PM; closed Sundays. 40 Novii Arbat St. (phone: 291-1421).

Philatelist Shop – A good stop for stamp collectors. Open daily from 1 AM to 7 PM. 1 Tara Shevchenko St. (phone: 243-0162).

Progress – Books written in and translated into English. Open from 10 AM to 7 PM; closed Sundays and Mondays. 17 Zubovskii Blvd. (phone: 246-9976).

Russkie Uzory **(Russian Patterns)** – Jewelry and handicrafts made in traditional Russian styles. Open from 10 AM to 7 PM; closed Sundays. 16 Petrovka St. (phone: 923-3964).

Russkii Suvenir **(Russian Souvenir)** – An offbeat shop offering the goods of

Russian "masters" of many trades. Open from 10 AM to 7 PM; closed Sundays. 9 Kutuzovskii Prospekt (phone: 243-6985).

Yantar **(Amber)** – Wide assortment of jewelry. Open from 10 AM to 7 PM; closed Sundays. 14 Gruzinskii Val. (phone: 252-4430).

Zenit – Sporting goods and photography supplies. Open from 11 AM to 7 PM; closed Sundays and Mondays. 9 Sokolnicheskaya Sq. (phone: 269-7111).

ZUM – Another big department store, near Red Square and about a mile from *GUM*. Open 8 AM to 9 PM. 2 Petrovka (phone: 292-7600).

 SPORTS AND FITNESS: Muscovites are avid sports fans, particularly of ice hockey, soccer, and horse racing. Attending such events is a good way to see Soviet citizens at leisure, enjoying themselves with exuberance and spirit. Schedules and tickets are available through the *Intourist* service bureaus. In addition to the *Olimpiiskii Sportivnii Complex* (Olympic Sports Complex; 16 Olimpiiskii Prospekt; phone: 288-3777), which was built for the *1980 Olympic Games*, there is a major sports facility across the Moskva River from Moscow State University: Luzhniki Park. The *Lenin Central Stadium Luzhniki* in Luzhniki Park (phone: 201-0155 or 201-0995) seats 103,000 people and is used for soccer matches and track and field meets, international competitions, and, occasionally, rock concerts. This stadium was the scene of the opening and closing of the *1980 Olympic Games*, and the principal athletic center for the games. Another sports complex built near Mira Prospekt for the *Olympics* has the largest indoor stadium in Europe.

Golf – At press time, final touches were being put on the Swedish-built *Golf Club Tumba* (1 Dovzhenko St.; phone: 147-6254) in the Lenin Hills near *Lenin Central Stadium Luzhniki* and Moscow State University. The 9-hole course is open to the public. The *Park* hotel's 18-hole Robert Trent Jones, Jr. course is slated to open this summer at Nahabino, 19 miles (31 km) west of the Kremlin (see *Checking In*).

Horse Racing – Harness and thoroughbred racing with low-stake pari-mutuel betting takes place each Sunday at 1 PM, as well as on Wednesdays in the summer at 6 PM at the *Hippodrome* racecourse (22 Begovaya St.; phone: 256-1562). At the *Ramensky Hippodrome* (about 31 miles/50 km from Moscow at Kazanskoe Shosse), there are races at 1 PM on Fridays. In winter, there are also exciting *troika* races held on the snow or ice.

Ice Hockey – The most popular ice hockey teams in Moscow are *Spartak, Dynamo, TSSKA,* and the *Red Army.* Ticket and schedule information is available from *Intourist.*

Soccer – This sport is a passion with many Muscovites. The *Dynamo Stadium* (36 Leningradskii Prospekt; phone: 212-7092 or 212-2252) holds 60,000 people and was built for one of Moscow's powerhouse teams, but the main events are held at the *Lenin Central Stadium Luzhniki.*

Swimming – The water for the *Moskva Open-Air Swimming Pool* (37 Kropotkinskaya Nab.; phone: 202-4725) is heated so the pool can be used all year. In winter, when the steam gathers over the pool, it may look like something from Dante's *Inferno,* but this steam layer protects the swimmers from the cold. There also are other pools and several bathing beaches in Moscow. Swimming competitions take place at the *Palace of Water Sports* (27 Mironovskaya; phone: 369-7444). The *Cosmos* hotel (150 Mira Prospekt; phone: 217-0785/6) has an indoor pool and a sauna, as well as a bowling alley.

 THEATER: *Intourist* service bureaus can provide schedules and tickets, but don't expect to get tickets for popular companies, such as the *Bolshoi Ballet,* unless you book well ahead of time. Muscovites used to look forward to a special treat at theater performances: the buffet during intermissions. These included caviar, sandwiches, chocolates, or delectable Russian ice cream, but the current food shortages make for disappointing fare. The most famous theater here is the *Bolshoi Theater* (Gosudarstvenni Akademichesky Bolshoi Teatr Soyuza SSR; 2

Teatralnaya Sq.; phone: 299-0050), which was preparing for renovations at press time. The *Bolshoi Opera* and the *Bolshoi Ballet* also perform at the 6,000-seat *Palace of Congresses Theater* (Kremlevskii Dvoretz Sezdov, inside the Kremlin Complex; enter through Kutafia-Troitsky Gate on Okhotnii Ryad St. and Arbat St.; phone: 227-8263). One of the oldest and most famous theaters in the Soviet Union is the *Moscow Feature Academic Theater of the USSR* (3 Hudojestvennogo Teatra Proezd; phone: 229-8760), which features classical and modern dramas. Other major theaters here are the *Maly Theater* (1-6 Sverdlova Sq.; phone: 925-9868), which stages Russian classics; *Moscow Drama and Comedy Theater*, known also as *Taganka* (76 Zemlyanoi Val St.; phone: 272-6300), is considered this city's most avant-garde; and *Stanislavsky and Nemirovich-Danchenko Academic Musical Theater* (17 Pushkinskaya St.; phone: 229-8388), which presents ballets as well as musical events. The *Gypsy Roman Theater* (32 Leningradskii Prospekt; phone: 250-7334) is the only theater of its kind in the Soviet Union. It features plays about the lives of Gypsies and their folk music; Shakespeare also is performed here. Two Jewish theaters offer productions in Moscow: the *Jewish Chamber Theater* (12 Taganskaya Sq.; phone: 272-4924) and *Shalom* (71 Varshavskoye Shosse; phone: 110-3758). Popular Soviet actors take the stage at the *Teatr Estrady* (Variety Theater; 20-2 Bersenevskaya Nab.; phone: 230-0444), while marionettes are featured at the *Theater-Studio Marionette* (37 Starokonushennaya Sq.; phone: 202-2483) and puppets at the *State Central Puppet Theater* (3 Sadovaya-Samotechnaya St.; phone: 299-3310).

MUSIC: Ticket and schedule information is available from *Intourist*. The three most important concert halls for music lovers in Moscow are the *Moscow State Conservatoire* (13 Gertsena St.; phone: 229-7412); the *Tchaikovsky Concert Hall* (20 Sadovaya Bolskaya St. in Mayakovsky Sq.; phone: 299-3681); and the *Hall of Columns* in the Trade Unions House (1 Pushkinskaya St.; phone: 292-0178). Opera is performed at the *Bolshoi Theater* and the *Stanislavsky and Nemirovich-Danchenko Academic Musical Theater* (see *Theater*). For something a bit lighter, try the *Moscow Operetta Theater* (6 Pushkinskaya St.; phone: 292-0405).

NIGHTCLUBS AND NIGHTLIFE: Nightlife in Western terms really doesn't exist here. A number of restaurants do have dancing each night (some also present shows), and some foreign-currency bars stay open for late drinkers. An all-night bar, the *Solaris*, features variety acts. Opened in 1989, the modest-by-Western-standards casino at the *Savoy* hotel (3 Rozhdestvenka St.; phone: 929-8674) was the first in the Soviet Union. Gamblers play with chips drawn on credit cards or non-ruble currency, and winnings are paid in checks drawn on a Finnish bank, cashable outside the country. Casino open from 8 PM to 4 AM. The *Casino Moscow*, open from 8 PM to 5 AM, is at the *Leningradskaya* hotel (21-40 Kalancheevskaya St.; phone: 975-1967); hard currency only is accepted. Gamblers at the new *Casino Royale* also use hard currency (22 Begovaya St.; phone: 945-1410). With the rich selection of theater, ballet, opera, music, the circus, and sports from which to choose, evenings need never be boring. And at any hour of the night, a walk in floodlit Red Square is a very special experience.

BEST IN TOWN

CHECKING IN: Hotel accommodations in the Soviet Union can be booked through *Intourist* or by a travel agent. You must apply for a visa listing all proposed stops and their duration, and once approved, deviations from your itinerary must be negotiated with a local *Intourist* representative. Visa applications also can be handled by your travel agency. Changes in your program can be requested at the *Intourist* service bureau in your hotel after you arrive, but do not count on the requests being approved. Usually, you will not be told the name of the specific hotel to which you have been assigned until you arrive in the city.

Accommodations in Moscow hotels usually are available in three classes: first class double rooms, deluxe 2-room suites, and deluxe 3-room suites. A few hotels also have spacious super-deluxe suites — usually with 2 floors. Brand new on the Moscow accommodations scene are several bed and breakfast establishments which offer foreigners a separate room and bath. Contact *IBV Bed & Breakfast Systems* (13113 Ideal Dr., Silver Springs, MD; phone: 301-942-3770; fax: 301-933-1124) or *ITS Tours & Travel* (1055 Texas Ave., Suite 104, College Station, TX 77840; phone: 409-764-9400 or 800-533-8688; fax: 409-693-9673). In addition, *American-Soviet Homestays* (Rte. 1, Box 68, Iowa City, IA 52240; phone: 319-626-2125) arranges stays with a Soviet family in Moscow, as well as several other Soviet cities. For more information, see *Accommodations* in GETTING READY TO GO.

The dramatically fluctuating Soviet economy makes it difficult to provide accurate rates for hotels; we suggest that you check costs — and the operative exchange rate — immediately prior to your departure (for more information see the *Soviet Union* in FACTS IN BRIEF). It is also often possible for rates to be guaranteed in US dollars (or you can prepay accommodations prior to departure) so there are no unhappy economic surprises. *Intourist* hotels usually include breakfast in the cost of the room. All telephone numbers are in the 095 area code unless otherwise indicated.

Cosmos – Built in 1979 by a French firm, this large and comfortable property has 1,777 rooms. It is near the Soviet Economic Achievements Exhibit, which is rather far from the city's center. Fortunately for its guests, there are 4 restaurants, 2 bars, a sauna, swimming pool, art and fur salons, and a car rental. Business facilities include 24-hour room service, meeting rooms for up to 1,000, English-speaking concierge, foreign currency exchange, secretarial services in English, photocopiers, translation services, and express checkout. 150 Mira Prospekt (phone: 217-1993, 217-1639, or 217-0785; fax: 288-9551; telex: 411489). Deluxe.

Intourist – Built some 20 years ago, this 22-story high-rise is just a short walk from Red Square. The 458 rooms are quite comfortable and you leave your room key at the front desk rather than with the floor matron, which is the typical procedure at hotels in Moscow. There are 5 restaurants, 2 cafés, a nightclub, hard currency shop, and an art salon. Business facilities include 24-hour room service, foreign currency exchange, secretarial services in English, photocopiers, cable television news, and translation services. The *Intourist* Central Excursion Bureau is right next door. 3 Tverskaya St. (phone: 203-6962; telex: 411823). Deluxe.

Metropol – Completely restored and renovated by *Intourist* and now managed by Inter-Continental hotels, this Moscow grande dame was due to reopen at press time. There are 400-plus rooms, 4 bars, 3 restaurants, and a coffee shop. The façade of this beautiful turn-of-the-century hotel is decorated with a marvelous majolica relief that reproduces Mikhail Vrubel's *Dream Princess.* There is a swimming pool and a sauna. It is close to the *Bolshoi* and *Maly* theaters on Sverdlova Square (see *Theaters*) and has a friendly outdoor café during warm weather. Business facilities include 24-hour room service, meeting rooms for up to 350, and a concierge. 1-4 Marksa Prospekt (phone: 225-6673 or 225-6212; in the US, 800-327-0200). Deluxe.

Mezhdunarodnaya I and II – Perhaps Moscow's best modern hotel, it was built specifically to receive foreign business travelers. It offers 540 rooms, 5 restaurants (serving Russian, continental, and Japanese food), 3 bars, an English pub, saunas, a swimming pool, a bowling alley, a variety of hard currency shops, and car rental. Business facilities include 24-hour room service, 3 meeting rooms (for up to 1,200),

English-speaking concierge, foreign currency exchange, secretarial services in English, audiovisual equipment, and translation services. *Intourist* does not provide reservations here, but many Western travel agencies do. 12 Krasnopresnenskaya Nab. (phone: 253-1391 or 253-1393; fax: 253-8260; telex: 411339). Deluxe.

Octyabrskaya I – Set on the banks of the Moskva River and originally reserved for Communist Party bigwigs and their guests, this hotel is rated by many as the best in the Soviet Union. There are 210 rooms, a restaurant, bar, sauna, hair salon, and a car rental. The exclusive property employs guards who check that all visitors coming and going on the grounds have hotel cards. And the tab may make you forget you're not in a capitalist country. Business facilities include meeting rooms for up to 210, photocopiers, and translation services. Reservations must be made directly through the hotel. 24 Dimitrova St. (phone: 239-3800 or 238-6558; fax: 230-2216). Deluxe.

Park – To escape from the city bustle, locals and foreign travelers alike stay at this hotel set in forested grounds at Nahibino, about 19 miles (31 km) west of the Kremlin. Along with a boat pond, the 4-story property offers 85 rooms, a restaurant serving Russian fare, a bar, billiards, sauna, massage, and a hair salon. An 18-hole Robert Trent Jones, Jr.-designed golf course is slated to open this summer. Business facilities include 24-hour room service, meeting rooms for up to 240, English-speaking concierge, foreign currency exchange, audiovisual equipment, photocopiers, computers, cable television news, and translation services. 1 Nahabino (phone: 563-0598 or 561-2975; fax: 563-3456). Deluxe.

Pullman Iris – Another recent addition (it opened last spring), this very comfortable property offers 155 rooms, 40 suites, and a Presidential Suite. There is a French restaurant (one of the *sous* chefs was trained by Paul Bocuse), a delicatessen, and a bar. Business facilities include 24-hour room service, meeting rooms for up to 500, secretarial services in English, and translation services. 10 Korovinskoe Shosse (phone: 488-8000; fax: 906-0105; telex: 413656). Deluxe.

Radisson Slavjanskaya – The Soviet Union's first American-managed hotel opened in July 1991 on the banks of the Moscow River. A joint venture of Radisson Hotels International, Americom International Corporation, and *Intourist,* the hotel has 430 rooms and 165 suites, 4 restaurants, a health club, swimming pool, shops, extensive meeting facilities, and direct-dial phone service (to the US and other European countries). Located at the Kiev railway station, near the former Ministry of Foreign Trade; 2 Berezhkovskaya Nab. (phone: 800-333-3333 in the US; or 240-2535; fax: 240-3217). Deluxe.

Savoy – Moscow's first real nod toward Western-style luxury was the $17 million renovation of the former *Berlin* hotel, now the number one stopping place for visitors with hard currency: no rubles accepted, and credit cards are preferred over cash. There are 86 guestrooms with tiled baths, a restaurant (see *Eating Out*), bar, the first gambling casino to open in the USSR, several hard currency designer shops, an art salon, and car rental. The surest way of obtaining a hard-to-get room reservation is to fly into Moscow via *Finnair* — which runs the hotel. Business facilities include 24-hour room service, meeting rooms for up to 600, English-speaking concierge, audiovisual equipment, photocopiers, computers, cable television news, translation services, and express checkout. 3 Zhdanova (phone: 929-8500; fax: 230-2186; telex: 411620). Deluxe.

Izmailovo – Owned by a group of Soviet trade unions, it was built as the *Olympic* village for the *1980 Summer Olympics.* The five buildings offer 1,100 rooms, 2 bars, 2 restaurants each, and car rental. Business facilities in each building include 24-hour room service, meeting rooms for up to 190, English-speaking concierge, foreign currency exchange, photocopiers, translation services, and express checkout. 71 Izmailovskoue Shosse (phone: 166-0109 or 166-4127). Deluxe to first class.

Olympic Penta – Opened during the spring of last year, this property is a joint venture of *Intourist* and the Penta group. The 12-story establishment has a sauna, swimming pool, solarium, and gym. There also are 2 restaurants, including a brasserie and a café. Business facilities include 24-hour room service, meeting rooms for up to 300, English-speaking concierge, audiovisual equipment, photo-copiers, cable television news, and express checkout. 18 Olimpiyski Prospekt (phone: 971-6101, or 800-225-3456 in the US; fax: 230-2597; telex: 411061). Deluxe to first class.

Rossia – Near St. Basil's Cathedral, this is Europe's largest hotel, with 3,090 rooms capable of accommodating 6,000 guests. It is so large that it has four separate wings, each with its own entrance and dining facility. On the top floor of the 21-story tower wing (room rates are higher here than elsewhere in the hotel), the *Rossia* restaurant provides a great view of the Kremlin and Red Square (see *Seeing the City*). The south wing has its own 3,000-seat concert hall and two cinemas. On the corner of the east wing is the entrance to an enormous foreign currency *Beriozka* shop. Business facilities include 24-hour room service, meeting rooms for up to 200, English-speaking concierge, foreign currency exchange, photocopiers, and translation services. North Wing, 6 Varvarka St. (phone: 298-5402); East Wing, 1 Moskvoretskaya Nab. (phone: 298-5531 or 298-1442). One fax and telex for entire hotel (fax: 298-5541; telex: 411641). Deluxe to first class.

Ukraina – One of the seven look-alike skyscrapers built during the late Stalinist period (Moscow State University is the largest), this city-owned property is on the banks of the Moskva, but is some distance from the center of the city. It offers 1,002 rooms, 5 restaurants, 2 galleries with art for sale, several hard currency shops, and a hair salon. Business facilities include 24-hour room service, meeting rooms for up to 200, foreign currency exchange, and audiovisual equipment. Kutuzovsky Prospekt (phone: 243-3030; telex: 411654). Deluxe to first class.

 EATING OUT: You may book prix fixe menu meals through the *Intourist* service bureaus for many Moscow restaurants. Payment to the service bureau usually is in foreign currency, and for most places the price includes appetizer, entrée, dessert, vodka, wine, fruit drinks, and coffee, as well as music and dancing, tip, and tax. A relatively new dining option exists in the form of private or cooperative restaurants and cafés, where prix fixe dinners are less common (ask about them at the service bureau in your hotel).

The advent of cooperatives has added a competitive edge to the city's restaurant scene, so food, service, and atmosphere in Moscow dining establishments are better than what had been common in years past. Making reservations at some cooperatives can be difficult, unless you speak Russian, but most of the better ones cater to foreigners and can assist people in English; the other option is to ask your hotel concierge to make reservations for you.

The restaurants will not fall into any fine dining category, but they do offer a wide variety of national foods from the various now predominantly independent regions and republics of the Soviet Union. If you like black caviar (called *ikra*), indulge yourself. If you like vegetables, you'll be disappointed; even in summer, vegetables are puny compared to any available in the West. In fact, it won't take long to figure out that Moscow is a center of cholesterol, with fatty sausages, salami, sour cream, butter, and eggs on menus in the better hotels — and that's just breakfast.

The dramatically fluctuating Soviet economy makes it difficult to provide accurate prices for restaurants; we suggest that you check costs — and the operative exchange rate — immediately prior to your departure. If you go to the cafés or restaurants on your own, you must pay in Russian currency, although credit cards are accepted in all *Intourist*-sponsored restaurants and some cooperative cafés. Most restaurants below accept rubles (some also accept hard currency or credit cards) and are open daily, unless otherwise indicated. All telephone numbers are in the 095 area code unless otherwise indicated.

Arlecino – A Soviet-Italian venture, this cozy eatery offers a menu of good Italian dishes, including *medalyony telyachyi po-milanski* (veal medallions fried with flour and served with spaghetti, grated cheese, and tomato sauce), *spaghetti nizza* (spaghetti with tomato sauce), and *salat Arlecino* (greens with olive oil). A variety show is featured in the evening. Open from noon to 3 PM and from 7 PM to midnight. Reservations advised. Credit cards only accepted. 15 Druzhinnikovskaya St. (phone: 205-7088).

Aragvi – Once the closest thing to luxury dining in Moscow, this bustling Georgian restaurant no longer is so exalted. But with its music and clientele heavily weighted on the tourist side, it still is popular. Georgian food is highly seasoned; specialties include a spicy meat soup called *kharcho;* skewered roast Georgian mutton, shashlik *po kharski;* and roast chicken pressed between scalding stones, *tsiplyata tabaka.* Open from 11 AM to 11 PM. Reservations necessary. Credit cards accepted. 6 Tverskaya St. (phone: 229-3762).

Arbat – With seating for 2,000 people, this spot is almost always filled with tourists who come to enjoy the floor show, as well as music and dancing. For a delicious hearty meal, order the *kotlety Arbatskie* (ground beef and pork roasted with a variety of ingredients and served with fried potatoes and marinated mushrooms). Open from noon to 11 PM. Reservations advised. Credit cards accepted. 29 Novii Arbat Prospekt (phone: 291-1445).

Atrium – A small dining establishment with decor reminiscent of 16th-century Rome, this cooperative specializes in Russian and continental fare. Fish eaters will enjoy the *sudak po-monastyrski* (a pike dish). Open from noon to 4 PM and from 6 to 10 PM. Reservations advised. Credit cards accepted. 44 Leninsky Prospekt (phone: 137-3008).

Baku – Good Azerbaijani food and music keep people coming back here. The food is similar to Turkish fare. Try *dolma* (meatballs in grape leaves) or the *dovta* (sour milk and meat soup). Open from 11 AM to 11 PM. Reservations advised. Hard currency accepted. 24 Tverskaya St. (phone: 299-2322).

Café 44 – Customers like to linger at this comfortable little eatery serving continental fare and featuring live music most nights. Try the *Govyadina 44* (the café's special beef dish). The cooperative also has a hard currency kiosk selling spirits and candy. Open from 11 AM to 11 PM. 44 Leningradskii Prospekt (phone: 248-4438 or 159-9951).

Café Kolkhida – A short walk from the *Tchaikovsky Concert Hall* and across the street from the *Puppet Theater,* this unpretentious cooperative is decorated in red and black, with crystal chandeliers and wall sconces. Live music is performed, and Georgian food is the specialty. Try the *harcho* (spicy tomato soup with meat), *lobiyo krasni* (peppery kidney bean salad), or the *satsivi* (chicken with nuts and a variety of spices). Open from noon to 11 PM. Reservations advised. If you pay by credit card rather than rubles, you could be charged about 10 times as much here. 6 Sadovo-Samotechnaya (phone: 299-6757 or 299-3111).

Glazur – An intimate eatery featuring live jazz, this Soviet-Danish joint venture specializes in such dishes as oyster, salmon, and pâté. Open from noon to midnight. Reservations necessary. Credit cards only accepted. 12-19 Smolensky Blvd. (phone: 248-4438).

Hermitage – The cooks here do their best to preserve the tradition of Old Moscow's best recipes. Open from 9 AM to 9 PM. No reservations. 3 Karetny Ryad (phone: 299-1160).

Kafé-Club Teatra Na Taganke – Frequented by actors, artists, and philosophers, this café features daily concerts, along with Russian and continental fare. Try the *sup joulien* (soup with vegetables). Open from 8 PM to midnight. Reservations necessary. Credit cards accepted. 19-3 Verkhnaya Radichshevskaya (phone: 272-6331).

Kropotkinskaya 36 – Inaugurated in 1986, this Soviet-Spanish venture is both the first and one of the best of the cooperative restaurants. The Russian food is good — try the caviar, *blini*, special salads, sturgeon — as is the atmosphere. Live music. Open daily from 8 to 10 AM and from noon to 12 midnight, Sundays noon to 11 PM. Reservations necessary. Credit cards accepted. 36 Kropotkinskaya St. (phone: 201-7500).

Lazania – For good Italian food, this comfortable eatery is the place to go. The cooperative's menu features over 50 items. Open from noon to 5 PM and from 7 to 10 PM. Reservations necessary. Hard currency and credit cards only accepted. 40 Pyatnitskaya St. (phone: 231-1085).

Likhobory – Especially popular with the younger set, it's a good spot to enjoy continental fare, such as suckling pig. Open from 2 PM to midnight. Reservations necessary. 27 Dmitrovskoe Shosse (979-7366).

Manila – Continental and — what else — Philippine fare is served in this cozy eatery, which offers a wide variety of à la carte items. Open from noon to 11 PM. Reservations necessary. Hard currency only accepted. 81 Vavilova St. (phone: 132-0055).

McDonald's – Soviets and foreign travelers alike can get their fill of *Big Mocs, kartotel-fries,* and *kokotels* (milk shakes), since the first of several franchises opened its doors in Moscow in early 1990. The grill and 29 computerized cash registers are manned by Soviet employees who wait on customers at what's now the world's largest branch, with seating for 700 people. It's the only eatery in town with a no smoking policy. At press time, the "golden arches" accepted only rubles (a burger, fries, and shake cost about 5.5 rubles). Open from 10 AM to 10 PM. Reservations unnecessary. In Pushkin Sq. (phone: 200-0590).

Mezhdunarodnaya I and II – Several good restaurants, cafés, and bars can be found at this hotel complex, also known as the International Trade Center. Although some do not accept rubles, all require reservations. Three of the better ones are the *Continental,* with a European atmosphere, soft music, and good food (phone: 253-1934); the *Russky,* for Russian cuisine and a Gypsy show in the evenings (phone: 253-1935); and *Sakura,* for authentic Japanese cuisine (foreign currency only; phone: 253-2894). 12 Krasnopresnenskaya Nab.

Muykhua – Chinese chefs prepare excellent dishes such as *rostki bambuka* (bamboo shoots) and *myaso po-suchuanski* (Szechuan meat). Open from 5 to 11 PM. Reservations necessary. Credit cards accepted. 2-1 Rusakovskaya St. (phone: 264-9574).

Pekin – About 70 different dishes are prepared by Chinese cooks at this 600-seat Soviet-Chinese venture. German beer also is available, and music and dancing provide entertainment. Open from noon to 11 PM. Reservations advised. 1 Sadovaya Bolshaya (phone: 209-2456).

U Pirosmani – Named after the Georgian primitivist painter Nikolai Pirosmanashvili, this cozy spot is decorated with copies of the painter's works, as well as wood beams and tables, stucco walls, an old piano and gramophone, and a fireplace. Ask for a table in the more attractive outer room. The menu offers spicy Georgian dishes and traditional Russian food. Open from noon to 11:30 PM. Reservations advised. Credit cards accepted; hard currency only for alcohol. In the southwest part of the city, across from Novadevichy Convent; 4 Novadevichy Proezd (phone: 246-1638 or 247-1926).

Pizza Hut – Another US fast-food eatery makes its way into the Soviet lifestyle (there are two branches in town). Open from 11 AM to 11 PM. Reservations unnecessary.

Credit cards and hard currency only accepted at 12 Tverskaya St. (phone: 229-2013). Rubles accepted at 17 Kutuzovskii Prospekt (phone: 243-1727).

Praga – Located in the center of Moscow, this is a good spot to dine after strolling along popular Arbat Street. Russian, Czechoslovakian, and other Eastern European dishes are served to up to 970 guests. A dance band plays in the evening. Open from noon to midnight. Reservations advised. Credit cards accepted. 2 Arbat St. (phone: 290-6171).

Razgulyai – Living up to its name, which means "cheer up," this dining place offers an amusing and interesting variety of rooms, creatively decorated. One room has Khokloma-style folk art, including red and gold paintings on Russian lacquerware. Another room, with a blue and white color scheme and wood-beam ceiling painted with blue flowers, is reminiscent of the Gzhel region, known for blue and white pottery. A third room, the Beresta, has red tablecloths, colorful paintings, and hanging baskets. A variety of traditional Russian dishes is served in each area. Live Russian and Gypsy music is performed. Open from noon to 11:30 PM. Reservations advised. Credit cards accepted. In the northeast part of the city; 11 Spartakovskaya St. (phone: 267-7613).

Rozak – A Soviet-Korean-Japanese venture, this romantic dining establishment serves continental fare to the accompaniment of live music. Open from 5 PM to 5 AM. Reservations necessary. Credit cards accepted. Shipkovsky Pereylok (phone: 235-1430).

Savoy – The luxurious dining room in the hotel of the same name is one of the best places in town to enjoy an elegant, quiet meal of Russian, Scandinavian, or international fare. Open from noon to 11 PM. Reservations essential. Credit cards accepted. *Savoy Hotel,* 3 Rozhdestvekna St. (phone: 929-8600).

Skazka – The name means "fairy tale," and if eating plus extravagant entertainment is what you're after, this is the spot. There's a very warm, candlelit, Russian atmosphere here. All kinds of acts, from acrobats to Gypsies to jazz musicians, perform, too. *Zakuski* (a spread brought to diners' tables, including herring, cold meat, tomatoes, deviled eggs, caviar, and a variety of vegetable salads) or single menu items are available. A gallery sells Russian art. Open from noon to midnight. Reservations advised. Credit cards accepted. 1 Tovarischcheskiyi Pereylok (phone: 271-0998).

Slavyansky Bazar – Originally opened in 1870, this always has been a favorite dining spot of writers and musicians who come to enjoy the traditional Slavic fare and music. Ten rooms, decorated in various traditional Russian styles, seat 450 guests. Open from noon to 4 PM and from 7 to 11 PM. Reservations advised. Credit cards accepted. 25-vo, 17 Oktyabrya St. (phone: 921-9833).

Slobodka – An unpretentious cooperative serving Russian food, it's a good place to stop in for a snack and a drink. Try the *Russkoye zaharkoye* (roast meat). Open from 1 to 11 PM. Reservations advised. 22-2 Gospitalny Val St. (phone: 360-7432).

Strastnoy-7 – Chic and expensive, the most elegant of Moscow cooperatives boasts a stark neo-classical decor, warmed by lavish table accessories, quiet music, and professional, friendly service. There is no menu; diners are served daily specials, which make the most out of limited ingredients. One such dish consists of tomatoes piled high with fresh herbed cream cheese, served with a tangy potato and cucumber salad or Old Moscow-style *roulette* — well-garnished platters of lightly fried, meat-and-ham–filled crêpes. The gallery sells Russian art. Open from noon to 11 PM. Reservations advised. Hard currency accepted at the bar. 7 Strastnoy (phone: 299-0498).

Tren-Mos – The name is a shortened version of Trenton-Moscow. Operated by a family from Trenton, New Jersey, this is a place where homesick Americans can relax over a good US meal. US state flags, along with other related memorabilia, cover the walls, and the menu offers familiar American dishes, such as chili and T-bone steaks. There's live piano music, too. Open from noon to 5 PM and from 7 to 11 PM. Reservations advised. Credit cards accepted. 21 Komsomolsky Prospekt (phone: 245-1216).

Tsentralynyi – Originally opened in 1865 as *Filippov's,* it serves traditional Russian food, such as beef Stroganoff and skewered mutton and onions (shashlik). A variety show is featured nightly, except Mondays and Tuesdays. Open noon to 3:30 PM and 6 PM to midnight. Reservations advised. Rubles only accepted. 10 Tverskaya St. (phone: 229-0241).

Vstrecha – A popular new cooperative serving Georgian and continental fare, it offers live music and a hard currency bar. Specialties include shashlik (mutton kebabs charcoal-roasted on a spit, served with marinated peppers, onions, and tomatoes) and *chakhohbili iz kuritzi* (stewed chicken with potatoes and tomatoes, cayenne, coriander, and saffron). Open 11 AM to 11 PM. Reservations advised. Rubles only accepted for food. 3 Gilyarovskogo St. (phone: 208-4597).

Yakimanka – Uzbek and continental fare are the specialties at this 70-seat cooperative with cozy furnishings — white wood furniture and Asian wooden ornaments. Try the sweet and sour *plov* (mutton, carrots, prunes, and onions mixed with rice) or the *lagman* (mutton, potatoes, and a variety of other vegetables served with noodles and gravy). A small band plays quiet music. Open from 2 to 11 PM (Sundays from 4 to 11 PM). Reservations necessary. Credit cards accepted; hard currency only for alcohol. 2-10 Bolshaya Polyanka St. (phone: 238-8888).

Zaydi-Poprobuy – The name of this café means "give it a try," which is fitting for a place that serves delicious Greek, French, and Georgian fare in two completely different settings. One room is decorated with copies of Georgian primitive art, while the other recalls Greece. Open from 11 AM to midnight. Reservations necessary. Credit cards accepted. Mira Prospekt (phone: 286-8165).

MUNICH

To many people, Bavaria is a place apart from the rest of Germany; gayer, more rosy-cheeked, less Teutonic. And Munich, the principal city of this southern region in the lap of the Bavarian Alps, is one of the jolliest cities in all Europe. It is renowned for two of the wildest, noisiest, fun-filled festivals anywhere. During *Oktoberfest* each year (held in September, oddly enough), hundreds of thousands of Germans and tourists celebrate the wedding of Crown Prince Ludwig to Princess Therese von Sachsen-Hildburghausen. The fact that the wedding took place in 1810 doesn't deter the crowd's enthusiasm one bit. Then, less than 4 months later, *Müncheners* go on another binge, called *Fasching*. Traditionally, all sorts of bizarre behavior is acceptable — and usually takes place — during this carnival season, preceding *Lenten* abstinence.

Even when there is no formal festival taking place, this is the beer capital of the world. Germans guzzle more beer than the people of any other country: 150 liters per person per year. But the Bavarians do even better, downing 250 liters apiece annually.

The thing that makes Munich so special, however, is that it is able to combine this earnest lust for life with modern sophistication. There is a pleasing blend of elegance and rustic charm, the naughty and the nice, here. Bavarian beer gardens and folk art coexist with Paris fashion, grand opera, and astrophysics, giving rise to such nicknames as "Village of a Million," and "Metropolis with a Heart."

As a cultural center, Munich has produced the largest number of German Nobel Prize winners; it is the home of the respected *Bavarian State Opera,* more than 60 legitimate theaters and cabarets, and important scientific institutes; and it is the largest university city in Germany, with more than 100,000 students in residence.

Statistics show that only one in three of Munich's 1.3 million citizens was born here, and one in ten is foreign-born. There is little wonder, though, that a cosmopolitan center that manages to retain a strong Alpine village flavor is so attractive to outsiders.

During the past 830-odd years, Munich has grown up along the banks of the Isar River, which flows down from the Bavarian Alps through forest and farmland before cutting a determined path through the eastern part of the city on its way to meet the Danube. On very clear days, the Alps, some 50 miles away, provide a stunning backdrop for the city.

Munich takes its name from the monks, *Munichen* in High German, who founded a Benedictine monastery in this area in the 9th century. The city itself was established beside the Isar River in 1158 by Henry the Lion, Duke of Saxony, who had been ceded part of Bavaria by Emperor Friedrich Bar-

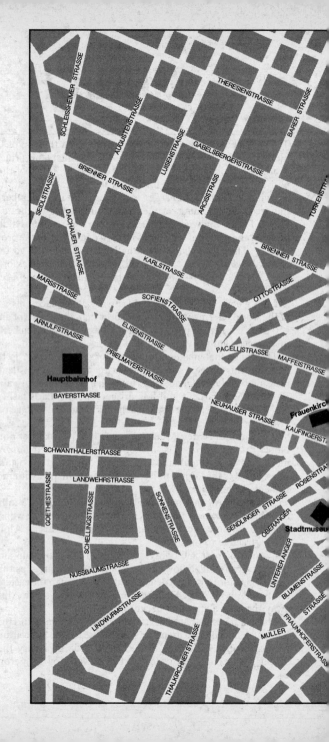

MUNICH

AMALIENSTRASSE

LUDWIGSTRASSE

KAULBACHSTRASSE

KÖNIGINSTRASSE

SKAR VON MILLER RING

VON DER TANN STRASSE

**Bavarian
National
Museum**

PRINZREGENTEN STR

WEINSTR   THEATINERSTR

Residenz

KARL SCHARNAGL RING

MARSTALL STR

**National
Theater**

MAXIMILIANSTRASSE

Rathaus

Hofbrauhaus

ktualienmarkt

WESTENRIEDERSTR

FRAUENSTRASSE

ZWEIBRUCKENSTR

STEINSDORFSTRASSE

KLENZESTRASSE

BAADERSTRASSE   KOHLER STR

LUDWIGS BRUCKE

REICHENBACHSTRASSE

CORNELIUSSTRASSE

ERHARDTSTRASSE

barossa. But in 1180 Barbarossa replaced Duke Henry with the Palatine Count Otto von Wittelsbach. From that time, the House of Wittelsbach was linked closely to Bavaria's and Munich's fortunes until the monarchy was replaced by a republic after World War I.

Toward the middle of the 19th century, Bavarian King Ludwig I put much of his energy into making Munich the most beautiful city in Europe. It was during his reign that many of the city's great buildings were erected and Ludwigstrasse was built. However, the king was forced to abdicate in 1848 when the scandal of his liaison with the Spanish dancer Lola Montez lent fuel to a revolutionary movement. His 18-year-old grandson, Ludwig II, became king in 1864 and carried out an even more grandiose building scheme. He ordered the construction of three extravagant castles and commissioned an array of phantasmagoria ranging from a boat in the shape of a huge shell to furniture, porcelain, and robes. Often called the Dream King, Ludwig II was much loved by his subjects, but court doctors declared him to be in an "advanced stage of mental disorder" and he was stripped of his powers shortly before he died by drowning at the age of 40.

After Germany's defeat in World War I, Munich was the center of the Nazi movement. Adolf Hitler and his National Socialists made an abortive attempt to seize power here in 1923 during the infamous Beer Garden Putsch. In 1938, Mussolini, Chamberlain, and Daladier met here with Hitler and agreed to let Germany annex the Sudetenland.

Much of the city was destroyed in bombing raids during World War II, but unlike some of its sister cities, Munich eschewed the modern and reconstructed its past. Except for the space-age architecture of the suburban Olympic Village, built for the 1972 summer games, and the *Gasteig Cultural Center,* Munich looks like a typical old European city. In some cases, original plans were used in the reconstruction or restoration of Munich landmarks. Today the city's public buildings reflect the many styles in which they were built over the centuries: late Gothic, Venetian Renaissance, neo-classical, rococo, and baroque. Church spires and bell towers, rather than high-rise office buildings, dominate the skyline.

Modern Munich is many things: an Old World city, a center of culture and sophistication, a city of gaiety, an intellectual center, and, with all its beer, *Wurst,* and *Gemütlichkeit,* a carnival of life.

MUNICH AT-A-GLANCE

 SEEING THE CITY: An exceptional view of Munich and the Bavarian Alps is available from the television tower (Olympiaturm) just northwest of the city at Olympic Village. The 943-foot tower was erected to facilitate televising the *1972 Summer Olympics.* A $3-elevator ride will take you to the tower terrace at 623 feet, with its impressive panorama of the city. There also is a dining room, the *Tower* restaurant, which revolves for a 360° view. Open daily 9 AM to 9 PM (phone: 306131).

SPECIAL PLACES: Marienplatz, with its tall white column of the Virgin, the city's patron, is the heart of Munich. Many of the streets leading from it have been closed to traffic and turned into a pedestrian zone called *Fussgängerbereich*. About 8 blocks west of Marienplatz is the central square, Karlsplatz, known locally as Stachus, where buses, trams, and subways to all parts of the city arrive and depart. Visitors often are confused because street names change abruptly in central Munich for no apparent reason. You always can get back to the center again, though, because there are numerous signs pointing the way and the spires and towers of landmark churches stand out above the lower red-roofed buildings that constitute the heart of Munich. The Isar River cuts through the city's eastern section, and a walk north along its banks will lead to a huge, lovely park, the English Garden. On the west side of the park lies the Schwabing district. Munich has a superbly integrated system of buses, trams, and subways to help you enjoy the city.

DOWNTOWN

Schwabing – At the turn of the century, it had a reputation as an artistic and intellectual center. Today this district to the north of the University of Munich is known to most visitors as the place "where the action is" in Munich. By day Schwabing resembles any other German residential district, but about 6 in the evening people swarm into its streets looking for a good time. The sidewalks along Leopoldstrasse, Schwabing's main street, and on Amalienstrasse and Türkenstrasse, take on a festive air. You'll see a confusion of sights: painters displaying their art, street musicians, poets offering their latest verses, barbers giving haircuts on the sidewalk, palm readers, quick-sketch artists. You can buy sandals, copper jewelry, ceramics, beads, belts — just about anything, in fact, including genuine and bogus antiques. Schwabing has more than 200 restaurants, with Greek, Yugoslavian, Italian, and Bavarian the most popular. There are countless discotheques, jazz *Kellers,* cafés, and boutiques.

Alte Pinakothek (Old Picture Gallery) – One of the world's great art galleries, this huge Renaissance building contains large and important collections of Dutch and Flemish painting from the 14th to the 18th century. The museum was built from 1826 to 1836 to house paintings gathered by the Dukes of Wittelsbach. Ludwig I made numerous other acquisitions that enhanced the museum's reputation. Among its treasures are important works by Albrecht Dürer and Peter Paul Rubens. Closed Mondays. Admission charge. 27 Barer Str. (phone: 238-05216).

Deutsches Museum (German Museum) – Considered the largest technical museum in the world, it sits on an island in the Isar River southeast of the city center. Included among its massive displays are the original 139-foot U-boat built in 1906, locomotives from the *Bavarian State Railway,* a collection of antique pianos and organs, a Messerschmitt 267 jet fighter from 1944, a planetarium, salt and coal mining exhibits in actual caverns, the aeronautical and space center, and much, much more. Unfortunately, detailed descriptions are available only in German, but it's still very much worth a visit. Open daily. Admission charge. Reached by subway (Isartor station) or by walking across one of several bridges connecting the island with the city. Isar Island (phone: 21791).

Gasteig Cultural Center – High on the right bank of the Isar River, just 400 yards from the *German Museum,* is one of Munich's newest attractions. It unites under one roof a philharmonic hall, two smaller concert halls, the Richard Strauss music conservatory, and the municipal library. The $130-million building has an ultramodern design, a sharp contrast to the surrounding neighborhood. 5 Rosenheimer Str. (phone: 480-98614).

Englischer Garten (English Garden) – This 18th-century garden, one of the oldest landscaped parks on the Continent, is a favorite meeting place. It has lakes, pavilions, riding trails, a site frequented by nude sunbathers, a Japanese teahouse, and Chinesischer Turm (Chinese Tower). At the base of the tower is the city's largest beer garden, where the favorite pastime is quenching one's thirst with a liter of beer while enjoying the passing scene. If you want to splurge, a pleasant carriage ride through the park will cost about $18 for a half hour. The park is northeast of the city's center, between Schwabing and the Isar River.

Frauenkirche (Cathedral of Our Lady) – The onion domes atop two 325-feet symmetrical towers have made this late Gothic cathedral Munich's most distinctive landmark. Its dull red brick façade was damaged extensively during air raids in 1944, but it has been rebuilt. The cathedral contains a rich depository of religious works of art, relics, sacred tombs, and the mausoleum of Emperor Ludwig IV. An elevator inside the south tower goes to the top of one of the towers, from which there is a good view of the city. 1 Frauenpl.

Residenz (Palace) – Although damaged during World War II, the royal palace has regained much of its glory. Built for the Dukes of Wittelsbach, the palace has been extended over the centuries to form a complex of buildings with seven inner courts. There are state rooms and royal suites in Renaissance, rococo, and neo-classical styles and displays of royal treasures. Closed Mondays. Admission charge. Entrance at 3 Max-Joseph-Pl. (phone: 290671).

Bayerisches Nationalmuseum (Bavarian National Museum) – The vast array of art and historical memorabilia from the Middle Ages to the 19th century on display here should give you an excellent introduction to Bavarian culture. The museum has what may be the most extensive collection of arts and crafts in the world. Along with its tapestries and woodcarvings, the museum is best known for its unique Krippenschau Collection of *Christmas* crèches (nativity scenes). Closed Mondays. Admission charge. 3 Prinzregentenstr. (phone: 21681).

Hofbräuhaus – This immense beer hall is a dance palace, a restaurant, and a national monument to the good life. In the beer garden, you'll be part of a scene people around the world associate with Munich: cheerful fräuleins carrying as many as 10 steins of beer at once, waitresses and waiters in peasant costumes moving through a noisy crowd selling pretzels stacked on long sticks, or white radishes cut into fancy spirals — both suitably salty to help you work up a thirst. It's not expensive, and is a must on any visitor's sightseeing agenda. Open daily. 9 Am Platzl (phone: 221676).

Neues Rathaus (New City Hall) – Munich's City Hall, built during the 19th century, dominates Marienplatz. Each day throngs of people peer up at its famous carillon (Glockenspiel), waiting to see the mechanical knights and their squires joust while the carillon signals to the city that it is 11 AM. It is a delightful diversion, not to be missed. Marienpl.

Viktualienmarkt (Victuals Market) – A few blocks south of Marienplatz, farmers, butchers, bakers, and other purveyors of food specialties set out their wares in an open-air market Mondays through Saturdays. It's the perfect place to browse, take pictures, and buy a snack or picnic fixings. Viktualienmarkt.

SUBURBS

Olympiapark (Olympic Village) – Built for the *1972 Olympic Games,* it also was the scene of the terrorist kidnapping (and later massacre) of Israeli athletes. The modern sports complex includes swimming pools, tracks, and gymnasiums. The park also has an 80,000-seat stadium — under an extraordinary skin-like roof — and an artificial lake. The housing built for Olympic athletes and officials is now a major residential suburb. Guided tours are available, and you even can swim in one of the pools that Mark Spitz made famous in his successful pursuit of seven gold medals. Admission charge. It can be reached easily by bus or subway. Oberwiesenfeld (phone: 306-13278 or 306-13424).

Schloss Nymphenburg (Nymphenburg Palace and Park) – Just west of the city limits stands a splendid 495-acre park with lakes and hunting lodges and Nymphenburg Palace, once the residence of the Bavarian kings. The great hall of the palace is decorated with frescoes by Johann Baptist Zimmermann, and a museum (*Marstall-museum*) in the south wing of the palace houses state carriages and sleighs. The *Nymphenburg China Factory,* with showrooms open to the public, is on the north crescent of the grounds. Concerts are presented on the grounds during summer months, and it is a particularly lovely spot to visit when the rhododendron are in bloom from May through June. Closed Mondays. Admission charge. Entrance from Menzingerstr. (phone: 170980).

Tierpark Hellabrunn (Hellabrunn Zoo) – Europe's largest zoo, Hellabrunn keeps its extensive collection of animals in a 173-acre natural setting of forestland and rivers. The zoo is famous for breeding rare animals and for its anthropoid ape section. Open daily; guided tours on Wednesdays. Admission charge. There is regular bus service from Marienpl. Four miles (6 km) south of Munich at 6 Siebenbrunnerstr. (phone: 625080).

Dachau – The name has evoked nothing but horror since this first Nazi concentration camp was built in 1933. Some 200,000 prisoners and deportees were received here. The number who died or disappeared is uncertain, although it is estimated that 32,000 may have perished. The magnitude of the atrocities committed is compounded by the natural beauty of the area: Dachau itself is a charming terraced town near a misty heath. The old administration building is now used as a museum where photos, memorabilia, and exhibitions document what transpired here. A film about the camp is shown twice daily (at 11:30 AM and 3:30 PM) in English. This is not a place for the fainthearted. Closed Mondays, December 24, and the afternoons of December 31 and *Shrove Tuesday.* No admission charge. Dachau, 14 miles (22 km) northwest of Munich, can be reached by Petershausen commuter train (*S-2*) from the main railway station. There is a direct bus (No. 722) from the station to the camp (phone: 8131-1741 or 8131-84566).

■**EXTRA SPECIAL:** It's said that over 650 kinds of beer are brewed in Bavaria, including those made privately. Munich is the home of six of Germany's major producers; one of them, Spaten (which alone makes nine different labels), will arrange tours upon request. During a half-hour walk through the plant, accompanied by an English-speaking guide, guests learn the various steps of beer making — from germination of the barley to bottling the brew. The tour is an essential preliminary to enlightened imbibing. 46 Marsstr. (phone: 5122 for reservations). Admission charge.

SOURCES AND RESOURCES

TOURIST INFORMATION: The Munich Tourist Office has information counters at the main railway station (Hauptbahnhof, Bayerstr.; entrance 2; phone: 239-1256), and at the Arrivals Hall of Munich-Riem Airport (phone: 907256); note that the Munich-Reim Airport will be closed permanently after May 16 (see *Getting Around,* below). Both offices are open daily until late evening. For information in English on museums and other sights, call the tourist office at 239162 or 239172.

The tourist office publishes an official monthly program, *München,* that lists theater, museum, and concert schedules, special exhibitions, hotels, camping facilities, and other useful information, but it is published only in German. However, many hotels provide literature in English focusing on Munich's activities and entertainment programs.

The US Consulate is at 5 Königinstr. (phone: 23011).

Local Coverage – The twice weekly *Munich Times* is an English-language newspaper.

Food – The *Munich Times* has restaurant listings, as does the tourist office's monthly *München,* in German.

TELEPHONE: The country code for Germany is 49; the city code for Munich is 89.

GETTING AROUND: Munich has an integrated rapid transit system, and the tickets that you buy from the blue dispensers at stations, streetcar stops, and on those vehicles bearing a white and green "K" sign can be used on buses, streetcars, subways, and local trains. You can cancel the tickets yourself in automatic canceling machines at the barriers of stations and in streetcars and buses bearing a yellow and black "E." There is a reduced-rate ticket for about $6 that permits unlimited transport in a 24-hour period. These special tickets are sold at the tourist offices and all ticket offices.

Airport – Through May 16 of this year, the Munich-Riem Airport will handle both domestic and international traffic. On May 17, the new Franz Josef Strauss Airport is scheduled to open as Munich's new terminus for all domestic and international flights. The Munich-Reim Airport, which will close when the new airport opens, is about a 30-minute cab ride to downtown Munich, and a taxi will cost from 25 to 30 deutsche marks ($15-$18). The airport's bus service to the city center leaves from in front of the main terminal; in the other direction, buses leave every 20 minutes from Munich's main train station (Hauptbahnhof), at Bahnhofplatz. For flight information, call 921-12127. The Franz Josef Strauss Airport (phone: 975360) is about 17½ miles (28 km) northeast of Munich. From downtown Munich the trip is about 30 minutes by rapid transit train or 45 minutes by taxi or bus (specific bus route information was unavailable at press time).

Bus and Streetcar – The Karlsplatz is the main junction for Munich's streetcars, and the East Railway Station (Ostbahnhof) across the Isar from central Munich is the terminal for many of the city's blue and white buses.

Car Rental – There are international and local rental firms in downtown Munich and at the airport. If you do drive, you should know that in some areas of Munich traffic-light poles contain two sets of lights: one on top for cars and a bottom set for bicycles. Munich also employs "motorbike" women, easily recognized by their light blue jumpsuits, who patrol the highways to aid lost or stranded motorists. Fluent in several languages, these women carry maps, tourist information, and other helpful material.

Subway and Train – Munich's subway is called the *U-Bahn.* It crosses the city in a north-south direction and has its central stops at Marienplatz and Hauptbahnhof. Like most European underground rail systems, the *U-Bahn* is clean, modern, and efficient. The *S-Bahn,* which connects with the *U-Bahn* at Marienplatz and Hauptbahnhof, is the interurban express line. It runs underground across the city in an east-west direction. Outside the city, it branches out over the whole national railway network. For information on *S-Bahn* trains, call 557575. For information on trains to other part of the country, call 19419 (schedules) and 554141 (fares).

Taxi – Munich's taxis are expensive. It will cost you nearly $3 just to have the driver flip down the arm of the meter. Taxis can be hailed on the street, or you can get one radio-dispatched by dialing 21610 or 19410.

LOCAL SERVICES: Dentist (English-Speaking) – Most German dentists speak English. However, the US Consulate (phone: 23011) has a list of English-speaking dentists (and physicians). For emergency service, call 723-3093.

Dry Cleaner/Tailor – *Paradies-Sofortreiningung* (11 Lerchenfeldstr.; phone: 223465); *Tommaselli* (102 Landsbergerstr.; phone: 505564).

Limousine Service – *Sixt,* 12 Baaderstr. (phone: 222829).

Medical Emergency – Munich's hospitals all have emergency rooms. For emergency service, dial 558661.

Messenger Service – *XP-Express Parcels Systems,* 94 Freischützstr. (phone: 956085).

National/International Courier – *DHL Worldwide Express,* 5 Carl-Zeiss-Str., Garching (phone: 320-8111).

Office Equipment Rental – *Bürozentrum Schulz* (192 Dachanerstr.; phone: 14820); *Pini,* for audiovisual equipment (Am Stachus; phone: 594361).

Pharmacy – *Bahnhof-Apotheke* (2 Bahnhofpl.; phone: 594119 or 598119). To find out which pharmacy is open at night, on weekends, or on holidays, call 594475.

Photocopies – *Cosinus,* 37 Königinstr. (phone: 282584).

Post Office – Open 24 hours daily. 1 Bahnhofpl. (phone: 538-82732).

Secretary/Stenographer (English-Speaking) – *International Business Services* (21 Kreillerstr.; phone: 431-3005); *Conference Hostesses* (15 Connollystr., Olympic Village; phone: 351-4374).

Telex – Post office, open 7 AM to 11 PM. 1 Bahnhofpl. (phone: 538-82732).

Translator – *Bundesverband der Dolmetscher und Übersetzer* (or *BDU,* the Association of Interpreters and Translators), 45 Amalienstr. (phone: 283330) and at 4 H.-Koob-Gentz-Str. (phone: 271-3154 or 271-3440).

Other – Tuxedo rental: *Cinyburg* (16 Lindwurmstr.; phone: 534412). Fur rental: *Astoria-Pelze* (3 Belgradstr.; phone: 309933).

 SPECIAL EVENTS: Munich is famous the world over for *Oktoberfest,* celebrated from late September through the first Sunday in October, and the pre-*Lenten* carnival, *Fasching,* which engulfs the entire city during the month preceding *Ash Wednesday* each February or March. *Oktoberfest* is 16 riotous days of beer drinking, sausage eating, and merrymaking at Theresa's Meadow, a fairgrounds where local breweries set up gaily decorated beer-garden buildings, brass bands oom-pah-pah continuously, and oxen are roasted on open spits. Unbelievable quantities of beer are drunk: Some 750,000 kegs are tapped. *Fasching,* which has been celebrated in Munich since the 14th century, hints more of indulgence in forbidden pleasures of the flesh (there is a traditional agreement that husbands and wives overlook one another's indiscretions during *Fasching*), but it, too, is characterized by lots of drinking and endless fun-seeking. The nonstop street reveling is all the more colorful for the outlandish costumes the celebrants don for fancy balls and an enormous parade through the city.

 MUSEUMS: Besides those mentioned in *Special Places,* notable museums in Munich include the following:

Antikensammlungen – Classical art, including Joseph Loeb's collection of Etruscan gold and silver. Closed Mondays. Admission charge. 1 Königspl. (phone: 598359).

BMW-Museum – Cars, motorcycles, and airplane engines of the Bavaria Motor Works. Open daily. Admission charge. 130 Petuelring (phone: 389-53307).

Glyptothek – Greek and Roman sculpture. Closed Mondays. Admission charge. 3 Königspl.(phone: 286100).

Jewish Museum (Jüdisches Museum) – Exhibits devoted to Jewish history, culture, and traditions. Open daily. No admission charge. 36 Maximilianstr. (phone: 297453).

Kunsthalle – Gallery used for temporary, visiting exhibitions. Closed Mondays. No admission charge. 15 Theatinerstr. (phone: 224412).

Münchner Stadtmuseum (City Museum) – Munich's history since the Middle Ages. Closed Mondays. Admission charge. 1 St.-Jakobs-Pl. (phone: 233-2370).

Museum in Stuck-Villa – Turn-of-the-century art. Closed Mondays. Admission charge. 60 Prinzregentenstr. (phone: 470-7086).

Neue Pinakothek – A collection of 19th- and early-20th-century art. Closed Mondays. Admission charge. 29 Barerstr. (phone: 238-05195).

Städtische Galerie im Lenbachhaus (Gallery in Lenbachhaus) – Kandinsky and the Blue Rider School are featured. Closed Mondays. Admission charge. 33 Luisenstr. (phone: 521041).

Staatsgalerie Moderner Kunst (State Museum of Modern Art) – A collection of 20th-century sculpture and painting. Closed Mondays. Admission charge. 1 Prinz-regentenstr. (phone: 292710).

Valentin Museum – Dedicated to one of Munich's legendary entertainers, Karl Valentin. Open daily. Admission charge. Gate Tower, Isartorpl. (phone: 223266).

 SHOPPING: Munich is such an elegant shopping city that some visitors confess to losing all sense of proportion once turned loose in the pedestrian zone. Shops tempt you with Bavarian beer steins, wonderful antiques, marvelous German porcelain, and items of German steel as well as Parisian fashions. Munich's most elegant shops can be found along Maximilianstrasse and Briennerstrasse and the small streets between Marienplatz and Odeonsplatz. Most of the antiques shops are concentrated in Neuturmstrasse, near Marienplatz. The city's leading department stores are *Kaufhof* on Marienplatz and *Karstadt,* near Karlsplatz. Most stores are open from 9 AM to 6 PM on weekdays (10 AM to 8:30 PM on Thursdays) and 9 AM to 2 PM on Saturdays. *Auer Dult* is a wonderful flea market for secondhand goods, antiques, and curiosities, set up three times a year — usually in April, July, and October at Mariahilfplat 2, across the Isar in the southeastern district of Au.

Alois Dallmayr – A world-famous fancy food store. 14-15 Dienerstr. (phone: 235100).

Anglia English Bookstore – The biggest selection of English-language paperbacks in southern Germany. 3 Schellingstr. (phone: 283642).

Beck – Famous for textiles, women's wear, and Bavarian handicrafts. Marienpl. (phone: 236910).

Biebl – Solingen carving sets and other items made of this renowned German steel. 25 Karlspl. (phone: 597936).

Dieter Stange-Erlenbach Pelze – Famed for its timeless and fashionable furs — for him and for her. 21 Maximilianstr. (phone: 535974).

Dirndlkönigin – An interesting display of Bavarian handicrafts, including the best selection of Bavarian folk costumes in Munich. 18 Residenzstr. (phone: 293804).

Kunstring – New and antique dinnerware. 4 Briennerstr. (phone: 281532).

Kurt Mory – A huge and varied stock of interesting beer steins, as well as a collection of pewter objets d'art. 18 Franenstr. (phone: 225931).

Loden-Frey – Men's and women's loden coats. 7-9 Maffeistr. (phone: 236930).

Maendler – High fashion for women. 7 Theatinerstr. (phone: 220437).

Moderne Creation München (MCM) – The latest in chic fashion accessories. 11 Nicolaistr. (phone: 331096).

Moshammer's – Clothing for men. 14 Maximilianstr. (phone: 226924).

Pini – The city's largest store for cameras and allied equipment. Am Stachus (phone: 594361).

Rosenthal – Home of the marvelous china, crystal, and cutlery. 8 Theatinerstr. (phone: 220422 or 227547).

Staatliche Porzellan Manufaktur – The main distributor of Nymphenburg porcelain. 1-2 Odeonspl. (phone: 172439).

Wallach Haus – Bavarian furniture, dirndls, and peasant dresses. 3 Residenzstr. (phone: 220871).

Walter – Leather clothing for men and women. 9 Amalienstr. (phone: 282294).

Wesely – Ornately decorated wax candles typical of this region. 1 Rindermarkt. (phone: 264519).

 SPORTS AND FITNESS: The excellent facilities built for the *1972 Summer Olympics* are used by a variety of professional teams in Munich, providing visitors with an opportunity to see everything from European soccer and basketball to ice hockey and track and field events. Sports schedules are listed in the monthly tourist office program, *München.* If you are a swimmer, you might enjoy using the *Olympic Swimming Hall* in Olympic Village. It's open to the public daily. The *Sportstudio* (16 Hansastr.; phone: 573479), is a fitness center open to nonmembers. For jogging, try the English Garden, which stretches north from Prinzregentenstrasse and is accessible easily from downtown. Cycling enthusiasts can rent bicycles at the entrance to the English Garden (at the corner of Königinstr. and Veterinärstr.; phone: 397016).

 THEATER: Munich has been known for centuries as a theater city. You can see everything from Greek tragedy to classical ballet to modern experimental drama in the numerous theaters here. The chief theaters are the *Residenz Theater* (1 Max-Joseph-Pl.; phone: 225754); the *Opera House, National Theater* (Max-Joseph-Pl.; phone: 221316); the *Cuvilliés Theater* in the Royal Palace (1 Residenzstr.; phone: 221316); *Theater in Marstall* (Marstallpl.; phone: 225754); *Prinzregententheater* (12 Prinzregentenpl.; phone: 225754); *Münchner Kammerspiele* in Schauspielhaus (26 Maximilianstr.; phone: 237-21328); the *Münchner Marionettentheater* (Munich Puppet Theater; 29A Blumenstr. at Sendlinger-Tor-Pl.; phone: 265712); and the *Münchner Theater für Kinder* (Munich Theater for Children; 46 Dachauer Str.; phone: 595454 and 593858), which reopened last year after extensive renovations.

 MUSIC: The first opera was performed in Munich in 1650, and the names of Wagner, Mozart, and Richard Strauss (Strauss was born in Munich) are linked closely with the *Bavarian State Opera,* which performs in the *National Theater.* Tickets are on sale at 11 Maximilianstrasse (phone: 221316). Opera also can be heard at the *Staatstheater an Gärtnerplatz* (3 Gärtnerpl.; phone: 201-6767). Hardly a day passes without a classical concert at one of the halls at the *Gasteig Cultural Center* (phone: 480-98614; see *Special Places*); jazz can be heard at clubs such as *Allotria* (33 Türkenstr.; phone: 285858); *Unterfahrt* (96 Kirchenstr.; phone: 448-2794); and *Jenny's Place* (50 Georgenstr.; phone: 271-9354). For rock and pop, try *Music Hall Epikero* (2 Detmoldstr.; phone: 351-0869) and *Schwabinger Podium* (1 Wagnerstr.; phone: 399482).

 NIGHTCLUBS AND NIGHTLIFE: Nightlife and Schwabing are almost interchangeable terms. You can dance over an aquarium filled with sharks at *Hamlet Light* in the *Holiday Inn* (194 Leopoldstr.: phone: 381790), disco at *Cadillac* (1 Theklastr.; phone: 266974) and at *Charly M.* (5 Maximilianspl.; phone: 448-4918), or rock the night away at the club in the *Bayerischer Hof* (2-6 Promenade Pl.; phone: 212-0994). Music and other entertainment is offered at *Clip*

(25 Leopoldstr.; phone: 394578), and *Domicile* (19 Leopoldstr.; phone: 399451) offers jazz and rock. One of the oldest Schwabing dance spots is *P-1* (1 Prinzregentenstr.; phone: 294252). There's always an interesting program of live music on tap at *MUH* (19 Innere Wiener Str.; phone: 448-9833), as well as at *Nachtcafé* (5 Maximilianspl.; phone: 595900), which offers jazz and more. A disco that appeals to "smart" Müncheners is *Bubbles* (25 Oscar-von-Miller-Ring; phone: 281182). At *Harry's New York Bar* (9 Falkenturmstr.; phone: 222700) you can gawk at the celebrities while imbibing one of 500 different drinks. Biting humor and satire are the offerings at the literary cabaret, *Lach und Schiessgesellschaft* (Ursulastr.; phone: 391997); and don't miss Gisela's vocal renditions at her bistro, *Schwabinger Gisela* (38 Herzog-Heinrich-Str.; phone: 534901). *Waldwirtschaft Grosshesselohe* (3 Georg-Kalb-Str.; phone: 795088) offers great Bavarian beer as well as live jazz.

If you prefer gambling, take the *Garmisch Casino's Blitz Bus* or one of the other buses the casinos run to bring players from Munich to the Garmisch area at the foot of the Alps, 54 miles (87 km) away. The buses leave from the north side of the main railway station at 5 PM on weekdays and at 2 PM Sundays. They leave Garmisch at 11 PM for the return to Munich. The trip takes about 1 hour and 35 minutes each way.

BEST IN TOWN

 CHECKING IN: Except during *Oktoberfest* and *Fasching,* there is plenty of hotel space in Munich, but prices are high any time of the year. Top hotels will cost a minimum of $105 a night for a double, and most of their rooms go for much higher prices; moderate-priced hotels charge between $60 and $105 a night; and anything below $60 must be considered inexpensive. And just so you don't forget, make reservations well ahead if you're coming for *Oktoberfest* or *Fasching.* Munich also has many delightful, inexpensive *pensions.* They don't have all the conveniences of a modern hotel, but they do have *Gemütlichkeit,* and that warmth and geniality is one of the best reasons to visit Munich. All telephone numbers are in the 89 city code unless otherwise indicated.

Bayerischer Hof-Palais Montgelas – Long considered Munich's landmark hotel, this 442-room property has managed to regain its reputation for excellent service and high standards. It always has had a top-drawer clientele, including Ludwig I, who favored it because the royal palace didn't have bathtubs. There's a *Trader Vic's* restaurant and a rooftop pool. Business facilities include 24-hour room service, meeting rooms for up to 1,200, English-speaking concierge, foreign currency exchange, secretarial services in English, audiovisual equipment, photocopiers, computers, cable television news, translation services, and express checkout. 2-6 Promenadepl. (phone: 21200; fax: 212-0906; telex: 523409). Expensive.

Grand Hotel Continental – A favorite of those who know the city well, it's close to the center of town and known affectionately as the "*Conti.*" Filled with flowers and priceless antiques, the hotel is part of a group of buildings known as the Kunstblock, the center of the Munich art and antiques market. Business facilities include 24-hour room service, meeting rooms for up to 60, English-speaking concierge, foreign currency exchange, secretarial services in English, audiovisual equipment, photocopiers, computers, cable television news, translation services, and express checkout. 5 Max-Joseph-Str. (phone: 551570; fax: 551-57500; telex: 522603). Expensive.

Hilton Park – Close to the picturesque English Garden, this 500-room hostelry is designed to meet the particular needs of the international business traveler. There are several restaurants, a pool, a sauna, a shopping arcade, and a massive underground garage. Business facilities include 24-hour room service, meeting rooms for up to 1,000, English-speaking concierge, foreign currency exchange, secretarial services in English, audiovisual equipment, photocopiers, computers, cable television news, translation services, and express checkout. 7 Am Tucherpark (phone: 38450; fax: 384-51845; telex: 521-5740). Expensive.

Holiday Inn – A 360-room hotel on Schwabing's main thoroughfare, the home of the *Hamlet Light* (see *Nightclubs and Nightlife*). Business facilities include 24-hour room service, meeting rooms for up to 600, English-speaking concierge, foreign currency exchange, secretarial services in English, audiovisual equipment, photocopiers, computers, cable television news, translation services, and express checkout. 194 Leopoldstr. (phone: 381790; fax: 381-79888; telex: 521-5439). Expensive.

Königshof – Despite its central location, this traditional and comfortable establishment is quiet. It also boasts one of Munich's best hotel restaurants, which has a great view of busy Karlsplatz. Business facilities include 24-hour room service, meeting rooms for up to 100, English-speaking concierge, foreign currency exchange, secretarial services in English, audiovisual equipment, photocopiers, computers, cable television news, translation services, and express checkout. 25 Karlspl. (phone: 551360; fax: 551-36113; telex: 523616). Expensive.

Penta – Part of a European chain and designed to cut down on rapidly soaring hotel prices, it caters to a predominantly business clientele. Guests carry their own baggage to their rooms. A unit in each room dispenses drinks, snacks, and even continental breakfast (eliminating the need for room service). There is an extensive shopping arcade and restaurant complex under the hotel, which is near the *German Museum*. Business facilities include meeting rooms for up to 600, English-speaking concierge, foreign currency exchange, secretarial services in English, audiovisual equipment, photocopiers, computers, cable television news, translation services, and express checkout. 3 Hochstr. (phone: 448-5555; fax: 488-8277; telex: 529046). Expensive.

Platzl – On the site of an old historic mill, this 270-bed hotel has modern conveniences. It is in the Old City center, across the street from the *Hofbräuhaus* (see *Special Places*). Business facilities include 24-hour room service, meeting rooms for up to 120, English-speaking concierge, foreign currency exchange, secretarial services in English, audiovisual equipment, photocopiers, computers, cable television news, translation services, and express checkout. 1 Platzl (phone: 237030; fax: 237-03800; telex: 522910). Expensive.

Queen's – Idyllically set on the right bank of the Isar River, near some of Munich's lushest greenery, this new property offers 150 tastefully furnished rooms. Business facilities include 24-hour room service, meeting rooms for up to 320, English-speaking concierge, foreign currency exchange, secretarial services in English, audiovisual equipment, photocopiers, computers, cable television news, translation services, and express checkout. 99 Effnerstr. (phone: 927980; fax: 983813). Expensive.

Rafael – Centrally located, this elegant establishment occupies a remarkable, 100-year-old building that formerly housed ballrooms, and most recently, the *Antik Haus* art galleries. The 74 rooms and suites, as well as the public rooms, are decorated in a luxurious, late-19th-century style. *Mark's* is the intimate hotel dining room. There is a rooftop swimming pool with a sweeping view of the Bavarian capital. Business facilities include 24-hour room service, meeting rooms for up to 100, English-speaking concierge, foreign currency exchange, secretarial services in English, audiovisual equipment, photocopiers, computers, cable television news, translation services, and express checkout. 1 Neuturmstr. (phone: 290980; fax: 222539; telex: 521-3666). Expensive.

Sheraton – East of the center of town, this 650-room property is clearly geared to the convention trade. Business facilities include 24-hour room service, meeting rooms for up to 1,200, English-speaking concierge, foreign currency exchange, secretarial services in English, audiovisual equipment, photocopiers, computers, cable television news, translation services, and express checkout. 6 Arabellastr. (phone: 92640; fax: 916877; telex: 523754). Expensive.

Vier Jahreszeiten (Four Seasons) – This is one of the great hotels of Europe, exuding opulence and elegance right through to its ultramodern wing and rooftop swimming pool. Its restaurant is wonderful (see *Eating Out*). Business facilities include 24-hour room service, meeting rooms for up to 450, English-speaking concierge, foreign currency exchange, secretarial services in English, audiovisual equipment, photocopiers, computers, cable television news, translation services, and express checkout. Owned by Inter-Continental and conveniently located only a few blocks from the glittering *Bavarian State Opera*. 17 Maximilianstr. (phone: 230390; fax: 230-39693; telex: 523859). Expensive.

Biederstein – Probably Munich's quietest hostelry, this charming place is on the fringe of Schwabing, next to the English Garden. Business facilities include 24-hour room service, foreign currency exchange, English-speaking concierge, secretarial services in English, and photocopiers. 18 Keferstr. (phone: 395072). Moderate.

Daniel – Plain, but clean and comfortable quarters; and a great location near the train station, subway, and within walking distance of most shopping. A good value. Business facilities include English-speaking concierge, foreign currency exchange, and secretarial services in English. 5 Sonnenstr. (phone: 554945; fax: 553420; telex: 523863). Moderate.

Intercity – In the main railway station building, but surprisingly quiet and comfortable. Business facilities include 24-hour room service, meeting rooms for up to 160, English-speaking concierge, foreign currency exchange, secretarial services in English, audiovisual equipment, photocopiers, computers, cable television news, translation services, and express checkout. 2 Bahnhofpl. (phone: 558571; fax: 596229; telex: 523174). Moderate.

Leopold – This 80-room hotel, on the fringe of Schwabing, is in an old 19th-century house. The back wing is quieter and faces a garden. Business facilities include 24-hour room service, foreign currency exchange, English-speaking concierge, secretarial services in English, and photocopiers. 119 Leopoldstr. (phone: 367061). Moderate.

Lettl – Centrally located, with breakfast included in the tariff. When reserving, ask for a room in the "new" wing. Business facilities include 24-hour room service, foreign currency exchange, English-speaking concierge, secretarial services in English, and photocopiers. 53 Amalienstr. (phone: 283026). Moderate.

Mariahilf – A particular favorite with English tourists, this 25-room pension is in a quiet sector of the city across the Isar from central Munich. Business facilities include meeting rooms for up to 50, English-speaking concierge, foreign currency exchange, and secretarial services in English. 83 Lilienstr. (phone: 484834). Moderate.

Uhland – A charming little hotel in a lovely old building on a street near Theresa's Meadow. Business facilities include 24-hour room service, meeting rooms for up to 60, English-speaking concierge, foreign currency exchange, and photocopiers. 1 Uhlandstr. (phone: 539277; fax: 531114; telex: 528360). Moderate.

Mariandl – This charming *pension* near Theresa's Meadow has not only 25 quiet rooms but also a restaurant famed for its evenings of free classical music. Business facilities include an English-speaking concierge and foreign currency exchange. 51 Goethestr. (phone: 534108). Inexpensive.

Theresia – Very close to the museums, this well-run establishment has 24 rooms. Business facilities include an English-speaking concierge and foreign currency exchange. In Schwabing, 51 Luisenstr. (phone: 5233081 or 521250). Inexpensive.

 EATING OUT: Bavarian cuisine is hearty and heavy, and most of it seems created to make you consume inordinate amounts of beer. Liver dumplings, *Leberknödel*, are the most famous of more than four score Bavarian dumplings. *Leberkäse* translates as liver cheese but is neither; it's a baked pâté of beef and bacon. Pork sausages and sauerkraut, *Schweinswürstl mit Kraut*, is another unforgettable local dish. Munich is the sausage (*Wurst*) capital of the world. *Weisswurst*, a veal-based white sausage, is sold throughout the city by street vendors as well as in beer gardens. It's best at about 11 AM. You'll also want to taste some of the local pretzels and salt rolls and sticks sold under such names as *Brez'n, Römische,* and *Salzstangerl.* Another specialty here is the large, tasty white radish, *Radi,* cut in spirals and sold with plenty of salt. If all of this makes you very thirsty, order *ein Mass Bier;* that's a liter. Otherwise, a half liter, *eine Halbe,* should suffice. If Bavarian food is too much for you every day, you can choose from a wide variety of other ethnic foods, especially in the conglomeration of foreign restaurants in Schwabing, some of them the best in Germany.

Like everything else in Munich, dining out can be very expensive. Even beer-hall fare, once the staple of budget-minded students, can add up quickly to $15, $18, or more. At expensive restaurants expect to pay a minimum of $60 for a meal for two; $30 to $60 in the moderate price range; and anything below that, inexpensive. All telephone numbers are in the 89 city code unless otherwise indicated.

Aubergine – This was Munich's (and Germany's) first Michelin three-star dining place. Chef Eckart Witzigmann insists on only the freshest ingredients, and his menu is sprinkled with dishes like venison with wild berries and lobster fricassee. Closed Sundays, Mondays, 2 weeks in August, and from December 24 to January 1. Reservations essential. Major credit cards accepted. 5 Maximilianspl. (phone: 598171). Expensive.

Boettner – A tiny wine restaurant in a high-ceilinged, paneled room behind a caviar-lobster shop. It has only about ten tables and always is crowded. The specialty here is lobster. Closed Sundays and holidays. Reservations necessary. Major credit cards accepted. 8 Theatinerstr. (phone: 221210). Expensive.

Kaferschänke – What started out as a corner grocery store has worked itself up to one of Europe's largest delicatessens and Germany's biggest catering service, and now includes a popular restaurant upstairs over the sprawling store. You can get anything from homemade head cheese (*Presskopf*), to bass from the Mediterranean. Closed Sundays. Reservations advised. Major credit cards accepted. 73 Prinzregentenstr. (phone: 41680). Expensive.

Sabitzer – A favorite of Munich's beautiful people, decorated all in white with turn-of-the-century art hung on the walls, this fine, small spot serves nouvelle cuisine. Closed Saturday afternoons and Sundays. Reservations advised. Major credit cards accepted. 21 Reitmorstr. (phone: 298584). Expensive.

Tantris – This fine restaurant in Schwabing serves some of the best of modern, light French cuisine outside France. Closed Sundays as well as Saturday and Monday afternoons; also closed for 3 weeks after *Pentecost.* Reservations advised. Major credit cards accepted. 7 Johann-Fichte-Str. (phone: 362061 or 362062). Expensive.

Vier Jahreszeiten (Four Seasons) – In the *Four Seasons* hotel, this dining room is quiet and ultra-elegant, and its delicious Bavarian cuisine is among the finest in

Germany. If you try the *Auszug aus schwarzen Trüffeln* (essence of black truffles), you're sure to agree. Closed Saturday lunch, Mondays, and August. Reservations necessary. Major credit cards accepted. 17 Maximilianstr. (phone: 230390). Expensive.

Bistro Terrine – The latest culinary vogue in Munich is the bistro, and this one is in the middle of swinging Schwabing. Its continental fare is complemented by the heady Mediterranean atmosphere. Closed Sundays and holidays; dinner only on Mondays and Saturdays. Reservations advised. Major credit cards accepted. 89 Amalienstr. (phone: 281780). Moderate.

Goldene Stadt – Bohemian dishes are served in the four adjoining dining rooms here. A photo-mural of a bridge over the Moldau in central Prague dominates the main dining room. Closed Sundays. Reservations advised. Major credit cards accepted. 44 Oberanger (phone: 264382). Moderate.

Halali – Not far from Schwabing, this unusually reasonably priced eatery serves quality nouvelle cuisine with a hearty Bavarian touch. Closed Saturday lunch and Sundays. Reservations advised. Major credit cards accepted. 22 Schönfeldstr. (phone: 285909). Moderate.

Joe Peña's – For those with a south-of-the-border craving, the Bavarian capital includes this remarkably good Mexican restaurant. The frozen margaritas are *delicioso*. Closed Sundays and holidays. Reservations advised. Major credit cards accepted. 17 Buttermelcherstr. (phone: 226463). Moderate.

Mifune – Ever since actor Toshiro Mifune opened this place, it's been a must for lovers of Japanese food. Closed Sundays and Saturday evenings. Reservations advised. Major credit cards accepted. 136 Ismaninger Str. (phone: 987572). Moderate.

Spatenhaus – A fine example of a typical Bavarian *Gaststätte* (inn), with its white-washed walls, pine tables and chairs, and many cozy niches. A delicious dinner here might include roast duck, suckling pig, or hare with mushrooms in cream sauce; dessert could be the flaky apple strudel or crisp apple fritters. Open daily. No reservations or credit cards accepted. 12 Residenzstr. (phone: 227841/2). Moderate.

Spöckmeier – This popular *Gasthaus* — which some say serves the best veal sausages in town — has two dining rooms: The vast, whitewashed and raftered hall downstairs bustles with shoppers and sightseers, and the smaller, paneled room upstairs hums with the quiet conversation of elegant drinkers. Closed Sundays from June to August. No reservations or credit cards accepted. 9 Rosenstr., just off Marienpl. (phone: 268088). Moderate.

Weisses Bräuhaus – Perhaps the most traditional of Munich's restaurants, this inn has been serving hearty food and wheat beer at the same site for over 400 years. A best bet is the roast pork with dumplings. Open daily. No reservations or credit cards accepted. 10 Tal (phone: 299875). Moderate.

Zum Alten Markt – Just a stone's throw from the colorful *Viktualienmarkt,* this downtown eatery is a must for lovers of good, but reasonably priced, continental fare with an emphasis on fish and veal dishes. Closed Sundays. Reservations advised. No credit cards accepted. 3 Dreifaltigkeitsplatz (phone: 299995). Moderate.

Bratwurstherzl – Around the corner from the *Viktualienmarkt* (see *Special Places*), this is one of the last truly Bavarian establishments in swinging Munich. Open for lunch only, but be seated by 11 AM, since it's very popular with Müncheners. Closed Sundays. No reservations or credit cards accepted. 3 Heiliggeiststr. (phone: 226219). Inexpensive.

Donisl – A visit here is a Munich must: This centuries-old beer hall is where many *Müncheners* come for their daily beer and sausage ration, especially in the late morning. Next to City Hall, the Neues Rathaus. Open daily. No reservations. Major credit cards accepted. 1 Weinstr., at Marienpl. (phone: 220184). Inexpensive.

Mariannenhof – At the edge of downtown Munich, this unpretentious place offers good food at reasonable prices in a comfortable atmosphere. The food is continental and traditional Bavarian. Attached to the restaurant is a bar and a tavern. Lunch and dinner on weekdays; dinner only on Saturdays and Sundays. No reservations or credit cards accepted. 1 Mariannenstr. (phone: 220864). Inexpensive.

Pfälzer Weinprobierstube – This tradition-laden wine cellar, in the former royal Residenz (see *Special Places*), features vintages from the Pfälz (Palatinate). The hearty food also is from that former Bavarian region. Open daily. No reservations or credit cards accepted. 1 Residenzstr. (phone: 225628). Inexpensive.

Weinstadl – Wine reigns supreme here, as does Munich *Gemütlichkeit*. It is in one of the city's oldest and most beautiful private buildings, built in the Gothic style in 1550. Open from 4 PM to midnight; closed Sundays. No reservations or credit cards accepted. 5 Burgstr. (phone: 221047). Inexpensive.

NAPLES

Naples, Gothic and baroque under an azure sky, intellectual capital of the Mezzogiorno, and Italy's third-most populated city, with nearly 1.7 million inhabitants, has often been described as one of the world's most beautiful seaports. Indeed, the magnificent Bay of Naples has long been lauded by its many illustrious visitors for its gently curving shoreline and palm-lined seaside avenues, its mild climate, sunny beaches, and romantic islands.

But Naples has always had a darker side. The brooding Mt. Vesuvius, "its terror and its pride," ever hovering over the city, buried neighboring Pompeii and Herculaneum when it erupted in AD 79. And the eerie Campi Flegrei (Phlegrean Fields), a steaming volcanic area just to the north, whose violent beauty inspired both Homer and Virgil, was regarded by the ancients as the entrance to the underworld. More recently, the earthquake that devastated southern Italy in November 1980 took a tragic toll in Naples, adding yet another major problem to the city's permanent ills of unemployment, crime, and disease.

For some visitors today, Naples is a disappointment. The old quarter is among the most densely populated areas in the world; infant mortality and unemployment rates here are among the highest in Italy — almost a fifth of the city's labor force is unemployed, and another estimated 40,000 persons derive their livelihood from smuggling. When a cholera outbreak in 1973 revealed that Naples had no sewers and was living on a beautiful but poisoned bay, "See Naples and die," once a popular saying beckoning visitors to the seductive charms of the city suddenly acquired a morbid and foreboding significance.

But the poor of Naples continue to survive with a surprising stoicism, and the people themselves are one of the city's attractions, laughing off their many problems, helping each other with an extraordinary sense of warmth and humanity — they are a people incapable of hatred, of any kind of discrimination, yet strongly emotional, sensitive, full of fantasy. Just remember the best movies of the postwar school of Italian neo-realism, directed by Roberto Rossellini, Vittorio De Sica, and Francesco Rosi, or the theatrical masterpieces of the famed Eduardo De Filippo, the voluptuous figure of Sophia Loren representing the Neapolitan woman — madonna, mother, and *puttana* (whore) all in one.

Watch them live: Naples is like a theater of life. Stroll along Via Caracciolo and see the fishermen pulling in their nets, oblivious to the traffic behind them; buy lemons and oranges or sulfur water from men and women who transact their business across 17th-century marble tabletops; give in to the importuning of pizza vendors hawking their wares; or, when the jostling of the-small, crowded streets becomes too much to bear, retire to a table in the elegant *Galleria Umberto I* or to the old *Caffè Gambrinus* on Via Chiaia and watch well-dressed Neapolitans socialize over an afternoon coffee or *aperitivo.*

Naples also is famous for its music, its festivals, its colorful arts. Neapolitan popular songs are, short of operatic arias, the best-known tunes to have come out of Italy; anyone who can strum a guitar or a mandolin knows at least one, and nearly everyone can sing along, at least the refrain. In the 17th and 18th centuries, the works of a Neapolitan school of composers — Alessandro Scarlatti was its leader — were just as well known; Pergolesi, Paisiello, and Cimarosa drew capacity crowds. The city's opera house, *Teatro San Carlo,* built in 1737, remains one of the world's finest. A Neapolitan school of painting, characterized by realism and warm colors, flourished in the 18th and 19th centuries. In the 18th century, too, the famous Capodimonte porcelain factory was turning out highly elaborate pieces for members of the royal court, while less exalted folk artists were raising the making of nativity scenes, or *Christmas* cribs, into an art. The shepherds and angels of many an *ignoto Napoletano* (unknown Neapolitan) live on in museums, and at *Christmastime,* an entire street — Via San Gregorio Armeno — is taken over by artisans selling their hand-crafted *presepi* or crèche scenes.

The city that was to spawn so much natural talent was founded as a Greek colony, probably in the 7th century BC, and was first called Parthenope, later Neapolis. Little remains of its earliest period. Then, along with the rest of the Italian peninsula, it became part of the great Roman Empire, and its intensely green countryside and sunny shores were soon studded with palatial villas of wealthy Romans who chose to spend the winters in Naples's milder climate.

But the tranquillity of the Roman period came to an end with the fall of the empire, and Naples sank into the abyss of the Dark Ages, as did all of Italy. The city came into its own again under the French rulers of the House of Anjou, who made it the capital of their Angevin kingdom of southern Italy in the 13th century and continued its progress under the Catalonian rulers of the House of Aragón, who took over in 1442. Then, in 1503, Naples (with Sicily) became a part of Spain, ruled for more than 2 centuries by Spanish viceroys who exploited the Italian provinces for the benefit of the Spanish treasury; so heavily taxed were the commoners (nobles and clergy were exempt) that in 1647 they rose up, led by Masaniello, but the revolution was crushed. After a short period under Austrian rule, it was the turn of the Bourbons, who arrived in 1734 and established the Kingdom of the Two Sicilies, with Naples as the capital. Its ancient dignity restored, Naples became one of Europe's major cities, attracting leaders in art, music, and literature until the unification of Italy in 1860. Economic and political problems gradually diminished its prestige, however, and damage from World War II dealt a severe blow to an already sick economy.

Today, thanks to a busy port, Naples is an important industrial and commercial center. It is a city both wise and violent, religious and pagan, magical and dirty, old and new. It attracts thieves, tourists, artists, and lovers of beauty with a contagious gaiety and exuberant, if chaotic, vitality. Its wealth of historical monuments; proximity to the Amalfi Coast, Capri, and the archaeological treasures of Pompeii and Herculaneum; and the magnificent — if somewhat tarnished — splendors of the romantic Bay of Naples, make it one of the world's great cities and a perennial tourist attraction.

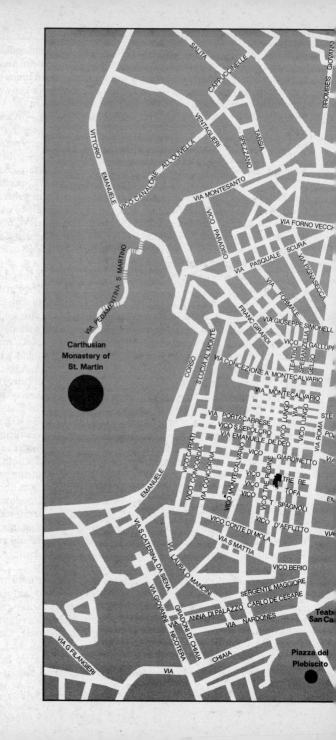

NAPLES AT-A-GLANCE

 SEEING THE CITY: Panoramic views of Naples and the bay are at every turn. Within the city, the outstanding view is from Room 25 of the *Certosa di San Martino* (Carthusian Monastery of St. Martin), now a museum. Depending on the weather and the visibility, however, the most spectacular view is from Mt. Vesuvius, some 15 miles (24 km) southeast of Naples. For more information on both these vantage points, see *Special Places,* below.

SPECIAL PLACES: To make sightseeing easier, think of Naples as divided into the following sections: In the area roughly between Piazza Municipio and Piazza del Plebiscito, there are monumental buildings and relatively wide-open spaces. The old quarter is near narrow Spacca-Napoli Street (the classic photos of streets strung with washing are taken here) and the historic center is to the northeast. Farther inland is Naples on the hills, the Vomero being the principal hill and an elegant residential district. To the west of the Piazza del Plebiscito area is Naples by the bay. Where the workaday port ends, a lovely promenade begins along the shore before the port of Santa Lucia and extends as far as another port area, Mergellina. Museums in Naples are open 9 AM to 2 PM Tuesdays through Saturdays, and 9 AM to 1 PM Sundays and holidays, unless otherwise noted.

DOWNTOWN

Castel Nuovo (New Castle) – This landmark on the Neapolitan waterfront, more often called the Castel Angioino (Angevin Castle) or Maschio Angioino, was built in the late 13th century by Charles I of Anjou, who modeled it on the castle at Angers. In the mid-15th century, Alphonse I of Aragón made substantial alterations. The triumphal arch sandwiched between two towers at the entry celebrates his entrance into Naples in 1443 and is an early example of Renaissance art in Naples. Inside the courtyard, the doorway to the Chapel of St. Barbara (or the Palatine Chapel), the only part of the castle remaining from Angevin times, is noteworthy, but the castle proper is not open to visitors. Piazza Municipio.

Palazzo Reale (Royal Palace) – Built in the early 17th century by Domenico Fontana for the Spanish viceroys, later enlarged and restored, this became the home of the Bourbon Kings of Naples and was then inhabited from time to time by the Kings of Italy. The niches on the façade contain statues of eight famous kings of the various dynasties that ruled Naples, including Charles I of Anjou, Alphonse I of Aragón, and Victor Emmanuel II of Italy. The palace is now a museum whose rooms contain original Bourbon furnishings, paintings, statues, and porcelain. Closed Mondays; in August and September, the museum stays open weekdays until 7:30 PM. Admission charge. Piazza del Plebiscito (phone: 413888).

Piazza del Plebiscito – This vast semicircle cut off on one side by the Palazzo Reale is the center of public life in Naples. Directly opposite the palace is the Church of San Francesco di Paola, a copy of the Pantheon in Rome, built by order of Ferdinand I of Bourbon in the late 18th century. Equestrian statues in the center of the square are of Ferdinand (by Canova) and Charles III of Bourbon.

Teatro San Carlo – Italy's second-most famous opera house is just off Piazza del Plebiscito and 40 years older than *La Scala*. Built under Charles of Bourbon in 1737 and inaugurated on the feast day of St. Charles Borromeo (whence its name), it was destroyed by fire in 1816 and thoroughly rebuilt in neo-classic style within 6 months, with Ionic columns, niches, and bas-reliefs on the outside and a fresco of Apollo and the Muses on the ceiling of the sumptuous auditorium — which seats 3,000 and has perfect acoustics. *San Carlo* audiences were the first ever to hear Bellini's *La Sonnambula,* Donizetti's *Lucia di Lammermoor,* and many other great works. Those not attending a performance can tour the theater in the morning, by prior arrangement. Closed Mondays. Via San Carlo (phone: 797-2111).

Galleria Umberto I – Across the street from *San Carlo,* this is the perfect place to sit down for a *caffè* or an ice cream. The Victorian arcade of glass and steel, topped with a cupola, was built from 1887 to 1890, and is younger than the one in Milan.

Chiesa di Sant'Anna dei Lombardi (Church of St. Anne of the Lombards) – This church was built in the 15th century and rebuilt in the 17th century. It is best known for its Renaissance sculptures, particularly for the eight life-size terra cotta figures of the *Pietà* (1492) by Guido Mazzoni — extremely realistic and rather eerie when seen from the main part of the church (it's in a chapel to the right at the far end). Via Monteoliveto.

Chiesa di Santa Chiara (Church of St. Clare) – The Church of the Poor Clares was built by order of Sancia of Majorca, wife of Robert I of Anjou, in the early 14th century. From the beginning, it was the church of the Neapolitan nobility. By the 18th century, it was covered with baroque decoration, but following serious damage in World War II, it has been rebuilt in its original Provençal-Gothic style. Be sure to see the 14th-century tomb of Robert of Anjou behind the altar and then go out to see the adjoining Chiostro delle Clarisse (Cloister of the Poor Clares). This unique 18th-century cloister is a lovely bower of greenery and flowers studded with columns and lined with seats entirely covered with majolica tiles — a colorful, welcome surprise. Via Benedetto Croce.

Chiesa del Gesù Nuovo – Just across the square from Santa Chiara on land surrounding the Palazzo Sanseverino. The interior of this late-16th-century church is full of baroque marblework and painting. The unusual façade originally was built in the 15th century for the palace. Piazza del Gesù Nuovo.

Chiesa di San Lorenzo Maggiore (Church of St. Lawrence Major) – One of the most important medieval churches in Naples, it was begun in the late 13th century by French architects, who did the polygonal Gothic apse, and was finished in the next century by local architects. Boccaccio fell in love with Fiammetta in this church in 1334 and Petrarch, who was living in the adjoining monastery, came here to pray during a terrible storm in 1345. Excavations at this site in 1990 uncovered some Greek and Roman ruins. Piazza San Gaetano.

Duomo (Cathedral) – The cathedral of Naples is dedicated to the city's patron saint, San Gennaro. It was built by the Angevins (in the late 13th and early 14th centuries) on the site of a previous basilica dedicated to Santa Stefania, which in its turn had been built on the foundations of a Roman temple dedicated to Apollo. It also incorporates a smaller basilica dating from the 5th century and dedicated to Santa Restituta. Rebuilt several times, the Duomo's 19th-century façade still sports 15th-century doorways. It contains the famous Chapel of San Gennaro (third chapel on the right), a triumph of 17th-century baroque art built in fulfillment of a vow made by Neapolitans for the passing of a plague. (The Latin inscription notes that the chapel is consecrated to the saint for his having saved the city not only from plague but also from hunger, war, and the fires of Vesuvius, by virtue of his miraculous blood.) Two vials of San Gennaro's dried blood are stored in a reliquary in the chapel, and twice a year, in May and September, all of Naples — or as many people as the church and the street in front can hold — gather to await the miracle of the liquefaction of the blood (see *Special Events*). If the miracle happens, all is well with the city. Via del Duomo.

Museo Archeologico Nazionale (National Archaeological Museum) – One of the most important museums in the world dedicated to Greco-Roman antiquity.

Among its precious artworks are sculptures collected by Pope Paul III of the Farnese family during 16th-century excavations of the ruins of Rome, including two huge statues found at the Baths of Caracalla: the *Farnese Hercules,* a Greek copy of a bronze original by Lysippus, and the *Farnese Bull,* a Roman copy of a Hellenistic bronze, carved from a single block of marble. The museum also is the repository of art and artifacts removed from Pompeii and Herculaneum since the 18th century. Most impressive of these are the exquisite mosaics from Pompeii and the bronzes from the Villa dei Papiri at Herculaneum, especially the water carriers (or dancers) and the two athletes. Other items removed from Pompeii and Herculaneum include silverware and glassware, combs, mirrors, and other toiletry articles, some furniture, and foodstuffs, such as carbonized bread, olives, grapes, onions, figs, and dates. Two other important collections to see in this 16th-century palace — which was first a barracks and then the seat of the university until the Bourbon King of Naples turned it into a museum in 1777 — are the Santangelo collection of ancient coins and the Borgia collection of Egyptian and Etruscan art. Closed Mondays. Admission charge. Piazza Museo (phone: 440166).

Catacombe di San Gennaro (Catacombs of St. Januarius) – The remains of San Gennaro lay in these catacombs from the 5th to the 9th century. On two levels, they date from the 2nd century and probably began as the tomb of a noble family that was later donated to the Christian community as a burial place. They are important for their early Christian wall paintings. Guided visits (most are in Italian, but some English-speaking guides are available) take place on Friday, Saturday, and Sunday mornings at 9:30, 10:15, 11:00, and 11:45. Admission charge. Off Via di Capodimonte, past the Church of the Madre del Buon Consiglio (no phone).

Museo e Gallerie Nazionali di Capodimonte (Capodimonte Museum and Picture Gallery) – One of Italy's best collections of paintings from the 14th through the 16th century is displayed in the grandiose 18th-century palace of a former royal estate on the hills in the northeastern part of the city. A Simone Martini panel (1317) of Robert of Anjou being crowned King of Naples is one of the museum's treasures; other masters represented are Bellini, Masaccio, Botticelli, Correggio, and Titian, among whose portraits of the Farnese family is a well-known one of Pope Paul III. The royal apartments on the first floor include a marvelous parlor, the Salottino di Maria Amalia, completely built and decorated in Capodimonte ceramics (some of which were shattered in the 1980 earthquake). In the park surrounding the palace a wedding party is often having pictures taken — it's one of the Neapolitans' favorite backgrounds. Open Tuesdays through Saturdays from 9 AM to 7:30 PM, June through September; 9 AM to 2 PM the rest of the year; and Sundays from 9 AM to 1 PM year-round. Admission charge. Parco di Capodimonte (phone: 741-0881).

Certosa di San Martino (Carthusian Monastery and National Museum of St. Martin) – Now a museum, this enormous monastery founded by the Angevin dynasty is beautifully situated on the Vomero Hill, next to an Angevin fortress, the Castel Sant'Elmo. The monastery was renovated in the 16th and 17th centuries (in the latter period by Cosimo Fanzago), so it is today a monument to the baroque. The church immediately to the left as you enter is lavishly done in baroque inlay of variously colored marbles and stones (see, too, the rooms behind the altar, including the one to the left with the intricate inlay of wood). In the museum, the marvelous view from the belvedere of room 25 is said to have inspired the saying "See Naples and die." The museum contains a collection of 19th-century Neapolitan painting, a naval section, a collection of memorabilia from the kingdom of Naples, and some striking 18th- and 19th-century *presepi,* or nativity scenes. The most famous is the Presepe Cuciniello, a room-size installation with countless figures and particularly graceful angels. Another *presepe* fits in an eggshell. Closed Mondays; in August and September it remains open until 8 PM Tuesdays, Thursdays, and Saturdays. Admission charge. Via Tito Angelini (phone: 578-1769).

Porto di Santa Lucia e il Lungomare (Santa Lucia Port and the Waterfront) –
One of the best-known Neapolitan songs has immortalized this tiny port abob with
picturesque fishing and pleasure boats. It is formed by a jetty that leads out from the
mainland to a small island entirely occupied by the Borgo Marinaro, a so-called fishing
village now populated largely with restaurants, and the Castel dell'Ovo (Egg Castle,
not to be confused with the Castel Nuovo, described above). The fortress dates from
the 12th century, but monks lived here even earlier, and in Roman times a patrician
villa occupied the site. Santa Lucia is the focal point of seaside Naples: Via Nazario
Sauro approaches it from the east; Via Partenope passes in front of it; and Via Caracciolo leads away from it to the west. The three together constitute Naples's *lungomare,*
a broad promenade along the water that is *the* place in Naples to take the early evening
passeggiata (stroll) and watch the sun go down. For at least a half mile of its length,
Via Caracciolo is backed by the greenery of the Villa Comunale, or public park, which
is stuffed with life — young lovers hugging, kids playing ball, grandparents taking the
air with the grandchildren, fathers renting miniature cars for mere toddlers who are
learning to become Neapolitan drivers. Ice cream is consumed by all.

ENVIRONS

Campi Flegrei (Phlegrean Fields) – Hot springs and sulfurous gases rise from this
dark, violent volcanic area that extends west of Naples from Capo Posillipo to Capo
Miseno, along the Gulf of Pozzuoli. Its name comes from the Greek, meaning "burning," and it is an area as rich in archaeological remains as in geophysical phenomena.
The remains of the Greek colony of Cuma, founded in the 8th century BC (the oldest
archaeological site in Italy), are about 12 miles (19 km) west of Naples (closed Mondays; admission charge), as are remains of Roman baths at Baia (closed Mondays;
admission charge). In Sophia Loren's hometown, Pozzuoli (8 miles/13 km west), the
third-largest amphitheater in Italy, built when the town was a major port in Roman
times, can be visited (closed Mondays; admission charge). Also in Pozzuoli is a Roman
temple, partially submerged in water, that reveals the effects of bradyseism, or "slow
earthquake," to which the whole area is subject; less or more of the pillars is visible
as the earth rises and falls. Lakes — such as Lago d'Averno (said to have been the
entrance to the underworld) and Lago Miseno — have formed in the craters of extinct
volcanoes in the Campi Flegrei, but the Solfatara crater just north of Pozzuoli is merely
dormant (its last eruption was in the 12th century). Full of steaming fumaroles and
containing the remains of a Roman spa, it is open daily (admission charge). Pozzuoli
is the last stop of the *metropolitana* from Piazza Garibaldi in Naples; Baia and Cuma
are stops of the Ferrovia Cumana suburban train line leaving from Piazza Montesanto.

Vesuvio (Mount Vesuvius) – This still-active volcano about 15 miles (24 km)
southeast of Naples last erupted in 1944 and has averaged one eruption every 35 years
over the past 300. Its most famous eruption was the one that buried Pompeii and
Herculaneum in AD 79 (see *Campania and the Amalfi Coast* in DIRECTIONS). That
explosion came from Monte Somma, 3,713 feet high, one of the volcano's two present
summits; some 200 years later, another summit, Monte Nuovo, 4,189 feet high, formed,
and this is the one that now is called Mount Vesuvius. There is no longer a chair lift
to the top of Monte Nuovo, but the ascent still can be made on foot along the path
that follows the edge of the crater, from which there are views down into the enormous
cavity or out toward the sea and the surrounding towns. All that is visible of Vesuvius's
cataclysmic power, however, are the vapors rising from fumaroles, and the guide
occasionally descends a bit into the crater for a better look at these vents. Take the
Naples-Salerno autostrada to Ercolano. From there it is an 8-mile (13-km) drive with
spectacular views. To reach Vesuvius by public transportation, take the *Circumvesuviana* railway (*Napoli–Barra–Torre del Greco–Torre Annunziata* line) from Stazione Circumvesuviana on Corso Garibaldi (it is reached by means of the down escalator
from the main train station in Naples). Get off at Herculaneum (Ercolano) or Pugliano,

then take a bus to the *stazione inferiore,* where an English-speaking guide may be hired. Be prepared for a long, steep climb; take comfortable shoes. Don't bother going on an overcast day.

■**EXTRA SPECIAL:** No stay in Naples is complete without a sunny drive up the famed promontory of Posillipo, a few miles southwest of the center, perhaps culminating in an alfresco lunch at Marechiaro (a most picturesque fishing village built high above the sea), which overlooks the southern end of the Bay of Naples. The road from Mergellina climbs past villas and fragrant gardens, becoming Via Nuova di Posillipo, which was begun by order of Murat, King of Naples, and completed in 1830. Don't miss the view of Cape Posillipo (from Via Ferdinando Russo just past Piazza Salvatore di Giacomo) before continuing up Via Nuova di Posillipo, which ends at Marechiaro. It was made famous by a song of the same name written by Salvatore di Giacomo, the first line of which is inscribed in the wall of an old house overlooking the water, marking the window celebrated in the song. On the way back, take Via Nuova di Posillipo, turn right onto Via Giovanni Boccaccio, and stop at the Parco della Rimembranza for spectacular views of the Bay of Naples on one side and the Bay of Pozzuoli on the other.

SOURCES AND RESOURCES

TOURIST INFORMATION: For general information, brochures, and maps of Naples and its environs, contact the Ente Provinciale per il Turismo (EPT; 58 Piazza dei Martiri, Scala B/Staircase B; phone: 405311); branches or booths are at the Stazione Centrale, the Stazione di Mergellina, and at the Aeroporto di Capodichino. The Azienda Autonoma di Turismo di Napoli (AAST), or local tourist office, is based in the Palazzo Reale (Piazza del Plebiscito; phone: 418744), but it has branches, including one at Piazza del Gesù Nuovo, one at the Castel dell'Ovo (phone: 552-3328), and one at the hydrofoil terminal in Mergellina (phone: 761-4585). The *Associazione Alberghi per la Gioventù* (Association of Youth Hostels) is at 40 Piazza Carità (phone: 551-3151).

The US Consulate is at Piazza della Repubblica (phone: 761-4303).

Local Coverage – Among its other brochures, the AAST puts out an interesting one entitled *Naples — The Old City: A Stratified Multiple Itinerary Map* that traces four itineraries through the historic center (roughly the area between Piazza del Gesù Nuovo and the Duomo), each route corresponding to a period in Neapolitan art: medieval, Renaissance, baroque, and rococo. The office also publishes a useful booklet, *Qui Napoli,* which is distributed monthly to the better hotels. Listings are in Italian and English. Another good monthly guide is *Napoli Top,* available in bars, hotels and at newsstands. The Neapolitans' daily newspaper is *Il Mattino.*

TELEPHONE: The country code for Italy is 39; the city code for Naples is 81. When calling from within Italy, dial 081 before the local number.

GETTING AROUND: Many of the major sights are easily accessible by foot. For others, such as the Parco di Capodimonte and sights on the Vomero, alternate means of transportation are desirable. Do everything you can to avoid driving in the city: Neapolitan traffic jams belong in the *Guinness Book*

of World Records. If you do drive, *never* leave anything in your car, even for the shortest period of time. Neapolitan car thieves are among the most resourceful in the world and can open and empty a car trunk in a matter of seconds.

Airport – Capodichino Airport serves mostly domestic and some international flights. A taxi ride from downtown takes anywhere from 15 to 45 minutes, depending on the traffic, and costs about $27; from the airport to downtown, the fare is double the meter. Night and holiday rides cost extra, as does baggage; ask to see the *tabella* (fare table). There is no special airport bus, but bus No. 14 from the main train station, Stazione Centrale, stops at the airport. The trip takes 30 minutes to an hour depending on traffic. Tickets cost about 75¢ and must be purchased in advance at a tobacco shop or newsstand.

Boats – Ferries and hydrofoils for Capri, Ischia, and Procida leave from the Molo Beverello, in front of Piazza Municipio and the Castel Nuovo, or from Mergellina's Porto Sannazaro. In summer, hydrofoils also depart from Mergellina to Sorrento, Positano, Amalfi, the islands of Ponza and Ventotene, Sicily, and the Lipari Islands. Sailing times are listed in *Il Mattino* and at tourist offices.

Bus and Tram – Main routes and schedules are listed in the supplement to the telephone directory, *Tutto Città.* Tickets cost 800 lire (about 65¢) and must be bought in advance at a tobacco shop or newsstand.

Car Rental – Major international firms are on Via Partenope: *Avis* (32 Via Partenope; phone: 764-5600); *Eurodollar* (14 Via Partenope; phone: 764-6364 or 764-5464); *Europcar* (38 Via Partenope; phone: 401454); *Hertz* (29 Via Partenope; phone: 764-5533, and 69 Piazza Garibaldi; phone: 206228); and *Maggiore* (92 Via Cervantes; phone: 522-1900, and the railway station). In addition, most of these companies have branches elsewhere in the city, including the railway station at Piazza Garibaldi and Capodichino Airport. Only a few gas stations are open at night. Check with your hotel or see the listings in *Qui Napoli* or *Napoli Top.*

Funicular – Four funicular lines connect lower-lying parts of Naples to neighborhoods on the hills. Of the three that go to the Vomero, the *Funicolare Centrale,* from Via Toledo to Piazza Fuga, and the *Funicolare di Montesanto,* from Piazza Montesanto to Via Morghen, are useful for visiting the Certosa di San Martino. The fourth funicular connects the Mergellina area to the Posillipo area.

Subway – The *metropolitana* runs from Napoli Gianturco to Pozzuoli Solfatara, making useful stops at the Stazione Centrale, Piazza Cavour (near the *National Archaeological Museum*), Piazza Montesanto and Piazza Amedeo (near funiculars), Mergellina, Campi Flegrei, and elsewhere en route.

Taxi – Taxis can be hailed while they cruise or may be picked up at any cabstand. For a radio-dispatched taxi call 556-4444 or 556-0202. Do not use unmetered taxis.

Train – Naples's main train station is Stazione Centrale (Piazza Garibaldi; phone: 553-4188). Trains to Herculaneum, Pompeii, and Sorrento, operated by the suburban railway, *Ferrovia Circemvesuviana,* leave from the nearby Stazione Circumvesuviana (Corso Garibaldi; phone: 779-2444), and can be reached by the down escalator from Stazione Centrale. Trains to Campi Flegrei points, operated by *Ferrovia Cumana,* another suburban railway, leave from Piazza Montesanto (phone: 551-3328).

 LOCAL SERVICES: Dentist (English-Speaking) – Dr. Antonio Siciliano (156 Via Toledo; phone: 552-2264); *Oral Rehabilitation Center* (141 Via Manzoni; phone: 640971 or 640932).

   Dry Cleaner – *Lavanderia Sanmarco,* 41 Via Santa Lucia (phone: 421396).

   Limousine Service – *Garage Dubbio* (6 Via Petronio; phone: 407138); *Autonoleggio Spigno* (13 Via Carrozzieri Alla Posta; phone: 552-4337).

   Medical Emergency – *Policlinico, Facolta di Medicina e Chirurgia* (5 Via Sergio Pansini; phone: 746-1111). One English-speaking doctor in private practice is Dr.

Vincenzo D'Antonio (5-8 Vico Satriano; phone: 414452); 24-hour ambulance service (phone: 752-0696); 24-hour medical service, doctor on call (phone: 751-3177).

Messenger Service – *Recapito Espresso Città,* 8 Via Nardones (phone: 418766 or 421904).

National/International Courier – *DHL International,* 94 Via Padula (phone: 540-1111).

Office Equipment Rental – *Aletta* (two locations: 6 Vicolo Campanile AI SS Apostoli; phone: 297100; and 130 Via Rossi; phone: 773-2976); *Scuotto,* audiovisual equipment (47 Via Padre Rocco; phone: 281073 or 734-9311); typewriters can usually be rented through your hotel concierge. Fully equipped offices for short-term rental (along with multilingual secretarial services, photocopy and telex machines, and meeting rooms) are available through *Centro Ufficio Attrezzati* (50/A Via Gianturco; phone: 205444) and *Tiempo Spa* (19-23 Via Sannio; phone: 785-9111).

Pharmacy – *Carducci,* open 24 hours daily (21-23 Via Carducci; phone: 417283); or dial 192 for recorded message of all-night pharmacies.

Photocopies – *Copy Rapid Galbiati* (18-20 Via S. Fusco; phone: 551-8437); and at most stationery shops.

Post Office – Central Post Office, open from 8 AM to 8 PM Mondays through Saturdays, to noon on Sundays. Piazza Matteotti (phone: 551-1456).

Secretary/Stenographer (English-Speaking) – *Tiempo Spa* (19-23 Via Sannio; phone: 785-9111); *Centro Ufficio Attrezzati* (50/A Via Gianturco; phone: 205444).

Tailor – *Ciardulli,* 109 Via Santa Lucia (phone: 421716).

Telex – Central post office, open daily from 8 AM to 8 PM; open 24 hours for telegrams. Piazza Matteotti (phone: 551-3446).

Translator – *European Secretarial Services* (126 Via Scarlatti; phone: 368925); *Associazione Interpreti e Traduttori* (88 Via Depretis; phone: 551-3507); *Centro Interpreti di Congressi e Traduttori* (63 Via Ventaglieri; phone: 412796); *Translation Center* (74 Via Cilea; phone: 647217).

Other – Convention equipment and personnel: *Centro Congressi Napoli* (146 Riviera di Chiaia; phone: 682420). Formal wear and costume rental: *Abiti Società* (6 Via Santa Brigida; phone: 323646).

 SPECIAL EVENTS: Twice a year (on the Saturday before the first Sunday in May and on September 19), Neapolitans crowd into the Duomo of San Gennaro and pray for the *Miracle,* the liquefying of the dried blood of their patron saint that is kept in two vials in a chapel of the church. The miracle is supposed to have first occurred on the hands of a bishop transporting the body after San Gennaro's martyrdom in Pozzuoli on September 19, 305, and it has been happening regularly since the first recorded recurrence in 1389 — regularly, but not *always.* The event is something of a mass fortune telling, because when it fails, some disaster is expected to befall the city — in the past it might have been plague, in the future it could be Vesuvius. (The blood failed to liquefy during the last eruption of Vesuvius in 1944.) The miracle lets Naples know that the saint still is with them, and nowhere is the atmosphere more alive with anticipation than in the chapel downstairs, where San Gennaro's bones are kept and the people plead for a sign. For information on details of the liquefaction, call 449097. Other important festivals celebrate the feast of *Santa Maria del Carmine* on July 16, and the *Madonna di Piedigrotta,* which lasts several days in early September.

 MUSEUMS: In addition to those mentioned in *Special Places,* a number of other museums and churches are impressive.

Aquarium – One of the oldest, if not *the* oldest, in Europe (1872), housing some 200 species of Mediterranean marine life, all collected from the Bay of Naples. Open daily except Mondays from 9 AM to 5 PM; admission charge. Villa Comunale (phone: 583-3111).

Cappella Sansevero (Sansevero Chapel) – The funerary chapel of the Sangro family, containing the *Veiled Christ* by Giuseppe Sammartino and many other 18th-century sculptures. Since its recent renovation, visits are by appointment only. 19 Via Francesco De Sanctis (phone: 454684).

Chiesa di San Domenico Maggiore (Church of St. Dominic Major) – A 13th-century church, frequently restored, containing the famous crucifix of St. Thomas Aquinas (who lived and taught in the adjoining monastery) and paintings by Titian, Luca Giordano, Solimena, Simone Martini, and others. Piazza San Domenico.

Chiesa di San Gregorio Armeno (Church of St. Gregory of Armenia) – A baroque church worth a visit for its famous nativity scene (only on view during the *Christmas* period). Via San Gregorio Armeno.

Chiesa di San Paolo Maggiore (Church of St. Paul Major) – A church of the late 16th century, wonderfully Neapolitan baroque in style, with paintings by Stanzione, Solimena, and Paolo de Matteis. Piazza San Gaetano.

Chiesa di Santa Maria del Carmine (Church of Santa Maria del Carmine) – Built in the 12th century and substantially reconstructed between 1283 and 1300, this church is home to a venerated image of the Madonna. An adjacent tower is the scene of a mock burning and other celebrations on the saint's day, July 16 (see *Special Events*). Piazza del Carmine.

Museo Civico Filangieri (Filangieri Civic Museum) – Arms, furniture, porcelain, costumes, and paintings, housed in the 15th-century Palazzo Cuomo. Open Tuesdays through Saturdays 9AM to 2PM; Sundays and holidays 9AM to 1PM. Admission charge. 288 Via Duomo (phone: 203175).

Museo Duca di Martina (Duke of Martina Museum) – Ivories, enamels, china, and majolica, European and Oriental, are displayed in the Villa Floridiana, a small neo-classical palace in the Vomero section, with splendid gardens and a panoramic view of the bay. Closed Mondays. Admission charge. Via Cimarosa (phone: 578-8418).

Museo Principe Aragona Pignatelli Cortes (Prince of Aragón Pignatelli Cortes Museum) – A collection of 19th-century furniture and china, plus a coach museum in the park's pavilion, with French and English carriages. Closed Mondays. Admission charge. Riviera di Chiaia (phone: 669675).

SHOPPING: For shopping purposes, Naples is commonly divided into a *zona elegante* (elegant zone) and a *zona commerciale* (commercial zone). The most fashionable shopping area, the *zona elegante,* is centered around Piazza dei Martiri, along Via Calabritto, Via Filangieri, Via dei Mille, and Via Chiaia. The latter leads to the more commercial zone between Piazza Trieste e Trento and Piazza Dante along Via Roma (also called Via Toledo after the viceroy who opened it in 1536) and toward the main railroad station along Corso Umberto I. Ceramics and porcelains have been sold here since the Bourbon kings founded the Capodimonte school and factory in the 18th century. Although original Capodimonte pieces are collectors' items and Capodimonte-style figurines are produced by companies all over Italy, the production of more traditional ceramics, in popular folk styles, continues to thrive in Naples and the vicinity. Another important product of the area is coral, much of which, it is said, is now imported from Southeast Asia but handcrafted nevertheless in nearby Torre del Greco, where there are several large factories and showrooms (*Giovanni Apa,* in Torre del Greco, just off the Naples-Pompeii Highway, is one source of coral and cameos). Neapolitan street markets are very colorful (always beware of pickpockets and *scippatori,* who speed by on motorbikes, grabbing bags and gold chains from shoulders and necks as they go). Markets are in the neighborhoods of Resina, for new or used clothing and fabrics; *Spacca-Napoli,* for books and silver objects; *Antignano,* for fabric, household goods, and food; and, at *Christmas,* Via San Gregorio, for traditional Neapolitan nativity figures. Antiques shops are found mostly in the area around Piazza dei Martiri and Via Santa Maria di Costantinopoli.

Baracca e Burattini – Opposite the entrance to the archaeological museum, an artisans' shop selling masks, marionettes, and lovely dolls. 2 Piazza del Museo (no phone).

Berisio – Antique books. 28 Via Port'Alba (phone: 544-7639).

Bowinkle – Lovely old prints of Naples — among other places — framed and unframed. 24 Piazza dei Martiri (no phone).

Chiurazzi – Bronze reproductions of sculptures in the archaeological museum. 271 Via ai Ponti Rossi (phone: 751-2685).

Coin – A good department store. 10 Via Scarlatti (phone: 578-0111).

Ospedale delle Bambole – Handcrafted dolls. 81 Via San Biagio dei Librai (phone: 203067).

La Rinascente – Another good and reasonably priced department store. 343 Via Roma (phone: 411511).

Il Sagittario – Curious leather goods (masks, sculptures). 10/A Via Santa Chiara (no phone).

Simplement – Top-quality women's shoes, ranging from classic to more unusual styles. 27 Via Calabritto (no phone).

La Soffitta – Hand-painted ceramics. 12 Via Benedetto Croce (no phone).

 SPORTS AND FITNESS: Most sports facilities belong to private clubs, so check with the concierge of your hotel about which may be open to the public.

Fitness Centers – *Athletic Club* for men and *Silhouette* for women, both at 21 Via Fiorentini (phone: 313160 or 313342).

Jogging – One good place to run is the *lungomare* (seafront promenade) along Via Caracciolo and Via Partenope from the port of Santa Lucia to the Mergellina. The Villa Comunale, the park behind Via Caracciolo, is another good spot.

Soccer – From September to May, *Napoli* plays at the *Stadio San Paolo* (Piazzale Vincenzo Tecchio, Fuorigrotta; phone: 615623 or 619205). Its capacity is 100,000 often fierce fans, although Neapolitans have the reputation of being the least rowdy among Italians.

Swimming – The polluted Bay of Naples is not the best spot for water sports, but there are fine seaside resorts on the nearby islands and along the Amalfi Coast.

Tennis – There are public courts at several tennis clubs, including the *Sporting Club Virgilio* (6 Via Tito Lucrezio Caro; phone: 769-5261); the *Tennis Club Vomero* (8 Via Rossini; phone: 658912); and the *Tennis Club Napoli* (Villa Comunale, Viale Dohrn; phone: 761-4656).

 THEATER: Even those who speak Italian probably won't readily understand the Neapolitan dialect, but just for the color and sheer vitality, take in a performance by the renowned *Repertory Group of Eduardo de Filippo* at the *Teatro San Ferdinando* (Piazza Teatro San Ferdinando; phone: 444500). A fine place to sample Neapolitan music and folklore is the *Circolo della Stampa* (reserve seats through your concierge). Other theatrical groups perform at the *Politeama* (Via Monte di Dio; phone: 764-5016); *Cilea* (Via San Domenico, at Corso Europa; phone: 656265); *Sannazaro* (157 Via Chiaia; phone: 411723); and *Bracco* (40 Via Tarsia; phone: 340234).

MUSIC: The season at the *Teatro San Carlo* (Via San Carlo; box office closed Mondays; phone: 797-2370 or 797-2111), one of the finest opera houses in the world, generally runs from December through most of June. Then, from mid-September through mid-November, the theater is the scene of a series of symphonic concerts, the *Concerti d'Autunno* (Autumn Concerts). The *Associazione Alessandro Scarlatti* performs at 58 Piazza dei Martiri (phone: 406011). Still more symphony and chamber concerts, by groups such as the *Accademia Musicale Napoletana* and others, are scheduled frequently at the *Auditorium RAI-TV* (Via Guglielmo Marconi; phone: 610122); in the church or cloisters of Santa Chiara (Via Benedetto Croce; phone: 522-6209); and in numerous other churches about town. The *Conservatorio di Musica* (Via San Pietro a Maiella; phone: 459255). In the summer, concerts are also held in the gardens at Capodimonte.

NIGHTCLUBS AND NIGHTLIFE: Like most port towns, Naples has a number of seedy bars and rip-off joints to be avoided. *Il Gabbiano,* near the principal hotels (26 Via Partenope; phone: 411666), is a piano bar that serves late snacks. One of the most elegant nightclubs in town is the *Virgilio* (6 Via Tito Lucrezio Caro; phone: 769-5261), up on the exquisite Posillipo Hill, one of the poshest areas in Naples. Another swanky nightspot is *Rosolino* (5-7 Via Nazario Sauro; phone: 415873), which also is a piano bar and restaurant. Worth looking into are *Chez Moi* (Parco Margherita 13; phone: 407526); *Boomerang* (Via Giotto; phone: 365185); *My Way* (Via Cappella Vecchia; no phone); *Casablanca* (101 Via Petrarca; no phone); and *Villa Scipione* (4 Via Scipione Capece; no phone).

BEST IN TOWN

CHECKING IN: An expensive hotel in Naples will charge from $145 to $220 a night for a double room; moderately priced hotels range from $100 to $145; and in the inexpensive category you'll be charged $45 to $100. All telephone numbers are in the 81 city code unless otherwise indicated.

Britannique – Offering Swiss management and efficiency, it's hospitable and very clean. Most of the 86 rooms in this old converted villa are large, and since it's set on a hillside up and back from the waterfront, most of them have attractive views. Business facilities include 24-hour room service, meeting rooms for up to 150, English-speaking concierge, foreign currency exchange, secretarial services in English, audiovisual equipment, photocopiers, computers, translation services, and express checkout. 133 Corso Vittorio Emanuele (phone: 761-4145; fax: 669760; telex: 722281). Expensive.

Continental – This ultramodern hotel has none of the charm of its older rivals, but what it lacks in style, it makes up for in efficiency. It is big (716 rooms), centrally located, and particularly geared to the business traveler. Business facilities include 24-hour room service, meeting rooms for up to 600, English-speaking concierge, foreign currency exchange, secretarial services in English, audiovisual equipment, photocopiers, computers, cable television news, translation services (including simultaneous interpreters), and express checkout. 46 Via Partenope (phone: 764-4636; fax: 764-4661; telex: 710244). Expensive.

Excelsior – Naples's only truly deluxe hotel, part of the reliable CIGA chain, it dominates the port of Santa Lucia, with terraced seaside rooms overlooking the 12th-century Castel dell'Ovo, the old fishing village of Borgo Marinaro, and the whole bay. The *Casanova Grill* takes some prizes, too (see *Eating Out*). There are 138 air conditioned rooms and a garage nearby. Business facilities include 24-hour room service, meeting rooms for up to 200, English-speaking concierge, foreign currency exchange, secretarial services in English, audiovisual equipment, photocopiers, computers, cable television news, translation services, and express checkout. 48 Via Partenope (phone: 417111; fax: 411743; telex: 710043). Expensive.

Miramare – Also conveniently located, with the added attraction of the waterfront, this hotel is reputable, comfortable, and small (30 rooms). Although it has no restaurant, there is a lovely breakfast terrace, and it is very near *La Cantinella* (see *Eating Out*). 24 Via Nazario Sauro (phone: 427388; fax: 416775; telex: 710121). Expensive.

Parker – This fine, renovated 96-room Belle Epoque-style property has a sweeping staircase, chandeliers, and old-fashioned elevators. Business facilities include 24-hour room service, meeting rooms for up to 220, English-speaking concierge, foreign currency exchange, secretarial services in English, audiovisual equipment, photocopiers, computers, translation services, and express checkout. 135 Corso Vittorio Emanuele (phone: 761-2474; fax: 663527; telex: 710578). Expensive.

Royal – Also on the Santa Lucia waterfront, this one is Naples's biggest (300 rooms). It's modern and busy, and it has a rooftop pool, garage, and air conditioning. Business facilities include 24-hour room service, meeting rooms for up to 550, English-speaking concierge, foreign currency exchange, secretarial services in English, audiovisual equipment, photocopiers, computers, cable television news, translation services, and express checkout. 38 Via Partenope (phone: 764-4800; fax: 764-5707; telex: 710167). Expensive.

Santa Lucia – This once shabby seafront property has been spruced up with considerable taste to match its smarter neighbors, which include the *Excelsior* and the *Vesuvio*. Old paintings and antiques lend an Old World touch to this 107-room hostelry, but the amenities are strictly 20th century. Business facilities include 24-hour room service, meeting rooms for up to 250, English-speaking concierge, foreign currency exchange, secretarial services in English, audiovisual equipment, photocopiers, computers, cable television news, translation services, and express checkout. 46 Via Partenope (phone and fax: 416566; telex: 710595). Expensive.

Vesuvio – Close to the *Excelsior,* Naples's second hotel also faces the picturesque port of Santa Lucia. It has 174 rooms, good baths, a decor ranging from period style to modern, a garage, and air conditioning. Business facilities include 24-hour room service, meeting rooms for up to 280, English-speaking concierge, foreign currency exchange, secretarial services in English, audiovisual equipment, photocopiers, computers, cable television news, translation services, and express checkout. 45 Via Partenope (phone and fax: 417044; telex: 710127). Expensive.

Paradiso – The breathtaking panoramic view of the entire Bay of Naples, seen from the front bedrooms and the roof terrace, make this place particularly appealing. Business facilities include 24-hour room service, meeting rooms for up to 35, English-speaking concierge, foreign currency exchange, secretarial services in English, audiovisual equipment, photocopiers, computers, translation services, and express checkout. 11 Via Catullo (phone: 761-4161; fax: 761-3449; telex: 722049). Expensive to moderate.

Mediterraneo – Not very romantic, but conveniently located in the commercial center of town, behind Piazza Municipio. More than 250 rooms, all air conditioned; garage. Via Nuova Ponte di Tappia (phone: 551-2240; fax: 552-5868; telex: 721615). Moderate.

San Germano – A few miles drive from the center of Naples, it's in rather nondescript surroundings at the crossroads for the *Ippodromo di Agnano* racecourse. This efficient hotel has some 100 pleasant rooms (each with TV set and air conditioning), a lovely garden, swimming pool, tennis courts, and a garage. 41 Via Beccadelli (phone: 570-5422; telex: 720080). Moderate.

Le Fontane al Mare – Nicely located (close to the seafront) and a very good value. Its 21 rooms are tastefully furnished in keeping with the 19th-century palazzo in which it is housed, but there's no restaurant. Be sure to keep a supply of coins on hand to feed the elevator. 14 Via N. Tommaseo (phone: 764-3470 or 764-3811). Inexpensive.

 EATING OUT: While Italian food is not all pasta and pizza, both originated in Naples and are a staple of southern Italy. Here pasta is almost always eaten as a first course at lunch, while it is usually replaced at the evening meal by a light broth or soup (if the evening meal itself hasn't been replaced altogether by a pizza, which is generally served only in the evenings). Naples is the home of *spaghetti c'a pummarola* (*spaghetti al pomodoro* in Italian), born of the mating of pasta with the tomato not too long after the latter arrived in Italy from South America in the 16th century. It is still the most popular pasta dish, easily prepared, vividly colorful, fragrant with additions of basil or parsley, oregano, and garlic, and topped with tangy parmesan cheese. Other Neapolitan favorites are *vermicelli con le vongole* (pasta with clams, with or without tomatoes, in a garlic and olive oil sauce), or *con zucchine* (with zucchini, garlic, and oil), and *pasta e fagioli* (a very thick white bean soup with short pasta).

As Naples is seafood country, the best main course here is simple fresh fish grilled and seasoned with olive oil and lemon. But if you're watching your budget, be careful. Most quality fish is sold by weight at restaurants, and you'd do well to avoid those whose prices are listed on the menu *al chilo* (per kilogram), which can turn an otherwise modest bill into a major monetary setback. Exceptions to this rule are lesser fish such as *alici* (anchovies), which, when fresh, can be tastefully prepared in oil, garlic, and parsley, and *fritto misto,* a mixture of fried shrimp, squid, and small local fish. One piece of advice: Don't ever eat raw seafood that may have come from the polluted Bay of Naples. Dinner for two with a house wine will run from $85 to well over $110 at a restaurant listed as expensive, from $55 to $85 at a moderate one, and from $25 to $55 at an inexpensive place. All telephone numbers are in the 81 city code unless otherwise indicated.

La Cantinella – A favorite of Neapolitans, visiting dignitaries, and tourists staying nearby along the picturesque port of Santa Lucia. Fresh fish, as everywhere, is at a premium, but local clams and mussels mated with a hint of garlic, parsley, and *pummarola* or tomato and lavished on a steaming plate of linguine constitute one of the great pleasures of southern Italian life, within reach of everyone's pocket. The service is friendly and efficient. Closed Sundays. Reservations advised. Major credit cards accepted. 23 Via Nazario Sauro (phone: 404884 or 405375). Expensive.

Casanova Grill – A delightfully intimate dining room for such a grand hotel as the *Excelsior,* it offers a wide selection of enticing antipasti, plenty of fresh fish, Neapolitan specialties such as pasta with seafood, a remarkable fish soup, and roast baby lamb with rosemary and garlic — all prepared and served with care and refinement. Open daily. Reservations advised. Major credit cards accepted. 48 Via Partenope (phone: 417111). Expensive.

Ciro a Mergillina – For 150 years, this has been *the* place to see and be seen in Naples. Its fish always is top quality, and the pizza is among the best in town. Closed Mondays. Reservations advised. Major credit cards accepted. 21 Via Mergillina (phone: 681780). Expensive.

Giuseppone a Mare – Traditionally one of Naples's best fish restaurants, with incomparable views from Cape Posillipo, it seems to have its ups and downs in quality, service, and price. Still, it's worth trying if you're in the Posillipo area. Closed Sundays and from *Christmas* through *New Year's.* Reservations advised. Major credit cards accepted. 13 Via Ferdinando Russo, Capo Posillipo (phone: 769-6002). Expensive.

Rosolino – An elegant supper club, piano bar, and nightclub in the Santa Lucia quarter, just a skip and a jump from the *Excelsior* and *Vesuvio* hotels. The restaurant is open at lunch, too; closed Sundays. Reservations necessary at dinner. Major credit cards accepted. 5-7 Via Nazario Sauro (phone: 415873). Expensive.

La Sacrestia – Dine alfresco here on delicious Neapolitan dishes such as homemade pasta stuffed with ricotta cheese, *scazzette di Fra' Leopoldo,* or any of the fresh fish dishes. On a hillside beyond Mergellina that affords splendid views from the terrace, it is closed Mondays from September through June, and Sundays in July and August. Reservations advised. Major credit cards accepted. 116 Via Orazio (phone: 664186). Expensive.

La Fazenda – Very Neapolitan, serving homemade garlic bread, wonderful pasta dishes, fresh fish, home-raised chickens, and exquisite desserts. In the Posillipo area, the surroundings are rustic, with spectacular views of the bay and flowers everywhere. Closed Sundays and 2 weeks in August. Reservations advised. Major credit cards accepted. 58 Calata Marechiaro (phone: 769-7420). Expensive to moderate.

Amici Miei – Traditional Neapolitan fare is served in a traditionally elegant ambience in one of the elegant residential zones of Naples, near the *Politeama Theater.* Closed Mondays and August. Reservations advised. Major credit cards accepted. 78 Via Monte di Dio (phone: 764-6063). Moderate.

La Bersagliera – In good weather, the Borgo Marinaro facing the Castel dell'Ovo can't be beat for local color. And this is the only one of these portside restaurants that makes it: Sometimes a dose of sun in a spectacular setting is worth more than a flawless meal. Specialties include good varied antipasti, fresh octopus salad, and a surprisingly inexpensive mixed grill of seafood that includes a tender and tasty fresh squid — a dish certainly worth a repeat visit. Naples' famous *scugnizzi* (streetwise waifs) ask for pieces of bread as they pass by between swims in the polluted bay. Closed Tuesdays. Reservations advised. Major credit cards accepted. 10 Borgo Marinaro, Santa Lucia (phone: 764-6016). Moderate.

Ciro a Santa Brigida – In the center of town, this has been one of the best and busiest of Naples' trattorie-*pizzerie* since the 1920s. Sample the great variety of fresh fish or pasta such as *lasagna imbottita* and *maccheroni alla siciliana.* This is also a good place for *pastiera,* a typical Neapolitan dessert made of ricotta cheese and wheat. Closed Sundays. Reservations advised. No credit cards accepted. 71 Via Santa Brigida (phone: 552-4072). Moderate.

Don Salvatore – It has been said that "Mergellina without Don Salvatore would be like Naples without Vesuvius." It's a longtime Neapolitan favorite where everything is good, from antipasto to pasta, fish, meat, and pizza (served evenings only). Closed Wednesdays. Reservations advised. Visa accepted. 5 Via Mergellina (phone: 681817). Moderate.

Dora – The ambience here is that of a small fishing boat and the fish served is first class. Try the *linguine all'aragosta* (pasta with crayfish). Closed Sundays and August. Reservations advised. No credit cards accepted. 30 Via Ferdinando Palasciano, Riviera di Chiaia (phone: 680519). Moderate.

Il Gallo Nero – Elegant dining in an antiques-filled 19th-century villa or on a terrace with a splendid view of Mergellina. Classic favorites as well as sensible innovations are on the menu, plus fresh fish and imaginative meat dishes. Open evenings only, except Sundays, when it's open for lunch; closed Mondays and August. Reservations advised. Major credit cards accepted. 466 Via Tasso (phone: 643012). Moderate.

Al Poeta – The Varriale brothers come from a long line of Neapolitan restaurateurs, and their flair has won them a dedicated following at this busy eatery, high up on Posillipo hill. The specialty is fish, and customers know it will be fresh (which is not always true in Naples). Closed Mondays. Reservations advised. Visa accepted. 134 Piazza Salvatore di Giacomo (phone: 769-6936). Moderate.

Osteria al Canterbury – Like many Neapolitan eating places, this one keeps its doors locked to ward off holdups. But don't be put off — inside, the atmosphere is warm and welcoming, with walls lined with wine bottles. Try the *maccheroni di casa Canterbury* (homemade pasta topped with mozzarella, eggplant, and a tomatoey meat sauce). The set lunchtime menu is particularly inexpensive. Closed Sundays. Reservations advised on weekends. Major credit cards accepted. 6 Via Ascensione a Chiajà (phone: 413584). Moderate to inexpensive.

Osteria Castello – This small trattoria beckons you with its terra cotta tile floors, cheerful red-and-white check tablecloths, and the wafting aroma of homemade pasta sauces. Owner Carmine Castello also waits on tables and is always ready to explain the menu, which changes every 3 days. The emphasis is on traditional, no-frills Neapolitan cooking, at down-to-earth prices. Closed Sundays. Reservations advised. American Express accepted. 38 Via Santa Teresa a Chiaia (no phone). Moderate to inexpensive.

Pizzeria Bellini – One of the city's oldest *pizzerie*. Besides a vast assortment of pizza (the most famous, with fresh basil and tomato), there are pasta, fish, and meat dishes. Closed Wednesdays. Reservations unnecessary. No credit cards accepted. 80 Via Santa Maria di Costantinopoli (phone: 459774). Moderate to inexpensive.

Il Pulcinella – A genuine family-style restaurant, cozy, friendly, and delicious. Closed Mondays and from July to September — but it's really a winter ambience anyway. Reservations unnecessary. No credit cards accepted. 4 Vico Ischitella (phone: 764-2216). Moderate to inexpensive.

Gorizia – One of the Vomero's older *pizzerie*, now a full restaurant with traditional Neapolitan cuisine. The pizza is still noteworthy (available evenings only). Closed Wednesdays and August. Reservations unnecessary. No credit cards accepted. 29 Via Bernini (phone: 644662). Inexpensive.

Vini e Cucina – The food is delicious — real home cooking, Neapolitan style — and so this little Mergellina restaurant is increasingly popular and often impossibly crowded. Closed Sundays. Reservations unnecessary. No credit cards accepted. 762 Corso Vittorio Emanuele (no phone). Inexpensive.

NICE

Those who remember the halcyon days of ornate villas, swaying palms, and languid luxury under an azure sky may shake their heads sadly at the Côte d'Azur of today: a symphony in cement, a real estate speculator's orgy of high-rise apartment blocks, pillbox hotels, honky-tonk pizza parlors, and shiny fast-food factories. Its once-quaint little marinas are linked by a permanent shoreline traffic jam, and some of its renowned beaches now look more like a horde of people dangling their feet from the edge of a freeway.

Although Nice has managed to keep its head above the concrete and retain its special flavor — a mixture of Marseilles, the *Mardi Gras,* and the Mediterranean, it slowly is becoming a place where tourism is more of a burden than a cultural exchange between visitors and natives. But at the first shine of sun, the café tables come out, the awnings unfurl, and strollers in sandals are back clacking along the Promenade des Anglais and, until the hordes of tourists invade its beach in July and August, you can enjoy the undeniable charms of the city. In the summer, the population of 340,000 burgeons with holiday makers from Paris, Piccadilly, and Peoria — though no longer from St. Petersburg — and an empty or moderately priced hotel room is harder to find than a winning lottery ticket. And a lot more scarce than a movie star. All the streets — particularly the Promenade des Anglais — are mobbed with traffic and the deafening noise competes with the burning sun, making summer in Nice a less than desirable experience. But in mid-autumn, when the locals and a few visitors take advantage of the last hot days to dip into the still-warm sea, you can again begin to feel that Nice is nice.

The Greeks from nearby Massalia (today's Marseilles) founded the city in 350 BC as a little market town and auxiliary port, and named it Nikaia. Continuous lootings by pirates from the Ligurian coast caused Nikaia's citizens to ask for military help from the Romans. They came, protected the city, and discovered the pleasures of the Riviera. The remains of their lavish colonization are evident today in the Arena and the Baths on the hill at Cimiez — the city's elegant residential section. During the fall of the Roman Empire, barbarians from the north and pirates from North Africa invaded Nice and brought about its decline. In 1388, the House of Savoy wrested the growing city from the Counts of Provence (who brought the city back to its former state) and retained almost unbroken possession of it for close to 500 years. Napoleon lived for a time at No. 6 on what is today the Rue Bonaparte, later on Rue St.-François-de-Paule by the opera house. In 1860, the head of the House of Savoy and King of newly unified Italy, Victor Emmanuel II, ceded the region to France in return for military support against an Austrian invasion (he did this after the citizens of Nice voted in favor of being under French control). Giuseppe Garibaldi, the Italian patriot, was born here, as was Masséna, the general Wellington admired most after Napoleon. In modern times, the beauty and climate of Nice have made it the amusement park of the European aristocracy, an off-season refuge from harsh northern climes and irritating revolutions. Today, the major portion of the city's income comes from various high-tech industries (e.g., electronics) rather than tourism.

The city, between Cannes and Monte Carlo, is one big easy-to-scan color postcard: the lapis lazuli of the Bay of Angels (Baie des Anges), the activity of the Vieux Port, and the timelessness of the towering Castle (Château) — the name given to the hill with the ruins of an old fortress that looms over the harbor. Along the bay runs the fabled Promenade des Anglais, a broad seafront avenue that resembles a mile-long outdoor café. At one end of the promenade is the city's pulse, Place Masséna: semitropical gardens set against crimson buildings and cool graceful arcades. Avenue Jean-Médecin (named after a former Mayor of Nice for 38 years, whose son — also a Mayor of Nice for 24 years — recently fled to South America to escape being arrested for tax evasion and fraud) is Main Street, bisecting the city in a straight line from the Place Masséna to the railroad station. The Old City, La Vieille Ville, is a little piano-shaped quarter — all narrow and cobbled and noisy, and pungently southern — that huddles in the shadow of the Château. La Vieille Ville's boundaries are the Quai des Etats-Unis and the Boulevard Jean-Jaurès beside the Paillon River, which is covered in parts by esplanades and divides the Old City from modern Nice to the west. In the past few years, Nice has spread farther to the west, past the airport that was expanded onto land reclaimed from the Baie des Anges.

Nice's heritage is culturally rich. Rodin, Modigliani, and Toulouse-Lautrec were among the numerous artists to have converged on the city starting in the 19th century. Matisse spent the last years of his life close to Nice, and for many years Chagall lived nearby; their works can be seen in the city's *Musée Matisse* and *Musée National Marc Chagall.* Music lovers flock to the renowned *Opéra de Nice,* and a variety of concerts are performed all year long throughout the city. And if you prefer fun and frolicking to art and music, Nice offers that too — not just with its usual festivities, but with a big bang during *Carnaval.*

NICE AT-A-GLANCE

SEEING THE CITY: The long azure sweep of the bay, the compact jumble of red tile roofs in La Vieille Ville, the foothills of Provence, and the Maritime Alps rising sharply just outside the city are best seen from a viewing platform at the summit of the 300-foot Château. It can be reached by an elevator — or a 300-step climb — at the end of the Quai des Etats-Unis, where the quay joins the Rue des Ponchettes. Now there is a train from the Promenade des Anglais that goes through La Vieille Ville en route to the hills of the Château; from there, an exceptional panorama of Nice's port and the Bay of Angels unfolds before you. For information and reservations, call *Les Trains Touristiques* (phone: 93-18-81-58).

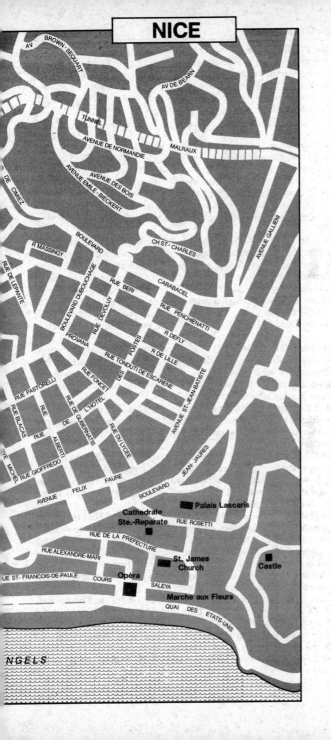

SPECIAL PLACES: Nice is a city to be seen casually, to be ambled through under a morning or late-afternoon sun, especially in and around the Old City and the renowned flower market, *Le Marché aux Fleurs.* Let your discoveries be guided by casual occurrences: the purchase of a peach in an open market, a cold glass of Corsican white wine at a portside café, the scent of thyme wafting from the flower market.

IN THE CITY

Promenade des Anglais – If you only have an hour in Nice, spend it strolling along this promenade from the Place Masséna to the *Négresco* hotel (see *Checking In*). Ornate hotels grace one side, and a narrow, crowded strip of pebbled beach separates you from the brilliant blue of the bay. The promenade takes its name from the city's English colony, which constructed the path (in the middle of the last century) that was the predecessor of this one. You can lunch in your bathing suit on several excellent private beaches along the Promenade des Anglais. Prices are moderate and carafe wines are good.

La Vieille Ville (Old City) – Old Nice is a tight labyrinth of winding streets and alleys, steep ascents between medieval buildings, and balconies festooned with rainbows of drying laundry. The character of the city as it grew down the slopes of the Château from the 14th to the 18th century is in striking contrast to the city of expansive patrician promenades that developed in more modern times. Of late, La Vieille Ville has shown indications of evolving into Nice's artists' quarter. Explore the Rue Rossetti, the Rue de la Boucherie, or the Rue du Collet. Crowd your way through the teeming street markets. Stop in at the Cathedral of Sainte Réparate and the 17th-century Church of St. James.

Le Marché aux Fleurs (Flower Market) – On the edge of the Old City, just behind the Quai des Etats-Unis, you'll find the wholesale flower market that offers one of Nice's most colorful spectacles. The varieties of blossoms are dazzling, the aromas heady, and there are a few well-placed cafés, where you can see, sniff, and sip, all at the same time. Closed Mondays and Sunday afternoons. Cours Saleya.

Le Marché de la Brocante (Antiques Market) – On Mondays, the huge square where the flower market is held becomes an antiques and bric-a-brac market of unusual allure. In the late afternoon on Wednesdays, local artisans and painters display their often-expensive works. Cours Saleya.

Palais Lascaris (Lascaris Palace) – A splendid private palace of the 17th century in Genoese style, this is the former residence of the Count Lascaris-Ventimiglia. It is noted for its ceilings with frescoes, its decorative woodwork, and its regal staircase. Closed Mondays in summer; Mondays, Tuesdays, and some public holidays in winter; and November. 15 Rue Droite (phone: 93-62-05-54).

Vieux Port (Old Port) – To the east of the Château, the harbor of Nice is an artful array of multicolored boats, from one-man dinghies and kayaks to the white steamers that make the crossing to Corsica. Excursion boats leave from the port and putter along to nearby Riviera towns. To reach the port, go out around the base of the Château at the far end of Quai des Etats-Unis or take Rue Cassini south from Place Garibaldi.

. **Cathédrale Orthodoxe Russe** – A reminder of the days when the royal Romanovs roamed the Riviera and the promenade bustled with grand dukes, ballerinas, and an occasional Bolshevik, the cathedral was built in the Belle Epoque of the 19th century, under the auspices of Czar Nicholas II himself. Built from 1903 to 1914, it is considered one of the most beautiful churches of its style outside of Russia. The church supports a bouquet of ornate onion domes in the ancient Russian style. Inside are a rich collection of icons and an impressive, carved iconostasis — the traditional screen that separates the altar from the nave in an Orthodox church. No visitors are permitted during the Sunday morning service. Admission charge. Bd. du Tzarewitch (phone: 93-96-88-02).

Musée National Marc Chagall – Built on a wooded hill in Cimiez in 1972, this modern museum houses works donated by Chagall, including the 17 canvases, painted over a 13-year-period, that make up his *Biblical Message*. In addition to the many fine paintings, the museum has sculptures, mosaics, sketches, and lithographs, all by Chagall. In summer, a tearoom is set up in the garden. Closed Tuesdays. Admission charge. Av. du Dr.-Ménard and Bd. de Cimiez (phone: 93-81-75-75).

Musée Matisse et d'Archéologie – Henri Matisse had his studio in the Cimiez section of Nice, and a representative collection of his work — canvases, drawings, and sculpture done at various stages of his career — along with some of the artist's personal effects and his private art collection, are in the village here. A separate building houses the collection of archaeological objects found at the Roman site of Cimiez. Matisse's tomb is at the north end of a nearby cemetery, where Raoul Dufy also is buried. Closed for renovations until the summer, when it will be open from 10 AM to noon and from 2 to 6 PM; closed Mondays and Sunday mornings. No admission charge. 164 Av. des Arènes de Cimiez (phone: 93-81-59-57).

Musée d'Art Moderne et d'Art Contemporain – The largest modern art complex in southern France, this museum offers not only excellent canvases, but good views of the city from the top of its four towers. Opened in 1990, it displays works from such world-renowned artists as César, Klein, Christo, Warhol, Lichtenstein, Morris, and Louis. Closed Tuesdays. No admission charge. Promenade des Arts (phone: 93-62-61-62).

ENVIRONS

Eze Village – Perched on a rock spike 1,550 feet above the sea, this unusual village — once a medieval fortress — offers a splendid panorama of the Riviera. It also has a tropical garden (Jardin Exotique) and a church with a beautiful 15th-century font. Nietzsche is supposed to have first worked out his masterpiece, *Thus Spake Zarathustra*, here. The walk from the Lower (Inferieure) Corniche up the Nietzsche Pass (Sentier Nietzsche) is picturesque and well worth the effort, and ends at Eze-Bord-de-Mer, by the water. Eze is less than 7 miles (11 km) from Nice, along the Middle (Moyenne) Corniche, on the way to Monte Carlo.

■**EXTRA SPECIAL:** The Chapelle du Rosaire (Rosary Chapel), designed and decorated by Matisse (who thought it his masterpiece) between 1947 and 1951, is the main reason so many people have rediscovered Vence, a picturesque old market town some 13½ miles (22 km) northwest of Nice (also see *France,* DIRECTIONS). The stunning stained glass windows (which Matisse executed to express his gratitude to the Dominican monks who protected him during World War II), the murals, and the church vestments created by Matisse may bring you here, but you'll also enjoy the setting — on a rock promontory, sheltered by the last foothills of the Alps — and the charm of the old town, enclosed in elliptical walls and entered through five arched gateways. Restricted access and the small dimensions of the chapel can result in its being crowded, however, especially when a tour bus unloads its contents. The chapel (on Av. Henri-Matisse) is open Tuesdays and Thursdays from 10 to 11:30 AM and 2:30 to 5:30 PM; other days by appointment made at least a day in advance (phone: 93-58-03-26). For those who are interested in exploring the town of Vence itself, a stop at the tourist office in the central plaza (Pl. du Grand-Jardin; phone: 93-58-06-38) will provide ample ideas about what to see and how to get there.

SOURCES AND RESOURCES

TOURIST INFORMATION: The Nice Office du Tourisme–Syndicat d'Initiative, whose hostesses speak English, has three branches: next to the railway station on Avenue Thiers (phone: 93-87-07-07), 5 Avenue Gustave (phone: 93-87-60-60), and at the Acropolis (open in summer only; 1 Esplanade Kennedy; phone: 93-92-82-82). There's also a welcome desk near the airport.

Local Coverage – The daily newspaper of the area is *Nice-Matin.* A free weekly directory of activities on the Riviera, *Sept Jours–Sept Nuits,* is distributed in the lobbies of most hotels. Also pick up the weekly *Semaine des Spectacles* for 5F. All are in French, but they're easy to decipher.

TELEPHONE: The country code for France is 33; the city code for Nice is 93, which is incorporated into all local 8-digit numbers. When calling a number in Nice from the Paris region (including the Ile-de-France), dial 16, wait for a dial tone, then dial the 8-digit number. When calling a number from outside Paris, dial only the 8-digit number. When calling from the US, dial 33 (which is the country code), followed by the 8-digit number.

GETTING AROUND: It's a good thing that central Nice is compact and easily accessible by foot, because traffic becomes ludicrous during the tourist seasons. Many areas have become pedestrian zones, such as Rue Masséna and some of its cross streets, as well as numerous streets in La Vieille Ville. If you want to move faster, rent a motorbike, moped, scooter, or bicycle from *Nicea Location Rent,* 29 Rue Paganini (phone: 93-16-10-30).

Airport – Nice–Côte d'Azur Airport (phone: 93-21-30-30), about 4 miles (6 km) west of the city, handles both domestic and international traffic. The approximately 10-minute taxi ride into town costs about 100F–150F (about $17–$25). The airport shuttle is part of the municipal bus network, *Transports Urbains de Nice* (24 Rue Hôtel des Postes; phone: 93-62-08-08). Leaving about every 20 minutes, it makes runs to the airport from 6 AM to 8 PM and continues to bring passengers into town (to Bd. Jean-Jaurès) from the airport until 11 PM. The shuttle leaves Nice from Avenue Félix-Faure next to the information office at the Gare Routière; some of the buses (such as the No. 23) into Nice go directly to the train station. The fare is 8F.

There also is a shuttle service from the Nice airport to Menton, which stops at the coastal resorts along the way — Villefranche, Beaulieu, Eze, Cap d'Ail, Monaco, Monte Carlo, and Roquebrune. Leaving approximately every hour from 7 AM to 8 PM, depending on the season, the trip takes about 1½ hours each way and costs 57F ($9.50) one way, 100F ($16) round trip (phone: 93-21-30-83). In addition, helicopter service to Monaco is available. For details, call *Héli-Air Monaco* (phone: 93-21-34-62 at the airport, 93-30-80-88 at the Héliport de Fontvieille in Monaco).

Boats – In summer, *Gallus* boats cruise along the Riviera. Apply to *SATAM* (Quai Lunel; phone: 93-55-33-33). For ferries to Corsica, inquire at *SNCM* (Quai du Commerce; phone: 93-89-89-89).

Bus – You can hop on a bus for outlying districts, such as Cimiez, at the Place Masséna. The central station for the urban bus network is at 10 Av. Félix-Faure (Traverse Flandres Dunkerque; phone: 93-62-08-08). Nearby, the main station for regional buses is the Gare Routière (Bd. Jean-Jaurès and Promenade Paillon; phone: 93-85-61-81).

Car Rental – Major international firms represented, both downtown and at the airport, are *Avis* (phone: 93-80-63-52 and 93-87-90-11); *Budget* (phone: 93-87-63-87 and 93-21-36-50); *Europcar* (phone: 93-88-64-04 and 93-21-36-44); and *Hertz* (phone: 93-81-51-21 and 93-21-36-72).

Taxi – Cabs are expensive, so watch the meter and remember streets often are clogged with traffic at certain hours. There usually are plenty of cabs at designated stands, and they also can be hailed in the streets; or call 93-80-70-70.

Train – The Gare *SNCF* is on Avenue Thiers (phone: 93-87-50-50). Another station, Gare de Provence (33 Av. Malausséna; phone: 93-84-89-71), belongs to the *Chemins de Fer de Provence* (Provence Railways), a narrow-gauge railway that operates on a scenic route between Nice and Digne, approximately 100 miles (160 km) to the northwest.

 LOCAL SERVICES: *Service 2A* (phone: 93-21-30-73), at Nice–Côte d'Azur Airport, is a general business service operated by the Nice Chamber of Commerce and linked to similar services at airports in Marseilles, Lyons, Paris, London, and Frankfurt. The staff can coordinate practically any kind of business need, including catering, secretarial assistance, telecommunications, and conference arrangements. Private offices and conference rooms (for up to 10 people) are for rent by the hour or day, and customized VIP services are available for individuals and groups.

Dentist (English-Speaking) – *Mme. Favot* (49 Rue Pastorelli; phone: 93-62-30-54 or 93-80-76-36); *Syndicat des Chirurgiens Dentistes des Alpes-Maritimes* (28 Bd. Raimbaldi; phone: 93-80-36-66 or 93-80-38-40).

Dry Cleaner – *Express Nettoyage,* 22 Av. Buénos Ayres.

Limousine Service – *Garage Plaza,* 12 Av. de Verdun (phone: 93-87-82-34 or 93-87-97-23).

Medical Emergency – *Hôpital St.-Roch,* 24-hour service. 5 Rue Pierre-Devoluy (phone: 92-03-33-33).

National/International Courier – *DHL International* is in Lyons, but serves Nice and surrounding municipalities (phone: toll-free in France, 05-20-25-25); *Chrono Post* is located in all branches of the post office.

Office Equipment Rental – *Ciné Photo-Technic* (2 Av. Aristide-Briand; phone: 92-09-03-03 or 92-52-52-52); *Bureco,* for typewriters only (53 Rue Rossini; phone: 93-87-20-80).

Pharmacy – *De Nuit,* open 24 hours. 7 Rue Masséna (phone: 93-87-78-94).

Photocopies – *Service 2A* at the airport (phone: 93-21-30-73); also at most photographic stores and hotels in the city, at all post offices, department stores and large supermarkets.

Post Office – There are two main post offices (23 Av. Thiers, near the train station; phone: 93-88-92-00; and at Rue de l'Hôtel des Postes and Pl. Wilson; phone: 93-85-94-20). Both are open weekdays from 7:30 AM to 8 PM and Saturday mornings.

Secretary/Stenographer (English-Speaking) – *Service 2A* at the airport (phone: 93-21-30-73) or through your hotel.

Teleconference Facilities – *L'Acropolis* is the best equipped (Esplanade Kennedy; phone: 93-92-83-00); *Palais des Congrès* (Av. Gallieni; phone: 93-92-80-80); *Nice Congrès at Palais des Expositions* (Esplanade de Lattre de Tassigny; phone: 93-92-33-33).

Telex/Telefax – At the post office (Rue de l'Hôtel des Postes and Pl. Wilson); also at major hotels.

Translator – *Denise Chabert,* 10 Av. Général Leclerc, Villefranche-Sur-Mer (phone: 93-01-80-25).

SPECIAL EVENTS: The Nice event par excellence is *Carnaval,* which begins 3 weekends before *Lent* and ends when His Majesty, King Carnival, is burned in effigy on *Shrove Tuesday.* The festivities include myriad parades and floats, marching bands and majorettes, fireworks and flowers, giant papier-mâché heads and masked balls. The *Fête des Mais* is a month of Sundays in May, with special merriment in the gardens of the *Roman Arena* at Cimiez. In July, the 10-day *Grande Parade du Jazz,* also in the Cimiez gardens, is the biggest jazz festival in Europe. In September, the *Triathlon de Nice* draws some of the world's best athletes who swim across the Baie des Anges for 3 miles (5 km), run in a 27-mile (42 km) marathon, and bicycle for 62 miles (100 km). To find out more about special events in Nice, contact *Comité des Fêtes* (5 Promenade des Anglais; phone: 93-87-16-28).

 MUSEUMS: The *Chagall, Matisse,* and *Modern Art* museums described in *Special Places* are the most impressive in Nice, but there are several others of interest.

Musée des Beaux-Arts Jules Chéret – Nice's municipal art museum, with works by Fragonard, Renoir, Degas, Picasso. This is one of the few authentic buildings remaining from *La Belle Epoque.* Closed Mondays. No admission charge. 33 Av. des Baumettes (phone: 93-44-50-72).

Musée d'Histoire Naturelle or Musée Barla (Natural History Museum) – Exhibitions on marine life, paleontology, and mineralogy. Closed Tuesdays. No admission charge. 60 *bis* Bd. Risso (phone: 93-55-15-24).

Musée International d'Art Naïf Anatole Jakovsky (Anatole Jakovsky International Museum of Naive Art) – Jakovsky's collection of almost 600 paintings documenting naive art from the 18th century to the present, representing some 27 countries. Closed Tuesdays. No admission charge. Château Ste.-Hélène, Av. Val-Marie (phone: 93-71-78-33).

Musée Masséna – Memorabilia of Napoleon's trusted marshal and exhibitions on the history of Nice. Closed Mondays. No admission charge. 65 Rue de France (phone: 93-88-11-34).

Musée Naval – From its perch atop the Tour Bellanda (a former residence of Berlioz), this museum overlooks spectacular grounds. It houses the expected — ship models, arms, navigation instruments — and the not so expected, such as models of the port at various times in its history. Closed Tuesdays. No admission charge. Tour Bellanda, Parc du Château (phone: 93-80-47-61).

Musée de Terra Amata – Artifacts from this excavated prehistoric site that is about 400,000 years old. Closed Mondays and 2 weeks in September. No admission charge. 25 Bd. Carnot (phone: 93-55-59-93).

SHOPPING: Street market shopping in La Vieille Ville is the least expensive and the most fun. Rue Masséna, Place Magenta, and Rue Paradis are the pedestrian zone of shops and cafés, with Rue Paradis noted for its elegant shops. There's also a flea market on Quai Infernet, Tuesdays through Saturdays.

Alziari – Oils, spices, rustic wooden kitchenware, and olive oil soap. 14 Rue St.-François-de-Paule (phone: 93-85-76-92).

Comtesse du Barry – Toulouse food delicacies of every description; 57 varieties of foie gras. 5 Rue Halévy (phone: 93-88-49-16).

Confiserie du Vieux Nice – A sweets factory with Provence specialties such as candied fruits and flowers. Watch the stuff being made downstairs, then buy it upstairs. 14 Quai Papacino and Rue Robilante (phone: 93-55-43-50).

Galeries Lafayettes – Part of a nationwide chain of department stores that has a

VAT rebate for tourists and an English-speaking staff. 6 Av. Jean-Médecin (phone: 93-85-40-21).

Louis Vuitton – Handbags, luggage, and other items with the status LVs. English spoken, prices high. Check erratic seasonal opening hours. 2 Av. de Suède (phone: 93-87-87-47).

Nice-Etoile – A shopping mall with clothing, shoe, and perfume shops, plus an art gallery on the second floor. 24 Av. Jean-Médecin.

Promenade des Antiquaires – Houses a complex of 22 antiques galleries. 7 Promenade des Anglais.

Riviera Bookshop – A wide choice of new and secondhand books in English. 10 Rue Chauvain (phone: 93-85-84-61).

Vogade – For chocolate lovers. 1 Pl. Masséna (phone: 93-87-89-41).

 SPORTS AND FITNESS: Boating – Various kinds of small boats are available for hire in the Vieux Port. Windsurfing craft, *planches à voile,* can be rented at bathing establishments along the promenade.

 Bowling – At 5 Esplanade Kennedy (phone: 93-55-33-11); open from 11 AM to 2 AM.

Fitness Center – The *Centre Profil* at the *Méridien* hotel (1 Promenade des Anglais; phone: 93-87-73-57) has an American instructor and is open to the public.

Golf – The most spectacular course is at Mont-Agel in the hills above Monte Carlo (phone: 93-41-09-11). There also are two good 18-hole courses near Nice — *Golf de Biot* (Avenue Jules-Grec, Biot 06410; phone: 93-65-08-48) and *Golf du Valbonne* (Château de la Begude, Valbonne 06160; phone: 93-42-05-30).

Horse Racing – Thoroughbred racing takes place at the *Hippodrome de Côte d'Azur* in nearby Cagnes-sur-Mer (phone: 93-20-30-30).

Horseback Riding – Horses can be rented at *Club Hippique de Nice* (368 Rte. de Grenoble; phone: 93-29-81-10); *Centre Regional de Randonnées et de Tourisme Equestre* (Rte. de Sain Cézaire St.-Vallier-de-Thiey 06460; phone: 93-60-73-48); and *Relais Equestre de la Ferme* (Rte. Nationale 98, Hyères 83400; phone: 94-66-41-78).

Jogging – The wide sidewalk on the sea side of the Promenade des Anglais is good for early morning jogging. The Parc de Vaugrenier, 5 miles (8 km) west of Nice on N7, has a jogging track equipped with exercise stations.

Skiing – From November to April, you can ski on the slopes at Valberg, Isola, Esteng d'Entraunes, Auron, and Gréolières-les-Neiges in the Alps, only an hour or two away.

Swimming – The Ruhl Plage is the most central of Nice bathing beaches. Castel Plage is set right into the rock of Pointe de Rauba Capeu below the Château. In winter, you can swim at *Piscine Municipale J. Médecin* (178 Rue de France; phone: 93-86-24-01) or try *Piscine Jean Bouin* in the *Palais des Sports* (next to the Acropolis, near the Palais de l'Exposition; phone: 93-13-13-13).

Tennis and Squash – Contact the *Nice Lawn Tennis Club* (Parc Imperial, 5 Av. Suzanne Lenglen: phone: 93-18-00-95). Squash is played at *Club Vauban* (18 Rue Mal-Vauban; phone: 93-29-09-78).

 THEATER: In summer, all of Nice's best theatrical experiences take place outdoors: cabarets, concerts, theater, and folkloric shows at *Théâtre de Verdure,* in the Albert I Garden (just off Place Masséna; phone: 93-87-77-39 or 93-82-38-68) and at the *Roman Arena* in Cimiez. Check with the tourist office or the *FNAC* record store (30 Av. Jean-Médecin; phone: 93-92-09-09) for more information. *Théâtre du Vieux Nice* (4 Rue St.-Joseph; phone: 93-62-00-03) is a music hall with operettas and dancing. The *Nouveau Théâtre de Nice* (Esplanade des Victoires; phone: 93-80-52-60) presents a season of plays in French from October through

April. For modern theater, try the *Théâtre de l'Alphabet* (10 Bd. Carabacel; phone: 93-13-08-88).

MUSIC: In addition to musical performances outdoors in summer, there is an opera season at the *Théâtre de l'Opéra* (Quai des Etats-Unis) from November through April. The box office is at 4 Rue St.-François-de-Paule (phone: 93-80-59-83 for information; 93-85-67-31 for reservations). The *Nice Philharmonic Orchestra* offers a musical spring and a musical autumn at the opera house. Jazz can be heard from October to June at Cimiez's *Centre de Diffusion et d'Action Culturelle de Cimiez* (49 Av. de la Marne; phone: 93-81-09-09).

NIGHTCLUBS AND NIGHTLIFE: Probably the best-known nightspot in Nice is the *Casino Ruhl*, on the ground floor of the *Méridien* hotel (1 Promenade des Anglais; phone: 93-87-95-87). Smaller than its counterparts in Monte Carlo, its only *jeux* are slot machines, but it does have a Las Vegas–style cabaret and a disco called the *Jok' Club*. *Gentry's* (29 Rue de Préfecture; phone: 93-62-28-62) hosts a cool crowd, features video clips, and serves breakfast from 5 AM on weekends. Gambling enthusiasts can also go to Cannes, 20 miles (32 km) southwest, or Monte Carlo, 13 miles (21 km) northeast.

BEST IN TOWN

CHECKING IN: Nice hotels can be divided into those along the Promenade des Anglais, with a view of the bay — and the traffic — and those set back on quieter streets. At an expensive hotel expect to pay above $150 per night for a double (although rates can be much higher for suites at hotels such as the *Négresco*); $100 to $150 at a moderately priced hotel; less than $80 is inexpensive. However, expect prices to leap upward by one-half in summer, and perhaps even double on the most expensive end. Do not show up in the summer high season without a reservation unless you want to become an expert in Riviera hotel lobbies. Be aware, though, that Nice has a good supply of furnished rooms for visitors who plan to stay a week or more; a brochure is available upon request from the Tourisme-Syndicat d'Initiative.

Beach Regency – A deluxe, modern, and fully air conditioned 332-room hotel. The management has established a very fine restaurant, *Le Regency* (closed in August), and such lively activities as *thés dansants* (tea dances) and festive buffet lunches on Sundays. And there's still a swimming pool on the roof as well as a good terrace restaurant, featuring Lebanese specialties, overlooking the bay. The location is a bit away from the center, toward the airport, but the street address still is right. Business facilities include meeting rooms for up to 400, English-speaking concierge, foreign currency exchange, secretarial services in English, audiovisual equipment, photocopiers, cable television news, translation services, and express checkout. Major credit cards accepted. 223 Promenade des Anglais (phone: 93-83-91-51; fax: 93-71-21-71; telex: 461635). Expensive.

Elysée Palace – This elegant hostelry boasts all the amenities desired by travelers on holiday or business. It's set 100 feet from the sea, yet is near the center of town, with 150 rooms and suites. Facilities include a rooftop swimming pool with a bar, a fitness room and sauna, a garage, 2 conference rooms, and an excellent restaurant. Outside, the hotel's signature is a 250-ton, 80-foot-high bronze statue of a woman by Sacha Sosno. Business facilities include meeting rooms for up to 25,

English-speaking concierge, foreign currency exchange, secretarial services in English, audiovisual equipment, photocopiers, cable television news, translation services, and express checkout. Major credit cards accepted. 33 Rue François-Ier (phone: 93-86-06-06; fax: 93-44-50-40; telex: 970336). Expensive.

Grand Hôtel Aston – Recommended not only because it is in the center of town, but also because it faces the fountains in the Place Masséna and has a good restaurant. Business facilities include meeting rooms for up to 180, English-speaking concierge, foreign currency exchange, secretarial services in English, audiovisual equipment, photocopiers, cable television news, translation services, and express checkout. Major credit cards accepted. 12 Av. Félix-Faure (phone: 93-80-62-52; fax: 93-80-40-02; telex: 470290). Expensive.

Holiday Inn – Opposite the airport, this place provides a regular free shuttle. Air conditioned throughout, it has modern luxury appointments, a pool, sauna, and solarium. Business facilities include meeting rooms for up to 150, English-speaking concierge, foreign currency exchange, secretarial services in English, audiovisual equipment, photocopiers, cable television news, translation services, and express checkout. Major credit cards accepted. Nice Airport, 179 Bd. René-Cassin (phone: 93-83-91-92; fax: 93-21-69-57; telex: 970202). Expensive.

Méridien – Above the *Ruhl Casino* near the Albert I Garden, this shiny, modern, somewhat impersonal hotel has lots of glass and escalators, and is luxurious in a more streamlined way than the Victorian dowager hotels that gave the Riviera its reputation. There's a good restaurant, piano bar, and health club, as well as an underground parking lot that offers access to the pedestrian zone. Business facilities include meeting rooms for up to 400, English-speaking concierge, foreign currency exchange, secretarial services in English, audiovisual equipment, photocopiers, cable television news, translation services, and express checkout. Major credit cards accepted. 1 Promenade des Anglais (phone: 93-82-25-25; fax: 93-16-08-90; telex: 470361). Expensive.

Négresco – One of those Côte d'Azur landmarks where everyone should stay at least once before doomsday. A great wedding cake hotel overlooking the promenade, with elaborately appointed rooms, a fine restaurant called *Chantecler* (see *Eating Out*), and staff in 18th-century rainment. In the central atrium, a ton of Baccarat crystal is suspended over what is allegedly the largest Aubusson carpet in the world (a similar chandelier is in the Kremlin). The building itself has been designated a national monument. Major credit cards accepted. Business facilities include meeting rooms for up to 400, English-speaking concierge, foreign currency exchange, secretarial services in English, audiovisual equipment, photocopiers, cable television news, translation services, and express checkout. 37 Promenade des Anglais (phone: 93-88-39-51). Expensive.

Plaza Concorde – A traditional palace, it is beautifully restored and in the center of town facing Albert I Garden and the sea. The view from the rooftop terrace is magnificent. Business facilities include meeting rooms for up to 550, English-speaking concierge, foreign currency exchange, secretarial services in English, audiovisual equipment, photocopiers, cable television news, translation services, and express checkout. Major credit cards accepted. 12 Av. de Verdun (phone: 93-87-80-41; fax: 93-88-61-11; telex: 460979). Expensive.

Pullman – In the center of town, this deluxe hotel is a 5-minute walk from Place Masséna. The rooms are air conditioned and soundproof. Among the hotel's attractions are a Polynesian bar, pool and sauna, exotic interior gardens, and a great view from the rooftop terrace. Business facilities include meeting rooms for up to 120, English-speaking concierge, foreign currency exchange, secretarial services in English, audiovisual equipment, photocopiers, cable television news, translation services, and express checkout. Major credit cards accepted.

28 Av. Notre-Dame (phone: 93-80-30-24; fax: 93-62-61-69; telex: 470662). Expensive.

Splendid-Sofitel – This 100-year-old dowager has been run by the same family for three generations, though it's been modernized, with television sets and air conditioning. One floor is reserved for nonsmoking guests. Only 500 yards from the sea, but it, too, has a pool as well as a sauna on the premises. Business facilities include meeting rooms for up to 100, English-speaking concierge, foreign currency exchange, secretarial services in English, audiovisual equipment, photocopiers, cable television news, translation services, and express checkout. Major credit cards accepted. 50 Bd. Victor-Hugo (phone: 93-88-69-54; fax: 93-87-02-46; telex: 460938). Expensive.

Westminster Concorde – Recently renovated, this old hotel is in the grand tradition, facing the sea. All the air conditioned rooms have mini-bars and color TV sets, and there's a good restaurant, bar, and disco. Business facilities include meeting rooms for up to 350, English-speaking concierge, foreign currency exchange, secretarial services in English, audiovisual equipment, photocopiers, cable television news, translation services, and express checkout. Major credit cards accepted. 27 Promenade des Anglais (phone: 93-88-29-44). Expensive.

Albert I – One of the best situated properties in Nice, it is 50 yards from the beach and Place Masséna and a 2-minute walk from the pedestrian zone. Good views of the sea and the gardens. Visa accepted. 4 Av. des Phocéens (phone: 93-85-74-01). Expensive to moderate.

La Pérouse – A charming small hostelry at the far end of the Quai des Etats-Unis, with a view of the entire bay, particularly spectacular at sunset. It offers gardens, pool, sauna. One drawback: traffic noise on an uphill curve outside. No restaurant. Business facilities include meeting rooms for up to 25, English-speaking concierge, foreign currency exchange, secretarial services in English, audiovisual equipment, photocopiers, translation services, and express checkout. Major credit cards accepted. 11 Quai Rauba-Capeu (phone: 93-62-34-63; fax: 93-62-59-41; telex: 461411). Expensive to moderate.

West End – Here is traditional elegance of a somewhat British flavor. A faithful clientele seems to have been coming back each year since the Crimean War. There are 101 rooms in this seafront location, but no restaurant. Business facilities include meeting rooms for up to 150, English-speaking concierge, foreign currency exchange, secretarial services in English, audiovisual equipment, photocopiers, translation services, and express checkout. Major credit cards accepted. 31 Promenade des Anglais (phone: 93-88-79-91; fax: 93-88-85-07; telex: 460879). Expensive to moderate.

Brice – This old hotel is 4 blocks from the Promenade des Anglais, in a delightful flower garden with orange and palm trees. Business facilities include meeting rooms for up to 30, secretarial services in English, audiovisual equipment, photocopiers, translation services, and express checkout. Major credit cards accepted. 44 Rue Maréchal-Joffre (phone: 93-88-14-44; fax: 93-87-38-54; telex: 470658). Moderate.

Frantour-Napoléon – This typical, gracious, Niçois building is on a quiet corner a few streets back from the beachfront, near the pedestrian zone. The owner also is the manager, and the atmosphere is warm and welcoming. Bar, but no restaurant. 6 Rue Grimaldi (phone: 93-87-70-07). Moderate.

Georges – Only 18 rooms, but each is comfortable, clean, well cared for, and looks as if it's been decorated with surplus *Négresco* furnishings. Rooms are understandably hard to come by in the summer, but it's well worth the necessary advance planning. Major credit cards accepted. 3 Rue Henri-Cordier (phone: 93-86-23-41). Moderate.

Grand Hôtel de Florence – Small, centrally located yet quiet, and air conditioned. There is no restaurant. 3 Rue Paul-Déroulède (phone: 93-88-46-87; fax: 93-88-43-65; telex: 470652). Moderate.

Primotel Suisse – A small hotel in the traditional style, close to the Old City. Its restaurant offers a panoramic view of the Bay of Angels. Visa accepted. 15 Quai Rauba-Capeu (phone: 93-62-33-00). Moderate.

New York – An old white building with tropical flora in its entrance court, on a side street off the busy Avenue Jean-Médecin. Centrally located and remodeled despite its elderly-looking exterior. Visa accepted. 44 Av. Maréchal-Foch (phone: 93-92-04-19). Moderate to inexpensive.

Résidencehôtel Ulys – Among the finest and most economical choices of Nice's many apartment hotels. The 88 studio and 1-bedroom apartments are clean, modern, and fully equipped with kitchens, and many have balconies overlooking the sea. Maid service by the day or week. Visa accepted. 179 Promenade des Anglais (phone: 93-96-26-30). Moderate to inexpensive.

Berne – Small, comfortable, and completely renovated, it is directly opposite the train station. No restaurant, but there's a pleasant cafeteria decorated in a rustic style. Visa accepted. 1 Av. Thiers (phone: 93-88-25-08). Inexpensive.

Impérial – In a garden with palm trees and exotic plants, this quiet hostelry is a bit out of town but close to the Exhibition Center and Congress Hall. Restaurant on the premises. Closed November through January. Visa accepted. 8 Bd. Carabacel (phone: 93-62-21-40). Inexpensive.

 EATING OUT: The food found in Nice is a curious mixture of Parisian, native Provençal, and neighboring Italian. However, the city can claim specialties of its own, and some are described in the popular *Cuisine of Nice* (Penguin) by the city's flamboyant former mayor, Jean Médecin, who is married to an American. Specialties include *pissaladière,* a kind of pizza topped with black olives, onions, and anchovies; *stocaficada,* a ragout of stockfish, served with potatoes, tomatoes, peppers, and zucchini; *gnocchi à la niçoise,* a kind of potato dumpling,; and *pain bagnat,* a loaf of French bread split down the middle, soaked in olive oil, and garnished with tomatoes, radishes, peppers, onion, hard-boiled egg, black olives, and parsley. *Soupe au pistou* is a vegetable bean soup with garlic, basil, and herbs. *Socca,* a popular dish in bars of the old town and port, is an enormous pancake made from chick-pea flour and olive oil, baked like pizza or fried in oil. It is usually washed down with a solid red wine or a little glass of *pointu* (chilled rosé). Fast food also has come to Nice; there are signs posted throughout the city giving directions to various quick eats.

Nice has the distinction of being the only major city in France, apart from Bordeaux, which grows its own Appellation Contrôlée wines within the city limits. These are the Bellet reds, whites, and rosés, which must be tried during your stay here. At a very expensive restaurant, expect to pay $200 or more for two for dinner; $100 to $150 at expensive restaurants; $50 to $100 at moderately priced restaurants; and less than $50 at inexpensive restaurants. Prices don't include drinks or wine; usually a service charge is included.

Chantecler – Since chef Jacques Maximin left, the expensive, elegant fare certainly is less thrilling, though such specialties as *gourmandise de foie gras* (a luxurious pâté), a fish fantasy called *charlotte de St.-Pierre,* and inventive dishes like lobster ravioli still are consistent and rate one Michelin star. The *menu dégustation* features tiny, elegant portions of a dozen different dishes. Closed mid-November to mid-December. Reservations necessary. Major credit cards accepted. 37 Promenade des Anglais (phone: 93-88-39-51). Very expensive.

Le Moulin de Mougins – One of the most extraordinary dining experiences on the

Côte d'Azur thrives in Roger Vergé's converted 16th-century mill in the charming market town of Mougins. The cuisine justifiably has earned three Michelin stars, and among the specialties to be enjoyed are braised slivers of Provençal duck in honey and lemon sauce, *escalope* of fresh salmon, lobster fricassee pâté of sole, and for dessert, cold wild strawberry soufflé. There also are 5 guestrooms. Closed Mondays, Thursday afternoons, and from January 29 to *Easter*. Reservations necessary. Major credit cards accepted. About 20 miles (32 km) west of Nice in Mougins (phone: 93-75-78-24). Very expensive.

L'Ane Rouge – Fine seafood specialties at this fancy restaurant include oysters in champagne, lobster, and bourride (fish stew) — or try the sweetbreads. Closed mid-July to September, Saturdays, and Sundays. Reservations necessary. Major credit cards accepted. 7 Quai des Deux-Emmanuels (phone: 93-89-49-63). Expensive.

Château de la Chèvre d'Or – For a special treat — one Michelin star — drive east out of Nice on the Moyenne Corniche to the perched village of Eze (see *Special Places*), where you will find this excellent restaurant in a restored medieval manor house with a garden. (It's also a hotel.) Dine on lobster mousse or rack of lamb, while enjoying a spectacular panorama of the sea. Closed from December 2 to March 2 and Wednesdays during off-season. Reservations necessary. Major credit cards accepted. Moyenne Corniche, Eze (phone: 93-41-12-12; fax: 93-41-06-72; telex: 970839). Expensive.

Coco Beach – A large fish restaurant a few yards from the sea that is popular with residents who appreciate good food. Renowned for its bouillabaisse, lobster, and grilled fish of all kinds. *Very* crowded during summer months. Closed Mondays and Sunday evenings and mid-September to mid-May. No reservations. Visa accepted. 2 Av. Jean-Lorrain (phone: 93-89-39-26). Expensive.

Colombe d'Or – This gallery–dining room in a small hotel (with a pool) just outside the gates of the old town in St.-Paul-de-Vence is most noted for its collection of post-Impressionist art. (It was here that the late Simone Signoret met Yves Montand, and later married him in the presence of the hotel owner.) Matisse and other artists sometimes paid their bills during the 1920s and 1930s with the paintings that now decorate the walls. The restaurant specializes in grills and roasts, and there is a lovely view from its terrace in summer. Closed early November to mid-December. Reservations advised. Major credit cards accepted. About 14 miles (22 km) northwest of Nice in St.-Paul-de-Vence (phone: 93-32-80-02; fax: 93-32-77-78; telex: 970607). Expensive.

Chez Don Camillo – A tranquil, intimate place that offers an appetizing taste of Italy (in case you're not going to make it across the border), but with a Niçois accent. Closed Sundays, Mondays, the second half of August, and school holidays in November and February. Reservations necessary. Visa accepted. 5 Rue des Ponchettes (phone: 93-85-67-95). Expensive to moderate.

Rôtisserie de St.-Pancrace – Dine on prawn stew, quenelles of salmon, roast squab, or ravioli stuffed with foie gras, among other dishes. A lovely view from the garden terrace. Closed Mondays except in July and August and from early January to early February. Reservations necessary. Visa accepted. In the village of St.-Pancrace, about 5 miles (8 km) north of Nice on D914 (phone: 93-84-43-69). Expensive to moderate.

La Toque Blanche – This 10-table spot offers magnificent fish dishes and has a fixed-price lunch weekdays. Closed Sunday evenings, Mondays, and mid-July through August 1. Reservations necessary. Visa accepted. 10 Rue de la Buffa (phone: 93-88-38-18). Expensive to moderate.

Auberge de Bellet – Beautifully decorated, it is the ideal place to sample the range of local Bellet wines. Accompany them with braised chicken with mint or the fricassee of fish with herb butter. In summer dine outdoors in the shaded garden.

Closed Tuesdays and the first 2 weeks in February. Reservations unnecessary. Major credit cards accepted. A mile (1.6 km) to the west of St.-Pancrace in the village of St.-Romans-de-Bellet (phone: 93-37-83-84). Moderate.

Bông Laï – For a change of pace, this Vietnamese-Chinese restaurant is quite good, especially the lacquered duck and the fish in ginger — even the chop suey. Closed Mondays, Tuesdays, and 2 weeks in mid-December. Reservations unnecessary. Major credit cards accepted. 14 Rue Alsace-Lorraine (phone: 93-88-75-36). Moderate.

Le Champagne – The emphasis is on fish, delicately prepared with fine sauces and served in a comfortable setting. Closed Sundays. Reservations unnecessary. Visa accepted. 12 Av. Félix-Faure (phone: 93-80-62-52). Moderate.

Au Chapon Fin – This charming place in the old quarter has a limited menu of delicious regional food. Closed Sundays, Monday lunch, holidays, mid-June to July 8, and 2 weeks at *Christmas.* Reservations unnecessary. Visa accepted. 1 Rue du Moulin (phone: 93-80-56-92). Moderate.

Chez Michel – Also called *Le Grand Pavois,* this place has very good seafood dishes, especially the fish soup, stuffed mussels, and the sole meunière. Closed Mondays. Reservations unnecessary. Visa accepted. 11 Rue Meyerbeer (phone: 93-88-77-42). Moderate.

Chez les Pêcheurs – The specialties of this seafood spot in the Old Port include fish pâté and grilled deep sea bass (*loup de mer*). Closed Wednesdays, Thursday afternoons, and from mid-November through December. Reservations unnecessary. Major credit cards accepted. 18 Quai Docks (phone: 93-89-59-61). Moderate.

Au Ciel d'Azur – Elegant dining where you'd least expect it — on the second floor of the airport. Very good fish, especially the sole, and luscious desserts. (There's a nonsmoking section.) And if you find yourself at the airport with time to kill but little appetite, the restaurant's adjoining bar is a comfortable refuge from the crowded self-service restaurant-bar on the third floor. Open daily. Reservations unnecessary. Major credit cards accepted. Aéroport de Nice (phone: 93-21-36-36). Moderate.

Au Passage – A Vietnamese eatery with French cooking, too. Excellent sauces; simple atmosphere. Closed Sundays and the last 2 weeks of August. No reservations. Visa accepted. 11 *bis* Bd. Raimbaldi (phone: 93-80-23-15). Moderate.

A la Ribote – The crazy-quilt menu lists oysters, fish, paella, and couscous, along with a daily special. Closed Saturdays. No reservations. Visa accepted. 5 Av. de Bellet, Pl. de Caserne des Pompiers Magnan (phone: 93-86-56-26). Moderate.

Ruhl Plage – The best of the beach restaurants along the Promenade des Anglais serves good grilled fish, salads, and carafe wines. A pool for children and all kinds of water sports facilities make it a popular summer lunch spot with the Niçois. Open from March through November, or as long as the weather stays warm. No reservations. Major credit cards accepted. Opposite the *Casino Ruhl,* which is at 1 Promenade des Anglais (phone: 93-87-09-70). Moderate.

L'Univers "César" – A great place for pasta, which is served in all shapes and styles. *Loup de mer* (catfish) with *cèpes* (mushrooms) and artichokes is another specialty of the house. The Niçois seem to come for the festive atmosphere as much as for the food, and at times it can be a bit of a circus. You might even bump into ski champion Jean-Claude Killy or some other French celebrity. Open daily until 2 AM. Reservations necessary. Visa accepted. 54 Bd. Jean-Jaurès (phone: 93-62-32-22). Moderate.

La Coquille – A popular, unpretentious seafood restaurant that displays its wares on the street and also prepares food to take out. Good for oysters. Closed Mondays. No reservations. Major credit cards accepted. 36 Cours Saleya (phone: 93-85-58-82). Moderate to inexpensive.

Rendez-Vous des Sportifs – A cheery family-run place specializing in Niçois cooking. Here you can sample the whole range of regional specialties, including *pissaladière,* stockfish, and *aubergine* (eggplant) fried in olive oil. Closed Sundays. No reservations. No credit cards accepted. 120 Bd. de la Madeleine (phone: 93-86-21-39). Moderate to inexpensive.

Bièrerie Chez Nino – You may find yourself the only out-of-towner in this small old bistro tucked away in a tiny street near the train station. The place features a hundred different beers (both bottled and draft) from 22 countries, and its friendly owner will help you choose the right one to accompany your meal. Good grills and stockfish. The pictures on display are painted by local artists and there's a guitarist singing songs by Jacques Brel and other *chansonniers.* The clientele is a democratic mix of business suits and leather jackets. Closed Sundays and August. No reservations. Visa and Carte Bleue accepted. 50 Rue Trachel (phone: 93-88-07-71). Inexpensive.

La Méranda – Simple and plain but highly recommended by the Niçois, this tiny, crowded place near the flower market is run by a husband and wife team. Service is a bit slow, as each dish is prepared to order. Tripes *niçoises* and pâtés *au pistou* are splendid choices. Closed February, August, Saturday evenings, Sundays, and Mondays. No reservations. Visa accepted. 4 Rue de la Terrasse (no phone). Inexpensive.

La Nissarda – In an attractive setting just a 10-minute walk from Place Masséna, serving many local specialties. Closed Wednesdays and for 2 weeks in July. No reservations. No credit cards. 17 Rue Gubernatis (phone: 93-85-26-29). Inexpensive.

La Pizza – The best pizza this side of Ventimiglia (and possibly Milan), and good pasta, too. Young folks congregate en masse here until 1 AM. Open daily from 11:30 AM. No reservations. Visa accepted. In the heart of the pedestrian zone, at 34 Rue Masséna (phone: 93-87-70-29). Inexpensive.

Rive Gauche – A small, friendly bistro with an Art Deco interior. Good food, like calves' liver and duck, and an excellent value. Closed Sundays, and August. No reservations. No credit cards. 27 Rue Ribotti (phone: 93-62-16-72). Inexpensive.

Taverne du Château – Good Niçois cooking in a lively family place in Old Nice. Open daily. No reservations. No credit cards accepted. 42 Rue Droite (phone: 93-62-37-73). Inexpensive.

 BARS AND CAFÉS: The *Scotch Tea House* (4 Av. de Suède; phone: 93-16-03-55) is very British and proper. *Café de France* (12 Bd. Gambetta; phone: 93-88-50-81) is a landmark where old and young Niçois alike, as well as out-of-towners, drink coffee or beer or dine from a light menu. An older crowd frequents *Le Mississippi* (5 Promenade des Anglais; phone: 93-82-06-61). At water's edge is *Le Queenie* (19 Promenade des Anglais; phone: 93-88-52-50), a café with a bamboo and glass decor. *Bar L'Hermitage* — also called *Bar des Oiseaux* (5 Rue St. Vincent; phone: 93-80-27-33) — is a colorful place where, legend has it, the owner carries a bird on her shoulder; ask for a *piconbière,* the house specialty. *Le Valentino* (3 Promenade des Anglais; phone: 93-87-09-27) features live music in decor centered on black lacquered wood. There's also live music at *Le Pam-Pam Masséna* (1 Rue Desboutin; phone: 93-80-21-60). *L'Isle Au Zebre* is a *cave* restaurant with French Caribbean music, a dance floor, and a billiard table (19 Rue Droite; phone: 93-80-56-27). Late-night places include *Bar-Tabac des Fleurs* (13 Cours Saleya), a bar near the *Marché aux Fleurs* that *opens* at 4 AM; and *Le Frog,* where you can drink, eat Tex-Mex food, and listen to live music after the restaurant closes (closed Sundays; Rue Milton Robbins; phone: 93-85-85-65). *Le Cheap* features spareribs, some French food, and good cocktails, and a great lineup of sounds from rock to jazz and soul (closed Sundays; 4 Rue de la Barillerie; phone: 93-80-46-76).

OSLO

The capital of Norway sits at the head of a 60-mile fjord on the country's southeastern coast, framed by a vast expanse of lakeland, woods, and moors, where fir-treed hills rise 2,000 feet. The oldest of the Scandinavian capitals, Oslo is enormous: 175 square miles, only a tenth of which is urban and town districts. The rest is a marvelous outdoor playground for Oslo's approximately 450,500 residents and its visitors from around the world.

Oslo today is a jumble of architectural styles, but each year more modern concrete and glass buildings replace old wooden structures. Multistory buildings and glass-roof atriums housing shops and offices are increasingly common. The Norwegian capital now boasts the tallest hotel in Scandinavia, the 37-floor *Oslo Plaza*. The city also has opened a mile-long tunnel that allows drivers access to the downtown harbor district, alleviating much of the once-heavy traffic.

Along with its attempts at modernization in this century, the city of Oslo has made a conscious effort to integrate art into the daily lives of its citizens. Frescoes and woodcarvings decorate public and private buildings, and sculpture is an integral part of public squares and parks. In spring and summer, all this colorful art, the small malls and shopping streets, and outdoor cafés give the center of the city the feeling of a medieval festival.

People are believed to have lived at the head of the Oslo Fjord 7,000 years ago. But the history of Oslo as we know it dates from 1048, when the Viking King Harald, called "Harald Hard Rule," built a commercial town in what is now east Oslo.

During the reign of Harald's successor, Olav Kyrre (1066–93), Oslo became an ecclesiastical center, its principal cathedral named after the city's patron saint, St. Hallvard. The foundation stones are all that remain today of this once mighty cathedral that served as the burial place of so many Viking kings.

Medieval Oslo reached its zenith during the reign of King Haakon V Magnusson (1299–1319), who built the majestic Akershus Castle and Fortress and decreed Oslo the capital of Norway. After Haakon's death the city went into decline. Many of its people were killed by the Black Death in 1349, and when Norway united with Denmark, Oslo lost its importance as a capital. Several times the city was devastated by fire, and in 1624 all of its wooden buildings succumbed to flames.

King Christian IV, who ruled Norway and Denmark at the time, ordered a new capital built somewhat farther west, behind the walls of Akershus. He named it Christiania, a name that was used until 1925, when the ancient name of Oslo was restored. The streets laid out by Christian IV are still the main streets of central Oslo. And a few of the stone and half-timbered buildings from this era can be seen today.

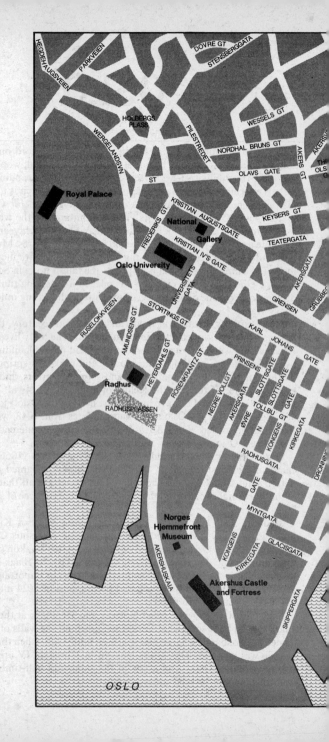

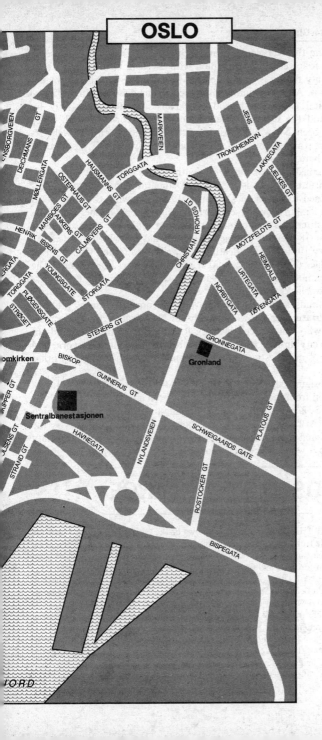
OSLO

In 1814, during the Napoleonic wars, Norway and Denmark were separated and there followed a 90-year union with Sweden. Oslo's main street, the hub of the city today, is named for the first of the Swedish-Norwegian kings, Karl Johan. After the union with Sweden was dissolved in 1905, the Norwegian capital entered a period of expansion, interrupted only by World War I and the German Occupation during World War II. Since 1917, Oslo has been Norway's most important maritime city as well. Its harbor has more than 8 miles of quays, and the world's largest tourist ships can dock here.

Norway is a constitutional monarchy with a parliamentary government whose current prime minister is the Social Democrat Gro Harlem Brundtland, who returned to power in December 1990, following the short-lived Conservative leadership of Jan Syse, who had taken over in October 1989. Ms. Brundtland's first term as prime minister began in 1981. The prime minister presides over an 18-member cabinet. King Harald V, who inherited the throne in January 1991 after the death of his well-loved father, Olav V, lives in the Royal Palace (with Queen Sonja) at one end of Karl Johans Gate. The Parliament meets in the century-old National Assembly building (Stortingsbygningen) a few blocks away.

When their minds aren't on business or government, chances are citizens are concentrating on snow. Virtually all Norwegians are avid cross-country skiers, who can be seen heading for any one of the thousands of trails within the city limits. Oslo residents often ski at night after work, and many of the city's most festive events are connected with skiing and other winter sports.

Ski jumping originated near Oslo in 1879. The Holmenkollen Ski Jump, which can be seen from most parts of Oslo, has been a landmark since it was built for the *1952 Winter Olympics*. The jumping tower itself is 184 feet high and its summit is 1,350 feet above the fjord overlooking Oslo. It is the combination of such manmade sights with an extraordinary natural beauty that makes Oslo a very special place to visit.

OSLO AT-A-GLANCE

SEEING THE CITY: Spectacular views of the city and the Oslo Fjord are available from several vantage points in the hilly, wooded area, Oslomarka, on the east, north, and west of the city. Perhaps the best panorama is from Tryvannstårnet, a 390-foot observation tower atop the 1,600-foot-high Tryvann Hill on the outskirts of Oslo. It is reached by taking the *Holmenkollen* suburban rail line to Voksenkollen. The *Summit 21 Lounge & Bar* on the top of the *Scandinavia* hotel offers a fine view of the city from downtown; it serves a buffet lunch in the afternoon and is a bar from 3 PM to 12:30 AM (30 Holbergs Gate; phone: 113000). Even more stunning is the *Plaza Sky Bar* on the 35th floor of the 37-story *Oslo Plaza* hotel (3 Sonja Henies Plass; phone: 171000); it's open daily, except Sundays, from 5 PM to 3:30 AM. After 9 PM, there's a cover charge (jackets required for men). To reach the top, take the exterior glass elevator.

SPECIAL PLACES: In Oslo the special places are not the museum and tourist sites but the different parts of the city that reflect its past. The once-controversial Vigeland Sculpture Park is a must for any visitor. History and architecture buffs will enjoy walking along Oslo harbor's bustling Rådhus Gate, whose buildings were among Oslo's finest private and public residences during the 17th and 18th centuries. Pause on the summit of nearby Akershus Fortress, dating from medieval times. For a feeling of Victorian Oslo, meander along the streets, such as Inkognitogata and Oscars Gate, directly behind the Royal Palace. The area known as Homansbyen is a protected historical enclave. In the latter half of the last century, the district's well-heeled residents tried to outdo each other by building houses grander and more unusual than those of their neighbors. The result is a pleasant mix of architectural styles. Today, some of the homes remain private residences, but many are embassies, consulates, or offices.

Travel out to Bygdøy peninsula for a glimpse of the good and easy life of many of modern Oslo's inhabitants with their expensive homes and swimming beaches side-by-side with Viking and polar ship museums. The peninsula, which juts into the fjord southwest of the harbor, can be reached by bus No. 30 or, in summer, by one of the ferries that leave from near City Hall. And by all means, take the tram up to Holmenkollen to experience the Oslo of the outdoor enthusiast — miles and miles of untouched forest and the widest network of ski trails in the world, over 1,300 miles worth. The Holmenkollen area also is the latest fashionable address, each new home bigger and more luxurious than its predecessor.

DOWNTOWN

Vaterland – Practically a city within a city, this major downtown development features the 37-story *Oslo Plaza* hotel and the luxurious *Royal Christiania* hotel; *Spektrum,* a 9,000-seat area for concerts and sporting events; and two major shopping complexes, *Oslo City* and *Galleri Oslo.* The ground floor of *Galleri Oslo* houses the "Oslo M" bus station, and the gallery is one stop on the shuttle from Fornebu Airport. The 5-story *Oslo City* complex has an underground area with ethnic food cafés. Shops in both complexes are closed Sundays; restaurants are open daily. 1 Stenersgt.

Oslo Harbor – Stroll along this busy, modern waterfront and you will see graceful white cruise ships that ply the fjords, small ferries, and private boats. Don't miss the chance to snack on tasty, tiny shrimp sold by fishermen who catch them at sea and cook them aboard their boats as they head back to the pier in front of city hall. For a bird's-eye view of the harbor, climb up to the ramparts of Akershus Fortress.

Rådhuset (City Hall) – A spacious square with fountains and sculpture separates this outstanding landmark from the harbor. Oslo's City Hall, although boxy, is lavishly embellished with contemporary Norwegian sculpture, woodcarvings, paintings, and tapestries. Guided tours available. Open daily. No admission charge. Rådhusplassen (phone: 861600).

Aker Brygge – Oslo's first "Fisherman's Wharf" opened 6 years ago, and has been a favorite waterfront gathering point for residents and visitors ever since. It features lots of little shops, boutiques, a theater, fast-food stands, ice cream parlors, bakeries, delicatessens, wine bars, and restaurants offering fare from Mexico, China, and other lands. There also is a multi-cinema complex with adjacent cafés, a major department store, and pricey penthouse apartments. Underneath it all is a huge parking garage. Open year-round, with jazz concerts featured outside in summer.

Domkirken (Oslo Cathedral) – Although both its exterior and interior have been restored since the cathedral was first built in the late 17th century, the altarpiece and pulpit are original, dating from 1699. Be sure to note the peculiar perspective of The Last Supper relief on the altar and the lamb on the table's platter. Also of interest are the bronze doors by Dagfinn Werenskiold, the stained glass windows by Emanuel Vigeland, and the modernist ceiling decorations by Hugo Lous Mohr, who used less conventional colors together, such as yellow, aqua, pink, orange, and chartreuse. Closed Saturdays from September to May. Regular services are held on Sundays at 11 AM and 7:30 PM (Stortorvet; phone: 413574). The old stables that were built around the cathedral have been converted to small shops. You can browse for antiques or watch silversmiths, weavers, potters, and other artists and craftsmen at work.

Minneparken (Ruin Park) – The foundation stones of St. Hallvard Cathedral can be seen in this park with a number of archaeological excavations from medieval Oslo. At the park's edge is Ladegård, a private residence built in 1725 on the ruins of the bishop's palace dating from 1200. Guided tours are offered May through September. Oslo Gate at Bispegata. It's best reached by taxi or by tram No. 9 (phone: 194468 or 557248).

Oslo's Markets – Three large, colorful outdoor markets are favorite spots for picture taking. Garden and greenhouse plants are sold in Stortorvet Square, near the cathedral; vegetables, fruits, and flowers are on sale in Grønland Torg and Youngstorget. All open daily, except Sundays.

Akershus Festning og Slott (Akershus Castle and Fortress) – Built originally by King Haakon V about 1300, this is one of the most important relics of medieval Norway. Rebuilt in Renaissance style under King Christian IV in the 17th century, it has been restored and now is used by the government for state occasions and festivities; there are Sunday afternoon concerts in the chapel. Buildings are open daily, May 2 to September 15; admission charge. The grounds are open year-round; no admission charge. Entrance from Rådhus Gate, a short stroll from City Hall (phone: 412521).

Norges Hjemmefront Museum (Norwegian Resistance Museum) – This stirring museum, on the grounds of Akershus Fortress, contains materials and memorabilia from the German occupation of Norway (1940-45) during World War II. Open daily. Admission charge. Akershus (phone: 403138).

Gamle Aker Kirke (Gamle Aker Church) – Built in 1100, this is by far the oldest building in Oslo and the oldest stone church in Scandinavia still in use as a parish church. Open Monday through Saturday afternoons or by appointment. Guided tours (usually in English) year-round. Evensong at 6 PM, and Sunday services at 11 AM. No admission charge. 26 Akersveien (phone: 693582).

Slottet (Royal Palace) – The residence of King Harald V and Queen Sonja is not open to the public, but you can visit the grounds. Get there in time for the changing of the guard each day at 1:30 PM. A brass band plays weekdays when the king is in residence, marked by the flying of his standard from the palace roof. At the west end of Karl Johans Gate.

Vigelandsanlegget (Vigeland Sculpture Park) – A world of people and animals sculpted in granite, iron, and bronze by Gustav Vigeland inhabit a lovely 80-acre park in the western section of Oslo. In 1921, the city of Oslo offered the brilliant, egocentric Norwegian sculptor a free hand in carving his masterwork in Frogner Park, a depiction of the whole cycle of human life. He was given a studio, workmen, assistants, and all the funds he needed — the cost ran into the millions by the time the job was finished in 1943. Vigeland takes on birth, growth, joy, suffering, and death in the 650-piece collection of huge, writhing, nude figures in metal and stone. Once considered controversial, the only thing controversial in the park today is its topless sunbathers. On the grounds there's also a statue of Abraham Lincoln, presented to Norway by the people of the heavily Scandinavian populated state of North Dakota on July 4, 1914. The park has a swimming pool, tennis courts, and a sports arena, and is a favorite spot for Oslo's residents summer and winter. In summer, there are two restaurants in addition to the year-round cafeteria. Open day and night all year. No admission charge. Frogner.

Vigeland Museet (Vigeland Museum) – Just across the road from the southern end of Vigeland Park is Vigeland's former residence and studio, which contains 1,650 sculptures, 420 woodcuts, hundreds of plates for woodcuts, and some 11,000 sketches by the eminent Norwegian artist. During the summer, concerts are held in the museum's courtyard. Closed Mondays. No admission charge. 32 Nobels Gate (phone: 442306).

Munch Museet (Munch Museum) – Edvard Munch, the Norwegian expressionist painter and graphic artist who died in 1944, bequeathed all his art to the city of Oslo. This light, airy, spacious museum was built in the eastern section of the city to house the almost 1,100 oil paintings, 4,500 drawings, 15,000 prints, and notes, letters, sketches, and other materials in the collection. Closed Mondays. Admission charge only from May 15 to September 5. 53 Tøyen Gate (phone: 673774).

Nasjonalgalleriet (National Gallery) – Norway's principal art collection. The emphasis is on Norwegian artists, but there is a representative sample of international artists, particularly the French Impressionists. Open daily. No admission charge. 13 Universitets Gate (phone: 200404).

Museet for Samtidskunst (Museum of Modern Art) – Inaugurated in 1989, this branch of the *National Gallery* is devoted to modern paintings, sculpture, and photography. The exciting and sometimes startlingly innovative collection is updated annually in order always to include works from the last 40 years; older acquisitions will revert to the *National Gallery.* Housed in a magnificent building, formerly a bank at 4 Bankplassen, downtown. Closed Sundays. No admission charge (phone: 335820).

Universitas Osloensis (Oslo University) – The main attraction for tourists at the university's downtown campus is the old festival hall, called the Aula, with its Munch paintings. This is where the award ceremony for the Nobel Peace Prize usually takes place (it's the only Nobel Prize awarded here; the others are presented in Stockholm). Open weekday afternoons in July. During the winter, admittance is upon request. No admission charge. 47 Karl Johans Gate (phone: 429091, ext. 756).

De Naturhistoriske Museer (Natural History Museums) – Visitors with children will especially enjoy this group of excellent museums, with displays and reproductions of Norwegian flora and fauna. Exhibitions are informative and interesting. Open every afternoon except Mondays. No admission charge. A short stroll from the *Munch Museum* through Oslo's Botanical Gardens, 1 Sars Gate, Tøyen (phone: 686960).

THE PENINSULA

Vikingskiphuset (Viking Ship House) – Three longships, the *Gokstad,* the *Tune,* and the *Oseberg,* from AD 800–900, will take you back to the days when Vikings roamed the seas. The upswept prow of the *Oseberg,* with a stunning pattern of carved animals, is an excellent example of the workmanship and beauty that characterized these vessels. The museum also has collections of utensils, gold and silver jewelry, and accoutrements from the Viking period. Open daily. Admission charge. 35 Huk Aveny (phone: 438379).

Norsk Folkemuseum (Norwegian Folk Museum) – Some 150 wooden buildings from all over Norway have been placed in a picturesque park near the *Viking Ship House* to provide a representative picture of Norway's past. One of the museum's treasures is a unique hand-hewn, wooden stave church from 1200. You also can see the last apartment of Norwegian playwright Henrik Ibsen, a collection of antique toys, and an exhibit about reindeer-herding. The gift shop sells guidebooks that provide descriptions, history, and maps of the area. Buildings open daily from March to November; park open year-round. Admission charge. 10 Museumsveien (phone: 437020).

Kon-Tiki Museet (Kon-Tiki Museum) – The balsa raft *Kon-Tiki,* used by Thor Heyerdahl and his crew on their 1947 voyage across the Pacific Ocean from Peru to Polynesia, is preserved here along with Easter Island statues and an underwater shark exhibit. Also on display is the papyrus boat *Ra II,* on which Heyerdahl traveled across the Atlantic Ocean from Morocco to Barbados in 1970. Open daily. Admission charge. Bygdøy; take the No. 30 bus from downtown or the ferry from City Hall (phone: 438050).

Norsk Sjøfartsmuseum (Norwegian Maritime Museum) – Norway's long maritime traditions are recalled by the collections inside this museum, a short walk from the *Kon-Tiki.* Outside the building, you can see Roald Amundsen's Polar ship, *Gjøa,* the first vessel to navigate a northwest passage in 1903–6. Guided tours (in English) are available. Open daily. Admission charge. Bygdøy (phone: 438240).

Polarskipet Fram (Fram Museum) – The third ship museum in the area houses the *Fram,* built for Fridtjof Nansen's Polar Expedition of 1893–96 and also used by Amundsen on his expedition to the South Pole in 1910–12. Open weekends only in November, closed December to April 15; otherwise open daily. Admission charge. Bygdøy (phone: 438370).

SUBURBS

Skimuseet (Ski Museum) – The world's oldest ski museum is inside the takeoff structure on the giant Holmenkollen ski-jumping hill. The collection outlines the history of skiing from the well-preserved tip of a ski found in a bog and believed to be some 2,500 years old to skis used in early Polar expeditions as well as modern equipment. Admission charge. A 20-minute ride by the *Holmenkollen Railway* from central Oslo and a 10-minute walk from the Holmenkollen Station. Holmenkollen (phone: 141690).

Frognerseteren – A 20- to 30-minute walk up the hill from the *Ski Museum* will take you 1,460 feet above sea level to a panoramic view of Oslo and the fjord. You also can stop in at the cozy lodge-restaurant here (see *Eating Out*). If you have the stamina, another 20 minutes of uphill walking (or go there directly by getting off at the Voksenkollen station on the *Holmenkollen Railway*) will lead you to the 390-foot Tryvannstårnet, the highest lookout tower in Scandinavia. Admission charge (phone: 146711).

Emanuel Vigeland Museet (Emanuel Vigeland Museum) – This small, two-room, church-like museum was built and decorated by Emanuel Vigeland, Gustav's younger brother. The main chamber's principal fresco, entitled *Vita,* has earned it the distinction of being Oslo's most controversial museum. Open Sunday afternoons only, year-round. No admission charge. A 7-minute walk from the Slemdal stop on the *Holmenkollen Railway* at 8 Grimelundsveien (phone: 149342).

Internasjonalte Barnekunst Museet (Children's Art Museum) – A very moving collection containing 70,000 children's drawings, paintings, ceramics, and sculpture from all over the world, in a former private home with a lovely garden. Open workshop and musical activities for children, but also wonderful for adults to visit. Closed Mondays and Fridays, during the school year, and Saturdays. 4 Lille Frøens vei (Frøen stop on the *Holmenkollen Railway;* phone: 468573).

Sonja Henie–Niels Onstad Art Center (Sonja Henie–Niels Onstads Kunstsenter) – The art center, 7 miles (11 km) west of Oslo near Fornebu Airport, was opened in 1968. It houses the permanent collection of 20th-century art donated by the international skating star and her husband. Included are works by Picasso, Miró, Villon, and Munch. Exhibitions and other events illustrating current trends and ideas in film, music, architecture, literature, and the applied arts are scheduled regularly. One room features Sonja Henie's trophies and prizes; otherwise the museum is dedicated to art. Open daily; during the summer old Sonja Henie movies are shown on Sunday evenings. Admission charge. Reached by bus from central Oslo. 1311 Høvikodden Høvik (phone: 543050).

Ekeberg Park – There's a fine view of Oslo and the fjord from the 685-foot hill in this lovely park just southeast of the city. It was on this hill that the oldest works of art in Oslo, Stone Age carvings some 3,000 years old, were found in 1915. These rock carvings can be seen between the Merchant Navy Academy here and Kongsveien. The park is easily reached by the Ljabru tram. With advance notice, the Oslo Tourist Board (see *Sources and Resources*) will arrange a torchlit sleigh ride through the Ekeberg woods.

Tusenfryd – The name of Oslo's amusement park means "A Thousand Delights." It has a roller coaster, clowns, music, miniature golf, movie theaters, restaurants, and other things to delight children of all ages. Open daily from 10 AM to 7:30 PM from June to mid-August. Call for hours during May and September. Admission charge. Dyreparken in east Oslo (phone: 09-946363).

■**EXTRA SPECIAL:** In the ancient fortress town of Fredrikstad, 60 miles (96 km) south of Oslo, you can watch craftsmen and designers at work in their quaint workshops, weaving and printing textiles, blowing glass, making silver jewelry, pottery, and furniture. *Plus Organization* operates a permanent exhibition and salesroom for the arts and crafts produced there.

Just over an hour north of Oslo, in the small Norwegian town of Jevnaker, lies Norway's most famous crystal factory, *Hadeland Glassverks.* Call ahead for tours (phone: 63-11000). A permanent glass museum and a "firsts" and "seconds" shop make a visit especially rewarding. The drive alone is worth the trip on a clear day, as it offers a peek into many cross sections of rural Norway — a crystal blue lake nestled in a picture-perfect valley, apple orchards, and farmlands. If you plan to take the bus, call 170166 for departure times.

The tourist board can arrange individually tailored full- and half-day Land Rover safaris in the Oslo forests (about $68 for 4 hours, $136 for 8 hours; meals and equipment included; discount available with the Oslo Card). Rambling, canoeing, and fishing are the diversions in the summer and skiing and snowshoe tours are the winter features. Be sure to dress warmly in the winter. Contact the tourist office at least 1 day ahead.

SOURCES AND RESOURCES

TOURIST INFORMATION: The Oslo Tourist Board and the Norges Information Sentret (Norwegian Information Center) operate a joint information office at Vestbanen (phone: 334386), formerly the West Railway Station, the large yellow building between Aker Bryugge and Rådhuset (City Hall). The office provides free information and maps and arranges tours and guide service. Open daily except during the winter, when it is closed Sundays.

The monthly guide *What's On In Oslo* lists special attractions such as concerts and sporting events. There's also the more comprehensive, but less timely, *Oslo Guide,* published annually. Both are available at most hotels, travel agencies, and at the tourist office.

The US Embassy is at 18 Drammensveien (phone: 448550).

Local Coverage – Oslo doesn't have an English-language newspaper, but American and British periodicals as well as the *International Herald Tribune* are widely available. Look for them at Narvesen kiosks. *Aftenposten,* one of Norway's most important newspapers, carries a summary of the day's news in English during the summer. Radio listeners can tune in to 93 FM on Sunday mornings for "Norway Today," an English broadcast with international news and features. Many large hotels have equipped all rooms with 24-hour English-text television, which provides international news and local information. Some have also introduced Cable News Network (CNN).

Food – Both *What's On In Oslo* and *Oslo Guide '92* have dining information.

TELEPHONE: The country code for Norway is 47; the city code for Oslo is 2.

GETTING AROUND: Airport – Fornebu Airport, which handles domestic and international flights, is a 20-minute trip from downtown. Taxi fare runs from 75 to 95 Norwegian kroner (about $11-$14). At a third of the taxi price, bus service operates between the airport and the Oslo M bus station at the ground floor of the *Galleri Oslo,* the central railway station, the Parliament, *Scandinavia* hotel, and the *National Theater* on Stortings Gate (phone: 424991).

Gardermoen Airport, 33 miles (51 km) north of the city, handles charter flights as well as all nonstop transatlantic flights. The trip downtown takes almost an hour, and taxi fare can run up to $100. Bus service between the airport and downtown Oslo is available for 60 Norwegian kroner ($9).

Bus, Tram, and Train – The main bus terminal is Oslo M at the *Galleri Oslo* shopping complex. Most of the buses running through the city center stop at Wessels Plass and by the University Square or at the *National Theater.* For information about timetables and fares, call Trafikanten, the transportation information center at the main entrance to the Oslo S at Jernbanetorget (phone: 177030).

Oslo now has only one railway station, Sentralbanestasjonen, or Oslo S, in the Jernbanetorget railway square at the end of Karl Johans Gate. It has a bank, post office, a tourism and accommodations center, a restaurant, cafés, and shops. The *National Theater* station and the main Stortinget subway station handle local trains to Skien, Moss, Eidsvoll, and other destinations. For all train information, call 171400.

Car Rental – All major American and European firms are represented.

Ferry and Local Boats – Boats and ferries leave from various piers along the harbor. For information on timetables, call the tourist office at 334386.

Taxi – You can call a taxi by dialing 388090, or find one at any taxi stand. Taxi stands are listed in part 1A of the telephone directory under the heading *Drosjer.* You also can hail a taxi on the street, but drivers are not allowed to pick up passengers near a taxi stand. To order a taxi for a later time, you must call at least an hour before you need it (phone: 388080).

Underground (T-Banen) and Suburban Tram lines – The *National Theater* and the Stortinget stations are the central stops for most electrified trams and the suburban railway to the forested park areas on the outskirts of Oslo. If you're planning to be in the city for 1 month, check with Trafikanten at Jernbanetorget (phone: 177030) about its Universal Card, to be used for travel on various buses, trams, the underground, and even some ferries. You'll need a pastport-size photograph for the card, which costs about $70 (phone: 177030).

Note: Short-term travel discounts also are available. A 24-hour Tourist Ticket costs about $8 and offers unlimited travel within a 24-hour period on local buses, trams, subways, suburban railways, and even local ferries. It is sold at all Narvesen kiosks (those marked with a large blue and white "N"), Innkvartering (the accommodations center) at Oslo S, the Oslo Tourist Board, main subway stations, post offices, and ticket offices. The first time the card is used it is stamped with the date and time. Another option is a *flerreisekort,* a card offering a 15% discount per prepaid trip. Cards may be purchased for 4 or 14 trips at Narvesen kiosks or from any conductor. Oslo also offers an extensive Oslo Card, which includes unlimited free travel on the city's trains, buses, underground, and boats; special prices at car rental firms; half price on trains to and from the capital; and admission to museums. It is valid for 1, 2, or 3 days. Single tickets may be purchased for about $2.50 per trip. Complete information is available at the tourist office or Trafikanten, located at Jernbanetorget.

Warning: Public transportation in Oslo operates on an honor system, with occasional spot checks. Travel without a valid ticket results in an on-the-spot fine of about $13. If you are using a discount card, be sure to validate it in the special machines on the waiting platforms and in the trams themselves.

 LOCAL SERVICES: Dentist (English-Speaking) – *Oslo Kommunale Tannlegevakt,* near *Tøyen Center,* offers emergency dental care from 8 to 11 PM, and also from 11 AM to 2 PM on weekends and holidays. 18 Kolstadgate (phone: 674846).

Dry Cleaner – Most Oslo dry cleaners take 7 to 10 days and are generally very expensive ($10 for a pair of pants). *Oslo American Rens* offers 24-hour service. 1 Griniveien (phone: 505741).

Limousine Service – *Bislet Limousine,* 70 Pilestredet (phone: 600000; fax: 800119).

Medical Emergency – *Legevakt,* open 24 hours (40 Storgata; phone: 117070). For ambulance service, dial 003.

Messenger Service – *Securitas Express A/S,* 51 Ostensjøveien (phone: 679010 or 680035).

National/International Courier – *DHL International A/S* (5 Fornebuveien; phone: 581700). Some Oslo hotels also offer courier service.

Office Equipment Rental – *Office for a Day-Oslo Business Center,* at Aker Brygge, offers equipment, office space, secretarial staff, and translators/interpreters on a short-term basis. 1 Stranden (phone: 830712).

Pharmacy – *Jernbanetorget Apotek,* open 24 hours; ring the doorbell at night. 4B Jernbanetorget (phone: 412482).

Photocopies – *Rank Xerox,* 3 Haslevollen (phone: 650427).

Post Office – The main post office is open from 8 AM to 8 PM weekdays and 9 AM to 3 PM Saturdays (15 Dronningensgt.; phone: 407823); there also is a branch at the Oslo S metro stop (phone: 407399).

Secretary/Stenographer (English-Speaking) – *Manpower A/S,* 10 Dronning Mauds Gate (phone: 835100).

Translator – *Forenede Translatorer* (15 Kongens Gate; phone: 425640); *Norsk Personal A/S* (4 Fr. Nansenspl.; phone: 330140).

Other – Business services/Convention information and facilities: *Manpower A/S* (15 Dronning Mauds Gate; phone: 835100); *Chamber of Commerce* (30 Drammensvn; phone: 557400); *Oslo Convention Bureau* (phone: 334386; fax: 334389). Formal wear rental: *Diva Utleiesalong* (3 Professor Dahls Gate; phone: 600002).

 SPECIAL EVENTS: In January, the *Monolith Meet,* a major cross-country ski race, takes place in the Vigeland Sculpture Park. The sporting calendar for January and February features a number of international speed-skating events, which often include the *European* or *World Championships.* The annual *Holmenkollen Ski Festival,* which attracts the cream of the world's cross-country skiers and ski jumpers, takes place in early March. *Holmenkollen Day* is the last Sunday of the festival, when up to 100,000 spectators make their way to the Holmenkollen Ski Jump to watch a special jumping competition. *Easter* is a special time of year for Norwegians, and most towns and cities are deserted over the long holiday weekend as the entire population takes off for its last fling on the slopes —

something a traveler should keep in mind. A few major hotels and restaurants may remain open, but the majority are closed. *Constitution Day,* May 17, is Norway's biggest holiday. One of the few days each year when national dress is worn, it is a photographer's delight. The children's parade up Karl Johans Gate to the Royal Palace is the highlight of the day, indeed, of any visit to Norway. Hotel reservations must be made very far in advance. Tourists in June will be treated to one of Norway's favorite events: *Sankthansaften,* or *Midsummer Night's Eve,* on June 23. Bonfires are lit everywhere on this festive evening, and a trip along the coastline, or out on the Oslo Fjord, is a special treat. Summer visitors have the opportunity to attend the famous *Bislet Games,* world class track and field events at *Bislet Stadium* that attract top international athletes. July is the main summer vacation month in Norway, and Oslo is pitiably void of Norwegians during these weeks. *Note:* On July 4, celebrations of American *Independence Day* are held, usually in Vigeland Park. Check with the Oslo Tourist Board for details.

MUSEUMS: In addition to those listed in *Special Places,* other notable Oslo museums are the following:

Historisk Museet (Historical Museum) – The university's collection of antiquities. Closed Mondays. No admission charge. 2 Frederiks Gate (phone: 416300).

Kunstindustrimuseet (Museum of Applied Art) – Applied art from the Middle Ages to the present. Closed Mondays. Admission charge. 1 St. Olavs Gate (phone: 203578).

Norsk Teknisk Museet (Norwegian Science and Industry Museum) – Science and technology, including many working models. No admission charge. 143 Kjelsåsveien, Etterstad (phone: 222550).

Norsk Tollmuseet (Norwegian Customs Museum) – The Customs House, depicted in exhibitions and models. Open Tuesday and Thursday afternoons from mid-May to mid-September; call for winter hours. Admission charge. 1A Tollbugt. (phone: 860300).

Postmuseet (Postal Museum) – Three centuries of communications. Open weekdays. No admission charge. 17 Tollbugt. (phone: 408059).

SHOPPING: Like other Scandinavian cities, Oslo is not a haven for bargain hunters. Prices are high, but you can get good value for your dollar if you concentrate on typically Norwegian items: arts and crafts, pewter, enameled silver, ski sweaters, and, if you are buying furs, Norwegian blue fox and black saga mink. Department stores like *Steen & Strøm* carry many of the same items as specialty shops do, but at lower prices. Several exhibition and sales centers have a wide range of Norwegian products on display, so you can get a good idea of what is available. Shops generally are open 9 AM to 5 PM on weekdays (department stores from 10 AM to 6 PM), but close at 1 or 2 PM on Saturdays and remain open until 6 or 7 PM on Thursdays. The city has relaxed its laws on opening hours, so you may find some shops open even later. The shopping complexes *Oslo City* and *Galleri Oslo* have extended hours; they are open weekdays from 9 AM to 8 PM and on Saturdays from 10 AM to 5 PM; their restaurants are open daily until 11:30 PM, Sundays until 10 PM.

These two shopping centers in the heart of the Vaterland development, together with the stores in Aker Brygge alongside the harbor, have become popular with Oslo residents — especially as places to look rather than buy. The three main traditional shopping areas are, perhaps, of more interest to visitors. The first is downtown Oslo, along Karl Johans Gate from Jernbanetorget to the Royal Palace and adjacent streets. If you're in this area, take a coffee break at the fashionable old *Theatercaféen* in the *Continental* hotel (phone: 419096) or the *Grand* hotel's *Grand Café* (try to get a table near the window; phone: 429390). There's much less expensive coffee to be had almost anywhere else, but the atmosphere at these spots is worth the price.

Another popular shopping district is Victoria Terrasse, called Vika by residents. Built just before the turn of the century, this plaza was named after England's Queen Victoria. Its government buildings, exclusive shops, and colorful boutiques make it a popular strolling area. This small shopping district is rather elite and attractive and just a few minutes' walk from downtown Oslo, south of the Royal Palace.

The third shopping district is along Bogstadveien Street, linking the northernmost corner of the grounds of the Royal Palace with Majorstua, a major transportation crossroads north of downtown. Its attractive shops and boutiques make the street a favorite with Oslo's well-to-do, and its site slightly off the beaten track means few (or no) tourist items and a more authentic atmosphere. Begin a morning by walking and shopping along this street, have an inexpensive lunch in one of the many salad bars, and then take the tram up to Holmenkollen and Frognerseteren (see *Suburbs*) to complete a full Oslo day.

Note too, that a new shopping center opened last year at Oslo's Fornebu Airport. In addition to very reasonably priced duty-free items, there are good selections of apparel, jewelry, and electronics.

Among the fine assortment of shops and boutiques in Oslo, we suggest the following — all of which accept major credit cards:

Brødrene Thorkildsen – For fine furs. 8 Ovre Slottsgt. (phone: 332105).

Brukskunstsentret i Basarhallene – A string of small craft stores and workshops behind the Oslo Cathedral. Dronningensgt. and Karl Johans Gate.

David Andersen – Synonymous with Norwegian silver, and particularly noted for enameled silver. 20 Karl Johans Gate (phone: 416955) or the branch in *Oslo City* (phone: 170934).

Erik W. Abelson – An elegant little boutique for Scandinavian crystal, bronze, and silver jewelry, as well as tableware, wooden items, fabrics, and more. 27 Skovveien (phone: 555594).

Freia – Norway's favorite chocolatier, it offers 30 different kinds, from the deluxe Kong Haakon assortment to the tiny 1-krone bars. 31 Karl Johans Gate (phone: 427466).

GlasMagasinet – One of Oslo's most tempting department stores, renowned for having the city's best selection of crystal and tableware. 10 Stortorvet (phone: 116350).

Husfliden – Norway's "official" arts and crafts shop offers homespun fabrics, hand-sewn clothing, wooden utensils, and pewterware. 4 Møllergaten (phone: 421075).

J. Tostrup – The capital's oldest silver shop. 25 Karl Johans Gate (phone: 423090).

Maurtua – A less expensive alternative to *William Schmidt* (see below), featuring hand-knit sweaters and a variety of Norwegian souvenirs. 9 Fr. Nansens Plass (phone: 413164).

Norway Designs – Ceramics, glassware, jewelry, clothing, and decorative art — all by Scandinavian designers. 28 Stortingsgate — downstairs (phone: 831100).

N.M. Thune – Pewter in every conceivable form. 12 O. Slottsgt. (phone: 414115).

Oslo Sweater Shop – For the largest selection of sweaters in town. In the shopping arcade of the *Scandinavia Hotel,* 5 Tullinsgt. (phone: 112922).

Steen & Strøm – The department store for everything from clothing and cosmetics to ski gear and Scandinavian deli items. 23 Kongensgate (phone: 416800).

Tanum – Oslo's best bookstore, with a huge English-language section. The place to buy travel guides, Scandinavian cookbooks, maps, translations of Norse sagas, and Norwegian classics. 43 Karl Johans Gate (phone: 429310).

William Schmidt & Co. – Norwegians think it's overpriced, but visitors love the wide quality selection — sweaters, gift items, and more. 41 Karl Johans Gate (phone: 420288).

 SPORTS AND FITNESS: Oslo considers itself the world skiing capital, but the city provides a natural playground for sports enthusiasts of all stripes.

Boating – Sailing or boating on the Oslo Fjord can be a delightful experience. *Norway Yacht Charter* (8 Skïppergt.; phone: 426498) offers large sailboats with crews. Smaller boats, sailboats, and canoes can be rented by the hour, day, or week. Inquire at the Oslo Tourist Board (phone: 334386) for current listings.

Camping – Three campsites are close to the city. *Ekeberg Camping* at Ekebergsletta is next to Oslo's largest natural park and less than 2½ miles (4 km) from the center of town. It has a riding school, a children's wading pool, a recreation and sports ground, a kiosk, and a shop and is open from June through August (phone: 198568). *Bogstad Camping,* near Bogstad Lake about 6 miles (10 km) from the city, is open all year and has winter-insulated cabins for rent. It also has shops, a cafeteria, a post office (open only during summer), a gas station, and other conveniences (phone: 507680). *Stubljan Camping* at Hvervenbukta is a third choice (phone: 612706), open June through August.

Curling – There are several curling clubs in Oslo, and members of foreign clubs are welcome to use their rinks. For information apply to *Oslo Curlingkrets,* attn: Stein-Erik Mattsson (phone: 229505) or contact the *Norwegian Curling Association* (phone: 518800).

Cycling – It is possible to enjoy cycling in the Oslomarka area without being unduly bothered by auto traffic. Suggested cycle tours of the area (some free) can be obtained from the *Norwegian Cycling Association* (60 Maridalsvn.; phone: 719293). Many local tourist offices and hotels rent bicycles for about $9 a day, as does *Den Rustne Eike,* behind the Royal Palace (32 Oscars Gate; phone: 441880), but be prepared to pay a hefty refundable deposit of 500 Norwegian kroner (about $76).

Fishing – There is good trout fishing in the hills north of Oslo. A fishing license is available at local sports stores (about $14 for adults; about $9 for children 16 years and under), but first a national permit must be purchased at the post office for about $9. *Pimpling,* or ice fishing, is popular in the Oslomarka area and on the Oslo Fjord whenever the ice is safe. You can't rent equipment, but if you have your own, you are in for a wonderful time. On the fjord's ice, you'll find marked trails to follow.

Fitness Centers – *Friskoteket A/S* (9A Bogstadveien; phone: 460090), has weights and exercise equipment, squash, a sauna, and a physical therapist on staff. *High Energy* (10 Osterhausgate; phone: 360600) is an American-style gym. For a low-impact workout or Tae Kwon Do, try *Fitness Network* (39 Maridalsvn.; phone: 206487). Larger hotels, like the *SAS Scandinavia,* have facilities on the premises. Guests at the *Oslo Plaza* hotel can enjoy fabulous views while working out on the 33rd floor, which has a sauna, solarium, pool, and fitness room.

Golf – The best-known links are the *Oslo Golf Club*'s *Bogstad* golf course, near Bogstad Lake and the Bogstad camping grounds (phone: 504402). To play, visitors must show membership in an established golf club and pay greens fees; equipment may be rented.

Hiking – In summer, there is a network of about 1,860 miles of paths for hikers in the Oslo area. July and August are the best months for mountain walking. Midtstuen and Frognerseteren stations on the *Holmenkollen Railway* are good starting points. *Den Norske Turistforening* (*DNT;* 28 Stortings Gate; phone: 832550) publishes excellent maps covering the mountain areas with suggested tour routes. If you'd prefer to hike with a group, *DNT* can organize conducted tours with guides and reasonably priced lodging in mountain huts.

Ice Skating – The skating season lasts from December until mid-March. Oslo prepares and maintains outdoor rinks in some 150 locations. There also is an artificial frozen rink open to the public at *Valle Hovin* from mid-October to mid-March. Admission to the rinks is free, but there is a small fee for the use of changing rooms. Ice hockey, speed skating, and figure skating competitions are held frequently at the *Bislett, Frogner,* and *Jordal Amfi* stadiums and the *Oslo Spektrum,* a 9,000-seat arena in the Vaterland development. Details of such events are listed in *What's On In Oslo.*

Jogging – A good choice is Frognerparken, 5 to 10 minutes from downtown. For a more rural setting, try any of the paths at Holmenkollen (*Holmenkollen Railway* to Frognerseteren stop). Many paths are clearly marked with destination and distance. Nordmarka, about 20 minutes north of Oslo, is a wilderness area ideally suited for joggers who wish to escape the crowds.

Skiing – Skiing is the national pastime in Norway, and the Oslo municipality maintains more than 1,300 miles of ski trails through the surrounding woods and hills of Oslomarka. These are primarily for cross-country skiing, but hills for ski jumping and alpine skiing are available, too. Most alpine hills are lighted for night skiing, which can be particularly exhilarating. There are even a few ski trails specifically for the blind. The best part is that many of the choice spots are only a short ride by bus or suburban railway from downtown Oslo. The *Sognsvann Railway* line goes to Lake Sognsvann, a popular starting point for ski tourers. Buses leave the capital about every hour for Skansebakken in the Sørkedalen district and Skar in the Maridalen district, two other convenient starting points for ski tourers. There also are buses to such slalom centers as Kirkerudbakken in neighboring Baerum and Ingierkollen at Kolbotn. *Tomm Murstad's* ski school (at Ovreseter, near the Voksenkollen terminal of the *Holmenkollen Railway;* phone: 144665) is one of several that rents equipment and provides instruction in cross-country and slalom during the winter months. Information on skiing and related activities in the Oslo area is available from the *Ski Association* (5 Kongev.; phone: 141690).

Swimming – Besides several beaches on the Bygdøy peninsula where you can swim in the Oslo Fjord, there are a number of public swimming pools, including an outdoor pool at Vigeland Park (see *Special Places*). The Vigeland Park pool has a wonderful, spacious lawn surrounding it and a slide complex that is a child's fantasy. Nudist bathing beaches are on the northeast side of Svartkulp, a small lake north of Oslo; outside the city on the south side of Langøyene in Oslo Harbor, reached by ferry from the Oslo docks; and on the south side of Bygdøy, near Huk. Three public baths and swimming pools near the center of the city are *Tøyenbadet* (90 Helgesens Gate; phone: 671889), *Bislet bad* (60 Pilestredet; phone: 464176), and *Vestkantbadet* (1 Sommerrog; phone: 440726). All have saunas.

Windsurfing – It's the craze in Norway, too. The most popular area is around Bygdøy peninsula. Rent equipment from *SeaSport Windsurfing Center,* 5 Elisenbergveien (phone: 447928).

 THEATER: Programs are published in the daily press and in *What's On In Oslo.* Most performances start at 7:30 PM and are in Norwegian. You can see an Ibsen play at the *Nationaltheateret* (National Theater), Norway's principal theater (15 Stortings Gate in Studenterlunden Park; phone: 412710). *Amfiscenen,* the experimental stage of the *National Theater,* is in the same building (phone: 410475), but up five flights of stairs. The *Dukketeatret* (Puppet Theater), in the same building as the *Oslo City Museum,* is a delight not only for children

(67 Frognerveien; phone: 429075); *Det Norske Teatret* (8 Kristian IV's Gate; phone: 424344) produces foreign plays and musicals in the language known as *ny norsk* or new Norwegian; *Oslo Nye Teater* features classic and modern comedy (10 Rosenkrantz Gate; phone: 421188); *Chat Noir* presents cabaret acts (5 Klingenberggt.; 832457); *ABC-teatret* is the place for light comedy and cabaret, including classics in summer (1 St. Olavsplass; phone: 112166); and the *Bryggeteatret* at Aker Brygge offers musicals and comedies (phone: 838820). Fine dining and revues are tastefully combined at Mølla (21 Sagveien; phone: 375450). Internationally famous shows such as *La Cage aux Folles* usually are performed at *Château Neuf* (7 Slemdalsvn.; phone: 693154 or 605424). Those in search of English-language productions must watch for special guest appearances by visiting groups. During the tourist season, there are occasional shows in English. All films shown in Norway are screened in their original language and subtitled in Norwegian. It may be tricky figuring out a movie's original title, however; newspaper listings sometimes carry the Norwegian title, usually followed by the country of origin.

 MUSIC: Music has deep roots in Oslo's cultural life. The *Royal Guard's* band plays outside the Royal Palace whenever King Harald V is in residence, usually between October 1 and June 24, at the changing of the guard at 1:30 PM, and museums and libraries arrange public concerts regularly. *The Oslo Philharmonic Orchestra* gives numerous concerts during the autumn and winter season. Many of the concerts are held in the university's festival hall or at the *Oslo Konserthus* (Oslo Concert Hall; 14 Munkedamsveien; phone: 834510); in July and August, the concert hall's *Lille Sal* is the site of Norwegian folk dancing on Mondays and Thursdays at 9 PM. *Den Norske Opera* hosts ballets as well as operas (23C Storgt.; Youngstorget; phone: for advance sales, 429475 or 427724). Oslo's newest concert hall, *Spektrum* at Vaterland, hosts both rock concerts and classical events; the ticket office is open Mondays through Fridays from 10 AM to 6 PM. *Note:* Tickets for most concert and theater performances also can be obtained at the *Billet-Service* (8 Stortorvet; phone: 423630) and *Ticket Master* (phone: 209333, 547008, or 930660).

 NIGHTCLUBS AND NIGHTLIFE: Oslo nightlife has blossomed in recent years, and the capital is losing its former sleepy reputation. Wine bars, discos, and supper clubs — offering fine dining at one level and live dance bands or cabaret shows at another — abound. *Humla* (26 Universitetsgt.; phone: 424420), is a popular supper club where even visitors over 40 won't feel out of place; at the same address (and phone number) are two other popular spots, *Barock,* a trendy restaurant and disco, and the *Exit* club. The disco *Bonanza* at the *Grand* hotel, the dance-restaurant *El Toro* in the *Bristol,* and the *Frascati Dancing Bar* (20 Stortingsgt.; phone: 336565) cater to more mature crowds, while *Galaxy* in the *Scandinavia* hotel and the *Comeback* (11 Rosenkrantzgt.; phone: 334640) are popular with the younger set. *Smuget* (34 Kirkeveien, near Karl Johans Gate; phone: 425202) is a 3-level establishment with an eatery, a disco, and a live jazz/blues/rock section. Yuppies gather for wine, beer, or dinner at *Josefine Vertshus* (16 Josefines Gate; phone: 603126), a pub housed in an old villa in historic Homansbyen. There are a number of good jazz clubs. Try *Oslo Jazzhus* (69 Toftesgt.; phone: 385963), or ask at your hotel for current clubs and nightspots. Two pleasant café–wine bars are *Fru Blom's* (41B Karl Johans Gate; phone: 427300), serving vintage wines by the glass, pâtés, cheeses, and other tasty snacks; and *Café Sjakk Matt* (5 Haakon VIIs Gate). After an evening zipping down the floodlit Trysvannskleiva ski run, skiers gather around the blazing log fire at the lakeside *Trysvannstua Lodge* (phone: 144134). On summer evenings, young people cruise the outdoor cafés at Studenterlunden, just off Karl Johans Gate. The *Plaza Sky Bar,* 35 floors up at the *Oslo Plaza* hotel in Vaterland, is a late-night must — for the view alone (phone: 171000); after 9 PM there's a cover charge, and jackets are required for men.

BEST IN TOWN

 CHECKING IN: Thanks to the addition of several major properties, Oslo is rife with good, modern hotels, but rates, unfortunately, remain high, and reservations must be made early if you plan to visit during the busiest ski periods (February, March, or *Easter*), May 17 (*Constitution Day*), or at the height of the summer tourist season. If you do arrive without a place to stay, *Innkvartering,* the accommodations center at Oslo S (Central Station), makes room reservations at hotels, *pensiones,* and private homes for a small fee and a refundable deposit; the service can apprise visitors of special rates. In general, however, no advance bookings are made, and you must show up at the center in person on the day you require the room. (It is worth writing at least 3 weeks ahead to *Innkvartering,* Oslo S, 1 Jernbanetorvet, 0154 Oslo 1.) For a double room with bath, expect to pay more than $225 a night at very expensive hotels; about $150 to $225 at an expensive hotel; from $90 to $145 in the moderate range; and less than $90, inexpensive. Tax and breakfast — usually a generous buffet — are included at all hotels, unless otherwise indicated. For budget travelers, some simple *pensiones,* two youth hostels, and many of Oslo's best hotels offer special weekend rates, sometimes up to 50% less, and even occasionally during summer. All telephone numbers are in the 2 city code unless otherwise indicated.

Continental – Centrally located, this first-rate property is a city landmark with 2 restaurants worth noting: *Annen Etage,* one of Oslo's best, and *Theatercaféen,* one of the city's most popular old-fashioned cafés (see *Eating Out* for both). Business facilities include 24-hour room service, meeting rooms for up to 300, English-speaking concierge, foreign currency exchange, audiovisual equipment, photocopiers, and cable television news. 24-26 Stortings Gate (phone: 419060; fax: 4219689; telex: 71012). Very expensive.

Grand – Oslo's most prestigious hotel: dignified, traditional, and offering excellent service. It has spacious rooms, 3 bars, 5 elegant restaurants — including *Etoile* and the *Grand Café* (see *Eating Out*) — a pool and exercise facilities, and a perfect downtown location. If money is no object, book the Tower Suite or the Nobel Suite, which houses each year's Nobel Peace Prize winner. Also 25 junior suites. Business facilities include 24-hour room service, meeting rooms for up to 300, English-speaking concierge, foreign currency exchange, secretarial services in English, audiovisual equipment, photocopiers, and cable television news. 31 Karl Johans Gate (phone: 429390; fax: 421225; telex: 71683). Very expensive.

Nobel – Convenience is a keynote here. Small, centrally located, and near the *Grand* hotel. Business facilities include meeting rooms for up to 14, photocopier, and cable television news. 33 Karl Johans Gate (phone: 427480; fax: 420519; telex: 71915). Very expensive.

Royal Christiania – Its mood and decor inspired by the 300-year history of Christiania (Oslo), this 539-room property features 90 suites, including the sumptuous 2-story Royal Suite. There are 3 restaurants — including the elegant *Christian den 4* (see *Eating Out*) — a wine bar, piano bar, and a café, which is housed in the spacious marble and brass atrium. Business facilities include 24-hour room service, meeting rooms for up to 700, English-speaking concierge, secretarial services in English, audiovisual equipment, photocopiers, computers, translation services, and express check-in/checkout for Sar Business Card holders (apply in advance). 3 B. Gunnerus Gate (phone: 429410 or in the US, 800-4UTELL; fax: 424622; telex: 71342). Very expensive.

SAS Scandinavia – A large, high-rise hotel near the Royal Palace, many rooms have lovely views of the city and the fjord. Facilities include a health club and swimming pool, 5 restaurants — including *Holberg's Scandinavia* (see *Eating Out*) — and bars, the most notable of which is the *Summit Bar* on the 21st floor. Business facilities include 24-hour room service, meeting rooms for up to 800, English-speaking concierge, secretarial services in English, audiovisual equipment, photocopiers, cable television news, translation services, express check-in/checkout, and express laundry. 30 Holbergs Gate (phone: 113000; fax: 113017; telex: 79090). Very expensive.

Oslo Plaza – With 712 luxurious rooms and suites, it's by far the country's largest hotel. The 37-story glass structure towers over Oslo, with the *Plaza Sky Bar* on the 35th floor. Business facilities include 24-hour room service, meeting rooms for up to 900, English-speaking concierge, foreign currency exchange, secretarial services in English, photocopiers, cable television news, and translation services. Sonja Henies Plass (phone: 171000; fax: 177300; telex: 11241). Very expensive to expensive.

Ambassadeur – This charming, small hostelry in the west end of the city is popular with diplomats and has suites and demi-suites, each tastefully decorated in a different motif ("Shanghai," "Roma," "The Captain's Cabin"). The *Sabroso* restaurant, open for lunch and dinner, serves "nouvelle Norwegian" cuisine at comparatively reasonable prices. There's also a small indoor pool. Business facilities include room service, meeting rooms for up to 25 (plus use of a nearby historic villa for up to 205), English-speaking concierge, and cable television news. 15 Camilla Collettsvei (phone: 441835; fax: 444791; telex: 71446). Expensive.

Bristol – A very traditional European stopping place, set right in the center of town, it offers pleasant, large rooms, an inviting lobby bar with comfy, deep, leather chairs, and a grillroom with Spanish decor and a dance floor. Business facilities include meeting rooms for up to 200, English-speaking concierge, foreign currency exchange, audiovisual equipment, photocopiers, and cable television news. 7 Kristian IV's Gate (phone: 415840; fax: 428651; telex: 71668). Expensive.

Gabelshus – A quiet, established hotel with a loyal clientele, the atmosphere of a stately home, and an impeccable restaurant. Business facilities include meeting rooms for up to 150 and a photocopier. A 15-minute walk from the city center. 16 Gabels Gate (phone: 552260; fax: 442730; telex: 74073). Expensive.

Holmenkollen Park Hotel Rica – Storybook-style, timber-beamed, with comfortable (but small) rooms, also distinguished by an excellent view of Oslo from its lovely setting on Holmenkollen Hill on the outskirts of the city. A huge fireplace dominates its public salon; some rooms have terraces, and its attractive restaurant (see *Eating Out*) features Norwegian specialties (try the salmon). Business facilities include 24-hour room service, a new conference center in a separate building for for up to 400, English-speaking concierge, foreign currency exchange, audiovisual equipment, photocopiers, computers, cable television news, and simultaneous interpretation facilities. Reached by car or the *Holmenkollen Railway* line. 26 Kongeveien, Holmenkollåsen (phone: 146090; fax: 146192; telex: 72094). Expensive.

Rica Hotel Oslofjord – Formerly the *Sheraton,* this large hotel is about 20 minutes from the city center and, as the name implies, overlooks the Oslo Fjord. Don't let the spartan exterior put you off; the interiors won't. The garden café is airy and pleasant, while the *L'Orchidée* restaurant (open for dinner only) is Art Deco in style. There also is a sauna and a fitness center. Business facilities include room service, meeting rooms for up to 350, English-speaking concierge, audiovisual equipment, photocopiers, and cable television news. 184 Sandviksveien (phone: 545700; fax: 542733). Expensive.

Rica Triangel – Now under the management of the Rica chain, this property is modest but modernized. Business facilities include meeting rooms for up to 20. Centrally located. 1 Holbergs Plass (phone: 208855; fax: 207825; telex: 19413). Expensive.

Rica Victoria – Conveniently located near the Parliament, this elegant new hotel opened in the spring of last year with 155 well-appointed rooms, plus 6 suites, a large restaurant, and bar. Business facilities include 24-hour room service, English-speaking concierge, and photocopiers. 13 Rosenkrantzgt. (phone: 429940; fax: 429943). Expensive.

Scandic Crown – Not far from the Royal Palace, west of the city center, it has been remodeled, and a wing was added, though all the rooms are quite small. There's a good restaurant and bar. Business facilities include meeting rooms for up to 200, audiovisual equipment, photocopiers, computers, and cable television news. 68 Parkveien (phone: 446970; fax: 442601; telex: 71763). Expensive.

Stefanhotellet – Centrally located, this clean, modest hostelry is best known for its restaurant (see *Eating Out*). All rooms have telephones. Business facilities include room service, meeting rooms for up to 70, audiovisual equipment, photocopiers, and cable television news. 1 Rosenkrantz Gate (phone: 429250; fax: 337022; telex: 19809). Expensive.

Cecil – Also centrally located, this no-frills property is geared toward the business traveler. One hundred of the 112 spotless, modern rooms are singles — all with full baths, extra-large desks, mini-bars, trouser presses, and hair dryers. There's a breakfast room, and lunch is served in the atrium, except Sundays. Business facilities include 2 meeting rooms for up to 6 and cable television news. Convenient to the Parliament and Karl Johans Gate, 8 Stortingsgt. (phone: 427000; fax: 422670; telex: 71668). Expensive to moderate.

Rica Triangel Apartments – Just around the corner from the *Rica Triangel* hotel, these 41 units have kitchenettes and are available for daily or monthly rentals. Monthly rates are very reasonable. 38 Pilestredet (phone: 208855; fax: 207825; telex: 19413). Expensive to moderate.

Munch – All the conveniences of a hotel in a far higher price range. No restaurant, but there is a breakfast room. 5 Munchs Gate (phone: 424275; fax: 206469; telex: 74096). Moderate.

Vika Atrium – A stone's throw from the harbor, Aker Brygge, and City Hall, it has 72 rooms and a restaurant open for breakfast, lunch, and dinner. It's not luxurious, but has high standards, and the location can't be beat. Meeting rooms can be arranged at the adjacent Norwegian Business College. 45 Munkedamsveien (phone: 833300; fax: 830957; telex: 79959). Moderate.

Hall Hotell-Pension – This basic, clean, small, west-end establishment caters to visitors who stay for several weeks or even months. No private bathrooms. No restaurant, and the only alcohol available is beer. Rates do not include breakfast. 21 Fritzners Gate (phone: 557726). Moderate to inexpensive.

 EATING OUT: As you might expect, Norwegian cuisine centers on a wide range of fish and seafood specialties in addition to game. Norwegian trout and salmon are not to be missed, but you also will find delicious meals of cod, haddock, and coalfish. *Gravlax* is one type of smoked salmon to sample, but if it is too hard on your pocketbook, try another Norwegian delicacy: warm smoked mackerel. Sample the beer: *brigg* and *lettøl* are the weakest, lager is called *pils,* and *export* or *Gold* is the strongest. *Akevitt* (the Norwegian spelling of aquavit), which is made from potatoes and herbs and spices, accompanies special meals (with a beer chaser). Both reindeer and moose steaks are excellent, especially in the fall during the hunting season. Breakfast can vary from the simple continental — coffee, rolls, butter, and marmalade — to the traditional Norwegian *koldtbord* — a buffet with everything from assorted herring dishes to salmon and paper-thin slices of roast beef. For a particularly good smorgasbord try the *Stefanhotellet* (1 Rosenkrantz Gate; phone: 429250) or the *Scandic Crown* hotel (68 Parkveien; phone: 446970).

Best bet for a quick and inexpensive lunch is a *konditori,* or bakery/tearoom, where the Norwegians tend to eat. Enticingly fresh noontime selections include sandwiches, cakes, coffee, and tea, to be enjoyed at small tables or counters. Or take them along to eat in a park.

For a large selection of restaurants offering a choice of different sorts of food in varying price categories, stroll around Aker Brygge at the harbor or the *Oslo City* or *Galleri Oslo* shopping centers, located near the central rail station.

Dining out in Oslo is expensive. Most visitors sample at least one *koldtbord* lunch, almost all of which include some hot dishes. A dinner at an expensive restaurant will cost $55 or more per person; moderately priced establishments charge about $30 to $50 a meal; and those in the inexpensive category charge less than $30. It's the price of beer and wine that can skyrocket the cost of a dinner for two into a $125 to $200 tab. All restaurants recommended below accept major credit cards. Many restaurants close during the *Christmas* and *Easter* holidays. All telephone numbers are in the 2 city code unless otherwise indicated.

Annen Etage – An elegant and traditional Norwegian-European dining room featuring French and Norwegian cuisine, on the second floor of the *Continental* hotel. Piano music. Open weekdays for lunch and dinner and Sundays for early dinner (closed Saturdays). Reservations advised. 24-26 Stortings Gate (phone: 419060). Expensive.

Bagatelle – The only Oslo restaurant to have a star in the Michelin guide, it serves fine French food and has a distinguished wine cellar. The menu is set; diners need only choose the number of courses: 5 or 7. Open Tuesdays through Fridays for lunch, and daily for dinner except Sundays. Closed July. Reservations necessary. 3-5 Bygdøy Allé (phone: 446397). Expensive.

Det Blåkjokken – Formerly *Tre Kokker,* nothing has changed about this intimate and elegant dining spot except the name. The traditional Norwegian menu features fish and game, and the food is excellent. The three chefs work in full view of diners. Open weekdays from 4 PM, Saturdays for dinner. Reservations necessary. 30 Drammensveien (phone: 442650). Expensive.

Christian den 4 – Named after the Danish-Norwegian king who relished good food and drink, this elegant establishment in the *Royal Christiania* hotel specializes in fish and game, followed by imaginative desserts such as passionfruit Charlotte. A good variety of wines is available from the cellar. Open for dinner only, Mondays through Fridays. Reservations advised. 3 B. Gunnerus Gate (phone: 429410). Expensive.

Etoile – On the sixth floor of the *Grand* hotel, with a glass roof and a beautiful view of the city, this first class kitchen serves French and Norwegian food. Open daily, noon to midnight. Lunch table (a buffet with seafood, herring, and cheeses) from noon to 2:30 PM. Reservations advised. 31 Karl Johans Gate (phone: 429390). Expensive.

Frascati – This popular old meeting and dining spot in downtown Oslo is open daily except Sundays from 3:30 PM to 4 AM. Live music and a disco nightly. Reservations advised. 20 Stortings Gate (phone: 336565). Expensive.

Holberg's Arstidene – An excellent grill restaurant with an international à la carte menu. It holds special gastronomical weeks in autumn and spring. Its decorations are from the Holberg *époque* by Bjorn Winblad. In the *SAS Scandinavia* hotel. Open Mondays through Saturdays from 5 PM. Reservations advised. 30 Holbergs Gate (phone: 113000). Expensive.

Kastanjen – An informal street-level brasserie, with a more elegant dining room downstairs, it features modern interpretations of Norwegian classics, especially fish dishes. The desserts are excellent. Open daily, except Sundays, from 2 to 10 PM. Reservations advised for downstairs only. 18 Bygdøy Allé (phone: 434467). Expensive.

La Mer – Perhaps the best fish and seafood spot in Oslo. Call 2 days ahead and order the house special, bouillabaisse. Open daily, except Sundays, from 4 PM. Reservations advised. 31 Pilestredet (phone: 203445). Expensive.

Mølla – In an old textile mill on the banks of the River Akerselva, this fine fish and game place was the setting for Oskar Braaten's novels about factory workers' lives in the beginning of the century. After dinner, there's dancing, and musical revues are presented in the bar area. Open daily, except Sundays, from 3 PM. Reservations advised. 21 Sagveien (phone: 375450). Expensive.

Najaden – A first class restaurant with a very pleasant atmosphere, in the *Maritime Museum*. It offers a special tourist's lunch with assorted herring, hot dishes, and cheeses. Open daily. Reservations advised. 37 Bygdøynesv., Bydgøy peninsula (phone: 438180). Expensive.

Blom – Charmingly decorated with the shields of members of the Norwegian Society of Artists (can you find Charlie Chaplin's and Liv Ullmann's?). The art and antiques on its walls are alone worth a visit. It specializes in fish and game, and has a popular lunchtime open-sandwich buffet, a favorite of businesspeople. Closed Sundays. Reservations advised. 41B Karl Johans Gate (phone: 427300). Expensive to moderate.

Bygdøystuene – Formerly the *Folk Museum Restaurant*, it has a classic interior and menu. In summer it becomes a charming open-air restaurant. Open daily. Reservations advised. Bygdøy peninsula (phone: 440080). Expensive to moderate.

Feinschmecker – A popular contemporary eatery, it features Norwegian and continental fare in a cozy setting of candlelight and antique wooden cupboards. The service is impeccable. Open daily. Reservations necessary. 5 Balchensgt. (phone: 441777). Expensive to moderate.

De Fem Stuer – Another of the city's top places for a fine lunch from a buffet that is one of the city's best. The decor is attractive, the view over the city and its environs outstanding. Open daily. Reservations advised. In the romantic *Holmenkollen Park Hotel Rica*, 26 Kongeveien, Holmenkollåsen (phone: 146090). Expensive to moderate.

Theatercaféen – This unrivaled Oslo favorite, much frequented by artists, is in the *Continental* hotel. The orchestra favors waltzes, but there is no dancing. A place to see and be seen. Window tables are the most fashionable. The lunch buffet, consisting mostly of open-face sandwiches, is very popular; ask to see the menu if you want a more filling dish. Open daily. Dinner reservations advised. 24-26 Stortings Gate (phone: 419060). Expensive to moderate.

Café Sjakk Matt – One of Oslo's most popular cafés, it's open midday for lunch and serves small snacks after 3 PM. Open daily. Reservations unnecessary. 5 Haakon VII's Gate, near Vika (phone: 423227). Moderate.

Costas – This large, trendy brasserie-cum-Italian eatery is always crowded. The pasta is not quite up to par with the sleek decor, but it's still *the* place to be seen in Oslo — and the desserts are delectable, especially the homemade sorbets. Open daily. Reservations necessary. 4 Klingenberggaten (phone: 424130). Moderate.

Grand Café – This busy dining place in the *Grand* hotel has large murals of life in

Old Christiania at the turn of the century, when it was Ibsen's destination twice daily. Music after 7 PM. Jazz brunch on Sundays. Open daily until 11:30 PM. Dinner reservations necessary. 31 Karl Johans Gate (phone: 429390). Moderate.

Håndverkeran Bar and Grill – A meeting place with a masculine atmosphere, for artists and journalists who flock to its special sandwich buffet from 11 AM to 2 PM each day. Closed Sundays. Reservations advised. 7 Rosenkrantz Gate (phone: 420750). Moderate.

Stefanhotellet – In the modest hotel of the same name, it serves excellent Norwegian food and offers a fine buffet. The new management has dropped the "no alcohol" policy established by the local Mission Society (the former owners), so guests now can enjoy wine with their meals. Open daily for dinner; lunch on Sundays. Reservations unnecessary. 1 Rosenkrantz Gate (phone: 429250). Moderate.

Tostrupkjelleren – The best of Oslo's basement restaurants, a meeting place for politicians, journalists, and businesspeople that serves international fare. Open for lunch and dinner daily except Sundays. Reservations unnecessary. 25 Karl Johans Gate (phone: 421470). Moderate.

Frognerseteren Kafé – Both à la carte restaurant and cafeteria, this establishment at Holmenkollen has the feel of a ski lodge. Try the fresh salmon or the "wild" stew of elk, reindeer, and berries. In summer, crowds gather on the terrace overlooking Oslo Fjord soak up the sun while enjoying apple cake served with mounds of fresh whipped cream; in winter, skiers flock to tables near the roaring fireplace. Open for lunch and dinner. Reservations unnecessary. 200 Holmenkollen (phone: 143736). Restaurant, moderate; cafeteria, inexpensive.

Chinatown Stortinget – Probably the best of Oslo's new crop of Chinese eateries, it has a slightly more formal atmosphere than Americans are used to at home. One side of the dining room serves very good Mongolian barbecue; the other features Cantonese dishes. Open daily. Reservations advised. Right beside the Parliament, at 19 Nedre Vollgt. (phone: 330800). Inexpensive.

Holmenkollen – The kitchen features Norwegian dishes, the dining room features a spectacular view of the city and fjord. Try the large lunch buffet. Open daily. Reservations unnecessary. Reached by the *Holmenkollen Railway* line. 119 Holmenkollveien, Holmenkollåsen (phone: 146226). Inexpensive.

Peppe's Pizza – Launched in 1969 by an American-Norwegian couple, the thin-crust pizza became an overnight success. A large pizza weighs in at a kilo (2.2 pounds), serves 3 to 4, and costs from $17 to $25. Decorated in a farmhouse motif — cozy, dark, filled with antiques — there are four branches in Oslo, including one in the city center at 4 Stortingsgt. (phone: 425418). Open daily. Reservations unnecessary, except for large groups. Inexpensive.

PARIS

It was Victor Hugo, the great French poet and novelist, who captured the true spirit of his native city when he called it "the heir of Rome, the mundane pilgrim's home away from home." If Rome, for all its earthly exuberance, never lets a visitor forget that it is the spiritual home of the West, Paris — with its supreme joie de vivre and its passion for eating, drinking, and dressing well — belongs unabashedly to the material world.

Like a magnet, Paris always has attracted visitors and exiles from all corners of the earth. At the same time, it remains not so much an international city as a very French one, and a provincial one at that. Paris has its own argot, and each neighborhood retains its peculiar character, so that the great capital is still very much a city of 20 villages.

But parochialism aside — and forgetting about the consummate haughtiness of Parisians (someone once remarked that Parisians don't even like themselves) — the main attraction of the City of Light is its beauty. When you speak of the ultimate European city, it must be Paris, if only for the view from the Place de la Concorde or the Tuileries up the Champs-Elysées toward the Arc de Triomphe, or similarly striking sights beside the Seine. Here is the fashion capital of the world and the center of gastronomic invention and execution. Here the men all seem to swagger with the insouciance of privilege, and even the humblest shopgirl dresses with the care of a haute couture mannequin. Paris is the reason "foreign" means "French" to so many travelers.

Paris is in the north-central part of France, in the rich agricultural area of the Seine River valley. With a population of over 2 million people, it is France's largest city, an industrial and commercial center, and an important river port. Roughly elliptical in shape, the city has more than doubled in size in the last century. Its limits now are the ring of mid-19th-century fortifications that once were well beyond its boundaries. At its western edge is the vast Bois de Boulogne and to the east the Bois de Vincennes — two enormous parks. Curving through Paris, the Seine divides the city into its northern Right Bank (Rive Droite) and southern Left Bank (Rive Gauche). The Right Bank extends from the Bois de Boulogne on the far west, through Place Charles-de-Gaulle (l'Etoile), which surrounds the Arc de Triomphe, and farther east to the Tuileries Gardens and the fabulous *Louvre*. North of the *Louvre* is the area of the Grands Boulevards, centers of business and fashion; farther north is the district of Montmartre, built on a hill and crowned by the domed Eglise du Sacré-Coeur, an area that has attracted great artists (and many of markedly less greatness) since the days of Monet and Renoir.

The Left Bank sweeps from the Eiffel Tower on the west through the Latin Quarter, with its university and bohemian and intellectual community. South of the Latin Quarter is Montparnasse, once inhabited jointly by artists and

PARIS

RUE D'AMSTERDAM
RUE DE CLICHY
RUE CAULAINCOURT
RUE DE CLIGNANCOURT

Basilique du Sacre-Coeur

MONTMARTRE

BD DE CLICHY
BD DE ROCHECHOUART

HAUSSMANN
RUE LA FAYETTE
RUE AUBER
Opéra
BD DES ITALIENS
BD ST DENIS

BD DE LA MADELENE
RUE DE LA PAIX
AV DE L'OPERA
PL DE L'OPERA
RUE DU QUATRE SEPTEMBRE

Place de la Madeleine
RUE ST-HONORE
RIGHT BANK
RUE REAUMUR

Place Vendôme

RUE DE RIVOLI
Palais Royal
Les Halles

Tuileries
QUAI DES TUILERIES
Louvre
RUE DE LOUVRE
RUE DES HALLES
Centre Georges Pompidou

QUAI DU LOUVRE
PONT DU CARROUSEL
PONT ROYAL

Musée d'Orsay
QUAI VOLTAIRE
QUAI MALAQUAIS
PONT NEUF
Palais de Justice

RUE DES SAINTS PERES
Church of St.-Germain-des-Pres
BD DU PALAIS
RUE DE LA CITE
Ile de la Cité

BD SAINT GERMAIN
Notre-Dame
Ile St.-Louis

BD RASPAIL
BD DE RENNES
RUE DE VAUGIRARD
RUE DES ECOLES
R SAINT JACQUES

Luxembourg Palace and Gardens

RUE MONGE

BD DU MONTPARNASSE
BD SAINT MICHEL

MONTPARNASSE
BD DE PORT ROYAL

intellectuals and laborers, now a large urban renewal project that includes a suburban-style shopping center around the Tour Montparnasse.

In the middle of the Seine are two islands, the Ile de la Cité and the Ile St.-Louis, the oldest parts of Paris. It was on the Ile de la Cité (in the 3rd century BC) that Celtic fishermen known as Parisii first built a settlement they named Lutetia, "place surrounded by water." Caesar conquered the city for Rome in 52 BC, and in about AD 300, Paris was invaded by Germanic tribes, the strongest of which were the Franks. In 451, when Attila the Hun threatened to overrun Paris, a holy woman named Geneviève promised to defend the city by praying. She succeeded — the enemy decided to spare the capital — and Geneviève became the patron saint of Paris. Clovis I, the first Christian King of the Franks, made Paris his capital in the 6th century. Relentless Norman sieges, famine, and plague curtailed the city's development, but at the end of the 10th century peace and prosperity came with the triumph of Hugh Capet over the Carolingians. Capet ascended the throne, the first of a long line of Capetian kings, and Paris became the "central jewel of the French crown," a great cultural center and seat of learning.

The Capetian monarchs contributed much to the growth of the city over the next few centuries. A defensive wall was begun in 1180 by Philip Augustus to protect the expanding Right Bank business and trading center, as well as the intellectual quarter around the newly formed university on the Left Bank. He then built a new royal palace, the *Louvre,* just outside these ramparts, but he never lived there. Medieval Paris was a splendid city, a leader in the arts and in the intellectual life of Europe. The Sorbonne attracted such outstanding scholars as Alexander of Hales, Giovanni di Fidanza (St. Bonaventure), Albertus Magnus, and Thomas Aquinas.

The Ile de la Cité remained a warren of narrow streets and wood and plaster houses, but the banks of the Seine continued to be built up in both directions. Renaissance kings, patrons of the arts, added their own architectural and aesthetic embellishments to the flourishing city. Major streets were laid out; some of Paris's most charming squares were constructed; the Pont Neuf, the first stone bridge spanning the Seine, was completed; and Lenôtre, the royal gardener, introduced proportion, harmony, and beauty with his extraordinary Tuileries.

Louis XIV, who was responsible for many of the most notable Parisian landmarks, including Les Invalides, moved the court to Versailles in the late 17th century. Paris nevertheless continued to blossom, and it was under the Sun King's rule that France and Paris first won international prestige. Visitors were drawn to the city, luxury trades were begun, and the Panthéon, Champ-de-Mars parade ground, and Ecole Militaire were built. In 1785, at age 16, Napoleon Bonaparte graduated from this military school with the notation in his report: "Will go far if circumstances permit!"

French history reflects the conflict between the two extremes of the French character, both equally strong: a tradition of aristocracy and a penchant for revolution. To the French aristocracy we owe magnificent palaces like the *Louvre,* the Luxembourg Palace, and Versailles, with their formal gardens. At the same time, the people of Paris have always been noisily rebellious and independent: from 1358, when the mob rebelled against the Dauphin, to the Fronde in 1648–49, the great French Revolution of 1789, the 1830 and 1848 revolutions that reverberated throughout Europe, the Paris Commune of 1870–71, and finally to the student rebellion of 1968, which nearly overthrew the Fifth Republic. The most profound one of all was the French Revolution at the close of the 18th century, the bicentennial of which was celebrated in grand style in 1989.

The excesses of the French court, the consummate luxury of the Versailles of Louis XIV, cost the French people dearly in taxes and oppression. The Parisians, fiercely independent, forced the French king to his knees with their dramatic storming of the Bastille in 1789. Inspired by the ideas of the French and English philosophers of the Enlightenment, just like the American founding fathers in 1776, the French subsequently overthrew their monarchy.

During the Revolution, unruly mobs damaged many of the city's buildings, including Ste.-Chapelle and Notre-Dame, which were not restored until the mid-19th century. Napoleon, who came to power in 1799, was too busy being a conqueror to complete all he planned, though he did manage to restore the *Louvre,* construct the Carrousel Arch and Place Vendôme victory column, and begin work on the Arc de Triomphe and the Madeleine. Though something of a tyrant, Napoleon's conquests spread the new ideas of the Revolution — including the Code Napoléon, a system of laws embodying the ideals of "Liberty, Equality, Fraternity" — to places as far away as Canada and Moscow.

Later in the 19th century, Paris was reorganized and modernized by a great urban planner, Baron Haussmann. He instituted the brilliant system of squares as focal points for marvelous, wide boulevards and roads; he planned the Place de l'Opéra, the Bois de Boulogne and Bois de Vincennes, the railway stations, the boulevards, and the system of 20 *arrondissements* (districts) that make up Paris today. He also destroyed most of the center of the old Cité, displacing 25,000 people.

During the peaceful lull between the Franco-Prussian War and World War I, the city of Paris thrived as never before. These were the days of the Belle Epoque, the heyday of *Maxim's,* the *Folies-Bergère,* and the cancan, whose spirit is captured so well in Offenbach's heady music for *Gaité Parisienne.* Montmartre, immortalized by Toulouse-Lautrec, was so uninhibited that the foreign press dubbed Paris the "City of Sin."

In the 2 decades before World War II, this free-spirited city attracted politically and socially exiled artists by the dozens: Picasso, Hemingway, Fitzgerald, and Gertrude Stein were just a few. Only in Paris could such avant-garde writers as James Joyce, D. H. Lawrence, and later, Henry Miller find publishers. And Paris, which witnessed the first Impressionist exhibition in 1874 — introducing Monet, Renoir, Pissarro, and Seurat — heard the first performance of Stravinsky's revolutionary "Sacre du Printemps" (Rite of Spring) in 1913, even though the baffled audience jeered loudly.

As the quintessentially beautiful center of intellectual life and home of the arts, Paris can claim to have earned its City of Light title. Even though it, like other modern cities, is troubled by a rise in crime — at *Maxim's,* for instance, a precautionary bulletproof window has been installed — its beauty and libertarian atmosphere remain. Its supreme talent for civilized living has made the city beloved by the French and foreigners alike. After all, these are the people who made food preparation a fine art, and despite the unfortunate presence of fast-food vendors on the Champs-Elysées, the French passion for haute cuisine remains unrivaled. And as the undisputed capital of fashion, male and female, Paris continues to be the best-dressed city in the world, and Rue du Faubourg-St.-Honoré remains the standard by which all other shopping streets are measured.

However avant-garde in dress, Parisians are a conservative lot when it comes to any changes in the appearance of their beloved city. When the Eiffel Tower was built in 1889, Guy de Maupassant commented, "I spend all my afternoons on the Eiffel Tower; it's the only place in Paris from which you can't see it." So today's Parisians grumble about the ultramodern *Centre Georges Pompidou,* a focus for every type of modern art: theater, music, dance, circus, painting, sculpture, photography, and film, and about *Le Forum des Halles,* a sunken glass structure filled with boutiques in what was once *Les Halles,* the bawdy produce market. They also don't seem especially thrilled by the I. M. Pei glass pyramids that form the new entrance to the *Louvre.*

Parisians accept innovations reluctantly because they want their city to remain as it has always been. They love their remarkable heritage inordinately, and perhaps it is this love, together with the irrepressible sense of good living, that has made Paris so eternally attractive to others.

PARIS AT-A-GLANCE

SEEING THE CITY: It's impossible to single out just one perfect Paris panorama; they exist in profusion. The most popular is the bird's-eye view from the top of the Eiffel Tower on the Left Bank; there are several places to have snacks and drinks and enjoy a view (on a clear day) of more than 50 miles. (There also are three restaurants where you can enjoy fine dining.) The tower is open daily, 10 AM to 11 PM; admission charge (Champ-de-Mars; phone: 45-55-91-11). From the top of the towers of Notre-Dame, eager spectators enjoy close-ups of the cathedral's Gothic spires and flying buttresses, along with a magnificent view of the Ile de la Cité and the rest of Paris. Start climbing the steps at the foot of the north tower; admission charge (Rue du Cloître Notre-Dame, 4e; phone: 43-25-42-92). On the Right Bank there's a stunning view from the terrace of Sacré-Coeur. The observatory on Tour Montparnasse also offers a striking panorama, as does the landing at the top of the escalator at the *Centre Georges Pompidou,* and the observation deck of *Samaritaine,* the 10-floor department store at the foot of the Pont Neuf.

The most satisfying view, if not the highest, is from the top of the Arc de Triomphe. The arch is the center of Place Charles-de-Gaulle, once Place de l'Etoile (Square of the Star), so called because it is the center of a "star" whose radiating points are the 12 broad avenues, including the Champs-Elysées, planned and built by Baron Haussmann in the mid-19th century. Open daily, 10 AM to 5:30 PM; admission charge (phone: 43-80-31-31).

SPECIAL PLACES: Getting around this sprawling metropolis isn't difficult once you understand the layout of the 20 *arrondissements.* We suggest that visitors orient themselves by taking one of the many excellent sightseeing tours offered by *Cityrama* (4 Pl. des Pyramides, 1er; phone: 42-60-30-14) or

Paris Vision (214 Rue de Rivoli, 1er; phone: 42-60-31-25). Their bubble-top, double-decker buses are equipped with earphones for simultaneous commentary in English and several other languages. Reserve through any travel agent or your hotel's concierge.

Once you have a better idea of the basic layout of the city, buy a copy of *Paris Indispensable* or *Plan de Paris par Arrondissement* at any bookshop or newsstand. These little lifesavers list streets alphabetically and indicate the nearest métro station on individual maps and an overall plan. Now you're ready to set out by foot (the most rewarding) or by métro (the fastest and surest) to discover Paris for yourself.

Street addresses of the places mentioned throughout the chapter are followed by their *arrondissement* number.

LA RIVE DROITE (THE RIGHT BANK)

Arc de Triomphe and Place de l'Etoile – This monumental arch (165 feet high, 148 feet wide) was built between 1806 and 1836 to commemorate Napoleon's victories. It underwent a major cleanup and restoration for the bicentennial of the French Revolution. Note the frieze and its 6-foot-high figures, the ten impressive sculptures (especially Rude's *La Marseillaise* on the right as you face the Champs-Elysées), and the arches inscribed with the names of Bonaparte's victories, as well as those of Empire heroes. Beneath the arch is the French Tomb of the Unknown Soldier and its Eternal Flame, which is rekindled each day at 6:30 PM. An elevator (or 284 steps) carries visitors to the top for a magnificent view of the city and the 12 avenues radiating from l'Etoile. Admission charge. Pl. Charles-de-Gaulle (phone: 43-80-31-31).

Champs-Elysées – Paris's legendary promenade, the "Elysian Fields," was swampland until 1616. It has come to be synonymous with everything glamorous in the city, though the "Golden Arches" and shlocky shops recently have replaced much of the old glamour (a commission was formed in 1990 to try to restore some of the old elegance). The Champs-Elysées stretches for more than 2 miles between the Place de la Concorde and the Place Charles-de-Gaulle (l'Etoile). The very broad avenue, lined with rows of plane and horse chestnut trees, shops, cafés, and cinemas, is perfect for strolling, window shopping, and people watching.

The area from the Place de la Concorde to the Rond-Point Champs-Elysées is a charming park, where Parisians often bring their children. On the north side of the gardens is the Palais de l'Elysée, the official home of the President of the French Republic. Ceremonial events, such as the *Bastille Day Parade* (July 14), frequently take place along the Champs-Elysées.

Grand Palais – Off the Champs-Elysées, on opposite sides of Avenue Winston-Churchill, are the elaborate turn-of-the-century *Grand Palais* and *Petit Palais* (Large Palace and Small Palace), built of glass and stone for the *1900 World Exposition.* With its stone columns, mosaic frieze, and flat glass dome, the *Grand Palais* contains a large area devoted to temporary exhibits, the *Palais de la Découverte* (the Paris science museum), and the planetarium. Closed Tuesdays; open Wednesdays until 9:45 PM. Admission charge. Av. Franklin-Roosevelt, 8e (phone: 42-89-54-10).

Petit Palais – Built contemporaneously with the *Grand Palais,* it has exhibits of the city's history, as well as a variety of fine and applied arts and special shows. Closed Mondays. Admission charge. Av. Winston-Churchill, 8e (phone: 42-65-12-73).

Place de la Concorde – This square, surely one of the most magnificent in the world, is grandly situated in the midst of equally grand landmarks: the *Louvre* and the Tuileries on one side, the Champs-Elysées and the Arc de Triomphe on another, the Seine and the Napoleonic Palais Bourbon on a third, and the pillared façade of the Madeleine on the fourth. Designed by Gabriel for Louis XV, the elegant square was where his unfortunate successor, Louis XVI, lost his head to the guillotine, as did Marie Antoinette, Charlotte Corday, Robespierre, and others. It was first named for Louis XV, then called Place de la Révolution by the triumphant revolutionaries. Ornamenting the square, the eight colossal statues representing important French provincial capitals were polished and blasted clean for the bicentennial celebration in 1989. The 3,300-year-old, 75-foot-high obelisk was a gift from Egypt in 1829.

Jardin des Tuileries – Carefully laid out in patterned geometric shapes, with clipped shrubbery and formal flower beds, statues, and fountains, this is one of the finest examples of French garden design (in contrast to an informal English garden, exemplified by the Bois de Boulogne). Along the Seine, between the Place de la Concorde and the *Louvre*.

Orangerie – A museum on the edge of the Tuileries gardens, it displays a series of large paintings of water lilies by Monet called the *Nymphéas* and the collection of Jean Walter and Paul Guillaume, with works by Cézanne, Renoir, Matisse, Picasso, and others. Open 10 AM to 5:15 PM; closed Tuesdays. Admission charge. Pl. de la Concorde and Quai des Tuileries, 1er (phone: 42-97-48-16).

Rue de Rivoli – This charming old street has perfume shops, souvenir stores, boutiques, bookstores, cafés, and such hotels as the *Meurice* and the *Inter-Continental* under its 19th-century arcades. The section facing the Tuileries, from the Place de la Concorde to the *Louvre*, is an especially good place to explore on rainy days.

Louvre – Built on the site of a medieval fortress on the banks of the Seine, this palace was the home of the French kings during the 16th and 17th centuries, until Louis XIV moved the court to Versailles in 1682. In 1793, it became a museum and now is one of the world's greatest art repositories. It's easy to spend a couple of days here, savoring treasures like the *Venus de Milo, Winged Victory,* the *Mona Lisa,* and the French crown jewels — just a few of the 297,000 pieces in six different collections.

Nor is the outside of this huge edifice to be overlooked. Note especially the Cour Carrée (the courtyard of the old *Louvre*), the southwest corner of which, dating from the mid-1550s, is the oldest part of the palace and a beautiful example of the Renaissance style that François I had so recently introduced from Italy. Note, too, the Colonnade, which forms the eastern front of the Cour Carrée, facing the Place du Louvre; fully classical in style, it dates from the late 1660s, not too long before the Sun King left for Versailles. Newer wings of the *Louvre* embrace the palace gardens, in the midst of which stands the Arc de Triomphe du Carrousel, erected by Napoleon. From here, the vista across the Tuileries and the Place de la Concorde and on up the Champs-Elysées to the Arc de Triomphe is one of the most beautiful in Paris — which says a lot. The glass pyramids — designed by I. M. Pei and opened in 1989 — sit center stage in the *Louvre*'s grand interior courtyard, and the largest of the intrusive trio now is the museum's main entrance. The controversial structure is the first step of a major expansion; when completed (the target date is 1993), the *Louvre*'s underground galleries, shops, and exhibit space will connect the North and South Wings, increasing museum exhibition space by almost 80%.

Good guided tours in English, covering the highlights of the *Louvre,* are frequently available, although not every day, so be sure to check in advance. Open from 9:45 AM to 6:30 PM; Wednesdays and Mondays from 9:45 AM to 9:45 PM; closed Tuesdays. Admission charge. Pl. du Louvre, 1er (phone: 40-20-51-51, for recorded information in French and English or 40-20-50-50, for more detailed information).

Place Vendôme – Just north of the Tuileries is an aristocrat of a square, one of the loveliest in Paris, the octagonal Place Vendôme, designed by Mansart in the 17th century. Its arcades contain world-famous jewelers, perfumers, and banks, the *Ritz* hotel, and the Ministry of Justice. The 144-foot column in the center is covered with bronze from the 1,200 cannons captured at Austerlitz by Napoleon in 1805. Just off Place Vendôme is the famous Rue du Faubourg-St.-Honoré, one of the oldest streets in Paris, which now holds elegant shops selling the world's most expensive made-to-order items. To the north is the Rue de la Paix, noted for its jewelers.

Opéra – Charles Garnier's imposing rococo edifice stands in its own busy square, its façade decorated with sculpture, including Carpeaux's *The Dance.* The ornate interior has an impressive grand staircase, a beautiful foyer, lavish marble from every quarry in France, and Chagall's controversially decorated dome. Until a few years ago, the opera house only could be seen by attending a performance (held September–June); now, however, visitors may explore its magnificent interior and enjoy its special exhibitions daily from 11 AM to 4:30 PM, except on the days when there are special performances. Admission charge. Pl. de l'Opéra, 9e (phone: 47-42-57-50).

L'Opéra Bastille – In sharp contrast to Garnier's *Opéra* is the curved glass façade of 20th-century architect Carlos Ott's new Paris opera house. Set against the historic landscape of the Bastille quarter, this austere, futuristic structure houses over 30 acres of multipurpose theaters, shops, and urban promenade. Inaugurated for the bicentennial of the revolution on July 14, 1989, the opera house opened in March 1990 with a production of Berlioz's *Les Troyens.* It looks a lot like the prison-fortress that started the French Revolution. Pl. de la Bastille, 11e (phone: 40-01-17-89).

La Madeleine – Starting in 1764, the Church of St. Mary Magdalene was built and razed twice before the present structure was commissioned by Napoleon in 1806 to honor his armies. The church is based on a Greek temple design, with 65-foot-high Corinthian columns supporting the sculptured frieze. From its portals, the view extends down Rue Royale to Place de la Concorde and over to the dome of Les Invalides. Nearby are some of Paris's most tantalizing food shops. Open from 7:30 AM to 7 PM as well as during concerts (held 4 PM Sundays) and other frequent musical events. Pl. de la Madeleine, 8e (phone: 42-65-52-17).

Sacré-Coeur and Montmartre – Built on the highest of Paris's seven hills, the white-domed Basilica of Sacré-Coeur provides an extraordinary view from its steps, especially at dawn or sunset. The area around the church was the artists' quarter of late-19th- and early 20th-century Paris. The more garish aspects of Montmartre's notoriously frivolous 1890s nightlife, particularly the dancers and personalities at the *Moulin Rouge,* were immortalized by the paintings of Henri de Toulouse-Lautrec. And if the streets look familiar, chances are you've seen them in the paintings of Utrillo; they still look the same. The Place du Tertre is still charming, though often filled with tourists and overly eager, mostly undertalented artists. Go early in the day to see it as it was when Braque, Dufy, Modigliani, Picasso, Rousseau, and Utrillo lived here. Montmartre has the last of Paris's vineyards — and still contains old houses, narrow alleys, steep stairways, and carefree cafés enough to provide a full day's entertainment; at night, this is one of the centers of Paris life. Spare yourself most of the climb to Sacré-Coeur by taking the funicular (as we went to press, it was being replaced by a more modern, glass contraption — bringing the *Louvre's* main pyramid to mind) or the Montmartre bus (marked with an icon of Sacré-Coeur on the front instead of the usual number) from Place St.-Pierre. Butte Montmartre, 18e.

Les Halles – Just northeast of the *Louvre,* this 80-acre area, formerly the *Central Market,* "the Belly of Paris," was razed in 1969. Gone are most of the picturesque early morning fruit and vegetable vendors, butchers in blood-spattered aprons, truckers bringing the freshest produce from all over France. Their places have been usurped by trendy shops and galleries of youthful entrepreneurs and artisans, small restaurants with lots of charm, the world's largest subway station, acres of trellised gardens and playgrounds, and *Le Forum des Halles,* a vast complex of boutiques, ranging from the superchic designer ready-to-wear to more ordinary shops, as well as concert space and movie theaters. Touch-sensitive locator devices, which help visitors find products and services, are placed strategically. A few echoes of the earthy past remain, however, and you can still dine at *Au Pied de Cochon, Pharamond,* and *L'Escargot Montorgueil,* or have a drink with the few remaining workmen (before noon) at one of the old brasseries.

Le Centre National d'Art et de Culture Georges Pompidou (Le Centre Georges Pompidou) – Better known as "the Beaubourg," after the plateau on which it is built, this stark, 6-level creation of steel and glass, with its exterior escalators and blue, white, and red pipes, created a stir the moment its construction began. Outside, a computerized digital clock ticks off the seconds remaining until the 21st century. This wildly popular museum brings together all the contemporary art forms — painting, sculpture, the plastic arts, industrial design, music, literature, cinema, and theater — under one roof, and that roof offers one of the most exciting views of Paris. The old houses and cobbled, tree-shaded streets and squares vie for attention with galleries, boutiques, and the spectacle provided by jugglers, mimes, acrobats, and magicians in the plaza out front. The scene in the courtyard often rivals the exhibits inside. Open weekdays from noon to 10 PM; 10 AM to 10 PM weekends. Closed Tuesdays; no admission charge on Sundays except for special exhibitions. Rue Rambuteau, at the corner of Rue St.-Martin, 4e (phone: 42-77-12-33).

Le Marais – Northeast of the *Louvre,* a marshland until the 16th century, this district became the height of residential fashion during the 17th century. But as the aristocracy moved on, it fell into disrepair. Recently, after a long period of neglect, the Marais has been enjoying a complete face-lift. Spurred on by the opening of the *Picasso Museum* in the Hôtel du Salé, preservationists have lovingly restored more than a hundred of the magnificent old mansions to their former grandeur. They now are museums of exquisite beauty, with muraled walls and ceilings, and their courtyards are the sites of dramatic and musical presentations during the summer *Festival du Marais.* Among the houses to note are the Palais de Soubise, now the National Archives, and the Hôtels d'Aumont, de Clisson, de Rohan, de Sens, and de Sully (*hôtel* in this sense means private residence or townhouse). The Caisse Nationale des Monuments, housed in the last one, can provide maps of the area, as well as fascinating and detailed tours. It also offers lectures on Saturdays and Sundays. 62 Rue St.-Antoine, 4e (phone: 42-74-22-22).

Place des Vosges – In the Marais district, the oldest square in Paris — and also one of the most beautiful — was completed in 1612 by order of Henri IV, with its houses elegantly "built to a like symmetry." Though many of the houses have been rebuilt inside, their original façades remain, and the recently restored square is one of Paris's enduring delights. Corneille, Racine, and Mme. de Sévigné lived here. At No. 6 is the *Maison de Victor Hugo,* once the writer's home and now a museum. Closed Mondays; admission charge (4e; phone: 42-72-10-16).

Musée Carnavalet (Carnavalet Museum) – Also in the Marais, this once was the home of Mme. de Sévigné, a noted 17th-century letter writer, and now its beautifully arranged exhibits cover the history of the city of Paris from the days of Henri IV to the present. Its recent expansion through the *lycée* next door and into the neighboring *Le Peletier* hotel doubled the exhibition space, making it the largest museum in the world devoted to the history of a single capital city. The expansion, done primarily to house a permanent major exhibit on the French Revolution, was part of Paris's celebration of the Revolution's bicentennial. Watch for special exhibitions here. The museum also rents out its concert hall to various music groups. Closed Mondays; no admission charge on Sundays. 23 Rue de Sévigné, 3e (phone: 42-72-21-13).

Musée Picasso (Picasso Museum) – This long-awaited museum (opened in 1986), which contains a large part of the artist's private collection, is at the Hôtel du Salé. To tell the truth, the building is at least as interesting as the artwork it houses — too many recent works, too few early ones — but a visit is worthwhile just to see Picasso's collection of works by other artists (the Cézannes are best). Open Mondays and Thursdays through Saturdays from 9:15 AM to 5 PM, Wednesdays from 9:15 AM to 10 PM. Admission charge. 5 Rue de Thorigny, 3e (phone: 42-71-25-21).

Cimetière Père Lachaise (Père Lachaise Cemetery) – For those who like cemeteries, this one is a beauty. In a wooded park, it's the final resting place of many illustrious personalities. A map is available at the gate to help you find the tombs of

Balzac, Sarah Bernhardt, Chopin, Colette, Corot, Delacroix, Héloise and Abelard, La Fontaine, Modigliani, Musset, Edith Piaf, Rossini, Oscar Wilde, and even Jim Morrison (of the *Doors* rock group), among others. Note, too, the legions of resident cats. Open daily from 8 AM to 5:30 PM. Bd. de Ménilmontant at Rue de la Roquette, 20e (phone: 43-70-70-33).

La Villette – The City of Sciences and Industry, a celebration of technology, stands in its own park on the edge of the capital and houses a planetarium, the spherical *Géode* cinema, lots of hands-on displays, and a half-dozen exhibitions at any given time. Restaurants and snack bars. Open 10 AM to 6 PM. Closed Mondays. 30 Av. Cotentin Cariou, 20e (phone: 40-05-70-00).

Bois de Boulogne – Originally part of the Forest of Rouvre, on the western edge of Paris, this 2,140-acre park was planned along English lines by Napoleon. Ride a horse or a bike, row a boat, shoot skeet, go bowling, smell roses, picnic on the grass, see horse races at *Auteuil* and *Longchamp,* visit a zoo, see a play, walk to a waterfall — and there's lots more.

Bois de Vincennes – As a counterpart to the Bois de Boulogne, a park, a palace, and a zoological garden were laid out on 2,300 acres during Napoleon III's time. Visit the 14th-century château and its lovely chapel; the large and lovely floral garden; and the zoo, with animals in their natural habitat. It's at the southeast edge of Paris (métro: Château de Vincennes).

Palais de Chaillot – Built for the *Paris Exposition of 1937* — on the site of the old Palais du Trocadéro left over from the *Exposition of 1878* — its terraces have excellent views across gardens and fountains to the Eiffel Tower on the Left Bank. Two wings house a theater (*Cinemathèque*), an aquarium, and four museums — *du Cinéma* (phone: 45-53-74-39), *de l'Homme* (anthropology; phone: 45-53-70-60), *de la Marine* (maritime; phone: 45-53-31-70), and *des Monuments Français* (monument reproductions; phone: 47-27-97-27). Closed Tuesdays and major holidays. Admission charge. Pl. du Trocadéro, 16e.

LA RIVE GAUCHE (THE LEFT BANK)

Tour Eiffel (Eiffel Tower) – It is impossible to imagine the Paris skyline without this mighty symbol, yet what has been called Gustave Eiffel's folly was never meant to be permanent. Originally built for the *Universal Exposition of 1889,* it was due to be torn down in 1909, but it was saved because of the development of the wireless — the first transatlantic wireless telephones were operated from the tower in 1916. Its centennial was celebrated with great fanfare in 1989. Extensive renovations have taken place, and a post office, three restaurants (*Jules Verne* is the best), and a few boutiques have opened up on the first-floor landing. On a really clear day, it's possible to see for 50 miles. Open daily from 10 AM to 11 PM; in the summer from 10 AM to midnight. Admission charge. Champ-de-Mars, 7e (phone: 45-50-34-56).

Chaillot to UNESCO – From the Eiffel Tower, it is possible to look out over a group of Paris's 20th-century buildings and gardens on both sides of the Seine, including the Palais de Chaillot, the Trocadéro and Champ-de-Mars gardens, and the UNESCO buildings. Also part of the area (but not of the same century) is the huge Ecole Militaire, an impressive example of 18th-century French architecture on Avenue de la Motte-Picquet. The Y-shaped building just beyond it, facing Place de Fontenoy, is the main UNESCO building, dating from 1958. It has frescoes by Picasso, Henry Moore's *Reclining Silhouette,* a mobile by Calder, murals by Miró, and Japanese gardens by Noguchi.

Les Invalides – Built by Louis XIV as a refuge for disabled soldiers, this vast classical building has more than 10 miles of corridors and a golden dome by Mansart. For yet another splendid Parisian view, approach the building from the Alexandre III bridge. Besides being a masterpiece of the age of Louis XIV (17th century), the Church of St. Louis, part of the complex, contains the impressive red and green granite Tomb of Napoleon (admission charge). Also at Les Invalides is the *Musée de l'Armée,* one of the world's richest museums, displaying arms and armor together with mementos of French military history. Open daily from 10 AM to 5 PM. Admission charge. Av. de Tourville, Pl. Vauban, 7e (phone: 45-51-92-84).

Musée d'Orsay (Orsay Museum) – This imposing former railway station has been transformed (by the Milanese architect Gae Aulenti, among others) into one of the shining examples of modern museum curating. Its eclectic collection includes not only the Impressionist paintings decamped from the once-cramped quarters in the *Jeu de Paume,* but also less consecrated academic work and a panorama of the 19th century's achievements in sculpture, photography, and the applied arts. Closed Mondays. Admission charge; reduced on Sundays. 1 Rue de Bellechasse, 7e (phone: 40-49-48-14).

Musée Rodin (Rodin Museum) – The famous statue *The Thinker* is in the garden of this splendid 18th-century residence. The chapel and the mansion also contain Rodin sculpture. Open daily except Mondays from 10 AM to 4:30 PM. Admission charge. 77 Rue de Varenne, 7e (phone: 47-05-01-34).

Montparnasse – Just south of the Luxembourg Gardens, in the early 20th century there arose an artists' colony of avant-garde painters, writers, and Russian political exiles. Here Hemingway, Picasso, and Scott and Zelda sipped and supped in places like *La Closerie des Lilas, La Coupole, Le Dôme, Le Select,* and *La Rotonde.* The cafés, small restaurants, and winding streets still exist in the shadow of a new shopping center.

Tour Montparnasse – This giant complex dominates Montparnasse. The fastest elevator in Europe whisks Parisians and tourists alike (for a fee) up 59 stories for a view *down* at the Eiffel Tower, from 9:30 AM to 9:30 PM daily; Fridays and Saturdays until 10:30 PM. The shopping center here boasts all the famous names, and the surrounding office buildings are the headquarters of some of France's largest companies. 33 Av. du Maine, 15e, and Bd. de Vaugirard, 14e (phone: 45-38-52-56).

Palais et Jardin du Luxembourg (Luxembourg Palace and Garden) – In what once were the southern suburbs, the Luxembourg Palace and Garden were built for Marie de Médici in 1612. A prison during the Revolution, the Renaissance palace now houses the French Senate. The classic, formal gardens, with lovely statues and the famous Médicis fountain, are popular with students meeting under the chestnut trees and with neighborhood children playing around the artificial lake. 15 Rue de Vaugirard, 6e.

Mosquée de Paris (Paris Mosque) – One of the most beautiful structures of its kind in the non-Muslim — or even in the Muslim — world, it is dominated by a 130-foot-high minaret in gleaming white marble. Shoes are taken off before entering the pebble-lined gardens full of flowers and dwarf trees. Inside, the Hall of Prayer, with its lush Oriental carpets, may be visited daily except Fridays, from 9:30 AM to noon and 2 to 6 PM. Admission charge. Next door is a restaurant and a patio for sipping Turkish coffee and tasting Oriental sweets. Pl. du Puits-de-l'Ermite, 5e (phone: 45-35-97-33).

Panthéon – This 18th-century "nonreligious Temple of Fame dedicated to all the gods" has an impressive interior, with murals depicting the life of Ste.-Geneviève, patron saint of Paris. It contains the tombs of Victor Hugo, the Resistance leader Jean Moulin, Rousseau, Voltaire, and Emile Zola. Open daily from 10 AM to 12:30 PM and 2 to 5:30 PM. Admission charge. Pl. du Panthéon, 5e (phone: 43-54-34-51).

Quartier Latin (Latin Quarter) – Extending from the Luxembourg Gardens and the Panthéon to the Seine, this famous neighborhood still maintains its unique atmosphere. A focal point for Sorbonne students since the Middle Ages, it's a mad jumble of narrow streets, old churches, and academic buildings. Boulevard St.-Michel and Boulevard St.-Germain are its main arteries, both lined with cafés, bookstores, and boutiques of every imaginable kind. There are also some charming old side streets, such as the Rue de la Huchette, near Place St.-Michel. And don't miss the famous *bouqui-nistes* (bookstalls) along the Seine, around the Place St.-Michel on the Quai des Grands-Augustins and the Quai St.-Michel.

Eglise St.-Germain-des-Prés (Church of St.-Germain-des-Prés) – Probably the oldest church in Paris, it once belonged to an abbey of the same name. The original basilica (AD 558) was destroyed and rebuilt many times. The Romanesque steeple and its massive tower date from 1014. Inside, the choir and sanctuary are as they were in the 12th century, and the marble shafts used in the slender columns are 14 centuries old. Pl. St.-Germain-des-Prés, 6e (phone: 43-25-41-71).

Surrounding the church is the *quartier* of Paris's "fashionable" intellectuals and artists, with art galleries, boutiques, and renowned people watching cafés such as the *Flore* (Sartre's favorite) and *Aux Deux Magots* (once a Hemingway haunt).

Musée de Cluny (Cluny Museum) – One of the last remaining examples of medieval domestic architecture in Paris. The 15th-century residence of the abbots of Cluny later became the home of Mary Tudor and now is a museum of medieval arts and crafts, including the celebrated *Lady and the Unicorn* tapestry. Open daily, except Tuesdays, from 9:30 AM to 5:15 PM. Admission charge. 6 Pl. Paul-Painlevé, 5e (phone: 43-25-62-00).

Eglise St.-Séverin (Church of St. Séverin) – This church still retains its beautiful Flamboyant Gothic ambulatory, considered a masterpiece of its kind, and lovely old stained glass windows dating from the 15th and 16th centuries. The small garden and the restored charnel house also are of interest. 3 Rue des Prêtres, 5e (phone: 43-25-96-63).

Eglise St.-Julien-le-Pauvre (Church of St. Julien le Pauvre) – One of the smallest and oldest churches (12th to 13th century) in Paris offers a superb view of Notre-Dame from its charming Place René-Viviani. 1 Rue St.-Julien-le-Pauvre, 5e (no phone).

THE ISLANDS

Ile de la Cité – The birthplace of Paris, settled by Gallic fishermen about 250 BC, this island in the Seine is so rich in historical monuments that an entire day could be spent here and on the neighboring Ile St.-Louis. A walk all around the islands, along the lovely, tree-shaded quais on both banks of the Seine, opens up one breathtaking view of Notre-Dame Cathedral after another.

Cathédrale de Notre-Dame de Paris (Cathedral of Our Lady) – It is said that the Druids once worshiped on this consecrated ground. The Romans built their temple, and many Christian churches followed. In 1163, the foundations were laid for the present cathedral, one of the world's finest examples of Gothic architecture, grand in size and proportion. Henri VI and Napoleon were crowned here. Take a guided tour (offered in English at noon Tuesdays and Wednesdays and in French at noon other weekdays, 2:30 PM Saturdays, and 2 PM Sundays) or quietly explore on your own, but be sure to climb the 225-foot towers for a marvelous view of the city and try to see the splendid stained glass rose windows at sunset. Admission charge to the towers. Pl. du Parvis, 4e (phone: 43-26-07-39).

Palais de Justice and Sainte-Chapelle – This complex recalls centuries of history; it was the first seat of the Roman military government, then the headquarters of the early kings, and finally the law courts. In the 13th century, St.-Louis (Louis IX) built a new palace and added Sainte-Chapelle to house the Sacred Crown of Thorns and other holy relics. Built in less than 3 years, the chapel, with its 15 splendid stained glass windows and 247-foot spire, is one of the jewels of Paris. Open daily from 10 AM to 4:30 PM. Admission charge. 4 Bd. du Palais, 1er (phone: 43-54-30-09).

Conciergerie – This remnant of the Old Royal Palace was used as a prison during the Revolution. Here Marie Antoinette, the Duke of Orléans, Mme. du Barry, and many others of lesser fame awaited the guillotine. It was restored extensively for the celebration of the bicentennial of the French Revolution, and the great arch-filled hall is especially striking. Open daily. Admission charge. 4 Bd. du Palais, 1er (phone: 43-54-30-06).

Ile St.-Louis – Walk across the footbridge at the back of Notre-Dame and you're in a charming, tranquil village. This "enchanted isle" has managed to keep its provincial charm despite its central location. Follow the main street, Rue St.-Louis-en-l'Ile, down the middle of the island, past courtyards, balconies, old doors, curious stairways, the Eglise St.-Louis, and discreet plaques bearing the names of illustrious former residents (Mme. Curie, Voltaire, Baudelaire, Gautier, and Daumier, for example); then take the quai back along the edge.

■**EXTRA SPECIAL:** Versailles, by far the most magnificent of all the French châteaux, is 13 miles (21 km) southwest of Paris, accessible by train or bus (also see *France*, DIRECTIONS). Louis XIV, called the Sun King because of the splendor of his court, took a small château used by Louis III, enlarged it, and really outdid himself. The vast, intricate, formal gardens, designed by the great Lenôtre, cover 250 acres and include 600 fountains, for which a river had to be diverted. At one time, the palace itself housed 6,000 people, and the court numbered 20,000. Louis kept his nobles in constant competition over his favors, hoping to distract them from any opposition to his rule. It's impossible to see all of Versailles in one day, but don't miss the Hall of Mirrors, the Royal Apartments, and the Chapel. Also on the grounds are the Grand Trianon, a smaller palace often visited by Louis XIV, and the Petit Trianon, a favorite of Marie-Antoinette, who also liked Le Hameau (the hamlet), a model farm where she and her companions played at being peasants. More than 20 additional rooms — the apartments of the dauphin and dauphine — are open to visitors Thursdays through Sundays. The gardens are open daily from 9 AM to 5 PM; the château and Trianons are closed Mondays and holidays. Guided tours in English are available from 10 AM to 3:30 PM. Admission charge (phone: 30-84-74-00). A spectacular illumination and display of the great fountains takes place on Sunday afternoons during the summer. For more information, contact the Versailles Tourist Office, 7 Rue des Réservoirs (phone: 39-50-36-22).

SOURCES AND RESOURCES

TOURIST INFORMATION: For information in the US, contact the French Government Tourist Office (610 Fifth Ave., New York, NY 10020; phone: 212-757-1125). In Paris, the Office du Tourisme de Paris (127 Champs-Elysées, 8e; phone: 47-23-61-72), open daily from 9 AM to 8 PM, is the place to go for information, brochures, maps, or hotel reservations. If you call the office, be prepared for a 4- to 5-minute wait before someone answers. Other offices are found at major train stations, such as the Gare du Nord (phone: 45-26-94-82) and the Gare de Lyon (phone: 43-43-33-24).

Local Coverage – *Paris Selection* is the official tourist office magazine in French and English. It lists events, sights, "Paris by Night" tours, places to hear jazz, some hotels, restaurants, shopping, and other information. Far more complete are three weekly guides, *L'Officiel des Spectacles, Paris 7,* and *Pariscope.* All are in simple French and are available at newsstands.

For insights on eating out and finding the best of French food and wine, consult *The Food Lover's Guide to Paris* (Workman, $12.95) by American-in-Paris Patricia

Wells. She also contributes a weekly column on restaurants to the *International Herald Tribune.*

 TELEPHONE: The country code for France is 33. All phone numbers in Paris begin with the prefix 4 (incorporated into the numbers given here); in the area surrounding Paris, they are preceded by either 3 or 6. When calling a number in the Paris region (including the Ile-de-France) from Paris, dial only the 8-digit number. When calling a number from outside the Paris region, dial 1, then the 8-digit number. When calling from the US, dial 33 (which is the country code), followed by 1, and the 8-digit number.

Many pay phones on Paris street corners accept only phone cards. They are available in 40- and 120-franc denominations at post offices and tobacco shops. Before dialing from a pay phone, put the card into the slot on the phone and close the hood. When the franc value remaining on the card is displayed, you can dial your call.

 GETTING AROUND: Airports – Charles de Gaulle Airport (Roissy, 16 miles — 25 km — northeast of Paris; phone: 48-62-12-12) has two terminals: Aérogare 1, for foreign airlines, and Aérogare 2, predominantly for *Air France* flights. The two terminals are connected by a free shuttle bus. *Air France* airport buses (phone: 42-99-20-18), open to passengers of all airlines for 40F (about $7), leave for the Palais des Congrès (métro station: Porte Maillot) every 12 minutes from 5:40 AM to 11 PM and take between 30 and 50 minutes, depending on traffic. City bus No. 350 between the airport and the Gare du Nord train station also is available, but it generally is slow, taking up to an hour. *Roissy-Rail* runs between the airport and the Gare du Nord every 15 minutes and takes about 35 minutes. (A shuttle bus connects the airport to Roissy station, and from there to the Gare du Nord is by train.) Taxis into town cost 160F (about $27) or more for most destinations.

Orly Airport (10 miles — 16 km — south of Paris; phone: 49-75-52-52) has two terminals: Orly Ouest, mainly for domestic flights and flights to Geneva, and Orly Sud, for international flights. The two terminals are connected by a free shuttle bus. *Air France* buses (phone: 43-23-97-10) leave for a terminus on the Esplanade des Invalides (métro station: Invalides) every 12 minutes and take from 30 to 45 minutes, depending on traffic. You can purchase tickets ($10 one way, $20 round trip) in the US from *Marketing Challengers International* (10 E. 21st St., New York, NY 10010; phone: 212-529-8484). City bus No. 215, which links the airport to Denfert-Rochereau, in southern Paris, takes about a half hour. *Orly-Rail,* a combination shuttle bus to Orly station and train to various stops in the city such as Luxembourg, St.-Michel, and Invalides, runs every 15 or 30 minutes depending on the time of day and takes 35 to 50 minutes, according to the stop. A taxi into town costs 100F (about $17) and up.

Buses linking Charles de Gaulle and Orly airports run roughly every half hour and take from 50 to 75 minutes.

Boat – See Paris from the Seine by day and by night for about 30F–35F (about $5–$6). Modern, glass-enclosed river ramblers provide a constantly changing picture of the city. Contact *Bateaux-Mouches* (Pont d'Alma, 7e; phone: 42-25-96-10), *Les Bateaux Parisiens* (Pont d'Iéna, 7e; phone: 47-05-50-00), or *Vedettes Pont-Neuf* (Sq. Vert-Galant, 1er; phone: 46-33-98-38). For 90F ($15), *Paris Canal* (phone: 42-40-96-97) offers a 3-hour barge trip starting on the Seine, then navigating through some of the city's old canals, locks, and a subterranean water route under the Bastille. An interesting commmentary is given in both English and French. There are two trips daily between the *Musée d'Orsay* and the Parc de la Villette — one leaves from the *Musée d'Orsay* at 9:30 AM and the other departs from the Parc de la Villette at 2:30 PM. Reservations are required.

Bus – They generally operate from 6:30 AM to 9:30 PM, although some run later.

Slow, but good for sightseeing. Métro tickets are valid on all city-run buses. Lines are numbered, and both stops and buses have signs indicating routes. One or two tickets may be required, depending on the distance traveled. The *RATP*, which operates both the métro and bus system, also has designated certain lines as being of particular interest to tourists. A panel on the front of the bus indicates in English and German "This bus is good for sightseeing." *RATP* has a tourist office at Place de la Madeleine, next to the flower market (phone: 43-46-14-14), which organizes bus trips in Paris and the region.

Car Rental – Book when making your plane reservation, or contact *Avis* (phone: 45-50-32-31), *Budget* (phone: 46-86-65-65), *Europcar* (phone: 45-00-08-06), or *Hertz* (phone: 47-88-51-51). Drivers should be aware that to reduce traffic jams, a 17-mile ban on parking on certain city streets (including the Champs-Elysées, Rue de Rivoli, and Boulevard Saint-Michel) is in effect from 8:30 AM to 8:30 PM on week days. Two routes are affected: north-south from the Porte de Clignancourt to the Porte d'Orléans and east-west, along the Seine from the Quai d'Issy to the Quai d'Ivry. Violators are subject to fines of up to $100.

Métro – Operating from 5:30 AM to about 1 AM, it is safe, clean, quiet, easy to use, and since the Paris rapid transit authority (*RATP*) began to sponsor cultural events and art exhibits in some subway stops in an effort to cut down on crime and make commuting more enjoyable, entertaining as well. The events have been so popular that so far they've been offered in about 200 of Paris's 368 métro stations.

The different lines are identified by the names of their terminals at either end. Every station has clear directional maps, some with push-button devices that light up the proper route after a destination button is pushed. Keep your ticket (you may need to show it to one of the controllers who regularly patrol the métro) and don't cheat; there are spot checks. In August 1991, the Paris Regional Transit Authority abolished the métro's long-standing first and second class system. There is now only one class of ticket.

A 10-ticket book (*carnet*) is available at a reduced rate. The Paris-Visite card, a tourist ticket that entitles the bearer to 1, 3, or 5 consecutive days of unlimited first class travel on the métro and on city-run buses, may be purchased in France upon presentation of your passport at 44 subway stations and 4 regional express stations, or at any of the 6 *French National Railroad* stations. In the US, the card is available by money order from *Marketing Challengers International* (10 E. 21st St., New York, NY 10010; phone: 212-529-8484) — $7.50 for a 1-day ticket, $20 for a 3-day ticket, and $30 for a 5-day ticket, plus $3 for postage and handling.

SITU – Handy streetside bus and subway directions are now available in some métro stations from *SITU* (*Système d'Information des Trajets Urbains*), a computer that prints out the fastest routing onto a wallet-size piece of paper complete with the estimated length of trip. The *RATP* (the rapid transit authority) service is free and augments the lighted wall maps that guide métro riders. High-traffic spots such as the Châtelet métro station, outside the Gare Montparnasse, and on the Boulevard St.-Germain, now sport *SITU* machines.

Taxi – Taxis can be found at stands at main intersections, outside railway stations and official buildings, and in the streets. A taxi is available if the entire "TAXI" sign is illuminated (with a white light); the small light *beside* the roof light signifies availability after dark. But be aware that Parisian cab drivers are notoriously selective about whom they will pick up, and how many passengers they will allow in their cab — a foursome inevitably has trouble. You also can call *Taxi Bleu* (phone: 49-36-10-10) and *Radio Taxi* (phone: 47-39-33-33). The meter starts running from the time the cab is dispatched, and a tip of about 15% is customary. Fares increase at night and on Sundays and holidays.

Train – Paris has six main train stations, each one serving a different area of the country. The general information number is 45-82-50-50; for telephone reservations, 45-65-60-60. North: Gare du Nord (18 Rue de Dunkerque; phone: 42-80-63-63); East: Gare de l'Est (Pl. du 11-Novembre; phone: 42-03-96-31); Southeast: Gare de Lyon (20 Bd. Diderot; phone: 40-19-60-00); Southwest: Gare d'Austerlitz (51 Quai d'Austerlitz; phone: 45-84-14-19); West: Gare Montparnasse (17 Bd. de Vaugirard; phone: 40-48-10-00); West and Northwest: Gare St.-Lazare (20 Rue de Rome; phone: 42-85-88-00). The *TGV* (*train à grande vitesse*), the world's fastest train, has cut 2 hours off the usual 4-hour ride between Paris and Lyons; it similarly shortens traveling time to Marseilles, the Côte d'Azur, the Atlantic Coast, and Switzerland. It leaves from the Gare de Lyon, except for the Atlantic Coast run which departs from the Gare d'Austerlitz; reservations are necessary. As we went to press, a new *TGV* station was scheduled to open in Massy, 16 miles (25 km) south of Paris. Located right near Orly, a 15-minute ride on the *RER* (suburban train), it is ideal for those who are traveling to other parts of France and want to avoid going into Paris.

 LOCAL SERVICES: Dentist (English-Speaking) – *Dr. Edward Cohen,* 20 Rue de la Paix, 2e (phone: 42-61-65-64 or 42-61-78-71).

Dry Cleaner/Tailor – Dry cleaners are available throughout the city. Note that many have two different price schedules, one for "economic" service, another for faster, more expensive service. The less expensive prices may be posted outside, but unless you specify, your clothes will be given the expensive treatment. *John Baillie, Real Scotch Tailor* (1 Rue Auber at Pl. de l'Opera, 2e; phone: 47-42-49-24 or 47-42-49-17) is a reputable firm that does tailoring French-style, despite its name.

Limousine Service – *Compagnie des Limousines* (26 Rue Armand-Silvestre, Courbevoie; phone: 47-89-43-08); *Executive Car/Carey Limousine* (25 Rue d'Astorg, 8e; phone: 42-65-54-20; fax: 42-65-25-93).

Medical Emergency – The *American Hospital* has 24-hour emergency service. The hospital also has a dental service and maintains an extensive network of English-speaking specialists. 63 Bd. Victor-Hugo, Neuilly (phone: 46-41-25-25).

Messenger Service – *Neuilly Courses,* 6 Villa des Sablons, Neuilly (phone: 47-45-54-00).

National/International Courier – *Federal Express* (*Copyshop,* 44 Rue du Colisée, 8e; phone: 40-85-38-88); *DHL International* (59 Av. d'Iéna, 16e; phone: 45-01-91-00 or 48-63-70-00).

Office Equipment Rental – *Chapchool Distribution,* for typewriters with English keyboards (minimum 2-week rental). 11 Rue Etienne-Marcel, Pantin (phone: 48-45-05-25).

Pharmacy – *Pharmacie Derhy* is open 24 hours a day, including holidays. Located in the *Galerie Les Champs,* 84 Av. des Champs-Elysées, 8e (phone: 45-62-02-41).

Photocopies – In addition to the numerous small outlets specializing in photocopies, facilities are available in many stationery stores and post offices.

Post Office – The main post office (52 Rue du Louvre, 1er; phone: 40-28-20-00) is open 24 hours a day; night hours are restricted to simpler operations such as posting a registered letter. Other branches are open from 8 AM to 7 PM on weekdays and until noon on Saturdays.

Secretary/Stenographer (English-Speaking) – *Multiburo* also rents office space. 17 Rue Galilée, 16e (phone: 47-23-47-47).

Teleconference Facilities – *Hôtel Méridien,* 81 Bd. Gouvion-St.-Cyr, 17e (phone: 40-68-34-34).

Telex – *PTT* (Postes et Télécommunications), open daily, including Sundays, from 8 AM to 7:30 PM, at 7 Rue Feydeau, 2e (phone: 42-33-20-12), and from 8 to 10:30 PM at 5 Rue Feydeau, just next door.

Translator – *Bilis Traduction,* 24 Rue Lafitte, 9e (phone: 47-70-50-80).
Other – Tuxedo rental: *Au Cor de Chasse,* 40 Rue de Buci, 6e (phone: 43-26-51-89).

SPECIAL EVENTS: After the *Christmas* season, Paris prepares for the January fashion shows, when press and buyers come to town to pass judgment on the spring and summer haute couture collections. (The general public can see what the designers have wrought after the professionals leave.) More buyers come to town in February and March for the ready-to-wear shows (fall and winter clothes), open to the trade only. March is the month of the first *Foire à la Ferraille et aux Jambons* of the year. This fair of regional food products held concurrently with an antiques flea market (not items of the best quality, but not junk, either) is repeated in September. The running of the *Prix du Président de la République,* the first big horse race of the year, takes place at *Auteuil* in April. From late April to early May is the *Foire de Paris,* the capital's big international trade fair. In late April or May there's the *Paris Marathon;* in late May (through early June), the *French Open Tennis Championships.* Odd years only, the *Paris International Air Show* is an early June attraction at Le Bourget Airport. Horse races crowd the calendar in June — there's not only the *Prix de Diane* at *Chantilly,* but also the *Grande Semaine* at *Longchamp, Auteuil,* and *St.-Cloud.* And in the middle of June, the *Festival du Marais* begins a month's worth of music and dance performances in the courtyards of the Marais district's old townhouses. *Bastille Day,* July 14, is celebrated with music and fireworks, parades, and dancing till dawn in every neighborhood. Meanwhile, the *Tour de France* is under way; the cyclists arrive in Paris for the finish of the 3-week race later in July. Also in July, press and buyers arrive to view the fall and winter haute couture collections, but the ready-to-wear shows (spring and summer clothes) wait until September and October, because August for Parisians is vacation time. Practically the whole country takes a holiday then, and in the capital the classical concerts of the *Festival Estival* (in July and August) are among the few distractions. When they finish, the *Festival d'Automne,* a celebration of the contemporary in music, dance, and theater takes over (from mid-September through December). The *Foire à la Ferraille et aux Jambons* returns in September, but in even-numbered years it's eclipsed by the *Biennale des Antiquaires,* a major antiques event from late September to early October. Also in even years, usually in November, is the *Paris Motor Show.* Every year on the first Sunday of October, the last big horse race of the season, the *Prix de l'Arc de Triomphe,* is run at *Longchamp;* and every year in early October, Paris holds the *Fête des Vendanges à Montmartre* to celebrate the harvest of the city's last remaining vineyard. On November 11, ceremonies at the Arc de Triomphe and a parade mark *Armistice Day.* An *International Cat Show* and a *Horse and Pony Show* come in early December; then comes *Christmas,* which is celebrated most movingly with a *Christmas Eve* midnight mass at Notre-Dame. At midnight a week later, the *New Year* bows in to spontaneous street revelry in the Latin Quarter and along the Champs-Elysées.

MUSEUMS: Some Paris museums (*musées*) are free or offer reduced admission fees on Sundays. "La Carte," a pass that can be used at over 60 museums and monuments in the city, is available at métro stations and at major museums (or in the US from *Marketing Challengers International,* 10 E. 21st St., New York, NY 10010; phone: 212-529-8484). Prices are the equivalent of $15.50 for a 1-day pass, $27.50 for a 3-day pass, and $37.50 for a 5-day pass. Note that "La Carte" is not valid for certain special exhibits. Museums of interest not described in *Special Places* include the following:

Archaeological Crypt of Notre-Dame – Under the square in front of walls and floor plans from later periods. Open daily from 10 AM to 4:30 PM. Parvis de Notre-Dame, 4e (phone: 43-29-83-51).

Catacombs – Dating from the Gallo-Roman era and also containing the remains of Danton, Robespierre, and many others. Bring a flashlight. Closed Mondays. 1 Pl. Denfert-Rochereau, 14e (phone: 43-22-47-63).

Egouts (Sewers of Paris) – Underground city of tunnels, a very popular afternoon tour, daily except Thursdays and Fridays, and on holidays and the days preceding and following them. Pl. de la Résistance, in front of 93 Quai d'Orsay, 16e (phone: 47-05-10-29).

Galerie Nationale de Jeu de Paume – Inaugurated in June 1991, this museum is devoted to contemporary art from 1960 on and includes paintings, sculpture, photographs, and videos, all installed in what was formerly the temple of Impressionism — the *Jeu de Paume,* at one end of the Tuileries. The interior has been redone to provide more and better exhibition space. Open Tuesdays, Thursdays, and Fridays from noon to 7 PM; Wednesdays from noon to 10 PM; and Saturdays and Sundays from 10 AM to 7 PM. Corner of the Tuileries Gardens at the Pl. de la Concorde.

Maison de Balzac – The house where the writer lived, with a garden leading to one of the prettiest little alleys in Paris. Closed Mondays. 47 Rue Raynouard, 16e (phone: 42-24-56-38).

Manufacture des Gobelins – The famous tapestry factory, in operation since the 15th century. Guided tours of the workshops take place Tuesdays, Wednesdays, and Thursdays from 2:15 to 3:15 PM. 42 Av. des Gobelins, 13e (phone: 42-74-44-50).

Mémorial de la Déportation – Set in a tranquil garden in the shadow of Notre Dame at the tip of Ile de la Cité, this monument is dedicated to 200,000 French women and men of all religions and races who died in Nazi concentration camps during World War II. Square de l'Ile-de-France, 4e.

Mémorial du Martyr Juif Inconnu – A moving tribute to Jews killed during the Holocaust, this 35-year-old, newly renovated memorial includes World War II documents and photographs. Open daily, except Friday afternoons and Saturdays, from 10 AM to noon and 2 to 5:30 PM. 17 Rue Geoffroy L'Asniers, 4e (phone: 42-77-44-72). The French Government Tourist Office has published a booklet, *France for the Jewish Traveler,* that describes these two memorials, as well as other places of interest to Jews visiting France. See "Tourist Information" in *Sources and Resources,* GETTING READY TO GO, for a list of the offices in the US.

Musée des Antiquités Nationales – Archaeological specimens from prehistoric through Merovingian times, including an impressive Gallo-Roman collection. Open daily, except Tuesdays, from 9:30 AM to noon and 1:30 to 5:15 PM. Pl. du Château, St.-Germain-en-Laye, 14e (phone: 34-51-53-65).

Musée des Arts Africains et Océaniens – One of the world's finest collections of African and Oceanic art. Closed Tuesdays. 293 Av. Daumesnil, 12e (phone: 43-43-14-54).

Musée des Arts Décoratifs – Furniture and applied arts from the Middle Ages to the present, Oriental carpets, and Dubuffet paintings and drawings. Galerie Art Nouveau–Art Deco features Jeanne Lanvin's bedroom and bath. It also houses 3 centuries of French posters formerly displayed in the now-closed *Musée de l'Affiche et de la Publicité.* Closed Mondays and Tuesdays. 107 Rue de Rivoli, 1er (phone: 42-60-32-14).

Musée Cernuschi – Art of China. Closed Mondays and holidays. 7 Av. Vélasquez, 8e (phone: 45-63-50-75).

Musée de la Chasse et de la Nature – Art, weapons, and tapestries relating to the hunt. Of particular interest is the courtyard where horses once were kept — it is decorated with sculpture. Open daily except Tuesdays from 10 AM to 12:30 PM and 1:30 to 5:30 PM. 60 Rue des Archives, 3e (phone: 42-72-86-43).

Musée Cognacq-Jay – Art, snuffboxes, and watches from the 17th and 18th centuries. Closed Mondays. 8 Rue Elzévir, 3e (phone: 40-27-07-21).

Musée des Collections Historiques de la Préfecture de Police – On the second floor of the modern police precinct, in the 5th *arrondissement,* are historic arrest orders (for Charlotte Corday, among others), collections of contemporary engravings, and guillotine blades. Open Mondays through Saturdays from 9 AM to 5 PM. 1 *bis* Rue des Carmes, 5e (phone: 43-29-21-57).

Musée Eugène-Delacroix – Studio and garden of the great painter; exhibits change yearly. Closed Tuesdays. 6 Rue de Furstenberg, 6e (phone: 43-54-04-87).

Musée Grévin – Waxworks of French history from Charlemagne to the present day. 10 Bd. Montmartre, 9e (phone: 47-70-85-05). A branch devoted to *La Belle Epoque* is in the *Forum des Halles* shopping complex. Open daily. Pl. Carrée, 1er (phone: 40-26-28-50).

Musée Guimet – The *Louvre*'s Far East collection. Closed Tuesdays. 6 Pl. d'Iéna, 16e (phone: 47-23-61-65).

Musée Jacquemart-André – Eighteenth-century French decorative art and European Renaissance treasures, as well as frequent special exhibitions. Closed Mondays and Tuesdays. 158 Bd. Haussmann, 8e (phone: 42-89-04-91).

Musée Marmottan – Superb Monets, including the nine masterpieces that were stolen in a daring 1985 robbery. Happily, however, all were recovered in a villa in Corsica and have been cleaned — some for the first time — before being rehung. Closed Mondays. 2 Rue Louis-Boilly, 16e (phone: 42-24-07-02).

Musée de la Mode et du Costume – A panorama of French contributions to fashion in the elegant Palais Calliéra. Closed Mondays. 10 Av. Pierre-I de Serbie, 16e (phone: 47-20-85-23).

Musée de la Monnaie – More than 2,000 coins and 450 medallions, plus historic coinage machines. Open daily, except Mondays, from 1 to 6 PM. 11 Quai de Conti, 6e (phone: 40-46-55-33).

Musée Gustave-Moreau – A collection of the works of the early symbolist. Closed Mondays and Tuesdays. 14 Rue de la Rochefoucauld, 9e (phone: 48-74-38-50).

Musée Nissim de Camondo – A former manor house filled with beautiful furnishings and art objects from the 18th century. Closed Mondays, Tuesdays, and holidays. 63 Rue de Monceau, 8e (phone: 45-63-26-32).

Musée de Sèvres – Just outside Paris, next door to the Sèvres factory, is one of the world's finest collections of porcelain. Closed Tuesdays. 4 Grand-Rue, Sèvres (phone: 45-39-99-99).

Musée du Vin – Housed in a 13th-century abbey that was destroyed during the revolution, the museum was restored in 1981. The history and making of wine is traced through displays, artifacts, and a series of wax figure tableaux. Open daily, except Mondays, from noon to 6 PM; Saturdays and Sundays to 5:30 PM. Admission charge includes a glass of wine. 5-7 Sq. Charles-Dickens, 16e (phone: 45-25-63-26).

Parc Océanique Cousteau – Based on the work of the French oceanographer, this museum houses ocean exhibits and interactive displays. Open Mondays, Tuesdays, and Thursdays from noon to 7 PM; Wednesdays, Saturdays, Sundays, and holidays from 10 AM to 7:30 PM. *Forum des Halles,* Pl. Carrée, 1er (phone: 40-28-98-98).

Pavillon des Arts – An exhibition space in the mushroom-shaped buildings overlooking the *Forum des Halles* complex. Presentations range from ancient to modern, paintings to sculpture. Closed Mondays and holidays. 101 Rue Rambuteau, 1er (phone: 42-33-82-50).

 GALLERIES: Few artists live in Montparnasse nowadays, as the center of the Paris art scene has shifted from the narrow streets of the Latin Quarter, which set the pace in the 1950s, to the Right Bank around the *Centre Georges Pompidou.* Here are some galleries of note:

Agathe Gaillard – Contemporary photography, including Cartier-Bresson and the like. 3 Rue du Pont-Louis-Philippe, 4e (phone: 42-77-38-24).

Artcurial – Early moderns, such as Braque and Sonia Delaunay, as well as sculpture and prints, with a fine art bookshop. 9 Av. Matignon, 8e (phone: 42-99-16-16).

Beaubourg – Well-known names in the Paris art scene, including Niki de Saint-Phalle, César, Tinguely, Klossowski. 23 Rue du Renard, 4e (phone: 42-71-20-50).

Claude Bernard – Francis Bacon, David Hockney, and Raymond Mason are among the artists exhibited here. 5 Rue des Beaux-Arts, 6e (phone: 43-26-97-07).

Isy Brachot – Master surrealists, American hyper-realists, and new realists. 35 Rue Guénégaud, 6e (phone: 43-54-22-40).

Caroline Corre – Exhibitions by contemporary artists, specializing in unique artists' books. 14 Rue Guénégaud, 6e (phone: 43-54-57-67).

Daniel Malingue – Works by the Impressionists, as well as notable Parisian artists from the 1930s to the 1950s — Foujita, Fautrier, and so forth. 26 Av. Matignon, 8e (phone: 42-66-60-33).

Darthea Speyer – Run by a former American embassy attaché, now an art dealer. Contemporary painting. 6 Rue Jacques-Callot, 6e (phone: 43-54-78-41).

Hervé Odermatt Cazeau – Early moderns — among them Picasso, Léger, Pissarro — and antiques. 85 *bis* Rue du Faubourg-St.-Honoré, 8e (phone: 42-66-92-58).

Maeght-Lelong – The great moderns on display include Chagall, Tapies, Bacon, Moore, Miró. 13-14 Rue de Téhéran, 8e (phone: 45-63-13-19).

Nikki Diana Marquardt – Spacious gallery of contemporary work opened by an enterprising dealer from the Bronx. 9 Pl. des Vosges, 4e (phone: 42-78-21-00).

Virginia Zabriskie – Early and contemporary photography by Atget, Brassaï, Diane Arbus. Also painting and, occasionally, sculpture. 37 Rue Quincampoix, 4e (phone: 42-72-35-47).

 SHOPPING: From new wave fashions to classic haute couture, Paris starts the trends and sets the styles the world copies. Prices are generally high, but more than a few people are willing to pay for the quality of the products, not to mention the cachet of a Paris label, which enhances the appeal of many things besides clothing. Perfume, cosmetics, jewelry, leather goods and accessories, wine and liqueurs, porcelain, and art are among the many other things for which Paris is famous.

The big department stores are excellent places to get an idea of what's available. They include *Galeries Lafayette* (40 Bd. Haussmann, 9e; phone: 42-82-34-56; and other locations); *Au Printemps* (64 Bd. Haussmann, 9e; phone: 42-85-80-00); *Aux Trois Quartiers-Madelios* (17 Bd. de la Madeleine, 1er; phone: 42-60-39-30); *La Samaritaine* (19 Rue de la Monnaie, 1er; phone: 40-41-20-20); *Le Bazar de l'Hôtel de Ville* (52 Rue de Rivoli, 4e; phone: 42-74-90-00); and *Au Bon Marché* (22 Rue de Sèvres, 7e; phone: 45-49-21-22). Two major shopping centers — *Porte Maillot* (Pl. de la Porte Maillot) and *Maine Montparnasse* (at the intersection of Bd. Montparnasse and Rue de Rennes) — also are worth a visit.

There are several shopping neighborhoods, and they tend to be specialized. Haute couture can be found in the streets around the Champs-Elysées: Av. George-V, Av. Montaigne, Rue François-Ier, and Rue du Faubourg-St.-Honoré; famous designers are also represented in department stores. Boutiques are especially numerous on Av. Victor-Hugo, Rue de Passy, Bd. des Capucines, in the St.-Germain-des-Prés area, in the neighborhood of the *Opéra,* in the *Forum des Halles* shopping center, and around the Place des Victoires. The Rue d'Alésia has several blocks devoted solely to discount fashion shops.

The Rue de Paradis is lined with crystal and china shops, and St.-Germain-des-Prés has more than its share of art galleries. The best and most expensive antiques dealers are along the Faubourg-St.-Honoré on the Right Bank. On the Left Bank there's Le Carré Rive Gauche, an association of more than 100 antiques shops in the area bordered by Quai Voltaire, Rue de l'Université, Rue des Sts.-Pères, and Rue du Bac. Antiques and curio collectors should explore Paris's several flea markets, which include the *Montreuil,* near the Porte de Montreuil; *Vanves,* near the Porte de Vanves; and the largest and best known, *Puces de St.-Ouen,* near the Porte de Clignancourt.

A few more tips: Sales take place during the first weeks in January and in late June and July. Any shop labeled *dégriffé* (the word means, literally, "without the label") offers discounts on brand name clothing, often last season's styles. Discount shops also are known as "stock" shops. The French value-added tax (VAT; typically 18.6% and as high as 33.33% on luxury articles) can be refunded on most purchases made by foreigners provided a minimum of 1,200F (about $200) is spent in one store. Forms must be filled out and the refund usually is mailed to your home. Large department stores and the so-called duty-free shops have facilitated the procedure, but refunds can be obtained from any store willing to cooperate. If the refund is not exactly equal to the tax — 15% to 25% refunds are common — it's because stores may retain some of it as reimbursement for their extra expense in handling the paperwork.

Here is a sampling of the wealth of shops in Paris, many of which have more than one location in the city:

Agnès B – Supremely wearable, trendy, casual clothes. 3 and 6 Rue du Jour, 1er (phone: 40-26-36-87 or 45-08-56-56); 13 Rue Michelet, 6e (phone: 46-33-70-20); 25 Av. Pierre-I-de-Serbie, 16e (phone: 47-20-22-44); and 81 Rue d' Assas, 6e (phone: 43-54-69-21). The latter store is for children only.

Alfred Dunhill – Menswear, toiletries, and luggage articles from the celebrated English tobacconist. 15 Rue de la Paix, 2e (phone: 42-67-57-58).

Arnys – Conservative and elegant men's clothing. 14 Rue de Sèvres, 6e (phone: 45-48-76-99).

Azzedine Alaïa – The Tunisian designer who brought the body back. 14 Rue de la Verrerie, 4e (phone: 48-04-03-60).

Baccarat – High-quality porcelain and crystal. 30 *bis* Rue de Paradis, 10e (phone: 40-22-11-00).

La Bagagerie – Perhaps the best bag and belt boutique in the world. 12 Rue Tronchet, 8e (phone: 42-65-03-40), and other locations.

Au Bain Marie – The most beautiful kitchenware and tabletop accessories, with emphasis on Art Deco designs. 10 Rue Boissy-d'Anglas, 8e (phone: 42-66-59-74).

Balenciaga – Ready-to-wear and designer haute couture. 10 Av. George V, 8e (phone: 47-20-21-11).

Beauté Divine – Antique perfume bottles, Art Deco bathroom accessories, glove stretchers, nail buffers, and mustache cups. 40 Rue St.-Sulpice, 6e (phone: 43-26-25-31).

Brentano's – British and American novels, critiques on the American arts, and a variety of books on technical and business subjects — in English. 37 Av. de l'Opéra, 2e (phone: 42-61-52-50).

Cacharel – Fashionable ready-to-wear in great prints. 34 Rue Tronchet, 8e (phone: 47-42-12-61), and other locations.

Cadolle – Founded in 1889 by the woman credited with inventing the brassiere, it still sells corsets as well as other items of frilly, pretty lingerie. 14 Rue Cambon, 1er (phone: 42-60-94-94).

Carel – Beautiful shoes. 12 Rond-Point des Champs-Elysées, 8e (phone: 45-62-30-62), and other locations.

Carita – Paris's most extensive — and friendliest — beauty/hair salon. 11 Rue du Faubourg-St.-Honoré, 8e (phone: 42-68-13-40).

Cartier – Fabulous jewelry. 11-13 Rue de la Paix, 2e (phone: 42-61-58-56), and other locations.

Castorama – One of 86 stores throughout France, this department store sells 45,000

European-designed housewares — from flowerpots to home security systems. 1-3 Rue Caulaincourt, 18e (phone: 45-22-07-11).

Céline – A popular women's boutique for clothing and accessories. 3 Av. Victor-Hugo, 16e (phone: 47-20-22-83).

Cerruti – For women's clothing, 9 Pl. de la Madeleine, 8e (phone: 40-17-03-16); for men's, 27 Rue Royale, 8e (phone: 42-65-68-72).

Chanel – Classic women's fashions, inspired by the late, legendary Coco Chanel, now under the direction of Karl Lagerfeld. 42 Av. Montaigne, 8e (phone: 47-20-84-45) and 29-31 Rue Cambon, 1er (phone: 42-86-28-00).

Chantal Thomass – Ultra-feminine fashions, 5 Rue du Vieux-Colombier, 6e (phone: 45-44-60-11); sexy lingerie, 11 Rue Madame, 6e (phone: 45-49-41-29), and other locations.

Charles Jourdan – Sleek, high-fashion shoes. 5 Bd. de la Madeleine, 1er (phone: 42-61-50-07), is one of many branches.

Charley – Excellent selection of lingerie at fairly low prices. 14 Rue du Faubourg-St.-Honoré, 8e (phone: 47-42-17-70).

Charvet – Paris's answer to Savile Row. An all-in-one men's shop, where shirts are the house specialty — they stock more than 4,000. Ties, too. 28 Pl. Vendôme, 1er (phone: 42-60-30-70).

Chaumet – Crownmakers for most of Europe's royalty. Expensive jewels, including antique watches covered with semi-precious stones. 12 Pl. Vendôme, 1er (phone: 42-60-32-82) and 46 Av. George-V (phone: 49-52-08-25).

Chloé – Designs for women. 3 Rue de Gribeauval and 60 Rue du Faubourg-St.-Honoré, 8e (phone: 42-66-01-39).

Christian Dior – One of the most famous couture names in the world. 28-30 Av. Montaigne, 8e; *Miss Dior* and *Baby Dior* for children also are at this address (phone: 40-73-54-44).

Christian Lacroix – The first major new fashion house to open in Paris in 2 decades. Offers the "hautest" of haute couture. 73 Rue du Faubourg-St.-Honoré, 8e (phone: 42-65-79-08).

Christofle – The internationally famous silversmith. 9 Rue Royale, 8e (phone: 49-33-43-00).

Claude Montana – Ready-to-wear and haute couture from this au courant designer. 31 Rue de Grenelle, 7e (phone: 42-22-69-56).

Commes des Garçons – Asymmetrical-style clothing for *des filles* and *des garçons.* 40-42 Rue Etienne-Marcel, 1er (phone: 42-33-05-21).

Courrèges – Another bastion of haute couture, with its own boutique. 40 Rue François-I, 8e, and 46 Rue du Faubourg-St.-Honoré, 8e (phone: 47-23-00-73).

Daniel Hechter – Sportswear and casual clothing for men and women. 146 Bd. St.-Germain, 6e (phone: 43-26-96-36) and other locations.

Destination Paris – Glittering selection of knickknacks, hand-painted T-shirts, scarves, picture frames, and souvenirs. 9 Rue du 29 Juillet, 1er (phone: 49-27-98-90).

Dorothée Bis – Definitely a trendsetter in women's wear. 33 Rue de Sèvres, 6e (phone: 42-22-02-90).

Les Drugstores Publicis – A uniquely French version of the American drugstore, with an amazing variety of goods — perfume, books, records, foreign newspapers, magazines, film, cigarettes, food, and more, all wildly overpriced. 149 Bd. St.-Germain, 6e (phone: 42-22-92-50); 133 Av. des Champs-Elysées, 8e (phone: 47-23-54-34); and 1 Av. Matignon, 8e (phone: 43-59-38-70).

E. Dehillerin – An enormous selection of professional cookware. 18-20 Rue Coquillière, 1er (phone: 42-36-53-13).

Emanuel Ungaro – Couturier boutique for women. 2 Av. Montaigne, 8e (phone: 47-23-61-94).

Erès – Avant-garde sportswear for men and women. 2 Rue Tronchet, 8e (phone: 47-42-24-55).

Fabrice – Trendy, fine costume jewelry. 33 and 54 Rue Bonaparte, 6e (phone: 43-26-57-95).

Fauchon – *The* place to buy fine food and wine of every variety, from *oeufs en gêlée* to condiments and candy. 26-30 Pl. de la Madeleine, 8e (phone: 47-42-60-11).

Fouquet – Beautiful displays of chocolates, fresh fruit candies, herbs, condiments, and jams. 22 Rue François-I, 8e (phone: 47-23-30-46), and other locations.

France Faver – Top-quality beautiful and comfortable shoes for women. 79 Rue des Sts.-Pères, 6e (phone: 42-22-04-29).

Fratelli Rossetti – All kinds of shoes, made from buttery-soft leather, for men and women. 54 Rue du Faubourg-St.-Honoré, 8e (phone: 42-65-26-60).

Freddy – A popular shop for gifts, perfume, gloves, ties, scarves, and other items at good prices. 10 Rue Auber, 9e (phone: 47-42-63-41).

Galignani – Recently renovated, this shop sells books in English and French. It has been run by the same family since the beginning of the 19th century. 224 Rue de Rivoli, 1er (phone: 42-60-76-07).

La Gaminerie – Reasonably priced, good sportswear; outstanding window displays. 137 Bd. St.-Germain, 6e (phone: 43-26-27-98).

Givenchy – Beautifully tailored clothing by the master couturier. 3 Av. George-V, 8e (phone: 47-23-81-36).

Le Gourmet – The *Galeries Lafayette*'s chic, new grocery featuring exotic and high-priced food, wine, and confections from around the world. 40 Bd. Haussmann, 9e (phone: 48-74-37-13).

Guerlain – For fine perfume and cosmetics. 2 Pl. Vendôme, 1er; 68 Champs-Elysées, 8e (phone: 45-62-52-57); 29 Rue de Sèvres, 6e; and 93 Rue de Passy, 16e.

Guy Laroche – Classic and conservative couture. 30 Rue du Faubourg-St.-Honoré, 8e (phone: 42-65-62-74), and 29 Av. Montaigne, 8e (phone: 40-69-69-50).

Hanae Mori – The grande dame of Japanese designers in Paris. 17 Av. Montaigne, 8e (phone: 47-23-52-03); 9 Rue du Faubourg-St.-Honoré, 8e.

Hédiard – Pricey but choice food shop, notable for its assortment of coffees and teas. Chic tearoom upstairs. 21 Pl. de la Madeleine, 8e (phone: 42-66-44-36).

Hermès – For very high quality ties, scarves, handbags, shoes, saddles, and accessories, though the prices may send you into cardiac arrest. 24 Rue du Faubourg-St.-Honoré, 8e (phone: 40-17-47-17).

Hôtel Drouot – Paris's huge auction house operates daily except Sundays. Good buys. 9 Rue Drouot, 9e (phone: 48-00-20-20).

***IGN* (French National Geographic Institute)** – All manner of maps — ancient and modern, foreign and domestic, esoteric and mundane — are sold here. 136 *bis* Rue Grenelle, 7e (phone: 42-25-87-90); 107 Rue La Boétie, 8e.

Issey Miyake – "In" shop, selling women's clothing made by the Japanese artist-designer. Classic, more expensive line at 201 Bd. St.-Germain, 7e (phone: 45-44-60-88); latest collections at 3 Pl. des Vosges (phone: 48-87-01-86).

Jean-Louis Scherrer – A top designer, whose clothes are favored by the Parisian chic. 51-53 Av. Montaigne, 8e (phone: 45-59-55-39).

Jean-Paul Gaultier – Designer clothes for men and women. 6 Rue Vivienne, 2e (phone: 42-86-05-05).

Kenzo – Avant-garde fashions by the Japanese designer. 3 Pl. des Victoires, 1er (phone: 40-39-72-02).

Lachaume – Stem for stem, the most beautiful flower shop in Paris. Buy a bouquet for an *ami(e)* or for *vous-même.* 10 Rue Royale, 8e (phone: 42-60-57-26).

Lalique – The famous crystal. 11 Rue Royale, 8e (phone: 42-65-33-70).

Lancôme – Cosmetics. 29 Rue du Faubourg-St.-Honoré, 8e (phone: 42-65-30-74).

Lanvin – Another fabulous designer, with several spacious, colorful boutiques under one roof. 15 and 22 Rue du Faubourg-St.-Honoré, 8e (phone: 42-65-14-40); 2 Rue Cambon, 1er (phone: 42-60-38-83).

Laura Ashley – The English designer's familiar Victorian styles. 94 Rue des Rennes, 6e (phone: 42-22-77-80); and 261 Rue St.-Honoré, 1er (phone: 42-86-84-13).

Louis Féraud – Couturier fashions for women at 88 Rue du Faubourg-St.-Honoré, and men at No. 62, 8e (phone: 40-07-01-16); and other locations.

Louis Vuitton – High-quality luggage and handbags. 78 *bis* Av. Marceau, 8e (phone: 47-20-47-00), and 54 Av. Montaigne, 8e (phone: 45-62-47-00).

Marché aux Puces – Paris's famous *Flea Market,* with 3,000 dealers in antiques and secondhand items. Open Saturdays, Sundays, and Mondays. Bargaining is a must. Porte de Clignancourt, 18e.

Marie Papier – Handsome marbled stationery and writing accessories. 26 Rue Vavin, 6e (phone: 43-26-46-44).

Marithé & François Girbaud – Not just jeans at this shop for men and women. 33 Rue Etienne-Marcel, 2e (phone: 42-33-54-69).

Maud Frizon – Sophisticated, imaginative shoes and handbags. 83 Rue des Sts.-Pères, 6e (phone: 42-22-06-93 or 42-22-19-86).

Missoni – Innovative, original Italian knitwear. 43 Rue du Bac, 7e (phone: 45-48-38-02).

Monique Germain – Unique hand-painted silk clothing at affordable prices: cocktail dresses, bridal wear, padded patchwork jackets. 59 Bd. Raspail, 6e (phone: 45-48-22-63).

Morabito – Magnificent handbags and luggage at steep prices. 1 Pl. Vendôme, 1er (phone: 42-60-30-76).

Le Must de Cartier – Actually two boutiques, on either side of the *Ritz* hotel, offering such Cartier items as lighters and watches at prices that, though not low, are almost bearable when you deduct the 25% VAT tax. 7 23 Pl. Vendôme, 1er (phone: 42-61-55-55).

Au Nain Bleu – The city's greatest toy store. 408 Rue St.-Honoré, 8e (phone: 42-60-30-01).

Nina Ricci – Women's fashions, as well as the famous perfume. 17 Rue François-I, 8e (phone: 47-23-78-88), and 39 Av. Montaigne, 8e (phone: 47-23-78-88).

Paloma Picasso – Perfume, clothing, and jewelry from one of France's preeminent designers and you-know-who's-daughter. 5 Rue de la Paix, 2e (phone: 42-86-02-21).

Per Spook – One of Paris's best young designers. 18 Av. George-V, 8e (phone: 47-23-00-19), and elsewhere.

Le Petit Faune – A marvelous place to buy children's things. 33 Rue Jacob, 6e (phone: 42-60-80-72), and other locations.

Au Petit Matelot – Classic sportswear, outdoor togs, and nautical accessories for men, women, and children. Especially terrific are their Tyrolean-style olive or navy loden coats. 27 Av. de la Grande-Armée, 16e (phone: 45-00-15-51).

Pierre Balmain – Couturier boutique for women's fashions, jewelry, and accessories. 44 Rue François-Ier, 8e (phone: 47-20-35-34), and other locations.

Pierre Cardin – A famous designer's own boutique. 83 Rue du Faubourg-St.-Honoré, 8e (phone: 42-66-62-94); 27 Av. Victor-Hugo, 16e (phone: 45-01-88-13); 14 Pl. François-Ier, 8e (phone: 45-63-29-13) and other locations.

Pixi & Cie – Terrific collection of dolls, toy soldiers, and antique windup cars. 95 Rue de Seine, 6e (phone: 43-25-10-12).

Porthault – Terribly expensive, but elegantly exquisite bed and table linen. 18 Av. Montaigne, 8e (phone: 47-20-75-25).

Puiforcat – Art Deco tableware in a beautiful setting. 22 Rue François-I, 8e (phone: 47-20-74-27).

Raymond – Charming and fairly inexpensive Porcelaine de Paris items. 100 Rue du Faubourg-St.-Honoré, 1er (phone: 42-66-69-49).

Romeo Gigli – Men's arty ready-to-wear and haute couture. 46 Rue de Sévigné, 3e (phone: 42-71-08-40).

Sabbia Rosa – Simple, chic, and sexy lingerie is sold in this tiny shop on the Left Bank. 73 Rue des Sts.-Pères (phone: 45-48-88-37).

Shakespeare and Company – This legendary English-language bookstore, opposite Notre-Dame, is something of a tourist attraction in itself. 37 Rue de la Bûcherie, 5e (no phone).

Sonia Rykiel – Stunning sportswear and knits. 70 Rue du Faubourg-St.-Honoré, 8e (phone: 42-65-20-81).

Souleiado – Vibrant, traditional Provençal fabrics made into scarves, shawls, totes, and tableware. 78 Rue de Seine, 6e (phone: 43-54-62-25), and *Forum des Halles,* Pl. Carrée, 1er.

Ted Lapidus – A compromise between haute couture and excellent ready-to-wear. 23 Rue du Faubourg-St.-Honoré, 8e (phone: 44-60-89-91); 35 Rue François-I, 8e (phone: 47-20-56-14); and other locations.

Thierry Mugler – Dramatic ready-to-wear for women. 49 Av. Montaigne, 8e (phone: 47-23-37-62).

Torrente – Women's fashions. 60 Av. Montaigne, 8e (phone: 42-56-14-14).

Upla – Sporty handbags, scarves, and casual clothing. 17 Rue des Halles, 1er (phone: 40-26-49-96).

Valentino – Ready-to-wear and haute couture fashions for men and women from the Italian designer. 17-19 Av. Montaigne, 8e (phone: 47-23-64-61).

Van Cleef & Arpels – One of the world's great jewelers. 22 Pl. Vendôme, 1er (phone: 42-61-58-58).

Vicky Tiel – Strapless evening gowns decorated with beads and bows, as well as contemporary sweaters and baseball-style jackets. 21 Rue Bonaparte, 6e (phone: 46-33-53-58).

Victoire – Ready-to-wear, with attractive accessories. 12 Pl. des Victoires, 2e (phone: 47-04-49-87), and other locations.

W. H. Smith and Sons – The largest (and best) Parisian bookstore for reading material in English. It sells the Sunday *New York Times,* in addition to many British and American magazines and books. 248 Rue de Rivoli, 1er (phone: 42-60-37-97).

Yves Saint Laurent – The world-renowned designer, considered one of the most famous names in high fashion. 38 Rue du Faubourg-St.-Honoré, 8e (phone: 42-65-74-59); 5 Av. Marceau, 8e (phone: 47-23-72-71); 6 Pl. St.-Suplice (phone: 43-29-43-00); and other locations.

BEST DISCOUNT SHOPS

If you're one of those — like us — who believes that the eighth deadly sin is buying retail, you'll treasure these inexpensive outlets.

Anna Lowe – Saint Laurent's styling, among others, at a discount. 35 Av. Matignon, 8e (phone: 45-63-45-57).

Bab's – High fashion at low — or at least reasonable — prices. 29 Av. Marceau, 16e (phone: 47-20-84-74), and 89 *bis* Av. des Ternes, 17e.

Boétie 104 – Good buys on men's and women's shoes. 104 Rue La Boétie, 8e (phone: 43-59-72-38).

Boutique Stock – A vast selection of big-name knits at less than wholesale. 26, 30, and 51 Rue St.-Placide, 6e (phone: 45-48-83-66).

Cacharel Stock – Surprisingly current Cacharel fashions at about a 40% discount. 114 Rue d'Alésia, 14e (phone: 45-42-53-04).

Catherine – One of the most hospitable of the perfume and cosmetics shops. A 40% discount (including VAT) is given on purchases totaling 1,500F (about $250) or more. 6 Rue Castiglione, 1er (phone: 42-60-81-49).

Catherine Baril – Women's ready-to-wear by designers such as Yves Saint Laurent and Jean-Louis Scherrer. 14-15 Rue de la Tour, 16e (phone: 45-20-95-21).

Dorothée Bis Stock – Ms. Bis's well-known designs at about 40% off. 74 Rue d'Alésia, 14e (phone: 45-42-17-11).

Drôles des Choses pour Drôles de Gens – Half-price clothes by Marithé and François Girbaud. 33 Rue Etienne-Marcel, 1er (phone: 43-72-15-23).

Emmanuelle Khanh – The designer's clothes at a substantial discount. 6 Rue Pierre-Lescot, 1er (no phone).

Griff 'Mod – Names like Laroche and Lapidus at sale prices. 20 Rue Petit-Champs, 2e (phone: 42-97-47-45).

Jean-Louis Scherrer – Haute couture labels by Scherrer and others at about half their original prices. 29 Av. Ledru-Rollin, 12e (phone: 46-28-39-27).

Lady Soldes – Prime fashion labels at less than normal prices. 221 Rue du Faubourg-St.-Honoré, 8e (phone: 45-61-09-14).

Lanvin Soldes Trois – Lanvin fashions at about half their normal retail cost. 3 Rue de Vienne, 8e (no phone).

Mendès – Less than wholesale prices on haute couture, especially Saint Laurent and Lanvin. 65 Rue Montmartre, 2e (phone: 45-08-52-62 or 42-36-83-32).

Michel Swiss – Huge selection of perfume, cheerful service, and discounts of almost 44% to American visitors who pay with cash or traveler's checks, and who buy more than 1200 frances ($200) of scents. 16 Rue de la Paix, 2e (phone: 42-61-71-71).

Miss Griffes – The very best of haute couture in small sizes (up to size 10) at small prices. Alterations. 19 Rue de Penthièvre, 8e (phone: 42-65-10-00).

Le Mouton à Cinq Pattes – Ready-to-wear clothing for men, women, and children at 50% off original prices. At 8, 10, and 14 Rue St.-Placide, 6e (phone: 45-48-86-26).

Pierre Cardin Stock – Terrific buys on the famed designer's men's clothing. 72 Rue St.-Honoré, 1er (phone: 40-26-74-73).

Réciproque – Billed as the largest *"depot-vent"* in Paris, this outlet features names like Chanel, Alaia, Lanvin, and Scherrer. Several hundred square yards of display area are arranged by designer and by size. 95 Rue de la Pompe, 16e (phone: 47-04-82-24); men's clothing and accessories next door at No. 101. New boutiques are at Nos. 89, 91, and 123 Rue de la Pompe.

Stéphane – Men's designer suits by Pierre Balmain, Ted Lapidus, and André Courrèges at 25% to 45% discount. 130 Bd. St.-Germain, 6e (phone: 46-33-94-55).

Stock Coupons – Features discounted Daniel Hechter for men, women, and children. 92 Rue d'Alésia, 14e (phone: 45-42-82-66).

Stock Griffes – Women's ready-to-wear apparel at 40% off their original prices. 17 Rue Vielle du Temple, 4e (phone: 48-04-82-34) and 1 Rue des Trois-Frères (phone: 42-55-42-49).

Stock System – Prêt-à-porter clothing for men and women at a 30% discount. 112 Rue d'Alésia, 14e (phone: 45-43-80-86).

Also, Rue du Paradis (10e) is the best area to shop for crystal and porcelain — Baccarat, Saint-Louis, Haviland, Bernardaud, and Villeroy & Boch — at amazing prices. Try *Cristalerie de Paris* at No. 10; *Boutique Paradis,* 1 *bis; L'Art et La Table,* 3; *Limoges-Unio,* Nos. 8 and 12; *Porcelain Savary,* 9; *Arts Céramiques,* 15; and *Cristallerie Paradis,* at No. 17.

■ *Note*: For a modest price ($15 and up), you can also take home a bit of the *Louvre*. The museum's 200-year-old Department of Calcography houses a collection of

16,000 engraved copper plates — renderings of monuments, battles, coronations, Egyptian pyramids, and portraits — dating from the 17th century. Prints made from these engravings come reproduced on thick vellum, embossed with the *Louvre*'s imprint. The Calcography Department (open daily, except Tuesdays, from 2 to 5 PM), is 1 flight up from the Porte Barbet de Jouy entrance on the Seine side of the *Louvre*.

 SPORTS AND FITNESS: Biking – Rentals are available in the Bois de Boulogne and the Bois de Vincennes, or contact the *Fédération Française de Cyclo-tourisme* (8 Rue Jean-Marie-Jégo, 13e; phone: 45-80-30-21); *Bicyclub* (8 Pl. de la Porte Champerret, 17e; phone: 47-66-55-92); or *Paris-Vélo* (2 Rue du Fer à Moulin, 5e; phone: 43-37-59-22). In addition to renting bicycles, *Paris by Cycle* (99 Rue la Jonquière; phone: 42-63-36-63) arranges guided group tours of the city, Versailles, and bike trips alternating with horseback rides. The world-famous *Tour de France* bicycle race takes place in July and ends in Paris.

Fitness Centers – The *Garden Gym* (26 Rue de Berri, 8e; phone: 43-59-04-58; and 123 Av. Charles-de-Gaulle, Neuilly; phone: 47-47-62-62) is open daily to non-members for a fee.

Golf – For general information, contact the *Fédération Française du Golf* (69 Av. Victor-Hugo, 16e; phone: 45-02-13-55). It usually is possible to play on any course during the week by simply paying a greens fee. Weekends may be more difficult. *Ozoir-la-Ferrière* (Château des Agneaux, 15 miles — 24 km — away; phone: 60-28-20-79) welcomes Americans (closed Tuesdays); and *St.-Germain-en-Laye* (12½ miles — 19 km — away; phone: 34-51-75-90) accepts non-members on weekdays only (closed Mondays). The *Racing Club de France* (La Boulie, Versailles; phone: 39-50-59-41) and *St.-Nom-la-Bretèche* (in the suburb of the same name; phone: 34-62-54-00) accept only guests of members. It's best to call at least 2 days in advance to schedule a time.

Horse Racing – Of the eight tracks in and around Paris, two major ones are in the Bois de Boulogne: *Longchamp* (phone: 42-24-13-29) for flat races and *Auteuil* (phone: 45-27-12-25) for steeplechase. *St.-Cloud* (phone: 43-59-20-70), a few miles west of Paris, and *Chantilly* (phone: 42-66-92-02), about 25 miles (40 km) north of the city, are both for flat racing. *Vincennes* (Bois de Vincennes; phone: 47-42-07-70) is the trotting track. Important races take place from spring through fall, but the *Grande Semaine* (Big Week) comes in mid-June, when nine major races — beginning with the *Grand Steeplechase de Paris* at *Auteuil* and including the *Grand Prix de Paris* at *Longchamp* — are scheduled.

Jogging – The streets and sidewalks of Paris may be ideal for lovers, but they're not meant for runners. There are, however, a number of places where you can jog happily; one of the most pleasant is the 2,500-acre Bois de Boulogne. Four more central parks are the Jardin du Luxembourg (reachable by métro: Luxembourg), the Champ-de-Mars gardens (just behind the Eiffel Tower; métro: Iéna), Parc Monceau (métro: Monceau), and the Jardin des Tuileries (métro: Tuileries, Louvre, or Concorde).

Soccer – There are matches from early August to mid-June at Parc des Princes (Av. du Parc-des-Princes, 16e; phone: 42-88-02-76).

Swimming – At the heart of Paris, rather unsuitably near the National Assembly, lies the *Piscine Deligny,* notorious in the summer for its acres of topless women bathers and, on the top deck, nude sunbathers of both sexes. The pool is set in a floating barge on the Seine beside the Concorde bridge; it is, says the sign, filled with fresh water. Open May to September. 25 Quai Anatole-France, 7e (phone: 45-51-72-15). Other pools include *Piscine des Halles* (10 Pl. de la Rotonde, 4e; phone: 42-36-98-44), *Pontoise* (19 Rue de Pontoise, 5e; phone: 43-54-06-23), *Butte-aux-Cailles* (5 Pl. Paul-Verlaine, 13e; phone: 45-89-60-05), *Keller* (14 Rue de l'Ingénieur-Robert-Keller, 15e; phone: 45-77-12-12), *Jean-Taris* (16 Rue Thouin, 5e; phone: 43-25-54-03), *Tour Montparnasse* (beneath the tower at 66 Bd. de Montparnasse, 15e; phone: 45-38-65-19), and *Neuilly* (50 Rue Pauline-Borghèse, Neuilly; phone: 47-22-69-59).

Tennis – For general information, call *Ligue Régionale de Paris* (74 Rue de Rome, 17e; phone: 45-22-22-08), or the *Fédération Française de Tennis* (*Roland Garros Stadium,* 16e; phone: 47-43-48-00). Americans who wish to attend the annual *French Open Tennis Tournament* may write in advance to the *Fédération Française de Tennis Billetterie* (Service Réservation, BP 33316, Paris 75767; phone: 47-43-48-00).

 THEATER: The most complete listings of theaters, operas, concerts, and movies are found in the *Officiel des Spectacles* and *Une Semaine à Paris–Pariscope* (see *Tourist Information,* above). The season generally is from September to June. Tickets are less expensive than in New York and are obtained at each box office, through brokers (*American Express* and *Thomas Cook* act in that capacity and are good), via your hotel's trusty concierge, or with the high-tech Billetels at the *Galeries Lafayette,* the *Centre Georges Pompidou,* and other locations. Insert a credit card into a slot in the Billetel and choose an event from among over 100 upcoming theater events and concert performances. The device will spew out a display of dates, seats, and prices, from which you can order your tickets — they will be printed on the spot and charged to your account. Half-price, day-of-performance theater tickets are available at the kiosks at the Châtelet-les Halles, 1er (Tuesdays through Saturdays from 12:45 to 7 PM), and at 15 Place de la Madeleine, 8e (Tuesdays through Saturdays from 12:30 to 8 PM, Sundays from 12:30 to 4 PM). The curtain usually goes up at 8:30 PM.

For those who speak French: Performances of classical plays by Molière, Racine, and Corneille take place at the *Comédie-Française* (Pl. du Théâtre, 1er; phone: 40-15-00-15). Two other national theaters are *Théâtre de L'Odéon* (1 Pl. Paul-Claudel, 6e; phone: 43-25-70-32) and *Théâtre National de Chaillot* (Pl. du Trocadéro, 16e; phone: 47-27-81-15). Last, but not least, the *Théâtre du Soleil,* in an old cartridge factory, La Cartoucherie de Vincennes (on the outskirts of Paris in the Bois de Vincennes, 12e; phone: 43-74-24-08), offers colorful productions ranging from contemporary political works to Shakespeare.

It's not really necessary to speak the language to enjoy the opera, dance, or musical comedy at *L'Opéra* (Pl. de l'Opéra, 9e; phone: 47-42-57-50 or 47-42-53-71), the new *L'Opéra Bastille* (120 Rue de Lyon in the Pl. de la Bastille, 11e; phone: 40-01-17-89 or 40-01-16-16), *Salle Favart–Opéra Comique* (5 Rue Favart, 2e; phone: 42-86-88-83), or *Théâtre Musical de Paris* (1 Pl. du Châtelet, 1er; phone: 40-28-28-40). Theater tickets can be reserved through *SOS-Théâtre* (73 Champs-Elysées, 8e; phone: 42-25-67-07).

For those who consider French their second language, Paris's many café-theaters offer amusing songs, sketches, satires, and takeoffs on topical trends and events. Among them are *Café de la Gare* (41 Rue du Temple, 4e; phone: 42-78-52-51) and *Café d'Edgar* (58 Bd. Edgar-Quinet, 14e; phone: 43-22-11-02).

 CINEMA: With no less than 200 movie houses, Paris is a real treat for film buffs. No other metropolis offers such a cinematographic feast — current French chic, recent imports from across the Atlantic, grainy 1930s classics, and the latest and most select of Third World and Eastern European offerings. In any given week, there are up to 200 different movies shown, generally in their original versions with French subtitles.

Film distribution is erratic, to say the least, so the French often get their *Silence of the Lambs* and *Goodfellas* flicks up to 6 months late. But the system works both ways: Many of the front-runners at Cannes first hit the screens here, which gives you a jump on friends back home.

Both *Pariscope* and the *Officiel de Spectacles,* which come out on Wednesday, the day the programs change, contain the full selection each week. *Pariscope* has thought of almost every possible way to classify films, sorting them into new releases and revivals, broad categories (for instance, the *drame psychologique* label means it will be heavier than a *comédie dramatique*), location by *arrondissement,* late-night showings, and so on.

Films shown with their original-language sound tracks are called VO (*version originale*); it's worth watching out for that crucial "VO" tag, or you may find yourself wincing at a French-dubbed version, called VF (*version française*). Broadly speaking, the undubbed variety of film flourishes on the Champs-Elysées and on the Left Bank, and it's also a safe bet to avoid the mostly French-patronized houses of les Grands Boulevards.

The timetables aren't always reliable, so it's worth checking by telephone — if you can decipher the recorded messages that spell out exactly when the five or so showings a day begin. A *séance* (sitting) generally begins with advertisements, and the movie proper begins 15 to 20 minutes later.

There's more room in the big movie houses on the Champs-Elysées, but the cozier Latin Quarter establishments tend to specialize in the unusual and avant-garde — often the only showing such films will ever get. For the ultimate in high-tech, the *Géode* offers a B-Max hemispherical screen, cupped inside a reflecting geodesic dome, at La Villette Sciences and Industry complex. The program is, however, limited to a single scientifically oriented film at any given time, whereas the *Forum Horizon,* in the underground section of the *Forum des Halles,* offers a choice of four first-run movies and claims to have one of the city's best sound systems. Some more out-of-the-way venues like the *Olympique Entrepôt* and the *Lucernaire* in Montparnasse are social centers in themselves, incorporating restaurants and/or other theaters.

Paris's *Cinémathèque* — at the Palais de Chaillot — runs a packed schedule of reruns at rates lower than those of the commercial cinemas. The *Videothèque de Paris,* in the *Forum des Halles,* was the world's first public video library. Visitors can select individual showings or attend regularly scheduled theater screenings of films and television programs chronicling Paris's history (phone: 40-26-34-30).

Then there are two period pieces almost worth a visit in themselves. *Le Ranelagh* (5 Rue des Vignes, 16e; phone: 42-88-64-44) has an exquisite 19th-century interior where films are screened and live theater performed. *La Pagode* (57 *bis* Rue de Babylone, 7e; phone: 47-05-12-15), with flying cranes, cherry blossoms, and a tearoom, is built around a Japanese temple that was shipped over to Paris by the proprietor of a department store in the 1920s.

MUSIC: The *Orchestre de Paris,* under the direction of Daniel Barenboim, is based at the *Salle Pleyel* — the *Carnegie Hall* of Paris (252 Rue du Faubourg-St.-Honoré, 8e; phone: 48-24-12-33). Other classical recitals are held at the *Salle Gaveau* (45 Rue La Boétie; phone: 49-53-05-07), at the *Théâtre des Champs-Elysées* (15 Av. Montaigne, 8e; phone: 47-20-36-37), and at the *Palais des Congrès* (Porte Maillot; phone: 46-40-22-22). The *Orchestre Philharmonic* performs at a variety of places, including the *Grand Auditorium* at *Maison de Radio France* (116 Av. du Président J.-F.-Kennedy; phone: 42-30-15-16 or 42-30-18-18). Special concerts frequently are held in Paris's many places of worship, with moving music at High Mass on Sundays. The *Palais des Congrès* and the *Olympia* (28 Bd. des Capucines; phone: 47-42-82-45) are the places to see well-known international pop and rock artists. Innovative contemporary music — much of it created by computer — is the province of the *Institut de Recherche et de Coopération Acoustique Musique (IRCAM),* whose musicians can be heard in various auditoriums of the *Centre Georges Pompidou* (31 Rue St.-Merri; phone: 42-77-12-33).

NIGHTCLUBS AND NIGHTLIFE: Organized "Paris by Night" group tours (*Cityrama, Paris Vision,* and other operators offer them; see *Special Places*) include at least one "Spectacle" — beautiful girls in minimal, yet elaborate, costumes, with lavish sets and effects and sophisticated striptease. Most music halls offer a package (starting as high as $120 per person), with dinner, dancing, and a half-bottle of champagne. It is possible to go to these places on your own, save money by skipping dinner and the champagne (both usually way below par), and take a seat at the bar to see the show. The most famous extravaganzas occur nightly at *Crazy Horse* (12 Av. George-V, 8e; phone: 47-23-32-32), *Folies-Bergère* (32 Rue Richer, 9e; phone: 42-46-77-11), *Lido* (116 *bis* Champs-Elysées, 8e; phone: 40-76-56-10), *Moulin Rouge* (Pl. Blanche, 18e; phone: 46-06-00-19), and *Paradis Latin* (28 Rue du Cardinal-Lemoine, 5e; phone: 43-29-07-07). An amusing evening can also be spent at smaller cabaret shows like *René Cousinier* (*La Branlette;* 4 Impasse Marie-Blanche, 18e; phone: 46-06-49-46), *Au Lapin Agile* (22 Rue des Saules, 18e; phone: 46-06-85-87), and *Michou* (80 Rue des Martyrs, 18e; phone: 46-06-16-04). Reserve all a few days in advance.

Discotheque or private club, there's one big difference. Fashionable "in" spots like *Le Palace* (8 Rue Faubourg-Montmartre, 9e; phone: 42-46-10-87), *Régine's* (49 Rue de Ponthieu, 8e; phone: 43-59-21-60), *Chez Castel* (15 Rue Princesse, 6e, members only; phone: 43-26-90-22), *Olivia Valère* (40 Rue de Colisée, 8e, members only; phone: 42-25-11-68), *Les Bains* (7 Rue du Bourg-l'Abbé, 3e; phone: 48-87-01-80), and *Elysées Matignon* (48 Av. Gabriel, 8e; phone: 42-25-73-13) superscreen potential guests. No reason is given for accepting some and turning others away; go here with a regular or look as if you'd fit in with the crowd. Go early and on a weeknight — when your chances of getting past the gatekeeper are at least 50-50. Don't despair if you're refused; the following places are just as much fun and usually more hospitable: *La Scala* (188 *bis* Rue de Rivoli; phone: 42-61-64-00), *L'Aventure* (122 Rue d'Assas, 6e; phone: 46-34-22-60), and *L'Ecume des Nuits* (*Hôtel Méridien,* 81 Bd. Gouvion-St.-Cyr, 17e; phone: 40-68-30-89).

Some pleasant, popular bars for a nightcap include *Bar de la Closerie des Lilas* (171 Bd. Montparnasse, 6e; phone: 43-26-70-50), *Harry's New York Bar* (5 Rue Daunou, 2e; phone: 42-61-71-14), *Fouquet's* (99 Champs-Elysées, 8e; phone: 47-23-70-60), *Ascot Bar* (66 Rue Pierre-Charron, 8e; phone: 43-59-28-15), *Bar Anglais* (*Plaza-Athénée Hôtel,* 25 Av. Montaigne, 8e; phone: 47-23-78-33), and *Pub Winston Churchill* (5 Rue de Presbourg, 16e; phone: 45-00-75-35).

Jazz buffs have a large choice with *Caveau de la Huchette* (5 Rue de la Huchette, 5e; phone: 43-26-65-05), *Le Bilboquet* (13 Rue St.-Benoit, 6e; phone: 45-48-81-84), *New Morning* (7-9 Rue des Petites Ecuries, 10e; phone: 45-23-51-41), and *Le Petit Journal* (71 Bd. St.-Michel, 6e; phone: 43-26-28-59).

Enghien-les-Bains, 8 miles (13 km) away, is the only casino in the Paris vicinity (3 Av. de Ceinture, Enghien-les-Bains; phone: 34-12-90-00). Open 3 PM to about 4 AM, it easily can be reached by train from the Gare du Nord.

BEST IN TOWN

CHECKING IN: Paris offers a broad choice of accommodations, from luxurious palaces with every service to more humble budget hotels. However, they all are strictly controlled by the government and must post their rates, so you can be sure that the price you are being charged is correct. Below is our selection from all categories; in general, expect to spend at least $300 and way up per night for a double room in the "palace" hotels, which we've listed as very expensive; from $200 to $300 in the expensive range; $100 to $200 is considered moderate; $50 to $100 is inexpensive; and $50 or less is very inexpensive (a miracle!).

Except for July, August, and December, the least crowded months, hotel rooms usually are at a premium in Paris. To reserve your first choice, we advise making reservations at least a month in advance, even farther ahead for the smaller, less expensive places listed. Watch for the dates of special events, when hotels are even more crowded than usual. The apartment rentals offered by *Paris Accueil/Paris Séjour* are an alternative to the hotel options listed here (see *Accommodations*, GETTING READY TO GO).

Street addresses of the hotels below are followed by the number of their *arrondissement* (neighborhood).

Bristol – A palace with a special, almost intimate cachet. Service is impeccable, as are the 188 spacious, quiet rooms and huge, marble baths. The beautiful little restaurant and comfortable lobby cocktail lounge are additional pleasures. There also is another wing with a heated swimming pool on the sixth-floor terrace. Business facilities include 24-hour room service, meeting rooms for up to 100, English-speaking concierge, foreign currency exchange, secretarial services in English, audiovisual equipment, photocopiers, computers, cable television news service, and translation services. Major credit cards accepted. 112 Rue du Faubourg-St.-Honoré, 8e (phone: 42-66-91-45; from the US, 800-223-6800; fax: 42-66-68-68; telex: 280961). Very expensive.

Crillon – No sign out front, just discreet gold "C's" on the doors, it is currently the only "palace" hotel in Paris still owned by a Frenchman. The rooms on the Place de la Concorde side, though rather noisy, have the view of views; rooms facing the courtyards are just as nice and much more tranquil. The popular bar and 2 elegant restaurants, *L'Obélisque* and *Les Ambassadeurs* (which rates two Michelin stars), often are frequented by journalists and US and British embassy personnel. Business facilities include 24-hour room service, meeting rooms for up to 150, English-speaking concierge, foreign currency exchange, secretarial services in English, audiovisual equipment, photocopiers, computers, cable television news, translation services, and express checkout. Major credit cards accepted. 10 Pl. de la Concorde, 8e (phone: 42-65-24-24; fax: 47-42-72-10; telex: 290204). Very expensive.

George V – This nonpareil pick of movie moguls and international tycoons has 288 elegantly traditional or handsome contemporary rooms and 63 suites: some, facing the lovely courtyard, have their own balconies; those on the upper floors, a nice view. And there are 2 recently renovated restaurants, *Les Princes* and a grill, as well as a tearoom. One of the liveliest and chicest bars in the city is here, with a bartender who mixes a mean martini. The patio is a summer delight. Business facilities include 24-hour room service, meeting rooms for up to 20, English-speaking concierge, foreign currency exchange, secretarial services in English, audiovisual equipment, photocopiers, computers, cable television news, translation services, and express checkout. Major credit cards accepted. 31 Av. George-V, 8e (phone: 47-23-54-00; fax: 47-20-40-00; telex: 650082). Very expensive.

Meurice – Refined Louis XV and XVI elegance and a wide range of services are offered at prices slightly below those of the other "palaces." The hotel, a member of the CIGA chain, has 187 rooms and especially nice suites, a popular bar, a restaurant, *Le Meurice* (which was recently renovated and moved to a *grand salon* overlooking the Rue de Rivoli), and the chandeliered *Pompadour* tearoom. The location and hospitality couldn't be better, and the first-floor public room has been restored. Business facilities include 24-hour room service, meeting rooms for up to 150, English-speaking concierge, foreign currency exchange, secretarial services in English, audiovisual equipment, photocopiers, computers, cable television news, and translation services. Major credit cards accepted. 228 Rue de Rivoli, 1er (phone: 42-60-38-60; fax: 49-27-94-91; telex: 220256). Very expensive.

Plaza-Athénée – One of the legendary hotels, this favorite of the sophisticated seeking serene surroundings and superior service has 218 rooms, some now being refurbished. This is an haute bastion that takes its dignity very seriously (a discreet note in each bathroom offers an unobtrusive route in and out of the hotel for those in jogging togs). The *Relais* tables are much in demand at lunch and late supper, and the two-star *Régence,* summer patio, tea tables, and downstairs English bar are places to see and be seen. Business facilities include 24-hour room service, meeting rooms for up to 120, English-speaking concierge, foreign currency exchange, secretarial services in English, audiovisual equipment, photocopiers, computers, translation services, and express checkout. Major credit cards accepted. 25 Av. Montaigne, 8e (phone: 47-23-78-33; fax: 47-20-20-70; telex: 650092). Very expensive.

Relais Carré d'Or – For those visitors who are in Paris for a long stay, this hostelry (with all the amenities of a luxury hotel) provides a variety of accommodations — from studios to multi-room apartments — all with modern kitchens, marble bathrooms, and lovely, understated furnishings. Most have a balcony overlooking the hotel's garden or Avenue George-V. Business facilities include 24-hour room service, meeting rooms for up to 30, English-speaking concierge, foreign currency exchange, secretarial services in English, audiovisual equipment, photocopiers, computers, cable television, translation services, and express checkout. Major credit cards accepted. 46 Av. George-V, 8e (phone: 40-70-05-05; fax: 47-23-30-90; telex: 640561). Very expensive.

Résidence Maxim's – Pierre Cardin's luxurious venture is located near the Elysée Palace. No expense has been spared here to create sybaritic splendor. The 40 suites range in style from sleek modern to Belle Epoque, with original Art Nouveau pieces from Cardin's own collections, and every bathroom has been individually designed. *Atmosphère,* its restaurant, has made a name in the city, and has a pleasant terrace in summer; *La Tonnelle* serves breakfast, and doubles as a tea salon; and the bar, *Le Maximin,* is open late. Business facilities include 24-hour room service, meeting rooms for up to 70, English-speaking concierge, foreign currency exchange, secretarial services in English, audiovisual equipment, photocopiers, cable television news, translation services, and express checkout. Major credit cards accepted. 42 Av. Gabriel, 8e (phone: 45-61-96-33; fax: 42-89-06-07; telex: 642794F). Very expensive.

Ritz – Optimum comfort, privacy, and personal service are offered here, in one of the world's most gracious and distinguished hotels. There is an extraordinary underground health club (with pool, sauna, squash courts, ozone baths, and massages), an extensive business center, and the Ritz Escoffier Ecole de Cuisine. The latest addition is the *Ritz Club,* a nightclub and discotheque on the hotel's lower level that is open to hotel guests and club members only. The 162 redecorated rooms still preserve their antique treasures. This turn-of-the-century monument is *the* place to splurge, and even its sale to Egyptian interests (some say the Sultan of Brunei is the real financial force) has not diminished the glow one iota. The bars are fashionable meeting places, and the two-star *Ritz-Espadon* restaurant carries on the tradition of the legendary Escoffier. Business facilities include 24-hour room service, meeting rooms for up to 150, English-speaking concierge, foreign currency exchange, secretarial services in English, audiovisual equipment, photocopiers, computers, cable television news, translation services, and express checkout. Major credit cards accepted. 15 Pl. Vendôme, 1er (phone: 42-60-38-30; fax: 42-86-00-91; telex: 220262). Very expensive.

Royal Monceau – This elegant, impeccably decorated property, not far from the Arc de Triomphe, has 3 restaurants — including one with an attractive garden setting — as well as 2 bars, a fitness center, pool, Jacuzzi, and beauty salon. Business facilities include 24-hour room service, meeting rooms for up to 250, English-speaking concierge, foreign currency exchange, secretarial services in English, audiovisual equipment, photocopiers, computers, translation services, and express checkout. Major credit cards accepted. 37 Av. Hoche, 8e (phone: 45-61-98-00; fax: 45-63-28-93; telex: 650361). Very expensive.

St. James's Club – Located in a château in a residential section of the city, this hotel is really a private club (there are others in the group: one in London, one in Antigua, another in Los Angeles). For an additional 50F ($8), non-members can stay here for a few nights and feel as if they are living in an elegant home. The penthouse suites have a winter roof garden. There's a health center, a 5,000-volume library, and 2 restaurants. Business facilities include 24-hour room service, meeting rooms for up to 30, English-speaking concierge, foreign currency exchange, secretarial services in English, audiovisual equipment, photocopiers, computers, translation services, and express checkout. Major credit cards accepted. 5 Pl. Chancelier Adenauer, Av. Bugeaud, 16e (phone: 47-04-29-29; in the US, 800-641-0300; fax: 45-53-00-61). Very expensive.

San Régis – This is an elegant place to feel at home in comfortable surroundings. Business facilities include English-speaking concierge, foreign currency exchange, photocopiers, computers, and cable television news. Major credit cards accepted. 12 Rue Jean-Goujon, 8e (phone: 43-59-41-90; fax: 45-61-05-48; telex: 643637). Very expensive to expensive.

Westminster – Between the *Opéra* and the *Ritz,* it was at one time quite prestigious, but declined somewhat before its recent renovation. The paneling, marble fireplaces, and parquet floors of its traditional decor remain; air conditioning has been installed; and a new restaurant, *Le Céladon,* and cocktail lounge replace the old grill and bar. Some of the 101 rooms and apartments overlook the street, some an inner courtyard. Business facilities include 24-hour room service, meeting rooms for up to 70, English-speaking concierge, foreign currency exchange, secretarial services in English, audiovisual equipment, photocopiers, and translation services. Major credit cards accepted. 13 Rue de la Paix, 2e (phone: 42-61-57-46; fax: 42-60-30-66; telex: 680035). Very expensive to expensive.

Balzac – Very private, this luxurious, charming hotel with 70 rooms and suites is ideally located off the Champs-Elysées. Another plus is that the Paris branch of the *Bice* restaurant (also of Milan and New York) is right here. Business facilities include 24-hour room service, English-speaking concierge, foreign currency exchange, and photocopiers. Major credit cards accepted. 6 Rue Balzac, 8e (phone: 45-61-97-22; fax: 45-25-24-82; telex: 290298). Expensive.

Colbert – Each of the 40 rooms in this Left Bank hostelry has a glass door leading onto a balcony. Decorated in pastel tones, there is a mini-bar and television set in each one. No restaurant, but breakfast included. Major credit cards accepted. 7 Rue de l'Hôtel Colbert (phone: 43-25-85-65; in the US, 800-366-1510). Expensive.

Grand – This renovated property, part of the Inter-Continental chain, has long been a favorite of Americans abroad, with its "meetingplace of the world," the *Café de la Paix.* It has 530 rooms and 10 luxurious suites, plus cheerful bars and restaurants — and a prime location (next to the *Opéra*). Business facilities include 24-hour room service, meeting rooms for up to 1,200, English-speaking concierge, foreign currency exchange, secretarial services in English, audiovisual equipment, photocopiers, cable television news, and express checkout. Major credit cards accepted. 2 Rue Scribe, 9e (phone: 40-07-32-32; fax: 42-66-12-51; telex: 220875). Expensive.

Holiday Inn Place de la République – In the heart of town, in a 120-year-old edifice that evokes the grandeur of the Second Empire — its façade is unlike any *Holiday Inn* you've seen before. Of the 333 pleasantly decorated rooms, those facing the courtyard are preferable to those facing the square. Restaurant, piano bar, and air conditioning. Major credit cards accepted. 10 Pl. de la République, 11e (phone: 43-55-44-34; fax: 47-00-32-34; telex: 210651). Expensive.

L'Hôtel – Small, but chic, this Left Bank hostelry is favored by experienced international travelers (Oscar Wilde died here). The 27 rooms are tiny, but beautifully appointed (antiques, fresh flowers, marble baths). The attractive restaurant, complete with waterfall, is flanked by a piano bar, and the location can't be beat. Business facilities include 24-hour room service, meeting rooms for up to 50, English-speaking concierge, foreign currency exchange, secretarial services in English, photocopiers, translation services, and express checkout. Major credit cards accepted. 13 Rue des Beaux-Arts, 6e (phone: 43-25-27-22; fax: 43-25-64-81; telex: 270870). Expensive.

Hôtel des Saints-Pères – In a great location in the heart of the Left Bank, its attractively decorated guestrooms, courtyard garden, and a charming bar make this one of Paris's best little hotels. Book far in advance — it's often difficult to get a room. Business facilities include English-speaking concierge, foreign currency exchange, and photocopiers. Major credit cards accepted. 65 Rue des Sts.-Pères, 6e (phone: 45-44-50-00; fax: 45-44-90-83; telex: 205424). Expensive.

Inter-Continental – The 500 rooms and suites have been meticulously restored to re-create turn-of-the-century elegance with modern conveniences. The top-floor Louis XVI "garret" rooms are cozy and look out over the Tuileries. There's an American-style coffee shop, a grill, and a popular bar. Business facilities include 24-hour room service, meeting rooms for up to 1,000, English-speaking concierge, foreign currency exchange, secretarial services in English, audiovisual equipment, photocopiers, translation services, and express checkout. Major credit cards accepted. 3 Rue de Castiglione, 1er (phone: 44-77-11-11; fax: 44-77-14-60; telex: 220114). Expensive.

Lancaster – Small and still smart, this recently renovated 57-room townhouse has quiet, comfortable accommodations. There are flowers everywhere, a cozy bar, a topnotch restaurant with courtyard service in summer, and underground parking. Run by London's Savoy group. Business facilities include 24-hour room service, meeting rooms for up to 20, English-speaking concierge, foreign currency exchange, secretarial services in English, audiovisual equipment, photocopiers, and cable television news. Major credit cards accepted. 7 Rue de Berri, 8e (phone: 43-59-90-43; fax: 42-89-22-71; telex: 640991). Expensive.

Lutétia – This recently renovated Belle Epoque hostelry is centrally located between Montparnasse and Odéon. Its 270 spacious and stylishly decorated rooms all have air conditioning. Its *Le Paris* restaurant has been awarded one Michelin star. Business facilities include 24-hour room service, meeting rooms for up to 450, English-speaking concierge, foreign currency exchange, secretarial services in English, audiovisual equipment, photocopiers, translation services, and express checkout. Major credit cards accepted. 45 Bd. Raspail, 6e (phone: 45-44-38-10; fax: 45-44-50-50; telex: 270424). Expensive.

Méridien – *Air France*'s well-run, 1,027-room, modern American-style property has all the expected French flair. Rooms are on the small side, but tastefully decorated, quiet, and with good views. There are 4 attractive restaurants, a shopping arcade, lively bars, and a chic nightclub, *L'Ecume des Nuits*. Business facilities include 24-hour room service, meeting rooms for up to 2,000, English-speaking concierge, foreign currency exchange, secretarial services in English, audiovisual equipment, photocopiers, translation services, and express checkout. Major credit cards accepted. 81 Bd. Gouvion-St.-Cyr, 17e (phone: 40-68-34-34; fax: 40-68-31-31; telex 651952). Expensive.

Méridien Montparnasse – With 952 rooms, this ultramodern giant is in the heart of Montparnasse. It has a futuristic lobby, efficient service, a coffee shop, bars, and the *Montparnasse 25* restaurant, with a view, and in summer, a garden restaurant. Business facilities include 24-hour room service, meeting rooms for up to 2,000, English-speaking concierge, foreign currency exchange, secretarial services in English, audiovisual equipment, photocopiers, computers, translation services, and express checkout. Major credit cards accepted. 19 Rue du Commandant-René-Mouchotte, 14e (phone: 43-20-15-51; fax: 43-20-61-03). Expensive.

Montalembert – Recently completely renovated inside (its lovely façade remains), this small and exquisite hotel is known for its privacy. The 51 rooms, suites, and public areas are decorated in Art Deco style. A favorite spot for the literary and artistic crowd. The menu at its restaurant emphasizes simplicity and freshness. Business facilities include 24-hour room service, meeting rooms for up to 30, English-speaking concierge, foreign currency exchange, secretarial services in English, audiovisual equipment, photocopiers, and express checkout. Major credit cards accepted. 3 Rue Montalembert, 7e (phone: 45-48-68-11; in the US, 800-628-8929; fax: 42-22-58-19; telex: 200132). Expensive.

Paris Hilton International – Its 474 modern rooms are only a few steps from the Eiffel Tower. Those facing the river have the best view. The glass-walled rendez-vous *Le Toit de Paris* has dancing and a glittering nighttime view; *Le Western* serves T-bone steaks, apple pie à la mode, and brownies (mostly to French diners). The coffee shop is a magnet for homesick Americans. Business facilities include 24-hour room service, meeting rooms for up to 1,000, English-speaking concierge, foreign currency exchange, secretarial services in English, audiovisual equipment, photocopiers, translation services, and express checkout. Major credit cards accepted. 18 Av. de Suffren, 15e (phone: 42-73-92-00; fax: 47-83-62-66; telex: 200955). Expensive.

Pavillon de la Reine – Supreme location for the Marais's only luxury hotel, owned by the management of the *Relais Christine* (see below) and similarly appointed. Its 49 spacious rooms look out on a garden or courtyard. The setting on the Place des Vosges is regal, and the *Picasso Museum* is only a couple of minutes away on foot. Business facilities include 24-hour room service, foreign currency exchange, and photocopiers. Major credit cards accepted. 28 Pl. des Vosges, 3e (phone: 42-77-96-40; fax: 42-77-63-06; telex: 216160). Expensive.

Prince de Galles – An excellent location (a next-door neighbor of the pricier *George V*) and impeccable style make this hostelry a good choice. All 160 rooms and suites are individually decorated. This Marriott member offers a restaurant and an oak-panelled bar; parking is available. Business facilities include 24-hour room service, meeting rooms for up to 150, English-speaking concierge, foreign currency exchange, secretarial services in English, audiovisual equipment, photocopiers, computers, translation services, and express checkout. Major credit cards accepted. 33 Av. George-V, 8e (phone: 47-23-55-11; fax: 47-20-96-92; telex: 800627). Expensive.

Pullman St.-Jacques – This four-star hotel has 797 up-to-date rooms, a nice shopping arcade, a cinema, 4 restaurants (one Japanese, one Chinese, one French, and an informal coffee shop), and the lively *Bar Tahonga*. A bit out of the way, but the métro is close by. Business facilities include 24-hour room service, meeting rooms for up to 3,000, English-speaking concierge, foreign currency exchange, secretarial services in English, audiovisual equipment, photocopiers, computers, translation services, and express checkout. Major credit cards accepted. 17 Bd. St.-Jacques, 14e (phone: 40-78-79-80; fax: 45-88-43-93; telex: 270740). Expensive.

Raphaël – A very spacious, stately place, with a Turner in the lobby downstairs and paneling painted with sphinxes in the generous rooms. Less well known among the top Paris hotels, but favored by film folk and the like. Business facilities include 24-hour room service, meeting rooms for up to 150, English-speaking concierge, foreign currency exchange, secretarial services in English, audiovisual equipment, photocopiers, computers, translation services, and express checkout. Major credit cards accepted. 17 Av. Kléber, 16e (phone: 45-02-16-00; fax: 45-01-21-50; telex: 610356). Expensive.

Relais Christine – This lovely small hotel, with modern fixtures and lots of old-fashioned charm, formerly was a 16th-century cloister. Ask for a room with a courtyard or garden view (we especially like No. 31); others tend to be small and noisy. Business facilities include meeting rooms for up to 20, foreign currency exchange, and photocopiers. Major credit cards accepted. 3 Rue Christine, 6e (phone: 43-26-71-80; fax: 43-26-89-38; telex: 202606). Expensive.

Le Relais Saint-Germain – In a 17th-century building, this 10-room hostelry is ideally situated on the Left Bank just steps from Boulevard St.-Germain and the area's best shops, eateries, and galleries. It is attractively decorated, and charming down to its massive ceiling beams and huge flower bouquets. A rare find. Major credit cards accepted. 9 Carrefour de l'Odéon, 6e (phone: 43-29-12-05; fax: 46-33-45-30; telex: 201889). Expensive.

Résidence du Roy – Within easy reach of the Champs-Elysées, this establishment offers self-contained studios, suites, and duplexes, complete with kitchen facilities. No restaurant. Business facilities include meeting rooms for up to 20, English-speaking concierge, audiovisual equipment, photocopiers, and express checkout. Major credit cards accepted. 8 Rue François-Ier, 8e (phone: 42-89-59-59; fax: 40-74-07-92; telex: 648452). Expensive.

Le Vernet – Recently totally renovated, this sister hotel to the elegant *Royal Monceau* has 36 modern rooms and suites and is located just a few steps from the Arc de Triomphe. Business facilities include 24-hour room service, meeting rooms for up to 15, English-speaking concierge, foreign currency exchange, audiovisual equipment, photocopiers, computers, translation services, and express checkout. Major credit cards accepted. 25 Rue Vernet, 8e (phone: 47-23-43-10; fax: 40-70-10-14; telex: 290347). Expensive.

Abbaye St.-Germain – On a quiet street, this small, delightful place once was a convent. The lobby has exposed stone arches, and the elegant public and private rooms are furnished with antiques, tastefully selected fabrics, and marble baths. There's a lovely garden and a bar, but there continue to be some complaints about the service. Business facilities include English-speaking concierge, foreign currency exchange, and photocopiers. No credit cards accepted. 10 Rue Cassette, 6e (phone: 45-44-38-11; fax: 45-48-07-86). Expensive to moderate.

Angleterre – Its 29 classic, clean, unpretentious rooms are in what once was the British Embassy, now a national monument. Business facilities include English-speaking concierge, foreign currency exchange, and photocopiers. Major credit cards accepted. 44 Rue Jacob, 6e (phone: 42-60-34-72; fax: 42-60-16-93). Moderate.

Britannique – Within minutes of the *Louvre* and Notre-Dame, this hotel was a Quaker mission house during World War I. All 40 rooms have been renovated and are equipped with mini-bars, hair dryers, and satellite television. Major credit cards accepted. 20 Av. Victoria, 1er (phone: 42-33-74-59; in the US, 800-366-1510). Moderate.

Danube St.-Germain – The rooms, with their four-poster bamboo beds, are comfortable, and some of them overlook an attractive courtyard typical of the Left Bank. Business facilities include foreign currency exchange and photocopiers. American Express accepted. 58 Rue Jacob, 6e (phone: 42-60-34-70; fax: 42-60-81-18; telex: 211062). Moderate.

Deux Continents – A cozy red sitting room looks invitingly onto the street here, in this 40-room establishment on the Left Bank. Major credit cards accepted. 25 Rue Jacob, 6e (phone: 43-26-72-46). Moderate.

Deux Iles – This beautifully redecorated 17th-century house is on the historic Ile St.-Louis. It has a tropical garden and the decor is in bamboo, rattan, and braided rope. The rooms have French provincial fabrics and Louis XIV ceramic tiles in the bathrooms. But there's one drawback: the rooms aren't very large. Business facilities include foreign currency exchange. No credit cards accepted. 59 Rue St.-Louis-en-l'Ile, 4e (phone: 43-26-13-35; fax: 43-29-60-25). Moderate.

Duc de St.-Simon – If you're in search of things past, this may be one of the best places in town, despite the rather small rooms. In 2 big townhouses in a beautiful, quiet backwater off the Boulevard St.-Germain, this elegant little spot veritably reeks of Proust. Just a 5-minute walk from the spectacular *Musée d'Orsay*. Business facilities include a foreign currency exchange and photocopiers. No credit cards accepted. 14 Rue de St.-Simon, 7e (phone: 45-48-35-66; fax: 45-48-68-25; telex: 203277). Moderate.

Grand Hôtel Taranne – Anybody anxious to get into the Left Bank scene should love it here, for the 35 rooms are literally on top of the *Brasserie Lipp*. Each room is unique: No. 4 has exposed beams, a TV set, and a mini-bar; No. 3 has a Louis XIII–style bed; No. 17, the oddest, has lights and a disco ball. Business facilities include foreign currency exchange and photocopiers. Major credit cards accepted. 153 Bd. St.-Germain, 6e (phone: 42-22-21-65; fax: 45-48-22-25; telex: 205340). Moderate.

Grand Hôtel de l'Univers – Modern and tucked away on a quiet street, it's also only 2 steps away from St.-Germain-des-Prés and the Latin Quarter. No restaurant. Major credit cards accepted. 6 Rue Grégoire-de-Tours, 6e (phone: 43-29-37-00; fax: 40-51-06-45; telex: 204150). Moderate.

Jeu de Paume – The architect-owner of this former *jeu de paume* (tennis court) has artfully married old and new in this newest addition to the exclusive Ile St.-Louis hotels. High-tech lighting, modern artwork, and a sleek glass elevator are set against ancient ceiling beams and limestone brick hearths. There's a country feeling here. Rooms are comfortable and reasonably priced. Business facilities include 24-hour room service, meeting rooms for up to 30, foreign currency exchange, secretarial services in English, and photocopiers. Major credit cards accepted. 54 Rue St.-Louis-en-l'Ile, 4e (phone: 43-26-14-18; telex: 205160). Moderate.

Lord Byron – On a quiet street off the Champs-Elysées, it has a pleasant courtyard and 30 comfortable, homey rooms. The staff is friendly and speaks good English, and a family atmosphere prevails. Major credit cards accepted. 5 Rue de Chateaubriand, 8e (phone: 43-59-89-98; fax: 42-89-46-04; telex: 649662). Moderate.

Lutèce – Here are 23 luxurious rooms (one split-level) on the charming Ile St.-Louis. Positively ravishing, with exquisite toile fabric and wallpaper and raw wood beams. 65 Rue St.-Louis-en-l'Ile, 4e (phone: 43-26-23-52; fax: 43-29-60-25). Moderate.

Madison – Offers 55 large, bright rooms, some with balconies and all with air conditioning. Major credit cards accepted. 143 Bd. St.-Germain, 6e (phone: 43-29-72-50; fax: 43-29-72-50; telex: 201628). Moderate.

Odéon – Small, modernized, and charming, it's in the heart of the St.-Germain area on the Left Bank. No restaurant. Major credit cards accepted. 3 Rue de l'Odéon, 6e (phone: 43-25-90-67; fax: 43-25-55-98; telex: 202943). Moderate.

Parc St.-Séverin – An interesting property in the heart of the 5th *arrondissement* on the Left Bank, it has a total of 27 rooms, including a top-floor penthouse with a wraparound balcony. The decor is modern but understated, and the overall ambience is appealing even though the neighborhood is less than the quietest in Paris. Major credit cards accepted. 22 Rue de la Parcheminerie, 5e (phone: 43-54-32-17; fax: 43-54-70-71). Moderate.

Regent's Garden – On a quiet street near the Etoile, it has 40 spacious rooms, some with large marble fireplaces. The property is run by young hoteliers who make you feel as if you are in your own home. A country atmosphere pervades. There's also a garden and parking. Major credit cards accepted. 6 Rue Pierre-Demours, 17e (phone: 45-74-07-30; fax: 40-55-01-42; telex: 640127). Moderate.

Résidence Charles-Dullin – In a sleepy corner of Montmartre, near the leafy square of the *Théâtre de l'Atelier,* this residential hotel charges nightly, weekly, and monthly rates. The apartments have kitchens, and some overlook a peaceful garden. Major credit cards accepted. 10 Pl. Charles-Dullin, 18e (phone: 42-57-14-55; fax: 42-54-48-87). Moderate.

Ste.-Beuve – A stylish place in Montparnasse with rooms and lobby designed by David Hicks. Major credit cards accepted. 9 Rue Ste.-Beuve, 6e (phone: 45-48-20-07; fax: 45-48-67-52). Moderate.

Le St.-Grégoire – A small 18th-century mansion on the Left Bank, this recently renovated hostelry has an intimate cozy atmosphere, a warm fire in the hearth, and 20 tastefully furnished rooms, some with terraces overlooking a garden. Major credit cards accepted. 43 Rue de l'Abbé-Grégoire, 6e (phone: 45-48-23-23; fax: 45-48-33-95). Moderate.

St.-Louis – On magical Ile St.-Louis, practically in the shadow of Notre-Dame, this small hotel will make the first-time visitor fall in love with the city forever. The 21 rooms aren't large, but they're pretty, and the 3 fifth-floor rooms under the eaves are enchanting, with tiny balconies overlooking Parisian rooftops. No TV sets, but baths are clean and modern, and there's a charming breakfast room and a warm welcome. No credit cards accepted. 75 Rue St.-Louis-en-l'Ile, 4e (phone: 46-34-04-80; fax: 46-34-02-13). Moderate.

St.-Louis Marais – On a quiet residential street on the edge of the newly chic Marais (Paris's oldest neighborhood), this tiny hotel is a short walk from the Place des Vosges, the *Louvre,* the quais along the Seine, and the Bastille nightclubs. Dating from the 18th century, when it belonged to the Celestin Convent, it has 14 small rooms, which were being remodeled as we went to press. Historical status has barred installation of an elevator, however. No credit cards. 1 Rue Charles-V, 4e (phone: 48-87-87-04; fax: 46-34-02-13). Moderate.

St.-Merry – A stone's throw from the *Centre Georges Pompidou* arts complex, this mock-medieval establishment may be the most bizarre hotel in Paris. It not only backs onto the Eglise St.-Merry, but it has a communion rail as a banister and ancient oaken confessionals as broom closets. The rooms, hung with dark, demonic oil portraits, have church pews for benches, and some rooms are even spliced by a flying buttress. In dubious taste, perhaps, but there's nothing else like it. No credit cards accepted. 78 Rue de la Verrerie, 4e (phone: 42-78-14-15; fax: 40-29-06-82). Moderate.

Tuileries – With a good location in a "real" neighborhood in the heart of the city, it has a well-tended look and attractive carved wood bedsteads. Major credit cards accepted. 10 Rue St.-Hyacinthe, 1er (phone: 42-61-04-17 or 42-61-06-94; fax: 49-27-91-56). Moderate.

L'Université – Its 28 charming rooms of all shapes and sizes are in a former 18th-century mansion. No credit cards accepted. 22 Rue de l'Université, 7e (phone: 42-61-09-39). Moderate.

La Villa – Popular with American fashion writers, this 35-room hostelry in the

St.-Germain area was completely renovated in post-modern decor. Although the rooms are incredibly small, the luxurious bathrooms alone are worth a stay here. Major credit cards accepted. Business facilities include an English-speaking concierge and foreign currency exchange. 29 Rue Jacob (phone: 43-26-60-00; telex: 202437). Moderate.

Vendôme – This older "house" has 36 immaculate high-ceilinged rooms with brass beds, and the location couldn't be better. There is a small restaurant with a limited menu, and a bar. Major credit cards accepted. 1 Pl. Vendôme, 1er (phone: 42-60-32-84; fax: 49-27-97-89). Moderate.

West End – Friendly, with 60 rooms, it's on the Right Bank. The front desk keeps a close, concerned watch on comings and goings, which some may find reassuring. Major credit cards accepted. 7 Rue Clément-Marot, 8e (phone: 47-20-30-78; fax: 47-20-34-42). Moderate.

Chomel – Sprucely decorated, this establishment is near the *Au Bon Marché* department store. Major credit cards accepted. 15 Rue Chomel, 7e (phone: 45-48-55-52; fax: 45-48-89-76). Moderate to inexpensive.

Ferrandi – Popular with international businessmen, this no-frills hostelry is done up in browns and blues, with a winding wood staircase and a quiet lounge. Major credit cards accepted. 92 Rue du Cherche-Midi, 6e (phone: 42-22-97-40). Moderate to inexpensive.

Des Marroniers – Good rates and an excellent location, in the heart of the Left Bank, makes this 37-room hotel a real bargain. It has a courtyard and pretty breakfast room. No credit cards accepted. 21 Rue Jacob, 6e (phone: 43-25-30-60). Moderate to inexpensive.

St.-Thomas-d'Aquin – Built in the 1880s, this unpretentious hotel is a simple, functional base from which to explore a shopper's paradise of new wave designer boutiques and tiny restaurants. The 21 rooms are clean and neat, and baths are modern (though tubs are half-size). Breakfast is included. Major credit cards accepted. 3 Rue d'Pré-aux-Clercs, 7e (phone: 42-61-01-22; fax: 42-61-41-43). Moderate to inexpensive.

Amélie – Centrally located, this comfortable spot has 15 rooms, each with color TV set, direct-dial telephone, and mini-bar. Breakfast is included in the rate, which makes this one of Paris's better bargains. Major credit cards accepted. 5 Rue Amélie, 7e (phone: 45-51-74-75; fax: 45-56-93-55). Inexpensive.

D'Argenson – The upper middle class residential district in which this hotel is located is off the typical tourist track but convenient to major department stores on the Bd. Haussmann and a 15-minute walk from the *Opéra*. The showplace rooms — Nos. 23, 33, 43, and 53 — feature fireplaces and up-to-date bathrooms. Room rate includes breakfast. Major credit cards accepted. 15 Rue d'Argenson, 8e (phone: 42-65-16-87). Inexpensive.

Bretonnerie – This restored 17th-century townhouse takes itself seriously, with petit point, dark wood furnishings, and several attic rooms with beams that overlook the narrow streets of the newly fashionable Marais area. Major credit cards accepted. 22 Rue Ste.-Croix-de-la-Bretonnerie, 4e (phone: 48-87-77-63; fax: 42-77-26-78). Inexpensive.

Ceramic – Close to the Champs-Elysées, the Faubourg St.-Honoré, and the métro, this 53-room establishment with an Art Nouveau façade has been designated a national historic treasure. Request a room facing the street, particularly No. 412 — enormous, with a crystal chandelier and wide bay windows. Room rates include breakfast. Major credit cards accepted. 34 Av. de Wagram, 8e (phone: 42-27-20-30; fax: 46-22-95-83). Inexpensive.

Delavigne – Good value and location (just down the street from the *Odéon* theater), it has an enlightened manager who says he isn't interested in simply handing out keys, but enjoys introducing foreigners to Paris. Major credit cards accepted. 1 Rue Casimir-Delavigne, 6e (phone: 43-29-31-50; fax: 43-29-78-56). Inexpensive.

Esmeralda – Some of the rooms look directly at Notre-Dame over the gardens of St.-Julien-le-Pauvre, one of Paris's most ancient churches. The oak beams and furniture round out the medieval atmosphere. Small and friendly, especially popular with the theatrical crowd. No credit cards accepted. 4 Rue St.-Julien-le-Pauvre, 5e (phone: 43-54-19-20). Inexpensive.

Family – A longtime favorite with Americans — you're treated just like part of the family. There are 25 small but comfortable rooms. Major credit cards accepted. 35 Rue Cambon, 1er (phone: 42-61-54-84). Inexpensive.

Grandes Ecoles – Just the sort of place that shouldn't appear in a guidebook (even the proprietress says so) and that people recommend only to the right friends. Insulated from the street by a delightful courtyard and its garden, it is a simple 19th-century private house with plain comforts, but it's long on atmosphere. There aren't many like it in Paris. Major credit cards accepted. 75 Rue Cardinal-Lemoine, 5e (phone: 43-26-79-23; fax: 43-25-28-15). Inexpensive.

Hôtel de Bellevue et du Chariot d'Or – Slightly eccentric, but friendly, this is the best of more than a score of tiny hotels in the wholesale garment district. Although the hallway carpets and wallpaper are in dire need of replacement, the rooms are clean and comfortable, and most of the baths have been redone. Room No. 110 is on the courtyard (which means it's quiet) and has twin beds, a pink bathroom, and a marble fireplace. Some rooms are large enough to sleep four. Breakfast included. Major credit cards accepted. 39 Rue de Turbigo, 3e (phone: 48-87-45-60; fax: 48-87-95-04). Inexpensive.

Le Jardin des Plantes – In addition to a magnificent setting across from the Parisian Botanical Gardens, near the Sorbonne, there are 33 airy, spotless rooms and baths, each with its own floral motif. The owner, a psychologist, has anticipated the traveler's every need: All rooms have mini-bars, TV sets, and hair dryers; some have alcoves large enough for extra beds for children; a sauna is available in the basement. Breakfast can be enjoyed in the sunny ground-floor coffee bar or on the fifth-floor terrace and rose garden. Art exhibits and classical music concerts are held on Sundays in the vaulted cellar. Major credit cards accepted. 5 Rue Linné, 5e (phone: 47-07-06-20). Inexpensive.

Jeanne d'Arc – This little place on a quiet street in the Marais doesn't get top marks for decor and its facilities are simple, but somehow its appeal has spread from Minnesota to Melbourne. It's well placed at the colorful end of the Rue de Rivoli, and the management is friendly and speaks English. Major credit cards accepted. 3 Rue Jarente, 4e (phone: 48-87-62-11). Inexpensive.

Lenox – Between the busy St.-Germain area and the boutiques nearby, it's small and very tastefully done, with a small bar. Popular with the fashion crowd. Major credit cards accepted. 9 Rue de l'Université, 7e (phone: 42-96-10-95; fax: 42-61-52-82). Inexpensive.

London – In the heart of the business district, this comfortable hotel has 50 rooms, each with color TV set and direct-dial telephone. Major credit cards accepted. 32 Bd. des Italiens, 9e (phone: 48-24-54-64; fax: 48-00-08-83). Inexpensive.

Prima Lepic – A 38-room hotel in Montmartre, a busy neighborhood of winding little streets that evoke the romance of *la vie bohème,* Utrillo, Picasso, Toulouse-Lautrec and the *Moulin Rouge.* Decorated by cheerful young owners, rooms sport pretty floral wallpapers and one-of-a-kind furnishings — a wicker chair, a mirrored armoire, a 1930s lamp. No. 56, on the top floor, looks out over Paris, and travelers with a child should make special note of room No. 2, which connects to another room. There's an elevator, and the public spaces are charming. Major credit cards accepted. 29 Rue Lepic, 18e (phone: 46-06-44-64). Inexpensive.

Prince Albert – Despite its unprepossessing aura of faded glory, this has its site to recommend it: just off the quiet and unspoiled Marché St.-Honoré and a hop, skip, and jump from the Tuileries. Major credit cards accepted. 5 Rue St.-Hyacinthe, 1er (phone: 42-61-58-36; fax: 42-60-04-06). Inexpensive.

St.-André-des-Arts – A rambling old favorite among the chic and hip whose purses are slim but whose tastes are discerning. No credit cards accepted. 66 Rue St.-André-des-Arts, 6e (phone: 43-26-96-16). Inexpensive.

Sévigné – If it's a little noisy (right on the Rue de Rivoli), the warm welcome and handy location make up for it. Major credit cards accepted. 2 Rue Malher, 4e (phone: 42-72-76-17). Inexpensive.

Solférino – A cozy place with Oriental rugs scattered about. The 34 tiny rooms have floral wallpaper, and there's a plant-filled breakfast and sitting room. Major credit cards accepted. 91 Rue de Lille, 7e (phone: 47-05-85-54). Inexpensive.

Le Vieux Marais – Near the *Centre Georges Pompidou,* this is one of the few agreeable hostelries in the Marais area, with brightly sprigged walls in the cheerful, if not very large, rooms. The breakfast room has an impressive wall-size engraving of the Place des Vosges, not far away. Major credit cards accepted. 8 Rue du Plâtre, 4e (phone: 42-78-47-22; fax: 42-78-34-32). Inexpensive.

Welcome – Recently renovated and overlooking the Bd. St.-Germain, it's simple but comfortable. No credit cards accepted. 66 Rue de Seine, 6e (phone: 46-34-24-80; fax: 40-46-81-59). Inexpensive.

Boucherat – A plain, friendly establishment with no airs and with a clientele that returns. Near the Place de la République. Major credit cards accepted. 110 Rue de Turenne, 3e (phone: 42-72-86-83). Very inexpensive.

Du Globe – Tiny and charming, it's on a quiet street in the heart of the St.-Germain area. No credit cards accepted. 15 Rue des Quatre Vents, 6e (phone: 43-26-35-50). Very inexpensive.

Henri IV – No one could call this modern — the fittings obviously haven't been changed for decades, and there's only a bidet and basin in the room, since the bathrooms are down the hall. But it has a reputation and a history, not least because it is the only hotel on the Place Dauphine on the Ile de la Cité — the real core of Paris. Prices are breathtakingly low. No credit cards accepted. 25 Pl. Dauphine, 1er (phone: 43-54-44-53). Very inexpensive.

 EATING OUT: Paris considers itself the culinary capital of the world, and you will never forget food for long here. Whether you grab just a freshly baked croissant and café au lait for breakfast or splurge on an epicurean fantasy for dinner, this is the city in which to indulge all your gastronomic dreams. Remember, too, that there is no such thing as "French" food; rather, Paris provides the perfect mosaic in which to try regional delights from Provence, Alsace, Normandy, Brittany, and many other delicious places.

Restaurants classed as very expensive charge $250 and way up for two; expensive is $150 to $200; moderate, $100 to $150; inexpensive, less than $100; and very inexpensive, $50 or less. A service charge of 15% is added to the bill, but most people leave a small additional tip for good service; wine is not included in the price. Street addresses of the restaurants below are followed by their *arrondissement* number.

Note: To save frustration and embarrassment, always *reconfirm* dinner reservations before noon on the appointed day. Also remember that some of the better restaurants do not accept credit cards; it's a good idea to check when making your reservations. It may come as a surprise to discover that many of the elite Paris restaurants close over the weekend; also note that many Paris restaurants are closed for part or all of July or August. It's best to check ahead in order to avoid disappointment at the restaurant of your choice, and it's also worth remembering that many offer special lunch menus at considerably lower prices. Here is a sampling of the best restaurants that Paris has to offer:

L'Ambroisie – Quietly elegant, beneath the arcade of historic Place des Vosges, this is the showcase for chef Bernard Pacaud's equally elegant cuisine. The menu is limited to only a few entrées, such as duck with foie gras, skate and sliced green cabbage in sherry vinegar sauce, veal sweetbreads with shallots and parsley on ultra-fresh pasta, delicately battered chicken thighs in a piquant sauce, and oxtail in a savory sauce, but the quality has earned the place three Michelin stars. Closed Sundays, Monday lunch, August, and holidays. Reservations necessary. Major credit cards accepted. 9 Pl. des Vosges, 4e (phone: 42-78-51-45). Very expensive.

Le Grand Vefour – Founded in 1760, this sedately elegant Empire-style establishment — with paintings on the mirrors — is known for refined menus (two Michelin stars) and perfect service. It's famous for toast Rothschild (shrimp in crayfish sauce set in a brioche) and pigeon Aristide Briand (boned roast pigeon stuffed with foie gras and truffles). Closed Saturdays at lunch, Sundays, and August. Reservations necessary. Major credit cards accepted. 17 Rue Beaujolais, 1er (phone: 42-96-56-27). Very expensive.

Jamin – Due to the culinary talents of owner-chef Joël Robuchon, this is one of the city's finest restaurants — with a three-star ranking by Michelin — and one of the most difficult to get into. Robuchon calls his cuisine "moderne," similar to but not always as light as nouvelle. The dining room is *very* small, so reserve far in advance. Waiting time is almost 8 weeks. Closed weekends and July. Reservations necessary. Major credit cards accepted. 32 Rue de Longchamp, 16e (phone: 47-27-12-27). Very expensive.

Lasserre – The ultimate in luxury, with a magical ceiling that opens periodically during dinner to reveal the nighttime sky. Equally sublime is the food, served in the *style Lasserre* — that is, vermeil dessert settings, plates rimmed in gold, and extravagant garnishes with each dish. The classic menu is heavy on foie gras, caviar, truffles, and rich sauces. Michelin downgraded the food to two stars a few years ago, but we think it's still topnotch. Closed Sundays, Monday lunch, and August. Reservations necessary. Major credit cards accepted. 17 Av. Franklin-D.-Roosevelt, 8e (phone: 43-59-53-43). Very expensive.

Lucas-Carton – Once proprietor of the Michelin three-star restaurant called *L'Archestrate,* chef Alain Senderens dropped that name (but not his triple-star rating) in 1985 when he moved to larger, more elegant quarters in a historic building that boasts a gorgeous Belle Epoque interior. Senderens enjoys the reputation as one of France's most innovative culinary talents, combining many tenets of nouvelle cuisine with Oriental and African influences. Closed Saturdays, Sundays, and most of August. Reservations necessary. Major credit cards accepted. 9 Pl. de la Madeleine, 8e (phone: 42-65-22-90). Very expensive.

Maxim's – A legend for its Belle Epoque decor and atmosphere. It's good for celebrations, but it's hard to feel comfortable if you aren't known here. Owned by fashion designer Pierre Cardin, this is one of the few places in Paris where you are expected to dress formally — on Friday evenings. There's an orchestra for dancing from 9:30 PM until 2 AM. Open daily. Reservations necessary. Major credit cards accepted. 3 Rue Royale, 8e (phone: 42-65-27-94). Very expensive.

Le Taillevent – Full of tradition, Louis XVI furnishings, 18th-century porcelain dinner service — all in a 19th-century mansion — this epicurean haven offers no-nonsense *cuisine classique,* which currently is the best in Paris. Try terrine of truffled sweetbreads, seafood sausage, duck in cider, and especially chef Claude Deligne's soufflés in original flavors like Alsatian pear and cinnamon chocolate. Three stars in the *Guide Michelin.* Closed weekends and August. Reservations necessary. Americans often have difficulty reserving here (although it's a bit easier if there are four in your party), and it's best to try at least 60 days ahead. No credit cards accepted. 15 Rue Lamennais, 8e (phone: 45-61-12-90). Very expensive.

La Tour d'Argent – Another of the five Parisian restaurants to be awarded three stars by the *Guide Michelin* and probably the best-known — though recent visits have not been up to the standards of years past. The spectacular view of Notre-Dame and the Ile St.-Louis competes with the food for the attention of a very touristy clientele. Pressed duck — prepared before you — is the specialty, but the 15 other varieties of duck are equally interesting. A single main dish here can cost $100, and to be quite frank, it just ain't worth it. Closed Mondays. Reservations necessary. Major credit cards accepted. 15 Quai de la Tournelle, 5e (phone: 43-54-23-31). Very expensive.

L'Ami Louis – This is the archetypal Parisian bistro, unattractive physically but with huge portions of food that we rate as marvelous. Though the original Louis is gone, his heirs have maintained the rough welcome and informal ambience. Specialties include foie gras, roast chicken, spring lamb, ham, and burgundy wines. A favorite among Americans, this is the place to sample authentic French fries. Closed Mondays, Tuesdays, and July and August. Reservations necessary. Major credit cards accepted. 32 Rue de Vertbois, 3e (phone: 48-87-77-48). Expensive.

Amphyclés – Since it opened in May 1989, Philippe Groult's tiny restaurant near the Arc de Triomphe has won praise and in 1991, a second Michelin star. A former student of star-chef Joël Robuchon of *Jamin,* Groult prepares wonderful dishes, including *crème de morilles au chou nouveau* (cream of mushroom soup flavored with new cabbage). Closed Saturday lunch and Sundays. Reservations necessary. Major credit cards accepted. 78 Av. des Ternes, 17e (phone: 40-68-01-01). Expensive.

Apicius – Jean-Pierre Vigato's highly original recipes have won him a reputation as one of Paris's finest chefs (and earned him two Michelin stars). Favorites include such delicacies as sweet-and-sour foie gras, *rougets* (a Mediterranean fish) with olive oil and potato purée, and a *panaché* of five mouth-watering chocolate desserts. Closed weekends and August. Reservations necessary. Major credit cards accepted. 122 Av. de Villiers, 17e (phone: 43-80-19-66). Expensive.

L'Arpège – Paris's current rage is two-star chef Alain Passard who prepares specialties such as *ris de veau aux truffes* (sweetbreads with truffles and chestnuts) and *lotte aux épices* (spicy monkfish). The prix fixe lunch at this eatery near the *Musée Rodin* is easily the best bargain around. Closed Saturdays and Sunday lunch and August. Reservations necessary. Major credit cards accepted. 84 Rue de Varenne, 7e (phone: 45-51-20-02). Expensive.

Le Carré des Feuillants – Alain Dutournier of *Le Trou Gascon* has set up shop right in midtown. The cuisine is still Gascon-inspired, but Dutournier is allowing his imagination more license with, for example, such creations as frogs' legs with watercress sauce and salmon served with braised cabbage and bacon. Michelin has awarded him two stars. Closed Saturdays for lunch and Sundays. Reservations necessary. Major credit cards accepted. 14 Rue de Castiglione, 1er (phone: 42-86-82-82). Expensive.

Castel – You might be able to get a reservation at this, one of the few private clubs in Paris, if you ask for help from the concierge at one of the town's grand hotels. The Belle Epoque interior is breathtaking, the cooking fine, and there's a disco in the basement. Specialties include lobster and chicken with cucumbers. Closed Sundays. Reservations necessary. Major credit cards accepted. 15 Rue Princesse, 6e (phone: 43-26-90-22). Expensive.

Chiberta – Elegant and modern, and boasting the acclaimed (two Michelin stars) nouvelle cuisine of Jean Michel Bédier. Try *bavarois de saumon au coulis de tomates frais* (salmon mousse with fresh tomato sauce) and *marbré de rouget au* *fenouil* (red mullet with fennel). Closed weekends and August. Reservations necessary. Major credit cards accepted. 3 Rue Arsène-Houssaye, 8e (phone: 45-63-77-90). Expensive.

Le Divellec – This bright and airy place serves some exquisitely fresh seafood. Try the sea bass, the *rouget,* and the sautéed turbot. The latter is served with "black pasta" — thick strips of pasta flavored with squid ink — an unusual and delicious concoction. Closed Sundays, Mondays, and August. Reservations necessary. Major credit cards accepted. 107 Rue de l'Université, 7e (phone: 45-51-91-96). Expensive.

Dodin-Bouffant – Popular because it was set up by the gifted, imaginative, and long-gone Jacques Manière, it still offers excellent seafood and inventive dishes (it has been awarded one Michelin star). Open late. Closed Sundays, 2 weeks at *Christmastime,* and August. Reservations necessary. Major credit cards accepted. 25 Rue Frédéric-Sauton, 5e (phone: 43-25-25-14). Expensive.

Drouant – Founded in 1880, this classic favorite reopened after an extensive face-lift, with an ambitious chef and menu. Michelin has awarded it one star. Open daily. Reservations necessary. Major credit cards accepted. 18 Rue Gaillon, 2e (phone: 42-65-15-16). Expensive.

Duquesnoy – Jean-Paul Duquesnoy, one of Paris's most promising young chefs, is in his element in nifty quarters. Warm carved woods and tasteful decor set the stage for specialties that include a new potato and caviar salad, terrine of leeks and langoustine, and a chocolate mousse and pistachio-filled *mille-feuille.* Two Michelin stars. Closed Saturday lunch and Sundays. Reservations necessary. Major credit cards accepted. 6 Av. Bosquet, 7e (phone: 47-05-96-78). Expensive.

Faugeron – Among the finest nouvelle restaurants, awarded two stars by Michelin, it rates even higher with us. Superb food, lovely service, and one of Paris's prettiest table settings in what once was an old school. Closed weekends and August. Reservations necessary. Major credit cards accepted. 52 Rue de Longchamp, 16e (phone: 47-04-24-53). Expensive.

Fouquet's Bastille – Sister restaurant to the Champs-Elysées institution (see *Wine Bars and Cafés*), this postmodern location next to Paris's new *Opéra Bastille* offers traditional fare with a modern touch. Closed Saturday lunch and Sundays. Reservations advised. Major credit cards accepted. 130 Rue de Lyon, 12e (phone: 43-42-18-18). Expensive.

Gérard Besson – Michelin has given this small and formal eatery two stars. The service is impeccable and the classic menu includes specialties such as fricassee of lobster. Closed Saturdays and Sundays July 13 to 30, and from December 22 to January 7. Reservations necessary. Major credit cards accepted. 5 Rue Coq-Héron, 1er (phone: 42-33-14-74). Expensive.

Jacques Cagna – The talented eponymous chef always provides an interesting menu at these charming premises on the Left Bank, very near the Seine. Michelin has awarded it two stars. Closed August, *Christmas* week, Saturdays, and Sundays. Reservations necessary. Major credit cards accepted. 14 Rue des Grands-Augustins, 6e (phone: 43-26-49-39). Expensive.

Lamazère – Truffle heaven. The menu is a triumph of rich products from the southwest of France. The owner is a magician in the real sense of the word, as well as with food. The elegant bar and salons are open late. Closed Sundays and August. Reservations necessary. Major credit cards accepted. 23 Rue de Ponthieu, 8e (phone: 43-59-66-66). Expensive.

Ledoyen – This grand dowager of Paris dining places received a major face-lift in 1988 when Régine, the capital's nightlife queen, took it over. Its look, and menus ordained by consulting chef Jacques Maximin, have received generally favorable reviews (one star from Michelin), particularly from high-powered businesspeople.

Closed Sundays and August. Reservations necessary. Major credit cards accepted. Carré des Champs-Elysées, 8e (phone: 47-42-23-23). Expensive.

Miravile – Gilles Epié, one of Paris's promising young chefs, recently moved across the river into larger quarters. He brought with him his customers, his Michelin star, and memorable dishes such as a lobster and potato cake. Closed Saturday lunch and Sundays. Reservations necessary. Major credit cards accepted. 72 Quai de l'Hôtel de Ville, 4e (phone: 42-74-72-22). Expensive.

Olympe – Owner and chef Dominique Nahmias is the first female chef to be awarded three toques — very high honors — by Gault Millau. Her nouvelle cuisine is painstakingly prepared and simply glorious; an excellent wine list adds to the meal's enjoyment. Closed Saturday and Sunday lunch, Mondays, and August. Reservations necessary. Major credit cards accepted. 8 Rue Nicolas-Charlet, 15e (phone: 47-34-86-08). Expensive.

Le Petit Montmorency – In his location near the Champs-Elysées, chef Daniel Bouché presents one of the most exciting and unusual menus in Paris. Very, very popular. Closed weekends and August. Reservations necessary. Visa and Carte Bleu accepted. 5 Rue Rabelais, 8e (phone: 42-25-11-19). Expensive.

Le Pré Catelan – It's the large restaurant right in the middle of the Bois de Boulogne, and believe it or not, the food here is very good. Ingredients are fresh and sauces are light. Specialties include four or five new dishes daily. Michelin has awarded it one star. Closed Sunday evenings, Mondays, and the first 2 weeks of February. Reservations necessary. Major credit cards accepted. Rte. de Suresnes, Bois de Boulogne, 16e (phone: 45-24-55-58). Expensive.

Régine's – The food actually is good in this beautifully decorated nightclub, which is frequented by Parisians as well as the chic international set. Ask your hotel manager to get you in because it's nominally a private club. Try the foie gras (made on the premises) and the goose. Closed Sundays. Reservations advised. Major credit cards accepted. 49 Rue de Ponthieu, 8e (phone: 43-59-21-60). Expensive.

Relais Louis XIII – Old-style decor and new cuisine in one of Paris's prettiest houses. Michelin has given it two stars. Closed Sundays, Monday lunch, and August. Reservations advised. Major credit cards accepted. 1 Rue Pont-de-Lodi, 6e (phone: 43-26-75-96) Expensive.

Tan-Dinh – The perfect pause from a constant diet of French specialties. Despite the loss of its Michelin star, its Vietnamese specialties are simply superb. Shrimp rolls, Vietnamese ravioli, and minced filet of beef are only three examples of the marvelous menu (ask for the version in English). Remarkable wine list. Closed Sundays and August. Reservations advised. Major credit cards accepted. 60 Rue de Verneuil, 7e (phone: 45-44-04-84). Expensive.

Le Toit de Passy – Not only is the food here good (Michelin has awarded chef Yann Jacquot one star), but the rooftop view in one of Paris's more exclusive districts is spectacular. Try specialties such as *pigeonneau en croûte de sel* (squab in a salt crust) while dining outdoors. Closed Saturdays (except for September through mid-December), Sundays, and holidays, 1 week in May, 1 week in September and *Christmas* week. Reservations necessary. Major credit cards accepted. 94 Av. Paul-Doumer, 16e (phone: 45-24-55-37). Expensive.

Vivarois – Claude Peyrot is one of France's finest chefs. Specialties in his small, elegant eating place include curried oysters au gratin, turbot, and assortments of desserts. Michelin has awarded it two stars. Closed weekends and August. Reservations necessary. Major credit cards accepted. 192 Av. Victor-Hugo, 16e (phone: 45-04-04-31). Expensive.

Auberge des Deux Signes – This place was once the cellars of the priory of St.-Julien-le-Pauvre; try to get an upstairs table overlooking the gardens. Auvergnat cooking à la nouvelle cuisine. Closed Sundays. Reservations necessary. Major credit cards accepted. 46 Rue Galande, 5e (phone: 43-25-46-56). Expensive to moderate.

Le Bistrot d'à Côté Flaubert – Michelin two-star chef Michel Rostang offers *cuisine de terroir* (uncomplicated, back-to-basics regional fare) in a turn-of-the-century bistro. Closed Saturday lunch, Sundays, and holidays. Reservations advised. Major credit cards accepted. 10 Rue Gustave-Flaubert, 17e (phone: 42-67-05-81). Expensive to moderate.

Brasserie Lorraine – Bustling and convivial until late at night, this place pulls in the neighborhood's bourgeoisie for animated evenings over the foie gras salads. Open daily from noon to 2 AM. Reservations unnecessary. Major credit cards accepted. Pl. des Ternes, 8e (phone: 42-27-80-04). Expensive to moderate.

La Cantine des Gourmets – This restaurant specializes in light, inventive creations of high quality (one Michelin star). Closed Sundays. Reservations advised. Major credit cards accepted. 113 Av. Bourdonnais, 7e (phone: 47-05-47-96). Expensive to moderate.

La Coquille – A classic bistro, where the service is unpretentious and warm, and the food consistently good. From October to May, the house specialty is *coquilles St.-Jacques,* a version that consists of scallops roasted with butter, shallots, and parsley. Closed Sundays, Mondays, holidays, and August. Reservations advised. Major credit cards accepted. 6 Rue du Débarcadère, 17e (phone: 45-74-25-95). Expensive to moderate.

Le Duc – The atmosphere is warm and comfortable, and Paul Minchelli is incomparably inventive with fish and shellfish (cooked and raw). Quality and variety are the rule here, with such specialties as curried oysters, tuna tartar, *coquilles St.-Jacques cru,* and an extraordinary seafood platter. Closed Saturdays, Sundays, and Mondays. Reservations necessary. No credit cards accepted. 243 Bd. Raspail, 14e (phone: 43-22-59-59 or 43-20-96-30). Expensive to moderate.

Faucher – Rising star Gérard Faucher opened this elegant restaurant 2 years ago and has drawn praise for his light touch with fish dishes and desserts ever since. Michelin awarded him a star this year. Closed Saturday lunch and Sundays. Reservations necessary. Major credit cards accepted. 123 Av. Wagram, 17e (phone: 42-27-61-50). Expensive to moderate.

Morot-Gaudry – On the top floor of a 1920s building with a great view of the Eiffel Tower, especially from the flowered terrace. Among the inventive dishes are calf's liver with raspberry vinegar, compote of chicken with leeks, and rice cake with ginger. One Michelin star. Closed weekends. Reservations necessary. Major credit cards accepted. 6 Rue de la Cavalerie, 15e (phone: 45-67-06-85). Expensive to moderate.

Pavillon des Princes – Under the direction of Pascal Bonichon, it serves delicious duck sausage salad with avocado, *coquilles St.-Jacques* with fresh pasta, and lamb nuggets with cabbage and tomatoes. On the edge of the Bois de Boulogne. Open daily. Reservations advised. Major credit cards accepted. 69 Av. de la Porte d'Auteuil, 16e (phone: 47-43-15-15). Expensive to moderate.

Au Quai d'Orsay – Fashionable, sophisticated, very French, and very intimate. Traditional copious bourgeois cooking and good beaujolais. Closed Sundays. Reservations advised. Major credit cards accepted. 49 Quai d'Orsay, 7e (phone: 45-51-58-58). Expensive to moderate.

Timonerie – Be sure to reserve 3 or 4 days in advance to dine at this one-Michelin-star restaurant. Specialties include *sandre rôti au chou et pommes de terre* (pike perch with cabbage and potatoes) and the chocolate tart. Especially recommended is the very affordable prix fixe lunch. Closed Mondays from March to August,

Saturdays from September to February, Sundays, and mid-February to mid-March. Reservations advised. Visa and MasterCard accepted. 35 Quai de la Tournelle, 5e (phone: 43-25-44-42). Expensive to moderate.

Le Trou Gascon – Alain Dutournier created the inspired and unusual cooking that features southwestern French specialties and a vast choice of regional wines and armagnacs. He has moved on to a more elegant neighborhood, but his wife holds down the fort at this one-Michelin-star restaurant. Closed weekends. Reservations advised. Major credit cards accepted. 40 Rue Taine, 12e (phone: 43-44-34-26). Expensive to moderate.

Allard – A very popular bistro with hearty country cooking and excellent burgundy wines. Snails, turbot, and *boeuf bourguignon* are the prime lures. Spring, when white asparagus and the new turnips arrive, is a special time here. Don't miss the chocolate charlotte for dessert. Closed weekends and August and for 10 days at *Christmas.* Reservations advised. Major credit cards accepted. 41 Rue St.-André-des-Arts, 6e (phone: 43-26-48-23). Moderate.

L'Amanguier – This series of garden restaurants serves an appetizing brand of nouvelle cuisine. Stick to a main course, which comes with a choice of appetizers, and the price is surprisingly low. The desserts are tempting. Open daily for lunch and dinner. Reservations advised. Major credit cards accepted. 51 Rue du Théâtre, 15e (phone: 45-77-04-01); 110 Rue de Richelieu, 2e (phone: 42-96-37-79); 43 Av. des Ternes, 17e (phone: 43-80-19-28); and 12 Av. de Madrid, Neuilly (phone: 47-45-79-73). Moderate.

Ambassade d'Auvergne – Its young chef creates delicious, unusual, classic Auvergnat dishes with a modern touch (try the lentil salad and the sliced ham). Also known for seasonal specialties and wonderful cakes. Open daily for lunch and dinner. Reservations advised. Major credit cards accepted. 22 Rue du Grenier-St.-Lazare, 3e (phone: 42-72-31-22). Moderate.

Astier – An honest-to-goodness neighborhood hangout that always is packed, because the clientele knows they can rely on it for the staples of bourgeois cooking, lovingly prepared. Closed Saturdays, Sundays, and August. Reservations advised. Major credit cards accepted. 44 Rue Jean-Pierre-Timbaud, 11e (phone: 43-57-16-35). Moderate.

Balzar – Perhaps because of its location right next to the Sorbonne, this mirrored brasserie has always attracted intellectuals. The steaks and *pommes frites* also are worth a visit. Open daily for lunch and dinner; closed *Christmas Week* and August. Reservations necessary. Major credit cards accepted. 49 Rue des Ecoles, 5e (phone: 43-54-13-67). Moderate.

La Barrière Poquelin – The excellent cooking *à la nouvelle cuisine* includes a splendid foie gras salad. Closed Saturdays for lunch, Sundays, and 3 weeks in August. Reservations advised. Major credit cards accepted. 17 Rue Molière, 1er (phone: 42-96-22-19). Moderate.

Bistro 121 – A hearty menu and excellent wines are offered in a modern setting that's always chic and crowded. Try *poisson cru mariné au citron vert* (seafood marinated in lime juice) and chocolate charlotte for dessert. One Michelin star. Closed Sundays, Mondays, and mid-July to mid-August. Reservations advised. Major credit cards accepted. 121 Rue de la Convention, 15e (phone: 45-57-52-90). Moderate.

Le Bistrot de Paris – Michel Oliver offers informality, original and classic bistro fare, and a good wine list, which attract a crowd. Closed Saturdays for lunch and Sundays. Reservations advised. Major credit cards accepted. 33 Rue de Lille, 7e (phone: 42-61-16-83). Moderate.

Le Boeuf sur le Toit – In the building that once housed a restaurant of the same name, a haunt of Jean Cocteau and other Paris artists in the 1940s, this eatery off the Champs-Elysées is managed by the Flo group, well known for good value in atmospheric surroundings. Open daily. Piano bar until 2 AM. Reservations advised. Major credit cards accepted. 34 Rue du Colisée, 8e (phone: 43-59-83-80). Moderate.

Bofinger – For magnificent Belle Epoque decor, this is the place; it's one of Paris's oldest brasseries and it is beautiful, even if the food is occasionally disappointing. Order onion soup and *choucroute* and you won't be unhappy. Open daily. Reservations advised. Major credit cards accepted. 3 Rue de la Bastille, 4e (phone: 42-72-87-82). Moderate.

Café de la Jatte – Only those in the know venture this far down the Seine for dinner. This leafy island, l'Ile de la Jatte, was ripe for a smart renovation, and this huge, high-ceilinged dining room, with half-moon-shaped windows and a pink floor, is now full of the chicest local clientele. The fare is healthy and simple: generous salads and roast chicken along with more nouvelle items. Open daily for lunch and dinner. Reservations advised. Major credit cards accepted. 60 Av. Vital-Bouhot, Neuilly, 15 minutes by car from central Paris (phone: 47-45-04-20). Moderate.

Chez André – A classic, bustling bistro near the chic shopping of Avenue Montaigne. Although a bit too noisy and crowded, it is quite popular with the well-heeled crowd, perhaps because it offers impeccably prepared *sole meunière, blanquette de veau, gigôt d'agneau,* and other traditional dishes. Reservations advised. Major credit cards accepted. 12 Rue Marbeuf, 8e (phone: 47-20-59-57). Moderate.

Chez Benoît – A pretty but unpretentious bistro with wonderful old-fashioned Lyonnaise cooking and exquisite wines. Just about at the top of the bistro list, it's rated one Michelin star. Closed weekends and August. Reservations necessary. No credit cards accepted. 20 Rue St.-Martin, 4e (phone: 42-72-25-76). Moderate.

Chez Georges – This narrow, old-fashioned bistro — with a whole platoon of matronly waitresses in starched aprons — is a bastion of traditional French cooking. Closed Sundays and holidays. Reservations advised. Major credit cards accepted. 1 Rue du Mail, 2e (phone: 42-60-07-11). Moderate.

Chez Josephine and **La Rôtisserie Chez Dumonet** – Two restaurants share the same building and the same management. *Josephine* is an old-time bistro with traditional cuisine and an excellent wine cellar; the *Rôtisserie* is lively and more modern, with steaks and grills over an open fire. *Josephine* is closed weekends and July; the *Rôtisserie,* Mondays, Tuesdays, and August. Reservations advised. Major credit cards accepted. 117 Rue du Cherche-Midi, 6e (phone: 45-48-52-40). Moderate.

Chez Maître Paul – The cooking of the Franche-Comté region is the specialty of this recently expanded restaurant with an *auberge* ambience. Try the *saucisse Montbéliard* (smoked garlic sausage), the *poulet au vin jaune* (chicken cooked in Jura wine), and the *gâteau aux noix* (nut cake). Closed Saturday lunch and Sunday. Reservations advised. Major credit cards accepted. The prix fixe menu is a good value. 12 Rue Monsieur-le-Prince, 6e (phone: 43-54-74-59). Moderate.

Chez Pauline – The perfect bistro. The tiny, wood-paneled downstairs room (ask to be seated there) is brightened by large mirrors and fresh flowers; the place settings look like Florentine marbeling. Try the oysters in a watercress sauce or the assortment of seafood with a saffron sauce, and save room for dessert — *mille-feuille* of orange with raspberry sauce is sublime. Closed Saturdays, Sundays, July, and from December 24 to January 2. Reservations advised. Major credit cards accepted. 5 Rue Villedo, 1er (phone: 42-96-20-70; fax: 49-27-99-89). Moderate.

Chez Pierre Vedel – Truly original cuisine. Closed weekends, from mid-July to mid-August, and at *Christmastime.* Reservations advised. Major credit cards accepted. 19 Rue Duranton, 15e (phone: 45-58-43-17). Moderate.

Chez René – This neighborhood bistro in the heart of the Left Bank offers hearty helpings of regional fare. Closed Saturdays, Sundays, August, and *Christmas Week*. Reservations advised. Major credit cards accepted. 14 Bd. St.-Germain, 5e (phone: 43-54-30-23). Moderate.

Chez Toutoune – This modest place specializing in Provençal dishes has become very popular for two good reasons: The food is tasty and the prices are fairly reasonable. The five-course, prix fixe menu features a rather short, but very interesting selection of appetizers, entrées, and desserts. Closed Sundays, Monday lunch, and mid-August to mid-September. Reservations advised. Major credit cards accepted. 5 Rue de Pontoise, 5e (phone: 43-26-56-81). Moderate.

La Coupole – A big, brassy brasserie, once the haunt of Hemingway, Josephine Baker, and Picasso, it is owned by the Flo group. The atmosphere is still great, the food still mediocre. Open daily until 2 AM. Closed August. Reservations advised. Major credit cards accepted. 102 Bd. du Montparnasse, 14e (phone: 43-20-14-20). Moderate.

Le Dômarais – This used to be the Crédit Municipal, or state pawnshop, and its elegant cupola now houses a sophisticated restaurant serving such inventions as camembert fondue, grilled Bayonne ham, and a *petit salé* of duck. Closed Saturdays for lunch and Mondays. Reservations advised. Major credit cards accepted. 53 *bis* Rue des Francs Bourgeois, 4e (phone: 42-74-54-17). Moderate.

L'Escargot Montorgueil – The polished wood paneling, the brass fittings, and the spiral staircase at this beautiful place, which dates from 1830, only add to the pleasure of a meal that might include snails in any of half a dozen styles or duck with orange sauce. Closed Monday lunch. Reservations advised. Major credit cards accepted. 38 Rue Montorgueil, 1er (phone: 42-36-83-51). Moderate.

La Ferme St.-Simon – Among our favorites for wholesome *cuisine d'autrefois* (old-fashioned cooking). Nothing very chi-chi here, just well-prepared, authentic dishes — the kinds you'd expect from a traditional Left Bank restaurant. Leave room for dessert; the owner once was a top assistant to Gaston Lenôtre. A perfect place for lunch. Michelin has awarded it one star. Closed Saturday lunch, Sundays, and August. Reservations advised. Major credit cards accepted. 6 Rue de St.-Simon, 7e (phone: 45-48-35-74). Moderate.

Au Gamin de Paris – Combines the coziness of a classic bistro with the chic of a historic Marais building and serves well-prepared, imaginative food. Open daily. No reservations after 8 PM. Major credit cards accepted. 51 Rue Vieille du Temple, 4e (phone: 42-78-97-24). Moderate.

Le Grand Colbert – Bright and brassy, with delightful polychrome, Belle Epoque motifs, and traditional offerings such as *boeuf gros sel* (boiled beef with coarse salt) and *merlan Colbert* (lightly breaded, pan-fried whiting), this renovated 19th-century brasserie is next to the Bibliothèque Nationale. Open daily. Reservations advised. Major credit cards accepted. In the *Galerie Colbert,* 2 Rue Vivienne, 2e (phone: 42-86-87-88). Moderate.

Jo Goldenberg – The best-known eating house in the Marais's quaint Jewish quarter, with good chopped liver and cheesecake and a range of Eastern European Jewish specialties. It's also a fine place to sip mint tea at the counter in the middle of a busy day. Open daily. Reservations unnecessary. Major credit cards accepted. 7 Rue des Rosiers, 4e (phone: 48-87-20-16 or 48-87-70-39). Moderate.

Julien – Belle Epoque decor with all the flourishes. Reliable, if uninspired, meals are served in a bustling atmosphere until 1:30 AM. Open daily. Reservations advised. Major credit cards accepted. 16 Rue du Faubourg-St.-Denis, 10e (phone: 47-70-12-06). Moderate.

La Manufacture – The second eatery of two-star chef Jean Pierre Vigato (of *Apicius*), this starkly modern place in an old cigar factory at the southern edge of Paris offers an excellent quality/price ratio. Closed Saturday afternoons and Sundays. Reservations advised. Visa accepted. 30 Rue Ernest-Renan, Issy-les-Moulineaux, 15e (phone: 40-93-08-98). Moderate.

La Marée – Unobtrusive on the outside, there is great comfort within — also the freshest of fish, the best restaurant wine values in Paris, and fabulous desserts. Michelin has awarded it one star. Closed weekends, holidays, and August. Reservations advised. Major credit cards accepted. 1 Rue Daru, 8e (phone: 47-63-52-42). Moderate.

Le Moulin du Village – Light and airy, especially in summer, when tables are put out on the cobbles of Cité Berryer, a tiny pedestrian alley very near the Madeleine, just off the Rue Royale. Cuisine is nouvelle and wines good. Closed Sundays. Reservations advised. Visa accepted. 25 Rue Royale, 8e (phone: 42-65-08-47). Moderate.

Le Muniche – St.-Germain's best brasserie is a bustling place with a rather extensive menu, and it's popular until 3 AM. Open daily. Reservations advised. Major credit cards accepted. 27 Rue de Buci, 6e (phone: 46-33-62-09). Moderate.

La Petite Chaise – Founded in 1680, it occupies 2 stories of a 17th-century stone house on the Left Bank. The intimate (and slightly run-down) atmosphere of the home of an ancient aunt characterizes this place, with brocaded walls, brass chandeliers, and antique oils contributing to the period decor. The trout you see swimming in a tank also are on the menu, as are specialties like shellfish crêpes and veal Pojarsky, in which the meat is combined with minced chicken. Always open. Reservations advised. Major credit cards accepted. 36 Rue de Grenelle, 7e (phone: 42-22-13-35). Moderate.

Au Pied de Cochon – No more *choucroute* on the menu (sob!). Crowded and colorful 24 hours a day, its customers enjoy shellfish, pigs' feet, and great crocks of onion soup, all in the old *Les Halles* area. Unfortunately, the food and service aren't what they used to be, and a garish redecoration has mangled most of the old atmosphere. But it still has local color. Open daily. Reservations advised. Major credit cards accepted. 6 Rue Coquillière, 1er (phone: 42-36-11-75). Moderate.

Pierre au Palais Royal – A delightful place with admirable bourgeois cooking (one Michelin star) and lovely chinon and saumur wines. Closed weekends and August. Reservations necessary. Major credit cards accepted. 10 Rue de Richelieu, 1er (phone: 42-96-27-17). Moderate.

Le Récamier – The so-called garden is actually a courtyard between a couple of high-rise buildings, but as the sun goes down, it's a very congenial place to dine in good weather. Martin Cantegrit is a perfect host, and the (one Michelin star) menu features first-rate fish dishes (try the turbot, if possible). The apple tart for dessert is special (order it warm), and the wine list is one of the most fairly priced on the Left Bank. Closed Sundays. Reservations necessary. Major credit cards accepted. 4 Rue Récamier, 7e (phone: 45-48-86-58). Moderate.

Restaurant du Marché – Cuisine Landaise, which means solid, country-style cooking — foie gras, *confits d'oie,* and fine wines from the Landes region in the southwest of France, near Bordeaux. An amazing choice of herb teas and a pretty terrace for summer dining. Open daily for lunch and dinner. Reservations advised. Major credit cards accepted. 59 Rue de Dantzig, 15e (phone: 45-32-26-88 or 45-33-23-72). Moderate.

La Rôtisserie du Beaujolais – A de rigueur spot for Paris's "in set" is Claude Terrail's recently opened casual canteen on the quai in the shadow of his three-star gastronomic temple, *Tour d'Argent*. Most of the meat, produce, and cheese served come from Lyons. Closed Monday and Tuesday afternoons. No reservations. Major credit cards accepted. 19 Quai de la Tournelle, 5e (phone: 43-54-17-47). Moderate.

Le Soufflé – On the street just behind the Rue Rivoli, not far from Place Vendôme, this is the place to enjoy an orgy of soufflés. We suggest crayfish soufflé for an appetizer, cheese soufflé as a main course, and chocolate soufflé for dessert — then head directly to your cardiologist! Closed Sundays. Reservations advised. Major credit cards accepted. 36 Rue du Mont-Thabor, 1er (phone: 42-60-27-19). Moderate.

Le Télégraphe – This former dormitory for female employees of the French post office attracts a trendy crowd, including Princess Stephanie of Monaco. The food is simple — *saumon unilatéral* (salmon filet cooked on one side with olive oil and herbs), and a good *crème brulée*. Open daily. Reservations advised. Major credit cards accepted. 41 Rue de Lille, 7e (phone: 40-15-06-65). Moderate.

Le Train Bleu – Fine food, good wine, and baroque decor so gorgeous it's been made a national monument. And it's in a train station. Open daily for lunch and dinner. Reservations usually unnecessary. Major credit cards accepted. Gare de Lyon, 20 Bd. Diderot, 12e (phone: 43-43-09-06). Moderate.

Ty-Coz – Breton cuisine features fish, cider, and crêpes; no meat, no cheese. Closed Sundays and Mondays. Reservations advised. Major credit cards accepted. 35 Rue St.-Georges, 9e (phone: 48-78-34-61). Moderate.

Le Zeyer – After a hard morning discount shopping on the nearby Rue d'Alesia, here's a good neighborhood place for mussels *marinière*, grilled *lotte* with sorrel, or platters of shellfish. Open daily. Reservations unnecessary. Major credit cards accepted. 234 Av. du Maine, 14e (phone: 45-40-43-88). Moderate.

Androuët – There's a great cheese emporium on the main floor and, upstairs, a unique restaurant where cheese is the base of every dish. In recent years the quality has slipped somewhat, but it still is a unique experience. Closed Sundays. Reservations advised. Major credit cards accepted. 41 Rue Amsterdam, 8e (phone: 48-74-26-90). Moderate to inexpensive.

Brasserie Lipp – This famous café is fashionable for a late supper of *choucroute* and Alsatian beer and for people watching inside and out. Closed 15 days at *Christmas*. Reservations advised. Major credit cards accepted. 151 Bd. St.-Germain, 6e (phone: 45-48-53-91). Moderate to inexpensive.

Chez La Vieille – Adrienne's cooking is simple, savory, and very popular. For lunch only. Closed weekends. Reservations necessary. No credit cards accepted. 28 Rue de l'Arbre-Séc, 1er (phone: 42-60-15-78). Moderate to inexpensive.

Clos de la Tour – This popular restaurant has "bistro moderne" decor. Closed Saturdays at lunch, Sundays, and August. Reservations advised. Major credit cards accepted. 22 Rue Falguière, 15e (phone: 43-22-34-73). Moderate to inexpensive.

Coup de Coeur – With a 2-level design reminiscent of Manhattan's stark Upper West Side eating establishments, this place features inventive cooking, eager waiters, and an interesting wine list. Closed Saturday lunch and Sundays. Reservations advised. Major credit cards accepted. 19 Rue St.-Augustin, 2e (phone: 47-03-45-70). Moderate to inexpensive.

Les Grandes Marches – Formerly the *Tour d'Argent Bastille,* though never related to Claude Terrail's 3-star temple overlooking the Seine, is a bustling, turn-of-the-century–style brasserie serving oysters and shellfish platters, fish, and grilled meat. Located next to the new *Opéra Bastille*. Open daily until 1:30 AM. Reservations advised. Major credit cards accepted. 6 Pl. de la Bastille, 11e (phone: 43-42-90-32). Moderate to inexpensive.

Joe Allen's – Just like the original on West 46th Street in New York City, it has good T-bone steaks, hamburgers, chili, and apple pie. Open daily till 1 AM. Reservations after 8 PM advised. Major credit cards accepted. 30 Rue Pierre-Lescot, 1er (phone: 42-36-70-13). Moderate to inexpensive.

Les Noces de Jeannette – Under new management, this place now offers inventive cuisine at reasonable prices. Closed Sunday evenings. Reservations advised. Major credit cards accepted. 14 Rue Favart, 2e (phone: 42-96-36-89). Moderate to inexpensive.

Le Petit Niçois – This tiny bistro, serving delicious bouillabaisse, is a favorite of French TV news crews who broadcast from a nearby building. A few good specials vary from night to night. Closed Sundays and Monday lunch. Reservations advised. Major credit cards accepted. 10 Rue Amélie, 7e (phone: 45-51-83-65). Moderate to inexpensive.

Au Petit Riche – Genuine 1900s decor, subtle Touraine cooking, and inexpensive vouvray, chinon, and bourgueil wines. Closed Sundays and August. Reservations advised. Major credit cards accepted. 25 Rue Le Peletier, 9e (phone: 47-70-68-68). Moderate to inexpensive.

Le Pharamond – Serves only the best Norman food in a beautiful Belle Epoque, timbered townhouse that has been declared a historic monument by the French government. Famous for *tripes à la mode de Caen* and *pommes soufflés* since 1862. Closed Sundays, Monday lunch, and July. Reservations advised. Major credit cards accepted. 24 Rue de la Grande-Truanderie, 1er (phone: 42-33-06-72). Moderate to inexpensive.

Atelier Maître Albert – Unlike most other eateries on the Left Bank, this one is pleasantly roomy, with a log fire in winter and an honest prix fixe menu year-round. Notre-Dame looms up in front of you as you walk out the door and onto the quai. Open daily except Sundays for dinner. Reservations advised. Major credit cards accepted. 1 Rue Maître-Albert, 5e (phone: 46-33-13-78). Inexpensive.

Aux Bigorneaux – A souvenir of the old *Les Halles,* this place is frequented by arty types and journalists. Especially recommended are the *foie gras frais maison,* the chicory salad, the steak au poivre, the Réserve Maison wine, and the sumptuous desserts. Closed Sundays, Mondays, and for dinner in winter. Reservations advised. Major credit cards accepted. 12 Rue Mondétour, 1er (phone: 45-08-49-33). Inexpensive.

Brasserie Flo – One of the last of the brasseries of the 1900s, owned by the enterprising Flo group. Hidden in a hard-to-find courtyard, it's excellent for oysters, foie gras, wild boar, and Alsatian specialties. Open daily and late. Reservations advised. Major credit cards accepted. 7 Cour des Petites-Ecuries, 10e (phone: 47-70-13-59). Inexpensive.

Brissemoret – Popular with Parisians, this eatery serves basic quality food at bargain prices. The tasteful ambience is a perfect setting for excellent foie gras, raw salmon marinated in fresh herbs, and great sauces (try the breast of duck in wine sauce). Closed Saturdays and Sundays. Reservations necessary. Major credit cards accepted. 5 Rue St.-Marc, 2e (phone: 42-36-91-72). Inexpensive.

Chez Fernand – A nondescript hole in the wall that produces surprisingly tasty dishes. *Pot au feu,* steaks with shallots, and fish pâté all are first-rate, but the real lure is the huge tub of chocolate mousse served for dessert — a chocoholic's fantasy come true. Open evenings only. Reservations advised. Visa accepted. 13 Rue Guirsade, 6e (phone: 43-54-61-47). Inexpensive.

Chez Jenny – A roisterous Alsatian brasserie, where the waitresses still wear white lace collars and dirndls. There are oysters year-round, though perhaps more in keeping with the place's character are the huge platters of *choucroute* (sauerkraut and assorted pork meat) accompanied by good riesling wine. Open daily. No reservations. Major credit cards accepted. 39 Bd. du Temple, 3e (phone: 42-74-75-75). Inexpensive.

Chez Marianne – A friendly Jewish delicatessen and restaurant; the falafels make nourishing fuel for any exploration of the Marais. Closed Fridays. Reservations unnecessary. Major credit cards accepted. 2 Rue des Hospitalières-St.-Gervais, 4e (phone: 42-72-18-86). Inexpensive.

Chez Yvette – This excellent, small, bourgeois restaurant has good home cooking, lots of choices, and great desserts. Closed weekends and August. Reservations advised. Major credit cards accepted. 46 *bis* Bd. Montparnasse, 6e (phone: 42-22-45-54). Inexpensive.

Chicago Meatpackers – If homesickness strikes, head here for hamburgers or chili; finish your American food fix with apple pie or chocolate chip cheesecake. Open daily. Reservations unnecessary. Major credit cards accepted. 8 Rue Coquillière (phone: 40-28-02-33). Inexpensive.

Gérard – A hearty *pot-au-feu* and other country favorites are served at this bistro. Closed Saturday lunch and Sundays. Reservations unnecessary. No credit cards accepted. 4 Rue du Mail, 2e (phone: 42-96-24-36). Inexpensive.

Le Jardin de la Mouffe – A choice of hors d'oeuvres, entrées, and desserts, plus a cheese course, half a carafe of wine, and a pretty garden view. Closed Mondays. Reservations unnecessary. Visa accepted. 75 Rue Mouffetard, 5e (phone: 47-07-19-29). Inexpensive.

Lunchtime – One of the few eateries in Paris that satisfies the desire for a light lunch, serving crispy mixed salads made with the freshest greens and a wide range of sandwiches, including blue cheese with cream, curried chicken with currants, and American standbys such as roast beef. The desserts are homemade and delicious. Lunch only. Closed Saturdays, Sundays, holidays, and August. Reservations unnecessary. No credit cards accepted. Two locations: 156 *bis* Av. Charles-de-Gaulle, Neuilly (phone: 46-24-08-99), and 255 Rue St.-Honoré (phone: 42-60-80-40). Inexpensive.

Moulin à Vent (Chez Henri) – Located across the street from what was once Paris's wine market, this bistro's decor has remained intact for over 40 years. The bar is adorned with half-barrels and small lights that are inscribed with the names of different wines and growers. The menu of meat (especially sausages from the Ardèche) and salads also has stayed the same. Try the frogs' legs and the steaks with shallots. Closed Sundays, Mondays, and August. Reservations necessary. Major credit cards accepted. 20 Rue des Fossés St.-Bernard, 5e (phone: 43-54-99-37). Inexpensive.

Paul – Once a secret bistro, it is now known by the whole world. There's good solid fare here, and the premises always are packed. Closed Mondays, Tuesdays, and August. Reservations advised. No credit cards accepted. 15 Pl. Dauphine, 1er (phone: 43-54-21-48). Inexpensive.

Petit Zinc – A popular late (3 AM) spot for fish, oysters, foie gras, and an ample, reasonably priced wine list. Open daily. Reservations advised. Major credit cards accepted. 25 Rue de Buci, 6e (phone: 46-33-51-66). Inexpensive.

Polidor – Regulars here keep their napkins in numbered pigeonholes, and the place's history includes frequent patronage by such starving artists as Paul Verlaine, James Joyce, Ernest Hemingway, and, more recently, Jean-Paul Belmondo. The College of Pataphysics, founded by Raymond Queneau and Ionesco, still meets here regularly for the good family-style food. Ask to see the house scrapbook. Closed in August. Reservations unnecessary. No credit cards accepted. 41 Rue Monsieur-le-Prince, 6e (phone: 43-26-95-34). Inexpensive.

Le Procope – One of Paris's oldest restaurants, where the food is reasonably good and the atmosphere couldn't be more Parisian; the service, however, leaves a lot to be desired. Open daily. Reservations advised. Major credit cards accepted. 13 Rue de l'Ancienne-Comédie, 6e (phone: 43-26-99-20). Inexpensive.

Relais de Venise – There's always a crowd waiting outside this place near the Porte Maillot, better known as "L'Entrecôte." The prix fixe menu includes free second helpings of steaks with pepper sauce and French fries. Fancy strawberry desserts cost extra. Open daily. No reservations. Major credit cards accepted. 271 Bd. Pereire, 17e (phone: 45-74-27-97). Inexpensive.

Robert et Louise – Family bistro, with warm paneled decor and a very high standard for ingredients and cooking. Try the *boeuf bourguignon* or the open-fire–grilled *côte de boeuf.* Also good are the *fromage blanc* and the wine *en pichet.* Closed Sundays, holidays, and August. Reservations unnecessary. No credit cards accepted. 64 Rue Vieille-du-Temple, 3e (phone: 42-78-55-89). Inexpensive.

Le Roi du Pot-au-Feu – A very good place to sample this delicious peasant dish. Closed Sundays. Reservations advised. Major credit cards accepted. 34 Rue Vignon, 9e (phone: 47-42-37-10). Inexpensive.

La Route du Beaujolais – It's a barnlike workers' bistro on the Left Bank, serving Lyonnaise specialties and Beaujolais wines. Don't miss the *charcuterie* and the fresh bread here, and try the *tarte tatin* (caramelized apple tart) for dessert. Closed Saturday lunch and Sundays. Reservations unnecessary. Visa accepted. 17 Rue de Lourmel, 15e (phone: 45-79-31-63). Inexpensive.

Le Trumilou – The formidable proprietress sets the tone of this robust establishment, which serves huge, steaming portions of boar, pheasant, and venison in season under a frieze of some excruciatingly bad rustic oils. Closed Mondays. Reservations unnecessary. Major credit cards accepted. 84 Quai de l'Hôtel-de-Ville, 5e (phone: 42-77-63-98). Inexpensive.

Vagenende – An Art Nouveau spot with fantasy decor that has changed little since it opened in 1898. It features adequate, filling meals at low prices. Open daily until 1 AM. Reservations unnecessary. Major credit cards accepted. 142 Bd. St.-Germain, 6e (phone: 43-26-68-18). Inexpensive.

Assiette au Boeuf – Steaks, salad, and *pommes frites,* with music in the evening. Open daily until 1 AM. No reservations. Major credit cards accepted. 123 Champs-Elysées, 8e (phone: 47-20-01-13). Very inexpensive.

Bistro de la Gare – Michel Oliver offers a choice of three appetizers and three main courses with *pommes frites.* Excellent for a quick lunch. Open daily. No reservations. Major credit cards accepted. Ten locations, including 73 Champs-Elysées, 8e (phone: 43-59-67-83); 59 Bd. Montparnasse, 6e (phone: 45-48-38-01); 38 Bd. des Italiens, 9e (phone: 48-24-49-61). Very inexpensive.

Chartier – Huge, turn-of-the-century place with lots of down-to-earth food for the money. Open daily until 9:30 PM. No reservations. No credit cards accepted. 7 Rue du Faubourg-Montmartre, 9e (phone: 47-70-86-29). Very inexpensive.

Drouot – The younger member of the Chartier family, but less known, and with more berets and fewer tourists. The waiters and waitresses, clad in black and white, look as if they emerged from a Renoir painting, although the decor is 1920s, with brass hat stands. The simple food is a bargain. To avoid a long wait for a table, arrive before 9 PM. Open daily. No reservations. No credit cards accepted. 103 Rue de Richelieu, 2e (phone: 42-96-68-23). Very inexpensive.

L'Etoile Verte – Not much to look at, but always full, it serves fresh and generous helpings of standard French classics — quenelles, seafood timbales, and so forth — at rock-bottom prices. Open daily. Reservations unnecessary. Major credit cards accepted. 13 Rue Brey, 17e (phone: 43-80-69-34). Very inexpensive.

L'Olympic Bar – Crowded at all hours, this popular hangout is open for meals at lunch only. Blue-collar workers, students, executives, fashionable women, and others eat and drink with pinball noise as a background. The decor is nothing to speak of, but the food is good, the portions huge, and the price is right. Closed

Sundays and sometimes for Saturday lunch. Reservations unnecessary. No credit cards accepted. 77 Rue St.-Dominique, 7e (phone: 45-51-75-87). Very inexpensive.

Le Petit Gavroche – A hole-in-the-wall bistro-cum-restaurant with a lively clientele, an inexpensive and classic menu, and the feeling that nothing has changed in years. Closed Sundays. Reservations unnecessary. No credit cards accepted. 15 Rue Ste.-Croix-de-la-Bretonnerie, 4e (phone: 48-87-74-26). Very inexpensive.

Le Petit St.-Benoît – French cooking at its simplest, in a plain little place with tiled floors and curlicued hat stands. Open weekdays. Reservations unnecessary. No credit cards accepted. 4 Rue St.-Benoît, 6e (phone: 42-60-27-92). Very inexpensive.

Au Pied de Fouet – This former coach house has had its habitués, including celebrities as diverse as Graham Greene, Le Corbusier, and Georges Pompidou. Service is fast and friendly, and it's a place to order the daily special. Desserts, such as *charlotte au chocolat,* are marvelous. Arrive early; it closes at 9 PM. Closed Saturday evenings, Sundays, 2 weeks at *Christmas* and *Easter,* and August. No reservations. No credit cards accepted. 45 Rue de Babylone, 7e (phone: 47-05-12-27). Very inexpensive.

■**EXTRA SPECIAL:** Although we've noted the existence of *Fauchon* in *Shopping,* we would be remiss in omitting it from the restaurant listings. Actually three spectacular stores stocking elegant edibles (at 26-30 Place de la Madeleine), *Fauchon* is considered so much a bastion of the privileged that one of its stores was bombed by radicals back in 1978. But the shops thankfully have long been back in full working order, which is a blessing for every abdomen in town.

One *Fauchon* shop specializes in the most beautiful fruits and vegetables available anywhere, plus pâtés, terrines, and as many other incomparable carryout items as even the most jaded gourmet's palate could conceive. If you're planning any sort of picnic, and are looking for something out of the ordinary, this is the place to pack your hamper. There also is a new grocery and sweet shop on the street level.

But it's across the narrow street in the far corner of the Place de la Madeleine that all of Paris congregates for nonpareil pastries, coffee, and an occasional snack or drink. Chocolate *opéra* cakes and macaroons in many hues, as well as *mille feuilles* and other custardy concoctions, are sold by the slice and can be sampled downstairs. Two years ago, the two original shops were joined by a *Fauchon* cafeteria/bar in the basement of the building located at 30 Place de la Madeleine and by a first class restaurant on the second floor. Breakfasts, lunches, snacks, and coffee are served downstairs throughout the day, while the restaurant upstairs is open for lunch and dinner. If you need a sugar surge during the course of your Paris meanderings, these are the places to take your high-caloric breaks.

For chocoholics: The very best hot chocolate in Paris (if not the universe) is served at *Angelina's* on the Rue Rivoli, 1er, and at its other location near the Porte Maillot métro in the Palais de Congrès. The best chocolate ice cream in the City of Light is at *Berthillon's* on the Ile St.-Louis (31 Rue St.-Louis-en-l'Ile, 4e). The best (and most generous) servings of chocolate mousse are offered at *Chez Fernand* (13 Rue Guirsade, 6e, on the Left Bank).

The name for the crusty sourdough loaf — *pain poilâne* — so beloved by the French comes from the tiny bakery, *Poilâne* (8 Rue du Cherche-Midi, 6e; phone: 45-48-42-59). Also be sure not to miss their flaky apple tarts, the hearty walnut bread, and take a peek at the chandelier made of bread dough that lights up M. Poilâne's office. It is open daily, except Sundays, from 7:15 AM to 8:15 PM.

WINE BARS AND CAFÉS: Choosing a place to drink is not a pressing problem in Paris. Following is a selection of watering holes to suit a variety of tastes and thirsts. Prices tend to be higher than in the United States, with a *café crème* or a glass of red wine costing $3 or more in the more expensive establishments. The moderate ones charge $2 to $3 for the same, and you pay less than $2 in the inexpensive spots.

Café Costes – Paris's glittering example of post-postmodernism and something of a pioneer on the scene. It has an impressive marble stairway, a clock inspired by Fritz Lang's film *Metropolis*, some wild high-tech restrooms, and a fashionable complement of lounge lizards. Open daily. Reservations unnecessary. Major credit cards accepted. Sq. des Innocents, 1er (phone: 45-08-54-39). Expensive.

Fouquet's – All the cafés on the Champs-Elysées are overpriced and most are nasty, so it may be worth paying the inflated tab for a coffee at this one (also a full-blown and overblown restaurant), which at least has more style than all the rest — as well as a large corner for outdoor tables in summer. Always open. Reservations advised for dinner; unnecessary for the café. Major credit cards accepted. 99 Champs-Elysées, 8e (phone: 47-23-70-60). Expensive.

Harry's Bar – The son of the original Harry, who opened this celebrated establishment in 1911, is still at the helm here. And the memories of past patrons like Ernest Hemingway, Gertrude Stein, and George Gershwin are almost as tangible as the university flags and banners that hang from the paneled walls. Open 10:30 AM to 4 AM every day but *Christmas*. Reservations unnecessary. Major credit cards accepted. 5 Rue Daunou, 2e (phone: 42-61-71-14). Expensive.

Willi's – An enterprising Englishman set up this smart little wine bar, a pleasant walk through the Palais Royal gardens and only minutes from the *Louvre*. The wine selection — a list of 150 — is one of the best in Paris, with an emphasis on Côtes du Rhône. The chef creates some appetizing salads as well as a *plat du jour*. Closed Sundays. Reservations unnecessary. Major credit cards accepted. 13 Rue des Petits-Champs, 1er (phone: 42-61-05-09). Expensive to moderate.

Blue Fox – On a cobbled market street behind the Madeleine, this wine bar has a list of about 20 reasonably priced wines by the glass that changes every 2 weeks. And there's good charcuterie to go with them. Closed Saturday evenings and Sundays. Reservations unnecessary. Major credit cards accepted. Cité Berryer, 25 Rue Royale, 8e (phone: 42-65-08-47 or 42-65-10-72). Moderate.

L'Ecluse – This unassuming wine bar looking onto the Seine has fathered five others, more sophisticated, in the Rue François-I, at the Madeleine, at the *Opera*, in *Les Halles*, and in Neuilly. Its red velvet benches and wooden tables — not to mention its bordeaux and its fresh, homemade foie gras — remain unchanged. Open daily. Reservations unnecessary. Major credit cards accepted. 15 Quai des Grands-Augustins, 6e (phone: 46-33-58-74), and several other locations in Paris. Moderate.

Le Pain et Le Vin – An imaginative wine bar with daily hot luncheon specials. It's operated by four Parisian chefs, including Alain Dutournier of the *Carré des Feuillants* and *Au Trou Gascon*. Closed Wednesday evenings. Reservations unnecessary. Major credit cards accepted. Several locations, including 1 Rue d'Armaille, 17e (phone: 47-63-88-29). Moderate.

Le Petit Bacchus – A wine bar specializing in unusual regional wines, displayed in crowded rows. You can buy wine by the bottle to take home or on a picnic, or sample them at the counter with cheese and charcuterie. Closed Sundays and Mondays. Reservations unnecessary. Major credit cards accepted. 13 Rue du Cherche-Midi, 6e (phone: 45-44-01-07). Moderate.

Taverne Henri IV – A selection of nearly 20 wines are offered by the glass, along with generous servings of simple food such as open sandwiches of ham, cheese, sausage, or a terrine of wild boar. You also can order cold food combinations by the platter. Closed weekends. Reservations unnecessary. No credit cards accepted. 13 Pl. du Pont-Neuf, 1er (phone: 43-54-27-90). Moderate.

Zimmer – Centrally located and with new moldings and chandeliers, this is the place to stop off for a drink before or after a show at one of the nearby theaters. Open daily until 1:30 AM. Reservations unnecessary. Major credit cards accepted. 1 Pl. du Châtelet, 4e (phone: 42-36-74-04). Moderate.

Au Duc de Richelieu – Specializes in the wines of Beaujolais, Chiroubles, Juliénas, St.-Amour, and so on. A cozy atmosphere and lots of wine tasting certificates on the walls. Closed Sundays and August. Reservations unnecessary. No credit cards accepted. 110 Rue de Richelieu, 2e (phone: 42-96-38-38). Inexpensive.

Jacques Melac – An old-fashioned wine bar run by a young, extravagantly musta-chioed man from the Auvergne, who bottles and sells his own rustic wines. Closed Sundays and Mondays. Open until 6:30 PM except Tuesdays and Thursdays when a set dinner is served. No reservations. No credit cards accepted. 42 Rue Léon-Frot, 11e (phone: 43-70-59-27). Inexpensive.

La Palette – This Left Bank hideaway on a quiet square, with outdoor tables during the summer, stays lively with a young crowd until 2 AM every morning except in August. Perhaps the monocled gentlemen on the 1930s tiles and the oils hung on the walls paid the bills of never-to-be-successful painters. Closed Sundays, holidays, and August. Reservations unnecessary. No credit cards accepted. 43 Rue de Seine, 6e (phone: 43-26-68-15). Inexpensive.

Le Rubis – A tiny corner bar with an old-fashioned atmosphere and a big selection of wines — about 30 in all. With your glass of wine try the pork *rillettes,* a savory meat paste made on the premises. Closed on weekends and 2 weeks in August. No reservations. No credit cards accepted. 10 Rue du Marché-St.-Honoré, 1er (phone: 42-61-03-34). Inexpensive.

Au Sauvignon – The no-nonsense couple in blue overalls who run this tiny corner bar look as if they just stepped in from the country. They seem to be in perpetual motion, pouring the white sauvignon and carving up chunky sandwiches from the famous *Poilâne* bakery not far away. Closed Sundays, 2 weeks in January, *Easter,* and August. Reservations unnecessary. No credit cards accepted. 80 Rue des Sts.-Pères, 7e (phone: 45-48-49-02). Inexpensive.

La Tartine – One of the old, authentic bistros, with a colorful local clientele and a good selection of wine by the glass. Closed Tuesdays and Wednesday mornings. Reservations unnecessary. No credit cards accepted. 24 Rue de Rivoli, 4e (phone: 42-72-76-85). Inexpensive.

La Tour de Monthlery – Hidden away on a small street near *Les Halles,* this animated bistro with sawdust on the floor and hams hanging from the rafters serves hearty, simple fare at bargain prices. Reservations unnecessary. Major credit cards accepted. 5 Rue de Prouvaires, 1er (phone: 42-36-21-82). Inexpensive.

PRAGUE

Goethe once called Prague "the most precious stone in the stone crown of the world." The beauty of Prague has remained legendary ever since the Middle Ages. And anyone who has ever seen the sun's rays lengthening across the city, skimming the gilded roofs and towers of Hradcanyand or skirting the banks of the Vltava where swans glide silently by, will agree that it is indeed *Zlata Praha,* Golden Prague.

In recent times, however, Czechoslovakia's physical allure often has been obscured by its political intrigues. And hardly a day goes by when, together with the other Eastern European countries making the arduous transition from state-run systems to market economies, Prague hasn't found its way into international headlines.

The country's problems probably began with the Yalta agreement among Roosevelt, Stalin, and Churchill in 1945, whereunder Czechoslovakia was agreed to be made part of the Soviet Union's sphere of interest. Although the Czechoslovakian Communist party got only minimal support in the 1946 elections, within the next 2 years the party had succeeded in nationalizing the country's entire economy, and by the early 1950s demonstrated (in the travesty of justice known as the "Prague trial") that a fully totalitarian regime was in power.

The following decade saw a certain easing of centralized political, cultural, and economic control, as more enlightened party members gained power. In 1968, this trend culminated in the rise to power of party chief Alexander Dubcek, who promised Czech citizens "socialism with a human face." But Russian tanks quickly dashed liberal hopes, and the joy of the so-called "Prague Spring" was very short-lived. During the period of "normalization" that followed the harsh Russian suppression, most of the proponents of freedom went to jail, were sent into exile, or accepted retirement — Dubcek himself was relegated to an obscure post in the forestry ministry. The final blow to enlightened leadership came on January 16, 1969, when Jan Palach, a despondent 20-year-old student, burned himself to death in Wenceslas Square.

Virtually all of Czechoslovakia spent the next 2 decades in a paralyzing stupor, relieved suddenly in November 1989 when Communist power in the country — and in most of the rest of Eastern Europe — collapsed like a punctured lung. The leadership vacuum temporarily was filled by brave "amateurs" led by playwright Vàclav Havel, the singleminded champion of human rights who headed a young protest movement called Civic Forum. Then, in June 1990, in the first free elections in Czechoslovakia since 1946, 96% of the eligible voters cast votes in an election that brought Civic Forum (and its Slovak twin, Public Against Violence) to formal power. President Havel earned the legal right to try to govern Czechoslovakia.

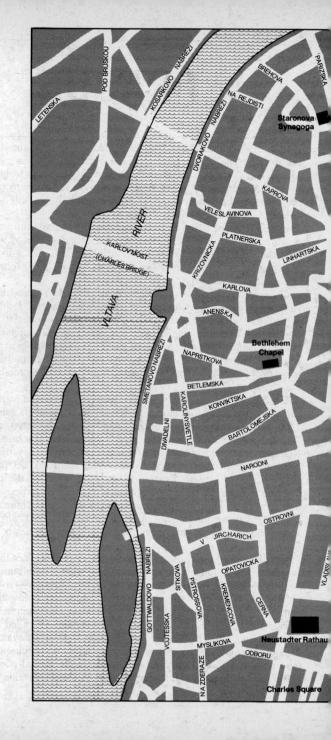

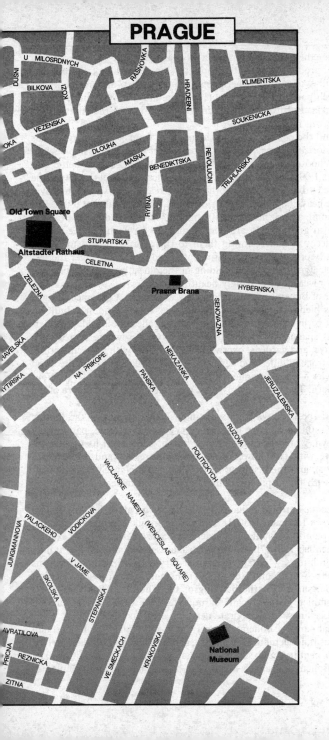

But then came the hard part; turning a mismanaged, state-owned economy into profitable, productive, private proprietorship. The role of the popular president is still evolving, and there continue to be deep disagreements between the Czech parts of the country (Bohemia and Moravia) and strongly Catholic Slovakia. Even the most optimistic Czech knows that the road to reconstruction will not be easy.

Yet despite all the convolutions on the political front, the country retains much of its historical perspective and flavor. And if you wish to step back in time, you can choose no better place than Czechoslovakia and no better city than Prague, its 1,000-year-old capital. The historical center of this city is the largest protected urban area in the world, for two reasons. First, Czechoslovakia escaped the heavy bombings of World War II, emerging almost unscathed physically. Second, almost half the 3,507 buildings now standing on Prague's original medieval ground plan are under landmark protection. The task of halting their decay — and restoring them to their former grandeur — is a dauntingly costly one, which only can be attacked piecemeal. Over the last couple of years, a good deal of scaffolding in the oldest parts of the city has come down to reveal breathtakingly beautiful façades.

In the center of Bohemia, Czechoslovakia's westernmost province, Prague is a sumptuous blend of nature and architecture. Like Rome, it is built on seven hills and is divided by a river, the Vltava (called the Moldau in German), which is spanned by 17 bridges. The city, everywhere dotted with parks, waterways, and gardens, overwhelms the visitor with its architecture. As in many European cities and towns, you can see layers of architectural periods and styles — Romanesque, Gothic, baroque, neo-classical, Art Nouveau, and modern. The Old Town is itself a course in the architecture of the last 500 years.

But Prague is best known for its distinguished examples of the Gothic and baroque. Gothic spires are literally everywhere in Prague, particularly in the Old Town, which boasts the Týn Church, 1365, with its Gothic exterior, complete with twin towers and flying buttresses (and, typically, a baroque interior), and the inspiring early Gothic Old-New Synagogue, majestically tall, with fluted pillars, pointed arches, and delicate stone embellishments.

Prague's baroque heritage includes the Wallenstein Palace, built by Italian architects between 1623 and 1630. It is an early baroque ensemble harmonizing sculptures, paintings, fountains, gardens, and a *sala terrena.* In an exuberant mood, Bohemia's rich 17th-century merchants and nobles invited Italian and German architects — notably the great Kryštof Dienzenhofer and his son, Kilián Ignaz — to decorate the capital in magnificent baroque style. First father, then son, supervised the building of the Church of St. Nicholas, a masterpiece complete with typically baroque features such as great curving forms, painted ceilings, and elaborate decorative effects.

The first inhabitants of Bohemia were a Celtic tribe called the Boïens, and the territory was Bolohaemom — hence the name Bohemia. The Slavs arrived during the 5th century, and settled in what is today known as Slovakia, Moravia, and Bohemia. Prague's history can be read not only in its buildings but also on the map of the city. The earliest settlements, first recorded in the 9th century, were at the foot of two ancient castles perched high on the tops of hills — Vyšehrad on the right bank of the Vltava and Hradčany on the left; after the fall of the great Moravian empire at the beginning of the 10th century, these strongholds became residences of the Bohemian kings On the right bank, a small settlement then formed a market center, which developed into the Old Town, and on the opposite bank, the Lesser Quarter grew up. Finally, Charles IV founded the New Town near the Old Town during the 14th century. The five royal towns of Prague, each retaining its distinct personality, officially became one in 1784.

Prague, first the seat of the Holy Roman Empire, then of the Hapsburgs, was the capital of the kingdom of Bohemia, coming into its full glory during the reign of Charles IV (1346–78). Charles, a man of culture and vision, founded the New Town, built Charles University (1348), reconstructed Prague Castle in the Gothic style, and initiated the construction of St. Vitus Cathedral. By then, Prague — with its 40,000 residents — was the third-biggest city in Europe, eclipsed only by Rome and Constantinople.

Beginning in 1402, John Huss preached his "fighting words" — advocating the reform of church abuses and the supremacy of Czech national aspirations in the face of German influences — from Prague's Bethlehem Chapel until he was burned at the stake in 1415; his martyrdom triggered the religious Hussite wars. In 1526, when Ferdinand I of Austria became king, the long oppression of the Czechs under the Hapsburgs began. His efforts to control the city were not only political in nature, but cultural as well. And he left his imprint on the architecture of the castle by having it rebuilt in Renaissance style. Vienna's efforts to reintroduce Catholicism and Germanization by force inspired the Czechs to passionate resistance — climaxed by the famous "defenestration" of two government officials: They literally were thrown out of the windows of Prague Castle in 1618, sparking a revolt by the Czech Protestant nobility and thereby central Europe's devastating Thirty Years War.

After the Czechs' defeat at the Battle of White Mountain (1620), and the public execution of 27 leaders, foreign nobles confiscated Czech lands, and Germanization reached its height under the Austrian Empress Maria Theresa in 1749, when German was made the official language. The Czech national spirit, however oppressed, never was vanquished; by 1918 the Republic of Czechoslovakia was born. But independence was tragically short-lived. Operating on the theory that their actions would keep Europe out of the war, France and England gave part of Bohemia to Germany during the infamous Munich Peace Conference in 1938. Hitler's troops occupied Bohemia and Moravia from 1939 until 1945, when the Czechs rose up against them in Prague, and held out bravely until the Soviet Army arrived 4 days later. (The Americans had already liberated western Bohemia, including Pilsen.)

The Communist state of Czechoslavakia was the result of a coup d'état in 1948, issuing directly from the Yalta agreement, and it ushered in a totalitarian regime from which it would take the country almost half a century to emerge.

Prague is a subtle and complex city, unfolding itself leaf by leaf, and then only to the most observant and curious visitors. To know the city, a visitor must amble through it slowly — discovering a palace here, a tower there, a decorative touch somewhere else, and now and then lingering at one of its numerous wine cellars and beer halls for refreshment.

Don't look here for the glitter of Parisian nightlife or the hurly-burly of London's Piccadilly Circus. Don't be deterred either by the networks of scaffolding crisscrossing the city's pollution-darkened buildings and monuments. They stand as proof that some much-needed metropolitan face-lifting is in progress, although, beware: In many places the scaffolding serves only to protect pedestrians from falling masonry. Do stop, look, and listen to Prague, because the city has much to tell, primarily through the rich blend of its architecture and its lovely natural setting.

Those who choose to stroll through the cobblestone streets, full of shadows at night, will follow in the footsteps of Mozart, Rilke, and Apollinaire, all of whom lived here, to say nothing of Franz Kafka, who was born here and who resided for a while in Golden Lane, a crooked little street behind the forbidding castle. In the words of another lover of Prague, the French poet Paul Valéry, "There is no city in the world in which magnificent wholes and valuable details and corners would be better combined, more happily situated."

PRAGUE AT-A-GLANCE

SEEING THE CITY: To catch the drama of Prague, visit the *Golden Prague* restaurant, on the eighth floor of the *Prague Inter-Continental* hotel (see *Best in Town,* "Checking In"), for a spectacular view of Prague Castle, particularly beautiful at sunset when the castle is a black silhouette and the last rays of the sun splash red and gold into the Vltava River. You'll know at once why this city is called Golden Prague. A view in the opposite direction opens out when traveling up Petřín Hill in the funicular (now open after decades of disuse).

SPECIAL PLACES: Any exploration should begin with a half-day tour of the city by motorcoach, with multilingual guide, offered by *Cedok,* the now privatized national tourist office. Buses leave from the *Cedok* branch office at 6 Bílkova, opposite the *Inter-Continental* (phone: 231-8255 or 231-9744). From then on, put on your walking shoes, and take in the city at a slow pace.

Historical Prague was originally five independent towns, and each of these five districts — New Town, Old Town, Lesser Town, Hradčany, and Vyšehrad — retains its individual character.

NEW TOWN (NOVÉ MĚSTO)

Prague's New Town dates from 1348, when it was established by King Charles IV. Wenceslas Square, with its profusion of shops, hotels, and restaurants, is the center of the modern city of Prague and a logical starting point for seeing the city.

Wenceslas Square (Václavské náměstí) – St. Václav ("Good King Wenceslas"), seated on his horse, guards this square, which is really a boulevard. Dominated by the

National Museum, Wenceslas Square — 2475 feet by 198 feet — is the central thoroughfare of the city, lined with Art Nouveau hotels, restaurants, cafés, and rather pricey shops.

National Museum (Národní muzeum) – The imposing neo-Renaissance façade and the interior decorations of this building reflect the spirit of late-19th-century Czech nationalism in which it was built. Its façade still bears the machine gun markings made by Russian troops, who mistook it for the Parliament during the 1968 invasion. Inside are paintings on Czech historical themes, fossils, stamps, and archaeological items. One of the few museums open Mondays (closed Tuesdays instead). Admission charge. 68 Václavské nám. (phone: 269451).

Flek's Inn (U Fleků) – Stop in and see one of Prague's most famous old pubs. No one knows quite how old it is, but it was in existence in 1499. Huge, with music and singing guests, *U Fleků* specializes in strong, dark beer, and is a big favorite among Germans and other tourists. 11 Křemencova (phone: 292436).

The Chalice (U Kalicha) – Another famous pilsner beer hall and restaurant, which is disappointingly modern in character (but full of literary allusions), where Jaroslav Hašek's Good Soldier Svejk set up a rendezvous "at 6 o'clock after the war." 12 Na bojišti (phone: 296017).

Slavia Café – Opposite the *National Theater* along the embankment, this is a gathering place for artists and intellectuals. 1 Národní (phone: 265616).

Charles Square (Karlovo náměstí) – Now a park surrounded by old buildings, the New Town's oldest square — and still Prague's largest — was the central market around which the town was proudly planned by Charles IV in 1348. On the north side is the oldest building in the New Town, the New Town Hall (Novoměstská radnice), site of its government from 1398 to 1784. On the south side of Charles Square, at No. 40, is an 18th-century baroque building known as Faust's House. Ever since the 14th century, houses on this site have been associated with alchemy and other occult practices. (The origin of the Faust legend is uncertain; it sometimes is said to have arisen from the strange adventures of a 16th-century English alchemist named Edward Kelley.)

Dvořák Museum – Once a summer residence called Villa Amerika (in the early 18th century), this lovely baroque building was designed by the noted architect K. I. Dienzenhofer. Fittingly, the building now houses mementos of Antonín Dvořák, the Czech composer of the great "New World Symphony" (which uses American folk tunes). In the sculpture garden in back of the house, Dvořák's music is performed during the summer. Closed Mondays. Admission charge. 20 Ke Karlovu, not far from Charles Sq. (phone: 298214).

OLD TOWN (STARÉ MĚSTO)

Walk here just before dusk, when the winding, narrow, cobblestone streets seem to merge into dim Gothic arcades. The Old Town, which contains most of the oldest buildings in Prague, dates from 1120. A great many medieval exteriors have been preserved in this area.

Powder Tower (Prašna brana) – This gate to the Old Town, used in the 17th century to store gunpowder, was first built in 1475, then rebuilt in the late 19th century. Here the Czech kings departed for the coronation route long ago. If you climb its 186 steps, the view is delightful. Na příkopě.

Celetná Street (Celetná ulice) – Renovated baroque townhouses line this curving street, once part of the royal coronation route. Today, visitors can follow it from the Powder Tower to Old Town Square, seeing the Carolinum, a 14th-century building that was part of the original university founded by King Charles IV (9 Celetná) along the way. Nearby is the *Tyl Theater* (11 Železná), where Mozart's masterpiece, *Don Gio-*

vanni, had its world première in 1787 and where scenes from the 1984 film *Amadeus* were shot. Theater renovations were completed last year, restoring the original magnificence and charm to this musical landmark. The theater is named for Josef Kateján Tyl, whose 1834 play, *The Fair* — and its provocative question, "Where is my home?" — inspired part of the Czechoslovakian national anthem.

Old Town Square (Staroměstské náměstí) – The center of Prague's Old Town, this important square was given a facelift in time for the 1988 celebration of the 40th anniversary of the Communist takeover. The monument to John Huss was erected in 1915, 500 years after the religious reformer was burned at the stake. Every hour on the hour, crowds gather to watch the astronomical clock (built in 1490) on the Old Town Hall as its mechanical figures of Christ, the 12 apostles, and allegorical *memento mori* figures perform their solemn march. The Town Hall itself was founded in 1338 and rebuilt many times (parts of it were destroyed by fire during the final days of World War II). The many treasures within include a dungeon and a well in the cellar, and a 15th-century council chamber adorned with 60 imaginative coats of arms belonging to the guilds of Prague and still used by the city government. Guided tours — some in English — are given hourly, following the clock's ritual.

On the east side of the square is the Church of Our Lady at Týn, dating from 1365, with its twin Gothic spires. Once the property of the Hussites and later of the Jesuits, this beautiful church combines a Gothic exterior with a baroque interior. Tycho de Brahe, the Danish astronomer, was buried here in 1601. A pretty little café, *U Týna,* is at 15 Staromětské náměstí. Nearby is the *House of the Bell* (Dům u Zvonu), a Gothic structure that serves as a municipal art exhibition hall, where concerts are performed.

This is "Kafka territory:" A bust of the writer commemorates the site of his birth in 1883, at 5 U radnice. He grew up in the graffiti-decorated house next to the Old Town Hall, and his father ran a shop on the ground floor of the rococo Goltz-Kinský Palace on the Old Town Square.

The Jewish Quarter – Walk north from the Old Town Hall on Pařížská Street and turn left on Cervená to see the Old-New Synagogue (Staronová synagoga), the oldest surviving synagogue in Europe (1270). One of Prague's most beautiful examples of the early Gothic style, it is truly inspiring, with its fluted pillars and sculptural decorations.

Jewish traders founded the Prague ghetto as early as the 9th century, and it became a center of Jewish culture by the 17th century. Parts of the ghetto were demolished in 1896 when Pařížská Street was being constructed. Only six synagogues and the cemetery remain. Visit the Old Jewish Cemetery, with its 12,000 15th- to 18th-century tombstones, several layers deep. It belongs to the *State Jewish Museum* (*Státni židovské muzeum;* 3 Jáchymova; phone: 231-0785), along with several former synagogues that now house exhibitions of religious articles and Hebrew manuscripts. In the restored Pinkas Synagogue (3 Siroká), the names of 77,297 Jewish men, women, and children murdered by the Nazis are painted on the interior walls. Ironically, during the war, the Nazis attempted to turn the entire Jewish quarter into a museum as a testament to the very culture they were seeking to destroy.

Convent of the Blessed Agnes – In a partly reconstructed Gothic convent, collections of 19th-century Czech paintings, porcelain, glass, silver, and pewter are on display. Closed Mondays. 17 U milosrdných.

Bethlehem Chapel (Betlémská kaple) – Here on the southern edge of the Old Town, the church reformer John Huss preached his revolutionary ideas from 1402 until his martyrdom in 1415. To the Czechs, Huss is a symbol of freedom from oppression and is revered as a national hero. The present chapel is a painstaking 1950-54 reconstruction of the original Gothic building, and the wooden threshold of the pulpit, once trod by Huss himself, is now protected under glass. 5 Betlémské nám.

Charles Bridge – One of the oldest and most beautiful bridges in Europe was built of stone in 1357 by Charles IV, between the Old Town and the Lesser Town. Lined on both sides by fine statues of the baroque period (1683–1714), its Lesser Town end has two towers; the higher one may be climbed for a spectacular view. The bridge is a favorite strolling place day or night, and it offers views of the castle, the Vltava River, and the lovely island of Kampa, with its chestnut trees. Vendors now sell trinkets and Soviet Red Army military wear along the bridge.

LESSER TOWN (MALÁ STRANA)

Sometimes called Little Town, this is Prague's baroque soul, founded in 1257 as the second of the royal towns (after the Old Town). During the 17th and 18th centuries, foreign noblemen and the Catholic church engaged some outstanding architects and artists to embellish what is the city's most picturesque quarter. Full of old palaces — including the magnificent Wallenstein Palace, where concerts are held during the summer — Lesser Town is a maze of little, crooked, cobblestone lanes full of old churches, museums, inns, wine cellars, and charming little parks. It is best just to wander around the town and discover its nooks and crannies for yourself.

Lesser Town Square (Malostranské náměstí) – Surrounded by 16th-century houses with arcades, the square — like the entire Lesser Town — is dominated by the Jesuit Church of St. Nicholas. Designed by famous 18th-century architects, the Dienzenhofers and Anselm Lurago, this is the finest baroque building in Prague.

Wallenstein Palace (Valdštejnský palác) – Northwest of St. Nicholas's Church is the magnificent baroque palace begun in 1624 by Italian architects for Albrecht Wallenstein, the great Hapsburg general. Unfortunately, the frescoes inside can't be seen because the building also houses the Ministry of Culture, but the public concerts in the garden are an experience that should not be missed. Valdštejnské nám.

Neruda Street (Nerudova ulice) – Leading from the Lesser Town to Hradčany Castle and lined on both sides by baroque façades is one of the most beautiful streets in the Lesser Town. Many townhouses on this street, named after Jan Neruda, the 19th-century writer, have preserved the old signs used before numbers were introduced: a red eagle, three violins, a golden goblet, and other quaint symbols.

HRADČANY

Near the castle of the same name, which probably was begun in the 9th century, is the Prague town of Hradčany, officially founded in 1320.

Prague Castle (Hradčany) – Today the seat of the government, this castle has been a Slav stronghold, residence of the Kings of Bohemia, and the seat of the President of the Republic; it is the history of the Czech nation in stone. With three walled and dizzyingly complex courtyards, the castle is best grasped with the help of a *Cedok* tour (see *Sources and Resources*). Perhaps most interesting is the interior of the vaulted, Gothic Vladislav Hall, where jousting tournaments once took place.

St. Vitus's Cathedral (Katedrála sv. Vita) – Dominating the castle is this Gothic mausoleum of the Czech kings and repository for the Czech crown jewels. (The jewels, however, rarely are shown to the public.)

Golden Lane (Zlatá ulička) – Just north of the castle, one of Prague's most charming cobblestone streets with little houses and shops is famous as the legendary street of alchemists who tried to turn lead into gold. Franz Kafka lived at No. 24 in 1917; it is now a bookstore.

National Gallery – From European Old Masters to Picasso, a very rich collection of paintings adorn the museum in the baroque Šternberk Palace on Castle Square. Closed Mondays. Admission charge. 15 Hradčanské nám. (phone: 352441).

St. George's Convent – An extensive collection of Czech Gothic art, which is superbly installed in the first convent founded in Bohemia. Jiřské nám.

The Loretto – Built in 1626 and so named because it was modeled after a pilgrimage church in Loretto, Italy. The church was declared a holy place after a house in Nazareth where Jesus and Mary had dwelt was miraculously transported there in 1299. It also is famous for the 1694 carillon in its clock tower and for the "Loretto treasury," a collection of extremely valuable 16th- to 18th-century jewelry and religious applied arts. Loretánské nám.

Strahov Monastery (Strahovský klášter) – West of the castle, high above the green slopes of Petřín Hill, is a gigantic monastery, built between 1140 and 1784, which once rivaled the castle itself in magnificence and whose garden provides a lovely view of Prague. Today, Strahov houses the *Museum of Czech Literature;* two baroque library halls also may be seen. Museum closed Mondays. Admission charge. Pohořelec (no phone).

VYŠEHRAD

High up on cliffs that rise above the Vltava on the side opposite Hradčany, this fortress and the town around it were probably founded in the 9th century. However, no one knows how old Vyšehrad really is; it may be much older.

Vyšehrad Fortress – Walk around the grounds, which include a park, the 11th-century Rotunda of St. Martin, and the Church of St. Peter and St. Paul.

Vyšehrad Cemetery – When you are in Vyšehrad, don't miss the burial place of the country's greats: Antonín Dvořák, Karel Capek, Jan Kubelik, Jan Neruda, and Bedřich Smetana are just a few.

■**EXTRA SPECIAL:** Kutná Hora, 42 miles (67 km) southeast of Prague, is a former silver mining town, which boomed in the 13th century, when its rich deposits were used to help create the splendor of the Bohemian court. During the 14th century, it was the second-largest town in the country. Here coins — including the thaler — were minted by craftsmen imported from Florence. Here also are the Vlašský Dvůr, a 13th-century palace where the craftsmen worked, a fine coin museum, a church whose vault is lined entirely with human skulls, and the unusual Gothic roof of St. Barbara's Church.

To see Ceský Sternberk, a 13th-century hilltop castle, as well, take *Cedok*'s 1-day bus excursion — "'Pearls of Czech Gothic Art" — on Thursdays.

Also of note nearby: The village of Lidice, 13 miles (21 km) from Prague, which was totally destroyed by the Nazis in 1942 in reprisal for the killing of a Nazi police governor. All local men were shot on sight, all women sent to concentration camps, and all young blond children shipped to the German Reich for adoption. Today the village (a national monument) has been preserved exactly as it was — so the ruins can serve as a "reminder" to the Czech people.

SOURCES AND RESOURCES

TOURIST INFORMATION: For general information, brochures, maps, and tour bookings, contact the now privatized *Cedok* (18 Na příkopě, Prague 1; phone: 212-7111), or Prague Information Service (20 Na příkopě; phone: 544444). The latter can arrange for private guides at its office (4 Panská; phone: 223411 or 224311), and as some people like to say, tourism in Czechoslovakia couldn't — or wouldn't — function without it. *Rekrea* (26-28 Parižska; phone: 231-

1192) is much smaller than *Cedok,* yet offers many services — and a much warmer welcome. And *IFB Bohemia* (25 Vaclavske Namesti; phone: 263747 or 262011), another private tourist agency, also is helpful. *Cedok* also can be contacted in New York (10 E. 40th St., New York, NY 10016; phone: 212-689-9720).

Note: In Prague there are still a number of black market money-changers. Their business has been drastically reduced, however, and they offer no better than 10% more than the official exchange rate. No matter how tempting they may seem, stay away.

The US Embassy is at 15 Třžistě (phone: 536641).

Local Coverage – You can find English-language newspapers in Prague in a few of the larger hotels or from street vendors in popular tourist areas. The *Prognosis* is a biweekly paper that includes local current events, and has excellent coverage of cultural events and nightlife in Prague. It can be purchased in major hotels, tourist offices, bookshops, and airline offices.

Food – Your best bet is to consult one of the tourist agencies.

TELEPHONE: The country code for Czechoslovakia is 42; the city code for Prague is 2.

GETTING AROUND: Airport – Praha-Ruzyně Airport, about 40 minutes from downtown by taxi, handles both domestic and international flights. Cab fare is about $10. Bus service connecting the airport and downtown leaves from Revoluční třída downtown and costs about 60¢; for more information, check with the *Czechoslovakia Airline* (*CSA*) counter at the airport. Shuttle bus service connecting the airport and major hotels costs about $5; more information can be obtained from the *Cedok* counter at the airport.

Bus and Tram – Though public transportation has been both inexpensive and good, bus and railway fares increased as the state began withdrawing its subsidies. You must buy a ticket at any newsstand or tobacco shop — not on the bus or tram. The ticket is punched once you are aboard. *Cedok*'s half-day motorcoach tour is a good introduction to the city and costs about $9.

Car Rental – At *Pragocar* (Nové Město, 42 Stěpánská; phone: 235-2825 or 235-2809 and Ruzyně Airport; phone: 367807); or *Europcar* (26 Parizska; phone: 213-0278).

Carriage Rides – A horse-drawn carriage ride, or *fiakr,* is a romantic way to see the city. The cost is about $40 per hour. You can find carriages drawn up at 5-13 Parizska; order them by phone (751489) or make reservations through *Cedok* or *Rekrea* (26-28 Parizska; phone: 231-1192).

Metro – Built in cooperation with the Russians and still expanding, the subway system is fast, safe, and clean. The same 4-koruna (about 12¢) ticket used for buses and trams can be purchased in metro stations.

Taxi – Reasonably priced taxis can be called at major hotels. Dial *Radio Taxi* at 203941 or 202951.

Train – The main train station is Praha Hlavní Nádraží, also called the Woodrow Wilson station in honor of the US president's efforts for peace at the end of World War I, and his subsequent involvement with negotiating the 1919 Treaty of Versailles, which officially recognized Czechoslovakia as an independent nation (Vítězného února; phone: 236-4441).

LOCAL SERVICES: Most hotels will try to arrange for any special services a business traveler might require.

Dentist (English-Speaking) – The number to call for emergency dental care is 261374, although English is not always spoken; it's best to ask the service desk at any major hotel to make the call for you.

Medical Emergency – The number to call is 155, although English is not always spoken; it's best to ask the service desk at any major hotel to make the call for you.

Pharmacy – Pharmacies alternate in staying open 24 hours a day; ask at your hotel desk about obtaining a schedule.

Post Office – Open from 6 AM to 6 PM weekdays, 8 AM to noon Saturdays. 1 Praha at 14 Jindřišská, Nové Město (phone: 264841 or 128).

Telex – Telex and telegraph service is always available at the post office at 14 Jindřišská, Nové Město (phone: 268301).

SPECIAL EVENTS: *Prague Spring* (Pražské Jaro), held every mid-May to early June since 1946, offers concerts, which include internationally known soloists, orchestras, chamber ensembles, and operas. Tickets are about $5. Every two years, one of the major European jazz festivals, *International Jazz Festival Prague* takes place. This year, concerts are held from October 25 to October 28; some of the performers scheduled include the legendary guitarist Joe Pass, the *Ambassador Big Band,* and the vocal group *Take Six;* previous festivals have included Chick Corea, Stéphane Grappelli, and Czech bands led by Gustav Brom and Milan Svoboda. For information, contact the *Czechoslovak Arts & Entertainment Agency Pragokoncert* (1 Maltézské nám.; phone: 533441). Prague also hosts several other smaller scale jazz events during the year — the *Prague Jazz Celebration Festival* in the spring, and the *Jazz on the Island Festival* in June. For further information, inquire at *Cedok* (see above) or *BTI* — a concert and tourist activities booking office (phone: 261889 or 231-8030).

MUSEUMS: In addition to the museums mentioned in *Special Places,* we recommend the following (all charge admission):

Antonín Dvořák Exhibition – Closed Mondays. 20 Ke Karlovu (phone: 298214).

Bedřich Smetana Exhibition – A museum devoted to the composer's life. Closed Tuesdays. 1 Novotného lavka (phone: 265371).

Bertramka – A 17th-century mansion in the Smíchov district, where Mozart stayed, now the *Mozart Museum.* Closed Tuesdays. 169 Mozartova (phone: 543893).

Museum of Musical Instruments – A must for music lovers, it has the second-largest collection of antique instruments in the world. Closed Mondays. 2 Lázeňská, Malá Strana (phone: 530843).

Museum of the Nation's Past – Its emphasis is on the baroque period. Closed Mondays. In the Lobkovic Palace, Jiřská St., behind Prague Castle (no phone).

SHOPPING: Bohemian glass and crystal are world famous. Especially recommended is *Moser* (12 Na příkopě). Also convenient is the *Bohemia* shop (2 Pařížská, on Old Town Square). Two doors away is a *Bižuteríe* (jewelry shop) aglitter with rhinestone tiaras and beaded necklaces.

Crafts can be bought in the Wenceslas Square area at *Slovenská Jizba* (40 Wenceslas Sq.) and *Krásná Jizba* (36 Národní třída); and at *Christmastime,* gingerbread tree ornaments are baked and sold at *Ceská Jizba* (12 Karlova). Contemporary artworks are sold at *Galerie Centrum* (6 ul. 28 října), and *Galerie Platýz* (37 Národní třída). For good recordings of Czech composers such as Smetana and Dvořák, browse through the record shop in the underground station at náměstí Republiky.

SPORTS AND FITNESS: Fitness Centers – The *Forum Praha* hotel (Kongresová ul.; phone: 410111), has a modern penthouse fitness center with gym, pool, squash courts, saunas, and solarium; there's a bowling alley in the hotel's pub. The *Inter-Continental* hotel (nám. Curieových; phone: 231-

9756) has exercise equipment and a sauna. The *Panorama* hotel (7 Milevská; phone: 416-1111) has a pool, sauna, and solarium. *Plavecký Stadión* (74 Podolská; phone: 439152), a 20-minute drive south of Prague in Podolí, has an Olympic-size pool, steamroom, and sauna.

Jogging – A good place is the Stromovka park, a 15-minute walk or 5-minute ride northeast from downtown.

Mini-Golf – At both the *International* hotel (1 nám. Družby, Prague 6-Dejvice; phone: 321051), and the *Forum Praha* hotel (Kongresova ul.; phone: 410111).

Soccer – Games are played at *Sparta Stadium* (98 Mílada Horaková, Letná). *Cedok* has tickets at its branch office (6 Bílkova) near the *Inter-Continental*.

Tennis – There are indoor and outdoor courts at *Sparta Stadium* (98 Mílada Horaková; phone: 325479) or *Centrálni Tenisový Dvorec* (7 Praha, Stavanice; phone: 213-6323 or 213-1270). Book court time through *Cedok* (18 Na příkopě; phone: 2127111).

 THEATER: Don't miss going to *Laterna Magika* (40 Národní; phone: 260033), a unique theater experience devised by the Czechs. It's not necessary to know Czech to enjoy this review, which includes dance, music, and film. Tickets cost about $3. Also popular with foreigners are the pantomime productions at the *Na zábradlí theater* (5 Anenské nám.; phone: 236-0449). Other theaters include the *National Theater* (2 Národní; phone: 205364), for the classics (in Czech), and the *New Stage* (phone: 205364), its architecturally controversial offshoot next door; and the *Smetana Theater* (8 Vítězného února; phone: 269746).

 MUSIC: Prague is a city that Mozart loved, where *Don Giovanni* had its world première; here Dvořák and Smetana lived and composed their music. Prague still is a very musical city. Concerts can be heard at the House of Artists, *Dvořák Hall* (nám. Jana Palacha; phone: 231-9164); Municipal House, *Smetana Hall* (5 nám. Republiky; phone: 232-5858); and *Palace of Culture, Congress Hall* (65 ul. 5 května; phone: 417-1111). Operas are performed at the *National* and *Smetana* theaters (see *Theater*).

During *Prague Spring,* concerts take place in various churches throughout the city. Several jazz festivals also take place in Prague, as well as a variety of other special musical events that vary from year to year. For specific information inquire at *Cedok* (see above).

 NIGHTCLUBS AND NIGHTLIFE: Prague is not a big nightclub town, but there are a few interesting after-dark places with live music and dancing. For jazz buffs, the *Reduta Jazz Club* (20 Národní St.; phone: 294340) has everything from Dixieland to swing to contemporary jazz-fusion nightly except Sundays. Plush furniture and a smoky, dark atmosphere grace this cozy jazz cellar. For teenage disco dancing try *Alfa* (28 Václavské nám.; phone: 223220) or *Jalta* (45 Václavské nám.; phone: 264683); *Est-Bar* (19 Washingtonova; phone: 222552) has dancing and entertainment; the *International Club* (1 nám. Družby; phone: 321051) also has dancing; *Lucerna* (61 Stěpánská; phone: 235-0888) and *Revue Alhambra* at the *Ambassador* hotel (5 Václavské nám.; phone: 220467) have entertainment. Those with a penchant for gambling can indulge themselves at *Roulette,* in the *Forum Praha* hotel (Kongresová ul.; phone: 410111), or at the casino at the *Ambassador* hotel (5 Václavské nám.; phone: 214-3111 or 221351). And if you're interested in a little pub crawling or wine tasting in the wee hours, ask *Cedok* about some of their latest after-dark tours. On your own, be sure to spend an evening at *U Fleků* (11 Křemencova; phone: 292436), one of Prague's oldest and most convivial pubs (see *Special Places*).

The biweekly English-language newspaper, *Prognosis,* includes listings of pubs, clubs, and other popular Prague hangouts.

BEST IN TOWN

 CHECKING IN: Most of the best hotels in Czechoslovakia belong to the Interhotel group and although a majority of them are now privatized, *Cedok* handles all bookings. One intriguing Prague option is called a "botel" (boat plus hotel), several of which are anchored in the Vltava River. For all hotels, advance bookings are essential, as the influx of tourists has created a greater-than-ever shortage of space in Prague. Interhotels are rated Deluxe, First Class (A), and Second Class (B); our categories of expensive, moderate, and inexpensive are roughly parallel. *Cedok* accepts bookings for non-deluxe hotels only on a half-board basis (meal vouchers can be used outside the hotel). Expect to pay from $70 all the way up to $200 for a double room in an expensive hotel; $40 to $70 for moderate; and $20 to $40 for the "botels," which are inexpensive. All telephone numbers are in the 2 city code unless otherwise indicated.

At the Three Ostriches (U tři pštrosů) – At the Lesser Town end of the Charles Bridge, this pretty 16th-century house now is Prague's most exclusive hotel, with a charming and first-rate restaurant. Its 18 rooms must be reserved at least a month in advance. 12 Dražického nám. (phone: 536151). Expensive.

Diplomat – Only a 10-minute drive from the city center, it's the most modern hostelry in town, with 387 rooms, 12 suites, and 5 business studios (each of which provides a bedroom and office space). There also are 4 restaurants and a nightclub, along with a sauna, whirlpool bath, and gym. Nonsmoking floors are available. Business facilities include meeting rooms for up to 250, audiovisual equipment, photocopiers, and cable television news. 15 Leninova (phone: 331-4111; fax: 341731; telex: 123280). Expensive.

Esplanade – Perhaps the most evocative of the pre–World War II hostelries in town, this Old World establishment has a very friendly family atmosphere and an excellent restaurant. There's a meeting room for up to 20. 19 Washingtonova (phone: 222552; fax: 265897). Expensive.

Forum Praha – Opposite the *Palace of Culture* conference center/concert hall, this is the most ambitious hotel in the country. It is a massive skyscraper with 492 doubles and 39 suites (including a "Presidential" suite), all of which have color TV sets featuring in-house movies. Only 5 minutes from downtown by taxi or subway. Other amenities include a fitness center, bowling alley, gift shops, elegant restaurant, nightclub, café, and the first casino in Prague. Business facilities include meeting rooms for up to 250, audiovisual equipment, photocopiers, cable television news, and translation services. Kongresová ul. (phone: 410111; fax: 420684 or 499480). Expensive.

International – This comfortable Soviet-style hotel is 15 minutes by subway from the center of Prague. In summer, Czech "beer party" and Slovak "wine party" entertainment programs are offered, which include dinner and folk songs and dances. (Tickets also are available at *Cedok.*) Business facilities include meeting rooms for up to 200 and cable television news. 1 nám. Družby (phone: 321051; fax: 311-6031). Expensive.

Jalta – A favorite of Americans, with 88 rooms, each with its own bath. The service staff is friendly and helpful, and the *Jalta Club* has disco music for dancing.

Business facilities include a meeting room for up to 20 and photocopiers. 45 Václavské nám. (phone: 226390; fax: 265541). Expensive.

Palace Praha – Recently renovated and deluxe, with Art Nouveau decor, it has 125 rooms and suites, a French restaurant, and a sauna. Business facilities include a meeting room for up to 60, audiovisual equipment, and photocopiers. In the heart of Prague, near the Old Town. 12 Panská (phone: 235-9394; fax: 235-9373). Expensive.

Prague Inter-Continental – This 11-story modern property, conveniently located on the edge of the Old Town, is sophisticated and has a very friendly staff. With 398 rooms, it offers superb views of the castle and the Old Town. Business facilities include 24-hour room service, meeting rooms for up to 100, audiovisual equipment, photocopiers, cable television news, and translation services. 5 Nám. Curieových (phone: 231-9756; fax: 231-9791 or 213-0500 for reservations). Expensive.

Ambassador – Exudes a somewhat faded Old World charm, with 115 rooms, a good restaurant, the *Pasáž Café,* and the *Embassy Bar.* Many of its rooms are furnished in Louis XIV style, with beautiful Czech crystal chandeliers. The hotel's casino offers blackjack and roulette. 5 Václavské nám. (phone: 214-3111 or 221351; fax: 236-7121). Expensive to moderate.

Panorama – Large, with 400 rooms, a pool and saunas, it's just four subway stops from the center of town. There's a meeting room for up to 15. 7 Milevská (phone: 416-1111). Expensive to moderate.

Paříž – This lovely 100-room *Jugendstil* (Art Nouveau) place has a café and a good restaurant decorated with blue mosaic tiles, and serving Czech specialties. Business facilities include a meeting room for up to 20, audiovisual equipment, and photocopiers. 1 U Obecního domu (phone: 236-2772; fax: 236-5948). Moderate.

■ **Note:** Three "botels" (ships built as hotels) are anchored in the Vltava River, with staterooms and bars; all are shipshape, lots of fun, and inexpensive. Each of them has about 80 rooms that are charming, though understandably somewhat cramped. They are: *Admirál* (Hořejší náb.; phone: 548685); *Albatros* (Náb. L. Svobody; phone: 231-3634); and *Racek* (Dvorecká louka; phone: 425793).

EATING OUT: Prague has thousands of eating places — outdoor cafés, wine cellars, pubs, and international restaurants. In most cases, reservations are advised, particularly during the *Easter* holidays and in summertime, but you would do well to note that they aren't always honored when you arrive. Czech cuisine is hearty and good, although it is weak on produce and fresh vegetables rarely appear on the menu. Specialties include *knedlíky* (dumplings), both plain and filled with fruit or meat; *knedlo-zelo-vepro* (baked pork with sauerkraut); *svíčková,* a beef marinated in spicy cream sauce; *uzené maso,* or smoked pork with potato dumplings and spinach; and roast goose or duck.

Wines from southern Moravia are the best; sample *tři grácie* in red, rosé, or white. In Prague, as elsewhere in the country, you have the choice of eating in either *pivnice* (beer halls), where the only drink is beer and dishes are quite basic, or in *vinarna,* where you can order wine and the food is a bit more distinctive. There also are the more traditional restaurants, where you have a multiple choice of drinks and food, and, interestingly enough, *dietni jedilna* (health food restaurants). But unlike those you are used to at home, these are designed for diners on special doctor's diets rather than those with health food or vegetarian tastes.

Restaurant prices in Prague generally are quite reasonable; we have rated a dinner for two at $30 and up as expensive; $20 to $30 as moderate; and $10 to $20 as inexpensive. Since businesses are now open to private enterprise, most eateries are converting to new ownerships. And since the Communist regime reduced most food to staple-Soviet cooking, better rated eateries usually signify a higher quality of interior design rather than cuisine. Remember, too, that you always can eat for almost nothing at a street stall, or "hall in the wall," a type of Czechoslovakian fast-food featuring grilled sausages. Note: Many restaurants do *not* accept credit cards. All telephone numbers are in the 2 city code unless otherwise indicated.

At the Golden Well (U zlaté studny) – Hearty fare is served at this stone-walled wine cellar with intimate niches for shadowy dining *à deux*. The building itself is famous for its gorgeous façade sculpture dating from 1714. Open daily. Reservations necessary. No credit cards accepted. 2 Karlova (phone: 263202). Expensive.

At the Painters' (U malířů) – A combination of 16th-century wall decorations and paintings and a 20th-century chef make this restaurant one of the finest dining experiences in Prague. This joint French-Czech venture opened in 1990, and has deliveries weekly from Parisian markets. French-style dishes are prepared superbly, with a choice selection of French wines available. Closed Sundays; open only for dinner. Reservations necessary. Major credit cards accepted. 11 Maltézské nám. (phone: 531883). Expensive.

At the Swans (U labutí) – This wine restaurant offers Czech specialties and atmosphere, with its old-fashioned nooks, vaulted ceilings, and window casings dating from the 14th century. Open daily for dinner. Reservations necessary. Major credit cards accepted. 11 Hradčanské nám. (phone: 539476). Expensive.

Chinese Restaurant (Cínská Restaurace) – Run by a Czech, this place serves some surprisingly good Chinese food in an atmosphere that is authentically Oriental. There are intimate booths for quiet dining. Closed Sundays. Reservations necessary. No credit cards accepted. 19 Vodičkova (phone: 262697). Expensive.

Diplomatic Club – A luxury establishment that caters to foreign visitors, it is complemented with a bar and a video room. Closed weekends. Reservations necessary. No credit cards accepted. 21 Karlova (phone: 261878 or 265701). Expensive.

Opera Grill – Most would agree that this is Prague's finest restaurant. Convenient to the *National Theater*, it offers excellent food and boasts a fine wine cellar. After dinner, a specialty is brandy served in a giant crystal snifter. Closed weekends. Reservations necessary. Major credit cards accepted. 35 Karolíny Světlé (another entrance at 24 Divadelni), in the Old Town (phone: 265508). Expensive.

St. Klara (Svatá Klára) – Three hundred years ago, Count Václav Vojtěch spent his evenings in his wine cellar a few steps below his baroque château. Today, foreign diplomats and others in the know frequent this *vinárna* (wine restaurant). It's cozier now than in the count's days, with its fireplace, fine service, accomplished cuisine, and selection of Moravian wines. Specialties range from fondue bourguignonne to *palačinky flambé* (crêpes), a classic Czech dessert. Open weekdays for dinner. Reservations necessary. No credit cards accepted. 9 U Trojského Zámku (phone: 841213). Expensive.

At the Spider (U pavouka) – When the dining room is full, as it usually is, ask to be seated in the elegantly appointed cocktail area. Open daily. Reservations necessary. Major credit cards accepted. In the courtyard of 17 Celetná (phone: 231-8714). Expensive to moderate.

Nabozízek – The funicular from Ujezd Street in Malá Strana brings diners to this pleasant restaurant with a terrace for good food and a gorgeous view. Open daily. Reservations necessary. No credit cards accepted. Petín Park (phone: 537905). Expensive to moderate.

At the Golden Stag (U zlatého jelena) – This small, intimate wine cellar has vaulted ceilings, tile floors, and wooden tables. Closed Sundays for lunch. Reservations necessary. No credit cards accepted. 11 Celetná (phone: 268595). Moderate.

At the Green Frog (U zelené žáby) – A favorite wine cellar among Americans, this place is more than 8 centuries old. The house specialty is grilled meat with sauerkraut. Open daily. Reservations necessary. No credit cards accepted. 8 U Radnice (phone: 262815). Moderate.

At the Red Wheel (U červeného kola) – In an open-air courtyard, it may take some effort to find this small spot — and even more to get in, since it is always crowded — but it is well worth the trouble. Closed Fridays. Reservations unnecessary. Major credit cards accepted. 2 Anežská (phone: 231-8941). Moderate.

At the 7 Angels (U sedmi andělů) – Furnished in a spare and elegant style — with a baroque accent. Try the *šíp amorův* ("arrow of love"), a specialty platter of grilled meat. Closed Mondays. Reservations unnecessary. No credit cards accepted. 20 Jilská (phone: 266355). Moderate.

Kóšer – A kosher restaurant located in Prague's Jewish Quarter. In the evening, alcohol is served, and a pianist plays. Open daily for lunch and dinner. Reservations necessary for dinner. No credit cards accepted. 18 Maislova (phone: 231-0909). Moderate.

Moskva – A Russian tearoom-restaurant located above a fast-food eatery called *Arbat.* Open daily. Reservations unnecessary. No credit cards accepted. In the pedestrian zone, at 29 Na příkopě (phone: 265821). Moderate.

Municipal House (Obecní dům) – On the left as you enter is an ornate *Jugendstil* (Art Deco) café and on the right an equally flamboyant restaurant, very convenient for lunch in the shopping area. Smoking is not allowed until after 2 PM. Open daily. Reservations unnecessary. No credit cards accepted. Nám. Republiky (phone: 231-8015). Moderate.

Pezinocká Vinárna – Beautifully designed, this Slovak wine restaurant features Gypsy music. Open daily. Reservations unnecessary. No credit cards accepted. In the House of Slovak Culture, 4 Purkyňova (phone: 291996). Moderate.

Praha Expo '58 – So named because it was the winner of the *1958 Brussels World's Fair* medal, this dining spot, in the Letenské Sády Park, between the Šverma and Hlávka bridges, offers diners a splendid view of the Vltava River and of the city. The food is excellent, particularly the pastries, which are a house specialty. Open daily. Reservations necessary. Major credit cards accepted. Letenské sady (phone: 374546 or 377339). Moderate.

U Golema – A good place to lunch before or after touring the *State Jewish Museum.* Popular with literary types, it has an elegantly simple decor. Try the veal with apple slices. Closed Mondays. Reservations necessary. Major credit cards accepted. 8 Maislova (phone: 231-0372). Moderate.

Vikárska – In the shadow of St. Vitus's Cathedral at Prague Castle, this small pub originally prepared meals only for church dignitaries. Now it is a favorite with locals and visitors. The restaurant specialty is called Bishop's Hat, a veal and cheese dish. Open daily. Reservations unnecessary. Major credit cards accepted. 6 Vikářská (phone: 535158). Moderate.

Vltava – A fish place that specializes in trout, prepared six different ways. Closed Mondays. Reservations unnecessary. No credit cards accepted. On the B. Engels Embankment, below street level (phone: 294964). Moderate.

At the Red Lobster (U červenéhoraka) – A small, pretty place for lunch or dinner. They serve an international menu, which includes steaks, seafood, lobster or shrimp cocktails, and a variety of desserts. Open daily. Reservations necessary. No credit cards accepted. 30 Karlova (phone: 265538). Inexpensive.

At the Town Hall (U Radnice) – Under the arcades just southeast of Old Town

Square, this typical beer cellar caters to businesspeople at lunch and dinner. It serves one of the best duck dinners in town. Open daily. Reservations unnecessary. No credit cards accepted. 2 Malé nám. (phone: 262822). Inexpensive.

Evropa Café – The pastries are only so-so, but the decor is a *Jugendstil* (Art Nouveau) feast for the eyes. Open daily. Reservations unnecessary. Visa only accepted. In the *Evropa Hotel,* 29 Václavské nám. (phone: 263720). Inexpensive.

U sv. Tomáše – Prague's oldest beer hall is huge, with vaulted ceilings. Populated by young students, the place offers plain wooden tables and huge steins of beer. The best dish is a plate of pork, sauerkraut, and dumplings. Open daily. Reservations unnecessary. No credit cards accepted. 12 Letenská (phone: 530064). Inexpensive.

ROME

If you're traveling from the north, you'll quickly understand why *Italia meridionale,* or southern Italy, begins in Rome: ancient stone ruins basking in the southern sun, baroque swirls teasing the senses at every turn, religious art exploding with color and Catholic sensuality — celebrating life with the conspicuous joie de vivre (here known as *gioia di vivere*) of southern Europe. Rome reaches out to your senses, blinding you with colors, beckoning you to stay. Its appeal is gripping and obviously romantic, inspiring throughout history many an illustrious northern visitor — such as Goethe, Keats, Byron, and Shelley — though today these romantic souls might be repelled by the insufferable noise, the screaming traffic, the exasperating strikes, political demonstrations, and general chaos of modern Rome. Yet despite the familiar symptoms of contemporary blight, Rome remains the Eternal City, ancient capital of the Western world, and center of Christianity for nearly 2,000 years.

Rome lies roughly in the center of the region of Lazio (Latium), just below the knee of boot-shaped Italy, between the Tyrrhenian Sea to the west and the Apennine Mountains to the east. The Tiber River gently curves through the city, with ancient Rome on its left bank, Vatican City and Trastevere (*tras* means across; *tevere,* Tiber) on its right. The original seven hills of Rome are all on the left bank, as is its modern center — the shopping areas that surround Piazza di Spagna (the so-called Spanish Steps), Piazza del Popolo, Via del Corso, Via del Tritone, and the legendary Via Veneto, celebrated in Fellini's film *La Dolce Vita.*

The 3rd-century Aurelian Walls still surround ancient Rome as well as most of papal and modern Rome. The city is unique because its fine buildings span so many centuries of history. There are Etruscan and ancient Roman remains, the most famous of which are the Colosseum and the Forum; buildings from the early Christian period such as the Castel Sant'Angelo; and a wealth of dazzling Renaissance and baroque architecture — from St. Peter's itself to Piazza del Campidoglio, the square designed by Michelangelo. The city abounds in churches, palaces, parks, piazze, statues, and fountains — all of which sparkle in the golden light and clear blue sky of the region.

Rome's beginnings are shrouded in a romantic legend that attributes the city's birth to Romulus and Remus, twin sons of the war god Mars and Rhea, a Vestal Virgin, who encountered Mars in a forest one day. The babies, left to die on the shore of the Tiber River at the foot of the Palatine Hill, were rescued and suckled through infancy by an old she-wolf and grew up to lead a band of adventurers and outlaws. Romulus, the stronger leader of the two, is said to have founded Rome in 753 BC, killing his brother to become its first king.

But earlier traces of habitation have been found on the Palatine Hill — one of the original seven hills — the site of Roma Quadrata, a primitive Rome

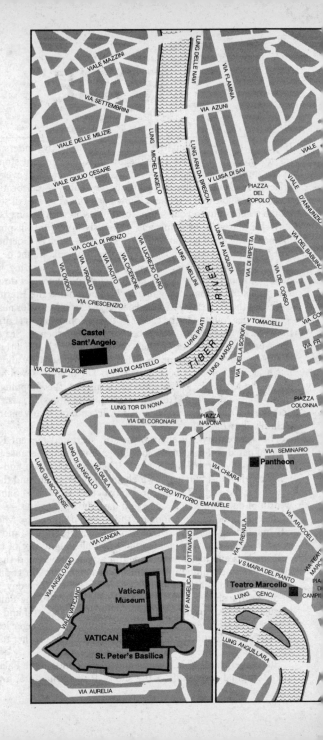

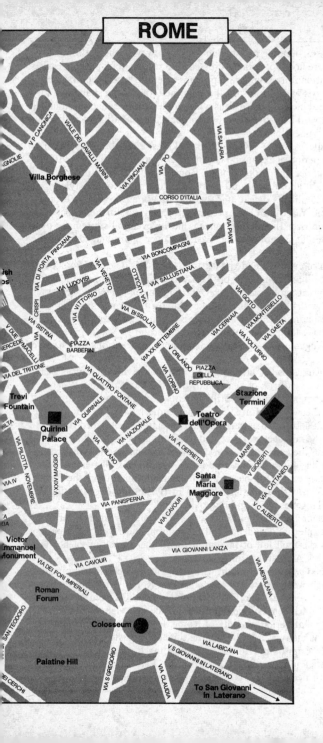

squared off by a surrounding rectangular wall. Below were the shallows of the Tiber River, where flocks of animals crossed, and trading took place in earlier times. The traditional founding date perhaps refers to when the first settlements of shepherds and farmers on the Palatine took on the shape of a city and the Latins, Sabines, and Etruscans who peopled the area had fused under one system of laws. The name *Roma* was probably a derivation of *Ruma,* an Etruscan noble name.

Following a succession of seven legendary kings, a republic was declared in 509 BC, and a period of expansion began. By 270 BC or so, the entire Italian peninsula was under the protection of Rome, and the resulting political unification brought about a cultural unity as well, a new Roman style in art and literature. Hannibal's defeat at Zama in 201 BC, an event that brought the Second Punic War to an end, prepared the way for further expansion: Rome's dominion over the Mediterranean and its eventual supremacy over Alexander the Great's empire in the East and over Spain and Gaul in the West.

A long period of civil war ended with Julius Caesar's defeat of Pompey in 48 BC, but the brilliant conqueror of Gaul was assassinated in the Senate 4 years later. His great-nephew and heir, Octavian, continued in the victorious vein, becoming, with the honorific name of Augustus, Rome's first emperor and one of its best administrators. Augustus is said to have found Rome a city of brick and to have left it a city of marble; the Theater of Marcellus and the Mausoleum of Augustus are among his many fine constructions that survive today.

The reign of Augustus (27 BC–AD 14) saw Roman civilization at its peak, and it ushered in 2 centuries of peace known as the Pax Romana. Wherever they went, the Romans introduced brilliant feats of engineering and architecture, as well as their own culture, government, and law. Persecution of the Christians, which had begun as early as Nero's reign — he blamed the burning of Rome on the new sect and executed large numbers of them in AD 64 — came to an end in the early 4th century, when Constantine the Great issued the Edict of Milan, guaranteeing freedom of worship for all religions. But Rome by now had become top-heavy with its own administration; the empire was divided in 395, with an eastern section in Byzantium (Constantinople, now Istanbul). This was the beginning of the end.

Rome's grandeur had long passed by the 5th century, when a series of economic crises, internal decadence and corruption, and repeated barbarian invasions led to the final fall of the empire with the deposition of her last emperor, Romulus Augustulus, in 476.

Thus began the Dark Ages, fraught with struggles between the empire and the church, which was centered in the papacy at Rome. Struggles between empire and papacy ensued. The Holy See, under Pope Clement V, actually fled Rome in the 14th century, taking up residence in Avignon, France, for 70 years. During that period, the city of Rome declined, and its population, which had been as many as a million at the time of Augustus, shrank to less than 50,000. The Capitoline Hill and once-bustling Roman Forum became pastures for goats and cows. Sheep grazed in St. Peter's.

The popes returned in 1377, and Rome again became the capital of the

Catholic world. Under papal patronage it was soon reborn artistically and culturally. During the 15th century, restoration of St. Peter's began, prior to its complete reconstruction; the Vatican complex was built; and new palaces, churches, and well-planned streets changed the face of the city. Powerful popes commissioned artists and architects to beautify Rome, and their genius created sumptuous palaces, splendid villas, and squares adorned with fountains and obelisks, until a second city grew out of the ruins of ancient Rome to match its former splendor. The 17th century brought the birth of baroque Rome, with its dominating figure, architect, sculptor, and painter Gian Lorenzo Bernini, whose masterpieces perhaps still best symbolize the spirit of this magnificent and undeniably theatrical city.

The comfortable security of the popes was shaken by the arrival of Napoleon Bonaparte in 1798. He soon set up a republic of Rome, deporting Pope Pius VI briefly to France, and in 1805 he was crowned King of Italy, proclaiming Rome a sort of second capital of the French Empire. In 1809, Napoleon declared the papal territories a part of France and in return was excommunicated by Pope Pius VII, who was deported to Fontainebleau. By 1815, the Napoleonic regime had collapsed, the papal kingdom was reconciled with France, and the pope was back in Rome, but the sparks of nationalistic passion had already been ignited in Italian hearts.

Friction between papal neutralism and patriotic fervor drove Pope Pius IX out of Rome to Gaeta in 1848. In 1849, Rome was again proclaimed a republic under the leadership of patriot Giuseppe Mazzini. Twice the French tried to restore the temporal power of the pope in Rome, meeting strong resistance from Republican forces led by Garibaldi. Finally, in 1870, the Italians entered Rome through a breach in the Aurelian Walls at Porta Pia and incorporated the city into the kingdom of Italy. That act dissolved the pontifical state and made Italian unity complete. A year later, Rome became the capital of the kingdom.

Mussolini's march on Rome in 1922 began the infamous Fascist regime that lasted until his downfall some 20 years later. The city was then occupied by the Germans until its liberation in 1944 by the Allies. In 1946, a referendum was held and Italy was declared a republic — just as it had been nearly 2½ millennia earlier.

Today, Rome is still the capital of Italy and of the Catholic church, as well as the home of some 3.5 million people (up from 260,000 inhabitants in 1870). Many Romans are employed in tourism-related industries and in government — in a city often strangled by bureaucratic problems. Besides filmmaking (in its cinematic heyday, Rome was called "Hollywood on the Tiber") and a certain amount of printing, there is some small-scale production of foodstuffs, pharmaceuticals, building materials, armaments, plastics, glass, clothing, religious articles, and handmade crafts. Thousands of artisans work in *botteghe* (shops) that open onto the streets in the area around Piazza Navona and in Trastevere.

For a society with significant problems — insufficient housing, impossible traffic, a soaring cost of living, and worrisome pollution — today's Romans still enjoy a relaxed way of life, as they have done for centuries. Perhaps nowhere north of Naples is the *arte di arrangiarsi* — the art of making do, or surviving with style — learned with such skill and practiced with such a timeless sense of resignation.

The *dolce vita* nightlife, more a figment of Fellini's imagination than a reality for any more than a handful of rich and/or famous Romans, has become subdued, but an unmistakable air of conviviality still prevails.

Not even soaring prices have limited the traditional Roman pastime of lingering lunches and late-night dinners at the city's 5,000 or so restaurants and trattorias. A sunny day at any time of the year still fills the cobblestone squares with diners at open-air eateries. They usually are engaged in animated conversation over their robust Roman food and inexpensive carafe wine from the Castelli (the surrounding hill towns such as Frascati). Most visitors are pleased to "do as the Romans do." No sense worrying about high prices and pollution if the inhabitants don't.

Roma, Non Basta Una Vita (Rome, A Lifetime Is Not Enough), by the late Italian author and journalist Silvio Negro, hints, with justification, at the impossibility of ever knowing everything about this city. For visitors who harbor the illusion of having seen all the ruins, churches, and monuments of Rome's glorious past, it may be time to begin discovering her countless hidden treasures, best done by walking the back streets and alleyways of the historic center (cars have limited access to many of them). Returning visitors will notice a spruced-up look — there are newly renovated palazzi everywhere, painted in the pale pastels popular in the early years of this century. And the *1990 World Cup* soccer games spurred on some transportation improvements as well — a new tram line and an efficient train service from Fiumicino Airport to downtown Rome.

If you feel suffocated by city life, try a day or two in the neighboring countryside. The surrounding Lazio region, sandwiched between the Tyrrhenian Sea and the Apennine Mountains, offers seaside resorts, rolling hills topped by medieval towns, picturesque lakes, rivers, and green meadows studded with umbrella pines, cypress trees, and wildflowers. Take an organized excursion to the Villa d'Este and Hadrian's Villa in Tivoli; to the Castelli Romani, or Roman hill towns, where the pope has his summer home; or to the excavations of Ostia Antica, the ancient port of Rome.

But take time to sit back and enjoy Rome. Visit the Forum and the Colosseum by day, and return at night when the ruins are bathed in gentler light to meditate over the rise and fall of ancient Rome. Watch the play of water in the Trevi Fountain or any of Rome's nearly 1,000 other fountains of every size and shape. See the ancient Roman Theater of Marcellus, which has been a Roman amphitheater, a medieval fort, a Renaissance palace, and which now contains apartments. Enjoy the savory cooking of the Lazio region. Ride a rented bicycle or jog in the Villa Borghese. Sip an *aperitivo* on the famed Via Veneto or at one of the many *caffès* that suddenly appear in unexpected corners of the historic city center.

Locally it is believed that on the last day of the world, while all the rest of humankind broods and repents, the Romans will throw a great farewell party, a gastronomic feast to end them all, with wine flowing from the city's many fountains. With the apocalypse not yet at hand, and despite the agonies besetting the country at large, the Eternal City remains eternally inviting.

ROME AT-A-GLANCE

SEEING THE CITY: Enjoy the magnificent view of all of Rome and the surrounding hill towns from Piazzale Garibaldi at the top of the Giancolo (Janiculum hill). It's best at sunset. Another panorama is visible from the top of St. Peter's dome. For a view of Rome dominated by St. Peter's, go to the terrace of the Pincio, next to the Villa Borghese, above Piazza del Popolo. And the most unusual view is of the dome of St. Peter's as seen in miniature through the keyhole of the gate to the priory of the Knights of Malta, on Piazza dei Cavalieri di Malta at the end of Via di Santa Sabina, on the Aventine hill. The picturesque piazza was designed by engraver Piranesi, a surrealist in spirit though he lived in the 18th century. For a real treat, a bird's-eye view of Rome is available via helicopter. Leaving from the Centro Sperimentale d'Aviazione at Urbe Airport (825 Via Salaria; phone: 812-3017), the $125 per-person fee yields 15 minutes of breathtaking spectacle. (Minimum of five passengers; reserve 1 week in advance.)

SPECIAL PLACES: Rome cannot be seen in a day, 3 days, a week, or even a year. If your time is limited to a few days, an organized bus tour is your best bet. (A quick and interesting one covers some 45 major sights in 3 hours. Although there is no guide, a short brochure gives the highlights. It leaves Piazza dei Cinquecento at 3:30 PM and, in winter, at 2:30 PM and costs about $6. Check the *ATAC* booth in the square for bus No. 110; it operates daily in season, weekends only out of season.) The Dutch Roman Catholic sisters of Foyer Unitas (30 Via Santa Maria dell'Anima; phone: 686-5951) lead free (though an offering is appreciated) tours to many sites around the city and the Vatican, and give slide presentations on various subjects (not always religious in nature). In addition, they offer information about Rome to anyone who drops in. Walking tours (usually in English) generally take place on Tuesdays, Thursdays, and some Saturdays. Then, when you've seen where your interests lie, grab your most comfortable walking shoes and a map. Most of historic Rome, which also is the city's center today, is within the 3rd-century Aurelian Walls and is delightfully walkable.

For practical purposes, the "must-sees" below are divided into ancient, papal, and modern Rome, but elements of two or all three categories often are found in one site — such as a sleek modern furniture shop in a Renaissance palace built with stones from the Colosseum. A further heading focuses on the palaces, fountains, splendid piazzas, and streets of Rome. The ancient center of the city is very close to Piazza Venezia, the heart of the modern city, and most of the sights of ancient Rome are around the Capitoline, Palatine, and Aventine hills. They can be seen on foot — though they were not built — in 1 day. Much of papal Rome is centered in the Vatican, but since all of Rome is a religious center, some of its many fascinating and beautiful churches are included under this heading. (For other churches, and for museums not mentioned below, see "Museums" in *Sources and Resources.*) Two bits of trivia worth noting: Throughout Rome, you will come across the initials *SPQR,* which stand for *Senatus Populusque Romanus* (the senate and the people of Rome). Ancient Romans used these letters to distinguish public works from private holdings, and as part of the city's inheritance they are still to be seen today — on everything from a magnificent monument to a mundane manhole cover. What's more, there really are seven hills of ancient Rome, and for the record they are called the Palatine, Capitoline, Quirinal, Viminal, Esquiline, Caelian, and the Aventine.

Virtually all the museums, monuments, and archaeological sites run by the state or city are closed on Sunday afternoons, and many on Mondays. Opening and closing hours change often (some are closed indefinitely because of strikes, personnel shortages, or restorations — it is estimated that only a third of Italy's artworks are exhibited), so check with your hotel, the tourist office, or the daily newspapers before starting out. Where possible, we have listed hours that seem relatively reliable.

Warning: Pickpockets work all around the city, but are especially numerous on such bus lines as the No. 56 to Via Veneto, and the Nos. 62 and 64 to the Vatican, and at the most popular tourist spots, even though plainclothes police scour these areas. Watch out especially for gangs of Gypsy children who will surround you and make straight for your wallet or purse. They haunt the Tiber bridges and the quayside walk to Porta Portese. Carry your shoulder bag on the arm *away* from passing vehicular traffic to avoid bag snatchers on motor scooters. Do not hang purses on café or restaurant chairs. Avoid carrying your passport and any significant amount of money around with you, and be sure to store valuables in a hotel safe-deposit box.

ANCIENT ROME

Colosseo (Colosseum) – It's said that when the Colosseum falls, Rome will fall — and the world will follow. This symbol of the eternity of Rome, the grandest and most celebrated of all its monuments, was completed in AD 80, and it is a logical starting point for a visitor to ancient Rome. See it in daylight, and return to see it by moonlight. The enormous arena, ⅓ mile in circumference and 137 feet high, once accommodated 50,000 spectators. To provide shade in the summer, a special detachment of sailors stretched a great awning over the top. There were 80 entrances (progressively numbered, except for the four main ones), allowing the crowds to quickly claim their marble seats. Underneath were subterranean passages where animals and other apparatus were hidden from view. In the arena itself, Christians were thrown to lions, wild beasts destroyed one another, and gladiators fought to the death. Gladiatorial combats lasted until 404, when Honorius put an end to them (possibly after a monk had thrown himself into the arena in protest and was killed by the angry crowd); animal combats were stopped toward the middle of the 6th century.

The Colosseum was abused by later generations. It was a fort in the Middle Ages; something of a quarry during the Renaissance, when its marble and travertine were used in the construction of St. Peter's and other buildings; and in the 18th century it even became a manure depot for the production of saltpeter. Yet it remains a symbol of the grandeur of Rome. Open daily. Admission charge for the upper level. Piazzale del Colosseo.

Palatino (Palatine Hill) – Adjacent to the Colosseum and the Roman Forum, the Palatine is where Rome began. Its Latin name is the source of the word *palace.* In fact, great men — Cicero, Crassus, Marc Antony — lived on this regal hill, and the Emperors of Rome — Augustus, Tiberius, Caligula, Nero, Domitian, Septimius Severus — built their palaces here, turning the hill into an imperial preserve. A 12th-century author called the spot the "palace of the Monarchy of the Earth, wherein is the capital seat of the whole world." In ruins by the Middle Ages, the ancient structures were incorporated into the sumptuous Villa Farnese in the 16th century, and the Farnese Gardens were laid out, the first botanical gardens in the world.

The Palatine is a lovely spot for a walk or a picnic. See especially the so-called House of Livia (actually of her husband, Augustus), with its remarkable frescoes; Domitian's Palace of the Flavians, built by his favorite architect, Rabirius; the impressive stadium; the view from the terrace of the Palace of Septimius Severus; and the remains of the Farnese Gardens at the top with another superb panorama of the nearby Forums. Closed Tuesdays; admission charge includes the Roman Forum. Enter at Via di San Gregorio or by way of the Roman Forum on Via dei Fori Imperiali.

Foro Romano (Roman Forum) – Adjoining the Palatine Hill is the Roman Forum, a mass of ruins overgrown with weeds and trees that was the commercial, civil, and religious center of ancient Rome. Its large ceremonial buildings included three triumphal arches, two public halls, half a dozen temples, and numerous monuments and statues. Set in what was once a marshy valley at the foot of the Capitoline Hill, the Forum was abandoned after the barbarian invasions and had become a cattle pasture by the Renaissance. When excavations began during the last century, it was under 20 feet of dirt.

Highlights of the Forum include the triumphal Arch of Septimius Severus, built by that emperor in AD 203; the Arch of Titus (AD 81), adorned with scenes depicting the victories of Titus, especially his conquest of Jerusalem and the spoils of Solomon's Temple; the ten magnificent marble columns — with a 16th-century baroque façade — of the Temple of Antoninus and Faustina; the eight columns of the Temple of Saturn (497 BC), site of the *Saturnalia*, the precursor of our *Mardi Gras;* three splendid Corinthian columns of the Temple of Castor and Pollux (484 BC); the Temple of Vesta and the nearby House of the Vestal Virgins, where highly esteemed virgins guarded the sacred flame of Vesta and their virginity — under the threat of being buried alive if they lost the latter. The once imposing Basilica of Maxentius (Basilica di Massenzio), otherwise known as the Basilica of Constantine, because it was begun by one and finished by the other, still has imposing proportions: 328 by 249 feet. Only the north aisle and three huge arches remain of this former law court and exchange.

As this is one of the most bewildering archaeological sites, a guide is extremely useful, especially for short-term visitors. A detailed plan and portable sound guide are available (in English) at the entrance. Open from 9 AM to 3 PM. Closed Tuesdays. Admission charge includes the Palatine Hill. Entrance on Via dei Fori Imperiali, opposite Via Cavour.

Fori Imperiali (Imperial Forums) – Next to the Roman Forum and now divided in two by Via dei Fori Imperiali is the civic center begun by Caesar to meet the demands of the expanding city when the Roman Forum became too congested. It was completed by Augustus, with further additions by later emperors. Abandoned in the Middle Ages, the Imperial Forums were revived by Mussolini, who constructed Via dei Fori Imperiali in 1932.

Two of the major sights are Trajan's Forum and Trajan's Market. Trajan's Forum, although not open to visitors, can be seen from the sidewalk surrounding it. It is memorable for the formidable 138-foot-high Trajan's Column, composed of 19 blocks of marble, now beautifully restored. The column is decorated with a spiral frieze depicting the Roman army under Trajan during the campaign against the Dacians — some 2,500 figures climbing toward the top where, since 1588, a statue of St. Peter has stood instead of the original one of Trajan. The Market (entered at 94 Via IV Novembre) is a 3-story construction with about 150 shops and commercial exchanges, some newly restored. Admission charge for Trajan's Market (closed Sunday afternoons and Mondays). Via dei Fori Imperiali.

Carcere Mamertino (Mamertine Prison) – Just off Via dei Fori Imperiali between the Roman Forum and the Campidoglio is the prison where Vercingetorix died and where, according to legend, St. Peter was imprisoned by Nero and used a miraculous spring to baptize his fellow inmates. From 509 to 27 BC it was a state prison where many were tortured and slaughtered. Much later, the prison became a chapel consecrated to St. Peter (called San Pietro in Carcere). To Charles Dickens it was a "ponderous, obdurate old prison . . . hideous and fearsome to behold." The gloomy dungeons below, made of enormous blocks of stone, are among the oldest structures in Rome. Via San Pietro in Carcere off Via dei Fori Imperiali.

Circo Massimo (Circus Maximus) – A few ruins dot the open grassy valley that once was the site of the great 4th-century BC arena. Originally ⅓ of a mile long and big enough to accommodate 250,000 spectators, the horseshoe shape of this racetrack served as a pattern for the other circuses that later arose in the Roman world. Today, the obelisks that decorated a long central shelf can be seen in Rome's Piazza del Laterano and Piazza del Popolo. The medieval tower that still stands is one of the few remains of the great fortresses built by the Frangipane family. Behind the Palatine Hill.

Pantheon – This, the best preserved of Roman buildings, was founded in 27 BC by Agrippa, who probably dedicated it to the seven planetary divinities, and rebuilt by Hadrian in AD 125. It became a Christian church in 606 and contains the tombs of Raphael and the first two Kings of Italy. The building is remarkable for its round plan combined with a Greek-style rectangular porch of 16 Corinthian columns (three were replaced in the Renaissance), for the ingenuity evident in the construction of the dome, and for its balanced proportions (the diameter of the interior and the height of the dome are the same). Closed Mondays. No admission charge. Piazza della Rotonda.

Terme di Caracalla (Baths of Caracalla) – These ruins are in the southern part of the city, near the beginning of the Appia Antica. Built in the 3rd century, they accommodated 1,600 bathers, but all that's left are sun-baked walls and some wall paintings. The vast scale makes a picturesque ruin, however, and Shelley composed "Prometheus Unbound" here. Operas are staged here in the summer. Baths open daily from 9 AM to 1:30 PM. Admission charge. Enter on Viale delle Terme di Caracalla, just short of Piazzale Numa Pompilio.

Porta San Sebastiano (St. Sebastian Gate) – This majestic opening in the 3rd-century Aurelian Walls (which encircle the city of Rome for 12 miles, with 383 defense towers) marks the beginning of the Appia Antica. It was, in fact, originally called the Porta Appia, and was rebuilt in the 5th century and restored again in the 6th century. Every Sunday morning, guided tours walk along the walls from Porta San Sebastiano to Porta Latina, affording good views of the Baths of Caracalla, the Appia Antica, and the Alban hills in the distance. The *Museo delle Mura* (Museum of the Walls), incorporated into the two medieval towers of the gate, contains local archaeological finds. Open Tuesdays through Saturdays from 9 AM to 1:30 PM; Tuesdays, Thursdays, and Saturdays from 4 to 7 PM; and Sundays from 9 AM to 1 PM. Admission charge. 18 Porta San Sebastiano (phone: 788-7035).

Via Appia Antica (Appian Way) – Portions of this famous 2,300-year-old road are still paved with the well-laid stones of the Romans. By 190 BC the Appian Way extended all the way from Rome to Capua, Benevento, and Brindisi on Italy's southeastern coast. Although its most famous sights are the Catacombs (see below), many other interesting ruins are scattered along the first 10 miles (16 km) of the route, which were used as a graveyard by patrician families because Roman law forbade burial (but not cremation) within the walls. Among the sights worth seeing is the Domine Quo Vadis chapel, about ½ mile beyond Porta San Sebastiano. It was built in the mid-9th century on the site where St. Peter, fleeing from Nero, had a vision of Christ. St. Peter said "Domine quo vadis?" ("Lord, whither goest thou?"). Christ replied that he was going back to Rome to be crucified again because Peter had abandoned the Christians in a moment of danger. Peter then returned to Rome to face his own martyrdom. Also see the Tomb of Cecilia Metella, daughter of a Roman general, a very picturesque ruin not quite 2 miles (3 km) from Porta San Sebastiano. Open daily from 9 AM to 1:30 PM. Admission charge.

Catacombe di San Callisto (Catacombs of St. Calixtus) – Of all the catacombs in Rome, these are the most famous. Catacombs are burial places in the form of galleries, or tunnels — miles of them, arranged in as many as 5 tiers — carved underground. Marble or terracotta slabs mark the openings where the bodies were laid to rest. Early Christians hid, prayed, and were buried in them from the 1st through the 4th centuries. After Christianity became the official religion of Rome, they were no longer necessary, but they remained places of pilgrimage because they contain the remains of so many early martyrs. St. Cecilia, St. Eusebius, and many martyred popes are buried here. Take a guided bus tour or a public bus. At the catacombs, guides, who are often priests, conduct regular tours in several languages. Closed Wednesdays. Admission charge. 110 Via Appia Antica.

Terme di Diocleziano (Baths of Diocletian) – West of the center of Rome, not far from the train station, are the largest baths in the empire, built in AD 305 to hold 3,000 people. The site now houses both the Church of Santa Maria degli Angeli, adapted by Michelangelo from the hall of the tepidarium of the baths, and the *Museo Nazionale Romano delle Terme* (National Museum of Rome of the Baths). The museum, one of the great archaeological museums of the world, contains numerous objects from ancient Rome — paintings, statuary, stuccowork, bronzes, objects of art, and even a mummy of a young girl. Admission charge to the museum, which is open Tuesdays through Saturdays from 9 AM to 1:45 PM and Sundays from 9 AM to 1 PM. The church is on Piazza della Repubblica; museum entrance is on Piazza dei Cinquecento (phone: 460530).

Castel Sant'Angelo – Dramatically facing the 2nd-century Ponte Sant'Angelo (St. Angelo Bridge — lined with statues of angels, including two originals by Bernini), this imposing monument was built by Hadrian in AD 139 as a burial place for himself and his family, but it has undergone many alterations, including the addition of the square wall with bastions at each corner named after the four evangelists. Later, as a fortress and prison, it saw a lot of history, especially in the 16th century. Some of the victims of the Borgias met their end here, popes took refuge here from antipapal forces (an underground passage connects it to the Vatican), and Benvenuto Cellini spent time as a prisoner on the premises. The last act of Puccini's opera *Tosca* takes place here. It is now a museum containing relics, works of art, ancient weapons, a prison cell, and a recently restored, 300-year-old papal bathtub. Open Mondays from 2 to 7:30 PM, Tuesdays through Saturdays from 9 AM to 7:30 PM, Sundays and holidays from 9 AM to 1 PM. Admission charge. Lungotevere Castello.

Teatro di Marcello (Theater of Marcellus) – Begun by Caesar, completed by Augustus, and named after the latter's nephew, this was the first stone theater in Rome and was said to have been the model for the Colosseum. It seated from 10,000 to 14,000 spectators and was in use for over 300 years. During the Middle Ages, what remained of the edifice became a fortress, and during the 16th century, the Savelli family transformed it into a palace, which later passed to the powerful Orsini family. The sumptuous apartments at the top still are inhabited by the Orsinis, whose emblem of a bear (*orso*) appears on the gateway in Via di Monte Savello, where the theater's stage once stood. Via del Teatro di Marcello. The palace can be visited only with a permit from City Hall: *Comune di Roma,* Ripartizione X, 29 Via del Portico d'Ottavia.

Largo Argentina – Just west of Piazza Venezia are the remains of four Roman temples, which, still unidentified, are among the oldest relics in Rome. It was at this site that Julius Caesar actually was assassinated (the Senate was meeting here temporarily because of fire damage to the Forum). The area, also the home of Rome's largest stray cat colony, is slated for much-needed archaeological excavation and restoration. Corso Vittorio Emanuele II.

Piramide di Caio Cestio (Pyramid of Caius Cestius) – In the southern part of the city, near the Protestant cemetery, is Rome's only pyramid. Completely covered with white marble, 121 feet high, it has a burial chamber inside decorated with frescoes and inscriptions. (Note: the interior can be visited only with special permission from the *Sovrintendenza Comunale ai Musei,* Monumenti, 3 Piazza Caffarelli.) Piazzale Ostiense.

PAPAL ROME

Città del Vaticano (Vatican City) – The Vatican City State, the world's second-smallest country (the smallest is also in Rome, the Sovereign Military Order of Malta, on Via Condotti), fits into a land area of less than 1 square mile within the city of Rome. Headquarters of the Roman Catholic church, the Vatican has been an independent state under the sovereignty of the pope since the Lateran Treaties were concluded in 1929. The Vatican has its own printing press and newspaper (*Osservatore Romano*), its own currency, railway, and radio station, as well as its own post office and postage stamps (thriving right now, with the surrounding Italian post offices functioning so badly, so do all your mailing from here! Vatican stamps may be used in Rome but not elsewhere in Italy, while Italian stamps may *not* be used in Vatican mailboxes). Souvenir packets of stamps can be purchased at the Philatelic Service in the office building on the left side of St. Peter's Church, entered under the Arch of the Bells. The Vatican's extraterritorial rights cover the other major basilicas (Santa Maria Maggiore, San Giovanni in Laterano, and San Paolo Fuori le Mura), the pope's summer home at Castel Gandolfo, and a few other buildings. It is governed politically by the pope and protected by an army of Swiss Guards (since 1506 when the corps was formed by Pope Julius II) whose uniforms were designed by Raphael. The changing of the guards takes place daily — at 9:30 and 11 AM, and 12:30, 2, 3:30, 4:30, and 5:30 PM.

General audiences are held by the pope every Wednesday on St. Peter's Square (at 10 AM during the summer; 11 AM in winter); in bad weather they are held in the Sala Udienza Paolo VI. Special audiences can be arranged for groups of 25 to 50 persons. Given John Paul II's propensity for travel, however, it is a good idea to check on his whereabouts before trekking off to the Vatican to see him. To arrange for free tickets to papal audiences, write to Bishop Dino Monduzzi (Prefettura della Casa Pontificia, Vatican City 00120, Italy). Be sure to include your address in Rome. Reservations will be confirmed by mail before the audience, but tickets will be delivered by messenger the day before. Last-minute bookings can be made in person from 9 AM to noon, up to 24 hours in advance, space permitting. They are available at the Prefettura office, located at the bronze doors of the right wing of the colonnade of St. Peter's Square.

Guided tours in English are offered year-round of Vatican City, including the underground excavations, the gardens, the Sistine Chapel, and the radio station. Sign up at the Ufficio Scavi (Excavations Office; near the Arch of the Bells; phone: 698-5318) for a 90-minute tour of the pre-Constantine necropolis in the Vatican, where it is believed that St. Peter is buried (closed Sundays; admission charge). Book a tour of the gardens at the *Vatican Tourist Information Office* (on the left side of St. Peter's Square, facing the church; phone: 698-4866). They are offered daily except Wednesdays and Sundays, from 10 AM to noon; in English on Thursdays. Admission charge. Also ask at the information office about tours of the Sistine Chapel (or make prior arrangements for a group visit through a travel agency). Weekdays from 8:30 AM to 1 PM there is a free 1-hour tour of Vatican Radio (3 Piazza Pia; phone: 698-34643), which broadcasts in 33 languages to 100 countries. Tickets also are available through Foyer Unitas (30 Via Santa Maria dell'Anima; phone: 686-5951) and Santa Susanna Catholic Church (14 Via XX Settembre; phone: 482-7510). Visits to the famous *Vatican Mosaic Workshop*, a school where students have been making miniature and full-size mosaic pictures for centuries, can be arranged by writing to Mons. Virgilio Noe (*Studio del Mosaico Vaticano,* Vatican City 00120, Italy; phone: 698-4466).

Piazza San Pietro (St. Peter's Square) – This 17th-century architectural masterpiece was created by Gian Lorenzo Bernini, the originator of the baroque style in Rome. The vast, open area is elliptical, with two semicircular colonnades, each four deep in Doric columns, framing the façade of St. Peter's Basilica. The colonnades are surmounted with statues of saints. An 83½-foot obelisk, shipped in a specially made boat from Heliopolis to Rome by Caligula, marks the center of the square and is flanked by two fountains that are still fed by the nearly 4-century-old Acqua Paola aqueduct which brings water from just north of Rome. Find the circular paving stone between the obelisk and one of the fountains and turn toward a colonnade: From that vantage point it will appear to be only a single row of columns.

Basilica di San Pietro (St. Peter's Basilica) – The first church here was built by Constantine on the site where St. Peter was martyred and subsequently buried. Some 11 centuries later it was the worse for wear, so renovation and then total reconstruction were undertaken. Michelangelo deserves a great deal of the credit for the existing church, but not all of it: Bramante began the plans in the early 16th century, with the dome of the Pantheon in mind; Michelangelo finished them in mid-century, thinking of Brunelleschi's dome in Florence. Giacomo della Porta took over the project at Michelangelo's death, actually raising the dome by the end of the century. In the early 17th century, Carlo Maderno made some modifications to the structure and completed the façade, and by the middle of the century Bernini was working on his colonnades. Open daily in summer from 7 AM to 7 PM, in winter from 7 AM to 6 PM. The vast dome of St. Peter's is visible from nearly everywhere in the city, just as the entire city is visible from the summit of the dome. For a fee, a visitor may go up into the dome by elevator, then take a staircase to the top for a panoramic view of Rome or a bird's-eye view of the pope's backyard. Also inside the basilica is the *Museo Storico* (Historical Museum; phone: 698-3410) which houses part of the Vatican's treasures. The dome and museum are open daily in summer from 8:30 AM to 5:30 PM, in winter from 8:30 AM to 4:30 PM. No admission charge.

The door farthest to the right of the portico is the Holy Door, opened and closed by the pope at the beginning and end of each *Jubilee Year,* usually only four times a century. The door farthest to the left is by the modern Italian sculptor Giacomo Manzù and dates from the 1960s. Among the treasures and masterpieces inside the basilica are the famous *Pietà* by Michelangelo (now encased in bulletproof glass since its mutilation and restoration a decade ago); the *Baldacchino* by Bernini, a colossal baroque amalgam of architecture and decorative sculpture weighing 46 tons; and the 13th-century statue of St. Peter by Arnolfo Di Cambio, his toes kissed smooth by the faithful. The interior of St. Peter's is gigantic and so overloaded with decoration that it takes some time to get a sense of the whole. Piazza San Pietro.

Musei Vaticani (Vatican Museums) – The Vatican's museum complex houses one of the most impressive collections in the world, embracing works of art of every epoch. It also contains some masterpieces created on the spot, foremost of which is the extraordinary Sistine Chapel, with Michelangelo's frescoes of the *Creation* on the ceiling (painted from 1508 to 1512) and his *Last Judgment* on the altar wall (1534 to 1541). The highly controversial restoration of the ceiling (sponsored by Japan's largest TV network) — only the first phase of the project — was completed 2 years ago after 10 years of work, and the removal of centuries of soot revealed unexpected vibrancy in Michelangelo's colors. A new lighting system also was installed in the chapel, and footnotes are being added to art histories. The second phase — restoration of the *Last Judgment* — is expected to take at least another year. The chapel is open in summer from 9 AM to 4 PM, the rest of the year from 9 AM to 1 PM.

While Michelangelo was painting the Sistine Chapel ceiling for Pope Julius II, the 25-year-old Raphael was working on the Stanza della Segnatura, one of the magnificent Raphael Rooms commissioned by the same pope, which would occupy the painter until his death. Also part of the Vatican museum complex are the *Pio-Clementino Museum of Greco-Roman Antiquities,* which houses such marvelous statues as *Laocoön and His Sons* and the *Apollo Belvedere;* the *Gregorian Etruscan Museum;* the *Pinacoteca* (Picture Gallery); the Library; and the Gregorian Profane, Pio-Cristiano, and Missionary-Ethnological sectors. Open 8:45 AM to 1:45 PM (longer in summer); closed Sundays except the last Sunday of the month, when the complex is open at no charge; other times there is an admission charge. Entrance on Viale Vaticano (phone: 698-3333).

San Giovanni in Laterano (Church of St. John Lateran) – Founded by Pope

Melchiades in the 4th century, this is the cathedral of Rome, the pope's parish church, in effect. It suffered barbarian vandalism, an earthquake, and several fires across the centuries; its interior was largely rebuilt in the 17th century by Borromini, who maintained the 16th-century wooden ceiling (the principal façade belongs to the 18th century). Older sections are the lovely cloisters, dating from the 13th century, and the baptistry, from the time of Constantine. The adjoining Lateran Palace was built in the 15th century on the site of an earlier one that had been the home of the popes from Constantine's day to the Avignon Captivity and that had been destroyed by fire. In front of the palace and church are the Scala Santa (Holy Stairs), traditionally believed to have come from the palace of Pontius Pilate in Jerusalem and to have been climbed by Christ at the time of the Passion. The 28 marble steps, climbed by worshipers on their knees, lead to the Sancta Sanctorum, once the popes' private chapel (not open to the public, but visible through the grating). Both the chapel and the stairs were part of the earlier Lateran Palace but survived the fire. Also in the piazza is the oldest obelisk in Rome. Piazza di San Giovanni in Laterano.

Santa Maria Maggiore (Church of St. Mary Major) – A 5th-century church, rebuilt in the 13th century, with an 18th-century façade and the tallest campanile in Rome. It has particularly interesting 5th-century mosaics and a ceiling that was, according to tradition, gilded with the first gold to arrive from the New World. Piazza di Santa Maria Maggiore.

PIAZZAS, PALACES, AND OTHER SIGHTS

Piazza del Campidoglio – The Capitoline was the smallest of the original seven hills, but since it was the political and religious center of ancient Rome, it was also the most important. When the need arose in the 16th century for some modern city planning, the task was given to someone worthy of the setting. Thus, the harmonious square seen today, with its delicate, elliptical, star-patterned pavement centered on a magnificent 2nd-century bronze equestrian statue of Marcus Aurelius (removed for restoration), is the design of none other than Michelangelo. The piazza is flanked by palaces on three sides: Palazzo Nuovo and Palazzo dei Conservatori, facing each other and together making up the *Musei Capitolini* (Capitoline Museums), and the Palazzo Senatorio, between the two, which houses officials of the municipal government. The *Capitoline Museums* are famous for an especially valuable collection of antique sculptures, including the *Capitoline Venus,* the *Dying Gaul,* a bronze statue (known as the *Spinario*) of a boy removing a thorn from his foot, and the *Capitoline Wolf,* an Etruscan bronze to which Romulus and Remus were added during the Renaissance. Open Tuesdays through Saturdays from 9 AM to 1:30 PM, and Sundays from 9 AM to 1 PM. Admission charge.

Piazza di Spagna (Spanish Steps) – One of the most picturesque settings of 18th-century Rome was named after a palace that housed the Spanish Embassy to the Holy See. The famous Spanish Steps actually were built by the French to connect the French quarter above with the Spanish area below. One of Rome's fine French churches, Trinità dei Monti, hovers over the 138 steps at the top, as does an ancient obelisk placed there by Pius VI in 1789. At the bottom of the steps — which in the spring are covered with hundreds of pots of azaleas — is the Barcaccia Fountain, depicting a sinking barge, inspired by the Tiber's flooding in 1589. Modern art historians disagree on whether this fountain, the oldest architectural feature of the square, was designed by Pietro Bernini or his son, the famous Gian Lorenzo Bernini.

Over the years, the steps have become a haunt of large crowds of young visitors, and all manner of crafts sales, caricature sketchers, and musicians contribute to the throng. The house where John Keats spent the last 3 months of his life and died, in February 1821, is next to the Spanish Steps at No. 26. It is now the *Keats-Shelley Memorial House* (phone: 678-4235), a museum dedicated to the English Romantic poets, especially

Keats, Shelley, Byron, and Leigh Hunt, with a library of more than 9,000 volumes of their works. Open weekdays from 9 AM to 5:30 PM (with a lunchbreak). Admission charge.

Via Condotti – A sort of Fifth Avenue of Rome, lined with the city's most exclusive shops, including *Gucci, Bulgari,* and *Ferragamo.* Only a few blocks long, it begins at the foot of the Spanish Steps, ends at Via del Corso, and is a favorite street for window shopping and the ritual evening *passeggiata,* or promenade, since it is — like much of the area — closed to traffic. Via Condotti's name derives from the water conduits built under it by Gregory XIII in the 16th century.

One of Via Condotti's landmarks is the famous *Antico Caffè Greco,* at No. 86, long a hangout for Romans and foreigners. Among its habitués were Goethe, Byron, Liszt, Buffalo Bill, Mark Twain, Oscar Wilde, and the Italian painter Giorgio de Chirico. The place is full of busts, statues, and varied mementos of its clientele, and the somber waiters still dress in tails. Another landmark, at No. 68, is the smallest sovereign state in the world, consisting of one historic palazzo. If you peek into its charming courtyard, you'll see cars with number plates bearing the letters SMOM (the Sovereign Military Order of Malta). Besides its own licenses, the order, founded during the Crusades, also issues a few passports and has its own diplomatic service and small merchant fleet.

Piazza del Popolo – This semicircular square at the foot of the Pincio was designed in neo-classical style by Valadier between 1816 and 1820. At its center is the second-oldest obelisk in Rome, dating from the 13th century BC. Twin-domed churches (Santa Maria di Montesanto and Santa Maria dei Miracoli) face a ceremonial gate where the Via Flaminia enters Rome. Next to the gate is the remarkable early Renaissance Church of Santa Maria del Popolo, an artistic treasure containing two paintings by Caravaggio, sculptures by Bernini, and frescoes by Pinturicchio, among others. The piazza's two open-air cafés, *Rosati* and *Canova,* are favorite meeting places.

Piazza Navona – This harmonious ensemble of Roman baroque is today a favorite haunt of Romans and tourists alike. It is also one of Rome's most historic squares, built on the site of Domitian's stadium. In the center is Bernini's fine Fontana dei Quattro Fiumi (Fountain of the Four Rivers), the huge figures representing the Nile, Ganges, Danube, and Plata. On the west side of the square is the Church of Sant'Agnese in Agone, much of it the work of a Bernini assistant, Borromini. There was little love lost between the two men, and according to a popular local legend, the hand of the Plata figure is raised in self-defense, just in case the façade of the church falls down, while the Nile figure hides under a veil to avoid seeing Borromini's mistakes. However, since the fountain was completed a year before the church was begun, the story doesn't hold water. From the 17th to the mid-19th century, the square would be flooded on August weekends, and the aristocrats of the city would cool off by splashing through the water in their carriages. Nowadays, during the *Christmas* season, until *Epiphany,* it is lined with booths selling sweets, toys, and nativity figures.

Piazza Farnese – This square is dominated by Palazzo Farnese, the most beautiful 16th-century palace in Rome. Commissioned by Cardinal Alessandro Farnese (later Pope Paul III), it was begun in 1514 by Sangallo the Younger, continued by Michelangelo, and completed by Della Porta in 1589. Opera fans will know it as the location of Scarpia's apartment in the second act of Puccini's *Tosca.* Today it is occupied by the French Embassy and can be visited only with special permission. The two fountains on the square incorporate bathtubs of Egyptian granite brought from the Baths of Caracalla.

Piazza Campo dei Fiori – Very near Piazza Farnese, one of Rome's most colorful squares is the scene of a general market every morning. In the center — surrounded by delicious cheeses, salamis, ripe fruit and vegetables, and *fiori* (flowers) of every kind — is a statue of the philosopher Giordano Bruno, who was burned at the stake here for heresy in 1600. Watch your wallet — this is a favorite hangout for thieves.

Piazza Mattei – A delightful clearing on the edge of the ancient Jewish ghetto, this small square's famous Fontana delle Tartarughe (Fountain of the Tortoises), sculpted in 1585 by Taddeo Landini, is one of Rome's most delightful. Four naked boys lean against the base and toss life-size bronze tortoises into a marble bowl above. The water moves in several directions, creating a magical effect in the tiny square.

Piazza del Quirinale – The Quirinal Palace was built by the popes in the late 16th to early 17th century as a summer residence, became the royal palace after the unification of Italy, and is now the official residence of the president of Italy. The so-called Monte Cavallo (Horse Tamers') Fountain is composed of two groups of statues depicting Castor and Pollux with their horses and a granite basin from the Forum once used as a cattle trough. The obelisk in the center is from the Mausoleum of Augustus. The square affords a marvelous view of Rome and St. Peter's. A band plays daily during the changing of the guard at 4 PM in winter, 4:30 PM in summer.

Fontana di Trevi (Trevi Fountain) – Designed by Nicola Salvi and completed in 1762, the Trevi Fountain (newly renovated after more than 2 years of work) took 30 years to build and is the last important monumental baroque work in Rome. Incongruously situated in a tiny square tucked away amidst narrow, cobblestoned streets, the magnificent fountain is quite striking when you suddenly come upon it at the turn of a corner. The colossal Oceanus in stone rides a chariot drawn by seahorses and is surrounded by a fantasy of gods, tritons, and horses. A low-voltage electronic field has been installed to discourage (but not injure) pigeons from perching on the fountain. According to legend, you will return to Rome if you stand with your back to the fountain and throw a coin over your left shoulder into the fountain. Young Roman men like to congregate in the small square on summer evenings, trying to pick up foreign women. Some prefer to pick your pocket — so be careful. Piazza di Trevi.

Piazza Barberini – At the foot of Via Veneto, this square in northern Rome has two of Bernini's famous fountains: the Triton Fountain in travertine, representing a triton sitting upon a scallop shell supported by four dolphins and blowing a conch shell; and the Fountain of the Bees on the corner of the Veneto, with three Barberini bees (of that family's crest) on the edge of a pool spurting thin jets of water into the basin below.

Villa Borghese (Borghese Gardens) – In the northern section of the city, this is Rome's most magnificent park, with hills, lakes, villas, and vistas. It is the former estate of Cardinal Scipione Borghese, designed for him in the 17th century and enlarged in the 18th century. Two museums are here: the *Galleria Borghese,* housed in the cardinal's small palace and noted for its Caravaggios, its Bernini sculptures, and Antonio Canova's statue of the reclining *Pauline Borghese;* and the *Galleria Nazionale d'Arte Moderna,* with its Italian modern works. Open Tuesdays through Saturdays from 9 AM to 2 PM, Sundays from 9 AM to 1 PM. No admission charge. The Villa Borghese is a wonderful place to sit and picnic in the shade of an umbrella pine on a hot summer day. Enter through the Porta Pinciana, at the top of Via Veneto, or walk up to the Pincio from Piazza del Popolo. The main entrance is at Piazzale Flaminio, just outside the Porta del Popolo.

Cimitero Protestante (Protestant Cemetery) – In the southern part of the city, behind the pyramid of Caius Cestius, the Protestant cemetery is principally a foreign enclave that harbors the remains of many adopted non-Catholics who chose to live and die in Rome: Keats, Shelley, Trelawny, Goethe's bastard son, and the Italian Communist leader Gramsci. There is nothing sad here — no pathos, no morbid sense of death — and few gardens are so delightful on a spring morning. 6 Via Caio Cestio.

Jewish Ghetto and Synagogue – On the banks of the Tiber River, near the Garibaldi Bridge, is this vibrant section of town, once a walled area, that is rich with restaurants offering Roman-Jewish specialties and tiny shops. The synagogue, located on the Lungotevere Cenci by the Tiber, houses a permanent exhibition of ritual objects from the 16th to the 19th century, plus documents of recent history. Open daily except Saturdays and on Jewish holidays.

Tiber Island – In the oldest part of the city, between Trastavere and the Jewish Ghetto, is this small, 900-foot-long island in the Tiber River. Roman legend has it that the island grew from a seed of grain tossed in after the Etruscan kings were forced out. Noteworthy is the Chiesa di San Bartolomeo (Church of St. Bartholomew) — set into its steps is a medieval marble font carved from an ancient column said to mark a sacred spring and early temple to Asclepius, the Greek god of healing. Victims of the city's 3rd-century plague were sent here and today a hospital here still cares for sick Romans. A small historical museum devoted to the island (*Museo Storico dell'Isola Tiberina*) was set to open as we went to press. There also is a tiny park on the marble-paved point of the island, a good spot to read or enjoy a picnic. The *Antico Caffè dell'Isola* has 2 rooms inside with tables for snacks. Next door is the popular trattoria *Sora Lella*.

MODERN ROME

Monumento a Vittorio Emanuele II (Monument to Victor Emmanuel II) – Sometimes called the Vittoriano, this most conspicuous landmark of questionable taste was completed in 1911 to celebrate the unification of Italy. Built of white Brescian marble and overwhelming the Capitoline Hill, it is often derided by Romans as the "wedding cake" or the "typewriter." It contains Italy's Tomb of the Unknown Soldier from World War I, and from the top you can see the network of modern boulevards built by Mussolini to open out the site of ancient Rome: Via dei Fori Imperiali, Via di San Gregorio, Via del Teatro di Marcello, and Via Nazionale — a busy and somewhat chaotic shopping street leading to the railroad station. Turn your back to the monument and note the 15th-century Palazzo Venezia to your left. It was from the small balcony of this building, his official residence, that Mussolini made his speeches. Piazza Venezia.

Via Vittorio Veneto – Popularly known as Via Veneto, this wide, café-lined street winds from a gate in the ancient Roman wall, the Porta Pinciana, down past the American Embassy to Piazza Barberini. The portion around Via Boncompagni is elegant, but the street also attracts a mixed crowd — from down-and-out actors and decadent Roman nobility to seedy gigolos and male prostitutes. Well-to-do Americans still stay in the fine hotels. The entire area, including the adjacent Via Bissolati with its many foreign airline offices, is well patrolled by police.

Porta Portese – Rome's flea market takes place on the edge of Trastevere on Sundays from dawn to about 1 or 2 PM. It's a colorful, crowded, and chaotic happening. Genuine antiques are few and far between, quickly scooped up before most people are out of bed. Still, you'll find some interesting junk, new and secondhand clothes, shoes, jeans, items brought by Eastern European immigrants, pop records, used tires and car parts, black market cigarettes — everything from Sicilian puppets to old postcards, sheet music, and broken bidets. Some say that if your wallet is stolen at the entrance, you'll find it for sale near the exit. Via Portuense.

OUT OF TOWN

Esposizione Universale di Roma (EUR) – Mussolini's ultramodern quarter was designed southwest of the center for an international exhibition that was supposed to take place in 1942 but never did. It's now a fashionable garden suburb and the site of international congresses and trade shows as well as of some remarkable sports installations built for the *1960 Olympic Games,* including the *Palazzo dello Sport,* with a dome by Pier Luigi Nervi. The *Museo della Civiltà Romana* (Museum of Roman Civilization) is worth seeing for its thorough reconstruction of ancient Rome at the time of Constantine. Open Tuesdays, Wednesdays, Fridays, and Saturdays from 9 AM to 1:30 PM, Thursdays from 4 to 7 PM, and Sundays from 9 AM to 1 PM. Admission charge. 10 Piazza Giovanni Agnelli (phone: 592-6135).

Ostia Antica – This immense excavation site about 15 miles (24 km) southwest of Rome was once the great trading port of ancient Rome, much closer to the mouth of the Tiber than it is today. The ruins — picturesquely set among pines and cypresses — first were uncovered in 1914 and new treasures are being discovered constantly. They have not had much chance to crumble, and they reveal a great deal about the building methods of the Romans and the management of a far-flung empire.

A visit takes at least half a day. Among the chief sites are the Piazzale delle Corporazioni (Corporations' Square), once 70 commercial offices, with mottoes and emblems in mosaics revealing that the merchants were shipwrights, caulkers, ropemakers, furriers, and shipowners from all over the ancient world; the capitolium and forum, baths, apartment blocks, and several private houses, especially the House of Cupid and Psyche; and the restored theater. Recent excavations have brought evidence of the town's Jewish community. Take the Decumanus Maximus to the end, turn left, and a few hundred yards away, on what was once the seashore, a synagogue stands, a moving testimonial to the Jewish presence in Rome in earliest times. Open daily except Mondays from 9 AM to 1 hour before sunset. A local museum (phone: 565-0022) traces the development of Ostia Antica and displays some outstanding statues, busts, and frescoes. Open daily except Mondays from 9 AM to 5 PM. Admission charge. To reach Ostia Antica, take the *metropolitana* from Stazione Termini, a train from Stazione Ostiense (the best choice), an *ACOTRAL* bus from Via Giolitti, or the *Tiber II* boat, daily from March through September (see *Getting Around*).

Lido di Ostia (also known as Lido di Roma) – Located 2½ miles (4 km) southwest of Ostia, it's a popular, polluted, and crowded seaside resort. Here and at other pleasant beaches both north and south of Rome, pollution has been so bad in recent years that swimming has been banned at many of them, but the view and the restaurants are pleasant, especially on summer evenings.

Castelli Romani – Rome's "castles" are actually 13 hill towns set in the lovely Alban Hills region southeast of Rome, an area where popes and powerful families of the past built fortresses, palaces, and other retreats. The mountains, the volcanic lakes of Nemi and Albano, chestnut groves, olive trees, and vines producing the famous Castelli wine continue to make the area a favorite destination of Romans who want to get away from the city on a fine day. Particularly charming are Frascati, known for its villas and its wines; Grottaferrata, famous for its fortified monastery, which can be visited; beautiful Lake Nemi, with its vivid blue waters and wooded surroundings, where Diana was worshiped; and Monte Cavo, a mountain whose summit can be reached by a toll road and which offers a panorama of the Castelli from a height of 3,124 feet. The Castelli Romani are best seen on an organized tour or by car — but beware of Sunday traffic. (For more information and a suggested itinerary, see Lazio in DIRECTIONS.)

■ **EXTRA SPECIAL:** Fountain fans should not miss Tivoli, a charming town perched on a hill and on a tributary of the Tiber (the Aniene) about 20 miles (32 km) east of Rome. It's famous for its villas, gardens, and, above all, cascading waters — all immortalized by Fragonard's 18th-century landscapes. Called *Tibur* by the ancient Romans, it was even then a resort for wealthy citizens, who bathed in its thermal waters, which remain therepeutic to this day.

The Villa d'Este, built for a cardinal in the 16th century, is the prime attraction — or, rather, its terraced gardens are. They contain some 500 fountains, large and small, including the jets of water lining the famous Avenue of the Hundred Fountains and the huge Organ Fountain, so named because it once worked a hydraulic organ. The villa and gardens are open to the public daily (admission charge). The fountains are gushing once again after being turned off because of fears that the water was polluted, but you'll have to look at them from behind a railing. On summer nights the fountains are beautifully illuminated, and there's a sound-and-light show. Nearby, the Villa Gregoriana, built by Pope Gregory XVI in the 19th century, has sloping gardens and lovely cascades (which are best on

Sundays, since most of the water is used for industrial purposes on other days), but it is definitely to be seen only after you have seen the Villa d'Este. It, too, is open daily; admission charge.

Only 4 miles (6 km) southwest of Tivoli is Villa Adriana (Hadrian's Villa), the most sumptuous of the villas left from ancient Roman times. It was built from AD 125 to 134 by the Emperor Hadrian, whose pleasure was to strew the grounds with replicas of famous buildings he had seen elsewhere in his empire. Extensively excavated and surrounded by greenery, the ruins of the villa include the Maritime Theater, built on an island and surrounded by a canal; the Golden Square in front of the remains of the palace; and the Terrace of Tempe, with a view of the valley of the same name. There are statues, fountains, cypress-lined avenues, pools, lakes, and canals. Closed Mondays; admission charge. You can see Tivoli with a guided tour or take an *ACOTRAL* bus from Via Gaeta or a train from Stazione Termini. Villa Adriana also can be reached by bus from Via Gaeta, but note that while one bus, leaving every hour, stops first at Villa Adriana and then at Tivoli, the other, leaving every half hour, goes directly to Tivoli and entails getting off at a crossroads and walking about a half-mile to Villa Adriana. If you rent a car (a wise choice), take the "autostrada per l'Aquila" to the Tivoli exit, then follow the signs.

SOURCES AND RESOURCES

TOURIST INFORMATION: The Ente Provinciale per il Turismo (EPT) for Rome and Lazio (headquartered at 11 Via Parigi; phone: 488-1851), has a main information office (5 Via Parigi; phone: 488-3748), with branches at Stazione Termini and in the customs area at Leonardo da Vinci Airport at Fiumicino. There also are branches at the Feronia "Punto Blu" and Frascati Est service areas of the A1 and A2 highways, respectively, for those arriving by car. All branches stock various booklets, maps, and hotel listings, all free. Ask for the English language monthly listing of events, *Carnet.*

The US Embassy and Consulate are at 119/A and 121 Via Vittorio Veneto respectively (phone: 46741).

For some good background material about Rome, see Georgina Masson's *Companion Guide to Rome* and Eleanor Clark's *Rome and a Villa,* both useful and amusing. A locally published book on the city's hidden treasures, *In Rome They Say,* by Margherita Naval, is also good reading; 30 walks through the city are described and mapped in *The Heart of Rome.* There are several English-language bookstores in the Spanish Steps area: the *Lion Bookshop* (181 Via del Babuino), *Anglo-American Book Company* (57 Via della Vite), and the *Bookshelf* (in the *Tritone Gallery,* 23 Via Due Macelli). The *Economy Book Center* (136 Via Torino) is particularly good for paperbacks.

For those especially interested in art history and archaeology, a team of professionals in both fields is available to take individuals or groups on private English-language tours of Rome, as well as 1- and 2-day trips outside the city. For information, contact Peter Zalewski (6 Via Cristoforo Colombo, Marcellina di Roma; phone: 774-425451; fax: 774-425122). An English-speaking German, Ruben Popper (12 Via dei Levii; phone: 761-0901), who has lived in Rome for 30 years, also leads tours (mostly walking) of the city.

Local Coverage – The *International Herald Tribune,* now also printed in Rome, is available at most newsstands each morning; it often lists major events in Italy in its Saturday "Weekend" section. *A Guest in Rome* is published by the Golden Key Association of Concierges. *La Repubblica, Corriere della Sera,* and *Il Messaggero* are daily newspapers that list local events on weekends; *La Repubblica* has an interesting Thursday supplement called "TrovaRoma" that lists the week's events, shows, theater, new movies, and more. *Wanted in Rome* is a useful handout found in American shops and schools.

Food – *La Guida d'Italia* — updated annually — is a comprehensive guide to restaurants and wine shops in Rome and throughout Italy. In Italian, it is published by *L'Espresso* and is available at newsstands. Another popular book — and with a fresher and zestier approach (but also in Italian) — is *Roma,* a restaurant guide published by Gambero Rosso.

 TELEPHONE: The country code for Italy is 39; the city code for Rome is 6. When calling from within Italy, dial 06 before the local number.

 GETTING AROUND: Airports – Leonardo da Vinci Airport in Fiumicino (phone: 601-24455 or 601-23640), about 21 miles (33 km) from downtown Rome, handles both international and domestic traffic. Check in at least 45 minutes before flights and allow waiting time in line, or you risk losing your reservation. In only moderate traffic, taxi travel time to the city is about 45 minutes and will cost up to $55, with additional costs for baggage, nighttime — after 10 PM — and holiday trips. The quickest and least expensive way to get to and from the airport is to take the train. Completed in 1990, an efficient and clean train line carries passengers between Leonardo da Vinci and the Piazza Piramide *metropolitana* station in Rome — 1 mile (1.6 km) south of the Colosseum — (where transfers can be made for *Linea A* and *Linea B*). The one-way fare is $5; service runs from 6:30 AM to 12:15 AM. A moving sidewalk from the airport's main terminal carries passengers to the *metropolitana*'s station near the airport. Taxis at the Piramide station can be hard to find; if you have lots of luggage, a better way to go is by cab from the airport. There no longer are any buses between the airport and the central railway station; however, from 6:30 AM to 12:15 AM, bus No. 176 departs from in front of the train station for Stazione Ostiense where it connects with the train to the airport. The fare is 1,000 lire (about 75¢). Ciampino Airport handles mostly charter traffic (phone: 794941). Urbe Airport is for private planes; it's a 15-minutes taxi ride from the center, and public transport (by bus) also is available from Piazza Vescorio; 825 Via Salaria (phone: 886-2075).

Bicycle and Moped – Pollution and insufferable traffic jams have made bicycling a popular, if sometimes dangerous, alternative to driving for many Romans. *Collati* (82 Via del Pellegrino; phone: 654-1084) rents bikes. Others can be found at Piazza San Silvestro, Piazza del Popolo, Piazza di Spagna, Piazza Augusto Imperatore, Lungotevere Marzio, and at Viale della Pineta and Viale dei Bambini in the Villa Borghese Gardens. To rent a moped, scooter, or motorbike, try *Scoot-a-long* (304 Via Cavour; phone: 678-0206); *Scooters for Rent* (66 Via della Purificazione, near Piazza Barberini; phone: 488-5485), which also rents bikes; and *St. Peter Moto* (43 Via Porta Castello, near St. Peter's; phone: 687-5714). By law, helmets must be worn while riding scooters or motorbikes.

Boat – From March through September, weather and water level permitting, the *Tiber II* carries 300 passengers on cruises along the river to Ostia Antica and back. It departs at 9:30 AM on Tuesdays, Thursdays, and Saturdays. For information and reservations, call *Tourvisa* at 445-3224 or the *Associazione Amici del Tevere* (Friends of the Tiber Society) at 637-0268. From May to September, the *Acquabus* plies the river daily, except Mondays, beating the road traffic, from Tiber Island to Duca d'Aosta Bridge near the *Olympic Stadium.* The trip takes 45 minutes each way and runs every

25 minutes. Pay the 1,000 lire (about 75¢) fare on board. Contact *Tourvisa* for information. For boat charters, contact *Aquarius* (32 Corso Vittorio Emanuele; phone: 687-1437).

Bus – *ATAC* (*Azienda Tramvie e Autobus Comune di Roma*), the city bus company, is the rather weak backbone of Rome's public transportation system. During August the number of buses in use is greatly reduced while drivers are on vacation. Most central routes are extremely crowded, getting off where you'd like is sometimes impossible, pickpockets are rampant, and some lines discontinue service after 9 PM, midnight, or 1 AM. Tickets, which currently cost about 75¢, must be purchased before boarding and are available at certain newsstands, tobacco shops, and bars. (Be aware that these outlets frequently exhaust their ticket supply, and the fine for riding without a ticket is about $40.) Remember to get on the bus via the back doors, stamp your ticket in the machine, and exit via the middle doors (the front doors are used only by *abbonati,* season ticket holders). There are no transfer tickets, but visitors can save money by buying 90-minute or full-day tickets, called "Big," at the *ATAC* information booth in Piazza dei Cinquecento or at principal bus stations, such as those at Piazza San Silvestro and Piazza Risorgimento. Tourists will appreciate the tiny, electric-powered No. 119, which loops through downtown Rome between Piazza del Popolo and close to Piazza Navona, passing the Spanish Steps. A weekly bus pass also is available, and route maps — *Roma in Metrobus* — are sold at the *ATAC* information booth and at the Ufficio Abbonamenti of *ATAC* at Largo Giovanni Montemartini and at some newsstands. For information, call 46951. Bus service to points out of town is run by *ACOTRAL* (including buses to Leonardo da Vinci Airport at Fiumicino). For information, call 593-5551. The Rome telephone directory's *TuttoCittà* supplement lists every street in the city and contains detailed maps of each zone as well as zip codes, bus routes, and taxi stands.

Car Rental – Major car rental firms such as *Avis* (38/A Via Sardegna; phone: 470-1229 in Rome, 167-863063 toll-free in Italy); *Budget* (24 Via Sistina; phone: 461905); *Europcar* (7 Via Lombardia; phone: 465802); and *Hertz* (156 Via Veneto; phone: 321-6831 or 321-6834); as well as several reliable Italian companies such as *Maggiore* (8/A Via Po; phone: 851620), have offices in the city and at the airport and railway stations. *Tropea* (1 Piazza Barberini; phone: 488-4682; fax: 482-8336) has rental and chauffeur-driven cars.

Leonardo da Vinci Airport (outside Rome) has desks at which tourists may buy coupons that can be redeemed at gas stations around Italy. Coupons must be purchased in foreign currency. Note that gas stations close for 2 hours at lunch and at 7 PM in winter, 7:30 PM in summer. Most are closed Sundays. Self-service stations operate with 10,000-lire ($8) notes. An efficient — and often economic — way to tour is by limousine. Hotels can suggest some, but a few to contact are *Capitol* (33 Via del Galoppatoio; phone: 360-5866); *Coop. UARA* (261 Via Panisperna; phone: 679-2320); and *Italo Mazzei Roma* (123 Via Trionfale; phone: 310963). Generally, it's not a good idea to hire free-lance taxis; drivers usually are unlicensed, and charge up to double the price of the regular taxi fare.

Horse-Drawn Carriages – Rome's *carrozzelle* accommodate up to five passengers and are available at major city squares (Piazza San Pietro, di Spagna, Venezia, and Navona), in front of the Colosseum, near the Trevi Fountain, on Via Veneto, and in the Villa Borghese. They can be hired by the half hour, hour, half day, or full day. Arrange the price with the driver before boarding — 1 hour currently costs about $50 minimum.

Subway – The *metropolitana,* Rome's subway, consists of two lines. *Linea A* runs roughly east-west, from an area close to the Vatican, across the Tiber, through the historic center (Piazza di Spagna, Piazza Barberini, Stazione Termini), and over to the eastern edge of the city past Cinecittà, the filmmaking center; a branch goes to the

Tiburtina train station, where numerous long-distance trains stop. *Linea B,* which is partly an underground and partly a surface railroad, runs north-south, from Stazione Termini to the Colosseum and, with a stop at the Ostiense station at Piazza Piramide to connect with the train to Leonardo da Vinci Airport, down to the southern suburb of EUR. The fare is about 80¢, and tickets are sold at certain newsstands, tobacco shops, and bars, as well as at most stations. Only a few stations are staffed with ticket sellers; there also are ticket-dispensing machines, but they only accept coins, so be prepared. Subway entrances are marked by a large red "M."

Taxi – Cabs can be hailed or found at numerous stands, which are listed in the yellow pages with their phone numbers. The *Radio Taxi* telephone numbers are 3570, 3875, 4994, and 8433. Taxi rates are increasing regularly, and drivers are obliged to show you, if asked, the current list of added charges. The current minimum fare is about $5 for the first 2 miles (3 km) or (if stalled in traffic) the first 9 minutes. After 10 PM, a night charge is added, and there are surcharges for holidays and for suitcases.

Train – Rome's main train station is Stazione Termini (phone: 4775 for information). There are several suburban stations, but the visitor is unlikely to use them except for Stazione Ostiense, from where trains depart for Ostia Antica and the Lido di Ostia (phone: 575-0732).

LOCAL SERVICES: Dentist (English-Speaking) – Dr. Peter Althoff (280 Via Salaria; phone: 844-3317); Dr. Charles Kennedy (29 Via della Fonte di Fauno; phone: 578-3639).

Dry Cleaner – *Tintoria Maddalena* (40 Piazza Maddalena; phone: 654-3348); *Minerva* (71/A Via del Gesù; phone: 679-2310); and *Mosca* (23 Via Belisario; phone: 482-7255).

Limousine Service – *Biancocavallo* (126 Via Tiburtina; phone: 520-2957); *Nazionale* (32/B Via Milano; phone: 481-8587; fax: 481-4530); *International* (60 Via Ludovisi; phone: 474-6078 or 475-0872); *Traiano* (19 Via Sant'Agata dei Goti; phone: 679-1518; fax: 678-7996).

Medical Emergency – *Policlinico* (1 Umberto, Viale Policlinico; phone: 492341); *Red Cross Ambulances* (phone: 5100). English-speaking physicians: Dr. Ettore Lollini (Salvador Mundi International Hospital, 67-77 Viale della Mura Gianicolensi; phone: 586041 or 839-3154); Dr. Frank Silvestri (36 Via Ludovisi; phone: 485706 or 332-2017); Dr. Susan Levenstein (Via Tritone; phone: 654-5708 or 475-8429); Dr. Vincenzo Baci (43 Via Cesare Balbo; phone: 474-1021). For an emergency house visit, around the clock, call 482-6741. In downtown Rome, the *San Giacomo Hospital* (off Via del Corso; phone: 67261) has an efficient first-aid service. The *Croce Rossa* (Red Cross; phone: 5100) provides ambulances.

Messenger Service – *Romana Recapiti* (two locations: 38 Via Vicenza; phone: 559-0917 or 559-0993; and 68 Via Palestro; phone: 495-6990); *Pony Express* (phone: 3309).

National/International Courier – National: *Carlo Ciucci* (18-20 Viale del Vignola; phone: 360-7803 or 360-5622). International: *DHL International* (two locations: Ciampino Airport, phone: 79491; and at the air terminal at the central railway station, 36 Via Giolitti; phone: 724-0641); *Stelci & Tavani* (103 Via Alessandro Severo; phone: 541-4460; fax: 541-1334); *Federal Express* will pick up at your hotel (phone: 675-2673; fax: 791-5831); *Fast Cargo* (141 Via dell'Omo; phone: 228-8305; fax: 228-8340); *XP-Express Parcel Systems Italy* (Ciampino Airport; phone: 796-0382); *Rinaldi* (34 Via Smerillo; phone: 410911; fax: 411-1565); *UPS/Alimondo* (329 Via della Magliana; phone: 527-3371; fax: 528-4859).

Office Equipment Rental – *Centro Macchina Ufficio* (48b-52 Via Tagliamento; phone: 867465 or 869233); *Executive Service* (68 Via Savoia; phone: 853241); *International Services Agency* (35 Piazza di Spagna; phone: 684-0287 or 684-0288).

Pharmacy – *Internazionale* (49 Piazza Barberini; phone: 462996); *Cola di Rienzo*

(213 Via Cola di Rienzo; phone: 351816). Both are open nights. To find out about drugstores open on Saturday afternoons and holidays, call 1921, or check the newspapers for their listings of *farmacie di turno.*

Photocopies – *Sandy* (58-59 Via San Basilio; phone: 475-8533 or 461346); *Centro Eliografico Prati* (7 Piazza dei Quiriti, near the Lepanto subway stop; phone: 389657 or 316643); *Centro Rank Xerox* (28 Largo delle Stimmate; phone: 654-1898; fax: 686-7542).

Post Office – The main post office (19 Piazza San Silvestro; phone: 6771) is open from 8:30 AM to 8 PM weekdays (until noon Saturdays). An express service called CAI (Corriere Accelerato Italiano) Post is now available at major post offices. Otherwise, Rome's most efficient post office for mail going out of Italy is the Vatican Post Office (Piazza San Pietro), open from 8:30 AM to 7 PM weekdays (until 6 PM Saturdays).

Secretary/Stenographer (English-Speaking) – *Rome At Your Service* (75 Via Orlando; phone: 484583 or 484429); *Executive Service* (78 Via Savoia; phone: 853241). Both can provide translation services. *Copisteria al Tritone* (17 Via Crispi; phone: 679-7190) has word processing facilities, fax machine, and secretarial services in English.

Tailor – *Cifonelli* (68 Via Sella; phone: 488-1827); *Caraceni* (two locations: 61/B Via Campania, phone: 488-2594; and 50 Via Sardegna, phone: 474-4023); *Coccurello,* for smaller budgets (7 Via Manfredi; phone: 802360 or 534-7038).

Telex/Facsimile Transmissions – Telexes and telegrams can be sent 24 hours daily from 18 Piazza San Silvestro (phone: 679-5530), next to the main post office. Fax service also is available there weekdays from 8:30 AM to 8 PM and from 8:30 AM to noon on Saturdays.

Translator – *World Translation Centre* (181 Via di Santa Maria Maggiore; phone: 475-5986, 461039, or 485922); *Agenzia Barberini* (5 Piazza Barberini; phone: 474-1738 or 488-1497; fax: 488-5491); *Alfa International* (29 Via Lucrezio Caro; phone: 323-0077; fax: 322-2038); *Rome at Your Service* (75 Via Orlando; phone: 484583); *Outer Relations Office* (123 Via Sistina; phone: 463951); *Executive Service* (78 Via Savoia; phone: 854-3241; fax: 844-0738). For simultaneous translations, contact *Centro Congressi* (23 Via Sallustiana; phone: 485990 or 465392); or *STOC* (two locations: 44 Via G. de Ruggiero, phone: 540-5621; and 203 Via Laurentina, phone: 540-3741).

Other – Convention Centers: *Palazzo dei Congressi* has 30 meeting rooms for up to 4,000 (Piazzale Kennedy in EUR; phone: 591-2735; fax: 592-4044); *Centro Internazionale Roma (CIR)* has 8 meeting rooms for up to 8,000 (619 Via Aurelia; phone: 6644; fax: 663-2689); *Palazzo dello Sport* has meeting rooms for up to 5,000 (Piazzale dello Sport; phone: 592-5107); *Palazzo Brancaccio* is available for conferences and is centrally located (7 Via Monte Oppio; phone: 487-3177). Also centrally located is the Renaissance *Palazzo Taverna* (37 Via di Monte Giordano; phone: 683-3785), which is available for receptions and business lunches. The Orsini-Odescalchi Castle (25 miles from Rome, in Bracciano) is a 15th-century castle, richly furnished and decorated with frescoes, that can be rented for receptions of up to 500. Office Space Rental (fully equipped): *Amministrazione Principe Livio Odescalchi* (80 Piazza SS. Apostoli; phone: 679-2154); *Executive Service* (68 Via Savoia; phone: 853241; fax: 844-0738); *International Business Centre* (121 Piazzale di Porta Pia; phone: 886-3051); *Tiempo* (50 Via Barberini; phone: 482-5151 or 482-1456); and *Center Office* (132 Via del Tritone; phone: 488-1995 or 474-7641). Desktop Publishing: *Scribe Desktop Publishing* (45 Via Paola Falconieri; phone: 531-5050). Tuxedo Rental: *Misano* (88 Via Nazionale; phone: 488-2005).

 SPECIAL EVENTS: The events of the church calendar — too numerous to mention here — are extra special in Rome. For *Natale (Christmas)*, relatively modest decorations go up around the city, almost all churches display their sometimes movable, elaborate *presepi* (nativity scenes), and a colorful toy and candy fair begins in Piazza Navona. The season, including the fair, lasts until January 6, *Epiphany,* when children receive gifts from a witch known as the Befana to add to those Babbo Natale (Father Christmas) or the Bambìn Gesù (Baby Jesus) brought them at *Christmas.* The intervening *Capodanno* or *New Year* is celebrated with a bang here as in much of the rest of Italy — firecrackers snap, crackle, and pop from early evening, and (though less than in the past) at midnight all manner of old, discarded objects come flying out of open windows. (Don't be on the street!) During the *Settimana Santa* (Holy Week), the city swarms with visitors. Religious ceremonies abound, particularly on *Good Friday,* when pilgrims, on their knees, climb the Scala Santa at St. John Lateran and the pope conducts the famous *Via Crucis* (Way of the Cross) procession between the Colosseum and the Palatine Hill. At noon on *Easter Sunday,* he pronounces the *Urbi et Orbi* blessing in St. Peter's Square. The day after *Easter* is *Pasquetta* (Little Easter), when Romans usually go out to the country for a picnic or an extended lunch in a rustic trattoria. The arrival of spring is celebrated in April with a colorful display of potted azaleas covering the Spanish Steps, and in May a picturesque street nearby, Via Margutta, is filled with an exhibition of paintings by artists of varied talents. (The Via Margutta art fair is repeated in the fall.) In May, too, Villa Borghese's lush Piazza di Siena becomes the site of the *International Horse Show,* and soon after that is the *International Tennis Championship* at *Foro Italico.* An antiques show also takes place in spring and fall along the charming Via dei Coronari (near Piazza Navona), and there's an *International Rose Show* in late spring at the delightful Roseto di Valle Murcia on the Aventine Hill. In late May or June the vast *Fiera di Roma,* a national industrial exhibition, takes place at the fairgrounds along Via Cristoforo Colombo. In mid-July the *Festa di Noiantri* is celebrated in one of Rome's oldest quarters, Trastevere. This is a great pagan feast, involving plenty of eating, music, and fireworks — as filmed by Fellini in his surrealistic/realistic *Roma.*

There are also innumerable characteristic *feste* or *sagre* (festivals, usually celebrating some local food or beverage at the height of its season) in the many hill towns surrounding Rome. The *Sagra dell'Uva* (Grape Festival) is the first Sunday in October at Marino celebrates the new vintage with grapes sold from stalls set up in the quaint old streets and wine instead of water gushing out of the fountain in the main square! Also worth seeing is the *Infiorata* at Genzano di Roma. On a Sunday in mid-June, a brightly colored carpet of beautifully arranged flowers is laid along the entire Via Livia. Both towns are about 15 miles (24 km) south of Rome in the *Castelli Romani* (see "Out of Town" in *Special Places*).

 MUSEUMS: Many museums are described in *Special Places.* Included in the following list of additional museums are churches that should be seen because of their artistic value. Many museums are closed on Mondays and some charge no admission on Sundays. Always check the hours before setting out (although most open at 9 AM and close for lunch).

Galleria Colonna – The Colonna family collection (in their home) of mainly 17th-century Italian paintings. Open Saturdays only, from 9 AM to 1 PM. Palazzo Colonna, 17 Via della Pilotta (phone: 679-4362).

Galleria Doria Pamphili – The private collection of the Doria family, housed in a sculpture hall and apartments, of Italian and foreign paintings from the 15th to the 17th century, including a portrait of Christopher Columbus. Open Tuesdays, Fridays, Saturdays, and Sundays, 10 AM to 1 PM. Palazzo Doria, 1/A Piazza del Collegio Romano (phone: 679-4365).

Galleria Nazionale d'Arte Antica (National Gallery of Ancient Art) – Recently renovated, this museum exhibits paintings by Italian artists from the 13th to the 18th century, plus some Dutch and Flemish works. Open Mondays through Saturdays from 9 AM to 2 PM, Sundays from 9 AM to 12:30 PM. Palazzo Barberini, 13 Via delle Quattro Fontane (phone: 481-4591).

Galleria Nazionale d'Arte Moderna (National Gallery of Modern Art) – Particularly noteworthy are the pre-World War I Italian painters and the futurists. Open daily from 9 AM to 1:30 PM; on Thursdays and Fridays, it also is open from 3 to 7 PM. 131 Viale Belle Arti (phone: 802751).

Galleria Spada – Renaissance art and Roman marble work from the 2nd and 3rd centuries; also two huge rare antique globes that were used on Dutch ships in the 16th century. Open Mondays and Tuesdays from 9 AM to 2 PM, Wednesdays and Saturdays from 9 AM to 2 PM and 3 to 7 PM, and Sundays and holidays from 9 AM to 1 PM. Palazzo Spada, 13 Piazza Capo di Ferro (phone: 686-1158).

Keats-Shelley Memorial House – A shrine to the romantics. Keats lived (briefly) and died here. Open weekdays from 9 AM to 1 PM and 2:30 to 5:30 PM. 26 Piazza di Spagna (phone: 678-4235).

Museo Napoleonico (Napoleonic Museum) – Memorabilia of the emperor's family during their rule in Rome. 1 Via Umberto I (phone: 654-0286).

Museo Nazionale d'Arte Orientale (National Museum of Oriental Art) – Pottery, bronzes, stone, and wooden sculpture from the Middle and Far East. Open Mondays through Saturdays from 9 AM to 2 PM, Sundays and holidays from 9 AM to 1 PM. 248 Via Merulana (phone: 737948).

Museo Nazionale Etrusco di Valle Giulia (National Etruscan Museum of the Giulia Valley – The country's most important Etruscan collection in a 16th-century villa by Vignola. Open Tuesdays through Saturdays from 9 AM to 7 PM, Sundays from 9 AM to 1 PM. 9 Piazzale di Valle Giulia (phone: 360-1951).

Museo di Palazzo Venezia (Palazzo Venezia Museum) – Tapestries, paintings, sculpture, and varied objects, as well as important temporary exhibits. Open Mondays from 9 AM to 2 PM, Tuesdays through Saturdays from 9 AM to 7 PM, and Sundays from 9 AM to 1 PM. 118 Via del Plebescito (phone: 679-8865).

Museo Preistorico ed Etnografico Luigi Pigorini (Luigi Pigorini Prehistoric and Ethnographic Museum) – A unique collection of objects from Italy's early history. Open Mondays from 2 to 7 PM, Wednesdays through Saturdays from 9 AM to 7 PM, and Sundays from 9 AM to 1 PM. 1 Via Lincoln (phone: 591-0702).

Museo di Roma (Museum of Rome) – Paintings, sculptures, and other objects illustrating the history of Rome from the Middle Ages to the present. Open daily from 9 AM to 1:30 PM. 10 Piazza San Pantaleo (phone: 687-5880).

Museo della Sinagoga (Synagogue Permanent Collection) – Adjacent to the synagogue is this small museum with exhibits on the arts and history of Rome's Jewish community through the centuries. Open Mondays through Thursdays from 9:30 AM to 2 PM and 3 to 5 PM, Fridays from 9:30 AM to 2:30 PM, and Sundays from 9:30 AM to 12:30 PM. Lungotevere Cenci (phone: 686-4193).

San Carlo alle Quattro Fontane (St. Charles at the Four Fountains) – A small baroque church by Borromini, it was designed to fit into one of the pilasters of St. Peter's. Via del Quirinale, corner Via delle Quattro Fontane.

San Clemente – An early Christian basilica with frescoes and a remarkable mosaic. Piazza di San Clemente.

San Luigi dei Francesi (St. Louis of the French) – The French national church, built in the 16th century and containing three Caravaggios. Piazza San Luigi dei Francesi.

Sant'Agostino (St. Augustine) – A 15th-century church containing the *Madonna of the Pilgrims* by Caravaggio and the *Prophet Isaiah* by Raphael. Piazza di Sant'Agostino.

Sant'Andrea al Quirinale (St. Andrew at the Quirinale) – A baroque church by Bernini, to be compared with Borromini's church on the same street. Via del Quirinale.

Santa Maria d'Aracoeli (St. Mary of the Altar of Heaven) – A Romanesque-Gothic church with frescoes by Pinturicchio and a 14th-century staircase built in thanksgiving for the lifting of a plague. Piazza d'Aracoeli.

Santa Maria in Cosmedin – A Romanesque church known for the *Bocca della Verità* (Mouth of Truth) in its portico — a Roman drain cover in the shape of a face whose mouth, according to legend, will bite off the hand of anyone who has told a lie. Piazza della Bocca della Verità.

Santa Maria sopra Minerva (St. Mary over Minerva) – Built over a Roman temple, with (unusual for Rome) a Gothic interior, frescoes by Filippino Lippi, and Michelangelo's statue of St. John the Baptist. Piazza della Minerva.

Santa Maria in Trastevere – An ancient church, the first in Rome dedicated to the Virgin, with 12th- and 13th-century mosaics. Piazza Santa Maria in Trastevere.

Santa Maria della Vittoria (St. Mary of the Victory) – Baroque to the core, especially in Bernini's Cornaro Chapel. Via XX Settembre.

San Pietro in Vincoli (St. Peter in Chains) – Erected in the 5th century to preserve St. Peter's chains, this church contains Michelangelo's magnificent statue of Moses. Piazza di San Pietro in Vincoli.

Santa Sabina – A simple 5th-century basilica, with its original cypress doors, a 13th-century cloister and bell tower, and stunning views of the city. Piazza Pietro d'Illiria.

 SHOPPING: Rome is a wonderful place to shop. You'll find the great couturiers, many of whom have boutiques as well, and most important Italian firms have branches here. While elegant clothing by top Italian designers will cost less here than back home, don't expect any bargain-basement finds. The best buys are in quality, hand-finished leather goods, jewelry, fabrics, shoes, and sweaters.

The chicest shopping area is around the bottom of the Spanish Steps, beginning with the elegant Via Condotti, which runs east to west and is lined with Rome's most exclusive shops, such as *Gucci* and *Ferragamo* for leather goods, and *Bulgari, Beltrami, Cartier, Di Consiglio, Massoni, Merli, Rapi,* and *Van Cleef* for exquisite jewelry. Via del Babuino, which connects the Spanish Steps to Piazza del Popolo, has traditionally been better known for its antiques shops, but is coming into its own as a high-fashion street, as is nearby Via Bocca di Leone, where there are such designers' boutiques as *Valentino, Ungaro, Versace, Trussardi,* and *Yves Saint Laurent.* Running parallel to Via Condotti are several more streets, most closed to traffic, with fashionable boutiques, such as Via Borgognona (*Fendi, Versace, Missoni, Laura Biagiotti,* and *Testa*), Via delle Carrozze, Via Frattina (for men's fashions at *Testa,* women's at *Max Mara,* as well as costume jewelry, lingerie, and some ceramics), Via Vittoria, and Via della Croce (known particularly for its delicious but pricey delicatessens such as *Ercoli,* or *Fior Fiore* for cheese, bread, and cookies). All of these streets end at Via del Corso, the main street of Rome, which runs north to south and is lined with shops tending to resemble each other more and more with their offerings of the latest fashions in shoes, handbags, and sportswear, particularly along the stretch between Piazza del Popolo and Largo Chigi, where Via del Tritone begins. There are some fine shops along Via del Tritone, Via Sistina, and in the Via Veneto area.

On the other side of the river toward the Vatican are two popular shopping streets that are slightly less expensive, Via Cola di Rienzo and Via Ottaviano. Also somewhat less expensive is Via Nazionale, near the railroad station. For inexpensive new and secondhand clothes, visit the daily market on Via Sannio, near San Giovanni, and the flea market on Sunday mornings at Porta Portese. For old prints and odds and ends, try the market at Piazza della Fontanella Borghese every morning except Sunday; antiques can be found along Via del Babuino, Via dei Coronari, Via del Boverno Vecchio, Via del Governo Vecchio, Via Margutta, and Via Giulia.

Fairly new on the Roman shopping scene is *Cinecittà Due,* an air conditioned shopping mall that has over 100 shops. Easily accessible by subway, it is open daily except Sundays from 9 AM to 8:30 PM.

Store hours are capricious. Shops usually are open in winter from 10 AM to 1 PM and 4 to 7:30 PM; closed Monday mornings. Summer morning hours are the same, but in the afternoon, stores are open from 4:30 to 8 PM; closed Saturday afternoons. A few, such as the popular department store *UPIM* on Via Tritone, are open all day.

The following are a few recommended shops in Rome:

Arte – Household and hope-chest linen, such as tablecloths, and hand-embroidered curtains at this shop near the Campo de' Fiori. 39 Via dei Giubbonari.

Balloon – Chinese silk is used to make Italian-style women's shirts in this store that is so popular that there are six in Rome and one in Paris. 35 Piazza di Spagna, 495 Via Flaminia Vecchia, and other locations.

Battistoni – Men's conservative clothing. The Duke of Windsor had his shirts made here — secretly, so as not to offend Britain's shirtmakers. 61A Via Condotti.

Bertè – Old and new toys. 108 Piazza Navona.

Bises – A place for fine fabrics. 93 Via del Gesù. *Bises' Boutique Uomo,* for men, is at 1-3-5 Corso Vittorio Emanuele.

Bomba e De Clercq – Exclusive sweaters and blouses with hand-crafted details. 39 Via dell'Oca, behind Piazza del Popolo.

Borsalino – World-renowned hats. 157/B Via IV Novembre.

Bruno Magli – Top-quality shoes and boots of classical elegance. 70 Via Veneto, 1 Via del Gambero, and 237 Via Cola di Rienzo.

Buccellati – For connoisseurs: A fine jeweler with a unique way of working with gold. 31 Via Condotti.

Bulgari – One of the world's most famous high-style jewelers, offering fabulous creations in gold, silver, platinum, and precious stones. 10 Via Condotti.

Capodarte – The latest styles in shoes and boots — many with matching bags — and some stylish fashions for women. 14/A Via Sistina.

Carlo Palazzi – Creative, high-quality fashions for men. 7/C Via Borgognona.

Carlo Pasquali – Old prints, engravings, original lithographs, and drawings. Near the Trevi Fountain. 25 Largo di Brazzà.

Cartoleria al Pantheon – Marbelized paper, some handmade and suitable for framing. Ask to see the one-of-a-kind paper mosaic-covered diaries and notebooks. Ideal for small gifts. 15 Via della Rotonda (phone: 687-5313).

Cascianelli – Old maps of Rome as well as prints and rare books. 14 Largo Febo.

Cerruti 1881 – Favorite fashions for Italian yuppies of all ages. Their jackets last a lifetime. 20 Piazza San Lorenzo in Lucina.

Cesari – Two locations, with fine household linen, including tablecloths and place-mats, lingerie and beachwear at 1 Via Barberini; exquisite upholstery fabrics by the meter at 96 Via Frattina.

Cicogna – The ultimate (or nearly) in children's clothing. 138 Via Frattina and 268 Via Cola di Rienzo.

Croff Centro Casa – Inexpensive household items and gifts, some of Italian design. 197 Via Cola di Rienzo, 137 Via Tomacelli, and 52 Via XX Settembre.

Davide Cenci – Classic elegance for men and women. Italian diplomats buy their pinstripe suits and trenchcoats here. 4-7 Via Campo Marzio.

Discount dell'Alta Moda – Last season's *alta moda* at discount prices. 16/A Via Gesù.

Discount System – A high-fashion discount store, featuring clothing, shoes, and leather goods up to 50% off retail. 35 Via Viminale.

Essences – Natural fragrances and the house's own blends of toilet water and perfume. 88 Piazza della Cancelleria.

Ex Libris – Antique books, prints, and rare maps are found in this charming shop. 77/A Via dell'Umiltà.

Fendi – Canvas and leather bags, luggage, and clothing. 39 Via Borgognona. Shoes and purse accessories. 4/E Via Borgognona and 55/A Largo Goldoni.

Ferragamo – For high-style women's shoes. 66 Via Condotti.

Filippo – An avant-garde boutique for men and women. 7 *bis* Via Borgognona and 6 Via Condotti.

Fiorucci – Famed, funky sportswear and shoes. 12 Via Genova, 19 Via della Farnesina, 236 Via Nazionale, 27 Via della Maddalena, and elsewhere.

Fornari – Fine silver and other gifts. 71-72 Via Frattina.

Franco Maria Ricci – Sumptuously printed books by a discriminating publisher, sold in an elegant setting. 4D Via Borgognona.

Funke – Top-quality shoes for men and women plus cordial service. Near the Pantheon. 52 Piazza della Maddalena.

Gabbiano – Modern artworks by Italians and others (there's also a branch in New York City). 51 Via della Frezza.

Galtrucco – All kinds of fabrics, especially pure silk. 23 Via del Tritone.

Genny – Ever-popular boutique for women. 27 Piazza di Spagna.

Gianfranco Ferré – High fashion for women. 6 Via Borgognona.

Gianni Versace – The Milanese designer's Rome outlets. 41 Via Borgognona and 29 Via Bocca di Leone.

Giorgio Armani – High fashion for men and women. 102 and 139 Via del Babuino.

Gucci – Be ready to wait in line for men's and women's shoes, luggage, handbags, and other leather goods. 8 Via Condotti.

Krizia – Elegant women's boutique. 11/B Piazza di Spagna.

Laura Biagiotti – Elegant women's wear. 43 Via Borgognona, corner of Via Belsiana.

Laurent – Good buys in leatherwear. 3 Via Frattina.

Libreria Archeologica – For the bookworm whose passion is the past. The specialty is Rome and Italy, but a few of the books on archaeology and ancient history have a broader reach. 2 Via Palermo.

Libreria Editrice Vaticana – A vast selection of art and archaeological books as well as books on religion and theology at the Vatican's own publisher's outlet. Next to the Vatican's post office in Piazza San Pietro.

Lio Bazaar – Amusing women's shoes. 35 Via Borgognona.

Lion Bookshop – The city's oldest English-language bookstore, chock full of volumes on Rome's history, travel, and food. 181 Via del Babuino.

Luna di Carta – All types of crafts made from paper — handmade papier-mâché fruit, small sculptures, and hand-colored prints. Il Vicolo dell'Atleta.

Maccalè – Yet another fine boutique for women. 69 Via della Croce.

Mail – English and western saddlery and other riding gear. 154 Via Germanico.

Marisa Pignataro – Outstanding knit dresses and tops in pure wool with interesting color combinations. 20 Via dei Greci.

Mario Lucchese – Everything for the golfer, including handmade spike-soled shoes and other tee-time apparel. 162 Via del Babuino.

Mario Valentino – Fine shoes and leather goods. 58 and 84 Via Frattina.

Maud Frizon – Highly original shoes for women, with corresponding prices. 38 Via Borgognona.

Miranda – Colorful women's woven shawls and jackets. 220 Via delle Carrozze.

Missoni – High-fashion knitwear in unique weaves of often costly blended yarns, such as linen with wool and silk. Via Borgognona 38/B. *Missoni Uomo,* for men, is at 78 Piazza di Spagna.

Ai Monasteri – Products ranging from bath oils to honey and liqueurs from more than 20 monasteries. 72 Corso del Rinascimento.

Moriondo & Gariglio – Delicious hand-dipped chocolates and violets crystallized in sugar. 2 Via della Pilotta.

Myricae – Hand-painted ceramics and such, made by Italian craftsmen from Sardinia to Deruta. 36 Via Frattina.

Naj Oleari – Famed cotton fabrics and accessories from bags to lampshades. 25A Via di San Giacomo and 32 Via dei Greci.

Nazareno Gabrielli – Excellent leather goods. 3-5 Via Sant'Andrea delle Fratte and 29 Via Borgognona.

Dell'Orologio – Decorative and figurative 20th-century art, including Art Deco, Futurist, and right now. 8 Piazza dell'Orologio.

Ottica Scientifica – Eyeglasses and contact lenses, fitted by one of Rome's best and most scrupulous optometrists; camera supplies and electronic equipment,too. 19 Via delle Convertite, near Piazza San Silvestro.

Ottocento Italiano – The 19th-century look in Italian furniture made from antique wood. They also make bookcases to order. 26 Via Nizza (near Piazza Fiume).

Perla – Avant-garde looks for young women. 88 Piazza di Spagna.

Perrone – Gloves — leather and other. 92 Piazza di Spagna.

Petochi – A treasure trove of fine jewelry and old and new tea services. 72 Piazza di Spagna.

Pineider – Italy's famed stationer. 68-69 Via Due Macelli and Piazza Cardelli.

Polidori – Exclusive menswear and tailoring at 84 Via Condotti and 4C Via Borgognona; finest pure silks and other fabrics at 4A Via Borgognona.

Le Quattro Stagioni – A delightful array of handmade ceramics by artisans from all over Italy. US shipping can be arranged. 30B Via dell'Umiltà.

Ramírez – Latest shoe fashions at reasonable prices. 73 Via del Corso and 85 Via Frattina.

Raphael Salato – For famous-maker Italian men's and women's shoes. 104 and 149 Via Veneto; 34 Piazza di Spagna.

Rinascente – One of the few department stores, offering good buys on gloves, scarves, and clothing for all ages. Piazza Colonna and Piazza Fiume.

Roland's – The specialty here is luxury coats for men and women. Piazza di Spagna.

Salotto – Made-to-order shirts for both sexes. 18 Via di Parione.

Sansone – Large selection of Italian and imported luggage, trunks, and travel bags, as well as wallets, purses, knapsacks, etc. Repairs and custom designs. 4 Via XX Settembre.

Schostal – Since 1870, traditional supplier of stockings (in silk, linen, cotton, etc.) and other undergarments for men and women. Moderate prices. 158 Via del Corso.

Soggetti – A 2-story showroom of Italy's famed high-style home furnishings and decorating objects — not easy to find in Rome. Near the Piazza Venezia on Via IV Novembre.

Al Sogno Giocattoli – Toys, including huge stuffed animals in amusing window displays. 53 Piazza Navona.

Spazio Sette – Two stories of Italian and imported fine design — everything from potholders to teapots, placemats, lamps, notebooks, quilts, and furniture. Just off Largo Argentina. 7 Via dei Barbieri.

Stefanel – Lively, youthful sportswear at a dozen branches, the most central of which are 148 Via del Corso, 31-32 Via Frattina, 41 Via Tritone, 227 Via Nazionale, and 191-193 Via Cola di Rienzo.

Testa – For offbeat, resort, and casual clothes for men. 13 Via Borgognona, and 42 and 104-106 Via Frattina.

Trevi Moda – Best buy for moderately priced, quality leather shoes and handbags, located in a favorite tourist area. 33 Via Lavatore.

Trimani – Founded in 1821, this is Rome's oldest wine shop. Its marble decorations are a national monument. 20 Via Goito.

L'Ulivo – Ceramics, handmade by the owner as well as by artisans from Puglia. 61 Via del Monte della Farina.

Valentino – Bold, high-fashion clothes for men and women. 13 Via Condotti for men, 15-18 Via Bocca di Leone for women; haute couture salon at 24 Via Gregoriana.

Vertecchi – Rome's most important stationer and artists' supplier, also gifts and design products. 38 and 70 Via della Croce, 18 Via Pietro da Cortona, and 12/F Via Attilio Regolo.

 SPORTS AND FITNESS: Auto Racing – The *Autodromo di Roma* (*Valle Lunga* racetrack, Campagnano di Roma, Via Cassia, Km 34; phone: 904-1027). Take a bus from Via Lepanto.

Fitness Centers – Rome has relatively few fitness centers and gyms, and those that exist tend to be cramped. An exception is the roomy, well-equipped, and (unusual for Rome) air conditioned *Roman Sport Center* (in the underground passage to the *metropolitana* stop at the top of Via Veneto in the Villa Borghese, 33 Via del Galoppatoio; phone: 320-1667). Although it is a private club, its American owner makes special arrangements for visitors to use the pool, squash court, aerosol room, sauna, Jacuzzi, and two workout gyms, as well as aerobics classes. Another private club, the *Navona Health Center* (39 Via dei Banchi Vecchi; phone: 689-6104), also will open its 3-room gym in an ancient historical palazzo to non-members. Fitness centers accessible to the public include: *Aldrovandi Health Center* (11 Via Michele Mercati; phone: 322-1435); *American Workout Studio* (5 Via Giovanni Amendola; phone: 474-6299), run by a former Jane Fonda Workshop instructor; and *Barbara Bouchet Bodyshop* (162 Viale Parioli; phone: 807-5049). Most others are by membership only.

Golf – Both the *Circolo del Golf Roma* (716/A Via Appia Nuova; phone: 794-6219), about 8 miles (12 km) from the center, and the *Olgiata Golf Club* (15 Largo Olgiata; phone: 378-9141), about 12 miles (19 km), have 18-hole courses and extend guest privileges to members of foreign clubs. The former is open to guests Tuesdays through Saturdays; the latter, Tuesdays to Fridays. There also is the 9-hole *Golf Club Fioranello* (Via Appia Nuova, Santa Maria delle Mole; phone: 608058). At *Acquasanta* (Via Appia Nuova; phone: 780-4307), visitors can play Tuesdays through Fridays (if they show a home club membership card) on an 18-hole course. Tee off with spectacular views of ancient ruins in the background; the club also has a lovely swimming pool and an excellent restaurant.

Horse Racing – Trotting races take place at the *Ippodromo Tor di Valle* (Via del Mare, Km 13; phone: 592-6786). Flat races take place at the *Ippodromo delle Capannelle* (1255 Via Appia, Km 12; phone: 799-3143) in the spring and fall.

Horseback Riding – For lessons at various levels of proficiency, rentals by the hour (sometimes a subscription for several hours is required), or guided rides in the country, contact the *Circolo Ippico Appia Antica* (Via Appia Nuova, Km 16.5; phone: 724-0197); *Società Ippica Romana* (30 Via dei Monti della Farnesina; phone: 396-6214); *Scuola d'Equitazione Le Piane* (Campagnano; phone: 904-2478 or 904-1925), or *Circolo Buttero Fontana Nuova* (near Sacrofano, outside Rome; phone: 903-6040). For weekend or week-long riding vacations, contact *Agriturist* (phone: 651-2342) or *Turismo Verde* (phone: 396-9931).

Jogging – There are two tracks at the *Galoppatoio* in the Villa Borghese; enter at the top of Via Veneto or from Piazza del Popolo. Villa Glori has a 1,180-meter track which is illuminated at night; the large Villa Pamphili has three tracks, as does Villa Ada, and Villa Torlonia has one pretty track flanked by palm and acacia trees; at *Acqua*

Acetosa there is also a dressing room open until 5 PM; and the Baths of Caracalla provide another good running spot (between the road and the Terme).

Soccer – Two highly competitive teams, *Roma* and *Lazio*, play on Sundays from September to May at the *Olympic Stadium* (site of the final game of the *1990 World Cup*), *Foro Italico* (phone: 36851).

Swimming – The pools at the *Cavalieri Hilton* (101 Via Cadlolo; phone: 3151) and the *Aldrovandi Palace* hotel (15 Via Ulisse Aldrovandi; phone: 322-3993) are open to non-guests for a fee. Public pools include the *Piscina Olimpica* (*Foro Italico;* phone: 360-8591, 360-1498) and the *Piscina delle Rose* (EUR; phone: 592-6717). Swimming in the sea near Rome has become dangerous due to very high levels of pollution; signs prohibiting swimming speckle many nearby beaches. The beach nearest Rome is at Ostia, and it's among the most polluted, very crowded, and strung from end to end with bathing establishments charging admission for entry and use of changing rooms. There are stretches of free beach at Castel Fusano and Castel Porziano, southeast of Ostia; the first is reachable by subway from Stazione Termini. Fregene, farther north along the coast, is very popular with fashionable (and mostly topless) Romans. There's also swimming at Lake Bracciano, about 20 miles (32 km) north of Rome, but no changing facilities. Avoid Sunday crowds.

Tennis – Most courts belong to private clubs. Those at the *Cavalieri Hilton* (101 Via Cadlolo; phone: 3151) and at the *Sheraton Roma* (Viale del Pattinaggio; phone: 5453) are open to non-guests for a fee. There are public courts occasionally available at the *Foro Italico* (phone: 361-9021). Also open to the public is the *Società Ginnastica Roma* (5 Via del Moro Torto; phone: 488-5566) which has 21 courts that are open from 9 AM to 9 PM; and in the Appia Antica area, the 4-court *Oasi di Pace* (2 Via degli Eugenii; phone: 718-4550), which also has a swimming pool.

Windsurfing – Windsurf boards and lessons are available at *Castel Porziano* (*primo cancello,* or first gate); at the *Stabilimento La Baia* (phone: 646-1647) and the *Miraggio Sporting Club* (in Fregene; phone: 646-1802); and at the *Centro Surf Bracciano* (Lake Bracciano; phone: 902-4568).

THEATER: During the theater season, approximately October through May, check *A Guest in Rome* or any daily newspaper for listings. Most theater in Italian consists of revivals of the classics (including Goldoni's and Pirandello's works and English and French classics in translation) and some lively avant-garde works. The principal theaters are the *Teatro Eliseo* (183 Via Nazionale; phone: 488-2114), the *Teatro Argentina* (Largo Argentina; phone: 654-4601), the *Teatro Valle* (23 Via Teatro Valle; phone: 654-3794), and the *Teatro Quirino* (1 Via Minghetti; phone: 679-4585). A season of classical drama (in Italian, and sometimes in Greek) is held in July each year in the open-air *Teatro Romano di Ostia Antica* (phone: 565-1913). The *Teatro Sistina* (129 Via Sistina; phone: 482-6841) is Rome's best music hall, offering top class, often imported, musical entertainment on Monday nights, when the regular rep is resting (in the fall, they usually run top-name Brazilian entertainment Monday nights). The charming, turn-of-the-century cabaret theater *Salone Margarita* (75 Via Due Macelli; phone: 679-8269) offers late-night shows and Sunday afternoon concerts. For films in English, check the newspapers for *Cinema Pasquino* (in Trastevere, Vicolo del Piede; phone: 580-3622) and the *Cinema Alcazar* (14 Via Merry del Val; phone: 588-0099), which often has English-language movies on Mondays and Thursdays.

MUSIC: Again, for current schedules, check *A Guest in Rome* or the daily newspapers. The regular opera season at the *Teatro dell'Opera* (1 Piazza Beniamino Gigli, corner Via Firenze; phone: 461755 or 463641), runs from December through May. The best way to get tickets for good seats is through

your hotel concierge or major travel agencies. If you choose to buy them yourself, go
to the box office at 10 AM, no more than 3 days prior to the performance. Be prepared
to wait — the line moves slowly. During July and August there is a summer opera
season at the Baths of Caracalla. (Tickets are on sale at the *Teatro dell'Opera* box office
or, on the day of performance, at Caracalla.) The *Rome Ballet* Company also performs
at the *Teatro dell'Opera*. Rome's *RAI* symphony orchestra, one of four orchestras run
by Radiotelevisione Italiana, the state television network, holds its concert season at
the *Auditorio del Foro Italico* (1 Piazza Lauro de Bosis; phone: 365625), from October
to June. At roughly the same time, the venerable *Accademia Nazionale di Santa Cecilia*
gives first class concerts with international guest artists, either at the *Auditorio Santa
Cecilia* (4 Via della Conciliazione; phone: 654-1044), or at the smaller *Sala Concerti*
(Concert Hall; 18 Via dei Greci; box office, 6 Via Vittoria; phone: 679-0389). Between
October and May, the *Accademia Filarmonica Romana* sponsors a series of concerts
at the *Teatro Olimpico* (17 Piazza Gentile da Fabriano; phone: 396-2635 or 393304) —
its summer season is held in the garden at the academy headquarters (118 Via Flaminia;
phone: 360-1752) — and the *Istituzione Universitaria dei Concerti* holds concerts at the
Auditorium San Leone Magno (38 Via Bolzano; phone: 853216), and at the university's
Aula Magna (1 Piazzale Aldo Moro; phone: 361-0051). Other concerts occasionally are
held at the *Auditorio del Gonfalone* (32 Via del Gonfalone; phone: 687-5952), and
around Rome by the *Coro Polifonico Romano*. Still other musical groups use the *Teatro
Ghione* (37 Via delle Fornaci; phone: 637-2294). Finally, there are concerts in many,
many churches throughout the year, especially around *Christmas,* and music festivals — classical, jazz, pop, and folk — outdoors in the parks and picturesque piazze
during the summer. For jazz and other modern music in clubs, see *Nightclubs and
Nightlife* below.

 NIGHTCLUBS AND NIGHTLIFE: Nightspots are born and die so quickly,
slip into and out of fashion so easily, so that visitors would do well to check
with Thursday's "Trova Roma" supplement to the daily *La Repubblica* for
an up-to-date idea of what's going on. Since the 1950s, the few nightclubs
are clustered around the big hotel/tourist office area of Via Veneto (although obviously
there are exceptions). By US standards, their prices are high. In most, the drink
minimum is about $25, and a bottle of champagne will cost at least $125. For the
younger set on the lookout for disco, jazz, and general hanging out spots with a few
extras — sometimes as much as a piano bar or as little as a dart board — a walk
through Trastevere or the Testaccio area around Rome's old general markets and
slaughterhouse (the newer bohemian area now that Trastevere has become gentrified)
will turn up a host of intriguing places.

Among the nightclubs, small, swanky, expensive *Tartarughino* (near Piazza Navona,
1 Via della Scrofa; phone: 678-6037) is popular with the political set. Everyone seems
to know each other, so it seems like a private club. A slightly younger crowd gathers
at *Gilda* (near the Spanish Steps, 97 Via Mario de' Fiore; phone: 678-4838), known for
its live music and pricey restaurant. *Cica Cica Bum* (pronounced *Chee*-ka *Chee*-ka
Boom (38 Via Liguria; phone: 464745), with 1940s decor and both easy listening and
disco music. Also fashionable are *Open Gate* (22 Via San Nicola da Tolento; phone:
474-6301), not far from the Via Veneto; and *Jackie O'* (11 Via Boncompagni; phone:
461401). Both are restaurants, but prepare to spend.

The disco *Piper '90* (9 Via Tagliamento; phone: 841-4459) has been packing people
in literally for generations. It changes its show every night, so be sure to call ahead to
find out if there's a fashion show or break dance demonstration. *La Makumba* (19 Via
degli Olimpionici; phone: 396-4392) plays African, Caribbean, and Latin music. The
Kripton (52 Via Luciani; phone: 870504) is very in with the gilded younger set. It has

a bar and restaurant. *La Tentazione* (Km 17.2 on Via Domentana; no phone) goes in for disco happenings, while *Vicolo delle Stelle* (22 Via Cesare Beccaria; phone: 361-1240) plays disco, rap, soul, and funk music until dawn. *Bulli e Pupi* (on the Aventine Hill, 11/A Via San Saba; phone: 578-2022) is not for executives, but for their offspring. The posh *Hosteria dell'Orso* (33 Via dell'Orso; phone: 656-4904) is a surefire and dignified solution to everyone's musical tastes — the dimly lit, comfortable *Blue Bar* on the main floor offers laid-back piano or guitar music, and *La Cabala* upstairs is a disco scene for title young Romans. It's in one of Rome's loveliest, centuries-old buildings, not far from the Piazza Navona (closed Sundays). There also is a restaurant (see *Eating Out*). *Hysteria* (3 Via Giovanelli; phone: 864-4587) is the newest "in" spot for dancing and drinking; it has the same owner as the swanky *Jackie O'*, Beatrice Jannozzi. There is live music some weekends and a VIP corner where only celebrities are seated. The locals love it. *Veleno* (27 Via Sardegna, off Via Veneto; phone: 493583) packs in the motorscooter crowd rather than the jet set. For live music and disco dancing in downtown historical Rome is the very special *Casanova* (36 Piazza Rondanini; phone: 654-7314). *Notorious* (22 Via San Nicola da Tolentino; phone: 474-6888) mingles disco with dining. *L'Incontro* (near Piazza del Popolo; phone: 361-0934) has a piano bar and disco.

Especially good jazz can be heard (despite the noise of diners in its restaurant) at *Saint Louis Music City* (13/A Via del Cardello; phone: 474-5076) and *Alexanderplatz* (9 Via Ostia; phone: 372-9398). Also try the well-regarded *Café Caruso* (36 Via Monte Testaccio; phone: 574-7720). *Yes Brazil* (in Trastevere, Via San Francesco a Ripa; phone: 581-6267) has live music from 7 to 9 PM and Latin disco after until 1 AM. Two other favorites for live music are *Caffè Latino* (96 Via di Monte Testaccio; phone: 574-4020) and *Grigio Notte* (30/B Via dei Fenaroli; phone: 686-8340) for jazz, salsa, and drinks.

If you're just an amiable barfly who might like to strike up a pleasant conversation in English, the place to go is the bar at the *Inghilterra* hotel (14 Via Bocca di Leoni; phone: 672161); there is no music except for the tinkling of ice cubes, but the bartender is the nicest in town. Also drop by another occasional American haunt, *Little Bar* (54/A Via Gregoriana — the street where the big fashion houses are located).

For those with a *funiculi funicola* idea of Italy as peasant exuberance expressed through music, you can spend an evening joining in with the singing waiters and waitresses at the twin restaurants (opened in the 1960s in Trastevere by two American brothers) *Da Meo Patacca* (30 Piazza dei Mercanti; phone: 581-6198) and *Da Cicerucchio* (1 Via del Porto; phone: 580-6046). You might think that you won't be able to stand all the noise, but the wine flows freely and fun is on the house; so take the kids along and enjoy.

BEST IN TOWN

CHECKING IN: Of the more than 500 hotels in Rome, the following are recommended either for some special charm, location, or bargain price in their category. Those without restaurants are noted, although all serve breakfast if desired, and all have heating and telephones in the rooms unless otherwise stated. In high season prices can be staggering; expect to pay from $550 up to $700 for a double room with bath in the hotels listed as very expensive, from $350 to $550 for hotels in the expensive price range, from $150 to $350 in the moderate category, and under $150 (to as low as $90) in the inexpensive category. Off-season rates are about 10% lower. All telephone numbers are in the 6 city code unless otherwise indicated.

Cavalieri Hilton International – Far from the historic center of Rome at the top of a lovely hill (Monte Mario) overlooking much of the city, with shuttle buses to Via Veneto and Piazza di Spagna running hourly during shopping hours only. But the swimming pool is especially desirable in summer, and the rooftop restaurant, *La Pergola* wins high praise from food critics. A resort property with year-round swimming, tennis, a sauna, and other diversions, it has 387 rooms. Business facilities include meeting rooms for up to 2,100, English-speaking concierge, foreign currency exchange, secretarial services in English, audiovisual equipment, photocopiers, cable television news, translation services, and express checkout. 101 Via Cadlolo (phone: 31511; fax: 315-12241; telex: 625337HILTRO I). Very expensive.

Eden – Among the most elegant in Rome, this hotel has excellent service, an intimate roof garden restaurant (see *Eating Out*), and a panoramic bar. There are 116 air conditioned rooms with TV sets. Business facilities include meeting rooms for up to 214, English-speaking concierge, foreign currency exchange, secretarial services in English, audiovisual equipment, photocopiers, cable television news, translation services, and express checkout. 49 Via Ludovisi (phone: 474-3551; fax: 482-1584; telex: 610567EDENRM I). Very expensive.

Excelsior – Big, bustling, but efficient, it dominates the Via Veneto, next to the US Embassy. It's a favorite with Americans, and the bar is a popular meeting place. There are 383 rooms in this member of the CIGA chain. Business facilities include 24-hour room service, meeting rooms for up to 400, English-speaking concierge, foreign currency exchange, secretarial services in English, audiovisual equipment, photocopiers, computers, cable television news, translation services, and express checkout. 125 Via Vittorio Veneto (phone: 4708; fax: 482-6205; telex: 610232EX-CEROI). Very expensive.

Grand – The pride of the CIGA chain in Rome, and traditionally the capital's most dignified hotel. It is truly grand — formal, well run, and elegant in style and service. It has 175 rooms and a central (if not exactly prime) location between the railroad station and Via Veneto areas. Its *Le Restaurant* is pretty near perfect (see *Eating Out*) and the two bars are cozy and chic — indeed, perfect, according to a recent industry poll on Roman watering holes. Afternoon tea also is served, with harp music. Business facilities include 24-hour room service, meeting rooms for up to 400, English-speaking concierge, foreign currency exchange, secretarial services in English, audiovisual equipment, photocopiers, computers, cable television news, translation services, and express checkout. 3 Via Vittorio Emanuele Orlando (phone: 4709; fax: 474-7307; telex: 610210GRANDRO I). Very expensive.

Hassler — Villa Medici – At the top of the Spanish Steps and within easy striking distance of the best shopping in Rome, favored by a loyal clientele. Guestrooms could stand some refurbishing, and the public rooms have seen better days. Each of the 108 rooms is individually decorated, and manager Albert Wirth is an attentive host. The roof garden restaurant has only so-so food, but splendid views, and offers Sunday brunch. Business facilities include meeting rooms for up to 180, English-speaking concierge, foreign currency exchange, secretarial services in English, audiovisual equipment, photocopiers, cable television news, translation services, and express checkout. 6 Piazza Trinità dei Monti (phone: 679-0770; fax: 678-9991; telex: 61028 HASLER I). Very expensive.

Aldrovandi Palace – Quiet, with 139 rooms in a fashionable residential area next to the Villa Borghese, and not far from Via Veneto, it has a delightful park with a swimming pool and a full-facility health club. Its restaurant, *Relais le Piscine,* is next door at 6 Via Mangili. Business facilities include 24-hour room service, meeting rooms for up to 400, English-speaking concierge, foreign currency exchange, secretarial services in English, audiovisual equipment, photocopiers, computers, cable television news, translation services, and express checkout. The hotel is at 15 Via Ulisse Aldrovandi (phone: 322-3993; fax: 322-1435; telex: 616141AL-DROV I). Expensive.

Ambasciatori Palace – Across the street from the US Embassy, it has 145 generally spacious rooms, old-fashioned amenities, and a very convenient location. Business facilities include 24-hour room service, meeting rooms for up to 200, English-speaking concierge, foreign currency exchange, secretarial services in English, audiovisual equipment, photocopiers, cable television news, translation services, and express checkout. 70 Via Veneto (phone: 47493; fax: 474-3601; telex: 610241HOTAMB I). Expensive.

Atlante Star – Near the Vatican, this large, modern hotel boasts a roof garden with a splendid view of St. Peter's dome, an excellent restaurant, and an efficiently equipped business center. Parking is available, as is the rental of a private plane for island-hopping. Business facilities include 24-hour room service, meeting rooms for up to 83, English-speaking concierge, foreign currency exchange, secretarial services in English, audiovisual equipment, photocopiers, computers, cable television news, translation services, and express checkout. 34 Via Vitelleschi (phone: 687-9558; fax: 687-2300; telex: 622355). Expensive.

Holiday Inn Crowne Plaza Minerva – The reopening of this 134-room, well-located hotel where Stendhal used to stay, was something of an event for downtown Rome. Its pricey restoration preserved the old baroque adornment. *La Cesta,* its restaurant (see *Eating Out*), has not yet won over all the food experts, but is quite good. Near the Pantheon. Business facilities include meeting rooms for up to 250, English-speaking concierge, foreign currency exchange, secretarial services in English, audiovisual equipment, photocopiers, cable television news, translation services, and express checkout. Piazza della Minerva (phone: 684-1888; fax: 679-4165; telex: 620091). Expensive.

Lord Byron – A small (47 rooms) first-rate place in the fashionable Parioli residential district, this once was a private villa, and it maintains the atmosphere of a private club. It has a celebrated restaurant, *Relais Le Jardin* (see *Eating Out*). Business facilities include 24-hour room service, meeting rooms for up to 100, English-speaking concierge, foreign currency exchange, secretarial services in English, audiovisual equipment, photocopiers, cable television news, translation services, and express checkout. 5 Via Giuseppe de Notaris (phone: 360-9541; fax: 322-0405; telex: 611216HBYRON I). Expensive.

Majestic – Completely restored with 100 rooms and suites, this air conditioned, century-old hostelry (the oldest on Via Veneto) is across the street from the American Embassy. Its opulently decorated reception room has a handsome fresco ceiling. There is a restaurant and the terrace bar offers a fine view of the Roman skyline. Business facilities include 24-hour room service, meeting rooms for up to 150, English-speaking concierge, secretarial services in English, audiovisual equipment, photocopiers, computers, cable television news, translation services, and express checkout. 50 Via Veneto (phone: 486841; fax: 488-0984; telex: 622262). Expensive.

Nazionale – Another old favorite (of Sartre and de Beauvoir, among others), the 86 renovated rooms here are very central, next to the Chamber of Deputies, between Via del Corso and the Pantheon. Business facilities include meeting rooms for up to 900, English-speaking concierge, foreign currency exchange, secretarial services in English, audiovisual equipment, photocopiers, and express checkout. 131 Piazza Montecitorio (phone: 678-9251; fax: 678-6677; telex: 6211427NATEL I). Expensive.

Parco dei Principi – This modern hotel is on the edge of Villa Borghese in the Parioli residential district, not far from Via Veneto. It has 203 rooms and a small swimming pool in a lovely garden. Business facilities include meeting rooms for up to 500, English-speaking concierge, foreign currency exchange, secretarial services in English, audiovisual equipment, photocopiers, computers, translation services, and express checkout. 5 Via Girolamo Frescobaldi (phone: 855-1758; fax: 884-5104; telex: 610517PRISOM I). Expensive.

Raphael – Behind Piazza Navona, it's a favorite of Italian politicians (it's near the Senate and the Chamber of Deputies), with 83 rooms. Some are small, some could use a bit of refurbishing, but loyal patrons love the antiques in the lobby, the cozy bar, and the location. The roof terrace has one of Rome's finest views. Business facilities include 2 English-speaking concierges, foreign currency exchange, secretarial services in English, photocopiers, cable television news, translation services, and express checkout. 2 Largo Febo (phone: 650881; fax: 687-8993; telex: 622396RHOTEL). Expensive.

Sheraton Roma – With 631 rooms and 25 suites, air conditioning, and a conference center that can handle up to 1,200 people, this modern, efficient hotel is also the one with the most sports facilities. Located in the suburb of EUR about 25 minutes south of central Rome, it has ample parking and regular shuttle-bus service to downtown and to the nearby Leonardo da Vinci Airport. There are 2 restaurants and a piano bar. Pluses include a health club, squash and tennis courts, outdoor pool, jogging circuit, sauna, and masseur. Business facilities include 24-hour room service, English-speaking concierge, foreign currency exchange, secretarial services in English, audiovisual equipment, photocopiers, computers, cable television news, translation services, and express checkout. Viale del Pattinaggio (phone: 5453; fax: 594-3281; telex: 626077SHEROM I). Expensive.

Sole al Pantheon – For those without a car, this 400-year-old, 25-room hostelry is in a perfect location. Lavishly renovated from the days when the poet Ariosto stayed here, today's conveniences include air conditioning and some spacious rooms (a few of the guestrooms have Jacuzzis). Shut your eyes to the garish decor in the lobby, and focus instead on the fine views from the upper rooms. Business facilities include an English-speaking concierge, foreign currency exchange, photocopiers, translation services, and express checkout. 73 Piazza della Rotonda (phone: 678-0441; fax: 684-0689). Expensive.

Cicerone – In the residential and commercial area of Prati on the Vatican side of the river, but convenient nevertheless because it's just across from Piazza del Popolo and the Spanish Steps. It has modern and spacious public areas, 237 well-appointed rooms, friendly, attentive service, and a large garage. Business facilities include meeting rooms for up to 200, English-speaking concierge, foreign currency exchange, secretarial services in English, audiovisual equipment, photocopiers, cable television news, translation services, and express checkout. 55/C Via Cicerone (phone: 3576; fax: 654-1383; telex: 622498CICER I). Expensive to moderate.

Columbus – In a restored 15th-century palace right in front of St. Peter's, this 107-room hotel offers antique furniture, paintings, and a garden — a lot of atmosphere for the price. 33 Via della Conciliazione (phone: 686-4874). Expensive to moderate.

Eliseo – Just off Via Veneto, this has traditional furnishings (with a slightly French air) in the public rooms and in some of the 50 guestrooms; others are super modern. A roof restaurant looks out over the tops of the umbrella pines in the Villa Borghese. 30 Via di Porta Pinciana (phone: 460556). Expensive to moderate.

Flora – At the top of Via Veneto, right next to the Villa Borghese, the 174 rooms are traditional, reliable, and not without charm. Business facilities include meeting rooms for up to 200, English-speaking concierge, foreign currency exchange, secretarial services in English, audiovisual equipment, photocopiers, computers, translation services, and express checkout. 191 Via Vittorio Veneto (phone: 497281). Expensive to moderate.

Forum – Built around a medieval tower in the middle of the Imperial Forums, this charming 79-room hotel is a bit out of the way but worth any inconvenience for the spectacular view of ancient Rome from its roof garden. The food here is less spectacular. 25 Via Tor de' Conti (phone: 679-2446). Expensive to moderate.

Inghilterra – Extremely popular with knowledgeable travelers, its 102 rooms have numbered Anatole France, Mark Twain, and Ernest Hemingway among many illustrious guests. Particularly attractive are the top-floor suites, some with flowered terraces. Be sure to ask for a spacious room; some are small, inevitable in older, downtown hotels. There is a small and simpatico restaurant (the *Roman Garden*), and the ever-crowded bar is a cozy haven for Roman patricians. Business facilities include meeting rooms for up to 50, English-speaking concierge, audiovisual equipment, photocopiers, computers, cable television news, and express checkout. Near the Spanish Steps, in the middle of the central shopping area. 14 Via Bocca di Leone (phone: 672161; fax: 684-0828; telex: 614552). Expensive to moderate.

Anglo-Americano – Just off Piazza Barberini, it has 115 rooms, and the back ones look out on the garden of Palazzo Barberini. Business facilities include English-speaking concierge, and photocopiers. 12 Via delle Quattro Fontane (phone: 472941; fax: 474-6428; telex: 626147ANCAM I). Moderate.

Degli Aranci – Small and quiet, it's in the Parioli residential district and has 48 rooms, a bar, and a lovely garden restaurant. Business facilities include 24-hour room service, meeting rooms for up to 40, English-speaking concierge, secretarial services in English, audiovisual equipment, photocopiers, translation services, and express checkout. 11 Via Barnaba Oriani (phone: 879774; fax: 879774; telex: 621071). Moderate.

Atlas – With 45 rooms and a flowered roof garden, this place has a central location. 3 Via Rasella (phone: 488-2140). Moderate.

Campo dei Fiori – Near the Campo dei Fiori square — a market area since the 1500s — the Renaissance palaces, the giant Palazzo Cancelleria, and the Palazzo Farnese (French Embassy), which was partly designed by Michelangelo, it is one of the coziest (and narrowest) in the area. The rustic rooms are small and sparsely decorated, but the exposed brick walls, hand-painted bathroom ceilings, and detailed architecture make up for the lack of space. For guests willing to climb 6 flights, there's a wonderful view of the city from the roof garden. No restaurant or bar. Business facilities include meeting rooms for up to 40, translation services, and express checkout. 6 Via del Biscione (phone: 687-4886). Moderate.

Cardinal – On Renaissance Rome's stateliest street, this restored 66-room palace (attributed to Bramante) is convenient for exploring some of the city's hidden treasures, but less so for shopping in the city center. No restaurant. 62 Via Giulia (phone: 654-2719). Moderate.

Fontana – A restored, air conditioned 13th-century monastery next to the Trevi Fountain, with cell-like rooms — though 10 of the 30 rooms have great views of the fabulous fountain — and a lovely rooftop bar. A bargain in every way. Business facilities include meeting rooms for up to 35, English-speaking concierge, and secretarial services in English. 96 Piazza di Trevi (phone: 678-6113). Moderate.

Pullman Boston – The roof garden is just one of the selling points of this carefully renovated 120-room hostelry, well located between Via Veneto and the Spanish Steps. Business travelers will appreciate the services. Business facilities include meeting rooms for up to 90, English-speaking concierge, secretarial services in English, audiovisual equipment, cable television news, translation services, and express checkout. The breakfast buffet is a serendipitous plus. Good value. 47 Via Lombardia (phone: 473951; in the US, 800-223-9862; fax: 482-1019; telex: 622247ETAPRM I). Moderate.

La Residenza – An exceptional bargain on a quiet street just behind Via Veneto. Old-fashioned and well-maintained, it has 27 rooms and feels much more like a private villa than a hotel. Book well in advance. Full American breakfast, but no restaurant per se. Business facilities include meeting rooms for up to 25, English-speaking concierge, foreign currency exchange, secretarial services in English, photocopiers, cable television news, and translation services. No credit cards accepted. 22 Via Emilia (phone: 488-0789; fax: 485721; telex: 410423). Moderate.

Santa Chiara – Beautifully renovated last year, this centrally located, 94-room hostelry has been in the Corteggiani family since 1834. No dining room, but close to many restaurants. Business facilities include meeting rooms for up to 40, English-speaking concierge, audiovisual equipment, photocopiers, cable television news, and express checkout. 21 Via Santa Chiara (phone: 683-3763; fax: 687-3144). Moderate.

Scalinata di Spagna – Tiny, but spectacularly placed overlooking the Spanish Steps, it's opposite the pricey *Hassler*. There are 14 rooms, no restaurant. 17 Piazza Trinità dei Monti (phone: 684-0598). Moderate.

Senato – Newly renovated, this 50-room hotel with delightful views of the Pantheon from the front rooms has air conditioning. A good value. Business facilities include English-speaking concierge, foreign currency exchange, photocopiers, and express checkout. 73 Piazza della Rotonda (phone: 679-3231; fax: 684-0297). Moderate.

Sitea – Gianni de Luca and his Scottish wife, Shirley, have bestowed the coziness of a private home on their 40-room, 5-floor hotel opposite the *Grand*. Rooms have high ceilings, crystal chandeliers, and hand-painted Florentine dressers. Other amenities: sitting rooms and a sun-drenched penthouse bar. 90 Via Vittorio Emanuele Orlando (phone: 482-7560). Moderate.

Trevi – Located in a recently renovated palazzo only a few steps from the fabled fountain. Tiny (20 rooms, all with private baths), this 4-story hotel offers many amenities, including air conditioning. 20 Vicolo del Babuccio (phone: 684-1406). Moderate.

Villa Florence – A charming 19th-century patrician villa in a residential area a few minutes' drive from the Via Veneto. The comfortable, modern rooms have TV sets, radio, and mini-bar, and are complemented by touches of ancient Rome in the public areas. Parking facilities and nice gardens. 28 Via Nomentana (phone: 440-3036). Moderate.

Aberdeen – Small and unpretentious, this completely renovated 26-room inn stars for its prime location near Parliament. Some rooms are air conditioned and there's a buffet breakfast. 48 Via Firenze (phone: 481-9340; fax: 482-1092). Moderate to inexpensive.

Canova – All 15 comfortable rooms in this quiet hostelry are air conditioned. There is a small café on the roof and an inexpensive restaurant next door. Well located between the Roman Forum and Santa Maria Maggiore. 10/A Via Urbana (phone: 481-9123; fax: 481-9123). Moderate to inexpensive.

Clodio – A modern 61-room hotel on the Prati side of the river, close to RAI's headquarters and to the *Foro Italico,* where the *International Tennis Championship* is held every May. 10 Via Santa Lucia (phone: 317541; telex: 625050). Moderate to inexpensive.

Coronet – Guests won't find luxurious accommodations at this pensione, but it is in a central area just a few blocks from the Piazza Venezia. Inside the Palazzo Doria, a palace which still is the home of the family who built it, some of its rooms have private baths. No restaurant. Business facilities include English-speaking concierge and foreign currency exchange. 5 Piazza Grazioli (phone: 679-2341). Inexpensive.

Dinesen – Off Via Veneto and next to the Villa Borghese, the 20 rooms in this charming place with a 19th-century air are a real bargain. Breakfast is included. No restaurant. 18 Via di Porta Pinciana (phone: 460932). Inexpensive.

Fabrello White – For basic, affordable accommodations, this pensione is a good bet. Not all of the 33 rooms have baths, but some have terrace views of the river. On the right bank of the Tiber, it's a 10-minute walk to the Spanish Steps. 11 Via Vittoria Colonna (phone: 360-4446/7). Inexpensive.

Gregoriana – On the street of the same name — high fashion's headquarters in Rome — this tiny (19 air conditioned rooms) gem attracts the fashionable. Its decor is reminiscent of Art Deco, with room letters (rather than numbers) by the late fashion illustrator Erté. No restaurant, though a continental breakfast is included. No credit cards accepted. 18 Via Gregoriana (phone: 679-4269 or 679-7988). Inexpensive.

King – The 61 rooms in this well-positioned, immaculate hotel are reasonably priced. No restaurant, though breakfast is served. Business facilities include English-speaking concierge, foreign currency exchange, secretarial services in English, photocopiers, cable television news, translation services, and express checkout. 131 Via Sistina (phone: 474-1515; fax: 487-1813; telex: 626236KINGHO I). Inexpensive.

Locarno – Near the Piazza del Popolo and the Spanish Steps, this Belle Epoque hotel often attracts artists, writers, and intellectuals. The 35 rooms have Victorian furniture, and many are large enough to include couches and desks. A clever touch here — guest bikes for getting around. During winter, a fire burns in the lounge, and in the summer drinks and breakfast are served on the terrace. Business facilities include meeting rooms for up to 15, English-speaking concierge, secretarial services in English, photocopiers, and express checkout. 22 Via della Penna (phone: 361-0841; fax: 321-5249; telex: 622251HOTLOC I). Inexpensive.

Margutta – Try for the two rooms on the roof (Nos. 50 and 51), complete with fireplaces and surrounded by a terrace. This 21-room hotel is near Piazza del Popolo and has an English-speaking concierge. No restaurant. 34 Via Laurina (phone: 679-8440). Inexpensive.

Sant'Anselmo – In a small villa on the Aventine Hill, this beflowered bargain has 26 rooms, a family atmosphere, but no restaurant. (Nearby are 4 other villas — with this one, totaling about 120 rooms — each with similar accommodations and prices, and all run by the same management.) Reservations necessary well in advance. Business facilities include meeting rooms for up to 50, English-speaking concierge, foreign currency exchange, secretarial services in English, and photocopiers. 2 Piazza di Sant'Anselmo (phone: 574-5174; fax: 578-3604; telex: 622812). Inexpensive.

Teatro di Pompeo – History, literally, is at the root of this hotel, as its foundation was originally laid in 55 BC and is said to have supported the Theater of Pompey, where Julius Caesar met his untimely end. On a quiet street, its 12 charming rooms have hand-painted tiles and beamed ceilings. No restaurant. Business facilities include meeting rooms for up to 20, English-speaking concierge, foreign currency exchange, audiovisual equipment, and photocopiers. 8 Largo del Pallaro (phone: 687-2566; fax: 687-2566). Inexpensive.

 EATING OUT: The ancient Romans were the originators of the first fully developed cuisine of the Western world. Drawing on an abundance of fine, natural ingredients from the fertile Roman countryside and influenced by Greece and Asia Minor, they evolved a gastronomic tradition still felt in kitchens the world over.

While the lavish and exotic banquets of exaggerated proportions described in detail by Roman writers such as Petronius and Pliny no doubt existed, they were relatively infrequent and probably more a vulgar show of *nouveaux riches* than typical examples of local custom. The old nobility, then as now, must have found such conspicuous consumption in poor taste, and in fact, the beginnings of genuine Roman gastronomic traditions were more likely among the humble masses, who dined on such staples as lentils and chick-peas, still regularly offered in Roman trattorias. Even the ancient Romans' beloved sauce of rotted fish, *garum,* is echoed in the olive oil, crushed anchovy bits, and garlic sauce that anoints the quintessential Roman salad green, crisp and curly *puntarelle.*

Unfortunately, today's authentically Roman kitchens are dwindling in number. One by one, the old-fashioned, inexpensive mamma-papa trattorias are becoming Chinese restaurants, of which Rome now boasts 140 — none of them too terrific. In addition, fast-food joints have arrived with a vengeance and with the *1990 World Cup* soccer games, every restaurateur renovated his or her locale — and the price list as well. So don't be surprised if an old favorite trattoria now is all tarted up and pricey.

Rome's traditional fare is further threatened by the standardized fad menus, which include such vogues as *rughetta* (arugula), tucked everywhere and often cooked to little effect. Watch out, too, for the new handy way to deal with leftover carpaccio (raw slivers of beef), sautéed *stracci* ("rags"). The trendy dessert continues to be *tiramisù,* a Tyrolean calorie bomb of mascarpone cheese, liqueur, and coffee. The very ease of its preparation, with no cooking involved, is elbowing out better and more interesting desserts.

The bright side is that a new generation of well-trained cooks is bringing back forgotten regional dishes and devising new versions of old standbys. These relative youngsters call their fare "creative cuisine," the fruit of their labors, and are well worth seeking out. The decreasing number of authentic Roman kitchens makes the survivors all the more precious, and it means that while a careful diner will test the new, he or she also will seek out and cherish the authentic old.

Real Roman cooking is quite like the real Roman people — robust and hearty, imbued with a total disregard for tomorrow. There's no room in the popular Roman philosophy of *carpe diem* for thoughts of cholesterol or calories or preoccupations with heartburn, hangovers, or garlic-laden breath. These considerations disappear before a steaming dish of fragrant *spaghetti all'amatriciana* (tomato, special bacon, and tangy *pecorino* — ewe's milk cheese), deep-fried *filetti di baccalà* (salt cod fillet), or *coda alla vaccinara* (oxtail stewed in tomato, onion and celery) — all accompanied by the abundant wines of the surrounding hill towns, the Castelli Romani.

Since Rome is close to the sea, its restaurants offer abundant fresh fish — particularly on Tuesdays and Fridays — but it is costly. All restaurants are required to identify frozen fish as well as other frozen ingredients. Don't hesitate to try the *antipasta marinara* (a mixture of seafoods in a light sauce of olive oil, lemon, parsley, and garlic), the *spaghetti alle vongole* (spaghetti with clam sauce — the clam shells come as well), and as a main course, trout from the nearby lakes or rock fish from the Mediterranean.

Veal is typically Roman, served as *saltimbocca alla romana* (literally, "hop-into-the-mouth," flavored with ham, sage, and marsala wine) or roasted with the fresh rosemary that grows in every garden. *Abbacchio al forno* is milk-fed baby lamb roasted with garlic and rosemary, and *abbacchio brodettato,* ever harder to find, is cooked in a sauce of egg yolks and lemon juice. *Abbacchio scottadito* ("finger burning") are tiny grilled lamb chops. On festive occasions, *maialetto* (suckling pig) appears on the menu; it is stuffed with herbs, roasted, and thickly sliced. Its street-stand version is eaten between thick slabs of country bread. Watch, too, for such Roman specialties as *tripa* (tripe flavored with mint, parmesan cheese, and tomato sauce), *coniglio* (rabbit), *capretto* (kid), *coratella* (lamb's heart), *animelle* (sweetbreads), and, in season, *cinghiale* (wild boar). Wild boar dried sausages are popular as an antipasto course, along with salamis; the local Roman salami is prepared with tasty fennel seeds.

Pasta dishes include the incredibly simple *spaghetti alla carbonara* (with egg, salt pork, and *pecorino* cheese). *Penne all'arrabbiata* are short pasta in a tomato and garlic sauce "rabid" with hot peppers. The familiar *fettuccine all'Alfredo* depends upon the quality of the homemade strips of egg pasta in a rich sauce of cream, butter, and parmesan.

Fresh, seasonal vegetables, which often are treated as a separate course, provide the base for many a savory antipasto, accompany the main dish, and are even munched raw — for instance, *finocchio al pinzimonio* (fennel dipped into the purest of olive oil seasoned with salt and pepper) — after a particularly heavy meal to "clean the palate." Several local greens are unknown to visitors, such as *agretti, bieta, cicoria,* and *broccolo romano* — the last two often boiled briefly, then sautéed with olive oil, garlic, and hot red peppers. Salad ingredients include red radicchio, wild aromatic herbs, and the juicy tomatoes so cherished during the sultry summer months when they are served with ultra-aromatic basil — the sun's special gift to Mediterranean terraces and gardens. Tomatoes are also stuffed with rice and roasted; yellow, red, and green sweet peppers, eggplant, mushrooms, green and broad beans, and zucchini are favorite vegetables for antipasto; while asparagus and artichokes are especially prized in season. The latter is stuffed with mint and garlic and is stewed with olive oil seasoning *alla romana,* or opened out like a flower and deep-fried *alla giudia* (Jewish-style).

After such a meal, Romans normally have fresh fruit for dessert, although there is no shortage of sweet desserts (such as *montebianco, zuppa inglese,* and, of course, *gelato* (ice cream). For a final *digestivo,* bottles brought to the table may include *Sambuca Romana* (it has an aniseed base), *grappa* (made from the third and fourth grape pressings and normally over 60 proof), and some sort of *amaro* (which means bitter, but is more often quite sweet).

A full meal, including house wine, may cost between $50 and $60 for two in a modest restaurant, while the same fare may cost twice that amount if the restaurant is even marginally fashionable. Most dining is à la carte, although a *menù turistico* is offered at some unpretentious trattorias for very reasonable prices, and a few tony establishments now serve sampler menus (*menù degustazione*) at a slightly lower price. Less expensive are the quick service, often cafeteria-style, *rosticcerie* and *tavole calde* (literally "hot tables"). A delightful novelty is the spate of small wine tasting establishments that offer light snacks at lunch with a glass of fine wine; some also provide pasta or a mixed vegetable platter. Most café-bars serve sandwiches as well as that delicious and filling health snack, *frullato di frutta* (a mixture of frothy blended fruit and milk). Be careful when ordering fresh fish or Florentine steaks *al chilo* — by weight — as this may swell a bill way out of proportion, even at average-priced restaurants. When in Rome, start your day as the Romans do with a tiny, but terrific cup of coffee at one of the many coffee-bars like *Antico Caffè Greco* (86 Via Condotti); *Rosati* (4-5 Piazza del Popolo); *Sant' Eustachio Il Caffè* (82 Piazza Sant' Eustachio); or *Tazzo a'Oro* (6 Via degli Orfani). Also, always ask prices when ordering wine. Good Italian wines can cost as much as $30 and up per bottle. Dinner for two (with wine) costs from $170 to $250 in restaurants listed below as very expensive, $100 to $175 in restaurants classed as expensive; $60 to $100 is moderate; and below $60 is inexpensive. All telephone numbers are in the 6 area code unless otherwise indicated.

Alberto Ciarla – Alberto, long an impassioned diver and spearfisherman, is another restaurateur who knows where to find fresh oysters (which he sometimes serves raw), lobster, and fish. Ciarla is rated one of Rome's finest chefs; the *L'Espresso* guide gives him its highest marks, three chef's toques. His herbed pasta sauces are a welcome change from the more usual ways of preparing Italy's favorite food. For meat lovers, the "Alter Ego" menu offers a pâté of wild pigeon, baby lamb, and game — including venison — in season. The ever-large, noisy crowd brightens up the black decor (even down to the tablecloths). In good weather, there's alfresco dining on a little piece of a Trastevere street. Dinner only; closed Sundays. Reservations advised. Major credit cards accepted. 40 Piazza San Cosimato (phone: 581-8668). Very expensive.

Il Pianeta Terra – This Planet Earth comes close to paradise. A young couple, half Tuscan and half Sicilian, has created an elegant, traditional, yet adventurous dining place in the heart of Rome. Starters such as ravioli stuffed with sea bass in a pistachio sauce or pasta with clams and broccoli lead to exciting main courses, such as the squab stuffed with artichokes or with oysters and clams, and to delicate desserts. The wine list is intelligently chosen. Note: the *menù degustazione* can cost more than an à la carte meal. Dinner only; closed Mondays and from mid-July through August. Reservations necessary. Major credit cards accepted. 94-95 Via Arco del Monte (phone: 686-9893 or 679-9828). Very expensive.

Relais Le Jardin – The sumptuous dining room of the *Lord Byron* hotel is still Rome's foremost restaurant. Chef Antonio Sciullo's creations blend the unlikely into the surprising and sometime sublime. The menu follows the seasons — you will find zucchini blossoms stuffed with bean purée, ravioli with a delicate pigeon ragout, and scallops lurking in a watercress flan. The dessert soufflé has a crunchy hazelnut topping. Service is appropriately sophisticated, as are the wines. Closed Sundays and August. Reservations necessary. Major credit cards accepted. *Lord Byron Hotel,* 5 Via Giuseppe De Notaris (phone: 322-4541). Very expensive.

La Rosetta – One of Rome's most famed fish restaurants, it is small, jam-packed, and chic. The chef grills, fries, boils, or bakes to perfection any — or a mixture of all — of the fish and seafood flown in from his native Sicily. A favorite specialty is *pappardelle al pescatore* (wide noodles in a piquant tomato sauce with mussels, clams, and parsley) or Sicilian-style *pasta con le sarde,* flavored with wild fennel. Closed Sundays, Mondays at lunchtime, and August. Reservations necessary. Major credit cards accepted. 9 Via della Rosetta (phone: 686-1002). Very expensive.

El Toulà – The well-heeled, well-traveled, and aristocratic assemble here for Cortina- and Venice-inspired fare; in winter that means hearty game dishes such as venison and, year-round, fish, such as the poppyseed-daubed salmon in oyster sauce. A favorite dessert is a large shortbread biscuit. There's an impressive wine list, but you might have to put up with hearing the man at the next table negotiating a major deal as the tables are quite close together. Closed Saturday lunch, Sundays, and August. Reservations necessary. Major credit cards accepted. 29/B Via della Lupa (phone: 687-3498). Very expensive.

Andrea – Tops for the Via Veneto area. In season, fettuccine with artichoke sauce; always on the menu, ricotta-stuffed fresh ravioli. Pleasant service, a serviceable house wine, and sweeties to sweeten the bill. Closed Sundays and 3 weeks in August. Reservations necessary. Major credit cards accepted. 26 Via Sardegna (phone: 446-3707). Expensive.

Le Cabanon – French and Tunisian food are served in an intimate ambience accompanied by Mediterranean melodies sung by the well-traveled owner, Enzo Rallo.

South American or French singers ably fill in the gaps. The usual onion soup and escargots, as well as a delicious Tunisian *brik à l'oeuf* (a pastry concealing a challengingly dripping egg within), couscous, and *merguez* sausages are among the choices. Open evenings only, and until late. Closed Sundays and August. Reservations necessary. No credit cards accepted. 4 Vicolo della Luce (phone: 581-8106). Expensive.

La Cesta – Centrally located in the *Holiday Inn Crowne Plaza Minerva* is this delightfully restored 19th-century restaurant. You can enjoy quiet dining for business as well as pleasure under splendid Venetian glass chandeliers. Beside a somewhat standard menu, there is a daily list of Roman and international specialties. The fare is excellent if not brilliant. Open daily. Reservations advised. Major credit cards accepted. 69 Piazza della Minerva (phone: 684-1888). Expensive.

Charles Roof Garden – A breathtaking view and creative Italian fare is offered at this restaurant on top of the *Eden* hotel. Regional specialties include homemade *tonnarelli* (thick noodles) with lemon sauce, while the café on the terrace offers a snacks menu. Open daily. Reservations necessary. Major credit cards accepted. 49 Via Ludovisi (phone: 474-3551). Expensive.

Il Convivio – A welcome addition on a street of artisans and antiques dealers, chef Angelo Trioiani and his brother Massimo have just 10 tables on which to lavish their version of "creative cuisine." A special menu (with lower prices) is available at lunchtime. A fine wine list. Closed Sundays. Reservations advised. Major credit cards accepted. 44 Via dell'Orso (phone: 686-9432). Expensive.

Girarrosto Toscano – Old fashioned and serious, it's a fine eatery for lovers of classic Tuscan fare. The sizzling Florentine steaks and fresh fish are grilled to perfection. The rest is perfect, too, but this is not always a restful place. Closed Wednesdays. Reservations necessary. Major credit cards accepted. 29 Via Campania (phone: 482-1899). Expensive.

Hosteria dell'Orso – Although this is widely known as a tourist place, the traditional Italian fare offered in an elegant 13th-century building is quite good. Upstairs is a disco (see *Nightclubs and Nightlife*), and downstairs is a piano bar. Closed Sundays. Reservations necessary. Major credit cards accepted. 33 Via dell'Orso (phone: 656-4904). Expensive.

La Lampada – This is the only Roman restaurant that specializes in truffles and wild mushrooms, but don't anticipate bargains, and don't expect the truffles to be fresh beyond the autumn/winter season. The risotto is made with white truffles, and the carpaccio with a grating of both black and white truffles (from Norcia and Alba, respectively). Closed Sundays. Reservations necessary. Major credit cards accepted. 25 Via Quintino Sella (phone: 474-4323). Expensive.

Papà Giovanni – It's small and intimate, with paintings and wine bottles lining the walls, and the bar is very well stocked — sip a *kir* as an *aperitivo* while choosing from over 700 wines. The highly praised fare is basically refined Roman, with truffles a seasonal specialty. Try *panzerotti al tartufo* (small ravioli with truffles). The interesting menu varies, so ask your waiter for current specialties. Closed Sundays. Reservations necessary. Major credit cards accepted. 4 Via dei Sediari (phone: 686-5308). Expensive.

Passetto – For classical Roman cooking, this Belle Epoque restaurant is a beloved local institution. In addition to the excellent antipasto, try the *filetto con carciofi* (steak with artichokes) and *porcini* mushrooms with asparagus, if they're in season. Closed Sundays and Monday afternoons. Reservations advised. Major credit cards accepted. 13-14 Via Zanardelli (phone: 654-0569 or 687-9937). Expensive.

Il Peristilio – The decor is sumptuous, with fine objets d'art, tasteful cutlery and china, and a refined aura. Air conditioning, a piano bar, and polite waiters complete the picture; the quality of the food may blur it. Closed Mondays. Reservations necessary. Major credit cards accepted. 6/B Via Col di Lana (phone: 322-3623). Expensive.

Pino e Dino – Although the founders have gone, current management continues their menu of interesting regional dishes. The restaurant is in one of Rome's more picturesque squares, but a cozy winter meal indoors, surrounded by wine bottles and artisan products from all over Italy, is just as enticing. Closed Mondays and most of August. Reservations necessary. Major credit cards accepted. 22 Piazza di Montevecchio (phone: 656-1319). Expensive.

Quinzi e Gabrieli – Seafood is a very serious subject here. It is prepared as naturally as possible for a maximum of 22 diners. In season, the oyster bar is popular. Closed Sundays and August. Reservations necessary. Major credit cards accepted. Near the Pantheon, at 5 Via delle Coppelle (phone: 687-9389). Expensive.

Le Restaurant – This elegant dining room at the *Grand* hotel serves continental cuisine and has a menu that changes with the season. Decor, flowers, and waiters in tails, all reflect the *Grand* approach to luxury. Open daily. Reservations necessary. Major credit cards accepted. 3 Via Vittorio Emanuele Orlando (phone: 4709). Expensive.

Ai Tre Scalini – Not to be confused with the renowned *gelateria* and café *Tre Scalini*, the food and wines here are special. Owners Roanna Dupre and Matteo Cicala change the menu frequently, but you'll be lucky if you find the fish soup or the fish-stuffed ravioli. A sampler menu is offered. The decor is simple; there are only seven tables, 30 diners in all, so reservations are necessary. Closed Mondays. Major credit cards accepted. 16 Via dei Santi Quattro (phone: 732695). Expensive.

Alvaro al Circo Massimo – Let Alvaro suggest what's best that day and you'll not go wrong, whether it's fresh fish, game such as *fagiano* (pheasant) or *faraona* (guinea hen), or mushrooms (try grilled *porcini*). The ambience is rustic indoors, and there are tables outdoors during the summer. Closed Mondays. Reservations generally are not necessary. Major credit cards accepted. 53 Via dei Cerchi (phone: 678-6112). Expensive to moderate.

Dal Bolognese – Strategically set next to the popular *Caffè Rosati* on Piazza del Popolo and with a menu nearly as long as the list of celebrities who frequent this fashionable eatery, it's run by two brothers from Bologna. Stargazers will still enjoy such specialties as homemade *tortelloni* (pasta twists stuffed with ricotta cheese) and the *bollito misto* (boiled beef, tongue, chicken, pig's trotter). There are tables outdoors in good weather. Closed Sunday evenings, Mondays, and most of August. Reservations necessary. Major credit cards accepted. 1 Piazza del Popolo (phone: 361-1426). Expensive to moderate.

Il Canto del Riso – There are two, actually — summer and winter. In warmer days it's a gussied-up river barge lurking under the Ponte Cavour, while in winter the restaurant makes its home in a historic building in old Rome. The name means "the Rice Song," and a northern connection (Veneto/Friuli) explains the preponderance of rice dishes: *risotto ai capasanti* (rice with scallops) is only one of more than a dozen rice starters. There is live music in the evening. Closed Sunday nights, Mondays, and in bad weather. Reservations advised in summer. Major credit cards accepted. Summer: Walk down to the river from Lungotevere Mellini, on the Vatican side (phone: 361-0430); winter: 21 Cordonata (phone: 678-6227) Expensive to moderate.

Cesarina – Year in, year out, here's the place to enjoy a well-prepared *bollito misto* from the rich cart of meat and sausage, with the green sauce *comme il faut.* In summer, the fresh fish may appeal more, as will the air conditioning. Year-round, the pasta Bolognese-style is a traditional favorite. Closed Sundays. Reservations necessary. Major credit cards accepted. 109 Via Piemonte (phone: 488-0828). Expensive to moderate.

Checchino dal 1887 – Among the most traditional of all dining places, it's renowned for its light touch with such Roman staples as oxtail, tripe, brains with artichokes, and *spaghetti con pajatta* (spaghetti in a tomato sauce with lamb's intestines). Try the *bucatini all'amatriciana* (a hearty pasta dish with bacon). Closed Sunday evenings and Mondays. Reservations advised. Major credit cards accepted. 30 Via Monte Testaccio (phone: 574-6318 or 574-3816). Expensive to moderate.

Comparone – Roomy and cheery, with plenty of tables outside in the piazza, this is an old favorite of *trasteverini* and visitors alike. The menu is traditional Roman. Closed Mondays. Reservations necessary. Major credit cards accepted. 47 Piazza in Piscinula (phone: 581-6249). Expensive to moderate.

Cornucopia – At this eatery in Trastevere, the few tables outdoors in this lovely piazza offer a view of medieval buildings. Inside, it is air conditioned, small, and inviting. The fare is seafood only, except in winter, when game also is on the menu. At lunchtime, a special limited menu (a choice of seven dishes with a glass of sparkling white wine, mineral water, and coffee) is available at an especially low price. Closed Mondays. Reservations necessary. Major credit cards accepted. 18 Piazza in Piscinula (phone: 580-0380). Expensive to moderate.

Cul de Sac 2 – On a tiny street in Trastevere, the owners of the wine shop *Cul de Sac 1* have created an elegant and attractive restaurant offering *cucina creativa*. Dishes such as lobster with creamed broccoli are carefully prepared, as is the wine list. Closed Sunday evenings, Mondays, and August. Reservations advised. Major credit cards accepted. 21 Vicolo dell'Atleta (phone: 581-3324). Expensive to moderate.

Fortunato al Pantheon – Barely a block from the Pantheon, this eatery is a favorite among politicos and writers. Fish in all ways — grilled, in risotto or pasta — is the specialty, and it is usually as fine as this eatery's long-standing reputation. Tables outside in summer. Closed Sundays and August 15–30. Reservations necessary. American Express accepted. 55 Via del Pantheon (phone: 679-2788). Expensive to moderate.

Al Gladiatore – This old-fashioned, cozy trattoria overlooking the Colosseum is known for its fresh fish. Closed Wednesdays. No reservations. Major credit cards accepted. 5 Piazza Colosseo (phone: 700-0533). Expensive to moderate.

La Maiella – On a delightful square colorfully illuminated in the summer for outdoor dining, this efficient organization with delicious food owes its fame and popularity to owner/manager Signor Antonio. The pope (while still a cardinal) was among his clientele, and the Roman-Abruzzian menu is nearly as long as the Bible. Fresh seafood, truffles, and the alfresco dining are the major attractions. Closed Sundays and a week in August. Reservations advised in the evenings. Major credit cards accepted. 45 Piazza Sant'Apollinare (phone: 686-4174). Expensive to moderate.

Nino – A reliable place, frequented by artists, actors, and aristocrats, and near the Spanish Steps, it is truly Tuscan. The cuisine is composed of the best ingredients, ably yet simply prepared, and the service is serious. Specialties: *zuppa di fagioli alla Francovich* (thick Tuscan white bean soup with garlic), *bistecca alla fiorentina* (thick succulent T-bone steak), and for dessert *castagnaccio* (semisweet chestnut cake). Excellent wine list. Closed Sundays. Reservations advised. Major credit cards accepted. 11 Via Borgognona (phone: 679-5676). Expensive to moderate.

Orient Express – Italians in the know dine here. Antique railway fixtures and menu items that track the famous route from Istanbul (shish kebab) to Paris (delicious onion soup) are what gives this small, pleasant eatery its name. The owners are a former Italian diplomat and his ex-schoolteacher wife. In Trastevere. Closed Sundays. Reservations necessary. American Express accepted. 80 Via Ponte Sisto (phone: 580-9868). Expensive to moderate.

Osteria dell'Antiquario – This small dining spot on a picturesque little square along the antiques-shop-lined Via dei Coronari prides itself on genuine Roman fare, well prepared with the finest seasonal ingredients. Alfresco dining in fine weather. Closed Sundays. Reservations advised. Major credit cards accepted. 27 Piazza San Simeone (phone: 687-9694). Expensive to moderate.

Paris – The Cappellanti family of chefs adds a creative zing to traditional Roman-Jewish and strictly Roman dishes such as *pasta e ceci* (pasta with chick-peas). Closed Sunday evenings, Mondays, and August. Reservations necessary. Major credit cards acepted. 7/A Piazza San Calisto (phone: 581-5378). Expensive to moderate.

Piccolo Mondo – Not exactly a "find," this cheerful and busy restaurant behind Via Veneto has been popular with Italians and foreigners alike for decades. Among the many varied antipasti displayed at the entrance are exquisite *mozzarellini alla panna* (small balls of fresh buffalo's milk cheese swimming in cream), as well as eggplant and peppers prepared in several tempting ways. There are sidewalk tables in good weather. Closed Sundays and the first 3 weeks of August. Reservations advised. Major credit cards accepted. 39 Via Aurora (phone: 481-4595). Expensive to moderate.

Piperno – A summer dinner outdoors on this quiet Renaissance *piazzetta,* next to the Palazzo Cenci — which still reeks "of ancient evil and nameless crimes" — is sheer magic. Indoors it is modern and less magical, and the classic Roman-Jewish cooking can be a bit heavy. The great specialty is *fritto vegetariano* (zucchini flowers, mozzarella cheese, salt cod, rice and potato balls, and artichokes — the latter *alla giudia,* or "Jewish-style"). Closed Sunday nights, Mondays, and August. Reservations necessary. Major credit cards accepted. 9 Monte de' Cenci (phone: 654-2772). Expensive to moderate.

Romolo – Summer dining is alfresco, in the dappled sunlight of a 450-year-old arbor, but eating is a delight year-round in this famed tavern in Trastevere where the painter Raphael courted the baker's daughter, la Fornarina. A favorite of Romans and tourists alike is the tasty *spaghetti alla bocaiola* (with a sauce of tomatoes, mushrooms, and tuna) and the grilled, herbed scampi kebabs. Another specialty is *mozzarella alla Fornarina* (melted cheese wrapped in prosciutto and accompanied by a fried artichoke). The wine list is excellent. Closed Mondays and August. Reservations necessary in summer. Major credit cards accepted. 8 Via di Porta Settimiana (phone: 581-8284). Expensive to moderate.

Taverna Flavia – It's been fashionable with the movie crowd, journalists, and politicians for over 30 years. Owner Mimmo likes autographed pictures — one entire room is devoted to Elizabeth Taylor — and the *Sardi's* style survives, despite the crash of "Hollywood on the Tiber" long ago. Near the *Grand* hotel, and open quite late. Good pasta dishes and fine grilled fish. Closed Saturday lunch, all day Sundays, and August. Reservations necessary. Major credit cards accepted. 9-11 Via Flavia (phone: 474-5214). Expensive to moderate.

Taverna Giulia – This reliable old favorite is set in a 600-year-old building. Genoese specialties include pesto served over the traditional *troffie* noodles, and smoked fish. Closed Sundays and August. Reservations advised. Major credit cards accepted. Vicolo dell'Oro (phone: 686-4089). Expensive to moderate.

Vecchia Roma – The setting is truly out of a midsummer night's dream on magical Piazza Campitelli on the fringe of Rome's Jewish quarter. The menu is traditional, the ingredients fresh, the salads pleasing, and the waiters courteous. We love it. Closed Wednesdays and 2 weeks in August. Reservations advised. No credit cards accepted. 18 Piazza Campitelli (phone: 686-4604). Expensive to moderate.

Apuleius – Near Rome's United Nations office complex, this tavern serves seafood in amiable, if kitschy, surroundings. Its Aventine hill location is a plus. *Spaghetti alla pescatore* (fish sauce) is special. Closed Sundays. Reservations advised. Major credit cards accepted. 15 Via Tempio di Diana (phone: 574-2160). Moderate.

La Campana – This unprepossessing, 400-year-old truly Roman restaurant, is favored by everyone from local folk to the stars and staff of RAI, Italian radio-television. Waiters help decipher the handwritten menu, which tempts most with *carciofi alla romana* (fresh artichokes in garlic and oil), *tonnarelli alla chitarra* (homemade pasta in an egg and cheese sauce), and lamb, and truffle-topped poultry dishes. Closed Mondays and August. Reservations advised. Major credit cards accepted. 18 Vicolo della Campana (phone: 686-7820). Moderate.

La Carbonara – On the square where Rome's most colorful morning food market has been held for centuries, this is where *spaghetti alla carbonara* (the sauce is eggs and bacon) is said to have been invented. The windows of the ancient palazzo look out over the scene; indoors is no less authentically Roman, from menu to decor. Closed Tuesdays. Reservations unnecessary. Major credit cards accepted. 23 Campo dei Fiori (phone: 686-4783). Moderate.

Il Cardinale – In a restored bicycle shop off the stately Via Giulia, decorated in a somewhat precious turn-of-the-century style, this popular evening spot specializes in regional dishes: pasta with green tomato or artichoke sauce, grilled eels, a sweetbread casserole with mushrooms, and *aliciotti con l'indivia* (an anchovy and endive dish). Closed Sundays and August. Reservations advised. Visa accepted. 6 Via delle Carceri (phone: 686-9336). Moderate.

Checco er Carettiere – In the Trastevere area — the Greenwich Village of Rome — this eatery has a large and friendly interior, with a garden in a courtyard, and a wood-paneled dining room. A guitarist strolls among the tables, a flower girl proffers blossoms, and a fledgling artist opens her portfolio to display sketches of surrounding landmarks. The food's super. An antipasto made entirely of seafood is a specialty, and there's a unique mixture of tomatoes and potatoes. Closed Sunday evenings and Mondays. Reservations advised in the evenings. American Express and Visa accepted. 10-13 Via Benedetta, Piazza Trilussa (phone: 581-7018). Moderate.

Le Colline Emiliane – With Tuscan inspiration and truffle toppings, an eatery like this is becoming a rarity. Service is prompt, decor simple, and the *maccheroncini al funghetto* delicious. It has a well-deserved reputation for consistency over the years. Closed Fridays and August. Reservations advised. Major credit cards accepted. Near Via Veneto. 22 Via degli Avignonesi (phone: 481-7538). Moderate.

Costanza – For those who prize a bit of history with their supper, these vaulted dining rooms are in a 2,000-year-old entryway to the ancient Theater of Pompeii. Now wildly chic, it has an interesting menu and is pleasant in winter; the service in summer is irritatingly slow. Closed Sundays and August. Reservations advised. American Express and Visa accepted. 63 Piazza Paradiso (phone: 686-1717 or 654-1002). Moderate.

Cuccurucù – A garden overlooking the Tiber provides one of Rome's most pleasant summer settings for dining alfresco, while inside it's cozy and rustic. The antipasti are good, and so is the meat grilled on an open fire. Ask for *bruschetta con pomodori* (toasted country bread smothered in fresh tomatoes and oregano), and a *spiedino misto,* a sort of shish kebab bearing great chunks of veal, pork, and sausage, all interspersed with onions and peppers and grilled. Closed Sunday evenings and Mondays year-round, Sundays in the summer, and August. Reservations advised. Major credit cards accepted. 10 Via Capoprati (phone: 325257). Moderate.

Il Dito e la Luna – Sicilian fare and *la cucina creativa* (Italy's answer to France's nouvelle cuisine) are featured at this lovely restaurant with white walls, terra cotta floors, and antique furnishings. Specialties include *lasagnette con scampi,* *pomodori, e zucchini* (flat pasta with shrimp, tomatoes, and zucchini), *anitra in pasta sfoglia* (duck in puff pastry with an orange sauce), and a good selection of homemade desserts. Open for dinner only; closed Sundays and August. Reservations advised. No credit cards accepted. 51 Via dei Sabelli (phone: 494-0276). Moderate.

Il Drappo – Drapes softly frame the two small rooms of this *ristorantino* run by the brother-sister team of Paolo and Valentina Tolu from Sardinia. They offer delicate dishes based on robust island fare, fragrant with wild fennel, myrtle, and herbs. The innovative menu, recited by Paolo and artfully prepared by Valentina, always begins with mixed antipasti including *carta di musica* (hors d'oeuvres on crisp Sardinian wafers). Closed Sundays and 2 weeks in August. Reservations necessary. American Express accepted. 9 Vicolo del Malpasso (phone: 687-7365). Moderate.

Giulio II – Fish baked in parchment and Sicilian-style stuffed swordfish are the specialties at this stylish new eatery in the Parioli quarter. It is within walking distance of the *Coppede'* fine arts complex, with its lovely fountain and architectural curiosities. Closed Saturday lunch, Sundays, and August. Reservations unnecessary. Major credit cards accepted. 80 Via Arno (phone: 841-5535 or 855-1002). Moderate.

Isola del Sole – A converted houseboat on the Tiber offers a variation on the theme of alfresco dining — with lunches under a welcome winter sun, or candlelit dining with the summer stars as backdrop. Try pasta with eggplant and ricotta, ravioli stuffed with *porcini* mushrooms, or carpaccio (thin slices of raw beef seasoned with olive oil, lemon, and flaked parmesan cheese). Extra-special chocolate mousse. From 11 PM to 4 AM there's a piano bar and dancing. Closed Mondays. Reservations advised (for best service, get there by 8:30 PM). Major credit cards accepted. Between Ponte Matteotti and the *metropolitana* train bridge; walk down to the river from Lungotevere Arnaldo da Brescia (phone: 320-1400). Moderate.

Mario – A Tuscan favorite, with the usual Tuscan specialties such as Francovich soup, Florentine steaks, and delicious game in season, all prepared with admirable care and dedication by Mario himself, but served by only three overworked waiters. Closed Sundays and August. Reservations advised. Major credit cards accepted. 55 Via della Vite (phone: 678-3818). Moderate.

Al Moro – Not far from the Trevi Fountain, this is a quiet, dignified place, very "in" with the theater crowd and the powers-that-be at the nearby Parliament. Traditional Roman specialties and seasonal dishes such as pasta with truffles are a must, as is the *fritta vegetariana,* a mix of deep-fried vegetables and cheeses. Closed Sundays and August. Reservations advised. No credit cards accepted. 13 Vicola delle Bollette (phone: 678-3495). Moderate.

Osteria Picchioni – The most expensive pizza in town, but it could also be the best, and it's a whole meal. Only top-quality ingredients are used in this family-style, old-fashioned trattoria, but the decor runs to plastic flowers. Fortunately, they don't tell the whole story. Watch out for the prices — a plate of spaghetti with truffles can run around $100! Be sure to make reservations — there are only 50 places. Closed Wednesdays. No credit cards accepted. 16 Via del Boschetto (phone: 465261). Moderate.

Osteria Sant'Ana – The locale was a convent in the 18th century, and Elio, the owner, is the third generation to run a restaurant. The vegetable hors d'oeuvres array is admirable, while carnivores will enjoy the charcoal grill; everyone likes the marron glacé ice cream, the location near Piazza del Popolo, the somewhat austere tone, and the moderate price considering the quality. Closed Saturday afternoons, Sundays, and 1 week in August. Reservations necessary in the evenings. Major credit cards accepted. 68 Via della Penna (phone: 361-0291). Moderate.

Otello alla Concordia – A delightful trattoria in the middle of the Piazza di Spagna shopping area, with certain tables reserved for habitués and a colorful courtyard for fine weather dining. The menu is Roman, and it changes daily, depending a great deal on the season. Closed Sundays, *Christmas* week, and the first week in January. No reservations. Major credit cards accepted. 81 Via della Croce (phone: 679-1178). Moderate.

Pierluigi – The fish is fresh, the piazza is charming, the price is a bargain, and in summer, the dining is alfresco. Reservations, therefore, are necessary at this popular trattoria in the heart of old Rome. Closed Mondays and Tuesday lunch. Reservations advised. Major credit cards accepted. 144 Piazza de' Ricci (phone: 686-1302). Moderate.

Al Pompiere – Visiting firemen and travelers adore this bright, old-fashioned restaurant in an ancient palazzo near the Campo dei Fiori, whose name means "The Fireman." The menu includes deep-fried artichokes and mozzarella-stuffed zucchini blossoms. Closed Sundays. Reservations advised in the evenings. No credit cards accepted. 38 Via Santa Maria Calderari (phone: 686-8377). Moderate.

Su Recreu – Finding this spot isn't easy, but the Sardinian food is worth the expedition. The large buffet antipasto is a "take all you want" affair, and there are about a dozen hot and cold choices. The authentic mozzarella (made with buffalo milk) is marvelous, as is anything cooked on the large wood fire right at the entrance. The fresh fish will add to the price. Closed Mondays. Reservations advised. Major credit cards accepted. 17 Via de Buon Consiglio; one block off the Via Cavour, not far from the Forum and the Via del Colosseo (phone: 684-1507). Moderate.

Shangri Là-Corsetti – In the EUR suburb, it's much favored by American businessmen who like the fresh fish. The public pool alongside can be agreeable despite the loud, loud music. Closed August. Reservations advised. Major credit cards accepted. 141 Viale Algeria (phone: 592-8861). Moderate.

Sora Cecilia – Founded in 1898, this modest trattoria offers homemade *agnolotti* (large ravioli) and good *penne all'arrabiata* (pasta with a peppery tomato sauce). Closed Sundays. Reservations advised. American Express accepted. 27 Via Poli (phone: 678-9096). Moderate.

Specchio Antico – Young people run this 6-year-old restaurant that is decorated with fine antiques from their father's prestigious shop. They have won kudos for the spaghetti with seafood *in cartoccio* (a paper bag), delicious array of vegetable hors d'oeuvres, and grilled meat. Closed Sundays. Reservations necessary in the evenings. Major credit cards accepted. 17 Via dei Pastini (phone: 679-7273). Moderate.

Toto alle Carrozze – It has hardly changed after all these years, but we liked it then and we like it now — a trattoria with a banquet spread of strictly Roman antipasti, good pasta, and Roman fish and meat dishes. This is a *giovedì gnocchi, sabato tripa* (Thursday gnocchi, Saturday tripe) kind of traditional Roman place. Closed Sundays. No reservations. Major credit cards accepted. Just off Via del Corso at 10 Via delle Carrozze (phone: 678558). Moderate.

Tullio – Up a narrow hill, just a few yards from the Via Veneto is this just refurbished Tuscan trattoria that serves superb *ribollita* (Tuscan vegetable soup) and baked beans *al fiasco* (in the bottle). It's a custom to place a straw-covered bottle of chianti on the table — diners pay only for what is drunk — and if you're not planning to visit Florence, this is a good place to try a grilled steak Florentine-style. Closed Sundays and August. Reservations advised. Major credit cards. 26 Via di San Nicola da Tolentino (phone: 481-8564 or 474-5560). Moderate.

Le Volte – Carlo Castrucci ran the renowned restaurant at the *Eden* hotel, and now has struck out on his own, in the 16th-century Palazzo Rondanini. Under its frescoed ceiling, diners can enjoy linguine in a lobster sauce, pizza baked in a wood-burning oven, and wild boar with polenta in autumn and winter. Closed Tuesdays and for 15 days in August. Reservations advised. Major credit cards accepted. 47 Piazza Rondanini (phone: 687-7408). Moderate.

Altrove – A new trattoria in the old Subura quarter between Trajan's Market and the Basilica of Santa Maria Maggiore. In one of the downstairs rooms, there is a patch of original Servian wall from ancient Rome. Open until 1 AM; closed Sundays. No reservations. Major credit cards accepted. 35 Via Cimarra (phone: 474-2923). Moderate to inexpensive.

Il Barroccio – *Pane rùstico,* crusty country-style bread, is made here every day, and beans are baked in a wood-burning oven. On a side street not far from the Pantheon, this is a prime place to try *crostini* in all its infinite permutations, and if you want to sample Roman-style pizza, do it here. Across the street at No. 123 is its twin, *Er Faciolaro,* owned by the same people. One or the other always is open. Reservations unnecessary. Major credit cards accepted. 13 Via dei Pastini (phone: 679-3797). Moderate to inexpensive.

Il Falchetto – Conveniently set off Via del Corso, with a few tables outdoors in fine weather, this might seem a tourist haven. But knowledgeable Romans fill the small rooms even in the gray days of winter. The imaginative game, veal, and fish dishes are delicious. Closed Fridays. Reservations advised. Major credit cards accepted. 12-14 Via Montecatini (phone: 679-1160). Moderate to inexpensive.

La Fiorentina – This favorite Roman pizzeria, with its wood-burning oven and grill, is in residential Prati on the Vatican side of the river. It serves pizza even at lunchtime, a rarity in Italy. Tables on the street in good weather. Closed Wednesdays all day, Thursdays at lunch. Reservations advised. Major credit cards accepted. 22 Via Andrea Doria (phone: 312310). Moderate to inexpensive.

Il Giardinetto – Not far from Piazza Navona is this quiet and charming newcomer with a few outdoor tables. The owner is Tunisian, speaks English, and cooks creditable Italian fare, including the ever-popular *spaghetti alla carbonara* (with egg and bacon), onion soup, and tiny *gnocchetti sardi* (an eggless Sardinian pasta with a sauce of fresh tomato and aromatic basil). A good value. Closed Mondays. Reservations necessary in summer. Major credit cards accepted. 125 Via del Governo Vecchio (phone: 686-8693). Moderate to inexpensive.

Giggetto al Portico d'Ottavia – In Rome's Jewish ghetto, this is the place to sample the delicious and well-prepared fried artichokes that most Roman menus identify as *alla giudeo,* "Jewish-style," as well as zucchini flowers stuffed with mozzarella and *crostini* (fried bread offered with an assortment of toppings). But don't take the waiters' occasional lack of attention personally; they ignore everybody. The food is first-rate and the experience absolutely authentic. Closed Mondays. Reservations advised. Major credit cards accepted. 21A Via del Portico d'Ottavia (phone: 686-1105). Moderate to inexpensive.

La Luna sul Tevere – A river restaurant, the "Moon on the Tiber" brought their chef from the Via Veneto's famed *Café de Paris.* Set on the banks of the Tiber, beneath the Duca d'Aosta Bridge, it has alfresco dining in summer and a rustic barge for indoor meals during inclement weather. Specialties include fettuccine with tuna and wild *porcini* mushrooms, breast of chicken with almonds, and petits fours of *tartufini* and *cremini.* Closed Mondays and the last 2 weeks of November. Reservations advised. Major credit cards accepted. Via Capoprati (phone: 323-6456). Moderate to inexpensive.

Le Maschere – For a taste of Calabria's Costa Viola, fragrant with garlic and devilish with red peppers, try this rustic and charming 17th- century cellar behind Largo Argentina. The fare is not for fragile stomachs: antipasti of tangy salamis, marinated anchovies, and stuffed, pickled, or highly seasoned vegetables of every sort; pasta with broccoli or eggplant, or the traditional *struncatura* (handmade whole-wheat pasta with anchovies, garlic, and breadcrumbs); fresh swordfish harpooned off the Calabrian coast, *stoccafisso* (salt cod stew with potatoes), or meat grilled on an open fire; pizza, southern sweets, 100-proof fresh fruit salad, and *tuma* (Calabrian sheep's milk cheese). Dinner only. Closed Mondays and part of August. Reservations necessary on weekends. Major credit cards accepted. 29 Via Monte della Farina (phone: 687-9444). Moderate to inexpensive.

L'Orso '80 – An old-fashioned trattoria close to Piazza Navona and with good traditional fare such as *spaghetti all'amatriciana* (with bacon, cheese, and tomatoes). Meats are grilled over a wood fire. Closed Mondays and August. Reservations unnecessary. Major credit cards accepted. 33 Via dell'Orso (phone: 686-4904). Moderate to inexpensive.

Al Piedone – Tiny and unpretentious, this spot is much favored by newsmen and politicos from nearby Parliament. Try the rigatoni with broccoli, sausage, and bacon, or the Puglia-style *orecchietti* (pasta) with hot red pepper, broccoli, and anchovies. When available, the roast veal stuffed with almonds, pine nuts, and raisins is truly special. A good wine list for a modest restaurant. Closed Sundays and late August. Reservations advised in the evenings. Major credit cards accepted. 28 Via del Piè di Marco (phone: 679-8628). Moderate to inexpensive.

Polese – This is a good value any time of the year, either outside under the trees of the spacious square or inside the intimate rooms of the Borgia palace. A great summer starter is *bresaola con rughetta* (cured beef with arugula, seasoned with olive oil, lemon, and freshly grated black pepper), and the *pasta al pesto* is fine year-round. Closed Tuesdays. Reservations taken reluctantly (come and wait your turn). Major credit cards accepted. 40 Piazza Sforza Cesarini (phone: 686-1709). Moderate to inexpensive.

Ponentino – A pizzeria in Trastevere, it has the ubiquitous wood-burning oven. The youthful owners also serve spaghetti old-Trastavere-style (with tuna, anchovies, and capers), vegetarian antipasto (the best choice), and grilled meat including lamb chops. Closed Mondays. Reservations necessary in summer for tables outside in the piazza. Major credit cards accepted. Off Via della Lungaretta near Tiber Island. 10 Piazza del Drago (phone: 588-0680). Moderate to inexpensive.

Sora Lella – In the heart of Rome on Tiber Island is this trattoria serving authentic Roman dishes such as *penne all'arrabiata* (quill-shaped pasta with spicy tomato sauce), *pasta e ceci* (pasta and chick-peas) with clams, tiny sautéed lamb chops, and beans with pork rind. Closed Sundays. No reservations. No credit cards accepted. 16 Via di Quattro Capi (phone: 686-1601). Moderate to inexpensive.

La Tavernetta – It looks like a take-out pasta shop, but there are actually four narrow dining rooms set one above the other. This is a tiny, tidy spot, barely a block from the Spanish Steps (toward the Piazza Barberini), where the homemade pasta is pretty near perfect and seafood is the specialty. Closed Sundays and August. Reservations advised. Major credit cards accepted. 147 Via Sistina (phone: 679-3124). Moderate to inexpensive.

Trearchi da Gioachino – Among the declining numbers of true Roman trattorias, this one stands out, thanks to Mamma Colomba Giammiuti's loving cooking. She comes from the Abruzzi region and specialties include homemade ravioli, *pappardelle* noodles with hare sauce and lamb, and other pasta made in various delectable ways. Closed Sundays and late August. Reservations advised. Major credit cards accepted. 233 Via dei Coronari (phone: 686-5890). Moderate to inexpensive.

Ettore Lo Sgobbone – A trattoria popular with newspaper and TV journalists, noted for its unpretentious northern Italian home-style cooking. Pasta and risotto courses are excellent: Try the simple *tonnarelli al pomodoro e basilico* (pasta with fresh tomato and basil sauce) or *risotto nero di seppie* (rice cooked with cuttlefish in its ink). Reservations advised for the few tables outdoors on the rather dreary, typically working class street. Closed Tuesdays. Reservations necessary. Major credit cards accepted. 8-10 Via dei Podesti (phone: 323-2994). Inexpensive.

Da Giulio – Another bargain for budget-minded travelers, on a tiny street off Via Giulia in a historic building. A few tables line the sunless street in the summer, but inside is most pleasant — if a bit noisy — with an original vaulted ceiling and paintings by local artists. Roman family-style cooking. Closed Sundays and late August. Reservations advised in summer. Major credit cards accepted. 19 Via della Barchetta (phone: 654-0466). Inexpensive.

Grotte Teatro di Pompeo – One of several places in this tiny, packed neighborhood that claims to be the place where Julius Caesar met his untimely end. On any chilly day, the *zuppa di verdura* (vegetable soup) can keep one's inner self warm, and the *fettuccine verdi alla gorgonzola* (green noodles in a rich cheese sauce) is a wonderful pasta choice. The colorful but unprepossessing premises don't bother guests. This is the perfect place for cost-conscious visitors to try *osso buco con funghi* (veal shank with wild mushrooms) and *saltimbocca alla romana* (small pieces of veal with prosciutto). Closed Mondays and August. Reservations unnecessary. Visa accepted. 73 Via del Biscione (phone: 654-3686). Inexpensive.

La Sagrestia – Lots of places claim the best pizza in town, and this one is a top contender, with pies fresh from the wood-burning oven. Good pasta, good draft beer, ever-crowded and cheery, with kitschy decor. Near the Pantheon. Closed Wednesdays and 1 week in mid-August. Reservations advised for large groups. Major credit cards accepted. 89 Via del Seminario (phone: 679-7581). Inexpensive.

Lo Scopettaro – On the Tiber River, right near the Porta Portese flea market, is this popular, noisy neighborhood spot that serves traditional Roman fare such as *pasta e fagioli* (pasta and beans) and simple grilled meat. Closed Tuesdays and August. Reservations unnecessary. No credit cards accepted. 7 Lungotevere Testaccio (phone: 574-2408). Inexpensive.

Settimio all'Arancio – Simple but good, right in the heart of downtown Rome, near the old Jewish ghetto. It's always crowded. Particularly noteworthy is the *fusili con melanzane* (pasta with eggplant). Closed Sundays and August. Reservations advised. Major credit cards accepted. 50 Via dell'Arancio (phone: 687-6119). Inexpensive.

La Villetta al Piramide – Near the Protestant cemetery and the marble pyramid, this cheery, large trattoria is run by owner-cook Ada Mercuri Olivetti, who once took first prize over 4,000 other Roman cooks for her *spaghetti all'amatriciana,* made with special bacon, tomato, and cheese. She serves other wholesome, hearty dishes, including vegetable antipasti. Closed Wednesdays. Reservations unnecessary. No credit cards accepted. 53 Viale Piramide Cestia (phone: 574-0204). Inexpensive.

A novelty for Rome are the less expensive eateries as an alternative to pizza; one such is the *Lucifero Pub* (28 Via dei Cappellari; phone: 654-5536), a fondue-and-beer tavern tucked into a side street off the Campo dei Fiori.

BARS AND CAFÉS: For lighter meals, Rome's many *caffès* are also well worth trying. The most fashionable spots for the lunch or pre-dinner *aperitivo* are the *Antico Caffè Greco* or the *Baretto* (Via Condotti), *Rosati* or *Canova* (Piazza del Popolo), and *Harry's Bar, Carpes,* the *Café de Paris, Doney's,* or others on Via Veneto. Best for light lunches are *Canova* and *Café de Paris. Babington's* (Piazza di Spagna) is an English tearoom that serves expensive snacks and luscious cakes. Currently *alla moda* is the little *Bar della Pace* (Piazza della Pace behind Piazza Navona), which is frequented by vendors from the nearby market in the morning and pre-lunch period, and then later in the day (until 3 AM) by all types, from artists and filmmakers to punks, poets, and students who, when the little marble tables fill up, rest their drinks and their bottoms on cars parked in the square.

At the tiny, busy Piazza Sant'Eustachio, the *Bar Eustachio* serves what is reputed to be the best coffee in town. It is an Italian-style espresso bar where a quick coffee is downed while standing. In the Jewish ghetto, lovers of sweets stand on line to get pastries fresh from an ancient oven, in the tiny, shabby, and excellent *Forno del Ghetto* (119 Via Portico d'Ottavia), where the production follows the religious holiday tradition.

As rising prices (and the influx of Chinese restaurants) oblige the more inexpensive trattorie either to upgrade to *ristorante* status or simply to disappear, they are being replaced by wine shops–cum–wine bars. In addition to being able to buy the traditional glass, bottle, or case of wine, these establishments also now offer a light lunch of artfully prepared vegetables or pasta and a glass of good wine (from November through March, try the wonders of the *vini novelli*) for $10–$12 per person. They are scattered all over old Rome, and are tiny and dark. Simply look for their sign — *Enoteca.* The shops have only a few tables, do not take reservations, honor no credit cards, and close before 8 PM. Try the *Bottega del Vino da Bleve* (9/A Via Santa Maria del Pianto; phone: 686-5970) in downtown Rome; the tiny *Cul de Sac I* (73 Piazza Pasquino; phone: 654-1094), which re-creates the atmosphere of an old *osteria; Il Piccolo* (74 Via del Governo Vecchio; phone: 654-1746) near Piazza Navona; and *Spiriti* (5 Via di Sant'Eustachio; phone: 689-2499).

On summer evenings, the after-dinner crowd often moves toward one of the many *gelaterie* in Rome, some of which are much more than ice cream parlors, since they serve exotic long drinks and *semifreddi* (like the famous *tartufo* — a double chocolate truffle — at Piazza Navona's *Tre Scalini,* where they sell 800 a day), and a few have lovely gardens and even live music. *Selarum,* (12 Via dei Fienaroli), and *Fassi* (45 Corso d'Italia), have both gardens and music. Perhaps the best-known *gelateria,* however, is the very crowded *Giolitti* (40 Via Uffici del Vicario), not far from Piazza Colonna — try any of the fresh fruit flavors; it boasts a tearoom (closed Mondays). Others are the sleek, high-tech *Gelateria della Palma* (which is also a piano bar, at the corner of Via della Maddalena and Via delle Coppelle); *Fiocco di Neve* (51 Via del Pantheon); and *Di Rienzo* (5 Piazza della Rotonda). They're all near the Pantheon; *Gelofestival* (29 Viale Trastevere, in Trastevere); and *Biancaneve* (1 Piazza Pasquale Paoli, where Corso Vittorio Emanuele II meets the Lungotevere dei Fiorentini). Favorites in the fashionable Parioli residential district are *Gelateria Duse* (also called *Giovanni;* 1 Via Eleonora Duse) and *Bar San Filippo* (8 Via San Filippo), both specializing in *semifreddi; Bar Gelateria Cile* (1–2 Piazza Santiago del Cile); the nearby *Giardino Ferranti* (29 Via Giovanni Pacini); and the *Casina delle Muse* (Piazzale delle Muse) for a fabulous *granità di caffè con panna* (coffee ice with cream). In the Jewish ghetto, try *Dolce Roma* (20/B Via Portico d'Ottavio; phone: 689-2196) for chocolate chip cookies and Austrian pastries. *Europeo Gran Caffè* (33 Piazza San Lorenzo in Lucina) is the place for indulging in high-calorie pastries.

ST. PETERSBURG

Imperial Russia: music, art, theater, ballet, literary salons, glittering court life. This city was the center of the lavish, reckless social milieu immortalized by Pushkin, Dostoyevsky, Tolstoy, and Turgenev. Almost inevitably, it was also the Cradle of the Revolution: Bloody Sunday, the storming of the Winter Palace, and Lenin's triumphant return from exile. St. Petersburg is relatively young for a European city of such rich cultural and political heritage — less than 290 years old — but what happened here has changed the course of world history.

In a city of such great beauty, where virtually every downtown building displays a plaque noting its historical significance, it sometimes is difficult to focus on the people who live here and the life of the city today. But St. Petersburg also is a city where a visitor from the West is immediately comfortable. When the days lengthen and dusk comes late, it is hard to resist walking among the people strolling arm in arm in the street, or relaxing in the parks in the fading light that casts its strange glimmer over the city. These glorious White Nights of summer are a consequence of St. Petersburg's location on the Gulf of Finland at about the same latitude as Helsinki. St. Petersburg is built on a series of islands, 403 miles (645 km) northwest of Moscow. Although its climate is less harsh than the Soviet capital's, the harbor is frozen 3 or 4 months of the year.

The hundreds of islands near the mouth of the Neva River, at a point where the Baltic Sea penetrates deepest into its eastern shore, were disputed for centuries by a succession of Finns, Swedes, and Russians. The Neva was an important early trade artery between Europe and Asia. In 1703, after defeating Sweden, Peter the Great built a fortress here to ensure against future invasions. Within 9 years, Peter had built a new city, his "window on Europe," and had moved the capital from Moscow.

St. Petersburg — Petrograd — as the new capital was originally called, was designed from the first to rival the beauty of Western Europe's finest cities. It developed in well-planned stages, acquiring an elegant façade as government buildings, cathedrals, and private residences of the nobility took their places along the Neva and the Fontanka and Moika rivers. Many of the most beautiful palaces were built in the last half of the 18th century under the direction of Catherine the Great's favorite French and Italian architects. As the excessive indulgence of the gentry increased, the lives of the czars' subjects became even more intolerable. Serfs were in semi-slavery. In St. Petersburg itself, overcrowded hovels where workers lived in miserable poverty surrounded the beautiful palaces, the lovely parks, and the great squares and avenues. This incredible contrast between the lifestyles of the nobility and the daily oppression of the workers was impossible to ignore. Change was inevitable.

On January 9, 1905, thousands of workers marched with their wives and children to the Winter Palace to petition Czar Nicholas II to intervene on behalf of better working conditions. The czar's troops opened fire at close range. The resulting massacre, known in Russian history as Bloody Sunday, was the spark that ignited the Revolution of 1905. Nicholas made some concessions that allowed him to survive the popular uprising, but only for a time. His inability to rule, further economic hardship brought on by World War I, and continued revolutionary activity brought down the whole structure of czardom in March 1917. A new era in Russian history began in November of that year when a Soviet government replaced the provisional government. It also meant a new era for this city: The capital was moved back to Moscow.

The city was renamed Leningrad in 1924 after the death of Lenin. Although its political importance diminished when Moscow became the seat of government, the city continued to grow as an industrial and commercial center until World War II. Almost 700,000 Russians lost their lives and some 10,000 buildings were destroyed during the 900-day German siege of Leningrad. But the city emerged from the war determined to restore its former beauty, and today St. Petersburg — its original name triumphantly restored after last summer's extraordinary overthrow of the Communist regime — remains the most European of Soviet cities.

The canals, rivers, and low buildings remind one of Venice, and Nevsky Prospekt has much of the air of the great boulevards of Paris. The parallels are reinforced by the 18th- and 19th-century baroque and neo-classical architecture that dominates the central city. The Sheremetyev Palace, Count Orlov's Marble Palace, Prince Potemkin's Taurida Palace and, especially the Winter Palace, are among the noble homes restored and used today as museums, offices, and meeting houses — lacking the grandeur of their original state, yet eminently more functional.

Even St. Petersburg's present modernization plan is designed to preserve the beauty of the city's past. New construction in the downtown area must be completed within existing façades. No skyscrapers are permitted to mar the horizon; glass and concrete structures are prohibited in central St. Petersburg. Modern building is allowed beyond the city center, however, and numerous large apartment complexes have been built to house the city's 4.5 million people. Most of the industrial expansion — from the shipbuilding industry to factories producing hydrogenerators — has taken place in outlying areas.

St. Petersburg has an extraordinarily rich cultural heritage, with direct links to the most fundamental changes in Russian political history. And though its citizens are well aware of the country's present and probable ferment, it is a city that speaks — not in name only — most eloquently of the Soviet past.

ST. PETERSBURG AT-A-GLANCE

SEEING THE CITY: There is no one vantage point that will provide a good view of the entire city. Peter the Great's decree that no structure should be taller than the spires of the Cathedral of Saints Peter and Paul (about 400 feet), along with the fact that the city is built on marshland, has created a relatively low skyline. However, if you stand beside the Neva opposite the Peter and Paul Fortress, you get a sense of where and how the city began. At the Admiral

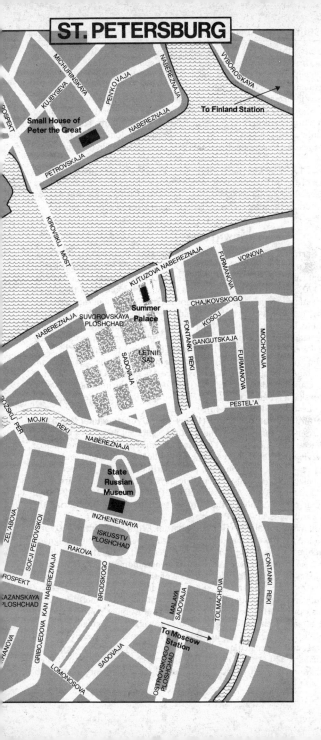

ST. PETERSBURG

To Finland Station

MICHURINSKAYA

KUJBYSEVA

PENKOVAJA

NABEREZNAJA

NABEREZNAJA

VYBOROSKAYA

Small House of Peter the Great

PETROVSKAJA

MOST KIROVSKIJ

KUTUZOVA NABEREZNAJA

FURMANOVA

VOINOVA

Summer Palace

CHAJKOVSKOGO

NABEREZNAJA

SUVOROVSKAYA PLOSHCHAD

KOSOJ

FONTANKI REKI

GANGUTSKAJA

FURMANOVA

MOCHOVAJA

LETNIJ SAD

SADOVAJA

PESTEL'A

MOJKI REKI

ROZSKIJ PER

NABEREZNAJA

State Russian Museum

INZHENERNAYA

ISKUSSTV PLOSHCHAD

ZEL'ABOVA

SOFJI PEROVSKOI

RAKOVA

BRODSKOGO

FONTANKI REKI

PROSPEKT

KAZANSKAYA PLOSHCHAD

GRIBOJEDOVA KAN NABEREZNAJA

SOFANOVA

MALAYA SADOVAJA

TOLMACHOVA

To Moscow Station

SADOVAJA

LOMONOSOVA

OSTROVSKOGO PLOSHCHAD

Building, where the city's three major avenues converge, you can grasp St. Petersburg's layout and planning. In Palace Square, the site of czarist splendor and bloody revolution, you get in touch with the city's history; on Nevsky Prospekt at Griboyedov Canal, you can feel the contemporary pulse of the city.

Note: The following information on sights and sites was accurate as we went to press, but it is more than possible that—given the current state of uncertainty in the entire Soviet Union—that statues will have been toppled, streets and squares renamed, and hotels and restaurants change hands. So do as the locals are doing: Watch history reform before your eyes and look upon a visit this year as an extraordinary experience.

 SPECIAL PLACES: The major sites of St. Petersburg are spread out over a number of the 101 islands that interconnect to form the city, but all are easily reached by public transportation. You can visit them on your own or arrange tours of the major sites with the *Intourist* travel service bureau (see *Sources and Resources*).

DOWNTOWN

Peter and Paul Fortress (Petropavlovskaya Krepost) – Before Peter the Great chose this site to build a new capital for Russia, he had ordered a fortress built to bar the Swedish fleet's approach. As St. Petersburg became secure from attack, the fortress, established in May 1703, came to be used more as a prison for opponents of the czarist regime. The list of political prisoners included Peter the Great's own son, the Czarevich Alexei; Dostoyevsky, before his exile to Siberia; and the anarchist Mikhail Bakunin. The Cathedral of Saints Peter and Paul (Petropavlovsky Sobor), with its tall, extremely slender golden spire, stands in the center of the fortress. It is the burial place of all the Russian czars from Peter I to Alexander III, with the exception of Peter II. In 1924, the Peter and Paul Fortress became a museum. (The main branch of the *State Museum of the History of Leningrad* is also on the premises; see *Museums.*) Open 11 AM to 6 PM (5 PM in winter). Closed Wednesdays and the last Tuesday of the month. Admission charge. 3 Petropavlovskaya Krepost, reached from Revolutsii Square on Peter and Paul Fortress Island (phone: 238-4540 or 238-4613).

Summer Palace and Garden of Peter I (Letny Sad; Dvorets-Musei Petra I) – Across the Neva from the fortress, on the Kutuzov Embankment (Nabereznaya Kutuzova), is a 30-acre park, laid out in 1704, and an unpretentious summer palace built in the Dutch style for Peter the Great. The park, filled with classical sculptures, is a favorite open space for St. Petersburgers, particularly during the summer's long White Nights. The palace is open daily, except Tuesdays, May through the first week of November from 11 AM to 6:30 PM. Admission charge (phone: 312-9436 or 312-9666). The park is open year-round, although the outdoor sculpture is covered during the winter. The park's entrance is at 2 ul. Pestelya.

State Hermitage; Winter Palace (Gosudarstvenni Ermitazh; Zimnniy Dvoryets) – Built as a home for the czars and czarinas during the 18th-century reigns of Elizabeth and Catherine the Great, the *Hermitage* was designed by the Italian architect Rastrelli. The grandiose baroque palace and four adjacent buildings now house one of the finest art collections in the world. The splendor of the room decorations — patterned parquet floors, molded and painted ceilings, furniture, and decorative objects of malachite, lapis lazuli, and jasper — dazzle the eye as much as the da Vincis, Raphaels, Titians, Rembrandts, and the Impressionist and post-Impressionist paintings. When you think you have already seen every richness and extravagance imaginable, arrange to take the special tour of the Gold Treasure Room, which holds the exquisite jewels of Catherine the Great and a spectacular collection of Scythian gold. Open from 10:30 AM to 6 PM (Thursdays: 12:20 PM to 8 PM) during the winter; from 10 AM to 5:30 PM in summer. Closed Mondays year-round. Admission charge. 36 Dvortsovaya Nab.

(phone: 219-8625 or 311-3420; or call the *Hermitage*'s excursion bureau at 219-8727).

Palace Square (Dvortsovaya Pl.) – Between the *Hermitage* and the great curve of the Admiralty Building, the former general staff headquarters, is the central square of the city. The red granite Alexander Column in the center was erected in 1832 as a monument to the victory over Napoleon in 1812. This square, the site of Bloody Sunday in 1905, is closely associated with the revolutionary movement. The climax of the October Revolution in 1917 was the storming of the Winter Palace from this square. Each year there are parades and demonstrations here to mark the event.

Peter the Great Monument – The famous bronze statue of Peter the Great, designed by the French sculptor E. M. Falconet, stands in the center of the grassy Decemberists Square (Dekabristov Pl.) to the west of the Admiralty Building. The statue, commissioned by Catherine the Great, depicts Peter astride a horse whose hoofs are trampling a writhing snake (said to be a symbolic representation of Sweden).

St. Isaac's Cathedral Museum (Isaakievsky Sobor) – St. Petersburg's largest church — and one of the world's largest domed structures — stands to the south of Decemberists Square. The cathedral is filled with mosaic and painted ceiling murals, decorated with 14 kinds of minerals and semi-precious stones. Malachite and lapis lazuli columns form a part of the massive gilded iconostasis before the altar. A Foucault pendulum that moves 13° each hour is suspended from the central dome. Open from 11 AM to 7 PM. Closed Wednesdays. Admissiom charge. Isaakievskaya Sq. (phone: 315-9732).

Alexander Nevsky Monastery (Aleksandr Nevskaya Lavra) – The monastery's Trinity Cathedral (Troitsky Sobor) was built in 1722 to house the remains of St. Alexander Nevsky, which had been brought here from Vladimir. In 1922, the silver sarcophagus containing the saint's ashes was moved to the *Hermitage*. The monastery also has ten other churches, four cemeteries (known here as necropolises), a seminary, and the *Museum of Urban Sculpture*. The 18th-century necropolis includes the graves of Peter I's sister and Mikhail Lomonosov, the scientist who founded Moscow University. The 19th-century necropolis includes the graves of Dostoyevsky, Tchaikovsky, Mussorgsky, Rimsky-Korsakov, and Borodin. You must buy a ticket to enter these cemeteries, but you may visit the interesting modern necropolis opposite the cathedral without charge. Note its unusual grave markers, such as the propeller of the plane in which a pilot met his death and a miniature oil rig for three oilfield workers. The *Museum of Urban Sculpture* has models and site photographs of most of the city's monuments. The monastery is closed Thursdays and the first Tuesday of each month; the museum is open from 11 AM to 6 PM (same closing days). Admission charge. Near the Aleksandra Nevskovo metro stop. 1 Aleksandra Nevskovo Sq. (phone: 274-2545, at the museum).

Volkovskoye Orthodox Cemetery – Affiliated with the *Museum of Urban Sculpture,* this necropolis (also known as Literatorskiye Mostki) holds the graves of several famous Russian writers (Alexander Kuprin, Ivan Turgenev, and Alexander Blok), scientists (Mendeleyev and Pavlov), and other prominent native sons. Open from 11 AM to 6 PM; closed Thursdays. No admission charge. 30 Rastanny Proezd (phone: 166-2383).

Russian State Museum (Gosudarstvenni Russky Musei) – Next to the *Tretyakov Gallery* in Moscow, this is the largest collection of Russian art in the world. There are some 300,000 examples of Russian painting, sculpture, decorative arts, and folk arts in this museum in the former Mikhailovsky Palace. Open 10 AM to 6 PM; closed Tuesdays. Admission charge. 4/2 Inzhenernaya St. (phone: 314-3448).

Ethnographical Museum of the Peoples of the USSR (Gosudarstvenni Musei Etnografii Narodov USSR) – In a wing of the *Russian State Museum* (but with its own entrance), this museum houses a beautiful collection of clothing, household goods, and folk articles associated with the daily life and customs of the peoples of the republics that currently make up the Soviet Union. Open 10 AM to 6 PM; closed Mondays and the last Friday of the month. Admission charge. 4/1 Inzhenernaya St. (phone: 210-3888).

Church of the Blood of the Savior (Khram Spasa na Krovi) – Built in the Old Russian style similar to St. Basil's in Moscow, this church was erected at the end of the 19th century on the spot where Alexander II was assassinated. The exterior is covered with mosaics. At press time, the church was temporarily closed for renovation, but it is scheduled to reopen sometime in the future as a museum of mosaic arts. Just north of the *Russian State Museum.* 1 Griboyedova Kan. Nab.

Bridges of St. Petersburg – From the ironwork of the large, impressive Kirov Bridge over the Neva to the multitude of small bridges connecting the islands, these structures are a natural museum of the city. The stone turrets and chains of the Lomonosov Bridge over the Fontanka are an example of the earliest bridges. This heavy style soon gave way to light, airy ironwork decorated with lions, gilded griffins, sphinxes, and other delightful creatures. There are hundreds of these bridges, large and small, and they create one of the unifying aspects of the city. The most famous, perhaps, is the Anichkov, which spans the Fontanka River at Nevsky Prospekt and has four sculptures by Peter Klodt. To allow ships to pass through, the bridges are raised at various times throughout the night.

Smolny Monastery and Institute – The cathedral and convent of the monastery were built in the 18th century by Czarina Elizabeth, and the institute was founded during the reign of Catherine II as a school for young ladies of the nobility. The room at the institute where Lenin later lived and worked now is a museum featuring paintings by St. Petersburg artists. Tours of the interiors are available by special arrangement, but the park may be visited at any time. Classical musicians and the church choir perform at the Smolny Cathedral and Exhibition Complex here beginning at 7 PM on Saturday and Sunday nights. The complex is open daily, except Thursdays, from 11 AM to 5 PM. Admission charge. 3 Rastrelli Sq. (phone: 311-3783 or 311-3560). The museum is open from 9:30 AM to 6 PM; closed Sundays (phone: 278-1461). Admission charge to the exhibitions. Along the Neva between Smolnovo St. and Smolny Prospekt, about 7 blocks east of the Cernysevskaya metro stop.

Piskarevskoye Memorial Cemetery – An eternal flame and small museum are at the entrance of these memorial grounds commemorating the 900-day siege of St. Petersburg (then called Leningrad) during World War II. Some 500,000 of those who died before the ring of the blockade was broken in 1943 were buried in mass graves here. The museum contains photographs and documents about the heroism of the city's residents during the blockade. North of the Smolny Monastery, across the Neva in the northeast sector of the city. Piskarevsky Prospekt.

Lenin Monument at the Finland Station – Lenin arrived at the Finland Station after 10 years in exile, and it was here, on April 3, 1917, that he spoke to workers from the turret of an armored car. In 1926, a statue of Lenin standing on an armored car was erected in a square in front of the railway station to commemorate the event and to mark the ninth anniversary of the revolution. Though still standing at press time, its fate was uncertain. Near the Lenina Sq. metro stop.

Cruiser *Aurora* (Creiser *Avrora*) – A blank shot fired from this cruiser signaled the beginning of the October Revolution. Now the cruiser is permanently moored in the Neva, opposite the *Leningrad* hotel (see *Checking In*). Open 10:30 AM to 4:30 PM. Closed Mondays and Fridays; admission charge. Petrogradskaya Nab. (phone: 230-8440).

ENVIRONS

Pushkin – Once known as the Czar's Village, this town is the site of the Yekaterinsky Palace, named for Peter the Great's wife, Catherine I. Built during the reigns of

Elizabeth and Catherine II in a 1,482-acre park, the palace has a stunning aqua façade, decorated with gold and white ornaments. Part of the palace now is a museum, with exhibitions of furniture, china, and the palace's history. The *Pushkinski Lizej Museum* (Lyceum for Noblemen's Children; 2 Komsomolskaya St.; phone: 276-6411) also is here, with manuscripts, rare books, and the personal belongings of Alexander Pushkin, who studied at the school for the nobility attached to the palace. The village was renamed for the poet in 1937, on the 100th anniversary of his death. Both museums are open from 10 AM to 5 PM; closed Tuesdays and the last Monday of the month; admission charge. Train service is available from the Vitebsky Station in St. Petersburg, with buses and taxis available at the station here. The palace is at 7 Komsomolskaya St., 14 miles (22 km) south of St. Petersburg along Moscow Prospekt.

Pavlovsk – One of the most beautifully restored palaces in the Soviet Union is less than 2 miles (3 km) from Pushkin. Originally hunting grounds that belonged to the Czar's Village, the palace grounds constitute one of the largest landscaped parks in Europe. The land and palace were a gift from Catherine II to her son Paul in 1777. You enter the 1,500-acre park on a road from Pushkin through cast-iron gates and over a wooden bridge. The palace is open from 10 AM to 5 PM; closed Fridays and the first Monday of the month; admission charge. 20 Revolutsii St. (phone: 470-2156). The palace grounds are 15 miles (24 km) south of St. Petersburg along Moscow Prospekt.

■ **EXTRA SPECIAL:** On the southern shore of the Gulf of Finland, Peter the Great built Petrodvorets, the Grand Palace, which he hoped would rival Versailles. He personally drafted the layout of the 300-acre park and gave detailed instructions on the design of the spectacular system of fountains that cascade through the park and gardens. The buildings were badly damaged during World War II but have been restored carefully, according to the original plans. Some 129 of the fountains in the system that begins on the Ropshinskiye Heights 13 miles (21 km) away are working today. The most impressive of these is the Samson Fountain, directly in front of the Grand Palace, which portrays Samson ripping open the jaws of a lion as a spray of water rises from the lion's mouth. Petrodvorets is about 20 miles (32 km) southwest of the city. It can be reached by leaving the city along Stacek Prospekt or, in summer, by hydrofoil down the Neva into the gulf. The palace is open from 11 AM to 5 PM; closed Mondays and the last Tuesday of the month. Admission charge. 2 Kominterna St. (phone: 427-5390 or 420-0079).

SOURCES AND RESOURCES

TOURIST INFORMATION: It is best to buy comprehensive guides to St. Petersburg before you leave the US. Although the country's politics have changed, two of the most useful are *The Complete Guide to the Soviet Union,* by Victor and Jennifer Louis (St. Martin's Press; $29.95), and the *Blue Guide to Leningrad and Moscow* (W. W. Norton; $19.95). *Leningrad: Art and Architecture,* by V. Schwartz (Moscow: Progress Publishers) is especially good and may be obtained in the US through stores that import Russian publications. *Leningrad, Its Monuments and Architectural Complexes* (Leningrad: Aurora Art Publishers) is a beautifully illustrated book sold in *Beriozka* stores (see *Shopping*) in St. Petersburg.

Although good transportation and city maps are available in hotels at news or book kiosks for very reasonable prices, it is helpful to take along a Falkplan map for Leningrad (Hamburg: Falk-Verlag; $6.95), available in the US. This pocket map is designed to be used in sections and includes a street name index and gazetteer for monuments, museums, hotels, and theaters. Again beware that in the wake of recent political events, many street and place names are changing.

Intourist (11 St. Isaac's Sq.; phone: 315-5129; fax: 312-0996; telex: 121509) deals with all foreign travel in the Soviet Union and provides English-speaking guides. Although you will have an English-speaking guide with you during tour activities, it would be helpful to learn the Russian (Cyrillic) alphabet and the sound for each of its characters. Many Russian words have English or French cognates, so once you sound out the words, life can become a bit simpler. Especially helpful is the Berlitz book *Russian for Travellers* ($5.95).

The US Consulate is at 15 ul. Petra Lavrova (phone: 274-8235).

Local Coverage – You can buy the *Moscow News,* an English-language weekly newspaper, or may occasionally find the *International Herald Tribune,* British daily newspapers, and some weekly magazines on sale in *Intourist* hotels.

 TELEPHONE: St. Petersburg cannot be dialed directly from the US. Calls must go through an international operator. When calling from other parts of the Soviet Union, dial 812 before the local number.

Phone books are nearly impossible to find in St. Petersburg, but you should be able to get directory assistance from the hotel desk or its service bureau. Telephones in hotel rooms are connected to the city system. To use a public pay phone, deposit a 2-kopeck coin in the pay slot before lifting the receiver, then dial when you hear a continuous buzzing sound. For long-distance calls, book them at least an hour ahead of time through the service bureau in your hotel.

GETTING AROUND: St. Petersburg has a small but exceedingly good subway system, called the metro, which is supplemented by a network of bus, trolley, and tram routes that enable you to move about the city with relative ease. Fares on each are less than a dime. Good, inexpensive, transportation maps are generally available in the hotels.

Airport – St. Petersburg's Pulkovo-2 International Airport is about 45 minutes from downtown by taxi; the fare is around 15 rubles. Transportation from the airport to downtown can also be arranged in advance through *Intourist* (see *Sources and Resources*). For information at the airport, call 311-5820.

Boats – In summer, hydrofoils and excursion boats ply the Neva River, the canals, and the smaller rivers. The fare usually ranges from 25¢ to 75¢, depending on the length of the trip.

Bus, Trolley, and Tram – The tram costs 10 kopecks per passenger; the bus and trolley 15 kopecks. Books of discounted tickets may be purchased at Soyuzpechat kiosks, which resemble newsstands, throughout the city. Bus stops are signposted with an A, trolley stops with a T, and tram stops with a T hanging from an overhead wire.

Car Rentals – Rentals can be made, with or without a chauffeur, through *Intourist* (phone: 312-1767). They must be paid for in Western currency or with a credit card. Rentals also are offered through *Sovinteravtoservice* (24 Malosetskoselsky Prospekt; phone: 292-1257 or 292-7718; fax: 292-0028); a chauffeur-driven Volvo costs about $16 an hour. Several hotels also have car rental facilities (see *Checking In*).

Metro – It runs daily from 5:30 AM to 1 AM, and fare is paid with a 15-kopeck coin. Since St. Petersburg is built on marshy land, the stations for the 25-mile metro are exceptionally deep. In fact, some escalator rides from the surface take 2 minutes — and escalators here move much more rapidly than they do in the US. Be warned: Stand to the right on down escalators; the left lane is for "runners." Coming up, however, you can stand on either side.

Taxi – Cabs are available at taxi stands or through hotel service bureaus, but they are expensive compared to other forms of transportation. Taxis and taxi stands can be recognized by a green "T" and a checkered pattern. The base fare is 40 kopecks, plus 40 kopecks for each additional kilometer. Private taxis do not have meters, and the fare is decided by the passenger and driver — be sure to agree in advance. If you call a taxi, there is an additional 5-ruble charge during the day, 10 rubles at night. For 24-hour service, call 312-0022.

Train – The five railway stations are Moscow Station (2 Vosstaniya Sq.; phone: 168-0111), Finland Station (6 Lenina Sq.; phone: 168-7685), Warsaw Station (118 Nab. Obvodnogo Kanala; phone: 168-2611), Baltic Station (120 Nab. Obvodnogo Kanala; phone: 168-2259), and Vitebsk Station (52 Zagorodny Prospekt; phone: 168-5390). For general information about departure and arrival times, call 168-0111.

 LOCAL SERVICES: Most hotels will try to arrange for any special services a business traveler might require, such as a translator or meeting facilities. Also see *Checking In.*

 SPECIAL EVENTS: *St. Petersburg Spring,* March 31–April 7, is a week of festivities celebrating the end of winter. The major annual arts festival in St. Petersburg is called *White Nights,* and is held June 21–29, when days here are so long that there is only a brief period of dusk each night. During the festival, there are performances by the *Kirov Opera and Ballet* (see *Theater*), the *Maly Theater Opera and Ballet,* and by various top Soviet singers and musicians. Here, as in Moscow, major celebrations are held on *International Labor Day,* May 1; *Victory Day,* May 9; *Constitution Day,* October 7; and *Revolution Day,* November 7. As proof of how things are changing, the official Soviet press published *Christmas* greetings for the first time in 1990. The Soviet government now recognizes *Christmas* as a public holiday (the Russian Orthodox *Christmas* falls on January 7), as well as *Easter Friday* (*Good Friday*).

 MUSEUMS: St. Petersburg is a major art center; many of the best-known museums are listed in *Special Places.* In addition, you may enjoy visiting — either individually or with an *Intourist* guided tour — some of the following. (Note: All museums listed below have admission charges with the exception of the *Lenin Museum.*)

Alexander Blok Memorial Flat-Museum (Musei-Kvartira A. Bloka) – The furniture and rooms have been re-created as they were when the distinguished Russian poet lived here; it was Blok's last flat. Open daily, except Wednesdays, from 11 AM to 6 PM. 57 Dekabristov ul. (phone: 113-8616 or 113-8633).

Anna Akhmatova Literary and Memorial Museum (Musei-Kvartira Anni Akhmatovoi) – Opened to the public in 1989, it's the flat where the famous Russian poetess lived for many years. Open from 10:30 AM to 6:30 PM; closed Mondays and the last Friday of the month. 34 R. Fontanki Nab. (phone: 272-5895).

Botanical Garden of the USSR (Botanicheskii Musei) – Founded in 1824, the garden has more than 3,000 varieties of tropical and subtropical plants. Open from 10 AM to 5 PM on Wednesdays, Saturdays, and Sundays. 2 Professora Popova ul. (phone: 234-1764 or 234-8470).

Brodsky House Museum (Musei-Kvartira I. I. Brodskovo) – Home of the portraitist of Lenin, it was closed for repairs at press time, but is scheduled to reopen later this year. 3 Iskusstv Sq. (phone: 314-3658).

Central Naval Museum (Tsentralny Voenno-Morskoi Musei) – A collection of ship models begun by Peter the Great in 1709, and more. Open 10:30 AM to 4:45 PM; closed Mondays, Tuesdays, and the last Thursday of the month. 4 Birzhevaya Sq. (phone: 218-2502).

Chinese Palace – Commissioned by Catherine the Great (who lived here for only 2 months), this exotically adorned building, located in the suburb of Lomonosov, is considered just as important — and impressive — as the Summer Palace. Open May 25 to September 30 from 11 AM to 5 PM; closed Tuesdays and the last Monday of the month (phone: 422-8016).

House Museum of Dostoyvsky – Home to the celebrated writer during the last years of his life. Open from 10:30 AM to 4:30 PM; closed Mondays and the last Wednesday of the month. 5/2 Kuznechny Per (phone: 112-0003).

House Museum of Peter I (Musei "Domik Petra I") – The dwelling used by Peter the Great while the Peter and Paul Fortress was being constructed. Open 10:30 AM to 5:30 PM; closed Tuesdays and the last Thursday of the month. 4 Birzhevaya Sq. (phone: 218-2502).

St. Petersburg Branch of the Central Lenin Museum (Petrogradsky Filial Tsentralnovo Muzeya V. I. Lenina) – Originally the Smolny nunnery, it was built in Russian baroque style by Rastrelli in 1764 and houses historical exhibitions. Open 10:30 AM to 6:30 PM; closed Wednesdays and the first Thursday of the month. 5/1 ul. Khalturina (phone: 312-9196).

Leningrad Museum of Theatrical and Musical Arts (Teatralnii Musei) – A variety of exhibits and descriptions of Russian theater and theatrical life. Open daily from 11 AM to 5 PM; closed Tuesdays and the last Friday of the month. 6 Ostrovskogo Sq. (phone: 311-1752 or 311-2195).

Literary Museum of the USSR Academy of Sciences Institute of Russian Literature (Pushkin House/Pushkinsky Dom) – The Soviet Union's most comprehensive collection of manuscripts of Russian poets from the 12th to the 20th centuries. Open daily, except Mondays, from 10:30 AM to 5 PM. Basil's Island, 4 Nab. Makarova (phone: 218-0502).

Menshikov Palace – St. Petersburg's most recently restored treasure, this branch of the *Hermitage* offers insights into the domestic scene — palatial-style — that shouldn't be missed. Open daily from 10:30 AM to 4 PM, Thursdays from noon to 4:30 PM; closed Mondays. 15 Universitetskaya Nab. (phone: 312-1112).

Museum of the Arctic and the Antarctic (Musei Arctici i Antarctiki) – The only museum of its kind in the world, it offers an introduction to the history of the exploration of the North and South Poles. Open Wednesdays through Sundays from 10 AM to 5 PM. 24 Marata St. (phone: 311-2549).

Museum of Artillery, Engineers, and Signals (Musei Artillerii, Ingenernikh voisk i voisk Sviazi) – A military museum of old arms, including a good collection of 16th-century weapons, which belonged to the czars. Open Wednesdays through Sundays from 11 AM to 6 PM. 7 Park Lenina (phone: 232-0209).

Museum of History of Religion and Atheism of the USSR (Gosudarstvenni Musei Istorii Religii i Ateizma) – In the Cathedral of Our Lady of Kazan, it is worth visiting for the architecture. Open 11 AM to 6 PM; closed Wednesdays and the last Thursday of the month. 2 Kazanskaya Sq. (phone: 311-0495).

Oreshek Fortress at Schlüsselburg (Crepost Oreshek) – Exhibitions devoted to the history and modern life of Schlüsselburg, a suburb of St. Petersburg. Take the train from the Finland Station to the Petrokrepost Station, or take the *Meteor* hydrofoil from the River Station (Rechnoi Vokzal). Open daily from May 15 to October 15, 10 AM to 6 PM (phone: 238-4686).

Peter the Great Museum of Anthropology and Ethnography (Musei Antropologii i Etnografii im. Petra Velikovo) – An exhibition of rarities, curiosities, and oddities of nature, started by Peter the Great, and occupying the building that formerly was the *Kunstkamera* (Chamber of Curiosities). Guided tours from 11 AM to 6 PM (tickets on sale from 10 AM to 11 AM). Closed Fridays, Saturdays, and the last Thursday of the month. 3 Universitetskaya Nab. (phone: 218-1412).

Pushkin Apartment Museum (Musei Kvartira A. S. Pushkina) – The house where Pushkin lived during the last months of his life. Open from 10:30 AM to 5:30 PM; Thursdays, from 12:20 PM; closed Tuesdays and the last Friday of the month. Tickets for guided tours (in English) go on sale during the first 40 minutes after opening. Visitors who arrive late will be turned away. 12 R. Moiki Nab. (phone: 311-3801).

State Museum of the History of Leningrad (Gosudarstvenni Musei Istorii Leningrada) – Founded in 1918 (and due for a name change), it depicts the city's history through exhibits, art works, and models. The main branch of the museum now is located in the Peter and Paul Fortress (phone: 238-4613). Open daily from 11 AM to 6 PM. Closed Wednesdays and the last Tuesday of the month. A subsidiary branch of the museum (at 44 Krasnogo Flota Nab.; phone: 311-7544 or 310-9065) currently houses an exhibition called "Leningrad During the Years of Soviet Power." Open Mondays and Fridays from 1 PM to 7 PM; Tuesdays, from 11 AM to 4 PM; and Thursdays, Saturdays, and Sundays from 11 AM to 5 PM; closed Wednesdays and the last Tuesday of the month.

Suvorov Museum (Musei Suvorova) – A must for the visitor who wants to know how the Russians won the wars in which they were involved of the 18th and 19th centuries. Open Wednesdays through Sundays from 11 AM to 6 PM. 43 Saltykova-Shedrina St. (phone: 279-3915).

Zoological Museum (Zoologichesky Musei) – Over 100,000 exhibits are in this former warehouse next to the stock exchange. Notable are the mammoths preserved in permafrost. Open from 11 AM to 6 PM; closed Fridays and Saturdays. 1 Universitetskaya Nab. (phone: 218-0112). Also of interest may be the Zoological Park at 1 Park Lenina (phone: 232-4828).

SHOPPING: For foreigners, the best buys usually can be found at the government-run hard-currency shops known as *Beriozka* (literally, "little birch tree"). These shops sell just about anything for which the Soviet Union is noted: furs, amber, jewelry, silver, balalaikas, vodka, caviar, wooden toys, and samovars. There are *Beriozkas* in most hotels, at a number of downtown locations, and at Pulkovo Airport (phone: 291-8848). Payment at these shops must be made in foreign currency or with traveler's checks or credit cards.

You also can shop where the Russians do, using Soviet currency. If you decide to go this route, select the item you want and take it to a clerk, who will give you a sales slip, which you take to the cash desk, the *Kacca*. When you pay, you'll receive a receipt, which you return to the clerk, who will give you your merchandise, already wrapped.

While food stores often remain open past 9 PM, most Soviet department stores are open from 10 AM to 9 PM. Some of the main department stores include *Dom Leningradskoi Torgovli* (*DLT*), which specializes in everything related to children, including clothes and toys (21-23 Zhelyabova St.; phone: 312-2627); *Gostiny Dvor,* a very large, old establishment (35 Nevsky Prospekt; phone: 312-4165); *Moskovsky,* not far from *Pulkovskaya* hotel (205-220 Moskovsky Prospekt; phone: 293-4455); and *Tsentr Firmennoi Torgovli* (Trade Firm Center; 1 Oktyabrsky Prospekt; phone: 352-1134). Except for department stores, most shops close for lunch from 2 to 3 PM.

Antiquarian Second-Hand Bookshop – Old and rare books in a variety of languages. Open from 11 AM to 7 PM; closed Sundays. 18 Nevsky Prospekt (phone: 312-6676).

Ariadne (Ariadna) – A cooperative that sells contemporary works by St. Petersburg artists. Open from 11 AM to 7 PM; closed Wednesdays. 32 R. Moiki Nab. (phone: 312-7831).

Dom Knigi – The largest bookstore in St. Petersburg, with posters, reproductions, and postcards on the second floor. The building itself is of interest because it was the

Russian headquarters of the Singer Sewing Machine Company early in this century; it has some wonderful Art Nouveau details as well as distinctive metalwork sculpture on its roof. Open from 10 AM to 8 PM; closed Sundays. 28 Nevsky Prospekt (phone: 219-9443).

Dom Muzyki i Radio **(House of Music and Radio)** – Recordings, videocassettes of Soviet films, and musical instruments (including balalaikas). Open from 11 AM to 8 PM; closed Sundays and Mondays. 15 Grazhdansky Prospekt (phone: 535-0314 or 534-4218).

Gallery **(Gallerya)** – Drawings, Russian boxes, wooden dolls, ceramic sculptures, painted samovars, and folk art by talented young Soviets. Open from noon to 7 PM; closed Mondays. 10 Pushkinskaya ul. (phone: 164-4857).

Gallery of the St. Petersburg Branch of the RSFSR Artists' Union – Pictures by professional artists. Open from 2 to 8 PM; closed Saturdays and Sundays. 38 Gertsena ul. (phone: 314-4815).

Globus – Prints, slides, and posters on local subjects. Open from 10 AM to 8 PM; closed Sundays. 78 Nevsky Prospekt (phone: 272-9598).

Hall of the Association of Amateur Artists – Attached to the Blok Library, the gallery features a good variety of works by amateur St. Petersburg artists. Open daily from 11 AM to 9 PM, to 6 PM on Saturdays and Sundays. 20 Nevsky Prospekt (phone: 311-0106).

Heritage **(Nasledie)** – The art shop of the St. Petersburg branch of the Soviet Cultural Foundation offers paintings, drawings, and sculpture. Open from 10 AM to 7 PM; closed Sundays and Mondays. 116 Nevsky Prospekt (phone: 279-5067).

Iskusstvo – Books, prints, and albums from Bulgaria, China, Czechoslovakia, Germany, Hungary, Mongolia, and Yugoslavia. Open from 11 AM to 8 PM; closed Sundays. 16 Nevsky Prospekt (phone: 312-8535).

Izdelia Hudogestvennikh Promislov – Traditional Soviet handicrafts including ceramics, wooden dolls, and lacquered boxes. Open from 11 AM to 8 PM; closed Sundays. 51 Nevsky Prospekt (phone: 113-1495).

Kikin Palace **(Kikiny Palaty)** – A salon featuring paintings from the Fund of Free Russian Modern Art. Open daily from 11 AM to 7 PM; closed Sundays. 9 Stavropolskaya ul. (phone: 271-2633).

Lancôme – A branch of the famous French cosmetics firm. Open from 11 AM to 8 PM; closed Sundays. 64 Nevsky Prospekt (phone: 312-3495).

Mir – More books from Bulgaria, China, Czechoslovakia, Hungary, Mongolia, and Yugoslavia. Open from 11 AM to 8 PM; closed Sundays. 13 Nevsky Prospekt (phone: 311-5146).

Narzan – For travelers who can't live without their daily supply of mineral water. All local brands, both flavored and not, but water is all that this store sells. Open 9 AM to 9 PM; closed Sundays. 34 Nevsky Prospekt (phone: 312-0206).

Norka **(Mink)** – A cooperative offering a wide choice of opulent fur coats, hats, and muffs, along with other small fur souvenirs — all made in the traditional Russian style. Open from 11 AM to 7 PM; closed Sundays. 34 Hertzena St. (phone: 273-4404).

Noty – For sheet music. Open from 10 AM to 7 PM. Closed Saturdays and Sundays. 26 Nevsky Prospekt (phone: 312-0796).

Palette **(Palitra)** – A cooperative selling works of fine and applied art. Open daily from 10 AM to 8 PM; closed Mondays. 166 Nevsky Prospekt (phone: 274-0911).

Passage – A very old, beautiful department store catering mainly to women. Open Mondays through Fridays, 10 AM to 9 PM; Saturdays, 10 AM to 6 PM. 48 Nevsky Prospekt (phone: 311-7084).

Planeta – A variety of books in English. Open from 10 AM to 7 PM; closed Sundays and Mondays. 30 Liteiny Prospekt (phone: 273-8815).

Podarki **(Gifts)** – For traditional Soviet items including beads, rings, brooches, vases, *matreshkas* (wooden dolls), fur hats and coats. Open from 11 AM to 7 PM; closed Sundays. 54 Nevsky Prospekt (phone: 314-1801).

Poliarnaya Zvezda – The shop's astounding choice of semi-precious stones — malachite, lazulite, tiger's-eye, amazonite, carnelian, agate — make it unnecessary to travel to the Ural Mountains or Siberia in search of fine jewelry. Open from 10 AM to 7 PM; closed Saturdays and Sundays. 158 Nevsky Prospekt (phone: 277-0980).

Prestige Gallery – A variety of goods hand-embroidered in the old Soviet style. Hard currency only accepted. Open from 11 AM to 8 PM; closed Sundays. 3 R. Moiki Nab. (phone: 273-9683).

Rapsodia – Musical paraphernalia, including recordings and books in Russian, German, English, and French. Open from 10 AM to 7 PM; closed Saturdays and Sundays. 13 Zhelyabova ul. (phone: 314-4801).

Sever – A popular pastry shop noted for its excellent tortes, cakes, and other sweets. 44 Nevsky Prospekt (phone: 311-2589).

Souvenirs – More traditional Soviet handicrafts. Open from 11 AM to 8 PM; closed Sundays. 92 Nevsky Prospekt (phone: 272-7793).

Viking – Artists of different bents and generations exhibit and sell their works here. Open daily from 10 AM to 9 PM; closed Sundays. 58 Nekrasova ul. (phone: 279-2480).

Vostochniye Sladosti – Specializing in Middle Eastern sweets, including that all-time favorite, halvah. Open 8 AM to 8 PM. 104 Nevsky Prospekt (phone: 273-7436).

 SPORTS: Hundreds of sporting events are held each year in St. Petersburg's major sports arenas: the *Leningrad Sports and Concerts Complex* (8 Yuria Gagarina Prospekt Park Pobedy; phone: 298-4847 or 298-4659), which seats 25,000; *Kirov Stadium* (1 Morskoi Prospekt; phone: 235-5169 or 235-2452); and *Yubileinaya Sports Stadium* (18 Dobrolyubova Prospekt; phone: 238-4122 or 238-4067), a sports and concert stadium that holds more than 6,000 spectators. St. Petersburgers are particularly fond of soccer and ice hockey. Schedules for current matches and events and tickets are available through your hotel service bureau. The world's only nighttime marathon is run on *White Night,* June 22, when the sky stays light well past midnight.

 THEATER: Your hotel service bureau will have tickets and information on performance schedules. For popular companies, such as the renowned *Kirov Ballet,* tickets will cost from $25 to $50. Performances begin early; usually 7 PM for the theater and 7:30 PM for the circus and puppet shows. During intermission, be sure to try the theater buffet, which includes open-faced salami and sturgeon sandwiches, cakes, cookies, soft drinks, and other snacks. Besides the *Kirov Academic Theater of Opera and Ballet* (Akademichesky Teatr Operi i Baleta im S. M. Kirova; 1 Teatralnaya Sq.; phone: 314-9083, 114-1211, or 114-5264), the major theaters in St. Petersburg include the *Maly Theater of Opera and Ballet* (Akademichesky Mali Teatr Operi i Baleta; Iskusstv Sq.; phone: 312-2040), *Bolshoi Puppet Theater* (Bolshoi Teatr Kukol; 10 ul. Nekrasova; phone: 273-6672 or 272-8215), *Leningrad State Circus* (Leningradsky Gosudarstvenni Tsirk; 3 R. Fontanki Nab.; phone: 210-4390), *Pushkin Academic Drama Theater* (Akademichesky Teatr Drami im. A. S. Pushkina; 2 Ostrovskovo Sq.; phone: 312-1545 or 311-6139), *Gorky Academic Bolshoi Drama Theater* (Akademichesky Bolshoi Dramatichesky Teatr im. M. Gorkovo; 65 R. Fontanki Nab.; phone: 310-9242), and the *Academic Theater of Comedy* (Akademichesky Teatr Komedii; 56 Nevsky Prospekt; phone: 314-2610 or 312-4555). Also noteworthy are the *Bolshoi Concert Hall* (Oktyabrsky; 6 Ligovsky Prospekt; phone: 277-7400 or 277-6960), the sure to be renamed *Lenin Komsomol Theater* (Teatr Leninskogo Komsomola; 4 Park Lenina; phone: 232-6244), *Lensovet Theater* (Teatr Lensoveta; 12 Vladimirsky Prospekt; phone: 113-2207), *Komissarzhevskaya Theater* (Teatr imeni Komissarzhevskoi; 19 Rakova St.; phone: 311-4252), *Maly Drama Theater* (Mali Dramaticheskii Teatr; 18 Rubinshteina St.; phone: 113-2094), *Derevo* (The Tree) *Studio-Theater* (47 Professora Popova St.; phone: 234-9895), and the *Shtern Jewish Theater* (Basil's Island, 83 Bolshoi Prospekt; phone: 217-2404).

MUSIC: Tickets and performance schedules for concerts can be obtained through your hotel service bureaus. Concerts usually begin at 7:30 PM. The major concert halls are the *Leningrad Philharmonic* (Leningradskaya Philarmoniya; 2 ul. Brodskovo; phone: 311-7353 or 312-2201), the *Glinka Small Hall* of the *Leningrad Philharmonic* (30 Nevsky Prospekt; phone: 312-4585), and *Glinka State Academic Chorus Kapella* (Gosudarstvennaya Akademicheskaya Khorovaya Kapella im. M. I. Glinki; 20 R. Moiki Nab.; phone: 314-1159). Other music venues include the concert hall at the *Leningrad* hotel (Conzertnii Zal Gostinnizy Leningrad; 5/2 Vyborgskaya Nab.; phone: 542-9056), the *Leningrad Concert Hall* (Leningradskii Conzertnii Zal, 1 Lenina Sq.; phone: 542-0944), *Jazz Center* (27 Zagorodny Prospekt; phone: 164-8565), *Leningrad Music Hall* (Leningradskii Muzik-Holl; 4 Park Lenina; phone: 233-0243), *Smolny Cathedral and Exhibition Complex* (Gosudarstvenni i Vistavochnii Compleks Smolnii Sobor; 3/1 Rastrelli Sq.; phone: 311-3560), and the *Lenin Sports and Concerts Complex* (298-4847 or 298-4659).

NIGHTCLUBS AND NIGHTLIFE: There are no Western-type nightclubs per se, but dancing is as much a part of an evening at a restaurant as the meal. Most nighttime activity here centers on one of the many theater or concert hall performances. There are late night, foreign-currency bars on the 10th floor of the *Leningrad* hotel, on the lower floor of the *Moskva,* and in the *Astoria* and *Pribaltiyskaya* hotels. The *Pribaltiyskaya* also has a nightclub which features live jazz; the *Karelia* has a discotheque (see *Checking In*). Casinos can be found in the *Chaika* hotel, and at the *Vostok* and *Vityaz* restaurants (see *Eating Out,* below). All gaming must be done with hard currency. In terms of big-city nightlife, this may be scant fare, but considering the range and quality of early evening entertainment, most visitors find it more than acceptable.

BEST IN TOWN

CHECKING IN: Hotel accommodations in St. Petersburg can be booked through *Intourist* or by a travel agent. You must apply for a visa listing all proposed stops and their duration, and once approved, deviations from your itinerary must be negotiated with a local *Intourist* representative. Visa applications also can be handled by your travel agent. Changes in your program can be requested at the *Intourist* service bureau in your hotel after you arrive, but do not count on the requests being approved. Usually, you will be told the hotel to which you have been assigned before you arrive in the city.

Accommodations in St. Petersburg hotels usually are available in three classes: First class double rooms, deluxe 2-room suites, and deluxe 3-room suites. New on the St. Petersburg accommodations scene are bed and breakfast establishments that can be booked by independent travelers. Visitors interested in staying with a local family can contact *IBV Bed & Breakfast Systems* (13113 Ideal Dr., Silver Springs, MD; phone: 301-942-3770; fax: 301-933-0024).

The dramatically fluctuating Soviet economy makes it difficult to provide accurate rates for hotels; we suggest that you check costs — and the operative exchange rate — immediately prior to your departure (for more information see FACTS IN BRIEF, *the*

Soviet Union). It is also often possible for rates to be guaranteed in US dollars (or you can prepay accommodations prior to departure), so there are no unhappy economic surprises. No meals are included in the advance payment plan. The hotels have banks, *Beriozkas,* postcard and stamp kiosks, service bureaus, beauty parlors, barber shops, and newsstands to serve most tourists' needs.

Astoria – Built in 1912 in the heart of downtown St. Petersburg, this five-star *Intourist* property reopened early last year after extensive renovations — and it is still St. Petersburg's best. The 436 rooms are decorated with antique furniture, and many provide good views of St. Isaac's Cathedral. Hitler planned to hold his victory banquet here after his armies captured the city; the framed invitation hangs in the lobby. There are 5 restaurants, 3 bars, 2 cafés, an art salon, a sauna, hair salon, and 3 hard-currency duty-free shops. Business facilities include 24-hour room service, meeting rooms for up to 180 and a banquet hall for 16, an English-speaking concierge, foreign currency exchange, secretarial services in English, audiovisual equipment, photocopiers, computers, cable television news, translation services, and express checkout. 39 Gertsena St. (phone: 311-4206; fax: 315-9668). Deluxe.

Evropeiskaya – One of St. Petersburg's small but grand old hotels, this *Intourist* property has been closed for renovations, but is slated to reopen early this year. Some rooms have balconies, and there are 22 penthouse suites (2-room duplexes) and 1 presidential suite (2 bedrooms, 2 bathrooms, and a living room). Guests can dine at the 3 restaurants and use the sauna and swimming pool. Business facilities include meeting rooms for up to 100, secretarial services in English, audiovisual equipment, photocopiers, and translation services. Located off Nevsky Prospekt, it is next door to the *Sadko,* one of St. Petersburg's best restaurants (see *Eating Out*). 1/7 ul. Brodskovo (phone: 217-8051; fax: 311-4611; telex: 121073). Deluxe.

Leningrad – Completed in 1970, this 736-room *Intourist* property overlooks the Neva River. There is an 800-seat concert hall, 2 restaurants (see *Eating Out*), 3 bars, a billiards hall, sauna, duty-free shop, car rental service, a plane/train ticket desk, and dry-cleaning facilities. Business facilities include 24-hour room service, 2 meeting rooms (seating 120 and 50), an English-speaking concierge, foreign currency exchange, secretarial services in English, photocopiers, translation services, and express checkout. 5/2 Pirogovskaya Nab. (phone: 542-9101, 542-9123, or 542-9411; fax: 542-9042; telex: 121366). Deluxe.

Mercury – Originally reserved for Communist party leaders, it is now a Soviet-British joint venture open to the traveling public. Housed in two locations less than a mile apart, the building on Tavricheskaya Street has 17 rooms, a restaurant, and a billiard room; the building on Tverskaya Street has 52 rooms, including several suites (one is a duplex), 3 restaurants, a billiard room, and car rental (chauffeur available). Business facilities for both hotels include 24-hour room service, meeting rooms for up to 90, English-speaking concierge, secretarial services in English, audiovisual equipment, photocopiers, computers, translation services, and express checkout. 39 Tavricheskaya St. (phone: 278-1221) and 22 Tverskaya St. (phone: 278-1468). Deluxe.

Moskva – Opened in 1977, this mammoth 770-room *Intourist* structure was built in typical Russian style. The staff is noted for its helpfulness, and the hotel is ideally located for connections with public transportation. There are 2 restaurants (one offers a variety show; see *Eating Out*), a sauna, duty-free shop, hair salon, car rental, a plane/train ticket desk, and dry cleaning service. Business facilities include 24-hour room service, a meeting room for up to 220, English-speaking concierge, foreign currency exchange, secretarial services in English, and translation services. 2 Alexandra Nevskogo Sq. (phone: 274-2115 or 274-2051; fax: 274-2130; telex: 121669). Deluxe.

Pribaltiyskaya – With 1,200 rooms — including a number of 3-room suites — and overlooking the Gulf of Finland, it is far from the city's center, but has several good restaurants (see *Eating Out*), a bar, nightclub with live jazz, sauna with massage room, beauty salon, duty-free shop, car rental, a plane/train ticket desk, and dry cleaning service. Business facilities include 24-hour room service, a meeting room for up to 400, English-speaking concierge, foreign currency exchange, secretarial services in English, audiovisual equipment, photocopiers, translation services, and express checkout. Operated by *Intourist.* 14 ul. Korablestroiteley (phone: 356-0158, 356-0207, or 356-0263; fax: 356-0094; telex: 122322). Deluxe.

Chaika – Formerly a city-owned apartment building, this 16-story property has been converted into a hotel. The accommodations, which still resemble Soviet flats, have 1 to 3 bedrooms, and each has a bathroom and kitchen. There is a Swedish restaurant and casino-bar, car rental, and a heated garage. Business facilities include 24-hour room service, a meeting room for up to 50, secretarial services in English, photocopiers, computers, cable television news, and translation services. 38 Serebristy Bulvar. (phone: 395-3085; fax: 301-5622; telex: 121037). First class.

Karelia – Situated in the northern part of town, a 30-minute drive from the city center, this property has 429 rooms, 2 restaurants (one Russian, one Scandinavian), 2 cafés, a disco, hair salon, and a plane/train ticket desk. Business facilities include 24-hour room service, a meeting room for up to 200, English-speaking concierge, foreign currency exchange, photocopiers, and translation services. 27/2 Marshala Tukhachevskogo St. (phone: 226-3277 or 226-3036; fax: 226-3556; telex: 122459). First class.

Oktyabrskaya – Located in the center of the city near the Moscow Station, this city-owned property accommodates 1,600 guests. There are 2 restaurants, a grill bar, café, hard-currency *Beriozka* shop, and dry cleaning service. Business facilities include 24-hour room service, a meeting room for up to 170, English-speaking concierge, foreign currency exchange, secretarial services in English, audiovisual equipment, cable television news, and express checkout. 10 Ligovsky Prospekt (phone: 315-5362 or 277-6330; telex: 122126 only in the Soviet Union). 11 Chernyshevskogo Sq. (phone: 296-7649 or 297-1902; fax: 296-3303). First class.

Olgino – Not far from the picturesque shore on the Gulf of Finland, this motel was built in 1980 for 600 guests. Cabins are available, too. There is a restaurant serving European fare, and a buffet. Business facilities include 24-hour room service, an English speaking concierge, foreign currency exchange, and translation services. 59 Primorskoe Shosse. (phone: 238-3484 or 238-3452; fax: 238-3954). First class.

Pulkovskaya – A mammoth, modern, Finnish-built property operated by *Intourist,* it is located between the airport and central St. Petersburg. Guests enter an impressive lobby and there are 800 serviceable rooms, 2 restaurants (see *Eating Out*), 2 bars, 2 saunas, a duty-free shop, hair salon, car rental, a plane/train ticket desk, and dry cleaning service. Business facilities include 24-hour room service, a meeting room for up to 500 and 12 rooms that hold up to 15, English-speaking concierge, foreign currency exchange, secretarial services in English, audiovisual equipment, photocopiers, translation services, and express checkout. 1 Pobedy Sq. (phone: 264-5122 or 264-5111; fax: 264-6396; telex: 321318). First class.

Sovetskaya – City-owned, this is a spacious and comfortable place, with the largest *Beriozka* shop in town. Less than conveniently located in the southwestern part of the city, it has 1,110 rooms, 3 restaurants, 2 bars and a grill bar, a hard-currency shop, hair salon, car rental, plane/train ticket desk, and dry cleaning service. Business facilities include 24-hour room service, meeting rooms for up to 180, and foreign currency exchange. 43/1 Lermontovsky Prospekt (phone: 259-2656 or 259-2552). First class.

EATING OUT: The food situation throughout the Soviet Union is poor, but the advent of independent cooperative restaurants has added a competitive edge to the city's restaurant scene; food, service, and atmosphere in St. Petersburg dining establishments are, perhaps, better than what was offered a few years ago. The prices are high at restaurants in *Intourist* hotels and at special hard currency bars and — except in the very best hotels — the ingredients still are often of mediocre or poor quality. Do sample the street food, however. Vendors sell tasty meat-, mushroom-, or cabbage-filled fried pastries (*pirozhki*), and the ice cream (*morozhenoye*) here is delicious. Try some *Kvass,* a drink made from fermented black bread and dispensed from small tanks on the sidewalks.

Wise travelers do not drink water from public fountains, tap water, or the water served at their restaurant table; a parasite, called *giardia lamblia,* is believed to be prevalent in the St. Petersburg water system. It can cause violent intestinal illness that can require hospitalization if not properly treated. There is an incubation period of about 2 weeks; therefore, this illness should not be confused with the usual travelers' maladies. You can avoid this parasite by taking minimal precautions; cooked food, tea, coffee, bottled water, and soft drinks are quite safe.

Meals at major restaurants in St. Petersburg can be booked in advance through your hotel service bureau, or you can book them on your own — that is, if you speak Russian. You can request a prix fixe menu, or you can order à la carte. Any drinks ordered in addition to the vodka and wine included in the prix fixe dinner must be paid for in Soviet currency. Most of the St. Petersburg hotels have dining rooms with live bands, dancing and, occasionally, a floor show. Reservations for hotel restaurants also should be made in advance with your hotel service bureau. There are also many cafés in St. Petersburg, providing a good opportunity to mix with local residents. The service bureaus won't make reservations for these cafés, so arrive early in case there's a wait. Payment in most cafés must be in Soviet currency.

Finally, as in other Soviet cities, private or cooperative cafés and restaurants have become popular; the service bureau at your hotel will provide addresses and phone numbers of the best of these. You can make your own reservations at co-ops — remember that English isn't always the lingua franca. Otherwise, book through *Intourist,* which will do the honors at some, if not all restaurants. All restaurants below are open daily and all variety shows are offered nightly, unless otherwise indicated. The dramatically fluctuating Soviet economy makes it difficult to provide accurate prices for restaurants; we suggest that you check costs — and the operative exchange rate — immediately prior to your departure. Some establishments only accept rubles, while others only accept hard currency.

Allegro – For traditional pizza, this small bistro is one of the best places in town. Alcohol and cigarettes available for hard currency. Open from 11 AM to 11 PM. Reservations advised. 73 Moskovsky Prospekt (phone: 298-9552).

Austeria – An eatery reminiscent of Peter the Great's time, it serves Old Russian fare. Try the *file austeria* (fried beef stuffed with onions and nuts and served with fried potatoes, onions, and carrots) or the *rulet starorusskii* (roast veal roll with hard-boiled eggs, onions, and carrots). Live music is played most nights. Open from noon to 11 PM. Reservations advised. Rubles only accepted. Ioannovsky Ravelin, Peter and Paul Fortress (phone: 238-4262).

Belaya Loshad – A favorite among locals — primarily for its convivial atmosphere — this spot serves good Russian beer and food. Try the *kolbaski okhotichi* (fried smoked sausage). Open from 11 AM to 4 PM and from 5 to 10 PM. Reservations unnecessary. 16 Chkalovsky Prospekt (phone: 235-1113).

Belye Nochi – Sit in the cozy booths for six and enjoy good continental fare, such as the cutlets *Belye Nochi* (fried pork brisket stuffed with mushrooms and onions and served with rice). Live music is played most nights. Open from noon to midnight. Reservations unnecessary. Rubles only accepted. 41 Mayorova Prospekt (phone: 314-9336).

Café Liana – A cozy cooperative serving good Armenian cooking. Specialties include shashlik (mutton roasted on a spit over charcoal) and *chahahbily* (stewed mutton served with roasted onion, tomatoes, and potatoes). Open from noon to 11 PM. Reservations advised. Rubles only accepted. 3 Sablinskaya St. (phone: 233-2005).

Chaika – A Soviet-German joint venture, it specializes in German fare (beef steaks and sausages) and German beer. Reservations necessary. Hard currency and traveler's checks only accepted. 14 Kanala Griboyedova Nab. (phone: 312-4631).

Daugava – Set in the *Pribaltiyskaya* hotel, this dining room with modern decor specializes in roast chicken and grilled meat. Open from noon to 11 PM. Reservations necessary. Hard currency and credit cards only accepted. *Pribaltiyskaya Hotel*, 14 ul. Korablestroiteley (phone: 356-4409).

Demyanova Ukha – A small spot with rustic decor, it's highly recommended for vegetarians; the menu consists primarily of fish and seafood. Open from noon to 10 PM. Reservations unnecessary. Rubles only accepted. 53 Maxima Gorkogo Prospekt (phone: 232-8090).

Fortezia – A Soviet-Belgian venture, this cozy spot has table lamps and etchings on the wall. Fried suckling pig and mushrooms from Altay are some of the tastier items on the menu of Russian fare. Open from noon to midnight. Reservations advised. Rubles only accepted for meals; alcohol and cigarettes must be paid for in hard currency. 7 Kuibysheva St. (phone: 233-9468).

Fregat – The food and decor here are right out of Peter the Great's era. Try the Russian specialties *miaso Fregat* (roast beef with cheese and mushrooms) or *kuri po-Kupecheski* (roast chicken in sour-cream sauce). Open from 11 AM to 10 PM. Reservations unnecessary. Rubles only accepted. 39 Bolshoi Prospekt (phone: 213-4923).

Goluboy Delfin – Specializing in a variety of fish dishes, this place is a favorite of seafood lovers and vegetarians. Open from noon to 11 PM. Reservations advised. Rubles only accepted. 44 Sredneokhtnisky Prospekt (phone: 227-2133).

Grill Bar – A good spot for a snack, this unpretentious bar serves tasty continental fare, including *rulet po-pushkarski* (grilled chicken) and shashlik (mutton roasted on a spit over charcoal). Open from noon to 10 PM. Reservations unnecessary. Rubles only accepted. 30 Bolshaya Pushkarskaya St. (phone: 232-8760).

Hermitage – For good traditional Russian fare and old-fashioned decor, stop in this café located in Pushkin, a mile from Yekaterinsky Palace and its park. Try the *zharkoye russkoye* (roast meat). Open from noon to 11 PM. Reservations advised. Major credit cards accepted. 27 Kominterna St. (phone: 476-6255).

Iveria – A small and cozy cellar, this co-op specializes in Georgian dishes such as *sazivi* (a piquant meat dish) and *chahahbily* (a chicken dish). Open from 11 AM to 10 PM. Reservations unnecessary. Rubles only accepted. 35 Marata St. (phone: 164-7478).

Kavkazky – This is the place to go for a taste of good Armenian, Azerbaijani, and Georgian fare. Try the shashlik *po-karski* (shish kebab) and the *sazivi* (a piquant meat dish). Have a glass of the good Georgian wine in the cocktail room. Live Caucasian (as in the republic of Georgia) music is played most nights. Open from noon to 11:30 PM. Reservations unnecessary. Rubles only accepted. 25 Nevsky Prospekt (phone: 311-3977).

Koyoga – A unique café with marble trimmings, it's a good place for dining on continental fare, and dancing. The *Koyoga* pork dish is especially tasty. Open from 9 AM to 5 PM. Reservations advised. Rubles only accepted. 15 Narodnaya St. (phone: 263-1893).

Leningrad – Located on Floor A of the *Leningrad* hotel, it offers a prix fixe menu of Russian and continental fare; menus on Wednesdays and Sundays are à la carte. Before dinner, have a drink at the hotel's beer bar. The restaurant is open from 8 PM to 11:30 PM. Reservations advised. Hard currency accepted at the bar. 5 Pirogovskaya Nab. (phone: 542-9155).

Literaturnoe Kafe – A gathering spot for St. Petersburg's "artsy" types, this literary café features classical musicians on the first floor, and many of St. Petersburg's best poets, writers, and artists congregate on the second floor. The food is delicious, too. Try *salat slavianskyi* (a salad of sliced boiled beef and potatoes mixed with a variety of fresh vegetables, hard-boiled eggs, and mayonnaise) or *selyamenin s gribami* (a mushroom dish). Open from noon to 10 PM; on Mondays, the second-floor hall is open from 7 to 11 PM only. Reservations advised. Rubles only accepted. 18 Nevsky Prospekt (phone: 312-6057).

Meridian – In the *Pulkovskaya* hotel, this 450-seat dinner-theater features a variety show, along with Russian and continental fare. The *schnitzel pulkovski* (pork fried in herbs and bread crumbs) is a specialty. Open daily, except Mondays, from 7 PM to midnight. Reservations advised. Rubles only accepted. 1 Pobedy Sq. (phone: 264-5134).

Metropol – One of St. Petersburg's oldest dining establishments, it was founded in the 19th century and still tries to maintain the era's charm. Continental fare prepared in the city is served in baroque surroundings where live music is played. Specialties include *cotlety po-Kievski* (chicken-fried steaks served with mashed potatoes) and *file pikantnoye* (beef stew served with boiled cabbage and carrots). Beware, however, food quality and the quality of service can be erratic. Open from noon to midnight. Reservations advised. Rubles only accepted. 22 Sadovaya St. (phone: 310-1846).

Moskva – Two large halls seating 570 and 620 feature variety shows nightly, except Wednesdays. The menu offers Russian and continental fare; one of the tastier dishes is *vyrezka files gribami* (meat with mushrooms). Open from 8 PM to midnight. Reservations advised. Rubles, hard currency, and credit cards accepted. 2 Alexandra Nevskogo Sq. (phone: 274-9503 or 274-2056).

Na Fontanke – Located in the center of St. Petersburg, it's one of the best cooperative dining spots in town. A variety show is featured in 19th-century surroundings. The menu offers such specialties as *langet Na-Fontanke* (fried beef served with boiled potatoes and peas) and the *salat St. Petersburzhskii* (salad prepared from an old Russian recipe). Open from 1 to 11:30 PM. Reservations necessary. Rubles only accepted. 77 Reki Fontanki Nab. (phone: 310-2547).

Neva – Particularly popular with Finns, the *Pribaltiyskaya* hotel's dining room offers continental fare and a dance orchestra. Try the *soodak* (pike and perch fried in butter and served with sour cream). Open from noon to midnight. Reservations necessary. Major credit cards accepted. 14 Korablestroiteley St., Floor 2 (phone: 356-1347).

Neva Café – A comfortable spot in the heart of Nevsky Prospekt, it serves good Russian dishes, accompanied by a variety show with live music. Try the caviar and the *cotlety po-Kievski* (chicken-fried steaks served with mashed potatoes). Open from noon to midnight. Reservations advised. Rubles only accepted. Operated by *Intourist*. 46 Nevsky Prospekt (phone: 110-5980).

Nevsky – For traditional Russian food and hospitality offered in modern surroundings, visit this first class dining establishment located in the city center. Specialties include *eskalop* (veal served with fried potatoes and olives). There's a variety show, along with live music performed by different orchestras in three separate dining rooms. Open from noon to midnight. Reservations necessary. Rubles only accepted. 71 Nevsky Prospekt (phone: 311-3093).

Okhotnichy Klub (Hunters' Club) – For those seeking hearty fare, this spot, decorated with hunters' trophies, serves a variety of·wild game. Try the *colbasky okhotnichy* (smoked sausages). Live music is played most nights. Open from noon to midnight. Reservations necessary. Rubles only accepted. 45 Dzerzhinskogo St. (phone: 310-0770).

Okolitza – The name means "Village Fence," and the rustic decor is reminiscent of a typical modest Russian wooden house. Dishes made from old Russian recipes comprise the menu. Open from noon to 11 ·PM. Reservations necessary. Rubles only accepted. 15 Primorsky Prospekt (phone: 239-6984).

Palanga – With seating for 400, this dining establishment features a touch of the Baltic; try the *rulet osoby* (sliced, boiled pork roll filed with carrot, eggs, garlic, and prunes) and the *blini po-pribaltiyski* (savory pancakes). There's a variety show. Open from noon to 11:30 PM. Reservations advised. Rubles only accepted. In the southwest part of the city. 127 Leninsky Prospekt (phone: 255-6417).

Petrovksy – Not to be confused with the floating restaurant of the same name (see below), this one is set in the *Leningrad* hotel with a wonderful view of the city. Live Russian folk music is performed while guests dine on Russian and continental fare. Open from 8 PM to midnight. Reservations necessary. Hard currency and rubles accepted. *Leningrad Hotel,* 5 Pirogovskaya Nab. (phone: 542-8092).

Petrovsky – An old ship has been turned into a restaurant and bar and now is permanently moored. The dark blue decor reflects the 18th century, as does the food. A house specialty is the *myaso po-preobrazhenski* (fried, beef-filled pastry, served with peas, onions, and tomato sauce). Open noon to midnight. Reservations advised. Rubles only accepted. Opposite house No. 3 on Mytninskaya Nab. (phone: 238-4793).

Pizza Express – A Soviet-Finnish venture, this eatery serves 13 kinds of pizza made from Finnish products and served in Russian surroundings. Paintings by local artists are for sale, too. Open from 11 AM to midnight. Reservations advised. Major credit cards accepted. 23 Podolskaya St. (phone: 292-2666).

Poles'E – A co-op which recently was awarded the Gold Medal of VDNKH (Exhibition of Economic Achievements) has earned a reputation for being one of the best eateries in the Soviet Union. The quiet, homey atmosphere is complemented by live music — Russian Gypsy folk songs. The fried suckling pig is especially tasty. Open from 12:30 PM to 11:30 PM. Reservations advised. Rubles and hard currency accepted. 4 Sredneokhtinsky Prospekt (phone: 224-2917 or 224-0227).

Polyarnoye – With candlelight and a relaxed atmosphere, this cozy spot is one of St. Petersburg's most romantic eateries. The menu features continental fare, including the tatsy *myaso na-skovorodke* (fried meat). Singers perform most nights. Open from 10 AM to 10 PM. Reservations unnecessary. Rubles only accepted. 79 Nevsky Prospekt (phone: 311-8589).

Sadko – One of the best restaurants in St. Petersburg, with traditional Russian fare, such as beef Stroganoff, skewered meatballs (called *lyulya kebab*), and *blinis* (crêpes stuffed with caviar, smoked salmon, or other delicacies). A balalaika orchestra, singers, and occasionally, folk dancers, provide entertainment. At press time it was closed for renovations and slated to reopen early this year. Next to the *Evropeiskaya,* ul. Brodskovo and Nevsky Prospekt (phone: 210-3198).

Schwabsky Domik – Also known as the "Schwäabisch Hut," this Soviet-German venture is a stylish eatery serving genuine Schwäbisch food and light German wines from Baden and Württemberg. There are two separate dining rooms with different menus and entrances; 90 seats are available to guests paying in hard currency (cash or traveler's checks). Open from 11:30 AM to 3:30 PM and from 6:30 to 10 PM. Reservations necessary. 28/19 Krasnogvardeisky Prospekt (phone: 528-2211).

Tbilisi Cafe – A cooperative serving excellent Georgian food, this interesting, intimate spot is decorated with ceramics and minatures from Georgia. Alcohol and tobacco are available for hard currency. Open from 11 AM to 11 PM. Reservations advised for dinner. Rubles only accepted. 10 Sytninskaya (phone: 232-9391).

Tete a Tete – The French accents are missing but this intimate place with many tables for two serves continental fare to the accompaniment of a jazz pianist. Sturgeon is one of the specialties. Jacket and tie are required for men. Open from 1 PM to 1 AM. Reservations necessary. Rubles only accepted. 65 Bolshoi Prospekt, Petrogradskaya Storona (phone: 232-7548).

Troika – Good food, from crabs to caviar, is served Russian-style in this baroque setting of gold and red, where variety shows are performed. Tickets are available for hard currency (about $20) from noon to 3 PM; after 3 PM, they are available for rubles only. Reservations necessary. 27 Zagorodny Prospekt (phone: 133-5343).

Turku – A Gypsy variety show is performed for up to 300 guests in this dinner-theater decorated in shades of red. The chicken leg stuffed with mushrooms is one of the best dishes offered on the continental menu. Open from 8:30 PM to midnight. Reservations necessary. Major credit cards accepted. *Pulkovskaya Hotel,* 1 Ploshchad Pobedy (phone: 264-5716).

U Petrovicha – Old Russian game dishes — elk, wild boar, and rabbit — are the specialties at this cozy little spot. Live music is performed most nights. Open from noon to 11 PM. Reservations necessary. Major credit cards accepted. 44 Sredneohtinksy Prospekt (phone: 227-2135).

Victoria – Located in the city center, this cozy new eatery with a fireplace is one of St. Petersburg's most popular. Continental fare is served (try the beefsteak Victoria), and there is a variety show, as well as a disco on Mondays. Open from noon to midnight. Reservations advised. Rubles only accepted. 24 Kirovsky Prospekt (phone: 233-3142 or 232-5130).

Vityaz – Not far from Yekaterinsky Palace in Pushkin, this Soviet-Italian venture offers Russian fare and a variety show (except Tuesdays). An especially tasty dish is the *miaso Vityaz* (beef sirloin covered with shredded onions and bread crumbs, fried in water and oil, and served with sour cream, fried potatoes, and whortleberries!). There also is a bar and a casino. Restaurant open from noon to midnight; casino, from midnight to 5 AM. Reservations advised. Major credit cards accepted at restaurant only. 20 Moskovskaya St., Pushkin (phone: 466-4316).

Volkhov – Situated in the city center, this unpretentious spot serves Russian food in a setting of traditional Russian decor. Try the *salat Volkhov* (house salad crowned with black caviar) or the *rulet Slavianskii* (roast pork roll stuffed with hard-boiled eggs and vegetables, and covered with mushroom sauce). Open from noon to 11:30 PM. Reservations advised. Rubles only accepted. 28 Liteyny Prospekt (phone: 273-4736).

Vostok – St. Petersburg's only dining establishment serving Indian fare at press time, this Soviet-Indian venture offers good dishes prepared over an open fire. There is a variety show and casino. Open from noon to 4 AM. Reservations advised. Major credit cards accepted. Primorsky Park Pobedy, near the lake (phone: 235-5984 or 235-4618).

Zhemchuzhina – Those who have a taste for Azerbaijani and Georgian fare will not want to miss this place. Good dishes are served with traditional hospitality. Try the *cutaby s myasom* (fried pastry filled with ground mutton and sprinkled with cinnamon) or the *dolma* (grape leaves stuffed with mutton, rice, mint, and onion). Open from 1 to 9 PM. Reservations advised. Rubles only accepted. 2 Shkipersky Protok St. (phone: 355-2063).

SALZBURG

For music lovers, Salzburg is mostly Mozart. But even those who are not enthralled by classical music are captivated by the charm of this almost picture-perfect small city in the mountains of west-central Austria.

Salzburg is a city of four distinct seasons and moods. Spring brings blossoms to the orchards, music to the theaters and churches, and wildflowers to the meadows within sight of the heart of the city. Summer is the exuberance of the renowned *Salzburg Music Festival,* lazy days sailing on lakes, hours spent nursing a glass of wine or iced chocolate in a terrace café. In fall, the foliage show can rival New England's, and the city seems to return to its birthright as the masses of tourists evaporate. Winter is, for some, the best season — almost romantically silent and personal as the snowflakes waft through wrought-iron shop signs onto twisting, cobbled streets.

The visitor is blessed with an astonishingly small area to get to know. Familiarity of place comes rapidly. The Old City — a maze of unsquared corners, labyrinthine lanes, curious steeples, and surprisingly spacious squares — is nestled between Mönchsberg (Monk's Mountain) and the Salzach River, which divides the city. On the right bank, modern Salzburg spreads east. The city's environs are breathtaking: azure glacial lakes, stunning châteaux, charming, timeless villages, and, always, the Alps.

An ancient Celtic settlement and then a Roman trading center, Salzburg was by AD 798 the seat of an archbishopric. The Salzburg archbishops also held the title of Princes of the Holy Roman Empire and were the leading ecclesiastics of the German-speaking world. They built a beautiful city, but some ruled with extreme intolerance, expelling Jews and persecuting Protestants. After Salzburg was secularized in 1803, it became part of Bavaria for a time, but was returned to Austria in 1818.

The economy here was long based on the salt from the mines of the region, hence the name of the city and province. Today, industry, farming, and the development of resorts and spas, as well as tourism, contribute to a comfortable standard of living for the more than 400,000 people of the province.

Although Wolfgang Amadeus Mozart was born here and it was here that his remarkable prodigy was first acknowledged, he was not really appreciated in Salzburg during his brief lifetime. Mozart left Salzburg for good at the age of 25, after breaking with Archbishop Hieronymus Colloredo, one of the last of the long line of autocratic archbishops who ruled Salzburg for nearly 1,000 years. Today, however, the apartment in which he was born (in 1756) and the house in which he and his family later lived are landmarks. There is a square bearing his name with a statue of the composer at its center. A music academy, the *Mozarteum,* honors him, and in its garden is a wooden pavilion in which Mozart is said to have worked on his last opera, *Die Zauberflöete* (The Magic Flute). The garden pavilion was brought here from Mozart's Vienna home a century ago.

The world-renowned *Salzburg Festival,* which draws thousands of visitors to the area in late July and August each year, often is dominated by his music. And there is a special *Mozart Week* festival during the last week in January.

Salzburg escaped serious damage during World War II while Austria was annexed to Germany. However, the *Salzburg Festival* — though it continued through 1943 — declined in significance because many musicians could not or would not participate. Following the Allied victory in Europe, the festival was revived under the baton of the late, legendary Herbert von Karajan, and continues to be one of the most important musical events in Europe. But whether you visit for the sounds of music or *caffè mit schlag,* Salzburg will enchant you.

SALZBURG AT-A-GLANCE

 SEEING THE CITY: The almost fairy-tale quality of Salzburg envelops you immediately as you approach the city from the east: the copper domes and belfries of the Old City outlined against a backdrop of mountains, the mighty fortress-castle (Festung Hohensalzburg) silhouetted against the sky. The terraces and the watchtower of the fort afford fine panoramas of the city and the Salzburg Alps to the south. It is reached by funicular (for a small charge) from Festungsgasse, near St. Peter's Churchyard at the foot of the mountain.

 SPECIAL PLACES: The Old City lies on the left bank of the Salzach River, girded by Hohensalzburg and the orchard-laden Mönchsberg (Monk's Mountain). The modern city, on the right bank, is bordered on the south by another mountain, Kapuzinerberg.

Hohensalzburg – The castle and fortress 400 feet above the city, atop a block of Dolomite rock, was begun in 1077 and completed in 1681. It was the stronghold, and sometime residence, of the Archbishops of Salzburg. The castle's staterooms retain original decorations of Gothic woodcarving, coffered ceilings, and intricate ironwork. Of particular interest are the huge porcelain stove (ca. 1501) in the Gilded Room and the hand-operated barrel organ dating from 1502. Guided tours. Open daily. Admission charge. From March through October and *Christmas* to mid-January it can be reached by funicular from Festungsgasse near St. Peter's Churchyard.

Old City – Beneath Hohensalzburg, crowded between the mountains and the river, are the colorful, narrow streets of the Old City. The main thoroughfare, Getreidegasse, is lined with quaint shops and charming 5- and 6-story houses. In the old patrician house at No. 9 is the third-floor apartment in which Mozart was born (*Mozarts-Geburtshaus*) and where he composed nearly all his early works. It is now a museum (open daily; admission charge). Getreidegasse leads into Judengasse, in the middle of what once was the Jewish ghetto. It, too, has shops adorned with medieval wrought-iron signs and picturesque buildings. The two streets meet near the Old Market Square (Alter Markt), with its colorful flower stalls, 16th-century fountain, and 18th-century pharmacy.

Dom (The Cathedral) – This fine early baroque cathedral with its two symmetrical towers, fine marble façade, and massive bronze doors was consecrated in 1628. When fire destroyed the previous late Romanesque cathedral in 1598, Archbishop Wolf Dietrich wanted to build a new one larger than St. Peter's church in Rome. But he was condemned for misconduct (he had 12 children by Salome Alt, his mistress) and died imprisoned in Hohensalzburg. His successors built a more modest, though quite beauti-

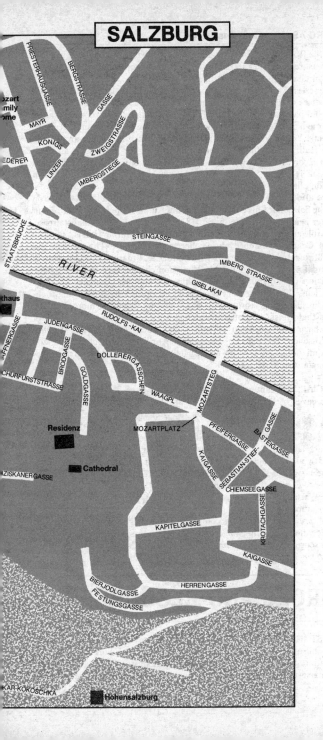

SALZBURG

Mozart
Family
Home

PRIESTERHAUSGASSE

BERGSTRASSE

GASSE

MAYR

KONIGS

ZWEIGSTRASSE

EDERER

LINZER

IMBERGSTIEGE

STEINGASSE

RIVER

IMBERG STRASSE

GISELAKAI

thaus

JUDENGASSE

RUDOLFS-KAI

AFFNERGASSE

BRODGASSE

DOLLERERGASSCHEN

CHURFURSTSTRASSE

GOLDGASSE

WAAGPL

MOZARTSTEG

Residenz

MOZARTPLATZ

PFEIFERGASSE

B. STEIGASSE

GASSE

ZISKANER GASSE

Cathedral

KAIGASSE

SEBASTIAN STIEF

CHIEMSEE GASSE

KROTACHGASSE

KAPITELGASSE

KAIGASSE

BIERJODL GASSE

HERREN GASSE

FESTUNGSGASSE

KAR-KOKOSCHKA

Hohensalzburg

ful, version. Note the Romanesque baptismal font where Mozart was baptized in 1756. The cathedral's treasure is on view in the museum, which is open daily from May to October. Admission charge for the museum. Dompl.

Residenz – The series of buildings on the north side of the Domplatz once comprised the ecclesiastical palace of the prince-archbishops. There are 15 staterooms, decorated with fine frescoes and paintings, on the third floor, and a gallery of European painting from the 16th through 19th century that includes the work of Rembrandt, Rubens, Breughel, and others. Young Mozart often played for guests of the prince-archbishop in the Conference Hall. Across the large square in front of the Residenz is an 18th-century *Glockenspiel,* or carillon, with 35 bells, played each day at 6 AM, 11 AM, and 7 PM. The Residenz is closed Sundays. Guided tours, except when events are in progress. Admission charge. 1 Residenzpl.

Mirabell Palace and Gardens – Archbishop Wolf Dietrich built a lovely palace on the right bank of the Salzach for his paramour, Salome Alt, in 1606. It was later rebuilt and remodeled after being destroyed by fire in 1818. The grand ceremonial staircase, decorated with marble angels, is of particular interest, and the Marble Hall is a favorite place for weddings. Candlelit chamber music concerts are held here. The gardens, laid out in the early 18th century, are adorned with statues and marble vases, flowers in abundance, and small pools. Open daily. No admission charge. East of Schwarzstr.

Schloss Hellbrunn (Hellbrunn Palace) – Once the summer residence of Archbishop Marcus Sitticus, this 17th-century castle is known primarily for its trick fountains, which spray unsuspecting visitors with water, and its theater of more than 100 mechanical figures that are set in motion by a clockwork movement to the music of an organ. Also on the grounds are a zoo (Alpenzoo) and the *Salzburg Folklore Museum* in the Monatsschlösschen. The palace is open daily, April through October; the zoo is open all year. Admission charge. At the end of Hellbrunnerstr., off Alpenstr., 3 miles (5 km) south of downtown Salzburg.

■**EXTRA SPECIAL:** The fantastic ice formations that have developed at the entrance to the caves of the Eisriesenwelt (World of the Ice Giants) are world renowned. The caves open at 5,459 feet on the western cliffs of the Hochkogel, some 30 miles (48 km) south of Salzburg. They may be visited from May through early October; detailed information is available from the state tourist information office in Mozartplatz (see *Sources and Resources*). You'll need warm clothes and sturdy shoes. If you drive there, stop at Hallein and visit the Dürnnberg salt mines, which have been worked since neolithic times, and the lovely Golling Waterfalls near the village of Golling. Leave Salzburg on Route 311 for Hallein, Golling, and the village of Werfen. The easiest route is to take the Werfen taxibus service to the cable car station for the caves.

American Express and several bus companies run a daily *Sound of Music Tour* of the film's locations, covering some 65 miles in 3 hours with the Rodgers and Hammerstein score playing on the bus's sound system. It's corny, but fun. Information: *American Express,* 5-7 Mozartpl. (phone: 842501).

SOURCES AND RESOURCES

TOURIST INFORMATION: The City of Salzburg Visitors' Bureau (Stadtverkehrsbüro), which can provide you with maps, brochures, and various information, has its main office at 7 Auerspergstrasse (phone: 8072-3462). There are several branches, including one at 5 Mozartplatz, in the Old City, and another in the main railway station. The tourist office for the province of Salzburg (Landestourismus) is also at 5 Mozartplatz (phone: 8042-2232 or 843264).

The US Consulate is at 51 Giselakai (phone: 28601).

Local Coverage – The *International Herald Tribune* and other major English-language newspapers can be purchased at newsstands downtown.

Food – *Restaurant Guide,* published by the tourist office, contains listings.

TELEPHONE: The country code for Austria is 43; the city code for Salzburg is 662.

GETTING AROUND: Just about everything of interest to the visitor is within easy walking distance of the Residenzplatz. The entire Old City and the Getreidegasse are pedestrian zones.

Airport – Salzburg Airport, which handles both international and domestic traffic, is a 10-minute drive from downtown; taxi fare should run about 150 Austrian schillings (about $12.50). City bus line No. 77 connects the airport with Salzburg's main train station on Südtirolerplatz (phone: 20551, for bus information).

Bus – There is quick, comfortable bus service. A "Salzburg Ticket," valid for 24 hours after its first use, allows access to the entire bus network, including the *Hohensalzburg Funicular.* It costs about $4 and is available at the Tourist Information Center, in the Transport Service ticket offices, and at *Tabak/Trafik* shops. Buses stop running at 11 PM.

Car Rental – Major international firms are represented.

Taxi – There are taxi stands at key spots throughout the city, and you may book one in advance by calling 74400. Fares, even though cabs are metered, can be high.

Train – Salzburg's main train station, the Hauptbahnhof, is on Südtirolerplatz (phone: 1717 or 71541 for information).

LOCAL SERVICES: Dentist (English-Speaking) – Dr. Glanschnig, 1 Münzgasse (phone: 842705).

Dry Cleaner/Tailor – Most hotels offer this service. If yours doesn't, call *Kleiderpflege* (Dry Cleaning Central; phone: 509354 for the nearest branch).

Limousine Service – *V.I.P. H. Pahovnikar,* 5 Linzer Bundesstr. (phone: 76515).

Medical Emergency – Call the *Austrian Red Cross* (phone: 144). The *Emergency Center* (8A Paris-London-Str.; phone: 141) is open from 7 AM Saturdays to 7 AM Mondays, and public holidays.

Messenger Service – Call the taxi service (phone: 76111) and ask for *Botendienst* (messenger service).

National/International Courier – *DHL International,* 1 Stöllnerstr. (phone: 845761).

Pharmacy – Pharmacy hours are from 8 AM to 12:30 PM and from 2:30 to 6 PM weekdays, to noon on Saturdays. They take turns for weekend and after-hours service; each pharmacy posts the name of the shops on duty in its doorway.

Photocopies – In any post office.

Post Office – The post office at the main railway station, Südtirolerplatz, is open 24 hours a day. All others are open until 6 PM weekdays; the one at 9 Residenzplatz also is open Saturdays from 8 to 10 AM.

Secretary/Stenographer (English-Speaking) – Inquire at the *Sheraton* hotel (4 Auerspergstr.; phone: 793210); or at the adjacent *Salzburg Conference Center* (Kongresshaus; 6 Auerspergstr.; phone: 73533 or 765110).

Telex – At the post office in the main railway station, Südtirolerplatz, if not at your hotel.

Translator – *Translingua,* 1a Hildwanpl. (phone: 8439420).

Other – Tuxedo rental: *Salzburg Kostümverleih,* 16 Bergstr. (phone: 73203).

 SPECIAL EVENTS: The major cultural (and social) event of *tout* Salzburg and the music world is the annual *Salzburg Festival,* beginning in late July. Programs for the festival are announced at the beginning of the year. Ticket requests must be addressed to: *Ticket Office of the Salzburg Festival* (Festspielhaus, Salzburg A-5010, Austria). It often is impossible to secure tickets to major events once the festival has begun. However, tickets may be available for chamber music concerts and outdoor performances. The festival takes place from the last week of July until the end of August.

Information about programs and tickets for the *Mozart Week* music festival, during the last week in January, the *Easter Festival,* and *Whitsun* concerts, also is available from the New York office of the Austrian National Tourist Office (500 Fifth Ave., New York, NY 10110; phone: 212-944-6880).

 MUSEUMS: In addition to those already mentioned in *Special Places,* Salzburg has several museums of interest. All of the museums listed below charge admission.

Burg Museum – Exhibitions about the city's development. Open daily. Hohensalzburg (phone: 8042-2123).

Carolino Augusteum – Named for Franz I's fourth wife, it contains artifacts from the Iron Age, Roman-era relics, Gothic sculpture, miniatures, furniture, musical instruments, paintings, and more. Closed Mondays. 1 Museumspl. (phone: 843145).

Haus der Natur (Museum of Natural History) – Dioramas that illustrate the earth's history, and exhibitions that trace man's relationship with nature. Open daily. 5 Museumspl. (phone: 842653).

Mozarts Wohnhaus (Mozart Family Home) – The composer's family lived here from 1773 to 1787. Closed Sundays. 8 Makartpl. (phone: 71776).

Salzburger Barockmuseum (Baroque Museum) – Kurt Rossacher's collection of paintings and sculpture from the baroque era. Closed Mondays. Mirabell Gardens Orangerie (phone: 77432).

Toy Museum – In St. Blaise's Church. Closed Mondays. 2 Bürgerspitalpl. (phone: 847560).

 SHOPPING: Loden coats and lederhosen, antiques, and handmade sweaters are good buys in Salzburg. Most department stores are open from 9 AM to 6 PM.

Art Galery Salis – Antiques, reproductions of 19th-century jewelry, and Fabergé. 13 Goldgasse (phone: 845434).

Jahn-Markl – Lederhosen and other leather garments. 3 Residenzpl. (phone: 842610 or 843153).

Jordis & Sohn – Hand-printed linens. Pausingerstr. 6 (phone: 72782 or 74066).

Lanz – Home of the internationally known line of cotton prints, dirndls, and other sporty women's clothes. 4 Schwarzstr. (phone: 74272).

Paul B. Burges – Antique small furnishings — reputedly a favorite shop of the Aga Khan. 31 Gstättengasse (phone: 848115).

Sine Tempore – Gifts and decorative articles. 11 Goldgasse (phone: 841276) and Neutorstr. 22 (phone: 846882).

Salzburger Heimatwerk – Handmade peasant crafts of the region. 9 Residenzpl. (phone: 84410 or 84419).

Street Markets – Fruits and vegetables are on sale at the *Grünmarkt* (Green Market) at Universitätsplatz and Wiener Philharmonikergasse every morning but Sunday (Saturday is liveliest) and on weekday afternoons. On Thursday mornings flowers and crafts, as well as a wide variety of edibles, are sold at the *Schrannenmarkt* near St. Andrew's Church.

 SPORTS AND FITNESS: Fitness Centers – The *Paracelsus Kurhaus* (2 Auerspergstr.; phone: 73200), is a medical spa that, in addition to peat mud and brine treatments by prescription, offers massage, breathing exercises, underwater gymnastics, and an indoor swimming pool with a solarium and sun terrace.

Golf – A 9-hole course is available at the *Klesheim Golf Country Club* (Klesheim, on the western outskirts of the city; phone: 850851). *Golf Club Gut Altentann* (851 Ignaz-Rieder-Kai; phone: 222222) also has a good course.

Jogging – Any of Salzburg's many parks is pleasant, but runners can exercise while sightseeing by circling the Mönchsberg, the mountain on which the castle is perched, or by following Hellbrunner Allee, the wide boulevard that leads to Hellbrunn Palace. There are fitness runs, ranging from a mile at *Naturpark Aigen* to the slightly more than 3-mile *Gaisberg Circular Run*. On both sides of the Salzach River are fitness trails where you pause every few yards to perform some diagrammed physical feat. On the commercial side of the river, the Fitnessparcour starts and ends at Schloss Aigen; it's just short of a mile long. On the scenic side, another course (about a half mile) starts just across a manmade lake from Schloss Leopoldskron, which served as Baron von Trapp's home in the film *The Sound of Music*.

Swimming – An indoor pool is at the *Kurhaus* in the Mirabell Gardens and there are outdoor pools, open May to September, in several parks. Bathing caps are a must for everyone.

Tennis – Courts are available at *Tennisklub Salzburg* (3 Ignaz-Rieder-Kai; phone: 22403), or the *Tenniscentrum* (Kasern, in the suburb of Lengfelden; phone: 50550).

 THEATER: The performance of *Everyman* (Jedermann), the morality play by Hugo von Hofmannsthal, each year in the forecourt of the cathedral is one of the few non-Mozart traditions connected with the *Salzburg Festival*. The famous *Salzburger Marionetten Theatre* (Salzburg Marionette Theater; 24 Schwarzstr.; phone: 72406) gives performances of operas and operettas. The season runs from *Easter* through September; events also take place at *Christmastime*.

 MUSIC: The most famous of all musical events is the *Salzburg Festival*, which takes place in the summer (see *Special Events*), but Salzburg is a city of music even in non-festival months. The *Landestheater* (City Theater; 22 Schwarzstr.; phone: 74086) schedules musicals, operettas, and operas as well as its regular diet of classical and contemporary drama from September through mid-June. There are organ concerts and other music at the *Mozarteum* (26 Schwarzstr.; phone: 73154), chamber music in the Residenz and Mirabell palaces, and more music in churches and parks throughout the year.

 NIGHTCLUBS AND NIGHTLIFE: Two pillars of Salzburg's late-night scene — where one can be bewildered by a maze of bars, discos, and night-owl cafés — are the *Saitensprung* (11 Steingasse; phone: 881377) and *Bazillus* (2A Imbergstr.; phone: 71631). If space to boogie is a priority, try *Friesacher Stadl* (57 Anif; phone: 6246-2411), in the suburb of Anif. And there is folk dancing at the *Sternbräu* beer garden (23 Getreidegasse; phone: 842140) every Friday night. If you see posters advertising that the *Salzburger Stierwascher* folkloric group is playing in town, be sure to go. You could gamble the night away at the elegant *Salzburg Casino* (on Mönchsberg; phone: 845-6560).

BEST IN TOWN

CHECKING IN: Salzburg has a rich range of accommodations, but it must be stressed that reservations should be made months in advance for the festival season. There is a hotel "finding service" at the railway station (5 Mozartpl.) and on the main entrance roads (look for the green and white "i" for information). The price of a double room with breakfast in an expensive hotel will range from $185 and up a night; in a moderately priced hotel, from $80 to $175; and in an inexpensive one, from $55 to $75. Note that the highest rates apply during the *Salzburg Festival*. All telephone numbers are in the 662 city code unless otherwise indicated.

Goldener Hirsch – A group of 800-year-old patrician houses have been joined to create an Old World, country inn ambience in the heart of the Old City. The 71 rooms vary in size; many have antique furnishings or native folk art hangings. The dining room serves some of the best food in the city (see *Eating Out*). Business facilities include meeting rooms for up to 100, concierge, and foreign currency exchange. 37 Getreidegasse (phone: 848511; fax: 848517; telex: 632967). Expensive.

Osterreichischer Hof – Across the Salzach River from the Old City near the *Mozarteum,* this traditional hotel, under the same ownership as the *Sacher,* in Vienna has an impressive skylighted central court. Each room is individually decorated, many have high ceilings, and all 119 are large, comfortable, and cheerful. Try to reserve a room overlooking the river. Its dining room serves excellent food (see *Eating Out*). Business facilities include meeting rooms for up to 1,000, secretarial services, audiovisual equipment, photocopiers, cable television news, and translation services. 5-7 Schwarzstr. (phone: 72541; fax: 75255; telex: 72541). Expensive.

Schloss Mönchstein – Situated in a park atop the Mönchsberg, in the center of Salzburg, this small, exclusive establishment has 8 rooms and 9 suites. Some consider it the most enchanting city hotel in the world. Business facilities include meeting rooms for up to 50. 226 Mönschberg Park (phone: 8485550). Expensive.

Sheraton – This hotel chain's Austrian base is perfectly situated downtown, beside the *Paracelsus Kurhaus* spa, the Mirabell Gardens, and the Salzburg Conference Center. Business facilities include meeting rooms for up to 130, foreign currency exchange, concierge, and cable television news. 4 Auerspergstr. (phone: 793210; fax: 881776; telex: 632518). Expensive.

Elefant – This ancient 38-room inn in the heart of the Old City is well kept and friendly. Folk art embellishes its basic simplicity. 4 Sigmund-Haffnergasse (phone: 843397; fax: 632725). Moderate.

Kasererbräu – The 43 rooms — some baroque or Biedermeier, others contemporary — are in a 13th-century house in the center of Old Salzburg. Business facilities include meeting rooms for up to 20. 33 Kaigasse (phone: 842406; fax: 842445; telex: 633492). Moderate.

Pitter – A rambling, cozy, family-run downtown hotel with 5 restaurants, of which the *Rainerstube* is most favored by natives in the know (see *Eating Out*). Business facilities include meeting rooms for up to 180. 6-8 Rainerstr. (phone: 785710; fax: 78571). Moderate.

Cottage – With 110 rooms, it's a large, but cozy hostelry near the route to the

Gaisberg (a mountain that affords good skiing and panoramic views of Salzburg), Berchtesgaden, and the Austrian and Bavarian Alps. 12 Joseph-Messnerstr. (phone: 659030; fax: 641833; telex: 63201). Moderate to inexpensive.

Weisse Taube – In the center of the city, this is a small 33-room place with rafters, wrought-iron, and all amenities. Business facilities include meeting rooms for up to 50. 9 Kaigasse (phone: 842404; fax: 841783; telex: 633065). Inexpensive.

 EATING OUT: Besides the breaded veal cutlet, called Wiener schnitzel, typical Austrian fare includes dumplings, *Knödel* and *Nockerl;* spicy stew, *Gulasch;* and, naturally, plenty of pastries. But the city's most famous dessert is an extravagant soufflé, called *Salzburger Nockerln,* that's like an immense, baked mousse, usually served with a dollop of raspberry or other fruit jam. Dinner for two with beer or house wine at an expensive restaurant will cost between $75 and $100; from $50 to $75 at a moderately priced restaurant; and from $30 to $50 at an inexpensive one. Although a 10% tip is included in most menu prices, an extra 5% gratuity is expected if service has been adequate. All restaurants below accept major credit cards. All telephone numbers are in the 662 city code unless otherwise indicated.

Café Winkler – The food is getting better all the time, but the view from Mönchsberg makes it even more worthwhile. Reached by lift from the foot of the mountain at Gstättengasse. Closed Mondays, except during the *Salzburg Music Festival.* Reservations necessary. 32 Mönchsberg (phone: 841-2150). Expensive.

Goldener Hirsch – The most discriminating palate will find satisfaction at this fine dining room in one of Salzburg's most attractive hotels. Its exciting and inventive kitchen prepares both continental dishes and Austrian specialties. As for dessert, it is noted for its supreme *Salzburger Nockerln.* Be sure to leave room for it. Open daily. Reservations necessary. 37 Getreidegasse (phone: 848511). Expensive.

Osterreichischer Hof – Some of the best dishes in Salzburg are prepared in the kitchen of this fine hotel restaurant. Specialties include *Hechtspatzen in Krebsensauce* (pike in crayfish sauce) and *Wildpastete* (venison pie). Open daily. Reservations necessary. 5-7 Schwarzstr. (phone: 72541). Expensive to moderate.

Rainerstube – A local favorite in the *Pitter* hotel, its atmosphere is pure *Gemütlich,* its specialties, typical Austrian fare. Closed Sundays. Reservations unnecessary. 6-8 Rainerstr. (phone: 845609). Expensive to moderate.

Alt Salzburg – The elegant red and gold interior of this excellent eatery merely adds to its cozy ambience. Closed Sundays except during summer festivals. Reservations necessary. 2 Bürgerspitalsgasse (phone: 841476). Moderate.

Purzelbaum – Very fashionable, good and centrally located, it is housed in one of the city's oldest inns and has a charming little garden for summer dining. Closed Sundays, except during the *Salzburg Music Festival.* Reservations necessary. 7 Zugallistr. (phone: 848843). Moderate.

Schlosswirt – In a suburb, about 4½ miles (7 km) south of Salzburg, this spacious place (with Biedermeier furnishings) is known for its delicious *Apfelstrudel.* Open daily. Reservations advised. 501 Anif (phone: 06246-2175). Moderate.

Festungsrestaurant – Good food and a view from the fortress-castle both are available here. Closed Tuesdays from October through May. Reservations necessary for large groups only. Festung Hohensalzburg (phone: 841780). Moderate to inexpensive.

Stiftskellerei St. Peter – A wine cellar in the 16th century, this popular spot, located in a former monastary, now serves local peasant dishes, such as *Bauernschmaus:* smoked pork, sausage, sauerkraut, and dumplings. The wine is from the abbey's own vineyards. In the summer, dine in the lovely courtyard. Closed Mcndays. Reservations advised. Next to St. Peter's Church (phone: 841-2680). Moderate to inexpensive.

Schloss-Restaurant Aigen – Near the Schloss (Castle) Aigen, this eatery has been here for 400 years, and is noted for its veal goulash. Closed Wednesdays. Reservations advised. 37 Schwarzenbergpromenade (phone: 21284). Inexpensive.

Stieglkeller – This beer garden, seat of the Stiegl brewery, is a beloved institution for natives as well as tourists, and folklore shows are presented between June and September. Closed October through April. Reservations advised. 10 Festungsgasse (phone: 842681). Inexpensive.

In addition to the restaurants listed above, Salzburg has numerous old-fashioned cafés that serve snacks and pastry. Especially recommended are *Café Bazar, Café Glockenspiel, Café Mozartkugel,* and *Café Tomaselli,* all of which are centrally located and fall into either the moderate or inexpensive categories. Also, be sure to indulge in fanciful pastries and ice-cream creations at one of Salzburg's delightful *Konditoreien,* such as *Schatz* (3 Getreidegasse; phone: 842792), *Bazar* (3 Schwarzstr.; phone: 74278), *Tomaselli* (9 Alter Markt; phone: 844488), or *Fuerst* — at several locations (5 Mirabellpl.; phone: 720347; 25 Roseggerstr.; phone: 35370; and 13 Brodgasse; phone: 843759).

STOCKHOLM

The Swedes have a favorite word, *lagom,* said to have been used by the Vikings as they passed a well-filled jug of spirits 'round the table at feast time. The word means "just enough" or "just right," a very fitting description of Stockholm.

What a big city offers by way of the good life is often tainted by the seamy side of urban society. But not so with Stockholm. The city is, indeed, *lagom.* Architecture, shopping galleries, entertainment, and cultural activities are available in a rich variety. And despite some concern over sporadic outbreaks of teenage violence and waves of graffiti, this still is a place where the streets are relatively safe and even downtown waterways are stocked with fish and clean enough for swimming. Here is that rarest of urban phenomena: one that improves with age.

More than 700 years old, Sweden's capital is, quite simply, one of the most beautiful cities in the world. From the winding, cobbled streets of its medieval district to the granite, marble, and glass of its modern downtown commercial centers, it exudes a serene majesty. While virtually every other city administration around the world struggles with the ubiquitous demons of traffic, pollution, and crime, Stockholm seems to grow stronger in its own quiet way.

Yet even as it forges its way into the 21st century, it remains mindful of its illustrious past. And for every ultramodern, glassed-in building complex that has sprung up in recent years, there have been several projects that called for the painstaking restoration of its magnificent historic buildings. Restored to pristine glory are classic restaurants such as *Riche* and *Den Gyldene Freden,* the palatial nightspot *Berns,* turn-of-the-century bathhouses *Central-badet* and *Sturebadet,* and the nearly 100-year-old *Royal Opera House.* The result: Materials such as gold leaf, brocade, marble, and crystal are almost as much in use today as chrome and concrete.

Stockholm was founded in the 13th century on a small, strategically located island on Sweden's east coast, where the waters of Lake Mälaren join the Baltic Sea. As Stockholm grew, the original Old Town (Gamla Stan) became known as the "City between the Bridges." Through the centuries, the number of bridges it was between proliferated as the city spread across wide bays, broad channels, and narrow waterways until today its population of 666,000 is spread over 14 islands. Stockholm's harbor opens into an archipelago of 24,000 islands, skerries, and islets. It is the Baltic's largest port, and yet it has no bawdy, tawdry waterfront quarter. And its encircling bracelets of water have freed Stockholm from the ugly collar of drab suburbs that blight so many of Europe's cities.

Not so many years ago, Stockholm was looked upon as a beautiful, romantic city, but sadly provincial by continental standards. Today, Stockholm

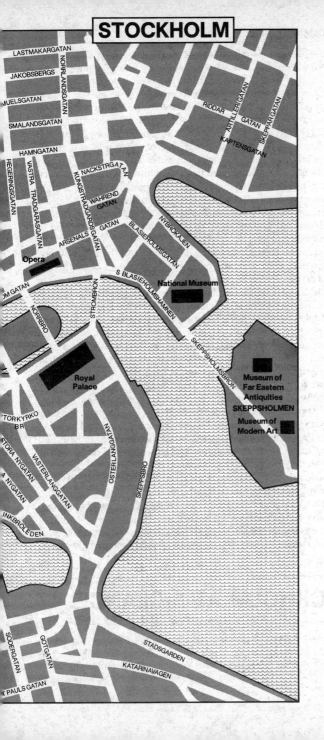

STOCKHOLM

LASTMAKARGATAN
JAKOBSBERGS
NORRLANDSGATAN
MUELSGATAN
SMALANDSGATAN
HAMNGATAN
REGERINGSGATAN
VASTRA TRADGARASGATAN
KUNGSTRADGARDSGATAN
NACKSTRGATAN
WAHREND GATAN
ARSENALS GATAN
BLASIEHOLMSGATAN
NYBROKAJEN

RIDDAR ARTILLERI GATAN
GATAN
SKEPPARGATAN
KAPTENSGATAN

Opera

S BLASIEHOLMSHAMNEN

National Museum

OM GATAN
NORRBRO
STROMBRON

SKEPPSHOLMSBRON

Museum of
Far Eastern
Antiquities
SKEPPSHOLMEN

Museum of
Modern Art

TORKYRKO BR

STORA NYGATAN
A NYGATAN
INKBROLEDEN
VASTERLANGGATAN
OSTERLANGGATAN
SKEPPSBRO

Royal
Palace

SODERGATAN
GOTGATAN
T PAULS GATAN

STADSGARDEN
KATARINAVAGEN

stands as the showpiece of Sweden's democratic socialism: a clean, well-planned metropolis as sophisticated, subtle, and savvy as any, whose people enjoy a high standard of living. Remote from the power blocs and conurbations of continental Europe, Stockholm has been content to pursue a slow, steady plan of development. Sweden's geographic and political isolation helped spare it the ravages of World War II, and public officials with a sense of aesthetics guided the city's growth to ensure a pleasing harmony of line and tone. The result has been a comfortable marriage of modern — and super-modern — architecture and restored historic façades. Once one of Europe's poor countries, its economy dominated by agriculture, Sweden has been transformed into a modern welfare state over the past 100 years. It is a constitutional monarchy with a parliamentary government system. Yet despite the obvious social equality of its citizens, the sober elegance of some of Stockholm's older districts still manages to convey an overall impression of bourgeois complacency.

There is one exception to the city's ultra-low profile on the international scene. In mid-December each year, the red carpet is taken out of mothballs, the silverware and crystal chandeliers are given a polish, and preparations are made to receive the annual crop of Nobel Prize winners (the Peace Prize is presented in Oslo; all the others in Stockholm). This is the one local event guaranteed to set teletype machines chattering in news agencies around the world. With its ancient streets and contemporary consciousness, Stockholm is a fitting place for such pomp and circumstance. Visitors who wonder how strict the formalities are at the traditional Nobel banquet are merely informed that all who seek admittance — right down to the hard-bitten press photographers — must wear full evening dress.

Yet the city's stuffy, elder statesman pose is quickly contradicted by manifestations of bustling commercialism and progressive liberal thought. Turning the next corner may delight or shock. Cabinet ministers have been known to ride the subway to Parliament. Palace guards wear shoulder-length hair, and the prime minister once donned a sequinned jacket to open a disco for the city's young set. One has come to expect the unexpected. Even so, the mood of calm can be shaken by the occasional incident. Zealous internal revenue investigators once triggered a public outcry by seizing the distinguished film director Ingmar Bergman and taking him "downtown for questioning" in a manner as dramatic as the plots of his own films. If nothing this exciting happens during your visit, however, there still is a wealth of historical buildings, museums, and monuments, not to mention uninhibited nightlife, to occupy your time.

STOCKHOLM AT-A-GLANCE

SEEING THE CITY: The very best aerial view of Stockholm is from planes circling the city before landing; if you can't have that, ascend to the observation gallery atop the 419-foot Kaknäs TV tower on the eastern edge of town. A bird's-eye view is the only way to comprehend fully the idyllic setting of the city. A mosaic of wooded islands and winding waterways enhanced by twisting copper spires and turreted roofs stretches almost as far as the eye can see.

 SPECIAL PLACES: Sightseeing tours by bus run regularly throughout the year, but most of central Stockholm can be explored on foot. The narrow lanes and charming squares of the Old Town especially reward the casual stroller. Sightseeing barges provide a fascinating "under the bridges" perspective on the city.

DOWNTOWN

Vasa Museet (Vasa Museum) – When the man-of-war *Vasa* was launched in 1628, she was intended as the flagship of the Royal Swedish Navy. But she foundered on the way out of Stockholm's harbor on her maiden voyage. This tragic — and embarrassing — mishap was but a dim memory when the wreck was rediscovered in 1956. During the next 5 years, a salvaging operation raised the remarkably well preserved warship and some 24,000 historic items aboard her from the harbor bottom. The *Vasa* (cleaned and refurbished) and her fittings now are housed in the museum. A short film detailing the salvage operation precedes regular guided tours in English. Open daily. Admisson charge. Djurgården (phone: 666-4870).

Skansen – This folklore center and summer meeting place for people of all ages is within walking distance of the *Vasa Museum.* Opened in 1891, Skansen was the prototype for outdoor museums now found throughout the world. More than 150 buildings of historic interest, brought here from various regions of Sweden, reflect the daily lives of rural and urban Swedes through the ages. In summer, craftspeople demonstrate glass blowing, weaving, and other traditional skills. Skansen's hilltop setting also houses a zoo; and concerts, open-air dancing, and shows here enliven the Stockholm summer scene. A traditional *Christmas* market is held at Skansen on three Sundays during *Yuletide.* The grounds are open daily in summer until 11:30 PM and in winter until 5 PM; buildings close earlier. Admission charge. Djurgården (phone: 663-0500).

Medeltidsmuseet (Stockholm Medieval Museum) – At Strömparterren Norrbro, this museum explores the development of Stockholm from 1250 to 1550. Closed Mondays (phone: 206168).

Gamla Stan (Old Town) – Birger Jarl founded the city of Stockholm on the central island of Gamla Stan in 1252. This Old Town district, a warren of small buildings jumbled together in crooked rows, is unmistakably medieval in character. Narrow lanes open onto market squares where merchants have traded since the 13th century. Even today, this remains one of the liveliest districts of the city. Careful and continuous renovation has preserved the buildings that now house about 300 small shops, restaurants, nightclubs, artists' studios, and boutiques. South of Stockholm's modern center; reachable by several short bridges.

Stockholms Slott (Royal Palace) – The royal family now resides at Drottningholm Palace (see below) to provide a greener environment for the children. Parts of the Royal Palace and the Royal Treasury with the crown jewels are open to the public, official engagements permitting. The palace, with its baroque and rococo furnishings and exquisite collections of tapestry and chinaware, was built during the late 17th and early 18th centuries. There is a small shop in one of the wings, where "royal" souvenirs can be purchased. A colorful changing of the guard ceremony takes place each midday in summer; 1 PM Sundays. Open until midafternoon; closed Mondays. Admission charge. At the foot of Norrbro Bridge, in Gamla Stan (phone: 789-8500).

Storkyrkan (Stockholm Cathedral) – A short walk from the Royal Palace, through the Old Town, takes you to Stockholm Cathedral, built in the 13th century and rebuilt between 1736 and 1742. Its ornate interior includes a masterful wood sculpture, *Saint George and the Dragon* by Bernt Nötke, dating from 1479. Behind the Royal Palace on Trångsund.

Stadshuset (City Hall) – The colonnaded red brick façade of this seat of Stockholm government is a masterpiece of architectural understatement. The building, dedicated in 1923, contains a spectacular Golden Hall, whose walls are covered with mosaics depicting Swedish history, made up of nearly 18 million gilded tiles. Guided tours (in English) are offered daily at 10 AM and noon, with additional tours offered May through September at 11 AM and 2 PM. The 320-foot City Hall tower (open from May to through September, 10 AM to 3 PM) offers an impressive panorama of the city. Admission charge. 1 Hantverkargatan (phone: 785-9060).

Postmuseum (Postal Museum) – A large and outstanding collection of postage stamps is housed in Gamla Stan in this lovely old building with an interesting history connected with the postal services. There is an authentic 19th-century mail coach, which has been modernized and extended. The prides of the collection are two rare 1847 Mauritius stamps and a quarter-sheet of 4-skilling banco. Don't bother making an offer, they're priceless. Closed Mondays. No admission charge. 6 Lilla Nygatan (phone: 781-1755).

Ostasiatiska Museet (Museum of Far Eastern Antiquities) – Surprisingly, Sweden has a long tradition in sinological studies. The Chinese exhibition here includes Stone Age ceramics from 2000 BC; a rich collection of jade pieces; carvings in wood, ivory, and horn; Chinese lacquer; and interesting everyday paraphernalia such as mirrors and dress hooks. The museum also has collections of fine arts and handicrafts from Japan, Korea, and India. Closed Mondays. Admission charge. Skeppsholmen (phone: 666-4250).

Ostermalms Saluhall – This large old covered market is where Stockholm's gourmets buy fresh meat, fish, and delicatessen goods. Steeped in atmosphere and rich in lively characters, the market offers visitors a taste of typical Swedish market trading from the past. Here, too, are salad bars and health food counters. Ask at *Lisa Elmquist's* for her recipe for *gravlax* (dill-cured salmon). A few blocks east of the city center on Ostermalmstorg.

Kungsträdgården – This broad, tree-lined avenue-cum-park with its dancing fountains in summer and ice skating during the winter months is an ideal place to engage in the pleasures of people watching. In the summer, there often is a show at the bandstand. Kungsträdgardsgatan.

Stockholm's Steamers – By the City Hall and opposite the *Grand* hotel one can catch sight of smart white steamships bobbing at their moorings. These genuine turn-of-the-century steam vessels are lovingly preserved and still contribute to the heavy summer traffic out to the archipelago. There is a powerful, romantic attachment to the islands they serve that stretch from Stockholm's doorstep right out to sea. You will not have touched the heart of the city until you have made the steamer trip out to an island paradise, such as the yachting center, Sandhamn. Several steamer operators offer frequent trips of varying lengths to the islands. Throughout the summer, daily ferry service to Sandhamn is run by *Strommakanal AB* (22 Skeppsbron; phone: 233375 for schedule information, 241100 for steamer rental). Local tourist offices have information on other schedules.

Waldemarsudde – This beautiful retreat in an exquisite setting was the home of the late Prince Eugen, an accomplished artist. His fine collection of paintings and sculpture is on exhibit here. Closed Mondays. Admission charge. Djurgården (phone: 662-1833).

Kulturhuset (House of Culture) – A modern center where exhibitions of art, handicraft, and design are featured and information is available on urban planning, history, culture, and Swedish social policies. Tourists may find its library and foreign newspapers particularly useful. There is a cafeteria on the top floor which overlooks the square. Open daily. 3 Sergelstorg (phone: 700-0100).

Moderna Museet (Museum of Modern Art) – Interesting special exhibitions of the work of contemporary artists complement the permanent collection of 20th-century art. Open from 11 AM to 9 PM; weekends until 5 PM; closed Mondays. Admission charge. Skeppsholmen (phone: 666-4250).

SUBURBS

Millesgården – Many of the finest works of sculptor Carl Milles are displayed in the terraced garden of his former home on fashionable Lidingö Island overlooking central Stockholm. The waterside residence also contains the sculptor's rich art collection, including some of the classical Greek and Roman statues that influenced his own work. Open daily, except Mondays, from 11 AM to 4 PM, to 5 PM May through October. Admission charge. Reached by subway to Ropsten, where buses leave frequently for Millesgården. 2 Carl Milles väg, on Lidingö (phone: 765-0553).

Drottningholm Palace – This 17th-century palace was built for dowager Queen Hedvig Eleonora on the island of Lovön just 5 miles (8 km) west of Stockholm. The French-style palace and its beautiful gardens suffer from the inevitable comparison with Versailles but deserve recognition in their own right. The Chinese Pavilion, a small, rococo summer house in the park, also is open to visitors. The palace and grounds are reached by road or by steamer that departs from Klara Mälarstrand near City Hall. Visitors also can take the subway to Brommaplan and then change to *Mälaröbuses,* which stop here. Palace open daily May through September; Chinese Pavilion open daily April to mid-October. Admission charge. Lovön (phone: 759-0310).

Drottningholms Slottsteater (Drottningholm Court Theater) – On the palace grounds, this superb rococo building fully deserves separate mention as one of the most perfectly preserved 18th-century theaters anywhere. During summer months, the theater's original stage sets and machinery are used for performances of period operas and ballets. But the 350-seat auditorium and theater museum are worthy of a visit at any time. Guided tours are available. Open May through September. Admission charge. Lovön (phone: 759-0406).

■**EXTRA SPECIAL:** The university and cathedral city of Uppsala lies less than 40 miles (64 km) north of Stockholm and offers much of historic interest to make the trip worthwhile. In addition to the medieval cathedral and fine 17th-century castle, the famous silver Bible, *Codex Argenteus,* is housed in the university library; Swedish botanist Carolus Linnaeus is honored with a museum at his former home; and there are burial mounds that represent the only Viking remains in this part of Sweden. Soak up the atmosphere as you down Viking mead, brewed from hops and honey and served in traditional ornamental horns at the pub near the mounds.

On the way to Uppsala, a short detour will take you to the oldest town in Sweden, Sigtuna. This small community once was immensely important, serving as the capital of the nation for over a century.

SOURCES AND RESOURCES

TOURIST INFORMATION: For general tourist information, call at Sweden House (Kungsträdgården; phone: 789-2000), where the Swedish Tourist Board and the Stockholm Information Service provide maps and literature. The $22-a-day Stockholm Card — valid for 1 adult and 2 children, and good for a free sightseeing tour in summer, unlimited use of public transportation, and admission to most museums — can be bought at Sweden House and several other locations, including Pressbyrån newsstands. Call *Frida,* an automatic information service (phone: 221840), for a summary of the day's events in English. Most hotels supply copies of *Stockholm This Week,* a free review of current activities in the city. During the winter, ask for the *Stimulating Stockholm* program.

A useful address for businesspeople is *Industrihuset* (19 Storgatan; phone: 783-8500), headquarters for the Swedish Trade Council and numerous other Swedish industrial organizations and export bodies.

The US Embassy is at 101 Strandvagen (phone: 783-5300).

Local Coverage – There are no English-language newspapers published in Sweden, though the *International Herald Tribune* and British papers are available at *Gallerian* (a shopping arcade) and at newsstands. National dailies sometimes produce English-language sections for tourists in summer.

Food – Consult the restaurant listings in *Stockholm This Week.*

TELEPHONE: The country code for Sweden is 46; the city code for Stockholm is 8. Stockholm is in the process of changing local phone numbers from 6 digits to 7; numbers listed in this chapter were the most current available at press time.

GETTING AROUND: Airports – Arlanda International Airport, which serves both domestic and international flights, is a 30- to 45-minute trip from downtown. The average taxi fare is 300 to 450 Swedish kronor (about $50 to $75); *SAS Limousine* (797-3700) charges about $60 per person to and from downtown. For other areas the price varies from about $30 to $83 per person (discounted for more than one passenger to the same address; a second person pays $15.50). The City Terminal, next to the Central Station, has regular airport bus service, with an intermediate stop at Jarva Krog; fare is about $6.60. There are two other airport bus routes serving Stockholm's northwestern (Kista) and western (Bromma) suburbs. A free bus service is operated between domestic and international terminals at the airport.

Bromma Airport, which serves a few local airlines as well as charter flights, is a 15-minute trip from downtown. The average taxi fare is 100 Swedish kronor (about $13). There is no bus service to the airport.

Subway, Bus, and Train – The Stockholm subway, with entrances marked by *tunnelbana* signs, is clean (except for graffiti), efficient, extensive, and by far the quickest means of intracity transportation. The newer stations have been designed by leading artists. The Kungsträdgården station downtown, for instance, has stone statues and miniature waterfalls. Some residents avoid the subway at night because of intermittent disturbances by homeward-bound revelers (harsh drinking-and-driving laws keep them off the roads). Note that considerable fare reductions often are in effect during the summer. Check with the tourist office or where you purchase your tickets.

All parts of the city are linked by bus routes, but during morning and evening rush hours progress can be slow despite special bus-only traffic lanes. Special tourist discount tickets (including the Stockholm Card; see above) for subways, buses, and streetcars can be purchased at major bus and subway stations as well as at Pressbyrån newsstands.

Central Station, the main railway (commuter and international trains), bus, and subway station, is at Vasagatan (phone: 248040 for information and reservations).

Car Rental – Major firms are represented at Stockholm-Arlanda Airport and at downtown locations.

Ferry Service – Small ferryboats operate regular services between Räntmästartrappan by the Old Town and Allmänna Gränd on Djurgården, and in summer between Nybroplan downtown and Allmänna Gränd. Cheap and great fun.

Taxi – Taxis are expensive but plentiful, except during rush hours and inclement weather. The break-up of Stockholm's taxi monopoly in 1990 did not produce the expected lower fares. The initial effect was an increase of some 10%, along with an additional government tax of 20% imposed in January 1991. The fare situation is now so complex that a pocket calculator is essential to anyone shopping around for the lowest rate. Taxi companies set their own tariffs. Some, but not all, companies include a tip in the metered fare. Prices start at 5 to 19 Swedish kronor (about 80¢ to $3) — just to get in. Nighttime rates are about 25% higher. When you call for a taxi, the pick-up fee can be up to 45 Swedish kronor ($7.40).

Licensed taxis now have yellow-number license plates and an authorization certificate displayed in the window. Taxis can be hailed in the street — an illuminated roof sign indicates they are available — but the easiest way is to call one of the major companies: *Taxi Stockholm* (phone: 150000 or 320000 in the suburbs; phone: 150400 for advance bookings or a tourist taxi with a bilingual driver); *Taxi Kurir* (phone: 300000); *Taxi Ett* (phone: 670000); or *Nya Top Cab* (phone: 200000). Both *Taxi Kurir* and *Nya Top Cab* offer a 15% discount to women from 6:30 PM to 6 AM; *Security Cab* (phone: 733-1500) offers a 35% discount to women between 7 PM and 6 AM, but the company has few vehicles, so be prepared for a long wait.

LOCAL SERVICES: Dentist (English-Speaking) – Marianne Dalheim, practice closed early July to mid-August (1 Kungsholmstorg; phone: 515252). For emergencies, the public dental clinic (22 Fleminggatan; phone: 6540590) is open from 8 AM to 7 PM daily. No appointments accepted.

Dry Cleaner – *Johansson & Källström*, 89-91 Drottninggatan (phone: 322790).

Limousine Service – *Limousine Service AB*, 20 Dannemoragatan (phone: 233345).

Medical Emergency – *City Akuten*, 3 Holländargatan (phone: 117177).

Messenger Service – *Adena Picko's* (phone: 730-0000); for delivery by taxi, call: 612-6000.

National/International Courier – *DHL International* (4 Lastbilsvägen, Sollentuna; phone: 359440 or 910151) is 40 minutes from the center of town, but they are the nearest and will send couriers. Express mail service to foreign destinations is available at post offices.

Office Equipment Rental – *Teco Kontorsservice AB* (25 Rålambsvägen; phone: 618-5400) rents electronic typewriters (1-month minimum); *Ljus & AV-teknik*, rents audiovisual equipment (40 Riddargatan; phone: 663-5255).

Pharmacy – *CW Scheele*, 64 Klarabergsgatan (phone: 218934).

Photocopies – *ABA Kopiering*, 67 Regeringsgatan (phone: 205042).

Post Office – The main post office (at 28-34 Vasagatan; phone: 781-2000) is open from 8 AM to 6:30 PM weekdays.

Secretary/Stenographer (English-Speaking) – *Proffice* (World Trade Center, 70 Klarabergsviadukten; phone: 787-1760); *Kontorsvikarien* (3 Jakobs Torg; phone: 247680).

Teleconference Facilities – *Swedish Telecommunications Administration Service Center*, 36 Kungsgatan (phone: 20-781110 or, for video conference reservations, 780-8283).

Telex – The main telecenter is in the Main Hall at the Central Railway Station (phone: 106439). To send a telex by phone, dial 0021 and ask for Phonotelex.

Translator – *Språktjänst* (Swedish Export Council), 42 Artillerigatan (phone: 783-8500).

SPECIAL EVENTS: *Walpurgis Night*, April 30, heralds the arrival of spring and is celebrated with bonfires in public places. *Labor Day*, May 1, is an occasion for parades and political speeches. *Midsummer* is a charming festival (originally pagan and very ancient) occurring in the third or

1030 STOCKHOLM / Sources and Resources

fourth week of June, when pagan rites are celebrated with folk dances, raising the Maypole, and general merrymaking. The month of July sees *Summer Stockholm,* a festival of athletic contests, music, and drama. The Nobel festivities take place annually in December, but access is difficult to everything but the public lectures of the prize winners. On *St. Lucia's* feast day, December 13, Swedish children traditionally wake their parents in the early morning hours to serve them saffron buns and coffee. Some of Stockholm's major hotels celebrate the day by sending blond *Lucia* maidens, wearing wreaths of candles on their heads, to serve the traditional breakfast to guests in their rooms. There also are special evening festivities at Skansen (see *Special Places*).

MUSEUMS: Stockholm has over 50 museums, art galleries, and historic buildings. Most museums are closed Mondays. Those of note not listed in *Special Places* include the following.

Armémuseum (Royal Army Museum) – Arms and artillery from the 16th century to the present. 13 Riddargatan (phone: 661-7602).

Hallwyl Museum – Collections of weapons, paintings, and Chinese porcelain. 4 Hamngatan (phone: 666-4499).

Historiska Museet and Kungliga Myntkabinettet (Museum of National Antiquities and the Royal Coin Cabinet) – Thirty rooms and 10,000 years of history. The second floor houses the coin collection. 13-17 Narvavägen (phone: 783-9400).

House of Nobility – In this historic, 17th-century building, exhibitions pertain to Swedish nobility. Riddarhustorget (phone: 100857).

Nationalmuseum (National Museum of Fine Arts) – Opened in 1794, it contains works by Breughel, El Greco, Rembrandt, Rubens, and Swedish artists. Södra Blasieholmshamnen (phone: 666-4250).

National Museum of Science and Technology – 7 Museivägen (phone: 663-1085).

Nordiska Museet – Over a million objects illustrate life in Sweden since the 16th century. Djurgården (phone: 666-4600). Closed Fridays.

Riddarholm Church – Founded in the 13th century, this pantheon contains the tombs of Swedish kings and other famous Swedes. Riddarholmen, across the bridge from the Old Town (phone: 789-8500).

Sjöhistoriska Museet (National Maritime Museum) – Exhibitions deal with the Swedish navy and merchant marine in a building designed by Ragnar Ostberg. Djurgårdsbrunnsvägen (phone: 666-4900).

Strindberg Museum – Sweden's most famous playwright lived here before his death in 1912. 85 Drottninggatan (phone: 113789).

Swedish Museum of Natural History – Frescati (phone: 666-4040).

Thiel Gallery – The private collection of Ernest Thiel; especially noteworthy are the late-19th-century paintings by Swedish artists. On Djurgården (phone: 662-5884).

Vin & Spirit Historiska Museet (Wine & Spirits Historical Museum) – The history of alcoholic beverages in Sweden: distillation, distribution, customs, and habits. 100 Dalagatan (phone: 333255).

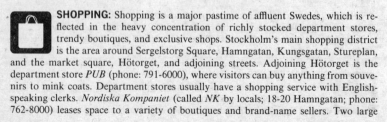

SHOPPING: Shopping is a major pastime of affluent Swedes, which is reflected in the heavy concentration of richly stocked department stores, trendy boutiques, and exclusive shops. Stockholm's main shopping district is the area around Sergelstorg Square, Hamngatan, Kungsgatan, Stureplan, and the market square, Hötorget, and adjoining streets. Adjoining Hötorget is the department store *PUB* (phone: 791-6000), where visitors can buy anything from souvenirs to mink coats. Department stores usually have a shopping service with English-speaking clerks. *Nordiska Kompaniet* (called *NK* by locals; 18-20 Hamngatan; phone: 762-8000) leases space to a variety of boutiques and brand-name sellers. Two large indoor shopping arcades downtown, *Sturegallerian,* at Stureplan, and *Gallerian,* accessible from Hamngatan and Regeringsgatan, save a tourist from getting a blue nose from window shopping outdoors in the depth of winter. Best buys are Swedish glass, textiles, ceramics, stainless steel housewares, furs, and Swedish crafts. Try the Old Town for antiques. Shopping hours generally are 9 AM to 6 PM weekdays and to 3 PM Saturdays. Some shops stay open an hour later during winter months. All stores listed below accept major credit cards unless otherwise indicated.

Amoress – Exclusive furs and leather jackets. 5 Norrlandsgatan (phone: 212200).

Carl Malmsten – The largest exponent of Swedish modern furniture. 5B Strandvägen (phone: 233380).

Casselryds – Elegant crystal and porcelain at favorable prices. A 25-minute drive south from downtown. 5 Storholmsgatan, Skärholmen (phone: 710-5116). *Casselryds* also has a small, centrally located branch at 11 Hamngaten (phone: 217034).

Duka Aveny – Stock of over 1,700 different glasses. 41 Kungsgatan (phone: 206041).

Georg Jensen Silver AB – Specializes in silverware, glassware, and porcelain. 13 Birger Jarlsgatan (phone: 213822).

Harald Westerberg Interior House – Three floors of quality furniture and home furnishings. 24 Norrlandsgatan (phone: 611-5200).

Hasselblads Foto – Home of the Swedish camera that American astronauts used in their space explorations. Three locations: 16 Hamngatan (phone: 214042), 71 Sveavägen (phone: 319799), and 21 Sergelgatan (phone: 218468).

Klockargården – An interesting range of Swedish folk handicrafts, including hand-painted cabinets, wall hangings from Dalarna (Dalecarlia), folk costumes, and handmade brushes. 55 Kungsgatan (phone: 214726).

Läns Hemslöjden – Center for Swedish handicrafts and souvenirs. 14 Drottninggatan (phone: 117549).

Nordiska Kristall – A wide selection of elegant Scandinavian crystal. The specialty is stemware. 9 Kungsgatan (phone: 104372).

Svensk Hemslöjd – More handicrafts, run by the Swedish Handicraft Society. 44 Sveavägen (phone: 232115).

Svenskt Tenn – Outstanding pewter designs and fabrics for the home. 5A Strandvägen (phone: 663-5210).

 SPORTS AND FITNESS: Stockholm has several soccer and ice hockey teams in the premier division of the league, and these are the major spectator sports. Schedules and ticket information are available from the tourist offices (see *Sources and Resources.*)

Basketball – Swedish basketball has had quite a lift from imported American players in recent years. Stockholm's top teams are *Solna* and *Alvik.* Games are played at various stadiums.

Fitness Center – *World Class Hälsostudion* (68 Luntmakargatan; phone: 345410) offers weights and exercise equipment, sunbeds, and massage.

Golf – There are some fine 18-hole courses in the Stockholm region: *Drottningholm* (phone: 759-0085), *Lidingö* (phone: 765-7911), and *Djursholm* (phone: 755-1477) are among the best. During the Swedish vacation month, July, foreign visitors may play these courses as guests, provided they show a membership card from their home club and evidence of their official handicap.

Ice Hockey – Swedish teams are very competitive internationally and players are known for their good skating ability. Stockholm's top teams *AIK* and *Djurgården* play at the *Globe Arena* (Johanneshov; phone: 600-3400) during the winter season, November through March.

Jogging – Djurgården Park, an island virtually free of buildings save museums, is a 10-minute walk from the center of town.

Soccer – The season is split into spring and autumn. *AIK* and *Djurgården* play at *Råsunda Football Stadium, Solna,* and *Hammarby* plays at *Söder Stadium.*

Tennis – Future Stefan Edbergs and lesser mortals can keep up their game at the *Royal Tennis Hall* (75 Lidingovagen; phone: 670350). The tennis hall also has squash courts.

Trotting – A popular spectator sport with gambling permitted. *Solvalla Stadium* at the border of the western suburbs of Bromma and Sundyberg (phone: 289630) has regular meetings during most of the year.

 THEATER: Few non-Swedish-speaking visitors would wish to sit through Strindberg in the original or hear *A Chorus Line* in Swedish, but those who do will find the current program at the *Dramaten* (Royal Dramatic Theater; at Nybroplan; phone: 667-0680) and other theaters in *Stockholm This Week.* The regular theater and opera season runs from the end of August to the middle of June.

 MUSIC: The *Operan* (Royal Opera House; just off Gustav Adolphs Torg; phone: 248240 for reservations, 203515 for other information) offers fine performances during the season, with local talent and prominent international singers. In summer there are performances at *Drottningholm Court Theater* (see *Special Places*). During the season there are also frequent concerts at the *Konserthuset* (Concert Hall; phone: 102110), *Berwaldhallen* (Berwald Hall; phone: 784-1800), and *Kulturhuset* (House of Culture; phone: 700-0100). In summer, there are outdoor concerts in several city parks and at Skansen. Recitals take place at the cathedral, Engelbrekts Church, Adolf Fredriks Church, Gustav Vasa Church, and St. Jakob's. Tickets and information can be obtained at a booth in the *Sturegallerian* arcade. Last-minute tickets are sold at the kiosk on Norrmalmstorg.

 NIGHTCLUBS AND NIGHTLIFE: Top discos are *Sturecompagniet* (4 Sturegatan; phone: 611-7800), *Café Opera* (Operahuset; phone: 676-5807), *Daily's Melody* (Kungsträdgården; phone: 215655), and *Valentino* (24 Birger Jarlsgatan; phone: 679-578022). These are the places to be seen; known habitués include royalty, pop stars, and international tennis aces. Otherwise the plethora of discos is a fast-changing scene. The palatial rooms of the classic nightspot in downtown Berzelli Park, *Berns,* have opened again after painstaking restoration (phone: 614-0550, restaurant; 614-0555, floor show). *Bacchi Wapen* (5 Järntorgsgatan in the Old Town; phone: 116671) is a nightclub with a cabaret featuring racy shows for tired executives and male striptease for ladies only (pick the right night!). *Hamburger Börs,* an exclusive nightclub that once tried to book the late Sammy Davis, Jr. and got the reply: "Mr. Davis doesn't play hamburger joints," has been renamed *Börsen* (6 Jakobsgatan; phone: 101600); Davis was among the many top artists to have performed here.

BEST IN TOWN

 CHECKING IN: Stockholm hotels have a high rate of occupancy all year round, so it's wise to arrange reservations well in advance of arrival. If you do arrive without a hotel reservation, *Hotellcentralen,* on the lower floor at the central railway station, is the official accommodations agency (phone: 240880, but note that only *advance* reservations can be made over the phone). Those visiting from mid-June through August and on weekends should ask about the special rates offered by most hotels. From June 18 through August 19, the Stockholm Package offers reduced rates of $62 to $110 — breakfast included — in first class hotels, with the Stockholm Card (see *Sources and Resources*). Rates quoted are per person in double rooms. The package is sold by travel agents in Sweden and *Hotellcentralen*. A double at one of the hotels listed below as expensive can cost $250 to $450; $135 to $245 at those classed as moderate. Although we don't list an inexpensive category, numerous pensions and youth hostels are available. (Contact *Sweden House,* Kungsträdgården; phone: 789-2000; or, in the US, *American Youth Hostels,* listed in GETTING READY TO GO, *Hints for Single Travelers.*) All telephone numbers are in the 8 city code unless otherwise indicated.

Diplomat – With 130 small, sophisticated rooms (with telephones) individually furnished in classic style, this place is centrally located at the edge of the fashionable diplomatic quarter in a building of historic significance and great character. There is a cocktail bar, and the elegant *Tea House* restaurant. Business facilities include meeting rooms for up to 12, English-speaking concierge, foreign currency exchange, secretarial services in English, photocopiers, cable television news, translation services, and express checkout. 7C Strandvägen (phone: 663-5800; fax: 783-6634; telex: 17119). Expensive.

Grand – Although renovated, this establishment remains steeped in European tradition and good old-fashioned luxury. Opposite the Royal Palace, it is the most exclusive hotel in town. If you are coming to collect a Nobel Prize, don't settle for anything less; there are 319 rooms, 2 restaurants, a winter garden, and a bar. Every room has a telephone. Business facilities include 24-hour room service, meeting rooms for up to 1,000, English-speaking concierge, foreign currency exchange, secretarial services in English, audiovisual equipment, and photocopiers. 8 Södra Blasieholmen (phone: 221020; fax: 611-8686; telex: 19500). Expensive.

Park – In a quiet spot but still close to the center of things, it is modern, exclusive, and not so large that it fails to offer attentive service. All 202 rooms have telephones, and a brasserie, piano bar, and first class restaurant are on the premises. Business facilities include meeting rooms for up to 70, English-speaking concierge, foreign currency exchange, secretarial services in English, audiovisual equipment, photocopiers, computers, cable television news, translation services, and express checkout. 43 Karlavägen (phone: 229620; fax: 216268; telex: 10666). Expensive.

Reisen – An interesting old building in the Old Town, it offers modern facilities and a fine view of the harbor. The hotel has 114 rooms with telephones, a grillroom, a piano bar, a sauna, and a small pool in its historic medieval cellar. Business facilities include meeting rooms for up to 62, foreign currency exchange, audiovisual equipment, and photocopiers. 12-14 Skeppsbron (phone: 223260; fax: 201559; telex: 17494). Expensive.

Royal Viking – The special features of this modern, 340-room property include 3 duplex suites with whirlpool bath and sauna, a glass-roofed winter garden with arcades and restaurants, and the *Sky Bar* on the top floor, with a lovely view. Business facilities include 24-hour room service, meeting rooms for up to 348, English-speaking concierge, foreign currency exchange, secretarial services in English, audiovisual equipment, photocopiers, computers, cable television news, and translation services. Near the Central Station. 1 Vasagatan (phone: 141000; fax: 108180; telex: 13900). Expensive.

Sergel Plaza – This elegant 406-room hotel — which includes 18th-century artwork and antiques — has much to recommend it. Along with being located in the heart of the city's business and shopping district, it offers a wide range of facilities: lobby bar, piano bar with nightly entertainment, and a beauty salon (with a sauna, massages, a solarium, and whirlpool baths — advance appointments advised).

Business facilities include 24-hour room service, meeting rooms for up to 200, English-speaking concierge, foreign currency exchange, secretarial services in English, audiovisual equipment, photocopiers, computers, cable television news, translation services, and express checkout. 9 Brunkebergstorg (phone: 226600; fax: 215070; telex: 16700). Expensive.

Sheraton-Stockholm – Fully renovated in 1990, this large, modern property is very much an American-owned, international-style place with an excellent location on the waterfront overlooking the Old Town. Its impressive lobby always is busy. The main restaurant, *Premiere,* has a rich ambience. The 459 rooms, of which 51 are in the top-floor Executive Towers section, all have telephones. Business facilities include 24-hour room service, meeting rooms for up to 700, English-speaking concierge, foreign currency exchange, secretarial services in English, audiovisual equipment, photocopiers, cable television news, translation services, and express checkout. 6 Tegelbacken (phone: 142600; fax: 217026; telex: 17750). Expensive.

Strand – On the waterfront, this delightful, old-fashioned place operated by *SAS* has high-ceilinged rooms (138 in all), which combine old Swedish furniture with new Italian textiles and lighting; the bathrooms are stunning. The atrium *Piazza* lounge and restaurant are fancifully designed to resemble the courtyard of an Italian palazzo. Business facilities include 24-hour room service, meeting rooms for up to 25, English-speaking concierge, foreign currency exchange, secretarial services in English, audiovisual equipment, photocopiers, computers, cable television news, and express checkout. 9 Nybrokajen (phone: 678-7800; fax: 611-2436; telex: 10504). Expensive.

Clas På Hörnet – A rarity in the city, this 18th-century country inn has 10 uniquely decorated rooms, each with its own name and furnished in period style. There is an excellent restaurant and a good smaller dining room (see *Eating Out* for both). 20 Surbrunnsgatan (phone: 165130; fax: 612-5315; telex: 14619). Expensive to moderate.

Continental – In an excellent central location, with 2 suites and 268 modern rooms with telephones, a cafeteria, a restaurant, bars, and a bistro. Business facilities include meeting rooms for up to 70, foreign currency exchange, audiovisual equipment, photocopiers, cable television news, and express checkout. 4 Klara Vattugränd (phone: 244020; fax: 113695; telex: 10100). Expensive to moderate.

Mälardrottningen – Formerly the luxurious private yacht of the late heiress Barbara Hutton, it's now an unusual 59-room hotel with an exclusive restaurant and cocktail bar on its bridge. Restaurant open weekdays for lunch, daily for dinner (except Sundays); a grill restaurant is open on the foredeck during May and June. Reservations necessary. Business facilities include meeting rooms for up to 18, foreign currency exchange, audiovisual equipment, and photocopiers. Moored at Riddarholmen (phone: 243600; fax: 243676; telex: 15864). Expensive to moderate.

Adlon – Centrally located, small, and unpretentious, it has 73 rooms, all with telephone. Three floors were fully renovated in 1991. Only breakfast is served in the dining room. Business facilities include English-speaking concierge, foreign currency exchange, photocopiers, and cable television news; the hotel can arrange for meeting rooms and secretarial services in English at the *Norra Latin Conference Center* nearby. 42 Vasagatan (phone: 245400; fax: 208610; telex: 11543). Moderate.

Flamingo – Pleasant, with 128 rooms, in a suburb that is 10 minutes from downtown by subway. Business facilities include meeting rooms for up to 120, English-speaking concierge, foreign currency exchange, secretarial services in English, audiovisual equipment, photocopiers, cable television news, and express checkout; translation services can be arranged. 11 Hotellgatan, Solna (phone: 830800; fax: 839814; telex: 10060). Moderate.

Prize – Centrally located in the World Trade Center, with nice accommodations, it keeps rates modest by dispensing with unnecessary frills and offering 188 (mostly single) pleasant, basic rooms, including 7 double-occupancy, all with telephone, TV set, and shower. Business and conference facilities can be arranged through the World Trade Center. 1 Kungsbron (phone: 149450). Moderate.

 EATING OUT: Swedish food was made famous by the smorgasbord, a seemingly endless array of delicacies from smoked salmon and dozens of varieties of herring to lingonberry jam and honey. If it's on the menu, you might want to try another Swedish specialty: elk steaks accompanied by red currant or rowanberry jelly. *Surströmming,* fermented Baltic herring, has as many detractors as fans. If you'd like to sample some in the traditional way, eat it on a slice of *norrland* bread with Swedish *mandel* potatoes and, perhaps, a glass of *snaps* to wash it down. Recent years have seen a great expansion of inexpensive, mass-production pizzerias, kebab and hamburger restaurants, and self-service cafeterias in Stockholm. But this new food culture has done little to harm the more established (and expensive) restaurants. A three-course dinner for two, with wine and service, can run $200 and up at an expensive restaurant, $100 to $175 at a moderately priced place, and $75 or less at an inexpensive one. It's possible to enjoy a good lunch at a modest price at restaurants all over Stockholm, while dining out in the evening tends to be more demanding on the wallet. One tip to help cut costs: Look for the words *Dagens rätt* on the menu. That means "today's special." Also worth noting: Don't be surprised if dining out costs a lot more than the last time you visited Sweden. Note that the sales tax on restaurant bills was doubled to 25% in 1990. Most restaurants accept major credit cards. All telephone numbers are in the 8 city code unless otherwise indicated.

Erik's – One of the newer restaurants in the Old Town, it's regarded by at least one local columnist as the best in Stockholm. It is an expensive and discreet haunt of those who love good food and have the means to enjoy it. Closed Sundays. Reservations advised. 17 Osterlånggatan (phone: 238500). Expensive.

L'Escargot – Traditional French cuisine in an elegant setting, with a brasserie downstairs and fine dining one floor up. Known for excellent service as well as an extensive wine list. Try the snails with roquefort sauce — one of the house specialties. Brasserie open Mondays through Fridays for lunch, daily for dinner; dining room closed Sundays. Reservations advised. 8 Scheelegatan — entrance on Bergsgatan (phone: 530577). Expensive.

Den Gyldene Freden – True to its name, "The Golden Peace," this elegant establishment — first opened in 1721, then closed for restoration in 1985, then recently reopened to enthusiastic acclaim — is a study in elegance and serenity. Rooms are named for famous Swedes who have dined here in the past. Food is strictly traditional — fish, game — and unforgettable. Closed Sundays. Reservations necessary. 51 Osterlånggatan (phone: 109046). Expensive.

Operakällaren – An institution in Sweden and a restaurant with a truly international reputation, it prepares the state banquets at the Royal Palace. Its kitchen sets the standard by which other restaurants all over the country are judged. It has palatial rooms with high ceilings and carved oak paneling hung with fine art, a baroque grillroom, and a magnificent smorgasbord. *Operabaren* and *Café Opera,* in the same building, are meeting places for Stockholm intellectuals. Open daily. Reservations necessary. Operahuset. (phone: 676-5800 or 111125, main dining room; 676-5800 or 110026, *Café Opera;* 107935, *Operabaren*). Expensive.

Riche – A ritzy up-market place, it features traditional Swedish dishes and nouvelle French cuisine. Closed Sundays. Reservations advised. 4 Birger Jarlsgatan (phone: 236840). Expensive.

Ulriksdals Inn – In the park of Ulriksdals Palace, it features a fine smorgasbord as well as French and international fare. Open daily for lunch and dinner; closes Sundays at 6:30 PM. Reservations necessary. Slottspark, Solna (phone: 850815). Expensive.

Aurora – An intimate hideaway that serves traditional Swedish fare. Closed Sundays. Reservations advised. 11 Munkbron (phone: 219359). Expensive to moderate.

La Brochette – Delightfully and authentically French: All the head chefs are French. The traditional but varied menu offers well-prepared food served in an inviting but constantly crowded dining room. A good selection of wines is available. Closed Sundays. Reservations advised. 27 Storgatan (phone: 662-2000). Expensive to moderate.

Clas på Hörnet – Delicious Swedish and international fare is served in the formal dining room of this 18th-century hostelry in the center of town. There also is a separate informal eatery, *Skänkrummet,* which offers a limited but good menu of traditional Swedish dishes at very reasonable prices. Both open daily. Reservations necessary in the formal dining room; no reservations at *Skänkrummet.* 20 Surbrunnsgatan (phone: 165130). Expensive to moderate.

Finsmakaren – A modest little place 15 minutes by taxi from downtown. The fine food and friendly service draw praise from all quarters. Closed weekends and July. Reservations advised. 9 Råsundavägen, Solna (phone: 276771). Expensive to moderate.

Latona – Swedish specialties in a medieval setting. Open daily. Reservations advised. 79 Västerlånggatan (phone: 113260). Expensive to moderate.

Martini – Centrally located, this fashionable dining room serves continental cuisine. Open daily. Reservations advised. 4 Norrmalmstorg (phone: 200420). Expensive to moderate.

Nils Emil's – The elegant decor and small size of this congenial spot conspire with the superb food to make dining here an intoxicatingly intimate experience. Closed Sundays and from late June to mid-August. Reservations necessary. 122 Folkungagatan (phone: 407209). Expensive to moderate.

Stortorgskällaren – Near the Royal Palace. Traditional Swedish dishes; verandah dining in summertime. Open daily. Reservations advised. 7 Stortorget (phone: 105533). Expensive to moderate.

Wärdshuset Godthem – A 100-year-old inn in the Djurgården. A good, varied menu, a pleasant view across the bay, intoxicating atmosphere, and a welcoming staff make this more a journey into 19th-century hospitality than just dining out. Open daily. Reservations necessary. 9 Rosendalsvägen (phone: 661-0722). Expensive to moderate.

Capri – One of the best of the wave of pizzerias that swept to popularity in Stockholm during the '70s. A mock grotto interior contrasts with the genuine Italian cooking; friendly and informal. Open daily. Reservations advised. 15 Nybrogatan (phone: 662-3132). Moderate.

La Famiglia – The name tells you that this neighborhood eatery is run by a family of Italians. Well-prepared pasta dishes are served in a friendly atmosphere. Open daily for dinner. Reservations necessary. 45 Alströmergatan (phone: 506310). Moderate.

De Fyras Krog – Four intimate dining rooms, each furnished in a different style reflecting various lifestyles of the past. Food is wholesome, traditional Swedish fare. Open daily for dinner. Reservations advised. 22 Tavastgatan (phone: 586405). Moderate.

Gässlingen – Somewhat off the main tourist beat, but worth the detour if you want to eat well and mingle with the locals — without denting a modest travel budget. Small, with a homey interior and a varied French and Swedish menu with a broad price range. Closed Sundays. Reservations advised. 93 Brännkyrkagatan (phone: 669-5495). Moderate to inexpensive.

Coco and Carmen – This lunch spot opened on the former premises of a bakery whose original ovens are preserved as a curiosity. The very tasteful interior has authentic 1920s furnishings. Serving reasonably priced light dishes such as cheese pie, toast *skagen,* soups, salads, and herring, it caters to a very genteel public but leans more toward friendliness than stuffiness. Closed weekends. Reservations advised. 7 Banergatan (phone: 660-9954). Inexpensive.

Restaurants of the Old Town – There are several cellar restaurants in the narrow lanes of the Old Town in centuries-old vaults, where every nook and cranny seem to have a story of its own. The proprietors are, for the most part, lively individuals whose feeling for haute cuisine is equaled only by their love of the Old Town and its medieval history. The food is excellent and the menus normally include delicacies from the traditional Swedish kitchen, perhaps raw spiced salmon or snow grouse.

Which one is best? Everyone has a favorite, but here are our two: *Diana* – Unconventional, mixed clientele. Closed Sundays. Reservations advised (2 Brunnsgränd; phone: 107310). Expensive to moderate. *Fem Små Hus* – Five interconnected buildings form a honeycomb of vaults, arches, and alcoves. Ideal setting for intimate dining. Open daily. Reservations advised (10 Nygränd; phone: 100482). Expensive to moderate.

VENICE

Venice is one of the world's most photic — and photographic — cities. As the sun sets, it burnishes the old buildings with a splendid, rosy glow that is reflected, then refracted, in the waters of the canals. The city is luminously beautiful, both in radiant, peak-season August and in bleak, wet November. And it is painfully beautiful when suddenly, on some late-winter morning, the rain trickles to a halt, the cloud curtains part, and trapezoids of sunlight reheat the ancient stones. Then there is an ineffable sense of renewal as the café tables are set up again in Piazza San Marco, and pigeons and waiters alike swoop out from the dark arcades while an orchestra begins another airy melody. Little wonder that, long before photography, Romantic painting flourished here.

Venice is 117 islets separated by 177 canals and joined by 400 bridges on Italy's northeastern Adriatic coast. A 3-mile bridge reaches across the Laguna Veneta (Venetian Lagoon), connecting it to the mainland near the small town of Mestre. The city is protected from the force of the Adriatic Sea by the natural breakwater of the Lido, a long, narrow sandbar that is one of the most fashionable resorts on the Adriatic.

The lagoon city began as a place of refuge from the violent barbarian invasions of the 5th century; mainland inhabitants fled to the isolated islands. As communities grew up, the islands became connected to one another, and Venice developed into a powerful, flourishing city-state. During the Crusades, this little maritime republic came to dominate the entire Mediterranean, and the winged Venetian lion, symbol of St. Mark, the city's protector, stood guard over a network of palaces from the Strait of Gibraltar to the Bosporus. This was the city of Marco Polo.

Renaissance Venice was the focal point for the great trade routes from the Middle East, and the markets beside the city's Ponte di Rialto (Rialto Bridge) were a pulse of European commerce. The doges — the city's rulers — celebrated their mastery of the Mediterranean with an annual ceremony of marriage to the sea, and the golden ducats that overflowed the city's coffers financed some of the world's most spectacular art and architecture. The Venetian school of painting, which produced magnificent colorists, began with Giorgione and achieved its apogee in the 16th century with Titian Vecellio, Paolo Veronese, and Jacopo Tintoretto. The proud, 1,000-year Venetian independence (La Serenissima) ended with the Treaty of Campoformio in 1797, when Napoleon traded the territory to Austria. In 1866, after nearly 70 years of Bonaparte and Hapsburg domination, the city was joined to newly unified Italy.

Today, Venice proper has a population of nearly 122,000 — 316,000 including the metropolitan area — which is steadily decreasing due to the city's extraordinarily high cost of living. The millions of tourists who swarm through its narrow streets and tiny squares make up Venice's chief industry — and they leave behind well over $100 million a year. A gaudy party atmosphere reigns from *Easter* to October, with a midsummer explosion sometimes as crass as it is colorful: the landing stages jammed and listing with tour groups, long lines waiting for frozen custard beside the Doge's Palace, and the big Lido ferries packed with sun-scorched day-trippers. Hawkers and hustlers populate every corner. (In 1990, after both national and international cries of outrage, Venice took itself out of the running as the site of *Expo 2000,* a proposed world's fair at the turn of the century that's expected to attract as many as 45 million visitors during a 4-month period!) In its way the scene is as vibrant, insistent, chaotic, and vulgar as anything from the days of the international market on the Ponte di Rialto.

And yet, even on *Ferragosto* weekend, Italy's state holiday in mid-August, it's still possible to turn deliberately from the main thoroughfare and string together a few random rights and lefts to find yourself in a haven of quiet back alleys, on a tiny bridge across a deserted canal, in the middle of a silent, sunbaked *campo,* with a fruit stall — and not a tourist in sight.

Venice in winter is a totally different experience: placid, gray, and startlingly visual. Suddenly, there is no one between you and the noble palaces, the soaring churches, the dark canals. Only the mysterious masked merriment of *Carnevale* (a month-long celebration, ending March 3 this year) interrupts the chilly repose of the time when Venice is most emphatically a community of Venetians.

Not everyone loves Venice. D. H. Lawrence called it "an abhorrent, green, slippery city," and it does have a dark, decadent quality, sometimes a damp depressiveness. (An inscription on a sundial says, "I count only the happy hours.") But few cities have attracted so many illustrious admirers. Shakespeare set one of his best-known plays, *The Merchant of Venice,* here. Galileo Galilei used the bell tower in Piazza San Marco to test his telescope. Richard Wagner composed here. Lord Byron and Henry James wrote here. It's not hard to feel the ghosts of these and others who, as James said, "have seemed to find [here] something that no other place could give."

VENICE AT-A-GLANCE

SEEING THE CITY: The traditional vantage point from which to admire Venice is the summit of the 324-foot red campanile (bell tower) in Piazza San Marco. The view on all sides is breathtaking — from the red-shingled rooftops and countless domes of the city to the distant islands that dot the wide lagoon. There's an elevator to the top or, for the heartier, a ramp. Open daily. Admission charge.

For a bird's-eye view of Piazza San Marco itself (and the rest of the lagoon city), take a short boat ride to the Isola San Giorgio (No. 5 ferryboat from the Riva degli Schiavoni — one stop) and ride the elevator to the top of the church tower. The church

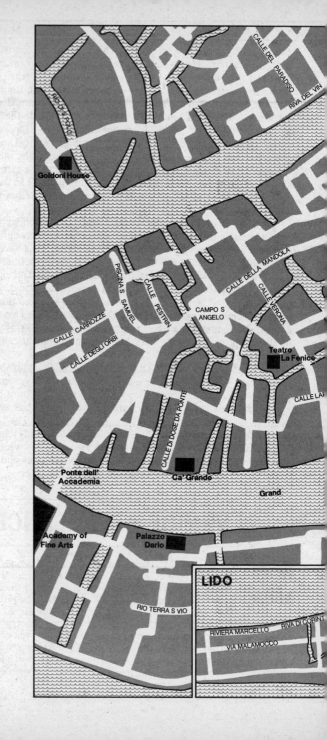

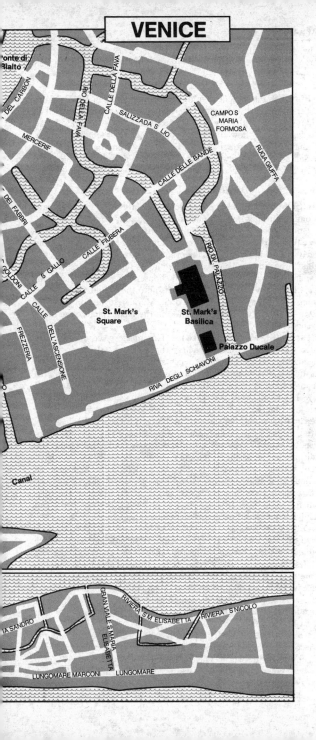

itself, a masterpiece by Andrea Palladio, contains two major works by Tintoretto. It also has beautiful carved wooden choir stalls depicting the life of St. Benedict. Open daily. Admission charge.

SPECIAL PLACES: Piazza San Marco is the center of life in Venice; from here sightseers can board steamers to the Lido and other islands as well as to the various quarters of the city. The Corso della Gente — a phrase Venetians use to describe the "flow of people" — is, in fact, the route that roughly parallels the Grand Canal, snaking through the heart of the city from the bridge (Ponte degli Scalzi) near the Santa Lucia railway station to Piazza San Marco and from there to the *Accademia.* You can follow it instinctively without once asking for directions.

DOWNTOWN

Piazza San Marco (St. Mark's Square) – Napoleon called this huge marble square the finest drawing room in Europe. Bells chime, flocks of pigeons crisscross the sky, violins play, couples embrace in the sunset — while the visitor takes it all in from a congenial café. A mere turn of the head allows you to admire St. Mark's Basilica, the Doge's Palace, the early 20th-century copy of the original 9th-century bell tower, the clock tower where giant bronze Moors have struck the hours for 5 centuries, the old administration offices, and the old library, which now houses the archaeological museum. In the *piazzetta,* through which the square opens onto the Grand Canal, there are two granite columns — one topped by the Lion of St. Mark (returned on April 25, 1991 — *St. Mark's Day* — after 6 years of restoration in the Netherlands), the other by a statue of St. Theodore.

Basilica di San Marco (St. Mark's Basilica) – This masterpiece of Venetian-Byzantine architecture was built in 830 to shelter the tomb of St. Mark, whose bones had been smuggled out of Alexandria. When first built, it was not a cathedral but a chapel for the doges. The present basilica was constructed during the 11th century, but the phenomenal decoration of the interior and exterior continued well into the 16th century. The basilica has a large dome and four smaller ones; its imposing façade of variegated marble and sculpture has five large doorways. The four famous bronze horses that have adorned the central doorway since 1207, when they were brought here after the sack of Constantinople, were removed in 1980 for restoration. Bronze replicas have taken their place in the doorway, and the originals are now on permanent display in the basilica's museum. Inside, the walls are encrusted with precious art, rare marbles, and magnificent mosaics. Behind the high altar in the chancel is the famous gold altarpiece, the *Pala d'Oro,* and the basilica's treasury includes rare relics as well as Byzantine goldwork and enamels. Much of the treasury has been on tour for some time. It is expected to be back in Venice at the end of this year. Open daily. Admission charge for the chancel and treasury. *Vaporetto* stop San Marco. Piazza San Marco.

Palazzo Ducale (Doge's Palace) – Next to the basilica is the pink and white palace with an unusual double loggia that served as the residence of the doges and the seat of government. The finest room in the palace is the Grand Council Chamber, containing paintings by Tintoretto and Veronese. You may also visit the doge's apartments and the armory. The palace is connected to the old prisons by the famous Ponte dei Sospiri (Bridge of Sighs), whose name comes from the lamentations of prisoners supposedly taken across the bridge to be executed. Open daily. Admission charge. *Vaporetto* stop San Marco. Piazza San Marco (phone: 522-4951).

Grand Canal – Lined with some 200 marble palaces built between the 12th and the 18th century, the occasionally drought-plagued Grand Canal has been called the finest street with the finest houses in the world. On the right (east bank) are the *Palazzo Vendramin-Calergi,* where Wagner died, now the winter home of the *Municipal Casino;*

the Ca' d'Oro (Golden House), so called because its ornate façade once was entirely gilded; the Palazzo Mocenigo, where Lord Byron lived; and *Palazzo Grassi,* an art museum bought and refurbished by the Agnelli family of Fiat fame. On the left (west bank) are the *Palazzo Pesaro,* which houses the modern art gallery, and the Ca' Rezzonico, an architectural jewel that contains the civic museum of 18th-century art. A good way to see all of these beautiful palazzi is to take a slow boat ride over the entire 2-mile length of the Grand Canal with the No. 1 line.

Chiesa di Santa Maria della Salute – Dedicated to the Madonna for delivering Venice from a plague, this 17th-century baroque church is just across the Grand Canal from Piazza San Marco. Its octagonal shape and white Istrian limestone façade are easily recognizable in innumerable paintings of Venetian scenes and panoramas. Inside are paintings of the New Testament by Titian and Tintoretto. *Vaporetto* stop Salute. Campo della Salute, Dorsoduro.

Chiesa del Redentore (Church of the Redeemer) – Also built to thank the Madonna for rescuing the Venetians from an earlier plague, and a must for architectural enthusiasts, this 16th-century church is known for its perfect proportions and remarkable harmony both inside and out. It was constructed by Andrea Palladio on a point of the Giudecca Island, a short ferry ride (take a No. 5) from St. Mark's by way of Isola San Giorgio. The yearly *Feast of the Redeemer* (the third Sunday in July; see *Special Events*) used to be attended by the doge, who reached the church across a bridge of boats. Open daily. *Vaporetto* stop Redentore. Campo Redentore. Isola della Giudecca, Dorsoduro.

Galleria dell'Accademia (Gallery of Fine Arts) – Brief but frequent visits are the best way to savor the rich contents of this great art gallery. Of particular interest are Veronese's *Supper in the House of Levi,* Titian's *Presentation of the Virgin,* Tintoretto's *Transport of the Body of St. Mark,* and Giorgione's *Tempesta.* The paintings of Venice by Antonio Canaletto, Francesco Guardi, and Gentile Bellini are the academy's most Venetian selections, both by subject and artist, and meld all impressions of the city. Open daily. Admission charge. *Vaporetto* stop Accademia. Campo della Carità, Dorsoduro (phone: 522-2247).

Museo del Settecento Veneziano (Museum of Eighteenth-Century Venice) – Built in the 17th century, Ca' Rezzonico — the palace that has housed the museum since 1936 — has a magnificent exterior that is best observed from the Grand Canal (in turn, its windows afford superb views of the canal). A splendid backdrop for some of the most sumptuous treasures of 18th-century Venetian art, the palace itself is known for its grandiose decor and its frescoes by Giandomenico Tiepolo and his son Giambattista. Closed Fridays. Admission charge. *Vaporetto* stop Rezzonico. Ca' Rezzonico, Dorsoduro (phone: 522-4543).

Scuola Grande di San Rocco (Great School of San Rocco) – The Venetian *scuola* was not a school, but something of a cross between a trade guild and a religious brotherhood that did works of charity and supplied wealthy patronage for the arts. San Rocco contains a rich collection of Tintorettos — some 56 canvases depicting stories from the Old and New Testaments. Open daily. Admission charge. *Vaporetto* stop San Tomà. Campo San Rocco, San Polo (phone: 523-4864).

Chiesa di Santa Maria Gloriosa dei Frari (St. Mary's Church) – Known simply as *Frari,* this Gothic Franciscan church is considered by many to be the most splendid in Venice after St. Mark's. It contains three unquestioned masterpieces: the *Assumption* and the *Madonna of Ca' Pesaro,* both by Titian, and Giovanni Bellini's triptych on the sacristy altar. An excellent way to appreciate its beauty is to attend an early morning mass before the tourists come. Open daily. Next to the *Scuola Grande di San Rocco. Vaporetto* stop San Tomà. Campo dei Frari, San Polo.

Chiesa di Santa Maria del Carmelo (Church of Our Lady of Mount Carmel) – Also known as the Chiesa dei Carmini (Church of the Carmelites), this 14th-century

Gothic church with a 17th-century campanile — crowned by a statue of the Virgin — still has original gilded wooden ornamentation in its nave. Also worthy of attention are the church walls, which are lined with many 17th- and 18th-century paintings. The cloister adjacent to the church (see the next entry) now belongs to the State Institute of Art. Open daily. *Vaporetto* stop Rezzonico. Campo Santa Margherita, Dorsoduro.

Scuola Grande dei Carmini (Great School of the Carmelites) – Next to the Carmelite church, this gracious 17th-century palace contains the most extensive collection of works by Giambattista Tiepolo anywhere in Venice. Paintings and frescoes adorn the interior. Closed Sundays. Admission charge. *Vaporetto* stop Rezzonico. Campo Santa Margherita, Dorsoduro.

Scuola San Giorgio degli Schiavoni (School of St. George of the Slavonians) – This small building, beyond Piazza San Marco in a part of the city most visitors do not tour, contains one of the city's most overlooked treasures: the frieze of paintings by Vittore Carpaccio depicting stories of St. George, St. Jerome, and St. Tryphon. Closed Mondays. Admission charge. *Vaporetto* stop San Zaccaria. Calle dei Furlani, Castello.

Jewish Ghetto – Venice's ghetto — the world's first — gave its name to all other confined Jewish communities. The word comes from *geto,* which in the Venetian dialect means foundry. Prior to 1516, when Venice's Jewish population was forced to move to an abandoned arsenal on a small, naturally isolated island in the *sestiere* of Cannaregio, they had lived predominantly on the island of Giudecca, "Island of the Jews." The 700 Jews who moved to the Ghetto Nuovo (New Ghetto) grew to 5,000 within a century. In 1541, an adjoining area, the Ghetto Vecchio (Old Ghetto) was annexed, followed by the Ghetto Nuovissimo (Newest Ghetto) in 1633. All three areas are characterized by "skyscrapers" — 7 stories high — that utilize the limited space. It was not until Napoleon arrived in 1797 that Venice's Jews were declared free citizens and allowed to live where they pleased. Five synagogues in the ghetto (the oldest is the German Synagogue — built in 1528 — and home of the *Museo Ebraico* — Jewish Museum) still stand in the three ghettos, where a small number of Jewish families continue to live. Take *vaporetto* No. 1 to San Marcuola. It's a 5-minute walk northeast from the train station.

ENVIRONS

Lido – For most of the 20th century, this shoestring island — across the lagoon from Venice proper — has been one of the world's most extravagant resorts. Indeed, the word *lido* has come to mean, in much of the world's lexicon, any fashionable, luxuriously equipped beach resort. There has always been a touch of decadence to the Venetian Lido with its elegant rambling hotels, sumptuous villas, swank casino, and world-weary, wealthy clientele. Thomas Mann used the Lido's posh *Grand Hotel des Bains* (see *Checking In*) as a background for his haunting novella *Death in Venice.* Today, hundreds of cabins and cabanas line the Lido's fine sandy beaches, and purists assert that the old resort has lost much of its glamour. But the tourists still come by the thousands — some drawn by the tinsel of an international film festival, others by the trendiness of a pop music celebration, but most lured by the legendary Lido ambience. There are buses on the island, which can be reached by frequent boat service from several different stops, including Riva degli Schiavoni (lines Nos. 1, 2, 6, and 34). There also is a car ferry (*tronchetto* No. 17) from Piazzale Roma.

Murano – This island has been the home of Venetian glass making since the 13th century. Visitors can watch the glass blowing and molding processes at one of the island factories but should be aware of the high-pressure tactics used to sell the glass. Murano is 15 minutes by the No. 5 or No. 12 *vaporetto* from Fondamenta Nuove.

Burano – The colorful homes, small boats, and nets and tackle of the fishermen who live here add charm to this little island, best known as a center of lace making, still practiced by some island women. Burano is 40 minutes by the No. 12 *vaporetto* from Fondamenta Nuove.

   Torcello – This was one of the most prosperous colonies on the lagoon in the 5th and 6th centuries, but as Venice grew, Torcello declined. The main square is overgrown with grass. Most of the cathedral, as it appears today, dates from the 7th to 13th centuries. It has several fine Byzantine mosaics, an interesting iconostasis, and a couple of noteworthy restaurants (see *Eating Out*). The island is 45 minutes by the No. 12 *vaporetto* from Fondamenta Nuove.

■**EXTRA SPECIAL:** West of Venice the so-called Brenta Riviera was where many wealthy Venetian merchants built luxury summer residences in the 16th century, many designed by Andrea Palladio or Andrea Sansovino. During the 17th and 18th centuries a luxurious barge, *Il Burchiello,* made a daily trip along the lazy Brenta, which links Venice and Padua. Today's tourist can enjoy the same cruise, from April through October, by motorized boat from Pontile Giardinetto near Piazza San Marco. The excursion, which includes lunch in Oriago and a bus return from Padua, takes a full day. The boat leaves from Venice to Padua on Tuesdays, Thursdays, and Saturdays, and it returns from Padua to Venice on Sundays, Wednesdays, and Fridays. Apply at *Compagnia Italiana Turismo* (*CIT*), open year-round (48 Piazza San Marco; phone: 528-5480), for information. (It also is possible to tour the area by car on a road that roughly parallels the canal.)

   South of Venice is the seaside town of Chioggia, once a major stronghold of the Venetian Republic. Now little more than a fishing port, it retains tantalizing traces of its past glory. The 13th-century Church of San Domenico displays works by Carpaccio and Tintoretto; the highly decorated baroque altar contrasts with its simpler surroundings. There are numerous other small churches in Chioggia, some in a poor state of repair, but all with significant works of Venetian art. The Duomo, or cathedral and bishopric, which stands at the end of Corso del Popolo, is a grandiose 17th-century building reconstructed on the ruins of the original 12th-century church. Inside are paintings that recount some of the history and sacred legends of Chioggia. Around the corner is the celebrated Piazza Vescovile. Bordered by plane trees and an ornamented balustrade, it has been a favorite subject for painters through the ages. Chioggia can be reached by boat, passing several other lagoon islands on the way, or by bus from the Piazzale Roma bus station. On the waterfront is *El Gato,* an excellent, inexpensive restaurant which specializes in local fish from the Adriatic Sea, served with fresh salads and local wines.

SOURCES AND RESOURCES

TOURIST INFORMATION: Stop in at the Azienda di Promozione Turistica in the southwest corner of Piazza San Marco (APT; 71/C Ascensione; phone: 522-6356) or the APT office at Santa Lucia train station (phone: 719078) for maps, and listings of hotels, museum hours, and special events. The Assessorato al Turismo (nearby in the Ca' Giustinian; phone: 522-4842) has information about the city's cultural events. The *Biennale* organization also is housed here. The *Associazione Guide Turistiche* (5267 Calle delle Bande, Castello; phone: 529-8730) has a list of multilingual tour guides whose fixed rates are approved by the local tourist board (about $90 for 3 hours, maximum 20 people). For information about winter activities, particularly cultural events, contact *Promove* (Corte del Teatro San Moisè, San Marco; phone: 521-0200).

The nearest US Consulate is in Milan, at 2-10 Piazza Amedeo (phone: 2-900-1841).

Local Coverage – The weekly *Un Ospite a Venezia* (A Guest in Venice) is a useful multilingual booklet published weekly and available at newsstands and hotels; it lists up-to-date museum schedules, special events, entertainment programs, and other activities. The glossy magazine *Marco Polo* covers all special events and cultural issues. Published monthly in Italian and English, it is available at newsstands and most hotels. *The Companion Guide to Venice* by Hugh Honour (London: Collins; $29.50) is a sensitive, well-written guide to the city; it is available in many bookstores.

TELEPHONE: The country code for Italy is 39; the city code for Venice is 41. When calling from within Italy, dial 041 before the local number.

GETTING AROUND: Losing yourself in Venice is inevitable — and recommended. However, major confusion can be avoided by knowing a few facts. Since 1711, Venice has been divided into six *sestieri* or wards, namely San Marco, Castello, Canareggio, San Polo, Dorsoduro, and Santa Croce. "Downtown" Venice — the largest of the six — is San Marco. The *sestieri* are used as points of reference and are part of a location's address. All locations have two: One is the official mailing address and the other is a specific street address. A store's mailing address, for instance, could be 2250 San Marco, while its street address is 2250 Calle dei Fuseri.

There are no cars in Venice. After crossing the Ponte della Libertà, visitors leave their cars in the lots and garages at Piazzale Roma. *Note:* don't leave anything in your car; even though there are attendants and a "security patrol" at the *piazzale,* things have been known to disappear. An even better idea for those arriving by car — to avoid the terrible congestion of the high season — is to park in mainland Mestre and catch the train to Venice, a journey of only 10 minutes or so. An added advantage of this strategy is that the sight of Venice has a far greater impact when one steps out of the train terminal into the midst of the city's beauty.

Airport – Marco Polo Airport (phone: 661111) serves both domestic and international flights. It is 8 miles (13 km) from the city and is reachable by *motoscafo* (motorboat) service, which leaves from the airport or Piazza San Marco and costs about $11 per person. A motorboat taxi (*taxi acquei*) for up to four people is about $60, including bags. *ATVO* bus No. 5 from the parking area of Piazzale Roma (across the Grand Canal from the Santa Lucia train station) costs about $4 per person. Ask for time schedules at Compagnia Italiana Turismo (CIT), Piazza San Marco, or at the tourist office in Piazzale Roma. Also consult the weekly booklet *Un Ospite a Venezia* (A Guest in Venice), available at newsstands and hotels.

Bus and Train – The bus station (phone: 528-7886) is at Piazzale Roma; the train station, Stazione Santa Lucia (phone: 715555), is on the Grand Canal not far from the bus station.

Gondola – A 50-minute tour of the city in one of these sleek, black boats will cost you as much as $60 (although five people can fit in each) and the price rises to $75 if you take one after 8 PM. Each additional 25 minutes will increase the bill by $30. Unless you give the gondolier specific directions, he will determine the route and may or may not play tour guide (at no extra cost). Sing, he won't. If you're looking for those romantic *barcaroli* you saw in Katherine Hepburn's *Summertime,* you'll have to sign up with *CIT* (48 Piazza San Marco; phone: 528-5480) or make arrangements through your hotel for a nighttime "Gondola Serenade" (about $25 per person). Depending on the request, a number of gondolas (from two to ten) will travel together, sharing the accordion music and Italian songs of an accompanying duo. It won't be intimate, but it will be fun. A less costly alternative is the gondola-ferry, called a *traghetto,* that crosses the Grand Canal at seven points for a bargain 50¢. The ride only lasts a minute, but it can be exciting as the drivers dodge *vaporetti* and *taxi acquei.*

Motoscafi and Vaporetti – The little steamers that make up the municipal transit system are inexpensive and fun. The *motoscafi* are express boats, making only a few important stops. The *vaporetti* are much slower; No. 1 chugs leisurely along the whole length of the Grand Canal, and No. 5 meanders for more than an hour through interesting parts of the city. Tickets cost between $1.50 and $2.50. If you're in a rush to get to the station or elsewhere, you can ask your hotel to call a *taxi acquei.* Although they're almost as expensive as gondolas, they're faster (phone: 522-2303). There is a movement afoot by environmentalists to replace them all with electric boats (sob!).

LOCAL SERVICES: Dentist (English-Speaking) – Dr. Pietro Ambrosini, Calle Bembo, San Marco (phone: 528-7736).

   Dry Cleaner/Tailor – *Centro Pulisecco,* 6262/D Calle della Testa, Cannaregio (phone: 522-5011).

Limousine Service – *International Rent-a-Car* (468/B Piazzale Roma; phone: 522-1159; fax: 520-8396); *Avis* (4964 Piazzale Roma; phone: 522-5825).

Medical Emergency – Ambulance service for *Ospedali Civili Riuniti* (phone: 523-0000). An English-speaking physician is Dr. Salvatore Saccardo (Calle Ostreghe, San Marco; phone: 522-1370).

Messenger Service – *Agenzia Espressi* (Ponte dell'Olio, San Marco; phone: 522-3719); *Nuova Serenissima* (496 Piazzale Roma; phone: 523-5415).

National/International Courier – *DHL International* (111 Via Torino, in Mestre; phone: 531-2666) will arrange hotel pickup.

Office Equipment Rental – *ENDAR* (*Centro Congressi,* Via Castello, Castello; phone: 523-8440); *Venezia Congressi* (1056 Accademia Dorsoduro, San Marco; phone: 522-8400) rents audiovisual equipment as well as other office equipment, and can help arrange meetings and conferences.

Pharmacy – Pharmacies take turns for 24-hour service; every week at least six stay open all night. Each pharmacy posts a list; dial 192 to find out which ones are on duty.

Photocopies – *Graphoprint* (Fondamenta Tolentini, Santa Croce; phone: 528-7035); *Christian Micoud* (Campo de San Luca, San Marco; phone: 528-9275).

Post Office – *PTT* (Rialto, Fontego dei Tedeschi; phone: 528-6212), open from 8:30 AM to 7 PM Mondays through Saturdays. More centrally located, though with shorter hours, is *PTT* (Calle Larga de l'Ascension, just off St. Mark's Square), open 8:10 AM to 1:40 PM weekdays, and from 8:10 AM to noon on Saturdays.

Secretary/Stenographer (English-Speaking) – *ENDAR* (*Centro Congressi,* Via Castello, Castello; phone: 523-8440); *Venezia Congressi* (1056 Accademia Dorsoduro, San Marco; phone: 522-8400).

Telex/Facsimile Transmissions – *PTT* (Rialto, Fontego dei Tedeschi; phone: 528-62320), open 24 hours daily.

Translator – *ENDAR* (*Centro Congressi,* Via Castello, Castello; phone: 523-8440); *Venezia Congressi* (1056 Accademia Dorsoduro, San Marco; phone: 522-8400); *TER* (3640/A Castello; phone: 528-9879).

Other – Formal wear and *Carnevale* costume rental: *Il Baule (di Pertini e Roditi),* Calle Lion, Castello (phone: 528-7788).

SPECIAL EVENTS: Starting about a month before *Ash Wednesday* (March 4, 1992), Venetians celebrate *Carnevale,* a pre-*Lenten* fete that includes outdoor masked balls, 24-hour street theater, and pop music. Every 4 years in June, the city hosts the *Regata Storica delle Repubbliche Mari-*

nare, the race and procession of historic boats and costumes that hark back to the 11th century when Venice was one of the ancient maritime republics (the others were Amalfi, Genoa, and Pisa). This year is Venice's turn, although there also will be a regatta in Genoa to commemorate the 500th anniversary of Columbus's discovery of America. On the night between the third Saturday and Sunday in July, illuminated gondolas glide along the canals while musicians play from barges on the lagoon and fireworks paint the sky. This is the *Festa del Redentore* (Feast of the Redeemer), one of the most special celebrations of the year in Venice. That Sunday, a "bridge" of boats from Dorsoduro to the Chiesa del Redentore commemorates the end of the 1576 epidemic. On the first Sunday in September, gondola races and a procession of decorated barges filled with Venetians in Renaissance dress highlight the *Regata Storica* (Historic Regatta) on the Grand Canal. The annual *International Film Festival* is held on the Lido in late August and early September, and in even-numbered years the important *Esposizione Internazionale d'Arte Moderna* (International Exposition of Modern Art), better known as *Biennale d'Arte,* takes place in a small park beyond the Riva dei Sette Martiri from June through October. Every September, there is a marathon that starts along the Veneto's Brenta Canal and follows the tow paths into and through the center of Venice, ending at the Basilica San Marco. To celebrate the *Festa della Salute* on November 21, another "bridge" of boats is formed from Santa Maria del Giglio to the Chiesa di Santa Maria della Salute.

MUSEUMS: Besides those mentioned in *Special Places,* Venice has a number of museums of special interest. The days and hours vary with the season. Check with the APT in Piazza San Marco (phone: 522-6356) for current schedules or look in *Un Ospite a Venezia.*

Civico Museo Correr (Correr Civic Museum) – A collection of historical curios from the Venetian Republic. Also, a picture gallery with works from the 13th to the 18th century, along with prints, sketches, and ceramics. Admission charge. *Vaporetto* stop San Marco. Piazza San Marco (phone: 522-5625).

Galleria Giorgio Franchetti (Franchetti Gallery) – Bronze sculpture from the 12th through the 16th century as well as an important collection of Renaissance paintings from Venice and Tuscany. Admission charge. *Vaporetto* stop Ca' d'Oro. Ca' D'Oro, 3932 Grand Canal, Cannareggio (phone: 523-8790).

Museo Archeologico (Archaeological Museum) – Recently reopened after extensive renovation, this museum houses ancient Greek and Roman statues, Greek and Etruscan vases, Egyptian and Assyrian jewels and antiques. Admission charge. *Vaporetto* stop San Marco. Piazza San Marco (phone: 522-5978).

Museo Ebraico (Jewish Museum) – A visit to the Jewish Ghetto is incomplete without time spent at this small museum that houses a collection of memorabilia from the ghetto's origins. The museum also organizes tours of the museum itself as well as to a number of the ghetto's synagogues otherwise closed to the public. Admission charge. *Vaporetto* stop Ponte delle Guglie or San Marcuola. 2902 Campo del Ghetto Nuovo, Cannaregio (phone: 715359).

Museo Fortuny (Fortuny Museum) – The sketches, pleated silk fabrics, and personal belongings of the Spanish-born material master Mariano Fortuny, who made this 15th-century Gothic palazzo his home for 42 years. Admission charge. *Vaporetto* stop Sant'Angelo. 3780 Campo San Benedetto, San Marco (phone: 520-0995).

Museo Guggenheim (Guggenheim Museum) – The private modern art collection of Peggy Guggenheim, including works from the cubist, abstract, surrealist, and expressionist movements. Artists represented include Picasso, Braque, Max Ernst (one of Peggy's husbands), and Jackson Pollock (her discovery). Admission charge. *Vaporetto* stop Accademia. Palazzo Venier dei Leoni, 701 Calle Cristoforo, Dorsoduro (phone: 520-6288).

Palazzo Grassi (also called Palazzo Fiat) – Splendidly restored, it's the site of important artistic expositions of international themes. Admission charge. *Vaporetto* stop San Samuele. 3231 Campo San Samuele, San Marco (phone: 523-1680).

 SHOPPING: Venetian glass is a seductive item, but most of it made today is of poor quality and design. Do a bit of comparison shopping first, and if you can, visit the museum and factories on Murano (see *Special Places*). With a keen eye to cut through the trinkets, you'll find winning souvenirs — from inexpensive necklaces of colorful Venetian glass beads to a simple, handsome decanter or perfume flacon. Other items worth purchasing are the traditional hand-made papier-mâché *Carnevale* masks, which have been enjoying a renaissance since the fete was reinstated in 1980. Almost all souvenir shops carry a sampling — from the authentic and historical to the modern and bizarre. Handmade lace can be exorbitantly expensive, but some of the smaller and simpler pieces can be charming and affordable. The widest selection can be found on Burano and in the shops around Piazza San Marco. In addition, marbleized paper products make lovely and easily transportable gifts.

Two of the city's most colorful outdoor food markets — the *Erberia* for produce and the *Pescheria* for fish — are near the Ponte di Rialto (Rialto Bridge). It is fascinating to wander here, even if you aren't shopping. During the Middle Ages, this area was the Wall Street of Europe, since Venice was queen of the seas and, therefore, queen of trade. In those days, spices, silver, and silks from the overland Eastern trade route all were sold here, and banks surrounded the area. Now it is more the staples of life that are sold from the small stalls — fruits and vegetables, coffee and cheeses, fresh game and seafood. The sounds and smells are pure Venice.

Venice's main shopping district is the area directly surrounding and west of Piazza San Marco or in the adjacent Mercerie to the north. While most shops are open in the mornings from 9 AM to 1 PM, they close for a long lunch, reopen around 3:30 PM, and remain open until 7 or 7:30. Most Venetian merchants accept major American credit cards.

Barozzi – Antique furniture, mainly 18th-century Venetian. One of the best in town. 2052 Calle delle Veste, San Marco (phone: 528-9615).

Domini – Fine silverware and china. 659-664 Calle Larga San Marco, San Marco (phone: 522-3892).

Al Duca d'Aosta – Sports clothes and accessories for men; women's wear is available across the street. 4946 Mercerie del Capitello, San Marco (phone: 534-4525).

Elysée – Elegant footwear and designer wear for men and women. 4485 Calle Goldoni, San Marco (phone: 523-6948).

Fendi – Chic clothing and leather goods for women. 1474 Salizzada San Moisè, San Marco (phone: 520-5733).

L'Isola – Contemporary museum-quality glassware designed by the Carlo Moretti firm — pieces are simple and lightweight. Some objects are displayed in the *Museum of Modern Art* in New York City. 1468 Campo San Moise, San Marco (phone: 523-1973).

Jesurum & Co. – Exquisite lace and other handmade needlework. Ponte Canonica, Castello (phone: 706177) and a much smaller selection at its branch in Piazza San Marco.

Libreria Antiquaria La Fenice – Old books and prints. Campo San Fantin and 1850 Piazza San Marco, San Marco (phone: 523-8006).

Luigi Bevilacqua – Silk brocade, damask, and printed velvet fabrics that have draped European courts, the Vatican, and the White House. 1320 Campiello Comare, Santa Croce (phone: 23384).

Mondo Novo – The city's best *mascheraio* (mask maker). Papier-mâché masks — alligators, camels, and mummies — for *Carnevale*. 3063 Campo Santa Margherita, Dorsoduro (phone: 528-7344).

Nardi – Beautiful high-quality jewelry in the Venetian tradition — both new and antique. 69 Piazza San Marco, San Marco (phone: 522-5733).

Paola Carraro – Unique oversize sweaters made of silk, mohair, or cotton that are hand-knit renditions of some of the world's great contemporary masterpieces — from Klee to Picasso, Magritte to Warhol. On the street from the *Accademia* to the *Guggenheim*, Dorsoduro (phone: 520-6070).

Pauly – Venetian glass by one of the star producers. Ponte dei Consorzi, Castello (phone: 529899).

Piazzesi – Notebooks, boxes, albums, and other gift articles crafted from handmade marbleized papers in classic Italian style. 2511 Campiello della Feltrina, San Marco (phone: 522-1202).

Rubelli – A Venetian landmark and one of Europe's most celebrated names in exquisite fabrics, some still made by hand on 15th-century looms. 1089 Campo San Gallo, San Marco (phone: 523-6110).

Salviati – A 100-year-old firm with the highest traditions of craftsmanship in Venetian glass. Largest collection at 195 San Gregorio, Dorsoduro (phone: 522-2523); other stores at 78 Piazza San Marco, San Marco, and the glassworks museum in Murano.

Veneziartigiana – A consortium of 60 local artisans housed in a beautiful wood-paneled building that used to be a pharmacy. 412 Calle Larga San Marco, San Marco (phone: 523-5032).

Venini – The only Venetian retail store for this world-famous glass design company of contemporary hand-blown glass. 314 Piazzetta dei Leoncini, San Marco (phone: 522-4045).

V. Trois – An exclusive representative of luxurious Fortuny fabrics as well as other exquisite new and antique Venetian fabrics. 2666 Campo San Maurizio, San Marco (phone: 522-2905).

 SPORTS AND FITNESS: The visitor to Venice gets plenty of exercise climbing up and down and across its hundreds of bridges. For more organized sports, one must move to the open spaces of the Lido, where the CIGA chain pretty much has the monopoly on sports activities. What they don't own, they manage, and with one phone call or fax, you can book tennis, windsurfing, water skiing, golf, or a beach cabaña. Contact them from April through October at 52 Lungomare Marconi, Lido (phone: 526-7194; fax: 526-0058).

Bicycling – A well-stocked place to rent bikes, including two-, three-, and four-seaters, as well as conventional two-wheelers, is *Giorgio Barbieri,* 5 Via Zara (no phone).

Fitness Center – *Palestra Europ* (6661/V Castello; phone: 520-7475), is the only fitness center in Venice open to visitors.

Golf – The *Golf Club Lido di Venezia* is a championship 18-hole course at the far southern end of the Lido (phone: 526-7194). It's reached by the *C* bus from the main Lido *vaporetto* landing or the No. 11 bus, just a block away.

Jogging – Just east of Piazza San Marco, the Riva degli Schiavoni runs southeast along the water toward the Riva dei Sette Martiri and the Giardini Pubblici (public gardens) — a good 20-minute jog. Runners also may jog on the Lido beach.

Sailing – If you arrive in Venice by boat, you can moor it at one of two marinas. The most picturesque is the *Marina San Giorgio* at the island just across from Piazza

San Marco. Renting a boat in Venice is almost impossible now because there have been too many accidents in the past with tourists at the helm.

Soccer – From September to May, *Venezia* plays at *Stadio Comunale P. L. Penzo,* S. Elena (phone: 522-5770).

Swimming – The northern end of the Lido has municipal beaches, all of which charge admission. Other beaches are the domain of the great luxury hotels of the Lido, but cabañas are available for an entrance fee. There is also a public pool at *Piscina Comunale Sacca Fisola,* Giudecca (phone: 528-5430).

Tennis – On the Lido, the *Tennis Club* (41/D Lungomare Marconi; phone: 526-7194) has 7 courts (2 covered; 2 lighted). Visitors also can play at the *Henkell Club* (Via Malamocco; phone: 526-0122) or the *Tennis Club Lido* (163 Via Sandro Gallo; phone: 526-0954).

THEATER: Music, rather than drama, is the performing art of Venice. If the language is not a problem, a pleasant theater for traditional and contemporary productions is *Teatro Goldoni* (4650/B Calle Goldoni, San Marco; phone: 520-5422). *Teatro Ridotto,* a delightful little rococo theater, hosts dance performances as well as drama. It's just off Piazza San Marco (Calle Vallaresso; phone: 522-2939).

MUSIC: Venice is a city with a rich musical tradition and a full calendar of musical events — as you will see from the wall posters that announce forthcoming concerts. *Teatro La Fenice* (1977 Campo San Fantin; phone: 521-0161), which celebrates its 200th anniversary this year, is the city's main auditorium. A first night at the *Fenice,* site of world premieres of opera classics by such composers as Verdi and Rossini, is a highlight of the social season. Its gold and pink plush interior is pure Venetian; tours are permitted when rehearsals are not in progress. In summer, there are concerts in various churches (where the acoustics are fabulous). If possible, attend a performance by either of the city's stellar chamber music groups: the *Solisti Veneti* or the *Sestetto a Fiati di Venezia* (Venice Wind Sextet). In winter, too, you can attend concerts in churches and in the ornate salons of palaces such as the 17th-century Palazzo Labia (now the Venice office of Italian state radio and television). Many church concerts are free, though contributions are welcome. The Chiesa della Pietà (Church of the Pietà), in the Castello *sestiere* where Vivaldi lived and worked, holds many concerts throughout the year featuring his music. Look for posters advertising these musical events along the main route between the Rialto and St. Mark's and in the weekly *Un Ospite a Venezia.*

NIGHTLIFE: *Martini Scala Piano Bar* (1980 San Marco; phone: 522-4121), is Venice's chicest nightspot and open until 3 AM. It has the same kitchen as *Antico Martini* (see *Eating Out*); the light fare is great and the prices much lower. Next to the *Teatro La Fenice,* which supplies it with a glossy, after-theater crowd, is *Antico Martini* (1983 Campo San Fantin; phone: 522-4121) a pleasant outdoor terrace and good, although very expensive, food. *Linea D'Ombra* is a lively jazz club (Fondamento Zattere, Dorsoduro; phone: 528-5295). As long as the weather holds, the city's best nightlife is the nonstop show in Piazza San Marco. Take up residence in one of the cafés, listen to the schmaltzy orchestra, and watch the world go by. Popular places for rock and disco are the *Acropolis* on the Lido (Lungomare Marconi; phone: 536-0466) and *El Souk Disco* (1056/A Accademia; phone: 520-0371). For gambling enthusiasts, the *Municipal Casino* (at the Lido; phone: 526-0626) is open from April through September — its winter home is the handsome *Palazzo Vendramin-Calergi* (on the Grand Canal; phone: 710211), open from October through March or April. Go for the opulent setting, if not to toss some chips. Both open 4 PM to 3 AM.

BEST IN TOWN

CHECKING IN: Your first decision is whether to stay out at the Lido or right in the center of town. Staying in the city might make your Venetian experience complete — you can look out onto a small picturesque canal or catch a sweeping view of the grand lagoon. But being on the Lido gets you away from the crowds. Be forewarned — Venice has some of Italy's most expensive hotels. Very expensive hotels here will charge $400 and up per night for a double; expensively priced hotels, $250 to $400; those in the moderate category, $150 to $250; inexpensive places, $80 to $150; and very inexpensive ones, $50 to $80. Most moderate hotels tack on a daily supplemental rate for air conditioning (about $15). Many hotels offer significant discounts in winter, and even in July and August.

During peak season (*Christmas* to January 6, around *Carnevale,* March 15 through June, and September and October), finding accommodations in Venice may be a problem. A pleasant solution is to stay in Padua, 20 miles and a 30-minute train ride away (see *Veneto,* DIRECTIONS) or in Ferrara, only slightly farther away (see *Emilia-Romagna,* DIRECTIONS). All telephone numbers are in the 41 city code unless otherwise indicated.

Cipriani – On the serene Isola della Giudecca, this luxurious, charming 3-acre oasis has a beautiful garden surrounding an Olympic-size swimming pool, and stunning views of the nearby Isola San Giorgio. Immaculate but relaxed service and such details as silk Fortuny wallpaper and heavy matching drapes are redolent of other times. Last year 9 private apartments in an exquisite old palazzo next door — each with a private butler — were added to the existing elegant rooms in the main building. All offer very formal, very capable service that's a throwback to a more formally opulent age. A sleek mahogany motorboat whisks guests to and from Piazza San Marco in 5 minutes, 24-hours a day. There is a fine restaurant in an idyllic setting. Open mid-March through mid-November. Business facilities include 24-hour room service, meeting rooms for up to 200, English-speaking concierge, foreign currency exchange, secretarial services in English, audiovisual equipment, photocopiers, computers, cable television news, translation services, and express checkout. *Vaporetto* stop San Marco. 10 Isola della Giudecca, Dorsoduro (phone: 520-7744; in the US, 800-524-2420; fax: 520-3930; telex: 410162). Very expensive.

Danieli – Once the residence of a 14th-century doge, this is one of Venice's largest hotels, with 222 rooms in three adjoining buildings. It is one of CIGA's crown jewels and you'll understand why just by walking into the historic palazzo's Gothic courtyard, now the hotel lobby in the Casa Vecchia. On the right is the Casa Nuova, where rooms are just as opulent but less theatrical, and on the left is the Danielino, which boasts a wonderful terrace restaurant on the top floor with a bird's-eye view of Isola San Giorgio. Service at times, however, can be less than gracious. Business facilities include 24-hour room service, meeting rooms for up to 300, English-speaking concierge, foreign currency exchange, secretarial services in English, audiovisual equipment, photocopiers, computers, cable television news, translation services, and express checkout. *Vaporetto* stop San Zaccaria. 4196 Riva degli Schiavoni, Castello (phone: 522-6480; fax: 520-0208; telex: 410077). Very expensive.

Gritti Palace – There are those — Ernest Hemingway was one, and we are two and three, as well as many crowned heads, film stars, and day dreamers — who would rather stay in this one-of-a-kind CIGA gem than anywhere else in Europe. Once the Renaissance residence of the Venetian doge Andrea Gritti who died here in 1538, it is one of the world's most celebrated hotels — famous for excellent service, a classic dining room (see *Eating Out*), and a beautiful dining terrace overlooking the Grand Canal. It also offers its guests use of the CIGA sports facilities — private beach, tennis, golf, and horseback riding — on the Lido. Exquisite interiors capture quintessential historical Venice at its best. Business facilities include 24-hour room service, meeting rooms for up to 80, English-speaking concierge, foreign currency exchange, secretarial services in English, audiovisual equipment, photocopiers, computers, cable television news, translation services, and express checkout. *Vaporetto* stop Santa Maria del Giglio. 2467 Campo Santa Maria del Giglio, San Marco (phone: 794611; fax: 520-0942; telex: 410125). Very expensive.

Locanda Cipriani – Even Venetians dream of honeymooning here on the peaceful, otherworldly island of Torcello, 40 minutes from Piazza San Marco. Most settle for a memorable meal (see *Eating Out*), for even though the inn's 6 country-style rooms are charmingly simple (so agreed Winston Churchill), obligatory half board makes this a costly escape. You'll never feel so removed from civilization, yet you'll have the luxury of first class dining just downstairs. Opened in 1936 by the man who gave the world *Harry's Bar* and now managed by his daughter and grandson. Closed in winter. *Vaporetto* stop Torcello. 29 Piazza San Fosca, Torcello (phone: 730150; fax: 735433). Very expensive.

Bauer Grünwald and Grand – Visiting royalty often stays in the poshest suites in this Grand Canal hotel, near Piazza San Marco. The hotel's other 200 rooms and junior suites are primarily populated by tour groups. There have been complaints recently about the service, but its roof garden, piano bar, and fine restaurant offer some of the loveliest vantage points from which to admire the city. Business facilities include 24-hour room service, meeting rooms for up to 160, English-speaking concierge, foreign currency exchange, secretarial services in English, audiovisual equipment, photocopiers, cable television news, translation services, and express checkout. *Vaporetto* stop San Marco. 1459 Campo San Moisè, San Marco (phone: 523-1520; fax: 520-7557; telex: 410075). Very expensive to expensive.

Monaco and Grand Canal – The intimate seclusion of this elegant yet homey hotel is just a minute's walk from Piazza San Marco and was constructed from three 18th-century family houses. Its acclaimed restaurant, suitably named *Grand Canal*, has a lovely flowered terrace directly across from the beautiful Chiesa di Santa Maria della Salute. Business facilities include 24-hour room service, meeting rooms for up to 50, English-speaking concierge, foreign currency exchange, secretarial services in English, audiovisual equipment, photocopiers, computers, cable television news, translation services, and express checkout. *Vaporetto* stop San Marco. 1325 Vallaresso, San Marco (phone: 520-0211; fax: 520-0501; telex: 410450). Very expensive to expensive.

Cavalletto e Doge Orseolo – Wonderfully situated two steps from Piazza San Marco, most of the 40 rooms overlook the colorful Bacino Orseolo, a kind of parking lot for gondolas (be sure to ask for one). Originally the home of Doge Orseolo, this completely restored 12th-century palazzo is stately and handsome and has a restaurant. Business facilities include meeting rooms for up to 40, English-speaking concierge, foreign currency exchange, secretarial services in English, audiovisual equipment, photocopiers, computers, translation services, and express checkout. *Vaporetto* stop San Marco. 1107 Bacino Orseolo, San Marco (phone: 520-0955; fax: 523-8184; telex: 410684). Expensive.

Excelsior Palace – This luxurious Old World property, refurbished in an exotic Hispano-Moorish style, established the Lido as a luxury seaside resort for Europe's monied set. Since 1937 it has played a key role in the prestigious *International Film Festival* held across the street. It has its own fine restaurant, private beach, tennis courts, and transportation to CIGA's horseback riding and a golf course off the hotel's property. Open *Easter* through October. Business facilities include 24-hour room service, meeting rooms for up to 600, English-speaking concierge, foreign currency exchange, secretarial services in English, audiovisual equipment, photocopiers, cable television news, translation services, and express checkout. *Vaporetto* stop Lido. 41 Lungomare Marconi, Lido (phone: 526-0201; fax: 526-7276; telex: 4210023). Expensive.

Grand Hotel des Bains – On the Lido, this stately, porticoed, luxurious, and gracefully old-fashioned hotel is where Luchino Visconti filmed much of *Death in Venice*. Its painstaking renovations were completed last year. It has spacious rooms and bathrooms, and is across the road from its private beach and luxurious cabañas. Part of the CIGA chain, it shares tennis, golf, and horseback riding facilities with the *Excelsior* down the road. Open *Easter* through October. Business facilities include meeting rooms for up to 400, English-speaking concierge, foreign currency exchange, secretarial services in English, audiovisual equipment, photocopiers, cable television news, translation services, and express checkout. *Vaporetto* stop Lido. 17 Lungomare Marconi, Lido (phone: 526-5921; fax: 526-0113; telex: 410142). Expensive.

Londra Palace – This charming place on a popular promenade offers the wonderful, romantic views of the Bacino di San Marco and the Byzantine Chiesa di San Zaccaria that inspired Tchaikovsky to write his *Fourth Symphony*. All 69 rooms have modern bathrooms, and a few have private balconies. Other amenities include a very good restaurant, an elegant bar, and a sixth-floor panoramic sun deck. Guests have a Mercedes at their disposal for a 1-day jaunt through the Veneto. Business facilities include meeting rooms for up to 200, English-speaking concierge, foreign currency exchange, secretarial services in English, audiovisual equipment, photocopiers, computers, cable television news, translation services, and express checkout. *Vaporetto* stop San Zaccaria. 4171 Riva degli Schiavoni, San Marco (phone: 520-0533; fax: 522-5032; telex: 431315). Expensive.

Luna Baglioni – Years of restoration have transformed this regal 115-room hotel into a cool marble palace with frescoed ceilings and imposing chandeliers made from Murano glass. Upper floors look out on the Giardinetti Reali (a lovely park) and neighboring *Harry's Bar* and over to the island of San Giorgio. There is a restaurant, and guests have access to numerous sports facilities on the Lido. Business facilities include meeting rooms for up to 150, English-speaking concierge, foreign currency exchange, secretarial services in English, audiovisual equipment, photocopiers, computers, cable television news, translation services, and express checkout. *Vaporetto* stop San Marco. 1243 Calle Vallaresso, San Marco (phone: 528-9840; in the US, 800-448-8355; fax: 528-7160; telex: 410236). Expensive.

Metropole – One of the last big hotels along the stretch of Riva degli Schiavoni toward the Arsenale, this hostelry offers exceptionally amiable service and an owner who is an avid antiques collector (each of the 64 rooms is decorated differently). Room 349 on the top floor may not overlook the lagoon as many of the others do, but a huge, elaborately hand-carved wooden bed and one of Venice's famed *altana* (wooden terraces) make you feel as if you're on top of the world. Vivaldi once lived here in far more monastic surroundings when the palazzo belonged to the adjacent Pietà Church. Free parking at the Piazzale Roma is available for hotel guests. Business facilities include 24-hour room service, meeting rooms for up to 80, English-speaking concierge, foreign currency exchange, secretarial services in English, audiovisual equipment, photocopiers, computers, translation services, and express checkout. *Vaporetto* stop San Zaccaria. 4149 Riva degli Schiavoni, Castello (phone: 520-5044; fax: 522-3679; telex: 410340). Expensive.

Bellini – Elegant Venetian decor replete with inlaid marble, matching silk wallpaper and drapes, authentic period pieces, and impressive Murano chandeliers. Just a block from the train station, this first class 70-room hotel was recently reopened after a major overhaul. It has a restaurant and sun deck with a view of the Grand Canal. Business facilities include meeting rooms for up to 80, English-speaking concierge, foreign currency exchange, secretarial services in English, audiovisual equipment, photocopiers, computers, cable television news, translation services, and express checkout. *Vaporetto* stop Ferrovia. 116 Lista di Spagna, Cannaregio (phone: 524-2488; in the US, 800-448-8355; fax: 715193; telex: 420374). Expensive to moderate.

Pullman Park – On the outskirts of the Papodopoli Gardens, this large, attractive hotel with efficient service is on a small canal. It is a very short walk from Piazzale Roma (the first stop for everyone en route from the airport by bus or car), the train station, and all the must-sees in the Santa Croce neighborhood. All 100 rooms are furnished in 18th-century Venetian style and those on the top floor have private balconies. It has easy access to the main *vaporetto* lines to all parts of Venice. Business facilities include 24-hour room service, meeting rooms for up to 110, English-speaking concierge, foreign currency exchange, secretarial services in English, audiovisual equipment, photocopiers, computers, cable television news, and translation services. *Vaporetto* stop Piazzale Roma. 245 Giardino Papadopoli, Santa Croce (phone: 528-5394; in the US, 800-223-9862; fax: 523-0043; telex: 410310). Expensive to moderate.

Accademia – In the 17th-century Villa Maravegie, this tranquil, rather stately, family-run establishment is near the *Galleria dell'Accademia.* It has a lovely garden where breakfast is served, with a view down a small canal to the Grand Canal. Wide vestibules, high ceilings, and the ambience of a private home from another era are slowly getting a much-needed uplift while leaving the informal *ambiente* intact. *Vaporetto* stop Accademia. 1058 Fondamenta Maravegie, Dorsoduro (phone: 523-7846; fax: 523-9152). Moderate.

Ala – In a charming *campo* directly behind its grand luxe neighbor, the *Gritti,* is this gracious and traditional hotel. Restoration of its 85 rooms is scheduled to be completed this year. It's about equidistant from Piazza San Marco and the *Galleria dell'Accademia. Vaporetto* stop Santa Maria del Giglio. 2494 Campo Santa Maria del Giglio, San Marco (phone: 520-8333; fax: 520-6390). Moderate.

Bisanzio – Although it is tucked away in one of the oldest and quietest corners of town, this hostelry is nevertheless close to everything. Of the 40 rooms decorated in the grand manner of Old Venice (Murano chandeliers, damask curtains, and so on), 6 of them have private terraces, some overlooking the nearby Chiesa della Pietà on the Riva degli Schiavoni. It has a private mooring for gondolas. *Vaporetto* stop San Zaccaria. 3651 Calle della Pietà, Castello (phone: 520-3100; in the US, 800-528-1234; fax: 520-4114). Moderate.

Bonvecchiati – Comfortable, with 86 rooms, midway between Piazza San Marco and the Rialto, it boasts an impressive collection of contemporary art. A bar and lovely terrace restaurant overlook a lively canal (as do 12 of the guestrooms). *Vaporetto* stop San Marco or Rialto. 4488 Calle Goldoni, San Marco (phone: 528-5017; fax: 528-5230). Moderate.

Cassiano – There are 36 rooms in this restored 15th-century Gothic palazzo on the Grand Canal; 6 of them (all triples, but they can be booked as doubles for a small supplement) look out on the *Canalazzo* (as the Venetians call their beloved canal).

Decor is the predictable 18th-century Venetian, but leave it all behind and bring your lemonade out on the hotel's private landing overlooking the glorious façade of the Ca' d'Oro. *Vaporetto* stop San Stae. On the Grand Canal, Santa Croce (phone: 524-1735; fax: 721033). Moderate.

La Fenice et des Artistes – Behind the *Teatro La Fenice* in a lively, popular neighborhood, this refined 61-room hotel has always appealed to opera buffs, performers, and musicians. There is a pretty garden, and marble, beam ceilings, and antique Venetian decor throughout. Its new management recently reopened the wonderful *La Taverna La Fenice* restaurant next door (see *Eating Out*). *Vaporetto* stop Santa Maria del Giglio or San Marco. 1936 Campo San Fantin, San Marco (phone: 523-2333; fax: 520-3721). Moderate.

Flora – This small jewel of a hotel (44 rooms) has a beautiful, flowered patio where you can eat breakfast or have afternoon tea or an evening *aperitivo*. Located 5 minutes west of Piazza San Marco, the atmosphere is tranquil and gracious. Ask for No. 47, a corner room on the top floor — it looks out onto Desdemona's palazzo (of *Otello* fame) with the dome of Santa Maria della Salute in the background. *Vaporetto* stop San Marco. 2283 Calle Larga XXII Marzo, San Marco (phone: 520-5844; fax: 522-8217). Moderate.

Giorgione – A top-to-bottom refurbishment completed last year (as well as the addition of more rooms this year) has left this 75-room hotel fresh, attractive, and inviting. It's located on a quiet side street off the popular Campo Santi Apostoli and is a minute's walk from the Ca' d'Oro and the Rialto. *Vaporetto* stop Ca' d'Oro. 4587 Salizada del Pistor, Campo SS. Apostoli, Cannaregio (phone: 522-5810; fax: 523-9092). Moderate.

Hungaria – Built in 1906, the mosaic façade of this 100-room hotel is a riveting focus of one of the Lido's main streets. The guestrooms are large, clean, and simple, and it has a comfortable Old World charm enlivened by a predominantly European clientele. A private beach shared by a number of the smaller hotels and the lagoon-side *vaporetto* dock are just 5 minutes away. Parking is available. *Vaporetto* stop Lido. 28 Gran Viale, Lido (phone: 526-1212; fax: 526-7619). Moderate.

Kette – Tucked in a quiet spot between *La Fenice* and Piazza San Marco, this charming and efficient hostelry is within strolling distance of everything, and has its own private dock for gondolas. *Vaporetto* stop San Marco. 2053 Piscina San Moisè, San Marco (phone: 522-7766; fax: 522-8964). Moderate.

Mapaba – There are 60 rooms in this property on the Lido. Your stay here will be tranquil and relaxing, whether reading in the hotel's wonderful garden or biking to nearby beach facilities arranged by the hotel. Open *Easter* to October. *Vaporetto* stop Lido. 16 Riviera San Nicolò, Lido (phone: 526-0590; fax: 526-9441). Moderate.

Panada – Renovations 3 years ago spruced up all of the 48 old Venetian-decorated rooms, 3 of which boast Jacuzzis. Common areas are modern and marble, all a minute's walk north of Piazza San Marco. There is no restaurant, but there is a cocktail lounge. *Vaporetto* stop San Marco. 646 Calle Specchieri, San Marco (phone: 520-9088; in the US, 800-221-6509; fax: 520-9619). Moderate.

Do Pozzi – Small, attractive, and just a minute west of Piazza San Marco, it has a pleasant atmosphere and a lively canalside restaurant, *Da Raffaele*. Breakfast is served in a charming courtyard. *Vaporetto* stop Santa Maria del Giglio or San Marco. 2373 Calle Larga XXII Marzo, San Marco (phone: 520-7855; fax: 522-9413). Moderate.

Quattro Fontane – Transformed from a 19th-century villa, this quiet 68-room hostelry with excellent service offers the peace of an English country garden. It still has the air of a family dwelling, with antique furniture of various origins and a pleasant alfresco restaurant. Set back from the main street, midway between the *Excelsior* and the *Grand Hotel des Bains*. Closed most of October through the end of April. *Vaporetto* stop Lido. 16 Via Quattro Fontane, Lido (phone: 526-0227; fax: 526-0726). Moderate.

Rialto – You can almost touch Venice's world-famous bridge from half of this hotel's 70 rooms; some of them with small wrought-iron balconies afford incomparable views. Double-paned windows and air conditioning (for an extra charge) keep out the inevitable cacophony of the busiest spot in town. The decor is a cross between modern and 18th-century Venice, with handsome beam ceilings; there is a restaurant. *Vaporetto* stop Rialto. 5149 Ponte di Rialto, San Marco (phone: 520-9166; fax: 523-8958). Moderate.

San Stefano – Last year's renovation of this former 15th-century watchtower-cum-hotel has created an intimate and immaculate oasis in one of the city's most elegant squares. There are only 11 rooms (8 overlooking the *campo*), each with brand-new, tiled bathrooms and lovingly decorated by the owner's wife. Very friendly service, excellent location, but no restaurant. *Vaporetto* stop San Samuele. 2947 Campo San Stefano, San Marco (phone: 520-0166; fax: 522-4460). Moderate.

Santa Chiara – With 28 rooms and a Grand Canal location — with beamed ceilings, antique furniture, and many views of the canal — it is particularly convenient for guests arriving by car (you can pull up to the back door before dropping it off at the car park across the street — a rare amenity in Venice). *Vaporetto* stop Piazzale Roma. 548 Piazzale Roma, Santa Croce (phone: 520-6955; fax: 522-8799). Moderate.

Savoia e Jolanda – This 78-room hotel, reopened last year after an extensive renovation, has two buildings. All the guestrooms in the main palazzo have a balcony and face the Grand Canal, but air conditioning hasn't been added yet. In the warm weather, you might want to stay in the *dependence* (where there is a cooling system) that overlooks a quiet piazza and the important Church of San Zaccaria. It has a restaurant. *Vaporetto* stop San Zaccaria. 4187 Riva degli Schiavoni, Castello (phone: 522-4130; fax: 520-7494). Moderate.

Seguso – Obligatory half board doesn't seem to daunt any of the regular guests, making this otherwise inexpensive family-run hotel moderate in price. Children are welcome in this 33-room hostelry on the sunny, Zattere promenade, with sweeping views of Giudecca island. *Vaporetto* stop Zattere. 779 Zattere, Dorsoduro (phone and fax: 522-2340). Moderate.

Torino – Tucked in a corner near fancier hotels, close to Piazza San Marco, this comfortable 20-room place located in a 16th-century palazzo is within easy reach of *La Fenice*. *Vaporetto* stop Santa Maria del Giglio or San Marco. 2356 Calle delle Ostreghe, San Marco (phone: 520-5222; fax: 522-8227). Moderate.

Campiello – In the shadow of big, well-known hotels sits this small family-run property in a quiet little piazza off the Riva degli Schiavoni. There are 15 clean and simple rooms. *Vaporetto* stop San Zaccaria. 4647 Calle del Vin, Castello (phone: 520-5764; fax: 520-5798). Inexpensive.

Canada – There's no elevator here, and the lobby is on the third floor, but if you have good legs, ask for either of the top floor's 2 rooms with beamed ceilings, a terrace, and roofscape. It is a minute's walk from the Rialto on one of the main arteries to Piazza San Marco. *Vaporetto* stop Rialto. 5659 Calle San Lio, Castello (phone: 522-9912; fax: 523-5852). Inexpensive.

Novo Teson – This 30-room hotel is located in a lively neighborhood near the Arsenale, across the street from the popular *Al Covo* restaurant (see *Eating Out*) and a stone's throw from the waterfront. Small, simple rooms with shower, though no air conditioning. *Vaporetto* stop Arsenale. 3980 Riva degli Schiavoni, Castello (phone: 522-9929; fax: 528-5335). Inexpensive.

Paganelli – This hostelry encompasses two buildings, each with 11 rooms. One has been renovated — all the rooms are air conditioned and have beautifully tiled bathrooms. In the other, less quiet half, the rooms offer character, wooden beams, occasionally a view of the Grand Canal, and air conditioning. Great value for Venice. *Vaporetto* stop San Zaccaria. 4183 Riva Schiavoni (phone: 522-4324; fax: 523-9267). Inexpensive.

La Residenza – A delightful 14th-century building that is little more than a stone's throw from the busy Riva degli Schiavoni. An enormous salon and 15 less dramatic guestrooms for lovers of faded grandeur and the drama of centuries past. Closed mid-November to mid-February. *Vaporetto* stop Arsenale. 3608 Campo Bandiera e Moro, Castello (phone: 528-5315; fax: 523-8859). Inexpensive.

Serenissima – Midway between the Rialto and Piazza San Marco, this hotel has 37 rooms, both with and without bath. Over 400 works of contemporary art make this place a magnet for those who appreciate the blend of modern painting and old-style decor. Closed mid-November to *Carnevale*. *Vaporetto* stop Rialto or San Marco. 4486 Calle Goldoni, San Marco (phone: 520-0011; fax: 522-3292). Inexpensive.

Locanda Montin – This 7-room place overlooking a charming stretch of canal with flower-covered balconies is ideal for those who want to spend little and be in a quiet, centrally located neighborhood. Ask for the room where Eleonora Duse and Gabriele D'Annunzio stayed. You'll sacrifice a private bathroom, but the payoff is the good food served in the far more expensive restaurant downstairs that used to be frequented by artists and intellectuals before it became trendy. There is a collection of original paintings by Venetian artists of the 1950s and 1960s, many of whom were regulars. *Vaporetto* stop Accademia. 1147 Fondamenta Eremite, Dorsoduro (phone: 522-7151). Very inexpensive.

Noemi – None of the 15 rooms here has private baths, but the shared facilities are clean and you'll feel as if you're visiting a dear Venetian aunt with your gracious octogenarian host, Signora Noemi. Downstairs is the well-known restaurant named after her (see *Eating Out*). Most guestrooms have impressive antique pieces that once graced the signora's home, and the stair's banister is an unusual tribute to Murano glasswork. *Vaporetto* stop San Marco. 909 Calle dei Fabbri, San Marco (phone: 523-8144). Very inexpensive.

 EATING OUT: One of life's great pleasures is dining out in Venice in good weather — alongside a canal on one of the wide, sunny squares, or in a little garden shaded by vine leaves. But in winter the crowded tables and warm interiors offer refuge from the misty, melancholy streets. As for the fare, everyone's perfect idea of Venice is eating a delicious seafood dinner and drinking a good wine from Veneto. It might be easier to find the idyllic setting than reliably good, fresh seafood dinners that have become quite expensive and hard to find. Frozen fish is too often served when an unknowing tourist doesn't ask about whether it is *fresco*, although a city law requires that menus specify which are *surgelato* (frozen) and which are fresh (often they don't). It is not uncommon to see Venetians at the next table eating fresher fish for lower prices. Be forewarned — the fish market is closed on Mondays, so the restaurant's pickings are slim. Prices for dinner for two, with wine, range from $150 to a whopping $225 at a very expensive restaurant; $100 to $175 at an expensive one; $50 to $100 at a moderate place; and $40 to $50 in the inexpensive category. Don't plan to linger too late; most restaurants take their last orders at about 10:30 PM or earlier. All telephone numbers are in the 41 city code unless otherwise indicated.

Antico Martini – One of Venice's classiest restaurants, across the square from the fabled *Teatro La Fenice*, serves both international and Venetian specialties in a

Belle Epoque setting. It has a fine wine list and the kitchen accepts orders until 11:30 PM for the sophisticated after-theater crowd. Closed Tuesdays, Wednesday lunch, and December to mid-March. Reservations necessary. Major credit cards accepted. *Vaporetto* stop San Marco. 1983 Campo San Fantin, San Marco (phone: 522-4121). Very expensive.

Club del Doge – In the *Gritti Palace* hotel, right on the Grand Canal, this is the place for a delicious selection of both traditional Venetian and continental dishes served in deluxe surroundings. In good weather, diners are served on a flower-bedecked canalside terrace across from the Chiesa di Santa Maria della Salute. Open daily. Reservations necessary. Major credit cards accepted. *Vaporetto* stop Santa Maria del Giglio. 2467 Campo Santa Maria del Giglio, San Marco (phone: 794611). Very expensive.

Harry's Bar – The original establishment to carry this moniker and long a Venetian landmark, it is also the city's only restaurant to be awarded one Michelin star. This popular spot is crowded with tourists in summer, and during the film and art festivals, it is the place to celebrity watch. The food is splendid, though it may be a bit overpriced. The Bellini cocktail was born here. Closed Mondays and most of January. Reservations necessary for the upstairs restaurant. Major credit cards accepted. Directly in front of the San Marco *vaporetto* stop. 1323 Calle Vallaresso, San Marco (phone: 523-6797). Very expensive.

Locanda Cipriani – The almost pastoral tranquillity of the garden makes this a perfect place for a leisurely lunch, or serene stay (see *Checking In*). The restaurant, under the same management as *Harry's Bar,* sits on an ancient piazza on the sleepy island of Torcello. Closed Tuesdays and in the winter. Reservations advised. Major credit cards accepted. *Vaporetto* stop Torcello. 29 Piazza San Fosca, Torcello (phone: 730757). Very expensive.

Quadri – A formal dinner here brings you back in time to the days of La Serenissima when lavish surroundings, deft service, and excellent *cucina veneta* was befitting a doge, with prices to match. Surprisingly, it is the only full-blown restaurant in the whole of Piazza San Marco. There also is a café downstairs. Closed Mondays. Reservations advised. Major credit cards accepted. *Vaporetto* stop San Marco. 120 Piazza San Marco (phone: 528-9299). Very expensive.

La Colomba – Sooner or later, everyone drops in at this favorite Venetian hangout near *La Fenice,* as folks have since the 1700s. Large, elegant, and always crowded, it has a lovely outside terrace, a renowned collection of modern art on the walls, and an equally creative array of meat and seafood specialties. Try *cartoccio Colomba,* Adriatic fish baked in a paper bag. Closed Wednesdays from November through June. Reservations advised. Major credit cards accepted. *Vaporetto* stop Santa Maria del Giglio or San Marco. 1665 Piscina di Frezzeria, San Marco (phone: 522-1175). Expensive.

Corte Sconta – Despite its steadily increasing prices, this old neighborhood *bacaro* (wine bar) has held onto its welcoming atmosphere. Old-timers still congregate at the bar, leaving the bare wooden tables to the savvy clientele who've found this hidden spot for inventive and traditional fish dishes prepared by the young chef. Closed Sundays, Mondays, January, and mid-July to mid-August. Reservations advised. Major credit cards accepted. *Vaporetto* stop Arsenale. 3886 Calle del Pestrin, Castello (phone: 522-7024). Expensive.

Da Fiore – This venerable establishment is a Venetian tradition for its simple treatment of fresh fish and shellfish, as well as fresh vegetable specialties and home-baked breads and desserts. Closed Sundays, Mondays, the last 3 weeks·of August, and from *Christmas* to January 6. Reservations necessary. Major credit cards accepted. *Vaporetto* stop San Tomà. 2202 Calle del Scaleter, San Polo (phone: 721308). Expensive.

Al Graspo de Ua – This colorful and popular place is in a 19th-century blacksmith's shop and has been a restaurant for over 100 years. It offers very good Venetian and regional dishes, fresh fish, and a good selection of wines. Closed Mondays, Tuesdays, mid-December to mid-January, and late July to mid-August. Reservations advised. Major credit cards accepted. *Vaporetto* stop Rialto. 5094 Calle Bombaseri, San Marco. (phone: 522-3647). Expensive.

Malamocco – A favorite of after-theater crowds (one of those rare few in town to stay open until midnight), it has elegant 18th-century decor, beamed ceilings, and is set in a pretty little square for outdoor eating. Closed Wednesdays, and early January to early February. Reservations advised. Major credit cards accepted. *Vaporetto* stop San Zaccaria. 4650 Campiello del Vin, Castello (phone: 522-7438). Expensive.

Taverna La Fenice – New management, young blood, undaunted enthusiasm, and a talented chef from the *Gritti* hotel promise to resuscitate this refined restaurant in the shadow of the *Teatro La Fenice.* For openers, try the *fettuccine alla Pavarotti* (with a cream base, escarole, and slivers of chicken breast and tongue), then move on to the fresh *sogliola alla Fenice* (filet of sole with zucchini, shrimp, and clams). There also are delicious meat entrées. Closed Wednesdays and January. Reservations advised. Major credit cards accepted. *Vaporetto* stop San Marco or Santa Maria del Giglio. 1938 Campo de la Fenice, San Marco (phone: 522-3856). Expensive.

Al Covo – Both owners — the Texan Diane and the Venetian Cesare — are reason enough to come here every night of your stay in Venice. She's as friendly and enthusiastic as he is talented and creative. Both are passionately dedicated to offering the freshest fish their suppliers can provide. Relatively new on the scene, the setting is handsome and relaxed and the staff exceptionally friendly. Although it is considered one of the best places in town for fresh fish and shellfish, carnivores will be just as delighted. Closed Wednesdays and Thursdays. Reservations advised. Major credit cards accepted. *Vaporetto* stop Arsenale. 3968 Campiello della Pescaria, Castello (phone: 522-3812). Expensive to moderate.

Osteria del Ponte del Diavolo – With two restaurants on the charming island of Torcello, it won't be hard to find this popular eatery owned by Corrado Alfonso, the former chef at the *Locanda Cipriani.* What's on the menu, from appetizers to desserts, is determined by what's in season. Open for lunch only, except June through August when dinner also is served; closed Thursdays. Reservations advised, especially on weekends. Major credit cards accepted. *Vaporetto* stop Torcello. Torcello (phone: 730401). Expensive to moderate.

Antica Bessetta – Venetian home-cooking is hard to beat, and here it is at its best in the fresh vegetable and homemade pasta dishes as well as in the more sophisticated (and expensive) fish specialties. Closed Tuesdays, Wednesdays, and mid-July to mid-August. No reservations. No credit cards accepted. *Vaporetto* stop Riva Biasio. 1395 Calle Salvio, Santa Croce (phone: 721687). Moderate.

Caffè Orientale – In a particularly delightful spot near the Chiesa Dei Frari with a romantic terrace on the Rio Marin, this family-run restaurant is as popular with the local Venetians as with foot-weary tourists for lunch. The menu (be prepared for Venetian dialect) includes reliably fresh Adriatic fish. Closed Mondays, January, and 2 weeks in August. Reservations advised. Major credit cards accepted. *Vaporetto* stop San Tomà. 2426 Calle dell' Olio, San Polo (phone: 719804). Moderate.

Ai Gondolieri – This dining spot serves a menu of traditional meat dishes to a full house of predominantly Italian patrons in a typical trattoria setting. The fresh pasta ushers in a memorable meal. Closed Wednesdays. Reservations advised.

Major credit cards accepted. *Vaporetto* stop Accademia or Salute. 366 Ponte del Formager, Dorsoduro (phone: 528-6396). Moderate.

Da Ivo – When Venetians can't look another sea bass in the face, they head here to enjoy chef Ivo's renowned *bistecca alla fiorentina.* If you've just come from Florence, the menu's specialties will look familiar — and inviting. Try the *pappardelle alla marinara* (thick, flat pasta in tomato, caper, and black olive sauce). Open until 11:30 PM. Closed Sundays and 3 weeks in January. Reservations advised. Major credit cards accepted. *Vaporetto* stop San Marco or Rialto. 1809 Calle dei Fuseri, San Marco (phone: 528-5004). Moderate.

Noemi – Salmon mousse, *risotto nero* (made with squid), and shrimp pâté are some of the many specialties at this well-known, family-run eatery. The elderly Signora Noemi now runs the show upstairs where 15 rooms are rented to lucky visitors (see *Checking In*), while her son efficiently takes care of things in the kitchen. Closed Sundays, Monday afternoons, and January 5 to February 15. Reservations advised. Major credit cards accepted. *Vaporetto* stop Rialto or San Marco. 909 Calle dei Fabbri, San Marco (phone: 522-5238). Moderate.

Riviera – Possibly the best restaurant on the wide Zattere promenade overlooking the Giudecca Canal. With decades of experience at the legendary *Harry's Bar,* the owner serves some homemade pasta that gives that institution a run for its money. The delicious *gnocchi alla gorgonzola* has a creamy cheese sauce with a bite. Closed Sunday evenings and Mondays. Reservations advised. Major credit cards accepted. *Vaporetto* stop San Basilio. 1474 Fondamenta le Zattere, Dorsoduro (phone: 522-7621). Moderate.

Da Valentino – On the Lido, this small dining spot with garden and terrace serves Venetian fish and meat specialties, including game in season. Homemade desserts and good local wines are an integral part of any meal here. Closed Mondays, Tuesdays, and Wednesdays during off-season, and October through mid-November. Seating is limited, so reservations are advised. Major credit cards accepted. *Vaporetto* stop Lido. 81 San Sandro Gallo, Lido (phone: 526-0128). Moderate.

Al Vecio Cantier – If you're on the Lido, it's worth the 10-minute taxi ride south to Alberoni and this lovely trattoria known for its fresh fish dishes. Try the enormous array of fish-based antipasti, or any of the daily specials, including *branzino,* sweeter than the American sea bass, expertly prepared *alla griglia* (grilled), and served outdoors when the weather is good. Closed Monday and Tuesday lunch, and November through January. Reservations advised. Visa accepted. *Vaporetto* stop Lido. 76 Via della Droma, Alberoni, Lido (phone: 731130). Moderate.

Alla Madonna – Brightly lit and lively, on a little side street on the San Polo (not San Marco) side of the Ponte di Rialto, it is a consistent favorite with Venetians because of its professional service (despite the bustle), reasonable prices, and reliably good food in unpretentious surroundings. Closed Wednesdays, 2 weeks in August, and December 24 to January 31. No reservations. Major credit cards accepted. *Vaporetto* stop Rialto. 594 Calle della Madonna, San Polo (phone: 522-3824). Moderate to inexpensive.

Al Mascaron – A great place for a meal after a visit to the nearby churches of Santa Maria Formosa or Santissimi Giovanni e Paolo. Join the food-wise habitués for a good, reasonably priced meal. Closed Sundays. No reservations. No credit cards accepted. *Vaporetto* stop Rialto. 5225 Calle Lunga Santa Maria Formosa, Castello (phone: 522-5995). Moderate to inexpensive.

Osteria Ca' d'Oro alla Vedova – This attractive place has successfully made the transition from *bacaro* (wine bar) to trattoria. It boasts a particularly well stocked wine cellar to accompany its Venetian fish and vegetable dishes, polenta (not always so easy to find in Venice), and Veneto cheeses. Closed Thursdays. No reservations. No credit cards accepted. *Vaporetto* stop Ca' d'Oro. 3912 Via Nova, Cannaregio (phone: 528-5324). Moderate to inexpensive.

Al Teatro – No place stays open so late (1 AM) and offers so much. Its neighbor, *Teatro La Fenice,* supplies much of the late-night crowd, but lots of others stop by for an *aperitivo,* a pizza, or full-course dinner. There is a piano bar, *Club la Mansarda,* on the top floor that stays open until 3 AM. Closed Mondays. No reservations. Major credit cards accepted. *Vaporetto* stop Santa Maria del Giglio. 1916 Campo San Fantin, San Marco (phone: 523-7214). Moderate to inexpensive.

Altanella – Four generations have been producing nothing but the freshest fish in a homey, no-frills ambience on the island of Giudecca, one of the least touristy areas of Venice. Try any of the daily specials, mostly grilled fresh fish, or the very light *fritto misto.* There are a few tables on a charming *altanella* (wooden terrace) over a small, pretty canal, so book in advance. Closed Monday evenings, Tuesdays, and most of August. No credit cards accepted. *Vaporetto* stop Redentore or Traghetto. 264 Calle dell'Erbe, Giudecca (phone: 522-7780). Inexpensive.

Al Bacareto – Near Campo Santo Stefano, this rustic trattoria has a few tables outside and a welcoming dining room inside where you can sample traditional local dishes, such as *bigoli in salsa* (whole wheat spaghetti with anchovy and onion sauce) or *fegato alla veneziana* (sautéed liver with onions). This is a home away from home for the artisans and residents of the Salizzada San Samuele area. Closed Saturday dinner and Sundays. No reservations. Major credit cards accepted. *Vaporetto* stop San Samuele. 3447 Calle Crosera, San Marco (phone: 89336). Inexpensive.

Dona Onesta – After a few hours at the Frari and the nearby Scuola di San Rocco, it's an easy walk to this congenial trattoria with simple, reliable food. The nearby university supplies a regular clientele of happy patrons. Closed Sundays. No reservations. Visa accepted. *Vaporetto* stop San Tomà. 3922 Calle de Dona Onesta, Dorsoduro (phone: 522-9586). Inexpensive.

Al Milion – Marco Polo's memoirs — he lived nearby — gave this *bacaro* (wine bar) its name. The food and *ambiente* are simple and unpretentious, yet enjoyable, and the selection of wines impressive. Closed Wednesdays and most of August. Reservations advised. No credit cards accepted. *Vaporetto* stop Rialto. 5841 San Giovanni Crisostomo, Cannaregio (phone: 522-9302). Inexpensive.

Pizzeria le Oche – With an incredible 40 varieties to choose from, this is the *Baskin-Robbins* of Venice's pizzerias. There's a pleasant garden in the back, but if you're lucky, there will be a free table out in front, the better to enjoy your *disco volante* (flying saucer) — two pizzas face to face like a giant sandwich — or the *mangiafuoco* with spicy salami and chili peppers. Closed Sundays. No reservations. Major credit cards accepted. *Vaporetto* stop San Stae or Rio Biasio. 1552 Calle del Tinto, Santa Croce (phone: 27559). Inexpensive.

Pizzeria alla Zattere – This is the favorite of pizza aficionados as much for its lengthy list of delicious pies as for its idyllic views of the Giudecca Canal. Closed Tuesdays. No reservations. No credit cards accepted. *Vaporetto* stop Zattere. 795 Zattere ai Gesuati, Dorsoduro (phone: 704224). Inexpensive.

Da Remigio – The food at this neighborhood trattoria is reliably good and the prices surprisingly low for a place so close to San Marco. Fresh fish, however, will hike your otherwise conservative bill. Closed Monday evenings and Tuesdays. No reservations. No credit cards aceptrd. *Vaporetto* stop Arsenale. 3416 Salizzada dei Greci, Castello (phone: 523-0083). Inexpensive.

Trattoria San Tomà – You might see pasta hanging out to dry in the sun, but most neighborhood regulars seem to return here for pizza while sitting in the lovely garden in the back. There also are a few tables in front in a charming little piazza.

Closed Tuesdays. No reservations. Major credit cards accepted. *Vaporetto* stop San Tomà. 2864 Campo San Tomà, San Polo (phone: 523-8819). Inexpensive.

La Zucca – The name, "The Pumpkin," hints at its vegetarian menu and some of its specialties, such as cream of pumpkin soup and pumpkin bread. It is always packed with a young, sophisticated, and interesting crowd that is mostly Venetian, as this place is off the tourist track. Desserts are homemade and delicious. Closed Sundays. No reservations. No credit cards accepted. *Vaporetto* stop San Stae or Rialto. 1761 Remo del Maggio, Santa Croce (phone: 524-1570). Inexpensive.

 WINE BARS AND CAFÉS: Join the Venetians in their ritual of drinking an *ombra* (a glass of wine) any time during the day from late morning to late at night at a *bacaro*, a pub named after a Pugliese wine once very popular in Venice, or an *enoteca*, a cheerful neighborhood wine bar usually offering simple hors d'oeuvres (*cichetti*) in the style of Spanish *tapas*. You'll also find hearty sandwiches, the occasional hot pasta dish, and if you're lucky, a few tables. *Bacari* are generally priced very modestly according to the wine choice — the reliable house wine (usually around 50¢ a glass) is de rigueur — while *enoteche* offer more extensive selections for some interesting wine tasting. Venice will sink before you can get to even a small sampling of these ubiquitous, unofficial social clubs. The following are the best known and most characteristic. None of the *enoteche* accepts credit cards. Also included are two of the most famous cafés in Venice, where you also can get a light meal.

Caffè Florian – Open since 1720, this beautiful, slightly frayed café looks out on the entire Piazza San Marco scene. It's the perfect site from which to watch the world go by while sipping coffee and nibbling a sandwich or sweet confection. Closed Wednesdays. No reservations. Major credit cards accepted. *Vaporetto* stop San Marco. 57 Piazza San Marco (phone: 528-5338). Expensive.

Lavena Caffè – One of the Piazza San Marco's historical cafés, it is said that Richard Wagner found inspiration here. Specializes in light food, but don't miss the "Lavena's Cup" ice cream extravaganza. An orchestra plays until midnight from early March through mid-November. Closed Tuesdays. No reservations. Major credit cards accepted. *Vaporetto* stop San Marco. 133 Piazza San Marco (phone: 522-4070). Moderate.

Leon Bianco – Grab a toothpick and spear any number of delicious potato, rice, or cheese croquettes. This is one of Venice's best-stocked sandwich bars, with a wine list to match. Closed Sundays. Near the busy Campo San Luca. *Vaporetto* stop Rialto. 4153 Salizzada San Luca, San Marco (phone: 522-1180). Inexpensive.

Do Mori – Open since 1750, this is one of the most characteristic of the traditional *bacari* — sandwiches, croquettes, and other fresh *cichetti*, but it's standing room only; there's no place to sit. Open daily until 10:30 PM; closed Wednesday afternoons and Sundays. *Vaporetto* stop Rialto. 429 Ramo Primo Calle Galiazza, San Polo (phone: 522-5401). Inexpensive.

Do Spade – This unspoiled, authentic *enoteca* is frequented by market vendors and high-brow connoisseurs alike. A variety of delicious sandwiches are made daily and there are a few wooden tables, although the crowd prefers to stand. Closed Sunday and most of July. *Vaporetto* stop Rialto. 860 Sotoportego delle Do Spade, San Polo (phone: 521-0574). Inexpensive.

Vino Vino – Purposely low-key and neighborhoody, this fashionable wine bar near *La Fenice* is owned by the upscale *Antico Martini*. Enjoy light meals at marble-top tables. Open until 1 AM for the after-theater set; closed Tuesdays. *Vaporetto* stop Santa Maria del Giglio. 2007 Ponte delle Veste, San Marco (phone: 522-4121). Inexpensive.

Al Volto – Considered the best in town, offering over 2,000 different wine labels from all over the world and 70 foreign beers. There are rare and costly wines as well as the more current and affordable vintages. Open until 9 PM; closed Sundays. *Vaporetto* stop Rialto. 4081 Calle Cavalli, San Marco (phone: 28945). Inexpensive.

On summer evenings, locals and visitors alike stroll through Venice, stopping for a gelato at one of the many ice cream shops in the city. Two that are worth a visit are *Paolin* (2962 Campo Santo Stefano, San Marco; phone: 25576), the oldest and best *gelateria* in town, and *Gelateria Nico,* behind the Accademia and on the Zattere promenade (922 Zattere ai Gesuati, Dorsoduro; phone: 25293), where gelato is made fresh daily.

VIENNA

For more than 600 years, Vienna was the glittering capital of the Hapsburg Empire. Its magnificent palaces and ballrooms are now active with tourists and special events when not housing ministries and other organizations, but the city lives on in a mood of genteel nostalgia. Although a quarter of its 1.5 million people are over 60, Vienna is experiencing a rejuvenation and is gaining an international character as it emerges as an East-West crossroads. Even with an influx of foreigners, however, the Viennese traditions of formality and hand kissing live on within an active social life that centers around the ubiquitous coffeehouses and a flourishing musical scene.

Vienna does not let you forget that it is the city of Mozart, Beethoven, Schubert, Haydn, Brahms, Johann Strauss, and so many other musical giants. Its major opera house, operetta theater, *Philharmonic* and *Symphony* orchestras, and *Vienna Boys' Choir* are as remarkable in quality as in popularity. And the richness of its cultural life is matched only by the richness of its divine pastries, strudel, and the legendary *Sachertorte.* Most endearing of all, perhaps, is the civilized indolence that is cultivated in the coffeehouses, where people read, converse, receive mail and telephone calls, or merely relax and slowly sip coffee.

Situated in the northeast corner of Austria, only 33 miles (53 km) west of Bratislava, Czechoslovakia, and a few hours' drive from Budapest, Vienna has a distinctly middle European flavor that sets it apart from such Western cities as Paris, Brussels, and Geneva. It's even a bit provincial. Women still wear the traditional gray and green hunting hat with a long, imperious feather, while men occasionally will sport capes, knickers, and green-trimmed Sunday-best uniforms. The mountains and the countryside never seem very far away. They aren't; the Vienna Woods begin at the city's western edge and are very much a part of the city life.

Downtown Vienna is not on the Danube; that river runs through its northeastern quarter, though the Danube Canal, diverted from the river, does touch the inner city. Vienna is easy to grasp geographically if you think of it from the inside out. Begin with the Stephansdom, the great cathedral that towers over the heart of the inner city. Its square, the Stephansplatz, is at the intersection of Graben and Kärntnerstrasse, and if you stand there, all Vienna eventually will pass by. Surrounding the cathedral, the Innere Stadt (Inner City) is a wobbly circle bounded on three sides by the Ringstrasse and on a fourth by the Danube Canal. The Ringstrasse changes names nine times, but all the versions end with the syllable "ring," which accurately describes its shape; it follows the outline of the Old City walls. Inside the Ring, the narrow winding streets seem in perfect harmony with the Old World charm and *Gemütlichkeit* (companionable coziness) for which Vienna is famous. The Hofburg, the old imperial winter palace, still sprawls impressively in the heart

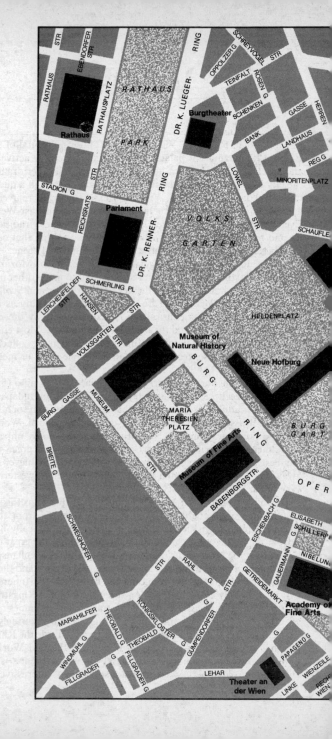

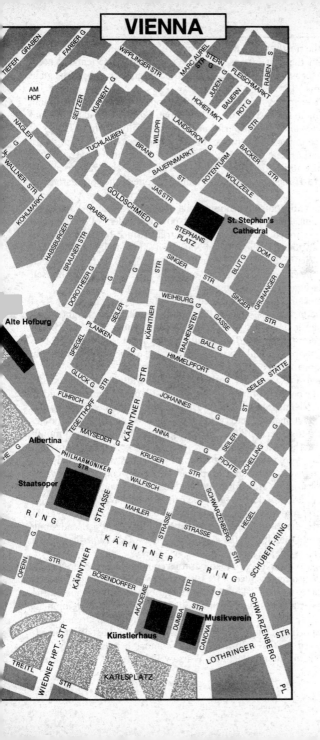

VIENNA

TIEFER GRABEN
AM HOF
FARBER G
WIPPLINGER STR
MARC AUREL STERN STR G
JUDEN G
FLEISCHMARKT
RABEN S
SETZER
KURRENT G
HOHER MKT
BAUERN
ROT G
STR
NAGLER G
G
TUCHLAUBEN
WILDPR
LANDSKRON G
STR
WALLNER STR
BRAND
BAUERNMARKT
ROTENTURM
BACKER STR
KOHLMARKT
GOLDSCHMIED G
GRABEN
ST
WOLLZEILE
HABSBURGER G
BRAUNER STR
JAS STR
STEPHANS PLATZ
St. Stephan's Cathedral
DOM G G
DOROTHEER G
SINGER
STR
BLUT G
SINGER
GRUNANGER
STR
Alte Hofburg
SPIEGEL
PLANKEN
SEILER
WEIHBURG
KÄRNTNER
RAUHENSTEN
GASSE
STR
G
BALL G
GLUCK G
STR
HIMMELPFORT
G
SEILER STATTE
FÜHRICH
TEGETTHOFF G
STR
JOHANNES
G
ST
SEILER
G
SCHELLING
Albertina
MAYSEDER G
KÄRNTNER
ANNA
G
FICHTE
G
PHILHARMONIKER STR
KRUGER
STR
SCHWARZENBERG
HEGEL
G
Staatsoper
WALFISCH
RING
STRASSE
MAHLER
STRASSE
STRASSE
KÄRNTNER
OPERN
STR
KÄRNTNER
BÖSENDORFER
RING
SCHUBERT-RING
SCHWARZENBERG
WIENER HPT. STR
AKADEMIE
DUMBA
STR
STR
G
CANOVA
STR
Künstlerhaus
Musikverein
LOTHRINGER
STR
TREITL
STR
KARLSPLATZ
PL

of the city. To the northwest is the little suburb of Grinzing, with its many wine taverns, and the vast expanse of the Wienerwald, the Vienna Woods. And to the east, across the Danube Canal, is the Prater Park, where the giant Ferris wheel turns.

Vienna — like so many of the cities of Europe — started as a Roman legionnaires' camp in the early years of the Roman Empire. It had a turbulent and violent history until the powerful and commercially oriented Dukes of Babenberg arrived in the 10th century. The city's modern history begins with the accession of the great Hapsburg dynasty in 1278, and the Hapsburgs dominated Vienna until the end of World War I. As the nucleus of the flourishing Austro-Hungarian Empire, Vienna was one of the cornerstones of Europe.

In 1814, in the ballrooms and dining halls of the Schönbrunn Palace, the Congress of Vienna, composed of the most powerful rulers of Europe and dominated by the shrewd negotiations of Austrian Prince Metternich, redesigned the map of Europe in the wake of Napoleon's downfall. Meetings were held in leisurely Viennese style, accompanied by receptions and balls, so that it was said that "the Congress doesn't advance, it dances." Beethoven himself conducted a gala concert for the dignitaries.

A few years later, in 1820, a new dance, the waltz, was introduced by Josef Lanner and Johann Strauss, senior. The waltz reached the height of its popularity during the days of Strauss's son, Johann Strauss, Jr., "the king of the waltz," who composed *The Blue Danube, Tales from the Vienna Woods,* and numerous other pieces, and who shuttled the 300 musicians in his employ from one ballroom to another.

Vienna's golden era coincided with that of the waltz and spanned the 68-year reign of the beloved Franz Joseph I (1848–1916). The emperor undertook to transform Vienna much as Baron Haussmann redesigned Paris during the same period. The medieval city walls were removed and the Ring boulevards constructed, together with trees, parks, gardens, buildings, and monuments. The *Opera,* the *Fine Arts Museum,* the *Burgtheater,* the Town Hall, and the Parliament were part of Franz Joseph's plan. And while the emperor was transforming the city, Sigmund Freud, an outwardly conventional Viennese doctor, was patiently transforming our ideas about the human mind.

Vienna began a period of decline after the end of World War I, the dissolution of the empire, and the ruinous worldwide depression. World War II brought the Nazis, drastic damage by Allied bombings, and a decade-long four-way division of the city by the Allied powers — a division that ended with the State Treaty of 1955.

Modern Vienna, the capital of a democratic republic, has recovered sufficiently to experience a renaissance of its 19th-century role as Europe's boardroom. Officially the world's "Third United Nations City," Vienna is the headquarters for a number of UN agencies, like the Industrial Development Organization and the Atomic Energy Agency; the home of the Organization of Petroleum Exporting Countries; and — because of its East-West straddle — it long served as the natural point of contact between the NATO countries and those of the now defunct Warsaw Pact. Today, Austria carefully protects its neutrality by law, allowing no military alliances and no foreign military bases. With the expansion of trade between East and West after the collapse of the Communist regimes behind the now raised Iron Curtain, Vienna's position as Europe's broker can only expand.

The period of postwar peace has brought about a resurgence of music and coffeehouses, the two basic ingredients of contemporary Viennese social life. The musical life of the city seems to involve everyone: Kiosks are plastered with notices of a cornucopia of concerts; the sounds of music being practiced seem to float from nearby open windows; many of the people in the street are carrying instrument cases. The great events of the social season revolve around the *Opera* and the *Philharmonic,* and people in dinner jackets and long gowns who glide past you in the early evening inevitably are going to *hear* something. But it is perhaps typical of Vienna that the finest places in the *Opera House* are the ten rows of standing room, dead center on a raised platform at the back of the orchestra. The houses of all of Vienna's great composers are carefully preserved and reverently visited. And a visit from Seiji Ozawa arouses far more passion than one from the US president.

Pastry eating is a national ritual that seems to be almost as important as Sunday morning mass. The windows of the city's bakeries and *Konditoreien* overflow with strudel, *Sachertorte,* cheesecakes, and nut horns, and the whipped cream (Schlag) flows like water. At teatime — and every other time — Viennese families stand with great seriousness beside the glass pastry altars choosing, after long reflection, the afternoon's 2,000 calories. When in Vienna, gorge as the Viennese do: If you start early and fit your last pastry in by five, you still should have room for dinner — and a little evening pastry.

Or if you are sated with pastries, just sit in a café, order coffee or wine, and drink in the spectacle of Old Vienna. Though it is a city haunted by the ghosts of the vanished Habsburg rulers, it also is blessed with their legacy of cultural brilliance, architectural splendor, and leisured living.

VIENNA AT-A-GLANCE

 SEEING THE CITY: The Donauturm — the Danube Tower — is an 846-foot-high column that was, in fact, built for seeing the city. Opened in 1964, across the river from the main city, it has two high-speed elevators that whisk you to the observation platform and the two revolving restaurants at the summit. From the tower you look over the green expanse of the Danube Park below, and the adjacent United Nations City, and across the river to the spires and domes of the Innere Stadt, and to the Wienerwald beyond. On a clear day, the horizon sweeps from the Alps to the plains of Hungary. Open from 9 AM until midnight, with winter times an hour shorter at each end. The last elevator leaves an hour before closing. In Donaupark, Wien XXII (phone: 235368).

For a more accessible view from an enchanting public garden across a Vienna that still resembles a Canaletto cityscape, stand on the terrace of the Upper Belvedere Palace. The entrance is from 27 Prinz-Eugen-Strasse, near the Südbahnhof railway station.

SPECIAL PLACES: The Innere Stadt (Inner City), encircled by the Danube Canal and the Ring boulevards, spans about 1 square mile and is best explored on foot. Its main street is the Kärntnerstrasse-Rotenturmstrasse, and its heart is the Stephansplatz, the cathedral square.

DOWNTOWN

Stephansdom (St. Stephen's Cathedral) – The most important Gothic structure in Austria, its soaring, ornate spire is a trademark of Vienna. Though called the Dom, its roof actually is a dramatically sloped wedge whose intricately patterned inlay gleams in the sun. The scene of some great events in Austrian history, the Stephansdom was the site of the famous double marriage of 1515 between the Hapsburgs and the Bohemian and Hungarian dynasties, a union that laid the foundations of the Austrian Empire. You can climb the staircase to the south tower or go down to the catacombs for a fee. An elevator will take you up the north tower to the cathedral's giant bell, the Pummerin, and another good view of Vienna. Noteworthy are the Romanesque west door, called the Giants' Doorway, the carved wood altarpiece in the left apsidal chapel, and the 15th-century red marble tomb of Friedrich III. 1 Stephanspl.

Spanish Riding School – The history of this most unique of Viennese institutions goes back some 400 years, when the first Spanish horses were brought to Austria under the aegis of Emperor Maximilian II. The imperial stud originated at Lipizza near Trieste; today its stunning white thoroughbred Lipizzaners are raised at Piber in southeastern Austria. The Riding School holds about 50 performances a year in Vienna on most Sundays at 10:45 AM and Wednesdays at 7 PM from March to June and September to December. Tickets are in fierce demand for the 600 seats and 275 standing places, and the rule of thumb for Sunday performances is to write *6 months ahead* to *Spanische Reitschule* (Hofburg, Vienna A-1010, Austria). Don't send any money; you pay when you pick them up. Or buy a ticket from a local travel agent for a 20% fee; try *Thomas Cook* (14 Kärmtmerring, Vienna A-1010; phone: 657631), or *Austrian Travel Agency* (3-5 Opernring, Vienna A-1010; phone: 588000). Tickets for Wednesday night performances and for a shorter program on Saturday mornings are available only through agencies.

Second best are the training sessions, usually held Tuesday through Saturday mornings from 10 AM to noon. There is a fee, but no advance reservations are taken — you stand in line in the Josefsplatz. The traditionally uniformed riders lead the majestic white stallions through their paces to the strains of classic Viennese music in a great baroque hall that is like an equestrian ballroom. The all-white building was designed in 1735 by the master Viennese architect Josef Fischer von Erlach. 1 Michaelerpl. (phone: 533-90310).

Stallburg (Imperial Stables) – A glassed-in passageway separates the riding school from the stables, which are seldom, if ever, open to the public, but the adjacent *Neue Galerie in der Stallburg* (New Stallburg gallery) houses some fine French Impressionists. Closed Tuesdays and some holidays. Admission charge, except on Sundays and holidays. 2 Reitschulgasse (phone: 533-6045).

Hofburg – This was the winter residence of the Hapsburgs, and, in fact, you will be inside it while you visit the Riding School and the Imperial Stables. It is an extensive architectural complex whose buildings range from early Gothic to turn of the century. The oldest part is the 13th-century Schweizerhof (Swiss Court), with the the Burgkapelle (Imperial Chapel), where Haydn and Schubert were choirboys and Mozart a young music master. Today, the chapel is the site of the Sunday morning masses sung by the *Vienna Boys' Choir.* You should also visit the sumptuous Imperial Apartments and the Treasury, which contains the fabulous crown jewels. Admission charge. 1 Michaelerpl. (phone: Apartments, 587-5554, ext. 515; Treasury, 533-7931).

Albertina – Near the Hofburg, the *Albertina* — whose name derives from its founder Duke Albert of Sachsen-Teschen — houses the world's greatest collection of graphic arts: etchings, engravings, color prints, sketches, woodcuts. The highlight is a complete collection of Albrecht Dürer's etchings, which are only a fraction, however, of the more than 1 million items housed here. Whatever is not on display can be studied in portfolios in the *Albertina*'s library. Closed Sundays in July and August and most holidays. Admission charge, except on Sundays from September through March. 1 Augustinerstr. (phone: 534830).

Kunsthistorisches Museum (Museum of Fine Arts) – One of the most dramatic experiences of painting in Europe is the roomful of Pieter Breughels (the Elder), which represents more than half the known body of work of this strange genius. *Children's Games, The Ascent to Calvary, Hunters in the Snow, Peasant Wedding, The Country Dance, Battle Between Carnival and Lent* — they're all here. Unlike the usual quick peek at an isolated world-famed canvas, this room provides a unified perception of the vision of a great creative mind; it's like reading Joyce's *Ulysses* or listening to Beethoven's "Ninth." The vision is dark, ironic, disturbing, almost satanic; the paintings are simply superb. Here, too, are some of Rubens's finest works — including the great Ildefonso Altar painting, the portrait of his second wife, Hélène Fourment, and a splendid self-portrait that is one of his last paintings. The museum also has works of Velázquez, Titian, Rembrandt, Holbein, Van Dyck, Giorgione, Cranach, and Raphael, as well as a Cellini salt cellar that is a Renaissance gold masterpiece. Closed Mondays and major holidays. Admission charge, except on Sundays from October through February. Certain collections are open Tuesday and Friday evenings from 7 until 9. 1 Maria-Theresienpl. (phone: 934541).

Viennese Cafés – If you only had an hour to see all of Vienna, you might get the best cross section of the city in one of its traditional cafés, sipping one of the ten-odd varieties of coffee you can order, munching a piece of *Apfelstrudel,* leafing through one of the newspapers the house provides, clipped onto a kind of short browsing pole. The Viennese café is a cross between living room, office, club, and enclosed street corner — where habitués lounge by the hour. *Jause* — the Viennese version of 5 o'clock tea — is generally the liveliest café hour.

Some of the city's most pleasant traditional cafés include *Café Corso* (1, Neuer Markt 8a); *Café Haag* (1, Schottengasse 2); *Hawelka* (6 Dorotheergasse); *Hummel* (66 Josefstädterstr.); *Kaffeerestaurant Bräunerhof* (1, Stallburggasse 2); *Landtmann* (4 Dr.-Karl-Lueger-Ring); and *Tirolerhof* (corner of Führichgasse and Tegetthoffstr.)

More pastry-oriented cafés or *Konditoreien* include *Bürgerhof* (127 Gentzgasse); *Demel* (14 Kohlmarkt); *Heiner* (21 Kärntnerstr.); *Lehmann* (12 Graben and 9 Wollzeile); and *Sluka* (8 Rathausplatz.)

Some of the most convivial coffeehouses include *Alte Backstube* (34 Lange Gasse); *Café Central* (14 Herrengasse); *Café Grünwald* (10 Bauernmarkt); *Café Museum* (6 Friedrichstrasse); *Café Rathaus* (5 Landesgerichtsstrasse); and *Sperl* (11 Gumpendorfer Strasse).

Cafés that regularly offer music to munch pastries by include *Café Prückel* (24 Stubenring); *Café Schwarzenberg* (17 Kärntner Ring); and the *Hotel Imperial* café (16 Kärntner Ring).

BEYOND THE CENTER

Schönbrunn – West of the center of town, this vast palace was the summer residence of the Hapsburgs, inevitably compared with the Bourbons' little country place in Versailles, which was built at almost exactly the same time. The palace itself has 1,441 rooms; the grounds are vast, and the sights various. There are the royal apartments and gala rooms, the delightful rococo palace theater (which was the stage for Max Reinhardt's world-famed acting school), the dazzling collection of imperial carriages, the beautifully groomed baroque park and gardens, the Pheasant Walk, the Tyrolean Garden, the Imperial Chapel, and the Gloriette — a colonnaded structure on the panoramic hill where the palace originally was meant to stand.

Also at Schönbrunn is the oldest zoo in Europe, once the imperial menagerie, with several thousand exotic animals centered around the graceful pavilion where the Empress Maria Theresa used to take her morning coffee. The palace itself is open daily and on summer evenings. During the summer, tours are frequently combined with concerts. The park and the zoo are open throughout the year; the Gloriette only from May through October. Separate admission charges to the zoo and palace. Schönbrunner-Schloss-Str. (phone: 833646).

Prater and Riesenrad – For a change of pace, visit this immense green space, northeast of the center of town. The Prater was once the private game preserve of the Hapsburg princes, but as early as 1766 the Emperor Joseph II opened the gardens to the public. Ideal for strolling or bicycling, the Prater's Hauptallée is a 3-mile-long boulevard, flanked by lovely chestnut trees and leading to the Lusthaus, once the imperial hunting lodge. In summer, veer left at the Lusthaus onto Aspernallee or Schwarzenstockallee and wend your way to *Gustav Lindmayer's Fischrestaurant* (closed Mondays; 50 Dammhaufen; phone: 218-9580), where you can sit on the banks of the Danube and enjoy a bowl of *Fischbeuschl* soup or a pilsener while barges and hydrofoils pass by.

At the entrance to the Prater amusement park stands the Riesenrad, the giant Ferris wheel, almost as much a symbol of Vienna as the Stephansdom spire. A landmark since the end of the 19th century, its great iron superstructure survived World War II, despite the bombs and fire that consumed most of the Prater. Only half as many of the bright red cars were replaced after the war, but the Riesenrad turns as ever. The panorama of Vienna is stunning as you swing to the top of the wheel's orbit — and *Third Man* devotees will remember Joseph Cotten and a menacing Orson Welles standing precariously by the open car door. Open April to November.

Grinzing – The place is a charming little suburb not quite half an hour north of downtown Vienna, but the name really stands for a whole aspect of Viennese life. Grinzing is where the Viennese go in the evening, in the summer, on Sunday afternoon — for food, wine, and merriment, and perhaps to remind themselves of the simple, hearty country pleasures that are at the root of so much of Austrian life. The food is the traditional *Brathendl* and *Backhendl* — tender young grilled and fried chicken; the wine is the *Heurigen,* which really means "from this year." In fact, *Heurigen* is the general name for the rustic taverns that dot Vienna's outskirts and specialize in the new wine, with old wooden tables and aging musicians. In warm weather there is a place to sit out under an arbor; in the winter there may be a crackling fire. Many of the Viennese arrive with elaborate box lunches from home or from richly stocked delicatessens. It is wise to take the No. 38 tram to and from Grinzing instead of driving.

■**EXTRA SPECIAL:** The Wienerwald, the Vienna Woods of the Johann Strauss waltzes, is a vast, unspoiled forest to the west and south of the city. The nearer edges are popular for Sunday outings, the deeper recesses fine for serious hiking or bike riding. (Bikes can be rented.) There are numerous well-marked trails.

At Mayerling in the Vienna Woods, on a snowy night in 1889, Crown Prince Rudolf — the only son of the Emperor Franz Joseph — and his lover, the Baroness Mary Vetsera, committed double suicide in a hunting lodge. The emperor, who had refused to allow the dissolution of his son's unhappy marriage, had the fatal bedroom torn down and a chapel built in its place.

A day's excursion also can take you to the ancient Cistercian monastery at

Heiligenkreuz, through the lovely wooded Helenental and Europe's largest underground lake, the Seegrotte, to the vineyards of Perchtoldsdorf and Gumpoldskirchen and past one of the Prince of Liechtenstein's Austrian castles. Rent a car, take a sightseeing tour offered by *Vienna Sightseeing Tours* (*Wiener Rundfahrten;* 4-11 Stelzhamergasse, Vienna A-1030; phone: 712-46830 or 715-11420), or take trolley No. 38 to Grinzing and continue by bus No. 38A to Kahlenberg and explore the many hiking trails in the woods.

Or take the No. 43 tram from downtown to Neuwaldegg and a 1½-hour hike (one-third of it uphill) to the *Sofienalpe* hotel (13 Sofienalpenstr.; phone: 462432), where you can stay the night or just dine on wild boar and *Millirahmstrudel,* a cottage cheese pastry served hot with vanilla sauce.

SOURCES AND RESOURCES

TOURIST INFORMATION: The Vienna City Tourist Office, in the underground passage by the opera (Opernpassage), is open daily (phone: 431608) and issues a free monthly program of all events of note in the city. A calendar of events is posted in every hotel and in other places throughout the city. Be sure to pick up a list of museum hours, as these are often subject to change. Freytag and Berndt publishes a good map of Vienna, which includes a brief guide to the city in English. The *Falk Plan* is a gorgeous, intricate, fold-out map that comes in two sizes. These maps are available at many of the city's bookstores.

The US Embassy is at 16 Bolzmanngasse (phone: 315511).

Local Coverage – *Vienna Life, Falter,* and *Wiener,* which list everything going on, are available at the *Shakespeare & Co.* bookstore (2 Sterngasse) and other outlets. Or tune in to Blue Danube Radio — in English, with news, pop music, and a list of events — at 102.5 on the dial between 7 and 9 AM, noon and 2 PM, and 6 and 8 PM.

Food – *Restaurant Guide,* published by the tourist office, contains listings, as does the monthly *Hallo Wien.*

TELEPHONE: The country code for Austria is 43; the city code for Vienna is 1 when calling from outside Austria, and 0222 when calling from within the country.

GETTING AROUND: Airport – Vienna's Schwechat Airport handles international and domestic flights. It is 20 minutes from downtown by taxi or bus, and taxi fare is about 320 Austrian schillings (about $27). Airport buses cost about 50 schillings ($4) and run to and from the City Air Terminal in the *Wien Hilton International* every 20 minutes during the day; at night they run according to flight schedules. There is also hourly bus service during the day from Vienna Airport to the Südbahnhof and Westbahnhof rail terminals (phone: 565-01717 or 565-05404, for more information). An hourly train runs from the airport to Wien-Mitte, a subway and rail station beneath the City Air Terminal in the *Hilton,* and Wien-Nord, a subway and rail station at the northernmost tip of the Prater; the trip takes a half hour and costs about 25 schillings (about $2).

Boat – Between April and October, the *Danube Steamship Company* (*DDSG*) provides sightseeing boat trips along the canal. Boats depart frequently for 1- to 2½-hour excursions from Schwedenbrücke on the canal. They also offer Hungarian-operated hydrofoil trips to Budapest (a 4½-hour trip; it's almost as fast as the train and much more scenic) as well as 10-hour excursions on a pleasure boat called the *Tancsics,* around the Danube Bend and past Bratislava, Czechoslovakia, and Hungary. For information, call 217100.

Car Rental – *Hertz* (24 Marxergasse; phone: 731596); *Avis* (33 Weyringergasse; phone: 655-8390); and *Inter-Rent Austria* (6-8 Bienengasse; phone: 565576).

Fiaker – A horse-drawn carriage, as Viennese as the Hapsburgs, is a favorite mode of transportation to weddings and carnival balls or just for trundling about the Old City. The public transport map marks Fiaker stands, and three reliable coachmen are *Martin Stelzel* (32 Gumpendorferstr.; phone: 566587); *Rudi Glück* (16/VII Gestetten-gasse; phone: 722-9804); and *Johann Paukner* (13/8 Mohsgasse; phone: 787918).

Shuttle Service – *Mazur Shuttle* is a minibus service that will drop you off or pick you up at your hotel. Make arrangements through the airline, the desk at the airport, or at your hotel (phone: 7770-2901); city office (phone: 604-2233).

Subway, Bus, and Train – Five efficient subway lines penetrate the heart of the Innere Stadt. Pleasant and quaintly Viennese are the lumbering red and white streetcars that weave through the city. For a few cents, the public transport office, in the underground passage by the *Opera,* will sell you a beautiful multilingual transport map that marks all the routes of the *U-Bahn, Stadtbahn, Schnellbahn,* tram, and bus, and explains the mysteries of tickets, passes, stamping machines, and the like. Buy tickets at any tobacconist's (Tabak Trafik) at reduced prices or from the machine. Tourists can buy discount full-day tickets, good for unlimited riding on all public transport, at tobacconists' counters in the airport and rail stations.

Taxi – You can call radio taxis at any of these numbers: 4369; 60160; 9101. Many taxi agencies now offer reduced rates to the airport.

Water Taxis – Vienna now has river taxis that ply the Danube. Each boat holds up to eight passengers, and clients with a motorboat license can hire a boat without a skipper. The hourly rate is about $95. These waterborne vehicles are moored on the canal near the Salztorbücke; call 639669 for information.

LOCAL SERVICES: Dentist (English-Speaking) – Peter Bischof, 16 Schwarzspanierstr. (phone: 422215).

Dry Cleaner/Tailor – Generally, this can be arranged through your hotel; otherwise, try the nearest *Phoebus Kleiderreinigung* (branches are listed by district in the city phone book).

Limousine Service – *Göth Car Hire,* 41 Ausstellungstr. (phone: 248303).

Medical Emergency – Dial 141 for medical emergency; dial 53116 for the *Medical Center.*

Messenger Service – *Funktrans Botendienst* (3 Hornbostelgasse; phone: 59909 or 567453); or call a taxi (phone: 4369, 60160, or 9101) and ask for *Botendienst* (messenger service).

National/International Courier – *DHL International,* two locations: Schwechat Airport (phone: 777-03631, 777-03632, 777-03633, 777-03634, 777-03635, or 777-03636) and at 59-61 Ungargasse (phone: 711810).

Office Equipment Rental – *Firma Dorfmeister,* 17 Kärntnerstr. (phone: 523607).

Pharmacy – English-speaking staff: *Cottage Apotheke* (1 Hasenauerstr.; phone: 342215); and *Internationale Apotheke* (17 Kärntner Ring; phone: 512-2825). *Apotheke zum roten Krebs* offers homeopathic as well as pharmaceutical medicines (4 Lichten-steg; phone: 533-6791 and 533-8540). All pharmacies take turns for the night shift.

Photocopies – *Wohlschlägl* has low rates (9 Stuckgasse; no phone); *Rank Xerox* (1 Karlspl.; phone: 505-5609).

Post Office – Daily, 24-hour service is provided at the main post office (19 Fleisch-markt; phone: 512-76810) and at the branches at Westbahnhof (phone: 832-6110) and Südbahnhof (phone: 501810) railroad stations. *Central Telegraphic Post Office* (1 Bör-sepl.; phone: 534160) is open daily until midnight.

Secretary/Stenographer (English-Speaking) – Contact Dr. Irene Voigt, *Translation Bureau and Congress Secretariat, Wien Hilton Hotel,* Am Stadtpark (phone: 754226 or 721479).

Teleconference Facilities – Contact the *Austria Center,* 23 Wagramerstr. (phone: 234-567300).

Telex – *Central Telegraphic Post Office* (1 Börsepl.; phone: 534160); your hotel also may have facilities.

Translator – Both translators (for the written word) and interpreters (for conversation) can be hired through Dr. Irene Voigt, *Translation Bureau and Congress Secretariat, Wien Hilton Hotel,* Am Stadtpark (phone: 754226 or 721479).

Other – Word processor services and rental: *Robert & Werner Tonko,* 3 Blindengasse (phone: 425451 or 421675).

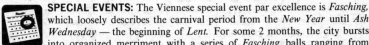

SPECIAL EVENTS: The Viennese special event par excellence is *Fasching,* which loosely describes the carnival period from the *New Year* until *Ash Wednesday* — the beginning of *Lent.* For some 2 months, the city bursts into organized merriment with a series of *Fasching* balls ranging from white-tie-and-champagne affairs like the *New Year's Eve Emperor's Ball* in the Hofburg to the *Vienna Plumbers Guild Ball* at a large hotel. The season's highlight is always the *Opera Ball,* which is held in the *Opera House* in February or March with the Austrian president on hand. Other old favorites: the *Wiener Philharmoniker Ball,* held in the *Musikverein* concert hall; the *Vienna Physicians Ball; Huntsmen's Ball of the Green Cross;* and the *Fool's Night of the Vienna Men's Choir.* The names are those of the sponsoring society, but they all are open to the general public, as is the *Champagne Ball* — begun in November 1986 — which now marks the opening of the European ball season. A complete schedule and ticket information are available from the Vienna Tourist Board, 5 Kinderspitalgasse, Vienna A-1095 (phone: 431608 or 435974).

The *Wiener Festwochen* is an orgy of music and theater, five festival weeks that generally run from mid-May to late June and attract internationally known musicians and theater groups. There is a garnish of side events: exhibitions, conferences, song festivals, and the like. For information and tickets: *Büro der Wiener Festwochen,* 11 Lehárgasse, Vienna-A1060 (phone: 586-1676).

■**EXTRA SPECIAL:** The ultimate *New Year's Eve.* If you've spent all your life hating *New Year's Eve,* there's a spectacular way to get over the grudge — spend it in Vienna. It requires substantial planning (and even more money) to motivate the concierge at your hotel to produce hard-to-get tickets to otherwise sold-out performances, but it's an event you will not soon forget.

A perfect *New Year's* celebration should begin with the annual exuberant performance of *Die Fledermaus* at the *Staatsoper* or *Volksoper* (see *Theater*). From there, move on to the *Imperial Ball* at the Hofburg Winter Palace for a glimpse of the old Imperial Ballroom (it's not worth staying, since the party has become too commercial). Then it's on to the *Hotel-Palais Schwarzenberg,* where 150 guests are entertained royally in the old palace ballroom and drinks are served in a small room notable for the two immense Rubenses on the walls. The Gobelin tapestries aren't exactly shabby, either. At midnight, the fireworks display rivals a *Fourth of July* extravaganza, and there's something special about dancing in the *New Year* to the strains of "The Blue Danube Waltz" (rather than "Auld Lang Syne"). At about 2 AM, a Tyrolean oompah band marches through the palace trumpeting away and all the guests march behind. Not bad.

Don't stay up too late, however, because the festivities begin again early on *New Year's Day.* At 11 AM in the *Musikverein,* the *Vienna Philharmonic* rouses celebrants from any morning lethargy with a program of Strauss (father and sons) waltzes and polkas that just about takes the roof off the hall. The flowers come from Holland, but the music is pure Vienna. If you can't get tickets for the performance, the next best thing is to buy a ticket for the sumptuous buffet brunch in the Johann Strauss Ballroom of the *Inter-Continental* hotel (28 Johannesgasse). Fill your plate with food, your glass with champagne, and then take them into the adjoining room where the concert is televised on a larger-than-life screen. The concert (*Neujahrskonzert*) is broadcast live to more than 25 countries. Tickets must be ordered a year in advance unless you are prepared to pay "scalpers" prices that may run three to four times the normal ticket prices — which themselves run from $25 to $300. For more information, contact *Musikverein,* 12 Bösendorferstr., Vienna A-1010 (phone: 658190).

Otherwise, *New Year's* lunch is at *Demel's* (for those who can get in), though any top coffeehouse will do. The late afternoon is for napping, and the *New Year's* climax is that evening, after a dinner of *Tafelspitz* (boiled beef with whipped horseradish cream sauce) at the *Sacher* hotel, when the *Vienna Symphony* performs Beethoven's "Ninth" in the *Konzerthaus* (see *Music*) where he first conducted it. Hearing the hundreds of voices sing the "Ode to Joy" last movement is quite a thrill.

MUSEUMS: Besides those mentioned in *Special Places,* Vienna has numerous other interesting museums. All of those listed below are closed Mondays and charge admission, unless otherwise indicated.

Historisches Museum der Stadt Wien (Historical Museum of the City of Vienna) – Three floors of exhibitions on the city's history and culture. Karlspl. (phone: 505-8747).

Johann Strauss Museum – 54 Praterstr. (phone: 240121).

Künstlerhaus (House of Artists) – Art exhibitions. 5 Karlsplatz (phone: 5879-6630).

Mozart Memorial – The composer's home from 1784 to 1787. 5 Domgasse (phone: 513-6294).

Naturhistorisches Museum (Museum of Natural History) – Closed Tuesdays. Maria-Theresien-Pl. (phone: 934541 or 930620).

New Hofburg Collections of Weapons and Ancient Musical Instruments and Ephesus Museum of Archeology – Closed Tuesdays. All at Heldenpl. (phone: 930620 or 934541).

Osterreichische Galerie des 19 und 20 Jahrhunderts (Austrian Gallery of 19th- and 20th-Century Art) – *Jugendstil* (Art Nouveau) painters and Austrian Expressionists, such as Oskar Kokoschka, Gustav Klimt, and others. 27 Upper Belvedere, Prinz-Eugen-Str. (phone: 784-1580).

Osterreichisches Barockmuseum and Osterreichisches Museum mittelalterlicher Kunst (Museum of Baroque Art and the Museum of Austrian Medieval Art) – Lower Belvedere, 6A Rennweg (phone: 784-1580).

Picture Gallery of the Academy of Fine Arts – 3 Schillerpl. (phone: 588160).

Schatzkammer (Treasury) – Completely restored in 1989, among other precious jewels it includes the custom-made imperial crown of Emperor Rudolf II, which is considered the most beautiful crown in existence. Closed Tuesdays. In the Hofburg; entrance by the Swiss Court (phone: 533-7931).

Schubert Museum – The composer's birthplace. 54 Nussdorfer Str. (phone: 345-9924).

Secession – Exhibitions in what was the meeting place and gallery of *Jugendstil* (Art Nouveau) artists, who seceded from the traditionalists in 1897. No admission charge. 12 Friedrichstr. (phone: 587-5307).

Sigmund Freud House – Freud's personal collection of books and photos, plus the famous couch, in the house in which he lived from 1891 to 1938. 19 Berggasse (phone: 311596).

Technisches Museum für Industrie und Gewerbe (Museum of Technology) – Closed Tuesdays. 212 Mariahilferstr. (phone: 934541).

Uhrenmuseum der Stadt Wien (Clock Museum of the City of Vienna) – Opened in 1921, it has over 900 timepieces. 2 Schulhof (phone: 533-2265).

Wagenburg (Carriage Museum) – More than 150 old carriages, many of them from the Imperial Court, dating back to the time of Maria Theresa (1740–1780). Schönbrunn Palace (phone: 823244).

SHOPPING: The center for shopping is the area around Kärntnerstrasse, Graben, and Kohlmarkt; most department stores are on Mariahilferstrasse. Some good buys are antiques, knitwear, glassware, crystal, porcelain, petit point, musical instruments and scores, fur hats, riding gear, and, of course, *Lederhosen* (leather pants), loden coats, and *Sachertorte* (chocolate cake).

The *Dorotheum* is the oldest auction house in Europe. Founded in 1707 by the Emperor Joseph I as a pawnshop for the poor, the *Dorotheum* is a city landmark and part of Viennese social life, even if you aren't interested in antiques. (You can pay a *Sensal,* a licensed bidder — who is absolutely honest — to bid for you at a small fee.) The Dorotheergasse, along with its surrounding streets, is one of Europe's finest streets for antiques. 11 Dorotheergasse (phone: 515600).

The *Naschmarkt,* an outdoor fruit and vegetable market, is not to be missed. It's held daily except Sundays south of the Opera Quarter, between Linke and Rechte Wienzeile. The *Flohmarkt,* a flea market, is held every Saturday near the *Naschmarkt.*

Note: You can avoid most of the 10% to 32% VAT if you are going to take your purchases out of Austria. In the shops, ask for the U34 form or for an ATS Tax Check and the ATS packet issued by the Austria Tax-Free Shopping Company; the packet includes directions for completing the refund form, plus a list of border points where refund offices are located. There are three offices at Vienna's Schwechat Airport. An alternative is to mail the slip and sales receipt, along with the address of your bank and your account number, either to the shop or to OAMTC Mehrwertsteuerverrechnung (1-3 Schubertring, Vienna 1010). Eventually you will receive a refund for the amount of the VAT.

Eduard Kettner – Hunting clothes and accessories, plus all types of hunting gear. 1, Seilergasse 12 (phone: 513-2239).

F. and J. Votruba – A century-old dynasty that deals in musical items, including instruments, scores, records, and anything you can think of. 4 Lerchenfelder Gürtel (phone: 936-8675).

Lanz – Known for dirndls and *Lederhosen* (leather shorts, often with suspenders). 10 Kärntnerstr. (phone: 512-2456).

Lobmeyr – Crystal. 26 Kärntnerstr. (phone: 512-0508).

Loden Plankl – A very reputable, if expensive, place for dirndls, *Lederhosen,* and other regional wear. 6 Michaelerpl. (phone: 533-8032).

Osterreichische Werkstätten – Austrian handicrafts. 6 Karntnerstr. (phone: 512-2418).

Polak – For riding gear. 17 Arnsteing (phone: 831238).

Resi Hammerer – The place for haute-couture loden and sports apparel for ladies. 29-31 Kärntnerstr. (phone: 512-6952).

Rosenthal-Studio – China and silver — and a beautiful wall mosaic outside. 16 Kärntnerstr. (phone: 512-3994).

Sacher – This has been the official chocolate cake (*Sachertorte*) outlet since 1832. You can eat one or have one of six different sizes shipped to the pastry lover of your choice. Kärntnerstr., around the corner from the main entrance of the hotel (phone: 51456).

Smejkal – One of the best of many places in Vienna that specialize in petit point embroidery. In the underground Opernpassage and at 9 Kohlmarkt. (phone: 587-2102).

Susi – Traditional Austrian clothing, including capes and hand-embroidered sweaters. 58 Währingerstr. (phone: 344-0992).

Trachten Tostmann – Dirndls (available off the rack or made to order) and other national costumes. 3a Schottengasse (phone: 533-5331).

W. F. Adlmüller – The highest fashion (and the most imaginative) in Vienna, for women and men. 41 Kärntnerstr. (phone: 512-6650).

SPORTS AND FITNESS: Golf – *Vienna Golfclub,* 65A Freudenau (phone: 218-9564).

Horse Racing – Year-round at the beautiful *Freudenau* (for flat racing and steeplechase racing) or *Krieau* (harness racing) tracks, both in the Prater.

Horseback Riding – If you want to be a participant rather than a spectator, this is the city in which to do it. A good riding center is the *Wiener Reitinstitut,* 17 Barmherzigengasse (phone: 713-5111).

Jogging – Stadtpark, which separates the *Inter-Continental* from the *Hilton* hotel, Volksgarten, and Burggarten are all good central parks. Farther out, but still within the city limits, are the Prater and the Lainzer Tiergarten. The latter — a 5,300-acre nature preserve — is closed Mondays and Tuesdays.

Tennis – The *Floridsdorfer Tennis Club* has 15 courts, an indoor hall, and no fee (5 Lorettopl.; phone: 381283). There's also *Vereinigte Tennisanlagen,* pleasantly situated in the Prater, with its own restaurant (Prater Hauptallée; phone: 246384); and *Reifen Tree* (Wien-Liesing, 370 Breitenfurterstr.; phone: 860637).

Walking – Virtually the Austrian national sport; there is a several-hundred-kilometer circuit of walking and hiking trails in the Vienna Woods, excellently marked and serviced by numerous inexpensive inns.

THEATER: Two famous old theaters are worth a visit, even if you have only a rudimentary knowledge of German: the beautiful *Theater in der Josefstadt* (28 Josefstädterstr.; phone: 402-5127); and the musical house *Theater an der Wien,* which played host to the world premieres of classics like Beethoven's *Fidelio* and Lehár's *The Merry Widow* (6 Linke Wienzeile; phone: 58830). Tickets for all Vienna productions also are available from the many agencies around town, but you will pay a 21.6% markup.

Vienna also has an English theater, which has been going strong since 1963 and is housed in a lovely neo-baroque building (12 Josefsgasse; phone: 421260). Its perennial attraction, Ruth Brinkmann as Ruth Draper, is a must. Last year, it was the venue for playwright Edward Albee's newest work.

MUSIC: The great Viennese musical experience is a concert by the *Wiener Philharmoniker,* whose headquarters are at the *Musikverein* (12 Bösendorferstr.; phone: 505-8681; daytime box office at 6 Karlspl.; phone: 505-8190; during July and August when the box office is closed, tickets can be ordered by fax: 505-9409). The other major concert hall, with three separate auditoriums, is the *Konzerthaus* (20 Lothringerstr.; phone: 721211). Also on any "must" list of Vienna musical experiences is the *Vienna Boys' Choir* (Wiener Sängerknaben). There is singing at mass in the Burgkapelle of the Hofburg most Sunday and religious holiday mornings at 9:15, though not in July or August. Tickets can be obtained by writing in advance to *Verwaltung der Hofmusikkapelle* (Hofburg, Schweizerhof, Vienna A-1010; phone: 533-9927); what's left is sold every Friday afternoon from 5 PM on (get there at least an hour before) at the Burgkapelle for the following Sunday morning.

The *Staatsoper* (2 Opernring) is one of the three or four most important opera houses in the world. During the course of a long season (September through June), most of the great names in today's opera world make an appearance. In addition to the opera, there are three other state theaters: the *Burgtheater* (2 Dr. Karl Lueger-Ring), which features classical repertory; the *Volksoper* (78 Währingerstr.), which specializes in light opera, Viennese operetta, and musicals; and the *Akademietheater* (1 Lisztstr.), which performs modern plays, using the *Burgtheater* company. Tickets for all four theaters are available from 15 days to 2 months ahead; write to *Bundestheaterverband* (1 Goethegasse, Vienna A-1010). Starting the week preceding a performance, you can buy tickets at the central state theater box office: *Bundestheaterkasse* (3 Hanuschgasse — in a courtyard just behind the opera house; phone for all state theaters: 514440).

Devoted music lovers might enjoy a visit to the old Bösendorfer Piano building (4 Canovagasse), back to back with the *Musikverein;* and, in summer, a tour of the homes of the great composers — Beethoven, Schubert, Mozart, Haydn, Strauss — who lived and worked in Vienna, organized by *Cityrama* (1 Börsegasse; phone: 534130), or by other major travel agencies.

NIGHTCLUBS AND NIGHTLIFE: The most traditional Viennese night on the town is at one of the *Heurigen* in Grinzing: lots of new wine to wash down dinner and a good dose of *Schrammelmusik* — Viennese folk music. Moored near the Mary Bridge (Marienbrücke) on the Danube Canal is the old riverboat called the *Johann Strauss;* a string orchestra provides music for dancing from 4 to 6 and 8:30 to 10:45 PM daily (phone: 639367). Cobenzlgasse is the main street of *Heurigen*-dom: try the *Altes Presshaus* (No. 15), *the Grinzinger Hauermandl* (No. 20), the *Grinzinger Weinbottich* (No. 28), or *Bach-Hengl* (a block away, at 9 Sandgasse). An "in" bar with music and a lively, classy crowd is the *Eden-Bar* (2 Liliengasse; phone: 512-7450), open until 4 AM. The reigning disco is the *Queen Anne* (12 Johannesgasse; phone: 512-0203). For floor shows, try *Renz* (50 Zirkusgasse; phone: 214-3151), near the Prater, or the *Casanova Erotic Revue Bar Theater* (6-8 Dorotheerg.; phone: 512-9845 or 512-9869). Vienna is one of the few major European cities with legal gambling. The *Casino Cercle Wien* is in the Palais Esterhazy (41 Kärntnerstr.; phone: 512-4836). In nearby Baden-bei-Wien, *Casino Baden* is bigger, flashier, and cash-ier (2 Arenastr., Baden-bei-Wein; phone: 2252-44496 or 2252-44497).

BEST IN TOWN

CHECKING IN: The nicest place to stay in Vienna is in the Innere Stadt — or just on the edge of it. Don't be put off by first impressions; many of the quaint hotels appear older than they do quaint — but they do have a particular Viennese charm. A double room with bath and breakfast costs from about $210 to $375 in hotels listed as expensive; $125 to $210 is moderate; and below $100 is inexpensive. All places below accept major credit cards, except where noted. Unless otherwise indicated, all telephone numbers are in the 1 city code when calling from outside of Austria, and 0222 when calling from within the country.

Bristol – It's just across the square from the *Staatsoper,* overlooking the Ring, with 152 rooms that are large and beautifully furnished. Lots of polished wood, black tile bathrooms with twin sinks, instant room service — and one of the great hotel bars of Europe. Business facilities include meeting rooms for up to 230, concierge, foreign currency exchange, secretarial services, audiovisual equipment, photocopiers, computers, cable television news, and translation services. 1 Kärntner Ring (phone: 515160; fax: 515-16550; telex: 112474). Expensive.

Imperial – This regal building, built in 1869 as a private palace for the Duke of

Württemberg, served as the Russian headquarters after World War II. It's more palatial in feeling and style than the *Bristol* and *Sacher;* its 158 rooms are superb and its service sublime. Wagner lived here for months during the production of his operas down the street. Business facilities include 24-hour room service, meeting rooms for up to 150, concierge, foreign currency exchange, secretarial services, audiovisual equipment, and cable television news. 16 Kärntner Ring (phone: 501100; fax: 501-10410; telex: 112630). Expensive.

Im Palais Schwarzenberg – Incomparably situated in its own manicured garden park in the center of Vienna, the 38 rooms are set in a section of the old palace and exude an incomparable aura of dignity and Old World character. With a prince of an innkeeper (Johann von Schwarzenberg), it's the only hotel in Vienna that's a member of the Relais & Châteaux group. The kitchen is one of the most elegant in the city (see *Eating Out*), and the service is first-rate. For those who overindulge, there's a fitness room. Business facilities include 24-hour room service, meeting rooms for up to 250, concierge, foreign currency exchange, and audiovisual equipment. 9 Schwarzenbergpl. (phone: 784515; fax: 784714; telex: 136124). Expensive.

Plaza Wien – Opened in 1988, this is a very "European" *Hilton,* with 252 large yet cozy rooms that offer bathrobes, hair dryers, fresh fruit, and the *International Herald Tribune* delivered every morning. There is a fitness room, and the sixth floor is reserved for nonsmokers. The cheery, bright *Le Jardin* restaurant serves continental, American, or Viennese breakfasts, lunches, and Sunday brunches. The Italian *La Scala* is a good dinner choice (see *Eating Out*). Business facilities include 24-hour room service, meeting rooms for up to 250, concierge, foreign currency exchange, secretarial services, audiovisual equipment, photocopiers, computers, cable television news, and translation services. 11 Schottenring (phone: 313900; fax: 313-90160; telex: 135859). Expensive.

Sacher – Over 100 years old, it's really a symbol of Vienna and a favorite of music lovers, listeners, and performers. Elegance, tradition, and the past are all in the air, in the ornate rococo decor, and in the faithful and distinguished clientele. The 126 rooms are modest but comfortable, and the service is impeccable. The concierge here is fabled for producing tickets (albeit sometimes at staggering prices) to Vienna's most noteworthy musical events. The hotel's restaurant is a center of Viennese social life (see *Eating Out*), and the elegant coffeehouse made the *Sachertorte* a legend. The *Staatsoper* is a 10-second walk away.Business facilities include 24-hour room service, meeting rooms for up to 255, concierge, foreign currency exchange, audiovisual equipment, and cable television news. 2 Philharmonikerstr. (phone: 51456; fax: 514-57810; telex: 112520). Expensive.

Vienna Inter-Continental – At one end of the elegant Stadtpark, this imposing member (498 rooms) of the worldwide chain has become a landmark where the Viennese love to eat, meet, dance, and gossip. Among its many virtues are imaginative and excellent Austrian and international cuisine in its *Four Seasons* restaurant (see *Eating Out*) and a special floor for nonsmokers. There also is a fitness room. Business facilities include 24-hour room service, meeting rooms for up to 1,000, concierge, foreign currency exchange, audiovisual equipment, and cable television news. 28 Johannesgasse (phone: 71122). Expensive.

Vienna Marriott – Glassy and modern, this American-style hotel on the Ring, opposite the Stadtpark, is an attractive oasis of openness in a city of fairly forbidding hotel lobbies. With a waterfall to sip drinks by, a swimming pool, whirlpool bath, sauna, and ice machines on every floor, modern conveniences abound. Of the 304 rooms, 22 are reserved for nonsmokers. Business facilities include 24-hour room service, meeting rooms for up to 1,000, foreign currency exchange, audiovisual equipment, and cable television news. 12A Parkring (phone: 515180; fax: 51518; telex: 12249). Expensive.

Wien Hilton International – Built directly across the Stadtpark, this 603-room high-rise quickly earned a loyal following for its turn-of-the-century *Klimt Bar;* the folksy, traditional *Vindobona Cellar; Park Café,* with good food and drink and a view; and *Rôtisserie Prinz-Eugen,* a fine restaurant that was the first in Vienna to win a Michelin star (see *Eating Out* for both restaurants). Business facilities include 24-hour room service, meeting rooms for up to 1,000, concierge, foreign currency exchange, secretarial services, audiovisual equipment, photocopier, computers, cable television news, and express checkout. Am Stadtpark (phone: 752652; fax: 784714; telex: 136124). Expensive.

Astoria – In the pedestrian haven behind the *Staatsoper,* this 108-room hotel has a lively international atmosphere in the lobby, and an upstairs restaurant (see *Eating Out*) that attracts a local crowd that enjoys the four-course Opera Menu (which can be taken in installments before and after performances). Business facilities include meeting rooms for up to 100, concierge, foreign currency exchange, audiovisual equipment, and cable television news. 1 Fürichgasse (phone: 51577; fax: 515-7782; telex: 112856). Expensive to moderate.

Mailbergerhof – Tucked quietly into a courtyard in the Annagasse with an unimposing entrance and a first-floor reception room, this is nevertheless a favorite of music and theater people, particularly for longer stays in one of its 6 lovely apartment suites. 40 rooms. 7 Annagasse (phone: 512-0641). Expensive to moderate.

SAS Palais – This Belle Epoque palace on the Ring has been lovingly restored by the *Scandinavian Airlines System* to create a luxury hotel with a fine restaurant, *La Siecle* (see *Eating Out*). Many jet-age amenities include airline check-in, a Royal Club, and a Business Club. There are fitness facilities and meeting rooms for up to 200. Parkring and Weihburggasse (phone: 515170). Expensive to moderate.

Biedermeier im Sünnhof – A charming hotel complex in several beautifully restored houses, complete with restaurants and shops on the premises. Business facilities include meeting rooms for up to 100 and audiovisual equipment. 28 Landstrasser Hauptstr. (phone: 755575; fax: 755-575503; telex: 111039). Moderate.

Graben – On a little dark street just off the Graben, but right in the middle of artistic and antiquarian Vienna. The 46-room building is a little drab, but just across the street is the city's liveliest hangout, the *Café Hawelka,* and the best sandwiches in Vienna are next door at *Tržesniewski.* Business facilities include meeting rooms for up to 60. 3 Dorotheergasse (phone: 512-1531; fax: 512-153120). Moderate.

Kaiserin Elisabeth – In a building that dates from the 14th century, just off the Kärntnerstrasse, this 66-room hotel is on the same street as several of Vienna's better restaurants, so you're always sure of a good dinner — come snow or high water. 3 Weihburggasse (phone: 51526; fax: 515267; telex: 112422). Moderate.

König von Ungarn – In one form or another, this fine old house has been in the hotel business since 1764. It boasts a glass-roofed atrium, a 3-story, century-old, indoor tree around which coffee and cocktails are served, and 32 rooms. The *King of Hungary* restaurant serves international fare. Business facilities include meeting rooms for up to 30, concierge, and cable television news. 10 Schulerstr. (phone: 51584; fax: 515848; telex: 116240). Moderate.

Römischer Kaiser – This handsome, baroque national trust building was erected in 1684 as the private palace of the imperial chancellor, then served as a military academy. It has been a hotel since the turn of the century. There are 24 rooms and a charming little café on the front doorstep. Business facilities include concierge and cable television news. 16 Annagasse (phone: 512-7751; fax: 512-775113). Moderate.

Stephansplatz – Just 5 paces across the pedestrian mall to the main portal of the

Stephanskirche, this may be the best location in town. It's also perched above a subway station that has a medieval chapel within; though the 72-room hotel's architecture is modern and without character, you are in the heart of Vienna, and the first-floor café is the heart of the heart. 9 Stephanspl. (phone: 534050; fax: 534-05711; telex: 114334). Moderate.

Pension Wiener – When Sam and Helen Thau retired, they sold their posh *Hôtel de France* on the Ring and opened this small 11-room hostelry atop a well-located, but quiet, downtown office building. If you like to take your Viennese *Gemütlichkeit* with a little Jewish mothering and all modern conveniences, this is the place. No credit cards accepted. 16 Seilergasse (phone: 512-33310 or 512-4816; fax: 513-9858; telex: 133658). Moderate to inexpensive.

Wandl – In the heart of Vienna, behind baroque St. Peter's Church (which has a famous crèche every *Christmas*), this pleasant, modest 138-room hotel has been family owned for generations. No credit cards accepted. 9 Peterspl. (phone: 534550; fax: 534-5577; telex: 115370). Moderate to inexpensive.

Schweizerhof – Just behind a marvelous clock on which statues of Vienna's greats — from Marcus Aurelius to Josef Haydn — march at midday, this 55-room hotel is very much a slice of old Vienna, with something rather pleasantly faded about its stylishness. 22 Bauernmarkt (phone: 533-1931; 630214). Inexpensive.

 EATING OUT: Viennese cooking ranks among the best in Europe. Don't eat for a week before; you won't be able to for a week after. Make sure, at some point, to have a stand-up sausage in the street (the safest and best *Würstelstand* is outside the main Creditanstalt-Bankverein, 6 Schotteng.) and to fit in at least one *Beisel,* one *Heurigen,* and one coffeehouse. A *Beisel* is like a bistro, a cozy inexpensive neighborhood restaurant, open all hours. A *Heurigen* is a tavern that specializes in wine of new vintage, sometimes has entertainment, and often offers food. It can be recognized by a tuft of greenery hanging over the door. And coffeehouses are a way of life in Vienna, a place to sit, read newspapers, converse, receive guests and mail, and make phone calls.

The highlights of Viennese cuisine include the *Wiener schnitzel,* ideally a lightly breaded veal cutlet. *Rindsgulasch* (beef goulash) also is popular, as is *Tafelspitz* (boiled beef with vegetables and horseradish sauce). Desserts in Vienna are positively sinful, especially baked ones such as *Strudel, Sachertorte,* and *Linzertorte* (a tart of raspberry jam and almonds). And there are always mounds of *Schlag* (whipped cream). Coffee is special in Vienna and it comes in many varieties, especially *Mokka,* which is black; *Brauner,* coffee with milk; *Melange* or *Milchkaffee,* frothing with hot milk; and *Einspänner,* with whipped cream in a glass.

A meal for two will cost from $70 to $140 or more in restaurants classed as expensive; $40 to $65 is moderate; and below $30 is inexpensive. Although a 10% tip is included in most menu prices, an extra 5% gratuity is expected if service has been adequate. All restaurants below accept major credit cards except where noted. Unless otherwise indicated, all telephone numbers are in the 1 city code when calling from outside of Austria, and 0222 when calling from within the country.

Altwienerhof – This place specializes in superb French food, and has one of the best wine cellars in town. Closed Saturdays and Sundays. Reservations essential. American Express only accepted. 6 Herklotzgasse (phone: 837145). Expensive.

Astoria – With a choice location in the heart of the city's cultural scene, this first class restaurant in the hotel of the same name is a local favorite. Specialties include Viennese dishes and local game in season; there's also a special four-course Opera Menu. Open daily. Reservations necessary. 1 Fürichgasse (phone: 51577). Expensive.

Four Seasons – The elegant dining room in the *Vienna Inter-Continental* hotel specializes in light versions of traditional Viennese and international fare. Closed Saturdays for lunch and Sundays for dinner. Reservations essential, except in July and August. 28 Johannesgasse (phone: 71122-143). Expensive.

Kervanseray – Many say this is the best fish restaurant in Vienna. Fresh fish, including lobster, is flown in daily. Turkish dishes also are a specialty. Enjoy a drink at the attached *Hummerbar*. Closed Sundays. Reservations essential. 9 Mahlerstrasse (phone: 512-8843). Expensive.

Korso – Possibly the best food in Vienna is served in this lovely dining spot fitted out with Art Nouveau decor. Closed Saturdays at lunch and 3 weeks during August. Reservations necessary. 2 Mahlerstr. (phone: 51516). Expensive.

Im Palais Schwarzenberg – Overlooking the formal gardens of the palace-hotel of the same name, this elegant dining room is a reflection of the establishment's status as Vienna's only member of the Relais & Châteaux group. The menu is French-flavored more than typically Viennese, and the service is merely perfect. A fine respite from an excess of *Schnitzels* and *Schlag*. Open daily. Reservations essential. 9 Schwarzenbergpl. (phone: 784515). Expensive.

Park Café – A pleasant place to see and be seen, it has a summer terrace overlooking the Stadtpark. There are luncheon buffets daily and brunch buffets on Sundays and holidays. Reservations advised. In the *Wien Hilton Hotel*, Am Stadtpark (phone: 752-652358). Expensive.

Rôtisserie Prinz-Eugen – The first among Vienna's dining establishments to earn a Michelin star, this excellent eatery in the *Wien Hilton* features game and other seasonal Viennese and international specialties. A business lunch is served Mondays through Fridays. Open daily. Am Stadtpark (phone: 752-652355). Expensive.

Sacher – There are those who would rather dine here than at any other place in Europe. It's superbly elegant, and it reeks of tradition — the zither music doesn't hurt. Dinner here before or after the opera is the quintessence of Vienna. Ordering *Tafelspitz* (boiled beef) and wearing a tie are mandatory, and will put the waiter on your side from the start. *Sachertorte* (the authentic article) is also a dessert must. Open daily. Reservations essential well in advance. 4 Philharmonikerstr. (phone: 51456). Expensive.

La Scala – Best for Italian dinners by candlelight, the aim of its famous chef Werner Matt (one of the most decorated chefs in Austria) is to turn it into Vienna's most outstanding restaurant; he's been having some success, since the restaurant was awarded a Michelin star last year, only 2 years after first opening. The Tyrolean-born Matt introduced nouvelle cuisine to Austria (at the *Wien Hilton*); his innovations continue here, as well as homemade pasta dishes and a marvelous *Tafelspitz*. Open daily. Reservations required. In the *Plaza Wien Hotel*, 11 Schottenring (phone: 313900). Expensive.

La Siecle – This impressive dining room, set in the *SAS Palais* hotel, serves Scandinavian specialties, as well as other international fare. Open daily. Reservations unnecessary in July and August, but are necessary the rest of the year. 32 Weihburggasse (phone: 51517-960). Expensive.

Steirereck – Set in an elegant old *Gasthaus* (small hotel), it's been rustically furnished and is now one of the best dining spots in town. The menu features refined dishes from the province of Styria. The lamb is very good, as are the venison, hare, and other game in season. Closed Saturdays and Sundays. Reservations advised. 2 Rasumofskygasse (phone: 713-3166). Expensive.

Zu den Drei Husaren – "The Three Hussars" has beautiful, typically Viennese decor in the old style, an abundance of plush velour and drapery. It's famous for the incredibly huge procession of hors d'oeuvres that is wheeled by your table (note that the charge is assessed by the piece). If necessary, don't eat all of your main course (this is the place to sample the definitive *Schnitzel*) to leave room for the special dessert, *Husaren Pfannkuchen* (crêpes). Open only for dinner; closed Sundays and often from mid-June to mid-August. Reservations essential. 4 Weihburggasse (phone: 512-1092). Expensive.

Zimmermann – This *Heuriger,* or tavern serving new wine, is absolutely charming. Its several cozy rooms surround a flower-filled courtyard and both the food and atmosphere are topnotch. Closed Sundays. Reservations advised. 5 Armbrustergasse (phone: 372211). Moderate.

Zum Weissen Rauchfangkehrer – A homey place — rustic furnishings, wooden benches, lovely hanging iron lamps, painted glass — on a street of elegant restaurants. The food is good, and for dessert take a deep breath and ask the waiter for *Brandteigschokoladecremekrapfen.* Your reward for saying that 31-letter mouthful will be one of the best chocolate cream puffs ever, preferably in the *Klavierzimmer* ("piano room"). Open daily. Reservations unnecessary. 4 Weihburggasse (phone: 512-3471). Moderate.

Figlmüller – A Viennese incarnation of a prewar Broadway eatery with waiters to match, who serve up platters overflowing with lusciously thin, tender pork schnitzels in a bustling but friendly atmosphere. A good place to sample traditional Viennese food and *Gemütlichkeit.* Closed Saturday nights, Fridays, Sundays, and August. Downtown: 5 Wollzeile (phone: 512-6177). In warm weather, try *Figlmüller*'s garden restaurant in Grinzing. Closed Fridays, Sundays, and January through March. Reservations unnecessary. 55 Grinzingerstr. (phone: 324257 or 323015). Moderate to inexpensive.

Griechenbeisl – Vienna's oldest pub: It's touristy, but oozes with charm. Viennese music is featured in the evenings. Open daily. Reservations advised. 11 Fleischmarkt (phone: 533-1977). Moderate to inexpensive.

Toni Wagner's Glacisbeisel – Inside the walls of the former imperial stables (now a trade fairgrounds), this *Beisel* near the *English Theater* boasts imaginative soups, good schnitzels, Czechoslovakian specialties, and vegetarian dishes. During summer, you can eat in a garden built into the ramparts. Open for lunch weekdays, for dinner daily; closed Fridays, Sundays, and January and February. Reservations advised. 1 Messepl. (phone: 930-7374). Inexpensive.

Tržesniewski – A must of musts. This isn't a proper restaurant, but is instead an ever-thronged sandwich bar, offering endless varieties of miniature open sandwiches from great bins of assorted Viennese goodies. Dark bread, draft beer, and *Apfelsaft,* apple cider. Open weekdays until 7:30 PM; closed Saturday afternoons, Fridays, and Sundays. No reservations. No credit cards accepted. 1 Dorotheergasse (phone: 512-3291). Inexpensive.

WARSAW

Warsaw, like its people, is a surprise, and it takes a little effort to get to know them both. On first impression, the capital seems as gray and forbidding as the poured concrete buildings with which the Poles quickly rebuilt their city after it was reduced to rubble during World War II. The skyline, dominated by the Stalinesque Palace of Culture and Science (built in 1950) and a few glass structures housing the city's latest hotels, seems as no-nonsense and functional as the 1.7 million inhabitants who go about their business each day in the Polish capital. Heavy pollution is a fact of Polish life.

Unlike other countries in Eastern Europe — most of whom decided to take their time about dismantling their centrally controlled economies — Poland chose a far more drastic route in 1989. Some industry pundits say they leaped into the water before they knew how to swim. Government subsidies were immediately removed to allow prices to rise to market levels, but average wages remained low, and it's not at all unusual to find a worker in Poland nowadays who earns as little as $50 a month. The country cracked down on the easy credit that previously had kept the antiquated Communist system afloat, but the result was not better times as expected. Instead inflation and a recessive economy, with output and production lagging behind by as much as 30% to 40%, unemployment on a rampage, and crime, drug use, shortages, and sporadic wildcat strikes crippling a country that for the first time in its much beleaguered history thought it would be tasting the sweet joys of Western freedom. So don't expect to find euphoria spontaneously erupting on every street corner.

What can you expect if you visit Warsaw today? Dramatic contrasts: A horse-drawn cart heading down the traffic-congested main thoroughfare to deliver a single crate of vegetables to a modern supermarket. Prices, not suprisingly, have skyrocketed compared to pre-free market days, but to the Western traveler they still will appear relatively low. Private enterprises greet the visitor on every side, especially "tailgate" enterprises that flourish out of the trunks of cars and the back doors of vans. But the most ambitious of these endeavors still are bogged down in the heavy bureaucracy that remains a carryover from the bad old days, not to mention the poverty level of the country as a whole. Under the Communist regime, the Poles had money to spend, but there were few goods to buy; today, the situation is nearly the opposite — inflation is soaring. Last year, however, Western banks agreed to cut Poland's debt in half, and the country's chances of economic recovery have taken a slight turn for the better.

Despite the precariousness of political fortunes, as President Walesa's Solidarity forces fragment and increasingly are pitted against Communist coalitions, pockets of the Old World curiously persist in Warsaw. A close look reveals the statuary of nymphs and satyrs in the 18th-century Saxon Gardens,

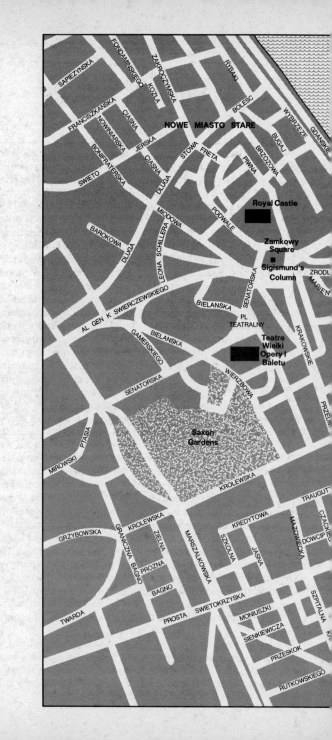

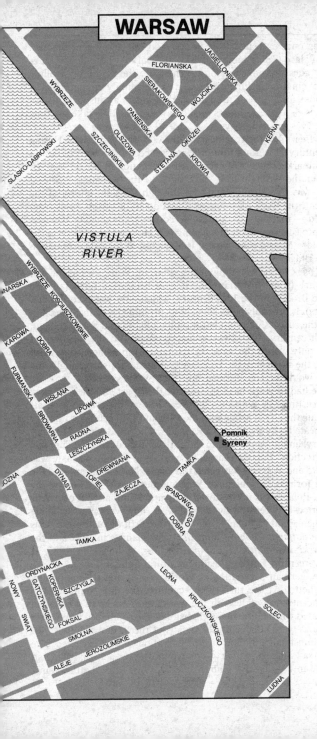

where cavalrymen once exercised their horses, and the elegance of the neo-classic Lazienki Palace (Palac Lazienkowski) and baths, where Polish kings entertained their guests. And, most of all, there are the smiles of strolling couples, the joy of children feeding ducks, and the seemingly ubiquitous little kiosks selling books and flowers, all combined to create an inspiring atmosphere. Varsovians — as the residents of Warsaw are called — take the time to beautify their lives in small ways.

Just a little farther on is the true heart of the city, the Old Town. Dating from the 14th century, it is a mixture of Renaissance and baroque buildings around a central marketplace. After the Nazi destruction of World War II, every detail, from the wrought-iron shop signs to the widening medieval streets, or *ulica,* was thoughtfully restored through the joint efforts of the Polish government, the work of volunteers, and donations from Poles from all over the world — particularly in the US. To some, the obvious newness of the buildings projects too much of a feeling of a Hollywood set. But to the Poles, the new Stare Miasto (Old Town) is a symbol of their determination to retain their heritage.

Warsaw dates back to the founding of the village of Warszowa at the end of the 15th century (some historians say it goes back even farther to the founding of Stare Brodno in the 10th century, which later was incorporated into the city limits). It probably owes some of its prominence to its protection by a castle, and the successful administration by a bailiff and a city council. In the early 16th century, Warsaw was incorporated into the kingdom of Poland, and not only would the *sejm,* or parliament, meet here, but, as of 1573, it would be the site where the kings were elected. Not surprisingly, the castle ultimately would be transformed into the royal residence.

The Poles have had to work hard to preserve their past and their identity as a people. Three times in Warsaw's 900-year history there have been attempts to annihilate the city. Throughout the 17th and 18th centuries, the city was occupied repeatedly by Swedes and Russians. The Swedes razed the city in the 17th century, and it was sacked in the 18th century during the suppression of an insurrection. Poland ceased to exist as a nation when it was partitioned in 1795 and Warsaw was given to Prussia. Napoleon captured the city in 1806 and formed the duchy of Warsaw, but it was retaken by the Russians in 1813. Poland was not restored as a nation until after World War I. During the period between the two world wars, however, Warsaw came into its own as the capital of Poland, and with the birth of such prestigious events as the *International Chopin Competition* for pianists in 1927 and the *Henryk Wieniawski International Competition* for violinists in 1935, it emerged as one of central Europe's leading cultural lights.

Then came the German occupation of World War II and the oppression of the Warsaw ghetto. At the turn of the century, the city contained the largest urban concentration of Jews in the world, and this large population was greatly increased when German and Polish Jews were shipped to Warsaw while Hitler's Nazis were pondering the details of the "Final Solution." In 1942 and 1943, almost half a million died of starvation or were executed. The Jews of the Warsaw ghetto, which was surrounded by a high wall, had inspired the world in 1943 by rising up in a fierce, albeit futile, battle against the Germans. The following year, all the underground groups in Warsaw united in a 63-day battle against the Nazis, which is remembered as the Warsaw Uprising. When it failed, the Nazis began the systematic destruction of the city. Hitler issued an order that not one stone of the city be left standing. More than 200,000 people were killed here; most of those who survived were deported.

Warsaw and its people were devastated by the war. And the city remembers. War plaques and monuments are everywhere; the *Historical Museum of the City of Warsaw* shows visitors captured Nazi film, documenting the destruction of the city. The city's great synagogue, near Swierczewski Avenue, which had been destroyed by the Nazis, was rebuilt. Today there is a new Warsaw, incorporating the past and looking with hope toward the future. After the war, the Polish Communist government took advantage of the rebuilding opportunity to move industrial and warehouse facilities to the outskirts. Park areas were tripled in size and streets were widened.

The Vistula (Wisła) River splits the city, with the downtown area on the left, higher bank, and the Praga housing suburb on the right. The symbol of Warsaw is Syrena, a winged mermaid armed with a sword and shield, whose statue guards the city from the Kościuszko embankment. For Varsovians, she personifies the city's proud motto: "Defies the Storm."

WARSAW AT-A-GLANCE

SEEING THE CITY: For a general sense of Warsaw's postwar reconstruction and continuing modernization, take the elevator to the 30th-floor terrace of the Palace of Culture and Science, on Defilad Sq. From here, on a clear day (rare in this heavily polluted city), you can see beyond the outskirts of the city, which are marked by heavy industry, modern buildings, and new housing estates. There is a small charge for the elevator. The best view of the Old Town and the castle is from the east side of the river.

SPECIAL PLACES: The Old Town is just north of the Slasko-Dabrowski Bridge (Most Śląsko-Dąbrowski). Most sights and activities of interest to tourists are to be found between this area and Lazienkowski Park south of Na Rozdrożu Sq.

Royal Castle – Warsaw's most important historical monument, its Royal Castle, built between the 14th and 18th centuries, was blown up by the Nazis in their campaign to wipe Poland off the face of the map. After a painstaking effort to rebuild this important symbol of the continuity of Polish history, it was opened to the public in 1983, and its imposing silhouette forms an impressive background to the King Sigismund's Column (Kolumna Zygmunta) in the middle of Zamkowy Square. The Royal Castle rejoins the ranks of the most beautiful palaces in Europe. Closed Mondays. Admission charge. Adjacent to Pl. Zamkowy (phone: 319197).

Old Town (Stare Miasto) – The Sigismund III Column, the oldest monument in Warsaw (1644), stands in the center of Zamkowy Square adjoining the Royal Castle grounds and at the edge of the Old Town. Nearby is the baroque, tin-roofed Pod Blacha Palace, noted for its attic crowned with a richly ornamented cartouche bearing coats-of-arms. The Old Town Market Square is the most beautiful square in Warsaw — enclosed by re-created 17th- and 18th-century baroque houses, filled with flowers, and alive with little shops and café life. Nearby is St. John's Cathedral, where Jozef Cardinal Glemp delivers the homily to the deeply religious, Roman Catholic Poles. Old walls that once fortified the city and the Barbican, a sort of tower house of the mid-16th century, have been reconstructed and add to the atmosphere of the district. West of the Vistula, north of the Sląsko-Dąbrowski Bridge.

World War II Monuments – So extensive was the heroic resistance to the Nazis that even the churches and cemeteries of Warsaw were scenes of fierce fighting. The city's Monument to the Heroes of Warsaw — Warsaw Nike — stands in Teatralny Square in front of the *Wielki Theater* (see "Music" in *Sources and Resources*). It is sort of a new version of the mermaid Syrena, a fighting goddess with sword raised. The *Pawiak Prison* (24-26 Ul. Dzielna), where 35,000 Poles were executed and another 65,000 were detained, now is a museum. The ghetto where the Jewish population was walled up in 1941 was not rebuilt. It is remembered by a Monument to the Heroes of the Ghetto on a small grassy square at Zamenhofa and Anielewicza Streets, and exhibits connected with the Ghetto Uprising at the Jewish Historical Institute (79 Al. Swierczewskiego; phone: 271843). The former Gestapo headquarters and prison (on Armii Wojska Polskiego Street near Pl. Na Rozdrożu) now is a Mausoleum to Struggle and Martyrdom. Across the river in Praga is a Monument to Brotherhood-in-Arms, celebrating Polish friendship toward the Soviet Union, whose soldiers liberated Warsaw. The monument is near the crossing of Targowa and Swierczewskiego Streets.

Lazienki Palace and Park – The splendid Palace on the Water in Warsaw's loveliest park was built in the 18th century for Stanisław August Poniatowski, last of the Polish kings. The Nazis plundered its collections and devastated the palace, but the interiors have been carefully copied and restored. There are some 18 other buildings and monuments in the spacious park, including the White House, once the residence in exile of the future King Louis XVIII of France. The monument to Chopin at the southern end of the park is the scene of Sunday afternoon Chopin concerts. At the southern end of the gardens is the conservatory, a place to enjoy the town's best cup of coffee, chocolate cake, and piano music. Park and palace closed Mondays. Admission charge to the palace. The Belweder Palace, official residence of the President of the State Council, is in Belweder Park, adjacent to Łazienki Park. Southeast of Pl. Na Rozdrożu, along Al. (for *aleje,* or avenue) Ujazdowskie (phone: 218212).

Saski Garden – In the center of the city, next to Victoria Square, this is the oldest garden in Warsaw. Built at the end of the 18th century in the style of an English garden, it has many rare trees and an artificial lake. Open daily. No admission charge.

Wilanów Palace and Park – This Polish version of Versailles was built in the late 17th century as a summer residence for King Jan Sobieski III, and is now a branch of the *National Museum.* Baroque terraces lead to a small lake. The baroque palace was restored after World War II and contains furniture, china, portraits, and other mementoes of the Sobieski family. The *Polish Poster Museum* (Museum Plakatu) is in a building on the palace grounds. The palace is closed Tuesdays; the poster museum, closed Mondays. Admission charge. Just south of the city, less than 6 miles (10 km) from the city center. Reached by express bus B or bus No. 180 from Ul. Marszałkowska (phone: 422606).

Father Popieluszko Tomb – Next to the Church of St. Stanislawa Kostki (on Koziedulskiego St. in the suburb of Zoliborz, due north of central Warsaw) is the tomb of Father Popieluszko, a 20th-century national hero and martyr, who fought for workers' rights and national independence. He was killed by the state police in 1984, and a simple granite cross has become a pilgrimage site for many Poles and visiting dignitaries.

■**EXTRA SPECIAL:** The manor house where Chopin was born in 1810 is now a museum. It is set in a lovely park in Żelazowa Wola, some 33 miles (53 km) west of the city. Chopin concerts are held on Sundays during the summer at the Chopin home. Six miles (10 km) to the north of Zelazowa Wola, in the village of Brochów, there is a mid-16th-century Renaissance fortified church where Chopin was baptized. The Chopin family birth certificates are in the parish church. Leave Warsaw by Route 1.

SOURCES AND RESOURCES

 TOURIST INFORMATION: Maps and information are available at tourist information centers, which can be recognized by their "IT" signs. The main centers in Warsaw are at 1-13 Zamkowy Square, across the street from the Royal Castle (phone: 270000), and at 16 Ul. Bracka (phone: 260271); another such center is open 24 hours a day, 7 days a week, at 16-22 Ul. Krucza (phone: 217823). The *Orbis* tourist office also is helpful (142 Ul. Marszalkowska; phone: 278031 or 273673). *Note:* Visitors would be wise to have single American dollars on hand, as they are accepted with regularity and great eagerness by cab drivers, shopkeepers, and street vendors.

It is almost impossible to find any of the few good guidebooks in English. Those to look for include *This Is Warsaw,* by Olgierd Budrewicz with photos by Jan Styczyński, a pocket-size guide (Wag Art Publishers; about $1.50), *Warsaw; A Concise Guide* by Wieslaw Glebocki and Karol Morawski (Krajowa Agencja Wydawnicza), or *A Guide to Warsaw and Environs* (Sport I Turystyka Publishers; under $1). The city map (*Plan Miasta*) is a detailed plan of Warsaw that, although in Polish, is extremely useful. It is published by PPWK and costs about $1.50, but it, too is difficult to find in Warsaw's bookstores. We also strongly recommend carrying a Polish/English dictionary; we bought a 2-volume paperback set for less than $4 from a street vendor in the Old Town.

The US Embassy is at 29-31 Aleje Ujazdowskie (phone: 283041 through -49).

Local Coverage – The *Warsaw Voice* is an English-language newspaper. The *International Herald Tribune, USA Today,* and *Time* magazine are available in the larger hotels.

Food – Your best bet is to consult the tourist information centers for dining recommendations.

 TELEPHONE: The country code for Poland is 48; the city code for Warsaw is 22.

GETTING AROUND: The Old Town, the Vistula embankment, and the whole route of Krakowskie Przedmieście, Nowy Swiat, and Ujazdowskie Streets are best seen on foot. But Poland's capital is a very big city, so at some point you will probably want to use cabs or municipal transportation.

Airports – Warsaw's domestic and international airports — collectively known as Okęcie (phone: 469996) — are placed together, connected by a 5-minute shuttle bus ride. Okęcie is a 20-minute cab ride from downtown; the fare is about $10 (dollars always are preferred). Bus service provided by the Polish airline *LOT* travels between the airport and the *LOT* office on Waryńskiego Street. Fare is about 50¢.

Bus and Tram – Avoid them if possible during rush hours, but they are the least expensive way to get around. Route signs are at each stop. Buy your ticket before boarding at a nearby tobacco or newspaper kiosk, called a *ruch,* then cancel it in a special machine on the coach. It's a good idea to buy extra tickets since *ruchs* often are closed.

Car Rental – The *Orbis*-run *Rent-a-Car* at the *Forum* hotel (24-26 Ul. Nowogrodzka; phone: 293875) and the *Victoria Inter-Continental* (11 Ul. Krolewska; phone: 274185) arrange for self-drive or chauffeur-driven car rentals. Arrangements also can be made at major hotels, at the airport, or before arrival through *Avis, Europcar,* or *Hertz.* Roman Cichecki has his own Mercedes cab and is a good English-speaking guide, as well. Contact him at *Taxi Osobowe* (18 Ul. Woronicza; phone: 625).

Taxi – Cabs may be hailed on the street, and rates are quite inexpensive. To order a taxi by phone, call 919. Make sure the driver turns on the meter at the onset of the ride. Be aware, too, that because of inflation, the price that appears on the meter is multiplied by 100 or 150; a sign on the taxi window will tell you which figure is used. Cabs also are fine for extended sightseeing surveys around the city; rates are reasonable if you agree on them before setting off.

Train – The main train station is at the corner of Emilii Plater and Aleje Jerozolimskie, in the center of town (phone: 200361 for local train schedules and information, 257554 for international trains). A PolRailPass is available in Poland at *Orbis* travel agencies; payment must be made in foreign currency. Beware of very rough, very professional bands of pickpockets who lie in wait for Western travelers as they board the trains.

 LOCAL SERVICES: Most hotels will try to arrange any special services a business traveler might require, such as a translator.

Dentist (English-Speaking) – It's best to ask the service desk at any major hotel to arrange this.

Medical Emergency – The number to call is 999, although English generally is not spoken; it's best to ask the service desk at any major hotel to make the call for you.

Pharmacy – Some pharmacies stay open 24 hours a day; ask at your hotel desk.

Post Office – The main post office on Święto-Krzyszka Street, in the center town, is open 24 hours daily.

 SPECIAL EVENTS: The holidays most important to the predominantly Catholic Poles tend to be religious, such as *Christmas, Easter,* and the *Feast of Corpus Christi* (in June). In addition, an *International Book Fair* is held here each May, and there is an *International Poster Biennale* in June of even-numbered years. The *"Warsaw Autumn" International Festival of Modern Music* is an important September event, and the *Jazz Jamboree* held in late October is the oldest jazz festival in central and Eastern Europe. The *International Chopin Competition* for pianists (held every 5 years) will next take place in October 1995 and the *Henryk Wieniawski International Competition* for violinists is held annually in September.

 MUSEUMS: In addition to those described in *Special Places,* Warsaw has a number of other interesting museums. All are closed Mondays and charge admission.

Archaeological Museum – Tools and other relics of prehistoric Baltic peoples. 5 Ul. Długa (phone: 313221).

Chopin's Drawing Room – Period furnishings. In the former Raczyński Palace (also once known as the Czapski Palace, now the *Academy of Fine Arts*). 5 Ul. Krakowskie Przedmieście (phone: 275471). (On the same street is the Holy Cross Church, where Chopin's heart is buried in one of its columns.)

Ethnographic Museum – Peasant life, folk art, and costumes. 1 Ul. Kredytowa (phone: 277641).

Jewish Cemetery (Cmentarze Zydowski) – Somehow this large cemetery survived the Nazi destruction of the city. Though overgrown, it is possible to walk among the headstones, many of which go back 2 centuries. Of the hundreds of thousands of Jews who once called Warsaw home, there are now only about 300 left, and visiting this final resting place, though heartbreaking, is a must. There is an English-speaking caretaker at the entrance. 49-51 Okopwa.

Historical Museum of the City of Warsaw – Pictures and exhibitions of Warsaw through the centuries. A 20-minute presentation compiled from captured Nazi film (narrated in English) shows the devastation of the city; shown daily at noon. Admission charge. 48 Old Town Market Sq. (phone: 310251).

Maria Skłodowska-Curie Museum and House – The chemist's home before she moved to Paris. 16 Ul. Freta (phone: 318092).

Municipal Building – Formerly the *Museum of Revolutionary Politics,* it now houses an exhibition of Old Masters' paintings contributed by the Porczynsky family. Pl. Bankov — once named, not so incidentally, Place Dzierzynskiego after the founder of Tcheka, forerunner of today's KGB (no phone).

National Museum – Poland's greatest art collection. Above all, don't miss the huge painting of the *Battle of Grunwald* by Jan Matejko, which shows the defeat of the Knights of the Teutonic order in the 15th century. During World War II, the Polish government ordered that the painting, like all other national treasures, be hidden, and though the Nazis offered a whopping reward for its return, there wasn't a single taker. 3 Al. Jerozolimskie (phone: 211031).

SHOPPING: Shops in Warsaw generally are open from 11 AM to 7 PM, but department stores open earlier and close later. Avoid the crowds by shopping before 3 PM. Leather, linen, and folk art, ranging from wonderful woodcarvings to handsome handwoven rugs, are good buys here. Amber and sterling silver jewelry are the best buys; if you're willing to pay in dollars, prices go down. A good place to look for old and new jewelry is along the side streets of the Old Town. Warsaw's Fifth Avenue is Ul. Nowy (New World Street), not terribly elegant by Western standards, but the best in the city. On Sunday mornings, there are some interesting flea markets around *Skra* and *Warszawa* soccer stadiums. (There are restrictions on the quantity and types of items you can take out of Poland; check with authorities before your trip.)

In 1989, the government introduced exit custom duties on all items bought in the country. The tax is from 100% to 300% of the value of the goods, except on those goods purchased in special shops that deal only in foreign currency, and must be paid upon leaving Poland. You should always keep receipts of the items, along with receipts proving that the zlotys were exchanged at official rates.

Art – Stylized folk art and works of modern art. 17 Ul. Krakowskie Przedmieście.

Canaletto – A good shop for amber and silver jewelry. Dollars are accepted happily. 89 Krakowskie Pzedmiescie.

Cepelia – Shops that sell souvenirs and folk art. Several locations: 2 and 5 Pl. Konstytucji, 8-10 Old Town Market Square, 23-31 Ul. Krucza, 99-101 Ul. Marszałkowska, and many others.

Desa – Three shops that specialize in old and contemporary Polish art. For posters, etchings, and woodcuts, the shop is at 30 Ul. Rutkowskiego; for coins and medals, 17 Ul. Nowotki; and for antique jewelry, 48 Ul. Nowy Świat.

Orno – Handmade artistic silverwork. 83 Ul. Marszałkowska, 52 Ul. Nowy Swiat, and 13 Ul. Swiętojańska.

Persian Market (Perski Rynek) – Each Sunday between 9 AM and 3 PM at this flea market, you can buy anything from antiques to homemade tripe soup to German war medals. Take bus A to the end of the line, then follow the crowd. Ul. Jana Kasprowicza at Ul. Przytyk.

Rózyckiego Market (Bazar Rózyckiego) – Capitalism ran rampant here long before the Communists lost power. Everything from fur coats and Western clothing to smuggled Russian caviar — all at negotiable prices — is for sale. Also available are homemade foods sold by the many elderly women who cater to both buyers and sellers from their sidewalk stands. At Ul. Targowa, two tram stops (on Nos. 9 and 13) from Pl. Zamkowy.

Supersam – A huge supermarket where locals often window shop; prices are very high by Polish standards. Near Pl. Unii Lubelskiej and Ul. Waryńskiego.

Szutka Polska – Sterling silver pins, earrings, and bracelets at very good prices. 15-17 Krakowskie Przedmieście.

Wactaw Okinski – Another good shop for amber and silver jewelry. Prices may go down if you offer dollars. 15 Ul. Piwna.

SPORTS AND FITNESS: Horse Racing – The *Suzewiec* race course, on the southern extremity of the city, is one of the largest in Europe. Races are held on Wednesdays, Saturdays, and Sundays in summer.

    Soccer – Played at *Skra* and *Warszawa* soccer stadiums. *Legia,* the best and most popular Warsaw team, also plays its matches at various stadiums around the country.

Swimming – In summer there is swimming at the *Legia* pool (Ul. Łazienkowska) or the indoor pool at the Palace of Culture and Science (6 Pl. Defilad). There are no public beaches, and you cannot swim in the river.

THEATER: Advance booking for theater or cinema tickets can be made through one of the tourist information centers (the branch at 1-13 Pl. Zamkowy; phone: 270000), or the *SPATI*F ticket office (25 Al. Jerozolimskie; phone: 285995, 219383, or 219454). The city's foremost drama theaters include *Polski* (2 Ul. Karasia; phone: 267992), *Dramatyczny* (in the Palace of Culture and Science, Pl. Defilad; phone: 200211), and *Ateneum* (2 Ul. St. Jaracza; phone: 267330 or 262421). There are several children's theaters in Warsaw, including the *Lalka* puppet theater (in the Palace of Culture and Science; phone: 200211).

MUSIC: Opera and ballet are performed at *Warsaw's Grand Theater of Opera and Ballet* (Teatr Wielki Opery I Baletu; Pl. Teatralny; phone: 263287). The prestigious international *Chopin Piano Competitions* are held every 5 years at the *Filharmonia* (12 Ul. Sienkiewicza; phone: 275712 or 267281), and there are operettas staged at the *Operetka* (49 Ul. Nowogrodzka; phone: 280360).

NIGHTCLUBS AND NIGHTLIFE: You'll need a fairly sophisticated knowledge of Polish to appreciate the humor at one of Warsaw's popular satirical cafés, but you might try one for the atmosphere.

    For jazz, try *Akwarium* (Ul. Emilii Plater; phone: 205072), a modern, glass nightspot near the Palace of Culture and Science. One of the city's best private clubs is *SARP* (13 Foksal), which is run by the association of Polish architects and artists. However, you must be taken there by a member. Young crowds frequent *Riviera Remont* (12 Ul. Waryńskiego; phone: 257497).

Though Las Vegas has nothing to fear, gambling is popular at the casinos at the *Orbis Forum, Mariott,* and *Victoria Inter-Continental* hotels. There is an admission charge: slot machines, blackjack, and roulette are available; gambling is in hard currency.

BEST IN TOWN

CHECKING IN: Since Warsaw is home to less than a dozen recommendable hotels, booking well in advance is strongly advised, especially during the summer. Expect to pay from $120 to $185 a night for a double in one of Warsaw's expensive hotels; from $70 to $100 in the moderate range. Prices include breakfast, and can be paid in hard currency or zlotys. All hotels listed below accept major credit cards.

Another housing option is the bed and breakfast type of accommodation, but in Warsaw, such places lack the breakfast. What they do provide, however, is an opportunity for a rare glimpse into the lives of typical Poles. Bookings and information are available through *Syrena* offices (17 Ul. Krucza; phone: 287540 or 217864). All telephone numbers are in the 22 city code unless otherwise indicated.

Marriott – The newest and best in town, it occupies the top 20 stories of a 40-story skyscraper. Its 525 rooms boast every Western comfort, from color TV sets (with CNN) to bathrooms complete with hair dryers. The English-speaking staff is extraordinarily polite and helpful, and keeps things running smoothly. There are several restaurants and the *Lila Weneda* coffee shop serves a first-rate buffet breakfast that is included in the room rate. There also is a casino. Business facilities include meeting rooms for up to 300, audiovisual equipment, photocopiers, and translation services. 65-79 Al. Jerozolimskie (phone: 306306). Expensive.

Orbis Holiday Inn – One of the first joint ventures of US and Polish capital, it boasts 338 rooms, spartan by most Western standards, but adequate. There also are 3 restaurants, a sauna, and a swimming pool. Business facilities include meeting rooms for up to 100, audiovisual equipment, photocopiers, cable television news, and translation services. 2 Ul. Zlota (phone: 200341; fax: 300569; telex: 817778). Expensive.

Victoria Inter-Continental – One of Warsaw's top hotels, it is close to the *Wielki Theater* and the Saxon Gardens. Its 370 rooms are comfortable (although the furniture is a little frayed at the edges), and the *Canaletto* restaurant specializes in Polish dishes. There is a swimming pool and a casino. Business facilities include meeting rooms for up to 50, audiovisual equipment, photocopiers, cable television news, and translation services. 11 Ul. Królewska (phone: 279271; fax: 279856; telex: 812516). Expensive.

Novotel – Near the airport, it's another joint venture, this one with the French hotel chain. The hotel offers comfortable rooms, along with shops and restaurants. Business facilities include meeting rooms for up to 50, audiovisual equipment, and cable television news. 1 Ul. Sierpnia (phone: 464051; fax: 463686; telex: 812525). Expensive to moderate.

Orbis-Europejski – For some sense of Old World Warsaw, it's the place to stay. The 279 rooms — including singles and doubles, with and without bath, and suites — are functionally modern in this 4-story building that is over 100 years old. A café looks out on the Saxon Gardens (Ogród Saski) and the Grób Nieznanegozolnieria (Monument to the Unknown Soldier). Business facilities include meeting rooms for up to 150 and cable television news. 13 Ul. Krakowskie Przedmieście (phone: 265051; telex: 813615). Expensive to moderate.

Orbis Forum – The Inter-Continental chain's second link in Warsaw is bigger, but not as nice. Its 751 rooms are of modest size and sparsely decorated. It has a casino and a central location, near the Palace of Culture and Science. Business facilities include meeting rooms for up to 200, audiovisual equipment, photocopiers, cable television news, and translation services. 24-26 Ul. Nowogrodzka (phone: 210271 or 280364; fax: 258517; telex: 814676). Expensive to moderate.

Orbis-Grand – The more than 410 rooms here are rather plain, but the midtown location is a plus. It has a rooftop café with glass-enclosed terrace and a swimming pool. On the eighth floor is a disco, making seventh-floor rooms places to be avoided, due to the noise. 28 Ul. Krucza (phone: 294051; fax: 219724; telex: 813422). Moderate.

Orbis-Solec – Somewhat away from the center, but nicely situated on the bank of the Vistula, it has 147 rooms with showers and toilets. The decor is minimal motel-modern. 1 Ul. Zagórna (phone: 259241; fax: 276442; telex: 814676). Moderate.

EATING OUT: Food shortages still are a fact of life in Poland, though not for visitors. A number of small, private, family-run restaurants now are slowly emerging on the scene. The best victuals usually go to the first class hotels, so local restaurants with character may not always have all the ingredients they need. They serve dinner relatively early, and by 10:30 PM most of the kitchens are already dark. Dinner for two, even with wine, at an expensive restaurant will be reasonable — $25 and up; a moderately priced restaurant will charge $15 to $25; and an inexpensive restaurant will serve meals from a dollar or two per person. Reservations are advised at all places listed below. Note that at press time *none* of the recommended restaurants accepted credit cards; check before you go. All telephone numbers are in the 22 city code unless otherwise indicated.

Zajazd Napoleonski – In a neighborhood not meant for strolling, this is a small, private hotel and restaurant. The uniformed, white-gloved staff serves superb food with great style. Dinner for two with wine will run $50 to $60. Open daily. 83 Ul. Ptowiecka (phone: 153454 or 153068). Very expensive.

Bazyliszek – Easily Warsaw's premier restaurant, best known for its wild game. It's on the second floor over a snack bar, and has an Old Warsaw ambience. The decor features hussars' armor and wooden beams. A horse and carriage usually is outside to take you for a romantic ride through the city after dinner. Open daily. Reservations necessary. 3-9 Rynek Starego Miasta (Old Town Market Sq.; phone: 311841). Expensive.

Lers – Good traditional Polish cooking is served at this dining establishment with attentive service. Open daily. Reservations necessary. 29 Ul. Dtuga (phone: 635-3888). Expensive.

Cristal-Budapeszt – Cristal and Budapeszt are two separate rooms in this popular Hungarian dining place. The Budapeszt room has a folk motif and Gypsy orchestra; the Cristal has a loud, modern Polish discotheque atmosphere. In either room, start with *zupa gulaszowa:* meat and vegetables in a delicious paprika-seasoned broth, served in steaming cauldrons. Open daily. 21-25 Marszałkowska (phone: 253433). Moderate.

Wilanów – Traditional Polish cooking served in a modern ambience. This lovely eatery is some distance from the town center, near the Wilanów Palace. Open daily. 27 Ul. Wiertnicza (phone: 421852). Moderate.

Karczma Slupskal – Traditional Kashubian — northern Polish — fare is served in a quaint regional restaurant with embroidered curtains and an unusual bar. The seats at the bar are carousel horses that move up and down, controlled from behind the bar. Among the specialties are the nut soup and boar pâté. Open daily. 127 Czerniakowska (phone: 414552). Moderate to inexpensive.

Dzik – You'll recognize this place by the mounted head of a wild boar, or *dzik,* outside over the front door. The specialty here, naturally enough, is wild game — when they have it. There are a number of rather threadbare stuffed animal heads mounted on the wall. Customers here tend to get a bit rowdy as the evening progresses. Open daily. 42 Nowogrodzka (phone: 219728). Inexpensive.

Rycerska – Good — yet popularly priced — Polish fare is served in a rustic atmosphere with medieval armor and oil-painted portraits. Open daily. 9-11 Ul. Szeroki Dunaj (phone: 313668). Inexpensive.

Staropolska – Near the university, this restaurant is a mainstay among academic types. Although the menu is limited, it has one of the best cold buffets in Warsaw, with veal in aspic and steak tartare. Also sample the broth with hard-boiled egg and sausage, called *zurek staropolski*. Old *Beatles* tapes or European disco music plays continuously. Open daily. 8 Krakowskie Przedmieście (phone: 269070). Inexpensive.

Special: One corner of the Old World still thrives in this otherwise drab culinary capital. It's called *E. Wedel* (8 Szpitalna; it's on the corner of Szpitalna and Wojciecha Gorskiego). The name is stenciled on the front window, and there is a sign that says "Pijalnia Czekolady," which roughly translates as "Chocolate Pumproom." The place consists of two small rooms right out of a *mittel* European stage set: one is mint green, the other is pink. The *only* thing served here is very good thick hot chocolate (in porcelain cups), for 22¢ per cup. No smoking is allowed. Right next door (on Szpitalna) is a faded, but still elegant (by local standards), candy shop, also owned by *Wedel*.

ZURICH

Zurich, long a stronghold of business and banking, is also an extraordinarily beautiful city — one of Europe's loveliest. Situated at the foot of the large lake that bears its name, the city spreads out along both banks of the Limmat River (which flows *out* of, rather than into the lake). Old Zurich, the well-preserved legacy of earlier times, remains the core of the modern city. The Limmat's right bank is lined with 16th- and 17th-century guildhouses that have been converted into private homes, still clustered around the medieval cathedral, the Grossmünster. On the left bank, the equally venerable Fraumünster, originally a convent dating from the 9th century, dominates narrow, winding streets of houses and shops with typical oriel windows and wrought-iron signs.

Only steps away is the Bahnhofstrasse, one of Europe's most elegant shopping streets and also the business heart of the city and of Switzerland. The world's image of Zurich is not mistaken. Business is indeed the city's forte, and behind many of the graceful façades of the buildings on the Bahnhofstrasse and adjacent streets, the "gnomes" of the international money market are discreetly at work. A center of the international gold market, Zurich guards fortunes in the vaults beneath its busy streets. The precious metal is also readily available for purchase in the shops above, in the form of jewelry of a quality not found elsewhere. All gold sold in Switzerland is 18 karat.

Situated on northern Switzerland's great plateau, Zurich nevertheless has an Alpine ambience, offering spectacular views of the glistening peaks on clear days. It owes its existence to ancient trade routes linking northern Europe with the Mediterranean world. Its recorded history goes back more than 2,000 years, but indications of human habitation that existed more than 6,000 years ago have been uncovered near the present opera house. As elsewhere in the Alpine region, the Romans found Celts here when they established an outpost they called Turicum. German tribes arrived with the fall of the empire and remained. Thanks to its strategic position, Zurich developed into a thriving commercial center during the Middle Ages. It was an independent city-state until joining the Swiss Confederation in 1351. Its prosperity and importance continued to grow, and it was the federal capital until 1848, when the seat of government was shifted to Bern.

Zurich is Switzerland's largest city, with some 800,000 people in the metropolitan area. The majority of them speak the Schwyzerdütsch dialect that you won't understand even if you speak German. Yet many will speak English, and tiny Switzerland always has been a country of many languages and many cultures; 70% speak Swiss German, 20% speak French, 9% Italian, and 1% Romansh. Although very conservative itself, the city has been a haven for revolutionary spirits from other countries. The social spirit of the Swiss has been one of wise tolerance and cooperation, and the justly celebrated Swiss political neutrality has made the city of Zurich a haven for such 20th-century greats as James Joyce, Lenin, and Thomas Mann.

Paradoxically, it was in Zurich, the most bourgeois of cities, that several revolutionary modern movements were nurtured: Here Lenin pored over Marx and Engels, wrote his famous essay, "Imperialism, The Highest State of Capitalism," and left in 1917 to organize the Bolshevik Revolution; here Ireland's James Joyce — when he wasn't romping through the streets and cafés — wrote that ultimate modern novel, *Ulysses;* and in the noisy *Cabaret Voltaire,* Tristan Tzara and Hans Arp formulated the ideas of the outrageous Dada movement, a vanguard of modern art. Harry Lime notwithstanding, the peaceful comfort of Zurich has harbored creations far more significant than the cuckoo clock.

ZURICH AT-A-GLANCE

SEEING THE CITY: No question, the most enchanting view of the city and lake is from Quai Bridge, where river and lake join. From here you can see both sides of the Old Town, with church towers, bridges, and medieval façades: this is a beautiful sight in daylight or at night. If you turn around, you can see the lake, dotted with sailboats — and on a Föhn (warm Alpine wind) day a picture-book view of the Alps.

To see the general layout of the city, try the Sonnenbergterasse, in front of the *Sonnenberg* hotel on Zurichberg, on the eastern edge of town, or have a drink or a meal at the *Sonnenberg* restaurant (98 Aurorastr.; phone: 262-0662), or try the terrace of the university *in* town. One note of caution: Although Zurich indeed is a strollers' city, visitors absolutley should avoid the Platzpromenade, a park north of the Hauptbanhof, which is the city's center of drug activity.

SPECIAL PLACES: On both sides of the Limmat, the Old Town has cobble-stone streets, narrow lanes, corners decorated by fountains, small antique shops, high fashion boutiques, and art galleries. Watch for the dates of the buildings, which are hewn into the stone doorways.

A good starting point is Münsterhof, a former pig market where recent excavations uncovered several layers of housing and burial, dating back to the 12th century.

DOWNTOWN

Fraumünster Church – This 12th-century church at Münsterhof is noted for its chapel, with marvelous stained glass windows created in 1970 and 1978 by Marc Chagall. Try to see them in the morning light. The organ here also is justly famous. Münsterpl.

Guildhouse "Zur Meisen" – A splendid rococo building with a wrought-iron gate houses the excellent ceramic collection of the *Historical Museum,* which is worth visiting if only for the marvelous view from its stuccoed rooms. Closed daily at lunch and Mondays. No admission charge. Münsterpl.

Lindenhof – This romantic, tree-covered lookout point, a few climbing crooked alleys away from the Fraumünster, was a fort in Celtic and Roman times; a Freemason lodge stands here now. Lindenhof offers a lovely view of the Old Town and is a favorite spot for lovers after dark.

St. Peterhofstatt – Another small, charming square surrounded by old buildings.

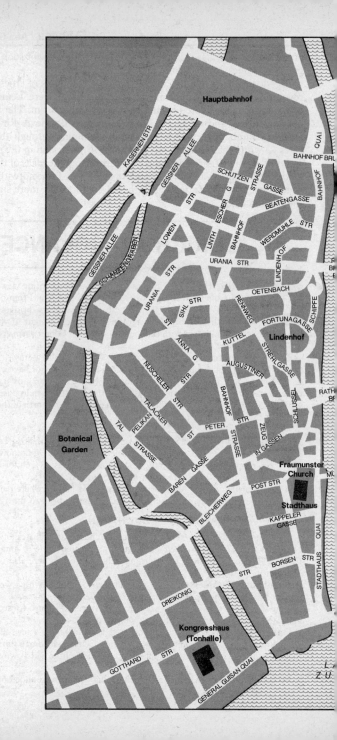

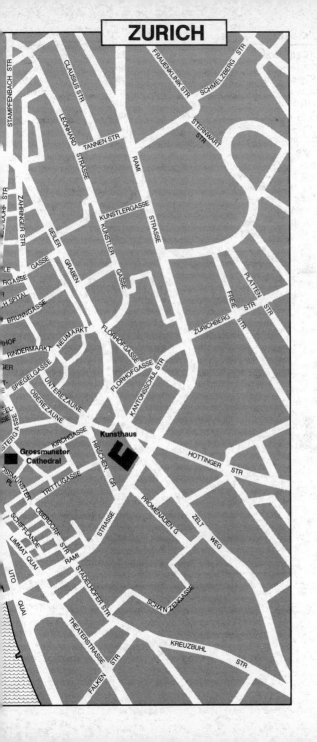

Grossmünster (Cathedral) – According to legend, this church was founded by Charlemagne, whose horse bowed down on the spot where the city's patron saints, martyrs Felix and Regula, died after walking from the river carrying their cut-off heads. This was the parish church of Ulrich Zwingli, one of the Reformation's most revered leaders, who converted Zurich to Protestantism in the mid-16th century. Its towers became a landmark of Zurich; the inside is rather cold and austere. 4 Zwinglipl.

Nägelihof – A delightful, small enclave, off 42 Limmatquai, this reconstructed square features cafés, amusing shops, two movie theaters, and a most unusual view of the Grossmünster towers.

Bahnhofstrasse – "The most beautiful shopping street in the world," and certainly one of the most expensive, Bahnhofstrasse was built on a site that was an ancient moat until about 100 years ago. Running from the lake to the main railway station, it's a shopper's and stroller's paradise — with rows of banks, shops, cafés for people watching — graced in summer with the intoxicating scent of linden trees and around *Christmas* with magnificent illuminations. There is a colorful flower and vegetable market at its lake end every Tuesday and Friday morning and a flea market every Saturday in summer.

Schweizerisches Landesmuseum (Swiss National Museum) – The largest and most complete collection of Swiss history is in a pseudo-castle behind the railroad station. Especially interesting are the prehistoric finds, the reconstructed Celtic tomb, Carolingian frescoes, and the treasury and some old paintings of Zurich. A brochure is available in English. Closed Mondays. No admission charge. 2 Museumstr. (phone: 221-1010).

Museum Rietberg – One of the most important collections of non-European art in Europe is set in the enchanting Wesendonck Villa, outside of the city center. Here Richard Wagner was often a guest, and his love affair with the hostess inspired *Tristan and Isolde.* The villa is surrounded by a magnificent private park, so bring a sandwich and you can spend a delightful day wandering in and out of the museum. The backbone of this collection is the donation of Baron von der Heydt, who had his world-famous treasures in 24 different museums before the *Rietberg* opened in 1952. The art items are mainly Indian, Southeast Asian, Chinese, Japanese, and African. The guidebook in English is recommended. Closed Mondays. No admission charge Wednesday evenings and Sundays. 15 Gablerstr. (phone: 202-4528).

Kunsthaus (Fine Arts Museum) – In 1976, the building was rebuilt in an "open museum" style, without rigidly dividing floors, walls, and stairs. The permanent exhibition includes an excellent collection of art from the Middle Ages until today, with emphasis on 19th- and 20th-century European works by Monet, Munch, Giacometti, Rodin, Chagall, and others. Closed Monday mornings. No admission charge Sundays. 1 Heimpl. (phone: 251-6755).

Boat Trip on the Lake – Don't miss this on a beautiful sunny day. Daily cruises vary in length from 1½ to 4 hours; the long one that includes the small town of Rapperswil is best. Boats depart from Bürkliplatz, at the lake end of Bahnhofstrasse. In summer there are special lunch cruises. For information call *Zurichsee Schiffahrtsgesellschaft* (phone: 482-1033) or the Zurich Tourist Office (phone: 211-4000).

Wohnmuseum – Two charming private houses from the 17th and 18th centuries display period interiors with interesting furniture; in the basement there is a collection of dolls made by the famous Swiss artist Sacha Morgenthaler. Closed at lunch hour in winter and Mondays. No admission charge. 22 Bärengasse (phone: 211-1716).

E. G. Bührle Collection – An extremely important private art collection, mainly from the 19th century, which includes French Impressionist paintings, medieval sculptures, and other items. The collection is in the private villa of the industrialist Emil Bührle, who died in 1956. Open on Tuesday and Friday afternoons only. Admission charge. 172 Zollikerstr. (phone: 550086).

Beyer's Watch & Clock Museum – The oldest watch shop in Switzerland. Inside is the private collection of the Beyer family — rare and interesting items dating from 1400 BC to the present. Closed weekends. No admission charge. 31 Bahnhofstr. (221-1080).

Botanical Garden – Rare plants from all over the world and a good cafeteria with a large terrace. The gardens could be combined with a visit to the nearby Bührle villa. Open daily. No admission charge. 107 Zollikerstr. (phone: 385-4411).

Zurich Toy Museum – The exhibits here are from the antiques collection of the same Franz Carl Weber who owns the famous toy shop (see *Shopping*). Closed mornings and Sundays. No admission charge. 15 Fortunagasse (phone: 211-9305).

OUT OF TOWN

Schaffhausen-Rhinefall and Stein am Rhein – Schaffhausen, 35 miles (56 km) north, is a wonderfully preserved medieval town, with a very photogenic fortress and the Rhinefall, Europe's largest waterfall (no match for Niagara); the best view is from Neuhausen, on the terrace of the *Bellevue* hotel. (Try their wine and fish while admiring the view.) Open daily (phone: 53-222121). Stein am Rhein, 13 miles (21 km) farther east, is a delight with its intricately painted housefronts and a museum in a former monastery. (You have to share it with loads of other tourists, though.) If possible, return through the gentle wine country around Stammheim, with villages of half-timbered houses, vineyards, and orchards.

St. Gallen and Appenzell – About 70 miles (112 km) northeast of Zurich is St. Gallen, a Swiss textile center, with a spectacular abbey-library in its cathedral (100,000 volumes of rare books and manuscripts). From here it is only a short drive into the country's most genuinely rural region, the Appenzell. (Its capital has the same name.) The region has farms, pastures, folk art (embroidery and woodcarvings), and lovely painted houses; around the Säntis (mountain) there is some high Alpine scenery, including a cable car that climbs to a 7,500-foot peak. Return via the picturesque road to Wattwil, with a stop in Rapperswil on the lake; then follow the shore to Zurich. This trip offers a good cross-section of the "real" but not so well known Switzerland.

■ **EXTRA SPECIAL:** Zurich is a perfect base for dozens of short and long excursions, easily accessible also by public transportation (or organized tours).

An excellent half-day trip would be to Einsiedeln, about 25 miles (40 km) southeast of Zurich, which offers Alpine scenery (splendid walks in summer, skiing in winter), and a world-famous baroque abbey, which is magnificent.

A cable car in Weglosen, only 10 minutes beyond Einsiedeln by car, takes you into the "real" mountains.

SOURCES AND RESOURCES

TOURIST INFORMATION: For general information, brochures, and maps, contact Verkehrsverein Zürich (Hauptbahnhof; phone: 211-4000). In the US, contact the Swiss National Tourist Office (608 Fifth Ave., New York NY 10020; phone: 212-757-5944). For business travelers, a good address to know is that of the Swiss-American Chamber of Commerce (41 Talacker; phone: 211-2454).

The best pocket guidebook in English is *Travel Guide Zürich,* published by Polyglot, available at any local bookstore. (It's also available at bookstores in the US, but be sure to get the latest edition.)

The *Zürich News,* which comes out every Friday, has a detailed listing of events for the coming week plus a 2-week forecast. It is available at all hotels and at the tourist office. The *Shopping Guide Zürich* is a monthly publication available at hotels and selected shops.

The US Consulate is at 141 Zollikerstr. (phone: 552566).

Local Coverage – There is no English-language newspaper, but for world news the best is the daily (except Sundays) *International Herald Tribune.*

Food – Consult the *Zürich News* for a rundown of restaurants in the city. For a description of regional cheeses and where they can be tasted, consult the *Guide Fromage Suisse,* available free from the Swiss National Tourist Office (see above).

 TELEPHONE: The country code for Switzerland is 41; the city code for Zurich is 1.

 GETTING AROUND: Airport – Kloten Airport, about 10 minutes from the center of town by train and 20 minutes by car, handles both domestic and international flights: Terminal A handles flights within Europe; Terminal B handles all the others. Trains to the airport leave every 20 minutes from the Hauptbahnhof, Zurich's main train station; the stop is called Kloten Airport (Flughafen). Cab fare from the city to the airport is about 40 Swiss francs (about $27).

Bus – The supermodern blue streetcar/trams (*VBZ*) are best. Automatic machines at every stop issue tickets for exact change. (You cannot pay on the tram and you are fined if found without a ticket.) The same applies to buses. If you intend to use them a lot, it is best to get a 1-day or a season ticket. An informative multilingual brochure, giving all the details, including rates and routes, is available at information booths marked "VBZ" in the underground *Shopville* at the main railroad station, at Paradeplatz and Bellevueplatz, or at the Zurich Tourist Office.

The in-season city tours by a golden tram, "Goldtimer," on Wednesdays, Fridays, and Sundays are lots of fun. Board them at the main train station (at Bahnhofpl.).

Bikes – Available for rent at most railroad stations, bikes provide a somewhat less expensive (and certainly delightful) means of getting where you're going. They can be taken onto passenger trains for a small fee and returned at any station.

Car Rental – All major firms are represented at the airport and in the city. *Avis* (17 Gartenhofstr.; phone: 242-2040); *Budget* (33 Lindenstr.; phone: 3831747); *Europcar* (53 Josefstr.; phone: 271-5656); and *Avag,* a local firm whose rates are sometimes lower (123 Sihlfeldstr.; phone: 242-8866).

Taxi – Among the most expensive in the world (tip is included in the fare), taxis can be flagged down; the light on top indicates availability. To call a cab: 271-1111 or 241-4100.

Train – The main train station is Hauptbahnhof, at Bahnhofpl. (phone: 211-5010 for information).

 LOCAL SERVICES: Dentist (English-Speaking) – Dr. Terance McDermott, 123 Klosbachstr. (phone: 252-4452).

Dry Cleaner/Tailor – *Terlinden* (29 Löwenstr. and other locations; phone: 211-0811); *Perma Clean* (26 Kreuzstr.; phone: 470505).

Limousine Service – *Welti Furrer Car Hire,* 31 Pfingstweidstr. (phone: 271-1442).

Medical Emergency – *University Hospital,* 100 Rämistr. (phone: 255-1111; the emergency phone number for the doctor on duty is 474700).

Messenger Service – *Kurier AG,* 49 Klausstr. (phone: 383-6666).

National/International Courier – *DHL International,* 56 Thurgauerstr. (phone: 301-1600).

Office Equipment Rental – *E. Brender AG,* for typewriters. 9 Bahnhofquai (phone: 211-7447).

Pharmacy – *Bellevue Apotheke,* open 24 hours. 14 Theaterstr. (phone: 252-4411).

Photocopies – *OK,* several locations, including 30 Uraniastr. (phone: 211-9242).

Post Office – The main post office is open from 6:30 AM to 11 PM Mondays through Saturdays, and from 9 AM to 11 PM Sundays. 95-99 Kasernenstr. (phone: 245-4111).

Secretary/Stenographer – *International Office,* 32 Rennweg (phone: 214-6111).

Telex – *International Office,* 32 Rennweg (phone: 214-6111).

Translator – *International Office* (32 Rennweg; phone: 214-6111); *Jean Paul Rochat* (108 Forchstr., Küsnacht; phone: 558090 or 910-7877).

Other – Office space rental, fully equipped: *International Office* (32 Rennweg; phone: 214-6111). Camera and photographic rental: *Foto Ganz* (40 Bahnhofstr.; phone: 211-7673). Men's and women's formal wear rental: *Atelier Claire Schärer* (134 Seefeldstr.; phone: 383-1206).

SPECIAL EVENTS: *Fasnacht* (the Zurich Carnival) is celebrated with masked processions and costume balls at the end of February or early March. The most typical and colorful event of all, the *Sechseläuten,* generally on the third Monday in April, celebrates the burning of winter on Bellevueplatz (a giant snowman is stuffed with firecrackers) as the 6 o'clock bells ring. This ceremony is preceded by a picturesque procession of medieval guilds in traditional costumes and carriages. These are members of fraternities, whose membership is inherited by the males in the best Zurich families.

There also is the yearly *June Festival,* with top musical and theatrical events. August 1 is a national holiday, commemorating the founding of the Swiss Confederation (last year marked its 700th anniversary); it is celebrated with fireworks and bonfires.

MUSEUMS: Most Zurich museums are described in *Special Places.* Also noteworthy is the *Museum Bellerive* (3 Höschgasse; phone: 383-4376), annexed to the *Museum of Applied Arts,* in a charming villa on Lake Zurich with excellent temporary exhibitions. The university has several interesting collections, among them the *Ethnological Museum* (non-European; 40 Pelikanstr.; phone: 221-3191), and the *Medicinhistorical Collection,* including items ranging from primitive instruments and techniques to present-day ones, (71 Rämistr.; phone: 257-2298). The *Foundation for Constructive & Concrete Art* (317 Seefeldstr.; phone: 533808) presents high-quality, international exhibits. The *Museum of Applied Arts* (60 Austellungstr.; phone: 271-6700) and *Helmhaus* (31 Limmatquai; phone: 251-6177) have interesting temporary exhibitions.

SHOPPING: It is hard to know where to begin in this shopper's paradise, with some of the best (and most expensive) merchandise in the world. The major hunting ground for shoppers is the ultra-elegant Bahnhofstrasse and its side streets (Storchengasse, In Gassen, and Rennweg).

The best buys in Switzerland are watches, which can be purchased here even though most are made in Geneva. Other interesting items are Swiss chocolate, embroidery and linen, optical instruments, and the wonderful (and inescapable) Swiss Army knives. *Jelmoli* and *Globus,* both on Bahnhofstrasse, are the two best-known department stores (the former with more solid quality and larger choice, the latter more "with it" and with lower prices); you can sample all Swiss wares here. General shopping hours are 9 AM to 6:30 PM during the week (to 9 PM on Thursdays), and 9 AM to 4 PM on Saturdays.

The Old Town is full of fashion boutiques, art galleries, and antiques shops, and there is more casual shopping along Limmatquai. In rainy weather, you might want to try *Shopville* under the main railroad station.

Albrecht-Schlapfer – Lovely eiderdowns and linen. 10 Lintheschergasse (phone: 211-5747).

Ariane Fluck – Quality handmade brass and tin bells, dishes, and figurines, Austrian dried-flower arrangements and wreaths, spice bouquets, and more. 2 Rennweg (phone: 211-7359).

Bally – Famous for shoes. 66 Bahnhofstr. (phone: 211-3515).

Bernhard Ilg – Jewelry. 128 Limmatquai. (phone: 252-2122).

Blumen Binder – For a wide variety of the freshest flowers. 10 Oberdorfstr. (phone: 472947).

Buch & Antiquariat Falk & Falk – Old books, prints, and manuscripts sold in a medieval house. 38 Kirchgasse (phone: 262-5657).

Bucherer – Large selection of fine watches and jewelry. 50 Bahnhofstr. (phone: 211-2635).

Café Schober – Cakes, cookies made in 16th-century molds, chocolates, and home-made marmalades. 4 Napfgasse (phone: 251-8060).

Cartier – Another magical name for watches and jewelry. 47 Bahnhofstr. (phone: 471141).

Daeniker's – The city's best and oldest English-language bookstore. Almost 150 years old, it has a terrific paperback selection. In Gassen, off the Bahnhofstr. (phone: 211-2704).

F. C. Weber – Toys and (yes) cuckoo clocks. 62 Bahnhofstr. (phone: 211-2961).

Fioramis – Interior design, silk flowers, and objects from the Engadine region of Switzerland. 30 Kirchgasse (phone: 252-1819).

Grieder – Women's and men's high-quality fashions. 30 Bahnhofstr. (phone: 211-3360).

Gübelin – More watches and jewelry. 36 Bahnhofstr. (phone: 221-3888).

Hannes B – Upscale menswear. 2 Wühre (phone: 211-8655).

Haus Zum Engel – Four floors of antiques, including furniture, first-edition books, and Napoleonic cavalry equipment. There's also artwork by Salvador Dalí. 24 Kirchgasse (phone: 251-3031).

Heimatwerk – Top-quality Swiss handicrafts. 2 Bahnhofstr. (phone: 221-0837).

Keinath – Fine, old silver and antiques. Near the *Storchen* hotel, 19 Wühre (phone: 211-9750).

Koch – Optical instruments. 11 Bahnhofstr. (phone: 221-2350).

Leinen Langenthal – Bed/table/kitchen linen from an old-established Swiss factory, plus gift items. 29 Strehlgasse (phone: 221-3104).

Medieval Art & View – Books on music, art, and food of the Middle Ages. 29 Spiegelg. (phone: 252-4720).

Meister – Crystal, silver, and jewels. 28 Bahnhofstr. at Paradepl. (phone: 221-2730).

Musik Hug – Musical instruments, including Alpine horns and wooden spoons called *Löffeli*. 28 Limmatquai (phone: 251-6850).

Operissimo – Everything to do with the opera — records, books, antiquarian items, opera glasses. 15 Färberstr. (phone: 252-9285).

Pastorini – Creative and educational toys. 3 Weinpl. (phone: 211-7426).

Paul Binder – Unique jewelry. 4 Storchengasse (phone: 211-7225).

Payot – Books in English. 9 Bahnhofstr. (phone: 211-5452).

Pic + Asso – A bewilderingly large selection of games, toys, and gadgets. 70 Hermetschloostr. (phone: 623500 or 628866).

Schade Uhren – Antique watches and clocks. 5 Waaggasse (phone: 221-1045).

Spitzenhaus – Handmade lace and embroidered organdy. 14 Börsenstr. (phone: 211-5576).

Sprüngli – More than a century old, this place is famous for chocolates and pastry. There also is a café here (see *Eating Out*). Bahnhofstr. at Paradepl. (phone: 221-17220).

Stäheli – Centrally located, this shop is another good source for English-language books. 70 Bahnhofstr. (phone: 201-3302).

Sturzenegger – Fine Swiss embroidery and linen. 48 Bahnhofstr. (phone: 211-2820).

Teehaus Wühre – An enchanting small tea shop with a wide selection of its own blends. 15 Wühre (phone: 211-6114).

Teuscher – Great chocolates. 9 Storchengasse. The company also has its own tea and coffee shop called *Schober,* on 4 Napfgasse (phone: 251-8060).

Tiffany – A branch of the well-known jewelry company, famous for its blue packaging. 14 Bahnhofstr. (phone: 211-1010).

Travel Book Shop – Books about all aspects of travel — many in English — sold by an informed staff. 20 Rindermarkt (phone: 252-3883).

Türler – And still more fine watches and jewelry. 28 Bahnhofstr. (phone: 221-0608).

Vogt – An antiques store in the Old Town that specializes in folk art. 13 Neumarkt (phone: 474155).

Wohnshop Bazar – Decorations, gadgets, gifts, bags, cards, and more. 32 Schifflände (phone: 261-8100).

SPORTS AND FITNESS: Fitness Centers – Both the *Atmos Fitness Club,* in the *Zürich* hotel (42 Neumühlequai; phone: 363-4040), and the *Town Squash Luxor Club* (35 Glärnischstr.; phone: 202-3838) offer onetime visits.

Golf – There are no public courses, but several clubs accept visitors: *Dolder Golf Club* (66 Kurhausstr.; phone: 475045); *Golf & Country Club Zumikon* (Zumikon; phone: 918-0051); *Golf & Country Club Schönenberg* (Schönenberg; phone: 788-1624); and *Golf & Country Club Breitenloo* (9 Untere Zäune; phone: 836-4080).

Hiking – Dozens of marked trails are on the outskirts of town.

Jogging – Run along Lake Zurich, on either side of Bellevue Bridge, or at Dolder in the Zurichberg forest.

Sailing and Rowing – Boats can be rented along Utoquai.

Skating – The ice rink at Dolder (36 Adlisbergstr.) is open only in winter.

Skiing – From December to March, nearby skiing is good; there are accessible runs within an hour of Zurich; equipment rental is available at all major ski shops, department stores, and ski resorts.

Soccer – Several national and international matches are played at *Hardturm* (321 Hardturmstr.) and *Letzigrund* (47 Herdenstr.) stadiums.

Swimming – Two good beaches are right on the lake (best is Tiefenbrunnen, popular with topless bathers), and there's an attractive pool at Dolder in the Zurichberg forest. In winter, several indoor public pools are open in town: *Blasi* (154 Limmattalstr.; phone: 341-9368) and *Oerlikon* (100 Wallisellenstr.; phone: 312-4690).

THEATER: Zurich has several small and large theaters. There are two main stages: *Schauspielhaus* (34 Rämistr.; phone: 251-1111) produces plays in classical German and *Theater am Neumarkt* (5 Neumarkt; phone: 251-1818) performs avant-garde works. There are twice-yearly productions of the *British Comedy Club* and also of guest companies — mainly during the *June Festival.* (See listings in local publications.) Movies are all in the original language with subtitles.

MUSIC: There is a variety to choose from. Top-quality operas, ballets, and operettas are presented at the *Opernhaus* (1 Folkenstr.; phone: 251-6922). Regular classical concerts of the *Tonhalle Orchester* and visiting orchestras are given at the *Tonhalle* (7 Claridenstr.; phone: 201-1580). There are also frequent concerts and recitals in several churches, mainly Fraumünster, Grossmünster, and St. Peter. Much less choice is available in jazz, rock, pop, and folk. The central ticket office for most cultural events is at Billetzentrale (Werdmühlepl.; phone: 221-2283); closed weekends.

NIGHTCLUBS AND NIGHTLIFE: The latest most public establishments can stay open is 2 AM (a few private clubs excepted, but outsiders cannot get in). *Diagonal* discotheque (Gen. Guisan-Quai; phone: 201-2410) is the best, and if you are the guest of the *Baur au Lac* hotel, you can get a temporary membership. The *Joker-Club* (5 Gotthardstr.; phone: 202-2262) has great live music and dancing; it often offers top shows as well. *Roxy* (11 Beatengasse; phone: 211-5457) and *Xenox* (43 Dufourstr.; phone: 251-9422) are very fashionable with young people. The *Birdwatcher's Club* (16 Schützengasse; phone: 211-5058) is a smart, semiprivate club that opens at 5 PM and becomes a lively disco by 9. The *Petit Prince* (21 Bleicherweg; phone: 201-1739) has disco dancing with international shows, and is open until 2 AM. For striptease with live music, try *The Red House* (17 Marktgasse; phone: 252-1110); the *King's Club* (25 Talstr.; phone: 211-2333) also offers good shows (mainly striptease) and dancing to disco music.

BEST IN TOWN

CHECKING IN: The following are our choices from an inventory of over 90 hotels. During the week, reservations are necessary. Continental breakfast or buffet is included at most hotels. All hotels listed have telephones in rooms; most also have radios.

Be warned that prices in Swiss cities are expensive. The range for a double room with a private shower or bath in the expensive category is $240 and up; in the moderate category, $100 to $180; in the inexpensive category, $65 to $80 (slightly less without a private bath). Several smaller hotels offer winter reductions. All telephone numbers are in the 1 city code unless otherwise indicated.

Baur au Lac – The most prestigious establishment in the city center, it offers understated Old World luxury, beautiful grounds, and a celebrity-dotted guest list; its 170 rooms always are full. It's set in its own gardens facing the lake and features adjacent parking. The *Grill Room* is a fashionable restaurant (see *Eating Out*). Business facilities include 24-hour room service, meeting rooms, English-speaking concierge, foreign currency exchange, secretarial services in English, audiovisual equipment, photocopiers, computers, cable television news, and translation services. 1 Talstr. (phone: 221-1650; fax: 211-8139; telex: 813567). Expensive.

Dolder Grand – A famous luxury property in the Zurichberg forest, built in fairy-tale-castle style, with a fabulous view, 200 antique and modern rooms, free transportation into town (a 10-minute ride), and a first class restaurant, *La Rotunda* (see *Eating Out*). Business facilities include 24-hour room service, meeting rooms for up to 895, English-speaking concierge, audiovisual equipment, photocopiers, computers, cable television news, translation services, and express checkout. 65 Kurhausstr. (phone: 251-6231; fax: 251-8829; telex: 816416). Expensive.

Carlton Elite – Long established, traditional, but modern, this hotel is on mid-Bahnhofstrasse, central to banks and shopping. It has Zurich's first pub, plus *Locanda,* an excellent Italian restaurant (see *Eating Out*). A few of the top-floor rooms have private roof gardens; split-level suites, too. Business facilities include meeting rooms for up to 300, English-speaking concierge, and audiovisual equipment. 41 Bahnhofstr. (phone: 211-6560; fax: 211-3019; telex: 812781). Expensive to moderate.

Central Plaza – Centrally located, this hostelry is bright and cheery, with pastel decor and palm trees. Several popular restaurants and bars create a lively ambience. 1 Central (phone: 251-5555; fax: 251-8535; telex: 817152). Expensive to moderate.

International – Within walking distance of the *ZUSPA Exhibition Center* and connected to downtown by several tram lines, this place offers a swimming pool, a fitness center and solarium, plus several restaurants and bars, one with a splendid panoramic view of Zurich and the Alps. Business facilities include 24-hour room service, meeting rooms for up to 700, English-speaking concierge, foreign currency exchange, secretarial services in English, audiovisual equipment, photocopiers, computers, cable television news, translation services, and underground parking. Am Marktpl., Zurich-Oerlikon (phone: 311-4341; fax: 312-4468; telex: 823251). Expensive to moderate.

St. Gotthard – In addition to its terrific location on the upper end of the elegant Bahnhofstrasse (near the railway station), this first class hotel has 140 modern rooms, the *Hummer Bar,* a very good seafood restaurant (see *Eating Out*), and a restored Art Nouveau café that serves snacks. 87 Bahnhofstr. (phone: 211-5500; fax: 211-2419; telex: 812420). Expensive to moderate.

Splügenschloss – A few steps from the lake, this charming member of the Relais & Châteaux group is in a turn-of-the-century building and has 55 cozy rooms and suites, all luxuriously furnished (some with balconies). There's a pleasant restaurant (see *Eating Out*) and bar, plus a meeting room for up to 30. 2 Splügenstr. (phone: 201-0800; fax: 201-4286; telex: 815553). Expensive to moderate.

Zum Storchen – Zurich's oldest (built in the 14th century) and most romantically situated hotel, in the heart of the Old Town on the Limmat River. Rooms, except for the corner ones, tend to be small and spartan, but those with a river view are much in demand (and require reservations far in advance). *La Patisserie* is a nice restaurant with a fireplace, and dining on the terrace in summer (see *Eating Out*). Business facilities include meeting rooms for up to 25, English-speaking concierge, audiovisual equipment, and cable television news. 2 Weinpl. (phone: 211-5510; fax: 211-6451; telex: 813354). Expensive to moderate.

Zurich – A modern high-rise, right behind the main railroad station on the riverbank. Rooms on the higher floors afford fabulous views of the city and the Alps. Indoor swimming pool, a bowling alley, and a fitness club are added features. Business facilities include meeting rooms for up to 250, English-speaking concierge, audiovisual equipment, and cable television news. 42 Neumühlequai (phone: 363-6363). Expensive to moderate.

Eos – This Art Nouveau villa in the green, exclusive residential area of the Zurichberg has a romantic little garden and 24 rooms, each with its own personality. 17 Carmenstr. (phone: 261-9060; fax: 261-9094). Moderate.

Florhof – A lovely old patrician building — renovation, unfortunately, destroyed the hotel's coziness. There is, however, a good restaurant. 4 Florhofgasse (phone: 261-4470; fax: 261-4611; telex: 817364). Moderate.

Helmhaus – Centrally located in a historic building, this is an excellent value (and superbly run) with 24 modern, cheerful rooms. No restaurant. 30 Schifflländepl. (phone: 251-8810; fax: 251-0430; telex: 816525). Moderate.

Nova Park – Catering mostly to business travelers, this place has a fitness club with everything from a Turkish bath and massages to a swimming pool. There are several restaurants, bars, a discotheque, and it is the headquarters of the *Backgammon Club of Switzerland.* Business facilities include meeting rooms for up to 600, English-speaking concierge, foreign currency exchange, secretarial services in English, audiovisual equipment, photocopiers, and cable television news. 420 Badenerstr. (phone: 491-2222; fax: 491-2220; telex: 822822). Moderate.

Opera – Next to the opera house (the best of the 67 modern rooms are on the top floor), it has a pleasant, large lobby/sitting room. No restaurant. 5 Dufourstr. (phone: 251-9090; fax: 251-9001; telex: 816480). Moderate.

Tiefenau – A private atmosphere prevails in this quiet, 150-year-old townhouse near the *Fine Arts Museum.* Accommodations are in 27 bed/sitting rooms (some very large), most furnished with antiques. There is a garden and a good, candlelit restaurant, *Au Gourmet* (see *Eating Out*). 8-10 Steinwiesstr. (phone: 251-2409; fax: 251-2476; telex: 816395). Moderate.

Limmathof – Perfectly located, and rather modest, it's near the railroad station, with 55 no-frills (but pleasant) modern rooms. No credit cards accepted. 142 Limmatquai (phone: 261-4240). Inexpensive.

EATING OUT: More than 1,000 restaurant choices flourish here in all varieties and price ranges. A service charge is included in all bills, but it is customary to leave a small tip anyway.

Switzerland is a country where the culinary traditions of Germany, Italy, and France meet, but there are specialties that are singularly Swiss. The people of Zurich — known for their interest in good food — like *geschnetzeltes Kalbsfleisch* (minced veal or calf's liver with cream) or *Leberspiessli* (roasted calf liver with bacon). Also local in Zurich is *Kalbsbratwurst,* a delicious veal sausage.

If you like cheese, try fondue, the national dish made with a combination of several Swiss cheeses and wine. Also try the crisp hash-brown potato "pancake" called *rösti.* Desserts feature fresh cream and delicious Swiss chocolate; try *Zuger Kirschtorte,* a cake soaked in kirsch, a cherry brandy. And visit at least one of the many tearooms for which Zurich is famous; they serve tea or coffee with a choice of pastries.

It also is rare to see plain water on the table, and as the only beverage ordered, it certainly is frowned upon. One American woman reports being threatened by a Swiss waiter who warned that if she drank only water with her fondue, all manner of ills would strike her digestion. Don't be intimidated; order mineral water (still or carbonated) if you wish. (Incidentally, most restaurants serve wine by the glass at reasonable prices.)

Like hotel prices, restaurant costs also can be stiff. Many places have less expensive luncheon menus. Our price range is for a three-course dinner for two without drinks, wine, or coffee. Count $90 and up as expensive; $70 to $90 as moderate; about $50 and under as inexpensive. In the better restaurants, reservations are necessary. All telephone numbers are in the 1 city code unless otherwise indicated.

Grill Room – One of several restaurants in the *Baur au Lac* hotel, this is one of Zurich's most elegant gathering places. As the name implies, this eatery specializes in grilled meat and fish — a favorite is the grilled turbot. There also are cold dishes, and don't leave without trying the house treat, the *Baur au Lac* dessert, a hot brandied apple tart. For summer dining there is also the open-air *Pavilion.* Open daily. Reservations advised. Major credit cards accepted. 1 Talstr. (phone: 221-1650). Expensive.

Kronenhalle – The best known place in Zurich, where "everybody" goes, from local artists to visiting celebrities; walls are covered with original Picassos, Mirós, and other works from the owner's collection. The menu offers international food with Swiss specialties. Try the chocolate mousse. Open daily. Reservations necessary. Major credit cards accepted. 4 Rämistr. (phone: 251-0256 or 251-6669). Expensive.

Kunststuben – Young, creative chef-owner Horst Petermann, who is rated among the top *toques* in the country, prepares memorable creations at this cozy, flower-filled place. The restaurant is the recent recipient of a second Michelin star. Closed Sundays and Mondays. Reservations essential. Major credit cards accepted. Located in the suburb of Küsnacht, 160 Seestr. (phone: 910-0715). Expensive.

La Rotunda – A fine eatery in the spectacular *Dolder Grand* hotel, serving superb international fare. Open daily. Reservations advised. Major credit cards accepted. 55 Kurhausstr. (phone: 251-6231). Expensive.

Les Vacanes – On the premises of the late lamented *Chez Max* in the nearby suburb of Zollikan, owner/chef Max Kehl has opened a new dining spot and the cuisine is now Japanese-French. The food is prettily presented and the decor is bright. Open for lunch and dinner. Closed Sundays. Reservations necessary. Major credit cards accepted. 53 Seestr., Zollikan (phone: 391-8887). Expensive.

Flühgasse – In an enchanting 16th-century inn, the food served here is among the best in Zurich. The emphasis is on light Swiss dishes. Closed Saturdays and Sundays. Reservations necessary. Major credit cards accepted. 214 Zollikerstr. (phone: 531215). Expensive to moderate.

Hummer Bar – Specializing in seafood as its name ("lobster" in German) suggests, this popular place is in the centrally located *St. Gotthard* hotel. Open daily. Reservations advised. Major credit cards accepted. 87 Bahnhofstr. (phone: 211-5500). Expensive to moderate.

Locanda – Located in the *Carlton Elite* hotel, Italian and French fare are the dual specialties here. Open daily. Reservations advised. Major credit cards accepted. 41 Bahnhofstr. (phone: 211-6560). Expensive to moderate.

La Rôtisserie – A charming eatery in the old *Zum Storchen* hotel. A fireplace in winter and open-air dining during the summer make it exceptionally pleasant. Their extensive menu features the Zurich specialty, *rösti,* and for chocoholics, the *Zum Storchen* mousse. Open daily. Reservations advised. Major credit cards accepted. 2 Weinpl. (phone: 211-5510). Expensive to moderate.

Splügenschloss – The menu has a French accent in this pleasant dining spot in the lakeside hotel of the same name. There's a definite emphasis on fresh herbs and sauces here with such choices as a rack of lamb with thyme sauce, a tarragon veal filet with homemade noodles, and their own "marriage of sole and scampi in marsala sauce." Open daily. Reservations advised. Major credit cards accepted. 2 Splügenstr. (phone: 201-0800). Expensive to moderate.

Zunfthaus zum Rüden – One of the most spectacular medieval guildhouses with a Gothic interior and a fabulous view on the Limmat offers delicious food. Open daily except Sundays in summer. Reservations advised. Major credit cards accepted. 42 Limmatquai (phone: 261-9566). Expensive to moderate.

California – This offbeat place has menus in English, California wines, and American food with an international touch. Informal, friendly atmosphere, and a small garden. Open daily; Saturdays and Sundays from 6 PM only. Reservations advised. Major credit cards accepted. 125 Asylstr. (phone: 535680). Moderate.

Au Gourmet – The place to go for intimate dining by candlelight. International fare is served in this dining spot at the charming *Tiefenau* hotel. Open daily. Reservations unnecessary. Major credit cards accepted. 8-10 Steinwiesstr. (phone: 251-2409). Moderate.

Mövenpick – Whether you want a good hamburger, some homemade cakes, or a full meal, the smart snack shop/restaurants in this chain are almost always open. Reservations advised. 4 Paradepl. (phone: 221-3252) and 1 Zeltweg (phone: 262-0444), among other branches (including the airport). At *Feldschlösschen Mövenpick,* the real highlight of this member of the chain is the Sunday brunch — the best bargain in town at about $18. Reservations necessary for brunch only. Major credit cards accepted. 81 Bahnhofstr. (phone: 211-5034). Moderate.

Oepfelchammer – In this historic house with an enchanting, cozy atmosphere, a special student fraternity room accepts anybody for a glass of wine at one long wooden table. The small restaurant has excellent "Old Zurich" specialties and other dishes; good open wines. Closed Sundays. Reservations necessary. Diners Club accepted. 12 Rindermarkt (phone: 251-2336). Moderate.

Sprüngli – For a tasty breakfast, snack lunch, or afternoon hot chocolate, this is the city's most famous and elegant café and candy shop — the chocolate truffles are delicious. Wonderful pastry to eat in or carry out. Closed for dinner and Sundays. Reservations unnecessary. Credit cards accepted in the retail shop only. Bahnhofstr. at Paradepl. (phone: 211-0795). Moderate.

Wolfbach – An excellent, small restaurant, specializing in freshwater fish. Closed Sundays. Reservations advised. Most major credit cards accepted. 35 Wolfbachstr., near the *Fine Arts Museum* (phone: 252-5180). Moderate.

Belcanto – In the city's *Opernhaus* (Opera House), this place (with an outdoor terrace) is open from morning to midnight and offers a menu ranging from light snacks to full meals. There's an interesting local cultural ambience, especially before performances. Open daily. Reservations advised for dinner before the opera only. Major credit cards accepted. Theater Pl. (phone: 251-6951). Moderate to inexpensive.

Blaue Ente (Blue Duck) – In an old grain mill, this is Zurich's liveliest and trendiest restaurant. The reasonable menu is devoted to adding fantasy to the meal. Open daily. Reservations essential. Major credit cards accepted. 223 Seefeldstr. (phone: 557706). Moderate to inexpensive.

Pinte Vaudoise – Swiss cheese specialties, like fondue and raclette (potatoes and cheese), are offered in a cozy, paneled tavern. Closed Sundays. Reservations advised. No credit cards accepted. 4 Kruggasse (phone: 252-6009). Moderate to inexpensive.

Tres Kilos – The first Mexican eatery in Zurich is extremely popular with locals. Very lively and noisy with a young, chic crowd. Open daily. Reservations necessary. No credit cards accepted. 175 Dufoursrt. (phone: 550233). Moderate to inexpensive.

Gleich – A vegetarian's delight, with dishes of great imagination and quality, this place is famous for homemade fruit tarts and special juices. No alcohol. Closed Saturday afternoons and Sundays. Reservations advised for lunch. No credit cards accepted. 9 Seefeldstr. (phone: 251-3203). Inexpensive.

Hiltl Vegi – The oldest vegetarian restaurant in town serves delicious salads, Indian curries, and other creative dishes. There are 55 varieties of fresh brewed tea in the upstairs restaurant's daily afternoon "tea buffet." Open daily. Reservations advised for lunch. No credit cards accepted. 28 Sihlstr. (phone: 221-3870). Inexpensive.

Kropf – An Art Nouveau beer hall, almost an institution, with good-and-plenty Swiss/German/Austrian food. Pleasant terrace in summer. Closed Sundays. Reservations advised. American Express accepted. 16 In Gassen, near Paradelpl. (phone: 221-1805). Inexpensive.

Select – The most popular meeting place for artists, students, and chess players serves good food and snacks (hearty hamburgers and outstanding ice cream), but no alcohol. Sidewalk tables. Open daily. Reservations unnecessary. No credit cards accepted. 16 Limmatquai (phone: 252-4372). Inexpensive.

Schober – A delight of gilded, picture-postcard charm, this is the oldest café in town. Cold snacks and marvelous sweets are available to eat here or to take with you. Open daily; closed evenings. Reservations unnecessary. No credit cards accepted. 4 Napfgasse (phone: 251-8060). Inexpensive.

DIVERSIONS

DIVERSIONS

Introduction

If you made random inquiries of passengers on any transatlantic flight and asked what they considered to be the most desirable things to see and do in Europe, the answers would vary enormously. The sportsperson — his thoughts lingering affectionately on a favorite fishing rod stored carefully in the hold — might select salmon fishing in Ireland or Scotland; the culture maven would more likely lean toward the most extravagant collections of art and architecture in the world; the gastronome would favor the restaurants of Alfred Girardet, Georges Blanc, and Michel Guérard; the hedonist, the beaches lining the Mediterranean from Gibraltar to Turkey; the mountaineer, the Alps; and the rest of the passengers, a wide combination of all these things and, perhaps, if it is a return visit, the guestroom of a favorite château in the Loire Valley or the view from a particular hill in southern Italy or a mountain in the Peloponnese.

What best characterizes Europe is not only its diversity, but also its density. Three-quarters of a continent and some 2,000 miles lie between America's highest mountains and the great urban cultural centers of the East Coast; but Basel, Switzerland, tucked between Germany's Black Forest and the foothills of the Alps, has one of Europe's finest small museums and is less than half a day's drive from Strasbourg, France, and the exquisite villages of Alsace. The number of activities that can be enjoyed within a day of Basel is simply staggering. And Basel is just one medium-size city near the center of Europe.

The unparalleled proximity of Europe's great cities and its historic countryside offers a variety of experience that couldn't be better suited to contemporary travelers. Certainly North Americans would travel to Europe under almost any conditions; to some degree the majority of us have an ancestral tie to Europe, and every trip carries with it something of a small celebratory homecoming. But today's travelers also are uniquely willing to take advantage of the enormous range of activities Europe offers, and of the fact that museum and mountain, ski slope and opera house, are virtually cheek by jowl.

Still, the sheer wealth of European attractions poses a challenge. Combining the right setting with the right activity is an art even back home, and facing a continent of 30-plus nations, dozens of enthralling cities, and hundreds of regions, districts, and areas — all with distinct cultural features — can cause even the savviest traveler some trepidation.

The pertinent question is: Where is the quality of experience highest? On the following pages we suggest the best places in Europe to pursue 20 different activities — from tennis, golf, and fishing to the abundant wildernesses of this most civilized of continents, the most accomplished theatrical and operatic performances, and we even assist in ferreting out auctions, flea markets, antiques shops, and Europe's finest shopping streets. Each section represents a distillation of the best in Europe, a selective guide to Europe at its most intriguing, calculated to make your visit an unparalleled experience.

For the Experience

Quintessential Europe

You've waited in line at the Eiffel Tower, and you've heard Big Ben. You've trekked through the *Louvre* to admire the *Mona Lisa*'s greenish complexion, and you've seen the Colosseum. No one who fancies him or herself a traveler could tour Europe and omit visits to these great sites and sights; their grandeur prevails — despite the tourist hordes and 20th-century tarnish. Yet there are scores of other spots in Europe that are not so celebrated and in their way deserve to be: Though not giants like the Eiffel Tower and the Colosseum, these somewhat lesser-knowns do offer an experience that is quintessentially European; here, the foreignness of the Continent and its traditions will come resoundingly home to you.

You will doubtless encounter dozens of these wonders on your own — but to get you started, here is our selection.

DINNER AT THE SACHER AND A PREMIÈRE AT THE STATE OPERA, Vienna, Austria: This is the happiness that money *can* buy — the most gracious, elegant, worldly evening in Europe. The *Sacher* hotel, aptly placed on Philharmonikerstrasse, has been the rendezvous of musicians, artists, and all Vienna since (it seems) the time of the pharaohs; and its own restaurant is among the best on the Continent. In the world of the *Sacher,* everything is just as it has always been — the decor as rich, the service as perfect, the clientele as brilliant, and the Wiener schnitzel, the *palatschinken,* and the *Sachertorte* as delectable as ever. Music is still an Austrian national religion, and the glittering *Staatsoper* is its temple. The frothy *Der Rosenkavalier* is the most Viennese of its productions, and if you can arrange it, *the* opera to hear (Beethoven's *Fidelio* is a close second choice). The black-tie *New Year's Eve* performance of *Die Fledermaus* is Europe's hardest ticket, though the concierge at the *Sacher* has been known to work even this miracle. Information: 4 Philharmonikerstrasse (phone: 1-514560).

CHRISTCHURCH COLLEGE MEADOW, Oxford, England: A beautiful, manicured English greensward, with the soft, rain-nurtured texture of a hill in the Cotswolds or the lawn at *Wimbledon,* this meadow was a greenhouse for the British Empire, and 8 centuries of the finest young people of England have strolled through the stone portals of the Great Quadrangle here and listened to the tolling of the evening bells from Tom Tower. Bolingbroke was at Christchurch before he became king; William Penn before he was expelled for "nonconformity;" Gladstone before he was prime minister; Lewis Carroll before he wrote *Alice's Adventures in Wonderland.* Walk slowly down the High Street. Two debating dons may sweep by you in their flowing black robes. Or there may be a game on *Merton Cricket Ground,* the players' uniforms a crisp white against the green velvet pitch. Have a pint of bitter and a pork pie at the *Turf Tavern* (Bath Pl. via St. Helen's Passage; phone: 865-243235). Browse in renowned *Blackwell's Book Store* (50 Broad St.; phone: 865-792792). And you, too, will listen to the bells of Tom Tower.

MIDNIGHT SUN IN LAPLAND, Finland: The Midnight Sun occurs between June and July. You must arrive in Rovaniemi, the capital of Lapland, and hope that there are no rains to make the normally magificent sunsets overcast. Otherwise, it is a memorable experience to be able to play golf, tennis, or take a hike after the midnight hour. The Northern Lights, which have been described as "nature's own light show," often are visible during November and December, but are as elusive as shooting stars.

BOULEVARD ST.-MICHEL, Paris, France: Essentially, this seething, vibrant merry-go-straight has changed very little since Ernest Hemingway and James Joyce and Co. discovered it in the 1920s. You still will find the endless ebb and flow of laughing, arguing students; the Africans and Orientals of every shade, height, and costume; the smells of street-corner crêpes, roasting chestnuts, nougat, and steaming *pommes frites;* the impromptu concerts by guitarists, bongo drummers, solo trumpeters, string quartets, their open instrument cases your invitation to drop in a franc. And there are art movie theaters showing four films in four basements in four different languages — and cafés by the score, their neat rows of seats the orchestra to the stage that is the Boul' Mich'. If you can manage to make the scene for *Bastille Day* — July 14 — by all means do so: The French really do dance in the streets.

OMAHA BEACH, Normandy, France: After the *D-Day* invasion, everything was different. One world ended, another world began. June 6, 1944, has come to be one of those watershed dates, like 1066 and 1775, that divide eras in human history. Here are the pyramids of the 20th century: the German pillboxes on the murderous cliff at Pointe du Hoc (dedicated as US soil), the landing craft and giant bulkheads sunk in the sands of Arromanches, the white crosses and stars and silent chapel at St.-Laurent-sur-Mer. Save a gray, blowy late afternoon. You can see it all panoramically, scanning the whole expanse of the coastline that was the site of the greatest mass military operation in history. Or you can find a way down to the beach somewhere along the peninsula, roll up your trousers, and wade through the shallow waters breaking on the sand flats. Whether you're 20 and read about Omaha Beach in a book or 80 and lost a son on these bloodied shoals, a visit here is the most strangely moving experience in all of Europe. In some way, we were all here.

ACROPOLIS OF LINDOS, Rhodes, Greece: Every day, the baking sun and corroding salt reclaim one more tiny particle of this ancient marble memory, a temple to Athena, set 30 miles (48 km) south of the island city of Rhodes, on a soaring promontory 400 feet above the sea. But below, and all around in every direction, the elements of the Greek islands that neither nature nor man has succeeded in eroding endure: the silent, craggy coves; the sweeping blond beaches, the white cottages gleaming against the cloudless sky; the olive groves and vineyards sloping down to the cobalt sea. A fishing boat cuts a momentary ripple in the glassy surface, the waters fold back into the timeless Aegean, and you think of Theseus skin diving and Sophocles grilling sardines. This is a place for dawns, for sunset, for solitude.

GALLERIA DELL'ACCADEMIA, Florence, Italy: On the quiet side street of Via Ricasoli, in a pleasant but uninspired building, are three of the greatest works of art of the Renaissance. Most famous is Michelangelo's stunning *David,* a colossus and a hymn to youth and power in its glorification of the human body. The *Prisoners* — a group of half-finished figures contorted as if to wrench their massive bodies free of the great marble blocks that imprison them — are among Michelangelo's most mature and disturbing works, as dark and yearning as the *David* is sunny and serene. They flank the corridor that leads to the *David.* And in the next room is the splendid *Cassone Adimari,* a 15th-century Tuscan wedding chest delicately embellished with paintings of lavishly robed and coiffed gentlewomen and graceful courtiers. Together, these three masterpieces embody the very spirit of the Renaissance: its boundless optimism and faith in mankind, its struggle toward freedom from the oppressive past, its festive joy in sheer physical beauty.

GRAND CANAL, Venice, Italy: The best way to come in is by train on the causeway across the lagoon. Walk out of the Santa Lucia Station to the head of the wide steps that lead down to the water. Stand still. And look. The whole lavish length of the Grand Canal is lined with a royal flush of Renaissance *palazzi* that make you feel as though all human endeavor that followed has been more or less superfluous. Take a gondola and have your driver pull over at the landing pier of the *Gritti Palace* hotel, and see it all again from the Gothic windows of your own top-floor suite. If it's your first visit and you don't have a lump in your throat, you have a stone for a heart. Didn't anyone ever say "See Venice and die"?

BULLFIGHT IN SEVILLE, Spain: "Sunday in Andalusia" is the title of this scenario. The morning is cool and quiet, with the southern sun and the heady odor of orange blossoms sliding in through the shutters, but you can feel the heat settling over the city, the excitement building. Follow the crowd to late-morning mass in the Gothic cathedral — one of the largest in Christendom — spectacular with its soaring columns, majestic vaults, rich stone and iron lacework; to the exotic tropical gardens of the Alcázar; to the shade of the riverside for an alfresco lunch of chilled gazpacho and manzanilla; and finally to the legendary *Plaza de la Maestranza* bullring. All your senses are assailed by the scene before you: the ocher turf glaring in the late afternoon sun; the tinny blare of the band; the procession's gaudy, spangled costumes; the *bandilleros'* ballet; the coarse, feverish crowd watering its passion with warm wine squirted from bulging skins; the black bull's thundering fury; the arrogant grace of the matador; the swirl of the red *muleta;* the flash of the sword blade. Death, triumph, idle amusement; blood, manhood, music, and sun: an age-old ritual, the core of Spain. At its worst, the *corrida* is a slaughterhouse. At its best, it can be a spectacle of unparalleled glory. Afterward, follow the crowd again: the evening *paseo* — the promenade — on the Sierpes, where all of Seville takes the air, arm in arm. And at night, somewhere in the maze of whitewashed walls and flowered patios in the Barrio de Santa Cruz, heels clack the torrid rhythms of the flamenco to the quivering sound of Spanish guitars.

GRINDELWALD, in the Bernese Oberland, Switzerland: At an altitude of 3,500 feet, the village of Grindelwald is the center stage for a great Alpine amphitheater. In the foreground are the sunny plateaus of the Grosse and Kleine Scheidegg and the ice-blue waters of the gleaming Bachsee. In the high distance, in a snowy military row, stand the five great rocky guards: the Wetterhorn, the Schreckhorn, Eiger, Monch, and — at 13,642 feet — the fabled Jungfrau: The rack railway of the Jungfraujoch is Europe's most spectacular transportation experience.

Like so many of the great Swiss and Austrian mountainscapes, this scene shades from the fairyland to the forbidding: from the charming town full of wooden chalets, puffing chimneys, and gaily splurging window boxes, to the craggy peaks and the ominous North Wall of the Eiger, which has taken the lives of so many climbers. If you visit in summer, trudge through the woods to the Bachsee or up the summit of the Faulhorn; from there, it seems that you can see the entire planet. If it's winter, step into your skis and swoop across the great snowfields of the Scheideggs. In any season, when the sun drops behind the peaks and a twilight chill comes over the town, have a steaming glass of *glühwein* and a languid nap under the feathery softness of a Swiss eiderdown.

WHITE NIGHTS OF LENINGRAD, Soviet Union: Once a year, during the last half of June, the sun leaves the horizon over one of the most beautiful of cities for only a few brief hours, and in place of the night, a mysterious chalky haze hangs over the horizon. The stolid Russians go giddy and sentimental, and in a sort of metropolitan tribal rite that celebrates the return of the White Nights, they flock to Strelka, at the prow of Vassilyevsky Island. The delicate pastel façades of structures put up along the entrancing canals of the Neva in the brilliant heyday of the court of St. Petersburg positively glow in this eerie light; and the great past of Mother Russia comes splendidly alive: the opulence of the czars' Winter Palace, the brooding mystery of Dostoyevsky in the Peter and Paul Fortress, the excitement of the revolution, the romance of Tchaikovsky.

Europe's Most Memorable Hostelries

 Europe is full of fascinating places to get a good night's sleep. In fact, some of the grandest of the world's grand hotels are here; they have the refinement and cachet that you'll find only in establishments that have spent centuries serving royalty and the rich. Other hostelries, as quaint as these grandees are luxurious, seem more like country homes; their atmosphere depends on whether you're in Sicily or Slovenia, the Cotswolds or Crete. A number of other lodging places are to be found in what were once spare monasteries or towering castles. The caravansaries we list below, by category, are sure to give you sweet dreams — and plenty of happy memories to look back on when your trip is over.

THE GRANDEST OF THE GRAND HOTELS

Like the great transatlantic liners that were once the centerpiece of European travel, the great hotels of Europe seem destined to disappear, to be gradually replaced by more practical concrete palaces. And when the world has finally been transformed into one gigantic *Holiday Inn*, we will look back longingly on the grand hotels' shimmering chandeliers, their lordly tail-coated concierges, the neat rows of shoes in their corridors awaiting morning massages. Already, these hotels belong more to the past than the present — still extant only by some strange quirk of fate. So enjoy them while you can, these gracious temples of excess, and damn the expense — which is usually monstrous. But don't think of it as just the cost of a hot bath, a night's sleep, a morning's coffee. A stay at a hotel such as Paris's *Ritz* is a concert, a visit to a museum, an evening at the theater, an experience seldom duplicated in the modern world. When you start your day with a turn through those historic revolving doors, you somehow see the whole of the surrounding city from a different, far more glittering perspective.

Some notes on getting the most from your stay: Remember that, as a rule, the more princely a hotel, the more regal the surcharges applied to telephone calls (300% is not unheard of) — so call collect when you can, use a phone credit card, or telephone from the nearest post office. You can dine out on the difference. Consider, moreover, the story of the irascible New Yorker, a guest at one of the Continent's most fabulous hostelries, who refused to pay the automatic 18% service charge because he said he hadn't had any service. And he won.

Here are some of the world's finest dormitories, on whose crested stationery there will be a good deal to write home about.

IMPERIAL, Vienna, Austria: Built more than a century ago as a private palace for the Duke of Württemberg, this establishment manages to be at once majestic and modern, and the impeccable, heel-clicking service that has always been a tradition here is not at all hard to get used to. The *Imperial* was, incidentally, a favorite of such discriminating egoists as Hitler and Wagner. Information: *Imperial,* 16 Kärntnerring, Vienna A-1015, Austria (phone: 1-501100).

SACHER, Vienna, Austria: The quintessential European hotel experience, this rococo monument to good living stands opposite the *Vienna State Opera House* and is a kind of "mission control" for Vienna's rich musical life. The rooms are not all elegant, but the service is uniformly superb, and the concierge is Vienna's prime source of otherwise unavailable opera and concert tickets. Its restaurant serves some of the finest food in Europe; the hotel's clientele has remained unchanged since, it seems, the rise of the Hapsburgs. Information: *Sacher,* 4 Philharmonikerstrasse, Vienna, Austria (phone: 1-514560).

LA RÉSERVE, Knokke-Heist, Belgium: In the country's finest beach resort, both on the shore of little Lake Victoria and a 2-minute stroll from Knokke's broad, sweeping beach, this is a model vacation hotel: Swimming pool, tennis courts, golf, horseback riding, sailing, and water skiing are on the property. A large bird sanctuary (to which the hotel's name refers) and a gambling casino are nearby. The food is wonderful, and an extensive art collection adorns the rooms. Information: *La Réserve di Knokke-Heist,* 160 Elizabethlaan, Knokke-Heist 8300, Belgium (phone: 50-610606).

CLARIDGE'S, London, England: With India and Australia gone, here is the final bastion of the British Empire. Its supreme, traditional elegance is as much a part of the London experience as the horse guards and the crown jewels. If it's winter, try for one of the suites with a working fireplace. Information: *Claridge's,* Brook St., London W1A 2JQ, England (phone: 71-629-8860; fax: 71-499-2210).

CONNAUGHT, London, England: Another stronghold of 19th-century Britain, luxurious and intimate, that soon will have you feeling like a distinguished guest at Lord Hyphen's townhouse. Small — with a tenaciously faithful clientele — it sometimes seems to be booked several generations in advance. Don't be put off by the hauteur; they've earned it. Information: *The Connaught,* Carlos Pl., Mayfair, London W1Y 6AL, England (phone: 71-499-7070; fax: 71-495-3262).

DORCHESTER, London, England: The grande dame is back after an extensive face-lift, and she never looked better. Once again, the faithful can flock to the heart of Mayfair and rest assured that all is even better than ever at "the Dorch." For those who require attention to the smallest detail, this is the place to feel pampered and protected. The renovation brought the return of Old World service schooled in the needs of today's travelers. All is well at teatime in the pillared *Promenade.* Thank heaven. Information: *Dorchester,* Park La., W1 London, England (phone: 71-629-8888; fax: 71-409-0114).

RITZ, London, England: The fellow who was heard to mutter snootily, "Nobody stays at the *Ritz* anymore," was off-base. The guestrooms and the decor are splendid and the service impeccable. Tea here is as vital a British ritual as the coronation. Information: *The Ritz,* Piccadilly, London W1, England (phone: 71-493-8181; fax: 71-493-2687).

SAVOY, London, England: This hostelry is to theater what the *Sacher* is to music. The *Savoy* is very near *Covent Garden* and Waterloo Bridge, and the lobby is often a *Who's Who* of the international entertainment world. The atmosphere is gently Edwardian, but the management is contemporary — and adept at catering to the demands of plutocrats from every part of the planet. The refurbished Thames Suites are London's most elegant address. Information: *The Savoy,* The Strand, London WC2R OEU, England (phone: 71-836-3719; fax: 71-872-8894).

LA RÉSERVE, Beaulieu, France: If thoughts of the French Riviera and Côte d'Azur awaken longings in you, you can get some satisfaction here at this luxurious seaside establishment graced by plenty of sun and surf, plus a sauna and swimming pool — and one of France's most renowned restaurants. The *Monte Carlo Casino* is just minutes away. Information: *La Réserve,* 5 Bd. Général-Leclerc, Beaulieu-sur-Mer 06310, France (phone: 93-01-00-01).

HÔTEL DU CAP-EDEN ROC, Cap d'Antibes, France: Over 100 years old, this Riviera landmark stands at the end of the Antibes peninsula in a lovely, semitropical park, looking out over the sea. An immaculately kept private beach, wisteria-rimmed tennis courts, and dinners on the patio of the patrician *Eden Roc* restaurant are highlights. Open from *Easter* to the end of October. Information: *Hôtel du Cap-Eden Roc,* Bd. Kennedy, Antibes 06604, France (phone: 93-61-39-01; fax: 93-67-76-04).

NORMANDY, Deauville, France: A great Norman mansion facing the sea in an urbane resort that is often called the Twenty-first Arrondissement of Paris, this hotel is a 5-minute walk from the *Deauville Casino,* which still has Europe's classiest casino clientele, most of whom catch a few hours' sleep at the *Normandy* between wagers. Fine at the height of the August racing season, and fine, too, for a winter weekend, when the rain and wind lash the Norman coast. Information: *The Normandy,* 38 Rue Jean-Mermoz, Deauville 14800, France (phone: 31-98-66-22; fax: 31-98-66-23).

NÉGRESCO, Nice, France: Something of an anachronism on the heavily trafficked and highly developed Riviera, this beautiful white Belle Epoque cream puff is still one of the shrines of European hotelkeeping. Its charming period rooms give you views over the ultramarine Baie des Anges and the long and lively Promenade des Anglais. Information: *The Négresco,* 37 Promenade des Anglais, Nice 06007, France (phone: 93-88-39-51; fax: 93-88-35-68).

CRILLON, Paris, France: Only the understated gold "C's" on its doors identify this grand example of Louis XV style, wonderfully situated right on Place de la Concorde. This is the only one of Paris's palace hotels still owned by a Frenchman. Once a private mansion, its interior is a regal assembly of 18th-century marble, carved and gilt-covered ornamentation, tapestries, and crystal chandeliers — luxe of the sort usually protected behind velvet cordons, but here eminently approachable. The *Crillon* has 136 large rooms and 27 suites. Those on the *place* have the best views; those on the courtyards are the quietest. Information: *Hôtel de Crillon,* 10 Pl. de la Concorde, Paris 75008, France (phone: 42-65-24-24; fax: 47-42-72-10).

GEORGE V, Paris, France: On the avenue of the same name that bisects the Champs-Elysées, this has been a favorite address of American travelers since the days of the Grand Tour. There is a prosperous, worldly air about its bustling halls, a feeling that things of continental importance are going on in the bar or under the sun lamps. The breakfast room serves some of the best warm croissants in town. Information: *George V,* 31 Av. George-V, Paris 75008, France (phone: 47-23-54-00; 800-225-5843 in the US; fax: 47-20-40-00).

PLAZA-ATHÉNÉE, Paris, France: The most exquisitely Gallic of Paris's major hotels, this one — Paris at its suave and urbane best — has attained such heights that among its regular guests are a few who look down their noses at the *Ritz.* Information: *Plaza-Athénée,* 25 Av. Montaigne, Paris 75008, France (phone: 47-23-78-33; 800-223-5843 or 800-223-6800 in the US; fax: 47-20-20-70).

RITZ, Paris, France: Perhaps the world's most famous hotel, beautifully positioned on Place Vendôme like the national monument it is. An 8-year-long overhaul has helped ease it out of French literature and into the 20th century with notable success, and its name is still synonymous with consummate luxury. Two floors (below street level) include a pool, a spacious spa, a cooking school, and a nightclub; the rooms and public spaces have been returned to their original elegance and opulence. Information: *Hôtel Ritz,* 15 Pl. Vendôme, Paris 75001, France (phone: 42-60-38-30; fax: 42-86-00-91).

BRENNER'S PARK, Baden-Baden, Germany: Overlooking the lushly pastoral Lichtentalerallée, this hotel has a setting like that of a Hapsburg summer palace and a wealth of balconies that make the most of it, offering views of particularly lordly trees and a romantic stream. The hotel has its own luxurious spa and a health clinic. The opulent *Baden-Baden Casino* and the wooded tennis club are an idyllic stroll away, as are all the other pleasures of this playground property. Information: *Brenner's Park Hotel,* Am der Lichtentaler Allee, Baden-Baden D-7570, Germany (phone: 7221-3530).

VIER JAHRESZEITEN, Hamburg, Germany: That rare combination of urban efficiency and countrified serenity, this fine hotel has a lovely lakefront setting with a view of the waterways that are so characteristic of the city, and all around are flowered promenades, gleaming yachts, and handsome villas. The hotel grill has a friendly fireplace and fine food. Among hotel people, this jewel is known as "the best Swiss hotel outside Switzerland." Information: *Vier Jahreszeiten,* 9-14 Neuer Jungfernstieg, Hamburg 36, Germany (phone: 40-34940).

CALA DI VOLPE, Costa Smeralda, Italy: The crown jewel of the complex developed by the Aga Khan on once-remote Sardinia, one of the Mediterranean's most fascinating islands. Rustic in style, like a Sardinian village, but deluxe in its comfort, it is discreetly tucked into a magnificent bright blue bay, just at the water's edge. Tennis, boating, swimming and skin diving, and glamorous nightlife are just outside your door, and it has served as the elegant background for some typical excess in a James Bond film. Open May through September. Information: *Albergo Cala di Volpe,* Costa Smeralda, Porto Cervo 07020, Italy (phone: 789-96083).

GRITTI PALACE, Venice, Italy: Dramatically situated on the Grand Canal, this Venetian-Gothic palazzo, a compact version of the Doge's Palace, has a dining terrace that floats on the water in the midst of the gondola traffic. If you just hang out of your window, you will see most of Venice float by in the course of a day. Information: *Gritti Palace,* 2467 Campo Santa Maria del Giglio, Canal Grande, Venice 30124, Italy (phone: 41-794611; fax: 520-0942).

DUE TORRI, Verona, Italy: A magnificent living museum fitted out entirely with antiques, this deluxe centuries-old hotel is *the* place to be during the open-air opera festival that takes place at the Arena di Verona each July and August. The management and the mood are elegant, and exquisite good taste has governed the selection of even the least important accessories. Information: *Due Torri,* 4 Piazza S. Anastasia, Verona 37121, Italy (phone: 45-595044; fax: 800-4130).

HÔTEL DE PARIS, Monte Carlo, Monaco: Across the square from the great *Casino,* this refurbished grand symbol of the era when money still bought happiness has been the winter palace for Russian grand dukes and English lords who have been coming to this petit principality for 3-month doses of sun and roulette for over a century. The hotel's elaborately painted and chandeliered dining room is an opera set — as is the whole regal, truly glamorous building. Be sure to sample the three-star cuisine emerging from the kitchen of the *Louis XV* restaurant. If, by chance, you cannot get a reservation, there is still the one-star grill on the top floor of the hotel, where the view is splendid. Information: *Hôtel de Paris,* Pl. du Casino, Monte Carlo 98000, Monaco (phone: 93-50-80-80).

REID'S, Funchal, Portugal: Set in extensive gardens on a promontory above the sea on the island of Madeira, this gracious lady offers a panoramic view of the picturesque bay and town of Funchal. Recently refurbished to commemorate its 100th anniversary, the friendly, personal service continues to make this charming hotel world-famous. There are 2 tennis courts, 2 heated seawater pools, and lift access to a private beach for sunbathing, swimming, and other water sports. Information: *Reid's,* Funchal 9000, Madeira, Portugal (phone: 91-23001; fax: 91-30499).

RITZ, Madrid, Spain: Ever since its regal inauguration in 1910, this impeccably maintained jewel has been a lavish landmark among the aristocracy of European hotels. Although this white castle is just a Goya's throw from the *Prado,* its marble terrace and chiaroscuro summer garden may be all you'll ever want to see of Madrid. Information: *Ritz,* 5 Plaza de la Lealtad, Madrid 28014, Spain (phone: 1-521-2857).

BELLEVUE PALACE, Bern, Switzerland: Having hosted the likes of Queen Elizabeth of England and King Baudouin of Belgium, this Swissôtel palace offers all its guests the royal treatment. Rooms 11-36 offer brilliant views of the Aare River and the Eiger, Mönch, and Jungfrau mountains; *La Terrasse* restaurant overlooks the Alps. Information: *Bellevue Palace,* 3-5 Kochergasse, Bern 3001, Switzerland (phone: 31-224581).

BÜRGENSTOCK HOTELS, Bürgenstock, Switzerland: This complex of three luxurious hotels (the *Grand,* the *Palace,* the *Park*) is in a 500-acre natural park that sprawls along a massive, wooded ridge some 1,500 feet above Lake Lucerne. Views from the hotel windows seem to take in half of Switzerland; rooms are hung with tapestries and Old Masters and furnished with lovely antiques. Information: *The Bürgenstock Estate,* Bürgenstock CH-6366, Switzerland (phone: 41-615545).

LE BEAU RIVAGE, Lausanne, Switzerland: A giant, queenly, Victorian manor set on 10 acres of lush private park on the shore of Lac Léman in Lausanne-Ouchy. The constantly tended grounds are like a botanical garden — with tennis courts — and you can come and go by boat to the front door. Information: *Beau Rivage,* Ouchy, Lausanne 1006 (phone: 21-617-1717).

LE LAUSANNE PALACE, Lausanne, Switzerland: Built in 1915, this palace has been the meeting spot for many international delegates, and during World War II it was used as the "exile" of choice for royalty and wealthy European families. Lush golds and blues, stately columns, chandeliers, and turn-of-the-century-style furniture are all part of the elegant, yet unpretentious, decor. The grand Rotonde, with a terrace offering wonderful views, is the perfect spot for a leisurely breakfast or tea. Information: *Le Lausanne Palace,* 7-9 Grand Chêne, Lausanne 1002, Switzerland (phone: 21-203711).

LE MONTREUX PALACE, Montreux, Switzerland: This hostelry has played host to Russian czars, as well as Russian novelist Vladimir Nabokov, who spent his summers here. Detailed frescoes and stained glass windows typify its elegant air, as do the white French doors and balconies in every room. For recreation, there's a heated outdoor swimming pool and a tennis court, or you might just want to relax and enjoy the views of Lake Geneva and France. Information: *Le Montreux Palace,* 100 Grand Rue, Montreux 1820, Switzerland (phone: 21-963-6373).

PALACE, St.-Moritz, Switzerland: Apprentices from all over the world come to this legend of Swiss hotelkeeping to learn to do things as perfectly as only the Swiss can. Stand on your sun-washed balcony on a crisp February morning, look out on the dazzling snows of the Engadine Valley and its high Alpine backdrop, and you will feel like the King of the Golden Mountain. Information: *The Palace,* St.-Moritz CH-7500, Switzerland (phone: 82-21101).

SUVRETTA HOUSE, St.-Moritz-Suvretta, Switzerland: The imposing 230-room stone "house" sits on a hill in the woods just outside of town and offers sweeping views of lakes and the piercing peaks of the Upper Engadine Valley. Perfection is found in the *Suvretta Club,* with its swimming pool and sauna, and in its several restaurants; a private ski school (in season), and a private ski lift that connects the hotel with the Corviglia slopes above the town. Families with children are particularly welcome. Information: *Suvretta House,* St.-Moritz-Suvretta 7500, Switzerland (phone: 82-21121).

DOLDER GRAND, Zurich, Switzerland: A romantic old Gothic fantasy on a forested mountainside 6 minutes by hotel car from downtown Zurich. Golf, tennis, woodland pathways, panoramic views over city and lake, world class cuisine, an ice rink, and an open-air pool with manmade waves are only a few of the delights that will make you want to settle down forever in the hotel's tower suite. Information: *The Dolder Grand,* 65 Kurhausstrasse, Zurich CH-8032, Switzerland (phone: 1-251-6231).

CASTLE HOTELS

Some of Europe's most fascinating hostelries started their lives as abbeys, baronial mansions, castles and châteaux, monasteries, and palaces. Most national tourist offices can tell you about those within their borders. *Europe's Castles and Palace Hotels* by Carole Chester ($9.95) offers a comprehensive listing. Also see *Relais & Châteaux,* published by the French organization of the same name, as a guide to a group of castle hotels, restaurants, and inns devoted to maintaining high standards of personalized service and cuisine. Here's our selection of some of the choicest.

SCHLOSS DÜRNSTEIN, Dürnstein, Austria: In northeast Austria, on a rocky plateau above the Danube, this baroque castle has been deftly transformed into a gracious modern hostelry. Formerly the summer residence of the Starhemberg princes, it now features a heated swimming pool, sauna and solarium, and first class Austrian cuisine. Open mid-March to mid-November. Information: *Schloss Dürnstein,* Dürnstein A-3601, Austria (phone: 2711-212).

PALAIS SCHWARZENBERG, Vienna, Austria: Small and exclusive, this establishment occupies a wing of a palace still owned by one of Austria's oldest families, in the middle of a 37-acre park close to the center of the city. The hotel is beautifully furnished, partly with antiques, and the atmosphere is perfectly sedate, totally calm. Information: *Palais Schwarzenberg,* 9 Schwarzenberghletz Pl., Vienna A-1030, Austria (phone: 1-784515).

CHÂTEAU DE NAMUR, Namur, Belgium: This 29-room château occupies a deep green private park at the summit of La Citadelle above Namur, overlooking the entire Meuse River valley. Swimming in the hotel pool and playing tennis on its courts will keep you busy between excursions to the Ardennes Forest. Information: *Château de Namur,* 1 Av. de l'Ermitage, Namur, Belgium (phone: 81-222630).

STEENSGAARD HERREGARDSPENSION, Millinge, Denmark: This half-timbered manor on the island of Fünen dates from the late 13th century and looks every bit its age, from the armor hall and the library to the ancient park that surrounds it and the vaulted cellar, now set up for billiards. You can play tennis, take horseback or carriage excursions in the wild countryside, or just enjoy the mile-long private beach. Each of the 15 rooms has a view of the lake or the park. Information: *Steensgaard Herregardspension,* Millinge, Denmark DK-5600 (phone: 62-619490; fax: 62-617861).

EASTWELL MANOR, Ashford, Kent, England: Set in some 3,000 acres of parkland picturesquely speckled with fluffy white sheep, this elegant, rambling stone country house was opened as a hotel just in 1980, but though the present house was rebuilt in 1926, its history can be traced back to the Norman Conquest; over the years it has had 20 owners, and Queen Victoria once made a visit here. The lavish use of space and splendid service reminds guests of an earlier, grander age: one visitor called it "the world's best twenty-room hotel." Though most of the rooms are absolutely huge, they are so cleverly decorated — with sitting areas, soft colors, and pretty fabrics — that they seem positively inviting. An oak-paneled bar lures guests down for drinks before dinner, which is served in a baronial dining room. The food is French, with an emphasis on nouvelle cuisine; there is also a short menu of local specialties — among them smoked eel and roast English lamb. Information: *Eastwell Manor,* Eastwell Park, Ashford, Kent TN25 4HR, England (phone: 233-635751 or 800-544-7570 in US; fax: 233-635530).

CHÂTEAU D'AUDRIEU, Audrieu, France: This magnificent 18th-century country house, preserved over the years by a single family, is set among lovely gardens in a 50-acre park crisscrossed by graveled pathways and scattered with trees that are almost as old as the house itself. The 24 sleeping rooms, which have retained their original paneling despite the ravages of the World War II battles fought in the area, are furnished with antiques, and the bathrooms are modern. Audrieu is halfway between Caen and Bayeux, a few miles from the historic beaches and just 2 hours' drive from Paris. Information: *Château d'Audrieu,* Audrieu (Calvados) 14250, France (phone: 31-80-21-52; fax: 31-80-24-73).

CHÂTEAU D'ARTIGNY, Montbazon, France: François Coty, the celebrated French perfumer, spent 2 decades building this opulent, mansard-roofed château on the site of another that had existed here since 1769 — so it isn't the oldest of castles. However, Coty had style and taste, and the château reflects this: The ceilings are almost as ornate as those you've seen at Versailles, and the bathtubs are real marble. There are 32 rooms in the main château; but the establishment's most notable sleeping quarters are on the top floor of the adjacent Pavilion Ariane, accessible via a lovely curved staircase. Information: *Château d'Artigny,* Route d'Azay-le-Rideau (D17) Veigné, Montbazon 37250, France (phone: 47-26-24-24; fax: 47-65-92-79).

DOMAINE DES HAUTS DE LOIRE, Onzain, France: Here is a Loire Valley château where you can spend the night. Once a hunting pavilion for a French count, this cozy country French establishment, its rooms papered with wonderful toiles and full of giant hand-hewn beams, feels like someone's home; everywhere there are gleaming antique copper pots and pans, often filled with fresh flowers, and the dining room is elegant and airy, so that you can watch the sun set as you wait for supper. Information: *Domaine des Hauts de Loire,* Onzain (Loir-et-Cher) 41150, France (phone: 54-20-72-57; fax: 54-20-72-23).

WALD UND SCHLOSSHOTEL FRIEDRICHSRUHE, Friedrichsruhe, Germany: One of the best country inns in Germany, this 18th-century baroque castle once served as a hunting lodge for Emperor Johann Friedrich I. Now in two buildings (one, the original castle itself), the 51-room property also boasts a 9-hole golf course, a tennis court, indoor and outdoor swimming pools, and a fine restaurant. Our favorite accommodation is No. 66, a corner room with a huge mahogany bed and the plushest eiderdown comforter under which we've ever warmed our toes. No. 55, with two beds and an overstuffed sofa, is equally appealing, and in the main building, we favor No. 35. Freshly squeezed orange juice, mineral water, and a bowl of fresh fruit is placed in the room each morning, and a dish of chocolates is set out before bedtime. It's enough to make one believe that the good life is still alive and well — at least here. Information: *Wald und Schlosshotel Friedrichsruhe,* Friedrichsruhe 7111, Germany (phone: 7941-60870).

SCHLOSSHOTEL KRONBERG, Kronberg, Germany: One of the finest castle hotels in a country that is full of them, this fairy-tale structure in the woods about a half hour from Frankfurt was built in 1888. It has housed French army officers, American soldiers and civilians, and assorted European bluebloods, and, in 1945, was invaded by jewel thieves who made a celebrated haul of heirlooms stored there. It is lovely — full of 19th-century furnishings and priceless paintings and tapestries. Information: *Schlosshotel Kronberg,* 25 Hainstrasse, 6242 Kronberg/Taunus, Germany (phone: 6173-7011). If you acquire the *schlosshotel* (castle hotel) habit, write the *Vereinigung der Burg und Schlosshotels,* an association of similar establishments (c/o Gast im Schloss, 1 Trendelburg 3526, Germany; phone: 6173-70101).

ASHFORD CASTLE, Cong, County Mayo, Ireland: At first glance this establishment looks like the progeny of a marriage between the last of the dinosaurs and the castle inhabited by Snow White's stepmother. The shape is long, low, and gray, with the battlements ridged like the scales down a dragon's back. The river in front is spanned by a stony bridge. Beside it, long Lough Corrib winds down to the sea at Galway. Not really homey, most would think, until they learn that in its present state, give or take a tower, it has been inhabited by several families, most recently by kin of the stout-brewing Guinnesses, in the persons of Lord and Lady Ardilaun. The 18th-century French château section in the middle was home to the Oranmore and Browne families, and the original hefty 13th-century section housed the Norman family known as the De Burgos, who conquered the surrounding land. Many of these illustrious occupants have left their marks. Apart from the fleeting resemblance to the Chartres Cathedral (the small dining room being about 45 feet high), the interior is in the comfortable-baronial school of design — just the thing for a comfortable baron who likes a bathroom in which a cocktail party for 30 could be given or who requires a bed the size of a tennis court. A hotel since 1939, unstintingly refurbished by a consortium of Irish-American owners, the place is luxury incarnate from the thick oriental-toned carpeting that hushes footsteps in salons and corridors to the Waterford chandeliers that sparkle in gilt mirrors. Fine paintings, sculpture, and uninhibited antique armor are artfully deployed around the public rooms, just to complete the picture. At least one real king has stayed and played here: Edward VII of England, for whom, they say, the billiard room was built. The recreation is of the outdoor kind. Angling for trout, pike, perch, char, rudd, and bream is in adjacent Lough Corrib (and the hotel kitchen, which has always been soundly middle-of-the-road, will prepare the catch). Shooting rights over 25,000 acres — 2,000 of which are a controlled area — provide the chance of bagging pheasant, teal duck, snipe, and woodcock; the lakeside chalet where Lord and Lady Ardilaun spent their wedding night is now in less romantic use as a sight for shooters' lunches. Golf and tennis are also part of the picture, and though there is not yet a jousting ground, hunting is an excellent alternative. The sedentary can ramble around the estate in jaunting cars and cruise up the lake in a boat that holds 50. It definitely isn't the place for those who like shops and shopping, although there is a crafts shop on the grounds and Cong, the nearest village, is a picturesque spot full of ruined abbeys. Nor is it one of the beacons of the Irish food scene, though the restaurant (which seats 180) has begun to win accolades. But despite the scope and the grandeur of it all, the castle is a delightful place, friendly and hospitable. It's easy to understand why King George V of England, who visited here often as the Prince of Wales, liked the place so much he could hardly be dislodged. Open year-round; 83 bedrooms and 6 suites, all with bath. Details: *Ashford Castle Hotel,* Cong, County Mayo, Ireland (phone: 92-46003 or 800-346-7007 in the US).

DROMOLAND CASTLE, Newmarket-on-Fergus, Ireland: The former seat of the O'Brien clan, this 16th-century conglomeration of turrets and towers — just a short drive from Shannon Airport — is stuffed with huge oil paintings and ornamented by handsome paneling, elaborate stone carvings, and picture windows that give out onto 500 acres of soft greenness; the chandeliered restaurant gleams sumptuously with its silk curtains and upholstery. Riding is a favorite activity, along with tennis, golf (on an 18-hole course), and fishing for trout and salmon. Information: *Dromoland Castle,* Newmarket-on-Fergus, County Clare, Ireland (phone in Shannon: 61-71144; in the US: 800-346-7007; fax: 61-363355).

VILLA D'ESTE, Lake Como, Italy: To visit here is to fall gently into a life lined with silk: The public rooms at this vast 400-year-old villa seem as fresh and opulent as when the villa was the home of a Renaissance cardinal, awash with antique chairs upholstered in deep blue brocaded silk, polished marble pillars, crystal chandeliers, winged stair-cases ascending to a balcony, handloomed carpeting, and arched leaded windows that open out to the cliffs and cypresses of the Como countryside. Breakfasts served at the lakeside dining room are a special treat: fresh grapefruit or orange juice (natural or mixed with champagne); freshly baked breads, rolls, brioches, and croissants; strong black coffee; cheeses; and hot baked Parma ham. Days are leisurely, filled with ambling along the marina, sitting in the sun, bathing in a pool built into the lake, and sipping a drink on the terrace. Information: *Villa d'Este,* Cernobbio, Lake Como 22010, Italy (phone: 31-511471; fax: 31-512027).

WINSELERHOF, Maastricht, Netherlands: This 16th-century farmhouse has been turned into a hotel-restaurant and is under the same management as the *Kasteel Erenstein,* a 13th-century Renaissance castle, and the fine restaurant *Château Neer-canne.* It's possible to arrange a package visit to all three, which are in close proximity to one another and a half-hour ride from the Maastricht airport. Ideal for a romantic weekend. Information: *Winselerhof* Cannerweg 800 Maastricht, Amsterdam, Nether-lands (phone: 43-251359; fax: 43-213406).

GLENEAGLES, Auchterarder, Scotland: "Heich abune the heich" — better than the best — might seem a grandiose claim to make about a hotel. But those who have experienced Britain's finest luxury resort — the Scottish Versailles of hotels — all agree with the decades of hoteliers who have believed the boast, from the early days when a chief point of pride was a private bath with every room, and on through the years, as crowned heads, aristocrats, and millionaires flocked to the establishment. *Gleneagles* has 242 rooms (20 of which are suites). Most guests rave about the golf courses, two of which are currently being combined under Jack Nicklaus' supervision to become their third championship course; it is due to open at the end of this year. But non-golfers will never be bored: The *Gleneagles Mark Phillips Equestrian Centre,* run by the estranged husband of Princess Anne, features two covered arenas and instruction in show, jumping, and dressage for everyone from the total novice to those involved in world class competition (Captain Phillips himself is available for instruction by arrangement). The 800-acre grounds also have facilities for fishing, clay-pigeon shooting, croquet, lawn bowling, miniature golf, Ping-Pong, all-weather tennis, squash, dancing, and billiards; plus a sauna and Turkish baths, hairdressing salon, Jacuzzi, swimming pool, and gymnasium. The gardens alone, spotted with bright-colored flowers, are a joy. The high-ceilinged rooms are spacious enough that guests don't trip over each other when room service sets up tea; the windows provide an eyeful of the lonely Scottish hills beyond the gardens; and the service can't be faulted, thanks to a better than one-to-one staff/guest ratio. When pipe bands set up on the velvety lawns, quite a few guests get goose bumps. Information: *Gleneagles Hotel,* Auchterarder, Perthshire PH3 1NF, Scotland (phone: 764-62231).

INVERLOCHY, Fort William, Scotland: At the foot of the mountain Ben Nevis, this century-old Scottish Highland castle — splendidly Victorian inside, with a magnificently frescoed great central hall — is surrounded outside by 50 acres of woods and a dramatic landscape. You can fish, golf, go riding, play tennis — or just sit around and sip the castle's private-label whisky. Queen Victoria slept here. Information: *Inverlochy Castle,* Fort William, Inverness-shire PH33 6SN, Scotland (phone: 397-2177).

SON VIDA, Palma de Mallorca, Spain: This spectacular 13th-century castle sits serenely atop a hill overlooking the Bay of Palma, with a breathtaking view of bustling Palma (15 minutes away) and the sea beyond. Tennis courts, a golf course, and riding stables spread out over the 1,400 acres of lavishly landscaped grounds. Information: *Son Vida,* Palma de Mallorca, Spain (phone: 71-451011).

LAKE, Llangammarch Wells, Wales: A truly luxurious country house hidden on its own 50 acres. Guests step out of a spectacular flower- and antiques-filled drawing room to enjoy a day of trout fishing, bird or badger watching, a set or two of tennis, or an afternoon in the nearby ultra-Victorian spa town of Llandrindod Wells. All that activity should stimulate a traveler's appetite, which is fine since the property also boasts one of the best dining rooms in Wales. The local lamb and fish are first rate, and the variety of herbed rolls (especially the rosemary) and the Welsh cheeses are very special. Try to book either the Badger or River suites, each perfectly decorated, with small but well done bathrooms. Information: *The Lake Hotel,* Llangammarch Wells, Powys, Wales (phone: 5912-202).

COZY INNS AND SMALL HOTELS

If your tastes run toward the rustic, you will be glad to know that Europe can lay claim to a super-abundance of small hotels and inns with the charm and ambience that only years of operation can produce. You can stay at Tuscan villas, half-timbered taverns, Swiss chalets, and Scottish country houses — as quaint as familiar American inns, but far more varied in their styles. Most — the last word in luxurious simplicity — will cost you as much as their multi-star urban cousins; at others, a night's lodging is quite reasonably priced.

JAGDSCHLOSS GRAF RECKE, Wald-im-Pinzgau, Austria: This lovely mountain lodge on the edge of the Hohe Tauern National Park makes a fine jumping-off spot for hunting, Alpine touring, and riding excursions in the Oberpinzgau. Information: *Jagdschloss Graf Recke,* Wald-im-Oberpinzgau 5742, Austria (phone: 6565-6417).

HUBERTUS KROEN, Feldballe, Denmark: A fine example of *kroer,* Danish country inns, this half-timbered building in the middle of a vast estate was built in 1710 on the site of a 13th-century castle and is today an important center of horse breeding and the preparation (for eating) of guinea fowl. Information: *Hubertus Kroen,* Mollerup Gods, Feldballe, DK-8410, Rønde, Denmárk (phone: 86-371019).

LYGON ARMS, Broadway, England: Though it isn't nearly as old as some buildings in the Cotswolds, 1532 seems a respectable enough birth date; that makes it old enough to have frequently welcomed Charles I as a guest and to have harbored Oliver Cromwell on the eve of the Battle of Worcester. And there are indications that the building itself is much older. A stone fireplace set into a 4-foot-thick wall, for instance, appears to have been crafted in the 14th century; and the rear courtyard door dates from the 15th century, the front door from the early 16th. All of the rooms are furnished with antiques of similar vintage, and a few pieces are of such high quality that they are illustrated in *The Dictionary of English Furniture.* The nine rooms in what is called the old wing are a study in Tudor, with rough beams, charmingly tiled oak floors, and dozens of blue Spode dishes on the fireplace mantels. The Great Chamber — one of the hotel's most famous rooms, known for its vaulted timber-crossed ceiling and its massive canopied bed — is No. 20. Bedrooms are constantly being refurbished, but the history ends at the bathrooms — all immaculate, modern, and with huge showerheads. The service is the equal of the surroundings: For example, a guest who shows a preference for Carlsberg lager on one visit will probably find a Carlsberg waiting when he returns. As for meals, prepared by chef Clive Howe, they are served in the Great Hall, with its barrel-vaulted ceiling and large fireplace. During the summer, guests can enjoy an alfresco dinner at the *Patio* restaurant in back. A new fitness center has opened with a pool, sauna, gym, solarium, snooker hall, and beauty salon. The wide, mile-long street on which the inn fronts is almost as pretty as the cream-colored stone hotel itself, and Stratford-upon-Avon is just 20 miles away. A member of the Savoy hotel group. Information: *Lygon Arms,* Broadway, Worcestershire WR12 7DU, England (phone: 386-852255).

GIDLEIGH PARK, Chagford, Devon, England: Take over 30 acres of secluded Devon woodlands, add a turn-of-the-century mansion built for consummate comfort and elegance, furnish it in impeccably good taste, and you have *Gidleigh Park.* American owners Paul and Kay Henderson have thought of everything to make guests feel elegantly at home. Each of the 14 rooms is special, but our favorites are Nos. 1, 2, and 3, which overlook the sweeping lawns and rushing brook. Tennis and croquet are popular here, too. A 3-room thatched cottage has been built on the grounds and is decorated in the same lovely country-English look as the hotel. As if all this weren't enough, there's superb food: Start with perfect pâté de foie gras or salmon tartare, then move on to sea bass with cucumber on a bed of fried noodles, among other choices. The foregoing, plus a distinguished wine list, have earned the dining room a faithful fan club. In 1990, tourism guru Egon Ronay also named it Hotel of the Year. Information: *Gidleigh Park,* Chagford, Devon, England (phone: 647-432367).

GRAVETYE MANOR, near East Grinstead, West Sussex, England: About halfway between London and Brighton, at the end of a meandering country road some 5 miles from East Grinstead, this ivy-covered Elizabethan manor house has become one of rural England's most impressive hostelries since its conversion to a hotel in 1958. Many of the oak-paneled rooms have fireplaces; all have thick carpets, soothing decor, and extras such as a fruit basket, an ice-water thermos, books, a hair dryer, and a special red telephone for emergencies — touches that have earned the hotel membership in the Relais & Châteaux group. Information: *Gravetye Manor,* East Grinstead, West Sussex RH19 4LJ, England (phone: 342-810567).

HAMBLETON HALL, Hambleton, Leicester, England: Set on a peninsula jutting into Rutland Water, only 10 miles off the A-1 Motorway, the main northward route from London, this beautifully restored and redecorated old manor house (Fern is our favorite room) has a dining room that's even better than its superb accommodations. In addition to admiring the scenic vistas over the lake and the surrounding countryside, guests can enjoy fishing, riding, or bicycling on the lake paths. But above all, *Hambleton Hall* provides its visitors with a genuine sense of English country life. Information: *Hambleton Hall,* Hambleton, Leicester LE15 8TH, England (phone: 572-756991).

CHEWTON GLEN, New Milton, Hampshire, England: The New Forest, which William the Conqueror named and claimed as a royal hunting ground in 1079, was already old when this brick mansion went up on 60 acres of peaceful parkland near its fringes. Rooms are done up with pretty, flowered fabrics that are frequently replaced to keep things looking fresh, and the color TV sets have been equipped to show a feature film every evening. A decanter of sherry is set out to greet arriving guests, and the bathrooms come furnished with fragrant bars of Roger & Gallet soap. The same perfectionism pervades the hotel's elegantly appointed restaurant, the *Marryat Room,* where a young French chef and his staff produce exquisite food. Those who recognize high standards and are irritated by expensive establishments that don't quite measure up will appreciate all that is here. Information: *Chewton Glen,* New Milton, Hampshire BH25 6QS, England (phone: 425-275341).

CLIVEDEN, Taplow, Buckinghamshire, England: One of England's great country estates, it stands majestically on 400 wooded acres beside the river Thames. Long the property of the legendary Astors — and the meeting place of the fabled "Cliveden Set" — it is now managed by Blakeney Hotels, who have preserved and classically redecorated the original rooms of the 17th-century mansion, retaining the works of art that reflect the lives of its previous owners. The incomparable grounds, which once received the attention of as many as 50 gardeners, include a sweeping pasture, dazzling flower borders, hanging woods, exquisite pavilions, temples, sculptures, 2,000-year-old Roman sarcophagi, and an amphitheater where "Rule Britannia" was first performed in 1740. In addition to beautiful walks, guests enjoy boat trips on the Thames, tennis (on both indoor and outdoor courts), swimming (in indoor and outdoor pools), squash, fishing, horse racing, polo, golf, and rowing. And there is a complete spa for men and women. Details: *Cliveden,* Taplow, Buckinghamshire SL6-OJF, England (phone: 6286-68561).

HORSTED PLACE, Uckfield, East Sussex, England: A stately Victorian mansion built in 1850 and until recently the home of the late Lord Rupert Neville, secretary to Prince Philip, it has 17 suites, a heated swimming pool, tennis court, croquet lawn, two 18-hole golf courses, and 23 acres of magnificent gardens. Furnished with beautiful antiques, the house is bright and cheery with chintz. Afternoon tea is served in the large, many-windowed drawing room, and an impressive library, complete with fireplace, overlooks the garden. As if all this were not enough to satisfy the most demanding of guests, the dining room, which serves very fine food, is especially popular for traditional British Sunday lunch. Here is precisely the kind of comfortable country elegance that travelers go to England to find. Only 90 minutes south of London, near Glyndebourne. Information: *Horsted Place,* Uckfield, East Sussex TN22 5TS, England (phone: 825-75581), or *Abercrombie & Kent International,* 1420 Kensington Rd., Oak Brook, IL 60521 (phone: 312-954-2922 in Illinois; 800-323-3602 elsewhere.).

MILLER HOWE, Windermere, Cumbria, England: If you tire of looking at the ever-changing light and shade over Lake Windermere in this lovely, Wordsworth-country hotel, you can play Scrabble, read a book from your private bookshelf, or listen to one of the cassettes on the stereo equipment in your room. There is something very personal about the rooms here, as though this is your own private domain for a day or two. You can wander into the kitchen to watch the friendly cooks prepare the treats that appear on the interesting menu. When you step out of your scented bath, you'll find morning tea waiting in pretty floral pots with lemon biscuits to sustain you before a substantial breakfast downstairs. Closed from early December through March. Information: *Miller Howe,* Windermere, Cumbria LA23 1EY, England (phone: 9662-2536).

OUSTAÙ DE BAUMANIÈRE, Les Baux-de-Provence, France: Famed primarily for its restaurant, still one of the very finest in France — though it lost one of its three Michelin stars in 1990 — the inn is beautifully set on an abandoned quarry in a wild Provençal valley and is elegantly furnished with local antiques. It offers tennis, swimming, and horseback riding to fill your time between elegant meals. Closed February. Information: *Oustaù de Baumanière,* Les Baux-de-Provence 13520, France (phone: 90-54-33-07; fax: 90-54-40-46).

BOYER "LES CRAYÈRES," Reims, France: With its move to a stunning 19th-century château, this three-star restaurant has added lodgings that match its food. Set on 19 beautifully landscaped acres, just a stone's throw from the twin Gothic towers of Reims Cathedral, it has 16 sumptuous 2-room suites, some of which open onto terraces overlooking the gardens and all of which are decorated differently, mostly in the style of the Louis Philippe era. *Boyer "Les Crayères"* is a member of the Relais & Châteaux group, and the main attraction is the food. The menu's offerings reflect a finely tuned balance between nouvelle and traditional cuisines, and service is helpful rather than overbearing. In support of the main local industry, the wine list includes more than 60 champagnes. Closed Mondays, Tuesday lunch, and mid-December to mid-January. Information: *Boyer "Les Crayères,"* 64 Bd. Henri-Vasnier, Reims 51100, France (phone: 26-82-80-80; fax: 26-82-65-52).

LE VIEUX LOGIS, Trémolat, France: France's beautiful Dordogne River valley is the setting for this unprepossessing inn, a former farmhouse that has welcomed guests since 1952, but has been in the family of the present owner, Mme. Giraudel-Destord, since it was built. It's a comfortable, enchanting place: The beds are covered with pristine white or bright floral spreads and vast down comforters (a rarity in this area); the cooks are generous with the ebony truffles that are sold in Scarlat, not far away. Information: *Le Vieux Logis,* Trémolat 24510, France (phone: 53-22-80-06; fax: 53-22-84-89).

VILLA SAN MICHELE, Fiesole, Italy: Formerly a Renaissance monastery with a façade designed by Michelangelo, this hotel (and Italian National Trust Monument) in the hills above Florence is surrounded by lovely gardens and seems like a gracious Tuscan villa. Open mid-March through mid-October. Information: *Villa San Michele,* 4 Via di Doccia, Fiesole 50014, Italy (phone: 55-59451).

POUSADA DO INFANTE, Sagres, Portugal: On the western end of the sunny, sandy Algarve coast, this small establishment is a handsome representative of the many official Portuguese inns *(pousadas).* Its 15 rooms must be reserved long in advance. Information: *Pousada do Infante,* Sagres, Algarve 8650, Portugal (phone: 82-64222).

PARADOR DE GIL BLAS, Santillana del Mar, Spain: The state-run Spanish *paradores* occupy elegantly restored old convents and castles along the sea, in the mountains, or on the outskirts of ancient villages. The *Gil Blas,* in the region of the beautiful Costa Cantábrica, is typical, with its heavy stone walls and arches, beamed ceilings, tile floors, and gracious rustic furnishings. Information: *Parador de Gil Blas,* Santillana del Mar, Santander, Spain (phone: 42-818000). The central *parador* office also handles bookings: *Red de Paradores del Estado,* 18 Calle Velázquez, Madrid 28001, Spain (phone: 1-435-9700). For a complete list of all the Spanish *paradores de turismo,* write the Tourist Office of Spain, 665 Fifth Ave., New York, NY 10022 (phone: 212-759-8822).

CHESA GRISCHUNA, Klosters, Switzerland: This establishment in the charming Alpine town of Klosters is as near perfect an Alpine chalet as you'll find: Riotous pink flowerfalls cascade over dark wooden balconies; pine-paneled rooms are warmed with crackling fires; fondue and *glühwein* are standard fare in the cozy dining room; and the eiderdown on your bed is as light as a dollop of whipped cream. Information: *Chesa Grischuna,* Klosters CH-7250, Switzerland (phone: 83-692222).

CHÂTEAU GÜTSCH, Lucerne, Switzerland: A few minutes by private cable car above Lucerne and its gleaming lake, this lovely turn-of-the-century mansion at the edge of the Gütsch woods has a heated swimming pool, public rooms decorated with suits of armor and old Swiss chests, a candlelit dining room in the wine cellar, and rooms fitted out with four-poster beds. The views from this elevation are spectacular — and in some rooms you can enjoy them from the bathtub. Information: *Château Gütsch,* Kanonenstrasse, Lucerne, CH-6003 Switzerland (phone: 41-220272). *The Swiss National Tourist Office,* 608 Fifth Ave., New York, NY 10020 (phone: 212-757-5944) has a listing of other Swiss inns and castle hotels.

AND NOW FOR SOMETHING REALLY RUSTIC

The Alps have their hikers' and climbers' huts, but for getting away from it all in the most styleless style, you can't beat:

ARCTIC, Narsarsuaq, Denmark: At the southern tip of Greenland, this no-frills establishment occupies an old World War II air base. There are ancient Norse settlements to explore, fjords for boating, the great ice glaciers for hiking adventures — so it doesn't really matter that you won't find a discotheque within 500 miles. Information: *Hotel Narsarsuaq,* Narsarsuaq, Greenland, DK-3923 Denmark (phone: 299-35253; fax: 299-35370).

The Shrines of European Gastronomy

In Europe, even ordinary food is very good by stateside standards; and the best attains an excellence only possible where the freshest and most flavorful ingredients are available to culinary artists who, working with the accumulated wisdom of centuries, cook with a religious devotion.

Such are the chefs behind the restaurants we've listed here, the places we prize most among European dining spots. They are not, we must emphasize, the kinds of places where you could eat three meals a day, every day. (That would be a bit like subjecting yourself to three consecutive Wagnerian operas without respite.) Nor are these shrines of European gastronomy meant for grabbing a quick bite on your way to another event; dinners are productions, worth planning for and taking the appropriate time to enjoy.

Reservations should be made several days (and sometimes weeks) in advance whenever possible, and in many cases, writing ahead is the only way to secure a table. But it's also a good idea (where realistic) to pass by the restaurant, choose a table, and look at the menu. Confirmation of your reservation, when you've arrived at your destination, is also wise.

Acquiring at least a rudimentary knowledge of wine also takes a little advance preparation, but is almost a prerequisite for eating in this type of establishment, since wines are as important as the food itself in the composition of your meal. The wine steward (sommelier) and the captain will help (so don't be afraid to ask), and afterward will monitor your bites and sips lest some selection falls short of the celestial. (If this happens, don't be bashful about returning it to the kitchen.)

A few more words of advice: Order what appeals to you, and don't be bullied into a rigid menu no matter how zealously it is pressed upon you. Daily specialties are usually good choices, and you should not be frightened off by multi-course epicurean feasts. In fact, these are very small samplings of the many dishes of which the chef is most proud, and can be an unforgettable treat. Prices will, inevitably, be high, but this is a once-in-a-lifetime thing. You should treat it (and enjoy it) as such.

Finally, a note on our choices. Nothing is quite so much fun (or as difficult) as putting together a list of Europe's most appealing restaurants. Actually, little could be more brazen. We could have played it safe by including only those establishments that hold multi-star recognition from other appraisers of haute cuisine, but we thought that was misleading at best. It would give short shrift to the enormous variety of cuisines that exist across Europe and to the many world class restaurants that operate across the Continent and that serve meals worth wandering for — but aren't French. So our reach is considerably wider, though we've noted our picks of the best Gallic tables; what follows is a true Europe-wide selection of restaurants that are, quite simply, nonpareil.

ZU DEN DREI HUSAREN (The Three Hussars), Vienna, Austria: This quintessentially Viennese establishment, in the heart of the Old City just off the bustling Kärntnerstrasse, offers a whole range of epicurean entrées and a vast selection of hors d'oeuvres. There's not a better place in the world to sample a classic Wiener schnitzel. Open for dinner only; closed Sundays and from mid-July to mid-August. Information: *Zu den Drei Husaren,* 4 Weihburggasse, Vienna, Austria (phone: 1-512-1092).

SACHER, Vienna, Austria: The venerable hotel restaurant has changed little since its kitchen confected the first *Sachertorte* — a rich, justly celebrated chocolate cake filled with apricot jam and coated with an equally sinful chocolate icing that is always served with a generous dollop of fresh whipped cream. The clicking of heels and the tinkling of crystal blend as naturally as ever into the harmonies of the *Vienna Opera* across the street, and only the ancient waiters belie the establishment's age. Epic *tafelspitz* (boiled beef) has been served for a century; don't miss it. And for dessert — since you can buy a *Sachertorte* to take out around the corner — have some *palatschinken* — thin pancakes rolled and filled with jam or chocolate and sprinkled with powdered sugar. Information: *Hotel Sacher,* 4 Philharmonikerstrasse, Vienna, Austria (phone: 1-512-3367).

COMME CHEZ SOI, Brussels, Belgium: As an alternative to the very grand country lodge above, we offer this very intimate urban restaurant, distinguished by a kitchen wholeheartedly devoted to modern culinary delights. The talented young chef here considers the "new" in nouvelle cuisine an invitation to experiment, and almost any one of his adventures will provide an evening's repast you will remember long and lovingly. Elegantly decorated and quietly friendly, nothing here will disappoint you. Closed Sundays, Mondays, *Christmas* week, and July. Information: *Comme Chez Soi,* 23 Pl. Rouppe, Brussels, Belgium (phone: 1-512-2921).

ROMEYER, Brussels, Belgium: Despite its rustic surroundings on the edge of the Soignes Forest about 6 miles (10 km) outside the city, this grand lodge offers one of the most cosmopolitan menus you'll find anywhere on the Continent: The restaurant's genial owner and namesake, Belgium's foremost chef, is wont to daub his Ostend oysters with caviar or to shape a mousse of pâté de foie gras like a porcupine and stud it profusely with black truffle "needles." Closed Sunday evenings, Mondays, February, and the first 2 weeks in August. Information: *Romeyer,* 109 Chaussée de Groenendael, Hoeilaart 1560, Belgium (phone: 657-0581).

CONNAUGHT GRILL, London, England: The *Connaught* is to London what the *Sacher* is to Vienna, and its *Grill* (one Michelin star) is every bit as well mannered as you'd expect of a place so thoroughly steeped in British tradition. The best dishes on the menu are those on which the Empire was founded: roast beef and Yorkshire pudding, Lancashire hot pot, gooseberry pie. After dinner, you will feel as if the gentlemen should retire to the library with a glass of port and a cigar. Closed weekends and bank holidays. Information: *The Connaught Hotel,* Carlos Pl., London W1, England (phone: 71-499-7070 or 71-492-0668).

LE GAVROCHE, London, England: After over 70 years of rating restaurants, the *Guide Michelin* gave its first three-star rating in Britain to this most French of restaurants. It is owned and run by Albert Roux, a former chef for the Rothschild family and once the chef in the royal household. The wine card is exceptionally long and inviting (listing over 400 items, including a 1945 Château Lafite Rothschild for about $1,000, though many modest vintages are available for less than $25). Closed weekends, and late December to early January. Information: *Le Gavroche,* 43 Upper Brook St., London W1, England (phone: 71-408-0881).

WATERSIDE INN, Bray-on-Thames, Berkshire, England: Three Michelin stars are still rare in England. Yet this establishment's claim to being one of the only two honorees is just part of the reason to make a detour to the village of Bray, not far from Windsor and 27 miles west of London. Michel Roux (the French chef with embassy experience and service for the best private families before he opened London's renowned *Le Gavroche* with his brother Albert) chose to open his Thames-side country restaurant in a setting that provides a feast for the eyes before the feast for the palate begins. In spring, enormous red tulips are in bloom all around, flowering cherry trees line the river, and swans circle past as though summoned by a magic wand. In summer, apéritifs are served on the terrace and in two delightful summer houses, and the sight of weeping willows and boats on the water may distract a diner — momentarily — from the extraordinary menu. Monsier Roux is ceaselessly inventive. Among his enduring specialties are *tronçonnettes de homard* (chunks of lobster in a white port wine sauce); warm oysters served in a puff pastry case, garnished with bean sprouts, raspberry vinegar butter sauce, and fresh raspberries; a medium-rare roast duckling pierced with cloves and served with a honey-flavored sauce; and a Grand Marnier–infused soufflé laid atop orange sauce and garnished with orange segments. The wine list, which counts no fewer than 400 bin numbers, is first rate, and some of the restaurant's personal touches are charming — for example, *foie gras tartelettes, gravlax* salmon, and haddock quiche served with cocktails. The cost of all this is "rather dear," as the British would say, but less than its equivalent in Paris and well worth it for a memorable occasion. Closed Mondays, Tuesday lunches, Sunday dinners from October through *Easter,* and from December 26 for 7 weeks. A private dining room, serving eight people, can be hired. No guestrooms. Details: *Waterside Inn,* Ferry Rd., Bray-on-Thames, Berkshire SL6 2AT, England (phone: 628-20691).

AUBERGE DE L'ILL, Illhaeusern (Alsace), France: There are those who claim that Alsace, not Paris, is France's culinary capital, and this establishment is their strongest piece of evidence. As run by the Haeberlin brothers — Jean-Pierre and Paul (the chef) — and Paul's son, Marc, the restaurant's menu is superbly Alsatian and impeccably prepared: wild hare salad, terrine of crayfish, peach salad with Burgundy. Closed Mondays and Tuesdays, most of February, and the first week in July. Information: *Auberge de l'Ill,* Rue de Collanges, Illhaeusern, Ribeauvillé 68150, France (phone: 89-71-83-23).

MOULIN DE MOUGINS, Mougins (Côte d'Azur), France: If your vision of the Riviera is dining in distinguished (or at least glamorous) company in a beautiful garden flooded with sunlight in an elegant country setting, what you've experienced is precognition, not hallucination. Just such romantic trances are regularly accomplished hereabouts, often accompanied by the smell of oranges; though far more likely in this case is the wafting aroma of heavenly fish soup, lobster grilled in basil butter, or fowl braised in port. Happy dreams. Closed Mondays (except mid-July to September), Thursday lunch, and the end of January to mid-March. Information: *Moulin de Mougins,* 424 Chemin du Moulin, Mougins, France (phone: 93-75-78-24; fax: 93-90-18-55).

ALAIN CHAPEL, Mionnay (Lyons), France: Among the flash and sizzle of the new styles of cuisine and the chefs perfecting it, don't fail to sample the fine dishes served at the late chef Alain Chapel's namesake. Lobster with noodles, stuffed calf's ear, and a fabulous lobster salad were among his most delicious stock in trade and his culinary traditions live on. Closed Mondays, Tuesday afternoons, and January. Information: *Alain Chapel,* RN 83, Mionnay 01390, France (phone: 78-91-82-02; fax: 78-91-82-37).

PAUL BOCUSE, Lyons, France: Out of the way though it may be, this city in what Parisians disdainfully label the provinces is home to one of the country's most honored restaurants, and travelers come from all over the world to sample its specialties — *soupe au potiron, loup au four, cassolette d'écrevisses.* In point of fact, the absence of large-scale tourism keeps Bocuse purer than its three-star *confrères* in the capital, which serve so many clients who barely know a *coquille St.-Jacques* from a cheeseburger. Information: *Paul Bocuse,* 50 Quai Plage, Collonges-au-Mont d'Or 69660, France (phone: 78-22-01-40; fax: 72-27-85-87).

TROISGROS, Roanne (Lyons), France: More than any other restaurant in France, this splendid house celebrates the land, changing the dishes on its menu season by season to use the area's fresh vegetables, poultry, shrimp, and snails to best advantage. Pierre Troisgros rejoices in the natural flavor of foods delicately enhanced and under-scored. A shopping trip with him is something of a lesson in local ecology, wildlife, biology, and topography all rolled into one. Renovations in 1990 included a gleaming glass and metal makeover of the once rather modest façade of the building. Closed Tuesdays, Wednesday afternoons, and most of January. Information: *Troisgros,* Pl. Jean Troisgros, Roanne 42300, France (phone: 77-71-66-97; fax: 77-70-39-77).

L'AMBROISIE, Paris, France: Promoted to three-star status by Michelin in 1988, this tiny, quietly elegant establishment on the ground floor of a mansion on one of Paris's most beautiful squares, is the showcase for chef Bernard Pacaud's equally elegant cuisine. The menu is limited to only a few entrées, such as duck with foie gras, skate and sliced green cabbage in sherry vinegar sauce, veal sweetbreads with shallots and parsley on ultra-fresh pasta, lightly battered chicken thighs in a piquant sauce, and oxtail in a savory sauce, but the dishes more than compensate for the limited number of choices with great portions of gustatory pleasure. Closed Sundays and Monday afternoons, August, February, and holidays. Information: *L'Ambroisie,* 9 Place des Vosges, Paris 75004, France (phone: 42-78-51-45).

GRAND VEFOUR, Paris, France: At the far end of Palais Royal's serene courtyard, this lovely, lavishly ornamented relic of old Paris is perhaps the most classically French of the great Parisian temples of gastronomy. Specialties of chef Fouché include *noisettes d'agneau à la vinaigre de basilic* and *soufflé antillais,* a bitter chocolate soufflé. Closed Saturday afternoons, Sundays and August. Information: *Grand Vefour,* 17 Rue de Beaujolais, Paris 75001, France (phone: 42-96-56-27; fax: 42-86-80-71).

JAMIN, Paris, France: Due to the culinary talents of owner-chef Joël Robuchon, *Jamin* is now one of Paris's finest restaurants with three stars from Michelin. Robuchon calls his cuisine "moderne," similar to but not always as light as *la nouvelle.* Closed Saturdays, Sundays, and July. Reserve 2 to 3 months in advance for dinner; 3 weeks to a month ahead for lunch. Information: *Jamin,* 32 Rue de Longchamp, Paris 75116, France (phone: 47-27-12-27).

LASSERRE, Paris, France: A friend once described a meal at *Lasserre* as similar to dining in one of those fabulous Fabergé music boxes, and so it is. The atmosphere in the plush upstairs dining room is very elegant, with waiters in white tie and tails. Service is swift and impeccable, and the cuisine sublime. Some special dishes include crab pâté *au Richard;* terrines of veal, duck, and chicken (served as one dish); eel pâté; frogs' legs in garlic; *rouget au sarriette;* and saddle of hare. Write at least a month ahead for reservations, offering a couple of dates; replies are prompt, and this slight effort will ensure a table in the elite center section of the dining room, where the ceiling opens during mid-meal, affording diners a view of the Paris sky. Closed Sundays, Monday lunch, and August. Information: *Restaurant Lasserre,* 17 Av. Franklin-Roosevelt, Paris 75008, France (phone: 43-59-53-43; fax: 45-63-72-23).

LE TAILLEVENT, Paris, France: Full of tradition, Louis XVI furnishings, 18th-century porcelain dinner service — all in a 19th-century mansion — *Taillevent* offers *cuisine classique* that is currently the best in Paris. Try terrine of truffled sweetbreads, duck in cider, and for dessert, one of chef Claude Deligne's unusual soufflés, like Alsatian pear or cinnamon chocolate. Three stars in the *Guide Michelin.* Closed weekends, part of February, and August. Reserve 2 weeks in advance for lunch; 6 to 8 weeks in advance for dinner. Note: It's easier to book a table for four people rather than for just two. Information: *Le Taillevent,* 15 Rue Lamennais, Paris 75008, France (phone: 45-61-12-90).

BOYER "LES CRAYÈRES," Reims, France: This three-star establishment is housed in a stunning 19th-century château, set on 19 beautifully landscaped acres, just a stone's throw from the twin Gothic towers of Reims Cathedral. The offerings, which include such dishes as mussel soup with saffron and orange, salmon with lemon and ginger, and standards like foie gras, bass with artichokes, and roast pigeon with garlic and parsley, reflect a finely tuned balance between nouvelle and traditional cuisines. Service is helpful without being overbearing. In support of the main local industry, the wine list includes over 60 champagnes. Closed Mondays, lunch Tuesdays, and mid-December to mid-January. Information: *Boyer "Les Crayères,"* 64 Bd. Henri-Vasnier, Reims 51100, France (phone: 26-82-80-80; fax: 26-82-65-52).

GEORGES BLANC, Vonnas, France: Set on the bank of the river Veyle in the picturesque Beaujolais village of Vonnas, this family-run restaurant-hotel has a history of excellence that goes back four generations. Great-grandmother Blanc, its founder, prepared simple country food. Her daughter developed the cuisine and came to be known all over France as "La Mère Blanc," or "Empress Blanc." Her daughter continued the tradition, and today Georges Blanc — the first male in the line and the first to have formal culinary and hotel schooling — offers an award-winning menu that combines both traditional regional cooking and nouvelle cuisine. There are two menus (two or four courses with cheeses and dessert), outstanding features of which are the braised sweetbreads in spinach, lamb tenderloin with fresh wild mushrooms, and a dessert cart brimming with 15 to 20 pastry selections. There are 23 charming rooms and 7 suites, a swimming pool, and tennis courts for guests who wish to make a real occasion of their dining experience. Closed Wednesdays, Thursdays, and January. Information: *Georges Blanc,* Vonnas 01540, France (phone: 74-50-00-10; fax: 74-50-08-80).

BAMBERGER REITER, Berlin, Germany: Traditional dark paneling and an old-fashioned homey atmosphere are surprising backdrops for the creative nouvelle Austro-French cuisine served at this dinner-only restaurant. For their more conservative guests, the Austrian owners, the Raneburgers, prepare such classic favorites as pot roast and dumplings; there is also a wide selection of French and German wines. In summer, eating in the front garden is very pleasant. Closed Sundays and Mondays. Information: *Bamberger Reiter,* 7 Regensburger Strasse, Berlin, Germany (phone: 849-244282).

VIER JAHRESZEITEN, Munich, Germany: Everything about it is tastefully discreet, from its half-lit glow to its creamy decor and hushed carpeting. This dining room in the *Vier Jahreszeiten* hotel offers Bavaria's most elegant and sophisticated cuisine, and when you've had the *Lachsforelle mit Kerbelsahne glaciert* (salmon trout glazed with chervil cream) or the *Kalbsfilet und Morcheln in Blätterteig* (filet of veal and morels in puff pastry in broccoli cream), you'll forget all about the last time you saw Paris. Information: *Restaurant im Hotel Vier Jahreszeiten,* 17 Maximilianstrasse, Munich 8000, Germany (phone: 89-230390).

TAVERNA TA NISSIA, Athens, Greece: One of the best restaurants in all of Greece is in the basement of the *Hilton* hotel. The decor, music, and food are Greek. Notable on the menu are the *kakavia,* a lavish bouillabaisse, and the spit-roasted Olympia lamb. The exotic Greek hors d'oeuvres and salads also are worth making room for. Information: *Taverna Ta Nissia,* 46 Vasilissis Sofias, Athens, Greece (phone: 1-722-0201).

GUNDEL, Budapest, Hungary: This magnet of Eastern European gastronomy is now under the ownership of legendary Hungarian-born, American restaurateur George Lang. The great Hungarian dishes so associated with the name Károly Gundel have returned, and the restaurant is once again the place where the elite meet; where the dessert crêpes are incredible, and the goose liver pie astounding. Information: *Gundel,* XIV, 2 Allatkerti út, Budapest, Hungary (phone: 1-122-1002).

ENOTECA PINCHIORRI, Florence, Italy: Michelangelo, Botticelli, and the *Enoteca Pinchiorri* — a perfect Florentine day. The edible art changes with the market's offerings but often exhibits such masterworks as foie gras with pomegranate salad, sole with onion and parsley purée, tiny *gnocchi* (potato dumplings) with basil, and veal with caper and lime sauce. The charming decor of a 15th-century palace and a flawlessly appointed table are all part of the artful setting. An *enoteca* is a type of wine merchant's showroom, which is how this place got its start. Closed Sundays, Mondays at lunch, and August. Information: *Enoteca Pinchiorri,* 87 Via Ghibellina, Firenze 50122, Italy (phone: 55-242777).

ANTICA OSTERIA DEL PONTE, Milan, Italy: Let owner Ezio Santin be your guide to the delectable dishes of this exceptional country inn where Santin's recipies combine Italian haute cuisine with French cooking techniques. Try the delicate pasta *fagotto* tied with leeks and tucked inside seafood tidbits such as lobster, crayfish, and caviar. Closed Sundays and Mondays and from December 25 through January 12, and August. Information: *Antica Osteria del Ponte,* Cassinetta di Lugagnano, Milan (phone: 2-942-0034; fax: 2-942-0610).

GUALTIERO MARCHESI, Milan, Italy: Owned and managed by the famous Italian chef, this spot is almost universally regarded as the single best restaurant in the country. Gualtiero Marchesi's dishes are works of art — all served in sophisticated contemporary decor. Closed Sundays, Mondays for lunch, and August. Information: *Gualtiero Marchesi,* 9 Via Bonvesin della Riva, Milan, Italy (phone: 2-741246; fax: 2-738-6677).

SAVINI, Milan, Italy: This beloved Milanese establishment famed for its rice dishes and fresh fish is in the fin de siècle *Galleria.* Beneath the elaborate crystal chandeliers statesmen, opera stars such as La Callas, and celebrities of all nations have dined. Go for the atmosphere; the cuisine is traditional Lombard, laced with international specialities. The wine list is appropriately grand with selections from the Napa Valley to the Loire. Closed Sundays and December 24 through January 6 and 15 days in August. Information: *Savini, Galleria Vittorio Emanuele II,* Milan (phone: 2-805-8343; fax: 2-807306).

RELAIS LE JARDIN, Rome, Italy: Not everyone agrees, but the understated elegance of the dining room of the *Lord Byron* hotel in Parioli helps make *Relais le Jardin,* for most Italian food critics, the foremost Roman restaurant. Chef Antonio Sciullo blends the unlikely into the often surprising and sometimes sublime. The menu follows the seasons: zucchini flowers filled with bean purée, ravioli stuffed with a delicate pigeon ragout, and scallops in watercress flan. Service is appropriately sophisticated, as are the desserts and wines. Closed Sundays. Information: *Relais Le Jardin, Hotel Lord Byron,* 5 Via Giuseppe de Notaris, Rome, Italy (phone: 6-322-4541).

EL TOULÀ, Rome, Italy: The well-heeled, well-traveled, and aristocratic assemble in the small, plush dining rooms here for Cortina- and Venice-inspired food. In winter, the menu features hearty game dishes such as venison, and the year-round specialty is fish (the poppyseed-daubed salmon in oyster sauce is especially good). A favorite dessert is the large shortbread biscuit. Good wines also are available. Closed Saturday lunch, Sundays, and August. Information: *El Toulà di Roma,* 29b Via della Lupa, Rome, Italy (phone: 6-873498).

TAMPAT SENANG, The Hague, Netherlands: The Hague boasts some of the best Indonesian restaurants in Europe, and this is one of the oldest and most elegant in the Netherlands. It's especially popular with embassy officials and local businesspeople. In the summer, guests can dine in the garden. Open daily for dinner. Information: *Tampat Senang,* 6 Laan van Meerdervoort (near the *Freedom Palace*), The Hague, Netherlands (phone: 70-363-6787).

AVIZ, Lisbon, Portugal: You will find Portuguese specialties on the menu of this Lisbon landmark, but the best dishes on the menu include *shashlik au riz,* smoked mallard, and other specialties that had their genesis all over the Continent. The restaurant's management and many of the staff are the legacy of the late, great *Aviz* hotel, once the *Waldorf* of Lisbon. Closed Saturday lunch and Sundays. Information: *Aviz,* 12-B Rua Serpa-Pinto, Lisbon, Portugal (phone: 1-342-8391).

HORCHER, Madrid, Spain: At this legendary establishment transplanted from prewar Berlin, game and fish are the specialties, but the ever-changing menu usually glitters with fanciful creations like asparagus mousse Cantábrica, pineapple lobster Titus, and crêpes Sir Holten, and no two meals here are ever quite alike. In Madrid, ten in the evening is considered a fine time to start dinner, and the service at *Horcher* is leisurely — so be sure to do enough cocktail-hour snacking to keep body and soul together. Closed Sundays and July. Information: *Horcher,* 6 Alfonso XII, Madrid, Spain (phone: 1-522-0731).

ZALACAIN, Madrid, Spain: The coveted third Michelin star that shines on this distinctively Spanish restaurant gives new status to Spain's often-deprecated cuisine. Visitors will find dishes prepared with the unabashedly Spanish flavorings of saffron, green pepper sauce, *escabeche,* and Basque cider served over Mediterranean seafood and broad beans. Though the menu changes with the season, the high quality of the food remains the same. Closed Saturday lunch, Sundays, *Easter Week,* and August. Information: *Zalacain,* 4 Alvarez de Baena, Madrid, Spain (phone: 1-261-4840).

OPERAKÄLLAREN, Stockholm, Sweden: Sunday — the traditional day to eat smorgasbord — is the best time to visit this large, beautifully designed dining palace facing the sea from inside the *Royal Opera House.* This is the particular smorgasbord, piled with seafood from all the waters of the North, that is the pride of Scandinavia. Information: *Operakällaren Opera House,* Box 1616, Stockholm S-11186, Sweden (phone: 8-111125 or 8-676-5800).

GIRARDET, Crissier (just northwest of Lausanne), Switzerland: Merely the best restaurant in the world. Alfred Girardet (known as Fredy) is one of the greatest culinary geniuses ever to put saucepan to fire, a master whose art is not wasted in pretensions of any sort, which makes a visit to his informal, comfortable restaurant a special joy. Girardet looks a little like a young, blond Orson Welles, and the only thing more attractive than he is his food. Closed Sundays and Mondays, the first 3 weeks of August, and from *Christmas* until January 10. Information: *Girardet,* 1 Rue d'Yverdon, Crissier, Switzerland (phone: 21-634-0505).

ARAGVI, Moscow, Soviet Union: One of the last oases of even moderate luxury left in the Soviet Union, this bustling Georgian restaurant crowded with commissars, foreign journalists, ballerinas, diplomats, and the like does a booming business in caviar (*ikra* in Russian) and icy vodka. The best dishes are hot and spicy, like *tsiplyata tabaka,* roast chicken pressed between scalding stones, and *shashlik po kharski,* skewered roast Georgian mutton. Sturgeon roasted on a spit is also excellent. Information: *Aragvi,* 6 Tverskaya St., Moscow, Soviet Union (phone: 095-229-3762).

Shopping Spree:
Europe for the Savvy

Shopping and Europe used to go hand in hand. You could buy things in Europe that you couldn't buy at home — or at least at prices far lower than you paid stateside. This is no longer quite so true nowadays, after years of galloping inflation and waltzing currencies. The extraordinary bargains of yore can be hard to find, though the most famous foreign merchandise — the coveted goods that bear the labels of such posh purveyors as Gucci, Louis Vuitton, Burberry, Saint Laurent, and the like — still costs considerably less than its inflated price in US shops.

Duty-free shops are another institution of which a wise shopper should beware: The only connection we have ever been able to see between *duty* and *airports* is that people feel they have a duty to buy something in them. One thing they certainly are is mostly bargain-free.

Furthermore, goods travel a great deal more than they used to, and a lot of the standard items that people used to stalk on the Champs-Elysées are available on Main Street. By the time you've traipsed, lugged, crammed, and declared, you're better off picking up Twining's tea and other such imports at the corner store.

The moral of the story is this: Shop as part of the *experience* of travel. Buy because it brings you into contact with people and places, customs and creation. Shop for things you couldn't find elsewhere, things that will remind you of those people and places when you are back home. Shop for things of very good quality, things you will use often. Then your purchase becomes an expensive snapshot, and the pleasure of the experience lingers.

BEST BUYS

What follows is a list of some of the great shopping experiences of Europe — its finest shops, its special products, small museums of commerce that will interest you even if you're not out to buy. We've indexed them not by place but by item on the theory that you may prefer to look for these purchases when you need them. Similar, more specific shopping lists are part of each individual city chapter in THE CITIES.

Antiques – The *Dorotheergasse* in Vienna; the auction houses in London: *Sotheby's* (34 New Bond St., W1; phone: 71-493-8080) and *Christie's* (8 King St., W1; phone: 71-839-9060); the giant *Louvre des Antiquaires* on the site of the old Magasins du Louvre in Paris; Via del Babuino, Via dei Coronari, and Via Giulia, Rome; Spiegel-straat, Amsterdam.

Birds – *Le Marché aux Oiseaux* — the bird market — held Sundays on Place Louis-Lépine, on the Ile de la Cité, Paris.

Books – The *Dorotheum* auction house, Vienna; *Blackwell's* (50 Broad St., Oxford, England; phone: 865-792792); *Maggs Bros. Ltd.* (50 Berkeley Sq., London W1; phone: 71-493-7160); *Foyle's* (119 Charing Cross Rd., London WC2; phone: 71-437-5660) and a number of other stores on Charing Cross Road; the *Dom Knigi* (26 Novii Arbat St., Moscow; phone: 95-290-4507).

Buttons – You'll find 10,000 different designs at *La Boutique à Boutons,* 110 Rue de Rennes, Paris.

Cameras – *Foto-Radio Wegert* (26-A and 157 Kurfürstendamm and at other branches) in Berlin; the stores of the *Interdiscount* chain in Lucerne (Pilatusstrasse and across from the main railroad station, plus other branches throughout Switzerland).

China – Augarten porcelain at the *Schloss Augarten* in Vienna; *Royal Copenhagen* (6 Amagertorv, Copenhagen); *Bing & Grøndahl* (4 Amagertorv, Copenhagen); *Rosenthal* (9 Kaiserstr., Frankfurt, and all over Germany); Delftware from *Focke and Meltzer* (124 Rokin or 65 P.C. Hooftstraat, Amsterdam); *Richard Ginori,* in major Italian cities; *Vista Alegre* porcelain (18 Largo do Chiado, Lisbon); slightly irregular name-brand china at *Reject China Shop* (33-35 Beauchamp Pl., London SW3; phone: 71-581-0737; and 134 Regent St., London W1; phone: 71-434-2502).

Coats – *Burberry's Ltd.* (18 Haymarket, London W1; phone: 71-930-3343); *Loden-Frey* (7-9 Maffeistr., Munich) for loden coats; *Davide Cenci* (Via Campo Marzio, Rome).

Copperware – "Dinanderies," hammered copper, from Dinant, Belgium. Villedieu-les-Poëles, a small farm town in Normandy, is wall-to-wall copper; *poëles* — frying pans — have been made there since the 17th century.

Crystal – You'll find Bohemian Moser crystal at 12 Na Příkopě in Prague; Waterford crystal all over Ireland; Venetian glass at *Pauly* (Ponte dei Consorzi, Venice); and *Baccarat* in Paris (30 *bis* Rue du Paradis).

Cutlery – *Henckels,* in all major German cities, including at 11 Rossmarkt, Frankfurt, and 33 Kurfürstendamm, Berlin.

Diamonds – *Amsterdam Diamond Center,* 1-5 Rokin, Amsterdam.

Eiderdowns – *Steen & Strøm,* 23 Kongensgate, Oslo.

Embroidery and Needlework – *Madeira Superbia* (75-A Av. Duque de Loulé, Lisbon) for Madeiran embroidery; *Casa Bonet* (3 Puig Dorfila, Palma de Mallorca, Spain).

Enamelware – *David Andersen,* at 20 Karl Johans Gate and in the *Oslo City Shopping Center,* Oslo.

Fabrics – *Galtrucco,* 23 Via del Tritone, Rome, and 27 Via Montenapoleone, Milan.

Food and Liquor – *Fortnum & Mason* (Piccadilly, London W1; phone: 71-734-8040); *Harrods* (87-135 Brompton Rd., Knightsbridge, London SW1; phone: 71-730-1234); *Fauchon* (Pl. de la Madeleine, Paris); *Alois Dallmayr* (14-15 Dienerstr., Munich); *Charlot* (83 Claudio Coello, Madrid); *Ka De We* (21-24 Tauentzienstr., Berlin); *Dispensa Gualtiero Marchesi* (6 Via San Giovanni sul Muro, Milan).

Furniture and Furnishings – Particularly in Denmark at *Illums Bolighus* (10 Amagertorv, Copenhagen) and *Paustian House* (2 Kalkbrændenløbskaj, Copenhagen).

Furs – *Birger Christensen* (38 Østergade, Copenhagen); *Revillon* (42 Rue de la Boétie, Paris); *Fendi* (4/E Via Borgognona, Rome); *Sistovaris and Sons* (14 Voulis, Athens); *Brødrene Thorkildsen* (8 Øvre Slottsgt., Oslo); *GUM* (3 Red Sq., Moscow; phone: 095-926-3471). In Russia, a *shapka,* the characteristic fur hat, is your best purchase.

Gloves – *Perrone* (92 Piazza di Spagna, Rome) and *Madova* (1r Via Guicciardini, Florence; phone: 296526).

Guns – *Holland and Holland* (33 Bruton St., London W1; phone: 71-499-4411); *James Purdey and Sons* (57 S. Audley St., London W1; phone: 71-499-1801).

Hats – *James Lock and Company, Ltd.,* men's hats since 1759 (6 St. James's St., London SW1; phone: 71-930-8874); *Bates* (21A Jermyn St., London SW1). For ladies, *David Shilling* (4 Chiltern St., London W1; phone: 71-935-8473). For men and women, *Herbert Johnson* (30 New Bond St., London W1; phone: 71-408-1174).

Haute Couture – The great Paris houses include *Christian Dior* (32 Av. Montaigne); *Yves Saint Laurent* (5 Av. Marceau); *Pierre Cardin* (83 Rue du Faubourg-St.-Honoré); *Courrèges* (40 Rue François-I); *Givenchy* (3 Av. George-V); and *Chanel* (29-31 Rue Cambon and 42 Av. Montaigne). For high fashion in Paris at discounted prices, try the following: *Boutique Stock* (26, 30, and 149 Rue St.-Placide); *Cacharel Stock* (114 Rue d'Alésia); *Club des 10* (58 Rue du Faubourg-St.-Honoré); *Dorothée Bis Stock* (74

Rue d'Alésia); *Drôles de Choses pour Drôles de Gens* (14 Rue des Colonnes-du-Trône);
Halle Bys (60 Rue Richelieu); *Le Mouton à Cinq Pattes* (6, 8, and 10 Rue St.-Placide);
Les Soldes Victor-Hugo (111 Av. Victor-Hugo); *Mèndes* (65 Rue Montmartre); *Miss
Griffes* (19 Rue de Penthièvre); *Olivieri Stock* (115 Av. Victor-Hugo); *Pierre Cardin
Stock* (11 Bd. Sebastopol); *Stéphane* (130 Bd. St.-Germain); *Stock Griffes* (17 Rue
Vieille-du-Temple); and *Stock System* (112 Rue d'Alésia).

Jewelry – In Vienna at *A. E. Köchert* (15 Neuer Markt), *Haban* (2 Kärntner
Strasse), and *Anton Heldwein* (13 Graben). *Wolfers* (82 Av. Louise, Brussels; phone:
511-6525) — especially for diamonds; *Asprey's* (165 New Bond St., London W1; phone:
71-493-6767); *Cartier* (7 Pl. Vendôme) and *Van Cleef & Arpels* (22 Pl. Vendôme), both
in Paris; the necklace of shops on the Ponte Vecchio in Florence; *Bulgari* (10 Via
Condotti) and *Buccellatti* (31 Via Condotti) in Rome; *Nardi* (69 Piazza San Marco,
Venice); *Bonebakker* (86-90 Rokin, Amsterdam); and various stores in Perth, Scotland,
for river Tay pearls.

Kitchenware – The premises of *E. Dehillerin* (18 Rue Coquillière, Paris) draws the
great French chefs. (No matter where you go, it's always nice to bring home the special
utensil used for national dishes — a fondue pot and forks from Switzerland; *paelleleros*
from Spain; escargot sets from France; and *moka express* from Italy.) In Milan a
must-stop is the ultra-chic *Officina Alessi* (9 Corso Matteotti).

Knitwear – *Westaway and Westaway* (65 Great Russell St., London W1; phone:
71-405-4479); *Albertina* (10 Via Lazio, Rome); in Oslo at *William Schmidt and Co.*
(41 Karl Johans Gate) and the *Oslo Sweater Shop*, in the *SAS Scandinavia* hotel's
shopping arcade (5 Tullinsgt.) for Scandinavian hand-knitted sweaters.

Lace – *Manufacture Belge de Dentelles* (68 Galerie de la Reine, near the Grand'
Place, Brussels; phone: 2-511-4477); many stores in the towns of Bruges and Malines;
Jesurum (Ponte Canonica, Venice); and, for Dalmatian lace, stores on the islands off
the coast of Yugoslavia.

Leather Goods – *Hermès* (24 Rue du Faubourg-St.-Honoré, Paris); *Ottino* (60 Via
Cerretani, Florence); *Fendi* (39 Via Borgognona, Rome); *Loewe* (8 Gran Vía or 26
Serrano in Madrid, and in other major cities in Spain); *Trussardi* (7 Via Sant' Andrea,
Milan); and *Gucci,* in Florence, Rome, Milan, and Montecatini. Suedes are a good
purchase in Yugoslavia: Try *Jugoexport* (2 Terazije, Belgrade).

Lenses – Contact, telescopic, binocular, or otherwise: In Munich, *Söhnges* (7 Briennerstr.), as well as in other German cities.

Linen – *Brown Thomas* (15 Grafton St., Dublin); *Podarki* (4 Via Gorky, Moscow).

Maps – *Edward Stanford,* 12 Longacre, London WC2 (phone: 71-836-1321).

Menswear – *Brioni* (79 Via Barberini) and *Carlo Palazzi* (7 Via Borgognona), both
in Rome, sell typically Italian garments — at the former they are more classic, at the
latter, flashier. Style at its highest: *Giorgio Armani* (102 Via del Babuino, Rome);
Valentino (13 Via Condotti, Rome). *Charvet,* Paris's answer to Savile Row (28 Pl.
Vendôme, Paris).

Music – *J. Votrüba* (4 Lerchenfelder Gurtel) or *Doblinger* (10 Dorotheergasse) in
Vienna; *Messaggerie Musicali* (2 Galleria del Corso, Milan). You'll find Russian records at *Melodye* in Moscow (40 Kalinina Prospekt; phone: 95-291-1421) — but the
sound quality is disappointing. Or get a harmonica from Trossingen, Germany, or a
violin from Mittenwald, Germany, or Cremona, Italy — where it all began.

Paintings – Works by contemporary artists will be found in Paris, at galleries along
Rue du Faubourg-St.-Honoré, Avenue Matignon, Rue La Boétie (on the Right Bank),
and scattered throughout the area around the Rue de Seine, Rue Bonaparte, and Rue
des Beaux-Arts (on the Left Bank). Berlin, as vital an art center nowadays as Paris, is
liveliest on and around the Kurfürstendamm; a complete directory of galleries is
available from *Arbeitsgemeinschaft Berliner Kunstamtsleiter* (56 Leibnizstr., Berlin;

phone: 849-882-7020). Do your browsing in Rome along the Via Margutta and the adjacent side streets in Milan in the Brera quarter. *Kreisler* (19 Serrano; phone: 1-576-5338) and *Kreisler Dos* (8 Hermosilla; phone: 1-576-1664) are your best bets in Madrid. The *Royal Society of Portrait Painters* (17 Carlton House Ter., London; phone: 71-930-6844) will help you choose an artist to execute your family's portrait.

Perfumes – *Floris* (89 Jermyn St., London SW1; phone: 71-930-2885) and *Penhaligon's* (at numerous branches, including 41 Wellington St., London WC2; phone: 71-836-2150); *Catherine* (6 Rue Castiglione) and *Michel Swiss* (Rue de la Paix) in Paris; and throughout the town of Grasse in the south of France, where you can sometimes visit the great perfume factories.

Pewter – Throughout the town of Huy, Belgium; *The Pewter Shop* (16 Burlington Arcade, London W1; phone: 71-493-1730); Nuremberg, Germany; and *N. M. Thune* (12 Ø. Slottsgate, Oslo).

Pharmaceuticals – The *Boots* chain all over England; the *Pharmacie Principale*, 11 Rue du Marché, Geneva.

Prints – In London: *Colnaghi* (14 Old Bond St., W1; phone: 71-493-4484). In Rome: *Ciambarelli* (143 Via dei Coronari).

Records – Collectors won't want to miss the *Saturn* record store (91 Hansaring; phone: 221-16160) in Cologne, Germany, reputedly the largest of its kind in the world. Its 3-floor inventory includes jazz, classical, pop, and a comprehensive selection of film soundtracks and Broadway cast albums.

Riding Equipment – *Der Reiter,* 43 Heinestr., Vienna.

Rugs – For *flokati* rugs in Athens: *Greco-Floc* (9 Adrianou) and *Karamichos* (3 Mitropoleos). For Orientals: *Alexander Juran* (74 New Bond St., London W1; phone: 71-493-4484) and *Luciano Coen* (65 Via Margutta, Rome). Also, the island of Sardinia in Italy (for expensive, but good-quality, handloomed pure wool carpets).

Shoes – Still in Italy, and still *Ferragamo* (66 and 74 Via Condotti, Rome). Bring gold. *Gucci* has its flagship store in Florence, and has branches in Rome, Milan, and Montecatini; *Tanino Crisci* (3 Via Montenapoleone, Milan).

Silver – *Georg Jensen* (40 Ostergade) and *Hans Hansen* (16 Amagertorv) in Copenhagen; *London Silver Vaults* (53-54 Chancery La., London WC2; phone: 71-242-3844); *Armaos* (22 Akadimias) and *Argiriou Bros.* (103 Kifissias), in Athens; and *Kurt Decker* (12 Biblioteksgatan, Stockholm).

Ski Equipment – All along the Maria-Theresienstrasse in Innsbruck; at *Steen & Strøm* (23 Kongensgate, Oslo); and at *Brigatti* (15 Corso Venezia, Milan).

Sporting Goods – *Lillywhite's,* Piccadilly Circus, London SW1 (phone: 71-930-3181).

Stamps – In London at the stamp auctions held by *Christie's* (8 King St., SW1; phone: 71-839-9060); in Paris at the outdoor stamp market at the corner of Avenues Gabriel and Marigny and extending to the corner of Avenues Ponthieu and Matignon (on Thursdays, Saturdays, and Sundays), or at the shops along the Rue Drouot; in Madrid on the Plaza Mayor, every Sunday from 10 AM to 2 PM, or the shops on Calle Felipe III; in Moscow at 16 Lybianskaya Square and at the *Philatelist Shop* (1 Taras Shevchenko St.); and at the *Ufficio Filatelico* of the Republic of San Marino.

Sweets – Belgian chocolates are the best at *Corné Toison d'Or* (12 Av. de la Toison d'Or; phone: 2-512-8947, and 24-26 Galerie du Roi; phone: 2-512-4984, and several other branches in Brussels). In Paris head to *Au Duc de Praslin* (33 Rue Vivienne) and *Maison du Chocolat* (225 Fg. du St.-Honoré and 56 Rue Pierre-Charron); and in Zurich to the *Confiserie Sprüngli* (21 Bahnhofstr.).

Tea – *King's Teagarden* (217 Kurfürstendamm, Berlin) has 170 different varieties to either take home or drink on the spot. The *Twinings* shop (216 Strand, London WC2; phone: 71-353-3511) sells a full range of the company's products for the lowest prices available anywhere. *Mariage Frères* (30 Rue Bourg-Tiboug, Paris) has imported and sold an impressive range of teas to the French for nearly 2 centuries. There's a retail counter and a tearoom, as well as a large array of tea pots and accessories.

Tobacco – *Dunhill* (30 Duke St., London SW1; phone: 71-499-9566). Cigar specialists: *James J. Fox* (2 Burlington Gardens, London W1; phone: 71-493-9009); *Davidoff* (2 Rue de Rive, Geneva); *Hajenius* (92-96 Rokin, Amsterdam).

Toys – The *Christkindlmarkt* (on the Rathausplatz in Vienna), at *Christmastime;* *Hamleys* (200 Regent St., London, W1); the city of Nuremberg in Germany (electric trains, *Christmas* tree ornaments, Steiff animals); port towns like Bremen and Lübeck (for ships in bottles); *Jouets Weber* (12 Rue Croix-d'Or, Geneva) for miniature replicas of trains and cars; *F.C. Weber* for toy trains and cars (62 Bahnhofstr., Zurich); *Dom Igrushki* (8 Kutuzovsky Prospekt, Moscow) for the nesting wooden dolls called *matryoshkas; Al Sogno Giocattoli,* for dolls and stuffed animals (53 Piazza Navona, Rome).

Tweeds – Ireland is still tops. Go to *Cleo Ltd.* for women (18 Kildare St., Dublin); *Kevin and Howlin* for men (31 Nassau St., Dublin); *Magee* (The Diamond, Donegal Town); and *Millars Connamara Tweeds* (in Clifden, County Galway).

Umbrellas – And canes, handles, pommels: *Madeleine Gély* (218 Bd. St.-Germain, Paris); *James Smith and Sons,* Europe's oldest umbrella shop (53 New Oxford St., London, WC1; phone: 71-836-4731).

Watches – *Bucherer* (5 Schwanenpl., Lucerne) and also sold all over Switzerland; *Patek Philippe* (41 Rue du Rhône, Geneva); *B&B* (1 Quai du Mont-Blanc, Geneva) specializes in Ebel timepieces; *Les Ambassadeurs* (39 Rue du Rhône, Geneva) specializes in Audemars-Piguet. Don't look for any bargains in classic Swiss watches: The several million handsome phonies ground out every year in Singapore and Taiwan are the only cheapies along the streets of Geneva. And if you're interested in knowing a little bit more than the time, don't miss Vienna's great *Uhrenmuseum* (clock museum), closed Mondays; admission charge (2 Schulhof; phone: 1-533-2265).

Wine – The wine auctions at *Sotheby's* (34 New Bond St., W1; phone: 71-493-8080) and *Christie's* (8 King St., SW1; phone: 71-839-9060) in London; *Fauchon* at Place de la Madeleine in Paris; *Weinhaus Schulmeister* (9 Langestr., Baden-Baden, Germany); *Buccone* (19 Via Ripetta, Rome); the *Madeira Wine Association* (Av. Arriaga in Funchal), and the wine lodges in Vila Nova de Gaia, across the river from Porto, Portugal.

Woodcarvings – All through the Tyrol district of Austria; in the town of Spa, Belgium; and in the town of Oberammergau, Germany.

HANDICRAFTS

Some countries now have exposition centers to display their handicrafts; often, the goods shown have been approved by a design board. For the best in Europe:

Finnish Design Center, 19 Kasarmikatu, Helsinki.

Gobelins looms (42 Av. des Gobelins, Paris) open Tuesdays, Wednesdays, and Thursdays; tours given at 2 and 3 PM.

National Organization of Hellenic Handicrafts, 3 Mitropoleos, Athens.

Husfliden (4 Møllergaten, Oslo); *Norway Designs* (28 Stortingsgaten, Oslo).

Artespaña (Empresa Nacional de Artesanía), 14 Hermosilla, 3 Plaza de las Cortés, or 32 Gran Vía, Madrid.

Svensk Hemslöjd, 44 Sveavägen, Stockholm.

Schweizer Heimatwerk, at various locations in Zurich: Rudolf Brun-Brücke, 14 Rennweg, 2 Bahnhofstr., and the Zurich Airport.

Craftcentre Cymru, in towns throughout Wales such as Betwys-Y-Coed; Chirk, Nr. Wrexham, Llangurig, Nr. Llanidloes, Machynlleth, and Porthmadog.

Narodna Radinost, throughout Yugoslavia.

DEPARTMENT STORES

Europe's greatest and grandest: *Harrods* (Knightsbridge, London SW1; phone: 71-730-1234); *Stockmann* (Helsinki); *Au Printemps* (Paris); *Galeries Lafayette* (Paris); *Kaufhaus des Westens,* known as *Ka De We* (Berlin); *Brown Thomas* (Dublin); *Switzer* (Dublin); *GUM* (3 Red Sq., Moscow; phone: 095-926-3471); *NK* (Stockholm); *El Corte Inglés* (Madrid); *De Bijenkorf* (Amsterdam).

SHOPPING STREETS

They vary in size and style — but are all worth a stroll. Take your shopping bag, and always keep an eye on your wallet and your handbag. The *Kärntnerstrasse* and *Graben,* Vienna; *Strøget,* Copenhagen; *Bond Street,* London; *Rue du Faubourg-St.-Honoré* and *Avenue Montaigne,* Paris; *Kurfürstendamm,* Berlin; the *Ponte Vecchio* and *Via Tornabuoni,* Florence; *Via Condotti,* Rome; the *Rialto Bridge* markets and the *Mercerie* — streets that lead from Piazza San Marco to the Rialto Bridge, Venice; elegant *P.C. Hooftstraat* near the museum quarter, and the *Rokin,* Amsterdam; the *Marktgasse,* Bern; the *Nevsky Prospekt,* Leningrad; *Grafton Street,* Dublin; *Bahnhofstrasse,* Zurich.

FLEA MARKETS

A country's junk is its life. And its past. And as a result, the myriad flea markets found scattered across the Continent are intensely direct experiences with the local culture. Some do a thriving trade in semi-fine antiques; others offer everything from torn inner tubes to inner tubes that are only punctured. Bargain like a Bedouin whether you're in Sicily or Switzerland. Go when it's raining, hang around until closing time, and you'll pay almost fair prices. Here are a few of the liveliest:

Flohmarkt, Vienna – Open Saturday mornings, Naschmarkt in the Sixth District, Vienna.

Marché des Antiquités et du Livre, Brussels – The antiques and book market, as this spot on the Place du Grand Sablon is called. Open all day Saturdays and Sunday mornings.

Marché de la Brocante, Brussels – Place du Jeu de Balle. Open every morning; busiest on Sundays.

Israels Plads, Copenhagen – Open Saturdays from 8 AM to 2 PM, May through September.

Camden Lock, London – Open weekends, 9 AM to 6 PM, and on holidays, except *Christmas* and *New Year.*

Camden Passage, London – Open Tuesdays through Saturdays, with open-air market on Wednesdays, Thursdays, and Saturdays all day. Islington.

New Caledonian (also known as the Bermondsey Market), London – Open Fridays from 6 AM to 2 PM. Bermondsey Sq. and Tower Bridge Rd.

Petticoat Lane, London – Open Sunday mornings until 2 PM. Middlesex St.

Portobello Road, London – Open Mondays through Saturdays (the best day); mornings only on Thursdays. Near Westbourne Park.

Forum de Dijon, Dijon – Held the last Sunday of each month. Rue de Général Delaborde.

Place de la Banque, Dijon – No town in France is without its *marché aux puces* (literally, "flea market"), and Dijon is no exception. This one is open on Tuesday and Friday mornings.

Villeurbanne, Lyons – Open all day Thursdays and Saturdays, Sunday mornings, and all day the first Sunday of every month, at Chemin de la Feyssine. Also, *Brocante*

Stalingrad (115 Bd. Stalingrad) is open Thursdays and Saturdays and Sunday mornings.

Boulevard Risso, Nice – Daily except Sundays from 8 AM to 5 PM.

Brocante de la Porte de Montreuil, Paris – Open weekends and Mondays from 7 AM to 7:30 PM; Saturday morning is best. This and the next market on the list are Paris's more rough-and-tumble *marchés*.

Brocante de la Porte de Vanves, Paris – Open weekends all day. Porte de Vanves.

Le Marché aux Puces de Clignancourt, Paris – Spread out over a vast area at the Porte de Clignancourt, this market is open from 7 AM to 7:30 PM on weekends as well as on Mondays (which is the best time). A detailed guide to this market can be purchased at the Paris Tourist Office on the Champs-Elysées.

Auer Dult, Munich – Held thrice annually in April or May, July or August, and October, for a full week each time at Mariahilfplatz.

Monastiraki, Athens – Open all day every day, with a special open-air bazaar — *Youssouroum* — on Sunday mornings. Althinas St. and Monastiraki Sq.

Piazza Grande, Arezzo – On the first weekend of every month.

Via Pietrapiana, Florence – Open every day during shopping hours.

Porta Portese, Rome – Off Viale Trastevere on Sunday mornings. Everything from old car parts to Russian army wristwatches and Calabrian country furniture.

Waterlooplein, Amsterdam – Open daily except Sundays, 10 AM to 4 PM. Also the colorful secondhand book market, *Oudemanhuispoort,* in the arcade at the entrance to the university; open daily except Sundays, 10 AM to 4 PM. There's also a flea market every Thursday during the summer in The Hague.

Feira da Ladra, Lisbon – This Thieves' Market is held Tuesdays, Fridays, and Saturdays in Campo da Santa Clara.

Els Encants, Barcelona – Open Monday, Wednesday, Friday, and Saturday mornings. Near the Plaça de les Glories. Also try the Thursday all-day antiques market in Plaça Nova.

El Rastro, Madrid – Sunday mornings from 10 AM to 2 PM (but some sections are open mornings all week long). At Plaza de Cascorro and along Ribera de Curtidores. There's also a stamp market from 10 AM to 2 PM on Sundays at the Plaza Mayor.

Marché aux Puces, Geneva – Held on Wednesday from 7:30 AM to 7 PM and Saturday from 6:30 AM to 5 PM, on the Rondpoint de Plainpalais.

Flohmarkt, Zurich – Saturdays from May to October, 7 AM to 4 PM on the Bürkliplatz. (Also try the *Rosenhof* market in the Niederdorf, open all day Thursdays and Saturdays from May to October.)

Auctions in Europe: Going, Going, Gone

 The auction world has always been something of a private club, where dealers stocked up in order to mark up and amateurs dared not tread. But during the inflation-ridden 1970s, the art market caught the public eye, and auction action became livelier than ever before. (At *Phillips* — London's number three firm — the year-end sales have increased fivefold in a decade.) Many dealers are now so sure of attracting consistently buy-happy crowds that they are also *selling* through the salerooms. So it goes without saying that the days when you could pick up an unnoticed Rembrandt for a song are long gone.

Nonetheless, there are still plenty of reasons to go to auctions: Aside from the fact that auction salerooms are among the best places in the world to learn about art, they are also great theater — high drama at low cost. The bidding has a seductive rhythm, and the tension has a way of catching you up even if you're not faintly interested in the lot on the block. The auctioneer — now more often a distinguished purveyor in pinstripes than the sort of fast-talking spieler who (as the American satirist Ambrose Bierce once noted) "proclaims with a hammer that he has picked a pocket with his tongue" — becomes a pied piper, with the bidders winking, blinking, and nodding in time to his music. As any addict will tell you, an auction is stock market, gambling casino, and living theater all rolled into one — the perfect answer to rainy day blues, more fun than watching the ticker tape, less decadent than an afternoon movie.

And though you can no longer expect to make a killing at an auction, there are good values to be found. Sales held when the weather is unspeakably foul may keep down the crowds — and the prices. Similarly, there are sometimes a few bargains at the beginning of a sale, before the bulk of the potential buyers have arrived and before the bidders have warmed up. In addition, prices can be low at the smaller London firms in August, when, because the big houses are closed for holiday, many dealers are on vacation. And in any event, you can usually buy an item on the block for about 30% off its price in a store — providing you know how to go about it.

Seasoned auctiongoers follow some important rules, the most important of which is to visit the exhibition of merchandise that takes place on the few days preceding the sale. ("If you can't be at the sale, you can leave a commission bid with the auctioneer, or even place an order by telephone — but if you can't be at the exhibition, you have no business buying," noted one expert.) Only there will you have the chance to examine the lots at close range, to inspect them for nicks, cracks, and other flaws that can affect their value and for signs that what you're paying for is what you're getting. Caveat emptor is the order of the day, and disclaimers are made by the score by nearly every auction house in the business. (One *Christie's* catalogue warned: "Each lot is sold by the Seller thereof, and with all faults and defects therein and with all errors of description, and is to be taken and paid for whether genuine and authentic or not, and no compensation shall be paid for same.") Consequently, it behooves you to make a pest of yourself: Have paintings moved so that you can look at them close up, and objects under lock and key removed from their cases. If you anticipate buying furniture, you'll have to know the dimensions of the empty spaces you intend to fill; take a measuring tape to the exhibition. If you're contemplating a large purchase, get an expert to accompany you.

Reputable houses make every effort to help their customers avoid mistakes, and publish lists of prices they estimate the lots will fetch — and, often, whole illustrated catalogues, full of carefully worded descriptions that can give you a great deal of information about the house's opinion of a lot's age and authenticity. (Here, too, there are disclaimers — that, for instance, the "origin, date, age, attribution, genuineness, provenance, or condition of any lot is a statement of opinion, and is not to be relied upon as a statement or representation of fact." But catalogue descriptions are usually accurate and in some cases are regulated by law.)

An elaborate lexicography prevails, and the catalogue can tell you that a phrase like "style of the 18th dynasty" in a sale of Egyptian statues denotes a fake, whereas a simple "18th dynasty" identifies the real McCoy. "Signed" means that the house believes that the signature on a painting is the artist's own, while "bears signature" indicates only the possibility. "Dated" means that the lot bears a date and that the date may be accurate. Even the typography of the catalogue can help you out. Descriptions that commence with capital letters refer to items that the house considers particularly valuable — but not so valuable as items allotted a whole page. Names of previous owners are also a clue to an item's value: Having belonged to a well-known collector is, for instance, a very fine pedigree indeed.

Once you've digested the catalogue and looked over the goods, you're ready for the auction. Based on your inspection, decide on your top bid (remembering to figure in the house's commission, up to 20%, and Value Added Tax where applicable) and don't allow yourself to be pushed beyond it. (It *can* happen, and often does, that in the excitement of the fray, people bid far out of their price range: Witness the poor Viennese student who, entranced by the bidding, kept raising his hand until he'd bought a Holbein; or the Swiss banker who attended the sale of his jade collection and ended up repurchasing every item from himself.) You will not, however, be held to a bid you regret if you call out promptly "withdrawn" in the appropriate language.

For all of its other troubles, London is still the world's auction capital, and the "market price" of a work of art or antique generally refers to what it (and others of its genre) have fetched in the London salerooms. Everyone knows about *Sotheby's* and *Christie's,* both over 200 years old and not far behind the Changing of the Guard and the red double-deckers as visitor attractions and symbols of the city. But fingers are rising and hammers are falling all over Europe. Here's a selection of the famous houses.

DOROTHEUM, Vienna: Founded by the Emperor Joseph I in 1707 as a pawnshop for the poor, the *Dorotheum* was already middle aged when *Sotheby's* and *Christie's* were born, and it's been in the Dorotheergasse, the center of Vienna's antiques district, since 1785. You should see it as a sort of national monument, even if you're not in the market. Besides the repertory of art and antiques auctions that are standard fare at all European auction houses, the *Dorotheum* stages eight major coin auctions a year and, after ignoring the 20th century for years, is rapidly expanding its modern art department. Branches of the *Dorotheum* can now be found in seven other Austrian cities. Information: *Dorotheum,* 17 Dorotheergasse, Vienna A-1010, Austria (phone: 1-515600).

GALERIE MODERNE, Brussels: This is the aristocrat among the many galleries in this city at the heart of the global art market. You'll find Oriental rugs by the kilometer, small pieces of sculpture, and ornate 18th-century furniture — all of consistently high quality. Information: *Galerie Moderne* has three salerooms; the headquarters is at 3 Rue du Parnasse, Brussels, Belgium (phone: 2-513-9010). Another Brussels auction house to inspect is *Nova,* with sales of jewelry, stamps, silver, and pianos, 35 Rue du Pepin, Brussels, Belgium (phone: 2-512-2494).

ARNE BRUUN RASMUSSEN, Copenhagen: This is strictly a fine arts house, with a large trade in Scandinavian valuables, antique Danish silver and bronze, rare books, rugs, fine wines, and a number of the sort of Russian items that tend to surface in all the Scandinavian salerooms. Ten-day sales take place every month, generally by category. Information: *Arne Bruun Rasmussen,* 33 Bredgade, Copenhagen DK-1260, Denmark (phone: 33-136911).

KØBENHAVNS AUKTIONER, Copenhagen: Spread out over approximately 63,000 square feet, this amalgamation of three old-city firms runs 150 sales a year of everything from heavy-duty machinery and motorboats to paintings and samovars. Items are displayed in the settings in which they'll end up: Machine tools in simulated workshops, Old Masters in elegantly furnished salons. Not on the regular circuit of continental dealers, *Københavns Auktioner* attracts just a small number of foreign buyers. Information: *Københavns Auktioner,* 4 Aebeløgade, Copenhagen DK-2100, Denmark (phone: 31-299000).

CHRISTIE'S, London: *Christie's* was founded in 1766, so that today an object's whole lineage can often be traced through the records of its appearances in *Christie's* sales; the motherhouse on King Street is a national landmark. Sales take place daily, and the exhibition rooms are a constantly changing museum. There are also branches in a dozen countries. The South Kensington saleroom handles items of recent vintage and generally lower value, such as toys, telescopes, and top hats. In Geneva, sales are generally at the *Richemond* hotel; the major emphasis is on more valuable silver, jewelry, clocks. In Rome, not a few sale items come from the hoards of Count X and

Princess Y, and there's an air of studied elegance about the salerooms in the glamorous Palazzo Lancellotti on Piazza Navona. Information: *Christie's,* 8 King St., St. James's, London SW1Y 6QT, England (phone: 71-839-9060); at 85 Old Brompton Rd., South Kensington, London SW7 3JS, England (phone: 71-581-7611); at 8 Pl. de la Taconnerie, Geneva CH-1204, Switzerland (phone: 22-282544); at 114 Piazza Navona, Rome 00186, Italy (phone: 6-864032); at 57 Cornelis Schuytstraat, Amsterdam, Netherlands (phone: 20-664-2011; and in Paris at 6 Rue Paul-Baudry (phone: 42-56-17-66).

PHILLIPS, London: Currently number three and trying harder and harder, it is the only top London house to maintain a full program of sales in the summer months, while its rivals are on holiday. It operates an extensive program of estate sales, often sparsely attended by the general public, so there's a good chance you'll find dealer-level prices. *Phillips* does a large volume in modestly priced lots; its employees are extremely helpful to auction novices. Information: *Phillips,* 101 New Bond St., London W1Y 0AS, England (phone: 71-629-6602).

SOTHEBY'S, London: When the city's oldest auctioneer, *Sotheby's,* merged with another royal auction house, New York's *Parke-Bernet,* in 1972, a sort of multinational corporation of art was born. Although you'll find *Sotheby* sales in many countries, its little white building on Bond Street is a kind of art world nerve center, with a roster of experts in every field that rivals that of the *British Museum;* an important sale of Old Masters, with hundreds of thousands of dollars riding on every twitch, beats an evening at the *National Theatre.* But it also does a thriving trade in lower-priced objects, Victoriana, and collectibles of every sort, from illustrated biscuit tins to yacht fittings. Branch salerooms in London, across Britain, and on the Continent (in Paris at 3 Rue Miromesnil; phone: 42-66-40-60; and in Amsterdam at 102 Rokin; phone: 20-275656) ensure that the sun never sets on a *Sotheby* auction. Information: *Sotheby's,* 34-35 New Bond St., London W1A 2AA, England (phone: 71-493-8080).

DROUOT, Paris: This venerable establishment occupies startling steel and glass quarters on the Right Bank street that was named for it and has 16 salerooms on three levels and parking space for 400 cars. Some 60 *commissaires-priseurs* (government-authorized auctioneers) form a kind of cooperative that handles the 600,000-odd lots that are sold here each year. In addition to the whole range of art objects, you can buy thirdhand TV sets, bottles of Château d'Yquem, and even an occasional horse. French auctioneers offer a unique, legal, 30-year guarantee on the authenticity of all purchases. Their sales, held irregularly but generally once a month, are becoming a Parisian institution. Information: *Drouot Richelieu,* 9 Rue Drouot, Paris 75009, France (phone: 48-00-20-20).

KUNSTHAUS LEMPERTZ, Cologne: A fourth-generation family business, founded in 1845 in one of Germany's richest cities, it specializes in Chinese, Japanese, and Southeast Asian art and also offers medieval work, sculpture, paintings by the Old Masters, and even 20th-century applied arts. New York's *Metropolitan Museum* is a customer at its sales (three in the spring and three in the fall). *Lempertz* maintains a US representative (*Werner Gallery,* 200 E. 97th St., New York, NY 10128; phone: 212-289-5666), to handle relations with its steady US customers. Information: *Kunsthaus Lempertz,* 3 Neumarkt, Cologne 1 D-5000, Germany (phone: 221-210251).

KARL UND FABER, Munich: Once auctioneers of antiquarian books and prints, *Karl und Faber* deals extensively in prints and drawings by the Old Masters, modern paintings and graphics, and top class 19th-century art. There are two principal sale periods annually, in June and November. This is a good place to start a collection of Dürer or Rembrandt etchings. Information: *Karl und Faber,* 3 Amirapl., Munich 2 8000, Germany (phone: 89-221865).

NEUMEISTER, Munich: This house's sales, which take place about once every 6 weeks, offer particularly good buys in faïence (a kind of crockery) and silver, German furniture, and 19th-century paintings. The catalogues are excellent and detailed and the subscription service efficient enough that you can prepare for the sales well in advance. Information: *Neumeister Münchner Kunstauktionshaus,* 37 Barerstr., Munich 40 8000, Germany (phone: 89-231-7100).

L'ANTONINA, Rome: The auctions at this house on Piazza Mignianelli are also cocktail-hour social events, presided over by superbly suited auctioneers and patronized by suntanned women in fancy jeans and simple mink. When you go, you'll find some good buys (primarily in Italian furniture and religious art) — and plenty of overpriced junk. The saleroom is small; arrive early or you'll be listening from behind a pillar. *L'Antonina* also occasionally auctions the contents of an entire villa, on location. The crowd is smaller, more professional — and the trip to the old estates can be a picturesque excursion into Italy's patrician past. Information: *L'Antonina,* 23 Piazza Mignianelli, Rome 00187, Italy (phone: 6-794009; fax: 6-795830).

DURÁN SUBASTAS DE ARTE, Madrid: Not really in the European big league — but then, Spanish art has a way of staying in Spain. You'll find attractively priced silver and porcelain items, a lot of ivory, and much early Spanish furniture that goes for considerably less than comparable Italian pieces — plus some of the world's most hideous paintings. Monthly sales except August and September. Information: *Durán Subastas de Arte,* 12 Serrano, Madrid, Spain (phone: 1-401-3400).

BUKOWSKI, Stockholm: Over 100 years old and highly respected in the trade, Scandinavia's foremost saleroom stages five sales annually — in May and November. They also run four annual sales in Helsinki, spring and autumn. It's not unknown for third-rate French and Italian canvases to be knocked down at vastly inflated figures, but you'll also encounter a good selection of Scandinavian paintings — which rarely drift south of the Baltic Sea. It's a refreshing change of scenery to auction eyes trained in London, Paris, or Rome. Information: *Bukowski,* 4 Arsenalsgatan, Stockholm 11147, Sweden (phone: 8-614-0800); or *Bukowski,* 22 S. Esplanadi, Helsinki 00130, Finland (phone: 0-640611).

GALERIE KOLLER, Zurich: As efficient, ethical, and expensive as Switzerland itself, *Koller* stages two 2-week series of auctions annually, one in fall and one in spring, plus a small sale on the first Tuesday of every month. Jewelry — an immense assortment of it — is a consistent highlight. As a sideline, *Koller* also maintains the 12th-century Château de Lucens, a vast living gallery in Lucens, with all furnishings for sale. Commissions charged to both buyer and seller are a hefty 18%. Information: *Galerie Koller,* 8 Rämistr., Zurich CH-8024, Switzerland (phone: 1-475040).

PETER INEICHEN, Zurich: The *Ineichen* salerooms, a Swiss national institution, are a carnival of antique watches and clocks, automatons, and weapons, and various and sundry other things Swiss: miniature Prussian cavalry officers, jeweled poignards, bioscopes, daguerreotypes, nickelodeons, and once, a ballerina clock that chimed the hour by cuckooing *Swan Lake.* Record price for a pocket watch: 650,000 Swiss francs; for a clock: 700,000. That's just in case you're cleaning out your closets. By appointment only. Information: *Peter Ineichen,* 75 Badenerstr., Zurich CH-8004, Switzerland (phone: 1-242-3944).

Spas: Europe's Unique Watering Spots

Long before travelers even dreamed of the pleasures of sea bathing and sun-tanning, spas like *Vichy* and *Badgastein,* blessed with mineral-rich waters thought to have healing powers, were important stops on the Grand Tour — every bit as important as Paris and Rome. Consequently, they all developed such a wide range of facilities over the years — fine hotels, golf courses and tennis courts, racetracks and bridle paths, gambling casinos, and elegant shops — that you can have a splendid spa vacation without taking so much as a sip of the waters that were their original raison d'être.

On the other hand, taking a cure — a favorite pastime of so many historic and fictional folk — is still a possibility, and you'll find baths of every tint and temperature, power showers, steamrooms and saunas, whirlpool baths and sprays, masseuses, mud tubs, paraffin packs, salt and honey rubs, infrared and ultraviolet treatments, facilities for vapor inhalations and gymnastics. And fountains — so that you *can* drink the water. Every resort has its specialty: Some specialize in water cures. (Some waters are good for arthritis, some for ailments of the liver.) Thalassotherapy — practiced at *St.-Malo, Pornichet, Quiberon,* and *Tréboul-Douarnenez,* all in Brittany — is a kind of marine approach to thermalism that emphasizes the benefits of salt water and sea air. (Grilled shrimp and oysters on the half shell are the extra added attractions.) Gerovital, a procaine derivative developed by a Romanian doctor named Ana Aslan and used in therapy centers like *Constanta, Eforie, Mamaia,* and *Mangalia* along the Romanian Black Sea coast, is claimed to retard the aging process dramatically. True or not, many European health insurance plans will cover the cost of a doctor-prescribed spa visit. While there is good deal of controversy about the real medical value of taking the waters, a visit to a spa is usually at least rejuvenating. All the national tourist offices of countries that boast major spas also maintain detailed lists of their facilities, indexed by the ailments that the waters are thought to cure. You can make your arrangements à la carte, or, through your hotel, you can buy a package that will allow you access to most spa facilities throughout your stay. You will, however, generally be required to have a checkup by a local doctor before being submerged, steamed, and pummeled.

Here's a selection of spots at which to sample the spa experience. The tourist offices in all these towns are active and informed, and a note to them should produce ample material on hotels and facilities.

BADGASTEIN, Austria: High in the Alps, some 50 miles (80 km) from Salzburg, this fine old spa was visited by Holy Roman Emperor Frederick III as early as the 15th century and eventually became known as the Spa of Kings. All the patrician elegance of the days of royalty is still very much in evidence, but there are all the facilities of this era as well: 3 swimming pools, tennis courts, golf courses, pathways for solitary rambles through the lush Alpine countryside. And sooner or later, everyone in *Badgastein* takes the flatcar rail ride through the galleries of the old Bockstein gold mine.

SPA, Belgium: Like a cathedral, the great bathhouse dominates the main square of this town, which lent its name to all of the world's watering spots, and the healthful waters of its mineral springs flow freely from fountains at every turn. The city of Liège is less than an hour away, and the road that takes you there leads past dozens of stately country mansions and lovely forests ribboned with scores of well-marked trails. You can go horseback riding in the woods, or swimming in the tranquil lake. Every August 15, there's the colorful, traditional *Battle of Flowers.* Long a favorite with the English, *Spa* retains a pleasant Anglo-Saxon air.

MARIENBAD, Czechoslovakia: *Mariánské Lázně,* as this spa is called in Czech, and *Carlsbad* (or *Karlovy Vary*) are central and Eastern European spa-dom's two centers — the grandiose *Esplanade* hotel, the pastel façades, the palms, and the crystal are all from another, more gracious period that is somehow at odds with the communized monotony of postwar Bohemia. The winds of political change have blown good news this way — particularly to *Carlsbad.* The *Pupp* hotel (renamed *Moskva* during the Communist years) and the *Imperial* hotel recently underwent rigorous renovations and returned each to its pre-Stalin splendor. There are beautiful tours in the nearby hills, and you can visit Prince Metternich's superb castle — though you'll have to go to Schloss Nymphenberg near Munich if you want to see where *Last Year at Marienbad* really was filmed. Bookings in Czechoslovakia are necessary well in advance since hotel facilities are limited. The most practical approach is to sign up for one of the comprehensive tours that include airfare, full room and board, and access to all health facilities, and which can be arranged through *Cedok* (10 E. 40th St., New York, NY 10016; phone: 212-689-9720). Prices are reasonable when compared to those at other major European spas.

EVIAN-LES-BAINS, France: On the south shore of Lac Léman, *Evian* attracts a large number of visitors from nearby Geneva — at least in part for the gambling in its busy casino. But there are also boat excursions and water sports of every sort on the great lake, and the high Alps and Italy are but an easy afternoon away. Like that of its thermal cousin, *Vichy, Evian's* mineral water has been exported around the world, spreading the fame of the spa. Convalescent vacationers guarantee return trips by gorging on pâté de foie gras, *fondue savoyarde,* and *mousse au chocolat;* most of the dieting is done between meals. Try to stay at the *Royal* (phone: 50-75-14-00; fax: 50-75-38-40), one of France's most luxurious hotels.

BADEN-BADEN, Germany: Since the Romans discovered the springs, which are so hot they are used in the town's central heating systems, this town, equidistant from Stuttgart and Frankfurt, has become so international that it's often called the "summer Paris." And it's still dotted with Russian chapels and villas from the high-living czarist days and the penultimate *Brenner's Park* hotel (phone: 7221-9000; fax: 7221-38772). The superbly tended Lichtentaler Allée (walkway) is one of the Continent's loveliest strolling places, and the glittering casino is an ancestor of Monte Carlo's. At cocktail hour in the high season, everyone who is anyone — and everyone *is* — gathers in the great frescoed *Trinkhalle* for a glass of warm water.

MONTECATINI, Italy: In the heart of Tuscany, *Montecatini* has a grandeur that makes it look more like a relic of the last days of the Roman Empire than a modern health resort. Its eight separate mineral springs feed into a cluster of buildings amid a vast area of parks and gardens, full of imperial-size pools, graceful colonnades and portals, and marble statuary and high domes. The *Grand Hotel e La Pace* (phone: 572-75801; fax: 572-78451) is a venerable hostelry on the same regal scale as the town. Open April through October, *Montecatini* is also an art center, with a colony of active galleries and antiques shops; in summer, it plays host to a roster of famous trotting races; and elegant boutiques line its prosperous streets. If that's not enough, Florence is only an hour away.

SATURNIA, Italy: This tiny place in the Tuscan hills, between the Aurelia coast road and the Via Cassia, near a less tiny place named Manciano (on Rte. 74), is not really a spa but a well-maintained, warm thermal waterfall with sitting places smoothed and hollowed out of the rocks by 2,000 years of bathers. You can swim and soak here comfortably even on a chilly *Christmas* holiday because it's open year-round. Archaeology buffs will enjoy the nearby Etruscan sites. A car is essential. If you prefer to soak in style, check into the only hotel, *Terme de Saturnia* (phone: 564-601061; fax: 564-601266).

Wheels of Fortune: Gambling in Europe

An old Napoleonic edict forbade roulette within 100 kilometers (62 miles) of Paris. Consequently, the casino of Forges-les-Eaux is exactly 110 kilometers (about 69 miles) from the city. Most other European governments still take a similar stance: Gambling frequently is discouraged in cities, where citizens are expected to be hard at work, but is permitted in spas, seaside towns, and other resorts, which are presumed to be frivolous by nature. In London — a notable exception to the rule — gaming is allowed only in private clubs, with absolutely no credit extended, and only to members of at least 48 hours' duration.

Restrictions notwithstanding, gambling is booming — and the whole casino scene is changing. Though splendid old dowager queens like Monte Carlo, Deauville, and Baden-Baden have retained their enormous cachet, they are as much national monuments as after-dark hot spots. Elsewhere, dress rules have eased or disappeared. Glossy new casinos are multiplying, and slot machines, craps, and junkets are being imported from America.

Casinos are almost but not quite like those in the US, and there are some things to remember:

When you go, be on the safe side, and — despite the new populism — dress with decorum or you may be turned away at the door (albeit with exquisite courtesy).

Take your passport. Most casinos require identification.

Don't be shocked when you're asked to pay an admission fee — it's customary in Europe. The sum may be small and usually includes a few free chips. Or it may be hefty and buy you a whole year's membership in a private club.

Remember that European casinos generally don't open until a discreet midafternoon hour and close at around 3 or 4 AM. Marathon games of chemin-de-fer, which can go on around the clock, are the only exceptions. The casinos are, however, open on Sundays and holidays.

If you're new to the games or their foreign terminology, ask at the admission desk for an explanatory booklet. And don't be shy about cross-examining the *chefs de partie* (the floor men). They are there specifically to provide you with every possible assistance in losing your money.

French is still the lingua franca of most continental roulette wheels. Remember the following: *faites vos jeux* (place your bets); *rien ne va plus* (no more bets); *rouge-noir* (red-black); *pair-impair* (even-odd); *passe-manque* (high-low); *jeton* (chip); *mise* (bet); *en plein* (single number, pays 35 times the *mise*); *à cheval* (two numbers, pays 17 to 1); *transversale* (three numbers, pays 11 to 1); *carré* (four numbers, pays 8 to 1).

With the exception of England, where it's forbidden by law, tipping usually is the croupiers' prime source of income. In roulette, the custom is to leave one of the 35 chips when you hit a number *en plein*. (You will not, however, be expected to tip for smaller wins or for a long period of residence at the table.)

Government regulation of gaming is particularly strict in France and England, less so elsewhere. But avoid semiprivate, semilegal, and uncontrolled clubs, lest you lose your shirt (and bankroll). For most games, the best odds are offered in England — thanks to the British Gaming Board.

Here's where you'll find the best and the brightest of the European casinos:

BADEN-BEI-WIEN, Austria: Vienna is one of the few European capitals that does have a casino. (You'll find it at the *Palais Esterhazy* on the Kärntnerstrasse.) But for the Viennese, who are forbidden to gamble here, a favorite evening's entertainment is the half-hour trip to nearby Baden — which has more space, more atmosphere, and fewer tourists.

LONDON, England: One European capital to offer gambling, London has a number of fine old clubs. *Crockford's,* (30 Curzon St., W1; phone: 71-493-7771) one of the most distinguished, occupies a beautiful mansion in the middle of Mayfair. Once the private reserve of half the aristocracy of England, it now boasts a membership that is overwhelmingly foreign. The membership fee, about $250 annually, gives you access to one other London casino, the *International Sporting Club* (45 Park La., W1; phone: 71-493-5362). Unless you can arrange to go as the guest of a member, a national law dictates that 48 hours must pass between your application for membership and admission to the club, and no credit at all may be extended. The same rules apply for admission to the *Ritz* (Piccadilly, W1; phone: 71-491-4678). London's major casino, in the basement of the *Ritz* hotel (although not owned or operated by the hotel) on Piccadilly. It has an exclusive membership, an elegant atmosphere, and an excellent restaurant. As at many London casinos, there are female croupiers, as deft as they are decorative; they wear richly colored designer gowns and rake in chips and deal blackjack decks with feline grace. Remember, the odds are better for the player in England, and the prohibition on tipping means that you can lose your money more slowly.

CANNES, France: The classiest of the Côte d'Azur casinos and a favorite haunt of vacationing sheiks and oil barons, the *Palm Beach* casino (phone: 93-43-91-12) is owned by the great Barrière chain. Its gross receipts always rank among the highest in Europe. Open summer and early fall only.

DEAUVILLE, France: Sometimes known as Paris's 21st Arrondissement, this attractive town on the coast of Normandy has been a playground of European royalty since the 19th century, when Napoleon III's half-brother brought horse racing here and put the place on the map. The casino (phone: 31-98-66-66) is a great, glittering wedding cake by the sea, sumptuously decorated, and is host to various social and cultural events during the fashionable summer season, which peaks with the August racing weeks. At that time, formal dress is still required in certain rooms. Stay in the beautiful *Normandy* (phone: 31-98-66-22; fax: 31-98-66-23) owned by the casino, stroll the boardwalk, and spend your winnings on lobster at the seaside *Ciro's* (phone: 31-88-18-10; fax: 31-98-61-67), also a casino property.

DIVONNE-LES-BAINS, France: Just outside wealthy, gambling-free Geneva, in a sleepy little border village, this most profitable of French casinos (phone: 50-40-34-37) attracts very big players from the foreign business and numbered-account community, and the sums that change hands on a single spin of the wheel in the handsome, hospitable casino could buy beach houses and thoroughbred race horses. Right beside the gambling tables, there's an excellent restaurant where you can dine until breakfast time. For more information on the casino, call the local tourist office (phone: 50-20-01-22).

FORGES-LES-EAUX, Seine-Maritime, France: Just outside the 100-kilometer roulette-free zone that Napoleon decreed must surround the country's capital, this place attracts Parisians who would rather not risk the wheels in that city's various clandestine gaming dives. Open daily from 3 PM to 3 AM. Try the *Continental* hotel (phone: 35-09-80-12; fax: 35-09-61-15) if you're dreading the pre-dawn drive back to Paris.

BADEN-BADEN, Germany: The biggest, oldest, richest, and most beautiful casino (phone: 72-212-1060) in Germany, it has been around for over 200 years. Its rooms are stunning and there is outdoor roulette on a vine-covered patio in summer. The town is one of Europe's most fashionable spas as well, and the Kurhaus next door is the site of countless business congresses and chamber music concerts.

BAD HOMBURG, Germany: A short distance northwest of Frankfurt, this casino (phone: 61-721-70170) occupies a special place in European gaming history: An early venture of the celebrated brothers Blanc, who went on to Monte Carlo 20 years later, it was the setting of that famous novelette of compulsive gambling, *The Gambler,* whose author, the great Russian master Feodor Dostoyevsky, managed to run through a nonfictional fortune of his own.

ATHENS, Greece: Fifteen miles (24 km) north of the city atop Pamitha Mountain, the *Mont Parnes* casino (phone: 246-9111) can justly claim a setting more spectacular than any other on the Continent. There's also fine Greek food, a nightclub, and, for those who don't feel like making the return trip to Athens, a hotel. It's more convenient to go by car, but public transportation is available from Syntagma Square. Some hotels provide a private minibus link.

CAMPIONE D'ITALIA, Italy: The casino (phone: 31-687921), whose name means "sample of Italy," is a delightful 20-minute boat ride across the lake from Lugano in Switzerland. The ferries operate frequently — to assure the Swiss of plenty of opportunity to sin on someone else's soil. Otherwise the crowd is largely Italian.

VENICE, Italy: From May through October the *Municipal Casino* (phone: 41-529-7111) is quartered out at the Lido, by the beach. But many prefer its winter setting on the Grand Canal, in the handsome *Palazzo Vendramin-Calergi* (phone: 41-524-0233; open November through April), where the composer Richard Wagner died. At night in the off-season, the streets of Venice can be quiet and bleak, but the *Palazzo* is always warm, gracious, and animated. There are several restaurants and a nightclub.

MONTE CARLO, Monaco: The queen of European casino cities now has three separate gaming establishments: the beautiful old *Casino* on the town's main square, with its fabulous, ornate decor and its sea-view picture windows; the Nevada-style *Loews* (phone: 93-50-65-00) in the lobby of the flashy *Loews* hotel — a joint undertaking between the American hotel company and the staid old Société des Bains de Mer, owner of most of Monaco; and the *Monte Carlo Sporting Club* (phone: 93-50-71-71), set on a spectacular manmade promontory by the shore (only open in July and August). During the winter, the high rollers crowd the old *salons privés* of the main casino, and in the summer the Rolls and yacht crowd moves down to the *Sporting* complex. The *Loews*, which offers free admission, teems with American junketeers, and the steady din from the neon slots and crap tables is miles away from the hushed elegance of the *salons privés*. Make the rounds of all three for a total picture of the European gambling scene today.

AMSTERDAM, Netherlands: Holland's newest casino, *Holland Casino Amsterdam* (phone: 20-664-9911), said to be the largest in Europe, opened its doors last year at the elegant *Lido* complex just behind the Leidseplein. Dress is casual, but sneakers are *verboten*.

ESTORIL, Portugal: This is certainly the gaudiest, flashiest, shiniest casino (phone: 1-468-4521) along the Iberian Peninsula. There is a big, slick floor show on double revolving stages and a marvelous seafood restaurant; the clientele is so well groomed and glittering that you can't help but wonder what they all do from 9 to 5. Probably nothing.

PONTEVEDRA, Spain: The *Casino de la Toja* (phone: 86-730025) at El Grove is the best of the country's many gaming houses. On an island near Pontevedra. A glamorous second is the *Casino Castillo de Perelada* (phone: 72-538125), dramatically set in the imposing Perelada castle, near Girona. The *Casino Gran Madrid* (phone: 1-859-0312) is at Torrelodones, about 17 miles (27 km) outside the capital on the highway to La Coruña. There's free transportation from Plaza de España in downtown Madrid.

PORTOROŽ, Yugoslavia: There's plenty of capitalist decadence in this flower-fragrant beach resort on the royal blue Adriatic. Try the *Metropol* hotel (phone: 66-75141) for raking in the dinars and for lovely swimming when you've had enough.

Offshore Europe:
Islands of Every Kind

With today's efficient transportation networks, it's getting harder to spot any difference between the center of Majorca and the center of Mykonos. But there are still many landfalls where you can find the solitude and isolation that have always characterized islands — and have, throughout the ages, constituted their main attractions. Herewith a selection of some of our favorites:

BORNHOLM, Denmark: The country's most easterly island is more like a part of Sweden — and, in fact, it takes less time to get to that nation's town of Ystad than it does to the homeland. A cross between a modern Scandinavian summer resort and a medieval Viking shrine, the island is full of attractions: one of Denmark's largest forests, at Almindingen; the spectacular National Trust white dunes at Dueodde; the mysterious grove of monoliths at Gryet; the great coastal cliffs of Helligdommen; plus peaceful old fishing villages like Hasle and Helligpeder, full of half-timbered houses; early medieval round churches like Osterlars near Gudhjem and Nylars near Akirkeby; Viking castles; and herring smokehouses. Rønne, an attractive old merchants' port, is the main town; you can get boats to Copenhagen (7 hours away) as well as Sweden and Germany. While you're there, visit one of the area's ceramic factories and the *Rønne Theater,* the oldest playhouse in Denmark. Clustered off the mother island are some 20 baby islands known as Ertholmene: Christiansø is well worth the 1¼-hour ferry ride it will take you to get there from the beautifully preserved old market town of Svaneke. Information: *Bornholm Tourist Office,* Havnen, Rønne, DK-3700, Denmark (phone: 53-959500; fax: 53-954131), or the *North Bornholm Tourist Office,* 4 Kirkegade, Allinge, DK-3770 Denmark (phone 53-980001; fax: 53-980226).

FAEROES, Denmark: Forty-seven thousand fiercely independent Faeroese (and twice that number of sheep) inhabit 17 of the rugged islands of this umbrella-shaped archipelago 300 miles from Iceland and 185 miles north of the Shetlands in the middle of the wild North Atlantic. A population of several million wild sea birds of every species — guillemots, gannets, fulmars, oystercatchers, and the *tjaldun* (the national symbol) — inhabit the towering shoreline cliffs. One startling island sight is the gathering of the prized guillemot eggs by Faeroese, who dangle by ropes over cliffside nests hundreds of feet above the swirling sea. Another is the *grindadráp,* a midsummer whale-slaughtering expedition, which turns the sea a violent red and ends with an all-night celebration. July 29 is the *Feast of St. Olav,* a gala event that has all the islanders converging on Torshavn for banquets of whale steaks, parades, concerts, and contests in ancient island skills. To get there, you can take the 2½-hour flight from Copenhagen to Vagar Airport — 2 hours by road from the capital of Thorshavn. Or go by sea: The romantic voyage lasts 35 hours; *DFDS Scandinavian Seaways* (phone: 33-156300) has sailings about once a week from Esbjerg between June and September. And bring your own liquor: The islands went dry a year before American Prohibition and never remoistened. Another sea route is from Scotland via the *P & O Ferry* (Orkney and Shetland Services, PO Box 5, P & O Ferry Terminal, Aberdeen AB9 8DL, Scotland; phone: 224-572615; telex 73344); or *Smyril Line* (PO Box 370, 25 Jonas Broncksgate, FR110 Thorshavn, Faeroe Islands; phone: 298-15900; fax: 298-15707). Information: *Danmarks Turistråd,* 22 Hans Christian Andersen Blvd., Copenhagen V DK-1553, Denmark (phone: 33-111325).

CORSICA, France: Most people can't remember anything more about Corsica than the fact that it used to belong to Italy (only 7½ miles north of Sardinia, it is also half as far from the Italian mainland as it is from France) and that Napoleon was born on the island in Ajaccio. "By the fragrance of its soil alone," wrote Napoleon, "I would know Corsica with my eyes closed." Since the French discovered it in force about a decade ago, however, it has become the country's classiest summer resort, and it's jammed in July and August. Yet in other months, and throughout the year when you get away from the main beach centers, Corsica is still a place of savage Mediterranean beauty and startling contrasts: There are deep forests covering more than half the island; 600 miles of coastline to explore; alpine landscapes like those at Monte Rotondo, Conte Cintro, and the little-known Ponte-Leccia; medieval cliff towns like Bonifacio; and a beautiful old port called Bastia. The dialect is a strange amalgam of French and Italian; the bouillabaisse is the fishiest and spiciest in France; and the *paghiella,* a haunting ancient harmony for three male voices, is still sung at all the island's religious festivals and by Corsican shepherds in the fields. Boat crossings from Nice, Toulon, and Marseilles take 6 to 12 hours, and there are frequent flights from Paris, Marseilles, and Nice. Information: *CRT de Corse,* 17 Bd. Roi-Jérôme, Ajaccio, 20176 BP 19 Corsica (phone: 95-21-56-56).

MONT-ST.-MICHEL, France: This spectacular granite monument about 2,000 yards off the coast of Normandy was, centuries ago, part of the mainland forest of Scissy. When the forest yielded to the sea, it became an island twice a day with the tides, and the rest of the time guides led visitors across the sodden shoals, between treacherous patches of quicksand. In the 8th century, the Bishop of Avranches built a shrine to celebrate a dream vision of the Archangel Michael, and in the 11th century, a Benedictine monastery was carved out of the natural granite. After the revolution, the Mont did a stretch as a state prison, and in 1877 a causeway — all that remains above water during the exceptionally high tides of the spring and fall equinoxes — was built to connect the island to the mainland. The Benedictines are in charge again, and Mont-St.-Michel is one of France's most stunning sights. Walk the single main street, flanked by timbered houses, to the abbey gate; lunch on one of the area's special plump, moist omelettes; and see both the original Romanesque monastery church and La Merveille, the Gothic 13th-century marvel. Rennes, 41 miles (66 km) away, is the closest large town. If you're at the Mont during low tide, there's also fine shrimping in the shallows.

ANDROS, Greece: Picking out just one of the magnificent islands of Greece is a little like trying to choose your favorite gold ingot at the Central Bank of Zurich. Lush, verdant Andros seems a fair compromise, situated, as it is, roughly in the middle of the three great island clusters: the Cyclades, the Sporades, and the Dodecanese. More wooded than some of its barren southern cousins and less touristy than crossroads like Rhodes and Mykonos, Andros has all of their magnetic Aegean virtues: a limpid sea and honey-colored beaches (Batsi, Korthion, Gavrio, Kapparia); evocative archaeological remains (ancient Palaeopolis); high mountain slopes (Mt. Petalo); plus pine woods and the fig and lemon groves of the valleys. A grilled *barbounia* (Aegean red mullet), a glass of ouzo, and the lilting music of a bouzouki in a *taverna* in the capital town of Andros, built on a promontory and capped with an old Venetian castle, and you will soon be mulling early retirement. Good reading matter for your visit: Thornton Wilder's beautiful novel, *The Woman of Andros.* Daily boats from Rafina and Karistos are available, and there are plenty of possibilities for island-hopping trips to Tinos, Siros, Paros, and Naxos. Information: *Greek National Tourist Organization,* 2 Amerikis St., Athens, Greece (phone: 1-322-3111); or the *Greek National Tourist Organization,* 645 Fifth Ave., Olympic Tower, New York, NY 10022 (phone: 212-421-5777).

CAPRI, Italy: The most famous, most expensive, and most crowded of all the Italian islands, Capri (*Ca*-pri, not Ca-*pree*) is also one of the most beautiful places in the world. To be sure, in July and August the little main square and the Marina Piccola beach are like cans of Mediterranean sardines, so you'd be wise to keep your distance if you're looking for peace and quiet. But Capri can be breathtaking with its sapphire sky and sea, its soft air scented with the heady aroma of the hillside lemon groves, and lush purple explosions of wisteria nearly everywhere you turn. Whenever you go, there's plenty to keep you busy: lazy morning orange juice in one of the Piazzetta cafés, funicular rides from the boat dock, afternoon jaunts down to the marina; rowboat rides around the grottoes; hair-raising minibus trips back up the hairpin road to town; and spooky moonlight rambles to the pagan shrine of the Matromania cave. The Roman Emperor Tiberius built 12 villas here to honor the 12 Olympian deities, and the area around his Villa Jovis — from which he ruled the whole empire for a decade — is a wonderful place to walk for fine views. A wide variety of boats, including the higher-priced, higher-speed hydrofoil, ply the waters between the island and Naples or Sorrento. Information: *Ente Provinciale per il Turismo,* Via Partenope 10 A, Napoli 80121,

Italy (phone: 81-764-6414); or the *Azienda Autonoma di Soggiorno e Turismo,* 1 Piazza Umberto I, Capri 80073, Italy (phone: 81-837-0634).

LIPARI, Italy: Italy's islands are places of summer and sun and sea — and many can be seriously overcrowded, not only by foreign tourists, but also by natives, who seem to prefer vacationing in throngs, in July and August. Among the most beautiful are the Aeolian Isles — a dramatic, volcanic cluster of seven landfalls off the northern coast of Sicily — fairly easily reached by hydrofoils, including one that departs from near Rome. (You may remember an old Roberto Rossellini–Ingrid Bergman film called *Stromboli,* which brought the islands some short-lived notoriety.) Lipari is the center of most activity — now as it once was, long ago, for the ancient Greeks, Romans, and Carthaginians — and the island is rich in archaeological relics, volcanic craters, and thermal springs. You can easily rent a boat to explore the empty coves that scallop the island's rocky shoreline. Regular ferry services are available from six mainland and Sicilian cities. Information: *Ente Provinciale per il Turismo,* Via Calabria, Isolato 301-bis, Messina 98100, Italy (phone: 90-675356); or *Azienda Autonoma di Soggiorno e Turismo,* 202 Via Vittorio Emanuele, Lipari (Messina) 98050, Italy (phone: 90-988-0095).

SARDINIA, Italy: Although largely overlooked by history due to its site well off the major trade routes, Sardinia is everyone's island. To the poet it is the picturesque fishing islet of La Maddalena, pointing offshore to the north of Corsica. To the international jet setter it is the Costa Smeralda, the Aga Khan's prohibitively expensive millionaire's playground, that cordons off one of Sardinia's most sublime corners, the northeastern tip. Here the water is emerald green, and the eerie wind-sculpted rocks and shoals and coves are of an unearthly beauty. Although seemingly all of Italy comes here in the summer, each Italian believes he is going to his own isolated atoll. Except during the first 2 weeks of August, privacy is paramount, as the vast stretches of beach, surrounded by strange and wonderful roseate cliffs and mountains, often appear almost empty. To the south, Cagliari, Sardinia's capital and main port, is unarguably Spanish in feel and architecture, and the physical features of its people testify to Spain's influence here. The stern fortress above the town is more reminiscent of the ancient kingdom of Aragón than present-day Italy. Inland, to the north, Sardinia's true identity — a mysterious, timeless one — unfolds at every mile, as prehistoric, conical stone fortress compounds, called *nuraghi,* still partially exist, recalling the island's inhabitants from neolithic times. Farther from the coast, great mountains loom, wild horses stampede across meadows, cork trees offer shade, and roast kid — not lobster — is served. On the western coast are the ruins of Tharros, the former Phoenician port, which lies beside marshes where flamingos congegate. Just inland, at Oristano, riders on horseback and wearing unique doll masks participate in the *Sa Sartiglia* race, part of the *Carnevale* celebration held every February. To the north, in Alghero, the people do not speak Sardo, the island's most popular and pervasive language; they speak a dialect based on Catalan. Ferries depart regularly for Cagliari and Oblia, in the northeast, from Genoa, Livorno, and Civitavecchia (near Rome). *Alisardo* (phone: 70-669161) runs an efficient regular air service to Cagliari, Alghero, and Olbia, from Rome, as well as a variety of other European cities. Book well in advance. Information: *Ente Provinciale di Turismo,* 9 Piazza Deffenu, Cagliari 09125 (phone: 70-668352); 19 Piazza Italia, Nuoro 08100 (phone: 784-30083); 276 Via Cagliari, Oristano (phone: 783-74191); or 36 Viale Caprera, Sassari 07100 (phone: 79-299544).

MADEIRA, Portugal: About 600 miles and 1½-hour's plane ride southeast of Lisbon, this semitropical paradise has not been a "discovery" since the inauguration in the mid-1960s of the airport at Funchal, but it is still a flowered and forested place of enormous serenity. The climate is a travel agent's fantasy, with year-round sea bathing, exciting skin diving, and impressive mountain walks. You can pluck bananas and nibble the sugarcane that grows in the fertile valleys; then drown any remaining sorrows in the fabled madeira wine. Funchal, the island's capital, is a gracious, manicured seaside city, where the flowers, the fruit, and the fish from all over the island tend to end up; *Reid's* hotel (phone: 91-23001) here is a splendid old relic of another era. You also will find a glittering casino. There is a good deal of ship traffic from Lisbon and points east. The spectacular Funchal fireworks display is one of Europe's great *New Year's Eve* celebrations. Information: *Direcção Regional de Turismo,* 18 Av. Arriaga, Funchal (Madeira) 9000, Portugal (phone: 91-29057).

ARRAN, Scotland, and ARAN, Ireland: Arran is a lovely clump of old Scotland set gently into the Firth of Clyde, about 13 miles from Ardrossan on the mainland; the Aran Islands are three rugged outposts of Ireland strung gently across the mouth of Galway Bay, about 35 miles from the mainland port of Galway. Yet, despite their relative proximity to their home countries, both Arran and the Arans have changed very little over the centuries, and their timeless landscapes and stubborn adherence to age-old traditions set the islands apart from their mainlands in time, if not space. In Brodick, Arran's fair city, you can visit baronial Brodick Castle; watch the *Highland Games* with the island athletes in their tartan kilts; join the bidding at the annual Highland sheep auction; fish for trout in the swift Machrie; or cross moors where red deer roam to the mysterious, prehistoric Standing Stones of Tormore. On the largest of the three Arans, Inishmore, there is Dun Aengus, a cyclopean fort with a circular tower that dates from the first century. The men still wear traditional vests and caps and Gaelic is spoken at home. The farming islanders grow potatoes in a homemade soil of sand and seaweed, while the fishing population sets out in wicker-framed, hide-covered *curraghs* (boats) to go lobstering and cockle picking. Information: For Arran, write to the *Information Centre,* the Pier, Brodick, Isle of Arran KA27 8AU, Scotland (phone: 99-770-2140). For Aran, contact *Ireland West Tourism,* Aras Fáilte, Galway City, Ireland (phone: 91-63081; fax: 91-6520); or the *Irish Tourist Board,* 757 Third Ave., New York, NY 10017 (phone: 212-418-0800; fax: 212-371-9052).

IBIZA, Spain: A hundred miles from both Alicante and Valencia, Ibiza is the smallest of the three principal Balearic Islands and the least affected by the burgeoning of everything that fuses Spain and the sea. Founded by the Carthaginians in the 7th century BC, you can feel the proximity of Africa in the baking sun, the tropical vegetation, the warm southern winds, the whitewashed Moorish houses, the green palms and pines, and the golden crescents of beach. The 1¼-hour boat trip to Ibiza's satellite, Formentera, is a pleasant way to get away from being away from it all. Boats leave regularly for Barcelona as well as for the two closer ports of Valencia and Alicante. Or you can fly from Barcelona (an hour away) or Valencia (a half-hour distant); the flight is especially pleasant for the view it gives you of the island, looking almost incandescent from on high. Information: *Oficina de Información de Turismo,* 13 Paseo Vara del Rey, Ibiza, Spain (phone: 971-301900).

HVAR, Yugoslavia: An elongated lobster claw of an island off the Dalmatian coast, Hvar has long been a haven for nudists, who control some of the best of the many splendid beaches. It also is known for having the highest percentage of cloudless days per year in the Adriatic, a statistic of which the natives are so proud that they will reimburse you for your room and board on days that it rains for 3 straight hours — and provide full refunds in the event of fog, snow, or subzero temperatures. The city, also called Hvar, is rich in architectural treasures from the palmy days of Venetian rule, and the lovely beaches face even lovelier beaches on tiny splinter islands like Palmižan and Biševo. Split is the closest port, though during the summer, a great variety of boats ply the Adriatic, from Venice on down, and many call in at the busy harbor. Information: *Tourist Office,* Hvar 58460, Yugoslavia (phone: 58-74005); or *Yugoslav National Tourist Office,* Rockefeller Center, Suite 210, 630 Fifth Ave., New York, NY 10020 (phone: 212-757-2801).

Classic Cruises
and Wonderful Waterways

 Whether you're dangling your hand from a dinghy or sitting at the captain's table on a transatlantic liner, being on a boat is something special. People wave and sing and talk to each other, the winds whip your hair, the waves rock you — gently or not — like a baby in a cradle. The pace seems closer to man's own than that of the *Concorde*.

The flip side is that ship or boat travel takes a relatively long time; that all water looks the same in the deep; that your fellow passengers aren't always congenial; and that the romantic winds can chill you to numbness while the waves make you sick. So it's always a good idea to bring a windbreaker, a pile of great books, and Dramamine. And if you're the restless type, don't set out on a long voyage until the sea has you hooked.

Here's an assortment of cruises in all styles and lengths that will put you in touch with the delights of putting out to sea:

ATLANTIC CROSSINGS: The days when the Atlantic could be crossed only by boat, when people talked about things like outside cabins and tipping the purser and sitting at the captain's table, and got a lump in their throats on seeing the white cliffs of Dover or the Statue of Liberty are not altogether past. There still is a way to enjoy all the things that made the *Ile de France* and the *Queen Mary* such legends: The *Queen Elizabeth 2* (*QE2*) makes the crossing from Southampton or Cherbourg to New York in 5 or 6 days, depending upon port of departure; *Cunard Line,* which runs her, offers a special package, in conjunction with *British Airways,* that includes return airfare — just in case you decide the sea voyage is really a *once*-in-a-lifetime experience. Some arrangements also include much-reduced fares for spouses and hotel accommodations throughout Europe. Information: *Cunard Line,* South Western House, Canute Rd., Southampton SO9 1ZA, England (phone: 703-634166); or *Cunard Line,* 555 Fifth Ave., New York NY 10017 (phone: 212-880-7500 or 800-528-6273). The *Royal Viking Line* occasionally offers a longer New York–Copenhagen run that includes a swing through the Norwegian fjords and stops in Amsterdam, Southampton, and Dublin. Information: *Royal Viking Line,* 95 Merrick Way, Coral Gables, FL 33134 (phone: 800-426-0821; in Florida, 800-422-8000). See also *Traveling by Ship* in GETTING READY TO GO.

NORWAY'S NORTH CAPE: This is the kind of scenery that inspired Sibelius's sweeping scores: There are shimmering fjords; angular, towering glaciers; deep evergreen forests; Arctic panoramas palely, eerily illuminated by the midnight sun. A typical cruise starts from Copenhagen or Oslo, takes in the magnificent Romsdalsfjord and Geirangerfjord, crosses the Arctic Circle, and eventually goes as far as Honningsvaag on Norway's North Cape, Europe's northernmost point. Shorter runs leave from Bergen on Norway's western coast for Kirkenes at the top of the cape (which is also accessible by air). Cruises of a variety of durations to the finest, deepest, and steepest fjords are offered by the *Royal Viking Line* (95 Merrick Way, Coral Gables, FL 33134; phone: 800-426-0821; in Florida, 800-422-8000) with stops in Helsinki and St. Petersburg. Other operators are *Bennett Tours* (270 Madison Ave., New York, NY 10016; phone: 800-221-2420 or in New York City, 212-532-5060); *Bergen Line* (505 Fifth Ave., New York, NY 10017; phone: 800-323-7436 or in New York City, 212-986-2711; fax: 212-983-1275; to request brochures only, 800-666-2374). Information: *Scandinavian Tourist Boards,* 655 Third Ave., New York, NY 10017 (phone: 212-949-2333).

MEDITERRANEAN: A Mediterranean cruise can be nothing more than a 30-minute hydrofoil ride between Naples and Capri — or a languid 14-day odyssey that includes every center of civilization in the ancient world from Alexandria to the Balearic Islands. One typical seven-country, three-continent cruise touches down at Dubrovnik, Kuşadasi, Rhodes, Cyprus, Haifa, Alexandria, and Venice. Another variety takes in the Dalmatian coast, Corfu, Malta, Tunis, Sardinia, Elba, Portofino, and Nice. *Sun, Chandris,* and *Costa* are three good, reliable lines with sleek ships and cheerful, accommodating staff. When you pick a cruise, don't be unduly influenced by mere quantity of ports on the itinerary: Four leisurely and sharply distinct courses usually beat eight hurried appetizers (and anyway, after a while, all handmade rugs, dockside taverns, and burly old seamen look the same). Most cruise space is booked through travel agents, but you can also write directly to the lines: *Sun Line Cruises* (1 Rockefeller Plaza, Suite 315, New York, NY 10020; phone: 212-397-6400 or 800-445-6400); *Chandris Shipping Lines* (95 Akti Miaouli, Piraeus, Greece; phone: 1-412-0932), or their *Chandris Cruises* office in the US (900 Third Ave., New York, NY 10022; phone: 212-223-3003); and *Costa Cruise Line* (World Trade Center, 80 SW 8th St., Miami, FL 33130; mailing address: PO Box 019614, Miami, FL 33101; phone: 800-462-6782; in Miami, 305-358-7330).

GREEK ISLANDS: Greek Islands cruises, which come in myriad styles, degrees of luxury (or not), and durations, show you a fascinating section of the marvel-filled Mediterranean. From Piraeus, you can make a quick run out to Aegina and Poros, or you can spend a week drifting out into the Dodecanese. Or you can sail from one wash-white-and-olive-green haven to the next until *you* have become a burly old seaman hawking handmade rugs at a dockside stand. Most cruises come as 3-, 4-, and 7-day packages, the most common ports of call being Santorini, Mykonos, Delos, Crete, Patmos, Rhodes, Kuşadasi, and Lindos. (If you're undecided about the detour Crete requires, remember that the Palace of Knossos is one of the great wonders of the Mediterranean.) Among the best companies are *Med Sun Cruises* (5 Sachtouri St., Piraeus, Greece; phone: 1-452-4726); and *Epirotiki Lines* (87 Akti Miaouli, Piraeus, Greece; phone: 1-452-6641 in Athens; or in the US at 551 Fifth Ave., New York, NY 10176; phone: 800-221-2470, or 212-599-1750 in New York). *Sun Line Cruises* and *Chandris* are both fine for the islands as well (see above). Alternatively, you can take a toothbrush, a bathing suit, and a copy of the *Odyssey* and do the whole thing on one of the hundreds of local ferries that link all the islands — or even charter your own yacht. You'll never want for bread and wine.

RHINE: The cruise down (or up) the Rhine, once an integral part of every American's Grand Tour, has gone a little out of fashion of late — but if you can afford it, this journey is still an experience of a lifetime. The banks of this *Alter Mann* ("Old Man River") as it cleaves Europe from Rotterdam to Basel are lined with ancient castles and villages that come straight from the fairy tales of the Brothers Grimm. The 160-year-old *KD German Rhine Line* has over a dozen ships, some functioning as waterborne buses and others (like floating hotels) that cover four countries in as many days. Information: *KD German Rhine Line,* 15 Frankenwerft, Cologne 5000, Germany (phone: 221-20880); the US representative is the *Rhine Cruise Agency,* at 170 Hamilton Ave., White Plains, NY 10601 (phone: 914-948-3600 or 800-346-6525 in the eastern US) or at 323 Geary St., San Francisco, CA 94102 (phone: 415-392-8817 or 800-858-8587 in the western US, including Alaska and Hawaii).

DANUBE: While it is certainly not blue, this celebrated waterway is long — twice as long as the Rhine — and immeasurably historic: When you've grasped the geography of the Danube and the Rhine, you've acquired the key to understanding much of the movement of European history. Meanwhile, the Danube offers an enormous variety of cruising possibilities. You can nip around Vienna waters for a mere 2½ hours; or you can ride a hydrofoil for 5 hours to Budapest. You can make a leisurely 4-day trip from Vienna to Passau and back. Or you can go through Hungary and Yugoslavia on the trail of the Hapsburg monarchy, a 7-day self-indulgence on a comfortable new ship,

MS *Mozart.* Information: *DDSG* (*Donaudampfschiffahrtsgesellschaft*), 265 Handelskai, Vienna A-1021, Austria (phone: 1-217500); or *Danube Cruises Austria,* 5250 W. Century Blvd., Suite 302, Los Angeles, CA 90045 (phone: 213-641-8001) or 241 East Commercial Blvd., Fort Lauderdale, FL (phone: 800-327-8223 in eastern and southern US; 800-999-0226 in western and central US).

CANAL AND RIVER CRUISING BY BOAT OR BARGE: There are two ways to cruise Europe's canals and rivers — by self-skippered boat or by joining a chartered cruise. We'll begin by describing self-skippered boat rentals. It works like this: You get a boat — a simple cabin cruiser. Someone shows you how to work the thing and tells you whom to call if you break down. You buy a pile of groceries, some fishing tackle, and a book of folk songs — and cast off for a floating holiday that will take you along as many of the hundreds of miles of the waterways that crisscross England, Wales, Holland, Italy, Spain, or France as you choose. There are plenty of places to moor, to walk and bicycle in the countryside (bring your own bike), to buy fresh piles of groceries (including local beer, ale, or wine). If you fear you'll feel as if you're driving at *Indy* after only an hour of Driver's Ed., hire a skipper to do the piloting. And if you don't feel like cooking, hire a whole crew (or stop in restaurants along the way). It's simple, idyllic, and expensive. And everyone who does it comes back talking about next year. For more information on self-skippered rentals (address of rental firms listed below): *British Waterways Board* (Melbury House, Melbury Ter., London NW1 6JX, England; phone: 71-262-6711), to find out about inland waterways in England, Scotland, and Wales; *Inland Waterways Association* (114 Regent's Park Rd., London NW1 8UQ, England; phone: 71-586-2510); *Anglo-Welsh Waterway Holidays* (Canal Basin, Leicester Rd., Market Harborough, Leicestershire LE16 7BJ, England; phone: 533-858-66910); *Frisia* (81 Oude Oppenhuizerweg, Sneek 8606 JC, Holland; phone: 5150-12814); *French Experience* (370 Lexington Ave., Suite 812, New York, NY 10017; phone: 800-28-FRANCE or 212-986-3800 in New York City).

If self-skippering sounds too intimidating or simply too troublesome, consider joining a charter barge along the canals and small rivers of England, Scotland, the Netherlands, or France. The sailing is handled by captain and crew and the most important person on the entire boat is the cook — ah, the cook. In the past decade there has been a proliferation of luxury barges and boats cruising the rivers of England's Cotswolds, across the best "eating" provinces of France, along Holland's wide, interconnecting system of canals. Usually barges are owned by the captain, who intimately knows the area being cruised, and bookings are arranged through larger companies. (Names and addresses of firms offering both self-skippered rentals and charter cruises are listed below.)

Barges are uniformly small — accommodating from 6 to 28 passengers and anywhere from 3 to 8 crew members, not counting dogs that regularly accompany such expeditions — and when not downright luxurious, they are always comfortable. They are also slow, cruising in a week of slow floating the distance a car would cover in a couple of hours of determined driving. They average about 5 miles an hour, but that doesn't account for the many planned and unplanned stops along the way while passengers shop in villages, explore nearby sites, bicycle along the towpath, or help with a lock — all of which happen all the time on any cruise.

And that leisurely pace, really, is the point of the cruise. Passengers see a small section of foreign countryside with an intimacy and warmth simply impossible through any other means of conveyance. Days are leisurely, punctuated by excellent meals (all food — but not drinks and wine — is included in the price of most cruises) cooked from provisions picked up along the way. Passengers can join the cook on shopping forays or spend their time wandering through villages, reading, sketching, biking, visiting nearby historic sites, or making longer half-day or day trips arranged by the captain, with the promise of a fine meal back on board at day's end.

Certainly some of the most luxurious and intimate cruises are those offered by *Abercrombie & Kent* and *Floating Through Europe* (addresses below), but numerous companies have charter cruises through the most inviting waterways of Western Europe. When reading a brochure, keep an eye on itinerary and routes as well as the boat's facilities (most have private cabins but shared bathrooms) and length of the cruise (3 days to a week is standard). The brochure should be specific about the kind of cruise it is (some are specifically "gourmet" fests, with emphasis on food; others make quite a point to visit historic sites along the river or canal or stop at the most beautiful châteaux; some seek out antiques areas for shopping) and give some idea of the activities possible along the route. And most important, the captain and crew should know well the area being cruised, and it should be an area you want to know well, for you will spend the duration of the cruise immersed in a riverside view of provincial life.

Some favorite English itineraries: The river Avon, from Stratford-on-Avon to Tewkesbury, through a string of delicious 16th-century villages, with stops for performances of the *Royal Shakespeare Company* in Stratford and antiquing in nearby Cotswolds' towns; the Thames, from Oxford to Windsor; and the Norfolk Broads, through John Constable country, with more than 200 miles of rivers, lakes, and connecting waterways.

In the Netherlands, cruises generally begin at Rotterdam, that active seaport, and proceed through the country's intricate system of canals to Gouda (home of the famous cheese) and Delft.

Favorite French routes are the canals and rivers of Burgundy, the province prized by lovers of good food and wine, the Canal du Midi in the Mediterranean province of Languedoc, and the canals and rivers of Brittany and Alsace.

These are only a few routes of the dozens offered by the cruise charterers listed below. Whether you do it yourself or join a well-skippered barge, it is the most intimate way to get to know Europe.

Abercrombie & Kent Travel, 1520 Kensington Rd., Oak Brook, IL 60521 (phone: 708-954-2944).

Anglo-Welsh Waterways Holidays, The Canal Basin, Market Harborough, Leicester LE16 7BJ, England (phone: 533-858-66910).

Bargain Boating, Morgantown Travel Service (PO Box 757, Morgantown, WV 26057; phone: 800-637-0782). Self-skippered, chartered boats and cruisers (for up to 8 passengers) in Belgium, Denmark, England, Holland, France, Ireland, Spain, and Scotland.

Blake's Holidays (Wroxham, Norwich NR12 8DH, England; phone: 603-782911). Self-skippered boats in France, Great Britain, Italy, and Spain.

Blake's Vacations (4918 Dempster St., Skokie, IL 60077; phone: 708-982-0561; 800-628-8118; fax: 708-982-0557). Books self-skippered boats in France, Great Britain, Belgium, Denmark, the Netherlands, and Yugoslavia.

Blue Line Cruisers (BP 21, Le Grand Bassin, Castlenaudary 11400, France; phone: 68-23-17-51). Chartered cruises in France.

Le Boat (PO Box E, Maywood, New Jersey 07607; phone: 800-922-0291). Charters motorboats and sailboats, and books barges in Belgium, England, France, Holland, Ireland, and Sweden.

Esplanade Tours (581 Boylston St., Boston, MA 02116; phone: 800-628-4893 or 617-266-7465). Books hotel-boat cruises throughout France.

Europ' Yachting (11 Bd. de la Bastille, Paris 75012, France; phone: 43-44-00-65). Chartered and self-skippered boats in France, England, Scotland, Yugoslavia, and Greece.

Floating Through Europe (271 Madison Ave., New York, NY 10016; phone:

212-685-5600 in New York City or 800-221-3140). Hotel-barge cruises in Belgium, England, France, Germany, and Holland.

French Country Waterways, Ltd. (PO Box 2195, Duxbury, MA 02331; phone: 617-934-2454 or 800-222-1236 in the continental US). Books luxury hotel-barge cruises in France; trips include hot-air balloon rides.

French Cruise Lines (FCL) (701 Lee St., Des Plaines, IL 60016; phone: 800-222-8664 or 708-824-4577). Offers inland cruises on the French Rhône, Saône, and Seine rivers, aboard two 100-passenger ships, the *Arlène* and the *Normandy*.

Hideaways International Travel Club (15 Goldsmith St., PO Box 1270, Littleton, MA 01460; phone: 800-843-4433 or 508-486-8955). Books skippered barge trips on the inland waterways of Europe for members only. (A $79 annual membership fee includes publications and other services for unique vacations.)

Hoseasons Holidays Ltd. (Sunway House, Lowestoft, Suffolk NR32 3LT, England; phone: 502-501010). Self-skippered boats in England, Scotland, Wales, and France.

Quiztour (19 Rue d'Athènes, Paris 75009, France; phone: 45-26-16-59). Chartered boats in France.

Skipper Travel (210 California Ave., Palo Alto, CA 94306; phone: 415-321-5658). Self-skippered and chartered boats in England, France, Holland, and Ireland.

LAKE LUCERNE: The German name of this body of water in central Switzerland — Vierwaldstätter See, or "Lake of the Four Forest Cantons" — refers to the way the lake's angular, bizarrely shaped arms and bays reach into a quartet of the tiny nation's 23 states. Seen from the sky, the lake looks like a missing piece in a jigsaw puzzle. Boats leave from the main landing stage near the railroad station in Lucerne and wander across deep blue green coves, so tiny they look like toys, and friendly open meadows, and up to the edge of some of the most breathtaking landscapes in the Alps. A full-day trip will give you time to stop for lunch and a cable car ride up the Rigi-Kulm that will give you a chance to look down on the lake and the mountains around it. Information: *Schiffahrtsgesellschaft des Vierwaldstättersees (SGV),* 5 Werftestr., Lucerne CH-6002, Switzerland (phone: 41-404540).

CANALS OF VENICE: It's hard to justify doing anything so expressly aimed at the romantic tourist as hiring a gondola. The experience is poetic and mysterious — and worth every one of the lire that you will be required to spend — particularly at night, when the pale moonlight silvers the city's medieval palaces, the island of San Giorgio Maggiore, and the Giudecca, and turns Venice into a heart-stopping stage that calls to mind Robert Browning's "In a Gondola" and Thomas Mann's *Death in Venice.* Rates — 30% higher after dark — are the same from one gondolier to another; choose one who is pleasant (and perhaps not overly talkative, since twisting around to keep up your end of the conversation can get uncomfortable). Five people can fit in a gondola, so the price ($68 an hour) is reasonable. But should you opt for another means of water transport, the *vaporetto* — the Venetian equivalent of a public bus — provides a less thrilling experience at a fraction of the cost. Or take a turn in one of the *traghetti* — gondola ferries — that make 2-minute, 50-cent trips across the Grand Canal at seven points, usually far from a bridge.

For the Body

Europe's Unparalleled Ski Scene

 Skiing is one of the most memorable activities any downhiller can enjoy during a European vacation. In the first place, no other mountains in the world are quite like the Alps and their surrounding ranges. America has peaks as high, but the valleys in Europe are generally lower, so that the ski runs in Europe tend to be longer and more diverse. And most of the prime European ski resort towns and villages possess an atmosphere that simply can't be found elsewhere.

Europe's ski centers come in all sizes and shapes. There are giants like St.-Moritz, Kitzbühel, and Chamonix, which offer vast assortments of runs and lifts, multilingual instructors, and facilities for a score of other winter sports, including — increasingly — cross-country skiing, plus well-equipped shops, fine hotels, lively nightlife, and all the other accoutrements required by the glossy good life of Europe's leisure classes.

Then there are the small resorts, with only a handful of lifts — but runs that go on and on, and an atmosphere that is less chaotic and more *gemütlich* (comfortable and cozy) than that of the majors. A good many of these smaller areas (and larger ones as well) have teamed up with similar sites nearby and installed a couple of extra lifts that enable guests to ski from one area to the other. These resort combinations often offer the ski facilities of far bigger areas, but with the pleasant, intimate après-ski life found only in small villages. It is also not unknown — as at Zermatt — literally to ski from one European country to another and then back again.

Almost everywhere in Europe, it's now possible to arrange for powder tours. There is, for example, helicopter skiing in many parts of Switzerland; the tours around Lauterbrunnen and Zermatt are especially beautiful. And a number of mountain tours are accessible via the various ski lifts. A cable car carries skiers to the top of the Aiguille du Midi, near Chamonix, in the French Alps, to begin the endless run down the glacier known as the Vallée Blanche — full of crevasses and melted-snow pools, surrounded by high peaks. The *Jungfraujochbahn,* the railroad that ascends the Jungfrau, one of Switzerland's highest mountains and leads to the start of a number of runs that will take you to the Concordiaplatz, where four glaciers cross. Best of all, there's no need to be a super-expert (just a strong intermediate whose knees will not go wobbly crossing a crevasse on a snow bridge scarcely wider than a pair of skis). Good skiers can tackle the Haute Route from Chamonix to Zermatt, overnighting on the way in mountain huts. (Information: *Hochalpine Bergsteigerschule,* Zermatt CH-39920, Switzerland; phone: 28-673456.) By the way, these excursions are mainly spring flings.

In summer, skiing continues on the tip-tilted glaciers — among others — at Zermatt and Saas Fee.

The list of ski resorts that follows includes some of the best of the Continent's offerings in all departments.

But first, some general hints for enjoying skiing in Europe:

If you possibly can, avoid skiing in Europe at *Christmastime.* Not only are the lift lines miserably long, but the weather conditions are also unreliable enough so that you might well end up learning how to make parallel turns on grass and mud. If you have no choice about when to go, at least try to get your skiing in before December 26, while European families are still sitting around their *Christmas* trees. Late January usually offers the best combination of good snow, slightly longer sunny days, off-peak prices, and manageable crowds.

Try, also, to hold out for a half-pension arrangement with your hotel. European skiers take lunch seriously, so there is lots of fine, uncrowded skiing possible while they are indulging in a long midday meal.

In virtually all the ski centers on our roster, the choice of hotels is large, and even the most modest little *gasthaus* usually offers cozy pine-paneled rooms, fluffy eiderdowns, and handsome Tyrolean furniture. We've included a few favorites in each price range: Expensive (E), Moderate (M), Inexpensive (I) — or, at least, more moderate. Each town, no matter how tiny, has a tourist office that can provide up-to-date information about hotel availability, unusual tours, ski schools, and so on. Take their reports of snow conditions with a grain of salt, however.

KITZBÜHEL, Austria: Don't be put off by the comparatively low altitude (2,642 feet). The region is a famous snow bowl that often has better ski conditions than resorts with twice its base elevation. The movie star of Austrian skiing, Kitzbühel is colorful, animated, international. The town is a kind of Tyrolean showpiece, with white peaks rising behind brightly painted buildings. Cable cars and chair lifts connect its ski areas with those of four neighboring towns to provide fantastic skiing possibilities. If you prefer less glitter, lodge a little way down the road in charming St. Johann-in-Tyrol, convenient to all Kitzbühel's facilities. Lodgings: *Klausner* (M); *Gasthof Eggerwirt* (I); *Weisses Rössl* (E).

OBERGURGL, Austria: One of the highest villages in the Alps, the town is far less known as a ski resort than as a mountaineering center. At the end of the 31-mile (50-km) Otztal Road (off the main Innsbruck highway), it has a pleasant Shangri-la quality. The 6,232-foot base elevation means both more sunlight and higher wind, and visitors return to the flatland a healthy-looking bronze. Evening pleasures are simpler than at the more cosmopolitan centers, but a day on the Gaisberg–Hohe Mut will send you to bed by 9:15 anyway. Lodgings: *Hochfirst* (E); *Enzian* (M); *Gasthof Gamper* (I).

ST. ANTON-AM-ARLBERG, Austria: Halfway between Innsbruck and Zurich on the main Arlberg road, St. Anton is a rather ordinary, heavily trafficked town. But the mountains above, rising from a 4,264-foot base, offer a vast network of lifts and superb skiing, ideal for vigorous skiers who like to spend most of the day on the slopes (as most St. Anton skiers do). The village is not the best for non-skiers. St. Christoph, about 4 miles (6 km) away near the top of the Arlberg Pass, is small, cheerful, and convenient to the high-altitude beginners' slopes. Lodgings: *Schwarzer Adler* (E); *Tannenhof* (M).

ZÜRS-LECH, Austria: Lech, a friendly, sunny mountain village on the shores of the river Lech, and Zürs, which grew up as a sort of hotel colony when skiing boomed in the Vorarlberg, share excellent, lift-linked slopes and broad snowfields that make intermediates look like experts. There's a wonderful run all the way down to St. Anton and the chance to make the return trip in a bright yellow Austrian postal bus. With a base elevation of 4,756 feet, this is a good area to try in early winter, when the rest of the countryside is still patched with green and brown. Lodgings: *Gasthof Post,* Lech (E); *Zürserhof,* Zürs (E); *Central,* Lech (M); *Ulli,* Zürs (M).

STARÝ SMOKOVEC, Czechoslovakia: Eastern Europe's best skiing is found in the heart of the High Tatras, in a national park in a region full of deep woods, frozen lakes, and craggy peaks. For skiing, there are jumps and slalom runs and long, gentle cross-country trails. The base elevation is 3,280 feet, and compared to the longtime centers of capitalist decadence in the West, the mood is pastoral and low-key; you won't feel out of place in last season's stretch pants. Lodgings: the fine old *Grand Hotel Starý Smokovec* (**E**); and at Novy Smokovec, the *Parkhotel* (**M**) and the *Bystrina* (**I**).

CHAMONIX, France: The presence of towering Mont-Blanc, the highest mountain in Europe, has made Chamonix, with a base elevation of 3,280 feet, the most famous resort in the French Alps (which now are connected to Courmayeur in Italy by the Tunnel du Mont-Blanc). The snowscapes amid the spires and glaciers of a whole range of 13,000-foot mountains are spectacular, and the *téléphérique* ride to the Aiguille du Midi is one of the great European experiences — with or without skis. The expert skiing is unexcelled anywhere, though even competent intermediates can make the magical 12.4-mile glacier run down the Vallée Blanche from the Aiguille. The lively nightlife, the fine French cuisine, and the busy gambling casino all make the resort a delight for non-skiers; the clientele is definitely sporty. Information: *Office du Tourisme,* Pl. Triangle-de-l'Amitié, Chamonix (phone: 50-53-00-24). Lodgings: *Mont-Blanc* (**E**); *Richemond* (**M**); *Roma* (**I**).

COURCHEVEL, Savoie, France: With 92 trails and some 380 miles of skiing, this resort, which actually is a collection of skiing centers named according to their altitude in meters (1,650, 1,550, and 1,300), offers some of the finest and certainly the most extensive skiing in France — lending credence to its sobriquet, "The Star." And there's a huge assortment of other activities to fill the time spent off the slopes: skating, swimming, hang gliding, concerts, language courses, and more. The resorts of Méribel, Les Menuires, and Val Thorens are linked with Courchevel by a network of 200 lifts and 311 miles of marked trails. Courchevel hosts the jumping and nordic combined ski events at this year's *Winter Olympics.* Information: *Office du Tourisme,* La Croisette, Courchevel 73120 (phone: 79-08-00-29). Hotels: *Byblos des Neiges* (**E**), *La Sivolière* (**M**), *Tournier* (**I**).

VAL-D'ISÈRE, France: Once a mountain resort and hunting village of the Duke of Savoy, this town built around a quaint 16th-century church lies on the Col de l'Iseran, the highest pass in the Alps; the base elevation is 6,068 feet. France's top skiers come here in preference to more chic centers like Mégève and Chamonix, and most of the evening talk at the town's modern, comfortable ski hotels is about trails and boots and bindings. The ski school has a fine reputation for serious, systematic instruction, and when the snow is deep or conditions are icy, the big runs are best left to the experts. Val-d'Isère is an ideal place for a long stay devoted to real improvement in the sport. Events at this year's *Winter Olympics* here include the men's downhill, giant slalom, and Super G races. Information: *Office du Tourisme,* Maison de Val-D'Isère (phone: 79-06-10-83). Lodgings: *Christiania* (**E**); *Santons* (**M**); *Bellevue* (**I**).

VALLOIRE, France: A great deal of lift building and trail making has taken Valloire dramatically out of the "Sleepy Alpine hamlet" class — the base elevation is now 4,592 feet. But it's still less international and far less congested than many centers with comparable facilities. Just near the Galibier Pass, the old part of the village centers around a large, friendly ice skating rink and an old church. There is a fine cross-country run through the Col du Mt. Tabor to the Italian town of Bardonecchia. Information: *Office du Tourisme,* Valloire (phone: 79-59-03-96). Lodgings: *Rapin* (**E**); *Les Carrettes* (**M**); *Centre* (**I**).

GARMISCH-PARTENKIRCHEN, Germany: Americans first got to know this Alpine ski resort back in the days when it was chiefly the US military that occupied the powdery slopes and a few dollars bought all the snow you could ski. The town itself is large, modern, and busy, and offers a whole range of winter sports activities, including curling and bobsledding. High above is the 9,840-foot Zugspitze, Germany's tallest mountain, whose peak, miraculously, is accessible by cog railway and cable car. There is a fine assortment of lifts and trails for every grade of skier, and the facilities are scrupulously maintained by a large local staff. Lodgings: *Dorint* (**E**); or, glamorously perched at 8,692 feet on the Zugspitzplatt, just under the summit, the *Schneefernerhaus* (E). *Wittelsbach* (E); *Bellevue* (M); *Edelweiss* (I).

REIT IM WINKL, Germany: A picturesque Bavarian town in the middle of a wide-open valley, with a base elevation of 2,296 feet, this is not the kind of place you're likely to see represented on bumper stickers and ski parka patches. Yet, with some 2 dozen tows and chair lifts fanned out on a cluster of broad plateaus and mild peaks under 6,560 feet, it's ideal for beginners and intermediates; the ski circus between Winklmoos-Alm, Dürnbachhorn, and Kammerköhr-Steinplatte is immensely satisfying and only of medium difficulty. There is a 2.5-mile toboggan trail, with a smaller version for children, and a fleet of horse-drawn sleighs for drives in the country, *Dr. Zhivago*-style — that is, with fur blankets wrapped around your knees. Evenings, sausage and sauerkraut are piled into small mountains on your dinner plate at any of the nearby restaurants. Lodgings: *Unterwirt* (E); *Altenburger Hof* (M); *Edelweiss* (I).

CORTINA D'AMPEZZO, Italy: Still the country's number one ski resort, which attracts a stylish, predominantly Italian crowd, it held Italy's first *Winter Olympics* back in 1956 and subsequently boomed, so that it is now one of the best-equipped ski towns in the Alps. One of its special pleasures is ice skating in the huge open shell of its *Olympic Stadium*, which you can have to yourself on virtually any early January morning. But whatever your sport, you're always surrounded here by the toothy spikes of the Dolomites. A lift network that links a series of high passes provides access to a great deal of terrain without ever doubling back, and a powerful sun is always there — even in February and March — to remind you that Venice and the Mediterranean are only a few hours away. Lodgings: *Cristallo* (E); *Concordia Parc* (M); *Menardi* (I).

LIVIGNO, Italy: The characteristic wooden houses of this curious, little-known village are strung out along about 7.5 miles of a valley near the Italian and Swiss frontiers. Not so long ago, cross-country skiers had these broad snowfields, the pretty lake, the gentle landscape, and the limitless horizons almost all to themselves. Now there's downhill skiing as well, including glacier skiing throughout the summer for the true enthusiast. The region's development has been enthusiastic but not excessive, and the area offers several hostelries and a number of attractive slopes with a base elevation of 6,068 feet. Lodgings: *Intermonti* (E); *Alpina* (M); *Verde Lago* (I).

SESTRIERE, Italy: Like Courchevel in France, this development of the Fiat company was built — expressly as a ski resort — on once-empty snowfields, so there's less of the cozy sense found in older ski towns. Nonetheless, there's a great deal of life here in season, along with superb high-altitude runs — rising from a base of about 6,560 feet — for every level of skier (it's possible to ski here for a week without ever repeating a run); a fine ski school (though a number of the instructors speak only rudimentary English); and lots of sun, evenly distributed between the slopes and the large terraces with deck chairs and umbrella tables. Sestriere is a marvelous place on weekdays, but impossible on weekends in high season, when big tour buses arrive by the score from Torino (Turin), about 51 miles (82 km) away. Lodgings: *Cristallo* (E); *Belvedere* (M), a local landmark; *Olimpic* (I).

LILLEHAMMER, Norway: Modern skiing was born in Norway and the site chosen for the *1994 Winter Olympics* is the charming east-central mountain village of Lillehammer, about 110 miles (176 km) from Oslo. There are numerous first-rate downhill trails, excellent cross-country skiing, and ski schools where instruction is available for all levels. Night skiing is popular, as are ice skating and sledding. For time spent away from the slopes, there are plenty of hotel nightclubs, discos, and shops. Lodgings: *Lillehammer* (E), *Oppland* (M).

KLOSTERS, Switzerland: Davos, some 7½ miles (12 km) away by road, is one of the Alps' finest ski centers, but it's a big, citified, not always attractive spot. By far the nicest place to stay in the region is the charming animated village of Klosters, which is connected to Davos by the ski lifts of the great Parsenn area. The Parsenn snowfields, with a base elevation of about 4,000 feet, are wonderfully varied, and while there are a number of areas that are rewarding for beginners, the area is also rich in challenging runs that are so long they make you feel as if you're crossing all of Switzerland. The Klosters Valley gets early shade — but its brisk nightlife starts just after twilight and seems to keep going until the tows open in the morning. Not a village of cowbells and milkmaids, Klosters is cosmopolitan, expensive — and great fun. Lodgings: *Chesa Grischuna* (**E**); *Sporthotel Kurhaus* (**M**); *Pension Soldanella* (**I**).

MÜRREN, Switzerland: Famous in the annals of ski racing as the site of the great Alpine-Kandahar course and the founding place of the *Kandahar Ski Club,* this sunny, romantic village, on a kind of balcony overhanging the Lauterbrunnen Valley, is little known among vacationing skiers and can still be a discovery even to Alpine veterans. Best of all, it's car-free. Some of the toughest, most exciting slopes in Switzerland, as well as countless simpler trails, rise above the 5,412-foot base; many runs end up within a few minutes' walk of the hotels. There's a spectacular revolving restaurant on the peak of the Schilthorn. Lodgings: *Mürren* (**E**); *Sporthotel-Edelweiss* (**M**); *Alpina* (**I**).

ST.-MORITZ, Switzerland: Possessed of such a long-standing, far-reaching reputation for being elegant, expensive, and sophisticated that a number of serious skiers spend years avoiding it — and years regretting their boycott when they finally do break down and go. The princes and the furs and the Lamborghinis are all here, but so are some of the finest, most exciting, best-maintained ski runs in Europe. It would take several days to ski them all just once. There is not just something for everybody — there's everything for everybody. The base elevation is 6,068 feet. The town has grown into a small ski city, and you can easily pick up a mink or a Matisse along with your boot wax. Make sure to have coffee and pastry at *Hanselmann*. Lodgings: *The Palace* (**E**) or *Suvretta House* (**E**), if you can afford it; *Neues Post* (**M**); *Languard* (**I**).

WENGEN, Switzerland: Like Zermatt, Wengen, in the middle of the Bernese Oberland, is car-free (with the nearest garages and parking lots a 15-minute train ride away at Lauterbrunnen). The town, which extends along a sheltered plateau at the foot of the imposing Jungfrau at 4,264 feet, shares a vast ski terrain with nearby Scheidegg and Grindelwald. There is a choice of mountain railways (including the renowned *Jungfraujochbahn*), which offer newer, higher ski trails at every stop. And the unparalleled Jungfrau Glacier runs are open from the middle of February until the end of May. In addition to all this skiing, there is a great deal of hockey, skating, curling, and just plain walking on well-packed, breathtakingly scenic snowy mountain paths. Lodgings: *Regina* (**E**); *Bellevue* (**M**); *Schweizerheim* (**I**).

ZERMATT, Switzerland: On a car-choked continent, the no-autos-at-all policy in Zermatt, at 5,248 feet, is especially delightful. And despite the town's international fame, it maintains a rustic village flavor. Zermatt also has that unique Alpine monument, the Matterhorn, looming above and a dazzling fishnet of cog railways, cable cars, gondolas, T-bars, and pommel lifts that serve an enormous variety of runs across snowfields and through the trees. And when you've done all that, there's a famous run over the Theodule Pass to Breuil-Cervinia in Italy. In addition, there's fine springtime skiing and regular town-to-glacier helicopter service. All in all, Zermatt probably offers Europe's most complete skiing experience. Lodgings: *Monte Rosa* (**E**); *Alpenblick* (**M**); *Chesa Valese* (**I**).

Tennis

Most American passions eventually sweep Europe as well, and tennis is no exception. The number of courts, players, clubs, and sleek designer outfits has been soaring in the last decade, so that tennis is now as much the sport of European butchers and bakers as it once was of barons. However, the groundswell started from a far narrower base than in America, and the sport still has a way to go. Facilities aren't as extensive as in the US, instruction isn't as expert, and there is still a shortage of high-powered accessories like videotape units, ball machines, and the like. The organized tennis vacation is still a comparative rarity. Still, the rapid rise of tennis champions all across the Continent is causing the number of players and facilities to increase exponentially.

If you were brought up in a world of tennis whites, "sorry, partner," and "take two, please," you may be put off by the noise level both on and off the courts, and by the general lack of Anglo-Saxon reverence for the game, particularly in Mediterranean countries. Nonetheless, a tennis match is still a fine, rapid way to escape the standard tourist circuit and get into local life. Travel with your tennis gear — and be sure to bring it all, so that your day need not be marred by the exorbitant cost of a Swiss T-shirt or a pair of German socks. Many clubs welcome brief visits by foreigners, so you suddenly may find yourself with a circle of Dutch or Danish friends. Like French in the gambling casino, English is the lingua franca of the tennis court, particularly among the well-to-do.

Synthetic court surfaces are still uncommon in Europe, so it's relatively easy to enjoy the pleasures of English grass courts and well-kept red clay ones — and often in spectacularly beautiful settings.

A cultural parenthesis: When Europeans kick back stray balls, it's not out of rudeness or impatience but because of their early soccer training.

Here are some good places to try a little serving and volleying on European tennis courts:

COPENHAGEN, Denmark: Ever since the success of Bjorn Börg, tennis has taken a great leap forward all over Scandinavia. The climate in Copenhagen in spring and summer is delightful for court capers, and a number of clubs offer temporary membership to visiting foreigners, including: *Boldklubben af 1893*, known locally as "B 93" (10 Per Henrik Lings Allé; phone: 31-381890); *Hellerup Idraetsklub* (37 Hartmannsvej, Hellerup; phone: 31-621428); and *Københavns Boldklub* (147 Peter Bangsvej; phone: 714180). You can get additional information about facilities, tournaments, and the like from the courteous *Dansk Tennis Vorbund, Brøndby Stadion*, 20 Idraettens Hus, Glostrup, DK-2600 Copenhagen, Denmark (phone: 42-455555).

BEDFORD, England: *Woodlands Tennis Centre* has a beautiful rural facility in Milton Ernest, one of the unspoiled villages along the river Ouse near Bedford. This tennis school offers courses for young people and adults at every level, from beginner to expert. Accommodations are either in the historic 17th-century center itself, with local families, or in a nearby hotel. Although summer is prime time, the school also runs weekend courses during the off-season. Fishing, boating, horseback riding, cycling, and squash are easily arranged. Information: *Tennis Coaching International, Woodlands Tennis Centre*, Milton Ernest, Bedford, England (phone: 2302-2914).

BODMIN, England: *Tennisville Holidays* in Cornwall is very British and very family oriented, with a cheerful atmosphere and excellent coaching. Courses are usually a week, but many guests stay longer. Both private and group instruction. Closed for a few weeks around *Christmas*. Information: *Tennisville*, Sunny Banks Farm, Fletchers Bridge, Bodmin, Cornwall PL30 4AN, England (phone: 208-75048).

HAILSHAM, England: *Windmill Hill Place Residential Tennis Centre* is 50 miles from London and 10 minutes from the sea, near the resort town of Eastbourne. There are 8 grass, 6 all-weather, and 4 indoor courts amid 20 acres of wooded grounds, and the main residence is an elegant Georgian mansion. Weekend and week-long sessions year-round. There also is a swimming pool and a 9-hole golf course. Information: *Windmill Hill Place Tennis Resort*, Windmill Hill, Hailsham, East Sussex BN27 4RZ, England (phone: 323-832552).

LA BAULE, France: Nestled in the lush but carefully groomed grounds of one of Brittany's star beach resorts, the *Tennis Country Club* at La Baule provides 30 courts, as well as accommodations in nearby luxury hotels. Facilities include a massage room and a heated, saltwater pool. It's pleasant to play 4 hours of tennis each day and spend the remaining 20 windsurfing, golfing, or gambling in the *La Baule* casino. Information: *Tennis Country Club,* 113 Av. de Lattre de Tassigny, La Baule Cedex 44504, France (phone: 40-60-23-44).

CAP D'AGDE, France: The *Club Pierre Barthès* is one of Europe's most dazzling complexes. Its 62 courts (6 covered and 16 lighted) are just a forehand away from one of the Mediterranean's choicest beaches. A lovely colony of guest villas and apartments and a small hotel. Open year-round; book well in advance, especially for summer. Information: *Club Pierre Barthès,* BP 547, Cap d'Agde 34305, France (phone: 67-26-00-06).

CARGÈSE, France: One of the very best spots to play tennis in Europe is at one of the many "vacation villages" of the *Club Med. Le Club,* as it's known in its native France, offers facilities that are extensive, instruction that is first rate, and settings that are consistently attractive and maintained with ecological fervor. The *Cargèse Club Med,* on the Gulf of Chiuni in Corsica, is a fine place to mix tennis and the sea. There are 10 courts with the green Corsican hills on one side and a rocky bay and wide, blond beach on the other. Accommodation is in very comfortable separate bungalows. And the *Club* organizes various excursions around the most inviting parts of Corsica. Open from mid-May to mid-September. Information: *Club Med,* Cargèse 20130, Corsica, France (phone: 95-26-40-01); or contact the *Club's* New York office at 40 W. 57th, New York, NY 10019 (phone: 800-CLUB-MED or 212-977-2100).

DEAUVILLE, France: The town itself owns 23 courts by the sea, and sponsors numerous tennis tournaments. But should you strike it rich at the world-famous casino, consider staying at one of the two classic Deauville hotels, the *Normandy* or the *Royal.* The former, an oversized Norman cottage in the heart of town, faces its own 21 tennis courts, as well as the Atlantic Ocean. If the weather is disappointing, jog through the underground passage to the casino or swim in the covered, heated, Olympic-size saltwater pool. Down the street is the *Royal* with 23 courts. Information: *Hotel Normandy,* 38 Rue Jean-Mermoz, Deauville 14800, France (phone: 31-986622; fax: 31-98-66-23); *Hotel Royal,* Bd. Cornuché, Deauville 14800, France (phone: 31-986633; fax: 31-98-66-34).

POMPADOUR, France: The super-efficient *Club Med* operation virtually guarantees a successful vacation, and this verdant paradise is no exception. There are 19 covered tennis courts, so even a rainy week in October won't dampen a tennis buff's dream holiday. And for those who need to rest their backhand, horseback riding along tree-lined paths, a 9-hole pitch and putt golf course, a heated swimming pool, and a pony club for children are also available. Information: *Club Med,* Domaine de Noailles, Arnac-Pompadour 19230, France (phone: 55-73-31-33); or in the US (see above).

VITTEL, France: This *Club Med* village — in the green French countryside — is the best of them all for tennis: There are 25 courts (17 clay), frequent tournaments, and instruction at all levels — and you'll never have any trouble finding partners on short notice. Accommodation is available in several of the gracious old spa hotels that went up here in the days when taking the waters was an indispensable interlude for the Parisian upper classes. Open May through September. Information: *Club Med,* Vittel 88800, France (phone: 29-08-18-80); or in the US (see *Cargèse, France*).

BADEN-BADEN, Germany: The main tennis club of Germany's most elegant spa has 9 carefully groomed courts in the middle of the lush Lichtentalerallée promenade. Giant ancient trees surround you and fine stately hotels like the *Brenner's Park* are just a hard forehand away. Information: *Tennis Club Rot-Weiss,* 5 Sekretariat, Lichtentalerallée, Baden-Baden D-7570, Germany (phone: 7221-24141) — and this is only one of several clubs in town. The visitors' bureau offers special all-inclusive tennis weeks, including instruction. General information: *Baden-Baden Verkehrsverein,* 8 Augustapl., Baden-Baden D-7570, Germany (phone: 7221-275200).

OBERLAHR, Germany: A highly professional setup split among three handsome resort hotels, *Hans Pötter's Tennis School* has videotape recorders, backboards, ball machines, and indoor and outdoor courts which are open for both day and night play through the year. You can sign up for special intensive weekend courses, or for more leisurely vacation weeks which will leave you time for excursions in the hill and lake country of the Rhine River valley. Information: *Waldbrunnen,* 7 Brunnenstr., Windhagen-Rederscheid 5469, Germany (phone: 2645-15582).

ATHENS, Greece: Athens is one of those enviable Mediterranean capitals where the weather is good for tennis all year long; though it's sometimes breezy and sometimes hot, it's always worth bringing your gear. Play and instruction are pleasantly inexpensive by US standards, and a strong American player is often treated as a kind of visiting apostle in Greek clubs. Courts and clubs to sample include the *Agios Kosmos Athletic Center* (phone: 1-894-8900); *Athens Tennis Club* (2 Vas. Olgas Ave.; phone: 1-923-2872); *Attic Tennis Club* (Dafni and Kalliga St., Filothei; phone: 1-682-5649); *Kifissia Athletic Club* (45 Tatoiou Rd., Strofyli, Kifissia; phone: 1-807-0100); and the *Glyfada Tennis Club* (Diadochou Pavlou Ave., Glyfada; phone: 1-895-3012). More detailed information is available from the *Greek Tennis Federation,* 89 Patission St., Athens 104, Greece (phone: 1-821-0478).

CORFU, Greece: Of the myriad Greek islands, this is the one where tennis has made the deepest inroads. *Club Med* has a seaside village at Ipsos with 15 courts that start to function in early May and attract a large assortment of first class vacation players. Accommodation is in simple but charming thatched huts, with communal dining areas. The sea is all around, and water skiing is also popular. Information: *Club Med,* Corfu, Ipsos-Corfu, Greece, or contact *Club Med* in New York (see *Cargèse, France*). Another spot where you'll find good players is the *Corfu Tennis Club* (4 Romanou St., Corfu, Greece; phone: 37021). The club, which has been around since 1896, retains its gracious, tennis-is-all-that-counts air. Good courts also are available at the *Hilton International* hotel, the *Roda Beach,* and the *Nissaki* hotels.

CAPO RIZZUTO, Italy: Following the French *Club Med* model of sports-oriented vacation villages, the 10 Italian *Valtur* complexes have cornered the market in the peninsula's glamorous locations. They guarantee luxurious accommodations and provide the same round-the-clock relaxing frenzy as their Gallic counterparts. Near Cefalu, on the northern coast of Sicily, is *Pollina,* with 8 tennis courts, 4 of them lighted so you can water-ski all day and save tennis for a nightcap. *Capo Rizzuto,* on the Ionian coast of Calabria, has 8 courts (5 lighted), and *Brucoli,* not far from the Sicilian city of Syracuse, has 6 courts (3 lighted). Special tennis weeks with top coaches are featured in June and July. *Valtur* summer holiday centers are open from May through September. Three other winter sports villages are open December through April: *Marileva,* for families with very young children; *Pila,* for families with children 5 to 12 years old; and *San Sicario.* Information: *Valtur Vacanze,* 42 Via Milano, Rome 00184, Italy (phone: 6-482-1000).

ROME, Italy: The town has been tennis mad ever since Italy won its Davis Cup, and there are some 50 clubs and centers, with almost exclusively clay courts. Among those that welcome transient players are the *Circolo Tennis Belle Arti* (158 Via Flaminia; phone: 6-360-6529); the *Circolo Tennis della Stampa* (Piazza Mancini at the Duca d'Aosta Bridge; phone: 6-396-0792); and the *Oasi di Pace* (2 Via degli Eugenii, Appia Antica; phone: 6-799-4550). For complete information and a list of every court in town contact the *Federazione Italiana Tennis,* 70 Viale Tiziano, Rome 00100, Italy (phone: 6-36851).

MONTE CARLO, Monaco: The host of the *Monte Carlo Open* every May, the *Monte*

Carlo Country Club (actually on French soil) has 23 splendid clay and synthetic courts, set into the rich surrounding greenery like precious stones. You'll also find a panoramic view of the bay and skilled multilingual instructors. Four courts are lighted; and from mid-April to mid-September, you can sign up for special 5-day courses. Two squash courts are available as well. Information: *Monte Carlo Country Club,* BP 342, Monte Carlo, Monaco (phone: 93-78-20-45).

VALE DO LOBO, Portugal: The *Roger Taylor Tennis Center,* run by Britain's former top star, is in the middle of an enticing resort area on the sunny Algarve coast. There are 12 courts (6 lighted; 2 covered) and a 5-hour daily clinic that starts off with seaside jogging. Superb golf and swimming are also available. Guest accommodations are in *Vale do Lobo* villas or the luxurious *Dona Filipa* hotel. The complex is only 9 miles (14 km) from Faro Airport. Information and reservations through the London office: *Roger Taylor Tennis Center,* Urbanizaçao de Luxo, 8100 Vale do Lobo, Algarve, Portugal (phone: 89-394779); or *Roger Taylor Tennis Holidays Ltd.,* 85 High St., Wimbledon, London SW19 5EG (phone: 81-947-9727).

MARBELLA, Spain: Lew Hoad — remember Hoad and Rosewall? — runs one of the best-known tennis schools in Europe here on the heavily developed Costa del Sol, with courses and programs for all kinds of players. You can lodge in apartments near the school, or, some 15 miles (24 km) away, at the deluxe *Los Monteros* hotel complex by the sea, whose spacious grounds are full of lawns, swimming pools, palm trees, and tropical foliage. There also are 10 additional tennis courts here along with 5 squash courts. Information: *Lew Hoad's Campo de Tenis,* Apartado 111, Fuengirola, Marbella (Málaga), Spain (phone: 474858). The area is also home to one of the biggest tennis operations of the *Club Med,* with 16 courts, 4 of them lighted, and accommodations in a large, comfortable hotel about 6 miles (10 km) from the beach. Shuttle service is provided. Open year-round. Information: *Club Med,* Don Miguel, Marbella (Málaga), Spain; or contact the *Club's* New York office (see under *Cargèse, France*).

GSTAAD, Switzerland: The dowager *Palace* hotel, the tennis hot spot in Switzerland, features the Roy Emerson Tennis Weeks in June and July as its main offering, back to back with the *Swiss Championships.* Emerson is not just a big name, his instruction is as exciting as his demonstrations. The prices are high, but the hotel and the tennis facilities are all spectacular — so if you can afford it, by all means go. Information: *Palace Hotel,* Gstaad 3780, Switzerland (phone: 30-83131). A number of other Swiss resort towns organize special tennis weeks in summer and offer packages that include rooms, meals, instruction, and unlimited play. Among those that combine the best facilities with the most attractive settings are the *Derby* hotel (Davos Dorf CH 7270, Switzerland; phone: 81-471166); and the *Tennisschule Laax, Sporthotel Signina* (Laax (GR) 7031, Switzerland; phone: 86-390151). Similar packages also are available in the snazzy towns of Ascona and St. Moritz. For details, contact the *Verkehrsbüro,* 6612 Via B. Papio, Ascona (TI) 6612, Switzerland (phone: 93-355544) or at St. Moritz 7500, Switzerland (phone: 82-33147).

THE GREAT EUROPEAN TOURNAMENTS

WIMBLEDON, Wimbledon, England: Still the world's number one tournament, this tourney, held in late June and early July, is an experience even if you've never held a racket. Grass courts, strawberry teas, and the legendary Centre Court are all high points, and the world class matches going on quietly on all the outlying lawns end up being merely side shows. Good seats for late-round matches are completely sold out months in advance, as are a good many seats throughout the tourney; and there are long lines for the tickets that are available. Also, a recent reduction in the number of attendees admitted — there is no more standing room — makes it even harder to get in. Good news: Current plans call for literally raising the roof to allow seating for another 1,000 fans. Centre Court and Court No. One seats are allocated by lottery. Send a self-addressed, stamped envelope with your request for an allocation form in October; you should receive it early in the new year. Information: *All-England Lawn Tennis Club,* Church Rd., Wimbledon, London SW19 5AE, England (phone: 81-946-2244). Tickets are available in the US as part of the tours offered by *Keith Prowse & Co.,* 234 W. 44th St., New York, NY 10036 (phone: 212-398-1430; 800-669-7469 outside New York) or *Traveltix International,* 400 Madison Ave., Suite 411, New York, NY 10017 (phone: 212-688-3700; 800-446-4943).

FRENCH OPEN, Paris, France: Held at *Roland Garros Stadium,* generally in late May and early June, this tournament's traditions go back to the great days of La Coste, Borotra, and Lenglen. The surface is authentic red clay, and it is a good notch above Rome in prestige and professionalism. Information: *Le Secrétaire Général,* Fédération Française de Tennis, Stade Roland Garros, 2 Av. Gordon-Bennett, Paris 75016, France (phone: 47-43-48-00).

ITALIAN INTERNATIONAL CHAMPIONSHIPS, Rome, Italy: Held in mid-May, this event, also known as the *Italian Open,* has a pleasant Tiber-side setting among the cypresses where many world class players participate. For exact dates and ticket information, in early spring contact the *Federazione Italiana Tennis,* 70 Viale Tiziano, Rome, Italy (phone: 6-396-2300).

Great Golf Courses

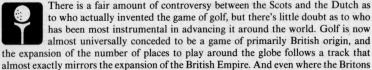

There is a fair amount of controversy between the Scots and the Dutch as to who actually invented the game of golf, but there's little doubt as to who has been most instrumental in advancing it around the world. Golf is now almost universally conceded to be a game of primarily British origin, and the expansion of the number of places to play around the globe follows a track that almost exactly mirrors the expansion of the British Empire. And even where the Britons did not actually annex territory, their vacation preferences clearly affected the construction of golf courses, as evidenced by the courses that exist in such exotic Eastern European spots as Karlovy Vary and Mariánské Lázně. Non-Czechs know them better as the historic spas of Carlsbad and Marienbad, the favorite haunts of the Hanoverian Kings of England, who were returning to visit their then-German homelands.

It will come as no surprise that the finest courses in Europe are found in England, Scotland, and Ireland, but what *is* surprising is the fact that these courses are almost always hospitable to visiting golfers. (See also "Scotland's Fabled Golf Courses," DIRECTIONS.) For the few private clubs among the best in Europe, it's always a wise idea to carry your home club membership card and a letter from your own club president or golf professional asking for hospitality. Europeans put great store in interclub reciprocity and will almost always honor such an official request.

Herewith, the best and most accessible golf courses in Europe:

ROYAL ANTWERP, Kapellenbos, Belgium: As its majestic name implies, this has long been a favorite of Belgian kings. The oldest club in Belgium, it was founded and laid out in 1888 by British immigrants. Set among beautiful pine and silver birch woods, this generally level course makes gauging distances a formidable challenge. The several long par 4's will force even a seasoned golfer to use a long iron to the green. Information: *Royal Antwerp Golf Club,* 2 George Capiaulei, 2950 Kapellenbos, Antwerpen LE2, Belgium (phone: 3-6668456).

SUNNINGDALE, Sunningdale, England: While the *Old* course is considered the championship layout here, the *New* is probably the harder of the two. When you play them, you will discover that the decision on difficulty is an arbitrary one at best. Fairways and greens are meticulously maintained, and this is perhaps the finest single set of courses in England. Private but visitors are welcome on weekends with a letter of introduction. Information: *Sunningdale Golf Club,* Ridgemount Rd., Sunningdale, Berkshire SL5 9RR, England (phone: 344-21681).

WENTWORTH, Virginia Water, England: The *East* course at *Wentworth* is gener-ally considered the prettiest of the three courses and can do wonders for a shaky backswing. (There's also a par 3 layout here.) But it's the *West* course that is sometimes not so affectionately called the "Burma Road." For a high-handicap player, the *West* is not unlike putting an innocent head into the mouth of an unfriendly lion. Again, *Wentworth* is a private club that's likely to offer access to traveling players on weekdays upon presentation of your own club membership card and a letter from your club president. Information: *Wentworth Golf Club,* Virginia Water, Surrey, England (phone: 9904-2201).

MONTE-CARLO, La Turbie, Cap D'Ail, France: On a clear day, this hilly 6,200-yard course has splendid views of Monaco and the coast from St.-Tropez to Italy. It hosts the annual *Monte-Carlo Open* on the PGA European Tour in June. A private club, visitors should call in advance to make arrangements. Greens fees range from $60 to $70. Information: *Monte-Carlo Golf Club,* La Turbie, Cap D'Ail 06320, France (phone: 93-41-09-11).

GOLF DE NÎMES CAMPAGNE, Nîmes, France: Built in 1968, these 6,800 yards are particularly challenging when the wind is blowing (which is quite often). In fact, the club suggests that only those with handicaps under 30 play at all. The 18th hole is next to a beautiful pond that is surrounded by weeping willows. The clubhouse is called the "White House," and is lined by a splendid alley of sycamore trees. Greens fees range from $40 to $80, depending on the time of year. Information: *Golf de Nîmes Campagne,* Rte. de St.-Gilles, Nîmes 30000, France (phone: 66-70-17-37).

GOLF DES BORDES, St.-Laurent Nouan, France: Texas architect Robert Von Hagge was asked to design a championship course that would respect the landscape. The result is this 7,100-yard layout, set 10 miles (16 km) southwest of Orléans. There is water on 12 of its 18 holes. Greens fees range from $50 to $100; electric cars are available. Information: *Golf des Bordes,* St.-Laurant Nouan 41220, France (phone: 54-87-72-13).

GOLF DE SEIGNOSSE, Seignosse, France: Completed in 1989 by designer Robert Von Hagge, this 18-hole track (6,800 yards, par 72) is considered one of the most spectacular courses in France. Beautifully set in the midst of the Landes pine forest, it is demanding and hilly (luckily, carts are available here). Greens fees range from $35 to $40. Information: *Golf de Seignosse,* Seignosse 40510, France (phone: 58-43-17-32).

ZUR VAHR, Bremen, Germany: On 220 acres of the thickly forested Garlstedter Heath, this course is full of tall, dense pine groves that surround players from tee to green, necessitating long, accurate drives and little need for bunkers, which number only 24. Rated as one of the finest championship courses in Europe by professionals. Information: *Zur Vahr Golf Club,* 15 Deliuswey, Bremen 33, Germany (phone: 421-236657).

BALLYBUNION, Ballybunion, Republic of Ireland: No less an authority than Tom Watson calls the old layout here one of the ten toughest courses in the world, and you will have no reason to disagree. The course is laid out at the point where the Shannon River estuary meets the Atlantic Ocean, and you should be not the least concerned that the out-of-bounds area beside the 14th hole is a graveyard. A Robert Trent Jones, Sr. 18-hole course has been added, but it is the old track that is the real attraction. Information: *Ballybunion Golf Club,* County Kerry, Republic of Ireland (phone: 68-27146).

ROYAL DUBLIN, Dollymount, Republic of Ireland: The "other" Dublin area golfing magnet that, though second to Portmarnock, still deserves a place among Europe's best. Again, the winds blow here and the rough grows to a size not normally known in the New World. Information: *Royal Dublin Golf Club,* Dollymount, Dublin 3, Republic of Ireland (phone: 1-336346).

KILLARNEY GOLF AND FISHING CLUB, Killarney, Republic of Ireland: There are two courses here beside the legendary lakes, and it's the older course that is the stronger. The scenery is startling in this fabled spot, and it may take an act of will to keep your head down, though it may not be worth the effort. The sight of the lakes framing the purple mountains is a once-in-a-lifetime experience. Information: *Killarney Golf and Fishing Club,* Mahoney's Point, Killarney, County Kerry, Republic of Ireland (phone: 64-31242).

LAHINCH, Lahinch, Republic of Ireland: This extraordinary course has been known to inflict players with every plague save famine and flood. It has one short par 5 that has been lengthened a bit by putting something that looks like the Great Wall of China in the middle of the fairway, and to add a little extra spice to your round, there's a 145-yard par 3 that's completely blind. Would you like to guess how they managed that? A small herd of goats crop the fairways, and golfers have been known to study their location and posture to gauge wind and weather. Our pick for the best in the west of Ireland. Information: *Lahinch Golf Club,* Lahinch, County Clare, Republic of Ireland (phone: 65-81003).

PORTMARNOCK, Portmarnock, Republic of Ireland: This fabled layout (just outside Dublin) is perhaps the best single course in the Republic. The short flag sticks, which are set on springs to let them swing freely in the breeze, tell you something about the wind hazards here, though again the quality of the course is superb. Be prepared for soaring scores but a bracing outing. Information: *Portmarnock Golf Club,* Portmarnock, County Dublin, Republic of Ireland (phone: 1-323082).

KENNEMER, Zandvoort, The Netherlands: Rated among the best golf courses on the Continent, this club offers the delightful surprise of rolling sand dunes, an unusual element in a country that is otherwise flat. Excellent, challenging play for the accomplished golfer. Information: *Kennemer Golf and Country Club,* 78-80 Kennemerweg, Zandvoort 2042 XT, The Netherlands (phone: 2507-12836).

ROYAL COUNTY DOWN, Newcastle, Northern Ireland: This is "where the Mountains of Mourne sweep down to the sea." They played the *British Amateur* championship here several years ago, and there are hazards in certain places that can prove rather startling to weak-kneed players. The minutes of the founding club meeting in 1889 reported that "the Secretaries were empowered to employ Tom Morris to lay out the course at a cost not to exceed £4." God alone only knows how old Tom hacked this course out of the rough sandhills for that price, but he sure made a beauty. Information: *Royal County Down Golf Club,* Newcastle, County Down, Northern Ireland (phone: 3967-23314).

ROYAL PORTRUSH, Portrush, Northern Ireland: Though the troubles in Northern Ireland persist, golf remains above the internecine disputes. The *Dunluce* course is the championship layout here and is named after the striking historic castle that is perched on steep seaside cliffs near the fairways of the only Irish links ever to host the *British Open.* Information: *Royal Portrush Golf Club,* Dunluce Rd., Portrush BT56 8 JQ, Northern Ireland (phone: 265-822311).

PENINA, Algarve, Portugal: Designed by Henry Cotton, who was three times the *British Open* champion, the course has managed to overcome the disadvantage of being set on very flat terrain. Literally hundreds of thousands of trees and shrubs were planted to provide a frame for the golf holes, and this former rice field is now a fine test of golfing skill. The large *Penina Golf* hotel adjoins the golf course. Information: *Penina Golf Club,* Monte de Alvor, PO Box 146, Penina, Portimao, Algarve 8502, Portugal (phone: 82-22051).

QUINTA DO LAGO, Algarve, Portugal: Now ranked among the top ten courses in the world, this relative newcomer — and site of the *1990 Portuguese Open* — basks under 300 days of sunshine a year. Even while most northern European courses are damp and dreary, the 27 holes here normally can be played in shirtsleeves in December. Designed by Bill Mitchell, the late American architect, *Quinta do Lago* spreads along the Algarve coast over undulating land fringed by umbrella pines. A newer course nearby, *San Lorenzo,* promises to be even more demanding — and serene. In the estuary beside its 6th and 7th holes, Portuguese women digging for seafood may be the only distractions of the day. Information: *Quinta do Lago Golf Club,* Almansil, Loulé 1800, Portugal (phone: 89-394529).

GLENEAGLES, Auchterarder, Scotland: The Scots tend to denigrate this superb group of courses because they do not conform to the treasured linksland tradition. But visiting golfers will fall prey to no such prejudice, and the *King's* course in particular is an absolute joy to play. It's also consistently in the best condition of any Scottish course and the extraordinary hotel here is reason enough for a visit. A visit during the month of June will allow play while gorse and broom are in bloom. A new course, the *Monarch,* designed by Jack Nicklaus, is scheduled to open late this year. Courses open to hotel guests only. Information: *Gleneagles Hotel Golf Course,* Auchterarder, PH3 1NF Perthshire, Scotland (phone: 7646-3543).

CARNOUSTIE, Carnoustie, Scotland: Just 5 miles from *St. Andrews* is this site of a half-dozen *British Open* golf tournaments. If the *Championship* course (the better of the two tracks here) is the least impressive of the championship Scottish courses at first glance, it takes only one round of play to appreciate its true value. It encompasses the very essence of what's best about playing golf in Scotland, and the back 9 in particular — with the famous 14th hole called "Spectacles" and the three backbreaking finishing holes — will leave you with memories (not necessarily pleasant) that you will not soon forget. Now that the course is off the *Open* rota (too few accommodations), access is easier. Information: *Carnoustie Golf Club,* Links Parade, Carnoustie, Tayside DD7 7JE, Scotland (phone: starter's box, 241-53249; or secretary, 241-53789).

MUIRFIELD, Gullane, East Lothian, Scotland: Home of the Honourable Company of Edinburgh Golfers and the oldest golf club in existence, Muirfield has provided challenging play to generations of golfers since 1744 and, as befitting a world class course, has been the scene of countless *British Open* tournaments; this year's championship takes place here. This may be the hardest course in Scotland to get to play; be sure to write well in advance asking for access; visitors are restricted to Tuesday, Thursday, and Friday mornings. Information: *Muirfield Golf Club,* East Lothian St., Gullane EH 31 2EG, Scotland (phone: 620-842123).

OLD COURSE, St. Andrews, Fife, Scotland: This is the prime magnet that draws the world's golfers, for this course dates, they say, from the 15th century. Its aura is only slightly diminished by the bathers and strollers who consistently cross the 1st and 18th fairways — it's the shortest route to the beach — though once out on the course, its extreme difficulty and careful design become more readily apparent. There are four other courses on the same site — the *Eden, Jubilee,* and *New* (which was opened in 1894) are best — but it's the *Old* that you *must* play. Plan your play date here carefully, because there's no golfing on the *Old Course* on Sunday, and applications for tee times on most days must be made months in advance. A "fiver" to the starter can, however, work wonders occasionally. A weekly ticket costs about $119 and allows unlimited play on the *New, Jubilee,* and *Eden* courses. Information: *Links Management Committee,* Golf Pl., St. Andrews, Fife, KY16 9JA, Scotland (phone: 334-75757).

ROYAL TROON, Troon, Scotland: Laid out along the beach, with the outgoing 9 heading virtually straight down the strand and the closing 9 paralleling it only a few yards inland, the prime distractions include the fact that the course lies directly below the flight path into Prestwick Airport and that there's a railroad track beside most of the back 9. So it sometimes seems as though players are about to be sucked up into the jet wash or run over by the 3:45 from Glasgow. Another classic *British Open* layout (and site of the 1989 tournament), playing privileges usually are made available to members of clubs in the US who can produce a respectable certificate of handicap. Writing ahead for a tee time is a good idea. Women are not allowed to play the *Championship* course. Information: *Royal Troon Golf Club,* Craigend Rd., Troon, Ayrshire, Scotland (phone: 292-311555).

TURNBERRY, Turnberry, Scotland: The two courses here, the *Ailsa* and the *Arran,* are quite close in quality, but it's the *Ailsa* on which the *British Open* was played in 1977 and again in 1986. The wind blows in from the sea, and it sometimes takes an act of courage just to stand up on the craggy tees and hit out into the teeth of what occasionally seems like a gale. The beautiful *Turnberry* hotel — built at the turn of the century in the Edwardian style — provides some respite from the elements, but the golfing challenge is the real lure here. Information: *Turnberry Hotel and Golf Courses,* Turnberry, Ayrshire, KA26 9LT Scotland (phone: 655-31000).

LA MANGA CAMPO DE GOLF, Los Belones, Spain: In a golf-mad country, where dozens of world class courses have been developed in recent years, *La Manga* remains one of the most superbly maintained. The two 18-hole championship layouts offer tantalizing views of the Mediterranean from nearly every tee, and the sights and scenery provide a sort of ancillary hazard. Information: *La Manga Campo de Golf,* Los Belones, Cartagena, Murcia 30385, Spain (phone: 968-564511).

TORREQUEBRADA, Benalmadena, Spain: Originally planned as a recreation center and golf course for vacationing German physicians, it's now a hotel, casino, and golf course open to the public, with a championship course designed by well-known Spanish golfer Pepe Gancedo. With the beautiful, sunny Costa del Sol as its backdrop, the course, though not long, is one of the most dramatic in Europe. About 15 miles (24 km) from Málaga. Information: *Torrequebrada,* PO Box 67, Carretera de Cádiz, KM 220, Benalmadena, Costa del Sol, Spain (phone: 52-446000).

FALSTERBO, Falsterbo, Sweden: Some 300 miles (480 km) from Stockholm and only 30 miles (48 km) from Copenhagen, it was founded in 1909 as a 9-hole course and expanded to 18 holes in 1930, making it one of the first full-fledged golf courses in Sweden. The exciting layout provides a fresh challenge with each wind change, and the naturally beautiful setting on a peninsula affords golfers stunning views across the sound to Denmark and along the Swedish shoreline. Information: *Falsterbo Golf Club,* Box 71, F-23011 Falsterbo, Sweden (phone: 40-470078; fax: 40-472722).

European Beaches:
Sun and Sand on Six Seas

When you look down on a teeming Riviera beach in the middle of July, it's hard to believe that it wasn't so many decades ago that the great Riviera hotels closed down for the season with the first searing rays of the midsummer sun. Nothing can turn back the clock, however, or dismantle the seafront condominiums and cement-block hotels, or banish the sun-seeking Nordic hordes.

But Europe has many beaches of great natural beauty, whatever their manmade garnish: beaches that offer a vast assortment of marine pleasures, beaches where the people are more fun to watch than the fish ever were.

Some caveats: The crowds during the first 3 weeks of August, when Europe's entire population seems bent on cramming in vacation, are too much of a good thing (late June and early September are the ideal times).

Also, though you will find surf far tamer here than in America, you will also find far less in the way of skilled lifeguard protection. And though the waves are gentle, the sun is fierce: Take it in carefully measured doses and keep smearing on that fancy French suntan goo.

KNOKKE, Belgium: The North Sea has a wintry sound to it, and, indeed, the area is briskly unlike that of the balmier Mediterranean. Nonetheless, the broad beaches along the Royal Road of the Belgian coastline are beautifully kept. Swimming here, however, is not advised along much of the coast due to the contaminated waters. Knokke, in the corner by the Dutch border, is the most complete of resorts: You'll find fine cuisine, ample sports facilities, gracious garden-rimmed villas, a gambling casino, and the country's most inviting hotel, *La Réserve* — lapped about by the sea, the swimming pool, and little Victoria Lake. But there are simpler pleasures as well, among them less-developed southerly beaches such as Blankenberge and Wenduine. You can walk along the dikes and the great empty dunes, go on pony rides and ride the traditional sail carts on the beach, or take in any number of the colorful folk festivals that take place all along the coast. And, in case of a cloudy day, there is a varied choice of easy excursions: the fish market at Zeebrugge, the bird reserve at Het Zwin, the lovely old village of Damme, and beautiful, canal-crossed Bruges.

LE CAP D'AGDE, France: The ancient Greeks used to anchor their ships off this jutting promontory. And a lot of modern French prefer its wide sandy beaches and deep calm coves to the overbuilt, overrun, overpriced Côte d'Azur. Unlike the Riviera, the development of this coastline from St.-Cyprien to Port Camargue has been carefully controlled to retain its natural beauty. There are good facilities for boating and for tennis (at the *Club Pierre Barthès*) and hills nearby that offer many wonderful walks. And the surrounding region is one of France's most attractive and least visited: You can day-trip to the walled towns of Carcassonne and Aigues-Mortes, the Roman theater at Nîmes, and the horse farms of the Camargue; and, at Béziers, take in bloodless bullfights.

PORTO-VECCHIO, Corsica, France: According to our First Law of Beaches, islands have the best ones, and the best of these are the least accessible. Witness Porto-Vecchio. A 5½-mile-long bay that gives its name to the small fishing port at its head, Porto-Vecchio plunges into the eastern coast of Corsica, just opposite the side where most boats and planes arriving from the French mainland discharge their passengers. The beaches predicted by the First Law are here in force — fine-sand strands like La Marine, Golfo di Sogno, St.-Cyprien, Pinarello, and Palombaggia, which flank the port town. The vegetation is subtropical; umbrella pines and conifers peculiar to the area line the coast. Other local specialties are lobsters and nudism. For information about the latter, contact the *Syndicat d'Initiative* (Porto-Vecchio, Place Hôtel de Ville, Corsica 20137, France; phone: 95-70-09-58). For off-beach entertainment, you can fly or sail to Bonifacio, a medieval fortress town at the southern tip of the island. And from there, it's only 7½ miles by ferry to Sardinia.

THASSOS, Greece: A Greek island, but not one of *the* Greek islands, Thassos lies in the northernmost part of the country, about an hour's ferry ride off the coast of Macedonia. Cooler than its sunbaked southern cousins, Thassos is also heavily wooded and its landscape is a study in greens — the silvery sage of the olive groves, the dark greens of the towering firs. Makriammos, a few kilometers south of Limenaria, the principal town, is the island's best beach, but if you drive the circular shore road, you'll find a dozen more: Skala Panagia, Kinira, Skala Marion, Skala Sotiros, Skala Rahoniou, and others. The quiet bays of Archangelos and Aghios Ioanis are also idyllic. The tree-covered ruins of the acropolis of ancient Thassos will remind you you're in Greece. Should there be a cloudy day, you can take the ferry back to Kavala and amble around the Byzantine fortress and the Imaret, a center of the country's Muslim culture.

GULF OF MIRABELLO, Crete, Greece: Crete's choicest beaches are on either side of the town of Aghios Nikolaos, known these days as the "the Cretan Riviera," which lies at the head of this deep bay (Kólpos Mirampelou in Greek) on the far eastern end of the island. Along with the beaches are some of the island's choicest beach hotels: the *Minos Beach,* the *Mirabello,* the *Elounda Beach,* the *Elounda Gulf Villas;* their most attractive accommodations are in Cretan-style bungalows right on the beachfront. Agios Nikolaos is full of animated taverns and fish restaurants, mainly along the docks and on the banks of Voulismeni, a tiny volcanic lake. Between sunbaths, you can hire a little boat to go out to the islet of Spinalonga, where you can explore a charming Venetian castle; drive or stroll to the village of Kritsa to have an ouzo, a game of backgammon, and a look at the frescoes in its 13th-century church.

FORTE DEI MARMI, Italy: The Italian Riviera della Versilia is really like a gigantic seaside café, and the chief amusement is watching the passing (or sprawling) parade: the phalanxes of multicolored umbrellas, deck chairs, and sentry-box cabins; the fleets of pedalboats; the sippers of Campari, builders of sand castles, players of volleyball, and scantily clad waders — out more to be seen than to enjoy the warm surf. The whole expanse between the Lido di Camaiore and the bustling resort town of Viareggio is really one long marina. Patrician families from Rome, Florence, and Milan have been coming here every summer for a century, though in recent years, many of their pined and palmed seafront villas have been transformed into small hotels. Never expect romantic solitude, and remember that all of Italy vacations in August.

COSTA SMERALDA, Sardinia, Italy: In the space of only a few years, $200 million and the Aga Khan transformed a rocky, primitive wasteland between the port of Olbia and La Maddalena at Sardinia's tip into the country's most glamorous beach complex. The boulders are still there and the water is a cloudless cobalt blue, but scattered from cove to cove are four elegant hotels, cleverly designed so that they seem to have grown out of the rocks: the *Romazzino,* the *Cervo,* the *Pitrizza,* the *Cala di Volpe.* The crowd can get very fancy, particularly when the yacht fleet is in — but the sun-and-sea life is superbly simple. There are boat and air connections from several mainland cities, but remember to reserve well in advance for a midsummer visit.

LIDO, Venice, Italy: Just a reminder that while you are visiting one of the most beautiful cities in the world you can also swim, sunbathe, and eat shrimp along the Lido, a long, skinny island bordered on the east side by the sea and on the west by the Venetian lagoon, just a 15-minute boat ride from downtown Venice. There is golf, tennis, horseback riding, boating, and plenty of beach life on the wide strands (some of them public, and some — immaculately groomed — the private reserves of the great seafront hotels, which sometimes can be used by non-guests for a hefty fee). When you've had enough of the sun, take the *vaporetto* back to the center of town for a stroll along the Venetian canals or to sip an *aperitivo* in the Piazza San Marco. Reserve accommodations well ahead for September, when visitors flock to see the *Venice Film Festival;* the antique gondola regatta, the *Feast of the Redemptor;* and every 2 years, the international art festival, *Il Biennale di Venezia.*

PRAIA DE ROCHA, Portugal: Some of Europe's finest beaches are along a 62-mile stretch of Portuguese coastline, between Faro and the Sagres promontory in the country's southernmost province, the Algarve. The strands face south toward Africa, and both the air and the water stay temperate most of the year. The heavy development that the area has undergone in recent years has taken its toll on the coast's raw natural beauty, but, in exchange, has provided it with an array of fine shorefront hotels: the *Algarve* at Praia de Rocha, the *Golf da Penina* at Penina, and the *Alvor Praia* at Prainha, to name just a few. Praia de Rocha has a beige yellow beach set against craggy red cliffs that erosion has sculpted into strange, exotic shapes: Rock spires, arches, and hollows make a kind of natural labyrinth on the sand. In the old fortress of St. Catherine, there is a good seafood restaurant (grilled sardines and *vinho verde* are local specialties) and stunning lookout point; the nearby port of Portimão gets a steady traffic of colorful fishing craft.

MAMAIA, Romania: The Black Sea is one of those bodies of water that Americans learn about in geography class, but never consider for swimming. Yet the Romanian and Bulgarian Black Sea coasts are to Eastern Europe what the Riviera is to France. Dr. Ana Aslan's discovery of the supposed wonder drug Gerovital has attracted a score of health-cure seekers to Romania. But there's still an immense gap between Techirghiol and St.-Tropez. Mamaia, a 5-mile strip of beach and rich vegetation between the Black Sea and Lake Siutghiol, offers a wide choice of hotels that — though the architecture is uniformly Moscow Modern — boast rooms and facilities fully as satisfactory as those of their Western counterparts. The crowd is international (with a preponderance of Eastern Europeans), and the nightlife and sports facilities are as abundant and varied as in the West — but prices are quite reasonable, and there's a refreshing plenitude of rustic Romanian restaurants serving wines and meals you'd never in an eon encounter in the Hamptons.

FORMENTOR, Majorca, Spain: First find the Balearic Islands, three and a half clumps of land about 100 miles off the eastern coast of Spain. The largest clump is Majorca; the thin tongue of land that runs off the top is Cape Formentor. Though honky-tonk Palma de Mallorca, its urbanized beaches, and its tour-bus traffic jams may mar the idyllic green countryside, the almond groves and wildflowers and the high shoreline cliffs that you see as you make the 40-mile (64-km) drive north from the capital to Formentor will give you entirely different feelings. Formentor's beaches — and those of Cala de San Vincente — are superb, and so is the *Formentor* hotel, surrounded by pine woods and looking majestically toward the sea, the bay, the mountains, the rust-colored bluffs. The cape ends with a dramatically positioned lighthouse. Not far away is the village of Puerto de Pollensa, where you can ingest a bowl of seafood stew and an *ensaimada* (the Majorcan pastry specialty), take a boat ride on the bay, and have a look at the hilltop Notre Dame de Puig.

DUBROVNIK, Yugoslavia: Far down the Dalmatian coast, not far from the Albanian border, this walled and turreted city is one of Europe's best preserved and most captivating — and it would be worth a visit even if it were in the middle of a desert. Instead, it juts out dramatically into the gleaming blue Adriatic. Inside the medieval walls is a collection of fine Renaissance palaces and churches, many dating from the great period of Venetian domination of the sea. The feeling of antiquity is heightened by the absence of cars and there's a wide flagstone main promenade that teems with life in summer, especially in July and August during a 6-week music festival. Out on both sides of the town are the beaches — long and bright, some of sand and others of scrubbed white pebbles; just across from the port is the tiny island of Lokrum, a wooded national park with fine swimming and skin diving and, hidden among the pines, a splendid outdoor restaurant installed in an ancient structure that began its life as a monastery. Big ferries, tiny dinghies, and just about any other kind of boat you can name putter up and down the coast in season, and you have a choice of a variety of maritime excursions from an hour's fishing offshore to a weekend cruise to Venice.

CLUB MED: *Club Med* isn't really a club at all, but a chain of over 100 vacation villages sited strategically on some of the most pleasurable parts of the planet. The idea started in France, and the head office is in Paris — but the clientele is, by now, thoroughly international. Guests usually are on the young side and interested in active vacations. There's always a variety of sports to enjoy, everything from judo to water skiing, and a *Club Med* vacation can be an exceptionally good deal for those who take advantage of the activities, because there's no extra charge. But the *Club's* settings are protected and beautifully landscaped and friendly (like a summer camp for big kids) and the outside world is kept at a distance, so you can enjoy yourself just as much if you do nothing more active than snooze in the sun. Accommodation at the *Club's* beach and seaside villages is usually in attractive, functional bungalows, and there are communal dining facilities. Two of the best *Clubs* for beach life include one in Pakostane in Yugoslavia and another on Corfu in Greece. You can get a complete list and information from the US office: *Club Med*, 3 E. 54th St., New York, NY 10022 (phone: 800-CLUB-MED or 212-977-2100).

The European Mountain Experience

Maybe Europe's mountains will look like its beaches in another decade, with vacationers climbing shoulder to shoulder past little men hawking alpenstocks and chocolate bars on each peak. But at least for now, the mountain country — often no more than a morning's drive from subways and stock exchanges — is still a wilderness paradise and has something to offer both pick-and-crampon types bound to scale the murderous North Wall of the Eiger and weekend enthusiasts accustomed to nothing more strenuous than strolls in the Vienna Woods.

There is a sense of good fellowship in the mountains: While beach people more often than not resent each other's territorial encroachment, mountain people share a sense of physical accomplishment that makes the trails and the Alpine huts very friendly places to be.

Though mountains are mountains — dangerous if you don't know what you're about — the Alps are for the most part as accommodating as the Continent itself. Europeans are great hikers, and there are miles and miles of well-marked trails. Most good European mountain areas are also liberally scattered with huts and refuges where climbers can get meals that, at the end of a day on the trail, taste better than a banquet at *Maxim's* and bunk on a mattress that feels as good as any at the *Ritz*. When the sun goes down, there's usually plenty of mulled wine and lusty singing. Many hikers spend weeks just trekking from one hut to the next. Some areas, especially in Teutonic countries, are so geared to entertaining hikers that they hand out small cards listing all the main huts, each of which is provided with a rubber stamp so that you can brand your card in the appropriate space. The goal is to end up with a stamp after the name of every hut on the card.

Whether you go out walking for a week or just a day, there are some precautions to observe. You don't have to outfit yourself for the conquest of Everest on your first stroll, but stout boots will certainly enhance the experience and a knapsack will come in handy. In it you should stuff a pocket flashlight and — no matter how hot the sun and cloudless the sky when you embark — a lightweight rain parka and a sweater. Alpine weather is enormously capricious and you can easily experience four seasons in a day. If you'll be out longer than that, you may want to bring a good long book. (Picking an area where excursions to the valleys are a possibility is a good idea if you're easily daunted by rain.)

And don't fail to buy a good map before you set out; take it to the local tourist office to find out about the relative hazards and pleasures of the local trails. Never start out knowing nothing. Be sure to tell someone where you're headed, and plan to be at your destination well before dark.

Here we've assembled a list of areas that will provide you with the most satisfying mountain experiences. Each item is keyed according to the activities you can enjoy there: Rambling (**R**), on walking paths that are easy enough to be pleasurable to children and beginning hikers; Trudging (**T**), on longer and steeper trails that will challenge intermediate hikers and adults; and Dangling (**D**), rope-and-crampon mountain goat stuff, suitable for trained climbers.

GROSSGLOCKNER and GROSSVENEDIGER, Austria: Austria's two star peaks both rise out of craggy ranges that offer a mountaineer's paradise of challenging climbs. The graves in the little mountain cemetery in the churchyard of Kals are grisly reminders of the perils of the Glockner, the tougher of the two. Experts can commence the ascent to its peak and to Grossvenediger's summit from a number of well-placed refuges throughout the area. For everyone else, there are *hütte*-to-*hütte* hikes that last several days and cover some of the Alps' most dramatic terrain. For information: *Tiroler Fremdenverkehrswerbung,* 6 Bozner Platz, Innsbruck A-6010, Austria (phone: 512-5320); or *Fremdenverkehrsbüro,* 90 Postfach, Lienz 9900, Austria (phone: 4852-4747). A good way to make either climb is under the auspices of the *Hochgebirgsschule Tyrol,* an Innsbruck climbing school and guide operation. To find out more, contact *Hochgebirgsschule Tyrol,* 3 Kaiser Josef-strasse, Innrain 67, Innsbruck A-6020, Austria (phone: 512-228900). **T, D**

OBERGURGL, Austria: On a wide, sunny plain at 6,560 feet in the middle of the Otztaler Alps, this town — one of the highest in Europe — offers a choice of accommodations that range from luxury hotels to simple wooden chalets, and the surrounding mountains are dotted with *hüttes* — refuges where hikers can find simple food and shelter. A great ring of glaciers and towering peaks and an abundance of high Alpine flora make for startling scenery, which can be seen from afar along easy trails a half hour from town, or conquered if you have the inclination and the skill. Obergurgl is a ski resort in winter; the town of Vent, on the other side of the Ramolkogl, is quieter and far less developed. It is also the jumping-off point for the ascent of the 12,464-foot Wildspitze. For information about instruction and guided climbs: *Hochgebirgsschule Obergurgl,* Haus Schönblick, Obergurgl 53, Tyrol A-6456, Austria (phone: 525-6251). **R, T**

HIGH TATRAS, Czechoslovakia: Like most of Eastern Europe, this magnificent mountain district is generally overlooked by Americans, though the resort areas are less developed and less expensive than their Western cousins. There is also a century-old tradition of climbing and a well-maintained network of huts and hotels. Starý Smokovec (3,280 feet), Strbske Pleso (4,428 feet), and Tatranská Lomnica (2,788 feet) are the main starting points for area excursions. The *Patria* hotel at Popradské Pleso (4,920 feet) is right by the lake, and is a fine springboard for trips into the popular Pic Rysy group. The *Sliezsky Dom,* a comfortable, modern hotel at 5,576 feet, has easy access to the Gerlachovský Stít and the whole Tatra range. Among the best high *chata* (mountain huts) are the *Zbojnícka,* the *Terryho,* the *Iames Pod Solískom,* and the *Pod Rysmi,* which at 7,380 feet is the highest *chata* in Czechoslovakia. Information: *Cedok,* 18 Na Příkopě, Prague 111 35, Czechoslovakia (phone: 212-7111); or *Cedok, (Czechoslovakia Travel Bureau)* 10 E. 40th St., New York, NY 10016 (phone: 212-689-9720). **R, T**

CUMBRIA and LANCASHIRE, England: From April through October, fell-walking and rock-climbing are favorite sports among the crags and crests of the Lake District counties, but it's certainly more Albion than Alpine. Centers for guided jaunts, rock-climbing courses, wildlife observation, and bird watching are *Footpath Holidays* (4 Holly Walk, Andover, Hampshire SP10 3PJ, England; phone: 264-352689); *English Wanderer* (13 Wellington Court, Spencers Wood, Reading RG7 1BN, England; phone: 734-882515). For more information on walking in Britain: *British Tourist Authority,* Thames Tower, Black's Road, Hammersmith, London W6 9EL, England (phone: 81-846-9000). **R, T**

MONT-BLANC, France and Italy: Though the highest mountain in the Alps is now pierced by a two-country tunnel that eliminates the need to climb over its majestic summit, it still provides some of the most challenging mountaineering in Europe. Chamonix — a classy ski resort town that attracts everyone from sun-deck loungers to helmeted, pick-toting rock climbers — is the principal center on the French side; the world-famous *Compagnie des Guides* (Maison de la Montagne, 190 Pl. de l'Eglise, Chamonix 74400, France; phone: 50-53-00-88) is the best source of information and assistance. Courmayeur, on the Italian side, basks in a great natural amphitheater bisected by the Dora River and sprinkled with picture-postcard Alpine hamlets. In summer, horseback riding through the valleys is popular. For details: *Azienda di Soggiorno,* Piazzale Monte Bianco, Courmayeur, Italy (phone: 165-842060). If the taming of Mont-Blanc by tunnel and cable car takes the romance out of the mountain for you, try going farther afield in the Valle d'Aosta to lesser-known centers like Paquier, Valtournenches, Cogne, and Valsavaranche in the Gran Paradiso National Park. For information on the whole area: *Ufficio Informazioni Turistiche della Valle d'Aosta,* 8 Piazza E. Chanoux, Aosta, Italy (phone: 165-35655). **R, T, D**

DOLOMITES, Italy: The hard hiking in this vast range south of the Brenner Pass — long a favorite region of expert and experienced climbers — has remained largely uncharted. The jagged brownish peaks of dolomitic rock, more dramatic still than the gray granite of the Alps, rise like giant, rusty, pink fangs above smooth snow meadows, forming one of the most awesome natural sights in Europe. If you ever cross the Sella, the Falzarego, the Pordoi, and the Pellegrino passes under a full moon, the rest of your life may seem anticlimactic. Cortina d'Ampezzo — a former site of the *Winter Olympics* and now a favorite summer resort of affluent Italians from the flatlands — is the classiest of a number of towns in the four Ladino valleys that are perfect places to begin mountain rambles; Corvara, Ortisei, and Canazei are equally beautiful and just as well placed. And because a large chunk of the Dolomites once belonged to Austria, the atmosphere in all these towns echoes the Teutonic era. The Marmolada and the Gruppo Sella are the major peaks, but there are dozens more. For information: *Azienda di Promozione Turistica,* 21 Via Pesaro, Belluno, Italy (phone: 437-970660); *Azienda di Soggiorno e Turismo,* 8 Piazza Walther, Bolzano, Italy (phone: 471-975656); *Azienda Autonoma per il Turismo,* 4 Via Alfieri, Trento, Italy (phone: 461-980000). **R, T, D**

MATTERHORN and MONTE ROSA, Switzerland: The car-free town of Zermatt, accessible only by railway, offers access to a dozen peaks of the "4,000 Club" — a sobriquet that refers to those mountain peaks over 4,000 meters (13,120 feet) high — representing five of the six highest mountains in Europe. If you don't want to be bothered with the Andes or the Himalayas this year, this area of the Swiss Alps will provide nine lives' worth of advanced climbing. The *High Alpine School,* which runs summer courses for experts, also can supply guides — advisable on these treacherous trails no matter how many times you have hopped up Mt. McKinley. Information: *Bergführerverein,* Zermatt 3920, Switzerland (phone: 28-673456); and *Verkehrsverein,* Zermatt 3920, Switzerland (phone: 28-661181). **D**

PONTRESINA, Switzerland: The Swiss take even their strolling seriously, and scores of footpaths are scrupulously marked by destination and estimated hiking time. That is especially true in the glorious Engadine Valley — one of those places that has everything for everybody. The 4.3-mile walk from Alp Languard to Muottas Muragl is a novice's dream: High but level, it offers spectacular vistas of the Engadine lakes and the whole Bernina Range. The area is also supplied with Alpine gardens and a game reserve, a choice of chair lifts and railways so that you can start your tour up high, plus huts with panoramic views, where you can savor three-star lunches. For experts, there's plenty of ice and rock climbing on the Piz Palu; and some of the most exciting climbing in Switzerland is on the 13,120-foot Piz Bernina. The fine *Mountain School* has a large team of expert guides and offers a variety of courses for aspiring mountaineers. Information: *Schweizer Bergsteigerschule,* Chesa Hotel Engadinerhof, Pontresina CH-7504, Switzerland (phone: 82-66444); and *Kur und Verkehrsverein,* Pontresina CH-7504, Switzerland (phone: 82-66488). **R, T, D**

STRADA ALTA LEVENTINA, Switzerland: Much to the delight of Alpine hikers, the Swiss government (which is never neutral about nature) has refurbished the old St.

Gotthard High Road, a medieval mule track and pilgrim's way. The whole trail, which runs 27.9 miles, makes a comfortable 3-day excursion, and there's plenty of fine food and comfortable shelter along the way. You start from Airolo, 3,772 feet, and on the first day travel via Brugnasco, Cresta, and Lurengo to Osco. The second day, you pass through Targuel, Rossura, Sorsello, Gianón, and Anzonico; and on the third day through Segno, Sobrio, Diganengo, and Pollegio Biasca. Just follow the red and white signs. Information: *Ente Turistico di Leventina,* Faido 6760, Switzerland (phone: 94-381616); or *Swiss National Tourist Office,* 608 Fifth Ave., New York, NY 10020 (phone: 212-757-5944). **R**

Going for Game:
Hunting and Fishing

With the growth of the "Green" environmental movement in Europe, fishing and hunting aren't the wide-open free-for-alls that they once were. Nevertheless, the possibilities for pursuing these sports are rich and extensive. From the Scottish Highlands to Poland's Mazur Lakes, from the Tatra Mountains of Czechoslovakia to the coasts of Brittany, there is an abundance of wildlife — often in spectacular settings.

THE HUNT

In the last 10 years, seasons have been shortened and are more rigorously observed. At the same time license costs have risen sharply: In Greece, for example, a 15-day hunting permit that cost $25 not long ago now sells for over $150. In some countries — Germany, Belgium, and Holland among them — you can hunt only as the guest of the owner of a private game reserve. (Foreigners may make contact through sporting magazines and clubs, but hired hospitality has a hefty price tag.)

Here are some of your best bets for unparalleled European hunting adventures.

ZIDLOCHOVICE, Southern Moravia, Czechoslovakia: This Eastern European country, practically one giant game reserve, offers some of the finest hunting in Europe; the pheasant preserve at Zidlochovice, near Brno, is one of its unique and richest areas, attracting hunters from all over the Continent by the hundreds every autumn. Northern Moravia also has two excellent reserves in the Jeseniky and Beskydy districts. For information: *Cedok-Lovy,* 18 Na Příkopě, Prague, Czechoslovakia (phone: 2-212-71111); or *Cedok (Czechoslovakia Travel Bureau),* 10 E. 40th St., New York, NY 10016 (phone: 212-689-9720). Prague, incidentally, has a number of specialty shops where you can buy excellent hunting equipment.

WEST COUNTRY, England: When the English say "hunting" they mean on horseback, with hounds; it is an activity as British as taking high tea. Two hotels in Devon specialize in arranging hunting for their guests: the *Crown* (Exford, Somerset, England; phone: 64-383-5545), and the *Arundell Arms* (Lifton, Devon, England; phone: 566-84666). You will surely need to be a proficient horseman to keep up with the Tallyho-Joneses. The *Arundell Arms* also arranges deer stalking and pheasant shooting, but its real specialty is fishing: The hotel has reserved rights to 20 miles of the Taymar River and its tributaries for salmon and trout fishing; the hotel also has its own well-stocked lake, as well as a fishing school where guests can receive instructions from local professionals. For information on hunting and shooting in Britain, contact: *British*

Tourist Authority, 40 W. 57th St., New York, NY 10019 (phone: 212-581-4700); or *British Field Sports Society,* 59 Kennington Rd., London SE1, England (phone: 71-928-4742).

CRETE, Greece: Quail and partridge hunting is a special experience in the wild and primitive parts of the island of Dia, across from Herakleion, but a far cry from the busy north shore beaches. This terrain is typical of the savage regions that served partisans so well during the island's German occupation. You will need a guide. The season begins on September 15 and lasts until the end of November. Hare and rabbit until the end of January. For more information: *Greek National Tourist Organization,* 1 Xanthoudidou, Herakleion, Crete, Greece (phone: 228203); or the *Forestry Office,* Dassarchio, 22 Iraklion Dedalou St., Herakleion, Crete, Greece (phone: 282776).

HIGHLANDS, Scotland: August 12, the "Glorious Twelfth," is the opening day of the 4-month grouse season, a national ceremony of sorts that takes place annually inside the triangle determined by Aberdeen, Perth, and Inverness. Braemar, Ballater, and Aboyne are among the more colorful spots. Hunters in the area also stalk roe, fallow, sika, and red deer at this time of year. The list of Scottish hotels that arrange for both grouse-shooting and deer-hunting expeditions for their guests includes *Raemoir House,* Banchory, Kincardineshire (phone: 3302-4884); *Kinloch House,* near Blairgowrie, Perthshire (phone: 250-84237); and *Knockie Lodge,* Whitebridge, Inverness-shire (phone: 463-923276). Contact them well in advance (before *Christmas* to participate the following summer), since you may need to write directly to the estates with hunting grounds. See if you can arrange to be there for one of the gatherings of the clans, Scottish ceremonies that also enliven the Highlands. For detailed information: *Highlands and Islands Enterprise,* Bridge House, 20 Bridge St., Inverness IV1 1QR, Scotland (phone: 463-234171).

COTOS OF THE PYRENEES, Spain: Under the administration of its National Institute for the Conservation of Nature, Spain has an extensive network of *cotos* — national hunting reserves. A number of the choices are clustered in the Pyrenees: Alto Pallars, Arán, Los Circos, Fresser, Cadí, Cerdaña, Vall Ferrera. Wild boar are profuse, and the Spanish specialize in tracking these harvest-plunderers; chamois, deer, roebuck, and grouse are also taken in the October to January season. Most big hunting areas have their *paradores* — picturesque state-run country inns and hotels. All foreigners planning to hunt in Spain should contact: *Administración Turística Española,* Sección de Caza, 25 Calle Velásquez, Madrid, Spain (phone: 1-435-6641). More information: *Federación Española de Caza* (National Hunting Federation), 53 Avenida Reina Victoria, Madrid 28006, Spain (phone: 1-253-3495); or travel agencies that specialize in hunting trips, such as *Cacerías Conde,* 7 Princesa, Madrid, Spain (phone: 1-247-1804); or *Promoción de Caza y Pesca,* 41 Duque de Sexto, Madrid, Spain (phone: 1-276-3661).

NOVI SAD, Vojvodina, Yugoslavia: The fertile wooded Vojvodine, north of Belgrade, is the nation's least exploited tourist area — and its richest hunting land. Near Novi Sad and the banks of the Danube, the Odzaci, Karavukovo, Bagremara, and Ristovaca reserves shelter a superabundance of wild hare, pheasant, and partridge. Information: *Lovoturs,* 26 Dr. Salvadora Aljendea, Novi Sad 21000, Yugoslavia (phone: 21-331277); and the *Yugoslav National Tourist Office,* Rockefeller Center, Suite 280, 630 Fifth Ave., New York, NY 10111 (phone: 212-757-2801).

FISHING HOLES

The best of Europe's fishing is some of the best on the planet. There are swordfish on the Costa Cantábrica in Spain, and carp and pike on Poland's Mazur lakes. The beaches of Brittany in France make for superb surfcasting. Britain lures anglers with the proximity of ancient hotels and quaint inns to its best fishing streams. (The booklet called *BTA Commended Country Hotels,* available from the *British Tourist Authority,*

40 W. 57th St., New York, NY 10019; phone: 212-581-4700, can provide the details.) Ireland is overflowing with hotels that offer summer fishing courses, and cater to novices as well as longtime fly-tiers. The *Irish Tourist Board* (757 Third Ave., New York, NY 10017; phone: 212-418-0800) can tell you more. Even the cities have their contributions: There's hardly a better way to spend a lazy Sunday than angling in the Belgian canals at Damme, near Bruges.

Here are some of the Old World's most celebrated fishing spots — worth every bit of the traveling you'll have to do to experience them.

  MARIAGER FJORD-KATTEGAT, Denmark: Fishing boats leave regularly from the fjord's three main towns — Hobro, Mariager, and Hadsund — to make for the open sea of the Kattegat, where cod, flounder, mackerel, sea trout, and plaice can be hauled out in an abundance as satisfying as the good fellowship aboard the ship. Information: *Turistbureauet* (Office of Tourism), 26 Adelgade, Hobro DK-9500, Denmark (phone: 98-525666). Other fine fjords for fishing are Roskildefjord, just west of Copenhagen, and Limfjorden, up north in Himmerland on Jutland. Information about Roskildefjord: the *Office of Tourism,* 3 Fondens Bro, Box 278, Roskilde DK-4000, Denmark (phone: 42-352700); or the *Office of Tourism,* 10 Tværstraede, Frederikssund DK-3600, Denmark (phone: 42-310685). Information about the Limfjorden: the *Office of Tourism,* 4 Havnen, Nykøbing Mors DK-7900, Denmark (phone: 97-720488). For general information: *Scandinavian Tourist Boards,* 655 Third Ave., New York, NY 10017 (phone: 212-949-2333).

  ITCHEN and TEST RIVERS, near Nether Wallop, Hampshire, England: For the outsider, topnotch fishing can be hard to find in Izaak Walton's home country: Most of the fishing rights to the best streams are controlled by associations and private citizens. However, there are also many country hotels that own equally productive fishing waters, and these establishments are British institutions. The Test River is a carefully managed, world-famous stream stocked with special fast-growing brown and rainbow trout. Information: *Southern Water Authority,* Southern House, Yeoman Rd., Worthing, West Sussex BN13 3NX, England (phone: 903-64444). In the same district, there is exceptional angling on a number of local rivers (practically in the shadow of Winchester Cathedral and Izaak Walton's burial place). The celebrated Itchen produces small, extra-wily wild trout; wild and unspoiled Itchen feeder streams are spring fed and good for large and exceptionally active trophy fish. Other well-known streams in the area include the Avon, the Derwent, the Dove (where Walton fished), the Eden, the Kennet, the Lune, the Ribble, and the Wharfe. They're all clear, fast flowing, and, because of their origins in Britain's chalk hills, highly alkaline; conditions, in other words, are ideal for nurturing big native brown trout that rise freely even when they reach 4 pounds or more. The British Tourist Authority's booklet *Commended Country Hotels,* cited above, provides information on a number of pleasant inns in the area. One of the best resources is *Orvis,* the well-known US fishing firm and school, near Stockbridge, Hampshire (phone: 264-781212; in the US, *Orvis,* Historic Rte. 7A, Manchester, VT 05254; phone: 802-362-3622). They run a fly-fishing school and own "beats" on both chalk streams.

  CORSICA, France: The fish that teem beneath the transparent blue water surrounding this Mediterranean island are even more varied and abundant than the sunbaked bathers who populate its sandy beaches. For information on lining up a seagoing craft and the necessary equipment for scuba diving and underwater fishing, contact the tourist office in each seaside town. Scuba diving clubs in each area will help too. Inland, trout and salmon fishing in lakes and streams can be arranged from nearby inns and farmhouses. Information: *CRT de Corse,* 17 Bd. Roi-Jérôme, BP 19, Ajaccio 20176, Corsica, France (phone: 95-21-56-56).

  LAKE CONSTANCE, Germany: One of the great lakes of Europe, the lovely Bodensee, as this body of water is called in German, is filled with a dozen different kinds of fish, including the prized *forelle* (trout). Ample facilities for boat hire are available both in Switzerland and in Germany (both of which touch the lake's shoreline); picturesque Lindau, a medieval German town on an island connected by bridge to the mainland, is a good place to base yourself. Information: *Lake Constance Tourist Office,* 8 Schützenstr., Konstanz D-7750, Germany (phone: 7531-24024).

CONNEMARA FISHERIES, Connemara, Ireland: Irish game fishing waters, among the finest in Europe, provide excellent and varied salmon and trout fishing on rivers and lakes, which are the cleanest in the European Community because of the Gulf Stream influence. The season opens as early as January 1, and the closing date is September 30 or October 12, depending upon the region. Some of the finest fishing opportunities are in the remote vastness of Connemara, which offers salmon and sea trout. An association of Irish fishery owners organizes bookings through the *Western Game Fishing Association.* Information: *Western Game Fishing Association* c/o Peter Mantle, Delphi Lodge, Connemara, County Galway, Ireland; or *Bord Failte* (Irish Tourist Board), Baggot Street Bridge, Dublin 2, Ireland (phone: 1-765871; fax: 1-764764).

BLACKWATER RIVER, near Youghal, Ireland: One of Ireland's most famous salmon rivers, rising near the border of Cork and Kerry, the Blackwater takes in 85 miles of long glides and deep pools. Salmon above 20 pounds are sometimes taken in the upper reaches; sea trout are taken lower down, closer to Youghal, where the river empties into the sea. Brown trout, weighing in at an average of about a half pound each, are fairly active on both wet and dry flies on the upper portion. Information: *Southern Fisheries Board,* Anglesea St., Clonmel, County Tipperary, Ireland (phone: 52-23971); or *Bord Failte* (see above).

SHANNON RIVER, Ireland: The 240-mile-long Shannon, the longest river in all of Britain and Ireland, drains a fifth of Ireland (about 6,060 square miles); its tributaries are 1,130 miles in length. It is slow moving, punctuated by numerous large lakes, and, for coarse fish (as bream, rudd, pike, perch, tench, and rudd/bream hybrids are collectively known), the Shannon has few equals anywhere; when the fish are biting, a catch of over a hundred pounds (mostly bream) is not unusual. On the Upper Shannon — that is, from the source to Athlone — Carrick-on-Shannon in County Leitrim is one of the best-organized fishing centers, and Strokestown, in County Roscommon, is a favorite destination of specimen rudd hunters. Particularly exciting lakes include Ree, which shelters all varieties of coarse fish; Lough Allen, which offers the best northern pike angling in all of Europe; and Lough Patrick, where two anglers once caught over 500 pounds of tench in one legendary session. On the Lower Shannon, Lough Derg is productive for pike, and the Plassey River — as the Shannon is called where it flows by Limerick City — is a coarse fisherman's dream. The Clare Lakelands, centered on the village of Tulla, are a must for the serious angler looking for a quiet vacation. Information: *Bord Failte* (above).

TROMS COUNTY, Norway: This is a place for serious fishermen to settle in for a month — or a summer. A hundred different rivers and watercourses, churning across a wild landscape, teem with salmon, sea trout, and sea char. You can fish in the lakes as well or in the saltwater fjords. June to early September is the season. The *International Sea Fishing Festival,* which includes 3 days of competition, takes place every mid-July in Harstad. Information: *Harstad Tourist Office,* 7C Torvet, Box 447, Harstad N-9401, Norway (phone: 82-63235); or the *Scandinavian Tourist Boards,* 655 Third Ave., New York, NY 10017 (phone: 212-949-2333. The book *Angling in Norway,* available from Arthur Vanus, PO Box 650279, Vero Beach, FL 32965, for $15, is detailed and helpful.) The *Fly-spesialisten Reisebyrå,* 1 Kronprinsesse Märthas Pl., Oslo N-0160, Norway (phone: 2-413870), specializes in setting up and booking salmon fishing trips and boat rentals.

Wild Europe

The air of the cities is sadly polluted, and the great monuments are crusted over with the grime of progress. Cement spreads along the seashores and through the countryside; crowds throng the museums, the ski slopes, and the beaches; and the seas are, it sometimes seems, increasingly stained with oil. But there are still places in Europe where times haven't changed: forests that are still dark and silent; Mediterranean coves that are still deserted; country roads that are still only dirt; high mountain paths where you can walk for hours without meeting another soul — or encountering a chewing gum wrapper. Germany's Wildpark Altenfelden-Mühltal; the plains of the Puszta and the great horse-farming area of Hungary; Italy's National Park of Abruzzo; and Krkonoše, Czechoslovakia's Mountain of the Giants National Park, are only a few examples.

To get away from it all, take a steamer along the Norwegian coast, traveling a silken black sea to the northernmost settlements in the world, past fjords and icebergs, past colonies of marine birds and the occasional whale. The hardy boats travel 365 days a year. Information: *Scandinavian Tourist Boards,* 655 Third Ave., New York, NY 10017 (phone: 212-949-2333), or *Bergen Line,* the general sales agent, 505 Fifth Ave., New York, NY 10017 (phone: 212-986-2711 or 800-323-7436; 800-666-2374 to request brochures; fax: 212-983-1275).

Or you can go bird watching in Scotland's Caerlaverock refuge, from September through April. Information: *Tourist Information Centre,* Whitesands, Dunfries, Scotland (phone: 387-53862).

In Greenland you can go on dogsled expeditions and drive with hunters and dogs across frozen fjords and lakes and through mountain passes to tiny hunting settlements. Information: *Ilulissat Tourist Office,* Box 272, Ilulissat DK-3952, Denmark (phone: 299-43222); or the *Greenland Tourist Service,* Box 1139, DK-1010 Copenhagen K, Denmark (phone: 33-136975).

Or, in France, you can take bicycle tours through the château-dotted Loire Valley. Information: *Fédération Française de Cyclotourisme,* 8 Rue Jean-Marie-Jégo, Paris 75013, France (phone: 45-80-30-21). Or the *Bicyclub de France,* 8 Pl. de la Porte de Champerret, Paris 75017, France (phone: 42-27-28-82).

You can even sit around on an empty beach in the altogether: There are scores of places for that, among them the sunny coast of Corsica, near San Nicolao or Porto-Vecchio. For details, contact the *CRT de Corse,* 17 Bd. Roi-Jérôme, Ajaccio BP 19 20176, Corsica, France (phone: 95-21-56-56); or the *Fédération Française de Naturisme,* 53 Rue Chaussée d'Antin, Paris 75009, France (phone: 42-80-05-21).

And that's only the beginning. Here are some more ideas for taking a walk on the wild side of Europe.

ARDENNES, Belgium: These deep, mysterious forests flanking the River Meuse, the picturesque valleys, and the lacy network of sparkling streams haven't changed all that much since Shakespeare wrote about them as the idyllic Forest of Arden in *As You Like It.* The manmade attractions are equally unspoiled: Dinant and Durbuy are the quaintest of villages; and the castles at Bouillon, Annevoie, and Spontin look like models for fairy-tale illustrations. You can explore underground grottoes at Han-sur-Lesse and Remouchamps or paddle a kayak down the Lesse or the Amblève, flanked by wild high cliffs. Namur is a good base of operations. For information: *Fédération du Tourisme de la Province de Namur,* 3 Rue Notre-Dame, Namur B-5000, Belgium (phone: 81-222998); or the *Belgian Tourist Office,* 745 Fifth Ave., New York, NY 10151 (phone: 212-758-8130).

CAMARGUE, France: A marshy triangle on the southern coast, bounded by the two branches of the Rhone and the sea, the Camargue is the closest thing in Europe to the Wild West: On some 50 *manades,* or ranches, cowboys called *gardians* ride herd on black bulls and wild white horses, who thunder across the swampy plains and salt flats and startle hundreds of pink-winged flamingoes into flight over the Etang de Vaccarès, the largest sanctuary of its kind in Europe. In Arles, the nearest large town, the bulls of the Camargue do bloodless combat in an ancient Roman amphitheater. And a little sea village called Stes.-Maries-de-la-Mer is the destination of a pilgrimage of Gypsies from all over Europe every May 24 and 25. Information: *Syndicat d'Initiative d'Arles,* Esplanade Charles de Gaulle, Blvd. de Lices, Arles 13200, France (phone: 90-96-29-35); and *Parc de la Camargue,* Le Mas du Pont-de-Rousty, Arles 13200, France (phone: 90-97-10-40).

NATIONAL PARK OF THE PYRENEES, France: A mountain range rising as high as the 10,820-foot summit of Mt. Vignemale, the Pyrenees are one of the wildest of Europe's uncharted landscapes; this national park, established in 1967 by the French government, covers a huge area extending from Mt. Lariste to Port Vieux and makes a common boundary on the south with the Spanish National Park of Ordesa. The French park teems with exotic wildlife, including brown bears, ibex, chamois, griffon, and the rare lammergeier, with its huge 9-foot wing span. There are information centers at Arrens, Cauterets, and Arundy, and a well-maintained network of high mountain refuges. Information: *Parc National des Pyrénées,* 59 Rte. de Pau, BP 300, Tarbes 65000, France (phone: 62-93-30-60).

WALES, Great Britain: The Pembrokeshire Coast National Park, extending from Amroth to Cardigan, takes in a breathtaking 150 miles of rocky cliffs, remote bays, sandy inlets, wild headlands, and, offshore, tranquil islets. You can walk the length of the coastline on a marked footpath. Or, to the north, explore Snowdonia National Park's 1,000 square miles of rugged mountains and moors, limpid lakes, and rolling green countryside speckled with hewn-stone hamlets. You'll want to see the Gower Peninsula, the Mawddach Estuary, and the great monolithic castles of Caernarfon, Caerphilly, Conwy, Harlech, and take one of Wales's eight narrow-gauge steam railways. (Try Llanberis to the summit of Mt. Snowdon.) Go pony trekking in Brecon Beacons National Park. And see if you can llearne just thryye llyttle wyrdds of ancient Welsh. Information: *Cardiff Tourist Information Centre,* 8-14 Bridge St., Cardiff, CF1 2EE, Wales (phone: 222-227281). Ask for leaflets on local walking tours (hundreds of different routes) and guides to accommodations in farmhouses, country inns, and campsites.

IOS, Greece: One of the outermost of the Cyclades island group, Homer's reported burial place, and a pirates' lair, Ios has the dazzling Aegean beauty of its sister islands Mykonos and Paros, but 50 years' less development. Gleaming white churches and chapels and windmills perch on rolling green hills high above secluded, sand-rimmed bays. There's a sleepy harbor village, a fine bathing beach in Milokotos Bay, the remains of a temple of Apollo at Psathi. Life is very simple. Information: *Greek National Tourist Organization,* 645 Fifth Ave., New York, NY 10022 (phone: 212-421-5777). For hotel reservations: *Hellenic Chamber of Hotels,* 6 Aristidou St., Athens, Greece (phone: 1-323-6962).

FINNMARK COUNTY, Norway: The northernmost province of the northernmost country in Europe, Finnmark is well above the Arctic Circle and even shares an odd 100-mile border with the top of Russia; though temperatures rise in summer to a temperate 86F (30C), they sometimes plunge in winter to a glacial −60F (−51C). Yet it is a beautiful land, full of peaceful fishing villages, great fjords, vast snowfields that you can cross on sleds, craggy cliffs teeming with wild birds. The Alta may be the best salmon river in the world. Go in midsummer, when the days are warm and the sun never drops below the horizon; or at *Easter* when, following a picturesque age-old custom, the Lapps who tend the country's 130,000 reindeer drive the animals down to the seacoast. Information: *Finnmark Tourist Board,* Postboks 1223, Alta N-9501, Norway (phone: 84-35041).

PUSZCZA BIAŁOWIESKA, Poland: One of the last strongholds of the majestic bison, this deep wilderness — the largest forest area in central Europe — also shelters wild boars, stags, lynxes, wolves, elk, and over 200 species of birds. Giant 500-year-old trees still flourish here, and in late September, during the mating season, the deer put on an enthralling spectacle. Culinary highlights of a visit to the area include mushrooms, wild blueberries, and Zubrowka, an aromatic vodka made from a local grass. Information: *Orbis,* 342 Madison Ave., New York, NY 10173 (phone: 212-867-5011) or from the *Polish National Tourist Office,* 333 N. Michigan Ave., Chicago, IL 60601 (phone: 312-236-9013).

PLITVICE LAKES NATIONAL PARK, Yugoslavia: Just 62 miles (100 km) from Zagreb, in the valley between the wooded mountains of the Mala Kapela and the Plješevica, 16 stunning emerald and turquoise lakes arranged in a series of terraces linked by churning cascades have left immense deposits of tufa and travertine, shaped into marvelous dams and stalactites. The primeval forests around them are fragrant with evergreens, and the sparkling lakes are filled with trout. And in the winter the ice skating can be a mystical experience. Local information is readily available from park attendants or hotel staff members. Or contact *Nacionalni Park,* 4823 Plitvička Jezera, Yugoslavia (phone: 48-76314); or the *Yugoslav National Tourist Office,* Rockefeller Center, Suite 280, 630 Fifth Ave., New York, NY 10111 (phone: 212-757-2801).

For the Mind

Twenty-Five Centuries of History: Europe's Great Museums

 Museum-going is a fine art — one essential to travel enjoyment, but one that few people seem able to master. On the one hand there are the camera-toting tourists like the one in the old *New Yorker* cartoon who accosts a *Louvre* guard: "Quick — where's the *Mona Lisa?* I'm double-parked." Then there are the "serious" tourists in sensible shoes who plod through the cluttered halls of the *Uffizi,* Baedeker in hand, trying to absorb 600 years of European paintings in an afternoon. Both groups would probably rather be somewhere else.

But museumgoing can be a great pleasure if you follow a few simple guidelines. First, make several short visits to a large museum rather than one long one. Stay just an hour and take in no more than a dozen really fine works. (You wouldn't try to skim 70 novels in a morning.)

There is no fatigue like aching, yawny museum fatigue and once it sets in, merely sitting for 3 minutes in front of a Rubens won't cure it. So go when you're fresh — preferably as soon as the museum opens, before the crowds have arrived, or at lunchtime, when the hordes are off refueling.

If possible, know what you want to see before beginning your rounds, so that you don't clutter your senses with bleeding saints and blustery seascapes. At the very least, stop on your way *in* to thumb the catalog and finger the postcards to get an idea of what there is to see and where you'll find it. And when you look at the paintings, don't look at the nameplate first. (You'll find out quickly enough what *you* really like as opposed to what you're *supposed* to like.)

Remember that a very personal experience of a minor museum can be more satisfying than an endless ramble through one of Europe's great warehouses of beauty. There is something essentially deadening about the format in which we are obliged to view the world's greatest art. Break away in any way you can: Take an hour's drive in the country just to see Piero della Francesca's *Madonna del Parto* in the cemetery of tiny Monterchi, 70 miles (112 km) southeast of Florence. Don't forget that single altarpiece in the empty village church, the grouping of portraits adorning the fireplace of the ancient mansion — art in the environment for which it was created. And visit a gallery or an auction house occasionally, just to remind yourself that once it was *all* for sale.

KUNSTHISTORISCHES (FINE ARTS) MUSEUM, Vienna, Austria: The heart of the great Hapsburg collection, opened to the public by Joseph II, the People's Emperor, survived two world wars intact and appears here today in most of its imperial glory. If you had an hour to devote to just one museum in Europe, you couldn't do better than to spend it in the room that this museum devotes to the work of Pieter Breughel, that dark Flemish Renaissance genius who executed the grotesque *Peasant Wedding,* the icily beautiful *Hunters in the Snow,* and the lunatic *Battle of Carnival and Lent.*

Elsewhere, you'll find a roomful of works by Rubens, including the famous portrait of a nude, fur-swathed Helene Fourment, and the Ildefonso altar painting as well as a stunning assortment of Albrecht Dürers and Jan van Eyck's *Cardinal of Santa Croce,* Giorgione's *Three Philosophers,* Titian's *Gypsy Madonna,* plus fine works by Cranach, Velázquez, Rembrandt, Holbein, Van Dyck, and Tintoretto. Open April through October, Tuesdays through Sundays from 10 AM to 6 PM; on Tuesday and Friday evenings parts of the museum are open until 9 PM, when illumination gives the paintings a special glamour. Closed Mondays and most holidays. Information: *Kunsthistorisches Museum,* Maria-Theresien-Pl., Vienna A-1010, Austria (phone: 1-934541).

BRITISH MUSEUM, London, England: Trying to knock off this gigantic storehouse of world culture in a single visit is like trying to master nuclear physics while in the barber's chair. The crown jewels of the collection, mainly devoted to archaeology and human history, are the renowned *Elgin Marbles* — the massive sculpture and relief saved from the ruins of the Parthenon and carted off to safe, civil England. Here, too, you'll find the *Rosetta Stone,* the black basalt tablet that provided the key to Egyptian hieroglyphics; the *Royal Gold Cup;* the *Portland Vase;* the *Sutton Hoo Ship Burial.* The collections of Greek, Roman, and Egyptian antiquities are unrivaled anywhere in the world, and one permanent display is devoted entirely to Etruscan civilization. "Man Before Metals" gives you an enthralling look at the art and technology of the Stone Age. The Near and Far Eastern departments are magnificent reminders of the time when Britannia ruled the waves. And at the library's checkout desk, you can ask to inspect one of Shakespeare's first folios. Open Mondays through Saturdays, 10 AM to 5 PM, and on Sundays from 2:30 to 6 PM. Information: *British Museum,* Great Russell St., London WC1B 3DG, England (phone: 71-636-1555).

NATIONAL GALLERY, London, England: Started by the British Government in 1824 with the purchase of 38 paintings, the *National Gallery,* including its newly opened Sainsbury Wing, houses one of the finest representative collections of European painting from the 13th to the 19th centuries. Among its masterpieces are the *Arnolfini Wedding* of Jan van Eyck; Piero della Francesca's *Baptism of Jesus;* Caravaggio's *Christ at Emmaus;* Botticelli's *Nativity;* Goya's *Dr. Peral;* and a moving, pitiless self-portrait by Rembrandt. Save for a rainy day the very best of British painting, from Hogarth to Turner, though even on your first visit you might catch a glimpse of Constable's *Hadleigh Castle* and Turner's *Fighting Téméraire.* Open weekdays 10 AM to 6 PM and on Sundays from 2 to 6 PM. Information: *National Gallery,* Trafalgar Sq., London WC2N 5DN, England (phone: 71-839-3321).

TATE GALLERY, London, England: A gift of Sir Henry Tate, built in 1897 on the site of Millbank Prison, the *Tate* is the national collection of modern painting and sculpture, but also contains British painting of the past. It boasts one of the world's best collections of French Impressionist and post-Impressionist works as well as excellent examples of the sculpture of Rodin, Maillol, Mestrovic, Moore, and Epstein. The British Department is the best place to see the work of William Blake, and the extraordinary Turner collection is in the Clore Gallery. The *Tate* is also very energetic about mounting vast special exhibitions of work on loan from abroad. Open weekdays 10 AM to 6 PM and Sundays 2 to 6 PM. Information: *The Tate Gallery,* Millbank, London SW1P 4RG, England (phone: 71-821-1313).

CENTRE GEORGES POMPIDOU, Paris, France: Known as the *Beaubourg* (after the plateau on which it is built), the most arresting thing here is the building itself — a multicolored carnival of tubes, girders, and transparent escalators that looks as though it were built with a giant Erector set. A modern Parisian landmark, this potpourri of ever-changing exhibitions spans world culture, covering everything from an Einstein memorial to the history of the jukebox. Crowded with visitors all day until its closing at 10 PM, it is probably the most successful attempt at museum making in years. Open weekdays except Tuesdays from noon to 10 PM; weekends from 10 AM to

10 PM. Information: *Centre Georges Pompidou,* Rue Rambuteau at the corner of Rue St.-Martin, Paris, France (phone: 42-77-12-33).

LOUVRE, Paris, France: This colossal haystack crammed with needles was initiated by François I in the 16th century with 12 paintings and the casts of a few of his favorite Greek sculptures. Today, a one-way stroll through each of its treasure-laden rooms would cover over 8 miles — and if you never saw the inside of another museum, you could still form a very complete picture of European, Oriental, and ancient art from a study of its collection. You couldn't miss the *Mona Lisa* or the *Venus de Milo* if you were dead set on doing so. But a few delights are easily overlooked in the lavish confusion: van Eyck's *Madonna of Chancellor Rolin;* Albrecht Dürer's *Self-Portrait;* Rigaud's portrait of the narcissistic *Louis XIV;* Ingres's *Turkish Bath;* Frans Hals's *Bohemian;* Memling's *Portrait of an Old Woman;* a small medieval gilded wood statuette of St. Stephen; and the *Handmaiden of the Dead,* a 4,000-year-old Egyptian wood carving of a young girl bearing food and wine for the banquet after death. Open from 9 AM to 5:45 PM (until 9:45 PM on Mondays and Wednesdays); closed Thursdays. Information: *The Louvre,* Place du Louvre, Paris 75001, France (phone: 40-20-50-50).

MUSÉE D'ORSAY, Paris, France: The Impressionist paintings that once crowded intimately into the joyfully informal *Jeu de Paume* museum have found a more spacious and sober home. The brilliant transformation of a vast turn-of-the-century glass and cast-iron train station into a museum has brought the best artistic production of France from 1848 to 1914 under one vaulted, translucent roof. Now Degas, Toulouse-Lautrec, Monet, and Renoir are hung in specially designed spaces within this railroad-cathedral, which they share with 600 fellow painters and sculptors. No detail of light, humidity, or acoustics has been left to chance, and visitors will make this voyage around the art world in perfect comfort and ease. The high point — the Van Goghs on the top floor, glowing under the northern Parisian skylight. Open from 10 AM to 6 PM (Thursdays until 9:45 PM); Sundays from 9 AM to 6 PM. Information: *Musée d'Orsay,* 1 Rue de Bellechasse, Paris 75007, France (phone: 45-49-11-11 or 40-49-48-48).

PERGAMON MUSEUM, Berlin, Germany: Among the impressive buildings on the Museuminsel (Museum Island) is this museum, the site of three astounding architectural feats: the *Pergamon Altar,* named after the ancient Greek city in which it was discovered (south of the historic city of Troy in what is now Turkey); the *Market Gate,* from a Roman settlement at Miletus (also in what is now Turkey); and the Babylonian *Ishtar Gate* and processional way. Each one is among the most imposing sights on view at any museum anywhere.

It's not just the extent or the age of these items, but their extraordinary size and scale that's overwhelming. The altar includes huge bas-reliefs of most of the major Greek gods, done in staggering detail, and the Roman agora gate stretches more than 2-stories high (it's easy to conjure up images of a Caesar or two strolling among its once filled space). Even more overpowering is the huge, 2,600-year-old entrance to the legendary city of Babylon, built by Nebuchadnezzar to demonstrate the greatness of the Babylonian empire and its gods. The walls of the *Ishtar Gate* are of brilliant blue and yellow kiln-baked brick, whose colors still dazzle. Open from 10 AM to 6 PM; closed Fridays. Information: *Pergamon Museum,* Am Kupfergraben, Berlin, Germany (phone: 9-203550).

DEUTSCHES MUSEUM, Munich, Germany: A change of pace, from the aesthetic to the technical. Unique in Europe, this huge complex on an islet in the Isar River covers the entire history of the development of man's knowledge of the natural sciences and his mastery of technology. Displays include everything from ancient compasses to modern aircraft. Some items are original, others are "faithful to the last detail" reconstructions. There are plenty of hands-on exhibits that can be activated by the spectator, and so children generally go gleefully out of their minds here. But even to diehards who ordinarily prefer Titian to fission, the museum is fascinating and you don't have to be a scientist to enjoy it. Open daily 9 AM to 5 PM. Information: *Deutsches Museum,* Museuminsel 1, Munich 22 D-8000, Germany (phone: 89-21791).

NATIONAL ARCHAEOLOGICAL MUSEUM, Athens, Greece: The nation's largest museum houses archaeological treasures found all over the country and from every period of ancient Greek history. Without a certain amount of scholarly preparation, you are not likely to be able to distinguish the Neolithic from the Cycladic from the Mycenaean — so just allow yourself to be overwhelmed by this matchless legacy of the most gifted civilization on record. You'll see sculptured bronze shields right from the pages of *The Iliad;* golden mortuary masks; Cycladic idols; Thessalian ceramics; the frescoes recently unearthed on the island of Santorini; and vast quantities of sculpture, including the *Philosopher of Antikythira,* the grave shrine of Aristonautes, the *Poseidon of Artemission,* and the *Dipylon Head.* Open 9 AM to 3 PM in winter, 8 AM to 5 PM in summer; Sundays 9:30 AM to 2:30 PM. Closed Mondays. Information: *National Archaeological Museum,* 1 Tositsa St., Athens, Greece (phone: 1-821-7717).

GALLERIA DEGLI UFFIZI, Florence, Italy: While you are hiking through the glowing rooms of the *Uffizi,* awash in the golden tides of the Italian Renaissance, just consider that a large portion of Italy's artistic patrimony is stacked in dingy storerooms, hanging in museum wings permanently closed for lack of personnel, and adorning the offices of petty bureaucrats in obscure ministries and consulates out of public view. Consequently, what you see here is the *crema della crema della crema* by Botticelli, Leonardo, Raphael, Piero della Francesca, Giotto, Caravaggio, and virtually every other major Italian artist. Particularly beautiful, and often overlooked, are the 13th- and 14th-century religious paintings on wood panels. Open from 9 AM to 6:45 PM; from 9 AM to 1 PM Sundays. Closed Mondays. Information: *Galleria degli Uffizi,* 6 Loggiato degli Uffizi, Florence, Italy (phone: 55-218341).

VATICAN MUSEUMS, Rome, Italy: The *Vatican Museums* attract not only the usual population of museumgoers, but also pilgrims and Vatican visitors — so crowding is a problem, and the Sistine Chapel, in particular, often has an aura of the subway in rush hour. (The first phase in the restoration of the chapel's ceilings was completed in 1989 after 10 years of work.) Early morning is probably the best time to go: Grab your ticket and dash past the papal robes, old maps, and tomb inscriptions, and you'll leave the school groups and convent delegations far behind. Your goals are the Raphael Rooms, the classical statuary (including the *Apollo Belvedere* and the *Laocoön*), the tapestry gallery, and the works of Fra Angelico, Giotto, and Filippo Lippi in the Pinacoteca (Picture Gallery). This is a difficult museum, and so a catalogue is a good investment. One more word to the weary: Don't combine the museums with a visit to St. Peter's. Open Mondays through Saturdays and the last Sunday of every month, from 9 AM to 2 PM (but no admittance after 1 PM); and until 5 PM (admission until 4 PM) from July to September. Information: *The Vatican Museums,* Viale Vaticano, Rome, Italy (phone: 6-698-3333).

RIJKSMUSEUM, Amsterdam, The Netherlands: The huge red brick building is one of a complex of three museums clustered around Museumplein. (The others are the *Van Gogh Museum* and the *Stedelijk.*) The star attraction at the *Rijksmuseum* is the incomparable Rembrandt collection, which includes *The Night Watch, The Anatomy Lesson, The Jewish Betrothal, The Drapers' Guild,* and a magnificent self-portrait. Here, there are Rembrandts by the roomful. But you'll also find lovely Vermeers, including the famous *Milkmaid,* along with works by Frans Hals, whose *Married Couple* ranks among northern Europe's greatest paintings. There's more — but stick with the Dutch masters on your first visit. Open daily except Mondays, 10 AM to 5 PM and Sundays 1 PM to 5 PM. Information: *Rijksmuseum,* 42 Stadhouderskade, Amsterdam, Holland (phone: 20-737538). Also visit Rembrandt's house at 4 Jodenbreestraat. Open daily 10 AM to 5 PM and Sundays 1 PM to 5 PM.

PRADO, Madrid, Spain: The heart of the *Prado* is the regal collection assembled by Spain's Bourbon and Hapsburg kings. Concentrate first on works by the four great Spanish masters: Velázquez, El Greco, Murillo, and Goya, whose progression from fashionable court painter to embittered madman is documented in breathtaking detail. Then turn to an excellent selection of works by another genius, Hieronymus Bosch, and to the fine Van Dycks, Titians, and Tintorettos — all hanging here as a result of Spain's royal ties with Flanders and Italy. Goya's *Maja Desnuda* is here, as is Velázquez's great *Las Meninas* (which you can view in a mirror, just as it was painted), and a delightful statue of a reclining Hermaphrodite. Thirteen rooms of Flemish masterpieces have opened up. (Picasso's fabled *Guernica* is housed nearby, in the Casón del Buen Retiro.) Another annex, the Villahermosa Palace — diagonally across Plaza Canovas del Castillo (the square with the Neptune Fountain) from the main building — now houses a major portion of the Thyssen-Bornemisza Collection, which many consider the most important private art collection in the world. Open 9 AM to 6:45 PM; closed Mondays. Information: *Museo del Prado,* Paseo del Prado, Madrid, Spain (phone: 1-420-2836).

HERMITAGE, St. Petersburg, Soviet Union: For a long time after its founding, the czars made the opulent *Hermitage* (the Winter Palace) the private preserve of themselves and their friends, and it was only with the revolution that the public got a look at the splendid contents — works on the order of Gainsborough's *Duchess of Beaufort;* Renoir's *Girl with a Fan;* Ingres's *Portrait of Count Guriev;* Breughel's *Fair;* Rembrandt's *Old Man in Red;* Titian's *Danaë;* Holbein's *Portrait of a Young Man;* and a wonderful, little-known Michelangelo sculpture, the *Crouching Boy.* As you might expect, a great deal of space is allotted to Russian history and culture, and exhibits run the gamut from exquisite antique silver and a map of the Soviet Union in semi-precious stones to "The Heroic Military Past of the Russian People" and turn-of-the-century paintings with fetching titles like *The Dairymaid Spurned* and *The Volunteer Shall Return No More.* The Indian and Oriental art collections are first rate — but unless you are wintering in St. Petersburg, stick to the magnificent European collection. Open from 10 AM to 6 PM (from 12:20 to 8 PM) during winter, and from 10 AM to 5:30 PM during summer. Closed Mondays. Information: *The Hermitage,* 36 Dvortsovaya Nab., St. Petersburg, Soviet Union (phone: 219-8625 or 311-3420).

MORE GREAT PAINTINGS

A number of the Continent's finest works of art will be found outside the museums listed above. Here's where you'll find a selection of the standouts.

Cathedral of St. Bavon, Ghent, Belgium – *The Adoration of the Mystical Lamb,* by Jan and Hubert van Eyck.

Musée des Beaux-Arts, Ghent, Belgium – *The Carrying of the Cross,* by Hieronymus Bosch.

Ny Carlsberg Glyptotek, Copenhagen, Denmark – Paul Gauguin's *Vahine No Te Tiare.*

Musée National Marc Chagall, Nice, France – Chagall's *L'Arc-en-ciel.*

Alte Pinakothek, Munich, Germany – Pieter Paul Rubens's *Rubens and Isabella Brant* and Albrecht Dürer's *Portrait of Oswolt Krel.*

Staatsgalerie, Munich, Germany – Edouard Manet's *Lunch in the Studio.*

Pinacoteca Comunale, Borgo San Sepolcro, Italy – Piero della Francesca's *The Resurrection.*

Museo Diocesano, Cortona, Italy – Fra Angelico's *The Annunciation.*

Palazzo Ducale, Mantova, Italy – *La Camera degli Sposi,* by Mantegna.

Cenacolo Vinciano, Milan, Italy – Leonardo da Vinci's *Last Supper.* (Currently being restored, its view is hampered considerably by scaffolding.)

Villa dei Misteri, Pompeii, Italy – The frescoes.

Cathedral of Siena, Siena, Italy – Duccio di Boninsegna's *The Maestà.*
Museo Correr, Venice, Italy – *The Courtesans,* by Vittore Carpaccio.
Munch Museet, Oslo, Norway – Edvard Munch's *Madonna.*
Kunstmuseum, Basel, Switzerland – Holbein's *Portrait of Boniface Amerbach.*

On the Boards: Theater and Opera in Europe

 London should be a first — and prolonged — stop on any theatergoer's itinerary; the stages here are some of the liveliest in the world — and there's no language barrier. Yet even on the Continent there is an old, established English-language company, the *English Theater* (12 Josefsgasse, Vienna, Austria; phone: 1-421260). The *Café Theater* in Frankfurt (45 Hamburger Allee; phone: 69-777466) has even sent a play to New York's off-Broadway; and the *English Speaking Theater Amsterdam* plays the *Bellevue* (90 Leidsekade; phone: 20-247248) in winter months and the *Stadsschouwburg* (26 Leidseplein; phone: 20-242311) in summer.

Besides which, some theatricals — among Europe's best — are largely nonverbal. And even when the language barrier does portend problems, you may encounter acting so compelling that you end up forgetting that you're not supposed to understand what's going on. In addition, many of Europe's great companies often perform international classics whose content is familiar. If you don't know the play, it's simple enough to search a city's largest bookstore for an English copy of the plays that are on. (Oddly enough, the simultaneous-translation earphone setups provided by some major theaters seem to create, rather than remove, a barrier between you and the players.)

What about tickets? Before leaving the US, pick up a copy of a local newspaper — the *Times* or the *Observer* is the best for London goings-on — and figure out what to see. You can buy tickets in advance for productions of the *Royal Shakespeare Theatre* in Stratford-on-Avon, and for the *Edinburgh Festival,* in the US at *Keith Prowse & Co.* (234 W. 44th St., New York, NY 10036; phone: 212-398-1430; 800-669-7469 outside New York), and at *Edwards & Edwards* (One Times Sq. Plaza, New York, NY 10036; phone: 212-944-0290 or 800-223-6108 outside New York), both of which can provide tickets for other London theater and cultural events as well. The *London Theatre News* is a monthly newsletter on London theater (annual subscription is $49). It also can provide help with ticket reservations and the like (12 E. 86th St., New York, NY 10028; phone: 212-517-8608). For tickets to performances in other cities, wait until you get there.

STEIRISCHER HERBST, Graz, Austria: This is a young, electric, eclectic arts festival (whose name translates "Styrian Autumn"); it generally plays from mid-September through early November. You'll encounter a good deal of experimental theater, mime theater, and film; and the performing groups are from all over Europe and America, so language is not a constant problem. The festival is increasingly important as a place to see what's fresh in European theater. Information: *Steirischer Herbst,* Palais Attems, 17/I Sackstrasse, Graz A-8010, Austria (phone: 316-730070).

BURGTHEATER, Vienna, Austria: Over 200 years old, this is one of Europe's great theaters and most accomplished companies. The repertory has a decidedly classical flavor, and sooner or later, every important play written in German for the last 300 years crosses the stage. The building (2 Dr. Karl Luegerringz) is an imposing, colonnaded baroque palace, and a première is a glittering Viennese social occasion. The same company performs a somewhat flashier repertory at the *Akademie Theater.* Tickets for both are available from 2 months to 15 days in advance from the *Osterreichischer Bundestheaterverband* (Austrian Federal Theater Association; Bestellbüro, 1 Goethegasse, Vienna A-1010, Austria). A week or less in advance, try the central box office (3 Hanuschgasse, behind the opera house; phone: 1-514440). Outside Austria, contact the *Vienna Ticket Service* (Postfach 160, Vienna A-1043, Austria; fax: 1-587-9844; telex: 135499).

LATERNA MAGIKA, Prague, Czechoslovakia: This amalgam of cinema, opera, theater, and circus offers you one of the most fascinating spectacles on the Continent; the name, which translates as "Magic Lantern," attempts to convey the swirling, kaleidoscopic style. Now you know less about it than you did before, so just go — and take children. Information: *Laterna Magika,* 40 Narodní, Prague, Czechoslovakia (phone: 2-260033). Prague also has a long tradition of mime, and a genius named Fialka, the Marcel Marceau of the East, performs regularly at *Na Zabradli.*

CHICHESTER FESTIVAL THEATRE, Chichester, England: Launched in 1962, this drama festival offers four plays between May and September, with topflight casts on a par with anything you'd see in London's West End. The theater, a striking hexagonal structure in the middle of a 40-acre parkland, lies just a 1½-hour train ride from Victoria Station. And during the main season, trains don't leave Chichester until the final curtain has fallen. Information: *Chichester Festivities,* Canon Gate House, South St., Chichester, West Sussex PO19 1PU, England (phone: 243-785718 or 243-781312, box office).

ROYAL COURT, London, England: Once termed experimental and even avant-garde, the *Royal Court* was where John Osborne introduced *Look Back in Anger,* where the Arnold Wesker trilogy was first performed, and where Harold Pinter vented his wrath on the English language. The audience is now very proper British and intermission crowds are indistinguishable from those, say, at the *Royal Ballet.* But the *Royal Court* is still *the* place to watch young England on stage. Information: *The Royal Court Theatre,* Sloane Sq., London SW1, England (phone: 71-730-1745).

ROYAL NATIONAL THEATRE, London, England: If English-speaking theater is your religion, the *National* should be your temple. It is, in fact, a complex of three theaters (the *Olivier,* the *Lyttelton,* and the *Cottesloe*) on the South Bank of the Thames. And it is the direct descendant of the nearby *Old Vic,* which was, for decades, London's crown jewel. Gielgud, Richardson, Ashcroft, Plowright, Scofield, Guinness, Finney, and all the other English theater greats have performed here — and the repertory knows no bounds of time, nationality, or style. Information: *Royal National Theatre,* South Bank, London SE1 9PX, England (phone: 71-928-2252; or, for recorded ticket information, 71-928-8126, 24 hours a day).

ROYAL SHAKESPEARE COMPANY, Stratford and London, England: This splendid company, which also picks its stars from the roster of English acting greats, performs in the splashy $280 million *Barbican Arts Centre.* In Stratford-on-Avon, its home is the *Royal Shakespeare Theatre,* set beautifully alongside the river, as well as the *Swan Theatre* and the tiny 150-seat *The Other Place.* The Stratford season runs from March through January. (Be warned that in midsummer busloads of holidaymakers, fresh from visits to see Anne Hathaway's chamber pot, turn the atmosphere a trifle frantic.) In London, you can generally buy tickets to a production with the same confidence that you'd pick up a Rolls or a Burberry. The company's specialty is breathing life into period pieces so obscure that even the boys at Eton don't have to read them. Information: *Royal Shakespeare Theatre,* Stratford-on-Avon, Warwickshire CV37 6BB, England (phone: 789-295623; or, for 24-hour booking information, 789-69191). In London: *Barbican Theatre,* 13 Cromwell Tower, Barbican EC2, England (phone: 71-638-8891).

HELSINKI FESTIVALS, Helsinki, Finland: More than a decade ago, Finland introduced over 800 summer festivals, produced and presented in various sections of the country. The idea was to attract foreign visitors and to familiarize them with the Finnish people and their achievements and, at the same time, to entertain them with local professional talent and international luminaries. The events range from symphonic concerts and opera performances in a 15th-century castle courtyard, to rock, folk, jazz, and pop music; to art exhibitions; to seminars on world problems — cultural fare for everyone, including the small fry. Information: *Finland Festivals,* 3A Vuorikatu, 17th floor, Helsinki, Finland (phone: 0-607386 or 0-669695).

The *Finland Festival* programs generally start in mid-June and run till mid-August. These are followed by the big *Helsinki Festival,* which stages as many as 100 events between late August and early September. For complete program information, contact *Helsinki Festival,* 28 Unioninkatu (phone: 0- 659688).

COMÉDIE-FRANÇAISE, Paris, France: As much a part of Paris as the *Louvre,* its next-door neighbor, and as French as the Académie Française, the *Comédie-Française* is as totally dedicated as either to the preservation of Gallic language and culture and its productions run to Racine and Corneille, frothy Molière, *Cyrano de Bergerac* done in the grand manner, and even *Waiting for Godot,* now that it's a classic. All the great names of French theater do a turn at the *Comédie,* and even if you know no more French than "La plume de ma tante," go. (Just think of it as a visit to another national monument.) Information: *Comédie-Française,* 2 Rue de Richelieu, Paris, France (phone: 40-15-00-15).

MARCEL MARCEAU, Paris, France: Just as the world had only one Edith Piaf and only one Maurice Chevalier, there is only one Marcel Marceau — and if you've never seen him, you're missing a treat. After a long struggle with the forces of anti-creation, he has opened his own school of mime, the *Ecole Internationale de Mimodrame,* and though much of the year sees him gesturing and grimacing his way around the world, he can be found here when he's in Paris. Information: *Ecole Internationale de Mimodrame,* 17 Rue René-Boulanger, Paris, France (phone: 42-02-32-82).

L'ODÉON, Paris, France: One of France's richly endowed (talent and money) national theaters, the *Odéon*'s style is more streamlined and flashy than some of its conventional cousins. Guest productions from the best French theatrical companies, as well as such glittering foreign attractions as the *Peking Art Theater,* the *Greek National Theater* performing *Euripides,* and Ingmar Bergman directing Shakespeare. Information: *L'Odéon,* 1 Pl. Paul-Claudel, Paris, France (phone: 43-25-80-92).

THÉÂTRE RENAUD-BARRAULT, Paris, France: This is the home theater of the reigning king and queen of the French stage — Jean-Louis Barrault and Madeleine Renaud. The repertory is diverse and far-ranging, but there's a good, steady diet of Beckett and Ionesco, as well as important new foreign plays. The theater is also a gathering place for stage personalities from all over Europe. Information: *Théâtre Renaud-Barrault,* 2 Av. Franklin-Roosevelt, Paris, France (phone: 40-76-00-29 or 45-62-08-95).

SCHILLER-THEATER, Berlin, Germany: With one of Europe's richest theatrical traditions, the Berlin stage nurtured half a dozen actors and actresses who later became major stars on Broadway and in Hollywood. The *Schiller,* the prince of German theaters, specializes in lavish, highly styled productions of the classics. Information: *Schiller-Theater,* 110 Bismarckstr., Berlin, Germany (phone: 849-319-5236). While you're in town, try to catch a political cabaret, another staple of the German theater scene. Best bets are *Die Stachelschweine* in the *Europa-Center* (phone: 849-261-4795) and *Die Wühlmause* (33 Nürnbergstr.; phone: 849-213-7047). And don't miss the famous *Berliner Ensemble* of Brecht-Weill-Lenya fame. Information: *Berliner Ensemble,* Bertolt Brecht Pl., Berlin, Germany (phone: 9-282-3160).

NATIONAL THEATER OF GREECE, Athens and Epidaurus, Greece: Productions here take you as close as you can get to the mysterious, ritualistic origins of the theater: where the national Greek company performs ancient Greek plays in their original settings. The *Athens Festival* runs throughout the summer in the Odeum of Herod Atticus at the foot of the Acropolis. The *Epidaurus Festival* spans July and August, set in the spectacular amphitheater of Epidaurus, about 90 miles (144 km) southwest of Athens. Information and tickets for both: *Greek National Tourist Organization,* 2 Spirou Miliou Arcade, Athens, Greece (phone: 1-322-1459). Tickets are on sale at the *Epidaurus* amphitheater only on the day of the performance (phone: 1-753-21005).

ABBEY THEATRE, Dublin, Ireland: The history of Ireland's national theater goes back into the last century, but its current $2.5-million home (the original "Shabby" having burned in 1951) was built in 1966. The pride of Dublin and the cradle of spirited Irish rhetoric, the *Abbey* is still home to Synge, Yeats, O'Casey, Behan — and the best in modern Irish drama as well. Catch an evening of *Playboy of the Western World* or *Juno and the Paycock,* have a quick whiskey around the corner at pubs named in honor of Barry Fitzgerald and Sean O'Casey in Marlborough Street, and, in the space of 3 hours, you can pretty much sense the essence of Ireland. Information: *Abbey Theatre,* Lower Abbey St., Dublin 1, Ireland (phone: 1-744505).

PICCOLO TEATRO, Milan, Italy: Founded just after World War II under the aegis of Giorgio Strehler, the *Piccolo* is Italy's number one company. The original mission was to take theater out of the idle hands of the elite and make it a vital instrument of popular culture — and the spirit still survives, though furs and jewels often clog its modest foyer. The repertory is international and imaginative, the production style original and intense. And there is always talk about keeping the *Piccolo* pure. Along with *La Scala,* this is the city's principal cultural institution. Information: *Piccolo Teatro,* Via Rovello 2, Palazzo del Broletto, Milan 20100, Italy (phone: 2-869-0631 or 2-657-1208).

EDINBURGH FESTIVAL, Edinburgh, Scotland: Founded in 1974, this is the largest arts festival in the world. It features music, theater, art exhibitions, and dance from mid-August to early September. Much of the festival's vitality comes from the four other festivals that run concurrently (although not always for the entire 3 weeks): the *Edinburgh Festival Fringe,* the *Edinburgh International Film Festival,* the *Edinburgh Book Festival,* and the *Edinburgh Military Tattoo. The Edinburgh Festival Fringe* evolved during the early years of the official *Edinburgh Festival* as a mixed bag of new theatrical and musical productions from around the world — some are scruffy, some super — remember *Beyond the Fringe?* Every year more and more amateur and professional groups are happy to perform "on the fringe." Not a single performing space in Edinburgh is left vacant; most companies aggressively advertise their shows, so be prepared to carry literally dozens of little posters and handouts as you perambulate through the town. For regular festival information and tickets: *Edinburgh International Festival,* 21 Market St., Edinburgh EH1 1BW, Scotland (phone: 31-226-4001). The *Fringe* has separate quarters: *Festival Fringe Society,* 180 High St., Edinburgh EH1 1QS, Scotland (phone: 31-226-5257). See also *Music Festivals,* below.

OPERA

Unlike theater, the great opera houses of Europe share a common pool of talent and music. A case in point was *Carmen* (French) at the *Vienna Staatsoper* (Austrian), conducted by Kleiber (German), directed by Zeffirelli (Italian), and sung by Domingo (Spanish) and Obrazova (Russian).

However, operas are generally best heard on their own territory — Wagner in Germany, Verdi in Italy, Bizet in France. Even if the soloists are of mixed nationalities, there is something about most productions that doesn't travel quite as well as you might expect. At any rate, if you are seeing a visiting team, ask what language the performance will be sung in: You might prefer not to hear a Sicilian Brunhilde or a Tyrolean Carmen.

The finely tuned tentacles of the German opera world extend far beyond the city limits of Munich, Berlin, and Frankfurt; in Germany, a sort of vast, well-managed farm system makes it possible to hear first-rate performances in any one of a dozen provincial centers.

Meanwhile, opera is most fun in Italy (even when questionably performed), and the 19th-century opera houses themselves are beautiful. Rather than the reverent silence of Teutonic audiences, you'll find zestful participation, and, in the south and the provinces, opera-goers sound catcalls for clinkers and hum along the rest of the time. And — either because of training methods or government subsidies — the most exciting new voices are turning up in Eastern Europe; and the unknown with the unpronounceable name you may hear in Prague or Warsaw may soon be getting top billing in London or New York.

In general, however, you'll see the best performances at the festivals of *Salzburg, Wiener Festwochen, Bayreuth, Berliner Festwochen, Munich,* and the *Maggio Musicale Fiorentino.* (See *Music Festivals* for descriptions.) From early July to late August, try the festival at the *Arena of Verona.* Information in Italian and English: *Ente Autonomo Spettacoli Lirici Arena di Verona,* 28 Piazza Bra, Verona 37121, Italy (phone: 45-590109; 45-596517 or 45-800-5151 for the box office). And, of course, don't miss these great European opera houses:

Staatsoper (State Opera), 2 Opernring, Vienna, Austria (phone: 1-51444). Great for Richard Strauss.

Volksoper (Folk Opera), 78 Wahringerstr., Vienna, Austria (phone: 1-51444). Good for Johann Strauss; specializes in Viennese operetta.

English National Opera Company, at the *Coliseum,* St. Martin's La., London WC2, England (phone: 71-836-3161). Great opera classics performed in English.

Royal Opera House, Covent Garden, Floral St., London WC2, England (phone: 71-240-1066, box office; 71-240-1911, other information).

L'Opéra Bastille, Pl. de La Bastille, Paris, France (phone: 40-01-17-89).

Deutsche Oper, 34-37 Bismarckstr., Berlin 1000, Germany (phone: 849-341-4449).

Bayerische Staatsoper, in the *National Theater,* 2 Max-Joseph-Pl., Munich 2 8000, Germany (phone: 89-221316).

La Scala, 2 Via dei Filodrammatici, Milan, Italy (phone: 2-807041).

San Carlo, Via San Carlo, Naples, Italy (phone: 81-797-2370).

Teatro La Fenice, 1977 San Fantin, Venice, Italy (phone: 41-521-0161).

Gran Teatre del Liceu, 65 Rambla Caputxins, Barcelona, Spain (phone: 3-318-9122; box office, 3-301-6787).

Bolshoi Opera, Bolshoi Theater, 2 Teatralnaya Sq., Moscow, Soviet Union (phone: 095-299-0050).

Europe's Magnificent Music Festivals

Every summer, Europe bursts into garlands of music festivals, looped in bright tones across the Continent in every direction. Some — like those at Salzburg and Bayreuth — are distinguished old celebrations of musical genius. Others are Ludwig-come-latelies whose thinly disguised purpose is to drum up tourist trade for otherwise quaint but hardly notable old villages. Still, they can make for a pleasant end to a day at the beach, and there will be plenty of last-minute tickets (or space for your blanket on the village green), though the major ones, serious musical pilgrimages, sell out months in advance.

Most of the festivals make inspired use of their home city's finest monuments — ducal palaces, castle courtyards, and Gothic cathedrals — so that concert-going becomes sightseeing. Moreover, music often acquires a new power outside the concert hall. Moreover, music often acquires a new power outside the concert hall. For events not listed here, a good source worth consulting is *Festival Europe!* by Margaret Johnson (Mustang Publishing, 1991; $9.95 in paperback).

SALZBURG FESTIVAL, Salzburg, Austria: Tickets to concerts of this generally recognized king of European festivals are high — but requests outnumber places by about four to one, and hotel accommodations during the run of the event, between late July and late August, are scarcer still. Still, if you can swing it and if you can afford it, there's nothing else quite like Salzburg. The performers are the best in the world, the audiences are distinguished and reverent, and you can't help but feel as if you are hearing Mozart for the first time. Write for a program in the fall and for tickets by *Christmas.* Bring dressy clothes: to Austrians, the marriage of Figaro is almost more important than their own. And if you happen to be cruising in the area, without any advance planning, give the festival a try anyway: Tickets for some of the delightful morning chamber concerts are often available. Or the concierge of the *Goldener Hirsch* may slip you one for *Don Giovanni* if you slip him $200; and if somebody dies, he may even let you share a room. Information: *Salzburger Festspiele,* Postfacha 140, Salzburg A-5010, Austria (phone: 662-842541).

WIENER FESTWOCHEN, Vienna, Austria: Music, as every schoolchild knows, was invented in Vienna; and for 5 weeks every year between early May and early June, the city holds a melomanic orgy to commemorate the event. Mehta, Levine, and Abbado come to town, with theater groups from all over Europe; and there are new productions at the *Staatsoper* (State Opera), premieres of new plays, art exhibitions, symposia, colloquia, and plain old songfests. And every one of the city's 23 *Bezirke* (districts) sponsors special district programs. Spring is a nice time to see the city. Information: *Wiener Festwochen,* 11 Lehárgasse, Vienna A-1060, Austria (phone: 1-586-1676).

FLANDERS FESTIVAL, Brussels, Belgium: The most important collection of musical events in Belgium, this festival is celebrated from spring into October in a number of Belgian towns — Ghent, Bruges, Mechelen, Antwerp, Leuven, and Brussels. Often concerts take place in the towns' most beautiful buildings. Information: *Festival van Vlaanderen,* 18 Eugeen Flageyplein, Brussels B-1050, Belgium (phone: 2-648-1484).

PRAGUE SPRING, Prague, Czechoslovakia: This doyen of European festivals has been around since 1945. Conductors and soloists from Eastern Europe are always on the program, along with some fine Russian artists whose performances usually sell out by the time they reach *Carnegie Hall.* Mid-May to early June. Information: *International Music Festival* "Prague Spring," Dum Umelcu, 12 Alsovo Nabrezi, Prague 1 CS-11001, Czechoslovakia (phone: 2-231-9307).

BATH FESTIVAL, Bath, England: The weeks between mid-May and early June are beautiful ones in this lovely Georgian town, and the festival offers music to match — a splendid selection classical music and jazz, plus walking tours, film shows, art exhibitions, and garden tours. Information (from January through June): *Bath Festival Office,* Linley House, 1 Pierrepont Pl., Bath BA1 1JY, England (phone: 225-463362). Booking in the US through *Edwards and Edwards,* One Times Sq., New York, NY 10036 (phone: 212-944-0290 or 800-223-6108).

CHELTENHAM FESTIVAL, Cheltenham, England: Founded just after World War II in this gracious Regency spa, the *Cheltenham Festival* exploits majestic settings like the Pittville Pump Room and the Victorian Town Hall to enhance a musical menu that can run from baroque to the best in contemporary, especially British. You also may hear the world première of works specially commissioned for the festival. Two weeks in July, with the enchanting Cotswold Hills and Severn Vale a short drive away. Information: *Cheltenham Festival Office,* Town Hall, Cheltenham, Gloucestershire GL50 1QA, England (phone: 242-521621; box office, 242-523690).

INTERNATIONAL FESTIVAL OF LYRICAL AND MUSICAL ARTS, Aix-en-Provence, France: This is one of the most attractive towns in the South of France, and the festival, which runs from mid-July to early August, uses several locations, including two cloisters, the Cathedral of St. Sauveur, the courtyard of the Archbishop's Palace, and the lovely Place des Quatres Dauphins. There is a strong emphasis on what the festival committee calls "the most beautiful instrument" — the human voice — but you'll hear works of all vintages, from early Corelli to late Stockhausen to Negro spirituals. Information: *Festival International d'Art Lyrique et de Musique,* Palais de l'Ancien Archevêché, Aix-en-Provence 13100, France (phone: 42-21-14-40 or 42-17-34-34).

INTERNATIONAL CHAMBER MUSIC FESTIVAL, Divonne-les-Bains, France: Held in a sleepy little village, a 15-minute drive across the border from Geneva (and the site of one of France's most profitable casinos), this connoisseur's festival presents chamber music (and only chamber music) of the highest caliber in the jewel-like *Théâtre de Divonne,* whose whimsical decor would enliven even an amateur bassoon recital. At the end of June or the beginning of July, an excursion here can be delightful, so delightful in fact that some particularly faithful patrons come all the way from Paris for a single concert. Information: *Syndicat d'Initiative,* Rue des Bains BP 23, Divonne-les-Bains 01220, France (phone: 50-20-01-22).

FESTIVAL DE STRASBOURG, Strasbourg, France: This 3-week event has been held annually in June and early July since 1938, and takes place mostly in the *Palais de la Musique et des Congrès.* But some events also are held in the town's majestic cathedral, as well as at other venues; succeeding days in one recent year saw performances by pianists Claudio Arrau and Vladimir Ashkenazy, violinist Itzhak Perlman, singers Pilar Lorengar and Marilyn Horne, and the *Juilliard Quartet.* Between concerts, you can eat yourself under the harpsichord: Strasbourg is generally acknowledged to serve some of the most luscious food in France (see *The Shrines of European Gastronomy*). Information: *Festival de Strasbourg,* 24 Rue de la Mésange, Strasbourg 67081, France (phone: 88-32-43-10).

BAYREUTH FESTIVAL, Bayreuth, Germany: This is the festival that Wagner built. A month-long orgy of Teutonic splendor that occupies the town every year beginning in late July, it features half a dozen Wagner operas presented in the theater that Wagner himself designed for this purpose, just down the road from a museum devoted to him. In their way, the audiences are as devoted as those who worshiped at Woodstock — different god, though, and a different crowd. Information: *Bayreuth Festival,* Postfach 100262, Bayreuth D-8580, Germany (phone: 921-20221).

BERLINER FESTWOCHEN, Berlin, Germany: Held every September during the crisp Berlin autumn, this eclectic festival offers a wide range of opera, orchestral music, chamber music, theater, mime, dance, and an assortment of art exhibitions. The roster of conductors who appeared here in one 30-day stretch not long ago — Böhm, Solti, Inbal, Stockhausen, Leinsdorf, Giulini, Abbado, the late Herbert von Karajan — reads like the list of graduates of Mt. Olympus Conservatory. Information: *Berliner Festspiele,* Postfach 301648, Berlin D-1000, Germany (phone: 849-254890).

MUNICH OPERA FESTIVAL, Munich, Germany: In early July, while most of Europe's opera houses sleep, Munich explodes for a melodious month with the music of Wagner, Strauss, Mozart, and, occasionally, the works of hot-blooded Latins like Verdi and Donizetti as well. Performances are held in the monumental *National*

Theater and the miraculous *Cuvilliés Theater* (also known as the *Altes Residenztheater;* 1 Residenzstr.; phone: 89-221316), perhaps the most beautiful auditorium in Europe. Information: *Münchner Opernfestspiele*, 11 Maximilianstr., *Bayerische Staatsoper*, Postfach 745, München 1 D-8000, Germany (phone: 89-21851).

MAGGIO MUSICALE FIORENTINO, Florence, Italy: Italy's answer to Salzburg presents artists just as fine, but programs so much more diverse that it seems a conscious attempt is being made to avoid musical chauvinism; you are as likely to hear Berg and Stravinsky as Rossini and Puccini. Some of the concerts are held in the magical Boboli Gardens — lovely and quintessentially Italian on a June evening. Despite its name, which translates as "Florentine Musical May," the festival continues right through June as well. Information: *Maggio Musicale Fiorentino*, Teatro Comunale, 15 Via Solferino, Florence 50123, Italy (phone: 55-27791).

INTERNATIONAL FESTIVAL OF THE TWO WORLDS, Spoleto, Italy: Founded in 1957 by Maestro Gian Carlo Menotti, this celebrated event, which begins in mid-June every year, brings together performers from both sides of the Atlantic for 3 weeks of dance, poetry readings, concerts, drama, opera, and art exhibits; the festival is celebrated for the diversity and high quality of its concerts and for the sizable number of premières of new works on its programs. However, the setting is equally noteworthy. Spoleto, which was the capital for the Dukes of Lombard between the 6th and 8th centuries, is a picturesque place, full of narrow vaulted passages and interesting nooks and crannies, quaint old shops and colorful markets. The final concert is traditionally held in front of the 12th-century cathedral, with the audience sitting on the majestic stairway that overlooks it — in the shadow of handsome palaces and hanging gardens. Menotti himself still participates. Information: *Festival dei Due Mondi*, 18 Via Beccaria, Rome, Italy (phone: 6-320-0747).

EDINBURGH FESTIVAL, Edinburgh, Scotland: Between late August and early September, the *Edinburgh Festival* presents a diverse, jam-packed program of music and theater that can include everything from the *Scottish Chamber Orchestra* playing in the stately 18th-century Hopetoun House to old-fashioned British military tattoos — although Frank Dunlop, the present festival director, tends to favor theater more and music less than have previous directors. An assemblage of innovative, low-budget productions known as *The Fringe* gives the festival its color. The substance derives from the first-rate program of superb operas, concerts, and recitals; and the *Edinburgh Festival* is one of Europe's major musical events. Information: *Edinburgh International Festival of Music and Drama*, 21 Market St., Edinburgh EH1 1BW, Scotland (phone: 31-226-4001).

MENUHIN FESTIVAL, Gstaad, Switzerland: Staged in August in the town of Gstaad-Saanen, among the towering peaks of the Bernese Oberland, this most personal of European music festivals is the work of the master violinist Yehudi Menuhin. The dozen-odd chamber concerts by celebrated virtuosos are held in the ancient church at Saanen. The rehearsals are open to the public, and one of the concerts is given by the top students of London's Menuhin School. Daytimes, you can enjoy spectacular Alpine rambles. Information: *Menuhin Festival*, Bureau de Renseignements, Gstaad CH-3780, Switzerland (phone: 30-41055).

INTERNATIONAL MUSIC FESTIVAL, Lucerne, Switzerland: Switzerland's major festival, held from mid-August to early September, has brought the likes of Rostropovitch, Richter, Milstein, Pollini, Von Karajan, Fischer-Dieskau, Barenboim, Arrau, and Dorati to this flowered, serene, lakeside town. (There was once a festival that featured appearances by all of them.) A special feature is the intensive program of advanced instrumental courses given by festival performers in collaboration with the Lucerne Conservatory. For program information: *Internazionale Musikfestwochen*, 13 Hirschmattstr., Lucerne 6002, Switzerland (phone: 41-233562). For course information: *Sekretariat der Meisterkurse im Konservatorium Luzern*, 93 Dreilindenstr., Lucerne CH-6006, Switzerland (phone: 41-367686).

MONTREUX-VEVEY MUSIC FESTIVAL and THE INTERNATIONAL JAZZ FESTI-VAL, Montreux, Switzerland: Montreux has two international festivals a month apart: the blaring, rocking *International Jazz Festival* in July, which attracts everyone from the likes of Herbie Hancock and Dave Brubeck to the *Brockville Junior High Half Time Stompers;* and, in September, the elegant *Festival de Montreux-Vevey,* featuring some of the world's major musical personalities — Weissenberg, Rostropovich, Milstein, Ashkenazy, and the Soloisti Veneti all took part in the 40th anniversary program 6 years ago in the shadow of the legendary lakeside Château de Chillon. The festival is also the site of the prestigious *Clara Haskil Competition,* to be held this year in August. Information: *Festival de Jazz,* Gd. Rue 42, Montreux CH-1820, Switzerland (phone: 21-963-1212); or the *Festival de Musique Montreux-Vevey,* 14 Av. des Alpes, Montreux CH-1820, Switzerland (phone: 21-963-1212).

DUBROVNIK SUMMER FESTIVAL, Dubrovnik, Yugoslavia: From mid-July to late August some 100 performances are presented in over 40 different places in this enthralling medieval walled city on the Adriatic. You can enjoy everything from Beethoven symphonies in the courtyard of the Rector's Palace to Dalmatian folk dances on the ramparts. Musically, it's not on a par with its Western cousins, but the setting can't be beat. Information: *Dubrovnik Summer Festival,* 1 Od Sigurate, Dubrovnik, Yugoslavia (phone: 50-27996).

Learning the Language

QUI?
WHO?
CHI?
QUIEN? Americans, in their splendid isolation, have always had reputations as poor learners of foreign languages, and we walk the world expecting universal mastery of English to have preceded us. If the natives didn't understand, the popular wisdom went, you were supposed to say it again, louder. In the years since World War II, this daydream has been approaching some kind of reality, with English emerging as the international language of trade and tourism. But no matter how many sales managers or desk clerks or headwaiters can answer your questions, there is no substitute for some knowledge of the local language as a way into a foreign culture. Without it, you only skim the surface of the country you visit; you read its dust jacket but never open the book.

The best method to acquire the language skills that will so greatly enhance your travel experience is an academic program in the country whose language you're trying to learn. The sounds and the rhythms of local speech will become a part of your own thought processes; every shop, every market, every street corner, is soon a language lab. Most European countries offer foreigners special courses lasting anywhere from 2 weeks to a full year, in settings as diverse as metropolitan capitals and Alpine castles. Here's *la crème de la crème:*

FRENCH

UNIVERSITÉ LIBRE DE BRUXELLES: Courses all year long — designed for everyone from the rank beginner to the college French instructor — with a Belgian accent. Information: *Université Libre de Bruxelles,* 50 Av. Franklin-Roosevelt, Brussels, Belgium (phone: 2-642-2030).

COURS POUR ETUDIANTS ETRANGERS, UNIVERSITÉ DE PROVENCE: A course in French civilization specifically designed for foreign students, under the auspices of the university, in one of the most gracious and charming towns in the south of France. University-age students tend to dominate, and the town is one large, animated campus. Information for both year-round and intensive summer courses (office closed during August): *Institut d'Etudes Françaises pour Etudiants Etrangers,* 23 Rue Gaston-de-Saporta, Aix-en-Provence 13625, France (phone: 42-23-28-43).

ALLIANCE FRANÇAISE: Exams at this venerable institution dedicated to the diffusion of French culture are a universal standard of French proficiency. The school is in the heart of the Parisian student quarter, and it has a clientele of all colors and tongues. Information: *Alliance Française,* 101 Bd. Raspail, Paris Cedex 06 75270, France (phone: 45-44-38-28).

CHAMBRE DE COMMERCE ET D'INDUSTRIE: The Chamber of Commerce sponsors programs in commercial French, with emphasis on understanding the life of the French business world. For details: *Chambre de Commerce et d'Industrie,* Direction des Relations Internationales de la Direction de l'Enseignement, 42 Rue du Louvre, Paris 75001, France (phone: 45-08-37-37).

FRANCE LANGUES: Courses at all levels in French language and civilization, with considerable use of audiovisual methods. Information: *France Langues,* 2 Rue de Sfax, Paris 75116, France (phone: 45-00-40-15).

SORBONNE: The University of Paris offers a variety of courses, during both the summer and the academic year, in French language and civilization. The *cours de civilisation française* — a potpourri of grammar, literature, history, and fine arts studies — is a model for courses at a number of other French universities that offer special programs for foreigners. Information: *Cour de Civilisation Française,* Galerie Richelieu, 47 Rue des Ecoles, Paris 75005, France (phone: 40-46-22-11, ext. 2670).

EUROCENTRE: An international foundation with head offices in Zurich, twenty schools distributed in seven European countries — and an outpost at Columbia University in New York City. The Paris branch — 16 classrooms, 2 language labs, a film room, and a library, set in the middle of the Latin Quarter — offers a program that blends excursions with course work. Information: *Eurocentre,* 13 Passage Dauphine, Paris 75006, France (phone: 43-25-81-40). For a complete list of all the Eurocentres, programs, and fees, contact *Eurozentren,* 247 Seestr., Zurich CH-8038, Switzerland (phone: 1-485-5040).

GERMAN

DEUTSCHER AKADEMISCHER AUSTAUSCHDIENST: This central office handles special courses for foreigners at a variety of German universities. The most desirable university towns are Munich, Hamburg, Augsberg, and Heidelberg (which offers a unique course in German literature, film and theater). Information: *DAAD,* 50 Kennedyallee, Bonn 2 D-5300, Germany (phone: 228-8820), or *German Academic Exchange Service,* 950 Third Ave., 19th Fl., New York, NY 10022 (phone: 212-758-3223).

GOETHE INSTITUT: Perhaps the most respected school of German language, the institute has some 16 centers in Germany and a number of foreign countries, promoting German culture abroad. Courses, which come in 3-, 4-, and 8-week packages, are intensive and include nearly 24 hours a week of instruction. Special new courses combine sports like sailing, riding, and skiing with language study. For complete information, contact the central office, *Goethe Institut,* Postfach 201009, 3 Lenbachpl., Munich 2, 8000 Germany (phone: 89-599-9200). Or write directly to either of the two big city centers at 7 Hardenbergstr., Berlin 12, 1000 Germany (phone: 849-881-3051); or 25 Sonnenstr., Munich 2 8000, Germany (phone: 89-592421).

HUMBOLDT INSTITUT: In the 16th-century castle of Ratzenried, deep in the Allgäu district, at the foot of the German Alps. Beautiful countryside, accommodations at the castle or in nearby private houses. Main courses start on the first Monday of each month, with special sessions available in summer and holiday periods. Information: *Humboldt Institut,* Schloss Ratzenried, Argenbühl/Allgäu 7989, Germany (phone: 7522-4044).

SALZBURG INTERNATIONAL LANGUAGE CENTER and IFK-INTERNA-

TIONALE FERIENKURSE: Salzburg, Austria, where the courses at these two schools are held, is one of the most charming towns in all of Europe, and so, though you may end up speaking the local Austrian dialect, the experience is worth it for the mountains, the music, and the *mohn strudel.* Information: *Salzburg International Language Center,* 106 Moosstr., Salzburg A-5020, Austria (phone: 662-844485); and *IFK-Internationale Ferienkurse,* 19 Franz-Josefstr., Salzburg A-5020, Austria (phone: 662-76595 or 662-846511).

GREEK

ATHENS CENTRE: In a residential area of Athens, the center offers year-round courses devoted to the intensive study of modern Greek as well as a special Translators' Seminar. Courses provide an insight into aspects of Greek culture, art, and history. The center assists students from abroad in finding accommodations, including summer sublets. Information: *The Athens Centre,* Greek Language Programs, 48 Archimidous St., Athens 11636, Greece (phone: 1-701-2268).

HELLENIC-AMERICAN UNION: Popular with Athens' resident American community as well as with locals who come to use the English library and read *The New York Times* on microfilm, the Hellenic-American Union offers courses in modern Greek for students of all proficiencies. Information: *The Registrar,* Academic Section, Hellenic-American Union, 22 Massalias, Athens, Greece (phone: 1-362-9886).

ITALIAN

EUROCENTRO: Eurozentren's sole center in Italy is in a Renaissance *palazzo* in the heart of Florence. In addition to providing first-rate Italian language instruction, the center puts a great deal of emphasis on teaching its students about Italian art and architecture, some of the finest of which can be seen from the school's windows. Information: *Eurocentro,* 9 Piazza Santo Spirito, Florence 50125, Italy (phone: 55-294605).

SOCIETÀ DANTE ALIGHIERI: The Dante is a worldwide organization for the diffusion of Italian culture, with some 400 branches teaching Italian to 50,000 students a year. The Rome branch offers courses in art, music, theater, furniture, and interior decoration; and sponsors films, concerts, lecture series, and assorted excursions. There are four 2-month terms from October to May, plus 2-month-long summer terms in June and July. Fees are quite low and instruction first-rate. Information about instruction in Rome and other Italian cities: *Società Dante Alighieri,* 27 Piazza Firenze, Rome 00186, Italy (phone: 6-687-3722).

UNIVERSITÀ ITALIANA PER STRANIERI: Founded in 1925 by the Italian government, this "University for Foreigners" is housed in the 18th-century Palazzo Gallenga of Perugia. Well run, with a diverse student body and nominally priced courses in subjects as varied as elementary Italian and Etruscology, it puts much of the country's regular university system to shame. Courses of varying lengths — from 2 weeks to 9 months — are offered throughout the year. Information: *Università Italiana per Stranieri,* Palazzo Gallenga, Piazza Fortebraccio, Perugia, Italy (phone: 75-58591).

SPANISH

CENTRO DE ESTUDIOS DE CASTELLANO: Founded in 1945, well before the Costa del Sol boom, and situated in a pleasant villa on a suburban street in Málaga, this school limits its classes to eight students each and offers month-long courses at four skill levels throughout the year. Dandy for keeping a winter visit to the sea from descending entirely into frivolity — but the beach is never more than an irregular verb away. Information: *Centro de Estudios de Castellano,* 110 Av. J. S. Elcano, Málaga 29017, Spain (phone: 52-290551).

COLEGIO DE ESPAÑA: In the noble and lively university town of Salamanca, the Colegio offers Spanish language and literature at every level, with special month-long immersion courses in the summer. Frequent excursions add color to the classroom routine. The university itself also offers excellent courses for foreign students in Spanish language and civilization. Information: *Colegio de España,* 65 Calle Compañia, Salamanca, 37008, Spain (phone: 23-214788); and *Secretaria de la Facultad de Filología,* Universidad de Salamanca, Plaza de Anaya, Salamanca 57001, Spain (phone: 23-216534).

ESADE IDIOMAS: Because this school is in Barcelona, you will hear a lot of the Catalan dialect in the city's shops and markets rather than the Castilian, which is spoken around Madrid and is the national language. Intensive month-long summer courses are offered in small groups. *ESADE* is also a school of business management, so practical Spanish is taught. Lodging with private families is available. Information: *ESADE,* Av. de Pedralbes 60, Barcelona 08034, Spain (phone: 3-329-3412; fax: 3-204-8105).

INLINGUA IDIOMAS: Part of a large European chain of effective language schools, Inlingua offers a wide variety of short intensive courses year-round. Housing is available on the school premises as well as with local families. Information: *Inlingua Idiomas,* 24 Arenal, Madrid 28013, Spain (phone: 1-248-0225).

TIPS ON OVERSEAS LANGUAGE PROGRAMS

Whether you're learning French or German, Italian or Spanish, be diligent about exposing yourself to the language you're studying. Read signs religiously, muddle through the newspaper daily, listen to the radio constantly, and eavesdrop on conversations. Stay with good solid lowbrow material — the local tabloid newspaper, not the local *Times.* Follow the latest murder and the hottest rock star romance. Watch the soap operas on television. Go back to comic books. Then hit the movies: Start with dubbed American films — even ones you've seen in English — where your familiarity with the settings, gestures, and lip movements will provide you with clues to the meaning of the lines. Then try out local films: If they're incomprehensible, see them again. And read books on subjects that really interest you; improve your tennis in German, or your lovemaking in French.

Speak with courage and without fear of error. Be zealous about putting yourself in situations that will demand that you communicate, and don't rely on friends who know the language better to help you do your daily business. Go shopping, talk to the chambermaid about her liver trouble, tell strangers the story of your life. The more you speak, the better you'll do it; 10 minutes in the street is worth an hour at home with chapter 6, exercise 17. Everybody is an expert in his or her own language, and most people are delighted to give free lessons in grammar or vocabulary while they repair your shoe or show you the way to the zoo.

Finally, remember that *accent* is as much a part of a language as its vocabulary. Listen to sounds and imitate them, and insofar as your ear and your tongue permit, try not to say everything as if you were reading from the Pittsburgh phone book.

Antiquer's Guide to Europe

Whether you're at Piccadilly Circus, on a dirt road in Andalusia, or in the throbbing heart of downtown Bratislava, sooner or later you'll see a sign that says "Antiques," and sooner or later you'll find yourself pawing over relics of the past as if in search of a gracious way to drain off excess capital. Europe has plenty to entice you — English silver, Persian rugs, fine painting and sculpture, and antique china, not to mention Venetian glass and French and English furniture.

For the most part, you'll do better buying such items in their country of origin — and at auction. Although every once in a while a dealer will underprice an item he doesn't love or understand, it's generally true that most will do the opposite, so that you're likely to pay unnecessarily high prices for Georgian sterling in Italy and Spanish paintings in Scandinavia. Antiques hunting in the auction houses ordinarily saves you about 30% — but only so long as you know the market. If you don't, stick to the shops, and just as auctiongoers are best advised to patronize the first-echelon salerooms, so should the less-than-expert buyer stick to reputable dealers, particularly when it comes to high-ticket items. With the booming of the art market, the forgery business has taken on the proportions of an industry. Conscientious dealers usually will guarantee in writing the authenticity of your purchase and often will accept its return, for the original price, if you change your mind. At the same time, a good dealer can advise novices about imperfections.

Ideally, you should buy only the best example you can find of a particular genre, in the best condition: Whether an item is damaged or not is a major factor in determining its market price (and should matter to you if you're buying as a potential investment); and in any case, a stain, a chip, or a warp will probably annoy you in the long run. Helpful antiques dealers also can provide you with the name of a good restorer, and, sometimes, can even arrange for you to pay the trade price for a restoration. Before you buy something that has been restored already, ask the dealer to explain what catchwords like "remodeled," "renewed," and "restyled" actually mean when applied to an item. You don't want to buy a Renaissance Tuscan armoire whose only original part is the keyhole.

You can learn something of what the dealers know at weekend courses that are available throughout the year at *Earnley Concourse* (Chichester, Sussex PO20 7JI, England; phone in Bracklesham Bay: 243-670392). *Christie's* in London offers a fine arts course that covers the subject in a year. Information: *Director, Christie's Education,* 63 Old Brompton Rd., London SW7 3JS, England (phone: 71-581-3933).

To find out where to buy, consult the *Weltkunst* (a world art review), published twice monthly and available at well-stocked newsstands in Germany (or through the magazine's office at 84 Nymphenburgerstr. (8000 Munich 19, Germany; phone: 89-126-9900); it contains a good Europe-wide auction calendar. So do the *Antiques Trade Gazette,* available at Metropress Ltd. (17 Whitcomb St., London WC2 H7PL, England; phone: 71-930-7192), and *Art and Auction* magazine (250 W. 57th St., New York, NY 10107; phone: 212-582-5633). Also see the art and auction page of the weekend edition of the *International Herald Tribune* and the *Guide Emer* (Emer Publicité; 50 Rue-Quai de l'Hôtel de Ville, Paris 75004; phone: 42-77-83-44), a specialized French publication aimed at the art and antiquity trade.

Some of the best hunting grounds are in Vienna, London, Paris, Berlin, and Rome; along streets full of antiques shops in other cities; and at a number of antiques fairs that take place all over Europe throughout the year.

ANTIQUES CAPITALS

VIENNA, Austria: Go straight to the Dorotheergasse, a lovely old street off the Graben where antiques shops have proliferated in the shadow of the great *Dorotheum* auction house at No. 17. The shops flow out into the side streets — the Braünerstrasse, the Spiegelgasse, and the Stallburggasse — and they devote themselves to every imaginable genre of antique. There are generalists who carry furniture, painting, and rugs; and specialists that stock only brocades, or crystal, or music boxes, or clocks and watches, or toy soldiers, and — because this is Vienna — a number that deal exclusively in collectors' instruments, manuscript pages of musical scores, composers' autographed letters, and the like. (Have a look at *Doblinger Musikhaus,* 10 Dorotheergasse; phone: 1-513030.) Also, call at the strongholds of the *Hofstätters,* Vienna's leading antiques dynasty: *Reinhold* (15 Dorotheergasse; phone: 1-533-5069), is the sculpture and furniture branch. Arrange also to attend at least one auction at the *Dorotheum* (17 Dorotheergasse; phone: 1-515600), a major source for dealers, which is always an education even if you never lift a finger. On Saturday, try the less rarefied end of the spectrum: The flea market at Naschmarkt in the 6th district is reached easily from the *Stadtbahn*'s Kettenbrückengasse station. And the city's big annual antiques fair, the *Wiener Kunst Und Antiquitätenmesse* (Vienna Art and Antiques Fair), runs for a week in November in the Hofburg. If you still haven't found anything, you're not really interested in antiques.

LONDON, England: The British Empire is the world's largest antique, but in its heyday the sun never set on the loot that flowed into its prosperous capital. And before that, during the French Revolution, the city was also a safe haven for things of value. Consequently, London has long been the unquestioned center of the antiques trade. Anything can be bought here, and everything has a market value and instant liquidity. The 10-day *Grosvenor House Antiques Fair,* held annually in June, is a sun in the antiques dealer's solar system; you'll find everything from Etruscan heads to Victorian bustles, and every piece has been authenticated by independent experts. The great auction houses, *Christie's* on King Street and *Sotheby's* on Bond Street, are instrumental in setting market prices; they're superb places to develop a feel for the market. Then there are the street markets that blossom and thrive in Camden Passage, Islington, on Wednesdays, Thursdays, and Saturdays (Wednesdays are best for antiques); at Bermondsey Square and Tower Bridge Road (known as the *New Caledonian* market), on Fridays beginning at 5 AM (the best time); and, on Saturdays, on Portobello Road, Westbourne Park, where you'll recognize as sellers the buyers of the previous day's *Caledonian.* All week long, you can browse in *Antiquarius* (131 King's Rd. SW 3; phone: 71-351-5353), *Chenil Galleries* (181 King's Rd. SW3; phone: 71-351-5353), the *Chelsea Antique Market* (253 King's Rd. SW3; phone: 71-352-9695), or *Gray's Antique Market* (58 Davies St. W1; phone: 71-629-7034). London's two renowned department stores, *Harrods* and *Fortnum & Mason,* both have excellent antiques departments that stock only the finest quality items. Antiques shops also can be found in quantity along Kensington Church Street, Fulham Road, Bond Street, Mount Street, Jermyn Street, Brompton Road, and the King's Road. Buy silver at the underground *London Silver Vaults* (Chancery House, Chancery La. WC2; phone: 71-242-3844); porcelain at the *Antique Porcelain Company Ltd.* (149 New Bond Street W1; phone: 71-629-1254); prints at *Colnaghi's* (14 Old Bond Street W1; phone: 71-491-7408); books at *E. Joseph* (1 Vere St. W1; phone: 71-493-8353); Oriental rugs at *Alexander Juran* (74 New Bond St. W1; phone: 71-491-7408); and Russian icons at the *Temple Gallery* (6 Clarendon Cross W1; phone: 71-727-3809). *Mallett and Sons* (40 New Bond St. W1; phone: 71-499-7411), is a miniature museum. Incidentally, if you've bought — or taken on approval — something you'd like an expert to examine, try the *British Museum* (where you'll never be quoted a value) or *Sotheby's* (where you'll be reminded that the house will be happy to sell it).

PARIS, France: Despite the ravages of the Revolution, you can still do some productive antiques hunting in Paris. The most fruitful market is the giant *Biennale Internationale des Antiquaires,* a marathon fair held in even-numbered years in mid-autumn at the *Grand Palais.* The rest of the time, visit the venerable *Hôtel Drouot* auction house, both in its quarters at 9 Rue Drouot on the Right Bank and in its other venue, the *Théâtre des Champs-Elysées* on stylish Avenue Montaigne. In addition, on the site of the old Magasins du Louvre there's an antiques shopping center with 250 shops: *Le Louvre des Antiquaires* (2 Pl. du Palais Royal; phone: 42-97-27-00), open daily except Monday, 11 AM to 7 PM). Two other important antiques centers are *Le Village Suisse* (78 Av. de Suffren and Av. de la Motte-Picquet; phone: 43-06-26-39), open every day except Tuesday and Wednesday; and *La Cour aux Antiquaires* (54 Rue du Faubourg-St.-Honoré; phone: 47-42-43-99), closed Sundays and Mondays. Saturdays, Sundays, and Mondays are the days to hit the *Marché aux Puces,* the huge flea market between the Porte de St.-Ouen and the Porte de Clignancourt, where some 3,000 shops, stalls, and blankets display everything from Renoir watercolors to 78 rpm records. The *Porte de Vanves* and the *Porte de Montreuil* markets also are in business on weekends only; you'll find more blankets, fewer shops, and better prices. And if you're in Paris in February or September, don't miss the semi-annual *Foire à la Ferraille* at the Parc Floral, Bois de Vincennes, where all the dealers stock up (phone: 42-62-44-44, for information). A number of streets are heavily populated with antiques shops. On the Right Bank, they include the Rue du Faubourg-St.-Honoré, Rue La Boétie, Rue de Miromesnil (especially for armor and toy soldiers), Avenue Victor-Hugo, Rue St.-Honoré, and Rue du Faubourg-St.-Antoine. On the Left Bank, prowl the Quai Voltaire, Rue de Grenelle, Boulevard St.-Germain, Rue Bonaparte, Rue de Beaune (scientific instruments), Rue du Bac (dolls, toys), Rue des Saints-Pères, Rue de Seine, and Rue Jacob. In addition, between the two banks, you'll find some pleasant shops in even more pleasant surroundings on the Ile St.-Louis. If you're a stamp fancier, don't miss the open-air stamp market — held on Thursdays, Saturdays, and Sundays at the corner of Avenue Gabriel and Avenue Marigny — or the countless shops along the Rue Drouot and in the arcades of the Palais Royal. Finally, to keep abreast of Parisian auction activities, pick up a copy of *La Gazette de l'Hôtel Drouot* at any Paris newsstand.

BERLIN, Germany: Berlin dealers have a long-cultivated and prized reputation for expertise and honesty, and you are likely to have a 30-year guarantee and an item's complete pedigree pressed upon you, even if you're running to catch a plane. And if you ever have any complaints, you can take it to a special court of arbitration established solely to handle antiques matters. The Keithstrasse is virtually one long row of antiques shops, with a variety of specialties. Some of the best include *Eva Lohmaier* (for silver and jewelry), *Hagen Jung* (for porcelain), *Karin Sonnenthal* (for Biedermeier furniture), and *Ruth Schmidt* (for really fine East Asian pieces). The area around Kurfürstendamm and Fasanenstrasse also is productive, as are Eisenacherstrasse, Winterfeldstrasse, Motzstrasse, and Fuggerstrasse. (*Joachim Schröder,* at No. 4, has fine silver and furniture). Bleibtreustrasse and Mommsenstrasse are the places to hunt for Jugendstil (Art Nouveau) and Art Deco pieces. You'll find a number of shops in the nearby Wilmersdorf and Charlottenburg sections of the city. Another sprawling secondhand market is on Saturdays and Sundays, 8 AM to 3:30 PM, in the Strasse des 17 Juni. Among other reputable and well-stocked dealers are the *Galerie Pels-Leusden,* on Fasanenstrasse, in the restored Villa Griesbach; *Wilhelm Weick,* on the Eisenacherstrasse (for paintings); *Werner Wormuth,* also on Eisenacherstrasse (for old frames and fine restoration); *Herbert Klewer,* on Viktoria-Luiseplatz (for furniture); and *Seidel und Sohn,* on Eisenacherstrasse (for 18th-century furniture and art). Berlin's giant department store, *Ka-De-We,* also has a first-rate antiques section.

ROME, Italy: The main artery for antiques hunters is the Via del Babuino; for junking, there's the sprawling Sunday morning flea market at Porta Portese; and for items in between there are middlebrow streets like Via dei Coronari (on the pricey side), Via del Governo Vecchio, Via di Panico, and Via Margutta (the site of an annual open-air art show). There is also an annual autumn fair in Via dei Coronari; all the shops are open at night and the strolling is delightful. And all week long throughout the year there is a pleasant collection of stands and stalls for old and new books and prints in Piazza Borghese. On the aristocratic Via del Babuino, the nobility includes *Di Giorgio, Amedeo di Castro, Apolloni, Olivi, Fallani* (for sculpture), *Luciano Coen* (for rugs), and *Sestieri* at Piazza di Spagna (for paintings). Two other fine Rome shops are

Tanca on the Salita dei Crescenzi, for antique jewelry and silver; and *Lukacs-Donath* on Via Veneto, for porcelain. It should be noted that Italy's antiques trade is lively in the Tuscan provinces, as well. The most important events are the sedate *Mostra d'Antiquariato*, held in Florence's Palazzo Strozzi in September and October of odd-numbered years, and Parma's booming *Mercanteinfiera*, a yearly October extravaganza. There are shops of national importance in Florence (*Bartolozzi, Bellini*); Milan (*Longari*); Turin (*Rossi*); and Venice (*Barozzi*). The best auction houses in Rome are *L'Antonina* on Piazza Mignanelli and the branch of *Christie's* at Piazza Navona. *Finarte* is tops in Milan. As a general rule, the antiques market in Italy is less richly international than in other European countries, and you should stick to local creations. Also tread with extreme caution when you inspect classical Roman and Greek pieces: There are enough of them around to fill the Roman Empire six times over.

MORE GREAT STREETS FOR ANTIQUES HUNTING

BRUSSELS, Belgium – Rue Watteau, Rue Lebeau, Rue Ernest-Allard, Chaussée d'Ixelles, and the Place du Grand-Sablon, which has a Saturday- and Sunday-morning antiques market.

COPENHAGEN, Denmark – All the side streets adjacent to Strøget, a half-mile-long pedestrians-only thoroughfare that runs through the city's center.

NICE, France – Village Segurane, at Rue Pierre Gautier, near the harbor.

MUNICH, Germany – The Ottostrasse, near Stachus.

ATHENS, Greece – Pandrossou, Solonos, Kriezotou, and Balaritou streets, and Kolonaki Square.

DUBLIN, Ireland – Grafton Street, Dawson Street, Francis Street, Patrick Street, Clare Street, Duke Street, Molesworth Street, and South Anne Street.

NAPLES, Italy – Via Domenico Morelli and Via Santa Maria di Constantinopoli, near the *Museo Nazionale;* Via Chiaia.

AMSTERDAM, The Netherlands – Nieuwe Spiegelstraat, near the *Rijksmuseum.* And nearly everywhere in The Hague; there are some 150 antiques shops in the city. *Christie's* is at 57 Cornelis Schuytstraat (phone: 20-664-2011) and *Sotheby's* is at 102 Rokin (phone: 20-275656).

WARSAW, Poland – Nowy Świat, Krakowskie Przedmieście.

MADRID, Spain – Calle del Prado, Plaza de las Cortés, Carrera de San Jerónimo, Calle Serrano, Mercado Puerta de Toledo, and the *Rastro,* a huge Sunday flea market.

BERN, Switzerland – The Kramgasse.

GENEVA, Switzerland – Rue de la Cité, Rue de l'Hôtel de Ville, la Grande Rue.

LAUSANNE, Switzerland – Cheneau de Bourg.

ZURICH, Switzerland – The Kirchgasse, Stüssihofstatt, Schipfe, Rindermarkt, and Oberdorfstr.

MOSCOW, Soviet Union – The state-run thrift shops, *Komissionyj, Bukinist,* or *Antikvar,* where you'll find everything from a piece of chipped crockery with a picture of a waving cosmonaut to a 17th-century icon of St. Dmitri (though most of the best items have been in London and Paris since 1917). Expect tricky export problems.

ANTIQUES FAIRS

SALZBURGER MESSE, Salzburg, Austria – Generally held in late March or early April in the *Residenz,* with dealers coming from all over the country.

LA FOIRE DES ANTIQUAIRES DE BELGIQUE, Brussels, Belgium – Held 2 weeks in February at the *Palais des Beaux-Arts.*

AUER DULT, Munich, Germany – A week-long flea market that takes place three times annually, in April or May, July or August, and October. Mariahilfplatz.

IRISH ANTIQUE DEALERS' FAIR, Dublin, Ireland – Held in July or August, at about the same time as the chi-chi Royal Dublin Society *Horse Show*.

ANTIQUES FAIR, Delft, The Netherlands – Held for 2 weeks every autumn (mid-October) in the *Prinsenhof Museum*.

SWISS ART AND ANTIQUES FAIR, Basel, Switzerland – An annual exposition generally held in the spring at the *Schweitzer Mustermesse*.

INTERNATIONAL ANTIQUES DEALERS FAIR, Lausanne, Switzerland – A November annual at the *Palais de Beaulieu*.

DIRECTIONS

Introduction

Fussy as they were, the Victorians were magnificent travelers: extremely thorough, compulsively curious, and driven by intense energy. Their Grand Tour of the Continent often took months, and led from Europe's major cities to the farthest outposts of civilization, wherever interest or curiosity directed.

Rare is the modern traveler who can spend more than 2 or 3 weeks at a time exploring Europe. As frustrating as this limit would seem to our Victorian predecessors, their alarm would be unfounded, for although today's trips are shorter, they are more frequent and aided by far faster and more efficient transportation alternatives. So the days when transatlantic visitors felt they had only one chance to "do" Europe in a lifetime are long over. Two weeks this year, 2 weeks next year, a hard-won month the year after — the North Americans' love affair with Europe intensifies with the frequency of acquaintanceship, not its duration.

Our indefatigable Victorian would be wrong to raise a skeptical eyebrow for another reason. Europe is especially well suited to a series of short visits precisely because of the cultural and historical density that makes it such a daunting prospect when contemplated as a whole. Spend 2 days touring a tiny area in depth or hopscotching the length of the Continent — the time will be equally well spent and the experiences, though very different, equally illuminating.

On the following pages are touring routes through 31 European countries. Organized to cover 3 to 5 days of traveling, they lead to Europe's areas of greatest scenic and historic interest. From the tiny villages of England's Cotswolds and its great cathedral cities, through France's wine country and the corniches of the Côte d'Azur, across the ancient Roman Via Emilia — used by Roman legions to conquer a continent, through fjords, moors, tors, and lava pours — this is Europe at its most intimate, historic, and dramatic.

Where possible, tours begin at major cities, and though our routes are most easily negotiated by car, tour operators with local buses often cover the same territory, freeing you from the necessity of driving. Entries are not exhaustive or comprehensive; they discuss the highlights of each route and can, in some sense, serve as starting points for longer journeys.

Entries are organized by country; an introduction provides some perspective and explains the routes that follow. The *Best en Route* section of each tour provides hotel and restaurant recommendations along the way (under each city, they are listed in order of expense). There is no effort to cover absolutely everything in these selections; our choices are made on the basis of places that offer the most memorable experiences. Since most countries are divided into several routes, it is often possible to string these together to form longer itineraries. But if you are pressed for time, you will find that by following any single itinerary you will see the most notable sites and sights (and attractive accommodations) in the area.

Andorra

A visit to the tiny principality of Andorra, 175 square miles nestled in the Pyrenees, used to be an adventure back in time to feudal Europe. Isolated by dramatic mountains, Andorra offered a picturesque setting that seemed far removed from the pace of the 20th century. In the last 2 decades, however, Andorra has leapt forward 400 years. Now, the quaint mountain villages are being renovated and, although farmers still work the tobacco fields by hand, their sons run computers in banks. As a tax-free enclave and a bargain haven, this is a favorite destination for the Spanish and French for wall-to-wall shopping, 7 days a week. In winter, good ski slopes and inexpensive après-ski amenities attract visitors from northern Europe (whiskey is $4 a bottle). But whatever the season, there is always a line of cars, buses, and trucks hauling visitors and goods to and from the principality on the one main road that wriggles through it from the north (France) to the south (Spain).

The most direct route to Madrid from Andorra, passing through the provinces of Lleida, Zaragoza, and Guadalajara, takes you through 325 miles (520 km) of diverse topography. The dramatic verticality of the Catalonian Pyrenees is softened by the rolling hills of agricultural Aragón and, finally, flattened by the dry, Central Meseta of Castile. Each region has a distinctive note of architecture, gastronomy, and language, and stops at such towns and villages as Lleida, Zaragoza, Calatayud, the Monasterio de Piedra, and Alcalá de Henares provide a varied itinerary to the capital of Spain from the remote land of Andorra.

The Catalonian region that includes Andorra was reconquered from invading Moors in the year 801 by the son of heroic Charlemagne, Louis I. This prince granted a small tract of his realm to the Spanish Bishop of Seu de Urgel. Successors to the bishop eventually felt their rule challenged by French noblemen and agreed to joint control over the area. The principality of Andorra was created under the tandem rule of the Count of Foix of France and the Spanish Bishop of Seu de Urgel. Andorrans first waved the country's blue, red, and yellow flag in 1298 and accepted an agreement whereby, in even-numbered years, the Spanish bishop would receive as tribute the equivalent of $12 in addition to six hams, six chickens, and six cheeses. In odd-numbered years, the French prince would be presented with a cash tribute of 960 pesetas.

Celebrating the 700th birthday of the nation in October 1978, Andorrans gathered to pay homage to their two (then current) liege lords, France's President Valéry Giscard d'Estaing and Spanish Bishop Joan Martí Alanis. It was the first time that both sovereigns ever had met on Andorran soil, and every indication was given that the feudal state would enjoy an updating of tradition in the future. At present, French and Spanish authorities oversee the justice and postal systems (all mail is delivered free within Andorra, and peseta or franc denominations of stamps are issued for mail outside the country). But since 1419 Andorrans have enjoyed free elections of their 24-member Council General and legislative head, the Sindic General, and are therefore proud to have one of the oldest parliaments in Europe. The total independence of the principality is not generally sought by the populace, whose national anthem underscores their present political feelings: "Faithful and free I wish to live, with my Princes as my protectors." Certainly only the unique political arrangement of joint rule provides Andorra with its privileged economic situation today. Originally dominated by a strictly agricultural economy, Andorra now is a model of modernization and growth.

Due to the influx of foreigners eager to establish residency in Andorra and enjoy its tax shelter, the country is attempting to restrict immigration and discourage speculators. In accordance with Andorran tradition, citizenship is acquired only after three generations of permanent residence or by the more expedient method of marriage to an *andorrano,* which is becoming the Catch-22 of the census bureau. At present, therefore, Catalan-speaking mountaineers, shepherds, and farmers share their nationality with savvy French- and Spanish-speaking hoteliers, real estate agents, and department store owners. Andorra is at the crossroads of time, perched in the Pyrenees, isolated from and dependent on the modern commercial world.

A visitor's first impression upon crossing the border into Andorra (a valid passport and the international insurance "green card" for drivers is required) is the monumental traffic jam of cars lined up to leave the country. This situation is evident in the French border town of Pas de la Casa in northeast Andorra (Rte. 20 from Toulouse), but much more so at the southwestern Spanish border hamlet of Farga de Moles (Route 145 from Lleida). This tie-up is created by the conscientious customs agents of each of the neighboring countries assessing the real value of duty-free purchases made in Andorra. This process is time-consuming since so many ingenious French and Spanish fill every imaginable cranny of their car, luggage, and personal attire with bargain-priced cameras, cosmetics, radios, watches, Scotch, pâté, skis, crystal, jewelry, perfume, and the like, that have not been listed on their customs declaration. In addition, the service stations just within the Andorran border are a mandatory last stop for motorists, since gasoline prices are often one-third less than those of Spain or France. We recommend that visitors entering or leaving Andorra do so during lunchtime (about 1 to 2 PM), when the lines at the border are shorter.

Once past the entry ordeal, the visitor to Andorra will be impressed by the dramatic landscape, racing rivers, and verdant meadows. The one major highway that crosses the country is excellent, and secondary roads to scenic lakes or hamlets are adequate. It is with a certain nostalgia that the visitor views the peaceful mountain villages and hears distant cowbells. Time definitely should be set aside for serenely experiencing the majesty of the mountains. Agencies in Andorra's capital, such as *Nadal* (94 Av. del Pessebre; phone: 21138) and *Lito* (63 Av. Meritxell; phone: 20000), offer half-day excursions to the most remote forests and peaks of the country. Day trips by private car or reasonably priced minibuses to the ski slopes of Arinsal and Pas de la Casa provide exhilarating encounters with nature at its most beautiful.

ANDORRA LA VELLA: Much therapeutic renewal of body and soul is needed after facing the bustle of Andorra la Vella, the nation's capital and the highest in Europe (3,000 feet). The modern, high-rise buildings almost block out the view of the surrounding peaks, and only the crisp mountain air suggests the splendor beyond the cement constructions. Spending money is the number one pastime, so travelers should come prepared with American dollars or Spanish or French currencies (almost anything is accepted), comfortable shoes, and a shopping list. All purchases on international name-brand items are bargains (up to 40% off), and many happy hours will be spent window shopping in the throngs of shops lining Andorra la Vella's streets. To recommend one store or another is futile, since most shops have standard prices and stock only the most marketable merchandise. This may prove less fun to the shopping enthusiast who loves to compare and haggle over the price, but it is infinitely more pleasurable to the buyer who knows the cost of the item at home and recognizes a bargain. Shopping hours are amenable even to late sleepers: 9 AM to 8 PM; most stores are open on Sundays.

A visit to the Casa del Vall, the Renaissance meeting house and seat of the Council General, is a cultural parenthesis in this shopping tour. In the small village of Encamp there is a surprisingly rich collection of antique cars, motorcycles, and bicycles at the *Museu Nacional de L'Automòbil* (64 Avinguda Príncep Episcopal, Encamp; phone: 32266). Open 10 AM to 8 PM. Closed during lunch and on Mondays. No admission charge.

Other adventures of a primarily cultural nature involve contact with the regional cuisine — a marvelous mixture of Spanish and French specialties, seasoned with that special Catalonian flavor. Fine French restaurants include *Molí dels Fanals* and *1900*, highly regarded by Spaniards. For those ready for a big splurge, fine eating and spectacular dining facilities are found primarily in hotels such as the *Andorra Palace* and *Roc Blanc*. See *Best en Route* for details on all four places. More modest eateries are abundant throughout the city as well, but most hotels will require that guests take full pension during tourist season; travelers should keep this in mind when checking in.

En Route from Andorra – Directly after leaving Andorra — calculating ample time to get through customs and replenish the gas tank — and heading south down Route 145 to Seu de Urgel, the traveler immediately senses the entry into Spain. The terrain becomes coarser, drier, and the towns less quaint. After passing Seu de Urgel, noted for its onetime bishop and co-prince of Andorra, follow Route 1313 along the Segre River past 77 miles (123 km) of farmland to Lleida. Route 1313 is a poor road, so this drive will take the better part of the morning. The villages passed along the way, however, are interesting and typical of the fertile Valley of Aran in western Catalonia. The medieval *Parador Jaime de Urgel* (phone: 73-445604) in the town of Balaguer, 5 miles (8 km) west of Route 148, 62 miles (100 km) south of Andorra, is a pleasant place for refreshment before continuing the remaining 16 miles (27 km) along Route 145 through the plains to Lleida.

LLEIDA: The capital of the province, with a population of 120,000, Lleida is built on a hill overlooking the Segre River. At the highest point of the city, the Gothic cathedral of Seu Vella can be admired and the remains of the ancient Arab fortress of La Zuda explored. The panoramic view of Lleida and the surrounding orchards is spectacular and well worth the drive up the hill. From this vantage point, the strategic importance of Lleida can be appreciated. Indeed, the city's name derives from the Latin word *ilerda,* or "stronghold," so named when the Roman troops of Caesar conquered the original Iberian fortress and, later, the rival army of Pompeii. The invading Moors made "Lareda" the capital of the *taifa,* or feudal realm, until the Christian armies came from the north to reconquer the region. Besieged by invading French troops at various times in its history, Lleida still presents itself as a well-fortressed city.

Due to its strong Catalonian ties, Lleida offers a cultural shock to visitors who think they can speak Spanish. The Catalán accent is more pronounced here than in Barcelona, but the warmth of the people compensates for the language barrier. Enjoy the Catalonian accent in the regional cuisine: the game dishes, *ensalada catalana* (salad with ham), *cassolada* (stew), and *caracoles* (the small striped, shelled snails from the fields). Order the regional wine from Raimat to accompany your meal. Fine restaurants include *Forn del Nastasi* (10 Salmerón) and *Moli de la Nora* (4 miles north of Lleida on the Seu road in the village of Vilanova de la Barca). Outside the city, on Route NII, the *Condes de Urgel* hotel has fine dining facilities in a picturesque setting (see *Best en Route* for all).

For further information regarding sights in Lleida, a map of the city and a brochure in English are available at the Office of Tourism, Edifici Pal-las (phone: 248120).

En Route from Lleida – Drive west on Route NII to Zaragoza, 86 miles (138 km) away. This is a better road, so the trip should not be very tiring. Also, the six-lane highway from Barcelona can be picked up just outside Lleida, further speeding the mainly uneventful journey past fertile valleys to Zaragoza, a city at the geographic crossroads of the Cantabric and Mediterranean seas and of the Pyrenees and the Central Meseta.

ZARAGOZA: The provincial capital and the largest city of the region of Aragón, with a population of 675,000, Zaragoza has been called the Lady of Four Cultures. The original Iberian city on the banks of the majestic Ebro River was conquered in 24 BC by Roman troops. The plan was to make it a city of peace for legion veterans. The name of the city derives from the Latin name Caesar Augustus, which, when pronounced rapidly, transforms to Zaragoza. The invading Arabs made the city, called Sarakosta by them, a cultural center and the seat of the regional King of Taifa until 1118, when the Christians reconquered Zaragoza for the crown of Aragón. These four cultures blend harmoniously to form the personality of Zaragoza, where Iberian and Roman ruins, Arab palaces, and Christian temples can be seen.

Zaragoza is a modern city today, important for its university and commercial vitality. Still, its main importance is for many visitors spiritual, since it was on a column of a Roman temple in Zaragoza that the Virgin Mary is said to have miraculously appeared to St. James with promises of salvation. The religious devotion to Nuestra Senora del Pilar is most profound in Spain and in Latin America, since the feast day coincides with October 12 celebrations of Hispanic culture. The monumental neo-classic Basilica del Pilar dominates the skyline from the Ebro River and is noted for its sculptured facade and interior frescoes by Goya, a native son. Most of the cultural sights of Zaragoza are within walking distance of the basilica, so it is a very good place to start a city tour.

Remains of Roman walls can be found west of the basilica. Farther west, the church of San Pablo can be seen, noted for its octagonal tower of the Mudéjar style, reflecting the design of Arab architects for Christian temples. A 10-minute walk farther, and not to be missed, is the Aljaferia, the spectacular Arab palace of the 11th century constructed by the Taifa king, Abu Chafar Ahmed Almoctadir-bilah. This pleasure retreat is the only example of Taifa architecture still standing and therefore has special artistic interest for those intrigued by Granada's Alhambra and Córdoba's mosque. Under restoration today, the Aljaferia is an unexpected treat for the visitor to Zaragoza. Other sights in Zaragoza are found east of the basilica and include the 16th-century Ayuntamiento, or government house; La Lonja, or market center; and the 14th-century Cathedral of La Seo, with its elaborate plateresque altar and baroque interior. The tourist office, near the old Roman walls, can provide brochures and maps that facilitate sightseeing.

Eating is excellent in Zaragoza, as in all of Aragón, and is characterized by simple but delicious preparation. The abundance of locally grown fruits and vegetables allows for great variety and selection in cooking. Such dishes as eggs *al salmorrejo,* chicken *a la chilindrón,* lamb *a la pastora,* or the *ternasco asado* are famed local delicacies, as are the sweets and candied fruits covered with chocolate. The robust table wines of Cariñena are outstanding.

When looking for a place to eat, do not be timid and miss out on the experience of exploring El Tubo, a winding labyrinth of streets in the area directly in front of the basilica. Row upon row of taverns and restaurants serve hearty regional fare in a rustic atmosphere. Since Zaragoza is a university town, there is always singing and guitar music in the air as students converge on their favorite haunt in El Tubo. There also is traditional singing at *El Plata* (23 4 de Agosto), one of the taverns in this maze of streets. Elsewhere, good cooking can be found at the *Costa Vasca, Asador Gayarre* (3 miles/5 km on the road to the airport), *Gurrea,* and *Horno Asador Gayesco.* The restaurant and *parilla,* or grillroom, of the *Corona de Aragón* hotel offer luxury dining at high prices (see *Best en Route* for details on the above restaurants).

Taking Route NII south out of the city, you drive past 50 miles (80 km) of orchards and vineyards before reaching Calatayud, the second largest city of the province.

CALATAYUD: The ancient Roman city of Bilbilis sat here, at the confluence of the Jalon and Jiloca rivers. Bilbilis flourished in pre-Christian times and is famous for being the home of the philosopher and writer Marcial. The city was renamed Zalat-Ayud by the Arabs, and ruins of the Moorish *ayud,* or castle, can be seen on the hilltop above the city. The many Mudéjar buildings such as the Colegiata de Santa Maria and the churches of San Andrés and San Pedro de los Francos are of artistic interest. Our itinerary takes you just past Calatayud, however, 12 miles (19 km) down Road 202 to the Monasterio de Piedra, founded in the 12th century by Cistercian monks.

MONASTERIO DE PIEDRA: The medieval monastery, today converted into a charming hotel, is an ideal place to stop and eat or spend the night (see *Best en Route*). In accordance with the original purpose of the monastery, the surroundings of the Monasterio de Piedra lend themselves to the monks' need for solitude and quiet contemplation. Of absolutely breathtaking beauty is the surrounding national park. It seems a wonder, in such an arid region, that the River Piedra could sculpt such spectacular caverns and create such dramatic cascades. The highlights of the park are conveniently indicated by arrows along a mile-long (2-hour walk) path. For those spending the night at the monastery, the evening itself will provide a memorable experience.

En Route from the Monasterio de Piedra – After winding your way back to Route NII, the remaining drive to Madrid includes a varied panorama of rural landscape and the opportunity for several brief stops in interesting towns. Fifty miles (80 km) from Calatayud is the ancient city of Medinaceli, the "city in the sky."

MEDINACELI: A drive to the top of the steep hill upon which the town was founded affords a magnificent view of the area and a chance to get close enough to admire the unique Roman arch that is unexpectedly perched on the edge of a plunging cliff. This 2nd-century construction is one of only two 3-tiered arches still in existence (the other one is in Rome) and seems to usher the traveler on toward the heavens — or at least on to the Central Meseta of Castile.

Returning to Route NII for 10 miles (16 km), you can take a short side trip down road C114 for 13 miles (21 km) to medieval Sigüenza.

SIGÜENZA: Built by the Romans on the banks of the Henares River in the 5th century, this picturesque town is best known today for its 12th-century Gothic cathedral. Here is the famous sculpture *El Doncel,* marking the tomb of the poetic and heroic nobleman slain in Granada in 1486, D. Martín Vázquez de Arce.

The remaining 80 miles (128 km) to Madrid, backtracking again to Route NII, bring you past Castilian towns large and small. Thirty-five miles (56 km) from Madrid you'll come to the city of Guadalajara.

GUADALAJARA: Today an industrial center, Guadalajara was at one time a Moorish stronghold, as its name, River of Stones, suggests. Later the feudal seat of the powerful Mendoza and Santillana families, it was an important center of Renaissance culture. The only vestige of this noble past, however, is the facade of the Infantado Palace, whose interior was totally destroyed during the Spanish Civil War.

Continuing the journey down Route NII for 14 miles (23 km) to Alcalá de Henares, one last stop can be made before reaching Madrid.

ALCALÁ DE HENARES: The highlights of a visit to Alcalá are the original Universidad Complutense, founded in 1508 by the humanist Cardinal Francisco Jiménez de Cisneros; the house where Cervantes was born; and the Municipal Hall, where an edition of the rare Polyglot Bible is displayed. You can have a medieval meal at the *Hostería del Estudiante,* next to the university (see *Best en Route*), or homemade candied almonds bought from a turntable from the cloistered nuns of the Franciscan Convent of Beaterio de San Diego.

En Route from Alcalá – Back on Route NII, the 21-mile (35-km) drive to Madrid, passing the American Air Force base at Torrejon de Ardoz and the international airport of Barajas, will take approximately half an hour.

BEST EN ROUTE

Hotels in Andorra and the northern provinces of Spain are moderately priced, running from as high as $70 a night, double occupancy, with private baths for expensive establishments, to around $50 in moderate ones, and as low as $30 and under (inexpensive). Restaurants also are inexpensive, and cost between $8 and $10 per person for a full-course meal. Most hotels, however, prefer their guests to take full-pension plans. Be sure to make reservations, particularly during the summer, at whichever hotel you intend to stay.

ANDORRA LA VELLA

Andorra Palace, Novotel, and Mercure – Linked by overhead walkways and centrally managed, these three properties offer modern accommodations. All rooms have a private bath, telephone, and TV set. Shared facilities include conference rooms, a pool, tennis courts, a sauna, gym, and boutiques. Good Spanish dishes are served in the *Andorra Palace*'s *La Truita;* the simpler French-style grill is in the *Novotel;* and the *Mercure* hotel has the coffee shop–style *Brasserie. Andorra Palace,* Prat de la Creu (phone: 21072); *Novotel,* Prat de la Creu (phone: 61116); *Mercure,* 58 Meritxell Av. (phone: 20773). Expensive.

Andorra Park – A view of the mountains as well as balconies, private baths, restaurant, and a swimming pool are found at this 40-room hotel. Roureda Guillemó (phone: 20979). Expensive.

Molí dels Fanals – A hotel with a restaurant specializing in French cuisine. Closed July. Reservations advised. Major credit cards accepted. Borda Casadet., Dr. Vilanova (phone: 24381). Expensive.

1900 – On a quiet side street, this place offers classy French fare, an excellent wine cellar, and nicely decorated dining rooms. Reservations advised. Unió II, Les Escaldes (phone: 26716). Expensive.

Roc Blanc – Since its refurbishment, this 240-room hotel now is the most modern in the area. Thermal therapeutic treatments are available. 5 Pl. Co-Princeps, Les Escaldes (phone: 21486). Expensive.

Flora – A bar and breakfast only are available at this 44-room hotel. 23 Antic Carrer Major (phone: 21508). Moderate.

Isard-55 – A 51-room hotel with its own dining room. 36 Av. Meritxell (phone: 20096). Moderate.

LLEIDA

Forn del Nastasi – For grilled meat and fish, as well as dishes baked in a wood-burning oven, this is the spot to go. Specialities include roast duck with peas, baked cod, and salmon served with mushrooms and crab. For dessert try the homemade ice cream or sorbet. Closed Sunday nights, Mondays, and the first 2 weeks in August. Reservations advised. Major credit cards accepted. 10 Salmerón (phone: 234510). Expensive.

Molí de la Nora – In an old windmill, decorated to look like an old barge inside, this restaurant offers specialties of fish and game in season. Closed Sunday nights, Mondays, and *Christmas Week*. Reservations necessary. Major credit cards accepted. 4 miles (6 km) north on the Seu road in the village of Vilanova de la Barca (phone: 190017). Expensive.

Condes de Urgel – This 105-room hotel features private baths, air conditioning, and a dining room. 17 Av. de Barcelona (phone: 202300). Moderate.

Ilerda – A small hotel that also offers dining facilities. Restaurant reservations advised. Barcelona Hwy. at Km 467 (phone: 200750). Inexpensive.

ZARAGOZA

Asador Gayarre – Salmon (in season) is especially good at this fish restaurant in an old, colonial-style house. Closed evenings during major fiestas. Reservations advised. Major credit cards accepted. 3 miles (5 km) out on the road to the airport. Ctra. Aeropuerto Km 4.3 (phone: 344386). Expensive.

Corona de Aragón – This 249-room hotel has a rooftop swimming pool and dining room. 13 Av. Cesar Augusto (phone: 430100). Expensive.

Gran – A 140-room hotel with a restaurant. 5 Costa (phone: 221901). Expensive.

Costa Vasca – The subtle use of fresh herbs with fish and meat, Basque cooking, and rioja wines make up the menu here. Open daily. Reservations unnecessary. Major credit cards accepted. 13 Teniente Coronel Valenzuela (phone: 217339). Moderate.

Goya – A 157-room hotel with private baths and a dining room. 5 Cinco de Marzo (phone: 229331). Moderate.

Gurrea – An international menu is offered in this centrally located restaurant. Closed Sundays and during August. Reservations unnecessary. Major credit cards accepted. 14 S. Ignacio de Loyola (phone: 233161). Moderate.

Horno Asador Gayesco – Nowadays, this place is much more than a grill. Try the imaginative fare, based on local produce. Closed Sundays and August 5–20. Reservations unnecessary. Major credit cards accepted. 44 Manuel Lasala (phone: 356870). Moderate.

El Plata – This tavern is in the famous El Tubo district, a winding labyrinth of streets in front of the basilica. No reservations (no phone). Inexpensive.

Ramiro I – Though it has no dining room, this 105-room hotel does have a bar. 123 Corso (phone: 298200). Inexpensive.

CALATAYUD

Calatayud – Private baths and dining services are provided in this 62-room hotel. Rte. NII, Km 237 (phone: 881323). Moderate.

MONASTERIO DE PIEDRA

Monasterio de Piedra – Housed in a former 12th-century monastery for Cistercian monks, this 61-room hotel has a swimming pool, bar, and a dining room. Nueralos, 15 miles (24 km) outside Calatayud (phone: 849011). Moderate.

GUADALAJARA

Pax – This 64-room hotel offers a swimming pool and dining room. Rte. NII, Km 57 (phone: 221800). Moderate.

ALCALÁ DE HENARES

Hostería del Estudiante – A fine restaurant with a medieval air, it specializes in roast meats. Open daily. Reservations advised. Major credit cards accepted. Next to the university, 3 Colegios (phone: 888-0303). Expensive.

Austria

Surrounded by Germany and Czechoslovakia to the north, Hungary to the east, Yugoslavia and Italy to the south, and Switzerland and Liechtenstein to the west, landlocked Austria (covering an area of about 32,375 square miles) is smaller than the state of Maine. Its geography, however, is more varied than perhaps any other European country. Moody plains with rocky outcroppings are crowned by castles and dense green forests evocative of medieval legends and fairy tales. The Danube flows for miles through the country's heartland, where robber-baron battlements still look down on waters that no longer are blue. In the Salzkammergut (Lake Region), ancient glacial waters lap calmly against the shores of little spa towns. There are acres of vineyards in settings more romantic than those in Burgundy or Bordeaux, and of course there are the Alps — some of the most breathtaking and dramatic peaks in the world.

Austria's 7.5 million people are spread out comfortably among city, town, spa, and farm, but the population swells annually by at least a million as tourists flock here to ski, sample the pastries, take the waters, listen to the music, or just generally absorb the splendor of this cultural jewel at the crossroads of Europe. If Vienna, Austria's capital, is the most distinguished city in the German-speaking world, Salzburg is certainly the most elegant; Innsbruck, high in the mountains, combines the best qualities of both and adds its own Alpine flavor; while Graz, to the south, is a medieval gem of an imperial city.

Location has made Austria a crossroads since ancient times. Some of the earliest evidence of human habitation in Europe has been unearthed around Hallstatt, in the Salzkammergut. In more recent times, the Celts and then the Romans lived here. For some 4 centuries, the Danube and the Rhine marked the northern boundary of their empire. Vienna was once Vindobona, a Roman frontier fortress. The Huns came this way, as have all conquerors since who have swept across Europe. In the 8th century, the country was Charlemagne's easternmost possession, hence its modern name: Osterreich, which in German means "Eastern Empire." The first indigenous monarchy was established by the Babenbergs in 976 at the town of Melk. Much of the country still was independently ruled (Salzburg was in the hands of the prince-archbishops long after this), and it wasn't until the 14th century, after the throne was moved to Vienna, that the Hapsburgs came from what is now Switzerland and became Dukes of Austria, a region then limited to the Danube Valley. They gradually extended their holdings, through advantageous marriages as much as military conquest, until they had amassed a patchwork empire that at one time included most of central Europe, Spain, the Low Countries, and much of Italy. In the 16th century, Austria was Europe's bulwark against Turkish expansion. Vienna withstood prolonged sieges in 1529 and 1683. (In retreat the Turks left their sacks of coffee outside the walls of Vienna and are therefore credited with the rise of the Viennese coffeehouse.) The last marked the end of the centuries-long Turkish threat, and Austria began its own steady expansion eastward, adding Hungary and large portions of present-day Czechoslovakia, Romania, and Yugoslavia to the Hapsburg realm. By 1700, Austria had become the great power of Europe.

Though the Hapsburgs reigned on, Austria's power was diluted during the 19th century, first by Napoleon and then by the revolution of 1848. The empire never regained its former prominence and was reduced to its present dimensions after World War I. Annexed by Hitler before World War II, Austria was occupied by the Americans, British, French, and Russians after Germany's defeat until 1955, when it once again became an independent state. The post–World War II years have been much kinder to the Alpine republic. Austrians at last found that sense of identity and purpose that is fundamental to the well-being of a nation, and have made rapid progress. A vigorously functioning democracy, Austria today is one of the most politically stable and economically prosperous countries in Europe and is moving to formalize its identity of interests with Western Europe by becoming a full member of the European Community.

Though the political names associated with Austria are sometimes notorious — Charlemagne, Richard the Lion-Hearted, Metternich, and Hitler — the musical names are the ones that spring more happily to mind — Beethoven, Bruckner, Haydn, Mahler, Mozart, Schubert, and the Strausses. And nearly every Austrian city boasts a festival in their honor.

Three Austrian routes are outlined below; two start from Vienna and one begins at Salzburg.

The Burgenland route is a 1- or 2-day drive south from Vienna through the quiet towns along the Hungarian border where the food — especially the wild game — is excellent and the wine is fresh. You follow the coast of the Neusiedler See down to the castle of Bernstein and come back north across the face of the Schneeberg, Vienna's Alp, to Baden and then back to the capital.

The trip from Vienna to Salzburg is one of the most picturesque in Europe, taking you through the famous Wachau wine-growing district, along the meandering Danube through Dürnstein to the historic golden abbey at Melk and on to the city of Linz. Then you head south through the beautiful lakes of the Salzkammergut, skirting the northern Alpine slopes and crisscrossing west to the elegant, three-hilled town of Salzburg.

The route south from Salzburg goes first to the spa town of Badgastein with its thundering waterfalls and then farther south to the Grossglockner Highway — the famous hairpin-turn road around one of the highest peaks in the Alps. From Lienz the route heads back north to Kitzbühel in the Tyrol and goes west along the Inn River, with mountains rising on both sides all the way up to Innsbruck, an urbane, medieval city where snow-capped peaks are visible from every corner. Through the Arlberg Pass to the Swiss border the Alpine landscape becomes more majestic, and the hillsides are clustered with white, spacious chalets. Our route gradually comes down out of the mountains and arrives at Bregenz, a neat resort town on Lake Constance at the western tip of the country.

Burgenland

This trip from Vienna into the province of Burgenland and back covers about 230 miles (368 km) and affords a look into the small towns that ring Vienna to the south and hug the Hungarian border to the east. It's a relaxing trip with good food, comfortable lodgings, and an uncrowded itinerary.

Burgenland itself actually was Hungarian until after World War I when the citizens voted to join with the new Austrian republic. The area boasts superb castles and estates, one of Europe's larger lakes, thousands of acres of prime vineyards, and probably the nation's finest regional cooking. It is difficult to find a really bad restaurant in Burgenland proper. Wild game, duck, and goose dishes, spicy homemade sausages, rich goulashes, and strudels of poppy seed and jam-filled crêpes highlight a cuisine that is at once hearty and still sophisticated enough for the most selective palate. The entire area was under Soviet occupation until Austria was granted its freedom in 1955. For many years people in the region hesitated to make improvements, but this has changed dramatically. Still, the region is not extensively toured, and the farther south from Vienna you get the more of a novelty a North American becomes.

In this section of Austria it is much wiser to follow "town to town" signs rather than highway signs. Many of the towns are so small that a quick stop is enough to absorb their flavor. Some of the highlights of these smaller towns have been lumped together, so, depending on how much time you want to spend, pick your stops in advance. From Vienna you drive east to the plains area of Marchfeld, then south to Rohrau, Haydn's birthplace, and on to the marshy lake country and bird sanctuary surrounding the Neusiedler See. From the lake town of Rust, you abruptly climb westward through low hills to Eisenstadt, the capital of Burgenland, and then south to Bernstein, the southern fulcrum of the trip and suggested evening stopover. Leaving this wooded plains area the route reenters Lower Austria and, driving north, encounters the Bucklige Welt ("Bumpy World"), a gentle pre-Alpine region of round hills covered with deep forests and orchards. At Puchberg you can climb the Schneeberg — called "our Alp" by the Viennese. Continuing north, the land flattens out as you reach the decorative spa town of Baden, the largest city on the trip and a stone's throw from the Vienna Woods.

VIENNA: For a detailed report on the city and its hotels and restaurants, see *Vienna,* THE CITIES.

En Route from Vienna – Leave Vienna by crossing the main channel of the Danube, noting the signs pointing right, to Grossenzersdorf, where you pick up Route 3 east. You have entered the plains of Marchfeld, an area fought over by the Romans, the Turks (they besieged Vienna from here in 1529), Napoleon (he suffered his first defeat near the village of Aspern), and the Red Army, who sliced through the retreating Nazis here during World War II on their way to liberate Vienna. Continue on through Orth, 17 miles (27 km) from Vienna, where you can stop at the huge, forbidding, 12th-century castle, now the *Austrian Museum of Fishery and Water Conservation* (1 Schlosspl.; phone: 2212-2555), and have fish soup and carp (daily except Wednesdays) at the nearby *Uferhaus.* Another 5 watchful miles (8 km) brings you to the tiny hamlet of Eckartsau.

ECKARTSAU: Here is the half-ruined château of Karl I, the last Austrian emperor, to which he fled in 1918 as his empire crumbled around Vienna. For a long time the Austrian government seemed satisfied to let this property crumble, too, but now it is possible to walk through the overgrown baroque gardens and the display rooms of the Imperial Hunting Lodge (1722) and think about the frightened and abandoned royal family hiding here.

En Route from Eckartsau – Make a 19-mile (30-km) deviation northeast on back roads to the little market town of Marchegg, which sits directly on the March (Morava) River, the Czechoslovakian border. (Americans no longer need a visa if they wish to visit Czechoslovakia). There's a castle here from the 13th century (it's since been more comfortably renovated to the spacious Renaissance proportions of the 17th century) that's now a hunting museum. Within are scenes depicting the onetime luxury of royal hunts, when the harsh outdoor life was softened for the nobles by the chamber orchestras that accompanied them and played as they beat the bushes. The area recently was acquired by the World Wild Life Foundation as a nature preserve. Head directly south on Route 49, and travel 12½ miles (20 km) to the Danube Bridge.

ROHRAU: On the south side of the river is the village of Bad Deutsch-Altenburg, where there is an 8,000-seat amphitheater and a museum; 9 miles (14 km) from Deutsch Altenburg are the remains of the Roman settlement of Carnuntum, which now is contained within the village of Petronell; 6 miles (10 km) farther south on Route 211 — you have to pick your way carefully — you'll find Joseph Haydn's birthplace, the village of Rohrau, on the Burgenland state line. The house where Haydn was born (No. 60, Rohrau A-2471; phone: 2164-2268) has been restored, showing off not only the musician's souvenirs but also the simplicity of his family's life. The thatch houses in the white-walled compounds of Burgenland are a counterpoint to the splendor of Vienna and quite simply different from the rest of the country. Rohrau also has a fine château of the Harrach family. When the occupation ended in 1955, the family's paintings, one of the outstanding private collections in the world, was moved here from Vienna. The *Harrach Collection,* in the Schloss Rohrau (Rohrau Castle; phone: 2164-22530), is open to the public from April through October (closed Mondays; admission charge); its Spanish and Dutch works are particularly fine. Also in the château is a good and surprisingly inexpensive restaurant.

THE NEUSIEDLER SEE: From Rohrau drive southwest on Route 211 and southeast on Route 10 to reach the reedy edges of the great Lake of Neusiedl at the village of Winden. This enormous lake, about half the size of Lake Geneva, is a geological freak of nature — it is so shallow that a tall person can literally walk across it. (Every year on the first or second weekend in August an organized walk takes place.) The lake dried up completely in the mid-19th century, filled again, and now has receded a bit. The lake's banks are covered with millions of reeds that give nesting and migratory protection to over 200 species of birds. Symbolic of the region are the cumbersome storks' nests found on top of many cottage chimneys. Used by the Viennese as a prime summer weekend retreat, the Neusiedler See often is filled with hundreds of sailboats.

RUST: As you travel south to the unofficial lake capital of Rust (25 miles/40 km from Rohrau), you cross very old vineyards that grow westward in the low hills surrounding the shore. The wine of the region, notably the unique blaufränkisch red (with the taste of a particularly robust burgundy), enjoys an excellent reputation worldwide. Many of the farmhouses in the region display green boughs on their doors, indicating that visitors may stop to taste and possibly purchase the wines. You also can visit a village market and buy a picnic lunch to take along to these alfresco taverns. Two of the most hospitable wine makers are *Just of Rust* (16 Weinberggasse; phone: 2685-251), which offers white wines, and the *Klosterkeller* (4 Rathauspl., in nearby Siegendorf; phone: 2687-252), for red wines. Both are closed Sundays. You won't have to carry your siegendorf wines home with you because they're distributed in the US by H&S (30 Somerset St., Belmont, MA 02178; phone: 617-484-5432).

Rust is a small, quiet town where German is spoken, but Hungarian lurks between the lines. Lucky travelers can hear Gypsy music in the taverns on summer nights and watch costumed, high-booted residents dance to it.

En Route from Rust – Less than 4 miles (6 km) south is the small village of Mörbisch on the Hungarian frontier (for entry requirements, see *Facts in Brief* in GETTING READY TO GO). There's good swimming and a midsummer music festival on a lakeside stage, where traditional Viennese operettas are performed outdoors on weekends (however, bring some insect repellent).

EISENSTADT: Some 12½ miles (20 km) west of Rust is Eisenstadt. The road here rises sharply, so you'll see some nice vistas as you arrive. The largest building in town is the hulking Esterhazy Palace, noted not so much for its architecture as for its history. Haydn was a member of Prince Esterhazy's court and, in 1766, was made musical director of the prince's orchestra and chorale. In return, the royal family named a room after Haydn. There are tours of this great hall, where the master nightly conducted his own compositions for the entertainment of his patrons (closed Mondays, *Christmas,* and *New Year's;* admission charge; Esterhazypl.; phone: 2682-3675). The rest of the château serves as administrative offices for the provincial government. (You also can see Haydn's house at 21 Haydngasse or his tomb at the Church of the Calvary.)

En Route from Eisenstadt – Drive south for 9 miles (14 km) to the large market town of Mattersburg. Turn west for a few miles at Mattersburg and follow signs to the imposing Forchtenstein Castle. This castle, sitting on a towering dolomitic rock, dates from the 13th century, and its vast rooms house good collections of medieval armor, weaponry, and hunting memorabilia. There's also a well almost 500 feet deep, dug by hand by Turkish prisoners of war in the 17th century.

BERNSTEIN: From Mattersburg drive south on Route 331 for 10½ miles (17 km) through Stoob. Continue south through Oberpullendorf and Lockenhaus, and 12 miles (19 km) from Stoob you'll find Bernstein, the southernmost point on the trip. There's a thriving serpentine jade business here and also the *Hotel Burg Bernstein* (1 Schlossweg; phone: 3354-220). The hill castle in Lockenhaus was built around 1200 by an itinerant Roman archbishop who liked the terrain. This castle also is a museum with a knights hall and a torture chamber. Indeed, one medieval lord of the manor, Graf Uilaky, is rumored to have come home from a 2-week plunder to find his wife's servant at her bedside. He knifed the servant immediately, but chose to brick up his beloved alive behind a handy castle wall. It is said that her ghost occasionally wanders the halls. In July, the castle is one of the sites of the *International Chamber Music Festival,* founded by Austrian violinist Gidon Kremer.

THE SCHNEEBERG TOWNS: The next morning, head north 7½ miles (12 km) to Kirchschlag, pick up Route 55 north, and watch for signs pointing northwest to Neunkirchen. There take Route 26 northwest, a road that runs through one of the finest wooded canyons in all of Europe, to Puchberg (29 miles/46 km from Kirchschlag). At Puchberg you suddenly find yourself in the Alps. The Schneeberg is one of the easternmost mountains, and you can catch a steam-driven, cog-wheel train here to its peak.

Four miles (6 km) east, at Grünbach, you can take a chair lift up to the Hohe Wand, a high plateau nature reserve. From Grünbach continue east another 4 miles (6 km) to Urschendorf and then follow back lanes for about 5½ miles (9 km) to the famous brewery town of Markt Piesting, where you have a chance to drink as many steins of Piestingerbräu as you can (or want). This famous brew is dark and a little bitter, like stout, and almost impossible to buy elsewhere.

BADEN: From Markt Piesting drive north 21 miles (34 km) through Bad Vöslau and 2.5 miles (4 km) farther to Baden (*Bad* is German for "spa"), the grandfather of all health resorts. The Romans called the town Aquae and used the sulfur thermal springs. Even the city's coat of arms depicts two people in a bathtub. Baden was Soviet occupation headquarters for Austria until 1955, and during this period the city's reputation as a resort suffered. Since the return of capitalism, however, the waters are bubbling again. There are a few historic highlights: Beethoven's house (10 Rathausgasse; closed Thursdays in summer; admission charge); the famous death mask collection at the *Städtisches Rollett-Museum* (1 Weikersdorferpl.); and the formal, triangular Hauptplatz with its ornate Trinity column commemorating the plague. But, for the most part, this is a place for vacationers. For those who can't wait for the waters to cure them there is more instant gratification (or demoralization) available at the *Baden Casino* in the *Spa Center*, where you can play roulette, baccarat, blackjack, or slot machines. There also are facilities for swimming, riding and cycling, saunas, and a host of other health-related activities. From here it's only 15½ miles (25 km) back to Vienna; the two cities are connected by showy old streetcars, by railroad, and by frequent buses.

BEST EN ROUTE

Expect to pay from $90 to $160 or more for a double room with breakfast per night in hotels listed as expensive; $65 to $85 in those listed as moderate; and $40 to $60 in the inexpensive places. Restaurant prices range from $85 to $125 for dinner for two in the expensive category; $50 to $75 in the moderate category; and $30 to $45 in the inexpensive category. Although a 10% tip is included in most menu prices, an extra 5% gratuity is expected if service has been adequate. Note: Many restaurants in the country are closed during the winter months.

GROSSENZERSDORF

Hotel am Sachsengang – This 100-room hostelry boasts one of the most remarkable and romantic restaurants in all of Austria. Grossenzersdorf is right outside Vienna, so you might want to include a stop here for lunch — outdoors, over a canal, when weather permits. The wild game is beautifully prepared, and trout or *Fogasch* (a sweet Hungarian fish resembling perch and pike) in *Blätterteig* (pastry dough) are specialties. On the main road, 60 Schlosshoferstr. (phone: 2249-2901). Expensive.

RUST

Nikolauszeche – Actually in Purbach, on the route from Winden to Rust, this restaurant in a 16th-century Renaissance building is the country cousin to Vienna's elegant *Zu den Drei Husaren*. It has the same ownership, but offers local wines and regional cooking at a much lower price. Specialties are *Grammeldaschel* (a ravioli-type dumpling filled with bacon), *Zander* (pike), and other fish fresh from the Neusiedler See. For dessert, try *Topfenknödel mit Zwetschkenröster* (cheese dumplings with plums). 3 Bodenzeile (phone: 2683-5514). Moderate.

Storchenmühle – The name means "storks' mill," and though it's in the minuscule village of Oslip, just outside Rust, it's one of the most famous places to eat in the Burgenland. *Fogasch* (pike/perch) is at its best here. Book your table well in advance. 4 Sportplatzgasse, Oslip (phone: 2684-2127). Moderate.

FORCHTENSTEIN

Reisner – In the village just below the castle sits an unpretentious little inn that might be the best in all of Burgenland. Be sure to reserve ahead and, when you do, someone who speaks German should tell Chef Johann Reisner your culinary likes and dislikes. He'll do the rest. Closed Wednesdays and half of January. 141 Hauptstr. (phone: 2626-3139). Moderate.

BERNSTEIN

Burg Bernstein – A famous old castle on top of a hill, it has only 10 rooms in a quiet setting. All the furniture is antique and the kitchen is excellent. It's closed in winter and still is undiscovered. 1 Schlossweg (phone: 3354-220). Moderate.

LOCKENHAUS

Burg Lockenhaus – Gidon Kremer's music festival, which runs for 2 weeks every July, has given the castle-restaurant in this medieval ruin a new lease on life. On Saturday nights, there is a six-course Robber Baron's Feast (*Raubrittermahl*) that includes wine, schnapps, live music, and a guided tour. Closed in winter. Reservations necessary (phone: 2616-2321). Moderate.

PUCHBERG

Puchbergerhof – A country hotel filled with folk art and hunting trophies, it has a good kitchen. Just east of the town center. 29 Wr.-Neustädter Str. (phone: 2636-2278). Moderate to inexpensive.

Forellenhof – This 145-bed hotel is a little higher up than Puchberg in the Alpine meadows near Losenheim. At the restaurant you can get marvelous mountain trout. 132 Losenheimer Str. (phone: 2636-220511). Inexpensive.

BADEN

Gutenbrunn – In a château, this 80-room hotel is one of the city's best. 22 Pelzgasse (phone: 2252-48171). Expensive to moderate.

Cholerakapelle – Just west of town, this restaurant in a striking gorge has good *Schnitzel* and game. 40A Helenental (phone: 2252-44315). Moderate.

Vienna to Salzburg

A traveler may speed along the autobahn between Vienna and Salzburg in 3 or 4 easy hours, yet this would be a mistake. The lands between the great Austrian cities offer some of the richest rewards in Europe. Spending 2 days on the route will give you time to experience some of the most beautiful countryside in the world; if you have even more time to spend, it wouldn't be wasted.

Our suggested route meanders north, south, and west, but, including side trips, it still is only about 310 miles (496 km) long. You'll drive through four Austrian *Bundesländer* (provinces): Wien (Vienna) is the capital province; Niederösterreich (Lower Austria) is the stable core of a nation whose boundaries and politics have played musical chairs for 10 centuries; Oberösterreich (Upper Austria) is where the Alps start to rise and the landscape becomes more severe and breathtaking with every kilometer; and Salzburg is another Alpine province bordering Germany on one side and the spa-studded Salzkammergut (Lake Region) on the other. A word here about Upper and Lower Austria: The names are confusing, for Lower Austria actually is northeast of Upper Austria. The logic behind this is the course of the Danube River: From

Germany it enters Upper Austria, continues into Lower Austria, and exits into Czechoslovakia and Hungary. (If you're still confused, just accept it and take solace in the fact that if you want to go from Virginia to West Virginia you probably travel north.)

This route offers a mix of history, culture, and physical beauty that is a great source of pride and enjoyment to the Austrian people. It's hard to turn down this opportunity to share it.

VIENNA: For a detailed report on the city and its hotels and restaurants, see *Vienna,* THE CITIES.

En Route from Vienna – Heading northwest from downtown Vienna, you cross the Danube and find yourself climbing into the quietly rolling hills of the wine district. Austrians like to drink their wine new, and the word for the current year's beverage is *Heuriger.* It's generally white, not too dry, strong, inexpensive, and good. Once you get over any "young wine" prejudice you may harbor, you'll find yourself stopping at the many *Heurigen* (wine taverns) along the route.

Take S3 northwest from Vienna to Stockerau, then pick up Route 4 and take it as far as Maissau. There, turn north on Route 35, and in about 5 miles (8 km) you'll be in Eggenburg.

EGGENBURG: Like many of the other Lower Austrian towns, this small medieval center used to be a walled fortress. Several of the 14th-century walls still are intact, and so are some of the towers that intersect them. In the Hauptplatz (Main Square) beside a Trinity column is a late medieval pillory, a squat, primitive reminder of the absolute power of the feudal lords and the circus-like quality of brutal, Gothic justice. Most of the houses are gabled, distorting their actual size and shape; for the church seekers there is Gothic St. Stephan's, with two Romanesque towers. The violence of the Middle Ages and the religious desire to continually redecorate created many churches like this, with different sections from different periods. The Romanesque style predates the Gothic and usually is simpler. (To distinguish between the two, the schoolboy maxim is: "Round arch, Romanesque; pointed arch, Gothic." Don't apply this rule to any later buildings because the romantic styles of the Renaissance took plans and details from every earlier movement and elaborated on them.)

Head west from Eggenburg on Route 303 for 9 miles (14 km) to Horn, the chief town and resort of the Forest District. Continue southwest another 4 miles (6 km) on Route 38 to the great abbey of Altenburg.

ALTENBURG: You've only driven 13 miles (21 km), but you've jumped a century or two into a new architectural style. The Benedictine abbey here was entirely rebuilt between 1650 and 1742, when baroque was the rage and the straight lines of Gothic discipline were softened by a multitude of curves as the vault gave way to the dome. Decoration was not only allowed but encouraged. The architects studied in Italy, but the abundance of bulbous church domes and tower topknots (there's a bulbous belfry here) were taken from more Eastern traditions like the Russian and the Greek. One look at the intricate, hand-carved, gilded woodwork on the church organ is proof that the craftsmen were encouraged to indulge themselves. The abbey library, ornamental staircase, and colorful grotesque baroque frescoes in the crypt also are interesting. It lost some of its collection during the Thirty Years War (1618–48) and even more when the Red Army used it for a barracks during World War II, but the structure itself has been artfully restored.

If you pick up Route 34 south out of Altenburg, you soon meet up with the beautiful Kamp River.

THE KAMP RIVER VALLEY: The trip south through the Kamp River valley is reason enough to travel north from Vienna. In a 30-mile (48-km) stretch you'll see castles and fortresses on either side of a quiet river that flows between flat and wooded banks, neatly planned towns, and occasional low, flat hills. The three towns not to be missed are Rosenburg, Gars, and Langenlois, but travel at your own pace and stop whenever something catches your eye. As you go south you reenter the wine district, so *Heurigen* will be popping up frequently.

Rosenburg is a good first stop because its castle is both magnificent and well-preserved (closed Fridays). Many of its rooms are fully furnished with sculpture, paintings, and weaponry, and there is a fine jousting yard.

The next stop on the way south is the pretty market town of Gars, with clean white buildings, small flowered plazas, and a neo-classic archway.

Langenlois, 13 miles (21 km) south of Gars, is a larger town, with the most wine-growers in Austria. (The best local wine is the dry white called grüner veltliner.) The houses are Renaissance, but the *Heimat Museum* (admission charge; phone: 2734-2101) deals mostly with earlier subjects, such as prehistory, regional folklore, and, of course, wine making. From Langenlois it's about 6 miles (10 km) to Krems, at the eastern end of the well-known Wachau.

THE WACHAU: You can practice your German pronunciation on this word — the *w* is a soft *v* and the *ch* is hard and guttural. However you pronounce Wachau, though, you'll still find it to be a series of river towns strung together on either side of the Danube. The area is steep and rocky but still manages to produce an abundance of wine, apricots, plums, and peaches. All this farming has kept the land rural and the towns thriving. The vineyard terracing neatly climbs the hillsides, and the hills themselves are topped by ruins of fortified castles. The Wachau has a rich folklore, with every town, castle, or church spinning its own heroic legend like that of the Kuenringer (10th-century lords), who blocked the Danube at its narrowest bend and extracted heavy tolls from all the unsuspecting merchantmen on the river. The aristocratic pirates are gone, but a sense of adventure and the beauty of the river landscape remain. Wander west along the river, stopping at Krems, Dürnstein, and Melk.

The city of Krems started doing business 1,000 years ago. Its business is wine, and a stop at the *Weinbaumuseum* (Viticulture Museum; admission charge; Dominika-nerpl.; phone: 2732-4927) is a good idea. Wine is so important to Krems that during the German occupation of World War II, the residents complained that, besides being Nazis, their captors were beer drinkers to boot.

There are some striking Renaissance houses in Krems: One good example is the building at 84 Steiner Landstrasse. The façade is at once Byzantine, Venetian, and German, with golden domed windows, layers of colored friezes, and an ornamentally columned stoa in front of the entrance.

On Route 3, about 4½ miles (7 km) west of Krems on the north side of the river, is Dürnstein, considered the most beautiful town on the Danube. If time permits you only one stop in the Wachau, this should be it. (The modern road bypasses this small town by tunneling under it, so be on the lookout.) Dürnstein's legend is that Richard the Lion-Hearted was imprisoned here in 1193.

The city is walled and filled with winepresses, ancient houses, and cafés. If Richard didn't enjoy his captivity, it probably was because he never got to sit in one of the cafés and watch the river flow by while sipping some of the strong regional specialty, apricot schnapps. (There are also, of course, gallons of *Heuriger* wine to be had.) There are tours of the parish church and a former Augustine monastery during the summer, both primarily baroque, but the more secular will appreciate the old wrought-iron signs hanging from the inns along the Hauptstrasse (Main Street).

Drive west on Route 3 another 19 miles (30 km), cross over to the south side of the Danube, and you'll be in Melk, a historian's paradise. Besides hosting Napoleon between 1805 and 1809 during one of his more successful jaunts, it was also the home of the first Austrian monarchy after 976. At the end of the 11th century, when Leopold III von Babenberg decided to move to Vienna, he presented his castle to the Benedictines, who converted it, after several renovations, into the finest baroque abbey north of Italy. The renovations were a result of various disasters that are recounted during the hour-long tours given in English. As it stands today, this huge, yellow abbey was designed by Jakob Prandtauer and completed by his son-in-law, Franz Munggenast (whose work you probably have already admired in Dürnstein and Altenburg). The interior of the church at Melk seems even grander and more spacious than it is because of its great dome, many windows, colorful frescoes, and statuary. The terrace of Melk's splendid baroque library affords a wondrous view of the Danube. Admission charge.

The town of Melk, though one of the largest in the Wachau, has resisted industrialization and kept its ancient plan intact and functioning. From Melk you can either continue west along the Danube or take E5 (the autobahn) into Linz.

En Route from Melk – About 55 miles (88 km) west is the ancient town of Enns, believed to be the oldest Roman settlement in Austria. In this century, it marked the dividing points of the American and Soviet zones of postwar occupation in Austria. If you get off the autobahn here and follow Route 337 and the Enns River north, you'll soon hit its confluence with the Danube, where you'll find a far more dramatic wartime reminder — the small quarry town of Mauthausen.

Until World War II, this town was on few travelers' itineraries. During the war the Nazis built a concentration camp here; the postwar Austrian government declared the campsite a national monument in 1949. Since then, Mauthausen has had many visitors. Outside the camp, memorials have been erected by the various countries of the 200,000 victims exterminated by the Nazis. There's a self-guided, tape-recorded tour (in English) of the camp that takes you through the memorials, the prisoners' huts, the gas chamber, and the notorious Steps of Death that lead into the quarry. This isn't average tourist fare, but most visitors find the trip very moving.

From Mauthausen it's a short jump on Route 3 west to Linz.

LINZ: Linz, a big city that straddles the Danube, is the capital of Upper Austria and a good place to stop. In the Hauptplatz (Main Square) there's a Trinity column that's as much a symbol of this city as the Statue of Liberty is of New York. The column is a baroque totem pole of white marble with cherubs adorning a twisting trunk and a Trinity capped by a golden sun on the top. Linz is also the home of St. Martin's, the oldest church in Austria. It is a simple church of stone with its original beams intact (there's not much in the way of vaulting) and some rare stained glass windows in the apse. The windows here probably were French inspired, for the church was built on Roman foundations by Charlemagne in the 8th century.

Besides preserving St. Martin's, the city has given its name to the *Linzertorte,* the crown prince of Austrian pastries (the *Sachertorte* is the reigning king). The *Linzertorte* is a far more complex affair, involving varying configurations of almond cake and raspberry jam, with or without *Schlag* — whipped cream.

Linz is a modern art center of Austria, and the *Neue Galerie der Stadt Linz* (15 Blütenstr.; phone: 732-239336; closed Saturdays, Sundays and most holidays; admission charge) exhibits works by Corinth, Klimt, Kokoschka, Kubin, Liebermann, and Schiele. There's also the *Francisco Carolinum* (Provincial Museum of Upper Austria; 14 Museumstr.; phone: 732-274482; closed Mondays, Tuesdays and holidays; admission charge), a fortress museum with a large collection of weaponry as well as folk art and musical instruments.

Every September, Linz holds a *Bruckner Festival* to commemorate the symphonies and choral work of Anton Bruckner, a notable native son. Bruckner actually was from St. Florian, a small town 11 miles (18 km) southeast of Linz on Route 1, where he was the organist at the famous St. Florian's Abbey during the 1840s and 1850s. He composed his greatest work there and actually wished to be buried beneath the organ. The pipe housing of the organ is another baroque masterpiece, with gilded angels and cherubs on neo-classic pilasters that run up to a red and gold cross and a ceiling painted with more angels over a fiery orange background. (St. Florian himself was drowned, but is the saint to be invoked in firefighting situations.) The organ appears in many art texts as the prime example of the baroque style in Austria. There are tours (in English) of the abbey that also take you through the library, the imperial apartments, and the *Altdorfer Gallery,* with paintings by the early 16th-century Danubian master Albrecht Altdorfer. Closed December through March; admission charge (phone: 7224-8903).

If you continue east on Route 1 back to Enns, you can pick up Route 337 south and drive 13 miles (21 km) to Steyr.

STEYR: At the confluence of the Enns and the Steyr rivers, this 1,000-year-old industrial center has a lovely Old Quarter that is a preserved wrought-iron wonder of enduring baroque, largely closed to cars. Besides exploring the Stadtplatz (Main Square), walk down Grünmarkt to the Neutor (New Gate), which looks out at the Enns River.

Just next door to Steyr is the tiny village of Christkindl (Christ Child), where on some *Christmas Eves* the midnight mass is televised to all of Europe. If you're here in December, a special post office with a special postmark will endorse and endear your mail to all your stamp collecting friends.

Head west out of Steyr on Route 122 through Bad Hall and pick up the autobahn west at Sattledt. Get off at Steyrermühl and drive south to Gmunden on the Traunsee, 45 miles (72 km) from Steyr and the easternmost lake of the Salzkammergut (Lake Region).

THE SALZKAMMERGUT: Every lake town here is a resort offering swimming, hiking, sailing, and fishing. Though the scenery is beautiful and there are landmarks and architecture to be seen, the accent here is more on vacationing than touring. These are the hills that Julie Andrews sang about, and though the Alpine vistas are special, the lakeside towns are fairly similar, so if you have time, pick one and vacation a little. If you don't, drive through them with the windows open to smell the wildflowers and absorb the good health (Salzkammergut means "district of salt mines," and the area is rich in minerals, with mines and health spas).

Gmunden has a mile-long esplanade with picturesque views of Lake Traun and the surrounding mountains. The town always has prospered (both from the salt trade and the upper class vacationers), and the lakeside is cluttered with expansive villas.

There is no lakeside at Bad Ischl, 20 miles (33 km) farther on Route 145, but there are two small rivers, the Traun and the Ischl. Between 1848 and 1914, Emperor Franz Joseph summered here with his entourage, so the town has a formal and imperialistic bearing. Franz Lehár also lived here, and there is operetta in summer. There are tours of the Kaiservilla (Emperor's Villa) or you can roam the park on your own and see the garden on foot or from a horse-drawn carriage.

En Route from Bad Ischl – A short detour south on Route 145 brings you to the old mining town of Bad Aussee, another fashionable resort. Turn west on Route 166 for Obertraun, on Lake Hallstatt. There's a funicular ascent here to the ice caves of Dachstein (the local Alp) that's one of the best in Europe. Follow 166 around the lake to the town of Hallstatt, one of the most ancient places south of Stonehenge. It gives its name to the Hallstatt period (1000–500 BC). The diggings in the area show that it was an Iron Age metropolis. You can go down into a salt mine or up another cable railway to a mountaintop inn. The town itself looks Swiss, with lakeside buildings of yellow stucco, vertical timber siding, and a solitary stone steeple. The return trip north to Bad Ischl makes a loop drive of about 40 miles (64 km).

Route 158 west from Bad Ischl goes to the base of the Wolfgangsee, where you turn right through Strobl and follow the road until it ends at the village of St. Wolfgang, on the north shore of the lake. Since the road ends so abruptly and the town is such a popular tourist attraction, parking is a major problem, so put your car in one of the two lots at the town entrance and walk. Besides the lake views, hiking paths, and brass band concerts, there's also a Gothic masterpiece in the town church and a long rack-railway ride up the side of the Schafberg (another Alp), from which you can see 13 lakes. The altar in the church is by Michael Pacher and was carved and painted on gilded backgrounds 500 years ago. A paddlewheel boat ride on this loveliest of lakes and a visit to St. Wolfgang's legendary *White Horse Inn* (see *Best en Route*) are highly recommended.

You follow the same road you entered on to Route 158, which you take west through St. Gilgen and on to the Fuschlsee, the smallest lake of the region and the last before you reach Salzburg, 35 miles (56 km) from Bad Ischl.

SALZBURG: For a detailed report on the city and its hotels and restaurants, see *Salzburg,* THE CITIES.

BEST EN ROUTE

Expect to pay $100 to $165 per night for a double room with breakfast in hotels listed as expensive; $65 to $85 in those listed as moderate; and $40 to $60 in the inexpensive places. Restaurant prices range from $50 to $90 for dinner for two in the expensive category; $30 to $50 in the moderate; and $20 to $30 in the inexpensive category. Prices do not include wine. Although a 10% tip is included in most menu prices, an extra 5% gratuity is expected if service has been adequate. All restaurants below accept major credit cards, unless otherwise indicated. Reservations are advised at all restaurants.

DÜRNSTEIN

Schloss Dürnstein – This 37-room hotel is a fine baroque castle overlooking the Danube. There are swimming and sauna facilities, and the management is especially welcoming. 2 Dürnstein (phone: 2711-212 or 2711-240). Closed in winter. Expensive.

Richard Löwenherz – A cozy inn in a former convent that has a swimming pool, a dreamlike garden, a terrace restaurant on the Danube, and, in every hallway, rustic furnishings worthy of a folkloric museum. Open mid-March to November. 8 Dürnstein (phone: 2711-222). Expensive to moderate.

STEYR

Minichmayr – Right in the middle of this small ancient town, is this renovated hotel with 105 beds and a very good restaurant (phone: 7252-23410). Moderate.

BAD ISCHL

Kurhotel – This large, modern hotel has every spa facility you can imagine available for its guests, and it's located in the center of town. 115 rooms. 10 Voglhuberstr. (phone: 6132-4271). Expensive.

HALLSTATT

Seehotel Grüner Baum – A family operation, its guests often stay for an entire vacation. It has 33 rooms (ask for one facing the lake) and an excellent kitchen. Closed November 1 to May 1. 104 Marktpl. (phone: 6134-263). Moderate.

SAINT WOLFGANG

Romantikhotel im Weissen Rössl (White Horse Inn) – The setting of a famous operetta is alive and well and thriving as a charming 129-bed resort hotel with lakeside eating facilities. Swimming in the lake or the indoor pool; there's also a sauna, a gym, and boating facilities. 74 Marktpl. (phone: 6138-2306). Expensive to moderate.

Gasthof Fürberg – Reached by boat from St. Wolfgang or St. Gilgen, and also by car from the latter, this rambling flower-lined inn has a sculpture of a fish over its door and features *Reinanke* and *Saibling,* the fish (distantly related to salmon) of the Wolfgangsee. Closed in winter (phone: 6227-385). Inexpensive.

Salzburg to Innsbruck to the Swiss Border

The trip from Salzburg through Innsbruck to the town of Bregenz on Lake Constance at the Swiss border runs in a relatively straight east-west line, but as routed here with north-south deviations it covers about 415 miles (664 km). The distance can easily be driven in about 2 days, but to enjoy the Alpine scenery and stave off fatigue, take at least 3 or 4. One of the joys of this trip is the combination of fairly short driving distances between stops, unretouched medieval towns, and the natural beauty of the Alps themselves.

This primarily is a trip through the Alps, and the views of craggy, snow-capped peaks rising dramatically around small, chalet-filled villages neatly set in mountain valleys are quite striking and unending. As you drive through the mountains you'll find each new vista more exciting than the last — the Alps are something you don't get used to. It's best to make this drive between June and October; the Alpine winters force road closings and the snows will abridge the route, cutting off some of the more breathtaking, twisting mileage. It's also best to start driving early in the day; as the valleys and lowlands heat up in the morning, the warm air rises and, meeting the cooler air around the mountaintops, shrouds the peaks in clouds by afternoon.

Before leaving the province of Salzburg you leave the city of Salzburg and drive south to Badgastein, Austria's premier spa, with health-giving, naturally hot water, an invigorating atmosphere, and cascading waterfalls in the center of town. From there you come back north a bit and dogleg west to the lakeside resort of Zell am See, the jumping-off point for the spectacular southern loop drive down the winding mountain highway around the Grossglockner, the highest Austrian Alp. This road links the provinces of Salzburg and Carinthia and ends at Lienz, the capital of the East Tyrol. From here you take the Felbertauern route back north, burrowing through the mountains this time instead of going over them. There are no mountain routes in the world that compare with these, and the sharp peaks and blazing glaciers both elate and chill the viewer with a majestic sense of natural history.

Your northern progress stops at Kitzbühel, a medieval town — filled with skiers but still picturesque — with tree-lined streets and large old houses. You're in the Tyrol now, and driving west you meet up with the Inn River and follow it, locked between high, green plateaus all the way to Innsbruck. No matter where you're from, Innsbruck is a town you won't want to leave. It combines rangy, Alpine scenery with formal, urban splendor and history — a resort city that hasn't lost its cultured, civilized charm.

From Innsbruck you continue west to the Arlberg region, your second twisting, heady mountain drive that's topped in altitude only by the Grossglockner. During the summer you can deviate south, around and over the peaks via the Silvretta road, and stop for a breather at the flat, manmade Vermunt Lake and Silvretta Dam. At other times of year travel is directly west over the Arlberg Pass or, when driving conditions are very poor, through the highway tunnel (toll) underneath the Arlberg between St. Anton and Langen. Both routes take you to Bludenz in the prosperous Vorarlberg, Austria's westernmost province, where the towns adopt a precise, Swiss mien. You drive on to Feldkirch with its rectangular towers and round turrets and turn north, following the Swiss border to the provincial capital of Bregenz. Here the route ends at the shore of the Bodensee (Lake Constance).

The provinces along this route blend a fierce, local patriotism with a sophisticated European worldliness that articulates itself through expressive folkways (the chalets here aren't just old houses but works of art, with painted and sculpted elevations) and proud, outgoing natives. If you like to ski, you've probably heard of almost every town along this route, but even if you think speeding down mountains is better left to goats, you'll find you won't have a dull moment from start to finish.

SALZBURG: For a detailed report on the city and its hotels and restaurants, see *Salzburg*, THE CITIES.

BADGASTEIN: From Salzburg drive south through Bischofshofen and Lend for 62 miles (99 km) to the elegant spa town of Badgastein. This is more of a spender's park than a town, with a curved strip of imperious shops and hotels that compete with each other for the most space. Badgastein is built into the north slope of the Tauern Range, and the Gasteiner Ache roars down this slope, creating an enormous waterfall in the middle of town. You can park your car and stroll up and down the Kaiser Wilhelm Promenade to see both mountains and town.

The Badgastein waters are world famous, and their therapeutic properties keep the money flowing through this town. The springs supply water that is naturally in the amazing range of 115 to 120F (about 47C). This thermal water is rich in radon, an element that the faithful claim eases (among other things) rheumatic complaints, circulatory problems, gout, and asthma. You can pay for a full cure with a lucky visit to the Badgastein casino; or, just to get your feet wet, there's a large open-air swimming pool fed by the thermal springs opposite the railway station.

THE GROSSGLOCKNER: From Badgastein, return to Lend and head west for 16 miles (26 km) on Route 311 to Zell am See, a resort town built on a flat tongue that extends off a wooded slope onto the Zeller See, a deep glacial ditch filled with blue Alpine water. There's a short cable car ride up the Schmittenhöhe that gives you a foretaste of the Grossglockner Highway. This is a good place to stop if you want to get an early morning start for the highway climb south. (In the winter, you skip this loop drive and just head 16 miles (26 km) west on 168 to Mittersill, the return point of this southern deviation.)

The Grossglockner Highway begins south of Zell am See at Bruck-an-der-Grossglocknerstrasse. This amazing tollway, completed in 1935, is the prototype for almost all mountain engineering, and if you could only drive a car for 1 day, this is the road you should take. You start out by going down into the dark Fusch Valley, but little by little you start ascending through a series of *Grand Prix* bends and hairpin turns that force you to take your time and pay homage to the immortal ledges and crags around you. There are car parks and overlooks for patient studiers, but even fanatical non-stoppers won't escape the hundreds of breathtaking panoramas.

You can stop at Edelweiss-Spitze and climb an observation tower to 8,453 feet or just keep driving to the Hochtor Tunnel, the high point of the roadbed at 8,216 feet. There's a cul-de-sac detour west on the Glacier road up to the Franz-Joseph-Höhe that ends in a terrace cut out of stone. Emperor Franz Joseph built a mansion here at the beginning of the Pasterze Glacier, Europe's largest. (In summer, you can walk on the glacier at your own risk.)

Back on the main road, you wind down and bear right for Lienz, the southern turnaround of the loop 56 miles (90 km) from Zell am See.

LIENZ: Lienz is an East Tyrolean town that has begun to crowd up in the summer since 1967, when the Felbertauern Tunnel was finished, opening a western route through the mountains. Now motorists can come through this hub from east and west, entering the Grossglockner road and leaving on the Felbertauern road or vice versa. This newer road has spawned speedy modernization in areas previously cut off from the rest of Austria by the imposing Alpine barrier. This toll road is open all year, and, though no match for its older brother to the east, the sights here are splendid.

En Route from Lienz – Start north from Lienz, again going down into a wooded valley; and then you rise to the resort of Matrei, a thriving ski spot since the road came through. Matrei is also the gateway to the Hohe Tauern National Park, comparable in size and beauty to Yosemite. Beyond Matrei, until very recently, no road at all existed, so that the last stretch of the highway toward Kitzbühel offers a particularly fresh view of virginal forests and once isolated folk life. From here you rise farther, passing deep gorges and hanging glaciers. The tunnel moles its way under a ridge of peaks to emerge on the north mountain slopes; you head downhill into Mittersill, 42 miles (67 km) from Lienz. Cruise through town and push on to Kitzbühel, 17 miles (29 km) up Route 161. You're officially in the Tyrol.

KITZBÜHEL: Kitzbühel's old streets are lined with cafés and pastel houses whose gables extend over the street with arrogant disregard for one-dimensional vertical planes. There are two churches here that are a nice manmade counterpoint to the mountains you just came from (the parish church is Gothic, but its shingled overhanging roof disguises it as yet another chalet).

En Route to Innsbruck – Leave Kitzbühel, driving west on 170 until you hit the Inn River; turn left on the southern bank, taking the local road if you're meandering or the Autobahn if you're in more of a hurry.

Rattenberg is the kind of tiny village you can tell your friends you "discovered" when you get home. The riverside buildings have high, flat, stucco faces that at first glance are reminiscent of the false fronts on movie sets. If you climb up to the fortified stone castle, you can look down and see the sloped roofs that the higher walls conceal. Just above Rattenberg is Alpbach, one of the loveliest resorts in the Tyrol. Spend a night here, and you'll be tempted to stay a week.

INNSBRUCK: Innsbruck is one of Europe's most delightful smaller cities. Particularly vital, it combines light industry, commerce (the main junction since almost prehistory for trade between Germany and Italy, France and Eastern Europe), learning (the university is over 300 years old), and tourism. Perhaps no city has a more dramatic setting, with towering, snow-capped Alps on display from almost every street corner. Stroll down the main shopping street, the Maria-Theresien-Strasse, walking from the Triumphal Arch (to celebrate a successful Habsburg marriage). You'll pass impressive patrician houses, then find yourself in the heart of an arcaded Gothic town with colorful detailing, various bulbous belfries, and intricate wrought-iron signs. The symbol of Innsbruck is the Goldenes Dachl (Little Golden Roof), an ornate Gothic balcony built in 1500 by Maximilian I, who used it to watch parades and concerts. The sculpted crests on the balcony and lower frieze and the heroic wall paintings give the façade an especially regal bearing. The golden roof that covers the balcony consists of over 3,000 gilded copper tiles. In the Hofkirche (Court Church), known as the Tyrolean Westminster Abbey, 28 larger-than-life statues of ancestors line the tomb of Maximilian, who, alas, isn't buried there.

If you momentarily forget you're in the mountains, hop on a No. 6 streetcar, and in a little while you'll feel a jerk as the city starts to fall away below you. The trolley has become a cog-wheel train and the conductor has become a tour guide, pointing out peaks and glaciers. The train will take you to the ski spa suburb of Igls (pronounced *Eagles*), but the destination isn't as important as the trip. You won't find a better vantage point from which to look at Innsbruck, an Alpine jewel. If you're tired of rides at this point, stay in town and sit in the Hofgarten under the weeping willows where you can listen to concerts on summer evenings.

From Innsbruck you continue west on Route 171 through Landeck into the Arlberg mountain region.

THE ARLBERG: At Landeck you have another seasonal choice: If it's summer, you can take another southern loop up and over the peaks on the Silvretta road; during the winter you must go directly west over the Arlberg Pass or through the Arlberg Tunnel, where you cross an interior border into the last Austrian province of Vorarlberg.

The northern route through the pass takes you by the austere Castle of Wiesberg, past the shimmering, reed-like span of the Trisanna bridge, and up to the posh, treeless slopes of St. Anton, where the Arlberg method of skiing (the art of snowplowing and parallel turning) was developed. As you continue the ascent, you reach the pass at 5,910 feet, just beyond St. Christoph. As the descent begins, the road over the Flexen Pass branches off to the right. Several scenic hairpin turns drop you into Stuben, and a few minutes later you reach Langen. This is also where you emerge if you decide to take the tunnel. From the western end of the tunnel, the route down to Bludenz becomes bleak, passing through a sparsely populated area that's punctuated only by an occasional power station.

The Silvretta route (not much longer than the Arlberg Pass road) is a tollway much more like the Grossglockner and affords the viewer another round of heart-stopping vistas. As you start the climb driving south (you take the left fork at Pians, under the Trisanna bridge), you pass through several neat ski villages with large farmhouse chalets characterized by long balconies, ornate window detailing, and little belfries on the roof peaks. The Silvretta and Vermunt lakes were created by modern dams, and either makes a good rest stop. The Silvretta is at the highest point on this winding road; you can walk across the dam either mulling over man's relationship with his environment or deciding what to have for lunch. On the downhill trip toward Bludenz you pass the ski and cattle town of Schruns, which Hemingway wrote about affectionately in *A Moveable Feast.*

THE VORARLBERG: The Arlberg and Silvretta routes converge at Bludenz, a busy valley town with ancient gates, cobbled plazas, and flowered, marble fountains. Depending on how long you've been driving, you might consider a night's rest here.

From Bludenz it's only 13 miles (21 km) to Feldkirch, a Gothic marketplace equidistant from Paris and Vienna. The Marktplatz (Market Square) is a square in which large houses with high, round-arched entries open onto the street, occasional bulbous belfries break up the roof lines, and wrought-iron signs with almost Art Nouveau spiraling hang from the fronts of the inns. The primitive, stone, 13th-century Schattenburg Castle is here, as are many Old Town walls, and it doesn't take much imagination to picture Feldkirch as a medieval armed camp. The castle is a museum now, with folk art from the Vorarlberg and the Tyrol well represented. It has an elegantly rustic cellar restaurant that serves a first-rate Schattenburg schnitzel.

Leaving town head north about 22 miles (35 km) through Dornbirn to Bregenz, the last leg of the journey, along the meadowlands of the Rhine Valley and the Swiss border.

BREGENZ: The Vorarlberg capital is a slick and classy lake resort that unfortunately is bisected by a railroad line separating the preserved upper town from the graceful shorefronts of Lake Constance. On the harbor side of the railway are relaxing walks, manicured gardens, and a lakeside stage, where the *Bregenz Festival* is held every summer. In case of rain, patrons withdraw to the adjoining indoor festival hall. On the inland side of the tracks in the upper town is the domed St. Martin's tower, quiet squares, and twisting streets that offer sanctuary when the beachfronts crowd up during the season. There's also a last-chance cable railway ride up the richly forested mountain slope of the Pfänder just outside the town. When you reach the peak, you'll find this last aerial view of the lake and the town is another beauty and one that brings back so many of the previous unforgettable vistas this journey offers.

BEST EN ROUTE

Expect to pay $100 to $175 or more per night for a double room with breakfast in hotels listed as expensive; $65 to $85 in those listed as moderate; and $40 to $60 in the inexpensive places. Restaurant prices range from $85 to $125 for dinner for two in the expensive category; $50 to $75 in the moderate; and $30 to $45 in the inexpensive category. Prices do not include wine. Although a 10% tip is included in most menu prices, an extra 5% gratuity is expected if service has been adequate. All restaurants accept major credit cards, unless otherwise indicated. Reservations are advised at all restaurants.

ZELL AM SEE

Grandhotel am See – This place is not only on the lake, it's also really grand. Rebuilt according to the original *Grand Hotel* plans (ca. 1500), it has a convivial café, a good restaurant, and large bedrooms. You'll feel as if you just stepped off a first class carriage of the *Orient Express.* On Vootsverleih off Esplanade (phone: 6542-2387 or 6542-2388). Expensive.

Berghotel Schmittenhöhe – Here's a place for the adventurous — the no sheet–woolen blanket set. It's at the top of the aerial tram with no-frill bedrooms, nourishing hot meals, and vertigo-inducing views (phone: 6542-2489). Inexpensive.

KITZBÜHEL

Tennerhof – Situated just outside the city center near one of Austria's most famous ski resorts, this elegant, family-owned establishment commands a beautiful view of the Tyrolean Alps and serves excellent food. There is a swimming pool on the grounds. The famous Hahnenkammrennen (downhill run) and several golf championships call this town home. (phone: 5356-3181). Expensive.

LIENZ

Traube – The bedrooms are comfortable and pretty, but the main attraction here is the restaurant in the cellar, the social center of the entire eastern Tyrol. 14 Hauptpl. (phone: 4852-2551 or 4852-2552). Moderate.

MATREI-IN-OSTTIROL

Rauter – This resort hotel is a longtime favorite of fishermen as well as skiers and other sports-minded people. It has been modernized in a manner that makes it one of the architectural wonders of Austria: Many of the rooms are spacious A-frame chalets *within* the main building. All offer splendid mountain and meadow views. 3 Rauterpl. (phone: 4875-6611). Moderate.

ALPBACH

Romantikhotel Böglerhof – Thomas Wolfe discovered this inn in 1936 when it was just a farmhouse that took in guests. He wrote home to mother that the Alpbach Valley had "some of the most beautiful mountains and villages" he'd ever seen. Today the inn is a thriving 88-bed hotel ablaze with geraniums and petunias. The surprisingly good room rate includes a breakfast buffet with fresh breads that are a feast in themselves (phone: 5336-5227 or 5336-5228). Moderate.

INNSBRUCK

Goldener Adler – This inn has actually been in business in the same building for over 600 years. During the *1976 Winter Olympics,* television coverage originated from this hotel's romantic *Stube.* It's in the heart of the Old Town, and if you really want to get into the spirit, request a room with traditional trappings and pretend you're Friar Tuck. 6 Herzog-Friedrich Str. (phone: 512-586-3340). Expensive to moderate.

Weisses Rössl – A comfortable hotel in the heart of town that was rebuilt, preserving its 15th-century architecture. Major credit cards accepted. 8 Kiebachgasse (phone: 512-523057). Moderate.

LECH

Gasthofpost – Lech, just outside St. Anton, is one of the great ski resorts of Europe. This hostelry is an easy pick because of its rich Vorarlberg folk decorations and chic international clientele. There's no pretense here, though, and the management is especially welcoming. Off-season the rates are reasonable, but when the skiers hit town the prices soar. 11 Haupstrasse-Nr (phone: 5583-2206). Expensive.

FELDKIRCH

Weisses Kreuz – This solid, well-run country-town hotel in the Old Quarter has an efficient management in the best Swiss tradition. The kitchen is excellent. Königshofstrasse (phone: 5522-22209). Moderate.

BREGENZ

Zoll – Since taking over this roadside inn, chef Ernst Huber has made it a shrine to gastronomy that lures pilgrims from nearby Germany and Switzerland as well as from all over Austria. Try the seven-course *Menü,* which features the freshest and most special of regional ingredients, carefully prepared and presented in manageable portions. 118 Arlbergstr. (phone: 5574-31705). Expensive.

Berghaus Pfänder – Open only from May until late September, this is a mountain restaurant with food as wonderful as the view. Try the *Hasenrücken pfänder,* saddle of hare served with *Spätzle,* potato croquettes, red cabbage, cranberries, and *Pfifferlinge* mushrooms. Adjacent to the Pfänder cable car station and a charming Alpine game preserve (phone: 5574-22184). Moderate.

Weisses Kreuz – The best hotel in town is an ancient, expertly run place that also serves as the town's prime social center. Breakfast only. 5 Römerstrasse (phone: 5574-22488). Moderate.

Belgium

The kingdom of Belgium is a tiny, industrious, and economically mighty nation about the size of Maryland jammed into the North Sea coast between France and the Netherlands. Belgium's 10 million people live on only 11,781 square miles — it's the second most densely populated country in the world — and they make every square meter count, from their ferociously productive factories, to their meticulously cultivated farmlands, to the tight and efficient network of roads, railroads, and inland waterways connecting it all. On a smaller scale, you can see how they make the most of space in the burgeoning flower gardens behind nearly every house. Close as things are, Belgium has forests that support a great variety of wild birds, such as avocets, shrikes, godwits, and grouse, and four-footed animals ranging from wild hamsters to wild boar.

Belgium is a constitutional monarchy, with power distributed among the king, his appointed cabinet, and the bicameral Parliament, consisting of a Senate and House of Representatives. The present king is Baudouin, a direct descendant of Belgium's first king, Leopold I, who took the throne in 1831.

Brussels is the capital, the center of business, industry, and culture; Antwerp is the most cosmopolitan city, one of Europe's greatest ports, a center of the world diamond market and the birthplace of Rubens; Liège is an important university and factory town and a world class maker of firearms; Bruges is famous for its handmade lace and the spectacle of its perfectly preserved medieval Flemish architecture; Ghent is another medieval city — larger, more gracious, and more commercial than Bruges; Ostend is a summer resort on the North Sea.

Julius Caesar found Celts in Belgium when he conquered Gaul in the 1st century BC. The Franks pushed in from Germany in the 3rd century; Belgium's northern people, the Flemish, are descended from the Franks, and the Walloons of the south from the Romanized Celts. The two groups have been squabbling ever since the Frankish invasion. Clovis and Charlemagne put Belgium under the Holy Roman Empire and Christianized it. The empire fell apart after Charlemagne's death in 814, and from the 9th century to World War II, the strategic land that now is Belgium was overrun almost continuously by the Vikings, French, Spanish, English, Austrians, Dutch, and finally twice by the Germans. National instability strengthened the economic self-reliance and chauvinism of the Belgian cities, which had to fortify themselves as best they could against invaders and to make protective pacts with one ruler to avoid being absorbed by another. In medieval and Renaissance times, Ghent, Bruges, Antwerp, and Ypres grew fat and powerful from the commerce passing through their ports, becoming great centers of art, architecture, and scholarship. The varying condition of Belgium's inland waterways has made their fortunes fluctuate wildly since the Renaissance.

In this century, Belgium was a trampling ground in both world wars and was occupied by Germany both times. During World War II, the Nazis bombed Belgium mercilessly, pilfered machinery, abducted laborers to work in Germany, and imposed general tyranny; the Battle of the Bulge, the German army's last stand before being decimated, took place in Luxembourg province, near the German border. Damage from both wars was so catastrophic that much of the country had to be rebuilt from scratch. Nevertheless, Belgium has recovered better than most countries in Europe, enjoying worldwide trade and the success of her chemical, metalwork, and food-processing industries.

Belgium has three official languages: of its 10 million inhabitants, some 60% speak Flemish, about 40% speak French, and a mere 0.7% speak German (in the southeastern cantons). Dutch is the official language in the northern four provinces, French in the southern four; the central province of Brabant, containing Brussels, officially is bilingual. For centuries, French was the official language of all Belgium, spoken by the wealthy and powerful throughout. However, as Flanders became richer and more industrial and Flemish nationalism acquired more political clout, the Dutch language was accorded more and more official respect; in 1962, Brussels was officially made bilingual as a concession to the northerners. Although political division in Belgium still tends to be along linguistic lines, the matter of Flemish equality is largely settled.

The country is almost entirely Roman Catholic, and about one quarter of the population attends mass regularly. Because of his staunch Catholic beliefs, in April 1990, King Baudoin abdicated for 42 hours rather than signing and giving royal assent to a law legalizing abortion. Religious tolerance is written into the constitution, and there are some Jewish and Protestant enclaves. Among the Walloons, there is a strong anti-Church movement; pro- and anticlerical feelings probably rank second, after the language question, as a source of political turmoil.

Belgians are contemptuous of authority, no doubt from centuries of foreign rule. The rights of the individual are considered more important than obligations to society; tax evasion, for example, has been developed to the level of an art. The Flemish in particular are highly independent, living mostly as small farmers and shopkeepers. They have the Teutonic bent for work, order, cleanliness, and conservative rectitude, and they tend to have large families. Walloons are more urbane and Gallic in their outlook, tending more toward radicalism, socialism, big government, and small families — although, like the Flemish, they are very industrious. Family life is a high priority with both groups; parents and grown children often live near each other. Belgians make no major decisions without consulting their families, and they spend most of their social lives with relations and the friends with whom they grew up. Households often do things as a group: Even a shopping trip is a family outing, with the father leading the brood.

In sports, Belgians love cycling best: Bicycles are used not only in races but also for commuting and recreation. Soccer is the most popular organized sport; pigeon racing also is important; and cockfighting, though illegal, still has a following. The annual auto races (held in May, August, and

September) at *Spa/Francorchamps* also draw huge crowds of enthusiasts.

Belgians are perhaps most passionate about good food, both at home and in restaurants. Belgian food, even in an inexpensive bistro, is plentiful, substantial, and good. Butter and rich sauces are used prolifically in pastries, vegetables, and meat dishes; the most popular meat is beef, and dessert is often made with chocolate or whipped cream. (It's not surprising that the nation has a high incidence of obesity, gout, and stomach and intestinal troubles.) Brussels is considered one of the two or three culinary capitals of the world, so prices for a meal in a top restaurant tend to be high. In addition to food, Belgians also take great pride in brewing beer; some brands to try are Orval, Gueuze, Kriek, Trappiste, and Rodenbach.

We've laid out two routes for visitors to follow through Belgium; they both begin in Brussels, which should be a major stop in its own right (see the city report in THE CITIES). The first route takes you through the Flemish-speaking north, to Antwerp, Ghent, Bruges, and Ypres, hotbeds of the great northern Renaissance in painting and architecture. Evidence of it — the churches, cathedrals, and guildhouses from the 12th to the 17th century — still tower over the narrow streets in many sections of Antwerp; inside are the huge, opulent paintings of the city's most famous son, Peter Paul Rubens. You drive west across the poppy-covered plains of Flanders to sights like the dank and massive forts of 'sGravensteen, in Ghent; Ghent itself has more historic buildings than anyplace else in Belgium. You'll visit the idyllic Princely Béguinage (a convent) in Bruges; you'll pass on to the white, sandy beaches of Ostend to swim or play tennis, where dikes, fences, dunes, and water pumps have conspired to hold back the North Sea for 700 years. At Ypres, farther south, is the reconstruction of the great Cloth Hall (a monument to medieval commerce) and the improbable *Festival of the Cat,* a vestige of a prehistoric culture.

The second route, for the nature lover as well as the history buff, goes through the pastoral, French-speaking area of southern Belgium known as the Ardennes. The countryside here is hilly and forested, less populous than the north, and the country's most scenic region. The trek is a long loop through the provinces of Liège, Luxembourg, Namur, and Hainaut, a green country of bluffs, valleys, and ancient armed citadels. The Ardennes is a hunter's paradise: Wild boar abound all year, and deer, pheasant, water birds, and wild sheep all have their season. If you like camping or hiking, allow several days for the wilderness of the Ardennes and the mysterious Belgian Lorraine, with its steep cliffs, dense woods, and lavish wildflowers. As you swing back north, you can witness dramatic folk pageants and tour exquisite country castles such as Annevoie and Beloeil.

Antwerp and Flanders

The western Flemish provinces of Antwerp, West Flanders, and East Flanders were one of the most important medieval and Renaissance art centers in the world. In Antwerp city, Ghent, and Bruges, much of the past still is standing and very much a part of daily life. It is to be expected that thousand-year-old churches still are in use; it's more surprising that many other ancient monuments still function as private houses and government buildings. Northern Belgium makes way for its teeming industries while it holds on to a rare respect for the past and local identity.

Antwerp is a center of publishing, the performing arts, and several industries — notably the diamond trade — and one of the major ports of Europe. Ghent is another industrial and cultural power, with its own port and more than its share of great Flemish art and architecture. Bruges is the preserved and polished medieval jewel of Belgium, having survived 400 years and two world wars with its ancient atmosphere intact. Ypres survived World War I with not much of anything intact and had to be completely rebuilt; it's now a modern city.

The rivers and canals connecting the interior with the ocean at one time made seaports of all the major Flemish cities. The Flanders terrain is so level you can smell the ocean 40 miles inland. The 41-mile shore, which actually sits below sea level, is mostly land reclaimed from the sea over the centuries for farming; the townspeople built dikes and windmills to keep the sea from taking it back. Although resorts and restaurants dot the white sand beaches, the ancient tradition of paying ceremonial homage to the power of the waters in a solemn Blessing of the Sea survives in many of the fishing villages from Knokke-Het-Zoute to the French border.

BRUSSELS: For a detailed report on the city and its hotels and restaurants, see *Brussels,* THE CITIES.

   En Route from Brussels – Head north from Brussels on Route E-19, out of Brabant and into the province of Antwerp. Your first stop, 15 miles (24 km) from Brussels, is the city of Mechelen, the religious capital of Belgium and the seat of the primate. Not only does Mechelen have a grand 49-bell carillon — which peals out concerts regularly — but also a school for *carilloneurs* (bell ringers) to perpetuate the art. Both school and carillon are in the Gothic cathedral of St. Rombout, begun in the 13th century and still not finished: Its great tower was supposed to be 551 feet high but never topped the mere 318 it is now — it's unlikely that anyone will suggest going ahead with those last 233 feet at this point. Inside, the cathedral is sumptuously baroque, with black and white marble and paintings by Van Dyck and other Flemish masters. For Rubens lovers, the Church of St. John in Mechelen has his famous *Adoration of the Magi.* Near Mechelen, in Muizen, is a "suburb" of the Antwerp Zoo called Plankendaal Park; it's a special breeding farm and resort for endangered animal species and a beautiful setting in which to see them (open in the warm weather).

   Some 10 miles (16 km) to the northeast is the charming, small Flemish town of Lier. Founded in the 8th century, it has produced a number of Belgium's more notable artists. The 13th-century cloisters, or *béguinage,* inside the town is a peaceful miniature of town life. Nearby, the Zimmer Pavilion houses the showpiece of the *1939 World's Fair* in New York City — an astronomical clock with 93 dials and 14 automata.

ANTWERP: Continue 10 miles (17 km) northwest to Antwerp. Founded in the 7th century by missionaries, it is now Belgium's second-largest city (pop. 785,000), the third-largest seaport in Europe, and a major producer of cars, petrochemicals, and cut diamonds. Seventy percent of the world's diamonds are produced here. The diamond trade goes back to the days of Charles the Bold, Duke of Burgundy, who reigned from 1467 to 1477. According to an old story, a young student invented a method of cutting and polishing stones; Charles entrusted him with three diamonds and was so pleased with the results that he presented one of the stones to the pope, another to King Louis XI of France, and kept the third for himself. Presumably, the student took the hint and went into business.

Most of the diamond trade today is clustered around the Central Station. Diamondland allows visitors to its showroom to watch the craftsmen at work. Tours are at 11 AM and 4 PM daily; closed Sunday. 33A Appelmansstr. (phone: 3-234-3612). The *Provincial Diamond Museum* (31-33 Lange Herentalsestr.; phone: 3-231-8645) features exhibits about diamonds, plus a treasure chamber of ancient and contemporary jewels. The museum is open daily, except January 1 and 2 and December 25 and 26; demonstrations on cutting and polishing are given on Saturdays from 2 to 5 PM.

Antwerp, the birthplace of the painter Peter Paul Rubens, celebrated the 400th anniversary of his birth in 1977. In a way, Rubens personified all that makes Antwerp what it is: art, international affairs, and wealth. He studied in Italy, became a diplomat, traveled widely, and brought an Italian touch to the Flemish painting tradition. His house (9-11 Wapper; open to the public daily from 10 AM to 5 PM) contains his own art and that of his contemporaries — as well as his furniture. Some of the pupils who studied here included Van Dyck, Jordaens, Snyder, and Jean Breughel. Besides painting prolifically, Rubens was a prominent politician, and his house gives you some idea of the private world of a public man in 17th-century Antwerp.

The Cathedral of Our Lady is the largest Gothic church in Belgium and Antwerp's major landmark, containing some of the world's greatest paintings — including Rubens's *Elevation of the Cross, The Descent from the Cross,* and *The Assumption.* It's open weekday afternoons until 5 PM, Saturdays from 12 to 5 PM, and Sundays from 1 to 4 PM.

Near the cathedral is the *Plantin-Moretus Museum* (open 10 AM to 5 PM daily; 22 Vrijdagmarkt; phone: 3-233-0294), site of the Plantin printing shop, famous all over Europe in the 16th century. In the richly furnished interior are Plantin's office and printing room, containing many first editions and engravings. Tapestries, gold-embossed leather bindings, the Biblia Regia, and 13 examples of the Gutenberg Bible are among its treasures.

The Stadhuis (City Hall; phone: 3-220-8211) built in a grand, far-flung style in 1564, faces the main square near the cathedral (closed Monday afternoons and Saturday mornings). Around it are the headquarters of Antwerp's rich tradesmen's guilds from the same period, furnished with sculpture, paintings, and tapestries.

Rubens is buried in the Church of St. James (St. Jacob), a Flamboyant Gothic edifice with a baroque interior. Built in 1491, St. James has an amazing inventory of art by Flemish masters: The marble communion table is by Verbruggen and Kerricx (late 17th century); the carving in the choir stalls is the work of Artus Quellin; there is a *Temptation of Saint Anthony* by Martin de Vos; and one of Rubens's own last works, *The Holy Family,* hangs in the chapel where he is buried. The church is open from 2 to 4 PM; closed Sundays and holidays.

Antwerp's *Royal Museum of Fine Arts* (L. de Waelplaats; phone: 3-238-7809; closed Mondays) often is called the richest museum in Belgium, a land of museums. There are about 2,500 paintings here, including a staggering collection of Rubens, Frans Hals, Van Dyck, Memling, and Rogier Van der Weyden. Even if you are not a student of art, you will be fascinated at the 800-year history of northern painting displayed here.

As in any seafaring country, *Belgium's Marine Museum* (1 Steenplein; phone: 3-232-0850), with ancient maps, ships, relics, and instruments, is worth a visit. The museum is in the Steen, a 10th-century fortress and the city's oldest building. For a relaxing cruise of Antwerp's famous harbor, take a *Flandria* sightseeing boat at Steenplein, a short walk from the Grote Markt.

A must-see is the world-famous Antwerp Zoo (next to the Central Station; phone: 3-231-1640). Check out the Reptile House and the Nocturama, a special darkened habitat for nocturnal animals.

If you are in Antwerp during *Lent*, make your way to a *Goose Race*, held on Sundays in several of the surrounding villages; it's just one of the many bizarre and dramatic traditions still thriving in this proudly parochial country. In a *Goose Race*, competing horsemen thunder along a track trying to snag the head of a dead goose suspended above them. The winner is proclaimed king, and festivities ensue in his honor.

Antwerp also is the home of the oldest golf club in Belgium, the *Royal Antwerp Golf Club* (2 George Capiaulei, Kapellenbos 2950; phone: 3-666-8456). The 27 holes are open to members only or guests of members.

The denizens of Antwerp are great beer lovers, and they know how to create the coziest watering spots (there are about 2,500 of them in town). During your sightseeing rounds, drop in at *De Pelgrom* (15 Pelgrimstr.; phone: 3-234-089)), a multi-chambered cellar featuring candlelight and classical music, near the cathedral.

En Route from Antwerp – Go west from Antwerp province into East Flanders (Oost-Vlaanderen), on the road to Ghent. You are entering the historic region of Flanders proper, which starts in the Netherlands and stretches down the North Sea coast into northern France. The poppies grow here, the sheep graze, and everything looks like a familiar landscape — which it is, because it's been painted hundreds of times by the Flemish masters whose works hang in museums all over the world; and centuries of armies have passed this way, leaving memories of the fields of Flanders in our collective consciousness.

If you are here in early September, try to arrive in time to watch the surreal, elephantine grace of the hot-air balloons in the international balloon race held every year in Sint-Niklaas, just west of the Antwerp border.

GHENT: Continue southwest to Ghent (pop. 236,000), the gracious and prosperous capital of East Flanders. Ghent has a long history of civic feistiness that put it in combat with a variety of governments and overlords from Burgundy, Flanders, Spain, and Holland. The city itself spawned an overlord in Charles Quint, the Holy Roman Emperor; King Edward III of England was living in Ghent when his son John was born, best known as John of Gaunt in Shakespeare's *Richard II*, who fathered a long line of English kings.

The center of Ghent is its medieval port, with more historic buildings than any other Belgian city. Surrounding the old quarter are the modern commercial and industrial sections.

The most dramatic introduction to Ghent is by way of 'sGravensteen, the formidable castle of the Counts of Flanders. Built in the 12th century over a 9th-century dungeon, it is a no-nonsense fortress, with walls 6 feet thick. Inside, the cold and damp of centuries hang in the air even in the summer. It has a small museum displaying instruments of torture. Visitors with small children must be on guard here, since there are many high, open walkways and steps. Open daily. Admission charge. Sint Veerle-plein; phone: 91-259306)

The most important medieval building in town is the cathedral of St. Bavo, a hybrid of Gothic, Romanesque, and baroque styles. The elaborately carved wood pulpit inside warrants a visit on its own. The four massive bronze candlesticks were ordered by Henry VIII of England for his tomb, but Cromwell got his hands on them after Henry's death and sold them to the Ghent clergy for the cash. In one of the chapels is the van Eyck *Mystic Lamb*, one of the world's most famous paintings. The history of this painting is a detective thriller in progress, for its origin still is vague. No one knows whether it was painted by both van Eyck brothers or by only one. Its panels have been cut off, buried, and returned several times. During the religious riots of the 16th century, the panels were hidden in the cathedral tower. They reemerged and were being sent to England as a gift to Queen Elizabeth I when they were intercepted by the family who originally had commissioned them. Two panels were stolen in 1934, and only one returned. Some believe the missing panel, *The Just Judge,* is hidden in the cathedral. The cathedral is closed at lunchtime.

Next door is the belfry, the rallying point for the people of Ghent in their many rebellions against their rulers. There is a fine view of the countryside from the tower. The sound and light show here (in English) is a must, as is the unique *Folklore Museum* (65 Kraanlei; phone: 91-231336); closed Mondays.

The *Museum of Archaeology* (2 Godshuizenlaan; phone: 91-251106), in the ancient Cistercian Abbey of Byloke, contains a rich assortment of art, glass, porcelain, weapons, and clothing. Closed Mondays. The *Museum of Fine Arts* has a splendid collection of Flemish primitives — such as *The Carrying of the Cross* by Hieronymus Bosch — as well as Dutch, German, French, English, Italian, and Spanish masters. The neighboring *Museum of Contemporary Art* focuses on post–World War II trends. Both museums are closed Mondays and located at the same address (3 Nicolaas De Liemaekereplein; phone: 91-211703).

Ghent has been noted for its horticulture industry for the last 200 years: It has historically been the center for the growing, breeding, and distribution of new varieties of flowers to all points of the globe. The flowering azalea, native to Korea, was developed in Ghent, and the city's nurseries supply 16 million plants a year — nearly half the world market. Coming in second, at some 80 million tubers a year, is the begonia, developed in Ghent into its present form from a South American flower. Hothouses dot the outskirts of the city. The town of Lochristi, 6 miles (10 km) outside Ghent, holds a begonia festival every August, when nurserymen put together floats and pictures using different-colored begonias.

A major event in Ghent is a mammoth flower festival held in the city every 5 years. (The next festival is scheduled for late April of 1995.) Over 450 horticulturists from all over the world will show their best plants in a 9-acre indoor expanse, with a total of 2 million Belgian francs offered in prize money. The first *floralies* (flower festival), in 1809 in the *Frascati Inn,* consisted of 50 potted plants arranged in front of a field of French tricolor flags around a bust of Napoleon.

In the 20th century the crowds are thick — 700,000 strong over the week-long run — peering at the likes of sweet peas and conifer arrangements to be judged by the Belgian Flower Arranging Society, blooming roses and daffodils, and every other conceivable plant presented to the Royal Society of Agriculture and Botany.

En Route from Ghent – Leaving Ghent, make a slight detour southeast to the 13th-century castle of Ooidonck on the river Lys (phone: 91-826123). Ooidonck is decorated with 17th- and 18th-century furniture, china, silver, and crystal (open only afternoons on some religious holidays and Sundays in July, August, and early September). The Lys borders the grounds on two sides, and a long avenue of linden trees links the castle with the Ghent road.

Ten miles (16 km) east of Ghent on Route 345 is the imposing Laarne castle with its treasures of silver and tapestries. Legend has it that a ghost still stalks the place. Closed Mondays. Admission charge (phone: 91-309155).

BRUGES: The main road leads directly to Bruges, the capital of West Flanders and the longtime rival of Ghent. Bruges is smaller (pop. 118,000), with a totally different appearance and atmosphere.

The city virtually is a moated museum of the Middle Ages, with stiff-gabled houses perched over cobbled streets and long-necked swans gliding along misty canals. For 200 years, Bruges was the most important commercial center in Western Europe, linking the Baltic and the Mediterranean seas. The riches of the world were piled high on its docks, and no king could equal the splendor of its court. The Counts of Flanders and their merchant princes brought artists and artisans from all over Europe to decorate their palaces, churches, and guildhalls. Their wives were so magnificently gowned that a visiting Queen of France once complained, "I thought that I alone was queen, but here I see hundreds of them around me."

But year after opulent year, the silt rose in the estuary linking Bruges with the North Sea until ships could no longer navigate the narrow, sand-choked waterway, and Bruges became landlocked. This put an end to the city's commercial importance, and Bruges was frozen in time, retaining its medieval atmosphere to this day. The 19th-century English poet Ernest Dowson called Bruges "this autumnal old city — the most medieval town in Europe."

Bruges must be visited on foot. The streets are narrow and twisting; some, like Stoofstraat, are only 3 or 4 feet wide. No skyscraper or high-rise blots the sky; for 7 centuries the highest point has been the 365-foot spire of the church of Notre Dame. For a beautiful view of the city, climb the steps of the belfry at one end of the Grote Markt (Main Square). On a clear day you can see Ostend and Zeebrugge and other towns along the coast as well as the maze of canals within Bruges itself. The canals that weave in and around the city give it a melancholy charm; lime trees and willows grow from the banks, and centuries-old buildings of faded brick are reflected in the silent waters. A few places in town offer canal boat tours.

Probably the greatest event in the city's long history took place in 1150, when Thierry d'Alsace, Count of Flanders, rode home from the Second Crusade. According to tradition, he brought with him some drops of Christ's blood, collected on Golgotha by Joseph of Arimathea and given to him by the King of Jerusalem. They are kept in a reliquary in the Basilica of the Holy Blood (around the corner from the town belfry) and every year are carried through the city in procession on *Ascension Thursday,* a religious holiday in May.

The churches of Bruges are as rich in history as they are in art, some with foundations going back to the 8th and 9th centuries. The dim, dusty-aisled crypt of the basilica, a 12th-century Romanesque chapel, is the oldest unaltered building still standing in Bruges.

The Cathedral of St. Salvator was begun more than a thousand years ago. It's hung with Gobelin tapestries, and some of its choir stalls are carved with the crest of one of Europe's oldest orders of chivalry, the Golden Fleece, founded in Bruges by Philip of Burgundy in 1429. It was in this cathedral that his knights assembled to worship.

Only a block away is the Church of Notre Dame, the site of Michelangelo's marble *Madonna and Child,* the 500-year-old Paradise Porch, and the magnificent mausoleum of Charles the Bold.

Even the former hospital is a museum. St. John's goes back to the 12th century. One of its 13th-century wards contains six paintings by Hans Memling; other wards have 12th-century frescoes of the Virgin Mary (phone: 50-332526; closed Wednesdays).

Scattered throughout Bruges (and other old cities in Flanders) are "God's houses," a series of compounds built by wealthy families or guilds for the poor and the old. The only requirements for residence are "honesty, good character, and a peaceable nature." There is one in Bruges built by the Meulenaere family in 1613 that has 24 one-story houses, each with its own garden. The community begins and ends each day with prayers for the generations that have lived and died there before them.

At the other extreme is the *Gruuthuse Museum,* the former home of one of the lords of Bruges. Its great hall, reception rooms, and collections of armor, porcelains, lace, coins, and furniture hint at the magnificence of private houses in the city's prime (closed Tuesdays; 17 Dijver; phone: 50-339911).

Next to it is the *Groeninge Museum,* housing some of the great masterpieces of Flemish art, including paintings by Jan van Eyck, Hans Memling, Hieronymus Bosch, and Pieter Breughel the Younger (closed Tuesdays; 12 Dijver; phone: 50-339911).

In all of Bruges there is probably no lovelier place than the Princely Béguinage, one of the convents of the peasant Béguines, who wore a *béguin,* or headdress, tied under the chin. There are *béguinages* throughout Belgium, famous for their manicured gardens. Today they are either maintained as museums or occupied, as in Bruges, by Benedictine nuns who still dress in the 15th-century style of their predecessors. To reach the Princely Béguinage, cross the Bridge of the Vine, which spans the Lake of Love, between the cloister and the main city. Across the lake, sunlight filters through the trees, and the only thing to break the peace is the song of a bird.

The miracle of Bruges is that it still stands, considering all the wars that have raged around it. The port of Zeebrugge, 8 miles (13 km) away, was seized by Germany during World War I and made into a U-boat base. When the British stormed the port, the Germans blew it up. It was rebuilt, destroyed again in World War II, and rebuilt once more.

When the 8th-century chapel of the ironmongers' guild was torn down to make way for a garage a few years ago, a preservation society was created to prevent further desecration. They named it the Marcus Gerards Foundation, after a 16th-century Bruges mapmaker who drew to scale every house and street in town. The foundation researches the history of the old buildings in this monumental city and keeps an eye on how they are maintained.

En Route from Bruges – Ostend and the 41-mile (66-km) stretch of Belgian coast are a short drive west of Bruges. There are resorts, casinos, and nightclubs from nearly one end to the other of this unbroken stretch of fine white sand. July and August are good for swimming, but beaches get very crowded with vacationing Belgians. If you avoid those peak months, you can still have a fine time playing tennis, breathing the sea air, and gambling away your money. At Ostend there is a long boardwalk along the North Sea, and the area is dotted with restaurants specializing in fresh fish, for this is Belgium's main fishing port.

The best areas in which to enjoy the sea away from honky-tonk civilization are in the extreme north and south of the coast. At the Zwin Bird Sanctuary up by the Dutch border, the sea lavender blooms on the marshes in July and August, where more than 100 species of birds make their home.

At Oostduinkerke, 12 miles (19 km) southwest of Ostend, a few fishermen still trawl for shrimp on horseback. Their annual shrimp fishing festival takes place the third weekend in June.

If you are in Ostend just before *Lent,* you will find yourself caught up in the *Masked Ball of the Dead Rat,* a stupendous carnival that occupies the entire town, but is concentrated in the casino. Candies in the shape of clogs are scattered to the throng at the festival's close. North of Ostend, at Knokke, an international fireworks festival is held every August on 5 nights spread out through the month.

On the final Sunday in May, a solemn procession in the town of Blankenberge culminates in the *Blessing of the Sea,* when seafaring people make a special peace with their ancient friend and enemy, a ritual that takes place at different times of the year along the coast.

Note: There now is daily jetfoil service from Ostend to Dover (it's a 1½-hour crossing), where trains to London are available. Ferries also operate daily from Ostend and Zeebrugge.

YPRES: Head south to Ypres when you have had your fill of the coast. One of the three great cities of Flanders in the Middle Ages, Ypres was razed in World War I, and a modern city has been built in its place. The 17th-century façades along many streets have been reconstructed, as have the city's two greatest buildings, St. Martin's Cathedral and the towering Cloth Hall — a monument to Ypres's textile industry built in 1214. Unfortunately, no medieval or later buildings survived the bombardment of 1914–18, but the region's red poppy fields, grazing animals, and pastoral countryside still are very much in evidence.

Ypres never fell in World War I, despite the bombardment, but the surrounding battles took over a quarter-million Allied lives. At the Menin Gate, a memorial to the soldiers of the British Commonwealth who died defending Ypres, traffic is stopped every evening for a few minutes while buglers blow a salute on silver bugles. The poem "Flanders Field," written by John McCrae, one of the soldiers who fought here, best expresses the mood of this place:

> In Flanders Field the poppies blow
> between the crosses row on row
> That mark our place; and in the sky
> the larks, bravely singing, fly
> Scarce heard amid the guns below.

On the second Sunday in May, Ypres holds what is possibly the strangest rite in all of Belgium, *Kattenwoensdag* (Festival of the Cats). Some 2,000 revelers dress up in gaudy costumes portraying cats, witches, and giants and march in procession accompanied by bagpipes. The parade has giant floats dedicated to feline folklore heroes, including Puss in Boots and Cieper, the king of the cats; Cieper has a wife, Minneke Poes, and a kitten-child, Piepertje. The culmination of the festival is when the town jester hurls little wooden cats to the crowd from the top of the town belfry (until 1817, he threw live cats). It is said that the holiday is a vestige of an ancient witch cult.

BEST EN ROUTE

All the major cities and towns in Belgium have comfortable hotels and first-rate restaurants. There also are several good *relais* (inns) in the countryside where you can spend the night or have a splendid lunch or dinner. It's wise to book ahead for a room in a hotel and essential to make a reservation for a meal or room at a *relais*.

Accommodations at an expensive inn will cost about $100 or more per night in a double for two; moderate, about $60; and inexpensive, about $40. A meal at an expensive restaurant will run about $50 or more per person for dinner, including tip, without wine; moderate, about $35; and inexpensive, about $20.

GHENT

St. Jorishof – Built in 1228, this 38-room hostelry is believed to be the oldest in northern Europe. It has a Gothic hall with a huge chimney. The interior is hung with the pennants of various clubs and organizations ranging from the medieval guilds to the Rotary Club. Napoleon Bonaparte was a guest. Closed the last 2 weeks in July and during the *Christmas* season. 2 Botermarkt (phone: 91-242424). Expensive to moderate.

BRUGES

Duc de Bourgogne – There are only 10 small rooms here, but the restaurant is the best in Bruges. Both the rooms and restaurant nearly always are booked. The dining room extends over a canal, and the area is most impressive at night, when it's floodlit. Near the entrance hall is a medieval version of a small cocktail lounge, where you wait for your table; its walls are hung with tapestries of saints and knights, the chairs and tables are heavy mahogany, and there is a huge fireplace. In the restaurant, order the North Sea fish and, if it's spring or summer, the asparagus. Closed Mondays, Tuesdays for lunch in summer, Sunday evenings in winter, and in July. Restaurant reservations necessary. 12 Huidevettersplein (phone: 50-332038). Expensive.

De Orangerie – A ravishingly charming 16th-century building turned into a cozy, 18-room hotel overlooking a canal. 10 Kartuizerinnestraat (phone: 50-34-16-49). Expensive.

Oud-huis Amsterdam – A handsomely converted townhouse, on a canal, with 17 rooms and a garden. 3 Spiegelrei (phone: 50-34-18-10). Expensive.

Pullman – Once a 17th-century convent, this link in the Pullman chain is in the heart of Bruges. 2 Boeveriestr. (phone 50-340971). Expensive.

ANTWERP

De Rosier – This work of hostelry genius, inconspicuously off a quiet side street, is one of those rare finds: an impeccably tasteful mansion-hotel (only 10 rooms) graced with antiques, a small indoor pool, and charming garden, run with the greatest discretion and style for its well-heeled clientele. Reservations are very hard to come by, but it's worth the wait. 21-23 Rosier (phone: 3-225-0140). Expensive.

Sir Anthony Van Dijck – A cobblestone passage marks the entrance to an ancient building housing the restaurant. The combination of fine food and a dramatic setting make this worth a stop, especially for lunch. Closed Saturdays, the second Sunday of each month, *Easter Week,* and the first 3 weeks of August. Reservations necessary. 16 Oude Koornmarkt Vlaaikensgang (phone: 3-231-6170). Expensive.

The Ardennes

South of Brussels is a world so different from Flanders that it's hard to believe they are part of the same country. This is the Ardennes — Shakespeare's Forest of Arden in *As You Like It* — stretching across the south of Belgium. The Ardennes extend into the three provinces of Namur, Liège, and Luxembourg (not to be confused with the Grand Duchy of Luxembourg, a separate country). It is gentle, green, and somehow a bit mysterious compared with the North, a countryside of legends and spirits, abbeys and castles. It is also the place to go if you want to spend your vacation skiing, hunting, hiking, or camping.

You can make a loop through the region by driving southeast of Brussels through Liège, Spa, and Malmédy, south to Bastogne and Arlon, west to Bouillon, north to Namur, west to Mons, and finally north back to Brussels.

BRUSSELS: For a detailed report on the city and its hotels and restaurants, see *Brussels,* THE CITIES.

    En Route from Brussels – Heading southeast to Liège, on the left you will pass Catholic University in Louvain, Belgium's oldest university, founded in 1425. Erasmus is one of its distinguished alumni. Architecturally, it ranges from the 15th to the 20th century. The town was badly damaged during the two world wars, but St. Peter's Church and the 15th-century Town Hall are worth visiting. Guided tours of the Town Hall are offered at 11 AM and 3 PM weekdays and Saturdays from April through September; weekdays only in winter. Like Oxford, Louvain has become somewhat commercial and industrial but basically preserves its clerical-academic serenity.

LIÈGE: Seventy miles (112 km) east of Brussels is Liège, Belgium's third-largest city (pop. 593,000) and a gateway to the Ardennes. Liège has been a prosperous industrial town since coal was discovered here in 1198. Most of the citizens are shopkeepers, artisans, miners, or steelworkers. (Val St.-Lambert crystal and sporting guns are produced here.) But above all, Liège — "'the Ardent City" — is a city that loves festivals, art, and music.

The streets of Liège are laid out as fitfully and capriciously as the local temperament, so don't plan your time here too closely. You should enjoy what you find, however. The skyline shows over 100 church spires, and the river Meuse winds its way through every quarter, which means you will often find yourself going over one nice little bridge or another. The city has one of Belgium's most important universities, the University of Liège, so the café life is well catered to.

In the center of Liège is a tiny island, Outre-Meuse (*Djus d'la Moûse* in the Walloon dialect), reminiscent of the Ile de la Cité in Paris. This "free republic" of garbled cobblestone streets and alleyways is best symbolized by Tchantchès, a beloved marionette character not unlike Punch, and the late Georges Simenon, the famed creator of Inspector Maigret and probably Liège's best-known native son. He lived here as a child at 25 Rue Pasteur. The tourist office runs tours of Simenon's Liège.

On Mont St. Martin are some particularly fine houses, with winding outdoor stairways and hidden gardens. The Place du Marché and the Place St.-Lambert are the heart of the city. The 11th-century Palace of the Prince Bishops (who ruled Liège until the 18th century) has two great courtyards. Each of the capitals atop the 60 columns of the portico is different from the others. Since the 19th century, the building has been used as the Palace of Justice.

One of Belgium's greatest art treasures is the baptismal font by Reinier van Hoei in the Church of St. Barthélemy, made of tin-coated brass sometime between 1107 and 1118. The Church of St. James is an old abbey with five Renaissance stained glass windows and an exquisite north portal. At the Church of the Holy Cross are a 12th-century enamel reliquary and an 8th-century key of St. Hubert. St. Hubert, the patron saint of hunters, established his bishopric at Liège in the 8th century; he is a very important saint in the Ardennes.

The city has a wide assortment of museums, but be sure to see the *Museum of Walloon Life* (Cour des Mineurs; phone: 41-236094; closed Mondays). In a 17th-century convent, it has, among other things, an amazing collection of musical instruments. There's also the *Curtius Museum* (13 Quai de Maestricht; phone: 41-232068; closed Tuesdays), with its unique glass and crystal collection, which displays the history of glassmaking. At the theater on the Rue Féronstrée, marionettes (large, intricate puppets) perform in Liège folklore pageants, religious plays, and sketches based on contemporary gossip. The characters include Tchantchès, biblical characters, and historical figures like Charlemagne and Napoleon. If you understand enough French to try to decipher Liègeois, the local dialect, you will appreciate a real folk art that is still very much alive. Liège is famous for its manufacture of guns, and the *Museum of Weapons* (8 Quai de Maestricht; phone: 41-233178; closed Mondays), with 12,500 pieces, is considered the best firearms collection in the world.

Before leaving, be sure to visit the site of the old Citadel; you can climb the 407 steps to the top or drive there. Although nothing remains of the Citadel, you will get a splendid view of the city and the surrounding countryside. The city's Sunday morning market along the quays even draws shoppers from neighboring Germany. A grand assortment of items is for sale, and it's a great meeting place for residents.

On the Sunday following *St. George's Day* (in May) in the neighboring town of Visé, the guild of crossbowmen, the Ancient Arquebusiers, wearing starched shirtfronts and stovepipe hats, celebrate St. George (the patron of archers) with a mass, procession, and an archery contest.

In the village of Rutten on May 1, the sanguine *Play of St. Evermeire* is performed in an orchard by the townspeople, just as it has been for over 1,000 years; it portrays the story of St. Evermeire and his fellow pilgrims, who were massacred by highwaymen in 699.

And you surely won't want to miss the *Pageant of the Flying Cat* in the town of Verviers on the third Sunday in June. An annual publicity stunt for the town, it commemorates the grand experiment of a chemist named Saroléa in 1641. Saroléa wanted to see if he could get his cat to fly, so he attached pig bladders filled with air to the luckless beast and dropped it off the tower of St. Remacle's Cathedral. Naturally, it plummeted like a stone — although it landed in good enough condition to scamper away and, being a wise cat, never returned. Every year the experiment is repeated (with a toy cat) at the Place du Martyr at 5:30 PM, accompanied by a triumphal procession with giant, confetti-belching cat floats. In this technological era the cat does fly successfully, since the bladders are now filled with helium.

>   **En Route from Liège** – Drive 24 miles (38 km) southeast to Spa, the site of the thermal spring from which all the spas in the world take their name. During the 18th and early 19th centuries, Spa was a favorite resort for the European nobility and royalty. The oldest spring is named for Peter the Great, who used to make his way from Russia to take the waters. Nowadays Spa is visited more for its grand hotels and wooded environs rather than the curative power of its waters. Every August 15, the colorful *Battle of Flowers* is held there.
>
>   Drive southeast to Malmédy, where the countryside is covered with alpine flowers in the summer and meadows and dense pine forests line the road. During the winter, this is a popular ski area. Malmédy, a monastery city founded in the 7th century, is best known today for its pre-*Lenten* carnival, which includes mass folk dancing and satirical plays in the local dialect. Nearby is the château of Reinhardstein, the ancestral home of the Metternichs and a completely furnished feudal stronghold.

BASTOGNE: Drive southwest, pick up the Liège road, and go directly south to Bastogne, 100 miles (160 km) from Brussels.

This is the site of the Battle of the Bulge, where the Nazis made their last stand as the Allies pushed toward Germany. The Germans launched their counteroffensive on December 16, 1944; the Americans holding Bastogne were hampered by snow and fog, which prevented any air support. On December 22 the Germans demanded an American surrender. The American General Anthony McAuliffe spurned their ultimatum with a single word: "Nuts." The next day the skies cleared, and Allied planes again took to the air; the Third Army, under General George Patton, counterattacked and reached Bastogne on December 26. Early in January, the First Army arrived from the north. By the end of the month, the Germans had been pushed back behind their own frontier, losing 120,000 men.

McAuliffe and his curt reply became part of Belgian folklore. There is a bust of him in town as well as a few derelict tanks scattered there and around the outskirts, mostly bearing the word "Nuts." The Mardasson American war memorial is laid out in the shape of a five-pointed star and inscribed with the names of the home states of the fallen GIs. Across from the Mardasson, also in the shape of a five-pointed star, is the *Bastogne Historical Center* (Colline du Mardasson; phone: 61-211413), with the largest collection of Bastogne battle relics in the world as well as a film of the battle in four languages; it's open daily from March through November (admission charge).

In the province of Liège, about 56 miles (90 km) north of Bastogne, some 8,000 American soldiers are buried at the Henri-Chapelle cemetery. Near the cemetery is a former monastery, the *Abbaie Val-Dieu,* now a modest but congenial cafeteria-style restaurant. Try the local specialty, *stron d'poye,* a tasty yeast-based spread served with whipped cream cheese on brown bread.

ARLON: Continue south to Arlon, the capital of the province of Luxembourg, where the great Roman road from Rheims intersected the road from the north. While the site of Arlon is the oldest settlement in Belgium, most of the buildings are new. The *Archaeology Museum* (13 Rue des Martyrs; phone: 63-226192) has a wealth of Gallo-Roman artifacts; the Church of St. Donat is built on the site of the castle of the Counts of Arlon, where Richard the Lion-Hearted set out for the Crusades. The church's terrace commands a sweeping view of the valley of the river Semois and Luxembourg, Germany, and France.

BOUILLON: Swing west to Bouillon, the home of Godfrey of Bouillon, a hero of the First Crusade and first King of Jerusalem. Looking out from his castle, it is easy to understand why whoever held this spot ruled the surrounding countryside: You can see a single figure approaching for miles in every direction. Be sure to see the Hall of Justice inside, with its gallows, and take a walk along the battlements (open daily, March through November; closed Mondays and Tuesdays in December; open weekends only, January and February).

En Route from Bouillon – Leave some time for hiking in the Ardennes and the Belgian Lorraine as you travel in this entire southeastern region. You can explore the densely wooded plateau country north of the river Semois all the way to Liège and the steep gorges and lush wildflowers of the Belgian Lorraine south of Arlon. Bring some sturdy shoes or boots, a compass, a light jacket or heavy sweater, and perhaps a camera. It's easy to get lost in this rolling landscape, so either stick to the trail markings or know where you are at all times — and beware of marshes after dark. The mountain peaks go to 2,000 feet, and the views are spectacular.

As you drive north, you'll be in the grotto district, where stalactites and stalagmites stretch from floor to ceiling in underground caverns. The most spectacular is the grotto of Han-sur-Lesse, which was sacred to a local prehistoric civilization.

North of Han-sur-Lesse, in the valley of the River Meuse, is the town of Annevoie, the site of one of Belgium's most beautiful castles. The Castle of Annevoie is relatively small and cozy, more like an 18th-century manor house than a fortress. Its gardens often are compared with those of Versailles, but in fact the gardens of Annevoie are prettier and less formal. There are fountains, pools, cascades, and canals, one after another, between avenues of trees and flowers. The castle is closed from September until *Easter;* the gardens are closed from November until April.

Only 10 miles (16 km) to the east is the Spontin château (phone: 83-699055), considered the most remarkable example of medieval military architecture in Belgium. Still inhabited, the château has stylishly furnished drawing rooms, tapestries, masterpieces of art, and an unusual square dungeon. It's in the charming village of Spontin (exit 19 of E411) and is open daily. Admission charge.

Namur is 20 miles (32 km) north, at the junction of the Sambre and Meuse rivers, a neat little city of 17th-century brick homes. Since the days of Julius Caesar, it has been blasted by one army after another. Louis XIV and William III of Orange fought for it; in both world wars the Germans sacked it and set fire to it. Yet many of its historic treasures have survived. Be sure to visit the House of the Sisters of Notre-Dame (15 Rue Julie-Billiart; phone: 81-230449; closed Tuesdays), with its magnificent treasury of art and relics. In particular, note the work of Hugo d'Oignies, who embellished his crosses and icons with figures of animals of the region.

Namur also has its own casino, *Casino de Wamin* (1 Baron de Moreau; phone: 81-223021). The Citadel, accessible by cable car or on foot, overlooks the Meuse and surrounding countryside.

THE MONS AREA: Mons lies west of Namur along the River Sambre; this region is an essential stop before you make your way back to Brussels.

Shrove Tuesday (before *Lent*) is celebrated in Belgium's usual splashy and improbable style in the town of Binche, near Mons. In a noisy carnival procession, the revelers, called Gilles, wearing bells, green glasses, and ostrich-plumed hats, perform rhythmic dances while marching and pelt the surging crowd with oranges. The onlookers then join in an increasingly frenzied circle dance with the Gilles. It is said that this pageant somehow portrays the Spanish conquest of the Aztec in the New World, with the Gilles playing the Indians, hurling gold (oranges) at the Spaniards. However, while the fruit is flying, the anthropology of it probably makes very little difference to the Binchois.

In Jumet, around July 21, an observance honors St. Mary Magdalene and celebrates the town's deliverance from the plague, dating from the epidemic of the 1380s. The procession begins solemnly until the chosen moment, when a messenger announces that the plague has ended because of their prayers to St. Mary; at this point, the entire parade, including the decorous clergy, breaks into a jubilant dance. In Belgian folk rites, the popular conscience exorcises the terrors and deliverances of the last 1,000 years to show the proper respect for fate so disaster will not strike again.

BELOEIL: It is a short drive from Mons to the castle of Beloeil (phone: 69-689655), a fitting culmination of this tour. For at least 10 centuries it has belonged to the family of the Prince of Ligne. The castle is virtually a museum of furniture, tapestry, paintings, sculpture, and porcelain. The family can trace its ancestry to the 7th century; the portraits in the castle are a history of Europe. The treasures of the house include memorabilia from Peter the Great and Catherine II of Russia and a lock of Marie Antoinette's hair. The formal gardens, laid out in the 17th century, feature a lake and tree-lined avenues and cover nearly 300 acres. There, among the flowers of the centuries, you may hope to lose yourself before finding your way home. There also is a Belgium-in-miniature exhibit, displaying the country's major historic sites and monuments on a scale of 1:25. Closed from November through March.

BEST EN ROUTE

Expensive accommodations will cost about $100 or more per night in a double for two; moderate, about $60; and inexpensive, about $40. A good meal in an expensive place will run $50 or more per person for dinner, including tip, but not wine; moderate, $35; and inexpensive, $20.

GENVAL

Château du Lac – Modeled after a Romanesque abbey but actually built around 1900, this is an ultramodern hotel-restaurant (38 well-appointed rooms) on the outskirts of Brussels. It overlooks Lake Genval and offers a variety of sports. 87 Av. du Lac, Genval (phone: 2-654-1122). Expensive.

DURBUY

Sanglier des Ardennes – The inn-restaurant on this picture-postcard town's main street is noted throughout the country for its fine food. The trout slices on lettuce and the roast squab are superb. Closed Thursdays and January. Restaurant reservations necessary. 99 Rue Comte Th. d'Ursel, about 20 miles (32 km) southwest of Spa (phone: 86-213262). Moderate.

LIÈGE

La Commanderie – A command post of the Knights Templar during the Middle Ages, this is now a small inn (14 rooms) with an excellent restaurant. The old stone buildings are in a private park a short drive southwest of Liège. Closed Wednesdays, except in summer, and weekdays in January and February. Restaurant reservations necessary. 28 Rue Joseph-Pierco, Villers-le-Temple (phone: 85-511701). Hotel, expensive to moderate; restaurant, moderate.

Mamé Vi Cou – This country-style restaurant, with its open fireplace and brick wall decorated with local marionettes, specializes in Liègeois cuisine. The *salade di "Djus d'la"* (bacon, green beans, and potatoes in vinegar), goose scallop, and blood sausage are particularly tasty, especially when washed down with a glass of *peket*, the local liqueur. Closed Mondays and mid-July to mid-August. Reservations advised. 9 Rue de la Wache (phone: 41-237181). Inexpensive.

MALMÉDY

Trôs Marets – Once a private house, this 11-room inn is surrounded by pine forests and has food that lives up to the lush setting. Closed mid-November to mid-December. 2 Rue des Trôs Marets (phone: 80-337917). Expensive.

Hôtel des Bains – A comfortable 15-room, lakeside hotel with an elegant restaurant that draws diners from neighboring Germany. Specialties include lobster and game (in season). Before dinner, sip an aperitif in the homey lounge that overlooks gardens and water. Closed Tuesdays and Wednesdays, the last week of August through the first week of September, and all of January. Restaurant reservations necesssary. 2 Lac de Robertville, Waimes (phone: 80-679571). Hotel, expensive to moderate; restaurant, moderate.

EREZÉE

Auberge du Val d'Aisne – Near Erezée, some 6 miles (10 km) west of the Liège road. Though the rooms are rustic, the nouvelle cuisine served at this 300-year-old inn is very fine; try the wild mushroom salad and the trout. From the cozy dining room, guests can gaze out over farmlands and a stream. It's worth a stop for the food alone. Closed Tuesdays, Wednesdays, Thursdays except in August, and from mid-December to mid-January and mid-June to mid-July. Restaurant reservations necessary. 15 Rue du Moulin-Fanzel, Mormont (phone: 86-499208). Moderate to inexpensive.

BASTOGNE

L'Air Pur – Off the road to Namur, this small hotel has 11 comfortable rooms but no atmosphere inside. Outside, the view of the valley of the Ourthe is dazzling, and the food is excellent. In winter, open weekends only. One and a half miles (2 km) from Houffalize. 11 Rte. de Houffalize, La Roche-en-Ardenne (phone: 84-411223 or 84-411503). Expensive.

L'Auberge du Moulin Hideux – Belgium's first Relais & Châteaux member, this 13-room inn, converted from an old mill, can be your base for Bastogne, Bouillon, and Annevoie. There is a tennis court, and a little pool by the mill where you can select the trout that will be on your plate for lunch. Even if you don't book one of its cozy bedrooms, try to have a meal; it is worth any inconvenience you may encounter getting here. Extensive wine list. Closed Wednesdays and from mid-November to mid-March. Restaurant reservations advised. 1 Rue de Dohan, Noirefontaine (phone: 61-467015). Expensive.

Château de Namur – This 29-room property is surrounded by a magnificent park at the summit of the Citadel above Namur, overlooking the entire Meuse River Valley. There are tennis courts and a swimming pool. The restaurant menu is seasonal (reservations advised). 1 Ave. de l'Ermitage, Namur (phone: 81-222630). Expensive.

Hostellerie du Prieuré de Conques – Between Bastogne and Bouillon on the banks of the Semois, this magnificent 18th-century priory now is a small (17-room) Relais & Châteaux hotel near the trout-filled Semois River; the chef here will prepare your catch. Closed Tuesdays and January to mid-March. Reservations advised. 176 Rue de Florenville, Herbeumont (phone: 61-411417). Expensive.

Bulgaria

Bordered by Romania, Yugoslavia, Greece, Turkey, and the Black Sea, Bulgaria is 325 miles wide and 250 miles long — slightly larger than Ohio — and one of the countries sharing the Danube River. Though it has a population of about 9 million, Bulgaria is the smallest Eastern European country, with an ancient history that predates even that of Crete.

Bulgaria is the rose capital of the world, exporting more than 80% of the world's supply of rose attar. It is credited with the discovery of yogurt, and its people until very recently were among the most long-lived anywhere in the world. In antiquity, the legendary Orpheus sang of Bulgaria's flower-covered meadows, the imposing Balkan and Rhodope massifs, and the deep forests of pine and walnut.

What is now Bulgaria was once the territory of Thracian tribes, whose 1,000-year-old civilization was influenced by the Greeks and the Persians before it eventually succumbed to Roman conquest and later, to successive waves of Slavic immigration to the Balkans.

The name "Bulgaria" comes from the Bulgars, a Turkish people from the steppes north of the Black Sea who preceded the Slavs by a century. Following the Slavs' arrival in the 7th century, Thracian assimilation into Slavic culture was complete. Today Bulgarians have a strong awareness of their Thracian heritage, as evidenced by the country's intense archaeological activity, yielding dazzling finds for its museums.

By the 9th century, Bulgaria was an empire and the cradle of Slav literature. The work of two Byzantine missionaries, the brothers Constantine (later Cyril) and Methodius, who spread the use of the Slavic vernacular in religious practice, found a warm reception in the Bulgarian state, which officially adopted Christianity in 865. The script that Cyril invented to transcribe church texts became the basis for the Cyrillic alphabet, used today by Russians, Ukrainians, Serbs, and Macedonians, in addition to the Bulgarians.

During the 14th century, when its arts and world trading flourished, Bulgaria was the most powerful country in southeastern Europe, largely because of its borders on the Black, Aegean, and Adriatic seas. Bulgaria was the envy of its neighbors, which led to its invasion and conquest by the Ottomans in 1396. Through the next 500 years, the Bulgarians tenaciously managed to hold onto their culture through a network of monasteries where artists and writers were sheltered, producing paintings, books, frescoes, icons, carvings, and musical scores. Today, about half a dozen of these former spiritual and cultural centers, the most famous of which is Rila, attract legions of visitors to their secluded mountain sites. One legacy of Turkish rule is the way Bulgarians shake their heads from side to side to express "yes" and nod for "no" — mannerisms that take some getting used to.

During the 15th century, to increase Bulgaria's revenues, the Turkish rulers encouraged the production of native crafts and improved trade. They also welcomed refugees, including Jews, from then intolerant Western Europe. Although most Jews settled in Constantinople and Salonika, many Bulgarian towns acquired small Jewish communities.

In the 19th century, the small but energetic Bulgarian intelligentsia propelled the development of a "National Revival" of culture and patriotism. Vasil Levski, one of the leaders of the anti-Turkish resistance, was caught and hanged in Sofia in 1866, thus becoming the greatest hero of the resistance. The "National Revival" eventually led to the April 1876 uprising against Ottoman domination. Although cruelly crushed, it provoked a larger conflict — the Russo-Turkish War of 1877, known in Bulgarian history as the War of Liberation. The 1878 Treaty of San Stefano gave birth to an independent state with strong bonds to Russia; in 1978 Bulgaria celebrated 100 years of independence. An interesting footnote is that the Bulgarian-Russian connection was well established long before the Russian Revolution, so the ties between the two countries are based not so much on ideology (although Bulgaria spent most of the post-World War II period as a Soviet satellite) as on invocations of "traditional friendship." They also share a similar Slavic language which uses the Cyrillic alphabet.

With the aid of the Soviet Red Army, the Communists took power in 1946, expelled the 9-year-old King Simeon II and his mother, and nationalized Bulgaria's economy. The new government "encouraged" some 50,000 Jews to emigrate to Israel, and forced 200,000 Turks to flee to Turkey. In 1984, the country's remaining 800,000 Turks were forced to "Bulgarize" their names. (Thousands more Turks have fled, but the recently elected government has begun to restore some of their civil rights.)

In an inevitable extension of the recent dramatic political changes in the rest of Eastern Europe, Todor Zhivkov, the former Communist (renamed Socialist) party leader, was ousted. Bulgaria's first free elections in 58 years were held in June 1990, but although there was stiff competition from the Union of Democratic Forces, the Bulgarian Socialist party won a majority of parliamentary seats.

After the elections, tens of thousands of Bulgarians marched in the streets of Sofia to protest the results, and just 1 month later Peter Mladenov — the newly elected president — was forced to resign. It appeared that the pro-democracy groups would not soon be appeased by their new government, which faced severe economic problems, including a $12 billion debt. The pressures — economic, political, and social — proved too great, and in August 1990, after a dizzying series of events, Zhelyu Zhelev, the head of the Union of Democratic Forces, became Bulgaria's first non-Communist president in 40 years, and Andrei Lukanov was made prime minister of the Socialist government. In November 1990, Lukanov resigned, however, after a series of protests and strikes by Bulgarians who were disgruntled with the faltering economy and the government's lingering ties to communism. Dimitar Popov became the new prime minister in December 1990, faced with the challenge of subduing a populace whose liberties and welfare have long been neglected.

In a move to encourage tourism, the Bulgarian government has re-evaluated the leva (the local currency) to give visitors more spending power and concurrently, help to eliminate the thriving black market. Unfortunately, this measure has not been of much help to the Bulgarian people, who still must stand in line for daily necessities and go for months without coffee or sugar. Gas lines last for hours when the few stations are open; travelers should fill up their tanks at any opportunity.

The first Bulgarian route starts with Sofia, on the western plain, climbs through the surrounding pine-forested mountains (with the beautiful Rila Monastery), then runs south and east to Plovdiv and Bachkovo, the historic center of the country, and farther east to the friendly city of Gabrovo, then finally to Veliko Tarnovo. The second route starts in Varna, Bulgaria's main port on the Black Sea, and discusses the new resorts that dot the coastline.

For specific information on traveling in Bulgaria, it's best to contact the official tour agency in the US, *Balkan Holidays* (41 East 42nd St., Suite 606, New York, NY 10017; phone: 212-573-5530). Make hotel reservations in advance (also book car rentals in advance, and be sure to agree on a fixed price; prices can fluctuate wildly if negotiated within Bulgaria).

Sofia and the Mountains

This route skirts the country's major ski resorts and takes you into the Rila Mountains, the highest range on the Balkan Peninsula and the fourth-highest in Europe. The route ends in the Thracian plains. This 200-mile (320-km) stretch plunges you into the heart of the country's dramatic and cultural past. While the asphalt roads are good (as they are throughout Bulgaria), go slowly to catch the elusive and mysterious notes of ancient history.

SOFIA: In the western part of Bulgaria, Sofia has been the nation's capital only since 1879, but it is one of Eastern Europe's most interesting cities. Nestled in a valley and dominated by the granite slopes of Mt. Vitosha (which is less than a half-hour away and offers good skiing until early May), it is known as the greenest city in Europe because of its 80 beautifully spaced parks. This ancient city, with a population of 900,000, clusters most of its hotels, department stores, outdoor markets, memorials, churches, theaters, and opera houses in a downtown area that can be seen on foot, making it an easy and pleasant city to explore on your own. "Ever Growing, Never Old" is the motto of Sofia, inscribed on its coat of arms. The city traces its beginnings to the 5th century BC, when it was settled by the Thracians, who left the country its beautiful gold treasures.

Sofia has gone through several name changes. Called Serdica under the Thracian Serdi, the settlement suffered invasion by the Greeks, Romans, Goths, and Huns, as well as by Byzantium. The Bulgars, who conquered the city in AD 809, called it Sredets, meaning "central," and in the 14th century it became known as Sofia, after the 6th-century Church of St. Sophia. Falling to the Ottoman Empire in 1386, Sofia was not liberated until almost 500 years later, when it was made the capital of the newly independent state. These various waves of conquest left their imprint on the city, creating a strange and exciting mix of Byzantine, Roman, Greek, and Turkish architecture, now interspersed among more modern hotels, department stores, and government offices. Sofia is a cosmopolitan city; besides many colleges and libraries, it has theaters, museums, and major art galleries, displaying the fine art of contemporary Bulgarian masters. Bulgaria is also known for its opera singers, and there are two fine opera houses here. Dancing is very close to the Bulgarian heart, and no visit could be complete without a stop at one of the folklore restaurants where you'll find young men and women in their blue and red sequined costumes kicking up their heels; it sometimes feels as if every night is Saturday night in Bulgaria.

While English is spoken in the major hotels and restaurants, visitors are confronted with the Cyrillic alphabet, making it a little difficult to know where you are at all times. A good map of the city will solve any problems. Your first stop should be at *Balkan Tourist* (37 Knjaz Dondukov, just behind the *Sheraton Sofia-Hotel Balkan;* phone: 884430), or at one of its branches in major hotels; the staff can provide maps of the city and country, as well as brochures, guides, tours, and even a translation of the Cyrillic alphabet into English, which you will find useful. You also can take a *Balkan Tourist* half-day motorcoach tour with a bilingual guide, or hire a guide for a walking tour. This will help you become oriented so you will be able to explore the city on your own. Use the *Sheraton Sofia–Hotel Balkan* as a focal point, even if you don't stay there, because it's in the very center of town at Sv. Nedelia Square (Sv. Nedelia means St. Sunday) — formerly Lenin Square — where Vitosha Boulevard meets Georgi Dimitrov Boulevard as they cross the end of the Largo, the area around the monumental headquarters of the Communist (now called Socialist) Party. Looking left from the *Sheraton,* there is the *National Historical Museum* (2 Vitosha Blvd.), with fascinating archaeological treasures and exhibitions of folk art; to the right is the *CUM* (pronounced *TSUM*) department store, across an underground passage, open in the middle, with a small flea market and half-closed shopping center and a church — the 14th-century St. Petka Samardjiiska, which can be visited in summer. While digging the underpass, the excavators unearthed Roman ruins that now are an integral part of the new passage, encased in glass. (Throughout this area, expect to be approached by people trying — illegally — to exchange money. Offers of these kinds should be answered with a firm *no.*) If time permits, make a worthwhile detour to the main outdoor market along Georgi Kirkov Boulevard to admire the produce on view, test the spices, and browse among the handmade woolen goods and ceramic pottery.

Following the example set by Vienna, Budapest, and Prague over the last few years, city planners have rid Vitosha Boulevard of automobile traffic between Sv. Nedelia Square and the gigantic Palace of Culture and have spruced up its shops and snack bars. The lovely folk art stores at No. 14 sell silver jewelry, leather goods, and embroidered blouses (in the left-hand shop), as well as rugs, wooden articles, ceramics, and copper coffee sets (in the right-hand shop).

Immediately behind the *Sheraton* (indeed, partly surrounded by it) is Sofia's most ancient building, the Rotunda of the Church of St. George, built by the Romans in the 4th century, restored much later, and containing three layers of 10th- to 15th-century frescoes.

As you go toward Ruski Boulevard, notice the ocher road tiles that make this street resemble something out of *The Wizard of Oz,* as well as the animated traffic police controlling pedestrian and vehicle flow from small towers at most intersections.

On your way, Democracy Square (formerly called Ninth of September Square) is dominated by the block-long marble mausoleum of Georgi Dimitrov, the international Communist hero (he stood up to the Nazis at the Reichstag Fire Trial) and Bulgarian premier from 1946 to 1949. This building was constructed in 6 days, following Dimitrov's death. Until 1990 his preserved corpse was on display here. Now he is buried in one of the city's cemeteries. Behind the mausoleum are the city gardens, a perfect place to sit and watch the people. On the other side of Ruski Boulevard is the former Royal Palace, now the *National Gallery of Painting and Sculpture* and the *National Ethnographic Museum.* Closed Tuesdays (phone: 883559).

Continuing down Ruski Boulevard, notice the first of many onion-domed Orthodox churches on the left. Along this street you can buy some of Bulgaria's best leather goods, baskets, and jewelry. Try *Mineralsouvenir* at No. 10 for marble ashtrays and gold and silver jewelry, the *Shop of the Union of Bulgarian Artists* at No. 6, and the *Souvenir Shop* at No. 4. Inexpensive opera and folk music records can be found at the *Maestro Atanassov Record Shop* at No. 8. At 147 Rakowski St. (turn right off Ruski), works by contemporary Bulgarian artists are for sale.

Ruski Boulevard leads to the modern, 6-story *Grand Hotel Sofia,* which forms a crescent on the Square of the National Assembly and faces a huge equestrian statue of Alexander II (the Russian czar who helped Bulgaria gain its independence from the Turks). Opposite the statue is the Parliament Building. Have a glass of Bulgarian wine or a cup of coffee on the terrace of the *Sofia* and be sure you are well rested before taking in the next — and most glorious — sight in the city: the magnificent neo-Byzantine Alexander Nevsky Memorial Church. Built during 1904–12 as a demonstration of the Bulgarians' gratitude to the 200,000 Russians who were killed while fighting to free them from Turkish rule, the cathedral, with its gold-leaf dome visible high in the air, attracts about 5,000 visitors a day. It has a museum in its crypt, which contains a remarkable, beautifully displayed collection of icons and church regalia; it is open daily.

If you continue along Ruski Boulevard, on your right is Freedom Park, with a zoo and a number of stadiums. Opposite are the college buildings of Sofia University. As you stroll around, look up often to catch glimpses of Mt. Vitosha's snow-tipped peaks looming over the city.

Sofia is most crowded during its *Music Weeks* (May 24–June 15), when it is filled with competitions, concerts, chamber music, and opera. Also, the *Kukeri Festival,* somewhat similar to Rio's *Carnaval* and definitely worth seeing, is held on the first day of *Lent.* For something a little different, attend a performance at the *Central Puppet Theater,* 14 Gurko St. (phone: 885416).

On the slopes of Mt. Vitosha, Boyana and its church make a pleasant half-day excursion. Leave the center on the road to Athens (Greece) and turn left over the tramlines up a road marked "To Boyana and Kopitoto." The road climbs steadily but easily for about 10 minutes through the Boyana district, where you turn left to visit the famous Boyana Church, hidden in the trees. The church may be entered by only six people at a time because the temperature and humidity have to be strictly controlled to preserve the murals that completely cover the walls and ceiling. Painted by the unknown Boyana Master in 1259, they are among the oldest murals in Bulgaria, depicting real people like King Constantine Assen and Queen Irina. Inquire at *Balkan Tourist* for opening hours. Back in the village, go up the hill again to a fork in the road and turn right to get to the *Kopitoto* hotel (phone: 571296) and restaurant, with wonderful views of Sofia. You also can continue farther to the *Golden Bridges* restaurant (in Bulgarian, *Zlatnite Mostove;* phone: 573004), just above a dramatic formation of huge boulders.

Longer excursions can be made to Melnik, a picturesque wine growing town near the Greek border, or to Koprivshtitsa, a rare gem of preserved folk architecture, where horse-drawn carts still clatter over cobblestones. Tours to most parts of the country can be arranged through *Balkan Tourist;* perhaps the most unusual one is devoted to Bulgarian yogurt-tasting.

En Route from Sofia – Heading southwest, you'll find the Rila Monastery 75 miles (120 km) from Sofia. Leave early in the day so you can enjoy Rila before proceeding to Plovdiv, which has better accommodations. Leave Sofia on the road for the Greek frontier and Thessaloníki. It's an easy route mostly through open rolling country, with the Rila Mountains beginning to appear on your left. In about 40 miles (64 km) you'll come to Stanke Dimitrov, where you turn left. On the way, you can visit the thermal hot springs of Sapareva Banja before continuing another 16 miles (26 km) and turning left for the monastery.

Here the road starts to wind and climb. The hills are thickly wooded, and the valley falls away below. Driving through these dark pine forests, you cross a bubbling brook, turn a bend, and high up, on the side of the mountain, you see an imposing stone wall over 80 feet high — your first sight of the Rila Monastery.

RILA: Founded in the 10th century by John of Rila, who fled the excesses of court life to found a hermitage, the monastery has always been the cultural shrine of Bulgaria, the defense of its cultural values against the pressures of the Ottomans. Destroyed several times, it was rebuilt in its present form after a devastating fire in 1833. Only Hrelyo's stone tower, built in 1335, remains of the ancient monastery; it dominates the huge inner courtyard of the 4-story, eccentrically shaped building.

Behind the imposing gates, the inside courtyard is an amazing scenario of delicate architecture, brightly painted porches, winding staircases, beautiful arches, frescoed walls, and a rectangular courtyard paved with slate. Look for the Chapel of the Transfiguration, with 14th-century murals, on the top floor of Hrelyo's Tower, and the monastery church in the courtyard, with its lovely woodcarvings and elaborate frescoes. For a small donation, visitors can light a candle on the elaborate candelabrum. The first level of candles are for happiness and good fortune, and the second level for remembering loved ones. The monastery houses a museum containing 16,-000 manuals, bibles written on sheepskin, icons, old weapons, coins, and a crucifix on which are carved 140 scenes with 1,500 figures — each no larger than a grain of rice — representing the decades of work by one monk, who became blind from his labors. For the practical-minded, there's a vast ancient kitchen (with a flue 62 feet high and a soup pot large enough to hold two oxen) that once catered to the brisk pilgrim trade. As you exit the monastery, there is a complex of bakeries and snack bars frequented by Bulgarians. The wood-oven baked bread is delicious, and there are fine cheeses, too.

To get to Plovdiv, you have to return to Stanke Dimitrov and take a crossroad via Samokov-Borovet to get to the main road to Plovdiv, International Highway A-80. A stopover could be made at the Borovets resort in the thickly wooded Rila Mountains, where accommodations include the *Rila* hotel (phone: 99725-350) winter sports complex, the *Sokoletz* hotel (phone: 99725-282), and the Finnish-designed *Yagoda* bungalow and sauna community (phone: 99725-343).

PLOVDIV: Bulgaria's second-largest city and home to many of the country's leading contemporary writers and painters, Plovdiv dates from Thracian times. Built on six hills, it is the gateway to the Rhodope Mountains. The *Balkan Tourist* office in Plovdiv is at 34 Moskva Blvd. (phone: 032-22-60-64).

By day, Plovdiv is a bustling, modern industrial city with an important annual trade fair; at night, it turns into a stroller's paradise — quiet and tranquil. Divided by the Maritsa River, Plovdiv boasts an old section reached by climbing hundreds of stone steps. At the top you first see the remains of a Roman amphitheater; today, visitors can attend opera, dance, and theater performances here. (You'd be well advised to wear sensible shoes; after the climb up, you've still got to negotiate the ancient cobblestone streets.) Going through the Hissar Kapiya gate, you enter a world of exquisite houses from the 19th-century National Revival period. Their façades are decorated with eaves in the form of waves and bay windows overhanging far into the streets, making the houses look top-heavy. The overhanging bays were a method of extending the house without impinging on pedestrian space in busy thoroughfares.

The *Charshiya* (Crafts Bazaar) on Strâmna Street is a group of five restored houses in which ten workshops sell handmade tufted rugs, embroideries, copper vessels, and carvings. You also can visit the *Argir-Koyumdjioglu House* (closed Monday and Friday mornings; 2 Dr. Chomakov St.; phone: 22-56-56), now an ethnographic museum with extensive displays of rare Thracian gold treasures. More gold artifacts are exhibited at the *Archaeological Museum* (closed Mondays; Sâedinenie Sq.; phone: 22-43-49). A nice ending to the tour is a stop at the open-air market for some peaches and cherries, typical native fruits. You can eat these comfortably ensconced on one of the terraces overlooking the city.

BACHKOVO: The 11th-century Bachkovo Monastery is 18 miles (29 km) from Plovdiv on the old Roman road connecting it to the Aegean coast, and is Bulgaria's second-largest monastery. This is Bulgarian wine country; you'll find both red and white wines, the best this side of France. The monastery complex is on the right bank of the Chepelarska River. Seen from the road, the monastery looks like an ancient fortress with two courtyards; in the center of each is a cruciform church. Founded in the 11th century, this massive building is decorated with frescoes of exceptional quality. The main Church of the Holy Virgin has rare, silver-clad icons and a wooden iconostasis of the finest workmanship.

KAZANLUK: Situated between the Balkan Range and the Sredna Gore Mountains, this city is the site of the Valley of the Roses, where traditional rose festivals are held at the beginning of June. Be sure to visit the *Museum of the Rose* (phone: 25170), where you can view exhibits describing the technology of attar extraction, and walk through the garden of "rosely" delights. Just up the road is the Kazanluk Tomb, a famous Thracian monument dating back to the 4th century BC. Now under the protection of UNESCO, a replica of the tomb — which can be visited — has been constructed nearby.

GABROVO: This town is worth a stop to visit the *Museum of Humor and Satire* (64 Brianska St.; phone: 27229), a former factory that now houses a collection of paintings and prints from artists around the world.

Just 5 miles (8 km) south of Gabrovo, hugging the banks of a mountain stream, is the *Etura Ethnographic Museum-Park,* Bulgaria's largest re-created historical village. Here, on cobblestone streets overhung with flower-filled balconies, dozens of handicrafts and trades are demonstrated — a fascinating display of the skills of the village artisans and 19th-century rural technology, from colorful textiles to copper and tin ware. Return to Gabrovo.

VELIKO TARNOVO: Truly the heart of Bulgaria, this medieval fortressed city was the country's capital for more than 200 years, and was a major political and intellectual center. The city suffered a major earthquake in 1908, but today it is surrounded by the churning waters of the Yantra River, and its distinctive houses are framed by verdant hills. Be sure to walk up Tsarevets Hill to see the archaelogical finds at this site where numerous 12th- to 14th-century city walls, buildings, and churches have been unearthed. During the 19th-century National Revival period, when the Bulgarians struggled against the Turks, the city also was an important political and cultural center. Bulgaria's first pharmacy was opened here in 1823. Now restored, it can be visited in the National Revival Quarter (at 13 Ivan Vazov St.). In the 1960s, Veliko Tarnovo was targeted by the government to become a showcase of traditional Bulgarian architecture. Today, the city is the country's best preserved 19th-century town.

BEST EN ROUTE

While Bulgaria used to be among the most inexpensive destinations in Europe, rates recently have risen dramatically. Double rooms are around $200 per night in expensive places (a bit higher during festival times) and about $100 to $150 in moderate places.

Meals, however, almost always are reasonable. Food and wine prices are much higher at hotels, but in the country you'll get more than you can eat and drink for just $5 to $10 per person. Bulgarians have hearty appetites, so don't be surprised to find meals consisting of at least five courses. All restaurants accept major credit cards, unless otherwise indicated. Reservations are advised at all restaurants, unless otherwise noted.

SOFIA

Forum – A handsome restaurant serving such Bulgarian and international classics as onion soup, omelettes, and leg of lamb. It also offers a wide selection of Bulgarian wines. 62 Vitosha Blvd. (phone: 521119). Expensive

Grand Hotel Sofia – This well-located modern hotel has a complex of shops and restaurants and a nightclub. 4 Narodno Sobranie Sq. (phone: 878821; fax: 881308; telex: 23405). Expensive.

Novotel Evropa – A French-built hotel close to the main railway station. 131 Georgi Dimitrov Blvd. (phone: 31261; fax: 32011; telex: 22051). Expensive.

Sheraton Sofia–Hotel Balkan – With its stately façade, this city landmark, a popular meeting place for visitors and locals alike, has undergone a complete renovation. It has 188 air conditioned rooms, 16 suites, restaurants, snack bars, and a Viennese-style café. The food is good, service excellent, management American; some people consider it the best urban hotel in the Balkans. In the middle of town. 1 Sv. Nedelia Sq. (phone: 876541; fax: 871038; telex: 23030). Expensive.

Vitosha New Otani – This Japanese-owned high-rise hotel has a Japanese restaurant called *Sakura,* as well as 3 other restaurants serving international and Bulgarian dishes. There is a nightclub, a casino, a Viennese café and garden, cocktail lounges, and everywhere, views of Mt. Vitosha and the surrounding forests. 100 Anton Ivanov Blvd. (phone: 624151; fax: 681225; telex: 22797). Expensive.

Bulgaria – In the *Bulgaria* hotel, where locals often go for dinner and dancing. 4 Ruski Blvd. (phone: 871977; telex: 22499). Moderate.

C.G. – Popular with hunters and anglers, this restaurant (still better known by its old name, *Lovno Rbarski Soious*) became a Bulgarian-Italian joint venture in 1990. It still offers the best game and fowl in town, fine wines, smiling service and a pleasant atmosphere. 31-33 Vitosha Blvd. (phone: 879465). Moderate.

Rodina – About a 10-minute walk from the town center, this Swedish-built hotel has a restaurant, several bars, a pool, saunas, a gym, and a solarium. 8 Totleben Blvd. (phone: 51631; fax: 543225; telex: 22200). Moderate.

Rubin – Another local favorite, with a 1960s decor and good wines. Dine at the restaurant or at the low-priced snack bar. Reservations unnecessary. Sv. Nedelia Sq. (phone: 874704). Moderate.

Zheravna – Bulgarian specialties served in a folk art atmosphere. Reservations unnecessary. No credit cards accepted. 26 Marshal Tolbuchin Blvd. (phone: 872186). Moderate to inexpensive.

BOYANA

Boyansko Hanche Tavern – Near the historic church, this dining spot has delicious specialties and Bulgarian wines. There's also a folk orchestra and a floor show (phone: 563016). Moderate.

RILA

Elesnica – This plain, clean restaurant serves excellent Bulgarian food. Try *shopska* salad with roasted sweet red peppers, cucumbers, small tomatoes, onions, olive oil and vinegar, topped with mounds of feta cheese or *tarator* soup (made of yogurt, walnuts, garlic, dill, and cucumbers). Main courses include grilled or roast beef, lamb, or pork. No reservations. On the left side of the road as you enter the Rila Monastery (no phone). Inexpensive.

PLOVDIV

Novotel Plovdiv – A member of the French chain, with pleasant accommodations, including a sports center, pools, outdoor tennis courts, saunas, and a nightclub. The dining room features a large selection of Bulgarian dishes. 2 Zlatyu Boyadjiev St. (phone: 55892 or 555171; telex: 44595). Expensive.

Alafrangite – Good Bulgarian dishes are served in an old house with a garden. It is in the old part of town. Reservations essential on weekends. 17 K. Nektariev St. (phone: 229809). Moderate.

Trimontium – A fine hotel with an Old World atmosphere, first class accommodations, and a garden; at the beginning of the pedestrian zone. 2 Kapitan Raicho St. (phone: 225561; telex: 44575). Moderate.

Zlatniya Elen – This folk tavern has good food and Bulgarian dancers. Reservations unnecessary. 13 Patriarch Eftimi St. (phone: 226064). Moderate.

KAZANLUK

Interhotel Veliko Tarnovo – Centrally located overlooking the old heart of the city and the banks of the Yantra River, this hotel has many modern conveniences. Complimentary breakfast is offered, and there is a dining room, bar, gym, swimming pool, and a sauna. 2 Emil Popov St. (phone: 30571). Moderate.

Kazanluk – Located in the center of town, there is a dining room, panoramic bar, swimming pool, sauna, and a hard currency shop. Complimentary breakfast is served and there is free parking. Svoboda Sq. (phone: 27210 or 27002). Moderate.

Veliko Tarnovo Yantra – Although the *Interhotel Veliko Tarnovo* offers more comforts, this charming hotel offers the best view — of an old fortress and the green hills. 1 Veltchova Zavera Sq. (phone: 30391). Moderate.

Bulgarian Black Sea Coast

The Greeks called it Pontos Euxinos — the Hospitable Sea — but the Turks, who feared its storms, renamed it the Black Sea. Whatever its name, the Black Sea coast of Bulgaria — a 235-mile stretch of sandy beach now boasting numerous hotel colonies — is fast becoming known as the Riviera of Eastern Europe. These modern resorts have sprung up relatively recently (most were built during the past 35 years), and today are frequented primarily by tourists from Eastern Europe, although visitors from Western Europe, the Soviet Union and the US also appear.

The major coastal town, however, is anything but recent. Varna, now an industrial center, is an ancient port and Bulgaria's main commercial outlet to the sea. Some 290 miles (464 km) from Sofia, Varna is Bulgaria's summer capital and is only a little more than an hour's drive south from the Romanian border. Varna is a perfect starting point for trips up and down the coast as well as for longer excursions across the sea to Istanbul or inland to the eastern monastery towns of Bulgaria.

Varna's original name was Odessos, and remnants of various past cultures are everywhere. Just outside the town are the remains of a Byzantine basilica, but predating this church is a large thermae built by the Romans that still stands in the middle of the city. Before the Romans, the Greeks were the masters here, having founded the city in 570 BC. Also outside town is the Aladja Rock Monastery, built in the Middle Ages.

Tours to the modern resort towns north and south of Varna should be booked through *Balkan Tourist* in Sofia (phone: 884430), in Varna (3 Musala St.; phone: 225524), or through *Balkan Holidays* (41 E. 42nd St.; New York, NY 10017; phone: 212-573-5530). For the most part, the hotels are quite similar — modern buildings facing the sea — but the amazing thing about these resorts is that in season, hotel accommodations right on the sea, including three meals a day, cost between $60 to $100 per day for a double room, and various package arrangements are offered. The beach towns are small and generally have uncomplicated layouts. (Unless otherwise noted, the address of a hotel or restaurant is nothing more than the establishment's name.) From Rusalka, north of Varna, to Nessebâr, to the south, the beach towns are all connected by International Highway E87, or by *Rometa,* a super speedboat.

RUSALKA: Near the Romanian border, this *Club Méditerranée* holiday village caters to families seeking sun and sports. There are three bays in which to swim, and 15 tennis courts on which to play, plus diversions for the kids. For information, contact *Club Med* offices (in the US, call 800-CLUB MED), a travel agent, or call 359-5184.

ALBENA: Albena was named after one of the most attractive female characters in Bulgarian literature. The town caters to a predominantly younger set, who crowd the many hotels, bars, folk taverns, and 4-mile-long beach. You can play tennis or golf or even brush up on your equestrian skills at the riding school. The town hotspot is the *Starobulgarski Stan* nightclub, with an architectural style that recalls old Bulgarian Gypsy tents. On the beach, it offers music and floor shows until 2 AM. The *Balkan Tourist* office is in the *Bratislava* hotel (phone: 2152 or 2930).

ZLATNI PYASÂTSI: Zlatni Pyasâtsi (Golden Sands) is about 8 miles (13 km) from Albena and probably the resort most popular with Americans, having often been compared to Long Beach, California. Again, you'll find an abundance of hotels and bars. The favorite here is a nightclub called the *Kukeri,* which has a wonderful view of the sea and entertainment by the *Kukeri Dancers,* masked men performing stylized pagan routines. For tourist information, call 855227.

DRUZHBA: This town, whose name means "friendship," is only 6 miles (10 km) from Varna. It's one of the older resorts, better suited to low-key revelers, and is the home of the Swedish-built *Grand Hotel Varna,* the most famous of all the Black Sea hotels, with a complex of restaurants and nightclubs and two sub-floors of spa facilities for exercise, massages, and pearl and mud baths (4 Chervenoarmeiski Blvd.; phone: 86-1491/8; telex: 77424). If the *Grand* is too expensive, consider stopping at the *Monastery Cellar,* a nightclub that serves a memorable wine called Monastery Whispers.

SLUNCHEV BRYAG: About 60 miles (96 km) down the coast from Druzhba, Slunchev Bryag (Sunny Beach) is a 2½-mile stretch of sandy shores surrounded by a deciduous forest on three sides. This family resort has day care facilities and supervised children's activities, which leave parents free to roam into places like *Khan's Tent Tavern,* another tent nightclub on the beach, or the *Pirate Ship,* a restaurant built like a ship and offering Bulgarian specialties and folk entertainment. Also worth a visit is the nearby city of Burgas and its international music and folklore festival, held every other year (in odd-numbered years) during the second half of June. An attractive alternative to the high-rise resort is the Finnish-built *Elenite Holiday Village* (phone: 554-2423), a hillside bungalow complex, including the 100-bed *Emona* (phone: 554-2325), about 6 miles (10 km) north of Sunny Beach (phone: 411-32423).

NESSEBÂR: Nessebâr is a vintage fishing village on a peninsula near Slunchev Bryag, where old Greek churches and wooden fishermen's houses along narrow cobblestone streets take you back in time. Nessebâr is an architectural gem and should be included on any Black Sea tour — but just for a visit, not an overnight stay. The *Balkan Tourist* office is at 18 Jana Laskova (phone: 554-2855).

SOZOPOL: Another charming collection of 19th-century houses with grapevine-shaded patios along winding lanes. There is a *Balkan Tourist* office (2 Chervenoarmeiska; phone: 5514-251), and several restaurants, but no major hotel. Stay at one of the three communities making up the *Djuni Holiday Village,* 6 miles (10 km) to the south. Like *Elenite, Djuni* was built by the Finns during the mid-1980s (phone: 5514-378).

Czechoslovakia

Located at the geographic heart of Europe, Czechoslovakia has long sat astride the historic crossroads over which conquerors and colonists have traveled. Sometimes, this meant being the unwilling recipient of these visitors' religious, cultural, and/or political domination.

Though Czechoslovakia was created as a more or less formal nation only in 1918, the historic entities of Bohemia and Moravia (mostly inhabited by the Czechs, who comprise 95% of the nation's population) and Slovakia (which is home to 5 million tenaciously Catholic Slovaks) have been around central Europe for as long as history has been recorded. The internecine disputes between the nation's two prime population groups — the remaining citizenry is mostly made up of a mix of Hungarians, Germans, Poles, Ruthenians, and Gypsies — is dramatically evidenced in demonstrations by the Slovaks who have advocated separatism since the communist government was overthrown in 1989. The "War of the Hyphen" (Czechoslovakia versus Czecho-Slovakia) brought about the adoption of the national moniker (however cumbersome), the Czech and Slovak Federative Republic, but many Slovaks remain unsatisfied with a mere name change.

Despite the demise of Communist party power and the nation's first free elections (in June 1990), Czechoslovakia is only slowly emerging from the torpor of collectivist administration. Václev Havel, the playwright-turned-president, has not had an easy time reconciling regional intrigues while he attempts to transform the old state-controlled systems into democratically administered free enterprise. Last year the government passed a series of laws to privatize state-owned enterprises, and they have since sold many small shops and businesses. Much of the existing industrial technology is antiquated, however, and there is little capital to prime the pumps of a capitalist rebirth. With all that has happened, Czechoslovakians retain little nostalgia about the past decades of repression; they look forward to a life of political and social freedom, with personal wealth a less compelling motivator.

Much that remains of Czechoslovakia's complicated past has been preserved. Indeed, although it is quite a small country — a little larger than New York State — it contains some 40,000 monuments, 2,500 castles (115 of them open to the public), and a number of old towns in which an attempt has been made to preserve their Gothic, Renaissance, and baroque architecture. Unfortunately, most Czechoslovakian towns and villages remain in a state of sorry neglect. The Communist regime that once kept train fares to an enviable 1945 level also cut off access to the builders' paint supply. As a result, this once colorful country now is a uniform gray, with carefully tended fields of green offering the only relief in the otherwise drab landscape. Hopefully, the recent political change will result in greater restoration and funds for adding much-needed variety and brightness to the countryside.

The country is composed of three areas: the Bohemian plateau in the west, the Moravian lowlands in the center, and mountainous Slovakia in the east. Each region has many historic sights. The territory of Bohemia and Moravia was the center of European culture in the 14th century, when Charles IV made Prague the capital of the Holy Roman Empire. He initiated a building boom that produced such Gothic wonders as the Charles Bridge in Prague and Karlštejn Castle, located south of Prague, near the town of Beroun. In Slovakia, historical monuments go back even farther, recalling the presence of Roman legions.

Despite its attention to the past, Czechoslovakia is a developed country, with the vast majority of the population of 15.3 million involved in commerce and industry and only 12.5% in agriculture. Czechoslovak companies produce everything from heavy machinery and Skoda cars (recently sold to Germany's Volkswagen) to bentwood chairs and Bohemian glass. Only 15% of the population lives in cities of more than 100,000 — Prague, the capital and largest city (pop. 1.2 million); Bratislava, the second-largest city (pop. 400,000) and the capital of the Slovak Socialist Republic; and Brno, the third-largest city (pop. 380,000) and the capital of Moravia. The rest of the population inhabits some 10,000 small towns.

This predominantly small-town culture opens up some appealing possibilities for those interested in folk traditions. If you visit in the spring and the summer, you will encounter (indeed, become part of) the numerous folk festivals in the small towns. While it is true that many of the festivals are organized entertainment events, featuring professional and semi-professional troupes wearing standardized folk costumes, they do attract folk enthusiasts from all over the world. They are a colorful blend of dance and music competitions, Maypole dancing, parades of the king, wine tastings, and open-air markets displaying handsome homemade crafts.

Spring and summer are also the most pleasant times for sightseeing and most sports. Being in the temperate zone, Czechoslovak springs and summers are warm and sunny, with average May temperatures in the high 50s F (15C) and summer temperatures in the high 60s and low 70s F (21C). Though Czechoslovakia is landlocked, it has thousands of ponds and lakes, many developed for swimming, boating, and fishing. A preponderance of these lakes are in southern Bohemia. In northeastern Bohemia stand the Krkonoše (Giant) Mountains, while the High Tatras — the highest mountains in the Carpathian chain — rise in Slovakia. Both regions are winter resort centers popular for downhill and cross-country skiing, tobogganing, and sleigh riding.

Czechoslovakia is a relatively easy country to explore. In the better restaurants and hotels English is understood, but German is the lingua franca for the tourist sector. Advance hotel reservations are essential even in the off-season (particularly in smaller towns) because the tourist traffic exceeds the population. Make arrangements through your travel agent or through the Czechoslovak National Tourist Office, *Cedok* (18 Na příkopě, Prague 1; phone: 212-27111), or in the US (10 E. 40th St., New York, NY 10157; phone: 212-689-9720).

The longest of the following three routes links Prague, the nation's capital, with Bratislava, the capital of Slovakia, passing through Bohemia, Moravia, and Slovakia, seeing the most famous spas, castles, and medieval towns. The remaining routes both start from Poprad, a city in eastern Slovakia. One route heads northwest into the High Tatras mountain resorts. The second runs east of Poprad, taking in the medieval towns and lovely landscapes of the Spiš region, where the country folk carry on the rural traditions of their ancestors in settings that have changed little over the generations.

Prague to Bratislava

This 227-mile (363-km) route links Bohemia, Moravia, and Slovakia — Czechoslovakia's three major regions — and takes in the country's capitals as well as its most famous spas, castles, and medieval towns. To follow the route, head northwest out of Prague, circle through Plzeň, south to Tábor, east to Brno, and farther south to Bratislava. You can spend several days touring, for all of the places along the route have reasonable overnight accommodations.

Since you will be passing through the three distinct areas of this country, be alert to subtle changes in traditions and customs. These regional differences will be most obvious at the folk festivals, held during the spring and summer in the small towns. You'll find that the cooking also differs: In Bohemia, try roast pork, goose, or duck with dumplings accompanied by pilsner or any other local beer. In the lake country of southern Bohemia, keep an eye out for menus offering fresh trout and carp. In Moravia, be sure to sample the local wines.

The highlights of the route include the renowned spa of Karlovy Vary; the Burgher's Brewery in Plzeň, where pilsner beer has been produced since the Middle Ages; the preserved historic town of Tábor; the formidable Spilberk Castle in Brno; and the capital of Slovakia, Bratislava. (It's possible to take a day-long excursion by bus to either Karlovy Vary or Plzeň. Inquire at *Cedok Tours*. (See "Sources and Resources" in *Prague,* THE CITIES.)

PRAGUE: For a complete description of the city and its restaurants and hotels, see *Prague,* THE CITIES.

    En Route from Prague – Heading northwest for 2 hours along Route 6, you pass through some of Bohemia's loveliest countryside — deep forests and rich farmlands, where hops are grown. Hillside castles dot the landscape.

KARLOVY VARY: In the narrow valley at the juncture of the Teplá and Ohře rivers lies Karlovy Vary, the most famous of Czechoslovakia's spas. It has 12 developed hot springs, and more than 100 springs in all. Legend has it that Karlovy Vary (Carlsbad in German) was discovered in 1358 by Charles IV — actually by the dog of Charles IV, who stumbled into a hot spring while chasing a stag. Although the stag is still the symbol of the spa, little of its former elegance has survived the years of Soviet domination. The fervent hope of the spa's managers is that with the country's new emphasis on free enterprise, the former "Queen of Central Europe" will be restored to her former position of eminence.

The huge spa building is reserved for guests taking the waters, but visitors can stroll along the ornate Colonnade, built in 1871–81, following in the footsteps of kings and queens and such notables as Beethoven, Goethe, and Mozart. The town still retains traces of its once-elegant atmosphere, but the surrounding area has been engulfed by industrial pollution.

While visiting the spa, indulge in a few Karlovy Vary rites: At the Gagarin Colonnade, built in 1975 to honor the world's first man in space, taste the hot bitter waters from a special mug with a long clay straw. Buy a box of *karlovarské oplatky* — delicious large round chocolate and vanilla wafers. Order *becherovka,* a liqueur also known jokingly as "the thirteenth spring." Visit the world-famous *Moser Glassworks* and the *Horní Slavkov* and *Stará Role* chinaworks, where you can buy fine Czech crystal and porcelain. In 1990, the city reinstated festivities commemorating Charles IV's discovery of the spa. A costumed procession heralds the reopening of the spa season in early May, led off by a 2-day feast of beer and sausages. Those interested in sports can enjoy swimming, hiking, golf, tennis, or fishing.

En Route from Karlovy Vary – Stop at the regal Kynžvart, the former summer residence of Count Metternich, the 19th-century Austrian statesman. Constructed in baroque and Empire styles, the château contains valuable collections of furniture, art, china, glassware, and arms.

MARIÁNSKÉ LÁZNĚ: Established in 1808, this spa (Marienbad, in German) was a favorite with such notables as Richard Wagner and King Edward VII. It is nicely designed, with parks and colorful façades lining Gottwald Square. The Russian writers Turgenev, Gogol, and Gorki also came here, along with composers like Chopin, Beethoven, Wagner, Liszt, Johann Strauss, and Dvořák. Spa yellow, the soft yellow of the exteriors of the major buildings and hotels, can be seen here and at spas throughout the country. Of the 40 springs here, the best known are Křížový, Lesní, and Rudolf. When you're not soaking, you can take advantage of the spa's many other recreational facilities: movies, concerts, a golf course, tennis courts, a pool, cafés, restaurants, and nightclubs. There also are numerous interesting 19th- and early 20th-century buildings: the Cross Spring Pavilion (1818), the Rudolf Spring Building (1823), the English church in neo-Gothic style (1879), the Maxim Gorki Colonnade in neo-baroque style (1889), and the Russian Orthodox church (1901). Take a side trip of 10 miles (16 km) east to Teplá to see the 12th-century monastery, with an impressive collection of rare books, manuscripts, and prints.

PLZEŇ: With large factories and a very smoky skyline, this city of 174,000 contrasts sharply with the other small Bohemian towns en route. But it is worth a visit to see the Burgher's Brewery, which has produced Pilsner Urquell beer since the Middle Ages. Begin the tour at the *Brewing Museum,* in an old brewing house on Roosevelt Street. It has a fine collection of beer mugs, jugs, pewter tankards, and glasses produced during the last 6 centuries. Also on display is an iron collar — the collar of dishonor — worn by brewers whose beer didn't make the grade. The town's beer stewards will tell you that pilsner should be drunk from a sparkling clean glass, accompanied by sharp cheese, smoked meat, and dark bread. And they're right.

Náměstí Republiky, the square in the center of town, is lined with houses that have Renaissance, baroque, Empire, and neo-Gothic façades. Two particularly lovely Gothic buildings are St. Bartholomew's Church, with its 340-foot tower, and the Abbey Church of the Virgin Mary.

In 1990, for the first time since World War II, Plzeň celebrated its liberation by American troops on May 5, 1945. This is now an annual event, with a number of breweries donating free beer to celebrants throughout the day.

TÁBOR: Set on the Lužnice River, amid the forests and lakes of southern Bohemia, this Gothic town is one of six historical reservations in Czechoslovakia. Tábor was founded in 1420 by the Hussites, an army of anti-church and -state rebels whose struggle was set off by the death of the Czech religious reformer John Huss (Jan Hus). Huss was burned at the stake as a heretic in 1415, but the Hussite struggle continued for the next 19 years. The saying goes here that "Nothing is mine and nothing is yours, because the community is owned equally by everybody." It is this laissez-faire philosophy that is said to have given rise to the — false — association between the term "Bohemian" and Gypsy, and led people to think of Bohemians as poor, homeless Gypsies or struggling artists.

Tábor now is a modern, growing town of 22,000, whose historic area is of greatest interest. An equestrian statue of military leader Jan Zižka, who commanded the Hussite forces, stands in the middle of Zižka Square. The most notable building is the Town Hall, which houses a museum documenting the Hussite movement (closed Mondays). Underneath the museum are 10 miles of medieval catacombs of tunnels and cellars, built as living quarters and later used to store beer and wine. The narrow, winding streets off Zižka Square, laid out to confuse attackers, lead to the Old Town. Originally surrounded by ramparts and bulwarks, the Old Town still has remnants of those fortifications, such as the Bechyně Gate and the adjacent Kotnov Tower, once part of a medieval castle that was turned into the town brewery in the 17th century.

If you want to spend some time here, stay at the inexpensive *Jordán* hotel (Zapotock-ého Nám.; phone: 23402), named for nearby Lake Jordán, where visitors can swim or fish.

BRNO: The capital of Moravia, Brno combines historic and contemporary Czechoslovakia. Here you'll find castles, museums, a baroque outdoor market, fairgrounds, a racetrack, and some of the hottest night spots around.

Spilberk Castle, which dates to 1287, was built as a fortress to resist invaders and was later turned into a sinister prison; it is deeply engraved on the collective conscience of the country. Here, political dissenters were detained and tortured by the ruling Hapsburgs. During World War II, Nazi forces reopened the prison, and Spilberk once again became a dungeon and death trap for the hapless. Instruments of torture are on display. The reconstruction of the castle, which started in 1990, is expected to continue a few years.

The castle restaurant offers a game menu, Moravian wines, and a view of the city (*Hradní;* phone: 26203, 24170). The park outside the castle has covered benches — a pleasant spot to rest.

The main streets in Brno all converge on Freedom Square (Náměstí Svobody), which is flanked by splendid baroque and Renaissance buildings. From the square you can see Petrov Hill, with the Cathedral of Saints Peter and Paul, a reconstructed Gothic structure built on the site of a Romanesque basilica. The cathedral on the hill is a welcome refuge from the urban bustle below. The nearby Capuchin Monastery, with its specially ventilated crypt containing the mummified bodies of monks and local nobility, is also of interest. Their bodies originally were preserved "naturally" by placing them on the monastery's cold floor, where the special flow of air, coupled with the building's unusual dryness prevented them from decaying. This practice was outlawed in 1784 for reasons of hygiene — as well as a general fear that the body of some local freedom-loving Moravian might wind up the object of an anti-Hapsburg pilgrimage.

From the cathedral, descend the steps to the outdoor Zelnýtrh cabbage market, sprawled over a steep cobblestone hill; you'll find hundreds of tables attended to by country men and women selling fruits, vegetables, handicrafts, and kitchen utensils. The market sprawls around Parnassas Fountain, which features a baroque sculpture depicting Cerberus, the Watchdog of Hell, and four continents (its designer, Johann

Fisher von Erlach, apparently was unaware of Australia). Among the area's other notable buildings are the old Town Hall and the Gothic Church of St. James, both in the Old Town. Also of note nearby is Slavkov, or Austerlitz, where Napoleon defeated an Austro-Russian/anti-French coalition in 1805. An enormous monument built in 1905 commemorates the event.

Brno's Exhibition Fairground, down the hill and past the railway station, is the site of events all year, highlighted by the *Consumers' Fair* in April. While here, have lunch at the *Myslivna* (Gamekeeper's Lodge), reached by crossing a wood on the south side of the Svratka River (12 Pisárky; phone: 335911 or 383247). Try the broiled trout à la Brno.

The city has few first class hotels, the newest and most convenient is the *International* (see *Best en Route*). Its bar, *Interclub,* is one of the most popular nightspots in the city (phone: 26411).

BRATISLAVA: Rising from the banks of the Danube, this capital of Slovakia was the capital of Hungary from 1541 to 1784, and 17 Hungarian monarchs were crowned here over the centuries. The Hapsburg royal family lived here for over 300 years. During the 1,000 years that today's Slovakia was known as "Northern Hungary," Bratislava was called "Poszony" in Hungarian and "Pressburg" in German. The city's population was predominantly Hungarian- and German-speaking until the 19th century, when an influx of Slovak industrial workers from the countryside began. In 1918, when Slovakia was incorporated into the new nation of Czechoslovakia, Bratislava officially assumed its Slavic name. It was here that, with the help of Nazi Germany, an independent Slovak Republic was proclaimed in 1939. The pro-Nazi clerical state headed by Archbishop Tiso expelled the Czechs and sent Slovak troops to fight the Russians. Although the Slovaks started to resist in 1943, an insurrection was repressed by the Nazis in August 1944.

Bratislava is a modern city (with modern pollution problems) that also boasts some 400 historic buildings, museums, monuments, and castles. BIPS (Bratislavská Informačná a Propagačná Služba), the city tourist office, is in the city center (1 Leningradská; which like many places bearing Lenin's name should be renamed by the time we go to press; phone: 334-370, 333-715, 334-415). It can provide information, guides, and translators, and it organizes walking tours of the city on summer weekends. The city's most noteworthy sight is Bratislava Castle, the 13th-century fortress that long guarded the city. Sunday concerts are held in the castle's Concert Hall. Sights in the Old Town that shouldn't be missed are the Gothic-baroque Old Town Hall; the Primatial Palace, with its famous Hall of Mirrors, where Napoleon and Emperor Franz II signed the Peace Treaty of Bratislava in 1805; St. Martin's Cathedral, the scene of many coronations; and *At the Red Crayfish,* a pharmacy museum with an interesting collection of apothecary jars. The *Slovak National Museum* (2 Vajanského nábr.; phone: 336551) has a special exhibition, "The Development of Man," which traces evolution from primitive times to the present. In the evening, stroll down to the *korzo* area near the Old Town Hall, and partake of the somewhat "Mediterranean" scene enjoyed by the city's youth.

If you've been eating the Bohemian and Moravian favorites of pork or roast duck with dumplings and sauerkraut, you'll find a marked difference in Slovak cooking. Its generous use of sour cream, paprika, and barbecued meat echoes the cuisine of neighboring Hungary. A few places in town that serve regional specialties are the restaurants in Bratislava Castle; *Kláštorná vináreň,* a wine tavern (1 Pugacěvova; phone: 338282) — especially its Detva stuffed steak; and the *Bystrica Café,* a revolving glass disk set on a 270-foot tower over the Slovak National Uprising Bridge, which spans the Danube. The *Koliba* (on Kamzík Hill), is one of the many shepherd's hut–style restaurants scattered throughout Slovakia that serve barbecued meat cooked over open pits, mulled wines, and Tatra tea. Gypsy violinists provide entertainment.

If you are visiting during the late spring or summer, you can take a day trip by hydrofoil to Vienna or Budapest.

BEST EN ROUTE

Expect to pay $70 to $110 per night for a double room in hotels in the expensive range; $40 to $60 in the moderate; and around $30, inexpensive. Prices, except at deluxe hotels, always include breakfast. (Meal vouchers can be used outside the hotel.) A dinner for two will cost $30 and up in the expensive range, between $20 and $30 in the moderate range. Reservations are advised for most hotel restaurants. All restaurants below accept major credit cards, unless otherwise indicated. Reservations are advised for all restaurants.

KRUŠOVICE

U Lípy – When he's not watching TV, owner Petr Novotný runs a country restaurant just off the main road to Karlovy Vary, 25 miles (40 km) from Prague. The homemade sausage with local relish and beer (dark or light) is a lot tastier than much of what you'll find in the fancy places in big towns. Closed Mondays. Pohostinstvi Krušovice (no phone). Inexpensive.

KARLOVY VARY

Pupp – Formerly known as the *Moskva* and once favored by Europe's elite, this now faded 168-room dowager is in the spa center — and about to undergo long overdue renovations. Among the facilities are golf, tennis, 6 restaurants including a French one, a bar, a nightclub, and a café. 2 Mírové náměstí (phone: 22121; fax: 240323; telex: 156220). Expensive.

Centrál – Built in 1910 and later renovated, this frayed hotel has 70 rooms, all with balconies. Restaurant and wine bar. No credit cards accepted. 17 Divadelni náměstí (phone: 25251). Moderate.

Parkhotel – Right behind the *Pupp,* and run by them, this old hotel (opened in 1885) has 117 rooms and a French restaurant. 2 Mírové náměstí (phone: 22121). Moderate.

MARIÁNSKÉ LÁZNĚ

Golf – A pretty and gracious hotel in a park setting, with a swimming pool. As the name suggests, there is a golf course on the property. In the city center. 55 Zaňub (phone: 26516). Expensive.

Esplanade – This 62-room hotel, opened in 1916 and later renovated, is near the spa center. There is a sauna, a fine restaurant, and a café; guests have golf privileges nearby. 43 Karlovarska (phone: 2162). Moderate.

PLZEŇ

Ural – Large and modern, this hotel, which has seen better days, is on the main square. 33 Náměstí Republiky (phone: 326858). Expensive.

BRNO

Grand – This first class, 114-room hotel has an excellent restaurant serving Moravian specialties and wines. The view, however, leaves something to be desired: The front overlooks a power plant and the city's southern industrial complex. The back faces out over an abandoned building site. 18-20 Tř. Benesova (phone: 23526). Expensive.

International – A deluxe modern hotel with 291 rooms, it has a good view of

Spilberk Castle and the Old Town. Among the facilities are 2 restaurants serving international and regional specialties, a bar, café, and a lively nightclub. 16 Husova (phone: 213-4111 or 26411). Expensive.

Continental – Favored by business travelers, this modern 228-room property has a restaurant, wine bar, and a summer garden. 20 Kaonecova (phone: 753121). Moderate.

Voroněž I & II – A two-building modern hotel with an excellent, beautifully designed restaurant that shouldn't be missed, *Moravská Chalupa*. The hotel also has a health club with pool and sauna. 47 and 49 Křížkovského (phone: 3735). Moderate.

Slovan – A smaller hotel with a pleasant restaurant. No credit cards accepted. 23 Lidická (phone: 5411). Moderate to inexpensive.

BRATISLAVA

Devín – In the center of town right on the Danube, this modern hotel has 103 rooms and a restaurant, café, wine bar, and terrace. 4 Riečná (phone: 330851). Expensive.

Forum Bratislava – One of the newest hotels in the country, it has 219 rooms and 11 suites, all with mini-bars and color TV sets. Other features: 3 bars, a Parisian-style café, a nightclub, French and Slovak restaurants (the latter is best), and a fitness center with pool, gym, and solarium. Rooms in the back are quieter. 2 Mierové nám. (phone: 348111; fax: 314645). In the US, Inter-Continental handles reservations (phone: 800-327-0200). Expensive.

Kyjev – The usual amenities are offered at this 217-room first class hotel: a restaurant, café, wine bar, nightclub, sauna, air conditioned recreation rooms, and shops. 2 Rajská (phone: 56341 or 52041). Expensive.

Vinárň Vel'ki Františkáni – Spend an entertaining evening at this historic tavern with its vaulted cellar and arcaded courtyard. Liter jugs of Slovak wine, generous helpings of hearty food, and a Gypsy orchestra add to the atmosphere. Closed Sundays. 10 Diebrovo nám. (phone: 333073). Moderate.

The High Tatras

Starting in Poprad, this route takes in the nearby resorts of the High Tatras, the highest mountains of the Carpathian range. In fact, the Tatras are not really that high (Mt. Gerlach, the highest, rises only 8,500 feet), but they soar dramatically from the surrounding plateau and their peaks etch themselves sharply against the skyline. The mountains are popular year-round — in the winter for skiing, tobogganing, and sleighing, and in the summer for hiking, boating, fishing, and swimming. The highlights of the route include the large resort center of Starý Smokovec, the beautiful mountain lake Strbské Pleso, and the best skiing in the area at Tatranská Lomnica.

POPRAD: The route begins here because the airport accommodates flights from Prague and Bratislava. Although dominated by modern, look-alike housing developments, Poprad has a few interesting sights; among them are the 13th-century Gothic Church of St. Egidius, which contains a fresco of a biblical scene with the Tatra

Mountains in the background, and the medieval streets of the Old Town, which are lined with baroque and neo-classical buildings. One note: Propad suffers from industrial pollution.

STARÝ SMOKOVEC: The largest of the resort centers, this is a complex of chalets, restaurants, and hotels at 3,280 feet, with facilities for downhill and cross-country skiing. In the summer, mountaineers can climb Mt. Gerlach or take a side trip to the Studenovodské (Cold Water) Falls. A railway leads up to Mt. Hrebienok, a small village with a toboggan run and a beginner's slope with night lighting. It's a great place for hiking — but watch out for sudden changes in the weather, especially in summer.

The most comfortable hotel in Starý Smokovec is the *Grand* (see *Best en Route*), which opened in 1898. Starting from the *Grand,* you can hike for 1 mile (1.6 km) into the forest to the *Koliba,* a rustic restaurant in a huge A-frame cabin.

STRBSKÉ PLESO: Translated as Lake Strba, this is a year-round, very modern resort town perched over 4,000 feet high in the Tatras. This spectacular mountain lake covers more than 40 acres. On its shore stands the finest of the hotels, the *Patria;* the rooms offer views of the lake or the mountains (see *Best en Route*).

TATRANSKÁ LOMNICA: The most elegant of the resort centers, this village is set in the second-highest park in the Tatras. Restaurants and hotels here are open all year; the favorite is *Grand Hotel Praha,* which opened in 1905 (see *Best en Route*). It offers sleigh rides in the winter and an excursion on the overhead cable railway — daily except Tuesdays — to Skalnaté Pleso (Rocky Lake) at an altitude of 5,255 feet. The downhill skiing on Lomnica Mountain is the best in the Tatras. The *Tatra National Park Museum* has excellent exhibitions documenting the area's past and its natural history.

BEST EN ROUTE

Expect to pay $60 and up per night for a double room with half board in hotels in the expensive range; $40 to $50 in the moderate; and around $30, inexpensive. A dinner for two will cost $30 and up in the expensive range; between $20 and $30 in the moderate; and $10 and under, inexpensive.

STARÝ SMOKOVEC

Grand – With a spa-yellow exterior, this large alpine chalet is the place to stay. The 103 rooms are first class and the atmosphere is old-fashioned. There are 2 restaurants and a wine bar. (phone: 969-2154). Expensive.

STRBSKÉ PLESO

Patria – Opened in 1976, this 11-story A-frame lakefront hotel either complements its mountain backdrop or wrecks the scenery, depending on your point of view. It has 151 rooms and 6 suites, all with private baths. Among the facilities are restaurants, a café, bar, snack bar, and nightclub. A fitness center includes a pool, sauna, gym, and a solarium. (phone: 969-92591). Expensive.

Panorama – Near Strbské Pleso, this modern, 106-room hotel has a restaurant, café, and gamerooms (phone: 969-92111). Moderate.

TATRANSKÁ LOMNICA

Grand Hotel Praha – Opened in 1905 and remodeled in 1973, this classic hotel is the favorite in the area. Its 98 rooms are convenient to ski lifts and many offer great mountain views. There's a restaurant, a wine bar, and a sauna. The *Zbojnická*

Koliba — a shepherd's hut restaurant serving barbecued meat, mulled wine, and tea — is nearby (phone: 967941). Expensive.

Spiš

This route links several small towns in the Spiš region. If you venture off the main roads into some of the remote rural villages, you may get a glimpse of life as it was centuries ago: People farm, weave, and make pottery using the methods of their ancestors. The Czechoslovak government still supports a cottage industry to keep its arts and crafts alive, and many of the cottages are here in eastern Slovakia. The highlights of the route include the lovely Gothic town of Levoča, Spiš Castle, the medieval town of Bardejov, and Hervartov, which has one of the oldest wooden churches in the Carpathians as well as many cottages producing crafts.

POPRAD: This is the starting point for trips to the Spiš towns. For details, see the Poprad in the *High Tatras* route.

KEŽMAROK: As an alternative, try using this historical town, with its restored Renaissance castle, as a base for touring.

LEVOČA: For centuries one of the most important commercial centers in Czechoslovakia, this small Spiš town has a treasury of Gothic architecture. The town is surrounded by 13th-century ramparts, and the older section has well-preserved buildings dating from the Middle Ages through the 16th and 17th centuries.

Laid out around a central square, the town plan still follows the chessboard pattern of its original design. Town Hall (1615) is outstanding, as are the old burghers' houses with arched Gothic entries. The Thurzo House (No. 7, on the main square) epitomizes the local Renaissance style, with characteristic elaborate balconies and loggias. The interior of St. James's Church on the main square has magnificent wooden altars. The celebrated main altar, carved in limewood by Master Paul of Levoča in 1507–17, depicts the Last Supper in fascinating detail.

En route from Levoča – The dramatic hilltop ruins of the 13th-century Spiš Castle, built to protect the inhabitants from Mongol invaders, are visible from the main highway (E85) from Poprad and Levoča, and the breathtaking view from the top is worth the trip up.

BARDEJOV: Tracing its history to the 12th century, this town was declared a "historical reserve" because of its notable Gothic and Renaissance architecture.

Bardejov looks medieval, with cobblestone streets, a checkerboard housing pattern, and ramparts begun in 1352, just before it became a free town in 1376. The main architectural monuments line the town square: The Gothic Church of St. Egidius, built in the 14th, 15th, and 16th centuries, has a splendid Gothic altar, intricately hand-carved pews, and shimmering rose windows. Constructed in 1506 at the dawn of the Renaissance in Slovakia, the Town Hall has an interesting transitional blend of Gothic and Renaissance features. Also notable is the Humanistic Gymnasium (1435). On the outskirts of town is *Bardejovské Kúpele,* a spa with an adjoining annex of folk architecture.

HERVARTOV: Five miles (8 km) southwest of Bardejov, this village has a beautiful 16th-century wooden church with its original painted ceiling. Ask a local for the house where the church keys are.

BEST EN ROUTE

If you plan to visit the Spiš region, check with *Cedok* in advance for listings of accommodations. The places we have listed below as moderate cost between $40 and $50 per night for a double room, MAP.

POPRAD

Európa – This modest 73-room hotel has 2 restaurants, a café, a wine bar, and a nightclub. Wolkrova (phone: 32744). Moderate.

KEŽMAROK

Start – A friendly place with a ski slope out back. No credit cards accepted. Lesopark (phone: 2915). Moderate to inexpensive.

Denmark

With low, rolling meadows, a countryside speckled with stately castles, charming provincial towns, and remnants of a Viking past, this smallest of the Scandinavian countries has all the enchantment of a Hans Christian Andersen fairy tale and the drama of a Shakespeare play. Once you have seen Denmark, it is not difficult to understand how Andersen, the 19th-century Danish poet, novelist, and author of children's stories, found his inspiration. But it is also here, at Kronborg Castle in Helsingør, that William Shakespeare installed his brooding Hamlet.

Denmark's 16,600 square miles include the large Jutland Peninsula north of Germany and some 500 islands, about 100 of which are inhabited. Several of the larger islands form stepping-stones across the Baltic Sea from Jutland to Sweden; the easternmost of these is Zealand, where the Danish capital, Copenhagen (København in Danish) is situated. Some of the smaller islands, such as Bornholm and Ærø, have picture-perfect provincial villages with quaint cottages and cobblestone streets. With all its islands, Denmark has 4,600 miles of coastline, although in total size the country is only one-third as large as New York State.

Traditionally an agricultural country, Denmark became more industrialized after World War II — accomplishing this in a more tasteful fashion than almost any other country in Europe. The country also is known for its advanced social planning. Social reforms were carried out in Denmark in the 18th century (serfdom was abolished in 1788), and a system of folk high schools was set up to reeducate Danish farmers. By the latter half of the 19th century, poor peasants were becoming prosperous small farmers. In 1914 and 1915, suffrage was extended to all adult Danes, and the cooperative movement flourished. During this century, further social welfare legislation has provided a wide variety of government services from day-care centers to housing and care for the elderly, though recent economic pressures have weakened these programs.

Denmark's royal family (the House of Glücksborg) represents the oldest continuous monarchy in the world. It is descended from the House of Oldenburg, which was established on the Danish throne in 1448, when Christian I became king. However, Denmark became a constitutional monarchy (and its monarchs are proclaimed, not crowned) governed by a bicameral parliament (the Rigsdag) in 1849. In 1953 it was replaced by a single-chamber parliament (the Folketing).

Denmark was first occupied 10,000 years ago by people who followed the receding glaciers north. These inhabitants left numerous dolmens, barrows, and other prehistoric monuments that still fascinate us, and archaeological finds from the Old and New Stone Ages and the Bronze Age are displayed in Danish museums. The country's recorded history dates from the time of the Vikings, about AD 800. These seagoing warriors conquered parts of England and Normandy, invaded the Mediterranean, and visited the coast of North America. From the 8th to the 11th century, they forged Denmark into the most powerful European empire of the era. The dramatic events and heroic figures of the Viking Age were often inscribed on runic stones, some of which may be seen today in forest clearings and along rural roadways.

The Middle Ages was a period of prosperity for Denmark. Beautiful castles with moats were built during this period. (The later Renaissance castles and manors are frequently noted for their beautifully landscaped gardens and grounds.) In 1397, Queen Margrethe I thought the time propitious to unite Sweden and Norway under the Danish crown. The union with Sweden dissolved in 1523, but Norway and Denmark remained united until 1814, a year after the state went bankrupt.

Nonetheless, the 19th century was a golden age for Denmark culturally; there was a flowering of literature and philosophy led by Andersen and the existential philosopher Søren Kierkegaard, and August Bournonville's choreography brought renown to the *Royal Danish Ballet.* Copenhagen blossomed into a culturally energetic and sophisticated capital.

Denmark was neutral in World War I, but although it had signed a nonaggression pact with Hitler, it was occupied by German troops from 1940 to 1945. Most of the Jewish population, as well as Jews fleeing from other countries, were helped to escape from the Nazis by the Danes, who also mounted a strong resistance movement.

In the postwar years, Denmark's bacon, beer and cheese, modern furniture, porcelain, and, more recently, electronics, textiles, and architectural and engineering skills have won world acclaim. The Danes, proud of their noble history and their country's well-groomed appearance, have also made tourism an important part of the country's modern economy. In 1991, gambling was legalized, and some half-dozen casinos, paying ample taxes to state coffers, sprang up around the country.

Our first Danish route explores Funen (Fyn, in Danish), the island between the mainland of Jutland and the island of Zealand, with stops at Odense, where Hans Christian Andersen was born; Ærø, a small island with cozy old villages; and Langeland, with its Viking burial grounds and small farming villages. Next visit the flat Jutland Peninsula, the country's heartland — an area of crystal fjords, stark moors, dense forests, sandy beaches, and small, medieval towns. The Zealand route from Copenhagen heads north around the large outer island past churches and castles that recall the warrior days of Viking rule and the splendor of the Renaissance.

Funen

This route follows small, well-maintained highways with bridge and ferry connections to various islands in the archipelago, taking you through the charming countryside known as Denmark's Garden. A tour of Funen is an easy 2- or 3-day swing, whether you're circling around from Copenhagen or on your way there from the Jutland Peninsula.

Hans Christian Andersen wrote about his birthplace: "Perhaps Odense will one day become famous and people from many countries will travel to Odense because of me." This was a daring prediction in the mid-19th century, but in fact, the Hans Christian Andersen museums and settings have prompted many people to make a special trip to Odense and the isle of Funen.

Along with literary and historical attractions, Funen and the islands are noted for their unhurried charm and subtle, disarming beauty. Centuries-old inns and museums are scattered throughout a landscape that alternates between gentle, rolling farmland and picturesque harbors, coastline, and beaches. While residents here are slightly less sophisticated than their compatriots in Copenhagen, they are more open to visitors and quite proud of their region.

To reach Odense from Copenhagen, you will have about a 1½-hour drive to the Korsør-Nyborg ferry, a 50-minute ferry ride, and another half-hour's drive from Nyborg to Odense. In peak tourist season, it's advisable to book the ferry in advance. Driving east from Jutland, take E20 or A1 across the island to Odense.

ODENSE: Denmark's third-largest city celebrated its 1,000th birthday in 1988. Odense has for centuries been the trade and transportation hub of Funen. Its university, theater, and orchestra also provide a solid cultural base, important for an area far from the nation's capital.

In addition, the white swan and little brown "ugly duckling" decorating most Odense posters and information brochures signify that Hans Christian Andersen still plays a major role in the life of the city. You can visit the storyteller's birthplace (at 37-45 Hans Jensensstræde; phone: 66-131372); the museum here has been open since 1908 and contains letters, manuscripts, published editions, and drawings that have illustrated his works. Next door is a delightful, intimate restaurant called, appropriately enough, *Under Lindetræt* (Under the Linden Tree; reservations advised; phone: 66-129286). Andersen buffs also will treasure his childhood home (3-5 Munkemøllestræde; phone: 66-129286), which no doubt inspired many of his children's stories.

Odense also is the home of delicious almond nougat and marzipan, exported around the world as traditional *Christmas* confections. These are sold by the loaf for baking or slicing.

To see one of the largest and most complete open-air museums in Denmark, head south from downtown on Sejerskovvej to Funen Village. The Odense Tourist Office, Rådhuset (phone: 66-127520) can provide bus information. In a peaceful, wooded setting, a cluster of farms, houses, mills, and brickworks re-create a village typical of the 18th and 19th centuries. Open daily during summer, weekends only during winter.

En Route from Odense – The perfect setting for a Danish *Alice's Adventures in Wonderland,* Egeskov is a 16th-century island fort 1 hour south of Odense, just off A9 on the way to Fåborg or Svendborg. The castle, encircled by a moat edged by gardens in various styles, boasts a maze of hedges from which little Alice would have had trouble escaping (taller visitors can see over the hedges). You also can visit the collection of vintage cars, carriages, and other antique conveyances at the adjoining museum. The castle park is open 9 AM to 5:30 PM daily, May through September. There is an admission charge. Concerts are held in the Great Hall during the peak season (phone: 62-271625).

The *Faldsled Kro*, outside Fåborg (see *Best en Route*), is more than a hotel; it is a trip back into 19th-century style and splendor. (It also is expensive, but worth an overnight stay.) Fåborg itself is a quiet town with many 18th- and 19th-century homes.

Depending on the direction of your travels, Svendborg can serve as the gateway either to the gardens of Funen or to the southern Danish archipelago. A market town since 1253, Svendborg and its port are still a center of trade. The town makes a good dining spot or resting place for 1 day of the journey. Drive across the bridge to the island of Tåsinge and climb the Bregninge Church tower for a remarkable view of Svendborg, Tåsinge, and the nearby islands.

ÆRØ: Still relatively well protected from modernization, Ærø has, among other things, several fine beaches and the old-fashioned port town of Marstal. Car ferries link "the jewel of the archipelago" to other islands, but the best way to visit is to leave your car in Svendborg and board the ferry as a foot passenger to explore the fairy-tale village of Ærøskøbing. As soon as you get off the ferry, the charm of cobblestone streets, narrow lanes, and half-timbered gingerbread houses tells you this Lilliputian town is something special. It is delightfully cozy and compact, and if the store you'd like to visit doesn't seem to be open, you probably just have to fetch the shopkeeper from down the block.

One unusual museum in the village is the home of "Bottle" Peter Jacobsen (22 Smedegade), the man who reputedly invented the art of building ships in bottles. Before his death in 1960, "Bottle" Peter crafted over 1,700 different bottled ships and 150 scale-model sailing ships. Also in Ærøskøbing are the *Ærø Museum* in the 1780 Bailiff's House (3-5 Brogade), and the furniture and tile display in Hammerich's House (22 Gyden). For more information on any of these sites, call 62-522950.

TÅSINGE: Elvira Madigan lived and died on this island, also known as Funen's Garden. Although A9 bisects Tåsinge, heading toward Langeland, your best bet is to crisscross it, making frequent stops. Almost in the shadow of the Bregninge Church is the tiny village of Landet and the medieval churchyard where Elvira Madigan and her lover, Count Sixten Sparre, were buried in 1889, when death ended the ill-starred romance of the Swedish officer and the beautiful performer.

Back across A9 the road leads to the seafaring village of Troense, with its small maritime museum and nearby Valdemar's Castle, which was built in 1644, then remodeled in the baroque style in 1754. The manor house is open to visitors, and the compound also includes a naval museum featuring royal barges and other vessels.

After Troense, just continue crisscrossing A9 through the farmland and small towns of Tåsinge at your leisure, stopping whenever the urge hits at a roadside *bageri* (bakery) for one of its fabled pastries.

LANGELAND: This "long island" (54 miles long and 5 miles wide), reached by one bridge and five ferries, offers both historical sites and places for relaxation. Coming from Tåsinge across Langelands Bridge you reach Rudkøbing, the island's capital. A town of half-timbered buildings, winding streets, and carved house doors, it was the birthplace of Denmark's famous physicist H. C. Orsted, discoverer of electromagnetism.

But in this region of manor houses and castles, it's best to stay outside the city in a place like the *Tranekær Gæstgivergaard* (see *Best en Route*), where a typical dinner might be leek soup, roast pheasant, fresh vegetables, and good Danish beer. Less than a mile (1.6 km) from the inn is Tranekær Castle. Although rebuilt extensively in 1863, the north wing with its 9-foot-thick walls, is thought to date back to 1160. Part of the castle grounds are open to the public.

Other attractions on Langeland include small farm villages, beaches, and pleasant rolling countryside. For the return trip to Copenhagen, a ferry goes from the fishing village of Spodsbjerg to Tårs, near Nakskov. (On the road back to Copenhagen, a detour at Vordingborg out to the majestic chalk cliffs of Møn is well worth the time.)

BEST EN ROUTE

Expect to pay at least $200 and up per night for a double room in the places listed as very expensive; $160 to $195 in those listed as expensive; $100 to $155, moderate; and less than $100 at inexpensive. Rates include tax and breakfast, unless otherwise indicated. Restaurant prices range from $60 and up for a meal for two in places listed as expensive and from $40 to $55 in those listed as moderate. Prices do not include drinks or wine. Tips are always included in the bill. All restaurants accept major credit cards unless otherwise indicated.

ODENSE

Sara Hotel Grand – A traditional old-style hotel, with furnishings representative of the 18th and 19th centuries. There's a fine restaurant, bar, café, sauna, solarium, and an inexpensive airport bus. 18 Jernbanegade (phone: 66-117171; fax: 66-141171; telex: 59972). Expensive.

H. C. Andersen – This is a fine example of modern Danish architecture as well as a first class hotel. There's an elegant restaurant, piano bar, sauna, solarium, and a casino. 7 Claus Bergsgade (phone: 66-147800; fax: 66-147890). Moderate.

Windsor – Simple Scandinavian rooms, a Victorian lobby, and a restaurant are found at this hotel. 45 Vindegade (phone: 66-120652; fax: 65-910023; telex: 59662). Moderate.

FALDSLED

Faldsled Kro – This inn was a former Royal Charter House (15th century) and is set in an exquisite garden and a romantic setting. Many of the 11 rooms and 3 suites have private entrances and courtyards. The restaurant serves superb international cuisine with a French accent. Closed from the third week of December through the first week of January. 513 Assensvej (phone: 62-681111; fax: 62-681162; telex: 50404). Very expensive to expensive.

SVENDBORG

Ærø – In the Ærø hotel, this restaurant provides good service and warm hospitality; the delicately sautéed fish could hardly be beat in a restaurant costing twice as much. 1 Brogade (phone: 62-210760). Moderate.

LANGELAND

Tranekær Gæstgivergaard – Built in 1802, it's intimate and homey; most of the pheasant, wild duck, and other game served at dinner has been bagged by a member of the innkeeper's family. Ten of the 15 double rooms have been modernized to make them more comfortable, and the service is very pleasant. Open year-round. Just around the bend from Tranekær Castle, 74 Slotsgade (phone: 62-591204). Inexpensive.

Jutland

The most direct road from southern Denmark to Skagen, the idyllic resort town on the North Sea, is Highway E45. Following this route, you can reach Skagen in a day or so, but you will be missing most of the special sights of Jutland, the ancient heart of Denmark, the world's oldest kingdom.

A long peninsula separating the North Sea from the Baltic, Jutland (or Jylland, as it is known in Danish) features a topography laced with charming fjords and trimmed with windswept moors, beaches, and forests. The only part of Denmark linked to the European continent, it is considerably larger than the 500 or so islands that make up the rest of the country. Thanks to its countryside, its farms and hamlets, and its magnificent, sandy coast, Jutland has been the major vacation spot for the Danes since the days of Hans Christian Andersen.

Andersen himself spent many summers here; and he wrote: "It was so beautiful out in the country. It was summer — the wheat fields were golden, the oats were green, and down among the green meadows, the hay was stacked. There the stork minced about on his red legs, clacking away in Egyptian, which was the language his mother taught him."

In addition to their passionate love for the countryside, the Danes have close ties with their historical tradition, one that has its roots in Jutland. By present dating methods, Jutland was settled about 12,000 years ago by nomadic hunters and fishermen who were following the receding Ice Age. Remains of this culture are scattered in peat bogs and burial mounds all over Jutland and include a wide variety of weapons, tools, and even several remarkably well preserved corpses a few thousand years old, now displayed at local museums.

For the Danes, however, history really begins around the 9th century, when the Danish Vikings, operating from bases in North Jutland, laid waste to England and Scotland, besieged Paris, and plundered towns as far south as Lisbon. King Gorm the Old and Queen Thyra built the Dannevirke Wall in this era, establishing Denmark's southern border, and their son, King Harald Bluetooth, introduced Christianity to the region in about 960. Harald's heirs, Swein Forkbeard and Canute the Great, ruled over an empire consisting of Denmark, England, Norway, and southern Sweden.

With the construction of Roskilde Cathedral and Copenhagen in the 12th century, the focus of Danish culture shifted to Zealand, the large island east of Jutland. Since then, aside from a few bloody Swedish invasions and a fierce border war with the Prussians in 1864, Jutland has been a tranquil repository of agriculture and traditional Danish mores.

The Jutland trip is a winding, 9-day excursion with many stops; it is divided into three sections. Should you need to curtail your vacation, you invariably will be within a short distance of E45 or a ferry to England, Sweden, or Norway.

En Route from Germany – If you are coming from Germany on the autobahn, you will probably need a break by the time you reach the Danish border town of Frøslev. If so, head east on A8, where, after a 12½-mile (20-km) ride on the northern shores of Flensborg Fjord, you will reach Gråsten, the site of Gråsten Castle, dowager Queen Ingrid's summer home. The present baroque palace dates from 1757; the castle church (ca. 1700) is open to visitors from April to September — provided that Queen Ingrid isn't vacationing here with her grandchildren.

If old battlefields are your cup of tea, 3 miles (5 km) east is Dybbøl, where the major battle of the 1864 war with the Prussians was fought. The Prussians took over Schleswig-Holstein, but the Danes' heroic resistance has been memorialized at the Dybbøl Heights, overlooking the old fortifications.

Next to Dybbøl is Sønderborg and the huge Sønderborg Castle, which dates to the 13th century. It was the prison of Danish King Christian II in the 16th century and was burned and looted by the Swedes in the 17th century. The castle, open daily, houses a museum of regional history. No admission charge for children under 16 (phone: 74-422539).

The road north to Abenrå runs from Augustenborg Fjord to Abenrå Fjord, and it should give you a feeling for Jutland's symbiotic relationship with the sea. Abenrå itself has a museum with an intriguing collection of maritime miscellany. Closed Mondays. No admission charge for children under 16. 33 H. P. Hanssens-gade (phone: 74-622645).

Ribe, a fairy-tale village, is the next destination, about 50 miles (80 km) north-west on A12. If you are interested in Viking lore, make a detour on Hærvejen, an old Viking road, and see the runic stone at Horslund.

RIBE: First mentioned in 850, Ribe was the site of a church built by St. Ansgar, the man who brought Christianity to Scandinavia. The dominant feature is the cathedral, Ribe Domkirke, built on the site of Ansgar's church and the first thing you see as you approach the town. Built in the first half of the 12th century, it is a striking mixture of Romanesque and Gothic elements and is full of legend and interesting architectural detail. The *Ribe Museum of Antiquities* also is worth a visit, and the town boasts over 100 protected houses from the 16th and 17th centuries. For a bit of local flavor, stop at the charming *Weiss Stue* (ca. 1600), near the cathedral, for a meal or a glass of "punch" (warmed aquavit, sweetened with a sugar cube).

The North Sea is just a few minutes away, and its tides are so strong that you may have to resist the temptation to drive across the mud flats of Vadehavet to the island of Mandø. Take the bus instead.

En Route from Ribe – About 15 miles (24 km) north of Ribe on A12 is the city of Esbjerg, the base for Denmark's fishing industry as well as the country's oil capital. Fishmeal plants, a busy international ferry terminal, and waterfront grain silos give Esbjerg a prosaic look, with none of the atmosphere of older Danish towns. (After all, it dates only to 1869.) Do drive down to the docks, however, and take the 20-minute ferry ride to the remarkable little island of Fanø.

FANØ: The ancestors of the 3,300 inhabitants of Fanø bought this island from the Danish crown in 1741, which explains the preservation of a unique culture on the island. Its lengthy beaches and grassy dunes make it a popular bathing resort, and on the southern spit of the island is the restored old fishing village of Sønderho. Fanø was once a prolific shipbuilding site. Today it has an important navigation school, but perhaps more writers and artists than seafarers make the island their home. Many people live in low houses with thatch roofs. On the first weekend in July, Nordby hosts the *Fanø Fair.* Sønderho's own festival is held the third Sunday in July. On these dates islanders dress in traditional costume and the past comes alive.

En Route from Fanø – Leave the west coast and get acquainted with another kind of scenery by cutting back across Jutland on the road leading northeast to Grindsted. The land changes noticeably as you leave the coast, and you will see some of the rolling farmland for which Denmark is famous.

If you are traveling with children, you might want to take the Vejle road 6 miles (10 km) to Billund and turn them loose on *Legoland* (phone: 75-331333; open from May 1 to the third week in September), a miniature world made from 15 million Lego toy bricks. There is a 40-foot replica of Mt. Rushmore, another of Cape Kennedy, and many activities for youngsters.

Another 19 miles (30 km) takes you to Vejle and the nearby village of Jelling, the ancient Viking capital, where you can see some of Denmark's most famous runic stones and the burial mounds of old King Gorm and Queen Thyra. (Denmark's current monarch, Queen Margrethe, is a direct descendant of Gorm.) The *Jelling Kro* (phone: 75-871006) is a fine place to sup with the ghosts of the Vikings.

The road north to Horsens via Juelsminde has a spectacular view of the coast and Palsgård Manor House, which is open to tourists.

HORSENS: Founded in the 12th century, this was a Franciscan abbey town during the Middle Ages before becoming a prosperous trading center in the 18th century. The old abbey church still exists, and many of the original decorations and carvings are still intact. The town itself is on a fjord and has many picturesque lanes and lovely 18th-century houses.

Horsens is the end of the first 3-day leg of the tour; you are now entering central Jutland, the second leg. Continuing north on E45, you leave the coast and approach Arhus. Here the landscape becomes more wooded, and you may even notice a slight elevation as you pass Yding Skovhøj Hills, the highest point in Denmark at 567 feet.

ARHUS: Denmark's second-largest city (pop. 250,000), Arhus is a major industrial and cultural center, thanks to its harbor and the University of Arhus. Among the city's many sights are the 12th-century Arhus Cathedral, which contains, among other things, Denmark's biggest church organ; the Old Town, a reconstructed 16th-century village (Viborgvej; phone: 86-123188); the *Viking Museum* (Clemens Torv; phone: 86-272433); and the *Museum of Prehistory,* with an Iron Age collection highlighted by the red-haired mummy of the Grauballe man, at the Moesgård Manor House (phone: 86-272433). The *Arhus Art Museum* (Vennelystparken; phone: 86-135255) is one of Denmark's most prominent, especially for modern paintings; closed Mondays; admission charge. The *Royal Scandinavian Casino* (4 Store Torv; phone: 86-120011) offers gambling in an elegant setting; open daily from 2 PM to 4 AM. If you visit in early September, be sure to catch the *Arhus Festival,* the biggest celebration of theater, dance, and music in Scandinavia.

SILKEBORG: Heading due west on A15, you reach the beautiful Lake District and, Silkeborg, in its center. The *Silkeborg Museum* (at Silkeborg Hovedgård; phone: 86-821578), is worth a stop, particularly if you want to see another early Dane, the 2,200-year-old Tollund man. Museum open Wednesdays, Saturdays, and Sundays; daily from April to mid-October; admission charge. The *Silkeborg Art Museum* (7 Gudenåvej; phone: 86-825388) has a memorable modern collection featuring work by native son Asger Jorn; closed Mondays; admission charge. Take a boat trip on the lakes, where you can relax and gaze at slender herons and other waterfowl. One of Denmark's great Resistance heroes, the poet and pastor Kaj Munk, was killed in 1944 by the Nazis at Hørbylund Bakke, 5 miles (8 km) west of Silkeborg.

En Route from Silkeborg – Drive west on A15 to Herning, the center of the Danish textile industry. Here you can get a good buy on a sweater or fabric design, and you can observe 19th-century peasant life and weaving techniques at the *Herning Museum* (1 Museumsgade; phone: 7-123266); closed Mondays, except in July. The town has fine modern art collections.

From Herning, A15 winds through the moors and lowlands of the west coast to Ringkøbing, a town economically ruined in the 18th century when accumulated silt deposits on Holmsland Klit cut off Ringkøbing Fjord from the North Sea. To prevent flooding, the Danes have built dikes similar to those in Holland. The area is thus undeveloped. Driving south on Holmsland Klit, you come to Tipperne Bird Sanctuary, the largest in Denmark.

HOLSTEBRO: North of Ringkøbing on A16, Holstebro is Jutland's center for theater and music. A depressed town some 25 years ago, it came into a windfall and spent the money on encouraging the arts. Today it has one of the leading experimental theaters in the world, the *Odin Theater* (Særkærparken; phone: 7-424212) and a lovely art museum, *Holstebro Museum* (3 Museumsvej; phone: 7-422923); open daily. Holstebro is a great example of creative city planning.

VIBORG: East on A16 is one of Denmark's oldest towns. Viborg dates to the

8th century, when it was the site of the Viking *ting* and various sacrificial rites, thanks to its placement at a critical crossroads. The Christians who later occupied the area decided to keep it as a religious center and in 1130 built a large cathedral; it was largely destroyed by fire but was restored in the 19th century. Today it is still the largest granite cathedral in all of Europe. It is decorated with a series of lavish frescoes, executed around the start of the 20th century by the painter Joakim Skovgaard. Open daily.

En Route from Viborg – The final leg of the Jutland trip covers the rugged scenery of North Jutland, which is virtually cut off from the rest of the peninsula by the Limfjord, a large body of water that was an important navigation route in Viking times. Here again, deposits of silt have wreaked havoc with maritime commerce, making the passage quite treacherous. Heading northwest on A26 toward Nykøbing and Thisted, you will first see the Limfjord at Skive, a small town with an interesting museum collection of Eskimo and prehistoric relics.

About 15 miles (24 km) northwest of Skive, connected by the Sallingsund Bridge, is the Limfjord island of Mors. Its largest town is Nykøbing Mors, the home of the Limfjord oyster industry and Dueholm Abbey, founded in 1377 by the Knights of St. John. Today the abbey houses the island's historical museum (phone: 97-723421). It is open daily; admission charge.

The best view on Mors is from the cliffs of Hanklit and Salgjerjøj, near the Thisted Bridge across Vilsund. Thisted itself is the principal town in northwest Jutland, in the Thy area. Nearby, at Hørdum, is a fantastic runic stone depicting Thor's epic struggle with the Midgård serpent.

Following A11 northeast along the northern banks of the Limfjord, you pass the promontory of Feggeklit on the island of Mors. According to the Danish medieval historian Saxo, this was where Hamlet avenged his father's death by killing his treacherous Uncle Fegge. From here, take the north road to Fjerritslev; stop for a swim and a look at the North Sea at Torup Strand.

From Fjerritslev, one can choose either A11 to Alborg, the next destination, or the southern route via Løgstør. The latter is slower but much more interesting; it passes the Viking town of Aggersborg as well as Løgstør, a fishing hamlet with a good museum on the history and culture of the Limfjord.

ALBORG: Denmark's fourth-largest city and Jutland's most important town, Alborg is the center of the tobacco, cement, and — as every good Dane knows — aquavit industries. Alborg will celebrate its 1,300th anniversary this year, with special cultural and sporting events. The official *Jubilee Day* is June 16. Like many Danish cities, Alborg has a well-preserved Old Town that must be explored on foot. Be sure to see Jens Bang's Stenhus, one of the finest Renaissance houses in Denmark, and have a drink downstairs in the cavernous *Duus Vinkjaelder* bar (9 Osteragade; phone: 98-125056), once a wine cellar. For a lively happy hour or night out on the town, head to Jomfru Ane Gade, a historic street lined with restaurants and pubs. The *Alborg Historical Museum* (48 Algade; phone: 98-124522) contains interiors from bourgeois homes of the 17th century, and the *North Jutland Museum of Art* (50 Kong Christians Allé; phone: 98-138088) houses a very modern collection in a marble structure designed by the Finnish architect Alvar Aalto. Also of interest are the Alborg Zoological Garden, Mølleparken, and a smaller replica of Copenhagen's *Tivoli* called *Tivoliland* (phone: 98-111255). Well worth a side trip is the annual celebration of the US's independence, held on July 4 at Rebild Hills, 20 miles (32 km) south of Alborg.

En Route from Alborg – Nørresundby, a suburb of Alborg on the northern side of the Limfjord, has the most important Iron Age and Viking burial ground in Scandinavia (Lindholm Høje). There are 682 graves as well as the ruins of a nearby settlement. The *Lindholm Høje Museum* (11 Vendilavej; phone: 98-124522) has exhibits about the site. Open daily. No admission charge.

From here, A17 runs northwest to Abybro, where it joins A11 running due north to Løkken and the coast. En route you may want to stop and see the famed church in Jetsmark or detour to swim at the small seaside town of Blokhus. Løkken itself is a popular summer resort, and you can drive the 10 miles (16 km) to Blokhus on the beach. Not far from Løkken is the 12th-century monastery and manor house at Børglum Kloster (phone: 98-994014); open daily from May 15 through September 16; admission charge.

The route leads next to the commercial center of Hjørring, a 13th-century town, which has a quaint historical museum, *Vendsyssel* (3 Museumsgade; phone: 98-920677), and St. Catherine's, a fine medieval church.

On the road north to Skagen, you'll see one of the most exotic sights in Denmark. Huge, shifting dunes up to 35 feet high that migrate 25 to 30 feet every year, the Råbjerg Mile is on the northern peninsula of Skagen, the juncture of the Baltic and the North seas.

SKAGEN: This charming little town by the sea became an artists' colony in the 1880s and has been a popular resort ever since. Paintings of people on the strand (the beach) by P. S. Krøyer have made Skagen known the world over. Artists' inspiration can be seen in the low, yellow-washed houses and in the town's various museums — the *Skagen Museum* (4 Brøndumsvej; phone: 98-446444), the *Museum of Old Skagen* (P.K. Nielsensvej; phone: 98-444760), *Drachmann's House* (21 Hans Baghsvej; phone: 98-445188), and the *Grenen Museum* (40 Fyrvej; phone: 98-442288), which houses contemporary art. Just west of town is the "church of the dunes," a 13th-century church that was abandoned to the sands in 1795. The history of Skagen's relationship with the sea is reflected in its five lighthouses, only one of which, Grenen, is still in use today. Skagen is the ideal place to end a tour of Jutland, and you may want to stay in one of its quiet little cottages for a while to digest your travels. If you find the area artistically inspiring too, it is possible to study painting. Consult the local tourist board.

BEST EN ROUTE

Expect to pay $100 and up per night for a double room in the places listed as expensive; $70 to $95 in those listed as moderate; and under $70, inexpensive. Rates include tax and breakfast, unless otherwise noted. Restaurant prices range from $65 and up for a dinner for two in the expensive category; $45 to $60 in the moderate category; and $40 and under, inexpensive. Prices do not include drinks or wine. Tips are always included in the bill. All restaurants accept major credit cards unless otherwise indicated. *Note:* Skagen and Fanø are very popular in the summer, so be sure to make bookings well in advance.

RIBE

Dagmar – On the main square of this beautiful little village, this is the best hotel in town, with 50 rooms and full accommodations. 1 Torvet (phone: 75-420033; Best Western in the US, 800-528-1234; fax: 75-423652). Expensive.

FANØ

Scan Club – Parents traveling with children may wish to try this beach hotel. All 27 rooms have kitchens, and special weekly rates are offered. Pool, restaurant. 52 Strandvejen, Nordby (phone: 75-163711). Expensive to moderate.

Sønderho Kro – A tiny, elegant, 7-room inn on the southern tip of the island. Full accommodations and a charming restaurant. Sønderho (phone: 75-164009). Moderate.

HORSENS

Snaptun Færgegård – Following the principle of sleeping near the sea, this 50-room inn gives you the chance to be lulled into slumber by the Baltic. Full accommodations. 11 Havnevej, Snaptun (phone: 75-683511; fax: 75-683909). Moderate.

SILKEBORG

Dania – A nice, respectable, businessperson's hotel on the main square of town, with 47 rooms, full accommodations. 5 Torvet (phone: 86-820111; fax: 86-802004; telex: 63269). Expensive.

RINGKØBING

Klitten – Right on the beach, this fine hotel has a restaurant. Open from June through August. Søndervig (phone: 97-339100). Moderate.

Strandkroen – This cozy little inn has 16 rooms and a restaurant. 2 Nordsøvej, Søndervig (phone: 97-339002). Inexpensive.

VIBORG

Missionshotellet – Somehow in this spiritual center it seems appropriate to stay in the inn with an ecclesiastical ring. Plenty of character can be found here. There are 60 rooms, 10 apartments with bath and kitchen, and full accommodations. 5 Sankt Mathiasgade (phone 86-623700; fax: 86-624046). Expensive to moderate.

THISTED

Limfjorden – This modern hotel has a good view of the Limfjord; 19 rooms and full accommodations. 39 Oddesundvej (phone: 97-924011; fax: 97-910666). Expensive.

ALBORG

Hvide Hus – A big-city hotel with all the trimmings, including a swimming pool, sauna, and 199 rooms with full accommodations. 2 Vesterbro (phone: 98-138400; fax: 98-135122; telex: 69690). Expensive.

SKAGEN

Skagen – The biggest place (and very modern) in this tiny town, with 83 rooms and a reputable seafood restaurant. 39 Gammel Landevej (phone: 98-442233; Best Western in the US, 800-528-1234; fax: 98-442134). Expensive.

Zealand

Tours from Copenhagen can be either 1-day loops or extended 2- to 3-day excursions that allow you to take greater advantage of the Zealand countryside and perhaps stay in a charming Danish manor house or traditional hotel.

While Copenhagen is considered one of the most modern and sophisticated cities in Europe, a half-hour drive transports you to an area of farmland and woods dotted with towns dating back more than 500 years.

Some of the high points of such tours are castles and churches that vividly re-create the time when kings ruled the realm we now call Scandinavia. You can visit a palace still used by the reigning monarch, a church with the tombs of almost all the royalty from the last thousand years, and the ramparts of Kronborg Castle in Helsingør (Elsinore), the scene of Shakespeare's *Hamlet*.

There is more to enjoy here, however, than colorful history. You also can stop at *Louisiana,* the modern art museum overlooking the sound, drive past a strip of posh shore homes known as the Danish Riviera, and relax on sandy beaches or in old fishing villages.

The most frequently traveled tour bus route is a 1-day loop that heads north from Copenhagen to *Louisiana* (at Humlebæk) and Helsingør, turns west to castles in Fredensborg and Hillerød, and then returns to Copenhagen. To get the most out of each stop, however, 1½ to 2 full days are recommended.

KLAMPENBORG: Heading north from Copenhagen off the coast road, the first stop is Klampenborg, which, in addition to a bathing beach, has Jægersborg Dyrehave, the royal hunting ground since the end of the 17th century. This is a favorite retreat for Copenhagen residents, where they can stroll among the old oak trees and watch the nearly tame deer. The highlight of the park between late March and the end of August is *Dyrehavsbakken* — or *Bakken,* as it's commonly known. Scandinavia's and perhaps Europe's oldest amusement park, *Bakken* is not unlike *Tivoli,* but set in the woods. There are enough attractions to merit a full day's visit and bicycles can be rented at the railroad station. Have lunch on the terrace of *Taarbæk Kro,* just off the beach; 102 Taarbæk Strandvej (phone: 31-630096 or 31-631596).

En Route from Klampenborg – While E47 is the fastest route to Helsingør, the 27-mile (43-km) Rte. 152 that winds along the Oresund coast really doesn't take much more time. Along the way are many elegant homes, fine examples of modern Danish architecture, that make it easy to understand why this stretch is known as the Danish Riviera. At the seaside town of Rungsted, about 15 miles (9 km) north of Copenhagen on Route 152, is the family estate of author Karen Blixen (Isak Dinesen), who wrote *Out of Africa.* She died in 1962, and her oceanside manor, Rungstedlund, has been preserved. It's open to the public, and houses the *Karen Blixen Museum* (111 Rungsted Strandvej; phone: 42-571057), exhibiting the baroness's (her title) writing room, bedroom, and mementos from her years in Africa. The old barn now houses a café, bookshop, and rooms for literary gatherings. Blixen's grave is nestled in a corner of the grounds, which serve as a bird sanctuary, according to her wishes. Open daily from May through September; closed on Tuesdays from October through April. No admission charge for children under 16.

HUMLEBÆK: About 22 miles (35 km) north of Copenhagen, this town is noted for the *Louisiana,* a museum and center for modern art. Established in 1958, the *Louisiana* stands majestically on the Oresund coast, looking over the sound toward Sweden. Not only does it have an outstanding collection of Danish and foreign art and sculpture, but the museum and gardens themselves are works of art.

HELSINGØR: About a half-hour north of Humlebæk, the coast road (Rte. 152) winds into Helsingør. According to the history books, people were living in the area before AD 1000, and Helsingør had already been named by 1231. But it wasn't until 1574, when Frederik II began the reconstruction of Kronborg Castle, that Helsingør took on strategic and historical importance.

Dating from around 1426, the castle had been completely rebuilt in its present Renaissance style by 1585. It houses collections of armor and Renaissance clothing and art; phone: 49-213078; closed Mondays October through April. There is a memorial to Shakespeare in the surrounding wall — this is presumed to be the Elsinore Castle that was home to Hamlet, the Melancholy Dane — and the castle itself is well preserved. Also on the Kronborg grounds is the *Mercantile and Maritime Museum* (phone: 49-210685), founded in 1915.

At Helsingør, Denmark and Sweden are less than 2 miles apart. It's worth making the 40-minute round trip by hydrofoil between Copenhagen and Helsingborg — if only to say you've been in Sweden.

To see the technological history of Denmark, visit the *Technical Museum* (23 Ndr. Strandvej.; phone: 49-217111), featuring Denmark's first airplane, railroad train, and trolley; open daily; admission charge.

HORNBÆK/GILLELEJE: From Helsingør, the longer tour of North Zealand continues up the coast to the resort towns of Hornbæk and Gilleleje. Both have picturesque fishing harbors and Hornbæk, in particular, a fine beach. Don't be surprised at the amount of nudity on the beaches or at the Danes' apparent nonchalance. The *Strand* in Gilleleje (4B Vesterbrogade; phone: 48-300512) and the *Trouville* in Hornbæk (20 Kystvej; phone: 42-202200; fax: 42-201827) are both well-known hotels that tend to fill up in summer months. Both towns also have campgrounds.

FREDENSBORG: Here is the Fredensborg Palace, the spring and fall home of the reigning monarch. The gardens were designed by the French landscape architect Jardin, who patterned them after those of Versailles. The castle is open only in July (when guided tours are given in English, French, and German), but the magnificent grounds are open year-round. Visitors sometimes run into dowager Queen Ingrid taking a stroll. She has apartments in a wing of the palace.

If you opt for the shorter circle route, a good place to stop for a late lunch is the *Store Kro* (see *Best en Route*), next to the palace. The inn has been around for centuries and serves typical Danish fare in traditional settings.

HILLERØD: Continuing west on A6, you come to Hillerød, one of the largest towns in North Zealand. Dominating the town is Frederiksborg Castle, which many people consider the most beautiful Renaissance castle in Europe. Built between 1600 and 1620 by Christian IV, it was reconstructed from the original drawings after fire gutted most of the structure in 1859. Since 1878 the castle has been the *National Historical Museum* (open year-round, though hours vary; admission charge); it contains collections of Danish artifacts, costumes, armor, and artwork. Particularly impressive is the chapel, which was largely spared by the fire, and the reconstructed Great Hall (directly above) is one of the most ornately impressive royal rooms in Europe. Adjacent to the edifice is the baroque Castle Park and the Badstuen, a country hunting lodge for royalty.

ROSKILDE: The focal point of Zealand tours west of Copenhagen is Roskilde, reached via A6. In the center of town is the Roskilde Cathedral, built in the 1170s, the final resting place of nearly all Danish royalty for the last thousand years. The church is a mélange of Romanesque and Gothic architecture, and its interior is rich in frescoes, monuments, sarcophagi, and art objects. On Saturdays in the summer, the Raphaëlis organ dating from 1555 is played at noontime.

By the harbor in Roskilde Fjord is the *Viking Ship Museum* (phone: 42-356555). Inside are five Viking ships, dating from around 1000, which were found in the fjord in 1962. In addition to the well-restored vessels, the museum offers an illuminating film describing the delicate, painstaking procedures used to excavate and restore the Norse relics. Open daily.

LEJRE: About 7 miles (11 km) southwest of Roskilde is Oldtidsbyen, the Historical-Archaeological Research Center at Lejre. The center is a working village, built to simulate conditions in the Iron Age, 3,000 years ago. The project, supported by the Carlsberg (beer) Foundation, as well as by the Danish government, is a favorite with youngsters. Open daily, May through September. Admission charge.

BEST EN ROUTE

Expect to pay $110 and up per night for a double room in the places listed as expensive. Restaurant prices range from $75 and up for a meal for two in the expensive category; $50 to $75 in the moderate category; and $50 and under, inexpensive. Prices do not include drinks or wine. Tips are always included in the bill. All places accept major credit cards unless otherwise indicated.

KLAMPENBORG

Taarbæk Kro – Offering fine dining right on the beach, this family-run inn features seafood prepared in the French style. Try the *carrelet à la ping,* local fish *meunière,* or, for lunch, the bountiful seafood plate; French and German wines. Seating is inside or on the terrace, and the service is congenial. 102 Taarbæk Strandvej (phone: 31-630096 or 31-631596). Dinner, expensive; lunch, moderate to inexpensive.

HELSINGØR

Marienlyst – Along the coast road just outside Helsingør, this is the premier hotel in North Zealand. Sitting by the pool, you can see Kronborg Castle in the distance. Superb international cuisine; 215 rooms and 7 suites. There's also an elegant new casino. 2 Ndr. Strandvej (phone: 42-101042; fax: 42-103530; telex: 41116). Expensive.

FREDENSBORG

Store Kro – A perfectly situated 49-room hotel on the road between Helsingør and Hillerød, just a short walk from Fredensborg Palace. One of its two buildings dates from 1723, and over the years the hotel has been the scene of receptions and royal weddings. The atmosphere is one of old-fashioned elegance. 1-6 Slotsgade (phone: 42-280047; fax: 42-284561; telex: 40971). Expensive.

SØLLERØD

Søllerød Kro – Only 10½ miles (17 km) north of Copenhagen but surrounded by woods is an inn dating from 1677. One of the most popular spots for the Danes' Sunday outings, the menu offers both French and Danish dishes; try the pickled salmon and the lobster bisque. After a meal, a walk through the woods is recommended. No overnight accommodations. 35 Søllerødvej (phone: 42-802505). Expensive.

Finland

Finland, a country of about 5 million people, is the easternmost Scandinavian landmass. Its southern end juts into the Baltic Sea to create two smaller bodies of water: the Gulf of Bothnia to the west, which forms a natural barrier with Sweden, and the Gulf of Finland to the south, which separates Finland from the Baltic state of Estonia. Finland shares its borders with Norway and Sweden to the west and north and with the Soviet Union to the east.

Finland's neighbors have dominated its history. First part of the Swedish Kingdom, then of the Russian Empire, Finland wasn't officially independent until 1917. This is important because anthropologically Finland is neither Scandinavian nor Russian. The language is Finnish, a Finno-Ugric language; and the people are Magyar-Estonian hybrids who migrated from the southeast.

This year Finland will celebrate its 75th anniversary of independence with folk festivals, sports events, cultural performances, art and architecture exhibits, and professional seminars. In conjunction with the anniversary celebration, 1992 has been declared *Homecoming Year;* a year-long series of events will encourage Finns living abroad to return to their family roots, strengthen their ties to the Old Country, and learn about the achievements of present-day Finland, as well as its many cultural offerings. For more information contact the Finland Society, 8 Mariankatu, Helsinki 00170, Finland (phone: 0-174255; fax: 0-654868).

Finland covers 130,500 square miles (about the size of New England plus New York and New Jersey), one-third of which is above the Arctic Circle. The southern two-thirds of the country are marbled with over 188,000 lakes dotted with more than 180,000 islands.

Wood-related and metal industries are the main Finnish occupations, but the national pastime is the sauna, and you'll miss something special if you leave Finland without trying one.

Helsinki, the capital, with a half-million people, is on the southern coast. It's a good starting point for any visit to the country. Finland's roads are good, as are the railway, bus, and airline connections. *Finnair* now serves 22 locations throughout Finland, and the railway offers special holiday tickets for unlimited travel within the country. Car rental is easy and uncomplicated as well. The first route takes you in and out of the beautiful southern lakeland. The waters are cold, clear, and shallow; the land is green and forested. There are also 2- to 5-day guided tours to the Lakelands by bus-boat-plane. The lake networks are vast and trafficked by romantic steamers, modern ferries, and hydrofoils.

The second route heads into the Arctic wilderness of Lapland, where the people are as much an attraction as the landscape. The fells (mountains raised from early glacial movement) make the land strangely beautiful, even where fir and birch forests end and the tundra begins.

The Lakelands

This long route (703 miles/1,132 km) takes you from Helsinki up, around, and through the beautiful Finnish lakeland. There are ten major towns along the way and many interesting stops that could take a week's meandering, but if you don't have time, you can get a good map and reroute, cutting across some of the larger lakes by ferry.

HELSINKI: For a detailed report on the city and its hotels and restaurants, see *Helsinki*, THE CITIES.

En Route from Helsinki – Leaving the capital for the lakeland, take Route 3 for 65 miles (104 km) to Hämeenlinna. The landscape is luxuriant farmland enriched by clear, blue waters. Before you reach Hämeenlinna, you pass through Riihimäki, site of the famous *Finnish Glass Museum* and a glassworks, where you can purchase samples of beautiful Finnish glassware (23 Tehtaankatu; phone: 914-741494; admission charge).

HÄMEENLINNA: Having received its royal charter in 1639, this is the oldest inland town in Finland. The city, which grew around the medieval Häme Castle in the northern part of town on Lake Vanajavesi, is a garrison town. Be sure to visit the *Art Museum* (2 Viipurintie) and Sibelius House (11 Hallituskatu) where the Finnish composer was born (admission charge for both). Hämeenlinna also is a terminal for the *Finnish Silverline* lake route; you can take a motorship or lake steamer to Tampere or Kangasala.

About 48 miles (77 km) along Route 3 and E79 is the town of Tampere. On the way you might stop for lunch at the Sääksmäki Bridge and eat on the picturesque lakeshore.

TAMPERE: The second-largest city in Finland, with 400,000 inhabitants, Tampere was founded 200 years ago on the banks of the Tammer River rapids on the isthmus between two big lakes, Näsijärvi and Pyhäjärvi. There also are some 180 lakes inside the city limits. Tampere is an industrial center known especially for metal, textiles, and footwear, but it also is famous for its theaters and other cultural activities.

Just before the center city, you cross a bridge; down to your right is the charming Koskipuisto (Rapids Park), where you can sit and watch the river flow. Here as well as in Hämeenpuisto (Häme Park), a little farther on, there are summertime folk dances and open-air concerts. There are several impressive churches, not all "15th-century stone" style: the Tampere cathedral is Gothic and built of Finnish granite, the Kaleva is Finnish modern, and the Eastern Orthodox Church of Tampere, with its bulbous towers, is the only neo-Byzantine church in Scandinavia. From Näsinneula, the highest observation tower in Finland, which also boasts the revolving *Restaurant Näsinneula,* you can drink in wide views of both the city and the lakes. Besides an aquarium, a dolphinarium, and a planetarium (all housed in the Särkänniemi recreation center; phone: 931-231333), Tampere also has one of Finland's best collections of 20th-century art at the *Sara Hildén-Museum* (Särkänniemi; phone: 931-231333); also visit the *Tampere Modern Art Gallery* (23 Palomäentie; phone: 931-31195) and the unique *Lenin Museum* (28 Hämeenpuisto; phone: 931-127313). Admission charge for all museums.

On a northern lake isthmus is Pyynikki Park, with a beautiful ridge of pine trees, calm lake views, and a revolving summertime theater. Kauppi Sports Park is the place to jog, swim, or play tennis. *Tampere Hall* (55 Ylioplokatu), the congress hall (the Finnish equivalent of "convention hall") and concert hall is on the edge of Sorsapuisto Park, opposite the university. Opened in 1990, the hall's dynamic architecture reflects Tampere's modern image.

JYVÄSKYLÄ: The trip from Tampere is 93 miles (150 km), but you can stop outside town at the industrial island commune of Säynätsalo on Lake Päijänne, the site of one of Alvar Aalto's famous buildings, the Säynätsalo Civic Center. If you're in a hurry, however, don't worry about missing it; the *Aalto Museum* (7 Seminaarinkatu; phone: 941-624809), where you can see most of the Finnish master's building plans, is in Jyväskylä, next to the university, with many other examples of Aalto's work. Admission charge.

Jyväskylä, one of the most popular tourist cities in the country and the capital of Central Finland, was founded in 1837 at the northern end of Lake Päijänne on the site of an ancient marketplace. Its importance as a cultural center is especially obvious in summertime, when various seminars, theater performances, concerts, and exhibitions are staged and well attended. For 10 days in early June, the *Jyväskylä Arts Festival* features Finland's longest-running annual multi-arts discussion forum; many musical events, seminars, and cultural programs are held (phone: 941-615624). More than anything else, though, this is a city of fine modern architecture, featuring a city theater designed by Aalto as well as the *Rantasipi Laajavuori* hotel (phone: 941-628211) with its *Sports Center,* just north of the city's center. The *Sports Center* is the site of the famous ski jump on which many Finnish athletes earned *Olympic* medals.

For information about lake cruises, sightseeing tours, or other activities, stop at the tourist office at 38 Vapaudenkatu (phone: 941-624903).

TURKU: Only 95 miles (160 km) west of Helsinki and easily reached by bus, train, car, or plane, Turku is Finland's oldest city. Though smaller than Helsinki and Tampere, its historical roots run deeper. Its trade and spiritual heritage once provided an important link that connected medieval Finland to the burgeoning sphere of Western culture.

In 1812, Turku lost its position as the country's capital when Czar Alexander I ordered the seat of government moved to Helsinki. Turku suffered another crushing blow in the fire of 1827, when virtually the entire city was razed. Architect Carl Ludwig Engel created a new master plan for the city in 1828, and today a visit provides a vivid glimpse into its significant past.

On this alternate route from Helsinki, begin with a visit to Turku Castle and Cathedral, two 13th-century monuments. Housed inside the restored castle (admission charge) is a historic museum, which shows medieval artifacts beside modern designs. Farther down the picturesque Aura River is the stone cathedral (Turku Harbor; phone: 921-30300), which was finished in 1300. Don't skip *Wäinoö Aaltonen Museum* (38 Itäinen Rantakatu; phone: 921-355690) where works by the renowned Finnish sculptor are displayed in a contemporary building designed by his son; it also has a pleasant café. Admission charge.

Nearby is the *Sibelius Museum* (17 Püspankatu; phone: 927-654494), with many orginal scores and unique musical instruments (admission charge). Concerts are held here regularly. This year from August 7 to August 16, a music festival will be held, featuring Renaissance and baroque pieces performed on period instruments (phone: 921-519450).

The Qwensel House, which dates to the 1700s, is a good example of how the middle class lived. Adjoining it is the *Pharmacy Museum* (13 Läntinen Rantakatu 13; phone: 921-303300), with mahogany fittings and an original restoration of an apothecary shop, complete with glazed earthenware jars and bottles dating to 1800.

If you want a change from Finnish food, visit *Pizzeria Dennis* (17 Linnankatu), a popular hangout for locals that serves inexpensive pasta dishes and plate-size pizza.

En Route to Kuopio – If it's July and you can't resist strawberries, stop at Suonenjoki, a small town that holds an annual *Strawberry Carnival.* If you have lots of time, you can continue this detour through the towns of Iisvesi, Tervo, and Karttula, where the lake scenery is unmatched.

KUOPIO: This capital of the Savo Province is a center of its culture, humor, and folklore. The city was founded about 200 years ago, and the old traditions are kept alive at the marketplace, where the high-tempered townsfolk meet to barter. You can buy a *kalakukko* (a tasty fish and pork pie), all sorts of vegetables, berries, and regional clothing and souvenirs. If you're not too full to keep exploring, try the *Orthodox Church Museum* (1 Karjalankatu), which has a unique collection of religious icons (admission charge). The revolving *Puijo Tower* restaurant at Puijo Panorama Tower (in Puijo; phone: 971-114841) gives a 360-degree view of the surrounding hills and lakes. For a glimpse of Kuopio's past, visit the open-air museum (22 Kirkkokatu; phone: 971-182685) with 19th-century buildings and a shoemaker at work. Admission charge.

En Route from Kuopio – To get to Joensuu the shortest way, take Route 17, which connects the two provinces and tourist regions of Savo and North Karelia. An alternate route goes south to the city of Varkaus, then northeast along Route 70 to Joensuu.

If you take the longer alternative you can stop at Varkaus, an industrial town at the junction of two extensive lake networks: Kallavesi to the north and Haukivesi to the southeast. The town's business is wood pulp and, except for a large Scandinavian altar fresco in the church, it is best explored by boat. Two-hour sightseeing cruises go through many idyllic channels and canals, the oldest of which, Taipaleen Kanava, was built in the 1830s.

Farther along this route is the village of Heinävesi, with the only cloisters in Finland, the New Valamo Monastery, with typically Russian cupolas built, oddly enough, out of copper, and the Lintula convent of nuns.

About 60 miles (96 km) north of Heinävesi on Highway 5 is the scenic harbor city of Lisalmi. Summer here is best; that's when the *Brewery Museum* of the Olvi Oy Brewery is open (11 AM to midnight, April 26 through September; no admission charge; Satama Harbor; phone: 977-14514). There's an exhibit of the history of beer, as well as a collection of some 900 beer cans from around the world. Enjoy the scenic Lake Porovesi and the museum restaurant, then drop in at the brewery for a tasting.

JOENSUU: The main town of North Karelia, Joensuu was founded in 1848 at the mouth of the Pielisjoki River. Its culture is documented at the *Karelia House Museum* (*Karjalan Talo;* 23 Kirkkatu; phone: 973-201634) in Ilosaari, where you'll also find a summer theater and restaurant serving regional fish and some of the best pastries in Finland. Again, there's an opportunity to take a lake cruise. Even the most inveterate landlubber shouldn't take the lakeland route without at least one boat trip.

A northern loop trip of about 185 miles (300 km) from Joensuu goes up and around Lake Pielinen. It takes you past the mountains of Koli, the old wooden houses and reconstructed log Bomba Castle at Nurmes, and the Ruunaankoski Rapids near Lieksa. Throughout the trip you might happen upon local bards, founts of indigenous lore who will be glad to sell you the best in regional handicrafts, from unique leather goods to fine linen tablecloths. There's a variety of wooden souvenirs fashioned from the knot and splint pieces that go unused in the forest industries. And in summer, there also are many *pradzniks,* religious Russian Orthodox festivals.

SAVONLINNA: From Joensuu, head southeast toward the Russian frontier on Route 6. It's possible to follow this road all the way to the border, but to get to Savonlinna you cut back west into the lakeland and eastern Savo region.

Savonlinna itself dates from 1475, when the Olavinlinna Castle was built. The medieval castle, ringed by lakes, was then a border fort manned by united Swedes and Finns on the lookout for czarist armies. The city that surrounds the castle wasn't founded until 1639, and today it is a beautiful lake and spa town. Again, you can take steamer cruises on the lakes from here. The boats leave from slips beside the marketplace and zigzag through the surrounding archipelagos. Shop at the market before cruising and pick up some fresh berries and local pastries. Try the savory ones, filled with smoked fish and meat. There are direct boats to and from Kuopio, Joensuu, and

Mikkeli. The castle, worth a visit, is the main site of the *Opera Festival,* which is always popular. If you're interested, tickets should be booked well in advance (for information, call 957-514700). Just outside Savonlinna is the small town of Kerimäki, with the world's largest wooden church. It holds 3,300 people, and during the summer the *Savonlinna Opera Festival* holds concerts here.

MIKKELI: Mikkeli, 64 miles (104 km) southwest of Savonlinna, is the main city of Savo province and is on the banks of the huge Lake Saimaa. It was the popular headquarters of the national hero Marshall C.G. Mannerheim. You can visit his headquarters, now a museum (1-3 Päämajakuja). Then walk north on Porrassalmen-katu to the church museum, where there's a stone sacristy dating from the 1320s. Those who crave more lake views can climb the Naisvuori observation tower and admire the various shades of green, blue, and white of the lakes and countryside.

En Route from Mikkeli – There's a choice of two picturesque routes to the town of Imatra, both of which return east toward the Russian border. The first is along Route 434, also called "the panoramic road of Savo," which passes over islands and straits on the shores of Lake Saimaa. The road wanders around hills and meadows with open lake vistas and at one point is punctuated by a short ferry ride.

The second, longer route goes back to Savonlinna (this is the route to take if you've skipped Mikkeli entirely) and takes you through the Punkaharju Ridge, a narrow Ice Age spit that separates Lakes Puruvesi and Pihlajavesi. Just off Pun-kaharju is *Retretti* (the Retreat), an amazing art center, completed in 1987, with an art gallery and an "acoustic" concert hall in a cave carved belowground.

IMATRA: Imatra is known mainly for the Vuoksi River rapids that roar through the center of town. On selected summer Sundays you also can see the release of the controlled Great Falls. Imatra is another good place to study Alvar Aalto's bold architectural creations, such as the Church of the Three Crosses. The town line is also the national border. As in most of the other lake towns, you can arrive or leave by boat, for Imatra is on the easternmost edge of Lake Saimaa.

LAPPEENRANTA: This city, only 23 miles (37 km) southwest of Imatra, is at the southernmost point of the Saimaa Lake network and has developed into Finland's biggest inland port. There's an involved channel and canal system from here to the Gulf of Finland that gives almost all the lakeland towns access to salt water. The channels, however, flow east through Russian territory before they reach the sea at Viborg. In 1968, Finland worked out a complicated leasing agreement with the Soviet Union that covers boat traffic along the system.

Lappeenranta was founded in 1649, and you can visit the Old Park, surrounded by an 18th-century rampart that encloses a fortress, various museums, and the oldest Orthodox church in Finland, dating from 1785.

En Route from Lappeenranta – About 56 miles (90 km) southwest on the Gulf of Finland is the small military town of Hamina. The entire town was planned and executed as a Renaissance fortress. Much of the 250-year-old wall still stands, enclosing the circular interior where you can see the old Finnish military traditions carried out at the Reserve Officers' Academy. There's also a bulbous Orthodox church dating from 1837.

KOTKA: Only 6 miles (10 km) from Hamina, Kotka lies on the peninsula between the two eastern tributaries of the Kymi River and stretches farther over Kotka Island. The Russians built naval fortifications here that were destroyed when the Russian fleet was overwhelmed by English sea power during the Crimean War. The only building left after the battle was the Orthodox Church of St. Nicolaus, which still stands and houses a collection of valuable icons.

The Finnish town was built in 1878 without Russian aid and now is an industrial center and a major port. You still can get a taste of Imperial Russia if you visit the czar's fishing lodge (now a museum) at the Langinkoski Rapids. If you want more naval history, there's a motorboat to Varissaari Island, where you can review the Battle of Ruotsinsalmi (between the Russians and the Swedes) of 1790. You can examine the cannon and the salvaged ships and plot how you might have guided one fleet or the other more strategically than their admirals did. Present-day Kotka was formed in 1977 with the merger of the nearby boroughs of Karhula and Kymi. The *Maritime Festival,* held every summer, preserves the tradition of the old seafaring ways and attracts a large number of participants from nearby Baltic regions.

PORVOO: Still farther west on the gulf and only 31 miles (50 km) east of Helsinki is Porvoo, the only Finnish city that still has an intact town plan from the 1700s. Porvoo's mercantile heritage goes back to the Middle Ages, when it was established as a trade center in 1346 by King Magnus Eriksson. It's got narrow winding streets, a town hall from 1764 in the middle of a quiet cobbled square, and an A-roofed cathedral built in 1418. The town's layout gives it a more southern European flavor, but the old pastel wooden houses and the brown and white wood detailing of the cathedral façade make it distinctly Scandinavian. Because of its style, Porvoo has always lured the more artistic and poetic Finns. You can visit the house (3 Aleksanterinkatu) where Finland's national poet, Johan Ludvig Runeberg, lived and worked. There's also an honorary residence for Swedish and Finnish poets called the Poet's House (also at 3 Aleksanterinkatu); it is easily confused with Runeberg's home but actually is an entirely different building near the cathedral. From this calm town, it's only a little more than a half-hour drive back to Helsinki.

BEST EN ROUTE

A double room in a good hotel in Finland costs $200 and up in those places classified as expensive. There are fancy places for less in the country, but not that much less — even in Lapland (tourism is one of its major industries), therefore a hotel in the moderate category will cost $110 and up; establishments in the inexpensive range will cost about $80 and up, but don't expect to find many of them. A first class meal in Helsinki, especially during the crayfish season, is at least $50 to $70, depending on drinks; again, we consider this expensive. Specialties in the smaller towns are less expensive; reindeer dishes are good, but usually expensive.

HÄMEENLINNA

Rantasipi Aulanko – This fancy hotel is next to a lake in a beautiful national park. There's a restaurant, a nightclub, a pool, and a beach, plus horses, golf, tennis, boats, bicycles, and whatever else you need for outdoor activities (phone: 917-58801; fax: 917-21922). Expensive.

TAMPERE

Ilves – An 18-floor super-hotel in the center of town with 336 rooms, 5 restaurants, and a rooftop sauna with a view of the city. It is connected to a glassed-in mall complex with cinemas, cafés, shops, and a medical center. 1 Hatanpäänvaltatie (phone: 931-121212; fax: 931-132565). Expensive.

Rosendahl – On the stately and beautiful Pyynikki Ridge, this luxurious hotel offers a variety of recreational activities. 13 Pyynikintie (phone: 931-112233; fax: 931-112233). Expensive.

Finlaysonin Palatsi – Built in 1899 as a private residence, this unique palace is now an elegant restaurant in the center of town. The menu changes daily and features fish and meat, including reindeer. In the summer months guests can dine outdoors among the greenery. Open daily. Reservations advised. 1 Kuninkaankatu (phone: 931-125905). Expensive to moderate.

JYVÄSKYLÄ

Laajavuori Summer Hotel – Next to the Sports Center, which is active year-round. 2 Auvilankujä (phone: 941-251323). Expensive.

Jyväshovi – This hotel has a cozy dining room, serving Finnish cuisine with a fine touch, and the obligatory sauna. Centrally located around shops and most of Alvar Aalto's early buildings. Sauna 35 Kauppakatu (phone: 941-630211; fax: 941-630290). Expensive to moderate.

Laajari Youth Hostel – A budget alternative for winter sports enthusiasts of all ages. 15 Laajavuorentie (phone: 941-253355). Inexpensive.

TURKU

Hamburger Bors – Modern and efficient, this hotel is opposite the city square in the middle of town. It has a sauna and a pool. 6 Kauppiaskatu (phone: 921-637381; fax: 921-311010). Expensive.

Marina Palace – On the Aura River, a luxury hotel with all the amenities. 32 Linnankatu (phone: 921-336300; fax: 921-516750). Expensive.

Park – A first class property which dates to the turn of the century with a distinctive Art Nouveau design. Its 20 rooms are well-furnished and comfortable. Restaurant and café. 1 Rauhankatu (phone: 921-519666). Moderate.

KUOPIO

Rivoli – This place offers a wide range of services, including sporting facilities, Jacuzzis, winter gardens, and sophisticated dining. 1 Satamakatu (phone: 971-195111; fax: 971-195170). Expensive.

JOENSUU

Kimmel – Here is a large but good hotel, with a nightclub and an excellent restaurant. 1 Itäranta (phone: 973-1771; fax: 973-177-2112). Expensive.

NURMES

Bombantalo – A huge, reconstructed Karelian "log castle," it has a good restaurant serving Karelian food. The rooms are in romantic log cottages with bath, phone, and TV sets. 1 Suojärvenkatu (phone: 976-22260; fax: 976-22270). Expensive to moderate.

SAVONLINNA

Spa Hotel Casino – This pleasant, 79-room lake resort has a private beach, tennis, boating, and other outdoor sports facilities. Kasinonsaari, PB 60 (phone: 957-22864; fax: 957-12524). Expensive.

Seurahuone – The 84 rooms in this centrally located hostelry have the basic amenities and are cheerfully furnished. Saunas have private terraces complete with lake views. 4-6 Kauppatori (phone: 957-5731; fax: 957-13918). Moderate.

Tott – Close to the harbor, this hotel was renovated in 1988 and offers views of the lake and Olavinlinna Castle. A buffet breakfast and morning sauna are included in the room rate. 1 Satamakatu (phone: 957-514500; fax: 957-514504). Moderate.

Snellman – This cozy eatery is a local favorite and besides its Finnish specialties like salmon soup and fried *vendace* (fish), it has international dishes and a salad buffet. Open daily during the summer for lunch and dinner; weekdays the rest of the year. Reservations unnecessary. Major credit cards accepted. 31 Olavinkatu (phone: 957-13104). Moderate to inexpensive.

Pavilionki – Operated by the catering department of the vocational training school, students are fully responsible for the cooking and serving at this comfortable eating place. Reservations advised. Major credit cards accepted. 4 Rajalahdenkatu (phone: 957-520960). Inexpensive.

KERIMÄKI

Herttua – This hotel/conference center is located in the ideal Finnish landscape of lakes and forests. The rooms are elegantly furnished and some have private saunas. There is a restaurant, café, and a bar, plus tennis and squash courts. Kerimäki (phone: 957-575501; fax: 957-541331). Expensive.

Savonlinna – Located 10 miles form the *Savonlinna Kerimaa Golf Resort*, this unique complex includes a driving range, tennis courts, stables, water sports in the summer, winter sports, and a restaurant. The comfortable wooden bungalows with saunas accommodate both large and small groups. Kerimäki (phone: 957-57511; fax: 957-575-1300). Expensive to moderate.

MIKKELI

Alexandra – A new hotel that features modern facilities, rooms for nonsmokers, a restaurant with a glass roof, sauna, and a heated garage. 9 Porrassalmenkatu (phone: 955-20201). Expensive.

IMATRA

Imatran Valtionhotelli – An island hotel almost in the midst of the Imatra Rapids, it's actually a stone castle with big rooms and first class food. 2 Torkkelinkatu (phone: 954-605111; fax: 954-61268). Expensive.

LAPPEENRANTA

Lappee – This 211-room hotel is well known for its excellent fitness centers, sauna, and pool. 1 Brahenkatu (phone: 953-5861 or 953-53295). Expensive.

PORVOO

Haikko Manor and Health Spa – A luxurious hostelry and convention center with complete health spa facilities and an acclaimed restaurant serving continental food. It's possible to take the hotel's cruiser to Helsinki during summer months. About 4 miles (6 km) from the middle of town (phone: 915-151-2201; fax: 915-153799). Expensive.

Wanha Laamanni – A visit to this restaurant in the heart of the Old City is a must. Housed in a 2-story, 18th-century complex, with a traditional menu of home cooking (on an open hearth), it will evoke memories of days gone by. Open daily. Reservations unnecessary. 17 Wuorikatu (phone: 915-130455). Moderate.

Lapland

Lapland is the great remaining wilderness of Finland. Covering the northern third of the country, almost all of it is above the Arctic Circle. This is truly the Land of the Midnight Sun, and in the northernmost town of Utsjoki, at the Norwegian border, there are 70 straight days of uninterrupted daylight that begin in mid-May. The Midnight Sun occurs between June and July. You must arrive in Rovaniemi, the capital of Lapland, and hope that there is no rain to make the normally magificent sunsets overcast. Otherwise, it is a memorable experience to be able to play golf, tennis, or take a hike after midnight. After a 50-day sunset, the sky gets dark at the end of November. The Northern Lights, which have been described as "nature's own light show," often are visible during November and December, but they are as elusive as shooting stars.

The roads across this wilderness run mainly north and south, with rather few connecting east-west arteries. The major routes have hard surfaces (black-top or concrete) and are plowed regularly through the winter. You'll notice many warning signs for reindeer crossings — pay attention to them. In the dark, surprised reindeer, like deer in the US, will often bolt directly into oncoming headlights. If you inadvertently hit a reindeer, you must inform the nearest police unit.

With the exception of its few urban centers, Lapland is a very sparsely populated area, with a density of only about two people per square kilometer. That leaves a lot of space for herds of roaming reindeer. You'll find fewer lakes here than in southern and central Finland, but there are many rivers, and between them are vast uninhabited areas. The topography varies greatly: low-lying swamps, river valleys with stands of pine and spruce, and regions of treeless tundra with an occasional scrub of birch on a low fell. (Fells are elevated plains that were left as high ground around gorges formed by retreating glaciers. The Lapp landscape is covered with these gently rounded, bare-topped hills.)

Along the northern highways of Finland, many roadside stalls sell authentic Lapp souvenirs. There are about 4,000 Lapps here, and their population is diminishing. Much like the American Indian, they were shunted off to less civilized terrain as the more industrialized Scandinavians, Russians, and Finns came to Finland. The Lapps live off the reindeer, and they use almost every part of the beast for clothing and food. They prize the antlers and make them into sculpture, as whalers do with whalebone. Some 200,000 reindeer wander freely but are owned by 5,800 Lapp families, who depend on them entirely for their living. Reindeer roundups take place from September to January and are colorful events. The Lapps dress in their traditional blue, red, and yellow outfits and their embroidered "caps of the four winds." Seventy-five miles (120 km) northeast of Rovaniemi, in Salla, is Scandinavia's first wildlife park devoted to reindeer husbandry. Visitors also can visit Santa Claus (no charge) at the Salla Reindeer Park year-round (phone: 692-37712). Contact the Finnish Tourist Office in Helsinki for information and reservations.

The shortest way from Helsinki to Rovaniemi, the capital of Lapland, is Route E4 through Lahti, Jyväskylä, Oulu, and Kemi — almost 520 miles (837 km). And this is before the main Lapland route through Rovaniemi, Sodankylä, Inari, and Utsjoki — another 284 miles (458 km). The thing to do is to take one of the car-sleeper trains. From Helsinki they take 12 hours, but they let you and your car off perfectly rested at the beginning of the route. There are several daily runs, which take about 1¼ hours.

ROVANIEMI: Though people have lived at the confluence of the Kemi and Ounas rivers just south of the Arctic Circle since the Stone Age, the Nazis, on leaving, torched the city and left it looking like a cigarette stub in the Arctic snow. As a result, the

"Gateway to Lapland" is an almost entirely new city, planned with meticulous and functional beauty by the Finnish architect Alvar Aalto. Since World War II, the population here has more than tripled. *Santa Claus Workshop* village (no admission charge) on the Arctic Circle is worth visiting, no matter what your age. The shops sell handicrafts unique to the region; you also can pet reindeer, sample reindeer milk, and sit on Santa's lap. A tourist lodge is on top of Ounasvaara, an Arctic hill overlooking the town that offers a wonderful urban/Arctic panorama. In town you can visit the *Lapland Provincial Museum* (admission charge) at the Lappia House and see the theater-convention building (11 Hallituskatu), designed by Aalto himself.

Rovaniemi is the administrative capital of Finnish Lapland as well as its most cosmopolitan city; consequently, it's the best place to sample a variety of Lapp delicacies. The dishes usually are based on local fish or game birds such as salmon, whitefish, ptarmigan, grouse, and capercaillie. There's also a wide variety of reindeer concoctions, such as reindeer stew, smoked reindeer, reindeer tongue, cutlets, steaks, and roasts. For dessert, try any of the cloudberry variations, often served over chewy Lapp cheese that has been warmed over a fire; afterward, a liqueur distilled from one of the native berries — bramble- or cranberry — is appropriate.

SODANKYLÄ: After an 80-mile (130-km) drive north through typical Lapland "fell" scenery (the roadbed curves between 1,640-foot hills) you reach the lively village of Sodankylä. Here is the oldest church in Lapland, an unpainted timber edifice in the middle of town.

Outside town you can stop at smaller villages, all of which are interesting. If it's July, hop south to Porttikoski and the annual lumberjacks' championships. Heading north, you pass between the two big artificial lakes of Lokka and Porttipahta on the way to Tankavaara, where you actually can pan for gold. If you don't want to get your feet wet, go to the *Gold Museum* (open year-round; admission charge) for the history of the Finnish gold rush. There are cozy cabins and a modern hotel here, as well as a café-restaurant serving Lapp specialties. For more information on the complex, call 9693-46158.

The scenery grows intensely beautiful as you pass wide fells and long vistas.

INARI: Not as much a town as a borough, Inari is classified as the Finnish city with the largest area. Of its 6,800 people, there are about 1,500 Lapps — or Sami, as they call themselves. Stretching to the northeast is the huge 50-mile-long Lake Inarinjärvi, with cold, exceptionally clear water and 3,000 islands.

At Inari Village is the outdoor *Inaria Lappish Museum* (actually more preserve than museum, it almost 2,500 acres), with exhibitions of Sami history and examples of Sami dwellings and towns (admission charge). In March there's a Lapland "rodeo," with reindeer races, lassoing, and relay skiing races. You also can take several different boat excursions on the lake.

UTSJOKI: As you continue driving north, you suddenly descend from the high fell plateau into the Teno River Valley. This area used to be crowded with birch trees, but maggots feasted on them for years before anyone thought about conservation. The experts say it's too late to reforest, and the region is fast giving in to encroaching tundra.

Utsjoki is the only city in Finland where the Lapps outnumber the Finns. It's an outdoorsman's town, so don't expect too much in the way of creature comforts. Also, don't assume that just because it's above the Arctic Circle it's always freezing. During the summer, Utsjoki can be one of the hottest places in Europe. The fishing here is great, but if it's not one of your first loves, Utsjoki won't be either.

BEST EN ROUTE

Lapland is a tourist area and therefore commands surprisingly high rates. An expensive room for two runs well over $100 per night, a moderate room will run from $80 to $100, and an expensive meal, between $40 and $60.

ROVANIEMI

Rantasipi Pohjanhovi – The city's most famous and traditional hotel, offering a wide range of outdoor activities such as reindeer sleigh rides, snowmobiling, and fishing safaris. The restaurant is known all over the province, generally is crowded, and probably serves some of the best reindeer dishes in the world. Pohjanpuistikko (phone: 960-33711; fax: 960-313997). Expensive.

Polar – A fine business hotel in the city center. Its excellent restaurant serves Lapp and continental delicacies. 23 Valtakatu (phone: 960-23751; fax: 960-16634). Expensive to moderate.

Erämaamaja Karhunpesä – "The Bear's Den" is a charming log hideaway by the lake in the midst of unspoiled wilderness. Sauna, boats for fishing, and snowmobiles are available. Approximately 20 miles (32 km) from Rovaniemi. Bookings should be made through the *Polar Hotel,* 23 Valtakatu (phone: 960-77250 or 960-23751). Moderate.

Sky Hotel Ounasvaara – A family hotel on the top of Ounasvaara Hill, overlooking Rovaniemi. Cozy rooms with private saunas, a panorama-view restaurant, and five downhill slopes and well-maintained cross-country ski tracks. Ounasvaara Hill (phone: 960-23371; fax: 960-318789). Expensive.

SODANKYLÄ

Kantakievari – This 53-room hotel has a restaurant with fine food, a bar, a sauna, and a pool, and a noteworthy variety of outdoor sports facilities. 15 Unarintie (phone: 9693-21926; fax: 9693-13545). Expensive to moderate.

Kantakievari Luosto – About 20 miles (32 km) from Sodankylä, a large lodge built of Lapp timber. Excellent outdoor sporting facilities, and a good variety of programs are offered. Kantakievari Luosto, PB 58 (phone: 9693-13681). Moderate.

IVALO

Ivalo – A hotel with modern comforts, an indoor pool, and gastronomic delights in the midst of the wilderness. Some 30 miles (50 km) before arriving at Inari. 34 Ivalontie (phone: 9697-21911; fax: 9697-21905). Expensive to moderate.

Riekonlinna – In the nearby village of Saariselkä, this hostelry is popular with skiers, be they families or singles (phone: 9697-81601; fax: 9697-81602). Expensive to moderate.

UTSJOKI

Utsjoki – By the shores of a famous salmon-fishing river, this rustic retreat offers everything you came this far north to see. The restaurant has fresh salmon and reindeer dishes. Utsjoki 99980 (phone: 9697-71121; fax: 9697-71126). Moderate.

France

Thomas Jefferson once said, "Every man has two countries — his own and France." The ideals of the French 18th-century Age of Enlightenment were embraced by the American founding fathers; in fact, Rousseau's theory of government by "social contract" formed the basis for the new kind of government boldly proposed in Jefferson's Declaration of Independence. The French inherited their love of reason from the Greeks and the Romans, and for many people, France represents an epitome of human achievement in 2,000 years of Western civilization. Paris is universally beloved as the City of Light, a leader in artistic and intellectual endeavors, and possibly the world's most beautiful city. Most significant, perhaps, has been the French talent for making art out of life. French food, wine, and fashion represent the ultimate in elegance, the perfection of civilized virtues.

To many, Paris is France. Almost 2.5 million of the nation's 53 million people live in the capital; Marseilles, which ranks second, has less than a million people; but neither Marseilles nor any other city can begin to compare with Paris's influence in French politics and culture. France is shaped like a star, with Paris at its heart. All roads and railroads lead to Paris, and anywhere else is regarded as provincial. Like the roads, the French Revolution radiated from Paris, and it is said that when Louis XIV made the mistake of building his palace at Versailles (only 12 miles/19 km outside Paris), he began to lose control over the entire country.

But visitors hardly can be expected to accept such a parochial view of national life. France, of course, is much more than Paris. Until the reunification of Germany in 1990, it was the largest nation in Western Europe, and it's a third larger than California, with an area of 211,208 square miles. To the delight of the French aesthetic sense of symmetry and balance, the country is shaped roughly like a hexagon, three sides bordering on land and three on water. It is a land blessed with great natural beauty and variety: southern sea and northern coast, high mountains and fertile valleys laced with rivers. The jagged Atlantic coastline of Normandy and Brittany forms its western border, and the sun-drenched bays and inlets of the Mediterranean lie to the southeast. The snow-covered Alps, which rise to the dramatic 15,771-foot peak of Mont-Blanc, form the Swiss and Italian borders to the east, and in the south, the high, rugged, olive-treed Pyrenees form a natural border with Spain. The gentle, pine-clad slopes of the Vosges are a continuation of Germany's Black Forest region to the northeast, and the fertile hills and valleys of Champagne and Burgundy are covered with priceless vineyards whose harvest is the source of the world's finest wines.

The French countryside is noted for its long stretches of straight, tree-lined roads, many of which date from Roman times. And although it is an industrial country, France also is a nation of many small privately owned farms.

Its rural population comprises 25% of its total population. A visitor often can catch a glimpse of a plow being drawn by horses or oxen. Thus it is not difficult to understand why the French people regard the soil of their country with an attachment that amounts to reverence.

Not only is their land remarkably beautiful, it has been inhabited since prehistoric times. Wall paintings at Lascaux and in other caves in the Dordogne are probably 20,000 to 30,000 years old. When the Celts migrated to the land they called Gaul sometime before the 7th century BC, it was inhabited by Iberians and Ligurians. Greeks colonized the area around Marseilles — which they called Massilia, founding the oldest city in France — and Julius Caesar conquered Gaul for Rome in 57–52 BC. During the 5th century AD, Germanic tribes invaded, especially the Franks, who converted to Christianity under Clovis I and established the kingdom that became known as France.

A unified national spirit was born in France on *Christmas Day,* 800, when Charlemagne, King of the Franks, was crowned by the pope in Rome as Holy Roman Emperor. Although Charlemagne's empire was short-lived, it left a lasting impression upon the French consciousness, even though the weakness of successive rulers allowed territorial princes, such as the Dukes of Burgundy and Normandy, to gain great power. In 987, however, the French nobility elected Hugh Capet King of France, and from this point, French national history is generally agreed to begin. Capet helped to centralize the monarchy, led in the Crusades and wars with England, and founded the Capetian dynasty. During the 12th and 13th centuries, trade flourished, craft guilds were established, and towns sprang up. Paris grew in importance as the royal city and as the intellectual center of Europe; the newly founded Sorbonne drew such teachers and philosophers as Abelard, Albertus Magnus, and Thomas Aquinas.

This time of peace was followed by the devastation and bloodshed of the Hundred Years War of 1337–1453 (the period covered by Barbara Tuchman's brilliant history, *A Distant Mirror*). Essentially a dynastic struggle with England, whose Norman kings held vast fiefs in France, this series of wars ended well for France, driving out the English and strengthening the power of the French monarchy. As in the days of Charlemagne, the French throne once again was endowed with a mystic aura, this time with the help of Joan of Arc, whose divine voices encouraged her to lead the French to victory at Orléans in 1429 and to champion Charles VII as King of France.

During the 16th and 17th centuries the Valois and Bourbon kings further increased the royal authority, moving the country toward absolute monarchy. The strong-armed rule of Cardinals Richelieu and Mazarin (1624–61) set the stage for their splendid successor, Louis XIV, whose reign was probably unequaled in the history of Europe for its elaborate and magnificent style. His attitude can be summarized in his famous remark, "*L'état c'est moi*" ("I am the state"). His was an age of brilliant achievements in art and literature, making France indisputably the intellectual capital of Europe. French became the international language for more than a century afterward. Frederick the Great of Prussia, who lived during the mid-18th century, spoke French, employed the French philosopher Voltaire as a tutor, and was rumored to have said that German was a language fit to be spoken only to horses and dogs.

The very magnificence of the French monarchy helped precipitate its downfall, for it was expensive to maintain and someone had to pay. The major cause of the French Revolution was the system of special privileges that exempted nobles and clergy from the taxes paid by the peasants and the middle class. In 1789, these latter groups rebelled against the monarchy in the person of Louis XVI, guillotined both the king and his queen, Marie Antoinette, and established the short-lived First Republic.

The chaos that followed the revolution resulted in the rise of Napoleon, who proclaimed himself emperor in 1804 and, though a dictator, undertook to spread the ideal of liberty to the world through his conquests. After his fall in 1814, the monarchy was restored. In the 19th century, France alternated between democracy and dictatorship and was characterized by the steady growth of a new French Empire (which disintegrated in the 20th century). A revolution in 1848 established a Second Republic, which was superseded by the dictatorship of Napoleon III, nephew of the emperor. Finally, a Third Republic emerged in 1870 that lasted until 1940, that saddest time in all French history when France capitulated to Nazi Germany. Between 1940 and 1945, the government was led by World War I hero Marshal Philippe Pétain, who, in collaboration with the Nazis, established a puppet government in Vichy in the South of France.

After World War II, the Fourth Republic was created; it collapsed in 1958 under the pressure of a revolution in Algeria. Although the Fifth Republic, engineered by Charles de Gaulle, has been threatened by the great number of political parties in France, it has managed to stand up in the face of such serious threats as the student revolt and general strike of May 1968.

The France of the past can, for the most part, still be seen today. The French preserve their old buildings well, be they the royal châteaux of Blois and Chambord in the Loire Valley or the magnificent cathedrals of Chartres and Reims. The landscapes of France are exciting, from the Pyrenees, the rugged mountains of southern France, and the snow-covered Alps farther north, to the luxuriant vegetation and posh villas of the sun-drenched Riviera on the Mediterranean coast, to the stark, chalk cliffs of Normandy's beaches. If you enjoy wine, you can tour the vineyards of Burgundy, Bordeaux, and Dordogne, and for food, every region of France has a different and highly developed style.

For the sports enthusiast, France is an especially exciting place to be this year, since it is hosting the *Winter Olympics* from February 8 to 23. Albertville will be the site of the opening and closing ceremonies, and the surrounding villages of the Savoie region will host various events. Although driving routes below do not cover the *Olympics* sites in the French Alps, if you wish to obtain more information, contact the official ticket and travel agent of the United States Olympic Committee, *Olson Travelworld Ltd.*, Olympic Division, 1334 Parkview Ave., Suite 210, Manhattan Beach, CA 90266 (phone: 800-US4-1992). *Powder Ski Adventures* (24196 Alicia Parkway, Suite E, Mission Viejo, CA 92691; phone: 800-888-6292) offers 7-night ski packages that include tickets to some of the ski events.

Our ten routes include Paris's weekend vacation land, a 50-mile radius called the Ile-de-France, extending north of the capital to Chantilly, west to Beauvais, and south to Chartres; it contains peaceful forests and valleys, châteaux and cathedrals. Paris itself is treated in detail in *Paris,* THE CITIES. From Paris you also can zigzag west into Normandy in the direction of Cherbourg, passing through green pastures and exploring the cheese industry, fashionable beaches, and busy harbors. Jutting out between the English Channel and the Bay of Biscay, Brittany's peninsula can be toured in a semicircular route from the magnificent shrine at Mont-St.-Michel west to Quimper and back east to the port of Nantes and its château. The Loire Valley, France's most splendid château country, extends east from Angers to Blois and includes some wine country as well. Two celebrated wine routes begin in the city of Bordeaux: The Dordogne lies east toward Rocamadour and Les Eyzies-de-Tayac, including fertile farmlands and prehistoric cave paintings, while Bordeaux runs north toward Pauillac and the fabled wine cellars of Lafite-Rothschild and Mouton-Rothschild.

Two of the most glorious areas in France, Provence and the Riviera, are adjacent to one another and can be seen together. Sunny Provence includes towns unmatched anywhere for their charm and beauty; they are set in the craggy mountains from Avignon southeast to Aix-en-Provence. Just south and west is the Riviera, stretching along the coast from Menton to St.-Tropez, a region beloved by modern painters like Picasso and Matisse for its dramatic cliffs overlooking the clear blue Mediterranean waters, its charming bays and fishing villages, its splendid villas and fashionable beaches.

Burgundy, yet another wine district, opens southward from Auxerre to Bourg-en-Bresse, passing through peaceful hills and valleys and ancient towns. Finally, there are the provinces of Alsace and Lorraine, with their strongly Germanic atmosphere and their beer as well as wine; when you travel east from Nancy to Strasbourg, it often seems that you're in Germany.

The Ile-de-France

The first thing you should know about the "island of France" (Ile-de-France) is that it is not an island. It is, in fact, the region surrounding Paris, and the name "Ile" comes from the rivers that form its boundaries: the Epte, the Aisne, the Marne, the Yonne, and the Eure, with the Seine and the Oise also running through the territory. Don't look for it on a map, though: legally, the region doesn't exist. Its population can't be counted, and neither train nor bus schedule knows it by name.

The Ile-de-France, extending around the city to a radius of roughly 50 miles (80 km), offers something for every visitor. Through this area traveled Charlemagne, St. Louis, Joan of Arc, Louis XIV and all the Kings of France, not to mention Emperor Napoleon, leaving memorials of their passing. The art lover is drawn to the magnificent cathedrals, beautifully preserved medieval abbeys, and sumptuous châteaux — architecture and design unparalleled anywhere else in France. For the nature enthusiast or the weary city dweller, the Ile-de-France has peaceful valleys, forests, and wildlife.

We suggest you make Paris your base for forays into the region. Every site on the route makes a comfortable day trip or can be combined with other stops to fill out a weekend jaunt. To strangers, Paris — the City of Light — can seem rather dark on Sundays and Mondays, when many shops and restaurants are closed. These are ideal days to visit this nearby countryside.

Telephone numbers in the Ile-de-France are dialed as Paris numbers, requiring no additional prefix when dialed from Paris and needing a 1 when dialed from outside Paris or France. Other numbers in this chapter fall outside the official Ile-de-France boundaries, and may need to be preceded by the prefix 16 when dialing from Paris.

CHANTILLY: Only 25 miles (40 km) from Paris via N16, Chantilly is famous for its château, its parks, and, of course, the racetrack. Five different châteaux have existed on this site in the last 2,000 years, but the present one was built only between 1875 and 1881 at the direction of the Duke of Aumale, a son of King Louis-Philippe. The château is small by French standards but exceptionally elegant. Inside is an excellent museum with over 2,000 artworks, including more than 600 oils by French, Flemish, and Italian masters of the 16th to 18th centuries (admission charge; open 10 AM to 6 PM; closed Tuesdays; phone: 44-57-03-62). Also visit the library, with its prodigious collection of rare books, and the chapel, where, to this day, the descendants of the last owner gather for Sunday services. The lordly 18th-century stables, which furnished mounts to the royal court in nearby Paris, are open to the public at the *Musée Vivant du Cheval* (Living Museum of the Horse); the stables house retired stallions from all the country's national stud farms, as well a unique collection of equestrian art (admission charge; phone: 44-57-40-40). Take time as well to wander through the gardens and the extensive forest which was a favorite hunting ground of the kings and nobles of France for 5 centuries.

En Route from Chantilly – A few miles southwest, taking D118 to D909, you'll come to Royaumont, one of the best-preserved medieval abbeys in France. Royaumont was founded by St. Louis in 1228, and the wealth and beauty that are still apparent attest to the protection lavished on it by successive Kings of France.

St.-Leu-d'Esserent lies 3 miles (5 km) northwest of Chantilly via N16 to D44. Its mellow and beautiful 12th-century stone church is renowned for its architectural excellence on a commanding site overlooking the Oise.

Route N924 east leads to the charming town of Senlis, dominated by the Ancienne Cathédrale de Notre-Dame (Pl. Notre-Dame), begun in 1153. Of particular interest is the portico, dedicated to the Virgin and the prototype for the porticoes of Chartres, Notre-Dame-de-Paris, and Reims. Also well worth a visit are the ancient Church of St.-Pierre (Pl. St.-Pierre), the Château Royal (for its Gallo-Roman walkway), and the hunting museum (*Musée de la Vénerie*) in front of the château (open 10 AM to noon and 2 to 6 PM; closed Tuesdays and Wednesday mornings; admission charge; phone: 44-53-00-80). The Gallo-Roman walkway, a defense wall around the château's perimeter, provides a good vantage point from which to view the principal monuments.

At Chaalis (7 miles/11 km south via N330) are the picturesque ruins of a 13th-century abbey and, in the park, yet another château in addition to a museum (no phone) that has three rooms devoted to the works of Jean-Jacques Rousseau, who died in nearby Ermenonville in 1778. You also can enjoy the countryside: There are numerous ponds, the famous Mer de Sable (Sea of Sand), and a small zoo at Ermenonville, 2 miles (3 km) south on N330.

COMPIÈGNE: On the banks of the Oise, 49 miles (78 km) north of Paris via N17, is this village, justly famous for its palace (Pl. du Palais). The palace's exterior is somewhat austere, but the exquisite interior decoration is beautifully preserved.

Compiègne has played a significant role in French history: Most of the Kings of France visited the town at one time or another, and Joan of Arc was taken prisoner here in 1430. In more recent conflicts, the armistice of November 11, 1918 was signed here (the exact site is marked in a clearing — Clairière de l'Armistice — in the woods surrounding the palace). In a sad footnote, from 1941 to 1944, Compiègne served as a deportation center for France's Jewish community en route to concentration camps.

The forest of Compiègne, with nearly 35,000 acres, has majestic avenues, pools (Etangs de St.-Pierre), and picturesque villages, such as Vieux-Moulin and St.-Jean-aux-Bois. Just beyond the forest, via D85, is the splendid 12th-century château-fortress of Pierrefonds, once the property of Napoleon.

BEAUVAIS: About 45 miles (72 km) from Paris via A15 and D927 lies Beauvais. Although the city is in one of the less attractive parts of the Ile-de-France, a visit to the imposing Cathédrale St.-Pierre makes the trip worthwhile.

The cathedral, whose Gothic style is in rather jarring contrast to that of the rest of the city, has had an erratic history, plagued by overambition and underfinancing. The soaring choir section, begun in 1247, was a challenge to architects throughout Europe. Unfortunately, they proved unequal to the challenge, and in 1284 the choir collapsed. In 1500, another generation of bishops decided to continue the work and undertook to finance it by the expedient sale of indulgences. But again the architects literally let Beauvais down: An experimental cross tower was constructed, but the supporting pillars gave way in 1573. Since then, the cathedral of Beauvais has remained a magnificent — but unfinished — monument.

The vaulted interior of the cathedral appears to rise to dizzying heights. The well-preserved stained glass windows give a luminous light that serves to illuminate the church's magnificent tapestries, attesting to the city's renown as a center of weaving.

Before leaving the city, look also at the Eglise St.-Etienne (Rue de l'Etamine and Rue de l'Infanterie). The stained glass of the choir section is among the most beautiful of the Renaissance.

En Route from Beauvais – Heading south toward Paris, take a detour west on D981 and D181 until you reach the town of Vernon. Nearby you'll find Giverny, the home of Impressionist painter Claude Monet from 1883 until his death in 1926. Forty years after Monet died, his home and its gardens were given to the Academy of Beaux Arts by his son, but they did not open to the public until 1980, after painstaking restoration of the grounds and structures according to Monet's many canvases of the place. Visitors can stroll through the exquisite flower-strewn French gardens and, across the road, the Oriental garden with its familiar Japanese bridge and lily pond, so often painted by Monet. The pink farmhouse and Monet's studio also can be visited. Open daily except Mondays from April to November 1 (phone: 32-51-28-21).

From Giverny, take N15 and N13 to St. Germain-en-Laye (from Paris, it's 13 miles/21 km west on N13). This former home of kings is today a favorite weekend retreat for Parisians. Its château was begun in the 12th century, but completely rebuilt in the 16th to bring it up to Renaissance standards. Two floors are occupied by the *Musée des Antiquités Nationales,* with displays of ceramics, glass, and jewelry through the time of Charlemagne (open 9 AM to 6 PM; closed Tuesdays; admission charge; phone: 34-51-53-65). The gardens and terraces are splendid, and the extensive forest surrounding the town offers all manner of recreational activities. The restaurants here include the well-regarded *Cazaudehore,* in the inn *La Forestière* (see *Best en Route*).

Continue west on N13 until you reach the château of Malmaison, bought by Napoleon as a gift to Josephine in 1799 and the place where she settled after her divorce in 1809. It's now a museum with many impressive artworks of the Napoleonic period, some of the house's original furnishings, and documents and mementos of battle tracing the era's history.

Return east on the N13 to N186. Following it south, you pass the most famous palace in all of France: Versailles, the crowning glory of Louis XIV. You will certainly want to stop here — and allow plenty of time; the palace and gardens are immense!

VERSAILLES: The building of this incredibly lavish palace nearly bankrupted the French monarchy. About 6,000 people once lived in the palace, and its vast gardens, designed by the famous royal gardener Le Nôtre in the formal French style, are spread out over 250 acres. A river was diverted to keep the 600 fountains flowing.

There is so much to see in Versailles that you might even want to spend more than 1 day here. On Sundays from May to October you can see the fountains illuminated in a splendid *Grandes Eaux Musicales* concert at 3:30 PM. On alternating Saturday evenings in July, August, and September, the *fête de nuit,* a striking sound and light show, is presented. Check with the Versailles Tourist Office (7 Rue des Reservoirs; phone: 39-50-36-22) for exact dates and times.

The highlights include the Royal Apartments, the Chapel, and the Hall of Mirrors. Don't miss the gardens and some of the smaller buildings on the grounds, including the Grand Trianon and the Petit Trianon, smaller retreats for kings, queens, and royal mistresses; and Le Hameau, Marie Antoinette's model farm, where she and her companions pretended to be peasants. Attractions include the apartments of the dauphin and the dauphine, which may be seen Tuesdays through Fridays; on Tuesdays and Fridays, there are guided tours in several languages, including English. The château is under continuous restoration, so be prepared for temporary closings of certain rooms from time to time. The château is closed on Mondays. Information is available from the Versailles Tourist Office (see above).

En Route from Versailles – Just south of Versailles via D91, you enter an area that many Frenchmen consider the prettiest countryside in the Ile-de-France — the Vallée de Chevreuse. Picturesque villages abound: Châteaufort, with its 12th-century fortress; St.-Rémy-lès-Chevreuse; St.-Lambert; Dampierre, the site of a 16th-century château; and Les Vaux de Cernay, one of the loveliest valleys in France. Just south of Les Vaux de Cernay on N306 is Rambouillet, the château that served as a rural retreat for Louis XVI and Napoleon, and still is used today by President François Mitterrand. Originally a medieval fortress, it retains its impressive 14th-century tower. You can tour the château whenever President Mitterrand is away — which is often (admission charge; phone: 34-83-00-25). From here, take N306 and then N10 straight to Chartres.

CHARTRES: Even though you may think you've seen enough cathedrals for a lifetime, Chartres remains a must. About 50 miles (80 km) southwest of Paris via D988 and N10, Chartres is without doubt the jewel of medieval cathedrals. The Portail Royal, portraying Christ in triumph, is one of the finest examples of French religious art. And Chartres is known above all for its stained glass windows. Dating mostly from the 12th and 13th centuries, with later replacements made from the original designs, they are considered the most beautiful in France, a country where exquisite stained glass has been preserved in remarkable quantity.

The city of Chartres, dotted with ancient gabled houses and charming corners, lives up to the beauty of the cathedral. Walk along the path from the cathedral to the St.-André church, for example, or, behind the bishopric, take the Tertre-St.-Nicholas (a short flight of steps) down to the river Eure with its series of bridges. As you head back toward the cathedral, wander along Rue Chantault, Rue aux Herbes, Rue de la Petite Cordonnerie, and the Place de la Poissonnerie, where curious old houses give one a sense of the medieval city come alive. The *Musée des Beaux-Arts* of Chartres (open 10 AM to 6 PM; closed Tuesdays; admission charge; right behind the cathedral; 29

Cloître Notre-Dame; phone: 37-36-41-39) houses some paintings and sculptures by the Fauvist artist Maurice Vlaminck.

En Route from Chartres – If you reached Chartres via Versailles and already have seen the sights there, you'll find little of interest on the road directly back to Paris. But if you've time for a detour east, you'll enter into the region of Fontainebleau, where there's plenty to see and do (from Chartres take D24 to N837; from Paris take N7 south).

FONTAINEBLEAU: Surrounding the fabulous Renaissance palace is a forest of 50,000 acres, the ancient hunting preserve of the Kings of France. Today, the grounds are open to the public, and picnicking, hiking, or horseback riding among the trees, ravines, and ponds makes a perfect counterpoint to a day of city sightseeing.

The palace itself was transformed from a 12th-century medieval château to a Renaissance palace by Francis I during the early 16th century. Later kings added further alterations and wings, including Napoleon, who lived here during much of his reign. Many people find Fontainebleau more beautiful than Versailles. It's open daily except Tuesdays (admission charge), and there's a guided tour through the Throne Room, the Queen's Bedroom, which was redone for Marie Antoinette, the splendid Royal Apartments with their Gobelin tapestries, the Council Room, and the Red Room, where Napoleon abdicated in 1814.

En Route from Fontainebleau – Just on the edge of the forest lies Barbizon, made famous as an artists and writers colony in the 19th century by the likes of Daumier, Troyon, Musset, and George Sand. You can visit Rousseau's house on the Grand Rue, just behind the Monument aux Morts, and you can stop for a drink at the celebrated *Bas-Bréau,* an elegant second home to many Parisians (see *Best en Route*).

Taking N5 out of Fontainebleau, you'll pass by the ruins of the ancient Abbaye-du-Lys. The next important landmark is Vaux-le-Vicomte, a 17th-century château and gardens that are among the most beautiful in Europe. The château was commissioned by Fouquet, a minister of finance under Louis XIV. Unfortunately, Fouquet's exquisite taste required greater resources than his personal fortune could accommodate, and access to state funds was all too simple. To build Vaux-le-Vicomte, Fouquet hired the greatest talents of the day: Le Vau as architect, Le Brun as decorator, Le Nôtre as landscape architect. A total of 5 years, 18,000 laborers, and the equivalent of $10 million later, the work was finished. But Fouquet had committed the fatal error of being grander in scope than his sovereign. In August 1661, he gave a fabulous dinner for Louis XIV. The decoration, the food, and the entertainment were so dazzlingly elegant that they provoked the king's jealous curiosity, and in no time Fouquet's embezzlement was exposed. A few days later, Fouquet was in prison and his property confiscated. But the magnificent château had whet the self-indulgent king's appetite, and, in the mid-17th century, Louis XIV employed the same team to build his own dream palace at Versailles, the site of his father's hunting lodge. Many of the splendidly decorated rooms of Vaux-le-Vicomte are open to the public from late March through October.

From Vaux-le-Vicomte, energetic travelers can take the A104 to the A4 to *Euro Disneyland* (exit is signposted) in Marne-La-Vallée (phone: 49-30-70-00); it is due to open in April. More than 11 million visits are expected to be made to the $4.5 billion European home of Mickey, Minnie, and Donald in the first year alone. Familiar Disney attractions include Main Street USA, Frontierland, Adventureland, Fantasyland, and Discoveryland, although there are some French additions, such as a fire-breathing dragon at Sleeping Beauty's castle and *Videopolis,* a theater which features both videos and live entertainment (it turns into a disco at night). There are themed hotels, a campground, restaurants, shops, an 18-hole golf course (a second course is planned), and *Festival Disney,* a nighttime entertainment center complete with a Wild West show. The site also can be reached by a 35-minute *RER* (regional express train) ride from Paris. There is a shuttle service from Charles de Gaulle and Orly airports (it lies between them) to carry visitors to the park's hotels.

From *Euro Disneyland,* take the A4 back to Paris.

BEST EN ROUTE

Because of their close proximity to Paris, country inns in the Ile-de-France tend to have city prices. Reservations almost always are required. Expect to pay $100 and up per night for a double room in hotels listed as expensive; $60 to $100 in those listed as moderate; and less than $60, inexpensive. The restaurants range in price from $100 and up for a dinner for two in the expensive range; $65 to $100 in the moderate range; and below $65, inexpensive. All places accept major credit cards, unless otherwise indicated.

CHANTILLY

Relais Condé – Small and bright, with a beamed ceiling and huge stone fireplace, this restaurant serves classic cuisine. Closed 2 weeks in February. Reservations advised. 42 Av. du Maréchal-Joffre (phone: 44-57-05-75). Moderate.

LYS-CHANTILLY

du Lys – A modest hostelry in a calm, beautiful park. 63 Av. Septième (phone: 44-21-26-19; fax: 44-21-28-19). Moderate.

TOUTEVOIE

Pavillon St.-Hubert – A small hotel in a relaxing setting overlooking a placid pond. Closed Janaury 15 to February 15. Av. du Toutevoie (phone: 44-57-07-04; fax: 44-57-75-42). Inexpensive.

ST.-JEAN-AUX-BOIS

La Bonne Idée – Fine inn and restaurant in a peaceful setting; 24 rooms available. Open daily. Reservations advised. Visa only accepted (phone: 44-42-84-09). Moderate.

BEAUVAIS

L'Esturgeon – Sturgeon are off the menu of this restaurant (they no longer frequent the Seine), but diners can get a good *coulibiac* of salmon, the house specialty. Closed Thursdays, August, and 1 week in February. Reservations advised. 17 miles (26 km) northwest of Paris via N190, at 6 Cours du 14-Juillet, Poissy (phone: 39-79-19-94 or 39-65-00-04). Expensive.

Mercure Beauvais – Comfortable hotel with modern facilities and an outdoor pool. 1 Av. Montaigne, ZAC Quartier St.-Lazare (phone: 44-02-03-36; fax: 44-02-12-50). Moderate.

ST.-GERMAIN-EN-LAYE

Le Forestière – This charming country inn with lovely gardens is a comfortable place for an overnight stay, but many visit simply for its *Cazaudehore* restaurant, which serves classical cuisine as well as several Basque specialties such as *pipérade* (eggs cooked with peppers, ham, and hot sausage). Closed Mondays. Reservations necessary. Most major credit cards accepted. 1 Av. Président-Kennedy (phone: 39-73-36-60; fax: 39-73-73-88). Expensive.

Pavillon Henri IV – An old-fashioned hotel with plush accommodations and a pleasant restaurant (where sauce béarnaise was invented) overlooking the gardens of the château. Restaurant open daily; reservations advised. 21 Rue Thiers (phone: 34-51-62-62). Expensive.

VÉSINET

Les Ibis – In a large park in an attractive residential area, the restaurant offers good food and a warm atmosphere. The rooms are simple but comfortable. Restaurant closed mid-July to September 1. Reservations advised. Ile du Grand Lac (phone: 39-52-17-41; fax: 30-53-20-80). Moderate.

ORGEVAL

Auberge Morainvilliurs – Formerly the *Auberge Provençale,* this attractive country inn and restuarant is set in private gardens. Closed Monday evenings and Tuesdays. Reservations unnecessary. Take N13 and D198 from St.-Germain-en-Laye (phone: 39-75-87-57). Expensive to moderate.

CHARTRES

Château d'Esclimont – Flanked by four towers and surrounded by a tranquil park, this elegant Renaissance château-hotel rates high in comfort, luxury — and expense. Most major credit cards accepted. St.-Symphoriem le Château (phone: 37-31-15-15; fax: 37-31-57-91). Expensive.

Grand Monarque – The town's fanciest hotel, it also sports a good restaurant serving nouvelle and classic cuisine and a bar. The lobby and dining room have been redecorated; 15 modern, elegant rooms have been added as well as meeting rooms and a winter garden. Restaurant open daily; reservations advised. 22 Pl. des Epars (phone: 37-21-00-72; fax: 37-36-34-18). Expensive.

La Vieille Maison – Elegant dining in an old house near the cathedral. Meals feature the freshest local produce. Closed Sunday evenings and Mondays. Reservations advised. 5 Rue au Lait (phone: 37-34-10-67). Expensive.

Boeuf Couronné – Half of the 26 spotless rooms here look over at the cathedral. There is a bar and outside terraces and a restaurant that serves local specialties with a reasonably priced menu. Open daily. Restaurant reservations unnecessary. 15 Pl. du Châtelet (phone: 37-21-11-26). Moderate.

Le Biniou – An unpretentious Breton *crêperie* that serves up everything on a pancake, using such imaginative ingredients as fried onions, scrambled eggs, and fresh cream for the savory versions and calvados and apple compote for the sweet ones. Taped and, occasionally, live music featuring the Breton bagpipes that give the restaurant its name provide the background. Closed Sundays and Mondays. Reservations unnecessary. 7 Rue Serpente (phone: 37-21-53-12). Inexpensive.

BARBIZON

Bas-Bréau – An elegant hotel that has welcomed well-heeled Parisians and celebrities since 1867. It has an intimate bar and a truly fine (it has earned one Michelin star) restaurant. A member of the Relais & Châteaux group. Closed January. Reservations necessary. Most major credit cards accepted. 22 Rue Grande (phone: 60-66-40-05). Very expensive.

EURO DISNEYLAND (MARNE-LA-VALLÉE)

Note: For hotel reservations information (in English), call 49-41-49-10 or send a fax to 49-30-71-00. Individual hotel telephone numbers were unavailable at press time.

Disneyland – This deluxe hotel, with 500 rooms and 25 suites, is reminiscent of a turn-of-the-century Victorian hostelry. There are 3 restaurants — the *California*

Grill, Inventions and *Café Français,* a bar, lounge, health club, swimming pool, and shops. Expensive.

New York – Perfect for the business traveler, this 574-room and 36-suite property was constructed to look like a cluster of Manhattan buildings — towers, row houses, and brownstones. There are several restaurants, including the *Rainbow Room* (for dinner and dancing) and the *Parkside Diner,* a huge convention center, a health club, 2 tennis courts, an indoor/outdoor pool, and a skating rink designed to resemble the one at Rockefeller Center. Expensive.

Sequoia Lodge – There are 1,011 rooms and 14 suites at this place which will open this summer. Built in a setting that resembles a national park in the US — it has 7 lodges, an indoor/outdoor swimming pool, 2 restaurants with views of a garden, a "winter room" with a fireplace, and 2 rivers. Other amenities include a health club, bar, and shop. Expensive.

Camp Davy Crockett – Four hundred-plus fully equipped units (each has a TV set and microwave oven) cater to those who crave an informal atmosphere. This campsite property has 181 hookups, a picnic table, and an indoor water park with waterslides, a river, spa, kids' pool, health club, and *Crockett's* restaurant. Moderate.

Cheyenne – More family-oriented (and lower-priced), the property will open this summer. It has 1,000 rooms (there are bunk beds for kids) scattered among 14 Wild West frontier-style buildings. There is a log fort with an observation tower, a corral, a covered wagon, and an indoor/outdoor swimming pool. The *Red Garter Saloon* features country music, and the *Chuckwagon Café* serves barbecue. There's a bar, too. Moderate.

Newport Bay Club – A touch of "down east" comes to Disney. There are 1,098 rooms and 15 suites, an indoor/outdoor pool, and 2 restaurants: the *Cape Cod* features fresh seafood, and the *Yacht Club* spotlights shellfish and clambakes. There also is a health club, a store, and several meeting rooms. Moderate.

Santa Fe – The architecture of this large property is pueblo-style. Its 1,000 rooms are spread among 42 separate buildings, reached by trails that use the flora, artifacts, and desert tones of the US southwest. *La Cantina serves* Tex-Mex fare, and if it's not hot enough, step outside and take a look at the smoldering volcano! There's an on-site drive-in movie, too. Moderate.

Normandy

Settled by successive waves of Celts, Gauls, and Britons, Normandy was the target of the Roman invasion in 56 BC. In the 9th century AD, the Vikings (north men, hence Normans) sailed from Scandinavia in their longboats — massacring, looting, burning, and taking possession of the land. Finally, in 911, the astute King Charles the Simple (whose name means "honest and straightforward" rather than "feeble-minded") and the Viking leader Rollo agreed to a truce, the terms of which granted to the "Normans on the Seine" the lands they already occupied in exchange for a permanent peace. Thus the duchy of Normandy was founded, and Rollo — later baptized Robert — was its first duke.

The erstwhile pirates proved to be adept both as farmers and as administrators in the rich and fertile valley of the Seine, and a prosperous, civilized state began to flourish within a century. The turbulent Norse blood rose one more time, however, when in 1066 William the Bastard, a direct — if left-handed — descendant of Rollo/Robert was thwarted by the Englishman Harold Godwinson in his claim to the throne of England on the death of Edward the Confessor. William enlisted the pope to his cause and, by September, was able to set sail for England with 12,000 men in almost 3,000 vessels. The English resistance was fierce, but on October 14, Harold lay dead on the battlefield near Hastings "with an arrow in his eye," and William — now no longer the Bastard but the Conqueror — was crowned King of England in Westminster Abbey on *Christmas Day*. A remarkable, graphic record of the conquest is preserved in the *Bayeux Tapestry*, on display daily at Centre Guillaume-le-Conquérant (Rue de Nesmond; phone: 31-92-05-48), across from the Bayeux Cathedral; open from 9:30 AM to 12:30 PM and from 2 to 6 PM; admission charge. Nine hundred years later, an invasion in the opposite direction was accomplished with equal success at the beaches on the coast of Calvados.

The landscape of Normandy is graced by a wealth of historic buildings that reflect the affluence and expansive generosity of the Norman people. Churches, abbeys, castles, and manor houses abound in styles that exemplify the finest of the last 10 centuries of European architecture. The materials for these buildings were delved from the land that supports them: soft, chalky stone in Rouen and the towns bordering the Seine; harder, fine-grained limestone around Caen. The simpler, half-timbered farmhouses and cottages of lower Normandy are typically constructed of whitewashed clay rammed between dark-stained lathes and topped with intricately woven thatch. In the Suisse Normande, an Alpine character is suggested by shale-covered cottages clustered against the hillsides. Sandstone and granite lend an austere effect to the time-weathered buildings of the Bocage and the Cotentin.

The seaside diversions of the Normandy coast range from the sophisticated glamour of the international resort of Deauville to the long, sandy stretches of Arromanches and Omaha (a name used only since the Allied landing of *D-Day,* June 6, 1944; the three beaches comprising Omaha were formerly called St.-Laurent, Colleville, and Vierville-sur-Mer). The hinterland offers grassy plateaus and undulating valleys threaded with freshwater streams.

The rolling green pastures of Normandy sustain horses ranging in size and temperament from spirited thoroughbreds to the massive Percheron draft-horses. Thousands of acres are given over to raising apples and flax. Most important, cows, goats, and sheep are raised for the cheese-making industry, for Normandy is the dairy of France. Norman cheeses such as camembert and pont l'Evêque are renowned the world over.

The cream of Normandy — like liquid ivory — complements the fine fish, vegetables, fruit, and game of the region, and for true Normans, of course, cider accompanies hearty dinners of regional specialties such as *tripes à la mode de Caen, pré salé* lamb from the salt marshes, or duck from Rouen. A pause is customarily taken in the middle of the Norman meal for the *trou Normand* — a quick gulp of the fiery calvados, applejack distilled from cider and aged for as long as 12 years to achieve a perfect fullness of flavor. An apple tart with cream is a memorable finish to any meal in Normandy.

Since the end of World War II, the Seine Valley and the Caen area have undergone dramatic industrial development. New industries such as motor vehicle assembly and oil refining have drawn workers away from the traditional Norman crafts of tanning and coppersmithing. The old *métiers* still survive on a reduced scale, however, and latter-day planners and developers have preserved — and often restored — the historic monuments and natural features of the landscape.

The arts have enjoyed a long and distinguished tradition in Normandy. The agonies suffered by France during the Hundred Years War inspired Olivier Basselin, a weaver from Les-Vaux-de-Vire, to write songs so spirited and timely that, although the songs themselves eventually passed from common currency, the name by which they were collectively known evolved from its original form to "vaudeville," passing out of the French language into English. Corneille, Flaubert, and Maupassant, among others, were natives of Normandy; Victor Hugo, although not a Norman, is bound inextricably to the province through his moving *Les Contemplations,* in which he mourns the tragic deaths by drowning of his daughter Léopoldine and her husband in the Norman village of Villequier in 1843. The village today is marked by a statue and a museum honoring the author. The luminous skies and delicate tints of the Norman countryside attracted the group of mid-19th-century painters who, in prefiguring the Impressionists, became known as the Barbizon School, so named after the village in the forest of Fontainebleau where they would meet. A few years later, the Impressionists — Monet, Renoir, the Englishman Sisley, and others — in turn took their inspiration from the light of Normandy. In the early 20th century, the province was a magnet for some of the finest painters of the period — Valloton, Van Dongen, and Dufy.

Only a half-day's drive from Paris, Normandy has beckoned tourists for generations, and its innkeepers and restaurateurs have maintained a tradition of comfort and hospitality at reasonable prices. The chic terrace cafés of Deauville and other coastal towns are full of Parisian weekenders and vacationers from May to September. Well-organized Syndicats d'Initiative (tourist offices) in the smaller towns will supply all the information you need to enjoy the countryside and its seasonal specialties.

You can drive to Normandy from any point in France, but since most visitors come from Paris, we'll give the quickest route from that direction: Take Autoroute A13 (Autoroute de Normandie) as far as the Chaufour exit, about 48 miles (77 km) from Paris. Then join route N13 for about 6 miles (10 km) to Pacy-sur-Eure; you're in Normandy.

PACY-SUR-EURE: Pacy is the commercial and service center both for residents and for Parisians with country homes in the area. The Gothic Church of St.-Aubin, remodeled in the 16th century, is worth a quick visit, and don't miss the well-known restaurant *Mère Corbeau* (phone: 32-36-98-49), across from the rail station.

En Route from Pacy-sur-Eure – Autoroute N13 toward Evreux takes you 22 miles (35 km) across the flat plateau of St.-André-de-l'Eure, which is strongly reminiscent of the plain of Beauce surrounding Chartres. Wheat and corn are the principal crops in this area of comfortable, conservative farmers.

About 4 miles (6 km) on the right before Evreux you'll see an air force base, built by the US after World War II and turned over to France in 1965. Signs reading Centreville (City Center) lead you off N13 and into Evreux along the Rue F.-D.-Roosevelt.

EVREUX: The religious and commercial capital of the Eure is a charming, typically Norman town too often neglected by travelers. The town has existed since Gallic times and has survived sacking and pillage by Vandals, Normans, English, and even fellow French. Evreux suffered heavy damage in the 1944 bombings, with the result that today its architecture is a medley of the very new cheek by jowl with ancient Norman half-timbered houses. Rue Chartraine, the main shopping street, is lined with elegant shops offering the products of local craftspeople. The many cafés are an important focus for business discussions and general "catching up" on market days.

If you park in the Cathedral of Notre Dame parking lot, you're in an excellent position to begin a walk at the foot of the Gallo-Roman ramparts along the Iton River, past the elegant 15th-century clock tower. The cathedral itself is a superb example of Gothic construction, with the earliest parts dating from the 12th century. English-language guides are available. In the former Bishop's House not far from the cathedral is a museum with displays of prehistoric and Gallo-Roman archaeology and artifacts of medieval Normandy.

En Route from Evreux – Taking N13 toward Lisieux leads you through the richest cultivated land south of the Seine, dotted here and there with picturesque country churches. At the intersection of N13 and D840, turn right for Neubourg, a pleasant rural town with a lively marketplace. At the market, turn left to enter D137. After about 6 miles (10 km) you come to Champ de Bataille, an imposing 17th-century mansion. A guided tour is well worth the 45 minutes, especially for art lovers, who will admire the fine paintings by Drouais, Van Loo, and Fragonard, among others, as well as sculpture by Canova, Lemoyne, and Pigalle.

Now you are in the heart of the region, the Normandy of legend. Drive carefully, keeping an eye out for the farmers who lead their herds back to the barns for milking in the late afternoon. Continue on D137 toward Brionne, once a medieval stronghold and now a living museum. From Brionne, N138 will take you on one of the most beautiful routes in France to the city of Rouen. Allow time to stop on the way, for every village is a gem. You should be prepared to spend at least a night and half a day in the picturesque and historic city of Rouen.

ROUEN: Though famous as the scene of the disgraceful trial and execution of Joan of Arc, quite independently of "the Maid," Rouen is renowned as a treasury of medieval architecture — the City of 100 Steeples. The capital of upper Normandy, Rouen has kept its ancient character, with houses dating from the 15th century still inhabited on narrow streets. The Syndicat d'Initiative (25 Pl. Cathédrale; phone: 35-71-41-77) can provide detailed tourist information in English. Be sure to see Rouen Cathedral, a fine Gothic structure built during the 11th and 12th centuries. Walk along the renowned Rue du Gros-Horloge (Street of the Great Clock), whose enormous clock is the best-known monument in the city. Two blocks away is the Place du Vieux-Marché (Old Marketplace), where Joan of Arc was burned at the stake in 1431. She is publicly commemorated at the site on the last Sunday of May.

Small shops in Rouen sell original drawings and paintings and the distinctive blue and white Rouen ceramics.

To reach the coast at Dieppe, take N27 north for 36 miles (58 km) through the Caux Plateau, a rich agricultural region.

DIEPPE: This ancient port has lost only a little of its character to the efficient modern harbor that has turned Dieppe into a large passenger port. Today the traffic through the harbor is likely to consist of fishing vessels or private boats, but in the 16th century the city was a major point of embarkation for explorers, privateers, and merchant ships.

A stroll through Old Dieppe is a little like opening a history book tracing 10 centuries of development. In the middle of the Fish Market is the ancient Place du Puits Sale

(Square of the Salty Well), a major crossroads. The Church of St. James was begun in the 13th century and has portions from the succeeding 3 centuries, and Dieppe Castle, built for the most part in the 15th century, was constructed around a much earlier tower fortification.

The beach along Maréchal Foch, at the foot of the castle, is extremely popular.

En Route from Dieppe – Travel along D75 and D79 via Fécamp toward Etretat. The road offers breathtaking views of the cliffs of the Côte d'Albâtre (Alabaster Coast). Fécamp is worth a stop for its typical Norman architecture and equally traditional ivory handicrafts. From Fécamp to Etretat, take D11, a pretty drive through the countryside, which alternates between dairy land and high cliffs.

ETRETAT: Etretat is famous for its high cliffs, which inspired many Impressionist painters, including Monet and Boudin. An 11th- and 12th-century church and a reconstructed market add charm and character to the town.

A drive via D910, N810, the Tancaxuitte Bridge, and Autoroute A1 takes you to the famous seaside resort of Deauville.

DEAUVILLE: This beautiful and elegant northern counterpart to St.-Tropez on the Riviera has all the accoutrements of a fashionable resort, complete with casino, lovely sailing harbor, and horse racing. Deauville life is marked by the activity on the boardwalk that runs the length of the beach. (Avoid the restaurants on the promenade, which are overpriced for the quality.) Hotels and restaurants here are very expensive, so travelers might prefer to spend the night at Honfleur, only 20 minutes away. Trouville is Deauville's twin city and a fishing town, where at sunset you can watch the fishermen bringing in the day's catch. An evening stroll along the harbor is lovely.

En Route from Deauville – The drive from Deauville-Trouville to Honfleur takes you along the Normandy Corniche, with breathtaking views of the sea. Take N834 through Trouville, past Touques, and into D288. At the David crossroads, bear left onto D279 for Honfleur.

HONFLEUR: Honfleur is a tiny, perfectly preserved old fishing harbor, with many monuments dating as far back as the 13th century. It was the base for the 17th-century voyages of discovery that led to the settlement of the most important French colonies, including Canada and Louisiana.

A 45-minute drive along A13 takes you to Caen.

CAEN: As the capital of lower Normandy, Caen is the region's agricultural and industrial center. Extensively damaged during World War II, Caen has been rebuilt with the traditional limestone to modern, urban plans.

Few monuments survived the 1944 shellings, but among those unscathed were the twin Abbaye aux Hommes and Abbaye aux Dames — reparation offerings of William the Conqueror and his wife, Queen Matilda. Restorations were carried out in the 17th century to replace areas damaged in the Wars of Religion.

In June 1988, the *Museum of Peace* opened in Caen (Bd. Montgomery; phone: 31-06-06-44). Its exhibits emphasize not the military victories but the sufferings of war. Open daily from 9 AM to 7 PM. Admission charge.

A "must" for gourmands is the local specialty: *tripes à la mode de Caen.*

Less than 20 minutes away on N13 lies Bayeux, another town intimately connected with William and his consort.

BAYEUX: This was the first town liberated after *D-Day.* The Gothic cathedral, built in the 11th century, is well worth a visit to see the extraordinary *Bayeux Tapestry,* at the Centre Guillaume-le-Conquérant in the Rue de Nesmond, which presents a blow-by-blow account of the decisive Battle of Hastings. (Recorded English-language tours are available daily except *Christmas.*)

To reach the historic *D-Day* shore of Arromanches, take a 15-minute drive on D156.

ARROMANCHES: "If we want to land, we must take our harbors with us." With these words, the historic decision was taken to build artificial harbors for the *D-Day* landing. Some parts of the harbor foundation built by the Allies can still be seen. The invasion museum provides an English-language commentary on the events of 1944.

En Route from Arromanches – The American Military Cemetery is about 1½ miles (3 km) beyond Colleville-sur-Mer (Omaha). A memorial fountain stands in front of the monument, surrounded by trees. The site commands an impressive view of the sea.

From the cemetery, take N13 to Cherbourg for the night.

CHERBOURG: When still a naval base, Cherbourg was an important harbor during World War II. The *War and Liberation Museum* at Fort de Roule (phone: 33-20-14-12) illustrates the progress of the war from the Allied landing on *D-Day* right up to the German capitulation in May 1945 (open 9:30 AM to noon and 2 to 5:30 PM; closed Tuesdays during winter). Admission charge. Technically speaking, Normandy ends with Cherbourg, although your visit is not complete without seeing the Monastery of Mont-St.-Michel, the romantic and beautiful peak that has been a source of dispute between Normandy and Brittany for centuries.

The drive from Cherbourg to Mont-St.-Michel — via D900, D971, and D973 — takes 2½ hours.

MONT-ST.-MICHEL: Atop soaring cliffs that rise from a flat, sandy marsh, the abbey of Mont-St.-Michel dates back to the 8th century, when it is said that the Archangel Michael appeared and commanded that a church be built on the spot. The archangel's footprint — admittedly vague in outline — is still shown to visitors. To tour the abbey, leave your car in one of the official parking lots and enter on foot through the outer gate of the ramparts. Don't miss the Lacework Staircase (Escalier de Dentelle), the superb Gothic buildings (Merveille), and the cloister, which seems suspended between sky and sea. The view from the North Tower is especially dramatic. The abbey is open from 9 AM to 6 PM daily. Admission charge.

BEST EN ROUTE

Expect to pay $130 and up per night for a double room listed as very expensive; $90 to $125 at hotels described as expensive; $60 to $90 in those listed as moderate; and less than $60, inexpensive. Note that hotels in Deauville are very expensive in July and August, often charging closer to $150 for a double room, and in any season, all along the Norman coast, a sea view can add $30 or more to a room's price. The restaurants range in price from $100 and up for a dinner for two in the expensive range; $60 to $100 in the moderate range; and less than $60, inexpensive. Prices do not include wine or tips. All hotels and restaurants accept major credit cards, unless otherwise indicated.

EVREUX

Normandy – Just off the main street, this hotel offers as a fine example of the best of Norman hospitality. A good restaurant features local specialties. Closed Sundays and in August. Reservations advised. 37 Rue E. Feray (phone: 32-33-14-40). Moderate.

ROUEN

La Couronne – With lovely old Norman decor, this is Rouen's most famous restaurant. Duck *à la rouennaise* is the famous dish here, but many regulars prefer other local classics such as *pieds de mouton* (sheep's feet) and *cassolette d'homard* (lobster casserole with fresh vegetables). Open daily. Reservations advised. 31 Pl. du Vieux-Marché (phone: 35-71-40-90). Expensive.

Pullman Albane – Part of the modern chain, but it fits astoundingly well into the old quarter, with 125 rooms with all the comforts. Rue de la Croix-de-Fer (phone: 35-98-06-98; fax: 35-89-41-46). Expensive.

Le Butte – Just 2 miles (1 km) outside of Rouen, this enchanting brick and beam country inn is decorated with traditional Norman furnishings. The inn has earned a Michelin star for its specialties such as *salade tiède d'homard frais* (warm lobster salad) and *assiette de foie gras d'oie aux trois façons* (fattened goose liver prepared three ways); chef Pierre Hervé is an expert at wedding traditional and modern cooking techniques. No guestrooms. Closed in August, *Christmas* holidays, Sundays, and Mondays. Reservations necessary. 69 Rte. Paris, Bonsecours (phone: 35-80-43-11). Expensive to moderate.

Colin's – A contemporary hotel tucked in a medieval courtyard and offering the city's most modern comforts: bar, garden court, garage, and a few steps away, one of Rouen's finest restaurants, *Bertrand Warin* (closed Sundays and Mondays; weekend reservations necessary; Visa accepted; 9 Rue de la Pie; phone: 35-89-26-69). Ask for a room with a view overlooking the city's rooftops. 15 Rue de la Pie (phone: 35-71-00-88; fax: 35-70-75-94). Moderate.

Le Manoir de Saint-Adrien – A few miles outside of Rouen, via the N15, this turn-of-the-century Anglo-Normande–style manor house with 18 rooms is located in a wooded setting overlooking the Seine. The exterior is half-timbered, and the inside is charming and cozy. Regional dishes are served. Open daily. Reservations advised. Most credit cards accepted. 6 Chemin de la Source, St.-Adrien (phone: 35-23-32-00). Moderate.

DIEPPE

Univers – A small and very popular hotel, it has 30 rooms, all furnished with beautiful antiques, and a restaurant on the premises. Be sure to make reservations well in advance. Closed mid-January to mid-February. 10 Bd. Verdun (phone: 35-84-12-55). Moderate.

DEAUVILLE

Normandy – Its half-timbered gables and balconies make this property one of Deauville's focal points. Inside it's as sumptuous as could be: huge plump pillows and soft velvet spreads adorn the beds in the 300 rooms and 20 suites. The tables and easy chairs are elegant reproductions of the Louis XVI era, and the bathrooms are spacious. Although the place has a reputation for snobbery, the staff seems pleasant enough. Open year-round. 38 Rue Jean-Mermoz (phone: 31-98-66-22; fax: 31-98-66-23). Very expensive.

Altéa – Overlooking the picturesque harbor, with 69 motel-style rooms. Reservations essential, especially in summer. Bd. Eugène-Cornuché (phone: 31-88-62-62; fax: 31-88-54-93). Expensive.

Spinnaker – With a Michelin star, this increasingly popular spot a little off the main drag is *the* place for gastronomes. Its young chef shows considerable promise. Closed Wednesdays and from mid-November to mid-December. Reservations advised. 52 Rue Mirabeau (phone: 31-88-24-40). Expensive to moderate.

Trophée – This hostelry offers modern rooms (some with balconies), a rooftop sun deck, a pleasant restaurant, and a complete range of services. In the middle of town, just a short walk from the beach. 81 Rue du Général-Leclerc (phone: 31-88-45-86; fax: 31-88-07-94). Moderate.

HONFLEUR

Ferme St.-Siméon – This half-timbered 17th-century inn (a member of the Relais & Châteaux group), overlooking the Seine estuary, was much frequented by the Impressionists. Now a modern, 19-room annex has been built, but the original 19 rooms are charming and cozy, and the kitchen turns out such well-prepared specialties as lobster stew, which won it a star from Michelin in 1990. Apéritifs are served on the terrace amid flower boxes and under colorful umbrellas. Open daily. Reservations advised. Most credit cards accepted. Rte. A.-Marais (phone: 31-89-23-61; fax: 31-89-48-48). Very expensive.

Lechat – A comfortable hotel with a restaurant in the heart of the old harbor district. 15 Pl. Ste.-Catherine (phone: 31-89-23-85). Hotel, moderate; restaurant, expensive to moderate.

Cheval Blanc – On the quai overlooking the port, this 15th-century inn has attractively refurbished rooms overlooking the water. In winter, the innovative owner offers weekend packages, including painting courses taught by Beaux Arts instructors. Visa only accepted. 2 Quai des Passagers (phone: 31-89-13-49; fax: 31-89-13-49). Expensive to moderate.

Ferme de la Grande Cour – In the middle of a beautiful orchard, this restaurant offers the best cider in the area along with a wide selection of local specialties. Closed 2 weeks during February. Reservations advised. Côte de Grâce (phone: 31-89-04-69). Moderate.

CAEN

Alcide – The place most recommended for sampling Caen's famous *tripe à la mode*, tripe simmered in calvados, the region's apple brandy, and served with boiled potatoes and a calvados chaser. Closed July and Saturdays. Reservations advised. Most credit cards accepted. Pl. Courtonne (phone: 31-93-58-29). Moderate to inexpensive.

BÉNOUVILLE

Manoir d'Hastings – Six miles (10 km) north of Caen, this restaurant is in an ivy-covered 17th-century priory with a garden. M. and Mme. Scaviner serve memorable lobsters with herbs, truffles, and foie gras in puff pastry. Closed 2 weeks in January. Reservations advised (phone: 31-44-62-43). Expensive.

BAYEUX

Lion d'Or – Particularly pleasant old Norman decor; the cuisine, which has garnered one Michelin star, is among the finest in the province. There are 30 clean, airy rooms upstairs, all with bathrooms. During the summer, half board is required. Closed mid-December to mid-January. 71 Rue St.-Jean (phone: 31-92-06-90; fax: 31-22-15-64). Moderate.

d'Argouges – An 18th-century mansion is now a simple and very comfortable hotel, a marriage of Old World charm and modern amenities. 21 Rue St.-Patrice (phone: 31-92-88-86). Moderate.

CHERBOURG

Mercure – This modern, comfortable hotel is managed by the Mercure hotel chain. Gare Maritime (phone: 33-44-01-11; fax: 33-44-51-00). Expensive to moderate.

Café du Théâtre – Excellent food served in attractive surroundings. Open daily. Most credit cards accepted. Reservations advised. Pl. du Général-de-Gaulle (phone: 33-43-01-49). Moderate to inexpensive.

MONT-ST.-MICHEL

Mère Poulard – This restaurant is famous for its huge omelettes, which are actually more like soufflés; the most dramatic version of *les omelettes à la Mère Poulard* is flambéed, for dessert. Another specialty is *agneau pré-salé* (lamb grazed in saltwater marshes) served with *flageolets* (beans). The dining room lives up to its location, with flagstone floors, a fireplace, and gleaming glassware. Open daily till

9:30 PM. Reservations necessary. Le Mont-St.-Michel (phone: 33-60-14-01; fax: 33-60-83-79). Expensive to moderate.

The Brittany Coast

The natives of France's northwestern peninsula consider their region a country apart, and with good reason. The vast, jagged coastline of Brittany resembles no other in France, and the tranquil interior, still primarily agricultural, seems to be part of another century. First inhabited by a mysterious race whose large, prehistoric megaliths can still be seen, the region was later invaded by the Gauls, the Celts, and finally the Romans. Brittany did not come under French rule until 1532, and even today, the Breton language and folklore are closer to the Celtic-based Welsh and Gaelic than to the French.

Brittany is a land of superstition sometimes verging on the mystical. It is the land that gave birth to the legend of Tristan and Iseult, to the tragic history of Peter Abelard and to the fabulous tales of Chateaubriand. But its traditions are living, as on feast days, when women still wear picturesque Breton costumes, complete with lace headresses.

The Breton peninsula reaches inland from a rocky, bay-lined coast with numerous excellent natural harbors and several stretches of treacherous rocks. The A11, a superhighway, cuts the travel time from Paris to Brittany. The route described below begins at St.-Malo and roughly follows the coast.

ST.-MALO AND DINARD: The beaches of the Emerald Coast and St.-Malo, a fortified island, city, and port dating from the 12th century, begin this route. The site is remarkable, and you'll appreciate it most from the ramparts (take the St.-Vincent gateway and then the stairway to the right). From inside the walls you can see the castle and the *St.-Malo Museum,* part of the castle structure. The tomb of the storyteller Chateaubriand lies on nearby Grand Bé Island, which can be reached only at low tide (take the Champs-Vauverts Gate out of town and cross the beach diagonally to the highway).

Across the estuary from St.-Malo is the elegant resort of Dinard, with an atmosphere of opulence topped off by the sparkling white casino (Plage de l'Ecluse). At Moulinet Point you'll have splendid panoramas of the coast. The Grande Plage is a popular beach for swimming and sunbathing.

En Route from St.-Malo and Dinard – From Dinard you can take a boat (or go by car via D766 inland for 18 miles/30 km) to the lovely old town of Dinan, boasting an impressive 14th-century castle overlooking the Rance. To see the old part of town, go along the Rue Ste.-Claire to the Rue de l'Horloge and Rue du Jerzual. (A good place for classic Breton crêpes: *Le Connétable,* 1 Rue Apport; phone: 96-39-06-74. Closed Monday evenings. Reservations unnecessary.)

The coastal road west (N786) goes to the resorts of St.-Lunaire and St.-Cast, both of which offer fine beaches and seascapes. Taking D13 to N786 and then following the coast on D16 takes you to Fort-la-Latte, a feudal castle begun in the 13th century and finished in the 14th and perched atop the cliffs like some pirate stronghold.

CAP FRÉHEL, LE VAL-ANDRÉ, ST.-BRIEUC: Just a few miles down the coast is Cap Fréhel, its spectacular red, gray, and black cliffs rising to a height of 229 feet above the sea. You can enjoy breathtaking views from the top of the lighthouse.

One of the finest sand beaches in Brittany is just along N786 at Le Val-André, and if you follow N786 to N12 you come to St.-Brieuc, the town that many Bretons consider the beginning of authentic Brittany. A short drive northwest on D6 brings you to Notre-Dame-de-la-Coeur, a lovely village noted for a serenely beautiful 15th-century chapel.

En Route from St.-Brieuc – Follow N786 along the coast for about 45 miles (72 km) to the busy resort of Perros-Guirec. Nearby are the lovely resorts of Ploumanach and Trégastel and the picturesque village of St.-Jean-du-Doigt, whose quaint name is derived from a prized relic — supposedly the finger of St. John the Baptist — which has been kept in the town church since the 15th century.

Along the coast at Carantec and St.-Pol-de-Léon (D786 to D73) and into the northwestern corner, the Coast of Legends, you'll travel windswept shores and be captivated by the typical Breton seascapes. If you find yourself in the area on the Sunday before September 8, drive inland to Le Folgoët (D788 from St.-Pol) for the annual public *pardon* ceremony. These *pardons* are the most characteristic expression of Breton religious fervor, when groups and individuals gather to do public penance, to fulfill a vow, or to seek divine favor. A colorful procession to and from the church is highlighted by the wearing of traditional Breton costumes — for women, a high lace cap of exceptional delicacy — afterward, the whole town takes part in a festival of dancing, feasting, and country games and competitions.

N788 south also will take you to modern Brest (or follow the coast via D27 to D28 and N789). This naval base also is a major urban center. There are numerous historical relics to be seen, and the arsenal and dockyards are worth a visit. A stroll along the 18th-century ramparts is especially interesting. However, it doesn't hold a candle to the smaller towns that lie farther south around the coast — in particular, delightful Locronan, once a center for the manufacture of sailcloth, now noted for well-preserved Renaissance houses built of granite and a marvelous central square (N170 to D7). If you see only one small Breton town, it should be this one. From here, D7 leads to D9 and the road to Raz Point, where deep, rocky chasms plunge down into the sea. It's a busy place, but the view is nothing short of spectacular.

A brief alternate route: If time prevents your going along the entire northwestern coast, we suggest turning inland at St.-Brieuc. Take N778 south and then follow D778 for a sample of the incredibly peaceful and generally unexplored countryside and a visit to the huge, magnificent castle at Josselin. From there you can reach the southern coast directly via N166 into Vannes. Or take D790 out of St.-Brieuc, then D3 and D15 through the Black Mountains for 84 miles (135 km) into Quimper.

QUIMPER: Thirty miles (48 km) from Raz Point via D784, 42 miles (67 km) south of Brest on N170, and 69 miles (110 km) east of Vannes (N165) is the prosperous old trading city of Quimper. In the fish market, the Breton costume often is still worn; there's a fine Gothic cathedral (Pl. St.-Corentin) with a superb organ, which can be heard on weekends, and a charming old quarter with streets such as the Rue Kéréon, the Rue du Guéodet, and the Rue du Sallé. Quimper is also a center of the manufacture of a distinctive style of blue or yellow pottery. On the fourth Sunday in July, the city hosts the colorful *Great Festival of Cornouaille.*

En Route from Quimper – Following the coast via D783 brings you to Pont-Aven, a flower-filled town with a small museum dedicated to the works of Paul Gauguin, who lived here and founded the Pont-Aven School of painting. A few miles east along D765 there's a wonderful secluded beach at Kerfany-les-Pins. A short detour north on D16 leads to Quimperlé, on the Ellé and Isole rivers. The "upper" town is centered around Notre-Dame-de-l'Assomption church (Pl. St.-Michel), and the "lower" town is grouped around the old Abbey of Ste.-Croix (Pl.

Hervo). The apse is an excellent example of Romanesque architecture, and the spooky crypt is well worth a visit.

QUIBERON PENINSULA AND BELLE-ILE: Still farther south and east along the coast, turn into D768 to reach the Quiberon Peninsula, whose myriad rocks, caves, and reefs make its stretch of surf-pounded coast one of the most exciting in the province. We suggest walking the Wild Coast (Côte Sauvage) from end to end and stopping at the Bull's Cave (Grottes du Taureau), the Window (Fenêtre), and the Old Woman (Vieille) — all well-marked sights. East and south of the coast are wide beaches and lively fishing ports, and there's a boat to take you to one of the major attractions of the southern coast: Belle-Ile.

The largest of the Breton islands, Belle-Ile is a landscape filled with picturesque whitewashed villages surrounded by farmland. You'll want to see the Apothicairerie Grotto, the Grand Lighthouse, and the boiling surf at Port-Coton. Leaving your car at the port, turn right and you'll come upon stone "needles" (Aiguilles), some of them like pyramids pierced by grottoes. At Port Donnant there's a fine sand beach between soaring cliffs; the setting is splendid but the swimming treacherous.

En Route from Belle-Ile – Regaining D768 north, turn onto D781 east into Carnac, a center for the curious prehistoric megaliths that dot Brittany, presumed to be druidic, though possibly much older. Of special interest are the Ménec Lines (Alignements de Ménec) 2 miles (3 km) outside town along D196. The Lines include more than 1,000 menhirs, as these prehistoric, upright monoliths are known. The spectacle of these stones, set in miles-long rows as straight as a single file of soldiers, is positively eerie.

Taking N781 and D28 north for 8 miles (13 km) brings you into Auray, one of the most enchanting towns in the region. There are wonderful views from Loc Promenade, and the St.-Goustan quarter is charming (access is through the 15th-century Place St.-Sauveur). From Auray, take N165 east for 10 miles (16 km) to Vannes.

VANNES AND THE GULF OF MORBIHAN: The Gulf of Morbihan is the tourist center of southern Brittany. An inland sea dotted with islands — many still privately owned — it is a place of extraordinary sunsets and the almost hallucinatory play of light on water. The best way to see this area is by boat, with excursions leaving from Vannes, Port Navalo, and Auray.

At the head of the gulf, Vannes has a picturesque old quarter enclosed by ramparts and centered around the Cathédrale St.-Pierre (Pl. Henri-IV). From the lower alley of the Promenade de la Garenne you see the most alluring corner of the city, where a stream flows at the foot of city walls built in the 13th century. Vannes makes an agreeable base for your tour of the area. Local cafés and stores can supply all your practical needs, and boat excursions start here for all other points on the gulf.

En Route from Vannes – The short boat trip to Monks' Island (Ile aux Moines) is highly recommended. You can cover the island on foot, exploring the old village where houses are nestled into winding hills overlooking the gulf.

Another stop on the boat tour is Locmariaquer, a village with some of the most important megaliths in Brittany (by car, take N165 west from Vannes and D28 and D781 south). The Great Menhir and the Merchants Table dolmen can be seen if you turn left before the cemetery as you leave town via D781. The island of Gavrinis also has an impressive collection of megaliths and is only a 15-minute boat ride from the colorful fishing village of Larmor-Baden (from Vannes, take D101 and D316).

NANTES: Leaving Vannes by N165 east, turn south at D774 for the chic, bustling resort of La Baule and the busy but unpicturesque seaport of St.-Nazaire. From there, N771 rejoins N165 to lead you into Nantes, once the capital of Brittany and today the major city on the river Loire. At Place de la Duchesse-Anne you can see the 15th-century château, with its low moat and wrought-iron cupola. The beautiful Gothic Cathédrale St.-Pierre et St.-Paul, badly burned in 1972, has been restored and is very much worth seeing (Pl. du Maréchal Foch). At Place Graslin, in the 18th-century section of the city, you can stop for a drink at *La Cigale*, a famous brasserie decked out with Art Nouveau murals and gilt woodwork. Rue Crébillon, toward Place Royale, leads you to the Passage Pommeraye, an interesting mid-19th-century shopping arcade with cast-iron railings and footbridges. And the *Fine Arts Museum* (Rue Clemenceau) is one of the best in France. Don't forget to try some of the food specialties in Nantes — the city is known for its crêpes and the muscadet wine that is bottled here. From Nantes, Paris is 237 miles (383 km) northeast via N23 and A11.

A final suggestion: Wherever possible, you should fill out the coastal routes by venturing into the interior of Brittany: towns such as Fougères, a favorite of Victor Hugo and Balzac; Vitré, 18 miles (29 km) south along N178, an enchanting Old World city; Les Rochers, Madame de Sévigné's château, 4 miles (6 km) southeast of Vitré; Lampaul-Guimiliau and St.-Thégonnec, the site of elaborately decorated Breton chapels; Tocky Questembert; Kernascléden; Le Faouet; Huelgoat; and hundreds of other towns and villages that make the Breton interior just as entrancing as the fabled coast.

BEST EN ROUTE

Expect to pay $90 and up per night for a double room in hotels listed as expensive; $65 to $90 in those listed as moderate; and under $65, inexpensive. The restaurants range from $100 and up for a dinner for two in the expensive range; $70 to $100 in the moderate range; and $70 and under, inexpensive. Prices do not include drinks, wine, or tip. Note that in summer, it is imperative to reserve hotel rooms and seatings at well-known restaurants far in advance. All hotels and restaurants accept major credit cards, unless otherwise indicated.

ST.-MALO AND DINARD

Central – The premier hotel in St.-Malo, in the Old Town, it has 46 large, attractively furnished rooms and a formal restaurant. (Restaurant closed January through mid-February; reservations advised.) 6 Grande-Rue (phone: 99-40-87-70). Expensive to moderate.

Duchesse Anne – This polished and gleaming turn-of-the-century restaurant specializes in seafood. Closed Wednesdays and in December and January. Reservations necessary. Most credit cards accepted. 5 Pl. Guy-La-Chambre (phone: 99-40-85-33). Expensive to moderate.

Elizabeth – A true gem in a town where sparkling exteriors usually conceal run-down guest quarters. 17 rooms; no restaurant. 2 Rue des Cordiers (phone: 99-56-24-98). Expensive to moderate.

Printania – A modest hotel in Dinard with a good view over St.-Malo and the Rance. Closed from November to *Easter*. 5 Av. Georges-V (phone: 99-46-13-07). Moderate to inexpensive.

DINAN

D'Avaugour – A delight of a hotel with 27 large rooms and an exceedingly good restaurant (closed Mondays in winter, 1 week in October, and 1 week in January; reservations advised). 1 Pl. Champs-Clos (phone: 96-39-07-49). Expensive.

PLEVEN (NEAR PLANCOET)

Manoir du Vaumadeuc – This sumptuous granite manor house-turned-auberge is one of Brittany's most luxurious hostelries. Closed early January to mid-March. Most credit cards accepted (phone: 96-84-46-17; fax: 96-84-40-16). Expensive.

VAL-ANDRÉ

La Cotriade – An excellent restaurant specializing in the local seafood. Closed early January to mid-February, Monday evenings, and Tuesdays. Reservations advised. Most credit cards accepted. Port de Piégu (phone: 96-72-20-26). Expensive.

PONTS-NEUFS

Lorand-Barre – Charmingly decorated in rustic Breton style, it features grilled lobster, sweetbreads in port wine, and delicious crêpes. Closed December to March, Sunday evenings, and Mondays. Reservations necessary. Eight miles (13 km) east of St.-Brieuc (phone: 96-32-78-71). Expensive.

TREBEURDEN

Ti al-Lannec – This handsome mansion now is an inn with capacious bathrooms, friendly management, very good nouvelle cuisine, and charm to spare. Closed mid-November to mid-March. Reservations advised. Allée de Mézo-guen (phone: 96-23-57-26; fax: 96-23-62-14). Expensive to moderate.

QUIMPER

Tour d'Auvergne – A modest hotel with modern facilities and a restaurant. Closed 2 weeks for *Christmas* and *New Year's;* restaurant open May to October. Reservations unnecessary. 13 Rue des Réguaires (phone: 98-95-08-70). Moderate.

PONT-AVEN

Moulin de Rosmadec – An excellent Breton restaurant set in a 15th-century stone mill amid beautiful gardens; there are 4 modern bedrooms next door. Restaurant closed Wednesdays, also Sunday evenings from October to June 1; hotel closed the last 2 weeks in October, and the month of February. Reservations advised. Most credit cards accepted. Near the bridge in the center of town (phone: 98-06-00-22). Expensive.

Taupinière – Graced by a beautiful garden and topped with a straw roof, this restaurant lacks nothing in the way of country charm. Specialties include giant crayfish grilled in the fireplace, raw tuna marinated in lime, and anglerfish served in butter and farmer's cider. Closed Monday evenings, Tuesdays, 1 week in March, and from mid-September to mid-October. Reservations necessary. Rte. de Concerneau, 1½ miles (2 km) from Pont-Aven (phone: 98-06-03-12). Expensive.

Manoir du Ménec – This hotel is situated in a gracious 15th-century stone manor northeast of Pont-Aven and has cozy individual cottages, each named for a famous painter. Also on the property are its own leisure center and 10 deluxe rooms. The restaurant, with ancient stone walls and elegant chandeliers, is in the oldest part of the manor; a heated pool, Jacuzzi, sauna, and multi-gym are in the newer section. There also are facilities for small conferences. Closed Sunday evenings and Mondays in winter. Most credit cards accepted. 29114 Bannalec (phone: 98-39-47-47; fax: 98-39-46-17). Expensive to moderate.

MOËLAN-SUR-MER

Moulins du Duc – A Relais & Châteaux establishment with a lake, swans, doves, comfortable cottage quarters, a covered swimming pool, a woodsy setting, and an inventive menu. Closed mid-January to March. Reservations advised (phone: 98-39-60-73; fax: 98-39-75-56). Expensive.

HENNEBONT

Château de Locguénolé – Elegant rooms, sumptuous food, and manicured, river-view grounds make this stately former castle one of the region's loveliest places to stay. Also a member of the Relais & Châteaux group. Closed January and Mondays from October to June 1. Off the D781 (phone: 97-76-29-04; fax: 97-76-39-47). Expensive.

QUIBERON

Sofitel – One in the ubiquitous French hotel chain, in a pleasant setting, it boasts a sparkling new saltwater spa (rated among the best in the region) and a very good restaurant. Closed January. Reservations advised (phone: 97-50-20-00; fax: 97-30-47-63). Expensive.

Ker Noyal – A lovely, well-kept, modern hotel with 100 rooms, only a short walk from the beach. Closed from November to March. Rue de St.-Clément (phone: 97-50-08-41). Moderate.

VANNES AND THE GULF OF MORBIHAN

Marébaudière – Set back from the road and quiet, it has 40 handsome rooms. 4 Rue Aristide-Briand (phone: 97-47-34-29). Moderate.

Richemont – Old-fashioned and charming, this hotel is right next door to a restaurant with an elaborate menu. Av. Favrel et Lincy (phone: 97-47-12-95). Moderate.

BELLE-ILE

Atlantique – Newly renovated, this hostelry between the port and the island's main square of Le Palais, capital of Belle-Ile, has a breezy, modern appeal. Ask for a room facing the sea. Quai de l'Acadie, Le Palais (phone: 97-31-80-11). Expensive to moderate.

PEN-LAN POINT (MUZILLAC)

de Rochevilaine – This hotel and restaurant (with one Michelin star) is housed in a beautiful old structure spectacularly set overlooking the sea. Closed January and February. Reservations advised. Three miles (5 km) from Muzillac, via the D5 (phone: 97-41-69-27; fax: 97-41-44-85). Expensive to moderate.

QUESTEMBERT

Bretagne – This old stone house wrapped in vines is a Relais & Châteaux establishment, with 6 rooms and an innovative young chef. Closed Sunday evenings and Mondays, except during July, August, and holidays. 13 Rue St.-Michel (phone: 97-26-11-12; fax: 97-26-12-37). Expensive.

NANTES

Domaine d'Orvault – Ten minutes from the center of Nantes, this luxurious Relais & Châteaux member has 30 rooms and is the logical choice for peace and quiet. Restaurant closed Mondays at lunch and February. Reservations recommended. Chemin des Marais-du-Cens, Orvault (phone: 40-76-84-02; fax: 40-76-04-21). Expensive.

Sofitel – Another in the modern chain dotting France. Ile Beaulieu, Rue Alexandre-Millerand (phone: 40-47-61-03; fax: 40-48-23-83). Expensive to moderate.

Rôtisserie de Palais – Small and unprepossessing but very popular eatery with a fairly substantial menu that changes with the market's offerings. Closed Sundays, 2 weeks in August, and a week in February. Reservations advised. 1 Pl. Aristide-Briand (phone: 40-89-20-12). Moderate.

O Cals Tell Nantais – A decidedly "unfancy" dining spot, but with superb food. Closed Sunday evenings and in August. Reservations advised. 161 Rue Hauts-Pavés (phone: 40-76-59-54). Moderate to inexpensive.

The Loire Valley

Early in the history of France, the mild climate and natural beauty of the provinces of Orléanais, Touraine, Maine, and Anjou — just southwest of Paris, slightly east of Brittany — attracted the pleasure-loving nobility. First they built feudal fortresses to protect themselves in an age of constant warfare; in more peaceful times — and as the Renaissance flowered in the valley of the Loire — watchtowers were softened with graceful Italianate spires, and windows were pierced in solid walls, the better to enjoy the terrain. Royalty raised pleasure palaces along the banks of the languorous river and its tranquil tributaries. Luxurious mansions and hunting lodges sprang up in the game-filled forests.

More than 7 centuries of architectural splendor are unfolded here, and at least five castles bring the past to life with son-et-lumière spectacles nightly in the summer. As spotlights play across façades, towers, and courtyards, voices re-create the bygone pageantry and intrigue of courtiers and their ladies.

All along the way, travelers will find pleasant wayside inns, frequently in historic residences. It's possible not only to see châteaux, but to sleep and dine in them as well. Don't try to see too many castles in 1 day: There are 120, plus 20 abbeys and 100 churches — all suffused with the royal "sweetness of life" of which court poets sang. Late spring or fall is the best time to visit, but if you must go in high (summer) season, stay off the main roads and go early everywhere to avoid buses crammed with tourists, for this is one of Europe's classic tourist circuits. Though schedules differ according to which castle you want to visit, most of them are open 7 days a week, from 10 or 11 AM, and close in the late afternoon, with a closed period in-between for lunch.

In the Loire, it is said, the purest French is spoken. The food of the region is superb and is perfectly complemented by the fresh and lively wines. The river and its tributaries are teeming with delicious freshwater fish, most of them familiar to Americans but masquerading on the menu under their French names. It may be useful to know that *alose* is shad; *brême,* bream; *brochet,* pike; *anguille,* eel; *truite,* trout; and *saumon* — well, you can guess that one. A *matelote* is a fish stew; a *friture de la Loire,* a plate of fried river fish; and a *quenelle,* a fish dumpling — usually of pike. Local chefs are fond of serving fish with a white sauce of butter whipped to a froth with a hint of shallots and vinegar (*beurre blanc*). Game is also plentiful: quail, pheasant, and partridge (*caille, faisan, perdreau*) and, of course, venison, called *chevreuil.* The lowly prune is an ingredient favored by Loire cooks. *Pruneaux* (prunes) come from *prunes* (plums), and the orchards are celebrated in the plum tarts of Anjou. The *charcuterie* of Anjou and Touraine is known for *rillons* and *rillettes* (potted and minced pork) as well as for the tripe sausages called *andouilles.*

The wide variety of local white, red, and rosé wines ideally accompany the regional cuisine. The celebrated whites of Vouvray (both still and sparkling), Sancerre, Muscadet, and Pouilly-Fumé are perfect with fish. The fragrant red wines of Bourgueil and Chinon should be sampled here, for they don't travel well. The white dessert wines of Anjou almost rival the more famous sauternes, and the champigny of Saumur is a red wine of rare quality. Don't forget the rosés of Anjou — light, dry, delicately perfumed, and wonderfully refreshing on a summer day.

ANGERS: Straddling the Maine River, this pleasant city is famous for fruit and wine and for having given rise to the Plantagenets, who became Kings of England.

High up on a hill, the moated, 17-tower Angers château gives a powerful impression of impregnable strength even in its current half-ruined state. A set of tapestries depicting the Apocalypse is the castle's main attraction. Woven in medieval Paris, the 70 pieces are over 550 feet long and more than 16 feet wide. They are magnificently displayed in a modern gallery in the former Courtyard of the King.

Other things to see in Angers include: the *Logis-Barrault Fine Arts Museum* (open daily; admission charge; 10 Rue du Musée; phone: 41-88-64-65); the Hôtel Pincé and the *Turpin de Crissé* museum (32 *bis* Rue Lenepeuu; phone: 41-88-94-27); the former Hôpital St.-Jean (4 Bd. Arago), housing ten contemporary tapestries and a small wine museum; the "Doutre" on the right bank, with lovely old houses dating from the 15th to the 18th century; Trinity Church (Rue Beaurepaire); and the impressive Cathedral of St. Maurice (Place de la Capital), which has three towers and fine stained glass. Each January the city hosts a wine fair lasting 2 weeks and, in June, an arts festival. Summer son-et-lumière performances are given at the château.

En Route from Angers – The 66 miles (106 km) between Angers and Tours offer many points of historical and scenic interest as well as several good inns for lunch, dinner, or overnight stays. To reach Saumur, follow D751 through Gennes and Cunault, with its fine church. Along the way you pass scattered dolmens and menhirs, relics of the Celts who lived here in early times.

SAUMUR: This charming town is famous for wine and for its world-renowned cavalry troupe, the Cadre Noir (exhibitions are given the last 2 weeks in July). The château, on a steep promontory, once was splendidly adorned with spires, pinnacles, gilded weathervanes, pointed dormers, and tall chimneys. It still is a majestic structure, with a particularly fascinating museum devoted to the history of the horse. From the watchtower, the view over the blue slate roofs and the Church of Notre-Dame-de-Nantilly extends to the vineyard-covered valleys of the Loire and the Thouet. This is rewarding country for antiques hunting. You should not miss a sunset over the Loire viewed from the superb restaurant of *Le Prieuré* (phone: 41-67-90-14) at nearby Chênehutte-les-Tuffeaux.

En Route from Saumur – Follow D947 along the Loire to Montsoreau, then turn south on D147 to Fontevrauld and its domed abbey. Here are the tombs of the Plantagenets (Henry II, Eleanor of Aquitaine, Richard the Lion-Hearted, Isabelle of Angoulême) and an extraordinary Romanesque kitchen with 5 immense fireplaces and 20 chimneys, unique in France. Continue east on Routes VO4, D117, D24, and N759 to Chinon, with a stop at La Devinière, the country house where Rabelais spent his childhood.

CHINON: Historic Chinon, overlooking the Vienne River, hasn't changed much since the Middle Ages. Above the town frowns the huge château, dramatically set on a high ridge. The ruins of three fortresses guarded by deep moats jut from the terrain, but only a hearth, now overgrown with ivy, recalls the great hall in which Joan of Arc recognized Charles VII. A steam train transports tourists back and forth to Richelieu, a model of classic 17th-century building.

En Route from Chinon – North on D7 about 9 miles (14 km) is the Château d'Ussé, said to have inspired Charles Perrault's fairy tale *Sleeping Beauty*. Bell turrets and towers rise delicately from flowering terraces against the rather somber background of the forest of Chinon. The chapel displays Aubusson tapestries depicting the life of Joan of Arc. Your next stop is Azay-le-Rideau; take Routes D7, then D17.

AZAY-LE-RIDEAU: The château here was constructed between 1518 and 1527 by Gilles Berthelot, treasurer under François I, and its fully furnished interior is a fascinating Renaissance museum. Bright white walls, four graceful corner turrets, and a slate roof of blue mirrored in the quiet river Indre form an enchanting backdrop for this fairy-tale castle's son-et-lumière performance.

Of interest in Azay are the Church of St. Symphorien, with its unusual façade, and the nearby Château Saché, which houses the *Balzac Museum* (open daily; admission charge; phone: 47-26-86-50).

VILLANDRY: North of Azay by about 6 miles (10 km) on Route D7, past poppy fields and rose-covered stone walls, is Villandry, "garden château of the garden of France." The famous triple-tiered gardens cover several acres and are best seen from a balustrade that runs along one side. The handsome Renaissance residence, constructed around the massive square tower of a medieval keep, was built by Jean le Breton, secretary of state to François I.

En Route from Villandry – Return to D57 and cross the Loire to Langeais, an impressive medieval fortress standing exactly as it was built. This château, where Charles VII married Anne of Brittany, was owned and occupied for many years by a millionaire who furnished it in exact detail to reflect 15th-century life.

Continue along the Loire on N152 to Tours.

TOURS: The capital of Touraine, in the heart of château country, is a major tourist center, with a charming old quarter, flowering parks and gardens, elegant shops, tree-shaded streets, and lively sidewalk cafés. No less appealing is the city's characteristically superb, refined cooking. In short, Tours offers everything the visitor needs for a taste of the good life typical of the area.

Among the special attractions of Tours are: St. Gatien Cathedral, as beautiful by night, when fully floodlit, as it is by day; the Basilica of St. Martin; St. Julien Church; and Charlemagne's tower. For a look at the balconies, stairways, and charming little courtyards of the Old Town, start with Place Plumereau's 15th-century wooden houses, then continue to the Maison de Tristan on Rue Briçonnet, then to Place des Carnes, Rue Paul-Louis Courier, Rue du Change, and the Hôtel Gouin's *Renaissance Museum* (open daily; admission charge; Rue de Commerce; phone: 47-66-22-32). Also of note are the *Musée des Beaux-Arts* (closed Tuesdays; admission charge; phone: 47-05-68-73) and the *Gemmail Museum* (closed Mondays; admission charge; phone: 47-61-01-19) on the terraces facing Pont Wilson.

LOCHES: About 25 miles (40 km) south of Tours, via N10 and N143 through the forest of Larçay, is the town of Loches. The château, once notorious as a top-security prison for the enemies of the king, is a fortified acropolis combining several buildings that are totally dissimilar in style and date from several centuries. Four thick walls supported by semicircular buttresses make up the enormous Romanesque keep — really three levels of dungeons — known as the Martelet. In these sinister premises, Louis XI and Louis XII kept such distinguished prisoners as Ludovico il Moro, Duke of Milan, whose paintings and inscriptions still can be seen on the walls. Evoking more pleasant memories are the recumbent statue of Charles VII's beautiful mistress, Agnès Sorel; Anne of Brittany's peaceful oratory; the folklore museum in the gatehouse; and the 11th-century collegiate Church of St. Ours, with two curious hollow pyramids roofing the nave. The château and dungeons are closed December and January and Wednesdays off-season. In mid-July, the town stages an old-fashioned "peasants' market," with natives in costume, artisans selling their wares, and singing and dancing in the streets.

VALENÇAY: Peacocks strut through the gardens of this romantic château, 30 miles (48 km) from Loches via D760 and D960. The castle still remains in the family of Talleyrand, who acquired it in 1803. Luxuriously furnished in Louis XVI, Regency, and First Empire styles, it has the charm of a much-lived-in home. The museum facing the château is devoted to souvenirs of Talleyrand's career and includes a reconstruction of his bedroom (open daily; admission charge; phone: 54-00-10-66). In the surrounding park, deer, flamingoes and llamas roam at liberty.

CHENONCEAUX: The château that many consider the most beautiful in the Loire lies about 34 miles (54 km) from Valençay via D956, then N76. Chenonceaux is certainly the most feminine and graceful of the castles of the Loire, and it is especially interesting because it was fashioned by and associated with some of the most fascinating and accomplished women in France. Thomas Bohier, controller of the Royal Treasury under François I, and his wife, Catherine Briçonnet, built the earlier part between 1513 and 1521. Bohier's official duties kept him away from home for long periods, and the responsibility for the design and construction fell to the capable Catherine. At Bohier's death, the château passed to the Crown in settlement of his debts. To mark the joyful occasion of his accession to the throne in 1547, Henri II presented Chenonceaux as a love token to his mistress, Diane de Poitiers, who commissioned a five-arch bridge to be built to the far bank of the Cher and planted fine gardens. When Henri died in 1559, his widow, the patient Catherine de Médici, saw her chance for revenge. Catherine forced Diane to vacate Chenonceaux in exchange for the much lesser château of Chaumont. Catherine then added her own touches, which included a magical 2-story, 197-foot gallery. Louise of Lorraine, Catherine's daughter-in-law, inherited the castle, which stood empty after her death until Madame Dupin arrived to enliven it with her famous salons. Madame Dupin's greatest fame, however, is derived from her position as grandmother of George Sand, née Aurore Dupin. The sixth mistress of Chenonceaux was the wealthy Madame Pelouze, who purchased the castle in 1864, then spent her life restoring it to its original grandeur. The property now belongs to the Menier family, chocolate manufacturers.

The château is approached by a long alley of towering trees. Two sphinxes guard the entrance, with Diane's gardens on the left, Catherine de Médici's on the right. The interior is richly furnished with tapestries, marble statues, and portraits. Allow time for a walk in the gardens and along the river for a splendid view of the castle reflected in the water below its arches in the late afternoon sun.

Within walking distance, in the village, are two good restaurants — *Hôtel du Bon Laboureur* and *Le Gâteau Breton* — (see *Best en Route*) where diners can enjoy dinner before the spectacular son-et-lumière performance, which dramatically unfolds the triumphs and defeats of the six chatelaines of Chenonceaux. Return to Tours via N76.

AMBOISE: On the left bank of the Loire, 18 miles (25 km) from Tours via N751, is Amboise. Charles VII was born here, and he died here of injuries sustained when he walked into the stone lintel of a low doorway. Charles was responsible for beautifying Amboise, importing Italian architects, sculptors, decorators, and gardeners to embellish the château. François I came to Amboise as a child and later gathered about him a court of artists and scholars. He was a patron of Leonardo da Vinci, who spent his last years here and was buried in the Gothic Chapel of St. Hubert. Clos-Lucé, the brick manor house where he lived, has an interesting exhibit of the models of his inventions. Nightly son-et-lumière performances at the château recount one of the more violent episodes in French religious history, the hanging of the Protestant conspirators of Amboise in the castle's courtyard. The château is open daily from 9 AM to 6:30 PM; admission charge (phone: 47-57-00-98).

The *Town Hall Museum* (open weekdays; no admission charge; 62 Rue de la Concorde; phone: 47-57-02-21) should be visited for its 14th-century sculpture, Aubusson tapestries, and royal autographs. The *Auberge du Mail* (see *Best en Route*) sets an excellent table.

Cross the river, take a last and best look at the château, and return via the Loire's right bank and Route N152. About 6 miles (10 km) from Tours, turn off on the Route du Vouvray through 3,000 acres of vineyards and stop for a sip of still or sparkling white wine at one of the tasting cellars along the way.

Take the quick A10 (Autoroute Aquitaine) 36 miles (58 km) east to Blois.

BLOIS: On the heights above the right bank of the Loire, the city of Blois clusters around the castle. The residence of kings, Blois is steeped in 4 centuries of history, and the castle provides a nutshell review of French architecture — a composite of the styles of several periods, from the massive simplicity of the Middle Ages to the classicism of the 17th century. The highlights are Louis XII's original brick and stone edifice; the François I wing, with its ornate, winding, exterior staircase; and the majestic western wing, a superb example of 17th-century refinement, built by Mansart for Gaston d'Orléans, the scheming brother of Louis XIII. The assassination of the Duc de Guise took place in Henri III's bedroom on the second floor, and the intrigues of Catherine de Médici are revealed by the 237 secret panels in her study. The Louis XII wing has a museum with 16th-century frescoes, furniture, paintings, and sculpture. Explore the castle's outer façades from the Place du Château; visit St. Louis Cathedral and the Old Quarter, St. Nicholas Church, and the Basilica of Notre-Dame. The former Bishop's Palace, now the Town Hall, has gardens and a terrace overlooking the hump-backed bridge across the Loire. On the terrace is a statue of Joan of Arc that is the work of the American sculptor Anna Hyatt Huntington.

CHAMBORD: Cross the river by N765, then drive upstream on D951 for 11 miles (18 km) to the largest of all the Loire châteaux. Built by François I as a pleasure palace, Chambord is set in a game reserve extending over 13,600 acres enclosed by the longest wall in France — 20 miles around. A striking feature of this extravagant 440-room hunting lodge is the roof — a bristling forest of spires, pinnacles, gables, turrets, and towers, including 365 chimneys. Behind the handsome Renaissance façade are well-maintained royal apartments. The palace has 74 stairways, including the ingenious double staircase, twin spirals constructed so that one person can ascend and another descend without meeting. Don't miss a promenade on the roof terraces, where the king's guests enjoyed a grandstand view of the progress of the royal hunts from a height of 80 feet. Take lunch or tea at the *Grand St. Michel* hotel (see *Best en Route*), next to the château. The first son-et-lumière performance was presented here in the spring of 1952, set to the music of Jean-Baptiste Lully, who composed and performed in this very château. At press time it was not certain whether the sound and light shows would continue this year. For current information, call 54-20-31-32. The château is open daily, except *Christmas* and *New Year's Day.* Winter hours: 9:30 AM to 1:45 PM and 2 to 4:45 PM; summer, until 5:45 PM (6:45 PM in August), with no midday closing. Admission charge.

CHEVERNY: Continue via D112 and D102 to Cour-Cheverny. Built in 1634 for the Counts of Cheverny, the castle now is occupied by a descendant of the original owner. Unlike the royal palaces, this less flamboyant yet handsome house has changed little over the centuries and still retains most of its original furnishings. A long avenue leads to the vast building, Louis XIII in style but already neo-classical. The splendor of the interior decoration and furniture make Cheverny a miniature Versailles, complete to a magnificently ornate king's bedroom. No monarch ever stayed at Cheverny, although the bedroom was kept in readiness in case the king should choose to exercise his right to stay. An outbuilding houses a hunting museum with 2,000 sets of antlers mounted on the walls, and the kennels are home to a pack of 70 hounds. Over 5,000 acres of forest belong to Cheverny; formal hunts are held twice a week from November to April. Non-members may join, but only the master of the hunt has the right to dispatch the quarry with a sword. *Hôtel des Trois Marchands* and the *St.-Hubert* restaurant, close to the château, are fine for lunch (see *Best en Route*). Return to Blois, about 8 miles (13 km) via N765.

CHAUMONT: This final castle to be visited is just over 10 miles (16 km) southwest of Blois on D751. A 10-minute walk up from the village along an avenue lined with venerable old cedars brings you to the château. Chaumont has much of the fortress about it — four wide towers, sentry walls, and a stern drawbridge — but ornamented windows lighten the façades, and the stonework is delicately carved. In the inner courtyard, the three façades opening onto the valley are ornamented by turreted staircases, dormers, and picturesque little bell towers. Catherine de Médici built an observatory at Chaumont, where, with her resident astrologer, she attempted to divine the future. Here, it is said, she foresaw the violent deaths of all three of her sons. At the beginning of the 19th century, Chaumont provided a haven, if not a home, for Madame de Staël when she was exiled from Paris by Napoleon.

En Route from Blois – Follow N152 east with short stops at Beaugency, known for its wine; Meung, with its tree-lined mall and pleasant riverside rambles; and historic Orléans. Each year this ancient city celebrates the victory of Joan of Arc with processions, bell ringing, and the illumination of the restored Cathédrale de St.-Croix. Few reminders of the Maid of Orléans survived World War II, but there are statues of Joan in Place du Martroi and on the porch of the Hôtel de Ville. Return to Paris, about 72 miles (116 km) via superhighway A10.

BEST EN ROUTE

Expect to pay $90 and up per night for a double room in hotels listed as expensive; $65 to $90 in those listed as moderate; and under $65 in the inexpensive ones. The restaurants range in price from $100 and up for a dinner for two in the expensive range; $70 to $100 in the moderate range; and under $70, inexpensive. All hotels and restaurants accept major credit cards, unless otherwise indicated.

ANGERS

Toussaint – This comfortable restaurant features simple and creative cooking — vegetable tart, foie gras à Layon, fresh fruit sherbets. Closed Sunday evenings and Mondays, late February, and 1 week in August. Reservations advised. Pl. Kennedy (phone: 41-87-46-20). Expensive to moderate.

Concorde – Modern convenience in the center of town, with 78 deluxe rooms and a pleasant restaurant open until 11:30 PM. Restaurant reservations advised. 18 Bd. Foch (phone: 41-87-37-20; fax: 41-87-49-54). Moderate.

Entr'acte – Popular rustic restaurant near the post office. Specialties include *coquilles St.-Jacques au champagne, saumon du Bourgueil.* Closed Saturday lunch and Sundays. Reservations advised. Most credit cards accepted. 9 Rue Louis-de-Romain (phone: 41-87-71-82). Moderate.

France – Opposite the train station and tourist office, with 61 attractive rooms. Its restaurant, *Plantagenets,* offers fine food and service (closed Saturdays; reservations advised). 8 Pl. de la Gare (phone: 41-88-49-42; fax: 41-86-76-70). Moderate.

Logis – Endowed with a Michelin star, it's known for seafood. Closed Sundays during summer, Saturday nights, and 2 weeks in July. Reservations advised. 17 Rue St.-Laud (phone: 41-87-44-15). Moderate.

Vert d'Eau – A well-known restaurant with original dishes. Specialties include *poissons de Loire beurre blanc, fricassée de poulet à l'angevine,* and *fraises Marguerite d'Anjou* in season. Closed Sunday evenings, Mondays, a week in February, and 2 weeks in August. Reservations advised. 9 Bd. G.-Dumesnil (phone: 41-48-52-86). Moderate.

SAUMUR

Le Prieuré – Gracious living and dining in an elegant Renaissance manor house — a member of the Relais & Châteaux group — in a 60-acre park. Its 35 rooms, 15 in the château itself, have period furnishings; there's a tennis court, a heated pool, riding, and golf nearby. Closed January 5 to March 5. Reserve well in advance for summer, at least 2 weeks other times of the year. Five miles (8 km) west of Saumur via D751 in Chênehutte-les-Tuffeaux (phone: 41-67-90-14; fax: 41-67-92-24). Expensive.

FONTEVRAUD-L'ABBAYE

Licorne – This small, elegant restaurant with a young, hospitable owner features Loire Valley fish with sorrel sauce, beef with tarragon sauce and homemade carrot-tinted noodles, and a scrumptious chocolate cake. In good weather, ask for a table outside. Closed Sunday nights, Mondays, and February. Reservations advised. Allée Ste.-Catherine (phone: 41-51-72-49). Expensive to moderate.

CHINON

Château de Marçay – Beautifully restored 15th-century château with 31 charming rooms, 4 suites, and a good restaurant, set in a park with terrace, pool, and a tennis court. Member of the Relais & Châteaux group. Closed from January to mid-March; restaurant closed Sunday evenings and Mondays from November to January. Reservations essential. About 4 miles (7 km) south of Chinon on Route D116 (phone: 47-93-03-47; fax: 47-93-45-33). Expensive.

La Poitevinière – A bit of home away from home in the Loire Valley, this château was purchased and renovated by Americans who fell in love with France. You can rent 1 of 5 large rooms (each with its own bath), or — for about $5,000 a week — the entire château if you like. Breakfast is included in the rates. There is no formal restaurant. Closed from the end of November through early April. No credit cards accepted. On D18 off D16, Avione (phone: 47-95-58-40; 415-922-4795 in the US; fax: 47-95-43-43; 415-928-2863 in the US). Expensive.

Gargantua – Brick and timber 15th-century mansion with 8 large, pleasant rooms and an excellent restaurant. Waiters are decked out in medieval garb twice a week. Specialties inlcude local fish and duck dishes. Closed from mid-November to April. Reservations advised. 73 Rue Voltaire (phone: 47-93-04-71). Moderate.

Giraudière – This picturesque manor house offers simple charm and 26 rooms, some with kitchenettes. No restaurant, but breakfast is served. Closed during January. Three miles (5 km) west of Chinon via the road to Bourgueil and the Savigny turnoff (phone: 47-58-40-36; fax: 47-58-46-06). Moderate.

AZAY-LE-RIDEAU

Grand Monarque – Peaceful little 29-room inn with a restaurant serving good local specialties and wines. Restaurant closed from mid-November to mid-March; hotel closed from mid-December to mid-January. Reservations necessary. Pl. de la République (phone: 47-45-40-08; fax: 47-45-46-25). Hotel, moderate; restaurant, expensive to moderate.

VILLANDRY

Cheval Rouge – A short stroll from the gardens of the château, this provincial restaurant features its own foie gras and smoked salmon, Loire fish, including *sandre* (perch-pike), and good regional wines. There also are 20 guestrooms. Restaurant serves until 9 PM. Closed Mondays, January, and February; open weekends only from November to January. Reservations advised. Most credit cards accepted (phone: 47-50-02-07). Moderate.

LANGEAIS

Hosten – Charming 14-room hostelry with an excellent restaurant. Specialties include lobster cardinal, salmon with sorrel, and crayfish vouvray. Closed Monday evenings, Tuesdays, December, January, and from June 20 to July 10. Reservations advised. 2 Rue Gambetta (phone: 47-96-82-12; fax: 47-96-56-72). Hotel, moderate; restaurant, expensive to moderate.

TOURS

Charles Barrier – This venerable chef has garnered top culinary ratings in Tours for decades and continues to merit two stars from Michelin for his refined versions of regional specialties. A prix fixe menu offers the pleasure of his elegant dining at a reasonable price. Closed Mondays, April through October, and Sunday evenings, November to March. Reservations essential. Most credit cards accepted. 101-103 Av. de la Tranchée (phone: 47-54-20-39; fax: 47-41-80-95). Very expensive to expensive.

Jean Bardet – In a grand old mansion in a park near the center of Tours, M. Bardet has quickly established his hotel/restaurant as one of the most outstanding in a region rich with luxurious hostelries. Specialties include fresh steamed salmon with soya (a soya bean purée), farm rabbit with artichokes, and oven-roasted lobster. Closed mid-February to mid-March; restaurant closed Sunday evenings and Mondays. Reservations essential. 57 Rue Groison (phone: 47-41-41-11; fax: 47-51-68-72). Very expensive to expensive.

Bordeaux – This 54-room hotel smack in the center of town, serves classic Touraine cuisine in its good, reasonably priced restaurant. Try the pike with *beurre blanc,* or the chicken in wine sauce. Open daily. Reservations advised. 3 Pl. Maréchal-Leclerc (phone: 47-05-40-32; fax: 47-64-05-72). Moderate.

Charmilles – A rustic restaurant with a lush garden that faces the Loire, its menu offerings include lobster salad and brill and turbot in béarnaise sauce. Open year-round. Reservations advised. Most credit cards accepted. 49 Quai des Maisons Blanches, St.-Cyr-sur-Loire (phone: 47-54-02-01). Moderate.

Poivrière – This restaurant, romantically situated in a 15th-century house, was recently taken over by a new chef/owner who specializes in fish dishes. Closed Saturday lunch and Sunday evenings. Reservations advised. 13 Rue du Change (phone: 47-20-85-41). Moderate.

Tuffeaux – Highly regarded, it boasts a special location near the cathedral in Tours's old quarter. Loire Valley fish are especially good here, as are puff pastry desserts. Closed Sundays, and Mondays for lunch. Reservations advised. Most credit cards accepted. 19 Rue Lavoisier (phone: 47-47-19-89). Moderate.

Royal – Modern conveniences and antique furnishings at a pleasant 32-room hotel. Bar, but no restaurant. 65 Av. Grammont (phone: 47-64-71-78; fax: 47-05-84-62). Moderate to inexpensive.

Chantepie – An intimate and comfortable hostelry with 28 rooms. No restaurant. Closed late December to early January. Most credit cards accepted. Joué les Tours, 4 miles (6 km) from Tours (phone: 47-53-06-09; fax: 47-67-89-25). Inexpensive.

CHÂTEAUX-HOTELS NEAR TOURS

Château d'Artigny – A stately château on a plateau above the Indre; it's the most luxurious hotel in the valley, in a 50-acre park with formal gardens, pool, tennis, riding, fishing, and golf nearby. The superb Touraine cuisine in the elegant restaurant is well known, and there's a 40,000-bottle cellar to choose from. Closed from November 27 to January 6. Reservations essential well ahead. About 1 mile (1.6 km) southwest by D17 from Montbazon; 7 miles (11 km) from Tours (phone: 47-26-24-24; fax: 47-65-92-79). Expensive.

Domaine de Beauvois – With 39 spacious rooms, a pool, tennis, horseback riding, fishing, and a popular dining room that serves pigeon, duck and fresh fish, as well as a hot apple tart and bourgueil and vouvray wines. Closed from January to mid-March. Reservations advised. Most credit cards accepted. Luynes, Rte. D49, about 7 miles (12 km) from Tours (phone: 47-55-50-11; fax: 47-55-59-62). Expensive.

Domaine de la Tortinière – Beautiful rooms and suites in the Belle Epoque manor house, plus a 2-story stable, and a cozy stone cottage. Peaceful, beautiful grounds, superb service, and perfect cooking, including specialties such as *saumon fumée* (smoked salmon), *meurettes d'anguilles au bourgueil* (eels in wine sauce), *filet aux truffes* (filet mignon with truffles), and oisly and montlouis wines. Open from March 1 to December 20. Reservations essential. Most credit cards accepted. One mile (1.6 km) north of Montbazon via N10 and D287 (phone: 47-26-00-19; fax: 47-65-95-70). Expensive.

VALENÇAY

Espagne – A former coaching inn with 11 lovely rooms and 6 suites. The restaurant features classic, regional specialties, including *terrine de foies de volailles aux truffes, noisettes d'agneau à l'estragon, delicieuse au chocolat;* valençay and chinon wines. Closed January and February, and Sunday evenings and Mondays in the off-season. Reservations advised. 9 Rue du Château (phone: 54-00-00-02). Expensive.

CHENONCEAUX

Bon Laboureur et Château – Pretty house covered with ivy and surrounded by a garden where meals are served in summer. The restaurant prepares pike in *beurre blanc, mousseline de brochet au coulis d'écrevisses,* and *tournedos mariné Vendôme;* try the montlouis and oisly wines. Recent additions include an outdoor pool with a bar and a grill restaurant. Open daily. Reservations advised. 6 Rue Dr.-Bretonneau (phone: 47-23-90-02; fax: 47-23-82-01). Moderate to inexpensive.

Gâteau Breton – In the heart of the village, this rustic Breton bistro offers simple home cooking and tasty pastries that are more than just good for the price. Closed Tuesdays. Reservations necessary. 16 Rue Doctor-Bretonneau (phone: 47-23-90-14). Inexpensive.

AMBOISE

Domaine des Hauts de Loire – Gracious 18th-century manor house in a 75-acre park with an 8-acre lake; 22 rooms and 6 suites in a separate but equally charming building have antique furnishings and modern bathrooms. There's a good, elegant dining room, and tennis courts to work off the damage. Closed from December to March. Reservations advised. Less than 10 miles (16 km) north of Amboise on N152, outside Onzain (phone: 54-20-72-57; fax: 54-20-77-32). Expensive.

Château de Pray – A lovely old château that has 16 guestrooms, a dining room, and a terrace for pleasant summer lunches. Linger over the salmon in sorrel sauce. Closed from mid-November to mid-February. Reservations advised. About 2 miles (3 km) northeast of Amboise via D751 (phone: 47-57-23-67). Moderate to inexpensive.

Auberge du Mail – The restaurant at this 12-room inn is considered the best in Amboise. *Confit d'oie au Vouvray,* poached salmon, *célestine de fruits de mer, filet en chevreuil,* and montlouis and chinon wines all are served. Closed Fridays from October to June 1. 32 Quai de Gaulle (phone: 47-57-60-39). Inexpensive.

BLOIS

Relais des Landes – A country inn with 20 pretty rooms and good food. Closed December. Ouchamps, about 10 miles (16 km) south of Blois by D751 and D7 (phone: 54-44-03-33; fax: 54-44-03-89). Expensive to moderate.

Novotel – Modern, air conditioned rooms, with a restaurant, a snack bar, and a pool. About 2½ miles (4 km) east of Blois by N152 at 1 Rue de L'Almardin, La Chaussée St.-Victor (phone: 54-78-33-57; fax: 54-74-25-13). Moderate.

CHAMBORD

Grand St.-Michel – This rambling place with 38 rooms provides a mesmerizing view of Chambord castle across the road. The dining room specializes in game during hunting season, but also has tasty *rillons* (spiced, cubed pork) and poached salmon and trout. The entire place shuts down from mid-November to late December. Reservations advised (phone: 54-20-31-31). Inexpensive.

COUR-CHEVERNY

St.-Hubert – A pleasant, provincial inn, it is close to the château and is known especially for its fine game (the specialty is venison). Closed Tuesday evenings, Wednesdays in off-season, and early December to mid-January. Most credit cards accepted. Rue National (phone: 54-79-96-60). Moderate to inexpensive.

Trois Marchands – Former coaching inn with sidewalk tables, 40 rooms, a courtyard, and good, fresh food. Closed mid-January to early March and Mondays from October to mid-January. Reservations advised. Pl. de l'Eglise (phone: 54-79-96-44; fax: 54-79-25-60). Moderate to inexpensive.

Bordeaux

The region of Bordeaux is known to America and most of the world by a litany of wine labels of renowned châteaux — Margaux, Mouton-Rothschild, Haut-Brion — and by famous place names such as Haut-Médoc, St.-Emilion, and Sauternes. To the French, however, Bordeaux simply means the river port itself, known for some of the finest 18th-century architecture outside of Paris as well as for a measured, contented style of living. As for the Bordelais, as the natives are called, they have been blessed beyond the measure of most people.

Until the middle of the 15th century, Bordeaux — and much of the southwest of France — was a privileged colony of the English, who for the most part let the local burghers have their way. Although the English influence waned after France's victory in the Hundred Years War, the long arm of the Parisian government did not make itself felt in any consistent way until the 18th century, when Louis XV ascended the throne. In the opinion of the king, Bordeaux's commercial and strategic importance made it necessary to assign special governors, called *intendants,* to manage affairs on the spot. It is to this era of the king's *intendants* that the city of Bordeaux owes the soberly elegant façades of its municipal buildings (the Bourse), monuments, and public buildings (the *Grand Théâtre*) as well as of the *hôtels-particuliers,* or townhouses (along the Allées Tourny).

The king often used these appointments to rid himself of overly ambitious men in his court. Such was the case of the Duc de Richelieu (1692–1788). A sometime general (he made a poor showing against Frederick II of Prussia in the Seven Years War), professional charmer, and jaded cosmopolite, Richelieu found the city of Bordeaux a maze of narrow alleyways and decrepit provincial buildings. He set out at once to change it, broadening streets into boulevards and commissioning a number of buildings, among them Bordeaux's *Grand Théâtre.* Successive *intendants* continued to reshape and refine the city's image, each trying to outdo his predecessors.

The sum of their legacy in design — beyond the monuments, the Allées Tourny, the Bourse, the Hôtel de Ville, and the numerous fine *hôtels-particuliers* — is greater than the whole of its elegant parts, for the overriding feeling in Bordeaux is one of order, calm, and refined well-being.

Though not exactly at the gate of the city, vineyards — the world's greatest for their variety and overall excellence — surround Bordeaux on all sides. A half-hour drive northwest puts you in the heart of the Médoc, with its aristocratic red wines. A 45-minute drive east is the medieval village of St.-Emilion, whose fine red wines are a fitting complement to the charms and attractions of the town itself. To the south of Bordeaux (actually in its southern suburbs) are found the reds and dry whites of Graves, while still farther south are the fine sweet wines of Sauternes and Barsac. Just a couple of miles southwest of downtown Bordeaux, in Pessac, is Château Haut-Brion, owned by a former US Ambassador to France, Douglas Dillon. This famous red wine was the only wine produced outside the Médoc to be classified in 1855.

The bounty to accompany all this drink comes from the farms, forests, and waters surrounding Bordeaux. Between the city and the Atlantic are the Landes, sandy plains, and pine barrens that stretch inland 90 miles or so, the source of excellent duck as well as of foie gras, the liver of fatted duck or goose. The ocean and the rivers provide oysters, mussels, fish, and lampreys — eels that are a local delicacy.

The well-fed Bordelais have any number of beaches at their disposal — from Biarritz, 110 miles (185 km) south, to the tip of the Médoc peninsula — along what they've rather fancifully called the Côte d'Argent. The favorite beaches are Cap Ferret, Le Porge, Carcans, and Montelivet. The last three, on the ocean side of the Médoc, are national parkland and still have many wild, undeveloped stretches.

The best road maps for the region are the *Cartes Touristiques* of the Institut Géographique National (IGN), scaled 1/100,000. For the Médoc, buy map No. 46; for St.-Emilion, No. 47; and for Graves and Sauternes, No. 55. Less detailed but very helpful are the IGN maps scaled 1/250,000. The regional map Bordeaux-Périgord (No. 110) also is good, as are the Michelin maps.

For a thorough tour of the vineyards, we recommend the late Alexis Lichine's *Guide to the Wines and Vineyards of France,* a comprehensive review of wine making throughout the country.

BORDEAUX: This city can be explored by foot, and the best place to start is at the Place de Comédie by the *Grand Théâtre,* whose location and grand scale make it the most impressive monument in the city. On the exterior balcony, 12 columns are surmounted by 12 goddesses and muses of the arts. The view from the theater along the Allées Tourny, with its broad promenade lined on either side by elegant shops and townhouses, gives a measure of the scale on which the Bordeaux *intendants* worked.

Walk along the Allées Tourny to the Place Tourny; a turn to the left will take you up Boulevard Clemenceau, where the smarter citizens of Bordeaux do much of their shopping for elegant clothes. At Place Gambetta is a small square park surrounded by cafés and pastry shops. Pause here for tea and a pastry at the fine *salon de thé* called *Darricau* (7 Pl. Gambetta; phone: 56-44-21-49); or continue through the square to Porte Dijeaux and Rue Bouffard, which leads to the Cathédrale St.-André (built from the 11th to the 15th century) and is a tiny street lined with shops selling antique porcelains, engravings, and prints, silver, furniture, and bibelots.

Rue Ste.-Catherine is a crowded pedestrian walkway and shopping artery that is impossible to avoid; it has a fine bookstore, *Librarie Mollat* (15 Rue Vital-Carles; phone: 56-56-40-40), but lacks the delights found elsewhere. More interesting are the small streets that branch off it toward the river leading to Old Bordeaux, with its tangle of shops, bistros, and galleries and an open-air market. The burgeoning restoration movement here makes this the most exciting area of the city.

The best-known (and purportedly the best) wine stores in Bordeaux are the small, discreet *Badie* (Pl. Tourny; phone: 56-52-23-72) and *La Vinotheque* (Cours du XXX Juillet; phone: 56-52-32-05). Also of note: *Bordeaux Magnum* (3 Rue Gobineau; phone: 56-48-00-06), and *L'Intendant* (2 Allées de Tourny; phone: 56-48-01-29), a striking establishment with a dramatic spiral staircase leading up along 4 flights of wine. Nor will you want to miss *Vignes et Vins de France* (4 Rue des Bahutiers), a tiny shop in Old Bordeaux. The Maison du Vin (1 Cours XXX Juillet; phone: 56-00-22-88) is Bordeaux's center for wine promotion. The bureau offers adequate maps for the wine regions of the Médoc, Graves, Sauternes, St.-Emilion, and Pomerol and has lists of which châteaux receive visitors and when.

Follow the Cour Intendance on the right side of the *Grand Théâtre* down to the quay and turn right, where you'll find the Place de la Bourse on your right. The building now houses the Chamber of Commerce of Bordeaux and is a magnificent example of 18th-century municipal architecture. The buildings that edge the quays from Place de la Bourse to St. Michael's Church are notable for the faces, called *mascarons,* carved over doorways and in walls, perhaps 200 in all and no two alike.

THE MÉDOC

You don't need to be a wine connoisseur to enjoy a tour of the Bordeaux wine country, especially of the Médoc. Of the hundreds of so-called châteaux in the Médoc, 65 were classified according to excellence in 1855, and these *grands crus classes* continue to demand top dollar today.

The special attraction of the Médoc — apart from its eminence as the source of exquisite, often expensive wine — is the incongruity of the flat, slightly undulating terrain carpeted with green vines. The landscape is dominated by the sky, and the whole vista is seen against the fantastic architecture and gentrified air of the wine châteaux. Some of these estates amount to no more than a good-size house with a surface cellar (here called a *chai*) where wine is made and stored. Others are grandiose affairs indeed, either built in a style consonant with their times, like Château Margaux (generally Empire) or Château d'Issan (17th century), or built only to express a 19th-century bourgeois conception of a château (Palmer, Lascombes, Cos d'Estournel). (Note that most châteaux are closed at lunchtime; it's always best to call ahead to arrange a visit).

In spite of its fame, the Médoc is not well marked from Bordeaux. From the center of town, follow the signs for Soulac or ask directions to the Barrière du Médoc. This will get you out of town in the right direction. About 2 miles (3 km) beyond the turnoff for the Paris Autoroute, the road branches to the right toward Pauillac. This is D2e, the vineyard road, which leads past the greatest of the Médoc châteaux.

Before heading up the vineyard road, golfing enthusiasts can detour west via D211 to the *Golf du Médoc* (Chemin de Courmateau, Louens; phone: 56-72-01-10), a course that is fast becoming known as France's most deluxe facility. Each of the 18 holes is sponsored by a different château, and bordeaux wines are served from these and other châteaux at minimum markup.

CANTENAC: About 9 miles (14 km) from the turnoff, just beyond a church on the left, is the entrance to Château Prieuré-Lichine. Park on the right side of the road opposite the archway and walk into the inner court. Once inside, on your left is a cloister decorated with antique firebacks; follow the gravel walk to the office, where you'll find an English-speaking guide to take you through the *chai.* This 16th-century *chai* is one of the oldest in the Médoc, but it has some of the newest wine making equipment. Tasting may be enjoyed for a small charge (about $5), and must be arranged with the château in advance. Wines also may be purchased. Open daily and during lunch (phone: 56-88-36-28).

Across the road from Prieuré-Lichine is the stone wall and gateway to Château d'Issan (phone: 56-44-94-45). Take a peaceful walk down a long alley of plane trees to the moated, turreted 16th-century château, which is privately owned. Visits to the *chai* can be arranged.

MARGAUX: Another three-quarters of a mile (1 km) up D2 from Cantenac will bring you to the turnoff on the right to the renowned Château Margaux. On the way you'll see signs for other prestigious châteaux, including Palmer and Lascombes. Château Margaux was rated a first growth (*cru*) in 1855 with only three others, and this privileged position is evident from the building and the grounds. The Empire château (built around 1802) has sober, classical lines and an imperial-looking stairway. The carefully laid out gardens include ponds where languid swans swim about — a present from Queen Elizabeth II. Although the château is privately owned and not generally open to visitors, a guide is available to take you through the *chai* if you write for an appointment to Château Margaux, Margaux 33460, France (phone: 56-88-70-28).

ST.-JULIEN: About 10 miles (16 km) beyond Margaux is St.-Julien. Here, Château Beychevelle is the main attraction; take a tour of the *chai* and of the impressive gardens in the rear. Appointments may be made to visit the château (phone: 56-59-23-00).

The grounds of the stately Château Ducru-Beaucaillou adjoin those of Beychevelle (phone: 56-59-05-20). Not far away is the fabled first growth, Château Latour, which actually straddles the boundary between St.-Julien and the commune of Pauillac. Today, all that remains of the ancient fortress that once stood here is the tower (phone: 56-59-00-51).

PAUILLAC: Pauillac as a wine district takes in more than just the town and includes two of the four first growths: Lafite-Rothschild and Mouton-Rothschild (elevated to first growth in 1973). Mouton "tried harder" during all its years as a second growth, but now, through the efforts of Baron Philippe de Rothschild and his late American wife Pauline, it has become the premier attraction of the Médoc and the second most popular tourist site in the southwest of France (after the shrine at Lourdes). An appointment is necessary, but worth making, to see the *Mouton Wine Museum,* the *chai,* and the cellars. The wine museum contains the Rothschilds' collection of paintings, tapestries, and art objects celebrating the cult of wine and the cultivation of the vine. This *chai* is the most impressive in the Médoc, with ten long neat rows of barrels stretching out for nearly 100 yards. On the far wall, perfectly centered and lit from behind, is the seal of Mouton carved in wood. The château is closed in August and on weekends. Call 56-59-22-22 for tour times.

Continuing up D2, Lafite-Rothschild is on your left. Its wine is said to have been the favorite of two royal mistresses, Mme. de Pompadour and Mme. du Barry. To visit the exquisite vaulted *chai,* call 56-73-18-18.

ST.-ESTEPHE: The 19th-century Château Cos d'Estournel (phone: 56-59-35-69) is the most exotic of all the Médoc châteaux, with its pagoda towers and massive carved wood doors. Although closed to the public at press time, check for current information. Also in St.-Estephe is Château Montrose (phone: 56-59-30-12) run by a mother-and-son team.

Continuing north, the flatness of the vineyards gives way to wooded slopes and fields of more conventional farm crops. A salty breeze is a reminder that this last stretch of the Gironde River is the estuary where fresh water meets the Atlantic.

ST.-EMILION AND POMEROL

The wine châteaux of St.-Emilion and Pomerol are more modest than those of the Médoc: The properties are smaller and the châteaux usually no more than houses, so there are few formalities when it comes to visiting.

The two regions border each other on the right bank of the Dordogne. To get there from the center of Bordeaux (a 45-minute drive), follow signs for Périgueux. This will put you on N89 to Libourne. At Libourne take D21e toward Montagne. Two interesting châteaux to visit in Pomerol are Vieux-Château-Certan (follow D21e past Catusseau and take the left-hand fork toward Néac) and Château l'Evangile (take the right-hand fork after Catusseau). To reach St.-Emilion from Pomerol or Libourne, take D17e or D670.

ST.-EMILION: One of the most picturesque wine villages in France, this is a medieval treasure perched on a small limestone plateau overlooking the valley of the Dordogne. In the 12th century, St.-Emilion was a stopping place for the pilgrims who wound their way on foot to the shrine of Santiago da Compostela in Spain. Pilgrims of one sort or another — for wine or for the love of old stones — have been passing through ever since.

Park your car at the Place des Créneaux and walk to the edge of the square for a view over the Dordogne Valley and the houses of the village below. At the nearby Syndicat d'Initiative (Pl. des Créneaux) you can pick up a map of the town with a list of tourist sites and wine châteaux, including visiting times.

St.-Emilion's charm is best appreciated in a leisurely amble through the town, which permits you to take in the sites as well as the peaceful, Old World feeling imparted by the narrow streets and small ocher stone houses with red tile roofs.

L'Eglise Monolithe is a 9th- to 12th-century church hewn into the side of the limestone cliff, the most important monolithic church in France. The Chapelle de la Trinité and the alleged Hermitage de St.-Emilion are part of the church.

Of less historical importance than L'Eglise Monolithe and the Chapelle, but no less compelling for their half-natural, half-manmade strangeness, are the remains of the Couvent des Cordeliers, a 14th- to 15th-century convent and cloister, now an overgrown shell of stone walls and stairways. In an interior court you can buy the locally made sparkling wine by the glass or bottle.

On the northern edge of town is Château Villemaurine. If you have time to visit only one of the almost countless châteaux in St.-Emilion, let this be it. The system of labyrinthine cellars scooped deep into the limestone is among St.-Emilion's (and even Bordeaux's) most dramatic. Philippe Giraud, the owner's son, speaks excellent English and can arrange visits for you (phone: 57-74-46-44). Closed mornings and Mondays.

BEST EN ROUTE

The city of Bordeaux offers a number of first class restaurants (the Médoc produces some of the greatest wines in the world) and hotels. The hotels we have listed as expensive will cost $95 and up for a double room per night; moderate, $60 to $95; and inexpensive, $60. In the restaurants we've mentioned, a meal for two without wine will cost $100 or more at an expensive place, $65 to $100 at a moderate one, and under $65 at an inexpensive one. Wine can cost as little as $5 a bottle or as much as you're willing to pay. All hotels and restaurants accept major credit cards, unless otherwise indicated.

BORDEAUX

Burdigala – This classic old edifice in the Mériadeck section has been transformed into an elegant four-star establishment. Its 71 rooms and 7 duplex suites offer modern comforts. 115 Rue Georges-Bonnac (phone: 56-90-16-16; fax: 56-93-15-06). Expensive.

Grand Bordeaux – A hotel since 1850 with a lovely façade that is a perfect counterpoint to the *Grand Théâtre* across the street. It was closed in mid-1990 for a complete renovation that should make it a super-deluxe 4-star property. At press time, reopening was slated for the middle of this year. 2-5 Pl. de la Comédie (phone: 56-90-93-44; fax: 56-79-25-04). Expensive.

Jean Ramet – Simple, intimate, friendly, and a favorite among the Bordelais. Open weekdays only. Reservations advised. Most credit cards accepted. Near Pl. de la Bourse, 7-8 Pl. Jean-Jaurès (phone: 56-44-12-51). Expensive.

Réserve – In the suburb of Alouette, this is the most pleasant of the Bordeaux hotels and also is blessed with an excellent restaurant, surrounded with gardens and trees. The restaurant alone is worth the trip (open daily; reservations advised). 74 Av. Bourgailh, L'Alouette Pessac, about 2 miles (3 km) southeast of the airport (phone: 56-07-13-28; fax: 56-07-13-28). Expensive.

Gambetta – Completely renovated and in the center of town. Each of the 33 rooms has a bath or shower and telephone; almost all have a television set. 66 Rue Porte-Dijeaux (phone: 56-51-21-83). Expensive to moderate.

Grand Hôtel Français – Totally renovated, this classic favorite achieves new heights of comfort and elegance. Though the grand stairway and gracious sitting rooms recall old Bordeaux, rooms are contemporary, service excellent. Buffet breakfast is provided by a well-respected local caterer. There is no restaurant. 12 Rue du Temple (phone: 56-48-10-35; fax: 56-81-76-18). Expensive to moderate.

Sainte-Catherine – Renovated deluxe accommodations in warm golden stone and wrought-iron, and including 91 spacious and comfortable rooms as well as a restaurant and piano bar. In the heart of Old Bordeaux at 27 Rue du Parlement Ste.-Catherine (phone: 56-81-95-12; fax: 56-44-50-51). Expensive to moderate.

Bistrot de Bordeaux – Tiny, attractive, and busy, this place has good fare, such as skate salad and duck filet, along with local wines. Closed Saturday afternoons. Reservations advised. Most credit cards accepted. 10 Rue des Piliers-de-Tutelle (phone: 56-01-27-96). Moderate.

La Ténarèze – An intimate little place on one of Bordeaux's loveliest public squares. Flavorful dishes of southwest France are served at both indoor and outdoor tables. Closed Sundays. Reservations advised. Most credit cards accepted. 18 Pl. du Parlement (phone: 56-44-43-29). Moderate.

Royal Médoc – A charming hotel with 45 modern, tastefully decorated rooms and a bar. 3-5 Rue de Sèze (phone: 56-81-72-42). Inexpensive.

Vieux Bordeaux – This renovated 18th-century gem has 11 clean, basic rooms. 22 Rue du Cancéra (phone: 56-48-07-27). Inexpensive.

MARGAUX

Le Relais de Margaux – In a 138-acre park, it has 28 rooms, 3 suites, tennis courts, a pool, and sauna. The restaurant is the best in the Médoc; try the dove or seafood specialties. Restaurant open daily; reservations advised. Rte. Vincent-Island (phone: 56-88-38-30). Expensive.

Savoie – Straightforward cooking and a wide variety of local wines are featured at this inn. When weather permits, dine in the garden. Closed Sundays and holidays.

Reservations advised. No credit cards accepted. Pl. la Trémoille (phone: 56-88-31-76). Moderate to inexpensive.

LAMARQUE

Relais du Médoc – A simple family-run restaurant, perhaps the best in the Médoc, serving hearty, satisfying lunches and dinners. Closed Mondays, Wednesday evenings, and the month of October. Reservations advised. Just off D2 between Margaux and St.-Julien (phone: 56-58-92-27). Moderate.

PAUILLAC

Château Cordeillan-Bages – A 17th century, elegantly renovated château complete with 18 rooms, and a restaurant noted for such specialties as *lamproie en remoulade bourgeoise* (lamprey eel in a remoulade sauce) and *noisette d'agneau de Pauillac à la citronelle* (medallions of lamb with lemon grass). Restaurant closed Mondays and Sunday nights; hotel is closed January. Reservations advised. Rte. du Château (phone: 56-59-24-24; fax: 56-59-01-89). Expensive.

Relais du Manoir – Modest as it is, this small, 8-room *relais* (a former *bordelle*) is making an honest attempt at refined and imaginative cooking. Good seafood. Closed Sunday evenings. Reservations advised. Less than a half-mile along the quay north of the center of Pauillac (phone: 56-59-05-47). Inexpensive.

GAILLAN EN MÉDOC

Château Layauga – An 18th-century château, converted into a small luxury hotel with 7 rooms decorated in Louis XV style. Its restaurant serves updated French classics prepared by chef/owner Philipe Gorand (open daily; reservations advised; major credit cards accepted). Gaillan en Médoc (phone: 56-41-26-83). Expensive.

Hôtel des Vieux Acacias – A pleasant 14-room establishment nestled among a peaceful park and gardens, and providing a perfect stopping point between the vineyards of Médoc and the Atlantic coast. Most credit cards accepted. Queyrac, Lesparre (phone: 56-59-80-63). Moderate.

ST.-EMILION

Hostellerie de Plaisance – Lovely little 12-room hotel with a cozy restaurant in the center of town. Closed January. Pl. du Clocher (phone: 57-24-72-32). Expensive to moderate.

Auberge de la Commanderie – Perched on a hill above Place du Marché, it has the look and feel of a French country house. There are 14 rooms (be sure to reserve in advance) and a very charming restaurant (closed Tuesdays). Most credit cards accepted. Rue des Cordeliers (phone: 57-24-70-19). Moderate.

Logis de la Cadène – This rustic place has 10 tables inside and another 6 outside under an arbor. Basic fare includes *entrecôtes* and omelettes. Closed Mondays and Sunday evenings. Reservations advised. Pl. Marché-au-Bois (phone: 57-24-71-40). Moderate to inexpensive.

The Dordogne

The appeal of the Dordogne is the attraction of extremes: This country of foie gras and truffles prepared with all the country cook's art is the same country whose long-hidden grottoes and secret caves have offered spectacular evidence of man's earliest organized societies — cave drawings, tools, and weapons thousands upon thousands of years old, a glimpse into the prehistory of humankind.

In southwestern France between the Massif Central and the Atlantic seaboard, the Dordogne includes the old and historic province of Périgord as well as parts of Limousin, Angoumois, and Saintonge. The entire region is endowed with luxuriant valleys, riverbanks lined with poplars and willows, vineyards, hillsides covered with walnut and fruit orchards, steep peaks crowned with medieval castles, and red-roofed fortified towns (*bastides*) perched above the half-dozen rivers that lace the terrain. Rugged granite and limestone plateaus and rocky outcroppings contrast with the fertile farmland to provide a profusion of natural beauty. The area includes the Périgord Blanc, named for the chalky limestone that imparts a whiteness to the countryside, and the Périgord Noir, which takes its name from the forests of dark oak.

To reap the fullest enjoyment from the Dordogne, equip yourself with a detailed map (Michelin No. 75 or IGN No. 47/48) and take your time. Just about every bend in the road (and there are plenty) offers a surprise to delight the eye and the imagination — a fisherman reeling in a trout; a perfect picnic spot; panoramas to photograph or paint; or cool forests inviting you to stroll where prehistoric man once hunted mammoth, bison, and deer.

Lingering over meals certainly will be a highlight of any itinerary. The Périgord's gastronomic glories are world renowned. In addition to the justly famed foie gras, *confit d'oie,* and truffles, the chefs of the Dordogne have almost infinitely subtle ways of preparing game, crayfish, trout, and other lake and river fish. Try *morilles* (morels) and *cèpes* (flap mushrooms); strawberries in season; jams and preserves from the native plums and walnuts. Among the wines to note are robust cahors; full-bodied white or red bergerac; pécharmant, a fruity red wine that goes well with game and poultry; and monbazillac, the fragrant sweet wine served as an apéritif with foie gras or with desserts.

The logical gateway to the Dordogne is Bordeaux, accessible by a 1-hour flight from Paris or an enjoyable 4-hour ride on one of Europe's fastest trains, which average speeds of 95 mph. Then it's just 145 miles (about 230 km) by car from Bordeaux to Rocamadour, the easternmost point on our itinerary. In between, however, is a good week's worth of wandering on well-maintained country roads with relatively little traffic, except in high season (July and August).

En Route from Bordeaux – For a description of Bordeaux, see the *Bordeaux* route. Leave Bordeaux by Route N89 via Libourne, an ancient stronghold founded by — and named for — Roger de Leybourne, an agent of the 13th-century King of England to whom the region belonged. Proceed along the course of the Isle River to Périgueux (about 75 miles/120 km), the capital of the Dordogne and a good place to make your headquarters for 1 or 2 nights.

PÉRIGUEUX: Once two towns separated by a wall, the lower section of Périgueux dates from the Roman era, with the remains of a 3rd-century Gallo-Roman amphitheater and the cylindrical shell of a pagan temple, the Tour de Vésone. The town was devastated in the Vandal invasion of the 4th century, and a new defensive wall was built with stones taken from the ruins. Portions of this fortification may still be seen near the Château Barrière and the Arena.

Two excellent examples of Périgord-Romanesque architecture remain from the Middle Ages: the Church of St.-Etienne-de-la-Cité (Rue de la Cité) and the Cathédrale St.-Front (Rue Taillefer). The latter, one of the largest churches in the area, also is one of the most unusual in all of France. The structure is built in the shape of a Greek cross; and the domes and cupolas show Byzantine influence. The bell tower, topped by a lantern-like structure supported by slender columns, is one of the finest Romanesque towers still standing. From the Barris Bridge, St.-Front looms huge and white above the upper town, but its impressive interior is well worth a close inspection, and the rooftop gives you a panoramic view of the town.

Browse for souvenirs and food specialties in the shops that line the square near the cathedral, then walk up Rue de la Clarté and Rue Limogeanne to the old quarter, with its fascinating late medieval and Renaissance houses, many with remarkable stairways, gates, and ornate façades. Near the cathedral *L'Oison* restaurant (31 Rue St.-Front; phone: 53-09-84-02) serves a classic fish mixed grill in the unique surroundings of an old hosiery workshop. Continue to Cours Tourny and the *Musée du Périgord* (phone: 53-53-16-42), which has a rich collection of more than 14,000 prehistoric artifacts as well as Gallo-Roman mosaics, ceramics, and bronzes. On the outskirts of town, *Marcel* (phone: 53-53-27-52) provides a seductive introduction to the gastronomic specialties of the region. *La Chocolathèque* (2 Rue Taillefer; phone: 53-53-40-48) satisfies any sweet tooth with *croquant du Périgord* or *nougatine au cognac.* Pick up additional tourist information at the Syndicat d'Initiative (1 Av. d'Aquitaine; phone: 53-53-10-63) and the Office Départemental du Tourisme (14 Rue du Président-Wilson; phone: 53-53-35-19).

A pleasant half-day excursion (via D710 and D78) can be made of a drive north through the valley of the Dronne River, taking in a visit to the Château de Bourdeilles and the town of Brantôme.

BOURDEILLES: The medieval ramparts of Bourdeilles enclose a double château built on a promontory: The first house is an imposing feudal fortress with a superb octagonal keep; the other is a 16th-century Renaissance palace with sumptuously decorated salons and a comprehensive collection of ancient furniture and tapestries. Open daily. Admission charge (phone: 53-03-73-36).

BRANTÔME: Brantôme is a delightful little town between two arms of the Dronne. Its fine 18th-century Benedictine abbey is now the Town Hall and houses the *Musée Desmoulin,* with an absorbing vignette of the town's history (open daily; admission charge; phone: 53-05-80-63). A stroll from the Renaissance Pavilion through the Monks' Garden and along the canalside quays past old houses with flowered balconies and terraces is a peaceful and reflective way to pass an hour or two. Lunch or dinner at the *Chabrol* (phone: 53-05-70-15) is highly recommended before the return to Périgueux via D939.

En Route from Périgueux – Start early in the morning heading east on N89 for Brive-la-Gaillarde. En route you will pass the partly restored, late Greek Revival Château de Rastignac. There's a striking similarity between its 18th-century semicircular Ionic peristyle and the southern portico of the White House.

South via Routes D65, 67, and 704 is Montignac and the celebrated caves of Lascaux, unfortunately closed to the public since 1963, when it was realized that the atmospheric imbalance created in the small space by the carbon dioxide exhaled by large numbers of visitors was causing bacteria to grow and gradually destroy the paintings. As a result, Lascaux was closed to the general public in 1963 and now can be visited only with special permission from local authorities (about five people a day are admitted). But in July 1983, Lascaux II, an exact replica of the most interesting sections of the original, finally was completed after 6 years of work. Artists from the Ecole des Beaux-Arts in Paris re-created the many hundreds of paintings in four chambers inch by inch, even using the same vegetable dyes and oxides that primitive man must have used. Lascaux II is open daily July and August, closed Mondays off-season. Tickets, which can be purchased only at the Montignac Tourist Office (Pl. Bertran-de-Born; phone: 53-51-82-60) during high season, include admission to Le Thot, in nearby Thonac, which offers a video presentation on prehistoric man and an exhibition on the construction and painting of Lascaux II.

Head back through Montignac to pick up D704 north and return to N89, following the course of the Vézère River to Terrasson, an active little city at the crossroads of three provinces and the scene of an important truffle and walnut market. From the ramparts of the 15th-century abbey, there's an excellent view over the slate-roofed houses down to the Vézère and the enchanting countryside dotted with poplars beyond. Continue on N89 through the Brive basin's rich plum orchards and vegetable gardens, and try to take time out at the *Château de Castel Novel* (see *Best en Route*), an old mansion in its own park with an excellent restaurant, just north of Brive at Varetz.

At Brive, turn south on N20 to Cressesac, then left on N140 for Martel and Rocamadour. At Réveillon, take D673 through the woods to the hamlet of l'Hospitalet. There's a spectacular vista over the narrow gorge of the Alzou, its rocky wall scaled by the extraordinary little fortified town of Rocamadour, the next stop. But be careful of roaming gaggles of geese along the winding country roads.

ROCAMADOUR: Rocamadour is built in superimposed tiers that literally are hewn out of the steep cliff face. Enter the town by the 13th-century Porte du Figuier near the Gendarmerie and you're on the principal thoroughfare, a narrow cobblestone street lined with souvenir shops. Continue down to the Porte Basse through a picturesque quarter of tiny houses clinging to the cliff, then return to Place de la Caretta and the Great Staircase, which pilgrims have been climbing on their knees each September since the Middle Ages. Some 141 steps up is Place Senhals, with the former clerics' quarters now converted into hotels such as the charming *Ste.-Marie,* with an attractive dining terrace. Near Place Senhals is Rue de la Mercerie, a tiny street lined with 16th-century houses. Climbing another 75 steps leads to Place St.-Amadour and the Basilica of St.-Sauveur with its crypt and chapels; Notre-Dame, with a shrine honoring an ancient miraculous Virgin and child carved out of walnut; and St.-Michel, with two fine exterior frescoes.

Less energetic travelers should take the elevator near the Porte Salmon to the château on the third level and work their way down. From the turrets of the château, built on a promontory and now the home of the caretakers of the shrines, you have an unforgettable view of the sheer drop over the gorge and the town.

From Rocamadour it's just 9 miles (15 km) to the Gouffre de Padirac, a 310-foot-deep gallery and caverns carved out of the limestone by a subterranean river. In an excursion lasting about 1½ hours, you can follow the course of the river for about ½ mile by a succession of narrow footpaths, switching to a boat that glides in and out of vast lakes and chambers and around bizarre rock formations.

En Route from Rocamadour – Route N673 twists and turns for about 13 miles (21 km) to Payrac. Turn left on N20 and head south for 2 miles (3.2 km), then pick up N673 again. At Gourdon turn north on D704 for Sarlat, stopping at the Grottoes of Cougnac. These clearly illuminated, accessible caves have prehistoric wall paintings of red ocher and black pigments that have been remarkably preserved.

SARLAT: Sarlat is a gem of a small, country town — a living museum with narrow, winding streets and ancient houses of gold-colored stone that painstaking restoration has returned to its original beauty. Don't be put off by the rather commercial, modern main street, Rue de la République. Get settled in one of the many pleasant hotels and head straight for the Syndicat d'Initiative (Pl. de la Liberté) for a walking tour map. If you happen to be there on Saturday morning, stop by the colorful street market in the same square.

The cathedral (Pl. du Peyrou) is a good central point for your explorations. Just across the way is one of Sarlat's most handsome Renaissance houses, the Maison de La Boétie, birthplace of the brilliant magistrate, author, and poet Etienne de La Boétie. Continue your visit to the Lanterne des Morts (Lantern of the Dead) behind the cathedral, the town's oldest and most curious structure; the Rue Montaigne, with a stop at the former coaching inn, now the *Galerie Montaigne,* displaying the works of local artists and craftsmen; the Présidial (the former Palais de Justice, now privately owned), with its splendid gardens, slate roof, and unusual lantern tower; Rue de la Salamandre and its rustic houses; and the Hôtel Plamon, a fascinating private home with three cathedral-like Gothic windows on the second floor. In the western part of town are steep, twisting streets such as Rue des Trois Conils, Rue du Siège, and Rue J.-J. Rousseau.

Sarlat also is the gastronomic capital of Périgord Noir, so stop by one of the inviting food shops for picnic makings or head for a restaurant such as *La Madeleine* (see *Best en Route*) to sample the foie gras that is a specialty of the town.

During the tourist season, guided tours of Sarlat are available; tours in English also are given, about once or twice a week. For more information, call 53-59-27-67. In August the town is host to a famous open-air drama festival, an antiques exhibition, numerous concerts at the cathedral, and important regional fairs.

> **En Route from Sarlat** – The day-long excursion through the Dordogne Valley between Sarlat and St.-Cyprien takes you along 40 miles (64 km) of meandering river, with great rocks towering high above and cliffs crowned with ancient castles and villages in the most romantic settings imaginable.
>
> Take D704 to Carsac; then follow D703 along the right bank of the Dordogne. The highlights include the Château de Montfort, destroyed and rebuilt four times, dominating a narrow loop of the river from its promontory; Dronne, a charming fortified town on the opposite bank with one of the more spectacular views of the valley from its ramparts and precipitous cliffside promenades; La Roque-Gageac, often called France's most beautiful village, especially when the stone houses are reflected by the late afternoon sun in the stream far below; and Beynac, clinging to another bend in the river with a château like an eagle's nest perched 800 feet above. This matchless setting overlooks another loop in the river as well as four more castles: the ruins of Beynac's great rival, feudal Castelnaud; Marqueyssac, with its lofty terraced gardens; Fayrac, the well-restored sentinel castle; and Les Milandes, once owned by the American singer and cabaret star Josephine Baker. Each has its own dramatic views and is of enough historical interest to merit a brief visit. A late lunch, dinner, or even an overnight stay at Beynac's *Bonnet* or St.-Cyprien's *L'Abbaye* is recommended (see *Best en Route*). Or you can continue to D49, then D706, and Les Eyzies-de-Tayac.

LES EYZIES-DE-TAYAC: This tiny village, hovering under a 600-foot overhanging cliff, is a prehistoric time capsule. Here, in 1868, skeletons dating from more than 30,000 years before were found in the Cro-Magnon Cave by railway workmen. Shortly thereafter, explorations of the nearby caves at Le Moustier and Madeleine uncovered other relics that are landmarks in the chronology of man. Organized tours with commentaries in French, English, and German depart from the Syndicat d'Initiative to the museum and the grottoes of Les Eyzies as well as to other important historical sites Mondays through Saturdays, June to September.

Halfway up the cliff in the center of town is the *National Museum of Prehistory,* in the former castle of the Lords of Beynac (closed Tuesdays; admission charge; phone:

53-06-97-03). There is a good view from the terrace with Dardé's larger-than-life 1930 sculpture of Cro-Magnon man. Inside are eight rooms with a fascinating collection of artifacts, art, skeletons, tools, weapons, and engravings from local excavations.

Within walking distance is the Font de Gaume cave, with over 200 red ocher paintings of animals. This art appears extraordinarily sophisticated to 20th-century eyes. Other nearby sites of interest include the troglodyte Madeleine deposit; Le Moustier; Grand Roc, with a garden of crystalline deposits; Les Combarelles, with more than 300 paintings of animals, including running mammoths; Laugerie; La Mouthe; and the Fish Cave, with a superb salmon figure.

En Route from Les Eyzies – As you head west on D706 and D703, the Vézère curves to Le Bugue, another lovely village with the excellent *Royal Vézère* hotel right on the river (see *Best en Route*); Limeuil, which clings to a hillside above the junction of the Dordogne and the Vézère, each river crossed by an arched stone bridge; and Trémolat, little changed from the Middle Ages, with a view of the sunlit valley and the loop of the river spread out below. From Trémolat to Lalinde, follow D31 along the river, then detour south on N660 for Monpazier, probably the best-preserved fortified town of the region. The great square is surrounded by covered arcades, ancient houses, and arched gateways.

Return to Beaumont and Lalinde, then proceed west on N660 to Bergerac, at the western edge of the Dordogne. This is an active, pleasant little town brimming with flowers. Its old quarter is a maze of twisting streets and Renaissance porches and façades. The elegant silhouette of the Château de Monbazillac dominates a nearby hill, and a tour of its massive round towers and battlements can also include a tasting of the products of the local wine cooperative, which now owns the château. A statue of Edmond Rostand's immortal Cyrano de Bergerac stands at Place de la Myrpe. From Bergerac, it's only about 57 miles (92 km) back to Bordeaux along Route 936, past tobacco fields and vineyards on the rich alluvial plain.

BEST EN ROUTE

Expect to pay $90 and up per night for a double room in hotels listed as expensive; $60 to $90 in those listed as moderate; and less than $60 for an inexpensive one. The restaurants range in price from $100 and up for a dinner for two in the expensive range; $70 to $100 in the moderate range; and under $70, inexpensive. Prices do not include drinks, wine, or tip. All hotels and restaurants accept major credit cards, unless otherwise indicated.

PÉRIGUEUX

Oison – Unusual setting in an old hosiery workshop; the fish mixed grill is especially good. Closed Sunday evenings and Mondays. 31 Rue St.-Front (phone: 53-09-84-02). Expensive.

Périgord – This member of the Logis de France association features 21 rooms, all with private bath, and a reasonably priced restaurant (closed Saturdays and Sunday evenings). Most credit cards accepted. 74 Rue Victor-Hugo (phone: 53-53-33-63). Inexpensive.

BRANTÔME

Moulin de l'Abbaye – A former mill on a gentle bend in the Dronne River, this is one of the most delightful inns in the region. It has 12 elegantly furnished rooms, a wonderful dining room (Chef Rabinel apprenticed with the Troisgros brothers), and a lovely riverside terrace. Closed Mondays and late October to early May. Rte. de Bourdeilles (phone: 53-05-80-22; fax: 53-05-75-27). Expensive.

Moulin du Roc – Another old mill that's now a friendly inn with 12 rooms. Its fine restaurant makes it worth a stop just for a meal (closed Tuesdays and Wednesday mornings). Four miles (6 km) northeast of Brantôme via D78, in Champagnac-de-Belair (phone: 53-54-80-36). Expensive.

Chabrol – Refined and comfortable and overlooking the Dronne. The 20 rooms are small but charmingly decorated, and the restaurant serves good regional dishes. Open daily. Reservations advised. Rue Gambetta (phone: 53-05-70-15). Hotel, moderate; restaurant, expensive to moderate.

VARETZ

Château de Castel Novel – Old mansion in its own park with pool and tennis. A member of the Relais & Châteaux group, it has 28 rooms and an exceptionally fine restaurant serving inventive regional dishes and cahors and bergerac wines. Open early May to late October. Reservations necessary in tourist season. Near Varetz, about 7 miles (11 km) northwest of Brive-la-Gaillarde on N901 (phone: 55-85-00-01; fax: 55-85-09-03). Expensive.

ROCAMADOUR

Château de Roumégouse – With 12 rooms and 2 suites in a wooded park with terraces overlooking Le Causse. Member of the Relais & Châteaux group. Riding and tennis nearby; pleasant restaurant (closed Tuesdays). Between Rocamadour and Gramat off N140 (phone: 65-33-63-81; fax: 65-33-71-18). Expensive.

Beau Site et Notre-Dame – In a restored 15th-century house with all modern comforts, 55 rooms, and a restaurant with a terrace that offers a beautiful view (closed mid-November to April). Rue Roland-le-Preux (phone: 65-33-63-08). Moderate.

Ste.-Marie – Small hotel with 22 comfortable rooms and a lovely, flower-lined terrace restaurant overlooking the Alzou Canyon. Closed November to April. Most credit cards accepted. Pl. des Senhals (phone: 65-33-63-07). Moderate.

SARLAT

Hostellerie de Meysset – Charming, ivy-covered manor house with 20 rooms, 6 suites, and a very agreeable restaurant. Closed October through April. One mile (1.6 km) northwest from town on Rte. de Eyzies (phone: 53-59-08-29). Expensive.

Hoirie – In a garden just outside town, this former hunting lodge now is a cozy, 15-room inn with lots of local atmosphere and a swimming pool. Closed mid-November to mid-March. 1½ miles (2 km) south of town at La Canéda (phone: 53-59-05-62; fax: 53-31-13-90). Moderate.

Madeleine – Restored, distinguished traditional hostelry; 19 well-kept rooms, 3 suites, and an excellent restaurant with hearty regional food. In high season, guests are required to take breakfast and dinner at the hotel. Closed November to mid-March. Most credit cards accepted. 1 Pl. Petite-Rigaudie (phone: 53-59-10-41; fax: 53-31-03-62). Moderate.

La Couleuvrine – Actually a restored 12th-century structure, it has 25 rooms with antique furnishings but all the modern amenities. Closed November 15 to December and January 10 to February. 1 Pl. de la Bouquerie (phone: 53-59-27-80). Inexpensive.

BEYNAC

Bonnet – Delightful small inn nestled in a grove of walnut trees on the banks of the Dordogne, with a wonderful view up to the castle of Beynac. There are 24 rooms, a pleasant staff, and a very popular restaurant. Closed from mid-October to mid-April. Most credit cards accepted (phone: 53-29-50-01). Moderate.

ST.-CYPRIEN

Abbaye – Small hostelry of 20 rooms, most with views down to the Dordogne River and an excellent restaurant. Open from mid-March to mid-October; closed Wednesdays in September. Rue Entrepot (phone: 53-29-20-48). Moderate.

LES EYZIES-DE-TAYAC

Le Centenaire – A sparkling 28-room hotel — more modern than the *Cro-Magnon* but equally worthy of praise — with a pool, a sauna, and a gym. Chef Roland Mazère, who apprenticed with a few of the country's best, takes an up-to-date approach to cooking that's won him two Michelin stars. Closed November to April. Most credit cards accepted. Les Eyzies (phone: 53-06-97-18; fax: 53-06-92-41). Expensive.

Cro-Magnon – Said to be where Cro-Magnon skeletons were found over 115 years ago, this delightful, vine-covered inn provides modern luxury and efficiency without forfeiting charm. There are 20 rooms, a swimming pool, extensive grounds, and a very good restaurant for classic traditional fare and some surprises. Closed mid-October to April. Rte. de Périgueux (phone: 53-06-97-06). Hotel, moderate; restaurant, expensive to moderate.

LE BUGUE

Royal Vézère – Comfortable and modern, this 48-room hotel sits on the bank of the Vézère with rooftop pool, sunny terrace, and a nightclub. Small, exclusive restaurant with well-prepared regional specialties. Open late April to early October. Pl. Hôtel-de-Ville (phone: 53-07-20-01). Expensive.

TRÉMOLAT

Le Vieux Logis – The epitome of rustic charm in an old house with antique furniture and lovely gardens. There are 20 rooms and a good restaurant, and nearby tennis, sailing, fishing, hunting, and horseback riding. Member of the Relais & Châteaux group. Closed mid-November to mid-December and mid-January to mid-February (phone: 53-22-80-06; fax: 53-22-84-89). Expensive.

BERGERAC

Château Rauly-Saulieut – This lovely 19th-century château amid vines, south of Monbazillac, now is a hotel/restaurant. Its 8 spacious rooms are exquisitely furnished with antiques belonging to the owner, who is also an antiques dealer. More of his items are on sale in a shop at the château. There also are gardens, a pool, a cozy restaurant, and conference rooms. Most credit cards accepted. Monbazillac (phone: 53-63-35-31). Expensive.

Le Cyrano – This unpretentious little restaurant serves the classics of the region. There are also 11 rooms, each with private bath. Restaurant closed Sunday evenings and Mondays, and June 26 to July 19. 2 Bd. Montaigne (phone: 53-57-02-76). Moderate.

Bordeaux – Modest, but with 42 adequate rooms and a restaurant. 38 Pl. Gambetta (phone: 53-57-12-83). Moderate to inexpensive.

Provence

As the French who flock here every summer know, one of the most charming regions in the country is Provence, the area along the southern banks of the

Rhône River, just north and west of the Riviera. Like the Riviera, Provence is known for its cloudless skies and brilliant southern sunshine. It also is known for its pretty little villages perched high up in the hills or nestled down in the valleys, with their typical red roofs and, in many cases, medieval stone walls intact. Small farms are plentiful here; typical crops are fruits and vegetables. Grapes are cultivated, and thyme, marjoram, and lavender grow wild. Olive groves are everywhere, and rows of tall cypress trees are planted to protect crops from the *mistral*, the powerful north wind of southern France.

The name "Provence" is derived from the historic fact that the region once was a Roman province; yet its history begins earlier, with the founding of Marseilles by the Greeks in 600 BC. The Romans invaded in about 125 BC and scattered traces of their stay everywhere. As a result, Provence is the section of France most renowned for its magnificently preserved Roman temples, arches, and amphitheaters. Its star attraction is the amazing 2,000-year-old, 3-tier Pont du Gard, between Nîmes and Arles, a Roman aqueduct that stands virtually intact.

In addition to Roman remains, Provence is dominated by Avignon, once the papal residence, with its impressive 14th-century Palais des Papes (Papal Palace), a vast stone fortress built during the schism within the papacy known to history as the Babylonian Captivity. The Pont d'Avignon, a bridge made famous in a French children's song, actually is called the Pont St.-Bénézet, and though partly destroyed, it still stretches picturesquely halfway across the Rhône. There's a fascinating side trip from Arles to the strange, marshy land of the Camargue, where bulls are raised for bullfights and wild horses, ducks, and flamingos roam free. At the eastern extreme of the route is Aix-en-Provence, which, except for its festival in July and August, is a quiet old university town adorned with boulevards, fountains, and cafés. Paul Cézanne lived here, and it's one of the loveliest towns in all of France.

Provençal cooking shows the Italian influence in its typical ingredients of garlic, tomatoes, and olive oil. The region produces the outstanding côtes du Rhône wines such as Châteauneuf-du-Pape, tavel, and rasteau.

Avignon, the starting point of the route described below, is a 7-hour drive from Paris along Routes A6 or N7; if you prefer, you can choose the more scenic itinerary along the Loire Valley and through Burgundy. The best maps of the region are the *Institut Géographique National's IGN* No. 115 or *Michelin* Nos. 83, 80, 81.

Note: Both Aix-en-Provence and Avignon host 3-week arts festivals in mid-July; both, but especially the one in Aix, are very popular, so make hotel reservations well in advance.

AVIGNON: The walled city of Avignon was the ancient seat of the papacy during the church's period of schism in the 14th century. Park near the train station (Bd. St.-Roch) and enter the city through the Porte de la République. As you walk straight along the tree-lined Rue de la République, you'll come to the Place de l'Horloge, a good spot to pause at an outdoor café and take in some of the local color. From here it's only a few steps to the Place du Palais, which is dominated by the immense, fortress-like stone walls of the medieval papal residence. Informative English-language tours are given twice daily through the vast interior halls of this historic palace. Admission charge.

Coming back out onto the Place du Palais, you'll see a toylike train. Take it. It will carry you up to the Rocher des Doms, a lovely park with a superb view of the Rhône River and its 12th-century bridge, Pont St.-Bénézet. For a better feeling of daily life in Avignon, wander into the pedestrian zone off Place de l'Horloge, browsing, for example, in Rue des Marchands and Rue des Fourbisseurs, then following Rue du Roi-René to the picturesque Rue des Teinturiers, beside a canal and old waterwheels. Avignon boasts elegant shopping, particularly for fine (but not cheap) regional antiques. Turn left anywhere off Rue de la République and you'll find many shops. Finally, cross the river to Villeneuve-les-Avignon. It is from this ancient city of cardinals, with Philippe le Bel's tower and the St.-André fort, that you'll get a spectacular view of Avignon at sunset.

En Route from Avignon – Take Route N100 directly west for 15 miles (24 km) to the Pont-du-Gard. This superb Roman aqueduct, some 2,000 years old, is almost completely intact. Standing 3 tiers high, it is a startling example of Roman engineering.

Doubling back a bit, you can follow N86 for 14 miles (about 22 km) directly into Nîmes, one of the major Roman cities of Provence, dating from the time of Emperor Augustus. Of principal interest are the Roman amphitheater (Pl. des Arènes — still used for bullfights) and Roman temple, the Maison Carrée (Bd. A.-Daudet just beyond Pl. Antonin). For a change of atmosphere, follow the Quai de la Fontaine along the canal to the 18th-century Jardins de la Fontaine. Here are the Temple de Diane and the Tour Magne, a Roman monument built about the end of the 1st century. The gardens offer a good look at the surrounding countryside and in summer are the setting for open-air art exhibitions.

Eleven miles (about 17 km) from Nîmes, via D42, is St.-Gilles, a good coffee stop. This typical Provençal town is known for the superb façade of its church (Pl. de la République), sculpted between 1180 and 1240.

Taking N572 east and N570 north brings you to Tarascon. The medieval château here is exceptionally well preserved, and its terraces, with a splendid view over the Rhône, make it one of the most beautiful feudal structures in France.

From here, taking N99 east, you are only 9 miles (14 km) from St.-Rémy-de-Provence, a lovely town with an active weekend open-air market and plenty of tree-shaded streets.

LES ANTIQUES and LES BAUX: Only half a mile from St.-Rémy, south along Route D5, is Les Antiques, yet another admirably preserved Roman site with a mausoleum — one of the finest Roman structures of its kind to be found today — a municipal arch, and the ruins of Glanum, a thriving city founded 6 centuries before Christ.

Five miles (8 km) farther down D5 is Les-Baux-de-Provence. In the Alpilles Mountains, this village presents an austere and almost lunar landscape of limestone hills. The view from the ancient fortress is breathtaking during the day and quite eerie at night. Understandably, Les Baux's unique beauty is no secret, and nestled into its haunting hills are some of the most fashionable and expensive restaurants and hotels in France. (One such is the Michelin two-star *Oustaù de Baumanière,* where you should try the red mullet mousse or the sweetbreads; see *Best en Route.*)

Taking D17 west for 11 miles (18 km) brings you to Arles, the next stop.

ARLES: Founded by the Greeks who settled Marseilles, Arles was a major capital during the Roman period, an important religious center during the Middle Ages, and today preserves its past in magnificent architectural ruins and relics. Of special interest are the amphitheater (Rond-Point des Arènes), the "sister" of the one at Nîmes, and the remains of a Roman theater, erected toward the end of the 1st century BC (leaving the amphitheater, take the tiny street right before Rue Porte-de-Laure to reach the theater). At the Place de la République is the Hôtel de Ville (Town Hall); the *Musée d'Art Paien,* containing antique statues, sarcophagi, and mosaics; and the Church of St. Trophime, founded in the reign of Charlemagne, with a magnificent portal and cloisters. Just to the right of the intersection of Rue du Président-Wilson and Rue de la République is the splendid *Musée d'Art Chrétien* (Museum of Christian Art). From its interior, you can descend into a subterranean gallery dating from the 1st century BC. Finally, visit Les Alyscamps (Av. des Alyscamps and Craponne Canal), which was used as a cemetery from Roman times to the end of the Middle Ages.

En Route from Arles – In this case it's more precisely "off the route" — an 82-mile (131-km) detour into the Camargue, a region whose landscape is unique in France: a vast, marshy delta of the two arms of the Rhône, where herds of wild bulls and horses run free and the terrain is dotted with the slender figures of herons stalking fish. In Stes.-Maries-de-la-Mer, the capital of the Camargue, Gypsies from all over Europe gather each May and October to honor their patron saint. From Arles, take N570 south. Come with the Gypsies; May and October are the recommended seasons.

Back in Arles, take N113 to N538 and the turnpike (A7, later becoming A8) for the 45-mile (72-km) trip into Aix-en-Provence.

AIX-EN-PROVENCE: Founded as Aquae Sextius (the Waters of Sextius) by the Roman consul Sextius in 122 BC, this ancient capital of Provence today offers a largely 17th- and 18th-century façade, with elegant private mansions, graceful squares, majestic avenues, and numerous fountains. It also is an intellectual center, having had a famous university since 1409.

The main boulevard — Cours Mirabeau — is bordered by towering, shady plane trees and lined with cafés, shops, and fine, aristocratic-looking townhouses. At each end of the Cours are the fountains that recall Aix's origin as a watering place for the Roman legions. This avenue is one of the most pleasant in Provence for strolling, café hopping, and window shopping.

At the Place de l'Hôtel-de-Ville there's a flower market and the remains of the old grain market. Enter the Hôtel de Ville to visit the remarkable 300,000-volume library founded in the 18th century by the Marquis de Méjanes, for whom it is named. Other points of interest can be found at the Place des Martyrs-de-la-Résistance: the *Musée des Tapisseries* (open daily; admission charge; phone: 42-23-09-91), the Cloître St.-Sauveur, and the Cathédrale St.-Sauveur, whose architecture runs the gamut of styles from the 5th to the 16th century. At 34 Rue Célony, the façade of the 17th-century Pavillon de Vendôme offers a fine example of Provençal decorative art. At the Place des Prêcheurs, there's the Eglise Ste.-Marie-Madeleine, containing important paintings, including a large work attributed to Rubens. You'll also want to see Paul Cézanne's studio (atelier) on Avenue Paul-Cézanne (closed Tuesdays; admission charge; phone: 42-21-06-53). The painter was born in Aix in 1839, and his studio has been reconstructed as it was found at his death in 1906.

In July and August, Aix holds an international music festival. This is the high season, action-packed and crowded: Last-minute reservations are risky. Open-air concerts are held in the archbishop's court as well as in the surrounding countryside.

En Route from Aix – Only a few miles outside Aix are several charming restaurants and hotels.

From Aix the route to Marseilles is simple: Just take N8 straight south for 19 miles (30 km). For a complete report on Marseilles, see *Marseilles,* THE CITIES.

BEST EN ROUTE

Expect to pay $100 and up per night for a double room in hotels listed as expensive; $60 to $100 in those listed as moderate; and less than $60 in the inexpensive. Restaurant prices are $110 and up for a dinner for two in the expensive range and $70 to $110 in the moderate range. Prices do not include drinks, wine, and tip. All hotels and restaurants accept major credit cards, unless otherwise indicated.

AVIGNON

Europe – A palace in the 16th century, it is now the best hotel in the city. Aubusson tapestries decorate the high walls in the antiques-furnished public rooms, the 50 bedrooms are richly appointed, and it has a pleasant restaurant. 12 Pl. Crillon (phone: 90-82-66-92; fax: 90-85-43-66). Expensive.

Hiély – Large and comfortable, it's the best restaurant in town. The choices are considerable and the value extraordinary. There are fine local wines from the côtes du Rhône. Closed Mondays (except in summer), Tuesdays, mid-June through early July, and 2 weeks at *Christmas*. Reservations necessary. Most credit cards accepted. 5 Rue de la République (phone: 90-86-17-07; fax: 90-86-32-38). Expensive.

Prieuré – The luxury hotel of the area, set in shady grounds with a pool and tennis courts and 36 exquisitely furnished rooms. It boasts a celebrated restaurant that specializes in grilled duck and tournedos with truffles. Closed mid-November through early March. 7 Pl. du Chapitre at Villeneuve-lès-Avignon (phone: 90-25-18-20; fax: 90-25-45-39). Expensive.

ST.-RÉMY-DE-PROVENCE

Hostellerie du Vallon de Valrugues – This establishment, in a beautiful setting, reopened after a change of management and extensive renovations, which included the addition of a sauna and golf facilities. Along with a remodeled restaurant headed by an ambitious young chef, there are 24 rooms and 10 apartments. Guests can opt for demi-pension or pension, taking either all or part of their meals at the hotel. Chemin Canto Cigalo (phone: 90-92-04-40; fax: 90-92-44-01). Expensive.

Antiques – Very attractive reception rooms, 27 guestrooms, a park, riding, and swimming. Closed late October to mid-April. 15 Av. Pasteur (phone: 90-92-03-02). Moderate.

Canto Cigalo – A modest hotel in quiet surroundings. No restaurant. Closed November through February. Most credit cards accepted. Chemin Canto Cigalo (phone: 90-92-14-28). Moderate.

Château de Roussan – A delightful hotel in an 18th-century mansion surrounded by a park. No restaurant. Rte. Tarascon (phone: 90-92-11-63; fax: 90-49-01-79). Moderate.

LES BAUX

Oustaù de Baumanière – The jewel of Les Baux, this hotel is elegantly furnished and offers flowered terraces, tennis, swimming, riding, and one of France's top restaurants (it has two Michelin stars). The building looks like a medieval castle and is decorated with antiques. Restaurant specialties include stuffed squab, duckling with lime, and *marrons glacés* (glazed chestnuts). Closed mid-January to March; restaurant open daily, except Wednesdays and Thursdays for lunch during the off season (phone: 90-54-33-07; fax: 90-54-40-46). Very expensive.

Cabro d'Or – A small hotel with a pleasant setting, it offers tennis, swimming, good views, and a fine restaurant. Closed mid-November through mid-December, Tuesdays at lunch, and Mondays mid-October through March (phone: 90-54-33-21). Expensive.

Mas d'Aigret – Very appealing, this modest hotel with 17 rooms offers swimming, a restful setting, and good views. Closed from early January to late February. D27 east (phone: 90-97-33-54; fax: 90-54-41-37). Expensive to moderate.

ARLES

Jules César – A former convent, this large, 60-room hotel still features cloisters and interior gardens. Its restaurant, *Lou Marquès,* serves very good regional cuisine. Closed November to December 20. Bd. Lices (phone: 90-93-43-20; fax: 90-93-33-47). Expensive.

d'Arlatan – Amazingly quiet though it's in the center of town. The 46 exquisitely furnished rooms in this half-medieval, half-Renaissance hotel overlook a garden. 26 Rue du Sauvage (phone: 90-93-56-66). Moderate.

AIX-EN-PROVENCE

Mas d'Entremont – In a typical Provençal setting is a tiny hotel with terraces, a park, a fine restaurant featuring seafood and other light dishes. Closed from November to mid-March, Sunday evenings, and Monday lunch, except holidays. Most credit cards accepted. Celony, 2 miles (3 km) north via N7 (phone: 42-23-45-32; fax: 42-21-15-83). Expensive.

Paul Cézanne – A very comfortable hotel with a beautiful interior. 40 Av. Victor-Hugo (phone: 42-26-34-73; fax: 42-27-20-95). Expensive.

Pigonnet – Framed by the beautiful grounds of the 50-room *Pigonnet* hotel, this terrace restaurant looks like a Renoir painting. Try the *noisette d'agneau au basilic* (medaillons of lamb with basil) and delight in the refuge from city life provided by the setting. 5 Av. du Pigonnet (phone: 42-59-02-90; fax: 42-59-47-77). Expensive.

Château de Meyrargues – In a restored 11th-century fortress, this hotel has a good restaurant. The rooms range from the simple to the "master bedroom," where you'll truly feel like a feudal lord. Closed late January to late February. Most credit cards accepted. Meyrargues, 10 miles (16 km) via N96 (phone: 42-57-50-32). Moderate to inexpensive.

The Riviera

The French Riviera, known in France as the Côte d'Azur, is the privileged Mediterranean coastline stretching from Menton in the east to St.-Tropez in the west and including such world-renowned resorts as Nice, Cannes, and Antibes. It is an area of spectacular beauty, with dazzling white cliffs rising from the sea, gracefully curved bays, and some of the most luxurious and palatial hotels and private villas anywhere in the world. The Riviera includes discreet corners and jet-set haunts, picturesque villages and major cities, but it all is a playground. This is the place for sunning, swimming, gambling, eating, nightclubbing, and, on the cultural side, for seeing some of the finest collections of paintings by modern masters in France (many of the most prominent figures in 20th-century art lived here at one time or another, drawn by the beauty of the terrain and the extraordinary clarity of the light).

Although the Riviera has the reputation of being the playground of the rich and famous (which indeed it is), you'll find a remarkably wide spread of prices. After all, this is the vacation paradise of the French themselves (the most demanding of peoples) who ritually crowd down here during the months of July and August. And you can be sure that they have contrived to keep standards high across all price ranges, from simple bistros and camping sites to the renowned gourmet restaurants and luxury hotels. Mind you, "expensive" can really mean just that — up to $400. And don't forget that in France it is usual to pay for the room, not the number of persons.

Many beaches are rocky or pebbly, but there are plenty of sandy beaches especially between Antibes and St.-Tropez. Some beaches are public and free of charge; others are "private," which usually means they belong to a restaurant or a hotel. But it's worth renting an air mattress and a beach umbrella at one of these for around $10 a day. Topless sunbathing (said to have originated at Tahiti Plage near St.-Tropez) is ubiquitous but hardly the rule. One of the great delights about the Riviera is that everyone does his or her own thing — the French are consummate individualists. So relax. High season is July and August when the inundation of tourists can make it a bit tacky. It's best to visit in May and June or even September and October. The temperatures will be cooler, of course, but still mild, and you'll be able to see something more than wall-to-wall people.

Nice–Côte d'Azur Airport is the busiest in France after Charles de Gaulle and Orly in Paris. It certainly is the most attractive. You come in over the sea to touch down on the edge of a bright white runway and step off the plane to palm trees and a fragrant breeze (called the *mistral* when it really blows). There's a fine restaurant (*Le Ciel d'Azur*) on the second floor of the airport. There are buses to Nice and many towns along the Riviera including Monte Carlo. A taxi to downtown Nice will cost you about between $8 and $10. There's also helicopter service to Monte Carlo.

You'll have no trouble finding your way around if you take along the *IGN* map No. 115 (Provence–Côte d'Azur) or *Michelin* map No.195 (Côte d'Azur–Alpes Maritimes). There is sun and sea and scenery wherever you turn, so stop anywhere and enjoy it. That's what the Riviera's all about.

LES CORNICHES: Nice is the usual starting point for the Côte d'Azur. (For a complete report on the city and its hotels and restaurants, see *Nice,* THE CITIES.) But the "real" Riviera begins once you leave the city. You don't have to go far. Between Nice and Menton, a 19-mile (30-km) trip, you'll travel by mountain passes, or *corniches,* that compel you to marvel at dramatic views of both sea and shoreline. From Nice you take N7 to the Grande Corniche. The ascent is quick, and especially magical views can be enjoyed as you pause briefly at Belvédère d'Eze, at La Turbie, at Vistaëro and its medieval château, and at Roquebrune-Cap-Martin. The old towns are enchanting and the landscape, superb. This road also leads to Monaco — where you'll certainly want to spend some time (see *Monaco,* DIRECTIONS) — and terminates in Menton, a city known for its excellent climate, tropical vegetation, and the international chamber music festival held each year in August.

On the return trip, take the lower pass (Corniche Inférieure) to enjoy panoramas that include bird's-eye views of some of the loveliest resorts in the world. At Beaulieu-sur-Mer, as you drive past *La Réserve,* the prestigious hotel and restaurant (see *Best En Route*), you begin to enter the "gold coast" ambience of the Riviera. Stop next at St.-Jean-Cap-Ferrat and visit the *Fondation Ephrussi de Rothschild,* set among exquisite gardens overlooking the sea. The splendid artworks and furniture date from the 14th to the 19th century. Just a few miles down the coast, the picturesque town of Villefranche is the classic model of a Mediterranean fishing port, with high cliffs that seem to fall into the sea. From here, return to Nice via N559.

   En Route from Nice – Between Nice and Cannes, half the fun is definitely getting there. Cagnes-sur-Mer, with its Renoir museum, is 8 miles (about 12 km) west via N7. St.-Paul, while not actually on the coast, is only a few miles inland and well worth the detour (take N7 west and N85 to D2). For lovers of the good life, there's the *Mas d'Artigny* hotel and *La Colombe d'Or,* a second home to some of France's best-known personalities (see *Best en Route*). For art lovers, this onetime home of Georges Braque boasts the *Maeght Foundation,* which houses one of the finest collections of contemporary art in France (open daily; admission charge; phone: 93-32-81-63). Nearby Vence (3 miles/5 km inland via D2) is Chagall's adopted city. The jewel-like Chapelle du Rosaire at Vence was designed entirely by Matisse, from the stained glass to the white ceramic walls (open Tuesdays through Saturdays June to mid-September; open Tuesdays and Thursdays only off-season).

   A few miles west back along the coast brings you to Biot, a medieval village perched on a hilltop. Visit the glassworks, where you can buy hand-blown glass and watch it being made. The *Fernand Léger Museum* also is worth a look (closed Tuesdays; admission charge; phone: 93-65-63-49). From Biot, the RN7 will take you to Antibes, where the *Château-Musée Grimaldi* houses a fine collection of the works of Picasso (closed Tuesdays; admission charge; phone: 93-34-91-91). Antibes, once the home of Monet, is a beautiful port with fortress walls and tiny, winding streets. Just beyond Antibes, you pass through Juan-les-Pins, somewhat gaudy, but a famous resort with good sand beaches.

   This is really the heart of luxury sun worship, and elegant private villas line the approach to Cap d'Antibes, one of the most exclusive spots on the Riviera. Take time just to walk around the *Hôtel du Cap d'Antibes* (see *Best En Route*) and enjoy a drink on the terrace. It's every glamorous story come to life and epitomizes the Riviera's status as a haven for the rich and famous. Napoleon's *Naval Museum* at Cap d'Antibes is well worth a visit (closed Tuesdays; admission charge; phone: 93-61-45-32). Follow the coast right around for 6 miles (10 km) to reach Cannes.

   CANNES: Unlike some of the earlier stops, Cannes is not quiet and discreet, but it too is the Riviera. The elegant (if sometimes noisy) Boulevard de la Croisette, with riotously colorful gardens tracing the line of the Gulf of Napoule, is the key to Cannes. Here are smart boutiques, myriad outdoor cafés, and the *Majestic* and *Carlton* hotels — the headquarters for international stars during the city's annual film festival in the spring (see *Best En Route*). As you follow the boulevard to Pointe de la Croisette you come to the famed (and original) Palm Beach, with your walk enhanced by constant views of the water. Take the boulevard in the opposite direction to get to the port, a harbor for the most extravagant yachts you could hope to see.

   Cannes is a chic city, with its café society, nightclubs, and two casinos. But it has more quaint charms as well — for example, the flower market in the Allée de la Liberté or the old city, centered around Place de la Castre. End your visit with a trip to the observatory of Super-Cannes, 3 miles (5 km) outside the city, north on Avenue Isola-Bella. It goes without saying that the panoramas are really sublime from here.

   En Route from Cannes – Excursions from Cannes offer some interesting stops for a change of pace. Take D803 to Vallauris, an important center for ceramic art; regular exhibitions are held in the summer. Via N567 and the Esterel–Côte d'Azur Autoroute you arrive at Mougins. This ancient fortified town, once Picasso's home, today houses one of France's finest restaurants, the *Moulin de Mougins* (see *Best en Route*). Seven miles (11 km) farther inland is Grasse, the perfume production center of France and a sought-after residential area as well. The perfume factories Molinard (52 Bd. Victor-Hugo) and Fragonard (Bd. Fragonard) are open to the public.

   Returning to Cannes, you can take a boat from the port to the nearby islands

(Iles de Lérins). The excursion takes half a day, including stops at Ile Ste.-Marguerite, fragrant with eucalyptus and pine forests, and at Ile St.-Honorat, the site of an ancient fortified monastery.

As you wind along the coast westward from Cannes (N559 to N98), the seascapes become vast leading into St.-Tropez, a distance of 45 miles (72 km).

ST.-TROPEZ: Rivaling Cannes as a jet-set favorite, St.-Tropez first became famous when Brigitte Bardot made it her home. Everything you've ever heard about this city is found at the port. You'll see starlets, swingers, spectators, and a whole coterie who'd give anything to be part of the action. The scene is hypnotizing, so settle back to watch with an early-evening Pernod (a licorice liquor) or blanc cassis at *Senequier's* in the port. Next day, take a trip out to Môle Jean Réveille (a jetty with a lighthouse) or to the Citadelle, built in the 16th and 17th centuries, which offers imposing views. Don't miss the *Musée de l'Annonciade* (Pl. Georges-Grammont), which has an outstanding collection of 20th-century art.

The best beaches at St.-Tropez are a few miles out on the Caps de St.-Tropez, du Pinet, and Camarat. Pampelonne Beach also is good, but the most chic is Tahiti Plage (strictly speaking, at Ramatuelle), where you can have a delicious and moderately priced lunch on the terrace overlooking the beach.

A warning: St.-Tropez has experienced a surge of construction — both residential and commercial — in the last several years. It is, of course, one of the "in" spots of the Riviera, but in the summer the congestion — both human and automotive — may be more than you care for. If frenzy is not your idea of vacation, you might prefer St.-Tropez in the off-season.

En Route from St.-Tropez – The heart of the Riviera ends at St.-Tropez, and although the region to the west offers fewer restaurants and hotels, the scenery is still dazzling. If you follow N98 to N559, you find high cliffs and expansive seascapes around Cavalaire-sur-Mer; at Lavandou, a longtime favorite of artists, good sand beaches and one of the loveliest fishing ports on the coast await you. From here, it's only 23 miles (37 km) back to St.-Tropez along the coast; but if you have time, take the mountain route (Rte. du Littoral) via the Corniche des Maures. It's twice as long, but the scenery is spectacular. The route ends in St.-Raphaël; from there just follow the coast 45 miles (72 km) east back to Nice.

BEST EN ROUTE

Expect to pay $150 and way up per night for a double room in hotels listed as very expensive; $115 to $140 at expensive; $75 to $115 in those listed as moderate; and under $75, inexpensive. The restaurants range in price from $115 and up for a dinner for two in the expensive range, $75 in the moderate range, and under $75 in the inexpensive category. Prices do not include drinks, wine, or tip. Service charge and tax invariably are included in the check. In high season, you may need to buy dinner or lunch in order to get a room.

Note: For the entire Riviera, reservations are necessary in high season. All hotels and restaurants accept major credit cards unless otherwise indicated.

ROQUEBRUNE-CAP-MARTIN

Vista Palace – This luxurious 68-room hotel set on a cliff has exceptional views of Roquebrune and the coast. A fine restaurant, a pool, gardens, and parking complete the amenities. Closed from mid-November to January, though the exact dates vary. About 2 miles (3 km) from downtown on the Grande Corniche (phone: 93-35-01-50; fax: 93-35-01-50). Expensive.

BEAULIEU-SUR-MER

La Réserve – One of France's top luxury hotels with an internationally known restaurant; heated swimming pool. Right on the sea. Closed mid-November to late December. 5 Bd. Mar.-Leclerc (phone: 93-01-00-01; fax: 93-01-28-99). Expensive.

Comté de Nice – A comfortable hotel (no restaurant). Closed for 2 weeks in January. 25 Bd. Marinoni (phone: 93-01-19-70; fax: 93-01-23-09). Moderate.

ST.-JEAN-CAP-FERRAT

Bel Air Cap-Ferrat – A luxury 59-room hotel right on the water, with lovely grounds, a beach, tennis, and a one-Michelin-star restaurant. Its "Club Dauphin" on the sea has a spectacular pool, sauna, restaurant (perfect for lunch), and a funicular to take guests back up to the hotel. Isolated and recently remodeled, this is arguably the finest hostelry on the Riviera. Open year-round. Bd. Gén.-de-Gaulle (phone: 93-76-00-21; fax: 93-01-62-49). Expensive.

Cappa – A top-rate seafood restaurant overlooking the port. Closed from November through January. Av. J.-Mermoz (phone: 93-76-03-91). Expensive.

Voile d'Or – This elegant hostelry has a fine restaurant, pool, and superb views of the port. Closed from November through February (phone: 93-01-13-13; fax: 93-76-11-17). Expensive.

ST.-PAUL-DE-VENCE

La Colombe d'Or – Luxury combining Provençal atmosphere and lush, beautiful gardens. This sumptuous, small hotel is famous for its collection of works by Miró, Calder, Picasso, and Chagall. Closed mid-November through mid-December (phone: 93-32-80-02; fax: 93-32-77-78). Expensive.

Mas d'Artigny – A stunning luxury hotel with 50 standard rooms that come with balconies, 25 suites with private swimming pools, and a dining room (one Michelin star) that serves fine seafood. Most credit cards accepted. Rte. de la Colle and des Hauts de St.-Paul (phone: 93-32-84-54; fax: 93-32-95-36). Expensive.

Hameau – This pleasant hostelry has 16 rooms but no restaurant. Closed from mid-November to February. 528 Rte. de la Colle, D7 (phone: 93-32-80-24). Moderate.

CAP D'ANTIBES

Cap d'Antibes – Truly grand, this luxury hotel has gorgeous grounds and views, swimming, and tennis. Its restaurant, *Pavillon Eden Roc,* serves delicious food. Closed from October to April. No credit cards accepted. Bd. Kennedy (phone: 93-61-39-01 or 93-61-56-63; fax: 93-67-76-04). Very expensive.

Bacon – From a terrace overlooking the sea, diners can enjoy very good bouillabaisse and excellent fresh fish. Closed Sunday nights, Mondays, and mid-November through January. Reservations advised. Bd. de Bacon (phone: 93-61-50-02). Expensive.

Gardiole – This simple, quiet hotel among the pines has 20 rooms, some of which face the sea. Chemin de la Garoupe (phone: 93-61-35-03). Moderate.

ANTIBES

Bonne Auberge – Fine Provençal cuisine and attentive service have won this elegant restaurant two Michelin stars. On the right-hand side of N7 coming from Nice. Closed from November 15 through December 15 and on Mondays (phone: 93-33-36-65; fax: 93-33-48-52). Very expensive.

Yacht – A charming pub-restaurant that caters to yacht crews who've put into Port

Vauban Harbor, with a grand view of the boats. A few rooms are available in the *Bellevue* hotel (same location as the restaurant). Closed Sunday nights, Mondays, and November through December 15. 15 Av. de la Libération (phone: 93-74-24-00). Moderate.

Mas Djoliba – This small, quiet hotel with 13 rooms has a beautiful park setting right in the center of town. Its restaurant is reserved for hotel guests only, and is open only for dinner. 29 Av. de Provence (phone: 93-34-02-48; fax: 93-34-05-81). Moderate to inexpensive.

L'Oursin – The best seafood in the downtown area is served at this popular but plain little restaurant. Closed Sunday nights, Mondays, and August. Reservations necessary. Most credit cards accepted. 16 Rue République (phone: 93-34-13-46). Moderate to inexpensive.

CANNES

Carlton – Numero uno in terms of old-fashioned prestige and glamour; 335 rooms provide traditional comforts. The view of the sea undoubtedly is the best in town. 58 Bd. de la Croisette (phone: 93-68-91-68; fax: 93-38-20-90). Expensive.

Gray d'Albion – This modern, comfortable, 174-room hotel has a restaurant that's quite good. 38 Rue des Serbes (phone: 93-68-54-54; fax: 93-99-26-10). Expensive.

Majestic – With the *Carlton,* one of the classic, glamorous hotels of Cannes. Closed 2 weeks in November. Bd. de la Croisette (phone: 93-68-91-00; fax: 93-38-97-90). Expensive.

Saint-Yves – A quaint and cozy old-fashioned villa in a delightful garden of palm trees, it has 8 rooms, plus 3 suites. Closed in November. 49 Bd. d'Alsace (phone: 93-38-65-29). Moderate.

MOUGINS

Le Moulin de Mougins – Set in a 16th-century olive oil mill with exotic plants outside the windows and original paintings on the walls, this is one of the most famous restaurants (three Michelin stars) in France. Chef Roger Vergé's specialties include lobster fricassee, pâté of sole, *escalope* of fresh salmon, and *salade Mikado* (with mushrooms, avocado, tomatoes, and truffles). The Réserve wine, a very fine rosé, comes from nearby vineyards, and the cold wild strawberry soufflé is delicious. (There are also 3 hotel rooms here that should be booked well in advance.) Closed Mondays, except in peak season, and from February to April. Notre-Dame-de-Vie; southeast 1 mile (1.6 km) via D3 (phone: 93-75-78-24; fax: 93-90-18-55). Very expensive.

Amandier de Mougins – Roger Vergé's *other* restaurant, also in a former olive oil mill, serves simpler and less expensive food. Closed Saturdays at lunch and Wednesdays. Pl. du Commandant-Lamy (phone: 93-90-00-91). Expensive.

Les Muscadins – If you can't get a room in *Le Moulin de Mougins,* this cozy inn in the heart of the old village supplies nearly equivalent charm and comfort. There are only 7 rooms, all beautifully furnished, so book well in advance. Closed mid-January to April; restaurant closed Wednesday lunch and Tuesdays. In the Old Town (phone: 93-90-00-43; fax: 92-92-88-23). Expensive.

ST.-TROPEZ

Byblos – A grand luxury hotel, decorated in Provençal style with some of the best food in town. Good views are matched by excellent swimming. Closed mid-October to late March. Av. Paul-Signac (phone: 94-97-00-04; fax: 94-97-40-52). Expensive.

Levant – On the road where Colette used to live, this hotel by the sea has 28 rooms, a pool, and a restaurant. Hotel closed October to April; restaurant closed mid-September to mid-June. Rte. des Salins (phone: 94-97-33-33). Moderate.

Sube – The most famous of the town's less expensive hotels is set right on the harbor. It has 26 unpretentious rooms. Open year-round. 15 Quai Suffren (phone: 94-97-30-04; fax: 94-54-89-08). Moderate.

Burgundy

Burgundy begins 100 miles (160 km) south of Paris and stretches almost to Lyons. The region has always been a place of passage, a transit zone between northern France and the Mediterranean south and between France and Switzerland. But Burgundy also is important in its own right because of its history, its produce, its art, and its architecture.

The region was conquered by the Romans in 52 BC, when Julius Caesar forced Vercingetorix, the Gallic ruler of the Arverni, to surrender at Alesia. A 5th-century invasion by the Burgundians, who came from the region of the Baltic Sea, gave Burgundy its modern name.

In 534, the Franks conquered the kingdom of Burgundy. The death of the great Frankish king Charlemagne in 814 heralded a 200-year period of chaos and turbulence. The long strife ended when the kingdom, by then reduced to a duchy, passed into the hands of King Robert II of France (known as Robert the Pious), who made his son Robert the first Capetian Duke of Burgundy.

Under the Capets, Burgundy became a bastion of Christianity. Monasteries were founded and magnificent churches built. But Burgundy's true golden age came when the Capets were succeeded in 1364 by the Valois — the grand dukes of Burgundy. During their reign, Burgundy spread well beyond its present borders and even beyond those of France to include most of Belgium and Luxembourg and part of Holland. It became a center of art and culture because of the many French and Flemish artists the dukes brought to Dijon, the capital. The Dukes of Valois ruled until 1477. After the death of the last duke, Charles the Bold, the duchy was taken by Louis XI of France as part of his kingdom.

Topographically, Burgundy is a land of hills and valleys laced with many streams. One-third of it is forested; in the rest, agriculture is the most important activity. Burgundy's agricultural products are world-famous — the mustard of Dijon, the beef of Charolais cattle, and, of course, the wine. Burgundy also has some industry — steel mills and glass and ceramic manufacturers — concentrated south of Dijon.

The wine country of Burgundy stretches from Dijon to the outskirts of Lyons, a treasure trove of beautiful medieval buildings. Because Burgundy was a center of monastic activity, most of these medieval remains are religious — either churches or abbeys. The predominant architectural style is Romanesque with a Burgundian accent, but there are Gothic structures and some Roman ruins as well.

Burgundy is crossed from north to south by Route A6, a major toll freeway.

Most of the other roads have only two lanes but are well paved and maintained. From Paris, take A6 due south to the exit of Auxerre-Nord to enter Burgundy at Auxerre. It's a distance of 104 miles (166 km).

AUXERRE: The gateway to Burgundy was first a Celtic settlement, then a Roman town, and later a religious center in the Middle Ages. The most impressive feature as you approach the town is the view of the Roman ramparts and the silhouettes of church spires above the Yonne River. Inside you get a closer look at the Gothic cathedral and Gaillarde clock tower.

Take N6, then D100 south about 30 miles (48 km) to Vézelay.

VÉZELAY: Once a pilgrimage center and now a Christian shrine, Vézelay began as an abbey in the 9th century. Its church became famous in the 11th century, when a monk associated with the abbey obtained relics reputed to be those of St. Mary Magdalene. Pilgrims flocked to Vézelay, and the town became prosperous. At the beginning of the 12th century, a modest Carolingian church was replaced by the present Romanesque basilica.

At the end of the 13th century, Vézelay declined. When other "relics" of St. Mary Magdalene were found in Provence, the pilgrims dwindled. Huguenots looted Vézelay in 1569, and part of the town was destroyed in the revolution. Not until 1859, after restorations by Viollet-le-Duc (who had achieved fame with his restoration of Notre-Dame de Paris) did Vézelay again become a pilgrimage site — for tourists.

Leave your car at the foot of the village and walk to the basilica, with a superb carving over its main door that represents the apostles' mission after the resurrection of Christ. Once inside, your first impression is one of light and airiness. Next, you notice details, such as the carved capitals on the columns. These figures, representing biblical characters, are very moving for their familiar, human facial expressions. If you want to know who's who, buy an English-language guidebook, on sale in the church.

The village of Vézelay has many shops selling the wares of local artisans. Unusual items include pewter jewelry in religious or zodiac designs and the blue, white, and gilt earthenware from nearby Clamecy.

Vézelay also is a good starting point for the rugged Morvan region just to the south, an area with many fine trout streams. You can get details on the fishing at any of the several charming country inns in the Vézelay region, the *Poste et Lion d'Or* in Vézelay, the *Moulin des Ruats* between Vézelay and Avallon, or the *Poste* in Avallon (see *Best en Route*).

En Route from Vézelay – The 52-mile (83-km) drive east to the Abbey of Fontenay is one of the most interesting on the whole Burgundy route. Take D457 to Avallon, a former walled town. Then follow D954 through the cheese making town of Epoisses — where you pass a castle with a water-filled moat — to Semur-en-Auxois.

Just before Semur you come to D980, a fork that takes you to Montbard and the Abbey of Fontenay. Pass the abbey for the moment and drive into Semur itself, once a feudal fortified town. It's worth a drive around to see the walls and towers where the townsfolk defied Louis XI's troops in 1478.

Return to D980 and, after driving through the industrial town of Montbard, take D905 and D32 to Fontenay.

FONTENAY: If you want an unspoiled picture of monastic simplicity not crowded by tourists, don't miss Fontenay. At first sight, the abbey looks like a large farm — which is just what a self-contained, self-supporting, 12th-century Cistercian monastery was supposed to be.

Fontenay was founded by Bernard de Clairvaux in 1118. The abbey prospered until the 16th century, at times with as many as 300 monks in residence. With the Wars of Religion, the institution declined and, by the time of the revolution, only three monks remained. They were driven out, and the buildings were sold and turned into a paper mill. In 1906, Fontenay was sold again, and the new owner set out to restore the buildings.

There are guided tours of Fontenay in French; even if you don't understand the language, you will understand more of medieval monastic life when you visit, in order, the church with its plain windows and dirt floor; the monks' dormitory; the arched cloister; the chapter house, or meeting hall; the scriptorium, where the monks wrote and illuminated manuscripts; the adjoining *caldarium* — the only heated room other than the kitchen — where the writing monks warmed their fingers to prevent frostbite; the prison, used for minor violators; and the forge.

If you visit Fontenay in the winter, don't go late in the day. There are no lights in the buildings, and late afternoon tours may be canceled because of darkness. There is an admission charge.

Take Route D905 and freeway A8 to Dijon, 52 miles (83 km) away.

DIJON: The capital of Burgundy reached the height of its glory under the four Valois Dukes of Burgundy — Philip the Brave, John the Fearless, Philip the Good, and Charles the Bold — who gave it its fine buildings. After Burgundy was annexed by France, Dijon declined for a time, but it revived after 1850 with the coming of the railroad. Today the city is an important industrial and commercial center. It is known especially for its gastronomic specialties: mustard, spice bread, black currant liqueur (*cassis*), and snails. An annual gastronomic fair is held in Dijon during the first 2 weeks in November.

Dijon's main tourist attractions are the former ducal palace and the streets around it. The palace now houses an art museum (closed Tuesdays; admission charge; Pl. de la Libération; phone: 80-74-52-70), with paintings and Burgundian sculptures. The most interesting parts of the palace, however, are the kitchen, with six fireplaces so large you can walk into them, and the guard room, housing the marble and alabaster tombs of Philip the Brave and John the Fearless.

En Route from Dijon – Route N74 leads 23.5 miles (38 km) south to Beaune through famous wine villages: Gevrey-Chambertin, Vougeot, Nuits-St.-Georges. Wherever you see a sign announcing *dégustation,* you can stop and taste the wines of the region.

BEAUNE: This town is the wine capital of Burgundy, and each year a famous wine auction is held on the third Sunday in November. All proceeds go to the hospital, the Hôtel-Dieu, a marvel of Flemish-Burgundian wooden architecture, founded in 1443 as a general hospital. It remained so until 1971 and is used as a geriatric institution. Parts of the building have been set aside as a museum. Most striking are the main ward — a perfect preservation of a medieval hospital — and an art masterpiece, Rogier van der Weyden's multi-paneled painting of the Last Judgment. In medieval times, this vivid depiction of heaven and hell stood in the main ward. There are guided tours in English; admission charge.

Wine lovers will want to visit the wine museum and the many cellars around the town's main square. Here you can taste and buy wine and wine accessories, including glasses, corkscrews, serving baskets, and tasting cups.

En Route from Beaune – You have several choices. Wine lovers can continue down N74 through Pommard, Volnay, Meursault, Puligny-Montrachet, and Mercurey, south toward Mâcon. Or you can make a 32-mile (50-km) side trip via D973 to Autun, a former Roman town now best known for its cathedral. However, this cathedral, with a Last Judgment panel over the main door and carved capitals inside, is much like the basilica at Vézelay, so you may just wish to continue down freeway A6 to Mâcon, via Tournus.

TOURNUS: An industrial town, it is worth a stop for its 11th-century Romanesque church. The austere arches and columns and the circular stairway to the bell loft give a special flavor of medieval piety.

You also can get an excellent meal here at *Greuze* (4 Rue A.-Thibaudet) before heading down A6 to Mâcon.

MÂCON: Though this is not a true tourist town, wine lovers may want to visit the *Maison Mâconnaise des Vins* (Av. Mae-de-Lattre-Tassigny; phone: 85-38-36-78) which sells burgundies at lower cost than in Beaune and offers a good inexpensive meal. Mâcon is a good base for side trips, west via N79 to Cluny and Paray-le-Monial or east on N79 to Bourg-en-Bresse and the church of Brou.

CLUNY: One of the most famous abbeys in France, Cluny was founded in 910 by Duke William the Pious of Aquitaine. In its heyday, from the 11th to the 14th century, the abbey exercised a widespread influence on religious, intellectual, artistic, and political life. Burgundian Romanesque architecture started at Cluny, and its abbey gave the church three popes. The city enjoyed enormous power and wealth. "Wherever the wind blows, there Cluny's wealth grows," the saying went.

And that, eventually, proved its downfall. The abbots became corrupt, and in 1790, during the Revolution, the abbey was closed. In 1798, the building was sold to a Mâcon dealer, who tore down parts of it for the stone. Fewer than half of the original abbey buildings remain today.

Because of the massive destruction that has taken place, a visit to Cluny may be disappointing. If you take the guided tour, buy a pamphlet in English and study Cluny's history before you begin. Then look for the two buildings that tell the whole story of Cluny's rise and fall: the south transept with its simple lines, all that remains of the great abbey church; and the Gothic chapel of Jean de Bourbon, with its heated side room where the privileged could worship in comfort while the ordinary monks braved the Burgundian winter chill.

PARAY-LE-MONIAL: This town, 43 miles (69 km) west of Mâcon, is dominated by its Romanesque Basilica of the Sacred Heart. Founded in 1109 by St. Hugues, founder of the great Cluny church, it is a smaller version of the Cluny building.

Because of the golden limestone used to build it, the basilica appears most impressive on sunny days at sunset. If the weather is poor, you may prefer not to journey out to Paray-le-Monial but turn east to Bourg-en-Bresse.

Go east on N79 from Mâcon for 21 miles (34 km) to D975 and Bourg-en-Bresse.

BOURG-EN-BRESSE: A chicken-raising and furniture making center, it is noted for its *appellation contrôlée* chickens. Ignore the town itself and go out the Bd. du Brou straight to the suburb of Brou and its church, the most beautiful in Burgundy.

Flamboyantly Gothic with a Renaissance cast, the church was completed in 1532. It was a work of love. In 1480, Count Philippe of Bresse was gravely injured in a hunting accident. His wife, Marguerite de Bourbon, vowed that if he recovered, she would turn the priory of Brou into a monastery. The count did recover, but Marguerite died before she could carry out her vow. The count and his son Philibert promised to fulfill it for her, but time passed and they forgot. Then Philibert, married to Marguerite of Austria, died unexpectedly of a chill. Marguerite saw his death as divine punishment and hastened to carry out the lapsed vow as a memorial to her beloved husband. For 400 years the church has stood as a symbol of married love.

Every part of this church — its golden light, its rich ornamentation — delights the eye. Most outstanding are the choir and the chapels. Note the realistic figures in the carved oak choir stalls (one even shows a naughty youth being spanked), the tombs of the two Marguerites and Philibert carved in Italian marble, the sumptuous stained glass windows, the white marble rood screen showing the seven joys of the Virgin.

There are guided tours of the church; the hours vary according to the seasons (phone:

74-22-26-55). The small charge also admits you to an art museum in the former monastery buildings.

Leave Burgundy via N83 for Lyons.

BEST EN ROUTE

Expect to pay $95 and up per night for a double room in hotels listed as expensive; $70 to $95 in those listed as moderate; and $70 and under, inexpensive. The restaurants range in price from $100 and up for a dinner for two in the expensive range; $70 to $100 in the moderate range; and $70 and under, inexpensive. Prices do not include drinks, wine, or tip. All hotels and restaurants accept major credit cards, unless otherwise indicated.

JOIGNY

A la Côte St.-Jacques – In a charming little cobblestone town 17 miles (27 km) north of Auxerre, this is an elegantly decorated restaurant known for its imaginative Burgundian food, which has garnered it three Michelin stars. Their selection of burgundy wines is one of the finest anywhere. Closed January. Reservations necessary. 14 Fbg. Paris (phone: 86-62-09-70; fax: 86-91-49-70). Expensive.

VÉZELAY

Espérance – This 22-room hotel provides lovely accommodations, but it's most notable for its restaurant, which has won high praise from many critics, including three stars from Michelin. Closed for lunch Wednesdays, Tuesdays, and from early January to early February. Reservations necessary. St.-Père-sous-Vézelay (phone: 86-33-20-45; fax: 86-33-26-15). Expensive.

Poste et Lion d'Or – At the foot of Vézelay village, with a view of rolling hills, 42 rooms, and a good restaurant featuring classic cuisine. Open from mid-April to early November (phone: 86-33-21-23). Expensive to moderate.

AVALLON

Hostellerie de la Poste – An atmospheric inn with 13 rooms and a very fine restaurant (closed Tuesday lunch and Mondays). Reservations necessary. 13 Pl. Vauban (phone: 86-34-06-12). Expensive.

Hostellerie du Moulin des Ruats – A charming former mill with a garden on the bank of a stream, where you can eat in pleasant weather. There are 24 rooms and a restaurant. Closed for a month and a half in winter, Mondays in off season, and Tuesday lunch. Most credit cards accepted. Two miles (3 km) southwest of Avallon in Vallée du Cousin (phone: 86-34-07-14). Expensive to moderate.

DIJON

La Cloche – The building dates back to 1424, but all that remains of the original structure are the exterior walls, including the façade. Following a complete renovation and takeover 2 years ago by the Pullman chain, it now ranks as Dijon's most elegant hostelry, with 80 attractively furnished rooms and suites enhanced by wonderful views of the Place Darcy park and the hotel's own peaceful little garden. A tea and coffee shop overlooks the garden; there's an excellent restaurant — *Jean-Pierre Billoux,* a bar, and a boutique. There are phones in the rooms, and in many of the bathrooms as well. 14 Pl. Darcy (phone: 80-30-12-32; fax: 80-30-04-15). Expensive.

Hostellerie du Chapeau Rouge – Recently redecorated, comfortable, and centrally located hotel with a good restaurant serving both regional and nouvelle cuisines;

excellent wines. 5 Rue Michelet (phone: 80-30-28-10; fax: 80-30-33-89). Expensive to moderate.

Thibert – Sophisiticated decor and refined cooking have won Jean-Paul Thibert a Michelin star. Situated on one of Dijon's most beautiful squares, it's a favorite with locals. Closed Sunday dinner, Monday lunch, 3 weeks in January, and 2 weeks in August. Reservations necessary. 10 Pl. Wilson (phone: 80-67-74-64). Expensive to moderate.

BEAUNE

Hostellerie de Levernois – Set in a 10-acre park just 2 miles (3 km) outside Beaune, this gracious 12-room hotel/restaurant was opened by Jean Crotet, former chef/ owner of the highly rated *Cote d'Or* in nearby Nuits-St.-Georges. The rooms, furnished by Mme. Crotet, are spacious and very comfortable, and the inviting, terraced dining room offers excellent cuisine for which Chef Crotet has gained two Michelin stars. Closed February, Wednesday lunch, and Tuesdays off-season. Three miles (5 km) southeast of Beaune, via the route Verdun. (phone: 80-24-73-58; fax: 80-22-78-00). Expensive.

Hostellerie du Vieux Moulin – Chef Jean-Pierre Silva's cooking has earned two Michelin stars for such creations as *estouffade de poireaux* and *jambonnette de grenouilles en meurette* (a delicate stew of leeks and frogs' legs), and so he well deserves. Located about 10 miles (16 km) outside Beaune in Bouilland, the hotel is closed Thursdays (for lunch), Wednesdays (except holidays), mid-December to mid-January, the last week of February, and the first week of March. Most credit cards accepted (phone: 80-21-51-16). Expensive.

Poste – A charming older hotel with a garden courtyard and what some feel is the best restaurant in Beaune. Closed mid-November to April. 1 Bd. Clemenceau (phone: 80-22-08-11; fax: 80-24-19-71). Expensive.

CHAGNY

Lameloise – Nine miles (14 km) south of Beaune, this restaurant is worthy of a detour. At this atmospheric, 15th-century country mansion, which has been rated three Michelin stars, Burgundian cooking is raised to a high art. Prices are pretty high, too, but the gustatory experience is worth it. Closed Wednesdays, Thursdays at lunchtime, and most of January. Reservations necessary. Most credit cards accepted. 36 Pl. d'Armes (phone: 85-87-08-85; fax: 85-87-08-85). Expensive.

TOURNUS

Greuze – Fine Burgundian food and beaujolais wines are offered at this charming country inn named for Jean-Baptiste Greuze, an 18th-century artist born in Tournus. Chef Jean Ducloux's efforts have earned him two Michelin stars. There are 21 rooms in the nearby *Greuze* hotel, owned by Ducloux. Closed the first week in December. 1 Rue Thibaudet (phone: 85-51-13-52; fax: 85-40-77-23). Expensive.

MÂCON

Château d'Igé – A remodeled 13th-century fortified castle in a village surrounded by vineyards not far from Cluny; 6 rooms and 6 suites. Hotel closed December to March; restaurant, to late January. In Igé, 8 miles (13 km) northwest of Mâcon via N79 and D85 (phone: 85-33-33-99; fax: 85-33-41-41). Expensive to moderate.

Altéa Mâcon – Modern motel with 63 rooms and a good restaurant. 26 Rue Coubertin, less than 1 mile (1.6 km) south via N6 (phone: 85-38-28-06; fax: 85-39-11-45). Moderate.

BOURG-EN-BRESSE

Auberge Bressane – Rustic inn specializing in local products, especially Bresse chicken. 166 Bd. de Brou (phone: 74-22-22-68). Expensive.

Le Logis de Brou – Comfortable, old-style hotel with a view of the park; 30 rooms. No restaurant here, but *Auberge Bressane* (above) is nearby. 132 Bd. Brou (phone: 74-22-11-55). Moderate to inexpensive.

Alsace-Lorraine

Since 1870, Alsace and part of Lorraine have spent almost equal time under the German flag and the tricolor. The two provinces are profoundly different from each other, yet their common destiny as "puzzle pieces" on France's northeastern border has caused them to be inextricably linked in people's minds. In Alsace particularly, there is much to make you think you are in Germany. Virtually all Alsatians speak French, but many of them also speak the local German dialect; folk dress appears at festivals celebrating the new wine; houses frequently are decorated with heavy timbered furniture and may even be heated by a ceramic stove in the main room. Indeed, if you had been traveling in Alsace or the Moselle area of Lorraine between 1870 and the end of World War I, you would have been in Germany.

Today, however, the provinces belong wholeheartedly to France even if there is some inevitable ambivalence in culture, language, customs, and accents. Its specialties — *choucroute garnie, kouglof* (*kugelhopf*), quiche Lorraine, Strasbourg sausages, and foie gras — are part of French gastronomic life, as are the magnificent white wines of Alsace and the *vin gris* of Lorraine. The Place Stanislas and the Cathedral of Strasbourg are works of French architecture, and who would deny Joan of Arc — the Maid of Lorraine — her French nationality?

With their turbulent history and strategic border position, Lorraine and Alsace offer a side of France that is very different from the sunny face of Nice or the craggy coast of St.-Malo. Here is a France whose citizens drink beer as often as they drink wine, that celebrates *Christmas* with decidedly Germanic *gemütlichkeit,* and that enjoys life with a heartiness which, on first acquaintance at least, bears little resemblance to the legendary refinement of French joie de vivre. An evening stroll around the Place Stanislas in Nancy or a stop in *La Petite France* in Strasbourg for a glass of framboise, the fragrant raspberry brandy customarily savored in large balloon glasses, testifies more to the particular charm of Lorraine and Alsace than any words. It is impossible not to be captivated.

Nancy, the starting point of our tour of Alsace-Lorraine, is 190 miles (360 km) east of Paris. For the fastest route from Paris, take A4 east to Metz; then take E12 south to Nancy.

NANCY: An old proverb says: "In Europe there are three magnificent ceremonies: the coronation of an emperor at Frankfurt, the investiture of a king at Reims, and the burial of a duke at Nancy." Founded in the 11th century, Nancy is the capital of

Lorraine and was a seat of power during the 17th and 18th centuries. The Dukes of Lorraine wielded international power until François III exchanged his duchy for that of Tuscany. In his place Louis XV installed Stanislas Leczynski, his father-in-law and the dethroned King of Poland, on the throne of Nancy in 1737. This was an astute political move, for on Stanislas's death, Nancy reverted to France.

Stanislas Leczynski is the man responsible for the glory of Nancy. He summoned artists and architects from all over France to celebrate his reign. The result is the Place Stanislas, a magnificent 18th-century square surrounded by seven pavilions decorated with wrought-iron grilles and balconies, all in a harmonious 18th-century style. This square is the center and soul of Nancy. The area around the Place Stanislas is also a part of Stanislas's urban plan. The Place de la Carrière, the Arc de Triomphe, and the Palais de Gouvernement all attest to the duke's refined architectural taste. Behind the Place de la Carrière, La Pépinière is an English garden and zoo. It's also a pleasant spot to while away an hour or two watching the Nancéiens at play.

Other spots of interest are the *Musée Historique Lorraine* (closed Tuesdays; admission charge; 64 Grande-Rue; phone: 83-32-18-74), which has a wonderfully rich collection relating to the history of Nancy. An archaeological garden displays Celtic, Gallo-Roman, and Frankish artifacts, and there's an almost complete collection of the engravings of Jacques Callot, numerous paintings of Georges de la Tour, a collection of furniture and folk art of the area, Judaica, and a museum of pharmacology.

The *Musée des Beaux-Arts* (closed Monday mornings and Tuesdays; admission charge; 3 Pl. Stanislas; phone: 83-37-65-01), in one of the pavilions of the Place Stanislas, is devoted to European painting from the 14th century to modern times. The museum displays works of Delacroix, Manet, Utrillo, Poussin, and Rubens, among others.

Nancy has numerous churches; two are well worth a visit: Eglise des Cordeliers (Grande Rue), burial place of the Dukes of Lorraine, and Eglise Notre-Dame-de-Bon-Secours (Av. Strasbourg), where Stanislas Leczynski and his wife, Catherine Opalinska, are buried.

For lovers of Art Nouveau, Nancy offers the *Musée de l'Ecole de Nancy* (closed Tuesdays; admission charge; 36-38 Rue du Sergent-Blandan; phone: 83-40-14-86), with objects from the workshop of Emile Gallé. The fluid lines of nature are captured in ceramic, glass, furniture, and other media.

LUNÉVILLE: Leaving Nancy by the southeast route, within about 20 miles (32 km) you come to Lunéville — '"little Versailles." Built by Léopold, Duke of Lorraine and an admirer of Louis XIV, the palace is a modest replica of the great palace of Versailles. Later, Lunéville became the favorite residence of Stanislas Leczynski, and its corridors resounded with the voices of such notables as Voltaire, Helvetius, and Diderot. There is a museum of military memorabilia and documents relating to Lunéville's history, but is better known for its collection of Lunéville porcelain. Closed Tuesdays. Admission charge (phone: 83-76-23-57).

BACCARAT: Southeast from Lunéville, it's 15 miles (24 km) to Baccarat, a name that has spelled fine crystal to lovers of the very best for more than 2 centuries. The *Musée de la Cristal* (admission charge; Rue du Cristalerie; phone: 83-75-10-01) displays antique and contemporary crystal works, some dating from the founding of the factory in 1764 (open weekends only, April 1 to June 15, from 2 to 6 PM; daily, June 16 to September 30, from 10 AM to noon and 2 to 6:30 PM). Although the factory itself is not open to the public, several shops in town display and sell Baccarat items.

ST. DIÉ: Continuing southwest from Baccarat, you come to St. Dié. It was in the *Cosmographiae Introductio,* printed and published in St. Dié in 1507, that the continent of America was so named for the first time. The town owes its origin and its name to a Benedictine monastery founded in the 7th century by St. Déodat. The Romanesque

Eglise Notre-Dame-de-Galilée and the 18th-century Cathédrale St.-Dié, which are united on the Rue Thiers by a 15th-century cloister, are the major points of interest.

En Route from St. Dié – From St. Dié, at the foot of the Vosges Mountains, head through the crest of the Vosges at Col Ste.-Marie and continue through Ste.-Marie-aux-Mines, then east through Fertrupt, winding to the Col du Haut Ribeauvillé and down to Ribeauvillé.

Ribeauvillé, at the base of the Vosges, is one of the many wine-growing towns in this area of Alsace. The town is noted for its gewürztraminer and its riesling. It is also noted for the *Pfifferday* (Day of the Fifes) festival, held on the last Sunday in August. If you're lucky enough to be in town, you'll see a historic parade, townspeople in regional costume, and folk dances. And you'll be able to drink wine from the "wine fountain" in front of the Town Hall. *John,* a pastry shop at 58 Grande Rue, sells *kugelhopf* by the slice.

From Ribeauvillé it's south to Riquewihr, a town that escaped war damage and remains today almost exactly as it was in the 16th century. There are no grand monuments to see in Riquewihr; you see, rather, a lifestyle, an era that has long since passed into history. The half-timbered houses, the old courtyards, the carved stone wells, and the fountains — all join to bring the past to life. If you are in town for the grape harvest in the autumn (usually October, occasionally September), you have the feeling of having stepped into a picture book.

From Riquewihr, continue south, then west, to Kayserberg. Known mainly as where Albert Schweitzer was born (in 1875), this farm town also is a delightful wine village filled with medieval houses. Sites include the ruins of an ancient castle, elegant 16th-century buildings, the Romanesque Eglise de la Ste.-Croix, and the Schweitzer birthplace (126 Rue du Général-de-Gaulle; phone: 89-47-36-55), now a museum (closed November to *Easter;* admission charge). A grape harvest festival is held here every 5 years.

COLMAR: From Kayserberg head east to Colmar. Unquestionably Alsace's most beautiful city, it is noted for its typically Alsatian character, for the Petite Venise section interlaced by a canal, for the old town with its 16th- and 17th-century houses, for the Eglise St.-Martin with its Gothic choir, and, most of all, for the *Musée d'Unterlinden* (open daily; admission charge; Pl. de la Sinn; phone: 89-41-89-23), in an old convent that was founded by two widows from a noble family. The 13th-century structure is entered through the cloister. In the chapel is the magnificent Issenheim altarpiece, painted in the 16th century by Mathias Grünewald. This masterwork alone is certainly worth a trip to Colmar, as it symbolizes the mysticism, the passion, and the fervor of the turbulent age from which it sprang. The chapel also has a 24-panel series of the Passion conceived by Martin Schongauer in the late 15th century. The rest of the museum contains diverse displays, including works by Picasso and Léger.

STRASBOURG: The sights are many and varied, but the number one spot for the visitor with only hours to spare is the cathedral, one of the glories of European medieval art and architecture. The original cathedral was begun in 1015 in the Romanesque style, but it burned several times; work on the present cathedral began in the 12th century, this time in pure Gothic. When complete in 1439, the lacy openwork spire made it the tallest building in Christendom. The cathedral has witnessed much of Alsace's turbulent history and has even served the Protestant faith, during the Reformation. Louis XIV and Louis XV worshiped here, and in 1770 Marie Antoinette was formally greeted here on the way to her wedding to Louis XVI. During the revolution, the spire was saved by being crowned by a huge, red Phrygian cap. The wars of the 19th and 20th centuries damaged the structure, but it survived to present the splendid sight we see today.

Before going inside, note the richly sculptured façade; its complex iconography alone almost sums up medieval religious belief. Stained glass is the marvel of the interior, whether richly colored as in the large rose window or in gray-green grisaille, as in St. Catherine's Chapel. Be sure not to miss the Pilier des Anges (Pillar of Angels) and the wonderful 16th-century astronomer's clock, both in the south transept. The latter is an ingenious device that goes into action at 12:31 PM each day — be on hand by 12:15 to catch the taped presentation which is available in English as well as other languages. Afterward, take a close look at the woodcarving of the *Maison Kammerzell,* the striking half-timbered house on the cathedral square. Now a restaurant and guesthouse (see *Best en Route*), it was built in the 16th century by a rich merchant.

The *Musée de l'Oeuvre Notre-Dame* (3 Pl. du Château; phone: 88-32-06-39), to the side of the cathedral, displays original working drawings of the raising of the cathedral as well as originals of many of its statues, which have been replaced by copies. The Château des Rohan, next door, built by a great French family that produced many statesmen and churchmen, is an 18th-century palace where private apartments can be seen, plus a decorative arts museum notable for its collection of ceramics, a fine arts museum, and an archaeological museum. Don't linger, however, because the city also has a historical museum, a museum of modern art, and the thoroughly charming *Musée Alsacien* of the folk art and traditions in rural Alsace.

The Petite France area is noted for its picturesque views of half-timbered houses reflected in the waters of small canals — this is a must. In the summer, you can take guided tours of Old Strasbourg by miniature train; boat trips are also available. Information can be obtained at the tourist office (Pl. Gutenberg; phone: 88-32-57-07) or at the train station (Pl. de la Gare; phone: 88-61-39-23). But remember that the best way to absorb the feel of a town is by sitting and watching. Find a suitable café, order a cold Alsatian beer, and relax as you savor the other side of France.

BEST EN ROUTE

Expect to pay $110 and up per night for a double room in expensive hotels; $75 to $110 in moderate ones; and less than $75, inexpensive. The restaurants run from about $100 for a dinner for two (excluding wine and other drinks) in the expensive range; $65 to $100 in the moderate range; and under $65, inexpensive. All hotels and restaurants accept major credit cards, unless otherwise indicated.

NANCY

Capucin Gourmand – The city's finest restaurant with some outstanding traditional dishes and some varied light specials. A less expensive prix fixe menu also is available. Closed Sunday evenings, Mondays, and August, and 2 weeks in January. Reservations advised. Visa only accepted. 31 Rue Gambetta (phone: 83-35-26-98). Expensive.

Grand Hôtel de la Reine – In a renovated landmark 18th-century building on Place Stanislas, this lovely hotel also houses the *Stanislas* restaurant, which has an excellent prix fixe menu and a very talented chef. 2 Pl. Stanislas (phone: 83-35-03-01; fax: 83-32-86-04). Expensive.

Altéa Thiers – Its 112 rooms are comfortable and nicely decorated, and it has a fine restaurant and bar. 11 Rue Raymond-Poincaré (phone: 83-35-61-01; fax: 83-32-78-17). Expensive to moderate.

Albert Ier Astoria – Quiet and comfortable, with 120 rooms but no restaurant. Close to the train station. 3 Rue de l'Armée-Patton (phone: 83-40-31-24; fax: 83-28-47-78). Moderate.

Excelsior – This Art Nouveau brasserie, classified as a historic monument, was taken over and renovated by the Flo group, which owns several lovingly restored classic bistros in Paris. The menu offers a large choice of seafood, fish, and regional items at affordable prices, all amidst beautiful surroundings. Reservations advised. Most credit cards accepted. 50 Rue Henri-Poincaré (phone: 83-35-24-57). Open daily. Moderate.

Gentilhommière – A charming provincial restaurant with very good meat and poultry dishes (veal, squab, duck) and excellent sauces. Closed weekends, August, and holidays. Reservations advised. Most credit cards accepted. 29 Rue des Maréchaux (phone: 83-32-26-44). Moderate.

RIBEAUVILLÉ

Des Vosges – This clean, modern hotel has 18 rooms and a good restaurant (one Michelin star) with an extensive menu that includes a three-course prix fixe meal for a reasonable price. 2 Grande Rue (phone: 89-73-61-39). Expensive to moderate.

Menestrel – Alsace's gently sloping vineyards surround this modern, flower-studded inn, owned by a pastry chef and his wife just outside Ribeauvillé. Closed mid-January to mid-February. Av. du Général-de-Gaulle (phone: 89-73-80-52; fax: 89-73-32-39). Moderate.

Tour – A picturesque, renovated old winery with 32 pleasant rooms. Most credit cards accepted. 1 Rue de la Mairie (phone: 89-73-72-73). Moderate.

Zum Pfifferhüs – An appealing *winstub* (German, for "wine pub") in a landmark building with very tasty *choucroute*. Closed Wednesdays, Thursdays, and in February. 14 Grande Rue (phone 89-73-62-28). Inexpensive.

RIQUEWIHR

Auberge de Schoenenbourg – Enjoy Alsatian food with flourishes of nouvelle cuisine while gazing at the vineyard behind the restaurant. The wines served are made from grapes grown here. Hotel and restaurant open daily. Most credit cards accepted. 2 Rue de la Piscine (phone: 89-47-92-28; fax: 89-47-95-88). Expensive.

KAYSERSBERG

Résidence Chambard – One of the best classic restaurants in Alsace, with a gracious dining room and specialties like foie gras in cabbage leaves. The annex behind the restaurant has a comfortable 20-room hotel. Hotel closed during *Christmas* and most of March. Restaurant closed Mondays and for lunch Tuesdays. 9 Rue du Général-de-Gaulle (phone: 89-47-10-17; fax: 89-47-35-03). Expensive.

COLMAR

Terminus-Bristol – A large old-fashioned establishment located across from the train station and remodeled in high style. Two added attractions: the Michelin one-star restaurant *Rendez-vous de Chasse* (phone: 89-41-10-10), featuring a talented young chef and one of the town's most fanciful menus; and a second, less formal, eatery next door, *L'Auberge,* offering more traditional fare. 7 Pl. de la Gare (phone: 89-23-59-59; fax: 89-23-92-96). Expensive.

Hostellerie "Le Maréchal" – At the water's edge in the charming Little Venice quarter, this sprawling collection of half-timbered houses with flower-strewn balconies and crooked stairways has a very individual charm. Rooms are named for composers — Mozart, Wagner, Beethoven — and each is decorated differently. The restaurant, overlooking the water, has tapestry, candlelight, and dark wood. Most credit cards accepted. 4-6 Pl. des Six Montagnes-Noires (phone: 89-41-60-32; fax: 89-24-59-40). Expensive to moderate.

Maison des Têtes – This simple brasserie is in an extraordinary 17th-century landmark building, where heads of people and mythical animals adorn the façade, imploring guests to enter. Closed from early January to mid-February, Sunday evenings, and Mondays. Reservations advised. 19 Rue de Têtes (phone: 89-24-43-43). Expensive to moderate.

Altea Champs de Mars – Comfortable accommodations and pleasant service. 2 Av. Marne (phone: 89-41-54-54; fax: 89-23-93-76). Moderate.

Le Petit Bouchon – Tucked away on a small square, this tiny upstairs eatery is decorated with flowers and varying shades of pink, operated by a Lyonnaise chef and his charming Alsatian wife, and offers a menu true to the owners' origins. Servings are generous and prices, reasonable. Closed Wednesdays and for lunch Thursdays. Reservations advised. Most credit cards accepted. 11 Rue d'Alspach (phone: 89-23-45-57). Moderate.

STRASBOURG

Buerehiesel – A beautiful dining room, very attentive service, wonderful fish and game dishes (in season), and a large list of fine wines. Closed Tuesday evenings, Wednesdays, 2 weeks in August, and for periods during the winter. Reservations advised. 4 Parc de l'Orangerie (phone: 88-61-62-24; fax: 88-61-32-00). Expensive.

Cathédrale Dauphin – An old building just in front of the cathedral now houses a hotel. Past the crisply modern lobby, and up a narrow stairway, are tastefully decorated rooms, many of them with fantastic views of the cathedral and square. Guests have access to a nearby health and fitness club. 12 Place de la Cathédrale (phone 88-22-12-12; fax: 88-23-28-00). Expensive.

Le Crocodile – Unquestionably one of the city's best restaurants (three Michelin stars), featuring French cuisine with an Alsatian touch; fish and game specialties are outstanding. Closed Sundays, Mondays, mid-July to early August, and a week at *Christmas.* Reservations necessary. 10 Rue de l'Outre (phone: 88-32-13-02; fax: 88-75-72-01). Expensive.

Holiday Inn – For those who seek a bit of home away from home, this modern hotel in the familiar chain offers familiar comforts including a health club with pool, sauna, steambath, and tennis courts. Near the Palais des Congrès, 20 Pl. du Bordeaux (phone: 88-35-70-00; fax: 88-37-07-04). Expensive.

Sofitel – A modern 163-room hotel with an excellent location, all the comforts of any first class establishment, and a good restaurant. Pl. St.-Pierre-le-Jeune (phone: 88-32-99-30). Expensive.

Dragon – This appealing addition to the city's hotels in a calm corner of town just slightly off the beaten track is 17th-century outside and Bauhaus modern inside. Rooms are in shades of gray with reproduction Mallet Stevens chairs and some have views of the cathedral. It's already a favorite with members of the European Parliament. 2 Rue de l'Ecarlate (phone 88-35-79-80; fax: 88-25-78-95). Expensive to moderate.

Maison Kammerzell – Occupying the best corner in town, this is a 16th-century architectural gem. The ground-floor dining rooms boast elaborate woodcarvings, and upstairs the restaurant overlooks the Place de la Cathédrale. Some claim the *choucroute alsacienne* here is the city's best. Last year, 9 guestrooms with modern decor were added. 16 Pl. de la Cathédrale (phone: 88-32-42-14). Expensive to moderate.

Maison des Tanneurs – Bedecked with balconies and flowers at the edge of a canal, this is the place to try *choucroute* (share it). Closed Sundays, Mondays, the first half of July, and late December to mid-January. Reservations advised. 42 Rue du Bain-aux-Plantes (phone: 88-32-79-70). Expensive to moderate.

Des Rohan – Completely modernized, though it looks like a historic landmark. The 36 rooms have private baths and are done in 17th- and 18th-century styles. No restaurant. Most credit cards accepted. 17-19 Rue du Maroquin (phone: 88-32-85-11; fax: 88-75-65-37). Expensive to moderate.

Vieille Enseigne – Once a mere *winstub,* this cozy restaurant with a club-like atmosphere, popular with politicians, has bettered its service and its food over the years, reaching a very high level in both. Closed Saturday lunch, Sundays, and from late July to mid-August. Reservations necessary. 9 Rue des Tonneliers (phone: 88-32-58-50). Expensive to moderate.

Nouvel Maison Rouge – This centrally located hotel was recently renovated in Art Deco style. It has a wide range of reception and conference rooms and an efficient and cooperative staff. No restaurant. 4 Rue des Francs-Bourgeois (phone: 88-32-08-60; fax: 88-22-43-73). Moderate.

La Petite Alsace – Rustic wood beams, white lace tablecloths, and a typically Alsatian menu characterize this pleasant spot in the heart of La Petite France. Reservations advised. 23 Rue du Bain-aux-Plantes (phone: 88-22-04-05). Moderate.

Chez Tante Liesel – It's friendly and cheerful with only nine tables and popular with diners for its family recipes and unexpected treats. Closed Tuesdays, Wednesday lunch, *Christmas,* and *New Year's Day.* Reservations advised. Most credit cards accepted. 4 Rue des Dentelles (phone: 88-23-02-16). Inexpensive.

Gutenberg – A small, simple, clean hotel in an old château. About one third of the 50 rooms come with a private bath, and many of them already have an extra bed for a third person or child. Most credit cards accepted. 31 Rue des Serruriers (phone: 88-32-17-15). Inexpensive.

Strissel – Good Alsatian food, wines, and atmosphere make this dining spot a local favorite. Convenient to the museums and the cathedral. Closed Sundays, Mondays, a week in February, and most of July. Reservations advised. Most credit cards accepted. 5 Pl. de la Grande-Boucherie (phone: 88-32-14-73). Inexpensive.

Germany

After two world wars, crushing defeat, foreign occupation, and division into hostile half-countries, there is again a united Germany at the center of Europe. *Wiedervereinigung* (reunification), the dream that postwar Germans for so long could only hope might be realized some distant day, suddenly came true in October 1990 with the absorption of the former German Democratic Republic in the east into the Federal Republic of the west.

The two parts of the new Germany remain, however, very disparate. The east, long touted as the "jewel" of the former Communist bloc, remains underdeveloped and inefficient by most Western standards. The economy has collapsed, a pollution problem of enormous proportions has been revealed, and the task of rebuilding the infrastructure is proving to be far more formidable (and expensive) than anticipated. It will be some time before conditions in the two parts of Germany come close to being equalized, especially for tourists. It is "pioneer work," say Germany's tourist authorities, "that is going very, very slowly."

Roads are a major problem. Despite a crash construction effort, it is expected to be at least 5 (and probably closer) to 10 years before the highway network in the east is on a par with the superb autobahns and secondary routes in the west. There also is some danger in the difference. The accident rate in the east has risen alarmingly with the arrival from the west of large numbers of drivers in high-powered cars, accustomed to burning up speed-limitless autobahns. Eastern drivers, accustomed to a pre-unification limit of 100 kilometers per hour (62 mph), are similarly a hazard in the west as they sputter along in their little "Trabis" with two-stroke engines — motors Americans more frequently encounter in lawnmowers.

With the exception of the largest cities in what was East Germany, travel services also are in short supply. At the time of reunification, the number of hotel beds in the east was estimated at 75,000, compared with 3.5 million in the west. There are some international class hotels in Berlin's eastern sector, Leipzig, and Dresden, built by the former Communist government for foreign guests paying in hard currency. Rates are comparable to similar accommodations in western cities. Elsewhere, choices remain limited. The best hotels in eastern Germany formerly were operated by a government agency, *Interhotel,* which has entered into a leasing arrangement with the western *Steigenberger* chain. (For information in the US, contact *SRS Hotels Steigenberger Reservation Service,* 40 E. 49th St., New York, NY 10017; phone: 212-593-2988.)

Reunited Germany, although considerably smaller than its prewar size, again is one of the larger countries in Europe; with 137,740 square miles, it is slightly smaller than the state of Montana. The landscape, however, is one of Europe's most diversified. Most of the renowned areas — the castle-crowned Rhine, the Black Forest, the Bavarian Alps and lakes — are in the west. Except for the Thuringian Hills, the east is largely flat, the beginning of the great Northern European plain that extends on eastward through Poland and Russia to the Ural Mountains.

Everywhere in Germany you encounter history as well as scenery. It goes back to at least the 7th century BC, when this heavily forested land was home to numerous Germanic tribes such as the Bavarians, Franconians, Frisians, Saxons, Thuringians, and Swabians, whose names survive as regional place names. In AD 9, these so-called "Barbarians" scored one of the most decisive victories in recorded history when they defeated three Roman legions in the Teutoburg Forest, southeast of the modern city of Bielefeld. That ended Roman expansion northward. The Rhine and Danube rivers became the empire's border for the next 4 centuries, and the Germans did not become "latinized," never adopting the Roman culture and language as did most other peoples of Western Europe. They were, however, gradually converted to Christianity (from the 5th through the 9th centuries).

In the 9th century, they came under the sway of Charlemagne (Karl der Grosse in German), ruler of the Franks, a kindred people who had migrated across the Rhine into present-day France. Although Charlemagne's empire soon disintegrated, the Germans perpetuated its memory until almost modern times in the Holy Roman Empire — a political fiction that supposedly united them but which the French philosopher Voltaire bitingly dismissed as "an agglomeration" that was "neither holy, nor Roman, nor an empire." He was right on the mark. In fact, feudalism reigned supreme. Germany was a bewildering patchwork of squabbling principalities and petty nobles who were often not much more than landed bandits, constantly in conflict with each other and with many foreign foes, including the pope in Rome.

While the rest of Europe was consolidating into nation-states, Germany remained divided, initially by politics and then, in the 16th century, by religion. The Reformation began here when Martin Luther (1483–1546), a priest and professor of theology, refused to renounce his denunciation of the corruption of the Roman church and his belief in individual salvation through faith. His excommunication in 1521 only exacerbated the conflict. Luther's forceful preaching and writing drew many in Germany (and elswhere in Europe) to the Protestant cause. The movement grew and the war that eventually broke out lasted for 30 years (from 1618–1648).

The image of Germany in modern times is of an aggressive country threatening its neighbors. For much of their history, however, the Germans have suffered from the aggressions of others, as French, Spanish, English, Swedish, and other foreign armies used German territory as their battleground. This was particularly true during the Thirty Years War; records dating from after that war describe vast areas of Germany as virtually depopulated wastelands. Germany was again a battleground during the Napoleonic Wars (1803–1815), after which its map was redrawn, eliminating the majority of its smallest states and preparing the way for a long-delayed unification.

Austria, the heir to the Holy Roman Empire (which had finally been put to rest by Napoleon), vied for leadership with Prussia, a military outpost on the eastern frontier that had developed into a particularly powerful entitity. A series of wars culminated in Prussia's victory over the German *"Erbfeind"* (hereditary enemy), France, in 1870. A German Empire uniting all states except Austria was proclaimed, with the Prussian ruler installed as kaiser. At first, Germany exerted a stablizing influence in Europe. Prince Otto von Bismarck, the imperial chancellor and architect of unity, sought to maintain the status quo through a network of alliances with other powers that effectively isolated the old enemy, France, still smarting from its defeat. It also was a period of rapid industrial growth, economic expansion, and social development. Although the government was autocratic, with little power delegated to an elected *Reichstag* (Parliament), it enacted the most advanced body of social legislation in any country of that day. The Bismarckian system remains the basis of the social welfare system of today's Germany. The period leading up to 1914 is still looked back upon by most Germans as a golden age.

But with the advent of a new emperor, Wilhelm II, in 1888, Bismarck was dismissed and a policy of colonial expansion led to friction with other powers, especially Britain, that culminated in World War I. Defeated, the empire collapsed and was succeeded by a republic, proclaimed in the university town of Weimar and since known to history as the Weimar Republic. It was unable to cope with the severe economic problems of the postwar years and was paralyzed by the rivalry of its many small political parties. Disunity and despair brought Adolf Hitler and his Nazi party to power in 1933. His Third Reich (the first having been the Holy Roman Empire, the second Bismarck's German Empire) quickly brought on another war, and after 6 years of incredible bloodshed and devastation, another absolute German defeat. In 1945, the victorious Allies met at Yalta and Potsdam and divided Germany into four zones — British, French, American, and Soviet.

The tension between East and West, aggravated by the Soviet blockade of Berlin in 1948–1949, resulted in the division of Germany into "East" and "West." The three Western allies soon merged their zones, turning over most powers to a new German government in 1949, which established a temporary capital in the university town of Bonn, on the Rhine. The next 2 decades saw the *Wirschaftswunder* (economic miracle) that not only rebuilt but transformed the country — actually, only half the former country — into the strongest economy in Europe and the third among all industrial democracies, after the United States and Japan.

A very different Germany emerged in the Soviet-occupied territories. A Communist state, the German Democratic Republic was established in 1949 in response to the merger of the western zones. It also made progress, especially after the construction of the Berlin Wall, in 1961, and the fortification of the entire zonal border with West Germany cut off the defection of large numbers of East Germans to the West. The GDR became the showcase of the Communist bloc, with an economy second only to that of the Soviet Union. It was regarded as the most stable of the Eastern European satellites, and enjoyed the highest standard of living.

But in 1989, the Wall sprang some leaks. It began with Hungary opening its border with Austria. East Germans took advantage of the opportunity to defect by detouring through a "brotherly socialist state." More sought to exit through Czechoslovakia. Then anti-government street demonstrations broke out in East German cities, especially Leipzig, and the Berlin Wall was breached by crowds from both sides. Events could no longer be controlled. Elections in the GDR led to an interim government, and with the approval of the four World War II powers, a decision to unite the two Germanys sooner rather than later. The West German deutsche mark became the common currency in June 1990, formal unification was declared in October, and the first all-German parliamentary election since 1933 took place in December.

Germany has been the cradle of heroes and monsters — a land of giants such as Bach, Brahms, Beethoven, and Wagner in music; Hegel, Kant, and Heidegger in philosophy; and Goethe, Schiller, and Thomas Mann in literature. Karl Marx and Friedrich Engels were the originators of modern Communist ideology, just as Einstein was the pioneer of modern physics. Paradoxically, it also was in Germany that Hitler came to power, and it was there, not so long ago, that this contradictory people nurtured the cancerous growth of Nazi fascism.

Many people fear a recurrence of the Nazi nightmare in Germany, and the recent increase of sporadic neo-Nazi incidents fuels that concern. The task of melding two regions that have had such very different experiences for almost half a century into one country is formidable, and there are many questions still to be answered. After 42 years as the "provincial capital," Bonn has been replaced by Berlin (the historic capital) as the seat of the federal government, although the cost of transferring the government will be immense. The division of the haves in the "west" and the have-nots in the "east" has spawned troubling new economic and sociologic friction.

These are, however, particularly exciting times in which to visit Germany and witness the rebuilding of a once great nation, set to benefit from the newly integrated European economy. The now-depressed east's future can be seen in the west's present. War-ravaged cities and towns have long since been rebuilt in modern style, but where possible the best of the old has been retained, or in some cases lovingly reconstructed. You still can see the fairy-tale castles of Bavaria's King Ludwig II. In fact, most of Bavaria still looks like the setting of a fairy tale by the Brothers Grimm with one medieval town after another — Rothenburg, Dinkelsbühl, Nördlingen — along the lovely *Romantische Strasse* (Romantic Road). Everywhere in Germany there are sleepy little villages with characteristic half-timbered houses, places where people sometimes still wear traditional costumes to markets and festivals.

Cologne Cathedral, virtually unscathed in World War II, towers over the ancient Rhineland city that began history as a Roman frontier post. Vibrant and exciting Berlin, in both sides of the once-divided city, contains some of the world's greatest art treasures. Munich is not only one of the world's most beautiful cities, but may well be the most livable. According to a poll some years back, two out of three Germans would prefer to live in the Bavarian capital if given the choice.

The former East Germany also has its showcase cities. Dresden, the capital of the Saxon kings and lavishly embellished by them over the years, was considered the most beautiful of Europe's Renaissance cities before World War II. It was heavily damaged by American and British air raids at the very end of the war, but some of its architectural treasures survived and others have been reconstructed. Leipzig, another beautiful Saxon city, was once the home of Johann Sebastian Bach and still claims one of the world's finest choirs. The Baltic Sea coast, a favorite prewar vacation spot, especially Rügen Island, does not yet have the facilities for large numbers of visitors, but can be expected to be an attraction again as redevelopment progresses.

The extraordinary variety of the German countryside, cities, and towns can be explored by following our nine routes (seven in the west and two in the east). In the north, a visitor can explore the Hanseatic cities of Bremen, Hamburg, and Lübeck and relax in the lake country of "little Switzerland," or on a beach such as at Travemünde on the Baltic Sea. The short, pleasant route from Frankfurt to Heidelberg follows the charming Main River Valley through the gentle wooded hills of the historic Odenwald and Spessart areas. Westphalia, land of ham and pumpernickel, castle-hotels and wayside inns, can best be seen in a circular route that begins in Dortmund. Castles, vineyards, and dramatic vistas mark the fabled Rhineland, which includes the area from Mainz to Koblenz, but can be extended to Cologne and Düsseldorf. Germany's Castle Road meanders along the Neckar River Valley, passing more than a dozen castles on the way from Heidelberg to Heilbronn. Rolling hills and thick forests characterize the Black Forest region, which extends from Basel, in Switzerland, to the exclusive German spa of Baden-Baden. The Romantic Road runs from Würzburg on the Main River to Füssen in the Alpine foothills, and passes through Bavaria's fabulous walled medieval towns.

In the east, there are two routes which may be combined if desired. Both begin in Berlin. The first goes west through Potsdam, across gently rolling hills to Magdeburg, over the Harz Mountains southward to the foothills of the Thuringian Forest, and then back north to Naumburg. From there, it is possible to return to Berlin or branch eastward to Leipzig and the second route, which includes the cultural center of Dresden; Meissen, where fine china has been manufactured since 1705; and the country of the Sorbs.

Northern Germany

Northern Germany, the area bounded roughly by Bremen, Hamburg, Lübeck, Kiel, and Schleswig, largely has remained undiscovered by modern American tourists. Yet it offers several lovely ocean beaches and some of its most historical cities. Relatively flat, the terrain of northern Germany is a pleasant blend of gently rolling hills, sunlit lake country, and fine sandy beaches.

Hamburg, a highly sophisticated city that is rarely on the usual tourist itinerary, is Germany's second largest, with a population of 1.6 million people. Bremen, with over half a million inhabitants, is the oldest German maritime city, having been a market port since 965; its 500-year-old medieval section still remains. You can vary your trip to northern Germany by visiting its important ports; exploring its tiny, undiscovered towns such as Stade and

Ratzeburg; and enjoying its ocean resorts such as Travemünde. For information and maps about the area, contact the regional tourist office in Oldenburg, just northwest of Bremen: Fremdenverkehrsverband, Nordsee-Niedersachsen-Bremen, 19-20 Bahnhofstr., 2900 Oldenburg (phone: 0441-14535).

The dominant force in northern German history was the Hanseatic League, a free association of medieval towns that concentrated on trade. Foremost in the league were the city-states of Bremen, Hamburg, and Lübeck. Since they paid taxes to no larger power, these cities became a powerful force in both domestic and foreign trade. Even today, people from the Hanseatic cities take immense pride in their localities, often identifying themselves as Lübeckers or Hamburgers before saying they are Germans.

Today, the Hanseatic League is mere history, although Germans still refer to the direct train line running from Bremen to Hamburg to Lübeck as the Hanseatic Line. This route is convenient, not only for travelers who choose to ride the modern, efficient railways of Germany, but for those who wish to tour northern Germany by car. The tour covers roughly 225 miles (360 km), so you will need at least 3 days.

BREMEN: The natural starting point for any tour of northern Germany, Bremen, along with its sister city of Bremerhaven, is the oldest seaport in Germany. Interestingly enough, it is because of Bremen that Bremerhaven exists at all. In the early 17th century, the merchants of Bremen noticed that their precious port was becoming clogged with mud from the Weser River that flows into it. Dredging operations were not then what they are now, so they simply moved the port downstream to Vegesack. Two hundred years later, Vegesack too became clogged with mud, so the merchants moved on to Bremerhaven, which now ranks as the largest container facility in Europe and Germany's second-largest seaport.

The tourist information service in Bremen, in front of the main train station, offers maps, brochures, and information about hotels and pensions (phone: 0421-36361).

Like most European cities, Bremen is best seen on foot. The heart of the city is the old medieval section surrounding the Marktplatz and most of the modern city has grown up around this area. The city used to be enclosed by a great wall, but the land where the wall used to stand is now a ring road that completely encircles the older part of the city.

Bremen's huge market square is worth a visit, if for nothing more than the delicious smell of roasting coffee from the surrounding coffeehouses or the lovely colors and shapes of fresh fruits and vegetables. The old Rathaus (Town Hall), on the market square, is well worth seeing; it houses the *Ratskeller,* an excellent restaurant with the largest wine list in Germany — more than 600 wines, all of them German.

Other sights in Bremen are the *Focke Museum* (240 Schwachhauser Heerstr.), renowned for its fine collection of historical artifacts from the north, and St. Peter's Cathedral, right on the market square. The 11th-century cathedral has an unusual cellar called the Bleikeller (lead cellar), where the lead slates for the roof were originally kept. A roofer who fell to his death was once put in the cellar for safekeeping, along with the roofing tiles. Everyone forgot about his body and it was some time before he was discovered, perfectly preserved. Apparently the air in the cellar is so dry that it mummifies anything that is put down there. Several mummified corpses are included in the collection, which is open on weekdays only.

While in Bremen, don't miss the old section of town referred to as the Schnoor, with its narrow 400- and 500-year-old streets, half-timbered houses, and quaint gabled roofs. There are many art galleries and crafts shops that offer some excellent buys on handmade items. Walk on the Rampart Walk (Wallanlagen), with its windmill and lovely green spaces. The *Café Knigge,* a lovely outdoor café with a terrace, is on an old pedestrian street (42 Sögestr.).

For people who have an undeniable urge to set out to sea, there are daily tours of the harbor area by boat, leaving the Martini jetty four times a day.

En Route from Bremen – It is only 75 miles (120 km) to Hamburg, little more than an hour's drive along the speedy German autobahns. If you have the time, the drive to Hamburg along the secondary highway that more or less parallels the autobahn (Rte. 75) is well worth the extra minutes, as it weaves through open moors and forests that are so common to this section of Germany. A good overnight stopping place is the little town of Rotenburg; it's just the place for a quiet rest.

STADE: About 25 miles (40 km) north of the autobahn, on Route 73, lies the town of Stade, which is starting to make a name for itself as a medieval city. Virtually unknown to most tourists, the quiet little town has some beautifully restored buildings, and restoration continues all the time. Be sure to see St. Cosmas Church, the Rathaus, the fish market, and the Bürgermeister Hintze Haus. At one end of the fish market is the restored Swedish warehouse that was built between 1692 and 1705 to serve as a supply depot for the Swedish troops that occupied the region at that time. Today, it serves as a regional museum for Lower Saxony.

HAMBURG: Hamburg is less than an hour's drive from Stade. Germany's largest seaport and second-largest city (after Berlin), Hamburg was an independent city-state in the Middle Ages, and even today the city exists both as a city and a state of Germany. Hamburgers always have been extremely proud of their independence, a pride that never showed more clearly than in 1871, when the Kaiser was going to raise a Hamburg merchant to the nobility. The Mayor of Hamburg informed the startled Kaiser: "It is impossible to raise a Hamburg citizen." That feeling still lingers today, and the citizens of this great harbor city are never so proud as when they can show off their city to visitors.

Hamburgers are quick to point out that the area the city now occupies has been inhabited continuously over the past 15,000 years, although permanent settlements can be traced back only 6,000 years. The first fortifications were built in 811, and although they were repeatedly pounded by the fierce Viking raiders of the north, the town continued to grow. In 1189, Frederick Barbarossa granted the city a charter as a free city and port, thereby exempting its ships from paying duty. After that, the merchants of the city prospered greatly. During the years of the Hanseatic League, no trading power on earth was the equal of Hamburg.

Despite the heavy bombing raids of World War II that all but flattened the city, it has recovered very well. Its port on the Elbe River is one of Europe's largest and it continues to grow. Though less popular with tourists than Munich or Berlin, today's Hamburg is an elegant and sophisticated modern city, with a 300-year-old opera and a renowned vaudeville theater, the *Hansa* (17 Steindamm; phone: 40-241414).

The tourist office at Bieberhaus (near the Central Station at Hachmannpl.; phone: 040-248700) can provide you with maps; the *Hamburg Guide,* a brochure containing a wealth of tourist information; and a fortnightly program guide, *Where to Go in Hamburg.* For hotel reservations and information, contact the Information Office (Hotelnachweis; phone: 300-51230), also at Central Station, Kirchenallee exit. There is a small fee for this service.

To get an idea of the layout of this large and sprawling city, take its excellent 2-hour bus tour, which begins at the train station daily.

Some of the sights that should not be missed are Europe's only privately owned zoo and the harbor, an incredible mélange of pleasure boats, oceangoing freighters, coal barges, tugs, and fishing boats. The harbor's 800th anniversary was celebrated in 1989. The fish market, where not only fish is sold, but just about every kind of ware, begins every Sunday at 5 AM near St. Pauli Landungsbrücken. Harbor tours are offered from entrance 2 to the St. Pauli landing by *Hadag Ships* (phone: 376-80024). The Aussenalster, a particularly wide and lovely branch of the Elbe that looks like a lake, is bordered by long, shaded avenues and green spots and makes a particularly fine place for strolling or boating. During the summer months, a very pleasant 50-minute Alster cruise departs from Jungfernstieg at frequent intervals and affords a lovely view of the city's towers and spires (phone: 341145). Also interesting are Planten en Blomen Gardens, a beautifully arranged park ideal for an afternoon's stroll, and St. Michael's Cathedral, a fine baroque church built in 1762, with a famous tower that offers a panorama of the city (admission charge).

For those who enjoy museums, Hamburg is just the place. An excellent art museum, the *Kunsthalle* (City Art Museum; closed Mondays; admission charge; 1 Glockengiesserwall) has a fine collection of paintings from medieval to modern; the modern section is best, with works by Klee, Munch, and others. There's the *Historical Museum* (Museum für Hamburgische Geschichte; closed Mondays; admission charge; 24 Holstenwall; phone: 349-122360), with an interesting collection relating to the ports and navigation; and the *Decorative Arts and Crafts Museum* (Museum für Kunst und Gewerbe; 1 Steintorpl.; phone: 248-252630), specializing in medieval gold and silver statuary, Renaissance furniture, clocks of northern Germany, and *Jugendstil* (Art Nouveau) items. The *Helms Museum* (2 Museumspl.) specializes in prehistory and early history of the Hamburg region. For a more up-to-date impression of this north German countryside and its residents, visit the *Altonaer Museum* (23 Museumstr.). For 20th-century north German art, visit the *Ernst Barlach Haus* (50 A Baron-Voght-Str.).

For Americans of German descent, Hamburg is an excellent place to do some genealogical research. The Historic Emigration Office in the *Museum for Hamburg History* has microfilm of nearly 5 million people who sailed from the port for the New World between 1850 and 1914. For further information, contact the German National Tourist Office (747 Third Ave., New York, NY 10017; phone: 212-308-3300); or Hamburg North America Representation (38 W. 32nd St., New York, NY 10001; phone: 212-967-3110).

Naturally it is impossible to overlook one of the most famous areas of Hamburg, the Reeperbahn. After dark, this area comes alive with neon lights, loud music, thick crowds, and barkers trying to attract those crowds to their establishments. Here sex shows, porno movies, strip clubs, and bars are the order of the day — or night, as the case may be. Many of these places are clip joints, pure and simple, but some of the better sexy stage shows are pretty safe bets. Among these are those at the *Regina Club,* the *Safari Club,* the *Colibri, Tabu,* and the *Salambo Cabaret.*

One of the best things about Hamburg is its restaurants. Everything is available, from haute cuisine to "rollmops" (pickled herring rolled in sour cream), in settings that vary from the crystal and china atmosphere of the top restaurants, to the beer and herring atmosphere of the waterfront snack bars (*Imbiss*). Because it's a port city, there are many fine foreign restaurants, the best of which is *Le Canard* (11 Martinistr.; see *Best en Route*). But Hamburg's specialty is fish, and its most famous specialties are *Finkenwerder Scholle,* (plaice), *Aalsuppe* (eel soup), and oysters, raw or baked with cheshire cheese. You can sample these and many other fine dishes right in the *St. Pauli* fish market at the Fischerhaus.

RATZEBURG: The distance from Hamburg to Lübeck is only 41 miles (66 km). Still, for the adventurous, the lovely island town of Ratzeburg on Route 208, in the middle of a lake to the south of the E22 autobahn, makes a lovely place to stay for a weekend, with plenty of swimming, boating, and fishing. The town is only a couple of kilometers from the former East German border, yet the easygoing way of life is so pleasant that it is hard to imagine that the border, which not long ago had its ghastly fences, mine fields, and machine guns, was less than 2½ miles (4 km) away. By all means see the local church, which has an interesting carved altar and is one of the largest brick churches in northern Germany.

LÜBECK: The capital of the Hanseatic cities during the Middle Ages, Lübeck retains the flavor of a medieval town, complete with towers, and old houses. The huge twin-towered gates at the entrance to the city — the Holstentor — hardly can fail to impress a visitor. These gates were built in 1477 as part of the fortifications, and today the massive towers serve as the symbol of Lübeck; they also house the *Municipal Museum.* Be sure to take a look at the old salt warehouses along one side of the Holstentor, a monument in the center of town, built in the 14th century to commemorate the merchants of the area.

Like most other German cities, Lübeck has an excellent tourist office (95 Becker-grubbe; phone: 451-122-8109), which can provide information and maps and will help arrange a room for the night in almost any price range for a small fee.

There are four museums in Lübeck, each a minor gem. Besides the *Municipal Museum,* there is *St. Anne's Museum* (15 St. Annenstr.), an old monastery that now houses local art and handicrafts; the *Behnhaus* (Königstr. at Glockenstr.), a perfectly preserved residence from 1780 that gives an excellent impression of how people lived then; and a museum in the cathedral that contains all the natural history discoveries from the area.

The Rathaus (Town Hall) is an unusual brick medieval building in the northern German style, on two sides of the Marktplatz. St. Mary's Church, a French Gothic structure that was built between 1251 and 1350, is known for its famed 17th-century organist, the composer Buxtehude.

The Haus der Schiffergesellschaft (2 Breite Str.), an old sailors' guild house dating from 1535, has an excellent restaurant inside, decorated with marine furniture and artifacts (see *Best en Route*). The *Buddenbrookhaus* (4 Mengstr.) was the family home of novelist Thomas Mann and the inspiration for his saga about the rise and decline of a Lübeck mercantile family.

One of the products for which Lübeck is most famous is the luscious marzipan candy, made from sugar and crushed almonds. It comes in virtually any shape, and you often see Lübeckers strolling along the streets, happily munching on a marzipan pig, pear, or apple. The best place in Lübeck, probably the best place in the world, to buy marzipan is the *I. G. Niederegger Konditorei and Café* (next to St. Mary's Church at 89 Breite Str.). Not only can you have a sinfully sweet piece of marzipan but a delicious cup of coffee to go with it. You can take some marzipan with you or mail it to friends as the perfect gift from Lübeck.

En Route from Lübeck – The drive from Lübeck to Kiel goes through what the Germans call the Holsteinische Schweiz, or little Switzerland, because of its numerous lakes and forests. It is best to take Route 76, which runs north through Plön and Preetz, rather than the faster, but more boring, Route 206 that runs through Bad Segeberg. If you are in the mood for an ocean beach, you can detour to Travemünde, just a few miles northeast of Lübeck, on the Baltic Sea; it's a fashionable resort with a casino. If not, your next stop might be either Plön, which is on the Plönersee, a large, scenic lake, or a bit farther north, Preetz, in the heart of the lovely and peaceful lake country.

KIEL: Kiel attracted a lot of attention when it hosted the sailing races that were part of the *1972 Olympics,* but as a center for tourism it leaves a lot to be desired. Most of Kiel was destroyed by the bombing during World War II, and the city has been rebuilt in modern style. It is a clean city, almost spotlessly so, but it has little to offer tourists, except perhaps for its bustling fish market, with an astonishing variety of fish. Besides the market, be sure to see the Kiel Canal, an outstanding engineering achievement that connects the North Sea and the Baltic and is the busiest canal in the world. Nearby, the Hindenburg Quay (Hindenburgufer), a 2-mile, tree-shaded promenade along the Kiel Förde, offers pleasant views of the harbor.

SCHLESWIG: About 31 miles (50 km) northwest of Kiel is Schleswig, the oldest town in the northern state of Schleswig-Holstein. It was founded by the Vikings and for many years it was a Viking stronghold; from here they plundered and looted the towns to the south, such as Hamburg and Bremen. Schleswig is well worth a visit, as it contains some of the richest Viking artifacts in northern Germany. By all means see the cathedral, built in 1100, with its incredible altarpiece carved elaborately in wood by Bruggeman in 1521.

Schleswig's other big attraction is the *Nydam* boat, an Anglo-Saxon vessel dating from the 4th century, one of the few of its type in the world. The boat is in a building near Gottorf Castle (admission charge). Built in the 12th century, the castle is the oldest in Schleswig-Holstein and is well worth a trip all by itself. It houses the *Schleswig-Holstein Museum,* containing fine exhibitions of folklore, art, and handicrafts (closed Mondays; admission charge). Just southeast of town on Route 76 is the open-air *Viking Museum* (at Haddebyer Noor), which contains fascinating artifacts that date from the 8th century AD.

Germans and Scandinavians have enjoyed the beaches, forests, lakes, cities, and towns of northern Germany for many years. Since Americans and other tourists have not yet discovered this area, it still is a good place for more adventurous souls to explore.

BEST EN ROUTE

Hotel prices vary a great deal along this route; costs generally are higher in the larger cities, especially in Hamburg, which is the site of the *Vier Jahreszeiten,* known as one of the world's most outstanding — and expensive — hotels. A double room with breakfast costs about $90 to $150 in the hotels listed as expensive; moderate is $65 to $85; and inexpensive is below $65. In an expensive restaurant, dinner for two without wine will cost $45 to $55; moderate, $30 to $40; and inexpensive, $15 to $30.

BREMEN

Park – Bremen's leading hotel is in an out-of-the-way spot, the lovely Bürgerpark. It has spacious, cheerful public rooms, a heated garden terrace, a fine restaurant, and many rooms with balconies overlooking the pond. Bürgerpark (phone: 421-34080). Very expensive.

Grashoff's Bistro – Don't be misled by the plain (but comfortable) surroundings; the kitchen here is very accomplished. Try the fish dishes, such as crab soup, haddock in mustard sauce, or turbot in baked pike mousse. Centrally located; closed evenings and all day Sundays. Reservations advised. 80 Contrescarpe (phone: 421-14740). Expensive.

Landhaus Louisenthal – A few miles northeast of the city center, in the suburb of Horn, this charming 1835 hotel is noteworthy for its quiet, Old World atmosphere. 105 Leher Heerstr. (phone: 421-232076). Expensive to moderate.

Übersee – This pleasant, 142-room hotel is near the market square. In addition to the usual amenities, it has a sauna and conference facilities. 27-29 Wachtstr. (phone: 421-36010). Expensive to moderate.

Ratskeller – Right in the 500-year-old City Hall, this place has lots of atmosphere and also serves good food. It's popular with the local folk, who meet here to sample its 600 German wines. Closed Mondays. Am Markt (phone: 329-0910). Moderate.

HAMBURG

Vier Jahreszeiten – Considered by some to be among the world's best hotels, this elegant and prestigious place is on Alster Lake in downtown Hamburg. It features conservative patrician furniture, streamlined modern facilities, and the atmosphere of a private home. There's an excellent restaurant, 2 bars, and a nightclub featuring international bands. 9-14 Neuer Jungfernstieg (phone: 403-4940). Very expensive.

Canard – Both the fine cuisine and the extraordinary selection of wines make this exclusive restaurant well worth a visit. Closed Sundays. Reservations recommended. 139 Elbchaussee (phone: 880-5057). Expensive.

Europäischer Hof – Facing the railroad station, this is Hamburg's second largest hotel and a pleasant, traditional establishment. There is a good restaurant (in the breakfast room, you can serve yourself from a marble fountain that spouts six different kinds of juices — and occasionally champagne). 45 Kirchenallee (phone: 402-48248). Expensive.

Landhaus Dill – A favorite of Hamburg gourmands, this charming eatery is located on the idyllic Elbe estuary. Specialties are lobster salad and roast lamb. Reservations necessary. 404 Elbchaussee (phone: 828443). Expensive.

Landhaus Scherrer – Its delicious north German cuisine and its lovely view of the Elbe make this another of Hamburg's fine dining spots. Closed Sundays. Reservations necessary. 130 Elbchaussee (phone: 880-1325). Expensive.

Prem – Successfully restored to its former grandeur, guests now can expect friendly service and tasteful decor, as well as excellent cuisine at *La Mer.* The rooms in front face Alster Lake; those in back overlook a charming garden. Reservations advised. 9 An der Alster (phone: 402-45454). Expensive.

Fischerhaus – This place specializes in absolutely perfect fish served in a very plain and unadorned atmosphere. Reservations advised. St. Pauli, 14 Fischmarkt (phone: 314053). Moderate.

Hafen Hamburg – Originally a seamen's home, this 155-room hostelry has a magnificent harbor view and a maritime motif. Rooms, although simply furnished, offer standard comfort. 9 Seewartenstr. (phone: 403-11130). Moderate.

Mellingburger Schleuse – An idyllic forest setting enhances this rustic-looking 28-room hotel. A small restaurant is on the premises. 1 Mellingburgredder (phone: 602-4001). Moderate.

City House – A small hotel — 24 rooms — very close to the train station. 25 Pulverteich (phone: 280-3850). Inexpensive.

RATZEBURG

Seehof – This quiet hotel is directly on the lake, and it would be hard to find a more charming place to spend a weekend. Even the restaurant is a bargain. 3 Lüneburger Damm (phone: 454-12055). Moderate.

LÜBECK

Lysia – The finest hotel in the city is on a canal at the edge of the Old Town. It has a sauna and an exercise room, a popular dance bar, a restaurant, and 2 conference rooms. Auf der Wallhalbinsel, corner of Holstentorpl. (phone: 15040). Expensive.

Wullenwever – In a former brewery, this fine restaurant is, at 400 years of age, one of Lübeck's best. Light, well-prepared food is served courteously amid a country ambience. Closed Mondays. Reservations advised. 71 Beckergrube (phone: 704333). Expensive.

Haus der Schiffergesellschaft – This historic sailors' guild house dates from 1535 and features nautical decor. A broad range of traditional German dishes is served

here. Closed Mondays. Reservations advised. 2 Breite Str. (phone: 451-76776).
Moderate.

Wakenitzblick – Quiet and comfortable, this hotel faces the canal. It has parking
and a restaurant. 30 Augustenstr. (phone: 451-791296). Moderate.

PREETZ

Landhaus Hahn – Just a mile (1.6 km) southeast of Preetz, in the village of Schell-
horn, this comfortable hostelry has 22 rooms and an excellent restaurant (dinner
only on Saturdays and Mondays). 12 Am Berg (phone: 4342-86001). Moderate.

SCHLESWIG

Waldhotel – Part of Gottorf Castle, this hotel is quiet, very well maintained, and
reasonably priced. The restaurant has a good and fairly inexpensive menu. If peace
and quiet are what you seek, look no further. 1 Stampfmühle (phone: 4621-23288).
Moderate to inexpensive.

Frankfurt to Heidelberg

If you drive the 59 miles (94 km) from Frankfurt am Main to Heidelberg on
the autobahn, the trip will take about an hour, but you won't see much more
than the backs and sides of huge high-speed trailer trucks. There's a lovely
alternate route, however, that wriggles its way south along the Main River
Valley, through charming old river towns with half-timbered houses, historic
churches and abbeys, romantic castles, gentle wooded hills, and fertile green
valleys.

Without any side trips, the Main River Valley route from Frankfurt to
Heidelberg covers about 107 miles (171 km); pleasant detours can add half
again as much to that distance. The whole route easily can be driven in a
single day, but it's far more pleasant to give yourself at least a day and a half.

The areas you'll be driving through are known as the Odenwald and the
Spessart. Prehistoric peoples lived along the banks of the Main, but there was
no real development until about AD 800, when many monasteries, like the one
you still can see in Seligenstadt, were established, and the monks began the
region's agricultural development.

Through the centuries, the Odenwald and the Spessart were the territories
of various bishoprics. They were shuttled more or less peacefully from one
owner to another. During the Thirty Years War (1618–48), these areas, like
most of Germany, were the scene of many bloody battles.

Although plans are vague and seem far in the future, the Main River is
slated to become part of an overall Rhine-Danube international waterway
system. Its banks are still relatively quiet and peaceful, even in Frankfurt and
in the other highly populated industrial areas, and the area is not touristy in
any way. Tourists in the Main Valley usually are vacationers from Frankfurt
and other German cities who are not partial to discos or pizza parlors.

Its small towns are unspoiled — like Michelstadt, with its lovely old
Marktplatz, or Wertheim, with its red sandstone castle. And Heidelberg may
well be the most beautiful city in Germany.

For maps, pamphlets, and information about the Frankfurt area, contact the tourist office in Wiesbaden, Hessische Landeszentrale für Fremdenverkehr (38-42 Abraham-Lincoln-Str., Wiesbaden W-6200; phone: 6121-73725); for the Heidelberg vicinity, it's Verkehrsverein Heidelberg (2 Friedrich-Ebert-Anlage, Heidelberg W-6900; phone: 6221-10821).

Before starting out for Heidelberg, take a look at Wiesbaden, a lovely spa city 19 miles (30 km) by autobahn to the west of Frankfurt. Its famous hot springs have been attracting visitors since Roman times. The mineral-laced waters are used for both bathing and drinking. A casino has been an added attraction in more recent times. The leafy Kurhausplatz in the center of town and elegant villas dating from the 19th century that were largely untouched during World War II also contribute to Wiesbaden's charm. If time permits, spend a night or two at the elegant *Nassauer Hof* hotel (3-4 Kaiser-Friedrichpl.; phone: 061-211330), and have dinner at its spuerb *Die Ente* restaurant.

FRANKFURT: For a detailed report on the city and its hotels and restaurants, see *Frankfurt,* THE CITIES.

En Route from Frankfurt – Take Route 43 east toward Mühlheim and Hanau. You might want to stop at Offenbach to see the *German Leather Museum* (86 Frankfurter St.; phone: 69-813021), containing leather objects from all over the world; open Mondays through Sundays; admission charge. Or at Hanau, you can see the birthplace of the Brothers Grimm and site of an interesting museum of local jewelry called *Goldsmith's House,* Schloss Philippsruhe, a baroque castle, and a monument to the celebrated brothers.

At the intersection of Routes 43 and 45, continue on the unnumbered road toward Hainstadt and Seligenstadt. Park before you reach the center of Seligenstadt, since parking usually is not permitted in the center of small villages in Germany.

SELIGENSTADT: Its principal attraction is a magnificently maintained former Benedictine abbey founded in AD 825 by Einhard, biographer of Charlemagne. However, the town itself is much older. It was a fortified castle on the *limes* — the wall built by the Romans through most of central Germany until the Romans were ejected from their fort by the Alemanni in AD 260. Only remnants are left of these walls, which traditionally were built around all castles.

Guided tours (in German) of the abbey are conducted year-round every day except Mondays. Don't let a German-only tour put you off; you'll understand more than you think you will.

Seligenstadt is a place where you can see the various architectural styles and periods of German history. The abbey itself has undergone many remodelings in a thousand years, and each remodeling has left traces of the style characteristic of the period.

From the abbey, walk toward the Main River. Then turn left and walk toward the ruins of the Kaiserpfalz, known also as the Palatium or the hunting lodge (*Jagdsitz*), built about 1235 for Holy Roman Emperor, Frederick II, who led a fascinating life that included no fewer than three excommunications.

Walk to the Marktplatz along the narrow Palatiumstrasse. All along the way and around the Marktplatz itself you will see some outstanding examples of the famous German *Fachwerkhäuser,* or half-timbered houses.

En Route from Seligenstadt – Leave Seligenstadt on the same road from which you entered, but this time head south toward Stockstadt. You may make a short detour to Aschaffenburg or continue on under the Mainhausen cloverleaf, pick up Route 469 at the Stockstadt autobahn exchange, and head for Miltenberg.

ASCHAFFENBURG: Chosen by the electors of Mainz as one of their residences, Aschaffenburg has beautiful parks, a large Renaissance castle, and an interesting church. St. Johannisberg Castle, built in 1605–14 for the powerful Archbishops of Mainz, is most impressive, shaped like a hollow square. See the palace and walk through its gardens to the Pompeianum, a reproduction of the Castor and Pollux house at Pompeii, built for the capricious Ludwig I of Bavaria. Then walk along the Landingstrasse behind the palace to the Stiftskirche, a 10th-century church that is an interesting mixture of baroque, Gothic, and Romanesque styles of architecture, but its real attraction is the exceptional church art. There is a Grünewald altarpiece and a Resurrection scene by Lucas Cranach the Elder (1520). To visit the lovely chapel, the altarpiece, and other treasures, look for the sexton. If he's not in the church, try at 1 Stiftgasse.

En Route from Aschaffenburg – Leave Aschaffenburg via Löherstrasse, the street directly behind the church, and watch for signs directing you to Schönbusch. This 18th-century park is one of Germany's most charming, with pools, islands, and a country house built for the archbishops in 1780.

Leave Schönbusch Park area on the south side (the one closest to the river) and follow the unnumbered road to its intersection with Route 469. Stay on 469 south for 22 miles (35 km) until you reach Miltenberg.

MILTENBERG: Again, park your car in the first convenient parking lot. Don't try to drive in or through the town center. You can walk from one end of Miltenberg to the other in 15 minutes.

The town showplace is its Marktplatz. It's triangular, relatively small, and surrounded by exceptional half-timbered houses; from the marketplace walk along the main street, the Hauptstrasse, which also is lined with fascinating houses.

The *Riesen* hotel is not as old as Miltenberg, which was little more than a wide spot in the Roman wall until the Thirteenth Legion was ousted by the Germanic tribes in AD 260. The Germans are avid record keepers, and there are files in Mainz, Munich, and Würzburg to prove that the *Riesen* was open and operating in the 12th century. A whole string of Holy Roman Emperors stayed here, beginning with Frederick Barbarossa who took shelter here in 1158 and 1168, and during the Thirty Years War it housed VIPs from both sides — depending on who was in control at the moment. It's still an ideal overnight stopping place (see *Best en Route*).

The tourist office (Städtisches Verkehrsamt) in the Town Hall (Rathaus) has an excellent walking guide to Miltenberg (phone: 9371-400119). It's in German only, but so clearly arranged that you can walk in sequence from one spot of interest to the next with no trouble.

En Route from Miltenberg – A worthwhile side trip from Miltenberg is the 18-mile (29-km) jaunt to Wertheim. The road parallels the Main River all the way, or if you want to take a rest from driving, leave your car in Miltenberg and go by boat from Wertheim.

The Main and Tauber rivers meet at Wertheim, and the town is dominated by a castle constructed of red sandstone, which is peculiar to the Odenwald and Spessart areas. A guide is available from the Wertheim Tourist Office (Fremdenverkehrsgesellschaft) in the Town Hall (phone: 9342-301230). The Marktplatz is worth seeing, with a Renaissance monument known as the Engelsbrunnen ("Angel's Well") at one end. The church has a number of unusually beautiful, well-preserved tombstones and memorials from the 16th century. You'll have to climb around to see the old castle, but the view of Wertheim and the rivers is worth a little puffing. Don't miss the opportunity to dine at *Schweizer Stuben* (see *Best en Route*), one of Germany's best restaurants.

Pick up Route 469 in Miltenberg again for 5 miles (8 km) to Amorbach.

AMORBACH: You'll notice the red sandstone towers of an abbey church that dominates Amorbach. It was built between 1742 and 1747 on the site of an earlier Romanesque church. The interior of this now-baroque abbey is worth seeing. Its chancel screen is one of the finest in Germany, and it has a justifiably well-known organ; concerts are held here during the high tourist season.

MICHELSTADT: Pick up Route 47, the Nibelungenstrasse, for 15 miles (24 km) to Michelstadt, the heart of Wagner country; this is where all the mythical action of his great operas was set. This is where the Nibelungen, evil guardians of a magic hoard of gold, are supposed to have done their hunting, and somewhat farther south, the great hero Siegfried went on the royal hunt during which Hagen killed him. Whether you are a true believer or not, the gently sloping countryside is lovely.

Michelstadt has what may be the most enchanting Marktplatz in the Odenwald, with a 16th-century fountain, a charming Town Hall, and many remarkable half-timbered houses. Notice especially the unusual design of the two bay windows in the Town Hall.

From Michelstadt it's about 42 miles (67 km) to Worms or 38 miles (61 km) to Heidelberg.

WORMS: This city is so packed with history and interest, visitors will want to take time to see as much as possible. It was destroyed in 436 by Attila the Hun, and in 1521 it was the scene of the famous Imperial Diet that passed judgment on Martin Luther. Worms became a Protestant city in 1525 and, as a result, was subject to heavy reprisals during the Thirty Years War. It was almost totally destroyed by the French in 1689, deprived of its free city status, annexed by France in 1801, and was returned to German rule by the Congress of Vienna in 1815. All of this major European history is written on its streets, its buildings, and on every street corner.

The tourist office (Verkehrsverein, 14 Neumarkt; phone: 6241-853560) has a great deal of helpful material and information in English. Look for it just opposite St. Peter's Cathedral, which is itself one of Germany's finest examples of 13th-century Romanesque architecture. The high altar is by Balthasar Neumann, a famous 18th-century master of German baroque architecture.

Worms is one of the oldest centers of Jewish culture in Germany and has the oldest synagogue in the country, founded in the 11th century. The ancient Jewish cemetery, just behind the cathedral, has been in use since the 11th century and is worth a visit. Worms also is the home area of liebfraumilch wine. Its name came from the Church of Our Lady (Liebfrauenkirche) at the city's northern end.

HEIDELBERG: Beautiful Old Heidelberg is surrounded by thickly wooded hills, which rise above its massive ruined castle. Beneath the castle, its old buildings with their red roofs and romantic towers face the peaceful Neckar River and its Old Bridge (Alte Brücke). The oldest university town in Germany, Heidelberg is still best known as an intellectual and cultural center. During the Middle Ages, the city was the political center of the Rhineland Palatinate. Heidelberg and its castle were destroyed by Louis XIV of France in 1689, and to make matters worse, the city was completely demolished by fire in 1693. After these disasters the electors turned their backs on Heidelberg and the town was rebuilt in baroque style.

Stop in at the local tourist office for maps, brochures, and all sorts of useful information. 2 Friedrich-Ebert-Anlage (phone: 6221-10821).

Both banks of the river afford excellent views of the town. Walk along the right bank, taking Neuenheimer Landstrasse, which runs west from the Old Bridge, and Ziegelhäuser Landstrasse, which runs east; then try the more ambitious Philosophers' Way (Philosophenweg) farther from the river, starting from Bergstrasse in the suburb of Neuenheim and ascending the slopes of the Heiligenberg.

Don't miss the castle, which can be reached on foot, by car, by escalator, or by cable car. See its 17th-century gardens, with their remarkable view from the Scheffel Terrace (named for a Heidelberg poet). You may want to take the guided tour (in English), offered daily at frequent intervals (admission charge). Be sure to see the Grosses Fass (Great Vat) here, made in the 18th century, with a capacity of 58,000 gallons and a stairway to the top. According to local lore, a dwarf named Perkeo once drank the whole thing.

Other sights in Heidelberg include the curious Students' Jail (2 Augustinergasse), where unruly students were incarcerated during the 18th and 19th centuries; the *Electoral Palatinate Museum* (Kurpfälzisches Museum; closed Mondays; admission charge; 97 Hauptstr.), in a baroque palace, containing a cast of the jaw of Heidelberg man (50,000 BC) and the great Altarpiece of the Twelve Apostles (Windsheimer Zwölfbotenaltar) by Riemenschneider (1509) among its treasures.

Heidelberg is a small city, well suited to walking and lingering about, especially in the streets of the old quarter and the quays along the river. Fortunately, it came through the Second World War unscathed. If the sun is shining, walk along the pedestrians-only Hauptstrasse, which leads to the Old City. It's the main shopping street, chockablock with boutiques and cafés. Stop in at *Seberer* for great doughnuts or pick up a pretzel from one of the ubiquitous vendors. At No. 178 is the *Ritter* hotel, a restaurant with a 16th-century façade. From Heidelberg, you can explore the scenic Neckar Valley to the east, its gorge surrounded by high, thickly forested hills.

BEST EN ROUTE

Prices along this route vary; they're significantly higher in the larger cities, so that you'll have to pay more for everything in Frankfurt and Heidelberg. Plan to spend $90 to $145 (more in Heidelberg) for hotels we have classified as expensive; $65 to $90 for moderate; and below $65, inexpensive. A dinner for two without wine will cost $75 to $150 in restaurants listed as expensive; $50 to $70, moderate; and $20 to $45, inexpensive.

SELIGENSTADT

Klosterstuben – Next to the church and the convent garden, this restaurant features excellent German cooking. It also serves a locally brewed beer (becoming increasingly rare in Germany as big breweries take over). Closed Sundays and Mondays. 7 Freihofpl. (phone: 6182-3571). Moderate.

AMORBACH

Schafhof – A romantic 16-room hotel in a former Benedictine monastery. It has an excellent restaurant, noteworthy for its lamb dishes. 2 miles (3 km) west in Otterbachtal (phone: 9373-8088). Expensive to moderate.

ASCHAFFENBURG

Romantik-Hotel Post – Not far from the Schloss Johannisberg, this hotel is beautifully decorated in the traditional sense of comfort and friendliness. The restaurant offers good continental food with a broad range of choices. 19 Goldbacherstr. (phone: 6021-21333). Expensive to moderate.

MILTENBERG

Gasthaus zum Riesen – In operation since the 12th century, this place claims to be Germany's oldest hostelry. Based on authenticated guest lists, the owner and restorer, W. Jöst, has furnished a series of bedrooms after the period of some famous visitors — Queen Christina of Sweden, for example. All furnishings are genuine antiques. Closed November to March. Reservations necessary — especially for the "name" rooms, but a good idea at any time. 97 Hauptstr. (phone: 9371-3644). Moderate.

WERTHEIM

Schweizer Stuben – Follow the signs to this truly excellent restaurant, featuring the finest Swiss-French-German cuisine in comfortable surroundings. It also has 16 rooms. Closed Mondays, Sundays, Tuesdays for lunch, and January. Reservations necessary. 11 Geiselbrunnweg (phone: 9342-3070). Very expensive.

HEIDELBERG

Der Europäische Hof – The leading hotel in Heidelberg consists of three wings, each from a different period. Centrally located facing a park, it's known for its service (the concierge is a gem) and for the fine French food in its *Kurfürstenstube* restaurant. There's a terrace for summer dining, a bar with dancing, conference rooms, and public rooms nicely furnished with antiques. Rooms are large and comfortable, and most have refrigerators and TV sets. 1 Friedrich-Ebert-Anlage (phone: 6221-5150). Very expensive.

Hirschgasse – This family-run place is opposite the castle in a building that dates from 1472. Tastefully restored, its rooms are modern and comfortable. The hotel, which is known for its romantic flair, has one of the best restaurants in town and a lovely, tree-shaded terrace for breakfast. Closed Sundays. 3 Hirschgasse (phone: 6221-403-2160). Very expensive.

Simplicissimus – Said to be the best restaurant in town, this pleasant establishment features nouvelle cuisine; its game and fish dishes are excellent. Open evenings only. Closed Tuesdays and from the end of July to August 20. Reservations advised. 16 Ingrimstr. (phone: 6221-13336). Expensive.

Weinstube Schloss Heidelberg – This restaurant, with a terrace right in the castle courtyard, offers a marvelous view of the castle and good food. The tasteful decor is that of a wine tavern, with an ornately paneled ceiling, natural wood tables, and framed engravings. Closed Tuesdays. Reservations advised. Schlosshof (phone: 6221-164294). Moderate.

Molkenkur – Nestled in the forest, and perched 300 feet above the castle, this quiet and charming small hotel can be reached either by car or cable car. It has a restaurant with a terrace. Closed from December 12 to January 1. 31 Klingenteichstr. (phone: 10894). Moderate to inexpensive.

Roter Ochsen – A famous student hangout dating from 1703, this place has students' initials on the walls, oak tables, and mementos of all sorts — like a set from *The Student Prince*. There's piano music in the evening, lots of beer, and typical German cooking. Open evenings only. Closed Sundays. 217 Hauptstr. (phone: 6221-20977). Inexpensive.

Westphalia

Though well liked by Germans and other Europeans, Westphalia, a dreamy area of castles, country inns, half-timbered houses, windmills, forests, hills, and mineral spas, has been little explored by Americans. (The proprietor of the noted *Schütte* hotel-restaurant in Oberkirchen tells us he has never had an American guest.) Perhaps Americans have shunned Westphalia because it contains the great industrial Ruhr Valley; in fact, Dortmund, Westphalia's principal city, is one of the major cities of the Ruhr. However, the well-heeled Ruhr residents like to have a peaceful, picturesque country area to which they can slip away for a weekend or a business conference.

Westphalia is a region of small, hedged-in farms that form a checkerboard pattern. Strict laws keep the villages small, the forests intact, and the air unpolluted. The castle-hotels and wayside inns have turrets and half-timbered exteriors, with baronial interiors and open fireplaces. Yet they also have indoor plumbing, central heating, and 20th-century mattresses. There is none of that run-down look found in Europe's more remote and poorer country areas.

In the northern part of Germany, Westphalia extends from the Rhine to the Weser River. For maps and information about the region, contact the tourist office, Landesverkehrsverband Westfalen E.V., 6 Südwall, 4600 Dortmund (phone: 231-527506/07).

The name Westphalia first appears in connection with a section of the duchy of Saxony in the 10th century. In the later Middle Ages, its major towns of Münster, Paderborn, Bielefeld, and others, were prosperous members of the Hanseatic League (an association of mercantile city-states). The Peace of Westphalia, which was signed in Münster in 1648 to end the Thirty Years War, gave Prussia a foothold in the area, which it maintained — except for the brief Napoleonic reign in 1808–13 — until 1945.

Westphalia is noted for its cuisine, which is the most distinctive in Germany. It starts with an ice-cold *Steinhäger,* a gin-like schnapps drink from the town of Steinhagen near Bielefeld; the drink is poured from a stoneware bottle into one of the deep pewter spoons Westphalians use as shot glasses. Then comes a chaser of cool Westphalian beer from Dortmund, which is second only to Munich as a German brewing city. Finally, there's pumpernickel — also Westphalian in origin — with butter, and justly famous Westphalian ham, eaten on a wooden board just as they do in this region.

You can enjoy the culinary and visual riches of Westphalia by touring the area in a circular route that begins and ends in Dortmund. The round trip is about 400 miles (640 km).

DORTMUND: Like all the cities in the Ruhr, Dortmund was leveled in World War II and rebuilt along coldly modern lines that are rather devoid of character. It is not dirty, however; the whole Ruhr has strict air pollution laws. Have a look at the Westfalenpark, with its German Rosarium (1,500 varieties of roses, half a million plants) and its TV tower topped by a revolving restaurant. Dortmund is best known as a beer-producing center; if you want to visit a brewery, contact the Verband Dortmunder Bierbrauer, 3 Ostenhellweg (phone: 231-525532).

Now head east into Westphalia proper, toward the Sauerland, an unspoiled region of woods and lakes to the east and south. The autobahn gets you out there quickly. Take the Sauerland Line (A45), following the signs to Siegen and Frankfurt, but leave at Olpe and follow the very scenic Route 55 north.

En Route from Dortmund – At this point you may wish to take a short detour to Attendorn, a place of lakes, a huge stalactite cave, and remarkable rock formations. The cave, called Attahöhle (follow the signs to Tropfsteinhöhle), is open daily; admission charge. Or continue on Route 55 to Lennestadt and then take the scenic Route 236 via the beautiful little village of Oberkirchen to Winterberg (one of the biggest German winter sports areas outside the Alps), and then drive north on Route 480.

OLSBERG: If they are so inclined, summer visitors can get a look at the Old West here at Fort Fun City, an "authentic" Western town, replete with saloon, jail, gambling hall, and a print shop where you can get a wanted poster with your own name on it.

Gevelingen Palace here is the starting point for Gypsy wagons, which you can rent for a tour of the Sauerland on "two horsepower." The wagons come complete with sleeping facilities for seven, blankets, linen, stove, dishes, pots and pans, gas lanterns, and gas heater. You follow a prescribed route and stop each night at a farm where they stable the horses. Continue on Route 480 via Brilon ("the most forested town in Westphalia") to Paderborn. Then take Routes 1 and 239.

DETMOLD: You now are in the middle of the Teutoburg Forest, another popular Westphalian district, which is famous to Germans as the place where the Romans were stopped in their northward march, in an epic battle in AD 9. Germanic tribesmen dealt them a stunning defeat, and the Roman Empire never extended any farther north in continental Europe. A giant statue to the tribal chief Hermann, who led the battle, commands a hill just 4 miles (6 km) outside the city at the village of Heiligenkirchen. It is 175 feet from Hermann's feet to the tip of his upraised sword. Not to be missed is the bird of prey sanctuary at nearby Bad Berlebeck. The eagles, vultures, and other big birds fly freely at 11 AM and 2:30 PM daily. Detmold also has an open-air museum, the *Lippisches Landsmuseum,* with typically Westphalian farmhouses, which usually combine red brick and half timbering. Continue on Routes 239 and 66.

BIELEFELD: One of Westphalia's larger cities, Bielefeld is coldly modern for the most part, but some fine patrician houses remain and there's also the Sparrenburg Castle (1 Am Sparrenberg), with a network of underground passages below. On the ground level is a museum devoted to playing cards and a good view of the Teutoburg Forest from the tower.

En Route from Bielefeld – From Bielefeld take Route 61 via Herford. On the way to Minden you pass the Porta Westfalica, where the Weser River suddenly emerges spectacularly from between two hills, out of the mountains, and on to the broad North German plain. One of the hills that has a fine view is topped with a monument to Kaiser Wilhelm.

MINDEN: Minden is a good place to board one of the old paddleboats that ply the Weser. See the outstanding Romanesque cathedral with its 11th-century crucifix and a 1480 painting of the Crucifixion by a Westphalian master. There's a bridge where the Mittelland Canal passes over the Weser. Also interesting is the Great Lock (Schacht-schleuse), just north of town; 279 by 33 feet long, it links the Mittelland Canal with the Weser.

En Route from Minden – Proceed along Route 65 to Lübbecke. (Once a year, during a festival in August, a fountain here bubbles with beer instead of water. You can help yourself if you can get near it.) Then take Route 239 south to Löhne, and take a short drive west on the autobahn.

BÜNDE: What is alleged to be the world's only tobacco museum (12 Funfhausen Str.) is in this cigar making town. When you pay your money you get, instead of a ticket, a cigar or a cheap clay pipe, which you can fill at a handy humidor. Displays include the world's largest cigar (5½ feet long, 20 pounds) and a pipe that was obviously highly prized by the infamous World War I German naval officer Count Luckner, the Sea Devil. He dropped it out of a train window and pulled the emergency brake so he could recover it. Continue on the autobahn to Osnabrück and head south on Routes 51 and 475.

WARENDORF: This is the horse capital of Germany, site of a state-operated stud farm, an important riding school, and the headquarters of the German Olympic Equestrian Committee. There are plenty of rental horses here and lots of riding paths; it is a good place to book a vacation in the saddle. Contact the local tourist office for more information on riding (phone: 2581-54222). There are big parades here on the last Saturday in September and the first Saturday in October, when horses are led by saddle masters in elegant uniforms. Drive from Warendorf along Routes 64 west to 51.

MÜNSTER: Westphalia's historic capital is the site of one of Germany's biggest universities. Every year, on May 15, Münster holds a festival to mark the Peace of Westphalia, negotiated here in 1648 to end the Thirty Years War. See the Prinzipalmarkt, the oldest and busiest street in town, with its elegant Renaissance houses. If you continue along Bogenstrasse, you'll see the Kiepenkerl, a statue of a peddler with his basket. The low-lying Romanesque cathedral is typically Westphalian, with its astronomic clock in the ambulatory and a glockenspiel that plays at noon.

The area surrounding Münster is known for its moated medieval castles, particularly the Castle of Vischering, set on an island, with an interesting interior and a prison beneath (closed Tuesdays). Also noteworthy are the castles of Hülshoff and Nordkirchen (the latter is now the university's School of Finance). Farther west is the medieval walled city of Coesfeld.

En Route from Münster – Continue along Route 51 through Dülmen; the estate of the Duke of Croy here is the only wild horse sanctuary (with 200 horses) in Europe. The event of the year here is the annual roundup on the last Saturday in May.

Take Route 51 to Recklinghausen and visit the *Icon Museum* (2A Kirchplatz), where icons are exhibited thematically (closed Mondays). In May and June, Recklinghausen is the site of the annual *Ruhr Festival* of music, theater, opera, and art exhibitions.

Next take the autobahn (Rte. A43) south to Bochum.

BOCHUM: This is the site of another unique museum, the *Museum of Mining* (Bergbau Museum; Wielandstr.). The big attraction is an actual coal mine below the building, with nearly a mile of shafts you can explore. Bochum also has Germany's best-known public observatory and planetarium (corner of Castroper Str. and Hagenstr.).

For an interesting detour, take the autobahn (Rte. A430) west to Essen.

ESSEN: The major metropolis of the Ruhr Valley, it is not the gritty industrial city a visitor might expect. The Minister (cathedral) is one of Germany's oldest churches, dating back to the 9th century, with some notable stained glass of a later date. The *Folkwang Museum* (41 Goethestr.) houses a collection of 19th- and 20th-century French and German art (closed Mondays, admission charge). On the city's southern outskirts is the Villa Hugel, the baronial former residence of the Krupp steel and arms dynasty. Resembling an elegant railroad station more than a home, it offers a somewhat grim glimpse of how the uppermost classes once lived (closed Mondays, admission charge). Return via the autobahn and Route 1 to Dortmund.

BEST EN ROUTE

Visitors to Westphalia will delight in the many charming hotels and inns to be found in the smaller towns. Prices here also tend to be lower than in the larger, more frequented city areas. A double room with breakfast in an expensive hotel will cost about $70 to 110; moderate is $40 to $65; and inexpensive is below $40. In the expensive restaurants, a dinner for two without wine will cost about $35 to $65; in moderate establishments it will be $20 to $30; inexpensive meals are under $20.

ATTENDORN

Burghotel Schnellenberg – This 13th-century castle in the middle of the woods has a commanding view of the town below. Many of the rooms are in the towers. You can dine in the rustic *Rittersaal Salon,* where game and fish dishes are especially recommended. Recreational opportunities here include tennis, hikes in the woods, and swimming in the Biggesee, 2 miles (3 km) away. Closed January 2–20 and December 20–28 (phone: 2722-6940). Expensive.

OBERKIRCHEN

Schütte – This former 18th-century coach house is in the middle of a Sauerland village of 800 inhabitants. It offers many miles of hiking paths in the surrounding woods, its own swimming pool, and its own stable, where visitors either rent horses or stable their own. Its restaurant's Westphalian food specialties include ham and *Pfefferpothast,* a very spicy stew. The game dishes are excellent: Try venison with red wine. The typically Westphalian interior is rustic, with an open fireplace. 2 Eggeweg (phone: 2975-820). Expensive to moderate.

PETERSHAGEN

Schloss Petershagen – A moated castle (built in 1306) on the Weser River, surrounded by meadows and parks, houses a small hotel (11 rooms) and an elegant restaurant with international fare. The restaurant has deep carpets, rich cloth on the walls, oil paintings, and linen tablecloths. It's not the place for Westphalian specialties, although it does feature fish from the Weser — smoked eel and trout soup. This palace also offers a "knightly banquet" for groups only, with waiters dressed in medieval costumes and menus offering old recipes. There's a bar in the cellar, and the surrounding park has tennis courts and a heated swimming pool. 5 Schloss Str. (phone: 5707-346). Expensive to moderate.

WARENDORF

Im Engel – Established in 1557, the hotel has been in the hands of the Leve family, the present proprietors, since 1692. It is right in the center of the Old City and has the usual rustic interior, with oak furniture, carved beams, pewter, old pictures, and the standard open fireplace. Westphalian specialties include mussel soup; steaks garnished with scrambled eggs; turbot served in white burgundy sauce; and *Schlachtplatte,* literally, "slaughter platter," consisting of Westphalian ham, sausages, and other smoked meat, heaped on a mound of sauerkraut. Facilities include a swimming pool, sauna, and solarium. Closed Fridays for dinner, Saturdays for lunch, and 3 weeks in July. 37 Brünebrede (phone: 2581-7064/65). Expensive to moderate.

MÜNSTER

Waldhotel Krautkrämer – About 4 miles (6 km) from the center of town, this 70-room hotel is on its own lake. It provides a rare combination of comfort, hospitality, sublime surroundings, and one of Germany's best restaurants. 173 Am Hiltruper See (phone: 2501-8050). Expensive.

Romantik-Hotel Hof zur Linde – A half-timbered former farmhouse 5 miles (8 km) from downtown, this 30-room hostelry has a tranquil location and an excellent restaurant. 1 Handorfer Werseufer (phone: 251-325002). Expensive to moderate.

Gasthof Stuhlmacher – This 17th-century restaurant has typical Westphalian decor and cooking, with ten famous beers on tap. The gabled exterior, right next to the Town Hall, displays a century-old metal figure of a professor and a worker sitting at a beer barrel, which means that the restaurant catered to all social classes. The interior is elaborately carved in wood and has stained glass windows, leather seats, and old pictures. Specialties include calf's head stew, homemade *Sülze* (pickled meat in aspic), homemade cheese, and Westphalian ham. Reservations advised. 6 Prinzipalmarkt (phone: 44877). Moderate.

Pinkus Müller – At this 19th-century student hangout, tourists, professors, and students sit side by side at long wooden tables on which every inch of surface has been carved with the initials of generations. Each regular customer has his own mug with his name on it, which hangs from a peg on the wall. The decor is German "schmaltz," with stained glass windows, overhead beams with painted mottoes in Low German, an open fireplace, a cannon, and a wooden board (no longer used) on which the names of those delinquent in their accounts were revealed to the public. The customary drink is *Altbier,* a heavy, somewhat sweet beer. You may want to start things off with a schnapps served from a deep spoon. Full meals can be had, but food specialties tend to be snacks that go well with beer, such as *Töttchen*, a small dish of veal and mustard, or a Westphalian stew of various smoked meat and sausages. Closed Sundays. Reservations advised. 4-10 Kreuzstr. (phone: 45151). Moderate to inexpensive.

ESSEN

Schloss Hugenpoet – In the village of Kettwig, off Route A52 (the autobahn) just south of Essen, this hotel and its restaurant are among the most charming in Germany. The property is surrounded by a moat, with parking in the courtyard which is reached by crossing a bridge and going through a gatehouse. The main dining room is in a glassed-in terrace overlooking the water and formal gardens. There have been castles on the site since AD 778, but the present building dates back only to the mid-17th century. The residence of a succession of noble families, it was converted into a luxurious hotel in 1955 with 18 modernized rooms and 1 suite. The "poetic" name means "Toad Pool," in the Low German dialect. 51 August-Thyssen-Str. (phone: 2054-12040). Expensive.

The Rhineland

Long before the autobahn and jetport, before the rail lines stitched the continent into a whole, the Rhine River was Europe's main street and prime commercial thoroughfare. Fed by melting Alpine snows in Switzerland and sharing frontage with France and the Netherlands, the Rhine is 820 miles long; it is nevertheless the section that flows through Germany that captures the imagination with its castles, vineyards, dangerous whirlpools, and legends of heroes, Rhine maidens, and Lorelei. The river flows steadily northward, broad, even-tempered, and unimpeded, in contrast with the tempestuous history of Germany, past and present.

Today as ever, the Rhine is a busy and important shipping route linking dozens of inland ports such as Ludwigshafen and Duisburg to the North Sea and the oceans beyond. However, this majestic river is also part playground, part historical monument, and part natural wonder. Despite the Rhine's more than 800-mile length, "the Rhineland" is a much narrower term, encompassing by common consensus only the 50-mile Rhine gorge between Mainz and Koblenz where the steep banks, striated by vineyards and crowned with castles, create the romantic picture most people associate with this famous river.

History, legend, and magnificent scenery have their attractions, but one cannot forget that the Rhineland is wine land. By most accounts, Germany's best wine district is the Rheingau, extending roughly from Wiesbaden to the mouth of the Lahn River near Kamp, only a few dozen miles downstream. Along this short stretch, a southern exposure ripens noble riesling grapes to perfection. For the confirmed wine connoisseur, a trip down the Rhine gorge is something of a pilgrimage. For the neophyte sipper, a few well-chosen stopovers here will provide a succinct introduction to the white wines many experts claim are the best in the world. For information about German wine, write to the *German Wine Information Bureau* (79 Madison Ave., New York,

NY 10016; phone: 212-213-0909), or the *German Wine Academy* (c/o Reisebüro A. Bartolomae, 8 Wilhelmstr., Wiesbaden D-62000, Germany). And the wine seems to impart an easygoing and fun-loving nature to the people in the surrounding countryside. Travelers can only agree that a relaxed and joyous outlook on life is an excellent one for hoteliers and restaurateurs. In fact, visitors often find that Rhinelanders cultivate their guests as attentively as they do their vines.

The Rhine can be explored by car, by rail, or by excursion boat. Multilingual bus tours also are available, and for these, contact the German National Tourist Office (Deutsche Zentrale für Tourismus; 69 Beethoven Str., Frankfurt am Main 6; phone: 69-75720); or stop at one of the city tourist offices — labeled Verkehrsamt or Verkehrsverein — along the Rhine route. They also provide maps and tourist information. The central tourist office for the region has two branches, one in Bad Godesberg, a suburb of Bonn, and the other in Koblenz: Landesverkehrsverband Rheinland e.V. (69 Rheinallee, 5300 Bonn–Bad Godesberg 1; phone: 362921); and Fremdenverkehrsverband Rheinland-Pfalz e.V. (103-105 Löhrstr., 5400 Koblenz; phone: 31079).

The above modes of travel can be combined, and the bearer of a Eurailpass can make as many stops as desired along the way to, say, Koblenz, and then use the pass at no extra charge on one of the many *Köln-Düsseldorfer* (*K-D*) or *Rüdesheim-Bingen* river steamers that ply this route, for a pleasant return trip. For information about boat trips, contact *K-D Schiffsagentur* in Köln (Cologne; 15 Frankenwerft; phone: 221-211864); or in Mainz (*Am Rathaus;* phone: 221-224511). Rail lines parallel the river on both sides, but the west bank affords the best scenery and most interesting stops. Travelers touring by car have the opportunity to stop and take pictures anywhere or to picnic at rest stops; the auto traveler can easily cross the Rhine at one of several bridges at Koblenz and made a round trip by returning along Route 42 on the east bank. Campgrounds are plentiful along both sides, and at several points car ferries, called *Autofähre,* will transfer you across the river for a nominal fee. The entire route covers about 143 miles (229 km) one way, but you'll want to spend at least 2 or 3 days in this glorious region.

MAINZ: This 2,000-year-old city founded by the Romans is most notable for its favorite son, Johannes Gutenberg, who invented movable type here in 1440. In the *Gutenberg Museum* (5 Liebfrauenpl.) you can see an original Gutenberg Bible and a replica of the famed printer's press, as well as an exhibition of printing through the centuries. Mainz also is the scene of a boisterous carnival, climaxing in the *Rosenmontag* parade on the last Monday before *Ash Wednesday.* Mainz Cathedral, though not architecturally impressive, is worth visiting for its art treasures, particularly the medieval sculpture by the Master of Naumburg in its *Diocesan Museum.* Closed Sundays. No admission charge.

RÜDESHEIM: It's downright touristy — and for good reason. Head straight for the Drosselgasse, a narrow, cobblestone alley lined with restaurants, wine taverns, and souvenir shops. Pick a pub where the oompah band isn't too loud, order yourself a *Römer* (a wine goblet with a bottle-green pedestal) of the local product, and get a taste of what the Rhineland is all about. This small city boasts rousing wine festivals in May and August and also has one of Germany's best wine museums, in Brömser Castle (closed Mondays), along Route 42 at the west end of town. For a small fee you can browse through 28 display rooms containing winepresses and various viticultural artifacts showing man's 6,000-year wine making tradition. A free brochure is available upon request. If you stop here, carry a jacket or sweater with you, for the cellar-like rooms are cool even in summer. To find a room or to collect a handful of brochures describing the sights ahead, contact Rüdesheim's city tourist office (16 Rheinstr.; phone: 6722-40831/32), where English-speaking personnel will answer all your questions. Another Rüdesheimer attraction is the curious Siegfried's Mechanical Music Cabinet, a collection of self-playing musical contraptions of the past, housed just off Drosselgasse.

Rüdesheim is a good place to catch a *K-D* river steamer. The trip to St. Goarshausen and back makes a nice afternoon jaunt, allowing plenty of time for wine sipping and a leisurely meal in the ship's surprisingly good restaurant.

En Route from Rüdesheim – Before crossing to Bingen and the more scenic left bank of the river, you might want to take a 9-mile (14-km) side trip north to Assmannshausen by way of Niederwald Hill. Just north of Rüdesheim along Route 42, you will pass the grim-visaged Amazon that is the Germania Monument, built on Niederwald Hill in the 1870s to commemorate the unification of Germany. You can get there from Rüdesheim by bus or by a chair lift, which carries you up the steep, vine-bearing slopes for spectacular views and picture taking.

On an island in the middle of the river is the Mouse Tower (Mäuseturm) — not to be confused with the Mouse Castle, encountered later — built centuries ago by the wicked Archbishop of Mainz as a stronghold for extracting tolls from passing ships. According to legend, the nasty archbishop ordered his henchmen to wipe out a band of beggars who came pleading for handouts. An army of mice rose up to avenge the slain beggars, chased the archbishop into the tower, and gobbled him up alive. One can readily see how the Brothers Grimm found plenty of fairy-tale material in Germany! There are short daily boat excursions from Rüdesheim to the village of Assmannshausen via the Mouse Tower.

Assmannshausen is an oddity because it produces only red wine, which comes from the burgundy-type (pinot noir) grape; however, only a local vintner with an exaggerated view of his own product would rank Assmannshausen red anywhere near the noble white rieslings from the surrounding area.

BINGEN: For the motorist, the left bank of the river affords the best view, so return to Rüdesheim and take the car ferry to Bingen, picking up Route 9 on the other side. In itself, Bingen is not especially interesting. But in common with nearby villages, it shares the typically relaxed Rhineland ambience. After a fine meal with wine, there's no better place in Germany for an evening stroll than through Bingen's narrow brick and cobblestone streets or along the riverfront of one of these delightful Rhineside towns.

En Route from Bingen – The stretch from Bingen to Koblenz is justly celebrated for its dramatic scenery, romantic castles, and legendary landmarks. The last section on the left bank, between Bacharach and St. Goar, is the narrow, steep road known as the Rheingoldstrasse. Just north of Bingen, several castles on the hills to the left invite you to do a little historical poking around. Especially worthy are Burg Rheinfels, perched on a rock, and Burg Reichenstein, set in a valley — both open to the public. It's useful to know the difference between the German words *Burg* and *Schloss,* both translated as "castle" by most dictionaries. A *Burg* is a fortified medieval structure, today often in ruins. Its military aspect is obvious. A *Schloss,* on the other hand, is more of a palace and is usually lavishly decorated and furnished. Many even offer guest accommodations.

The towns of Bacharach and Oberwesel bid the traveler to stop and explore. There are more castles in the area than one could comfortably see in a week, so don't feel bad about passing up most of them. The Jost family in Bacharach runs a justly famous antique porcelain and glassware shop called *Trödel's* (7 Oberstr.).

On the right, between Bacharach and St. Goar, are the Rhine gorge's two most distinctive landmarks — one might even say trademarks. Die Pfalz is a squat, dome-roofed medieval toll station in the middle of the current between Bacharach and Oberwesel. In the romantic past, Die Pfalz had chains stretched across the river to stop passing ships, and cannons were leveled at stubborn river captains. This fortified structure did a brisk business until an international agreement in 1868 eliminated all such extortion on the Rhine. Try to get a photo of Die Pfalz when an especially colorful river barge is passing in the foreground or background. Seven miles (11 km) downstream from Die Pfalz is the legend-haunted Lorelei, a sheer outcropping of rock forever immortalized by the poem of Heinrich Heine. According to the sagas, a blond maiden — a Germanic version of the Sirens — lured sailors to their deaths with song from her perch on this rock. As *K-D* excursion boats pass this point, strains of Schumann melodies are played on a sound system, and the German tourists on board suddenly look very reverent indeed — understandably so, because the Lorelei is as characteristically German as Old Faithful is American. It's a "must" stop, and today a road runs to the top.

ST. GOAR and ST. GOARSHAUSEN: These twin towns face one another across a broad, lake-like expanse of the Rhine. St. Goar's castle, Burg Rheinfels, is worth a stop.

A few steps beyond the St. Goar Tourist Office (120 Heer Str.; phone: 6741-383) is the shop of *Doris Mühl*, which offers an incredible array of cuckoo clocks, beer steins, quality glassware, and famous Hummel figurines. Three decades of American GIs have helped this shop thrive, and its English-speaking proprietors gladly welcome Americans.

You can take the car ferry across to St. Goarshausen, which is as delightful as its sister village on the left bank. Travelers with children may find the carnival rides set up near the *K-D* steamer dock a welcome distraction. St. Goarshausen is the scene of the majestic *Rhine in Flames* fireworks and spotlight extravaganza on the third Saturday in September. But alas! (for St. Goarshausen-ites): The spectacle is best seen from St. Goar across the river. Just south of St. Goarshausen is the Lorelei.

The steep-sided Rhine gorge ends beyond the village of Boppard, a residential valley town with a particularly pleasant promenade aptly, but not too imaginatively, named Rhine Promenade (Rheinallee). At Koblenz, the Rhine is joined by the Moselle River, a famous wine river route well worth a side trip.

En Route from Koblenz – Though less dramatic than the stretch between Bingen and Koblenz, the area north of Koblenz has many intriguing features. Continuing up the left bank, take a look at the Abbey of Maria Laach, a Benedictine monastery, with its Romanesque basilica. It's a short detour of 9 miles (14 km) west of the river at Andernach. The abbey is most interesting for its location on the Laacher See, the largest of the volcanic lakes in the Eifel plateau, a peaceful, wooded area.

Farther north along the Rhine is the Rheineck, a *Burg* with a view of the surrounding valley. Still farther, on the slope of a former volcano, is the Rolandsbogen (Roland's Arch), the ruins of the castle of the knight Roland, hero of the "Chanson de Roland."

Southeast of Bonn, on the right bank (there's a car ferry from Bad Godesberg to Königswinter), is the Drachenfels, a romantic, rocky summit with a ruined tower and a panoramic view that includes the Eifel plateau, Bonn, and Cologne. It's in the Seven Mountains (Siebengebirge) range, whose low summits, once crowned with castles, now are crowned with forests; the whole area is a national park. The Drachenfels was named for the legendary dragon slain by Siegfried, the hero who became invincible by bathing in its blood. The area also is known for its wines, the best of which is called *drachenblut* (dragon's blood). Excursions for Drachenfels (15 minutes by cog railway) leave from Königswinter at frequent intervals.

BONN: In June 1991, Bonn lost its status as Germany's "provisional" capital to Berlin, the historic capital 350 miles (560 km) to the east. The postwar Germans must have wanted the capital of the new Germany in a place where nothing exciting ever happens, for after its spirited street carnival on *Weiberfastnacht* and *Rose Monday* (the dates vary with the calendar), the city goes back into hibernation. Its loss as the seat of government will mean an enormous financial drain on the city, but Bonn retains one claim to fame: The composer Ludwig van Beethoven was born and spent his early years in this Rhineside city. The excellently restored *Beethoven House* (20 Bonngasse; phone: 228-632500) deserves a stop. See also the Alter Zoll, a bastion with a view of the Rhine, and stroll along the promenade on the banks of the river, past the Bundestag, where the Parliament met before its move to Berlin.

COLOGNE (KÖLN): The silhouette of Cologne's great Gothic cathedral dominates the city's skyline; it's one of the world's finest. Begun in 1248, the cathedral was an on-again, off-again project not completed until 1880. Although 90% of the city was leveled by World War II bombing, the cathedral escaped virtually intact. See the 14th-century stained glass windows, the altarpiece, and the Magi's Shrine. The Cologne Tourist Office, off the cathedral square (phone: 221-3345), has a good selection of tourist brochures covering the cathedral and other sights. Cologne's Roman beginnings are on display at the *Roman-Germanic Museum* (closed Mondays; admission charge) opposite the cathedral, where one may see the striking 1-million-piece *Dionysus Mosaic*, dating from AD 200. Other museums include the modern *Wallraf-Richartz und Ludwig Museum*, between the cathedral and the Rhine, with an excellent collection of old Dutch and Flemish paintings as well as old and modern German works; the modern and contemporary section is outstanding, with a large collection of pop art. The *Käthe Kollwitz Museum* (Neumarkt-Passage; phone: 208-5899), is the first in Germany devoted to this great painter and sculptress.

After a round of sightseeing, you can take a cable car (near the zoo) over the Rhine, enjoy an excellent view of the cathedral, and relax in the Rheinpark. Nearby is the city exposition center, site of *Photokina*, the world's fair of the photographic industry, held during September in even-numbered years. There's shopping galore along Hohe Strasse and Schildergasse, where every major German department store chain seems to be represented. In the evening, this shopping district blossoms with street vendors and musicians. Other evening entertainment is offered by the pubs of Cologne's modest Altstadt (Old Town), which is nevertheless lively with music. Finally, the carnival here is reputed to be the best in Germany, with events reaching their highest pitch during the weekend before *Ash Wednesday*.

DÜSSELDORF: The residents have a saying: Düsseldorf is not on the Rhine, it's on the Kö. Certainly, Düsseldorf turns its back on the river and faces instead Königsallee — Kö for short — an elegant, kilometer-long promenade whose fashionable shops are a major center of German haute couture. The Kö is jewelry, furs, fine silverware, art, rare books. But the Kö also is restaurants and friendly open-air cafés, where you can sip a drink and see and be seen.

At night the spotlight shifts to Düsseldorf's other center, the lively Altstadt (Old Town), where some 200 pubs and inns jump to the sounds of live music. Nightlife here is rollicking rather than vulgar. But proof that the mellow Rhineland wine villages are far away may be seen in what Düsseldorfers are drinking, for this is beer country, and the local specialty is Altbier or Düsseldorfer Alt, a dark lager brew. The many Yugoslavian, Japanese, Italian, Argentinian, and other ethnic restaurants indicate that this is a city of international business and the business center for the Ruhr region.

Though a very modern city, Düsseldorf has a distinguished history that dates from the 13th century. The city has been known for its prominence in the arts since the 19th century, when Napoleon made it the capital of the grand duchy of Berg; among those who lived here were Heinrich Heine, Robert Schumann, and Felix Mendelssohn. The *Hetjens Museum* (Palais Nesselrode, 4 Schulstr.; phone: 899-4210) has a large collection of ceramics; *Kunstsammlung Nordrhein-Westfalen,* in its beautiful new building (5 Grabbe Pl.; phone: 133961), has some fine works of modern art, especially those by Paul Klee; and the *Goethe Museum* (2 Jacobistr.; phone: 899-6262) has an extensive collection of the writer's manuscripts and memorabilia. The opera house (Heinrich-Heine-Allee) is also an interesting place, as is Schloss Benrath (closed Mondays; admission charge; 104 Benrather Schlossallee; phone: 899-7271).

For maps and further information about Düsseldorf, contact the tourist office, 12 Konrad-Adenauer-Pl. (phone: 211-350505).

BEST EN ROUTE

The Rhineland is prime tourist country, and has been for over a century. Good hotels abound (little Rüdesheim alone has over 60), though in the wine villages the best were built in an age when guests arrived with servants and steamer trunks. Today they are like faded aristocrats and seem somewhat overpriced by American standards. Hotel restaurants can be excellent, however, and a continental breakfast — often augmented by eggs or sausage — invariably is included in the overnight price. Good double rooms may be found all along the river at prices ranging from $30 to $50 and up — though private bathrooms may not be included, so make sure you get what you want before booking. Our advice is to arrive early and head for the city tourist office, whose personnel can find a room without language problems. In the Rhenish cities, the top hotels meet the highest international standards and command prices to match; here, English is the second language. Below are just a few of the top hotels to choose from. Modest *Gasthäuser* and *pensions* are plentiful everywhere.

We have classified hotels that charge $85 to $125 for a double room with breakfast as expensive; moderate is $50 to $85; and inexpensive, below $50. A dinner for two without wine will cost $60 to $100 in an expensive restaurant; $35 to $60 is moderate; and $20 to $35, inexpensive.

RÜDESHEIM

Waldhotel Jagdschloss Niederwald – Here's a true *Schloss* hotel high on the Rhine hills, 3 miles (5 km) northwest of Rüdesheim, with an imperial view of the river. The restaurant features wine tasting and game in season — as well it should, for this was part of the former hunting lodge of the Archbishop of Mainz. Closed in the winter. Auf dem Niederwald (phone: 6722-1004). Expensive to moderate.

ASSMANNSHAUSEN

Krone – Overlooking the Rhine, this 400-year-old inn has a museum in the second-floor lounge, with letters and manuscripts by famous people who have stayed here. The spacious bedrooms have traditional furniture (favorites are No. 71 and No. 77) and the public rooms are oak-paneled and full of antiques. The food in the restaurant is outstanding; try especially the turtle soup, fresh salmon, or eel. Closed in the winter. Breakfast not included. 10 Rheinuferstr. (phone: 6722-2036). Expensive to moderate.

BINGEN

Römerhof – Across the narrow Nahe River, in the suburb of Bingerbrück, is this charming, tranquil hotel. The view is bewitching, and the site historic. Among the features are a garden and a lovely Rhenish wine tavern. The restaurant is closed

Saturdays, and the entire establishment is closed during the winter months. 10 Rupertsberg (phone: 6721-32248). Moderate.

ST. GOAR

Schlosshotel auf Burg Rheinfels – Tucked in the picturesque ruins of a medieval castle, this hotel looks out over St. Goar, the Lorelei rock, and the Cat and Mouse castles. It has an open-air terrace with a spectacular view, an indoor pool, a sauna, a museum, a conference room, and a restaurant specializing in venison. 47 Schlossberg (phone: 6741-2071/3). Expensive to moderate.

Zum Goldenen Löwen – Overlooking the Rhine, this small hotel has a restaurant with an outdoor terrace where the view is excellent. Closed January to March. 82 Heerstr. (phone: 6741-1674). Expensive to moderate.

Hauser – With a lovely view of St. Goarshausen across the river, this small, modest hotel has a café and a terrace. Restaurant closed Tuesdays. 77 Heerstr. (phone: 6741-333). Inexpensive.

BONN

Steigenberger Venusberg – Bonn's newest hotel, opened in 1989, is on Venusberg Hill. It offers a good view of Bonn and the Rhine Valley. Designed in the style of a French country mansion, this luxurious hostelry has 80 rooms and 6 suites as well as 2 restaurants. 1 An der Casselsruhe (phone: 228-2880). Very expensive.

COLOGNE (KÖLN)

Excelsior Ernst – Opposite the cathedral and near the train station, this establishment is everything you would expect from an Old World hotel. Its rooms radiate an aura of luxury, comfort, and charm; the service is very efficient, although not ostentatious. *Hansa-Stube* is its very well regarded restaurant. 1 Trankgasse (phone: 221-2701). Very expensive.

Goldener Pflug – Exquisite house specialties are served at this fine restaurant in a pleasant setting. Service is first rate. Closed Sundays and in July. Reservations advised. 421 Olpener Str. (phone: 221-895509). Very expensive.

Altstadt – This small hotel is in the Old City near the landing dock for Rhine boats. Herr Olbrich, the owner, once was a steward for the *German-American Line.* His tastefully decorated rooms are impeccable, and the personal service is outstanding. Rooms have bars and refrigerators. Closed December 20 to January 6. Reservations advised. 7 Salzgasse (phone: 221-234187/88/89). Moderate.

Fruh – This bustling restaurant-beerhall near the cathedral is a tradition in Cologne. Not as vast or as noisy as most of its kind in Germany, it is a favorite of captains of finance as well as taxi drivers. Waiters are caled *kobus* (for *Jakobus*) and supposedly won't respond to anything else, but have been known to make exceptions for visitors in town. The beer is a very dry local brew called *Kolsch* and menu specialties include *Rheinischer sauerbraten* (Rhineland pot roast) and *kassler ripchen* (smoked pork cutlet), which is served with mountains of sauerkraut and mashed potatoes. 12-14 Am Hof (phone: 221-212621). Moderate.

Weinhaus im Walfisch – Seafood dishes and some of the best German wines are the specialty here. The building predates the last war by more than 300 years, a rarity in hard-hit Cologne. Closed Sundays and in July. Reservations advised. 13 Salzgasse (phone: 219575). Moderate.

DÜSSELDORF

Breidenbacher Hof – Convenient to both the activities of the downtown area and the Old World charms of the Altstadt (Old Town), this recently renovated hotel is one of Germany's best addresses. Tradition, luxury, and elegance combine well with very efficient service in its 151 rooms. Its *Grill Royal* restaurant ought not to be missed. Closed Saturdays and Sundays for dinner. 36 Heinrich-Heine-Allee (phone: 221-13030). Very expensive.

Zum Schiffchen – Don't miss the jovial atmosphere and hearty food of this beer garden that's a favorite town haunt. Napoleon is said to have dined here, as well as Heinrich Heine and Arthur Miller. Closed Sundays. 5 Hafenstr. (phone: 211-132422). Moderate to inexpensive.

The Neckar River Valley

This route along the meandering Neckar River follows Germany's Castle Road (Die Burgenstrasse) from Heidelberg to Heilbronn. More than a dozen castles and strongholds can be found along this road, some of which housed aristocratic families during the Middle Ages. Many of the princely feudal dwellings are in ruins; others are intact and have been restored as museums, hotels, inns, and wine taverns. Zwingenberg Castle, for example, still is inhabited by royalty — by relatives of Britain's Prince Philip — but Hirschhorn and Hornberg castles now are hotels.

One of Germany's wine districts, producing mainly red wines, the scenic Neckar River Valley is surrounded by high, forested hills crowned with castles, fortresses, and quaint old towns. Beginning in Heidelberg (see *Frankfurt to Heidelberg*), this 1- or 2-day drive runs 50 miles (80 km) south to the wine producing town of Heilbronn, where the Castle Road ends. From here it's an additional 32 miles (51 km) through the Swabian Hills to the major industrial and cultural center of Stuttgart, home of the *Stuttgart Ballet* and Mercedes-Benz. Finally, you can drive yet another 27 miles (43 km) south to see Tübingen, a charming old university town.

Well-marked hiking trails connect towns and castles, and the forested castle areas generally are honeycombed with quiet, scenic trails. Boat trips leave from many locations on the Neckar; passenger and car ferries transport you to interesting sites on the opposite bank. A bicycle lane runs along most of the route. The valley also has health spas and resorts for the recreation-minded. For maps and further information about the region, contact the tourist office in Stuttgart (Landesfremdenverkehrsverband Baden-Württenberg, 23 Bussenstr., Stuttgart 7000; phone: 711-481045; or Fremdenverkehrsverband Neckarland-Schwaben, 21 Lohtorstr., Heilbronn 7100; phone: 7131-69061).

En Route from Heidelberg – Neckargemünd, a 1,000-year-old town by the winding Neckar, features old inns such as the *Ritter* (40 Neckarstr.), with open-air terraces overlooking the valley (see *Best en Route*). A church steeple rises over half-timbered houses and the old Town Hall. Neckargemünd also has the only parachute museum in Western Europe (7 Bach Str.). From here Dilsberg is a short detour of 3 miles (5 km).

Dilsberg, a fortified hamlet high above the Neckar River, resisted Imperial General Tilly and his Bavarian men during the Thirty Years War. The stout ramparts and lookout towers of this walled city are visible from both banks. If you park your car outside the town walls and enter the town on foot, you can explore the fortress, a mysterious subterranean tunnel, and the castle ruins (Burgruine). The tower (open summers only), with almost 100 stairs, offers a panoramic view of the river. Return by the same route to Neckargemünd, take Route 37 to the north bank, and drive toward Neckarsteinach. You'll spot castle ruins on the ridge as you approach the town, which is 3 miles (5 km) from Neckargemünd.

NECKARSTEINACH: Also known as the Four Castles Corner (Vierburgeneck), this town boasts four medieval citadels built in the 12th and 13th centuries. On the left side of Route 37, shortly before you reach the town, a parking area marks the start of a wooded trail that connects Vorderburg, Mittelburg, Hinterburg, and Schadeck castles. The walk takes about 45 minutes and ends in the town itself, not far from the parking area. On many summer evenings, the town holds the *Four Castles Festival,* in which the castles are illuminated and fireworks are exploded. Neckarsteinach's center is carefully preserved, so you also may want to stroll around the town. From here follow Route 37 to Hirschhorn, approximately 6 miles (10 km) away.

HIRSCHHORN: This town is dominated by its impressive castle fortress, *Hirschhorn Castle,* which now is part of the *Schloss-Hotel* (see *Best en Route*). The towered defenses were built in the 13th century, but the castle itself dates from the 16th century. For a small fee you can climb the 121 steps of the tower, which lead to a magnificent view of the sharp Hirschhorn bend in the river. Below the castle, the walled village still holds the remains of a deep moat. Historic Ersheimer Chapel is across the river; from there you can have a good view of the castle. From Hirschhorn continue up the north bank for about 7 miles (11 km) to Eberbach.

EBERBACH: This ancient imperial city has fortress ruins that date from the 11th century. Four powerful towers attest to its medieval beginnings. The old Deutscher Hof, the medieval center of town, is alive with colorful inns, half-timbered houses, and cobbled streets. In the old market square, the town's eventful history is recorded in 14 scenes painted on a front wall of the *Karpfen* hotel. You can see other engraved murals on the oldest inn in the city, the *Gasthaus zum Krabbenstein,* and at the Hay Market (Heumarkt).

After a walk in the Old City, stop at the large red and white *Victoria Café* (5 Friedrichstr.) and choose from an immense assortment of confections, candies, and desserts. The town also has a health resort park, large forested reserves, indoor and outdoor swimming pools, tennis courts, and is Germany's acupuncture center.

ZWINGENBERG: Continue on Route 37 for 7 miles (11 km) to Zwingenberg. Follow signs to the train station (Bahnhof) and park your car. A short distance up the road, a paved path leads to the Zwingenberg Castle, one of the most magnificent of the castles on the Castle Road. The interior of the residence of the Battenbergs, relatives of Britain's Prince Philip, is only open to the public from May 1 to September 30, Tuesdays, Fridays, and Sundays from 2 to 4:15 PM. The fortress has been spared by war and almost untouched by renovation. The Lords of Zwingenberg, its first owners in the 13th century, supplemented their income by imposing customs fees on shipping on the Neckar River. Two more castle ruins — Stolzeneck and Minneburg — are on the opposite bank of the river.

NECKARZIMMERN: From Zwingenberg, drive on Route 37 to its junction with Route 27 at Neckarelz, a distance of about 10 miles (16 km). Then follow Route 27 a few miles to Neckarzimmern. Look for the sign for Burg Hornberg and follow the paved road to the left to the *Schloss Hornberg* (Hornberg Castle, now a hotel).

Overlooking vineyards sloping to the river's bank, this castle was once the home of the Knight of the Iron Fist, Götz von Berlichingen, who wore an artificial hand after losing his right hand in the Bavarian War of 1504. For a small charge, you can explore the castle ruins, visit the museum with its medieval armor and implements, and climb the watchtower (almost 140 wooden steps) for a commanding view of the Neckar

Valley. This castle was first mentioned in a document in 1184. Since that time it has changed hands several times; it has been sold, given away, and even pawned during its colorful history.

You may want to pause for a meal or a drink in the castle's former stable, now converted into a restaurant and bar. The windows of the restaurant look out over the valley, and you can sample wines that come from the slopes below.

NECKARMÜHLBACH: From Hornberg drive on Route 27 to Gundelsheim (an interesting historical town with its Castle of Horneck). At Gundelsheim, drive over the bridge across the Neckar and follow the marked road near Neckarmühlbach to Burg Guttenberg (Guttenberg Castle), one of the very few medieval German castles that have not been destroyed; it is, in fact, still a residence.

Dating from the 12th century, this castle offers more than just historical and architectural interest. It also houses an extensive collection of live birds of prey, many uncaged, from throughout the world. Here, amidst the stately castle fortifications, stand eagles, vultures, and other predators. The birds entertain visitors during a show in which vultures swoop down over the heads of the audience.

The museum also displays historical remnants, such as a skillfully crafted Madonna, medieval books and documents, instruments of torture, woodcuts, engravings, copper etchings, jewelry, kitchenware, porcelain, and glass. An old spiral stairway takes you to the different floors of the museum and leads to a door marked "zum Turm" (to the tower). If you decide to climb the more than 100 steps to the open tower, you'll be rewarded with a sweeping view of the countryside.

From here, continue on the left side of the river to Bad Wimpfen.

BAD WIMPFEN: This royal city of the Castle Road was the imperial residence of the Hohenstaufens in the 13th century. The Upper Town (Bad Wimpfen am Berg), as the old part of Bad Wimpfen is called, is marked by the towers, spires, and red tile roofs that crown its half-timbered structures.

A short walking tour of the old section takes about an hour and is well worth it. You can see the Town Hall, market square, the Blue Tower, the picturesque house of Mayor Elsesser, the Steinhaus (Romanesque, from about 1200), the imperial chapel, and the Red Tower, the emperor's refuge in times of danger. A walk down Klostergasse passes half-timbered houses with gardens, the Mansion of the Knights, and the former bathhouses dating from 1543.

En Route from Bad Wimpfen – You can continue on the left bank of the Neckar to Heilbronn or cross the river to Route 27 and drive a short distance to Bad Friedrichshall, a spa town with salt mines. Here you can arrange a tour of the saltworks or visit the local castle-hotel, *Schloss Lehen* (Hauptstr. 2). Then drive along the right bank to Neckarsulm, a town that will interest automobile and motorcycle buffs. You can tour the NSU Automobile Factory weekdays at 10 AM and 2 PM or visit the *Zweiradmuseum,* in the former Castle of the Teutonic Order. This exhibition shows the development of original models of bicycles and motorcycles. Follow either the left or right bank to reach Heilbronn.

HEILBRONN: In the midst of forests and vineyards, this is one of Germany's major wine producing towns. You can sample the fine wines at the *Heilbronn Harvest,* a traditional wine festival in early September; *Wine Village,* a festival centered around the Town Hall, also held in September; or at any time in any of Heilbronn's inns such as the *Insel* (see *Best en Route*) at Friedrich Ebert Brücke, on an island in the river.

Formerly a free imperial city, Heilbronn has many interesting buildings. The 1315 Tower of the Church of St. Kilian was Germany's first Renaissance structure. Also in the city's center, the 15th-century Town Hall with its ornamental clock, made in 1580, and the 14th-century Gothic Käthchenhaus, a patrician dwelling in the market square.

En Route from Heilbronn – If you have additional time, you may want to continue along the Neckar, taking Route 27 on the right bank, for 32 miles (51 km) to Stuttgart, passing through gently rolling vineyards and small, picturesque medieval towns such as Lauffen, Kirchheim, and Besigheim. You may want to stroll along some of the streets in these old towns.

STUTTGART: A city of more than half a million people, Stuttgart is more than an industrial center. Besides being the headquarters of Mercedes, Stuttgart is home of the highly acclaimed *Stuttgart Ballet* as well as the *State Opera* and a *Philharmonic Orchestra.* Surrounded by the wooded Swabian Hills, Stuttgart has devoted two-thirds of its land to green spots, including vineyards that are near the business district and the main railroad station. It is also the capital of the federal state of Baden-Württemberg.

Enjoy the view of Stuttgart and the Swabian Jura from the Television Tower (Fernsehturm) south of the city on Bopser Hill. Built in 1956 from a unique design by Dr. Fritz Leonhardt, the tower has an observation platform and a good restaurant, the *Turmrestaurant.* Then visit the Old Town where, on the Schillerplatz, you can see Stuttgart's Old Palace, built in both 14th-century Gothic and 16th-century Renaissance styles, with a courtyard surrounded by galleries. It now houses the *Württemberg Regional Museum,* devoted to regional history. Schillerplatz also is the site of a vegetable and flower market on Tuesdays, Thursdays, and Saturdays. Nearby, the ultramodern Rathaus (Town Hall) also is of interest, with its glockenspiel that plays folk songs.

The *Stuttgart State Gallery* (Alte Staatsgalerie; 30-32 Konrad-Adenauer-Str.) houses a fine collection of paintings from the Middle Ages to the 19th century. The ultramodern *Neue Staatsgalerie* next door displays 20th-century art, including works from the German Expressionist and Bauhaus movements. Both closed Mondays. No admission charge. The most popular museum here, however, is the *Daimler-Benz Museum,* in the Mercedes-Benz plant in the suburb of Untertürkheim. Accessible by bus Line 56 from the bus station, or by Line 5 from the central train station, it contains displays of cars, car engines, and other motors — racing car, boat, airplane, motorcycle — in addition to the history of the venerable firm, which began in 1900 (closed Mondays; no admission charge).

Stuttgart is graced by parks, the most beautiful of which is Killesberg Park, on a hill in the northern part of town. Another park worth a visit is the Cannstatter Wasen, where a popular festival is held every year for 2 weeks at the end of September. Like the *Oktoberfest* in Munich, it is one of Germany's biggest, most popular festivals. Stuttgart also is known for its modern buildings, particularly the asymmetrical *Liederhalle* near the town center, designed in 1956 by Adolf Abel and Rolf Gutbrod. The concrete exterior of the *Liederhalle,* containing three concert halls with excellent acoustics, is enlivened with mosaics, glazed brick, and quartz.

Stuttgart's Tourist Office is below the main railroad station (Arnulf-Klett-Passage; phone: 222-8240). There is now direct train service between the main station (Hauptbahnhof) and the Stuttgart Airport. On Saturdays at 10 AM, free walking tours (in English) leave from Schillerplatz.

TÜBINGEN: From Stuttgart it's 27 miles (43 km) to this lovely old university town. The University of Tübingen, founded in 1477, still uses the town's Renaissance castle, whose terraces, bastions, and gardens offer a fine view of the Neckar and the Old Town. Nearby is the Marktplatz, which is especially colorful on market days — Mondays, Wednesdays, and Fridays — when you can see peasants in regional dress selling produce.

Don't miss the famous Platanenallee, an avenue of plane trees on a manmade island in the Neckar, a pleasant place both day and night. The Platanenallee may be reached by the Eberhard Bridge. Both the bridge and the island offer excellent views of the town, with its river, its old houses, and its willow trees.

BEST EN ROUTE

On this, Germany's Castle Road, hotels and inns — even those in the castles — are surprisingly reasonable. The most expensive places are in the larger cities such as Stuttgart. A double room with private bath, breakfast, tax, and service included in the price will cost $85 to $150 in hotels listed as expensive; $45 to $80 is moderate; and under $45, inexpensive. Many of the restaurants along this route are in the hotels and inns. A dinner for two will cost $60 to $100 in an expensive restaurant; $30 to $55 is moderate; and below $30 is inexpensive.

NECKARGEMÜND

Zum Ritter – This charming inn has 41 rooms, a terrace with an extraordinary view, and a good restaurant. 40 Neckarstr. (phone: 6223-7035). Moderate.

HIRSCHHORN

Schloss-Hotel – A hilltop castle-hotel with 15 rooms, it overlooks the Neckar River valley and the small town below. Dining facilities include indoor restaurants and an outdoor terrace with an excellent view. Accommodations in the guesthouse annex are less expensive than those in the castle (*Hirschhorn Castle*). Closed in December and January. Auf Burg Hirschhorn (phone: 6272-1373). Moderate.

NECKARZIMMERN

Götzenburg Hornberg – Another, equally interesting castle-hotel high above the river, this place has 27 rooms and a terrace with a view of the river valley. The restaurant serves regional specialties (don't miss the mushrooms) and wines from the castle vineyards below. The atmosphere is informal. Open March to November (phone: 6261-4064/65). Expensive to moderate.

NECKARMÜHLBACH

Burgschenke Burg Guttenberg – This fine restaurant, within the castle grounds, offers game dishes such as venison, good desserts, and local wines. The view of the valley is memorable. Closed Mondays. Burg Guttenberg (phone: 6266-228). Moderate.

HEINSHEIM

Schlosshotel Heinsheim – This baroque manor and guesthouse has its own palace chapel, a swimming pool, gardens, and a vineyard. Indoor and outdoor dining and a classic drawing room provide the final touches. It has excellent service, a friendly atmosphere, and good food. In Heinsheim on the left bank, near Bad Wimpfen (phone: 7264-1045). Moderate.

BAD FRIEDRICHSHALL

Schloss Lehen – A quiet, elegant house set back from the road, this hostelry is surrounded by greenery and gardens. Built in the 1400s, it offers a homelike atmosphere and a good restaurant. 2 Hauptstr., on the edge of town on the right bank (phone: 7136-4044). Expensive.

HEILBRONN

Insel – In the heart of the city, this 120-room hotel with its own park actually is on a small island in the middle of the Neckar. The modern hotel has a café terrace, a restaurant offering Swabian specialties, and a French restaurant. Most of its rooms have balconies. Friedrich-Ebert-Brücke (phone: 7131-6300). Expensive.

Wirtshaus am Götzenturm – The idols' tower (Götzenturm) in the medieval city wall gave this restaurant its name. Try the fish and the local Württemberg wines. The owner also runs the *Beichtstuhl* wine cellar around the corner. Open evenings only. Closed Sundays. 1 Allerheiligenstr. (phone: 80534). Expensive to moderate.

STUTTGART

Graf Zeppelin – Near the main railroad station, this hotel is the city's largest. It has an indoor swimming pool, sauna, health club, disco, and a pleasant dining room. 7 Arnulf Klett Pl. (phone: 7131-299881). Very expensive.

Alte Post – In a comfortable old tavern, this inn provides regional cuisine and seafood. Among the specialties are medallions of veal, filet of sole in lobster sauce, shrimp cocktail, and fresh oysters when in season. The service matches the high standards of the kitchen. Closed Saturdays, Sundays, and early August; open Mondays for dinner only. Reservations advised. 43 Friedrichstr. (phone: 711-293079). Expensive.

Am Schlossgarten – Completely renovated, this centrally located property offers above-standard comfort. Two restaurants, one with a terrace view, are next door. 23 Schillerstr. (phone: 711-20260). Expensive.

Goldener Adler – Regional Swabian dishes — *Maultaschen, Spätzle,* and fresh mussels — are the specialties of this downtown restaurant. Also, try a bottle of its red wine from Württemberg. Closed Mondays. 38 Böheimstr. (phone: 711-640-1762). Moderate.

TÜBINGEN

Krone – With tasteful traditional furnishings, modern facilities, and an international menu, this 55-room hotel fits well into the atmosphere of the old university town. 1 Uhlandstr. (phone: 7071-31036). Expensive.

Hotel am Schloss – Just outside the gate of the castle that looks down on the town, this small hotel has 23 rooms, some furnished with antiques, window boxes overflowing with flowers, and an excellent small restaurant serving Swabian specialties. 18 Burgstr. (phone: 7071-21077/78). Moderate.

The Black Forest

The Black Forest (Schwarzwald, in German) lies in southern Germany, bounded roughly by a rectangle made from the cities of Rastatt, Basel, Schaffhausen, and Pforzheim. It is inappropriately named, as the forests are no darker or blacker here than any other forests in Germany; in fact, the whole area receives considerably more sunshine than the overall average for the rest of the country. It is a bright, open land of tree-covered mountains, rolling hills, and intermittent pine and birch forests. There are ski resorts and spas. The ordinary mountain towns are small, rustic, and colorful, often tucked away in valleys of stunning serenity and beauty. Some of the larger cities, such as Baden-Baden and Freiburg, are renowned as cultural centers, but many of the small towns are quaintly provincial in their outlook — in fact, some of the people still wear their regional costumes.

Throughout its history, the Black Forest region has clung tenaciously to its own identity. During the Thirty Years War, the area passed from the hands of the Austrians to the French and then to the Bavarians. The French got it back again for a short time in 1679, then the Austrians returned in 1697, after which the area remained in the Austrian sphere of influence. It became part of the German duchy of Baden and the kingdom of Württemberg in 1815. Now it's part of the state known as Baden-Württemberg. All of this turbulent history has given the Schwarzwalders a strong sense of their own identity; indeed, they revel in their own customs and manners.

There's hardly a section of the Black Forest that is lacking in beauty and charm. If you take the autobahn from Basel to Baden-Baden, the distance is 102 miles (163 km); our incomparably more scenic byway climbs over the 4,898-foot Feldberg Mountain peak and runs along the renowned Schwarz-wälder Tälerstrasse (Rte. 294), just to name two of its highlights. The tour could be made in as little as 1 day, but you'll probably prefer to spend 2 or 3.

To hurry through an area like the Schwarzwald is to miss such delights as staying in half-timbered little *Gasthäuser* (hotels) with warm smoky dining rooms where the locals drink their nightly beer and *kirschwasser,* a fiery local distillation made from cherries. The speedy traveler would also miss such regional specialties as *Schwarzwälder Schinken,* a smoked ham sliced so thin it is transparent; or the luscious taste of fresh mountain trout, cooked with almonds, with heaps of boiled salted potatoes as the perfect side dish. Brochures, maps, and information about the region are available from the tourist office, Fremdenverkehrsverband Schwarzwald e.V., 45 Bertholdstr., Freiburg 7800 (phone: 761-31317/18).

En Route from Basel (Switzerland) – Starting from the southwest corner of the Black Forest, near the Swiss border city of Basel, it is only a quick 15-minute drive north to Lörrach on Route 317. There are some interesting ruins above Lörrach called Burg Rötteln, and the town museum contains many fine examples of Black Forest handiwork, such as woodcarving, clock making, and religious figurines.

Continuing on Route 317, it is a 25-mile (40-km) drive to the village of Todtnau, at an altitude of 2,169 feet. The air here is so clean and pure that Todtnau has been recommended as a resort for people with respiratory ailments. There are not many manmade attractions in the area, but there still is plenty to do. In the winter, the area is renowned for its skiing (both downhill and cross-country) and in the summer, the hikers come out in droves to tramp through the woods and valleys that make up the region surrounding the town. For summer visitors, there is also swimming (both indoor and outdoor pools available), miniature golf, and open-air concerts.

At Todtnau the road splits, with Route 317 continuing east to Titisee via the route over the Feldberg, the highest mountain peak in the Black Forest (4,898 feet). This is a very scenic drive, well worth the time. The Feldberg offers the best skiing in the Black Forest, and during the summer the views from this mountain area are unequaled in the entire region.

As magnificent as the drive over the Feldberg may be, there is an equally attractive way to the city of Freiburg from the turnoff at Todtnau. The road is narrower, and closed in the winter, but the mountain scenery is superb. This is the Schauinsland Strasse, over the Schauinsland peak, which at 4,212 feet is one of the taller mountains in the Schwarzwald.

FREIBURG: Freiburg is a modern, bustling city of more than 180,000 people, yet it maintains its sense of Old World charm as surely as an aged Schwarzwälderin with her round *Bollenhut* on her head. As the Freiburgers say, it is Germany's smallest "big town," and where else can you find a modern city that has the cleanest and most sparkling gutters in Europe, with fresh mountain water running through them continuously?

Freiburg was badly damaged during bombing raids in World War II, yet today all of the damage has been repaired, and the famed cathedral, with its 386-foot Gothic tower and spectacular stained glass windows, is the equal of any European church. This is the only Gothic cathedral in Germany that was totally completed during the Middle Ages. (The cathedrals in both Cologne and Ulm were not finished until the 19th century.) Opposite the south side of the cathedral stands the 16th-century *Kaufhaus,* originally erected as a merchants' hall but now used as a festival hall on special occasions. Its shocking color — a cross between blood red and gallbladder yellow — only makes it stand out from the rest of the buildings in the Münsterplatz. Nearby is the Rathausplatz, which contains an unusual Rathaus (Town Hall), formed by joining two old patrician houses that stood beside each other. Other important sights in the city are the *Haus zum Walfisch* (Whalehouse) near the Rathaus and the *Augustiner Museum* (Augustinerpl.), which contains medieval and baroque art of the Upper Rhine region.

Freiburg also is known for its cozy little wine taverns, with many of them dispensing local vintages that have been grown and cultivated within the city limits. For a good local wine, try a Freiburger Schlossberg (though perhaps the best wine in the entire Baden region is made a few miles to the west in the village of Ihringen, where the Doktorgarten and Winklerberg are both considered excellent vineyards).

FURTWANGEN: From Freiburg it is a short drive along Route 31 to the turnoff for Route 500 (north). There are several scenic overlooks along this road, each one of them worth a stop. During the summer, the mountain valleys will be alive with little white and blue flowers, and the tiny villages, many of them nothing more than a handful of houses with barns attached, all seem too perfect to be real.

Furtwangen is worth a stop because of its excellent clock museum *Uhrenmuseum* (11 Gerwig Str.), which is open daily from April through October; closed weekends from November through March. Here, virtually anything that can be made to tell time has been garnered into the museum and displayed. There are cuckoo clocks of every shape, size, and description, from a tiny clock that would fit into the palm of the hand and gives off a cuckoo like a canary with laryngitis to a monstrous old wall-hanger with a cuckoo that still sounds like a canary with laryngitis. There are grandfather clocks, grandmother clocks, and clocks that are simply grand.

TRIBERG: Just before Route 500 winds its way down into Triberg, there is a turnoff with a magnificent view of the surrounding valley. This also is the entrance to the Triberger Waterfall, the highest waterfall in all of Germany at 492 feet. An interesting walk begins at the top of the waterfall and continues down the path beside it to the town of Triberg, a distance of about 3 miles (5 km), all on carefully manicured trails with handrails. Sections of the waterfall are beautiful, but don't expect anything on the scale of Niagara or Victoria Falls: It simply is not that kind of waterfall.

Triberg itself is both pretty and interesting. No visitor should miss the *Heimatmuseum* (Wellfahrts Str. 4), a collection of local handicrafts and woodcarvings. There also is a fine collection of clocks in the museum, and a room completely decorated with woodcarving — walls, ceiling, benches, everything. Also in the museum is a collection of old mechanical musical instruments, including player pianos and an old pipe organ that still plays with the loudest racket imaginable. Children of all ages will be entranced by the moving characters in the mechanical band.

NIEDERWASSER: Just outside Triberg, Route 500 intersects Route 33 and continues north. There is an excellent restaurant in the tiny village of Niederwasser, the *Gasthaus Rössle* (see *Best en Route*). Directly across the road from the restaurant is a gift shop selling everything from cuckoo clocks to hand-carved wooden plates, all at prices much lower than at the main tourist centers in Germany. The gift shop accepts major credit cards, a rarity in this part of Germany. Both the restaurant and the gift shop can hardly be missed, as they are the *only* things on the road near Niederwasser.

ALPIRSBACH: At Hausach, Route 33 intersects Route 294, the famous Schwarzwälder Tälerstrasse, which continues on up to Freudenstadt. Along the way, it passes through the charming village of Alpirsbach, with its Benedictine monastery, built in the year 1095.

FREUDENSTADT: Freudenstadt has one of the most elegant new market squares in all of Germany. The original market square was destroyed during the war, but the reconstruction has been well done. Aside from the Marktplatz, there is little to see in Freudenstadt, but it is an excellent town for shopping for such things as clocks and woodcarvings. There also are more than 560 miles of hiking trails leading through the woods and valleys around the town. The small *Ratskeller* restaurant (8 Marktpl.) is one of Germany's best.

En Route from Freudenstadt – From Freudenstadt, there are two roads to Baden-Baden. One is called the Schwarzwälder Hochstrasse, or the High Road, and the other is the continuation of the Schwarzwälder Tälerstrasse, or the Low Road. Both are beautiful at any time of year, but the Hochstrasse probably has a slight edge in natural scenery; the Tälerstrasse is easier and smoother driving, with fewer curves and hills. The two roads intersect at Baiersbronn, where the magnificent restaurant at *Kur und Sporthotel Traube* (237 Tonbachstr.) is well worth a visit.

BADEN-BADEN: Baden-Baden is internationally famous for its casino and its baths, which have been in operation since Roman times. During the 19th century, this was the most famous spa in Europe, and kings and emperors from all over the world came here to gamble by night and nurse their hangovers the next day. Though royalty is no more, Baden-Baden remains one of the most exclusive resort towns in all of Europe.

The casino at Baden-Baden is one of the most formal and elegant in all of Europe. By all means stop to admire its crystal chandeliers and oh-so-deep carpets. James Bond would feel right at home here. The castle, the Neues Schloss, also is worth a visit. Be sure to see Lichtentaler Allee, Baden-Baden's lovely and fashionable promenade along the Oos.

Baden-Baden is directly beside the main A5 autobahn, one of the major north-south arteries in Germany, and from this point the rest of the country can easily be reached in a few hours.

BEST EN ROUTE

Because it is an area of small towns, the Black Forest (except for Baden-Baden) is generally less expensive than many other parts of Germany. A double room with breakfast will cost $80 to $130 in expensive hotels; $50 to $75, moderate; and below $50, inexpensive. A dinner for two without wine runs $50 to $90 in expensive restaurants; $30 to $45, moderate; and below $30, inexpensive.

FREIBURG

Colombi – Near the Old City, opposite a park, is Freiburg's top hotel, with fine service, a comfortable and inviting lobby, a good restaurant, and a popular wine tavern. Many rooms have balconies. 16 Rotteckring (phone: 761-31415). Expensive.

Oberkirchs Weinstuben – The place for regional cooking (and comfortable guest-rooms in the hotel as well). It's on a little square adjoining the lovely old department store *Kaufhaus*. The restaurant is an old, dark-paneled place with rustic wooden chairs. Try game dishes here: pheasant, wild boar, deer, and rabbit — all deliciously prepared. Closed Sundays. 22 Münsterpl. (phone: 761-31011). Expensive to moderate.

Zum Roten Bären – Directly on the Schwabentor, the old gate that still guards the entrance to the city, this is one of the oldest *Gasthäuser* in Germany, founded in 1227. Its charming Old World rooms and its excellent food at moderate prices are hard to beat. 12 Oberlinden (phone: 761-36913). Expensive to moderate.

Zähringer Burg – Jürgen Kavelmann, one of Freiburg's best chefs, has quickly succeeded in restoring the fine culinary tradition of this restaurant. Don't miss the fish dishes. Closed Sunday evenings and Mondays. Reservations advised. 19 Reutebachgasse (phone: 761-54041). Moderate.

FURTWANGEN

Ochsen – A quiet place to spend the night, with good simple rooms and inexpensive food, served in truly gargantuan portions. Closed Mondays. 7 Marktpl. (phone: 7723-2016). Inexpensive.

TRIBERG

Park Hotel Wehrle – One of the finest hotels in the Black Forest (set in a lovely park) offers good service, a swimming pool, sauna, solarium, and an excellent restaurant known for its trout dishes (20 different kinds are listed on the menu). It has comfortable period furniture and lots of atmosphere. Major credit cards accepted. 24 Gartenstr. (phone: 7722-86020). Expensive.

NIEDERWASSER

Gasthaus Rössle – In a tiny village, this excellent and reasonably priced restaurant specializes in *Rinderroulade* (small rolls of beef in a tasty brown sauce) and tender veal steaks served with fresh peas and carrots. There also are 6 guestrooms. Closed Wednesdays. 26 Freiburgerst (phone: 7808-2272). Inexpensive.

ALPIRSBACH

Löwen Post – In the marketplace of a charming village, this is a comfortable and pleasant hotel with a good restaurant. Closed Tuesdays. 12 Marktpl. (phone: 7444-2393). Inexpensive.

FREUDENSTADT

Kurhotel Sonne am Kurpark – This small hotel, in a park opposite the spa center, not only has comfortable accommodations but also boasts one of the Black Forest's best restaurants, featuring regional dishes. 63 Turnhallestr. (phone: 7441-6044). Expensive.

BAIERSBRONN

Schwarzwaldstube – The irresistible combination of excellent food and rustic splendor, as well as a fine French menu, make this one of Germany's most highly regarded restaurants. Being part of the elegant 200-year-old *Kur und Sporthotel Traube* doesn't hurt, either. Closed Thursdays and Fridays for lunch, and most of July. Reservations advised. 237 Tonbachstr. (phone: 7442-4920). Expensive.

BADEN-BADEN

Brenner's Park – One of Germany's (and the world's) most luxurious hotels, it's very expensive but worth it. Here kings mingle with celebrities and lions of industry. It has everything — indoor and outdoor pools, a complete spa and a health clinic, gracious service, public areas with river views, music, dancing, miniature golf, and riding. There is a formal restaurant and a grill. Reservations advised. 4-6 Schillerstr. (phone: 7221-3530). Very expensive.

Pospisil's Restaurant Merkurius – This is the place to sample baby lobster or leg of lamb: inspired, inspired. Closed Mondays, and for lunch Tuesdays and Saturdays. Reservations advised. 2 Klosterbergstr., in nearby Varnhalt (phone: 7223-5474). Expensive to moderate.

The Romantic Road

The so-called Romantic Road (Romantische Strasse) runs south through Bavaria, from the imperial city of Würzburg on the Main River to the mountain frontier town of Füssen in the foothills of the snow-clad Bavarian Alps. It is romantic, not for any dramatic scenery on the road itself, which traverses gentle, wooded hills and quiet valleys, but for its glorious medieval towns, some of which are 2,000 years old, and many of which have survived much as they appeared in the Middle Ages.

The wealth of sights along this route almost defies belief. In Würzburg and some of the other towns a visitor can see the incomparable works of Tilman Riemenschneider, Master of Würzburg, a 16th-century Gothic woodcarver and sculptor with a very distinctive style. There's Rothenburg ob der Tauber, Germany's best-preserved medieval city, with its walls, fountains, and gabled patrician houses, and Augsburg, once the richest city in Europe, with elegant avenues, lovely fountains, and mansions of the rich, as well as what is probably the world's oldest extant housing project for the poor, dating from 1519. Also not to be missed are the Wies Church, the rococo masterpiece of Dominikus and Johann Baptist Zimmermann, set in the midst of meadows, and Germany's two most magnificent castles, called the Royal Castles. During the summer, the area has folk festivals, open-air operas, concerts in royal palaces, and traditional centuries-old plays.

This 215-mile (344-km) route begins in Würzburg, taking Route 27 south to Tauberbischofsheim, Route 290 to Bad Mergentheim, and Route 19 to Igersheim. It follows the Tauber River through Weikersheim and Creglingen to Rothenburg, then takes Route 25 through central Bavaria, shifts to Route 2 to Augsburg and Route 17 to Füssen in the Alpine foothills.

Although much of the route follows principal highways, some portions are on small, winding, two-way roads that pass through tiny villages. Look out for signs, because the route is not always clearly marked. In the towns, narrow, cobblestone streets make driving difficult, so you may want to look for a parking area (marked with a large, white *P* on a blue background), and then walk into the Old City areas. Since there aren't many gas stations along this route, keep an eye on your gas gauge.

For information and maps of the region, contact the tourist office in Rothenburg: Arbeitsgemeinschaft "Romantische Strasse," Fremdenverkehrsamt, Rothenburg ob der Tauber 8803 (phone: 9861-40492).

WÜRZBURG: Set amid the vine-clad hills of the Franconian wine country, this is Germany's outstanding baroque city. Though bombed heavily during World War II, it has been completely restored. Würzburg, which remained staunchly Catholic throughout the Reformation, is known as the "city of the Madonnas," for more than 300 statues of the Virgin stand in front of its houses. The early history of the town was dominated by the prince-bishops who lived there, first in the Marienberg Fortress and later in the Residenz, both of which still are standing. Würzburg also is famous for its art treasures, most of which are the creations of two men: the 16th-century Gothic sculptor Tilman Riemenschneider, known as the Master of Würzburg, and the 18th-century German baroque architect Balthasar Neumann, court architect to the prince-bishops.

The fortress and the palace, on opposite banks of the Main River, are still the major sights in the city. High above the town is the Marienberg Fortress, which now houses the fine *Franconian Museum of the Main* (Mainfränkisches Museum), with its extraordinary sculptures by the Master of Würzburg. Near the fortress is the Käppele, a baroque chapel with rococo decorations and a lovely view of the town, the river, and the fortress. Cross the old bridge (Mainbrücke), dating from the 15th century and decorated with statues of 11 saints, to the Residenz, where you can see the court gardens, the imperial hall (Kaisersaal), the church (Hofkirche), and the grand staircase (Treppenhaus). You also might want to see the Cathedral of St. Kilian, a Romanesque church with sculptures by Riemenschneider, and such secular baroque buildings as Zum Falkenhaus; both are near the Marktplatz on the palace side of the river.

While in this city, stop in one of the restaurants or wine taverns offering Franconian wine and *Mainfischli* (little fish from the Main River).

TAUBERBISCHOFSHEIM: This lovely little town with a 1,200-year history has several focal points: the Palace of the Prince Electors of Mainz, the Manor House and watchman's tower, the double Gothic Chapel of St. Sebastian, and the baroque Church of St. Lioba. Half-timbered buildings and baroque courtyards lend this valley township the tranquil atmosphere of the past. The town has garnered fame as a center for fencing enthusiasts. From here drive 11 miles (18 km) on Route 290 to Bad Mergentheim.

BAD MERGENTHEIM: This small town is both a spa resort and a historical center. The Order of Teutonic Knights was based in the magnificent Renaissance Mergentheim Palace from 1525 until it was dispossessed by Napoleon in 1809. Founded in 1128, during the Crusades, this religious and military order wielded considerable political power in the surrounding area. You might want to take a look at the palace with its noteworthy baroque church, which was redesigned by Balthasar Neumann during the 18th century.

En Route from Bad Mergentheim – Continue for 9 miles (14 km) to Weikersheim, where the Renaissance castle of the Princes of Hohenlohe is worth a stop for its remarkable 16th- to 18th-century furniture, tapestries, porcelain, and sculptures of emperors and empresses. Continue from Weikersheim about another 9 miles (14 km) to Creglingen and its Church of Our Lord (Herrgottskirche), about a half-mile outside the town on the Blaufelden Road. This little church in the countryside, completed in 1389, contains many art treasures, among them the masterpiece of woodcarver Tilman Riemenschneider (the 16th-century Gothic Master of Würzburg), the altar of the Virgin Mary. It's 14 miles (22 km) from here to Rothenburg. To get in the right mood for this medieval walled town, park outside the walls and walk through a gate into the medieval fortress.

ROTHENBURG: Overlooking the steep, beautiful Tauber River Valley, Rothenburg ob der Tauber is the best preserved example of a medieval town in Germany. This former imperial residence has remained intact largely because it failed to recover economically from the Thirty Years War, so it is still a typical 16th-century town, its gabled houses retaining their steep Gothic roofs and oriel windows. Its huge encircling fortress walls and watchtowers are straight out of a fairy tale, and the town inside the walls is intriguingly medieval as well, with its narrow, cobblestone streets and graceful, flowing fountains. Historic inns here display skillfully crafted wrought-iron signs, and horse-drawn carriages still carry visitors through the central area of the city.

According to legend, Rothenburg was saved from destruction during the Thirty Years War by the drinking prowess of its leading citizen. When Tilly, commander of the Imperial Army, threatened to destroy the town, the burgomaster, Nusch, offered him a cup of the best local wine, after which Tilly agreed to spare the town if someone could quaff 6 pints all at once. Nusch obliged, and this tale is reenacted seven times a day when the clock on the *City Councillors' Tavern* (Ratstrinkstube) strikes 11 AM, noon, and 1, 2, 3, 9, and 10 PM. The doors on each side of the clock open to reveal two figures — a disbelieving General Tilly watching the town mayor empty a more than 3-liter bumper of wine in one draught.

The Town Hall, also in the market square, has two sections, one of which is 14th-century Gothic and the other 16th- and 17th-century Renaissance. You can climb its tower for a spectacular view of the city fortifications, which are shaped like a wine goblet. From the Town Hall you can walk to the Herrngasse, the widest street in the city, which begins at the market square. The Herrngasse is lined with stately patrician houses, which are decorated with a variety of gables. It's a short walk to the city's oldest and mightiest gate tower, the Burgtor, which leads into the Burggarten, a lovely public garden with a view of the Tauber bend, the curious medieval two-tier bridge called the Topplerschlösschen, and the village of Detwang.

Within the city's walls, countless streets and alleyways beckon you to explore shops, galleries, restaurants, taverns, and museums.

There are festivals here at *Whitsuntide* (seven Sundays after *Easter*) and in September, and throughout the year the community sponsors cultural events, concerts, and historical plays. Information about such events usually is posted in the market square, or contact the tourist office (2 Marktplatz; phone: 40492). There is much to see and do in Rothenburg, so this is a good place to spend at least 1 night.

En Route from Rothenburg – Drive 19 miles (30 km) on Route 25 to Feuchtwangen, where you might want to see the excellent *Heimatmuseum,* with its fine folklore collection, including Franconian costumes, crafts, and furniture. From here it's 8 miles (13 km) to Dinkelsbühl.

DINKELSBÜHL: Here is yet another beautifully preserved medieval city, complete with walls, towers, and gateways — all mirrored dreamily in the green waters of the town moat.

This is a sleepy 16th-century town, except during a week-long festival in mid-July known as *Children's Treat* (Kinderzeche). The festival celebrates the children of the town, who during the Thirty Years War induced the Swedish invaders to spare Dinkelsbühl. During the summer there is also an outdoor theater, performances by the Dinkelsbühl *Boys' Band,* and a night watchman who makes his rounds.

Take the time to wander around the Old Town, with its unpaved medieval streets lined with 15th- and 16th-century houses, which are decorated with hand-carved signs and with flowers hanging from their balconies. Segringer Strasse and Nördlinger Strasse are particularly interesting, as is the Deutsches Haus on Martin-Luther-Strasse, with its elaborate Renaissance decorations. St. George's Church, in the center of town, is a 15th-century Gothic structure with remarkable carvings and a Romanesque tower. It's about 19 miles (30 km) from here to Nördlingen on Route 25.

NÖRDLINGEN: Known as the living medieval city, this fortified town has retained not only its ancient buildings and city walls, but medieval customs and costumes as well. In the Rübenmarkt in the center of this circular town, the peasants still wear traditional dress on market days. The town is completely encircled by roofed parapet walks that pass the wall's many towers and gates. A watchman still surveys the town, calling out at night from the top of the tower of the late Gothic Church of St. George. The 15th-century church, with its tower of volcanic rock and its lavishly decorated interior, is worth seeing; its lovely painted altarpiece by Friedrich Herlin, however, is in the town museum.

En Route from Nördlingen – It's 11 miles (18 km) to Harburg, where a castle stands guard over a lovely hamlet on the Wörnitz River. The Harburg Castle is worth a stop for the art treasures in its museum — illuminated manuscripts, engravings, Gothic tapestries, and woodcarvings by the incomparable Riemenschneider.

At Donauwörth, yet another medieval town 6 miles (10 km) farther, the Wörnitz River meets the Danube; here our route continues along the Lech River on Route 2 for the 27 miles (43 km) to Augsburg.

AUGSBURG: Historical buildings of every style and epoch grace this, Bavaria's third-largest city, the oldest on the Romantic Road. Founded in 15 BC, Augsburg was a Roman provincial capital for 450 years and a free imperial city for 500 years. Two fabulously wealthy families dominated Augsburg during the 15th and 16th centuries, making it a major trading and banking center. The Fuggers, financiers of the Hapsburg dynasty, wielded enormous power and influence; the Welsers once owned most of Venezuela.

During and after its Renaissance heyday, Augsburg attracted artists and humanists. Both Holbeins were born here as was the architect Elias Holl, who created the Town Hall (1620) and other Renaissance buildings. Later, Leopold Mozart, father of the great composer, was born here, and his house still stands as a museum (30 Frauentorstr.; phone: 324-2196). Not far from here, in a side street off Leonhardsberg Street, is the house in which the late German playwright Bertolt Brecht was born, in 1898. It, too, is now a museum (phone: 324-2799).

Start at the huge Town Hall; in front is the impressive Fountain of Augustus, created in 1594. Walk south on the beautiful, wide Maximilianstrasse, the main street, decorated with fountains and lined with mansions built by the wealthy Renaissance burghers. Behind the lovely Hercules Fountain is the very attractive Church of St. Ulrich and St. Afra, built in 1500. Since the 1555 Peace of Augsburg between German Catholics and Protestants, it has contained a Catholic and a Protestant church.

Also worth seeing is the town cathedral, north of the Town Hall, which has 11th-century bronze doors, the oldest stained glass windows in Germany (12th century), and paintings by Holbein the Elder. The Schaezler Palace (46 Maximilianstr.) contains a magnificently decorated rococo banqueting hall and works by such German masters as Hans Holbein the Elder and Dürer and by non-Germans such as Rembrandt, Rubens, and Veronese. Take a look at the Fuggerei, east of the town center, a housing project for the poor, built by the Fugger family in 1519 and still in operation today; it includes 4 gates, a church, 8 streets, and 66 gabled houses.

For more information about Augsburg, contact the tourist office, Verkehrsverein, 7 Bahnhofstr. (phone: 821-36024).

En Route from Augsburg – Continue on Route 17 for about 24 miles (38 km) to Landsberg where there are many works of the rococo (18th-century) master architects, the brothers Johann Baptist and Dominikus Zimmermann, including the Rathaus, the Johanniskirche, and the Ursulinenkirche. See the lovely Hauptplatz (Main Square) with its fountain and the 1425 Bavarian Gate (Bayertor) with its turrets and sculptures.

Continuing toward Füssen on Route 17, don't miss the short detour at Wies to see the marvelous Wies Church, acknowledged as the greatest achievement of rococo art in Germany, the work of Dominikus and Johann Baptist Zimmermann. Set in the meadows, surrounded by woods, this magnificently ornamented structure was so lovingly built between 1746 and 1754 that Dominikus Zimmermann spent the last 10 years of his life nearby, unwilling to leave his finest creation. The simple exterior stands in marked contrast to the rich interior, with its oval cupola, elaborate woodcarvings, paintings, frescoes, and giltwork — all beautifully lit by many well-placed windows. Time has taken its toll, however, and the church has been renovated.

SCHWANGAU: Near this small town just 2 miles (3 km) east of Füssen are the two most impressive castles in all Germany, Hohenschwangau and Neuschwanstein, called the Royal Castles (Königsschlösser). Originally a 12th-century castle, Hohenschwangau was restored in 1832-36 by Maximilian II of Bavaria, father of King Ludwig II, "Mad King Ludwig," who grew up here, befriended Richard Wagner, and later created the far more extravagant Neuschwanstein in 1886.

Hohenschwangau is in neo-Gothic style, furnished with cherry and maple Biedermeier furniture and decorated with many heavy royal art objects, including a piano on which Wagner played. Neuschwanstein was designed to look like a fairy tale, with its gables, turrets, and pinnacles, perched on a hill overlooking the forests and lakes of the Füssen region. Many of its interiors are made to recall Wagner operas, including an artificial stalactite grotto straight out of *Tannhäuser*. The furnishings are so fabulous as to appear unreal, with tapestries, carvings, chandeliers, gilt, and marble — all on a grand scale. Unfortunately King Ludwig lived here for only 102 days before he committed suicide.

FÜSSEN: This mountain frontier town, once the summer residence of the Augsburg bishops, includes a palace and church high above the River Lech. The majestic wall of Alps behind the town provides a fitting setting for this spa and winter-sports resort. The medieval stone buildings of the town lend a picturesque quality to this, the final stop on the Romantic Road. From here, you can cross through mountain passes into the Austrian portion of the Alps.

BEST EN ROUTE

Even though the Romantic Road is very popular with tourists, its hotel and restaurant prices are rather reasonable by German standards. Rooms with baths are often much more costly then those without. Prices quoted here are for a double room, with bath, breakfast, and service included. On this route, expensive hotels will charge $85 to $140; moderate prices are $40 to $80 and inexpensive is $25 to $35.

A dinner for two will cost $60 to $90 in an expensive restaurant; $30 to $55 in a moderate one; and below $30 in an inexpensive place. Note that many of the restaurants on this route are in the hotels and inns, and are described in the hotel listing.

WÜRZBURG

Rebstock – Once a palace, now a modern hotel with more than 80 rooms, it has a neo-classic façade and is furnished with a harmonious mixture of traditional and modern pieces. It has an attractive terrace, 2 restaurants, and comfortable rooms. Closed Sundays for dinner. 7 Neubaustr. (phone: 931-30930). Moderate.

Bürgerspital Weinstuben – This traditional wine tavern is a must. The wines are almost impossible to find elsewhere, and Franconian dishes, like *Bratwurst mit Kraut*, are hearty. Closed Tuesdays and mid-July to mid-August. 19 Theaterstr. (phone: 931-13861). Inexpensive.

ROTHENBURG OB DER TAUBER

Burghotel – A large half-timbered house at the Old City wall, this hotel also offers a good view at somewhat less expense than the hotels noted above. It's charmingly set in a small garden with a pool, is attractively decorated, and offers friendly service. 1 Klostergasse (phone: 9861-5037). Expensive.

Eisenhut – A colorful, historical inn, this luxurious 86-room hotel is actually several medieval patrician houses joined together. This also is Rothenburg's top restaurant, with prices to match. Excellent international cuisine and wine can be enjoyed in the richly paneled, galleried dining hall or on the garden terrace overlooking the Tauber River. Try the trout specialties in season. 3-5 Herrngasse (phone: 9861-7050). Expensive.

Goldener Hirsch – In a quaint section of the city, this 80-room hotel is a remake of a 17th-century inn. A comfortable hotel with traditional taste and good service, it features the *Blaue Terrasse* (Blue Terrace) restaurant, with a panoramic view of the river valley. 16 Untere Schmiedgasse (phone: 9861-7080). Expensive.

Baumeisterhaus – Right off the marketplace in a patrician residence built in 1596, this restaurant has a beautiful courtyard, good German food, and reasonable prices. 3 Obere Schmiedgasse (phone: 9861-3404). Moderate.

Ratsstube – Also on the marketplace and very popular, this tavern-style restaurant features such regional dishes as blood sausages with sauerkraut and Bavarian mixed grill. Don't miss the white asparagus dishes in season (May-June). 6 Marktpl. (phone: 9861-5511). Inexpensive.

Zur Höll – A wine tavern — in the town's oldest house (1222) on the town's oldest street — that's well worth a visit, both for its Franconian wines and regional dishes. Open evenings only; closed Tuesdays. 8 Burggasse (phone: 9861-4229). Inexpensive.

BAD MERGENTHEIM

Victoria – This 100-room hotel-spa has bath, massage, and swimming facilities, as well as an excellent restaurant, *Zirbelstuben*. Guests also can dine on the attractive rooftop garden terrace, where there is a heated, glassed-in swimming pool. Rooms have baths and glassed-in balconies. 2 Poststr. (phone: 7931-5930). Expensive.

DINKELSBÜHL

Deutsches Haus – A half-timbered house dating from 1440, this 13-room inn, decorated with richly painted designs and woodcarvings, is elegantly furnished. Its restaurant serves local specialties. 3 Weinmarkt (phone: 9851-2346). Moderate.

Goldene Rose – In the heart of town, this pretty, 6-story inn dates from 1450. The 20 rooms are modernized, though furnished with antiques, and the hotel offers a homey atmosphere at a reasonable rate. It also has a good restaurant. Closed January and February. 4 Marktpl. (phone: 9851-831). Moderate.

NÖRDLINGEN

Sonne – Next to the Town Hall and the cathedral, this Old World inn, dating from 1477, has been modernized. It offers 40 comfortable rooms, good service, and a choice of dining rooms. Restaurant (all rooms) closed Fridays. 3 Marktpl. (phone: 9081-5067). Moderate.

AUGSBURG

Drei Mohren – Combining contemporary with traditional decor, this rebuilt 110-room hotel, famous since 1723, was destroyed in an air raid in 1945. Rebuilt in a somewhat overly opulent style, it still offers first class accommodations. Its formal dining room serves international dishes and features such specialties as venison and filet of sole with white wine sauce. It also has an attractive garden terrace. 40 Maximilianstr. (phone: 821-510031). Expensive.

Fischertor – This restaurant is one of Augsburg's finest. Nouvelle cuisine reigns supreme here. Try the duck with shrimp and avocado cream or the calf's liver with mushrooms. The wines and the service are equally topnotch. Closed Sundays and Mondays. Reservations advised. 16 Pfärrle (phone: 821-518662). Expensive.

Gunzenlee – Six miles (10 km) southeast of town, this restaurant has an extensive international menu. The charcoal-grilled meat is among the best bets. In warm weather you can dine on a pleasant garden terrace. 14 Münchner Str., Bad Kissing (phone: 971-823-36139). Moderate.

Fuggerkeller – Noted not only for its setting — vaulted, cave-like rooms below street level in the former Fugger residence — but also for its fine food and drink. The strong, dark Fugger beer is an experience. Closed Sunday evenings and in August. 38 Maximilianstr. (phone: 821-516260). Moderate to inexpensive.

Ratskeller – This Town Hall restaurant has particularly good, solid German food at reasonable prices. Closed Mondays, Sunday evenings, and in June. 2 Rathauspl. (phone: 821-154086). Moderate to inexpensive.

HOHENSCHWANGAU

Schlosshotel Lisl und Jägerhaus – Near the two royal castles, this 60-room spot is comfortable and offers a spectacular view. The graciously styled hotel has a terrace and is surrounded by its own gardens. Its dining rooms serve local and international fare. Closed January and February. 1 Neuschwansteinstr. (phone: 8-1006). Expensive to moderate.

FÜSSEN

Hirsch – This 48-bed hotel, centrally located, has a large restaurant. Closed from December to mid-February. 2 Augsburger-Tor-Pl. (phone: 8362-5080). Expensive.

Sonne – Also in the center of Füssen, this hostelry has 32 comfortable, rustic rooms and a café. 37 Reichenstr. (phone: 8362-6061). Moderate.

Pulverturm – In the idyllic spa center, it serves both continental and regional dishes. You also can dine on the pleasant terrace. Closed in November. 1 Schwedenweg (phone: 8362-6078). Moderate to inexpensive.

The Harz Mountains and the Thuringian Forest

Shaped like a large slanted block, the rugged Harz Mountains in the southwest corner of what was East Germany are silent witnesses to much of German history. The region, pocked by limestone caves and pierced by tall mountain peaks, is dotted with numerous castles, churches, and fortresses built during the Middle Ages. Our route runs through several cities of import: Potsdam, a residence of Frederick the Great during the 18th century as well as the site of the conference in which Churchill, Stalin, and Truman decided the fate of postwar Germany; Eisenach, birthplace of Johann Sebastian Bach; and Weimar, the home of Goethe and Schiller and namesake of the short-lived republic that fell with the rise of Hitler. Near Weimar is a memorial to Buchenwald, a notorious concentration camp during World War II.

The route begins in Berlin, then goes to Potsdam, Magdeburg, and the Harz Mountain towns of Quedlinburg and Wernigerode. From Wernigerode it continues southwest to Eisenach, after which it swings eastward to Erfurt and Weimar; this is the area known as the Thuringian Forest, its gentle wooded slopes rounded rather than jagged, peaceful rather than dramatic. After turning northward to Naumburg, you can go on to Leipzig and our second route, or you can return to Berlin.

Maps, brochures, organized tours, and other information are available from the tourist offices in each of the cities and some of the towns. In Berlin, inquire at the *Europäischer Reisebüro,* 5 Alexanderpl. (phone: 2-215338 or 2-153565).

POTSDAM: Most people know Potsdam as the place where the four victorious powers of World War II — Russia, Britain, the US, and France — signed the 1945 agreements that split Germany and Berlin into four zones of occupation. But Potsdam has been known since 1660, when the Princes of Hohenzollern chose it as their country residence and began a palatial building program that ended only in the late 19th century. The 18th century saw the city develop as the military center of Old Prussia, boasting at one time a ratio of 8,000 soldiers to just 17,000 inhabitants. Since World War II, shapeless modern architecture and now-regretted demolition programs have destroyed some of Potsdam's old charm, but the palaces and the parks still are as delightful as ever. Potsdam was East Germany's Hollywood, producing feature films at its DEFA studios.

The road from Berlin leads southeast of the town, near the *Interhotel Potsdam.* You might start with a walk round the Old Town, centering on Klement-Gottwald-Strasse, now a pedestrian precinct with small cafés, shops, and an information bureau (at 5 Friedrich-Ebert-Str.). From here it's an easy walk along the Allée nach Sans Souci to Potsdam's main attraction, the Sans Souci Park and the baroque Sans Souci Palace (built on Frederick the Great's orders in 1745–47). In August 1991, Frederick's remains, which for many years had been in Stuttgart, were reinterred at the palace. Next door is a picture gallery with works by Rubens, Van Dyck, Tintoretto, and others; the ornate Chinese teahouse; statues; shrubberies; and at the end, the New Palace (1769), another creation of Frederick's 46-year reign. Never actually lived in, it was intended to demonstrate the Prussian state's unbroken might after the Seven Years war.

In the northeastern part of town, the *Cecilienhof* hotel, at Neuer Garten, built during World War I in the style of an English country mansion, is where the 1945 conference took place. The *Cecilienhof* also houses an interesting museum devoted to the conference, which includes the original furniture. Ironically, as if to remind visitors of the consequences of that conference, a stretch of the Berlin Wall, sealing "West" Berlin from surrounding "East" Germany, once stood just 200 yards away, in full view at the bottom of the garden. By the way, *Cecilienhof* also is an excellent hotel with a good restaurant (see *Best En Route*).

En Route from Potsdam – Route F1, part of the main trans-European artery intended by Hitler to link Paris with Berlin in the 1930s, leads out of town into the farmland along the Havel River. If you are here in spring, the cherry blossoms on either side of the two-lane highway are breathtaking. Brandenburg, 25 miles (40 km) along the route, was the capital of the Prussian state for centuries, but it declined as Berlin took over the role of administrative center. Another hour's drive along the tree-lined F1 brings you via sleepy villages to Magdeburg, on the Elbe. You now are entering the Harz (Woodland) Mountains, a region of rugged, weather-beaten rocks, medieval churches and castles, rich woodlands, and fertile farm country.

MAGDEBURG: The heavy machineworks, the Ernst Thälmann Engineering Combine (SKET), has its headquarters here, a fitting location since this is where Magdeburg's most famous citizen, former mayor Otto von Guericke (1602–86), proved the power of vacuum and invented the "Magdeburg Hemispheres." Sadly, Magdeburg has had a history of destruction. It burned down almost totally during an attack in 1631, and more than 90% of the rebuilt inner city was razed by Allied bombing in January 1945. Only parts of the city center have been reconstructed as they once were. If you begin with the Old Town Hall (the *Rathaus*), you'll notice the famous 13th-century statue of the *Magdeburg Rider* on his horse facing the building from the square. He's only a copy of the original statue, sculpted in 1240, but now in the city museum on Otto von Guericke Strasse. A 10-minute walk through what's left of the Old Town leads to the mainly 12th-century Cloister of Our Dear Lady, possibly one of the best-restored architectural ensembles in Germany. Next door is the cathedral, with quaint cloisters around the side entrance; it was first recorded as a place of worship in 955. In the northern transept a group of six wooden figures by Germany's highly regarded 20th-century sculptor, Ernst Barlach, memorializes starkly and impressively the dead of World War I. The Nazis had it removed from the cathedral, but the ensemble was reinstalled in 1957.

En Route from Magdeburg – You can take Route F81 out of Magdeburg, through Egeln and Halberstadt, but for a taste of the small country roads almost completely free of traffic, bear right on the outskirts of the town to head for Wanzleben. You'll pass through typical German provincial towns, hardly changed since World War II. From Kroppenstedt the route goes over the top of a small range of hills, a foretaste of things to come. At Halberstadt, drive farther on F79.

QUEDLINBURG: Hardly hit by the war, the town of Quedlinburg still boasts hundreds of picturesque half-timbered houses, many with the old signs of their former owners. Head for the marketplace, where restorers have done an impressive job on the Renaissance Town Hall and on the colorful woodcarvings on the façades of the surrounding 16th-century houses. Looking away from the Town Hall is the Schlossberg, crowned by a cathedral with its 19th-century towers resting on a medieval body. (Guided tours in German are given on the half-hour until 3:30 PM; during the summer, tours in English also are available on request.) From the balustrade of the castle (*Schloss*) there's a stunning view of Old Quedlinburg, with its tiled roofs tilting at all angles. The restaurant in the castle complex serves a respectable lunch, outside if the weather's good, and fine afternoon coffee. It's worth a stop before continuing to drive along the northern base of the Harz Mountains, taking the minor road to Weddersleben and Thale.

En Route from Quedlinburg – After Thale you pass through Blankenburg. Stop briefly at the Regenstein Castle just out of town to the right. It was chiseled out of sandstone and was first used as a fortress in the 5th century.

WERNIGERODE: Nine miles (14 km) farther on is the center of the Harz vacation area. Its colorful and half-timbered 16th-century Town Hall at the crossing of Marktstrasse and Breite Strasse looks like something out of a fairy tale by the Brothers Grimm. Unfortunately, 40 years of neglect by the former East German authorities allowed many of the town's quaint buildings to deteriorate. Much of the town center looks as if it had been bombed, even though Wernigerode emerged unscathed from World War II. There is an unusual feudal museum here, in the medieval castle that overlooks the town; its exhibits include medieval furniture and objects illustrating daily life in the Middle Ages and the history of the Harz region. Wernigerode is also the northern terminal for a narrow-gauge steam railway that links the northern and southern Harz. If you have time, take a trip (it costs only a few pfennigs) up through Drei-Annen-Hohne and past the Brocken, which at 3,747 feet is the highest peak in the Harz. It was chosen by Johann Wolfgang von Goethe for the *Walpurgisnacht* scenes in *Faust*.

En Route from Wernigerode – Take Route F244 toward Elbingerode. On the left toward Rübeland there are some impressive limestone caves worth seeing — if you have the patience to join the long lines. Then head along F81 to Hasselfelde and down through deep leafy gorges along F4 to Nordhausen, southern terminal of the railway from Wernigerode. Nordhausen is the town that produces Germany's famous schnapps, Nordhauser Doppelkorn. Most goes for export, so you'll probably find there's not much to buy here.

The Kyffhäuser Mountain 15 miles (24 km) southeast of Nordhausen rises 1,565 feet out of the north Thuringian plain, and is shrouded in legend. One was that Emperor Redbeard, or Barbarossa, would sleep in his underground cave here until the time came to unite the German people. With the proclamation of the united German Reich in 1871, formed by joining the 24 previously independent German states, Kaiser Wilhelm I had a monument erected on the Kyffhäuser Mountain peak, representing himself as a glowering and mighty Barbarossa in red sandstone. In good weather, the view from the top of the mountain is breathtaking, extending northward to the Harz and westward across the former border between East and West Germany.

Now you have a choice. You either can go to Eisenach, Erfurt, and Weimar by way of Bad Frankenhausen, Route F85 to Sachsenburg, and Route F86 to Straussfurt — it's 54 miles (86 km) to Eisenach — or, if you wish, skip this section and head for Leipzig and the second route.

EISENACH: In recent times known as an automobile manufacturing center, Eisenach (pop. 50,000) is better known as the site of the *Wartburg,* a castle dating from 1067, now a museum. It was the home of the medieval Minnesänger poets immortalized by Richard Wagner in his opera *Tannhäuser.* It also served as Martin Luther's retreat in the 16th century, when he translated the Bible into German, laying the foundations for today's spoken language. The composer Johann Sebastian Bach was also born in Eisenach, and the family home (21 Am Frauenplan), houses a fascinating collection of musical instruments and Bach family memorabilia.

En Route from Eisenach – Route F7, with views of the hills on the right, takes you 34 miles (54 km) east to Erfurt. On the way, a half-hour excursion southeast to Arnstadt is very rewarding (head for the autobahn in Gotha): This is one of the oldest towns in this part of Germany (first mentioned in 704). Bach was an organist here from 1703 to 1707. Besides a beautifully restored marketplace, Arnstadt also has a 200-year-old doll collection in the Neues Palais (New Castle). From here, Erfurt is a 20-minute drive north.

ERFURT: A provincial capital and major industrial center, Erfurt with its 220,000 inhabitants is the only sizable town in central Germany that was not largely destroyed in World War II. It was liberated by the Americans in April 1945, but was handed over to the Russians under the agreements that divided Germany into occupied zones. Dominating Erfurt are two Catholic churches side by side on the Domberg. The walls of the cathedral and those of St. Severi (both finished by the 15th century) lie just a few feet apart at their closest point. In town, a walk down the Marktstrasse leads to the Krämerbrücke, a 14th-century ensemble of houses on a bridge over the Gera River. Formerly houses of petty traders, they were restored in the 1960s as delightful little antiques shops, book stalls, and cafés. This is a good place to find that unusual souvenir.

WEIMAR: Thirteen miles (21 km) east of Erfurt on Route F7 lies Weimar, today a town of just 65,000 people but one of the most important centers of German history and culture. Goethe and Schiller both wrote their greatest works here in the 18th and early 19th centuries. In 1919, the first German Republic, also known as the Weimar Republic, proclaimed its constitution in the town's now reconstructed *National Theater;* the Weimar Republic fell during the world economic crisis in the early 1930s, when the ferociously nationalistic Nazi party rose to power. The homes of Goethe and Schiller (the former on the Frauenplan and the latter on the Schillerstrasse) now are open as museums. A short walk from Goethe's house past the *Interhotel Elephant* brings you to a park now named after the poet, a place where he used to walk. Across the river is the garden house he used in the summer, now an extension of the main museum.

BUCHENWALD: Before leaving the area, take a detour to Buchenwald, 4 miles (6 km) northwest. Now run as a national memorial, it's the site of one of Hitler's most notorious concentration camps, opened in 1937. Here 56,000 people, including Jews, Communists, and prisoners of war, died before the surviving inmates were freed by the Americans in April 1945. The contrast between the barbarities once perpetrated here and the humanistic ideals of nearby Weimar is chilling.

En Route from Weimar – Route F7 (we purposely have kept off the autobahns, as these show travelers so much less of the countryside than the quieter country roads) takes you toward Jena, but turn left at F87 and head past Apolda to Naumburg.

NAUMBURG: If, after Magdeburg and Erfurt, you can still take some more medieval architecture, the cathedral has to be seen. The town was a major trading and religious center in the Middle Ages. The Cathedral of St. Peter and St. Paul has been beautifully preserved, and its earliest parts date from 1210. Inside are realistic and humorous carved figures of ordinary folk of the time, installed in the late 13th century. Before you leave Naumburg, visit the *Ratskeller* in the Town Hall (Wilhelm Pieck Pl.), where with any luck you'll find a bottle of excellent and very dry local wine. Try it; it's little known outside this part of the country.

En Route from Naumburg – Taking Route F87 again out to the east, you pass through Weissenfels 11 miles (18 km) away, before reaching the main north-south autobahn. That's the end of this route, and you can return to Berlin or drive south toward Nürnberg in Bavaria. But if you've developed a taste for more, take the slightly shorter tour through Leipzig and Dresden, with many attractive tidbits along the way.

BEST EN ROUTE

Although hotel reservations in what was East Gremany no longer have to be made in advance through a state-owned travel agency, travel and accommodations in this part of the country are still in a state of flux, so a tourist office can be helpful. A good idea is to check on hotel information before leaving Berlin. Contact the Europäischer Reisebüro at 5 Alexanderpl. (phone: 2-215338 or 2-153565).

Prices have been climbing steadily here since unification, and better hotels and restaurants in the cities may now be at or close to those in western Germany. There are, however, a few bargains to be found in smaller towns. Dinner for two, with drinks and wine, costs about $55 or more at expensive restaurants; between $25 and $50 in the moderate range; and under $25 in inexpensive places. Tips are included in the bill.

POTSDAM

Interhotel Potsdam – This large high-rise hotel, at the entrance to town nearest Berlin, is one of the most prestigious in the east, with prices to match. It has a sauna, dancing, entertainment, a restaurant, and a bar. Lange Brücke (phone: 23-4631). Expensive.

Cecilienhof – Set in a 20th-century version of an English country house, this historic building was the site of the Potsdam conference in 1945. As a hotel it's smaller and less luxurious than the *Potsdam,* but it has a restaurant, a café, and some rooms with baths. Neuer Garten (phone: 33-3141). Expensive to moderate.

Klosterkeller – A comfortable restaurant with decent food. 94 Friedrich Ebert Str. (no phone) Inexpensive.

MAGDEBURG

Interhotel International – This big hotel (358 rooms) has private baths in all rooms, a restaurant, a café, and dancing. Some might consider it modern and character-less, as are many of the better hotels in the country's eastern region. 87 Otto von Guericke Str. (phone: 91-3840). Expensive.

QUEDLINBURG

Schlosskrug – Set in the castle forecourt, this restaurant serves good lunches and afternoon coffee. No reservations. 1 Schlossberg (phone: 455-2838). Expensive to moderate.

EISENACH

Auf der Wartburg – In Wartburg Castle, the 30 rooms here are in the usual German-modern style, and there is a restaurant. Wartburg (phone: 623-5111). Expensive.

Stadt Eisenach – This 85-bed hotel has a restaurant and parking. 11-13 Luisenstr. (phone: 623-3682). Moderate.

Hohe Sonne – Just outside the city, this dining place is in a lovely rustic area with a view of the Wartburg. Regional Thuringian dishes are its specialty. Open daily. No reservations. Am Rennsteig (phone: 623-2903). Inexpensive.

ERFURT

Erfurter Hof – Opposite the railroad station is one of the best kept and most distinguished hotels in what was East Germany. It has all conveniences and an excellent restaurant serving interesting culinary inventions. The rooms in the back are quieter than those facing the station. Bahnhofsvorpl. (phone: 61-51151). Expensive.

Bürgerhof – Centrally located, this hostelry is as comfortable as it is unpretentious. 35 Bahnhofstr. (phone: 61-21307). Inexpensive.

Hohe Lilie – A popular eatery, it occupies the first 2 floors of a building that dates from 1540. Spicy Balkan dishes are the house specialty. Closed Mondays. Reservations advised. 31 Dompl. (phone: 61-22578). Inexpensive.

Tourist – Though characterless, this hotel is modern. 158 Yuri Gargarin Ring (phone: 61-1076). Inexpensive.

WEIMAR

Belvedere – A newer luxury hotel (by former East German standards), this 290-room establishment is idyllically located opposite Goethe's Park on the river Ilm. The atmosphere is quiet, dignified, and historical. Among the many modern facilities are 3 restaurants. Belvederer Allee (phone: 621-2429). Expensive.

Elephant – Centrally located and extensively remodeled, this place dates from 1696, but has most of the facilities you could want and some extras, such as horseback riding and dancing. There's a fine restaurant in the basement. Am Markt (phone: 621-1471). Moderate.

Leipzig, Dresden, and Sorb Country

This short but quite interesting route (in the former GDR) connects Leipzig and Dresden, eastern Germany's two major cities after Berlin, both of which were heavily damaged during the war and have since been restored. Leipzig, long known for its medieval trade fairs, still hosts two important international fairs in November and March. And amazingly enough, you can still eat and drink here in *Auerbachs Keller,* the restaurant and tavern where Goethe had Faust and the Devil meet in *Faust* (see *Best en Route*). Dresden is the place for great art treasures, both in the Zwinger fortress and in the *Albertinum,* and its restaurants are among the best in the region.

You can begin your drive in Berlin or in Naumburg, where the previous route ended. For maps, brochures, and further information, contact the local tourist offices (in Dresden at 22 Ernst Thälmann Str.; phone: 48650; in Leipzig at 1-3 Katharinenstr.; phone: 79210).

LEIPZIG: It was here that the freedom revolution of 1989 got its start, through mass protest demonstrations. In the past, East Germans called this city of 565,000 people the secret capital of the GDR. It is the country's second most important industrial and commercial center, hosting a week-long trade fair twice a year that attracts exhibitors from up to 60 countries at a time. Leipzig, its name derived from the Slav *Lipsk,* "place of the lime tree," also is the site of a large printing industry, of the second-largest university in the old GDR, and of a sports institute. Bach spent his most creative years, from 1723 to 1750, as choirmaster at the St. Thomas Church here. Leipzig was badly damaged by World War II bombing, but architects have succeeded here better than elsewhere in restoring its former character. The Old Town Hall (16th century) and the Thomaskirche (1494) have been completely restored; the newer Rathaus (19th century), on the edge of the neatly circumscribed Old Town, was hardly touched. (It has an excellent restaurant in its basement.) Grimmaische Strasse leads to Karl-Marx-Platz, the new university, and the opera, and it's lined with souvenir and book shops. The *Gewandhaus* concert hall was rebuilt in 1987.

A short walk back across the market square brings you to the Thomas Church, where the boys' choir, which Bach used to conduct, still gives free concerts of motets every Friday evening and Sunday morning when they are not on tour. Bach lies buried at the eastern end of the church. More than any other former East German town, Leipzig abounds in good eating and drinking places. Apart from the main hotels, the *Kaffeebaum,* on the corner of Kleine Fleischergasse and Barfussgässchen, has been serving beer and food for centuries.

Before leaving Leipzig, follow the Strasse des 18 Oktober to the memorial to the Battle of the People (Völkerschlachtdenkmal). You will pass the fairground and a fine Russian Orthodox church erected in 1913. The memorial to the 1813 victory of Russian and German troops over Napoleon's Grande Armée is a monstrous, 300-foot-high edifice completed the same year as the church. The view of Leipzig, and the remarkable acoustics inside, are worth the climb to the top of the monument.

En Route from Leipzig – Route F6 leads to the cathedral, wine, and porcelain town of Meissen, 53 miles (85 km) east, through rolling farming landscapes; later it joins up with the Elbe, one of Europe's greatest rivers. Where the Elbe winds between the cliffs of Saxonian Switzerland, between Dresden and the Czech border, visitors might think they are on the Rhine.

MEISSEN: This is the town that gave the world Dresden china, and it is a must on any tourist's itinerary in Germany. The first porcelain was produced here in 1710, in the 15th-century *Albrechtsburg Castle* that dominates the town. Dresden china was ideally suited to the extravagant rococo style in 18th-century art, and for the first few years the Meissen princes kept their craftsmen virtual prisoners here, lest rivals learn the secret of the "white gold." But it got out, needless to say. Today the factory in the *Triebischtal* (the castle's stable) produces china mainly for export, and can be visited during the week.

The town itself, founded in 929 and once the seat of the Saxonian bishops, is one of the best preserved in eastern Germany. Visit the *Albrechtsburg Castle,* now a museum, and the delightful and still privately owned wine house of Vincenz Richter, just off the market square at 12 An der Frauenkirche. A good lunch can be had in the cafés in the courtyard of the *Albrechtsburg;* be sure to sample the local wines, especially the rare Meissner Domherr.

En Route from Meissen – Rather than go straight along Route F6 to Dresden, take the road north across the river in Meissen and follow the signs to Weinböhla along a small country road. Continue through Auer and in 10 miles (16 km) you come to one of the most beautiful of the country residences built around Dresden by Saxon Prince Frederick Augustus (the Strong) in the 18th century. *Schloss Moritzburg* is a museum of baroque porcelain, furniture, and hunting weapons.

Another way to reach Moritzburg is to leave the car in nearby Radebeul and take a narrow-gauge steam railway for five stops. The East Radebeul train station is located on the corner of Thiermannstrasse and Pestaroccistrasse.

DRESDEN: One of the high points of any visit to now-united Germany, this city is alive with cultural tradition and political history. Its many art collections rank among the most valuable in the world, and Dresden is today one of Germany's larger cities, with a population of over half a million. To visitors from Britain and America, its name, like that of Hiroshima, is synonymous with the horrors of modern warfare. Up to 35,000 people are believed to have died in the Anglo-American bombing raids on February 13 and 14, 1945, and some 80% of the town center, with its narrow old streets and passageways, was razed to the ground. The Schlosskirche, the *Semper* opera house, and the galleries along the Brühlsche Terrasse have been rebuilt to restore to Dresden the silhouette made famous by the 18th-century painter Canaletto. Behind that waterfront, the rest of the city center has been rebuilt in characterless concrete and glass. However, work is in progress to restore Old Dresden to its former baroque and rococo splendor.

The city was founded in about 1200, and it remained a trading city until it was chosen by the lavishly spending Saxon princes for their court in the 17th century.

Pragerstrasse, once Dresden's most fashionable street, is now flanked by blocks of flats and shops, but it's pleasantly landscaped with fountains and benches. Past a new cinema and department store, you reach the Old Market (Altmarkt) with the restored Kreuzkirche (Church of the Cross), home of the world-renowned *Kreuzchor* (a boys' choir) on the right. Straight ahead is the Palace of Culture (1969), and behind that the memorial ruins of the Frauenkirche that once bore one of Europe's most famous cupolas. You are now in the heart of Old Dresden, surrounded by car parks and bomb sites that drive home the devastation of that terrible time in 1945. Follow on toward the river and up the steps, and you come to the *Albertinum* (1559) with its glass dome and exhibitions of state art collections within (closed on Thursdays). There are 19th- and 20th-century German paintings, French Impressionist works, and the famous Green Vault (Grünes Gewölbe) with works of goldsmiths and jewelers from the 15th to the 18th centuries. The Zwinger, a fortress built between 1711 and 1722 at the height of Augustus's reign, was lovingly restored in the postwar years. In magnificent baroque style, with lovely sculptures and chimes of Dresden porcelain, it houses one of the world's most stunning art collections, the *Picture Gallery of Old Masters,* which includes Raphael's *Sistine Madonna* (1513). Also visit its unparalleled collections of china, coins, and hunting weapons.

En Route from Dresden – You can return directly to Berlin via the autobahn, a distance of about 122 miles (195 km). Or you can spend some time in the Spreewald, a 93-square-mile network of canals, woods, and pastures along the Spree River southeast of the capital. Get off the autobahn at Lübbenau. Carved wooden road signs indicate the way to the port (*Hafen*) where you either can take a leisurely 3-hour ride in a punt along the slowly flowing canals or hire a canoe if you feel energetic. That's the best way to do it, and try the private boat rental establishment of *Herr Franke* (72 Maxim Gorki Str.), down a small unpaved road before you reach the main harbor. The prices are still very low.

During your excursion, possibly poled along by a Sorb woman in national dress (all the punt owners are private, incidentally, and pool only their passengers in a punting collective), don't miss the waterside cafés along the route. They generally serve good coffee and cakes in the afternoon.

BEST EN ROUTE

As advised in the previous route, it's still a good idea to check on hotel information in this part of the country before leaving Berlin. Contact Europäischer Reisebüro at 5 Alexanderpl. (phone: 2-215338 or 2-2153565).

For a double room in expensive hotels, expect to pay $125 and up; $75 to $120 in the moderate category; under $75, inexpensive.

Dinner for two, with drinks and wine, costs about $40 or more at expensive restaurants; between $30 and $35 in the moderate range; and under $30 in inexpensive places. Tips are included in the bill.

LEIPZIG

Merkur – The best hotel in town, it has 4 restaurants, a swimming pool, a sauna, and a nightclub on the 27th floor that offers a breathtaking panorama of the city. And it's away from the downtown area, so it's quiet. *Sakura,* with its Japanese cuisine, is well worth a visit. 15 Gerberstrasse (phone: 41-7990). Expensive.

Astoria – An excellent hotel, elegantly furnished in traditional late-19th-century style, with all the modern conveniences. It has a good restaurant, a pleasant terrace, a café, and dancing. Like the other big hotels here, it's much used by visiting businesspeople for the trade fairs in March and September. Platz der Republik (phone: 41-71710). Moderate.

Auerbachs Keller – Goethe made this tavern famous in *Faust,* and the place is decorated with sculptures and paintings inspired by that drama. It's a beautiful restaurant, which serves excellent food, beers, and wines. No reservations. Mädlerpassage (phone: 41-209131). Moderate.

Kaffebaum – The oldest coffeehouse in Leipzig dates from 1694 and was frequented by many famous people: Goethe, Lessing, Wagner, and Liszt among others. Its original decor includes lovely old wooden tables. The food is basic but good; the beer is good, and the place is very popular. Lunch only on Saturdays and Sundays. Reservations advised. 4 Kleine Fleischergasse (phone: 41-200452). Moderate.

Stadt Kiew – In the middle of town opposite the Old Town Hall, this popular restaurant specializes in Ukrainian dishes. Markt Peterstr. (phone: 41-295063). Moderate.

Stadt Leipzig – Opposite the main railway station, this is a first-rate hotel by former East German standards. All guest facilities are available, including a barber shop and a sauna. The front rooms do tend to be noisy. Richard Wagner Str. (phone: 41-288814). Moderate.

Stadtpfeiffer – Excellent food is served here in the *Gewandhaus* concert hall complex. Lunch only in July and August. Karl-Marx-Pl. (phone: 41-713-2389). Moderate.

Ratskeller – A wonderful student haunt in the basement of the New Town Hall. Its specialty is a fine potato omelette (*Bauernfrühstück*). Martin Luther King (phone: 41-791-3591). Inexpensive.

DRESDEN

Bellevue – The city's second-largest (330 rooms) hotel. Guestrooms have a magnificent view, across the Elbe, of the Old City center. Quiet, pleasant atmosphere. Köpckestr. (phone: 51-56620). Expensive.

Dresdner Hof – This newer hostelry overlooks the historic city center. The 335 rooms and apartments are decorated in Bauhaus-style. Facilities include a swimming pool, sauna, solarium, bowling alley, and 10 restaurants (try *Le Gourmet* and *Ristorante Rossini*). Ander Frauenkirsche (phone: 51-20920). Expensive.

Aberlausitzer Töpp'l – A rustic eating spot featuring the hearty fare of the Lusatia area, home of the Sorbs. The dishes are reminiscent of Bohemian cuisine. Try the remarkable dark beer, a traditional Lusatian delicacy. Reservations advised. Str. der Befreiung (phone: 51-55605). Moderate.

Astoria – A small, comfortable hotel in the city center known for its friendly atmosphere. Not every room has a private bath. Ernst-Thälmann-Pl. (phone: 51-48560). Moderate.

Gewandhaus – This hotel has a fine restaurant, one of the most pleasant and popular eating places in Dresden. Reservations advised. 3-7 Gewandhausstr. (phone: 51-4952342). Moderate.

Königstein – On Dresden's main shopping street, this large hostelry is less pretentious, less luxurious, and more popular with local and East European tourists. Pragerstr. (phone: 51-48560). Moderate.

Secundogenitur – Though this eatery offers only one dish a day, the quality is excellent, and it's in the old baroque city center. No reservations. Brühlsche Ter. (phone: 51-496147). Moderate.

Ratskeller – As in most German towns, the Rathaus (Town Hall) here has its own restaurant, and like most Ratskellers, it's a good value, unpretentious and noisy. It's great for meeting townsfolk and sampling the atmosphere. Reservations advised (phone: 51-493212). Moderate to inexpensive.

Kügelgen-Haus – Behind the baroque façade is a gastronomic complex consisting of several restaurants and a beer cellar where good food and drink can be found at good prices. The *Meissener Weinkeller* features some very rare regional wines. Reservations advised. 13 Str. der Befreiung (phone: 51-52791). Inexpensive.

Gibraltar

Whether approaching by land or sea, most first time visitors are mesmerized immediately by the Rock of Gibraltar, surely one of the world's most famous natural landmarks. "Gib" stands there, just as strong and steady as it's supposed to, thrusting up defiantly from the Mediterranean like a clenched fist. It's no wonder that this British Crown colony of more than 30,000 residents is anathema to Spain. The reasons for this go back to 1713 and the Treaty of Utrecht, which ended the War of Succession between rival French and Austrian (the Hapsburgs) pretenders to the Spanish throne. At that time, Bourbon King Philip V gained the crown of Spain but was forced to cede Gibraltar to England. To this day, Spaniards will find every fault with the present British rule of the Rock and insist that Gibraltar must be returned to its rightful owners. The issue over tiny Gibraltar became so bitter that the single point of entry by land, over an isthmus between La Linea on the Spanish mainland and the Rock itself, was closed for a number of years to all vehicular and pedestrian traffic. And that's quite a controversy when you consider the size of the place — 3 miles long and three-quarters of a mile wide.

On February 4, 1985, Spain reopened its border with Gibraltar, making it vastly easier on travelers who, until then, had to take a ferry or hydrofoil from Málaga or Algeciras to Tangiers, then ferry from the North African port across the Strait of Gibraltar. The crossing took several hours.

Now that the border is open, however, Gibraltar attracts plenty of foreign visitors. All purchases are VAT free, so many people come here just to shop. Others come to bask in the sun: Gibraltar has a mild climate throughout the year, as does the southern Spanish coast. There are yachting marinas, other water facilities, and deep-sea fishing. And, in addition to the historic interest, Gibraltar's very British atmosphere exists in striking contrast to the neighboring Spanish communities and the Moroccan cities across the Strait. The Union Jack flies over photographs of the queen that are emblazoned with the slogan: "Keep the Rock British." Gib is very much a part of the British Empire.

Conflict over who owns the Rock goes back many centuries. In the year 711, the Moorish commander Tarik ibn Ziyad landed on the Rock and gave his name to the promontory that was to be the stepping-off point of his invasion of Spain. The pronunciation of Jabal al Tariq (Tarik's Mountain) was modified over the 7 centuries of Moorish rule to become "Gibraltar." Queen Isabel herself personally led Christian troops to capture Gibraltar in 1462 as part of her strategy to weaken the Moors' supply route from nearby Morocco and definitively reconquer all of Spain. The Peñón de Gibraltar, or Rock of Gibraltar, was an integral part of peninsular Spain until the early 18th century, when the Rock was ceded to Britain. During the Great Siege of 1779–83, the Strait of Gibraltar was the battleground of rival European navies. As later proved by the Battle of Trafalgar, the British fleet led by Admiral Nelson was far superior to the Hispano-French armadas, and Gibraltar was retained by the victorious British.

The border was closed in 1969 by Generalisimo Francisco Franco, and the Spanish government issued a strong protest to the UN against the British colonial "occupation" of a territorial possession of Spain. The countries of the NATO Pact repeatedly vetoed attempts to challenge British control over the vitally strategic air and naval bases that are on the Rock of Gibraltar. However, the Brussels Agreement of November 1984 paved the way for the full opening of the frontier in February 1985, allowing people and goods to cross the border. Under this agreement, the British and Spanish governments decided to discuss all differences over Gibraltar, including sovereignty.

THE ROCK OF GIBRALTAR: Surging from the sea to a height of 1,400 feet, the Rock looms up like some familiar life insurance company's advertisement. Originally, the Romans believed the Rock to be one of the two Pillars of Hercules, the entryway to the Mare Nostrum (literally, "Our Sea," or the Mediterranean) and gateway to Western civilization. Beyond the pillars to the west was the Unknown, the end of the world. What was unknown has long since passed into the domain of knowledge, and you can gaze upon it by taking a cable car to the summit of the Rock. The view on a clear day extends north to Granada's Sierra Nevada, south to the glimmering Strait of Gibraltar, and beyond to the Atlas and Rif mountains of Morocco.

Halfway up the hill, the Apes' Den is the home of the only wild simians of Europe. The mystery surrounding the presence of these tailless monkeys on the Rock has given rise to several theories. The one most generally accepted is that the monkeys found subterranean caves in Morocco and followed the passageways 10 miles under the Strait to emerge on Gibraltar. Recent legend has it that as long as the monkeys stay, the Rock will remain British. In any event, by order of Sir Winston Churchill many years ago, the apes were declared a protected species. A word of warning for your own protection: Do not feed the apes — they are fond of human fingers and they spit.

At another ridge of the Rock, the ruins of the 14th-century Tower of Homage are a reminder of the original Moorish castle overlooking this strategic strait. You can reach the tower via winding Willis' Road; inexpensive minibus tours of the Rock leave from Gibraltar Town or cars can be rented. When hiring a car, remember that traffic stays to the right. Since blowing your horn is forbidden, it is customary to pound on the side of the car to warn other drivers of your approach or to signal danger.

GIBRALTAR TOWN: The town has a museum containing intact Moorish baths and two marinas. For nightlife, there's the *International Sporting Club of Gibraltar* (phone: 350-72228), better known around town as simply "the casino," and there are several nightclubs, including the *Buccaneer* (phone: 350-74945), *Penelope's* (phone: 350-77582), and *Chimney Corner Club* (phone: 350-75201).

The *Week of the Sea* sailing competitions lure planeloads of English visitors every summer, as do the July concert festivals. Shoppers always crowd Gibraltar Town's Main Street to take advantage of VAT-free prices on brand-name and luxury items or to barter for Moroccan handicrafts at the Oriental bazaars.

THE GALLERIES: Northeast of town, farther up Queen's Road, are 'the galleries'. Carved out of the Rock by the British during the Great Siege and expanded by Allied engineers during World War II, some sections of the 30 miles of tunnels can be visited today. Labyrinths winding 370 feet deep remain off-limits to civilians.

THE CAVES OF ST. MICHAEL: First explored in 1936, these caves are testimony to the extraordinary geological formation of Gibraltar. Some 1,000 feet above sea level, they feature an underground lake, an amphitheater with wonderfully illuminated stalactites, and an eerie subterranean breeze that could well come from Africa. Almost as enthralling is the drive to the caves, up steep Queen's Road, to the southwest of Gibraltar Town.

BEACHES: The best swimming and fishing spots are at Catalán Bay, a village first founded by Italian immigrants on the eastern side of the Rock. Other Mediterranean swimming sites are Eastern Beach and Sandy Bay. On the Bay of Gibraltar, there are two rocky beaches — Camp Bay and Little Bay.

EUROPA POINT: Marking the very tip of continental Europe, this is a good spot to view Africa, to the south. The lighthouse, which dates from 1841, is near the Shrine of Our Lady of Europe and guides mariners to safe port. Driving back to Gibraltar Town along Europa Road, stop off at the Alameda Gardens, where there is a monument to General Elliot, the British commander during the Great Siege.

BEST EN ROUTE

Expect to pay at least $110 for a double room at either hotel and between $50 and $60 for a meal for two at the *Rock*. The pubs are inexpensive, about $20 for a meal for two, and the best places to eat on Gibraltar. They have English beer, such as Watney's Red and Guinness, plus a full complement of munchies — Scotch eggs, sausages, and cheese.

Holiday Inn – Centrally located, its facilities include a rooftop swimming pool, sauna, dining room, and coffee shop. Airport transportation is provided and pets are welcome. Major credit cards accepted. Governor's Parade (phone: 350-70500). Expensive.

Rock – Overlooking the town on the western slopes, this hotel has views across the bay. There is a saltwater pool and a playground on the premises. The dining room is quite modern and features international, predominantly European, cuisine. Roast beef with Yorkshire pudding is on the menu. Major credit cards accepted. 3 Europa Rd. (phone: 350-73000). Expensive.

The Terrace Room – In a lush setting at the *International Sporting Club* overlooking the bay, diners can choose from among a variety of international dishes. Open for dinner only from 9 PM to 2 AM. Reservations advised. Most credit cards accepted. 7 Europa Rd. (phone: 350-76666 or 350-72200). Expensive.

The Spinning Wheel – A special favorite among Gibraltar businessmen, this place offers international food served in cushy surroundings. We suggest you try the lamb. Closed Sundays and Saturday lunch. Reservations advised. Major credit cards accepted. 9 Horsebarrack La. (phone: 350-76091). Moderate.

Strings – English and Moroccan food — at a price most travelers can afford. Closed Sundays, Mondays, and Saturday lunch. Reservations advised. No credit cards accepted. 44 Cornwall La. (phone: 350-78800). Moderate.

Royal Calpe – Stop in for lunch — from 12 PM to 3 PM — and enjoy some of the best pub food on Gibraltar: shepherd's pie, steak-and-kidney pie, salads. The location is handy, the atmosphere lively. No credit cards accepted. 176 Main St. (phone: 350-75890). Inexpensive.

Other local pubs to investigate: *The Angry Friar* (Main St.), *The Bull and Bush* (Irish Town), *The Horseshoe* (Main St.), and *Ye Olde Rock* (off the Piazza).

Great Britain

The term Great Britain properly refers, not just to England, but also to Scotland, Wales, and Northern Ireland — the northeastern tip of the island of Ireland that lies to the west of England and Wales, across the Irish Sea. In more recent years the name United Kingdom has become popular, supplanting the Victorian conceit of Great Britain as the heart of an empire that, until World War II, dominated 40% of the planet. Even today, the British influence, from language to such idiosyncratic sports as cricket and rugby, is found worldwide. The British parliamentary system is the midwife, if not the mother, of all modern democracies. The Industrial Revolution was born here.

The semantic change from Great Britain to the United Kingdom reflects the growing nationalist movements England has been forced to accommodate, particularly in Scotland and Wales, where an emphasis on rediscovering, saving, and developing "lost" traditions and language has found a strong resurgence. In Ireland, this changing relationship is one of the underlying causes of the present "troubles" (the British are nothing if not masters of understatement) with Protestant Loyalists (that is, loyal to the British Crown), who are fighting a rear-guard action to maintain control of Northern Ireland when the majority of the population is Catholic.

England, the largest landmass of the four "states" of the United Kingdom, has dominated and controlled the others for centuries. Ireland and Wales were joined to England by the end of the 13th century (which is why, today, the eldest son of the reigning monarch is made Prince of Wales); the English and Scottish thrones were joined at the death of Elizabeth I, in 1603, in the person of James I of England and James VI of Scotland. To a great extent, the history of Great Britain is the history of England, its kings and queens and its parliament. Indeed, the average American is not aware that while the British constitution has never been set down on paper, British Common Law, which goes back to 1066 and William the Conqueror, is England's constitution and has provided a sound basis for the American and other legal systems. Where the US has its Supreme Court as the final arbiter of constitutionality, Great Britain has the House of Lords.

Caught between a reverence for tradition and history that sometimes stifles innovation and the fear that clinging slavishly to the past will turn the country into a "Third World has-been," the UK has painfully discovered that it can no longer compete on the world stage alone. Thus, it became a reluctant member of the European Economic Community (the so-called Common Market) and has drawn toward a federation of European states that this year will be the economic equal of the United States and Japan.

It is now clear that Britannia no longer rules the waves, and the British have been adjusting to that hard fact since World War II. Like the Romans, who also once dominated most of the world, the British possess a talent for government. Since 1215, when the nobles forced King John to sign the Magna Carta, rulers have wisely recognized the rights of their subjects. With no written constitution, the complicated British system of Common Law has also long contained safeguards for individual liberties. Above all, the English system is stable, and its revered institutions and traditions have survived the vicissitudes of history with only a single brief civil war. Since revolution just isn't the English way, the people have incorporated changes into their existing institutions by yielding certain rights to the nobles in 1215, to Parliament in 1660, to the middle class in 1832, and to the working class in 1867. Characteristically, the English never abandoned their aristocracy as other European monarchies did; instead, they kept augmenting its ranks by admitting wealthy or accomplished men and women to the peerage.

English people are known for their reserve. Foreigners often have viewed them as silent, cold, morose, melancholy, or just plain snobbish. Many writers, English and foreign, have wondered about the British character. Some have claimed that the British silence stems from a need, as inhabitants of a crowded island, for solitude and peace. Others have claimed they are merely shy. George Santayana, the Spanish-born philosopher, suggested that the Englishman is governed by an "inner atmosphere, the weather in his soul"; similarly, J. B. Priestley, the English novelist and critic, asserted that the English are suspicious of the purely rational and rely upon instinct and intuition more than other Western Europeans do. Their reliance upon intuition might be one clue to the extraordinary wealth and beauty of English literature, which — unlike the stereotypical and probably mythical Englishman — tends to be exuberant and romantic, as the plays of Shakespeare amply testify. The more one examines the English character, however, the more elusive and contradictory it appears; for if the English are traditional and conservative, they are also a nation of eccentrics. If they're gloomy, they are also well known for their marvelous senses of humor, as evidenced by the English comedies that continue to delight audiences of stage and screen.

The British inhabit, in the words of poet William Blake, a "green and pleasant land." Their plentiful rainfall makes for grass that is greener than that of most other countries. Because of the warming effects of the Gulf Stream, roses often bloom until *Christmas*. Moderation, a keynote of the British character and climate, extends also to the islands' geography. Both are moderate in size, with Great Britain the 8th largest and Ireland the 20th largest island on earth. Compared with other places, Britain has no dramatic geographical features; its mountains and lakes, though lovely, are not unusual in magnitude.

With Northern Ireland, Britain occupies a total of 94,196 square miles, a few miles off the northwestern coast of Europe. The island of Great Britain is not much larger than the state of Arkansas. Most of southern England, except Devon and Cornwall, is lowlands, while the Lake District, Scotland, and Wales are chiefly mountainous. Much of northern England consists of rolling upland scenery. England is divided from Scotland to the north by the Tweed and Liddel rivers and the Cheviot Hills; Wales is a landmass on England's west coast.

The British are a nation of city dwellers; 81% of Britain's 56 million people live in urban areas. London, the capital of England (Edinburgh is the capital of Scotland; Cardiff, of Wales; and Belfast, of Northern Ireland), is by far Britain's largest city, with a population of over 7 million. Birmingham and Manchester, English industrial cities farther north, rank second and third, with 1 million and half a million respectively.

If you have come in search of the "merrie England" of endless villages and farms, you will be disappointed, because relatively little of that remains; nevertheless, mementos of earlier days are everywhere, for the British love history and tradition. Stonehenge and Avebury stand as awesome reminders of a prehistoric Britain, occupied by Bronze Age people even before the Celts arrived in the 5th century BC. Later invaders included the Romans in 55 BC, the Germanic tribes of the Angles, Saxons, and Jutes in the 5th century AD, and, finally, the Normans in 1066.

When the Angles and Saxons invaded, the Celts retreated to Wales, Cornwall, Scotland, and Brittany (France), where they remain to this day. Both Welsh and Gaelic are linguistic outgrowths of a Celtic tongue; English, however, is based upon the Germanic Anglo-Saxon, with the addition of a heavy sprinkling of Norman French. Besides French vocabulary and manners, William the Conqueror brought feudalism to England. Nearly 2 centuries later, in 1215, powerful nobles forced King John to sign the Magna Carta in recognition of their feudal rights.

The next important event in English history was the Hundred Years War, a dynastic struggle with France from 1337 to 1428 punctuated by outbreaks of the Black Death. As England recovered from these disasters, its wool trade prospered and towns grew, along with their new merchant and artisan classes.

The central government expanded under the great Tudor monarchs, particularly Henry VIII and Elizabeth I, who ruled an increasingly strong and prosperous nation from 1485 to 1603. In 1529, Henry VIII broke with the pope, who refused to grant him a divorce, and established the Church of England. Elizabeth was queen during England's golden age, when Sir Francis Drake and Sir John Hawkins (and the weather) defeated the Spanish Armada, and when Christopher Marlowe, William Shakespeare, Ben Jonson, John Donne, and many other great poets and playwrights illumined the English scene.

Although James I united England and Scotland with his ascent to both thrones in 1603, the 17th century brought England to civil war, with the parliamentarians defeating the royalists in 1649, beheading Charles I, and creating the Commonwealth that lasted for 11 years under Oliver Cromwell. The monarchy that was restored in 1660 was different from the earlier one, for this time Parliament had summoned the king; from then on, kings were forced to cooperate with Parliament.

During the 18th century, the British Empire expanded to places as remote as India and North America. Britain became the world's greatest power for 200 years — this despite the loss of the 13 American colonies in 1776.

The Industrial Revolution transformed England late in the 18th century; as a result, the landed aristocracy was joined by a newly powerful middle class that was enfranchised by the Reform Bill of 1832. During the long era of Queen Victoria (1837–1901), Britain led the world in commercial, industrial, and political power. Military and economic rivalry with Germany resulted in World War I. Hitler's rise plunged Britain into World War II, when Britain had to fight Germany alone for an entire year after France fell in 1940 (Russia joined the war effort in 1941). During the heavy night bombings of its cities and the long and lonely Battle of Britain, the nation marshaled truly remarkable courage and strength. The war destroyed large urban areas, including vast chunks of London and Birmingham.

Like the Green Knight in the medieval tale *Sir Gawain and the Green Knight,* who walked off after a duel bearing his chopped-off head under his arm, the British nation has survived and renewed itself. It has transformed its colonial empire into an extensive commercial network, the British Commonwealth of Nations, and it has joined the European Common Market. Since the war it has also nationalized the Bank of England, coal, steel, and the railways, and in 1948 it established a system of socialized medicine. Under former Prime Minister Margaret Thatcher, however, increasing numbers of nationalized industries were "privatized" — returned to non-governmental ownership.

John Major became the new prime minister in November 1990, and he quickly addressed widespread complaints by British citizens about such issues as the now-defunct poll tax. The prime minister is obligated to call national elections no later than July of this year. At press time, Major had still declared no date, since his conservative government was still lagging behind in the by-elections. It will probably take a marked improvement in employment and general economic conditions for Mr. Major to win a fourth consecutive term for the Tories.

Although Britain today is struggling with the same economic pressures as the rest of the world, it is a wonderful place to visit because, among other things, Britons speak our language — or, rather, we speak theirs. Visitors will notice, however, that their English is different from that heard in America. George Bernard Shaw described the US and Great Britain as two nations separated by a common language. But whether you dream of seeing the changing of the guard at Buckingham Palace, touring the still-rural Shakespeare country, walking through the mountainous Lake District as Wordsworth and Coleridge did, surveying the English moors or the Scottish Highlands, drinking Scotch whisky at its source, watching the sun set in a sleepy Welsh fishing village, or making idle conversation in an authentic Irish pub — these joys and many other surprises await you in Britain.

Any trip to Great Britain should begin in London, one of the great cities of the world. From here you can explore Britain, using any or all of our suggested tour routes. You can see southeast England by starting near London in Canterbury, proceeding to the coast at Dover, and from there southwest to the resort of Brighton. Traveling farther west, our tour of southwest England begins at the ancient religious site of Stonehenge and continues west to the rocky peninsula of Devon and Cornwall, past Exeter, the wild and forbidding plain of Dartmoor, and the castle at Tintagel, where the legendary King Arthur is said to have been born. Also to the west is Wales, with its three national parks (Snowdonia, Pembrokeshire, and Brecon Beacons) and its jagged coast sprinkled with charming fishing villages.

Southeast of Wales, the Cotswolds, Shakespeare's country, is one of the prettiest rural districts in England; our circular route, which begins at Bath and ends in Oxford, includes the lovely Cotswolds and Stratford-upon-Avon, Shakespeare's birthplace. Farther north, the Lake District, where the 19th-century Lake Poets — William Wordsworth and Samuel Taylor Coleridge among them — loved to roam, has been preserved as a national park, with lovely mountains, lakes, and fields bounded by dry stone walls.

Crossing England's narrow waist to the opposite coast, our tour of northeast England begins at York, circling through the Yorkshire moors before heading north along the coast, then branching inland through Durham and Newcastle upon Tyne to Berwick-on-Tweed at the Scottish border. It's easier to explore Scotland in three parts: the Lowlands, or southern section, including Edinburgh, Glasgow, and Abbotsford — the site of Sir Walter Scott's house; the Highlands, the eastern and central region of magnificent mountains and moors; and finally, western Scotland, Robert Burns country — a coastal route, a place of resorts, and an ideal departure point for the Hebrides, the rugged islands off Scotland's western coast. The last route goes through Northern Ireland, the ancient province of Ulster, with its uncrowded beaches, bays, cliffs, and castles and its two highest ranges, the Mountains of Mourne in the southeast and the Sperrin Mountains in the north. Though the violence in Northern Ireland is sporadic, coverage of it since the late 1960s has dampened tourism considerably, which means that no crowds will interfere with your pleasure.

Southeast England: Kent, Canterbury, and the Coast

For better or worse, geography conspired to make Kent and east Sussex — the broad foot of land that spills out below London to form the bluff-lined and beach-speckled coast of southeast England — the only welcoming mat England has ever extended to the Continent. It is country suited to landing parties, Kent's rich orchards, hop fields, thatched barns, and high-hedged roads giving way to Sussex's high South Downs, from which one can see for miles in all directions. To the north is the wide estuary of the Thames; to the south, the English Channel; and to the east, where England and France are only some 20 miles apart, the Straits of Dover.

Such an invitation has been hard for European warlords to resist, and for 2,000 years attempts have been made to enter England through the southeast. Some have been successful. The Romans established an administrative center in London, and the Normans conquered all of England after their decisive victory at the town of Battle, near Hastings, in 1066, when William the Conqueror killed King Harold. Others' attempts have failed. From August to October 1940, Britain stood virtually alone against the full weight of the Nazi war machine as the Battle of Britain raged over the Weald of Kent. But each of these efforts has left some mark on this extraordinarily rich part of

England. Kent, labeled the Garden of England, nurtures as much history as fruit and hops in its fertile countryside.

The major sites along England's southeast coast — as well as Canterbury, Dover, Hastings and Battle, and Brighton — can be visited on day trips from London. Travelers with little time should certainly choose the most appealing destination and make the journey (by car or, even faster, by train). But more rewarding is a perambulation through the countryside, following the coast as a rough guide, and seeing sites great and small along the way. The route outlined below runs clockwise from Canterbury to Brighton.

This route begins south of London at Westerham, near Winston Churchill's home, Chartwell, and tours some of the estates and castles in the area as it moves east to the cathedral city of Canterbury. Here, within the city's ancient walls, are the cathedral and shrine associated with St. Thomas à Becket, who was murdered here in 1170 by four knights after he defied his old friend and former lord, King Henry II.

The historic ports of Sandwich and Deal are a short drive east of Canterbury, and the famed white cliffs of Dover are just to the south. This scalloped shore, across the narrow Straits of Dover from the French coast, has been the target of invading armies from Caesar to Hitler. Along the coast are layers of fortifications, rebuilt and enlarged by successive generations, and castles and seawalls that seem ageless. The narrow channel invited smuggling during more peaceful days, and coastal marshes bred stories of betrayal and death. Read a gentle primer of gothic horror tales before you journey forth — the legends of pre-Roman and Roman blood sacrifices will come alive for you. Perhaps a little inquisitive exploration will lead you to solve the mystery of the skulls in Hythe's church.

Farther south and west, Pevensey Bay was the site of William the Conqueror's landing, and nearby is the town of Battle, where he fought Harold's army. His defeat of King Harold at the Battle of Hastings (October 14, 1066) marked the beginning of a new era for England; it is a date no English schoolchild ever forgets. Farther along the coast is the Royal Pavilion at Brighton, and the trip ends with a visit to the springs at Royal Tunbridge Wells. Its medicinal waters prompted Edward VII to elevate the town to royal status, and its charming atmosphere makes it still popular today. It is just a short drive north from here to London. For more information, contact the South East England Tourist Board, The Old Brew House, 1 Warwick Park, Tunbridge Wells, Kent TN2 5TU, England (phone: 892-540766).

LONDON: For a complete description of the city and its hotels and restaurants, see *London,* THE CITIES.

En Route from London – Take Route A21 south through Bromley, continuing as far as the A233 cutoff. Follow A233 south to its junction with A25 near Westerham.

WESTERHAM: *Pitt's Cottage* (Limpsfield Rd.; phone: 959-62125), a timbered house used as a summer cottage during the late 1700s by William Pitt the Younger, stands on the outskirts of town. Pitt was well regarded as a wartime prime minister and was a motivating force behind two anti-Napoleonic coalitions involving several European nations as well as Russia and England. The cottage has since been converted into a restaurant serving traditional English roasts.

Westerham is the birthplace of General James Wolfe, whose victory over the French troops under the Marquis de Montcalm at Quebec on September 13, 1759, gave England control of Canada. A statue of Wolfe, who was mortally wounded during the decisive battle, stands in the village green not far from his childhood home, now called Quebec House. The statue of a more recent war hero, Prime Minister Winston Churchill, shares the town center with Wolfe. Churchill's country home, Chartwell, is about 2 miles south of town (via Route B2026) on a wooded hillside terraced with a series of gardens. The study where Churchill worked remains as he left it. Open Tuesdays through Thursdays from 12 to 5 PM and Saturdays, Sundays, and holidays from 11 AM to 5 PM, April through October; Wednesdays, Saturdays, and Sundays from 11 AM to 4 PM, March and November. Admission charge (phone: 732-866368).

En Route from Westerham – Take Route A25 east about 6 miles to the village of Sevenoaks. Knole, one of the largest and most magnificent baronial mansions in England, lies just off A25 on A225. The building, referred to by Virginia Woolf as "a town rather than a house" in her novel *Orlando,* sprawls over 3 acres and includes (according to legend) 7 courtyards corresponding to the days of the week, 52 staircases for the weeks, and 365 rooms — one for each day in the year. The house was begun in 1456 by Archbishop Thomas Bourchier and was held by the Archbishops of Canterbury until turned over to Henry VIII. The estate, named for the grassy knoll on which it stands, was given to the Sackville-West family by Queen Elizabeth I in 1603, the year she died. The house was enlarged, and over the years the estate acquired an incredible art collection, including canvases by Gainsborough, Van Dyck, Reynolds, and others. Today the interior is furnished entirely in the Elizabethan mode, with furnishings virtually untouched since the family was first given the house Open Wednesdays through Saturdays from 11 AM to 5 PM and Sundays from 2 to 5 PM, April through October. Admission charge (phone: 732-450608).

Return to Route A25, traveling east about 2 miles to the cutoff to Ightham Mote. The stately 14th-century manor house, encircled by a moat, contains a beautiful Tudor chapel (open Mondays, Wednesdays, Thursdays, and Fridays from 12 to 5 PM and Sundays from 11 AM to 5 PM, April through October; admission charge; phone: 732-810378). If you find yourself working up a thirst, travel a bit farther to the *Crown Point Inn* (phone: 732-810669), a comfortable paneled pub with its own garden in the tiny village of Seal Chart, outside Plaxtol. Route A25 becomes M20 and leads directly into Maidstone.

MAIDSTONE: Many historic buildings line the streets of Maidstone, the bustling capital and agricultural center of Kent. Several streets in the High Street area have been closed to vehicular traffic in an effort to preserve these fine examples of early architecture. Near the town's 14th-century Church of All Saints is a tithe barn of the same period, part of the palace of the Archbishop of Canterbury, when it was used as a stable. It's now the home of the *Tyrwhitt-Drake Museum,* displaying a fine collection of ornate horse-drawn carriages. Open 10 AM to 5:30 PM year-round. Admission charge. Archbishop Stables, Mill St. (phone: 622-754497).

Chillington Manor, an Elizabethan mansion on St. Faith's Street, is now the home of the *Museum and Art Gallery* (open Mondays through Saturdays from 10 AM to 5:30 PM; admission charge; phone: 622-754497), which contains the memorabilia of essayist William Hazlitt, a native of Maidstone. North of town, on A229, is the Carmelite retreat at Aylesford Priory (open daily; no admission charge).

En Route from Maidstone – Readers of Charles Dickens will enjoy a short (8 miles) side trip north to Rochester, which appears so often in his work and, thinly disguised, is the city of Cloisterham in his last story, *The Mystery of Edwin Drood.* Dickens's home at Gad's Hill is not open, but the food, drinks, and atmosphere at the author's favorite inn, *The Leather Bottle* (in Cobham; phone: 474-814327), are ample recompense. You can visit other buildings in Rochester that figure in his work — Eastgate House (now the Dickens Centre; phone: 634-44176), the cathedral (phone: 634-43366), and Guild Hall (phone: 634-48717). All open daily; admission charge to Dickens Centre and Guild Hall.

Rochester Castle, a massive Norman fortress, was erected late in the 11th century and partially rebuilt during the 14th century. The castle is 120 feet high and has walls 12 feet thick. Rochester Cathedral incorporates architectural styles from several periods, from the crypt and tower built in 1082 and the decorative mid-14th-century doorway to the Chapter Room. Open daily. No admission charge (phone: 634-42852).

Route A20 continues east-southeast from Maidstone toward Ashford, passing Leeds Castle. This fairy-tale fortress stands in the middle of a lake — no mean task in the 1200s, when it was built. It was the home of Lord Culpepper (Governor of Virginia, 1680–83) and later his grandson, Lord Fairfax. Open daily from April to October; weekends only November through March. Admission charge (phone: 622-65400).

The remains of a palace of the Archbishops of Canterbury lie within the ancient village of Charing, about 13 miles from Maidstone. Pick up A28 eastbound from Ashford to Canterbury, a distance of about 14 miles across the meadowy downs that extend through Kent from the outskirts of London to the coast at Dover.

The main road neatly bypasses the delightful village of Chilham, so keep an eye open for the turnoff. The gardens and grounds of Chilham Castle contain a raptor center and a "pets' corner" (open daily from March to October; admission charge; phone: 227-730319). Bird-handling demonstrations, with falcons and eagles, are held most afternoons. The atmosphere of the *White Horse Inn* (The Square; phone: 227-730355) will confirm the feeling of earlier times; it has often been used in movies because of its virtually unchanged 15th-century appearance inside and out. The food is as enjoyable as the fireplace on a chilly evening, so reservations are advised.

Continuing east on Route A28, a glimpse of the three pinnacled towers of Canterbury Cathedral heralds the ancient city.

CANTERBURY: This approach leads into the heart of Canterbury through the massive West Gate used by countless pilgrims traveling to the shrine of St. Thomas à Becket. It was the murder of Archbishop Thomas à Becket in 1170, and his canonization 2 years later, that elevated the cathedral to its status as a shrine. Following 9 centuries of pilgrims, make your way along the main street and then turn left into the narrow course called Mercery Lane. Straight ahead is Christ Church Gate, leading to the cathedral precincts (or close). Give yourself plenty of time to explore the cathedral treasures — the glowing medieval stained glass windows, the ancient paintings in the crypt, and the elaborate vaulted cloisters; but there is much more to see here.

The Romans built the fortress of Durovernum on this site in AD 43. The remains of the city walls are visible near the Dane John Gardens, and the characteristic mosaic Roman roadway can still be seen at Butchery Lane.

St. Martin's Church, one of the ancient landmarks mentioned in the rhyme in George Orwell's *1984,* is one of the oldest functioning churches in England. Christian services were held here as early as AD 500, and the present building may have evolved from 4th-century Roman villas on the same site. The ruins of St. Augustine's Abbey, established by St. Augustine in AD 602 with the support of King Ethelbert, lie outside the city's East Wall, near the foot of St. Martin's Hill along Longport Street.

The Canterbury Tales Visitors' Centre features an elaborate multimedia show featuring figures dressed as pilgrims in 14th-century costumes (open daily; admission charge; St. Margaret's St.; phone: 227-454888). The *Canterbury Heritage Museum* features a steam-powered locomotive designed by George Stephenson (closed Sundays, November through May; admission charge; Stour St.; phone: 227-452747).

There are several inviting inns for food and drink, such as the *Three Tuns* (Watling St.) and the bow-windowed *Olive Branch* (in Burgate).

En Route from Canterbury – Route A257 leads due east from Canterbury to the medieval port of Sandwich, one of the original Cinque (Five) Ports (see *En Route from Deal*). As Sandwich's harbor became clogged with silt in the 16th century, the city lost importance. It gained lasting fame, however, when the fourth Earl of Sandwich invented the world's most popular and enduring meal — the sandwich. According to legend, the earl was loath to leave the gaming tables to eat and asked that a concoction of bread and meat be made for him. The earl — who was infamous for being in charge of the admiralty when Britain lost its North American colony — was a dissolute man, and the story has something of the ring of truth about it. Two inns, the *Bell* (The Quay, Sandwich; phone: 304-613388) and the *Kings Arms* (High St.; phone: 304-890216), will be glad to provide a sample of this handy bar snack and something with which to wash it down. Richborough Castle, just off Route A257 1½ miles north of Sandwich, was established by the Romans around AD 43 and added to by the Saxons during the 3rd century (open daily; admission charge; phone: 304-612013). Route A258 leads to Deal, about 6 miles south along the coast.

DEAL: Deal was an important shipping center through the early 19th century. Under Henry VIII, three castles were erected here: Deal Castle (open daily; admission charge; phone: 304-372762), Walmer Castle (open daily except January and February and when Lord Warden is in residence; admission charge; 1 mile south on A258; phone: 304-364288), and Sandown Castle (since washed away). There is a good possibility that Caesar's forces landed along this shore when the Romans invaded Britain, and here Henry VIII feared the pope would launch a Holy War against him as the self-proclaimed head of the Church of England. The coast off Deal, called Goodwin Sands, is a complicated series of sandbanks that are exposed at low tide. Lighthouses and lightships illuminate the area after dark, but maritime accidents persist. The narrow roadstead formed between Goodwin Sands and the coast, not the safest anchorage for shipping, is popularly known as The Downs.

En Route from Deal – Traveling south on A258 toward the busy port of Dover, Walmer Castle is only 1 mile from Deal. The castle has been the residence of the Lord Warden of the Cinque Ports since the mid-1700s. This association of seaports began in the 11th century, when five principal ports (Hastings, Hythe, Dover, Sandwich, and Romney — now New Romney) banded together to provide England with a makeshift navy. Later this was formalized by a charter that granted certain privileges in exchange for the pledge of supplying ships and men for the country's defense. Other ports along this southeast foot of England, the part closest to France, became involved in this arrangement during the dangerous period from the 13th to the 16th century. Following the establishment of the Royal Navy, the importance of the association and the post of Lord Warden declined drastically. Dover is only 7 miles farther south on A258.

DOVER: The chalky white cliffs of Dover have been a strategic landmark ever since the early Iron Age, when a settlement was established here. Roman invaders quickly erected a fortress and an octagonal lighthouse, or pharos, that still stands beside the more recently built Norman Dover castle (open daily; admission charge; phone: 304-205830). The castle keep surrounds a 240-foot-deep well, and the underground passages — formerly used as a World War II military base — now serve as a museum covering British defense since Napoleonic times. The Saxon Church of St. Mary-in-Castro, within the castle walls, is England's oldest. The ancient Roman roadway called

Watling Street begins here and leads to London via Canterbury. On clear days, France is easily visible across the Straits of Dover, 20 miles away, and the view from the battlements of Dover Castle atop the 400-foot bluff overlooking the city and sea is magnificent. Dover is one of the main embarkation points for ferries to France (Calais, Dunkirk, and Boulogne) and Belgium (Ostende and Zeebrugge).

During both world wars, Dover again rose to prominence as a point of departure for troops bound for the Continent and as the goal of planes straggling back from the fighting. The city was pounded by long-range artillery during World War II, and the thick castle walls sheltered the population through the 4-year bombardment.

En Route from Dover – The famous cliffs extend southwest toward Folkestone, neatly trimming the coastline with a tall white chalk sea wall for almost 7 miles. Beyond this point the cliffs fall away, exposing the shore. Stretching westward is a double line of defenses constructed in the early 19th century against the threat of an invasion by Napoleon: a series of 74 small coastal fortresses — circular Martello towers — reinforced by a Royal Military Canal a short distance inland. Additional defenses were erected in 1940 when Hitler massed his forces along the French coast. Take Route A20 southwest along the coast from Dover to Folkestone before picking up Route A259 for the additional 4 miles to Hythe.

If you're favored with good weather in Folkestone, take a stroll on the Leas — a broad, mile-long, grassy walkway on the crest of the cliffs just west of the harbor. From here the coast of France unfolds in a beautiful panorama 22 miles distant. On the east side of the harbor is the Warren, where a section of the chalk cliff has crumbled and fallen on the beach — a great hunting ground for fossils.

HYTHE: Three Martello towers still guard the former Cinque Port of Hythe, although the harbor has long since silted up and the sea receded. There are also fortifications from other periods, including the ruins of a Roman castrum, Stutfall Castle, near the Royal Military Canal that bisects the city. Lympne Castle, a residence of the Archdeacons of Canterbury until the mid-1800s, incorporates a square 12th-century Norman tower into its otherwise 14th- and 15th-century construction (open May to September; admission charge; phone: 303-67571). The castle overlooks Romney Marsh, a sparsely populated, low-lying pasture full of memories of the old smuggling days, when untaxed (and often illegal) cargoes were unloaded here. The fields and marsh grass support a large number of Romney Marsh sheep. A miniature steam railway (open daily *Easter* to September, and weekends in March and October) runs a 13-mile course from Hythe to New Romney along the fringe of the marsh. The presence of over 1,500 human skulls in the town church has never been explained.

En Route from Hythe – Route A259 parallels both the coast and the railway, passing through Romney Marsh as it travels to New Romney. Dymchurch, halfway between the two closed ports (New Romney lost the use of its harbor in the 13th century), is a popular weekend resort with a 5-mile beach. The small village itself lies in the shelter of a 3-mile fortified seawall built by the Romans to prevent the marshes from flooding. The wall has been continuously improved, and the fortifications were added in 1940. At New Romney the road bears inland, crossing the border of Kent and heading toward the ancient towns of Rye and Winchelsea (21 miles and 24 miles from Hythe, respectively) in neighboring East Sussex.

RYE: The receding sea and centuries of silt buildup have obstructed the port of Rye — like so many of its neighboring ports — limiting traffic to small coastal vessels and fishing boats. The town was razed by the French in 1377 and again in 1448, destroying the most historic buildings, but many of the houses erected during the late 15th century still grace Rye's cobblestone streets. The town retains the atmosphere of that medieval time and a measure of its former bustling activity within its crumbling 14th-century walls.

Both the *Mermaid Inn* (Mermaid St.; see *Best en Route*), rebuilt during the 15th century and rumored to have been a smugglers' rendezvous, and the timbered 15th-century *Flushing Inn* (Market St.; phone: 797-223292) are excellent haunts for travelers. The works of the great clock (ca. 1560) in the 12th-century Church of St. Mary are thought to be among the oldest still functioning in England, though the originals of these golden cherubs with hammers are in the Town Hall, while the operative ones are a reproduction. The cherubs are known as the Quarter Boys because they strike at 15-minute intervals past the hour but not on the hour. Lamb House was the residence of novelist Henry James from 1898 until his death in 1916 (open Wednesday and Saturday afternoons, mid-April through October; admission charge; West St.; no phone). The 16th-century dramatist John Fletcher's birthplace, a vicarage near Lion and Market Streets, is now a tea shop called *Fletchers House.* The de Ypres family purchased the 13th-century tower that bears its name in the early 14th century; it is now a museum (open daily; admission charge; phone: 797-223254).

Winchelsea, also added to the Cinque Ports alliance before the changing coastline ruined its harbor, was completely relocated to its present site in 1283 by Edward I. The church, begun soon afterward, is dedicated to St. Thomas à Becket. Parts of William Thackeray's *Denis Duval* are set in the two towns.

En Route from Rye – South of Winchelsea, Route A259 descends toward the shore. At Hastings, 9 miles from Rye, the road regains the coast. The strategic and psychological importance of this area to England becomes clear when viewed against the historic background of this section of coastline.

Following Edward the Confessor's death in January 1066, Harold ascended to the throne of England, but his claim to the monarchy (through his mother's bloodline) was weak. Duke William of Normandy felt his kinship to Edward (his father had been Edward's cousin), coupled with the oath Harold had sworn in support, justified his claim to the throne.

It was just a few miles west of Hastings, at Pevensey Bay, that William landed his forces on September 28, 1066.

King Harold and his men were busy fighting Tostig in the north and had to march southward from the Battle of Stamford Bridge. He gathered additional support as he traveled but it was not until the morning of October 14 that Harold's army, perhaps 10,000 ax- and spear-carrying foot soldiers, formed a shield wall along a ridge just north of Hastings. William's force was composed of a few thousand archers and several thousand mounted knights and armed men. Norman arrows rained on the defenders, and cavalry charges broke on the wall of spears and shields. In the late afternoon William faked a retreat, drawing many of the inexperienced English militiamen from their positions, and decimated them with his cavalry. King Harold and the remainder of his army were soon slaughtered. On the spot where Harold planted the Royal Standard, where he and his closest followers actually died, William the Conqueror erected Battle Abbey. By *Christmas,* William was crowned King of England in Westminster Abbey.

HASTINGS (ST. LEONARDS and BATTLE): Although Hastings and adjoining St. Leonards now form a popular resort area, the original Cinque Port city stagnated after the harbor became clogged with silt during the late 12th century. This 600-year sleep kept the Old Town beautifully intact. Narrow streets and age-old houses characterize the east end of town, where Hastings began as a fishing village. Even the tall, skinny sheds used to store the fishnets, built during the 16th century, have survived, as did the 14th-century St. Clement's and the 15th-century All Saints' churches. The fishermen's "net shops," set along a part of the beach called the Stade, are near the *Fisherman's Church,* also known as the *Shipwreck Heritage Centre,* a museum (open late May to late September, weekdays and Sunday afternoons; phone: 424-424787). Next door is the *Sealife Centre* (admission charge).

The ruins of Hastings Castle, erected around the time of William's invasion, overlook the 3-mile beach area. The magnificent homes in this section of town reflect the resurgence of Hastings as a resort during the late 18th and early 19th centuries. An amusement pier adds to the gaiety of the promenade along the beach, but the most beautiful aspect of the town is natural — the cliffwalks to the east of Hastings and St. Clement's Caves (below the castle), once used by smugglers. Take the 100-year-old *West Cliff Railway* (an antique elevator) up to the castle and caves to see the *Smugglers' Adventure,* a wax museum in the caves which tells the history of the smugglers through the 18th and 19th centuries (open daily, except Mondays in winter; admission charge; phone: 424-63721) and the "1066 Story" nearby — a video show of the history of Britain from the 1066 invasion of William the Conqueror to the present (open daily; admission charge; phone: 424-422964).

The nearby small town of Battle, which derives its name from the famous Battle of Hastings, includes the abbey founded by William the Conqueror. The battle site, from the ridge where Harold formed his lines to the heights of Senlac and Telham on the far side of the valley, where William's forces gathered, is just southwest of the town. The abbey gatehouse faces Market Square, and the ruins of the abbey church (destroyed around 1540) center on the spot where Harold fell. Those sections of the abbey that survived intact and those added in later years are now used as a school. (The abbey ruins are open daily). The horrors of the clash of forces come vividly to life in the *Battle Museum* (open weekdays, *Easter* through September; admission charge; High St.; phone: 424-63721).

      En Route from Hastings – Continue southwest along the coast on Route A259 toward the popular seaside resort of Brighton, a distance of about 45 miles. Since this coastal road may be clogged with traffic during the summer months, it might be a good idea to take the inland route, A27, which veers off from A259 at Pevensey.

BRIGHTON: The flow of travelers and bathers to the shore at Brighton started in the mid-18th century, when a local doctor began recommending the salt water and sea air to several members of England's fashionable elite. It hasn't stopped. By 1783, the Prince of Wales (later George IV) made his home here and ordered the construction of the Royal Pavilion. In 1817, he had the building altered to a more Oriental style; by that time the carnival atmosphere of the resort was well established. Even a partial listing of those who frequented Brighton would sound like a *Who's Who* of English history and literature: Lewis Carroll, Sir Winston Churchill, Arthur Conan Doyle, William Gladstone, and Herbert Spencer. Aubrey Beardsley was born here, and George Holyoake died here. By 1929, Brighton had tripled in size, sprawling from Hove to Rottingdean (a 7-mile seafront) and several miles inland.

An esplanade stretches the length of the beach, and two piers, including the Palace amusement pier, extend from it at either end. Madeira Drive leads on to Black Rock, where the Brighton Marina, one of the largest in Europe, opened in 1979. The older section of Brighton forms a permanent bazaar in the area known as the Lanes, bounded by the Old Steine (near the pavilion) and West Street. The Royal Pavilion and the Royal Stables, now the *Dome Theatre,* mark the inland border of this shopping haven featuring jewelry shops, art galleries, and antique shops. Around the corner on Church Street is the *Museum and Art Gallery* (closed Mondays; admission charge; phone: 273-603005). The Sussex Room at the museum contains a thorough history of the area and a fabulous collection of English ceramics (the Willet Collection). And the Royal Pavilion is itself a living museum of one of the most vivid periods in English taste (open daily; admission charge; phone: 273-603005).

Brighton is not, however, the place for spending your days indoors or even out shopping. Virtually every holiday sport is available here, and if none of the active amusements (sailing, golf, tennis, and such) is to your taste, there are the shows at the *Dome Theatre,* the greyhound racing, cricket, and football at Hove, or the horse racing at the *Brighton Races* (Freshfield Rd.). Then there's the *King Alfred Leisure Centre* (in Hove) and during the summer, the *Volk's Electric Railroad* (Madeira Dr.) from Palace Pier to Black Rock (admission charge). Many theater productions open here before going to London's West End.

En Route from Brighton – Route A23, aided by the M23 motorway, makes a beeline for London, 60 miles due north of the beaches. A more entertaining route is A27 northeast from Brighton to Lewes and A26 from there to Royal Tunbridge Wells, the health resort that has been extremely popular since the discovery of the "healing powers" of its chalybeate mineral waters in 1606. It's about 30 miles from Brighton at the junction of A26 and A21. A promenade called the Pantiles, designed as a shopping and visitors' area in 1638, is just as popular today. The mineral waters can be sampled from the springs at the far end of the walkway, and the *Duke of York* pub (phone: 892-30482) serves those looking for something a little stronger at the tables outside its Victorian building in the center of the Pantiles promenade. Route A21 leads north toward Westerham and Sevenoaks, about 10 miles away.

BEST EN ROUTE

The roads from the coast to London have been lined with inns and guesthouses for centuries, and many of those available to modern travelers are the same ones patronized by kings' messengers (and murderers) 6 centuries ago. The degree of comfort has increased a good deal in the intervening years, however, and you should have no complaints about the quality or range of accommodations available. Expect to pay $200 or more for a double room in those places categorized as very expensive; between $100 and $175 at an expensive hotel; $75 to $95 at moderate places; and under $75 in any hotel or guesthouse listed as inexpensive. Full English breakfast usually is included in the overnight charge. A meal for two, excluding drinks, wine, or tips, will run about $70 to $80 in places listed as expensive; $40 to $70 in moderate; and under $40 in inexpensive.

WYE

New Flying Horse Inn – A 17th-century coaching inn with oak beams, gleaming brasses, 10 rooms, and good food. Upper Bridge St. (phone: 233-812297). Inexpensive.

Wife of Bath – Five miles south of the tiny town of Chilham is Wye, a village that would escape notice altogether if it weren't for this very fine restaurant with English and French cuisine. Weekly menus change with the season to ensure absolutely fresh food. Closed for Sunday dinner and for a week at *Christmas*. Reservations essential. 4 Upper Bridge St. (phone: 233-812540). Inexpensive.

CANTERBURY

County – Although this 16th-century hotel has been refurbished in the name of creature comforts, it retains the feel of its older rooms. The original timbers and exposed beams are still there, but certain modern niceties (like private baths in all rooms) have been added. High St. (phone: 227-766266; fax: 227-451512). Expensive.

DOVER

Dover Moat House – A large, modern, 79-room hotel that's conveniently close to the ferry terminals. Amenities include a restaurant and a heated indoor pool. Townwall St. (phone: 304-203270; fax: 304-213230). Expensive.

RYE

Mermaid Inn – This beautifully preserved 15th-century inn is one of the most charming old hotels in England. Its walls still conceal the priest holes and secret staircase used to avoid arrest in the old days of pirates and smugglers. Mermaid St. (phone: 797-223065). Expensive.

HASTINGS

Beauport Park – Set off in a beautiful park area, the stately Georgian hotel has a formal garden to add to the timeless atmosphere. The service is in keeping with that feeling of another age, and the heated outdoor pool is a bonus during the summer. Battle Rd. (phone: 424-851222; fax: 424-52465). Expensive.

BRIGHTON

Grand – Right in the center of the seafront, this is an old and very attractive establishment with Victorian architecture at its best in the lobby and landings. Reopened in 1986, the hotel was lavishly restored following an IRA bombing in 1984. King's Rd. (phone: 273-21188; fax: 273-202694). Very expensive.

Hospitality Brighton – A relative newcomer on the seafront, with an imposing atrium overlooking the sea. King's Rd. (phone: 273-206700; fax: 273-820692). Very expensive.

Old Ship – On the seafront close to the Lanes, much of its original style and charm remains, especially in the 200-year-old banqueting room used by the prince regent. The rooms vary from simple singles to lavish antique-four-poster-bedded delights. King's Rd. (phone: 273-29001; fax: 273-820718). Expensive.

ROYAL TUNBRIDGE WELLS

Spa – A posh Georgian mansion set in an exclusive part of town, this family-run establishment offers traditional hospitality and modern facilities such as a Jacuzzi and gym. Ask for a room overlooking the grand gardens, thick with rhododendrons. The *Chandelier* restaurant is closed Saturdays at lunchtime. Reservations advised. Major credit cards accepted. Mt. Ephraim (phone: 892-20331; fax: 892-510575). Expensive.

Southwest England: Devon and Cornwall

Its atypically warm climate is not all that distinguishes southwest England from the rest of Great Britain, although it is the feature of this thumb of land stuck into the Atlantic that most attracts other Britons. With coasts on the English Channel and the Atlantic Ocean and weather that at its most extreme approaches the subtropical (indefatigable Cornish gardeners have been known to grow palms, much to the consternation of unsuspecting passersby, who find palm trees in England a touch surreal), popular resorts like Torquay and Newquay are full all summer long.

But there is a mysterious quality to Devon and Cornwall born of centuries of relative isolation that is both fascinating and a little frightening. It is this quality — not its reputation for warm weather or seaside frolics — that draws most foreign visitors. For the distinction between rural Somerset and Dorset and Devon's famous moors couldn't be more pronounced. Dartmoor — now a protected national park — is a vast sparse expanse of exposed rock and chalk, eerie and mystical at night, yet beautifully trimmed in a verdant layer of wild grasses and purple heather that glow in the sunlight by day. Across them sweep sudden storms and lashing gales of wind and rain, and from them have come stories of the hounds of hell, dark demons, and druids. The coasts of Cornwall, isolated for centuries, bred generations of sea scavengers as well as culture, language, and customs unlike any others in England.

In Plymouth, Sir Francis Drake busied himself with a game of bowls as the Spanish Armada gathered offshore; from this same port the Pilgrims departed for the New World. Pirates and scavengers alike took delight in hiding among the coves and inlets that line both the north and south coasts of the region, preying on shipping by force and luring their victims to destruction on unmarked rocks and shoals.

From London to the ancient religious site of Stonehenge, the route we offer below bears south into Salisbury and then Dorchester before heading west to Exeter. The district is scattered with Roman ruins, and some of this ancient architecture can still be seen. Farther west, across the wilds of Dartmoor, lies Plymouth, a major port of the British navy since the days of wooden ships. Cornwall's twin peninsulas of Land's End and the Lizard form the southwestern tip of England, and in the bay between these outstretched arms of land is Penzance, a resort and a point of departure for the offshore Isles of Scilly. Nearby is one of England's most spectacular castles, St. Michael's Mount, on a mountain rising 200 feet from the sea.

Returning east along the north coast of Cornwall and then Devon, the route passes the island-fortress of Tintagel, claimed to be the birthplace of King Arthur, and the surfing resort of Bude before ending in the forests and valleys of Exmoor National Park. For more information write to the West Country Tourist Board, Trinity Court, 37 Southernhay East, Exeter EX1 1QS, Devon, England (phone: 392-76351).

LONDON: For a detailed report on the city and its hotels and restaurants, see *London,* THE CITIES.

En Route from London – It's about a 2½- to 3-hour journey to Stonehenge via either the M3 motorway or Route A30, but switch over to A30 at exit 8 of the motorway and follow it until the point where A303 originates and A30 bears south. Take A303 into Amesbury, which marks the eastern entrance to the Salisbury Plain, about 120 miles west of London. This windblown 200-square-mile table of chalk and rock is the bedrock of English history.

STONEHENGE: The best known of almost 80 ancient religious sites in the area, Stonehenge lies 2 miles west of town just off Route A303 (open daily year-round; admission charge; phone: 980-623108). An earthwork 300 feet in diameter raises the crude formation above the plain and sets it apart from its surroundings. Although the site was used by the druids for their sun-based festivals beginning around 250 BC, computer evidence supports the theory that these circles served as an astronomical calendar for timing the movements of the moon and stars — and predicting eclipses — around 1500 BC. That anyone could have moved and placed these massive chunks of stone at any time, let alone in 1500 BC, is an incredible act of faith in itself. Scientists remain baffled as to how it was done.

The stone monoliths, mined, shaped, and moved to this spot, are arranged in two concentric outer circles with two interior horseshoes. The uprights in the outer circle are 13½ feet tall and linked by fitted capstones; the inner circle is slightly smaller. Many segments of both circles remain intact. The two horseshoes are formed of unconnected trilithons (two uprights supporting a single capstone) in a concentric pattern. The largest of the five still standing is over 20 feet tall and extends 8 feet below ground.

En Route from Stonehenge – Backtrack into Amesbury and stop at the *Antrobus Arms* hotel to discuss the druids (see *Best en Route*). The present hotel, which evolved from a coaching inn for passengers on the London-Exeter coach, carries its age well. On a cold night its roaring fireplaces (and a whiskey) will chase the chill as well as ever. The abbey at Amesbury was founded by the widow of King Edgar the Peaceful after his death in 975, although parts of the structure date from the 7th century. It was here, according to the tales of King Arthur, that Queen Guinevere took final refuge after the death of Arthur. Route A345 leads directly south to Salisbury, just a few miles away, but there is a much nicer, smaller road running through the Avon Valley, via Wilsford and Middle Woodford, slightly west of the main route.

SALISBURY: The 400-foot spire of Salisbury Cathedral, the tallest in England, dominates the entire plain on which the city is located. Salisbury was established and construction of the cathedral began in 1220, when religious jurisdiction over the area was transferred here from the ancient city of Old Sarum. The remains of Old Sarum — which began as a crude earthwork, grew to a Saxon town, and later became a Norman fortress — lie on a hill north of Salisbury. On the banks of the Avon, the *Rose and Crown* provides comfortable accommodations (see *Best en Route*); and you're bound to feel welcome at one of the three bars at the *Haunch of Venison* (Minster St.; phone: 722-22024).

Take Route A354 southwest from Salisbury to Dorchester, about 40 miles distant, across the hills of Dorset Downs. South of Puddletown lies the countryside Thomas Hardy called Egdon Heath in his novels; Salisbury appeared as Melchester.

DORCHESTER: Thomas Hardy transformed this quiet agricultural center where he was born into the city of Casterbridge for his Wessex novels, but Dorchester has withstood much greater alterations throughout its existence. Maiden Castle, a pre-Roman earthwork, is a magnificent ruin left by the native neolithic Britons. Later, under the Romans, this was a crossroads called Durnovaria, and the nearby Maumbury Rings was the site of an amphitheater. King John later used the town as a hunting center. Today, the *Dorset County Museum* (closed Sundays; admission charge; High West St.; phone: 305-62735) displays finds from the nearby Iron Age fort, Maiden Castle, and a reconstruction of Hardy's study taken from his house at Max Gate; there are also some of his original manuscripts, notebooks, and drawings. In the 17th century, Judge Jeffreys held his Bloody Assizes in Dorchester, consigning some 200 men to the gallows in the wake of the Duke of Monmouth's failed rebellion in 1685. Jeffreys was a notoriously cruel man, and the High West Street building where he roomed is said to be haunted; if you spot the judge, don't speak. The *Royal Oak,* a pub right up the street, should be your next port of call. Hardy's cottage and the fringes of Egdon Heath are accessible from Route A35 about 3 miles east of town. The current tenant will open the cottage by appointment (admission charge), and the gardens are open to the public daily, except Tuesdays, from April to October (no admission charge; phone: 305-62366).

En Route from Dorchester – Route A35 leads west, cutting across the hills and farms of beautiful Dorset Downs. Bridport, about 16 miles from Dorchester, was Hardy's Port Bredy; it has a good beach on West Bay. The town achieved some notoriety as a major producer of rope and netting, leading to the designation of a hangman's noose as a "Bridport dagger". West of Bridport the road divides, and A3052 leads southwest to the resort town of Lyme Regis, on the coast.

LYME REGIS: The steep streets of Lyme Regis lead downhill from the coastal farmlands to the old stone pier known as the Cobb, famously portrayed in *The French Lieutenant's Woman.* It was here that the Duke of Monmouth landed to raise an army among the men of southwest England in his attempt to wrest the crown from James II in 1685. Jane Austen kept a cottage called Wings atop the promenade overlooking the area; she used the setting for Louisa Musgrove's accident in the novel *Persuasion.* The worn chalk cliffs are studded with fossil formations, and an ichthyosaurus was recovered here in 1811 by Mary Anning.

Route A3052 continues west through Colyford to the resort area of Sidmouth and goes on to Exeter, a total distance of 32 miles.

EXETER: The strategic and historic city of Exeter, dominated by beautiful Exeter Cathedral, stands on the banks of the Exe River, guarding the neck of the southwest peninsula containing Devon and Cornwall. It is the county town of Devon. The Romans created a fortified city here, Isca Dumnoniorum, and the crumbling walls that once marked its boundaries can still be seen. Over the years, this site has been besieged, stormed, taken, and sometimes held by and against a long series of attackers. The Saxons called the town Escanestre and founded a monastery in 680. The ruins of Rougemont Castle, erected by William the Conqueror after he seized the town in 1068, testify to the area's military importance.

Exeter Cathedral (High St. near South St.), which evolved from a Norman structure begun in 1112, includes only the massive towers from that period, having been continually rebuilt and altered for almost a century from 1270 until the late 14th century. Intricate construction details, like the vaulted roof and elaborately carved figures on the west façade, contribute to its appeal. The 14th-century Guild Hall, decorated inside and out with coats of arms and the insignia of various trade guilds and individuals, may be the oldest municipal building in England (closed Sundays; no admission charge; phone: 392-265500).

Exeter has several good museums covering the 11th century: St. Nicholas Priory's remaining wing, furnished as a medieval great hall with kitchens (open Tuesdays through Saturdays; phone: 392-265858); the *Maritime Museum* (open daily; phone: 392-58075); the *Royal Albert Memorial Museum and Art Gallery* (open Tuesdays through Saturdays; phone: 392-265858); and the *Museums of Costume and Lace* in Rougemont House (closed Sundays; phone: 392-265858). Admission charge for all.

In its younger days Exeter was a port city, accessible from the English Channel via the navigable Exe River. Several of Queen Elizabeth's favorite sea captains, Sir Francis Drake and Sir Walter Raleigh among them, docked at Exeter and often stepped into *Mol's Coffee House* (now a silver- and goldsmith's shop) in the Cathedral Close. Drake is also thought to have had a few at the *Ship Inn* (Martins La.; phone: 392-72040), which still serves thirsty travelers.

En Route from Exeter – Pick up Route B3212 on the western outskirts of the city, leading into the heart of Dartmoor National Park. The magic of the wild and rugged moors has fascinated English authors, their readers, and travelers for centuries. The bleak windswept hills, capped by high outcroppings of granite called tors, and coarse wild grasses are the home of wild ponies, grazing sheep, literary pilgrims, and even tales of the "hounds of hell," adapted from older legends of the "beast from below" left over from pre-Roman druidic cults. Ruins of ancient religious sites and bits of Roman construction are scattered about the 300-square-mile area punctuated by tors that reach as high as 2,000 feet. The peaceful air and quietude of the moors make them ideal for an afternoon's tramp or horseback ride, but remember Sherlock Holmes's admonition to Sir Henry Baskerville: "Don't go out upon the moors at night!" Even if the hounds of hell don't get you, the moors are interspersed with spots of soggy marsh and dotted with tiny lakes, and more than one wanderer has been lost here. Also, be wary when setting off on daytime hikes; take along a compass, map, some food, and extra clothing, since Dartmoor can quickly become enshrouded in mist and cold even in summer.

The *Warren House Inn* (near Postbridge; phone: 822-88208), about 18 miles from Exeter, once quenched the thirsts of tin miners walking home across the moor. The structure dates from the early 18th century but has since been rebuilt. (Locals claim the fire in the hearth has been burning continuously since 1845.) Pause for a bracing Scottish & Newcastle ale before continuing to the intriguing early granite bridge that leads toward Dartmoor Prison (closed to the public). Princetown, the highest town in England and administrative headquarters for the dark-walled prison, is only 6 miles beyond the bridge. The prison was established for captured French soldiers in 1809 and was used for American prisoners during the War of 1812. The facility began over a century of service as the Dartmoor Convict Prison in 1850, although sections were destroyed by fire during an insurrection in 1932.

Continue southwest on Route B3212 about 5 miles to Yelverton, and take A386 the remaining 8 miles into Plymouth.

PLYMOUTH: A principal English seaport for over 500 years, Plymouth dominates the mouths of the Plym and Tamar rivers at Plymouth Sound. This natural harbor, protected by rocky headlands on either side, has been an important military installation since it was fortified during the early 1400s, and many of the famous English privateers used Plymouth as their base for shipping raids. It was here that the outnumbered English fleet awaited the Spanish Armada in 1588.

English naval legends say that Sir Francis Drake was in the middle of a game of bowls on Plymouth Hoe when the Armada was sighted — and calmly finished his game before the battle. A statue of Drake and several other memorials stand on the Hoe's green lawns today, on the southeastern point of the waterfront near the Citadel. The Citadel, part of the fortifications erected under Charles II in the 1660s, currently is used by the British military. Also on the Hoe is the *Plymouth Dome Heritage Centre* featuring audiovisual displays that bring Plymouth's exciting history to life (open daily; admission charge; phone: 752-600608 or 752-603300).

The *Mayflower* colonists set sail from Plymouth's pier at the Mayflower Steps, on the west side of the point near Sutton Pool. Near Barbican Quay, at the foot of Lambhay Street, is the ruin of a gatehouse, part of a 14th-century castle. Large sections of this historic city were damaged by bombs in World War II, but the Barbican area survived in its Elizabethan purity. It is now a lively area full of antiques shops, art galleries, restaurants, and pubs, and the narrow cobblestone streets are overhung by the timber frames of merchant homes. Note the Elizabethan House on New Street, beautifully furnished with 16th-century pieces, and the Merchant House (also on New St.), with its social history exhibition (both open Tuesdays through Saturdays, and Sunday afternoons with an admission charge; phone: 752-264878 for both). Other parts of Plymouth have been extensively rebuilt, and, together with the adjoining communities, have grown into a single maritime center. The Royal Dockyards, established by William of Orange at Devonport, a mile west of Plymouth, contributed heavily to this effect. Entrance to the dockyards is restricted.

The Plymouth Tourist Office is at the Civic Centre on Royal Parade (phone: 752-264849).

Just outside Plymouth is Saltram House, an 18th-century mansion with a collection of fine paintings by Sir Joshua Reynolds (open Sundays through Thursdays, April through October; admission charge; off the A374, east of the city; phone: 752-336546). Also visit the Cotehele House, a well-preserved medieval residence with a working mill (open daily, except Fridays, April through October; admission charge; off the A388, northwest of the city; phone: 579-50434).

En Route from Plymouth – The River Tamar marks the boundary between Devon and Cornwall, and Route A38 crosses Plymouth Harbour on the Tamar Suspension Bridge, traveling 30 miles toward the town of Bodmin. Much of the china and raw china clay shipped through the port of Plymouth comes from this area, evidenced by the chalky white piles of mining waste lining the roadways. The route bears north to Liskeard, and then turns west again to Bodmin, skirting the southern fringe of Bodmin Moor. There are some interesting stone formations on this edge of the moor: three odd stone circles known as the Hurlers and a 30-foot mound of granite blocks dubbed "the Cheesewring." If you have some extra time, detour south from Liskeard on B3254 to visit the picturesque fishing ports of Looe, Polperro, and Fowey; then take B3269 into Bodmin.

BODMIN: On the steep western slopes of the rocky tablelands of Bodmin Moor, this agricultural center is a natural touring base for the entire moors area. St. Petroc's Church, rebuilt during the 15th century, is the largest medieval church in Cornwall, and the nearby waters of St. Guron's Well are reputed to have brought about miraculous cures for eye troubles and blindness. If you'd like the mud in your eye to be a little stronger, make your way to the *Hole in the Wall* (Crockwell St.; phone: 208-72397) — through a hole in the wall! The building may have been a debtors' prison during the 18th century. In addition to the stoneworks found in the southern area on the approach to Bodmin and the Roman ruins scattered about, Dozmary Pool (off A30 in the northeast sector) is deep with legends. In the legend of King Arthur, the sword Excalibur was cast into the lake, where it was caught by a single arm extended from beneath the surface. Cornish legends also tell of Jan Tregeagle, who was condemned for his sins to the task of emptying the pool with a leaky shell. Perhaps Tregeagle has escaped his doom, because these days the waters are not deep, and periods of drought dry the lake. The grouping of houses that surround the turnoff to Dozmary Pool is the village of Bolventor, the pirate rendezvous in Daphne du Maurier's *Jamaica Inn.*

Arrange to have tea in *Lanhydrock House,* an impressive estate of woods and gardens covering over 400 acres, about 2½ miles south of Bodmin on Route B3269. Both the gatehouse and the portrait gallery in the north wing are remnants of the original 17th-century construction; other sections of the house were rebuilt in 1881. The elaborate plaster ceiling of the gallery depicts scenes from the Old Testament. Open daily, except Mondays, *Easter* through October; the gardens are open year-round. Admission charge (phone: 208-73320).

En Route from Bodmin – Take Route A30, then A391 south 12 miles through Cornwall to St. Austell, an attractive industrial center bounded by both stark moorlands and sandy beaches. Just outside town are the Medacuddle Holy Well and an ancient stone formation called the Stone Chair.

It is 14 miles farther on A390, then A39, to the market town of Truro, the administrative center of Cornwall, officially established in 1877. The Georgian edifices along Truro's Lemon and Prince's Streets and Trafalgar Row attest to the town's earlier prosperity. Small wonder that when the See of Cornwall was reestablished in 1876, the city was chosen for the first cathedral to be erected since the Reformation. Its bold early Gothic design, added to the site of a 16th-century church, was completed shortly before World War I.

Route A39 leads southabout 11 miles from town to the intersection with A394. A short side trip from here along A39 descends to the port of Falmouth and Pendennis Castle. It's only 13 miles west, from the intersection to Helston, at the base of the broad promontory called the Lizard, via A394. Every year in early May, Helston's residents dance through the town's streets in their traditional *Flora* or *Furry* celebration. Popular legends say that this is related to the death of a dragon that dropped a huge rock on the town, but a more likely hypothesis is that it is the remnant of druidic spring fertility rites.

THE LIZARD: This broad peninsula, varying from 200 to 400 feet above sea level, is the place to go for dramatic views of England's rugged southernmost shore. On the west side of the Lizard is Mullion Cove, where many caves cut into the cliffsides are exposed during low tide — a find for spelunkers and treasure seekers. The colorful cliffs of Kynance Cove lie farther south along the western shore. Lizardtown itself is less than a mile from the lighthouse that marks the southernmost spot in England, Lizard Point; the lighthouse is open to the public from 11 AM to 6 PM (admission charge). On the eastern shore (off B3293) is the port of Coverack, once a base for smugglers. It is partially protected by the Manacles Rocks, an offshore hazard that has wrecked many a ship.

Penzance, the principal town of the western peninsula known as Land's End, is 13 miles west of Helston on A394.

PENZANCE: The fishing and seaport center of England's southwestern extremity, Penzance is well sheltered within Mount's Bay, which splits the tip of Cornwall into the Lizard and Land's End peninsulas. The mild climate here has attracted travelers for centuries, and the city has become a popular resort and shopping center. In bygone days, the town was often sacked by pirates, and it was virtually destroyed by Spanish raiders in 1595. The 1836 Market House (Market Jew St.), now a bank, is worth seeing, but a far greater rarity in England are the subtropical plants and flowers in Morrab Gardens; only the exceptionally warm climate of this distant area allows these plants to survive in Britain (open daily; no admission charge; no phone).

Frequent departures from the port by both boat and helicopter shuttle visitors to the Isles of Scilly (pronounced *Silly*), an archipelago of over 150 islands and rocky outcroppings about 30 miles southwest of Land's End, near where the Atlantic meets the English Channel. Only five islands are large enough to support populations, but there are several interesting forts and religious sites spread throughout the chain. On St. Mary's there's Star Castle, erected in 1593. Other attractions on the island include the *Longshore Heritage Centre,* a history museum covering shipwrecks and British newspapers; Bants Carn, a Bronze Age village and burial chamber; and the *Isle of Scilly Museum* (all open daily, *Easter* through October; admission charge for each; phone: 720-22536). Tresco Abbey on Tresco Island has lovely gardens (open daily), with between 3,000 and 4,000 varieties of plants, and the gardens' *Valhalla* is an outdoor collection of ships' figureheads (admission charge covers all; phone: 720-22849). St. Helen's has two ancient ruins: a church and a monastery; and there are numerous other structures on the islands. Legends are the only firm evidence that these islands are the mountaintops of the lands of King Arthur, Lyonnesse, although some of the earlier fortifications could be from that semi-mythical period.

One of the most spectacular visions in all of England is St. Michael's Mount, standing majestically about one-quarter mile off the sandy shore of Marazion, a tiny market town 3 miles east of Penzance. In 495, fishermen claimed to have seen a vision of St. Michael appear on the 200-foot mountain that rises from the calm waters of Mount's Bay. In the 11th century the grounds were used for a priory. The castle (open weekdays and many weekends for charity, April through October; Mondays, Wednesdays, and Fridays, November through March) can be reached by a causeway during low tide or by ferry from either Penzance or Marazion at highwater periods. Note that in winter, ferry service is irregular, and visits are by guided tour only. Admission charge for castle and boat (phone: 736-710507).

En Route from Penzance – A generous coastal esplanade leads south to the picturesque fishing villages of Newlyn (1 mile) and Mousehole (pronounced *Mowzal;* 3 miles), sheltered in the lee of Mount's Bay — perfect material for a beautiful morning's walk. In Mevagissey, 5 miles outside of St. Austell, be sure to stop at the *Ship Inn* (Fore St.; phone: 726-843324) for a taste of a local beer, and prevail upon the publican to tell you the story of fisherman Tom Bowcock. Save your evenings for viewing the sunsets from the western tip of Land's End — they're incredible!

About 10 miles southwest of Penzance (via either B3315 or an extension of the esplanade, the cliff path) are the sandy beaches of Porthcurno, the cultural hub of Land's End. Here, on a cliff west of the village, is the open-air *Minack Theatre,* which uses its vast panorama of the Atlantic for a backdrop and presents anything from *Macbeth* to, naturally, Gilbert and Sullivan's *Pirates of Penzence* (open late May to mid-September; phone: 736-810694). On the village's east boundary is Logan's Rock, a delicately balanced 65-ton granite boulder that can easily be rocked in place — however, local custom insists that if it falls over, you've got to replace it.

LAND'S END: This immense granite ridge extending into the sea is the westernmost point of England. Once called Penwith in Cornish, the area is privately owned, and features a popular Lost Labyrinth Exhibition, children's playground, and video displays (open daily; admission charge; phone: 736-871501). Slip out onto the point just before dawn or, even better, at dusk for fantastic views of the sun. The Isles of Scilly are easily visible on a clear day, and lighthouses illuminate the most treacherous rocks after dark. Afterward, stop at the *Old Success Inn* overlooking Sennen Cove before heading on.

Inland (from the villages of Zennor, Morvah, and St. Just — all on the B3306 north) are several Stone Age quoits, or dolmens — burial chambers formed by laying a top, or capstone, across stone uprights. Chysauster is the site of an Iron Age village of huts used by Roman and British miners until about AD 100.

The resort of St. Ives, on the north coast of the peninsula, is only 7 miles northeast of Penzance. Here the narrow cobblestone streets are lined with the cottages of fishermen. The town, long popular with artists, swells with summertime painters each year. You'll find St. Austell lager in pubs throughout town, as well as national brews.

En Route from Land's End – Traveling northeast from Penzance, Route A30 runs parallel to the coast, gradually bearing inland toward the village of Fraddon, 35 miles away. All of the small roads to the left (north) of the highway lead to the coast, and many run along the shoreline before returning to A30. The region is edged with tiny coves and long strands of beach, which can stretch to 4 or 5 miles during low tide. At Fraddon, the *Blue Anchor* (Draycott Ter.; phone: 726-860352) deserves a pause for a beer before taking A39 through the attractive countryside of the Vale of Mawgan to Camelford, a trek of some 23 miles. Then follow B3266 a mile north to B3263, which brings you into Tintagel.

TINTAGEL: Along the craggy slate cliffs of the western Cornish coastline are the ruins of one of the most famous castles in England, Tintagel Castle, which legend says is the birthplace of King Arthur, born to Uther Pendragon and his queen, Igerne (closed Mondays during winter; admission charge; phone: 840-770328). The castle sits on a headland of slate, called Tintagel Head, high above the Atlantic cove. The ancient village of Tintagel (now quite touristy), at one time known as Trevena, is on the mainland less than a mile away. The cave in which Merlin is said to have woven his spells (and perhaps to have been sealed) is at the foot of the castle's steep cliffs, accessible only at low tide. The castle was built in the 12th century on the ruins of an earlier Celtic monastery. The mainland fortifications were added during the following century to protect the natural rock bridge that once served as the castle entranceway; it has since collapsed and a new bridge built. The 14th-century thatch cottage, which now serves as Tintagel's post office, is also worth seeing.

En Route from Tintagel – Continuing east on Route B3263 returns you to A39 headed north and east to Bude, an attractive resort about 14 miles up the coast.

Bude's sandy beaches, though lightly laced with rocky headlands, are famous for both swimming and surfing, and the festive atmosphere of this summer resort has also spawned a golf course and tennis courts.

Route A39 makes it way north about 30 miles from Bude to the huge bay (known both as Bideford and Barnstaple Bay) formed at the mouth of the River Taw. The beautiful fishing village of Clovelly, deeply set in a cleft face of the cliffs that line the western curve of the bay, has been fairly inundated by artists and travelers. At one time Bideford, perched on the hills that overlook the mouth of the Torridge River on the west side of the bay, was one of England's busiest seaports, frequented by Sir Walter Raleigh, Sir Francis Drake, and Martin Frobisher. Many fine homes, built by wealthy merchants in the 17th century, still line the town's main street, Bridgeland Street. The town Westward Ho! was named for Charles Kingsley's 1855 novel (3 miles northwest of Bideford); but, in fact, parts of the book were actually written in Bideford (it's the "little white town" in the book) at the *Royal* hotel. Take a moment to examine the 24-arch bridge in the center of town — it was built in 1460 (and altered slightly in the 1920s). Barnstaple, although no longer the bustling seaport that thrived for 1,000 years, is still a busy market town for the surrounding area. Relieved of the pressures of constant growth, Barnstaple has become a delightful town to visit and a pleasant base for touring the north coast and Exmoor. The *Three Tuns* (High St.; phone: 271-71308), more than 500 years old, is an excellent place for meeting people. The downstairs attracts younger drinkers; the upstairs bar tends to be a bit quieter and conservative.

EXMOOR: The twin resorts of Lynton and Lynmouth, both within the boundary of Exmoor National Park, lie another 20 miles northeast along A39. Approaching from the lower coastal area of Barnstaple, the rising granite and slate hills of Exmoor are a grand sight. Lynton is the higher of the two resorts, on a cliff almost 500 feet above the sea; Lynmouth lies at the water's edge, where the East and West Lyn rivers join the sea. Coastal walking paths lead both east and west through beautifully wooded rocky high ridges and combes. Inland, the moor's gentle ridges create a maze of valleys and vales.

The Doone Valley, setting for Richard Blackmore's novel *Lorna Doone,* is about 4 miles south (inland) from the resort areas. The story is in part an amalgamation of tales about the outlaw band that terrorized the moor for several decades during the 17th century, and Blackmore drew heavily upon both factual events and local legends as well as places in his work.

Route B3223 leads inland from the resorts, through the very heart of Exmoor. Simonsbath (9 miles southeast of Lynmouth) lies just a few miles from the head of the Doone Valley. Time has almost obliterated the ruins at this end of the valley, which are thought to have been occupied by the outlaw band. Route B3223 joins B3224 east of Simonsbath and continues to the hunting and fishing center of Exford. Here the staghounds that track Exmoor's famed wild red deer are kenneled, and anglers by the score test their skills against elusive trout. Check with the proprietor of the *Crown* hotel (Sinai Hill; phone: 598-52253) about obtaining a horse for an afternoon ride through the moors, then head off about 4 miles northeast to Dunkery Beacon. The beacon is the highest point on the moor, 1,705 feet, and the view extends almost 100 miles in good weather. A healthy trek of about 4 miles north across the moors returns you to near the coast at Porlock. This village lies right on A39, about 6 miles east of Lynmouth, and somewhere in the intervening stretch may well be the cottage "twixt Porlock and Lynton" where Samuel Taylor Coleridge had the opium vision that resulted in "Kubla Khan." Some sources claim, however, that the vision occurred in his home at Nether Stowey, about 35 miles east of Lynton on A39.

BEST EN ROUTE

Southwest England is amply provided with small inns and historic accommodations, and the traveler so inclined can spend just about every night holed up with the ghosts of his or her choice, though in most cases the accommodations are not going to be modern or splashy. On the other hand, in the major resort areas, every kind of guesthouse, hotel, motel, and rental is available, though reservations are advisable in summer. Expect to pay $240 (or more) a night for a double in the hotels listed as very expensive; from $180 to $230 in the expensive range; $100 to $175 in the moderate range; and under $95 in the inexpensive category. You will find good food at reasonable prices in most places, but for a really excellent dinner for two with wine, expect to pay about $75-$90, considered moderate.

AMESBURY

Antrobus Arms – This former vicarage has combined modern comfort with its antique style quite nicely. The hostelry's features include both log fires and central heating, plus a walled garden with a fountain and Cedar of Lebanon tree. Church St. (phone: 980-623163). Moderate.

SALISBURY

White Hart – A blend of Georgian and modern styles heightens the delightful atmosphere of this well-aged hostelry. Three bars to fit your moods, traditional English fare, and a warming fire on chilly days complete this comfortable nest. St. John St. (phone: 722-27476; fax: 722-412761). Expensive.

Rose and Crown – On the banks of the Avon, this hotel is a happy amalgam of ancient inn and contemporary hostelry. There are four-poster beds in the half-timbered old inn and comfortable modern rooms in the annex. Harnham Rd. (phone: 722-27908). Moderate.

EXETER

Royal Clarence – This historic building with 63 rooms overlooks the cathedral in the city center. Cathedral Yard (phone: 392-58464; fax: 392-439423). Expensive.

Buckerell Lodge Crest – When built in the 13th century, this building served as a hunting lodge. Now it has 54 rooms and wonderful views. Topsham Rd. (phone: 392-52451; fax: 392-412114). Moderate.

PENZANCE

Lamorna Cove – Although the modern additions can't compare with the original granite house or its lovely setting above a tranquil wooded cove, the hotel is a delight. Lots of tasty seafood is served in its restaurant. Lamorna, 5 miles from Penzance (phone: 736-731411). Expensive.

Lesceave Cliff – White walls and Mediterranean arches, combined with beach views, belie this hotel's location in England. The staff is exceptionally helpful, and can arrange fishing trips. Praa Sands, 7 miles from Penzance (phone: 736-762325). Moderate.

ISLES OF SCILLY

Island – On a wonderfully quiet island (no cars!), this place combines old and new architectural styles into a beautiful beach resort. The hotel also has a good restaurant, and arranges fishing charters; sailboats are available too. Closed early October to mid-March. Tresco (phone: 720-22883). Very expensive.

St. Martin's – Opened in 1989, this is the only hotel on the island of St. Martin's (it has just 60 permanent residents). The cottage-style property has 24 individually designed rooms, and the setting in the cove by the sea is superb. There's an indoor pool and subtropical gardens. St. Martin's, Isles of Scilly (phone: 720-22092; fax: 720-22298). Expensive.

ST. IVES

Garrack – Set on a hill above St. Ives, this eccentric, family-run hostelry provides a totally British experience. The cheerful hospitality makes guests feel they're visiting a real home. There are log fires and an indoor pool. The restaurant serves lobsters fresh from a tank. Burthallan La. (phone: 736-798955). Expensive.

Tregenna Castle – Perched above the old fishing village, this 18th-century home certainly offers the grandest view of the bay available. It is something of a resort, with tennis, golf (18 holes), squash courts, a pool, and more. St. Ives (phone: 736-795244). Expensive.

BARNSTAPLE

Imperial – In the center of Barnstaple's charming waterfront, the older parts of this hotel are quite beautiful. Taw Vale Parade (phone: 271-45861). Moderate.

Wales

Like all mountainous countries, Wales has been slow to react to outside change. In part this has been due to poor communications; the roads here rise and fall sharply, twisting and turning around the mountainsides, making contact with the outside world rather difficult. In part, however, it has been due to the character of the Welsh people, who, throughout 5 centuries of Roman occupation, brutal conquest by the Normans, and 700 years of uninterrupted English rule, have managed to hold on to a unique culture, age-old customs, and their own ancient, sonorous language (it is estimated that about one quarter of the population still speaks Welsh). Although technically and for all practical purposes a British principality whose 2.5 million people are governed from Westminster, Wales has retained a distinct identity and an aura of legend and mystery even in the eyes of its English neighbors.

While the scenery here is always marked by its grandeur, it is more diverse than one might imagine. Occupying an 8,000-square-mile landmass that juts west from England into the Irish Sea, Wales is divided informally into three areas — South, Mid, and North Wales — each possessing distinctive topography and points of interest. The route described below covers all three, beginning in the South, at the bustling capital of Cardiff, and threading its way some 275 miles north, first through the grassy mountains and wild moorlands of Brecon Beacons National Park, then west toward the coast. After visiting some of the loveliest seaside resorts and coastal villages of Mid Wales, the route enters the rugged mountain country of the North, passing through the towering beauty of Snowdonia National Park, in the northwest corner of the country. Snowdonia's range is capped by the 3,560-foot peak of Snowdon itself, the highest point in Wales, the summit of which can be reached on the *Snowdon Mountain Railway* from Llanberis (mid-March through October; phone: 286-870223). This rack-and-pinion line is one of many still powered by steam engines, all of which operate on extremely narrow-gauge track using small locomotives and carriages, known locally as "the great little trains of Wales."

Wales is renowned for its castles, huge, warlike bastions, many of which were built by Edward I in the 13th century to demonstrate the supremacy of the English Crown over the Welsh. Some of the greatest of these fortresses are along our route in North and South Wales, where they stand, often overlooking the sea, as impressive reminders of the country's turbulent past.

The Wales Tourist Board puts out three excellent publications covering North, South, and Mid Wales. In addition to extensive gazetteers and a regional map, each gives details on activities, nature trails, good beaches, and so forth. For more information, contact the tourist board at Brunel House, 2 Fitzalan Rd., Cardiff CF2 1UY, Wales (phone: 222-499909).

CARDIFF: Connected to London and the rest of the outside world by the M4 motorway, high-speed train service, and its own small airport, Cardiff, formerly one of Britain's most important seaports, is an ideal starting point for a tour of Wales. With a population of 300,000, it is the capital and largest city in Wales. Spacious and dignified, the city is also thoroughly cosmopolitan, with large, covered shopping arcades and excellent sports facilities, including that holiest of places for rugby fans, Cardiff Arms Park, the national rugby stadium.

Among the city's chief attractions for visitors are its castle and the *National Museum of Wales,* both near the center of town. Cardiff Castle (open daily; no admission charge; phone: 222-31033) was begun by the Normans in the 11th century on the site of an old Roman camp. A thin layer of brown stone can still be seen running through the castle's surrounding wall, marking the spot where the Roman defenses left off and, centuries later, the Norman work began. The original castle keep stands on a small, moated mound, an example of the Norman motte and bailey. Expanded over the years, the castle was reconstructed in 1865 by the third Marquis of Bute, a young man with a passion for architectural fantasy. Although the ornate Victorian exterior is not to everyone's liking, the castle's interior, with its lavish reproduction of medieval decorations and rich historical murals, is fascinating. The *National Museum of Wales* (open daily; no admission charge; Cathays Park; phone: 222-562400) displays interesting Welsh archaeological finds, handicrafts, and folk art and is especially noted for its collection of French Impressionist paintings, the centerpiece of which is Renoir's *La Parisienne.* The Cardiff Tourist Information Office is at 8-14 Bridge St. (phone: 222-227281).

Two miles from the city center, on the banks of the River Taff, is the village-like suburb of Llandaff, home of the 12th-century Llandaff Cathedral, with its striking modern sculpture, *Christ in Majesty,* by Jacob Epstein.

Five miles west of Cardiff at the village of St. Fagans is the *Welsh Folk Museum* (open daily April through October, otherwise closed Sundays; admission charge; phone: 222-569441). This open-air museum is in a woods and garden. Many old houses, mills, farms, and a chapel have been moved from all over Wales and rebuilt on the site to illustrate early Welsh life. Caerphilly, with its 13th-century castle, is 6 miles north on A469. The castle is the second-largest in Britain (open daily; admission charge; phone: 222-883143). A fine white cheese is named after the town, where it is still made by traditional methods at the *Court House* (phone: 222-888120), now a pub and restaurant.

En Route from Cardiff – Route A470 takes you through Tongwynlais, home of the Victorian extravaganza Castell Coch, another fairy-tale edifice built by the young Marquis of Bute. From the outside this castle looks like an ornate French château, and its interior is lavishly fitted. Open daily. Admission charge (phone: 222-810101).

BRECON: The major center for touring the 519 square miles of Brecon Beacons National Park, Brecon sits at the junction of the rivers Usk and Afon Honddu. It has a massive 13th- and 14th-century fortified priory that stands high above the Afon Honddu on Priory Hill. The town's castle, in the garden of the *Castle of Brecon* hotel (see *Best en Route*), was dismantled by the townsfolk during the 17th-century civil war in an attempt to avoid the bloodshed necessary to defend it.

The *Brecknock Museum,* in the old County Hall in Glamorgan Street, displays interesting examples of Welsh folk art and local crafts, such as the hand-carved wooden "love spoons" young Welshmen used in bygone days to plight their troth (closed Sundays; admission charge; phone: 874-4121). Just west of the town is the Mountain Centre of Brecon Beacons National Park (phone: 874-3366). The center, located out in the wilds, is a friendly, informal place where the park's staff is keen to help in your exploration of the mountains. Use the center as a base for walking, for picnicking, or for just sitting and staring (highly recommended).

En Route from Brecon – Route A40 follows the girth of the Brecon Beacons, three red sandstone peaks, the highest of which looms nearly 3,000 feet high through scenery that is inspiring at any time of year. Often mist rolls downward from the Beacons and the nearby Black Mountains, creating an atmosphere of eerie solitude.

Anglers may want to stop at Llandovery, an important market town well known in the area for its excellent salmon fishing.

CARMARTHEN: Carmarthen is the administrative hub of the southwestern corner of Wales. Its large covered market draws crowds every Wednesday and Saturday, and behind it the cattle market holds sales each Monday, Wednesday, and Thursday.

In Nott Square stands a monument to Dr. Robert Ferrar, Bishop of St. David's, who was burned at the stake on this site in 1555. Also of interest is the *Carmarthen Museum,* in the former Bishop's Palace at Abergwili on the outskirts of the town (closed Sundays; admission charge; phone: 267-231691).

En Route from Carmarthen – Fans of the poet Dylan Thomas may want to divert onto A4066 at the village of St. Clears for a side trip to Laugharne, where Thomas lived and wrote and where he lies buried in a simple grave in the village churchyard. The Boathouse was the poet's residence (open daily to the public from *Easter* to October; admission charge; phone: 994-427420). Otherwise, take the A477 to Tenby.

TENBY: This ancient walled town stands on a rocky peninsula at the western edge of Carmarthen Bay. With two sandy beaches and a pretty harbor, it makes a delightful base for touring the Pembrokeshire coast. Some 2½ miles offshore is Caldey Island, the home of an ancient but still functioning monastery where Cistercian monks make perfume from the island's flowers.

There are many good hotels within the town's 14th-century walls, including the *Imperial* (see *Best en Route*), which actually incorporates parts of the walls in its structure. Local events include golf tournaments (*Tenby Golf Club*'s 18-hole course is at South Beach; phone: 834-2787), *St. Margaret's Fair* (with an amusement park and open-air stalls selling a variety of goods), and a lively regatta and carnival, all of which occur in August.

Local pottery and paintings are for sale in the many art shops of Upper Frog Street.

CARDIGAN: Another market town also popular with visitors, Cardigan (north of Tenby via the A478) has a number of cafés and restaurants and a good number of accommodations, mainly in small guesthouses. Its chief attraction is salmon fishing. There are good catches to be had on the Afon Teifi, which flows from here into

Cardigan Bay. Some fishermen still use coracles — homemade boats of intertwined willow and hazel that look rather like wicker shopping baskets; they have been used for salmon fishing for over a thousand years. Coracle races are held at the Teifiside village of Cilgerran in August.

Three-quarters of a mile away, across Cardigan Bridge, is St. Dogmael's, an old Welsh house that was sacked by the Norse and later claimed by the Normans, who turned it into an annex of the Abbey of Tiron in France. The church contains the ancient Sagranus Stone, whose inscriptions in Latin and old Gaelic served as a key to the language of the tribes of the Dark Ages.

En Route from Cardigan – Head north on Route A487 for the 39-mile drive along the coastline to Aberystwyth (pronounced *Aber-ist-with*).

From this road you can reach many of the small coastal villages, including New Quay, which some say is the setting of Dylan Thomas's play *Under Milk Wood* (others claim it's Fishguard). You pass through the popular yachting center of Aberaeron, a 19th-century Georgian town, many of whose buildings are of special architectural or historic interest.

ABERYSTWYTH: A popular seaside resort with both sand and pebble bathing beaches, Aberystwyth is also the seat of the University of Wales and the administrative center for Cardigan Bay. Its lively seafront promenade (now a bit touristy) is lined with hotels and has a pier, bandstand, and the ruins of a castle, which stand sentinel on the headland.

History is carefully preserved at the National Library of Wales, which houses some of the earliest Welsh manuscripts (closed Sundays, bank holidays, and the first week in October; no admission charge; Penglais Hall; phone: 970-623816); and the past is still very much alive at Alexandra Station, where the *Brecon Mountain Railway's* last steam-powered service departs for the spectacular falls at Devil's Bridge, high in the Vale of Rheidol, which according to legend was built by the devil himself (railway open *Easter* through October; phone: 685-4854). Closer to home, the town's cliff railway carries visitors to the peak of Constitution Hill, where they have a splendid view of the bay and the town from the Camera Obscura, the world's largest lens. Local folk history is recorded in the *Ceredigion Museum* in the *Edwardian Coliseum Theatre* (open daily; admission charge; phone: 970-617911).

Concerts and evening shows are regular summer features along the promenade, and at the *Arts Centre* on the university campus. The *Arts Centre* also holds frequent exhibitions, and the *University Theatre* presents a summer season of plays (box office phone for both: 970-623232).

En Route from Aberystwyth – Route A487 skirts the base of the mountains, heading up into the Dovey Valley to Machynlleth, a market town that was made capital of Wales by Owain Glyndwr in the 14th century, during the great Welsh hero's drive to rid the country of English rule. As you drive through town, you pass an immense clock tower, standing like a rocket ready for launching, a gift from the Marquess of Londonderry in 1873. Plas Machynlleth, also in the town, was formerly the Londonderry residence and now houses the local Council.

DOLGELLAU: At the head of the lovely Mawddach Estuary and almost at the foot of the famous Cader Idris Mountain, scenic Dolgellau is an important market town for the many small mountain villages in the vicinity. It makes an ideal base for walks and excursions into the lake and mountain country to the east.

The customs and speech here remain distinctly Welsh, but thanks to its large number of visitors, you should have no trouble being understood. The town itself is quite old and is built largely of the native gray stone. Its bridge, crossing the Afon Wnion, was built in 1638 and is now an officially protected structure. Close to the primary school is an old tollhouse left from the days of turnpikes.

In the Mawddach Valley close to the town you can try your luck panning for gold;

gold has been excavated in the surrounding mountains since Roman times, and it is this Welsh gold that was used in some royal family wedding rings, including those of Queen Elizabeth II and the Princess of Wales, in 1981.

HARLECH: Still a small village, Harlech is dominated by its immense gray stone castle, another of the chain of fortifications ordered by Edward I. It was this massive stronghold, the last to yield to the Yorkists in 1468, that provided the inspiration for "Men of Harlech," one of the best-known traditional Welsh songs. Standing high on a rocky promontory, Harlech Castle offers extensive views of land, sea, and mountains (open daily; admission charge; phone: 766-780552). Those with no fear of heights can walk all around the castle on its unfenced, 10-foot-thick walls and climb the 143 steps to the top of its gatehouse. Look toward the sea, half a mile away, and recall that when the castle was built in 1283 it actually stood on the shore. Since that time, however, the sea has receded.

En Route from Harlech – The private village of Portmeirion, near Penrhyn-deudraeth, was built by architect Sir Clough Williams-Ellis, who died in 1978. Portmeirion (with its beautiful hotel; see *Best en Route*) is a strange, pastel dream world built in an Italianate style (admission charge to the village).

CAERNARFON: Still mostly enclosed in its 13th-century town walls, Caernarfon is perhaps the best-known Welsh town since the 1969 investiture of Prince Charles as Prince of Wales in its beautiful castle. The castle stands defiantly at the junction of the River Seiont and the Menai Strait, overlooking the Isle of Anglesey. Begun, like Harlech Castle, in 1283, it took 37 years to build, and today it is regarded as a masterpiece of medieval architecture. Inside is the Prince of Wales' Exhibition, along with the *Museum of the Royal Welsh Fusiliers,* complete with an audiovisual presentation on the town's heritage. Open daily. Admission charge (phone: 286-3094).

In addition to being a market center (on Saturdays in Castle Square), Caernarfon also boasts two yacht clubs, tennis, golf, and bowls facilities, and good river and sea fishing. In Castle Square is a statue of Prime Minister David Lloyd George, who was instrumental in securing a future for Caernarfon Castle: He spent his boyhood in the village of Llanystumdwy, near Criccieth. The Caernarfon Tourist Office (in the Oriel Pendeitsh building; phone: 286-672232) offers information on the *Maritime Museum* (admission charge) and the trawler located alongside Victoria Dock.

Near the town is the Roman fort of Segontium, a military center founded in AD 78. A museum here displays the area's archeological finds. The town of Llanberis, 8 miles southeast of Caernarfon is the base station for the *Snowdon Mountain Railway* (April–September). Or follow the spectacular Llanberis Pass, a winding road flanked by steeply rising mountains and the debris of rock slides, to the village of Beddgelert. From the top of the pass, known locally as Pen-y-Pass, you can walk up to the summit of Snowdon.

BEST EN ROUTE

During the peak summer months, a few of the famous *Eisteddfodau* — festivals of music and poetry — are held in towns and villages throughout Wales. If your trip will coincide with any of these, make sure you book hotel reservations well in advance. Note, too, that drinking laws can be idiosyncratic in Gwynedd, in the northwest, where you cannot drink alcoholic beverages on Sundays except as a guest in a hotel. Under the Taste of Wales scheme inaugurated by the Wales Tourist Board, hotels and restaurants are being encouraged to serve traditional Welsh fare. Look for the round Taste of Wales sign, indicating a participating establishment. In the listing below, any establishment charging under $80 per night for a room for two persons is considered inexpensive; $85 to $110, moderate; $115 to $145, expensive; and more than $150, very expensive; prices are slightly higher in Cardiff. You will find good food at reasonable prices in most places, but for a really excellent dinner for two with wine, expect to pay about $65, considered moderate.

CARDIFF

Angel – Right near Cardiff Castle, this is the best hostelry in town, with a palatial style, especially in the main restaurant. There are 250 rooms (phone: 222-232633; fax: 222-396212). Expensive.

Park – A beautifully appointed 108-room hotel combining the traditional air of a country house with the luxury and comfort of a modern hotel. Two good restaurants. Park Pl., in the center of town (phone: 222-383471; fax: 222-399309). Expensive.

Armless Dragon – Bright and cheery, this eatery combines European and Asian dishes, such as shark curry, laverbread balls, wild rabbit, and rack of Welsh lamb. Closed Saturday lunch and Sundays. Reservations essential. Major credit cards accepted. 97 Wyverne Rd., Cathays (phone: 222-382357). Moderate.

Blas ar Gymru – This cozy eatery, whose name means "Taste of Wales," serves up generous helpings of good, wholesome, traditional Welsh dishes like cawl (a thick vegetable, leek, and lamb soup) and gower cockle and bacon pie, all washed down with local wine or mead. Closed weekends for lunch and Sunday dinner. Reservations advised. Major credit cards accepted. 48 Crwys Rd. (phone: 222-382132). Moderate.

New Harvesters – Be sure to bring a robust appetite — the food here is British with a Welsh flavor, that is, hearty but rather plain. Try the homemade soup and the delicious casserole. Open Tuesdays through Saturdays for dinner, Sundays for lunch. Reservations advised. Major credit cards accepted. 5 Potcanna St. (phone: 222-232616). Moderate.

BRECON

Castle of Brecon – Pleasant surroundings attached to an old castle overlooking the River Usk. Good restaurant. Castle Sq. (phone: 874-4611; fax: 874-3737). Expensive.

Lansdowne – This simple but comfortable Georgian hotel has 12 bedrooms, most with bath, and a restaurant. 39 The Watton, Brecon (phone: 874-3321). Inexpensive.

CARMARTHEN

Ivy Bush Royal – Thoroughly streamlined, this historic 80-room hotel offers saunas, a choice of cocktail lounges, and a good restaurant with Welsh cuisine. Spilman St. (phone: 267-235111; fax: 267-234914). Expensive.

TENBY

Imperial – Immediately above the beach, with fabulous views of St. Catherine's and Caldey islands from most of the rooms. The hotel's terrace incorporates part of the medieval town walls. Two restaurants offer traditional British and French fare. There also are dinner dances. The Paragon (phone: 834-3737; fax: 834-4342). Moderate.

Royal Lion – Overlooking Tenby Harbour, this modernized 17th-century coaching inn has 36 rooms, 22 with bath. Basically a family hotel, open April through September, with a residents' dining room and a seafood restaurant. High St. (phone: 834-2127). Inexpensive.

ABERYSTWYTH

Belle Vue Royal – A comfortable hotel overlooking Cardigan Bay, with a restaurant and 42 rooms; there's also complimentary golf for residents on weekdays on an 18-hole golf course nearby. Marine Ter. (phone: 970-617558; fax: 970-612190). Inexpensive.

DOLGELLAU

George III – This 300-year-old hotel with a restaurant is delightfully situated at the head of the Mawddach estuary. Freshly caught fish is the dining room's specialty in summer, and in winter, the menu turns to local game. Most of the 13 rooms have views of the estuary and the mountains. Just out of town on the A493 in Penmaenpool (phone: 341-422525; fax: 341-423565). Expensive.

HARLECH

Maes-y-Neuadd – Pronounced *Mice*-er-*Nay*eth," this establishment, run by two families, is one of Wales's most charming country-house hotels. The front bedrooms have the best views, overlooking Snowdon and Tremadog Bay. Expect superbly cooked Welsh specialties from the kitchen: lamb in honey, cider, and rosemary; herrings with apple and sage; and Welsh amber pudding. Closed the first 2 weeks in December. Reservations necessary for non-guests at Sunday lunches. At Talsarnau, 3 miles north of Harlech (phone: 766-780200; fax: 766-780211). Very expensive.

PORTMEIRION

Portmeirion – The site of this magical place overlooks Cardigan Bay, and each of the 14 bedrooms is distinctly decorated. Decor in the main hotel includes hand-embroidered white crewel work from Kashmir for the dining room curtains, and antiquities found in Rajasthan for the main bar. This is ornate Victoriana at its very best, including an outdoor swimming pool and spacious lawns. As close to a fantasy hotel as exists in Wales; perhaps that's why such creative types as Noel Coward, George Bernard Shaw, and Orson Welles spent significant time here. Portmeirion, Gwynedd (phone: 766-770228; fax: 766-771331). Expensive.

CRICCIETH

Bron Eifion – A country-house hotel, conveniently close to Portmeirion and within sight of Cardigan Bay. Lots of Oregon pine paneling, a wood-beam roof, granite walls, and a minstrel's gallery distinguish the interior. Near Criccieth Castle (phone: 766-522385; fax: 766-522003). Expensive.

CAERNARFON

Royal – A historic coaching inn with 58 rooms that's been updated and made very comfortable. Its good dining room specializes in local produce. North Rd. (phone: 286-673184). Moderate.

Black Boy Inn – Within the town's medieval walls, this inn dates from the 14th century. Oak beams and inglenooks abound, and the cooking in its restaurant is simple but good. North Gate St. (phone: 286-673023). Inexpensive.

Chocolate House – Guests stay in the private studio cottages that hug the pleasant courtyard and dine on the house specialty — chocolate desserts. Open year-round. Plas Treflan, Caeathro (phone: 286-672542). Inexpensive.

The Cotswolds

Less than 100 miles west of London is the region known as the Cotswolds. It encompasses about 450 square miles of rolling limestone upland of the Cotswold Hills, punctuated by charming, carefully preserved medieval towns and villages built from the hills' honey-colored stone, which gives the region its character. The Cotswolds themselves stretch northeast in a curving 60-mile arc from Bath to the vicinity of Stratford-upon-Avon. Along their western edge they form a steep ridge of solid limestone, and their crest is the Thames-Severn watershed. But the overall character of the countryside is tranquil and picturesque, like a rich tapestry. Much of this land is a great, sweeping pasture for the famous Cotswold sheep, with their heavy ringlets of fleece that once upon a time brought wealth to the area.

This is the England of the imagination: rolling hills covered by copses of ancient oaks, a landscape scaled to size for country walks and bird watching. Towns are tied to one another by twisting country lanes that carry a constant commerce of farmers and sheepers, postmen, parsons, and pubgoers. The vista from any hill is as likely to include the square tower of a Norman church as a far field of cropping sheep, and any church is likely to be surrounded by the stone tile roofs of a tiny village, now no longer populated by farm workers but by retired folk, weekenders, and commuters to the larger towns. Village cemeteries are shaded by yews and village streams guarded by weeping willows. Nothing is very far from anything else, but privacy and protective isolation are accentuated by the quiet and country peace that settles over all. Although relatively few ancient customs have survived, village names are remnants of an earlier language and a younger England: Wyck Rissington, Upper and Lower Slaughter, Oddington, Guiting Power, Clapton-on-Hill, Bourton-on-the-Water, Chipping Campden.

The Cotswolds provided a rich agricultural center for the Romans until the 5th century, and the Roman presence is still visible in many places, such as the roads in Cirencester and the baths in Bath. The Romans left, the Danes took over, the Saxons routed the Danes, and the Normans routed the Saxons; and they all left their mark. But when the Cotswold sheep began to pay off, it was the wool merchants of the Middle Ages who built the symbols of the area that have endured — magnificent churches like the 15th-century one at Northleach and the 14th-century one at Cirencester.

The route described below begins in Bath, 115 miles west of London, goes north through the heart of the Cotswolds to Stratford, and returns to London by way of Oxford. Starting from London, take the southwesterly Route M3 and the A303 past Stonehenge and swing northwest on A36 to Bath.

An eminently English way to see the Cotswolds is to take to Shanks' mare and walk all or part of the 107-mile Cotswold Way, a series of well-marked and easily negotiated paths that follow the crests of the Cotswold hills from Bath to Chipping Campden in the north. Parts of the Way were first used by travelers 3,000 years ago, and later by medieval traders moving from village to village, the same villages that dot its course today. One need not be an accomplished hiker to follow the Way for a distance, and the weak of spirit can take heart in the thought that village and pub are never far apart. The benefits are multiple: Immersed in the countryside, you have a walking-pace view of the villages, buildings, cottages, churches, Roman ruins, Iron Age hill forts, and barrows — Stone Age burial mounds — that dot the region (the barrow at Belas Knap, between Cheltenham and Winchcombe, is one of the most impressive specimens in England).

The Way is maintained by the Gloucestershire County Council, which marks its course with large yellow arrows to make hiking easier. Thornhill Press publishes an excellent guide, *The Cotswold Way,* by Mark Richards, available throughout the area. A detailed guidebook, *The Way of the Cotswolds,* is available from the Heart of England Tourist Board, Woodside, Larkhill, Worcester, Worcestershire WR5 2EQ, England (phone: 905-763436).

BATH: In the southwest corner of the Cotswolds region, Bath is Britain's oldest and most famous spa, where each day over 250,000 gallons of water from the mineral springs gush to the surface at a temperature of 120F (49C). The city's popularity through the ages is reflected in its architectural styles. Many quarters were built and rebuilt to suit the tastes of successive generations who came to "take the waters." But in a tremendous urban planning effort in the 18th century the whole was unified, laid out along classical lines in tier upon tier of Georgian crescents, terraces, and squares up the steep sides of the wooded hills along the winding Somerset Avon. Today it is an elegant Georgian spa that proudly calls itself the best-planned town in England.

According to legend, Bath was founded by the father of Shakespeare's King Lear, who was expelled from court as a leper, became a swineherd, and regained his health by imitating his swine and rolling in the warm mud of the mineral waters. In reality, it was probably the Romans who founded the town when they established an elaborate system of baths here in AD 54 and named the place Aquae Sulis, after a local god.

In the 5th century, after the Romans departed, the town fell into ruin. It was not until the 10th century that the region regained some prominence, when a newly built abbey was chosen for the coronation in 973 of King Edgar as the first King of England. Its fame was short-lived, and it didn't regain its reputation as a spa until the early 17th century, when the ailing Anne of Denmark, the wife of King James I, visited the baths. Kings and queens and their entourages, members of court, country gentry, and notables from all walks of life followed her lead to take the cure or just luxuriate. The baths became so popular that diarist Samuel Pepys wondered how the water could be sanitary with so many bodies jammed in it.

Today's city of elegant squares and exquisite crescent streets is the labor of love of two 18th-century architects, father and son, both named John Wood. They oversaw the rebuilding of the fashionable resort town, built the now-famous Pump Room, with its terrace restaurant, and the Assembly Rooms that today house one of the largest costume collections in the world. (The entire complex, including the Roman baths — which took archaeologists 250 years to uncover — the Pump Room, and the Assembly Rooms, is open daily; admission charge; phone: 225-61111.) Near the baths is the 15th-century Abbey Church.

But the Royal Crescent is the ultimate expression of Bath, a beautiful scimitar of street with 30 pale amber Georgian stone houses whose 114 Ionic columns, like soldiers on parade, support a continuous cornice the length of the street. It is considered the handsomest street in England. Visitors can see the interior of 1 Royal Crescent, perfectly restored in its Georgian splendor (open Tuesdays through Saturdays, and Sunday afternoons, March through October; Tuesdays through Saturdays, November and December; admission charge; phone: 225-28126). Landsdown Crescent is another testament to the elegance of the Regency period. At Great Pulteney Street is the *Holburne Museum and Crafts Study Centre* (closed Mondays and January and February; admission charge; phone: 225-66669), with a superb collection of silver, glass, porcelain, miniatures, and paintings by English masters.

To see Bath as the Georgian era left it, it is best to go by foot, and because Bath is a small city, this is no hardship. Start with a map at the Colonnades (Bath St.), site of the tourist office (phone: 225-462831). Here you can also get complete information on the city and its environs, including a detailed plan of the baths. Guided tours are available.

About 2 miles east of the city, on A36, is Claverton Manor, home of the *American Museum in Britain,* near Bathwick Hill, which has 18 rooms with period furnishings from the 17th to the 19th century. Open daily from 2 to 5 PM, April through October. Admission charge (phone: 225-60503).

> **En Route from Bath** – Route A46 north takes you immediately into the hills, lifted by an enormous underpinning arm of limestone tilting south and east, where the road winds left and right with the contours of the terrain. It is a particularly beautiful road, lined with hedgerows and trees and many wild flowers in early spring. After about 11 miles turn right onto B4040, marked Malmesbury. This narrow road passes close to the village of Badminton, the site of the Duke of Beaufort's stately mansion and the birthplace of the game that bears its name. The 15,000-acre estate of Badminton House is the scene of the renowned horse trials every late April or early May; the Badminton House itself is not open to the public, but the horse trials are. To get to Badminton village, turn left at Acton Turville for about a mile. Ten miles farther is Malmesbury.

MALMESBURY: This pleasant little town high above the river Avon is the site of a magnificent Norman abbey with a most unusual history. During the dissolution under King Henry VIII in the 16th century, the building was sold to a clothier for £1,500. The man promptly brought in his weaving machinery and converted it into a factory. It was not until 1823 that a restoration effort was begun. Despite the many years of decay, the restoration was eminently successful, and today the abbey represents the finest example of Norman building remaining in Britain. The richly carved south porch and the musicians' gallery are especially impressive.

The town has two special connections with aviation. The first was at Malmesbury Abbey in the 11th century, when Elmer, a monk, attempted to defy gravity by leaping from the tower wearing a pair of homemade wings. He survived the leap but was lame ever after. And at Kemble, 6 miles north of Malmesbury, the Royal Air Force aerobatic team, the *Red Arrows,* practice their aerial formations.

Malmesbury is one of the oldest boroughs in England and a very well planned medieval city; it was already an important town before the Norman invasion. Some medieval remains are still extant, including fragments of walls and ruins of a 12th-century castle that can be seen today at the *Old Bell* hotel (see *Best en Route*). Six bridges lead to the Market Square, at whose center is an impressive octagonal Tudor market cross. There are several lovely 17th- and 18th-century houses built by rich weavers on the adjoining streets. George Washington's ancestors appear to have come from this region, since at least five Washington predecessors are buried in a churchyard in Garsdon, 2 miles east of Malmesbury.

At Kemble, 8 miles after leaving town on A429, the road crosses a frail stream that rises to the surface only a few hundred yards away. This trickle is the mighty River Thames, just starting on its epic journey to London and the sea. Four miles farther is the ancient Roman town of Cirencester.

CIRENCESTER: A bustling market town (there is a market on Fridays in Market Place), Cirencester (pronounced *Siren*-cester) was called Corinium when it was the capital of the Romans' first province in Britain and second in size only to London. Three Roman roads — Akeman Street, Fosse Way, and Ermine Street — radiated from the town, and are still used by traffic today. Mosaic floors, sculpture, and pottery recovered from the digs now form the extensive collection of Roman relics in the *Corinium Museum* (closed Sunday mornings from April to October; closed Mondays from November to March; admission charge; Park St.; phone: 285-655611). Just outside town, on Quern Hill, are the remains of a Roman amphitheater, just as one would expect in a major provincial capital. Don't miss the magnificent array of medieval stained glass in the 15th-century parish church. A number of events are staged in Cirencester each year, including horse trials, hot-air balloon meetings, polo competitions in May, June, and August, the street market on Mondays and Fridays, and a cattle market every Tuesday.

En Route from Cirencester – Take Route A429 out of town. If time permits, travel the more circuitous route to Fossebridge via Barnsley and Bibury. The latter is a most attractive Cotswold village with a trout farm and an interesting folk museum in an old watermill whose moving parts still work. At Fossebridge, 7 miles north, there is excellent trout fishing. This is also the turnoff for Chedworth Roman Villa, which has some of the best-preserved remains of a Roman house in England. The villa displays mosaic pavements and the hypocaust, or central heating system — an underground fire chamber and a series of tile flues for distributing heat. In season, there is a display of lilies of the valley in the garden, thought to have been originally planted by the Romans (closed Mondays in summer, Mondays and Tuesdays in winter, the last 3 weeks in December, and all of January and February; admission charge; phone: 242-89256).

Continuing north on A429 for 5 miles, you come to the junction with A40 and the town of Northleach. You can stop at this picturesque old coaching town before going 9 miles farther to Bourton-on-the-Water.

NORTHLEACH: Important in the wool trade in the 15th century, this village of winding streets has changed little. Its proud church with its richly carved south porch is one of the finest built by the medieval wool merchants. Unlike many others in the region, this church miraculously escaped defacement by the Puritans. For a glimpse of the Cotswolds farming history, visit the *Cotswold Countryside Collections,* a museum housing old farm tools (admission charge; on the main road through the village, A429; phone: 451-60715). Also worth seeing from the outside are lovely Tudor almshouses in the village and the Blind House, the windowless 18th-century jail, next to the town post office on Market Place.

BOURTON-ON-THE-WATER: With the River Windrush flowing gently beside the main street, this village is sometimes called the Venice of the Cotswolds. It has a picture-postcard quality: The stream is so clear, the banks are so green, and the tiny 18th-century stone bridges are so picturesque — it all seems like a tableau. A good starting point for a walking tour is the *Old New Inn,* which has a scale model of the village at one-ninth the original size. Don't miss the quaint old house on Sherborn Street, built in 1650 with dovecotes set right into the wall. *Dial House,* now a hotel, is another old farmhouse, built in 1698 (see *Best en Route*). Most other houses in town date from the 18th century.

Another attraction is Birdland, a bird garden, which contains more than 600 exotic species from all over the world (open daily; admission charge; phone: 451-20480). Much of the Cotswolds is a bird watcher's paradise, and the English pursue this favorite pastime with single-minded vigor. A midsummer walk down any wooded lane or along the Cotswold Way is likely to turn up magpies, rooks, or ravens; larks, thrushes, or blue tits; blackbirds, wood pigeons, and the English robin. You might want to take a pair of binoculars and a field guide.

En Route from Bourton-on-the-Water – This is the heart of the Cotswolds, a series of tiny villages signposted along unclassified roads that lead to an England long gone elsewhere. The Rissingtons — Wyck, Little, and Great — are three quiet villages on the western slope of the Windrush Valley. All have the Norman churches so commonly found in Cotswold towns, though Wyck Rissington's is perhaps the oldest, with remnants of an earlier Saxon church incorporated in the structure of its Norman edifice.

More famous than the Rissingtons are the Slaughters — Upper and Lower — if fame is the correct word to use for a village of 165 people (in the case of Upper Slaughter), a crystal-clear stream full of watercress and crossed by a ford and a tiny stone bridge alongside. The village center lies behind an old castle mound, and from the byroad to Lower Slaughter, down an avenue of evergreens, you can see the magnificent Upper Slaughter Manor House, with Elizabethan front intact. Opposite the church is the entrance to the *Lords of the Manor* hotel (see *Best en Route*). Lower Slaughter is one of the most renowned villages in England. The footbridge over the gently curving stream has provided a subject for countless artists and photographers. Pick up A436 to Stow-on-the-Wold, now a quiet hill town but once the bustling, prosperous center of the Cotswold wool trade because of its location at the junction of several main roads. The market square is a jumble of old inns and houses, among them the fine St. Edward's Hall, which contains a collection of armor. Continue to Moreton-in-Marsh.

MORETON-IN-MARSH: The town astride the Roman Fosse Way has a medieval stone tower on its main street that was used as a jail; a bell in the tiny tower once sounded curfew. One of the town's most interesting houses is 17th-century Creswyke House (closed to the public); the mulberry tree in its garden is said to have been grown from a cutting of Shakespeare's tree in Stratford. Take A44 west for about 6 miles, then turn right onto B4081 for Chipping Campden.

CHIPPING CAMPDEN: This town was restored carefully by the Campden Trust, a group of people mindful of the past; as a result, it is remarkably well preserved. If you can ignore the traffic — mostly visitors looking for a parking place — the main street looks just as it did hundreds of years ago. And Chipping Campden's many fine old buildings are a delight. The church, though heavily restored by the Victorians, is one of the best in the Cotswolds. Built in the Perpendicular style by the town's wool merchants in the 15th century, it is unusually large and contains several fine brasses. Near the church are almshouses dating to 1612. All along High Street, you'll see many houses built with warm Cotswold stone; also stop at the handsome bow-windowed Grevel House (the former home of a wealthy woolman) on Church Street. Across the way is Woolstapler's Hall, a 14th-century house where wool merchants traded; it's now a museum of the town's history and a tourist information center (no admission charge; phone: 386-840289). The Market Hall, a solid yet graceful structure composed of 14 stone arches built in 1627, was where the area's farmers sold their dairy products. Pick up A46 and proceed south to Broadway.

BROADWAY: Here the diverse elements of Cotswold life come together in perfect harmony. The uniform honey-colored stone buildings lead to the inevitable cricket green; on any afternoon of a match you will hear the distinct Cotswold accent rollicking back and forth from players to spectators in support or friendly raillery. Behind a yew hedge is Abbot's Grange, a 14th-century house with its own chapel. Lording over all is the splendid *Lygon Arms* (see *Best en Route*), a coaching inn visited by Charles I and Cromwell, today one of England's finest hostelries and kitchens. The famous hotel has even brought some industry to Broadway. The workshop set up in 1904 to repair the inn's antique furniture today exports its products worldwide to collectors. The village has many lovely old buildings, among them the three-gabled Tudor House, the Prior's Manse, and Court Farm, with its garden of rare shrubs, an English passion. If Broadway is an attractive base for Cotswolds' exploration, it is only half the attraction. The other half is Stratford-upon-Avon, only 15 miles away.

STRATFORD-UPON-AVON: This illustrious town, forever synonymous with William Shakespeare, is the place of his birth and burial. England carefully guards this image, and the whole town is something of a shrine to Shakespeare's memory, an international center of pilgrimage administered by an official body called the Shakespeare Birthplace Trust. And yet around and beside the thousands of visitors that come to see plays at the *Royal Shakespeare Theatre* and to make the rounds of the Shakespeare sites, Stratford's ancient existence as a very lively market town continues unabated. The town received its first market charter in 1196 — fully 368 years before Shakespeare's birth — and still holds an open market and one important cattle market a week. As has happened for centuries, once a week Cotswold farmers bring their produce into this charming town filled with half-timbered early-16th-century buildings, set in peaceful countryside of green fields, the gentle Avon, and lovely old halls, castles, and churches.

Stratford is best explored on foot, with a walking map available at the tourist office, Judith Shakespeare House (1 High St.; phone: 789-293127). Inevitably, most of the sites you will want to visit are related to the playwright. So perhaps the best place to start is at his birthplace, a half-timbered 16th-century building with a lovely garden in back (closed Sunday mornings and during winter; admission charge; Henley St.; phone: 789-204016). The house has been furnished in the style of the period and contains memorabilia, including books and manuscripts. Going along Bridge Street, you come to the river Avon and to the lovely 14-arch Clopton Bridge, dating from the 15th century. Spacious riverside gardens lead to the *Royal Shakespeare Theatre,* which in itself draws many visitors. The season runs from April through January, and tickets should be bought as far in advance as possible from the box office (*Royal Shakespeare Theatre,* Stratford-upon-Avon, Warwickshire CV37 6BB, England; phone: 789-295623; for 24-hour booking information, 789-69191). Adjoining the theater is the picture gallery and exhibition of portraits and relics of famous Shakespearean players (open daily). A pleasant riverside path leads to Holy Trinity Church, where Shakespeare and his family are buried. Nearby is Hall's Croft, once the home of Shakespeare's daughter Susanna and one of Stratford's finest Tudor townhouses (closed Sundays during winter; admission charge; phone: 789-204016). In the center of town and dating from 1596 is Harvard House, the home of the mother of John Harvard, benefactor of Harvard University (admission charge; High St.; phone: 789-204507). The half-timbered house, once owned by the university, has reverted to its former owner, the Shakespeare Birthplace Trust. A few yards away is New Place (admission charge; Chapel St.; phone: 789-204016), all that remains of Shakespeare's last home — the foundation — and in the fine Elizabethan garden is the venerated mulberry tree said to have been grown from a cutting planted by Shakespeare himself. Thomas Nash's house next door, which once belonged to the husband of Shakespeare's granddaughter, is now a museum of local history (admission charge).

Close to Stratford are several other Shakespearean landmarks. Anne Hathaway's Cottage in Shottery, 1 mile west, is a well-preserved English thatched farmhouse that was the early home of Shakespeare's wife (closed Sunday mornings in winter; admission charge). Mary Arden's House in Wilmcote, north of Shottery, was Shakespeare's mother's home before her marriage. It is one of the outstanding farmsteads in Warwickshire (closed Sundays during winter; admission charge; phone: 789-204016). Most of the 16th-century buildings are made of close-timbered oak beams and native stone, an ideal setting for the museum of rural life they now house. Within the pleasant countryside north of Stratford via A46 is Charlecote Park, where young Will was allegedly caught poaching. The massive Elizabethan mansion, fronted by an avenue of lime trees, is now a museum of historic carriages (closed Mondays and Thursdays, April through October; admission charge). Farm buildings near the picturesque gatehouse have been converted into an attractive restaurant with a walled garden (phone: 789-840277).

From Stratford, take Route A34 to Oxford, 40 miles away through rich farmland.

OXFORD: A much-quoted description of Oxford by the 19th-century poet Matthew Arnold — "'that sweet city with her dreaming spires" — is still apt today, at least from afar when one first sees the university's towers, domes, and pinnacles rising impressively above the skyline. But it soon becomes clear that today a busy industrial city surrounds the ancient university community. In fact, town preceded gown. Oxford the city was established in about 912, the university 250 years later. Relations between the two were hostile, and after a series of riots the university took virtual control of the town — for 600 years. But peace was eventually made, and now town and gown work closely together to guard the character of the city and keep the historic core of Oxford intact. This core — one of the great living architectural treasures of the world — contains examples of every style of building from Saxon times in less than a square mile.

To do Oxford justice, spend at least one full day, during most of which you will be on foot. The city's charm is in its streets: High Street, with its sweeping curve and magnificent skyline; lovely 17th-century Hollywell Street; and ancient, cobblestone Merton. Peace and quiet here collect in out-of-the-way places: alleyways such as Magpie Lane and Logic Lane off busy High Street; the well-kept college gardens and quadrangles along the banks of the city's two rivers — Thames and Cherwell; the green open spaces in the heart of the city, including Christ Church Meadow, only a few hundred yards from High Street and St. Aldate's. The latter is a good starting point for a walking tour of the historic buildings. A first stop should be the information center in St. Aldate's, opposite Town Hall (phone: 865-726871), which arranges sightseeing tours and provides maps.

More than 600 buildings in the city are considered of outstanding architectural or historic merit. Most belong to the university, and among those you should not miss are Christ Church, established by Henry VIII in 1546, with Tom Tower, which dominates St. Aldate's; Tom Quad, the largest quadrangle in Oxford, and the college chapel, which is Oxford Cathedral; Magdalen (pronounced *Mawd*-lin) College, dating from 1458; Merton, the oldest college, built in 1264, which also has the oldest library and Mob Quad, the oldest complete quadrangle; New College, founded in 1379, which contains parts of the ancient city wall; twin-towered All Souls College, which has a sundial by Christopher Wren; St. John's College with the Canterbury Quadrangle, a masterpiece of 17th-century architecture; the circular *Sheldonian Theatre* (phone: 865-27729), designed by Wren and completed in 1669, used for university ceremonies; St. Mary the Virgin, the university church dating from the 13th and 14th centuries; and the *Ashmolean Museum,* the first public museum in Britain (open daily; no admission charge; phone: 865-512651). Another attraction for families is the Oxford Story, a realistic animated history of the city (open daily; admission charge; Broad St.; phone: 865-790055.)

An easy 8-mile drive north of Oxford is Blenheim Palace (ancestral home of the Dukes of Marlborough), a huge estate with 2,000 acres of parkland, the birthplace of Sir Winston Churchill, and now the home of the 11th duke. Open daily, mid-March through October. Admission charge (phone: 993-811325).

From Oxford, London is a distance of 57 miles away.

BEST EN ROUTE

The Cotswolds are inn country. There is a plethora of coaching or posting inns, converted manor houses, and small historic hostelries. Someone famous has invariably slept in every one of them, and it's often a matter of deciding whether you would rather put your head on a pillow where Cromwell slept before a great battle or rest in a former royal stopover.

The places listed here have a common denominator best described by the word "outstanding," but the outstanding feature may range from the architecture, history, or location of a building to the quality of service, degree of comfort, or price of the establishment. Generally, expect to pay at least $180 or more per night for a double in those hotels we've listed as very expensive; from $130 to $175 in the expensive category; $80 to $125, moderate; and under $75 in the inexpensive range. The Cotswolds are chockablock with small bed and breakfast houses in which a bed and a meal can cost $65 to $75 for two, and though we've restricted the listings below to the more historic and intriguing hostelries, don't overlook these homey, comfortable places while you travel. Expect to pay as much as $80 or more for two for a meal in the expensive restaurants; $55 to $70 in the moderate; under $55, inexpensive.

BATH

Royal Crescent – Forming the impressive center of the famous Royal Crescent, this elegant Georgian hotel occupies an unrivaled location. With commanding views, it is within walking distance of the Assembly Rooms, the Roman baths, the Pump Room, and the abbey. It has 36 super-deluxe rooms and some extra-special apartments. There are magnificent Georgian public rooms, a good restaurant, and on long, lazy hot days, tea is served in the attractive gardens. 15-16 Royal Crescent (phone: 225-319090; fax: 225-339401). Very expensive.

Pino's Hole in the Wall – This restaurant sounds like a cellar but in fact is a beamed and flagstone room, an altogether delightfully civilized place to have dinner. The Italian dishes are enticing and there is great variety. Closed Sundays. Because it seats only 40 people, reservations are necessary, especially for Saturday night. Major credit cards accepted. 16 George St. (phone: 225-425242). Expensive.

Pratt's – Equally historic, this hotel is in a quiet cul-de-sac of the South Parade near the River Avon and the city center. It has 48 modern, comfortable rooms, all with a private bath. The restaurant serves traditional English meals. South Parade (phone: 225-460441; fax: 225-44807). Expensive.

MALMESBURY

Old Bell – This is a fabulous 13th-century inn, a wisteria-clad gabled building, originally the guesthouse of a famous Norman abbey. It still retains a medieval spiral staircase and part of the castle wall. There are 18 rooms, all with central heating. The inn has pretty gardens, a good restaurant, and the charming *Castle Bar*. Abbey Row (phone: 666-822344; fax: 666-825-1145). Expensive.

CIRENCESTER

Fleece – Dating from the time of Henry VIII, this hotel has an attractive black and white timbered frontage. Inside the downstairs rooms, lounge, and bar have Cotswold stone walls, fine open fireplaces, and low beamed ceilings. A Jacobean staircase leads upstairs to 25 suites, some with teak furniture. The restaurant specializes in nouvelle cuisine. Real ales (try the local brew, the Three B's ale) are served. The staff is helpful and pleasant. Market Pl. (phone: 285-658507; fax: 285-651017). Expensive.

King's Head – Opposite the famous parish church in the attractive marketplace, this 15th-century coaching inn has been completely modernized without losing its charm. Amenities include 70 well-appointed suites and an elegant restaurant offering high-quality, extensive à la carte and table d'hôte menus. Market Pl. (phone: 285-653322; fax: 285-655103). Moderate.

NORTHLEACH

Wickens – Set in a centuries-old stone house, this dining place offers an elegant yet homey atmosphere. Owners Christopher and Joanna Wickens see to it that the freshest of local products are used for their English cuisine with a French touch. There is an extensive wine list. Open daily. Reservations advised. Visa only accepted. Market Pl. (phone: 451-60421). Expensive to moderate.

BOURTON-ON-THE-WATER

Dial House – Converted to a hotel in 1989, this gem is in the heart of the village, with an acre of walled gardens where guests can enjoy cream teas while watching croquet. Four of the 10 rooms have four-poster beds. The *Inglenook* restaurant serves fine English and French fare. The Chestnuts, High St. (phone: 451-22244). Expensive.

UPPER SLAUGHTER

Lords of the Manor – If Upper Slaughter didn't have a beautifully preserved 17th-century manor house and surrounding grounds as a hostelry for visitors, it would be necessary to invent one. Luckily it was done some 300 years ago, and you need only call for reservations. Just outside town (phone: 451-20243; fax: 451-20696). Very expensive.

STOW-ON-THE-WOLD

Fosse Manor – An ivy-covered manor house with 23 spacious rooms and a restaurant serving English country fare. Fosse Way (phone: 451-30354; fax: 451-32486). Moderate.

King's Arms – So named because King Charles spent a night here in 1645, this 500-year-old inn offers simple lodgings. Market Sq. (phone: 451-30364). Inexpensive.

MORETON-IN-MARSH

White Hart Royal – If you stay here, you will have shared a place with royalty — Charles I spent the night in this half-timbered posting inn in 1644. The hotel has 18 rooms (9 with bath) and a small timbered dining room. High St. (phone: 608-50731; fax: 608-50880). Moderate.

BROADWAY

Dormy House – Originally a farmhouse built on an escarpment above Broadway, its ancient beams and exposed stone walls prove its historic pedigree while open fires, wood paneling, and cozy bedrooms bring contemporary warmth. So does the cheery staff under the skipperdom of Harvey Pascoe. Willersey Hill (phone: 386-852711; fax: 386-858636). Very expensive.

Lygon Arms – This is one of England's fine old inns. The main building dates from 1530, though parts of it are more than 600 years old. It was frequented by Charles I and Oliver Cromwell, and rooms named after each have been carefully preserved or restored. There is also a well-designed modern extension, and the harmonious relationship of old and new gives the inn a vivid and lively air. There are 61 beautifully appointed rooms (all with bath) with classic antique furnishings. The magnificent Tudor dining room serves expensive meals, but they're worth it. The inn also has a tennis court and fitness center. High St. (phone: 386-852255; fax: 386-858611). Very expensive.

STRATFORD-UPON-AVON

Moat House International – Behind the somewhat pedestrian façade are all the comforts expected of a major hotel chain. The hotel has 250 rooms, all elegant, many with marvelous views. Guests have free access to an adjacent leisure center. Bridgefoot (phone: 789-414411; fax: 789-298589). Expensive.

Grosvenor House – On the main Warwick Road, this hostelry is actually several large houses imaginatively linked into one comfortable hotel which features a restaurant serving British fare. Close to the center of town. 12 Warwick Rd. (phone: 789-69213; fax: 789-266087). Moderate.

Payton – A well-maintained little hotel with a homelike atmosphere in a quiet part of town, though only a short walk from the back gate of Shakespeare's birthplace. There are 5 rooms, all with private bath, 1 with a four-poster bed. Big British breakfasts are served. 6 John St. (phone: 789-66442). Moderate.

OXFORD

Le Manoir aux Quat' Saisons – At the top of the country-house hotel league, this dining-and-lodging establishment, 12 miles from Oxford, boasts a two-Michelin-star restaurant, and is a member of the Relais & Châteaux group, too. The 10 luxurious guestrooms feature half-tested beds and views overlooking nearly 30 acres of meadows and gardens. It is possible for two people to spend as much as $800 a night half board, but this discourages few, as booking months in advance is a necessity. Church Rd., Great Milton (phone: 844-278881; fax: 844-278847). Very expensive.

Randolph – The best in town, with Victorian-Gothic charm, an efficient staff, and a very good location directly opposite the *Ashmolean Museum.* There are 104 rooms, a restaurant with continental cuisine, a snack shop, and a bar. Cream teas are served every afternoon in the lounge. Beaumont St. (phone: 865-247481; fax: 865-791678). Very expensive.

Studley Priory – A marvelous alternative to an indifferent overnight stay in town is this excellent hotel that was once a 12th-century Benedictine priory, later an Elizabethan manor house. On 13 acres amid rural peace and quiet, it is only 7 miles from Oxford. Filmgoers will recognize it as Thomas More's Tudor manor in *A Man for All Seasons.* The 19 rooms provide modern comfort in harmony with period furnishings. There are log fires in the public rooms and good food in the lovely dining room. The easiest approach is from the Headington roundabout on the A40 bypass east of Oxford. Horton-cum-Studley (phone: 86735-616; fax: 86735-613). Very expensive.

The Lake District

The drive from London to Scotland can hit some heavy weather in the western Midlands, where the concentration of heavy-duty industrial cities is particularly high. Stoke-on-Trent, Manchester, Liverpool — these names reverberate with the crash of the mill and the roar of the factory. A well-meaning Londoner might urge you to stay steadfastly to the east, ensuring that you encounter the more bucolic pleasures of Cambridge, Lincoln, York, and Northumberland (see the *Northeast England* route). And indeed, so splendid are those towns and the country around them that it would be hard to argue with such advice.

Unless it meant forgoing forever that crumpled, rumpled, well-watered mountain country known as the Lake District, squeezed tarn, mere, beck, and fell into the small county of Cumbria, just an hour or so north of Manchester.

Only 30 miles across in any direction, there is a special intensity in the beauty of the Lake District, as if nature were offering a unique reward for the sprawling rigors of the industrial belt. No part of England is so universally loved by Britons — for the purity of its meres, clearwater mountain lakes; its almost vertical fields filled with grazing sheep, each field carefully delineated by painstakingly maintained stone walls; its sharp rocky peaks; and the thousands of tiny lakes (tarns) fed year in and year out by innumerable waterfalls and streams — the becks. What is earth-loving and ancient in the English spirit is drawn irresistibly to the uncompromising beauty of the Lake District.

Small wonder that the Lake District is primarily associated with a group of poets of the late 18th and early 19th centuries who not only celebrated the beauty of the region, but discovered here values to stand against the encroaching horrors of the Industrial Revolution. Chief among these poets was William Wordsworth, who lived here for most of his life, but others are equally well-known: Robert Southey, Samuel Taylor Coleridge, and writers John Ruskin and Thomas De Quincey. Much of what you see and do in the region is associated with the Lake Poets.

One of the most surprising things about the Lake District is how small this famous area really is. You can drive right through it in less than an hour and yet spend a month without ever seeing half of what time and nature have created here. Looking at a map, you see that the principal lakes — Derwentwater, Ullswater, Windermere, wild Wastwater, Buttermere, Crummock Water, Tarn Hows, Grasmere, and Rydal Water — radiate from a central mountain mass like the spokes of a wheel. The distances between these postcard-perfect lakes are short, but each of the larger lakes provides a good base for exploring the nearby area. You could easily spend 2 days around each major lake — Derwentwater, Windermere, and Ullswater especially — before moving on, allowing time for some hiking as well as exploring the towns and villages of the district.

The route described below actually begins in the northeastern corner of the Lake District, at the town of Penrith near Ullswater, and cuts a deep V into the heart of the area. From Windermere, in the south-central section of the lakes, there is easy access to the challenging mountain peak of Helvellyn (3,113 feet). The next leg of the trip, north from Windermere to Derwentwater, crosses the paths of the Lake Poets. For the last 37 years of his life Wordsworth lived at Rydal Mount, just a few miles from Ambleside. The home he had occupied previously, Dove Cottage, is a few miles farther north, at Grasmere. Thomas De Quincey, author of *Confessions of an English Opium Eater,* took over the cottage when Wordsworth moved. At the north end of this leg is Derwentwater — perhaps the most beautiful of all the lakes. Robert Southey made his home here, in the town of Keswick, where he frequently was joined by Percy Bysshe Shelley and Coleridge. The twins, Buttermere and Crummock Water, are just a short drive southwest of Keswick, and beyond them, in the northwest corner of the Lake District, is Cockermouth. Wordsworth and his sister Dorothy were both born and raised here, and the family home and nearby fields became part of the joyous imagery of the poetry that introduced this area to readers everywhere. From Cockermouth, the route follows the western boundary of the Lake District, heading south, and numerous small roads lead into the heart of the mountains and the area's best climbing. The route cuts across the base of the Lake District to return you to the main highway and London, north to Scotland, or east to Yorkshire.

LONDON: For a complete description of the city and its hotels and restaurants, see *London,* THE CITIES.

En Route from London – Leave London on either the M4 west (through the Cotswolds) to the M5 and north into the M6, or by taking the M1 north to Rugby and picking up the M6 westbound, later bearing north at Birmingham. Beyond Manchester and Liverpool lie the beautiful Forest of Bowland, and, just beyond, the fringes of the Lake District. Drive along the edge of this mountainous area to Penrith (exit 40), at the northern end of the district.

PENRITH: The charming town of Penrith has withstood time and the onslaught of travelers comfortably. The oldest section of town has grown up around the 13th-century Church of St. Andrew (rebuilt in the early 1700s) and the nearby 16th-century schoolhouse. Several conflicting legends surround the presence of the two stone formations on the church grounds, known as Giant's Grave and Giant's Thumb. One version holds that this is the burial place of an ancient king. The ruins of Penrith Castle are now a town park, but two excellent 16th-century pubs, both on Great Dockray, are still thriving: the *Gloucester Arms* (phone: 768-62150) and the *Two Lions,* which has a restaurant (phone: 768-63511).

En Route from Penrith – Just outside Penrith on B5320 is the village of Tirril. A few minutes' drive beyond is Pooley Bridge, at the northern end of Ullswater, the second largest of the region's lakes. It is possible to arrange a day's boating or fishing at Pooley Bridge, a fine way to explore this beautiful lake; ask the boat owners on the pier. And keep an eye out for the elusive wild red deer that frequent the southeastern shore of Ullswater. A worthwhile diversion from Pooley Bridge is the secondary road along the southern shore of the lake past the *Sharrow Bay Country House* hotel (see *Best en Route*), which surveys the most scenic views in the district; the road dead-ends ultimately in the peaceful valley of Martindale. Route A592 continues to skirt the northwestern bank of Ullswater, bypassing Gowbarrow Park. This grassy fell comes alive with daffodils each year, and traveling poets can, as Wordsworth did, pause to write about the yellow blooms.

The village of Glenridding, at the head of Ullswater Lake, has a pier to match that of Pooley Bridge, 13 miles away by road. (By water, the lake is only 7½ miles long.) Patterdale, which shares the head of the lake, is only a mile farther.

From here the roadway crosses over the Helvellyn mountain range through Kirkstone Pass. There are several good climbing trails through these hills, and some of the most challenging paths lead to the peak of Helvellyn Mount (3,113 feet). But the ascent of Kirkstone Pass (1,489 feet), though fairly steep in some places, certainly holds no difficulties for drivers. At the summit is *Kirkstone Pass Inn* (phone: 5394-33624), which has the distinction of being one of the highest taverns in England, and a wide choice of whiskies. On the far side of the pass the road leads down to Troutbeck Valley and the small town of Troutbeck. At the southern end of Troutbeck is the 17th-century Townend House, used as a residence by the family of Yeoman Browne. The interior and furnishings remain intact, as does the timbered barn (open April to October; closed mornings, Mondays, and Saturdays; admission charge; phone: 5394-32628).

WINDERMERE AND BOWNESS: The adjoining resort areas of Windermere and Bowness mark the middle of Lake Windermere's east bank. The view of the lake from the town is unimpressive, but if you climb to the peak of Orrest Head (just north of the railroad station) you'll get a far better perspective of the lake and its surrounding mountains. Virtually every recreational activity imaginable — fishing, boating, sailing, golf, tennis, scuba, and even pony trekking — is available in this busy visitors' center.

Charles Dickens is known to have spent many hours in the *New Hall Inn* (phone: 9662-3488); founded in 1612 in the center of Bowness near the lakefront, it is still known locally as the "Hole in the Wall." When Dickens visited, the proprietor was Thomas Longmire, a well-known wrestling champion (which may account for the lack of damage inflicted on the pub over the years).

Lake Windermere, the largest of the lakes (10½ miles long), has a much softer aspect than most of the lakes in the region, the happy product of its luxuriantly wooded banks, filled with rhododendrons that burst into flaming color each June. The best way to see it is to take one of the regular cruises that operate between Lake Side in the south and Bowness and Waterhead at the lake's northern end (May through September). There are several small islands in Windermere; on one of them, Belle Isle, is a magnificent 18th-century mansion that is unfortunately not open to the public. Seen from Bowness and other points along the more civilized side of Windermere, the western shore has all the lure of undiscovered territory. Fortunately for intrepid explorers, there is a ferry from Bowness to the far side that deposits travelers on a secondary road leading to the village of Near Sawrey, the site of Hilltop Cottage. This quaint 17th-century house was the home of Beatrix Potter, the author and illustrator whose Peter Rabbit, Squirrel Nutkin, and other characters have been loved by generations of children. A collection of her drawings is on display, and children will be pleased to find the setting of most of her tales right around the house and grounds (open 11 AM to 5 PM; closed Thursdays; admission charge; phone: 9666-269). The road passes a small lake, Esthwaite Water, and continues into Hawkshead, just under 6 miles from the ferry.

HAWKSHEAD: Far from the resort mood of Windermere, this quiet little village beyond Esthwaite Water offers an introductory course in Lake District life that begins in the center of the village at the 17th-century *Queen's Head Inn* (phone: 9666-271), where you can get a pint of ale to fortify you for a stroll through the stone cottages of the town. Start at the schoolhouse, founded in 1585 by native son Edwin Sandys, Archbishop of York, and attended by Wordsworth between 1778 and 1783. You'll find his name scratched in one of the desks. Wordsworth may have lodged at Ann Tyson's cottage, on a lane off Red Lion Square. Northwest of Hawkshead, a steep byroad leads to Tarn Hows, a small fir-fringed lake high in the hills that has the best views of the surrounding countryside, especially of Coniston Water to the south and the mountain called the Old Man of Coniston, which lords it over the lake. John Ruskin is buried at Coniston Church; his home at Brantwood can be visited (open daily, March through November; Sundays, December through February; admission charge; phone: 966-41396). Take the northbound secondary road out of Hawkshead to nearby Ambleside.

AMBLESIDE: Just under a mile from the north end of Lake Windermere, Ambleside is an excellent touring base for climbers eager to explore the lakeland's hills and forests. Wordsworth's famed Scafell Pike (3,210 feet) is a considerable hike from Ambleside, but other peaks are more accessible. It is best to obtain detailed maps of trails and to make proper arrangements before starting any trek. The local information center is in Ambleside's old Court House in the Market Square (phone: 5394-32582). A short distance away, up the lane past the *Salutation* hotel, is Stockghyll Force, a beautiful waterfall cascading 70 feet to rocks below. St. Mary's Church, erected in 1854 by Sir Gilbert Scott, has a memorial to Wordsworth and a mural of the village's rush-bearing festival, still held yearly on the last Saturday in July. The festival is thought to descend from a Roman harvest ceremony. Just 2 miles north of Ambleside on A591 is Rydal.

RYDAL: William Wordsworth, with his wife, three children, sister, and sister-in-law, moved to this village in 1813 and lived here until his death in 1850. His home, Rydal Mount, contains a large collection of memorabilia, including several portraits of his family and friends, and his personal library (open daily 10 AM to 5:30 PM, March through October; Wednesdays through Saturdays from 10 AM to 12:30 AM, November through February; admission charge; phone: 966-33002). Wordsworth drew heavily on the surrounding countryside for inspiration and poetic images, and the mute crags and flowered hillsides around his home appear repeatedly in his work. His love of nature is reflected in the 4½-acre garden he grew around Rydal Mount, as attentively cared for today as by the poet.

Just a short distance up the road is Nab Cottage, occupied briefly by Thomas De Quincey (1806) and later by Samuel Taylor Coleridge's eldest son, Hartley. Skirting the north bank of Rydal Water (which, together with the Rothay, links Grasmere and Windermere lakes), the roadway continues to the village of Grasmere.

GRASMERE: Grasmere Lake, just a mile long and half as wide, is almost too perfect for words, complete with an emerald green island in its center. Wordsworth and his sister Dorothy lived on the lake at Dove Cottage from 1799 until 1808. After William married (and fathered three children), he and his family moved to Rydal Mount, turning the cottage over to their friends Thomas De Quincey and his wife, who had been living at Nab Cottage. The *Wordsworth Museum* (open daily *Easter* through October; admission charge; phone: 9665-544), across from Dove Cottage, is really a tribute to Wordsworth and his circle. Pages and materials from many area writers, famous and obscure, are displayed along with some interesting relics.

Although August is the most crowded month in which to visit the Lake District, it is also the month of the *Grasmere Sports,* usually held on the third Thursday of the month. The games feature traditional Lakeland sports, such as fell racing, an all-out dash to the top of the nearest mountain and back, and Cumberland wrestling. Until Cumberland and Westmorland were combined into Cumbria County, competition between these rivals was intense, and the administrative alteration hasn't changed anything; these games have been held every year since 1852. While you're in town, stop in at the Church of St. Oswald (parts of which may be from the 13th century) and, in the yard, at the graves of William Wordsworth, his wife and sister, and Hartley Coleridge.

En Route from Grasmere – Continuing north along the Rothay on A591 toward the wooded shores of Thirlmere, Helvellyn Mount rises to the right. The tiny 17th-century chapel at Wythburn is worth a visit and always is open. Its parking lot is the starting point of a climbing trail to the peak of Helvellyn (the parking lot at the north end of Thirlmere is the start of a gentler forest trail). Keswick, 13 miles from Grasmere, is just a few miles beyond the north end of the lake. You'll get an excellent view of the area from the crest of Castlerigg, and a road on the right leads to the Castlerigg Stone Circle.

KESWICK: Sheltered by the towering Skiddaw (3,053 feet), this ancient market town sits near the shore of beautiful Derwentwater, 3 miles long and a mile wide, surrounded by a delightful mixture of bare rock, grassy banks, and forested glens and crowned by a wreath of tiny islands. One of these, Floating Island, is no more than a tangled mass of lake weeds riding on a bubble of swamp gas. The other islands, however, are more substantial, and several support beautiful homes; the remains of a 7th-century retreat are on the island of St. Herbert.

Many poets, including Shelley, Southey, Wordsworth, and Coleridge, were drawn here, and the *Keswick Museum and Art Gallery* displays some of their manuscripts, letters, and personal effects (open April through October, closed Sundays; admission charge; Station Rd.; phone: 7687-73263). Southey's home, Greta Hall, has become Keswick School; his body lies at the Crosthwaite Churchyard. Southey, Wordsworth, and Coleridge all patronized the bar at the *Georgia* hotel (St. John's St.; phone: 7687-72076), which claims to be the oldest inn in town. Judging by the crude stone masonry and faded walls, it may well be. On a rainy day (a not infrequent occurrence) visit the *Cars of the Stars Motor Museum,* which features, among other autos, James Bond's Lotus from *For Your Eyes Only* (open *Easter* through October; admission charge; phone: 7687-73757).

Two of the best points for viewing Derwentwater and its environs are at Castle Head (529 feet), just south of Keswick, and at Friar's Crag, a rocky headland on the lake. John Ruskin was particularly enamored of this spot, and there is a memorial to him here. Southey favored the view from the hill near Greta Bridge.

En Route from Keswick – Drive south along the eastern shore of Derwentwater on B5289 to the incredibly beautiful Borrowdale Valley. Here the Bowder Stone, a huge boulder that tumbled from some nearby height, stands precariously on edge near Castle Crag, a 900-foot-tall rock cone that can be climbed without too much effort in under half an hour. Great Gable, a little farther along the route, is a more challenging target — 2,949 feet of tough climbing. It takes about 3 hours to ascend this monster, but the view is well worth the effort. The entire area from Skiddaw to Windermere, and even the Isle of Man are visible from the crest.

Continue on B5289, crossing over Honister Pass, then dropping through some rough territory until you reach the farm of Gatesgarth. The placid waters of Buttermere come into view as the roadway curves in a giant U, first west and then north. Buttermere's nearby twin, Crummock Water, lies just beyond to the northwest. Scale Force, a lively waterfall with a drop of over 120 feet, is not far from the pretty village of Buttermere. The easiest access is by crossing the stream between the two lakes and following the path on the far side. It will be muddy, so wear boots or hiking shoes. A few miles farther north, B5289 intersects B5292; you can either take B5292 east toward A66, Keswick and Penrith, or extend your trip by heading west toward Cockermouth.

There is no direct road across the mountain barrier in the western half of the Lake District, making it a particularly appealing area for experienced and properly equipped backpackers and hill walkers.

COCKERMOUTH: Strategically placed at the junction of the Cocker and Derwent rivers, Cockermouth is a pre-Roman community, though little remains from its earliest period. Even its 12th-century castle was destroyed during the violence of the mid-1600s. Wordsworth House was built in 1745 (open daily, except Thursdays and Sunday mornings, from April through October; admission charge; Main St.; phone: 900-824805). This house, in which Dorothy and William grew up, is a fairly simple, countrified example of Georgian architecture that has survived intact. The furnishings used by the Wordsworth family, however, are long gone. William's father is buried in the churchyard. Fletcher Christian of *Mutiny on the Bounty* was born at nearby Moorland Close (1764).

En Route from Cockermouth – Take A5086 south from Cockermouth along the western fringe of the Lake District. Ennerdale Water, perhaps the least visited of the larger lakes, lies about 10 miles away, on a secondary roadway to the east. A similar turnoff about 10 miles beyond leads to Wastwater, the deepest of the lakes, set among a group of stern and savage-faced mountains. The contrast to gentle Windermere is marked. The village of Wasdale Head, a mile beyond the lake, is an excellent climbing center, but strictly for experts.

Returning to the main road (A5086 becomes A595 near Ennerdale Water), you arrive at Ravenglass, a port at the mouth of the Esk River about 25 miles from Cockermouth. The Eskdale Valley can be explored either by road or on the narrow-gauge, steam-powered, 7-mile-long *Ravenglass and Eskdale Railway* (phone: 6577-278). "Narrow" is an understatement; 15 inches make it positively skinny. The train runs daily from April through October, with reduced service in winter (admission charge).

Overlooking the river Esk, just beyond the town, is Muncaster Castle, the seat of the Pennington family for 700 years (open afternoons, *Easter* through September; closed Mondays; admission charge; phone: 6577-614). Farther on, at Broughton, another secondary road (A593) leads up the Duddon Valley toward Coniston Water and Hawkshead. Just east of Broughton, A595 bears south along the coast, and A590 continues east toward A6, the city of Kendal, and the M4 motorway.

BEST EN ROUTE

Travelers to the Lake District have a wide choice of excellent accommodations, varying from some of the best hotels in the country to small (but comfortable) inns and bed and breakfast spots. Any number of inns and homes that provide the basics — a warm room and breakfast for a modest price — are hidden among these wooded hills. Expect B&B charges for two to run about $60 to $75. Expect to pay $170 and up per night for a double room with breakfast in inns listed as very expensive; between $120 and $160 for those in the expensive range; $80 to $115 for moderate; and $75 and under for inexpensive. The hostelries listed below are a selection of our choices for the area; there are many other inns along the roads you'll be traveling, and the experience of exploring an unknown inn should be all your own. Dinners at the expensive to moderate establishments in the area are about $70 to $95 for two people.

ULLSWATER

Leeming House – Commanding fine views over the lake, it's a gracious country-house hotel and restaurant. Closed early December to early March. Watermillock (phone: 7684-86622; fax: 7684-86443). Very expensive.

Sharrow Bay Country House – Partners Francis Coulson and Brian Sack have spent 40 years making this one of the most respected and attractive hotels in Britain. Rates include dinner, a pleasure at this establishment's restaurant. Closed December to early March (phone: 7684-86301; fax: 7684-86349). Very expensive.

Old Church – With the Ullswater lapping on their front lawn, owners Kevin and Maureen Whitemore offer an enormous range of sporting activities in the surrounding area, along with good food and comfortable accommodations. Closed December through February. Watermillock (phone: 7684-86204; fax: 7684-86368). Expensive.

WINDERMERE

Miller Howe – Is it the beautiful view of placid, tree-lined Lake Windermere or the impeccable service that makes this hotel seem such a bastion of calm? In either case, there is hardly a better headquarters for touring the area. It's one of Britain's best country-house hotels. Closed mid-December through February. Rayrigg Rd. (phone: 9662-2536; fax: 9662-5664). Very expensive.

Belsfield – A magnificent Georgian mansion overlooking Lake Windermere with an interesting blend of period pieces and modern furnishings. A wing (in the garden) has been added, making a total of 66 rooms, and there's a jogging trail that winds through 6 acres of grounds. Bowness on Windermere (phone: 9662-2448; fax: 9662-6397). Expensive.

Rothay Manor – This elegant hotel near Ambleside has its own croquet lawn and excellent cuisine. Closed early January to early February. Rothay Bridge (phone: 5394-33605; fax: 5394-33607). Expensive.

Quarry Garth – A solid, no-nonsense mansion, typical of scores of private retreats built in the lakes by wealthy industrialists, with just 11 bedrooms, a cozy paneled lounge, and an elegant dining room. Troutbeck (phone: 9662-3761; fax: 9662-6584). Moderate.

Lowick House – Dorothy Sutcliffe takes a few guests into her beautiful Lakeland farmhouse (and puts whiskey in your porridge if the weather looks grim). Bedrooms are beautifully furnished, and dinners are multi-course feasts. Lowick, near Ulverston (phone: 229-85227). Inexpensive.

GRASMERE

Michaels Nook – A charming Victorian country home furnished by the proprietor, Reginald Gifford, with many beautiful antiques. Some of the bathrooms have been "modernized," but the older ones are more fun. There is also a fine restaurant on the premises; reservations essential. Rates include dinner (phone: 9665-496; fax: 9665-765). Expensive.

Swan – Immortalized by Wordsworth, this very friendly 36-room hotel is admirably managed and has a good restaurant featuring a number of vegetarian dishes (phone: 9665-551; fax: 9665-741). Expensive.

KESWICK

Lodore Swiss – On the edge of Derwentwater, with glorious views of the lake and Lodore Falls. Though the building is fairly large and very grand in appearance, it is run by a staff trained under the family (the Englands) who owned the hostelry before the Stakis chain bought it, so the atmosphere remains warm and friendly. Closed January through mid-February (phone: 7687-77285; fax: 7687-77343). Expensive.

Mary Mount Country House – Also on the shores of Lake Derwentwater, 3 miles south of Keswick and under the same management as *Lodore Swiss,* this comfortable and cozy hotel is set in beautiful woodlands. Closed November through March (phone: 7687-77223; fax: 7687-77343 at the *Lodore Swiss* hotel). Inexpensive.

Pheasant Inn – This old coaching inn with 20 rooms still retains its traditional atmosphere. On Bassenthwaite Lake near Thornthwaite Forest (phone: 59681-76234). Inexpensive.

Northeast England

Between the Midlands and the border of the Scottish Lowlands, where England narrows to a tight, trim waist of land, lies a section of exceptionally rugged and beautiful geography. The Pennine Chain — a group of hills that reach only 3,000 feet above sea level at their highest — runs straight down the center of this neck of land, dividing east and west as neatly as a surgeon's blade. To the west falls the Lake District and Cumbria (see *The Lake District* route); to the east, stretching across chasms and caves, are the dales and moors of Yorkshire and a long coast on the North Sea.

At England's narrowest point, Roman legions were once posted in an uneasy vigilance against the raids of marauding Pict warriors from the north. In AD 122, goaded past endurance, Emperor Hadrian ordered the construction of an immense wall, to reach from the North Sea at the River Tyne to Solway Firth on the Irish Sea coast, to discourage the savage northerners. The high, parapeted wall, 6 feet high and 8 feet thick, stretched for 73½ miles and was punctuated at every mile by a guard station filled with Roman soldiers — still uneasy. What remains of this magnificent effort are various ruins across Northumberland and many mile stations still standing.

Later, with the coming of the Normans, a network of castles was built across this area. Many of these medieval fortresses are also extant, as obdurate and impregnable as ever, firm against age. Others have crumbled, leaving the history of their passing in broken walls and weary battlements.

It is rather apt that the gateway to this country of rocky moors, forested dales, and sandy resort beaches on the North Sea coast is the ancient city of York, home of York Minster, one of Great Britain's most beautiful cathedrals. As wild as the country is, it has always been a center of British religious experience, and Christianity actually came to Britain through the coastal island of Lindisfarne (Holy Island).

The route described below is circular, leaving York for the journey north through the North York moors to Durham, dominated by Britain's finest Norman cathedral, and then on to Newcastle upon Tyne and along the coastline to Berwick-upon-Tweed on the Scottish border. Here the route turns south again to wander through the central highlands of the Pennines, the moor, and Yorkshire dales on its way back to York. For more information, contact the Northumbria Tourist Board (Aykley Heads, Durham DH1 5UX; phone: 91-3846905), and the Yorkshire and Humberside Tourist Board (312 Tadcaster Rd., York YO2 2HF, England; phone: 904-707961).

LONDON: For a complete description of the city and its hotels and restaurants, see *London*, THE CITIES.

En Route from London – Take the M1 motorway directly north from London to Leeds and pick up A64 going northeast to York. It's a fairly long journey, about 225 miles all told, and will take about 4 hours.

YORK: Its very name has the ring of ancient authority about it, and well it should. The Romans established York — then called Eboracum — in AD 71 as a garrison town and the seat of the province. A succession of Roman emperors visited, and it was here, in 306, that Constantine the Great was proclaimed ruler of the known world. Such is the fleeting nature of glory that the Romans abandoned the town only 75 years later, and it slipped quietly from history until the Anglo-Saxons moved 3 centuries later. It was a walled city when King Harold II was in the area in 1066, fighting the Scandinavians, only to be called back to the south of England on the double to meet the forces of William the Conqueror.

The section of the city within the ancient walls is perhaps the best-preserved medieval city in Great Britain, and from its heart rises the largest Gothic cathedral in the country, York Minster. Begun in 1081 on the site of a series of earlier churches, it was not completed until the 15th century. More stunning than its awesome proportions are its stained glass windows, the largest concentration of stained glass in Great Britain. The giant Great East Window is the size of a tennis court.

The medieval heart of the city is girdled by 3 miles of defensive wall, and the most interesting parts of the city are within them. Just as in the Middle Ages, the quirky, timbered, slightly akimbo buildings in the Shambles — once the butchers' quarter — are devoted to shops, though the butchers have given way to boutiques, galleries, and crafts shops, most with original butcher's block and meat hooks intact. Goodramgate is another medieval shopping area, and Micklegate, the central highway of yore, is lined with much later but very beautiful Georgian homes and buildings. Other required stops are the pillared Assembly Rooms (Blake St.; phone: 904-613161), evoking the elegance of the 18th century, and the medieval timberwork of the Merchant Adventurers' Hall (Fossgate; phone: 904-645818). If you don't mind long lines, visit the popular *Jorvik Viking Centre* (Coppergate; phone: 904-643211); electric cars take visitors underground to see a fascinating excavation site and exhibition, including a reconstructed 10th-century Viking village. Then relax at the *Black Swan* (in Peasholme Green); in 1417, the Lord Mayor of York lived in the house. Definitely worth seeing are the reconstructed period scenes at the *Castle Museum* (open daily; Tower St.; phone: 904-653611) and *National Railway Museum* (open daily; Leeman Rd.; phone: 904-621261), which houses a history of the railroad; natives come from all over Britain to see it. (All museums above charge admission.) The York Tourist Information Office, always phenomenally busy, is in the De Gray Rooms (St. Leonard's St.; phone: 904-621756).

En Route from York – Take A64 northeast toward the North York Moors National Park, about 40 miles away. A roadway about 15 miles outside York leads to Castle Howard, a palatial mansion topped by a gilded dome that was used as the setting for the television production of Evelyn Waugh's *Brideshead Revisited*. Sir John Vanbrugh designed the central structure, erected early in the 18th century. A wing was added in the 1750s. A collection of period clothing is on display; the house is magnificently decorated and furnished. The grounds, including a lake, complete the image of luxuriant living (open daily from *Easter* through November; admission charge; phone: 65-384333).

Rejoin A64 and continue to the small market town of Malton. Then go north on A169 through Old Malton to Pickering.

PICKERING: This little town is on the fringe of the national park, a vast expanse of rolling hills and valleys that becomes a purple sea abloom with heather during the late summer. Pickering is well suited to the quiet atmosphere of the moor — time has not altered either appreciably. Relax at the *Black Bull Inn* (Malton Rd.; phone: 751-75258), an ancient stone tollhouse, before exploring the moors. An easy way to view these beautiful valleys and ridges of exposed rock is aboard the *North Yorkshire Moors Railway* (phone: 751-72508), a steam-powered line built in 1836 by George Stephenson that runs between Pickering and Grosmont in summer.

En Route from Pickering – Route A169 cuts right through the moorlands to the coast at Whitby. This delightful old port is overlooked from a cliff by the impressive ruins of Whitby Abbey, established in 657 and extensively rebuilt around the 12th century (closed Mondays, October through March; admission charge; phone: 904-22902). Long associated with the sea and sailing ships, the older parts of Whitby still consist of cobbled streets and the red tile cottages used by fishermen and shipwrights. *Dracula* also has made the town famous; Bram Stoker summered here, and set the story's first three chapters in Whitby. A resort area has grown on the town's West Cliff.

Just a few miles south of Whitby along the coast (off A171), clinging to the cliffs, is the village of Robin Hood's Bay. Here the tall cliffs drop to their lowest point, creating a beautiful setting for the picturesque fishing settlement.

The leading resort town on the Yorkshire coast, Scarborough, lies about 15 miles farther south. The cliff-top ruins of a 12th-century castle and the Church of St. Mary (also 12th century) separate the two sandy bays that are Scarborough's principal attractions. The shrinking old sector, near the harbor, still preserves its crafts and fish markets and several early homes. The bluff, now the site of a castle ruins, once held an Iron Age lookout-earthwork, a Roman fire beacon, and later a chapel. Beyond is South Bay and a spa with beautiful gardens. This is a residential area, reflected in stately homes and abundant gardens.

Return to Pickering on A170 westbound, skirting the southern fringe of the moors. Having traced a circle northeast of Pickering, continue west on A170 past the town toward Kirkbymoorside and Helmsley.

HELMSLEY: The ruins of a 12th-century castle dominate this small town at the foot of the ridges where the valleys of Pickering and Rye meet. Just 2 miles away, in the

Ryedale Valley, are the magnificent ruins of Rievaulx Abbey, built over a period of almost 200 years in the 12th and 13th centuries. The terrace above the abbey overlooks the ruins themselves and offers a fine view of the pastoral vale (open year-round; admission charge; phone: 4396-228). In 1990, Duncombe Park, a stately home boasting the tallest ash and lime trees in England, reopened (open *Easter* through September; admission charge; phone: 439-70213). If staying overnight, try the *Black Swan* hotel (see *Best en Route*), a 400-year-old Georgian and Tudor building with a modern wing.

En Route from Helmsley – Route A170 goes west, descending to Thirsk in the southwest corner of the moors. From Thirsk, take A19 north toward Middlesbrough and look for signs for A177, which leads northwest to Durham. The whole drive from Helmsley to Durham is about 50 miles.

DURHAM: Whether it was worship of God or defense against the Scots that was uppermost in the minds of the builders of Durham's magnificent cathedral and equally dramatic castle, the two buildings, facing each other across the Palace Green on a wooded gorge literally hanging over the River Wear, make Durham one of the most dramatically situated cities in Great Britain. When the cathedral was built in the 11th century, the bishop was responsible for the physical as well as the spiritual well-being of his flock, and defense was certainly part of his purpose. The original castle, built about 100 years later at the insistence of William the Conqueror, was replaced by the current keep in the 14th century and the Great Hall added at the same time (the castle is part of Durham University today). The two buildings are breathtaking, with the triple towers of the cathedral visible. Altogether, Durham Cathedral is one of the finest Romanesque-style churches in Europe. Not to be missed in Durham is the *University of Durham Museum of Art,* on Elvet Hill, with an incredible collection of Eastern art forms spanning many centuries (open November to February; closed weekends; admission charge; phone: 385-66711). After a culturally enhancing day of touring, have a beer at the old *Market Tavern* (Market Pl.).

En Route from Durham – Route A167 leaves Durham at a leisurely pace, going north about 15 miles toward Newcastle upon Tyne, or take the A1, a four-lane motorway. A few miles before Newcastle lies Washington, once a small mining town. The town's Old Hall, erected early in the 17th century, incorporates parts of an older structure — the 12th-century home of the family of George Washington (closed Fridays, *Easter* through September; open Wednesdays, Saturdays, and Sundays in winter; admission charge; phone: 91-416-6879).

NEWCASTLE UPON TYNE: This lively industrial center of the northeast first became famous as an exporter of coal during the 13th century. Today, Newcastle's steel and petroleum industries lead the city's current redevelopment phase. Originally this site was called Pons Aelius, one of the guard stations of Hadrian's Wall — a massive line of fortifications which defined the limit of Roman Britain when it was built.

Robert Curthose, son of William the Conqueror, erected a castle here late in the 11th century. The "new" castle (now gone) was constructed over a century later, between 1170 and 1250. The *Hancock Museum* (at Barras Bridge) is one of the best natural history museums in England (closed Sundays during winter and Sunday mornings during summer; admission charge; phone: 632-322359). The towering spire of St. Nicholas's Cathedral is 194 feet tall and reinforced by flying buttresses. Plan to visit the *Beamish* open-air "living museum" of the region's past ways of life near Stanley, a short bus ride from the city center. Named European Museum of the Year in 1987, it is still widely considered one of the most interesting collections in Britain (open daily from *Easter* through mid-October; Tuesdays through Sundays the rest of the year; admission charge; phone: 207-231811).

En Route from Newcastle upon Tyne – Take A1 north, traveling between the coast and the forested hills of Northumberland National Park, one of the wildest and least traveled areas in England — a good spot for experienced hikers to get a taste of the country through which Romans and Picts warred. Nearer the roads are fine spots for the more civilized pleasures of a quiet picnic. Some 35 miles away is Alnwick, an attractive old town outside the gates of the Duke of Northumberland's Alnwick Castle. These stern walls, reinforced between 1310 and 1312, when its towers were erected, mask an interior of truly ducal magnificence (open daily except Saturdays, May through September; admission charge; phone: 665-602207). A secondary roadway leads northeast from B1340 to the tiny fishing village of Craster, about 6 miles from Alnwick. Treat yourself to a breath of sea air: Park the car and walk 1½ miles along the coast path to the ruins of Dunstanburgh Castle. This dramatic 14th-century structure, perched on a cliff 100 feet above the sea, was hotly contested during the Wars of the Roses (open daily; admission charge; phone: 66576-213).

The popular resort of Seahouses, with an excellent beach area, is only a few miles farther along the coast. Take a National Trust boat (contact N.T. Information Centre; phone: 665-721099) to Inner Farne, a sanctuary for birds (puffins, terns, guillemots, kittiwakes, and others) and gray seals (open April to September).

Bamburgh Castle, one of the largest and most imposing medieval castles in Britain, still stands on a craggy headland overlooking the beach. Built in the early 12th century, the fortress was extensively restored at the beginning of the 20th century. Open afternoons, *Easter* through last Sunday of October. Admission charge (phone: 668-4208).

Continue north along the coast to Beal, where a 3-mile causeway (usable only at low tide) connects the mainland to Holy Island.

LINDISFARNE, or HOLY ISLAND: Here, in the 7th century, St. Aidan established the missionary center from which Christianity spread to the mainland. The ruins of the 11th-century Benedictine priory, including a red sandstone church, and a small castle stand among the picturesque fishermen's cottages on the island today (open daily; admission charge; phone: 289-89200). Lindisfarne is known for the brewing of mead, a potent honey-based liquor. Pick up an extra bottle for yourself before returning to the mainland and the northbound coast road.

BERWICK-UPON-TWEED: The heavily fortified city of Berwick-upon-Tweed shifted between Scotland and England 13 times before being settled in England in 1482. The 16th-century ramparts ringing the Old City are in excellent condition and create a massive circular 2-mile promenade. Several well-preserved 18th-century buildings, including the Town Hall and Barracks, are open for inspection (all closed Mondays during winter; admission charge for all). Charles Dickens is said to have read poetry in the 18th-century *King's Arms* hotel, on a rise above the dockyards (see *Best en Route*).

En Route from Berwick-upon-Tweed – Edinburgh is about 60 miles northwest along the coast road. If, however, you're returning south, follow the bank of the River Tweed on A698. The ruins of Norham Castle, on the riverbank, are just off the main road 7 miles from Berwick (open daily October through March; admission charge; phone: 28982-329). Continue south on A698 to Cornhill on Tweed, and there pick up A697 southeast to Wooler, at the foot of the Cheviot Hills on the fringe of Northumberland National Park. There you can call for refreshments at the creeper-clad *Tankerville Arms* (Cottage Rd., Wooler; phone: 668-81581). The Earl of Tankerville's 14th-century Chillingham Castle is about 5 miles east of the village. A unique herd of pure white wild cattle have grazed the castle grounds for 700 years (open April through October; closed Tuesdays; admission charge; phone: 6685-213).

Return to A697, veering southeast away from the border of the Northumberland Park to the junction with B6341. Take B6341 southwest to Rothbury, deep in the wooded valley of the river Coquet, then continue south on the B6342 until it becomes A6076 leading into Hexham.

HEXHAM: The beautiful priory church typifies the town of Hexham. Little remains of the original structure, but some interesting 12th-century sections are in good shape. There is a 13th-century stone chair used as a frithstool: a sanctuary for whoever sat in it. The present Manor Office (at Hall Gate), which houses the tourist information bureau, is a 14th-century prison, and the 15th-century Moot Hall was used by the court bailiff (admission charge; phone: 434-605225). The town is well situated for a detailed look at the Roman Wall: It sits just about halfway along the wall's length.

En Route from Hexham – Richmond lies about 70 miles southeast of Hexham. From Hexham, forsaking the main highways for a spell, take the hill road (B6306) that climbs up from the Tyne Valley to the village of Blanchland, built around the site of a 12th-century abbey; part of the original church now serves the parish. In the heart of the Pennine Hills, the road makes a switchback on the B6278 to Barnard Castle, an agreeable little town named for its ruined 12th-century castle (open daily, admission charge; phone: 833-38212), from which there is a great view over the River Tees. Just off A66 and just east of the town center (Market Square) is the *Bowes Museum* (open daily; admission charge; phone: 833-690606), which looks exactly like a French château. John Bowes built it in 1869 in honor of his French wife. It houses a fine collection of paintings, furniture, and porcelain, hardly to be expected on the outskirts of a such small country town. The art collection at Lord Barnard's splendid 14th-century Raby Castle is also quite notable and worth the 6-mile drive from the main road (open Wednesday and Sunday afternoons, May and June; closed mornings and Saturdays, July through September; admission charge; phone: 833-60202). Take B6277, then A66 east to B6274, which leads into Richmond.

RICHMOND: Here the great ruins of Richmond Castle stand precariously above the River Swale, guarding Swaledale and the eastern access to the Yorkshire dales. The original fortress was erected in 1071, and the keep added about 100 years later. The *Georgian Theatre Royal* (Victoria Rd.; phone: 748-3021) is open to the public after a century of gathering dust; built in 1788, it is one of the oldest theaters in England.

Explorers will find a tour of the dales, a series of beautiful valleys in the Pennine Hills, a delightful activity. They are filled with small villages and warm Yorkshire stone houses. Swaledale, deeper and wilder than most other valleys, is worth following for the village Thwaite at the far end. Here the steep Buttertubs Pass (the buttertubs are circular holes in the limestone) leads over the hills to Hawes, a noted cheese center in pastoral Wensleydale.

En Route from Richmond – Take A6108, then B6270 and a secondary road to Hawes. Stay on the secondary road leading southeast from Hawes toward the villages of Grassington and Burnsall. Visit the ruins of Bolton Abbey just a few miles farther south (open daily; admission charge; phone: 75671-227).

From here a bona fide main road (A59) goes east to the resort town of Harrogate.

HARROGATE: Now a thriving convention center due to its hotels, parks, and shops, Harrogate had been noted for its mineral waters and clean mountain air (atop a plateau 500 feet above sea level). The 200-acre common, called the Stray, is still the town center. The *Royal Pump Room* (opposite the Valley Gardens), where the public baths were located, is now a museum (closed Mondays and February; admission charge; phone: 423-503340).

En Route from Harrogate – York is only 23 miles east of Harrogate on A59, but be prepared to stop at the old town of Knaresborough. Chief among the local sights is the celebrated Mother Shipton's Dropping Well (Mother Shipton was a witch), which has petrifying properties — you can leave something here and come back in a few years to find it turned to stone. Open daily April through October.

BEST EN ROUTE

Some of the nicest places to stay in northeast England are not the larger hotels but the small inns and private homes that offer bed and breakfast. In general, they are undistinguished places — roomy, warm, and comfortable — and they provide a basic level of service at a moderate price. Expect to pay $150 and up (including breakfast) for two in establishments classified below as very expensive; $120 to $150 in those listed as expensive; $80 to $120 in the moderate category; and $80 and under at places in the inexpensive category. (Prices in York are slightly higher.)

Bear in mind that these ranges are expressed in American dollars and that the currency exchange market is far from stable. You will find good food at reasonable prices in most places; a really excellent dinner for two with wine will cost about $60 to $80, considered moderate.

YORK

Royal York – A magnificent Victorian structure, this railway hotel has been operating for just over 100 years. Although certain necessary steps toward modernization have been taken, the traditional air remains, especially at teatime in the high-ceilinged lounge. Other features include a fitness room and a putting green in the formal gardens. Station Rd. (phone: 904-653681; fax: 904-623503). Very expensive.

Viking – Large and centrally located, this modern hotel stands out because of its excellent service. The interior is quite pleasant, and if you can get a room overlooking the river, it will add immeasurably to your stay. North St. (phone: 904-659822; fax: 904-641793). Expensive.

Hill – This Georgian establishment is family run, and since it has only 10 rooms, staying here is like staying in a private home — with your own bath or shower, use of a delightful garden, and traditional cuisine. About 2 miles from the city center. 60 York Rd., Acomb (phone: 904-790777). Moderate.

Hudson's – A large Victorian hostelry, a few minutes' walk from the city center. All 28 bedrooms have a private bath and a TV set, and good traditional English dishes are served in the restaurant "below stairs." 60 Bootham (phone: 904-621267). Moderate.

PICKERING

Forest and Vale – In summer the walled garden is a joy, and in winter curling up by the fireplace in this comfortable Georgian inn is the ultimate expression of quiet and cozy. Malton Rd. (phone: 751-72722). Moderate.

SCARBOROUGH

Royal – Truly a luxury liner among the resort hotels dotting this small town, this is a picture-perfect example of how the good life should be led. In this aged structure, the idea of ornate decoration comes back to life and blends well with the artwork on display. St. Nicholas St. (phone: 723-364333; fax: 723-500618). Expensive.

HELMSLEY

Black Swan – As traditional a northern inn as it is possible to find, this hotel was built in the 16th century of local stone, with public rooms of old wood and large fireplaces. Market Pl. (phone: 439-70466; fax: 439-70174). Very expensive.

Feversham Arms – Built of Yorkshire stone with 18 pretty bedrooms, the hotel also has an enjoyable restaurant. 1 High St. (phone: 439-70766; fax: 439-70346). Moderate.

DURHAM

Royal County – The aviary in the public area must have been added since this inn's days of catering to the horse and carriage set, and it's only one of the many tasteful improvements made over the years. A newer wing of rooms and a sauna have been added. Old Elvet (phone: 9138-66821; fax: 9138-60704). Expensive.

NEWCASTLE UPON TYNE

Gosforth Park – One of the very modern, very luxurious establishments in the area, this one is set in a wooded sector close to the racetrack about 4 miles north of the city. With 178 rooms, there is no shortage of facilities, and the service is excellent. High Gosforth Park (phone: 91-236-4111; fax: 91-236-8192). Very expensive.

County – An airy Victorian railway hotel, with just enough modernization to make you comfortable, but not so much that the hotel's own personality doesn't show through. The grand central staircase says it all. Neville St. (phone: 91-232-2471; fax: 91-232-1285). Expensive.

BERWICK-UPON-TWEED

King's Arms – This lovely Georgian coaching inn has a walled garden, 2 restaurants (one is a coffee shop modeled on an 18th-century stagecoach), and 2 bars (one in the converted stable block). Hide Hill (phone: 289-307454; fax: 289-308867). Moderate.

BLANCHLAND

Lord Crewe Arms – The medieval atmosphere at this hostelry isn't surprising, since the building includes parts of an 11th-century monastery that once occupied the site of the village. It's haunted, not by a monk, but by the ghost of a pretty girl, one Dorothy Foster, who has apparently been trying to deliver a message for the past 285 years. Near Consett (phone: 434-675251; fax: 434-675337). Moderate.

HARROGATE

Old Swan – A charming building, dating from 1700, that prides itself on old-fashioned comfort and service. The rooms are large, and the manners of the staff belong to the time when graciousness was a way of life rather than a business. Swan Rd. (phone: 423-500055). Expensive.

Drum and Monkey – A truly fish-only restaurant, even its walls are decked out with mounted fish. Enjoy a plate of Pacific oysters, a bowl of stewed mussels, or a hearty serving of grilled sole — along with a selection of good white wine. Closed Sundays. Reservations advised. Major credit cards accepted. 5 Montpellier Gardens (phone: 423-502650). Moderate.

The Scottish Lowlands: Sir Walter Scott Country

The Scottish Lowlands — the central and southern parts of the country — are, in the international popular imagination, at variance with the Highlands in almost every way. Whereas Highlanders are thought to be romantic, Catholic, Celtic, and volatile, Lowlanders are thought to be practical, Presbyterian, steady, and narrow. There is a grain of truth in this, but only a grain. The Lowlands are nothing if not romantic. They include Scotland's two best-known battle sites, for instance, each of them a mile from Stirling Castle: Stirling Bridge, where William Wallace drove back the English forces in 1297, and Bannockburn, where Robert the Bruce was victorious in the same cause in 1314.

The Scottish Borders, where Sir Walter Scott lived for most of his adult life, are noted for their peaceful rivers and famous ruined abbeys, to say nothing of numerous literary landmarks, including Scott's baronial country house at Abbotsford. The Trossachs, where so much of Scott's writing is set, are known as the Gateway to the Highlands (a title also claimed by Stirling) and are very lovely. Loch Lomond is there. And Glasgow, though inferior to Edinburgh in glamorous topography, is superior in theater and the arts; in recent years it has been transformed into an exceptionally attractive modern city.

An important tip for the unsuspecting motorist: Don't wait for good weather before setting off in your car in the morning — you might be a grandparent by the time it arrives. Pack snacks, bought from your hotel or a local bakery, for everybody (there are tearooms in the palatial *Gleneagles* hotel in Perthshire — see *Best en Route* — but precious few anywhere else). Scottish bakeries sell milk, sandwiches, and stuffed rolls as well as cakes and buttered scones. Try to tour Scotland in April and May or September and October, when crowds are thinner, the air crisper, and colors brighter. If you go in midsummer you will miss the beauteous yellow gorse (spring) and purple heather (autumn).

Your best bet in maps comes in a Scottish Tourist Board kit called *Enjoy Scotland*, which includes a small book listing 1,001 Scottish sights. All are marked on the map, along with golf courses, picnic tables, information centers — everything that legibly fits. The kit costs about $14 from the Scottish Tourist Board (23 Ravelston Ter., Edinburgh EH4 3EU, Scotland; phone: 31-332-2433; fax: 31-344-1513). It also is available from the tourist office at Waverley Market (3 Princes St., Edinburgh; phone: 31-557-1700 or 557-2727).

EDINBURGH: For a detailed report on Edinburgh and its hotels and restaurants, see *Edinburgh*, THE CITIES.

En Route from Edinburgh – Seventeen miles west of Edinburgh on the M9 is Linlithgow Palace, on the south shore of Loch Linlithgow. This breathtaking piece of fairy-tale architecture was the birthplace of Mary, Queen of Scots in 1542 and is one of Scotland's four royal palaces (the others are Falkland Palace in the kingdom of Fife, Stirling Castle, and Edinburgh's Holyrood House). James I of Scotland built it in the 15th century; later rulers extended it (open daily; admission charge; phone: 31-226-2570). Adjoining the palace is St. Michael's, one of the finest medieval parish churches in Scotland (open daily, June through September; weekdays the rest of the year; admission charge; phone: 506-842195).

STIRLING: If you want to see into Scotland's soul, stand on the heights of Stirling Castle Rock behind any of the castle cannonades and gaze northeast to the Grampian

Mountains, northwest to Stirling Bridge, or south to Bannockburn. Here, for centuries, was Scotland's sole defense against any English invasion of northern cities like Perth (an important medieval Scots town) and the Highlands. Whoever controlled Stirling Castle controlled the only route north across the River Forth. Scots patriot Sir William Wallace (1272–1305) and King Robert Bruce — known to history simply as the Bruce — had to hold the castle against the English to hold Scotland. They succeeded, though after years of intermittent battle, brave Wallace was betrayed to the English and hanged, drawn, and quartered in London. Since that time, all kinds of psychological and historical defense mechanisms against the English have become deeply rooted in Scottish hearts. The castle also houses the *Argyll and Sutherland Highlanders* military museum.

Once a residence for Stuart kings, the palace section of the castle is intriguing. Mary of Guise, the wife of James V, employed stonemasons from her native France to decorate its façade with Bacchanalian stonemasonry figures, providing a touch of Renaissance French fancy that is amusingly out of place in such a stern Scottish context. Both Mary, Queen of Scots and King James VI were crowned at Stirling Castle (open daily; admission charge; phone: 786-50000).

Surrounding the castle are many impressive buildings from the 16th and 17th centuries as well as the visitors' center (open year-round; admission charge; phone: 786-62517) with a multi-screen show and an imaginative picture gallery (there's also a bookshop, crafts shop, and tea garden).

A mile away, at Bannockburn, is another exhibition on Robert the Bruce, organized by the National Trust for Scotland. Open March through October. Admission charge. Off the A9, south of Stirling (phone: 786-812664).

DOUNE: The 14th-century castle here is pure picturebook stuff. Owned since the 16th century by the Earls of Moray, one of whom was a half-brother to Mary, Queen of Scots, this stark, towering edifice in a woodland between two streams has survived more or less in its original form, a rarity in Scotland. And it is so medieval that no one lives in it today. Also at Doune, 2 miles past the castle on A84, is the present earl's collection of vintage, veteran, and modern cars, the *Doune Motor Museum,* next to Doune Park Gardens, an idyllic 60 acres of woodland walks and flowering shrubs. The castle and gardens are open daily; the museum from April through October. Separate admission charges for each (phone: 786-841203 for all).

TROSSACHS: Scott made this part of Scotland famous with his narrative poem *The Lady of the Lake,* set at Loch Katrine, and with his novel *Rob Roy.* He encouraged his London acquaintances to visit the area until so many came that he complained, "Every London citizen makes Loch Lomond his washpot and throws his shoe over Ben Nevis." Yet today the Trossachs are curiously underdeveloped, which adds to their beauty but makes it difficult to find adequate hotels and restaurants. You will want to drive north on A84 from Callander past Loch Lubnaig to Rob Roy's grave at Balquhidder, a route almost smothered in wild primroses. Turn left onto A821 just north of Callander to tour Lochs Katrine, Achray, and Venachar. Then follow A81 from Callander southwest to A811 and on to the famous Loch Lomond itself.

LOCH LOMOND: Loll on the beach on the eastern shore, gazing at purple mountains studded with rivulets and waterfalls. A tourist center at Balloch, on the southern tip of Loch Lomond, will provide plenty of information to inspire you (open year-round; phone: 389-53533).

GLASGOW: Although this preeminently industrial city had fallen on hard times since the great days of the "tobacco lords" (merchants involved in trade with America) in the 18th century and the Clydeside shipbuilders in the 19th, in the mid-1970s the city witnessed a rebirth of cultural productivity and awareness when street after street of houses began major renovations, revealing a splendor few realized existed. Indeed, there has been talk all over Britain of a Glasgow renaissance, arising from the city's claim to such fine additions as the *Burrell Collection* (see below) and, most of all, the European Parliament's selection of Glasgow as the Cultural Capital of Europe for 1990, which featured an array of cultural events, attracting travelers from all over the world. Today a brighter-than-ever spotlight shines on the city.

Nowhere in Scotland is the spirit more indomitable or the humor more pungent, as you'll quickly learn when you talk to Glaswegians. The city is medieval — like so many medieval cities, growing up around a 13th-century cathedral. Its most imposing architecture is Victorian, and the buildings around George Square could provide a primer in Victorian excess and excellence. The interior of the city, however, has been redesigned to produce an effective and attractive modern landscape. Glasgow Dockland, in particular, on the river Clyde, has undergone a near-miraculous transformation. After a stroll through George Square and surrounding streets and environs, make for the Glasgow University area in Kelvingrove. The *Glasgow Art Gallery and Museum* here is studded with the work of French Impressionists and of talented Scots Impressionists who were influenced by them (open daily; no admission charge; phone: 41-357-3929). Treat yourself to a stroll through Kelvingrove Park along the River Kelvin. The *Burrell Collection* (in Pollok Country Park) has become Scotland's most popular tourist attraction, with its 19th-century French paintings and its art objects, ceramics, furniture, and stained glass (closed Sunday mornings; no admission charge; phone: 41-649-7151).

At night the excellent *Scottish Opera Company* performs at the *Theatre Royal* (Hope St.; phone: 41-331-1234). The *Glasgow Citizens' Theatre Company* (119 Gorbals St.; box office phone: 41-429-5561 or 41-429-0022) stages avant-garde productions of traditional plays that make off-Broadway look like a vicar's tea party.

NEW LANARK: The old mills here and the town that is an integral part of them are one of the earliest experiments in progressive labor management. In 1799 the Welsh socialist Robert Owen bought the mills at New Lanark and went about creating a humane work situation. He stopped child labor, instituted a program of health insurance for workers, built clean, livable housing, and opened schools and recreation facilities. In 1829, after disagreements with his partners (one of whom was Jeremy Bentham), he withdrew, but in the meantime he financed a new utopian experiment in New Harmony, Indiana, that was far less successful (in part, because it was a community of intellectuals committed more to ideology than cooperation). History buffs will want to follow the Heritage Trail; for more information contact the tourist information center (phone: 555-61345).

PEEBLES: This pleasant old wool manufacturing town by the River Tweed is an excellent base for exploring the Borders. Adjoining Peebles on the west is Neidpath Castle, a striking, 13th-century stronghold with walls 11 feet thick (open *Easter* through mid-October; admission charge; phone: 8757-201).

En Route from Peebles – Seven miles east of Peebles on A72 is Traquair House, dating from the 10th century, the oldest continuously inhabited dwelling in Scotland. Twenty-seven Scottish and English monarchs have visited it. Ale is still produced at its 18th-century brewhouse. Open every afternoon, *Easter* through mid-October, and daily, July through mid-September. Admission charge (phone: 896-830323).

ABBOTSFORD: No visit to Scott country would be complete without a stop at Scott's home on A72, 12 miles east of Traquair House. Scott built this ornate mansion between 1817 and 1822, using the most romantic materials he could find. He made a special trip to attend the razing of Edinburgh's 14th-century tolbooth, for instance, known as "the Heart of Midlothian" (also the title of a Scott novel), in order to make off with its front door, which he then had incorporated into the design of his new abode.

A guide will take you through from March through October, daily, except Sunday mornings. Admission charge (phone: 896-2043).

Nearby are Melrose and Dryburgh abbeys, two famous border abbeys dear to Scott's heart. Melrose Abbey, founded in 1136, is renowned for its traceried stonework; Dryburgh Abbey, which also dates from the 12th century, houses Scott's tomb. Both are below Abbotsford, on A6091. For more information, contact the tourist information office (phone: 89682-2555).

BEST EN ROUTE

From May through September it is advisable to book ahead, as accommodations are often hard to find on the spot. Lunches in Scottish hotels are served approximately between noon and 2 PM, dinners approximately between 7 and 9 PM unless otherwise noted. Establishments charging $120 and up per night for two occupants with breakfast are listed as expensive; those with rates from $85 to $120 are considered moderate; and those charging under $85, as inexpensive. For dinner for two with wine, expect to pay about $90 in expensive restaurants in the area; $75 to $90 in moderate restaurants; and less than $75 in those listed as inexpensive.

STIRLING

Golden Lion – Though now clinging for dear life to its immaculate historic pedigree, this 84-room hotel is nonetheless the best of Stirling's lately rather dubious center-city bets. Robert Burns, the royal family, and a host of film stars have all stayed here. 8 King St. (phone: 786-75351; fax: 786-72755). Moderate.

CALLANDER

Roman Camp – There are 14 bedrooms and a few very decorative and very alive peacocks trailing across the lawn of this 17th-century hunting lodge. English and Scottish dishes are served in its restaurant. Reservations necessary. Off Main St. (phone: 877-30003; fax: 877-0764). Moderate.

KILLEARN

Black Bull – Famed for its food as far afield as Glasgow, the cuisine is traditional English and Scottish and perfectly wonderful. High tea also is served. Reservations necessary May through September, especially on weekends. Major credit cards accepted. Off Main St. (phone: 360-50215). Inexpensive.

GLASGOW

Albany – Glasgow's finest business-center-cum-hotel where the visiting pop stars stay in the uneasy company of executives. This is a slick, 251-room, flat-topped box with a big-city image. Inside, it's soft lights, carpets, and chrome. One of the 2 dining rooms is a popular carvery with Scottish traditional cooking. Rates are lower on weekends. Bothwell St. (phone: 41-248-2656; fax: 41-221-9202). Expensive to moderate.

Hospitality Inn – A modern, 316-room hotel in the heart of Glasgow, its *Garden Café* serves dinner from 5 to 11 PM for "a taste of Scotland." Rates are lower on weekends. 36 Cambridge St. (phone: 41-332-3311; fax: 41-332-4050). Expensive to moderate.

Stakis Grosvenor – This modernized Victorian residence has 95 attractive and comfortable bedrooms. Dinner from 5 PM. Rates are lower on weekends. Grosvenor Ter. at Great Western Rd. (phone: 41-339-8811; fax: 41-334-0710). Expensive to moderate.

Babbity Bowser – A hotel-cum-restaurant with a sense of humor, this 1790 building (attributed to Robert Adam) hosts poetry readings and folk evenings. There are 6 simple rooms, and real Scottish fare is served. Open daily. Restaurant reservations necessary. Major credit cards accepted. Central location at 16 Blackfriars St. (phone: 41-552-5055). Moderate.

Central – It's comfortable in an old-fashioned way. There are 219 sumptuous bedrooms and 2 restaurants, the *Entresol* and the *Carvery* (open for breakfast and dinner; reservations required). Major credit cards accepted. Gordon St. (phone: 41-221-9680; fax: 41-226-3948). Moderate.

PEEBLES

Park – Ideal for fishing, riding, golf, and tennis; its paneled dining room, bar, and lounge look out over landscaped gardens and Cademuir Hills. There are 26 rooms. Innerleithen Rd. (phone: 721-20451). Moderate.

Peebles Hotel Hydro – This palatial estate stands by a lovely waterfall in one of Scotland's most historic areas. There's a swimming pool, squash court, and parkland offering a variety of activities. English and Scottish traditional cooking are the dining room's features. Off A702, on Innerleithen Rd. (phone: 721-20602; fax: 721-22999). Moderate.

Scotland's Fabled Golf Courses

If you're a golfer and haven't played in Scotland, you haven't seen where it all began and where it's still mostly "at." Assuming your plane lands at Prestwick, just above the old market town of Ayr, you are already in the heart of Scottish golf country. There are eight championship courses in the Prestwick area, including the course at Prestwick itself, the site of the first-ever *Open* in 1860. All the courses on the tour outlined below (except *Gleneagles*) are links courses, which means they consist of tough seaside dunes riddled with furzy clumps and covered by the merest modicum of grass (except, of course, for the bunkers). Americans aren't used to playing on links courses; for a few tips see the *Useful Hints* at the end of this route.

TURNBERRY: This massive vacationers' paradise, which looks like a landlocked ocean liner, has as its front lawn the world-famous *Ailsa and Arran* courses. If you can afford it, stay at this elegant hotel for 2 or 3 days and use it as a base to make the rounds of the six neighboring championship links (the desk clerk will give you directions).

The 9th hole of the *Ailsa,* Bruce's Castle, has a tee isolated on a promontory, complete with a picturesque lighthouse, that juts into the Firth of Clyde. You'll need a crack shot over the water to get your ball back on the mainland. The *Turnberry* hotel caters to golfing needs, at a reduced rate for residents. Handicap certificate required. *Turnberry Hotel,* Turnberry, Strathclyde KA26 9LT, Scotland (phone: Turnberry 655-31000). For more information on the hotel, see *Best en Route* below.

ROYAL TROON: There are two courses here, the *Portland* and the *Old,* the latter a championship course. The *Old* course is out along the beach, with the outgoing nine heading virtually straight down the strand and the closing nine paralleling it only a few yards inland, the only distraction — aside from the view of the Firth of Clyde, the Isle of Arran, and flaming sunsets — is the course's location directly below the flight path into Prestwick Airport. So it sometimes seems as though players are about to be sucked up into the jet wash. Another classic *British Open* layout, it is one of the few important private clubs in Scotland, though playing privileges are usually made available to visitors who are members of clubs in the US. The *Old* Course is open to women on Mondays, Wednesdays, and Fridays. No visitors on Fridays or weekends. Advance booking necessary. *Royal Troon Golf Club,* Craigend Rd., Troon, Strathclyde, Scotland KA10 6EP (phone: 292-311555).

PRESTWICK: Now considered too old-fashioned for the *British Open* rota because of its small, whimsical fairways and limited facilities for handling crowds, this tough, historic course, the scene of 24 *Opens,* is nonetheless full of hidden surprises and is worth playing at least once. This course also gets its share of racket from Prestwick Airport. Visitors can play on weekdays, by application only. There are no ladies' tees, but women are welcome in the Cardinal Room for light refreshments. Bookings must be made well in advance. *Prestwick Golf Club,* Links Rd., Prestwick KA9 1QG, Ayrshire, Scotland (phone: 292-77404).

THE OLD COURSE, ST. ANDREWS: St. Andrews is the world's "home of golf," a shrine to which all serious golfers should eventually make a pilgrimage. The *Old Course,* famous since golf was played with knives and forks, is on the West Sands at the junction of Golf Place and the Links. It is shaped as God made it, bunkers and all, even where, as on Heathery Hole (the 12th), the bunkers are in the middle of the fairway and not seen from the tee. The *Old Course* is full of bad kicks and subject to capricious changes in the direction of its high winds. It never plays the same way twice and can damage your ego, yet such is its magic that golfers who begin by hating it invariably end loving it. There are four other courses on the same site — the *Balgove* (a 9-hole beginners' course), *Eden, Jubilee,* and *New* (which was *opened* in 1894), but it's the *Old* that any dedicated golfer must play.

Just behind the *Old*'s first tee is the stately, sacrosanct clubhouse headquarters of the *Royal and Ancient Golf Club* (known as the *R & A*). Its members, a kind of board of directors of world golf, gaze at you sardonically from the "Big Room" through a bay window as you tee off. Pay no attention to them. Don't miss the displays of old clubs, trophies, films, and quizzes at the excellent new *British Golf Museum* behind the *R & A* (open daily, March through September; closed Mondays the rest of the year; admission charge; phone: 334-78880). For a real slice of local color, try to get a caddie from the Caddie Master opposite the *R & A* clubhouse. The true Scottish caddie, now a dying breed, is most often a mature gentleman of modest size with a 10-day growth of beard who is too old to lift a club but too young to forget when he could. He knows each blade of grass on the course by heart, and has seen innumerable *Opens.* His accent sounds like a pneumatic drill. He'll advise what club you need for every shot, then stand aside implacably while you sklaff into the wee burn. Clubs and carts are also for hire.

It's a good idea to contact the Links Management Committee of *St. Andrews* at least 8 weeks (though a year is not too early) before your visit to apply to play on the *Old Course* (phone: 334-73393). Otherwise you may find you can't get near it. Forms are not issued for Saturdays or Thursday afternoons. The *Old Course* is closed Sundays. Handicap certificate required. Write to *Links Management Committee of St. Andrews,* St. Andrews, Fife, KY16 9JA Scotland (phone: 334-75757).

En Route from St. Andrews – Take A91 west across Fife, past peaceful Loch Leven, to the Yetts of Muckart (about 37 miles), where you'll join A823. Follow it north 9 miles into Perthshire to the *Gleneagles* hotel. About 5 miles beyond the Yetts of Muckart you'll be high above Glen Devon, with a panoramic view southwest across Stirling Plain. Go slowly and enjoy it.

GLENEAGLES: This is Scottish heaven for American golfers, not only because championships are played here, but also because the moist, thick turf on its greens is comfortably like the turf at home. There are two 18-hole golf courses, the *King's* and *Queen's,* and the 9-hole *Monarch Wee. Gleneagles* is also a luxury hotel, even grander than *Turnberry* (see *Best en Route*) and with almost as many ballrooms as tearooms — plus an Equestrian Centre, of which the queen's estranged son-in-law, Mark, is co-proprietor, and former racecar driver Jackie Stewart's shooting school, reputed to be the biggest and best in Europe. The golf courses are open to visitors, but hotel guests have priority. *Gleneagles Hotel,* Auchterarder, Perthshire PH3 1NF, Scotland (phone: 764-62231; fax: 764-62134).

Useful Hints: To play on links courses you need a wedge, a brush-up on your pitch-and-run technique, and a canny way of sizing up the wind, which can change a par three to a par five. Bring a nylon rainsuit that fits over your clothes, wear dark colors if you don't want to be stared at, and take note that women are not allowed in many clubhouse bars. Cut down the number of clubs you carry, and most important of all, speed up your game. Only at *Turnberry* and *Gleneagles* dare you pause to make bets, drink beer, or tell jokes. No four-ball games are allowed at private clubs on weekends. A letter of introduction from your home club secretary must be handed to the secretary of any private club a day in advance. Order lunch in advance in clubhouse dining rooms and wear a shirt and tie.

Listed below, area by area, are suggestions for family outings while the golfers are slamming balls down the fairways.

At St. Andrews:
The West Sands, the town's lovely, long, clean beach.
The *St. Andrews Woollen Mill,* just by the *Old Course* on the street called the Golf Links. Fair Isle and Shetland knitwear is sold at factory prices. Closed Sundays.
St. Andrews University, the oldest in Scotland (1412). Its buildings dot the town's central shopping area (South St. and district).
Falkland Palace, one of the homes of the Stuart kings, built 1501–1541, 15 miles west of St. Andrews on A91, then 2 miles south on A912. Open daily, *Easter* through September; weekends only in October. Admission charge (phone: 33-757397).

At Gleneagles:
The town of **Auchterarder,** a mile away, famed for its antiques shops (the hotel desk clerk will give you directions).

In Ayrshire:
See the *Western Scotland* route, Ayrshire section.

BEST EN ROUTE

Expect to pay $200 and up per night for a double room with breakfast in those establishments we list as very expensive; between $130 and $190 at expensive places; $85 to $125, moderate; and $80 or under at inexpensive hotels. For restaurants, the ranges are $45 and up for a dinner for two in the expensive category; $25 to $45 in the moderate; and $25 and under in the inexpensive category. Prices do not include wine, drinks, or tip.

PRESTWICK

Carlton – A modern, 39-room hotel near shopping centers and featuring free live entertainment. Dinner from 6 PM. 187 Ayr Rd. (phone: 292-76811; fax: 292-76811, Ext. 249). Moderate.

TURNBERRY

Turnberry – Catering to golf enthusiasts (see above), the hostelry's 115 rooms are all uniquely decorated in an Edwardian style. In addition to the two 18-hole championship golf courses, there are 2 tennis courts, a swimming pool, a sauna, and 12 horses for riding. A new multimillion-dollar health spa completes this resort where even non-athletic visitors can relax. The hostelry's restaurant features French fare, in addition to English and Scottish traditional cooking, served in a lavish Edwardian atmosphere, in a lovely setting overlooking the sea. On A77, off A719, by Turnberry Lighthouse (phone: 655-31000; fax: 655-31706). Very expensive.

TROON

Marine Highland – Overlooking the 18th fairway, this is Troon's finest hotel. In addition to the distinguished restaurant, there's an outstanding health and leisure club. Reservations necessary May through September. Crosbie Rd. (phone: 292-314444; fax: 292-316922). Expensive.

ST. ANDREWS

Old Course – Completely refurbished and the only luxury hotel *in* the home of the *Old Course* golf course (at the edge of the 17th fairway), this hostelry has stylish rooms. No golf on Sundays. Old Station Rd. (phone: 334-74371 or *Preferred Hotels Worldwide,* 800-323-7500; fax: 334-77668). Very expensive.

Rusack's – Set beside the 18th hole of the *Old Course,* this hotel, established in 1887, offers 50 comfortable rooms, off-season golf packages, and full clubhouse facilities. St. Andrews (phone: 334-74321; fax: 334-77896). Expensive.

St. Andrews Golf – The view here, through bay windows adorned with flower boxes and looking out to sea, is completely delightful. So are the resident owners. English and Scottish traditional cooking. The Scores (phone: 334-72611; fax: 334-72188). Moderate.

AUCHTERARDER

Gleneagles – Pleasingly palatial, with incomparable service and decor and a menu that is a magnum opus. It's a haven for golfers, with 3 of the best courses in Scotland. There's also a domed leisure center with a pool, squash court, and sauna, along with facilities for shooting and horseback riding. Off A823; 2 miles from Auchterarder (phone: 7646-3543). Very expensive.

Scottish Highlands: Edinburgh to Inverness

The Scottish Highlands, scene of some of the most barbaric events in the history of Britain, are also full of some of the most breathtaking scenery in the world. Highlanders, many of whom are pure Gaels, have the lilting voices and mercurial natures associated with their Irish cousins. Like the peasant Irish, Highlanders were victimized and exploited by an ascendancy class. During the so-called Highland Clearances, which began in the late 18th century, crofters were driven from their homes so that landowners could replace them with sheep, at that time a more lucrative proposition. Those who refused to go had their houses and worldly goods burned. Hundreds of families fled south, jobless and possessionless, at the mercy of fortune, speaking only their native Celtic tongue.

Today 10% of the Scottish population owns 84% of the land, which shows how little things have changed since the 18th century. Great regions of lonely moors and mountains remain in the grip of a handful of aristocrats who live in London and come north to hunt, shoot, and fish. You can see them in droves in the spring at 9 AM in the *Station* hotel dining room in Inverness, just off the London train, madly excited by the chill Highland air, dripping with tweeds, and all barking at once for kippers and cream at shy native waitresses. Nowadays, wealthy travelers from Germany, Japan, and the US fly into Inverness, dressed in tweeds and leather. "Gillies" (guides) accompany them on hunting expeditions, stalking deer, shooting grouse, and catching salmon.

The Edinburgh-to-Inverness route described here takes you through the eastern and central Highland regions, which are lusher, more prosperous, more forested, and less Gaelic than the western regions. Some west Highland areas (not Gaelic ones) are included in the *Western Scotland* route.

EDINBURGH: For a complete description of the city and its hotels and restaurants, see *Edinburgh,* THE CITIES.

En route from Edinburgh – From the west end of Princes Street, follow Queensferry Road north across the Forth Road Bridge to the two-lane M90 (about 13 miles). Three miles farther is Dunfermline, the capital of Scotland in the early Middle Ages, when Edinburgh was a mere castle.

DUNFERMLINE: Dunfermline Abbey is a royal imperative for tourists. King Robert the Bruce was buried in the abbey choir in 1329 and King Charles I, born in the abbey guesthouse in 1600. An attractive modern brass marks Bruce's grave, now under the roof of the parish church, the Norman nave of which is built over the abbey ruins. Parts of the original 11th-century monastic buildings can still be seen here (closed Sunday mornings; admission charge; Monastery St.).

The American steel king and millionaire Andrew Carnegie (1835–1919) is a third major personage associated with Dunfermline. He was born here in a damask weaver's cottage on Moodie Street (open daily, April through October, from 11 AM to 5 PM, except Sunday mornings; daily from 2 to 6 PM, November through March; no admission charge; phone: 383-724302).

En Route from Dunfermline – Twelve miles beyond Dunfermline you might stop for a *coup d'oeil* at the Moors of Kinross and peaceful Loch Leven, on your right. Mary, Queen of Scots was imprisoned in Loch Leven Castle — on the island in the center of the lake — for 11 months in 1567 (open daily April through September; admission charge). You can visit the castle by getting off the M90 at the Kinross interchange and taking a ferry from Kinross pier. For more information contact the Kinross Tourist Information Centre (phone: 577-63680).

DUNKELD: Want a taste of paradise? Have a picnic on the Dunkeld Cathedral grounds by the bonnie banks of the river Tay. (You can get sandwiches at the *Country Bakery* on Atholl St.) This idyllic spot was the ancient capital of the Picts and Scots from AD 850, and the bones of the great St. Columba of Iona, founder of the Celtic Christian church, were lodged at Dunkeld Cathedral for a time after the Vikings raided Iona in 597. Along with the charming cathedral, you'll love the 40-odd 17th-century row houses (admission charge), restored by the National Trust for Scotland, that make up the main part of the village. For details contact the Dunkeld Information Centre (phone: 3502-688).

PITLOCHRY: It seems a veritable Brigadoon with its storybook array of gabled houses and country churches rising sharply up the Tummel River valley brae only to be locked in by giant heather-covered mountains. The town is beautifully situated and consequently a famous resort with many activities, including the *Pitlochry Festival Theatre,* bagpipe and drum pageants, *Highland Games* (mid-September), mountain climbing, pony trekking, organized nature trail hiking (with Scottish National Forest brochures on plants, birds, and animals), golfing, and salmon fishing.

Use Pitlochry as a base for a couple of side trips. A couple of miles north of Pitlochry on B8019 is the entrance to the famed Queen's View above Loch Tummel, where Queen Victoria used to picnic. As you leave Loch Tummel, look to your left for Mt. Schiehallion, the conical peak so perfect in shape that scientists used it to compute the earth's mass. At the village called Kinloch Rannoch, follow the small, unnumbered road around Loch Rannoch's south shore. Here is the beautiful Black Wood of Rannoch, the last piece of medieval forest in Scotland.

South of Pitlochry, cross the River Tay and follow the A827 and then B846 to the turnoff for Glen Lyon (follow the signs for Fortingall). Glen Lyon is the longest glen in Scotland, beloved for its sun-speckled, wooded glades and the plethora of legends associated with it.

En Route from Glen Lyon – At the Bridge of Balgie, over the river Lyon, an unnumbered road runs south to join A827 beside Loch Tay. Take this and turn right at the junction. In 6 miles you'll be at Killin, famous for its lake view and dazzling waterfall, a typical example of Highland scenery at its finest.

PASS OF KILLIECRANKIE: At this luscious wooded gorge, on A9 north of Pitlochry, especially beautiful in autumn, Viscount Claverhouse ("Bonnie Dundee") and his Jacobite army routed the English troops of William III in 1689. The National Trust for Scotland has a visitors' center and a battle display here (open *Easter* to mid-October; phone: 796-3233).

BLAIR ATHOLL: Nearby is Blair Castle, the family seat of the Dukes of Atholl, head of the Clan Murray. The present duke lives in Blair Castle, where he keeps the last and only legal private army in Europe, the Atholl Highlanders (about 65 men). Thirty-two rooms of his 700-year-old abode are awash in Chippendale, Limoges, Zoffany, and Jacobite relics. Open daily, including the attractive tearoom, from *Easter* through mid-October; closed Sunday mornings. Admission charge (phone: 79681-207).

En Route from Blair Atholl – The A9 runs near Newtonmore, known throughout the Highlands for its shinty team (shinty is a faster, fiercer form of hockey). You pass the usually bustling shinty field as you enter town.

KINGUSSIE: The ruins of rocky Ruthven Barracks are visible from the main road. These were maintained by English forces as a defense against Jacobite uprisings between the rebellions of 1715 and 1745. (The fact that there *was* a Jacobite Rebellion in 1745 may say something about their effectiveness.) Visit the Highland folk museum called *Am Fasgadh* ("The Shelter" in Gaelic) by the river. It has a furnished thatch cottage that illustrates how bleak life in northern Scotland once was (open daily April through October; weekends November through March; admission charge; phone: 5402-307).

AVIEMORE: Several top class, formal hotels, such as the *Stakis Coylumbridge* and the *Aviemore Highlands* (see *Best en Route*), overlook this popular ski resort's snow-studded Cairngorm Mountains. Slalom into the sunset above an incredible view at 11 o'clock at night! The slopes are rough but cheap. Information about prices, opening times, equipment rental, and so forth is available at the Spey Valley Tourist Organization (Aviemore; phone: 479-810363).

En Route from Aviemore – Detour off A9 to the town of Carrbridge, nip into the *Landmark Visitor Centre,* the first exhibition of its kind in Europe (open daily; admission charge; phone: 3384-334). Ten thousand years of Highland history are surveyed entertainingly in a triple-screen audiovisual theater.

If time isn't pressing, take the B970 along the valley of the River Spey, passing the Loch Garten Nature Reserve where, in 1959, ospreys (long extinct in Scotland) returned to nest (open daily; admission charge; phone: 479-83694). From Speybridge, follow the signs on the A939 and the B976 to Braemar. Here sits Balmoral, the royal family's summer home since 1852. The estate consists of 11,000 acres beside the delightful River Dee. Only the grounds and a portion of the house are open to the public (Mondays through Saturdays, May through July), and then only when no royalty is in residence (admission charge; phone: 3384-334).

INVERNESS: Despite its glamorous site on the Moray Firth, Inverness is the Plain Jane of Scottish cities. It won't make you wish you were a painter, but it *will* give you a center from which to strike out in all directions for Scotland's most ethereal parts. Ideas for day trips are legion at the Inverness, Loch Ness and Nairn Tourist Board (23 Church St.; phone: 463-234353). Musts are Culloden Moor, where Bonnie Prince Charlie's army was decimated in the famous Jacobite uprising of 1746, and Loch Ness, whose 22-mile length can be scouted for the monster by driving south on A82. The first recorded sighting of the monster was by St. Columba nearly 1,500 years ago; it continues to be at home to visitors, but with no formal hours. Culloden's *Old Leanach Farmhouse,* now a battle museum, also is worth seeing (open daily, *Easter* through October; admission charge; phone: 463-790607).

BEST EN ROUTE

Expect to pay about $200 per night for a double room with breakfast in hotels classified as very expensive; $140 to $195 in the expensive category; $85 to $135 in the moderate category; and under $80 in the inexpensive category. For restaurants, the ranges are $45 and up for a dinner for two in the expensive category; $25 to $45 in the moderate; and $25 and under in the inexpensive category. Prices do not include wine, drinks, or tip.

DUNFERMLINE

King Malcolm Thistle – Dunfermline's finest hostelry is named for the Malcolm who overthrew Macbeth (his wife, Queen Margaret, founded Dunfermline Abbey). Modern by design, but with English and Scottish traditional cooking. Queensferry Rd., Wester Pitcorthie, just south at A823 (phone: 383-722611; fax:; 383-730865). Moderate.

PITLOCHRY

Atholl Palace – This turreted Victorian monster with a glowingly comfortable interior and sweepingly glorious view was built in 1880 as a health resort alongside some healing spas. More soothing today is its fine Scottish cooking, including grouse and other game. It's on its own secluded grounds on Atholl Rd.; look for the sign at the turnoff south of Pitlochry on A9 (phone: 796-2400; fax: 796-3036). Expensive.

Green Park – Its very beautiful setting — on Loch Faskally overlooking the mountains — is much admired by the outdoorsy people who visit this hotel to fish, hike, or ski. There are 37 rooms, each with private bath and television. The restaurant serves traditional Scottish fare, and there is a bar. Clunie Bridge Rd. (phone: 796-3248). Moderate.

AVIEMORE

Stakis Coylumbridge – Very modern and plush, it offers a variety of athletic activities, including a gym, 2 indoor pools, and tennis. English and Scottish traditional cooking in the dining room at the usual hours and snacks in the coffee shop from 10 AM to 10 PM. Rates are lower the longer you stay. At Coylumbridge, on A951 en route to the Cairngorms from A9 (phone: 479-810661; fax: 479-811309). Expensive.

Aviemore Highlands – Every morning the chef at this hotel decides what will be on the evening's menu; try requesting your favorite dinner dish at breakfast by getting your waitress to carry a message on a paper napkin. On the road to the Cairngorms just past Aviemore Centre; follow the signs from A9 (phone: 479-810771). Moderate.

BALLATER

Craigendarroch – Half hotel and half time-share, this former baronial mansion is set in some of Scotland's most breathtaking highlands, overlooking the River Dee. Guests can use the country club facilities, including a pool, sauna, gym, snooker table and even a dry ski slope. Braemar Rd., Ballater, Royal Deeside (phone: 3397-55858; fax: 3397-55447). Very expensive.

INVERNESS

Culloden House – *The* place to stay at Inverness, in rural splendor below Culloden Moor. The light, spacious rooms of this beautiful 18th-century palace are full of ornate plasterwork and priceless antique furniture. On Culloden Moor (phone: 463-790461; fax: 463-792181). Very expensive.

Station – The Victorian decor of this 59-room relic is comfortably plush. Its restaurant serves good traditional English and Scottish fare. Academy St. (phone: 463-231926; fax: 463-710705). Expensive.

Kingsmills – Ten minutes' walk from downtown, this striking, white, 200-year-old time capsule with its front door in an architraved turret has 70 rooms, a swimming pool, squash courts, and 4 acres of gardens. Culcabock Rd. (phone: 463-237166; fax: 463-225208). Moderate.

Cummings – In spite of the complete ordinariness of this 38-room rectangle, this place somehow manages to be endearing. Nightly Scottish cabarets here have been wowing audiences from June to September for years. Church St. (phone: 463-232531). Inexpensive.

Western Scotland

Ayrshire is famous for its golf courses, its cattle, its golden beaches and quaint Victorian resort towns, its comparatively dry climate, and its view of the Isle of Arran. It is even more famous, however, as the home of Robert Burns, the 18th-century rustic bard who heralded poetry's Romantic Age. Scotland may be the only country in the world to celebrate its national identity by paying homage to a poet. On February 22, when Americans are sedately eating cherry pie in memory of George Washington, the Scots are just beginning to surface after the revels of *Burns Night* (January 25). The festivities include elaborate banquets of Scottish dishes, innumerable toasts, poetry recitals, and piping, singing, and dancing till dawn. This night (together with *New Year's Eve*) is traditionally a time for the wild side of the Scot, seemingly shrouded the rest of the year in rock-ribbed Presbyterianism, to come out, as it were, for Ayr.

North of Ayrshire is world-famous Inveraray Castle, the seat of the Dukes of Argyll. About 40 miles farther up the coast is lovely Oban, a starting place for the Western Isles and a good point of departure for touring the western Highlands.

Assuming you have arrived at Prestwick Airport, take the coast road, A79, 5 miles south to Ayr past a succession of Victorian villas that are now small hotels specializing in malt Scotch whiskies.

AYR: This cozy harbor and market town was chartered in the 13th century and is now a popular resort, with a marvelous beach and a nationally famous racecourse. The only architectural relics left in the town are the Tower of St. John, which is believed to date from the 13th century (Citadel Pl. and Eglinton Terr.); the Auld Brig, which Burns praised in his poem *The Twa Brigs* (High St.); 16th-century Loudoun Hall, townhouse of the hereditary sheriffs of Ayrshire (Boat Vennel); and the Auld Kirk, built by Oliver Cromwell in 1654, in which Burns was baptized (off High St., diagonally opposite Newmarket St.). For more information on all these historical sites, call 292-284196.

South of the town, off B7024, you might want to spend a happy hour or two at Belleisle Park, which has a zoo, nature trail, gardens, and a championship golf course (phone: 292-41258).

ALLOWAY: Burns's birthplace is a tiny, pastoral village on the River Doon, a leafy haven dominated by the rather incongruous Corinthian columns of the Burns Monument, which makes you feel as though you'd wandered into a painting by Fragonard. The only evidence of time's incursion into Alloway is the *Land O'Burns Centre* (open daily; phone: 292-43700), featuring a visual display, crafts shop, bookstall, cafeteria, and landscaped gardens with picnic tables. Across the street, the humble, whitewashed cottage in which the poet was born in 1759 has been preserved intact (open daily, except Sundays, November through March; phone: 292-41215). Adjoining the cottage is the *Burns Museum.* (The museum, crafts shop, and gardens are open daily *Easter* through October; admission charge to all Burns buildings; phone: 292-41321.) A little farther up the road is the 700-year-old Brig O'Doon, the arched bridge where the witch in Burns's poem "Tam O'Shanter" caught hold of Tam's mare's tail, and Auld Alloway Kirk, the scene of the witches' revels in the poem. If you have a day to spare, you can follow the Burns Heritage Trail, visiting every place Burns ever went, from Ayr to Dumfries in the next county. Details are available at the *Burns Museum.*

  En Route from Alloway – On A719, heading south toward Culzean Castle, there's a sign marking the Croy Brae, also known as Electric Brae. As you climb it, shift gear into neutral: you will then coast *uphill!* Coming down the other side, shift into neutral again: Now you are coasting uphill backward! Natives swear it is an optical illusion.

CULZEAN CASTLE: Standing on a cliff overlooking the Firth of Clyde, this breathtaking edifice is one of Scotland's most-visited castles. Culzean Castle (the name, pronounced *Cul*-lane, refers to the caves over which the castle is built) was for centuries the seat of the Kennedy family, later the Kennedys of Cassilis. Most of the present structure was designed for the tenth Earl of Cassilis in the late 18th century by the famous Scottish architect Robert Adam. Adam's achievements here include the much-admired oval staircase and his remarkable drum-shaped drawing rooms (with curved fireplaces) giving onto the sea. The uppermost apartments were given to President Eisenhower to use as his Scottish residence as a token of appreciation after World War II. The castle's portrait of Napoleon was a gift from Josephine, a relation of the Kennedys. Castle open daily 10:30 AM to 6 PM (5 PM during winter). Admission charge (phone: 6556-274).

En Route from Culzean Castle – Return to Ayr by A77, past the ruins of Crossraguel Abbey, founded in 1244, whose last abbot was roasted by the Kennedys in the 16th century until he signed away his lands. Closed Thursdays evenings and Fridays. Admission charge (no phone).

Beyond Ayr, traveling north on A78, you come to the sailing towns of Irvine, Saltcoats, and Largs. You can rent boats at the latter (contact the Largs Tourist Information Office; phone: 475-673765). At Gourock, also a seaside holiday center, hop a ferry for Dunoon, the main town across the firth on the Cowal Peninsula. Ferries run every hour, and the ride is 20 minutes (phone: 475-33755).

DUNOON: This burgeoning vacationland has a 4-mile waterside promenade running alongside piers, gardens, amusement arcades, amazing views, and fancy hotels. On summer nights in the gardens there are band concerts, model boat displays, variety shows, flower shows, dances, tournaments, and Highland games. It's a good place to spend a night if you like crowds and gaiety. Holy Loch, with its US submarine base, is just beside it.

INVERARAY: Far more peaceful than Dunoon and more beautiful as well, the hereditary seat of the Dukes of Argyll, chiefs of the powerful Clan Campbell, is ethereal in its isolation by the quiet waters of Loch Fyne. The original village was destroyed in 1644 by the royalist Marquess of Montrose, then rebuilt by the third Duke of Argyll; successive dukes have lavished a great deal of money on preserving its 17th- and 18th-century architecture. The 140-foot bell tower, part of the Episcopal Church of All Saints (the Avenue), houses the world's second-heaviest ring of ten bells, which are chimed during *Inverary Fortnight,* around the end of July. The view from the top of the tower is glorious. The Victorian jail here has been opened to visitors (admission charge; phone: 499-2063).

For centuries, the Dukes of Argyll lived in the famous Inveraray Castle nearby. The present castle, which dates from the early 16th century, was replanned and rebuilt from 1743 to 1770. Its unusual mixture of neo-Gothic and Scottish baronial styles and its strange colors and conical towers make it look for all the world like a *Disneyland* castle. The castle's roof caught fire in 1975, but is now fully restored. The interior contains a wealth of 18th-century ornamentation and architectural curiosities, portraits by Gainsborough and other great artists, and a collection of historical relics that provide virtually a crash course in Highland history. A guided tour is available (apply to the estate's "factor"; phone: 499-2203). Open April to mid-October. Admission charge.

En Route from Inveraray – Following A819 north, you'll pass through Glen Aray and along the south shore of Loch Awe. The islands in the loch are the traditional Clan Campbell burying ground. It's romantic to imagine those stark, ancient funerals, in which only the father, brothers, and a lone piper accompanied the dead in a small boat across the waves.

Visible on your left, as you join A85 for Oban and skirt the north tip of Loch Awe, is the impressive ruin of Kilchurn Castle, a Campbell stronghold since 1440 (closed to the public). Six miles farther on, on the right, at Cruachan Waterfall, is the Cruachan Underground Visitor Centre. This is a 4-million-kilowatt power station in a vast cavern inside Ben Cruachan, run by Scottish Power using water pumped from Loch Awe to a reservoir 1,200 feet up the mountain. Guides and a minibus tour are on hand. Open from *Easter* through late October. Admission charge (phone: 8662-673).

West of Ben Cruachan is the Pass of Brander, where the Clan MacDougall tried unsuccessfully to ambush Robert the Bruce in 1308.

OBAN: Oban was set up as a fish market by a government agency in 1786. Today it is a bustling holiday spot with a picturesque circular harbor, quaint, wedding cake hotels, and a distinctly Highland flavor. Fish auctions are still held on the docks every Tuesday and Thursday evening, weather permitting.

As you waft down the town's mile-long esplanade with a couple of glasses of the local whisky inside you, gaze across the firth to the sun-studded Hebridean islands for a true glimpse of heaven.

There's a variety of good boat trips, including day cruises to the island of Iona, the first Christian settlement in Scotland, famous for its association with St. Columba, who founded a monastery here in 563. Forty-eight Scottish kings lie buried on the island, including Macbeth. Wear a sweater for the boat ride; it's an open craft. For details, contact the Oban, Mull, and District Tourist Board, Argyll Sq. (phone: 631-63122).

GLENCOE: This ominous, mist-enshrouded glen was the scene of a famous massacre in 1692, when a government force of Campbells wiped out an entire branch of the Clan Macdonald — who had received them as guests — by stabbing them in their beds at daybreak. To learn more details, visit the *Glencoe and North Lorn Folk Museum* (open *Easter* through September; closed Sundays; admission charge) off A82 just past Balla-chulish, Glencoe's only village. The visitors' center (phone: 8552-307) offers information on Glencoe and the surrounding area.

En Route from Glencoe – The small resort town of Fort William is popular and bursting with hotels, but its setting is drab and moorish. The shopping here is quite good, however, and about 5 miles beyond the town, on the right, is Ben Nevis, which at 4,406 feet is Britain's highest mountain.

At Loch Oich you can either take A87 west for 50 miles to Kyle of Lochalsh or continue up A82 along Loch Ness to Inverness. From Inverness you can follow the Highlands tour route backward to Edinburgh.

If you head west, as you approach Kyle of Lochalsh you pass Loch Duich and, just offshore, Eilean Donan, one of Scotland's most-photographed castles (open daily *Easter* through September; admission charge; phone: 599-85202). Macreas, McReas, and McCraes from all over the world come here to visit their clan war memorial. Try to be there at sunset, when all is bathed in unearthly light. Then suddenly you come upon the sea and, opposite you, the fabled Isle of Skye, the largest and most famous of the Hebrides, with its dark, jagged Cuillin hills. You may never want to go home.

BEST EN ROUTE

Expect to pay $120 and up per night for a double room in hotels classified as expensive; $80 to $115 in the moderate category; and $75 or less in the inexpensive category. For restaurants, the ranges are $50 and up for a dinner for two in the expensive category; $30 to $50 in the moderate; and $30 and under in the inexpensive category. Prices do not include wine, drinks, or tip, and will vary with the dollar, to some extent.

AYR

Belleisle House – Once the property of the Magistrates of Ayr, who evidently saw no reason to stint themselves, this delightful 19-room hotel retains such personal embellishments as engraved fireplaces. (It lends some credence to fellow Ayrshire-man Burns's poetic attacks on the divisions between rich and poor, powerful and lowly.) Elegant traditional dishes are served in one of two dining rooms, one a replica of Marie Antoinette's music room, the other modeled after her bedroom.

Inside Belleisle Park grounds on Doonfoot Rd. (phone: 292-42331; fax: 292-45325). Expensive.

Fairfield House – A truly blue-ribbon Scottish hotel in the center of town, its interior was redesigned by Lady Henrietta Spencer-Churchill, daughter of the present Duke of Marlborough. There are 30 sumptuous rooms and a restaurant with a varied menu. 12 Fairfield Rd. (phone: 292-267461; fax: 292-261456). Expensive.

Pickwick – One of the best of a seafront string of Victorian villas specializing in pure malt whiskies and Scottish foods. Most of the 15 rooms have baths. 19 Racecourse Rd. (phone: 292-260111). Moderate.

OBAN

Alexandra – A modernized, well-furnished 56-room hotel with magnificent views over the harbor, Oban Bay, and the Firth. The Gorran Esplanade (phone: 631-62381; fax: 631-64497). Moderate.

Caledonian – There are excellent sea views from this grand old Victoria Station hotel; Scottish and English food are served in its dining room. Station Sq. (phone: 631-63133). Moderate.

GLENCOE

Ballachulish – This modernized hotel has retained its family atmosphere and is singled out by the knowledgeable for particular praise. It has 28 rooms, baronial lounges, and a restaurant serving a remarkable blend of traditional and international dishes. Through the Pass of Glencoe (on A828 at the Ballachulish Bridge), dominating Loch Linnhe (phone: 8552-606; fax: 8552-629). Expensive.

Kings House – Scotland's oldest licensed inn, this 22-room hotel on Rannoch Moor stands on an old drovers' road, along which cattle were once herded to market. A great base for climbers, anglers, skiers, and hikers. On the A82 (phone: 8556-259). Inexpensive.

KYLE OF LOCHALSH

Lochalsh – A comfortable resort hotel just beside the ferry to the Isle of Skye, with glorious views from most of the 40 rooms. English, Scottish, and French cuisines are served here. Ferry Rd. (phone: 599-4202). Expensive.

Northern Ireland

Northern Ireland's troubles have given it bad press. This has had two effects: People know Northern Ireland is part of the United Kingdom (it was separated from the rest of Ireland in 1921), and sporadic violence has discouraged visitors. Those who do come, however, find any hostility confined mostly to certain economically depressed residential neighborhoods in the two large urban centers of Belfast and Londonderry and directed mainly at members of the police, British army, and paramilitary — all of whom usually maintain low visibility. They also find unspoiled coastline and countryside, empty beaches, uncrowded roads, fine accommodations, and friendly people.

Northern Ireland — virtually synonymous with the ancient province of Ulster and still often so referred to — covers about one-sixth the total area of Ireland. The province is so compact — about 70 miles at its widest by about

100 miles long — that in a short tour of 3 to 4 days you can crisscross its six counties and take in most of their highlights. Among these are several hundred miles of bay-indented coast, with coves, cliffs, castles, and beaches; many lovely inland lakes and scores of rivers and streams; two great mountain chains — the fabled Mountains of Mourne, sweeping down to the Irish Sea in the southeast, and the Sperrin Mountains in the northwest.

The tour described below begins in Belfast, the capital of Northern Ireland, and makes a clockwise circle around the province, following the southern part of Ulster's long coastline that encircles County Down. County Down has its share of resorts and fishing villages along the winding shore but is dominated by the Mourne Mountains in the south, where Slieve Donard rises from the sea to 2,796 feet.

County Down is bordered by Armagh to the west, the county whose rich northern fruit-growing area has earned its title as "the garden of Ulster."

County Fermanagh, the farthest west, is "the lakeland of Ulster." The River Erne winds through its center, separated by the town of Enniskillen into two large lakes, Upper and Lower Erne, both with many islands.

The inland county of Tyrone has a fine variety of scenery — gentle hills, glens, river valleys, moors, and small towns. But the bulk of the land piles up to the 2,000-foot peaks of the Sperrin Mountains.

The county of Londonderry, in the northwestern corner, is an interesting mix: To the south are the Sperrin Mountains (shared with County Tyrone); to the north is the Atlantic coast, fringed with magnificent beaches of surf-washed sands. The county's boundary with County Antrim in the east is the River Bann; in the west the River Foyle borders the Irish Republic.

Antrim forms the northeastern corner, with the southeastern end buttressed by Belfast. Its magnificent east coast curves around the base of steep headlands, between which the beautiful nine green glens of Antrim open to the sea. Almost every bay along the coast is a link in a chain of fine seaside resorts, tiny ports, and picturesque cliff-top ruins. Near the northernmost point, Torr Head is only 13 miles from Scotland. On the northwestern end of Antrim's coast is the Giant's Causeway, a curious volcanic rock formation that's a celebrated natural wonder and UNESCO World Heritage site. The River Bann and Lough Neagh, the largest lake in Ireland and Britain, form the western boundary.

BELFAST: This is a fairly new city that grew rapidly during the 19th-century shipbuilding and linen production boom. Belfast was dubbed "the Athens of the North" during a great cultural blooming in the late 18th and early 19th centuries, when prominent citizens became patrons of learning and art. In the same period the shipbuilding industry grew by leaps and bounds, and new machinery and processes helped Belfast gain a position of supremacy in the linen industry. When the six Ulster counties were separated from the rest of Ireland by an act of the British Parliament in 1921, Belfast became the capital of the province of Northern Ireland.

The port city, with a greater-city population of 500,000, is on the River Lagan where it joins the sea. Its center is Donegall Square, dominated by the large City Hall, a Renaissance-style building with a tower at each corner and a graceful dome in the center (tours available Wednesdays at 10:30 AM and by arrangement; advance booking required; no admission charge; phone: 232-320202, ext. 227). On the east side stands a sculpture commemorating the 1912 *Titanic* disaster — the largest ship of its time was built here.

Other impressive buildings are St. Anne's Cathedral and the *Ulster Museum,* with collections of Bronze Age, Celtic, and early Christian artifacts (open weekdays 10 AM to 5 PM; Saturdays 1 to 5 PM; Sundays 2 to 5 PM; no admission charge; Stranmillis Rd.; phone: 232-381251). Also visit the Palm House, an 1839 cast-iron glass house in the Botanic Gardens (no admission charge; phone: 232-324092). The ornate Edwardian *Grand Opera House* (Great Victoria St.; phone: 232-240411) has been restored and stages all kinds of entertainment. Belfast has three theaters, two universities, and excellent shops in the center of town. The port has 7 miles of quays. The shipyards of Harland and Wolff include the largest shipbuilding dock in the world. All can be viewed from the crest of Cave Hill, where the Belfast Zoo (phone: 232-776277; admission charge) also is located. There are acres of parkland on the outskirts of the city, including Dixon Park, with its 20,000 rose bushes.

Six miles east of Belfast on Route A2 is the small residential town of Holywood beside Belfast Lough.

HOLYWOOD: Although the town has a good promenade, a golf course, and tennis and yachting facilities, the main reason to stop here is the *Ulster Folk and Transport Museum,* which spreads over 180 acres and faithfully re-creates 19th-century life — from a blacksmith's forge to a weaver's house. There are farms and craftsmen working at their craft. You can buy their products (open Mondays through Saturdays from 11 AM to 5 PM, Sundays 2 to 5 PM, to 6 PM May through September; admission charge; Cultra Manor; phone: 232-428428).

BANGOR: Ulster's chief yachting center, Bangor is well laid out, with fine promenades, gardens, and recreation grounds. Yacht races go on all the time, setting out from the *Royal Ulster* (phone: 247-465002) or the *Ballyholme* clubhouse (phone: 247-271467).

En Route from Bangor – Take A21 south to Newtownards, at the northern end of Strangford Lough, a busy marketing and industrial town. Continue to Comber, where flax yarn for linen is spun. Go south on A22 along Strangford Lough passing Killyleagh, with Ulster's finest residential castle (closed to the public), en route to Downpatrick. St. Patrick is reputed to be buried in the nearby Down Cathedral churchyard in Downpatrick; the gravesite is marked by a huge slab of Mourne granite, and on *St. Patrick's Day,* pilgrims scatter daffodils over the spot. The life and influences of Ireland's patron saint are documented at the nearby *St. Patrick's Heritage Centre* (open weekdays 11 AM to 5 PM, weekends 2 to 5 PM; closed weekends September through June; no admission charge; phone: 396-615218). Halfway between this quiet hilly town and the pretty village of Strangford, 9 miles east, lies Saul (signposted), a place with a special meaning for Irish everywhere, for it was here that St. Patrick landed in 432 to begin his Irish mission and build his church. Although the church was destroyed several times, fragments of earlier buildings remain, as well as the little memorial church of St. Patrick (Church of Ireland), built in 1932 to mark the 1,500th anniversary of Patrick's arrival here. The Shrine of St. Patrick, a mile farther west of the prominent hill of Sliabh Padraig, is a place of pilgrimage. A granite figure of the saint stands on the summit.

Continue to Strangford, on the western shore of the strait connecting Strangford Lough with the sea. There is a car ferry every half hour to the village of Portaferry on the opposite shore (phone: 39686-637). This area is noteworthy for the many castle and monastic ruins around the Lough's indented shore, including Portaferry and Strangford castles, large rectangular structures built by the Anglo-Normans to guard the strait entrance. Castle Ward, a National Trust House, is 1 mile from

Strangford village (open April and October; admission charge; phone: 39686-204). Portaferry also has Northern Ireland's only aquarium and the Queen's University Marine Biology Station, which is worth a visit for its ecological interest (admission charge; phone: 2477-28062).

From Strangford, take A2 around Dundrum Bay all the way to Newcastle, driving toward the impressive Mourne Mountains looming to the southwest.

NEWCASTLE: This seaside resort is beautifully situated along the sandy beach that fringes Dundrum Bay, with the great bulk of Slieve Donard filling the skyline behind the town.

Two miles west, at Bryansford, is scenic Tollymore Forest Park. There are many planned walks here along the Shimna River and on the mountainside. Three miles north of Tollymore is another forest park — Castlewellan — with an outstanding arboretum.

Extending southwest for nearly 15 miles are the Mourne Mountains.

En Route from Newcastle – The scenery along the Mourne coastline, Route A2, is superb, particularly at Annalong, a tiny, picturesque fishing harbor with an early 1800s water-powered corn mill, herb garden, and a visitors' center (phone: 3967-68736). About 13 miles from Newcastle is Kilkeel, the headquarters for a large fishing fleet. The town is a good center for exploring the Mournes and the coast of south Down.

The coast road continues through the charming little resort towns of Rostrevor and Warrenpoint on the edge of Carlingford Lough, where you look across the water to the shores of the Irish Republic and on to the "frontier" town of Newry. This industrial center and port, in a hollow among hills at the head of the Newry River estuary, has been important from ancient times because of its strategic position at the "gap of the north" — the main crossing into Ulster from Dublin and the south. Take A28 into County Armagh and to the town of Armagh, about 20 miles northwest.

ARMAGH: This ancient city — once the seat of Ulster kings — has been the ecclesiastical capital of Ireland for over 1,500 years. It was here in 443 that St. Patrick established a cathedral and monastic school, which have been destroyed and rebuilt many times. The Church of Ireland cathedral now occupies the site. The Catholic cathedral stands imposingly on an adjoining hilltop, approached by a long series of steps with terraces. Its inside walls are covered with mosaics, including medallions of the saints of Ireland. Marble is used for everything from altars to pulpit.

The city has an air of quiet dignity. Its well-laid-out streets are dominated by the two cathedrals, both named for St. Patrick. At the center of town is the Mall, a pleasant green lined by fine Georgian houses, the small but excellent *Armagh County Museum,* with exhibits on prehistoric artifacts, Viking raids, local natural history, Irish lace and linen, and Black Bog jewelry (open Mondays through Saturdays from 10 AM to 1 PM and 2 to 5 PM; no admission charge; The Mall East; phone: 861-523070). Also worth visiting are the courthouse in the town center, the 17th-century Armagh Royal School (College Hill; phone: 861-522807), and the 18th-century observatory of the Hall of Astronomy at the *Armagh Planetarium* (admission charge to planetarium shows; College Hill; phone: 861-523689).

Take Route A28 to Augher and join A4 to Fivemiletown, where you cross into County Fermanagh. Continue to Enniskillen, the center of Northern Ireland's scenic lakeland.

ENNISKILLEN: Between the Upper and Lower Lough Erne, the town is a convenient base for exploring this peaceful countryside on roads along the wooded lakeshores or by boat on the lakes. Abundant fishing and the availability of modern boats for rent have made these lakes very popular. Notable National Trust properties in the area include Castle Coole, Ireland's finest neo-classical house, now restored (phone: 365-

322690), and Florence Court, a mid-18th-century Irish Georgian home (phone: 36582-249). Both are open from the end of March through September (closed Thursdays); call for hours; admission charge.

The Marble Arch Caves, 3 miles out on the A4, contain a fascinating underworld of lakes, weirs, waterfalls, and lofty chambers. Well-lit walkways are maintained for visitors. Open daily *Easter* to October, from 11 AM, but it's wise to call ahead because water levels sometimes rise in the caves. Admission charge (phone: 36582-8855).

En Route from Enniskillen – Take Route A46 to Belleek, the westernmost point of Ulster. This border town, where Northern Ireland meets the Republic, is known for its lovely handmade eggshell-thin pottery. The world's most extensive collection of Belleek lusterware is for sale at *Belleek Pottery Ltd.* (Fermanagh); factory tours also are available (admission charge; phone: 36565-501).

From Belleek take A47 to Kesh, and A84 into County Tyrone until it joins A32 to Omagh. The Ulster-American Folk Park, 4 miles north of Omagh, re-creates bygone rural life in Northern Ireland and illustrates the notable contributions of Ulster men and women to US history, including the ancestors of a dozen US presidents. There is a reconstructed 19th-century emigrant ship and harbor master office with costumed interpreters (open daily 11 AM to 6:30 PM *Easter* through early September; Mondays through Saturdays from 10:30 AM to 5 PM the rest of the year; last admission 1½ hours before closing; admission charge; phone: 662-243292).

LONDONDERRY: This ancient seaport, which stands on a commanding hill overlooking a broad tidal curve of the River Foyle, was founded as a monastic settlement in 546. Although it was never occupied by the Anglo-Normans, it was the scene of many struggles between Irish forces and a succession of invaders. In 1608, with the English in control, the land was granted to the citizens of London (thus, Londonderry). A large colony of Protestants was imported and the walls were fortified. These walls withstood several sieges; the most famous occurred in 1689, led by England's Roman Catholic King James II, from which came the still widely used Protestant response "No surrender." The siege lasted 105 days.

The Old Walls, the city's most prominent feature, are in excellent condition. They are now laid out as a promenade, with many of the old cannons still standing where they once stood, by the four old city gates. Information about guided tours of the city walls can be obtained from the tourist information center (Foyle St.; closed Sundays; phone: 504-267284). The O'Doherty Fort serves as an interpretive and exhibition center for visitors (admission charge; phone: 504-265238, ext. 205).

In Shipquay Place is the Guild Hall, an impressive modern Gothic structure with a fine series of stained glass windows illustrating events in the city's history. It was partly destroyed in the disturbances of 1972 but is now mostly restored (phone: 504-365151). Shipquay Street leads to the 17th-century Protestant cathedral. Outside the city walls is the 19th-century Catholic cathedral, on James St. in Bogside.

En Route from Londonderry – Take Route A2 out of the city; you are in for a 74-mile treat of the most scenic coast road in Northern Ireland, which leads all the way into Belfast. The road goes east to Limavady, then curves northeast to hug the shore and pass through two noted County Derry resorts: Castlerock and Portstewart. They offer what all resorts on the north coast have in common: excellent beaches, good sea and river fishing, and several fine golf courses. Continue 4 miles to Portrush in County Antrim.

PORTRUSH: This resort has an outstanding golf course — the *Royal Portrush*, the only Irish course ever to host the *British Open*. Call in advance to play (phone: 265-822311). Nearby are the romantic ruins of Dunluce Castle (open daily, April through September, from 10 AM to 7 PM; Sundays from 2 to 7 PM; closes at 4 PM on

Mondays and from 1 to 1:30 PM the rest of the year; admission charge). During summer there is bus service to the Giant's Causeway, the absolute must-see on this route.

Often called the eighth wonder of the world, and now a UNESCO World Heritage site, the causeway is an intriguing rock formation on the coast near Bushmills. It was formed by cooling lava that burst through the earth's crust in the Cenozoic period as long as 70 million years ago. Here the basaltic lava split into prismatic columns as it cooled. And there they stand, about 40,000 basalt columns, mostly hexagonal, packed together in a shape so regular they seem cut by hand. The Interpretive Visitors Center (on Causeway) has exhibits and a restaurant (open daily from 10 AM to 7 PM July and August; earlier closing the rest of the year; admission charge for the audiovisual program; phone: 2657-31855).

En Route from Portrush – Continue east to Portballintrae and Old Bushmills, home of the world's oldest licensed whiskey distillery. Tours and tastings require booking during the summer (phone: 2657-31521).

Continue past resorts with wide beaches separated by cliffs — white, black, and red — fretted by the sea into strange shapes. Ballycastle is the point of departure for white-cliffed Rathlin Island, the haunt of millions of sea birds. For year-round ferry schedule call 2657-63907. (A minibus to Rathlin Nature Reserve meets ferries in the summer.) About 3 miles east of here a signposted road leads to Fair Head, the northeastern extremity of Ireland, which rises to 636 feet of sheer cliffs of columnar basalt and offers a fabulous view of Rathlin Island and Scotland. The road goes on to Torr Head, the closest point to the Scottish coast. Rejoin Route A2 near Cushendun, a lovely hamlet preserved by the National Trust, and enter the area of the nine glens of Antrim. Continue to Glenariff.

GLENARIFF: Here is the most famous of the Antrim glens. Formed by the Glenariff River at Red Bay, the glen stretches inland for about 5 miles between steep mountains. It has signposted walking trails and a nature information center (open daily from 10 AM; phone: 26637-232).

En Route from Glenariff – The coast road takes you past more glens and beautiful sea views to Larne, the crossing point for car-ferry service from Stranraer and Cairaryan in Scotland, the shortest cross-channel passages between Ireland and Britain. Continue south for 21 miles to Belfast.

BEST EN ROUTE

Northern Ireland has an adequate supply of comforatble hotels and restaurants. Hotels and guesthouses are generally clean and fairly inexpensive. The more expensive ones may have a special feature, such as an unbeatable location or generous amenities, which include a full Irish breakfast. At hotels listed below as very expensive expect to pay $240 or more; at expensive, $100 to $150; moderate, less than $100. All hotels recommended have well-respected restaurants open to guests and non-guests alike.

BELFAST

Culloden – This sumptuous Victorian mansion is set amid gardens and woodlands 6 miles east of Belfast on the A2 at Cultra, across from the *Ulster Folk Museum*. Once the palace of the Bishops of Down, its Gothic arches and stained glass are still intact. All of the 92 comfortable rooms are furnished with antiques. The elegant restaurant has traditional international cuisine. Cultra (phone: 2317-5223; fax: 2317-6777). Very expensive.

Europa – With the most central location in the city, it has 200 pleasant, well-equipped rooms. It's also next door to the *Grand Opera House* and a favorite gathering place for locals. *Bewley's Coffee Shop* and *Harper's Bar,* on the ground floor, have been renovated; a cocktail and piano bar and a more formal restaurant are upstairs. There's live music nightly, except Sundays. Great Victoria St. (phone: 232-327000; fax: 232-327800). Very expensive.

Dunadry Inn – Once a linen mill, then a paper mill, this charming 67-room hostelry offers good service as well as a bird's-eye view of a bygone era, with converted old mill cottages, the lawn where linen was once laid out to whiten in the sun, and original mill fixtures, including beetling machines, which now adorn the bar. Near Belfast International Airport, 19 miles from downtown Belfast, 2 Islandreagh Dr. in Templepatrick, Co. Antrim (phone: 8494-32474; fax: 8494-33389). Expensive.

Wellington Park – In south Belfast, it is close to Queen's University, the Botanic Gardens, and the *Ulster Museum.* The decor includes a permanent display of contemporary Irish painting and sculpture. 21 Malone Rd. (phone: 232-381111; fax: 232-665410). Expensive.

CRAWFORDSBURN

Old Inn – This partly thatched attractive village inn, a few miles east of Belfast, dates from 1614. Its 32 bedrooms have many charming Old World features. There is a lovely garden, and very good food is served. 15 Main St. (phone: 247-853255; fax: 247-852775). Expensive.

NEWCASTLE

Burrendale – Offering the most modern comforts in the area, this hostelry has a country club with health club and spa, including a heated pool, Turkish steambath, sauna, solarium, Jacuzzi, exercise room, massage, and a beauty salon. 51 Castle Wellan Rd. (phone: 3967-22599; fax: 3967-22328). Expensive.

Slieve Donard – On the Irish Sea, in the shadow of the magnificent Mourne Mountains, and next to the renowned *Royal County Down Golf Club,* this grand hotel of the railway era has been refurbished. All of its 120 rooms have private baths. There is an indoor swimming pool. Downs Rd. (phone: 3967-23681 or 3967-24830). Expensive.

ENNISKILLEN

Killyhevlin – This stately mansion overlooking Lower Lough Erne, with lawns sloping down to the waterside, provides a very special overnight stay. There are fine views from the 22 spacious rooms; some have balconies. Dublin Rd. (phone: 365-323481; fax: 365-324726). Expensive.

LONDONDERRY

Everglades – On the river Foyle on the outskirts of town, this upscale hotel has 38 rooms, a dining room, and live piano music. Prehen Rd. (phone: 504-46722; fax: 504-492000). Expensive.

BLACKHILL, NEAR COLERAINE

Blackheath House – A charming Georgian home with 6 double-occupancy rooms and a fine restaurant, *MacDuff's.* 112 Killeague Rd. (phone: 265-868433; fax: 265-732048). Moderate.

BUSHMILLS

Bushmills Inn – A 200-year-old coaching inn, it has 11 rooms in country-style decor with Ulster charm — pine floors and peat fires. Main St. (phone: 2657-32339). Moderate.

CARNLOUGH

Londonderry Arms – Once the property of Sir Winston Churchill, the great-grand-son of the original owner, this 19th-century building is in a seaside village at the mouth of Glencloy, one of the nine glens of Antrim. There are only 14 rooms in this family-run hotel, so make reservations. 20 Harbour Rd. (phone: 574-885255; fax: 574-885263). Moderate.

BALLYGALLY

Ballygally Castle – Northern Ireland's only plantation-era hotel property (built in 1625 but with modern extensions) has some atmospheric turret rooms. This mostly modernized 30-room establishment faces the sea. Antrim Coast Rd. (phone: 574-83212; fax: 574-583681). Expensive.

Greece

At the southern tip of the Balkan Peninsula, Greece occupies a prominent position on the Continent and in European history. Greece covers some 50,944 square miles; the mainland spreads between the Ionian Sea on the west, the Aegean on the east, and the Sea of Crete to the south; more than 3,200 islands lie in the surrounding seas. Because of its island territory (170 of the islands are inhabited), Greece is actually larger than it appears, exceeding neighboring Bulgaria in size.

The sea is a major influence on life in Greece. The Greeks have been seafarers throughout their history, and today their shipping industry, although severely affected by the last decade's shipping crisis, still is one of the world's largest. The 9,300-mile coastline is one of the world's longest, and Greece is known for the beauty of its many beaches.

Greece's terrain is quite rugged; some 80% of the land is mountainous. Mt. Olympus, the legendary home of the gods, rises 9,570 feet and is one of the highest peaks in the country. Only 30% of the land is arable. The fertile plains of Thessaly support the country's major crops, wheat and tobacco, though plenty of olives, fruits, and vegetables are grown on Crete and other areas.

Greece has a population of 10 million, 53% of which is urban. Athens is the capital and largest city (pop. 3.27 million in greater Athens); the other major cities are Thessaloníki (pop. 1 million) and Patras in the Peloponnese (pop. 209,387). Most of the people are Greeks, with Turks and Vlachs — an ancient people speaking a language akin to Romanian — making up the largest ethnic minorities — and Slavs, Albanians, and Jews forming smaller groups.

The very cradle of Western civilization, Greece has an extremely rich history. Traces of a neolithic population in Greece date from 6000 BC, but sometime around 3000 BC a more advanced civilization lived on Crete, which was followed by the development of tribes on the mainland. Some of these tribes banded together to form city-states and eventually developed the more sophisticated social structure of democracy, Greece's greatest contribution to the civilized world. Hellenistic culture reached its apex in the 4th century BC in Athens, where democracy nurtured the works of Plato and Aristotle. Later, in the 3rd century BC, Alexander the Great confederated numerous city-states and conquered new territories, creating a large empire. Greece subsequently became part of the Byzantine Empire (AD 395) and still later (in the 15th century) was conquered by the Ottomans. Not until the early 19th century did most of the country again regain its independence.

The heritage of ancient Greece is the legacy of all contemporary Western nations, but it is a special source of pride to modern Greeks. Numerous vestiges of it remain — Greek, Roman, and Byzantine ruins, from the majestic Acropolis in Athens to the extremely well preserved Theater of Epidaurus on the Peloponnese, where visitors still can see ancient Greek drama as it was performed millennia ago.

In addition to sites of great historical significance, Greece has an extraordinarily beautiful countryside. The Mediterranean landscape dominates the southern mainland, much of the Peloponnese peninsula, and many of the islands. Rocky hills drop down to long stretches of coast and seas of deep blue and aquamarine. In the north, the vegetation is denser, similar to that found elsewhere on the Continent. The summers are hot, sunny, and dry; winters, cool and damp, and, in the north, snowy. Spring is warm and pleasant, a time when the hills come to life with colorful wildflowers, though Greece in summer reaches its most basic state — sun, rock, and sea. Greece's low prices are another attraction; in fact, prices still are considerably lower than in other European countries.

But in many ways, Greece is not European at all. Four centuries of occupation by Turks left a strong Middle Eastern flavor in many aspects of Greek life — from relations between the sexes to food, folklore, and an exasperatingly Byzantine notion of bureaucracy. In planning your stay, bear in mind that many archaeological sites and museums close at 3 PM, the Greeks generally take a siesta between 3 and 6 PM, so unless you're on a beach or simply like walking, there may be little do during the afternoons.

In addition, air and ferry service among the islands, and guided tours, are cut back sharply during the colder, grayer winter months. By contrast, the hotels, beaches, and ruins are packed solid with tourists in summer. To avoid the crowds, travel during the shoulder seasons — spring and fall — is highly recommended, as the weather still is lovely.

The following routes originate in Athens except for the tours of the islands, which are accessible by sea and air from Athens or major island ports. The route through northern Greece heads to Thessaloníki by way of Mt. Olympus and Meteora, then branches off, east to the Turkish border and west to the Yugoslavian border. A short route leads through the Parnassus mountain region to Delphi, once the home of the most celebrated oracle of all time. Island routes focus on Crete, Greece's largest island; the Dodecanese Islands, of which Rhodes is the largest and most popular; the Cyclades, including Mykonos and Delos, which offer everything from varied nightlife to magnificent archaeological sites; the Eastern Aegean islands, of which Lesbos is the most prominent; and Corfu to the west, considered by many to be the most beautiful of all. Another route loops around the Peloponnese peninsula, taking in 4,000 years of history scattered over 8,000 square miles.

Northern Greece

Northern Greece is markedly different from the rest of the country in both geography and history. Nature seems to have acted more intensely here; the climate is continental rather than Mediterranean, as is the vegetation. The region's history has been turbulent from ancient times through World War

II and the civil war of 1946. Perhaps as a result, the people are less outgoing than other Greeks, though they are still warm and hospitable.

You need time to explore this area. The two suggested routes, from Athens to Thessaloníki and then either west to the Yugoslavian border or east to the Turkish border, take from 3 to 5 days each. To cut the trip shorter, you can fly to Thessaloníki from Athens and rent a car for the rest of your touring. You also can take a plane to Ioannina, a must for those who do not want to miss the climb up Mt. Olympus and a visit (by bus from Ioannina) to Meteora, a fascinating monastic community built on huge rocks, which look as if they are suspended in midair. Set behind the town of Kalambaka, this is a most impressive site, dating possibly to the late 13th or early 14th century. From Meteora, we suggest an overnight side trip to the charming village of Metsovo, which is steeped in Balkan ambience. You can get another plane at Ioannina or rent a car there for the trip to Thessaloníki; though the drive along mountain roads is arduous, the views are superb. To follow the route outlined below, get an early start driving from Athens.

ATHENS: For a complete description of the capital and its hotels and restaurants, see *Athens* in THE CITIES.

En Route from Athens – Take a break at Kamena Vourla, about 100 miles (160 km) from Athens. You can go for a swim in this attractive resort town or have some refreshments. Between here and Larissa, the route crosses one of the most fertile plains in Greece. Stop at one of the restaurants just before Larissa for lunch. Heading for Meteora, turn west on the road for Trikala for 36 miles (58 km), where a 12-mile (19-km) drive leads to Kalambaka.

METEORA: Rising 1,820 feet high, the 24 formidable rock pillars stand isolated in space. On these precipitous cliffs, 14th-century Byzantine monks built a monastic community that became a sanctuary for the persecuted and the devout. Some centuries later, the community started to deteriorate, and today only 4 of the original 24 monasteries are inhabited, 2 of them by nuns. You can spend the night in Kalambaka. The hotels are small, however, so book ahead during the summer. An excellent, superbly hospitable restaurant — *The Meteora* — is right on the square in Kalambaka (phone: 432-22316).

En Route from Meteora – Back on the National Road, you can break for an excellent seafood meal at Platamon. Turn off the road 12 miles (19 km) farther at the village of Plaka to start the ascent to Mt. Olympus, Greece's tallest mountain (9,620 feet) and home of the Olympian gods. A paved road leads to Litohoron, 1,150 feet up the mountain, and on to the chalet at 4,290 feet. From here it is possible to hike to the highest refuge at 6,930 feet. The climb is a rewarding one, especially in spring, when there is still snow but the weather is mild.

METSOVO: This tiny village in the province of Epirus — to which Albania once belonged — is a stunning place that seems more Balkan than Greek. It is carved into a piece of the Pindus mountain range, and its ubiquitous white stucco houses are trimmed, chalet style, with finely carved wooden balustrades and balconies and roofed with red tile or gray slate. Here live the Vlachs, an ancient people of obscure origin who still speak an archaic language resembling Romanian; few residents speak English. Elders dress in richly embroidered costumes. Metsovo, aside from its beauty, is renowned for the quality of its handicrafts: woven goods, filigree jewelry, carved wood, leather, and fur. There is a folklife museum in town, and a 20-minute hike out of town leads to the gorgeous Byzantine frescoes of the former St. Nikolaos monastery. Metsovo is also a ski station; its traditionally decorated hotels are wonderfully cozy in winter. From Kalambaka, head west on Route E-87 for about 93 miles (149 km).

THESSALONÍKI (Salonika): Established in 316 BC and named after the stepsister of Alexander the Great, Thessaloníki provides all the amenities of a modern coastal city while preserving its notable past. When Macedonia became a Roman province in 148 BC, Thessaloníki was made its capital. Touring Greece's second-largest city today, you'll see numerous Roman remains in the walled-in "acropolis," or high part of the Old City, and interesting Byzantine churches, among them the remarkable Church of St. Dimitri, Thessaloníki's first Christian martyr. The *Archaeological Museum* (YMCA Sq.; phone: 31-830538) contains magnificent golden treasures from the tomb of Philip II, father of Alexander the Great. Discovered in 1977, it was the first unlooted tomb found in Macedonia and confirms the theory that Vergina, where it was found (48 miles/77 km from Thessaloníki), was the burial ground of Macedonian kings. Don't miss a visit to the *Byzantine White Tower.* Built around 1430, it is the symbol of this historic city and is now a museum housing a small but interesting Byzantine collection; the top of the tower offers fine views of the city. A fascinating and beautiful collection of northern Greek costumes and traditional objects is displayed in the *Folkloric/Ethnological Museum* (at Hanth Sq.; phone: 31-830591). Admission charge to all three museums.

For a break in sightseeing, there is shopping at the clothing, book, and folkcraft stores on Tsimiski and Aristotelous Streets. Then, have a drink and some seafood at *Tottis'* ouzo bar, on central Aristotelous Square, overlooking the quay. Among the most popular restaurants in town are *Olympos-Naoussa* (located in the center of town), where you can have excellent meals in a simple setting; *Krikelas* (in the center of town), where the parade of appetizers leaves little room for the main course; and *Mandragoras* (also in the center of town), complete with hanging puppets and imaginative cooking. Thessaloníki, perhaps because of long (nearly 500 years) Turkish domination, is known for its fine food. So a potluck stop at any of the quayside restaurants in town, or on the winding seaside road north of the city, is likely to produce memorable results.

From Thessaloníki, *men* can make a fascinating side trip.

MT. ATHOS: The grounds of the 1,000-year-old monastic republic are forbidden "to any woman, to any female, to any eunuch, to any smooth visage," according to an edict issued by Emperor Constantine IX in 1060. There aren't many eunuchs around these days, and it's no longer necessary to grow a beard, but females still are excluded.

Mt. Athos, or Aghion Oros (Holy Mountain), the easternmost of the three peninsulas of the Halkidiki, is reached from Thessaloníki by the road to Poligiros, the local capital. At Paleocastron, 35 miles (56 km) from Thessaloníki, the road branches right and left; head left via Arnea, a small village that produces excellent wine and handwoven textiles, and Stagyra, the birthplace of Aristotle. The road leads down the coast along the Bay of Ierissos and on to Ouranoupolis, a lovely seaside town. This is as far as women and cars can go, but there are several good hotels on the beach.

From Ouranoupolis, a short boat ride leads to the port of Daphne; from here a cobbled path ascends through thickets of oleanders to Kariés, capital of the autonomous Mt. Athos community. The imposing monasteries are scattered — sometimes a 5-hour walk from one another — among the lush vegetation of the valley. In the 16th century, Athos accommodated about 40,000 monks in 40 monasteries; today the number has dwindled to 1,500 monks in 20 large monasteries and monastic hermitages. In recent years, however, there's been a reviving interest in monastic life, and those numbers are increasing slightly now. Athos is a living Byzantine museum, and its treasures are priceless.

Visit as many of the monasteries as you care to; hospitality is always extended to the visitor, though it is customary to leave a contribution. A permit from the Foreign

Ministry in Athens (phone: 1-362-6894) or the Ministry of Northern Greece in Thessaloníki (phone: 31-270-092) is needed to enter Mt. Athos; Americans first must obtain clearance from the US Embassy in Athens (phone: 1-721-2951).

En Route from Mt. Athos – On the way back to Thessaloníki, you can stop off and relax for a few days at one of the lovely beach resorts of Kassandra, the westernmost of the Halkidiki peninsulas. Back in Thessaloníki, there are two alternative routes: west to the Yugoslavian border or east to the Turkish border.

THESSALONÍKI TO THE YUGOSLAVIAN BORDER: About 25 miles (40 km) from Thessaloníki en route to Edessa, make a slight detour to see the remarkable ruins of ancient Pella, the birthplace of Alexander the Great. The remains cover an extensive area, including entire streets with buildings that had courtyards surrounded by peristyles. Well-preserved pebble mosaics on the floors depict mythological scenes. The small museum houses many of the finds.

At Edessa, the original capital of ancient Macedonia, stop and buy the enormous juicy peaches known as *yarmades.* Some 42 miles (67 km) farther you'll reach Florina, which is only 10 miles (16 km) from Yugoslavia. Vendors in the open-air market speak Serbo-Croatian as a second language. While dining in Florina, try the local specialties made of sweet red peppers.

Take a side trip to Prespes Lake, a resort and wildlife preserve whose shores are skirted by Greece, Yugoslavia, and Albania. You can spend some time on a nicely laid-out beach, have some refreshments at the tourist pavilion, and get a glimpse of the off-limits coast of Albania.

The road to Kastoria passes through spectacular mountain scenery (note: the route can be hazardous in the winter). Once in this lakeside town — the fur center of Greece — you can watch furriers turn scraps into luxurious coats and jackets, which are available at some of Europe's lowest prices. Take a boat ride around the lake and stop at the Monastery of Mavrotissa, with its interesting frescoes.

THESSALONÍKI TO THE TURKISH BORDER: If you're traveling through the area from May 20 to 23, take a side trip to the village of Langadhás, about 13 miles (19 km) northeast of Thessaloníki. Here are the *anastenarides* (firewalkers), who dance on burning embers, apparently transported and oblivious to the pain. The tradition originated as a pagan rite but is now a Christian ritual, performed in honor of St. Constantine.

Some 45 miles (72 km) farther, the road climbs high before zigzagging down to Kavala, opening up a sweeping view of the harbor town and the nearby island of Thassos. Kavala is a large, picturesque town, built around the harbor. Among its highlights are the Roman aqueduct that curves through the center of town and the Byzantine fortifications above the decidedly Oriental eastern section. Mohammed Ali, founder of the Egyptian royal line, was born in an old Turkish building in this area in 1769.

Several waterfront *tavernas* specialize in fresh fish. If you have time, take a boat to Thassos, a lush green island whose serene beauty is a scenic counterpoint to the oil derricks drilling offshore at Prinos, Greece's only commercially exploited oilfield.

You can take a side trip to Philippi, built by Philip II in 356 BC. The extensive remains of the town lie on both sides of the road.

A good road leads to Xanthi and Komotini. Both towns have a strongly Oriental flavor: Mosques with minarets and black-veiled women wearing Turkish pants attest to the Muslim minority living here since the exchange of citizens between Greece and Turkey in 1923. In Xanthi, stop at the lovely Porto Lagos beach for a swim and some lunch.

En route to Alexandroupolis, you'll probably encounter a few oxcarts. The town is pretty, but not particularly interesting. A short drive leads to the west bank of the Evros River, which separates Greece from Turkey. Soldiers of each nationality guard either side of the bridge.

BEST EN ROUTE

Expect to pay $80 and up per night for a double room in hotels listed as expensive, around $60 in the moderate category, and $30 or so in the inexpensive category. Note that in Thessaloníki, rates rise as much as 20% during September's *International Trade Fair*.

LARISSA

Divani Palace – Each of the 77 air conditioned rooms has a telephone and a radio. Al. Papanastasiou (phone: 41-252791). Moderate.

KALAMBAKA

Divani – This motel has gardens, a large pool, a restaurant, bar, and 165 air conditioned rooms, each with a telephone and a radio. Below the Meteora (phone: 432-23330). Moderate.

METSOVO

Bitouni – Filled with the warm, rich hues of handwoven pillow covers and handsomely carved pine ceilings, this 24-room hotel is a study in Greek hospitality. In winter, the owners serve tea before a crackling fire in the hearth. The tiny, but adequate rooms look right out onto the town and the mountains beyond it. On the main road heading out of town (phone: 656-41545). Moderate.

THESSALONÍKI

Electra Palace – A stylish Art Nouveau hotel that has plenty of atmosphere, very good views of the city's Aristotelous Square and the well-kept waterfront, and 131 air conditioned rooms. 59 Aristotelous Sq. (phone: 31-232221). Expensive.

Macedonia Palace – This large property on the quay provides luxurious modern accommodations in 287 rooms; those with sea views are in demand. Megalou Alexandrou Ave. (phone: 31-837520). Expensive.

Amalia – Part of the reputable Greek chain, this centrally located hostelry has 70 air conditioned rooms with private bath and telephone. 33 Ermou St. (phone: 31-268321). Moderate.

Capsis – In the commercial section of town, this 428-room hotel has a friendly atmosphere. 28 Monastiriou (phone: 31-521421 or 31-521321). Moderate.

OURANOUPOLIS

Xenia – A pleasant place to spend the night before taking off for Mt. Athos. Accommodations are in a 42-room hotel or in bungalows. In town (phone: 377-71202). Moderate.

FLORINA

Ligos – The 40 rooms here are simple and comfortable. There's a bar, restaurant, and roof garden. In town (phone: 385-28322). Inexpensive.

KALITHEA

Pallini Beach – A large hotel (495 rooms and bungalows), with its own beach and pool. Facilities include tennis, boating, water skiing, horseback riding, and a sauna.

There is also a seafood restaurant, a cafeteria, and a bar (phone: 374-22480). Moderate.

KAVALA

Lucy – Each of the 450 rooms at this new hotel has a private bath and telephone. There also is a restaurant and bar. Kalamitsa Beach (phone: 51-832600). Moderate.

ALEXANDROUPOLIS

Astir – A cozy and comfortable 53-room hostelry. On the beach (phone: 551-24571). Moderate.

Delphi and the Parnassus Region

Even if you're spending only a few days in Greece, the trip to Delphi is a must. Rising from the heart of the mountainous Parnassus region, Delphi is the home of the most celebrated oracle of all times — awe-inspiring in its beauty and austerity. The best time to visit is in the spring or fall, when the wild flowers bloom in colorful variety on the hills and the tourist flow is limited. In the summer, avoid the climb in the early afternoon; the heat and intense sunlight can be exhausting. At all times, Delphi leaves a profound impression on the visitor.

ATHENS: For a complete description of the capital and its hotels and restaurants, see *Athens,* THE CITIES.

En Route from Athens – For a cold drink, stop at the tourist pavilion in Levadia, 70 miles (112 km) from Athens, and sit by the waterfall.

ARACHOVA: Perched over 3,000 feet high on a winding mountain road, this town has cobblestone streets and neat stone houses with pots of aromatic basil and lavender out front. For lunch, have lamb roasted on the spit and the potent local wine, then browse in the shops featuring the splendid multicolored fabrics woven by the townswomen.

You can climb up to the nearby Corycian grotto, dedicated in ancient times to Pan, the god of shepherds, and to the forest nymphs. In ancient times, women from Athens, Boeotia, and Delphi gathered here every 5 years, dressed in animal skins and carrying torches, to dance all night in celebration of the Bacchanalia.

To reach the highest peak of Mt. Parnassus, get set for 3 more hours of climbing. Mountain refuges are available at Kontokedro and Yerondovrahos. In winter, buses take visitors to the Mt. Parnassus ski center, which offers the best skiing in Greece.

DELPHI: The road, winding through olive groves and vineyards, suddenly opens up on the awesome site of the ancient oracle's temple. In this setting, you can understand why the ancient Greeks regarded Delphi as the "navel of the earth." Such is the magnificent isolation of the site, with golden-red cliffs looming around it, the serenity of the sacred valley below, and, in the distance, the Gulf of Itea sparkling in the sunlight. At the center of Delphi stands the sanctuary of Apollo; from here the narrow Sacred Way zigzags past treasury buildings of the ancient Greek city-states to the ruins of the Doric Temple of Apollo. After being purified with water from the nearby Castalian spring, the priestess, dressed in full ceremonial robes, would utter her prophecies.

Above the temple rises the 4th-century BC theater; the high tiers command a panoramic view of the sanctuary and the profoundly secluded landscape. At sunset, when a soft blue light spreads over the glowing pinkish mountains, the feeling that you're alone in the world can be complete — unless a busload of tourists has joined you.

The ruins of the Marmaria (the Marbles), dedicated to the goddess Athena, lie below the main road. Midway between the Marmaria and the sanctuary is the Castalian spring, where you can stop for a drink under the huge plane trees.

The museum on the main road between the village and the sanctuary contains numerous pieces found in the sanctuary and the Marmaria or nearby. The highlight of the collection is a bronze statue known as *The Charioteer,* dating from 478 BC. Among the other displays are the pediments from the Temple of Apollo, several exquisite archaic statues, and statuettes of gold and ivory.

BEST EN ROUTE

Expect to pay $50 and up per night for double rooms in the hotels listed below.

DELPHI

Amalia – This large hotel has 185 elegant rooms with air conditioning, a pretty, airy restaurant, a huge lobby with a fireplace (for those who come for the winter skiing), and good views. In town (phone: 265-82101).

Vouzas – Closer to the ruins, this 58-room hotel has good service and spectacular views from private balconies and the roof garden restaurant. 1 Rue Frederique (phone: 265-82232; in Athens, 1-775-2733).

Crete

Equidistant from Europe, Asia Minor, and North Africa, Crete has a special location, history, and heritage. Legend has it that Zeus, supreme god of heaven and earth, was born and raised here. The myths of the labyrinth, the minotaur, and the wings of Icarus originated on Crete. And from 3000 to 1400 BC the Minoans flourished here, leaving behind remnants of the first great civilization in Europe. Crete was ruled by Romans, Arabs, Venetians, and Turks at different times until it finally was united with Greece in 1913.

The natural setting of Crete, Greece's largest island and the southernmost point in Europe, is truly magnificent. Rugged mountains rise in the center, east, and west. Between them stretch fertile plains and valleys. At the coasts, the mountains drop down to the sea, forming stretches of sandy beaches and secluded coves.

The best way to see Crete is to rent a car, although regular bus service connects the various towns on the island. Daily air and sea connections link the mainland and other islands with Heraklion and Khaniá. You can begin your tour in either city; the route outlined here starts in Khaniá.

To get a full taste of Crete, try the local specialties: cheeses, ranging from the mild manouri to the stronger graviera, a gruyère-type cheese mellowed in caves; honey from Sfakia usually served over thick yogurt; and figs and pomegranates. Sample *raki,* a sort of home-brewed ouzo, or *tsikoudia,* the gin-based aperitif served in tiny glasses. Cretans down these drinks in one gulp. They're strong stuff, so don't get carried away when they start offering rounds in honor of the foreigner enjoying their favorite drinks.

KHANIÁ: The capital of Crete, Khaniá is an interesting mixture of Venetian and Oriental influences. It is divided into two sections — the old Venetian town of narrow streets which includes the 17th-century mosque (now housing the tourist office), and the horseshoe-shaped harbor area. A fruit and vegetable market dominates the center of town, with open stalls and lively scents and colors. Buy *diktamo* here, a rare herb that can be used to brew a delicious tea, considered a panacea by the islanders. After browsing around, have a cold drink at the town square before going down to the charming harbor, with its arched buildings, cobblestone streets, and Venetian lighthouse. After lunch at any of the fish restaurants on the quay, spend the afternoon at the beach and return to the harbor in the evening for a leisurely dinner at a *taverna* on the quay. Get a good night's rest before starting out the next day for an adventurous all-day hike through the Samarian Gorge.

SAMARIAN GORGE: Reputed to be the longest in Europe, this gorge can take anywhere from 5 to 8 hours to cross. Pack a picnic lunch. Take a bus or drive the 25 miles (40 km) to Omalos. From here you start the descent on a path that zigzags down into the gorge. At this point the hike may seem awesome, but it's actually quite manageable if you're wearing comfortable shoes. The next 11 miles (18 km) are filled with fascinating scenery — mysterious shadows; unusually shaped rocks; and pine, cypress, and fig trees scattered among myriad wildflowers. The hike ends at the fishing village of Aghia Roumeli, where you can take a boat across to Chora Sfakion, a rugged, mountainous area that claims to produce the tallest and longest-living Greeks. Spend the night here on the shores of southern Crete, where Zorba woke the passions of a young English intellectual, in the famous novel by Nikos Kazantzakis. In the morning, you can take the bus to Khaniá.

RETHYMNON: Attractive Venetian and Turkish architectural styles predominate in Crete's third-largest and most Oriental city. Though severely damaged during World War II, the fortress (1574) is the best-preserved Venetian building on the island. Inside is a mosque, and nearby is a Venetian fountain and small archaeological museum with a collection of bronze pieces from a Roman shipwreck. There is a sandy beach in town and a tiny Venetian harbor, which, though neglected these days, remains charming.

If you are visiting Rethymnon on *St. George's Day* (usually April 23, sometimes later), don't miss the celebration at the mountain village of Asi Ghonia, about an hour's drive away, where flocks of sheep are brought to the churchyard to be blessed; then they're milked and the milk is distributed to visitors. A traditional Cretan *glenti* with songs and dances follows. While here, buy the pungent graviera cheese that is allowed to mellow in the many nearby caves.

En Route from Rethymnon – Before the next few days of sightseeing, you can relax for a day or two in the beach resort of Aghia Pelagia, 12 miles (19 km) before Heraklion.

HERAKLION: Begin your tour of Crete's largest, but certainly not most attractive, city at the Venetian port, where you can walk beside the fortified walls to the 16th-century Venetian castle. Stroll around the marketplace and have a typical Cretan lunch in one of the many *tavernas* in the area. The *Heraklion Museum* (admission charge; at Eleftherias Sq.; phone: 81-282305) has the world's greatest collection of Minoan treasures, including the famous *Disc of Phaestos*. Also of interest is the *Historical Museum* (near the *Xenia* hotel), with exhibitions covering the early Christian, Byzantine, Venetian, and Turkish periods.

You can take several interesting side trips from Heraklion. The restored Palace of Knossos, home of the legendary King Minos 4,000 years ago, is a few miles southwest.

Plan to arrive early so you can spend a few hours here (guidebooks — in English — can be purchased at the entrance).

For a glimpse of village life, drive up to Anoghia in Mt. Idi, 21 miles (35 km) from Heraklion. From here, dedicated climbers can attempt to reach the Idian Cave, where legend says Zeus grew up. Farther up from Anoghia is the village of Axos. Stunning handmade crafts can be purchased in both villages.

Another must in the area is a visit to the Minoan site of Phaestos, 37 miles (59 km) from Heraklion (a guidebook available on the site is recommended). For a relaxing break, drive 6 miles (10 km) to Matala to swim in the warm waters of the Libyan Sea and lie on the sandy white beach surrounded by caves. Once inhabited by early Christians, the area has attracted the free-spirited from all over the world who come to bask under the magical, mystical Greek sun.

En Route from Heraklion – On the way to Aghios Nikolaos, stop at Malia with its Minoan palace, narrow winding alleys, and lovely beach. Break for lunch near Malia beach at *Taverna Kalypso,* which serves award-winning specialties using succulent Cretan produce, fresh herbs, and virgin oil from the olive trees next door.

AGHIOS NIKOLAOS: This chic resort town is a place to sit back, relax, and enjoy the sun and sea. The area has luxury accommodations, and the harbor is packed with *tavernas,* discos, and souvenir shops.

For a change of pace, visit the village of Kritsa, 7½ miles (12 km) away, with a superb view of the bay below. Every year, on the last Sunday in August, an old Cretan wedding is performed here, with festivities lasting well into the night.

Another worthwhile side trip is to the Diktaion Cave, the legendary birthplace of Zeus. The hike entails a drive to the Lasithi Plain, famous for its windmills and handwoven textiles, and a climb to the cave, starting from the village of Psychro. The cave has stalactites and stalagmites over 200 feet long. If you're up to the arduous 6-hour climb to the summit, start out in the village of Aghios Georgios, 2½ miles (4 km) before Psychro, and hire a guide in the village. The hardships of the climb are rewarded by a spectacular view of the entire island.

En Route from Aghios Nikolaos – The 44-mile (70-km) drive to Sitia passes through whitewashed villages set among orchards and olive groves. Next to the road there's a terrifyingly sharp drop to the sea. Don't attempt the drive if you've been drinking.

SITIA: This lovely town has many beautiful beaches, the best known of which is Vai (a few miles out of town), a long sandy beach with a dense growth of palm trees. It's a romantic spot to camp out; you can also stay at one of the hotels in town.

IERAPETRA: The largest town in southern Crete, Ierapetra retains an Oriental flavor with Venetian touches here and there. The coast is lined with *tavernas,* discos, and a few hotels where you can spend the night before crossing Crete at its narrowest point to return to Heraklion or Khaniá.

BEST EN ROUTE

Expect to pay $100 and up per night for a double room in hotels listed as expensive; around $60 for those in the moderate category; and about $30 for those in the inexpensive range.

KHANIÁ

Amphitriti – At the old Venetian port, this modern hostelry has magnificent views and comfortable rooms. 33 Lithinon St. (phone: 821-56471). Moderate.

Panorama – In an ideal spot with 167 rooms, each with a balcony overlooking the water. The property has 2 swimming pools. Kato Galatos (phone: 821-54200). Moderate.

RETHYMNON

El Greco – Right on the beach, this resort has a pool, tennis, mini-golf, Ping-Pong, a playground for children, and all water sports. The 307 rooms are in hotel accommodations or bungalows (phone: 831-71281 or 831-71102). Moderate.

AGHIA PELAGIA

Capsis Beach – On a lovely stretch of beach 15 miles (24 km) from Heraklion, this hotel has gardens, 3 pools, and 2 sandy beaches. There are 191 hotel rooms and 354 bungalows (phone: 81-233395). Expensive.

HERAKLION

Dolphin Bay – Comfortable rooms or bungalows on Amoundra Beach, 2 swimming pools, tennis courts, restaurants, and a bar (phone: 81-1103). Moderate.

Knossos Beach – Only 7 miles (11 km) from town in Kokkini Hani, this hotel has 106 pleasant rooms and bungalows (phone: 81-761000). Moderate.

AGHIOS NIKOLAOS

Astir Palace – A deluxe resort complex with 297 rooms and bungalows overlooking two private beaches. There also are tennis courts and 2 swimming pools. Elounda (phone: 841-41580; fax: 841-41783). Expensive.

Elounda Mare – Overlooking the sea, this deluxe resort has a pool, tennis, putting green, and water sports facilities. The only hotel in Greece that is a member of the prestigious Relais & Châteaux group, it has 297 bungalows set in an attractive wooded area. Dine in the intimate tavern where the ambience is delightful and the service good. No beach (phone: 841-41512). Expensive.

Minos Beach – On the beach, this luxurious resort has 118 bungalows facing the sea, an outdoor pool, and good recreational facilities (phone: 841-22345). Expensive.

Cretan – Though some dishes here are only fair, the hors d'oeuvres and grilled items are tasty, and the harbor view is glorious. Reservations advised (phone: 841-28773). Moderate.

IERAPETRA

Atlantis – A comfortable 69-room hotel that is a good place to spend the night before heading back to Khaniá or Heraklion. Aghios Andreas (phone: 842-28555). Inexpensive.

The Dodecanese Islands: Rhodes, Kos, Patmos, and Karpathos

Southeast of the Greek mainland, off the coast of Asia Minor, the 12 islands of the Dodecanese group offer a wide variety of natural attractions and historical ruins. Lying relatively close to one another, the islands have similar histories but diverse personalities. Rhodes is the largest and most popular of the group, with Kos running second in tourist flow and amenities. Two of the less frequented islands — Patmos and Karpathos — are included here for those who want a taste of simple island life. The most rewarding aspect of spending some time on the smaller islands is the genuine warmth and hospitality extended by the islanders.

RHODES: Rhodes has something for everyone: sites of great historic interest, a wealth of natural beauty, accommodations ranging from luxury hotels to simple rooms in village houses, a variety of sports facilities, and a large casino. Because Rhodes is the favorite of sun-worshiping Scandinavians, it can be very congested from June through August. May and September, also hot months, are much more relaxing on Rhodes.

According to Greek mythology, the island sprang out of the sea and was offered as a gift by Zeus to Apollo, the sun god, who named it after his current fling, Rhodos, daughter of Aphrodite. Archaeological evidence indicates that Rhodes was originally settled by the Minoans and Myceneans. The island prospered in the 11th century BC under the Dorians, who founded Ialysus, Kamiros, and Lindos; in 408 BC these three cities united to form the city of Rhodes.

Incorporated into the Byzantine Empire in AD 395, Rhodes was sold by its Genoese masters to the crusading Knights of St. John in 1306. During their 200-year rule, they converted the island into a Christian stronghold; they were finally forced out by the Ottomans, who controlled Rhodes until 1912, when the Italians seized the island. Rhodes finally was reunited with Greece and the other Dodecanese islands in 1947.

The most striking reminders of this diverse history can be found in the town of Rhodes. The Old City has remnants of the Crusaders and the Middle Ages — narrow streets; 13th-, 14th-, and 15th-century buildings adorned with coats of arms; and powerful walls built by the Knights of St. John. Visit the *Archaeological Museum* (Street of the Knights), housed in the 15th-century Hospital of the Knights, and the massive Palace of the Grand Masters, a 14th-century fortress with underground passages and chambers. The Turkish quarters are nearby, marked by mosques and old Ottoman homes.

Surrounding the Old City is the modern section, a cosmopolitan Greek island capital with fine hotels, a myriad of duty-free shops, and the *Grand* hotel casino. According to legend, the harbor entrance of Mandraki was once straddled by the immense bronze Colossus of Rhodes, one of the Seven Wonders of the World, which towered 126 feet and weighed 300 tons.

You can take side trips to the three Dorian cities from the capital. Little remains of ancient Ialysus, 10 miles (16 km) from Rhodes, but there's a good view from the acropolis. Kamiros, 22 miles (35 km) from town, has more of interest, including a 3rd-century BC temple and colonnade, a 5th-century cistern, and the agora, or ancient marketplace. Lindos, 32 miles (51 km) from Rhodes, is an attractive old village that can get very busy in summer, and unless you visit off-season, it's not really worth fighting the crowds. The acropolis (which can be reached on foot or by hired donkey) dominates the ancient city, which was once the center of the cult of the goddess Athena. A 4th-century temple dedicated to her still stands and was being restored to its original grandeur at press time. Many 15th-century houses, built when the Knights of St. John converted Lindos to a fortress, line the narrow streets of the town. There also is a long beach where St. Paul is said to have landed on his way to Rome.

Petaloudes (Valley of the Butterflies), 16 miles (26 km) south of Rhodes, is one of the island's most stunning locales. Each spring, thousands of butterflies (actually moths) nestle in the trees of this narrow, thickly wooded valley. If you stir the branches, the creatures fill the air in a bursting reddish-gold cloud.

In Rodini, 2 miles (3 km) south of Rhodes, an annual wine festival is held from mid-July to the end of September. Visitors can sample the local wines to their hearts' content and watch musicians and dancers perform late into the night.

Fine beaches line the shores of the island. Good fishing grounds are found near the villages of Kamiros, Lindos, Kallithea, and Gennadi.

KOS: The birthplace of Hippocrates, the father of medicine, this island, second in size to Rhodes, has a history similar to that of Rhodes but a quieter atmosphere. The town of Kos is quite attractive, with white, arched houses set in lovely gardens. The coastal road to the port of Mandraki is particularly pleasant for a walk or a bicycle ride. Beaches are excellent all over the island, as are the accommodations.

Historical highlights include the Castle of the Knights of St. John, the ancient agora, the Temple of Dionysus, the Roman baths, the gymnasium, and the town museum, with a statue of Hippocrates, which dates to the 4th century BC. Famous South African doctor Christiaan Barnard established an international health center on Kos.

PATMOS: The northernmost of the Dodecanese, Patmos is known primarily for its associations with St. John the Divine, who received the Revelations and dictated them to a disciple in the Sacred Grotto, which lies between the harbor and the capital. The massive, elaborately decorated Monastery of St. John, which has also served as a fortress, is the principal historic site.

Patmos has fine sandy beaches (many of which are reached by taking a local boat) and the white architecture characteristic of many Greek islands. You can do some challenging hiking here, too. Every year on August 15 (*Feast of the Assumption*) there's an all-out celebration with food, music, and dancing.

To really get away from it all, take a caïque (small fishing boat) to the small nearby island of Lipsi, with isolated beaches, good *tavernas* lining the harbor, and hardly any tourists.

KARPATHOS: Midway between Rhodes and Crete (and accessible from both), Karpathos is a folklorist's paradise. In the densely forested north, people maintain centuries-old traditions. In the village of Olympus (reached by a poor road from the little harbor of Diafani), the women till the fields and do most of the heavy chores. They work in long, dark blue coats worn over bright tops and white breeches, with brightly patterned scarves covering their heads. Bear in mind that this is not a tourist attraction but a way of life.

If you are in Olympus after *Easter* or in late summer (August 15 and 29 or September 8), you can watch and perhaps participate in a traditional celebration, with plenty of wine, songs, and dances. If a wedding is to take place, the villagers hold an extravagant *glenti*, or feast — 3 days of music, dance, food, wine, and strictly observed customs.

There are several good beaches on the island near the capital, Pigadia. You can take interesting side trips by motorboat to the nearby uninhabited islets of Saris and Armathia.

BEST EN ROUTE

Expect to pay $100 and up per night for a double room in hotels listed as expensive; $80 and up for those in the moderate category; and under $30 for those in the inexpensive range. Most of the bigger — and better — hotels are found on the east coast around Faliraki. Homeowners on the smaller islands rent clean, comfortable rooms at modest prices.

RHODES

Rodos Bay – Set on a hillside, this modern resort has all recreational facilities. Most of the 330 rooms and bungalows are in the main building — best of all are the maisonettes, split-level bungalows facing the sea with spectacular views. Ixia Trianda (phone: 23661). Expensive.

Rodos Palace – The tallest building on the island, this luxury resort has all the amenities and then some — outdoor and indoor pools, tennis, mini-golf, sauna, restaurants, disco, shops, nightclub, and bowling alley. The 610 air conditioned rooms are fashionably decorated and comfortable; some have gardens or sea views. Ixia, 2½ miles (4 km) from town (phone: 241-25222). Expensive.

Alexis – This is the place for excellent seafood. Have lunch or dinner on the patio, but take a peek inside at the display of fresh fish. The eatery serves some of the best Greek salads around, and the house specialty is a delicious prawn soup with feta cheese. Reservations advised. 18 Socrates (phone: 241-29347). Expensive to moderate.

Chevalier Palace – A good bet for those who prefer to be in town, as it is within walking distance of the historic town center. Facilities include 188 rooms, a pool, sauna, nightclub, and a fine self-service restaurant. A casino is just across the street, and a beach is nearby. 3 Stratigou Griva (phone: 241-22781). Moderate.

Qupia – A 20-minute drive off the beaten path and into the hills above Rhodes, this place is very popular with Greeks. Dine on the terrace or in one of several cozy dining rooms with exposed stone walls and beamed wood ceilings. There is no menu, but English-speaking waiters will bring dish after dish to your table. Reservations advised. At the turnoff for Tys (phone: 241-91824). Moderate.

Xenia – Each of the 26 rooms offers private bath and balcony. There's also an 18-hole golf course and good sea views. Paralia Afantou (phone: 241-51121). Moderate.

KOS

Dimitra Beach – Right on the beach, this resort has 134 rooms and bungalows, restaurants, bars, a lounge with dancing, and a snack bar. Aghios Fokas (phone: 242-28581). Expensive.

PATMOS

Xenia – Simple and comfortable accommodations in a 35-room hotel with fine views in breathtaking surroundings. In town (phone: 247-31219). Moderate.

KARPATHOS

Porfyris – This comfortable 22-room hotel is one of the few around. In town (phone: 245-22294). Inexpensive.

The Cyclades: Mykonos, Delos, Paros, Naxos, and Santorini

In Greece, a group of islands called the Cyclades form a rough circle around the sacred island of Delos, a religious, cultural, and commercial center of the ancient world. Apart from their archaeological interest, each of the 39 islands comprising the group (24 are inhabited) has much to offer the visitor, from the intense nightlife of Mykonos to the isolated beaches of Kimolos, where there are no hotels but plenty of hospitality. Some of the best-known Cycladic islands are described below.

MYKONOS: "Is Greece near Mykonos?" the American tourist is said to have asked his travel agent; though it's probably apocryphal, the question is indicative of the island's fame — and perhaps notoriety.

You name it, and Mykonos is bound to have it: a harbor teeming with luxury yachts and fishing boats; more discotheques, bars, and restaurants than all the other Greek islands put together; narrow cobblestone streets lined with art galleries and chic boutiques; officially designated nude beaches; many windmills; and over 300 churches.

The most outstanding feature of this island is its dazzling brightness; blazing sunlight reflects off the always freshly whitewashed houses and churches. Practically everything is white — even the trunks of the few trees in town are painted white. This brightness makes getting up in the morning a pleasure; it seems a shame to sleep at night, especially when the full moon illuminates the island. Actually, hardly anyone turns in before the early morning hours, so the popular beaches don't get crowded before noon. These are to the south and are accessible by bus, taxi, or boat. For nude swimming, try Paradise, Super Paradise (preferred by homosexuals), or Elia.

When night falls, Mykonos comes alive with activity to suit every taste. You can watch the colorful international set that frequents the island, have a drink at a bar in Little Venice overlooking the sea, take your time over dinner (try the local tangy cheese called *kopanisti* and *amygdalota,* tasty crushed almond sweets), then head to one of the current hot spots. Many say Mykonos has the best nightlife in Greece.

If possible, avoid Mykonos in August; the *meltemi,* or north wind, can be annoying, and the island is most crowded then.

DELOS: No one should leave Mykonos without taking the half-hour boat trip to Delos (except when the high winds of *meltemi* are blowing). First settled some 5,000 years ago, Delos became the religious, cultural, and financial center of the Aegean around 1000 BC. It remained prominent until 454 BC, when the island treasury was moved to the Parthenon for safekeeping. In Hellenistic times, Delos revived as a commercial center.

Many of the island's temples and shrines are extremely well preserved. Highlights include the Terrace of the Lions, the Sanctuary of Apollo (according to mythology, the sun god was born here), the smaller Temple of Artemis, an agora, other sanctuaries, and a museum. Spend the night in the small hostel and take an evening walk in the moonlight. Delos is nearly uninhabited, and the solitude can be deeply moving.

PAROS: An island of undulating hills, it became famous for its fine white marble used in ancient times by sculptors. Approaching Parikia, the main port and capital, visitors will catch sight of local fishermen and native islanders enthusiastically and politely seeking guests for small hotels and pensions. The main part of town has a wide variety of shops for every taste, but the ancient city here is the main attraction. Follow the narrow stone alley to the legendary Katapoliani Church, which dates from the 6th century; the Byzantine collection here includes precious relics, icons, frescoes, and woodcarvings. Every August 15 a major celebration takes place here.

While on Paros, take a day trip by bus, car, or the ubiquitous scooter. (Be careful riding the scooters, which have sent many a visitor home on crutches.) A half-hour drive from the town of Paros is Naoussa, a picturesque port with a medieval castle. Directly opposite is Kolimbithra where strangely carved rocks enclose inlets with golden sands and the deep blue sea. Paros is dotted with a number of delightful little villages: At Lefkes, almost in the center of the island, beautiful pottery is made; Marpissa is dominated by a Venetian Castle; long sandy beaches are found at Drios, Aliki, and Pisso Livadi. Across from Paros is the island of Antiparos, where buses take visitors to stalactite-filled caves. If you prefer, just hike around the island on your own. Ferry service between Paros and Antiparos runs daily during the summer months from 8 AM to 7 PM, with boats leaving hourly. Check ahead for the hours during other times of the year with the ferry service (phone: 284-22079).

NAXOS: About 6 miles east of Paros, this island is the largest and most fertile of the Cyclades. The expansive harbor and the picturesque town of Naxos, combined with extensive stretches of beach, are what attract visitors year after year. The island's impressive history is everywhere, too. According to mythology, it was on Naxos that the god Dionysus sprang from the thigh of Zeus. Today, the majestic Temple of Apollo is on the tiny islet of Palatia, linked to the main island by a causeway. On Naxos, there are Mycenaean tombs, a museum of rare finds from the tombs, a castle, historic churches, and two ancient quarries — one at Apollonas and the other at Melanes. The village of Halklo has medieval fortresses and several Byzantine churches. The village of Filoti also has a beautiful church adorned with Byzantine icons. In Sangri, visit Himaros Tower, one of the best-preserved monuments of the Hellenistic period. Once you've had your fill of sightseeing, relax at the sandy beaches of Apollonas, Kastraki, Vigia, or Aghios Georgios.

SANTORINI: Known in Greek as Théra, this striking island is of volcanic origin. Some believe that a massive volcanic eruption here in the 16th century BC caused the decline of the Minoan civilization, centered on Crete, to the south. Santorini often is associated with the legendary Atlantis.

Santorini is a crescent-shaped mass of rock with precipitous cliffs up to 1,000 feet high. Donkeys and a special railway wind up the cliff from the harbor, where the cruise ships dock, to the island capital of Fira, with its narrow, cobbled streets and medieval quarter. Ancient Théra was inhabited at various times by Phoenicians, Dorians, Romans, and Byzantines, and some impressive ruins remain. You can swim at one of the island's black (lava) sand beaches just outside Oia, or take a motorboat excursion to the volcano, on an adjacent islet.

BEST EN ROUTE

Expect to pay $100 and up per night for a double room in hotels listed as expensive and about $40 for those in the inexpensive range.

MYKONOS

Chez Ketrin – A longtime favorite of Greeks and visitors, the dining room is romantically lit and offers excellent service. Try the *spanakopita,* spinach pie, and the charcoal-grilled veal chop. Reservations unnecessary (no phone). Expensive to moderate.

Philippi – Romantic and elegant, with comfortable dining rooms, this dining establishment serves delicious fish and eggplant salad. Reservations unnecessary (no phone). Expensive to moderate.

Santa Marina – Located on a private beach, it's an apartment-style complex ideal for families. Each apartment has a patio with a view. Only 15 minutes from town. Ornos Bay (phone: 289-24002). Expensive to moderate.

Petinos – Right on the beach, this 29-room hotel has a *taverna.* Plati Yalos (phone: 289-22127). Inexpensive.

Poseidon – A no-frills hostelry within walking distance of town and at the water's edge, it is well-maintained and friendly. Room 17 has a balcony overlooking the sea (phone: 289-22437). Inexpensive.

DELOS

Xenia – Since this is the only place on the island to spend the night, you have to be lucky to get one of the few beds available. It's worth a try to experience the solitude after dark. Some camping is also permitted, and there's a very simple restaurant (phone: 289-22259). Inexpensive.

PAROS

Xenia – On a hill overlooking Parikia's beach, this comfortable hotel has a restaurant and bar, convenient for guests who don't feel like strolling into town (phone: 284-21394).

Arian – Just up the road from the main harbor of Parikia, this is a charming, family-run hostelry. Rooms are small but well-furnished with balcony, private bath, and telephone. The patio is a nice place to have breakfast (phone: 284-21490). Inexpensive.

NAXOS

Mathiassos – Overlooking the beach, it has 204 modern, comfortable rooms, many with a terrace (phone: 85-22200). Moderate.

SANTORINI

Atlantis – Overlooking the sea, this stately hotel — a favorite of many Santorini regulars — offers comforts not normally found at island hostelries (phone: 286-22232). Expensive.

Kastro – An upscale eatery open for dinner only, it's food is fair, but the view is magnificent. Try the grilled swordfish kebab — order it under-cooked. Reservations unnecessary (no phone). Expensive.

Atlantis Villas – Not to be confused with the *Atlantis* hotel, this unusual white-stucco hostelry overlooks the Aegean Sea and has charming rooms filled with Greek antiques and traditional artifacts. Have breakfast on the terrace, and jump in the saltwater swimming pool. Beware that the rooms are really too cold for comfort from September through June. Oia, Santorini (phone: 286-71214). Expensive to moderate.

Delfini II – Just above the sea and the landscape of Fira, these new apartments are furnished traditionally but have modern facilities, including kitchens (phone: 286-22780). Moderate.

Selene – An elegantly eccentric restaurant and bar that attracts an interesting mix of locals and tourists. Open daily, except during off-season months. Reservations advised. In Fira (phone: 286-22249). Moderate.

Finikia – Run by a friendly Greek who formerly worked in several American hotels, it has large rooms, along with a restaurant serving excellent Greek dishes and continental fare. Just outside Fira, before the village of Oia (phone: 286-71372; fax: 286-71118). Moderate to inexpensive.

Kukumarlos – Have lunch on the terrace above the sea here, and if you're ready for a break from Greek cooking, try a cheese pizza with a glass of retsina. No reservations (no phone). Inexpensive.

Laokasti – Though the service is minimal, this pleasant eatery near the *Atlantis Villas* serves tasty grilled octopus and chicken. No reservations (no phone). Inexpensive.

The Islands of the Eastern Aegean: Lesbos, Samos, and Chios

Lush green vegetation in parts, crystal-clear waters in every shade of blue, and small villages clinging to tradition characterize the islands of the northeastern Aegean Sea. The three described here can be reached by air from Athens or by boat from Piraeus, northern Greece, and Rhodes.

LESBOS: In the time of Sappho (600 BC), Lesbos was probably the most advanced city in the world, with its intellectual life at a remarkably high level. It was here that the world's first known great woman poet sang her poems to the young girls she loved; the passion of her descriptions was such that the term "lesbian" has been used to denote love between women ever since. Lesbos was also the birthplace of Aesop, one of the most famous storytellers of all time.

Today Lesbos (also known as Mytilene) preserves little of its ancient glory, but it's a marvelous place for sunning, swimming, hiking, and exploring ancient and Byzantine ruins.

From the island's capital, Mytilene, good roads lead to practically all parts of the island. On the northern tip is Molivos, or Mithimna, reached by a lovely coast road. En route, stop at Thermi to see an excavated prehistoric settlement. Swim at the excellent beach in Aghios Stephanos, and have lunch at one of the numerous *tavernas*. The road passes through extensive olive groves — the island is famous for its olives and olive oil — until reaching Molivos. Set over the beach and fishing harbor, this attractive town seems to grow right out of the surrounding hills. A 17th-century Genoese castle dominates the town and offers a fine view of the Turkish coast. There also are stone tower houses dating from that period.

SAMOS: Inhabited since 3000 BC, Samos was the birthplace of the great mathematician Pythagoras (6th century BC) and also, according to mythology, of the goddess Hera, sister and wife of Zeus. The landscape is quite striking — golden beaches, blue sea, and mountains in the east and west. About 10% of the island is cultivated with vineyards that produce a very aromatic white wine. Flowers bloom everywhere.

Vathi is the capital and tourist center of the island. The *Archaeological Museum* and *Museum of Byzantine Art* both have interesting exhibitions. You can hike up to the monastery of Zoodohos Pighi for a sweeping view of the Turkish coast, only a few miles away, and accessible by boat from Samos.

Samos is a great place for hikes and excursions. Buses link different towns on the island and travel on good roads. There are several lovely beaches with diverse landscapes to explore, including Kokari, Marathokambos, Pirgos, Kootso, and Platanakia. Take a break at any of the fishing villages along the way; most offer comfortable hotels or rooms in private houses.

Visit Pithagorio, once the island's capital and now an enchanting fishing village, 10 miles (16 km) south of Vathi. Natives call the town Tigani ("frying pan") because of its shape. Here you can see the remains of an ancient wall, a theater, and an aqueduct that was built through the mountain in the 6th century BC. The view of nearby Asia Minor is superb. Less than a mile away is a monastery constructed deep inside a cave surrounded by a natural cistern. The Heraion, 3 miles (5 km) from Pithagorio, is the site of a temple dedicated to Hera that was considered one of the Seven Wonders of Antiquity.

CHIOS: Like Samos, the crescent-shaped island of Chios is fertile and beautiful, and many of its inhabitants are rich: A number of the Golden Greek shipowners come from the island that Homer referred to as "the rocky realm" (according to one legend, the island is his birthplace).

Chios is the original chewing gum producer. For centuries the island's prosperity was based on the cultivation and sale of mastic gum, popular with the courtesans of antiquity for the pleasant aroma it gave their breath. Today, you can buy it wrapped in cellophane or drink it in the form of *mastiha* — but go easy, it's very potent.

You can take a pleasant walk through the pine trees to the Nea Moni (New Monastery), a fine example of Byzantine architecture. The mastic gum tree area spreads south from the monastery of Aghios Minas. Villages in the area retain a medieval character, with stone houses, narrow arcaded streets, and interesting churches.

While on Chios, take a boat to the five small Oinoussai Islands off the northeastern coast. They have good fishing and hunting grounds and sandy beaches. The rich Greek shipowners who were born here return frequently with their families, filling the harbor with luxury yachts. A regular boat service links Chios to the nearby Turkish coast.

BEST EN ROUTE

Expect to pay $80 per night for a double room in hotels listed as expensive; $50 and up for hotels in the moderate category; and about $30 in the inexpensive range.

LESBOS

Lesbion – On the harbor of Mytilene, this hotel has 38 comfortable rooms. In town (phone: 251-22038). Moderate.

Lesbos Beach – Outside town, the accommodations consist of 39 furnished apartments. Neapolis (phone: 61531). Moderate.

Sappho – Also on the harbor, this place offers 31 standard rooms at modest prices. In town (phone: 28415). Inexpensive.

SAMOS

Doryssa Bay – An attractive hotel with 252 rooms. Pithagorio (phone: 273-61390). Expensive.

Xenia – The most comfortable of the accommodations in town, with 31 rooms. Vathi (phone: 273-27463). Moderate.

Merope – The attraction here is the lovely view; 80 rooms. In Karlovassi (phone: 273-32650). Inexpensive.

CHIOS

Chios Chandris – On the port, this branch of the quality hotel chain is well run and the 156 rooms are nicely appointed. In town (phone: 271-25761/6). Moderate.

Corfu

The second-largest and most populous of the Ionian islands, Corfu is considered by many to be the most beautiful of the Greek islands. It has has been praised by Homer in the *Odyssey,* chosen by Shakespeare as the setting for *The Tempest,* and extolled by Henry Miller in *The Colossus of Maroussi,* and by Laurence Durrell in *Prospero's Cell.* Many prominent Greeks frequent Corfu, known locally as Kérkyra.

In the North Ionian Sea, Corfu marks Greece's westernmost point. The semi-mountainous terrain supports more lush vegetation than any other Greek island. Millions of olive trees grow on the gentle slopes. Orange, lemon, cypress, acacia, and plane trees take root here, and the fragrance of a wide variety of flowers fills the air.

Good roads leading to all parts of the island start from the capital, the town of Corfu on the east coast. You can tour by car, bus, or taxi, or, if you're taken with the island's romantic atmosphere, horse and carriage. For sunning and swimming, you can head to the beaches of the luxury resorts or find isolated beaches and coves all over the island.

Corfu is an entry point into Greece from other places in Europe. The island is accessible by ferry from Brindisi, Ancona, and Otronto, Italy, and from Dubrovnik, Yugoslavia, or by air from most European capitals. Daily flights link Corfu and Athens, and the island also can be reached by ferry from Igoumenitsa in western Greece or Patras on the Peloponnese.

CORFU: The cosmopolitan seaport capital of this island is also called Corfu. With its many main and side streets, squares, and churches, the city is a delight to explore on foot. It has an interesting architectural style incorporating Byzantine, Venetian, French, Russian, English, and Italian elements, with the medieval section comprising narrow Italianate alleyways, flanked by shuttered tenements with laundry lines flying between them. Even the Greek spoken here is laced with Italian borrowings, such as *nonna* (grandmother) and *pomedor,* from the Italian *pomodoro.* One of the best introductions to the spirit of the Corfiots is to spend an evening at a *taverna* or *cafenion* on the Spianada (Esplanade), Greece's largest public square, formerly the Venetian parade ground. On summer evenings, open-air concerts are given by earnest local bands.

Corfu is an old town, and you can see the remnants of the civilizations that have played a role in its history. At the tip of Aghios Nikolaos, the northern section of town, is a Venetian fortress, which many historians identify with the Heraion Acropolis, mentioned by Thucydides. Corfu's Town Hall (1663) is a splendid example of Venetian architecture. Mon Repos, the former royal palace, is a neo-classical structure with a Doric portico; it now serves as a summer villa for Greek commissioners. Britain's Prince Philip was born here. Other highlights include the *Archaeological Museum* (5 Vraila), with finds from excavations; the *Museum of Asiatic Art* (Kato Platia), with a rich collection of Chinese, Japanese, and Indian art and a very un-Greek, enormous relief carving of the Gorgon; and Kanoni, 2½ miles (4 km) south of town, a semicircular terrace that commands an excellent view of the harbor and provides access to two little islets with monasteries.

The town has excellent facilities for sports and recreational activities. The major resorts have mini-golf, tennis, water skiing, and swimming at their own beaches. There's a public beach and a pleasant garden-lined promenade at the Mon Repos palace; the most popular beaches on the island are Roda, 22 miles (35 km) north of town, and Glyfada, 10 miles (16 km) west of town. Tennis is available at the *Tennis Club* (Vraila and Romanou) and golf, at the 18-hole course near the village of Vatos. Corfu is also good for other activities — fishing, hiking, and even cricket, an odd relic of British rule, at the *Corfu Cricket Green.* You can go horseback riding at the stables in Gouvia, 5 miles (8 km) from town right on the Spianada, in Alikes, 3 miles (5 km) from town, or on the west coast, in Paleocastritsa about 24 km (15 miles) away.

In the evenings there is ample entertainment at the hotel clubs and the discos around town. In 1891, Empress Elizabeth of Austria had her summer palace built in Gastouri, 5 miles (8 km) south of town, and named it the Achilleion after her favorite hero with the vulnerable heel. It now houses a casino. The structure itself is considered amusing by some and an atrocity by others, but the lovely gardens stretching down to the sea are appreciated by most everyone for evening strolls.

MT. PANTOCRATOR: Rising 3,000 feet in the northern section of the island, Corfu's highest summit commands an excellent view of the surroundings. To the south spreads the city of Corfu and the rest of the island. To the east lies Albania (only a mile away at the closest point). On a clear day, the coast of Italy is visible to the northwest. The monastery on the mountain dates back to 1347.

PALEOCASTRITSA: On a small bay surrounded by hills, this popular resort, 16 miles (26 km) west of Corfu, is popular for its clear water, good fishing, and excellent seafood. Local *tavernas* specialize in lobster.

PAKI: Less than 8 square miles in area, this islet, 2½ hours by motorboat from Corfu Harbor (boats leave twice daily except on Sundays), is a great place to spend a serene day or two. Covered with dense vegetation, including olive trees and vine plants, the island is unique in its underwater caves and excellent lobsters. You can stay in bungalows on the beach or rent rooms in islanders' houses.

BEST EN ROUTE

Prices for double rooms per night in the hotels listed below range from $100 and more (expensive) to around $60 (considered moderate). As on Rhodes, most of the luxury hotels on Corfu are not actually in town, but shuttle bus service is provided.

CORFU

Astir Palace – Overlooking Komeno Bay, this modern resort attracts an international clientele. It has 184 rooms and 124 bungalows. Facilities include a sauna, swimming pool, tennis courts, private beach, shopping arcade, restaurants, and a *taverna*. At the beachfront (phone: 661-91490; fax: 661-91881). Expensive.

Corfu Hilton – This attractive resort has fine facilities — indoor and outdoor pools, tennis, a disco, bowling, several restaurants, bars, and 256 rooms and bungalows. The landscaped beachfront gardens are very pleasant. The hotel provides shuttle service to town and the golf course. Kanoni (phone: 661-30041; fax: 661-36551). Expensive.

Bella Venezia – The best, and newest, of the hotels in town, 2 blocks from the Spianade. Price includes breakfast; no credit cards accepted. 4 Zambeli (phone: 661-46500). Moderate.

Hermones Beach – Sloping down to a private beach, this first class facility has 272 hotel rooms and bungalows. Among the amenities are a pool, restaurants, bars, and a lounge with music. 8½ miles (14 km) from Corfu just before Paleocastritsa (phone: 661-9-4241). Moderate.

The Peloponnese

Separated from mainland Greece by the Gulf of Corinth, the Peloponnese peninsula encompasses more than 8,000 square miles of varied and impressive scenery. Much of the peninsula is mountainous, though the different ranges are separated by sweeping, fertile plains, and the low-lying coastal regions give way to some fine beaches. The area is rich in archaeological ruins. Its history has been traced back some 4,000 years through excavations at Mycenae, a great capital of the ancient Hellenic civilization.

The route spans large distances, historically and geographically, and requires about 5 days, though you could easily spend more time. Starting in Athens and heading west to Corinth, the itinerary loops around the peninsula. Among the highlights are Olympia, the site of the first *Olympic Games;* Vassai, with the 5th-century BC Temple of Apollo Epicurus; Mistra, a wonderfully preserved former Byzantine settlement on a mountainside; Mycenae; and Epidaurus, where you can watch a performance of an ancient drama in a huge open-air amphitheater.

ATHENS: For complete details on the capital and its hotels and restaurants, see *Athens,* THE CITIES.

En Route from Athens – It's best to start out in the morning on the Athens-Patras National Road. Stop at the Corinth Canal, about an hour's drive away, and look at the isthmus that connects the Peloponnese with mainland Greece.

CORINTH: Once the largest city of Greece, Corinth was prosperous to the point of decadence when it was destroyed by the Romans in 146 BC. The area remained uninhabited for the next 100 years until a Roman colony was founded by order of Julius Caesar. Corinth regained its former prominence, though earthquakes and a series of barbarian invasions eventually brought about its decline. The modern town has little of interest. The 6th-century BC Temple of Apollo, in the Old Town, is the only Greek ruin in ancient Corinth. The museum opposite the temple contains primarily Roman exhibitions. Beyond the Old Town, the mountain Acrocorinth rises 1,885 feet. Easily reached by car, the summit is topped by an ancient fortress, commanding a spectacular view of the Saronic and Corinthian gulfs. The original Hellenic fortress was later expanded, in succession, by the conquering Franks, Venetians, and Turks.

En Route from Corinth – Head to Patras along either the National Road or the narrower but infinitely more attractive coastal road, which winds its way between a plain of olive trees and the blue waters of the Corinthian Gulf. The largest town along the way is Aegion, designed attractively on three layers above the sea. Stop for a fresh fish lunch here or at one of the smaller villages on the road.

PATRAS: Greece's main western port is a well-laid-out town with arcaded streets and large squares at the harbor. Ancient ruins are scarce, though the history dates back to Mycenaean times. The main sights are the Odeion, built in Roman times; the *Archaeological Museum;* and the Church of St. Andrew, the largest church in the country. From Patras, you can make connections to the Ionian islands (see the *Corfu* route) or Italy. You can spend the night at a hotel in town or, better yet, at Loutra Kilini, 50 miles (85 km) southwest, where there are excellent accommodations right on one of the loveliest, whitest beaches in Greece (see *Best en Route*).

OLYMPIA: This fertile valley is the home of the *Olympic Games,* held in honor of Zeus, their legendary founder. In the first games (776 BC) the gods were pitted against human heroes. Some 200 years later, the games were instituted on a regular, 4-year basis. Events included competitions in wrestling, foot racing, chariot racing, horse racing, the pentathalon, and various artistic contests. The games were discontinued when the Romans conquered Greece. In 1896, they were reinstituted in Athens. Although Athens had vied to host the *Golden Olympiad* in 1996 (the centenary of the modern *Olympics*), after a vigorous and much-publicized attempt, the city lost out to Atlanta, Georgia.

The Olympic ideal, combining strong physical development with high intellectual achievement, has been universally adopted. The sacred flame burning at the Altis, symbol of this ideal, has never been extinguished and is still carried to wherever the games are being held.

Some of the best-known Greek myths originated in Olympia. According to legend, Apollo and Herakles were among the first winners. After a questionable victory in a chariot race, Nero introduced a singing contest to display his artistic talents. Statues of the victors were erected in the Altis sanctuary, which contains the ruins of many buildings, including the 5th-century BC Temple of Zeus. The gold and ivory statue of Zeus was destroyed in a fire, but the pediments of the temple are displayed in the *Museum of Olympia.* The ruins of the stadium, which could seat 20,000 spectators, also are here.

En Route from Olympia – If you want to do some alpine exploring or just relax amid mountain scenery, take a side trip to Vytina, 60 miles (96 km) west of Olympia. You can stay at a hotel built right on the cliff (see *Best en Route*), with spectacular views of the surrounding area. The food and wine are excellent, and there are good buys in woodcarvings made by local craftsmen.

VASSAI: The road ascends to a plateau on which the splendid Temple of Apollo Epicurus sits in awesome solitude. Built in 420 BC by Ictinus, the architect of the Parthenon in Athens, the temple was erected as a token of gratitude after the population was spared decimation by a cholera epidemic. It is made of gray stone indigenous to the area and is unusually designed with elements of three architectural styles — Doric, Ionic, and Corinthian. Before or after the ascent to Vassai, stop at the village of Andritsaina below for a cool drink.

En Route from Vassai – Stop in the seaside town of Kalamata for a meal of fresh fish. There are lovely silk kerchiefs for sale at the monastery in town. Visitors also can witness, firsthand, the devastating effects of the strong earthquake that shook Kalamata literally to pieces in late 1986.

PYLOS: This attractive little town rises from the Bay of Navarino, where, in 1827, the allied fleets of Great Britain, France, and Russia destroyed the Turkish and Egyptian forces to ensure Greek independence. Remains of the sea battle can still be seen from the harbor on a clear day. A memorial to the British sailors stands on the low rock in the center of the harbor.

King Nestor of Pylos, who aided the Achaians in their campaign against Hektor's Trojans, dwelt in a palace above the road south of town. The remains of the palace are quite impressive, particularly the throne room and the monumental entrance on the southeastern side. On a hill, the palace also commands a superb view of the area.

METHONI: Seven miles (11 km) south of Pylos, this small town on the west of the peninsula, along with Coroni on the east of the peninsula (linked by a dirt road), were known as the Eyes of Venice. The towns were the first Venetian foothold on the Greek mainland; the Venetian fortress still stands in Coroni. Nice beaches line the shores, and fishing is good in the area.

SPARTA: The drive to Sparta is delightful, particularly in spring when the wildflowers on Mt. Taygetus are in full bloom. The contemporary town of Sparta is an agricultural center of the Eurotas Valley and a convenient place to spend the night. Little remains of the ancient town, situated north of the modern town, except for the scant ruins of an acropolis and theater. However, ancient Sparta became the greatest military power in Greece after the Spartans defeated the Athenians in the Peloponnesian War. The term "spartan" still is used to denote fierce discipline and endurance. Visit the small archaeological museum on Lakougou Street (open 8 AM to 3 PM; closed Mondays; admission charge).

MISTRA: This deserted medieval town, built as a fortification on the side of a steep hill, has some of the best-preserved examples of Byzantine architecture in Greece. The narrow winding streets are lined with 14th- and 15th-century churches and houses.

For dinner, go to the *Kotopouladiko* in the tiny village of Mistra, below the ruins. Here you can get delicious fried chicken served with salads and bread.

THE MANI: This highland region is the most austere and isolated in the country. Its proud inhabitants live in small villages and in the tall, castle-like houses that have fortified the Mani for centuries. They have always resisted rule by foreign powers, and the many fortified towers seen in the area attest to the Maniots' independent spirit.

At Diros, you can explore caves with impressive stalactites and stalagmites (admission charge). Have lunch at a *taverna* on the picturesque quay at Gythion, the port of the Mani.

Kythera: From Gythion, take a ferry to the least known and most southerly of the Ionian islands, which is actually closer to the Peloponnese group. Also known as the island of Aphrodite, Kythera is about 19 miles (30 km) long and has a beautifully varied landscape of sandy beaches, green valleys with waterfalls, groves of olive and almond trees, high mountains, and low-lying plains. Aghia Pelagia is the arrival point on the island; from here, drive a car or take a taxi (about 3,000 drachmas/$16) to the capital of Chora on the southern tip of the island, about 17 miles (27 km) away. (Bus service is only available to school children.) Chora is home to a Venetian castle, built in 1502 (the site dates to 1150), overlooking the sea; it has an impressive gate with a tunnel-like entrance. Within the castle grounds are several post-Byzantine churches with violets and yellow semberviva flowers growing around them. Down the hill 2 miles (3 km) away is the port of Kapsali, a charming fishing harbor with several restaurants and apartment complexes. Before leaving the island, be sure to explore Panagia, the largest of a number of monasteries on the island, located in the tiny village of Mirtidia, and visit the caves with folk wall paintings and stalactites in Milopotamo.

If you wish to bypass the trip to Kythera, about 15 miles (24 km) past Diros is the small port of Gerolimenas with brightly painted caïques (fishing boats). Have lunch at a *taverna* and watch the waves crash against the rocks. Later, move on to the village of Vathia 5 miles (8 km) away, where 17th-century gray stone towers loom in the hills, overlooking the valleys and sea. Managed by the Greek Tourist Office, these towers offer overnight accommodations. Vathia is a wonderful place for hiking and discovering secluded beaches. Five miles (8 km) farther on, at the southernmost tip of Greece is Porto Kagio, a seaside refuge for quail and storks, where travelers can climb to the church on the hill or watch the fishermen preparing their freshly caught octopus, drying them out in the sun.

MONEMVASSIA: In Greek, the word means "one entrance," and from afar Monemvassia looks like an island, with only one narrow causeway joining it to the mainland. This Byzantine town on a great island-rock repulsed numerous attacks thanks to its strategic location and almost impregnable Byzantine and Venetian fortifications. It is still dominated by the ruins of a castle and ramparts, old mansions, small houses, narrow lanes paved with stone, churches with crumbling façades, and old low archways. Unspoiled by tourism, it is a charming retreat from the busy islands and city life.

MYCENAE: This ancient city was the center of the Hellenic civilization, and the presumed capital of Agamemnon. Archaeologists maintain that Mycenae was first inhabited around 3000 BC, but its great significance was not discovered until 1874, when Heinrich Schliemann began excavating five of six shaft graves rich with golden treasures, now on display at the *Archaeological Museum* in Athens. The principal points of interest are the six shaft graves, the city walls, a theater, cemetery, and several giant *tholos,* or beehive-shape tombs, with stone-flanked approaches. One of these, originally called the Treasury of Atreus by historians, may actually be the tomb of Agamemnon. But all *tholos* tombs, unlike the shaft graves, were looted, leaving little material to prove this theory.

> **En Route from Mycenae –** Take a short detour to Tyrins, the birthplace of Herakles. The palace and cyclopean walls made of huge stone blocks date from Mycenean times.

NAFPLION: According to legend, this pretty town was created by Palamidi, son of the sea god Poseidon. Set amid orchards on the Bay of Nafplion, the town was the first capital of Greece after the War of Independence. Visit the restored castle of Palamidi (reached by road or a 1,000-step footpath), and the Bourtzi fort, built by the Venetians on an islet in the bay. The nearby beaches of Assini and Tolo are very pleasant, as is a lunch of freshly caught fish at one of the waterfront *tavernas.*

EPIDAURUS: Once the sanctuary of Asklepios, the god of medicine, this ancient site includes the Doric Temple of Asklepios, the Tholos with its Corinthian columns, notable Greek and Roman baths, and a small museum containing finds from the area.

Spend the evening at the open-air theater, where you can experience a memorable performance of ancient tragedy or comedy. In stunning natural surroundings, the theater, designed by Polycleitus the Younger, is one of the best-preserved structures of ancient Greece. Its seating capacity is 14,000; despite its size, the theater's acoustics are remarkable — even on the last of its 55 tiers you can hear every word uttered onstage. The annual festival of ancient drama lasts from early July to late August. Performances finish at about 11 PM, so you either can spend the night or make the 2-hour drive back to Athens.

BEST EN ROUTE

Expect to pay around $50 per night for a double room in hotels listed as expensive; $25 and up for those in the moderate category; and about $20 for those in the inexpensive range.

PATRAS

Astir – This comfortable 120-room hotel is in the center of town. 16 Aghiou Andreou (phone: 61-277502). Expensive.

Galaxy – Also convenient, this 53-room hotel offers standard accommodations. 9 Aghiou Nikolaou (phone: 61-278815). Moderate.

Thraka – A good place for tasty Greek specialties such as stuffed tomatoes or *youvetsi* (baked beef with noodles). Open daily. Barkopannou St. (phone: 624-22575). Inexpensive.

OLYMPIA

Amalia – Not far from the archaeological site, this extremely pretty, all-white hotel, set amid wooded hillsides, has 147 rooms as well as convention facilities (phone: 624-22190; fax: 624-22444). Expensive.

Europa – Another comfortable hotel, this one is set on a hill above town and the pine-covered slopes of Cronus, the promontory that protects the famous ruins (phone: 624-22650). Expensive.

Spap – Just outside town; most of the 51 rooms have lovely views of the ancient site and the surrounding area. Above the site (phone: 624-22514). Expensive.

VYTINA

Xenia – Right on the cliff, this 20-room motel offers a fantastic panorama of mountain scenery. Good food and wine also are available. In town (phone: 795-21218). Inexpensive.

LOUTRA KILINI

Xenia – This 80-room resort hotel is convenient to the beaches (phone: 623-96270). Moderate.

SPARTA

Menelaion – The 48 high-ceilinged rooms here are decorated with antique furniture. 91 Paleologou (phone: 731-22161). Moderate.

GYTHION

Gythion – In the center of town overlooking the harbor, it offers picturesque views, especially from room No. 15 and No. 16, which are fully furnished apartments with kitchen and private terrace. Breakfast is not included in rates. 33 V. Pavlou St. (phone: 733-23523). Moderate to inexpensive.

Saga – Farther along the harbor, nearly opposite the dam to Marathonisi, this small new pension has modern rooms at reasonable prices. On the main harbor street, Khanae (phone: 733-23220). Moderate to inexpensive.

KYTHERA

Marou – A luxury hotel overlooking the sea, above the ferry port. Suites are available, along with a bar and tennis courts. Aghia Pelagia (phone: 735-33466). Expensive.

Margarita – A beautiful small hotel with stone floors and modern Greek furnishings. Each room has a telephone and TV set. There's also a bar and restaurant. Chora (phone: 735-31711; fax: 735-31325). Moderate.

Kalokerines Katikies – This small hotel complex offers comfortable accommodations, including some fully furnished apartments overlooking the harbor. The owners, Mr. and Mrs. Rigas, speak English well and provide friendly service. Open late May to late October. Kapsali (phone: 735-31265). Moderate to inexpensive.

Pierros – Open year-round, this *taverna* attracts locals who wander into the kitchen and choose from a varied selection of terrific Greek dishes, including stuffed tomatoes, fresh fish, and meat pastries. Comfortable air conditioned rooms, traditionally furnished, also are available above the restaurant. Livadi (phone: 735-31014). Moderate to inexpensive.

KALAMATA

Avra – A small pension with 7 comfortable rooms. 10 Santaroza, Paralia (phone: 721-82759). Inexpensive.

Filoxenia – On a secluded beach, this attractive hotel has 155 rooms and reasonable prices (phone: 721-23166). Inexpensive.

GEROLIMENAS

Akrogiali – Overlooking the small fishing port, this hostelry and restaurant offers comfortable rooms, some with a private terrace; there are also four private apartments available. The restaurant serves a half-dozen Greek specialties (phone: 733-54204). Moderate to inexpensive.

MONEMVASSIA

Byzantino – The rooms are antiques-filled and cozy at this hostelry opposite the small square and facing the sea. Request room No. 1, which has a private terrace and terrific view. Conveniently located on the main street with shops and restaurants. Matoula Ritsou (phone: 732-61660). Moderate.

To Kanoni – Guests can dine in several rooms, inside or out, at this busy restaurant, located in the *Castro* (Castle), along the only shopping area of the town. The service is a bit slow but well worth the wait for traditional dishes such as moussaka or *pastitsio*. The local fresh red mullet also is good. Reservations unnecessary. Major credit cards accepted (phone: 732-61387). Moderate.

Matolya – Also situated within the castle complex, this family-run eatery serves guests in a garden terrace or the rustic dining room. The kitchen is visible, so guests can see what is offered. Try the fresh zucchini salad, stuffed grape leaves in lemon sauce, or veal with eggplant. Open daily for dinner. No credit cards accepted (phone: 732-61660). Moderate to inexpensive.

NAFPLION

Xenia's Palace – Overlooking the Bourtzi fortress from a hill called Akronafplion, this luxury 54-room hotel offers pleasant, comfortably furnished accommodations and an excellent restaurant. (phone: 752-28981). Expensive.

Xenia – Many of the rooms in this 58-room hotel have balconies overlooking the bay. The food and service are good. Above town (phone: 752-28991). Moderate.

Agamemnon – About a mile (1.6 km) from the ruins, this 8-room hostelry has modest prices. In the village (phone: 721-66232). Inexpensive.

EPIDAURUS

Xenia II – Accommodations are in 24 comfortable cottages near the ancient theater (phone: 753-22003). Moderate.

Hungary

This small, landlocked country near the geographic center of Europe, with a blend of Eastern and Western traditions, has long appealed to travelers. It is a land of beautiful landscapes, romantic music, decorative folk art, historic monuments, and excellent — if occasionally heavy — food.

Despite its size — it is not quite as big as Indiana — and its relative flatness, the country has an extremely colorful and varied landscape. Hungary is bisected by the Danube River (called Duna in Hungarian), which rushes south after carving a sharply angled route through mountains along the country's northwestern border.

To the west of the Danube is Transdanubia, a picturesque area of rolling hills, cultivated vineyards, old towns, and Balaton, Europe's largest warmwater lake. Within the Great Hungarian Plain, east of the Danube, are abundant fruit orchards, fields of waving wheat, sunflowers, and corn, and the prairie-like *puszta*. This vast granary is the historic home of Hungary's famous whip-cracking herdsmen on horseback. In addition to the scenic mountains of the Danube Bend in the northwest, there are low, forested mountains along the northeastern frontier, which is also famous for its wine-growing regions. Deer, wild boar, and spiral-horned moufflon roam freely in state game reserves.

Hungary is bordered on the west by Austria, on the north by Czechoslovakia, on the east by the Soviet Union and Romania, and on the south by Yugoslavia. Foggy weather is common in fall, and winters can be bone-chillingly damp or Siberian-cold with much snow; summers are hot and dry.

The fact that Hungary has an extremely homogeneous population today — 96.6% of its 10.6 million people are ethnically Hungarian or, in their language, Magyar (the rest are Slavs, Serbs, Croats, Slovaks, and Gypsies), is the result of this century's two world wars. On the losing side in World War I, Hungary was forced to give up vast territories that had been part of its kingdom. Some 600,000 Jews, nearly two-thirds of the country's Jewish population, were murdered during World War II.

Adding to Hungary's singularity is its language, which is unlike any other in Europe although, as part of the Finno-Ugric language group, it is distantly related to Finnish and Estonian. The first inhabitants of this part of Europe were the Celts, who were conquered by the Romans in AD10. The Romans founded Aquincum (Budapest) as a frontier post; they also were founders of the thermal baths, making them precursors to modern-day spas. The ancestors of today's Magyars were fierce hordes of mounted tribesmen from the Ural Mountains who staged forays deep into Western Europe. Seven of their tribes, under the leadership of Arpád, were checked by the forces of the Holy Roman Empire in the 9th century, and they eventually settled in the general area of what now is Hungary.

Stephen (or István), a descendant of the almost legendary Magyar leader Arpád, became the first King of Hungary in AD 997 and worked strenuously to convert his people from paganism to Catholicism. For his efforts, he received a crown from the pope and later was canonized. St. Stephen's Crown has been a symbol of Hungarian nationhood ever since. (The crown was taken to the US for safekeeping during World War II, but was only returned in 1978, some time after tensions between the church and the local Communist government were eased.) About two-thirds of Hungary's population is at least nominally Roman Catholic, and the majority of the rest are Protestants.

After the Arpád line died out in 1301, various royal houses of Europe struggled for control of Hungary. The coronation of Mátyás Hunyadi (known as Matthias Corvinus) as king in 1458 brought prosperity and national glory to Hungary. This Renaissance king, famous for his dazzling court at Visegrád, restored public finances and reduced the power of masters over serfs. But after his death, central Hungary fell under the yoke of the Turks for some 150 years, while the northern and western sections were drawn into the Austrian Hapsburg domain. When the Turks were finally forced to withdraw from the capital of Buda in 1686, the Hungarians were compelled to accept Austrian succession to the Hungarian throne. The Hungarians rose up against Austrian absolutism several times. They succeded in establishing the first Hungarian republic in 1848, but were defeated the following year. The repression that followed caused the first mass exile of thousands of Hungarians. In 1867, however, their persistent battle for more independence led to the establishment of a dual monarchy in which Austria and Hungary were partners.

After the fall of the Austro-Hungarian Empire in World War I, Hungary was governed by Admiral Horthy, an authoritarian regent, from 1920 to 1944. Its alliance with Nazi Germany was followed by German occupation, which lasted until the liberation of Budapest, after a horrendous 2-month battle, by Soviet troops in 1945. In 1949, the government was taken over by the Hungarian Workers party (which later changed its name to Magyar Szocialista Munkáspárt — MSZMP, the Communist party in Hungary), and Hungary became politically, economically, and militarily aligned with the Soviet Union. In 1956, Soviet forces were called in to help crush an uprising, and 200,000 Hungarians fled into exile. However, starting in the early 1960s, the government of János Kádár enacted a number of reforms that took some of the sting out of the defeat of liberal elements. Since the end of the Kádár era in 1988, the pace of political and economic change has quickened.

This was especially true in 1989, when Hungary made a dramatic dent in the Iron Curtain by opening its borders to East German refugees who wished to emigrate to West Germany. Seeing that their policies had led the country to near economic and political ruin, the Communist authorities decreed political change. While changes in other Soviet-controlled countries resulted in protests in the streets, the Hungarian Communists sensed the inevitability of their demise, and in March 1990 organized the first free elections since 1947 — only to lose them. In August 1990, Hungary's first post-Communist right-of-center Parliament elected Arpad Goncz president (a 5-year term). Goncz, a writer and translator, had been a prisoner of the Communist government.

The country today, very much aware of its economic shortcomings, is attempting to introduce and develop free enterprise as quickly as possible. Many Hungarians fear, though, that change might be happening too quickly, and that the country's industries might be sold to Western investors for far too little. Hungarians also fear that inflation and a 10% unemployment rate could further destabilize the country, but pragmatism dictates no other choice but to pursue the road to free enterprise and democracy.

A visit to today's Hungary is an intellectually heady experience, as well as a pleasure for the senses. Two sensory pleasures are particularly indulged, and even may be combined: eating and listening to music. The latter experience can be rewarding in a restaurant, where a Gypsy orchestra often is as accomplished as it is in a concert hall.

The Magyar musical heritage comprises classical as well as folk music. It was dramatically expressed in the romantic rhapsodies of Ferenc (Franz) Liszt in the 19th century and in the modern music of the 20th-century masters Béla Bartók and Zoltán Kodály, both of whom devoted years of intensive study to Hungarian folk songs.

The special Hungarian harmony of flavors has made the country's cuisine, based on a superb marriage of meat, spices, and fresh vegetables, internationally appreciated. The special sweet Hungarian paprika is one of the world's most versatile condiments.

This wealth of historical, cultural, and culinary interest, coupled with the fact that Budapest is the brightest and most romantic capital of central Europe — indeed, one of the loveliest cities in Europe — has increased tourism to the point where the number of visitors to Hungary each year exceeds the country's population.

For those who would like to see more of the country than its wonderful capital, we have provided three tour routes. If you have only a short time to spend outside Budapest, a visit to the nearby Danube Bend offers an opportunity to enjoy some of the country's most breathtaking scenery while encountering its royal and ecclesiastical past. Our second route, into Transdanubia, is through a softer landscape, also rich in history, to Hungary's busiest center of recreation and relaxation, Lake Balaton. The final route, through the Great Hungarian Plain, allows you to explore the Hungary of peasant folk legend and to see some of Europe's most desirable farmland.

The Danube Bend

As it heads east from its route along the Czechoslovak border, the Danube River makes an elbow bend through the wooded Pilis and Börzsöny hills, divides into two channels that will unite again at Budapest, and gracefully curves south on its long journey to the Black Sea.

This scenic, history-rich area about 31 miles (50 km) north of Budapest is called the Danube Bend and is a favorite place for excursions for residents, many of whom have built small weekend homes there, as well as visitors. Its picturesque environs can be explored leisurely, and most pleasantly, by steamer on the river or by car. The main towns along the route also can be reached by train.

If you drive north, Route 11 follows the general contour of the right bank of the river between Budapest and Esztergom, an early seat of Hungarian kings and an ancient ecclesiastical center. To the west, all along the route, is the Pilis Park Forest, which harbors wild boar and deer. You can make the trip upriver along one bank and downriver along the other, or you may prefer to crisscross the river, visiting key cities on either bank as they appear on the route. For the purposes of description, this route will take the latter course, beginning at Budapest and ending at Esztergom, 40 miles (65 km) away.

BUDAPEST: For a detailed report of the city and its hotels and restaurants, see *Budapest,* THE CITIES.

En Route from Budapest – The highway leaves the capital on the Buda side of the Danube, which divides into two channels around the huge Szentendre Island just north of the city. The route upriver along the Szentendre channel, to the west of the island, offers the most rewards for tourists and is one of the busiest roads in Hungary on weekends.

SZENTENDRE: This old market town, where the great Hungarian painter Károly Ferenczy worked for the greater part of his life, is filled with interesting churches and art museums. Many artists have settled here in the old merchant houses of the original Serbian and Dalmatian settlers, who came here during the 17th century, fleeing the Turkish occupation. Today, the city's character largely reflects the 18th and 19th century, with distinguised Serbian architecture and color.

The small main square, Fő tér (formerly Marx tér), is lined with lovingly restored, 18th-century baroque houses. Each summer a theater festival is held in the square. The *Ferenczy Museum* (6 Fő tér) contains works by the Ferenczy family as well as paintings by members of the artists colony established here in 1928. Another museum (1 Vastagh György utca) displays the ceramics of Margit Kovács, and a collection of paintings and drawings by Lajos Vajda is on view at 1 Hunyadi János utca.

An open-air *skansen,* the *Outdoor Village Museum* (open from April through October), in the north of town contains original examples of folk architecture, brought here from Hungary's 23 regions. Craftsmen here demonstrate milling, candlestick making, scone and honeycake baking, and so forth, on the first Sunday of each month. There also is a very good restaurant, *Uj Etterem,* in the surrounding park. To reach the museum, follow Szabadság forrás utca uphill.

The *Serbian Museum of Ecclesiastical History* (5 Engels utca) contains Eastern Orthodox religious art from the 14th through the 18th century, and you can see one of the finest iconostases (wonderful woodcarvings and old manuscripts) in Hungary in the Greek Orthodox Belgrade Church on Alkotmány utca. There is an interesting medieval Roman Catholic parish church on Templom Hill, near the main square. This church was rebuilt in 1710, but parts of it date from the 12th century. A panoramic view of red rooftops and the Danube River is offered from the square surrounding the church.

Traces of Stone Age men have been found in caves in the vicinity, and the largest Bronze Age cemetery in central Europe was excavated in nearby Budakalász.

En Route from Szentendre – At Pomáz, an unnumbered road in the direction of Esztergom leads to the popular mountain resort of Dobogókő in the Pilis forest. At Leányfalu, you can stop and hike to the 1,500-foot Red Stone Cliff (Vörös-kő Szikla) for a wonderful panoramic view of the plain and the Danube Bend.

The town of Tahitótfalu spreads along both sides of the channel, and the bridge here is a good place to cross over to the island if you want to stop for some swimming, canoeing, or rowing. The river is quite shallow near the village of Kisoroszi, at the northern tip of the island. It has a good beach and and a ferry can take you back across the channel.

You now are leaving the plain and entering the mountain area, and the two channels of the Danube reunite as the river is forced into a more constricted course.

VISEGRÁD: The setting of this small village among the mountains at the center of the Danube Bend, and the relics of its illustrious past as a royal stronghold during the Middle Ages, make Visegrád an immensely popular tourist center.

During the past few decades, a magnificent summer palace that flowered during the reign of King Matthias Corvinus (1458–90) has been excavated and reconstructed on a hillside on the main street (27 Fő utca). A fine Renaissance fountain of red marble in the ceremonial courtyard bears the king's coat of arms.

You also can see the remains of the citadel (Fellegvár) on Castle Hill and the hexagonal Salamon Tower, a typical 13th-century fortified dwelling built by King Bela IV, with walls 9 feet thick to resist prolonged attacks. On a clear day, the view over the Danube to Czechoslovakia is absolutely spectacular. On another hill (Sibrik) are the remains of a Roman camp from about the 4th century.

Some of the discoveries of modern excavations and exhibitions of Visegrád's royal past can be seen at the *King Matthias Museum* (Mátyás Király Múzeum; 41 Fő utca), in an 18th-century baroque mansion that once was a royal hunting lodge.

En Route from Visegrád – Dömös is at the southernmost point of the bend the Danube makes around the southern foothills of the Börzsöny Mountains. From the slopes of the little town's hills, there is an impressive view of the V-like path of the river. This popular resort is frequently used as a starting point for hiking into the Pilis Mountains.

Pilismarót, near the start of the Danube Bend, has a wonderful 2-mile beach and numerous small bays. The picturesque town across the river, Zebegény, is an artists' colony and popular summer resort that can be reached by ferry.

Up stream from Zebegény is the frontier station of Szob, on the Czechoslovak border. You can visit two baroque castles or enjoy the town's pleasant beach before taking the ferry back to the right bank of the Danube and the last few miles to Esztergom.

ESZTERGOM: The philosopher-emperor Marcus Aurelius is said to have written some of the books of his *Reflections* here when this was an important Roman outpost. But Esztergom is best known as the residence of Magyar kings in the 12th and 13th centuries and the seat of the primate of the Hungarian Catholic church.

The largest cathedral in Hungary (390 feet long) was built here, on Castle Hill (Várhegy), between 1822 and 1856. Liszt's *Esztergom Mass* was performed at the cathedral's opening. A Renaissance chapel adjoins the south side of the cathedral, whose treasury includes numerous works of art, including a 13th-century gold cross upon which the Kings of Hungary took their coronation oaths. Behind the cathedral is the *Treasury Museum,* full of religious relics, including objects used by the archbishops during the past 800 years, and a small-scale model of the cathedral complex. In May 1991, the body of Hungary's Cardinal Jozsef Mindszenty was buried here. He died in 1975, in exile because of his fierce nationalism and anti-communism.

The *Castle Museum* next to the cathedral contains fragments of a royal palace that had been destroyed during the Turkish occupation and nearly forgotten until this century, when large-scale excavations were undertaken. The palace was begun in 972 by St. Stephen's father, but its most glorious period came in the late 12th century, during the reign of King Béla III.

The *Christian Museum* (Keresztény Múzeum; 2 Berényi Zsigmond utca) contains one of Hungary's most important fine arts collections. It includes excellent examples of Hungarian paintings, minor medieval Italian works, fine Flemish and French tapestries, and a remarkable 15th-century altar.

Esztergom actually sits on a narrow side channel of the Danube, separated from the main stream by a long island connected to the city by bridges.

BEST EN ROUTE

Hotels in the Danube Bend area are relatively simple places, charging about $25 or $35 a night for a double room with breakfast. There are a number of excellent camping sites along the route, including one on Pap Island, near Szentendre, which accommodates up to 500 campers. For restaurants, expect to pay $10 to $12 for a dinner for two without drinks, wine, or tip. All restaurants below accept major credit cards, unless otherwise noted.

SZENTENDRE

Rab Ráby – The name means "prisoner Ráby" (a 19th-century local literary figure), and the house, which is now an eatery, was built by a Serbian merchant about 150 years ago. Each table is graced with a unique piece of 19th-century memorablilia, such as an 1843 newspaper, an old teapot, a bronze sculpture, or a pair of prison foot chains. The menu includes Hungarian fish and meat dishes. Closed Mondays. Reservations necessary during summer. 1 Péter Pál utca (phone: 26-10819).

DOBOGÓKŐ

Nimród – A modern hotel with 78 rooms set high in the woods of the Pilis Mountains. The restaurant serves game in season. Reservations advised. 2 Eötvös sétány (phone: 26-27644).

VISEGRÁD

Fekete Holló – A good, private restaurant near the Danube. Reservations advised. No credit cards accepted. 12 Rév utca (phone: 26-26166 or in in Budapest, 611-136036).

Pecsenye Grill – In front of the church is this small hole in the wall offering homemade Hungarian-style grilled food. Open daily until 4 PM. Reservations unnecessary. No credit cards accepted. Rév utca (no phone).

Silvanus – Modern and well-designed, this hotel on top of a mountain has a good restaurant, specializing in game, and a bar. Fekete-hegy (phone: 26-136063).

ESZTERGOM

Esztergom – This small hotel overlooking the Danube has its own sports center. Primás Sziget (Primate Island), Nagy-Duna sétány (phone: 33-12883).

Fürdő – An 89-room hotel near the spa with swimming pools, a restaurant and bar, and central heating. 14 Bajcsy-Zsilinszky utca (phone: 33-11688).

Halászcárda – On the island (Esztergom-sziget), this is the classic "seedy" place where Hungarians come to eat delicous fish soup and to listen and dance to the music of Vajda Pál's electric organ. Open all night. No credit cards accepted. Szabad Május sétány (phone: 33-11052).

Korona Kávénóz – A pleasant coffeehouse, it serves a variety of rich Hungarian cakes and pastries, along with coffee, tea, and wine. No credit cards accepted. Széchenyi tér (no phone).

Sötétkapu Söröző – Situated at the foot of the basilica, this recently opened eatery offers traditional Hungarian dishes. No credit cards accepted. Béke tér (phone: 33-13495).

Lake Balaton

The sandy beaches of Lake Balaton, where water temperatures range from 68F (20C) to 79F (26C) in the summer, attract a solid stream of vacationers, both Hungarian and foreign, from May to September. Since World War II, the Hungarian government has developed the area around Balaton — central Europe's largest lake — into a mass recreation center; the 122-mile shoreline is virtually one continuous resort. For visitors, a knowledge of German is extremely useful here.

The southern shore generally is flat, with only an occasional steep hill overlooking the lake, and the water is extremely shallow, making it an ideal beach for families with small children. The north shore is characterized by a chain of long-extinct and now-eroded volcanoes. Gently undulating vineyards cover the basalt hills, producing the grapes for some of the finest wines of Hungary. The area is also known for its effervescent mineral springs.

If you don't like crowds, it is best to visit the lake area in early spring or fall — rates are cheaper then, too. There are good rail connections for most of the larger resort towns, and in summer there are frequent fast trains from Budapest. The following route, beginning and ending in Budapest, explores the various resort areas around the lake.

BUDAPEST: For a detailed report of the city and its hotels and restaurants, see *Budapest,* THE CITIES.

En Route from Budapest – The outskirts of Budapest give way to undulating hills as you travel southwest on Highway 70. The Brunswick Mansion, a must for music lovers, is located in a beautiful old park at Martonvásár, about a half hour from Budapest. It is preserved in memory of Ludwig van Beethoven, who composed some of his important works while visiting here in the early 1800s; the *Moonlight Sonata* purportedly was composed here. Concerts of his music are given here during the summer, and there is a *Beethoven Museum.*

Almost one-third of Lake Velence, which begins some 6 miles (10 km) beyond Martonvásár, is thick with reeds and dotted with swampy, marshy islets. In spring and autumn its grassy knolls are stopping places for scores of thousands of migrating birds, including rare waterfowl. The 6-mile-long and very shallow lake is a rapidly developing holiday resort, with good beaches, yachting facilities, hotels, restaurants, and camping sites, particularly along the southern shore near Gárdony and Agárd. The northern shore attracts anglers, hunters, and other sportsmen. It also is possible to drive directly to Székesfehérvár from Budapest on the M7 motorway.

SZÉKESFEHÉRVÁR: Called Alba Regia by the Romans, during the Middle Ages this town was a thriving royal seat where Hungarian kings were crowned and, later, buried. Hungarian legend says that the country's very first prince, Great Magyar Prince Árpád, set up camp near or in the city and claimed the territory for his tribe. Today, it is an important industrial center in the Meadowland (Mezöföld), where three-fourths of the population is engaged in agriculture. Most of the medieval town was destroyed during the Turkish occupation (1543–1688). However, a number of interesting buildings remain in the inner city. The main square of the inner town is Szabadság tér, site of the 17th-century baroque Town Hall, the former Zichy Palace, with its attractive rococo and baroque interior, and the Garden of Ruins (Romkert), on the site of the excavations of the former cathedral, where 37 coronations were held.

The *King Stephen* (István Király) *Museum,* at the corner of Gagarin tér and Népköztársaság, has interesting exhibitions of local archaeology, history, and folklore.

Siófok, the biggest tourist center on Lake Balaton, is about an hour's drive from Székesfehérvár on the M7 motorway — or somewhat longer if you follow Highway 70 through a number of small towns.

SIÓFOK: The shores of Lake Balaton are virtually one long string of beach resorts, but Siófok is the largest town on the southern shore and is continually expanding to take in neighboring communities. It has the most sophisticated tourist operations, some of the best beaches, and crowded facilities from *Easter* till the season ends in September.

Although the obvious attraction of Siófok is its long sandy beach, there are a few interesting churches and an excellent riding academy nearby. For more information, contact the *IBUSZ* office (Kele utca 123, Siófok; phone: 84-12011 or 84-13412). There also is an open-air theater in Dimitrov Park and many pleasant garden restaurants in which to relax. The *IBUSZ* office here can even arrange for you to take a cooking class with a chef from one of the top resort hotels.

There are ferries to the north shore peninsula of Tihany from Szántód Harbor, near Siófok. Inland from the lake, on Highway 65 at Ságvár, are interesting ruins of a fortified Roman camp, dating from the 3rd century. The Romans also built the Sió Canal that connected Lake Balaton to the Danube near the Yugoslav border.

En Route from Siófok – The shore road winds through numerous resort towns, but at Balatonföldvár a road south leads to Kőröshegy, where many of the original features are retained in a 15th-century, single-naved Gothic church, despite restoration work in the 18th century. The taverns here are good places to sample the regional wine and listen to Gypsy music.

After carefully negotiating several dangerous sudden curves through the town of Balatonszemes, the shore road reaches Fonyód, the site of Stone and Bronze Age settlements and now a busy resort area. At Balatonkeresztúr, Highway 7, which has paralleled the lake since Zamárdi, veers south, and Highway 71 serves the north shore.

KESZTHELY: The largest of the lake towns, Keszthely has been a municipality since the early 15th century. Its charming old streets create a pleasant ambience, and there are a number of interesting sights to divert you from the pleasures of the beaches. The Georgikon (on Georgikon utca) was founded in 1797 and was the first agricultural college established on the European continent. The first inhabitants of the area were neolithic peoples, followed by Celts and Romans, who built a bridge across the lake near here. In 1742, Count György Festetics, who was of Serbian origin, bought 250,000 acres around Lake Balaton and developed the land into one of Europe's largest stud farms, supplying various royal houses on the Continent, as well as the Republican Cavalry of the US. Festetics built himself a palace, the third-largest in Hungary, which is as fine as any built in Europe. Its wonderful Helikon Library has some 90,000 books representing most European languages. A visit to the palace (at 1 Szabadság utca) is a must to see the valuable antiquities, art (paintings and sculpture), a wonderful park, and the impressive view from the terraces (closed Mondays.) The *Balaton Museum* (2 Múzeum utca) has interesting historical and ethnographical exhibitions.

Hévíz, the most famous spa in Hungary, with its own freshwater lake (Lake Hévíz, Europe's largest warmwater lake — 82–93F) and indoor and outdoor thermal baths, is a few miles west of here. The spa offers medical and cosmetic advice.

En Route from Keszthely – The shore road passes through the Badacsony, a district of basalt terraces where lava from long-extinct volcanoes has created bizarre rock formations. The area also is known for its fruit growing and for the excellence of its vineyards. The ruins of Szigliget Castle, dating from the 13th century, stand on a hill just west of the town of Badacsony.

Beyond Balatonszepezd, a favorite retreat of artists and writers, a mile-long road leads up a hillside to Zánka, where there is a fisherman's lodge in the woods and a 13th-century church that was remodeled in the baroque style in 1786. Medieval pageants are sometimes held in summer in the 15th-century castle in Nagyvázsony, a town about 10 miles (16 km) farther north.

TIHANY: The small peninsula of Tihany, a series of hills covered with poplar and acacia trees and the scent of lavender, is one of the loveliest spots on Lake Balaton. Its long history as a stronghold can be read in the remains of a 3,000-year-old earthenwork fortification and in Celtic and Roman ruins. A beautiful yellow abbey church with twin spires stands on a hill overlooking the peninsula. Several peasant houses that once belonged to the lake fishermen now make up the *Open-Air Museum of Ethnography* (11 Pisky sétány). Closed Mondays and in off-season. Exhibits of furniture, costumes, and art create a rich testimony to the local history of Lake Balaton.

There is excellent fishing in Lake Belső, high on a hill above Balaton — in effect, a lake within a lake; and the villagers' unusual thatch-roofed houses of dark gray volcanic tufa add charm to the landscape. Government institutes have been set up on Tihany to study its wealth of geological and botanical rarities. A family holiday village occupies the tip of the peninsula (see *Best en Route*). The *Tihany Tourist Center* (20 Kossuth utca; phone: 86-48519) rents sailboats, among other services.

BALATONFÜRED: The oldest and one of the most renowned health resorts in the area, Balatonfüred is the last large town on Lake Balaton. There are several large and recently built hotels here, an attractive poplar-lined promenade along the lake, and an inviting central park. There is also a neo-classical Round (Kerek) Church on Blaha Lujza utca, built in 1846. Yachting races frequently are held here, and the harbor is the busiest on the lake.

In the main square, Gyógy tér, there is a colonnaded pavilion built over the bubbling waters of a volcanic spring. In all, the town has 11 medicinal springs that for hundreds of years have been attracting those seeking cures (particularly for heart and nerve disorders). Hills around the city are covered with vineyards that produce very drinkable wines.

En Route from Balatonfüred – The shore road can be followed through a dozen or so small communities around the lake back to a connection with the M7 motorway or Highway 70 to return to Budapest. Another alternative is to take Highway 73 north from Balatonfüred into the Bakony hills to Veszprém before heading back to Budapest.

VESZPRÉM: Built on five hills, this picturesque town of cobblestone streets, old gateways, and arches is Bakony's cultural and economic center. It is an old settlement rich in historical monuments. The *Castle* (Vár) *Museum,* in the Heroes' Gate (Hősök kapuja) near Vörös Hadsereg Square, contains old weapons, armor, and historical documents. The late 18th-century baroque Episcopal Palace (12 Tolbuhin utca) is next to the early Gothic Gizella Chapel, built in the 13th century.

The *Bakony Museum,* in Lenin Park on Kálvária Hill, has exhibitions that detail the Bakony region's history, customs, and crafts.

BEST EN ROUTE

Lake Balaton is Hungary's most popular resort, so hotel reservations should be made well in advance if you plan to visit during the summer. A double room will cost between $20 and $45 per night, depending on the month and resort chosen. All the hotels listed are open from May to September unless otherwise noted. It also is possible to rent cottages or apartments on the lake, and *IBUSZ* (phone: 84-12011, 84-13412, or 84-

13955) can arrange for the rental of sailboats that can sleep four at $200 to $400 per week. Restaurants range in price from $25 and up for a dinner for two in the expensive range; around $15 in the moderate; and $10 and under, inexpensive. Prices do not include drink, wine, or tip. All restaurants below accept major credit cards, unless otherwise indicated. Reservations are advised at all restaurants.

The wines of the Balaton region, particularly the spicy white ones, are justly famous. Among the best are the badacsony blue stalk (*Badacsonyi kéknyelü*), gray friar (*Badacsonyi szürkebarát*), and riesling (*Badacsonyi rizling*). The food specialty is the perch-pike-type fish *fogas*.

SIÓFOK

Balaton – On the lake with a private beach. All rooms have balconies, and the hotel has a nightclub and an espresso bar. 9 Petőfi sétány (phone: 84-10655). Moderate.

Európa – Lakeshore setting and private beach, pool, sauna, a restaurant and an espresso bar are among this hotel's amenities. 17 Petőfi sétány (phone: 84-13411). Moderate.

Fogas – Excellent food served in a garden setting. 184 Fő utca (phone: 11405). Moderate.

Hungária – Balconied rooms, a private beach, a restaurant, and a bar are offered here. 13 Petőfi sétány (phone: 84-10677). Moderate.

Ménes Csárda – Very good — and very spicy — local specialties are served in this restaurant, actually a restored old stable decorated with antique folk art. In Szántódpuszta, about 6 miles (10 km) west of Siófok on the main highway to Balatonföldvár (phone: 84-31352). Moderate.

Napfény – A small, family-type hotel near the beach, with balconied rooms. 2 Petőfi sétány (phone: 84-11408; fax: 84-10612). Inexpensive.

KESZTHELY

Helikon – Facing the beach, with its own "island," connected to the hotel by a bridge. There are spa facilities, a restaurant and bar, tennis courts, and a yacht marina. The service is very friendly. 5 Balatonpart (phone: 82-18944 or 84-11330; fax: 84-18403). Expensive.

Fishermen's Inn (Halász Csárda) – Fish specialties. South of Keszthely on the lakeshore (phone: 82-12751). Moderate.

Helikon Tavern – Good food and wine and Gypsy music. About 5 miles (8 km) east of town. Make reservations through the *Helikon* hotel (see above). Moderate.

Hévíz Aqua Thermal Hotel – The place to come for a variety of treatments. A large modern hotel spa with 213 rooms set in a calm, wooded area. 13-15 Kossuth Lajos U. Hévíz (phone: 82-18947; fax: 82-18970; telex: 82-35247). Moderate.

Hullám – This flower-bedecked small hotel, with a pool and wide-ranging sports activities, consciously tries to evoke the leisurely atmosphere of bygone days (phone: 82-19850). Moderate.

Park – The Horuath family converted their 1949 house into one of the first private restaurants to open in the Balaton area. Today, it's a very pleasant eatery serving a rich variety of Hungarian dishes. During the summer the garden is a favorite of natives and tourists alike. Reservations necessary during summer. Vörösmarty (phone: 82-11654). Moderate.

TIHANY

Club Tihany – Along with 161 Scandinavian-style bungalows, this 330-room hotel is part of Hungary's first vacation village, which offers families a private beach, pool, boutiques, and all kinds of sports activities. 3 Rév utca (phone: 86-48088 or 86-44170). Expensive.

Fogas Csárda – Excellent fish dishes served on a terrace or in one of four dining rooms — with Gypsy music. Off Hwy. 71 (no phone). Expensive to moderate.

Sport – Enjoy excellent food as well as a panoramic lake view. Fürdőtelep (phone: 86-44016). Expensive to moderate.

BALATONFÜRED

Annabella – A modern hotel with picturesque surroundings on the lakeshore; private beach, restaurant and terrace, nightclub, and pool. Open April 15 to October. 25 Beloiannisz utca (phone: 86-42222). Expensive.

Marina – On the lake with a private beach, this hotel has a pool, a health club, a nightclub, and a restaurant with Gypsy music. Open May to October. 26 Széchenyi utca (phone: 86-43644). Expensive.

Baricska Csárda – The perfect spot to sample *halászlé,* an all-fish chowder with paprika, or baked *fogas,* the local fish specialty. No credit cards accepted. On the lakefront (phone: 86-43105). Moderate to inexpensive.

The Great Hungarian Plain

The Great Hungarian Plain (Nagy Alföld), east of the Danube, is the heart of Hungary and one of Europe's richest larders. During the past century, the thousands of acres of the drifting sand and needle grass that characterized this seemingly endless flat expanse, called the *puszta,* have been transformed into lush orchards and vineyards, and modern machinery now cultivates the corn and wheat fields.

But the government has taken steps to preserve the heritage of the rural Hungarian peasant, long romanticized by poets and painters: the isolated whitewashed crofts, the special *puszta* gray cattle and herds of horses, the traditional arts and crafts. They still can be seen in places such as the National Park of Hortobágy, although like the American prairie the reality of that heritage has vanished completely.

This circular route from Budapest takes you to some of the most important towns of the area of the Great Hungarian Plain, sometimes referred to as Little Cumania, and to some of its art centers. Most of the towns are on main railway lines and can be visited on a train journey through the region. There also are bus connections.

BUDAPEST: For a detailed report on the city and its hotels and restaurants, see *Budapest,* THE CITIES.

En Route from Budapest – About an hour's drive southeast on the E60 motorway, Highway 40 heads to Cegléd, an old peasant community that was the birthplace of István Tömorkény, one of the great chroniclers of peasant life. The *Lajos Kossuth Museum* (on Rákóczi utca and Marx K. utca) contains the patriot's death mask. Farther south is Nagykőrös, the center of a rich market-gardening region famous for its Kőrös Morello cherries and other fruit. A splendid morning market is held here. Or, if you are driving directly to Kecskemét on the E75, consider stopping off at Lajosmizse, 13 miles (21 km) before Kecskemét, to visit the *Farmhouse Museum,* or watch the horse shows at the *István Széchenyi Riding Club,* a castle-hotel (see *Best en Route*).

KECSKEMÉT: This is the hometown of Zoltán Kodály, the famous composer of modern music who also collected and wrote about Hungarian folk music. And this sprawling town of 100,000 people itself seems to blend two worlds.

Since World War II, Kecskemét has become an important food-processing center, and modern housing estates have replaced many single-story dwellings. But the old peasant architecture can be seen along Bánk Bán and János Hoffman Streets. Two examples of Hungarian Art Nouveau that should not be overlooked are the Town Hall on Kossuth Lajos tér and the Ornamented Palace (Cifrapalota) on Szabadság tér. On the Kossuth Lajos tér there are three churches: the 15th-century Franciscan church, the 17th-century Protestant church, and the late 18th-century Catholic church. A bit southwest of Kossuth Square, behind the 16-story county council building, is a unique double-gated peasant house with a fine verandah. Beautiful examples of shepherds' cloaks and embroidered clothing of the region are on display at the *József Katona Museum* (1 Bethlen Krt.). The *Szórakaténusz Toy Workshop and Museum,* (11 Gáspár utca) is a must for children. At the same address is the *Museum of Native Artists,* which features the works of Hungarian naïf artists from 1910.

An artists colony, where many of Hungary's best painters and sculptors of the 20th century have worked, is in a large park on Mártírok utca, southeast of the center.

The Kecskemét area is famous for its apricots and apricot brandy, called *barack,* and a grape harvest (Kecskeméti Szüret) is held each September. In odd-numbered years there is a *Kecskemét Folk Music Meeting* of singers and musicians and the International Kodály Seminar for music teachers; an International Creative Camp of Musicians takes place every July. A more recent event is the March music festival held in conjunction with the *Budapest Spring Festival.*

The Kecskemét riding school, just outside the city on Highway 44, has excellent horses selected from the famous stud farms of the *puszta.*

En Route from Kecskemét – Heading south on the E5 motorway you reach Kiskunfélegyháza, an important cultural center of Kiskunság (Little Cumania). The *Kiskun Museum* has a good archaeological collection and an interesting penology display.

A road to the west of town will take you to the Kiskunság National Park and its major section, the Bugacpuszta. The gray cattle and branch-horned *racka* sheep of the region graze here in pastures surrounded by trees, marshes, and sand dunes. The *Shepherd Museum,* a glass-walled, circular building resembling a Mongolian yurt, has displays that detail the old nomadic way of life and animal breeding in the *puszta.* Nearby, a refurbished old inn called *Tanya-Fogado,* provides an ideal setting for sampling Hungarian specialties and regional wines (phone: 76-62455).

Another detour off the E5 motorway, this one to the east just before you reach Szeged, leads to Lake Fehér (Fehér-tó), the home of red heron, ducks, and other fish-eating birds. (Permission to visit the bird sanctuary must be obtained in advance; travel agents usually can make these arrangements.)

One of the typical sights of the Great Hungarian Plain is storks nesting in the chimneys of farmhouses along the road.

SZEGED: The economic and cultural center of the southern region of the Great Hungarian Plain straddles the Tisza River near the Yugoslav border. Every May the international *Hungaropan Cup,* featuring kayak-canoe races, is held on the Tisza River. The present town was laid out after a devastating flood in the last century, but Szeged has a long, rich history.

The town was occupied by the Ottoman Turks for 144 years, until the end of the 17th century, and it was plundered and burned in 1704 in retaliation for its support of the freedom struggle against the ruling House of Hapsburg of Austria. During the 1848–49 war of independence from the Hapsburgs, Szeged was, for a short time, the capital of the country. During the great Tisza flood of 1879, the town was almost completely swept away.

The central town square, Széchenyi tér, has a pleasant promenade of old plane trees and is lined by a number of various public buildings. A few blocks south is the impressive Dóm tér, a square surrounded by arcaded buildings of dark red brick and dominated by the twin-spired 19th-century Votive Church at its center. The neo-Romanesque church has the second-largest organ in Europe (the largest is in Milan's cathedral). The church was built by survivors of the 1879 flood. The medieval tower of St. Demetrius is at its side. Part of the huge square is the site of the *Szeged Open-Air Theater,* where the *Szeged Festival* (Szegedi Szabadtéri Játékok) of opera, drama, and ballet is held every year in July and August. Hungary's finest Serbian Orthodox church, known for its outstanding iconostasis, is on the north side of the square.

Szeged is famous for its salami products, beautifully embroidered slippers, and a delicious fish soup, *szegedi halászlé.* Visit the *Salami Factory Museum,* open Tuesdays and Thursdays (10 Felsö-Tiszapart; phone: 62-26033). In Tápé, an outer district of the town noted for the artistic mats woven by its women, villagers have retained their picturesque folkways and dress. A collection of folk dress and everyday articles can be seen at 4 Vártó utca. A park 3 miles (5 km) outside Szeged, inhabited by monkeys and crocodiles as well as by animals native to Hungary, was designed with young visitors in mind.

Traditional as well as newer styles of pottery are made in workshops at Hódmezővásárhely, a small town 16 miles (26 km) northeast of Szeged on Highway 47. Modern and traditional ceramics are displayed and sold at *Lajos Gulácsy Gallery* (17 Kárász utca). The *János Tornyai Museum* (16-18 Szanto Kovacs utca) has interesting archaeological and ethnographical collections.

En Route from Szeged – About halfway to Baja on Highway 55 you can turn north on Highway 53 to reach Kiskunhalas, home of the famous Halas lace, *halasi csipke.* You can see the lace makers at work at the *Cottage Industry Cooperative,* and the *Lace House* (Csipkeház) has a large exhibition of the fine craft that has won the town a worldwide reputation.

BAJA: This picturesque town on the banks of the Danube and Sugovica rivers has numerous islands with sandy lidos and fine parks, lovely old churches, and an artists colony in a former nobleman's mansion at 1 Arany János utca. It also has one of the few bridges over the Danube south of Budapest. The folklore and folk art collections of the *István Türr Museum* (on Béke tér) are typical of the region.

KALOCSA: This town, 21 miles (34 km) north of Baja on Highway 51, is one of the most important centers of folk art in Hungary. The women of the town are famous for the primitive, ornamental painting with which they decorate the walls of their homes and for the designs they paint on furniture and door panels. The finest examples of their work can be seen at the Népművészetiház (1-3 Tompa Mihály utca), in the same building as the *Folk Art Cooperative,* where some of these "painting women" work with outsiders interested in learning this folk art. The *Károly Viski Museum* (25 Szt. István utca) exhibits folk art of the Kalocsa Sárköz region.

In quaint little villages nearby, whitewashed houses often are strung with garlands of the red peppers that are grown in the area and used to make fine Hungarian paprika. The *Paprika Museum* (on Marx tér) is at Kalocsa's open-air vegetable market.

Northeast of Kalocsa is Kiskőrös, home of the 19th-century revolutionary poet Sándor Petőfi.

The highway back to Budapest parallels the Danube, passing through Dunapataj, a village near pleasant Szelidi Lake, and through two towns where the poet Petőfi lived and worked — Dunavecse and Szalkszentmárton.

BEST EN ROUTE

First class hotel accommodations are limited, but prices are relatively low. At the places mentioned, a double room with bath and breakfast will cost about $26 to $30 a night. Meals also are quite inexpensive in the towns of the Great Hungarian Plain. Dinner for two, with a local wine, will cost between $10 and $12 at most good restaurants. All restaurants below accept major credit cards, unless otherwise indicated. Reservations are advised at all restaurants.

KECSKEMÉT

Aranyhomok – This 5-story modern hotel on one of Kecskemét's central squares is the best in the area. It has a large restaurant that features excellent goose liver, a coffee shop, and a bar. The hotel also organizes horseback riding. 3 Széchenyi tér (phone: 76-20011). Moderate.

Gerébi Country House and Motel – Situated in a park with a pool, tennis courts, and a riding club, this 18th-century mansion has been converted into a hotel with 11 double rooms and 2 suites; there is also a motel with 39 rooms. In Lajosmizse, on Highway 5, 13 miles (21 km) north of Kecskemét. 224 Alsólajos (phone: 76-56045). Moderate.

Gúnár – A 34-room hotel, converted from an old inn. 7 Batthyányu (phone: 76-27077). Moderate.

Szélmalom Csárda – This restaurant is in a replica of the traditional whitewashed windmills of the Great Hungarian Plain. Just outside town on the E5 motorway, in the direction of Szeged. No credit cards accepted. 167 Városföld (phone: 76-22166). Moderate.

SZEGED

Alabárdos – Set in a cellar, this eatery provides a romantic atmosphere, including Gypsy music, with your food. No credit cards accepted. 13 Oskola utca (phone: 62-12914). Moderate.

Hungária – Near a shady park on the bank of the Tisza River, next to the *Szeged National Theater*. All the hotel's rooms have private baths. 2 Komócsin Zoltán tér (phone: 62-21211). Moderate.

International 1st Class Camping Site and Motel – The name says it all. No credit cards accepted. 2 Dorozsmai utca (phone: 62-61255). Inexpensive.

Virág Café – Pastries and ice cream are served in an elegant, old-fashioned setting. Klauzál tér (phone: 62-11459).

Iceland

An extended trip to Iceland is a strange blend of culture shock and geological field trip. Though this country might be the world's largest small town (there are only 253,480 people on the whole island, and almost half of them live in Reykjavik), the natives are among the most sophisticated of Europeans, aware of the latest in both fashion and culture. Though Iceland has the oldest republic in the world (founded by Norse wanderers in AD 870), the country is a geological infant, still growing steadily from fissures, lava flows, earthquakes, and volcanoes.

In the North Atlantic between the Denmark Strait to the west and the Norwegian Sea to the east, Iceland measures 190 miles from north to south and 300 miles from east to west. Because it's partially ringed by the warm currents of the Gulf Stream, the island is habitable — barely. Its weather is abruptly changeable, and its terrain is unlike any other country on Earth. More than 10% glacier and 10% lava, it's a land of hot and cold. The word "geyser" is Icelandic, and geothermal water is everywhere. Some of this naturally hot water has been harnessed, and one hot spring, Deildartunguhver, has been so pressurized and heated by the earth's interior turbulence that boiling water flows through it at 40 gallons per second. Amazingly, this boiling water flows completely naturally, close to the Arctic Circle, in the Land of the Midnight Sun. There are volcanic eruptions on an average of one every 5 or 6 years, but the Icelanders have started to adapt to even this. (In 1973, when a volcano erupted on the inhabited offshore island of Heimaey, the entire population was evacuated in a matter of hours. Though the eruption lasted from January to May, Icelandic scientists were able to cool and reroute the lava flows with ocean water so that most of the town was saved and the harbor left open.)

The countryside is hauntingly beautiful, with an almost treeless landscape of stark lava fields, awesome glaciers, lakes, mountains, and a fjord-indented coastline. There are rivers in Iceland, but they aren't navigable because of their breakneck currents caused by a combination of rainfall and melting glaciers that also leave the riverbeds strewn with debris. The price of this stark, natural beauty is the need to import almost all raw materials and staples from wood to fruit to fuel. Iceland raises sheep and cattle (also reindeer have been imported and bred); lamb is the staple in the Icelanders' diet. The life here is hard, but the people of Iceland have one of the longest life expectancies in the world.

Outside Reykjavik, the capital, there's not too much in the way of town life. A ring road around the island was completed in 1974, but if you want to travel north, it's best to fly to Akureyri, the northern city of 14,000 staunch citizens who live on Arctic banks and make wry New Englanders seem like outgoing Texans.

Because of its need to import almost everything, Iceland is generally expensive, but a trip here can be a special experience, one in which you can't help both marveling at the people and becoming keenly aware of the power and life of the earth itself.

REYKJAVIK: Many people stop over here on transatlantic flights, but few have the foresight to stay and explore Iceland's capital and commercial and maritime hub. A good place to start an exploration is the Austurvöllur, the quiet central square at the intersection of Kirkjustraeti and Posthusstraeti. This was the reputed home site of Iceland's first settler, a Norwegian Viking named Ingólfur Arnarson, who arrived in 874. The republic's early history was not all rosy — Iceland was long dominated by both the Norwegians and the Danes. In the 19th century, however, there was a successful independence movement led by Jón Sigurdsson, Iceland's national hero, whose statue stands here in the grassy quadrangle. The city surrounds this square with neat, multi-storied buildings topped with red, white, and green roofs, all scrupulously crisp and clean. On the edges of the square are the imposing Parliament House and the stone Cathedral of Reykjavik. Also near the square is the Tjörn, the town pond and summer home for many wheeling Arctic terns.

It's an easy city to walk around in, and though the signs are generally incomprehensible, most of the people speak English. The Iceland Tourist Board is located here (3 Laugavegur; phone: 27488) and is generally very helpful. The *Thjodminjasafnid* is the national cultural museum (closed Mondays; no admission charge; 7 Frikirkjuvequr, at the corner of Sudurgata and Hringbraut; phone: 1-28888). At the same location is the *National Museum of Art* (closed Mondays; no admission charge; phone: 1-621000). Even before the Norse, Irish monks came to Iceland as early as the 8th century. After the establishment of the Althing (the governing body) in 930, art flourished and Icelandic literature — the most sophisticated writings of the Middle Ages — is still preserved in illuminated manuscripts. You'll find a sampling of the precious "saga" manuscripts at the *Arnagardur* (Manuscript Institute of Iceland), an unassuming modern building (closed Sundays; no admission charge; in the *Arnastofnun,* on Sudurgata; phone: 1-25540). In nearby Laugardalur you can take a swim and sauna in the city's open-air pool, naturally heated year-round by hot springs.

A circle route from Reykjavik east can, in 1 day, encompass the country's most famous natural and historic attractions: the Geysir hot spring area, the Gullfoss waterfall, and Thingvellir, the site of the ancient parliament. There aren't that many roads, but it's still a good idea to get a clear map and trace your route before you start east from the capital through Hellisheidi to Hveragerdi.

HVERAGERDI: This town is important for its many greenhouses, which Iceland depends on year-round for such warm-weather crops as tomatoes, bananas, and grapes. The greenhouses are heated entirely from the active hot springs of the area. Continue past the towns of Selfoss, Hraungerdi, and Húsatoftir, where you turn north to Flúdir. You can stop at the Skalholt Cathedral here, where there are outdoor concerts on summer Sunday afternoons.

THE GREAT GEYSIR AND THE GULLFOSS: Continue north to two of the most famous natural sights in Iceland. The world "geyser" originated with the Icelandic Great Geysir, a sprouting hot spring that gives its name to similar springs all over the world. The original only rarely performs now, but nearby is another old regular known as Strokkur.

Another 16 miles (26 km) east is the Gullfoss, the Golden Waterfall. Considered to be one of the world's most beautiful, this fall plunges down a series of cascades into a deep gorge of the Hvítá River. Now return west across the Brúará River, past Middalur, to the Laugarvatn Lake area. This is a deep glacial lake and a popular resort area, with hotels, campsites, an indoor swimming pool, and a steambath built directly over the hot springs.

THINGVELLIR: From Laugarvatn, continue west across Lyngdalsheidi to Thingvellir. This Plain of National Assembly, or Althing, was named for the country's first open-air legislative assembly, which was established here in AD 930. The Icelandic Parliament had its roots in these annual 2-week summer confabs, which were attended by tribal chieftains from throughout the country. Thingvellir is starkly and beautifully situated on an immense lava plain intersected by rock fissures and surrounded by a craggy distant horizon. To the northeast is an extinct shield volcano, Skjaldbreidur, at the northern end of Lake Thingvallavatn. Since there are few visible remains of the early meetings, it's best to visit Thingvellir with a knowledgeable guide, but even on your own you can savor the peacefulness here. You can camp at one of the sites in the surrounding national park.

From here travel south to Ulfljótsvatn Lake and the Ljosafoss waterfall via the Thrastalundur woods. The drive goes alongside the Sogid River, popular with the salmon-fishing set, and heads south past Ingólfsfjall Mountain. The secondary road rejoins the main route (just west of Selfoss), which goes back to Reykjavik.

BEST EN ROUTE

Everything in Iceland is expensive — there's no getting around it. A cup of coffee can cost as much as $1.50 (refills usually are included), a short cab ride, $4 or $5. The best food and lodgings are in Reykjavik. The ptarmigan (called *rjupa* here) is very good; it's served in a delicious sauce called *rjupusosa*. Expect to pay about $130 for a room for two at hotels and around $50 for dinner for two at restaurants in Reykjavik. There is no tipping in Iceland. For further information on restaurants, nightlife, galleries, and museums, pick up a copy of *What's On in Reykjavik* at your hotel.

REYKJAVIK

Fógetinn – Reykjavik's oldest house is a popular restaurant serving traditional Icelandic dishes, including lamb, game, and seafood. The atmosphere is warm and rustic, and there is live music nightly. 10 Adalstraeti (phone: 91-16323). Expensive.

Holiday Inn – A new modern link in the ubiquitous chain with 100 rooms and a restaurant. Rates include breakfast. 38 Sigtún (phone: 1-689000). Expensive.

Holt – Tucked away on a quiet residential street, this hotel has what many consider the city's best restaurant. 37 Bergstadastraeti (phone: 2-5700). Expensive.

Loftleidir – Right at the Reykjavik Airport, it has 221 rooms, a restaurant, and pool. Rates include breakfast (phone: 1-22322). Expensive.

Naust – A seafood restaurant in a former fish warehouse — what could be more atmospheric? It has a small dance floor and very good food and is very popular with the residents. 6-8 Vesturgata (phone: 1-7759). Expensive.

Odinsvé – A friendly hostelry in the heart of the city, it has 28 rooms and a good restaurant. 1 Pórsgata (phone: 1-25224 or 1-25640). Expensive.

Saga – Not far from shops and other sights in the city center, this modern hostelry offers 218 well-appointed rooms, a sauna, Jacuzzi, solarium, and exercise equipment. There also are several bars and restaurants, including the top-floor *Grill*, which serves traditional Iceland dishes, as well as international fare. Hagatorg (phone: 1-623980). Expensive.

Ireland

Whether you come for the salmon and trout that jump onto your line; to share a "jar" at a pub while you listen to traditional music played on pipe and fiddle and old tin whistle; to clamber over craggy mountains or ponder prehistoric monuments; to capture the varied greens of the landscape on canvas or film; to rent a cottage and write a novel; or to visit relatives or make new friends, your welcome in Ireland will be warm.

The Republic of Ireland, across the narrow Irish Sea from England, has few natural resources, but it has two that make it a "little bit of heaven" for travelers: enchanting beauty and charming, friendly people. Since it must import more than it can export, Ireland depends heavily on income from tourism.

It may be the lyricism that first attracts people to this island on the western fringes of Europe — all those songs about the "lilt of Irish laughter" and the way place names roll off the tongue: the Gap of Dunloe, the River Liffey, Galway Bay, Kilkenny and Kildare. The Irish seem born with a love of language, and the poet-philosopher has always been the real king of Ireland, even in ancient times when poets or seers called *fili* preserved Celtic laws and history orally. This is the land that produced the towering artistry of William Butler Yeats, James Joyce, and Samuel Beckett (never mind that the latter two had to leave the country to find full expression). And though Beckett wrote in French, there is no doubt he was Irish. Today, Ireland gives special tax breaks to artists and writers.

Although English is the everyday language of most people in the Republic, Irish, a form of Gaelic, is actually the national language. Irish was, in fact, the vernacular outside the cities and larger towns until the early nineteenth century. But with the establishment of a national system of schools, English spread to a point where today there are only pockets of Irish-speaking people. You are more likely to see the Irish language than hear it; public signs frequently are posted in both English and Irish. In Irish-speaking districts near the west coast, signposts are sometimes in Irish only, but most maps published in Ireland provide place names in Irish and English.

Many of the people who believe that the Irish language is an essential part of Irish nationality also work to preserve national games and dances and other riches of Ireland's Celtic past. The best way to hear traditional music and song and to see Irish dancing is to attend one of the frequent sessions held by the more than 200 branches of Comhaltas Ceoltoiri Eireann, the central organization for the promotion of these arts (inquire at any tourist information office). An important 3-day festival of traditional music and song, the *All-Ireland Fleadh,* is held on the last weekend of August each year in a different town.

The Celts came to this island from central Europe sometime after 600 BC, but it is believed that there were inhabitants here as early as 6000 BC. Ireland has the richest concentration of prehistoric monuments in Western Europe, including numerous megaliths known as dolmens. Most often they are three huge boulders standing upright to support a heavy capstone, and they usually mark an ancient burial site.

The prehistory that has been preserved in Ireland's epic tales, legends, and poetry is a marvelous mixture of myth and fact. There are story cycles dealing with kings — some of them belonging to history, others to legend — like the Fenian cycle, which tells of the deeds of the giant Finn MacCool and his band of warriors, the Fianna. There are stories of the Little People, leprechauns and the like, who, according to folklore, were related to the Tuatha De Danann, an early Irish race with magical powers driven underground by Celtic Milesians, the predecessors of the current Irish, said to come from Spain. It is, perhaps, a measure of how integral fairies and spirits are to the Irish culture to note that this country's greatest poet, William Butler Yeats, once devoted himself to a study of Irish folklore and an extensive classification of the Little People.

When St. Patrick brought Christianity to Ireland in the 5th century, he found an island country of small, separate kingdoms united in language and culture. The development of the church in Ireland along monastic rather than ecclesiastic lines reflects to some extent the development of the country itself. In its early days there were no towns or villages, just simple dwellings with cattle enclosures scattered over the countryside.

Norsemen raided the island repeatedly from the 9th century until their defeat in 1014 at Clontarf, near Dublin, by the High King Brian Boru. The defeat did not promote Irish unity, however, because Brian died soon after, and when his sons initiated wars over the division of his lands, it ultimately gave the Normans, newly arrived in England, an opportunity to land troops in Ireland.

During the next 700 years, the Norman and then Tudor conquests spread over the whole of Ireland. Irish landlords were systematically supplanted by English and Scottish settlers, many of whom were Protestant. Ulster became the stronghold of these settlers, and that northeastern province grew different in character from the rest of the island. With the Irish parliament in the hands of the British-Protestant minority, stiff penal laws were enacted to deprive Catholics and dissenters of civil and religious rights.

Inspired by the American and French Revolutions, followers of Wolfe Tone and other leaders challenged the British in 1798, but the uprising was crushed, and in 1801, Ireland became part of the United Kingdom. The great potato famine (1845–48) added to the miseries of the Irish people. During a 5-year period, the population was reduced from 8 million to 4 million, through starvation, disease, and emigration, which many saw as the only hope for a decent life. Such extreme conditions led to the formation of the Irish Republican Brotherhood in 1858 and a renewed sense of Irish nationalism.

In 1914, Parliament passed a Home Rule bill for Ireland (that Protestants in the north opposed), but suspended its implementation on the outbreak of the First World War. Two years later, impatient and distrustful, Patrick Pearse and James Connolly led the Easter Uprising, proclaiming Ireland a

Republic. Although the rebels only held out a week, the British aroused the feelings of the whole country by executing 15 of the leaders. At the next general election, 73 of 105 seats in the Irish parliament were won by a militant independence party called Sinn Fein. These Sinn Fein members met in Dublin on January 21, 1919, to issue a declaration confirming the Republic proclaimed in 1916 and to constitute themselves as the National Parliament (Dail).

The attempt by the British to suppress the parliament and the military wing of republicanism, the Irish Republican Army (IRA), led to a guerrilla war for independence, euphemistically referred to as "the Troubles." Britain granted dominion status to the Irish Free State, but Northern Ireland had the option to get out, and the country was partitioned. In 1937, a new constitution declaring Ireland to be a sovereign, independent, democratic state was approved by plebiscite.

The ultimate reunification of Northern Ireland with the Republic is still a major goal of many Irish Catholics. The Irish parliament has outlawed the IRA, but that organization has continued its campaign of violence in England and Northern Ireland, with financial aid from US citizens, since hostilities broke out over demands for just treatment of Catholics in Northern Ireland. Since 1969, thousands of people have been killed and injured in the fighting in Northern Ireland. But although there has been some minor terrorist activity in the Republic, there is little likelihood a visitor will encounter any unpleasantness. Political attitudes in Ireland seem to have grown somewhat more liberal in recent years, as was illustrated in the December 1990 election of Mary Robinson as Ireland's first woman president. Though the presdent functions mainly as a ceremonial head, Ms. Robinson hopes to play a role in challenging traditional Irish beliefs and laws.

The Republic of Ireland is only a bit larger than the state of West Virginia. At its widest east-west point it is 171 miles across, and at its greatest north-south length it stretches 302 miles. The warm, damp air from the Gulf Stream along its west coast in the Atlantic Ocean combine to keep the weather mild. Temperatures only rarely drop to freezing during the winter, and summer temperatures usually range from 57F to 61F, but can reach 70F to 75F at times. Except for a strip along the east coast, the country receives some rain at least 200 days a year. This climate is responsible for Ireland's remarkable verdant beauty.

Ireland's natural beauty should be explored leisurely. Do it by car if you must, but consider the alternatives. Go on foot along the stone-walled lanes wherever they may lead or take a small map and compass and wander through the hills. There are over 100 centers throughout the country that rent bicycles and provide maps and time estimates for excursions.

The range of accommodations in Ireland is one of the most varied in Europe. There are hotels in castles, in fine old Georgian mansions, in farmhouses, and in old inns. You also can stay in private homes that offer bed and breakfast or rent your own Irish cottage; information is available from the Irish Tourist Board or *Rent an Irish Cottage, Ltd.* at Ballycasey House, Shannon, County Clare, Ireland (phone: 61-61988).

The routes we have outlined are designed to afford maximum exposure to the wonders of Ireland. The initial route takes you along the coast from Dublin to Cork through the Wicklow Mountains, the pretty villages and rich farmland of County Wexford and County Waterford, to Blarney Castle and Ireland's second-largest city. The second route, from Cork to Killarney, traverses an area of lakes and mountains long celebrated for its beauty by poet and painter alike. It is a fisherman's paradise and a golfer's heaven as well, so it should come as no surprise that it is the area of Ireland most popular with tourists in the summer.

From Killarney to Galway, our third route passes through the rich agricultural area of the Midwest Counties, along the lovely River Shannon and on to the starkly beautiful Cliffs of Moher and the gray rock of the Burren country and then to Galway Bay. From Galway, our fourth route takes in the rugged Aran Islands, then heads north through the austere Connemara Mountains to Sligo and Yeats country. The final route, from Sligo to Donegal, travels through a rugged area dominated by limestone hills — the Ireland of myth and legend.

Southeast Ireland: Dublin to Cork

A scenic 160-mile coastal route can take you from Dublin to Cork in 4½ leisurely hours. But to savor the changing moods and character of the Irish scene you must meander. The route you should consider to get a feel for southeast Ireland wanders over more than 250 miles in seven counties; it snakes south from Dublin through Wicklow, Wexford, and Waterford, angles north to take in the countryside of Kilkenny, arcs west into legendary Tipperary, and veers south again to Cork and the coast. Ideally, this tour should be spread over 3 days.

It will seem incredible, but a mere half-hour's drive from the city center of Dublin brings you to the splendid isolation of the Wicklow Mountains. Here, great valleys with melodious names like Glenmalure, Glendalough, Imaal, Clara, and Avoca wind through heather-covered hills. Uncrowded roads pass unforgettable sights — a high waterfall, an ancient monastic settlement, a splendid estate.

To the south lies the friendlier, less dramatic landscape of County Wexford; fertile farmland is served by picturesque villages and the historic, narrow-streeted town of Wexford itself. Just to the west is Waterford, a name synonymous with the fine crystal whose renown has tended to overshadow the scenic beauty of the county. Thirty miles north of Waterford is ancient Kilkenny, the town dominated by magnificent Kilkenny Castle along the River Nore. The rich pasturelands of Tipperary and the Golden Vale continue into Cork. It is quiet scenery, without the brooding grandeur of the west; rolling hills rise behind ancient towns; Norman castles sit on riverbanks shared with roofless, ruined abbeys.

The suggested stopping points in a 3-day tour are Wexford, Waterford,

Kilkenny, or Cashel. If your schedule allows only 2 days for the route, skip Kilkenny.

DUBLIN: For a detailed report on the city and its hotels and restaurants, see *Dublin,* THE CITIES.

En Route from Dublin – The coast road from Dublin leads past two famous resorts: Dún Laoghaire (pronounced Dun *Leary*), on the south shore of Dublin Bay, a residential town on a magnificent harbor; and Sandycove, the site of the Martello tower where James Joyce once lived, today open to the public as a Joyce museum (open Mondays through Saturdays from 10 AM to 5 PM, April through October; make appointment with the curator at other times; phone: 1-280-8571). Continuing to Dalkey and Killiney, one enters George Bernard Shaw territory. Shaw had a cottage on Dalkey Hill that he described as commanding "the most beautiful view in the world." Follow signposts to Bray, which will bring you on to N11. Just before entering that seaside town, swing right, following the Wexford signpost. After 2 miles, another right turn takes you through hills into a wooded hollow where you come upon Enniskerry, one of the prettiest villages in Ireland, renowned for the estate of Powerscourt.

ENNISKERRY: Near the village, signs point the way to Powerscourt (phone: 1-867676; fax: 1-863561), one of Ireland's great estates. Its beautiful Georgian mansion was gutted by fire in 1974, but its substantial skeleton attests to its former grandness. Also remaining are 14,000 acres of resplendent grounds, including gardens with fountains, statuary, and rare shrubberies along the River Dargle; a deer park; and the 400-foot Powerscourt Waterfall, the highest on these islands. The gardens are open from *St. Patrick's Day* to October; admission charge. The Waterfall Gate is open throughout the year.

From Powerscourt, driving through the Wicklow Hills, you come to Roundwood, the highest village in Ireland, and just beyond is Laragh, the gateway to Glendalough.

GLENDALOUGH: This deep glen, set in the Wicklow Mountains between two lakes, is a very special place with a very romantic history. In the 6th century, when St. Kevin came to Wicklow in search of tranquillity, he found it here. But the hermit's sanctity attracted so many disciples that, almost unwittingly, he founded a great monastery that eventually became one of the most renowned centers of learning in Europe. The visitor today sees the remains of many buildings from the 9th through the 13th century, including a perfect example of a Round Tower. There are wonderful nature trails in the valley's forest park.

En Route from Glendalough – Return to Laragh. Following Route R755 to Rathdrum, then R752, you pass through the densely wooded vales of Clara and Avoca. (The latter is the beauty spot where the Avonmore and Avonbeg rivers join to form the River Avoca. Here the poet Thomas Moore wrote his hymn to the vale, "The Meeting of the Waters.")

Heading back to the coast, you come to Arklow, an important fishing port and boatbuilding center. *Gypsy Moth III,* the yacht that took Sir Francis Chichester around the world (now docked at Greenwich, England), was built in an Arklow shipyard.

At Arklow, pick up N11 into County Wexford, through the towns of Gorey and Ferns, to Enniscorthy.

ENNISCORTHY: In a picturesque part of the Slaney Valley, this small town clings to steeply sloping ground along both banks of the river. The object of many attacks throughout history, including seizure of the lands by Oliver Cromwell and his forces in the 17th century, this was the site of a famous rebellion against the British in 1798. The insurgents made their last stand on Vinegar Hill, at the eastern end of the town, and were forever commemorated in the ballad "Boulavogue."

Enniscorthy Castle, dating from the 16th century, is excellently preserved and now is a folk museum (admission charge; phone: 54-35926). St. Aidan's Cathedral is a fine example of neo-Gothic architecture, made all the more impressive by its commanding site overlooking the River Slaney.

WEXFORD: Also on the River Slaney, along its estuary, is hilly Wexford, settled in 850 by the Vikings, who gave it its name, Waesfjord ("the harbor of the mud flats"). This is where the Anglo-Normans got their first foothold in Ireland. They established a walled town and built Selskar Abbey. Henry II of England spent *Lent* of 1170 there in penance for the murder of Thomas à Becket. At the *Bull Ring,* in the center of town, bullfights were staged for the Norman nobles. In 1649, Oliver Cromwell captured Wexford, massacred the townspeople, and destroyed 13 churches. The house where he stayed is now a *Penney's* department store. Other historic Wexford houses, dealt with more fairly by fate, include the birthplace of Sir Robert McClure, the Arctic explorer who discovered the Northwest Passage, and the home of Lady Wilde, mother of Oscar Wilde (closed to the public). A statue to Commodore John Barry, "Father of the American Navy," stands on the quays.

The best way to see the town is on one of the daily walking tours organized by members of the Old Wexford Society. Tours are offered without charge, although contributions are always welcome; detailed information is available at the tourist office on Crescent Quay (phone: 53-23111).

In October or November, Wexford holds the acclaimed *Wexford Opera Festival,* including a program of exhibitions, concerts, recitals, and films.

From Wexford, take Route N25 to New Ross.

NEW ROSS: On a hill overlooking the River Barrow, New Ross is the home of lovely St. Mary's Abbey, a relic of Norman times. Five miles south, on R733, is the John Fitzgerald Kennedy Memorial Park, a splendid arboretum commemorating the president, whose ancestors came from nearby Dunganstown. Try the *New Ross Galley* — the restaurant on a boat — where you can combine a good meal with a superb cruise between New Ross and Waterford (see *Best en Route*).

WATERFORD: Route N25 leads to Waterford, another former Viking settlement. Reginald's Tower, a fortification built by Reginald the Dane in 1003, is now a museum on the Quay. Beautiful 18th-century Christ Church Cathedral is also a tourist attraction (open Monday, Wednesday, and Friday afternoons in the summer). Above all, the city is famous for the crystal that bears its name, and a visit to the Waterford glass factory (Cork Rd.) is a must. The original plant opened in 1783, and the fine glass, exported throughout the world, quickly made its reputation. There was a 100-year hiatus in production when the industry as a whole went into decline, but in 1951 the factory reopened and has since outgrown its buildings several times. Today the company employs 2,000 people and hosts an average of 3,000 visitors a week who watch the master blowers, crystal cutters, and engravers in action (open weekdays; closed the first 2 weeks in August; children under 12 not admitted; phone: 51-73311).

From Waterford take Route N9 to Kilkenny.

KILKENNY: This ancient and historic city is dominated by two beautifully preserved major buildings. The 13th-century Cathedral of St. Canice marks the spot of an even older monastery from which the city grew, and a climb up the Round Tower beside the cathedral offers fine views of the city and surrounding countryside. Dominating the view and everything else in sight is the magnificently preserved Norman palace on the banks of the River Nore, Kilkenny's second treasure. Before the Normans came, the city was the capital of the kingdom of Ossory. In the 14th century, the existing Ossory palace was taken over — and then taken apart — by the Normans, who raised in its place the castle that has stood, defiant of time, ever since. Kilkenny has traditionally been associated with high-quality crafts. Across the road from the castle is the *Kilkenny*

Shop (Castle Parade), one of the finest stores in Ireland for Irish crafts, from textiles to silverware. As in Wexford, there are marvelous walking tours of the city. Ask at the tourist office at Shee Alms House, Rose Inn St. (phone: 56-21755).

Take Route N76 going south from Kilkenny and join R691 at Ballymack (about 6 miles out), continuing to Cashel in County Tipperary.

CASHEL: Dominating the market town that bears its name is the Rock of Cashel — Cashel of the Kings — the history of which spans 16 centuries. From the 4th century, the kings of the province of Munster were crowned on this 300-foot limestone rock and had their palace here. St. Patrick preached Christianity on the site in 450. In the 12th century, King Murtagh O'Brien gave the Rock to the church and began a period of great ecclesiastical building. Even the now roofless buildings retain their grandeur, but Cormac's Chapel, still roofed, is a gem of 12th-century Hiberno-Romanesque architecture (open daily; small admission charge). The lovely Queen Anne deanery, built for the archbishop in the 18th century, is now a hotel — the *Cashel Palace* — with a fine restaurant (see *Best en Route*). The shop/studio of silversmith Pádraig O Mathúna, near the hotel, is worth visiting. There is excellent trout fishing on the River Suir (permits can be obtained at the tourist office, Town Hall). From Cashel, Route N8 leads south to Cahir.

CAHIR: Cahir Castle, dominating the Suir, is one of the largest and most splendid medieval castles in Ireland. Restored, it is open to the public.

En Route from Cahir – Follow Route N8 out of Cahir to Mitchelstown and N73 to Mallow. To the left rise the Knockmealdown Mountains; on the right are the Galtees. The rich fishing waters of the Blackwater make Mallow a popular angling and hunting center. From Mallow, N20 goes south to Cork city.

CORK: The name Corcaigh means "marshy place," an apt description of its state for centuries after St. Finbarre founded a monastery here in the 6th century where Cork University now stands. (Cork's patron saint is honored in the lovely neo-Gothic Protestant Cathedral of St. Finbarre.) It is a city of 175,000 people, the Republic's second largest metropolitan area. Today the city straddles the two branches of the River Lee without getting its feet wet. Cork's excellent shopping center offers many goods. Major department stores are on Patrick Street; one of the best is *Cash's.* Small shops and boutiques abound on Prince and Oliver Plunkett Streets. A particularly good crafts shop is *Crafts of Ireland* (Winthrop St.; phone: 21-275864), opposite the post office. Walking tour maps are available from the tourist office (Grand Parade). The city also has an active cultural life: the *International Choral Festival* in April–May, the *Cork International Film Festival* in September, and the *Guinness Jazz Festival* in October, which draws huge crowds. The *Triskel Arts Centre* (Tobin St., off S. Main St.; phone: 21-272022) has exhibitions of local contemporary paintings and sculpture, readings, and a small restaurant.

Two trips from Cork should not be missed, one to Blarney Castle and the other to Kinsale.

BLARNEY: Route R617 (start off on N20 toward Mallow and Limerick) leads to Blarney, only 6 miles away. Few people in the English-speaking world have not heard of the Blarney Stone, which is said to confer the gift of eloquence on all who kiss it. The gift is well earned, however, for the stone juts out just under the battlement, which means you have to lie on your back far above a sheer drop and, with a guide holding your legs, stretch to your utmost to touch lips to stone. The view of the pretty castle park from the tower is better than the kiss. Both castle and park are open daily (open daily from 9 AM to dusk; admission charge to castle; phone: 21-385252). Also open to the public is the "new" Blarney Castle House, adjoining the old one (open Mondays through Saturdays from noon to 6 PM, June to mid-September; admission charge; phone: 21-385252). It is the house of the Colthursts, to whom the Blarney connection descended after Cromwell wrested it from the MacCarthys. The small village of Blarney, attractive in its own right, boasts a craft shopping center offering fine products at reasonable prices.

KINSALE: Take the airport road out of the city to get to Kinsale. With its narrow streets, tall houses, and stormy history, this attractive harbor town 17 miles south of Cork is an essential stop for lovers of good food — "'the culinary capital of Ireland." There is, for the town's size, an extraordinary range of really top restaurants whose proprietors have banded together in a Good Food Circle, which holds an annual *Gourmet Festival* in September.

BEST EN ROUTE

The southeastern region has some very good hotels and restaurants and a great many that are fair to mediocre. The listings here consider only the best in both accommodations and cuisine.

Expect to pay about $120 per person per night in one of the hotels or inns listed as expensive; from $50 to $100 in the moderate range; under $50 in those places listed as inexpensive. Meals at even the best restaurants are reasonable. We have categorized as expensive a meal for two that costs $90; $40 to $70 falls into the moderate range; and you can have quite good meals for as little as $30 for two at inexpensive spots. The restaurants below accept most major credit cards. Reservations for hotels are a must everywhere during the tourist season and at other times when there are special festivals.

GOREY

Marlfield House – On an estate with woodlands and gardens, this fine Regency-period country house offers 19 rooms, all with private bath or shower. The restaurant is highly recommended. Courtown Rd. (phone: 55-21124; 800-223-67664 in the US; fax: 55-21572; telex: 80757). Expensive to moderate.

WEXFORD

Talbot – Overlooking Wexford Harbor, this waterside hostelry has 99 rooms, all with private bath and some with hair dryers, 2 restaurants, a leisure center with indoor heated pool, gym, saunas, squash courts, and a solarium. The *Tavern* offers live music from traditional to jazz, and there's a weekly Irish cabaret in the summer. Trinity St. (phone: 53-22566; fax: 53-23377; telex: 80658). Moderate.

White's – Originally opened in 1779 as a coaching inn, it has 76 elegant rooms (all with bath), 2 restaurants, and 2 bars. Both taverns — the *Old Wexford* and the *Shemalier* — are popular for sing-along sessions. George's St. (phone: 53-22311; fax: 53-45000; telex: 80630). Moderate.

Killiane Castle – Kathleen Mernagh runs this gracious guesthouse set on 230 acres. In addition to the 8 rooms with shared baths, apartments are available, and there's a 17th-century tower on the grounds. Open March through October. Off the Rosslare Harbour Rd., Drinagh (phone: 53-58885). Inexpensive.

NEW BAWN

Cedar Lodge – In a lovely rural setting among rolling hills, halfway between Wexford and New Ross, this low, modern building has 13 rooms (all suites). Its bar is good for lunchtime snacks, and the restaurant has a very good reputation. Carrigbyrne, near New Ross (phone 51-28386; fax: 51-2822). Moderate.

NEW ROSS

Galley Cruising – This intriguing restaurant on a boat prepares fresh produce with appealing flair, but much of the appeal is the cruise itself — a long munch through the New Ross–Waterford River valleys. Reservations essential. Bridge Way (phone: 51-21723). Moderate.

WATERFORD

Waterford Castle – Set on its own landscaped island 2 miles downstream from the city, the 12th-century castle reopened in 1988 with 19 rooms (all with private bath), a heated indoor pool, horseback riding, and a variety of other sports. The *Munste Room* offers Irish fare enlivened by French sauces. Cross the bridge from Waterford to the island of Balinakill (phone: 51-78203; fax: 51-79316; telex: 80332). Expensive.

Jurys – In this modern hotel on a hill on the northern side of the River Suir, all 100 rooms have views that are especially striking at night, when the lights of Waterford are twinkling. Amenities include private baths, air conditioning and central heating, a fine restaurant with panoramic city vistas, a heated pool, golf on an adjoining 18-hole course, and 38 acres of gardens. Ferrybank (phone: 51-32111; fax: 51-70129; telex: 80684). Moderate.

Tower – Centrally located on The Mall near historic Reginald's Tower, this 125-room hotel has been tastefully refurbished, with an emphasis on brickwork, mirrors, and flowering plants in the public rooms and eclectic furnishings in the bedrooms. Waterford chandeliers sparkle in the pink-toned dining room, known for its local river trout. The Mall (phone: 51-75801; fax: 51-70129; telex: 80699). Moderate.

KILKENNY

Mount Juliet – A 1,400-acre walled park is the setting for this 18th-century country house, just 12 miles south of Kilkenny City. The 32 beautiful rooms all have private bath, and most country sports are available, including a new 18-hole golf course and fishing on the River Nore. Thomastown (phone: 56-24455; fax: 56-24522; telex: 80355). Expensive.

Hotel Kilkenny – Ten minutes' walk from the city center, this refurbished hotel and leisure complex has 60 suites, a conservatory, indoor swimming pool, Jacuzzi, and sauna. College Rd. (phone: 56-62000; fax: 56-65984). Moderate.

Newpark – On the north edge of the city, this Victorian country house has been skillfully combined with modern extensions and converted into a comfortable hotel with 60 rooms (each with private bath and phone). Facilities include a first-rate dining room, a noon-to-midnight grillroom, an excellent leisure complex, Irish musical entertainment, and twice-weekly discos. The staff is efficient and enthusiastic. Beside the 18-hole *Kilkenney* golf course, Castlecomer Rd. (phone: 56-22122; fax: 56-61111). Moderate.

CASHEL

Cashel Palace – This elegant Queen Anne building, formerly an archbishop's residence, is set amid beautiful formal gardens in the town center. It has 20 rooms with bath. The *Bishops Buttery* features light meals all day, and the *Four Seasons* is a fine dinner spot. Main St. (phone: 62-61411; fax: 62-61521; telex: 20638). Expensive.

Chez Hans – An attractive dinner spot, picturesquely set in an old converted church, with pointed windows and doors, right under Cashel's Rock. Chef-proprietor Hans prides himself on what he calls Irish-German cuisine. Reservations necessary. Rockside (phone: 62-61177). Expensive.

MALLOW

Longueville House – This very elegant 16-bedroom Georgian mansion with a genial host overlooks the lovely River Blackwater, where guests may fish. The restaurant features homegrown produce superbly cooked by the owner. Reservations essential (phone: 22-47156; 800-223-6510 in the US; fax: 23-47459). Expensive.

CORK

Fitzpatrick Silver Springs – A modern hotel on the city's fringes. All 100 rooms have a private bath. If you are lucky, yours will have a delightful view of the river with its passing ships. There is a handy coffee shop, a restaurant, and a sports complex. Glanmire Rd. (phone: 21-507533; fax: 21-507641; telex: 76111). Expensive to moderate.

Arbutus Lodge – Those who want to get as close as possible to what some consider the best restaurant in Cork, and perhaps in Ireland, should head for this elegant mansion overlooking the city and the river. The Georgian decor is enhanced by a collection of modern Irish art. There are 20 small but good rooms, all with bath. Restaurant reservations essential. Montenotte (phone: 21-501237; telex: 75079). Moderate.

Jurys – On the banks of the River Lee with views of St. Finbarre's Cathedral, this modern establishment has 185 rooms with private baths, a seafood restaurant (*Fastnet*), a sing-along bar, and an atrium-shaped pavilion with indoor-outdoor heated pool, saunas, squash courts, and a gym. Western Rd. (phone: 21-276622; fax: 21-274477; telex: 76073). Moderate.

Rochestown Park – Set in large gardens on the south side of Cork City, it has 33 rooms. The staff is amiable and attentive, and Blarney Castle is close by. Rochestown Rd., Douglas (phone: 21-892233; fax: 21-892178; telex: 75825). Moderate.

KINSALE

Acton's – This member of the Trusthouse Forte family has a terrific location facing the harbor, extensive rose gardens, a seafood restaurant, and a nautical tavern. There are 55 rooms, all with private bath. The Waterfront (phone: 21-772135; fax: 21-772231; telex: 75443). Expensive.

Man Friday – Beautifully situated in its own garden, this friendly restaurant has a rustic decor and a menu ranging from prawns Napoleon and Polynesian chicken to shellfish nouvelle. Reservations necessary. Scilly (phone: 21-77-22-60). Expensive to moderate.

Vintage – This vine-covered, beamed little restaurant stands in a winding street near the harbor. The cooking is imaginative, with particular emphasis on local produce. Choices include noisettes of lamb, free-range duckling, medallions of monkfish, and Wiener schnitzel. Reservations necessary. Main St. (phone: 21-772502). Expensive to moderate.

Blue Haven – In the middle of the village, this small, cozy hotel has 10 individually decorated rooms, 7 with bath. But the star attractions are the dining room's huge platters of local crab, mussels, and lobster and its fish casseroles, veal *Cordon Bleu*, and duck baked in brandy. The paneled bar, with a wood-burning fireplace, serves seafood soups and sandwiches. Restaurant reservations necessary. Pearce St. (phone: 21-772209). Moderate.

Southwest Ireland: Cork to Killarney

Artists and writers have for centuries celebrated the beauty of the "Kingdom of Kerry," where the majesty of Ireland's highest mountains contrasts starkly with its romantic glens and the splendor of the rugged coastline gives way to glorious lakes and luxurious forests. It is a landscape of infinite variety and constantly changing colors. Basically, the mountainous southern part of Kerry consists of the three large peninsulas of Beara, Iveragh, and Dingle; the smaller northern part is an area of undulating plain that stretches as far as the Shannon estuary. Along the coast, sandy bays alternate with cliffs and rocky headlands; the inland scenery includes the beautiful lakes of Killarney.

But scenic beauty is by no means Kerry's only attraction. Its many coastal resorts, climbable mountains, excellent fishing waters, good golf courses, and a wealth of ancient monuments make the southwest a paradise for sightseeing or sports-loving travelers.

There are lively, cheerful towns where pub regulars have formed semiformal singing groups, small fishing towns where the lilt of the ancient Irish tongue is on most lips, remote and lovely places where time has stood still.

This route concentrates on Kerry's great peninsulas: Beara, which it shares with Cork; Iveragh, famous for the Ring of Kerry, the complete scenic circuit around the peninsula; and Dingle, the most northerly promontory, which stretches 30 miles west from the low-lying country around Tralee to mountain ranges that turn to wild, deserted hills and lead to magnificent coastal scenery. You should allow 3 days and nights for the tour. If your time is limited, make sure you don't miss the Ring of Kerry, roughly a 110-mile round trip from Killarney. To see it leisurely will take most of 1 day.

CORK: For a description of the city, see the previous route.

En Route from Cork – Route R618 takes you along the north bank of the River Lee and passes through the picturesque villages of Dripsey, with its woolen mills, and Coachford.

MACROOM: This thriving market town, worth a quick visit, is set amid a large Irish-speaking district, and on market day Irish can be heard here and there. The gateway of the ruined castle, reached via the market square, stands at the center of town.

En Route from Macroom – Go back one-half mile on the Cork road (N22). Keep right at this first fork, following the signpost for Bandon and Cork, and very shortly turn right onto R584. Pass the Lee Valley Reservoir, continuing to Inchigeelagh and Ballingeary. Between these two villages the road skirts lovely Lough Allua. A circuit of the lake is recommended for those who have a lot of time to spare. Next, make a right turn 4 miles beyond Ballingeary where the sign reads: Gougane Barra.

GOUGANE BARRA: The mountain-encircled lake of Gougane Barra, source of the River Lee, is where St. Finbarre, the founder of Cork, had his hermitage in the 6th century. It has a splendid forest park with extensive nature trails.

Return to R584. Continue southwest as the road descends via Keimaneigh Pass and the Ouvane Valley to Ballylickey and Glengarriff.

GLENGARRIFF: The name means "the rough glen" and is only partially true of this lovely village on the Beara Peninsula snuggled into a deeply wooded glen. There is nothing rough about this glen, and sheltered as it is from any harsh winds, the village has a justly famous reputation for mild weather and tropical vegetation. Some of the plants and trees that flourish here are arbutus, eucalyptus, fuchsia, rhododendron, and blue-eyed grass. There is excellent sea and river fishing in and around the town, and bathing is good along the nearby coves, one of which, Poulgorm ("blue pool"), is a picturesque spot with a fine view — just a 2-minute walk from the village post office. There are tennis courts, a golf course, and unlimited terrain for riding and walking.

If time permits, a visit to the lovely Italian Gardens on Garinish Island is recommended (open daily; admission charge). There are plenty of boats and boatmen available for a small charge.

En Route from Glengarriff – If pressed for time, continue directly to Kenmare via N71. Otherwise follow the spectacular Healy Pass road, which is 17 miles longer. From Glengarriff this follows R572 along the south coast of mountainous Beara, the least-frequented of the three great southwestern peninsulas. At the foot of the Caha Mountains is Adrigole village. Hungry Hill, from which Daphne du Maurier took the title of her novel, looms to the northwest. At the schoolhouse in Adrigole turn right when you come to the sign: Healy Pass.

HEALY PASS: This road, opened in 1931, was built at the direction of Tim Healy, the first Governor-General of the Irish Free State. It climbs to a height of 1,084 feet as it crosses the Caha Mountains, the border between County Cork and County Kerry, and provides magnificent views over Sheep's Head and Mizen Head to the south and Kenmare River and the mountains of the Iveragh Peninsula to the north.

LAURAGH: The Healy Pass road descends to join the scenic sea road, R571, at Lauragh. Not far from Lauragh are the Cloonee Lakes, stocked with salmon and sea and brown trout. Route R571 continues along the coast to Kenmare.

KENMARE: This small town, at the head of the Kenmare River where the Roughty River meets the sea, has the mild climate common to the south coast. It is an excellent center from which to tour both the Beara and Iveragh peninsulas. There is bathing in the sheltered coves west of the town, salmon and brown trout fishing, and boating in the bay. Kenmare is also noted for its lace making, where the traditional point lace is still made.

Kenmare is the site for the *Fruits de Mer Festival* (usually in September), which features deep-sea fishing, seafood exhibitions and banquets, and a wide range of entertainment.

Kenmare's tourist information office is open from June through September, at 18 Main St., County Kerry (phone: 64-41233).

The most direct road to Killarney is Route N71, over the mountains to Molls Gap, via Ladies View, a lookout point with a panoramic view of the wonderful lakes of Killarney before entering the town. A more circuitous route is the famous Ring of Kerry road that encircles the Iveragh Peninsula by way of Waterville and Cahirciveen, about 100 miles in all. Take N70 from Kenmare.

PARKNASILLA: Renowned for its lush vegetation, this estate is the grounds of the beautiful *Great Southern* hotel (see *Best en Route*), a favorite holiday place of George Bernard Shaw.

SNEEM: This pretty town, where the Dutch royal family has vacationed, lies amid equally pretty scenery at the head of the Sneem River estuary. There is very good fishing here: Brown trout, salmon, and sea trout abound in the river and nearby mountain lakes. You'll want to stop at the *Blue Bull* — a quiet pleasant country pub and restaurant (see *Best en Route*) — if only for a quick drink to see its collection of prints and paintings.

STAIGUE FORT: Beyond Sneem, the Ring of Kerry road winds inland for a few miles through wild scenery, meeting the coast again at Castlecove, a peaceful retreat near a fine sandy beach. Here, make a right turn at a small sign: Staigue Fort. About 1½ miles north are the imposing ruins of a circular stone fort, one of Ireland's finest archaeological remains, which could date back as far as 1000 BC. Its rough stones are held in place without mortar.

CAHERDANIEL: Back on the coast road, past Westcove, is the village of Caherdaniel, near the shore of Derrynane Bay. In the vicinity is the curious hermitage of St. Crohane, hewn out of solid rock. Nearby is Derrynane House, once the home of Daniel O'Connell, "the Liberator," who gained the emancipation of Irish Catholics in 1829.

The house, now restored, contains a museum with O'Connell's personal possessions and furniture (admission charge to house only; phone: 667-5113). The house is part of Derrynane National Historic Park, with a nature trail through fine scenery. It is open to the public all year.

En Route from Caherdaniel – Route N70 climbs to a height of 700 feet at the Pass of Coomakista and offers a superb view. While the inland mountains rise sharply on one side, the lonely Skellig Rocks can be seen on the other in the open Atlantic. Skellig Michael bears the remains of a 6th-century monastery; it can be reached on a calm day from Portmagee. On the descent from Coomakista, Ballinskelligs Bay comes into view, with the village of Waterville nestling in its curve.

WATERVILLE: This small, unspoiled village lies between the Atlantic and beautiful Lough Currane on the eastern shore of Ballinskelligs Bay. On the east and south, mountains rise from Lough Currane, reaching 2,000 feet on the east side; in the lake itself float several islands, and in addition to Currane, there are many smaller lakes in the vicinity. With all this water, Waterville is a famous angling center almost by default, and no aquatic pursuit is ignored. There is boating, bathing from the fine sandy beach on the bay shore, and, for resolute landlubbers, golfing on a championship course.

En Route from Waterville – Follow either the coastal Route N70 to Cahirciveen and on to Glenbeigh or take one of the spectacular mountain roads to Glencar and thence to the coast. The latter is recommended. At New Chapel Cross, 1½ miles outside Waterville, leave N70 for an unclassified road to the Pass of Ballaghisheen. At a point between Bealalaw Bridge and Lough Acoose, a left turn leads to Caragh Lake and descends to rejoin N70 at Caragh Bridge. A left turn brings you to Glenbeigh after 2 miles (see below). Alternatively, a right turn continues to Killorglin, famous for its *Puck Fair*. (Every August the town holds a 3-day festival during which a goat is enthroned as King Puck to preside over a cattle, sheep, and horse fair. Shops are open day and night. Thousands of people come from all parts of Kerry.) From Killorglin, you may take R562 to Killarney, or continue northward to the Dingle Peninsula.

GLENBEIGH: At the entrance to a semicircle of mountains known as the Glenbeigh Horseshoe, where the Behy River flows into Dingle Bay, the town nestles at the foot of Seefin Mountain (1,621 feet). The scenery here is magnificent, and the circuit of hills from Seefin to Drung Hill (the horseshoe) is one of Kerry's finest mountain walks, with glacial corries and lakes throughout and fabulous trout fishing in innumerable rivers and lakes. Its other glory is nearby Rossbeigh strand, a 3-mile tongue of fine sand and dunes reaching out into Dingle Bay.

En Route from Killorglin – Follow N70 to Castlemaine, where R561 takes you into the Dingle Peninsula, a thriving center of Gaelic language and culture, rich in archaeological remains. This peninsula has been the setting for movies and should be familiar to filmgoers who have seen *Ryan's Daughter*.

INCH: Not far from the head of Dingle Bay, on the south side of the peninsula, lies the sheltered seaside resort of Inch. Its name to the contrary, the village has a 4-mile strip of firm golden sand that provides excellent bathing. The beach is backed by dunes that have yielded evidence of very early habitations.

DINGLE TOWN: The peninsula's chief town lies at the foot of a steep slope on the north side of the harbor and is bounded on three sides by hills. It was the main port of Kerry in the old Spanish trading days, and in the reign of Queen Elizabeth I it was important enough as an outpost to merit a protective wall. It has always been a fishing town; deep-sea fishing facilities are excellent. There is also good bathing and pony trekking into the surrounding hills. It is the gateway to the West Kerry Gaeltacht, the Irish-speaking district, and a good base for extended exploration of this rich area. A must stop is *Doyle's Seafood Bar* (see *Best en Route*).

En Route from Dingle – The road continues to Ventry, with its delightful beach. To the right of the road beyond Ventry are signs for "beehive huts." These lead to groups of small stone buildings shaped like beehives, constructed without mortar on a corbel principle. They generally served as monks' cells in early Irish monasteries. Since the ancient method of construction is still in use, it is often difficult to distinguish the old from the recent.

The road from Dingle continues to Slea Head at the tip of the peninsula, where the view of the Blasket Islands, the westernmost point in Europe (except for Iceland), is spectacular.

THE BLASKETS: This is a group of seven islands in the Atlantic. The largest, the Great Blasket, is about 4 miles long and three-quarters of a mile wide. Now uninhabited, it used to be known as "the next parish to America" when it had a village settlement. The Blaskets were inhabited from prehistoric times by an Irish-speaking community that gradually thinned out until, in 1953, the last islanders moved to the mainland. Many islanders were exponents of the art of *Seanachai,* or storytelling. Several books have been written about island life, among them: *Twenty Years A-growing,* by Maurice O'Sullivan; *The Islander,* by Thomas Crohan; and *Peig,* by Peig Sayers — all Blasket islanders. Boats to the Blaskets can be hired in Dunquin, north of Slea Head.

En Route from Slea Head – The road continues through Dunquin and Ballyferriter. About 1½ miles northeast is Gallerus Oratory, one of the best-preserved 9th-century buildings in Ireland (no admission charge). Although it is built of unmortared stone, it is completely watertight after more than 1,000 years.

Return to Dingle via Ventry. To get to Tralee, go over the Connor Pass if it's a clear day. Driving this road demands great care; it should be avoided in bad weather. Leave Dingle by the unclassified road marked Connor Pass, climbing northeasterly between Brandon and Slievenea mountains. At the summit (1,500 feet) is a breathtaking view: the bays of Brandon and Tralee to the north, Dingle Bay and Dingle town to the south, and the lakes in the deep valley to the left. The road then winds down along the base of great cliffs and ultimately goes through a valley of boulder-strewn wilderness. Incidentally, Brandon Mountain is named for Saint Brendan the Navigator who, according to tradition — and some scholars — reached America from here long before Columbus. In the town of Camp, take adjoining R559 for Tralee.

TRALEE: This friendly, busy trading center is one of the most active towns in southern Ireland. There is salmon and trout fishing in its rivers, excellent deep-sea fishing, a choice of superb beaches, sailing, skin diving, riding, and golf. Throughout the summer, the *Siamsa* (pronounced *She*-amsa) brings to life, through mime, music, song, and dance, the customs of the Irish countryside at *Siamsa Tíre Godfrey Place* (phone: 66-23055). Inquire for details at the tourist office (32 The Mall; phone: 66-21288). The greatest attraction of the town, however, is undoubtedly the *Festival of Kerry* at the end of August. This week-long event is described as "the greatest free show on earth." Its highlight is the crowning of the Rose of Tralee, from contestants from all parts of the world. Throughout the festival the town is brilliantly lit; every street is the scene of some outdoor entertainment or sporting event.

KILLARNEY: This is one of the major destinations of most visitors, because of the unrivaled beauty of its location. Three main lakes are in a broad valley stretching south between mountains. Closest to town is the Lower Lake, the largest of the three; the peninsula of Muckross separates it from the Middle Lake, which is connected with the Upper Lake by a narrow strait called the Long Range. The lakes are surrounded by luxuriant woods of oak, arbutus, birch, holly, and mountain ash, among which grow masses of rhododendron as well as ferns, mosses, and other plants. Besides the three main lakes, there is Lough Guitane, 4 miles southeast, and innumerable small tarns hidden in the folds of mountains and in rockbeds.

Part of Killarney's lake district lies within the 11,000-acre Bourne Vincent Memorial Park, once a private estate and in 1932 presented to the government, which promptly made it a national park. *Muckross House,* a 19th-century manor, is now a folk museum (open daily, admission charge; phone: 66-31440; fax: 66-33926) located in Memorial Park but still part of the estate.

South of the town is the Gap of Dunloe, a magnificent gorge that runs for 4 miles between MacGillycuddy's Reeks and Purple Mountain. Tours through the gap are made on ponies or on foot. In the town and the park, horse-drawn jaunting cars are available. A full day's tour includes a boat ride that, in turn, requires some shooting of rapids to traverse the three lakes.

There are two championship golf courses, the *Killeen* golf course and *O'Mahony's Point* golf course, adjacent to each other and served by the same clubhouse (phone: 64-31034). There is also a racetrack nearby and salmon and trout fishing on the lakes and nearby rivers; the highest mountain range in Ireland, the MacGillycuddy's Reeks, offers superb walking and scrambling possibilities to the experienced.

BEST EN ROUTE

The southwest is the most visited area in Ireland. That means that hotels of all degrees from luxurious to plain are plentiful, but rooms are always in demand. Book well in advance, and expect to pay somewhat more than in other parts of Ireland. The good news is that the hotels in the area are excellent (the one exception is Tralee, where neither accommodations nor restaurants warrant a lot of enthusiasm, but where the pubs are simply wonderful) and well versed in dealing with excited and overawed visitors. Many activities associated with the southwest — pony treks and fishing, long hikes in the mountains and deep-sea expeditions — can be arranged through hotels.

There is a wide range of prices among the hotels and restaurants. Certainly there are many lovely bed and breakfast houses with extremely reasonable rates, but at the luxurious resorts that are scattered around the route (such as the *Park* in Kenmare), rates can jump to $200 per night per person for a double in the middle of summer.

In general, expect to pay around $100 per person per night for a double in those places listed as expensive; from $50 to $90 in the moderate range; and under $45 in the inexpensive. A restaurant listed as expensive will charge as much as $90 for a meal for two; between $35 and $55 in the moderate range; and under $30 in the inexpensive category. Prices don't include wine, drinks, or tips. Restaurants recommended accept most major credit cards.

KENMARE

Park – Widely recognized as one of the country's finest hotels (Ireland's first to win a Michelin star for its dining room), the hotel is on its own palm tree–lined grounds on Kenmare Bay, just at the edge of the village. Guests are greeted like royalty as they sit down to register at an antique stockbroker's desk in the lobby. There are 48 rooms, all with bath, including 6 master suites with four-poster beds and hand-carved armoires. The restaurant, with romantic bay views on long summer days and candlelight in winter, specializes in seafood, especially salmon and shellfish. Restaurant reservations essential (phone: 64-41200; 800-223-6764 in the US; fax: 64-41402; telex: 73905). Very expensive.

Sheen Falls Lodge – Overlooking the Sheen River, this beautifully restored country house offers 40 fine rooms en suite, a fitness center, good restaurant, and a 1,000-book library, with special emphasis on Irish topics. Horseback riding also is available, along with salmon and sea trout fishing in the Sheen. Open from *Easter* through *New Year*'s (phone: 64-41600; 800-221-1074 in the US; fax: 64-41386; telex: 73820). Expensive.

Purple Heather Bistro – Seafood is the specialty of the house, with meals served

in the comfortable bar. Closed Sundays and *Christmas.* Reservations advised.
Henry St. (phone: 64-41016). Moderate.

Kenmare Bay – A pleasant hotel with 68 airy and modern rooms, a lively bar, and
a good restaurant. During the *Fruits de Mer Festival,* it can be very crowded.
Closed November through March. Sneem Rd. (phone: 64-41300; telex: 73880).
Inexpensive.

PARKNASILLA

Great Southern – One of George Bernard Shaw's favorite vacation spots, this
beautiful hotel on a lush estate is splendid all around. There are 60 rooms with
bath, a private golf course for guests, a heated indoor swimming pool, and fishing
or boating on the bay. The food is superb. Closed November through March
(phone: 64-45122; fax: 64-45323; telex: 73899). Expensive.

SNEEM

Blue Bull – A charming pub made up of three different rooms decorated with
fascinating prints of County Kerry scenes and, appropriately, an attention-getting
straw blue bull's head. In the summer, a back room becomes a seafood restaurant.
Restaurant reservations advised. Square (phone: 64-45231). Moderate.

WATERVILLE

Butler Arms – At the edge of the Atlantic, this grand old hotel has been owned by
the Huggard family for over three generations. The fine dining room specializes
in locally caught seafood dishes. There's also a *Fisherman's Bar.* Closed mid-
October to mid-April (phone: 667-4114; fax: 667-4520). Expensive to moderate.

GLENBEIGH

Ard na Sidhe – Elegant, quiet, and beautifully secluded in the forest at Caragh Lake,
this was once a private home. Now, there are 20 rooms, all with private bath. To
find *Ard na Sidhe,* "hill of the fairies," look for the signs on N70 between Killorglin and Glenbeigh. Open May through August. Killorglin (phone: 66-69105; fax:
66-69282; telex: 73833). Moderate.

Towers – This is a popular 28-bedroom family-run hotel; good food is a tradition
here, and during the summer season there is Irish entertainment nightly in the bar.
Glenbeigh (phone: 66-68212). Moderate.

DINGLE

Doyle's Townhouse – In the heart of town sits this little gem, an outgrowth of the
very successful *Doyle's Seafood Bar* next door. The public areas are rich in Victorian and Edwardian antiques, while the 8 rooms of varying sizes all boast telephones, TV sets, adjustable beds, and modern bathrooms of Italian marble. The
establishment provides all the comforts of a fine hotel with a homey ambience.
Open mid-March through mid-November. John St. (phone: 66-51174; fax: 66-
51816). Moderate.

TRALEE

Brandon – One of the largest hotels in County Kerry, this is standard modern in
style but genial in operation. All 154 rooms have a private bath. There's also a
dining room, a coffee shop, and a nightclub with dancing. Princes St. (phone:
66-23333; fax: 66-25019; telex: 72130). Expensive to moderate.

Ballygarry House – A country inn with a private garden and an Old World look,
complete with open fireplaces. All 16 of the individually decorated rooms have a
private bath. The restaurant serves mostly continental dishes. One and a half miles

from town on the Tralee-Killarney road. Leebrook (phone: 66-21233; fax: 66-31670). Moderate.

Tralee also has plenty of pubs to attract the thirsty or weary traveler. Some of the best include *The Abbey Inn* (Bridge St.; phone: 66-22084); *Bridge Inn* (Bridge St.; phone: 66-21827); *Brogue Inn* (Rock St.; phone: 66-22126); *Oyster Tavern* (The Spa, west of Tralee; phone: 66-36102); *Pig & Whistle* (Rock St.; phone: 66-21894); and *The Tavern* (Boherbue; phone: 66-21161).

KILLARNEY

Dunloe Castle – This is a sister to the *Europe* (below) and is not an old Irish fortress but a modern German-owned château-style hotel near the Gap of Dunloe. All 140 rooms have private baths, and other amenities include an excellent restaurant, a heated indoor pool, sauna, tennis courts, horseback riding, fishing, croquet, putting green, fitness track, tropical gardens, and nightly entertainment. Open April through September. Beaufort (phone: 64-44111; fax: 64-44583; telex: 73833). Expensive.

Europe – Like its name, this hotel is more European than Irish. (It is owned by Germans, which may explain it.) With a marvelous location on the shore of one of the Killarney lakes, it has all the amenities of a luxury hotel — a heated indoor pool in a health complex that includes a sauna. The 176 rooms vary in size and degree of luxury, but most have spectacular views and balconies. The *Panorama* restaurant has an international menu with views befitting its name; the *Tyrol* offers faster fare in a skylit alpine setting. Open during March and from May through October. Fossa (phone: 64-31900; 800-221-1074 in the US; fax: 64-32118; telex: 73913). Expensive.

Great Southern – The grand old lady of Killarney hotels has 180 comfortable rooms, but some in the modern wing are smallish. The public rooms are very elegant. The ballroom-size dining room is quite handsome, with a dome and pillars (phone: 64-31262; 800-223-1588 in the US; fax: 64-31642; telex: 73998). Expensive.

Cahernane – This was once the home of the Herberts, the family who owned Killarney. It is a mile outside town, near the famous lakes, with 52 gracious bedrooms, log fires, 2 restaurants, and a fine wine cellar. Muckross Rd. (phone: 64-33936; fax: 64-34340). Expensive to moderate.

Aghadoe Heights – A modern hostelry with 60 rooms that are less than luxurious, but the fine lake views make up for their shortcomings. The *Rooftop* restaurant dispenses exceptionally good local seafood as well as traditional Irish dishes, and the *Abbey Room* provides musical entertainment and dancing every summer evening except Sunday. Amenities for guests include salmon fishing on a private stretch of river and special arrangements at Killarney's golf courses. Closed mid-December to mid-January. Aghadoe (phone: 64-31766; fax: 64-31345; telex: 73942). Moderate.

The Midwest Counties:
Limerick and Clare

Limerick is a county of rolling grassland south of the River Shannon estuary. It is a rich agricultural area, particularly in the east, where it is known as the Golden Vale. The majestic Shannon drains the fertile pasturelands, making them ideal for dairy farming. This is countryside with a quiet beauty: Low hill ranges dot the plains; small towns rise here and there, each with its ruined castle or abbey and ancient bridge. Some of Ireland's best fox hunting is in this county, home also of many stud farms.

The huge Shannon estuary separates Limerick from County Clare to the north. Clare provides a stark contrast to the rural beauty of Limerick. Stone is the keynote of the landscape; it predominates everywhere. Along the west coast, spectacular slate and limestone cliffs drop to the incoming Atlantic, forming a coast of spectacular bluffs. To the north this rugged coast rises nearly 700 feet above the sea in the sheer Cliffs of Moher. Inland rises the Burren, an area of bare limestone terraces that shelter many caves and underground streams and a rich profusion of both Arctic and Mediterranean vegetation, which is usually not found in these latitudes.

Limerick is the gateway to the Irish Republic for travelers landing at Shannon International Airport, only 15 miles away (in County Clare), 30 minutes by car or bus. Many tourists are routed to the southwest or midwest from Dublin via Limerick. The Dublin to Limerick leg is 123 miles, a drive of about 3½ hours.

The following route starts at Killarney, going generally north, with some backtracking and detours. It can be done in 2 days with time planned for one of the medieval Shannon castle banquets, which must be booked in advance (phone: 61-61788). The overnight stay could be in Limerick or Ennis.

KILLARNEY: For a description, see the previous route.

En Route from Killarney – You have a choice of two equally pleasant routes: through Listowel, Tarbert, and Askeaton — the Limerick road along the Shannon — or the inland route through Newcastle West and Adare. You can also combine the routes to see the most interesting parts of each. The route that follows is a combination: the estuary road to Askeaton, turning inland at Askeaton to Adare.

Leave Killarney on N22 for Tralee. Continue on N69 through literary Listowel, where a writers' workshop is held for a week every June, with performances of plays by Kerry authors and literary get-togethers. About 11 miles north, at Tarbert, you meet the 60-mile-long estuary of the River Shannon. (A car-ferry operates from here to Killimer in County Clare on the north side of the estuary.) Continuing on N69, you enter County Limerick at the dairy town of Glin, the site of beautiful 18th-century Glin Castle, which has a crafts shop and tearoom. Askeaton is another picturesque old town with some notable ruins: 15th-century Askeaton Castle straddles the steep banks of the River Deel; a Franciscan friary stands on the banks of the river, and in its Protestant cemetery are the chancel and belfry of St. Mary's Church.

From Askeaton, turn off the main road onto R518, going inland through Rathkeale, a busy market town. On the way out of Askeaton, on the right, are the ruins of the 13th-century Franciscan Friary of St. Mary's.

At Rathkeale, turn east onto N21. About 7 miles northeast is the enchanting village of Adare, its thatched cottages and lichened medieval churches surrounded by woods on the River Maigue. The finest of the monastic ruins here is the 15th-century Franciscan friary on the estate of the Earl of Dunraven. (The 19th-century manor house and grounds, home of the Earls of Dunraven, have been converted to an impressive castle-style hotel; see *Best en Route.*) Among other noteworthy ruins are the 14th-century Adare Castle, 13th-century Trinitarian

Abbey (incorporated into the town's Catholic church), and the 14th-century Augustinian priory, now part of the town's Protestant church. Route N21 continues northeast to Limerick, about 11 miles.

LIMERICK CITY: The fourth-largest city in Ireland (pop. 76,000) offers an appropriately engaging introduction to the country for those many, many visitors who begin journeys here after the short half-hour trip in from Shannon Airport.

Limerick is a city of wide streets, handsome Georgian houses, and impressive public buildings such as the Custom House and the Town Hall. But this gracious architecture hardly reflects its violent history. It was occupied by the Danes in the 9th century and taken by the Anglo-Normans toward the end of the 12th century. In 1210, King John ordered the building of a strong castle and Shannon Bridge to control the crossing point of the river. In later centuries the city walls were extended for security. In the 17th century the city was torn between revolts by the Irish who seized the city and sieges by the English to bring them to their knees. The Treaty of Limerick in 1691 was to end hostilities and grant political and religious liberty to the Irish and the Catholics, but repeated violations of the treaty forced thousands into exile. The Treaty Stone, on which the pact was signed, stands on Thomond Bridge near King John's Castle. The 300-year anniversary of this event was celebrated in 1991 with a major renovation of the medieval precinct around the castle and bridge. Beside the castle is 12th-century St. Mary's Cathedral. This Church of Ireland structure is architecturally interesting; inside is an unusual collection of 15th-century misericords, oak carvings from choir stalls. Remnants of the old city walls, bearing the marks of cannon, can be seen near St. John's Hospital. Also worth a visit is the Limerick lace collection in the Good Shepherd Convent (Clare St.).

Activities include greyhound racing three times weekly at the city track; salmon and trout fishing at Castleconnell, 8 miles away, and brown trout and grilse fishing on the River Mulcair, 4 miles away; horse racing at *Greenpark* on Lower Killarney Road and Limerick Junction, 21 miles out of town; golf at *Ballyclough* and at *Castletroy,* 3 miles away; and swimming and boating on the River Shannon.

En Route from Limerick – As soon as you leave the city on N18 going west, you are in County Clare. Some 12 miles from Limerick you pass *Bunratty Castle.* This splendidly restored 15th-century castle is open to the public daily, as is Heritage Park on the castle grounds, where visitors can see typical Shannon houses through the ages and watch traditional skills such as candle making, bread baking, and iron forging. Raucous medieval banquets — food and entertainment — are held nightly in the castle. These require reservations. For more information on the castle or to make banquet reservations contact *Shannon Castle Tours* (phone: 61-61788).

Beyond the castle, just before the road turns north, N19 branches off to the left to Shannon Airport. Continuing on N18 to Ennis, another 12 miles, you pass through Newmarket-on-Fergus.

ENNIS: Friendly, narrow-streeted Ennis is County Clare's capital. It is a progressive business and marketing center, but of greater interest to the visitor are the remains of several abbeys in and around town: Ennis Abbey, built in the 13th century and remodeled through the 15th century, a mixture of architectural styles; Clare Abbey, a 12th-century Augustinian priory; and Killone Abbey, from the same period.

En Route from Ennis – Take Route N85 west through hilly Ennistymon, where the little River Cullenagh falls in cascades through the town center. Here join N67 to get to Lahinch, a resort with a mile-long beach, excellent for bathing and surfing. There is a challenging golf course, and periwinkles and dilisk are sold in twists of newspapers along the promenade. Route R478 in Lahinch leads to the fishing village of Liscannor and 3 miles west (a sign indicates the turnoff) are the Cliffs of Moher, one of the outstanding features of County Clare. Rising nearly

700 feet above the sea and extending about 5 miles along the coast, they provide magnificent views — especially from O'Brien's Tower (a short climb from the car park) at their northern end. From here you can see the Aran Islands to the north and, on a clear day, across Galway Bay all the way to Connemara.

DOOLIN: From the Cliffs of Moher, continue along the coastal road to this hamlet on the edge of the Atlantic. The town is well-known in the folk music world, so bring your fiddle, your flute, or just a pair of open ears to enjoy the good music. There are only a few houses, a shop or two, and a pub (maybe two), but people have been known to take up to 3 days just to pass through Doolin.

Near Doolin is the Burren (meaning "great rock"), the strange lunar-like region of bare, silvery limestone hills, caves, underground waterways, and *turloughs* (intermittent lakes, sometimes called disappearing lakes because the water is absorbed by the porous limestone, acting like a drain). Several routes crisscross the Burren. Though naked and treeless, the Burren is a naturalist's delight because of its rare, low-growing flora, such as Irish orchid and blue spring gentian, scattered over rock and sod. There are about 500 ring forts, or *caher,* where inhabitants of the Burren lived in about 600 BC. The most spectacular of these is Caherdoonerish, 600 feet up on Black Head with 18-foot walls and a view of the Aran Islands.

Just outside Ballyvaughan, you can stop to see the impressive stalactites in Aillwee Cave (open to the public) where there also is a restaurant and a good crafts/souvenir shop (phone: 65-77036; fax: 65-77107). At Rinn Point in Ballyvaughan, there is shore fishing for flatfish and mullet, while the bay affords bottom fishing for bass, flounder, and dogfish.

From Ballyvaughan, continue on N67 through Kinvara, and on into County Galway, past *Dun Guaire,* another castle in which medieval banquets are held (see *Best en Route*). At Kilcolgan turn left onto N18 for Galway city.

Beyond Kilcolgan is Clarinbridge, the heart of oyster country and the scene of an oyster festival in September. Route N18 leads to Oranmore, where it becomes N6 into Galway city.

BEST EN ROUTE

Perhaps because County Limerick and County Clare are close to Shannon International Airport, the area offers unusual accommodations along with the somewhat inventive entertainment-cum-restaurant fare offered as medieval castle banquets. Depending on your state of mind, these can be fun, but if you hate crowds, avoid the banquets, particularly the one at *Bunratty Castle; Dun Guaire* is a little more intimate as medieval banquets go, but that's not going very far. Don't make the mistake, however, of writing castles completely off your itinerary. Only 8 miles from Shannon Airport is *Dromoland Castle,* one of the finest hotels in Ireland. The Irish do this sort of thing extremely well (there are several of these castle-hotels in Ireland) and if you want to spend the money, *Dromoland* and *Adare Manor* are each unique experiences (see below for both).

Price ranges for hotels, including castles, are $130 and up per person for a double, very expensive; $70 to $90, expensive; $50 to $70, moderate; below $50, inexpensive. For restaurants, expect to pay about $80 for two in the expensive category; $45 to $65, moderate; under $30, inexpensive. Prices don't include wine, drinks, or tips. Restaurants recommended accept most major credit cards.

ADARE

Adare Manor – Opened in 1988, it's in the same tradition as the luxury hotels *Ashford Castle* and *Dromoland Castle.* The splendid, ornate, Tudor Revival manor — formerly the private home of the Earls of Dunraven — occupies 840 acres of parkland and gardens near the salmon-filled Maigue River, beside the prettiest village in Ireland. There are a total of 64 rooms, including 12 that provide garden views. Traditional Irish fare is offered in the restaurant. Adare (phone: 61-396566; 800-462-3273 in the US; fax: 61-396126). Very expensive.

Dunraven Arms – It's hard to say which is more beautiful, the ivy-covered Old World hotel with its charming garden or its location on Adare's cottage-lined main street. Both are lovely. The hotel has 44 bedrooms, all with bath. It also has a very good restaurant (reservations advised). Main St. (phone: 61-396209; fax: 61-396541; telex: 70202). Moderate.

LIMERICK

Dromoland Castle – For true luxury, you must go outside Limerick to Newmarket-on-Fergus, about 16 miles away (8 miles from Shannon Airport). This is another one of Ireland's castle-hotels. Unadulterated luxury prevails in its regal public rooms and 73 guestrooms. It offers 18 holes of golf, riding, tennis, fishing, and, in season, pheasant shooting within spacious grounds. The dining room is formal, as befits a palace, and its food is excellent. Restaurant reservations essential. Newmarket-on-Fergus (phone: 61-71144; fax: 61-363355; telex: 70654). Very expensive.

Fitzpatrick Shannon Shamrock Inn – This establishment — not the best of the Fitzpatrick chain, but conveniently near Shannon Airport — has 100 rooms, 10 river suites, a heated indoor pool, a sauna, a French/Irish restaurant, and a bar. It's next to *Bunratty Castle* and *Durty Nelly's* pub. About 10 miles from Limerick in Bunratty (phone: 61-361177; fax: 61-61252; telex: 72114). Expensive.

Limerick Inn – A modern, comfortable motel with 133 rooms, a commendable continental restaurant, and above average service. Amenities include a leisure center with a swimming pool and a gym, plus tennis courts and a putting green. Ennis Rd. (phone: 61-51544; fax: 61-326281; telex: 70621). Expensive.

MacCloskeys – Encompassing the former mews and wine cellars of Bunratty House, a restored 1804 mansion, this appealing candlelit restaurant is the creation of Gerry and Marie MacCloskey, who describe their menu as "French with an Irish flair." Specialties include Dover sole, rack of lamb, pheasant, and lobster. Closed Sundays, Mondays, and *Christmas*. Reservations necessary. Bunratty Folk Park, Bunratty (phone: 61-74082). Expensive.

Jurys – Just over the bridge from the Limerick city center, overlooking the River Shannon, this modern hotel offers efficient service and 95 well-appointed rooms. There is a pub and coffee shop, but the restaurant, the *Copper Room,* is noteworthy. Small but attractive, it offers excellent French cuisine. Service is efficient and friendly. Open for dinner only. Ennis Rd. (phone: 61-55266; fax: 61-326400; telex: 70766). Expensive to moderate.

ENNIS

Old Ground – An ivy-clad, centrally located hotel dating from the 17th century. One of its rooms used to be Town Hall and another one the jail. It now has 61 rooms with bath, some with antiques and others more modern in decor. There is a warming fireplace in the lobby and the *Poet's Corner* bar. O'Connell St. (phone: 65-28127; fax: 65-28112; telex: 70603). Expensive.

COROFIN

Maryse & Giblin – Beside the lake in its own grounds, this restaurant specializes in French and Italian dishes at modest prices. Open *Easter* to October. Reservations necessary (phone: 65-27660). Moderate.

LAHINCH

Vaughan's Aberdeen Arms – An oasis of comfort, this hostelry has 55 rooms with bath. The bar serves periwinkles rather than peanuts, and the restaurant offers some very fine seafood. Open April to October (phone: 65-81100; fax: 65-81228; telex: 70132). Moderate.

BALLYVAUGHAN

Gregan's Castle – Since the spa of Lisdoonvarna has only mediocre hotels, it is advisable to come to this charming, homey, antiques-filled castle at the foot of Corkscrew Hill, overlooking the Burren country and Galway Bay. There are 16 cozy bedrooms, all with bath. Open March through October. The restaurant is excellent; reservations necessary (phone: 65-77005; 800-223-6510 in the US; fax: 65-77111). Moderate.

KINVARA

Dun Guaire – This castle serves more intimate, but not less enjoyable, medieval banquets than *Bunratty*. The food is Irish and good; the entertainment, "literary" — featuring recitations from the work of famous Irish writers such as Yeats. Open May through October. Call *Shannon Castle Banquets* for reservations (phone: 61-61788; fax: 61-62256; telex: 72122).

KILCOLGAN

Moran's Oyster Cottage – A popular stop that vies with *Raftery's* (see below) for the "best oysters" designation. What makes it attractive above and beyond the food is its Old World air and grassy setting on the shores of Galway Bay. People love to sit outside or lounge on the grass in the summer months. Reservations advised. The Weir (phone: 91-86113). Moderate.

Paddy Burke's Oyster Inn – This internationally famous oyster tavern offers high-quality bar food along with its *Cordon Bleu* fare in the restaurant. It has a warm, relaxed atmosphere. Reservations advised. Clarinbridge (phone: 91-96107). Moderate.

Raftery's – In the heart of oyster country, you won't find better oysters and seafood generally than in this country pub with restaurant. And it's less expensive than most of its kind. Reservations advised. At the junction of Rtes. N67 and N18 (phone: 91-86175). Moderate.

The Irish West: Galway to Mayo to Sligo

Galway is a large county divided into two contrasting regions by the expanse of Lough Corrib. To the west, lying between the lake and the Atlantic, is Connemara — a region of scenic grandeur dominated by the rocky mountain range known as the Twelve Bens. Connemara — with a kaleidoscope of mountain and valley, lake and stream, bog and sea — has inspired many painters. They've painted the sparkle of water in deep valleys, tiny whitewashed cottages against purple mountains, great castles on the shores of calm and wooded lakes, fields the size of pocket handkerchiefs, and immense skies.

The region east of Lough Corrib is more subdued; it is a fertile limestone plain, partially covered with bogs, that extends to the Galway-Roscommon border and the River Shannon.

The people of Connemara and of the Aran Islands, west of Galway Bay, are an ancient people with ancient ways. They still fish the wild seas in their frail boats called *curraghs,* pasture their sheep on the green and golden mountainsides, and speak mostly Irish, the language of the Celts. Galway city is an important tourist center and the gateway to the scenic areas of the county.

GALWAY CITY: On Galway Bay at the mouth of the River Corrib, Galway is a busy seaport, a thriving city with good hotels and stores and a fine university.

The Magnata mentioned by Ptolemy in the 2nd century AD is thought to have been Galway. The city evolved from a fort built in 1142, then was seized by the Anglo-Normans, who converted it into a walled town by the 13th century, a powerful western stronghold. While they isolated themselves from the native Irish population, the Normans engaged in active trading with the rest of the world. Much of their commerce was with Spain and some intermarriage occurred, which accounts for the dark hair and coloring of many Galway people and the Iberian influence in some of the city's architecture.

Since historic Galway is compact, with narrow streets, it is best seen on foot; walking tour maps, with an interesting path through old Galway clearly laid out, are available at the tourist office (Eyre Sq.; phone: 91-63081). There are several sights that should not be missed. Lynch's Castle (Shop St.), now a bank, is a fine old mansion, and the 14th-century Church of St. Nicholas (Lombard St.) is supposed to be the last place Christopher Columbus worshiped before sailing for America. Near the fish market is the Spanish Arch leading to Spanish Parade, so named because it was the favorite promenade of Spanish merchants. The Salmon Weir Bridge spanning the River Corrib draws many visitors during the spawning season, when hundreds of salmon can be seen stacked on the riverbed waiting to leap upriver to their spawning grounds in Lough Corrib.

Because of its proximity to the Aran Islands, Galway is the ideal place to purchase Aran sweaters; one of the best shops for sweater and tweeds is *O' Máille's* (Lower Dominick St.). For crystal and porcelain, the *Treasure Chest* (William St.) is good; for books, including fine bindings and artwork, try *Kenny's Bookshop and Art Gallery* (High St.); the *Bridge Mill* (Bridge St.) has a variety of small shops and art galleries, and here you can also sip a cup of coffee to the soothing swish of the mill-wheel.

Since Galway is the gateway to Gaelic country, it is only fitting that an authentically Irish — that is, Gaelic — entertainment should flourish here. The folk theater, *Taibhdhearc* (pronounced *Tive* — rhyming with "dive" — *yark*), operates year-round (Middle St.; phone: 91-62024). It puts on special variety shows with music and dancing, called *Seoda,* for visitors three times a week in July and August. Galway's other theatrical company, *Druid,* has won international renown; the company performs at the *Druid Lane Theatre* (phone: 91-68617).

Several summer events attract big crowds and fill hotels and guesthouses nearby: the 5-day *Galway Races* in July and August; the weekend *Galway Oyster Festival* in September; and an annual ceremony called the *Blessing of the Sea,* which takes place one day between late July and the end of August, at the beginning of the herring season. During festival weeks the town is jammed and accommodations are impossible to find; reservations are a must.

West of the city, on Route R336, close to the shore of Galway Bay, is Salthill, a resort suburb of pastel houses and a long boardwalk with a stunning view. Thirty miles out to sea from Galway are the three Aran Islands — Inishmore, the largest with 7,635 acres; Inishmaan; and Inisheer. These rugged and barren chips of land immortalized in Robert Flaherty's film *Man of Aran* offer an interesting side trip. You can reach the islands by boat from Galway in 3 hours or by air in 20 minutes. Flight and boat schedules as well as booking information for both transportation and accommodations for an overnight stay on the islands are available at the tourist office at Eyre Sq. (phone: 91-63081).

On the islands you will be transported back in time to a primitive way of life. The language is Irish, and some of the people still wear homespun clothing. You can watch the islanders create soil from sand and seaweed to grow feed for their livestock and meager produce for themselves; fishermen put out to sea in *curraghs* (boats made of narrow strips of wood and tarred canvas no different from those their ancestors used); and the women knit garments in intricate patterns.

If you go for the day, you can tour the island in a jaunting car. If you stay overnight, you can wander the rocky paths in splendid isolation or explore the ancient ruins — forts and churches.

Boats from Galway land at Kilronan, the main town on Inishmore. They sometimes call at the other islands as well, but cannot dock there, so if you want to visit you must disembark into a *curragh* on the high seas for transporation ashore. Another way to get to the smaller islands is to take a *curragh* from Kilronan.

En Route from Galway – North on the main road is Sligo, about 86 miles away. Our route, designed to cover as much as possible in 1 day and still see the outstanding sights of Connemara, is roughly twice that distance. Good bases for extended exploration are Cashel, at the head of Bertraghboy Bay on the west coast, and Clifden, farther up the coast on the edge of the Atlantic. Both places have good hotels (see *Best en Route*).

Leave Galway on N59, going northwest a few miles until you come to Moycullen. On the left side of the road is a Connemara marble factory where you can observe marble being worked — shaped, ground, carved, and polished. Both the plant and a shop that sells finished objects are open daily. Continuing on N59, you are actually parallel to Lough Corrib, but you don't see much of the lake until you get to Oughterard, a lovely trout and salmon angling center.

From Oughterard, N59 curves west through Maam Cross and passes the shores of some of Connemara's lovely lakes — Lough Shindilla, Oorid Lough, beautiful Lough Glendalough at Recess, and Lough Derryclare. This stretch of road has some of the best scenery in Connemara, with the lakes on one side and the Twelve Bens looming majestically ahead. The mountains are conical, with precipitous slopes distinctively colored by lichens and mosses.

Beyond Recess, the first turn to the left is R340, marked Carna. Take this road for about 5 miles to an unmarked right turn, which leads to Cashel.

CASHEL: This little angling resort is beautifully situated on the waters of Bertraghboy Bay. Cashel (not to be confused with the town in County Tipperary) is little more than the fine *Cashel House* hotel (see *Best en Route*), a post office, a school, and a couple of shops — and that's it. The village is idyllic for the gardens that thrive in this wooded, sheltered bay amid peace and quiet. There is also ample opportunity for outdoor activities, from freshwater and sea fishing to horseback riding and mountain climbing.

The next stop on our route is less than 5 miles west on R341.

ROUNDSTONE: A charming fishing village with whitewashed houses overlooking a tranquil harbor, Roundstone is known for its fine beaches, particularly Dog's Bay, a magnet for naturalists and geologists interested in studying foraminifera — unusual, large-shelled amoeboid protozoa. Towering over the village is isolated Urrisbeg Mountain, which provides a splendid view of the surrounding lake-dotted countryside and the splendid, irregular coastline.

En Route from Roundstone – Continue around the promontory on coastal Route R341, known as "the brandy and soda road" because of the bracing quality of the air. It passes through Ballyconneely on the remote shores of Ballyconneely Bay, where golfers can play the 18-hole *Ballyconneely* course (phone: 95-23602). There are glorious beaches everywhere, including the lovely Coral Strand on the shores of Mannin Bay. Deep-sea fishing can be arranged in many villages along the way.

CLIFDEN: The main town of Connemara, Clifden is an ideal center for exploring the glorious scenery of the region. The busy little town nestles on the edge of the Atlantic against a superb backdrop of mountains. The *Connemara Pony Show* held here each August attracts buyers from throughout the world.

En Route from Clifden – Route N59 leads north to Moyard and then through Letterfrack (visit the new National Park there) to the romantic Kylemore Pass, a beautiful valley dominated by the 19th-century castellated mansion *Kylemore Abbey* (phone: 95-41146), now a girls' school run by Benedictine nuns; they also manage a pottery and restaurant open to visitors (phone for both: 95-41113).

Beyond Kylemore, the road follows the southern shore of Killary Harbour, a magnificent fjord-like arm of the sea that runs inland between steep mountains rising like enormous walls. Near the head of Killary Bay is the village of Leenane, another angling resort and an excellent center for mountain climbing.

From Leenane, take Route R395 into County Mayo. Go past the Asleagh Falls, heading west on the north shore of Killary Harbour, where the road turns inland and the landscape alternates between dramatic lakefront and brooding mountains. Gold deposits have been discovered in this remotely beautiful valley; it remains to be seen whether mining activities will be allowed to mar its splendor. From Louisburgh, near the coast, continue on R395, going east to Westport. Along the way is Ireland's "holy mountain," Croagh Patrick, an isolated conical peak rising 2,510 feet from the shore of Clew Bay and one of the most conspicuous features of western Ireland's landscape. On this mountain, St. Patrick is said to have fasted 40 days during *Lent* in 441, praying that Ireland would never lose the Christian faith. According to tradition, he summoned all venomous creatures in Ireland to the summit and then cast them out. (To this day there are no snakes in Ireland.) Every year, on the last Sunday in July, thousands of pilgrims — many barefooted — climb the mountain. Throughout the day, masses are celebrated in the little chapel at the top.

WESTPORT: The town is charmingly laid out on an arm of Clew Bay in a hollow surrounded by trees and groves. In recent years, it has become a deep-sea fishing center, and the annual June festival draws many fishermen. The main tourist attraction, however, is Westport House, a beautiful estate less than 2 miles miles from town. The fine Georgian mansion overlooking the bay is the home of the Marquess of Sligo (open to the public April through mid-October; phone: 98-25141). The house is a treasure of fine paintings, silver, Waterford glass, and exhibits of historical interest. There is also a small zoo on the grounds, as well as a camping site and a caravan park (single admission charge to the house and zoo).

En Route from Westport – There are a number of routing alternatives from Westport. If you want to base yourself for several days in a fairy-tale setting in County Mayo, you must stay at *Ashford Castle* (see *Best en Route*) in Cong, roughly halfway between Galway and Westport, on the north shore of Lake Corrib. The 13th-century fortress, the former home of the Guinness family, is now a luxury hotel with elegant rooms and suites overlooking either the lake, the river

Cong, or the landscaped gardens that stretch over several hundred acres. It is a sporting paradise — for hunting, fishing, golf, and tennis.

From Westport to Sligo you have a choice of routes. If you're pressed for time, take N60 east 11 miles to Castlebar, a small bustling town in the heart of the limestone plain; continue on N5 to Charlestown and join N17 going northeast until you bump into N4, which will take you into Sligo. This route is roughly 53 miles.

A more scenic alternative from Castlebar is Route R310 north to Pontoon, a picturesque angling resort between Lough Conn and the smaller Lough Cullen, both of which are full of salmon and trout. Cross the isthmus between the lakes and continue north to Ballina, County Mayo's largest town (pop. 6,000), on the salmon-rich River Moy.

From Ballina, take shore Route R297 into County Sligo through Enniscrone and Easkey. Join the main Sligo road, N4, at Ballisodare.

BEST EN ROUTE

The best accommodations in the west are set in some of Ireland's most beautiful countryside and have some of the finest restaurants. Romantic, luxurious *Ashford Castle* is very expensive, from $140 and up for two. The price range for a double room in the area's other hotels is $80 to $90, expensive; $60 to $80, moderate; below $40, inexpensive. For a meal for two, $75 and up is considered expensive; $35 to $50, moderate; under $35, inexpensive. Prices don't include wine, drinks, or tip. Restaurants listed below accept most major credit cards.

GALWAY CITY

Drimcong House – A lovely old country house now serves as the backdrop for one of Ireland's most accomplished restaurants. Like the decor, the food is elegant yet unpretentious, the service efficient yet unobtrusive. Specialties include wild game, spiced beef, salmon, and oysters. It is a dining experience not to be missed. Closed *Christmas* through January. Reservations essential. One mile past Moycullen village on N59 (phone: 91-85115). Expensive.

Great Southern – A superior hotel, with 120 of the most comfortable rooms in Galway. Its elegant foyer is the center of social life in the city, perfect for striking up new friendships. A heated swimming pool and sauna are welcome bonuses. Eyre Sq. (phone: 91-64041; fax: 91-66704; telex: 50164). Expensive.

Ardilaun House – Once the stately home of an aristocratic scion, the building and grounds still retain a patrician aura. It's hidden among trees and shrubs on Taylor's Hill, the best address in town. Salthill (phone: 91-21433; fax: 91-21546). Moderate.

Anno Santo – For those who prefer the quiet life, here is a classy, intimate place with 14 rooms in a relaxed atmosphere. Threadneedle Rd., Salthill (phone: 91-22110). Inexpensive.

OUGHTERARD

Connemara Gateway – An efficiently run motel, it has 62 rooms with private bath, a leisure center, indoor pool, 18-hole golf course, and first class dining (phone: 91-82328). Moderate.

Currarevagh House – An aristocratic home on Lough Corrib, now a peaceful and relaxing guesthouse. The 15 rooms are old-fashioned and comfortable. Open from April to October. Reservations essential. Four miles north of town (phone: 91-82313; fax: 91-82332; telex: 50905). Moderate.

CASHEL

Ballynahinch Castle – A glamorous castle-hotel in a wonderful lake and mountain setting. It has 28 rooms (all suites), a good wine cellar, and open fires. At Ballinafad (phone: 95-31006; fax: 95-31085). Expensive.

Cashel House – This Georgian country house has 30 bright, pleasant bedrooms, 27 with bath. Its dining room fare is cooked by the owner. Closed December to mid-February. Restaurant reservations necessary (phone: 95-31001; 800-223-6510 in the US; fax: 95-31077). Expensive.

CLIFDEN

Abbeyglen – The proprietor sees to it that the hotel is warm and friendly and that the cuisine is of a high standard. There are 42 rooms, 40 with bath, and a heated outdoor swimming pool. Closed December through January. Sky Rd. (phone: 95-21201; fax: 95-2797; telex: 50866). Moderate.

Renvyle House – Elegant and convivial, rambling and gracious, this 60-room paneled haven, once the home of writer St. John Gogarty, is perched on the edge of the Atlantic shore. Log fires add extra comfort, and manager Hugh Coyle might even sing to you in the evening. The restaurant features Irish fare (reservations necessary). Closed January to mid-March. Ten miles north of town, turn left at Tully Cross (phone: 95-43511; fax: 95-43515). Moderate.

Rockglen Manor – Once a shooting lodge, now a small, elegant hostelry (30 rooms) with a reputation for fine food. Closed November through February. Restaurant reservations necessary. On the coastal road (phone: 95-21035; 800-223-1588 in the US; fax: 95-21737). Moderate.

WESTPORT

Newport House – If you go out of town 8 miles from Westport, there is a delightful, rambling Georgian mansion set in its own wooded estate. It has everything the town hotels don't have: 19 great rooms and delicious cuisine. Closed October to mid-March. Newport (phone: 98-41222; fax: 98-41613; telex: 53740). Expensive to moderate.

Westport Ryan – A member of the dependable Ryan chain, in a quiet woodland setting, all 56 rooms have color TV sets and telephones. Video films, tennis courts, and other amenities are available. Louisburgh Rd. (phone: 98-25811; fax: 98-26212; telex: 53352). Moderate.

CONG

Ashford Castle – This 13th-century castle is considered by many to be Ireland's finest castle-hotel. Beside Lough Corrib in beautiful grounds, it has 83 rooms and suites with views of the lake or the gardens. The guestrooms are beautifully appointed, as are the public rooms, with their views over the landscaped gardens. It is a fairy-tale castle, splendidly run. The superb cuisine often features the day's catch of fish. It is possible to dine at the castle even if you aren't staying here, but reservations are essential. On 98A just east of Cong (phone: 92-46003; 800-346-7007 in the US; fax: 92-46260; telex: 53749). Expensive.

The North: Sligo to Donegal

The northwest is rugged country. County Sligo is a healthy mix of mountain, lake, and coastal scenery. In the western part, the Ox Mountains form a background to the coastal plain, while north of Sligo town the landscape is dominated by steep, flat-topped limestone hills. The low-lying coast is fringed by sandy beaches and low cliffs.

Sligo is extraordinarily rich in archaeological remains and places associated with the heroes and heroines of the ancient Irish epics and sagas. Inextricably linked to this area and its Celtic tradition is the poet William Butler Yeats. His poems, particularly the early ones, create a haunting picture of ancient Ireland, the Ireland of myth and legend, and you won't regret having his cadences and images in your mind's eye when you come to Sligo.

Donegal, the most northerly county in the Republic, extends along much of the northwest coast. Despite patches of tasteless "modernization," it is one of the wildest, loveliest, and most remote parts of Ireland, with distinctive scenery — a bay-indented coast, great areas of blue and purple mountains, deep wooded glens, and many lakes. All kinds of stone, from cave-riddled limestone to mixtures of igneous rocks, make up the foundation of the land and give the scenery its form and color.

SLIGO TOWN: Although Sligo is northwest Ireland's most important town, its population is only 14,000. It is picturesquely situated on the estuary of the Garravogue River on a wooded plain between Lough Gill and the sea. If the lake, with its scattered islands, is not one of Ireland's loveliest, it is most certainly its most famous, immortalized by one of Yeats's best-known poems, "The Lake Isle of Innisfree." The town itself contains some fine buildings, the most notable being the 13th-century Dominican friary, Sligo Abbey. Although the building was sacked in 1641, the ruins — a nave, choir, and central tower — are magnificent. From June to August, guided walking tours of Sligo leave every day at 11 AM from the tourist office (Temple St.; phone: 71-61201).

Sligo is an excellent angling center for game fish. There are fine beaches close to town at Strandhill and Rosses Point. The latter also has a splendid golf course, *Rosses Point.*

A short tour of Yeats country should certainly include a trip along the shore of Lough Gill. Three-hour boat tours leave from Doorly Park (Riverside Quay).

Another site that should not be missed is the archaeologically rich area west of town, bounded by its main natural feature, the Hill of Knocknarea (1,078 feet), on whose summit Ireland's ancient warrior queen Maeve reputedly lies buried beneath an immense cairn. Between Knocknarea and Sligo town is Carrowmore, the "graveyard of the giants," a site containing the greatest concentration of megalithic burial stones in Ireland.

En Route from Sligo – Route N15 goes north through Bundoran and Ballyshannon — wild country scarcely touched by time, where small whitewashed, thatch-roofed cottages huddle together against the fierce Atlantic gales. A few miles from Sligo, the road passes Ben Bulben, known as the "table mountain" for its curious shape. On its slopes, 1,730 feet high, the great warrior and ill-starred lover of Irish myth — Diarmuid — met his death; and at its base is buried Yeats, who celebrated Diarmuid's exploits in poetry. Yeats's grave by the little Protestant church in Drumcliffe lies exactly as he had willed it in his 1938 poem "Under Ben Bulben." The tombstone bears the poem's famous last stanza: "Cast a cold eye/On life, on death/Horseman, pass by!"

Farther along the coast is Bundoran in County Donegal, a popular resort on the south shore of Donegal Bay. Bundoran has a fine bathing beach with a promenade, excellent freshwater and sea fishing, and a championship golf course. It also has one of the best views in the area: the Sligo-Leitrim Mountains to the south, the Donegal hills to the north, and, along the beach, a range of cliffs carved into fantastic shapes by the waves.

A few miles up the coast is the lively hilly town of Ballyshannon, on the banks of the River Erne, reputedly the oldest settlement in Ireland. According to tradition, Parthalon, a Scythian, settled on the islet Inis Saimer in the Erne estuary at Ballyshannon in 1500 BC. Stop in *Donegal Irish Parian China* (phone: 72-51826) and select a piece of the hand-crafted, wafer-thin Donegal Parian tableware.

A short detour from Ballyshannon leads to one of Donegal's most spectacular bathing and surfing beaches, a 3-mile-long strand surrounded by gentle hills at Rossnowlagh. Return to N15 to continue to Donegal town.

DONEGAL TOWN: This thriving market town at the head of Donegal Bay and the mouth of the River Eske is an excellent touring center because of its location where the main roads from Derry, West Donegal, and Sligo converge. *Magees,* which manufactures the celebrated Donegal tweed, is in the town, and its mills are open to the public on weekdays (no admission charge; phone: 73-2100; fax: 73-21283). Visitors can watch the distinctive technique of close weaving and the use of the plant dyes that produce the tweeds' famous heather tones. The retail store is on the Diamond, the central square; the factory is on Milltown. The imposing ruin of 16th-century Donegal Castle stands on the bank of the River Eske near the Diamond. South of the town are the remains of the 15th-century Donegal Abbey.

En Route from Donegal – Take Route N56 west to Killybegs, one of Ireland's most important fishing ports on a fine natural harbor. Killybegs was once noted for the greatly valued Donegal carpets, but in recent years the industry has declined, and finding these hand-knotted carpets for sale is rare; the White House, Buckingham Palace, and Dublin Castle all have Donegal carpets in their ceremonial rooms.

From Killybegs, continue on R263 west to Carrick, a good starting place for the ascent of Slieve League (1,972 feet) and for exploring the magnificent cliff scenery of the adjoining coast. In Carrick, make a 2-mile detour south to Teelin. From here, a mountain track leads over Carrigan Head to the secluded Lough O'Mulligan and the sheer cliffs of Bunglass, which rise out of the water to a height of 1,024 feet. The view from the point, named Amharc Mor ("the great view"), lives up to its name: It is among the most magnificent in Donegal. Experienced climbers can go farther along the cliff edge to One Man's Pass, a narrow ledge with a precipice of more than 1,800 feet on one side, dropping sheer down to the sea, and on the other an almost equally precipitous escarpment falling down to a lonely mountain lake. From there it is not far to the summit of Slieve League, at 1,972 feet the highest maritime cliff in Europe, against whose base the Atlantic hurls powerful crashing waves. The path along the mountaintop is very rough and dangerous.

Retrace your steps from Teelin to Carrick and continue west on R263 to Glencolumbkille.

GLENCOLUMBKILLE: In the heart of the Irish-speaking area of South Donegal, this glen runs into the hills from Glen Bay. Many houses dot its slopes in surroundings at once peaceful and strikingly picturesque. On the north side rises the cliff of Glen Head. The coast has splendid rock scenery and there is a beautiful beach, and it is a popular family vacation spot. Glencolumbkille is rich in monuments dating from pre-Christian times as far back as 5,000 years ago.

Adjacent to the holiday village is a folk village re-creation of cottages representing different periods of Irish life.

En Route from Glencolumbkille – An unclassified road leads to Ardara. This road rises to spectacular Glengesh Pass at 900 feet, then plunges in a steep descent to the valley below. Ardara, in a pretty valley at the mouth of the River Owentocher and Loughros More Bay, is another important center for the manufacture of Donegal homespun tweeds. Route N56 leads north to the Gaelic districts of Dungloe and Gweedore. In Gweedore, make a left turn along R257 until you meet T72, which will take you north to Bloody Foreland, the cliff that takes its name from the warm, ruddy color of its rock in the setting sun.

Route R257 curls eastward along the coast to Gortahork, near Ballyness Bay. For the traveler who wants to spend several days in the area, the town of Gortahork, with *McFadden's* hotel and fine restaurant (see *Best en Route*), is a good center for touring the north — to Horn Head, Melmore Head (both north of the villages of Dunfanaghy and Port-na-Blagh), and Fanad Head (from which the R247 brings you south by lovely Lough Swilly to Rathmullan and Letterkenny). Then head on to the Inishowen Peninsula with Malin Head, the northernmost point in Ireland. This northland of the Republic consists of spectacular peninsulas ringed by misty, craggy, windswept cliffs rising straight from the water, with dramatic views of the boundless Atlantic Ocean broken by numerous islands and headlands.

An unclassified mountain road will bring you to Glenveagh National Park, which is not to be missed. It has a spectacular lake situated between rugged mountains, with a romantic castle, deer herds, and superb formal gardens which gradually merge with the wild mountainsides (open daily year-round). This is a truly magical place, developed with great care. There is an interpretive center, which offers fascinating information on the social and natural history of this part of Donegal (open daily, *Easter* through September; admission charge). Nearby is the *Glebe Gallery* with a fine collection of paintings by contemporary Irish painter Derek Hill and works by the Tory Island primitive painters (admission charge).

You can then join the R251 to Letterkenny, the principal town of County Donegal, which overlooks Lough Swilly where the River Swilly empties into the lake. From here there is a selection of routes across the interior of the county to the west coast, all of them passing through superb mountain scenery. Route N56 descends through the twin towns of Stranorlar, where it joins N15, and Balleybofey through the wild and lonely Barnesmore Gap back to Donegal town.

Donegal town is 138 miles from Dublin through the inland counties and 176 miles from Shannon Airport.

BEST EN ROUTE

Because the north country has spectacular vistas, so do many of the hotels (the vistas are often better than the accommodations themselves). But the north has come a long way, and things are getting better all the time. Still, because hotels and restaurants are rather isolated and some are fairly small, it is necessary to make reservations. Expect to pay $140 and up for a double room in the expensive range; $70 to $120 in the hotels we list as moderate; under $70 in the inexpensive category. For meals, $50 for two is expensive; $25 to $40, moderate; under $20, inexpensive. Prices don't include wine, drinks, or tip. Restaurants recommended accept most major credit cards.

SLIGO

Ballincar House – Manager Helen O'Brien will make you feel welcome and well cared for in this gracious, small hotel halfway between Sligo town and the sea at Rosses Point. She is particularly proud of the fish menu, which is based on the day's catch. Rosses Point (phone: 71-45316; fax: 71-44198; telex: 91297). Expensive.

Cromleach – A country house at Castlebaldwin, it has 10 rooms, modern facilities, and caters to nonsmokers. The food is delicious. Ten miles south of Sligo town, well signposted off the N4 (phone: 71-65155; fax: 71-65455). Expensive.

Coopers Hill House – Set on 500 acres in Riverstown, 11 miles south of Sligo, the O'Hara family has lived here since 1774. They offer 6 guestrooms with four-poster or canopied beds and furniture and fittings to match. The food is splendid. Keep an eye out for Cyril, the resident peacock. Open mid-March through October. Reservations essential. On the N4 to Dublin turn left; there is a signpost about 10 miles from Sligo (phone: 71-65108; 800-223-6510 in the US; fax: 71-654566). Moderate.

Reveries – Good food and enchanting views of Sligo Bay draw guests here. Specialties include fresh fish and other dishes creatively prepared with fresh local ingredients. You can spend an entire day attending one of their regular cooking exhibitions. Closed Sundays and Mondays. Dinner only, except at the cooking demonstrations. Reservations advised. Right in the middle of Rosses Point village, just 6 miles north from Sligo town (phone: 71-77371). Moderate.

Sligo Park – A reasonably good modern hotel with 59 comfortable rooms, all with phone, TV set, bath, and shower. It's hidden among trees, surrounded by an expanse of green pasture. Pearse Rd. (phone: 71-60291; fax: 71-69556; telex: 40397). Moderate.

Glencarne House – You might find it worth the 30-mile drive south of Sligo for the absolute charm of this lovely stone farmhouse where Agnes Harrington and her farmer husband Pat make guests feel very welcome. Fresh flowers and log fires are throughout the house, which has 6 rooms, 3 with private bath. Polished antique furnishings make up the decor, and the food is served fresh from their organic farm. 5 miles south of Boyle on the Dublin road, Ardcarne, Carrick-on-Shannon (phone: 79-67013). Inexpensive.

ROSSNOWLAGH

Sand House – Spectacular beachside setting marks this hotel. Of its 40 rooms (all with bath), many overlook the sea. The public rooms are elegantly furnished, and the entire place exudes a feeling of peaceful rest. The dining room is good, and a golf course adjoins the grounds. This is surfing territory, and surfboards are available. (phone: 72-51777; 800-233-6764 in the US; fax: 72-52100). Expensive to moderate.

DONEGAL TOWN

St. Ernan's House – A small, graceful hostelry set on its own tidal island just on the outskirts of Donegal town — and joined to the mainland by a causeway — it offers sea views and tranquillity. All 13 rooms have private bath. St. Ernan's island (phone: 73-21065; 800-223-6510 in the US; fax: 73-22098). Expensive.

GORTAHORK

Arnold's – Run by the same family for three generations, it offers 34 rooms, good food, friendly atmosphere, and good views of Sheep Haven Bay and Horn Head. In the village of Dunfanaghy (phone: 74-36208; fax: 74-36352). Moderate.

McFadden's – If a hotel can ever be described as sociable, this is it. There are 16 rooms with bath. It has a good reputation for food. Main St., Gortahork (phone: 74-35267). Moderate.

Port-na-Blagh – In another fine location on a Port-na-Blagh cliff overlooking Sheep Haven Bay, this is called a welcoming hotel for its friendliness. It has 45 comfortable rooms, most with bath. The seafood is particularly good. Port-na-Blagh (phone: 74-36129). Moderate.

RATHMULLAN

Rathmullan House – Guests come here for the log fires, comfort, good food, views of the hills and the lough, and walks down to the secluded beach. There are 16 rooms and a heated indoor pool. On the shores of Lough Swilly, about 20 miles southeast of Gortahork (phone: 74-58188; fax: 74-58200; 800-233-6510). Expensive to moderate.

Water's Edge – Seafood, steaks, and vegetarian dishes comprise the menu at this wonderful waterfront setting where the food is consistently good. Reservations advised. About 20 miles southeast of Lough Swilly (phone: 74-58182). Moderate.

Italy

Italy has played a prime role in forming Western European culture, but paradoxically, the modern nation of Italy, established in 1870, is still in the process of coming into its own. The dual nature of its history is both a burden and a blessing. As Italy experiences uneven industrial development between its north and south, the country's often-paralyzing bureaucracy hinders widespread economic growth. This factor only accentuates the north-south division, even as the country prepares for the further challenge of the new European Community. Nevertheless, not since the glorious age of Rome, when the city was the core of a world empire, has Italy experienced such peace and prosperity. And not since the Renaissance have its artistic and cultural achievements attained such great heights.

This heritage is one of which the Italians are justly proud. The brightest jewels of the Renaissance still glow in Italy — the Foundling Hospital by Brunelleschi in Florence that revolutionized architectural design; the anatomically accurate portrayal of the human form in works by Leonardo da Vinci; Raphael's lifelike Madonnas; and Michelangelo's monumental Sistine Chapel ceiling in Rome.

This rich heritage is one of the major forces unifying the Italian people. Italians take pride in the national treasure of their cultural legacy. This, their common language, and their religion (97% of all Italians are Roman Catholics) are what Italians share, whether they come from Milan, Rome, or Palermo.

Italy's boot-shaped peninsula covers 116,318 miles, stretching from the mainland of southern Europe 745 miles into the seas of the Mediterranean, with 5,280 miles of coast. The country has a confusing maze of borders — France on the northwest, Switzerland and Austria to the north, Yugoslavia to the northeast, the Ligurian Sea to the northwest, the Tyrrhenian Sea to the west, the Ionian Sea to the southeast, and the Adriatic Sea on the east. This country of coasts and water is strung out on a T-shaped frame of mountains: the highest peaks are in the Alps of the north — Mont Blanc at 15,771 feet and the Matterhorn at 15,205 feet; but along the spine of country run the Apennines, a rocky backbone that goes the entire length of the Peninsula. The climate varies with the topography. Along the seacoast, winters are temperate and summers are hot. In the mountains, summer days are warm, nights cool, and winters cold and snowy.

As the climate varies with topography, so do the economics. The south — rocky, devoted to citrus crops and olive growing — still suffers from underdevelopment, and the region's unemployed youth are easy prey for organized crime, an increasing problem. The north, comprising a vast plain drained by the Po River, is far richer, with great industrial centers, such as Milan, Genoa, and Turin, and agricultural areas devoted to rice, wheat, and especially grapes, which find their way into a variety of fine Italian wines.

Italy is the home of 57.6 million people, 92% of whom live in its cities. Throughout history, Italians have been urban animals, viewing cities as centers of culture and civilization and settling them with great energy and ingenuity. Even agricultural workers tend to live in cities or towns, preferring to travel long distances to the fields rather than live in them. Some 3 million people live in Rome, the capital and Italy's major cultural and historical center. In Rome is Vatican City, an independent enclave in which the pope is sovereign. Other major cities are Florence, Milan, Turin, Venice, Genoa, Naples, and Palermo, Sicily. Ethnic and linguistic minorities comprise less than 5% of Italy's population. Of these, the major groups live in border regions: Slovenes in Friuli-Venezia Giulia, German speakers in Trentino-Alto Adige, and French speakers in Valle d'Aosta. Some inhabitants of Calabria and Sicily speak Greek and Albanian dialects.

Some of these different groups are actually descended from people who inhabited the country during Italy's long and complicated history. Recorded civilization in Italy dates back to around 2000 BC, when the peninsula was settled by fair, blue-eyed Ligurians, ancestors of the Latins. Around the 9th century BC, the Greeks sailed to Italian shores, and Italy became a setting for the myth of Ulysses and other legends. The Greeks settled southern Italy and Sicily during the 8th century BC, establishing colonies of city-states known as Magna Graecia. The Greek civilization thrived in the 6th and 5th centuries BC, declining in the 4th century BC. While the Greeks were colonizing the south, the Etruscans, a highly artistic civilization from Asia Minor, settled central Italy.

In the 3rd century BC, the Romans conquered Italy, subduing and incorporating the Etruscan league of cities, and establishing a great empire from Rome. Julius Caesar reigned during the 1st century BC; his conquest of France — Gaul — made Rome supreme over much of the barbaric as well as the civilized world. Under Caesar, Roman culture flourished, enriched by an infusion of Greek elements. After Caesar's assassination, his nephew Octavian (later known as Augustus) succeeded him and instituted the Pax Romana, 200 years of peace when the Roman Empire extended from Britain to Asia Minor and its wealth, industries, professional institutions, and culture flourished.

At the end of the 2nd century AD, the Bishop of Rome gained supremacy as the head of the new Christian religion. Rome declined in the years following the Pax Romana, and Italy was torn apart by invading groups. It was briefly reunited when Charlemagne was named Holy Roman Emperor in 800, but the ensuing century saw the country disintegrate into conflicting groups seeking control of provincial kingdoms. Italy was ravaged by battles between different city-states until Napoleon came to power in the early 19th century.

Despite this internal strife, Italian civilization and culture were maintained by the development of the monastic movements of the 12th and 13th centuries, which preserved ancient Roman texts of history, literature, and philosophy and developed religious thought. This laid the foundation for the Renaissance in the 15th and 16th centuries. The independent city-states established a delicate balance of power, and rich patrons such as the Medici family of Florence supported the arts. The humanistic secular atmosphere encouraged worldly life and human endeavor. This age spawned some of the greatest artists of Western civilization — Leonardo da Vinci, a genius in many fields, the personification of the Renaissance man (1452–1519); the architect Brunelleschi (1377–1466); Michelangelo (1475–1564); Raphael (1483–1564); and Galileo Galilei (1564–1642).

Napoleon annexed large sections of Italy, including Rome, in the early 19th century. A long tradition of disunity and foreign domination brought about the Risorgimento, the movement for political unity in Italy, that gathered broad support under the popular leader Giuseppe Garibaldi. Italy was finally united under King Victor Emmanuel II in 1870.

The country was ruled as a monarchy and joined the Allies in World War I. Benito Mussolini rose to power during the early 1920s and ushered in one of the darkest periods in Italy's history. Il Duce, a leader of the National Fascist party, promised a vague program of order at home and greater prestige abroad, though what he actually delivered was a totalitarian state controlled by the militia. Mussolini formed an alliance with Hitler and fought against the Allies during World War II. Under his rule, the National Racial Code was implemented, and more than 10,000 Italian Jews were killed in Nazi concentration camps. A small Italian Resistance Movement fought Mussolini and the Nazis, but reprisals took a heavy toll on Italy. Large parts of the country were in ruins, 400,000 people were killed, hundreds of thousands were left homeless, and half of all industrial plants were destroyed, leaving the economy sharply disrupted. Mussolini was captured by partisans in 1945 and executed.

The experience of World War II and fascism deeply scarred Italy. Though the country was declared a republic in 1946, during the postwar era Italy was divided by extreme political differences. Some 40 governments have risen and fallen since the war. The leading parties are the centrist Christian Democrats and the Partito Democratico della Sinistra (PDS), the formerly named Italian Communist Party. Factionalization of Italian politics continues today. The socialists — more akin to the Social Democrats in other countries — have managed to grow progressively as the two other major parties see their strength being whittled away — all owing to the changing, but less radical, face of today's Italian society. None of the parties has managed to gain a clear majority. In the most recent national election the Christian Democrats led by a comfortable margin, and they currently govern in coalition with other centrist and center-left parties.

From the early 1970s to 1982, terrorist acts aimed at political leaders and wealthy industrialists plagued the country, along with strikes and double-digit inflation. Today, political violence has diminished, but Italy still has many problems. In part, these are caused by the staggering socioeconomic discrepancy between the rich industrial north and the poorer, rural south. Up to the past decade, this gap caused great internal migrations from south to north and village to city. The biggest economic problems of the 1990s are widespread unemployment among Italian youth and ongoing inflation, caused by massive government deficits and dependence on foreign energy sources. Though Italy is ranked as the fifth-largest industrial power of the non-Communist world, its economy is still underdeveloped in many respects, and promises of vital institutional reform drag on from one government to the next as the country's debt continues to grow. Structural imbalances, an inefficient administrative system, and political fragmentation have made it difficult to proceed with economic and social reforms.

Family ties are particularly strong in Italy. Although divorce was introduced in 1973, a relatively limited number of Italians so far have made use of it, although separation, seen as a compromise rather than a means to an end, has now firmly taken hold. It is common for offspring to live at home until they marry, and often married couples unable to find affordable housing will remain with one set of parents. Feminism has made some inroads (more in the north than the south), but the number of women who pursue careers is still lower than in most other Western countries. While children are highly valued, economic considerations, birth control availability, and the lack of public family services have led to a declining birth rate. Nevertheless, enduring traditions and widespread frustration with a malfunctioning government have helped maintain the family as the root of Italian society.

Italians, especially in the north, love opera, and all seem to be passionate soccer fans and avid filmgoers, although the cinema has been dealt a blow by television, where a plethora of channels fight for broadcast space. Neorealism in cinema, which has had a profound influence on contemporary film, was developed in Italy. This movement aimed to portray real life in films by setting them in the streets with amateur casts. Luchino Visconti's *Ossessione,* Vittorio de Sica's *Bicycle Thief,* and Roberto Rossellini's *Open City* exemplify this movement. In the 1960s and 1970s, Italian cinema moved away from neorealism. The films of Federico Fellini became increasingly surreal, and Michelangelo Antonioni explored existentialist themes. A younger generation led by Bernardo Bertolucci produced films of social and political comment. The tradition of *cinema d'autore,* films written by one writer-director, continues to bring forward new movie makers.

The area in which Italian differences shine most brightly is food. The concept that most people carry of Italian food is hopelessly limited. Italy is made up of 20 different regions, each with its own distinct cuisine. The best way to enjoy the delights of Italy's regions is to eat your way through them, sticking to regional specialties and experimenting with new dishes rather than going for a known quantity. In Piedmont, for example, Italy's mountainous northwest corner, the cuisine has been deeply influenced by France and Switzerland. Specialties are exquisite white truffles and *grissini,* crisp bread-sticks, as well as the Turin cheese, fontina, that is used in a fondue-like dish called *fonduta.* In late summer and early fall a favorite Piedmont dish is the huge, fresh mushrooms called *porcini;* for dessert have zabaglione, the rich whipped pudding made of egg yolks, sugar, and marsala wine.

Milan, the capital of the Lombardy region, sits on a vast marshy plain north of the Po River better suited to rice and cattle than to wheat and olive trees. Thus rice and butter, rather than pasta and oil, are the basis of Lombard cuisine. Its most famous dishes are *cotoletta alla milanese,* a thin scaloppine of fine Lombardy veal lightly breaded, and *risotto alla milanese* (creamy rice tinted gold by saffron). A favorite *Christmas* dessert is *panettone,* a brioche-like cake stuffed with candied fruit. Another good dessert is a pear with gorgonzola cheese.

Tuscan food centers around finely grilled and spitted meat in such dishes as *bistecca alla fiorentina, capretto* (suckling kid), and *cinghiale* (boar). Rich soups are popular, such as the *zuppa di verdure* (vegetable soup), bean soup with garlic bread, and *acquacotta* (literally, "cooked water," a mixture of bread, broth, pasta, vegetables, eggs, and cheese so thick that it can be eaten with a fork).

In Rome, the food harkens back to ancient times. Dishes such as *pasta e ceci* (chick-peas), salt cod, and the springtime favorite, chicory, have imperial ancestors. The food is not light — oxtail stew, tripe, and fennel-laced salami — but it is dearly loved.

Sicilian cuisine is based on seafood, and tuna, sardines, mullet, octopus, porgy, and salt cod are likely to turn up at any meal. Sicily is the home of cannelloni, however, the wonderful squares of noodles rolled into tubes and filled with ricotta cheese and ground meat that are now popular worldwide. And delicious salads, using much eggplant, are ubiquitous. *Caponata* is a cold salad that incorporates eggplant, onions, olives, celery, and capers; *melanzane alla trapanese* is fried eggplant seasoned with rosemary, tomato purée, and garlic.

More recently, restaurateurs and chefs throughout Italy have sought to enliven their menus by using lighter ingredients and fewer heavy sauces, rediscovering and reinterpreting centuries-old regional recipes. Current Italian cookbooks describe food as "traditional" or "creative," the latter being a modified version of the Italian nouvelle cuisine developed in Milan.

Italians eat their main meal in the afternoon around 1 PM. The meal follows a traditional pattern; however, most menus are à la carte, so you can order as much or as little as you want. The opening course is generally antipasto, a mixed platter of cold hors d'oeuvres — cooked vegetables, salami, and prosciutto — or another appetizer. Soup or pasta follows and you can eat pasta in any of its various forms — macaroni (in soup or on a plate), spaghetti, lasagna, or vegetable soup. The entrée consists of meat — veal, lamb, or chicken are best, or fish in coastal areas — accompanied by a green salad or vegetable. Sauces vary widely but tend toward butter and garlic in the north and tomato bases in the south. Drink Italian wines with the main course. The fruit course follows — peaches, apricots, grapes, wild berries, or figs, depending on the season; the final course is *dolci,* or sweets, anything from rich Italian pastries to *gelato,* ice cream, or *sorbetto,* refreshing ices. Then try some espresso, strong Italian coffee sometimes served with a touch of anisette. Though Italian cuisine is rich in variety, it is usually hearty and tasty. Wherever you are in Italy, it's hard to go wrong.

In the following pages we outline ten driving routes that cover Italy's major areas of interest, from the Alps along the country's northern border with France and Switzerland, the Italian Riviera, to the islands of Sicily and Sardinia in the Tyrrhenian Sea. The routes are by no means comprehensive, but they offer an introduction to the incredible diversity and the awesome beauty of the Italian countryside and the people. The routes are the Lombardy lake region from Milan to Sirmione and the Italian-Swiss border to the Po Valley; Emilia, through the Po Valley and western Apennine Mountains from Milan to Ferrara; Piedmont and Val d'Aosta from Entrèves to Turin through the foot of the Alps; the Italian Riviera; the Dolomites from Bolzano to Trento, passing through the eastern Alps near the Austrian border; rugged, central Tuscany from Florence to Cortona through the Apennine Mountains; Campania on the southwestern coast around Naples and Paestum; Calabria, the southern toe of Italy's boot; and Sicily and Sardinia.

■**Note:** All museums and archaeological sites mentioned below charge admission, unless otherwise indicated.

The Lombardy Lakes (including Lugano, Switzerland)

The northwestern border of Italy and Switzerland — rent by the jagged peaks of the Alps and laced together again by a healing series of spectacular, deep lakes — has been a play area since the Romans conquered Gaul and Cicero set up a summer house on Lake Como. The Lombardy lakes were originally formed by the same glaciers that cut the peaks and valleys of the nearby Alps into such fine relief, but Lombardy itself is a great deal larger than just its lake area. Below this stitching of lakes spread 9,000 square miles of gradually flattening land, flowing around Milan from the foothills of the Alps to the green fertile plains of the Po River valley.

Once the center of Roman Gaul, Lombardy suffered a long and turbulent history, during which it was inexorably caught between the forces of northern and southern Europe. Buffeted between one ruling power and another for centuries, it came under the influence of the German Empire, the Bishops of Milan, and Venice, France, and Austria. During the Middle Ages, Lombardy was controlled by powerful families, often cultured and worldly and almost always unprincipled and ruthless. As a result the Lombard heritage includes as much German and French medieval art and architecture as homegrown bloodshed and mayhem.

The dynasties lost their power to Venice in the 15th century, only 100 years before a French invasion swept Lombardy into the Austrian Hapsburg empire. It joined the new Italian kingdom in 1860. Much of this history is revealed in the accumulation of architecture around the lakes, from Roman ruins to elegant 18th-century villas. The area's warm climate and fertile soil are responsible for the wide variety of luxuriant Mediterranean flowers, cypress trees, and other flora.

Since Milan is the most central Lombard city, easily accessible to major highways, it is here that the 5-day route begins. The trip first takes you north toward Lake Maggiore and magnificent views of the distant Alps, along lakeside roads to Lake Lugano and a brief visit to the Swiss town of Lugano. Heading back toward Italian Lombardy again, the route travels down to Lake

Como, then cuts across the plains and valleys, past several resort towns, in a southeastern direction. On the last segment of the trip, more time is spent in the cities themselves. Bergamo, the 2-tiered city; Brescia, a commercial center; and Garda, site of Italy's largest lake, are some of the stops made on the final portion of the trip.

MILAN: For a detailed report on Milan, and its hotels and restaurants, see *Milan,* THE CITIES.

   En Route from Milan – Pass the industrial suburbs of Lainate and Saronno, where the flat plains around the city begin to give way to mountainous terrain. In the Valley of Olona, surrounded by mountain peaks, lies the town of Castiglione Olona. The art treasures of Olona are the work of the medieval Cardinal Branda Castiglione, who embellished his hometown with Renaissance houses for himself and his relatives and his cathedral with a famous series of frescoes by Renaissance artist Masolino da Panicale. See the Castiglione Mansion and its small church in the main square.

VARESE: This is now a center of Italy's shoe industry, but its pleasant hillside surroundings have made it popular as a summer resort as well. From the gardens of the 18th-century Palazzo Comune (City Hall) you get a fine view of the distant Alps, and at nearby Villa Mirabella is the *Museo Lodovico Poglighi,* a good museum of prehistoric finds from the lake district at Villa Poglighi; open 10 AM to noon and from 2:30 to 5:30 PM; closed Mondays (phone: 332-281590).

LAVENO: Commanding an outstanding view of Lake Maggiore, the second-largest and what some regard as the most beautiful of the Italian lakes, Laveno is now known primarily for its ceramic industry.

From here take a steamer over to the famous lakeside town and resort of Stresa on the Piedmontese side of the lake, 27 miles (43 km) away.

STRESA: On the edge of the Pallanza Bay, Stresa abounds in 18th-century villas and gardens, many of them now luxurious hotels. Among the villas worth noting are Villa Ducale, the Villa Pallavicini, and the Villa Vignola.

   En Route from Stresa – Continue north on the lakeside road to Luino, a small industrial town and resort near the mouth of the Tresa River, which runs into the lake. At Ponte Tresa you are on the tip of Lake Lugano, more than half of which is in Italian-speaking Switzerland. Lake Lugano is wilder than Lake Maggiore, with a more exotic beauty. From Ponte Tresa, itself half Swiss, follow the lakeside frontier to Porto Ceresio for the 70-minute ferry ride to Lugano, Switzerland.

LUGANO (Switzerland): Lugano was ceded to the Swiss by Milan in the early 16th century and has remained so despite Italy's attempts to regain it in 1798. Lugano seems modern until you reach the heart of the Old City, which is entirely Italian. On Via Cattedrale is the 16th-century cathedral, with some excellent early frescoes and a Renaissance tabernacle. In the Old City, right on the lake, is Villa Favorita, which houses one of the finest private art collections in the world, collected by Baron Heinrich Thyssen-Bornemisza, with works from the 16th through the 18th century and some later French Impressionists. (Note: much of the collection is on long-term loan to the *Prado* in Madrid.)

The boat between Lugano and Porto Ceresio stops at Campione d'Italia, a tiny medieval town that, although geographically in Swiss territory, is an enclave answering to Rome. The birthplace of artists and sculptors since the early Middle Ages, it now has one of Italy's four legal casinos.

The road south backtracks to Varese, from which Route 342 leads to Como on beautiful Lake Como.

COMO: Originally settled by the Romans, this ancient city on the southern tip of

Lake Como has for centuries been the home of Italian silk manufacturing. Of greater interest to the visitor is the wealth of its architecture, much of which is clustered around the Piazza del Duomo, where the lovely Pretorian palace known as Il Broletto (1215) stands next to the Palazzo del Comune of the same period and the Duomo, begun in Renaissance Gothic style in 1396 and finished by baroque artists in 1750. Along Via Vittorio Emanuele visit the fine Romanesque Church of San Fedele. And for those in pursuit of things material, *Ratti* (19 Via Cernobbio; phone: 31-233262; open Mondays through Saturdays) is a terrific outlet for designer silk scarves and fabric.

CERNOBBIO: This lakeside resort, right next to Como, is dominated by the magnificent 16th-century *Villa D'Este,* once the home of the powerful Dukes of Ferrara, now a magnificent hotel. The villa stands near a beautiful park on the shores of Lake Como (see *Best en Route*).

    En Route from Cernobbio – Before you leave the western end of Lake Como, you can drive around the lake to Varenna or take a steamer directly to Bellagio, leading to the southbound portion of the route. The extra drive of approximately 48 miles (77 km) around the lake is well worth the trip.

GRAVEDONA: This is the principal town on Lake Como's northern shore and one of the three cities that remained independent from the Middle Ages to the late 16th century. In the town center stands the massive square Palazzo Gallio and the small 12th-century Church of Santa Maria del Tiglio.

BELLAGIO: The town of Bellagio, sometimes called the Pearl of the Lake, sits at the point where the main part of Lake Como intersects with the leg commonly called Lake Lecco. The narrow streets and ancient buildings make for a lovely, relatively easy walk, full of every sort of diversion. There's a bathing beach beside the Villa Serbelloni, in the middle of town, and the lovely gardens at the Villa Melzi are worth a visit — especially for the marvelous view across the lake toward Tremezzo.

LECCO: The western branch of Lake Como is also known as Lake Lecco, named for this industrial town at its southern tip. Lecco is also the scene of the famous novel *I Promessi Sposi,* by Alessandro Manzoni, whose 18th-century villa still stands in the area.

BERGAMO: The 2-tiered city of Bergamo, straddling a hill overlooking the Lombardy plain, is divided into a modern, busy lower center and a silent, medieval upper one. The Lower City, Città Bassa, was almost entirely built in 1924 by Piacentini, the main architect of the fascist period. Visit the Palazzo dell'Accademia Carrara, with a worthwhile collection of Italian furniture of the 16th and 17th centuries. It also has a good collection of Rubens, Van Dyck, and Clouet.

The Upper City, Città Alta, is reached by a funicular that drops its passengers in Piazza Mercato delle Scarpe, inside the medieval walls of the Old City. Bergamo was originally an Etruscan city; then it became a Roman town, a Lombard duchy, and finally part of first the Venetian and then the Austrian dynasties. At the heart of the Città Alta is the Piazza Vecchia amid a breathtaking collection of medieval buildings including the severe 12th-century Palazzo della Ragione and its massive tower. Through the archways of the palace you can see the cathedral square, with the 15th-century Cappella Colleoni, whose façade is a striking composition of colored marbles and delicate carving. The Romanesque basilica Santa Maria Maggiore, to which the chapel is attached, was begun in the 12th century. Also on the square is the small 14th-century baptistry (which was once inside the basilica) and the cathedral, which has a 19th-century façade. Make your way back to Piazza Mercato delle Scarpe, from which Via Rocca leads off to the medieval lookout post, La Rocca, in the middle of a spacious park. From its height there is a glorious view of the surrounding Bergamasque valleys.

    En Route from Bergamo – Cross the industrial Seriana Valley via the tiny sulfur bath resort of Trescore Balneario and the neighboring spa of Gaverina. Stop in the principal resort of Lovere when you reach Lake d'Iseo, one of the smallest and least developed of the Lombard lakes. The road from Lovere to Sornico is the most scenic along the lake's western bank.

BRESCIA: Badly bombed during World War II, this commercial and industrial city on Lake d'Iseo has been largely restored so that its Renaissance and medieval piazza and buildings are visible once again. Its central Piazza della Vittoria is one of the few comparatively modern constructions. Also visit the original Roman center of the city and the Capitoline Temple, which dates to AD 72 and houses examples of Roman art.

From Brescia take Route 45B through Rezzato and Tormini to Lake Garda.

LAKE GARDA: This is the largest and most spectacular of the Italian lakes. Its northern shores are surrounded by wild mountain scenery while the broader southern part of the lake lies in lower, softer green countryside. Most famous of its lakeside resorts is Gardone Riviera, where the proto-fascist poet Gabriele D'Annunzio lived and died at the *Vittoriale degli Italiani,* a curious complex of memorials, gardens, and memorabilia, all collected by D'Annunzio himself and left as a museum for future generations. Closed Mondays (no phone).

BEST EN ROUTE

Endearing, gracious, and elegant hotels and inns are found throughout the Lombardy lake region. Fine restaurants that serve excellent, classic European country cooking are also a hallmark of the area. Expect to pay $250 or more per night night for a double room at those hotels we've categorized as very expensive; from $170 to $220 in those places listed as expensive; between $80 and $150 at hotels in the moderate category; and under $75, inexpensive. Expect to pay $200 or more for a meal for two at expensive restaurants; between $100 and $200 at restaurants in the moderate category; under $75, inexpensive. Prices do not include drinks, wine, or tip.

VARESE

Lago Maggiore – This excellent, small restaurant in a fine old palazzo serves some of the finest and most creative examples of Lombard cuisine — fillet steaks with cream truffles, roast meat, and game. The selection of wines is excellent. Closed Sundays, Mondays for lunch, and 3 weeks in July. Reservations advised. Most major credit cards accepted. 19 Via Carrobbio (phone: 332-231183). Expensive.

Il Sole – One of the best restaurants in all of Lombardy, it offers a beautiful lakeside view, plus a few delightful rooms. It also has its own beach facilities. Closed Mondays and January. Reservations advised. About 14 miles (22 km) north of Varese in Ranco. Piazza Venezia (phone: 332-976507). Expensive.

STRESA (PIEDMONT)

L'Emiliano – The culinary repertoire — filet steaks with truffles, grilled fish, perfectly cooked vegetables, mushrooms in season, and a select choice of wines — is among the most inventive and refined in town. Closed Tuesday evenings, Wednesday lunch, and in January and February. Reservations necessary. 48 Corso Italia (phone: 323-31396). Expensive.

Grand Hôtel et des Iles Borromées – This turreted baroque villa is the quintessential luxury hotel. Owned by the CIGA hotel chain, its well-furnished, spacious rooms all have private baths. It has a private beach on Lake Maggiore, an incomparable view, superb gardens, swimming pool, tennis courts, and restaurant. 67 Lungolago Umberto (phone: 323-30431). Expensive.

Regina Palace – Grand, elegant lakeside hotel with breathtaking gardens, a heated swimming pool, fitness center, tennis, squash, and the *Charleston* restaurant for fine dining. Lungolago, Corsa Umberto (phone: 323-30171). Expensive.

Villa Aminta – Though less extravagant, this recently refurbished hotel has tasteful gardens, a private beach, tennis courts, and a good restaurant. Closed from November through mid-March. 123 Via Nazionale del Sempione (phone: 323-32444). Expensive to moderate.

Du Parc e Villa Pineta – This secluded hotel stands in a lovely garden. Closed October through March. 1 Via Gignous (phone: 323-30335). Inexpensive.

LUGANO (SWITZERLAND)

Bellevue au Lac – A spacious hotel in a garden setting overlooking Lake Lugano and the surrounding mountains, it has a swimming pool, car park, and a good restaurant. Closed from mid-October to mid-March. 10 Riva Caccia (phone: 41-91-543333). Expensive.

Bianchi – A traditional and friendly top-quality restaurant in Old Lugano, recently restored to its grandeur of 200 years ago. Specialties include cold antipasto, veal and fish dishes, and truffles. Closed Sundays and 3 weeks in August. Reservations advised. Major credit cards accepted. 3 Via Pessina (phone: 41-91-228479; fax: 41-91-233868). Expensive.

De la Paix – This hotel has a heated swimming pool, 3 restaurants, and enviable views of the lakes and mountains. Closed in January. 18 Via Cattori (phone: 41-91-542331). Expensive.

Villa Principe Leopoldo – The former residence of royalty, it's now a charming, sophisticated retreat with tennis, gym, sauna, swimming pool, tearoom, piano bar, and restaurant. All 24 spacious suites are elegantly appointed and have views of Lake Lugano. 5 Via Montalbano (phone: 41-91-558855). Expensive.

CERNOBBIO

Villa d'Este – The most elegant retreat in the lake district. Stay in the main building, the 16th-century cardinal's former palace, awash in marble pillars, crystal chandeliers, and winged staircases, or in the more secluded "annex," a 19th-century villa. In either case, guests luxuriate in the midst of acres of park, with superb formal gardens landscaped right to the edge of the lake. The 180 rooms and suites are opulently decorated with period furniture and 19th-century antiques. There are multiple restaurants (the *Grill/Sporting Club* is best), tennis courts, 3 pools (an indoor pool and 2 outdoor, one of which floats in the lake), and facilities for water sports. A new heating system has been installed to offset any chill in the off-season months. Open March through November. 40 Via Regina (phone: 31-511471; fax: 31-512027). Very expensive.

Terzo Crotto – Dine indoors or alfresco at this spot on Lake Como, one of the best places in town for northern cuisine — a wide variety of soups, excellent meat, fresh mushrooms, truffles, wild strawberries, and blueberries in their respective seasons. Also a small hotel. Closed Thursdays and November. Reservations advised. 21 Via Volta (phone: 31-512304). Moderate.

Trattoria del Vapore – Small, informal, and friendly, this is a fine dining spot for the freshest fish or pasta. Closed Tuesdays. Reservations advised. Visa only accepted. 17 Via G. Garibaldi (phone: 31-510308). Moderate.

Albergo Giordino – Though a variety of entrées are available, the varieties of perfect pizza (try more than one) make this place a must for dinner. Open daily. Reservations advised. 22012 Cernobbio (phone: 31-511154). Moderate to inexpensive.

COMACINA ISLAND

Locanda dell'Isola Comacina – On the only sizable island in Lake Como, at the end of a winding, narrow path, this place features a menu that hasn't changed in many years. And why should it, when the feast served up includes "Smuggler's

Trout" (perfectly grilled fish splashed with olive oil), pressed roast chicken, a huge antipasto (the marinated carrots are especially delicious), and a dessert of home-made vanilla ice cream atop fresh orange slices, doused in banana liqueur. Open March through October; closed Tuesdays, except in June and July. Reservations advised. To get here, take a motorized *lucia* from the tiny town of Sala Comacina directly to Comacina Island on Lake Como (phone: 344-55083). Expensive.

COMO

Sant' Anna – Several charming wood panelled rooms offer intimate and delicious dining. The bill of fare lists unpretentious *Nova cucina* — try the fresh lake fish or taglialini with salmon and peppers, and the veal cutlet covered with diced tomato looks almost too good to eat — but not quite. The young waiters couldn't be more helpful. Closed Fridays and Saturday at lunch. Reservations advised. Major credit cards accepted. 1/3 Via Turati (phone: 31-50-52-66). Expensive.

MENAGGIO

Victoria – Delightful Belle Epoque hotel with 50 refurbished rooms, many of which overlook the lake. There's also a garden, swimming pool, and elegant restaurant. Menaggio (phone: 344-32003). Expensive to moderate.

BERGAMO

Taverna del Colleoni – In a 16th-century palace in the old quarter, this place serves traditional dishes with imaginative variations. Polenta (maize pudding) with fried egg and white truffles, fresh mushrooms, truffles, smoked ham, and meat are all delicious. Pasta dishes are light and appetizing. Closed Sundays, Mondays, and August. Reservations advised. 7 Piazza Vecchia (phone: 35-232596). Expensive.

Tino Fontana Excelsior San Marco – This first class hotel has 150 rooms, all with private bath and air conditioning. Ask for a room off the busy main street. There's also an excellent restaurant with a fine view (closed Sundays; most major credit cards accepted). 6 Piazza Repubblica (phone: 35-232132). Expensive.

La Vendemmia – Exquisitely prepared Bergamasque dishes — smoked goose breast, local salami, and cheese fritters — are served in the garden of this 17th-century house, weather permitting. Closed Mondays. Reservations necessary. 17 Via Fara (phone: 35-221141). Expensive.

Da Vittorio – Renowned for its young chef Enrico Cerea, who has prepared exquisite dishes for international heads of state, this spot should not be missed. The fish and meat dishes are deliciously prepared and beautifully presented. Closed Wednes-days and during August. Reservations necessary. Most major credit cards ac-cepted. 21 Viale Giovanni XXIII (phone: 35-218060). Expensive.

Cappello d'Oro e Del Moro – The restaurant at this unpretentious hotel is excellent. Reservations advised. Some major credit cards accepted. 12 Via Papa Giovanni XXIII (phone: 35-232503). Moderate.

Emilia

Stretching from the southern end of the flat and fertile Po Valley and the western Apennine Mountains north of Tuscany, Emilia only came into exis-tence as a region in 1860 with the unification of Italy. The name originates from the Roman road, the Via Emilia, which runs in a straight line from Milan to Rimini on the Adriatic coast; it was built by Aemilius Lepidus to connect the Roman Empire with its newly acquired northern European lands. Since that time, the road has been responsible for much of the region's trade development and was an important communication line throughout the various Roman and medieval conflicts that swept through Emilia's cities and countryside. During World War II, it was used by the Allied forces occupying Italy.

Emilia is a small region, but its culture and customs are the product of 20 centuries of densely packed history. Most of its cities — Parma, Bologna, Ferrara — were medieval and Renaissance duchies or principalities and are replete with architectural memorials of long and eventful histories. But it is a rich area to visit for more than its history, for a good part of its cultural distinction is expressed in its cuisine, the richest cooking in Italy. Bologna is known as Bologna the Fat, and for good reason. Emilia is where tortellini, those delicious pasta pockets filled with meat or cheese, and *tagliatelle,* golden flat egg noodles, are served wrapped in dense *ragù bolognese,* the traditional meat sauce made with pork, beef, chicken livers, vegetables, butter, and cream. Here is where mortadella (the grandfather of American bologna) and salami originated. And here is where Parma, one of Italy's most beautiful cities, inspired delectable Parma ham and world-famous parmesan cheese.

Although pork is the most popular meat in Emilia, veal is deliciously transformed in Bologna to create *lombatini di vitello* — veal chops wrapped in prosciutto with a cream sauce. The major wines of the region are the frothy lambrusco and a fruity red called sangiovese.

It is also a region of geographic contrast — mountainous in the west, where the Apennines shoot down central Italy; flat in the northeast, where a broad expanse of flatlands surrounding the huge Po River cradles some of Italy's best agricultural soil. In the mountains south of Bologna, the Emilian capital, ancient watchtowers still stand atop nearly inaccessible peaks; they were built by medieval warlords to keep constant vigil for enemies approaching in the strife-torn region. These strategic towers were used again by the Allies during the last war.

A logical starting place for a 4-day tour of this region is on the northwestern tip, where the Via Emilia connects Milan to the town of Piacenza. Caught between the Po River and the Apennine foothills, Piacenza is an important trade center. It also offers a first glimpse of the medieval Gothic and Romanesque styles of art and architecture found throughout the cities on this route. Heading south, the other major cities on the route include Parma; Modena, a well-endowed agricultural area as well as an artistic center claiming one of the finest galleries in the country; Bologna, a major hub of commerce and learning, renowned for its ancient university; and Ferrara, a former cultural enclave for artists, writers, and philosophers, now turned toward agriculture and industry.

MILAN: For a detailed report, see *Milan,* THE CITIES.

PIACENZA: The original Roman city is long gone, destroyed by invading barbarian tribes at the dissolution of the Roman Empire, but much of the medieval town that flourished from the 12th century remains, even though Piacenza today is thoroughly modern, caught up in the production of methane gas from the rich fields buried beneath the flatlands of the Po River valley. Wheat, hemp, and corn are traded here in a thriving agricultural market, but the Old City, centered around Piazza Cavalli, captures the essence of medieval Emilia as well as any town in the region. Dominated by two statues of medieval rulers belonging to the Farnese family, which held the duchy of Piacenza from the 16th to the 18th century, the piazza is surrounded by the graceful Gothic Palazzo del Commune, known as Il Gotico, on one side; inside is a newly reopened museum of paintings with works by Peter Paul Rubens and others. On the other side stands the 13th-century Church of San Francesco, at the beginning of Via Venti Settembre, which ends in front of the Duomo, a rather majestic cathedral in Lombard-Romanesque style built between the 12th and 13th centuries.

En Route from Piacenza – Travel on the Via Emilia through pleasant green countryside to Salsomaggiore, the second-largest spa town in Italy. It has saline waters, which are good for rheumatism, as well as the natural sulfur pools in nearby Tabiano.

PARMA: In the middle of the vast plain south of the Po River, Parma is acclaimed for its architectural beauty and gastronomic delights. It abounds with excellent restaurants, so when exploring, stop in almost any section of town for a satisfying meal. Pork meat cuts in Emilia are generally the most famous in Italy; in Parma, the specialty is prosciutto, which, combined with its prized aged parmesan cheese, often garnishes many dishes.

Despite heavy bombing in the last war, Parma still retains much of its splendor as the former capital of the duchy of the Farnese. The old center of the town is Piazza Garibaldi, bounded by the governor's palace, clock tower, and the Town Hall. More spectacular, however, is the Duomo, the cathedral with its baptistry, bishopric, and campanile and their interior frescoes, including the Duomo's cupola painted by Correggio. From the Via del Duomo it is a short walk to Piazza Marconi and the majestic 16th-century Church of Madonna della Steccata, which was damaged by bombs in the last war but admirably restored. Next, visit the *Palazzo della Pilotta,* one of the unfinished buildings begun during the reign of the Farnese dukes. It's now a museum, with exhibitions spanning the city's history from prehistoric times to the late Renaissance as well as collections from ancient Egypt and the Far East. Equally interesting is the *National Gallery,* with rooms devoted to Emilian artists, especially the school established in Parma by Correggio, and Italian artists from other regions from the 14th, 15th, and 16th centuries. Closed Mondays.

MODENA: Originally a Roman colony, this city fell under the control of powerful ducal dynasties in the early Middle Ages, later passing to Austrian dominion. The medieval period proved the strongest influence on Modena's artistic development and today remains the dominant presence in the city's role as a center of art.

For a rich sampling of Gothic and Romanesque design, begin a city tour at the cathedral in the Piazza Grande. Begun in 1099 and finished 3 centuries later, its architecture is mainly early Gothic; inside, frescoes and statues date from the 15th century. Outside the cathedral, notice the tall, graceful Lombard bell tower known as the Ghirlandina, the city's best-known monument. Going down the Via Emilia, be sure to stop at the *Palazzo dei Musei,* which houses one of Italy's finest art galleries. Closed Mondays (no phone).

BOLOGNA: You would not be a hopeless romantic to see something of the fate of all Italy in the varying fortunes of this city. Built by the Etruscans (who called it Felsina), it was conquered by the Gauls, invaded by the Romans, sacked by northern tribes during the dissolution of the Roman Empire, and finally, in the 12th century, plunged into the interminable internecine warfare of the Guelphs and Ghibillines, who represented no ideology beyond their allegiance to various personalities and vague identification with pro- and antipapal forces. It was not until the Guelphs prevailed in the middle of the 13th century that Bologna came to full flower and the form of the city as it exists today was established — red slate roofs, long arcades, distinctive elliptical domes. During this period the university — the oldest in Europe, founded in

1076 — flourished, and in the 16th century, when the city became associated with several ruling families (of whom the Bentivoglio were the most famous), the city became a center of art, literature, and learning. Today, Bologna is a major industrial town that crosses Italy from Tuscany through Emilia.

In the center of town is the traffic-free Piazza Maggiore, where three Gothic structures stand within a few steps of one another. The Palazzo Comunale is the most complicated, a group of palaces incorporated into one beautifully proportioned complex. It houses a small but fine municipal art collection of works by some of the finest Renaissance and 18th-century artists. A similar architectural plan, involving seven separate churches of different periods joined together, exists at the church of Santo Stefano complex. This consists of the 11th-century Church of the Crucifix, the octagonal Church of the Holy Sepulcher (where St. Petronius is buried), and the Church of St. Peter and St. Paul. Several other small chapels and churches are housed in this medieval complex as well.

FERRARA: To reach this city, you finally leave the Via Emilia at the Bologna highway junction and head north. Autostrada A15 takes you to new Emilian territory — one of very green countryside dotted with vines and trees. Ferrara itself sits on drained and filled-in marshland. It is now an agricultural and industrial center that once flourished as a commercial and cultural stronghold during the Renaissance. As an independent duchy under the Dukes of Este and their rich courts, it was a haven for some of the most highly talented artists, philosophers, humanists, chefs, and writers of the age.

When you arrive, first visit the Castello Estense, a fortress with massive corner towers and a surrounding moat built in the 14th and 15th centuries. Many of the inside rooms are open to the public — some with majestic interiors and frescoed ceilings. The castle chapel and dungeons are open as well (closed Mondays; no phone) . Nearby is the 12th-century Romanesque-Gothic cathedral and marble bell tower facing the 13th-century Palazzo Comunale, which had to be restored in 1924. Along Via Scandiana visit the 14th-century *Palazzo Schifanoia,* which the fabled dukes used for their many amusements. Now a museum, its interior walls have frescoes with scenes from the life of Duke Borso D'Este (open daily; 532-64178). A short distance away, in the Via Settembre, stands the unfinished but splendid Renaissance *Palazzo di Ludovico il Moro,* now an archaeological museum full of Etruscan and Roman treasures. Closed Mondays (phone: 532-66299).

BEST EN ROUTE

In Emilia you'll find some pleasant if not outstanding hotels and some truly splendid restaurants. Expect to pay $250 or more per night for a double room at those hotels categorized as very expensive; between $150 and $250 at hotels in the expensive category; between $80 and $150 for moderate category; under $80, inexpensive. Expect to pay $100 or more for a meal for two at those restaurants we've classified as expensive; between $60 and $100 at restaurants in the moderate category; under $60, inexpensive. Prices include wine but not drinks or tip.

PARMA

Palace Hotel Maria Luigia – In the town's historic center, this hotel has 90 rooms, elegantly furnished with all modern conveniences. The very good *Maxim's* restaurant is here — but it's no relation to the one in Paris (closed Sundays and in August). Private parking available. 140 Viale Mentana (phone: 521-281032). Expensive.

Park Hotel Stendhal and Ristorante La Pilotta – This elegant modern hotel in an old piazza stands in a small square in the old quarter. Its good and reliable restaurant is closed during August and on Sundays. Reservations advised. 3 Via Bodoni (phone: 521-208057). Expensive.

Park Hotel Toscanini and Ristorante al Torrente – Somewhat less fancy, and in the center of town, this hotel has a very good restaurant (closed Mondays and August). 4 Viale Toscanini (phone: 521-289141). Expensive.

Angiol d'Or – Here you'll find excellent beef and veal dishes. Closed Mondays for lunch and Sundays. Reservations advised. Most major credit cards accepted. 1 Via Scutellari (phone: 521-282632). Moderate.

La Filoma – The decor is not as lavish as that of the *Angiol d'Or,* but the stuffed veal and *tortelli alla parmigiana* make up for it. Closed Sundays and July 20 to August 20. Reservations advised. Most major credit cards accepted. 15 Via Marzo XX (phone: 521-234269). Moderate to inexpensive.

MODENA

Fini – Roast and mixed boiled meat is brought to your table and carved to your liking at this excellent, elegant restaurant owned by the Fini family, whose food company is one of the region's major producers of salami and sausage. Restaurant closed Mondays, Tuesdays, and August. Reservations advised. Most major credit cards accepted. Largo San Francesco (phone: 59-214250). Expensive.

Oreste – Considerably less ornate than the *Fini,* it serves terrific pasta and poultry. Closed on Wednesdays, Sunday nights, and July.' Reservations advised. Most major credit cards accepted. 31 Piazza Roma (phone: 59-243324). Expensive to moderate.

Bianca – This simple and homey trattoria serves delicious Modenese dishes, and is extremely popular — mainly because Bianca herself has been running its kitchen for over 35 years. Summer dining is in the garden. Closed August and for lunch Saturdays and Sundays. Reservations advised. Most major credit cards accepted. 24 Via Spaccini (phone: 59-311524). Moderate to inexpensive.

BOLOGNA

Baglioni – This 17th-century palace-turned-hotel, the grande dame of Bologna, is exquisitely decorated and offers impeccable service and the superb *I Carracci* restaurant (closed Sundays), one of the city's finest. Reservations advised. Most major credit cards accepted. 8 Via Indipendenza (phone: 51-225445). Very expensive.

Grassilli – *Risotto alla chef* and filet steaks with bacon and champagne are the specialties at this small, low-key eatery. Closed Sunday evenings, Wednesdays, July 15 to August 15, and the last week of December. Reservations advised. Most major credit cards accepted. 3 Via del Luzzo (phone: 51-222961). Expensive.

Al Pappagallo – Housed in a 700-year-old building, this well-known, traditional establishment is known for its filet steaks cooked in flaky pastry. Closed Sunday evenings, Mondays, and the first 2 weeks in August. Reservations advised. Most major credit cards accepted. 3 Piazza Mercanzia (phone: 51-232807). Expensive.

FERRARA

Astra – A centrally located hotel with first class accommodations; 82 rooms and a good restaurant (closed Wednesdays and August). 55 Viale Cavour (phone: 532-206088 or 532-47002). Expensive to moderate.

Ripagrande – In a Renaissance palazzo, this elegant hotel is decorated in a striking blend of antique and modern; the rooms on the upper levels have a lovely view. There is a good bar and restaurant with summer dining in the charming courtyard. Restaurant closed Mondays and in August. 21 Via Ripagrande (phone 532-765250; fax: 532-764377). Expensive to moderate.

Buca San Domenico – The pizza here is the best in town, but there are also many other good dishes. Closed Thursdays and July. Reservations unnecessary. No credit cards accepted. 22 Piazza Sacrati (phone: 532-20008). Moderate.

Grotta Azzurra – A popular downtown place specializing in northern Italian cuisine. Closed Thursdays, the first 2 weeks of January, and July. Reservations advised. Most major credit cards accepted. 43 Piazza Sacrati (phone: 532-37320). Moderate.

La Provvidenza – A rustic atmosphere and lovely garden provide a perfect setting in which to enjoy mountains of fresh pasta (including the classic pumpkin-stuffed ravioli, *capellacci di zucca*), grilled meat, and delicious desserts. Closed Mondays and July. Reservations advised. Most major credit cards accepted. 92 Corso Ercole D'Este (phone: 532-205187). Moderate.

Europa – On the main street, this 46-room hostelry set in a Renaissance palazzo has a somewhat worn, but authentic, charm and a secluded garden. Parking area, too. 49 Corso Giovecca (phone: 532-33460). Moderate to inexpensive.

Vecchia Chitarra – This unpretentious place serves solid Ferrarese cooking. Closed Mondays and Tuesdays. Reservations unnecessary. 13 Via Ravenna (phone: 532-62204). Moderate to inexpensive.

Ferrara – The hotel's excellent location provides easy access to the city's attractions. 4 Piazza Repubblica (phone: 532-33015). Inexpensive.

Piedmont and the Val d'Aosta Region

Piedmont, the northwesternmost region of Italy is one of the shortest routes on our tour of the country. As its name implies, it lies mostly at the foot of the Alps, which surround it on three sides, and borders on France and Switzerland. Its eastern portion is within the outer limits of the great Po River valley.

This route also includes the adjacent region of Val d'Aosta — Italy's smallest, least populated area — formed by valleys surrounded by the high peaks of Mont Blanc, the Matterhorn, and Mt. Rosa in the north and Gran Paradiso in the south. One of Italy's semi-autonomous regions, stretching from Courmayeur to Pont St. Martin, it consists of largely French-speaking mountain villages closely bound by mountain traditions and customs. The mountains surrounding Val d'Aosta are interspersed with medieval castles and a smart set of resorts, many open year-round for skiing.

A tour of both regions begins at Entrèves-Courmayeur, where a modern tunnel connects France and Italy. It continues south through Courmayeur proper and other Val d'Aosta resorts until it enters Piedmont territory. The final portion of the trip is spent in Turin, the capital of Piedmont and an industrial and cultural center.

Piedmont, with access to France, played an important role in Rome's control of its empire, and there are important ruins from the Imperial Age at Aosta (once known as "the Rome of the Alps"), Susa, and Turin. But its richest period was under the Dukes of Savoy, from the 16th through the 19th century. The House of Savoy filled Turin with Renaissance, baroque, and rococo palaces and the countryside with castles and hunting lodges such as

Stupinigi, now a museum of decorative arts (at Ville Reale), and sanctuaries such as La Superga. In the 19th century, Piedmont was the moving force behind the unification of Italy under the House of Savoy.

In 1861 Turin became the capital of Italy and remained so until 1865, when the entire area turned from politics to industrial and resort operations. Today the Turin area has become one of the chief industrial zones of the country, supported by Fiat, Olivetti, and other major corporations, while the mountain areas, particularly the Val d'Aosta, have developed into prosperous resorts for both winter and summer sports.

From Roman times, Val d'Aosta's strategic position — guarding one of the main approaches to Italy from northern Europe — has been its source of power. Hannibal is known to have crossed the Alps here in the 3rd century BC (with elephants in tow), and in 1800 Napoleon I led his army over the Great St. Bernard Pass. Today a tunnel under the same pass assures year-round entry from Switzerland to Italy and the 15 mile (24 km) tunnel under the Mont Blanc range carries very heavy international traffic from France. Both tunnels lead to Aosta, from which autostrada A5 runs to the north Italian plain. There are several other transalpine passes through this region that are open only in summer, including Little St. Bernard, the Mont Cenis, and Mont Genèvre from France, and the Simplon from Switzerland.

ENTRÈVES: The first in a series of mountain resorts that mark the Piedmont–Val d'Aosta range, Entrèves, which nestles alongside Courmayeur, making the two hardly distinguishable, best serves the area as a base of operations.

You can travel by cable car from Entrèves across four different sections of the Mont Blanc range (the highest in Western Europe) to Chamonix in France. At its summit of 15,771 feet above sea level, the Mont Blancs open to a sensational panorama of peaks and glaciers — but go only in good weather, otherwise the view is badly obstructed.

Another scenic excursion can be made to the head of the Val Ferret as far as Arnouva. If you are really energetic, hike the mule track to the Pre' de Bar, about a half mile (1 km), an Alpine rise 6,767 feet above sea level with superb views of the surrounding peaks.

COURMAYEUR: This village in the upper Dora Baltea Valley, 3 miles (5 km) from Entrèves, is the largest resort in the Val d'Aosta. A fashionable summer resort, it's also popular for winter skiing, boasting some of the country's finest chair lifts, cable cars and tows, plenty of tearooms, nightclubs, discotheques, and all the usual resort paraphernalia.

AOSTA: The regional capital of Val d'Aosta and the Italian connection for the Great St. Bernard Pass road into Switzerland, Aosta is an ancient town, founded by the Romans in 25 BC. It combines interesting Roman remains (the Arch of Augustus, the Pretorian Gate, sections of the Roman walls and theater), with evidence of a prosperous medieval society. The latter gave rise to the Church of Sant' Orso, founded in the 10th century. Its cloister, cathedral, and apse towers were built over a period of three centuries. Aosta is also the starting point for the Gran Paradiso National Park, a nature preserve comprising the Cogne and Valsavarenche valleys.

BREUIL-CERVINIA: Once a summer pasture for cattle from nearby villages, Cervinia is now a completely modern center, with 40 hotels, 28 chair lifts, cable cars and tows, skating rinks, bobsled runs, bowling alleys, swimming pools, and saunas. Towering to the north is the Matterhorn (Il Cervino in Italian) and to the west the Jumeax precipices, making it one of the most beautifully situated resorts in the Val d'Aosta. It is a year-round resort, with winter skiing on the Plateau Rosàglacier, summer hiking excursions into near and far mountains (including the Matterhorn and Preithorn), and spectacular views anytime.

The town, however, is not inexpensive, but within the reasonable to expensive price range, you'll find a wide selection of hotels.

AYAS-CHAMPOLUC: At the foot of the Preithorn and the western peaks of the Monte Rosa massif, this town is a popular winter sports resort, but it's even more pleasant and quiet in the summer. Hotels here are unpretentious and set amid refreshing pine forests or atop mountain slopes.

GRESSONEY VALLEY: Within this valley are a number of year-round resorts, the main ones being Gressoney St. Jean and Gressoney La Trinité. Either one can serve as a starting point for a climb up Monte Rosa, at 15,203 feet the second highest peak in the Alps.

En Route from Gressoney Valley – Beyond Pont St. Martin, the two main southbound highways, A5 and SS26, leave the mountain region of the Val d'Aosta and enter Piedmont proper, marked by the more level area of the north Italian plain. The SS26 highway runs to Chivasso, where it forms a junction with SS11 for Turin. This route is not advisable since it runs through the northern suburbs of Turin, generally congested with very heavy traffic. Instead, take A5, which leads to the city's north end.

TURIN (TORINO): The capital of the Piedmont region, Turin is one of the great industrial centers of Italy, with a population of 1.2 million. Founded by the Romans, it didn't acquire prominence until the 16th century, when the reigning Dukes of Savoy filled Turin with fine baroque palaces and churches. These now stand in the old section of town, the heart of which is the Piazza Castello, a handsome, arcaded square with the former Royal Palace at the north end and the Palazzo Madama on the east. Parts of the Palazzo Madama are Roman, parts medieval, though the elegant façade on the piazza is a baroque addition of the 18th century. On the northeast side of the piazza is the *Teatro Regio* (phone: 11-88151), the opera house, also with a baroque façade but with an ultramodern interior, the product of a 1973 restoration. One of the liveliest city streets is the arcaded Via Roma, which leads to the Piazza San Carlo, a cultural and commercial haven that contains the great *Egyptian Museum* (open daily; phone: 11-544091 or 11-513157) and the *Galleria Sabauda (open daily; 11-547440),* both in the baroque *Palace of the Academy of Sciences.*

Near the riverbanks in the east is the most peculiar edifice, which has become the emblem of the city. Known as Mole Antonelliana, it was originally a synagogue built in 1863. Its tower ends in a spire 548 feet high and now serves as a lookout point.

Farther east is the Po River, lined with handsome and fashionable residential buildings. Upstream is Valentine Park, laid out in 1830 with an imitation medieval castle and an exhibition village. The park's modern exhibition center is the site of the annual *Automobile Show;* farther upstream is the *Automobile Museum* (40 Corso Unità d' Italia; closed Mondays and Tuesdays in winter; Mondays in summer; phone: 11-677666), with a good collection of antique cars. Car buffs will also want to visit the huge auto factory *Il Lingotto,* which was recently converted by the Fiat Foundation into an interesting exhibition complex, Fiat Lingotto (only open during the annual exhibition in the spring; 294 Via Nizza, Turin; phone: 11-69391). On the city's west side is the *Gallery of Modern Art* (Via Magenta; phone: 11-6961131), well worth a stop.

Since the traffic problem in Turin is particularly bad and parking is a great problem, it is best to tour the city on foot. Also, it's advisable to book rooms in hotels that have garages or reserved parking lots. But beware: Turin fairly sprawls, and getting around can be confusing and tiring. Arm yourself with a bus map and tickets.

Downtown Turin and its green suburbs offer some of Italy's finest dining spots, second only to the Emilia-Romagna region in quality and creativity. For a gastronomically rewarding excursion on the outskirts of Turin, drive to Alba, a small town in the hilly country known as Le Langhe, the center of one of the great wine producing regions of Italy.

Since Turin is at the center of a network of highways leading in all directions, it's a convenient starting point for trips throughout Italy and to France. Main roads lead to the Riviera, Genoa, Florence, Rome, Milan, and the Italian lakes.

BEST EN ROUTE

Accommodations in the Piedmont and Val d'Aosta range from elegant urban and resort establishments to rustic and Alpine spots. Expect to pay $300 or more per night for a double room at those hotels classified as expensive; between $120 and $150 for a double room at hotels in the moderate category; under $100, inexpensive. Resort prices can increase by 30% in the ski season. Expect to pay $200 or more for a meal for two at those restaurants categorized as expensive; between $100 and $200 in the moderate category; under $60, inexpensive. Prices do not include drinks, wine, or tip.

ENTRÈVES-COURMAYEUR

La Clotze – This place serves some of the best Piedmontese cooking around; it also has a fine view of Mont Blanc. Closed Wednesdays and from mid-June to mid-July. Reservations advised. Most major credit cards accepted. About 4 miles (6 km) from Entrèves on the Ferret road at Plampincieux (phone: 165-89928). Moderate.

Maison de Filippo – A charming, rustic village restaurant, this is a good place for hearty, filling fare. Closed Tuesdays, May, and November. Reservations unnecessary. Most major credit cards accepted (phone: 165-89968). Moderate.

Pilier d'Angle – This modest, 12-room hotel (an additional 8 rooms are available nearby) in the middle of the village has a pleasant garden and restaurant. Rooms include half board — breakfast and dinner. Open December through March. Most major credit cards accepted (phone: 165-89129). Moderate to inexpensive.

Portud – Most of the 36 rooms have private baths. Although the view isn't quite as spectacular as that at the *Val Veny* (below), it is quite pretty. An additional 25 rooms are available nearby. Open summers only. At Portud, 4 miles (6 km) on the Val Veny road (phone: 165-89960). Moderate to inexpensive.

Astoria – Reasonably priced and centrally located, this hotel has 33 rooms, a garden, a restaurant, and a garage. Closed mid-September to mid-December, May through June. A la Palud N (phone: 165-89910). Inexpensive.

Val Veny – Beyond the town limits, with a dazzling view of Mont Blanc, this 20-room hotel is open only in the summer. Only 5 of the rooms have private baths. There is a garage. About 2½ miles (4 km) from Entrèves on the Val Veny road, Plan Ponquet (phone: 165-89904). Inexpensive.

COURMAYEUR

Palace Bron – Overlooking the village, it has striking surroundings that help to compensate for its relatively isolated setting (though it does provide transport to and from cable car stations). There are 27 rooms, many with views of the lovely garden and grounds, and a restaurant. Closed October to mid-December, and May through June. 37 Via Plan Gorret (phone: 165-842545). Expensive.

Royal e Golf – Facilities at this classy 80-room hostelry include a heated swimming pool, garden, and an excellent restaurant (dinner only, closed Mondays; most major credit cards accepted). The hotel is closed in September. In the center of town, at 83 Via Roma (phone: 165-843621). Expensive.

Cadrant Solaire – These former huge, old stables have been converted into an eatery providing a genuine country feel. The food is a happy marriage of French cuisine and Italian traditions. Excellent for lunch. Open daily in August; closed Mondays the rest of the year. Reservations advised. Most major credit cards accepted. 122 Via Roma (phone: 165-844609). Expensive to moderate.

K2 – Although it's named after the second-highest mountain peak in the world (climbed in the 1950s by a Courmayeur citizen), this down-to-earth restaurant on the road to Mont Blanc serves well-prepared dishes, including hearty soups and game, as well as a variety of salamis and cheeses. Closed Mondays, May, June, and November. Reservations unnecessary. Villair (phone: 165-842475). Moderate.

Vieux Pommier – In the center of town, this restaurant serves good regional French and Italian fare. Closed during October and on Mondays. Reservations unnecessary. Most major credit cards accepted. 25 Piazzale Monte Bianco (phone: 165-842281). Moderate.

Cresta et Duc – Comfortable, with 39 rooms, it's open from December through April and from June through September. 7 Via Circonvallazione (phone: 165-842585). Moderate to inexpensive.

AOSTA

Cavallo Bianco – This former carriage house in the middle of town combines to perfection the rustic and the refined. Try the game (quail or squab) or the filet of beef with red wine. Closed Sunday evenings, Monday lunches, and mid-June through mid-July. Reservations necessary. Most major credit cards accepted. 15 Via Aubert (phone: 165-362214). Expensive.

Valle d'Aosta – This modern, 100-room hotel has lovely gardens and a garage. Its restaurant, *Grill le Foyer,* is closed Tuesdays and November. Near the autostrada exit at 146 Corso Ivrea (phone: 165-41845). Expensive to moderate.

Rayon de Soleil – A comfortable, 39-room hotel on a broad avenue in the center of town. Its restaurant is closed on Fridays. Viale Gran San Bernardo, Località Saraillon (phone: 165-362247). Moderate to inexpensive.

BREUIL-CERVINIA

Cristallo – In addition to 85 well-appointed rooms, there are tennis courts, a covered swimming pool, and a garage. Closed September through November and May through June. In the center of town (phone: 166-948121). Expensive.

Neiges D'Antan – An excellent eatery at the entrance to town. The menu includes delicious fondues. Closed Mondays and July. Reservations unnecessary. Most major credit cards accepted. Frazione Cret. Perreres (phone: 166-948775). Expensive to moderate.

Residence Alto Cielo – This modern 35-room hotel has both indoor and outdoor swimming pools, tennis courts, and a garage. In the center of town (phone: 166-948759). Expensive to moderate.

Grotta – A good dining spot in the center of town. Closed Thursdays. Reservations unnecessary. Most major credit cards accepted. Contrada Montabel (phone: 166-949492). Moderate.

Pavia – Good, plentiful fare served in a friendly environment. Closed Thursdays, mid-May through mid-July, and September 15 through November. Reservations unnecessary. No credit cards accepted. In the village (phone: 166-949010). Moderate.

Chalet Valdotain – Set amid quiet countryside, with a good view of Lac Bleu, this unpretentious 35-room hotel is closed in May and November. About 1 mile (1.6 km) from town at Lac Bleu (phone: 166-949428). Moderate to inexpensive.

AYAS-CHAMPOLUC

Anna Maria – In a pine forest, this 20-room charmer is open *Christmas* through mid-April and mid-June through August. Full board is available. (phone: 125-307128). Moderate to inexpensive.

Genzianella – Splendidly situated in a mountain valley on the banks of a clear, well-stocked stream, this 20-room hotel offers simple accommodations. Closed in October. Two miles (3 km) from Champoluc. St. Jacques (phone: 125-307156). Inexpensive.

TURIN (TORINO)

All hotels listed have parking facilities or garages.

Del Cambio – A historical restaurant with classic Victorian design, its cuisine matches the ambience. The house specialties are fondue with truffles, pot roast in barolo, and mixed boiled meat. Closed Sundays and August. Reservations necessary. Most major credit cards accepted. 2 Piazza Carignano (phone: 1-546690). Expensive.

Jolly Ambasciatori – The largest hotel in town, it has 197 air conditioned rooms and a restaurant. Near the train station and airport at 104 Corso Vittorio Emanuele (phone: 1-5742). Expensive.

Jolly Hotel Principi di Piemonte – One of the leading hotels in town, its 105 rooms have air conditioning and it has a good restaurant. 15 Via Gobetti (phone: 1-519693). Expensive.

Sitea Grand – Excellent service, comfortable rooms, and a central location. 35 Via Carlo Alberto (phone: 1-5570171). Expensive.

Turin Palace – Kings, queens, and pop stars stay in this century-old, recently renovated hostelry. Continental breakfast is included with the price of one of its 125 rooms, and the restaurant is excellent. Next to the railway station, at 8 Via Sacchi (phone: 1-515511). Expensive.

Villa Sassi-El Toulà – Set in an 18th-century villa with a large garden, this luxurious, fashionable restaurant also has 12 rooms with private bath for overnight stays. Restaurant closed during August, Sunday evenings, and Mondays. Reservations necessary. Across the Po River, 47 Via Traforo del Pino (phone: 1-890556). Expensive.

Alexandra – The best thing about this modern, 48-room hotel is its site on the Dora River. 14 Lungodora Napoli (phone: 1-858327). Expensive to moderate.

Al Gatto Nero – The specialties are Florentine steaks, grilled fish, and meat. There is an excellent wine cellar. Closed Sundays and August. Reservations necessary. Most major credit cards accepted. 14 Corso Filippo Turati (phone: 1-590414). Expensive to moderate.

Vecchia Lanterna – The best in town for classic Piedmontese food — risotto with barolo, *agnolotti* (a kind of pasta) stuffed with duck, and saddle of venison. There's a fine wine selection. Closed Saturdays for lunch, Sundays, and August. Reservations necessary. Most major credit cards accepted. 21 Corso Re Umberto (phone: 1-537047). Expensive to moderate.

Montecarlo – The mixed menu here offers classic Italian dishes, superb wild mushrooms, and nouvelle cuisine concoctions such as duck with blueberries. Desserts are delicious and the wine list select. Closed Saturday lunchtime, Sundays, and July 15 to August 18. Reservations advised. Most major credit cards accepted. 37 Via San Francesco da Paola (phone: 1-830815). Moderate.

President – Centrally located, this 72-room hotel has a lovely terrace and enclosed garden. Service is courteous, and the atmosphere is pleasantly friendly. 67 Via Antonia Cecchi (phone: 1-859555). Moderate.

Victoria – Recently restored, this 75-room hostelry combines Art Nouveau decor with modern comforts. It's conveniently located on a quiet downtown street. 4 Via Costa (phone: 1-553710). Moderate.

Tre Galline – A classic Piedmontese trattoria in the city's historic quarter, it enjoys a solid reputation. Closed Sundays, Mondays, and August. Reservations advised.

No credit cards accepted. 37 Via Bellezia (phone: 1-546833). Moderate to inexpensive.

Il Blu – A large, lively place, with quick service and a good selection of salads as well as grilled meat and locally produced sausages. Closed Sundays and August. Reservations unnecessary. Most major credit cards accepted. 15 Corso Siccardi (phone: 1-545550). Inexpensive.

The Italian Riviera

The Italian Riviera stretches in an arc across the northwestern part of the Mediterranean coast of Italy, bordered by France on the west and Tuscany on the east; its apex is just west of Genoa. The Riviera is traversed by two main roads: the Via Aurelia and the autostrada, both running an average distance of 164 miles (262 km). The autostrada generally runs a few miles inland from the coast, with exits for the most important towns. Since the coast is mountainous and generally very steep, the views are often spectacular, although sometimes interrupted by tunnels. In fact, take caution when driving in high winds along roads that pass over gulleys, especially when issuing from tunnels. The Via Aurelia runs entirely along the shoreline, passing straight through coastal towns and villages. Although picturesque in spots, the road is narrow and twisting and the traffic usually heavy. The best plan is to take the autostrada, exiting only at the places you wish to visit.

The warm climate, clear air, and scenic mountain backdrop of the Italian Riviera have made it one of Europe's leading resorts. It is wise, therefore — and during the high summer season essential — to make hotel reservations well in advance. The best seasons for the Riviera are spring (March through June), autumn (mid-September through October), and possibly *Christmas* week (although it is too cold for swimming). July and August are best avoided because of the crowds, noise, and heavy traffic. Each town has a tourist information office, generally called Azienda di Turismo or Pro Loco, that can provide detailed information on hotels, restaurants, sites, and activities.

There are two border crossing points from France. The autostrada is reached from Monte Carlo or Menton (an extension from Nice was under construction at press time, but the date of completion was unknown), with the actual border in the middle of a tunnel. Passport and customs control is on the Italian side of the tunnel. The French shore road runs into the Italian Via Aurelia at Ponte San Ludovico, just outside Menton. Border formalities for tourists are usually perfunctory, but on weekends and during the high season lines can be long. If you travel on the shore road, stop directly after the border crossing to visit the Balzi Rossi caves, where traces of prehistoric human habitation have been discovered. Also explore the Hanbury Gardens of La Mortola, one of the most famous botanical gardens in Europe. From here you can join the autostrada at the Ventimiglia exit and either stop in the town — set, in part, on a hill with narrow streets and Roman remains — or continue directly to Bordighera.

BORDIGHERA: This is one of the older resort towns on the Riviera, patronized in the late 19th century by the English and by various European royalty. The Italian Riviera was settled not by Latins but by Ligurians, a fair northern race, and like many Ligurian towns, Bordighera consists of an older center on a hill with a newer section along the shore. Between the two are villas, hotels, and beautiful gardens centered along the old Roman road. Bordighera is famed for its palm trees and has held a monopoly for the supply of palms to the Vatican for *Palm Sunday* since 1586.

Many of the large hotels in town, which in the past catered to dowager duchesses and retired Indian major generals, are now closed or were turned into apartment houses, but a few still exist in their original form. Bordighera has 64 hotels, so there is considerable choice.

SAN REMO: This is the largest resort on the Riviera, with a resident population of over 60,000 that is at least quintupled in the summer. It is a noisy, overcrowded, and overbuilt town whose major attraction is the *Municipal Casinò* (Casinò Municipale, 18 Corso Inglesi), where you can win a fortune or (more likely) lose your shirt at roulette, baccarat, and other games of chance. You also can get a very fine (but expensive) dinner in the casino restaurant. There are dozens of restaurants, pizzerias, and snack bars in town; for recreation try sailing, water skiing, shopping, and golf; the 18-hole *San Remo* course (phone: 184-67093) can easily be reached by cable car.

Several excursions can be made from San Remo. The best is to Monte Bignone, which offers a superb view over the coast and a nearby pine forest. It can be reached by either road or cable car. Another worthwhile trip is to the artists' colony at Bussana Vecchia, an old town destroyed by an earthquake in 1887 and abandoned until the 1950s, when it was taken over by a group of artists who settled among the ruins.

En Route from San Remo – Beyond San Remo, for the next 30 miles (48 km) or so, the coast isn't particularly interesting, and it is a good section to cover on the autostrada until you reach the Andorra exit and there rejoin the coastal road, following the signs for Laigueglia and Alassio. (There is a bad section of road around Cape Mele with alternating one-way traffic.)

LAIGUEGLIA: This small resort at the southern end of the Bay of Alassio has a good beach and several hotels. A picturesque old town, it also has many fine old houses and a large baroque church.

ALASSIO: This is one of the oldest resort towns on the Riviera and, despite a good number of unaesthetic modern buildings, it is still quite attractive, with a fine sandy beach over 1½ miles long. The Old Town along the beach consists of one narrow street (now a pedestrian zone) with shops, taverns, restaurants, and cafés. The town hills rise steeply into the villa district, which has many gardens laid out by the original winter residents, mostly English. At Garlenda (11 miles/18 km distant) is the *Garlenda Golf Club* (phone: 182-580012) with an excellent 18-hole course, a country club, and bungalows for rent. Good skiing is available at Monesi, about 31 miles (50 km) away, making Alassio a year-round resort. The high season, though, is from April to the end of September.

Alassio is an excellent base from which to explore the churches and ancient monuments of nearby villages. Stop at Moglio, Vegliasco, and Testico, all within a distance of 12 miles (19 km).

ALBENGA: Once an important Roman port, Albenga is now a busy market town for the produce of the hinterland (fruit, particularly peaches, and early vegetables). However, testaments to its interesting history, such as the 5th-century baptistry and fine tower houses, abound. Visit the *Roman Naval Museum,* with the remains of a Roman ship sunk in Albengan waters in the 1st century BC. Open daily (in the Palazzo Peloso-Cepolla; no phone).

From Albenga you can take an interesting excursion inland through the Aroscia Valley past Villanova, an ancient walled town, to Ortovero, a region famous for the red pigato wine. You can continue on through the pleasant countryside to Ponte di Nava, where you'll find the object of this jaunt, *Beppe's* (32 Via Nazionale; phone: 174-391924), a fine restaurant specializing in snails, game, trout, and, in season, raspberries. Before turning back, visit Ormea, a pretty summer resort; Garessio, known for its mineral springs; and, finally, the romantic village of Castelvecchio.

Except for the charming historic section of Finale Ligure, the shore road from Albenga is unattractive, and it is advisable to transfer to the autostrada as far as Genoa.

GENOA (GENOVA): The greatest port in northern Italy and the main outlet for the "Industrial Triangle" (Turin, Milan, and Genoa), this city (pop. 750,000) rises like an amphitheater from its semicircular port into the hills above the city. Surrounding the harbor is the oldest (medieval) section, with steep and narrow streets and arcades and medieval houses and churches (a total of about 200). Above the port is Renaissance Genoa, consisting of fine palaces built by rich Genoese merchants and great seafarers such as Andrea Doria, once the rivals of the Venetians in cultivating trade with the East. Then, on the higher slopes and in the flat area to the east, is modern Genoa, with wide streets and boulevards, squares and public gardens. Still higher is the Circonvallazione a Monte, a panoramic boulevard winding in and out among the hills, with fine views over the city. The layout of the city is very confusing since it follows no recognizable plan: Visitors would be well advised to buy a city map, available at any newspaper kiosk. Fortunately, the principal sights and monuments are well marked, and many are being spruced up for this year's 500th anniversary of the discovery of the New World by native son Christopher Columbus. Contact one of the tourist offices for information: 10 Via Porta degli Archi (phone: 541541), open weekdays from 8 AM to 1:30 PM and 2 to 5 PM, Saturdays from 8 AM to 1:30 PM.; 18r Piazza Verdi, near the Stazione Brignole (phone: 562056), open Mondays to Saturdays from 8 AM to 8 PM.

The 16th and 17th centuries saw a flurry of artistic activity in this wealthy shipping city. The impetus was provided by a number of Flemish artists — Rubens and Van Dyck among them — who were invited to come to the city to work for wealthy merchant families, primarily making portraits. To form an image of what the city was like in this grand period, stroll down Via Garibaldi (known as Via Aurea before the last century), lined with 16th-century palaces of elaborate design. The frescoes and gallery of Palazzo Cataldi, the art gallery in Palazzo Bianco (with fine collections of Genoa's adopted Flemish sons), and the antiques in Palazzo Doria Tursi tell reams about the life in Renaissance Genoa.

For one of the best panoramas of the city, take a cable car from Largo della Zecca up to the town of Righi.

Genoese cuisine features a number of specialties, such as *trenette al pesto* (noodles and a sauce flavored with basil, garlic, and pine nuts); fish ravioli; a vegetable pie known as *torta pasqualina* (an *Easter* specialty of vegetables, eggs, and ricotta in a pie crust); *cappon magro* (a mixed salad of vegetables and fish with a mayonnaise sauce — very rich); and, of course, fish of all kinds.

En Route from Genoa – From Genoa, continue east on the autostrada until you reach Camogli, a picturesque small port with tall houses, a favorite residence for sea captains. On the second Sunday in June, a gigantic fish fry is held here.

Continue on the autostrada to the Rapallo exit, where you get on the shore road leading to Santa Margherita and Portofino on the Tigullo Gulf, one of the most scenic sections of the Riviera. Rapallo itself is grossly overbuilt. It has some 50 hotels, a yacht harbor, and the *Rapallo Golf Club* (phone: 185-50210) with an 18-hole course. The beaches are barely adequate, but many of the better hotels have swimming pools.

SANTA MARGHERITA LIGURE: This is the best resort in the Tigullo area since it is neither overbuilt nor underdeveloped — perfect for a comfortable stay. The resort has 34 hotels, some situated on the waterfront or overlooking the sea and others above the town, with a view.

PORTOFINO: Considered by many to be the "pearl" of the Italian Riviera, it was originally a small fishing village enclosed in a bay. It has grown into a very exclusive (and expensive) resort, retaining its original atmosphere and charm by very stringent zoning regulations. Take a walk to the lighthouse past the Church of San Giorgio for a fine view over the whole bay (total walking time is 1 hour). And don't miss the nearby hamlet of San Fruttuoso, reached by motorboat in 20 minutes.

En Route from Portofino – To get back to the main roads, you must backtrack to Rapallo. Beyond Rapallo, the autostrada runs almost entirely inland until it reaches the La Spezia exit and continues into Tuscany.

The Via Aurelia follows the coast, past Chiavari and Sestri Levante; then it, too, moves inland, climbing through fine scenery to the Bracco Pass. The coast from here to La Spezia is very steep, rugged, and very beautiful. Unfortunately, except for Monterosso, the other villages of the Cinque Terre, or "Five Lands" — Vernazza, Corniglia, Manarola, and Riomaggiore — the most unspoiled part of the whole Riviera, are difficult or impossible to reach by road. These small fishing and wine growing towns cling to the rocky coast and are more easily reached by train or from La Spezia on the finished portion of the shore road. (The railroad works its way mostly through tunnels, but each town has a station.)

LERICI: Sailing back from a visit to Leigh Hunt in Pisa, headed for his home in Lerici on the Gulf of Spezi, Percy Bysshe Shelley was capsized and drowned here in 1822; his body, found washed ashore, was burned in a funeral pyre by his wife and companions. This romantic and tragic event has marked this attractive little town ever since, drawing both historians and simple romantics to spend some time here. Lerici serves as a stop on the Riviera route, though short excursions to Tellaro, Montemarcello, and Bocca di Magra on the estuary of the Magra River are possible from here.

BEST EN ROUTE

Since the Italian Riviera is a resort area, you will find many fine hotels and restaurants, and high seasonal prices. Expect to pay as much as $225 and up per night for a double room at those hotel categorized as very expensive; between $150 and $225 at those places listed as expensive; between $85 and $150 for hotels in the moderate category; under $85, inexpensive. Expect to pay $200 or more for a meal for two at those restaurants categorized as very expensive; $100 to $200 at expensive; between $50 and $80 at a restaurant in the moderate category; under $50, inexpensive. Prices do not include drinks, wine, or tip.

MORTOLA INFERIORE–Ventimiglia

Balzi Rossi – One of the Riviera's finest restaurants, it offers dining on the terrace in the summer. Closed Sunday evenings, Mondays (except during summer), and in November. Reservations necessary. Most major credit cards accepted. Piazzale de Gaspari, San Ludovico, Ventimiglia (phone: 184-38132). Expensive.

BORDIGHERA

Del Mare – A pleasant 104-room hotel that stands in a park, it boasts a private beach, swimming pool, and tennis court. Closed from mid-November through mid-December. Most major credit cards accepted. 34 Via Portico della Punta, about 1 mile (1.6 km) from town at Capo Miliarese (phone: 184-262201). Expensive.

Cap Ampelio – In a park, this old, established, 100-room hotel has a swimming pool and a restaurant. Closed from mid-October to mid-December. 5 Via Virgilio (phone: 184-264333). Expensive to moderate.

Le Chaudron – This charming restaurant offers very good Italian and French food. Try the spaghetti with lobster and the irresistible homemade desserts. Closed Mondays, January 15 to 30, and July 1 to 15. Reservations unnecessary. Most major credit cards accepted. 2 Piazza Bengasi (phone: 184-263592). Moderate.

Chez Louis – An eclectic assortment of tasty Italian and French dishes characterizes the culinary repertoire. Try the shellfish soup *en croûte.* Closed Tuesdays (except in summer) and November. Reservations unnecessary. Most major credit cards accepted. 30 Corso Italia (phone: 184-261602). Moderate.

Reserve Tastevin – The menu at this excellent restaurant contains an interesting selection of Mediterranean specialties. Closed Mondays and Sunday evenings (except during summer for both), and from the second week in November to December 20. Reservations advised. Most major credit cards accepted. 20 Via Arziglia (phone: 184-261322). Moderate.

Romano – Here, the accent is on pasta and other Italian dishes. Closed Wednesdays. Reservations unnecessary. No credit cards accepted. 15 Piazza del Popolo (phone: 184-265734). Moderate.

Astoria – This well-maintained hotel in the villa district has 24 rooms and a garden. Most major credit cards accepted. 2 Via Tasso (phone: 184-262906). Inexpensive.

SAN REMO

Royal – San Remo's classic luxury establishment has 140 rooms, most overlooking the beach or surrounding park. There is a heated swimming pool and tennis courts. Closed mid-October to mid-December. Most major credit cards accepted. 80 Corso Imperatrice (phone: 184-5391; fax: 61445). Very expensive.

Astoria–West End – This 120-room hotel is set among spacious gardens near the sea. 8 Corso Matuzia (phone: 184-667701). Expensive.

Casinò – You won't have to gamble on the high quality of food or service here. Many rate both as consistently superb, though a bit pricey. Reservations necessary. Most major credit cards accepted. 3 Corso Inglesi in the *Municipal Casinò* (phone: 184-79901). Expensive.

Da Giannino – Simplicity and good taste characterize this restaurant; owner and chef Signora Gasperini prepares some very fine fish and squid dishes. Try one of the local ligurian wines. Closed Monday lunches, Sundays, and the first half of December. Reservations necessary. Most major credit cards accepted. 23 Lungomare Trento e Trieste (phone: 184-504014). Expensive.

Londra – Set in a park, this 127-room hotel has a heated swimming pool. Closed October through mid-December. 2 Corso Matuzia (phone: 184-668000). Expensive.

Osteria del Marinaro – You will find any number of fish dishes (but only fish) on the menu at this centrally located eatery with 20 tables. Reservations necessary. Closed Mondays and late October through November. Most major credit cards accepted. 28 Via Gaudio (phone: 184-501919). Expensive.

Pesce d'Oro – House specialties are *lasagne al pesto,* fish soup, and grilled scampi. As seating capacity is limited, reservations are necessary. Closed Mondays and mid-February to mid-March. Most major credit cards accepted. 300 Corso Cavallotti (phone: 184-576332). Expensive.

Méditerranée – Overlooking the yacht harbor, it has 70 tastefully furnished, modern rooms, a swimming pool, and fragrant gardens. Closed November through mid-December. 76 Corso Cavallotti (phone: 184-571000). Expensive to moderate.

Résidence Principe – If you plan to stay in town for a while, consider booking one of the 52 rooms in this residential hotel, with very pretty gardens, swimming pool, and a lovely view. 96 Via Fratelli Asquasciati (phone: 184-83565). Moderate.

U'Nostromu – Excellent risotto and well-prepared fish are served here. Closed

Wednesdays and November. Reservations unnecessary. No credit cards accepted. 2 Piazza Sardi (phone: 184-501979). Moderate.

Villa Maria – The most attractive feature at this quiet 19-room hotel is its flower garden. 30 Corso Nuvoloni (phone: 184-531422). Moderate.

Europa e Della Pace – More than half the 70 rooms in this unpretentious but comfortable hotel have private baths. Many have windows overlooking the sea. Near the *Municipal Casinò,* 27 Corso Imperatrice (phone: 184-578170). Moderate to inexpensive.

LAIGUEGLIA

Laigueglia Residence – This restored old mansion on the shore has 55 rooms. Closed from November through March. 14 Piazza Libertà (phone: 182-49001). Moderate.

Splendid – Aptly named, this 14th-century palazzo has 50 well-appointed rooms, many of which overlook the beach. There is also a swimming pool. Closed November through March. 4 Via Badarò (phone: 182-49325). Moderate.

Residence Paradiso – Some of the 32 units at this unpretentious hotel have kitchenettes. 1 Via dei Pini (phone: 182-49285). Inexpensive.

ALASSIO

La Palma – Don't miss the special fish soup and the wonderful *pasta al pesto* served in this superb restaurant. Reservations necessary. Most major credit cards accepted. Closed Tuesdays and November. 5 Via Cavour (phone: 182-40314). Expensive.

La Vigna – Be sure to make reservations before heading for this popular terrace restaurant. Closed Wednesdays. Most major credit cards accepted. 1 Via Lepanto Solva (phone: 182-43301). Expensive.

Diana Grand – Although some of the 77 rooms have beachside balconies, those at the back of the hotel are noisy. In addition to a private beach, there is a swimming pool, a sauna, and restaurant. Closed December and January. 110 Via Garibaldi (phone: 182-42701). Expensive to moderate.

Méditerranée – It overlooks the sea and has its own beach. All 75 rooms have private baths. Closed from October 20 through March. 63 Via Roma (phone: 182-42564). Expensive to moderate.

Caffè Roma – You can easily while away a few hours at this pleasing café with adjoining snack bar. Closed Mondays. Reservations unnecessary. No credit cards accepted. 316 Via Dante (phone: 182-40188). Moderate.

Excelsior – The restaurant in this small *pensione* is a good place to sample French and Italian cuisine. Closed Wednesdays. Reservations advised. No credit cards accepted. Via Robutti (phone: 182-40454). Moderate.

Regina – Although not lavish, 31 of its 39 rooms have private baths. Closed October through March. 220 Via Garibaldi (phone: 182-40215). Moderate.

Lido – This substantial, 52-room hotel is on the beach. Closed October through March. 9 Via Novembre IV (phone: 182-40158). Moderate to inexpensive.

GENOA (GENOVA)

There are more than 200 hotels, many in each price range, and innumerable restaurants and pizzerias in the Genoa area.

Antica Osteria del Bai – It doesn't look like much from the outside, but the inside of this eatery is warm and cozy with windows overlooking the sea. Try the ravioli stuffed with fish. Closed Mondays and August 1 to 20. Reservations advised. Some credit cards accepted. 12 Via Quarto (phone: 10-387478). Expensive.

Le Fate – Considered by many to be the best dining place in town, especially for fish — often cooked in herbs. Closed Saturday lunchtime and Sundays. Reservations necessary. Some credit cards accepted. 31 Via Ruspoli (phone: 10-546402). Expensive.

Jolly Hotel Plaza – This 100-room establishment is in the most fashionable part of town, near the Piazza Corvetto, and has a classy restaurant. The staff, however, is less than friendly. 11 Via Martin Piaggio (phone: 10-893642). Expensive to moderate.

Savoy Majestic – While not as elegant as some hotels in town, it is conveniently close to the train station, and the 116 rooms are extremely comfortable. The restaurant is also very good. 5 Via Arsenale di Terra (phone: 10-261641). Expensive to moderate.

Astoria – Although this simple hotel near the Brignole railroad station does not have its own restaurant, 60 of its 74 rooms have private baths. 4 Piazza Brignole (phone: 10-873316 or 10-873991). Moderate.

Del Mario – Classic Genoese cooking and a wide choice of good wines. Dinner reservations advised. Closed Saturdays and August 10-25. Dinner reservations advised. Most major credit cards accepted. 33 Via Conservatori del Mare (phone: 10-298467). Moderate.

Gran Gotto – Genoese specialties, starting with perfect pasta sauces, prevail at this popular, upscale eatery, which offers guests a "Piatto del Buon Ricordo" (souvenir plate). Closed Saturday lunch, Sundays, and August. Most major credit cards accepted. 11r Via Fiume (phone: 10-564344). Moderate.

Nino – This place serves Ligurian and Piedmontese specialties. Closed Sundays and July. Reservations advised. Most major credit cards accepted. 20 Salita del Fondaco (phone: 10-205884). Moderate.

Vittorio Al Mare – A seaside restaurant with a beautiful view, this place specializes in fish and risotto dishes. However, the general consensus is that the quality that once distinguished it has diminished. Closed Mondays and August. Reservations advised. Most major credit cards accepted. 1 Belvedere Firpo, at Boccadasse (phone: 10-312872). Moderate to inexpensive.

Agnello d'Oro – The "Golden Lamb" is a bargain; one of Genoa's better hotels for the price. The 38 relatively quiet rooms have air conditioning and telephones. There is also a restaurant. Closed October through March. No credit cards accepted. 6 Vico delle Monachette (phone: 19-262084). Inexpensive.

CAMOGLI

Cenobio dei Dogi – Its terraced gardens overlook the 88-room hotel's private beach and the bay. It also has a private 17th-century chapel, as well as a tennis court, a swimming pool, and an excellent restaurant (closed Fridays and from January 7 through February). 34 Via Cuneo (phone: 185-770041). Expensive.

Da Rosa – A wonderful port restaurant with great views and excellent seafood. Closed Tuesdays and from November to mid-December. Largo Casa Bona (phone: 185-771088). Expensive to moderate.

RAPALLO

Bristol – Many of the 91 rooms in this modern hotel overlook the gardens, private beach, and heated swimming pool. There is also a pricey restaurant. Closed January and February. 369 Via Aurelia Orientale (phone: 185-273313). Expensive.

Rapallo Eurotel – This good, 64-room hotel has a garden, a swimming pool, and a restaurant. 14 Via Aurelia Poniete (phone: 185-60981). Expensive to moderate.

Da Ardito – This popular dining spot has maintained its high standards for the last 50 years. It serves tasty regional dishes and wonderful local wines. Closed Tuesdays. Reservations advised. No credit cards accepted. 9 Via Canale, San Pietro di Novello (phone: 185-51551). Moderate to inexpensive.

Da Monique – Here, too, you'll find imaginative fish and seafood dishes. Closed Tuesdays and from January 20 through February 20. Reservations unnecessary. Most major credit cards accepted. 6 Lungomare Vittorio Veneto (phone: 185-50541). Moderate to inexpensive.

Riviera – All 20 rooms overlook the sea, and there is a good restaurant. Closed from November through mid-December. Piazza Novembre IV (phone: 185-50248). Moderate to inexpensive.

SANTA MARGHERITA LIGURE

Imperial Palace – In a spacious park, this outstanding luxury hotel in a former patrician villa has 96 rooms, a heated swimming pool, and a restaurant. 19 Via Pagana (phone: 185-288991). Very expensive.

Miramare – Many of the 79 rooms at this highly reputable establishment face its private beach. There is also a garden, a heated swimming pool, and a restaurant with a buffet in season. 30 Via Milite Ignoto (phone: 185-287013). Expensive.

Laurin – Near the harbor, it has 41 recently refurbished rooms, a swimming pool in a garden, and a restaurant, *La Broche*. Closed from November through *Christmas*. 3 Corso Marconi (phone: 185-289971). Expensive to moderate.

Da Alfredo – This lively fish restaurant and pizzeria is popular not only with the locals, it's also a favorite of tenor Luciano Pavarotti. Closed Thursdays. Reservations unnecessary. Most major credit cards accepted. 38 Piazza Martiri Libertà (phone: 185-288140). Moderate.

Metropole & Santa Margherita – Most of its 48 rooms have private baths, and its century-old garden overlooks a private beach. Closed November through mid-December. 2 Via Pagana (phone: 185-286134). Moderate.

Paranza – Another fine fish restaurant. Closed Thursdays and mid-January to mid-February. Reservations unnecessary. Most major credit cards accepted. 46 Via Jacopo Ruffini (phone: 185-283686). Moderate.

Beppe Achilli – A wide selection of roast meat and fowl are served here. Closed Wednesdays and December. Reservations unnecessary. Most major credit cards accepted. 29 Via Bottaro (phone: 185-286516). Moderate to inexpensive.

Vela – This remodeled old villa overlooking the bay has 16 rooms, a garden, and a restaurant. 21 Corso Cuneo (phone: 185-286039). Moderate to inexpensive.

PORTOFINO

Splendido – The most fashionable, exclusive hotel in town has 65 rooms, a heated swimming pool, and tennis courts. Half pension (one meal daily) is required. Reservations are essential at the pricey restaurant. Closed November through March. On the hillside above the village, 10 Salita Baratta (phone: 185-269551). Very expensive.

Nazionale – On the harbor, it has 13 rooms and a restaurant (phone: 185-269575). Expensive.

Pitosforo – On the waterfront, it serves some of the best fresh fish and seafood in town. Closed Tuesdays, Wednesday lunchtime, January, and February. Reservations advised. Most major credit cards accepted. On the harbor at Molo Umberto I (phone: 185-269020). Expensive.

Piccolo – Smaller than the *Splendido* and considerably less extravagant, this 26-room hotel has a garden, parking area, and an outdoor restaurant. Closed from November to late February. On the hillside above the village, below the *Splendido*, 31 Via Provinciale (phone: 185-269015). Moderate.

Eden – This economical 9-room hostelry in the center of the village also has a restaurant. 21 Vico Dritto (phone: 185-269091). Moderate to inexpensive.

LERICI

Byron – This comfortable, 26-room hotel overlooks the water. 25 Lungomare Biaggini (phone: 187-967104). Moderate.

Calata – Fine fresh fish can be sampled here, on the waterfront. Closed Tuesdays and November. Reservations advised. No credit cards accepted. 4 Via Mazzini (phone: 187-967143). Moderate to inexpensive.

Golfo dei Poeti – Another good seafood restaurant with a nautical atmosphere. Closed Tuesdays. Reservations advised. Most major credit cards accepted. 19 Via Mazzini (phone: 187-967414). Moderate to inexpensive.

Shelley e delle Palme – Most of the 50 rooms overlook the enchanting bay. 5 Lungomare Biaggini (phone: 187-968204). Moderate to inexpensive.

The Italian Dolomites

One of Europe's most beautiful and striking mountain ranges is the Italian Dolomites, part of the eastern Alps, from the central northern region of the Trentino–Alto Adige east to the Veneto region and the Piave River, both only a short distance from the Austrian border. The range continues south to the fringe of the fertile Po Valley. It is the home of some of Italy's most popular ski resorts, including Cortina d'Ampezzo and Val Gardena, site of the *1970 World Cup Ski Championship.*

The Dolomites have a fascinating geological history. Their unique formations of pinnacles and sheer rocks are the result of huge prehistoric eruptions from the sea that covered the area millennia ago. Sea fossils are found in the highest peaks, and Stone Age and Iron Age implements have been found in the Alps overlooking Bolzano, indicating that the Dolomites may have been one of the earliest inhabited areas in Europe.

The geologic structure of these mountains — limestone and porphyry — give them their famous rose-pink hue that deepens to an almost fiery red at sunset. Most towns in the Dolomites are a delightful mixture of Roman ruins, medieval fortifications and castles, early medieval buildings decorated with frescoes, and baroque churches. The Dolomites stand at a European crossroads, the meeting point of different peoples, languages, and cultures; and they have become battlegrounds innumerable times, from invasions by Roman legions and Emperor Charlemagne's campaigns to battles between the Austrian Empire and the Italian states. At the end of the ruthless conflicts of World War I, much of the Dolomites were handed over to Italy by Austria, and so Alto Adige — South Tyrol until 1918 — though Italian, is predominatly German-speaking.

The climate is typical of mountainous regions throughout Europe — snow on high ground from November to April, spring rain through June, and hot, sunny weather in the summer — though summer is infamously unpredictable, with sudden rains and fogs likely anytime.

To see as much as possible, travelers must zigzag through the Dolomites, stopping for cable car climbs or walks through interesting towns. The route described below begins at the Brenner Pass, on the Austrian border, at the

Italian town of Bolzano in the eastern Dolomites and follows a very crooked and irregular path until it returns to its starting point. By following it, you will have meandered completely through the eastern portion of the mountains, stopping in such towns as Bressanone, Ortisei, Brunico, Cortina, and San Martino di Castrozza. To cover the western part of the Dolomites, you again begin at Bolzano, but this time travel in the opposite direction, following the twisted southbound route to Trento. Each portion takes a few days, so allow a total of about 6 days. One encouraging factor: The Dolomites have one of the most efficient and dense networks of mountain roads in Europe and offer a wide variety of accommodations at every level.

BOLZANO: An important gateway to northern Europe in ancient times, Bolzano, called Bozen by its German-speaking population, reflects a predominantly Austrian character in its language and culture. It is the traditional capital of the Alto Adige area of the Dolomites.

The old center of Bolzano is entirely Tyrolean (the Alto Adige region was Austrian-controlled South Tyrol until 1918). The 13th-century Gothic cathedral stands in Piazza Walther. Medieval arcades flank Via dei Portici, the narrow main street, along which modern shops have been built. This long street runs into the market square at Piazza delle Erbe, where a lively and colorful fruit market is held daily. Visit the *Museo Civico* (Civic Museum), which houses a rare collection of local wooden sculptures and paintings as well as a vast archaeological and ethnographic collection (closed holidays; 14 Via Cassa di Risparmio; phone: 471-974625). Then cross the Isarco River for a short walk to the tiny, picturesque village of Gries. Don't miss its charming Gothic parish church.

En Route from Bolzano – For one of the less frequented, romantic routes to the Dolomites, take the northbound road No. 508 for 41½ miles (66 km) to Vipiteno. The drive unwinds along the narrow yet lovely green Sarentina Valley, where many medieval castles dominate the scenery. Some are in ruins, others still inhabited, but the renowned Castle Roncolo can be visited Tuesdays through Saturdays, 10 AM to noon and 3 to 5 PM, and well deserves to be seen for its 13th-century frescoes and its dramatic location right on the edge of a gorge.

BRESSANONE: One of the most charming Alto Adige towns, Bressanone claims an eclectic combination of Gothic, Renaissance, and baroque architecture. Its 13th-century cathedral cloister and the tiny chapel with a fresco of St. Christopher are worth a visit, but even if you see nothing else here, you must stop at the *Elefante* (see *Best en Route*), a beautifully preserved 16th-century hotel with original furnishings and one of the best restaurants in the Dolomites.

ORTISEI: At the foot of the grassy slopes of the Alpe di Siusi, Ortisei is a summer and winter resort. It's the chief town of the Val Gardena, one of the most romantic valleys of the Dolomites, carpeted with wildflowers that attract hikers every spring, and the paths are well-marked for hiking at every level. A 6-minute cable car ride from the town takes you to the upper slopes of this range, opening up to incomparable views of the neighboring Catinaccio (or Rosengartens) and the long, pointed outline of the Sassolungo (Langkopf) Mountain. Back in town, to learn about Val Gardena's folklore and culture, take time to visit the *Ladin Museum* (usually open weekday afternoons; phone: 471-76245). The artistry of local woodcarvers can be viewed at the *Permanent Exhibition of Groden Handicrafts* (no admission charge; at the Congress Hall; phone: 471-77620). The tourist board is also here (phone: 471-76328).

En Route from Ortisei – Drive for 6 miles (10 km) to Selva di Val Gardena, a skier's and climber's paradise. Travel past the resort of Arabba, then head north through the Val Badia, yet another Dolomite ski valley and one of the few places where the ancient language of Ladino (a derivative of Latin) is still spoken.

BRUNICO: The capital of the Pusteria Valley and almost entirely Austrian in character, Brunico is famous for the spacious and gentle slopes that surround it. It is dominated by the Tyrolean castle of Bishop Bruno of Bressanone, built in 1251, but the area's greatest attraction is a half-hour's walk away — the breathtaking panorama from the Plan di Corones. Guided tours of this lovely town are offered each Wednesday and Friday at 5 PM, from mid-June to September (for information, contact the tourist board, phone: 474-85722).

En Route from Brunico – Follow Route 49 toward the Lake of Misurina, one of the most romantic spots of the Dolomites. Near the lake are the Tre Cime di Lavaredo Mountains, a popular Dolomite climb. Follow Route 48 to Auronzo di Cadore. You are now in the Veneto region, a more sparsely populated area of the Dolomites.

CORTINA D'AMPEZZO: In a sheltered basin surrounded by pine forests and some of the most spectacular Dolomite peaks, Cortina is probably the best-known and best-loved (or at least the most posh) mountain resort in the entire Dolomites. It offers a huge variety of ski runs as well as walking and climbing trails and is well supplied with hotels and restaurants in every category. Book many months ahead for winter; January bookings are the easiest to come by.

SAN MARTINO DI CASTROZZA: This is not merely another popular ski resort. San Martino di Castrozza, surrounded by tall peaks and pine-wooded slopes, is a local scenic wonder. Pale di San Martino, the group of Dolomite pinnacles that dominate the city, are famous for their intense rose-pink glow at sunset. There are many available chalet-style hotels, typical of the region.

En Route from San Martino di Castrozza – Travel north past Predazzo and Moena and on to Vigo di Fassa, the capital of the lovely Fassa Valley and another Ladino-speaking area. To complete the eastern portion of the trip, follow Route 241 back toward Bolzano. It leads into the famous Strada delle Dolomiti, the most popular Dolomite road. Make a few short stops along the strada at the Passo di Costalunga, the small Lake of Carezza (Karersee), whose water, for geological reasons, is a deep siena red. The route then descends into the wild, romantic Ega Valley. After passing beneath the main Brenner Pass highway, you are back in Bolzano.

Here again is your starting point, but this time for a trip through the western Dolomites, which lie primarily in the Trentino region. These are marked by local mineral spring waters that course through the lake and mountain areas and by architectural monuments of the medieval and Renaissance ages. You begin this western Dolomite route with Merano.

MERANO: This old-fashioned spa town is typical of the south Tyrol's special charm. Its inner core is small, quaint, and Tyrolean while the outer town is marked by massive, somber, 19th-century Austrian hotels.

CLES: This pretty, medieval village in the heart of Val di Non was once the home of the Clesio family, medieval rulers whose ancestral castle dominates the town. A small Renaissance parish church also stands in the village center.

MADONNA DI CAMPIGLIO: Now one of Italy's biggest mountain resorts, Madonna di Campiglio offers countless excursions in summer and winter into the two ranges — Brenta and Adamello. Although mountain climbing in this region is geared to veteran hikers, there are several less challenging trails for beginners.

En Route from Madonna di Campiglio – As you head toward Trento, the road winds through some of the most attractive countryside of the region. You will come upon the spa center of Comano, the romantic lake and castle at Toblino,

Lake Santa Massenza (which runs through the tiny spa town of Vigolo Baselga), and the peaceful lakeside village of Terlago.

TRENTO: Only 18½ miles (30 km) south of Bolzano, this city served, for the same strategic reasons as its northern neighbor, as an important Roman town on the Brenner Pass. In the years following Roman rule, Trento fell into relative obscurity, but it once again gained fame in the mid-16th century as the seat of the famous Council of Trent, held by church authorities to consolidate church power and curtail abuses in the face of the Protestant Reformation. With more than 2,000 participants, the Council formed the single largest gathering of European church authorities at the time. Trento has always been Italian in character and language, despite its position in Austrian territory until 1918.

Some city highlights include the Via Belenzani, one of Trento's most beautiful streets, lined with Venetian and Renaissance palaces with frescoed exterior walls; the baroque Church of San Francisco Saverio; and Trento's most celebrated monument — Il Castello di Buon Consiglio (the Castle of Good Counsel) — the original dwelling place of the Bishops of Trentino–Alto Adige, built in the 13th century. Also of special interest is the Duomo (Cathedral) whose style spans the 12th and 13th centuries, Lombard Romanesque to Gothic.

BEST EN ROUTE

Grand old Tyrolean hotels, inns, and converted castles stand on mountainsides and in the center of town in this part of the country. Expect to pay between $100 and $180 per night for a double room at those places categorized as expensive; between $50 and $100 at hotels in the moderate category; under $45, inexpensive. Hearty country fare and local wines are served in any number of pleasant restaurants. Expect to pay $60 or more for a meal for two at those restaurants categorized as expensive; between $40 and $50 at restaurants in the moderate category; under $35, inexpensive. Prices do not include drinks, wine, or tip.

BOLZANO

Da Abramo – A fine restaurant housed in a building that was once the Town Hall of Gries; the interior is enlivened by a multitide of flowers and plants. Traditional and Italian dishes are served. Closed Sundays and July. Reservations necessary. Most major credit cards accepted. 16 Piazza Gries (phone: 471-280241). Expensive.

Grifone-Greif – There are some beautiful furnishings on the large landings and in the upstairs reading rooms at this traditional Austrian hotel on the central piazza. There is a swimming pool, and the restaurant is excellent. 7 Piazza Walther (phone: 471-977056). Expensive to moderate.

Luna-Mondschein – A somewhat less refined but nonetheless characteristically Tyrolean hotel with a garden and a restaurant specializing in local cuisine. Most major credit cards accepted. 15 Via Piave (phone: 471-975642). Expensive to moderate.

Scala-Stiegel – On the edge of the Old Town, this old-fashioned Tyrolean hotel has gardens, a swimming pool, and a restaurant. 11 Via Brennero (phone: 471-976222). Moderate.

BRESSANONE

Elefante – In a secluded corner of town with a garden and a heated swimming pool, the inside of this well-run, beloved hotel has changed little over the past 400 years except for essential modernization such as heating. It's filled with genuine 16th-century furnishings. The restaurant, also called *Elefante,* serves local dishes prepared with great care and the freshest ingredients. Try the house specialty, *piatto Elefante* — a mountainous variety of cold meat served with appropriate sauces. Restaurant is closed Mondays and during most of the winter. Hotel is closed January 7 to March 3. 4 Via Rio Bianco (phone: 472-32750). Expensive to moderate.

Corona d'Oro – More modest by comparison, this hotel in the old, porticoed center of town has a modern, pleasantly furnished restaurant where simple Tyrolean dishes, wine, and beer are served. Closed December 15 to *Christmas* and January 1 to February 15. 4 Via Fienili (phone: 472-35154). Moderate to inexpensive.

ORTISEI

Aquila-Adler – This modern hotel in a medieval setting has a restaurant with a garden, swimming pool, and garage (phone: 471-796203). Expensive.

Hell – Don't be deceived by the name. This hotel offers typical Tyrolean comfort in its 27 rooms, international cuisine, hearty breakfasts, a sauna, and a solarium. 3 Via Promenade (phone: 471-795270). Moderate.

SELVA DI VAL GARDENA (WOLKENSTEIN)

Tyrol – One of Selva's chalet-style hotels has some of the most superb views of the Dolomites. The restaurant is known for good country food and friendly service. Closed from October through mid-December and from mid-April through mid-June (phone: 471-75270). Expensive to moderate.

Dorfer – Small and relatively isolated, this hotel has a private garden and a decent restaurant. Closed October through mid-December and May through mid-June (phone: 471-75204). Moderate to inexpensive.

BRUNICO (BRUNECK)

Royal Hinterhuber – Set on a hill with an impressive, wide-angle view of the surrounding valleys, this hotel has gardens, tennis courts, swimming pool, parking area, and a fine restaurant. Closed mid-October to mid-December and mid-April to mid-May. Nearly 2 miles (3 km) southeast of Brunico (phone: 474-21221). Expensive to moderate.

Andreas Hofer – Pine walls and typical Tyrolean furniture are the most distinctive decorative features of this modern hotel. Fresh mushrooms in season are the chef's specialty. Closed the first half of December. 1 Via Campo Tures (phone: 474-85469). Inexpensive.

AURONZO DI CADORE

Al Lago – A pretty little hotel above Santa Caterina Lake, it has quite a good restaurant. Closed from October through May. 14 Via Piave (phone: 435-9314). Inexpensive.

CORTINA D'AMPEZZO

De la Poste – This century-old, luxury, chalet-style hotel has spacious rooms and a well-known restaurant. Closed October 20 to December 20. 14 Piazza Roma (phone: 436-4271). Expensive.

El Toulà – In Ladin dialect, a *toulà* is a wood-paneled, convivial room, and this *toulà* is just the right place to refresh your spirits and palate after a day of hiking, strolling, or skiing. The country-Venetian specialties are very good. Open December 3 through April 2 and July 15 through September 15. Reservations advised. Most major credit cards accepted. 123 Località Ronco (phone: 435-3339). Expensive.

Capannina – Although not a luxury hotel, it is well situated and has one of the best restaurants in town. The Venetian and Tyrolean cooking is superb, as is the selection of wines. Closed from October through mid-December and mid-April until July. 11 Via della Stadio (phone: 436-2950, hotel; 436-2633, restaurant). Expensive to moderate.

Franceschi – In addition to a restaurant, it has tennis courts, a parking area, and a fine garden. Closed from mid-April to mid-June and October to December 20. 86 Via Cesare Battisti (phone: 436-867041). Expensive to moderate.

Menardi – This rustic, 48-room hotel on the northern outskirts of town has a pleasant restaurant and a private garden from which you can see the Dolomites. Closed from October through mid-December and April to June 19. 110 Via Majon (phone: 436-2400). Moderate to inexpensive.

SAN MARTINO DI CASTROZZA

Birreria Drei Tannen – Lively and elegant, this little restaurant serves hearty mountain food and local wine at tables set around a fireplace; dinner only. Closed mid-September to mid-December and mid-April through June. Reservations advised. Most major credit cards accepted. 233 Via Passo Rolle (phone: 439-68325). Moderate.

San Martino – Modernized and enlarged, this is actually one of the oldest hotels in the area. Most of its rooms have retained their balconies, from which you can see the entire valley. A swimming pool, tennis court, and restaurant round out the facilities. Closed from mid-September through mid-December and mid-April through June. 279 Via Passo Rolle (phone: 439-68011). Moderate to inexpensive.

Rosetta – Not as lavish as the *San Martino*, it, too, maintains an aura of classy tradition and has a garden, parking area, and restaurant. Closed mid-September through mid-December, and mid-April through June. Via Passo Rolle (phone: 439-68056). Inexpensive.

MERANO

Castel Freiberg – A 14th-century former castle, about 4 miles (6 km) southeast of Merano, with 36 rooms. Facilities include tennis courts, an indoor swimming pool, a sauna, and a solarium (phone: 473-44196). Expensive.

Andrea – Here you'll find well-prepared Tyrolean fare in a friendly, refined atmosphere. Upstairs is an authentic *Stube* (paneled room) from the 17th century. Closed Mondays and mid-January to mid-March. Reservations advised. 44 Via Galilei (phone: 473-37400). Expensive to moderate.

MADONNA DI CAMPIGLIO

Golf – This large, well-maintained country hotel has a 9-hole golf course, garden, and parking area. Service is friendly and efficient. The pricey restaurant is excellent. Closed April through June and September through December. Campo Carlo Magno (phone: 465-410035). Expensive.

Caminetto – The gardens at this comfortable hotel overlook the Dolomites, and the restaurant serves well-cooked Tyrolean meals. Closed from April to mid-July and September through November. 38080 Madonna D'Campiglio (phone: 465-41242). Moderate.

TRENTO

Accademia – In a beautifully restored inn with about a dozen rooms, it features a fine restaurant serving traditional Trento specialties, refined and lightened (reservations advised; most major credit cards accepted). The inn's top-floor suite is worth reserving well in advance. 4 Vicolo Colico (phone: 461-981580). Expensive to moderate.

Chiesa – Near the castle in a 16th-century setting, this reliable dining establishment features appealing local specialties, and the pasta is particularly good. Dinner only; closed Mondays and during late summer. Reservations unnecessary. Most major credit cards accepted. 64 Via San Marco (phone: 461-985577). Expensive to moderate.

Villa Madruzzo – This converted 18th-century villa has comfortable rooms and a pretty garden. Nearly 2 miles (3 km) east of town in Cognola. 38050 Cognola (phone: 461-986220). Moderate to inexpensive.

Birreria Forst – Don't miss the chance to eat in this very popular beer hall. The food is regional as are the wines. Closed Mondays. Reservations unnecessary. Most major credit cards accepted. 38 Via Oss Mazzurana (phone: 461-35590). Inexpensive.

Tuscany

Extending from the snow-capped Apennines north of Florence to south of the Maremma plains, Tuscany is probably Italy's wealthiest region. Its riches lie in a cultivated diverse land that has prospered since the early Etruscan, Roman, and later medieval periods, with a gastronomical discipline that rivals the finest on the continent. But even more important, Tuscany's art, architecture, and age-old traditions reflect an illustrious history now deeply embedded in its modern culture. Some of its cities and villages number among the oldest in central Italy.

Tuscany derives its name from the Roman Tuscia. Its original inhabitants were the pre-Roman Etruscans, a peaceful, progressive, and artistic people whose origins are obscure, but who spread through an area of Italy between Naples and the northern Po Valley. Eventually overrun by the Romans in 40 BC, the heart of Etruscan civilization — the land between the Tiber and Arno rivers — became a province of the Roman Empire. The Etruscans were wise in agricultural ways, and it's undoubtedly to them that Tuscany owes its reputation as a producer of some of the best wine and food in Europe.

Despite modernization in the past few decades, Tuscany holds fervently to its medieval past. Every year long-standing traditions — such as a 13th-century horse race, the *Palio,* in Siena; a Saracen jousting tournament in Arezzo; and a medieval football game in Florence — are re-enacted by Tuscans, all of which allow them to remember their roots and relive their past.

The logical starting point for a Tuscan itinerary is Florence, the leading cultural and commercial hub of the region. Slightly west of central Italy, the Tuscan route curves under the cross-country sway of the Apennines. It travels seaward to Pisa, then inland and south to Siena, down toward the marshlands of Maremma, and finally northeast to Arezzo and Cortona, 50 miles (80 km) south of Florence. Between the large cities, it passes through hilltop villages, seafaring towns, and sites of ancient ruins. This is a route on which one could tarry happily for weeks, but properly organized, it can be covered in about 4 or 5 days, hitting the highlights and getting a feel for the area and its people.

From Florence (for a complete report on the city, see *Florence,* THE CITIES), the route goes to Lucca, where the tour really begins.

LUCCA: Striking because of its unusual architectural character, Lucca is marked by a mixture of styles that date from the 6th century. The town is surrounded by 16th-century ramparts, and a short walk shows a predominance of Romanesque and Pisan influence. Visit the huge 18th-century Piazza Napoleone, at the center of town, and the *National Art Gallery of Lucca* in the historic Villa Guinigi in Quarchiona (closed Mondays; phone: 583-46033). Also worth seeing is the cathedral begun in the 6th century; it stands in the stately Piazza di San Martino.

Also a rich architectural center famous for its olive oil, Lucca's market comes alive every morning. Townspeople crowd the vast squares surrounding the Church of St. Michele.

PISA: An important Italian port in the early Middle Ages, Pisa was a much-sought-after center of trade until 1405, when it became a Florentine city. Recognizable from afar for its fabled leaning tower, Pisa is a delight of Romanesque architecture. Her builders and stone carvers were among the finest of the Renaissance period.

When you enter Pisa, head for the Piazza del Duomo, where the famous tower stands beside a cathedral and baptistry, richly decorated with carving by the Pisano family. The tower itself was begun by Bonanno Pisano in 1174 and, despite the sinking foundations, was completed in 1350. For safety reasons, the tower can no longer be climbed. Visit the nearby Campo Santo, a 12th-century cemetery built by the Crusaders, and its surrounding Gothic galleries.

   En Route from Pisa – Turn inland on Route 67, past the industrial town of Pontedera, and veer off at San Miniato Basso to visit the art-filled hilltop town of San Miniato. There, from a castle above the town's 12th-century cathedral, you can look out over the whole Arno Valley. From San Miniato, take a minor road south through unspoiled vine-clad Tuscan hills past the villages of Casastrada, Mura, and Il Castagna. Continue for 31 miles (50 km) to San Gimignano, the town of medieval towers. Looking out from the hilltops of this city, it might as well be the 14th century. The lookout posts built for prestige by noblemen during the early medieval wars still offer magnificent views of the surrounding Col d'Elsa Valley. Leaving San Gimignano on the main Siena highway (Rte. 68), turn left and drive through the characteristic wine country of the Chianti Valley to Poggibonsi, a wine trading town. From there, turn south for the last 15½ miles (25 km) to Siena.

SIENA: After Florence, Siena has probably the richest artistic heritage in Tuscany. An important agricultural town, the medieval spirit of Siena is almost entirely preserved. Originally an Etruscan city later taken over by the Romans (who named it Sena Julia), it was a much-contested territory through the medieval wars between the Italian states. After many vicissitudes, including the plague in 1348, Siena became part of the duchy of Tuscany in 1559.

The city is laid out over three hilltops surrounded by walls. Begin a tour of Siena at the Piazza del Campo, the heart of the city and the scene of the famous *Palio,* when 10 of the former medieval districts are represented by a horse and bareback rider in a mad race around the piazza. The *Palio,* held on July 2 and August 16 every year, is the highlight of a magnificent festival carried out with color and fervor by the Sienese — not as a staged tourist attraction but as a celebration of their heritage.

In the sloping Piazza del Campo stands the graceful Gothic town hall with its bell tower, accessible to the public. Then make your way to the Piazza del Duomo, where the cathedral dedicated to the Madonna stands on a raised marble platform. Visit the baptistry, which seems to form the crypt of the cathedral, and browse through the

Pinacoteca Nazionale — the art gallery at Palazzo Buonsignori — for a fundamental knowledge of Sienese art.

Walking along the narrow streets of Via di Città and Via Banchi di Sopra, both of which skirt the Piazza del Campo, you will come to the Chigi-Saracini Palace. Now a music academy, it houses some beautiful Renaissance apartments displaying a gallery of Tuscan paintings, open to the public upon request. Along the same row is the Loggia dei Mercanti, the merchants' center, which once served as the center of commerce. Farther along are the Piazza Salimbeni and its four palaces, which were built over a period from the 13th to the 16th century. The palace designs reflect the progression of architectural styles over the years from the medieval to the Renaissance and finally, the baroque.

You can spend days in Siena simply wandering through the medieval streets soaking up the atmosphere of the city. Siena is also one of the greatest wine centers in the country. For some of the best chianti around, buy a bottle at *Cantina Del Brunnell* (20 Via Paradiso; phone: 577-48446), and for some excellent cooking, frequent the local trattorias. You can stay at hotels converted from Renaissance palaces or at modest but charming hostelries in the outlying country overlooking the Chianti hills.

October draws the most visitors, so book ahead in early autumn. In summer, Siena is searingly hot: Look for hotels with swimming pools.

En Route from Siena – Take the Porta S. Marco and Route 73 for Grosseto, 58 miles (94 km) away. This route is in complete contrast to the gentle, vine-clad hills of central Tuscany. Sparsely populated, wild and uncultivated, this is an introduction to the Maremma marshland. Travel past the small villages en route until a vast panorama opens out over the Maremma plains to the sea and the Argentario Peninsula. This gives way beyond Grosseto, the capital of Maremma, to green coastal plains until it reaches the forests and green hills of the national park known as the Uccellina.

UCCELLINA: The home of the original flora and fauna of Maremma, the Uccellina National Park features grasslands and beaches. One example of an Uccellina beach, and generally characteristic of the Tuscan shoreline, is Marina di Alberese, where a long stretch of white sand faces the edge of a pine forest. Visits to the park can be arranged through *Le Cannelle* (Parco dell'Uccellina, Talamone; phone: 564-887020) some 3 miles (5 km) away in the village of Alberese.

Out of the Maremma region grew an unusual heritage when it became famous in the 18th century as a kind of "Wild West" of Italy. Herds of cattle and wild horses ran free through the plains, and cattle rustlers and bandits abounded.

SATURNIA: A tiny village on a hilltop, it's surrounded by countryside of Etruscan necropolises. In the village lie the remains of a Roman road, the Via Claudia, as well as a reconstructed 12th-century castle. Named Aurinia by the Etruscans, the later name of Saturnia is said to be derived from the Roman god Saturn. In the valley below the village swirl the steaming sulfur springs of the ever-popular Terme di Saturnia.

En Route from Saturnia – From Saturnia take the road for Sovano and Sorano; these two special villages are perched atop hills of *tufo* — the soft brownish stone of Etruria — surrounded by Etruscan tombs. Transfer to the Roman road, the Via Cassia, then turn north for the first time along the route, leaving the Etruscan hills behind and heading back for the fertile green of central Tuscany. Along this final meandering segment of the drive you'll come across many small towns in medieval settings. Follow the turns on the highway that lead to Route 327, and follow it until you reach the town of Arezzo.

AREZZO: The Romans called it Arretium — a town that lies in the middle of olive- and vine-covered hills in a valley where the Chiana and Arno rivers meet. Today it is Italy's gold manufacturing capital. At the center of town is the 14th-century Church of St. Francis, which contains a remarkable fresco cycle (look behind the high altar) by Piero della Francesca, a native of Arezzo; though under restoration at press time, most of the fresco is visible. Nearby is the sloping Piazza Grande, the focus of urban life for centuries, which is surrounded by buildings in a variety of architectural styles. Note especially the 16th-century Palazzo delle Logge, with its open portico of shops, flanked by Renaissance palaces and medieval homes, as well as the magnificent Pieve di Santa Maria, a Romanesque church that backs onto the square, its tall bell tower of "100 holes" (it actually has 40 mullioned windows) standing alongside. The first weekend of every month, an important antiques fair is held in Piazza Grande, and on the first Sunday in September it is also the scene of the annual *Joust of the Saracen —* an exciting reenactment of a medieval tournament on horseback.

From the piazza, walk through the old quarter of town to the Ponte Solesta, which spans the Tronto River. Across the bridge is a magnificent view of the town, with its medieval towers and churches.

CORTONA: A visit to Cortona, on the border of Tuscany and Umbria, is like a step back in time to the early Renaissance. Secluded and silent, atop a hill covered with olive trees and vineyards, the walled city of Cortona is characterized by steep, narrow streets that open onto uneven piazzas. Its cathedrals and palaces display masterpieces, and the Palazzo Pretorio (Casali) houses a rich Etruscan museum.

BEST EN ROUTE

In this part of Italy you will find some very pretty hotels and reasonably priced restaurants where regional cuisine is nothing less than a fine art. Expect to pay $125 or more per night for a double room at those hotels categorized as expensive; between $60 and $125 in the moderate category; under $50, inexpensive. Expect to pay 80 to $140 for a meal for two at those restaurants classified as expensive; between 50 and $80 at restaurants in the moderate category; under $50, inexpensive. Prices do not include drinks, wine, or tip.

LUCCA

Buca di San Antonio – Steeped in history, this former 19th-century post office offers some of the best Lucchese cooking in town in a friendly atmosphere. Risotto and game dishes are specialties. Closed Sunday evenings and most of July. Reservations advised. 1-3 Via della Cervia (phone: 583-55881). Moderate.

PISA

Buzzino – Here is some of the best Pisan cooking, especially mixed grilled fish and roast veal with herb and mushroom sauce. Chianti wines are plentiful and excellent. Closed Tuesdays and November. Reservations necessary. Most major credit cards accepted. 44 Via C. Cammeo (phone: 583-562141). Expensive.

Sergio – Despite its unpretentious surroundings, this place overlooking the Arno River is probably the best restaurant in town, serving plentiful Pisan food and wine. It is decorated with antique objects, and one wall is 1,000 years old. Closed Sundays, Monday lunchtime, and July 15 to August 16. Reservations necessary. Most major credit cards accepted. 1 Lungarno Pacinotti (phone: 583-48245). Expensive.

D'Azeglio – One of the better small hotels, it offers inviting decor and good service. 18-B Piazza Vittorio Emanuele (phone: 583-500310). Moderate.

Arno and Ristorante da Antonio – This reconstructed 13th-century building is now a hotel and restaurant near the banks of the Arno, within walking distance of the *National Museum.* 6 Piazza della Repubblica (phone: 583-501820). Inexpensive.

SAN GIMIGNANO

La Cisterna and Ristorante La Terrazza – In the medieval town square, this 50-room hotel is known for its large, wooden-balconied rooms overlooking the valley that surrounds this quiet hilltop town. The restaurant on the top floor serves excellent Tuscan cuisine. Hotel and restaurant closed from early November to early March; restaurant also closed Tuesdays and Wednesdays at lunchtime; most major credit cards accepted. 23 Piazza della Cisterna (phone: 577-940328). Hotel moderate; restaurant expensive.

SIENA

Certosa Di Maggiano – What was a convent for 7 centuries is now a richly appointed hostelry with 14 carefully decorated rooms and a small, splendid restaurant. There's also a tennis court and swimming pool. A short ride from town, 82 Via Certosa (phone: 577-288180). Very expensive.

Park – Set in a beautiful park on the outskirts of town, this elegant 16th-century villa has tennis courts, a heated pool, spacious rooms, and a fine, very expensive restaurant, *L'Olivo.* It is part of the CIGA hotel chain. 18 Via di Marciano (phone: 577-44803). Expensive.

Garden – This pleasant, 67-room hotel has lovely gardens, a swimming pool, and a restaurant. 2 Via Custoza (phone: 577-47056). Moderate.

Grotta di Santa Caterina – You'll find a wide selection of Sienese chianti wines at this characteristically medieval tavern, which is very popular with the *Palio* crowd. Closed Sunday evenings and Mondays. Reservations unnecessary. Most major credit cards accepted. 26 Via della Galluzza (phone: 577-282208). Moderate to inexpensive.

Chiusarelli – At the edge of the Old City, this 50-room hotel has a restaurant, a small garden, and a parking area. 9 Viale Curtatone (phone: 577-288234, restaurant; 577-280562, hotel). Inexpensive.

Mariotti–da Mugolone – Hearty home-cooked meals are served in a simple setting. Closed Thursdays and most of July. Reservations unnecessary. Most major credit cards accepted. 8 Via dei Pellegrini (phone: 577-283235). Inexpensive.

SATURNIA (GROSSETO)

Terme di Saturnia – This large, peaceful, luxurious country hotel, popular even in winter, has a natural sulfur swimming pool and falls, gym, tennis courts, and a good restaurant offering diet menus. Full pension is required. The hotel owns a nearby ranch, with horseback riding and hunting (phone: 564-601061). Expensive.

CORTONA

San Luca and Ristorante Tonino – The setting is undeniably charming — on the fringe of a medieval town with tranquil, rural surroundings. The restaurant is closed for Monday dinner and Tuesdays. Reservations necessary. Most major credit cards accepted. 2 Piazza Garibaldi (phone: 575-603100). Hotel expensive to moderate; restaurant expensive.

La Fonte dei Frati – In a renovated, centuries-old *casa colonica* (farmhouse) just outside Cortona, this restaurant offers well-prepared simple fare indigenous to the area, and rustic but sophisticated ambience. Closed Tuesdays. Reservations advised. Most major credit cards accepted. 234 Case Sparse, Località Camucia (the periphery of Cortona; phone: 575-601370). Moderate.

Oasu G. Neumann – Insiders know what a find this tidily run former monastery is, with its clean, simple rooms, quiet garden, and fine view across cypress trees to the valley below. No TV sets. 1 Via Contesse (phone: 575-603188). Inexpensive.

Campania

Campania has long lured enthusiastic visitors with its spectacular natural splendors, its unparalleled wealth of archaeological excavations and historic monuments, and its people, who have cheered the world with their music and their food.

Two picturesque gulfs (Naples and Salerno), three promontories (Phlegrean Fields, the Sorrento Peninsula, and Cilento), a massive volcano (Vesuvius), a forest-covered mountain at the edge of the blue Tyrrhenian Sea (Mt. Faito), and several romantic islands (Capri, Ischia, and Procida) are sufficient reason to tour this region. Add to this plenitude one of the greatest concentrations of archaeological excavations in the world — at Pompeii, Herculaneum, and Paestum, as well as others scattered around the region at other points — unforgettably romantic towns of historical and mythological importance such as Sorrento, Amalfi, Ravello, Positano, and Naples itself, and the region becomes a journey of compulsive interest.

Dominated by the cities of Naples, Amalfi, and Sorrento, the area consists primarily of three sections, each with a splendor of its own. There's the Bay of Naples in the north, a volcanic area with steaming natural hot springs first used by the ancient Romans as thermal spas; a series of three romantic islands off the coast of Naples, including the international resort of Capri; and the Amalfi Coast, the picturesque rocky mountain region winding along the Tyrrhenian Sea from Sorrento to the Gulf of Salerno.

Vesuvius, one of the few volcanoes in Europe still active, stands poised between the northern and southern edges of the Campanian route. Its fiery lava, which buried Pompeii and Herculaneum in AD 79, has not erupted with force since 1944. However, the twin peaks still emit trails of smoke at periodic intervals.

The November 23, 1980, earthquake that devastated vast parts of Campania struck the interior Apennine zone in the southeast, leaving the coast practically untouched. Thus, the islands and the popular Amalfi Coast were spared damage. In Naples, several buildings received dangerous cracks and two collapsed altogether, but the major hotels and restaurants were not damaged. The Pompeii ruins were closed temporarily for repairs but reopened shortly after the quake. Sorrento suffered some minor damage, and the few hotels that were affected merely used the situation to their advantage and did some repainting and renovating.

The route begins in Naples, the regional capital and the center for fascinating tours to the volcanic region.

NAPLES: For a complete report on the city, see *Naples,* THE CITIES.

    En Route from Naples – While in Naples, take an excursion to the eerie Phlegrean Fields, a steamy volcanic zone of dark, violent beauty about 12½ miles (20 km) from the city. It extends along the Gulf of Pozzuoli on a promontory from Cape Posillipo to Cape Miseno. Visit the semiactive crater of Solfatara near Pozzuoli, then continue to the Lake Avernus crater, regarded by the ancients as the entrance to the Underworld. Continue on to Baia, noted for its ancient Roman baths, and Cape Miseno. The cape has wonderful views of the islands of Ischia and Procida. From Cape Miseno, travel up the outer edges of the promontory to the ruins of Cumae, an 8th-century Greek colony, where Virgil's verses were written in the Cave of the Sibyl. Then drive the 15½ miles (25 km) to Pompeii. If time is a factor, do a combined Pompeiian-Herculaneum day tour. Both of the two Roman cities, buried in the AD 79 eruption of Vesuvius, are fascinating. The ruins of Herculaneum are less extensive because they have been less thoroughly excavated. If, however, you have time to do the whole thing properly — and it's worth making time — start with the excellent *Museo Archeologico Nazionale* (National Museum; 19 Piazza Museo) in Naples the day before, where the majority of the Pompeii treasures are exhibited, and at the sites use the guidebooks published by Libreria dello Stato called *Pompeii* and *Herculaneum.*

Take a trip to Vesuvius itself, now a desolate and barren landscape overlooking the Bay of Naples and the rest of Campania.

THE ISLANDS: There is frequent ferryboat and hydrofoil service among the islands of Capri, Ischia, and Procida and the mainland cities as well as helicopter transport from the Naples-Capodichino Airport to Capri and Ischia. Even on a limited schedule, spend at least a day on Capri, and if time is no problem, visit Ischia as well. Procida is the least attractive of the three islands — it's very volcanic, with four craters and black sand.

CAPRI: The gem of the bay, sunny Capri (pronounced *Kah*-pree) was a favorite resort for the Phoenicians and ancient Romans as it is today for international jet setters, day-trippers, and shoppers (but don't expect bargains). It is not a swimmer's paradise; there are few beaches on Capri's dramatic, almost inaccessible coastline. But Capri is a place for walkers. Visits in May, June, early autumn, and even *Christmastime* are rewarding, though be aware that most hotels are closed in winter. Its villages consist of small public squares, villas and white houses, set amid varied subtropical vegetation. Visit the towns of Capri and Anacapri, the Marina Piccola and Marina Grande, and the famous Blue Grotto sea cave. Also, stop at the ruins of Villa Jovis (one of many resorts built by the Emperor Tiberius) and the Villa San Michele at Anacapri, celebrated by Swedish physician and writer Axel Munthe in *The Story of San Michele.* Spectacular views of the Faraglioni (rock islets) are seen from the Punta Tragara belvedere.

ISCHIA: Twice the size of Capri but half as crowded, Ischia is of volcanic origin (its source, Mt. Epomeo, hasn't erupted in nearly seven centuries, and its slopes now produce the renowned Epomeo wine). Sandy beaches, thermal hot springs, and lush green scenery all contribute to the enduring popularity of this Emerald Isle, as it is known. Porto d'Ischia is the charming island harbor town, south of which is Ponte d'Ischia (named for an Aragonese-built bridge), the site of a 15th-century castle. Casamicciola and Lacco Ameno are favorite resorts, and Sant' Angelo is one of the island's several picturesque fishing villages.

AMALFI COAST (COSTA AMALFITANA): Stretching from Sorrento to Salerno along the gulf of that name, the Amalfi Coast is one of the most spectacular drives on any Italian route. On a peninsula, the northern portion around Sorrento has been exploited in recent years, but the southern half of the peninsula remains a romantic paradise — sun-warmed rocks and terraced gardens, lemon and olive groves overlooking sparkling blue bays and coves, flowered promontories and secret beaches. In *The Immoralist* André Gide said that the road from Sorrento to Ravello "was so beautiful that I had no desire . . . to see anything more beautiful on earth."

Although the Amalfi Coast actually begins at Sorrento, a couple of preliminary stops en route make the drive from Naples more interesting. Pick up the Autostrada del Sole (A3) as far as Castellammare di Stabia, less than 31 miles (50 km) from Naples, which was, like Pompeii and Herculaneum, destroyed by Vesuvius in AD 79. Then, take the scenic road (SS145) that curves around the northern coast of the peninsula and stop a short distance farther at Vico Equense. It offers good views of the coast, inexpensive boat service to Capri, and delicious pizza, sold, like textiles, by the yard — actually, by the meter. Look for a large sign, "Pizza al Metro," towering over some of the town's cliff-hanging white houses. Prepare yourself for hairpin curves and an unhurried drive.

SORRENTO: Tourists return time and again to Sorrento, a legendary resort amid beautiful gardens. Its cliff-top setting is its main attraction, but it features several architectural points of interest, including its Duomo, which has a 13th-century cloister with distinctive pointed arches, reflecting the Moorish influence.

En Route from Sorrento – Be prepared for a treacherous slice of highway that continues clear around the mountains until you reach Positano. To avoid the entire scene, drive back north to Gragnano (famous for its red wine) and take an inland route to Positano.

POSITANO: John Steinbeck once described Positano as "a dream place that isn't quite real." Its white houses and terraced gardens cling gently to slopes that roll into the sea, all around a picturesque port dotted with small fishing boats.

During the 10th century, it was one of the most important mercantile cities in the world, but more recently it has become a refuge for writers and artists, who derive inspiration from its natural and architectural settings. Positano is a particular favorite among the younger set, not only because its vertical architectural plan makes frequent climbing necessary in daily living, but also because its fashions center around original and inexpensive boutique wear designed by local artisans. These items, which are displayed temptingly along narrow cobblestone streets, set the fashion pace for summerwear throughout Italy. Good bargains also can be found on locally made ceramics.

En Route from Positano – The road continues past many fishing villages and Saracen towers — once the haunts of pirates — perched on peaks and reefs above the sea. The cliffside corniche then passes over the great gorges of the Valley of Furore and carves into the rocky walls of the Lattari Mountains east to Amalfi.

AMALFI: A Moorish-looking town with white houses and a curiously Oriental church, Amalfi was originally an important maritime republic loyal to Byzantium. Its greatest period of prosperity was during the 11th century, when the Amalfi Navigation Tables, the oldest maritime code in the world, regulated shipping in the entire Mediterranean. Amalfi's cathedral is worth a stop; its bronze doors were cast in Constantinople in 1066.

RAVELLO: This is by far the most picturesque spot along the Gulf of Salerno. When you arrive in Ravello, first visit the Villa Rufolo, whose gardens so inspired Richard Wagner, then stroll through the gardens of the Villa Cimbrone to the belvedere for a spectacular view of the entire gulf. Ravello's cathedral has a fine set of bronze doors and two famous pulpits.

PAESTUM: This ancient Greek city by the sea is one of the finest archaeological sites in the world, with three temples standing nobly among asphodel, oleander, and aromatic herbs. The basilica and the so-called Temple of Neptune, side by side, were both probably dedicated to Hera. The latter, dating from the 5th century BC, is one of the most beautiful Doric temples in Italy or Greece and one of the best preserved. A third temple, the Temple of Ceres, was actually dedicated to Athena. Don't miss the museum, particularly the paintings from the Diver's Tomb and the metopes from the sanctuary of Hera Argiva, found nearby.

If returning to Rome by car, pick up the autostrada via Nola, bypassing Naples, at Salerno.

BEST EN ROUTE

Some of the most truly charming hotels and restaurants in Italy are tucked away in Campania. Expect to pay $150 to $350 or more per night for a double room at the hotels categorized as expensive; between $80 and $150 in the moderate category; under $80, inexpensive. Expect to pay $100 or more for a meal for two at those restaurants classified as expensive; between $60 and $100 in the moderate category; under $50, inexpensive. Prices do not include drinks, wine, or tip.

LUCRINO (LAKE AVERNUS)

Ninfea – On a lake that was once part of the Bourbons' hunting reserve, this restaurant is renowned for its fresh fish. Closed Tuesdays and from September 15 to June 15. Reservations advised. 1 Via Italia (phone: 866-1326). Expensive to moderate.

CAPRI

Canzone del Mare – This pleasant afternoon restaurant on the beach is a favorite with swimmers and sunbathers, who come for a relaxing meal and a drink before the restaurant closes at dusk. The specialty is fresh fish. Closed October to *Easter*. Reservations advised. Most major credit cards accepted. Marina Piccola (phone: 81-837-0104). Expensive.

La Capannina – Sporting a Michelin star, this rather chic restaurant's specialties are fish and pasta. Try the green *gnocchi* with salmon and the *penne* with eggplant. Closed Wednesdays (except in August), and November through March. Most major credit cards accepted. 12 *bis* Via delle Botteghe (phone: 81-837-0732). Expensive.

Europa Palace – Terraces brimming with flowers, and a swimming pool are among the charms of this modern, spacious 100-room hostelry, one of the best on the island. Closed November to March. 2 Via Capodimonte (phone: 81-837-0955). Expensive.

Da Luigi – Frequented by yachtsmen, since it's accessible by sea, it's considered one of the top restaurants on the island. Lunch only. Closed October to *Easter*. Reservations unnecessary. Most major credit cards accepted. On the Strada dei Faraglioni (phone: 81-837-0591). Expensive.

Luna – The garden terraces at this lovely and comfortable 48-room hotel have a fine offshore view of the Faraglioni. The interior decor is tasteful, service is good, and there is a swimming pool. Closed November through March. 3 Via Matteotti (phone: 81-837-0433). Expensive.

Punta Tragara – Designed by the French master architect Le Corbusier, it has a splendid view of the Faraglioni. In addition to antique furnishings in the 41 rooms, it has a swimming pool, spa baths, and hydromassages. Closed October 15 through March. 57 Via Tragara (phone: 81-837-0844). Expensive.

Quisisana e Grand – This deluxe, 143-room hotel caters to a well-heeled, well-traveled crowd. It has tennis courts and a swimming pool. Closed January through March. 2 Via Camerelle (phone: 81-837-0788). Expensive.

Scalinatella – An elegant, small hotel overlooking the sea. Closed November through March 15. 8 Via Tragara (phone: 81-837-0633). Expensive.

La Pigna – This well-run restaurant is also frequented by yachtsmen, and owners of neighboring villas. A few minutes' walk from the center of town on the road to Marina Grande. Closed Tuesdays in low season and from mid-October through March. Reservations advised. Most major credit cards accepted. 30 Via Roma (phone: 81-837-0280). Expensive to moderate.

Da Gemma – Not far from the *piazzetta,* this convenient restaurant with a pleasant outdoor terrace is another of Capri's favorite eateries. Closed Mondays and November. Reservations advised. Most major credit cards accepted. 6 Via Madre Serafina (phone: 81-837-0461). Moderate.

Flora – A 14-room hotel with romantic appeal but no restaurant. Closed November through March. 26 Via Serena (phone: 81-837-0211). Moderate to inexpensive.

ISCHIA

L'Albergo della Regina Isabella e Royal Sporting – A deluxe, super-comfortable 133-room spa hotel, owned by the excellent CIGA chain, it has a swimming pool, private beach, tennis court, and gardens. Closed November through March. 4 Piazza S. Restituta at Lacco Ameno (phone: 81-994322). Expensive.

Excelsior Belvedere – This extravagantly decorated 67-room Excelsior chain hotel is noted for its excellent service. The building is set among landscaped gardens with a swimming pool and a nearby beach. Closed November to March. 3 Via Emanuele Gianturco (phone: 81-991020). Expensive.

Jolly – With 200 comfortable rooms, this hotel at Porto Ischia features thermal spa treatments. There is also a swimming pool and an excellent restaurant. Closed January and February. 42 Via de Luca (phone: 81-991744). Expensive.

Il Moresco – An old Spanish-style building smothered in bougainvillea. It has 63 rooms, a swimming pool, tennis courts, gardens, and a solarium. Closed November through March. 16 Via Emanuele Gianturco at Punta Molino (phone: 81-981355). Expensive.

Punta Molino – An elegant 88-room hotel overlooking the sea with lovely gardens and a swimming pool. Half-pension (at least one meal) required. Closed November to late April. Lungomare Telese già Colombo (phone: 81-991544). Expensive.

Damiano – The specialty is fish in this modern-looking restaurant with a glass-enclosed terrace. Lunch served only on Sundays. Closed October through March. Reservations advised. Most major credit cards accepted. Via della Vigna, Porto Ischia (phone: 81-983032). Expensive to moderate.

Bristol Palace – This 39-room hotel has a restaurant, thermal bath facilities, swimming pool, and gardens. Closed November through March. 10 Via Marone (phone: 81-992181). Moderate.

Di Massa – The specialties of the house are honest Ischitana dishes — including *coniglio* (fresh rabbit). Closed Tuesdays and winters. Reservations advised. Most major credit cards accepted. 29 Via Seminario, Porto Ischia (phone: 81-991402). Moderate.

Gennaro – It has a central location and authentic island decor, and it's known for its fish soups and antipasti. Closed Tuesdays in winter and November through March. Reservations unnecessary. Most major credit cards accepted. 66 Via Porto, Porto Ischia (phone: 81-992917). Moderate.

Pensione La Villarosa – A charming, family-style, 37-room villa that has a splendid garden fragrant with gardenias, and a swimming pool. It is known for friendly, personal service and comfort. Closed November through March. 13 Via Giacinto Gigante (phone: 81-991316). Inexpensive.

GULF OF NAPLES COAST

Axidie – Occupying a former monastery, it's furnished with antiques and has 29 balconied rooms with delightful views of the sea. On the grounds are tennis courts, a swimming pool, and a beach. Marina Aequa, Vico Equense (phone: 89-879-8181). Moderate.

Da Gigino – Pizza is sold by the meter in a spacious, open-air garden in the center of town. Reservations unnecessary. No credit cards accepted. 10 Via Nicoteria, Vico Equense (phone: 89-879-8426). Inexpensive.

SORRENTO

Excelsior Vittoria – This old-fashioned 125-room member of the Excelsior chain is surrounded by orange and lemon groves. The panoramic terraces overlook well-kept grounds with a swimming pool. An elevator whisks guests down to the hotel's private beach. Open year-round. 34 Piazza Torquato Tasso (phone: 81-807-1044). Expensive.

Minerva – Somewhat out of the way, it's worth it because of its lovely position on the sea. With only 50 rooms, this family-style *pensione* has charm and a good seafood restaurant, *La Minervetta.* Closed in winter. 30 Via Capo (phone: 81-878-1098). Expensive.

Bristol – This pleasant, 130-room hotel has a swimming pool, restaurant, and a terrace with a beautiful view of the gulf. 22 Via Capo (phone: 81-878-4522). Expensive to moderate.

Imperial Tramontano – In the heart of town, this 119-room hotel is surrounded by nice gardens. Many of the rooms overlook the gulf and beach, and there is a swimming pool. Closed January and February. 1 Via Veneto (phone: 81-878-2588). Expensive to moderate.

Kursaal – This very popular spot in the center of town turns out good seafood and pizza. Reservations unnecessary. Most major credit cards accepted. Via Fuorimura (phone: 81-878-1216). Expensive to moderate.

Parco dei Principi – A 173-room hotel that was once a Bourbon family villa, it has a stupendous park and a view of the gulf. It, too, has a swimming pool and beach. An excellent place, especially for the price. Closed November through March. Most major credit cards accepted. 1 Via Rota (phone: 81-878-4644). Expensive to moderate.

President – Set high on a bluff amid a pine grove overlooking the bay, this 82-room hotel has a swimming pool and gardens outside Sorrento on Colle Parise. Closed November through March. Via Nastro Verde, Colle Parise (phone: 81-878-2262). Expensive to moderate.

Antico Francischiello – Cheerful and hospitable, with genuine local cooking. Closed Wednesdays except in summer. Reservations unnecessary. No credit cards accepted. 27 Via Villazzano, about 4 miles (6 km) from Sorrento (phone: 81-877-1171). Moderate.

Bellevue Syrene – Converted from an 18th-century villa, it has 50 rooms in a charming setting. There's an elevator to a private beach. 5 Piazza della Vittoria (phone: 81-878-1024). Moderate to inexpensive.

La Favorita o' Parrucchiano – An authentic Sorrentine restaurant that serves fresh local cheeses — *trecce, burielli* — vegetables, and fish. Try the very good fish soup. Closed on Wednesdays during winter and spring. Reservations advised. Most major credit cards accepted. 71-73 Corso Italia (phone: 81-878-1321). Moderate to inexpensive.

La Tonnarella – An unpretentious 11-room pension on the outskirts of town that overlooks the sea, and has a hilltop restaurant in a lemon- and oleander-filled garden. Closed December through February. 31 Via Capo (phone: 81-878-1153). Inexpensive.

POSITANO

Sirenuse – Author John Steinbeck once stayed in one of the 65 rooms of this converted 18th-century villa, now a superb hotel with a good swimming pool and view of the sea. Open year-round. 30 Via Colombo (phone: 89-875066). Very expensive.

Buca di Bacco – Traditionally Positano's favorite restaurant of the yachting crowd. Try the fish and you might well understand why. Closed mid-October to March 24. Reservations necessary. Most major credit cards accepted. Via Marina, opposite the port (phone: 89-875699). Expensive.

Miramare – This first class 14-room hotel has a distinctive warmth despite its small size. Closed mid-November to mid-March. Viatrara Gencino (phone: 89-875002). Expensive.

Poseidon – The 50 rooms in this elegant establishment offer a lovely view of the sea and coastline. There is also a swimming pool. Closed October 14 through *Easter*. 148 Via Paitea (phone: 89-875014). Expensive.

San Pietro – Built into a cliff next to the sea, this 55-room hotel has an elevator to a private beach, a swimming pool, and tennis courts. Closed January through March. Less than 1 mile (1.6 km) south of town (phone: 89-875455). Expensive.

Palazzo Murat – The 18th-century palace of Gioacchino Murat (a King of Naples and Napoleon's brother-in-law) has been tastefully restored with some period furniture and beamed ceilings. All of the 28 rooms have a certain magic, but especially those overlooking the courtyard filled with purple bougainvillea. Open year-round. 23 Via dei Mulini (phone: 89-875177). Expensive to moderate.

La Cambusa – A very good restaurant that gets better all the time. It goes so far as to employ its own fishermen, and it also turns out Positano's best spaghetti with zucchini (the town's most characteristic dish) and an excellent fish soup. A lovely verandah overlooks the *piazzetta* and the beach. Closed from mid-January through March. Reservations advised. Most major credit cards accepted. Piazza Amerigo Vespucci (phone: 89-875432). Moderate.

Chez Black – A favorite of bathers taking a lunch break. Try the spaghetti with clams or the mixed fish fry. Closed November through January. Reservations necessary. Most major credit cards accepted. 19 Via del Brigantino (phone: 89-875036). Moderate.

Casa Albertina – A small and attractive family-run hotel with personal service. All rooms have terraces overlooking the sea. 4 Via della Tavolozza (phone: 89-875143). Moderate to inexpensive.

La Bougainville – In the center of town, this 14-room hotel is clean and convenient. Closed December through February (phone: 89-875047). Inexpensive.

Da Vincenzo – Less glamorous than some other dining spots but a favorite of Positanesi. Local fare is featured, including lots of fresh vegetables and baked pasta. Reservations unnecessary. No credit cards accepted. Up the hill on the Casa Soriano curve, at 172-178 Viale Pasitea (phone: 89-875128) Inexpensive.

AMALFI

Santa Caterina – This 42-room hotel stands atop a cliff with an elevator leading to a beach. There is also a saltwater swimming pool. Open year-round. 19 Via Nazionale (phone: 89-871012). Expensive.

Cappuccini Convento – An old monastery converted into a splendid 48-room hotel. High on a cliff, it has sensational views of the coast; also a solarium and a private beach. Open year-round. 46 Via Annunziatella (phone: 89-871008). Expensive to moderate.

Belvedere – It's cut into a cliff so that the series of terraces appear to be growing downward. Naturally, it overlooks the sea, with dazzling views from its 36 rooms. There is also a swimming pool. Closed November through March (phone: 89-831282). Moderate.

Excelsior Grand – Modern and efficient, this 85-room link in the Excelsior chain has a beach, a swimming pool, and gardens. Closed mid-October to mid-April. Three miles (5 km) outside Amalfi in Pogerola (phone: 89-871344). Moderate.

Da Gemma – A homey trattoria featuring outdoor dining in summer. Seafood specialties include spaghetti with clams and linguine with scampi. Good local wines. Closed Thursdays and January to mid-February. Reservations advised.

Most major credit cards accepted. Via Cavalieri di Malta (phone: 89-871345). Moderate.

Luna Convento – This converted 13th-century convent has 42 rooms, lovely cloisters, a restaurant, and a swimming pool. Open year-round. 19 Via Amendola (phone: 89-871002). Moderate.

La Caravella – Genuine southern Italian home-style cooking — both seafood and meat dishes. Closed Tuesdays and November. Reservations unnecessary. Most major credit cards accepted. 12 Via Camera (phone: 89-871029). Moderate to inexpensive.

Miramalfi – Featuring an elevator to the beach, a swimming pool, and 45 rooms (phone: 89-871588). Moderate to inexpensive.

RAVELLO

Palumbo al Confalone – This utterly romantic 19th-century villa, now a hotel is in a unique setting. It is built on the ruins of the 13th-century Confalone, perched 1,200 feet above the Amalfi Drive. Its fine restaurant offers specialties such as *fusilli al gorgonzola* and *crostini* of mozzarella. Be sure to have lunch in the beautiful garden overlooking the Gulf of Salerno — a special delight. Open year-round. 28 Via San Giovanni del Toro (phone: 89-857244). Expensive.

Caruso Belvedere – Formerly the 11th-century Palazzo D'Afflitto, it has been transformed into a delightful, 26-room hotel. Its restaurant is deservedly famous. It produces its own wines and a curious house soufflé — half lemon, half chocolate. Not only is the food delicious, the setting is gorgeous. Hotel open year-round. Restaurant closed Tuesdays during winter. 52 Via San Giovanni del Toro (phone: 89-857111). Moderate.

La Colonna – An attractive restaurant with whitewashed walls and vaulted ceilings. Owner Alfonso Sorrentino makes daily changes to the menu. His wife, Carmela, runs a ceramics shop in the main piazza. Closed Tuesdays. Reservations advised. Most major credit cards accepted. 20 Via Roma (phone: 89-857411). Moderate to inexpensive.

Cumpà Cosimo – Home cooking, Ravello-style — fresh fish and vegetables. Specialties include minestrone, bean soup, and pizza. Closed Mondays in winter. Reservations unnecessary. Most major credit cards accepted. Via Roma (phone: 89-857156). Moderate to inexpensive.

Parsifal – Not as elegant as the others but nonetheless tasteful, this 20-room hotel is in a section of a 13th-century convent. Closed October through March. 5 Via d'Anna (phone: 89-857144). Moderate to inexpensive.

Calabria

Calabria, the sunny toe in the boot that is Italy, is a strangely beautiful land. It is neither the average tourist's idea of southern Italy (as all sun, song, and smiles) nor is it the strictly dreary picture of a depressed people in a depressed part of the Mezzogiorno forever brooding on their not insignificant problems. Calabrians have the knack — learned perhaps out of necessity — of living reality rather than worrying about it.

It's a land rich in natural scenery, from the rugged, vineclad slopes of the northern Sila Mountains to the white sandy beaches at the southern tip of the Tyrrhenian Sea. A warm climate produces an abundance of ancient olive, lemon, and orange groves as well as bergamots, figs, and chestnuts that dot the mountains and central plains. But it's more the picturesque towns and the old-fashioned warmth of the Calabrians that set this region of Italy apart.

This is a land of hospitable people who welcome visitors with genuine cordiality, a jug of wine, a home-cooked meal, and a zest for living. Tradition is elemental to the Calabrians and embraces all areas of life. These southern Italians are also a superstitious people, celebrating their many religious feasts with pagan rites and wailing laments reminiscent of ancient Greece — no surprise in an area once known as Magna Graecia.

The region is divided into three provinces named after their capital cities: Cosenza, the inland section in the north; Catanzaro, farther south, near the eastbound Ionian coast; and Reggio di Calabria, at the tip of the toe, separated by only a narrow strait from Sicily.

If you're making your first visit to Calabria, we suggest driving from central Italy. Although you can fly to Lamezia Terme or Reggio di Calabria and rent a car there, the 248-mile (397-km) drive from Salerno (403 miles/645 km from Rome) on the Autostrada del Sole (A3) is unforgettable. You'll wind through some of Italy's most spectacular scenery: through tunnels carved out of the mountains, with views of medieval hill towns, pine forests, and glistening sea below.

The autostrada (one of the few toll-free *autostrade*) extends into Reggio di Calabria in southern Italy, but there is an alternative in Route 18. You can pick that up by leaving the autostrada at Lagonegro for Praia a Mare. Remember, though, that in the south of Italy, points of interest are much more widely separated than in the north, and driving is very difficult except for stretches of Route 18, which follow the coast quite closely.

The Calabrian portion of this trip begins in Praia a Mare, at the northern edge of the region. The route proceeds down the coastline, making several stops along the way at resort beaches and inland medieval towns. The part of the coastline that best captures the essence of Calabria is the Costa Viola (Violet Coast) in the southern province of Reggio. The Costa Viola extends some 31 miles (50 km) from Gioia Tauro to Santa Trada, just north of the provincial capital of Reggio di Calabria. Named for the violet hue that the land and turquoise Tyrrhenian Sea take on at sunset, the Costa Viola consists of a strip of small towns and sandy beaches, the latter interrupted by dramatic cliffs and grottoes. Many of the beaches are accessible only by boat, and the larger ones have only recently been provided access with roads and are indiscriminately dotted with *pensioni* and *trattorie*.

While the towns of this region have been reconstructed in a rather nondescript fashion following the 1908 earthquake, each still has its classic *corso* (main street), which provides the setting for the ritual evening *passeggiata* (promenade) and a favorite *caffè* or bar on the main piazza where townspeople gather to exchange gossip over a coffee, ice cream, or pastry.

From the Costa Viola you drive to Reggio di Calabria, the most modern city of the region, and continue inland toward the eastern coast and the Ionian Sea. There you'll find Italian towns still rich in Greek heritage as well as remnants of medieval architecture.

En Route from Salerno – On the drive south toward the Costa Viola from the beginning of Route 18, make your first stop at Paria a Mare or at Diamante, a bit farther along. Either provides a fine introduction to the province of Cosenza, with its wooded plains and beaches, many of which are becoming popular as year-round resorts. H. V. Morton's *A Traveller in Southern Italy* noted: "From Pizzo southward there is an additional clarity in the air, a bluer sea, beautiful clouds . . . one thinks a landscape like this could produce only poets and artists."

Continue right around the cape (Capo Vaticano) past Nicotera (where wonderful terra cotta masks are made — they ward off evil spirits), returning to Route 18 south. Now you begin the itinerary along the Costa Viola, with the first stop at Gioia Tauro.

GIOIA TAURO: Although this town is not a spectacular entry to the Costa Viola, it does boast some magnificent olive trees on the Plain of Gioia, said to be the oldest and largest in Europe, supposedly dating back to the time of Christ.

PALMI: Beyond the silvery flicker of olive groves along the coastline, the road suddenly opens to the largest of Palmi's sandy beaches, La Tonnara. At the southernmost point of the beach, on a rock jutting out of the sea, stands a solitary ancient olive tree. When the town council declared it Palmi's symbol a few years ago and began fertilizing and doctoring it, *l'olivo* suddenly wilted, demanding to be left once again to its own resources.

Like its symbol, Palmi thrives when left to follow its natural course. Physically lush subtropical plants and uncultivated flora — jasmine, bougainvillea, prickly pears, and of course the bergamots — fill the air with a sweet fragrance; culturally, Palmi's inhabitants continue to follow ancient beliefs and customs. You'll find living proof of the latter at the *Calabrian Folklore Museum,* which has fine collections of old and new masks from Seminara, Greek-style ceramics from the Ionian coast, pastoral art from the Aspromonte, and a number of religious and superstitious objects used to ward off evil spirits (open daily; in the Casa della Cultura Leonida Repaci; phone: 966-23530).

Before leaving Palmi, don't miss a trip up to the top of Mt. St. Elia, "the balcony over the Tyrrhenian." The magnificent view includes Mt. Etna and Messina in Sicily, the Aeolian Islands, and the Calabrian coast as far north as Cape Vatican. And be sure to take a drive to La Marinella, a tiny fishermen's cove, Palmi's bathing beach before the road to La Tonnara was built some 20 years ago. It's not a very comfortable pebble beach, but the area is good for snorkeling.

BAGNARA: South of Palmi, beyond the famous Zibibbo vineyards clinging to rocky terraces that descend toward the sea, you reach the swordfishing center of the Costa Viola. Activity hasn't changed in this town since the days of the early Greeks. Life centers around the capture, sale, and preparation of swordfish, at least between April and late July or August, when the fish come to spawn from colder Arctic waters. The fishermen harpoon the swordfish by hand as they did in ancient times.

Once ashore, the heavy catch is carried on the heads of the *bagnarote* (women of Bagnara) to the market for sale. Many are also exported to the larger cities and show up in restaurants throughout Italy. (They appear as *pesce spada* on the menu.)

Swordfish serves as the main diet staple for the southern Calabrians nearly 4 months a year; it is cooked in so many different ways that no one seems to tire of the meaty morsels. Most often, they are grilled and dowsed with *salmoriglio,* a tasty sauce of garlic, oregano, and olive oil.

SCILLA: As you drive south on the coastal highway with the Aspromonte Mountains to the left, the dramatic indented coastline on the right suddenly gives way to the huge rock of Scilla, recalling the myth of Scylla and Charybdis, which inspired poets from Homer to Schiller.

The town named for the rock of Scilla again brings to mind the ancient Greeks and their ancient rituals. This is never more evident than in Scilla's picturesque fishermen's quarters, known as the Chianalea. Here, a narrow cobblestone road lines the houses rooted to the famous rock. Fishermen's wives sit on small chairs outside their doorways when the swordfish aren't running, mending the great nets that provide their livelihood. When walking through the area, stop for lunch in a typical Scillan house, now a restaurant, *Da Glauco* (see *Best en Route*).

Before you even begin to approach Chianalea, you come upon an impressive medieval castle, seemingly sculpted out of the rock of Scilla itself. The foundations date from 493 BC, only it now hosts a youth hostel, *Ostello Murat Castello Di Pizzo* (phone: 965-754033) — one of the best of its kind — and a discotheque. This, as well as the grand terrace of the main town square, is worth a visit. Now a favorite promenade for residents and tourists, the terrace overlooks the rooftops of the Old Town and the beautiful sandy Sirens Beach.

SANTA TRADA CANNITELLO: The Costa Viola ends with this town, the peninsula's closest point to Sicily. For years there has been talk of a gigantic bridge being built that would eventually connect the town to Sicily, but at press time construction had not begun. The treacherous tidal currents of the Strait of Messina recall the plight of the ancient mariners. In fact, the currents are so strong and the water so cool that swimming between here and Reggio is nothing less than exhilarating, although the calm lukewarm waters between Palmi and Scilla are generally preferable.

VILLA SAN GIOVANNI: From this point there is frequent car ferry and hydrofoil service across the strait to Messina. Similar transport to Messina is also available regularly from Reggio, making a day trip to Taormina, only 31 miles (50 km) from Messina, almost irresistible.

REGGIO DI CALABRIA: A modern city almost entirely rebuilt following the earthquake of 1908, Reggio di Calabria is the gateway to Sicily. Although surrounded by a somewhat unattractive coastal shelf and numerous factories, Reggio has its high points. These include an elegant seaside boardwalk (Lungomare Marina) and the interesting *National Museum* (open daily; 26 Piazza de'Nava; phone: 965-754033), housing artifacts from the archaeological excavations in the region — especially of the early Greek and Roman civilizations — and the recovered and restored bronzes of Riace.

GERACE: You'll recognize Gerace well before you arrive, perched high on a sharp rock overlooking Locri. This solemn medieval town has a richness of art treasures unequaled in the region.

LOCRI: Your arrival in Locri itself may be less inspiring, since this flat modern town is more reminiscent of the dry and dreary Far West than of any Greek city you've ever seen. Don't despair. Drive a few miles south to the ruins of the ancient city of Epizephyrii. Take care not to miss the Greek-Roman theater and *Antiquarium* (museum) at Locri (closed Mondays; phone: 964-20844).

En Route from Locri – Rather than retrace your route across the rugged Aspromonte mountain chain, if it's early enough in the day, you can return to Reggio and the Costa Vióla by driving clear around the "toe" on Highway 106 along the Ionian or Jasmine Coast. This will take you past the Bovalino Marina on the slopes of the Aspromonte, Capo Spartivento, and the picturesque locality of Pentidattilo. While this area is particularly enticing for its traditional Indian summer during September and October, the months of June through August are more interesting for the student of folk customs. During this time feasts are celebrated in towns throughout the area, many concluding with elaborate fireworks displays.

BEST EN ROUTE

Hotels have improved a lot in Calabria over the past few years and you won't have much trouble finding comfortable accommodations in the bigger towns, though you won't find extremely luxurious establishments, either. Expect to pay $150 and up for a double room at those hotels categorized as expensive; between $80 and $150 at those in the moderate category; under $80, inexpensive. Expect to pay $100 or more for a meal for two at restaurants in the expensive category; between $50 and $100, moderate; under $50, inexpensive. Restaurants serve generous portions of southern cooking. Prices do not include drinks, wine, or tip.

GIOIA TAURO

Euromotel – This simple roadside hotel has adequate accommodations. Via Nazionale, about 1 mile (1.6 km) southeast of the city (phone: 966-52083). Moderate.

Park – Near the autostrada, with 44 rooms, it's modern, comfortable and convenient for passing travelers. 21 Via Nazionale (phone: 966-51159). Moderate.

Buco – Northern Italian dishes, primarily from Emilia, share the menu with local fare. Reservations unnecessary. No credit cards accepted. 116 Via Lo Moro (phone: 966-51512). Moderate to inexpensive.

PALMI

Arcobaleno – This 50-room hotel is on the road between Palmi and the Taureana Beach and has a restaurant, a swimming pool, and tennis courts. Via Taureana (phone: 966-46315). Expensive to moderate.

Centro Residenziale Costa Viola – A quiet, countryside hotel set among olive groves. The rooms have a lovely sea view. Open year-round. Località Torre (phone: 966-22016). Expensive to moderate.

La Lampara – Rustic in atmosphere, it serves excellent fish dishes, especially *involtini di pesce spada* (swordfish rolls) in season. Closed November and December. Reservations advised. Some credit cards accepted. Lido Tonnara (phone: 966-46332). Moderate.

La Marinella – The chef Salvatore's special pasta with tomato sauce, local *pecorino* (sheep's milk cheese), and good fresh fish are your best culinary bets here. Reservations advised. Some credit cards accepted. Marinella Cove (no phone). Moderate to inexpensive.

Pizzeria La Margherita – Specialities here are *pizza alla pioggia* and homemade whole wheat pasta in anchovy sauce. Open summers only. No reservations. No credit cards accepted. Across the road from the northern end of the Tonnara Beach (no phone). Moderate to inexpensive.

Miami – Although not as sophisticated as its name suggests, this hostelry is on a big local beach. Tonnara (phone: 966-46396). Inexpensive.

Oscar – In the heart of town, this hotel offers modern conveniences. Via Roma (phone: 966-23293). Inexpensive.

Pinewood Pizzeria (La Pineta) – Pizza is served under pine trees at St. Elia. No reservations. No credit cards accepted (phone: 966-22926). Inexpensive.

SCILLA

Ulisse – Excellent seafood — the chef used to work at London's *Savoy* — served in elegant surroundings. Closed Mondays. Reservations advised. Most major credit cards accepted. 1 Via Omiccioli (phone: 965-790190). Moderate.

Alla Pescatora – Run by a former fisherman, it serves fine seafood. Closed Wednesdays and mid-December to mid-March. Reservations advised. Some major credit cards accepted. 32 Via Colombo (phone: 965-754147). Moderate to inexpensive.

Da Glauco – A typical former house with a magnificent terrace overlooking the fishermen's houses, the port, and the Mediterranean, its special dish is Signora Pontillo's spicy dried tomatoes and pickled eggplant antipasto. Open daily. Reservations advised. Some major credit cards accepted. Take the road to La Chinela (Via Chinela) and turn off at the sign for *Da Glauco;* ring the bell marked "Samigila Pontina" (phone: 965-46330). Moderate to inexpensive.

Sirene – This hotel-restaurant on the beach serves fresh fish alfresco, near the sea. It has only 7 rooms. At the lower end of town; 57 Via Nazionale (phone: 965-754019). Inexpensive.

VILLA SAN GIOVANNI

Castello Altafiumara – This restored castle by the sea has tennis courts and a swimming pool. Near Villa San Giovanni–Cannitello (phone: 965-759061). Expensive.

Piccolo – Simply, the best hotel in town. Its restaurant has delicious antipasti, good wine, and homemade sweets and ice cream. Piazza della Stazione (phone: 965-751410). Expensive to moderate.

REGGIO DI CALABRIA

Baylik – A trattoria serving pasta and all kinds fish dishes from the Ionian coast. Closed Thursdays and mid-July to mid-August. Reservations advised. Most major credit cards accepted. 1 Via Leone (phone: 965-48624). Expensive.

Excelsior – Member of the deluxe Excelsior chain, this is *the* hotel in the capital, though some of its rooms and furnishings have seen better days. 66 Via Vittorio Veneto (phone: 965-25801). Expensive.

Miramare – Completely remodeled, it's now an excellent 96-room hostelry. The fine restaurant serves swordfish specialties and game in season. Excellent desserts. Restaurant closed Sundays. 1 Via Fata Morgana (phone: 965-91881). Expensive.

Palace Hotel Masoanri's – Slightly less deluxe than its sister hotel, the *Excelsior,* but still very comfortable. 95 Via Vittorio Veneto (phone: 965-26433). Expensive.

Bonaccorso – This well-respected restaurant near the station has fine pasta and boiled meat. Closed Fridays and August. Reservations advised. Most major credit cards accepted. 8 Via Cesare Battiste (phone: 965-96048). Expensive to moderate.

Primavera – A simple but comfortable hotel with 62 rooms. 177 Via Nazionale (phone: 965-47081). Expensive to moderate.

Collina dello Scoiattolo – Classic Calabrian dishes served artfully. Closed Wednesdays. Reservations advised. Most major credit cards accepted. 34 Via Provinciale (phone: 965-682255). Moderate.

Conti – One of the best dining spots for local antipasto, macaroni, and fish. The house wine, pellaro, is excellent. It also has a new, adjacent pizzeria. Closed Mondays, except in summer. Reservations advised. Most major credit cards accepted. 2 Via Giulia (phone: 965-29043). Moderate.

LOCRI

Demaco – A modern 37-room seafront hotel in the main town with polite management. Hotel open all year; restaurant closed in winter. 28 Via Lungomare (phone: 965-20247). Moderate.

Faro – If you want to spend some additional time exploring the Greek-Roman theater of Locri, you'll find these accommodations convenient. Closed Mondays and late October to late November. Portigliola, on Rte. 106 (phone: 965-390005). Inexpensive.

Rocco Simone – Peasant cooking in this small, welcoming trattoria near the Greek ruins. No reservations. No credit cards accepted. Piazza Contrada Moschetta (phone: 965-390005). Inexpensive.

Sicily

The largest island in the Mediterranean (9,925 square miles), Sicily is probably the least "Italian" of Italy's regions. Because of its strategic position among Europe, Africa, and Asia, Sicily has been invaded, conquered, and settled by many peoples during the last 3,000 years. Each group left traces of its civilization, both in the character of the Sicilians and in the architectural remains of its town churches, temples, and villas.

Originally part of Magna Graecia (Greater Greece), Sicily (and Siracusa, on the southeastern coast, in particular) was a great cultural center until it fell to the Romans and became an exploited colony. With the fall of the Roman Empire, Sicily became open territory, invaded by a succession of armies from barbaric northern tribes and Saracens to Byzantines. Finally, in the 11th and 12th centuries, the Normans brought a period of political peace to the island, and Sicily became an autonomous state whose power extended halfway up the Italian peninsula. Beginning in the 13th century, however, it fell back under foreign rule, to be controlled by France, Spain, and the Bourbon Kings of Naples until the arrival of Garibaldi, who began his campaign for the unification of Italy in Sicily. The island became part of Italy in 1860.

While by nature an agricultural land, Sicily has over the last 20 years or so developed some industry in the form of oil refineries and chemical plants. The island's natural wealth, though, lies in its citrus fruits, olives, and vineyards, with the most fertile land on the slopes of Mt. Etna. At 10,902 feet, Mt. Etna dominates eastern Sicily.

A common means of access to Sicily is by ferryboat or hydrofoil from the southern tip of the mainland at Reggio di Calabria or Villa San Giovanni across the Strait of Messina. This brings you to the starting point of the Sicilian route at the northeastern end of the island. The route zigzags along coastal roads and inland highways, covering the island in a fragmented, but often-traveled pattern that covers the most interesting towns and villages.

When visiting Sicily, try to arrive in spring or early fall; the climate is closer to that of North Africa than Europe, so it is advisable to avoid the intense heat of July and August.

MESSINA: The main port of Messina, founded by the Greeks in the 8th century BC and occupied by the Carthaginians and then the Romans, was rebuilt after the disastrous earthquake of 1908 and again after the bombardments of World War II.

Perhaps Messina's most unusual feature is a curious mechanical and astronomical clock, the biggest in the world, built in Strasbourg and brought to the town in 1933. Housed in the bell tower of the town's 13th-century Norman cathedral, the mechanism activates various carved figures, and evangelical scenes move into an intricate series of acts at midday that lasts for almost an hour. The clock and cathedral are in the central Piazza del Duomo. Just east of the cathedral is the church of the Annunziata dei Catalani, another Norman construction, and at the end of Viale della Libertà is the *National Museum,* with a choice selection of Renaissance and post-Renaissance art (open daily; phone: 90-355333).

TAORMINA: Twenty centuries ago this tiny, well-developed resort town (with only 5,000 full-time residents) was popular with the Greeks and Romans. It gained international fame early in the 20th century, when it was rediscovered by a group of English and German aesthetes. The draw has always been the same: its year-round mild climate and its spectacular position overlooking the bay and the rocky coast below. Best of all, in spite of the quite heavy tourist traffic in the summer, the town has lost none of its historical charm.

The first stop on any tour of Taormina should be the Greek theater, carved out of a natural cavity on the hillside and dominated by the smoking peak of Mt. Etna in the distance. It must be the most dramatic setting for a theater in the world. It is still used for modern productions of Greek tragedy as well as for summer festivals.

In the central Piazza Vittorio Emanuele stands Palazzo Corvaja, the site of Sicily's parliament in the 14th century.

Stroll down the nearby Corso Umberto, the main shopping street, to Piazza IX Aprile, a terrace surrounded by cafés where you can sit and enjoy a local almond wine aperitif and an incomparable view of the bay. Farther along is the medieval Convent of San Domenico, now one of the most beautifully situated hotels in Taormina (see *Best en Route*). At the end of Corso Umberto I is a tiny funicular station where a cable car takes you down to the beach of Mazzarò in the summer.

In addition to restaurants and hotels, Taormina is also full of nightclubs where Sicilian folklore is reenacted in song and dance by local groups.

CATANIA: Repeatedly destroyed and rebuilt after violent eruptions of Mt. Etna, Catania is a thriving commercial center originally founded as a Greek colony in the 8th century BC. Since the last eruption of Etna to affect Catania was in 1693, the Old City center has a 17th- and 18th-century air. In the heart of the city, at the Piazza del Duomo, stands the symbol of Catania — an elephant sculpted out of lava with an obelisk on its back. To the left of this structure is the Chierici Palace; nearby, a small river flows from its underground course along the slopes of Etna.

Catania serves not only as an economic and architectural center but as the starting point for a trip to the top of Mt. Etna. This takes at least half a day (preferably morning) and requires appropriate dress — heavy mountain shoes and some warm clothing. Leave the city along the long, straight main street, Via Etnea, which takes you through a landscape of burned-out craters and lava rocks past a mountain hotel (20 miles/32 km) to a cable car to the top, central crater. There you will see a large sea of magma heaving and bubbling with sulfur fumes. It is advisable to take along a guide from town. *CIT Tours* (phone: 95-327240 in Catania; 95-341411 at the airport) conducts tours (in English) of the area. Make sure to start your trip back to town at least 2 hours *before* sunset.

En Route from Catania – Follow Route 114 some 35 miles (56 km) south to Siracusa, passing as you do the bridge over the Simeto River, 5 miles (8 km) from Catania, where English and American troops fought bitterly against the Germans and Italians at the beginning of the Allied advance through Italy in 1943. Several war cemeteries dot the area.

SIRACUSA (SYRACUSE): More than any other Sicilian town, Siracusa shows archaeological evidence of the ancient Greek and Roman civilizations. Although now it has the air of a quiet provincial town, Siracusa was once a major cultural and political center on a par with Rome, Athens, and Carthage. One of the many legends surrounding it involves a Roman attack by sea and an ingenious defense planned by Archimedes, a native of Siracusa. He devised a system of setting fire to the enemy Roman ships by means of reflecting sun rays onto their sails. Siracusa was eventually captured by the Roman fleet, however, and Archimedes killed. Excavations around both Siracusa and Ortigia, the island site of the city's original settlement, now reveal much of its early Greek and Roman foundations.

Before you explore the city's archaeological remains, visit the *Archaeological Museum* in Villa Landolina Park (closed Mondays; phone: 931-66222). It is one of the most important museums in Italy and necessary for a basic knowledge of Sicily's history and prehistory. In its collection is the magnificent Greek statue, *Venus Anadyomene* (Venus from the Sea), discovered in 1804. The archaeological zone stands behind the present city. Its main highlight is the Greek theater, probably the largest and most complete monument of its type in the ancient world left to us. Sculpted out of rock probably in the 3rd century BC, the theater found frequent use under its main patron at the time, Aeschylus, a prolific playwright. Under his influence, Siracusa saw the birth of Greek drama. The theater is still used today for performances of Greek plays in the late spring of even-numbered years.

Opposite the Greek theater stands the Ara di Ierone II (Hieron II), a huge altar built for public sacrifices. From here it is a short walk to the Roman amphitheater, constructed in the 4th and 3rd centuries BC for the spectacle of Christians fighting lions. Although now planted with cypress and oleander trees, you can still clearly see traces of the original structure.

AGRIGENTO: Its hillside position on the southern coast overlooking the surrounding valley and sea earned for Agrigento the praise of the ancient Greeks and the poet Pindar, who named it "the most beautiful city of mortals." It is the site of the Valley of Temples, a magnificent complex of temples and impressive columns built in the 5th and 6th centuries BC as well as the birthplace of both the ancient philosopher-scientist-priest Empedocles and the modern playwright Luigi Pirandello.

PALERMO: The capital of Sicily and the seat of the regional Sicilian government, Palermo was known by the Greeks as Panormos — all port — for its gulf location, and today it still ranks as the most important seaport on the island.

Architecturally, Palermo is divided into a modern north side and an historic south side. The core of the old quarter is a crossroads known as the Quattro Canti di Città — the Four Corners of the City — bounded by a group of baroque buildings built in 1609. Nearby is the Piazza Pretoria and a 16th-century fountain, decorated by statues of pagan gods and nicknamed Piazza della Vergogna — Square of Shame.

Many of the beautiful palaces and churches for which Palermo is often recognized are of Norman design. This is true of the Church of the Martorana (Piazza Bellini) and the cathedral along Corso Vittorio Emanuele (a street flanked by baroque palaces). The latter houses five royal tombs.

BEST EN ROUTE

In Sicily you will find a number of luxury hotels, converted historic villas, and many smaller, simpler hotels. Expect to pay over $400 for a double room at those hotels categorized as very expensive; $250 to $350 at expensive; between $100 and $200 at those in the moderate category; under $90, inexpensive. Fish and seafood are the major ingredients in Sicilian cooking, and you can sample them at quite a few good restaurants. Expect to pay $100 or more for a meal for two at those restaurants categorized as expensive; between $70 and $100 at those in the moderate category; under $70, inexpensive. Prices do not include drinks, wine, or tip.

MESSINA

Alberto – The most elegant restaurant in town, it serves such delicacies as spaghetti *en papillote*. Closed Sundays and August 5 to September 5. Reservations necessary. Most major credit cards accepted. 95 Via Ghibellina (phone: 90-710711). Expensive.

Jolly Hotel dello Stretto – Part of the well-known, comfortable Italian chain, with views of the straits. Reservations necessary. 126 Via Garibaldi (phone: 90-43401). Expensive to moderate.

Pippo Nunnari – A pleasantly rustic place, decorated with antiques, and ideally suited for an introduction to Sicilian cooking. *Pasta alla Norma* (pasta with tomato sauce topped with slices of eggplant), *pesce spada* (swordfish), available in May and June, and the Sicilian dessert *pignolata* are served along with robust Sicilian wines. Closed Mondays and early July. Reservations advised. Most major credit cards accepted. 157 Via Ugo Bassi (phone: 90-293-8584). Expensive to moderate.

TAORMINA

San Domenico Palace – A former convent dating from 1400, this is one of the world's most beautiful hotels, providing wonderful views of Mt. Etna. Its spacious rooms, furnished in antiques, were once monastic cells. Low entrances and thick walls help cool the interiors during oppressively hot summers. It has a swimming pool and a restaurant. 5 Piazza San Domenico (phone: 942-23701). Very expensive.

Grande Albergo Capo Taormina – This large, modern hotel has a private beach, a swimming pool, and a well-run restaurant. Closed December through February. Mazzarò (phone: 942-24000). Expensive.

Granduca – Delightful and elegant, this restaurant is one of the most popular in town. Il Cavaliere (Sir) Gaetano Li Greggi, Sicily's galloping gourmet, presides over the kitchens. Closed Mondays (except during summer). Reservations necessary. Most major credit cards accepted. 170 Corso Umberto I (phone: 942-24420). Expensive.

Villa Sant'Andrea – Overlooking a small bay, this little hotel has its own private beach, a colorful garden, and a restaurant. Closed January and February. 137 Via Nazionale, Mazzarò (phone: 942-23125). Expensive.

Pescatore – Taormina's best trattoria stands against a hill above the rocky bay. The simple but well-chosen menu mainly features fish. Closed Mondays and November through February. Reservations advised. Most major credit cards accepted. Via Nazionale, Isolabella, Mazzarò (phone: 942-23460). Expensive to moderate.

CATANIA

Catania Sheraton – Just 7 miles (11 km) north of Catania, this large hotel complex has a private beach, swimming pool, tennis court, and seaside buffet service, as well as a restaurant. Cannizzaro (phone: 95-271557). Expensive to moderate.

Pagano – A homey, casual restaurant near the courthouse, it serves a wide variety of Sicilian specialties, as well as some innovative local dishes. Closed Saturdays and August. Reservations advised. Some major credit cards accepted. 37 Via de Roberto (phone: 95-322730). Moderate.

Siciliana – This family-style restaurant is Catania's best and has a garden for outdoor dining. The menu includes traditional Sicilian dishes like roast kid, risotto with squid ink, and mixed fish grill as well as heady regional wines. Closed Sunday evenings and Mondays. Reservations advised. Major credit cards accepted. 52-A Viale Marco Polo (phone: 95-376400). Moderate.

SIRACUSA

Jonico (a Rutta e Ciauli) – One of the few places in Sicily where the meat is as delicious as the fish. The restaurant's terrace has a great view of the sea and cliffs. Closed Tuesdays, mid-August, and the first half of September. Reservations advised. Most major credit cards accepted. 194 Riviera Dionisio il Grande (phone: 931-65540). Moderate.

Villa Politi – This converted 19th-century villa surrounded by gardens was one of Winston Churchill's favorite vacation spots. Near the archaeological zone, it isn't nearly as grand as it once was, but at press time full restoration was slated to begin by September of last year and scheduled to be completed this year. It has a good restaurant, a swimming pool, and tennis courts. 2 Via M. Politi Laudien (phone: 931-32100). Moderate.

AGRIGENTO

Mosè – Traditional Sicilian cuisine served in a pleasant atmosphere. Closed Mondays and August. Reservations unnecessary. Some major credit cards accepted. 6 Contrada San Biagio (phone: 922-26778). Moderate.

Villa Athena – Built at the turn of the century, this charming hotel has a swimming pool, a garden, an excellent restaurant, and a great view over the Valley of Temples. The restaurant, one of the best in the area, serves meals where the Arab culinary influence is noticeable. The staff, however, could be a little friendlier and the walls between the guestrooms a little thicker. Via dei Templi (phone: 922-586288). Moderate.

PALERMO

Charleston – One of Sicily's most famous restaurants because of the consummate excellence of its food. Closed Sundays and from mid-June to late-September. 30 Piazzale Ungheria (phone: 91-321366). During summer, a branch that serves excellent fish and wonderful dessert is open at Mondello Beach. Viale Regina Elena (phone: 91-450171). Reservations advised for both. Most major credit cards accepted at both. Expensive.

Gourmand's – One of Palermo's most popular dining spots, it serves and occasionally invents its own classic Sicilian dishes. Closed Sundays and mid-August. 37/E Via della Libertà (phone: 91-323431). During summer, there's a branch open on Via Torre in Mondello. Reservations advised for both. Most major credit cards accepted at both (phone: 91-450049). Expensive.

Villa Igiea Grand – This classic Sicilian hotel, a short taxi ride from the downtown area, stands on a private beach and has a swimming pool and tennis courts. Both the hotel and its fine restaurant, *La Terrazza,* are renowned for excellent service. 43 Via Belmonte (phone: 91-543744). Expensive.

A'Cuccagna – A lively city restaurant that excells in regional dishes, especially seafood. Closed Mondays and August. Reservations advised. Most major credit cards accepted. 21-A Via Principe di Granatelli (phone: 91-587267). Expensive to moderate.

Grande Albergo e delle Palme – Large, old-fashioned, and centrally located, this hotel has an appropriately seductive touch of decadence, which acted even on Wagner, who composed here. The renowned restaurant, *La Palmetta,* perched atop the roof garden, is excellent. 398 Via Roma (phone: 91-583933). Expensive to moderate.

Scuderia – Traditional Sicilian dishes are prepared with love and imagination in this modern establishment, one of Palermo's best, located on the outskirts of town near the racetrack. You can dine in the garden. Closed Sunday evenings. Reservations advised. Most major credit cards accepted. 9 Via del Fante (phone: 91-520323). Expensive to moderate.

Excelsior Palace – A comfortable hotel near the fashionable Via della Libertà. 3 Via Marchese Ugo (phone: 91-625-6176). Moderate.

N'Grasciata – Good home cooking is found at this typical dockside trattoria off the beaten tourist track. Well known for its seafood. Try the *bottarga* (pressed tuna eggs) by itself or as a sauce for pasta. Closed Sundays. Reservations advised. Most major credit cards accepted. 12 Via Tiro a Segno (phone: 91-6161947). Moderate to inexpensive.

Il Dottore del Brodo – This small tavern becomes the gathering place of Sicilian men and women of letters in the evenings. You can order regional soup and pasta dishes according to the season and sometimes grilled fish, meat, and good local wine. Closed Sundays. Reservations unnecessary. No credit cards accepted. 5 Vicolo Paterna (phone: 91-320138). Inexpensive.

Sardinia

Floating in the Tyrrhenian Sea 116 miles from Italy's western coast and 130 miles from Africa's northern coast lies the rugged, sunwashed island of Sardinia. Originally inhabited in neolithic times, Sardinia had an early history of invasion by Phoenician and Punic forces who, in addition to warfare, brought the island trade, language, writing, and, of course, art, of which many examples are on exhibit today in the capital city, Cagliari. In the later Roman-Punic wars, Sardinia was conquered by the military forces of the Roman Empire. During the Middle Ages and Renaissance, Sardinia was the object of intense rivalry between various Italian city-states, and its relationship to the rest of Italy was only resolved when it joined the unification in 1860 as a region. Here, on the tiny island of Caprera off Sardinia's northern shore, Giuseppe Garibaldi is buried.

With a population of about 1.5 million, Sardinia is one of the most sparsely populated Italian regions, although it is the second largest island in the Mediterranean. Its people have been firmly planted on their home ground for centuries and are something of a race apart from Italian mainlanders and even the Sicilians, whose island has also been crossed and conquered continuously through the centuries. Sardinians are a hardy, withdrawn, but hospitable people. They believe strongly in an independent economy based on agriculture and fishing, despite the gradual development of industry on the island. For those who live off the land, life is hard even today, and the sight of a lonely shepherd eking out a living on some stony hilltop is still fairly common. Once Sardinia was the main supplier of timber for the Italian mainland; now the land is bare, covered by olive trees, juniper, myrtle, asphodel, and wild roses, the odor of which covers the island in spring. Typical handicrafts include handloomed carpets, ceramics, and coral jewelry.

There are still few roads in Sardinia and not more than half a dozen large towns on its 9,300 square miles. These few towns, though, are invested with a history that makes them well worth visiting. And for those interested in prehistoric ruins, there are many *nuraghe,* prehistoric stone defense towers, some surrounded by several rings of stone fortifications. If you plan to visit in August, check with the local authorities about possible danger from fires in the areas, a recurring yearly problem.

Start your tour of the island in Cagliari, and drive along the western coast past fishing villages, new resorts, and coal mining towns until you reach the unspoiled northern tip of the island at Santa Teresa. Then head back south to Cagliari, but this time along the eastern coast, Costa Smeralda, a sometime haven for jet setters and Italian business barons. The trip forms a complete loop in approximately 5 days.

CAGLIARI: The city can be reached by the daily car ferry from Civitavecchia, a little over an hour's train journey going north from Rome. Cagliari is to all appearances an unattractive, modern town and a busy port. It has an old center, however, surrounded by 13th-century walls built by the Pisans. When you enter the medieval core of the town, explore the cathedral and then walk to the Terrazza Umberto I — all that is left of a 16th-century Spanish fortification. The terrace offers a splendid view of the harbor and nearby pine forests. Be certain to visit the Roman amphitheater, Sardinia's largest Roman monument, and the Botanical Gardens, with its display of Mediterranean and tropical plants.

    En Route from Cagliari – Before beginning the northward climb up the Sardinian coastline, drive south along the SS 195 for 18 miles (30 km) to Nora. En route you pass Sarroch and Villa St. Pietro, and nearby *nuraghe* colonies. These groups of circular stone structures are considered to be the earliest signs of civilization on the island. Nobody has yet determined whether they indicate dwelling places, burial grounds, or fortifications. Nearby is the Church of Sant'Efisio, honoring the patron saint of Cagliari. It's enlivened by a colorful traditional religious procession on May 1.

SAN ANTIOCO: This ancient port, reached by continuing along the SS 195, is now connected by a bridge to the Sardinian mainland. In its old center (where a Genoese dialect is still spoken), visit the *Museum of Ancient Artworks* and the nearby necropolis of Sulcis. Its long sandy beaches and spectacular rocky coastline are an added attraction. From the port of Calasetta (known for its wines) at the north of the island, take the short car-ferry ride to Carloforte on the neighboring island of San Pietro.

SAN PIETRO: Lined with beaches and undulating rock-hewn inlands, Isola San Pietro is the tuna center of Sardinia. Here the killing (called *mattanza*) of huge tuna fish, during May and June, is a major event and provides, along with agriculture, one of the island's main sources of income. From San Pietro's Carloforte take the ferry to Portovesme (an hour's crossing) and continue to Iglesias, 18 miles (30 km) inland.

IGLESIAS: This is the capital of the coal mining area and the home of a museum for other mineral specimens found in Sardinian soil. Its architecture reflects a Spanish influence, evident in the town's two Gothic cathedrals. Heading north for 15 miles (24 km), you come to the Roman temple at Antas.

ORISTANO: Along the Gulf of Oristano and the mouth of the river Tirso, this town survived centuries of foreign invasion. Remains of its original medieval defense walls — the Porta Manna — stand in the central Piazza Roma. In town, visit the *Antiquarium Arborense* (open Tuesdays through Saturdays; 8 Via Vittorio Emanuele; phone: 783-70422), a museum containing archaeological findings from the neolithic age.

THARROS: Originally a Carthaginian, then a Roman port, this town was probably abandoned around the 11th century. Its ruins reveal something of each age, from Punic waterworks and temples, to Roman baths and houses, to early Paleo-Christian churches and a Jewish temple.

BOSA: On one of the hills surrounding the fishing village of Bosa Marina, this small town at the mouth of the Temo River is dominated by the medieval castle of Serravalle. Primarily Spanish in character, the town's residential section is replete with 16th- and 17th-century façades and wrought-iron balconies. About 1 mile (1.6 km) outside town stands the Church of San Pietro Extramuros, the oldest Romanesque church in Sardinia, built in the 11th century.

ALGHERO: Set amid olive and eucalyptus trees, Alghero, on the Coral Coast (as it is called), combines a long stretch of beachland with an old town center clearly Catalan Spanish in character. Many Catalan customs are practiced here to this day. The morning fish market is a spectacular sight.

On your tour, follow the ancient defense walls until you near the town center, then walk toward the stocky round tower, Torre Sulis, for a splendid view of the surrounding coast. Don't miss the side trip by boat across the bay to the dramatic Capo Caccia and the Grotta di Nettuno, a series of underground caves that have, over the ages, formed crystalline stalactites and stalagmites. Much of the grotto is yet unexplored. Nearby is Porto Conte, a resort that offers fine free beaches for swimmers; follow the coastal road, Route 127 *bis,* west for about 8 miles (13 km).

En Route from Alghero – Travel north (direction Porto Torres) 7 miles (11 km) to the prehistoric (Bronze Age) necropolis of Anghelu Ruiu in the heart of Sardinian wine country (Tenuta dei Pini). From the necropolis, continue north several miles and then east on the SS 291 to Sassari.

SASSARI: This is Sardinia's second capital, founded in the 11th century by coastal inhabitants seeking a more secure dwelling place inland. A relatively independent locality, its citizens are renowned for their courage in resisting the Austrians in World War I.

Sassari's history is best traced by a visit to the *Sanna Museo Archeologico Etnografico* (closed Mondays; 64 Via Rome; phone: 79-272203). It contains archaeological findings from prehistory to the Middle Ages as well as some fine examples of Sardinian art and craftsmanship. Walk through town past the Fonte Rosello, a stone fountain built by the Genoese in 1605, and the remains of the medieval defense walls and towers. Climb the steep slope of Corso Vittorio Emanuele II to the Church of Santa Maria di Betlemme, with its Romanesque façade and baroque interior. This church hosts the concluding ceremonies of Sassari's *Feast of Candlesticks* procession, which is held on August 14 to commemorate the end of an outbreak of the plague in 1580.

CASTELSARDO: Tourist development in Castelsardo hasn't spoiled the loveliness of this former fishing village. The remains of a medieval castle on a high rock overlooking the town still offer an unparalleled view of the Costa Paradiso to the northeast and the Gulf of Asinara to the west, and the old part of the town with its steep winding streets and 16th-century cathedral still stands intact. Castelsardo is also known for craftsmanship, especially basketwork made from the fronds of the dwarf palm trees that abound in the area.

En Route from Castelsardo – Take a leisurely drive north from Castelsardo to Santa Teresa, enjoying the Costa Paradiso, with its red cliffs and fantastic rock formations jutting into a vivid blue sea. The ride is 40 miles (64 km) on route SS 200.

SANTA TERESA DI GALLURA: Santa Teresa, on the farthest northern tip of Sardinia, is another small fishing village developed for tourism but still unspoiled. Surrounded by sheltered bays, it's an ideal stopping place. A trip also should be made to the Capo Testa Peninsula, about 3 miles (5 km) outside town, and its amazing rock formations. From there, Corsica appears to be only a stone's throw away.

En Route from Santa Teresa di Gallura – As you travel around the northern cap of Sardinia, the coastal road brings you to a pair of islands — Palau and Capo Orso, opposite the archipelago of La Maddalena — that are barren, but beautiful. Accompanied by many other islands surrounding the archipelago, these are rich fishing grounds and renowned tourist spots. One of the most famous islands nearby is Caprera, where Garibaldi is buried. The southbound route along the eastern coast of Sardinia begins here.

COSTA SMERALDA: Called a millionaire's playground, Costa Smeralda (the Emerald Coast), on the northeastern edge of Sardinia, has been transformed by the Aga Khan into one of the most fashionable resorts in Europe. Hotels built in a rustic,

Moorish style border private secluded bays (*Cala di Volpe* is an example; see *Best en Route*), and fishing villages have been transformed into quaint towns with very pricey cafés, restaurants, and boutiques. Stop in Porto Cervo and nearby Porto Rotondo, with its terrace overlooking the huge harbors.

For a taste of local fare, it is more advisable, and probably less expensive, to go to Olbia, 11 miles (18 km) south of Porto Rotondo.

OLBIA: One of the main ports that connect Sardinia to Italy, Olbia is easily the prettiest, surrounded by a ragged coastline and picturesque little islands dotted here and there in the gulf.

NUORO: Almost devoid of monuments, churches, or remains that mark its origins, Nuoro is nevertheless worth an overnight stay just to see something of the wild interior of Sardinia. On a hill, it overlooks a vast expanse of woodland and barren mountains, favorite grounds for hunters. It is also the hometown of two of Sardinia's greatest writers — poet Sebastiano Satta and Nobel Prize winner Grazia Deledda, whose house is now preserved as a tiny museum on Via Deledda.

En Route from Nuoro – This final portion of the Sardinian route takes you along southeastern coastal roads and then inland to Cagliari. You pass through a wide, green, and prosperous valley until you reach Oliena, at the bottom of a craggy mountain, the Sopromonte, famous for its vineyards. Continue on to Tortoli and Arbatax, resort towns renowned for their beauty.

Continue south through the coastal plains of Sardinia, past several *nuraghe* excavations, and on to Muravera, an agricultural town, once surrounded by orange groves, now surrounded by a few discretely placed tourist hotels. On route SS 125, turn inland for the last 39½ miles (64 km) to Cagliari, where the road winds through forests and mountain gorges to the Quartu Sant'Elena, a suburb of Cagliari. There, some interesting 15th-century Sardinian paintings are displayed in the parish church. Returning to Cagliari proper, there should be time for a last Sardinian meal before the night ferry leaves for Civitavecchia.

BEST EN ROUTE

Accommodations on Sardinia range from sleek coastal resorts to simpler establishments, but most share a greater or lesser proximity to the sea. Restaurant reservations are necessary on the Costa Smeralda, and for dinner at all seafood restaurants in July and, especially, August. Expect to pay $170 or more per night for a double room at those places categorized as expensive (much higher on the Costa Smeralda where prices can be as high as $800); between $90 and $150 at those in the moderate category; under $65, inexpensive. Expect to pay $50 or more for a meal for two at those restaurants categorized as expensive; between $50 and $90 at restaurants in the moderate category; under $50, inexpensive. Prices do not include drinks or tip.

CAGLIARI

Dal Corsaro – Fresh and imaginatively cooked lobster, eel, shrimp, and fish are all well worth trying. There are also traditional Sardinian meat dishes and a large selection of robust Sardinian wines. Closed Tuesdays and from December 22 to January 4. 28 Viale Regina Margherita (phone: 70-664318). During the summer, the restaurant opens another branch at Poetto (phone: 70-370295). Reservations necessary for both. Most major credit cards accepted at both. Expensive.

Regina Margherita – This very comfortable hotel is the only truly superior establishment in town. Some of its 100 air conditioned rooms have views of the port; all have private baths. *La Cascata Terrace Café* is in a garden with a fountain. 44 Viale Regina Margherita (phone: 70-670342). Expensive.

Sa Cardiga e Su Schironi – The front of this small, unpretentious restaurant is a grocery store; the back houses a homey restaurant with good local wine and food. Closed Mondays and from late October to late November. Reservations advised. Most major credit cards accepted. On the Pula Road, SS 195, at the Capoterra intersection (phone: 70-71652). Expensive.

Mediterraneo – One of Cagliari's few first-rate establishments, it boasts 136 rooms, a lush garden, and a restaurant, *Al Golfo*. Lungomare Cristoforo Colombo (phone: 70-653971). Expensive to moderate.

Panorama – A modern hotel with 97 air conditioned rooms, swimming pool, and penthouse restaurant (closed Sunday evenings and Mondays). 231 Viale Armando Díaz (phone: 70-307691). Expensive to moderate.

Italia – Modern and absolutely central, this hotel has 113 rooms and a coffee shop open until reasonably late. Closed August 2 through 23. 31 Via Sardegna (phone: 70-655772). Moderate.

ISOLA SAN PIETRO

Hieracon – Romantics will enjoy this hotel/*ristorante* with panoramic views of the water and tranquil gardens. All rooms include private bath, a telephone, air conditioning, and heating. True Sardinian ambience, 5 minutes from the ferry. Open year-round. 62 Corso Cavour (phone: 781-854028). Moderate.

ORISTANO

Faro – Considered the town's best dining spot, specialties here include lobster salad, spaghetti with *bottarga* (pressed tuna eggs), *penne* (tubelike pasta) with *pecorino* cheese, and mixed fish grill. Closed Sundays, Mondays, the first half of January, and the second half of July. Reservations advised. Major credit cards accepted. 25 Via Bellini (phone: 783-70002). Expensive to moderate.

Forchetta d'Oro – Fish features prominently on the menu, especially the Sardinian *bottarga*. Its terrace and garden contribute to the restaurant's popularity. Closed Sundays and the last half of August. Reservations advised. Most major credit cards accepted. Via Giovanni XXIII (phone: 783-302731). Moderate to inexpensive.

Mistral – A well-maintained modern hotel near the center, with a reasonably attractive lounge and bar. The hotel's restaurant turns out some of the best food in town, thanks to the eye for detail and service of the German management, and the chef, a Sardinian, tempted back from one of Berlin's top Italian restaurants. Via Martiri di Belfore (phone: 783-302445). Moderate to inexpensive.

Nicolò – The island's Arab connections are celebrated in this jolly trattoria, where couscous appears on the menu along with local fare. Closed Fridays except in summer. Reservations unnecessary. Some major credit cards accepted. Via Dante Carloforte (phone: 783-854048). Moderate to inexpensive.

ALGHERO

Villa Las Tronas – On a promontory overlooking the sea, with its own fine restaurant, this was once a summer residence of the Italian royal family. Only 30 rooms, so book ahead. Hotel open year-round; restaurant closed Wednesdays and from mid-September to mid-May. 1 Lungomare Valencia (phone: 79-975390). Expensive.

Carlos V – A swimming pool, tennis court, and garden are among the facilities at this functional, modern hostelry on the waterfront. 24 Lungomare Valencia (phone: 79-979501). Expensive to moderate.

Lepanto – This warm, traditional restaurant (the busiest in town and also claimed to be among the best) faces the sea. When available, fresh lobster is the specialty.

Caviar usually is on the menu. Closed Mondays during winter. Reservations necessary. Most major credit cards accepted. 135 Via Carlo Alberto (phone: 79-979116). Expensive to moderate.

Pavone – Great soup, antipasto, risotto, and seafood are served at this small, family-run restaurant. Many think it's the best in town. Closed Wednesdays and January. Reservations advised. Most major credit cards accepted. 3-4 Piazza Sulis (phone: 79-979584). Expensive to moderate.

Del Mare da Uccio – All the local specialties — spaghetti with squid, sea bass, lobster, and crab — are available, as are the best local wines. Closed Tuesdays and November. Reservations advised. Some major credit cards accepted. 8 Via Liverno (phone: 79-979238). Moderate to inexpensive.

SANTA TERESA DI GALLURA

Shardana – This secluded hotel and restaurant have a private beach, swimming pool, garden, and tennis courts. Although its isolation is now threatened by encroaching development, its position on the sea is still lovely. Closed from October to late May. Santa Reparata (phone: 789-754031). Expensive to moderate.

Canne al Vento da Brancaccio – The owners of this simple restaurant are also farmers, which accounts for the freshness of the meat and cheese. The wine selection is very good. Guestrooms are available, too. Closed Saturdays (except in summer) and from October through November 15. Reservations unnecessary. No credit cards accepted. 23 Via Nazionale (phone: 789-754219). Inexpensive.

Nibbari – In a field between the main road and the rocky Santa Teresa beach, this 38-room quiet, comfortable hotel has a good restaurant. Closed October through May. About 1 mile (1.6 km) south of town, Località la Testa (phone: 789-754453). Inexpensive.

COSTA SMERALDA

Cala di Volpe – Owned by the Aga Khan, this extravagant hotel has served as a background for James Bond movies and is the jet set headquarters on Sardinia. The 123 rooms are rustic in decor but luxurious in appointments. Open May through September (phone: 789-96083). Very expensive.

Cervo – A large, elegant hotel with a heated freshwater swimming pool. Closed November through mid-March. Porto Cervo (phone: 789-92003). Expensive.

Le Ginestre – This 64-room hotel has a restaurant and a freshwater swimming pool and is a short walk from a small beach. It's a good choice if you don't care about being directly on the water. Closed October through mid-April. Golfo Pevero (phone: 789-92030). Expensive.

Mola – Long considered by many to be the best restaurant in the area, it has successfully resisted the moneyed winds of change — everything is still good. Closed November to March. Reservations advised. Most major credit cards accepted. Piccolo Pevero (phone: 789-92436). Moderate.

Lu Stazzu – Here's where to sample Sardinian specialties like *maloreddus* (dumplings with a tomato and sausage sauce) and *porcetto al mirto* (suckling pig roasted on a spit and served on a bed of myrtle leaves). Lu Stazzu Picuccia, on the road from Porto Cervo to Arzachena. Reservations advised. Most major credit cards accepted (phone: 789-82657). Moderate.

Pomodoro – A chic *pizzeria/ristorante* just behind the *Cervo* hotel. Excellent antipasto and mouth-watering pizza in an attractive rustic setting indoors or outside under a grape arbor. Open year-round. Reservations unnecessary. Some major credit cards accepted. Porto Cervo (phone: 789-92207). Moderate to inexpensive.

OLBIA

Gallura – This small, humble dining establishment conceals an excellent kitchen that serves traditional Sardinian dishes. Closed Mondays, October 15 to 30, and during the *Christmas* holidays. Rooms are available, too. Reservations essential. Most major credit cards accepted. 145 Corso Umberto (phone: 789-24648). Expensive to moderate.

Tana del Drago – The nearby Golfo degli Aranci keeps this place well supplied with fresh fish. Closed Mondays and November. Reservations unnecessary. Some major credit cards accepted. About 1 mile (1.6 km) northeast of town in Fruttuosu (phone: 789-58632). Moderate.

NUORO

E.S.I.T. – This place offers genuine hospitality and home-cooked food. Monte Ortobene, about 5½ miles (9 km) east of town (phone: 784-33108). Moderate.

Fratelli Sacchi – Here you'll find a limited but well-prepared menu. Pasta with asparagus and roast wild boar are house specialties. There also are 21 guestrooms. Closed Mondays and from October through April. Restaurant reservations advised. Some major credit cards accepted. Five miles (8 km) east of town at Monte Ortobene (phone: 784-34030). Hotel inexpensive; restaurant moderate to inexpensive.

Grazia Deledda – The largest hotel in town, it has a fine restaurant where the service is good, as is the cooking. 175 Via Lamamora (phone: 784-31257). Inexpensive.

Liechtenstein

Liechtenstein is not the obscure, lunch-stop country it's often made out to be. Almost three times the size of Bermuda, it's a fairy-tale land of medieval castles, lush Rhine meadows, ivy-clad chalets, vineyards, and quaint villages clinging to the Alps. Although Liechtenstein borders Switzerland and Austria and is quite close to one of the most popular tourist circuits in Europe, this 62-square-mile principality of 28,500 residents still has the virtue of being off the beaten track of most travelers.

From 1938 until his death in 1989, the country was ruled by Prince Franz Josef II Maria Alois Alfred Karl Johann Heinrich Michael Georg Ignatius Benediktus Gerhardus Majella, the Twelfth Ruling Prince of Liechtenstein, Duke of Troppau, Duke of Jägerndorf, Count of Reitberg, and Knight of the Golden Fleece; he had been the longest-reigning ruler in the world. In contrast to the pomp of his name and titles, Franz Josef, one of the wealthiest men in Europe, dressed casually and drove around in his own, medium-priced car. All of Liechtenstein shed tears at his passing and that of his wife, whose death he survived by only a month. His son, Crown Prince Hans Adam (who had substituted for his father since 1984), now is the ruling Prince of Liechtenstein. The royal family still lives in the 13th-century castle perched about 300 feet above Vaduz, the country's main city, and Prince Hans Adam presides over a land that has been continuously inhabited for more than 5,000 years. In the late 1600s, a wealthy Austrian, Prince Liechtenstein, bought out two bankrupt counts with property in the Rhine Valley and created the principality in 1719.

Today, it is an industrial nation producing an array of items from pharmaceuticals to false teeth, yet its factories are virtually impossible to find because they're in low-profile buildings in vineyards, polluting neither the air nor the water. Liechtenstein's people — none of whom is unemployed — enjoy one of the highest standards of living in the world and pay very low taxes. The country is without an army, university, or hospital. Liechtenstein is represented worldwide by the Swiss National Tourist Offices (there are US offices in New York City, Chicago, and San Francisco).

There are several ways to get to the principality: A 5-minute drive or a train ride from Buchs, Switzerland, brings you to the village of Schaan, and it's a half-hour drive from Feldkirch, Austria. Both Buchs and Feldkirch are stops on the *Paris-Innsbruck-Vienna* express; local trains on the same route stop at three Liechtenstein villages — Schaan, Nendeln, and Schaanwald. A convenient and enjoyable entry route is the hour-long train ride from Zurich on the *Zurich-Chur* line. The train glides through spectacularly beautiful Swiss countryside along the western shores of the Zurich and Walen lakes to the medieval Swiss town of Sargans. A 15-minute ride by the Swiss *Postbus* or by taxi takes you from one of the oldest democracies in the world to Vaduz, the capital of monarchal Liechtenstein, one of the last remnants of the Holy Roman Empire.

Vaduz is a convenient base for successive explorations of the northern lowlands, eastern mountain region, and southern Rhine Valley; this 50-mile (80-km) route takes about 2 or 3 days of leisurely travel. If you enter from Switzerland, you won't have any border-crossing headaches because Liechtenstein and Switzerland have the same currency and customs authority. If you enter from Austria, Switzerland's formalities apply. The people of the principality speak the Swiss brand of German.

VADUZ: Most of the highlights in Vaduz (pronounced Va-*dootz*) are in the main street area (the Städtle). Head for the Liechtenstein National Tourist Office (37 Städtle; phone: 21443; fax: 20806) and arm yourself with free brochures and guides and a detailed map of the principality (about $1). There are two major attractions in the same building as the tourist office: the *Postage Stamp Museum,* featuring changing exhibitions from the collection of the Princes of Liechtenstein (open daily; no admission charge; phone: 66259) and the *Liechtenstein State Art Collection* (open daily; admission charge; phone: 22341). The art collection is packed with priceless objets d'art, including one of the most impressive Rubens collections in the world. In addition, there are Rembrandts, Botticellis, Pieter Breughels, and Van Dycks. Many of the paintings are reproduced on Liechtenstein's postage stamps, which can be seen (and purchased) in the *Postage Stamp Museum.* The museum is known to philatelists the world over, as the stamps are among the most decorative and valuable in the world. Right next door is the *National Museum* (open daily; admission charge; 43 Städtle; phone: 22310). Get your passport stamped with the impressive crown insignia at the museum's boutique on the first floor. The museum has local artifacts dating from the Iron Age and a vast collection of medieval weapons, sculptures, and paintings.

The boutiques, souvenir shops, and sidewalk cafés in this area are worth a browse. You can find good buys in leather and wooden handicrafts, local wine, art books, chocolates, and domestic liqueurs. Treat yourself to the local grilled game meat, soufflés, and hearty stews served at one of Europe's most celebrated restaurants, in the *Real* hotel (see *Best en Route*), next door to the tourist office. Felix Real, the owner-chef, and his brother, Emil, who operates the posh *Park Hotel Sonnenhof* (in a mountainside vineyard half a mile away on Mareestrasse; see *Best en Route*) learned how to cook in their native Italy. They perfected their skills at *Maxim's* of Paris, and have been catering to royalty ever since.

No visit to Vaduz is complete without a trip to the palace, and the most enjoyable way to get there is by taking a leisurely, 20-minute stroll up a wooded footpath from the tourist office. Or take a bus from the Städtle or rent a bicycle from *Hans Melliger* (10 Kirchstr.; phone: 21606). Although the castle itself is not open to the public, the terraces and rolling meadows around it are perfect picnic spots, and the elevation provides a panoramic view of Vaduz, the Rhine Valley, and the surrounding Alps. You can drive, cycle, or take the *Postbus* (the Swiss Rail Pass is good on them) from Vaduz north to Schellenberg. It's a half-hour trip.

SCHELLENBERG: Sprawled over wooded hills and lush meadowlands, this community has several archaeological sites dating back to the New Stone Age. In addition, the partially restored ruins of two medieval castles are worth a visit. If you take a walk along the marked Eschnerberg mountain trail, you'll see the historic areas as well as the beautiful woods. The next community to the south — the villages of Mauren and Schaanwald — virtually is in another era.

MAUREN and SCHAANWALD: Bordered by gentle meadows to the south and west and mountains to the east, Mauren and Schaanwald are two villages about a mile (1.6 km) apart. Archaeological excavations in Mauren have unearthed the remains of a Roman bath and warehouse dating from the 2nd century. The village has a beautiful parish church and a vicarage erected in 1787. The most popular attraction here, however, is the bird sanctuary–nature path that extends from Mauren east to Schaanwald. From Schaanwald, head west about 3 miles (5 km) to Gamprin-Bendern.

GAMPRIN-BENDERN: The Rhine flows gently past this area of rolling pastures and picture-postcard farmhouses. Here are the remains of a church built around AD 500 and a large building constructed after the Reformation that today serves as a vicarage; the church and vicarage, on a hilltop, can be seen from afar and are favorites with visitors and photographers. It's about a mile (1.6 km) southeast to the next area.

ESCHEN and NENDELN: The village of Eschen was first documented in the Carolingian estates registry (ca. 831), but excavations reveal that it was inhabited as far back as 5000 BC. Visit the prehistoric settlements of Malanser and Schneller in Eschen and the medieval Holy Cross, St. Sebastian, and Rochus chapels in Nendeln. Then take the road leading up through Eschen to the posh neighborhood of Schönbühl and view the houses of the most desirable residential area in Liechtenstein. From Nendeln drive south along the twisting mountain road, about 4 miles (6 km), to Planken.

PLANKEN: This little village of about 300 people was settled in the 13th century by immigrants — called Walser — from Upper Valais in Switzerland, who populated big areas of the Alps and kept their distinct heritage alive. The dialect used here is drastically different from that of the rest of the Rhine Valley, as are the culture, cuisine, and costumes. It's a beautiful village of meadows and quaint inns. The views of the mountains, villages, and the Rhine Valley are excellent from the road south to Schaan.

SCHAAN: Two miles (3 km) north of Vaduz, this village of trim gardens, flower-decked homes, cafés, and colorful shops features a 12th-century Romanesque church and an imposing 18th-century chapel. Return to Vaduz and head south about 3 miles (5 km) to Triesen, where you can begin exploring the Liechtenstein Alps.

TRIESEN: At the foot of the Alps and on the Rhine, Triesen once was inhabited by Roman nobility as a result of its convenient location. Especially interesting are the Roman section of the village (the Oberdorf) and the Maria and St. Mamerten chapels.

En Route from Triesen – Several hiking paths fan out to the Liechtenstein Alps and south across the Rhine Valley into Switzerland. From Triesen take the excellent road north into the mountains. After twisting and turning for about 4 miles (6 km), the road arrives at the idyllic village that gives the community its name.

TRIESENBERG: The residents of this tiny village (also called Walser) dress in colorful costumes and build their wooden homes in a decorative, regional style that's been in vogue since 1300. At the *Walser Heimatmuseum,* an interesting folklore museum, a slide show tells about the history and life of the Walser community (closed Mondays; admission charge). At its altitude of 3,000 feet, Triesenberg seems nailed to the side of the Alps and commands an excellent view of the misty Rhine Valley below and the Alpine pine forests behind the village. Here you may see chamois and deer darting out of the woods or view the cattle, sporting enormous bells, grazing in the lush meadows.

En Route from Triesenberg – The Rhine and Samina valleys are connected by a 2,800-foot mountain tunnel. Excellent roads and cross-country hiking trails (the distances usually are marked in approximate walking times) zigzag through the Samina. Even if you're pressed for time, instead of proceeding directly east and up to Malbun, give yourself another hour or two and make your way via Masescha, Gaflei, and Steg.

MASESCHA: A quaint hamlet, 4,100 feet high and about 3 miles (5 km) north of Triesenberg, Masescha provides a breathtaking panorama and Theodul's Chapel, a restored medieval monument. If you want to spend some time hiking or mountain climbing, Gaflei, about a mile (1.6 km) farther north, is a good bet. One of several mountain paths starting here is the Prince's Climb (Fürstensteig), which follows a high ridge between the Rhine and Samina valleys; originating at 4,900 feet, the path weaves around several peaks up to an altitude of 7,000 feet. Only experienced hikers need attempt it. From Gaflei, there's an excellent road as well as several mountain paths to Steg, where you can visit the chapel of St. Wendelin, honoring the patron saint of shepherds. From Steg the road meanders southeast along the icy Malbuner Bach (Malbun Brook) about 2 miles (3 km) before reaching Malbun.

MALBUN: At the base of a bowl of mountains, Malbun rapidly is becoming one of the most popular winter ski centers in the eastern Alps. Take the chair lift up to the Soreiserjoch Peak at 6,400 feet — again, for experienced hikers only; a steep ridge road leads from here to the Bettlerjoch (the low point in the mountain range, similar to a valley), where in summer the *Alpine Club* operates the *Pfälzerhütte* (phone: 23679 or 29587), which offers a restaurant and accommodations. If you have time, hike from Malbun to the Sareiserjoch border pass into Austria; this adventurous jaunt takes about 2 hours. From Malbun, head back down the road to Triesen and proceed south into Balzers.

BALZERS: Amid rolling meadows, vineyards, and medieval castles, Balzers is dominated by the impressive Gutenberg Castle, built on a prehistoric mound; from 1314 to 1824 it belonged to the Hapsburgs. Near the castle and worth visiting are the Mariahilf and St. Peter chapels, the parish church, and the old vicarage. Another attraction here is the Elltal nature preserve and its collection of rare Alpine flora.

BEST EN ROUTE

One good reason for spending time in Liechtenstein is that the prices of its hotels and restaurants are generally more reasonable than those of Switzerland. We've rated hotels charging more than $165 a night for a double room with bath and breakfast as very expensive; $130 to $165 as expensive; from $80 to $130 as moderate; and under $80, inexpensive. (Note that at the *Parkhotel Sonnenhof* rates can be as high as $250 for two.) Many of Liechtenstein's best restaurants are in the hotels; a meal for two in an expensive restaurant will run $75 to $140; $55 to $75 in the moderate category; inexpensive restaurants run under $55. Prices do not include taxes, wine, or tips. All restaurants listed below accept major credit cards unless otherwise indicated.

VADUZ

Parkhotel Sonnenhof – Possibly one of the best small hotels in Europe. The cuisine is regional and French and prepared by celebrated chef Emil Real. The dining room is open to hotel guests only. Reservations advised. Mareestr. (phone: 21192; fax: 20053). Very expensive.

Löwen – This historic landmark inn, surrounded by hilly vineyards and with a view of the castle, has 7 rooms with modern baths, all uniquely furnished with antiques. Its elegant restaurant serves dinner, and the cozy bar serves lunch; both feature excellent local and continental dishes, as well as wines from the hotel's own vineyards. Restaurant reservations advised. 35 Herrengasse (phone: 21408; fax: 20458). Expensive.

Real – Hearty and well-prepared regional and international fare is featured at this hotel's restaurant. Reservations essential. 21 Städtle (phone: 22222; fax: 20891). Expensive to moderate.

Torkel – In the Princely vineyards, this charming, paneled inn has outstanding food, prepared by chef Rolf Berger. A giant, 17th-century winepress (*Torkel*) is also here. Wine tastings can be arranged. Closed Sundays and Mondays. Restaurant reservations necessary. 9 Hintergasse (phone: 24410). Expensive to moderate

Landhaus Prasch – Some of the best regional fare in the area is served at this small, modern hotel. Closed November through March. Reservations advised in summer. 16 Zollstr. (phone: 24663 or 23140; fax: 25486). Moderate.

Engel – This small hotel offers French cuisine in its dining room. Open daily. Reservations advised. No credit cards accepted. Städtle (phone: 20313; fax: 81159). Moderate to inexpensive.

SCHELLENBERG

Wirthschaft zum Löwen – A gem of a restaurant and a protected historical monument, found on the most beautiful lookout point of Liechtenstein, surrounded by splendid hiking trails. A "secret," as you find it only by knowing about it: Outside the village, near the Austrian border, it is indicated only by a discreet sign on the building. Simple food with local specialties seldom found anywhere else is offered. Closed Sunday evenings and Thursdays. Reservations advised. No credit cards accepted. Im Winkel (phone: 31162). Inexpensive.

ESCHEN-NENDELN

Engel – Lamb and venison are the specialties in this hotel's popular restaurant. Closed Sundays and Mondays. Reservations advised. 9491 Nendeln (phone: 31260). Moderate.

PLANKEN

Saroja – Small and homey, this hostelry is one of the best deals in the principality. Closed Mondays and Tuesdays until 6 PM. Reservations advised in summer. 9494 Planken (phone: 31584). Inexpensive.

SCHAANWALD

Waldhof – An unpretentious, pleasant little restaurant, it serves some of the best food in Liechtenstein. Traditional and local dishes are prepared from the freshest of products. Closed Sundays. Reservations necessary. No credit cards accepted. 296 Vorarlbergerstr. (phone: 31338 or 33498). Expensive to moderate.

SCHAAN

Dux – There's an excellent restaurant in this hotel serving Swiss, French, and regional cuisine. The house specialty is fondue. Closed Wednesdays. Reservations advised. 9494 Schaan (phone: 21727). Moderate.

TRIESEN

Meierhof – Fish dishes are the specialty in this hotel's excellent restaurant. Dinner only on Saturdays. Reservations advised. 9495 Triesen (phone: 61282; fax: 82359). Moderate.

TRIESENBERG

Martha Bühler – The terrace restaurant of this inn offers a fine view. Closed Wednesdays. Reservations necessary. 9497 Triesenberg (phone: 25777; fax: 82861). Moderate to inexpensive.

MALBUN

Alpenhotel Malbun – A good, moderately priced, medium-size hotel that serves both continental and local food. Reservations advised. No credit cards accepted. 9497 Malbun (phone: 21181). Moderate.

BALZERS

Engel – This old inn, in the oldest part of Balzers, is well known for good, simple food, with house specialties. Closed Mondays. Reservations advised. No credit cards accepted. 18 Im Höfle (phone: 41201). Inexpensive.

Luxembourg

Bordered by France, Germany, and Belgium, the Grand Duchy of Luxembourg calls itself "the green heart of Europe," for fully one-third of the country's 999 square miles still is unspoiled forest. Geographically, there are two regions: in the north, the hilly, picturesque uplands of the Ardennes; in the south, rolling farmlands and woods bordered on the east by the grape-growing valley of the Moselle. Flowers are everywhere. Fields are sprinkled with wild poppies, daisies, clover, and buttercups — the perfect Impressionist landscape. White and purple lilacs outline the roadways, and in early summer the hillsides blaze with yellow gorse bushes. Storybook villages nestle beside peaceful rivers. Castles — some restored and others in ruins — cap the mountaintops.

Luxembourg's hotels and inns are clean and relatively inexpensive, and its restaurants combine the subtleties of French cooking with the heartiness of German food. The local white wines are fresh, light, and tart, and they are served with both fish and meat (red wines are not produced here).

The nation's history is dense with traces of all the armies that have marched across Europe. Once part of the Roman Empire, the country has been manipulated by dukes and dictators, princes and potentates, knights and nobles. France, Spain, Prussia, Bohemia, Austria, and the Netherlands have all had their fingers in its political pie, and for hundreds of years Luxembourg was involved in one alliance, treaty, or confederation after another. Twice in this century the country has been invaded by Germany, but peace and relative prosperity have reigned since the Allies liberated the area in September 1944. Today, Luxembourg is a constitutional monarchy with a bicameral legislature. The Parliament is elected by popular vote; the ministers are appointed by the monarch. The present ruler is the Grand Duke Jean, who is married to the Princess Josephine Charlotte of Belgium.

With a population of 377,000, Luxembourg is one of the few nations with a declining birth rate, low unemployment, and virtually no poverty; its gross national product is estimated to be the equivalent of $3 billion. Roman Catholicism is the prevalent religion, but the country also has Protestant and Jewish communities.

Iron mining and steel production in the southwest of Luxembourg are the major industries, followed by banking, and television and radio production. Agriculture, including the cultivation of grapes, and cattle raising are also important, and a number of major US corporations have subsidiaries in Luxembourg. Tourism is an increasingly valuable revenue producer (Luxembourg hosts 2 million visitors per year); the country's appeal to those who love camping and hiking is on the upswing. And lovers of good food appreciate Luxembourg's many top restaurants — among them 11 establishments with Michelin stars.

Most international travelers arrive at Luxembourg Airport in Luxembourg City. (For years the city was the European gateway for millions of Americans taking advantage of *Icelandair's* low transatlantic fares, but vacationers now are urged to stay and see the country.) A valid passport is the only document required for citizens of the US and most other nations. There's a national tourist office in Luxembourg City (Pl. d'Armes; phone: 22809 or 27565), at Findel Airport, at the Air Terminus (near the railway station), and in many other towns.

Using Luxembourg City as a base, you easily can reach any other part of the country within hours, and all of Luxembourg can be covered without strain in a week to 10 days. It's a good idea to spend several nights in smaller towns like Echternach and Vianden to experience the charm of their small inns and hotels and the distinctly medieval atmosphere of the country; in these villages you'll find rebuilt feudal battlements, ancient abbeys, and patrician houses in quiet, verdant settings. You'll find an interesting mixture of Gallo-Roman and Germanic cultural influences as well as three major languages: German, French, and Luxembourgeois (a combination of the other two). It's customary to speak French with waiters. Many people, however, speak English.

LUXEMBOURG CITY: Luxembourg's over-1,000-year-old capital has an exciting location: The oldest part of the city is actually a high plateau whose steep cliffs plunge into the beautifully landscaped valleys of the Alzette River. Some 98 old and modern bridges connect this central plateau to other parts of the city on surrounding hills and plateaus. If you suffer from vertigo or acrophobia, proceed cautiously as you cross the dizzying bridges or the steep precipices.

Winding around the edge of Luxembourg City's central plateau is the celebrated Promenade de la Corniche, a walkway offering breathtaking views of the city. For centuries this area was a fortress of great strategic importance. Although the military fortifications were dismantled from 1867 to 1883, the Casemates — a 13-mile network of underground passages — remain just below the promenade; cut into the solid rock of the plateau, they could shelter thousands of soldiers. Exploring these dark and damp tunnels can be fun for the nimble (open daily; admission charge; enter at Place de la Constitution). As you stroll through the Old City, note the Renaissance Grand Ducal Palace, constructed from the 16th to the 18th century (Rue de la Reine), and the Foreign Ministry, built in 1751 (Rue Notre-Dame) adjoining the Cathedral of Notre-Dame (1613–1621), with its fine sculptures and crypt. The *National Museum* (closed Mondays; Rue de la Boucherie; phone: 93301) features interesting archaeological and sculpture exhibitions (closed Mondays). Place d'Armes, in the heart of the city, is a popular public square with outdoor cafés and a bandstand for concerts.

On the second and fourth Saturday of the month, a flea market is held at Place d'Armes where all kinds of collectors' items can be found, especially porcelain, books, and toys. For good buys on good china, visit the *Villeroy & Boch* outlet (330 Rullingergrund; no phone).

Just 10 minutes east of the city, near Hamm, is the US Military Cemetery. Over 5,000 American Third Army soldiers who died during the Battle of the Bulge are buried here. Later, when General George S. Patton was killed in an automobile accident, he, too, was buried here.

MONDORF-LES-BAINS: Eleven miles (18 km) southeast of Luxembourg City, on the French border, is Luxembourg's famous spa. In an 89-acre public park, it is renowned for its foul-tasting but supposedly curative waters. The warm water has been used to treat rheumatism, liver, and gall bladder problems, and it is a powerful laxative when imbibed. The park has a large, lovely rose garden. The town also boasts a casino, *Casino 2000* (Rue Flammang; phone: 661001), as well as tennis, boating, fishing, and miniature golf.

The charming architecture here, from Art Nouveau houses to restored churches, is worth seeing, too. From May through August St. Michael's Church (1764–1766) offers guided tours focusing on the frescoes and furniture (open Saturdays 6 to 7 PM and Sundays from 8 AM to noon; no admission charge; 1 Allée Jean-Linster).

ECHTERNACH: This medieval village lies along the Sauer River on Luxembourg's eastern border; its name means "the place where horses are brought to drink." There are hundreds of footpaths in the surrounding woods. Across the river is Germany and the mountains that once held the Siegfried line between France and Germany from 1933 to 1938. (You still can see the bunkers on the hill.) Heavily damaged during World War II, Echternach has been restored meticulously. The Town Hall, which dates from 1328, is the centerpiece of the charming main square. Nearby, beside the river, is the imposing Benedictine Abbey that was founded in the 7th century by a Northumbrian monk, St. Willibord, whose remains are buried in a white marble sarcophagus in the crypt of the abbey's basilica. Among the abbey's treasures are its impressive 12th-century frescoes and the brilliant, modern, stained glass windows. The *Abbey Museum* was opened in 1989, and exhibits facsimiles of manuscripts from the 11th-century book printing school (open daily, May 19 through August, from 10 AM to noon and from 2 to 6 PM; open weekends from 2 to 5 PM the rest of the year; admission charge; 2 Rue des Tanneurs; phone: 72296). The basilica is the terminus of the famed dancing procession, held every *Whittuesday* (usually in mid-May). Religious in origin — it is an act of penance, an expression of pious fervor — the event is celebrated by the entire village. Swaying, jumping, and dancing, the crowd moves through the streets as a haunting repetitive tune is played, paying homage to the English saint.

LITTLE SWITZERLAND: Hiking is a top sport throughout Luxembourg, but nowhere is it better — or more beautiful — than in the Moellerdall (Miller's Dale) section of the Ardennes that's also known as Little Switzerland. Just a few minutes north of Echternach, it comes as a complete surprise. After parking your car, you walk through gently rolling fields into a forest, and suddenly you're on a narrow path leading up and down through deep gorges, across bubbling streams, and beside (and through) enormous bolders. The whole area is dense with the kinds of tall straight trees Cézanne loved to paint. Although the area isn't as wild as it looks and the main hiking path is only about 2 miles (3 km) long and fairly well defined, you're strongly advised to have either a guide or a very good map of the area. Comfortable clothes and hiking boots are also musts.

VIANDEN: This village on the Our River (an extension of the Sauer) near the German border, a short drive northwest of Echternach and the Little Switzerland area, is one of Europe's more romantic spots. A charming small bridge arches over the river, connecting the two parts of the town, and a formidable castle stands guard high on an overhanging hill. Restored in the 1980s, it is the largest feudal castle in the Ardennes region. The narrow streets — parts of which date from the 9th century — slope down to the river, where graceful promenades line both banks. Next to the bridge is the little house where French writer Victor Hugo spent part of his exile. The house is now a museum and a tourist information office (both open daily, April through October, from 9:30 AM to noon and from 2 to 6 PM; near the bridge; phone: 84257). A more recent addition to the village is the *Doll Museum,* which displays some 200 dolls made from 1860 to 1960 (open daily, *Easter* to mid-October, from 10 to noon and from 2 to 6PM; admission charge; 98 Rue Grande). On the second Sunday in October, a festival celebrating the nut harvest takes place here.

BOURSCHEID AND DELANNOY (CASTLE AT CLERVAUX): Two of Luxembourg's most interesting castles lie just northwest of Vianden; you can stay there and visit both castles in a day's outing, driving out one way and returning another. Bourscheid, an 11th-century walled castle, is perched on a mountaintop overlooking the hills, valleys, and waters of the Ardennes region. The extensive ruins here are restored (open March 1 to September 30; admission charge). The 11th-century castle at Clervaux, home of Franklin D. Roosevelt's ancestors, stands in the center of Clervaux, another charming village surrounded by mountains. The castle is open from *Whitsun* (the eighth Sunday after *Easter*) to mid-September (admission charge). Three important permanent exhibitions are housed in the castle: photographer Edward Steichen's "Family of Man" collection, scale models of Luxembourg's medieval castles, and a Battle of the Bulge display. Those particularly interested in the battle can visit the *Battle of the Bulge Museum* in Wiltz (open June to September 15 from 10 AM to noon and from 1 to 5 PM; admission charge; Rte. du Château; phone: 957444), which has numerous monuments and remnants of World War II. Also worth seeing is the church made of local stone, built in the Rhenish-Romanesque style in 1910.

BEST EN ROUTE

This small country has a fairly wide range of hotel prices. The nightly cost of a double room with bath or shower can range from $30 to $250. Accommodations priced from $100 to $250 are considered expensive; those from $60 to $100 are termed moderate; and those under $60 are rated inexpensive. Restaurant prices range from $65 and up for a dinner for two in places listed as expensive; around $40 for those in the moderate category; and $20 in the inexpensive category. Prices do not include drinks, wine, or tip. German, French, Chinese, Indian, Thai, Yugoslav, Russian, and Portuguese are among the types of restaurants found here. Most major credit cards are accepted at the restaurants below, unless otherwise indicated.

LUXEMBOURG CITY

Aérogolf-Sheraton – This ultramodern hotel near the airport — it's totally soundproof — serves fine food. Its top-floor *Crossroad Bar* offers light entertainment. Rte. de Trèves, Senningerberg (phone: 34571). Expensive.

Cravat – Luxembourg's most elegant hotel overlooks the Petrusse Valley. There are 59 rooms in this romantic, 100-year old establishment. 29 Bd. Roosevelt (phone: 21975). Expensive.

Inter-Continental Luxembourg – The country's largest hotel is in Europa Park, just minutes from the center of town. A wide range of services are available for both the business and vacation traveler, including a complete health club with an indoor pool. Handicapped accessible. 12 Rue Jean-Engling (phone: 43781). Expensive.

Pullman – Formerly a *Holiday Inn,* this 260-room property is on the "new plateau" near the European Parliament and European Court of Justice buildings and the Trade Fair Building, overlooking the old part of the city. Handicapped accessible. Rue de Fort Niedergrunewald, Kirchberg (phone: 437761). Expensive.

Le Royal – In the heart of the historic Old City, this thoroughly modern establishment is complete with swimming pool, sauna, and solarium. Handicapped accessible. 12 Bd. Royal (phone: 41616). Expensive.

Arcade – Part of the French chain, this new 68-room hotel attracts a young crowd, as well as groups. Near the railway quarter and convenient to the main shopping area. 30 Rue Joseph-Junck (phone: 492496). Moderate.

Ibis – Located between the Luxembourg airport and town, it has 120 rooms, 4 of which are specially designed for the handicapped. Conference facilities; free parking available. Rte. de Trèves, Senningerberg (phone: 438801). Moderate.

Saint Michel – Set in a beautiful 17th-century house behind the Grand Ducal Palace, this 2-star Michelin restaurant specializes in fish dishes prepared by French chef Pierrick Guillou. Closed Saturdays and Sundays. Reservations advised. 32 Rue de l'Eau (phone: 23215). Moderate.

EHNEN (near MONDORF-LES-BAINS)

Simmer – This old one-star inn on the Moselle River has long been famous for fine food. Try the pâté, stuffed Luxembourg trout, and charlotte russe. Closed January and February. Reservations advised. 117 Rte. du Vin (phone: 76030). Expensive.

ECHTERNACH

Bel-Air – A winding road leads you up to this lovely, secluded inn above the river. Surrounded by its own park, it has a gracious dining room and a delightful cocktail lounge. Open daily. Reservations advised. 1 Rte. de Berdorf (phone: 729383). Expensive.

Eden au Lac – Recently expanded, this property now has 69 rooms, many with splendid lake views (phone: 728282). Moderate.

Grand – On the Sauer River overlooking the hills of Germany and the old Siegfried Line, is a modern hotel with small but well-designed rooms and large modern bathrooms. Excellent cuisine is served on the enclosed porch facing the river. Open daily. Reservations advised. 27 Rte. de Diekirch (phone: 729672). Moderate.

Marco Polo – This intimate 10-room hostelry recently opened in a central location, just a 10-minute walk from the Old City. Rue du Fort-Neipperg (phone: 404880). Moderate.

MONDORF-LES-BAINS

Mondorf – A comfortable, 113-room hotel at the famous spa. Each room has a bath, TV set, mini-bar, and balcony. Guests have free access to the spa's sauna, solarium, and Turkish and whirlpool baths; there's a small fee for tennis and squash. Mondorf-les-Bains (phone: 670ll). Expensive.

VIANDEN

Oranienburg – For three generations this family-operated inn has provided comfortable rooms, good service, and a friendly atmosphere. The adjoining *Le Châtelain* restaurant offers first-rate food and a fine wine cellar (closed Mondays; reservations advised). 126 Grande Rue (phone: 84153). Hotel, moderate; restaurant, expensive to moderate.

Heintz – A historic landmark that is a superb small hotel. Once part of the adjoining medieval Trinitarian monastery, it's a delightful place presided over by the warm and expansive Madame Hansen. Each room is individually decorated. And the food is excellent; a typical meal might consist of ham or mushroom quiche, smoked tongue with béarnaise sauce, beans wrapped in bacon, raspberry sherbet with whipped cream, and a carafe of the house wine. Restaurant open daily; reservations unnecessary. 55 Grand Rue (phone: 84155). Inexpensive.

WILTZ

Hôtel du Commerce – Situated in the center of the upper town, this charming hotel has been family-run for three generations. All rooms have bath or shower, telephone, and television. The proprietor personally presides over the restaurant, where guests are pampered with fine food and drink. 9 Rue des Tondeurs (phone: 95670). Inexpensive.

The Maltese Islands

The sun-drenched Maltese Islands — an archipelago comprising the main island of Malta, its smaller sister island of Gozo, the islet of Comino, and two large rocks, Cominotto and Fifla — are near the very center of the Mediterranean some 60 miles south of Sicily. Because of their strategically important location, the islands always have attracted foreign powers. In recent years, Malta was the site of the 1989 summit meeting between Presidents Bush and Gorbachev, and in 1990 both Pope John Paul II and Britain's then–Prime Minister Margaret Thatcher visited. For centuries the Maltese Islands have possessed a wealth of history out of all proportion to their size. From megalithic temples and Roman remains to medieval towns and villages, the foremost of which is the citadel of Mdina; from religious traditions dating to AD 60, when St. Paul is said to have been shipwrecked here, to the enormous artistic achievements of the Knights of St. John of Jerusalem in the 16th, 17th, and 18th centuries, Malta's successive occupants have left behind a rich cultural tapestry set against a backdrop of honey-colored hills and azure sea.

Starting with the Phoenicians, Malta was occupied successively by the Romans, Byzantines, Arabs, Sicilians, and the Knights. Napoleon was here briefly in 1798, and the island passed to British rule in 1800. Nevertheless, the tiny nation, now an independent republic within the British Commonwealth, has remained intensely individualistic. Its 350,000 inhabitants have managed to combine a cosmopolitan attitude with a strong sense of tradition and national pride; along with their own basically Semitic language, nearly all Maltese speak English, Italian, and often French as well. Malta attained its independence from Britain in 1964, and from 1971 to 1987 was governed by hardline Socialists who were a little too friendly for comfort with neighboring Libya. The present administration is more pro-West and anxious to encourage investments and develop the country's industries and tourism. Accordingly, new air terminals are under construction (due to be completed sometime this year), and air service and hotel inventory are being expanded. Flights are now regularly scheduled from all European gateways, and a hydrofoil runs between Malta and Sicily in just 2½ hours. Overall, some $300 million is being spent on basic infrastructure improvements, focusing on the island's antiquated telecommunications network, roads, and water supply.

Today, Malta is an ideal vacation spot, offering a near-perfect Mediterranean climate, picturesque beaches and lovely harbors, a fascinating variety of architectural and historical treasures, and a genuinely warm and welcoming people. Malta is deluged with package tourists, primarily from Britain and Germany, during the peak summer months. Some great bargains are available on all-inclusive tours if you happen to be flying in from London. Given the warm year-round temperatures as well as the lower shoulder season rate, visitors might consider traveling in the spring or fall. For a wide range of facilities, the *Marsa Sports Club* (phone: 233851) is easy to reach by public transportation from the capital, Valletta.

Driving on Malta and Gozo can be a challenge, particularly for Americans. Driving is on the left-hand side and there are no highways, just plenty of good, tarmac roads. Since the total area of Malta and Gozo is barely 119 square miles (Malta itself is only 17 miles long) and the distance between points of interest is very short, you may be tempted to jog rather than drive, but the steep, hilly roads of both islands will soon dispel such notions. Try the private taxi services, such as *John's Garage* (phone: 238745), for reasonable rates to the airport or to the Gozo ferry connection. Or rent a car from a local agency, such as *United Car Rental* (phone: 556291). Note: Rental cars have yellow license plates to forewarn locals to be patient!

Our route starts out at Malta's capital, Valletta, proceeds inland to the ancient walled city of Mdina (part of the old capital), and crosses finally, after several short but interesting detours, to the town of Marfa at the northwest tip of the island, from which point you can take the ferry for a 1- or 2-day visit to Gozo You also can take a hydrofoil to Sicily for a day tour. The trip there takes just 90 minutes. For tickets, call *Virtu Rapid Ferries Ltd.* (phone: 232522).

VALLETTA: The island's capital was built by Jean de la Valette, Grand Master of the Order of Knights of St. John, after the epic siege by the Turks in 1565. Rising dramatically from the water, in one wide sweep, the city dominates the island's historic Grand Harbor, one of the finest natural ports in Europe and also one of the least polluted; people still swim here. For an excellent introduction to Malta's history, begin a tour of Valletta with *The Malta Experience,* a 40-minute audiovisual presentation given hourly in the *Mediterranean Conference Center* (Mondays through Fridays, shows every hour from 11 AM to 4 PM; Saturdays at 11 AM and noon only; admission charge; on Merchants St.). This complex was first built by the Knights of Malta in the 16th century as one of the most advanced hospitals of its time, and boasted close to 1,000 beds and an important school of anatomy. Today, it still features the longest corridor in Europe — a passageway nearly 2 city blocks long in the lower level — and functions as a site for many international conferences.

Although Valletta today is a mixture of old and new, the city retains much of its original baroque flavor, and a restoration project is in the works to ensure that it stays that way. You will have no trouble exploring the town on foot; it is only about 1,000 yards long and is built in a regular grid around the main street, now called Republic Street, where many of the better shops are found. Also on Republic Street is the *National Museum of Archaeology* in the 16th-century Auberge de Provence, one of seven palaces built by the Knights of St. John of Jerusalem (closed public holidays; admission charge; phone: 239545 or 237730). Inside, important collections of prehistoric pottery, statuettes, stone tools, and ornaments recovered from Malta's many prehistoric sites are exhibited. Another majestic monument is St. John's Co-Cathedral, historically and artistically one of the most important monuments on the island. Completed around 1577, it was designed by Gerolamo Cassar, chief engineer of the Order, who was also responsible for building much of Valletta itself. Each of the cathedral's chapels was allotted to a national group of the Order and each is notable in its own way. Caravaggio's masterpiece, *The Beheading of St. John* was recently restored in Rome and once again is hanging in the oratory. The Palace of the Grand Masters, an imposing edifice built around two courtyards off Palace Square, was also designed by Cassar. Many of the State apartments are decorated with friezes depicting episodes from the history of the Order. Running along the back of the building is the Armoury, two halls containing a fine collection of arms and armor. Notice the beautiful marble tombstones — more than 400 of them — covering the cathedral floor. These bear the escutcheons of the Knights, Latin inscriptions, and graphic renderings of the Grim Reaper. The National Library of Malta (Old Treasury St.) is a veritable treasure trove for the bibliophile, though sadly many rare editions printed before 1500 currently are in a state of decay. The building itself is an architectural jewel.

The *National Museum of Fine Arts* (South St.; phone: 225769) is in an 18th-century palace; it houses paintings, sculpture, furniture, and objects connected with the Order of St. John. A section of the museum is reserved for works by Maltese artists. Also worth a visit is the *Manoel Theatre* (Theatre St.; phone: 222659), built as a court theater in 1731 and now one of the oldest in use in Europe. From the Upper Barrakka Gardens, on the edge of the city, visitors are rewarded with a magnificent view of Grand Harbor and, across the harbor, the ancient cities of Vittoriosa, Cospicua, and Senglea. The best way to explore the harbor and the Three Cities, as they are called, is in one of Malta's brightly colored *dghajjes* (pronounced *die-yes*), or water taxis, available for hire at the Old Customs House. One of the *Captain Morgan* harbor tours (phone: 331961 or 336981), though a bit pricey, offers an informative 1½-hour narrative journey and is worthwhile just to get a closer look at the three ancient cities and the imposing ships docked in the harbor. For tickets, drop in at the tour headquarters down by the waterfront in Sliema, or purchase them through any tourist office in the city.

As you leave Valletta, and its suburb of Floriana, take a look back at the city's once-formidable 16th-century fortifications. Built to resist attack from non-European invaders, they served most recently to shelter the Maltese population from the determined bombing of Hitler's Luftwaffe.

En Route from Valletta – South of the city in the village of Paola is the Hypogeum, an underground monument built around 2400 BC and consisting of a system of caves, passages, and cubicles cut from the rock. Guided tours are available. Nearby are three well-preserved historic temples that were discovered in 1915; they have been certified as the oldest self-standing buildings in the world.

MDINA: Towering upon a 700-foot plateau, Mdina was once part of the island's capital during the Romans' stay in Malta (218 BC–AD 270). According to tradition, it was here that St. Paul converted the Roman Governor Publius to Christianity and consecrated him the first Bishop of Malta. In 870, the Arab conquerors walled up a small section of the plateau and named it Mdina, the Arab word for a walled city. When Arab rule ended in 1090, Count Roger of Sicily started a building program within the city walls, and between that time and the coming of the Knights of St. John, Mdina was the capital of Malta. Today it also is known as Città Vecchia, the Old City, and the Silent City; it is the finest and best-preserved city on the island. Historically the home of the Maltese nobility and the archbishopric, it has retained its Maltese flavor and has remained virtually unchanged for centuries. No cars are allowed in the city, so park outside the ramparts.

On entering the city, you soon come to St. Paul's Square, which is dominated by the baroque façade of the Cathedral of St. Peter and St. Paul, built on the site of an older church in 1694. The cathedral museum houses such treasures as the painting of the Madonna and Child attributed to St. Luke, who was shipwrecked in Malta with St. Paul; a flagon by Cellini; engravings by Dürer; and the cross carried to Godfrey of Bouillon in the first crusade to Jerusalem in 1099. The Vilhena Palace, on the right of the square, now houses the *Museum of Natural History* (closed public holidays; admission charge). Follow Villegaignon Street to the city's northern bastion, which offers superb views of the island.

En Route from Mdina – Across the moat from Mdina is the suburb of Rabat, famous for its catacombs and the island's only remaining Roman villa.

To the south lies Verdala Castle, a traditional fortified palace designed by Cassar in 1586 as a summer palace for Grand Master Verdala (open Tuesdays through Fridays 9 AM to noon and 2 to 5 PM; admission charge; phone: 454021). The palace grounds, known as the Buskett Gardens, served as hunting grounds in the days of the Knights, and unfortunately, still are haunted in the springtime by Malta's overzealous bird hunters. The grounds also are the scene of the *Mnarja,* the traditional folk festival held June 28-29 and characterized by singing, feasting, and dancing. Horse, mule, and bareback donkey races are held near Mdina during the afternoon of June 29.

MOSTA: This is the site of the Church of St. Mary, known as the Rotunda. A massive structure built in 1860 and over 200 feet high, it boasts the third largest dome in the world and can accommodate up to 12,000 people at a time. On April 9, 1942, a German bomb pierced the dome and landed among 300 people. Fortunately, it failed to detonate, and no one was hurt.

En Route from Mosta – The north road leads to St. Paul's Bay, where St. Paul is said to have been shipwrecked. To the northeast stands Mellieha, towering on a high ridge overlooking Ghadira Bay. Here, in a grotto, is the church where St. Luke is supposed to have taken shelter and painted the Madonna.

After skirting the spectacular beach of Ghadira Bay, the road winds up the hills to Cirkewwa, where, depending on weather conditions and public demand, a ferry usually leaves every hour carrying people, cars, and provisions to the sister island of Gozo. Taxi and — sporadic — bus service also are available.

MARSAXLOKK: This fishing village on the coast, southeast of Valletta — the name means "South Harbor" — made international headlines in 1989 when it set the stage for the famous Bush-Gorbachev summit talks (ultimately disrupted by a series of equally publicized storms). At any other time, it is best noted as the spot where many of the capital's residents go on Sunday afternoons. Fishermen are out touching up the paint on their colorful boats, (called *luzzus,* for the Phoenician craft from which they were inspired) and decorating them with the eyes of Osiris, the Egyptian god of the Underworld. Farther along the waterfront, octopus, rockfish, shrimp, and lobster are sold in the fish market, as well as local crafts such as mesh shopping bags and lacework. Watch it, though — the fishermen's knit sweaters appear to be machine-made these days. For an excellent seafood lunch, stop off at *Ruzzu* on the waterfront (phone: 871569).

En Route from Marsaxlokk – A few miles out of town is the giant, ancient Ghar Dalam cave, housing stalagmites and the bones of countless elephants, hippopotami, and red deer — evidence of the land bridge that once connected Europe and Africa. Those with an interest in prehistory might also consider stopping at the megalithic temples of Tarxien (on the way back to Valletta) and Hagar Qim (southwest of the airport), which predate Stonehenge and the Pyramids. Overlooking the sea, it is a wonderful spot to hike and marvel at the historic setting.

GOZO: This is the legendary isle of Calypso, from which Ulysses found it so difficult to tear himself away. The Maltese like to say that a sea divides the islands of Malta and Gozo, although in reality they are only about 4 miles apart. In fact, Gozo does have a character all its own, noticeable the moment you set foot here. The tiny island, only 9 miles long and 4½ miles wide, seems immune to the passage of time; it is sleepy and rural, greener than Malta, a bit more picturesque, and more dominated by its hilltop villages, with their quiet squares. It is a special place — to be discovered leisurely.

En Route from Mgarr – It is only a 5-minute ride from the port of Mgarr to the capital, Victoria, but you can make a short detour to visit the village of Xaghra, with its subterranean caves full of stalactites and stalagmites. A short walk brings you to the famous Ggantija Temples, which predate Stonehenge and the Pyramids (admission charge). Visit Gozo Heritage, a touristy but informative walk-through "experience" of the island's past.

VICTORIA (RABAT): The center of communications for the island, this is nonetheless a quiet, charming town. The *Gran Castello* (Citadel) was the medieval capital and is built much like Mdina, on a hill overlooking the surrounding countryside. Inside the Citadel is an interesting folklife museum. The town has a modest but graceful cathedral, which, instead of a dome, has a clever perspective painting that simulates one. Victoria's quaint Old Town centers around its main square, It-Tokk. In the early evening it is filled with people strolling, talking, and drinking the good local wine. Try the peppery local cheese, *gbejniet* — it's especially good with a slice of crusty bread; and be sure to taste the local honey.

   En Route from Victoria – Just north of the road leading to San Lawrenz is the Basilica of Ta' Pinu, a simple, lovely church that has become a pilgrimage center. To the west, along the coast, is the Inland Sea and Window, a natural pebbly bathing pool with crystal-clear water and sheer cliffs hanging over it dramatically. Heading north from Victoria, in a few minutes you arrive at Marsalforn, which, in summer, is a popular seaside resort and, in winter, a quiet fishing village. Also on the north coast is Calypso's Cave, with its magnificent view over the red sands of Ramla Bay. The cave itself is not particularly exciting, and there are no traces of the nymph Calypso, who, according to ancient myth, once lured Ulysses here. A short distance southwest of Victoria lies Xlendi Bay. The small village of Xlendi has the cozy, picturesque charm of many European seaside spots, but it is growing quickly. Local crafts such as lace, pottery, and Mdina glass can be purchased here at bargain prices, and the disarmingly simple *St. Patrick's* hotel (phone: 556589) is right on the water. We also suggest the fresh fish at nearby *Joe's Paradise,* a local hangout that features Elvis memorabilia as well as memorable eats (see *Best en Route*).

   COMINO: Only 1 mile square, Comino has one hotel, about 14 inhabitants, no cars, and, needless to say, an authentic get-away-from-it-all atmosphere. There are, however, plenty of pigs — survivors of the African swine fever that devastated most of Malta's porcine population in the early 1980s. The boat trip from Malta takes 20 minutes and operates regularly from April to October. This is an ideal spot for snorkeling and windsurfing.

BEST EN ROUTE

Malta is striving to be a resort, and a few of the best hotels still have an upper-crust British Empire flavor to them. The government classified lodgings aren't economical by Italian standards (Malta's nearest neighbor), except for hotels offering off-season packages. Many new properties have been built in recent years, but the older, more historic parts of the island often are more charming than some of the overpopulated tourist areas such as St. Julians, with its many discos and self-consciously chic restaurants. Among the islands' restaurants the competition is fierce; consequently many good meals are available on romantic seaside terraces or in atmospheric cafés for reasonable prices. There are restaurants on Malta with Chinese, Japanese, Malaysian, Indian, Turkish, Italian, Viennese, and British menus. The best dishes, though, are local and are Mediterranean-inspired with a special nod to Italy. Much of the meat is shipped frozen from Australia, but the rabbit is fresh and cooked over an open fire in a stew called *Stuffat Tal Fenek.* The seafood dishes made from fresh Mediterranean catches also are excellent. Many hotel restaurants advertise a per-head flat rate that's usually a good deal, but due to the longtime British influence, don't be surprised to find "chips" served in even the finer establishments. For an

appetizer or snack, try *hobz biz-zejt,* chopped tomatoes, garlic, olive oil, and anchovies (optional) spread on crusty bread. And do stop in at one of the *Maxim's,* a
local chain of fast-food shops which specialize in delicious ricotta-filled pies called
pastizzi (about 15¢), or pizza slices, or *timpana,* a macaroni dish covered with
puff pastry. The crusty Maltese bread, baked in wood-burning ovens, rivals San
Francisco sourdough for excellence, and for sweets lovers, the nougat is not to be
missed.

Expect to pay more than $120 to $200 per night for a double room in hotels listed
as expensive; about $60 to $110 for those in the moderate category; and $35 to $60 for
those in the inexpensive range. Most room prices include breakfast; half-board also is
common. A bounteous Maltese lunch or dinner in an expensive restaurant, including
wine, tax, and tip, will cost about $25 per person; about $15 per person in a moderate
eatery.

VALLETTA-FLORIANA

Giannini – A very elegant restaurant with a wonderful view of Manoel Island,
overlooking Hastings. It attracts mainly businesspeople at lunchtime. Open Mondays through Thursdays for lunch only; Fridays and Saturdays dinner only, except
during summer when dinner is served every evening. Reservations advised. Most
major credit cards accepted. 23 Windmill St., St. Michael's Bastions (phone:
227121). Expensive.

Bologna – Old World service and atmosphere, coupled with excellent Italian cuisine.
Serves lunch and dinner. Closed Sundays. Reservations necessary. Most major
credit cards accepted. 59 Republic St., Valleta (phone: 246149). Moderate.

Bon Appetit – Featuring simple Maltese dishes at absurdly low prices, this ordinary
looking café is a real sleeper. They serve a marvelous *hobz biz-zejt,* a tuna sandwich
on crusty bread soaked in fresh tomato sauce with lettuce, olive oil, and capers.
The *timpana* is another treat. Open daily for lunch and dinner. Reservations
unnecessary. No credit cards accepted. 19 St. Anne St., Floriana (phone: 242764).
Inexpensive.

British Hotel – Situated in one of Valletta's quaint terraced streets, this family-run
hotel has a breathtaking view of the old harbor, which makes up for its otherwise
rustic accommodations. The restaurant offers Maltese specialties, and there is a
bar with its own terrace. Reservations unnecessary. Ursola St. (phone: 229022 or
224730). Inexpensive.

Café Cordina – An elegant café where the staff is as interesting to watch as are the
other diners. Ice cream and other desserts are served with style. Open daily.
Reservations unnecessary. Most major credit cards accepted. 244 Republic St.,
Valletta (phone: 234385). Inexpensive.

Café La Veneziana – A modern Italian-style ice cream parlor/bar/pizzeria, where
locals like to drop in after dinner. The pastries are hard to pass up. Open daily.
Reservations unnecessary. No credit cards accepted. 29-30 Melita St. (phone:
222513). Inexpensive.

Castille – Talk about faded elegance! The rooms are dark and narrow and the
fixtures archaic. Nevertheless, this plucky old hotel has a certain charm to it, an
unbeatable location right on Castille Square at the entrance to town, a rooftop
restaurant with a magnificent harbor view, and a bar that is very popular. Castille
Sq., Valletta (phone: 243677). Inexpensive.

Spinella Café – Where the Maltese come before and after taking a stroll along
Republic Street. Sandwiches, pizza, and tasty cheese pastries are the big draw, with
espressso to wash it all down. Open daily from 8 AM to 8 PM. Reservations
unnecessary. No credit cards accepted. 24 Republic St., Valletta (phone: 237124).
Inexpensive.

RABAT-MDINA

Bacchus – Housed within the fortifications of the ancient city of Mdina in two chambers where grapes were once pressed, this still is a good spot for tasty local wines. Weather permitting, opt for a table on the terrace and sample the fresh fish of the day. Open daily from 10 AM to midnight. Reservations advised. Most major credit cards accepted. Inguanez St., Rabat (phone: 454981). Moderate.

Grand Hotel Verdala – There is a pleasant, airy feeling to this place, where the public spaces have checkered marble floors. The 164 rooms were recently upgraded and now each one offers a color TV set, mini-bar, and telephone; all have balconies, many with a spectacular view of the surrounding valley. There are 2 swimming pools, a health club, 2 tennis courts, 3 restaurants, and 2 bars. Room service is available around the clock. Inguanez St., Rabat (phone: 641700). Moderate.

Medina – For good local fare such as Maltese fish soup, grilled *lampuki* (a local seasonal fish), and Maltese potatoes dine at this converted Norman townhouse. Open for lunch and dinner; closed Sundays. Reservations advised. 7 Holy Cross St., Mdina (phone: 454004). Moderate.

Xara Palace – If you're staying inland, this hostelry might be an interesting choice. It doesn't have much in the way of facilities, but it's air conditioned and it's dripping with atmosphere. At press time, renovations were being planned. St. Paul's Sq., Mdina (phone: 450560). Moderate.

SLIEMA–ST. JULIANS

Barracuda – For fresh seafood and warm hospitality. Open daily. Reservations advised. Most major credit cards accepted. 194-195 Main St., St. Julians (phone: 331817). Expensive.

Holiday Inn Crowne Plaza – One of the best hotels on Malta, it offers 182 rooms — ask for one that overlooks the sea — along with a gym, sauna, 2 restaurants, and a pizzeria. A huge old gun turret has been transformed into a pool. Tigne St., Sliema (phone: 341173; 800-465-4329, in the US; fax: 311292). Expensive.

Malta Hilton – Set among landscaped gardens by the sea, it offers 201 rooms with color TV and mini-bar, a private beach, large pool, tennis courts, 2 restaurants, shops, business facilities, and parking for 250. St. Julians (phone: 336201; 800-445-8667, in the US; fax: 341539). Expensive.

Sheraton Dragonara Palace – There are more hotels in the Sliema area than anywhere else on the island, but this has always been one of the fanciest among the more antiquated properties. Recently taken over by Sheraton, it is due to reopen this year with 350 suites and extensive business facilities. Overall, it has a very romantic setting. St. Julians (phone: 336421). Expensive.

Park – A new property just off Sliema's waterfront and 5 miles (8 km) from the airport, it has 144 tastefully decorated rooms with private bath, telephone, and air conditioning. There is a restaurant, bar, and coffee shop. Graham St., Sliema (phone: 319810). Moderate.

Lion Court – Away from the noisy city center where discos blare, this small, unpretentious hostelry has 16 comfortable rooms — some with balconies, all with private bath and telephone. The restaurant serves modest home-cooked Maltese dishes. Minutes from the sea promenade and bus stops. 9 Nursing Sisters St., St. Julians (phone: 336251). Inexpensive.

GOZO

Charles Bar and Restaurant – The owners at this unpretentious spot bottle their own wine and raise the rabbits that go into the delicious *fennick* (stew). Portions are very generous, and the food is excellent. Open Tuesdays through Sundays. Reservations advised. No credit cards accepted. On the church square, Mgarr (phone: 473235). Expensive.

Ta' Cenc – Formerly a farmhouse, it's now a charming hostelry, renovated and expanded to 85 rooms. All but two rooms have private terraces, and all have color TV sets, mini-bars, private bath, telephone, and air conditioning. The restaurant is open daily. Reservations advised. Major credit cards accepted. It's out of the way but relaxing. Sannat (phone: 556830). Expensive.

Cornucopia – This innovative hotel complex (40 rooms) combines elements of Maltese farmhouses, such as pine furniture, with modern conveniences. There are 2 swimming pools and an excellent restaurant. There also is a private farmhouse with a kitchen and full amenities. It's just a 10-minute walk from the center of town and a short drive to the beaches. 10 Gnien Imrik, Xaghra (phone: 556486). Moderate.

Marsalforn – A simple family-run hostelry, it's just minutes from the beach where guests can enjoy sailing, windsurfing, and scuba diving. The restaurant serves Maltese dishes, as well as English breakfasts. Marsalforn Bay (phone: 556147). Moderate to inexpensive.

Jester – Just across the square from the *Oleander* (below), this eatery is operated by two aunts, Jessie and Esther, with cooking strictly a family affair. Open for lunch only Mondays through Saturdays. No reservations. No credit cards accepted (no phone). Inexpensive.

Joe's Paradise – Do drop in at this unassuming bayfront "dive," and try the fresh catch of the day served with a crisp helping of *pommes frites*. Or the pasta marinara. Or *both*. The ambience is provided by Elvis memorabilia — as well as what's on the cassette player. Open daily for dinner. Reservations advised. No credit cards accepted. Xlendi Bay (phone: 556878). Inexpensive.

Oleander – Here's where the locals drop by for fresh fish, rabbit stew, pasta, delicious soup, or whatever owner Mario and his sister decide should be set on the table that day. Good local wines. No menu. Open daily for dinner. Reservations advised. No credit cards accepted. 10 Victory Sq., Xaghra (phone: 557230). Inexpensive.

Monaco

The principality of Monaco, although one of the smallest states in Europe, is, at the same time, one of the most famous because of its wealth and glamour. Today's Monaco is a mixture of old and new, with sleek modern buildings next door to the pastel stucco and tile of traditional 19th-century French Mediterranean architecture. The emphasis everywhere is on sumptuous elegance. Yachts of the rich and famous fill the port, the shops display the wealth one dreams of — vintage wines, rare jade and ivory, costly jewels, couturier clothes and furs. Tourists, dazzled by the display, may sometimes forget that Monaco, with its rare climate and its turbulent history, has other resources besides manmade riches.

The climate is much like southern California's: Winters are mild; summers warm, with little rain. The vegetation, too, is like southern California's, with orange and lemon trees, palms, and live oaks. The water temperature of the Mediterranean is ideal for swimming. The only drawback is the beaches, all rock in their natural state. The few sand beaches here are all manmade, and Monaco's most exclusive stretch of beach is actually just over the border, in France.

The oldest part of Monaco, the Rock, was first colonized in the 6th century BC by a Ligurian tribe called the Monoikos, hence the probable origin of the name Monaco. The principality is ruled by the Grimaldi family, one of whose ancestors (Francesco Grimaldi, a Ligurian nobleman immortalized as Malizia, the Cunning One) wrested control of the territory from the Republic of Genoa in 1297. For more than 100 years, the family fought Genoa to maintain control of its conquest, and once that matter was settled, it still had to contend with other occupying foreign powers — Spain from 1524 to 1641, France from 1641 to 1814. When the Grimaldis regained sovereignty in 1814, Monaco was larger than it is today and included the cities of Roquebrune and Menton, which separate the principality from the Italian border. These two cities grew discontented under the yoke of Monaco and seceded in 1848, reducing the state to its present size.

Modern Monaco, with an area of only 482 acres, is divided into four parts: Monaco (the Old City); Monte Carlo (the New City); La Condamine (the port); and Fontvieille (the industrial district, where Monaco brews its own beer). But, in comparison to tourism, industry is of minor importance to Monaco. The tourist business was given a major overhaul by the present ruler, Prince Rainier III, and his American wife, Princess Grace (the former actress Grace Kelly), who died in 1982. Banks, modern hotels, and convention centers have been built. Monaco maintains extensive public tennis courts and an 18-hole golf course, and the harbor offers superb sailing and water skiing.

Among special events are the *Monte Carlo Rally* (since 1911) in January and the famous *Grand Prix* auto race in May. There also is the *International*

Tennis Championship, held at the *Monte Carlo Country Club* in late April, and the *Monaco Golf Open,* held in July. The summer months also are enlivened by the *International Fireworks Festival.* In February, the *International Circus Festival* is held. The *Monte Carlo Philharmonic Orchestra* can be heard practically year-round; the *Monte Carlo Opera's* season is from January through March.

Although Monaco is a sovereign state (it has an elected national council), with its own postage stamps (favorites with collectors) and car license plates, it is politically bound to France. There are no formalities crossing the border — you may not even realize when you've done it. And French money is the medium of exchange.

Because Monaco is so small, you don't need a car. There is a good internal bus system, which also takes side trips to some interesting neighboring towns. But if you prefer to be independent, you can rent a car from a number of international agencies.

You'll have no language problem in Monaco. English is widely spoken, and lots of English books and magazines are available at newsstands and bookstores. Information can be obtained at the tourist office at 2A Bd. Des Moulins (phone: 93-50-60-88 or 93-30-87-01).

MONACO

GRAND CASINO: A world-famous landmark. Even if you're not a gambler, you shouldn't miss the casino, where the legend of glamorous Monaco really began. The secession of Menton and Roquebrune reduced the revenues as well as the size of the principality, and when Prince Charles III came to the throne in 1856, he took up his father's idea of opening a gambling casino like the fashionable and successful one at Baden-Baden. A casino was built and struggled along until 1862, when the prince hired an expert manager, François Blanc, who had run the casino in Bad Homburg. Blanc hired boats and carriages to bring people from up and down the coast to Monaco's casino. At the same time, he spurred construction nearby of Monaco's first luxury hotel, the *Hôtel de Paris* (see *Best en' Route*). Through Blanc's efforts, the casino became fashionable and by 1869 was bringing in such large sums that the prince was able to abolish all taxes for his citizens. In 1878 Charles Garnier, the architect of the *Paris Opera House,* was commissioned to design the casino building you see today.

Stop for a minute in front of the casino to absorb the drama of the setting: the sea in the background; lush gardens with sculpture exhibitions; the building itself, with its copper roof enhanced by a green patina; and always, the coming and going of elegant limousines and sports cars carrying glamorous patrons from all over Europe. When you enter, you can go as far as the American Room and White Salon (slot machines and American-style games) without restriction, though you may have to show a passport to prove you're 21. A passport and an entrance fee are required for the European gaming rooms, such as the Touzet Rooms and Salons Privés. Most rooms open daily at either 10 AM or 3 or 4 PM. The casino is closed on May 1. Pl. du Casino (phone: 93-50-69-31).

PRINCE'S PALACE: With its crenelated tower sporting a rather incongruous clock and its Louis XIV cannons complete with neat stacks of cannonballs piled like apples in a market, the palace looks like an operetta castle, perfect for a miniature monarchy. At the sentry boxes, the guard changes each day precisely at 11:55 AM. The picture is so quaint you may not wish to risk destroying the illusion by going inside.

You can go inside, however, from June through September. You'll see the Court of

Honor, surrounded by mainly 17th-century frescoes, the State Apartments, and the Throne Room. Admission charge (phone: 93-25-18-31).

EXOTIC GARDEN: A cactus garden, but much more, this was a project of Prince Albert I. It clings to the side of a cliff at the western approach to Monaco, more than 300 feet above the sea. The inclination of the cliff provides protection from northern winds and maximum exposure to the winter sun, so the 7,000 species of cacti and succulents from semi-arid climes around the world thrive as well here as in their native habitats. Equally impressive is the view, a sweeping one that embraces the whole principality. Bd. du Jardin Exotique (phone: 93-30-33-65).

Within the garden, at the base of the cliff, are the Observatory Caves. Although today you're most likely to notice the stalagmites and stalactites, at one time the caves housed prehistoric man, whose bones have been found here. You can take a guided tour of the caves, but note that the climb up and down totals 558 steps. If this seems too much, the nearby *Museum of Prehistoric Anthropology* (Bd. du Jardin Exotique) safeguards what has been found on the site (and elsewhere in the principality and environs). Open daily. A single admission fee covers the garden, caves, and the museum (phone: 93-30-19-21).

OCEANOGRAPHIC MUSEUM: Not only a museum, but a working scientific research institute, this was another brainchild of Prince Albert I, called the "scholar prince" because of his passionate interest in oceanography. Prince Albert wanted a museum to house the results of his scientific expeditions around the world and to promote the science of oceanography. The building on the rock of Monaco, at the edge of a sheer drop, was a bold construction for the time. Pillars had to be built from sea level to support the building, and the rocks below had to be hollowed out to let in sea water for the aquarium. Though the work began in 1899, the inauguration did not take place until 1910.

Start your visit on the lowest level, with the aquarium. It's one of the finest in Europe — not surprising when you learn that the director of the museum is Jacques-Yves Cousteau. Films made by Cousteau are shown in the conference hall. On the ground floor are zoological exhibits, skeletons of large marine mammals, and specimens that Prince Albert brought back from his travels. The top floor is perhaps the most interesting. Here are kept Prince Albert's whaleboat, 19th-century brass navigational instruments, and, in complete contrast, ultramodern diving equipment. Open daily, except on the Sunday of the *Grand Prix de Monaco*. Admission charge. Av. St.-Martin (phone: 93-15-36-00).

OUTSKIRTS

LA TURBIE: Take the winding Route de la Turbie from Monaco to the Grand Corniche, and turn west (5 miles/8 km). This is the highest of the three corniches, offering spectacular views of coast and mountains. Built by Napoleon on the site of the ancient Roman Aurelian Way, its highest point is at La Turbie, 1,475 feet above Monaco.

The town is best known for its Roman relic, the Trophy of Augustus. It is worth a visit because there are only two structures of this kind still standing (the other is in Romania). The Trophy was built in 6 BC to commemorate Augustus Caesar's victory over the Gallic tribes of the region. The round pillar originally stood 160 feet high. On the base was engraved a list of the 44 conquered tribes, and above, between Doric columns, were statues of the generals who took part in the campaign. The top was surmounted by a statue of Augustus himself, flanked by two prisoners. A large part of the monument was destroyed by the Lombards in the 6th century, and villagers took much of the fallen stone for their houses. Now it is being restored.

You can climb up on the ruins for some spectacular views and interesting camera shots. If you'd rather, go to the terraces below the Trophy, where you have a panoramic view of Monaco and can see down the coast as far as Bordighera, Italy. In some spots, though, the view disappoints: Trees have been charred by fires that hit the French coastal regions in recent summers.

End your visit with the *Trophy Museum* (Pl. du Palais). The display includes a model of the Trophy in its original form as well as interesting photographs of the restoration, much of which was sponsored by an American, Edward Tuck. The Trophy and museum are open daily. Admission charge (phone: 93-25-18-31).

ROQUEBRUNE: Take the Grand Corniche east 4 miles (6 km). At the *Vistaëro,* stop to enjoy the view from this hotel perched right at the edge of a cliff.

The medieval village of Roquebrune is clustered around the oldest castle in France; you should be sure to see it for its very evocative picture of life in the Middle Ages. The village is typical of the medieval architecture all along this coast. The streets are narrow and steep; some are actually stairways, or vaulted passages. The buildings are made of rough stone with red tile roofs. The doors and windows are small to conserve heat in winter and keep the houses cool in summer.

Start from the Place de la République, once the advance defense post for the castle. Walk along the Rue Raymond-Poincaré to the Place des Deux-Frères, up the Rue Grimaldi, then left into Rue Moncollet. Here you see medieval residences cut right into the rock. Guests of the castle were accommodated here.

The castle itself was built at the end of the 10th century by Conrad I, count of Ventimiglia, for defense against the Saracens. Its ownership was bounced back and forth among Italy, Monaco, and France. It was used as a fortress, a manorial home, and even a prison under the French directorate.

Start your visit in the great Ceremonial Hall. The well in the center was fed by rainwater, a vital detail in this dry countryside. You'll also see the niche for the lords' throne, a 15th-century mullioned window, and, slightly lower, a storeroom. Climb the stairs to the three upper levels. On the first are a small guardroom, the former prison, and the archers' dormitory. On the second are the lords' living quarters, bedrooms, dining room, and kitchen with a primitive bread oven. These rooms have been restored and furnished. From the top level — the artillery platform — there's a glorious view of the red-roofed village, with Monaco and the Mediterranean beyond.

Roquebrune is a pleasant spot for lunch. You can also find some attractive handicrafts by artisans in Roquebrune — colorful pottery, and trays and salad bowls made of olivewood.

You can return to Monaco via Cap Martin. Take the Grande Corniche to the Moyenne Corniche, then go east to D52, where you will cut back west. D52 winds among the magnificent villas of the aristocracy (Empress Eugénie of France once lived here) before joining the Corniche Inférieure, which takes you back to Monaco through Monte Carlo Beach.

EZE-VILLAGE: Take the Moyenne Corniche about 5 miles (8 km) east. It's a better road than the Grand Corniche, but more crowded and less scenic. A cliff-perched town, like Roquebrune, Eze-Village has winding streets, a cactus garden, and a sweeping view of the Mediterranean from the ruins of the castle. It's less historic than Roquebrune, but has two superb restaurants (see *Best en Route*). Eze is also a good place to buy locally made copper and enamel jewelry.

BEST EN ROUTE

Expect to pay $250 and up per night for a double room in hotels listed as very expensive; $130 to $250 for those in the expensive category; $75 to $125 at a moderate place; and less than $75 for a very adequate double room in a small, inexpensive hotel. Restaurants range in price from $100 and up for a dinner for two in the expensive category; $50 to $100 in the moderate; and less than $50 in the inexpensive category. Prices usually include service charges, but not drinks or wine. The establishments listed below accept all major credit cards, unless otherwise indicated.

MONACO

Hermitage – Opened in 1899, it still looks like a fit setting for a turn-of-the-century grand duke. A winter garden, a restaurant with Belle Epoque decor and food to match, and 200 luxurious rooms. More sedate than the bustling *Hôtel de Paris*. Pl. Beaumarchais (phone: 93-50-67-31 or 93-50-67-38; fax: 93-50-47-12; telex: 479432). Very expensive.

Hôtel de Paris – Like the casino across the square, its contemporary, this is a historic landmark that is *the* address in Monaco. It has 300 luxuriously refurbished rooms as well as the regal *Salle Empire* dining room, the three-star *Louis XV* restaurant, and the *Grill,* a swank rooftop restaurant (see below for the latter two) that are among Monaco's best. Pl. du Casino (phone: 93-50-80-80; fax: 93-25-59-17; telex: 469925). Very expensive.

Beach Plaza – The other hotel on a private beach, this one is modern, with some 320 air conditioned rooms, swimming pools, and an open-air grill restaurant. 22 Av. Princesse-Grace (phone: 93-30-98-80; fax: 93-50-23-14; telex: 479617). Expensive.

Bec Rouge – Fans of its classic cuisine and elegant air consider it the best in town. The *blinis* with smoked salmon or caviar are a specialty. Closed January. Reservations advised. 11 Av. de Grande-Bretagne (phone: 93-30-74-91). Expensive.

Grill – A panoramic location atop the *Hôtel de Paris,* excellent *grillades,* a remarkable wine list, and exquisite raspberry soufflés all conspire to provide a memorable evening at this one-Michelin star dining establishment. Closed Mondays and the first half of December. Reservations advised. Pl. du Casino (phone: 93-50-80-80). Expensive.

Loews Monte Carlo – An ultramodern polygon right at the edge of the water, with 600-plus rooms, its own American-style casino, swimming pool, disco, nightclub, and several restaurants including the *Pistou* (see below). Av. des Spélugues (phone: 93-50-65-00; fax: 93-30-01-57; telex: 479435). Expensive.

Le Louis XV – Chef Alain Ducasse won this fine establishment its third Michelin star in 1990. In the *Hôtel de Paris,* it's one of the best places to eat in the Mediterranean — or any other — area. Closed November 20 to December 25, and Tuesdays and Wednesdays, February 26 to March 13. Reservations essential. Pl. du Casino (phone: 93-50-80-80 or 43-30-23-11). Expensive.

Mirabeau – Elegant, yet less expensive than the other Société des Bains de Mer hotels (*Hermitage, Paris, Monte Carlo Beach*). This is in a modern high-rise, with its own pool, restaurants, and 113 rooms. 1 Av. Princesse-Grace (phone: 93-25-45-45; fax: 93-50-84-85; telex: 479413). Expensive.

Monte Carlo Beach – Right on a beach at nearby Roquebrune-Cap-Martin. Small (46 renovated rooms) and charming (the terra cotta–roofed building dates from 1928), it's east of town at the exclusive *Monte Carlo Beach Club.* Closed from November to mid-April (phone: 93-78-21-40; fax: 93-78-14-18; telex: 462010). Expensive.

St. Charles – The maritime decor suggests the specialty here: fine seafood. Closed Tuesdays and from November 20 to December 25. Reservations advised. 33 Av. St.-Charles (phone: 93-50-63-19). Expensive.

Alexandra – There are 55 rooms, each with a bath or shower, in this modest hotel. No restaurant. 35 Bd. Princesse-Charlotte (phone: 93-50-63-13; telex: 489286). Moderate.

Pistou – On the roof of *Loews Monte Carlo* hotel and serving specialties of Provence — lamb with a sauce of vegetables and garlic; local cheeses. Reservations advised. Av. des Spélugues (phone: 93-50-65-00). Moderate.

Polpetta – This café specializes in Italian and southern French cuisine. Closed for lunch on Saturdays, 2 weeks in October, and 3 weeks in February. Reservations advised. Visa only accepted. 2 Rue Paradis (phone: 93-50-67-84). Moderate.

Terminus – These 54 rooms, each with a bath or shower, a TV set, and a radio are near the train station. There is a restaurant. Reservations unnecessary. Visa only accepted. 9 Av. Prince-Pierre (phone: 93-30-20-70). Inexpensive.

Nightclubs – Although Monaco's nightlife has traditionally been monopolized by the *Casino de Monte Carlo* (phone: 93-50-69-31), you can also try your luck at the casino in *Loews Monte Carlo* (phone: 93-50-65-00) or at the one in the *Monte Carlo Sporting Club* (phone: 93-30-71-71), open summers only. Then squander your winnings or drown your sorrows at *Jimmy'z* or *Parady'z,* both in the sporting club (phone: 93-50-31-66). In winter, *Jimmy'z* moves to the Pl. du Casino (phone: 93-50-80-80).

ROQUEBRUNE

Roquebrune – The place to go for delicious bouillabaisse. Closed November, 1 week in January and Wednesdays out-of-season. Reservations necessary. 100 Corniche Inférieure (phone: 93-35-00-16). Moderate.

Lucioles – There's a delightful view of the sea from an open terrace and a fixed-price menu. Closed Mondays and from November to March. Reservations unnecessary. No credit cards accepted. 12 Av. Raymond-Poincaré (phone: 93-35-02-19). Inexpensive.

EZE-VILLAGE

Château de la Chèvre d'Or – A restored medieval manor house in the heart of the village, it offers splendid views of the sea. There are 10 rooms, a pool, and a dining room that serves classic one-star French fare. Hotel closed from December 4 to March 1; restaurant closed Wednesdays from December to March. On the Moyenne Corniche at Rue Barri (phone: 93-41-12-12; fax: 93-41-06-72). Expensive.

Richard Borfiga – More one-Michelin-star French cuisine, with especially fine sauces. Closed Mondays and 3 weeks in January. Reservations unnecessary. Pl. de Gaulle (phone: 93-41-05-23). Expensive.

The Netherlands

The Netherlands is a small country — smaller than most American states — and can be crossed by car in a couple of hours. Packed into this tiny area, however, is an astonishing array of things to see and do. The country's compactness, combined with its excellent freeway system and efficient rail service, is handy for visitors since most points on the recommended tour routes can be reached easily in day trips from Amsterdam.

The unique geography of the Netherlands has shaped the country's history and the character of its people. Named for its unusually low (nether) geographic location — all of western Holland is below sea level — the Netherlands has risen literally from the sea to become an affluent, intriguing nation. During the last Ice Age, a great glacier shaped much of Holland into flat land. As the climate warmed and the glaciers melted, millions of tons of melting ice increased the water level of the North Sea (bordering the Netherlands on the west), causing the sea to inundate these low-lying lands. The land was not flooded evenly, because sand dunes acted as natural breakwaters and this brought about the development of lagoons and swamps. Much of the Netherlands is land reclaimed from the sea by various advanced draining techniques. The Dutch were pioneers of dike building and drainage canals, and their history is a continuous battle with the sea over which they have triumphed. On lands that once were flooded stand the country's greatest cities — Amsterdam, Rotterdam, and The Hague. Perhaps the Dutch people's constant struggle with water — exemplified by the mythical Dutch boy who stuck his finger in the leaking dam and saved his town from flooding — have made them tenacious and successful. What they have accomplished with almost negative natural resources is proof of their success. Well-designed cities with stunning architecture, neat polder fields of the rural landscape, and the enduring works of art of the Netherlands's Golden Age, the 17th century, are among the spoils for the native and the traveler.

Before you go, contact the *Netherlands Board of Tourism* (355 Lexington Ave., New York, NY 10017; phone: 212-370-7367) for information about travel, accommodations, tourist activities, and cultural events. They can supply you with a number of informative brochures, including *Unique Hotels of Holland,* and sell the Holland Leisure Card, which provides vouchers for a variety of activities. Once in Holland, stop first at the local VVV tourist office for information. The toll-free VVV central number is 6-340-34065; their offices offer a wealth of brochures and services. There are VVVs in practically every town and village, with offices located at or near railway stations in larger cities, and near the center of town in smaller villages. Each one specializes in its own region, though most also carry the standard literature on the rest of the country issued by the National Tourist Office (phone: 70-370-5705). These brochures, maps, and pamphlets are the best local guides. The Dutch automobile association, *ANWB,* has the best detailed road maps, and also publishes a large number of specialized touring maps on different themes and regions. You can pick up maps at the *ANWB* office in The Hague (220 Wassenaarseweg; phone: 70-314-7147) or in Amsterdam (5 Museumplein; phone: 20-730844). Falk-Verlag also publishes a multilingual road map of the country, available at any newsstand.

As you enter towns and cities, follow the *Centrum* signs to reach the center. *Doorgaand Verkeer* indicates the route for through traffic.

Our first route leads you through Randstad, where the major cities are concentrated. Though the cities are quite close together, they offer remarkable diversity, from the well-preserved old town of Haarlem to the extremely modern-looking Rotterdam. The northern Netherlands route takes in the typical Dutch polder landscape of the North Holland province, and heads over the immense Enclosing Dike, which contains the North Sea. The southern Netherlands route passes through the most geographically varied area of the country, through moors and forests, and the hill country of north Brabant and Limburg — the most French of the country's provinces. The last itinerary takes in the eastern region, where medieval castles and fortified towns lie amid forests and purple heathland.

The Randstad:
From Amsterdam to Rotterdam

This region, much of it below sea level, exemplifies Holland's compact diversity. Although the Randstad refers to a sort of supercity bounded by Amsterdam, Utrecht, Rotterdam, and The Hague, the greatest distance between any two of these cities is a mere 47 miles (75 km), from Amsterdam to Rotterdam. No four cities, as their inhabitants are quick to point out, could be more different. Nor is it the intention of planners that the four simply expand until they merge in an unbroken mass of concrete. Though this area is the most industrialized and densely populated in the country (60% of Holland's inhabitants live here), villages, farms, and rural and recreational areas are carefully preserved to maintain the variety and livable quality of the megapolis. All the sophisticated attractions of modern urban life can be found here, as well as miles of unbroken flower fields, lush pastures with grazing cows, and small historic towns. The route leaves Amsterdam on the Haarlemmerweg, which becomes the N5 state highway leading to Haarlem, and winds its way south through the bulb fields to Leiden, The Hague, Delft, and Rotterdam.

AMSTERDAM: For a complete report on the city and its hotels and restaurants, see *Amsterdam,* THE CITIES.

HAARLEM: This 900-year-old town has one of the country's best-preserved historic centers. An important city when Amsterdam was only a sleepy fishing village, Haarlem is still remembered for its heroic resistance during Holland's 80-year revolt against Spain, when it was besieged in 1572 for 7 months and finally largely destroyed, along with much of the population.

Haarlem's central square is the medieval Grote Markt, ringed by a number of noteworthy buildings including the 14th-century Stadhuis (Town Hall), originally a hunting lodge of the Counts of Holland; the ornate *Renaissance Meat Market*, built in 1603 (now a museum); and the Grote Kerk or Church of St. Bavo constructed between 1390 and 1520. The church also is known for its Müller organ, built in 1738. With 68 registers and 5,000 pipes, the organ has lured the likes of Mozart and Handel to Haarlem. Every June, it is the centerpiece of an annual improvisation competition that draws top organists from all over the world. From the beginning of April until mid-October, public concerts are given on Tuesday evenings and Thursday afternoons. On the first weekend of November a large annual antiquarian book fair is held at Baynes Hall, just outside the train station. Of special interest is the *Frans Hals Museum* (62 Groot Heiligland; phone: 23-319180), originally a home for old men built in 1608. Be sure to visit *Teylers Museum* (16 Spaarne; phone: 23-320197), said to be the oldest in the country. From March 1 through September 30, the museum is open Tuesdays through Saturdays from 10 AM to 5 PM, and from October 1 through February 28 it is open Tuesdays through Saturdays from 10 AM to 4 PM; throughout the year, the museum also is open the first Sunday of every month from 1 to 4 PM. On spring and summer evenings, romantic candlelight concerts are performed in the museum. Haarlem is the starting point of the annual spring flower parade through the bulb district, which takes place on the fourth Saturday in April at 10 AM. It is only a 20-minute train ride from Amsterdam.

En Route from Haarlem – A short detour 6 miles (10 km) west leads to Zandvoort, a popular resort, with its 5½ miles of sandy beaches (including a nudist beach). There's also a great restaurant in Bloemendaal, very close to the Haarlem train station (see *Best en Route*).

Just outside Heemstede you'll find the *Heemstede Cruquius Museum* (27 and 32 Cruquiusdijk), which houses one of the three original steam-driven pumping stations that drained the immense Haarlem Lake from 1849 to 1852. From April to September, the museum is open Mondays through Saturdays from 10 AM to 5 PM, and on Sundays and public holidays from noon to 5 PM; during October and November, it is open Mondays through Saturdays from 10 AM to 4 PM, and on Sundays and public holidays from noon to 4 PM. Groups with reservations may visit the museum between December and March. Today, that lakebed holds the Schiphol International Airport, 13 feet below sea level and probably the only airport in the world built on the site of a naval battle. The teahouse next to the museum is a handy place for a break.

At the world's largest flower auction in Aalsmeer some 10 million cut flowers are sold daily (except weekends) in the 75-acre auction hall (313 Legmeerdijk). Tours are available between 8 and 11 AM. Arrive early to see the operation at its blooming best. On the first Saturday in September, Aalsmeer is the starting point of the world's biggest floral parade, which travels to Amsterdam and back. Floats are on view in the auction halls the days before and after the parade.

Nieuw-Vennep is the modern site of the famous Bols Company (7 Lucas Bolsstraat). After more than 4 centuries in business, this is the world's oldest distiller of liqueurs.

In April and early May, Holland's vast bulb fields are in brilliant bloom. If you visit at this time, take a mini-tour by turning south at Hillegom toward Lisse, and follow the signposted flower route. In Lisse, don't miss the Keukenhof (Stationsweg), a spectacular 70-acre garden featuring some 7 million bulbs and 5,000 square yards of greenhouses, open only during the blooming period. Bus tours (about $20) depart daily from Amsterdam. For information call *Lindbergh Excursions* in Amsterdam (phone: 622-2766).

LEIDEN: Dating from Roman times, Leiden is one of Holland's oldest towns. For a long time, it also was one of the most important. It is the site of the country's first university, established in 1575 in recognition of the town's heroic role in the revolt against Spain. Part of the university still is housed in the former convent chapel (73 Rapenburg), where it has been since 1581. The *Grande Café in den Leidschen Salon* (2 Steenstraat; phone: 71-130335) is a perfect spot to enjoy a light lunch (try the smoked eel) in the company of students. The lifting of the siege of Leiden in 1574 is celebrated every year on October 3. America's Pilgrim ancestors took refuge here from 1608 to 1620, and you should not miss the chance to visit the Pilgrim Fathers Documents Center (45 Vliet) or the restored St. Pieter's Church, where they worshiped. Also worth a look is the *De Valk Windmill Museum* (1 Tweede Binnenvestgracht; phone: 71-254639), which is in an 8-story brick windmill dating from 1743; a miller's lifestyle of that period is depicted here; admission charge. For a light lunch, try some Dutch pancakes, which come in a variety of flavors, at the *Oud Leyden* (51-53 Steenstraat; phone: 71-133144); more elegant dishes are served in the Michelin-starred restaurant of the same name and under the same management next door.

THE HAGUE: Once a hunting resort of the Counts of Holland, its original name was 's Graven Hage, or Den Haag (the Count's Hedge). Today, this city of half a million, the third-largest in the Netherlands and the country's political capital and seat of government (Amsterdam is the official capital), provides an excellent capsule illustration of the varied character of the Randstad.

As befits a major world capital housing more than 60 foreign embassies, The Hague is a smart, sophisticated, and cosmopolitan city, known for its beauty, elegance, and stateliness. The city contains three Royal Palaces — in tow of which the royal family reside and hold functions — and retains a distinctively regal air. The daily business of government is carried on in the historic Binnenhof (Inner Court) or Parliament House complex of buildings in the ancient heart of the city, dominated by the magnificent 700-year-old Ridderzaal (Knights' Hall). It was here that the village of Die Haghe grew up around a hunting lodge built by the Count of Holland in the 13th century. Summer offers special treats. The imposing 15th-century Church of St. Jacob or Grote Kerk (the Kerkplein) features carillon concerts at noon on Mondays, Wednesdays, and Fridays, while the mansion-filled and tree-lined Lange Voorhout is turned into an open-air books and antiques market every Thursday and Sunday during the summer. The *Mauritshuis Museum* (8 Korte Vijverberg; phone: 70-346-9244), a former 17th-century palace housing one of the world's best collections of paintings from the Dutch school, is also close by. The museum is open Mondays through Saturdays from 10 AM to 5 PM, and on Sundays from noon to 3 PM.

An entirely different side of The Hague is presented by the city's lively seafront, Scheveningen, which has long been one of Europe's major resorts. Features include an attractive promenade and pier, dozens of beachfront cafés, a nudist beach, and one of Holland's major casinos in the landmark *Kurhaus* hotel (see *Best en Route*).

The Hague has more than a score of museums. Principal among these is the *Gemeente* (City) *Museum* (41 Stadhouderslaan) designed by the famous Dutch architect H.P. Berlage. It features a collection of period costumes, rare musical instruments, paintings by masters of The Hague School, works by Dutch artist Piet Mondrian, and changing exhibitions of contemporary art. Open Tuesdays through Sundays from 11 AM to 5 PM, Sundays from 1 to 5 PM, and on Wednesday evenings from 8 to 10 PM. In the adjacent building in the same complex is the *Museon* (phone: 70-338-1338) which showcases popular science exhibitions of interest to visitors of all ages. The *Panorama Mesdag* (open April 1–September 30, weekdays from 10 AM to 5 PM, and Sundays from noon to 5 PM; open November 1–February 28, weekdays from 10 AM to 3 PM, and Sundays from noon to 3 PM; during October and March, open weekdays from 10 AM to 4 PM, and Sundays from noon to 4 PM; 65B Zeestraat) has the world's largest painting, completed in 1881 and depicting Scheveningen life at the time. The *Gevangenpoort* (Prison Gate) *Museum* (open year-round, Mondays through Fridays from 10

AM to 4 PM, and, from April through September, open Saturdays and Sundays from 1 to 4 PM; 33 Buitenhof) is a medieval horror chamber with torture rooms and instruments still intact. Other notable museums include the Hague's *Historical Museum* (open daily from 10 AM to 5 PM; 7 Korte Vijverberg; phone: 70-364-6940) and the *Museum Scheveningen* (open Tuesdays through Saturdays from 10 AM to 5 PM; 92 Neptunusstraat; phone: 70-350-0830), illustrating the history of Scheveningen as a fishing village.

The Hague is well known for its unique miniature city, Madurodam, 5 acres of meticulously crafted reproductions of real structures done on a scale of 1:25. Everything works, too, from the 2-mile railway network to the canal locks and harbor fire boats. Nearly 50,000 tiny lights come on at dusk. At 175 Haringkade in the Scheveningse Bosjes woodland park; open from March 28 to January 5, with varying hours (phone: 70-355-3900).

Other Hague sights include the Royal Residence at Huis ten Bosch Palace, the home of Queen Beatrix, on the Bezuidenhoutseweg in the Haagse Bos (Hague Woods), and the Peace Palace (Carnegieplein), a gift of the American millionaire and philanthropist Andrew Carnegie and now the site of the International Court of Justice.

With its many woods and parks, The Hague also lays claim to being Holland's greenest city. Worthy of special attention are the 19th-century Japanese Garden, Clingendael Park, open during the blooming season from about mid-May to mid-June, and the world-famous rosarium in the 50-acre Westbroekpark in the Scheveningse Bosjes, with its roses in full glory during August.

The Hague's special combination of city, woodland, seaside, and dunes is reflected in the wide range of recreational facilities available. Greyhounds race at *Clingendael* on the Rijksstraatweg, and the horses run at *Duindigt* in Wassenaar (29A Waalsdorperlaan). Nearby Duinrell has a campground, recreational area, and amusement park, where you can even ski on artificial slopes (and snow) in the wintertime. You can swim there year-round and enjoy the thrills of the largest indoor/outdoor waterslide in Europe, or else try the glass-covered surf pool on the Promenade in Scheveningen. In warm weather, there's the North Sea, and for deep-sea fishing or a cruise, try *Rederij Jacq. Vrolijk* (Doorniksestraat; phone: 70-351-4021).

Special Hague events include the ceremonial opening of Parliament on the third Tuesday in September, when the queen sets out in her golden coach, and the week-long annual *North Sea Jazz Festival* in July, which attracts top performers from all over the world. A modern concert building, *Dr. Anton Philips Zaal Concert Hall*, is divided into two theaters, for dance and music events (phone: 70-360-9810). If hunger strikes, cross the street to the *Markt Hof* (Farmers' Market), and sample some Chinese food at the stands.

Vlaggetjesdag (Flag Day), celebrated late in May when the colorfully bedecked herring fleet sets out from Scheveningen for the first catch of the new season, is also a special event. This year *Floriade,* a special world horticultural exhibition, will be held in Zoetermeer, about 7 miles (11 km) outside the center of The Hague, from April 15 through October 11. (Take the main A12 Highway or the train.) Dubbed "the greatest flower show on earth," it will be set in a 50-acre park with theme pavilions, international exhibitions, and a fruit and vegetable auction (phone: 79-681992).

DELFT: This town, dating from 1246 with its architecturally splendid 300-year-old center, is best known outside Holland for the famous pottery that has become synonymous with its name. The Porceleyne Fles (196 Rotterdamseweg; phone: 15-602358) is the only factory that still makes Delftware in the traditional way (others churn out machine-made imitations). You can watch the company's 300 artists painting the entirely handmade Delft Blue. Closed Mondays. No admission charge.

To the Dutch, Delft is most important for its historical associations. William the Silent of Orange, the country's founding father and precursor of the present royal family, was assassinated here in 1584. Some bullet holes from that attack still can be seen in the walls of the beautiful 15th-century *Prinsenhof Museum* (Agathaplein), William's residence at the time. The museum itself is devoted primarily to the history of Delft and the Netherlands' long struggle for independence from Spain.

Delft is the traditional burial place of the royal family. Tombs are not on public view, but you can visit the mausoleum of William at the New Church, on the Markt, built in 1496. If you have the stamina, climb the tower for a spectacular view of the city.

ROTTERDAM: Holland's second-largest city, with a population of about 580,000, Rotterdam once rivaled Amsterdam in beautiful old buildings but was devastated by a Nazi air raid in 1940. The city was rebuilt and is today extremely modern — well designed and attractive. Air and light sometimes seem to have been used as purposefully as glass and steel in its reconstruction. The broad 1¼-mile pedestrian shopping precinct, Lijnbaan, is an attraction in its own right, as are the unique pencil-shape houses and the Cubist architecture by the waterfront, which still is referred to as Oudehaven, or Old Harbor. For a glimpse of the past visit the "white house" building, which was the sole postwar survivor. The 600-foot Euromast (20 Parkhaven) is worth a visit for its panoramic restaurant, cafeteria, observation tower, and an airborne ship's bridge manned by retired officers who are happy to explain the instruments.

Don't miss the opportunity to tour the large, modern port complex by boat from Spido at the Willemsplein. Greenery is well provided for by the beautiful Kralingse Bos woodland park, and the *Boymans–van Beuningen Museum* (18-20 Mathenesserlaan; phone: 10-4419400) has a fine collection of modern and traditional art; admission charge. The *Volkenkunde* (Ethnological Museum; 25 Willemskade; phone: 10-411-1055) focuses on cultures of other countries of the world, and exotic foods are served in the museum's restaurant (phone: 10-404-5871), which specializes in Caribbean cooking; open from 10 AM until 10 PM (closed Sundays). The highly respected *Rotterdam Philharmonic Orchestra* offers the best in classical music at the *Doelen Concert Hall* (50 Schouwburgplein). For live jazz, stop by *Dizzy's* (15 Houttuinen; phone: 15-122125), not far from the train station. The *Doelen* also offers a number of special cultural activities, including the *International Poetry Festival* every June. In early February, the annual *International Film Festival* is held in the city center.

Rotterdam is not all modern, however. Miraculously spared the Nazi bombs was the historic port of Delfshaven, from which America's founding Pilgrim fathers sailed on the first leg of their voyage to the New World in 1620. A painstaking 20-year project restoring Delfshaven's 110 buildings was completed in 1980, and many of these now belong to artists and practitioners of traditional crafts. Of special interest is the Guild House of the Sack Carriers who unloaded the ships (13-15 Voorstraat), where you can buy — at bargain prices — new pewter objects cast in original 17th- and 18th-century molds and watch how they are made. *De Dubbelde Palmboom* historical museum (10-12 Voorhaven; phone: 10-476-1533) is devoted to old crafts. If you want to see the Pilgrim Fathers' Church, call first or check next door (18 Voorstraat; phone: 10-477-4156). A special commemoration service is held here every *Thanksgiving Day.*

Close to Rotterdam is Kinderdijk, with Holland's greatest concentration of windmills. On Saturday afternoons July and August, weather permitting, all 19 mills are turning.

Also outside Rotterdam is the town of Gouda; its *Cheese Market* is held in the 17th-century weigh house in the central Markt on Thursday mornings from 9:30 AM to noon, June 30 to August 31. Nearby is Holland's oldest (1448) and most beautiful Town Hall, which lures marriage-minded couples from all over the country. On a selected evening in mid-December, the entire square is illuminated by candlelight until the magnificent town *Christmas* tree, a gift from Norway, is switched on. Carol singing and a concert in the church follow.

BEST EN ROUTE

In The Hague, expect to pay $110 and up for a double room in the expensive range, $70 to $90 in the moderate range, and under $60 in the inexpensive category. Dinner for two should cost from $75 to $125 in expensive restaurants, from $40 to $60 in those listed as moderate, and under $30 in the inexpensive ones. Prices include drinks and wine. Indonesian restaurants are particularly good in The Hague.

HAARLEM

Lion D'Or – Built in 1850 and now operated by the Golden Tulip chain, this small, intimate hostelry is near the train station, minutes from the city center. 34-36 Kruisweg (phone: 23-321750). Moderate.

La Pêcherie – A popular fish restaurant in the city center. Reservations advised. Oude Groenmarkt (phone: 23-314884). Moderate.

Bistro Jacques – A cozy French-style eatery near the Grote Kerk (Big Church). Reservations advised. Grotemarktplein (phone: 23-322398). Inexpensive.

BLOEMENDAAL

De Bokkedorans – Just minutes by taxi from the Haarlem train station, this one-Michelin-star restaurant is well worth a detour to or from the beaches at nearby Zandvoort. French cooking is a specialty, as is the personal service. Open Tuesdays through Fridays for lunch and dinner, Saturdays for dinner only; closed Mondays. Reservations advised. 53 Zeeweg (phone: 23-26300). Expensive to moderate.

THE HAGUE

Hotel des Indes – Formerly a residence for royalty, this elegant property operated by Inter-Continental hotels offers efficient service and excellent accommodations. It is surrounded by embassies near the House of Parliament in the picturesque city center. 54-56 Lange Voorhout (phone: 70-346-9553). Expensive.

Kurhaus – Originally opened in 1885, this historic beachfront hotel was completely rebuilt and re-opened in 1979. Dominating the seaport resort area of Scheveningen, the hotel has a classical façade that is an exact replica of the original. Inside, there's modern luxury, centered around a vaulted dome reception area with old paintings and inlaid mosaics. The most elegant of the Netherlands' casinos is here, along with a first class French restaurant called *Kandinsky* and 2 bars. Adjacent to the hotel is an all-weather recreation center with a pool, sauna, and solarium. 1 Kurhausplein (phone: 70-352-0052). Expensive.

Corona – Elegant and luxurious, it has only 26 rooms, and service is outstanding. The excellent restaurant attracts a discerning clientele. Just opposite the House of Parliament, 39-42 Buitenhof (phone: 70-363-7930; fax: 70-361-5785). Expensive to moderate.

Garoeda – An elegant yet unpretentious 2-story restaurant in the center of town, near the American Embassy. Excellent rijsttafel (an Indonesian feast featuring some 20 dishes served with an abundance of rice). Reservations advised. 18A Kneuterdijk (phone: 70-346-5319). Moderate.

Park – In the old center of town near the Royal Palace and the chic shopping district. Rooms have direct-dial telephones, cable TV, writing desks, and luxurious marble bathrooms. Rates include buffet breakfast. 350 Molenstraat (phone: 70-362-4371). Moderate.

Tampat Senang – Dating from 1929, this is not only one of the oldest Indonesian restaurants in The Hague, it's also the most elegant. Rijstaffel, with 10 to 30 dishes, is served exclusively. Popular with the political and business movers-and-shakers.

Open daily for dinner. Reservations necessary. 6 Laan van Meedervoort (phone: 70-363-6787). Moderate.

Westbroekpark – This restaurant is in an open glass pavilion in the middle of a beautiful park. You can dine on French specialties while looking at the hundreds of roses growing outside. Try the four-course Golden Rose menu. From June to September, dining is outside in the midst of a blaze of color. Reservations advised. 35 Kapelweg (phone: 70-354-6072). Moderate.

Café Schlemmer – A must for a cappuccino or light meal. Its muted colors and distinct furnishings remind one of Schlemmer's paintings from the 1930s. Live music is often played on Sunday afternoons. Reservations advised. 17 Houtstraat (phone: 70-360-9000). Moderate to inexpensive.

Kantjil – A helpful staff ensures that guests at this modern, no-frills eatery enjoy a good rijsttafel. For a true adventure in Indonesian fare, ask for several à la carte specialties offering a combination of sweet, sour, and spicy tastes. Reservations advised. 121 Torenstraat (phone: 70-365-6131). Moderate to inexpensive.

DELFT

De Prinsenkelder – In a medieval cellar with Gothic arches, old wood, and antique tables, this chic and atmospheric restaurant specializes in French fare. Its specialty menus change weekly. Reservations advised. 11 Schoolstraat (phone: 15-121860). Expensive.

De Zwetheul – This picturesque spot, between Delft and Rotterdam, is run by a couple that presides over the traditional Dutch kitchen. Terrace dining in good weather. Lunch served Tuesdays through Fridays; dinner Saturdays and Sundays. Reservations necessary. 480 Rotterdamseweg (phone: 10-470-4166). Expensive to moderate.

Café de Kerk – A traditional café in the center of town, with tasty soup and sandwiches. 20 Kromstraat (phone: 15-141474). Inexpensive.

Dekok – Near the station, this small hostelry has 14 rooms, most with private bath and shower, color TV sets, telephones, and mini-bars. A buffet breakfast is included in the rates. 15 Houttuinen (phone: 15-122125). Inexpensive.

ROTTERDAM

Atlanta – In the town center, opposite City Hall, this hotel offers all modern amenities in a traditional Dutch setting. 4 Aert van Nesstraat (phone: 10-411-0420). Expensive to moderate.

De Unie – A restaurant done in Art Nouveau style and serving fine Dutch and French fare, with an eclectic clientele. Reservations unnecessary. 430 Mauritsweg (phone: 10-411-7394). Moderate to inexpensive.

Loos – Near the river Maas, not far from the central station, this Art Nouveau café, inspired by architect/designer Adolf Loos, serves excellent reasonably priced food. It's a good spot to people watch. Open daily. Reservations advised for dinner. 1 Westplein (phone: 10-411-7723). Inexpensive.

The Northern Netherlands

This 155-mile (248-km) route travels through the typical Dutch polder landscape of North Holland province, across the immense Enclosing Dike, which holds back the North Sea, into Friesland, the Netherlands's most unusual province. North Holland is characterized by its flat, rustic meadowlands reclaimed from the sea and sprinkled with church spires and thatch-roofed farmhouses, but it also possesses dreamy fishing villages, as well as the country's most beautiful beaches.

Friesland, particularly the Wadden Islands just off the coast, is a nature-lover's paradise, containing one of Europe's most important bird sanctuaries and wildlife preserves, as well as the country's best facilities for water sports. With its own language, history, and cultural traditions, passionately clung to by the majority of its half-million residents, Friesland gives the impression of being more of a tiny republic than a Dutch province. Its history is in fact older than Holland's; so fierce were the early Frisians that even the Roman legions were unable to subdue them. The Frisians literally built their country with their bare hands, doggedly constructing huge mounds of earth called *terpen* to protect them from the sea. More than 100 million cubic yards of earth (the equivalent of 21 Great Pyramids) were shifted this way. The Frisians, who also have a sense of humor, have made something of a joke out of their legendary pride and stubborn independence by issuing "passports". Pick one up at one of the tourist offices. They make intriguing souvenirs and also offer valuable reductions on many attractions.

ZAANDAM: In Zaandam (24 Krimp), only an 11-minute train ride from Amsterdam, you can see the cottage where the eccentric Russian czar, Peter the Great, disguised as a shipyard worker, stayed while on a state visit in 1697. Just outside of town is De Zaanse Schans, a village constructed in 1948 from threatened historic mills and houses that were transported to the site and painstakingly reassembled. It is now a living museum occupied by families, but the windmills — as well as an antique clock museum and an old bakery — are open to the public (open daily; no admission charge; phone: 75-162221). In nearby Koog aande Zaan (18 Museumlaan) is a windmill museum with models demonstrating how the mills work.

    En Route from Zaandam – The stretch of coastline a few miles west of the route is among the most unspoiled in the country. There is a magnificent 12,500-acre dune reservation with entrances at the villages of Wijk aan Zee, Heemskerk, Schorl, Castricum, Bakkum, Egmond, and Bergen. The last village is an artists' colony with charming shops and cafés. Rent a bike from one of the cycling shops here, such as *Busker* (1 Kerkstr.; phone: 2208-95196), and tour the scenic dunes.

ALKMAAR: This picturesque town is especially famed for its cheese market on the central Waagplein. On Friday mornings at 10 AM in the spring and summer, a colorful early-17th-century tradition continues as the cheeses are auctioned off and carried to the 14th-century weighing house by members of one of Europe's few surviving medieval guilds.

HOORN: Like others along what was once the Zuider Zee, this historic port town on the shore of Lake Ijssel has adopted tourism and water sports since being cut off from the ocean. Summer is the season for a folklore market that gives demonstrations of traditional crafts, and the historic triangle tour, which includes a trip by steam train to Medemblik, and by boat to Enkhuizen. At the last stop, the *Zuiderzee Museum,* a reconstructed — and inhabited — village of 130 homes and shops depicts the area's turn-of-the-century fishing culture (admission charge; 18 Wierdijk; phone: 2289-18260). If hunger calls, the fish restaurants along the quay by the inner harbor offer hearty local dishes that fill your stomach without emptying your purse. Try some steamed mussels in season (the best time to sample them is from September through April).

The villages of Marken and Volendam, where the locals still wear traditional costumes (mainly as a draw for tourists), and the little-changed 17th-century cheese town of Edam lie 12½ miles (20 km) south of Hoorn. A rather strange museum in Edam (8 Wowneerstraat) is in a 16th-century house that has a cellar that actually floats; at different times, the house has been occupied by a man famed for his beard, which reached down to his toes and back up to his shoulders; a woman nearly 9 feet tall; and another man who weighed over 500 pounds! Exhibits focus on them and other local curios (closed Mondays; admission charge).

En Route from Hoorn – At Den Oever you might like to make a side trip by heading 16 miles (26 km) to Den Helder, where you can catch a ferry to Texel, the largest and most popular of the Wadden Islands. Although Texel is swamped with campers in the summer, all of the islands are beautiful and undeveloped, and there are small hotels where you can stay — check with the VVV.

Back en route, you cross the Afsluitdijk, a massive 12-mile-long dike separating the North Sea from freshwater Lake Ijssel. Stop at the monument, 4 miles (6 km) from Den Oever, and climb up for a view of the surrounding water. If this dike ever springs a leak, it'll take much more than a boy's finger to plug it up.

A short way up the coast is the seaport town of Harlingen, originally a Norman settlement, now a jumping-off point for the attractive islands of Vlieland and Terschelling. Cars are banned from Vlieland.

Franeker features an unusual working planetarium with a model, created by a craftsman in 1781, that demonstrates the solar system as it was known in the 18th century (open Mondays through Saturdays; daily during summer; admission charge; 3 Eise Eisingastraat; phone: 5170-00070). A short way off the road at the next junction at Dronrijp is Winsum, the center of a uniquely Frisian sport — pole-vaulting over canals. Developed from the practical need of a means of crossing the canal-laced fields, this sport is interesting because most of the contestants end up in the water rather than on the far bank. Championships are held on Saturdays in August.

LEEUWARDEN: Built on three *terpen,* this city is the capital and heart of Friesland. The notorious spy Mata Hari was born here. A statue of her stands on the Korfmaker-spijp. The house where she grew up is now occupied by the *Museum of Frisian Literature* (28 Gröte Kerkstraat). The *Fries Museum* (24 Turfmarkt) has English-speaking guides (available by appointment), who provide some insight into the history and culture of this unique province. The *Princessehof Museum* (11 Gröte Kerkstraat) has an excellent ceramics collection, including many one-of-a-kind pieces. From the 16th-century Oldehove Tower (Oldehoofster Kerkhof), you can view the city from May through September (Tuesdays through Saturdays from 9:30 AM to 12:30 PM, and from 1:30 PM to 4:30 PM). The *Taveerne De Waag,* in the weighing house, built in 1568, is an interesting place to eat. Admission charge to all museums.

Another unique form of recreation that is rapidly gaining in popularity with tourists is *wadlopen* — walking through the shallows. The Wadden Sea between the mainland and the islands is so shallow that it is actually possible to walk to three of the islands when the tide is out. Organized treks are an absolute must for bird watchers. They require a day, an experienced guide, suitable clothing and equipment, and some advance planning. Departures are from Holwerd or Wierum on the coast to the north. For information contact the VVV in Leeuwarden (1 Stationsplein; phone: 58-132224). The hamlet of Hoogebeintum stands on the highest (40 feet) *terp* in the province. To view the 13th-century church, get the key from the minister.

SNEEK: This popular yachting center is the site of a major international regatta in August. In the lake district, Friesland is Holland's prime location for all water sports.

SLOTEN: This walled town with a population of 700 is the smallest in Friesland. Resembling a movie set, this popular center for water sports is worth seeing.

En Route from Sloten – In Wolvega there's a statue of the founding father of New York, Peter Stuyvesant, who was born in the adjoining community of Weststellingwerf.

Zwarlendijkster: Between the villages of Een and Bakkeveen are these preserved fortifications dating from 1593, on which Stuyvesant based New York's defenses. It was this first wall that gave Wall Street its name. The wooded area is an attractive place to walk or bicycle. From here you can return easily to Leeuwarden via Drachten or extend your tour by continuing north to the university city of Groningen, and looping back down to Amsterdam through a few pastoral provinces.

BEST EN ROUTE

Expect to pay $100 and up for a double room in an expensive hotel, $60 to $80 in the moderate range, and about $50 in the inexpensive category. Dinner for two should cost $40 to $50 in the restaurants listed as expensive, $20 to $30 in those listed as moderate, and under $15 in the inexpensive places. Prices do not include drinks or wine.

HOORN

De Oude Rosmolen – Elegantly situated in a 16th-century building, this dining place offers French cooking, fine wines, and attentive service, under the direction of owner/chef Constant Fonk. Open for lunch and dinner; closed on Thursdays. Reservations necessary. 1 Duinsteeg (phone: 2290-14752). Expensive to moderate.

Petit Nord – Near the train station, the 34 rooms in this modern hostelry have private bath, phones, color TV sets, and radios. Breakfast is included in the rates. 53-55 Klien Noord (phone: 2290-12750; fax: 2290-15745). Inexpensive.

LEEUWARDEN

Oranje – This completely rebuilt, reasonably priced hotel in the center of town has 78 rooms and a good restaurant specializing in Dutch and international dishes. 4 Stationsweg (phone: 58-126241; fax: 58-121441). Expensive to moderate.

GROUW

Oostergoo – Cozy, simple but comfortable, this 24-room hotel on the lake about 6 miles (10 km) from Leeuwarden has a restaurant serving Dutch food and fish specialties. 1 Nieuwe Kade (phone: 5662-1309). Moderate to inexpensive.

The Southern Netherlands

This 225-mile (360-km) route, bordered by Belgium to the south, passes through the most geographically varied part of the Netherlands, from the estuaries and islands of Zeeland (Sea Land) on the North Sea coast, through the moors and forests of North Brabant, to the hill country — the only hill country in Holland — of Limburg province in the southeastern pocket between Germany and Belgium. These last two, the country's Catholic provinces, are notorious among their sterner Protestant brethren for the annual carnival madness that sweeps the southeast for 3 days in February. The festivities, which include parades, colorful costumes, street music, round-the-clock opening of cafés, and general hysteria, are at their most frenetic in the larger towns, particularly Bergen op Zoom, Den Bosch, Breda, and Maastricht. North Brabant and Limburg are the least Dutch of the country's provinces, with closer cultural, historic, religious, and geographical links to the south. Limburg in particular has a distinctive French flavor.

ROTTERDAM: For a complete description of Rotterdam, see *The Randstad: From Amsterdam to Rotterdam.* Then, head west to the old fortified town of Brielle, the first town to go over to the Protestant cause after being taken by privateers in the service of William the Silent on April 1, 1572. The event is celebrated every year on this date.

STELLENDAM: On the night of January 31, 1953, freak conditions combined to fulfill the worst of Dutch nightmares. Some 300 miles of dikes stretching from Rotterdam southward were overwhelmed by a raging North Sea, resulting in the flooding of 4.5% of the nation's total land area, and the deaths of nearly 2,000 people. The Dutch answer to this disaster was the daring Delta Plan. Completed in 1986, after 31 years of work, this engineering feat closed off the huge estuaries dividing Zeeland, transformed recreation areas, and eliminated more than 400 miles of coastline. Most of the time you travel through Zeeland, you will be driving over water. These roads, linking the formerly isolated province to the rest of the country, were created by the Delta Plan. The *Delta Expo,* which explains this enormous project with the help of films, mock-ups, a tour of the interior workings of the barrier, and a boat ride, is open daily from March 31 to October, Wednesdays to Sundays the rest of the year. Burgh-Haamstede (phone: 1115-2702).

    En Route from Stellendam – The route passes through a region that has become an important center for water sports, with its beach resorts, campgrounds, dunes, and woods, and its excellent facilities for sailing, fishing, windsurfing, and so on. Zierikzee and Veere are particularly attractive towns. An intriguing place to eat or stay in Veere is *De Campveerse Toren* (see *Best en Route*), originally part of the town fortifications and now a monument. It has also been an inn since 1558 and was selected by William of Orange for his wedding feast, which is the Dutch equivalent of "George Washington slept here."

MIDDELBURG: The completely reconstructed medieval center of this small provincial capital won the title of "model center" during Europe's *Architectural Heritage Year* in 1975, and some of Holland's most interesting old buildings are to be found here. Most famous is the abbey dating from 1120, with its complex of churches, a 1,280-foot tower known as Long John that can be climbed in the summer, a museum depicting Zeeland's history and culture, and a distinctive restaurant done in period decor. If you find the wealth of architectural treasures somewhat overwhelming, visit Miniature Walcheren (Molenwater) where they are all meticulously reproduced on a scale of 1:20. In the summer you can tour the city by horse-drawn tram or attend a Thursday market with residents in regional costume. Surrounded by lovely countryside and coastline, Middelburg is a good place in which to stay over.

    En Route from Middelburg – At the seafront city of Vlissingen, you can lie on the beach and watch an incessant stream of passing ships making their way to and from the major Belgian port of Antwerp. A steam train in Goes makes daily tours of the region in the summer. The old center of Bergen op Zoom, on the Ooster Schelde inlet from the sea, is worth a stop.

BREDA: Principal sights of this historic town, beautifully situated amid moors and woodlands, are the market square and Grote Kerk on the Grote Markt, and nearby Breda Castle, originally dating from 1350. The castle, home of the Royal Military Academy since 1828, also is where the Dutch signed New Amsterdam (later named New York) over to the British in 1667. Two-hour guided tours (in English) are given Tuesdays through Fridays in the summer at 2 PM. Breda hosts a popular 1920s-style jazz festival every May, and on Saturdays from April through September there is a curiosities and crafts market on the Havermarkt. The VVV (17 Willemstraat) conducts a historic-mile walking tour of the center in the summer. The *Casino Breda* is open from 2 PM to 2 AM and features French and American roulette, blackjack, slot machines, a bar/restaurant, and a 5-guilder chip with admission (30 Bijster; phone: 76-227600). Near the A27 Breda-Utrecht Highway.

About 12½ miles (20 km) north of Breda lies the unique marshland nature preserve of Biesbosch, a fisherman's and bird watcher's paradise of tangled creeks and waterways. Boat tours of the area are available in summer from *Zilvermeeuw Cruises* (3 Weitjes) in the tiny village of Drimmelen, near Made, site of Europe's largest inland yacht harbor. The *Biesbosch* restaurant has fish specialties and provides an unrivaled view of the watery terrain (open from *Easter* until mid-October; phone: 1626-2608).

TILBURG: This town is a handy jumping-off point for a number of interesting side trips. If you pass town and turn right toward Hilvarenbeck, you will come to the turnoff for the *Beekse Bergen* amusement and safari park. Also interesting is the crazy-quilt village of Baarle-Nassau, which has two of nearly everything, including mayors. Many of the residents cross the international frontier between Holland and Belgium every time they go from one room of their homes to another. About 7½ miles (12 km) north of Tilburg on the road to Waalwijk is the enchanting fairy-tale park of *Efteling* (at Kaatsheuvel); it's Holland's largest amusement park and is considered a Dutch *Disneyland*. The *Tilburg Textile Museum* (96 Goerkastraat; phone: 13-367475) has exhibitions on the history of the textile industry, as well as historical and contemporary textile art. The *Autotron* in Roosmalen, near 's-Hertogenbosch, has a fine collection of over 400 antique cars. Admission charge to all museums and amusement parks.

's-HERTOGENBOSCH: This mouthful, usually known by the more manageable name Den Bosch, is the provincial capital of North Brabant. So taken with the city was the 15th-century painter Hiëronymus Bosch that he adopted it as his last name. His ardor was understandable, as Den Bosch is especially famed for its romantic antique center. Its market square (markets are on Wednesday and Saturday mornings) and the 14th-century St. Janskerk Cathedral are among Europe's most beautiful. Even the VVV, housed in a small 13th-century castle (77 Markt), is an attraction in this surprising city.

Weight-watchers can eat in peace at the medieval *Dry Hamerkens* (57 Hinthamerstraat), which features calorie-conscious menus as well as fuller selections. Just outside town in neighboring Vught, on the E9 south, it is an impressive restaurant in the 16th-century Maurick Castle, complete with drawbridge.

En Route from 's-Hertogenbosch – Eindhoven is the home of Holland's giant Philips Electronics Company, but also the site of the *Von Abbé Museum* (10 Bilderdijklaan; phone: 40-389730), which is known throughout Europe for its collection and changing exhibitions of 20th-century art.

From here you can drive direct to Maastricht on E9, or take the more leisurely alternative — E3 east to Venlo on the German border, and south from there. This route passes through Limburg's loveliest countryside, dotted with churches and castles. The landscape actually resembles the popular (and largely prewar) picture many people have of Europe. On the way to Venlo detour north via Venray to the village of Overloon, the site of a unique and disturbing war museum, the *National War & Resistance Museum* (1 Museumpark), which includes a 35-acre park still littered with the battered tanks, field guns, and other weapons left behind after the 3-week Battle of Overloon. Closed weekends. Admission charge.

MAASTRICHT: Dating originally from pre-Roman times, this provincial capital is Holland's oldest city. Maastricht was besieged 21 times; 9 of the 100 castles of Limburg province can be found here, as well as myriad historical monuments. One of Europe's finest restaurants, *Château Neercanne* (see *Best en Route*), is in Holland's only terraced castle. The 40,000-bottle wine cellar is kept at optimal temperature in a grotto beneath the castle. For a lighter touch in haute cuisine, try *Au Coin des Bons Enfants* (4 Ezelmarkt; phone: 43-212359). Its French owners are particularly well known for their seasonal specialties, including wild game.

The heart of Maastricht is its central square, 't Vrijthof, ringed by numerous cafés and monuments including the 10th-century St. Servaas Church, and *In Den Ouden Vogelstruys*, a café opened in 1312. A good place for a snack, the café is said to be the oldest in Holland. The stone bridge spanning the Maas River, constructed in 1298, is even older.

A unique sight nearby is the 120-mile network of manmade tunnels beneath nearby St. Pietersberg hill, 2 miles (3 km) south of the city. Begun by the Romans in search of marl for building stone, the tunnels have also provided a handy refuge during the city's frequent times of trial. Parts of this subterranean realm date from the French occupation of 1794 and include a World War II treasure room, where Rembrandt's immortal *Night Watch* was preserved from the Nazis. Note the signatures of Sir Walter Scott and Napoleon, among countless others, on the tunnel walls. Enter via Châlet Bergrust, 71 Luikerweg.

VALKENBURG: This hill town is a popular vacation spot among the Dutch. Approximately 40 more miles of tunnels lie beneath the ruins of Holland's only hilltop castle. Several entrances lead to a coal-mine museum, a mysterious underground lake, and an exact replica of the Roman catacombs. Aboveground is the province's largest casino at Odapark.

HEERLEN: The *Thermen Museum* (9 Coriovallumstraat), built over an excavated Roman bath in this ancient town, contains many indigenous Roman artifacts. Open daily. Admission charge (phone: 45-764581).

VAALS: At 1,000 feet, this is the highest point in the Netherlands and the meeting point of Holland, Belgium, and Germany.

BEST EN ROUTE

Expect to pay $100 and up for a double room in the expensive range, $60 to $80 in the moderate range, and about $50 in the inexpensive category. Breakfast generally is included. Dinner for two should cost $40 to $50 in the restaurants listed as expensive, $20 to $30 in those listed as moderate, and under $15, inexpensive. Prices do not include drinks or wine.

VEERE

De Campveerse Toren – Close to Middelburg, this historic inn — which has been catering to tourists for 5 centuries — has 19 rooms as well as a restaurant specializing in fish dishes. 2 Kade (phone: 1181-291). Expensive to moderate.

d'Ouwe Werf – A waterside restaurant offering unusual fish dishes, a good wine list, and a harbor view. Closed Mondays, 2 weeks in February and part of July and August. Reservations advised. 2 Bastion (phone: 1881-1493). Moderate.

VLISSINGEN

Britannia Watertoren – This pleasant seaside hotel with 35 rooms has 2 restaurants, both of which offer local fish specialties and lovely wide-angle views of ships sailing to and from foreign ports of call. 244 Blvd. Evertsen (phone: 1184-13255). Moderate.

's-HERTOGENBOSCH

Chalet Royale – Located just minutes from the train station in the city center, the owner, Mrs. Van den Boer, attracts a varied clientele to her highly rated restaurant. Closed Saturday lunch and Sundays. Reservations necessary. 1 Wilhemina-pliam (phone: 73-135771). Expensive to moderate.

WEERT

l'Auberge – Located 15 minutes out of Eindhoven en route to Roemond is a restaurant that is definitely worth a stop. Chef Emannuel Mertens presides over this intimate dining room with pride and great cooking. Closed Saturday lunch, Sundays, Mondays, and from mid-July through early August. Reservations necessary. 101 Parallelweg (phone: 49-503-1057). Expensive to moderate.

MAASTRICHT

Château Neercanne – Under the same management as the *Kasteel Erenstein*, a 13th-century Renaissance castle, and hotel-restaurant *Winselerhof*, a 16th-century farmhouse. It's possible to arrange a package visit to all three chic hostelries, which are near one another and a half-hour ride from the Maastricht airport. The complex has become very popular with business travelers due to its location near Germany, Belgium, and Luxembourg. Full business services and meeting rooms are available. Ideal for a romantic weekend as well. 800 Cannerweg (phone: 43-251359; fax: 43-213406). Expensive.

WITTEM

Kasteel Wittem – Dating from the 10th century, this 12-room castle-hotel is on its own private grounds, and just north of Maastricht. Inside is a Michelin-starred restaurant. 3 Wittemmerallee (phone: 4450-1208). Expensive to moderate.

GULPEN

Kasteel Neubourg – This moated castle, surrounded by woods, features 25 spacious rooms and a French restaurant. Located in the neighborhood of Maastricht. Closed in January and February. 1 Rijksweg (phone: 4450-1222). Expensive.

Utrecht and the East

Of special interest to nature lovers, this 109-mile (174-km) route passes through some of Holland's loveliest countryside, from the forests and purple heathland of the 240-square-mile Veluwe nature preserve with its wild deer and boar, to the farmlands and great country estates of bordering Achterhoek. With a turbulent history stretching back to Roman times, this area is rich in castles and fortified towns, and has some of the best-preserved medieval structures in the country.

En Route from Amsterdam – Take the A1/E35 to Hilversum where you pick up the A27 to Utrecht. This takes you past Muiden on the former Zuider Zee, a popular water sports center famous for its 13th-century castle, and moat-ringed Naarden, a beautifully preserved old fortress town. On the opposite side of Hilversum are the Loosdrecht Lakes, a major center for water sports and recreation.

UTRECHT: Founded by the Romans in AD 47, this ancient city is the geographic and historical center of the Dutch nation. Today it has a population of about 234,000 and is Holland's fourth-largest city. Worthy of special attention is the medieval city center and the unique canalside wharves and cellars (now shops and cafés) lining the Nieuwegracht and Oudegracht. At the heart of the old center is the Domplein, a square containing one of the country's most magnificent cathedrals. Work on the church was begun in 1254, and required over 250 years to complete. The 350-foot church tower, constructed separately and completed in 1382, is the tallest in the Netherlands and offers rewarding views for the hearty (May–September).

Utrecht is also the convergence point of the *Dutch Railway System* and there is a fascinating railway museum in a former station (6 Johan van Oldebarneveltlaan), exhibiting old steam locomotives and models. The *Music Box Museum* (10 Buurkerk-hof) has a collection of mechanical music makers dating from the 18th century, ranging from singing birds and a violin- and piano-playing monstrosity to musical chairs and street organs. The *Centraal Museum* (1 Agnietenstraat) contains historical displays, including an authentic Viking ship. Take a short side trip to the village of Haarzuilens and the spectacular De Haar Castle, set in an artificial lake amid grounds modeled after Versailles (3 miles/5 km on E9 toward Amsterdam). The castle still is occupied, but parts of it frequently are open to the public.

En Route from Utrecht – A slight detour to Soest on the road leading through De Bilt and Bilthoven leads past Soestdijk Palace (actually a 17th-century hunting lodge), home of former Queen Juliana.

AMERSFOORT: This town has walls, four city gates, and double moats still ringing it, as well as a wealth of architectural treasures within its medieval center. In summer, canal cruises offer a leisurely view of the city, while day-long boat trips up the nearby Vecht River recapture the flavor of Holland's Golden Age. Boats for both trips leave from behind Utrecht's General Post Office, at the Vieburg.

APELDOORN: From here you can tour the wooded Veluwe region by steam train. Trains leave in the summer (daily, except Saturdays) from 13A Stationsplein. The museum at *Het Loo Palace* (1 Koninklijk Park) was formerly the royal residence and includes many displays about the royal family. Admission charge.

OTTERLO: The Hoge Veluwe National Park is here, and in the center of the lovely woodland setting is the *Rijksmuseum Kröller-Müller,* with its renowned collection of Van Gogh paintings and drawings and modern sculpture garden. When the weather is good, a walk through the woods is memorable. Or pick up one of the free bicycles at the main gate and tour the woods a while. It is a 1½-hour train ride from Amsterdam (via Arnhem or Edam), followed by a short bus or taxi ride — and well worth it. Closed Mondays. Admission charge. Otterlo (phone: 83-821241). *De Koperen Kop* is a restaurant in the park, where you can watch the deer being fed. Pick up a park map at the entrance.

ARNHEM: This attractive town had the misfortune to be the scene of Operation Market Garden in 1944, a serious defeat of the British airborne troops, which was portrayed in the film *A Bridge Too Far*. Important mementos of that heroic and desperate battle are the Airborne Cemetery at nearby Oosterbeek and the *Airborne Museum* in Grote Hartensteyn in the same town. The nearby 12th-century *Doorwerth Castle* houses a hunting museum. Immediately north of the city at 89 Schelmseweg is the 100-acre *Openlucht* (Open-Air) *Museum,* in which actual farms, mills, and homes have been reconstructed to give a complete picture of traditional Dutch country life. There's also a costume museum and a zoo and safari park, where you can drive or take a mini-train through 60 acres of free-roaming lions, giraffes, and other beasts of the wild. A pleasant place for a meal during summer is the farm restaurant *Boerderij Rijzenburg* at nearby Schaarsbergen, also an entrance to the Hoge Veluwe National Park. Admission charge at all museums, including a combined fee for the zoo and safari park.

ACHTERHOEK: Extending eastward from the Veluwe, this is a protected, rustic region of farms, woodlands, and great country estates. The VVV in Zutphen, 16 miles (26 km) from Arnhem on the A48, has maps for do-it-yourself bike tours through the castle-filled countryside.

BEST EN ROUTE

Expect to pay $110 and up for a double room in the expensive range, $60 to $80 in the moderate range, and about $50 in the inexpensive range. Dinner for two should cost $40 to $50 in the restaurants listed as expensive, $20 to $30 in those listed as moderate, and under $15 in the inexpensive. Prices do not include drinks or wine.

UTRECHT

Café Polman – An elegant open dining room and bar with an interesting bistro-style menu. 2 Kaesstraat (phone: 30-313368). Moderate.

Pays Bas – In the heart of the city near the Jans Kerk, the hotel's classic building dates from the 17th century but has modern facilities. The rooms all have bath or shower and TV sets. 10 Janskerkhof (phone: 30-333321). Moderate.

Smits – Located in the *Vredenburg* shopping and theater complex, this modern hotel provides friendly service and comfortable lodging. Rooms have private bath, color TV sets, and telephone. 14 Vredenburg (phone: 30-331232). Moderate.

APELDOORN

Astra – Simple but comfortable accommodations are offered at this cozy pension converted from two 19th-century homes in the garden district. 12-14 Bas Backerlaan (phone: 55-223022). Inexpensive.

Oranjeoord – A converted 1880 Victorian hunting lodge–manor house that was owned by old Queen Wilhelmina (grandmother of the present queen) until her death in 1962. The cozy bedrooms with terrace or balcony overlook the herb or rose gardens. 134 Hoog Soeren (phone: 57-691227). Inexpensive.

OTTERLO

Jagersrust – The place to stay if you want to make a leisurely visit to the renowned *Rijksmuseum Kröller-Müller* (see above) in the Hoge Veluwe National Park. The 100-year-old hostelry has been renovated and has 19 well-appointed rooms. There is a restaurant, and breakfast is included in the rate. Bikes are available for rental. 19-21 Dorpsstraat (phone: 8382-1241). Inexpensive.

ARNHEM

Groot Warnsborn – Surrounded by forest, this lovely 29-room former manor house is only a few minutes from the center of town. The restaurant features seasonal menus, continental style. 277 Bakenbergseweg (phone: 85-455751). Expensive.

HEELSUM

Klein Zwitserland – Just west of Arnhem, this 61-room chalet-style hotel has an indoor pool, a sauna, a solarium, tennis courts, bike rentals, and miniature golf on the premises; horseback riding is available nearby (phone: 8373-19104). Expensive.

De Kromme Dissel – An attractive restaurant is noted for its candlelit, Old World ambience. Within the Klein Zwitserland complex. 5 Klein Zwitserlandlaan (phone: 8373-19104). Expensive.

Norway

The kingdom of Norway stretches along the western edge of the Scandinavian peninsula, bordering Sweden, Finland, and the Soviet Union to the east. Norway has a 1,700-mile coastline on the North Atlantic, raggedly indented with inlets, fjords, peninsulas, and islands. Because the coast is so well sheltered, and most of the country's land area is so rocky and mountainous, Norwegians have taken to the sea since prehistoric times.

Today's Norway numbers only 4 million people — half of the population of New York City — rattling around over a spacious 149,158 square miles. The country is not particularly urban, and the major cities would be considered large, pleasant villages by most countries' standards. Oslo, the capital and biggest of the towns, has a population of less than half a million; Bergen (pop. 208,400) is an important cultural center, famous for its beautiful fjords; Trondheim (pop. 134,200) is a major center for trade, shipping, and industry; Stavanger (pop. 96,000) is another industrial outpost, handling fish processing, shipbuilding, and pumping Norway's North Sea oil. Other large towns include Kristiansand, Drammen, Skien, Tromsø, Alesund, and Bodø.

Norway is a constitutional monarchy, ruled by King Harald V, plus Prime Minister Gro Harlem Brundtland, the *storting* (parliament), and supreme court. The present independent government was installed in 1905, although the apparatus of state has been developing since the early 19th century, heavily inspired by the constitutions and ideals of the American and French revolutions.

Possibly the most important question on the minds of all those who have never been to Norway is: What is a fjord? A fjord is a long, narrow inlet of the sea, cutting through very steep, nearly parallel cliffs that extend below the surface of the water. A land area with a fjord looks like a macrocosmic cheesecake from which a long, narrow slice has been cut. Norway's Sogne Fjord runs over 100 miles inland from the North Sea, with walls that plunge 4,000 feet to the ocean floor. The sight from the top of the fjord of tons of ice-blue water roaring and foaming between the rocky walls is one of the most spectacular wonders in nature.

About one-quarter of Norway's land area is above the Arctic Circle, yet the climate of Oslo averages only about 12 degrees colder than that of New York. The North Atlantic drift keeps Norway's harbors free of ice.

Rivers like the Glomma and the Rana run through the mountains and valleys and provide much hydroelectric power. In fact, 99% of Norway's electricity is generated by hydropower. One-quarter of the country is forested, and the timber industry is big. Fish is exported all over the world; iron, nickel, and aluminum are mined. Community, social, and personal services is the biggest single employer, manufacturing second, employing about one-third and one-fifth of the working population respectively. About 6% of the work force is in agriculture, about 16% in trade. Norway's merchant fleet, once the pride of the nation, has been reduced considerably in the past few years. Shipping is still important in Norway but is being overshadowed by North Sea oil production. Norwegians are largely responsible for one of today's most glamorous, exciting, and profitable seagoing industries — cruising. Visionary entrepreneurs from Norway have been behind such developments as launching Caribbean cruising, ordering the world's biggest and most luxurious vessels, and marketing cruising to "the masses." Norway is now moving away from the heavy industry of the past into the field of sophisticated technology. The country's GNP per capita is the seventh-largest in the world.

Most Norwegians are of Scandinavian stock — like the Swedes — but in the county of Finnmark in the north live Samis (Lapps). There are two official languages, *bokmål* ("book language"), the language of literature and wealth, a vestige of Danish rule, and *nynorsk,* a language developed by a 19th-century nationalist, based on rural dialects. Both *bokmål* and *nynorsk* are used in the media, but *bokmål* still prevails. In the far north, the Sami dialect also is spoken.

Considering Norway's rough-hewn and beautiful countryside, it isn't too surprising that Norwegians are very outdoors-oriented. Like the Swedes, they have a reputation for having blond hair, robust health, and good looks. They do a lot of walking, as befits a country where distances are great, roads often are rough, and fuel is expensive. The population density is scant, and even cities are laid out with lots of elbow room. Oslo is touted by the city fathers as one of the biggest cities in Europe, since it covers 175 square miles, but it includes vast areas of farmland and forest.

Norwegians get used to snow in winter, and are less likely to burrow inside when the weather is cold than people from warmer climates. The word *ski* is Norwegian, and Norwegians like to joke that they are born with skis on their feet. Both cross-country and downhill skiing are avidly pursued by large numbers of people, and a Nordic specialty is ski jumping. Speed skating also has a long tradition and strong following. Soccer, as in the rest of Europe, is the biggest organized sport. Popular indoor activities include handball, boxing, gymnastics, and ballroom dancing. Oslo draws skiers from all over Europe and has seen more national ski championships than any other Norwegian city. Lillehammer (pop. 22,000), 110 miles (177 km) north of Oslo, has been selected as the site of the *1994 Winter Olympics.* Many facilities are being built in connection with the games, including a ski jump, ice rink, and an Olympic Village that will accommodate 3,000 athletes. The total budget approved by the Norwegian government is a staggering $1 billion.

The arts in Norway are encouraged by heavy state subsidies, particularly in film and book publishing. One of the most striking examples of government-sponsored art is the 650-piece sculpture park near Oslo by Gustav Vigeland, built at the city's expense. Norway has produced artists of international renown: painter Edvard Munch, composer Edvard Grieg, and dramatist Henrik Ibsen. It is interesting to note that a brooding, death-obsessed spiritualism pervades the work of the nation's three greatest cultural figures. Some say the stark seasonal contrasts in the land of the midnight sun have a profound effect on the national psyche. On a brighter note, actress Liv

Ullmann also is Norwegian, as is the marathon runner Grete Waitz and the pop rock group *A-ha*.

Norwegian folk art is highly practical, using fine handwork in the making of furniture, embroidery, weaving, and silver. The expression *arts and crafts* is based on the Scandinavian concept of *brukskunst;* Norway has several museums devoted to applied art.

The area of Norway was just an agglomeration of small Viking kingdoms until Harald Haarfagre ("fair hair") united them at the end of the 9th century, based on the model of a northern British kingdom he recently had pillaged. Missionaries from Britain brought Christianity to Norway in the 10th and 11th centuries.

Leif Eriksson, a Viking émigré living in Iceland, became the first European to reach America, touching down in Newfoundland in AD 1000. The Vikings established settlements in the northeastern US — some say they got as far south as Massachusetts.

Norway prospered as an independent country until the Black Death of 1349 wiped out half the population. The German Hanseatic League assumed Norway's trade in Bergen and the rest of the country slipped into 400 years of Danish rule. Sweden took over Norway when Denmark was defeated with its ally Napoleon in 1814. During the 19th century, 880,000 Norwegians emigrated elsewhere, mostly to the US. In 1905, the nation finally broke off from the Swedes and set up their own kingdom, appointing Carl, the second son of the King of Denmark, who took the Norwegian name Haakon VII. Haakon's son Olav took the throne at his father's death in 1957. King Olav V was a well-loved figure, who died at the age of 87 in January 1991. His son, Harald V, and Queen Sonja, now serve as the country's monarchs. Sonja is the first queen in 3 decades to sit on the Norwegian throne.

Norway stayed neutral in World War I, although half her merchant fleet was sunk. The Nazis invaded on April 9, 1940, and occupied Norway until May 1945, bringing with them concentration camps, political executions, and economic disaster. The king and most of the fleet escaped; Norwegian ships were vital to Allied operations in the North Atlantic, and Norwegians at home sabotaged the German occupiers courageously and ruthlessly. The leader of the collaborationist forces in Norway, Vidkun Quisling, whose name has come to be a synonym for *traitor*, was executed at the war's end.

Although Norway joined NATO in 1949, it remains fiercely independent on economic matters. In 1972, a majority of the population voted against joining the European Economic Community (EEC). Since World War II, Norway's wealth of trade, industry, and cheap hydroelectric power have given its citizens one of the highest standards of living in Europe, and with the discovery of large oil and gas deposits off the North Sea coast, the future seems promising.

Over 80% of Norway's land area is taken up by mountains and forests. Norway is somewhere you go to see natural beauty, rather than the marvels of civilization: mountains, valleys, fjords, moors, lakes, forests, waterfalls, and, in general, the absence of other people. The weather is often beautiful, just right for as brown a tan as you can get anywhere, but be ready for rain — make good use of clear days.

There are three routes below for exploring Norway. The first begins in Oslo, possibly the least hectic capital city in Europe, and winds down the Oslo Fjord through prime beach and sun country, cuts west through pine-scented forests to the barren Telemark plateau, and finishes in a burst of fjords and flowers in Bergen, on the Atlantic coast. The second route is a 1,000-mile adventure to the point farthest north on the continent of Europe, beginning by road in Trondheim, switching to a coastal steamship from Bodø to Tromsø to take you through the sheer cliffs of the western islands, and finishing again by car to the barren North Cape, far above the Arctic Circle. The last trip we recommend is to Lillehammer, the *1994 Winter Olympics* host. From Oslo, it's an easy day trip, but if you want to try out the slopes before the world's best skiers do, plan for an overnight or weekend trip. There's plenty to do, too, even if you don't ski, skate, or toboggan.

Oslo to Bergen

This scenic route begins with the calm and pastoral capital of Norway, Oslo, a city of a mere 450,500 inhabitants and many clapboard houses, farms, and forests, is also the seat of the Norwegian parliament. From here, you'll drive down the Oslo Fjord, west to the rococo church in Kongsberg, and across Telemark, where you'll find farms, beautiful stave churches, an old canal system still in operation, and barren heaths. The last stop is Norway's pride, fjord-bound Bergen, a graceful 11th-century city that has played host to Viking, merchant, and warships, art, and industry during its 1,000-year history.

Another way to travel this route is via the *Bergen-Oslo Railway*. Providing a dramatic 280-mile (451-km) day trip across Norway's rooftop, this classic line spans desolate Hardanger plateau, climbs above the timber line to a peak altitude of 4,267 feet, and stops at the old alpine and cross-country ski resorts of Geilo and Voss. You can make reservations in advance at one of the branches of the Norwegian National Tourist Office in the US. In addition to the ticket price, a seat reservation is purchased separately for a few dollars.

OSLO: For a complete report on the city and its restaurants and hotels, see *Oslo,* THE CITIES.

En Route from Oslo – Along the coast south of Norway's oldest city, Tønsberg, on the Brunlanes Peninsula, are good beaches and quiet coves for swimming and sailing, from Stavern to Nevlunghavn. Historic Tønsberg is worth a visit. Founded by King Bjørn Farmand, the seafaring merchant son of King Harald Haarfagre, the city was mentioned in sagas dating to 872. Norway's largest castle was built here during the Middle Ages and its ruins are among northern Europe's most impressive. The shoreline twists and turns on itself often, creating many protected beaches along the small towns in the area. The waters are quite warm in July and August. Take Route 8 through Larvik north toward Kongsberg; you'll be driving along the Laagen River through a valley of cornfields and bright red and white farmhouses.

KONGSBERG: Kongsberg, "the king's mountain," was founded by King Christian IV when silver was discovered here in 1624. The city flourished and became the second largest in Norway, but declined as the silver output fell in the 19th century. The last mine was abandoned in 1957. The 18th-century rococo church in Kongsberg is worth seeing; its exterior is unprepossessing brick, with a copper cupola, but inside all is rich and elaborate. The ceiling is covered with paintings and hung with crystal chandeliers; the pulpit, altar, choir balcony, and organ are carved with great enthusiasm, and painted in golds and blues. There are 3 tiers in the gallery, and box seats for the king and lesser dignitaries. Kongsberg is a major ski area, with four T-bars, five giant slalom courses (lighted until 9 PM weekdays for night skiing), and touring trails as well as a ski school. Call the *Ski Center* (3-731755) for information about weather conditions and equipment rentals. The abandoned silver mines also are worth a visit, and the town runs a special little railway into the mines for sightseers. A museum at the entrance to the mines displays silver in a variety of forms.

TELEMARK: West of Notodden begins the county of Telemark, a wild, often barren area of mountains, valleys, and plateaus that stretches all the way to the fjord district. The first inhabitants here were hunters; small, single-family farms followed, in the style of the American prairie. It is thought that skiing was invented here, and today, "Telemark Swing" is used to describe a particular style of skiing. The towns and villages exist mostly in the south and east; this is the prime area for a characteristic feature of rural Norwegian architecture, the *stabbur* or storehouse. In a countryside of individual farms, there was no town warehouse in which to store grain, so a story was added to each house to tuck away surplus for the lean years. Much care was lavished on the building and ornamentation of these houses, from elaborate wall hangings to beautifully carved joists and furniture, intricate "rose painting" on walls, doorways, clocks, and pottery.

As you proceed west, you'll pass through more valleys, farms, and villages, and by quite a few roadside cafés. Just west of Notodden is Heddal Stave Church, the country's largest stave church. It was built in 1242 and restored in 1954.

A very worthwhile diversion is a cruise on the Telemark Canal, between Notodden and Skien, which travels along 93 miles of waterways. Trips are available on either the small motorized cruiser *Telemarken* or the remodeled *Victoria,* which is more than a century old. Both boats travel through 18 locks, past tranquil countryside, ancient wooden farmhouses, and green and golden fields. The entire trip takes a day, but passengers can get on and off at any of a half-dozen points. To book a cruise, write to *Telemarksbåtene* A/5, 3812 Akkerhaugen, Norway (phone: 3-958211; fax: 3-958296).

At Eidsborg, south of E76, is another fine example of a stave church, which is believed to have been built in 1354 or earlier. Nestled on a hill, the outside walls of the church are covered with a sheath of hand-carved tiles that overlap each other like the leaves of an artichoke, giving the whole building the look of a single, living plant. Note the elaborate woodcarvings on the columns in the doorway and the interior.

The route now cuts through the heart of the Hardangervidda, a nearly uninhabited plateau of lakes and moors, where the elevation is about a mile. Several thousand years ago, a glacier came through here, ripping away everything in its path, leaving the wet, mossy, treeless landscape you see before you. An impressive waterfall, Vøringsfossen, drops 540 feet through a rocky chasm in this plateau. Lakes, boulders, heather, and an awesome bleakness extend left and right until you arrive at the fjords.

LOFTHUS: Turn north onto E47 toward the industrial town of Odda and the Sørfjorden. The road skirting the precipice is both narrow and scenic, burrowing through mountains, and passing over towering waterfalls. The hamlet of Lofthus, which is past Odda on the eastern edge of the fjord, was a favorite retreat of Edvard Grieg. The place has a mystical peacefulness; it is surrounded by snow-capped mountains and the Folgefonn glacier in the distance, and crowded with blossoms in the summertime.

En Route from Lofthus – Continue up to Kinsarvik. About 15 miles (24 km) north is a pretty little gem of a fjord, Eidfjord. A few miles east on Highway 7 is Vøringfoss, a spectacular waterfall. Back at Kinsarvik, take the ferry across the mouth of the Sørfjorden to Kvanndal, on the western edge of the great Hardanger Fjord. Drive south along the fjord toward Bergen, as waterfalls spawn rainbows, and mountains rest against each other like the backs of huge sleeping animals. This is one of the most spectacular regions of what is considered by some the most scenic country in the world. Once you arrive in Bergen and find a place to roost, you must, without fail, drive, ferry, and walk through as much of this titanically beautiful region as possible. The best time to go is May and early June, when the fruit trees are in bloom.

BERGEN: Looking like a crowded gingerbread village, Bergen sits in a harbor under Mt. Fløyen, protected and hidden from the North Sea by a peninsula. It is one of Norway's most worldly, cultural, and physically beautiful cities. The people speak with a distinctive accent that even non-Scandinavians can detect, and their proud and independent spirit can be summed up in the local saying, "I'm not Norwegian; I'm from Bergen."

Vikings used to set out from the coves around Bergen to the lands now known as England, Europe, and Iceland. The city was founded in 1070 by King Olav the Peaceful, who thought it would make a good center for trade with Europe and northern Norway. During the 12th and 13th centuries, it was the country's capital. In 1349 the Black Death came to Norway, destroying over half the native population. Norway's crippled economy enabled the German merchants who had been trading with the city for centuries to gain control of the city's commerce. The Germans held on for 200 years, making the port a major trading center of the Hanseatic League and the richest city in Norway. Finally, in 1559, the Danish authorities trained their guns on the Hanseatic buildings and offered the Germans citizenship or oblivion; some left, others became Norwegians. The *Hanseatic Museum* (1A Sinnegdardsgaten; phone: 5-314189) is a reconstructed 16th-century Hansa merchant's house, smelling of cool wood in some rooms and dried cod in others. Norwegian cod was an important item of trade for Catholic Europe, as it often provided Friday's dinner. At the museum you can see the scales the merchants used for weighing goods — one scale for buying, and another for selling. Be sure to visit the lesser known, but equally fascinating, Schøtstuene, where the merchants gathered to socialize, and the waterfront section of town, called Bryggen (meaning "the wharf"), where they came to conduct business. Now, painters, weavers, and artisans have set up workshops in the restored medieval wooden houses. Guided tours (in English) are offered in the summer. Tickets are sold at the *Bryggens Museum* (beside the *SAS Royal* hotel; phone: 5-316710), which includes the remains of medieval Bergen — cooking implements, games, musical instruments, and other objects used in daily life.

Overall, Bergen has an 18th-century grace, with a skyline of close-packed mansard roofs punctuated by church steeples. The best view of the city is from the funicular that goes up Mt. Fløyen (1,050 feet), which operates until midnight. Get on at Ovregatan and Vetrildsalm. At the summit, paths lead through lakes, flowers, pine, and heather.

In late May and early June is the *Bergen International Festival,* featuring music, drama, opera, ballet, art, and folklore. A lot of the music, understandably, is by local hero Edvard Grieg, and concerts are held every day at *Grieg Hall* in town and in the suburb of Hop at his old residence, Troldhaugen, a pastoral Victorian estate on a lake. World-renowned conductors and soloists are featured. Concerts also are held at Haakonshallen and St. Mary's Church. Plays are performed at *Den Nationale Scene* — Ibsen predominates — and folk plays and dances take place outdoors. Reservations must be made far in advance for a visit during festival time.

Haakonshallen and St. Mary's Church are both worth seeing in their own rights; the 13th-century hall, plainly visible from the harbor and Bryggen area, was badly damaged in World War II when a Dutch ship carrying nitroglycerin blew up in the harbor, but the restoration of the massive medieval construction was well done. Bergen's oldest building is St. Mary's Church (Romanesque Mariakirke), built in the early 12th century. It is considered Norway's most beautiful church, with an intricately carved and painted baroque pulpit, donated by the Hansa in the 16th century. Note the tortoise-shell inlay on the unusual lectern, which is adorned with carvings and astrological symbols (the church is next door to the *Bryggens Museum* and the *SAS Royal* hotel). The Fantoft Stave Church, built in 1150, also is aesthetically pleasing. Its sharply peaked roofs and Viking dragons trim are reminiscent of Thai temples. To visit the church, take any bus leaving from platforms 18, 19, or 20 at the station; get off at the Fantoft stop and make the 10-minute walk up the hill.

With the wealth brought in by trade, art was sure to follow, and industrialist Rasmus Meyer's private collection of paintings, drawings, and furniture (at the the waterfront mansion on Rasmus Meyers Allé; phone: 5-311130) is probably the best in Norway outside the *Oslo National Gallery*. Meyer lived from 1858 to 1916, and his particular zest was for native Norwegian painters: lots of Munch, of course, plus Nikolai Astrup, Harriet Backer, Gerbard Munthe, and J. C. Dahl. Admission charge in the summer. Next door is the *Bergen Art Gallery* (5 Rasmus Meyers Allé; phone: 5-321460), with its more contemporary, though, somewhat limited, collection. Admission charge.

Only a 10-minute walk from the downtown area, the *Bergen Aquarium* (2 Nordnes-parken; phone: 5-320452) is open year-round. During your wanderings, be sure to try some of the local fish dishes and the local beer, Hansa, considered among the world's best. Bergen has one of Norway's most picturesque open-air fish markets in the harbor in the center of the city, said to be the most photographed in Europe; open daily except Sundays from 8AM to 3 PM.

If you have an interest in Victorian houses, climb up the hill from *Grieg Hall* to Parkeveien, the lane skirting the university district, where the last century's elite built their "castles." The exteriors are well-preserved, though few of the homes are single-family residences today.

Music lovers may wish to make the short 16-mile (26-km) trip south to Lysøen to visit the home of Bergen's other musical native son, Ole Bull. The world-famous violinist (1810–1880) built his summer villa, Little Alhambra, with a distinctive Arabian flavor. Open afternoons daily from mid-May to mid-September. Admission charge. From Bergen, take 553 in the direction of Fana (south). Stay on 553 to Fana, passing Fanafjell to Sorestraumen. Follow the signs to Buena Kai; at Buena Kai, catch the *Ole Bull* ferry, which leaves hourly when Lysøen is open. Or take bus No. 20, "Lysefjordruta," from the bus station located in central Bergen at 8 Stromgaten.

Another site worth visiting outside the city is Gamle Bergen (Old Bergen; phone: 5-256307), a preserved town of wooden buildings and cobblestone streets that features the original architecture and furnishings of the homes of a baker, a merchant, and others. Open May through August. To reach Gamle Bergen, drive north from Bergen on Road 14 and follow the signs. Or take bus Nos. 1 or 8 from downtown Bergen.

BEST EN ROUTE

Hotels along this route are rather pricey, around $155 and up for a double room at an expensive tourist hotel, which provides meals, entertainment, and bars; more moderately priced accommodations are available for $100 to $150; under $100 is inexpensive. Breakfast and tax are included. Look for reduced rates on weekends and during the summer. Rooms in guesthouses, which are smaller and may not have a private bath or shower, start at about $30 and are scattered throughout villages and towns. All you have to do is ask at a local tourist information center, or flag down a passing Norwegian. If you prefer, you can camp out on one of the many campgrounds in the countryside for about $10 a night; chalets can be rented for $125 to $425 a week, depending on the season (based normally on a minimum occupancy of four), and there are a number of youth hostels, open mostly during the summer, for $10 a night. Again, tourist information centers in the villages can direct you. The *Royal Norwegian Automobile Club* huts are offered to all *AAA* members: For further information, contact *KNA Auto Club* in Oslo (20 Drammensv.; phone: 2-561900). Expect to pay more than $60 per person at restaurants we list as expensive; $30 to $60 for moderate; and less than $30 for inexpensive. Restaurants listed below accept major credit cards *only* when indicated.

KONGSBERG

Grand – The best in the city provides small comfortable rooms and good meals in a fine restaurant or an easy-going cafeteria. Facilities include an indoor swimming pool. Christian August, Gate 2 (phone: 3-732029). Moderate.

Skikroa – A large eatery popular with the young ski crowd, this lodge offers sandwiches and snacks in an informal setting. Reservations unnecessary. By the Kongsberg ski lifts (phone: 3-731628). Inexpensive.

BERGEN

Admiral – Right next to the scenic harbor, this hotel has 107 elegant, ultramodern rooms and 12 suites, many with harbor views. There's also a piano bar and a reasonably priced restaurant serving both meat and seafood dishes; flaming "Lobster Emily" is the specialty. 9 Sundtsgt. (phone: 5-324730; fax: 5-229280). Expensive.

Neptun – All the rooms at this 120-room hotel are being remodeled, floor by floor, so ask for a new one when booking. There is a French restaurant, a pub, bar, and café. 8 Walckendorffs Gate (phone: 5-901000; fax: 5-233202; telex: 40040). Expensive.

Norge – In an excellent location, this classic 348-room luxury hotel offers a full range of room categories, from singles and doubles to demi-suites and full suites. It has several restaurants, a summer garden café, disco, bars, and a large indoor swimming pool. 4 Ole Bulls Plass (phone: 5-210100; fax: 5-210299; telex: 42129). Expensive.

Rosenkrantz – A lively piano bar just off the lobby perks up this 129-room hotel, which is a popular nightspot. Convenient to Bryggen, the waterfront area. 7 Rosenkrantzgt. (phone: 5-315000; fax: 5-311476; telex: 42427). Expensive.

SAS Royal – The wood and brick design of this 300-room, first class hotel fits well into its location in the Bryggen section of the harborfront. It has an executive floor that offers special services and deluxe suites; and a restaurant, café, nightclub, and bar. 5003 Bergen (phone: 5-318000; fax: 5-324808; telex: 40640). Expensive.

Suitell Edvard Grieg – At the airport, this luxury hotel is the country's first all-suite property and has 148 suites and 2 restaurants, one more formal than the other, but both featuring Norwegian specialties. There also are 2 large, elegant bars with dancing on Saturday nights to live bands. 50 Sandsliasen (phone: 5-229901; fax: 5-229985). Expensive.

Bellevue – An old Bergen dining establishment with an elegant interior and a spectacular view over the fjord. Open for lunch, dinner, and after-theater meals. Downstairs, there's an informal terrace grillroom, with dancing from 10 PM on. Dinner reservations advised. Major credit cards accepted. 9 Bakken (phone: 5-310240). Expensive to moderate.

Banco Rotto – This spacious restaurant in a former bank is built in the Italian Renaissance style. High ceilings, marble walls, and parquet floors would make this spot a treat even if the food weren't remarkable — but it is. A self-serve pâtisserie is available from 11 AM. The extensive à la carte menu of Norwegian and international dishes is offered from 3 PM. Dinner reservations advised. A pub and piano bar complete the venue. Major credit cards accepted. In the city center, near the Bank of Bergen. 16 Vaagsalmenningen (phone: 5-327520). Moderate.

Bergen Airport – Convenient to the airport and about 8 miles (13 km) from the city center, its 239 rooms include several suites, and many rooms have kitchenettes. There is an indoor swimming pool, squash courts, and a fitness center. A restaurant serves Norwegian specialties and is open for breakfast, lunch, dinner, and late-night snacks. 3 Kokstadveien (phone: 5-229200; fax: 5-229280). Moderate.

China Palace – An elegant Chinese restaurant with a plush red and gold decor. Try the jumbo prawns. Open for lunch and dinner. Reservations unnecessary. Major credit cards accepted. Upstairs at 2 Strandgt. (phone: 5-326655). Moderate.

Dreggen – A new addition among the budget hotels, this spotless, 31-room property is located on 2 upper floors of a commercial building, overlooking Haakonshallen and the harbor. All rooms have TV sets and hair dryers. If you're on a tight budget, ask for a room without a private bath. No restaurant, but there is a breakfast room with a view. 3 Sandbrugatan (phone: 5-316155; fax: 5-315423). Moderate.

Enhjørningen – The name means "Unicorn," and this cozy old seafood eatery is indeed a rare find. A cold seafood buffet is offered at lunch. Open daily. Reservations advised. Major credit cards accepted. At Bryggen (phone: 5-327919). Moderate.

Munkestuen Café – Cozy and family-run with only 5 tables, it boasts a short but superb menu that changes daily. Deliciously prepared steaks, game, and fish are fresh from the market, and the wine cellar is stocked with 200 fine vintages. Open from 4 PM. Closed Saturdays and all of July. Reservations necessary well in advance. Major credit cards accepted. 12 Klostergaten (phone: 5-902149). Moderate.

Villa Amorini – Next to the *Bergen Art Gallery,* this casual, youth-oriented wine bar features snacks and live music from 11 PM. Open daily from 9 PM to 3 AM. No reservations. 5 Rasmus Meyers Allé (phone: 5-310039). Moderate.

Park Pension – A charming converted townhouse near the university, it offers rooms with baths at budget prices by Norway's standards. Reserve well in advance. 35 Harald Haarfagres Gate (phone: 5-320960; fax: 5-310334). Inexpensive.

Trondheim to the North Cape

This is a trail for the adventurous. We don't mean that it's physically dangerous, but that it requires an active spirit and a zest for exploration. It's an expedition to the Nordkapp, the northernmost point in Europe. If you drive, you must go in June, July, or August, so the roads will be clear of snow and you can see the midnight sun. If you choose to cruise all the way on a coastal steamer, you can travel year-round, as the coast remains ice-free thanks to the North Atlantic Drift, an extension of the Gulf Stream. But remember that the daylight hours during winter at these latitudes are very short. However, if conditions are right, you may see the spectacular Northern Lights in the night sky. The north of Norway is big, wild, and exotic, but no one can tell you what the beautiful sights are. Here, you write your own guidebook and judge each towering cliff, deep-blue lake, and clump of flowering heather with your own eyes. This is a trip for the young and the young at heart; it's popular with hearty French, German, and Italian adventurers.

Start your trip in a rented car from Trondheim, the capital of the province of Trøndelag, at the threshold of the Arctic. Founded in the 10th century, Trondheim is now a commercial city, with a growing number of high-tech industries, and the seat of one of Norway's biggest universities. It also has an important cathedral, Nidaros. You'll take the Arctic Highway (E6) north from here through lakes and river valleys past Mosjøen and Mo-i-Rana to cross the Arctic Circle into the land of the midnight sun at the top of a barren plateau.

At Bodø, you'll hop on the coastal steamer, which will take you between the sheer cliffs of the Lofoten and Vesterålen islands to Tromsø, the oil boom town, and launching base for many North Pole expeditions. Pick up a car here for the rest of your own expedition: A ferry will carry you across the last strait to Honningsvåg, so you can drive to the North Cape, and look down on all of Europe.

Another way to explore this part of the Norwegian coast is to take the express steamer from Bergen to Kirkenes — 1,500 miles, 6 days one-way or 11 days round-trip. The steamer calls at about 30 fishing villages and towns, including Trondheim, Bodø, Lofoten and Vesterålen, Hammerfest and Honningsvåg. The northeastern terminus, Kirkenes, is on the Russian border. The steamers are small and clean, with ample deck space, hearty buffet-style meals, and a bar. Dress is informal; the sea air, invigorating; and the scenery, breathtaking. Tickets may be purchased for any segment of this trip, but reservations for the entire voyage in the peak summer season must be made months in advance. Contact the Norwegian National Tourist Office (phone: 212-942-2333) or *Bergen Line* (505 Fifth Ave., New York, NY 10017; phone: 800-323-7436 or 212-986-2711; to request brochures, 800-666-2374; fax: 212-983-1275).

Thanks to an agreement between Norway and the Soviet Union, the *Finnmark Shipping and Transport Company* (*FFR*) is offering 1-day tours by high-speed catamaran from Kirkenes to Murmansk, June 15 to August 31. Contact *FFR* at PO Box 308, Hammerfest N-9601, Norway (phone: 84-11655; fax: 84-14655; telex: 64257).

TRONDHEIM: Trondheim is the home of Norway's major technical university and is a big trading town, exporting timber, fish, and farm products. A major shipbuilding and transportation center, it is a pleasant and useful city, but not stunning. Its buildings draw on a tradition of the ordinary from the 19th and 20th centuries: solid stone office buildings and glass and steel cheeseboxes. There also are some old narrow streets of small, pastel wooden houses.

Trondheim's Nidaros Cathedral, built for St. Olav, has attracted pilgrims from all over Europe. It was badly battered during the Reformation and nearly destroyed by fire several times, so a lot of the Gothic-Romanesque hybrid that stands now is 20th-century restoration work. Norway's Gustav Vigeland, creator of the mammoth sculpture garden in Oslo's Frogner Park, carved the gargoyles and grotesques for the head tower and north transept. The stunning stained glass is the work of artist Gabriel Kielland, who won a competition to design one window and then devoted his life to creating all of them. Note the breathtaking "rose window" with its brilliant cerises and cobalt blues. The façade of the cathedral includes a mix of heroic figures, among them Viking kings, Adam and Eve, and various saints. Behind the cathedral is the restored Knight's Hall of the 12th-century Archbishop's Palace. From here, late Viking kings ruled Norway's Christianized colonies in Britain, Iceland, and Greenland.

Be sure to see the *Ringve Museum of Musical History* (phone: 7-922411) in a manor house at 60 Lade Allé, in the eastern suburbs. During the tours, the guide plays the well-preserved instruments from time to time: spinets, harpsichords, and pianos, and some vintage string and wind instruments as well. (Tours are available in English from late May through September; in winter at 1:30 PM on Sundays.) On the walls all around are paintings and photographs of famous composers and musicians. Admission charge.

As you wander along Trondheim's streets, you are likely to pass one of the largest wooden buildings in Scandinavia — Stiftsgaarden, built in rococo style from 1774 to 1778. Located on Dronningens Gate, between Munke Gate and Nordre Gate, it is used as the royal residence when the king and queen are in town.

Two of the best features of modern Trondheim are the fish market on the docks and the fruit stands in the Torvet (marketplace). If you visit the city during the summer, take the ferry from downtown Trondheim out to Munkholmen, the small island in the harbor containing the remnants of a Benedictine monastery. In the summer months it serves as Trondheim's most popular swimming and outing choice, so pack your swimsuit, camera, and a picnic lunch, or dine at the local restaurant.

En Route from Trondheim – Just northeast of the city in the Stjørdal Valley, near the village of that name, is the ruin of the fortress of Hegra Festning, built in 1910 as a bulwark against the Swedes (the border is 49 miles/78 km to the east). The fort became a symbol of the Norwegian Resistance in World War II when a German force was badly mauled trying to take it in 1940. Peace has reigned over the fort since then; bushes and flowers now are crowding the barbed wire, gun ports, and blasted walls; the view of the surrounding hills and the valley 1,000 feet below is splendid. Wild strawberries, raspberries, and blueberries grow in the vicinity.

In the village of Hegra, on the other side of the valley, are the Leirfall rock carvings, one of the most prolific sites in Norway, chiseled in 500 BC. They are said to be the religious art of an agricultural civilization, designed to increase fertility; they are symbolic and simple of line, showing stylized ships, and people and animals, some with erect phalluses — as well as circles, dots, swastikas, and footprints. Move on up the highway through the low, wooded Lake Snåsa region; you'll pass near Børgefjell National Park on the right.

About 60 miles (96 km) north of Mo-i-Rana you cross the Arctic Circle in the valley of the great, green Rana River; snow-covered bluffs 4,000 feet high lie to the left and right as you climb to the top of an empty plateau, and into the land of the midnight sun (66°32'N). The line of the Arctic is marked by a stone monument; there is a post office offering Arctic Circle postmarks nearby, and a café with the inevitable souvenir shop.

The countryside following the circle, near Rognan, is some of the most spectacular you will see along this route: The road passes high above the Saltfjord, which is sometimes covered with a light mist, past snow-covered mountains hulking behind.

BODØ: Bodø is the capital of Nordland province; the sun doesn't go down here from June 3 to July 7. It's warm, considering the latitude, sitting at the mouth of the Vestfjorden, sheltered by the Lofoten Islands. Add to this the opportunities that lurk everywhere for fishing, climbing, bird watching, or just walking around gaping at the scenery, and you can understand why tourists by the droves come here to soak up the midnight sun. Do not miss the famous cathedral, built in 1956: The tall bell tower is separate from the rest of the structure; the main roof is copper, the outer walls concrete, and the inside wonderfully large and airy, with a high ceiling, reddish-brown woodwork, handmade wall hangings, and delicate stained glass windows at each end of the building. The *Nordlands Museum* (116 Prinsensgt.; no phone) has exhibitions of tools, fishing industry items, and a terrarium.

Burned and bombed to the ground at the beginning of World War II, Bodø has long since recovered its position as a leading fishing and Arctic communications center.

Visitors can try their hand at fishing at Saltstraumen, the world's most powerful maelstrom, 20 miles (32 km) outside town. Millions of gallons of water rush through the narrow passage, guaranteeing catches of cod, halibut, and salmon. No license is required; rent tackle at any Bodø shop. Buses to Saltstraumen depart several times a day from the terminal at 2A Sungt. (phone: 81-21240).

For more information on Bodø, contact the tourist office (phone: 81-24406).

Just south of Bodø is Svartisen, Norway's second-largest glacier. On Saturday afternoons in the summer, there are boat tours to this tremendous hulk of ice. Tickets are purchased on board. For more information, contact *Saltens Dampskibsselskab* (phone: 81-21020).

LOFOTEN AND VESTERÅLEN: Now begins the marine portion of your expedition to the Nordkapp; turn in your rented car and claim your bunk on the coastal steamer at Bodø to make the 23-hour passage to Tromsø, threading through the steep cliffs and fishing villages of the Lofoten and Vesterålen islands. The steamer is a functional ship, a cargo and mail vessel that can also take about 200 passengers. It's not the *QE2*, but it's clean, it's only for 23 hours, and you'll get more of the incredible scenery than you could playing chemin de fer on some cushy cruise ship. The islands present a wall of snow-capped mountains and cliffs that rise suddenly from the shore to heights of 2,000 to 3,000 feet. It's particularly dramatic as the steamer slips into a narrow strait between two peaks and seems about to be swallowed in their immense shadows. The ship departs at 3 PM and arrives at Tromsø 23 hours later.

HARSTAD: En route you'll pass through Harstad, a modern town in the heart of Norway's largest island, Hinnøya. Harstad holds the *North Norway Festival,* with historical plays, folkloric programs, and musical performances, each summer for a week around *Midsummer's Day,* June 23. Internationally known artists are always among the performers.

TROMSØ: Disembark at Tromsø and pick up your car. An ancient whaling capital, Tromsø was also base of operations for North Pole explorers and polar bear hunters. Much of its frontier atmosphere has been retained, and it's now something of a boom town. It rather arrogantly refers to itself as "The Paris of the North," a claim made only half in jest. Tromsø has doubled in population to about 49,800 in the past decade, with the advent of a medical school and regional hospital specializing in Arctic ailments. All the establishments in town — restaurants, brewery, pubs, and pizzerias — claim to be the world's northernmost. Worth a look are the *Polarmuseet* (Polar Museum; 11B Søndre Tollbugt.; phone: 83-84373), devoted to Arctic exploration; the aquarium; and the Arctic Cathedral, whose design is reminiscent of an iceberg. The cable car affords a bird's-eye view of Tromsø and its fjord, where in World War II the German battleship *Tirpitz* was finally sunk by British bombers.

En Route from Tromsø – The last leg in this trek is the shortest, about 280 miles (448 km) over dry plateau, as the Arctic Highway winds around fjords and inlets, and passes a few villages. Lyngen Fjord between Tromsø and Alta is thoroughly alpine, with jagged peaks and hairpin turns. Alta, once little more than an airport and a trading town, is becoming more important as tourism to the North Cape increases. Before turning north, consider a day trip south through Europe's deepest canyon and up across the plateau to Kautokeino, the major center for the nomadic Lapp reindeer herders. The Sami, as they prefer to be called, congregate here to trade and worship, and they have built a church and a hotel in the style of a Sami hut. The town silversmith, whose shop you can visit, makes jewelry in ancient Sami designs. Karasjok, another Sami community, lies just to the north. A new exhibition center, near the *SAS Karasjok* hotel (see *Best en Route*), features traditional Sami turf huts and reindeer, as well as artists working with silver, stone, textiles, and crafts for the home. If you cross the nearby Tana River, you'll be in Finland.

Back in Alta, continue north to Hammerfest. The world's northernmost incorporated town, it was the first Norwegian town to get electric street lights. Stop at the Town Hall to join the Royal and Ancient Society of Polar Bears, testifying to your northerly adventure. From here you can take an excursion boat directly to the North Cape, or you can drive and ride the ferry up to Honningsvåg, the largest fishing port in Norway.

The first man to reach the North Cape is said to have been a Viking named Ottar, who sailed around it in AD 880, bound for the White Sea. England's King Alfred the Great met Ottar and had his story of the voyage "beyond the known world" set down in writing. The account sits in the *British Museum* today.

Another 21 miles (34 km) will bring you from Honningsvåg to the black cliff that Ottar signed more than 1,100 years ago. Keep your eyes peeled; you are likely to see herds of reindeer grazing beside the road, but their coloring sometimes enables them to blend into the tundra. The *British Museum* probably won't keep your tour diary, but you certainly will; and the Nordkapp post office will also issue you a special certificate testifying that you've been there and mail your postcards to boot. It may be stretching the truth a little to call Nordkapp the most northerly point in Europe, but not much.

The sun shines continuously here from May 14 to July 30; the farther south you travel, the shorter this period will be, and, conversely, the farther north you travel, the longer the period will last. The most beautiful sight, however, is in early August, when the sun dips below the horizon for a few minutes of night, in a spectacular glow of red and purple.

Facilities at the North Cape have been upgraded and expanded. In addition to a café, an enlarged souvenir shop, and a video presentation on a giant screen, there now is a tunnel leading down into the cliff itself. The tunnel opens into a grotto with panoramic windows overlooking the sea, historical displays, and exhibits. One ticket provides admission to all the attractions.

BEST EN ROUTE

Most hotels in the Arctic Circle region cost over $150 for a double room that we list as expensive; moderate, $100 to $145; inexpensive, $100 and under. Rates, however, drop substantially on weekends and during the summer. Nearly all establishments offer private baths and/or showers, plus other amenities found in luxury hotels; breakfast usually is included. Make reservations beforehand: 200,000 visitors a year come to Nordkapp. Expect to pay more than $40 per person in restaurants we list as expensive and $20 to $40 in moderate places. Drinks are not included. Restaurants listed below accept major credit cards *only* when indicated.

■ **NOTE:** Surprisingly, northerly nightlife is often very exuberant. Hotel nightclubs compete with nearby beer halls, and both should be sampled for a complete picture of life in the North. Unlike their Oslo relatives, citizens up here are quite outgoing, and travelers may find themselves swapping stories with fishermen and petrochemical geologists before the night is through.

TRONDHEIM

Britannia – A classic hotel dating from 1897, it has large and comfortably furnished remodeled rooms. The dark wood bar is inviting and the spacious *Palm Garden* restaurant, serving Norwegian and continental specialties, is simply splendid. 5 Dronningensgt. (phone: 753-0040; fax: 751-2900; telex: 55451). Expensive.

Gran Hotel Olav – The most luxurious and priciest in town, it has spacious rooms decorated in 27 unique styles. There are 9 suites, including the fabulous Milano penthouse, and all baths have marble fittings. Located in a concert hall/dining/ and shopping complex. 48 Kjøpmannsgt. (phone: 753-5310; fax: 753-5720; telex: 65035). Expensive.

Residence – An old, established hotel, right in the city center. It offers 66 rooms, a restaurant serving Norwegian specialties, plus a café and bar. 26 Munkegt. (phone: 752-8380; telex: 55372). Expensive.

Royal Garden – This large, ultramodern hotel has a striking multilevel atrium. Several of the new suites are multilevel and richly decorated. Facilities include an elegant restaurant, an indoor swimming pool, and a gymnasium. 73 Kjøpmannsgt. (phone: 752-1100; fax: 753-1766; telex: 55060). Expensive.

Bryggen – Some consider this the best restaurant in town. Fish is the house specialty, but the other Norwegian and international dishes also are tasty. Special fixed menus are available, starting at 6 PM; in addition, there are à la carte items. Open daily, except Sundays, from 4 PM. Reservations advised. Major credit cards accepted. On the water near the Old Town Bridge (phone: 752-0230). Expensive to moderate.

Havfruen – An elegant seafood restaurant occupying 2 levels in an old warehouse. There's a large main dining room downstairs, and a more intimate dining room upstairs. Open daily, except Sundays, from 4 PM. Reservations unnecessary. Major credit cards accepted. 7 Kjøpmannsgt. (phone: 753-2626). Expensive to moderate.

Vertshuset Tavern – Built in 1739, this wooden tavern offers mountain-style cooking (smoked ham, diced meat, salami, mutton with garnishes) and also more conventional food. Open April to October. Near the *Folk Museum* at Sverresborg (phone: 752-0932). Moderate.

Augustin – A little gem of a hotel for budget-conscious travelers, it has 75 rooms, all decorated in cheerful colors. Amenities include trouser presses and hair dryers. Guests have access to the *Residence,* the sister hotel down the block. 26 Kongensgt. (phone: 752-8348; fax: 751-5501; telex: 55578). Inexpensive.

BODØ

SAS Royal – This 13-story, 184-room hotel is the largest in the city and offers a fine restaurant plus a pizza place in the cellar, coffee shop, cafeteria, bars, and a disco. The top-floor nightclub affords a great view. 2 Storgaten (phone: 81-24100; 800-44UTELL in the US). Expensive.

Norrøna – A bed and breakfast establishment that has a cozy café facing the main street, a restaurant, and the *Piccadilly Pub,* which also serves light fare. 4B Storgt. (phone: 81-25550). Expensive to moderate.

Bodø – The city's newest hotel has a comfortable atmosphere and such special features as rooms which are suited especially for people suffering severely from allergies, rooms accessible to handicapped guests, and a bridal suite. The *Skagen Bistro* specializes in fish dishes. 5 Prof. Schyttesgt. (phone: 81-26900; fax: 81-25778; telex: 64560). Moderate.

Grand – A 48-room hotel that offers baths and showers, double and single rooms, and a dining room. 3 Storgaten (phone: 81-20000; fax: 81-22709). Moderate.

Normandie – An interesting restaurant with a Viking decor, it specializes in pizza and quiche. 1 Havnegt. (phone: 81-21832). Moderate.

HARSTAD

Grand Nordic – Next to the *Viking Nordic,* it has comfortable rooms and a restaurant. 2 Strand Gate (phone: 82-62170; telex: 645152). Moderate.

Viking Nordic – The biggest hotel in town, with a restaurant, lounge, and indoor swimming pool. 2 Fjord Gate (phone: 82-64080; fax: 82-64210; telex: 64322). Moderate.

LOFOTEN AND VESTERÅLEN

For the 23-hour steamer trip from Bodø to Tromsø, you must reserve a berth 2 to 3 months in advance in the summer season. A couple can reserve a private cabin, but singles room with strangers, usually of the same sex. Contact *Bergen Line* (505 Fifth Ave., New York, NY 10017; phone: 800-323-7436 or 212-986-2711). Various packages available.

TROMSØ

Arctandria – A rustic and cozy restaurant featuring both seafood and meat dishes; the special is a platter consisting of three kinds of fish and two or three kinds of shellfish. Dinner from 6 PM; Sundays from 3 PM. 1 Strandtorget (phone: 83-82020). Expensive.

Grand Nordic – In a class with the *SAS Royal* (below), it has modern rooms and all the basic amenities. There is a health club, restaurants, and a bar. 44 Storgaten (phone: 83-85500; fax: 83-85500; telex: 64204). Expensive.

SAS Royal – One block from the steamer pier, this large (195 rooms) and convenient hotel has a fine harbor view and several restaurants, including the elegant *Caravel*, which features Norwegian and international dishes. There also is a popular nightclub, *Charly* and a friendly pizza bar. 7 Sjøgata (phone: 83-56000; fax: 83-85474; telex: 64260). Expensive.

Scandic – Near the airport, this property has 147 rooms (2 of them suites) and a fine view of the fjord. Its restaurant serves international dishes, and there's a nightclub, bar, pool, and sauna. 23 Heilou, Langnes (phone: 83-73400; fax: 83-81905; telex: 64036). Expensive.

Saga – Simple but good, and near the harbor, it has 52 rooms, all with showers. There also is a cafeteria and a typical Norwegian restaurant. 2 Richard Withsplass (phone: 83-81180; fax: 83-81180; telex: 64220). Expensive to moderate.

Branko's – This charming, intimate restaurant, owned and operated by Yugoslavian restaurateur Branko and his Norwegian wife, has become a Tromsø favorite; many consider it the best in town. One flight up on the main street, it's open for lunch and dinner. 57 Storgaten (phone: 83-82673). Moderate.

Peppermøllen – Here you can sup on fresh, well-prepared fish, reindeer, and grouse. 42 Storgaten (phone: 83-86260). Moderate.

ALTA

SAS Alta – The biggest and the best in town, complete with a café, bar, entertainment, disco, sauna, solarium, and a jogging track. Centrally located at Løkkeveien (phone: 84-35000 or 800-44UTELL in the US; fax: 84-35825). Expensive.

HONNINGSVÅG

Rica Hotel Nordkapp – A new 240-room hotel located just outside of town in the direction of the North Cape, it offers modern rooms, a restaurant, several lounges, and a shop in the lobby. Skipsfjorden (phone: 84-73388; fax: 84-73233). Expensive.

SAS Nordkapp – This 174-room establishment offers private baths and/or showers and 2 restaurants: the *Carolina,* featuring Norwegian specialties, and a grillroom for less formal dining. There also is a pub/disco. Centrally located on the busy harborfront (phone: 84-72333; fax: 84-73379). Expensive to moderate.

KAUTOKEINO

Kautokeino Tourist – A small (46-room) lodge-style establishment with a large fireplace, restaurant, bar, disco, sauna, and solarium. Ask at the reception desk about seeing reindeer herders at work or taking snowmobile safaris. On the bluff just outside town (phone: 84-56205; fax: 84-56701). Expensive.

KARASJOK

SAS Karasjok – This 38-room basic, clean hotel has a ski lodge atmosphere with wooden beams and a fireplace. There's a restaurant, sauna, and bar (phone: 84-66203; 800-44UTELL in the US; fax: 84-66802; telex: 64346). Expensive.

Lillehammer and Environs

Lillehammer, 111 miles (178 km) miles north of Oslo, makes for a pleasant day trip from the capital. Skiers and hikers may want to take advantage of 2- or 3-night lodge packages. Drive along the E6, skirting the western shore of fjord-like Mjøsa, Norway's largest inland lake, past rolling farmland that becomes increasingly hilly. A few miles beyond the town of Gjøvik you'll cross the bridge to Lillehammer, the gateway to Ibsen's Peer Gynt country, nestled on the eastern shore. An enchanting town of church steeples and big wooden houses silhouetted against a backdrop of mountains crisscrossed by ski runs; Lillehammer's ski facilities will be used for the *1994 Winter Olympics*. Just to the east are the alpine centers of Nordseter and Sjusjøen.

Although Lillehammer is small (pop. 22,000), its winter sports facilities are well known throughout Europe; in fact, it has hosted more national skiing championships than any other Norwegian city. Reputed to be the only place in the world with a skier in its coat of arms, Lillehammer boasts 312 miles of marked cross-country ski tracks; 6 tracks near town are floodlit for night use. Slalom enthusiasts can choose from runs with lifts in Lillehammer and neighboring Oyer (12 miles/19 km north), Nordseter, Sjusjøen (14 miles/22 km southeast), and Brottum. There are several schools — for both cross-country and downhill — and skiers can rent or buy equipment.

If you aren't an avid skier, there are a variety of other activities to enjoy in the area. Lillehammer has two outdoor skating rinks, or you may try a hiking trip; if you're more adventurous, arrange a sleigh ride, or tour the *1994 Winter Olympics* district with a team of huskies. You can command your own team or ride in a sled. Half-day, full-day, and overnight trips are available. During the summer, the area offers windsurfing, sailing, canoeing, and swimming at Lake Mjøsa; walking and horseback riding in the moutains. Contact the Lillehammer Tourist Office (2 Jernbanegt.; phone: 62-59299) for more information on these activities.

Most of the action at Lillehammer centers around the outdoors; it's not a place for the traveler seeking a wide variety of fine restaurants, shops, or clubs. Nightlife can be found at the hotel restaurants that offer dancing. During the summer, *Maihaugen,* an open-air museum with its 130 historic buildings spread over a 95-acre park, is well worth a visit. There are craftsmen plying their trades and farmers doing their chores at the houses, barns, and shops. The park is open year-round, but the buildings are closed during winter; admission charge. Be sure to stroll up Nordseterveien to Bjerkebaek, the house where the Nobel Prize–winning writer Sigrid Undset lived from 1921 until her death in 1949. The privately owned home is closed to the public.

The Lillehammer Tourist Office (at the railway station, 2 Jernbanegt.; phone: 62-59299 or 62-51098) has information about hotels, ski lodges, and attractions in the area; the office is closed Sundays. For information on the *1994 Olympics* stop in at the Olympics Information Center (19 Elvegt.; phone: 62-71900; fax: 62-71950). There are a variety of choices for accommodations in and around Lillehammer (our recommendations follow), but if you're thinking ahead to 1994, be aware that 100,000 spectators are expected to be on hand for the most popular *Olympic* events. Note that almost all available lodging in Lillehammer and its environs already has been reserved for the *Olympics* personnel, officials, and VIPs; spectators should plan to stay in Oslo and at other locations. Train and bus connections to Lillehammer will be stepped up during the games.

BEST EN ROUTE

Except for Lillehammer's hotels, most accommodations in the area are in mountain lodges. Book rooms well in advance for winter weekends, the *Christmas* and *Easter* holidays, and July and August when most Norwegians leave the cities for vacations in the countryside. Hotel and lodge rates vary greatly according to the season, but generally expect to pay $125 and up for a double room in the places we list as expensive, $80 to $125 for a room in the moderate category, and less than $80 for an inexpensive room. These prices include breakfast only, but most lodges have half- (breakfast and lunch) or full-board rates available. Keep in mind that lodges often require weekend or 3-day minimum stays. Inquire about discounts for longer stays.

LILLEHAMMER

Lillehammer – Set in a private park, this comfortable, elegant property is just a 5-minute walk from the *Lillehammer Ski Center*. The restaurant has live music and dancing nightly. There also is an indoor and outdoor pool, a fitness room, and several lounges (phone: 62-54800; fax: 62-57333; telex: 19592). Expensive.

Rica Victoria – The town's foremost business hotel, right in the city center, has 105 rooms offering mountain or lake views. There are 2 restaurants, a dance bar, disco, and a spacious terrace that's popular during the summer. Guests have access to the nearby city swimming pool. 84B Storgt. (phone: 62-50049). Expensive.

Lundehaven – A new 77-room inn with traditional furnishings and regional antiques. There's a fitness center with a whirlpool bath and a breakfast room. Located right in the center of town, on Storgate. For bookings, call the Lillehammer Tourist Office (phone: 62-59299). Moderate.

Oppland – At press time this comfortable hotel, part of the Best Western chain, was expanding from 83 rooms to 100. Some of them have balconies and views of Lake Mjøsa. The restaurant has music for dancing 6 nights a week, and the bar has a fireplace. There's also an indoor pool. 2 Hamarveien (phone: 62-58500 or 800-528-1234, Best Western in the US; fax: 62-55325; telex: 74869). Moderate.

OYER

Hafjell – This new independently owned property offers 138 rooms — including several suites — a restaurant, cafeteria, and a coffee shop. Close to the Hafjell ski area. Make reservations through the Lillehammer Tourist Office (phone: 62-59299). Expensive.

Oyer Gjestegård – A 61-room ski lodge at Hafjell. There's a cafeteria, restaurant, bar with dancing, and an indoor pool with a water slide (phone: 62-78335; fax: 62-78050). Moderate.

NORDSETER

Lillehammer Høyfjellshotell – Guests can cross-country ski right outside this lodge, and the alpine runs are just a bit farther away. There are 46 rooms and 4 apartments, a restaurant with dancing, and a bar; there also is an indoor pool, a miniature golf course, and many other outdoor activities (phone: 62-64004; fax: 62-64080). Expensive.

SJUSJØEN

Sjusjøen Fjellstue – A simple, family-style lodge, it has 69 rooms, most of them with private showers. There's also a dining room, bar with dance floor, and children's playroom (phone: 65-63413). Moderate.

Panorama – The best hotel in the area, this recently renovated and well-maintained property offers 50 rooms, fine views, and a cozy decor with a fireplace. There's also a restaurant and a dance bar. The town's post office and a few shops are nearby (phone: 65-63451; fax: 65-63560). Inexpensive.

Rustad – The focus is on outdoor activities at this rustic lakeside lodge. There are 90 rooms, some with private bath. The dining room serves tasty Norwegian dishes (phone: 65-63408). Inexpensive.

Poland

A visit to Poland nowadays offers a chance to see history in the making. For the first time since the end of World War II, Poland has a non-Communist government; and although Soviet troops are still on Polish soil, the Curtain has been lifted. People speak their minds — without worrying whether they'll still have a job — or be in jail — the next day. Censorship of the press has been abolished, and though Russian and German still are spoken more frequently than English, there's little difficulty making yourself understood.

This is not to say that the transition from a closely controlled, state-run system to one of free-enterprise has been easy. The Solidarity trade union, led by the charismatic leader Lech Walesa in Gdańsk, gave birth to the dominant ideological movement in Poland; Walesa was elected the country's president in December 1990. The economic difficulties — and differences — have not been so neatly resolved, and the country has endured inflation and rising unemployment. Factories have closed; shortages of food and other basic living necessities continue; strikes erupt; crime has skyrocketed. Many small, private businesses around the country have closed almost as quickly as they opened, but there is still broad hope that the new market economy will improve, with experience. The Poles have begun to enjoy freedom of the press and unfettered travel, the sort of self-determination that was unknown only a few years ago.

From the imperial rule of kings and princes to present-day politics passionately debated in smoky coffeehouses, Poland has rarely known a day free from strife. But in spite of a succession of invasions since the beginning of its history — and its seeming disappearance from the collective consciousness — this 120,727-square-mile country has managed to survive, with both its spirit and identity intact.

The Poles are descended from tribes of western Slavs, who were unified in the 10th century by a plains-dwelling tribe, the Polanie, in order to resist increasing invasions from the west by Germanic tribes. In 966, Duke Mieszko I put the new state under the protection of the Holy Roman Empire and accepted Christianity for himself and his people. From almost the very beginning of the country's thousand-year history, Roman Catholicism has been virtually synonymous with Polish nationhood.

Most of Poland lies in the north European plain. It stretches south from the Baltic Sea to the Sudety and Carpathian mountains, which separate it from Czechoslovakia. It is bordered by Germany on the west; and the Soviet Union on the east. Temperatures are higher than normal for Poland's latitude, but weather conditions vary from region to region. Winters can be severely cold, and there are frequent showers in summer. However, pleasant warm weather continues through October, but often under heavy (and widely polluted) gray skies.

Prevailing winds and tidal action have resulted in few good harbors along the Baltic coast, but they have created wonderful long sandy beaches that attract tens of thousands of vacationers to the 325-mile seacoast. Below the sand dunes and forests of the coastal belt, there is a stunning postglacial region of thousands of lakes and heavily wooded hills rich in wildlife. Poland has 13 natural parks and some 500 wildlife preserves. The wild European bison is protected here, along with chamois, bear, grey wolf, moose, boar, elk, wildcat, and the swift, dun-colored tarpan, one of the smallest horses in the world.

The central lowlands are mostly flat and, although they do not have the richest soils, are the most extensively cultivated areas. About 45% of Poland's 37 million people live in rural areas. Poles privately own 80% of the country's arable land, but mechanization has been slow. In general, heavy industrial development was emphasized by the former Communist government at the expense of agriculture. The foothills region paralleling the two mountain ranges along the southwestern border contains most of the country's mineral wealth and its best agricultural land. The Upper Silesia region is the most industrial, the most heavily populated, and the most polluted area of the country.

The mountains themselves are not particularly rugged, except in the High Tatra range of the Carpathian Mountains, and have long been populated by farmers and shepherds. Outdoor activities, the beauty of the scenery, and the charm of local folk art, particularly woodcarving, make the mountains an important tourist destination.

The borders of modern Poland are strikingly similar to those of the first Polish state, although the country's history has been one of constant struggle to hold its own against larger, more aggressive neighbors. At one point — from 1795 to 1918 — Poland ceased to exist as an independent state, having been partitioned by Austria, Prussia, and Russia. During that 123-year period and throughout Communist rule, the Roman Catholic faith has served as an element of cohesion and unity for the Polish people.

World War II began with the German invasion of Poland on September 1, 1939. After 6 weeks of fierce resistance by Polish horse cavalry against German armored cavalry, the country was conquered and occupied. Poland remained under foreign occupation for 5½ years. The devastation and loss of life were among the worst suffered by any of the war's victims. It was in Poland that the Nazis started their Final Solution, subjecting all European Jews to mass genocide. Cracow, nearly alone among Polish cities, escaped massive destruction, but 6 million Poles — half of them Jews — were killed in Nazi concentration camps. Today, these camps (including Auschwitz) are maintained as museums, and serve as constant reminders of the war's horrors.

In the early 14th century, Jews had been welcomed into Poland as immigrants, during the reign of Casimir III (Casimir the Great), one of Poland's greatest rulers; and before World War II, they numbered some 3 million residents — Europe's largest Jewish population. After the war, most of those who survived the Holocaust emigrated to Israel. The few who stayed behind soon followed after an anti-Semitic campaign became virulent in 1968. It is estimated that there are now only about about 4,000 Jews in all of Poland.

Throughout the war, Jews and other Poles resisted the Nazis through various resistance organizations. The culmination of the Jewish struggle was the uprising in the Warsaw Ghetto in April 1943, when 60,000 Jews were killed and 100,000 survivors were sent to concentration camps. The following year the Polish Home Army organized the Warsaw Uprising, in which more than 200,000 Poles were killed. After their defeat, Hitler gave instructions for the total annihilation of the city. The Red Army entered on January 17, 1945 to liberate what had become a city of smoldering ruins.

The postwar Provisional Government of Poland was formed in Lublin in 1944. The August 2, 1945 Potsdam peace conference established Poland's western frontiers along the Oder-Neise line, and in August 1945 Moscow's Polish-Soviet Treaty confirmed the 1918 Curzon Line (drawn by British diplomat George N. Curzon at the Versailles conference in 1919) as the country's eastern frontier. Poland lost 69,290 square miles on the east and gained 39,596 square miles on the west. Consequently, 3,300,000 ethnic Germans left Poland, joining some 4,000,000 who already had left these territories ahead of the advancing Red Army during the closing days of World War II.

After the war, Stalin undertook the sovietization of Poland through the puppet leadership of Boleslaw Bierut. Farms with more than 124 acres of land were expropriated, and all businesses with more than 50 workers were nationalized. A Soviet marshal, Konstantin Rokossovsky, who had liberated Warsaw, became Poland's defense minister from 1949 until 1956. The 1947 elections were rigged and "won" by a coalition led by the Polish Communist party. On July 22, 1952 a Soviet-type constitution was installed and the People's Socialist Republic of Poland proclaimed.

The people's republic, though, did little to please the people, and Poles took to the streets in 1956, 1970, 1976, and again in 1980 to protest their living conditions. In 1980, a strong independent union, *Solidarnosc* (Solidarity), was founded in Gdańsk's Lenin Shipyards, under the leadership of Lech Walesa, an apprentice electrician. Within months, 10,000,000 workers became members, while 3,000,000 peasants joined Rural Solidarity. The strength of Solidarity and the recurrent strikes and demonstrations led to a serious threat of Soviet invasion, which, in turn, prompted the head of the government, General Wojciech Jaruzelski, to impose martial law. Lech Walesa and all Solidarity leaders were jailed.

In July 1983, once the threat of a Soviet invasion had passed, martial law was lifted, and the union again was legalized. Government-opposition round-table talks were held in 1988, followed by free elections in 1989. Tadeusz Mazowiecki became prime minister and General Jaruzelski became president of the country whose official name is now the Republic of Poland. A Solidarity-controlled parliament started a series of reforms that Poles hope will lead the country to economic recovery. Popular elections were held again only a year later: In December 1990, Lech Walesa became president. Parliamentary elections were held in January 1991; the Libertarian party, led by Jan Krzysztoph Bielecki, won control and Bielecki became prime minister. Because of the continuing election reforms, yet another parliamentary election was scheduled as we went to press.

Poles are understandably proud of both their heritage and their pantheon of authentic heroes: Nicolaus Copernicus, whose theories about the universe provided the foundation for modern astronomy; Marie Skłodowska-Curie, whose research with her husband led to the discovery of radium; Frederick Chopin, whose mazurkas and polonaises seem to embody the Polish spirit; the Nobel Prize winners Lech Walesa, Henryk Sienkiewicz, Wladislaw Reymont, and Czeslaw Milosz; and the former Karol Cardinal Wojtyla of Cracow — who became Pope John Paul II in 1978.

The religious shrine of Our Lady of Częstochowa, Cracow — Poland's second-largest and loveliest city — and the breathtaking Tatras draw hundreds of thousands of visitors to southern Poland each year. The route south from Warsaw — through heavily industrialized Upper Silesia to the medieval beauty of Cracow, and beyond to the serenity of the mountains where centuries-old traditions of farmers and herdsmen are intact — offers the traveler a continuum of Polish history. By car, the route from Warsaw to Częstochowa is about 135 miles (216 km), from Częstochowa to Cracow approximately 90 miles (144 km), and from Cracow to Zakopane, some 66 miles (106 km). There also are rail connections.

WARSAW: For a detailed report on the city and its hotels and restaurants, see *Warsaw,* THE CITIES. The capital is the usual point of departure for tours to other parts of Poland.

CZĘSTOCHOWA: The huge monastery complex on top of Jasna Góra (Shining Mountain; phone: 45087) has dominated this drab Warta River town since Paulist monks founded it in 1382. The monastery is the focal point of a religious cult devoted to Our Lady of Częstochowa, the so-called Black Madonna.

Each year, enormous numbers of pilgrims come to pay homage to the sacred portrait of the Madonna, said to have been painted by St. Luke and brought here in 1384. In 1430 the painting was attacked by dissident Protestants, and to this day the Madonna still has a scar on her face. The portrait, with its darkened paint, hangs over an exquisite altar of wrought silver and ebony wood in a chapel in the monastery church. It can be viewed only during religious services. In 1665, when the monastery was under seige from Swedish invaders and the force was held off by the heroic efforts of Polish soldiers and monks, legend says that the defense was aided by the Black Madonna. In the following months, the Poles rallied together and drove the Swedes out of the country. More than 300,000 people take part in the two pilgrimages each year in August: the *Feast of the Assumption,* August 15, and *St. Mary's Day* for the Black Madonna, August 26. Over the centuries, monarchs and others seeking blessings from Our Lady of Częstochowa have donated priceless art, jewelry, and heirlooms to swell the monastery's treasury. Many of the offerings are on permanent exhibition. Only VIPs, by special permission, are allowed to visit the monastery library, which contains some 20,000 valuable documents and records pertaining to Polish history.

Częstochowa itself is one of the chief towns of Poland's largest iron-ore mining region and an important textile industry center. Since World War II, there has been extensive urban and industrial development here.

En Route from Częstochowa – Heading south on E16, you pass some of the region's iron-ore mines before reaching Siewierz, where you can visit the ruins of the medieval castle of the Bishops of Cracow who once ruled here. Katowice, the capital of the Upper Silesia industrial region, is a modern industrial center and home of the renowned *Grand Symphony Orchestra* of the Polish radio. The route continues south to Tychy, once a popular resort center on nearly dry Lake Po-procanskie, then turns east to Oswiecim (Auschwitz), site of the largest Nazi concentration camp of World War II.

AUSCHWITZ: The Poles call it Oświęcim, but whatever the name, there is no mistaking that here lies the largest of all the Nazi concentration camps. Some 4 million people (most of them Jews), representing 28 nationalities, were exterminated at the two camps that the Nazis operated here from 1940 to 1945. The site of Auschwitz (less than an hour's drive from Cracow) has been made into a national museum. Pictures of the victims, the gas chambers in which they died, and the enormous display cases containing their personal belongings — even hair shorn from prisoners and destined to be sold as pillow stuffing — are a chilling reminder of the grisly crimes committed here. A film about Auschwitz (narrated in English) and the starving inmates who were alive the day the camp was liberated is shown at the museum several times a day. Equally shattering is a trip to Birkenau, some 2 miles (3 km) away, the site of the largest crematoria. After a visit to either site — regardless of background or belief — you will never be quite the same. Because of the increasing number of visitors, reservations are required to visit the camp. For information, call 23132.

CRACOW: Cracow (Kraków) is almost everyone's favorite Polish city. Travelers destined for the Tatra resorts to the south almost always stay here longer than they had planned. Unlike Warsaw and other Polish cities, Cracow was untouched by bombs and other massive destruction during World War II. Its medieval charm is still apparent on every tree-shaded street, although the pollution caused by the nearby Nowa Huta steelworks is almost overpowering.

Poland's third-largest city was founded in the 9th century. An early Polish king, Wladyslaw I (Casimir III's father) — commonly known as King Wladyslaw the Short — made Cracow Poland's capital after he unified the country in the early 14th century; it remained preeminent for some 3 centuries, until the honor was passed to Warsaw. Cracow lately has attracted international attention because it was the see Karol Cardinal Wojtyla served before becoming Pope John Paul II, the first Roman Catholic pope from a then-Communist country.

Wawel Hill, with its fortified castle and cathedral, dominates the skyline, while Rynek Główny, one of the largest town squares in Europe, is the center of city life.

The hill was first fortified to defend a crossing of the Vistula River beneath it. The stately Gothic cathedral was built from 1320 to 1364, and by the time of King Casimir the Great (1333–1370), Wawel was the center of state authority and culture. In the 16th century, King Sigismund the Old had a beautifully proportioned Renaissance palace built as his residence. The north wing was later renovated in accordance with the baroque spirit.

Although the royal court was moved to Warsaw in 1609, Wawel remained the coronation site of Polish kings. The inhabitants of Cracow have never really accepted Warsaw as the capital and today they often say that Warsaw may be the head of Poland but Cracow is the heart. During the 17th century, Poland was almost strangled economically by the Swedish wars, but even when it was occupied by the Austrians between 1795 and 1918, Wawel was considered a national treasure that symbolized the country's independence. During World War II, the Nazis had plans to blow up the castle and the cathedral, but a surprise offensive by the Russian army prevented this destruction. There is a fine panorama of the Old City below Wawel Castle, including its green promenades, monuments, and fortifications.

You enter the castle through an arcaded courtyard that is now used for open-air concerts. The castle's 71 rooms are high and airy and richly appointed. Among its treasures is a collection of 136 rare 16th- and 17th-century Flemish tapestries. The Chamber of Deputies has an unusual coffered ceiling that features heads carved and painted in the 16th century to represent members of the royal court. Several chambers are covered entirely in Spanish leather, which has been embossed and hand-painted with fine designs. There is an admission charge to the castle.

The elaborate tomb of St. Stanislaus, Poland's patron saint, stands in the middle of the nave of the adjacent cathedral (the current pope's former parish), and two chapels are particularly noteworthy. These are the Chapel of the Holy Cross, decorated with colorful, 15th-century frescoes, and Sigismund Chapel, in which red marble tombs are set strikingly against white marble walls. An 11th-century crypt, incorporated from an earlier cathedral on this site, is crammed with the tombs of kings, queens, bishops, and Polish national heroes.

Splendid old mansions of noblemen and merchants are clustered on streets at the bottom of Wawel Hill. Grodzka street leads right to the main town square, but along the way there are dozens of narrow passageways between shops that open onto tiny courtyards with workshops and balconied houses.

Most of the buildings in the main square were built between the 14th and 16th centuries. The huge white and brown Cloth Hall (Sukiennice) was built in the 14th century, but was renovated in the Renaissance style during the 16th century. Always a center of commerce, the building now contains dozens of small craft and souvenir shops, which are housed in a colonnaded wooden arcade on the ground floor, as well as the *Gallery of Polish Painting,* with a fine collection of 18th- and 19th-century work on the second floor.

St. Mary's Church (Mariacki), opposite the Cloth Hall, was built in the 15th century and is best known for the magnificent altarpiece carved by Wit Stwosz in late Gothic style. This medieval triptych of life-size figures in gold raiment depicts the assumption of the Virgin Mary. A series of 14th-century stained-glass windows above the triptych take up its themes and colors. The altar opening takes place daily except Sundays at noon.

Diagonally across the square from the church is the Old Town Hall tower, the only reminder of the Town Hall that was demolished in 1820. The tower houses a branch of the *National Museum,* and its dungeon has been turned into a wine cellar.

The red brick of St. Florian's Gate, the Barbican, and some town walls and towers are all that remain of the medieval fortifications that protected Old Cracow. Today, the limits of the older parts of the city are marked by a green belt of gardens, known as Planty.

Another important landmark is Jagiellonian University, founded in 1364 by King Casimir the Great and one of the oldest centers of learning in Europe. During the war, the Nazis executed the university's entire teaching staff. Today, some 50,000 students study here. A prized possession in its museum is the world globe on which Nicolaus Copernicus, a former student here, first acknowledged America. The country is indicated by the words, "America New Discovery."

Europe's second-oldest synagogue, built in the 14th century for exiled Spanish Jews, is on Ul. Szeroka, in the old Jewish quarter. During the war, the Nazis desecrated the synagogue, using it to stable horses. Now a Jewish museum, it is being refurbished by the government.

There were about 60,000 Jews in Cracow before the war; today there are perhaps 200. Remu'h Synagogue, nearby (24 Ul. Szeroka), is the only one of the city's eight surviving synagogues still open for worship. In a cemetery near the synagogues (at 40 Ul. Szeroka) there is a lovely memorial: Salvaged pieces of desecrated tombs (with fragments of Hebrew inscriptions and carved decorations) have been fashioned into a wall creating a great stone collage. Ask the guardian at the Remu'h Synagogue for information regarding visits.

Cracow boasts a long and rich theater tradition. The city's eight repertory theaters are well known for the quality of their productions. One of the best is *Helena Modrzejewska Stary Theater* (1 Ul. Jagiellonska) and almost every premiere at its branch,

Kameralny Theater, is of national interest. The *J. Slowackiego Theater* (1 Pl. św. Ducha), which shares the premises with the *Cracow Opera House,* also is highly regarded.

In even-numbered years, the *International Biennale of Graphic Arts* (4 Ul. Szczepanski) is held here. Works of art by contemporary artists and folk artists are on view and for sale at branches of *Cepelia,* the folk arts and crafts cooperative, and *Desa,* antiques and art shops. There are several *Cepelia* branches (12 Ul. Karmelicka; 22 Ul. Szewska, Sukiennice; 7 Rynek Główny; and 1 Pl. Mariacki). *Desa* branches include the *B Gallery* (2 Ul. Bracka); the *Modern Art Gallery* (Nowa Huta-Osiedle Kościuszkowskie, pavilion 1A; and the *Contemporary Art Gallery,* 3 Ul. św. Jana).

For those who are interested, the Wieliczka salt mines are 8 miles (13 km) south of Cracow. Visitors can tour a museum located 150 yards underground, with sculptures, tiles, chandeliers, and many other objects carved from salt. The salt mines were first discovered and used in the 13th century. There also are underground tennis courts, a giant chapel, and a clinic for the treatment of respiratory illnesses. Tours are conducted daily — the last one leaves at 2 PM.

For general tourist information, check with the Wawel Tourist Information and Advertising Center (8 Ul. Pawia; phone: 220471 or 226091). Excursions can be arranged through various tourist offices, including *Orbis,* the Polish Tourist Office (1 Ul. Puszkina; phone: 224746; fax: 222885) in the *Orbis-Cracovia* hotel (Orbis Szczepaánskiego Sq. 3; phone: 221298).

ZAKOPANE: Nestled between the Gubalowka Ridge and the towering Tatras, this popular town is an extremely charming, always lively, holiday center. In winter, skiing and ski jumping are important added attractions, but all year, it is the beauty of the mountains and valleys and the rich folk culture preserved by the highlanders that draw Poles to Zakopane.

Fir, beech, and spruce grow in the subalpine woods of the Tatras. As you go higher, there are spruce forests and stone pine, dwarf mountain pine, and alpine pastures with little vegetation. Edelweiss and stone pine are among the 260 species of plants here, and the region is a natural habitat for lynx, marmot, chamois, brown bear, various deer, and, sometimes, the golden eagle.

The town itself is a museum of regional folk culture. The wooden gingerbread houses are similar to Norwegian stave churches, but more complicated in design. The lacy look of the carved façades is reminiscent of Victorian valentines. Against the backdrop of pine forests and snow-peaked mountains, these homes seem most idyllic. At the lower end of Ul. Krupówki, near Kościeliska, there are a small mid-19th-century church, several typical highlanders' houses, and a cemetery where nearly every monument is a masterpiece of folk art. The local museum, *Dr. Tytus Chalubinski Tatrzanskie Museum* (10 Ul. Krupówki), includes a reconstruction of a highlander's cottage interior, specimens of plants, birds, and animals native to the Tatras, and a collection of local costumes. *Tea Cottage* (39 Ul. Bulwary Stowackiego) is another museum with typical regional flavor.

Many men of the area still wear white woolen trousers with distinctive black and red embroidery called *parzenica,* and richly embroidered, cape-like outer garments, known as *cucha,* to the delight of the tourists. In the outdoor market, country women sell hand-knitted mohair cardigans, the primitive leather moccasins worn by highland people, and special local cheeses.

There are horse-drawn carriages available to take visitors to the surrounding areas, such as the village of Jaszczurówka, where a small wooden church stands as an almost perfect example of elaborate Zakopane architecture, and Harenda which has an 18th-century church built of squared larch trunks.

For a magnificent panorama of the town and the Tatras, you can take a chair lift from near the *Orbis-Kasprowy* hotel to the top of Gubałowka Hill. At Kuźnice, a little more than 2 miles (3 km) south of Zakopane, there is a funicular to Kasprowy Wierch

(6,451 feet), the region's most famous ski mountain. Come early or reserve through *Orbis* (22 Ul, Krupówki, Zakopane; phone: 5051; in the US, 212-867-5011). There are ski routes down to Zakopane and to Kuźnice. At the southeastern corner of the Tatra National Parks complex are two beautiful lakes — Morski Ono and Czarny Staw — and Mt. Rysy, which, at 98,386 feet, is the highest peak in the Polish Tatras.

The Dolina Białego Valley, where the crystal Bialy Potok stream flows through steep crags, is just a 15- or 20-minute walk from the center of Zakopane.

Some hotel restaurants serve such regional specialties as braised boar, elk, and rabbit. Nighttime entertainment in Zakopane ranges from folk music and dancing to discotheque.

BEST EN ROUTE

Rooms may be hard to come by at the height of the tourist season, and impossible to get at Częstochowa during the August pilgrimage. If you can book one, a double will cost from $70 to $150 a night at an expensive hotel; $40 to $70, at a moderately priced one; and $30 to $40 at an inexpensive hotel.

In Zakopane, non-*Orbis* hotels can arrange accommodations in private homes in the area.

Dinner for two with wine at an expensive restaurant will cost $20 to $35; at a moderately priced restaurant, $15 to $20; and at an inexpensive one, as little as $5.

You can pay for meals at restaurants and cafés in zlotys, but hotel rooms must be paid for in dollars or other hard currency.

The introduction of private enterprise has allowed Poles to venture into the hotel and restaurant trades, and many new establishments are beginning to flourish in tourist regions. Local tourist offices usually supply their addresses and will assist in making reservations.

CZĘSTOCHOWA

Orbis-Patria – A modern, medium-size hotel (180 rooms) on the main avenue to Jasna Góra. Its restaurant and nightclub are good bets for dining. Major credit cards accepted. 1 Ul. Starucha (phone: 47001/9; fax: 46332; telex: 37269). Expensive.

Motel–Orbis – Austere — yet inviting — this small hostelry is about 1½ miles (2 km) from the monastery. 287 Ul. Wojska Polskiego (phone: 57233; telex: 37605). Moderate.

CRACOW (KRAKÓW)

Orbis-Cracovia – Centrally located, with 427 rooms, a restaurant, café, and several shops. Major credit cards accepted. 1 Ul. Puszkina (phone: 228666; fax: 219586; telex: 322341). Expensive.

Orbis–Forum – Though physically unattractive, this undistinguished 1987 addition to the hostelry scene offers 284 rooms — all fully air conditioned with bath, mini-bar, and color TV set. Half of the rooms overlook the Vistula River and Wawel Castle. It is the equivalent of a mid-range motel in America. There also are a restaurant, a nightclub, 3 bars, and a rooftop café. Major credit cards accepted. 28 Ul. Marrii Konopnickiej (phone: 669500; telex: 322337). Expensive.

Orbis–Holiday Inn – Although all *Orbis* hotels in Cracow are listed as first class, the description comes closest to accuracy here as a result of the decor, restaurant, and general ambience. Totally air conditioned, it has 304 double rooms and 2 suites, as well as a swimming pool. However, it is a 10-minute bus ride or a 5-minute drive to Rynek Glówny. Major credit cards accepted. 7 Ul. Marsz. Koniewa (phone: 375044; fax: 375938; telex: 325356). Expensive.

Wierzynek – Cracow's attempt at haute cuisine, in a centuries-old home on Market

Square. Interesting, but hardly memorable meals. The menu goes on for pages. Reservations necessary. No credit cards accepted. 15 Rynek Główny (phone: 221035). Expensive.

Pod Kopcem – A 19th-century Austrian fortress, this hotel/restaurant is perched on the top of a hill and offers the best view in town. Major credit cards accepted. Ul. Waszyngtona (phone: 220355; telex: 221035). Expensive to moderate.

Balaton – Hungarian-style food and music and a convenient downtown location. No credit cards accepted. 37 Ul. Grodzka (phone: 220469). Moderate.

Centrum – A non-*Orbis* hotel — that is, not run by the tourist bureau — so standards may fluctuate. At least it's downtown. 59-63 Ul. Kilinskiego (phone: 328640). Moderate.

Dniepr – Also conveniently situated, it specializes in Russian food. 55 Ul. Stycznia (phone: 337214). Moderate.

Europejski – Worth investigating — if for no other reason than it's a hotel without "Orbis" in its name. 5 Ul. Lubicz (phone: 20911). Moderate.

Krak – The best camping site and motel near Cracow. Major credit cards accepted. 99 Ul. Radzikowskiego (phone: 72122; telex: 325698). Moderate.

Orbis-Francuski – Built just after the turn of the century, this centrally situated hotel has 57 very good rooms. Major credit cards accepted. 13 Ul. Pijarska (phone: 225122 or 225270). Moderate.

Swiatowid – Another non-*Orbis* hotel. 68 Ul. Kościuszki (phone: 363044). Moderate.

U Wentzla – Another downtown eatery, this one features Polish fare, such as *vigos,* a dish of sausage with sauerkraut. Reservations advised on weekends. No credit cards accepted. 19 Rynek Główny (no phone). Moderate.

Wanda – A motel located next to the Holiday Inn. Built in 1982, it has 80 spare and simple rooms. 9 Ul. Koniewa (phone: 371677). Moderate.

Polonia – Unadvised unless you're desperate for a room. 38 Ul. Narutowicza (phone: 331896). Inexpensive.

Staropolska – Considered one of the best eateries in the country, Polish specialties here include several types of wild game. Service is sometimes slow; order and then relax. Reservations advised on weekends. No credit cards accepted. 4 Ul. Sienna (phone: 225821). Inexpensive.

ZAKOPANE

Orbis-Kasprowy – Beautifully situated on a mountainside, this 288-room establishment is only a 10-minute drive (half-hour walk) from town. Each room has a terrace with a lovely view. Rooms are small, but modern and bright. The restaurant is attractive and serves excellent food. Major credit cards accepted. Polana Szymoszkowa (phone: 4011). Expensive to moderate.

Gazda – A hotel with a restaurant. No credit cards accepted. 1 Ul. Zaruskiego (phone: 5011). Moderate.

Orbis-Giewont – Built in 1910 in the center of town, this hostelry has 48 rooms, a restaurant, and a cocktail bar that serves good tap beer. Major credit cards accepted. 1 Ul. Kościuszki (phone: 2011). Moderate.

Gubatówka – A restaurant that is 5 minutes, by funicular, up Gubatówka Hill. No reservations or credit cards accepted. (no phone). Moderate.

U Wnuka – This café is in an old inn that has typical regional decor. No credit cards accepted. 8 Ul. Kościeliska (no phone). Inexpensive.

The best campground in the Zakopane area is south of the city on Ul. Zeromskiego (phone: 2256). Inexpensive.

Portugal

To most people Portugal means either Lisbon — the charming capital city, rich in monuments, museums, and churches — or the Algarve — the famed vacation area, with its congenial mixture of sea, beaches, luxurious hotels, and varied cuisine. However, beyond Lisbon's city limits and away from the southern shore lies a country of ancient towns, walled villages, and captivating scenery.

Portugal's history goes back 3,000 years, to the time when Greek and Phoenician traders established settlements here. Later, Portugal became part of the Roman Empire (the country was then known as Lusitania), and many remains of the Roman occupation survive. Following the decline and fall of Rome, Portugal was subject to invasions by Visigoths from the north and by Moors from the south. By the mid-12th century, Portugal had expelled the Moors and emerged as a nation with its own culture and language. By the 16th century, following the great age of discoveries, it held title to the most extensive empire in the world. Though the empire has disappeared, the past is still very much alive among Portuguese people today. Many historic buildings, unfortunately, are falling into ruin, as efforts to restore them have been minimal, but the country's handicrafts, colorful costumes, festivals, and music continue to reflect a cultural heritage almost unchanged, in spite of much evidence of modern progress.

Portugal is rectangular, bordered on the north and east by Spain and on the south and west by the Atlantic Ocean. With an area of some 35,553 square miles, Portugal is a relatively small country. Its major cities are Lisbon (pop. 827,800) and Porto (pop. 450,000). The landscape encompasses a wide variety of contrasts — the lush green valley of the Minho River, the rugged mountains of the Tràs-os-Montes region, the steep-hilled vineyards of the Alto Douro, and the Beira flat coast. In the south the pale gold wheat fields and olive and cork groves of the Alentejo give way to the cosmopolitan resorts of the Algarve, where beaches and imposing cliffs are washed by the warm waves of the Gulf Stream.

The summer's heat is moderated along the coast by sea breezes. Days can be quite hot but the temperature drops in the evening. Winters are mild and snow seldom is seen except in the high mountains. The climate is most pleasant for driving trips in the spring and fall, but travel in the southern region also is comfortable during the winter.

Road development, although fast improving, still is somewhat rudimentary in country areas. A fast toll highway is gradually closing the distance between Lisbon and Porto and should be completed in the next few years. Away from the coast, a program is under way to widen and improve main roads linking the biggest towns, but much of the network still consists of narrow, poorly surfaced byways. Road signs are fairly obvious, but a good road map is a necessity. While driving, watch out for donkeys and oxen. They were on the roads long before the automobile and are still there. Gasoline is expensive, but Portugal is still a bargain in other respects, relative to most European countries. Well-maintained hotels and *pousadas* (government-owned inns in buildings of artistic or historical interest) as well as excellent restaurants are found throughout the country. Accommodations generally are good and plumbing is modern and clean. Tap water is considered safe to drink but most people prefer bottled mineral water. Grapes are grown in many areas and the regional wines are excellent. When dining out, request the house wine if one is available.

Perhaps the most interesting accommodations available are at the many country manor houses that offer bed and breakfast. At the moment there are about 200, mainly in the north of the country, and they are invariably fascinating — and comfortable — places to stay. There are three types: *paços,* houses where royalty have stayed; *casas antigas,* houses that have been in the family for more than 300 years; and *quintas,* old farmhouses. Many of the houses belong to aristocrats, and in the evening travelers often can chat with a count or other scion of an old family. The accommodations are always of a high level, but prices usually are moderate. Central booking and information is available through *Turihab* (Ponte de Lima; phone: 58-941864 or 58-942729), *A.C.T.* (Cascais; phone: 1-284-4464), and *Privetur* (Lisbon; phone: 1-654953). *Pousadas* also can be booked centrally in Lisbon at *Enatur* (phone: 1-848-9070 or 1-848-9078/9).

Two weeks is sufficient to travel around most of Portugal. Our first route originates in Lisbon and heads north through Porto, the second-largest city; from here it loops around the mountainous northern region to Guimarães, the cradle of the Portuguese nation, and Vila Real, home of Mateus rosé wine. The next route starts in Lisbon, circles around the central region taking in the towns of Elvas, Estremoz, and Evora, which are rich in historic sites. The last itinerary focuses on the Algarve, Portugal's southern coast and beach resort area.

The Northern Coastal Region and Western Mountains

This route covers a lot of territory, temporally as well as geographically, starting at the modern capital of Lisbon, traveling through Porto, industrial center and second-largest city, to Guimarães, birthplace of Portugal's first king.

The route from Lisbon to Porto in the western part of the country along N1 is heavily trafficked. Though the route links Portugal's most densely populated areas, it passes through small towns, forests, farms, woods, olive groves, and a few popular beach resorts on the Atlantic. Many of the highlights of the route below are architectural — the extravagant mountaintop castle built by Ferdinand Saxe-Coburg-Gotha between 1846 and 1850 in

Sintra; the imposing marble monastery in Mafra built in 1717 for King João V; the walled town of Obidos; and the splendid abbey Mosteiro de Santa Maria, which contains the tombs of two ill-fated 14th-century lovers. Dating even farther back are the ruins of Conímbriga, one of the most important Roman settlements on the Iberian Peninsula.

Leaving Porto, the route heads north, then east and south, circling through the mountainous northern region. The road is a little bumpy, but not unacceptably so. The old road links small fishing villages, and then travels along the Minho River, Portugal's northernmost natural border with Spain. Highlights along the way are Braga, an ancient city founded by the Romans with monuments from the 12th century through ornate 18th-century baroque styles. Guimarães and Vila Real, home of the famous Mateus wine, are set amidst the deep vales and terraced mountain vineyards of the great port wine producing region. If you want to avoid the rutted roads and traffic (but miss some of the old charm), take the new A4, which links Porto to Campo, about 5½ miles (9 km) from Braga.

LISBON: For a detailed report on the capital, its hotels and restaurants, see *Lisbon,* THE CITIES.

QUELUZ and SINTRA: Depart from Lisbon on N249 heading west and drive 7 miles (12 km) to Queluz for a look at its 18th-century pink rococo palace, surrounded by formal gardens (open 10 AM to 5 PM; closed Tuesdays; admission charge). Sometimes described as Portugal's Versailles, the palace was built by Pedro III for his "mad queen" Maria, and although it is still used — to house visiting dignitaries — it is also open to the public. Another 9 miles (15 km) west of Queluz, in the verdant hills of the Serra da Sintra (Lord Byron sang its beauty, calling it a "glorious Eden"), is a wealth of palaces, including the National Palace of Sintra, built by several Portuguese kings and reflecting styles from Moorish through Gothic, Manueline, Renaissance, and baroque. Another palace open to visitors is the Pena Palace, a 19th-century Bavarian fantasy, while still another, the Palácio dos Seteais, is now a luxury hotel. (For more information on sights, hotels, and restaurants in Queluz and Sintra, see *Lisbon,* THE CITIES.) A slight detour to the coast west of Sintra leads to Cabo da Rocha, where there is a view of cliffs, coast, and sea, plus a lighthouse marking Europe's westernmost point. Retrace the road to Sintra and pick up N9 to Mafra, 14 miles (22 km) away.

MAFRA: The imposing marble Mosteiro rises from the road without preamble. Erected in 1717 for King João V by German architect Friedrich Ludwig, the great edifice contains a monastery, basilica, palace, and once housed a school of sculpture. Its library houses 20,000 volumes of 17th- and 18th-century works on theology, geography, and military theory. The façade alone demands attention with its baroque decorations, columns, statuary, and ornate belfries. You can purchase lovely pale blue and white pottery in the shops facing the monastery or just 3 miles (5 km) away in the town of Sobreiro, where it is made.

En Route from Mafra – At Torres Vedras, 21 miles (34 km) along N9, you'll see distant windmills outlined on the rolling hilltops, vineyards, and apple and pear orchards set out in neat fields. You'll also see the Torres Vedras, lines of earthen battlements incorporating castles and fortresses built by the Duke of Wellington to stave off Napoleonic troops during the Peninsular Wars; some of the fortifications have been restored and can be visited. At Bombarral, 16 miles (26 km), take N8 7 miles (11 km) to Obidos.

OBIDOS: This walled town is dominated by the old castle's keep and towers. Taken from the Moors in 1148 by Afonso Henriques, the little city so captivated Queen

Isabella in 1228, that her consort, King Dinis, presented it to her. Pass through the double-arched gateway, follow the narrow main street to Igreja de Santa Maria, and park below in the square. Proceed on foot to Igreja de São Tiago where a path on the left leads to the ramparts. On the right is the *Pousada do Castelo,* once the royal palace (see *Best en Route*). The serene dining room inside serves a pleasantly formal lunch. Shops in town offer a wealth of handicrafts: lace, embroidered tablecloths, basketry, fashionable heavy knitted sweaters. Don't miss the octagonal church standing alone in a field below the town. Built by Philip II of Spain, it contains a 14th-century onyx statue of a black virgin which resembles the Black Virgin of Monserrat in Spain.

   En Route from Obidos – Caldas da Rainha, on N8, is a large commercial center noted for its spa dating back to 1485. It was founded by Leonor, the wife of King João II, who believed in the curative power of its waters. The city's hospital and park still bear her name. Traditional regional ceramics are on sale in the town's shops and factories, and an annual ceramics fair draws large crowds.

   Veer left at Alfeizerão and head for São Martinho do Porto, a typical beach resort. From the promenade you can see an unusual saltwater lake connected to the ocean through a rift between high coastal cliffs. If you like quiet beaches with good fishing and clean water, try Foz do Arelho Beach on a small, pine-covered peninsula, just 2 miles (3 km) from Caldas.

   A short drive north on N242 leads to the famous fishing port of Nazaré, where the beach is lined with brightly painted, high-prowed fishing boats. Nazaré has become a rather touristy beach resort, but some customs survive: Men still wear traditional plaid shirts and black caps, and women, black capes. They still dance the *vira* — a spirited folk dance — and cook their tasty fish stew, *caldeirada.* For an excellent view, drive or take a funicular to the Sítio, a section in town perched high above the beach. There is a spectacular view from the belvedere, and on the cliff just below you can see a hoof print. According to legend, it was made by the horse of Portuguese nobleman Dom Fuas Roupinho, who accidentally rode off the cliff while pursuing a deer. He prayed to Our Lady of Nazaré and was saved; in gratitude he built the little Chapel of Memory, which is perched on the cliff. *Mar e Sol* or *Riba Mar* serve good meals along the seaside. Though the shops appear rather touristy, they sell handsome hand-knit fishermen's sweaters at moderate prices.

ALCOBAÇA: Constructed by Cistercian monks in 1178, the Mosteiro de Santa Maria is one of Portugal's most splendid abbeys. The building has been altered and restored, but the interior retains its uplifting spaciousness. The church contains the Flamboyant Gothic–style tombs of Inês de Castro and Dom Pedro, ill-fated lovers of the 14th century. (Dom Pedro's father, King Afonso IV, ordered his nobles to murder Inês to prevent Prince Pedro from marrying her. When Pedro became king, he ordered the execution of the murderers, after forcing them to pay homage to her dead body dressed in the garb of a queen.) In the cloister you can visit the monks' kitchen with its enormous chimneys and marble tables; a stream of the River Alcoa flows underneath this kitchen. In the Middle Ages the stream provided fresh fish for the royal table. On the Rossio, the sweeping square before the abbey, the distinctive pottery and ceramics of the region are displayed for sale (open 9 AM to 7 PM).

BATALHA: A masterpiece of Portuguese Gothic and Manueline (after Manuel I, during whose reign the transition from Gothic to Renaissance styles gave birth to an original artistic form of decoration in Portugal) styles, the town's church is an awesome monument. Embellished with flying buttresses, turrets, and tracery, it was erected between 1402 and 1438 to commemorate the victorious battle of Aljubarrota, which ended Castilian domination of Portugal. The stark, soaring interior of the nave is offset by a richly decorated cloister and lavabo. The small Founder's Chapel contains the tombs of King João I, Queen Philippa of Lancaster, and their children, most notably

Prince Henry the Navigator. The beautiful, unfinished Manueline chapels are at the back of the church. The square adjacent to the monastery is lined with small shops and cafés.

FATIMA: A side trip can be made from Batalha to Fatima — a distance of 20 miles (32 km) — the world-famous shrine where the Virgin Mary appeared in 1917 to three shepherd children. The pilgrimages on May 13 and October 13 often bring several hundred thousand pilgrims from all over the world. The town has several hotels.

LEIRIA: This pleasant town is just 7 miles (11 km) from Batalha on Route 1. In its center on a volcanic hill stands the Castelo, built in 1135 by Afonso Henriques, from which you have a panoramic view of the picturesque Old Town and the charming countryside. Leiria is most appealing for a stroll at twilight — when the old streets and houses seem to blend with the modern. A festival held during the last 2 weeks of March features exhibitions and folk dancing. Another worthwhile side trip can be taken to Marinha Grande, 8 miles (13 km) from Leiria. This glass making center was founded around 1730, and the glass factory was built by the Stephens brothers, Englishmen who later donated it to the state. You can visit the factory, in an old pink mansion in the center of town, as well as the glass museum on the premises.

En Route from Leiria – The main road to Coimbra, N1, leads through 45 miles (72 km) of farms, olive trees, and pine woods. About 9 miles (14 km) below Coimbra, an archaeological dig has uncovered the foundations of a large Roman town, Conímbriga, inhabited first by Celts in neolithic times. Guided tours allow visitors to see the remains of what was once the most important Roman settlement in Portugal. A museum at the site, the *Museu Monográfico,* displays objects unearthed here — coins, pottery, cloth, lamps, games, jewelry, sculpture, murals, and mosaics. The museum is open from 10 AM to 1 PM and from 2 to 6 PM, June through September (to 5 PM the rest of the year); closed Mondays and holidays. The site itself is open daily from 9 AM to 1 PM and from 2 to 8 PM, June through September (to 6 PM the rest of the year.) There are admission charges to both the ruins and the museum; there is also a restaurant with a panoramic terrace.

COIMBRA: Beginning as a Roman settlement, suffering invasions by barbarians and Moors, taken by Christians in 1064, Coimbra finally came into its own as a cultural and artistic center after the founding of its famed Universidade Velha in 1290. Climb the steep narrow cobbled way through the Old Town to the university courtyard for a tour of the ancient buildings. The magnificent Biblioteca Joannina (Joannine Library) is decorated in carved and gilded baroque-styled wood with intricately painted ceilings; it contains an enormous collection of old books. The Ceremonial Hall hung with portraits of the Kings of Portugal and the beautiful Manueline ornamented chapel are still in use today. A former Episcopal palace nearby holds the *Museu Machado de Castro* (Rua de Borges Carneiro) where one is led from room to room by guides determined to explain everything about each of the collections' gold objects, sculptures, paintings, and ceramics. Beneath the palace, and forming part of the museum, is the cryptoportico — a series of underground passages built by the Romans and now housing a collection of ancient relics and Roman sculpture. Also worth visiting are the 12th-century Sé Velha, one of the country's greatest Romanesque cathedrals, with its Flamboyant Gothic altarpiece; the 16th-century Mosteiro de Santa Cruz and its lovely Manueline cloister; a 12th-century Cistercian convent, Mosteiro de Celas; and across the river in the Santa Clara area, the Convento de Santa Clara-a-Nova. Children will enjoy the nearby Portugal dos Pequenitos, a beautifully constructed village with replicas of all of the country's famous buildings scaled down to a child's size. Nearby is the Quinta das Lagrimas, where the ill-fated Inês de Castro lived with her Prince Pedro. Now a private estate, its gardens are open to the public daily.

En Route from Coimbra – Follow N1 18 miles (29 km) to Luso, a lovely spa situated in the midst of forested rolling hills. An Olympic-size swimming pool in the gardens behind the *Grande Hotel das Termas* (see *Best en Route*) is open to the public. Admission charge.

BUÇACO: Take the winding road through Buçaco Forest, a park founded in 1628 by Carmelite monks. In the center of the forest a royal hunting lodge, built from 1888 to 1907 by Carlos I, has been transformed into the *Palace* hotel (see *Best en Route*). This incredible structure was designed in a pastiche of Manueline styles and is highly ornamented. A table on the round, elaborately decorated porch overlooking the gardens provides an enchanting setting for lunch or dinner. Adjacent to the hotel stands a 17th-century Carmelite monastery, chapel, and cloister open to visitors. The olive tree in the driveway marks the spot where the Duke of Wellington tied up his horse on the eve of winning a great victory over French invaders in 1810. The well-maintained forest has myriad trails for good hiking.

En Route from Buçaco – Retrace through Luso to Mealhada to pick up N1 north. Along the way you'll see numerous shops carrying copper and brass wares. On the road from Buçaco there are more than a dozen restaurants which specialize in *leitão a bairrada* (suckling pig roasted on a spit) accompanied by a variety of regional vegetables. Also offered is a champagne-like wine called *espumante* — both white and red — which is delicious when chilled. If you have time turn off at Agueda for a side trip to Aveiro. This coastal fishing village, inhabited since the 11th century, is on a saltwater lagoon, crisscrossed by canals and surrounded by weedy marshes and sand flats. Fishing, seaweed gathering, and ceramic and china manufacturing are the chief industries. During July and August, there are colorful *moliceiro* (seaweed-gathering boat) races on the lagoon. Aveiro also has one of Portugal's most impressive museums, the 15th-century *Convento de Jesus*. It contains many paintings and religious artworks, as well as the tomb of Princess Joana, a member of the convent famed for her piety.

Some 34 miles (54 km) farther up the coast on N109 is the popular resort, Espinho. Featuring a vast swimming pool complex, facilities for all water sports, a fine golf course, clay pigeon shooting, and a casino, Espinho is purely for fun. N109 leads into the superhighway approach to Porto, the second largest city in Portugal.

PORTO: Its history dating from the 8th century BC, the region known as Portucale was given to Henri of Burgundy in 1095 as part of the dowry of Princess Teresa. Developed as an important trading center with northern Europe, the area of Portucale eventually gave its name to the entire country after figuring prominently in the struggle for independence. Porto, known as Oporto in English, became the base of the Portuguese shipping fleet, which evolved into a formidable maritime power.

Cross the Douro River via Ponte Dom Luis I; the lodges of Vila Nova da Gaia, storehouses of the world-famous port wine, lie below the bridges. Narrow streets, heavy traffic, and many one-way signs contribute to the difficulties the driver may encounter in trying to find the way to the central parking location, Praça do Humberto Delgado. The easiest, most comfortable way to see this tightly built industrial town is to take a *Cityrama Bus* tour, which will include a stop at the wine center across the Douro. Principal places of interest include the 12th-century cathedral, Terreiro da Sé (on Cathedral Sq.); the Igreja de São Francisco, a Gothic church with a richly decorated interior (Rua Infante Dom Henrique); and the *Museu Soares dos Reis* (Rua de Dom Manuel II; open 10 AM to noon and 2 to 5 PM; closed Mondays and holidays; admission charge except on weekends), where the exhibits include early paintings, sculpture, pottery, and religious works of art. Many shops display silver, gold, and filigree jewelry, leather goods, and locally made ceramics. Some of the best restaurants are *Portucale, Orfeu, Escondidinho,* and the *Comercial* (see *Best en Route*). With meals, everyone drinks the ultra-dry *vinho verde* wines from the Minho region and the fuller, red table wines from the Douro and Dão regions. For before and after meals, there are various ports.

En Route from Porto – The N14 heads north 20 miles (32 km) through vineyards and cornfields to Vila Nova de Famalicão, where you pick up N103 to Barcelos. This attractive town is known for its painted rooster, which has become a popular symbol of Portugal. According to legend, a pilgrim from Galicia, Spain, was staying at the home of a Barcelos judge when the house was robbed. He was unjustly accused of the crime and sentenced to hang. He asked to see the judge who was at dinner and eating a rooster. The pilgrim said to the judge: "May that rooster rise up and crow if I am innocent." It did, and he was set free. Barcelos has a lively Thursday market where you can buy handmade rugs, laces, ceramics, brightly enameled figurines, as well as housewares and blue jeans. The ruined Ducal Palace houses an archaeological exhibit and ceramics museum (open 10 AM to 6 PM; until 5 PM in the winter). The 17 miles (27 km) along N14 to Viana do Castelo is a lovely drive. The entire region is known for its good hunting and fishing as well as for its fairs and religious pilgrimages. A list of these activities is available at the Barcelos Tourist Office (phone: 53-811882), on Largo da Porta Nova.

VIANA DO CASTELO: This fishing port and holiday resort is nicely situated, with a seascape, river bank, and hillside. One of the most famous festivals in the country, *Festa da Nossa Senhora da Agonia,* is held here each year during the third week of August, when the townspeople don their colorful embroidered costumes and gold jewelry to take part in the activities. A former 18th-century palace, the *Museu Municipal* (Rua Manuel Espregueira; open 9:30 AM to noon and 2 to 5 PM; closed Mondays and holidays; admission charge) houses a fine exhibit of tiles, furniture, pottery, and ceramics. The cobbled Praça da República holds some of the city's most impressive buildings, including the delightful, 16th-century Renaissance Igreja da Misericórdia. Follow the signs for Santa Luzia, up a winding road through pine and eucalyptus, to the Basilica of Santa Luzia for a dazzling view of the entire region.

En Route from Viana do Castelo – Follow Highway 203 along the Lima River to Ponte de Lima, a town with a fine Roman and medieval bridge and many 16th- and 17th-century manor houses. Some of these — the Conde de Aurora, for example — are open to the public. For dinner, try lamprey stuffed with rice, a regional specialty.

VALENÇA: In spite of strong fortifications, this town of old stone houses and cobblestone streets was once at the mercy of Spanish invaders. The 13th-century castle at the far end of town has been handsomely reshaped into a modern inn, *Pousada de São Teotónio* (see *Best en Route*). The 17th-century ramparts open on an incomparable view of the Minho Valley and the Spanish mountains beyond. Shops in town carry a good selection of sweaters and embroidered bedspreads.

En Route from Valença – Passing through the gate, turn left down the hill to N101, then it's 11 miles (18 km) to Monção. This walled town is an attractive base from which to explore the Peneda-Gerês National Park. The National Forest Department can arrange guided excursions through the park, so you can see its many wild horses and boars. Nearby at Bretiandos and Briteiros there are pre-Celtic, Iron Age ruins. A comfortable inn, *Albergaria Atlántico* (13 Rua General Pimenta de Castro, Monção; phone: 51-652355), has a decent dining room with a nice view. There is also a pleasant *pousada, Pousada de São Bento* (see *Best en Route*), at Caniçada at one of the entrances to the park.

The N101 now begins its journey 46 miles (74 km) south to Braga. Take a look at the stately palace of Brejoeira, before the ascent on the shady mountain road, and stop off in Ponte da Barca to sample its white, dry, "green" wines. For a more comfortable if less adventurous ride, the new A4 leads from Porto to Campo, 5½ miles (9 km) from Braga.

BRAGA: Founded in the 5th century by the Romans, conquered by Visigoths and Moors, this ancient city has developed into a visibly prosperous industrial center. Liberated from the Moors by a Spanish king and French crusaders, Braga became part of the dowry of the king's daughter, Dona Teresa, when she married a French nobleman in 1095. Early on, it became the religious center of Portugal, home of its archbishops. Over the centuries many monuments, churches, and palaces were erected by the bishops; during the 18th century Braga became the center of baroque art in Portugal. The highly decorated 12th-century Sé Catedral contains a museum of sacred art and the tombs of its founders, Henri of Burgundy and Dona Teresa. Among the buildings of notable architectural design are the Antigo Paço Episcopal church overlooking the Jardim de Santa Bárbara, the nearby Town Hall, and the 13th-century castle and keep. Many of the old buildings are artfully lit in the evenings. A religious festival is held during *Holy Week,* and the *Nativity of St. John* is celebrated for 3 days starting on June 23. Every Tuesday there is a market on the edge of town where you can buy handcrafted articles from artisans of the region.

En Route from Braga – Some 3 miles (5 km) from Braga on N103.3 is the monumental baroque staircase that leads to the 18th-century sanctuary of Bom Jesus do Monte. This curious stairway is adorned with chapels and statuary depicting figures from the Passion. Mount the steps as the pilgrims do or reach the top by funicular or motor car for a spectacular view from the church plaza. Take N101 south to Guimarães.

GUIMARÃES: This attractive, busy town is known as the cradle of the Portuguese nation. Foundations for the village were begun in the 10th century with the construction of a monastery. In 1095 the village was presented to Henri of Burgundy by his father-in-law Alfonso VI, King of León and Castile. The great Castelo, whose keep dates from the 10th century, was the birthplace of Afonso Henriques who became the first King of Portugal. Nearby is the tiny Romanesque Church of St. Michael and beyond, the 15th-century palace of the Dukes of Bragança. Visit the Romanesque Igreja Nossa Senhora da Oliveira and its cloister exhibition, *Museu Alberto Sampaio.* Just below the town park lies the Igreja São Francisco whose interior flaunts an ornately carved and gilded baroque altar; old tiles decorate the walls of the chancel. Walk to the old section of town on the Rua Santa Maria, lined with 14th- and 15th-century houses. Hand-embroidered linen is a specialty of this area.

En Route from Guimarães – This 22-mile (35-km) stretch of N101 to Amarante is populated by lace makers whose wares are spread out at the side of the road. Located along the banks of the Tamega River, Amarante is the home of a 13th-century saint, Gonçalo; the town boasts many old churches, the most impressive of which is the Church and Monastery of São Gonçalo beside the 18th-century stone bridge of the same name. After crossing the Tamega River, turn left onto N15, which wends slowly up into the stern but grand Serra do Marão. Halfway (18 miles/29 km) to Vila Real is the *Pousada de São Gonçalo* (phone: 55-461113), a good place for a lunch break.

VILA REAL–MATEUS: Proceed through Vila Real, following the signs for Murça and Sabrosa on N322 to Mateus, home of the famous rosé wine. At the Mateus Manor, visit the imposing 18th-century baroque residence, so familiar from the label on its wine bottles. Still owned by the Counts of Vila Real, the manor contains old Portuguese furnishings, family portraits, and cases full of mementos, memorabilia, toys, and personal effects. Visitors can see the chapel and gardens, but the vineyards can only be viewed from a distance.

En Route from Vila Real – There are a few alternatives from here. If you have a flexible schedule, the N2 north of Vila Real links notable spa towns — Vidago, with its parks and woodland and the *Vidago Palace* hotel (see *Best en Route*); and Chaves, an old town with a Roman bridge, 17th-century ramparts, a castle with a 14th-century keep, and a spa.

A longer drive on N15 from Vila Real ambles through a vast mountain region for 86 miles (138 km) to Bragança, whose walled medieval city and towering 12th-century castle keep dominate the lower modern town. Just outside the town is the *Pousada São Bartolomeu* (phone: 73-22493), pleasant for an overnight stay.

If your time is more limited, continue on N2 into the deep vales and terraced mountain vineyards of the great port wine producing region. Cross the Douro River at Régua, and wind your way through the valley where the grapevines cling to the nearly perpendicular terraced hillsides that drop down to the river to Lamego.

LAMEGO: This is a neatly arranged town of 16th- and 18th-century houses. The Cortes, a representative body of nobles, clergy, and townspeople, met here in 1143 to acknowledge Afonso Henriques as King of Portugal and implement the royal right of succession to the throne. In the *Museu de Lamego*, a former 18th-century bishop's palace, early paintings, tapestries, and 16th- to 18th-century tiles are on display. Several churches of note are the Sé, which dates from the 12th century; the Igreja do Desterro, with fine interior decoration (ask for admission at 148 Calçada do Desterro); and the Santuario Nossa Senhora dos Remédios, a baroque edifice whose impressive staircase is embellished with an unusual arrangement of pinnacles and ornamental tiling. Lamego also is known for its smoked ham and all kinds of sausages.

VISEU: Farther south on N2 is this important agricultural and crafts center. Sixteenth-century residences and 18th-century balconied town houses line the narrow streets of the old section. The cathedral on the Praça da Sé has an interesting cloister and gallery of sacred art. Also worth a look is the *Museu Grão Vasco* (Baço dos 3 Ascaloes; phone: 32-26249), which contains paintings from the 16th-century Viseu school and representative works of old and new Portuguese artists.

En Route from Viseu – The best route to complete the circle to Porto is N16 west to N1 north at Albergaria-a-Velha and straight on to Porto (84 miles/134 km). Otherwise you can head south to Tomar along N2, N234, N1, and N110, where you can pick up the central route at its northernmost point.

BEST EN ROUTE

Expect to pay $90 to $150 for a double room per night in a hotel in the expensive category, $40 to $90 in the moderate, and $30 to $40 in the inexpensive category. A dinner for two people with local wine will cost $70 and up in the expensive range, about $50 in the moderate, and $30 in the inexpensive range. Prices do not include drinks, wine, or tips.

OBIDOS

A Ilustre Casa de Ramiro – Decorated in Moorish style with an open hearth, this very special eatery serves steaks, codfish, and a variety of international dishes. Closed Wednesdays. Visa and American Express accepted. Rua Porta do Vale (phone: 62-959194). Expensive to moderate.

Estalagem do Convento – A delightfully converted convent, it has 13 rooms with antique-style furnishings. The beamed-ceiling dining room specializes in regional fare. Open daily. Reservations advised. Major credit cards accepted. Rua Dr. João de Ornelas (phone: 62-959217; fax: 62-959159). Moderate.

Pousada do Castelo – Originally a 16th-century palace, this inn on the ramparts has regional decor, 6 rooms, and a rustically elegant dining room with country and international cooking; bar. Open daily. Reservations advised. Most major credit cards accepted. Paço Real (phone: 62-959105 or 62-959146). Moderate.

SÃO MARTINHO DO PORTO

Parque – This spacious mansion-style hotel has 44 rooms in a garden setting. Only breakfast is served; no restaurant. Avenida Marechal Carmona (phone: 62-989506). Inexpensive.

NAZARÉ

Mar Bravo – It has regional fare and good (but expensive) seafood, plus a panoramic view to recommend it. Open daily. Major credit cards accepted. Praça Sousa Oliveira (phone: 62-551180). Expensive to moderate.

Nazaré – A modern 50-room hotel with a restaurant (open daily), bar, and a nightclub. Largo Afonso Zuquete (phone: 62-661311; fax: 62-553238). Inexpensive.

Praia – Another modern hotel (with 40 rooms), it is on a main street near the beach. Breakfast only. 39 Avenida Vieira Guimarães (phone: 62-551423). Inexpensive.

LEIRIA

Dom João III – Near the market, this 64-room hotel has a restaurant (open daily) and bar. Avenida Heróis de Angola (phone: 44-812500; fax: 44-812235). Moderate.

Euro-Sol – Nicely landscaped, this attractive, modern, 54-room hilltop hotel has an outdoor pool, an exceptional top-floor dining room (open daily), and a bar. Rua D. José Alves Correia da Silva (phone: 44-812201; fax: 44-811205). Moderate.

BATALHA

Pousada do Mestre Afonso Domingues – Sparkling and gracious, this inn near Batalha's church — one of Portugal's most renowned monuments — has 21 rooms, air conditioning, and a pleasant dining room (open daily). Reservations advised. Major credit cards accepted. Batalha (phone: 44-96260). Moderate.

COIMBRA

Dom Luis – Located on a hill across the river from the city, this new hostelry has 105 rooms and suites, satellite TV, and a restaurant (open daily) offering fine food and a panoramic view. Banhos Secos (phone: 39-442510; fax: 39-813196). Moderate.

Dom Pedro – Good regional and international cuisine is served at this elegantly rustic restaurant. Open daily. Reservations unnecessary. MasterCard and Visa accepted. 58 Avenida Emidio Navarro (phone: 39-29108). Moderate.

LUSO

Estalagem do Luso – This lovely guesthouse has 7 artfully furnished rooms and a dining room (open daily). Rua Dr. Lúcio Pais Abranches (phone: 31-93114; fax: 31-93668). Moderate.

Grande Hotel das Termas – Surrounded by gardens and parks, this large resort hotel has 157 rooms, a spacious dining room (open daily), and a bar. Facilities include a huge outdoor pool, a spa, tennis, a casino, and a nightclub. Open from June till mid-October. Major credit cards accepted. Rua dos Banhos (phone: 31-93450; fax: 31-93668). Moderate.

BUÇACO

Palace Hotel do Buçaco – Forest, park, and gardens surround this magnificent former royal hunting lodge that features Manueline decorations, fine furniture, 70 luxurious bedrooms, a bar, and a splendid dining room (open daily). Floresta do Buçaco (phone: 31-93101). Expensive.

AVEIRO

Pousada da Ria – Overlooking the lagoon and town, this balconied inn has 10 comfortable rooms, a swimming pool, a dining room with regional cooking (open daily), and bar. Torreira-Murtosa (phone: 34-48332; fax: 34-48333). Moderate.

ESPINHO

Praiagolfe – A modern beach hotel with 199 air conditioned rooms, restaurant (open daily), bar, nightclub, a large outdoor pool, and an adjacent golf course. Rua 6 (phone: 2-720630; fax: 2-720888). Moderate.

PORTO

Infante de Sagres – An oasis in the midst of a busy city, this luxury hotel has 84 pleasant rooms, a grand dining room with attentive service(open daily), and elaborately decorated lounges. 62 Praça Dona Filipa de Lencastre (phone: 2-200-8101; fax: 2-314937). Expensive.

Sheraton – With 253 rooms and all the customary amenities of the chain, this is away from the town center. 1269 Avenida Boavista (phone: 2-668822; fax: 2-691467). Expensive.

Portucale – On the 13th floor of the *Albergaria Miradouro*, this first-rate restaurant offers splendid views and international and regional cuisine. Open daily. Reservations necessary. Major credit cards accepted. 598 Rua da Alegria (phone: 2-570717). Expensive.

Orfeu – A modern surf and turf establishment with wood paneling and soft piped-in music. It's favored by fish lovers, particularly cod enthusiasts. Open daily. Reservations advised. Most major credit cards accepted. 928 Rua Júlio Dinis (phone: 2-64322). Expensive to moderate.

Escondidinho – The best regional food in the city is served at this popular restaurant. Tiles, marble, and local crafts decorate the inside, while outside it looks like a typical country house — which makes it stand out in an otherwise modern urban street. Closed Sundays. Reservations necessary. Visa and MasterCard accepted. 144 Rua Passos Manuel (phone: 2-200-1079). Moderate.

Tivoli-Porto-Atlántico – A supermodern complex beyond the city center, it has 58 air conditioned rooms, indoor and outdoor pools, shops, and restaurants. 66 Rua Afonso Lopes Vieira, off E5 (phone: 2-694941; fax: 2-667452). Moderate.

Tuela – An excellent modern hotel with 200 air conditioned rooms, a restaurant, and bar, it's in a reasonably central location. 200 Rua Arquitecto Marquês da Silva (phone: 2-600-4744; fax: 2-610-3709). Inexpensive.

VIANA DO CASTELO

Parque – This modern 120-room hotel overlooking the Lima River has inviting grounds, spacious lounges, a heated pool, a rooftop restaurant with regional and international cuisine (open daily), and a bar. Praça da Galiza (phone: 58-828605; fax: 58-828612). Moderate.

Santa Luzia – High above town, this 42-room hotel surrounded by a park and gardens has an Old World atmosphere and modern amenities — heated pool, tennis courts, excellent restaurant (open daily), terrace with a stunning view, and a bar. Monte de Santa Luzia (phone: 58-828889; fax: 58-828892). Moderate.

VALENÇA

Pousada de São Teotónio – This modern inn at the edge of a walled town has 16 nice rooms, an airy dining room (open daily), good food, and a bar. There's a gorgeous view from the terrace. Valença do Minho (phone: 51-824242; fax: 51-824242). Moderate.

BRAGA

Do Parque – Set in the woods near the Bom Jesus Sanctuary, this 49-room hostelry has been nicely restored to its original 9th-century style and furnished with unique paintings and antiques. Its restaurant is open daily. Bom Jesus do Monte (phone: 53-676548; fax: 53-676679). Moderate.

Inácio – Tasty regional cooking is served in this popular restaurant, whose ambience is enhanced by stone walls and rough beams. Open daily. Reservations advised. Major credit cards accepted. 4 Campo das Hortas (phone: 53-13235). Moderate.

Turismo – Conveniently located on a main street, this modern hostelry has a spacious interior, 93 air conditioned rooms, a pool, a bar, restaurant (open daily), and shops. Avenida da Liberdade (phone and fax: 53-612200). Moderate.

CANIÇADA

Pousada de São Bento – Stone walls, spectacular views, 10 rooms with rustic decor, a dining room with good, hearty, regional cooking (open daily), and an outdoor pool are found at this inn. Cerdeirinhas-Soengas Caniçada (phone: 53-647190; fax: 53-647867). Moderate.

GUIMARÃES

Pousada de Santa Marinha da Costa – A 15th-century royal country palace with 59 rooms, immaculately restored and furnished, on a hill overlooking the town. Banha de Guimarães (phone and fax: 53-418453). Expensive.

Jordão – Below the movie theater of the same name, this spacious, busy restaurant serves a variety of international and regional dishes. Closed Monday evenings and Tuesdays. Reservations advised. 62 Avenida Afonso Henriques (phone: 53-40198; fax: 53-516498). Moderate.

VIDAGO

Vidago Palace – This pleasant, turn-of-the-century, 122-room hotel is in a tranquil setting with gardens, a pool, tennis, and a golf course. Breakfast is served. Parque (phone: 67-97358). Inexpensive.

LAMEGO

Parque – Set on the grounds of the Nossa Senhora dos Remedios Sanctuary above the city is this completely renovated 19th-century hostelry. There's an excellent restaurant that's open daily (phone: 54-62105; fax: 54-65203). Moderate.

VISEU

Grão Vasco – In attractive gardens in the town center, this spacious hostelry has 86 rooms (with another 24 under construction at press time), an outdoor swimming pool, a discotheque, and central heating. The restaurant (open daily) serves meals on the garden terrace in good weather. Rua Gaspar Barreiros (phone: 32-423511; fax: 32-27047). Moderate.

O Cortiço – An excellent restaurant in the medieval part of town, it serves dishes based on old local recipes, whose details are kept secret. Specialties include *arroz caqueirado,* a veal-and-rice dish; *coelho bêbado,* made from wine-fed ("drunken") rabbits; and *bacalhau podre,* a tasty dish worthy of a better name than this, which means "rotten codfish"! Open for lunch and dinner daily except *Christmas.* Reservations necessary. Major credit cards accepted. 43 Rua Augusto Hilário (phone: 32-423853). Moderate.

Central Portugal

This route originates in Lisbon and loops around central Portugal through an area of rolling plains crisscrossed by rivers and known for cork and olive oil production. The bold reds of the stripped tree trunks along the way attest to the wealth of cork growing here. Central Portugal offers much of interest. In Tomar the magnificent Convento de Cristo, a fortified castle and convent, blends styles of architecture from the 12th through the 17th century. Next, the route swings through Marvão, a medieval village, and through three of Portugal's most engaging towns: Elvas, where a 15th-century aqueduct still carries water to the town; Estremoz, whose artisans are famous for their pottery figurines of people and animals; and Evora, where you can see a Roman temple dating from the 2nd century.

LISBON: For a detailed report on the capital, its hotels and restaurants, see *Lisbon,* THE CITIES. From Lisbon pick up the A1 toll highway for the 41-mile (65-km) trip to Santarém.

SANTARÉM: Founded in 10 BC by Iberian King Abidis, taken from the Moors in 1147 by Afonso Henriques, Santarém once was the royal residence. This busy little district capital now is the center of bull breeding for Portugal's bullfighting. The *Igreja de São João de Alporão* (Rua Serpa Pinto) serves as an archaeological museum with a diverse assortment of Arabian and Romanesque objects, sculpture, coats of arms, and the Flamboyant Gothic tomb of the Count of Viana (open 10 AM to noon and 2:30 to 5 PM; closed Mondays; admission charge). The 14th-century Gothic Igreja da Graça has a particularly attractive carved doorway crowned by a magnificent rose window.

En Route from Santarém – Cross the Tagus River on N114 for Alpiarça in order to visit the lovely *Museu Casa dos Patudos,* former residence of José Relvas, statesman and art patron. The collection includes 17th- and 19th-century tapestries and carpets, china, paintings, and furnishings (open Thursdays, Saturdays, and Sundays from 10 AM to 12:20 PM and 2 to 6 PM; admission charge). Follow N118 to N243, recrossing the Tagus to N365. Turn onto N113 for the 35 miles (56 km) to Tomar.

TOMAR: Founded by the Order of the Templars on the River Nabão, this town is crowned by the magnificent Convento de Cristo. The Templars started building the fortified castle and convent in 1160 but construction was not completed until the 17th century. This beautiful monument combines several styles of architecture with the ornate Gothic entrance, the rotunda modeled after the Holy Sepulcher in Jerusalem, the Italian Renaissance cloister, and the fanciful Manueline window seen from an upper terrace of the Cloister Santa Bárbara. Halfway down the hill from the convent, there is a good view from the plaza of the Renaissance Capela de Nossa Senhora da Conceição. The 15th-century Igreja de São João Baptista (Praça República) has a Manueline belfry and a notable interior. Tomar also has a lovely city garden with a lagoon for boating and an old water mill.

En Route from Tomar – The village of Abrantes has a ruined castle-fortress with a splendid view from its belvedere.

CASTELO DE VIDE: This is an appealing spa town of prehistoric origins with whitewashed houses and winding alleys. Because of the supposedly wondrous quality of the waters and the lack of intense heat, it is popular with tourists. The castle, rebuilt in 1299 and restored in 1710, provides a marvelous view from its keep. The old Judiaria

(Jewish) quarter has many houses with interesting Gothic doorways, and there are numerous charming 17th- and 18th-century buildings.

MARVÃO: Firmly established atop a rough hill sits the medieval village of Marvão, a stronghold fought over during the civil war of 1828–34. Follow signs to Marvão-Beria, wending up the steep incline to the rampart gateway. Either park outside the walls or drive to Pillory Square. Walk to the summit, enter through four gateways, and climb the stairs to the parapets leading to the castle keep. On the hilltop, *Pousada de Santa Maria* is a simple friendly inn with a dining room overlooking a panorama of mountains and the Spanish border (see *Best en Route*).

PORTALEGRE: Once a center of tapestry manufacturing and silk production, the 17th- and 18th-century mansions of this attractive town attest to past prosperity. Notable buildings include the cathedral, Largo da Sé, and the tapestry workshops in the old Jesuit monastery (Rua Guilherme Gomes Fernandes).

ELVAS: The great Aqueduto da Amoreira joins the impressive ramparts of this old village and carries water to the inhabitants as it has since the 15th century. Turn into the viaduct gateway and proceed to the mosaic tile, tree-lined Praça da República. Walking around this area, you can see the Igreja de Nossa Senhora da Assunção with its imposing marble chancel, the tile-faced Igreja Nossa Senhora da Consolação, and the castle in the northwest corner of the ramparts, which dates from Moorish times. The military bastion of Forte de Nossa Senhora da Graça on a hill north of the town and the Forte de Santa Luzia to the south complete the fortifications.

ESTREMOZ: This old hilltop village of red-roofed white houses rises from the plains. The ancient cobbled streets, 13th-century keep, tiled castle chapel, 17th-century walls, and Igreja Santa Maria's collection of primitive paintings are of greatest interest. The village is a fine place for an evening walk.

The artisans of Estremoz, a well-known pottery center since the 16th century, are especially recognized for their unusual pottery figurines depicting people and their animals in scenes of everyday life. You'll also see beautiful objects made of marble from the local quarries.

EVORA: This town is one of the oldest settlements on the Iberian Peninsula. Follow the "centro" signs and park on the Praça do Giraldo or continue on to the *Pousada dos Lóios* (phone: 66-24051 or 66-24052) and park there. The 2nd-century Templo Romano is one of the most remarkable reminders of the Roman past in Portugal. Evora was a center of learning in the 15th century. Its old university — now a public high school — has an *aula magna* (large assembly hall) entirely covered with 17th-century tiles. The Sé (Cathedral) is particularly interesting for its variety of architectural styles and adornments and for the contents of the treasury. This rich collection includes ecclesiastical objects and old illuminated books and manuscripts. The *Museu Regional,* adjacent to the Sé in a former 16th-century episcopal palace, houses ancient sculpture and primitive paintings (open 9 AM to noon and 2 to 5 PM; closed Mondays; admission charge). The venerated 16th-century Igreja de São Francisco on Praça 28 de Maio, built in the Gothic Manueline style, has a chapel constructed of human skulls and bones. This oddity was conceived by the Franciscan monks as an incentive to their fellow brothers to meditate on the transitory nature of life.

En Route from Evora – From here you can complete the circle by returning to Lisbon or heading south for the Algarve. If you are returning to Lisbon, go via Setúbal to Palmela and Sesimbra for visits to their three castles, for swimming and deep-sea fishing, and for splendid views from the Arrabida Mountains. The entire Arrabida Peninsula once belonged to the Dukes of Palmela, but it is now a national park. Its flora is unique in Europe, somewhat comparable to Corsica and the Ardennes.

SETÚBAL: For centuries an important commercial port, Setúbal sits at the mouth of the Sado River, which is noted for its extensive beds of giant oysters. The *Castelo* *de São Filipe* (see *Best en Route*), built during Spanish domination, sits above the city and now is a fine *pousada*.

Just across the water and easily reached by car ferry or Hovercraft is the Troia Peninsula with 20 miles of fine sand beaches for swimming, surfing, and skin diving. A tourist complex with hotels, nightclubs, modern shops, and a golf course bustles, but doesn't intrude upon upon what Hans Christian Andersen once called "a terrestrial paradise." The Troia Peninsula is steeped in history and legend — ruins of a Roman fish factory and chapel have been excavated.

PALMELA: Located 6 miles (10 km) above Setúbal in a region famous for its muscatel wines, Palmela has a royal residence and a 12th-century fortress, transformed into a splendid 25-room *pousada* (see *Best en Route*).

SESIMBRA: At the southern foothills of the Arrabida Mountains facing south on a wide bay lies Sesimbra, an old fishing village with the amenities of a modern tourist resort. Unfortunately, unbridled development has destroyed much of the fishing village ambience, and summers are very crowded. There are very good fish restaurants, however, which specialize in grilled red mullet, sea bass, and sardines. If you prefer to catch your own dinner, rent a boat with a professional guide at the docks. The ruins of Sesimbra Castle, overlooking the town, were once a Moorish stronghold.

En Route from Sesimbra – Stop off in Vila Nogueira de Azeitão, home of Lancers rosé wines and, more importantly for wine buffs, the home of one of Europe's finest sweet dessert wines — Fonseca's Setúbal muscatel. You can sample both at the Lancers winery and at the company's old wine cellars down the road where Setúbal muscatels are aged.

BEST EN ROUTE

Expect to pay $110 and up per night for a double room in a hotel in the expensive category, $60 to $110 in the moderate, and $55 and under in the inexpensive category. A dinner for two people with local wine will cost $70 and up in the expensive range, about $40 to $60 in the moderate, and $35 in the inexpensive range. Prices do not include drinks or tips. Major credit cards are accepted at all places below, unless otherwise indicated.

SANTARÉM

O Mal Cozinhado – One of Santarém's most popular and attractive restaurants, where the food and atmosphere are regional. Open daily. Reservations advised. No credit cards accepted. Campo da Feira (phone: 43-23584). Inexpensive.

TOMAR

Pousada de São Pedro – Overlooking Portugal's largest reservoir, 8 miles (13 km) from Tomar, this quiet inn has 15 rooms, a dining room with views of the dam and Zêzere River. Castelo do Bode, on N358 (phone: 49-381159). Moderate.

Templários – On landscaped grounds next to a river park, this modern hotel with small town tranquillity has 84 air conditioned rooms with balconies, a swimming pool, tennis, very good food, and a bar. Reserve odd-numbered rooms for fabulous evening views. 1 Largo Cândido dos Reis (phone: 49-312121; fax: 49-312191). Moderate.

MARVÃO

Pousada de Santa Maria – On a mountainside in an ancient walled town, this inn has 9 small, neat rooms, country decor, and a dining room offering wide views, simple regional cooking, and a bar. Marvão (phone: 45-93201). Moderate.

ELVAS

Pousada de Santa Luzia – Just off the main road stands this attractive air conditioned inn with 11 rooms and an inviting dining room serving fine regional and international cuisine; bar. Avenida de Badajoz, on N4 (phone: 68-622128). Moderate.

ESTREMOZ

Pousada da Rainha Santa Isabel – In a medieval palace in the Old Town, this grand luxury hotel has 23 large rooms with spectacular views and canopy beds, a lofty dining room with excellent regional food, a bar, a chapel, and an inner patio. Largo Dom Dinis (phone: 68-22618; fax: 68-23982). Expensive.

EVORA

Cozinho de Santo Humberto – The regional dishes and game are excellent here. Open daily. Reservations advised. 39 Rua da Moeda (phone: 66-24251). Expensive.

Fialho – The most celebrated restaurant in the region, it's especially renowned for its game dishes. Closed Mondays. Reservations advised. 16 Travessa das Mascarenhas (phone: 66-23079). Expensive.

Pousada dos Lóios – This elegantly restored convent still has many original details and 28 compact, attractively furnished rooms. The dining room (built around the cloister) serves regional food prepared according to old convent recipes. There's also a breakfast room and a bar. Largo Conde de Vila Flor (phone: 66-24051; fax: 66-27248). Expensive.

BEJA

Luís da Rocha – A busy but simple restaurant that serves decent food at modest prices. Open daily. Reservations advised. 63 Rua Capitão João Francisco de Sousa (phone: 84-23267). Inexpensive.

SETÚBAL

Pousada de São Filipe – Built within old castle walls, this rustically furnished inn has 15 rooms, a dining room serving regional specialties, and a bar. Setúbal (phone: 65-523844). Expensive.

A Roda – A small place, it serves some of the best regional cooking in town. Closed Sundays. Reservations advised. 7 Travessa Postigo do Cais (phone: 65-29264). Moderate.

PALMELA

Pousada de Palmela – In an imposing 12th-century castle that stands on the crest of a high hill, this flagship of the state-owned *pousadas* has 27 air conditioned rooms, each with a spectacular view of the sea and the countryside. There is a fine restaurant, serving excellent game dishes, and a bar. Castelo de Palmela (phone: 1-235-1395; fax: 1-235-0410). Expensive.

SESIMBRA

Espadarte – A 79-room hotel right on the beach, convenient for fishing. Esplanada Comandante Tenreiro (phone: 1-223-3189). Moderate.

Mar – Built into the side of a hill overlooking the sea, there are 120 rooms with private baths and balconies, a commanding view, plus a swimming pool, bars, and a disco. 10 Rua General Humberto Delgado (phone: 1-223-3326; fax: 1-223-3888). Moderate.

The Algarve

The Algarve has been a favorite holiday area with Europeans for many years, and now beach-loving Americans have begun vacationing on the southern coast of Portugal. Fine sandy beaches, edged by gigantic sandstone cliffs, offer long stretches of untrammeled shore, as well as tiny hidden coves. Strung along the coast are luxury hotels and attractive first and second class establishments. In addition to resort complexes there are small fishing villages and simple residential areas.

The best of many worlds is available in the Algarve, from sophisticated nightlife to seaside solitude. The sports enthusiast will find excellent facilities for tennis, golf, riding, fishing, water skiing, windsurfing, and boating. Shoppers will find a wide selection of fine hand-crafted articles — pottery, embroidery, knitwear, and jewelry. Festivals take place throughout the year. There are many excellent restaurants that serve seafood and regional specialties as well as international cuisine.

The best time to visit the Algarve is from the end of January, when the almond trees are in blossom, through the summer until the end of October. But the Algarve really is a year-round resort, as the weather never is very cold by European standards.

The route traced below follows the coast from Vila Real de Santo António in the east to Cabo de São Vicente in the west along N125 for a distance of some 100 miles (160 km). The two-lane road is not a coastal route — in order to reach the beach resorts turn off at the sign for each destination. Although little byways sometimes lead from one beach settlement to another, they often are poorly marked and surfaced.

The most interesting features of the Algarve lie west of Portimão, where the landscape softens into tree-covered rolling hills dotted with small farms. You pass little painted donkey carts on the road and catch glimpses of the sea. As you approach the turnoff for Sagres, N268, the terrain becomes more rugged. At this spectacular route's end lies the famous school of Henry the Navigator.

PRAIA DE MONTE GORDO: A long flat stretch of beach and several first class hotels make this town a great place to vacation. The early-14th-century ruined castle of the Knights of Christ is an interesting historical site in Castro Marim, west on N125.6.

TAVIRA: This fishing village is built on both shores of the Rio Gilão. A Greek settlement in 380 BC, the town was later conquered by the Goths and Moors. The foundations of the bridge date from Roman times and there is a ruined 13th-century castle. Thanks to a local council that banned construction that might erode the historic quality of the town, expanded tourism hasn't changed Tavira's charm.

OLHÃO: Founded by fishermen in the 18th century, life in this town of cube-shape white houses revolves around its fishing port. Fresh produce and local handicrafts are sold in the local market.

FARO: The capital of the Algarve was an important Moorish city, taken by Afonso III in 1249 to end Arab domination in Portugal. The Old Town, surrounded by ancient houses and parts of the defensive walls, has two museums and the Sé (on Largo da Sé), the interior of which is decorated with 17th-century tiles. In the *Ethnological Museum* (Rua Ataide de Oliveira), an English-speaking guide gives explanations of the historical and folkloric displays. The *Museu Marítimo,* in the old office of the captain of the port on the *Doca* (marina), exhibits model ships and fishing boats. If possible, take a boat excursion through the Ria Formosa marshlands of Faro, where a guide will point out fiddler crabs, egrets, storks, and other beach denizens. Day trips include bird watching and lunch on Ilha de Faro, an island beach.

LOULÉ: High in the hills above Faro, this little center of handicrafts is a good place to shop for pottery, brassware, copper, basketry, and so on. A market in the center of town (open mornings, except Sunday), has tackier items than in recent years (e.g., Rambo dolls), but unbelievable bargains still are available. *La Réserve,* in Santa Bárbara de Nexe, off the road between Faro and Loulé, is a good place to dine (see *Best en Route*).

ALMANSIL–VALE DO LOBO: This lovely recreation area surrounds one of the Algarve's most illustrious resort hotels, *Dona Filipa* (see *Best en Route*). There's also a well-designed residential area.

QUARTEIRA: Once a quiet fishing village, this is now a busy, fast-growing resort town with a superb beach.

VILAMOURA: This highly developed vacation and tourist center stretches from the sea to N125. Vilamoura has a large yacht marina and an excellent golf course.

ALBUFEIRA: The heart of the tourist's Algarve, this large resort town has a Moorish ambience that belies its diverse resort activities and sophisticated nightlife. The last town to be taken from the Moors in 1250, there is nothing left here of historical value but it is pleasing to walk around town or watch the return of the fishing boats and explore the caves and grottoes along the beach. There's good shopping for handicrafts and antiques.

ARMAÇÃO DE PERA: This old fishing village lies between sandstone cliffs. You can take boat excursions to the caves and grottoes along the shore.

LAGOA: A typical Algarvean market town, founded in the 15th century on the site of a much earlier Roman settlement. Shopping is the highlight at this crafts center; you also can visit the Lagoa winery. *Toji* is an inviting restaurant with a spectacular view of the sea. At Algar Seco, Carvoeiro Beach, south of Lagoa.

SILVES: This ancient hill town was once the Moorish capital of the Algarve. All that remains from that time is the impressive, restored castle-fortress. The parapets command a panoramic view, and in the evenings the lighted battlements are a memorable sight. The 13th-century Gothic cathedral, the Sé, contains the remains of a Moorish mosque and tombs presumed to be those of Crusader soldiers.

PORTIMÃO: The largest fishing town on the Algarve has lots of activity, many tourists, and heavy traffic. The approach to the port from the bridge across the Arade River opens up a captivating view of the bay with its boats and quays. The town itself is pleasant for walking and there are many good shops on the Rua Santa Isabel and the Rua do Comércio. Just southeast, before crossing the bridge, is the seaside village of Ferragudo, a small fishing hamlet with a ruined 16th-century castle. There are several luxury hotels along the beach in Praia da Rocha and Praia dos Três Irmãos. For the best in golfing, head to the fine *Penina Golf* hotel in Penina (see *Best en Route*).

LAGOS: Founded by the Carthaginians in 350 BC, this is the most attractive harbor town in the Algarve. The walls around the old section are traces of Roman occupation. From this port, the caravels of Henry the Navigator embarked on many voyages of exploration and discovery. The 17th-century Forte do Pau da Bandeira still dominates the harbor. The chapel of Igreja de Santo António (on Rua General Alberto da Silveira) has a baroque interior with much gilded statuary and a painted trompe l'oeil ceiling.

Adjacent to the chapel is a museum containing extensive folkloric and archaeological exhibits and sacred art. The Igreja São Sebastião (Rua Conselheiro J. Machado) has some features of artistic merit including a Renaissance door and tiled walls. Shops sell antiques, brass and copperware, and embroidery. For excellent dining try the distinctively decorated *Pousada do Infante* (see *Best en Route*).

Stop off at Ponta da Piedade, a colorful site of caves, beach, and sea, west of town.

En Route from Lagos – The landscape from Lagos to Sagres on N125 becomes grandly severe, supporting a handful of tiny villages ending abruptly at Vila do Bispo. Turn left onto N268 for a few kilometers; you'll come to a right turn leading to the lighthouse overlooking Cabo de São Vicente — allegedly the landing place of the boat containing the martyred body of St. Vincent.

SAGRES: On this windy, solitary headland, Prince Henry established a navigation school in the 15th century, which enabled the Portuguese to maintain naval supremacy for almost 2 centuries. The old building here now is a hostel. From the cliff tops, you can do some challenging fishing or watch the boats as they trawl the deep for a rich variety of fish. The area is a very dramatic land's end.

BEST EN ROUTE

Expect to pay $110 and up per night for a double room in a hotel in the expensive category, $65 to $85 in the moderate, and $40 to $50 in the inexpensive category. A dinner for two people with local wine will cost $70 and up in the expensive range, about $30 to $70 in the moderate, and under $30 in the inexpensive range. Note that for accommodations in July in August, it is advisable to book well in advance. All restaurants and hotels below accept major credit cards, unless otherwise indicated.

MONTE GORDO

Alcazar – An attractive, modern, air conditioned hotel with 95 rooms, a restaurant, bar, and pool. Rua de Ceuta (phone: 81-52184). Moderate.

Vasco da Gama – This comfortable beach hotel has 182 rooms and suites, a spacious restaurant, bars, a pool, and tennis. Avenida Infante Dom Henrique (phone: 81-44321). Moderate.

TAVIRA

Eurotel Tavira – In a beautiful setting with a sea view, this hotel is one of the best in the eastern Algarve. It offers 80 rooms, a dining room, and its own pool and sports facilities. Quinta das Oliveiras, 2 miles (3 km) east of town (phone: 81-22041). Moderate.

SÃO BRÁZ DE ALPORTEL

Pousada de São Bráz – This inn in the hills north of Faro has 21 rooms, a dining room, and a bar. São Bráz de Alportel (phone: 89-842305). Moderate.

FARO

Cidade Velha – Discreetly elegant, this restaurant is in the old walled city. Excellent Portuguese and international cooking. Closed Mondays. Reservations advised (phone: 89-27145). Expensive.

Casa de Lumena – This attractive former family mansion has outdoor patio dining and a varied Portuguese menu. Open daily. Reservations advised. 27 Praça Alexandre Herculano (phone: 89-801990). Moderate.

Eva – On the marina, this popular modern hotel has 150 air conditioned rooms, a top-floor dining room, rooftop terraced swimming pool, nightclub, and several bars. Courtesy bus service to the beach is provided. Avenida da República (phone: 89-803354). Moderate.

Roque – Popular with the locals for its fresh sea fare and low prices, it is on the Ilha de Faro, a short drive from town on the airport road and then across a long, low bridge. The restaurant faces the beach on the marshland side of the island, with a large outdoor dining area. Closed Wednesdays in winter. Reservations unnecessary. Ilha de Faro (phone: 89-817868). Inexpensive.

SANTA BÁRBARA DE NEXE

La Réserve – Off the road between Loulé and Faro (6 miles/10 km from the coast), this is an elegant, modern, and luxurious establishment (the only Portuguese member of the prestigious Relais & Châteaux group). It offers 20 suites, all with bedroom, bath, and living room, plus a verandah with sea view; the grounds are endowed with a swimming pool and a tennis court; and the Michelin-starred restaurant is highly praised. Closed from early September to mid-December (restaurant closed Tuesdays; reservations advised). No credit cards accepted (phone: 89-90234). Expensive.

ALMANSIL–VALE DO LOBO

Dona Filipa – This superbly run and maintained hotel overlooking the beach has 129 attractive air conditioned rooms with large balconies, a terrace with a pool, and tennis courts. The dining room has fine continental cuisine and excellent service. A buffet lunch is served in a terrace area. There's a lively bar, an inner patio, and a golf course next to the hotel. Make reservations well in advance. Vale do Lobo (phone: 89-394141). Expensive.

O Elegante – On the waterfront, this restaurant offers first class Portuguese food. Closed Tuesdays. Reservations. Avenida Infante de Sagres (phone: 89-314225). Expensive.

Isidoro – A spacious dining room done in nautical decor, overlooking the sea, that serves good seafood and regional dishes. Open daily. Reservations unnecessary. Avenida Infante de Sagres (phone: 89-315219). Moderate.

VILAMOURA

Dom Pedro – Close to the beach, this attractive modern hotel has 260 air conditioned rooms with balconies, a swimming pool, tennis, a golf course, and a bar. Vilamoura (phone: 89-388-9802). Expensive.

Vilamoura – An extensive resort complex that includes 40 villas, 52 hotel rooms and suites, a restaurant, bars, shops, and a spacious pool. In town (phone: 89-380088). Moderate.

ALBUFEIRA

Balaia – Surrounded by green lawns on a cliff overlooking the beach, this nicely designed modern hotel run by Club Med has 193 rooms with balconies, 12 family villas, an inviting dining room, a luncheon terrace, bar, a large swimming pool, and boutiques. Praia Maria Luisa (phone: 89-586681). Expensive.

Borda d'Agua – A few kilometers east of Albufeira, this attractive complex of restaurants overlooking the beach serves excellent seafood and continental dishes. Open June through September; closed Mondays. Reservations advised. Praia da Oura (phone: 89-512045). Moderate.

A Ruína – On the edge of Fishermen's Beach in an old building, this restaurant has very fresh fish and a terrace bar with a marvelous view. Reservations unnecessary. Rua Cais Herculano (phone: 89-52094). Moderate.

ARMAÇÃO DE PERA

Vilalara – Just a mile (1.6 km) west of town, this luxurious resort village has 65 beautifully furnished apartments and villas, appealing indoor and outdoor restaurants, a pool, tennis, a bar, and a private beach. Armação de Pera (phone: 82-314190). Expensive.

Garbe – A first class, cliff-top hotel with 103 rooms and suites, and a dining room and terraced pool overlooking the beach; also a bar and shops. Avenida Marginal (phone: 82-312194 or 82-312195). Moderate.

PORTIMÃO

Old Tavern – Good English and continental dishes are served in an old Portuguese atmosphere. Closed Saturdays. Reservations advised. 43 Rua Júdice Fialho (phone: 82-23325). Moderate.

PRAIA DA ROCHA

Algarve – This establishment has a Moorish-inspired modern decor and furnishings, 219 air conditioned rooms and suites, and a giant pool set amid green lawns and gardens. There's also an intimate grillroom and bar, a dining room with a sea view (reservations advised), a nightclub, and shops. Probably the best first class hotel buy in the Algarve. Avenida Tomás Cabreira (phone: 82-415001). Expensive.

PRAIA DOS TRÊS IRMÃOS

Alvor Praia – In a spectacular beach setting, this hotel has 201 attractive air conditioned rooms and suites. The sparkling split-level dining room has an international menu and an outdoor buffet lunch. There's also a large pool, tennis, fishing, an excursion boat, shops, a bar, and a nightclub. Praia dos Três Irmãos (phone: 82-458900). Expensive.

PENINA

Golf da Penina – One of Europe's best golf resorts, the 27-hole championship course was designed by Henry Cotton. Facilities include a driving range, tennis courts, and a huge pool with sun decks and bar. There are 202 air conditioned rooms and suites, nicely decorated lounges, a dining room, a grillroom, and a bar with dancing. Penina Portimão (phone: 82-415415). Expensive.

LAGOS

Alpendre – This well-staffed first class restaurant has an extensive menu, including local specialties, and an impressive wine list. Closed Wednesdays. Reservations advised. 17 Rua António Barbosa Viana (phone: 82-62705). Moderate.

Lagos – Buses take guests to the beach at this attractive, 273-room hotel with a fine restaurant. Rua Nova da Aldeia (phone: 82-769967). Moderate.

Lagosteira – Under the same management as *Alpendre,* this eatery specializes in seafood. Closed Tuesdays. Reservations advised. 26 Rua 1 de Maio (phone: 82-62486). Moderate.

SAGRES

Pousada do Infante – On the cliffs with an incredible view, this attractive inn has 33 rooms, a dining room with a sea view, and a terrace. In town (phone: 82-64222). Expensive.

Baleeira – A simple, comfortable hotel that is extremely popular because of its prime seaside location; its 120 rooms look out on the sea. There is a saltwater pool, a bar, and a pleasant dining room with smashing views. It also has its own tennis court and bikes for hire. In town (phone: 82-64212). Moderate.

Tasca – This fishermen's restaurant serves good seafood, regional dishes, fresh salads, and has a good wine list. Guests staying at the nearby *Baleeira* hotel receive a 10% discount upon presentation of their check-in card. Closed Saturdays from mid-January to mid-February. Reservations unnecessary. In town (phone: 82-64177). Inexpensive.

Romania

Romania covers some 91,700 square miles, bordered by the Soviet Union to the north, the Black Sea to the east, Hungary and Yugoslavia to the west, and Bulgaria to the south. Its population is almost 23 million (under its Communist rule, Romania had the highest growth rate in Eastern Europe due to a Ceauşescu regime policy that outlawed birth control), of which the largest concentration (2.2 million) is in the capital city of Bucharest.

There are three major historic and geographic areas in Romania. Walachia is on the flat Danube plain in the south. The Danube itself is a natural southern border with Bulgaria, and historically the river brought trade and culture to the valley from the west. Bucharest sprang up here as a major center of government and industry. The Danube flows into the Black Sea, and the only Romanian seacoast stretches below the river delta there, primarily a resort area with many beaches. There is a major seaport at Constanţa.

The country is fairly mountainous, north of the Danube plain. Transylvania is encompassed by the Carpathian Mountains, crossing the country's center from north to southwest. The area has had a turbulent history, having been overrun from time to time by various hordes — the Germanic and Magyar from the west and the Ottoman from the south. During more peaceful times, however, the Transylvanian rulers often invited the Germans and Magyars to share their trading knowledge and other business skills in order to help local economic development. As a result, the historical centers of most Transylvanian towns are inhabited by German or Hungarian minorities, while the suburbs and surrounding villages are populated by Romanians. At present, there is a large Hungarian population (2 million), and remnants of a German minority depleted by postwar emigration.

The Romans probably coined the expression *divide e impera* (divide and rule) when they attempted to conquer the Thracian tribes north of the Danube and south of the Carpathian Mountains. Once they succeeded in acquiring those areas, however, *divide e impera* was practiced through the centuries by all successful invaders of present-day Romania. Romania's frequent internal feuding helped the Turks, Hungarians (and Austro-Hungarians), Nazis, and Russians, to divide and rule with relative ease.

The Greeks operated a trading center along the Romanian coast of the Black Sea and began to exploit the Thracian tribes who lived there. They recruited Thracians for their armies, and when the first Thracian slaves were brought to the Athens slave market in the 4th century BC, they were named *Daos* (Latin, *Davus*) — a name frequently used for slaves in Greek tragedies and the name known by Romans as Dacia and Dacians.

Various Roman generals waged wars and Roman consuls practiced politics against the Dacians from 112 BC until AD 16, when the emperor Trajan finally succeeded in subduing the entire area. His success was marked by two celebrated columns, one in Rome and one (the Tropaeum Trajani) in Adamclisi in the Dobrogea area in east Romania. Although the Romans left the country after the collapse of their empire, their language, though somewhat modified, endures. Romanians claim to be descended from Latin-speaking Daco-Romans, and the Romanian language is a romance tongue, akin to French and Italian.

Since the end of the Roman Empire, many tribes and nations have influenced Romania — culturally, socially, and economically. Goths and Slavic tribes were the first, Hungarians and Russians, the last. Christianity was introduced by the Bulgarians in 846. Magyars invaded Romania during the 9th century before settling down farther west (in present-day Hungary). They returned with King Stephen in the 11th century, and a Tatar-Mongol invasion destroyed the country in 1241. Around the same time, Vlach tribes, who lived south of the Danube, moved north and became integrated with Daco-Roman inhabitants and acquired their language.

At the end of the 13th century, they split into two groups — one settling in Moldavia and the other in Walachia. Until 1859, when the autonomous Danubian principalities formed Romania, the area's inhabitants lived more separately than together, divided and ruled by different neighbors. The Turks fought hardest, intrigued the most, and stayed the longest. It was during the 14th and 15th centuries, at the time of Mircea the Old, Vlad (the Impaler) Tepes, Michael the Brave, and Stefan the Great that the foundations for the Romanian nation were established. Vlad became known as the Impaler when his custom of cutting off the heads of his defeated enemies and putting them on stakes became infamous throughout the Ottoman Empire and the Hungarian kingdom. Nicknamed Count Dracula, he became the widely known vampire after stories were written about him by Bram Stoker, the 19th-century Irish novelist.

Although Moldavia and Walachia were reunified in 1859 under the leadership of Prince Alexandru Ioan Cuza, Romania still was prey for its neighbors. The country managed to maintain its autonomy much of the time, and even augmented its territory after the dissolution of the Austro-Hungarian Empire in 1918, at the end of World War I. Transylvania and Bukovina (in Moldavia) were a "prize" granted to Romania for entering the war in August 1916 on the side of the Entente, even though Romania's army was soundly beaten by German troops in August 1917.

At the advent of World War II, Romania's King Carol II's reign was marked by continued attempts to please both Germany and Russia. Eventually, Romania (with the strong-arm help of the pro-Nazi Iron Guards) fell into the pro-German camp. Half a million troops were allowed to enter the country in 1940, and in June 1941 the Romanian army joined the Germans in their attack on the Soviet Union. However, on August 23, 1944, victorious Soviet troops invaded Romanian soil. King Michael, son of the by-now exiled King Carol II, organized a coup, captured more than 50,000 German troops, joined the Allies, and declared war on Nazi Germany.

The prewar National Peasant, Liberal, Social Democratic, and Communist parties formed the National Bloc, and in 1946 their coalition won 71% of the Romanian peoples' votes. The Communists "secured" key ministries, and through a wave of arrests, intimidations, and party mergers (with Social Democrats), and by outlawing the National Peasant party, they forced King Michael into exile after his abdication in 1947. The following year the new People's Democratic Front won the majority of seats in parliamentary elections. A constitution was adopted on March 28, 1948.

The Communist regime nationalized all of Romania's industry and agriculture, and created a nation of uniform wage earners. The peasant population was employed in huge factories built in the suburbs of all Romanian cities, and all the land was collectivized and converted into enormous agro-industrial complexes.

When Nicolae Ceausescu was elected leader in 1974, the pace of industrialization increased, and his megalomaniac visions turned the country into Europe's largest unfinished work site. The country experienced shortages in every part of its economic, social, cultural, and private life. Romania was culturally and politically strangled, but any growing dissent was quashed quickly by the all-powerful Securitate, the feared secret police. Virtually all of Romania's ties with the outside world were cut off during Ceausescu's last 10 years.

At the end of 1989, the Romanian army organized a coup d'état, after popular uprisings had wracked the nation for weeks and hundreds had been killed. Ceausescu and his wife, Elena, were captured while trying to flee the country and quickly executed on *Christmas Day.* The National Salvation Front, headed by Ion Iliescu, was installed, as political parties were revived. In May 1990, the first free elections since 1937 were held; Iliescu was elected president by a landslide. Many Romanians, however, were suspicious of the election results since there were reports of threats and even several deaths at some polling places.

Many are suspicious, too, of Iliescu's political intentions, since the main party, the National Salvation Front, is comprised mostly of former Communist party members — including Iliescu himself — who served under the Ceausescu government. In the month following the elections, pro-democracy groups raided state-operated television stations and burned down the police headquarters, after the police in Bucharest raided the demonstrators' tent camp where they had been demanding that Iliescu and other top government officials, former members of the Communist party, be replaced. The political dispute led to the most violent confrontation in Eastern Europe since the December 1989 coup.

Despite accusations against the president, Iliescu claims that he no longer abides by Leninist doctrine, and that he wishes to lead Romania into a more democratic future. Today, a sort of creative anarchy prevails in this country where the people are trying to improve the quality of their personal lives while attempting to improve the country's economy. Many Romanians feel (and act) like orphans, searching for the right direction, while fearing they may further harm the already precarious social structure and unleash the divisive ethnic strife that has hampered the country so often in the past. However, the long lines for basic living supplies have not disappeared, and economic recovery has barely begun, and the country's internal conflicts are far from over.

Our first route in Romania starts with a tour from Bucharest, the spacious capital city with parks and lakes, and then leads north to Brasov, a well-preserved medieval city in Transylvania. The route goes west to Sighisoara and Sibiu (also Transylvanian cities), then on to Hunedoara, Arad, and Timisoara (the latter two located on the Banat plain).

The second route is a tour of the famous monasteries of Bukovina, a small area near the Soviet frontier and the historic seat of the Moldavian monarchy. These folk churches, adorned with dazzling 16th-century wall paintings and nestled in isolated valleys, are not easy to reach. But their unique beauty rewards those who seek them out.

Travel in Romania during the winter months can be very uncomfortable because of lack of food and energy shortages (resulting both in underheated rooms and in the undependable availability of gasoline). The better hotels in the capital are always well heated, and their restaurants operate reasonably well at any time of the year. When traveling through the Romanian countryside, plan to arrive at your destination at least 1 hour before sunset, since street lights are extremely rare — or often nonexistent. Note too that restaurants close very early, so if you're planning to arrive late at night, you might want to bring along something to eat.

Bucharest to Timisoara
From Walachia to the Banat Plain

This route passes between two of Romanian's larger urban centers, Bucharest and Braşov, as well as some interesting cities farther west, including Timisoara. Bucharest and Braşov are separated by about 105 miles (168 km) of good road, which passes through countryside of seemingly endless wheat and cornfields, and hills covered with apple, plum, and pear orchards. There are endless groups of athletes, in fashionable warm-up suits, jogging along the roadside (there's a long list of famous Romanian sports heroes from Nadia Comăneci to Ilie Nastase, and the whole country is very sports conscious), but in the more rural areas you still can see groups of women laundering the week's wash in the streams. There also are cows, water buffaloes, herds of geese, and sheep tended by lonely shepherds wrapped down to their ankles in wool cloaks. Handmade clothes with beautiful embroidery can be bought from roadside vendors. Drive carefully, especially at night, because roads are crowded with animals, Gypsy wagons, and people walking to work. Chronic gas shortages lead to endless lines at those pumps that are working, but foreigners (who must buy gas coupons at the border or in hotels) can jump the queue. Take care not to let the tank run low, or you may end up stranded. Gas stations usually close between 7 and 8 PM.

Bucharest is a flat and friendly city on the northern Danube plain, but the drive north to Braşov ascends the Carpathian Mountains of Transylvania, where the skiing is good and the winter resorts are plentiful. Later on, driving west, you will arrive at Banat, the "bread basket" of Romania. For a complete report on the capital and its hotels and restaurants, see *Bucharest,* THE CITIES.

BRAȘOV: From Bucharest, drive north on Route 1 (E15) to this early medieval city at the foot of Mt. Tímpa in the Carpathians. The road leads along the Prahova and Timis river valleys, and passes through old Dacian settlements (founded as early as 70 BC) that now are winter ski spas. Brașov is a red-roofed town with winding streets, small squares, and a cable car ride up the mountainside that lets you absorb all the views. When it was known as Kronstadt, Brașov was a prosperous trading center inhabited by Transylvanian Saxons, Protestant merchants who had emigrated from German lands. It's now one of the nation's chief industrial centers (pop. 320,000), but you wouldn't guess it after a walk through the Old Town. Behind an imposing Gothic façade, the Black Church (closed Sundays) houses, unexpectedly, a collection of Oriental rugs, and the *Casa Sfatului,* or *Council Hall* (now a museum, 23 Piața August) dates from 1420; the large square that surrounds it is an inviting pedestrian hub.

The best day trip from Brașov is up into the Carpathian Mountains to the resort town of Poiana Brașov and the 14th-century Bran Castle. Bran is mistakenly touted as Dracula's home base, but in truth Vlad only occasionally vacationed there (generally depending on how much of a lead he had on his pursuers). Still, the hilltop castle is worth a visit, with its thick, fortified walls, dramatic peaked towers, and clammy, narrow passageways. Poiana Brașov ("Sunny Glade") is a wonderful stop for summer hikes or winter skiing and skating. The restaurants here feature hot, homemade dishes cooked over open fires.

SIGHISOARA: From Brașov, drive 76 miles (121 km) northwest on the road marked Tirgu Mures to Sighisoara. This medieval town has a beautifully preserved historical center within its intact city walls and 11 watch towers. Sighisoara also is the birthplace of Vlad Tepes, and the town flourished during Tepes's rule when he invited German (Saxon) and Hungarian traders and artisans to help develop his country's economy. Here the Saxons developed the iron mines and foundries, and laid a base for the town's present-day porcelain industry. Even today, the German-speaking population is very proud of its Saxon origins.

Entry to the Old Town is through the gate under the monumental 14th-century *Clock Tower,* now a museum (closed Mondays). Nearby is a 1515 monastery church with fine hanging Oriental rugs, and across Piața Muzeulii (Museum Square) is the house where Vlad Tepes lived from 1431 to 1435; it's now a restaurant (see *Best en Route*). Just behind Tepes's house, in the center of the Old Town, the Strada Scolii leads from Piața Cetatii (Citadel Square) to the covered wooden stairway (1642) with its 172 stairs leading to the Gothic Bergkirche (Mountain Church), built in 1345. After the Reformation, the fine frescoes in the church were covered with plaster (at press time the frescoes and the church's façade were being restored). The church keeper, who lives in a cottage in front of the church, has the keys and offers guided tours (in German only). In front of the church is an old German cemetery with fascinating tombstones under centuries-old trees.

SIBIU: To reach this city, take the road marked Sibiu 58 miles (93 km) southwest. Originally a Roman colony called Cibinum, Sibiu was refounded and named Hermannstadt by Germans from Saxony during the 12th century. Today, it is one of the most beautiful places in Transylvania. Its Piața Republicii (Republic Square) displays a beautiful collection of painted pastel baroque façades. On the square is the city's *Historical Museum* and Council Tower, as well as the *Brukenthal Museum,* Romania's oldest and, perhaps, finest art gallery (closed Mondays). Behind the Piața Republicii is the Piața Grivita with the Gothic Evangelical Church (1300–1520), which has an interesting 1772 organ with 6,002 pipes, as well as a beautiful Crucifixion fresco (1445). In front of the church is a 13th-century staircase passage leading into the picturesque lower part of town. Before heading down, admire the rooftops of the houses below.

Near Sibiu are the Fagaras Mountains, with some of Romania's best hiking grounds.

HUNEDOARA and DEVA: Located 10 miles (16 km) from each other, these two cities were Transylvania's gateways to the west. They can be reached from Sibiu by taking the road marked to Hunedoara west for 81 miles (130 km). In Deva, the 13th-century citadel is worth seeing. Beware that you must pass through some of the country's most polluted areas on the way from Deva to Hunedoara. Romania's first "modern" iron mills were built here in 1750, and the industry still exists. The pride of Ceausescu's industrial development, the Hunedoara steel mills are spread over 6 miles of land north of the city. Brace yourself for almost deafening noise, black smoke, and red sparks emitted from the mills, which at night resemble Dante's *Inferno*. But if you can find your way along the disasterously marked roads, Hunedoara's 15th-century castle definitely is worth seeing. The castle's walls, almost 100 feet thick in some sections, were built by Turkish prisoners. Its Gothic architecture, high towers, and fancy drawbridge are among Romania's finest.

ARAD: From Hunedoara, drive 98 miles (157 km) west (and slightly north) on the road marked "to Arad." Built on the Mures River, the city has an attractive neo-classical *State Theater* (103 Bd. Republicii) and an interesting *History Museum* (in the Palace of Culture, 1 Enescu Sq.).

After Arad, take the road marked to Timisoara 32 miles (51 km) south.

TIMISOARA: The December 1989 uprising against Ceausescu's Communist regime began in Timisoara. Inhabited by a mixture of Hungarians, Germans, and Serbians, the city is a showcase of Banatian baroque architecture, with its wide squares and streets and low, colorful houses. The capital of Romania's agricultural region of Banat, Timisoara has a variety of cultural monuments that reflect the town's ethnic population.

At Piața Unirii (Unity Square) is the baroque Catholic cathedral (1754), attended by the German speaking population, and on the opposite end is the Serbian church (1774). At the nearby Piața Libertatii (Liberty Square) is the Old Town Hall (1734), and just south of it is Hunaides Palace, with the local history museum (closed Mondays). Two blocks east of Hunaides Palace is Opera Square, with the *Opera House* and the Serbian Orthodox cathedral (1936). In the middle of the square is a column with figures of Romulus and Remus, a gift from Rome. Opera Square, with its restaurants and shops and surrounded by turn-of-the-century buildings, is the heart of the city today. It was here in Opera Square that the first demonstrations were held in December 1989 against the Communist regime. Behind the Serbian Orthodox cathedral is a lovely park on the banks of the Bega Canal.

BEST EN ROUTE

Expect to pay anywhere between $90 and $150 per night for a double room in hotels listed as expensive, between $30 and $75 for those in the moderate category. Meals are a much better deal. Most restaurants charge only about $12 for even the most lavish, three-course extravaganza for two; for a restaurant we've listed as moderate, expect to pay between $6 and $8. Be aware, though, that unless you travel in summer, the choice of dishes will be severely limited. Prices do not include drinks, wine, or tips. In most places, restaurant reservations always are necessary. Also, it is best to eat dinner early, since Romanian cooks are known for running out of ingredients as the evening wears on.

BRAȘOV

Carpați – The hotel of choice in Brașov. It's very fancy, with big comfortable rooms and a well-supplied restaurant. Major credit cards accepted. 9 Gheorghe Gheorghiu-Dej Blvd. (phone: 921-42840; telex: 33260). Hotel: expensive; restaurant: moderate.

Cerbul Carpatin – Housed in a 16th-century building that once belonged to a wealthy merchant, this many-roomed establishment offers well-heeled residents and tourists grilled meat platters, good wine, and a "folklore" floor show, as well as music and dancing. No credit cards accepted. 14 Piața 23 August (phone: 921-43981 or 921-42840). Moderate.

Chinezesc – If you tire of eating Romanian food, try this Sino-Carpathian eatery operated by the *Carpați* hotel (3 blocks away). Formerly a palace and then a bank, it has been converted into a pleasant restaurant. No smoking allowed. Closed Wednesdays. Major credit cards accepted. 2 Piata 23 August (no phone at restaurant; for information, call the *Carpați* hotel at 921-42842). Moderate.

Postavarul – Built in 1906, this hotel was expanded in 1926 and now has 160 rooms, 80 with private bath. It's located in the pleasant pedestrian part of town, and unlike many of the city's other establishments, this one has some character. Major credit cards accepted. 62 Strada Republicii (phone: 921-44330). Moderate.

Orient – There's a café on the left (where for a fixed price you get the best cup of coffee in town along with a cold drink and a pastry) and a teahouse on the right (where for the price of tea you also get hors d'oeuvres and cakes). It opened in 1987, but the lovely decor has a 1930s and turn-of-the-century feel. Don't miss it. No smoking allowed. No reservations or credit cards accepted. Strada Republicii, a main shopping street off Piața 23 August (no phone). Moderate.

POIANA BRAȘOV

Sport – Modern and pleasant, this hostelry near the ski lifts has a restaurant, bar, disco, and shops. Major credit cards accepted (phone: 92-262313). Expensive.

Sura Dacilor – This restaurant, which looks much older than it is, is surrounded by grassy mountain walks at a Transylvanian ski/summer resort. The pleasing aroma from the kitchen will whet even the most reluctant appetite. No reservations or credit cards accepted. In the middle of town (no phone). Moderate.

SIBIU

Imperatul Romanilor – Just off the Piața Republicii, this 1895 building recently was renovated and now offers 102 rooms, a sauna, a gym, and a billiard room. The restaurant serves Romanian and continental fare. 4 Strada N. Bălcescu (phone: 924-16490). Expensive to moderate.

SIGHISOARA

Cetate – From 1431 to 1435, Vlad Tepes lived in this house with thick walls and small doorways. On the first floor is an eatery serving good Romanian food, and there is a beer cellar downstairs (phone: 950-71596). Inexpensive.

TIMISOARA

Continental – A modern cement structure that dominates the city, this hotel has all the basics. A black market and a money exchange function at nearby parking lots. Major credit cards accepted. 2 Blvd. 23 August (phone: 961-34144; telex: 71266). Moderate.

Cofetaria Unirea – Adjacent to the baroque Catholic cathedral, this recently redecorated coffeehouse serves ice cream and a variety of cakes. Pleasant outdoor tables offer a grand view of the Piața Unirii. No smoking allowed inside. No reservations or credit cards accepted. 13 Piața Unirii (no phone). Inexpensive.

The Moldavian Monasteries: Bukovina

Bukovina is a small tract of land in the northern Carpathian foothills that gradually rise from the Siret River Valley farther north and east. The area, in the northeast corner of Romania, is a Moldavian reservation of beautiful mountain scenery with knobby, green-carpeted hills spotted with dense fir stands. The Moldavians still sport their traditional dress whites, and the almost total lack of English-speaking people (except for tour guides) makes a trip here adventurous. Bukovina is not heavily visited and is not really convenient to any place that is. There's minimal nightlife, few wines of distinction, and travelers are advised to bring along extra canisters of gasoline and food supplies. The five churches and monasteries here, with exterior walls covered by frescoes, are like no other structures in the world.

The buildings all are relatively simple and took months rather than generations to build. They are, however, the epitome of folk architecture, built to an unwieldy and large scale that makes them look from a distance like squat, one-story bungalows. It is only when you approach them that you realize how enormous they are. They have few windows and are covered by peaked-cap roofs that descend steeply and then suddenly bow out, creating wide eaves over thick walls, the outsides of which are covered with artwork. Virtually every façade is bathed in color with frescoes illustrating the Bible, classical philosophy, and local folklore — a historic library of pictograms.

Moldavian history's medieval golden era was overseen by its greatest monarch, Stephen the Great, who, though he never rated a title higher than prince, reigned from 1457 to 1504. Because of the turbulence of the times and the violence of the populace, the length of Stephen's reign was unheard of (and even today ranks with Joe DiMaggio's 56 consecutive, safely hit-in games as a feat of longevity). He was a master tactician who encouraged cultural pursuits, and all the churches were built during his era or shortly thereafter. He is credited with the development of the Moldavian style, which is a blending of rough-hewn, hand building techniques (that were at the same time structurally primitive and colorfully folksy) with the far more sophisticated architectural concepts of the southern Byzantine and the European Gothic. The frescoes on the church walls served the dual purposes of being a showcase for the area's unified cultural expression and a schoolroom, teaching history and religion to a predominantly illiterate constituency. These priceless frescoes have been preserved outside although exposed to the elements since the mid-1500s. Their colors are so rich and true that the blue on the sides of the Voroneţ Church has been given a name of its own, Voroneţ blue. Though the art world has many times attempted to copy it, this blue has never been accurately duplicated in its total richness.

It's best to plan your tour with the Romanian Tourist Board in Bucharest (7 Magheru Blvd.; phone: 145160), where you can arrange to hire an English-speaking guide, or just get a good road map of Bukovina and wander on your own.

If you have a lot of time, sufficient gasoline, and extensive food supplies, consider extending your tour of northern Romania westward to the Maramureş region, near the Soviet border. The villages dotting the hilly green countryside are of special interest to ethnographers; here folk art and traditional customs have been preserved as nowhere else in Europe. Only in Maramureş do so many people wear their handmade folk costumes, not only at festivals and on special occasions, but every day. Friendly villagers may invite visitors into their wooden houses for home-distilled spirits and a glimpse of a way of life that has hardly changed for centuries.

SUCEAVA: This town of 100,000 is the major hub of the area — and very polluted. It's the jumping-off point for any tour of the monasteries. Suceava is 270 miles (432 km) from Bucharest, and the distance can be covered in 1 hour by plane or 6 hours by train (arrangements for a car and driver can be made in Bucharest), or you can drive the distance yourself in a day. This was the seat of Moldavian power from 1388 to 1566, and there are still vestiges of the medieval citadel — which often was attacked, but never conquered — not even by the Ottoman armies commanded by Mohammed II after they overran Constantinople.

There are several interesting churches in town, but since the rest of the route is predominantly architectural, time here would be better spent browsing through the more secular folkwares — mostly spin-offs of the handmade fabrics and local pottery industries — for which Bukovina is famous. In the 16th-century *Princely Inn* you'll find the *Folk Art Museum,* with a restoration of the interior of an authentic peasant house and exhibitions of national costumes, dolls, masks, wedding regalia, and carpets (5 Ciprian Porumbescu Str.).

The monasteries are spread out over the 56 miles (90 km) or so directly west of Suceava; to stop at all five, plan on a day out and a day back. If you want to spend less time, make sure to route yourself carefully so that you don't get lost and find night falling in a town where nobody speaks a language you can understand and it takes you an hour to find out that there aren't any hotels in the vicinity. Most important of all, start out with a full tank of gas. Driving northwest out of Suceava on Route 2, turn left at Milişăuţi and you'll soon come to Arbore, the first of the famous churches.

ARBORE: This is the smallest and the simplest of the 16th-century churches. Though the interior is only dimly lit, the outside walls are covered with frescoes that tell the story of Genesis and also depict the lives of the saints. The predominant color here is green, and there are five distinct shades of it that mix with reds, blues, and yellows. In the courtyard there are two stone slabs with 15 even gouges that the artists used for holding and mixing their paints. The best-preserved works are on the western wall and the buttressing. Unlike most primitive wall painting, there is an abundance of detailing here involving the use of perspective, animated figures, and literal facial expressions.

SUCEVIŢA: Continuing west from Arbore, you come to the town of Solca and turn north through Clit to Marginea. From there it's only another 6 miles (10 km) west to Suceviţa. The 1586 monastery here is surrounded by thick stone walls and guarded by five imposing towers. There are more well-preserved frescoes here than at any of the other churches, and they are everywhere, inside and out, except on the northern wall, where the painter fell off his scaffold and died. (Legend has it that the wall was left blank as a tribute to him.) In addition to the religious paintings, there also are portraits of Sophocles, Plato, and Aristotle along with more Eastern images from the *Arabian Nights.* The village of Suceviţa is one of the most picturesque in all of Romania — the houses' verandahs have carved wooden pillars, and townspeople dress in national costumes.

MOLDOVIŢA: About 18 miles (29 km) west of Suceviţa on Route 17A is the commune of Vatra Moldoviţei, in the shadow of Rarău Mountain. Moldoviţa has another large monastery (1532) in the center of the town. The paintings here have a less religious flavor. The most striking series is of the siege of Constantinople, with detailing that outlines the entire city. There's a museum here where you can see engraved and painted furniture, including Prince Petru Rareş's black ornamental throne. The manicured grounds are neatly laid out with flagstone paths that run from fortification to castle to church.

If you continue south you'll come to the town of Cîmpulung Moldovenesc, where you might consider stopping over before returning east to Suceava on the southern half of the route.

VORONEŢ: Driving east along the Moldova River on Route 17, the route passes through the towns of Vama, Molidu, and Frasin, stopping at Gura Humorului (18 miles/29 km from Cîmpulung), where you can go north to the Humor Monastery or south to Voroneţ. Voroneţ is the most famous and the oldest of the monasteries (1488) and was built by Stephen the Great himself. The 16th-century paintings here began a style that took from the Byzantine art of the south and mixed with it a more Gothic flavor. The building itself is the most elegant of all these structures, more involved and animated, with rows of repeating pilasters capped by round arches, crenelated friezes, and round windows. The famous blue is breathtaking, and the paintings, especially those of the Last Judgment, are simultaneously humane and barbaric, with pretty women, musicians, and people being torn apart by wild beasts.

HUMOR: Less than 4 miles (6 km) north of Gura Humorului, the Humor Monastery is the last of the churches. It was built in 1530 and is unique in that it has a large open verandah, arched on three sides. It's also interesting to note that in one of the frescoes the devil is portrayed as a woman with wings. From here it's only another 22 miles (35 km) back to Suceava on Route 17.

BEST EN ROUTE

Expect to pay anywhere between $20 and $30 per night for a double in the hotels listed below. Meals are a much better deal. Most restaurants charge about $12 for even the most lavish, three-course extravaganza for two. Prices do not include drinks, wine, or tips.

SUCEAVA

Arcaşul – You might be a little wary of a place that brags about its parking lot, but if you've just driven 8 hours from Bucharest, you'll find this conveniently located hotel is just what you want. Besides comfortable rooms with big, soft beds, it's also got a disco/bar and a good restaurant. Major credit cards accepted. 4-6 Mihai Viteazul Str. (phone: 987-10944).

Căprioara – This rustic restaurant sits in the Adîncata forest just outside of town. Beautiful surroundings for some good Moldavian fare of hearty goulash, with brandy to wash everything down. No reservations or credit cards accepted. 5 miles (8 km) from Suceava (no phone).

SUCEVIŢA

Suceviţa – Close to the monastery, this first class inn with rooms as well as small bungalows has a restaurant that's small but serves great food. The people will make you feel as if you are Prince Stephen's long-lost brother-in-law (no phone).

The Black Sea Coast

The Romanian coastline on the Black Sea stretches for about 150 miles from the Danube Delta at the Soviet border, all the way south to the Bulgarian frontier. Roughly 165 miles (264 km) east of Bucharest, this area can be reached by plane in about half an hour or by train or car in about 3 hours. (You ferry across the Danube at the midpoint of the trip.) Sandy beaches and fancy resorts (the most famous is Mamaia) line the coast; the tideless sea assures delightful swimming. And should you tire of toasting yourself on the Black Sea's strands, you can drive into Constanța for a shot of civilization or cruise into the Danube Delta for a whiff of wilderness.

CONSTANȚA: Romania's main port city occupies the site of the ancient citadel, Tomis, founded by Greek merchants during the 6th century BC. The city is a mix of the early Greek, the Roman (Ovid was exiled here, and the square bearing the poet's name features his pensive statue), and the Byzantine. There's also a mosque here with an Arabian mosaic dome and a lighthouse-like minaret. Part of the sand here is flanked by a hedge and tree line that combines with the ornate façades of the older buildings to give this resort a mellow air.

THE DANUBE DELTA: The 2,500-year-old town of Tulcea is 77 miles (123 km) north of Constanța on Route 22, where the Danube trisects and fans into its delta. The Greeks called the city Aegyssus, and the *Danube Delta Museum* (32 Progresului Str.) chronicles their coming and going. The town is now the main departure point for tourists who want to take river cruises into the delta to see the nature preserve (tours can be arranged by the Carpați National Tourist Office, *Delta Hotel,* 2 Isaccei Str.). The land is wildly beautiful here: marshes crisscrossed by canals and brooks; islands bristling with rushes and reeds; clumps of trees sheltering otters, foxes, wildcats, and boars. During migratory periods, over 300 species of birds nest in the delta.

BEST EN ROUTE

The hotel and restaurants listed below are moderately priced; accommodations will probably run about $30 per night for a double room, dinner for two, about $12.

CONSTANȚA

Casa Cu Lei – This hotel's restaurant is an architectural monument, and each of its dining rooms has a different structural design — Brancovan (a particular Romanian style), Venetian, and Spanish. It's worth having a meal here simply for the atmosphere. There also are a few rooms which must be reserved well in advance. 1 Dianei Str. (phone: 916-17416).

Cazino – This ornate restaurant that used to be a casino is on the seawall (you can't miss it), with huge, round, arched windows, an eating terrace on a promontory stretching out over the water, and fine food (no phone).

Continental – An adequate downtown hotel that offers a private bath, telephone, and TV set in every room and boasts its own wine cellar. 20 Bd. Republicii (phone: 916-15660; telex: 14237).

San Marino

Every year, more than 3 million tourists visit San Marino, the oldest and smallest republic in the world. You might think that this number would overwhelm the country — considering that it has a population of only 23,000 and an area of only 23 square miles — and to a certain extent it does. At high noon on a midsummer day, it is sometimes hard to see San Marino's quaint charm beyond the droves of day-trippers and the gaudy displays of countless souvenir shops vying for their attention. But if that day is a clear one, look again. From any number of points in San Marino, the panorama embraces not only the Apennines to the south, the expansive plains and hills to the north, the brilliant blue Adriatic to the east, but also the Yugoslav coast, 156 miles away. No doubt about it, San Marino's mountaintop setting is spectacular, and it is this, along with interesting historical sites and colorful remnants of the republic's long past, that makes a visit worthwhile.

San Marino lies 11 miles from the Adriatic coast of north-central Italy, bordering the regions of Emilia-Romagna to the north and the Marche (Marches) to the south. Most visitors arrive from the coastal town of Rimini, and as you approach from this direction, the republic's distinctive "skyline" comes into view dramatically: Monte Titano (Mt. Titanus), at a height of 2,470 feet, with its three fortified peaks. The territory of San Marino consists of this mountain, with the capital, San Marino city, on top, and the surrounding hills, scattered with eight small villages or "castles" (*castelli*). The climate is temperate, thanks to its altitude and the ever-present "garbino" wind, with summer temperatures that rarely exceed 80F.

According to tradition, San Marino dates back almost 1,700 years, to AD 301 and the arrival of a Christian stonecutter from Dalmatia named Marinus. Fleeing the religious persecution of the Roman Emperor Diocletian, Marinus sought out the secluded safety of Monte Titano, where he built a chapel and began to live a saintly life. Other Christians soon followed him, giving rise to a free community that very early in its history developed the democratic institutions still governing it today.

San Marino's inaccessibility protected it throughout the period of the downfall of the Roman Empire and the subsequent barbarian invasions. Later, when covetous neighbors did cast eyes in its direction, it struggled valiantly to remain independent. Only twice was it unsuccessful, once in the 16th century, when it was occupied by Cesare Borgia, and again in the 18th century, when Cardinal Giulio Alberoni, legate in Romagna, took it upon himself to annex it to the Papal States. In each case, the loss of liberty lasted only a few months.

Along with its freedom, the country prides itself on a long tradition as a place of asylum. The Italian patriot Giuseppe Garibaldi was one of the most famous figures to have found refuge here, in 1849. During World War II, there were 100,000 refugees within the borders. Sadly, the republic was bombed in 1944, despite its proclaimed neutrality.

San Marino does have a small, picturesque, volunteer army. The blue uniforms, blue and white plumed headgear, and old-fashioned muskets and sabers of the militia and the Guardia del Consiglio Grande e Generale (the latter serves as an honor guard to the country's rulers) can be seen on special occasions. Guardsmen of the Guardia di Rocca, however, are on regular duty at the entrance to the government palace, and their green jackets, red trousers, red and white feathered caps, and vintage pistols are no less decorative.

The economy of the country is based on tourism, light industry, some farming, and the sale of postage stamps, which have considerable philatelic value. While the Italian lira is the local currency in common use, the minting of coins, mainly for collectors, is another source of revenue.

San Marino is accessible by bus, car, and even helicopter. The year-round bus service from Rimini leaves frequently from several stops including the Rimini train station and takes about 45 minutes. Buses arrive in San Marino at either Piazzale della Stazione or Piazzale Marino Calcigni, both within easy walking distance of the walls of the historic center. In summer, a helicopter service connects Rimini with Borgo Maggiore, one of San Marino's *castelli*, from which San Marino City is reachable via a cable car ride. The nearest airports are at Miramare di Rimini (9 miles/14 km away) and Forlì (38 miles/61 km away). The nearest train station is in Rimini. Travel by car is scenic on the four-lane highway from Rimini, though you also can reach the border along other well-paved but more sinuous routes. The San Marino Tourist Office, in the centrally located Contrada Omagnano (phone: 549-882998; closed weekends), produces an excellent free guide in English, the *Practical Guide to San Marino,* covering everything from cable car timetables to advice on how to cope with an overheated engine in traffic jams on the town's steep and narrow streets.

En Route from Rimini – The border is marked by a banner proclaiming, in Italian, "Welcome to the Ancient Land of Liberty." A passport is not needed to enter, and there is no customs control, despite the customs station.

Within minutes you are in Serravalle, the most populous of the *castelli.* Here there is evidence of industrial growth alongside one of the country's oldest and best-kept castles. Since the bestowal of Serravalle to San Marino in 1463, the republic's territory has not grown by a single inch. Not even Napoleon's offer to extend its borders in 1797 was accepted.

Continuing along the winding road, you will see Domagnano, another of the "castles," to the left before arriving at Borgo Maggiore.

BORGO MAGGIORE: A market town established in the 12th century, and worth a stop. Originally known as Mercatale, its weekly open-air market, held on Thursdays, has been taking place since 1244. The porticoed Piazza di Sopra remains practically unchanged. Just off the main square, Piazza Grande, is one of San Marino's most important museums, the *Museo Postale, Filatelico e Numismatico* (open daily; admission charge; phone: 549-903958). It contains examples of all stamps and coins issued by the republic, along with stamps from other countries. Nearby is the *Museo delle Armi da Fuoco* (Firearms Museum), whose collection spans the 14th through 19th centuries and includes a section dedicated to Garibaldi (open daily; admission charge; phone: 99-1295). Stop also for a look at the ultramodern Santuario della Beata Vergine della Consolazione (Sanctuary of the Blessed Virgin of Consolation), which was built in the 1960s and contrasts sharply with the town's medieval appearance.

En Route from Borgo Maggiore – From Borgo Maggiore you can reach San Marino by foot along the shortcut called the Costa, by car, or by cable car.

SAN MARINO: Proceed along the highway toward San Marino City and leave the car in one of the several parking areas near the historic center. The Old City within the walls is entered through the Porta di San Francesco (St. Francis's Gate), begun in the 14th century as the doorway to a convent. Once inside, to the right is the convent and the small Chiesa di San Francesco, both founded in 1361. Though this is the oldest church in the republic, only its façade gives away its age; much of the original character of the interior was lost in 17th- and 18th-century restorations. The cloister next door houses a gallery of changing exhibitions and a museum with some noteworthy old paintings, including one of St. Francis by Guercino.

From the Porta di San Francesco, San Marino's narrow streets must be explored on foot, and the ascent can be quite steep at times. Via Basilicius leads upward to the tiny Piazzetta del Titano, one of the social centers of the town. Not far off the square, on Contrada Omerelli, is the Palazzo Valloni, a structure partly of the 15th and partly of the 18th century. It houses the state archives, with documents dating from 885, as well as the government library. Until recently, it also contained the *Museo Pinacoteca di Stato*, whose collection of paintings and objects of historical and archaeological interest are in storage, pending a decision on a new, permanent home. The collection had been displayed temporarily in the Chiesa di Santa Chiara, farther along on Contrada Omerelli. The street ends with the Porta della Rupe, the gate through which you enter the city if you take the shortcut from Borgo Maggiore.

To continue the ascent, return to Piazzetta del Titano and take the short walk up the hill to Piazza Garibaldi and the government stamp and coin office (Azienda Autonoma di Stato Filatelica e Numismatica). Then turn and follow Contrada del Collegio up to Piazza della Libertà, the largest and most elegant of San Marino's squares. It takes its name from the 19th-century statue of liberty in the middle, but it's also known as the Pianello, since it's one of the few flat spaces within the walls. Off to the left is the mountain shelf and a spectacular view, while directly in front of you, dominating the square, is the Palazzo Pubblico, or government palace.

Although there has been a public building here since the early 14th century, today's Palazzo Pubblico dates only to the end of the 19th century, but it was built in an old-fashioned neo-Gothic style. If you want to arrive for the changing of the guard, stop at the nearby tourist office on Contrada del Collegio for information on the time. (For a fee, this office will also stamp your passport with an unnecessary, but official, San Marino visa.) Open April through October only (phone: 549-991435).

San Marino is governed by two Captains Regent chosen twice a year for 6-month terms by the Great and General Council, whose 60 members, in turn, are elected by popular vote and hold office for 5 years. When parliament is in session, visits to the palace are limited; otherwise, you can see its most important chamber, the richly decorated Sala del Consiglio, with the double throne of the two rulers at one end beneath a large allegorical painting featuring San Marino at its center. Two other rooms usually are on view, in addition to the atrium and the grand staircase, whose walls are covered with busts and inscriptions, works of art as well as symbols of the republic's past.

Among them is a bust of Abraham Lincoln, who was made an honorary citizen of San Marino in 1861. The *sammarinese* (as the natives are called) are proud of the thank-you letter, preserved in the state archives, in which he said. "Although your dominion is small, nevertheless your State is one of the most honoured throughout history . . .."

Beyond the Palazzo Pubblico, Contrada del Pianello leads to the cable-car station.

En route, it passes the Cava dei Balestrieri, the field on which the *Palio delle Balestre Grandi*, a crossbow competition complete with Renaissance costumes, is held each year on September 3, in celebration of the founding of the republic. Don't assume that this colorful event is staged only for tourists — it was mandated by law in the early 17th century, even as crossbows were beginning to be superseded by more modern weapons. Exhibitions are held at other times of the year, but if you miss them, you may still see one of San Marino's crack crossbowmen engaged in target practice.

From here, you can continue the climb by following Contrada Omagnano or by returning to Piazza delle Libertà. Either way, follow signs to the Basilica di San Marino. The mortal remains of the republic's founding saint are buried under the altar of this neo-classic church, which was built in the 19th century to replace an older church that stood on the spot.

From the basilica, more signs point through the oldest quarter of the city to the first of the three fortified towers that figure on the country's coat of arms. The tower, known as the Rocca or Guaita, dates from the 11th century, although in its overall appearance it is of the 15th century. San Marino is 2,465 feet above sea level at this point. For a splendid view, climb to the top of the tower and enjoy the cool breezes blowing off the Adriatic.

The Rocca is joined by a watch path to the second tower, the Fratta or Cesta, on the highest point of Monte Titano (2,470 feet). This tower dates from the early 14th century and contains a museum of arms and armor dating from medieval times to the 20th century. The tower's lookouts provide more magnificent views.

If your legs have held out thus far, you may want to go along the less beaten path to the third tower, the Montale, although it is not open to the public. This narrow, graceful structure was in use from the 13th to the 16th century.

From the Montale tower, a path leads down the slope to the modern Congress Palace. Turn back toward the center along Viale J. F. Kennedy, Via Giacomo Matteotti, and Viale Antonio Onofri, and you will see other modern buildings and, just up the hill, tennis facilities, all evidence of the present in this most ancient of states.

For automobile enthusiasts, the *Museo Auto Ferrari* (Via Tonnini; phone: 990390) is a must. It is small, but well designed and contains a collection of gleaming Ferraris, from the earliest models to the famous Testarossa. Closed Mondays; admission charge.

San Marino is at its traditional best during its holidays. Besides September 3, celebration of the founding of the republic, two choice days to be on hand are April 1 and October 1, when the elaborate, centuries-old investiture ceremony of the newly elected captains regent takes place.

A note to shoppers: Souvenirs of a very pedestrian nature are the most conspicuous items for sale in San Marino. Nevertheless, there are some legitimate buys. These include stamps and coins, of course, as well as local wines and liqueurs. San Marino produces some excellent wines: sangiovese, a rich, robust red, and a naturally fermented sparkling dry white called grilét. Local wines can be sampled and purchased at the cooperative *Consorzio Vini Tipici* (Strada Serrabolino, 87 Valdragone, Borgo Maggiore; phone: 549-902124). For an idea of crafts products available, go to the *Mostra dell'Artigianato* (Handicraft Exhibition) above the Piazzale Mario Giangi parking area, just off Viale Federico d'Urbino. If you've brought serious spending money, have a look at *G. Arzilli* (1 Via Donna Felicissima) a large jewelry store on par with the best in Italy.

BEST EN ROUTE

Expect to pay $50 or more per night for a double room in hotels rated as expensive; about $40 to $50 in those listed as moderate; and about $35 in inexpensive hotels. A meal for two will cost from $40 to $60 in expensive restaurants and from $30 to $40 in moderate ones. All restaurants serve an economical tourist menu whose fixed price is prominently displayed. Note that most San Marino hotels and restaurants close for a month or two in winter. All restaurants listed below accept major credit cards, unless otherwise indicated.

Grand Hotel San Marino – Just outside the Old City walls, this modern hotel is probably the most comfortable in San Marino. Each of the 54 rooms has a private bath or shower and each of the front rooms has a balcony with a beautiful view of the Apennines. There is a restaurant, the *Arengo* (reservations advised), and a garage. Viale Antonio Onofri (phone: 549-992400; fax: 549-992274; telex: 505555). Expensive.

Righi-La Taverna – In summer, the tables right on Piazza della Libertà are filled with tourists feasting on one-dish platters and the grand view of the Palazzo Pubblico. But the local specialties and pizza also served at this 2-story restaurant make it very popular with the *sammarinese* year-round. Open every day in summer; closed Wednesdays in winter and from mid-December through January. Reservations advised. Piazza della Libertà (phone: 549-991196). Expensive.

Il Beccafico – Centrally located closed to the Rocca, or Tower, this eatery is decorated with crossbows and other ancient weapons. Specialties include such typical local dishes as ravioli stuffed with ricotta cheese and herbs, and *caciatello,* a dessert not unlike crème caramel and just as tasty. Reservations unnecessary. 35 Via Salita alla Rocca (phone: 549-992430). Moderate.

Bolognese – There are only 5 rooms in this small, family-run hotel, but each is furnished with character, including solid wood antique bedsteads in some cases. The restaurant has a terrace for outdoor dining on warm summer evenings. 28 Via Basilicius (phone: 549-991056). Moderate.

Buca San Francesco – Straightforward cooking of San Marino and the neighboring Romagna region. Pasta dishes include *tagliatelle,* tortellini, and green lasagna, while second courses range from *scaloppine al formaggio e funghi* (with cheese and mushrooms) to grilled and mixed roast meat. Open daily from March through October. Reservations unnecessary. 3 Via Orafo (phone: 549-991462). Moderate.

Excelsior – Not as grand as its name suggests, but nevertheless a clean, comfortable hotel with an award-winning restaurant and parking facilities. Viale J. Istriani (phone: 549-991163 or 549-991940; fax: 549-990399). Moderate.

La Fratta – This busy, cheerful restaurant specializes in spit-roasted meat. It also turns out very fine homemade *tagliatelle.* The decor is rustic, and a terrace offers a panoramic view for alfresco dining. Open daily. Reservations advised. Salita alla Rocca (phone: 549-991594). Moderate.

La Grotta – This charming hostelry has 14 rooms, all with private bath or shower, and a pleasant restaurant. Contrada Santa Croce (phone: 549-991214). Moderate.

Joli – Just outside the city walls, this small hotel is comfortable and friendly, with the added bonus of a garage to help solve parking problems. 38 Viale Federico D'Urbino (phone: 549-991008). Moderate.

La Rocca – A small, pleasant hostelry on the way up to the Rocca, or castle, it has 10 rooms, each with a bath and most with private balconies offering good views. It also boasts a small swimming pool, an uncommon luxury at San Marino hotels. Salita alla Rocca (phone: 549-991166). Moderate.

Titano – San Marino's first hotel, it opened in the 1890s, just a few steps from Piazza della Libertà. It has 50 rooms, all with bath or shower and some with a view. The panoramic terrace restaurant is one of the loveliest spots in town. 21 Contrada del Collegio (phone: 549-991006; fax: 549-991375; telex: 505444). Moderate.

Vecchia Stazione – Owned and operated by the Andreani brothers, who also operate the *Joli* hotel next door, this eatery has acquired a reputation for good traditional San Marino cooking. Try *nidi di rondine* (pasta rolls stuffed with ham, cheese, and tomato and baked in a bechamel sauce) and *coniglio porchetta disossato* (oven-roasted rabbit stuffed with fennel). Reservations unnecessary. Viale Federico D'Urbino (phone: 549-991009). Moderate.

Diamond – Here are 7 inexpensive rooms for guests and one of the best restaurants in town. The building is quite unusual — it's been dug out of a rock. Open daily from mid-March to mid-October. Contrada del Collegio (phone: 549-991003). Hotel, inexpensive; restaurant, moderate.

The Soviet Union

Today's Soviet Union is an amalgam of disparate elements. We see history unfolding daily, as the effects of the death of Communism are felt and a new political order emerges. There is, on one hand, the surviving awesome beauty of Russian churches and religious icons, the music of Peter Ilyich Tchaikovsky and Nikolai Rimsky-Korsakov, and the art treasures of the now renamed St. Petersburg's *Hermitage;* on the other, is the technology of space exploration, the ultra-efficiency of Moscow's metro, the frustration of long shopping lines, and the coordination of Soviet industrial companies with a host of foreign firms. The Soviet Union is Stalin's purges, vodka and caviar, a *troika* ride across the snow in bitter cold, and the warmth of a family gathering around the samovar. It is the "Song of the Volga Boatman," the voices of Leo Tolstoy and Fyodor Dostoyevsky, and the Kremlin clock chimes ringing out across Red Square. It is borscht and ballet, balalaikas and bureaucracy, and renegade republics; no longer can it lay claim to Estonia, Latvia, and Lithuania — they are now free and separate states. It also is a state of intellectual, political, religious, financial, and ethnic ferment — an ever-changing economic order, with peasant women in babushkas still peddling their garden vegetables from roadside tables, while *McDonald's* is selling more *Big Mocs* daily in Moscow than in most of its other franchises around the world.

For the visitor to the Soviet Union, *glasnost* (openness), the disintegration of the Communist Party , and the debut of democracy have inaugurated many new options. Until recently, for example, most foreigners arriving in St. Petersburg or Moscow saw little more than these two cities. Now visitors are free to enter the Soviet Union at any number of gateways, such as Torfianovka, Bursnichnoye, Chop, Brest, Shegini, or — an increasingly popular point of entry — Tallinn, the capital of Estonia that was part (reluctantly) of the Soviet Union for over 50 years.

Still other travel options are being made available. *Finnair* flies from Helsinki to Tallinn in about 20 minutes, while the government-run *Aeroflot* flies from Helsinki to St. Petersburg in about an hour. Or, if you prefer to travel in a more leisurely fashion, ferry across the Baltic in less than 4 hours. *Aeroflot* and *Scandinavian Airlines System* (*SAS*) now provide service from Stockholm to Tallinn, and from both Stockholm and Copenhagen to Riga, capital of Latvia, another gateway eager for Western tourism. The venturesome are even entering through Erevan, on Turkey's northern border, driving all the way up to Finland.

Further helping to ease travel snags is the Soviet Union's increased receptiveness to tourism by car. Whereas only two routes were open to rental cars in the recent past, today's travelers can drive on more than 12,000 miles of main and secondary roads, and in major cities such as Moscow and Tallinn, cars can be rented through *Auto Europe, Hertz,* or *Intourist* (see *Traveling by Car* in GETTING READY TO GO). Bear in mind, however, that Soviet traffic regulations are strictly enforced, and violators — particularly drunken drivers — are subject to stiff fines or jail.

Despite the many real rewards of *glasnost,* and the recent political upheavals, not everything — and anything — goes. You must still register the route you choose to take with *Intourist,* as well as clear any hotel and transportation reservations through them. You also must allow at least 6 weeks for your visa — especially if you plan to travel on your own — and though state-run tourism organizations have lost some 15% to 20% of their business to new private, cooperative, or autonomous industries, you still may find that you need *Intourist* — or at least a US travel agent specializing in Eastern European tours — to make all the reservations you want (see *Package Tours* in GETTING READY TO GO).

So far from throwing caution to the wind and kicking up your heels, the best rule of thumb is to play it conservatively. Before arranging your itinerary, always check the US State Department's latest Soviet Union travel advisories to find out how the current political situation may — or may not — affect your plans. In addition to its warnings about an increase in crime (mainly pocketpicking and mugging), the State Department has been advising travelers in frail health not to visit the Soviet Union. Organized tours are strenuous, basic medical supplies (such as disposable hypodermic needles) are in short supply, and health care and hygiene are seldom up to the standards back home. But for those who are stout of heart and sturdy of health, adventurous in spirit and, more important, eager to become a part of living history, there's no question that illumination, stimulation, and insights by the cartload await in the Soviet Union.

The rapidly altering borders of the Soviet Union nominally stretch some 6,800 miles from the Baltic Sea in the west to the Bering Strait, which separates it from Alaska, in the east, and extends north-south nearly 3,000 miles. Its 7.9 million square miles (the defection of the Baltic States reduced its size by less than a million square miles) represent more than one-sixth of the earth's total landmass, covering the eastern half of Europe and the northern third of Asia. Winters can be long and severe, and the short growing season and erratic rainfall have hindered agricultural development.

This vast country recently consisted of 12 separate republics — at least 8 of which have declared themselves independent and its 272 million people represent more than 90 (the combined populations of Estonia, Latvia, and Lithuania have lessened the number by only 7.7 million) ethnic groups — although Russians, Ukrainians, and Byelorussians make up about half the total. Russian is the official language, but the use of local minority languages is encouraged.

The so-called European part of the Soviet Union, ranging from the country's western borders to the Ural Mountains, is the area of densest population and the area most often explored by tourists. We also have included the several southern republics of the Transcaucasus between the Black and Caspian seas, which, though less often visited, offer a most interesting look at a section of the Soviet Union influenced more by the Middle East than Europe.

The tensions between West and East were important in shaping the development of this country. The evolution of the territory commonly known as Russia is a complex amalgamation of the histories of several distinct nationalities.

The Slavic tribes who lived in the Kiev and Novgorod areas from earliest times were relatively peaceful, but were preyed upon often by Asian and Germanic tribes. In the 9th century, the Viking Varangians were invited by the Novgorod republic to come and restore order; their reign lasted until the 13th century. The Greek Orthodox religion, adopted from the Byzantine Empire, was introduced in Kiev Rus, the first East Slavic principality, and was to remain a dominant theme of East Slavic life until the Bolshevik Revolution proclaimed official atheism in this century.

The Tatar-Mongol invasions began in the 13th century. Kiev Rus was conquered and held in bondage for some 250 years until another east Slavic principality, Muscovy, became strong enough, under Ivan IV (also known as Ivan the Terrible) to break the Mongol stranglehold. It was during the Tatar period that the institution of serfdom took hold.

In the 16th century Russian history was dominated by Ivan the Terrible, who built a powerful united state but also imposed a reign of terror. A period of strife and upheaval followed his death. Then Michael Romanov, the first of the dynasty that would rule Russia for over 300 years, was elected czar. Peter the Great, the first powerful Romanov, came to the throne at the end of the 17th century. He introduced Western customs, culture, and technical achievements that transformed his country from a backward principality to a powerful empire. But neither he nor Catherine the Great, widow of his grandson and the next powerful Russian ruler, dealt with the system of serfdom that enslaved tens of thousands of Russian peasants. Russia's most famous serf rebellion, the Pugachev revolt, occurred during her reign.

In the wake of the French Revolution and the Napoleonic wars, a wave of liberalism spread over Europe, but the czars of Imperial Russia continued to run their country like a private estate. When Czar Alexander I died in 1825, there was an abortive revolution known as the Decembrist uprising, which, although crushed, became a symbol for liberals, radicals, and revolutionaries for the remainder of the century. After Russia was defeated by the French and British in the Crimean War, Czar Alexander II found it practical to issue a proclamation freeing the serfs, but the evils of the system continued. When the czar was killed by a terrorist's bomb in 1881, any gains that had accrued to the peasants were lost and a reactionary attitude set in that would dominate the remaining years of czarist rule.

Still, the 19th century had been an extraordinary one for the arts in Russia. Literature flourished, beginning with Alexander Pushkin, and including Nikolai Gogol, Ivan Turgenev, Dostoyevsky, and Tolstoy. In music, Russia produced Tchaikovsky, Modeste Moussorgsky, Alexander Borodin, and Rimsky-Korsakov. Toward the end of the century, there was a flowering of the dramatic arts with the plays of Anton Chekhov and the staging of Konstantin Stanislavsky. And by the early 20th century, Russia had become preeminent in ballet.

At the turn of the century, however, the conditions of the peasants deteriorated further in the wake of a staggering depression and Russia's defeat in the Russo-Japanese War. When a peaceful group of workers and their families tried to petition the czar for relief, the soldiers opened fire on them. This massacre, known as Bloody Sunday, was the first act of violence in the 1905 Revolution, which led to the establishment of a more democratic form of constitutional monarchy. However, Russia's entry into World War I imposed further hardships on the country. In March 1917 (February by the new calendar), a bourgeois democratic revolution brought down the entire structure of czardom, and a provisional government was formed. Then, on November 7, the Bolsheviks, V. I. Lenin's Communist party, replaced the provisional government with the first Soviet state. A full-scale civil war raged until 1922, when the Red Army triumphed and the Union of Soviet Socialist Republics emerged.

After Lenin died, the Soviet leadership passed to Joseph Stalin, and the country moved into a period of rapid industrialization and brutal collectivization of agriculture. Stalin was a ruthless leader in absolute control of the Communist Party. When he purged the party of those he considered unworthy of membership, they were not merely expelled; they were executed.

Economic development was interrupted by World War II, in which the Soviet Union was allied with Britain, France, and the United States. The people of the Soviet Union suffered extraordinary losses during the war. Huge areas of the country were destroyed, and some 20 million soldiers and civilians were killed. Following the war, Soviet power extended into neighboring countries of Eastern Europe, and by 1946, the Cold War between the Soviet states and the Western powers was a fact of life. A so-called Iron Curtain separated the West from the xenophobia of the Communist bloc.

After Stalin's death, his excesses were denounced by Nikita Khrushchev, who, as premier, preached peaceful coexistence with the West. But his tenure also saw the widening of an ideological rift between the USSR and mainland China, which lessened Soviet influence in some parts of the world. Conflicts with the US, especially over Cuba, kept the Cold War icy. Khrushchev was forced into obscurity in 1964, and ultimately was succeeded by Leonid Brezhnev, who, until the Soviet invasion of Afghanistan, presided over a period of détente with the West — as well as years of domestic economic and political stagnation.

Mikhail Gorbachev represented the first generation of Soviet leaders who were not born until after Lenin's death, and the first President of the USSR to wield real power. And until the free election of Boris Yeltsin as President of the Russian Republic in June, 1991, Gorbachev's power — though challenged — was pretty much intact.

Then in the summer of 1991, an abortive 72-hour coup led by the KGB and other right wing hardliners turned out to be the death knell for the Communist old guard and signaled the disintegration of the Soviet Union as it has existed since the 1917 Revolution. Although Gorbachev managed to remain in office, Yeltsin's voice was heard loud and clear.

The subsequent end of 74 years of Communist rule, coupled with the inroads made by *glasnost* and *perestroika* (restructuring), have created a new atmosphere for intellectuals (and others) that is reflected in the theater, the art world, on television, and in the press, and most of all, in Soviet political perspectives. The effort to change and renew the moribund Soviet economic system now is the country's primary priority, and observing the process is stimulating and thought-provoking.

The Soviet Union is different things to different people. In truth, the recent dramatic changes have not yet changed the nation's basic image with outsiders; it remains neither a workers' paradise nor an authoritarian land of automatons. Where it currently fits on such a continuum is something for individual assessment. But for the visitor willing to set preconceptions aside for the duration, this huge, important country has much to recommend. It has a splendid cultural history and an impressive record of modern technical and scientific achievement.

Traveling in the quiet countryside provides the perfect opportunity to meet and get to know the Soviet people. A surprisingly high percentage of Soviet citizens speak English, German, or French. For the most part, they are proud of their country and interested in yours. You may learn more about the Soviet Union from such personal encounters than from any other aspect of your trip.

The following routes have been designed to introduce you to some of the most interesting places in the European part of the Soviet Union, and to permit you to experience the cultures of several different ethnic groups. With the first route, you can start out — or wind up — in Finland. The route goes to St. Petersburg and Moscow, and offers a taste of the typical Soviet countryside: picturesque villages of fancifully painted peasant cottages; lush backyard vegetable gardens providing vivid contrast with mile after mile of lifeless collective farms; vast pine forests alternating with dreary factory towns; walled kremlins (fortresses) and gold-encrusted churches dating back to the Middle Ages, yet as vital as if they had just been erected yesterday.

The second route leads down the mighty Volga River from Kazan to Rostov-on-Don, and provides a window on the history of Russia.

The third route actually is an exploration of two of the Soviet Union's most important cities — Kiev and Odessa — and introduces Ukrainian culture.

For rest and relaxation, we also have provided a tour of Black Sea resorts. This route runs from Yalta (in the Crimea) along the eastern shore to Sukhumi (in the Republic of Georgia). Our last tour, from Batumi on the Black Sea coast through snow-peaked Caucasus Mountains to Vladikavkaz (formerly Ordzhonikidze), will acquaint you with the several distinct national groups that populate Georgia.

■**Note:** In addition to our choices for hotel accommodations listed in *Best en Route* at the end of each driving tour, travelers now have the option of staying at bed and breakfast establishments in many parts of the Soviet Union. *IBV Bed & Breakfast Systems* (13113 Ideal Dr., Silver Springs, MD; phone: 301-942-3770; fax: 301-933-0024) makes arrangements for foreigners to book a room and bath with a local family. *IBV* also can arrange rentals for furnished apartments and summer resort cottages throughout the Baltics.

From Finland, Tallinn or Vyborg to Novgorod

Make the Baltic crossing from Helsinki to Tallinn during the summer, on any day of the week but Wednesday. (Sailings are less frequent during the other seasons.) From the Estonian capital to Moscow by way of St. Petersburg and historic Novgorod, you'll be covering 680 miles (1,088 km). Another option: Travel by train from Finland, then rent a car in the Soviet Union at Vyborg, close to one of the border-crossing towns. From Vyborg to St. Petersburg and on to Moscow is 582 miles (931 km).

TALLINN: The city's primarily Estonian people are closely related ethnically, linguistically, and culturally to the Finns. Stroll through Tallinn's Old Town over crooked cobblestone streets and between wonderfully preserved Hanseatic buildings with their red tile roofs, turrets, spires, and ancient steeples. The city's fortifications date back to the Danish conquerors of the 13th century and the Teutonic knights of the 14th century. The triumphal arch in Town Hall Square was erected in honor of the visit of Peter the Great in the 1700s. Visit the palace built by Peter for his wife Catherine (not to be confused with Catherine the Great, who appeared on the scene much later). Here in the palace you'll note a disturbing collection of stylized paintings which artists were forced to create under Stalin's regime, "idealizing" what actually was the painful surrender by peasants of their animals to collective farms. This collection has been preserved in its original form to serve as a "reminder" to all who see it of those suppressive days of not so long ago.

The *Dragon Gallery* (18 Pikk St.; phone: 142-601979) is Tallinn's most interesting place for art. Should you need to exchange currency, the Tartu Commercial Bank (9 Dunkri St. in Old Town) can help you.

En Route from Tallinn – The trip to St. Petersburg (250 miles/400 km) is a full-day's drive.

VYBORG: The other point-of-entry option from Finland, Vyborg boasts fewer than 80,000 inhabitants, but due to its important role during the Communist Revolution, it is worth a visit. It was here that contraband Marxist literature and weapons were smuggled into imperial Russia from abroad. It was also here that Lenin went into hiding in September 1917, working underground to mastermind the Bolshevik uprising the following month in St. Petersburg. Besides Lenin's house, located downtown, which has been turned into a musueum (*Intourist* offers a 4-hour tour for $50), you'll want to see Vyborg's Scandinavian-style castle and the city's early Novgorodian settlement, as well as a handful of other historical buildings dating back to the 13th, 15th, 16th, and 18th centuries.

En Route from Vyborg – The trip from Vyborg to St. Petersburg (125 miles/ 200 km) is an easy half-day's drive.

After your visit to St. Petersburg (see also *St. Petersburg* in THE CITIES), take another half-day's drive down the not yet renamed Leningrad-Moscow Highway to Novgorod.

NOVGOROD: Roughly translated as "New Town," Novgorod is a cultural and crafts center. It was founded by the Slavs more than 1,100 years ago, and is one of the oldest cities in the Soviet Union. From the 12th to the 15th century, Novgorod was a feudal republic run by a legislature of merchants and princes, whose domain extended from the Arctic and Baltic seas to the Ural Mountains. Karl Marx called it "Russia's first republic," though Novgorod lost its independence to czarist conquerors in 1471, then was nearly destroyed during World War II by the Nazis. Fortunately, many of its treasures have been skillfully restored.

Like Moscow, Novgorod has a walled kremlin, housing St. Sophia Cathedral, built in 1045 and one of Russia's oldest churches. Its center dome is a giant replica of a warrior's helmet, topped by a brass dove and cross. Local legend has it that Novgorod will survive as long as that dove never flies away. The kremlin's art museum contains fine collections of early religious hand-lettered manuscripts and gold icons.

From Novgorod on to the capital of the Soviet Union (219 miles/350 km) is another full day's drive. (See *Moscow,* THE CITIES.)

BEST EN ROUTE

Hotel prices throughout the Soviet Union will be determined more by your specific travel plans, the time of the year you choose to go (with summer the most expensive season), and the class of accommodations you pick (*Intourist* rates hotels — and in some cases, rooms — according to 2, 3, and 4 stars, with 4 stars the most comfortable). A tourist selects the level of luxury (a relative term in the Soviet Union), rather than an individual hotel. Western tourists will discover that lodging is about as expensive as in major American cities. Economy options do not exist per se — unless you decide to go camping. Keep in mind that *Intourist* and establishments run by them accept hard currency only.

Although *Intourist* once ran virtually all the hotels and restaurants in the Soviet Union, 15% to 20% of this business now is run by private enterprises, cooperatives, and autonomous regional organizations. This can be a mixed blessing, since the newer travel resources often book the least modern hotels. By contrast, the new cooperative restaurants usually boast better and more varied menus (often at higher prices). Please note that the rate of failure is high among these new ventures. It still is advisable to make your arrangements through a US travel agent specializing in Eastern European travel.

Restaurants generally open in late morning and close by midnight. The price of meals is relatively low, compared to what you'd have to pay for something similar in the US. Reservations usually are not required, but it's wise to double-check with your hotel's *Intourist* desk before heading off to dine. *Intourist* also can provide the names and addresses of private or cooperative cafés and restaurants that offer local and European cuisine. You may have to make your own reservations here, however — that is, if you speak Russian, or have an interpreter on hand.

Tallinn's cuisine reflects Slavic, Germanic, and Hungarian influences. Try the *sult* (jellied veal), *pirukad* (meat-filled pastry), *rosolje* (beet vinaigrette), *mulgi kapsus* (meat with sauerkraut and barley), and the Estonian version of goulash. Vyborg was part of Finland until World War II, but its food is basically Russian today.

TALLINN

Gloria – The medieval town wall is part of the entrance to this large and respectable restaurant. A variety show is performed daily, except Mondays, and dance music is played. Hard currency accepted for alcohol. 2 Müürivahe (phone: 142-446950).

Gnoom – A snug, medieval-style dining establishment that has a cellar with recorded music, a grillroom with live music, and a bar. 2 Viru (phone: 142-442488).

Kannike – A cozy cooperative where a sauna, beer, and snack can be enjoyed. 108 Vabaduse Puiestee (phone: 142-447888).

Kirole Grill and Bar – Another cooperative dining place, this one specializes in seafood. 19 Pärny Maantee (phone: 142-446550).

Kungla – An unpretentious hostelry built about 20 years ago in the center of Tallinn. It has 160 rooms, a restaurant with a variety show, café, hard currency bar, and hair salon. 25 Kreutzwaldi St. (phone: 142-421460).

Maiisnokk – The oldest tearoom in Tallinn, with a fine sampling of pastries. 16 Pikk St. (phone: 142-601396).

Nord – Seafood and Estonian fare are served in a house set in the Old Town. 3-5 Rataskaevu (phone: 142-443170).

Olympia – A 26-story modern hostelry with a splendid view of the Old Town. There are 378 rooms, a restaurant with a variety show, café, grill-bar, sauna, souvenir shop, hair salon, car rental service, and currency exchange. 33 Kingissepa St. (phone: 142-602436 or 142-602438; telex: 173165).

Palace – Modernized tastefully in a joint venture with Finland's *Arctia* chain, it offers 92 rooms, all with private bath, mini-bar, phone, satellite color TV, and even a trouser press. Two of the 5 suites have their own sauna. There also are 2 restaurants on the premises — *Linda* with first class food, and the cozy street-level *Pizzaria Margareta* with Italian fare. There's also a casino, car rental, and currency exchange. 3 Voidu Valjak (phone: 142-444540).

Peoleo – An Estonian-Canadian venture with 22 double rooms, a restaurant, bar, hard currency shop, tennis courts, and an English-speaking concierge. 555 Pärny Maantee, Laagri (phone: 142-444761; fax: 142-443098; telex: 173247).

Rataskaevu – Newly restored, this cozy hostelry in the Old Town hosts guests of the government. There are 19 rooms and a restaurant. 7 Rataskaevu St. (phone: 142-441939).

Submonte – A popular new Old Town eatery where continental fare is served. An Estonian-Finnish joint venture. 4 Rüütli (phone: 142-666871).

Tallinn – Not quite on a par with the *Viru* or *Palace*, but offering 202 rooms, a restaurant, and 4 bars. English-speaking concierge. 27 Toompuiestee St. (phone: 142-604332).

Viru – A high-rise hotel on Viru Square that is both Finnish-built and furnished. Among its attractions: a supper club with a floor show and dancing, as well as *Restaurant 22* on its top floor (yes, the 22nd) with good continental food and an even better view of the Old Town below. 4 Viru Sq. (phone: 142-652093; fax: 142-448423).

VYBORG

Druzhba – One of the city's newer hotels — it was built in 1982 — it offers 102 rooms, a swimming pool, and a sauna, plus a restaurant featuring a choice of European, Asian, or Russian food. Car rental and hard currency exchange are on the premises. Located near the railroad station, it's particularly handy if you plan on arriving by rail. 5 Zheleznodorozhnaya (phone: 81278-25744).

NOVGOROD

Intourist – Offering 122 rooms, and a restaurant with both European and Russian food. Also, a hard currency bar, hair salon, and currency exchange office. 16 Dmitriyevskaya (phone: 81622-75089 or 81622-74235).

Russki Chai – A tea house across the kremlin park, serving caviar, sandwiches, and pastries, plus a selection of teas poured from samovars. 1-4 Leningrad St. (phone: 81622-92488).

The Volga

The Volga is a river the size and strength of Russia itself, a waterway that crosses a continent, a river the Russians call "mother." Tourists who travel its route by steamer come closest to feeling the real spirit of the Russians. The timeless atmosphere of quaint rural villages is juxtaposed with the modern technology of hydroelectric installations and automobile plants. The Volga is a mighty river: 2,300 miles long, from Volgoverkhvoye northwest of Moscow to Astrakhan, a delta city on the Caspian Sea.

Since earliest times, the Volga has carried Finns, Slavs, Turks, Mongols, and Tatars; Jews, Christians, and Muslims, all seeking trade and conquest. In 1552, Ivan the Terrible opened the Volga to the Russians by defeating the Kazan Tatars. The most recent conflict over the Volga came from Hitler and the German army. During the months between August 1942 and February 1943, the Nazis ravaged Stalingrad (now Volgograd) in an unsuccessful attempt to subdue Russia and reach the oil-rich Caspian.

Today, the Volga region hosts thousands of tourists from around the world each year. This river route goes from Kazan to Ulyanovsk, Togliatti, Volgograd, and Rostov-on-Don, 900 miles (1,440 km) to the south. You can reach Kazan by plane, train, or car. *Intourist* can arrange a Volga River cruise for you. The entire trip from Kazan to Rostov-on-Don takes 11 days, but you may select a shorter itinerary. Cruise boats provide complete accommodations, including meals and lodging.

KAZAN: The capital of the Tatar Autonomous Republic also is the cultural center of the Tatars (or Tartars), one of the many distinct nationalities that make up the Soviet Union. The city dates from the 15th century. It was the center of a typical medieval Muslim state with many internal conflicts as well as struggles with the Russians. In 1552, Czar Ivan the Terrible and the Russian army captured Kazan. Today, the city is half Russian and half Tatar.

A good place to begin a tour of the city is the Kazan Kremlin (Pervomaiskaya Pl.; phone: 8432-327466), which dates from the 15th and 16th centuries. The kremlin, near where the Kazanka River enters the Volga, is an architectural monument (*kremlin* means "fortress" in old Russian) with marvelous towers and churches. There is an impressive panorama of the kremlin from the Spassky (Spasskaya) Tower. Across the square from the Spassky Tower is the *Tatar State Museum* (2 Lenina St.; phone: 8432-327162), with a good collection of information about the Volga region. Near Lake Kazan there are two imposing 18th-century mosques: Mardzhani, open for services (17 Nasiri) and Apanayevskaya (29 Nasiri).

During the 19th century, the University of Kazan (18 Lenina; phone: 8432-321549) was a center of liberal ideas in eastern Russia. V. I. Ulyanov-Lenin was expelled from law school here in 1887 for taking part in student riots. Although a statue of Lenin as a student stood in front of the university as we went to press, and a Lenin Monument sat in Svodbody Place (the main square of Kazan), both may have been toppled by the time you read this.

An important collecting and processing point for Russian furs, Kazan is a major rail junction and one of the largest industrial centers in the Volga basin.

The main shopping street, or *ulitsa*, is Bauman. You can relax in Gorky Park on Ershova, or at the zoo and botanical gardens (112 Taktasha; phone: 8432-375032 for both). For entertainment, visit the *Musa Dzhalil Opera and Ballet Theater* (Svodbody Pl.; phone: 8432-324328) or the puppet theater (21 Lukovskova; phone: 8432-389272).

En Route from Kazan – By boat, the trip to Ulyanovsk takes about 12 hours. The boat passes through the Kuybyshev Reservoir and valleys, where, depending on the season, you may see fruit trees in bloom or fields of wheat, sunflowers, or potatoes. Coriander is grown and processed in one of these valleys. Approaching Ulyanovsk, you pass the popular bathing beach on Paltsensky Island, which can be reached by boat from Ulyanovsk.

ULYANOVSK: This small city on a high hill on the Volga-Sviyaga watershed was called Simbirsk until 1924, when it was renamed for its most famous son: Vladimir Ilich Ulyanov, known to the world as V. I. Lenin. Lenin was born here on April 22, 1870.

The *Lenin Museum* (58 Lenina St.; phone: 8422-312222), which contains mementos of Lenin's youth, is in the house where the family lived in the 1880s before Lenin left to attend the University of Kazan. Nearby a huge Lenin Memorial Complex, including the house in which he was born, his grammar school, and other buildings associated with his life, was opened in 1970 to commemorate the 100th anniversary of his birth. A statue of Lenin as a schoolboy is in front of the railway station.

There are a number of interesting old, low, wooden houses along the narrow streets of the city. The main shopping street is Goncharov.

■ **Note::** Given today's anti-Lenin sentiment, it is not inconceivable that the above-mentioned sites and streets will be renamed, and that Ulyanovsk's original name be restored.

En Route from Ulyanovsk – The journey to Volgograd takes about 36 hours by boat and is full of fascinating sights. Shortly after leaving Ulyanovsk, you pass Vinnovskaya Grove, a popular recreation park.

If you made the river journey in the mid-1960s and came back today, you would be struck by how much the Volga bears witness to Soviet progress. The former town of Stavropol, south of the Kuybyshev Reservoir and Hydroelectric Plant, has become the new city of Togliatti. This industrial center was renamed for a former leader of the Italian Communist Party when the Volga Automobile Factory was built and equipped in cooperation with the Italian firm, Fiat. Excursions to Togliatti can be made by hydrofoil from Ulyanovsk. Nearby you can see the Lenin Hydropower Works.

Now the Volga winds around the Zhiguli Mountains. Forests and small settlements of Russian vacation homes, *dachas,* line the banks.

VOLGOGRAD: Historically, this city has been important as a southern outpost to protect Russia from invasions. It was founded in the 16th century as the fortress town of Tsaritsyn to guard the Volga route.

The city made its greatest mark on history during the period in which it was called Stalingrad (1925–61) by handing the German army one of its most significant defeats of World War II. Stalingraders fought the Nazis house to house for a full year until Soviet troops could encircle and defeat them. The Victory Monument to the heroism of Stalingrad's people, on the ancient Mamaev Kurgean hill, is one of the most moving war monuments ever built: Scenes of battle are depicted on the steps leading up from Lenin Prospekt. An eternal flame burns in the circular Hall of Military Glory. Slogans of the street-fighters are carved into the walls, and the names of all the war dead are inscribed on mosaic plaques.

Volgograd stretches along the river for 43 miles. It is the administrative and economic center of the lower Volga region.

There is a planetarium (on Yuri Gagarin; phone: 8442-363483), a circus (on Volodarsky; phone: 8442-363106), a musical comedy theater (on the Central Quay; phone: 8442-363105), and a puppet theater (15 Lenin Prospekt; phone: 8442-330649). Shopping is concentrated in the area around the city's center, Fallen Fighters Square (Pavshikh Bortsov Pl.) and the Alleya Geroyev.

En Route from Volgograd – The boat goes west here through the canal connecting the Volga with the River Don.

To reach the Don, your boat passes through a number of locks and the Tsimlyansk Reservoir, which feeds the canal and irrigates the steppe.

ROSTOV-ON-DON (Rostov-na-Dony): If you have come the entire way from Kazan, you may notice the difference in the appearance of this southern city, the gateway to the Caucasus. The area of Rostov-on-Don beyond the central Theater Square (Teatralnyi Pl.) was once the Armenian town of Nakhichevani, and the houses here are typically low, old Armenian dwellings.

Rostov-on-Don became a city in 1797, having grown up around a fortress built to defend Russia from the Turks. Its importance as a port city and trade center was enhanced by the completion of the Volga-Don Canal in 1952. The city now has a population of 1 million.

Shopping and museums are along Engelsa. There are four theaters, a racecourse, a regional philharmonic orchestra, a bathing beach, a sports stadium, and several parks here.

Some 42 miles (67 km) to the east in the industrial town of Taganrog on the Azov Sea, is the *Chekhov Museum* in the house where the great Russian writer and dramatist was born.

Moscow is about 2 hours by plane from Rostov-on-Don, if you are at the end of your tour. On the other hand, it is a good starting place for a tour of the Black Sea coast. You also can return to Moscow by way of Kiev.

BEST EN ROUTE

The cuisine of the Volga region is wholesome and hearty. You might begin your meal with an array of hot and cold appetizers called *zakusky*. Baked fish stuffed with buckwheat groats and *solyanka,* a fish or meat stew made tart with salted cucumbers and olives, are delicious entrées.

KAZAN

Kazan – Run by *Intourist,* this restaurant offers live music. 9 Bauman St. (phone: 8432-320930).

Mayak – For continental fare. 185 Dekabristov St. (phone: 8432-535482).

Tatarstan – Centrally located, this dining spot serves local dishes, and live music is played. 1 Kuybysheva St. (phone: 8432-323533).

Vostok – Located in the center of town, this restaurant specializes in Uzbek food. Reservations advised. 13 Kuybysheva St. (phone: 8432-323533).

ULYANOVSK

Venets – Run by *Intourist,* it has 480 rooms, a restaurant, and hard currency shop. 19 Sovietskaya (phone: 8422-394880).

Volga – With 350 rooms, a restaurant, hair salon, and television sets. 3 Goncharov (phone: 8422-314577).

VOLGOGRAD

Intourist – A comfortable hostelry with a restaurant, hard currency bar, and hair salon. 14 Mira St. (phone: 8442-364553; fax: 8442-339175; telex: 117116).

Tashkent – Russian and Uzbek food are served at this spot on the Volga Embankment, along with live music (phone: 8422-363636).

Volgograd – More Russian fare and live music. 12 Mira St. (phone: 8442-361116).

ROSTOV-ON-DON

Moskovskaya – Another *Intourist* property, it has 179 rooms, a restaurant and hair salon. 62 Engelsa St. (phone: 8632-388700).

Rostov – With 400 rooms, a restaurant (serving Russian food along with a variety show), a sauna, bar, and hair salon. 59 Budyonovsky Prospekt (phone: 8632-391670).

Tsentralny – Russian food and live music. 36 Engelsa (phone: 8632-666916).

Volgodon – Popular dishes here include fried chicken, steaks, and *salat Slaviansky* (sliced boiled beef, potatoes, fresh cucumbers, peas, and hard-boiled eggs covered with mayonnaise). 31 Beregovaya (no phone).

Kiev and Odessa

Two of the most important cities in the Soviet Union are in the Ukrainian Soviet Socialist Republic, which lies between Russia, to the east, and Poland, Czechoslovakia, Hungary, and Bulgaria to the west. Kiev is the third-largest city in the Soviet Union, and Odessa, on the Black Sea, is one of the Soviet Union's major ports.

The Ukraine slopes down from the Carpathian Mountains in the west to rolling hills with beautiful oak and beech forests, and broad plains where the soil is rich and black. It is well developed agriculturally as well as industrially, and is sometimes called the breadbasket of the Soviet Union.

Although the sentiment for Ukrainian nationalism has remained strong, Ukrainians have long been considered junior partners in governing the Soviet Union. Leonid Brezhnev, the late general secretary of the Soviet Communist Party, was born here and held important party posts in the Ukraine earlier in his career. Khrushchev, Russian by birth, was a party official here and carried out Stalin's purges in the Ukraine.

Kiev is some 532 miles (851 km) southwest of Moscow. It can be reached by plane, train, or road. Odessa, almost due south of Kiev — about 303 miles (485 km) — also is linked by rail, air, and road, and can be reached by sea. You can sail between Kiev and Odessa on the Dnieper River.

KIEV: The capital and cultural center of the Ukraine is a picturesque city that grew up on a series of wooded hills overlooking the Dnieper. Poplar and chestnut trees along the streets soften the effect of the rather undistinguished buildings built after World War II. Parks and gardens make up nearly 60% of Kiev.

Before the Golden Horde, led by a successor of Ghengis Khan, destroyed the city in 1240, Kiev had been the leading East Slav principality. Christianity had been introduced to the East Slavs through Kiev in the 10th century. After 300 years of repeated invasion by Lithuanians, Crimean Tatars, and Poles, the Ukraine was united with Russia in 1654. After the 1917 Russian Revolution, the Ukraine declared independence in January 1918; Soviet troops took over the area 2 years later, and in 1922, the Ukraine became one of the original republics of the Soviet Union. Kiev suffered severely during World War II; only one-fifth of its prewar population was found alive when Kiev was liberated from the Nazis in 1943. Following the lead of other restless Soviet republics and the formation of a new democratized Ukrainian Parliament, the Soviet Union's second-largest republic declared sovereignty in July of 1990.

The oldest monument in the city is the Golden Gate (Zolotye Vorota), built in 1037 as the main entrance to the city at Bolshaya Podvalnaya and Volodimirska Streets. St. Sophia Cathedral (Sofiisky Sobor) with its 13 cupolas and impressive interior frescoes and mosaics is nearby, at 24 Volodimirska. It now is a state museum.

Kiev is a wonderful city to explore, particularly in light of recent political changes, which have placed the city in a continuous state of flux. *Glasnost* and *perestroika* have heightened Ukrainian national consciousness and eliminated former taboos. For instance, centuries-old churches, once shuttered, are being reopened and services resumed. There's also been a revival of folk art and song; visitors can catch sight of impromptu performances at street corners, parks, and underground subway passages. Rock 'n' roll music, too, is popular with the younger crowds. Along broad boulevards, such as Kreshchatik, you're likely to come across scenes reminiscent of London's Hyde Park, as debates rage on between old-style Communists and independence-minded firebrands. At night, much of Kiev seems to be glued to television sets, watching the Ukrainian Parliament proceedings over the latest political conflicts. Kiev also has splendid opera and ballet, which can be seen at the *Shevchenko Opera and Ballet Theater* (50 Vladimirskaya; phone: 44-208754); otherwise, nightlife is mainly sought in bars and hotel restaurants that feature live — and loud — music. On a night out, Kievans seem to eat and dance with an abandon that suggests greater change is near. The mood among the people, unfortunately, is tinged with skepticism; the hope is that positive changes will come soon — and peacefully.

One of the most fascinating places in Kiev is the Monastery of the Caves (Pecherskaya Lavra; 211 Sichneve Povstannya), which was founded in 1051 by two monks. This complex of churches, cathedrals, and monuments was built in and around a series of caves on the high right bank of the Dnieper. Mummified bodies of monks can be seen in the tombs of the Nearer Caves, also known as St. Anthony's Caves (Blizhshie Pechory). Just outside the monastery is the Church of the Redeemer of the Birchwood (Tserkov Spasa-na-Berestove), where Yuri Dolgoruki, founder of Moscow, and other Princes of Kiev are buried.

Pushkin and Gogol are among the Russian writers who lived in Kiev for a time, and Taras Shevchenko, the poet and artist looked upon as the father of the Ukrainian national literature, was born here. You may visit the house in which he was born (8A Shevchenko); the *Shevchenko Museum* (12 Shevchenko Prospekt; phone: 44-242556) houses his art and literary work. (A memorial park has been established where this great figure of Ukrainian romanticism is buried, about 92 miles/148 km downriver from Kiev near the town of Kanev. The trip can be made by boat.)

To sample the rich Ukrainian culture, visit the *Museum of Ukrainian Art* (6 Kirova; phone: 44-286462), which includes the work of Ukrainian artists from the 15th to the 19th century and Soviet Ukrainian artists. Examples of handiwork and folk art, such as the intricately painted eggs called *krashenki,* dating from the 16th to the 20th century, are displayed in the *Historical Museum* (2 Volodimirska; phone: 44-284864). Also not to be missed is the open-air *Folk Architecture Museum* (no phone), a 200-acre area where some 400 old houses, churches, and other structures from all over the Ukraine have been reconstructed.

The controversial World War II monument at Babi Yar, "to the Victims of Fascism," is worth seeing. The ravine where more than 100,000 residents — many of them Jews — and prisoners of war were murdered by the Nazis has been landscaped into a park on the outskirts of Kiev, off Artyomov Street.

The park on Volodimirska provides a marvelous view of the river, and the promenade along the Dnieper is a wonderful place for a summer evening stroll. The city's most popular bathing beach, on Trukhaniv Island in the river, can be reached by a footbridge, Parkovyi Most. There are several theaters, a horse racing track, a circus, and numerous parks. Kalinin Square, off the Kreshchatik opposite the *Moskva* hotel, is the place to go in the evening for a sample of local nightlife. (At press time officials were planning to rename the square.) Young people gather around the square in warm weather to sing, recite poetry, and dance. Shopping is concentrated near Kreshchatik Prospekt, but there also is an interesting outdoor market (17 Vorovskov), and a large covered market, *Bessarabka* (on Shevchenko Prospekt). In the lower town, known as Podol, are artisans and old merchant quarters. An interesting way to reach the Podol district is to head down the steep Audreyevsky Spusk, an ancient cobblestone road lined with galleries and cafés, including the popular *Art Café* (no phone).

Besides the usual forms of public transportation — trams, subway, buses, and trolleys — Kiev has a funicular railway connecting Vladimir's Hill Park (Volodimirska Girka) with Podol.

ODESSA: Although a settlement and port had flourished here on the north shore of the Black Sea for centuries, Odessa itself is a relatively young city. It was built by order of Catherine the Great after the Russian army captured the entire region from the Turks in 1789. Its favorable location and special privileges granted by the czar enabled the city to quickly become one of the greatest ports in Russia.

The magnificent, wide, granite steps of the Potemkin Staircase, which lead up from the embankment, present an impressive entrance to the city for visitors arriving by sea. The staircase is named for the well-known battleship *Potemkin,* whose sailors mutinied, then stormed up the steps to join Odessa workers in an unsuccessful attempt at revolution in 1905. There are several monuments to the men of the *Potemkin* in the city.

Odessa withstood a 69-day siege by the Nazis during World War II. Later, along with St. Petersburg, Volgograd, and Sevastopol, Odessa was accorded the title of Hero City by the decree of the Praesidium of the Supreme Soviet. *Intourist* (26 Lenina; phone: 482-245246) can arrange tours of the catacombs, part of several hundred miles of caves in the area that served as hiding places for World War II partisans (as well as revolutionaries and criminals, at other times).

Primorsky Prospekt, at the top of the Potemkin Staircase, is a main street and popular seaside promenade; the heart of the city is October Revolution Square (Oktyabrskoi Revolutsii Pl.). Poplars, chestnuts, and white acacia trees grow along the avenues.

The façade of the five-domed Assumption (Uspensky) Cathedral (Sovietskoi Armyiyi) is a combination of Russian and Byzantine styles. The *Opera House* (8 Lastochkina St.; phone: 482-291324), one of the country's most beautiful theaters, has an Italian Renaissance façade and resembles the Vienna opera house. You can trace the history of the people who have lived along the north coast of the Black Sea through exhibits at the *Archaeological Museum* (open 11 AM to 6 PM; closed Mondays; 4 Lastochkina St.; phone: 482-226302).

For entertainment, there are several theaters, a concert hall, a circus, and a race track. There are several excellent bathing beaches, including one in Shevchenko Park, and numerous spas along the coast. *April Fool's Day* is celebrated with a carnival and variety shows in the streets and concert halls.

From Odessa, many tourists visit the Crimea and the resorts along the eastern coast of the Black Sea.

BEST EN ROUTE

Hotels are owned and run by *Intourist,* cooperatives, or other professional organizations. Reservations for *Intourist* establishments can be made only through *Intourist*-appointed travel agencies. To contact *Intourist* headquarters in Kiev, call 44-245246. If you prefer to stay in the sometimes superior cooperative hotels, contact a travel agency that specializes in the area. If you are traveling on your own, you could luck out and get a room the same day you arrive, but hotels are often fully booked months in advance.

As elsewhere in the Soviet Union, the price of hotel accommodations is related to the season, the class of accommodations you choose, and your travel plan, rather than to individual hotels. For Western tourists, lodging is at least as expensive here as in major American cities. Economy options usually do not exist, except perhaps for camping facilities.

Hard currency *only* is accepted at most hotels in this region (few accept credit cards), and rates continue to rise. Most travelers to the Ukraine are on package tours. Rates at most hotels include two meals.

In spite of the high prices, hotel service continues to be only fair. A few rubles or a dollar bill, though, are bound to produce a gold-toothed smile — as well as hot tea, bottles of Pepsi, or mineral water — from the floor attendant, usually a robust woman who keeps track of guests' comings and goings.

Service in restaurants is generally equally listless, but again, a single dollar bill will produce a waiter on the double, and the bottle of vodka you were told was impossible to find in all of Kiev will suddenly arrive at your table.

Because of severe food shortages around the country, many private or cooperative cafés and restaurants have been driven out of business, at least temporarily, so it is important to call ahead. The *Intourist* office in your hotel can provide the names and addresses of cooperative cafés and restaurants. Unless you are traveling with a tour group or know someone with connections, however, it is difficult to get into many cooperatives. Reservations are highly recommended at all establishments. If the meal plan at your hotel includes breakfast and lunch, don't assume you will automatically be seated for dinner. Restaurants that cater to foreign visitors (mostly in hotels) have better access to delicacies and are thus a magnet for Kievans with money to spend. Meals are paid for in local currency, and prices are very low by Western standards. Restaurants open in late morning and usually close by midnight.

You must try chicken Kiev in Kiev, though you will find it well prepared in Odessa as well. Beef Stroganoff and various concoctions of ground meat mixtures, called *kotlety,* are good entrées, while *blini* — thin, rolled pancakes with cheese, meat, or vegetable fillings — make good snacks or entrées. The best tortes and sweetcakes in the Soviet Union are baked in the Ukraine.

KIEV

Bratislava – One of the larger *Intourist* hotels, with 363 rooms, it's clean but void of character like most modern hostelries here. The restaurant serves excellent Ukrainian dishes, such as stuffed dumplings and smoked fish, and a lively folk band plays. Away from the center of town on the left bank of the Dnieper River, but near the subway. 1 Malyshko (phone: 44-551744).

Dnipro – Conveniently located near shopping and sightseeing, this 190-room *Intourist* establishment was under renovation at press time but still open to the public. Good restaurant. 1 Leninsky Komsomol Sq. (phone: 44-296569 or 44-914829).

Intourist – This new 370-room property is the very best that *Intourist* has to offer in Kiev. Although the restaurants are inconveniently located in a separate section of the main building, the property itself is centrally located near the *Rus* hotel (phone: 44-245246).

Khata Karasya – For good Ukrainian food and folk entertainment. Make reservations at your hotel's *Intourist* desk. Svyatoshino, on the northwestern outskirts of Kiev (no phone).

Kiev – Despite the cafeteria-style decor, it's a very good spot to eat; the cold meat platters are delicious, and they serve the best chicken Kiev in town. Live music draws floor-stomping crowds. On the second floor of a cooperative hotel; 26 Kirova (phone: 44-930155).

Kureni Tavern – Good Ukrainian food, served during summer only. Make reservations through *Intourist.* Near the Dnieper (no phone).

Lybid – An 18-story *Intourist* hotel with 280 rooms. The restaurant serves mediocre Ukrainian and continental food, and folk dances are performed. Away from the city center but with good bus connections; Victory Sq. (phone: 44-740063).

Maxim – A cooperative bistro with romantic Slavic music and candlelight, it's among the best dining places in town. Try any dish that is prepared with wild mushrooms. Reservations essential. Near the opera house, 21 Lenina (phone: 44-241272).

Mlyn – Ukrainian food served in a converted mill set on an island in the Dnieper River. Open during summer only. Make reservations through *Intourist.* Near the Hidropark metro station (phone: 44-245246 for *Intourist*).

Moskva – An imposing, 16-story, 200-room cooperative hotel, right across from the city's liveliest square. 4 October Revolution St. (phone: 44-292804).

Prolisok – A 105-room *Intourist* motel and campsite on the city's outskirts, a 15-minute drive from downtown. The restaurant with Ukrainian specialties makes it worth the trip. Svyatoshino, 1 Brest-Litovskoye Hwy. (phone: 44-440093 or 44-441293).

Rus – A modern, 22-story *Intourist* property with 477 rooms near the city center. The restaurant serves Ukrainian and continental fare. There are bars, a bowling alley, and a hard currency souvenir shop. Be aware that the slot machines in the lobby sometimes draw an unsavory crowd. 4 Gospitalnaya (phone: 44-204255 or 44-204226).

Zhovtenvyj – Privately managed and starkly decorated, this modern property was formerly a very exclusive Communist party hotel. Expensive but well worth it. Among the best features: the deep bathtubs. Down the block from the *Kiev* hotel, 5 Roza Luxemburg.

ODESSA

Casino – Specialties at this Ukrainian dining establishment include *soodak* (roasted pike and perch pieces fried in butter and served with sour cream sauce and potatoes). There also is a variety show. Open 1 PM to 1 AM; closed Mondays. 16 Stantsia Bolshogo Fontana (phone: 482-471582).

Gambrinus – A beer cellar, popular for its *basturma* (smoked meat) and fish dishes. Open 10 AM to 8 PM. 31 Deribasovskaya St. (phone: 482-212911).

Kavkaz – A cooperative eatery serving Caucasian fare and featuring a variety show. Open noon to 5 PM and from 7 to 11 PM. 10 Halturina St. (phone: 482-236173).

Londonskaya – Still the best hotel in the city, this *Intourist* property has a casino, private beach, grill-bar, and car rental. 11 Primorsky Blvd. (phone: 482-255393; telex: 232132).

Ukraina – A large eatery serving Ukrainian and continental fare. Variety show nightly, except Wednesdays and Thursdays. Open 11 AM to 11 PM. 1 Martynovskogo Sq. (phone: 482-257105).

U Pechesskago – Another cooperative eatery, this one serves continental fare. There's a variety show, too. Open noon to 11 PM. Halturina St. (phone: 482-250395).

Georgia

From the subtropical climes of its Black Sea coast to the snow-peaked Caucasus Mountains, the Republic of Georgia is one of the most delightful — and least explored — areas of the Soviet Union. In few other corners of the world are the trade and migration routes of the past better represented by the present than in this republic.

Mountain and valley communities settled by various nationalities throughout the centuries cling tenaciously to their identities, resisting assimilation. These groups — Imeretians, Abkhazians, Svanetians, Kabards, Ossetians, Daghestanians, and others — speak dozens of different languages and dialects, in some cases unintelligible to their nearest neighbors. They are Muslim, Christian, and Jew, though their religion now is not emphasized. The predominant language of the region is Georgian; the official language at press time, was still Russian.

This route takes you from Batumi on the Black Sea — only miles from Turkey — to Tbilisi, the capital of Georgia, and north through the highest points of the Caucasus Mountains to Vladikavkaz. The route is only about 341 miles (546 km) long, but it leads through rugged mountains, narrow valleys, and over winding roads. The scenery, cuisine, and friendly people will more than compensate for the inconvenience of the terrain.

BATUMI: Magnolias, palms, and other subtropical trees grace this important resort and port city on the Black Sea close to the Turkish border. Situated along one of the best bays of the Black Sea, Batumi's beaches of sand and small pebbles attract sun-worshipers from April to November, despite the intense summertime humidity. Extension of an oil pipeline from Baku in the early part of this century made Batumi part of the oil export trade, increasing its importance as a port.

Batumi's location has led to its occupation at various times by Romans, Greeks, Byzantines, and Turks. For 300 years before it was placed under Russian authority in 1878, Batumi had been dominated by the Turks. During that time, the local population was forced to adopt Islam. The Muslim Georgians are called Ajars and Batumi is the capital of the Ajar (Atchar) Autonomous Republic.

You can still discern the Oriental and Muslim character of the city in parts of the old town, and the Mosque (6 Chkalov) is open for services. The local museum (4 Dzhinzaradze; phone: 34611) has an interesting exhibition of national costumes; there are also a circus, an aquarium, and several theaters. The *Summer Theater,* built in the Georgian style in 1948, is in Primorsky Park, next to a wide beach. Another pleasant green space is the 45-acre Young Pioneers' Park.

For shopping, there is a market and a department store on Chavchavadze. The many small cafés throughout the city are good places to sample the mouth-watering, spicy Georgian cuisine.

En Route from Batumi – There's a good beach less than 4 miles (6 km) north of Batumi at Makhindzhauri. The name means "place of the maimed," which refers to the Georgian Christians who were tortured into accepting Islam by the Turks. A little farther along the coast is the Green Cape (Zelyoni Mys) resort; the botanical garden here is said to be the most beautiful in the Soviet Union.

The route inland to Gori passes through a valley where collective farms cultivate tea and tangerines, and bamboo grows beside the road. The valley ends at Dioknisi, where you pass over a low range of mountains to Adigeni. A road to the north takes you to a mineral springs resort, Abastumani. Continuing on the main road, you come to Akhaltsikhe (Ahalcihe), a town famous for an old fortress and its silver filigree. About 37 miles (60 km) farther east is Borzhomi, another warm springs resort. There's a 6th-century monastery here, and numerous spas and vacation homes in the area.

About 24 miles (38 km) to the southeast is a ski resort, Bakuriani, but you'll need to make reservations well in advance if you plan to stop there.

Returning to the main road, you pass through Khashuri (Haøuri) and then Kareli, where you begin to see the high peaks of the Caucasus in the distance.

GORI: This is the town where Stalin was born in 1879, and it's the only place in the Soviet Union that still has a statue of the dictator standing in the town's main square. The *State Museum of I.V. Stalin* describes Stalin's rise to power and his role as a Communist dictator (no admission charge for tour-group members; 32 Stalin Prospekt; phone: 22681). There also are ruins of a 12th-century fortress, Goris-Tsikhe, on a hill overlooking the town, but the town itself dates from the 16th century.

Gori was inhabited by refugee Armenians in the 12th century, and later occupied by Turks, Georgians, and Persians until it was taken by Russia in 1801. An earthquake in 1920 severely damaged the town.

On a hill above the right bank of the Kura River, opposite Gori, there is a 16th-century church dedicated to St. George, the Goris-Dzhavri Monastery. According to legend, it was founded by Queen Tamara in thanksgiving to the saint for rescuing her favorite falcon.

En Route from Gori – The resurfaced road along the Kura River east of Gori leads to the ancient cave town of Uplis-Tsikhe (also known as Troglodite Town), which was inhabited before the time of Christ. The town was organized in tiers, and the houses, streets, and markets are distinguishable today. North of the town is the village of Didi Ateni, which has an important Georgian monument: the 7th-century Sioni Church, decorated with 10th-century frescoes.

Heading toward Tbilisi, the capital of Georgia, the scenery begins to change from lush, wooded slopes to barren, almost monotonous cliffs above the raging Kura.

TBILISI: There is a distinctly Mediterranean flavor to this city of olive-skinned Georgians, Azerbaijan peasants, Asian Kurds, and others. Food, drink, and celebration are integral parts of the spirit of Tbilisi and its million inhabitants. On the right bank of the Kura, since ancient times Tbilisi has been a key point on the trade routes from the Caspian to the Black Sea, and from Armenia across the Caucasus to Russia.

The city is bounded on the west by Mt. David (Mtatsminda Mountain), on the east by the Makhat Range, and on the south by the Sololax. It was built on a series of hills in the 5th century on the right bank of the river. This old part of town, or *stary gorod,* is a series of narrow, winding streets where the houses seem to hang from the hills. Now restored, the Old Town has a number of small cafés and restaurants where traditional gaiety and friendliness enhance the zesty Georgian cooking. *Tbilisoba,* a folk-art festival, is held here during the last week of October. The Georgian word *tbili* means warm, and the city has long been known for its warm sulphur springs, some of which are still active along the banks of the river. You can visit some of the bathhouses in the Old Town. The oldest is the Erekle Bath at 2 Bannaya St. (phone: 8832-722633).

There are a number of interesting churches in the city and the *Georgian Art Museum* (1 Ketskhoveli; phone: 8832-996635) has an excellent collection of icons, frescoes, china, and Georgian paintings. For musical performances, there's the *Georgian State Philharmonic Concert Hall* (123 Plekhanov Prospekt; phone: 8832-363309). This is the home of the Georgian national dance ensemble, which has won an international reputation, as well as of the *State Symphony Orchestra* and other musical groups. There are a number of other important theaters here, including the *Georgian Puppet Theater* (37 Rustaveli Prospekt; phone: 8832-951713).

Several farmers' markets selling fresh produce and, occasionally, crafts of the province dot the city. Rustaveli Prospekt is the main street and the place for shopping. *Tsitsinatella* (23 Rustaveli; phone: 8832-935688) is a hard currency shop open from 11 AM to 8 PM (closed Sundays); and handicrafts are on sale at *Art Salon* (19 Rustaveli; phone: 8832-934689). The city's largest park is atop Mt. David, 1187 feet above the town. You'll find the *Funicular* restaurant on the top floor of a 3-story house in the park.

Average temperatures here in July and August are well above 90F (32C).

MTSETA (MTSKHETA): A short distance north of Tbilisi is the cradle of Georgian culture, the ancient capital of Mtseta on the slopes of the holy Mt. Kartli. According to legend, the Sveti Tskhoveli Cathedral here is built on the spot where the robe that Christ had worn to his crucifixion was rediscovered in AD 328. It supposedly had been brought here by a Jew who had won it when lots were drawn for Christ's garments. The present version of the cathedral is a perfect example of 15th-century Georgian architecture. This is also the city of St. Nina's good works and miracles, and the main church of the Samtavra Convent is dedicated to her. Near the convent is an ancient cemetery that was used from the Iron Age until the 11th century.

En Route from Mtseta – The Georgian Military Highway north through the

Caucasus to Vladikavkaz wanders through some of the most beautiful landscape in the Soviet Union. The highway follows the Aragvi River through the villages of Natakhtari and Zhinvali where you can see the ruins of castles and watchtowers. From Tzilkani, Mt. Kazbek begins to appear intermittently in the distance. After you pass through Ananuri, known for its 16th-century fortress, the road becomes more winding. Pasanauri, at the confluence of the Black Aragvi and the White Aragvi (3,335 feet), is an area of alpine meadows, wild game, and river trout. From Mleti, the road begins a steep ascent via sharp curves around what seem to be perpendicular rock walls. The views are spectacular as you approach Gudauri, where snow is often still deep in June. You reach your highest point at Krestovi Pass (7,700 feet), where avalanches are a problem at certain times of the year, when the snow starts to melt.

As you descend toward Vladikavkaz, you pass through the town of Kazbegi in the shadow of Mt. Kazbek's snowy peak (16,545 feet). The road follows the Terek River down to Gveleti through the Daryal Gorge to Lars and Balta, and finally to Vladikavkaz (2,345 feet), the capital of the North Ossetian Autonomous Republic.

VLADIKAVKAZ: Lime trees and 19th-century houses line the main street — Mira Prospekt — of this strategically located town, north of the snow-covered Caucasus Mountains. In 1931, the town was renamed Grigory Ordzhonikidze, in honor of a prominent Communist and statesman. Recently, though, the town took back its original name of Vladikavkaz, which means "mistress of the Caucasus."

On both sides of the river Terek and protected by rocky cliffs, Vladikavkaz is especially important because of its position on the Georgian Military Highway, which leads south through the mountains to Tbilisi. At the entrance to the highway, at Tbilisskoye Chaussee, there is a 79-foot granite obelisk in memory of the 17,000 Red Army soldiers who lost their lives in battles with the White Guard during the civil war of 1919.

Exhibitions at the local museums and performances at the *Ossetian Music and Drama Theater* (18 Naberezhnaya; phone: 86722-34902) will give you a good picture of Ossetian life. There is a local *Intourist* office (19 Mira Prospekt; 86722-33552).

BEST EN ROUTE

Once again, hotel prices have more of a relationship to the travel package or class you choose and the season than they do with the specific hotel. Lodging usually is at least as expensive in the Soviet Union as in major American cities, and economy options rarely exist. Most restaurants open in late morning and close at 11 PM or midnight. Reservations usually are not necessary for restaurants along the route, and prices are relatively inexpensive.

Addresses and reservations for Old Town restaurants, as well as for cooperative and private cafés, can be provided by the Service Bureau at your hotel.

The most famous Georgian dish is shashlik: skewered bits of meat — frequently lamb — marinated in pomegranate juice. A good snack or entrée is the unsweetened pastry filled with meat, cheese, or cabbage, called *pirozhki*. *Kachapuri* is a delicious cheese-filled pie which varies a bit, according to local traditions within the region. A good baked egg, cheese, and meat dish is called *cheezhi-peezhi*. The favorable climate means that many fresh vegetables are available year-round. When available, caviar from the Caspian Sea and trout from Armenia are prized delicacies.

BATUMI

Intourist – Hotel, plus a restaurant with both Russian and European food, a sauna, and a hard currency shop. 11 Ninoshvili (phone: 32211).

TBILISI

Adzharia – A 22-story hotel with 309 rooms, located close to both the zoo and circus. There's a hard currency bar. 1 Constitution Sq. (phone: 8832-369822; fax: 8832-997828).

Aragvi – Somewhat formal restaurant, serving typical Georgian food. 6 Naberezhnaya (phone: 8832-934423).

Café Actress Margarita – Besides serving coffee, fruit drinks, and pastries, it also offers a contemporary art gallery to feed the soul. 187 Nutsubedze (no phone).

Intourist – Hotel-cum-restaurant. 7 Rustaveli Prospekt (phone: 8832-832881).

Iveria – Considered the best in town, this 22-story hotel with 278 rooms is on the Kura River. There are 3 restaurants, including a cooperative, which has excellent food, folk music, and perhaps best of all, explanations in English of how the dishes and wine have been made. Two unexpected bonuses: an *Intourist* office and a rooftop pool. Also, a hard currency bar and shop, and a currency exchange. 6 Inashvili (phone: 8832-997089 or 8832-930488; fax: 8832-997828).

Mukhambani – While you sample the regional food, you also can watch Georgians dance on the tables, throw knives, and otherwise create a vibrant atmosphere. Try the dry red mukhuzani wine or the semisweet kinzmaruli, Stalin's favorite. 15 Rustaveli (phone: 8832-931769).

Odsahury – A cooperative specializing in home cooking, and offering seating outside. Paleashveli St. (phone: 8832-670889).

Tbilisi – Some say this 77-year-old hotel, close to the opera and ballet, is the best in the city. There are 138 rooms, 2 restaurants, 2 bars, a hard currency shop, swimming pool, sauna, and winter garden. The nightclub features a folkloric show. 13 Rustaveli Prospekt (phone: 8832-997829; fax: 8832-997828).

Daryal – Georgian fare made with food fresh from the market. Hard currency and rubles accepted. 22 Rustaveli Prospekt (phone: 8832-997075).

GORI

Intourist – Considered one of the "newer" entries on the hotel scene, it was built in 1959 and boasts 54 rooms. 26 Stalin Prospekt (phone: 22676).

VLADIKAVKAZ

Gorny Orel – Serving typical Georgian food, and offering a postcard-perfect view of the city from the slopes of Mt. Lysaya. About 7 miles (11 km) from town (no phone).

Kavkaz Hotel – 47 Vatutin (phone: 34926).

Otdykh Restaurant – In Hetagurov Park (no phone).

Vladikavkaz – A modern hotel on the Terek River, near the century-old Sunnite mosque. 75 Kotsoyev (phone: 50700).

Black Sea Resorts

The seaside towns and holiday resorts along the Black Sea are almost perfect places to strike up acquaintances with Soviet (Ukrainian and Russian) citizens, who vacation here, too. It's easy to begin a casual conversation on the beach or in the relaxed atmosphere of an outdoor café. Actually, vacationers here are an international lot. In addition, many foreigners come to take cures; the area is renowned for its mineral spas.

The resort towns of the Crimea and the eastern coast of the sparkling blue Black Sea are all the more beautiful because the Caucasus Mountains serve as their backdrop. The scenery varies from rocky cliffs to sloping foothills lush with subtropical vegetation, and rare and unusual plants flourish in the marvelous climate.

Cool water temperatures and the high salt content make swimming in the Black Sea an exhilarating experience, and most of the beaches are composed of pebbles and small stones. Nonetheless, many vacationers prefer Black Sea resorts to those of the Mediterranean, which is connected to the Black Sea by the Bosphorus. The climate along the Caucasian coast is similar to that of the French Riviera, which is why some people call this area the Soviet Riviera. Temperatures are a few degrees cooler on the Crimean coast.

A visit to the Black Sea is most enjoyable if made in a leisurely fashion, with stops at various resorts. The entire trip can be done by Black Sea steamer or by car, or in combination with the air service between Adler on the Caucasian coast and Simferopol in the Crimea.

YALTA: All passenger ships sailing to the Crimea and the Caucasus stop at Yalta, a charming resort town that lies in a natural amphitheater formed by mountains as high as 4,500 feet.

Yalta is best known to Westerners as the scene of the 1945 conference attended by US President Franklin D. Roosevelt, British Prime Minister Winston S. Churchill, and Soviet Premier Joseph Stalin during the last stages of World War II. The conference was held at Livadia, the former residence of the czars, a few miles east of Yalta.

One of the special attractions in Yalta is the *Chekhov Museum* (112 Kirova; phone: 654-325042), in the 2-story white house in which the great writer lived during the last 6 years of his life. It was here that Chekhov wrote two of his most brilliant plays, *The Cherry Orchard* and *The Three Sisters*.

Another favorite tourist stop is the Wine Tasting Hall (1 Litkins) where talks on Crimean wine production are followed with free samples of the product. The wine making center of the Crimea is just northeast of the city at Massandra. Beyond Massandra, off the road to Simferopol, is the 80,000-acre Crimean Game Preserve. Guided tours can be arranged through the *Intourist* office at your hotel. The Nikitsky Botanical Garden (phone: 654-335575), near the seashore east of Yalta, contains the world's largest rose garden, with over 1,600 varieties.

Yalta was first mentioned in chronicles in the early 12th century. Once a colony of Genoa, it was under Turkish domination for centuries until it became part of Russia at the end of the 18th century. Another 100 years later, it had become a popular resort. There are scores of sanatoriums along the coast, including dozens in Yalta itself. It is estimated that over a million people vacation in this area each year. The best bathing beach in the Crimea is Golden Beach (Zolotoi Plyazh), southwest of Yalta between Livadia and Miskhor. Alupka, a bit farther to the southwest, is one of the most beautiful resort towns in the Crimea. Its Vorontsov Palace (10 Dvortzovoye Shosse; phone: 654-722281 or 654-722951), surrounded by a 100-acre park here, was designed by Edward Blore, one of the architects of Buckingham Palace.

East from Yalta, you can visit Feodosiya, famous in the 13th century as a slave market town, and Kerch, an industrial center and fishing base on the Kerch Straits. There is a railroad from Kerch across the straits to the Caucasian coast. You can also travel to the Caucasian coast from here by boat.

En Route from Yalta – There are car ferries and passenger boats to take visitors from the Crimea to the Greater Sochi coast, and air connections between Simferopol and Adler, the Sochi air terminal. If you prefer, it is possible to drive around the Sea of Azov, from the Crimea to Zhdanov, Rostov-on-Don, and Krasnodar and pick up the coastal route at the port city of Novorossysk.

As you head south, the road passes between bays and beaches to the west and the foothills of the Caucasus Mountains on the east. The first village of note is Gelendzhik, one of the oldest settlements on the Black Sea coast. Burial monuments over 4,000 years old have been found in this area. The coast road gradually climbs to about 2,625 feet, then, after cutting through the Mikhailov Pass, descends to Archipo-Ossipovka at the mouth of the Vulcan River.

Tuapse, an important port that handles crude oil that is piped here from the northern side of the Caucasus, is the last good-sized town before entering Lazarevskoye, the northernmost district of greater Sochi. Ashei, a pleasant little seaside resort just north of the village of Lazarevskoye, is known for its excellent beaches and the nearby mountains which are popular with climbers.

The Memedoo Gorge in the Ashei range near Lazarevskoye has a number of small waterfalls and grottoes.

Dagomys, the northern district of Sochi, is well known as a terminus for hiking routes through the Caucasian State Preserve, and it now has the city's best hotel complex. From a park on the western slopes of Mt. Armyanka, there are stunning views of the Greater Sochi area, the sea, and the mountains.

SOCHI: This is the most important resort in the Soviet Union. Sheltered by mountains, which seem to descend right into the sea, Sochi is favored by a climate similar to that of Nice or San Remo, and is considered the heart of the Soviet Riviera.

Although there was a fortress here in the mid-19th century, the town didn't begin to grow until the area's potential as a health resort, because of its mineral springs, was recognized in 1893. By 1909, the first of the grand spa hotels had been opened; today there are nearly 60 and most of the 250,000 people who live in greater Sochi are employed in some facet of the health or holiday industry. About 2 million people visit greater Sochi each year.

Spectacular panoramas of the town, the sea, and the mountains are available from an observation tower atop Mt. Bolshoi Akhun, about 14 miles (22 km) from the center of Sochi. The viewing platform stands 2,155 feet above sea level, and there is a restaurant nearby. Bus No. 39 from the Riviera section of the city goes to the mountaintop.

The 25-acre Riviera Park, with its charming outdoor cafés, scores of sports grounds, and an open-air theater, is the center of Sochi life. Kurortny Prospekt, the main street, runs south from the park, paralleling the sea. A 114-foot spire with a star on top, on the roof of the main seaport building, provides an unusual landmark for boats miles at sea.

The public beaches are south of the center of the town.

Some of the sanatoriums that have been built on the hills and cliffs have funicular railways or elevators. One of the most beautiful of these is the Ordzhonikidze Sanatoria, which was built in Italian Renaissance style during the 1930s. The interior was decorated in traditional Russian style by local artists.

In addition to the beautiful mimosas, oleanders, magnolias, and palms that grow along Sochi's streets, there are specimen trees and shrubs from all over the world in the local botanical garden, Dendarium (74 Kurortny Prospekt; phone: 862-923602).

Traces of prehistoric man have been found in some of the caves of the Caucasus. Two, Vorontsovskiye and Kudepstinskiye, are near Sochi, but they should only be visited with an experienced guide.

Other short excursions can be made to the Agur waterfalls near old Matsesta, to the yew and boxtree grove on the eastern side of Mt. Akhun in the Caucasian National Preserve, and to one of the large tea plantations in the area.

En Route from Sochi – About 13 miles (21 km) south of Sochi is the town of Khosta, famous for its health treatment centers and as a hiking station. Then comes Adler, where the central airport for the entire region is located. An extensive drainage system has helped turn Adler, once merely marshland, into a sunny, subtropical garden noted for its health spas and campgrounds.

As you leave the Krasnodar region and enter Abkhazia, an autonomous region that is part of the Republic of Georgia, you may sense differences in the language and culture. The first Abkhazian resort you encounter is Gagra where, thanks to its marvelous climate, roses bloom in winter. The next resort is Pitzunda, with its prehistoric flora reserve. If you leave the coast road, heading northeast, you can visit Lake Ritsa, at 2,860 feet above sea level one of the most beautiful in the Caucasus. The drive, about 38 miles (61 km), takes you through a deep canyon and past forests of spruce, pine, and beech.

Back on the road south, the beaches become more sandy and less pebbly, as you approach Sukhumi. One of the most beautiful beaches on the entire coast is at Gudauta, about 27 miles (43 km) north of Sukhumi.

SUKHUMI: The city seems to be one big park: its avenues lined with lovely laurels, palms, and Himalayan cedars; its gardens rich with eucalyptus, citrus, and banana trees. There is a botanical garden (18 Chavchavadze) with rare and unusual flowers, and the plants in the 80-acre forest-park on the slopes of Sukhumi Hill have been selected so that the garden is always in bloom.

Sukhumi, which lies between the mouths of the Gumits and Kelasuri rivers, is the capital of Abkhazia. The settlement was built by the Romans in about the 2nd century, and was one of the chief slave markets on the Black Sea under the Turks, before Abkhazia freed itself with the help of Russia. There are a number of interesting ruins, including the 11th-century castle of King Bagrat in the southeastern part of the city. A short distance from the castle ruins is Shrom Cave, a wonderland of stalactites and stalagmites.

Another unusual attraction is the monkey-breeding farm maintained on the slopes of Mt. Trapetsaya under the auspices of the Academy of Sciences of the Soviet Union. The animals, primarily baboons and macaques, are used for scientific research purposes.

Many visitors to the Black Sea resort areas end their trip here, but it is also a starting point for tours of Georgia.

BEST EN ROUTE

The price of your accommodations has less to do with the hotel you choose than with the travel package plan or class you select, or whether you visit the Black Sea by cruise ship. Lodging for all Western tourists is at least as expensive in the Soviet Union as in major American cities, and there are not many economy options, other than camping.

Most restaurants open late in the morning and close at 11 PM or midnight. Reservations may be advisable at the better restaurants in the most popular resort areas. Food prices are relatively low. Your hotel Service Bureau will supply the names and addresses of new private and cooperative cafés and restaurants in the resort areas.

Some of the best renditions of Russian, Ukrainian, and Caucasian food are found in Black Sea restaurants. Sample the beef Stroganoff, chicken Kiev, and Caucasian shashlik (skewered lamb). The semitropical climate means fruit and fresh vegetables are available year-round. And dairy products such as the feta-like *sulguni* cheese, sour cream or *smetana,* and yogurt, called *matsoni,* are excellent.

YALTA

Brigantina – A cozy eatery in the heart of the city, serving delicious Russian food. Live music (phone: 654-320171).

Dzalita – Serves Ukrainian fare to tourists groups only. 8 Moskovskaya (phone: 654-342595).

Espanola Bar – Fish dishes are served in this grounded schooner, opposite the *Oreanda* hotel (phone: 654-317106).

Oreanda – A renovated European-style establishment, run by *Intourist,* with marble floors, 121 rooms, a restaurant, bar, sauna, hair salon, tennis court, billiards, car rental, and currency exchange. Located less than 100 feet from the sea, and close to a Crimean wine tasting hall and artisans' pavilion. 35-2 Lenin Embankment (phone: 654-328276).

Ukraina – Serves nutritionally balanced, traditional Ukrainian fare in a relaxed atmosphere. 34 Promenade (phone: 654-316057).

Yalta – Run by *Intourist* and Hilton hotels, it's the best in Yalta, with a private beach, a number of restaurants and bars, a heated swimming pool, tennis courts, sauna, and currency exchange. Masandra Park, 50 Draziinski (phone: 654-350150 or 654-325594; telex: 654-187112).

SOCHI

Akhun – An eatery with a great view of the slopes of Mt. Bolshoi Akhun (no phone).

Dagomys – Built in 1982, it has 1,007 rooms and a large private beach. Facilities include 7 restaurants, 7 bars, an 18-hole practice golf course (bring your own clubs and balls), billiards, bowling, a sauna, hair salon, car repair, a currency exchange office, and helicopter pad. 7 Leningrad St. (phone: 862-321275 or 862-325400; telex: 862-191214).

Kamelia – A seafront property with 150 rooms, 2 restaurants, a sauna, and car rental. 91 Kurortny Prospekt (phone: 862-990992 or 862-990201).

Magnolia – A 400-room hostelry with a restaurant, bar, casino, and sauna. 50 Kurortny Prospekt (phone: 862-929594).

Primorye – Continental fare is served in a dining room with seating for 120. 1 Sokolova St. (phone: 862-923730).

Zemchuzhina – The name means "pearl," and the hotel is one of the city's best. The 19-story high-rise complex on the waterfront has 1,004 rooms, 7 restaurants (serving Russian and Georgian fare and seafood), 4 hard currency bars, a private beach, heated swimming pool, tennis courts, hard currency shop, car rental, and currency exchange. Art is sold in the salon. Helicopter service transports guests to the mountains for skiing, about 37½ miles (60 km) away. 3 Chernomorskaya St. (phone: 862-926084 or 862-927364; fax: 862-992099; telex: 862-412614).

SUKHUMI

Amra – Caucasian specialities prepared especially for lovers of piquant food. Rustaveli Prospekt, by the sea (phone: 88122-22412).

Amza – Georgian dishes prepared according to old recipes. Sukhumskaya Gora, on Sukhumi Hill (phone: 88122-24914).

Dioscuria – Georgian fare served in a setting of traditional Georgian decor. Rustaveli Prospekt, in the ruined fortress (phone: 88122-26716).

Sinop – Decorated in traditional Georgian style and serving Caucasian food. Tbilisskoye Hwy. (phone: 88122-22033).

Spain

Spain has marvelous beaches, castle-hotels, glorious art, stirring music, sophisticated cities, excellent food, wonderful wines, joyous religious festivals, and the drama of the bullfight. There are items of the highest quality leather and lace for the shopper as well as unique inexpensive souvenirs. There are cultural differences that add special interest to the various regions, and there are churches of astounding beauty.

It is a country whose various layers of civilization can be seen in monuments, architecture, and art: dolmens and cave paintings from prehistoric times; the rounded arches that tell you the Moors were here; Romanesque and Gothic churches from the European Christian period; lavishly ornamented cathedrals from Spain's own golden age; and magnificent paintings by a parade of geniuses from El Greco in the 16th century to Velázquez in the 17th, Goya in the 18th, and Picasso in our own century.

In short, Spain seems almost to have been designed with the tourist in mind. You can explore charming typical villages, virtually unchanged by the passage of time, or head for renowned resort areas like the Costa del Sol, which has become more international than Spanish.

With an area of 194,883 square miles, mainland Spain occupies most of the Iberian Peninsula, which lies to the south of France between the Atlantic Ocean and the Mediterranean Sea and is separated from North Africa by the Strait of Gibraltar. (Much smaller Portugal, along the west coast, shares the peninsula.) Spain is the third-largest country in Europe (after the Soviet Union and France) and is more mountainous than any other European country except Switzerland. It also has 2,475 miles of coastline, and it is possible to ski in the Sierra Nevada, less than 50 miles (80 km) from the Costa del Sol. The Balearic Islands in the Mediterranean, and the Canary Islands, just off the coast of Africa and almost 1,000 miles southeast of the peninsula, are worlds apart, yet thoroughly Spanish.

Provinces near the Pyrenees are green and lush, with meadows and fields bordered by trees and hedges. A high (2,000-foot), dry plateau, the *meseta,* dominates central Spain, its brown earth sometimes awash with golden cereal grains; and, to the south, along the Mediterranean, the land supports vineyards and olive groves, as well as lemon and orange trees. Except in the higher reaches of the mountains and in the northern *meseta* during the winter months, temperatures remain relatively high throughout the year in Spain. In the southeast, for instance, temperatures range from 55F (13C) to 60F (15C) in January. The extreme south (away from the coast) is the hottest in summer, with thermometers registering above 100F (38C) in some places.

When Phoenicians first came to Spain in the 11th century BC, they found Iberian tribes already living in the eastern parts of the country. It was the Phoenicians who gave the name Hispania to the peninsula, known to them as "Land of Rabbits." Greeks, Celts, Carthaginians, Romans, and Visigoths also invaded the country before the Moors conquered Spain in AD 711 and imposed an Islamic culture. Christianity had spread across Spain as early as the 1st century; eventually there ensued a 700-year Christian campaign to reconquer Spain. It was not until the late 15th century that King Ferdinand and Queen Isabella were able to drive the last enclave of Moors from Granada and unite Spain.

Isabella and Ferdinand had instituted the cruel court of the Inquisition to discover and punish converted Jews and later Muslims, who were insincere. Christians also were investigated for heresy. The court lasted until 1834. In the same year as the reconquest of Granada, the Catholic monarchs expelled all Jews who would not convert. Interestingly, the year was 1492, and across the Atlantic Ocean, Christopher Columbus, outfitted by the same monarchs, was opening a new era for Spain, as well as the rest of the world, by discovering America. (This year Spain will celebrate the 500th anniversary of the discovery of America.)

By the 16th century, Spain was a major colonial power. Spanish conquistadores plundered Latin America in search of gold and silver and declared the New World to be part of Spain. Precious minerals were shipped to the homeland by galleons, and Spain's naval prowess became so great that its fleet was known as the Invincible Armada until its defeat, in 1588, by Great Britain. Spain's subsequent military losses in the Thirty Years War, which ended in 1643, further contributed to its decline as a powerful nation.

During the 19th century, Spain suffered a series of internal conflicts, which were, in essence, protests against a foreign monarchy. The three Carlist wars, which actually revolved around pretenders to the throne, finally resulted in the creation of a republic in 1873, but it lasted only a year before the monarchy was restored. At the same time, Spain's Latin American colonies were struggling for autonomy, and Cuban independence at the end of the Spanish-American War in 1898 spelled the end of the Spanish overseas empire.

The bitter division between monarchists and republicans continued well into the 20th century. In 1923, King Alfonso XIII appointed a military dictator, who was so unpopular with the masses that he was forced into exile. The king finally abdicated to avoid a civil war. But when the elections that followed produced a socialist republican majority and the government initiated reforms, it engendered such right-wing opposition that civil war erupted. Francisco Franco, who had led the victorious Nationalist forces, became dictator of Spain. Under his regime, Spain remained neutral in World War II. Political dissent in Spain was suppressed and civil liberties were stifled until Franco's death in 1975, at which time Juan Carlos ascended the throne and undertook a policy of liberalization.

Our six Spanish routes are northern Spain along the Cantabrian seacoast from the Basque Country west to Santiago de Compostela; Castile, which passes through central Spain's most important historic cities; the Costa del Sol, with Spain's most famous resort towns; Andalusia, which has retained more Moorish traditions than any other part of Spain; the Canary Islands, off the northwest coast of Africa; and the Balearic Islands.

Note: If you have always dreamed of castles in Spain, you can now make reservations easily at 83 historic or resort *Paradores de Turismo* through *Marketing Ahead* (433 Fifth Ave., New York, NY 10016; phone: 212-686-9213). Information is also available at the Tourist Office of Spain in the US (see *Sources and Resources,* GETTING READY TO GO).

Northern Spain

The north coast of Spain extends from the Basque Country at the foothills of the Pyrenees, to the country's most westerly reaches on a little ledge above Portugal. This tour begins in the Basque Country, follows the coast to La Coruña, and then turns inland to the south to end in Santiago de Compostela, the spiritual capital of Spain.

The Basque region, which resembles the lower Alpine section of Austria, deserves special attention because the Basque people are very possibly the oldest surviving ethnic group in Europe. (They predate the ancient Iberian tribes of Spain.) The Basques have a strong sense of political and cultural autonomy and, when waxing most poetic, claim direct descent from Adam and Eve via the lost city of Atlantis. Most serious scholarship on the Basques offers no definitive answers as to their ethnic origins, and early Basque history remains something of a mystery.

The Basque language is not Indo-European in origin; it is something of a linguistic missing link, thought to date from the very beginning of the use of language itself. Non-Latins, the Basques are fair-skinned and live in both Spain and France. Their motto "Four Plus Three Equals One" refers to the four Spanish and three French Basque provinces, and the desire for political self-determination. (After the democratic constitution of 1978, all 52 Spanish provinces were organized into 17 *comunidades autónomas,* of which the Basque Country — País Vasco in Spanish; Euskadi in Basque — is one.)

Our route begins on the Basque part of the coast, due north of Pamplona, at Fuenterrabía (Hondarrabia in Basque), a resort town near the French border and just south of Biarritz. It continues to the charming city of San Sebastián (Donostia in Basque), a world-renowned summer resort. Following the coast through lovely old Spanish towns like Santillana del Mar, the route includes such natural wonders as the Picos de Europa mountain range, with snow-capped peaks as high as 8,688 feet and the *rías* of northwest Spain, which are inlets similar to the fjords of Norway and the lochs of Scotland. The final stop is Santiago de Compostela, a fascinating historical city that has been a shrine for a thousand years, the destination for pilgrims honoring St. James, the Apostle, whose remains are said to rest there.

FUENTERRABÍA: This popular seaside resort and fishing port has steep streets and tiny houses with flower-bedecked, wrought-iron balconies. Because of its strategic position near the frontier, it was the target of attack by the French for centuries. Each September 8, Fuenterrabía celebrates the *Feast of Our Lady of Guadalupe,* who is said to have saved the town after a 2-month siege by the French in 1638. The town is also noted for its excellent seafood.

PASAJES DE SAN JUAN: This village is best reached via Pasajes de San Pedro, from which launches cross regularly. Pasajes de San Juan is a tiny town with brightly painted houses squeezed together, rowing clubs, good restaurants, and a central plaza of unparalleled charm. Notice how the freighters and tankers entering the straits dwarf the quayside houses. French author Victor Hugo lived and worked here during his exile in the winter of 1843; his house (59 Calle San Juan) is open to the public.

SAN SEBASTIÁN: On three hills, cut by the Urumea River, and graced with the lovely scallop-shaped bay, the Bahía de la Concha, beautiful San Sebastián with its sandy beaches is one of the major summer resorts of Europe, attracting visitors from all over the world who seek the Belle Epoque charm lacking in many other Spanish beach resorts. It's also a major Basque city and the capital of Guipúzcoa, the smallest province in Spain. Although the Old Town (Parte Vieja) at the foot of Mt. Urgull was burned down by the Duke of Wellington's British troops, as Napoleon's forces fled in 1813 during the Peninsular War, it has been rebuilt — narrow streets and all — and is worth exploring, especially at about 8 PM, when the bars and restaurants of its central square, Plaza de la Constitución, are crowded. The balconies around this charming square have numbers because they were ringside seats for bullfights once held here.

The *San Telmo Museum,* on the Plaza de Zuloaga at the foot of Mt. Urgull, is set in a 16th-century Renaissance monastery, and has interesting Basque memorial crosses, an ethnographic exhibit, and strange old Basque headdresses. You can drive or walk to the top of Mt. Urgull for a fine view of the town and the bay from the public park at the top. The building there is a chapel topped by a huge statue of Christ.

Also be sure to stroll along the Paseo Nuevo, the wide promenade that encircles Mt. Urgull and offers fine vistas of the bay and the sea beyond. For a truly spectacular panorama of the city, the bay, and the sea, drive 3 miles (5 km) west along the Concha beach to Mt. Igueldo.

The Basque Country, and particularly San Sebastián, is a place where good eating assumes major importance. The city has a Gastronomic Academy and very exclusive, male-dominated eating societies that sponsor cooking contests, but the flair for good eating spills over into the local restaurants, the most modest of which is likely to serve outstanding food. Seafood is especially good here.

During the summer season San Sebastián holds a 2-week international jazz festival, an international film festival, and a folklore festival called *Basque Week* (Semana Grande). The posh casino, *Nuevo Grand Casino del Kursaal,* located in the *Londres e de Inglaterra* hotel (2 Calle Zubieta), is a traditional highlight. For further information, contact the tourist office in San Sebastián (13 Calle Andia; phone: 943-426282), or the Tourist Office of Spain in the US.

GUERNICA: Heading west from San Sebastián along the Cantabrian coast road, you reach the town of Guernica, whose wretched decimation during the Spanish Civil War (2,000 died in 3 hours) was immortalized by Picasso in one of his greatest paintings. (The original canvas, which once hung in New York's *Museum of Modern Art,* was returned to Spain for display in the Casón del Buen Retiro — part of the *Prado* — in Madrid.) The town has been rebuilt in traditional style. A few miles farther west, the beach at Baquio is worth a stop.

BILBAO: The largest city of the autonomous community of the Basque Country, which comprises the provinces of Alava, Vizcaya, and Guipúzcoa, Bilbao is primarily an industrial city. It is lively in the summer during *Semana Grande* and the August bullfights, when you will see some serious animals, feisty matadors, and a spirited festival. Bullfight critics and the matadors themselves stay at the *Ercilla* hotel (see *Best en Route*).

SANTANDER: Proceeding west on the E-50 highway leads to the autonomous region of Cantabria and its capital city, Santander, sometimes called the intellectual and cultural capital of Spain because of its courses at the International Menéndez Pelayo

University and the *International Festival of Music and Dance,* usually held in late July through early August. It is also a summer magnet for tourists, who come to enjoy the exceptional variety of beaches, including El Sardinero, with its casino. El Sardinero and several other beaches extend so far out during the spectacularly low tide that they blend into one continuous stretch of sand on which fishing boats tilt in temporary dry dock. The town is divided into an old section — much of which was wiped out during a tragic fire in 1941 — and a new area near the harbor devoted to shops and restaurants.

SANTILLANA DEL MAR: This is a lovely, beautifully preserved medieval Spanish town renowned for its Collegiate Church, which dates from the 12th century; here the relics of St. Juliana (Santillana is a contraction of Santa Juliana) are enshrined. See the Romanesque church with its magnificent sarcophagus honoring the saint and the impressive cloisters, memorable for their capitals, which were carved by a master craftsman during the 12th century. Also noteworthy are the town's old patrician houses, dating from the 15th to the 17th century, particularly the *Villa House,* now an inn, with its semicircular balconies, and the houses along the Calle de las Lindas and the Calle del Río. (The latter street has a stream running down its center.)

En Route from Santillana del Mar – Just west of Santillana are the phenomenal Caves of Altamira, the famed 15,000-year-old "Sistine Chapel of prehistoric stone painting." The main cave is open to the public on a limited basis. Written permission must be requested 6 months in advance from the Director, *Centro de Investigación y Museo de Altamira* (Santillana del Mar, Santander, Spain; phone: 942-818102). The adjacent museum and the Cave of the Stalactites are open Mondays through Saturdays from 10 AM to 1 PM and 4 to 6 PM and on Sundays and holidays from 10 AM to 1 PM.

Continue west and you will reach the massive Picos de Europa mountain range, where breathtaking gorges have been carved by the mountain streams. These spectacular snow-capped mountains rise between Santander and Oviedo, and their highest peak is 8,688 feet. A good place to stay between Santander and Oviedo is the typically Spanish resort town of Llanes. From here, if you wish, you can catch a glimpse of the mountains, by taking a detour of 11 miles (18 km) to Covadonga, turning south just before the town of Cangas de Onis. Here a shrine was erected in a most dramatic mountain setting, commemorating the reconquest of Spain from the Moors, which began in Covadonga in 718. The road is steep and narrow, but passable.

OVIEDO: Oviedo is the capital of Asturias, a regional entity that was originally a separate kingdom. Known primarily as a cider producing and mining region, Asturias has a rugged seacoast, a mountainous interior that has been compared to the Swiss Alps, and a natural greenness of exceptional depth and intensity. Salmon and trout, deer and mountain goat populate the Asturian streams and mountains. The coastal villages produce ample seafood. The Oviedo market held daily in the Plaza de Daoiz y Velarde and the Cathedral Square are the main attractions in this small town. Don't miss the matchless 12th-century sculpted columns at the Cámara Santa (Holy Chamber) inside the splendid Gothic cathedral (Pl. de Alfonso II), where the gold and silver items in the treasury are also very fine and very old (9th century).

En Route from Oviedo – Continuing along the coast, you enter the region of Galicia in the northwest corner of the Iberian Peninsula. Because of its geographic isolation, Galicia has remained the least developed part of Spain. Its ocean waters are sparkling clean, but there are few tourist accommodations. Life in Galicia is very basic, and its fishermen battle daily with poverty and the dangers of the sea.

An unusual geographic feature here is the *rías* — inlets similar to the sea lochs of Scotland and the fjords of Norway. The Rías Altas extend along the north coast from Ribadeo to La Coruña and the Rías Bajas continue along the west coast from La Coruña to Pontevedra.

On this route you might want to look for the *cetarias,* seafood pounds, where lobsters and other crustaceans can be bought alive. Nearby open-air restaurants will cook and serve your acquisitions.

The area is also known for the ribeiro wines; the red is very dark and fruity; the white, champagne-like.

LA CORUÑA: This town, from which Philip II's Armada set sail in 1588 to be defeated by England's Drake and Hawkins, is now called the San Sebastián of Galicia for its lovely beaches. The town itself is also charming, with its medieval walls and its 2nd-century Roman lighthouse, the Hercules Tower, which still functions.

Along the harbor in the park of San Carlos are the 18th-century San Anton and San Carlos forts. The old section of La Coruña, called La Ciudad Vieja (the Old City), has lovely cobbled streets and little squares like the Plaza de Santa Bárbara. The cafés in the old part of town are social centers, and the Plaza de Maria Pita is a good place for eating, drinking, and strolling.

SANTIAGO DE COMPOSTELA: Santiago's only rivals are Rome and Jerusalem, and the shrine here attracts pilgrims from all over the world. Santiago is the contraction for *San Diego,* or St. James. A legend says that St. James the Apostle landed here to proselytize and then died in Judea at the hands of Herod. His body was buried here, lost, and rediscovered by a miracle wrought in the 9th century. It is said that the night sky showered stars upon his grave to reveal its whereabouts to the faithful. The name *compostela* refers to the land (*campo*) of stars (*estrellas*). St. James is still honored by pilgrimages, with very special ones in years when his holy day falls on a Sunday, usually every 5, 6, or 11 years; the next year is 1993. The famous Way of St. James (El Camino de Santiago), extending from Paris through Pamplona, Burgos, and León to Santiago, and marked with monasteries and churches, is one of the world's oldest tour routes; one early guidebook dates from 1130.

The center of attraction in Santiago is the cathedral, built from the 11th through the 13th century. It can be seen from plazas on all sides, the chief of which is the Plaza del Obradoiro. The magnificent Obradoiro façade is a 1750 baroque creation by Fernando Casas y Novoa. Richly ornate, it is sculpted in a blend of straight and curved lines characteristic of the baroque style. Be sure to see the wonderful 12th-century Romanesque Gate of Glory, the Romanesque Goldsmith's Door, and the 17th-century Holy Door — all inside the cathedral.

Santiago (pop. 106,000) is also the site of one of Spain's earliest universities. The student quarter and the old neighborhood between the cathedral and the university are the most popular strolling and dining areas in town. The summer music school headed by the late Andrés Segovia, the great guitarist, is another attraction.

Explore the Plaza del Obradoiro fronting the cathedral and the Plaza de la Quintana at its east end, and wander along such medieval streets as the Rúa Nueva, Calle del Franco, and Rúa del Villar. On the western side of town is the Paseo de la Herradura, a pleasant promenade along a wooded hill, which offers a fine view of the cathedral and the city.

The annual *Festival of Santiago de Compostela* is celebrated on *St. James's Day,* July 25, with grand processions and much feasting. When the date falls on a Sunday, as it will in 1993, there are special celebrations, so be sure to make hotel reservations in advance. For more information about the city, contact the local tourist office (43 Rúa del Villar; phone: 981-584081) or the Tourist Office of Spain in the US.

BEST EN ROUTE

Expect to pay $145 or more for a double room in those hotels we've categorized as expensive; between $80 and $140 at a hotel in the moderate category; under $80, inexpensive.

Basque gastronomy is a high art, renowned throughout the world. Here, you will find several restaurants of supremely high caliber where every meal is truly unforgettable. Expect to pay $80 or more for a meal for two at those restaurants we've categorized as expensive; between $60 and $80 for a meal for two in the moderate category; under $60, inexpensive. Prices do not include drinks, wine, or tips. All restaurants listed accept major credit cards, unless otherwise indicated. Reservations are advised at all restaurants.

FUENTERRABÍA

Kulluxka-Zeria – A genial place that serves fish and seafood prepared according to Basque recipes. Closed Sunday evenings, Tuesdays in winter, and during December. 19-23 Calle San Pedro (phone: 943-642780). Moderate.

Parador El Emperador – This should be your first stop in Spain as you cross the border from France; it is scheduled to reopen this year following extensive renovation. Check in advance with the central *paradores* office in Madrid (91-435-9700). Not only is the Basque cooking good, but this former medieval castle-cum-fortress with real cannonball holes in the façade has an interesting art gallery. Plaza de Armas (phone: 943-642140). Moderate.

PASAJES DE SAN JUAN

Casa Cámara – Renowned as one of the most important centers of new Basque cooking, the cuisine here features natural ingredients with traditional and innovative recipes. Lobster dishes are the house specialty. Closed Sunday evenings and Mondays. 79 Calle San Juan (phone: 943-523699). Expensive.

Txulotxo – Here you'll find a splendid selection of Basque seafood and fish dishes. Closed Sunday evenings, Tuesdays and mid-October to mid-November. 76 Calle San Juan (phone: 943-523952). Moderate.

SAN SEBASTIÁN

Akelarre – Delicate Basque and French cuisine carefully prepared and served in a lovely setting atop Monte Igueldo. Closed Sunday evenings, Mondays, and the first 2 weeks of June and December. Barrio Igueldo (phone: 943-212052). Expensive.

Arzak – The high priest of the new Basque cuisine, owner-chef Juan Mari Arzak has won Spain's National Gastronomy Prize. His river crabs with truffles and lobster sauce, pastries, apple pudding with strawberry cream, and mousse are considered among the most delectable culinary creations in the country. Closed Sunday evenings, Mondays, 2 weeks in June, and 3 weeks in November. 21 Calle Alto de Miracruz (phone: 943-285593). Expensive.

María Cristina – The past splendor of this Belle Epoque hotel (a member of the CIGA group) has been restored by a thorough refurbishing. The lounges and spacious rooms, now modernized, are elegant, with original antiques. Paseo República Argentina (phone: 943-293300; fax: 943-423914). Expensive.

Londres e Inglaterra – Standing on the beach, all wood on the inside, complete with creaking floors and elevators, this 120-room hotel is an incomparable Old World establishment. 2 Calle Zubieta (phone: 943-426989; fax: 943-420031). Expensive to moderate.

Rekondo – Farm-fresh produce enhances the rich meat and fish dishes. Closed Wednesdays and November 1-22. Paseo de Igueldo (phone: 943-212907). Expensive to moderate.

Aldanondo – This unpretentious chophouse has a distinct rural sporting flavor. Closed Tuesdays. Visa accepted. 6 Calle Euska-Erria (phone: 943-422852). Moderate.

Casa Paco – Another bastion of new Basque cooking, it is known for its sea bream, baby eels, and anchovies. Closed Sundays and Monday lunch. 31 Calle de Agosto (phone: 943-422816). Moderate.

GUETARIA

Kaia and Kaipe – *Kaia,* upstairs, and *Kaipe,* downstairs, serve some of the best seafood on the Basque coast. From the upstairs, you can see the port, across the Bay of Biscay, all the way to Biarritz, France. Be sure to sample txakolí, a typical white wine made from sweet-sour grapes grown on the hillsides overlooking the sea. This two-in-one restaurant is on the port. Closed October. 10 Calle General Arnao (phone: 943-832414). Expensive to moderate.

GUERNICA

Zimela – This simple restaurant is a good place for a filling meal. Closed Tuesday nights and February. 57 Calle Carlos Gangoiti (phone: 94-685-1012). Moderate to inexpensive.

BILBAO

Ercilla – Crossing the time warp from Old World style to New World comfort, this centrally located hotel is the traditional favorite of matadors and bullfight critics. Its *Bermeo* restaurant is excellent. Closed Saturday lunch, Sunday dinner, and weekends in July and August. 37 Calle Ercilla (phone: 94-443-8800; fax: 94-443-9335). Expensive.

Guria – Here, diners feast on prized Basque delicacies prepared according to traditional recipes. Codfish and steaks are house specialties. Closed Sundays, the last week of July and first week of August. 66 Gran Vía (phone: 94-441-0543). Expensive.

Carlton – Adequate if hardly luxurious lodging, this is a pleasant alternative to the *Ercilla,* which might well be full during the bullfight season in August. Part of the HUSA chain. 2 Plaza Federico Moyúa (phone: 94-416-2200; fax: 94-416-4628). Moderate.

Gredos – Though not as lavish as *Guria,* this restaurant offers traditional Basque dishes at reasonable prices. Closed mid-July to mid-August. 50 Calle Alameda de Urquijo (phone: 94-443-5002). Moderate.

Excelsior – Another good choice for comfortable sleeping quarters in Bilbao. 6 Calle Hurtado de Amézaga (phone: 94-415-3000). Inexpensive.

SANTANDER

Real – This large Belle Epoque hotel, an aristocrat atop the city's highest hill, offers true Old World charm plus the modern luxuries of its refurbishment. 28 Paseo de Pérez Galdós (phone: 942-272550; fax: 942-274-573). Expensive.

Ferry – A fine seafood restaurant along the port with a good harbor view. Open daily. Estación Marítima (phone: 942-213445). Expensive to moderate.

Casa Valentín – Fish and seafood are served in a modest setting at reasonable cost. 19 Calle Isabel II (phone: 942-227049). Inexpensive.

SANTILLANA DEL MAR

Parador Gil Blas – This converted medieval villa provides enchanting accommodations in a remarkably picturesque medieval village, near the prehistoric Altamira Caves. Plaza de Ramón Pelayo (phone: 942-818000; fax: 942-818391). Expensive to moderate.

Altamira – Since the *Gil Blas* has a limited number of rooms for guests, this is an alternative in town. It's not nearly as spectacular, but quite charming in its own way. 1 Calle Cantón (phone: 942-818025; fax: 942-840136). Inexpensive.

COMILLAS

El Capricho – This imaginative *modernista* landmark private villa near the beach was designed by the famed Catalán architect Antoni Gaudí in 1885. After a major refurbishment, it opened in the summer of 1989 as a deluxe restaurant specializing in Cantabrian and international dishes. A separate cafeteria serves more economical fare. Closed Mondays. On the road between Santillana del Mar and Llanes (phone: 942-720365). Expensive to moderate.

LLANES

Don Paco – A comfortable Spanish-style resort hotel, modest and quiet, with 42 rooms with baths. Closed October through May. Parque de Posada Herrera (phone: 985-400150). Inexpensive.

Montemar – Similar to the *Don Paco,* this place has a cafeteria and 40 rooms. Open daily from June 1 through September 30. Calle Jenaro Riestra (phone: 985-400100). Inexpensive.

OVIEDO

Reconquista – Unquestionably the best place for an overnight stop in Oviedo. 16 Calle Gil de Jaz (phone: 985-241100; fax: 985-241166). Expensive.

Casa Fermín – Oviedo's most notable restaurant is acclaimed for its venison in season, (October through March) and Asturian codfish. Closed Mondays. 8 Calle San Francisco (phone: 985-216452). Expensive to moderate.

Principado – Traditional Asturian cooking. The desserts and pastries here are especially good. Open daily. In the hotel of the same name, 6 Calle San Francisco (phone: 985-217792). Moderate to inexpensive.

RIBADEO

Parador de Ribadeo – Built in the 1950s, this well-kept, government-run hostelry overlooks the mouth of the Eo River from a good location near the Santander–La Coruña Highway. Its restaurant, which serves Galician dishes — boiled ham with greens, fresh fish, and *empañada* (fish or meat pie) — has a fine reputation. Open daily. Calle Amador Fernández (phone: 982-110825; fax: 982-110346). Moderate.

LA CORUÑA

Rápido – The best selection of seafood in the city, as well as some Galician dishes, both complemented by ribeiro and albariño wines. Open daily. 7 Calle Estrella (phone: 981-224221). Expensive.

Fornos – Here you'll find well-prepared regional dishes and a good selection of hearty local wines. Closed Tuesdays. 25 Calle Olmos (phone: 981-221675). Moderate.

VILLALBA

Parador Condes de Villalba – Between Ribadeo and Santiago, this small, 6-room hotel is set in a vine-covered medieval tower and furnished with authentic antiques. Its fine restaurant specializes in *zarzuela,* assorted fish, and *fillaos,* custard-filled crêpes. Closed during December. Calle Valeriano Valdesuso (phone: 982-510011; fax 982-510090). Moderate.

SANTIAGO DE COMPOSTELA

Parador de los Reyes Católicos – This immense and magnificently restored monument was originally founded as a royal hospice in 1499 by King Ferdinand and Queen Isabella. Now a deluxe property of the government's *paradores* group, it is one of the most memorable inns in northern Spain. Open daily. Plaza de España (phone: 981-582200; fax: 981-563094). Expensive.

Don Gaiferos – One of the best restaurants in town. Closed Sundays and 2 weeks from *Christmas Eve* to January 7. 23 Rúa Nova (phone: 981-583894). Expensive to moderate.

El Franco – A fine restaurant specializing in Galician cuisine. Open daily. 28 Avenida del Generalísimo Franco (phone: 981-588814 or 981-581234). Expensive to moderate.

Peregrino – You won't be disappointed at the quality of this elegant old hotel. Avenida Calle Rosalía de Castro (phone: 981-521850; fax: 981-521777). Moderate.

Castile

Although the term *Castile* is used to denote a region embracing 15 provinces (including the autonomous community of Madrid) in the mountainous central plateau, the area is actually divided into two large administrative regions (*comunidades autónomas*) — New Castile (Castilla–La Mancha) and Old Castile (Castilla y León). New Castile comprises the provinces of Albacete, Ciudad Real, Cuenca, Guadalajara, and Toledo. Old Castile, which lies northwest of New Castile and north of the Guadarrama and Somosierra ranges of the Cordillera Central, includes the provinces of Avila, Burgos, Segovia, Soria, Palencia, Valladolid, León, Zamora, and Salamanca. In the geographic center of Spain, the *comunidad* of Madrid is surrounded by these two regions.

Our itinerary goes from Madrid south to Toledo, then northwest to Avila with a side trip to Salamanca, then northeast to Segovia, Valladolid, and Burgos. From Burgos, you can continue northeast to Pamplona, site of the running of the bulls immortalized by Ernest Hemingway in *The Sun Also Rises*.

MADRID: For a complete report on the capital and its hotels and restaurants, see *Madrid,* THE CITIES. Two small Castilian towns that you might visit as side trips before beginning our tour are Aranjuez and Chinchón, both within about 30 miles (48 km) of Madrid.

Just off Route N-IV, Aranjuez is famous for its spring strawberries and asparagus. Its cool shady boulevards and plazas draw many a Madrid family for Sunday promenades. Aranjuez's main sites of interest (follow the signs) are the Royal Palace (El Palacio Real), begun by King Philip II; the Sailor's House (Casa de Marinos), which displays the royal boats; the Prince's Garden; and the Farmer's House (Casa del Labrador); all-inclusive admission charge for all sites. This romantic town inspired the haunting, lyrical "Concierto de Aranjuez," by composer Joaquín Rodrigo. A classical guitar concerto, it has also been interpreted by many jazz artists, the late Miles Davis among them.

The central plaza of Chinchón is one of the best-known small-town squares in central Spain, and is the site of bullfights during the summer season.

The best way to begin our tour of Castile is to head south from Madrid on the N401 highway for 44 miles (70 km) to Toledo.

TOLEDO: Master artist El Greco's painting *View of Toledo* depicts this 16th-century city standing atop green, windswept hills, under fiercely tormented stormy skies.

Whether or not you happen to catch similar climatic forces at work during your visit, you will be inspired anyway by the beauty of Toledo's palaces, private houses, and courtyards, as well as the view of the city itself from the Circunvalación road which runs parallel to the Río Tajo.

A center of Spanish civilization from as far back as the 8th-century Moorish era, Toledo has enough important sites to keep anyone engrossed for a good number of days. Dominating the skyline is the Alcázar, the now-dour fortress where the Spanish hero El Cid governed after conquering the Moors in the late 11th century. The reconstructed Alcázar is open daily (the original building was destroyed during the Spanish Civil War) and houses the *Museum of the Spanish Civil War.*

The cathedral, at Arco de Palacio, in the center of the city, dates from the 13th century and contains ornate artwork, sanctuaries, chapels, and bell towers, representing literally hundreds of years of devoted, inspired craftsmanship. You can ascend the bell tower, where an 18th-century bell is still in use.

The Church of St. Thomas (Iglesia Santo Tomé), at Angel Santo Tomé, houses El Greco's famous painting *The Burial of the Conde de Orgaz.* A few blocks away, on Paseo del Tránsito and the corner of Calle Reyes Católicos, is the 14th-century synagogue El Tránsito (it no longer functions as a Sephardic Jewish house of worship). During the Inquisition, the synagogue became a church, and the Jews who prayed there became Christians. Many of those who refused to convert fled the country. Part of the synagogue houses a museum that is open daily and contains Sephardic religious articles.

The *Casa y Museo de el Greco* (El Greco House and Museum; 3 Calle Samuel Ha-Levi; phone: 925-224046) contains some of the 16th-century artist's paintings and memorabilia. It is across and up the street from the synagogue.

From Toledo, take N403 northeast to Avila.

AVILA: This city was one of the strongholds of the reconquest of Spain from the Moors by the Christians, a 700-year conflict that finally ended in 1492 when King Ferdinand and Queen Isabella seized Granada and united Spain. Standing at almost 4,000 feet above sea level, the city is famous for its walled battlements. You can get the best view of the walls from the western section of the city, where they overlook the Río Adaja. Guided tours of some sections of the wall and walks along several sentry paths are available, or you can freely roam the parapets. The battlements at Avila are considered to be among the best existing examples of medieval fortifications. The cathedral at the foot of Calle Tostado; the *Deanery Museum* (Casa de los Deanes), containing Flemish and Spanish art (Calle de Eduardo); and the Convent of St. Teresa of Avila, the Christian mystic (Calle Marcelino Santiago), are the main sites in town.

Not far from Avila stands El Escorial, a palace and monastery built by King Philip II in a near-record 21 years. An austere, classical monument, it achieves a rare architectural consistency and contains paintings by Bosch, El Greco, and Velázquez, among others, in addition to its remarkable library and Royal Mausoleum (for complete details on the palace/monastery, see "Extra Special" in *Madrid,* THE CITIES).

> **En Route from Avila –** If you wish to make a side trip to Salamanca, simply follow N501 northwest. Salamanca is a university town with a Plaza Mayor that is more elaborate than the one in Madrid. You can walk around the city's major sites in about 3 hours; these include the university, the new and old cathedrals, and the Church of San Esteban — all with wonderful Plateresque façades. Surrounding Salamanca is an agricultural region where bulls are raised and their hides tanned to produce Spanish leather. From Salamanca, you may press on past Avila for 18 miles (29 km) to Villacastin and pick up A-6 freeway heading east. Turn off at exit N-603, which leads north to Segovia, 18½ miles (30 km) away.

SEGOVIA: In the city's main square, in 1474, Isabella la Católica was proclaimed Queen of Castile. Segovia's major sites are the Roman aqueduct and 14th-century alcázar (palace) with 19th-century modifications. In the center of town stands the cathedral (the last Gothic one built in Spain), plus numerous Romanesque churches. On the road south of Segovia you'll find the stone bridge that Ernest Hemingway described as a steel bridge and used as a setting in his novel *For Whom the Bell Tolls*.

Continue on the N601 highway from Segovia to Valladolid.

VALLADOLID: A university city, Valladolid claims to speak the purest Castilian Spanish. The house of 16th-century author Miguel de Cervantes, who wrote *Don Quixote* and who is known as the father of the modern novel, is near the Plaza Zorrilla, just off Calle Miguel Iscar. The other important sites in town are the cathedral; the 16th-century cloisters of San Gregorio College (Colegio San Gregorio; Cadena de San Gregorio Valladolid; phone: 983-250375), which also includes a renowned museum of Spanish sculpture; and the university (Universidad de Valladolid).

Take N620 to Burgos.

BURGOS: It was in Burgos, the 10th-century capital of Castile, that Francisco Franco was declared the *caudillo* (military commander) in 1936. The city holds a permanent place in Spanish military history, and none other than El Cid, the 11th-century warrior who became a legend, is buried in the Burgos Cathedral. (El Cid's exploits inspired Spain's first epic poem, "El Poema del Cid," written in the early 12th century.) The cathedral — with its slender, openwork spires — is the main reason for stopping here. After the cathedrals of Toledo and Seville it is the third largest in the country, dating as far back as the 13th century. The city's riverside promenade, the Paseo del Espolón, is particularly attractive, and two monasteries within walking distance of the center — the Monasterio de las Huelgas Reales and the Cartuja de Miraflores — are rich in artworks.

En Route from Burgos – The wheat fields and lush pine woods that surround Burgos were the inspiration for poet Antonio Machado. After Spain's loss of her last colonial possessions in the Spanish-American War, Machado and a group of writers, called the Generation of '98, turned to celebrate the most characteristically Spanish (really Castilian) countryside. A visit to the town of Soria on N234 will acquaint you with the pastoral landscape. Some fine examples of Romanesque architecture can be seen here, and there are interesting, burnt sienna–colored houses built by successful sheep ranchers and a 16th-century cathedral. Northeast of Soria on N111 are the ruins of the city of Numantia, whose citizens, according to legend, committed mass suicide rather than capitulate to the Romans in 133 BC.

Stay on N111 all the way to Pamplona.

PAMPLONA: Not actually in Castile, this city in the province of Navarre is one of the most famous in Spain. In *The Sun Also Rises*, Ernest Hemingway describes the annual *Festival of St. Fermín* (Fiesta de San Fermín), July 6–20, when full-grown, half-ton bulls are allowed to run through the streets in the early morning hours. The afternoon bullfights are among the most spectacular in the world. The city's main sites are the 14th-century cathedral and the *Navarre Museum* (Museo de Navarra), housing murals and religious sculpture (Calle Santo Domingo; phone: 948-227831).

BEST EN ROUTE

Decent and frequently even sumptuous accommodations at reasonable prices can be found throughout Castile, especially at one of the numerous government *paradores*. But it's necessary to make reservations months in advance for many of them. Expect to pay over $90 for a double room listed as expensive; between $60 and $85 at a moderate hotel; and under $45 in an inexpensive one.

Castilian restaurants provide gracious, aristocratic atmosphere as well as fine food. Expect to pay more than $80 for a meal for two at those restaurants we've listed as expensive; between $45 and $80 at those restaurants in the moderate category; under

$45, inexpensive. Prices do not include drinks, wine, or tips. All restaurants below accept major credit cards, unless otherwise indicated. Reservations are advised at all of the places listed.

TOLEDO

Parador Conde de Orgaz – A low, 2-story hotel commanding a sweeping view of the city, this is generally considered to be one of the most stunning *paradores* in the national chain. All rooms have air conditioning. The restaurant serves international as well as Manchegan fare. Paseo de los Cigarrales (phone: 925-221850). Expensive.

Hostal del Cardenal – With unquestionably the best restaurant in town, this small *hostal* is set in a restored 18th-century Toledan palace that once served as a cardinal's residence. It has a lovely garden and 27 charming rooms. 24 Paseo Recaredo (phone: 925-220862). Expensive to moderate.

Carlos V – If the *Conde de Orgaz* is fully booked, this is a fine alternative in the center of town. 1 Calle Trastamara (phone: 925-222100). Moderate.

Chirón – This restaurant is known for the splendid scenery and surroundings, as well as good regional dishes. The building stands across the Puerta de Chambron gateway through the city's walls overlooking the Río Tajo. Closed Mondays. 1 Paseo Recaredo (phone: 925-220150). Moderate.

Maravilla – Another good, centrally located hotel. It, too, is definitely worth considering if you can't get a room at *Conde de Orgaz*. 7 Calle Barrio Rey (phone: 925-223304). Moderate.

Venta de Aires – A leading restaurant with a tree-shaded terrace for summer dining. Closed Sunday dinner. Reservations unnecessary. 25 Circo Romano (phone: 925-220545). Moderate.

ARANJUEZ

Casa Pablo – Local asparagus and strawberries in season are served at this pleasant Castilian restaurant. Closed during August. Reservations unnecessary. 20 Calle Almíbar (phone: 91-891-1451). Moderate.

CHINCHÓN

Parador de Chinchón – This deluxe member of the *parador* chain was originally a 17th-century monastery. Its restaurant serves fine Castilian dishes, and the cloisters are now glassed in to form a delightful lounge decorated with antique furniture and superb tapestries and overlooking the gardens, fountain, and swimming pool. Travelers often prefer this as a tranquil base from which to visit Madrid, just 28 miles (45 km) away, as well as nearby Aranjuez and Toledo. 1 Avenida Generalisimo (phone: 91-894-0836). Expensive.

Mesón Cuevas del Vino – The best restaurant in town is in an old mill. Here — and everywhere else in town — you can sample the potent licorice-flavored liqueur called *chinchón*. Open daily. 13 Calle Benito Hortelano (phone: 91-894-0206). Moderate.

AVILA

Parador Raimundo de Borgoña – This grand old building was actually a 15th-century palace where Raymond of Burgundy (Raimundo de Borgoña) lived during a military crusade against the Moors. The exterior of the castle is bleached white stone; inside, the rooms have whitewashed walls and tile floors and are artistically furnished. Marqués de Canales y Chozas (phone: 918-211340). Expensive.

Mesón del Rastro – An old inn that is now a charming restaurant. Open daily. 1 Plaza del Rastro (phone: 918-211218). Moderate.

Parador de Gredos – In an old lodge with a new wing added in 1975, it stands in a wooded section of a plateau with excellent views of the Gredos mountain peaks, about an hour's drive from Avila. Inside, the atmosphere is similar to a hunting lodge. Fresh trout is the dining room's specialty. Navarrendonda de la Sierra (phone: 918-348048). Moderate.

SALAMANCA

Parador de Salamanca – This is a modern *parador* across the river, overlooking the city's Gothic skyline. It offers very good accommodations, conscientious service, and an outdoor swimming pool. Just off the Salamanca-Valladolid road, 2 Calle Teso de la Feria (phone: 923-268700). Expensive.

SEGOVIA

Arcos – Near the colossal Roman aqueduct, this built-for-convenience small hotel also serves as a mini-convention center. Its popular restaurant, *La Cocina de Segovia,* features excellent Castilian specialties. 24 Paseo Ezequiel González (phone: 911-437462). Expensive.

Parador de Segovia – A *parador* with a deluxe rating. It has a swimming pool, gardens, and a fine view of the city from its hilltop site. Outside of town on the road to Valladolid. Carretera de Valladolid (phone: 911-430462). Expensive.

Mesón de Cándido – Segovia's finest restaurant, set in a 15th-century house, specializes in Castilian delicacies — roast suckling pig, lamb roast, veal chops, and a special soup made according to the master chef's recipe. Open daily. 5 Plaza Azoguejo (phone: 911-425911). Moderate.

Mesón Duque – This noted restaurant is *Cándido*'s main rival, serving typically Castilian food. Open daily. 12 Calle Cervantes (phone: 911-430537). Moderate.

VALLADOLID

Mesón de la Fragua – Of the many restaurants and cafés around Plaza Mayor, this is the best. Closed Sundays. 10 Paseo Zorrilla (phone: 983-337102). Moderate.

BURGOS

Landa Palace – This splendid castle-hotel has a very fine restaurant that turns out delicious French dishes along with equally appetizing local specialties. On the Madrid-Irun highway (phone: 947-206343). Expensive.

SORIA

Parador Antonio Machado – The contemporary hilltop building overlooks the mountains and the Río Duero Valley. The dining room is noted for its Castilian game dishes and rich rioja wines. Parque del Castillo (phone: 975-213445). Expensive.

The Costa del Sol

The Costa del Sol is Spain's answer to Acapulco and Rio de Janeiro: miles upon miles of high-rise hotels, condominiums, bungalows, and campsites overlooking the azure Mediterranean. In fact, it is one of Europe's most developed and most popular beach and golf resort areas. Many people look upon the Costa del Sol as an international playground rather than part of Spain. Some argue, incontestably, that the original character of the area —

dry, hilly land sprinkled with whitewashed villages — has been changed forever by the resorts that provide accommodations, nightlife, and other recreational opportunities for tourists — about 6 million every year.

The Costa del Sol extends from Almería on the easternmost part of the southern Mediterranean Coast to Algeciras, 236 miles (378 km) to the west. The center of the coast is the city of Málaga, an important port. Both Algeciras and Málaga have ferries connecting Spain with Tangiers, Morocco, and the Spanish Moroccan port towns of Ceuta and Melilla. In the 84 miles (134 km) between Málaga and Algeciras are the most developed (and crowded) of the Costa del Sol resort towns — Torremolinos, Fuengirola, and Marbella. Along this stretch of road (or beach) you are more likely to hear Swedish, German, French, Arabic, and English spoken than Spanish.

Though not always so named, the Costa del Sol has been attractive to foreign visitors ever since the Phoenicians landed on its shores in about the 6th century BC. They were followed by the Greeks, Romans, and Moors. The Moorish influence, although considerably more visible in the inland villages, can still be seen along the coast. Fortresses and the ruins of guard towers stand on cliffs near the sea. In contrast to the modern, white high-rises that line much of the dry, hilly coast are villages of whitewashed cottages and colorful gardens.

The best time of year to visit is around March and April, before the hordes descend. The temperatures tend to be in the 60s F (mid-teens to low 20s C) with clear, sunny skies. In the summer, the mercury climbs into the 80s and 90s F (20s and 30s C), but because the heat is dry and breezes from the Mediterranean cool the air, few hotels other than expensive ones have air conditioning.

Although you can plan to visit every resort along the Costa del Sol, we recommend that you choose one spot as a base and make 1- or 2-day trips to other towns. The N340 highway runs the entire length of the Costa del Sol and all you need do is follow it.

ALMERÍA: Just beyond the town, the Almería desert contains some of the world's most famous sand dunes. Certainly, they are among the most filmed — *Lawrence of Arabia, The Good, the Bad, and the Ugly,* and *Reds* were made here, to name a few. Residents claim that so many film crews have drifted through town over the years, that they no longer remember the titles of the movies that were (and are) being made. In the 1960s, Almería was known to thousands of young people who were on the road in Europe as the place where you could make a few bucks as an extra in a Western. All you had to do was join the Spanish actors' union, sign on with a film company, and be willing to spend 8 or 9 hours in the sweltering heat dressed as a cowboy or Indian. You can find out which movies are being filmed in the neighborhood by stopping at Almantur, the official tourist board (Carretera de Málaga; phone: 951-234859), where you can get maps directing you to the film locations in the area.

In town, the main place of interest is the Alcazaba, a Phoenician castle that was converted into a fortress by the Moors. The site of music festivals during the second half of August, the castle stands on a hill. You can't miss it.

The cathedral is another building that has lived through various incarnations. Originally a mosque, it was Christianized in the 16th century; however, architecturally, it has retained something of a Moorish character.

ALMUÑECAR: This town — one of those clean coastal villages that smell of orange blossoms — dates from the Phoenicians, who called it Sexi. But don't get your hopes up. Although the nearby beaches of San Cristóbal, Punta del Mar, La Herradura, and Berenguel can be as sexy as the bodies languishing on them at the moment, Almuñecar itself offers only a Roman aqueduct and a Moorish fortress as sightseeing attractions. As in Almería, the fortress here, too, is called the Alcazaba.

NERJA: Discovered by two youngsters who were poking around the countryside in 1959, the caves for which this little town is world famous were opened to the public in 1960. Since then, visitors have come to wander through the mazes, gazing at the underground waterfalls, crypts, and the stalactites and stalagmites that adorn ceilings and floors, and are lit by multicolored lights. Adjoining the caves is an anthropological museum with prehistoric paintings said to be 20,000 years old. A music and dance festival is held in the caves every year during the first 2 weeks in August.

Apart from its caves, Nerja is known for a natural promontory overlooking the Mediterranean called El Balcón de Europa (The Balcony of Europe). If it sounds like a promising title for a best seller, perhaps you'll be inspired to start writing after contemplating the stunning seascape.

This is also a good town for festivals. In addition to the music festival in August, there is a procession of boats honoring the Virgin of Carmen on July 16, a series of parades with fireworks honoring San Isidro (St. Isidore) on May 15, and a 4-day bash in honor of Nerja's patron saint, from October 9 through October 12.

   En Route from Nerja – Take an interesting side trip to the village of Frigiliana, only 3 miles (5 km) inland from Nerja in the surrounding Almijara mountains. This tiny Andalusian town (pop. 2,160) of winding streets, red tile–roofed cottages, tropical flowers, and enchanting views of the neighboring mountains and valleys may be declared a national monument in order to protect it from possible ravishment by 20th-century developers.

MÁLAGA: The center of the Costa del Sol is known as the place that gave the world sweet málaga wine. The vineyards that produce the wine grapes cover the hills on the outskirts of town. You can sample málaga wine at any one of the small *bodegas* (taverns) in the center of town.

In addition to its prized vineyards, Málaga has a few other spots of interest. Overlooking the city, the Gibralfaro Castle spreads along a reddish cliff covered with ivy and cypress trees. The castle dates back to the Phoenician times, and has Moorish modifications that were added in the 8th century. The castle adjoins the Alcazaba where the Arab monarchs resided during the 11th century. (It now contains an archaeological museum, which is open daily.) They are both on a hilly park accessible by Calle Mundo Nuevo or Calle Victoria to Ferrandiz.

Málaga's cathedral a 16th-century building with a truncated bell tower, has an ornate interior. The adjoining museum is open daily except Sundays and holidays. The cathedral, not surprisingly, is on the Plaza de la Catedral.

The *Museo de Bellas Artes* (Fine Arts Museum), in an old palace (6 Calle San Agustín), contains an eclectic collection of Roman artifacts, Moorish art, and paintings by El Greco, Murillo, and Picasso, a native son of Málaga. (His birthplace is at 16 Plaza de la Merced.)

To get a feeling for the town, take a carriage ride along the Paseo del Parque, a promenade near the waterfront lined with tropical gardens and sidewalk cafés. Or amble down Calle Marqués de Larios, Málaga's main shopping street. At the Plaza de Toros, at the end of the Paseo del Parque, you can take an English guided tour and get a glimpse of what goes on behind the scenes of a bullfight. The most important bullfights of the year take place on *Easter Sunday,* during the *Corpus Christi* festivities in June, and during the first week in August. For more information about bullfights and other events, contact the Tourist Information Office, 5 Calle Marqués de Larios (phone: 952-213445).

Málaga is an excellent jumping-off point for trips to Africa. The ferry and hydrofoil to Tangiers and Ceuta (Spanish Morocco) leave from the Estación Marítima along Muelle Heredia. (Note that the ferry and hydrofoil service operates year-round, except when waters are too turbulent.)

TORREMOLINOS: This is the busiest resort on the Costa del Sol. Not so very long ago, Torremolinos was a quiet little fishing village visited by handfuls of European tourists. You would never know it to look at the place today: White high-rise hotels and apartment complexes, many with tennis courts and swimming pools, line the coast. In town are restaurants, supermarkets, nightclubs, discotheques, and boutiques. Nearby is a hotel and golf course, the *Parador Nacional de Golf* (see *Best en Route*), and the 20-acre *Tivoli Amusement Park.* And of course, there always is the Mediterranean.

In the summer, Torremolinos is jam-packed with tourists from all over the world. In November, when the *Benalmádena Film Festival* is held, the town is even more hectic, if that's possible.

BENALMÁDENA COSTA: Although it is difficult to see where Torremolinos ends and Benalmádena Costa begins because the scenery is the same, Benalmádena has a somewhat more subdued atmosphere and a less frenetic nightlife than the super-resort next door. A casino with a 9-story apartment complex has opened at Torrequebrada outside Benalmádena.

FUENGIROLA: A family resort area of seaside villas and campsites overlooking the sea, Fuengirola is quieter than Torremolinos or Benalmádena. Here you'll find pleasant little beach cafés, bars, and quiet coves as well as wide, white stretches of sand. Overlooking Fuengirola is a 10th-century Moorish castle, Sohail. A few miles north of the coast, in the hills, Lew Hoad, a former Australian tennis star and *Wimbledon* champion, runs a tennis camp called *Rancho de Tenis.* The 18-hole *Club de Gold de Mijas* (phone: 952-476793) is nearby.

MARBELLA: The chicest of the towns along the Costa del Sol, Marbella is also the most expensive and has retained more of its traditional architecture than any of its neighbors. Many oil sheiks and movie stars have homes here, and the prices in the picturesque little bistros and designer boutiques reflect it. Not far from Marbella are several golf courses: *Marbella Golf,* designed by Robert Trent Jones, Sr. (phone: 952-830068); *Golf Nueva Andalucía* (phone: 952-780300); *Aloha Golf* (phone: 952-812388); *Golf Guadalmina* (phone: 952-781377 or 952-780008); and *Golf Atalaya Park* (phone: 952-781894).

NUEVA ANDALUCÍA: This community is actually a section of Marbella. It has a smashing marina — Puerto José Banús, where hundreds of yachts from all over the world dock. Nueva Andalucía is also the home of the Costa del Sol's first casino at *Hotel del Golf Plaza* (Urbanización), which offers roulette (European and American), blackjack, baccarat, chemin de fer, and *punto y bancca.* The casino is part of a leisure complex also containing 4 swimming pools, a nightclub, 3 bars, and 3 restaurants.

ESTEPONA: Although developers are starting to build here and the beachfront has become more commercial, the surrounding mountainous area of Estepona has managed so far to retain its traditional character, with fishermen, goatherds, and farmers living as they have for centuries. Not far from Estepona is the *Club de Golf Valderama,* designed by Robert Trent Jones, Jr. (phone: 956-792775).

ALGECIRAS: Most people don't really get acquainted with this sleepy little port on the southernmost peninsula of Spain. Although it has a few hotels, it is mostly known for its port, from which ferries leave for Tangiers, Morocco, and Ceuta, Spanish

Morocco. The people in Algeciras are very friendly and the town market is a fascinating bustling center of peddlers, greengrocers, and butchers.

BEST EN ROUTE

The Costa del Sol has some 300,000 hotel beds, ranging from comfortable to elegant. There are apartment houses, hostels, inns, *paradores* (inns owned by the Spanish government), and government-run campsites that cater primarily to families with recreational vehicles or large tents. The biggest bargain here might be renting a villa, condominium, or apartment. Ask a travel agent or write to Sara Burns (Urbanización Los Monteros, Marbella, Spain), or José Juan Abrines (Costa del Sol Tourist Promotion Board, PO Box 298, Palacio de Congresos, Torremolinos — Málaga, Spain). Expect to pay over $115 for a double room at places listed as expensive; $75 to $115 is moderate; under $60 is inexpensive.

Service, atmosphere, and presentation of food are almost always pleasant on the Costa del Sol. Expect to pay more than $60 for a meal for two at those restaurants listed as expensive; between $35 and $55 at those restaurants in the moderate category; under $35, inexpensive. Prices do not include drinks, wine, or tips. All restaurants below accept major credit cards, unless otherwise indicated. Reservations are advised at all restaurants, except where noted.

ALMERÍA

Almería – There's no shortage of hotels in Almería, but this — clean, modern, with a swimming pool and a fine view of the harbor — is one of the best. In the center of town. 8 Avenida Reina Regente (phone: 951-238011). Moderate.

NERJA

Parador de Nerja – From its hilltop vantage point, this 2-story resort overlooks the mountains and the Mediterranean. Its swimming pool and tennis courts are in a garden setting, and its restaurant serves international as well as Andalusian cuisine. El Tablazo (phone: 952-520050). Moderate.

MÁLAGA

Málaga Palacio – A large, traditional establishment with a central location between the park and the cathedral. There are views of the nearby port from the upper rooms, the rooftop pool, and the restaurant. 1 Cortina del Muelle (phone: 952-215185). Expensive to moderate.

Antonio Martín – This simple restaurant near the harbor serves fresh fish, seafood, and paella. It has a view of the harbor. Closed Mondays. Reservations unnecessary. 4 Paseo Marítimo (phone: 952-211018). Moderate.

Café de París – Hot and cold soups and smoked meat and fish are the specialties of this centrally located restaurant. Closed Sundays. Reservations unnecessary. Vélez Málaga (Malagueta; phone: 952-225043). Moderate.

Parador Gibralfaro – With only 12 rooms in its luxuriously appointed interior, this inn is constantly booked. The terrific site — overlooking the sea next to Gibralfaro Castle — makes the restaurant and bar popular spots. Reservations necessary (phone: 952-221902). Moderate.

Casa Pedro – Your best bet for a hearty seafood meal served up in an unpretentious spot by the ocean. At El Palo Beach, just outside the city. Closed Monday dinner. No reservations. 112 Calle Almería Quitapenas (phone: 952-298396). Inexpensive.

Marisquería Noelia – This seafood *tasca* can't be beat for the variety and freshness of its catch-of-the-day delicacies, which are on colorful display. Small and unpretentious, it is always crowded with friendly *malagueños* at *tapas* time. In a charming central section of town. No reservations. 138 Calle La Victoria (phone: 952-260246). Inexpensive.

TORREMOLINOS

Casa Guaquín – This is a family restaurant in every sense; the owner's family even catches the seafood served. Closed Thursdays and December. Reservations unnecessary. 37 Calle Carmen, Playa Carihuela (phone: 952-384530). Moderate.

Chalana – Continental dishes share the menu with paella and fresh fish. Closed Tuesdays and November through mid-December. No reservations. Paseo Marítimo (phone: 952-384956). Moderate.

Meliá Torremolinos – This 283-room resort is one of the largest on the Costa del Sol. A member of the Spanish Meliá chain, it offers everything from 2 nightclubs to Sunday morning mass. And it's about 5 minutes' walk from the beach. 109 Avenida Carlota Alessandri (phone: 952-380500). Moderate.

Parador del Golf – Contemporary in design and on an 18-hole golf course, this is a 40-room link in the Parador chain. In addition to a beachfront location, it has a swimming pool and a restaurant. Halfway between Málaga and Torremolinos (phone: 952-381255). Moderate.

Camping Torremolinos – If you're traveling on a budget, but would like to be close to Torremolinos's nightlife and social scene, this is a good alternative to costly hotels. How much you actually have to rough it depends on the kind of RV, camper, or tent you bring; facilities include a swimming pool and showers. It's about a 10-minute walk to the beach; Carretera Torremolinos–Benalmádena, Km 228 (phone: 952-382602). Inexpensive.

Hong Kong – Egg-roll addicts can get their fix here, Torremolinos-style. The Cantonese cooking is generally pretty good. Closed during the first 3 weeks of November. Calle Cauce (no phone). Inexpensive.

Portofino – This terrace that has been built on the beach serves seafood that couldn't taste any fresher if you caught it yourself. Playa Montemar (no phone). Inexpensive.

BENALMÁDENA-COSTA

Torrequebrada – A luxury beach resort complex on a 15,000-acre estate, with one of Europe's largest casinos, a complete health spa, nightclub, championship golf course, tennis courts, swimming pools, tropical gardens, 4 restaurants, and views of the Mediterranean and the ancient, white mountainside town of Benalmádena. Carretera de Cádiz, Km 220 (phone: 952-446000). Expensive.

FUENGIROLA

Casa Zafra – Unmistakably nautical in atmosphere, the inside of this seafood restaurant has been built to resemble a ship. 6 Calle Perla (no phone). Expensive to moderate.

Langosta – Still another fine seafood establishment. Closed Mondays and December through mid-January. 1 Calle Francisco Cano (phone: 952-475049). Moderate.

Olla – You can choose from Spanish, Basque, or international dishes at this beachside restaurant with a terrace facing the sea. Closed Mondays. Paseo Marítimo, Los Boliches (phone: 952-474516). Moderate.

China – For hefty Indonesian meals or old-fashioned Cantonese dishes, this restaurant can't be beat. Closed Thursdays. 27 Calle Ramón y Cajal (phone: 952-472993). Moderate to inexpensive.

MIJAS

Byblos Andaluz – This sparkling deluxe resort has tennis courts, fabulous swimming pools with poolside bars and buffets, and a complete health spa housing the Luison

Bobet Institute of Thalassotherapy. The Andalusian-style hotel and villas with patios and fountains overlook 2 Robert Trent Jones, Sr. par 72 golf courses. Three restaurants serve haute cuisine, regional dishes, and special dietetic meals. Nearby is the picturesque 2,500-year-old town of Mijas. Three miles (5 km) from Fuengirola in Urbanización Mijas-Golf (phone: 952-473050). Expensive.

MARBELLA

Marbella Club – Dazzling and sleek, this expanded resort put Marbella on the map. Here you can rub elbows with the jet set — if you're willing to pay for the privilege. Carretera de Cádiz, Km 184 (phone: 952-771300). Expensive.

Los Monteros – A 171-room complex of 3 buildings spread over the grounds of a former estate, it has 5 swimming pools, 10 tennis courts, a golf club, horseback riding, beachfront, and lots of trees. Urbanización Los Monteros (phone: 952-771700). Expensive.

Puente Romano – These sun-drenched, palm-studded villas lounge beside the Mediterranean. Each of the 200 airy rooms has a private terrace. Four restaurants, tennis courts, and a *Regine's* discotheque. Carretera Cádiz, Km 184 (phone: 952-770100). Expensive.

NUEVA ANDALUCÍA

Golf Hotel Nueva Andalucía – A sparking white building set among floral gardens, this 21-room hotel is close to three Robert Trent Jones, Sr. golf courses. Equipment can be rented and lessons are available. There is a heated pool, dining room, shopping arcade, and a discotheque. Nueva Andalucía (phone: 952-780300). Expensive to moderate.

ALGECIRAS

Camping Costa Sol – A hilly plot of land given over to tents and campers, its main blessing is its proximity to a stretch of beach offering a fine view of the Rock of Gibraltar. It's about a 20-minute bus ride from town on the Carretera Cádiz-Málaga (phone: 956-660219). Inexpensive.

Marea Baja – The menu here offers a large variety of fish and seafood entrées, and ice cream crêpes for dessert. Closed Sundays. 2 Calle Trafalgar (phone: 956-663654). Inexpensive.

Andalusia

The Andalusian region is, in a very real way, the heart of Spain. Indeed, Andalusia is home to that which most people think of as Spanish: the flamenco, a flamboyant music and dance that's so identified with the Gypsies of Granada and Seville; Spain's many famous matadors — El Cordobés, Manolete, and Lagartijo; the traditional flower-draped, whitewashed cottages clinging precariously to rocky hillsides; and the stunning Moorish palace and garden complex, the Alhambra.

A mountainous region in the southern part of the country, Andalusia comprises eight provinces: Almería, Cádiz, Córdoba, Granada, Huelva, Jaén, Málaga, and Seville. The Sierra Morena, Sierra Nevada, and Sistema Penibética mountain ranges take up large sections of the interior. Much of the land is given over to the cultivation of olives, oranges, sunflowers, and grapes. Andalusia is bordered on the west by the Gulf of Cádiz and on the south and east by the Mediterranean Sea. Andalusia's major cities are Córdoba, Granada, Málaga, and Seville.

The recorded history of the region dates back to the arrival of the Phoenicians between the 11th and 5th centuries BC. Around the same era, the Celts, who migrated south from northern Europe, intermarried with the native Iberian residents; their offspring, the Celtiberians, are the ancestors of today's Spanish. Around the turn of the millennium, the Romans arrived, bringing their culture, politics, and philosophy. They built cities at Itálica (Seville), Córdoba, and Baelo-Claudia, as well as roads, aqueducts, and monuments. The Romans were followed by the Christian Visigoths around the 5th and 6th centuries AD, who were, in turn, vanquished by the Moors in 711. The Moorish era is known as the golden age of Andalusia. During this period, the region was the seat of an independent caliphate that thrived while the rest of the European continent remained in the Dark Ages. The most important Andalusian monuments — the Mezquita of Córdoba, the Giralda of Seville, and the Alhambra of Granada — date from this epoch.

In 1492 the Muslim empire in Spain, already reduced to the kingdom of Granada, was conquered by the Catholic monarchs Ferdinand and Isabella. In the same year, the adventurer Christopher Colombus set off from Palos de la Frontera, an Andalusian port, to discover the New World.

Nowadays, people from the New World travel to discover Andalusia. The best time to visit is in March and April, when the temperatures are in the 60s and 70s F (15 to 21C) and it is not yet crowded. June, July, and August are peak months. It tends to rain in the winter.

Our tour starts in Córdoba, and heads southwest to Seville and Jerez de la Frontera, before winding northeast through the mountains to Ronda and Granada. If you are driving remember that the countryside is very rugged and so are the roads.

CÓRDOBA: Founded by the Romans in 151 BC, it was a city popular with Julius Caesar, Pompey, and Agrippa. Both Senecas were born here. Ruins of Roman walls and a Roman stone bridge reconstructed by the Moors still span the Río Guadalquivir. The former capital of Moorish Spain during the 8th century, it was governed as a separate emirate until the 10th century when the Caliphate of Córdoba was established. During the 10th-century reign of Abderramán III, the city had 500,000 inhabitants and some 300 mosques. It was at that time one of the leading cities in Europe and also one of the leading cities of the Muslim world. Today the population numbers only 285,000, but in many areas of the town the mystery of the Córdoban past is still very much alive.

While you are in Córdoba, be sure to see La Mezquita (follow the signs), a masterpiece of Moorish–early Spanish architecture that was first a mosque, then a cathedral. During the 8th century, the Muslims shared the mosque with the Christians. After passing through the Patio of the Orange Trees (Patio de los Naranjos) you enter a forest of columns — alabaster, jasper, and marble — topped by ocher and tan horseshoe arches. The columns come from as far away as North Africa where they were taken from Roman, Visigoth, and Phoenician ruins. One testimony to the size of the mosque is the fact that the Christians built a full-size cathedral in its center after Córdoba was reconquered in 1236. La Mezquita is open daily (Cardenal Herrero; phone: 957-470512).

Surrounding La Mezquita is the oldest part of the city. Called the Judería, it contains the Jewish quarter to the northwest. On Calle Judíos, there is a 14th-century synagogue with segregated men's and women's sections. Nearby, on Calle Averroes and Calle Judíos, is a patio where flamenco dancers perform during the summer months. Across the street from the synagogue is the *Museo Municipal* (Municipal Museum), which contains early Córdoban artifacts, and the *Museo Taurino* (Bullfighting Museum), which has articles that belonged to some of Córdoba's major matadors — Lagartijo, Manolete, El Cordobés, and Guerrita. Both are at 5 Plaza Maimónides.

Along the banks of the Río Guadalquivir, the Alcázar, a group of splendid Moorish gardens of pools, towers, fountains, and terraces, is open daily. If you are a fan of Don Quixote, be sure to visit Plazuela del Potro, where an inn mentioned in Cervantes's novel is still standing.

About 4 miles (6 km) west of town is the Medina Azahara, the remains of a Moorish city built in the 10th century. It's worth a side trip, especially for the pleasant country-side surroundings.

Although you can shop for souvenirs in the area around La Mezquita, the really worthwhile items are Córdoba embossed leather and filigree silver. There are plenty of little cafés where you can sip coffee and relax.

The main tourist office is at the Palacio de Congresos y Exposiciones (10 Torrijos; phone: 957-471235); a smaller municipal office is on the Plaza Juda Levi (phone: 957-472000).

Now take the N-IV highway southwest to Seville.

SEVILLE: According to legend, Seville was founded by Hercules the Greek. Although the city shares a similar pattern of earlier history with Córdoba, Seville came into its own after the Christian reconquest of Andalusia in the 13th century. The cathedral contains some of the treasure that Spanish conquistadores brought back from the New World.

The cathedral and Alcázar complex (Av. Queipo de Llano) is the most impressive site in the city. The 15th-century cathedral is the third largest in the world, after St. Peter's and St. Paul's, and the largest Gothic structure in the world. Like the cathedral of Córdoba, it is built on the site of a former mosque adjoining a Patio of the Orange Trees. All that remains of the original mosque is a statuesque 322-foot Moorish tower, La Giralda, which is now the symbol of Seville. After touring the opulent 15th- and 16th-century interior of the cathedral, take the exit called Puerta de los Naranjos, which opens onto the patio. Walk to the Puerta Oriente, across a plaza, and you will find yourself at the Alcázar, the Moorish fortress that was modified by the Christians in the 14th century to resemble the Alhambra in Granada.

After touring the Alcázar, have lunch at the *Hostería del Laurel* (5 Plaza de las Venerables), where none other than Don Juan is supposed to have eaten before or after he went a-wooing. It's still in service and the food is quite good (see *Best en Route*).

After lunch, take a walk through the Barrio de Santa Cruz or down Calle Sierpes, the shopping street reserved for pedestrian traffic. Be sure to spend some time strolling through Parque María Luisa along the banks of the Río Guadalquivir and Avenida María Luisa, and take a boat ride at the Plaza de España. After such a pleasant afternoon, you'll know why Bizet's *Carmen* and Rossini's *Barber of Seville* are set here.

Unlike Córdoba, Seville has maintained its prominence as the spiritual center of Andalusia. In fact, the most exciting times to visit Seville are during *Semana Santa* (Holy Week) and during the *Feria de Sevilla* (Spring Fair) following *Easter.* During *Easter,* many holy images are paraded through the streets; the religious processions are world famous. During the *feria,* the city becomes a nonstop fiesta. Hotel reservations often are made a year in advance.

Speaking of reservations, this year Seville expects millions of visitors at its colossal *Expo '92* (April 20 to October 12), celebrating the 500th anniversary of the discovery of America. Seville played an important role in the discovery and colonization of the New World as a seaport connected to the Atlantic by the Guadalquivir River. The

1,000-acre Island of Cartuja, formed by two branches of the river, is the site of the fabulous fairgrounds. The Carthusian Monastery of Santa María de las Cuevas, for centuries the only structure on the island (now known for its fine ceramics), has been transformed into Spain's royal and government pavilions. For information, contact *Expotourist Services,* Isla de la Cartuja, Seville 41010, Spain (phone: 95-446-1992).

For year-round nighttime entertainment in Seville, visit the *Arenal* (7 Calle Rodo; phone: 95-421-6492), which features some of the best and most authentic flamenco performers in Andalusia, in the colorful setting of a 17th-century mansion. Unlike many others, this *tablao* is a favorite of locals and dancers as well tourists.

The E25 highway leads south to Jerez de la Frontera.

JEREZ DE LA FRONTERA: The town that first gave the world sherry is still producing it. Guided tours are conducted through Jerez's wine cellars with wine sampling offered afterward. You can buy sherry on the spot if any particular brand appeals to you. If you imbibe a bit more sherry than you're accustomed to, be sure to spend the night in Jerez before tackling the roads to Ronda, as they twist around cliffs and are difficult to navigate. You can also rent a chauffeured car or take an organized bus tour.

En Route to Granada – Set in the hills of the Serranía de Ronda, one of the oldest cities in Spain, Ronda is divided into two sections by a gorge more than 300 feet deep. South of the gorge is the old Moorish section, with its narrow, curving streets and alleyways. In this part of town is found the Casa del Rey Moro (Palace of the Moorish King); the Church of Santa María la Mayor, which was a mosque in an earlier incarnation; and the Moorish baths. The Plaza de Toros is said to be where Pedro Romero started modern bullfighting in the 18th century. The best way to see Ronda is on foot. The splendid views of the surrounding hills and the gorges are truly impressive. Don't expect the Rondeños to welcome you with wide open arms; they are less exuberant than their other Andalusian neighbors. This may have something to do with the fact that the Serranía de Ronda used to be a refuge for bandits and *contrabandistas.*

Ronda can be reached from Jerez by heading east on N342. This road continues to Granada but it is a tortuous, time-consuming route. Scenic, yes; but you'll probably spend so much time praying that you won't enjoy the views. Alternatively, you can take N344 south to Fuengirola and follow the coastal route (N340) through Málaga to Motril, heading north on N323 to Granada. It gets you there without the agony.

GRANADA: To most people, Granada is synonymous with the Alhambra, a lavish fortress-palace-garden complex built on a mountain overlooking the city. Built by the Nasrid royal family (an Islamic group that fought the Christians in the 13th century), the Alhambra is one of the best preserved of all Moorish palaces in the world. It consists of three main areas: the Alcazaba and watchtower that date from the 9th century; the Alhambra itself; and the Generalife, or summer gardens. Within the Alhambra is the 14th-century palace, which has many spacious courtyards and patios decorated with mosaic arches, fountains, columns, and gardens. A visit to the Alhambra is a dazzling, sensual experience: color, texture, sound, and smell intermingle.

Down the hill from the Alhambra, on Calle San Jerónimo in the cathedral quarter, is the Capilla Real (Royal Chapel), where the Catholic monarchs King Ferdinand and Queen Isabella are buried on the site of their victory over the Moors.

Opposite the Alhambra, the hilly Albaicín neighborhood is an intriguing maze of cottage-lined streets and patio gardens that sprout, like miniature Generalifes, in the middle of each house. The Sacromonte, at the summit of Albaicín, has some Gypsy caves where flamenco dances are performed. Be forewarned that they are overpriced; the shows in town are usually at least as good (if not better) and much less expensive.

For a list of reputable flamenco clubs and information on festivals, contact the Andalusian Tourist Office (2 Libreros; phone: 958-225990), or the city's tourism office (10 Plaza Mariana Pineda; phone: 958-226688).

In winter, from November to May, you can ski at the Solynieve ski center in the Sierra Nevada range, a few miles from Granada. Facilities include a chair lift, 8 ski lifts, and 2 cable cars. For details, see the tourist office listed above.

BEST EN ROUTE

Accommodations range from modern hotels to historic *paradores* (government-run inns). Expect to pay $115 or more for a double room at those places we've listed as expensive; between $55 and $110 for a room in the moderate category; under $55, inexpensive.

Andalusian restaurants are known for their pretty flowers, music, and artistic presentation of food that add sparkle to the atmosphere. Expect to pay more than $70 for a meal for two at those restaurants we've listed as expensive; between $45 and $70 at those restaurants in the moderate category; under $45, inexpensive. Prices do not include drinks, wine, or tips. All restaurants below accept major credit cards, unless otherwise indicated.

CÓRDOBA

El Caballo Rojo – Córdoba's leading restaurant serves Andalusian gazpacho, tortillas, and Valencian paella. Open daily. Reservations advised. 28 Calle Cardenal Herrero (phone: 475375). Moderate.

Meliá Córdoba – What this hotel lacks in charm it makes up for in modern amenities and a very convenient location in the center of town. It has a nightclub, bar, dining room, swimming pool, and a shopping arcade. Jardines de la Victoria (phone: 957-298066). Moderate.

Parador la Arruzafa – On the outskirts of town, this *parador* is not in a historic building but in a fairly ordinary-looking, relatively recent structure. The dining room serves game in winter and gazpacho with almonds in summer. Avenida de la Arruzafa (phone: 957-275900). Moderate.

Albucasis – Close to the Mezquita, this delightful little newcomer occupies an old mansion that has been stylishly restored in Mudéjar fashion. Spotlessly clean, with friendly service, it has 15 rooms and a charming patio. Breakfast only. 11 Calle Buen Pastor (phone: 957-478625). Moderate to inexpensive.

El Churrasco – Various styles of steaks are served, with potatoes, rice, and/or eggs. Closed Thursdays and August. Reservations necessary. 16 Calle Romero, 1 flight up (phone: 957-290819). Moderate to inexpensive.

Residencial Maimónides – A small hotel right across the street from La Mezquita offers modest accommodations and the most scenic location in town. In the old section. 4 Calle Torrijos (phone: 957-471500). Moderate to inexpensive.

SEVILLE

Alfonso XIII – Seville's most elegant establishment (now part of the CIGA chain), this palatial *gran lujo* hotel was built for the *1929 Ibero-American Expo* in neo-Mudéjar style, with tiles, grillwork, marble, arches, and columns galore. There is sun and socializing at the garden pool and bar and a grand atmosphere in the lobby, lounges, and restaurant. It's a great place to visit even if you're not staying here. 2 Calle San Fernando (phone: 95-422-2850). Expensive.

Sevilla Sol – This deluxe hotel is part of the Sol chain, Spain's biggest. Centrally located near the Plaza de España, it features a swimming pool, physical-fitness center, squash courts, convention facilities, fine restaurants, and the special Club Elite services. 3 Avenida de la Borbolla (phone: 95-442-2611). Expensive.

Doña María – Directly across the street from the cathedral in the Barrio de Santa Cruz, this small hostelry has received good reviews from just about everyone who's crossed its threshold. There's a rooftop swimming pool but no restaurant. 19 Calle Don Remondo (phone: 95-422-4990). Expensive to moderate.

La Dorada – Both the restaurant and the clientele are casually elegant, and the seafood and service are excellent. Closed Sunday evenings and July 15 to August 15. Across the river at 6 Calle Virgen las Aguas Santas (phone: 95-445-5100). The proprietors also operate *La Taberna Dorada,* at José Luis de Casso (phone: 95-465-2720), as well as a seafood restaurant in Madrid. Expensive to moderate.

Inglaterra – Another top contemporary hotel in the center of the city, behind the Town Hall. Many of its comfortable rooms have large balconies. It's a short walk from here to the cathedral and Calle Sierpes. There's a sunny second-floor restaurant. A good buy for Seville. 7 Plaza Nueva (phone: 95-422-4970). Expensive to moderate.

Oriza – One of the fanciest restaurants in town, this is a favorite of the local aristocracy and visiting European epicureans. The Biscayan seafood is excellent, and the unusual decor is highlighted by Eiffel-wrought ironwork. Closed Sundays and August. 41 Calle San Fernando (phone: 95-422-7211). Expensive to moderate.

El Burladero – The name refers to the bullfighter's protective barrier at the entrances to the arena, and this eatery is decorated in a taurine theme. It's very popular with the Spanish. Start with *angulas de Aguinaga* (baby eels), or gazpacho, then have meat, poultry, game, or paella. Service, food, and wine are excellent. Open daily. Reservations necessary. 1 Calle Canalejas (phone: 95-422-2900). Moderate.

Hostería del Laurel – After touring the Alcázar, have lunch where the infamous Don Juan dined. Open daily. Reservations advised. 5 Plaza de los Venerables (phone: 95-422-0295). Moderate.

La Isla – Extraordinary seafood, including fish and shellfish flown in from Galicia, is served at this eatery with high-backed, black-lacquer chairs and salmon-colored tablecloths. Closed in August. 25 Calle Arfe (phone: 95-421-5376). Moderate.

Mesón Don Raimundo – In a former convent with antique furnishings, this restaurant has plenty of atmosphere and good seafood. Closed Sunday nights. Reservations advised. 26 Calle Argote de Molina (phone: 95-422-3355). Moderate.

Parador Alcázar del Rey Don Pedro – Originally a 14th-century Moorish fortress, this is a triumph of architectural restoration, with all the modern luxuries, including a restaurant, bar, and swimming pool. In the historic town of Carmona, just 18 miles (29 km) east of Seville, it is well worth the commute. Carmona (phone: 95-414-1010). Moderate.

Río Grande – Here, wide terraces flank the riverbanks, and the architecture of the building is lovely in its own right. There's a rich paella, perfect gazpacho, and *salteado de ternera a la sevillana* (diced veal with local green olives, carrots, and potatoes). Open daily. Reservations necessary. 70 Calle Betis (phone: 95-427-3956). Moderate.

JEREZ DE LA FRONTERA

Sherry Park – On an elegant tree-lined avenue — the town's main drag — this ultramodern establishment has 300 air conditioned rooms, a restaurant, and a swimming pool to help beat the summer heat. 11 Avenida Alvaro Domecq (phone: 956-303011). Expensive.

Avenida Jerez – Less sumptuous than its neighbor, *Sherry Park,* across the street, this modern high-rise offers comfort and a good location, if not a lot of atmosphere. There are 95 air conditioned rooms. 10 Avenida Alvaro Domecq (phone: 956-347411). Moderate.

El Bosque – On the main avenue near several hotels, it's said to cater to the local sherry aristocracy. Exotic Andalusian dishes on the menu include items such as a shellfish-and-salmon salad. Closed Mondays. Reservations advised. 28 Avenida Alvaro Domecq (phone: 956-303333). Moderate.

Gaitán – This small place with rustic decor and photos of famous guests on the walls serves savory Andalusian stews and soups complemented by delicious original dishes and tempting desserts. Closed Sunday nights, Mondays, and August. 3 Calle Gaitán (phone: 956-345859). Moderate to inexpensive.

GRANADA

Alhambra Palace – If you can't get a room in the *Parador San Francisco* (below) and still want to stay near the Alhambra, this is a fine alternative. It, too, stands on the Alhambra hill, with great views of the Alhambra and the city. Built in 1910 with design and decor blending with the Moorish-Andalusian architecture of the Alhambra, it has been refurbished and 11 deluxe suites have been added. 2 Calle Peña Partida (phone: 958-221468). Expensive.

Bobadilla – Rambling over 1,500 acres of countryside, this magnificent resort-hotel-ranch complex is midway between Granada, Córdoba, and Seville. The epitome of luxurious Andalusian ambience, it has a Mudéjar-style main lobby reminiscent of the Moorish mosque of Córdoba, and no two of its exquisitely decorated rooms are alike. Fountains, patios, and gardens are everywhere, and the central gathering place is a 16th-century–style chapel with a 1,595-pipe organ. A choice of restaurants includes the elegant *La Finca*. A fitness club, lake-size swimming pool, and conference rooms round out the facilities. Loja (phone: 958-321861). Expensive.

Parador San Francisco – This one tops the list of *paradores*. In a restored 15th-century section of the Alhambra itself, it commands magnificent views of the Generalife, the city, and the Sierra Nevada. Its restaurant features topnotch Andalusian cuisine. Reservations are required at least 8 months in advance, especially for the peak months of May, June, September, and October. Alhambra (phone: 958-221443). Expensive.

Torres Bermejas – One of the best restaurants in town for Andalusian cooking. Closed Sundays. 5 Plaza Nueva (phone: 958-223116). Moderate.

Washington Irving – Named for the American writer whose *Tales of the Alhambra* helped rekindle foreign interest in the place, this hotel is near the Alhambra and offers decent, reasonably priced accommodations. 2 Paseo del Generalife (phone: 958-227550). Moderate.

Cunini – Granada's most prominent seafood restaurant features fresh catch of the day flown in from the Cantabrian coast. Closed Sunday evenings. Reservations advised. 14 Calle Pescadería (phone: 958-250777). Moderate to inexpensive.

Colombia – Next door to the Alhambra, meals are served to the accompaniment of flamenco guitarists. Closed Sundays. Calle Antequeruela Baja (phone: 958-227434). Inexpensive.

The Canary Islands

A cluster of seven major and six minor islands in the South Atlantic, the Canary Island archipelago lies about 65 miles off the northwest coast of Africa. Spread across the 28° north latitude line, just 4° north of the Tropic of Cancer, the Canaries have a springlike climate throughout the year — in the 70s F (21–31C). The major islands are Tenerife, Gran Canaria, Fuerteventura, La Gomera, El Hierro, and La Palma.

Although legends suggest that the Canary Islands are the remains of the lost continent of Atlantis, history indicates that the first recorded visit occurred during the 1st century AD. According to Roman historian Pliny the Elder, it was explorers from Roman Mauritania who first visited the islands. They found the islands full of wild dogs, two of which they took back to their king, Juba II. Accordingly, Juba dubbed the islands *insulae canariae* — the islands of dogs. The descendants of these original inhabitants, a type of mastiff known as *verdino,* still live in the Canaries.

Other sources maintain that the islands derived their name from a variety of finch (*Serinus canarius),* found living in the trees. Whatever the etymology, the mainland Spaniards who conquered the seven cone-shaped volcanic islands during the 15th century adapted the Latin name to the Spanish *Isla Canarias.* To add to the confusion, there was a Berber-speaking tribe in nearby Morocco known as the Canarii, and some scholars believe it was they who gave their name to the islands.

Acquiring mastery over this domain was not easy, as the Spaniards faced fierce resistance from the original inhabitants, the Guanche cave dwellers. Although the islands were rediscovered in 1402, it took until 1496 to conquer the Guanches.

Little is known about the Guanches, who were eventually decimated by the Spanish armies, the bubonic plague, locust-induced famine, and volcanic eruptions. Traces of their crude existence, however, remain all over the archipelago, in the form of ceramic and leather artifacts, geometrical cave paintings, mummies, language, and traditions. A tall, fair-skinned, and light-haired people, the Guanches were probably of Phoenician and/or Berber stock. It is believed that they had no boats; how they reached the islands, and from where, is still a mystery.

Today's Canary Islanders are peaceful, friendly, artistic people, who make their living farming, fishing, and producing handicrafts — as well as by working at various jobs in the modern resort developments. Though only recently discovered by American tourists, the Canaries have long been popular with vacationing Europeans. The villages of white cottages with red-tile roofs sprinkled throughout the mountainous interior of the volcanic islands make the archipelago inviting to travelers who enjoy exploring unusual places and discovering the distinctive character of each island.

GRAN CANARIA

As you fly into Gando International Airport, south of Gran Canaria's capital, Las Palmas, the island looks like Mt. Everest rising from the Sahara. The stark, rugged landscape becomes greener and soon you can distinguish banana trees, coffee groves, sugarcane, almond trees, and tomato farms. Each village is actually an oasis.

LAS PALMAS: The capital city of this 592-square-mile island is a duty-free port; Europeans from all over the Continent flock here for the bargains in furs. *Voula Mitsakou* (28 Calle Luis Morote, at the junction of Calle Sagasta and Avenida General Vives; phone: 928-267636), a well-known furrier with shops in half a dozen European cities, charges 30% to 50% less for their sable, ermine, and other skins in Las Palmas than in their other branches. In addition, there are plenty of shops selling Chinese silks, Indian marble, cameras, tape recorders, liquor, shoes, clothing, jewelry, and souvenir items. Bargaining or "negotiation," as it is otherwise called, is highly appropriate, but you have to be good at it to best the Indian, Pakistani, and Lebanese merchants who own most of the stores. It is a good idea to know the range of prices of items you are considering throughout the city before you actually buy. And if you're in the market for a camera, be sure you know the exact model number: It can make a big difference in price.

Las Palmas covers a strip of seafront on the northwest tip of the island. A natural depression in the coastline has provided a sheltered bay for the beach called Playa de las Canteras. The rocky breakwater, shaped rather like an arm, extends almost around the bay and makes it as calm as a lake. Running parallel to the beach, the 2-mile Paseo de las Canteras promenade boasts numerous restaurants: Swedish, Italian, Chinese, Finnish, Mexican, Indian, German, and Spanish, as well as a few of the sit-down or stand-up fast-food variety. In addition, there are many bars, cafés, and bistros.

The rhythm of life in Las Palmas is determined by the sun. Visitors often spend the day lying in the sun from 8 or 9 AM until 4 or 5 PM. Then, in the cool of the evening, they head for the outdoor cafés, shops, restaurants, and bars of the Paseo. Shops remain open until dusk, about 9 PM. If clouds or mist interfere with the sun, people stroll or shop — but only until the sun reappears.

Sometimes people go for a walk in Parque Santa Catalina where Canarian families often come for their evening strolls. It's very pleasant, as local guitarists play impromptu serenades for passersby. To get to the park, walk along Calle Padre Cueto 4 blocks to Castillo, then head right along Castillo for 2 blocks. Note, however, that crime is on the rise and it's best not to visit the parks at night.

The public market is a good place for taking photographs of people engaged in the ordinary everyday commerce of buying and selling foodstuffs and other provisions. It occupies an entire block at the corner of Calles Néstor de Torre and Galicia. From the Paseo, walk up Calle Thomas Miller, the street with the statue of the dolphin. Take it straight to the market.

Doramas Park (Parque Doramas) contains a zoo, swimming pool, and an unusual model of a Canarian village designed by local painter Néstor de la Torre. The park is easy to get to: Any bus traveling along Calle León y Castillo at Parque Santa Catalina also goes to Parque Doramas. After a visit to the park, the *Bodegón* restaurant (Parque Doramas) is a good place to taste Canarian food (see *Best en Route*). But watch out; first encounters with Canarian food can be explosive. The ubiquitous sauce called *mojo picón* is an *amigo falso* (false friend). Its seemingly benign aroma belies its true nature. *Mojo picón* is not just a hot sauce, it's an incendiary concoction of chili peppers, garlic, oil, vinegar, salt, and pepper. But don't hesitate to order either the *cazuela canaria* or *sancocho de pescado,* a fish casserole and stew, respectively. Try them both — they're delicious.

TEJEDA: About 25 miles (40 km) southwest of Las Palmas along narrow, mountain roads lies the petrified forest, which the Spanish poet Unamuno (1864–1936) called a "petrified storm." It lies about 4,800 feet above sea level amid a bleak, awesome, volcanic landscape. Be sure to take advantage of the sensational lookouts (*miradores*) along the route. Bus excursions and English-speaking taxi drivers also cover this route. The concierge at any hotel will help you arrange transportation.

MASPALOMAS: On the southern edge of Gran Canaria, about 35 miles (56 km) from Gando Airport, lies Playa del Inglés, an ocher strand of beach that curves around a palm-fringed lagoon, looking like a setting from *The Arabian Nights.* Just 1 mile (1.6 km) to the west of the Maspalomas lighthouse, Playa Pasito Blanco has a deepwater harbor with a marina where deep-sea charters can be hired. There is an 18-hole golf course at *Iberotel Maspalomas Oasis* (Playa de Maspalomas; phone: 928-760170), a resort (see *Best en Route*).

PUERTO RICO: Just 20 miles (32km) west of Maspalomas, this apartment-condominium complex is great for families and couples who want to spend a month, a summer, or the entire year in a setting complete with marina, beach, swimming pools, restaurants, shopping, nightclubs, and playgrounds. The complex is pretty big, but the design of the community is not overwhelming. (This area is not particularly recommended for single travelers.) You can find out about booking space in Puerto Rico from the tourist office in Las Palmas (Parque de Santa Catalina; phone: 928-264623) or at the Tourist Office of Spain in the US (665 Fifth Avenue, New York, NY 10022; phone: 212-759-8822).

SAN BARTOLOMÉ DE TIRAJANA: Another day trip from Las Palmas or Maspalomas takes you to this town at the bottom of a huge crater at the foot of the central mountains. At 6,500 feet, the snow-capped Pozo de las Nieves ridge is the highest point on the island. It's a 2-mile hike, straight up, from San Bartolomé to the peaks.

TENERIFE

Only 20 minutes by air from Las Palmas, Tenerife, spread over 793 square miles, is the largest of the Canary Islands. (It also can be reached by flights from Madrid in a little over 2 hours.) Lusher, with more forest, colorful vegetation, and a somewhat higher rate of rainfall, Tenerife is called the island of "eternal spring." It is also one of the archipelago's main agricultural centers. Most vegetables grown in the Canaries come from Tenerife's soil.

SANTA CRUZ DE TENERIFE: A duty-free port, the capital of Tenerife is more Spanish in character and aesthetically more pleasing than Las Palmas. However, it has no beaches to speak of and is primarily a city of shops. The streets bounded by Calle del Castillo, Calle Valentín Sanz, Calle Emilio Calzadillo, and the ocean form a square within which are literally hundreds of shops selling everything. As in Las Palmas, the Indian, Pakistani, Lebanese, and Spanish shopkeepers are willing to negotiate but they are not about to give anything away. Calle del Castillo is closed to traffic from the Plaza de España to the park at the end of the street. Plaza de España is noteworthy because of its memorial and monument to the men of Tenerife who died in the Spanish Civil War. Due to its height, the monument can be seen from quite a distance, so try to use it as a directional marker as you head into the shopping district, which is almost always jammed with hordes of shoppers.

PLAYA LAS TERESITAS: With barren volcanic cliffs for a backdrop, this beach, about 10 minutes from the center of town along the road to San Andrés, resembles a moonscape. In fact, you would think you were swimming in a moon crater if the moon had water. Only one-quarter of a mile long and about 150 yards wide, the beach is totally protected from the open Atlantic by a stone jetty. You can reach the beach by taking a bus from the Plaza de España.

LA OROTAVA: One of Tenerife's prettiest towns, La Orotava is across the neck of the island from Santa Cruz and overlooks Puerto de la Cruz, 1,000 feet below. This is the best place to shop for indigenous crafts. Be sure to visit the *Artesanía La Casa de los Balcones* (3 Calle San Francisco; phone: 928-380629), one of a national chain of arts and crafts centers established by the Spanish government. It is in an old house with a flower-filled patio. Here you will find the delicate *calado,* drawn-thread embroidery, used for everything from handkerchiefs to tablecloths, manufactured by women working at wooden looms. The women speak English and they are glad to answer questions. In addition to local crafts, ceramics from Seville and leather from Barcelona are also on sale.

The annual *Corpus Christi* festival in June is a celebration of the religious fervor, energy, and artistry of the people of La Orotava. Before the festival's procession, the town's squares and streets are covered with carpets of brilliant flowers and colorful sand designs. The largest and most intricate sand carpet is laid on the Plaza del Ayuntamiento, across town from the *Artesanía.* On other streets around town carpets made from hundreds of thousands of flower petals — bougainvillea, dahlias, geraniums, carnations — as well as crushed leaves and pine needles depict a variety of biblical scenes. Although the *Feast of Corpus Christi* is at its most colorful in La Orotava, it is celebrated throughout the Canaries, floral carpets and all.

PICO DEL TEIDE: There are few places on earth where you can explore volcanic craters. Even fewer give you the chance to stand more than 2 miles above sea level and look in all directions, unhindered. El Pico del Teide, a crater more than 40 miles in circumference and more than 6,600 feet above sea level, is one of those rare places. Just beyond the crater stands the highest mountain in Spain, El Teide, at 12,200 feet. Parque Nacional Las Cañadas del Teide has a cable car to the top of the mountain. The 15-minute ride to the summit is breathtaking enough to make even the most avid photographers gaze at the scenery and forget about taking pictures. When there are few clouds, the six other major Canary Islands and the coast of Africa are clearly visible. At dawn, the sun touching the mountains creates splendid shadows that blend with the different shades of lava and ash. The stillness and barrenness is intensely moving.

PUERTO DE LA CRUZ: Considering that Puerto de la Cruz has no beach worthy of its name, it is reasonable to wonder why it is one of the major tourist centers of Tenerife. Put simply, Puerto is pure resort — an enclave of shops, hotels, restaurants, bars, and discos. There is hardly anything else. The town has been given over to strolling, shopping, and eating. To compensate for no beach, clever architects and engineers have built seawater pools, promenades, manmade lakes, and lounging areas into and around the rocky volcanic outcroppings that extend offshore for hundreds of yards.

The best way to get to know Puerto is on foot. A walk through the most interesting part of town should begin at Plaza de Concejil on Calle San Juan. Head right on Calle de Santo Domingo, then left on Calle de San Telmo. San Telmo, the main drag, runs along the waterfront. It's an elegant street with a bevy of fine shops and hotels to match. Follow San Telmo until it becomes Avenida de Colón and runs parallel to Playa Martiánez. Take it to Calle de Aguilar y Quesada, then back to the Plaza.

Puerto de la Cruz is about a half-hour bus or car ride from the Los Rodeos Airport, near Santa Cruz de Tenerife, which serves other Canary Islands. On the south coast of the island, the Reina Sofía Airport is the one most used for Madrid and international flights.

LANZAROTE

An eerie, burnt-out island punctuated by hundreds of extinct volcanoes, Lanzarote is the most physically astonishing of the Canaries. Its scenery is so unusual that people who fly in from Tenerife or Las Palmas always describe the place as unforgettable.

ARRECIFE: The island's capital is actually a fishing town with an airport. Two castles, San Gabriel and San José, stand guard on a hill. Arrecife itself is not particularly interesting, but a drive north to Teguise, the former capital set on top of an extinct volcano, gives you a splendid view of some of the smaller Canaries: La Graciosa, Montaña Clara, Alegranza, Roque del Este, and Roque del Oeste. The highlight of Teguise is Guanapay Castle, perched on top of the cone. Not far from Teguise, the kaleidoscopic Verdes Cave tunnels for miles inside the Corona Volcano labyrinth. Connecting underground is the Jameos del Agua lagoon, a huge grotto with a restaurant-bar-nightclub (phone: 928-835010) and a unique pool designed by the island's internationally famed architect César Manrique.

Heading into the interior from Arrecife takes you through the terrace farms of La Gería. Here, farmers spread over their fields a layer of fine volcanic ash, which absorbs the nightly dew and provides moisture for the plants. Out of this bizarre agricultural technique, sumptuous melons, watermelons, figs, onions, tomatoes, and grapes are grown. The grapes are fermented to produce malvasía wine.

Continuing west farther into the interior of the mountain brings you to the Parque Nacional Timanfaya, also known as La Montaña de Fuego, the most stunning of the island's natural attractions. From the top of the mountain, you can see hundreds of extinct volcanoes in the surrounding countryside. The summit is accessible by camel;

you ride in chairs slung over either side of the hump. Camel processions leave from Arrecife for the 2-hour trip.

Heading south from Arrecife you will find the Tías resort development, which can accommodate 1,000 visitors in small hotels, cottages, and apartment houses. There is a marina with deep-sea fishing charters available. Puerto del Carmen is now one of the largest vacation centers, located at the Tías resort, cluttered with hundreds of white-washed bungalows and cottages and several high-rise hotels. Farther south still, there is a pleasant little village at Plaza Blanca, from which ferries depart to the island of Fuerteventura.

ISLA GRACIOSA

To the north of Lanzarote, this tiny, 17-square-mile island has one small mountain, La Montaña de las Agujas. There are also two fine beaches, Caleta del Sebo and Las Conchas.

FUERTEVENTURA

Fuerteventura has the longest shoreline of any of the islands, with plenty of spacious, empty beaches and some really dramatic sand dunes à la Sahara. If you really want total seclusion, this is a good spot for it. Playa de Jandía at the southern end of the island and Gran Tarajal have good fishing: Sardines, swordfish, and tuna are quite plentiful and easily caught. The capital, Puerto del Rosario, has an airstrip and not much else.

LA PALMA

Known as "the green island," La Palma covers 281 square miles. Its capital, Santa Cruz de la Palma, slopes along the eastern side of a crater called La Caldera de Taburiente. Approximately 17 miles in circumference, La Caldera is ringed with pine trees and has been declared a national park. You can explore it to a depth of 2,500 feet. The city itself has some 16th-century buildings, including the church of San Salvador and the Ayuntamiento (city hall); a natural history museum containing aboriginal artifacts; and traditional village architecture, featuring ornately hand-carved balconies protruding from the second and third stories of adjoining whitewashed cottages.

At the southernmost tip of the island is the vineyard district of Fuencaliente. To the north of the capital is the forest of Los Tilos, where the thick tropical vegetation includes giant ferns.

Although facilities and services for tourists are not as well developed as on Gran Canaria or Tenerife, La Palma does attract good numbers of Europeans who prefer quiet vacations.

LA GOMERA

The craggy seacoast and mountainous terrain of this 146-square-mile island have made transportation difficult. To compensate, the islanders have developed over the centuries a system of communication based on whistling, with which they can "speak" to each other from hilltop to valley.

About 20 miles by ferry from Tenerife's Playa de los Cristianos, La Gomera is the site of the Church of the Asunción where Columbus and his crews heard mass before setting off for parts unknown. The house in which he lived, the *Casa de Colón-Museo de Bellas Artes,* is on the main street, near the post office (open daily 9 AM to 2 PM; admission charge; Torre del Conde; no phone). The Torre del Conde, an old fortress, has been declared a national historic monument, and the island's Garanjonay National Park (open daily 9 AM to 2 PM; admission charge) is a UNESCO Natural World Heritage Site.

Apart from San Sebastián, the capital, and the whistling Gomera islanders themselves, the island has several banana plantations, orchards, a fishing village called Playa Santiago, and a good, tawny beach on Valle Gran Rey. The island has no airport, but *Ferry Gomera* (Avenida Tres de Mayo, Santa Cruz de Tenerife; phone: 922-219244) makes three trips daily from Tenerife. *Transmediterránea* (35 Calle General Franco, San Sebastián de La Gomera; phone: 922-871300) also operates hydrofoil service, four times daily.

EL HIERRO

The smallest major island of the archipelago (less than 107 square miles), El Hierro is called "the island of iron." It is the harshest of all, with black volcanic soil, steep massifs, deep craters, and barren mountains. About 3,500 of the island's 7,000 residents live in the capital, Valverde, the central town of an agricultural area where wine is the major product. In the southern part of El Hierro, there is good fishing at La Restinga.

BEST EN ROUTE

With plenty of hotels to choose from, the choices listed below represent those that have some particularly appealing quality — location, service, or aesthetic design. Expect to pay $110 or more for a double room at those places in the expensive category; between $55 and $90 at a hotel in the moderate category; under $55, inexpensive.

Restaurants in the Canary Islands span the culinary spectrum from sleek international dining spots to funky regional places where you can sample local cooking. Expect to pay $60 or more for a meal for two at those places we've categorized as expensive; between $25 and $55 at those restaurants in the moderate category; under $25, inexpensive. Prices do not include drinks, wine, or tips. All restaurants below accept major credit cards, unless otherwise indicated.

GRAN CANARIA

Iberotel Maspalomas Oasis – The center of the action, this busy, large resort is popular with European tour groups. It has a nightclub, golf course, horseback riding, tennis, health club, shopping arcade, and a number of other facilities. Playa de Maspalomas (phone: 928-760170). Expensive.

Meliá Las Palmas – Right on the Las Canteras beach, this property is large and luxurious, with swimming pools, fine restaurants, a disco, and lovely gardens. 6 Calle Gomera, Las Palmas (phone: 928-268050). Expensive.

Meliá Tamarindos – Although far from the fashionable, sophisticated cities of Europe, this hotel rivals the best of them in decor, grounds, and amenities. Its 2 swimming pools and beach make it a good place for simple lounging in the sun. There is even a full buffet alongside one of the swimming pools, as well as several bars and a disco. On the hillside across the highway, the huge, white, cast-concrete object with a pole in its center is a sundial — a gift from the Swedish people. And you can set your watch by it. 3 Calle Retama, Playa San Agustín (phone: 928-762600). Expensive.

Reina Isabel – Right on the beach at Las Canteras and relatively modern in decor and furnishings (although it could stand some renovations), its facilities include a fine restaurant, swimming pool (with adjoining disco), beachfront nightclub, and solarium. 40 Calle Alfredo L. Jones, Paseo Playa de las Canteras, Las Palmas (phone: 928-260100). Expensive.

Santa Catalina – Of Las Palmas's more than 100 hotels, this one has the most intriguing atmosphere. An imitation Moorish palace standing in the middle of the flowers of Parque Doramas, it has a casino, large swimming pool, miniature golf, shopping arcade, and fireplaces in the public rooms. Parque Doramas (phone: 928-243040). Expensive.

Bodegón – Our favorite place for Canarian food. Try the seafood; specialties include *cazuela canaria* (fish casserole) and *sancocho de pescado* (fish stew). Reservations unnecessary. Parque Doramas, Las Palmas (no phone). Moderate.

El Pote – Excellent fish, seafood, and lamb as well as Galician specialties and fine ham are found here. Closed Sundays. Reservations unnecessary. 41 Calle José María Durán (phone: 928-278058). Moderate.

San Agustín Beach Club – With African decor in a strikingly contemporary setting, this spot is renowned for topnotch international fare. Closed during May and June. Reservations advised. 1 Playa de los Cocoteros, San Agustín (phone: 928-760370). Moderate.

Camping Guantánamo – At Mogán, or more specifically on the beach at Tauro, this campsite is about 60 miles (96 km) from Las Palmas. Although it can accommodate 1,500 people, food, beverages, and other supplies are not available on the site. But if you're interested in spending your time on the beaches of the south coast or visiting Cruz de Tejeda, this is your best bet (phone: 928-241701). Inexpensive.

Camping Temisas – This one is relatively small as campsites go, but then so is the demand. It's built to accommodate about 50 campers. For food, beverages, and other supplies, Aguimes is the closest town. Lomo de la Cruz (phone: 928-241701). Inexpensive.

Puerto Rico – A decent little eatery that serves local food, particularly fish and seafood. No reservations. Playa Mogán, Puerto Rico (phone: 928-745181). Inexpensive.

TENERIFE

Meliá San Felipe – A convenient, comfortable establishment with a freshwater swimming pool, tennis courts, and a nightclub featuring flamenco dancers. But we think the service could be spiffier, especially in the huge dining room. 22 Avenida de Colón, Puerto de la Cruz (phone: 922-383311). Expensive.

Mencey – This charming old yellow building has retained some of its former grandeur, enhanced by renovations. Set in lovely gardens, its rooms have been splendidly refurbished and a wing with motel-type units has been added. Part of the elegant CIGA hotel chain, its facilities include 2 swimming pools, tennis courts, a bar, and a poolside buffet. 38 Avenida José Naveiras, Santa Cruz (phone: 922-276700). Expensive.

Parque San Antonio – If you want to get away from the madding throngs of tourists in Puerto de la Cruz, but wish to be close enough to the center of town to make quick forays, consider this as your first choice for accommodations. Tucked away in a veritable botanic garden all its own, it is merely 5 minutes by bus from the center of town. Carretera de las Arenas, Puerto de la Cruz (phone: 922-384851). Expensive.

Semiramis – Puerto's futuristic centerpiece must be seen to be believed. Imaginative architecture makes it appear to be built from top to bottom, running down a mountain. All rooms overlook the ocean and have refrigerators; some have kitchens. It also has 2 swimming pools, tennis courts, a lounge area with games, and a good dining room. 12 Leopoldo Cologán, Urbanización La Paz, Puerto de la Cruz (phone: 922-385551). Expensive.

Parador de las Cañadas del Teide – Ideal for catching the sunrise over the Pico del Teide. In fact, your hosts won't allow you to oversleep. The wooden inn is modeled after a Swiss chalet with a swimming pool and a lounge with a fireplace. All is surrounded by nature trails. Reservations required well in advance. 20 miles (32 km) outside of La Orotava on the Carretera Vilaflor — Highway C-821 (phone: 922-232503). Moderate.

El Pescado – The name means "the fish" and that's what you'll find on the menu, prepared in a variety of intriguing ways. Closed Wednesdays and May through September. Reservations unnecessary. 3-A Avenida Venezuela, Puerto de la Cruz (phone: 922-371008). Moderate.

La Riviera – Snazzy continental dishes are the hallmark of this chic, tastefully decorated restaurant. Closed Sundays and mid-August through mid-September. Reservations advised. 155 Rambla General Franco, Santa Cruz de Tenerife (phone: 922-275812). Moderate.

Mesón del Teide – In Las Cañadas National Park, its unparalleled location on the 2,000-foot mountain El Portillo makes this worth the trip, even if you only sip a glass of wine and snack on a sandwich. Reservations unnecessary. La Orotava (no phone). Inexpensive.

LANZAROTE

Casa Salvador – Tucked away in one of the quieter corners of the island, this lovely seafood restaurant stands right on the beach. Playa Blanca de Yaiza (no phone). Expensive.

Castillo de San José – In the cellar of a medieval castle that is now a contemporary art museum, this is one of the most beautiful restaurants on the island. Open daily. Reservations advised. One mile (1.6 km) northeast of Arrecife on the road to Las Caletas (phone: 928-812321). Expensive.

Meliá Salinas – Looking like a giant spacecraft newly touched down in a tropical paradise, it offers 310 modern rooms, each with a private terrace facing seaside. Outdoor delights such as tennis, diving, and sailing abound, as do indoor pleasures — restaurants, bars, massage, sauna, cinema, and disco. Calle Sur Teguise, Costa Teguise (phone: 928-813040). Expensive.

Arrecife Gran Hotel – Although standing smack in the middle of a village, there is no way this contemporary resort could be considered to be in the center of the action. Its most astounding feature is a restaurant on an island in the middle of a small lake that can only be reached by boat. It also has a pool, cheerful dining room, and lots of flowers. Avenida Mancomunidad, Arrecife (phone: 928-811254). Moderate.

El Diablo – Another dramatically located dining spot, it stands amid the volcanic mountains of the interior and serves lunch only. Open daily. No reservations. Montaña del Fuego, Tinajo (phone: 928-840057). Inexpensive.

Yaiza – There is no menu; excellent seafood dishes depend on the catch of the day. Open daily. No reservations. Playa Blanca (phone: 928-830141). Inexpensive.

FUERTEVENTURA

Parador de Fuerteventura – Standing on the edge of the ocean, this modern *parador* is the best hotel on the island. Puerto del Rosario, Urb. Playa Blanca (phone: 928-851150). Moderate.

LA PALMA

Parador de Santa Cruz de la Palma – Another addition to the national chain. It, too, rates top marks. 34 Avenida Marítima, Santa Cruz de la Palma (phone: 922-412340). Moderate.

LA GOMERA

Parador Conde de la Gomera – Built in the unique Canarian manorial style, this inn is surrounded by lush tropical gardens. In addition to beautiful ocean views, guests enjoy a swimming pool. It's much in demand, so make reservations early. Calle Llano de la Villa (phone: 922-871100). Moderate.

The Balearic Islands

The Balearic Islands lie 90 miles southeast of Barcelona in the Mediterranean Sea. The major section of the archipelago consists of two pair of islands: Mallorca and Minorca (in Spanish, *Menorca*), and Formentera and Ibiza. Many smaller islands of lesser significance complete the archipelagic structure. Of the four major islands, Mallorca (whose name means "the larger") is the largest, best known, and best equipped for tourism. Minorca (whose name means "the smaller") receives fewer foreign visitors and, consequently, has retained its tranquil, seaside communities. Ibiza is home to jet-setters, artists, and pseudo-artists. Formentera is undoubtedly the most secluded of the four islands.

The Balearic Mountains are thick with ancient fig and olive trees while the beaches are shaded by evergreens. The surrounding seas are exceptionally calm and clear despite the prevailing winds.

The Balearic language is a dialect of Catalán, the language of Cataluña, the Barcelona region of mainland Spain. Catalán is a Romance language that resembles Provençal French with some vestiges of colonial Latin as it was spoken in the Roman Empire.

Remnants of human habitation date from the Bronze Age. In different parts of the islands are large stone pyramids, thought to be Bronze Age tombs, called *talayots*. Later Balearic islanders were mercenaries and seamen in the armies and navies of Rome and Carthage. The Moors reigned from AD 902 until 1229 when the Aragonese reconquest converted the Balearics into a prosperous center of Mediterranean trade. In the 16th century, Spain's attention shifted to the New World and the Balearics fell into the hands of the Turks and the Barbary pirates, whose influence can still be seen in the walls and watchtowers of Mallorca.

During the 18th century, Father Junípero Serra set forth from the Balearics, where he was born, to found the string of missions along the California coast known as El Camino Real, the Mission Trail. In the 19th century, composer Frédéric Chopin and his mistress, author George Sand, chose Mallorca as their island retreat.

Twentieth-century visitors find that May, early June, and September are the best months for a quiet, relaxing visit. The weather is sparkling clear, with temperatures in the 70s and 80s F (21-26 C). July and August are the most intense, active months. The Balearic Islands have a climate temperate enough for year-round water sports: sailing, swimming, diving, and deep-sea fishing for sole, perch, and bream. There is a racetrack in Palma, the capital of Mallorca, and plenty of golf courses and tennis courts.

MALLORCA

PALMA DE MALLORCA: Between June and September the airport of Palma, the Balearics' and Mallorca's capital, is one of the busiest in the world. With thousands of hotel rooms and hundreds of restaurants, Palma is one of the world's most bustling resort centers.

The Bay of Palma is protected from the wind and weather by the Puig Mayor mountain range which lies to the northwest of the city. Palma Nova and Magaluf beaches are the only two sandy areas to the west of Palma, although there are hotels along the sheer coastline. To the east of the city, although there is less protection, there are miles of excellent beaches and resorts known as the Playas de Palma. With 76,000 residents, the city of Palma contains almost one-third of the island's population (236,000).

Known as the Ciutat de Mallorca after the liberation from the Moors in 1229, the town was colonized by Jews and Genoese and subsequently prospered. James II and his successors were able to build majestic Gothic buildings and Italian-style villas. Mansions were erected in the 15th and 16th centuries by descendants of merchants and landed gentry. The typical Mallorcan *casa* (with an interior patio framed by marble columns) developed in the 18th century can be seen in many parts of Palma.

The heart of the city is the wide promenade, or *rambla,* known as the Borne (open market).

In the old part of town east of the Borne are shops that specialize in crafts, filigree, embroidery, world-famous pearls, and glasswork. A morning walk might begin at the Ayuntamiento (City Hall) at 2 Plaza Cort. Here you'll find the Van Dyck painting *The Martyrdom of San Sebastián* hanging on the first floor. Continue 1 block south to the Church of Santa Eulalia (Iglesia Santa Eulalia). Across the street stands the Casa Vivot, one of the best examples of 18th-century Palma townhouses with an inner court and paintings by Breughel, Ribera, and others. At Plaza San Francisco, the Church of San Francisco contains the tomb of Ramón Llull, famed Doctor Illuminatus, philosopher and humanist of cosmopolitan 13th-century Mallorca. One block south of the Plaza, Casa Palmer is a fine example of 16th-century Gothic and Renaissance architecture. The Moorish Baths, intact from the era of the Caliphate, can be found on Paseo Umjuay. Liberally sprinkled along this route are cafés and saloons for late breakfasts and early aperitifs.

Casa Oleza (2 Calle Morey) is another example of the famous Mallorquín patios or interior courtyards. The Oleza patio is an extraordinarily well-balanced composition, which includes an iron-topped well, typical wide arches, and short marble columns supporting a balcony.

To the west of El Borne are the three palaces: Palacios Morell, on Calle San Cayetano; Palacio Sollerich, on the Borne itself, with one of the best patios in the city; and Palacio Montenegro, on the street of the same name.

Other important sights include the cathedral; the Spanish Pueblo (Pueblo Español), which includes exact reproductions of famous houses representing different regions, epochs, and architecture from all parts of Spain; La Almudaina, a Moorish fortress just off Plaza de la Reina; La Lonja, a 15th-century structure built by Guillermo Sagrera to house an exchange; the fishing neighborhood of Puig San Pere; and Bellver Castle, overlooking Palma in Parque Bellver.

For maps and brochures about places of interest, hotels, and restaurants, contact the Tourist Information Office at the airport (phone: 971-260803) or 10 Avenida Jaime III (phone: 971-712216) in the center of town.

With 250 miles of coast broken into dazzling coves, inlets, and beaches, Mallorca has much to explore. Because the narrow roads snaking around cliffs with precipitous drops are a legitimate driving hazard, we recommend that you hire a chauffeured car with an English-speaking guide to get to the fishing villages, resorts, and other sites of interest described below. The classic seascapes and mountain scenery deserve to be enjoyed fully, and if you are unused to the surprisingly rugged dips and turns of the roads, chances are you will be too preoccupied with safety to savor the sights. From Palma, there are five distinct touring routes: (1) from Palma north to Valldemosa, Deya, and Sóller; (2) from Palma north to Manacor and the caves; (3) from Palma northeast to Pollença and Formentor; (4) from Palma to the eastern coves; and (5) from Palma to the southwest peninsula.

PALMA TO SÓLLER: The 46-mile (74-km) Valldemosa-Deya-Sóller tour is a relaxed, 1-day trip from Palma. Valldemosa and Deya may be seen in the morning with a late lunch at the Puerto de Sóller. You can stop for coffee in the mountain pass on the road back to Palma.

Valldemosa's main attraction is the Carthusian monastery in which George Sand and Chopin passed the winter of 1838–39. Beyond Valldemosa the road runs along thousand-foot cliffs to San Marroig. The former resident, Archduke Luis Salvador, had a fine view of the Foradada, a famous rock with a doughnut-like perforation.

The village of Deya is surrounded by hills and evergreen forests. Known for its large colony of British artists and bohemians, Deya perches loft-like over the sea. Below the village is a stream outlet, tiny cove, Cala Deya, and beach.

The town of Sóller lies a few miles inland from the port. The road back to Palma over the Alfabia Sierra offers excellent views of the sea and sunset to the west.

PALMA TO THE DRACH CAVES (CUEVAS DEL DRACH): The second recommended route through Manacor, Artá, and the Drach Caves covers 109 miles (174 km), about 3 hours' driving time. Manacor is 30 miles (48 km) from Palma. From the city of Manacor, it is a short distance to Porto Cristo and the caves. Las Cuevas del Drach consist of four chambers of polychromatic pools and stalactite columns spreading over a distance of just over 1 mile. The tour takes 90 minutes and costs about $2. Other caves can be found in Artá and in the city of Manacor. In fact, the Artá Caves are said to have inspired Jules Verne to write *Journey to the Center of the Earth.*

Also on this route are found the *talayots,* megalithic stone structures thought to be Bronze Age burial markers. The village of Capdepera is the site of a fortress high over the Mediterranean. Cala Ratjada is a fishing town with small streams and ocean beaches. On the way back to Palma, you can stop at the town of Petra, birthplace of Junípero Serra (1713–1784), the Franciscan monk whose Californian and Mexican missions developed into San Diego, Monterey, and San Francisco.

PALMA TO FORMENTOR: The third route, to Cape Formentor, northernmost point of the island, covers between 109 and 124 miles (175 and 198 km), passing through Pollença and Alcudia, and other points of interest along the way. You can stop at Selva to see the San Lorenzo Church; at Campanet to see the caves; and at Alcudia where old Roman ramparts and a Roman theater still stand. Puerto de Pollença is a well-entrenched artists colony with a sheltered bay and fine harbor. Stop in at the museum of the painter Anglada Camerasa (open 4 PM to 7 PM summer months, to 6PM winter months; closed Sundays, Wednesdays and holidays; admission charge; 87 Paseo Anglada Camerasa; no phone), which features the island's most representative artists. Puerto de Pollença has become the home of many Europeans and Americans; you can purchase a cottage for around $30,000 to $50,000 or rent one for anywhere between $200 and $1,000 a month.

The road from Puerto de Pollença to Formentor passes one genuinely overwhelming vista after another. The best places to stop for a look are Es Colomer Belvedere lookout and the Cape Formentor lighthouse. The golf course in Formentor at the *Formentor* hotel (Playa de Formentor; phone: 971-531300) is made all the more challenging by the constant winds.

PALMA TO EASTERN COVES: The fourth route, which covers the coves or *calas* of the island's east coast, is a 100-mile (160-km) run with stops at Campos, Felanitx, Porto Colom, Cala Mitjana, Cala D'Or, Porto Petro, and Cala Santañyi. For a shorter trip, proceed directly to Santañyi and spend the day visiting only the *calas* of Santañyi, Figuera, and Llombarts.

PALMA TO SOUTHWEST PENINSULA: The fifth and last route is a Palma–Palma Nova–Paguera–Andraitx–Estallenchs– Bañalbufar–Esporlas–Palma circuit of 56 miles (90 km). The southwest coast has a fine selection of beaches and the island's most intense concentration of hotels. Santa Ponsa, Cala Fornels, Camp de Mar, Puerto de Andraitx, Estellenchs, and Bañalbufar are the main sites of interest.

MINORCA

Minorca, the second-largest Balearic Island, measures 271 square miles, numbers just under 50,000 inhabitants, and is less tourist-oriented than Mallorca. The British occupation of the islands during the 18th century left discernible traces in the architecture: guillotine windows, rocking chairs, folding wing Pembroke-style tables, and stand-up clocks with Queen Anne inlay work. The heath-like countryside, swept by the north wind, is lightly wooded, with wind-bent wild olive trees, low stone walls, and small fields.

Cows and sheep provide the basis for the island's two main industries, shoes and cheese. Mayonnaise owes its name and creation to Mahón, the island's largest city (pop. 21,000).

Minorca is a place where people go to spend a few weeks or months, as opposed to Mallorca, which caters to shorter-term vacationers. Developments such as Binibeca and Punta Prima near Mahón, and Cabo Dartuch near Ciudadela, Minorca's second-largest city, usually offer lodgings for periods of weeks, rather than days.

The spots to visit on the island of Minorca include Ciudadela and Mahón on the western and eastern ends, respectively; Cabo de Caballerias and Fornells to the north; and Cala de Santa Galdana to the south. Mercadal is in the approximate center of the island and was once the site of the island government. Monte Toro, the island's highest point and a religious sanctuary, is 2 miles (3 km) from Mercadal.

Minorca can be reached by air from Palma or Barcelona. The island's airport is at Mahón. Boat service connects Ciudadela to Palma and Alcudia, Mallorca. The Tourist Information Center is in Mahón at 13 Plaza de la Constitución (phone: 971-363790).

MAHÓN: A gleaming little port that somehow manages to retain an innately unobtrusive air, Minorca's largest city has one of the best sheltered harbors in the Mediterranean with excellent anchorages. The main site of interest is the Finca San Antonio, former residence of British Admiral Nelson. About 1 mile (1.6 km) from town near Trepuco village stand several *talayots.*

CIUDADELA: Minorca's second-largest city is surrounded by exceptionally fine beaches: Cala Santandria, Algañares, Cala Blanca, and Cala Blanes. Boiled lobster with mayonnaise sauce and *mahón* cheese with sausages are the tastiest local dishes.

FORNELLS: At first glance this is merely a modest fishing village standing in a grove of evergreens, but its appearance masks its popularity as a resort.

IBIZA

The 209-square-mile island of Ibiza lies 70 miles southwest of Palma de Mallorca. Ibiza rose to prominence in the Mediterranean region during the years of Carthaginian hegemony (7th century BC), and to this day, the predominant influence in the island's architecture is North African.

Accessible by air from Barcelona, Madrid, Palma, and Valencia, or by sea from Barcelona, Palma, Valencia, Alicante, and Denia (the closest point), Ibiza attracts a well-heeled, international crowd who tend to stay on the island for months or years at a time.

IBIZA: The island's capital is divided into an Upper Town (Dalt Vila) and a harbor by an ancient 16th-century wall. Sights in the Dalt Vila include the Las Tablas Gateway, the cathedral, and the *Archaeological Museum* (open daily 10 AM to 1 PM; admission charge; 3 Plaza de la Catedral; phone: 971-301771), containing Punic ruins excavated from Ibizan sites. The town is compact, and you should find these special places easily. From the belfry in the Dalt Vila, there is an excellent view of the town and port. The Tourist Information Office is at 13 Paseo Vara de Rey (phone: 971-301900).

The Marina Quarter explodes into sound and color as you enter from the sedate Dalt Vila. Every afternoon (except Wednesdays), the narrow streets are packed with portable shops where vendors sell nearly everything — shell and silver jewelry, watercolors, leather goods, terra cotta figurines, and other items — and music blasts from the innumerable indoor-outdoor pubs featuring exotic mixed drinks and even more exotically garbed waiters and waitresses. The streets in this section are lined with boutiques featuring the local fashions for which Ibiza is famous.

Among Ibiza's most popular beaches are Ses Figuretas, Talamanca, and Playa D'En Bossa. Several of Ibiza's beaches have gone "naturalist" (nude), although there is some shedding of bikinis on nearly all of them. About 9 miles (14 km) northwest of Ibiza, the town of San Antonio Abad overlooks the rock island called Isla Conejera. The Church of Santa Inés, which has been declared a national monument, sits atop ancient catacombs.

FORMENTERA

Formentera — whose name means "the wheat island," from the Latin "frumentum" — is the smallest of the Balearics, covering 32 square miles. Lying 11 miles south of Ibiza, it is significantly more tranquil than the other three Balearic Islands. It has 4,500 year-round inhabitants, but attracts few tourists.

Boat service across the Es Freus channel connects La Sabina, Formentera's harbor, with Ibiza. The tiny capital of the island, San Francisco Javier, has a population of around 1,187 and is a cluster of sparkling white cottages. Topographically, the island consists of a string of beaches with Berberia Cape on the southern end of the island and La Mola Cape, guarded by a lighthouse, on the eastern end. Pine forests and salt flats take up much of the interior.

Although Formentera is a great place for relaxing by the sea or participating in water sports, there is no nightlife to speak of.

BEST EN ROUTE

Hotel prices are comparable to those along the Costa del Sol. You can expect to pay $120 to $255 for a double room at those places we've listed as expensive; between $45 and $110 for a double room in a hotel we've classified as moderate; under $45, inexpensive.

There are literally dozens of restaurants on Mallorca, the largest and busiest island, but considerably fewer restaurants of note on Minorca, Ibiza, and Formentera. Expect to pay $55 or more for a meal for two at those restaurants we've categorized as expensive; between $35 and $55 at those restaurants in the moderate category; under $35, inexpensive. Prices do not include drinks, wine, or tips. All restaurants below accept major credit cards, unless otherwise indicated. Reservations are advised at all restaurants.

MALLORCA

Caleta – The most elegant of the capital's many restaurants serves continental and Mediterranean food. 19 Calle Federico García Lorca, Palma (phone: 971-232751). Expensive.

Formentor – In a pine grove, its extensive gardens, terraces, swimming pool, anchorage, and overall environment make it the most luxurious of the island's hotels. Its restaurant is also excellent. Playa de Formentor (phone: 971-531300). Expensive.

Meliá Victoria – On the western side of Palma's bay with stunning views, this hotel, built in the 1920s, has recently been modernized, and the atmosphere is pleasant. 21 Calle Joan Miró, Palma (phone: 971-232542). Expensive.

Porto Pi – For outstanding French Basque cuisine. Closed Sundays. 174 Calle Joan Miró, Palma (phone: 971-400087). Expensive.

Son Vida Sheraton – This converted 18th-century palace, about 4 miles (6 km) from

Palma on the road toward Andraitx, stands on a hill with splendid views of the bay, city, and mountains. Activities include swimming, golf, tennis, boating, and horseback riding. Its luxury attracts the international jet set, who enjoy each other's company in the baronial dining room. Castillo de Son Vida, Palma (phone: 971-790000). Expensive.

Caballito del Mar – Befitting its location near the *lonja* on Paseo Marítimo, this eatery serves superb seafood in generous portions. Closed Sundays. 5 Paseo Sagrera, Palma (phone: 971-721074). Expensive to moderate.

Bec-Fi – Argentinian *parrillada* (barbecued mixed grill) and lobster are the specialties. Closed Mondays. 91 Avenida Anglada Camerasa, Pollença (phone: 971-531040). Moderate.

Ca'n Pacienci – Start a meal here with the tomato soup (made with fresh cream) or a pâté, then try the stuffed chicken or one of the traditional Mallorquín dishes. Open for dinner only. Closed Sundays and from November to March. Carretera del Puerto, Pollença (phone: 971-530787). Moderate.

Chez Sophie – Here the French cuisine is exquisite. Closed Sundays and December. 24 Calle Apuntadores, Palma (phone: 971-226086). Moderate.

Club Náutico – Fresh seafood and fish are served in a nautical atmosphere. Closed Tuesdays. Muelle Viejo, Pollença (phone: 971-531010). Moderate.

Estación Marítima Stay – *The* place for succulent crab creations, other seafood dishes, and the most potent Irish coffee on Mallorca. Open daily. Malecón del Puerto Pollença (phone: 971-530013). Moderate.

Jardín Chino – As its name, "Chinese Garden," suggests, this is Palma's finest Chinese restaurant. Open daily. 2 Plaza Mediterráneo, Palma (phone: 971-230053). Moderate.

Lonja del Pescado – This dining spot prepares the finest bouillabaisse with fresh lobster on the island. Closed Wednesdays; open daily in July and August. Muelle Viejo Pollença (phone: 971-530023). Moderate.

Mi Vaca y Yo – A roadside *tavernita* that serves hearty meals of typical Mallorquín cuisine. Closed during July. Playa de Canyarnel, Capdepera (phone: 971-384247). Moderate.

Puerto – This notable seafood eatery serves excellent food. Closed Tuesdays. 3 Paseo de Sagrera, Palma (phone: 971-221104). Moderate.

Tablita – Another little eatery in a tiny pocket of the island. Closed Wednesdays and from January 10 to March 10. Cala Ratjada (phone: 971-639021). Moderate.

Las Tinajas – Nonstop *tapas* from 10:30 AM to 11 PM, and fruit meringue pie as well. Closed Sundays and Saturday dinner. 13 Calle Berengario de Toramira (behind *Galerías Preciados*), Palma (phone: 971-718786). Moderate.

Casa Gallega – Although the Balearic Islands are a long way from the northwest corner of mainland Spain, this place specializes in Galician cooking. Open daily. 6 Calle Pueyo, Palma (phone: 971-721141). Moderate to inexpensive.

Daina – Large enough to be spacious, yet small enough to know you're here, this excellent hostelry commands a view of Pollença's Bay. 2 Calle Atilio Boven, Puerto de Pollença (phone: 971-531250). Moderate to inexpensive.

Petit Celler Carnete – The best restaurant in the center of town. 5 Calle Cetre, Sóller (no phone). Moderate to inexpensive.

Celler Ca Vostra – One of the best *tavernitas* in Pollença. Camino Alcudia, Pollença (phone: 971-531546). Inexpensive.

Celler El Puerto – A good place for a hefty seafood lunch. Closed Wednesdays from September 30 to April 1; open daily other times. 22 Plaza Almirante Oquendo, Pollença (no phone). Inexpensive.

Celler Sa Premsa – *Celleres* (cellars) and *tavernitas* (taverns) serve Mallorquín food, primarily combinations of *lechona* (pork), fresh fish, seafood, plenty of squid, and paella. This place is a favorite. Closed Saturdays and Sundays. 8 Plaza Obispo Berenguer de Palou (phone: 971-723529). Inexpensive.

MINORCA

Casa Manolo – This little café on the docks serves boiled lobster with mayonnaise sauce and *mahón* cheese with sausages. Open daily. Cuidadela (phone: 971-380003). Moderate.

Port Mahón – The best hotel in Mahón. Fort de l'Eau, Paseo Marítimo (phone: 971-362600). Moderate.

Rocamar – For good seafood, especially typical Minorcan *caldereta* (lobster stew), this is a good choice. Open daily May through October; closed Sunday dinners and Mondays from December to May; closed during November. 32 Cala Fonduco (phone: 971-365601). Moderate.

El Greco – Another good place for Mediterranean fare. 49 Calle Doctor Orfila, Mahón (phone: 971-364367). Moderate to inexpensive.

Casa Diego – Near *D'Es Port,* this place features similar local fare at bargain prices. Ciudadela (no phone). Inexpensive.

Casa Riera – For fresh fish and seafood, this is the best in town. 7 Plaza Generalísimo, Fornells (no phone). Inexpensive.

Chez Gaston – Here you can get continental dishes along with fresh fish and seafood. Closed Sundays and from December 15 to January 15. 13 Conde de Cifuentes (phone: 971-360044). Inexpensive.

Mare Nostrum – For a generous Minorcan meal, visit this eatery on the beach. Playa Santandria (no phone). Inexpensive.

Ses Set Voltes – Still another seafood "find" on the beach. Playa Santandria, Ciudadela (no phone). Inexpensive.

IBIZA

Hacienda Na Xamena – One of the most magnificent hotels in all of the Balearics. On the northern part of the island, it commands breathtaking views of the coastline from its cliff-top swimming pools, terraces, and luxurious rooms. Superb food is graciously served at the poolside patios and the hotel restaurant. There are tennis courts plus an indoor pool, gym, and sauna, and the charming village and beach cove of San Miguel are a short way down the pine-forested hills. San Miguel (phone: 971-333046). Expensive.

Pikes – An exclusive, free-wheeling hotel, it has 7 luxury suites and 10 double rooms. The original building, about 600 years old, was an olive and grain mill. Some of the more exotic rooms have sunken tubs and harem-style touches. Other features include 3 restaurants, 2 dining terraces, a video room and film library, a tennis court, and a tile pool. The beach is 10 minutes away. A week's stay is required during summer months. Camino Sa Vorera, San Antonio (phone: 971-342222). Expensive.

Masía d'En Sord – In a lovely old Ibizan house with a magnificent garden, it offers grilled meat and international dishes. Closed Saturday lunch and November. Ibiza–San Miguel Hwy. (phone: 971-310228). Moderate.

Torre del Canónigo – Though this 15th-century bishop's mansion has been renovated thoroughly and divided into independent private apartments with modern conveniences, it retains its noble ambience and decor. From its hilltop setting in Ibiza's Dalt Vila, the views are breathtaking; it's easy to recapture the tranquil medieval mood while strolling through the narrow cobblestone streets. Open May through October; reservations are necessary, and there is a minimum stay requirement of 3 to 7 nights, depending on the season. Apartments accommodate from 2 to 4 guests. 8 Calle Obispo Torres (phone: 971-303884). Moderate.

Mar Blau – A truly fine budget-priced hotel in relaxed, shady surroundings. Its 15 rooms have windows overlooking the sea. Near the marina, it also has a good seafood restaurant. Los Molinos (phone: 971-301284). Inexpensive.

Ses Figueres – One of the smaller Ibiza hotels on the beach, it has splendid views of the bay and offers excellent value. Playa de Talamanca (phone: 971-301362). Inexpensive.

Campsites – The Spanish government runs three campsites on Ibiza: *San Antonio* and *Cala Bassa* at San Antonio Abad, and *Florida* at Santa Eulalia del Río. For information contact the Tourist Office of Spain in the US (phone: 212-759-8822). Inexpensive.

FORMENTERA

Sa Volta – Good local food served in a pleasant environment (it's also a small hotel). Es Pujols (phone: 971-320120). Moderate.

Voramar – A quiet oasis on Es Pujols Beach, protected from the wind by Cape Punta Prima, this hostelry looks across the water to Ibiza. Its restaurant is one of the best on the island for fresh fish and other seafood. Playa Es Pujols (phone: 971-320121). Inexpensive.

Sweden

The images of Sweden that are universally recognized are a kind of code to this complex Scandinavian culture. Fierce, bearded Vikings; healthy, blond youths; dense silent forests; sparkling blue lakes and crystalline fjords — the fascination of a visit is learning just how these particular images have come to represent Sweden, and in what ways they are a true picture. As always, the truth will prove twice as fascinating as anything you could imagine.

As in any country, history and culture start with geography. Occupying the eastern half of the Scandinavian Peninsula, the country shares borders with Norway to the west and Finland to the northeast. The more populous southern third of the country juts into the Baltic Sea; the northern end creeps over the Arctic Circle. Parts of Sweden are still glacier-bound; several thousand years ago, *all* of Sweden was covered with ice. However, for the most part, Sweden's landscape is now speckled with lakes and carpeted with meadows and forests. Sweden has a temperate climate with warm summers and cold winters. The generally poor soil and rocky terrain have led Swedes to turn to forestry, mining, and steel production for their major industries.

The earliest settlers in Sweden appeared in about the 3rd century BC; these people were mostly farmers and fishermen. Many years later, in the 1st century AD, a seafaring tribe, that turned to plunder and trade, grew very powerful and began to control what is now Sweden. This tribe — the Svea, forefathers of the Vikings — initiated trade, as well as conflict, with parts of Europe and Britain. Sweden was well situated for trade and as it became more lucrative, the Hanseatic League became interested in the country. Soon several German merchants came to live in Visby, a prosperous walled town on the island of Gotland, and in Stockholm, which was then a port and fortress on Lake Mälaren. By the 14th century, the Hansa merchants controlled Sweden; in an effort to resist the Hanseatic influence, Norway, Sweden, and Denmark joined together as the Union of Kalmar. The center of government for this union was in Denmark. Eventually the Swedes began to resent even the Danish rule, and in the 16th century Gustavus Vasa, a Swedish noble, led a rebellion. In 1523, victorious, he was elected king, and thereafter the influence of the Hanseatic League waned.

For several hundred years, until the early 19th century, Swedish kings were constantly at war with their neighbors, including Germany, Denmark, Poland, Finland, and Russia. As a result, Sweden annexed as well as lost many territories in Europe, Scandinavia, and even America (there was a small Swedish colony on the Delaware River from 1638 to 1655). In 1809 Sweden enacted a series of reforms, making the king a ceremonial figurehead and conferring the powers of government on an elected parliament. Later in the 19th century, Sweden declared itself a neutral country, a policy that remained in effect throughout the two world wars.

The Swedish Welfare System was born during the depression of the 1930s and grew up during and after World War II. Basically a system for the redistribution of income, the plan attempts to provide every Swede with a minimum and satisfactory standard of living — food, housing, education, and medical care. The price tag for these humane policies is a staggering 50% to 80% personal income tax.

Sweden is among the world's leaders in the exploration of and experimentation with design. Based on the concept that functional things must also be graceful, Swedish design has influenced or changed the appearance of many everyday items, such as furniture, glassware, ceramics, and textiles.

A strong folkloric heritage provides Sweden with rich cultural texture. In the summer numerous festivals are held, for which men and women don their native costumes and dance around traditional Maypoles — made of detailed wrought iron or wood and decorated with intertwined sprigs of flowers and forest greenery. In the Dalarna region, *spelmänslag* (fiddlers) often entertain at the festivals, playing ancient folk tunes and ballads.

Our tours of Sweden each offer you a taste of new and old Sweden: the Dalarna and Värmland route runs through dense forests and medieval towns; the Gothenburg route takes you north from Sweden's second largest city and maritime capital through the fishing villages and along the dramatic fjords of Sweden's granite coastline; the historic walled city of Visby is the highlight of the Gotland route; and the Lapland route ventures into one of the last unspoiled and uncivilized areas on earth — the Lapp wilderness. *Note:* The numbering of highways in various parts of Sweden was changed in 1985. Therefore use only those maps published *after* 1985.

It is easy to get around on your own, as over 80% of the Swedish people speak and understand English. Foreign television programs are broadcast in their original language with Swedish subtitles.

Dalarna and Värmland

The trip up from Stockholm northwest to Mora and back down to Karlstad covers roughly 520 miles (832 km) and takes you through the Swedish heartland provinces of Dalarna and Värmland. The route meanders through seemingly unending forests that break unexpectedly to reveal breathtaking lake expanses. The roads occasionally rise, resting at overlooks where the landscape unfolds beneath you in long, floating lines. The major towns are clustered around the two great lake districts, Siljan in Dalarna and the Fryken group in Värmland.

The dense Dalarna forests were first cut back for settlement in the 16th century, when rich veins of iron ore and copper were discovered and mined under the leadership of King Gustavus Vasa. The Dalarna route from Stockholm goes first to the mining town of Falun and then on to the picturesque Siljan Lake towns of Leksand, Rättvik, and Mora, where it turns south for Värmland. As you travel, you'll notice the landscape changes: the deep forests and weathered wooden sheds of Dalarna give way to Värmland's wide verdant fields and country villas.

Värmland has been home to some of Sweden's "greats": famous writers Erik Gustaf Geijer and Selma Lagerlöf (a 1909 Nobel laureate in literature), as well as John Ericsson who, after emigrating to New York, changed the concept of sea power with his design for the USS *Monitor,* the first successful ironclad warship. From Mora you can plunge farther west and then south to the Fryken Lake towns of Torsby, Sunne, and Arvika. Or you can follow the Klarälven River directly south through Ransäter to Karlstad, the major city of Värmland on the vast Vänern Lake.

STOCKHOLM: For a detailed report on the city and its hotels and restaurants, see *Stockholm,* THE CITIES. The great city of Stockholm originated as a modest 13th-century Viking fortification built on an island where Lake Mälaren meets the Baltic Sea. As was often the case, the military installation grew into a civilized center of art and commerce, but Stockholm's transition was perhaps more dramatic than that of other cities that developed in this way. Far from the usual random urban sprawl, Stockholm spread over 14 islands into one of the most beautiful and certainly the most ordered city in the world. Stockholm is the home of the Swedish monarch, but the real ruler of the city is design. Streets, buildings, and squares are preserved with religious respect. Trees are judiciously planted along cobbled boulevards, and flower urns are artistically arranged in quiet plazas flanked by pastel-colored 3- and 4-story buildings capped with elegant and varied entablatures — a stepped arch on one house, a rounded, baroque detail on another, and a rose-windowed gable on a third. The Swedish design concept is evident everywhere and is typified in glassware that developed from involved Venetian decoration into the simpler Scandinavian look of utility with no loss of grace. Utility and grace are carried through from town plan to individual buildings to the furniture inside the buildings and finally to the people themselves.

En Route from Stockholm – Falun is a 3- or 4-hour drive from Stockholm on Routes 70 and 60 and the largest town in Dalarna. The main point of interest here is the Falun Copper Mine that's been in operation since the Vikings forged swords and shields — long before Sweden was even a country. This mine was the Renaissance world's major source of copper, and places like Versailles were roofed with its output. There's a tour of the mine that takes you down an elevator to the winding shafts and cavernous spaces below. While here, note the rock wall autographed by touring royalty and the massive 650-foot timber wall — a marvel of carpentry and probably the tallest wooden edifice in the world. At nearby Sundborn, visit the home of artist Carl Larsson in an idyllic rural setting.

SILJAN LAKE TOWNS: Lake Siljan is a blue glacial lake surrounded by lush evergreen forests and towns that look much as they did in the early Middle Ages. From Falun, you can either proceed directly to Lake Siljan on Route 80 or double back onto Route 70, where the first lake town you come to is Leksand, a thriving, woodsy resort. On the first Sunday in July there's a boat race here that's a hotly contested national event. The vessels used are called "church boats" and they look like mastless, tiny Viking ships. They widen from a sharp prow and sit low in the water as they glide across the lake, each propelled by 20 oarsmen dressed to the nines in native finery. The boats don't sit idle the rest of the year, so if you can't get there for the race, you might see them taking worshipers to Rättvik's church for Sunday service from midsummer through the third week in August. Boat races also are held at Siljansnäs, Tällberg, Mora, and Sollerön during late June and early July. In late spring, there's a folk dance festival replete with *spelmän* — fiddlers dressed in the traditional high socks, white shirts, and ornate black vests with red piping. There's also an annual folk miracle play, *Himlaspelet* (The Road to Heaven), that's performed outdoors in late July. The House of Culture (on Kyrkallén) shows folk works painted by wandering peasant artists who went door to door, depicting religious scenes on the residents' ceilings. The biblical heroes in these paintings are invariably clothed in Dalecarlian costume.

If you prefer a thorough and organized view of the lake towns, you can pick up a boat lake tour at Rättvik, only 7½ miles (12 km) from Leksand. If you just want a quick but comprehensive peek at the region, there's an old wooden tower (just outside of town at Vidablick) that you can climb for free. From the top you can reconnoiter at will. Rättvik also has a Cultural Center (2 Stor Gatan; phone: 248-70195) with a library and two museums as well as a preserved farm complex called Gammelgård. Many of the wooden structures here were built in the 16th century with incredible care and skill. The tongue and grooving at the corners is so perfectly executed it looks as if the beam ends were machined. The original shingles look more durable than space-age plastics and the fences are marvelously designed to adapt to changing terrain.

Mora is the last lake town and the last stop in Dalarna. It's the finishing point of the *Wasa Ski Race,* the longest cross-country skiing competition in the world, annually attracting more than 10,000 entrants who challenge the grueling 53-mile run. Like the other Siljan towns, Mora celebrates the past in summer festivals and Maypole dancing. The most famous of all Swedish painters, Anders Zorn (1860–1920), lived here and many of his portraits are on display in the *Zorn Museum* (36 Vasagatan) along with Scandinavian sculpture, furniture, textiles, and other examples of local crafts. You can also visit the artist's home and studio. There's another lakeside open-air museum that depicts the indigenous rural life of the Middle Ages. Just east of Mora in the town of Nusnäs you can watch craftsmen fashioning the traditional Dala Horse souvenirs that are sold all over the country.

En Route to Karlstad – There are many small destinations in Värmland that take you off the main southern route along the Klarälven River that you pick up at Stöllet. Instead of heading directly south to Karlstad, you can cut back north and take a canoe trip through beautiful scenery at Sysslebäck. The fishing here is great and you can rent tackle along with your canoe. If you head west from Stöllet, you hit Route 234, which you can take south through the Fryken Lake towns of Torsby — a traditional Norwegian/Swedish trading center — and Sunne — the nearest town to the two mansions associated with Selma Lagerlöf, who is perhaps Sweden's most famous author and her home in the town of Mårbacka, just east of Sunne, is now a museum. Ten minutes south of Sunne is the Rottneros Manor, which she used as a model for the Ekeby mansion in her best-known work, *The Saga of Gösta Berling.* Rottneros Manor is now a sculpture park and garden with wildlife and a terrarium; it's one of the most beautiful spots in all of Sweden, displaying the works of many prominent Scandinavian artists. As a last stop on this Värmland detour, you might want to continue southwest to Arvika, a small town of 16,000 on the Glafsfjorden Lake where you can take a boat tour of the area or listen to a summer concert at the Ingesund Music College. This lake area is wonderful for hiking and there are more than 125 miles of marked trails across fields, along lakeshores, and through forests.

RANSÄTER: If you drive directly south from Stöllet along the Klarälven River on Route 62, "The Pilgrim's Way," you go through the prosperous and quiet little river town of Ransäter, once the home of dramatist Erik Gustaf Geijer. In midsummer, the *Värmlänningarna,* a Swedish *Romeo and Juliet,* is performed outdoors. His home also is open to the public.

The village surrounding the open-air theater is an example of more affluent country habitats, dating back to the time when timber cut from the area started fetching good prices in Great Britain during the end of the Industrial Revolution. The timber was used for props in English coal mines. It was floated down the Klarälven River, and even today tugboats with half-mile-long batches of timber in tow slowly descend the river to Karlstad — the main city of the province — where the timber is processed. Ransäter also is the site of the *Hembygdsgård* (open-air museum) where fiddlers in folk costume gather for music festivals in summer.

KARLSTAD: This is the capital of the province and the home of the *Värmland Museum,* which has exhibitions of textiles, painting, and crafts as well as historic displays. The museum is centrally located in a manicured park on Sandgrundet. The Marieberg Forest is the town's other large park; here you can listen to music or dance at one of the pavilions. Karlstad is a commercial center and the main northern port on the Vänern, the largest lake in Western Europe. The port itself is on the Klarälven River and you can take a tour boat at Residenstorg for a leisurely sail around the city's waterways. Just outside of town in Skutberget there is a campground (phone: 54-35139) and lakefront open-air baths. If you are of Swedish descent or interested in Swedish emigration to North America, trace your heritage at the Emigrant Register at 4 Norra Strandgatan (phone: 54-159269).

From Karlstad, you can take an interesting side trip to Filipstad, 25 miles (40 km) to the northeast. Filipstad is the birthplace of John Ericsson; you can visit his mausoleum in the churchyard in the center of town, behind the *Scandic* hotel. As we have said, Ericsson migrated to Brooklyn, New York, where he became an ironmonger and builder. At the outbreak of the American Civil War he implemented a visionary plan to combine the new diesel engine with a screw propeller for the design of the Union's ironclad ship, the *Monitor.* This ship soundly defeated the Confederate's ironclad entry, the *Merrimack,* winning Ericsson an honored place in naval history. In 1890, the US Navy returned his body to Filipstad where it was entombed and the mausoleum was built. On *Swedish American Day,* at the end of July, there is a mock battle on the lake at Filipstad in his honor.

BEST EN ROUTE

A number of hotels offer special weekend discounts and low summer rates. An expensive hotel can run anywhere from $150 to $250 per night for a double room. The moderate establishments charge $100 to $150. It's wise to make reservations in advance or to use one of the "check" systems operated by some hotel chains. This can be arranged through any travel agent. If you are traveling on a low budget, try the so-called motoring lodgings offered by 200 hotels. You pay about $25 to $35 per bed in a double room; breakfast is extra. For information, contact *Biltur-Logi* (Siljansgården, Tällberg S-79303, Sweden; phone: 24-750925), or *Cole Travel Service* (310 W. State St., Geneva, IL 60134). Thirty-nine Best Western hotels offer reduced rates from June 1 through August 31. Contact the national office for more information (phone: 800-528-1234).

TÄLLBERG

Klockgården – In a village-like setting, these timber buildings with 36 rooms are scenically situated beside Lake Siljan, between Leksand and Rättvik, a region with strong folkloric traditions. There also is a small restaurant with a much-vaunted smorgasbord (phone: 247-50260). Expensive to moderate.

MORA

Mora – A small, clean hotel with 140 neat, comfortable rooms. It's easy to find in the center of town at 12 Strandgatan (phone: 250-11750). Expensive to moderate.

RANSÄTER

Uddeholms – Four rustic buildings with 59 rooms are located in the town of Uddeholm, between Stöllet and Ransäter, in an idyllic lakeside setting. 6 Hotelvägen, Hagfors (phone: 563-23600). Expensive.

KARLSTAD

Stadshotellet – This stately 143-room hotel is in a large yellow building overlooking the river. You can sit in the nearby café, play tennis or golf nearby, or take a dip in the pool. 22 Kungsgatan (phone: 54-115220). Expensive to moderate.

FILIPSTAD

Hennickehammars Herrgård – A superb, tastefully decorated lakeside hostelry with 57 rooms in an 18th-century manor. Period furniture fills the lounges. 3 miles (2 km) south of Filipstad (phone: 590-12565). Expensive.

Gothenburg and the West Coast

The west coast of Sweden, with Gothenburg at its center, is very popular with Scandinavian vacationers but often neglected by international tour operators. This is surprising because the scenic coastal strip combines most of the features the foreign visitor looks for in a typical Scandinavian vacation.

South of Gothenburg is an almost continuous ribbon of sandy beaches and summer resorts, but this trip takes you in the opposite direction — north, toward the Norwegian border. You follow a craggy, granite coastline that breaks up into skerries toward the sea and opens into fjords and lakes toward the land. The whole coast is dotted with tiny isolated fishing villages and peaceful yacht harbors tucked away in rocky coves.

The area attracts many visitors from Scandinavia and northern Europe during the summer months (June through August), yet once away from the busy camping sites and major highways you enter an intimate, peaceful world of great natural beauty that seems untouched by modern industrialization.

Many visitors live the nomadic life in trailer homes or under canvas at the many campsites. Youth hostels, rented summer chalets, or fishermen's cottages are ideal accommodations for overseas visitors. They're plentiful and reasonably priced.

One interesting aspect of this route is its flexibility. You can head directly up the map to the Norwegian border or meander in and out of the windswept coastal indentations, stopping at any fjord or island that catches your eye. You'll find the drive is at least 200 miles (320 km) long and probably longer if you do a lot of island and fjord hopscotching. You'll also find that the dramatic coastal roadside scenery is as much of an attraction as the stops along the way.

GOTHENBURG: Though this is the principal seaport of Scandinavia and the home of some of Sweden's major industrial concerns, don't make the mistake of hurrying through here without pausing to get acquainted with this friendly unsophisticated city of 700,000. Despite being Sweden's second major city, with a busy downtown commercial area, Gothenburg has a relaxing pace and there are plenty of entertainment spots where the tourist can mix with the native. The *Liseberg Amusement Park* (on Oregrytevägen) attracts 3 million visitors annually. Its roller coaster climbs to a height of 150 feet and reaches speeds near 50 mph. Open daily from early May to late August, and weekends only during the second half of April and all of September.

The city was built in the early 17th century by Dutch architects (King Gustav Adolf II granted its first charter in 1621), but also has drawn on the influence of Germans and English over the ensuing centuries. Gothenburg quickly reveals itself to be a garden city with well-kept canals, parks, and botanical gardens like Trädgårdsföreningen and Botaniska Trädgården. Take a *Paddan* boat canal tour that takes you under 20 bridges to soak in the Dutch influence, and the short boat excursion to Elfsborg Fortress to learn about the great naval battles of the 17th century between Swedish and Danish forces.

Kronhuset (Kronhusgatan) is the oldest building in Gothenburg and has a museum recording the history of the city, as well as reconstructions of turn-of-the-century shops. The *Sjöfartsmuseet* (Maritime Museum; on Lilla Bommen; phone: 31-611000) displays ship models from Viking times to the present and richly illustrates the maritime traditions of this major port.

The main drag in Gothenburg is Kungsportsavenyn, referred to simply as Avenyn (Avenue). It's a wide, tree-lined boulevard with cafés, shops, elegant buildings, and nightclubs. There are restaurants that serve Italian, Scottish, German, and Chinese fare, and even a smattering of American fast-food favorites. The cafés here are the best places in town to sit and watch people go by — during the day, the shoppers and tourists, and during the evening, the local young folk who cruise up and down, finally congregating at the Poseidon Fountain (a work by Carl Milles) in the Götaplatsen, the large square at the end of the avenue. At one side of the fountain is the Stadsbiblioteket (library), where you can check on the progress of your favorite baseball team or get the latest on the US political scene by looking at one of the American newspapers available in the reading room.

The *Gothenburg Art Gallery,* also in the Götaplatsen, has an amazingly good collection of art, including work by Cézanne, Van Gogh, Rodin, and Picasso. There's also work by modern Scandinavian masters like Anders Zorn, Edvard Munch, and Carl Milles.

One place not to be missed here is the Feskekörka, or "fish church," next to the fish market in Gothenburg Harbor. The "church," built about 100 years ago, resembles any other normal Lutheran church until you step inside and discover it's actually a fish market, filled with some 20 booths where merchants offer every kind of seafood, from lobsters to herring, fresh and smoked salmon, eels, sole, flounder, crabs, shrimp, and many others. An auction is held at the harbor Tuesdays through Saturdays at 7 AM for the day's fresh catches. There are inexpensive day trips via ferry from Gothenburg to Denmark.

In order to plan your route up the coast in detail, you might want to stop at the Gothenburg Tourist Office (2 Kungsportsavenyn, in the city center; phone: 31-100740). To start the trip north, leave town on the main highway, E6, and after a short drive along the Göta River Valley, get off the main road and you enter Kungälv, a 1,000-year-old town with a turbulent history.

KUNGÄLV: A merchant town occupied this site as early as the 10th century. Three hundred years later, the location had gained significance strategically as a border stronghold between Norway and Sweden (the present border runs more than 100 miles to the north), and work began on the impregnable Bohus Fortress. This mighty stronghold was subjected to many sieges through the centuries but was never taken by force of arms. The ruined structure still stands proud and impressive, jutting up amid the trees on a now placid island.

Across the river in the old part of the town, around Västra Gatan, are several interesting old wooden buildings, mainly from the 18th century, and an exquisite church dating from 1679, which has a richly adorned baroque interior.

Leaving Kungälv, avoid the main highway and make your way northwest on winding country roads, heading for the bridge to Tjuvkil on the island of Koön. From here there is a small passenger-only ferry to Marstrand, a yachting harbor and fashionable summer resort on a small wooded island dominated by the 17th-century Carlsten Fortress.

MARSTRAND: Herring fishing made this island village a prosperous one during the 16th century, but then the lucrative herring shoals moved away and there followed a history of mixed fortunes with periodic devastation by fire and pestilence. Today, the picturesque white-walled timber buildings and crooked alleyways belie this troubled past, never more so than on international regatta days in July or August, when tall-masted yachts swarm the quayside and suntanned visitors stroll the waterfront.

En Route from Marstrand – Make your way back to the mainland and, still keeping to the small country roads, follow the winding coast north until you reach Stenungsund, less than an hour's drive away. Here you sweep to the left and up onto the impressive Tjörn Bridges, spanning three beautiful sounds and linking the mainland with the idyllic islands of Tjörn and neighboring Orust. The Tjörn Bridges are a tourist attraction in themselves, offering a splendid vantage point for panoramic views over rocky, heather-clad isles and often a colorful procession of yachts passing through the sound below.

On the seaward fringes of Tjörn Island, there is a fairy-tale world of refreshingly unsophisticated fishing communities such as Rönnäng and Skärhamn, where red timber cottages huddle together on rocky headlands or perch precariously on tiny skerries. Rows of stockfish are hung out to dry on large tent-shaped racks, and pleasure boats and round-hulled fishing vessels line the wooden jetties. The area also is rich in Stone Age relics. The northern edge of Tjörn Island is linked by bridge to the neighboring island of Orust, where you can explore more ancient relics and quaint fishing villages, notably the lobster harbor, Mollösund, tucked away on a peninsula in the southwest corner of the island.

Continue to the northwest corner of Orust to Ellös, where a car ferry transports you across to Rågårdsvik on the island of Skaftö. Head north across the island to the attractive seaside resort of Fiskebäckskil where you can stroll at the harbor, enjoy a swim, fish, sail, or try the 9-hole golf course.

A few miles northeast of Fiskebäckskil, at Skår, a car-ferry goes to Finnsbo, a couple of miles from Lysekil.

LYSEKIL: Once the center of the local stone-quarrying industry, this small village of 7,000 now is a popular resort and yacht harbor with many diversions for the summer tourist. By day you can enjoy tennis or swimming, and at night, the area's many restaurants and discos. Boat excursions for sea fishing or general exploration in the surrounding waters are available at the harbor.

At Brastad, some 10 miles (16 km) north, stop to view the remarkable ancient rock carvings, then follow Route 162 again, turning left onto Route 163 at Hallinden. Proceed to a fork in this highway, and turn left toward the coast again in the direction of Åby and Kungshamn.

KUNGSHAMN: Kungshamn and neighboring Smögen are two of the finest and most interesting fishing ports on this coast. Kungshamn has a modern fishing harbor. Nearby Smögen can be reached by way of the Smögen Bridge, and is a lovely, picturesque fishing hamlet with quite an international atmosphere in summer. Stroll the long wooden quayside lined with timber boathouses and souvenir shops and admire the elegant pleasure craft and rugged fishing vessels crowding every inch of mooring space. Fishing trips are arranged to go out to the best fishing grounds in the archipelago for whiting, cod, and mackerel. If you stay until evening, you can watch the shrimp auctions and enjoy a fresh seafood supper.

En Route from Kungshamn – Follow the coast road north past fjords, wide bays, and rocky inlets until you join Route 163 again at Bottne Fjord. Drive north through Hamburgsund and Fjällbacka until you reach Grebbestad. This route shows the rugged, sculptured coastline at its best and all along the way there are places where you can linger awhile for some angling or bathing.

A couple of miles east of Grebbestad lies Tanumshede, the best known of all Sweden's rock carving sites. The strange figures and symbols you see here were carved in the granite rock some 3,000 years ago and are still legible. The most impressive of the carvings is at Fossum and depicts a battle scene.

The route continues north on main Route E6, reaching the Norwegian border at the Svinesund Bridge, some 60 miles (96 km) from Oslo.

BEST EN ROUTE

Expect hotels in Sweden to be priced as high as those in the US. Very expensive hotels, which have single and double rooms, run anywhere from $100 to $195 a night. More modest in price are those first class tourist hotels with full accommodations (private baths in most; in some you may have to opt for a bathroom in the corridor); these run $50 to $100 (expensive), for a single or double room. Other hotels, smaller in size, can run from $40 to $80 (moderate). Reservations are recommended.

There are hotel check systems covering all of Sweden. Consult the Swedish Tourist Board (655 3rd Ave., New York, NY 10017; phone: 212-949-2333), for details (ask for the free booklet *Hotels in Sweden*). Information on these check systems as well as Swedish summer chalets is available from the Gothenburg Tourist Office (2 Kungsportsavenyn, S-411 10 Gothenburg, Sweden; phone: 31-100740).

GOTHENBURG

SAS Park Avenue – A 318-room property offering banquet facilities, a bar, restaurant, swimming pool, sauna, and secretarial services (if you need them), among other amenities. 36-38 Kungsportsavenyn (phone: 31-176520; fax: 31-169568). Very expensive.

Sheraton – This 343-room establishment is opposite Central Station and has a swimming pool. 59-65 Södra Hamngatan (phone: 31-806000; fax: 31-159888). Very expensive.

Windsor – Smaller, 91-room hotel with a bar and an English-style restaurant. 6 Kungsportsavenyn (phone: 31-176540; fax: 31-113439). Expensive.

KUNGÄLV

Fars Hatt – A pleasant 130-room hotel in a convenient location. Torget (phone: 303-10970; fax: 303-19637). Expensive.

MARSTRAND

Alphyddan – Modest 37-room hostelry in the center of this small island town. 6 Långgatan (phone: 303-61030; fax: 303-61200). Moderate.

LYSEKIL

Lysekil – A 50-room hotel with a restaurant and a nightclub. 1 Rosvikstorg (phone: 523-11860; fax: 523-15520). Expensive to moderate.

TANUMSHEDE

Tanums Gestgifveri – This old country inn serves very good food and is an ideal overnight spot for soaking up the historic ambience of this ancient region. Rte. E6 (phone: 525-29010; fax: 525-29571; telex: 42031). Expensive to moderate.

Gotland

In the time of the Vikings, Gotland was the gateway to Scandinavia. It's Sweden's largest island, off the east coast in the Baltic, and, because of its location, it was historically the guardian of the Scandanavian peninsula. It began as a strategic military base for a succession of Viking kings bent on plundering the lands to the east (now Russia) and later became a trading point and an economic and cultural center. The history of Gotland still is visible all over the island in Stone Age cave dwellings, picture stones, and medieval churches.

After the decline of the Vikings and the development of more civilized methods of international trade, Visby, Gotland's main city, became the center of the Hanseatic League, a Germanic trade association. In the 13th century, the burghers of Visby built an intricate limestone wall modeled on the effective Roman civil defense perimeters. As the town grew prosperous with trade, the people built an affluent city within the wall, out of the marble and the sandstone they found in abundance on their flat, fertile island.

Gotland was civilized long before the Swedish mainland and became one of the wealthiest and most powerful states in Europe, but in 1361 Danish King Valdemar Atterdag invaded. (Legend has it that the king's lover, the treacherous daughter of Visbian Nils the Goldsmith, opened the city gate and let the Danes in.) In any case, Visby fell and never regained its imperial stature.

Today Gotland is a land of beaches, spas, and sailing, with a beautiful landscape and a warmer climate than the rest of Sweden so that, aside from tourism, farming is the mainstay of the island's economy. Gotland is 78 miles long and 25 miles wide with plenty of room for Gotland sheep — a black-wooled variety — to graze all year round. In the Lojsta Hajd woodland you also can see the wild Gotland Russ ponies, small and temperamental from inbreeding, but unusual looking and still friendly.

Geologically, the most remarkable features of this island are the "marine stacks" or *rauker* — nature's own sculptures of limestone, formed by eroding winds and waters — that give Gotland's lovely sandy beaches a character all their own. The stacks are formed at the stony edges of the slopes leading to the sandy beaches.

You enter Gotland through Visby. In the summer, there are car ferries from Nynäshamn and Oskarshamn on the mainland. If you bring your own car, make sure to book tickets well in advance as the auto berths are often sold out. Even without a car, advance booking is required since the summer ferries are usually packed with travelers. Flights are available to Visby Airport from Stockholm-Arlanda, Norrköping, and Kalmar.

VISBY: This is one of the oldest cities in Sweden and its wall alone would make it worth the trip. The wall is about 2 miles long and is capped by 44 towers with crenelated turrets and long, thin archer's windows. Some towers are also gateways. Inside the walls you can see gleaming whitewashed stone houses with shiny red tile roofs; the city has a sort of southern European look. Eventually, Visby grew too large for its surrounding wall and was forced to build up, around, and over itself. It's now a town of romantic arches and alleyways with clinging vines and bushes growing out of every wall cranny. The red roofs are punctuated by stepped gables, and bicycles are the preferred mode of transportation over the cobbled streets. Visby has been called the city of roses and there are colorful blossoms everywhere. The Almedalen old harbor, lifted by land augmentation over the centuries, has been transformed into a botanic oasis with many varieties of flowers. A special *Medieval Week* is held in the first week of August, with colorful pageants and jousting tournaments.

There are 100 churches and chapels on Gotland; only 9 of them were built after 1350. Some of them are in ruins, but there's still more stained glass here than anywhere else in Scandinavia. A vivid glimpse into the past is outside the wall at the Galgberget (hanging mound), which was a raised medieval execution area whose stone gallows you can still examine.

Visby also is a tourist town with good restaurants, shops, and comfortable hotels. If you want to rent a bicycle, ask at the tourist office (9 Strandgatan; phone: 498-10982). They'll also tell you where you'll find the best sailing, skin diving, and surf.

En Route from Visby – The Väte, a 14th-century stone church, is 18 miles (29 km) south of Visby on Route 142.

From Väte, the route continues along the highway into the Lojsta Hajd woodlands — the home of the Gotland ponies. Half wild, half domestic, the ponies are left to roam around for 3 years before they are rounded up to be broken in.

Turning east at Fride, you pass the Etelhem Church, go through the village of Hemse, and arrive at Holmhällar fishing village on the southeastern tip of Gotland.

HOLMHÄLLAR: The beaches around Holmhällar are splendid, and here samples of the typical marine stacks can be seen. You'll also find several caves with stalagmites like frozen curtains of stone, formed by millennia of dripping water seeping through the limestone bedrock.

Farther south, the Hoburgen man — a marine stack shaped like a head — marks the island's southernmost point. The view across the Baltic is breathtaking.

En Route from Holmhällar – Returning north to Visby along the coast, stop over at Djupvik fishing village. According to legend, it was here that invading Danes landed. Back in Visby, you can head north on the island, but avoid the uppermost part of Gotland, which is a restricted area.

The Lummelunda Cave and the *Lummelunda Geological Museum,* a 20-minute drive north along the coast of Visby, are recommended sites, as is a drive across the island to Slite. Beaches at Slite are excellent, and the Slite Strandbad beach, on a little island off the harbor, is especially enjoyable.

BEST EN ROUTE

Just because you're off the mainland doesn't mean hotel prices will be lower. On the contrary, they're about the same or higher than those on previous routes: $180 to $250 (very expensive) for a double room, $150 to $180 (expensive), and $100 to $160 (moderate). Every hotel has double and single rooms, and it's not a bad idea to reserve beforehand, especially during the summer months.

You also can rent private rooms and cottages on the island. Contact *Gotlandsresor AB* (Box 2081, Visby 621 02, Sweden; phone: 498-19010), or call one of the following: *Gotlandsturist Service* (phone: 498-49050), *Gotlandsturist Center* (phone: 498-79095), or *Visby Resebyrå* (phone: 498-17050). Cottages also can be rented through *Turistcentralen* (phone: 498-18951).

VISBY

Strand – Situated smack in the center of this picturesque city, this 110-room hotel is within walking distance of the sea. Other amenities include a sauna, a solarium, a sun terrace, and a small swimming pool. 34 Strandgatan (phone: 498-12600; fax: 498-78111). Expensive.

Villa Borgen – Pleasant, 18-room hotel, with a garden. 11 Adelsgatan (phone: 498-71170; fax: 498-49300). Expensive to moderate.

HEMSE

Hemse – This 20-bed hotel is small but pleasant and has a restaurant. 58 Storgatan (phone: 497-80151; fax: 497-80796). Expensive to moderate.

BURGSVIK

Sallmundsgårds – A 19th-century farmstead converted into an 18-bed hotel that reflects Gotland's rural culture. Hamra (phone: 497-99120). Moderate.

Lapland

For many travelers, Lapland, sprawling across the wild regions of Arctic Scandinavia, has the same sort of fascination usually reserved for remote, isolated destinations like Samarkand, Tibet, and Katmandu.

There is indeed a certain romance about an area still unconquered by man and civilization, a domain of awesome proportions where reindeer roam free and fast-disappearing wildlife such as the bear and golden eagle still hold their own. Man has made but small inroads here: The nomadic Lapps, who are believed to have migrated to Scandinavia from Russia, accepted the hardy lifestyle that Arctic conditions imposed in making this their home, following the migratory reindeer herds. In recent decades, the quest for iron ore and the need for electrical power generated by the mighty rushing rivers has given rise to industrialization in the wilderness. It is the development of modern towns like Kiruna that has made conventional tourism possible in these parts. Of course, along with modernization comes the breaking down of old traditions and it isn't uncommon now to see snowmobiles during reindeer round-ups and Lapps wearing blue jeans instead of their ancient colorful outfits fashioned almost entirely of reindeer hides.

When contemplating a vacation trip, bear in mind that the unique rewards of travel in these regions, the joy of experiencing vast tracts of unspoiled nature and of living under the midnight sun, must be paid for in the form of a few discomforts. Your accommodations may be a well-equipped but simple mountain cabin instead of a luxury hotel, and you might suffer a few insect bites if you forget your repellent, but this doesn't mean that you have to be an athlete and outdoorsman to venture this way. Time your visit, however, during the warm summer months of June, July, and August, and possibly even May and September if you do not like cold weather. Winter days are short and temperatures can fall many degrees below freezing, but life goes on here, and the dry cold air means the crisp days can be enjoyed despite the sinking mercury.

The route takes you through a landscape where birch-clad valleys and vast pine forests give way to mountain plateaus, waterfalls, river rapids, and primeval moss-covered fens; where herds of reindeer follow age-old migratory paths, swimming bravely across broad rivers to reach their mountain grazing lands; where the fisherman, naturalist, and amateur photographer have more excitement in one week than friends back home might experience in a lifetime.

The numerous rivers of the region snake down in valleys from the mountainous northwest to spill out finally into the Gulf of Bothnia. Roads tend to follow these river valleys, each ribbonlike highway reaching up into the mountains and, in some cases, winding as far as the Norwegian coast. Each road is a tour route in its own right. They pass fish-rich lakes, vast national parks, snow-capped mountain ranges, and Arctic tundra. Fittingly, each road has a romantic name, like the Blue Road, Way of the Four Winds, the Midnight Sun Road, or the Linné Route.

The following tour route, designed to give visitors a varied and, as far as possible, complete picture of these northern wilds, traces a winding path northward into the mountains.

For the most part, the roads are modern with hard metal surfaces, but in some of the more remote stretches, you may find yourself driving on well-kept dirt roads.

Our starting point is Luleå, the Baltic port that can be reached by regular air service, railroad, or by main highway E4 from Stockholm, an ideal gateway into the region. At the tourist office here, Nordkalottresor/Norrbottens Turistråd (53 Sandviksgatan, phone: 920-94070), you can collect a useful brochure covering Swedish Lapland. From Luleå, follow Route 97 northwest and you will soon pass the garrison town, Boden. At Boden turn left and drive southwest on Route 356 heading for Alvsbyn some 30 miles (48 km) farther on — a market town on the Pite River deservedly known as the "land of the rapids." At Alvsbyn, turn right onto Route 374, traveling northwest to Storforsen, Europe's largest unrestricted waterfall and last untamed giant rapids. See the Pite River crash and rumble its way at breakneck speed down the hillside, falling 252 feet over a stretch of 3 miles. There is a forestry museum here with tar-works and charcoal stacks in operation so you can see what a Swedish lumber camp looked like in days gone by.

Leaving Storforsen, you continue northwest through lake-dotted open moorland, passing over the Arctic Circle (there's little more than a signpost to mark the crossing), and finally reaching the Lapp center of Jokkmokk.

JOKKMOKK: Here at the *Ajtte* (Lapp Museum) you will receive your first insight into the rich and colorful culture of the hardy, nomadic Lapps. The museum displays more than 2,000 Lapp objects, including life-size old storehouses, folk costumes, sleighs, delicately carved wooden utensils, and an array of exquisite silver jewelry. From now on you will become increasingly aware of your presence in the wild domain of the Lapps and their precious reindeer, for you are certain to meet them face to face from time to time during your tour. Since the reindeer herds are nomadic and unpredictable, it is not possible to set dates and places when and where you can see the migration or the summer musters. It's possible to get help and guidance from a friendly Lapp, but don't make the mistake of insulting these taciturn folk by approaching them as some sort of curiosity or tourist attraction. They are a proud people whose labor is honest and whose lifestyle is hard, a nomadic race who are making the difficult transition into 20th-century civilization as their native region, Lapland (an area that cuts across Scandinavian national boundaries), becomes less and less remote. Today, there are only 50,000 Lapps left in Scandinavia, 17,000 of whom live in Sweden.

After you visit the museum, call at the tourist office (4 Porjusvägen) to collect your Polar Certificate recognizing your crossing of the Arctic Circle (for a small charge), and then take a look at the Gamla Kyrkan (The Old Church), a small timbered building dating from 1753 (damaged by fire in 1972). Postcards mailed at the post office are canceled with a special Arctic Circle stamp.

The county of Jokkmokk contains the vast, wild, and unforgettably beautiful national parks, Sarek, Padjelanta, and Stora Sjöfallet. These provide a worthwhile detour for the experienced outdoorsman through the last true wilderness in Europe. The 100 glaciers and 20 towering peaks of these wild preserves are the haunt of the osprey, loon, wild goose, and golden eagle. The stepping-off point for hiking expeditions into Sarek and Padjelanta National parks lies about 80 miles (128 km) northwest of Jokkmokk along highway 805 at Kvikkjokk. Here you can pick up the famous King's Trail, a hiking route laid out by the *Swedish Touring Club* and marked by cairns. There are mountain chalets at suitable intervals along the route, but don't attempt this hike unless you know what you're doing. From Kvikkjokk, there are aerial connections by light aircraft to scenic points in the surrounding region as well as aerial sightseeing trips over the mountains.

En Route from Jokkmokk – Take Highway 88 north for about 30 miles (48 km), crossing the Lule River and reaching Porjus, a community developed in conjunction with the hydroelectric project harnessing the Porjus Falls. East of Porjus is the Muddus National Park, an area of virgin pine and spruce forest, untouched swamplands, and undulating granite mountains. Muddus is a nature reserve for bear, elk, marten, and weasel, and the home of many rare migratory birds. Unfortunately, this is also wild country, difficult to penetrate and more for the avid bird watcher and naturalist than the conventional tourist, although some trails have been laid out with raised wooden duckboards to improve accessibility.

Continue on Highway 97 for about another 30 miles (48 km) and you enter Gällivare, passing Thunder Mountain, which rises some 2,699 feet above sea level.

GÄLLIVARE: This is a flourishing mining community and trading center where you will have much to do: join one of the daily tours to the nearby iron mines at Malmberget; visit the local museum at Vasara with 2,000-year-old skis on display; and view the 18th-century Ettöre Church. A modern building here of considerable interest to the tourist is Björnfällan (The Bear Trap), a 54-square-foot log cabin said to be the largest in the world, built with 80 tons of stone and 230,000 feet of timber, most of which is 400-year-old gray pine. The building acts as a service center for a holiday village of log cabins clustered in the surrounding countryside, and it contains two saunas, a swimming pool, meeting rooms with open fires, shops, and restaurant. This vantage point also provides a spectacular view of the surrounding area. From Gällivare, you can book transportation by seaplane or helicopter to mountain fishing camps such as Tjuonajokk, where grayling, char, and salmon trout provide the challenge for the keen angler. Gällivare Airport has daily scheduled air service to Stockholm.

En Route from Gällivare – Follow Highway 98 north through moorland and forest, passing scenic lakes and rivers. After some 50 miles (80 km) you reach Svappavaara and, 30 miles (48 km) farther west, Kiruna, a mining town with modern accommodations. Here you can get a wonderful meal of local delicacies such as white grouse (ptarmigan) followed by cloudberries and cream for dessert. Kiruna also has tours into the world's biggest underground mine, which extracts up to 30 million tons of iron ore annually.

En route from Kiruna – Continue northwest on the newer section of Highway 98 over the mountains to Narvik in Norway. This spectacular scenic route takes you through the truly wild Abisko National Park and along beautiful Torne Lake.

Alternatively, you can drive from Kiruna back to Svappavaara, then east to Vittangi. From here it's 65 miles (104 km) to Karesuando, a church village on the border of Sweden and Finland. The road is through a tundra region of countless lakes and rivers where the subsoil is permanently frozen. From here the lunatic fringe may choose to continue northward via Kautokeino and Alta in Norway all the way up to North Cape, a magnificent precipice that marks the northernmost tip of Europe. Another alternative is to follow Route E78 southeast into Finland. Our less ambitious but nonetheless spectacular route proceeds northwest from Karesuando on Route E78 — the beautiful "Way of the Four Winds," running parallel with the Könkämä River along the Swedish-Finnish border.

Seventy miles (112 km) farther on as you climb steadily into an alpine region, you cross the border into Norway at Siilastupa, finally reaching Skibotn on the Lyngen Fjord. Your first breathtaking glimpse of the awe-inspiring fjord, its sheer rock walls rising nearly vertically, unbroken but for the odd frothy waterfall crashing into the still waters below, tells you have reached the rocky, skerried coastline of northern Norway. Follow the road southwest along the scenic fjord passing Kvesmenes, where you might join a deep-sea fishing trip to the shark waters of the Arctic Ocean. On either side of the Lyngen Fjord rise the ragged peaks of the Lyngen Alps, spewing impressive blue white glaciers right down to the surface of the water. The faces of the glaciers sparkle like diamonds in the sun. Leaving the fjord, follow Route E78 looping northwest onto a large peninsula toward the Arctic fishing port of Tromsø in Norway.

TROMSØ: Your first impression of Tromsø — apart from the obvious beauty of its coastal setting and backdrop of blue mountains — will be the lush green vegetation that contrasts strongly with the Arctic tundra you have recently passed through at similar latitudes. The rich flora and mild climate on this coast are explained by the Gulf Stream that washes warm currents onto these northern shores.

Tromsø is the largest city in northern Norway (see *Norway* in DIRECTIONS), often called the gateway to the Arctic because of the many expeditions that have set out from here. Take the 2½-hour sightseeing tour that leaves from the *SAS Royal* hotel (7 Sjøgata), showing you the best of Tromsø Island, on which most of the city is situated, and the *Tromsø Museum,* just outside of town, which traces the history of the region from the Stone Age through Viking times and up to the present. The museum also has a section devoted to Lappish ethnography. At the end of the tour you are dropped near the cable car ride up to Storsteinen Mountain, where you receive a sweeping panoramic view over the green city, its wide fishing harbor, and the gentle mountains beyond. Here in Tromsø is your chance to enjoy the more conventional tourist pursuits of a shopping spree and an evening out.

Our route ends in Tromsø but there are possibilities to continue south along the coast passing the fishing harbor of Narvik and the wild and beautiful Lofoten Islands.

BEST EN ROUTE

Accommodations are sparse in Lapland, and range from $150 or more for a double room (very expensive) to $100 to $150 (expensive) and $75 to $100 (moderate). In Lapland, prices usually include three meals. Again, make reservations before you come.

ABISKO

STF Abisko – Scenically located at the start of the King's Trail (Kungsleden), it has 165 rooms and cottages. Near the lift (phone: 980-40000). Moderate.

BJÖRKLIDEN

Fjället – A comfortable hotel with 51 rooms and well-equipped cottages overlooking Lake Torne and Lapp Gate (phone: 980-40040 or call the reservations office in Stockholm: 8-248360). Expensive to moderate.

GÄLLIVARE

Dundret Holiday Village – First-rate resort made up of log cabins and a service center that includes saunas, a swimming pool, meeting rooms with open fires, shops, and a cafeteria. It also has an impressive view of the surrounding area. 1 Per Högströmsgatan (phone: 970-11040). Very expensive.

Nex – Opposite the railway station, this 97-room hotel offers both dining and dancing. 1 Lasarettsgatan (phone: 970-11020; fax: 970-15475). Expensive.

Polar – A 52-room hotel in the center of Gällivare, close to the railroad station. Facilities include a restaurant and a sauna. 9 Per Högströmsgatan (phone: 970-11190). Moderate.

KIRUNA

Ferrum – This 170-room property provides rooms with private baths, a dining room and dancing. 15 Lars Janssonsgatan (phone: 980-18600). Very expensive.

Kebne – A 54-room hotel near the railroad station. 7 Konduktörsgatan (phone: 980-12380; fax: 980-14505; telex: 980-8211). Expensive.

TROMSØ, NORWAY

SAS Royal – This 195-room hotel has excellent accommodations (private baths) and a very good restaurant. 7 Sjøgata (phone: 83-56000). Very expensive.

Switzerland

Switzerland is virtually synonymous with the Alps, yet only three-fifths of its territory is mountainous. The northeastern part of the country, where the population is concentrated, is largely plateau. Switzerland does, however, have the lion's share of the greatest peaks in the Alpine range — 11 of the 12 soar above 14,000 feet, including the awesome Matterhorn. Interlacing the peaks are valleys and gorges gouged out by glaciers, not all of which are ancient history. Several are still at work, including Europe's largest, the Aletsch, in central Switzerland near Interlaken, and the Jungfrau. The variety of Switzerland's scenery is enormous and almost everything is within easy reach. Its people are also incredibly diverse: Four ethnic and linguistic groups — German, French, Italian, Romansh — maintain their characteristics, culture, and independence under the aegis of one central government. Not only do the 26 cantons (states) guard their individual rights fiercely (until 1848 some even had their own money), but so does every community within the cantons. This is why it's possible to pay twice as much in taxes in one village as in another a mile away.

Switzerland's low-profile observance of its 700th anniversary in 1991 was entirely in character. While the Swiss possess some of the world's most spectacularly scenic real estate, they have little in the way of natural resources. Consequently, they have had to make their way in the world through industriousness. Their focus is on results, which have been considerable. With a population less than that of New York City, Switzerland has an important industrial economy. Its currency is rock solid. And it is banker to the world.

Geographical or historical necessity played less of a part in the formation of the Confederation Helvetica (Swiss Confederation) than did the will of the people. In prehistoric times most of the territory was inhabited by Celts (the Helvetians were one of the main Celtic tribes). Later it was ruled by the Romans, who brought cultural and economic prosperity, and then it was overrun by Germanic tribes. The latter included the Alamans, who settled in what is today the German area of the country, and the Germanic Burgundians, who settled west of the Sarine River and adopted the speech that eventually became French. The Alamans retained German, and today the Sarine remains the dividing line between French- and German-speaking Switzerland. In feudal times the territory was part of the Holy Roman Empire, and was later ruled by princely families or bishops, who often fought each other for supremacy. It was against the Hapsburgs that the original three forest cantons (Uri, Schwyz, Unterwalden) rebelled, and they eventually formed an alliance, marking the birth of the nation on August 1, 1291. It did not happen as dramatically as the famous legend of William Tell has it, but the spirit of freedom was the same, and Tell and his apple still are revered today. (This story of Swiss nationhood arose in the 15th century and was made world-famous by the German poet Schiller in the 18th century. It tells of a conspiracy, solemnly sworn among representatives of the three cantons, to overthrow the evil Bailiff Gessler, who had subjected the archer Tell to his famous ordeal.) One by one, all the cities and cantons joined or were acquired by the confederation; the last one was Jura in 1979.

The country now is ruled by a federal government, similar to that of the US, which wields executive and legislative power. The executive branch is controlled by a federal council consisting of seven members and headed by a president serving a 1-year term. Since the head of the council also is the country's president, most Swiss don't know who their government's chief executive is for a given year. The voting age recently was lowered from 20 to 18, adding some 160,000 voters to the electorate, and at long last, in February 1991, women were given the right to vote in all areas of Switzerland.

The rapid approach of a fully integrated European Community also is forcing the Swiss, who take their neutrality so seriously that they have never joined the United Nations, to re-evaluate their aloofness from economic as well as political alliances.

You generally will find the Swiss very friendly and helpful. In most hotels, there is always somebody who speaks English. The best times for motoring are June, September, and October, when the high passes are open but the roads aren't clogged with travelers. Despite the changeable weather, any time is good — in recent years, for example, November has been a particularly beautiful month for touring the mountains. Roads are good, but the German Swiss in particular tend to be cautious (and very law-abiding) drivers. Road numbers often exist only on maps and not on road signs. Also, note that a SFr.100 fine is imposed if you are caught driving on most Swiss autobahns without the special car sticker that is used in lieu of tolls. Rental cars usually have these stickers; if you're driving into Switzerland, they are available for about $20 at border crossings or at service stations.

The best maps are *Michelin No. 427,* Switzerland, and the Michelin regional maps. For city maps, ask at the tourist offices. The best quick reference is the green Michelin guidebook *Switzerland;* for statistics and general information, there's a small red paperback, also called *Switzerland,* published yearly by Kümmerly and Frey. The *Swiss Hotel Guide,* available at the tourist offices, also is helpful.

The four itineraries described below take you through the most important regions and cities, giving a good cross section of the country. Three of the four routes originate in Zurich, the largest city and industrial and financial center of Switzerland. The Zurich to Geneva route passes through some of Switzerland's most historic towns, including Murten and Fribourg. The Zurich to Lugano route travels the high Swiss Alps, running through mountain passes famous for their breathtaking scenery. Another routing from Zurich to Lugano, via the Engadine, cuts through the heart of Swiss tourism, with stops at Bad Ragaz and St. Moritz, the famous health spa and resort. The last route, Bern to Montreux, is typical of diverse Switzerland: It connects the Alps with Lake Geneva and en route you will savor subtropical vegetation as well as glacial vistas.

Zurich to Geneva

This itinerary, which stresses culture and cities, is more idyllic and peaceful than the mountain routes. Starting with Zurich, the route goes west along the Rhine to Basel, then proceeds southwest through the country's oldest mountain range, the Jura (where the language changes from German to French), then to the basin of the Biel and Neuchâtel lakes and gentle, pastoral countryside, to its climax, radiant Lake Geneva with its crown of Alps. The trip includes stops in culturally vibrant Basel; charming Neuchâtel; the "museum town" of Murten; historic Fribourg; enchanting Gruyères; and the university town of Lausanne. Any season is good for this 260-mile (416-km) route. Count on doing it in 3 fairly leisurely days; it's possible to do it in 2 by leaving out some museums.

ZURICH: For a complete description of the city and its hotels and restaurants, see *Zurich,* THE CITIES.

En Route from Zurich – Take the scenic (and actually shorter) Route N7, which passes the airport and proceeds along the Rhine, which is not yet navigable here. Tiny Kaiserstuhl, just off the main road, is worth a short stop, as it has kept its medieval look. Across the old bridge is Germany. After Zurzach, which features a spa with hot springs, the Aare — the largest all-Swiss river — joins the Rhine in a picturesque confluence at Koblenz. All along the other side of the Rhine loom the Gothic towers of small German towns. Soon after pretty Laufenburg, the road divides; head for Rheinfelden, with its old spa and famous brewery. From here take Route 3 to Augst, site of the impressive ruins of Augusta Raurica, the oldest Roman settlement on the Rhine. Much has been restored, and you can see some of the artifacts found — including silver plates decorated with mythological details — on display at the museum. It's only a few more minutes from here to Basel.

BASEL: Although it's Switzerland's second city (after Zurich) in terms of population and business, Basel is first in culture — a traditional patron of the arts. Of Celtic Roman origin, the city later was ruled by a prince-bishop for over 1,000 years. (This explains the bishop's staff in Basel's coat of arms.) The town joined the Swiss Confederation in 1501, and became Protestant soon after. It always has had major importance as a port (the Rhine is navigable from here on down) and as a road junction, especially after the river's first bridge, the Mittlere Brücke, was built in 1225. It remained the only one to span the Rhine for centuries, and it still stands.

It's easy to get lost in Basel, so park in the center of town and do your exploring on foot. A walk along the Obere Rheinweg, a promenade following the Rhine's right bank, will give you a good overall picture of Old Basel; it's also nice to take the ferry across. On the other side of the Rhine is the 12th-century cathedral (Münster), which provides another fine panorama of the town from its twin Gothic towers. Nearby you'll find some interesting patrician townhouses. The Town Hall, on Market Square (still the site of a daily market), is an impressive 16th-century sandstone building that's adorned with frescoes. The metal fountain designed by Swiss artist Jean Tinguely, mechanically rattling and wending (when it works) in a pool next to the Kunis, is a sample of some of the new art on public display.

And, of course, there are the museums — more than 30 of them! The *Kunstmuseum* (Fine Arts Museum; St. Albangraben), one of the most remarkable of its kind in the world, features the Amerbach Collection. It includes outstanding examples of early

German and Flemish art and the largest group of paintings by the Holbein family assembled anywhere. (Amerbach was a friend of the Holbeins.) There are also French Impressionist works and modern abstracts. The *Kirschgarten* (Cherry Orchard Museum; 27 Elizabethenstr.), in a lovely old patrician mansion, has period furniture, magnificent porcelain, antique watches, and a delightful exhibition of old toys. It also contains a substantial part of the collection of the *Historical Museum;* the latter is in the Gothic Barfüsser Church, on Barfüsserplatz.

This Week in Basel, a booklet published by the tourist office, provides an excellent suggested walking tour of the Old Town, complete with a map. While you're here, stop at "three-countries corner," a spot marked by a spire, where the Swiss, German, and French borders all converge, and take in the excellent view of the port and city from the terrace (reachable by elevator) of the Swiss Navigation Companies' silo. And be sure to sample the local cookie specialty, *basler leckerli.* In addition, you can take in a free concert, given in a number of different churches year-round. It's a good idea to visit Basel on the Monday after *Ash Wednesday,* for that's when the town really comes alive in an annual carnival called *Fasnacht.*

En Route from Basel – Take the road parallel to Route 18 south; just off the road and near Basel's city limits is Arlesheim, with its charming baroque church and famous Silberman organ. On a mountain overlooking this town is the fortress-like Goetheanum, the center of the Anthroposophical Society. The structure was built according to exacting esoteric rules — for example, no right angles. Goethe's scientific theories strongly influenced the movement, and his plays often are performed here.

At Laufen, you enter the pastoral Jura range. The region becomes French-speaking as you drive along the Birs River to Delémont, former summer residence of the Prince-Bishops of Basel. The lovely baroque palace is now the seat of the Jura government, established in 1979. Nearby is Courfaivre, with its remarkable modern stained glass windows created by Fernand Léger in the village church. Continuing on Route 6 for 10 miles (16 km) and then on a smaller road for 4 miles (6 km), you come to St. Ursanne, a medieval gem, complete with city gates, a Romanesque basilica, and a stone bridge across the Doubs River.

Following the scenic "Corniche de Jura" Road, join Route 18A. You'll pass through the most unspoiled section of the Jura, the Franches Montagnes; as you ride the high plateau, it's easy to feel on top of the world. Here are lovely natural parks, pastures with grazing horses (this is the major horse-breeding region), low farmhouses, and little inns that serve good local trout and ham. Saignelégier, the sleepy regional center, comes to life with the annual horsemarket and show in August. At Le Roselet (off Les Emibois) you can visit a "home" for old horses. La Chaux de Fonds is the center of Swiss watch manufacturing, and there is a truly fabulous underground watch museum: On view in specially lit sections is the world's most comprehensive collection of timepieces, from sundials to atomic clocks, *Musée International d'Horlogerie* (21 Rue des Musées). A scenic mountain pass road ascends to Vue des Alpes, where there's a lookout point at 4,209 feet. On clear days the panorama of the Bernese Alps and Mont-Blanc is overwhelming. Descending toward Lake Neuchâtel, you come to Valangin, a charming little town with an old castle that's now an interesting regional museum. From here, it's a short ride to Neuchâtel, a honey-colored university town on a peaceful lake.

NEUCHÂTEL: Some claim that the purest French in the world is spoken in this aristocratic city; after the 11th century, it belonged successively — and by inheritance — to the House of Orléans and the King of Prussia. The intellectual and cultural heritage can be felt in a walk through the Old Town, especially in the 12th-century University Church and the castle. The *Ethnographic Museum* is outstanding for its Egyptian and African collections and thematic display rooms (4 St.-Nicolas). The

Museum of Art and History (Rue des Beaux-Arts) features ingenious automatons invented in the 18th century and has public demonstrations the first Sunday of each month at 2, 3, and 4 PM.

En Route from Neuchâtel – Cross the canal connecting the Neuchâtel and Biel lakes north of the city, and head for Murten, on the far side of the lake of the same name.

MURTEN (MORAT): This enchanting town is a museum in itself, having retained most of its medieval ramparts and towers. A historic battle was fought here in the 15th century between the Swiss Confederates and the army of the Duke of Burgundy, and it's still commemorated today. A walk around the ramparts provides picturesque views of the old roofs, the lake, and the castle. Hauptstrasse (Main Street) displays a pleasing harmony of design, with its arcaded, geranium-covered houses, fountains, and city gate; a row of restaurants and cafés makes it even more inviting. It's a short drive southeast to Fribourg.

FRIBOURG: You enter one of the most picturesque and interesting cities of the country through an old gate; strangely, it's often bypassed by tourists. Its river, the Sarine, is a true dividing line between the French and German parts of Switzerland. Fribourg is a historical Roman Catholic bastion, and the site of a renowned Catholic university established in 1889. Founded in 1157, the city was ruled by different families until it joined the confederation in 1481. Several major religious orders, such as the Franciscans, Cistercians, and Jesuits, have settled here in the course of centuries.

Eglise des Cordeliers (the Franciscan church on Rue de Morat), completed in the 13th century and rebuilt in the 18th century, retains its original chancel and stalls, as well as its splendid St. Anthony altarpiece, painted by two artists whose signatures were red and white carnations. In addition, bridges on the winding Sarine offer marvelous views of the town. The river itself swirls around Fribourg's unusual spur-like rock formations. You also should see the Gothic towers and elaborately decorated interiors of St. Nicholas' Cathedral; the turrets and belfry of the 16th-century Town Hall; and the excellent collection of sculpture, furniture, and jewelry in the elegant *Museum of Art and History* (all on Rue de Morat).

En Route from Fribourg – Continue along the pretty, manmade Lake Gruyères; for a more scenic route, don't take the freeway or the main road, but the smaller one that goes via Marly and Corbières (stop at the bridge for a good view) through regions of pastoral scenery where folklore is still alive. Then proceed via Broc directly to Gruyères.

GRUYÈRES: This hilltop town, definitely one of the route's highlights, appears to be preserved against time — it could be the setting for medieval fairy tales. Cars are prohibited within the town's walls for a good part of the year, so leave yours in one of the lots on the outskirts. Then take a leisurely stroll down the wide, cobblestone main street that's lined with old houses, observing the house on the left with the gracefully carved 16th-century window frames. Proceed up to the castle, the former abode of the benevolent Counts of Gruyères, and view the collection of tapestries, furniture, and medieval war booty housed in the impressive 15th-century edifice. Gruyères is, of course, an excellent place to sample fondue; also try the local heavy cream with berries. In the morning, pay a visit to the cheese factory at the bottom of the hill and watch the product being made. Later, there's an audiovisual show.

En Route from Gruyères – Head north to Bulle, featuring the *Gruèrien Museum,* with its fine collection of regional costumes and furniture. Next, turn south to Châtel St. Denis on the same road, and begin the magnificent descent to Lake Geneva; from here the road to Blonay is more scenic and less direct. The lake begins to come into view here, with the grandiose high Valais Alps providing a beautiful backdrop. Whether you come from the Blonay road or Route 12, you end up near Vevey, a pleasant resort that's the headquarters of the Nestlé Company. Be sure to visit the *Alimentarium* (Food Museum), part of the Nestlé

Foundation, with exhibits on food production and processing, the diets of various countries, and tools and utensils from the 18th to the 20th century. Also see the *Old Vevey Museum* (43 Rue Italie; phone: 29-921-0722), where the Wine Growers Fraternity displays models of its costumes dating back to the last century. Although the new freeway to Lausanne is particularly scenic, it's still better to drive there through the vineyards on the specially marked Wine Route (Route de Vignoble) through old villages like Chexbres, Riez, and Grandvaux. On this route, you'll drive along narrow roads, passing old castles (many of which are privately owned), and small pubs and inns that serve regional specialties and their own homegrown white wine. The lake is always in view, and the drive is especially beautiful in late fall when the vineyards turn yellow. Several wine caves are open to visitors. Take the lake road at Lutry and enter Lausanne by way of the port of Ouchy.

LAUSANNE: The route climbs steeply from Ouchy to the Old Town of this youthful, upbeat university city. Recent excavations of neolithic skeletons have dated habitation of the area to the Stone Age, and part of the late Roman city of Lousonna has been unearthed slightly west of here. Starting with its consecration in 1275, however, the cathedral has been the center of town and is closely connected with its history.

It is the most beautiful Gothic building in Switzerland with its picturesque towers, sculptured doors, and relief work; a museum containing some of its treasures is in the splended Bishop's Palace next to it. An unusual, fascinating collection of works by mentally deranged artists, donated to the city by the French painter Jean Dubuffet, is nicely exhibited in an 18th-century palace (*Collection d'Art Brut*, Château de Beaulieu, Av. de Bergières). Farther up the hill, in a lovely villa with a park, is the Hermitage Foundation, which stages important art exhibitions every summer (mainly of the Impressionist and later periods). From the center of town, take a funicular down to Ouchy, a bustling port with lovely views of Lake Geneva and the mountains. Stop into one of the cozy pubs here and sample the raclette — a melted cheese specialty served with small potatoes and pickles.

En Route from Lausanne – A worthwhile, short sidetrip is picturesque Romainmôtier, nestled in a valley some 22 miles (35 km) north of Lausanne via Route 9. Its honey-colored medieval houses are dominated by the oldest and most important Romanesque church in Switzerland. While in town, try the outstanding *tartes* of Madame Pittet at *Café Le Môtier* (closed Mondays; 1323 Romainmôtier; phone: 24-531429). Return to Lausanne and take Route 1 toward Geneva; you'll pass through Morges, a pleasant little town with an excellent view of the lake's widest point, as well as the *Vaud Military Museum*, which displays arms and uniforms dating from 1798. Along the way, Nyon is worth a stop.

NYON: This delightful port, lined with flowers, served Caesar as a base for his Helvetian couriers, and it still bears some traces of Roman times; for example, the god Attis is represented on Caesar's Tower here. The *Roman Museum*, built on the ruins of a recently discovered basilica, is considered the best of its kind in the country. Open daily; closed during lunchtime. The town's ramparts also are worth seeing.

En Route from Nyon – Before reaching Geneva, you may find a stop at Coppet enjoyable; this town features the château where Germaine de Staël, a French-Swiss novelist, lived after Napoleon's affections for her cooled. It's elegantly furnished in Louis XVI style, and has some fine portrait paintings. The best way to enter Geneva is along the lake. (For more information see *Geneva,* THE CITIES.)

BEST EN ROUTE

Although we haven't listed them, there are many small inns in the Jura region that offer good local food and acceptable lodgings. Accommodations on this route tend to be more costly from mid-June through September, and drop off — sometimes significantly — from November through March. We've assigned an expensive rating to hotel rooms costing $180 and up in high season. Accommodations are moderate if they run from $95 to $150. And we've rated rooms inexpensive if they cost $60 or less. Rates are for a double room with a shower. Restaurant prices range from $100 and up for a dinner for two in places listed as expensive, $55 to $85 in those listed as moderate, and around $40 in the inexpensive category. Prices do not include drinks and wine or coffee; tips are included. All restaurants below accept major credit cards, unless otherwise indicated.

BASEL

Bruderholz – In recent years, this elegant restaurant has become one of Switzerland's finest. Outside the center of town, it specializes in French food. Closed Mondays. Reservations essential. 42 Bruder-holzallee (phone: 61-358222). Expensive.

Drei Konige (Three Kings) – The oldest luxury hotel in the country, it boasts a historic guest list — from emperors to authors. It's directly on the Rhine and has 145 excellent rooms and a good restaurant on the terrace. 8 Blumenrain (phone: 61-255252). Expensive.

Schloss Bottmingen – A delightful baroque castle with a moat and a lovely garden is the setting for excellent food and service. Closed Sundays and Mondays. Reservations necessary. 9 Schlossgasse, Bottmingen (phone: 61-471515). Expensive to moderate.

Der Teufelhof – This unusual hostelry is set in an old house near the Kunsthalle. Each of the 8 rooms is decorated by a different artist. There's a restaurant, wine bar with patio, café, and bar, plus 2 small theaters. 47 Leonhardsgraben (phone: 61-251010). Expensive to moderate.

Confiserie Tea Room Schiesser – Basel's most traditional café overlooks the famous 16th-century Town Hall and serves excellent pastries and light snacks. Closed Sundays (and Mondays in summer). Reservations unnecessary. No credit cards accepted. 19 Marktplatz (phone: 61-256077). Moderate.

Krafft am Rhein – In the Klein (small) Basel section, this hotel has a fine view of the cathedral. 12 Rheingasse (phone: 61-691-8877). Moderate.

Kunsthalle – The favorite of many artists, this place is lively and has good food (primarily Italian). Closed Sundays. Reservations unnecessary. No credit cards accepted. 7 Steinenberg (phone: 61-234233). Moderate.

Zum Goldenen Sternen – In Basel's restored, picturesque St. Alban section, Switzerland's oldest pub lacks for nothing in the way of charm. No credit cards accepted (phone: 61-231666). Moderate.

NEUCHÂTEL

Beaulac – A modern hotel beautifully situated on the lake harbor. No credit cards accepted. Quais Léopold-Robert et du Port (phone: 38-258822). Moderate.

Maison des Halles – This popular restaurant is in an ancient building in the Old Town. No credit cards accepted. Rue du Trésor (phone: 38-243141). Moderate to inexpensive.

MURTEN

Vieux Manoir – Set right on the lake with its own private beach, this slightly pretentious hotel has pleasant rooms and an excellent restaurant. Closed mid-December through mid-February. No credit cards accepted. 3280 Meyriez-Morat (phone: 37-711283). Expensive to moderate.

La Channe Valaisanne – Good, reasonable food served in a medieval room that could pass for a small museum. The cellar has vintage wines on exhibit. Closed Mondays. 51 Grande Rue (phone: 37-712565). Moderate to inexpensive.

GRUYÈRES

Chalet – This cozy, rustic restaurant is near the castle. It serves fine fondue, raclette, and other Swiss specialties. 1663 Gruyères (phone: 29-62154). Moderate.

Hôtellerie des Chevaliers – Modern, yet cozy, this hotel just beyond the medieval ramparts offers wonderful views. The rooms feature rustic or period furnishings and fresh flowers. There also is an excellent restaurant. 1663 Gruyères (phone: 29-61933). Moderate.

Hôtellerie de St.-Georges – The windows of this charming, antiques-furnished, old inn face the open country below. There's a big terrace, and an elegant, cozy rotisserie with excellent food. Closed November through March. No credit cards accepted. 1663 Gruyères (phone: 29-62246). Moderate.

LAUSANNE

Beau Rivage Palace – This splendid establishment has been offering elegant lodging for over 100 years. Separated from the lake by a large park, it has an indoor and outdoor pool, tennis courts, and several restaurants. Most of the luxurious rooms have balconies and lovely views. Its *Café Beau Rivage* has become the hottest place in town. 1000 Lausanne-Ouchy (phone: 21-617-1717). Expensive.

Girardet – Managed by chef Fredy Giradet, this restaurant serves the best food in Switzerland — and perhaps in the world! Plan to stop here for a leisurely meal, but be sure to make reservations far in advance — for dinner, 2 months before; for lunch, several weeks before. About 4 miles (6 km) from Lausanne. Closed Sundays and Mondays. No credit cards accepted. 1 Rte. d'Yverdon, Crissier (phone: 21-634-0505). Expensive.

Grappe d'Or – The best place in town for both food and atmosphere; its specialty is meat grilled over a wood fire. Closed Saturdays and Sundays. Reservations necessary. 3 Cheneau de Bourg (phone: 21-230760). Expensive.

Lausanne Palace – Built in 1915, this Swissôtel palace is one of Lausanne's most elegant hotels. On a clear day many of the 167 rooms offer fine views of Lake Geneva and France's Savoy Alps. The *Rotonde,* with marble columns and chandeliers, is a fine place to have tea or breakfast and to people-watch, and *Le Relais* restaurant is the place to go for a romantic dinner. 7-9 Grand Chêne (phone: 21-203711). Expensive.

Alpha – This cheerful, modern 240-room hotel in the heart of Lausanne has a good coffee shop and a cozy cellar restaurant featuring local cheese specialties. Free parking. 34 Rue du Petit-Chêne (phone: 21-230131). Expensive to moderate.

Résidence – Combining two charming old villas, each of the 94 rooms is different. Owned by the same owners as those of the *Beau Rivage* hotel. 15 Pl. du Port (phone: 21-617-7711). Expensive to moderate.

Château d'Ouchy – A romantic hotel in a 12th-century fortress, it provides 85 rooms right on the lake. Pl. du Port (phone: 21-267451). Moderate.

Goya – Here you can find an inexpensive café as well as a more elegant restaurant; both are intimate and good. Reservation unnecessary. No credit cards accepted. 18 Rue de Grand-St.-Jean (phone: 21-312-0266). Moderate to inexpensive.

NYON

Clos de Sadex – This 18th-century lakeside manor house is now a charming, relaxed hotel. No credit cards accepted. Du Clos de Sadex, 131 Rte. de Lausanne (phone: 22-612831). Expensive to moderate.

COPPET

Du Lac – An enchanting small hotel on the lake, it has rustic yet elegant rooms, an outstanding restaurant, and a garden. Coppet 1296 (phone: 22-776-1521). Expensive to moderate.

Zurich to Lugano
via the Four Passes

This, the most scenically spectacular route, with one dramatic highlight after another, takes you zigzagging from north to south through the geographical and historical center of Switzerland, covering eight cantons. The views are often breathtaking: sparkling lakes, snowy peaks, flowery chalets, and pastures with bell-tinkling cows. Although the route is primarily scenic and historical, Lucerne and Lugano offer some points of cultural interest. The Four Passes portion of the trip is possible only in June through October and is closed for the rest of the year; it's advisable to travel here in good weather only. Spend at least 3 days on this 233-mile (373-km) route. You can do it in 2 days if you leave out Lucerne, but even then it would be impossible to absorb everything. It's best to start on the Four Passes circuit in the morning, driving with the sun at your back wherever possible.

En Route from Zurich – Leave Zurich (for more information, see *Zurich*, THE CITIES) on the heavily traveled road to Switzerland's most popular tourist town, Lucerne, then drive along the strangely shaped, highly scenic Lake Lucerne, through the sanctuary of the country, where William Tell shot his legendary apple and the Swiss Confederation started in 1291. (It will help you enjoy all the spots of historical interest on this route if you read Schiller's *William Tell* or a synopsis of it.) You gradually ascend on new, excellent roads into the highest Swiss Alps. The route makes a rough circle through three of the mountain passes, proceeding up and down through frequent hairpin curves and great scenery, and then continues south on the fourth, the St. Gotthard Pass road. This was developed in the 13th century after the frightening Schöllenen Gorge was conquered. It has since become a vital artery for tourist trade and military use. By the way, the 6,940-foot-high St. Gotthard Pass is a favorite maneuver area of the Swiss army, and in spring and fall you are bound to see soldiers. Population is scarce and life extremely difficult in these high regions, but you never have to drive too long before you spot an inn, small village, or service station. On the Gotthard Pass you cross the great north-south divide and the scenery soon becomes different; this is also a weather divide and you often pass from clouds into brilliant sunshine. (Strangely, it is seldom the other way around.) The old inn on the pass, *Vecchia Susta,* was restored and now is a museum, with historic documents, vehicles, and a multimedia show. Another part of the building still houses an inn. The route continues down the Leventine Valley along the Ticino River, which gave its name to the canton, and passes through vineyards, past campaniles and places with Italian names — it's like a different country, though it has been part of Switzerland since 1803. After Bellinzona, the first sturdy palm trees appear and beautiful Lugano is close by. Although the roads are excellent throughout, they're narrow at certain points; at times, they widen into freeways. There's a great deal of traffic in summer and on weekends, so try to avoid it. And don't rush. A rule of the mountain roads is that the ascending car has the right of way, though on this route roads are wide enough for two.

Take the main road to Lucerne along the pleasant, verdant Sihl Valley. The freeway after Sihlbrugg eliminates a slow and uninteresting stretch between Baar and Zug. (If time permits, a short detour to Zug is worthwhile, for its placid lake and charming Old Town.) The main road is nothing special, but it gets you to Lucerne in about an hour.

LUCERNE: This most photographed Swiss city is truly beautiful, even in the bad weather, which it often has. Once a modest fishing village, it became famous and rich as the bridgehead of the important Gotthard route, opened in the 13th century. In 1332, it was the first city to join the Swiss Confederation, then consisting of only the three original cantons. Parts of impressive fortifications, like the Musegg tower and wall, are still standing. The Reformation, which swept most of 16th-century Switzerland, never succeeded in Lucerne, which remains today a Roman Catholic bastion. The yearly mid-August *Music Festival* is one of the most important in Europe. Lucerne deserves several days, but if you only have time for the main sights, start with the town symbol: the famous Kapellbrücke, a covered bridge that spans the Reuss River. Along with the flanking Wasserturm (Water Tower), the bridge served as a fortification against attack. The inside partitions of the bridge are graced with 120 paintings, done in the 16th to 18th centuries, which illustrate Lucerne's history. The tower served as a lookout point, a prison, and an archives, and now belongs to the Artillery Club. Other important sights of Lucerne's Old Town section are the Town Hall (with its historical museum) on Kornmarkt Square, Weinmarkt Square with its lovely painted houses and Renaissance fountain, and the Spreuerbrücke, a covered bridge which has macabre Dance of Death paintings. A walk along the lakeshore quais also is interesting, but another famous Lucerne sight, the Lion Monument (Löwendenkmal; Denkmalstr.) could be left out without much loss. The Gletschergarten (Glacier Garden) next to it is interesting, with its Ice Age glacier potholes and giant stones; there's also a museum containing prehistoric specimens, the first relief map of Switzerland, and some furnishings of old Lucerne. The Cathedral Hofkirche (Leodegarstr.) has an especially atmospheric courtyard, with tombstones in the walls, and the baroque Jesuit Church has been splendidly restored, cheerfully serene in coral and white. The *Verkehrshaus* (Swiss Transport Museum; Lidostr.) is much more interesting than its name indicates: There's a lively exhibition of the development of ships, trains, cars, and planes displaying the oldest specimen of each. The museum also has a marvelous model of the Swiss railway crossing the Gotthard, with 12 trains simultaneously in motion. Also on the premises is the *Hans Erni House,* containing works by the famous Lucerne artist. The *Richard Wagner Museum* is in the southern suburb of Tribschen (in an idyllic villa with a lovely view about 2 miles/3 km from Lucerne). The composer lived here for years and wrote some of his major works. Letters, photographs, and Wagner's original scores can be seen at the museum. The villa also houses an interesting collection of old musical instruments from all over the world. (In winter, it's closed Mondays, Wednesdays, and Fridays.)

Shopping is easy and seductive: Watches and clocks, jewelry, handicrafts, embroidery, and souvenirs all can be bought. Most of the shops are around Schwanenplatz or on the way to the cathedral. To find the largest selection of jewelry, pay a visit to *Bucherer* (5 Schwanenpl.). Nearby, there's a good place to shop for embroidery: *Sturzenegger* (7 Schwanenpl.). Souvenirs also abound near the Lion Monument.

If you spend an evening in Lucerne, don't miss the night boat; it's garish but fun, and the view of the brightly lit town alone makes the trip worthwhile. You can have a fondue dinner or just wine on board, and dance to live folk music. For the best view of the town, have a drink in the pleasant garden of the *Château Gütsch* hotel (Kanonenstr.); the cafés along the Reuss near the Kapellbrücke are also nice stops.

En Route from Lucerne – Drive along Lake Lucerne (also called Vierwaldstättersee, or the Lake of the Four Forest Cantons), with its several distinct branches ("as a handkerchief waving good-bye in four different directions," a poet said), to Meggen. There's an interesting modern church right off the main road. Don't be put off by its exterior: The transparent marble walls inside are wonderful, especially in sunshine. You'll pass Merlischachen and its steep wooden houses with their first floors elevated high above the ground; these houses, accessible only by stairs, are typical of this region. Here also is the Astridchapel, built where Queen Astrid of Belgium had a fatal car accident in 1935. Küssnacht, a little town with an important role in early Swiss history, features the *Engel* hotel, a most remarkable historic building on its main square. Only a mile (1.6 km) outside town, on Route 2, is the famous Hohle Gasse; park your car and walk the short sunken road where, according to the legend, William Tell waited to kill Bailiff Gessler. There's a small chapel at the end of the road commemorating his success. Route 2 continues on the shore of Lake Zug to Arth and Goldau, under the slopes of Mount Rigi, with extraordinary views all along, then passes charming little Lauerzer Lake. The *Insel Schwanau* (see *Best en Route*) is a good place to stop for lunch or a drink beneath the ruins of a former fortress. You have to ring the bell on shore for a boat to pick you up. From here, it's only 3 miles (5 km) to Schwyz, which is not on the main road, but worth a short visit. (The fast freeway from Arth bypasses Lauerz. If you want to travel really fast, the freeway from Lucerne, on the alternate lakeside through the long Seelisberg tunnel, takes you directly to Altdorf.)

A more scenic and longer road from Küssnacht to Schwyz follows the sometimes rocky shores of the lake on the "Lucerne Riviera," where flowers blossom early in the season, through the resort areas of Weggis and Vitznau. Vitznau has Europe's oldest rack-and-pinion railway to Mount Rigi. Built by its inventor in 1871, the railway still has over 95% of its original cog racks; the ride up the steep slope is filled with wonderful views. Several lakeshore restaurants along the way specialize in fish. A high, rocky road leads to Gersau, a tiny sovereign republic for more than 425 years (1390–1817); the lake is deepest here, and has lovely underwater scenery.

If you want to leave Lucerne out of your itinerary, you can proceed directly from Zurich on the freeway to Arth and Schwyz or Brunnen; it's also very scenic.

SCHWYZ: This town provided Switzerland with its name and flag, and its Archive of Federal Charters (off Bahnhofstr.) preserves the original Covenant of Confederation of 1291. The 16th-century Town Hall, in picturesque Town Hall Square (Rathauspl.) has paintings of historical scenes on its exterior walls. Schwyz, a predominantly Catholic town, supplies the Vatican with some of the Swiss Guard.

BRUNNEN: Many famous guests, including Queen Victoria and Richard Wagner, have visited this old-fashioned resort. It used to be a shelter from the ferocious *föhn* storms, which can whip up the water into 400-foot spouts. Across the lake is Treib, another old storm refuge and a traditional asylum for fugitives. It was the meeting place of the first Confederation of Switzerland; you can still see the first house of parliament, the parlor of a local inn.

En Route from Brunnen – The magnificent Axenstrasse is a road hewn in rock high above the fjord-like Urner Lake (still part of Lake Lucerne), and for 10 miles the view of the steep wild shores across, the deep blue water below, and the Alps ahead is unforgettable. In season, the traffic is quite heavy, but the scenery compensates for everything. Several lookout points between Brunnen and Sisikon provide views of historic Rütli Field, where the representatives of the original cantons took a solemn oath of independence from the Hapsburgs, according to Schiller. Each year, on August 1, speeches and celebrations are held here in commemoration of a national holiday. After Sisikon, a tunnel replaces the open mountain road — it's safer for cars, but takes away the view. Leave your car at the south end of the tunnel and walk along the old road, a perfect place to take pictures. The William Tell Chapel (Tellskapelle) commemorates another dramatic event in the Tell legend: Held captive on his enemies' boat, Tell took advantage of a sudden storm and leaped to shore. A short, steep path leads down to the chapel from the roadside parking area. The lake ends at Flüelen and you can continue on the new freeway or drive through Altdorf, the small capital of Uri Canton (one of the original three) and see the statue of William Tell in the main square. Erected in 1895, it has since been made famous by its representation on Swiss postage stamps. Both roads follow the Reuss Valley and slowly start to climb the St. Gotthard massif. If you're interested in trains, drive through Erstfeld; the model in the *Lucerne Transport Museum* is based on the busy railroad station here (see *Lucerne*).

AMSTEG: This is the last village before the big climb starts, and if you haven't stopped yet, the *Stern and Post* hotel is ideal; it has served as a stopover for travelers on stagecoaches and other vehicles for over 150 years (see *Best en Route*).

En Route from Amsteg – The smooth freeway takes you up to Wassen effortlessly. There's a remarkable waterfall, Pfaffensprung, nearby, but you have to park off the old road before Wassen to see it; the cascading waters produce some marvelous rainbows as they hit the rocks. From Wassen, take the old road to Göschenen; this should give you a good idea of how difficult it was to build a road up the Gotthard massif 600 years ago. Göschenen's lively railroad station is found at the north end of the two tunnels that convey trains and cars through the pass. From here, you can get a good view of the Upper Dammastock ice field. Next you pass through the Reuss Valley with its smooth, granite walls culminating in a legendary bottleneck, The Schöllenen Gorge. This narrow passage made the development of a route southward through the Gotthard Pass impossible until the 13th century, when a road was driven through the gorge. The new road diminishes the contemporary traveler's feeling for the eeriness of the place. To recapture some of that awe, park your car near Devil's Bridge (Teufelsbrücke) and take a short walk on the old road. The bridge itself replaced another bridge here, which, according to legend, was built with the aid of the Devil, who asked to be paid with the soul of the first creature to cross it. The result angered the Devil a great deal — the creature turned out to be a goat. The enraged Devil then heaved a huge stone into the valley; one of the large rocks a short distance before the gorge is called the Devil's Stone.

After the gorge, head for Andermatt, a popular ski resort and a true crossroads of the Alps. The Furka and St. Gotthard roads have their junction here. Driving back to Wassen, you get a completely different view of the scenery than you had on the way to Andermatt. At Wassen, take the Susten road going west, unless it is afternoon and the light is against you.

The Susten Road, finished in 1945, was the first Swiss mountain road built especially for motorists. As it starts its steady climb, the route presents an interesting view of the jagged crests of a group of mountains called the Five Fingers. Driving through the upper hairpin bends, you'll see the panorama widen to a final view of the valley. Before you reach the tunnel through the road's crest, you can stop and survey the peaks from a viewing table. Walk to the road's highest point — 7,411 feet — from the large parking lot at the tunnel's west end. The view for the next few miles is the most magnificent the route offers: You'll see an arctic landscape at the foot of the Stein glacier, including a small lake complete with miniature icebergs. You can park at several road bends to enjoy views of the steep descents (from the *Susten Pass* hotel, a short "glacier road" leads even deeper into ice, snow, and rocks). After passing through some fertile valleys, you'll reach Innertkirchen, where you can pick up the Grimsel Road; the ancient *Tännler Inn*, before the junction, is a good place to rest.

The Grimsel Road first passes through pastoral scenery with some huge escarpments. (The avalanches are fierce here in the winter.) Then the views become more and more Dantesque — enormous granite rocks, slabs, and walls polished smooth and shiny by glacier action. Park your car for a view of the spectacular Handegg Waterfall cascading into a narrow gorge. Next, after a small, turquoise lake is the surrealistic Lake of Grimsel — an elongated reservoir created by two dams. The steep upward bends provide the best view of the lake; at the road's crest there's another small lake where a battle between the Austrians and the French took place in 1799. From here you can turn down to Gletsch, where the Furka Road begins, and catch a first glimpse of the Rhône glacier.

Although Gletsch itself consists of only a few houses, it's a good place to view the constantly receding glacier. Today, the glacier isn't in the basin, but photos of 100 years ago show it reaching the valley. This is where the Rhône, one of the longest rivers of Europe, starts its course. As you climb the Furka, every bend supplies another view of the glacier; the best one is just before the now defunct *Belvedere* hotel. Even though it's disappointingly gray and dirty on the surface because of the heavy flow of traffic, the glacier still is impressive. Stop at the *Belvedere,* which has enough parking space and is the best point from which to view the panorama of the Bernese and Valais Alps. But the main attraction is the ice grotto that's cut into the glacier: Its transparent walls glitter with an unbeliev- able bluish light as the sun comes through the crevasses. A few miles beyond is the highest point of the Furka Pass, measuring 7,975 feet, with the Galenstock peak hovering above. The road skirts the Alps descending, first gently, then steeply, toward Realp, providing a sweeping view of the barren valley below.

If you don't want to make another stop at Andermatt, turn off at Hospenthal (marked by an old watchtower) to pick up the Gotthard Road. After a few steep turns, the scenery becomes desolate; the road's crest at 6,919 feet has rocks and glacial ponds that are very uninviting. The pass owes its name to a chapel of the patron saint that was built here in about 1300. From here, you can take either the new freeway through the tunnel and viaduct, or the smaller, steeper, somewhat more scenic one through the Tremola, with its view of the Leventine Valley below, to Airolo, a tunnel exit station and tourist resort. Take the freeway from here, as the smaller road (Route 2) is not as scenic.

The Leventine Valley is not very interesting compared to all you have already seen, but the driving's quite fast. Rough stone houses, chestnut trees, and the campaniles of the Ticino River area appear; there are several rushing waterfalls and, a little farther on, vineyards. Giornico has a remarkable Romanesque church, San Nicolao, and charming houses off the main road. You may want to stop at Bellinzona or bypass it and Monte Ceneri on the new but unscenic autobahn.

BELLINZONA: This administrative center of Ticino Canton has guarded the valley for centuries with three old castles. One of them, Castello Montebello, now houses the excellent historical and archaeological *City Museum.* Castello di Sasso Corbaro has a beautiful view and a café.

En Route from Bellinzona – The plain widens and soon Route 2 starts a steep but short climb up Monte Ceneri and offers wonderful glimpses of the Lago Maggiore below. It's about 10 minutes to Lugano from here. For a more scenic approach, take the exit marked "Lugano Süd (south) and Paradiso."

BEST EN ROUTE

Accommodations on this route tend to be more costly from mid-June through Septem- ber, and drop off — sometimes significantly — from November through March. We've assigned an expensive rating to hotel rooms costing $170 and up in high season. Accommodations are moderate if they run from $100 to $150. And we've rated rooms inexpensive if they cost $80 or less. Rates are for a double room with a shower. Restaurant prices range from $100 and up for a dinner for two in places listed as expensive, $50 to $85 in those listed as moderate, and around $40 in the inexpensive category. Prices do not include drinks and wine or coffee; tips are included. All restaurants below accept major credit cards, unless otherwise indicated. Reservations are advised at all restaurants.

LUCERNE

National – Known for its comfortable and luxurious rooms with views of Lake Lucerne, the hotel also has a popular Viennese café with a terrace that's open in summer months. 4 Haldenstr. (phone: 41-501111). Expensive.

Palace – Lucerne's other high-quality hotel, it also has very comfortable accommodations with lake views. 10 Haldenstr. (phone: 41-502222). Expensive.

Raben – In a medieval building in the Old Town, this is one of Lucerne's best restaurants. It is owned and run by cookbook author Marianne Kaltenbach, who presents delicious, inventive dishes. Major credit cards accepted. Kornmarkt (phone: 41-515135). Expensive.

Des Balances – On the Reuss River in the Old Town, this hotel is furnished with antiques. Weinmarkt (phone: 41-511851). Expensive to moderate.

Old Swiss House – This famous restaurant near the Lion Monument has lovely rustic decor and serves Swiss and international fare. Closed Mondays. 4 Löwenpl. (phone: 41-516171). Expensive to moderate.

Château Gütsch – Featuring a fabulous view from its hillside perch, the hotel has a good restaurant in a rustic setting and serves drinks and snacks in its garden. Since it's a bit difficult to find the place at first, the hotel runs a private cable car from the center of town. Kanonenstr. (phone: 41-220272). Moderate.

Wilden Mann – Owned by the same family for over 100 years, this establishment in an ancient house has small but very charming rooms. Its tavern and elegant restaurant serve excellent food. 30 Bahnofstr. (phone: 41-231666). Moderate.

Royal – This pleasant spot, a bit away from the center of town, offers magnificent views and comfortable rooms — an excellent value. 22 Rigistr. (phone: 41-511233). Moderate to inexpensive.

Pickwick – An informal little hotel on the river in the Old Town that has an amusing custom: Each patron gets an apple at night. Breakfast vouchers for a nearby restaurant are supplied on request. No credit cards accepted. (Since it's difficult to find the entrance, ask at the *Pickwick Club*.) 6 Rathausquai (phone: 41-515927). Inexpensive.

Weinhof – A typical Swiss restaurant, small, cozy, and reasonably priced. Closed Saturdays. No credit cards accepted. 12 Weystr. (phone: 41-511251). Inexpensive.

MERLISCHACHEN

Swiss Chalet – This touristy but very attractive motel-restaurant on the main road serves good snacks. The attached, charming *Schloss* hotel is directly on the lake. Rte. 2 (phone: 41-371247). Moderate.

KÜSSNACHT

Gasthof Engel – A splendid example of old local architecture, this hotel was the site of the Helvetian Confederation's sessions from 1423 to 1712. Closed in winter. No credit cards accepted (phone: 41-811057). Inexpensive.

VITZNAU

Park – An Art Nouveau castle directly on the lake, with Old World atmosphere and a big park — in good weather, a fairy tale come true. The hotel's spacious rooms have marble baths, and there's also a good restaurant. No credit cards accepted. Kantonsstr. (phone: 41-830100). Expensive.

LAUERZERSEE

Insel Schwanau – In a highly romantic setting on a tiny island after which it's named, this restaurant serves good food. You must ring the bell on the lakeshore to be picked up by a boat. Closed in winter. No credit cards accepted. Insel Schwanau (phone: 43-211757). Moderate.

BRUNNEN

Waldhaus Wolfsprung – This small chalet-hotel furnished with brass beds and Persian rugs is in a forest above an Alpine lake and has a private beach. Closed in winter. No credit cards accepted. 12 Axenstr. (phone: 43-311173). Moderate.

ALTDORF

Goldener Schlüssel – A small hostelry in a charming historic house in the center of town. No credit cards accepted. Altdorf 6460 (phone: 44-21002). Inexpensive.

AMSTEG

Stern and Post – A comfortable old stagecoach inn, it features excellent food and paneled, antiques-filled rooms (phone: 44-64440). Moderate to inexpensive.

INNERTKIRCHEN

Gasthof Tännler – In a lovely old farmhouse, the hotel's rooms are comfortably appointed, but don't have separate baths. No credit cards accepted. Susten Pass road (phone: 36-711427). Inexpensive.

Zurich to Lugano
via the Engadine

This 204-mile (325-km) route contains scenery that's dotted with architectural jewels, and takes you through the center of Swiss tourism, the Graubünden (Canton Grisons). Romansh, a language stemming from Illyrian and Latin, is still spoken here; sections of the canton once formed part of ancient Rhaetia, a province of the Roman Empire. The Rhaetians resisted both the Celts (who, in pre-Roman times, occupied all of present Switzerland except Grisons) and the Germanic tribes, who came after the Romans. Rhaetia completely controlled the north-south Alpine crossings before the Gotthard Pass was opened. Ruled by feudal lords and bishops, the Rhaetians formed an alliance with three other groups in the 15th century. Wars, Hapsburg rule, and more wars typify the ensuing history of the area, and the many castles and ruins are vivid signs of this. The canton joined the Swiss Confederation in 1803, but Romansh officially became the country's fourth national language in 1938. Swiss German also is spoken here.

This is the region of Switzerland that's known as the Engadine, a particularly pastoral, scenic stretch, full of images straight out of "Heidi." Somehow, the sight of beige-colored cows grazing with large bells clanging around their necks, set against an Alpine background, is simply perfect for the scenery-lovers in the crowd. Although the passes of the route are open year-round, September is perhaps the best time to take the trip because the special light of the Engadine is most evident then. Spring, when you can see the over-whelming contrast of snowy Grisons with blossoming Ticino, is also a good time to go. Though it's almost as mountainous, this route has scenery that's quite different than that of the central Alps — it's less forbidding, and has more color and variety. Starting again from Zurich in the north, you drive southeast, passing by Lake Walensee, to Chur, the artistic, cultural, and administrative center of the canton; then you climb through spruce-covered mountains to the ancient Roman Julier Pass and descend into the extraordinary Engadine Valley. Here are Switzerland's most famous resorts, including St. Moritz, the queen of them all. From here, the route proceeds down to warmer regions and chestnut groves, dipping briefly into Italy along Lake Como, and turns back into Switzerland's Tessin (Ticino), a cheerful canton that has retained its Lombardian culture since becoming part of Switzerland in 1803.

Although the roads are always excellent, on weekends they're usually crowded. This is a perfect route for seeing the high mountains in winter, as most other crossings are closed, and the skiing is unequaled anywhere. Your car will need winter equipment into late spring. Spend at least 3 days and 2 nights — and preferably more. And don't miss Grisons' culinary specialties of *Bündnerfleisch* (paper-thin slices of air-dried beef that are eaten with the fingers) and rich, delicious nutcake; with a glass of wine, the two make a perfect light meal.

En Route from Zurich – Drive along the highway running adjacent to Lake Zurich; there's a lovely view of the lake and the distant mountains. Traffic gets very heavy at Lake Walensee, but the grand scenery of sheer rocks, waterfalls, and the characteristically jagged peaks make up for it. The lake is treacherous, with sudden storms that take their toll in damages each year. The fortress of Sargans, visible from afar, looms over this important medieval trading route. Soon afterward is Bad Ragaz — the best-known health spa in the country: Its mineral waters have been in use since the 11th century. (In the old days, patients were lowered down with ropes to springs located a little farther on in the Tamina Gorge.) It has elegant hotels, lovely parks, and an 18-hole golf course. Next is Maienfeld, a charming, sleepy little town with beautiful patrician houses. The valley here follows the Rhine, the longest river in Europe, as it flows down the Alps. And the pastures are "Heidi country" — they served as the setting for the famous book.

CHUR: Recent excavations here date the city back to 3000 BC. After the Roman period, Chur was a center of Christianity. Walk the narrow streets of the enchanting old town with its medieval houses, and after crossing under an old gate, climb the steps to the cathedral; there's a famous Gothic triptych inside, as well as a pre-Christian sacrificial stone, near the altar. The splendid baroque Bishop's Palace (Hof), next to the cathedral, is still the bishop's residence. The *Hofkellerei* (see *Best en Route*), a pub in the Bishop's Palace, is a good place for some *Bündnerfleish* or other refreshments. The *Rhaetian Museum,* set in a 17th-century mansion on Hofstrasse, has many prehistoric, Roman, and medieval treasures.

En Route from Chur – Leaving Chur, Route 3 climbs steeply, offering a wonderful view of the city and its many spires. The road leads through scented, moss-covered woods to Lenzerheide, a popular resort with one of the most unusual hotels, *Guarda Val;* the hotel's Alpine barns make it worth a stop, even if you don't spend the night (see *Best en Route*). In Lenz (Lantsch), the language changes from

German to Romansh and road signs are bilingual. The village itself has an interesting cemetery with ornate iron crosses. This lovely drive through meadows, rounded hillsides, distant chapels, and sweeping views steeply descends toward Tiefencastel, in the Albula Valley. A white church tower marks Tiefencastel, but the real attraction is the Carolingian Church of St. Peter of Mistail, built in AD 926. Ask townspeople for directions to the church; they'll also tell you where to get the key if the church is closed. Castle ruins dot the slopes along the road from here, reminders of a turbulent past; you'll pass through Savognin (a resort with three notable baroque churches), to the Marmorera Dam Reservoir, which has flooded two tiny hamlets. Bivio has a jewel of a Catholic church with Renaissance and baroque interiors. The ancient Roman Septimer road branches off from here, and is open only to hikers. The austere Julier Pass, 7,494 feet, used by the Romans, is still the main entrance to the Engadine. Its Latinate name recalls the important role of the Romans in the early Swiss history — two roadside markers are parts of a former Roman temple. From the final steep bends of the now-descending road there's a wonderful panorama of almost the entire Engadine Valley. Its clear sky, beautiful lakes, charming architecture, and extraordinary scenery justify its fame. Excursions in the valley are easily taken; Silvaplana is the first village in the Engadine, and a few minutes away is glittering St. Moritz.

ST. MORITZ: The town itself is disappointing, as its urban streets and houses are without charm or character. But the lakeside setting, excellent climate, mineral spas, and jet-set guests have made it famous. The Mauritius Springs have been in use here for about 3,000 years. Don't miss the *Engadine Museum* (on the road to the baths), a delightful reconstruction of local architectural styles, including typical *sgrafitti* (plaster decorations) and a wide-ranging collection of furniture, illustrating the domestic life of farmers, bishops, and lords. The *Segantini Museum* (30 Via la Somplaz) contains works of the Engadine's most famous painter, Giovanni Segantini, an Italian of the late 19th century. Winter is the best time for celebrity watching, and the *Palace* hotel (27 Via Serlas; see *Best en Route*) is a good place to do it — its *King's Club* is a center of nightlife here, but activities don't start until midnight. For more moderate fare, try the charming *Chesa Veglia* (also in the *Palace* hotel) for tea or dinner. Or check out the excellent nutcake at *Café Hanselmann,* (8 Via Maistra). Though recent winters have been unprecedently mild, skiing usually is superb, snow and sun almost guaranteed; and, at sporting events and on the slopes, you can rub elbows with active and inactive royalty and movie stars who generally have their own homes up here. There are opportunities for dozens of excursions and walks, but there are two things you should do even if you have little time at your disposal: a cable car ride up Muottas Muragl (8,084 feet) for a spellbinding view of the upper Engadine Valley, and a walk along the Sils Lake on a well-kept footpath. On the latter walk, stop at the Italian-speaking hamlet of Isola for delicious, homemade cheese and a drink. The German philosopher Friedrich Nietzsche spent much time around here, and his house in Sils is now a small museum. A ride up the Corvatsch, 10,840 feet, from Silvaplana takes you to eternal snow and summer skiing. In season, there are many cultural events in St. Moritz, featuring famous artists. Golf, horseback riding, tennis, swimming (in pools, because the lakes are too cold), sailing, and windsurfing also are available.

You also can catch the *Glacier Express* here. Every day one train heads out of St. Moritz at exactly 10:10 AM, heading east for Zermatt and the Matterhorn. At the same time, its sister train pulls away from Zermatt, heading for St. Moritz. Between the two nonpareil Swiss resorts, riders spend just under 6½ hours passing through scenery that just might comprise the world's longest snow-covered postcard. The *Glacier Express* honors the unlimited-mileage SwissPass and Swiss Flexipass, but reservations must be made well in advance. For more information contact the Swiss National Tourist Board, 608 5th Avenue, New York, NY 10020 (phone: 212-757-5944).

En Route from St. Moritz – After driving along the Silvaplana and Silser lakes you come to the Maloja Pass, which is not really a pass at all (as it's lower than St. Moritz), but the upcoming sharp drop and curving steep road make it look like one. At the peak of the road, opposite the *Maloja Kulm* hotel, there's a beautiful lookout over the Bergell Valley ahead. This valley has its very own characteristics: It's still Alpine but has undeniably southern traits that become more and more pronounced with every turn. Sections of the old Roman road interlace it.

In Vicosoprano, a medieval tower attached to the Town Hall was a prison and torture chamber used for witch trials in the 16th century. (If it's closed, ask at the office.) A short detour to Soglio is a must: Taking the narrow, winding road through chestnut groves, you reach this spectacular little village on a ledge, with its palaces of the once powerful and still prominent Salis family. The best known of the palaces, the charming *Palazzo Salis* hotel, has a romantic garden (see *Best en Route*). There's also a magnificent view from the little cemetery. At Castasegna, the Alpine vegetation is left behind as you cross into Italy, and vineyards and fruit trees appear, and the architecture becomes distinctly southern. After Chiavenna, take the narrow principal road along the western side of Lake Como toward Como and Lugano; although the road periodically has heavy traffic, the lake is beautiful. At Menaggio take Road 340 right — watch for the tricky turnoff, it's easy to miss — to Lake Lugano (Italians call it Lago di Ceresio). The lake is narrow and finger-shaped here, and there are steep, wooded, roadless slopes on the other side. Near Lugano, between the principal road and the lake, is Gandria, a charming village that's worth a side trip.

GANDRIA: Explore the village by climbing up and down its steps, going under its arches, and walking between its old arcaded houses. It has many boutiques and is a typical artist's village. Sit on the terrace of a café hanging out over the water, and gaze at rows of pastel houses rising directly from the lake. The *Smuggler's Museum,* in an original hideaway on the other side of the lake, is approachable by boat only. Boats usually leave twice a day from Gandria.

En Route from Gandria – At Castagnola the bay opens out and you get the full visual impact of Lugano, one of Switzerland's most picturesque towns.

LUGANO: This cultural center of Ticino is ideal for a spring or fall sojourn. It features a palm tree–lined lakeshore promenade, arcaded streets, sunny piazzas with cafés, and the beautiful old church of Santa Maria degli Angioli with its famous 16th-century frescoes. The main artistic attraction is the *Villa Favorita,* a splendid private art collection of European masters in the owner's residence (if you happen to have $30 million, the villa is for sale) on Castagnola Road (open daily except Mondays from 10 AM to 5 PM; admission charge). Part of the collection is in the *Prado* (see "Twenty-Five Centuries of History: Europe's Great Museums" in *For the Mind,* DIVERSIONS). A 10-minute funicular ride from the Paradiso quarter up Monte San Salvatore provides a fabulous circular panorama of lakes and Alps. You can get an even more sweeping view from Monte Bré on the other side of Lugano. It's possible to drive there via a very narrow, very steep road, but it's easier to take the funicular from Cassarate Road. Boat trips on the lake run frequently and are highly recommended. In the Italian village of Campione, 10 minutes away by boat or car, the casino has craps and blackjack.

BEST EN ROUTE

Accommodations on this route can be costly, especially in famed resorts and health spas like St. Moritz and Bad Ragaz. Hotels that charge $200 to $300 and up for a double room with shower for a night get an expensive rating; extremely elegant resorts, like the *Palace, Suvretta, Kulm,* and *Carlton* hotels in St. Moritz, are considerably more expensive. Accommodations ranging from $100 to $200 are moderate, and those costing below $90 for two for a night in high season are rated inexpensive. Most of these hotels only have half-board plans. Restaurants range in price from $100 and up for a dinner for two in places listed as expensive, $55 to $85 in those listed as moderate, and around $40 in the inexpensive category. Prices do not include drinks, wine or coffee; the tip is included. All restaurants below accept major credit cards, unless otherwise indicated. Reservations are advised at all restaurants unless otherwise noted.

BAD RAGAZ

Quellenhof – The most elegant hotel at the spa. No credit cards accepted. Bad Ragaz 7310 (phone: 85-90111). Expensive.

Schloss Ragaz – A small château with a few charming rooms, plus several modern bungalows. It's in a large park and has a swimming pool. Bad Ragaz 7310 (phone: 85-92355). Moderate to inexpensive.

CHUR

Hofkellerei – In the Bishop's Palace, this old pub features regional furniture and serves local specialties. Reservations unnecessary. No credit cards accepted. 1 Hof (phone: 81-233230). Moderate to inexpensive.

Stern – This 300-year-old inn serves outstanding cuisine, including Grisons specialties. No credit cards accepted. 11 Reichsgasse (phone: 81-223555). Moderate to inexpensive.

LENZERHEIDE

Guarda Val – All the modern comforts are provided at this hotel despite its rustic, Alpine, barnlike exterior. Its enchanting restaurant is on a big terrace. Coming down from Chur, turn right as you enter Lenzerheide (phone: 81-342214). Expensive to moderate.

ST. MORITZ

Badrutt's Palace – It looks like a gingerbread castle, on a hillside with lake and mountain views, and draws a jet-set crowd. They come for the luxurious rooms (270 in all), the spacious French restaurant, the renowned wine cellar, the fitness center, and, presumably, for that seductive well-pampered feeling. Via Serias (phone: 82-21101). Very expensive.

Suvretta House – "What the *Palace* strives for, the *Suvretta* has already achieved," says one guest. This very exclusive hotel attracts old money. A 9-story castle of a building, it is off the beaten track — a self-sustaining resort with its own ski school and private lift, not to mention 2 bowling alleys and an award-winning restaurant. Note: They now accept credit cards. Off Via Suvretta (phone: 82-21121). Very expensive.

Chesa Veglia – Owned by the *Palace* hotel, this restaurant-café has a delightful Grisons interior and serves dinner, afternoon tea, and snacks. No credit cards accepted (phone: 82-33596). Expensive.

Steffani – A cozy family hotel in the center of town that serves Grisons specialties in its restaurant. Open daily (phone: 82-22101). Expensive to moderate.

Café Hanselmann – This popular watering hole serves the best cakes in town. No credit cards accepted. Via Maistra (phone: 82-33864). Moderate.

Veltinerkeller – A perfect place for sampling local specialties, especially grilled meat and homemade pasta dishes. Open daily. No credit cards accepted (phone: 82-34009). Moderate.

SILVAPLANA

La Staila – A small hotel in a historic house; a good value (phone: 82-48147). Moderate.

SOGLIO

Palazzo Salis – In one of the Old Town palaces, this establishment affords a very exclusive atmosphere, even if the comfort isn't always perfect. There's a small garden and a good restaurant. Closed in winter. In high season, reservations are advised. No credit cards accepted (phone: 82-41208). Inexpensive.

LUGANO

Bianchi – Reopened last year and restored to its grandeur of 200 years past, this fabulous eatery specializes in fresh fish dishes and meat entrées with an Italian flair. Closed Sundays and 3 weeks in August. 3 Via Pessina (phone: 91-228479; reservations: 91-234203; fax: 91-233868). Expensive.

Splendide Royal – Featuring Old World elegance, modern comfort, and excellent service, this hotel has rooms with fabulous terraces on the lake. A good value. 7 Riva A. Caccia (phone: 91-542001). Expensive.

Villa Principe Leopoldo – This former residence of the Hohenzollern princes overlooks the town and lake. Its luxurious junior suites are furnished in cozy pastels. There also is an excellent restaurant (open daily). 5 Via Montalbano (phone: 91-558855). Expensive.

Al Portone – This little restaurant serves outstanding Italian food. Closed Sundays and Mondays for lunch. 3 Via Cassarate (phone: 91-235995). Expensive to moderate.

Europa Grand – On the central lake promenade, this comfortable, modern place has spacious rooms, some with balconies and all with color TV sets and air conditioning. There is an indoor pool with a sun terrace and several restaurants. 1 Via Cattori (phone: 91-550171). Moderate.

Grand Hotel Villa Castagnola – This venerable (100-year-old) establishment recently re-emerged in renewed splendor after a thorough restoration. Most rooms face the pleasant park and lake. There is a covered pool, a beach, tennis courts, and a fitness room. Within walking distance of the famous Thyssen Collection in *Villa Favorita*. 31 Viale Castagnola, Lugano-Cassarate 6906 (phone: 91-512213). Moderate.

Romantik-Hotel Ticino – In an old Tessin palazzo, the rooms surround a charming inside patio. A small, vine-covered terrace and rustic pub are attached. Closed for 6 weeks during the winter. 1 Piazza Cioccaro (phone: 91-227772). Moderate.

Antico – A restaurant featuring a vine-covered dining terrace overlooking the lake. Closed in winter. Gandria (phone: 91-514871). Inexpensive.

Bern to Montreux

Starting in Bern, the capital of Switzerland and one of Europe's loveliest cities, this 184-mile (294-km) route first proceeds east and south to the mountainous Bernese Oberland and then into the unique Valais region, ending up in Montreux, a popular resort on Lake Geneva. Count on 3 days for the tour; the best time to see Valais is in October, when its colors are most beautiful.

This route combines scenic, historical, and cultural attractions, and is passable all year round. To climb to the eternal snows of the impressive Jungfrau, however, you have to take a special train.

Although you'll see some lovely pastoral scenery, replete with flowers and clear blue lakes, in the Bernese Oberland, it's the Alpine triumvirate of Eiger, Mönch, and Jungfrau that make the area exceptional. With Interlaken as the jumping-off point, this is one of the world's most famous mountain recreational spots. The upper Rhône Valley, forming part of the canton of Valais, is an altogether different world. Isolated from the rest of the country by the steep mountains, its warm climate and abundant vegetation make it reminiscent of Provence; indeed, the Valais is Switzerland's main wine growing region. Ruins and castles dot the slopes, and numerous museums and churches bear witness to the canton's historical importance. And the amazing lateral valleys, ascending quickly to more than 6,000 feet, should definitely be explored.

The Bernese and Valais people share a similar history; the region was ruled successively by Celts, Romans, Germanic tribes, and the Holy Roman Empire. Then came the rapid expansion of German-speaking Bern, which eventually dominated more than one third of present Switzerland. The Valais, where the Romans first settled, was later divided between German and French influence and today the eastern part is still German and the western part French. Napoleon temporarily annexed Valais for France and began building the Simplon Pass Road (a passage already used by the Romans), but he did not live to see it in use.

BERN: Built on a peninsula of the winding Aare River, this enchanting capital has kept its character intact. The Duke of Zähringen established the city in 1191 on his thickly wooded hunting ground. It was agreed that the first animal caught on a particular hunt would supply the new city with its name; when the creature turned out to be a bear, the duke dubbed the town Bärn, from which its present name derives, and placed a bear on its coat of arms. In 1353 Bern joined the confederation and later became extremely powerful because of its aggressive expansionist policies. The canton has tenaciously held onto its annexed territories — Jura broke away as recently as 1979. In 1848 Bern was chosen as the seat of the federal government, replacing Zurich.

The arcaded streets of the Old Town are the city's true main attraction, featuring the Gothic and baroque façades of homes that are often incredibly luxurious inside. (Take a look at the houses on Junkerngasse, for example — it's the city's most prestigious street address.) In 1405, the wooden houses of the Old Town were completely destroyed by fire; but by the 18th century, they were completely rebuilt in the yellow green sandstone you see here today. Modern Bern simply grew up around the older city, and the aristocratic tradition contrasts nicely with a youthful spirit that also characterizes this university town. Somewhat typically, recently discovered medieval fortifications are structurally integrated with an underground passage in the main railroad station, and explanatory notes have been supplied. All of Old Bern's significant sights are within walking distance of each other, and the tourist office (in the main railway station; phone: 31-227676) provides an excellent map of the center of town.

Walk to the Nydegg Bridge for a good view of the irregular group of roofs atop the houses at the bend of the Aare River; as a result of a law quite unusual for the symmetry-minded Swiss, these domiciles could not be built at the same size and height. A few steps across the bridge, you'll find the Bärengraben (Bear Pit), which houses a number of the city's symbolic animals. Across the bridge in the opposite direction, and a short distance down Junkerngasse, the high tower and flying buttresses of the cathedral of St. Vincent (Münster) come into view. The main portal of this impressive Gothic church features several old statues (some of them still painted) depicting aspects of the Last Judgment and dating from the beginning of the 16th century. And if you don't mind climbing the 254 steps to the tower's platform, you'll be rewarded with an excellent panorama of the town and the Bernese Alps. Farther west is the Zytglocke (Clock Tower), first built in the 12th century and restored in the 16th; at regular intervals during the day, large groups of people cluster to view the mechanical jesters, bears, and kings perform at 4 minutes before the hour in the tower of the astronomical clock. For souvenirs bearing Bern's bear symbol, visit *Heimatwerk,* which carries Swiss crafts (61 Kramgasse), or the *Abegglen* bakery, which sells chocolates and honey cakes (36 Spitalgasse).

The dignified, domed Parliament Building is in the Florentine Renaissance style, and one of its regular guided tours can provide some idea of the workings of Swiss government. Every Tuesday and Saturday, there's a lovely flower market in front. Walk along the high Kirchenfeldbrücke for a different view of town around the Parliament building.

The museums of Bern are worth a separate trip; the *Kunstmuseum* (Fine Arts Museum), for example, has the largest collection of works by Paul Klee, a native of Bern, and a great number of modern French paintings (Hodlerstr.). The *Kunsthalle* (Helvetiapl.) houses temporary exhibitions of the latest in international art. The *Bernese Historical Museum* features booty from the Burgundian wars and from other expansionist escapades, including arms, standards, tapestries, and manuscripts, as well as beautiful furniture from later periods (Helvetiapl.). Others are the *Natural History Museum* (Bernastr.) with its imaginative display of animals in natural surroundings; the *Swiss Alpine Museum* (Helvetiapl.), which has models of early alpinism and skiing, and reliefs of the Alps; and the *Swiss Postal Museum,* in the same building as the *Alpine Museum,* with one of the largest permanent stamp collections of the world. The National Library has one of the most extensive Bible collections anywhere (Hallwylstr.).

Cellars are as characteristic as arcades in the Old Town, and they now serve mainly as art galleries, boutiques, theaters, and restaurants. One of the most interesting cellar attractions is the oldest wine tavern of Bern, the *Klötzlikeller* (6 Gerechtigkeitgasse). Bern's nightlife is surprisingly vibrant, featuring dozens of pubs and nightclubs. It was at the city beach, right under the Parliament windows, that the first topless bathers appeared, igniting a national controversy.

En Route from Bern – The autobahn goes directly to Thun, but if you have time and the weather is good, take the lovely country road via Riggisberg, with its checkerboard fields and wide vistas. On summer afternoons, you can see a most extraordinary private collection of old textiles at the Abegg Foundation in Riggisberg. A short distance east of the freeway, at Kiesen, is an interesting cheese museum with a reconstruction of a workroom and a multilingual audiovisual show. Soon comes Thun, an attractive town on the lake of the same name; its medieval castle has a historical museum containing impressive tapestries, as well as a toy collection. Take the road along the scenic north shore through the resorts of Hilterfingen and Gunten, sometimes passing high over the cold, blue green lake that's one of the country's favorite spots for sailing. Interlaken is highly overrated and not really worth a stop, unless you're interested in the souvenir shops or the especially good pastry served at *Café Schuh;* continue to Grindelwald, a bustling resort village in a glacier with the Alps' Eiger peak hovering above it.

JUNGFRAU (VIRGIN): This is the only one of the three peaks that non–mountain climbers can reach. Count on a minimum of a half-day for the railway climb up to the

11,336-foot Jungfraujoch, the "saddle" of the mountain, and back. In good weather, the high transportation price (around $70 per person) is justifiable, but don't bother taking the trip at all if the visibility is questionable. The train ride itself provides spectacular rocky views, lookout stops, and multilingual explanations. Besides the incredible panoramas to be seen from its terraces, the Jungfraujoch features summer skiing, dogsled riding, and mountain climbing. The Aletsch glacier — the largest in the Alps — can be seen from here. It's also possible to take the train back to Lauterbrunnen, site of a grand waterfall on the other side of the mountain, using circular tickets.

En Route from Grindelwald – Head back to Interlaken and proceed along the south side of Lake Thun (not on the freeway) to picturesque Spiez, which has a lovely view from the railroad station. From here you begin the journey into the Kander Valley, heading south on the main road toward Kandersteg; the route, narrow at first, passes under steep peaks. Then it widens, and weather-beaten, carved wooden houses with large roofs come into view. Stop at Blausee, a small jewel of a lake with extraordinary clear, blue water set in a moss-covered forest; there's a trout hatchery here, and the *Blausee* restaurant, which serves trout specialties. Soon you'll reach Kandersteg, a small resort, where a railway takes cars through the Lötschberg Tunnel in about 15 minutes; from Goppenstein on the other side, a narrow road leads down to Route 9, and the wide, sunny Rhône Valley. (If you're interested in a pilgrimage to the Matterhorn, you can reach Zermatt — closed to autos — via a train from Täsch, which is over an hour's drive south from Goppenstein.) Turning west, you'll soon reach Sierre, the first stop in Valais.

SIERRE: The language changes from German to French within this lovely town, reputed to be the sunniest in Switzerland. In *Château de Villa,* an old castle under huge trees, there's a combination museum and restaurant, serving excellent raclette (a Valais cheese specialty served with potatoes) and wine from local vineyards. There is a unique pewter museum in the former *Château Bellevue* hotel.

En Route from Sierre – Proceeding west on Route 9, just before Sion, you'll reach St. Leonard, site of the largest subterranean lake in Europe.

SION: The two peaks that dominate this 2,000-year-old town give it a sense of history. The ruins of a medieval stronghold rest atop the hill called Tourbillon, and a fortress-like church, completed in the 15th century, crowns the Valère peak. The latter structure, Notre Dame de Valère (Our Lady of Valère), is well worth the climb; park your car in the lot between the two hills. An excellent panorama of the lower Valais can be viewed from the terrace. Inside, there are splendid 17th-century stalls with panels that portray scenes from the life of Christ, and the oldest functioning organ in the world (built in 1390). Each year, international organ concerts are held here. The attached museum contains Romanesque furniture that belonged to the Bishops of Sion and Valais embroidery and lace. In town, the magnificent Supersaxo mansion, built in 1505, features a wooden ceiling with a huge rose depicting the Nativity. A short distance away is the 17th-century Town Hall (Hôtel de Ville, Rue de Grand Pont) with its richly ornamented wooden door. Also interesting is the 3,500-piece glass collection on display at the *Archaeological Museum* (Grange à l'Eveque at Majoria).

For an outstanding view of Sion, drive 5 miles (8 km) to Savièse, an ancient-looking mountain village. Sion itself is a good place to start from in exploring the valleys that extend south below the Rhône. These are typified by extreme, rocky landscapes graced with small barns and chalets; two that are particularly interesting are the Hérens and Hérémence valleys.

HÉRENS AND HÉRÉMENCE VALLEYS: Cross the Rhône south from Sion, and take one of the secondary roads that climbs the steep ledge toward Vex, where Dent Blanche, one of the highest peaks in Switzerland, comes into view. From Vex, the road passes high over a stream and later through a tunnel underneath the Pyramids of Euseigne — bizarre, crowned columns formed by the erosion of the rock. The valley narrows and deepens as the road ascends to Evolène, a pleasant mountaineering resort known for its tall, wooden houses filled with flowers. Women of this village still wear local costumes. Head back for Euseigne and drive up from there through the desolate, eerie scenery of the Hérémence Valley. The road ends at the enormous Grand Dixence Dam; a height of 935 feet makes it the tallest dam in the world. Completed in 1966, it's the most formidable construction task yet undertaken by the Swiss. An elevator ascends from the parking lot to water level, and there's a walking path along the top. Return to Sion on the route that passes through the villages of Hérémence and Salins.

En Route from Sion – Take Route 9 until just beyond Ardon, then turn right onto the secondary road through the vineyards; you'll pass through small wine growing communities like Chamoson, Leyron, and Saillon, which are protected by sunbaked rocky slopes. Saillon features the ruins of an impressive castle as well as picturesque old houses. In this region, you can visit wine caves, and small inns serve local food. At Martigny, called Octodurus by the Romans, the starkly modern Pierre Gianadda Foundation also is interesting. Built over the ruins of a Gallo-Roman temple, it houses a small archeological museum, a collection of vintage cars, and changing exhibitions of modern art. Take Route 9 again, following the Rhône as it turns sharply north. St. Maurice, the capital of Valais under the Romans, is worth a stop. Take a guided tour of the church's treasury, one of the most opulent in the Christian world; among the items on view here are a gold casket decorated with pearls and cameos and a golden ewer that reputedly belonged to Charlemagne. Farther north, near Bex, you can stop for a good meal at *Rôtisserie St. Christoph,* a restaurant and motel in a medieval fortress. Aigle, renowned for white wine, features a 15th-century castle with a *Wine and Salt Museum.* Continue along the freeway for the best view of Montreux.

MONTREUX: Cypresses, fig trees, magnolias, climbing vines, and other Mediterranean forms of vegetation flourish in Montreux, Lake Geneva's most popular resort; its climate is mild all year long. Musical events — including the famous summer jazz festival — enliven the quiet atmosphere here.

Walk through Old Montreux — up the hill, with its interesting houses and crooked streets, to the terrace of the Church of St. Vincent. From here you can get a good view of the towers of Château Chillon, about 2 miles south. The fortress on Chillon rock was initially constructed in the 9th century to defend the major road to Italy, but its present form dates from the 13th century. Its recurrent use as a prison was made especially famous by Byron's poem "The Prisoner of Chillon."

Montreux also offers other attractive side trips: The spectacular train ride to the Rochers de Naye, for example, shouldn't be missed. The trip affords excellent views of Lake Geneva, the Alps, and the Jura. And for more entertainment, Lausanne is only 20 minutes away.

BEST EN ROUTE

There are some good budget accommodations on this route; a number of hotels charge as little as $55 for a double room with shower for a night. Hotels charging $185 to $270 and up in high season are rated expensive. Those asking $100 to $180 are moderate. We've rated those establishments charging $90 or less as inexpensive. Restaurants range in price from $100 and up for a dinner for two in those places listed as expensive, from $60 to $85 in those listed as moderate, and from $35 to $55 in the inexpensive category. Prices do not include drinks and wine or coffee; the tip is included. All restaurants below accept major credit cards, unless otherwise indicated.

BERN

Bellevue Palace – In the center of Bern, adjacent to the grandiose Parliament buildings, this Swissôtel palace is where visiting kings and queens stay. All rooms have just been renovated; many offer spectacular views of the Aare River and the Eiger, Mönch, and Jungfrau mountains. There is a fitness center with an indoor swimming pool, and a fine restaurant, *La Terrasse.* Have a drink on the terrace for the view and atmosphere. 3-5 Kochergasse (phone: 31-224581). Expensive.

Schweizerhof – Next to the railroad station, this very comfortable hotel has genuine antique furnishings that have been collected by its owners, the Gauer family. Its fine restaurant, the *Schultheiss-Stube,* is the best dining place in town; it's cozy and has superb food. 11 Bahmhofpl. (phone: 31-224501). Expensive.

Della Casa – A gathering spot for politicians and ambassadors, this Italian restaurant, which also serves a variety of Swiss dishes, is one of Bern's most popular spots to have a hearty cassoulet. Closed Saturdays and Sundays. Reservations advised. 16 Schauplatzgasse (phone: 31-222142). Moderate.

Kornhauskeller – Set in a cellar (once a granary) this lively place specializes in *Berner platte,* an assortment of boiled meat and sausage served with sauerkraut that's much lighter than it sounds. A brass band entertains at night. Closed Mondays. Reservations unnecessary. 18 Kornhauspl. (phone: 31-221133). Moderate.

City – A modern, cozy hotel, across from the railroad station. Bubenbergpl. (phone: 31-225377). Moderate to inexpensive.

Goldener Schlüssel – This small place is popular because of its good food. Reservations unnecessary. 72 Rathausgasse (phone: 31-220216). Moderate to inexpensive.

Goldener Adler – In the heart of the Old Town, this beautiful old inn provides adequate comfort and a friendly, family atmosphere. 7 Gerechtigkeitsgasse (phone: 31-221725). Inexpensive.

Klötzlikeller – Over 300 years old, this wine tavern also serves snacks. Closed Sundays and Mondays. Reservations advised. 62 Gerechtigkeitsgasse (phone: 31-227456). Inexpensive.

■ **A note on nightclubs:** There are several nightspots in town. *Mocambo* (61 Aarberggasse; phone: 31-225041) and *Chikito* (28 Neuengasse; phone: 31-222680) are the best, offering daily floor shows. Reservations are necessary at both.

GRINDELWALD

Grand Hotel Regina – One of the best in the Bernese Oberland; it is quite luxurious and serves excellent food. Closed in November. Reservations advised. Grindelwald 3818 (phone: 36-545455). Expensive.

Spinne – This modern hotel has a casual atmosphere. Closed in November. Reservations advised (phone: 36-532341). Moderate.

BLAUSEE

Blausee – In a fabulous setting on Blue Lake, this restaurant offers trout specialties. Closed in winter. Reservations advised (phone: 32-711641). Moderate.

SIERRE

Relais du Manoir – Run by local wine growers, this eatery serves and sells outstanding wines; a few local food specialties, including raclette, are also available. It's set in the 16th-century Château de Ville. Reservations advised. 4 Rue Ste.-Catherine (phone: 27-551896). Moderate.

Grotte – As its name implies, this small hotel is built into the rocks, on the shore of Lac de Géronde, in the suburb of Chippis. The restaurant here is very popular; reservations advised. Closed in November. Lac de Géronde (phone: 27-554646). Inexpensive.

SION

Caves de Tous Vents – In a 13th-century wine cellar, in the shadow of the Valère church, this restaurant serves excellent Valais specialties (dinner only). *L'Enclos de Valère,* in a lovely garden setting next door, is under the same management and specializes in French food. Both closed Mondays. Reservations advised. 16-18 Rue des Châteaux (phone: *Caves,* 27-224684; *L'Enclos,* 27-233230). Expensive to moderate.

La Pergola – This small modern hotel is a very good value. Its restaurant specializes in Italian dishes. 116 Rue de Lausanne (phone: 27-224641). Inexpensive.

BEX

Rôtisserie and Motel St. Christoph – Rustically attractive, the restaurant serves charcoal-grilled specialties. It's in a small medieval fortress; all rooms have individual terraces and exits to the garden. Reservations advised (phone: 25-652977). Hotel, inexpensive; restaurant, expensive to moderate.

MONTREUX

Montreux Palace – Vladimir Nabokov used to spend summers at this luxurious Swissôtel palace overlooking Lake Geneva and facing France across the water. The beautiful frescoes, chandeliers, and French doors enhance the already romantic surroundings. Dine in *Le Restaurant Français,* serving Swiss and French fare. 100 Grande Rue (phone: 21-963-5373). Expensive.

Pont-de-Brent – This little country inn has become known as one of the great places to dine in Switzerland. Closed Sundays and Mondays. Reservations necessary. In Brent, just above Montreux (phone: 21-964-5230). Expensive.

Eden au Lac – The hotel retains its turn-of-the-century charm. There's a garden right on the lake, where a luncheon buffet is served. Except for the 2 weeks of the jazz festival (usually held July 7-22), it is quiet. Restaurant reservations advised. 11 Rue du Théâtre (phone: 21-963-5551). Expensive to moderate.

Caveau du Museum – You also can dine in this lively discotheque, with its cozy, rustic atmosphere, in the center of Old Montreux. Swiss fare and grilled meat are the specialties. Closed Sundays. Reservations advised. 40 Rue de la Gare (phone: 21-963-1662). Moderate.

Europe – A typical old "grand hotel," with a lovely lake view, it is a very good value, but it is now a hotel school with 100 students, and it's sometimes overrun with groups. There are 170 rooms and although there is no restaurant, breakfast is served in the rooms. 15 Av. des Alpes (phone: 21-963-7404). Moderate.

Victoria – In the suburb of Glion-sur-Montreux, this charming old hotel on a 16-acre park was renovated recently, and its rooms offer spectacular panoramic views. There is an outdoor swimming pool and tennis courts. A member of the prestigious Relais & Châteaux group (phone: 21-963-3131). Moderate.

Vieille Ferme – It's a charming farm, very rustic, slightly out of the center of town, and it serves local specialties. Try the raclette — while listening to country music. Closed Mondays. Reservations advised. Montreux-Chailly (phone: 21-964-6465). Moderate.

Yugoslavia

The long-smoldering ethnic and nationalistic turmoil among the Serbs, Croats, and Slovenes (among others) erupted dramatically during the past year. As a result, the US State Department issued a warning to US visitors against travel to Yugoslavia. Prospective travelers should check with the US State Department's Citizens' Emergency Center (202-647-5225) prior to departure. What's more, the Yugoslavia National Tourist Office in New York City closed indefinitely last summer. We offer the following in the hope that Yugoslavia's problems will end sometime soon, and that it once again becomes a safe place to visit.

The Socialist Federal Republic of Yugoslavia is the remarkable conglomeration of six republics, four major languages, two alphabets (Latinate and Cyrillic), and the cultures of a dozen different empires from all over world history. Stretched along the Adriatic Sea between Europe and Asia, the area has been ruled and changed for a time by everybody from the ancient Celts to the Ottomans; from the marauding Goths to the stately Austrians; and from Jove to Muhammad to Jesus Christ. Monuments of the different empires are in every part of the country. Its Seven Sights (Dubrovnik, Split, Kotor, Ohrid, the Monastery of Sopocani, and the national parks at Plitvice Lakes and Durmitor Mountain) are on UNESCO's official list of the world's natural and cultural heritages.

The southern Slavs came to present-day Yugoslavia during the 6th and 7th centuries, when Serbs, Croatians, and Montenegrins established kingdoms that flourished for more than 3 centuries. After the Battle of Kosovo in 1389, the eastern parts of present-day Yugoslavia fell under Turkish rule for almost 500 years. Although many southern Slavs defended their territory in the battle, the Turks conquered Serbia and Macedonia, and later they took parts of Croatia, Montenegro, Bosnia, and Herzegovina. The western parts of present-day Yugoslavia were first conquered by Magyars, who took Croatia in 1102, and the Hapsburgs, who took Slovenia in 1278 and Croatia in 1527.

Between 1805 and 1815, Napoleon's Illyrian provinces were established in parts of Croatia and in Slovenia, but they were ruled by the Hapsburgs again after the 1815 Battle of Waterloo. It was in the middle of the 19th century that the idea of a a union of southern Slavs was born in Croatia. Meanwhile, the Serbs and Montenegrins won their independence from the Turks in 1878. The Balkan Wars (1912–13) liberated the Macedonians from the Turks, but resulted in the partition of Macedonia among Serbia, Greece, and Bulgaria. The assassination of Austro-Hungarian Crown Prince Francis Ferdinand in Sarajevo in 1914 resulted in the outbreak of World War I and the end of the Hapsburg Empire; Yugoslavia was formed on December 1, 1918. The new kingdom of Serbs, Croats, and Slovenes was proclaimed in Belgrade; it included the former kingdoms of Serbia and Montenegro, Bosnia, Herzegovina, Croatia-Slovenia, and Dalmatia — all previously under the authority of

Austria, Hungary, or both. King Peter I of Serbia (who had been King of Serbia since 1903) became the first monarch of the united Serbs, Croats and Slovenes, and his son, Alexander of Yugoslavia, was made the regent. The reign of King Alexander exacerbated the Croats' nationalist feelings; under the direction of Nazi Germany and Fascist Italy, right-wing Croatian Ustashi terrorists assassinated him in Marseilles in 1934. When Germany occupied Yugoslavia in 1941, the Ustashi were given Croatia and free rein to terrorize anyone who was not a Croat nationalist.

For more than 4 decades, Yugoslavia was governed by a Communist party, which came to power after resisting German occupation, and liberating the country, during World War II. However, long before the recent upheavals within Eastern Europe and the Balkans, the state was tolerant of religion, linguistic diversity, and a degree of local autonomy. Despite ties to Stalin during the war, the late Marshal Tito pulled Yugoslavia away from the USSR's influence in 1948 and forged his own alliances.

In Yugoslavia, you'll find that the language, festivals, costume, religion, and cooking style change wherever you go. The land of Yugoslavia is surprisingly varied over its 99,000 square miles. There are the snowy Julian Alps in the north and the warm Adriatic coast in the south, with its 1,000 offshore islands, 66 of them inhabited. Dense forests in several regions still harbor bear, wolves, wild boar, and deer; and the central plains are as low, flat, and lush as medieval Flanders. Hills or mountains cover most of Yugoslavia except for the north central region; rail and road transportation are not very extensive or sophisticated yet. The interior is full of large, clear lakes and warm mineral springs. The biggest river is the Sava (600 miles), which meets the trans-European Danube at Belgrade.

Yugoslavians travel freely at home and abroad. The press is no longer subject to censorship, and there is easy access to foreign publications of all kinds in the major cities.

During the 1980s, Yugoslavia experienced deep economic, political, and ethnic crises that included a decline in the standard of living, triple-digit inflation, and the introduction of wide economic reforms. Steps are being implemented, however, to try to encourage private enterprise, foreign investments, and political democratization in order to better integrate the country with the Common Market in Western Europe. In 1990, free elections were held in all six republics and right-of-center governments were elected in four; the Communists retained power in Serbia and Montenegro. The wave of change recently has brought to the surface pent-up nationalist feelings that have culminated in clashes between Orthodox Serbs and Islamic Albanians in the province of Kosovo. Emotions between the Serbs and Croats, and the Serbs and Slovenes also are quite tense as both the Croats and Slovenes seek confederation instead of federation. In June of 1991, two of the wealthier republics, Slovenia and Croatia, declared independence, throwing the country into civil turmoil. The attempt by the Yugoslav government to control the separatist schism by force did little to ease tensions. As we went to press, this volatile federation appeared to be on the brink of disintegration.

Belgrade is the capital and the center of commerce, industry, and communications. The main cultural and economic centers are Zagreb, Dubrovnik,

Ljubljana, Sarajevo, and Skopje. Other large cities include Split, Novi Sad, Rijeka, and Titograd.

About one-third of the population works in agriculture, the rest in service and industry. Although the nation is becoming more urban and cosmopolitan, the different ethnic groups in Yugoslavia have a powerful folk tradition, which you will notice wherever you go: Dances, folklore plays, and mystical pageants are celebrated in every region and are taken quite seriously.

Roads in Yugoslavia have improved considerably in recent years. The Adriatic Highway (Jadranska Magistrala) runs along the coast, and is one of the most scenic roads on the Continent. The major route that links the country from the northwest to the southeast is the Autoput Bratstva i Jedinstva (Highway of Brotherhood and Unity), and it is being turned into a major four-lane thoroughfare. The unfinished sections, however, are in treacherous condition. These two routes link up with a number of lateral roads. The Ibarska Magistrala (Ibar Highway), which runs from Belgrade to Skopje in the south, leads through the heart of the ancient Serbian kingdom.

We've laid out three routes for exploring Yugoslavia. The most popular is the coastal route, which begins near Trieste, Italy, and winds south along the Adriatic Sea through the cities of Portoroz, Opatija, Rijeka, Zadar, Split, and Dubrovnik. This coastal area is full of beach resorts, Roman ruins, steep bluffs, cultural festivals, and fine seafood. The second trek begins in Podkoren, in the Julian Alps in northwestern Yugoslavia. Bring your skis. The drive goes south through mountains to Ljubljana and Zagreb and on to the capital city of Belgrade. Belgrade has over 30 museums and galleries, hosts symphonies, opera companies, and film festivals, and serves foods of every nationality. The third route starts 3 miles (5 km) from the Greek border and winds north through Macedonia, where you can see Turkish mosques, Byzantine frescoes, and Bohemian folk festivals, and stop for fishing and swimming at lakefront resorts. The route continues through Pristina to Kraljevo.

Trieste to Dubrovnik

Guiding a reader on an auto tour of the Yugoslav Adriatic is different from giving advice on an artistic, historical, or skiing tour. There are no complicated directions; after the first 25 miles (40 km), you'll be going southeast on the Adriatic Highway (Jadranska Magistrala), overlooking the incredibly blue Adriatic Sea — if the water isn't on your right, you took a wrong turn. The areas along the coast are quite diverse, but we're only going to mention a few spots in any detail, since your reasons for driving the coast are probably going to be the same all the way along — sun, rocks, sand, and sea — and you'll know them when you find them. The wonderful thing about this coast is that you'll stumble on what you're looking for everywhere. So, this tour will give you some idea of what you're passing through, tell you about some interesting sights, and give you some broad tactics on where to find your piece of sand.

The most important advice is this: The resort cities are crowded at high season — June, July, and August — so if you want privacy and you don't want to spend too much money, go to the small village beaches (which are as beautiful as any), and stay at pensions or private houses. Then go into town to take your pulse-quickening excitement whenever you're ready for it. If you can travel in May, September, or October, you'll find the tourist population comparatively low, and your lodging costs likewise: Prices drop up to 50% in those months, and the climate is just as fine as at high season.

The northern half of this journey, from Trieste (on the Italian border) to Zadar, goes over a predominantly rocky shoreline, with good pebble beaches. South of Zadar is where the lush Mediterranean vegetation begins, with palm, pine, and hibiscus. Throughout, the beaches are lovely and the weather quite dependably sunny and warm except for a few months in winter, when it sometimes rains. The coastline is among the most jagged in Europe. If you measured its length as the crow flies, it would be 390 miles (624 km); when you follow the contours of all the bays, inlets, and peninsulas, it measures 1,125 miles (1,810 km). You will be driving along the coast, following almost every twist, for a total of 530 miles (848 km).

Yugoslavia's Adriatic coast is known for its nudist colonies; this is more or less the center for organized nudism, or "naturism," in southern Europe. Generally speaking, nudism is a very health-oriented, bring-the-kids kind of lifestyle. The philosophy is that clothes give us dirty minds; most nudist camps are notoriously nonsexual. Naturist resorts (marked with FKK signs) are open to anyone, and there are at least 30 well-known ones between Trieste and Ulcinj; some are near large cities, some near small villages, and many on islands. If you don't need a lot of fancy facilities, every seaside village has its own informal nude bathing area.

Over the millennia, sailors, conquerors, and adventurers have left behind their houses, their ships, and their descendants to stay along the Adriatic coast and its islands. However, many of the 1,000 islands off the coast are still inhabited only by seagulls; this applies to many in the Kornati chain off Zadar. Perhaps you'll take some time out to visit a timeless desert island away from your car and your hotel, and listen to the silence.

The route begins in the Slovene greenery around Trieste (Italy) at the Lipica horse farm, breeding ground of the proud Lipizzaner horses, and descends to the seaside for a taste of Austro-Hungarian grandeur near the old resorts of Portoroz and Opatija. You will see the Roman amphitheater arena of Pula, still used for theater and film presentations, sample two sets of sun-soaked islands at Brioni, a favorite site of the late President Tito, and watch the coast go greener and more lush as you drive south. The pandemonium of Rijeka and Zadar may dizzy you, and Diocletian's palace in Split will certainly awe you; for relief, you can poke along the beach in small Dalmatian villages. The last stop is the cultural and Bohemian capital of the coast, Dubrovnik, where you can, particularly during the summer season, take in some of the best art, music, and nightlife the 20th century has to offer, inside the walls of a 16th-century town. You may want to take your trip farther down the coast, and there are some suggestions for places to see.

Although hundreds of hotels have been built on the Yugoslav coast since the 1950s, demand for accommodations frequently outruns supply. Since private enterprise was encouraged — and today, capitalism is the name of the game — bed and breakfast establishments can be found in every town, city, and village along the coast. These lodgings can be booked through either the local tourist offices or travel agencies, or just look for the vacancy signs in different languages among any group of houses along the road and bargain with the owners. Speaking and understanding German helps, since Germans form the largest group of foreign visitors. Prices at these places are much lower than in hotels — $10 to $20 per day per person — and you can really get a better feeling for the country and its people.

The culinary specialties are so varied in Yugoslavia — a blend of East and West, of central Europe and the Mediterranean — that they are sure to satisfy all tastes. Although international cuisine is available in the big hotels, the national dish is *cevapcici* — grilled, sometimes spicy, minced meat — and the national drink is *sljivovica* — rather potent plum brandy. Other local delights are *sarma* (mixed minced meat and rice in sauerkraut), stuffed peppers, *duvec* (baked vegetables and meat), *bosanski lonac* (stewed beef, lamb, vegetables, and spices), *kajmak* (a cheese-like cream from boiled milk), and, for dessert, apple *strudla* (paper-thin pastry stuffed with grated apples, nuts, and sultanas).

TRIESTE: Get on the highway northeast toward Sezana, to cross the border into Yugoslavia just before you reach that town. The approach from Trieste brings you into Yugoslavia's contentious Republic of Slovenia, an area ruled by the Austrian nobility from the time of Charlemagne until World War I. Slovenia was the lush, hilly playground of the Austro-Hungarian Empire, with grand, lakefront resorts.

LIPICA: Off the highway past Sezana is the 4-century-old horse farm at Lipica, the original stud farm of the Lipizzaner horse, founded in 1580 by Archduke Charles of Austria. Lipica supplied the horses for the Austrian cavalry and the famous Spanish riding school of Vienna. All this wouldn't be half so interesting except that they'll let you ride them. For the rest of your days, you'll probably never ride such a thoroughly blue-blooded, beautiful, well-brought-up horse. Instruction is available daily if you need it at *KTC Lipica* (phone: 067-73781 or 067-73792) and at *Club Hotel Lipica* (phone: 067-73597 or 067-73541). Reservations are advised. For spectators there are shows in the indoor riding ring at 11 AM and 1:30 PM.

En Route from Lipica – Before heading out to the sun and the sea, take a detour to Postojna, 25 miles (37 km) north of Lipica toward Ljubljana. Postojna is renowned for its complex of caves, which are among the largest in Europe. A miniature train takes visitors through concert halls, around underground lakes, and between dazzling and colorful stalactites and stalagmites. Not far from Postojna (about 6½ miles/10 km) is Skocjanska Jama, with the same natural beauty as Postojna but less crowded and better preserved. Return to Lipica and continue east to Divaca, where you will intersect a highway; turn south toward Kozina and go beyond it about 20 miles (32 km), until you meet up with the road you will follow the rest of this trip, the Adriatic Highway.

Go south to Portorož, the largest and best-known seaside resort in Slovenia; flowers grow in abundance in this former Old World bastion — Portorož means "Port of Roses." Sailing and parachuting competitions, cultural events and folklore plays take place here in the summer. Flying lessons are available at *Sports Airport Portorož* (phone: 066-79617 or 066-79710). In the neighboring town of Seca, there is a permanent outdoor exhibit of stone sculpture called Forma Viva.

Near Seca is Umag, where visitors can play tennis at *Stella Maris,* Yugoslavia's largest tennis center, which hosted the first *Yugoslavian Open* in May 1990.

Stop at Piran, on a peninsula about 5 minutes outside Portorož. This is an old Mediterranean town with narrow streets, and small churches with Renaissance and baroque paintings. Piran's city walls are still standing, as is a fragment of a Byzantine wall.

On the way to Pula, the compact stone houses and red roofs of the town of Rovinj are a must-see. This medieval fishing and trading village has been an artists' colony since the 1950s and is one of the most beautiful cities on the Adriatic. The baroque Church of St. Euphemia dominates the town and nearby islands.

PULA: From Portoroz, the highway continues down the coast to Pula, a major coastal city built on an ancient Illyrian settlement dating from the 5th century BC. It became a Roman colony; the Roman amphitheater in Pula, which seats 23,000, has lasted better than the one in Rome. Pula's amphitheater is still in use: The annual *Festival of Yugoslav Films* (among other events) is held here. Other Roman buildings include a 1st-century temple to the Emperor Augustus, and the 4th-century Hercules gates. During the time of the Austro-Hungarian Empire, Pula's bay served as the empire's major military harbor, and the world's first torpedo was produced at the shipyard here. Close to Pula is Medulin, a small seaside village with good beaches.

Another place that should not be overlooked is the Brioni Islands National Park, a short boat ride from Fazana, a small port near Pula. Littered with Greco-Roman and medieval ruins, the 14 islands are famous as the residence of former President Tito and as the meeting place of world leaders. Their exceptional natural and cultural beauty are now accessible to visitors. Lodging on the islands consists of 350 beds in hotels and villas. On the island of Venga, a small train goes through a zoological garden filled with animals that were given to Tito by Third World countries. Authorities have built a golf course and and are planning to open polo grounds; for information call 052-22455.

En Route from Pula – The road continues through a number of fishing villages. From one of them, Brestova, travelers can take a car ferry to the resort islands of Cres and Losinj; see more on the resort islands below.

OPATIJA: Opatija, at the foot of Mount Ucka, 40 miles (64 km) along the coast, was a popular resort among the Austro-Hungarian nobility. Its streets still have a 19th-century air, with elegant shops and luxury hotels with formal gardens and tropical trees; they also have casinos. For culture, see a play at Opatija's summer theater.

En Route from Opatija – Near Opatija is the medieval village of Volosko. A sand walk stretches along the beach for 6 miles (10 km), and goes through the nearby fishing villages of Ika and Icici.

RIJEKA: From Opatija it is 10 miles (16 km) to Rijeka, the largest Yugoslavian port, at which all ship, railway, and bus routes leading to this part of the Adriatic coast converge. It has museums, art galleries, theaters, a library, a university, a 15th-century clock tower, a Benedictine church, and a Croatian fortress from the Middle Ages built by the Frankopans, one of the ruling families in medieval Croatia.

En Route from Rijeka – From Rijeka to Split, 240 miles (384 km), the coastal highway affords spectacular views of the sea, Kvarner Bay, and various coves, villages, and islands. Most of the islands visible from the coastal road appear barren, inhospitable, and sun scorched; they are rendered infertile by the strong northerly winds that sweep their flanks year-round, spraying them with tiny drops of salt water. However, the protected sides of the islands, not visible from the mainland, often are rich with vegetation and are usually inhabited. At the entrance of the Bay of Bakar is the town of Kraljevica and its early baroque castle. Nearby is the *Uvala Scott* hotel complex (phone: 051-801226) and "vacation village."

Krk is the largest island in Kvarner Bay, and the largest in the Adriatic, with sand and pebble beaches, and lush vegetation. Near the *Uvala Scott,* a new bridge connects Krk with the coast. There are ancient forts and medieval castles as well.

Crikvenica, 9 miles (14 km) from Kraljevica, is a famous seaside resort and medical center that uses thalassotherapy — treating ailments ranging from nervous tension to heart disease with sea water. The small resort of Selce is 2 miles (3 km) from Crikvenica; 4 miles (6 km) farther on is Novi Vinodolski, with a sandy beach.

RAB and LOŠINJ: The island of Rab, in Kvarner Bay between Krk and Pag, is one of the sunniest spots in Europe, with abundant foliage and a mild climate. The main town, also called Rab, was an ancient Greek and then a Roman settlement; at times it becomes a crowded bathing resort. Four bell towers rise above the town walls. In the town is a 14th-century palace and the 7th-century Church of St. John.

Lošinj is farther out in the bay, beyond the island of Cres, and is extraordinarily green but is also crowded at peak times.

PAG: The island of Pag, famous for its fine (and expensive) *paški sir* (sheep's milk cheese), is just as pretty as the more touristy islands, but more rural, and with fewer hotels and tourism facilities. If you don't mind staying in a pension, you can avoid the crowds here. Its many restaurants, called *konoba*, always offer sheep's milk cheese hors d'oeuvres before the traditional grilled fish.

ZADAR: An ancient city, Zadar is the southernmost point of the Kvarner Bay area. Settled well before the 1st century — with surviving buildings, gates, and other relics of the Roman Empire and the Venetian period (15th to 18th century) — Zadar is the center of 20th-century, bustling, hard-and-fast tourism for the northern half of the coast. There's an airport just north of town, rail service toward the east, and ferry and hydrofoil service leading from Zadar to everywhere. It's not a quiet place. There are lots of high-rise hotels, pleasure boats, and populous beaches. There is also a lot of functional activity on the water: Fishing is done with nets from small boats.

For those feeling adventurous, hire a water taxi or a fisherman to take you out to one of the uninhabited Kornati Islands, which are set aside as a national park, for the day or the week or longer. Be sure to make arrangements to be picked up. Or consider renting a boat in town; you can leave your car with the boat rental people. This could be the most exhilarating part of the trip; it's not often in this life you can rule your own island in the sea. If you have a tent, it's possible to camp out on the sand under the stars for as long as you like. The undisturbed sound of lapping waves is good for the spirit. Come with supplies, though; there's no fresh water anywhere. If you prefer to sightsee with a group, there are regular excursions to the islands from Zadar.

Stop by the town's museums and treasuries — it's had an interesting past — and visit the 9th-century Church of St. Donat.

En Route from Zadar – About 40 miles (64 km) south of Zadar is Sibenik, founded in the 10th century at the estuary of the Krka River. Take a boat tour of the port; the view of Sibenik's white-domed medieval and Renaissance palaces from the water is grand. The best way to explore the area is by walking its narrow stone streets. In the center of the city is Saint Jacques Cathedral, perhaps the finest on the whole coast. The Romanesque cathedral was built between 1431 and 1536 by sculptors Juraj Dalmatinac and Nikola Florentinac. A nice highlight is to take an excursion to Skradin to see the waterfalls of the Krka.

Primosten, a small peninsula town, is 5 miles (8 km) south of Sibenik. Lodging is found mainly in private houses, although a hotel complex, the *Marina Lucica* (phone: 59-70022), is nearby. There is also a nudist beach.

Do not fail to see Trogir, a "museum town" on an island (reached by bridge) about 20 miles (32 km) before Split. The animals in the carvings and reliefs of the Cathedral of St. Lovro are so vivid they look as if they may drool on you at any moment. There is one ancient Roman relief, the *Diety and Petronius,* and several medieval buildings, including the cathedral, the Lucic Palace, and the Pamfogna Palace.

SPLIT: On the opposite end of the peninsula, 55 miles (88 km) from Sibenik is Split, one of the two or three towns on the Adriatic that shouldn't be missed. The present administrative center of the region of Dalmatia, it was founded in the 4th century AD by the Roman Emperor Diocletian as his retirement home. The titanic palace and enclosed town he had built make up the old quarter of modern Split. The palace has four gates: gold, silver, iron, and bronze. The chambers are so huge that many of them were made into entire houses in later years; the corridors are now streets in the Old Town. Symphony concerts, opera, dance performances, and plays take place inside the walls, and the palace basement houses several art and historical galleries.

In the town that grew up outside the walls, there is a 16th-century synagogue and cemetery. Although Split is a big industrial center, there are resort areas along the coast just southeast of the city, with hotels, heated swimming pools, and a good supply of places to go. At the western part of town, just past the *Museum of Ivan Mestrovic Sculptures,* is Marjan, a small pine-tree-covered hill that offers one of the most spectacular views of Split.

You can book an excursion from Split to the inland town of Sinj, where the Alka medieval jousting tournament is held every August, featuring knights on horseback.

En Route from Split – Along the coast from Split to Dubrovnik, 134 miles (214 km), is an area of shimmering blue coves, sandy and pebbled beaches sheltered by pine trees, and balmy offshore islands, all overlooked by the 5,000-foot peaks of the coastal mountains; it is known as the Makarska Riviera, and is the lushest and sunniest area on the Adriatic. Unfortunately, some of the pine forest has been destroyed by fire in the past few years. In this Makarska region are the towns of Brela, Baska Voda, Makarska, Tucepi, and Podgora, and the fishing villages of Drasnice, Igrane, Zivogosce, Drvenik, and Zaostrog. Some 56 miles (90 km) before Dubrovnik, the road forks; one branch leads toward Mostar, with its elegant 16th-century stone bridge over the Neretva River. Halfway to Mostar is Medugorje, a pilgrimage destination where the Virgin Mary is said to regularly visit one of the village girls. The place is to be avoided in July and August, when thousands flock here from all over the world.

SOUTHERN ISLANDS: The islands at this southern end of the coast are the main tourist attractions in Yugoslavia. The most popular ones as well as those less traveled are characterized by a consistently warm, sunny climate, good beaches, thick vegetation, and ancient forts and dwellings.

Brac, a popular island, has extensive pine woods in its hills, good for walking. At Bol is the baroque Church Gospa od Kamena and a beautiful sandy beach called Zlatni Rat (Golden Cape). Brac also is known for its white marble, which was used for the construction of the Diocletian Palace in Split and the White House in Washington, DC.

Hvar is a year-round resort that welcomes many tourists. The main town, also called Hvar, has the oldest theater in Europe, built in 1612; performances are still held there. Hvar's hotel managers are so confident of the weather there, they say that from November through March their guests will not pay rent for any day the temperature goes below freezing, or if it snows or fogs over; they allow 50% off if it rains more than 3 hours, providing a guest stays at least 7 days. Paklenski Otoci, the island group opposite Hvar's harbor — a nudist paradise — has wonderful beaches and tropical vegetation. Good swimmers can even swim to the islands.

Korcula claims Marco Polo as a native son. The town of Korcula has its own cathedral, St. Marco's, built between the 13th and 16th centuries, which contains paintings by Tintoretto and Bassani.

Mljet is an out-of-the-way spot, very wild and forested, and is considered the most beautiful of these islands. It has two hotels, lots of private houses with rooms for rent, a national park, plus a large lake dotted with small islands. Mljet is definitely for the slightly adventurous.

Solta (near Split) is also off the beaten track, and consequently never gets very crowded. There are lots of boardinghouses where visitors can stay and get to know the islanders.

DUBROVNIK: The city of Dubrovnik, the last stop on our route, looks like the same powerful, grandiose, and magnificent city it was during the 16th century. Formerly the Free Republic of Dubrovnik, it was a center of art and commerce, and gaudy rival to another city-state on the Adriatic, Venice. Dubrovnik was almost completely destroyed by an earthquake in 1667, but was totally rebuilt and prospered until Napoleon overtook it in 1806. Now the city, preserved in its medieval splendor, is considered the most beautiful in Yugoslavia.

Seen from above, the roofs of the city make up a sea of red orange tile, dotted with the white domes of a few particularly grand edifices. The buildings are constructed on a huge scale, with rows of pillars and sweeping arches, imperious towers, gorgeous stonework façades, and momentous fortifications bristling with cannons. And, of course, there are fountains, courtyards, gardens, and bell towers. Particularly awesome sights are the Rector's Palace, Onofri's Fountain, the cloisters of Franciscan and Dominican monasteries, and the baroque Church of St. Vlaho.

The first thing to do when you get into town is to get a view of the whole place — by walking around the city on top of its thick walls, this will take about 2 hours (it's best to walk in the late afternoon, when the sun is not so strong). You might want to take a cable car tour as well, to see the bright colors of the landscape from above.

Dubrovnik's summer festival, from mid-July to late August, brings in world class performers of symphonic and chamber music, opera, ballet, drama, and folklore to play in the palaces, gardens, and courtyards. Nightlife in Dubrovnik is either bohemian, cosmopolitan, expensive, or, frequently, all three. The city has several superb restaurants (see *Best en Route*), and there are gambling casinos in three hotels — the *Belevedere* (phone: 50-28655), the *Libertas* (phone: 50-27444), and the *Imperial* (phone: 50-23688). The best entertainment in Dubrovnik, however, is a stroll along Stradun (Main St.), in the Old Town. Regardless of the tourists — or the season — inhabitants of all ages take to the street at sundown to greet friends and exchange gossip.

Dubrovnik's 15th-century synagogue, on Zudioska (Jewish) Street, is the third-oldest in Europe. The *Maritime Museum* has artifacts and historical background on the city's 16th-century heyday; there tends to be a museum or gallery on just about every corner. The museum is located in the Fortress of St. Ivan on the first and second floors (phone: 264650).

The island of Lokrum is a particularly good (and popular) bathing spot and park just south and east of the town's mainland. If you feel up to it, you can pick your way through the foliage to the Adriatic side of the island for a more private swim. There is a nudist beach on Lokrum known for its friendly atmosphere.

En Route from Dubrovnik – You may feel like going down the coast from Dubrovnik all the way to the Albanian border. Besides stopping along the way at whatever little beach grabs your fancy, we recommend a visit to Cavtat, which has ancient Greek and Roman monuments, and the *Croatia* (see *Best en Route*), one of the swankiest hotels on the coast. A small population of blacks, descendants of slaves who escaped the wreck of a pirate ship in the 18th century), lives in Cavtat. Sites to see include Herceg-Novi, with its lovely flower gardens; Igalo, Yugoslavia's best-known seaside spa; Budva, founded in the 14th century BC, with Greek and Roman monuments and long, sandy beaches (the spa was partially destroyed by a recent earthquake and has yet to be fully reconstructed); Sveti Stefan, a tiny medieval village on an island connected to the mainland by a causeway, converted entirely into expensive deluxe tourist housing; and Ulcinj, with a long and inviting sandy beach. A worthwhile day trip is a visit to the inland site of the Yugoslav partisans' greatest battle, the Valley of Heroes, and also to the virgin forest of Perucica. On the rugged sides of Sutjeska River Canyon, visitors are awed by the centuries-old, 100-foot-tall pine trees, which seem to grow out of sheer rock at the most inaccessible and windswept heights.

BEST EN ROUTE

Accommodations for two people in an expensive place will cost $100; moderate, $25 to $60; inexpensive, $15 to $25. Restaurants in the expensive category charge $6 to $15 per person for dinner, including wine; meals that cost less than $6 per person are considered moderate.

LIPICA

Club – All the modern comforts are offered at this hostelry with 120 rooms and a restaurant (phone: 67-73597). Moderate.

PORTOROŽ

Bernardin Complex – Comprising the *Bernardin,* the *Grand Emona,* and the *Villas Park,* this complex offers splashy, angular, modern hotels, embracing a small marina. Major credit cards accepted. 66320 Portorož (phone: 66-75271; fax: 66-75491). Expensive to moderate.

Palace – In front of the beach and in the city center, this is an old-time palace with an indoor swimming pool (phone: 66-73541; fax: 66-76188). Expensive to moderate.

Rovinj Park – A modern hotel on the port, it offers the best accommodations in town. Major credit cards accepted (phone: 52-811077; fax: 52-813497). Moderate.

OPATIJA

Kvarner-Amalia – A turn-of-the-century European hotel and restaurant, with banquet halls, chandeliers, and flowered terraces facing the sea. Good continental food and entertainment every night. Major credit cards accepted. Park 1, Maja 4 (phone: 51-271233). Moderate.

Učka – On the road that leads to the top of the Učka Mountains, this lovely place offers a beautiful view over Kvarner Bay. The restaurant serves game. Reservations necessary. No credit cards accepted. (phone: 51-713450). Moderate.

ISLAND OF KRK

Ribarsko Selo Haludovo – A deluxe hotel complex with apartments and villas built as a Mediterranean fishing village with red tile roofs; constructed originally as a playground by *Penthouse* magazine. Malinska, Krk (phone: 51-859111). Moderate.

SPLIT

Bellevue – This turn-of-the-century establishment is one of the town's most charming. Although small (just 86 beds), it's centrally located, overlooking the old port and neo-baroque Prokuratives Square, which is popular with evening strollers. 2 A. Jovica (phone: 58-585655). Moderate.

Lav – The name means "lion," and it's the best hotel complex in the Split area, albeit rather ultramodern and concrete. It's 6 miles (10 km) south of Diocletian's palace. Miljevac (phone: 58-551444). Moderate.

Marjan – Overlooking the old port and Diocletian's Palace, this glass hostelry offers a wonderful view of the city. 5 Obala JNA (phone: 58-42866). Moderate.

DUBROVNIK

Argentina – With its villas — Sheherezada and Orsula — this hotel has one of the best views of the Old City and the port. The Villa Orsula has only 9 rooms and

3 suites, and provides some of the most luxurious accommodations in Dubrovnik. Built in 1936 and fully renovated in 1989, it has a piano bar, garden café, and a tavern called the *Victoria*. There are also swimming pools, tennis courts, a sauna, and a massage. Closed from January to March. 14 Frana Supila (phone: 50-23855 or 50-22540; fax: 50-32524; telex: 27558). Expensive.

Atlas Club Nautika – Housed in a beautiful old building situated near the Pile Gate, there is an excellent piano bar on the ground floor, and a restaurant on the first floor that serves a wide range of seafood dishes. It also has an extensive wine list and perhaps the best service in Dubrovnik. The restaurant is open daily until midnight. Reservations advised. 5 Brsajlje (phone: 50-27292 or 50-27333; fax: 50-28342). Expensive.

Babin Kuk Holiday Park – This complex contains 4 ultramodern hotels designed by Edward Durrell Stone, the architect of the *Kennedy Center* in Washington, DC. Every conceivable facility is available; the *Dubrovnik President* (50-20265 or 50-22666; fax: 50-20269) is the most elegant of the hotels. 9 Ivana Lola Ribara (phone: 50-25644). Expensive.

Belvedere – Overlooking the Adriatic, this first-rate establishment has 200 rooms (on the small side) and 20 suites. The atmosphere is friendly and relaxed throughout. There are indoor and outdoor pools, shops, 2 formal restaurants, a casino, and an informal seaside tavern. Major credit cards accepted. V. Bukovca (phone: 50-28655; fax: 50-21772). Expensive.

Croatia – Tucked into the cliffs overlooking the Adriatic in the tiny town of Cavtat, near Dubrovnik, this hostelry is as good as any in the city. It also has a casino. Major credit cards accepted. Cavtat (phone: 50-78022; fax: 50-78213). Expensive.

Libertas – A multi-tiered modern structure built into the side of a hill overlooking the beach and the city ramparts. There's a pool, sauna, solarium, restaurant, and a nightclub. 1 Lavcevicera (phone: 50-27445). Expensive.

Domino – Perhaps the best eatery in Dubrovnik, it offers a rich variety of meat and fish dishes. Closed December to February. Reservations necessary. 3 Od Domine (phone: 50-32832). Expensive to moderate.

Esculap – Another excellent restaurant in Cavtat. It has a nice terrace with a view of the Adriatic. Closed from November to March. Reservations advised. 1 Trubicev Put, Cavtat (phone: 50-478666). Expensive to moderate.

Imperial – Built in 1897, this large hotel is the oldest in Dubrovnik. Located in the vicinity of the Old City walls, it is considered one of the best in town. Although it does not have its own beach, there is a garden and a casino. Closed from December to April. 2 M. Simoni (phone: 50-23688 or 50-23689; fax: 50-23074; telex: 27639). Expensive to moderate.

Maestoso – A lovely intimate place that is famous for its fresh fish and meat dishes. The restaurant has a terrace and its own parking. Open daily till 1 AM. Reservations advised. 1 Bulevar Lenjina (phone: 50-20986). Expensive to moderate.

Excelsior – An old grande dame of a hotel, popular with Americans. On the water, with the best view of the walled city. 3 Fran Supila (phone: 50-23566). Moderate.

Konavski Dvori – Twenty-two miles (35 km) east of the Old City, this restaurant serves freshwater trout from the nearby source of the Ljuta River, and lamb on the spit. Gruda (phone: 50-79039). Moderate.

Orsan – Only a 15-minute drive (12 miles/20 km) north from Dubrovnik is probably the best restaurant in Yugoslavia, located in a converted peasant house made of stone. Famous for seafood. Closed December through March. Reservations advised in July and August. No credit cards accepted. 2 T. Kikerja, Zatonmali (phone: 50-89267). Moderate.

Piccolo Mondo – Specializing in local dishes and good seafood, this dining place is conveniently located in the center of the Old City. Major credit cards accepted. 18 Prijeko (phone: 50-26015). Moderate.

Domizana – This place outside of town in Cavtat is well worth the trip. Decorated like a traditional Dalmatian wine cellar, it offers good national food. Open daily till 1 AM. Reservations unnecessary. Major credit cards accepted. 2 Zal, Cavtat (phone: 50-478539). Moderate to inexpensive.

SVETI STEFAN

Sveti Stefan – A 16th-century fishing village and pirate stronghold turned deluxe hotel. It completely occupies a small island, connected by a causeway to the mainland. All cars are parked on shore. The cottages' exteriors were preserved intact, and given plush, air conditioned innards. Reservations necessary. Major credit cards accepted (phone: 86-62242 or 86-41333; fax: 86-62223). Expensive.

Milocer – The former residence of the Queen of Montenegro, it has a mansion and 6 villas, its own beautiful pebble beach, and mountains and a pine forest as a backdrop. Major credit cards accepted (phone: 86-62242 or 86-41333; fax: 86-62223). Moderate.

Podkoren to Belgrade

This tour of the heartland begins in the Julian Alps, which are shared by Italy, Austria, and Yugoslavia, in the Yugoslav mountain town of Podkoren. Bring your skis or your hiking clothes, and prepare to take in some heavenly Alpine air. The route covers natural inland beauties such as the Martuljk waterfalls, Lake Bled, and the limestone caves at Postojna. Plan to spend some time at Lake Bled for swimming, rowing, fishing, or skating, depending on the season. As the elevation drops, you'll tour the cultural centers of Ljubljana and Zagreb, where we recommend you see what sports the natives are playing and what concerts they're attending — and also, where they've been going to church for the past 700 years or so. There's an optional side trip to the Plitvice Lakes National Park that would add about 160 miles (256 km) to the total; the Plitvice Lakes form a natural staircase of 16 cascading lakes.

A long drive through a forest full of wild animals such as fox, elk, grouse, and wild boar ensues after Zagreb, followed by the green fertile plains. This grain belt of Slavonija is a good place to meet rural people and get a sense of what it's like to live away from the shrillness of cities; it's exhilarating to get attuned to a place where time does not seem manmade.

Belgrade, the capital, is the end of the journey, the city with the most hustle and bustle in Yugoslavia. Here in the center of Yugoslav industry, commerce, and communication, you can get the best possible sense of what Yugoslavia thinks it's about; everything from industrial fairs to film festivals is held in Belgrade; there are Gypsy street-singers in Skadarlija, the bohemian and theater district; buy a souvenir from a sidewalk craftsman. For a complete report on the capital, its hotels, and restaurants, see *Belgrade,* THE CITIES.

PODKOREN: Start at the mountain town of Podkoren, near the Austrian border on Route E94, a main tourist road, and drive south through the blue green Julian Alps at 2,700 feet. Skiers can stop at the winter resort at Ratece-Planica, where there are ski slopes, five jumps, and lifts; there are several other resorts in the area: Kranjska Gora (one of Yugoslavia's most developed winter sports centers), Mt. Vitranc, and Gozd Martuljk. If you don't know how to downhill ski, this might be a good time to cross-country ski or learn how — it's not hard to pick up, and there can't be many better spots in the world to begin. Near Gozd Martuljk are the huge Martuljk waterfalls at the foot of Mt. Spik, and the Pericnik waterfall at Mojstrana. There are several hiking trails passing through these Slovene mountains, one extending all the way from the Baltic Sea in northern Europe to Yugoslavia's Adriatic. The water of the nearby Sava River is a brilliant metallic blue, and the air is Alpine-clear.

BLED: The mountain resort of Bled is 25 miles (40 km) in from Podkoren, sitting on Lake Bled in a valley surrounded by the snow-capped Alps. The 11th-century *Castle of the Bishops of Brixen* (phone: 64-77103), overlooking the lake from a sheer cliff, has been converted into a museum and inn. Lake Bled's waters are restricted to bathing and rowing (no motorboats to break the peace), and skating and curling in the winter. In the area are hunting grounds, fishing spots, tennis courts, riding facilities, and Yugoslavia's only 18-hole golf course, *Golf Club Bled* (phone: 64-78180).

En Route from Bled – A detour of 19 miles (30 km) to the southeast will bring you to Lake Bohinj, another mountain lake area good for skiing and hiking.

LJUBLJANA: About 55 miles (88 km) down from Podkoren is Ljubljana (pronounced *Lyoob*-lyana), the capital of the Republic of Slovenia, and the cosmopolitan and economic center of the state as well. Expositions, concerts, festivals, exhibits, and major sporting events (basketball, hockey, soccer, Ping-Pong) all take place here. Ljubljana's museums are particularly worth a look; the *National Museum* (20 Presernova) is one of the oldest in Europe. The city is also the center of all official and non-official countercultures, with unorthodox happenings taking place all year round. The city's architecture spans the 15th to the 20th century, with many baroque buildings and 30-story modern monoliths. Do not miss the works of Joze Plecnik, the city's (and Yugoslavia's) best-known architect; visit the *Architecture Museum* (Plecnik's former home) and the private chapel — both at 4 Karaunova — the neo-Byzantine church on Emonska, and the marketplace at Liberation Square. A block down the hill is Plecnik's Shoemaker's Bridge; to the left is his Triple Bridge; and near the *Jugendstil* (Art Nouveau) shops in the mew quarter are two pedestrian bridges that he added to a stone bridge. Finally, visit the Municipal Cemetery with several chapels designed by the Art Nouveau master; it's a 15-minute ride from downtown by car or bus.

En Route from Ljubljana – Worth a detour is a visit to the Postojna Caves in Postojna, where in towering chambers of limestone, the dripping water has formed shapes in stalactites and stalagmites, more magnificent and improbable than anything in Minimal Art. Take E70 from Ljubljana; it's just a 40-minute drive.

Highway E94 out of Ljubljana passes through woods, with no intersections. At 39 miles (62 km) south of the city is a turnoff for Novo Mesto, on the Krka River, where you can go swimming or trout fishing. Back on the main highway you will reach the 13th-century castle of *Otocec* (phone: 51-21830; fax: 51-22590), on an island in the Krka. Like many Yugoslav monuments, the castle is now a hotel and restaurant.

The mountains give way to hills and wide river valleys between Ljubljana and the next major Yugoslav city, Zagreb, 93 miles (149 km) away. This region has several spas dedicated to treating a wide range of complaints, from neuralgia to heart disease: Dolenjske Toplice, Smarjeske Toplice, and Cateske Toplice are on or near the main highway. Most spas offer the use of their hotels and hot springs to the healthy as well as the sick.

You will cross the Slovenia-Croatia border on very bumpy E70 about 16 miles (26 km) from the Croatian capital of Zagreb, Yugoslavia's second-largest city and its artistic center.

ZAGREB: Zagreb comprises what is now really three cities: the Upper Town (Gornji Grad), the oldest part of Zagreb, with many buildings from the 13th century; the Lower Town (Donji Grad), built at the turn of the 19th century; and New Zagreb (Novi

Zagreb), built since World War II, very stark and square, with wide parking lots. The Upper and Lower towns are protected as national monuments. The oldest parts of the city have undergone massive restoration; many turn-of-the-century buildings now have a warm, pastel-colored glow. Particularly pleasant is Trg Republike, the city's main square, with its newly restored figure of Ban Jelačić, a 19th-century Croatian national hero.

Today, Zagreb is an important locale on the world cultural circuit: Major opera companies and symphonies play here, and the *International Festival of Contemporary Music* takes place in odd-numbered years; *I Solisti di Zagreb* is one of the world's foremost chamber groups; Zagreb hosts the *World Festival of Animated Cartoons*, held in even-numbered years; and there is the *International Folklore Festival* every July.

In 1987, Zagreb was enriched by the opening of a world class museum, the *Mimara* (on Rooseveltov Trg). Housed in a converted 19th-century high school, the museum's 3,750-piece collection was donated by Ante Topic-Mimara, who died a few months before its opening. On view are Byzantine and Russian icons; paintings by Raphael, Michelangelo, El Greco, Velázquez, Murillo, Goya, Rembrandt, Rubens, Renoir, Manet, Degas, and many others; medieval sculptures; one of the world's most important glass-object collections, with items dating from 3000 BC; and an impressive Far East art collection. All in all, this place is a small-scale Balkan *Louvre*.

A permanent exhibition of the so-called Hlebine School of Native Painters is mounted at the *Gallery of Primitive Art* (3 Cirilometodska). A visit will give you some idea of this movement. And while you're here, check out any of Zagreb's numerous other museums, galleries, and private collections.

Be sure to see the 19th-century *Croatian National Theater* (15 Trg Marsala Tita) at night, if possible, for its sturdy, majestic exterior and beautiful music-box interior: plush red seats, inlaid wooden booths, huge fresco ceiling, and splendid chandelier.

Zagreb's churches are well worth a tour: St. Mark's, a 13th-century church (Tadicev Trg), has medieval coats of arms in mosaic on its tile roof; St. Stephen's Cathedral (Kapitol) has intricate stonework towers, over 300 feet high, and thick fortifications.

As Yugoslavia's most culturally sophisticated city, Zagreb has the country's most cosmopolitan nightlife; although most cafés and restaurants have an Old World Austro-Hungarian style, there are some modern ones, too.

The city's environs offer more things to do: In the immediate vicinity are enough woods for walking, hunting, and fishing. Marshal Tito's birthplace in Kumrovec, 28 miles (45 km) away, is done up as a museum dedicated to him — it looks rather Early American, with the exposed cross-beamed ceiling and a rough-hewn rocking cradle in the corner.

At Belec, 22 miles (35 km) from the city, is a baroque church decorated inside with carvings and figurines of diabolical inventiveness, with an altar like a three-dimensional Hieronymus Bosch painting.

En Route from Zagreb – Be sure to make time for a side trip to the Plitvice Lakes National Park, 80 miles (128 km) south of Zagreb. Take E70 out of the city, and when the road forks at Karlovac — 30 miles (48 km) on — turn due south (toward Tusilovic); the road signs will direct you as you get near. Plitvice Lakes form a natural staircase of 16 emerald lakes, each cascading down into the next in the middle of a virgin forest. There are hotels near the park and quite a few tourists.

It is 240 miles (384 km) from Zagreb to Belgrade on the main highway, which passes through dense forests, on the Slavonian plains, populated principally by elk, grouse, wild boar, and hunters. The Srem plains follow, the most fertile cropland in Yugoslavia. If you're sick of castles by now, you won't find many here — only sugar beets, green hills, and rustic farm folk who might have stepped out of a painting by Pieter Breughel the Elder.

BEST EN ROUTE

Accommodations for two people in an expensive place will run $50 to $100; moderate, $25 to $50; inexpensive, $15 to $25. At the restaurants listed below expect to pay between $20 and $40 per person, including wine, at an expensive place; $10 to $20 at moderate.

BLED

Villa Bled – The former Alpine retreat of President Tito is now a small luxury hotel. For big spenders and name-droppers who enjoy luxuriating in the living quarters of world leaders. Major credit cards accepted. 26 Cesta Svobode (phone: 64-77436). Expensive.

Toplice – A beatifically elegant hotel on Lake Bled in the Julian Alps, with crisp mountain air, damask sofas, Persian rugs, and finely tailored guests. Ask for a quiet room overlooking the lake, since rooms facing the street are quite noisy. Swimming, fishing, and hunting are available nearby. Major credit cards accepted. 20 Cesta Svobode (phone: 64-77222; fax: 64-78897). Moderate.

Blejski Grad – Set in the *Castle of the Bishops of Brixen,* it's the oldest tavern in the city, with heavy, rustic wooden furnishings. The cooking is Viennese style. No credit cards accepted (phone: 64-77103). Inexpensive.

LJUBLJANA

Holiday Inn – This European link in the ubiquitous chain is Yugoslavia's first. In the middle of town, with a full-size swimming pool on the roof. Major credit cards accepted (phone: 61-211434). Expensive to moderate.

Paulin – Just off the Ljubljana-Zagreb Highway and next to the 18th-century church, this pleasant place offers traditional food and local specialties. It also has a pool hall. Closed Tuesdays. Reservations advised. 31 Mačkovec (phone: 61-22308). Moderate.

Pri Zabarju – This traditional house, whose name means "Frog Hunter," offers local dishes in a rustic setting. Reservations necessary. Major credit cards accepted. On the road to Postojna; 50 Viska Cesta (phone: 61-261204). Moderate.

ZAGREB

Esplanade – An Art Deco masterpiece, with huge rooms, crystal chandeliers, and black marble walls. Good service, and painstaking 19th-century elegance. Though the establishment rates an "A" by Yugoslav government standards, it has no swimming pool and is somewhat small; it's still considered the best deluxe hotel in the country. The restaurant matches its style and quality. Major credit cards accepted. 1 Mihanoviceva (phone: 41-512222 or 41-435666; fax: 41-428721). Expensive.

Inter-Continental – Glassy and modern, with Yugoslav paintings on the walls, the hotel has big rooms, a swimming pool, and a health club, but service is slow and unfriendly. Major credit cards accepted. 1 Krsnjavoga (phone: 41-453411; fax: 41-444431). Expensive.

Dubravkin Put – Located in the forest just beyond the Lower Town, this chalet-type dwelling specializes in traditional fare from Zagreb and the surrounding area. The terrace is very pleasant during the summer. Reservations advised. Major credit cards accepted. Dubravkin Put B.B. (phone: 41-278118). Moderate.

Gradski Podrum – The name means "the city cellar," and to enter you descend from the street into a large restaurant that preserves its intimacy by the use of partitions. Continental cooking, elegant atmosphere, and crisp service. Next to *Gradska Kavana,* the town's finest 1920s café — also a must! Reservations unnecessary. Major credit cards accepted (phone: 41-274920). Moderate.

Kaptolska Klet – Two steps from the cathedral, this place offers a rich variety of local dishes and wines. Service is friendly and fast. Reservations necessary. 5 Kaptol (phone: 41-275200 or 41-276550). Moderate.

Korčula – Set in a pleasant cellar, this eatery offers the best fish dishes in Zagreb. For hors d'oeuvres try the Dalmatian smoked ham; it's on a par with the best Italian products from Parma. Reservations necessary on summer weekends. Major credit cards accepted. 17 Nikole Tesle (phone: 41-422658). Moderate.

Kulusic – With modern decor and friendly service, this café and bar is a popular hangout with Zagreb students and artists. A jazz fair is featured here in October. No reservations or credit cards accepted. Hrvojeva (no phone). Moderate.

Opera Rooftop – Despite its pretentious interior, the huge sweeping windows offer nice views of the New and Old cities. Try the prune-garnished Dalmatian pot roast or the Bosnian stew served in earthenware pots. Reservations advised. Major credit cards accepted. At the *Inter-Continental;* 1 Krsnjavoga (phone: 41-443411). Moderate.

Drina – Traditional cooking, with dishes not often found in other Zagreb eating places and generous servings. A specialty is Bosnian pot, three kinds of meat stewed with vegetables in an earthenware dish. Major credit cards accepted. 11 Preradoviceva (phone: 41-422654). Moderate to inexpensive.

PLITVICE LAKES

Jezero – Perhaps the best hostelry in the Plitvice Lakes region, it has a swimming pool and a sauna (phone: 48-76526). Moderate.

Lika – Tucked away in the park itself, it offers homemade bread and brandy, local trout and cheese, and lamb on the spit (no phone). Moderate.

Bitola to Belgrade

This is a short tour of some of Yugoslavia's most famous art treasures, found in the churches, mosques, monasteries, and excavated towns of Macedonia and Serbia. This eastern part of the country was ruled, in order, by the Greeks, Romans, Byzantines, Serbian medieval kings and Turks. The Greeks and Romans contributed marble statues and tile mosaics; the Byzantines and Serbians covered the walls of their churches with religious frescoes; and the Turks, forbidden to represent life in art, built magnificent mosques and forts decorated inside with abstract patterns. Art lovers should visit because they can't see these objects in their original state anywhere else — no museum in New York or Chicago can ever remove or borrow the frescoes of Sopocani, or the floor from the Imperial Mosque of Pristina, or the mosaic water nymph from the bath in the Roman town at Gamzigrad. And besides, these objects are in their original setting, where the original purpose is a little nearer to the observer's reach than it could be hanging on a wall in a strange city.

Our tour starts at the ruins of the ancient Greek city of Heraclea near Bitola and finishes at Belgrade, traversing the works of the Byzantine and Turkish empires en route. Some of the sites are far-flung; monasteries in particular tend to be secluded; the beautiful lake and mountain settings should make up for the inconvenience of reaching some of them. All of the sites are well known and well marked.

July and August are the peak months for folk festivals; ask the Yugoslavia

National Tourist Office for a listing for this region (630 5th Ave., Suite 280, New York, NY 10111; phone: 212-757-2801). Note: Because of the country's ethnic unrest at press time, there was some question as to whether this tourist office would remain open.

BITOLA: We begin 3 miles (5 km) from the border of Greece, near the Yugoslav city of Bitola, in the Republic of Macedonia. About 2 miles (3 km) south of town are the ruins of the ancient Greek city of Heraclea, which was an important commercial and strategic center linking Constantinople to the Adriatic coast. (A road, the Via Aegnatia, was built by the Romans in order to connect Heraclea to Salonique, Dyrrachium — in Albania — and Constantinople.) Particularly beautiful is the mosaic tile floor in the foundations of the basilica uncovered here and the life-size marble statues. There is also a partially unearthed Roman theater. At the end of July a folk festival, *St. Elia's Days,* features songs and dances from all over Yugoslavia.

En Route from Bitola – Proceed west on E5S, a main tourist highway, toward Ohrid. About 15 miles (24 km) along this road, take the left-hand turnoff and head for the church of St. George in Kurbinovo, near the town of Pretor on the eastern shore of Lake Prespa. The church itself is rather unassuming, but the frescoes inside, painted in 1191, are striking — take note particularly of the Assumption and the Annunciation.

OHRID: Go back up to the main highway and continue to Ohrid, the city on the shores of Lake Ohrid. The Church of St. Sophia in Ohrid is the most famous and sumptuous medieval monument in Macedonia, built in the 11th and 14th centuries. When the Turks moved in, they covered up the church's dramatic frescoes with mortar — since images of life are forbidden in Islam — but these were carefully uncovered in the 1950s. The Ascension is particularly expressive: note the dour, attentive angels in the friezes, crouching in a background of quiet green and blue. Classical music is played here during the *Ohrid Summer Festival* (for information, call 21204).

There are brilliantly colored frescoes at another Ohrid monument, the Church of St. Clement, including an athletic angel in the Annunciation who is about to touch Mary in midstride, as well as a beautiful wooden statue of St. Clement.

En Route from Ohrid – Take a detour south along Lake Ohrid toward St. Naum's monastery on the Albanian border. The lake will be on your right, and a national park on your left. Take the opportunity to go for a swim in the clear waters and a hike in the park. Naum's, when you reach it, is extraordinary for its beautiful setting on the lake, and the state of its preservation. It was here, in the 10th century, that St. Naum and St. Clement wrote liturgical services in the old Slav language, which still survive among Orthodox believers today; St. Naum and St. Clement were disciples of Constantine Cyril (who created the Cyrillic alphabet) and his brother St. Methodius, Greek priests who Christianized Slavs from Macedonia to Moravia in Czechoslovakia. Next, drive the 19 miles (30 km) back north to the main highway and take it all the way to Skopje.

SKOPJE: Macedonia's capital was badly damaged in an earthquake that killed 1,070 people in 1963, so most of its new buildings, designed by Japanese architects, are modern. Ironically, Skopje was founded in 518 by refugees from the ancient town of Scupi (3 miles/5 km from modern Skopje), which had just been destroyed by an earthquake; they named the new settlement after their former home.

There is much to see, despite both quakes, in Skopje and its environs. A magnificent 15th-century medieval footbridge spans the Vardar River, and is still very much in use. The great Mustafa-pasha Mosque and the Daut-pasha bath were built in the 15th century by the Turks.

The Church of St. Panteleimon in Nerezi (just south of the city) is the place to see, if you see no other church in Macedonia. The fresco of St. Damian, painted in 1164, is remarkable for its somber dignity in color composition and graceful lines. Experts rank the Lamentation, the Nativity, the Visitation, and the Transfiguration as among the finest in Byzantine art.

Marko's Monastery, properly called the Church of St. Demetrius (14th century), is just south of Nerezi, and has frescoes of biblical subjects not conventionally treated in ecclesiastical art. A moving example is Rachel's Tears.

En Route from Skopje – Head north on E27 out of Skopje toward Pristina. Just short of Pristina is the monastery at Gracanica (13th to 14th century); the stones making up the structure are red and yellow, giving the effect of gold. The top of the building has rows of ascending arches and towers, gathering to one pinnacle tower on the roof — it is considered the most beautiful early Serbian building anywhere. The frescoes inside are perfectly preserved, displaying in lively fashion the horrors and glories of this world and the next, sort of an illustrated Dante.

The Roman ruins of Ulpiana, near Gracanica, contain mosaics, tombstones, and a basilica.

PRISTINA: This is the capital of Kosovo, and is a mixture of old Eastern architecture with ultramodern. The most important monument is the Imperial Mosque, built in 1461 by Sultan Mehmet II; there are also several 19th-century Turkish buildings standing in the town. The collection in the *Museum of Kosovo* (2 Miladina Popovica) tells the Oriental history of the town in detail.

NOVI PAZAR: Go northwest out of Pristina on E27 toward Titova Mitrovica, following the road past that town to Novi Pazar. Novi Pazar is also being built up in modern style, but the Alem-Altum Turkish mosque (16th century) is worth seeing.

The real attraction is 10 miles (16 km) west of the town in the hills at Sopocani. The monastery there was built in 1265 by King Uros I to house his own tomb. The frescoes of Sopocani, with those of Nerezi, are said to be the best in Byzantine art. Using yellow, green, violet, and gold leaf (which has by now peeled away), the artist here painted with great feeling the nobility and tragedy of man. See in particular the Dormition of the Virgin and the saints' portraits.

En Route from Novi Pazar – Take the highway north out of Novi Pazar, and on the way to Kraljevo you will pass the Monastery of Studenica, Serbia's most prestigious holy place. Next to the river Studenica (the Cold One) the monastery still has three of its original churches — all built during the 12th century by Prince Stefan Nemanja. The main church is Sveta Bogorodica (Holy Virgin), built with Italian marble. Its frescoes, particularly the crucifixion, are perhaps the most expressive artistic works of their kind in all of Serbia. There is also a treasury and dining room worth visiting.

KRALJEVO: Continue north about 38 miles (61 km) from the monastery to Kraljevo to see the restored monastery of Zica, painted bright earthen red, as it was in medieval times. Built from 1208 to 1220, it was here at the seat of the Archbishopric of Serbia that the medieval Serbian kings were crowned. The remaining frescoes here are few, but of beautiful quality and color, particularly the Resurrection, depicting a robed angel seated at the side of the open tomb.

At Visegrad, 100 miles (160 km) east of Kraljevo on the river Drina, you will come upon Yugoslavia's oldest bridge. Built of stone by the Turks in 1571, this graceful, historic span connects Belgrade and Dubrovnik and inspired Ivo Andric, Yugoslavia's only Nobel Prize winner for literature, to write an epic novel about it — *The Bridge on the Drina*.

The Kalenic Monastery near Kraljevo is constructed with graceful and detailed relief in its arches; its architecture is among the best in the Serbian style.

En Route from Kraljevo – Get on the highway east for a final stop before Belgrade. About 22 miles (35 km) after the town of Krusevac, after the highway has turned north and converged with the highway from Nis, take an eastward turnoff (toward Romania) and drive until you get to the town of Zajecar, just shy of the Bulgarian border. Near town are the excavations of the late Roman fortress of Gamzigrad (3rd and 4th centuries). There you will find the palace ruins, a huge Roman bath, and mosaics with a grace, sumptuousness, and eroticism that will refresh you.

Gaze at the splendid city gates of Gamzigrad, which no longer keep anyone in or out; whenever you feel ready, get back on the highway west via Zajecar towards Despotovac, a 15th-century capital of King Stephan Lazarević, who built a walled monastery called Manasija, which is well worth a visit. To reach the Danube, turn north at Niš-Belgrade Highway and head to Belgrade and civilization, where the Gamzigrads of the future wait their turn. For a complete report on the capital and its hotels and restaurants, see *Belgrade,* THE CITIES.

BEST EN ROUTE

Accommodations for two people in a moderate hotel will cost $30 to $45. Expect to pay $20 to $40 per person, including wine, in restaurants listed as expensive, and between $10 and $20 in moderate places.

PRISTINA

Grand – A modern hotel in the city center, it offers grand views of the town. Major credit cards accepted (phone: 38-20211).

OHRID

Desaret – On Lake Ohrid, this modern hotel has a wooden Macedonian-style exterior — which might look Scandinavian to Western eyes. Major credit cards accepted (phone: 96-24040; fax: 96-35460). Moderate.

Inex Gorica – This modern hotel has the region's best restaurant; it serves Ohrid trout — found only in Lake Ohrid. Major credit cards accepted (phone: 96-22020). Moderate.

DESPOTOVAC

Sindelić – This small-town eatery that caters to locals specializes in grilled meat and wonderful roasted spring lamb. 35 Maršalatita Str. (phone: 35-611778). Inexpensive.

Index

America's Favorite Travel Guides Give You More, and Save Money, Too.

BIRNBAUM TRAVEL GUIDES are full of details found in no other guides, plus data about discounts that can make an otherwise unaffordable trip possible. Only we tell you how to find the best restaurant on the entire Continent (see GENEVA/Eating Out), give you the address of the car rental company that offers only top-of-the-line BMWs, Porsches, or Mercedes in which to test the autobahns (see GETTING READY TO GO/Traveling by Car), or plan the perfect New Year's Eve (see VIENNA/Extra Special).

What's more, savvy travelers can enjoy all this while saving lots of money by dealing with consolidators, last-minute travel clubs, bucket shops, net fare outlets, and the like. No other travel guide names all these sources!

STEPHEN BIRNBAUM is America's leading travel authority. His television appearances, daily radio newscasts, and magazine and newspaper columns have made him the most recognized travel expert in the country. He's known to millions for his lively reporting on what's best (and what's not). His best-selling travel guide series shows travelers how to find the highest quality of experience at the lowest possible cost.

ALEXANDRA MAYES BIRNBAUM is the former marketing director of *Glamour* magazine, managing editor of *Seventeen* magazine, and editor-in-chief of *Good Food* magazine. She adds a unique woman's point of view that no other guide provides.

More Discounts and Details Than Any Other Travel Guide

HarperPerennial

A Division of HarperCollinsPublishers

A Stephen Birnbaum Travel Guide
Cover Design © Drenttel Doyle Partners
Front Cover Photo © Mitch Epstein
Back Cover Photo © Lisa Kahane

| USA | $17.00 | UK | £11.99 |
| CANADA | $23.00 | AUSTRALIA | A$24.95 |

ISBN 0-06-278016-6

51700>

9 780062 780164